Badger
STATE ANIMAL

Muskellunge
STATE FISH

Sugar Maple
STATE TREE

Wood Violet
STATE FLOWER

State of Wisconsin

2005-2006 Blue Book

Compiled by the
Wisconsin Legislative Reference Bureau

JULIE LASSA

STATE SENATOR • 24TH SENATE DISTRICT

State Capitol, P.O. Box 7882
Madison, WI 53707-7882
1-800-925-7491
sen.lassa@legis.state.wi.us

WISCONSIN STATE REPRESENTATIVE
Louis J. Molepske, Jr.
71ST ASSEMBLY DISTRICT

P.O. Box 8953
Madison, WI 53708-8953
Rep.Molepske@legis.state.wi.us

Toll-free: (888) 534-0071
District: (715) 342-8985
FAX: (608) 282-3671

12

The following LRB Reference Section staff members produced the *2005-2006 Wisconsin Blue Book:*

Lawrence S. Barish, editor
Lynn Lemanski, lead publications editor
Kathleen Sitter, photo editor

Jason Anderson, legislative analyst
Shanin R. Brown, legislative analyst
A. Peter Cannon, legislative analyst
Anthony Gad, legislative analyst
Lauren Jackson, publications editor
Michael J. Keane, legislative analyst
Robert A. Paolino, legislative analyst
Clark G. Radatz, legislative analyst
Daniel F. Ritsche, legislative analyst
Richard L. Roe, legislative analyst

ISBN 0-9752820-1-8

Front cover: Mosaics by Kenyon Cox in State Capitol: "Justice", Legislation", Government", Liberty". Photographs and design by Kathleen Sitter, Legislative Reference Bureau.

Back cover: Images of historic county courthouses from the collections of the State Historical Society of Wisconsin.

JIM DOYLE
GOVERNOR
STATE OF WISCONSIN

July 2005

Dear Readers:

Wisconsin's progressive tradition has created close ties between its people and their government. Residents of our great state expect their leaders to look out for their interests and protect their civil liberties. Elected officials in state government work hard to do just that: passing and signing into law legislation that strives to improve the quality of life in Wisconsin. However, it is the third branch of government – the court system, composed of non-elected officials – that works diligently, and often in obscurity, to uphold those laws, the rights of the people of Wisconsin, and the purest pursuit of justice.

Statesman and philosopher Edmund Burke once said that justice is the "great standing policy of civil society." Indeed, the noble pursuit of justice is the underpinning of every level of government and would not be possible without the judicial branch, as illustrated in this year's feature article, "The Wisconsin Court System: Demystifying the Judicial Branch." I am especially pleased to write the introductory letter for this edition of the *Wisconsin Blue Book* because, as a former Attorney General and the son of a judge, my respect for the law runs deep; and as Governor, I have seen first-hand the invaluable role Wisconsin's courts play in upholding and advancing for our liberties, freedom, and democracy.

I believe that our Justice system only works when it works for all of us, and to do that, it must reflect the great diversity and the boundless optimism of Wisconsin's people. This past year marked a new beginning for the Wisconsin Supreme Court with the appointment of Justice Louis Butler, the first African-American Justice in Wisconsin history. Justice Butler joins a Supreme Court composed of three other men and three women, including the first-ever woman appointment, Chief Justice Shirley Abrahamson. Now, more than ever before, our highest court is more representative of our great state, our communities, and our people.

Every two years, our state publishes this *Blue Book* – an invaluable resource for citizens who wish to be well informed and actively engaged in the entire democratic process. It is the story of Wisconsin, its government, and its people, and I hope that you will not only use it, but enjoy it.

Sincerely,

Jim Doyle
Governor

P.O. BOX 7863, MADISON, WISCONSIN 53707-7863 • (608) 266-1212 • FAX: (608) 267-8983 •
WWW.WISGOV.STATE.WI.US

$\mathfrak{State}$ of $\mathfrak{Wisconsin}$
LEGISLATIVE REFERENCE BUREAU

INTRODUCTION

The production of each edition of the *Wisconsin Blue Book* is a cooperative undertaking made possible by the combined efforts of many individuals throughout state government. Although the Wisconsin Legislature publishes the *Blue Book*, and responsibility for editing the book is assigned to the Legislative Reference Bureau, individuals in all 3 branches of government contribute to the final product. Legislators and legislative staff contribute biographical information and photographs; executive department personnel describe the organization and functions of their respective agencies and compile a wide variety of statistical data; and judicial branch staff help profile the judicial branch of government.

This, the 87th edition, is no exception. The feature article in the *2005-2006 Blue Book* exemplifies the cooperative approach. The aptly titled article, "The Wisconsin Court System: Demystifying the Judicial Branch", is coauthored by Robin Ryan, legislative attorney with the Legislative Reference Bureau, and Amanda Todd, public information officer for the Wisconsin Supreme Court. The authors describe in considerable detail the structure and functions of the judicial branch. However, the article offers more than a description of offices, officials, and officialdom. By outlining the relationship among the various courts and the roles that judges, attorneys, and jurors play in the judicial system, it provides readers with a readable and comprehensive primer on our legal system and an understanding of how the judicial branch of government impacts our lives and safeguards our shared values. The text is augmented by a generous number of photographs, charts, and graphics which were largely the work of LRB photo editor Kathleen Sitter. As the first *Blue Book* main article to focus exclusively on the court system, it occupies a unique place in the historical series of articles on Wisconsin state government. As such, it is a valuable addition to our knowledge of the judicial branch.

The covers and divider pages that introduce each section of the book continue the judicial theme. The front cover design highlights the four mosaics depicting Justice, Government, Legislation, and Liberty, which adorn the rotunda in the State Capitol Building. Each of the 12 divider pages include a photograph of a county courthouse and reveal a diverse and eclectic range of architectural styles. Several of the photos by L. Roger

Turner were originally published in *Wisconsin's Historic Courthouses*. A montage of historic county courthouses reflecting the grandeur of an earlier age graces the back cover.

As noted, many people, including the LRB staff, work together to produce the *Blue Book*. Legislative attorneys, in addition to coauthoring the main article and contributing articles on significant court decisions and significant legislation, edit and review large portions of the text. Publications editors format text, take photographs, and incorporate graphics to create the final layout of the *Blue Book*. The legislative analysts compile the statistical section and are involved in almost every part of the production of the *Blue Book*. Two recently retired members of our research staff who shared a combined 48 years of experience merit special mention. Richard Roe, *Blue Book* associate editor, compiled and edited the executive branch agency descriptions, among other responsibilities, for a number of editions. He tackled this daunting task with perseverance, aplomb and good humor and amassed an encyclopedic knowledge of state government organization in the process. Peter Cannon, senior legislative analyst, resident historian and computer expert applied his considerable expertise to designing legislative district maps and compiling the history and population and vital statistics sections of the *Blue Book*. Both Rich and Pete will be missed not only for their contributions to the *Blue Book* but for the dedication and professionalism they demonstrated throughout their careers in support of the Wisconsin Legislature. We wish them both a happy and fulfilling retirement.

As always, we hope that you find the latest edition of the *Blue Book* a useful and valuable resource. The editors encourage readers to contact us with comments and suggestions on how to make the next edition even better.

Lawrence S. Barish
Blue Book Editor
July 2005

TABLE OF CONTENTS

Biographies

Biographies and photos: Wisconsin constitutional executive officers, Supreme Court justices, members of the U.S. Congress from Wisconsin, and legislators (also includes congressional and legislative district maps)

Lincoln County Courthouse

L. Roger Turner

ALPHABETICAL INDEX TO BIOGRAPHIES

GOVERNOR

Jim Doyle (Dem.): Born Washington, D.C., November 23, 1945; married; 2 children. Graduate West H.S., Madison 1963; attended Stanford U. 1963-66; B.A. UW-Madison 1967; J.D. (*cum laude*) Harvard U. Law School 1972. Attorney. Former Madison law firm partner; lecturer, UW Law School; attorney for a federal legal services office on Navajo Indian Reservation in Chinle, AZ (1972-75). Served in Peace Corps. Member: Amer. Bar Assn., State Bar of Wis. and Arizona and Dane Co. Bar Assns. Dane Co. District Attorney 1977-83.

Elected governor 2002. Member: State of Wisconsin Building Comn. (chp.); Public Records Board; Women's Council; Information Technology Management Board; Transportation Projects Comn. (chp.); Council of State Governments; National Governors' Assn.; Democratic Governor's Association; Council of Great Lakes Governors; Midwest Governors' Assn.; Education Comn. of the States; Midwestern Higher Education Commission.

Elected attorney general 1990; reelected 1994 and 1998. Member: State Board of Commissioners of Public Lands; State Board of Canvassers; State Council on Alcohol and Other Drug Abuse; Judicial Council; National Assn. of Attorneys General (president, 1997-98) and member of its committees on Antitrust, on Civil Rights, on Criminal Law, on Environment, and on Energy Consumer Protection (exec. com.), member of its task forces on Juvenile Justice, on Health Care Fraud and Elder Abuse, and on Youth Violence and School Safety, and member of its working groups on Indian Gaming, on the Internet, and on Utility Deregulation (chp.).

Telephone: Office: (608) 266-1212; Fax: (608) 267-8983; E-mail address: governor@wisconsin.gov

Mailing address: Office: 115 East, State Capitol, Madison 53702.

LIEUTENANT GOVERNOR

Barbara Lawton (Dem.): Born Milwaukee, July 5, 1951; married; 2 children. Graduate Waterford Union H.S., Waterford; B.A. Lawrence University, Appleton 1987; M.A. University of Wisconsin-Madison 1991. Member: Greater Green Bay Area Community Foundation (founding trustee); Women's Political Voice (advisory board); League of Women Voters; American Association of University Women; National Women's Political Caucus. Former member: Educational Resource Foundation (founding director); Entrepreneurs of Color (advisory board); Latinos Unidos (founding director); Governor's Commission on Campaign Finance Reform; Greater Green Bay Multicultural Center (adv. bd.); Northeast Wisconsin Technical College Educational Foundation (board of directors); Planned Parenthood Advocates of Wisconsin (director).

Elected lieutenant governor 2002.

Telephone: Office: (608) 266-3516; Fax: (608) 267-3571; E-mail address: ltgov@ltgov.state.wi.us

Mailing address: Office: 19 East, State Capitol, P.O. Box 2043, Madison 53701-2043.

Governor
JIM DOYLE

SECRETARY OF STATE

Douglas J. La Follette (Dem.): Single. B.S. in chemistry Marietta College 1963; M.S. in chemistry Stanford U. 1964; Ph.D. in organic chemistry Columbia U. 1967. Former director of training and development with an energy marketing company; assistant professor, UW-Parkside; public affairs director, Union of Concerned Scientists; owner and operator of a small business; research associate, UW-Madison. Member: Amer. Solar Energy Society; Audubon Society; Friends of the Earth; Phi Beta Kappa. Former member: Council of Economic Priorities; Amer. Federation of Teachers; Federation of American Scientists; Lake Michigan Federation; Southeastern Wis. Coalition for Clean Air; Clean Wisconsin (formerly Wis. Environmental Decade, founder).

Elected secretary of state 1974 and 1982; reelected since 1986. Member: State Board of Commissioners of Public Lands (chp.).

Elected to Senate 1972.

Telephone: Office: (608) 266-8888; Fax: (608) 266-3159.

Mailing address: Office: 30 West Mifflin Street, 10th Floor, P.O. Box 7848, Madison 53707-7848.

STATE TREASURER

Jack C. Voight (Rep.): Born New London, December 17, 1945; married; 2 daughters. Graduate New London Washington H.S.; B.S. UW-Oshkosh 1971. Insurance agency owner. Vietnam veteran; Army sergeant 1968-70. Member: Appleton Northside Business Assn.; Appleton Optimist Club; Appleton Taxpayers Assn.; Fox Cities Chamber of Commerce; American Legion (life member); Rotary Club of Appleton; VFW (life member); Fox Valley Vietnam Veterans; Midwest State Treasurers Assn. (pres. 1997); National Assn. of State Treasurers. Appleton City Council 1983-93 (pres. 1992-93).

Elected state treasurer 1994; reelected 1998, 2002. Member: State Board of Commissioners of Public Lands; State Depository Selection Board; Insurance Security Fund (bd. of dir.); State of Wisconsin Investment Board (treas.); Wisconsin Retirement Fund (treas.).

Telephone: Office: (608) 266-1714; Fax: (608) 266-2647.

E-mail address: Jack.Voight@ost.state.wi.us

Mailing address: Office: 1 South Pinckney Street, 5th Floor, P.O. Box 7871, Madison 53707-7871.

ATTORNEY GENERAL

Peggy A. Lautenschlager (Dem.): Born Fond du Lac, November 22, 1955; married; 3 children, 2 stepchildren. Graduate L.P. Goodrich H.S. 1973; B.A., Phi Beta Kappa, Lake Forest College (IL) 1977; J.D. UW-Madison 1980. Attorney. Former U.S. Attorney, Western District of Wis. (1993-2001); Winnebago County District Attorney (1985-88); interim Winnebago County Court Commissioner. Former adjunct faculty member of the UW-Madison Law School, UW-Oshkosh, and Ripon College. Member: State Bar of Wis.; Dane County Bar Assn.; Fond du Lac County Bar Assn.; Legal Assn. for Women; Law Enforcement Training Officers Assn.; Wis. Association of Women Police; Blandine House, Inc. (bd. of dir.). Former member: Democratic National Committee; Wisconsin Elections Bd.; Fond du Lac Morning Optimist Club; Governor's Council on Domestic Abuse; Fond du Lac Big Brothers and Big Sisters; Oshkosh Area Big Brothers and Big Sisters; Oshkosh Rape Crisis Center; United States Attorney General's Advisory Committee (lst Wisconsinite to serve on committee); Wauburn Girl Scout Council; former Girl Scout Troop Leader.

Elected attorney general 2002. Member: State Board of Commissioners of Public Lands; State Board of Canvassers; State Council on Alcohol and Other Drug Abuse; Judicial Council.

Elected to Wisconsin Assembly 1988, representing the 52nd Assembly District and serving in the 1989 and 1991 sessions.

Telephone: Office: (608) 266-1221; Fax: (608) 267-2779.

Mailing address: Office: 114 East, State Capitol, Madison 53702.

STATE SUPERINTENDENT OF PUBLIC INSTRUCTION

Elizabeth Burmaster (nonpartisan office): Born Baltimore, MD, July 26, 1954; married; 3 children. Graduate Governor Thomas Johnson H.S., Frederick, MD; B.M. UW-Madison 1976; M.S. UW-Madison 1984; honorary doctorates, Beloit College and Edgewood College 2004. Former music and drama teacher, district fine arts coordinator, and principal in Madison Metropolitan School District (Madison West High School).

Elected state superintendent 2001; reelected 2005. Member: UW Board of Regents; Educational Communications Board (vice chp.); Wisconsin Technical College System Board; Governor's Economic Growth Council; Governor's Council on Workforce Investment; Council of Chief State School Officers and its Task Force on Early Childhood Learning (chp.); National Center for Learning and Citizenship (chp.).

Telephone: Office: (608) 266-1771; (800) 441-4563 (toll free).

E-mail address: state.superintendent@dpi.state.wi.us

Mailing address: Office: 125 South Webster Street, P.O. Box 7841, Madison 53707-7841.

**Lieutenant Governor
LAWTON**

**Secretary of State
La FOLLETTE**

**State Treasurer
VOIGHT**

**Attorney General
LAUTENSCHLAGER**

**State Superintendent
of Public Instruction
BURMASTER**

SUPREME COURT JUSTICES

Mailing address: Supreme Court, P.O. Box 1688, Madison 53701-1688. Telephone: (608) 266-1298.

CHIEF JUSTICE

Shirley S. Abrahamson: Born New York City, December 17, 1933; married; 1 child. Graduate Hunter College H.S. 1950; B.A. N.Y.U. 1953; J.D. Indiana U. Law Sch. 1956; S.J.D. UW Law Sch. 1962; D.L. (honorary) Willamette U. 1978, Ripon College 1981, Beloit College 1982, Capital U. 1983, John Marshall Law Sch. 1984, Northeastern U. 1985, Indiana U. 1986, Northland College 1988, Hamline U. 1988, Notre Dame U. 1993, Suffolk U. 1994, DePaul U. 1996, Lawrence U. 1998, Marian College 1998. Member: American Philosophical Society (elected 1998); American Academy of Arts and Sciences (fellow 1997). Recipient: American Judicature Society *Dwight D. Opperman Award* 2004 and *Herbert Harley Award* 1999; ABA Commission on Women in the Profession *Margaret Brent Women Lawyers of Achievement Award* 1995; UW-Madison *Distinguished Alumni Award* 1994; Wisconsin Communication Association *Wisconsin Outstanding Communicator Award* 1992.

Appointed to Supreme Court August 1976 to fill vacancy created by death of Chief Justice Horace W. Wilkie; elected to full term 1979; reelected 1989 and 1999. Became chief justice August 1, 1996, upon the retirement of Chief Justice Roland B. Day.

JUSTICES

(In Order of Seniority)

Jon P. Wilcox: Born Berlin, September 5, 1936; married; 2 children. Graduate Wild Rose H.S.; B.A. Ripon College 1958; J.D. UW-Madison 1965. Former practicing attorney; faculty, Wis. Jud. College 1985-96. Served in Army 1959-61. Member: Phi Alpha Delta; State Bar of Wis. and its Media and Law Relations Com., its Bench Bar Com., Jurist Award Subcom. (co-chp.), Senior Lawyer Div.; Amer., Dane, and Tri-County Bar Assns.; Wis. Law Found. (bd. of dir.); The Fellows of the Amer. Bar Found.; Amer. Bar Assn. Appellate Judges Conf. Com. on Continuing Appellate Education; Masons; Rotary International; Trout Unlimited; Ducks Unlimited. Former member: Wis. Trial Judges Assn.; State-Federal Jud. Council; Amer. Judicature Soc.; Amer. Trial Lawyers Assn.; UW Law Sch. Bd. of Visitors (1970-76); State Bar of Wisconsin's Jud. Clerk Utilization Com., Jud. Substitution Com., and Dist. Bd. of Professional Responsibility; Natl. Conf. of Christians and Jews (1980-84); Prison Overcrowding Task Force (1988-90); Wis. Conservation Congress (1975-80); Comn. on the Judiciary as a Co-Equal Branch of Government (co-chp.); Wis. Jud. Council. Recipient: *Outstanding Jaycee Award* 1974 (Wautoma); Ripon College *Distinguished Alumni Award* 1993.

Waushara Co. Family Ct. Commissioner 1978-79; Waushara Co. Circuit Ct. Judge 1979-92; Chief Judge, 6th Jud. Dist. 1985-92; Wis. Sentencing Comn. 1987-92 (chp.). Presentation at Natl. Inst. for Justice Conf. on "Judicial Discretion and Sentencing Guidelines", 1987; Contributor: Wis. News Reporters Handbook, "Courts and Court Procedures" 1987; Wis. Chief Judges Com. 1990-92 (chp.).

Served in the Wisconsin State Assembly 1969-75, representing Green Lake-Waushara Counties and 72nd Assembly District.

Appointed to Supreme Court September 1992 to fill vacancy created by the retirement of Justice William G. Callow; elected to full term 1997.

Ann Walsh Bradley: Born Richland Center, July 5, 1950; married; 4 children. Graduate Richland Center H.S.; B.A. Webster College (St. Louis, MO) 1972; J.D. UW-Madison (Knapp Scholar) 1976. Former high school teacher, practicing attorney, and Marathon Co. circuit court judge. Member: National Conference on Uniform Laws; elected member of the American Law Institute; Wisconsin Bench Bar Committee; UW Law School Board of Visitors; Amer. Judicature Soc.; American Bar Assn.; State Bar of Wis.; elected fellow of the American Bar Foundation, Wisconsin Legal History Committee; Rotary International; lecturer for the ABA's Asian Law Initiative. Served on Wis. Task Force on Children in Need. Former member: Wis. Judicial College (associate dean and faculty); Wis. Rhodes Scholarship Com. (chp.); Wis. Equal Justice Task Force; Wis. Jud. Conference (chp. and legis. com.); Civil Law Com. (exec. com.); Task Force on Children and Families; Wis. State Public Defender Board (bd. of dir.); Com. on the Admin. of Courts. Recipient: American Judicature Society's *Herbert Harley Award* 2004; *Business and Professional Woman of the Year* 1993; *Woman of Distinction Award* 1993; *Business Woman of the Year Athena Award* 1990.

Elected to Supreme Court 1995; reelected 2005.

**Justice
WILCOX**

**Justice
BRADLEY**

**Justice
CROOKS**

**Chief Justice
ABRAHAMSON**

**Justice
PROSSER**

**Justice
ROGGENSACK**

**Justice
BUTLER**

N. Patrick Crooks: Born Green Bay, May 16, 1938; married; 6 children. Graduate Green Bay Premontre H.S. 1956; B.A. (*magna cum laude*) St. Norbert Coll. 1960; J.D. U. of Notre Dame Law Sch. 1963; Army Judge Advocate General's School at U. of VA 1963-64; Natl. Jud. Coll. at U. of Nevada-Reno May 1984; Inst. of Jud. Admin. at N.Y.U. Law Sch. 1996. Former practicing attorney (1966-77); business law instructor, UW-Green Bay (1970-72); faculty, Wis. Jud. Coll.; attorney, Military Affairs Div., Army Judge Advocate General Office, Pentagon (1964-66); legal intern, Internal Security Div., U.S. Dept. of Justice (1962). Vietnam Era vet.; served in Army (capt.) 1963-66. Member: Amer. Bar Assn. and law school evaluator in its judicial division; State Bar of Wis. and its Media and Law Relations Com.; Dane Co. Bar Assn.; Brown Co. Bar Assn. (pres. 1977); Assn. for Women Lawyers of Brown Co.; Notre Dame Law Assn. (bd. of dir.); Wis. Law Foundation (exec. com.). Former member: Wis. Judicial Council (1998-2002); Juvenile Justice Study Task Force (1994-95); United Way of Brown Co. (pres. 1976-78); East Central Criminal Justice Planning Coun. (1973-85); Brown Co. Legal Aid (chp. 1971-73); Fed. Bar Assn. (1964-65). Recipient: Notre Dame Academy *Distinguished Alumnus of the Year Award* 2002; Amer. Bd. of Trial Advocates *Trial Judge of the Year* 1994; St. Norbert Coll. *Alma Mater Award* 1992 and *Distinguished Achievement Award in Social Science* 1977; U. of Notre Dame *Award of the Year* 1978; Army Judge Advocate General *Commendation Medal* 1966. Author of works in *Notre Dame Lawyer* 1961-63; *Judges Bench Book-Juvenile.* Brown Co. Ct. judge 1977-78; Brown Co. Circuit Ct. judge 1978-96.

Elected to Supreme Court 1996.

David T. Prosser, Jr.: Born Chicago, IL, December 24, 1942; single. Graduate Appleton H.S.; B.A. DePauw Univ. 1965; J.D. UW-Madison Law School 1968. Former practicing attorney; admin. asst. to U.S. Congressman Harold V. Froehlich 1973-74; attorney-advisor, U.S. Dept. of Justice 1969-72; lecturer, Indiana U.-Indianapolis Law School 1968-69. Member: Judicial Coun.; State Bar of Wis.; Dane Co., Milwaukee Co., and Outagamie Co. Bar Assns. Former member: Wis. Coun. on Criminal Justice 1980-83 (exec. com.); Judicial Coun. Com. on Prelim. Examinations 1981; Wis. Sentencing Comn. 1984-88 and 1994-95; Wis. Sesquicentennial Comn. 1993-99; National Conference of Commissioners on Uniform State Laws 1983-96.

Outagamie Co. District Attorney 1977-78.

Elected to Wisconsin Assembly 1978. Speaker of the Assembly 1995-96; Minority Leader 1989-94.

Commissioner, Wis. Tax Appeals Comn. 1997-98.

Appointed to Supreme Court September 1998 to fill vacancy created by resignation of Justice Janine P. Geske; elected to full term 2001.

E-mail address: david.prosser@wicourts.gov

Patience Drake Roggensack: Born Joliet, IL, July 7, 1940; married; 3 children. Graduate Lockport Township H.S.; B.A. Drake University 1962; J.D. UW-Madison Law School 1980 (*cum laude*). Former practicing attorney. Member: State Bar of Wis.; American Judicature Soc.; American Bar Assn.; Dane Co. Bar Assn; American Bar Foundation (fellow); American Judges Assn.; Legal Assn. of Women; Bar Assn. for the Western District of Wisconsin (past president). Board service on: YMCA; YWCA; Wisconsin Center for Academically Talented Youth; Olbrich Botanical Society; International Women's Forum (past president).

Court of Appeals Judge, District IV (1996-2003). Served on Judicial Conference (legislative liaison); Committee for Public Trust and Confidence in the Courts; Publication Committee for the Court of Appeals; State Court/Tribal Court Planning Committee (co-chair); Personnel Review Board (appeals court delegate).

Elected to Supreme Court 2003. Service on Personnel Review Board (supreme court delegate); 2005 Statewide Bench Bar Conference (co-chair).

Louis B. Butler, Jr.: Born Chicago, Illinois, February 15, 1952; married; 2 children. Graduate Chicago South Shore H.S. 1969; B.A. Lawrence University 1973; J.D. UW-Madison Law School 1977. Member: State Bar of Wisconsin; Milwaukee County Bar Association; National Judicial College (faculty member); National Association for the Advancement of Colored People (NAACP) (former bd. of directors; former co-chair, Political Action Committee); Wisconsin Association of African-American Lawyers (former president and treasurer); Community Brainstorming Conference (bd. of directors; former chair). Former member: Bench Bar Criminal Committee; Criminal Judicial Benchbook Committee; Criminal Law Section (bd. of directors) and Individual Rights and Responsibilities Section (bd. of directors; chair) of the State Bar of Wisconsin; Legal Action of Wisconsin (bd. of directors), Legal Services to Indigents Committee (bd. of directors); Milwaukee Area Television Access (bd. of directors); Milwaukee Trial Judges Association; Stephen Avery Task Force; Urban Initiative Task Force on Public Education; Wisconsin Municipal Judges Association (president, legislative trustee, bd. of directors); Wisconsin Sentencing Commission.

Assistant State Public Defender (1979-92); Milwaukee Municipal Court Judge (1992-2002); Milwaukee County Circuit Court Judge (2002-04).

Appointed to Supreme Court August 2004 to fill vacancy created by the appointment of Justice Diane Sykes to the Federal Court.

WISCONSIN MEMBERS OF THE 109th CONGRESS
2005-2006

MEMBERS OF THE U.S. SENATE

**U.S. Senator
KOHL**

Herbert H. Kohl (Dem.)

Born Milwaukee, February 7, 1935; single. Graduate Milwaukee Sherman Elementary School; Milwaukee Washington H.S.; B.A. in Business Administration, UW-Madison 1956; M.B.A. Harvard U. 1958; honorary L.L.D. Cardinal Stritch College 1986. Businessman; president of an investment company; owner of a professional basketball team; part owner of a professional baseball team. Former president of a business corporation. Served in Army Reserve 1958-64. Member: Democratic Party of Wisconsin (state chp. 1975-77). Recipient: Pen and Mike Club *Wisconsin Sports Personality of the Year* 1985; Wisconsin Broadcasters Assn. *Joe Killeen Memorial Sportsman of the Year* 1985; Greater Milwaukee Convention and Visitors Bureau *Lamplighter Award* 1986; Wisconsin Parkinson Assn. *Humanitarian of the Year* 1986; Kiwanis *Milwaukee Award* 1987.

Elected to U.S. Senate 1988; reelected since 1994. Committee assignments: **109th Congress** — Appropriations Committee (since 103rd Congress) and its Subcommittees on Agricultural Appropriations (ranking member), on Commerce, Justice, and State, on Homeland Security Appropriations, and on Labor, Health and Education; Judiciary Committee (since 101st Congress) and its Subcommittee on Antitrust, Competition Policy and Consumer Rights (ranking member); Special Committee on Aging (ranking member, mbr. since 101st Congress). **102nd Congress** — Governmental Affairs Committee (also 101st Congress) and its Subcommittee on Government Information and Regulation (chp.); Select Committee on POW/MIA Affairs.

Telephones: Washington office: (202) 224-5653, TTY: (202) 224-4464; District offices: Appleton: (920) 738-1640; Eau Claire: (715) 832-8424; La Crosse: (608) 796-0045; Madison: (608) 264-5338; Milwaukee: (414) 297-4451; Toll free: (800) 247-5645.

Internet address: www.kohl.senate.gov

E-mail address: senator_kohl@kohl.senate.gov

Voting address: 929 North Astor, Milwaukee 53202.

Mailing addresses: Washington office: 330 Hart Senate Office Building, Washington, D.C. 20510-4903; District offices: 4321 West College Avenue, Suite 235, Appleton 54914; 402 Graham Avenue, Suite 206, Eau Claire 54701; 425 State Street, Suite 202, La Crosse 54601; 14 West Mifflin Street, Suite 207, Madison 53703; 310 West Wisconsin Avenue, Suite 950, Milwaukee 53203.

U.S. Senator
FEINGOLD

Russell D. Feingold (Dem.)

Born Janesville, March 2, 1953; 2 children. Graduate Janesville Craig H.S. 1971; B.A. with honors (Phi Beta Kappa) UW-Madison 1975; B.A. in law with first-class honors Oxford U. (Rhodes Scholar, Magdalen Coll.) 1977; J.D. with honors Harvard U. Law Sch. 1979. Former practicing attorney 1979-85; visiting professor Beloit Coll. 1985. Member: Wis. and Dane Co. Democratic Parties; Amer. Bar Assn., State Bar of Wis., and Dane Co. Bar Assn.; Phi Beta Kappa; Amer. Assn. of Rhodes Scholars. Recipient: ABATE of Wis., Inc.'s Award 1994-1996; Concord Coalition *Deficit Reduction Honor Roll* 1993-95, 1997-2004, and *Deficit Hawk Award* 1994 and 1997; Long Term Care Campaign *Claude Pepper Legislative Award* 1997; Milwaukee Minority Business and Development Center Award 1992; National Assn. of Police Organizations *Senator of the Year Award* 1997; National Fair Housing Alliance *Award for Excellence* 1996; University of Illinois *Paul H. Douglas Ethics in Government Award* 2000; Rated Best Voting Record in the U.S. Senate by League of Conservation Voters 1994-2000; John F. Kennedy Library Foundation *Profile in Courage Award* 1999; Taxpayers for Common Sense Action *Taxpayer Hero* 1997-98 and 2000-03; Wis. Dept. of Public Instruction *Friend of Education Award* 1992; Wis. State Council of Vietnam Veterans of America *Distinguished Achievement Award* 1993 and *Legislator of the Year* 1997; Consumer Federation of America *Philip Hart Public Service Award* 2003; Panetta Institute *Jefferson-Lincoln Award* 2002; Wis. Primary Health Care Assn. and National Assn. of Community Health Center, Inc. *Community Health Super Hero Award* 2002; Wis. Civil Liberties Union *William Gorham Rice Civil Libertarian of the Year Award* 2001; Friends of Libraries *Public Service Award* 2004; National Association of Consumer Bankruptcy Attorneys *Champion of Consumer Rights* 2004; Rotary International *Polio Eradication Champion* 2004; National Farmers Union *Golden Triangle Award* 2004; National Guard Association of the United States *Charles Dick Medal of Merit* 2004.

State legislative service: Elected to Senate 1982-90 (served through 1/5/93).

Elected to U.S. Senate 1992; reelected 1998. Committee assignments: **109th Congress** — Foreign Relations Committee and its Subcommittees on African Affairs (ranking member), on East Asian and Pacific Affairs, and on European Affairs; Budget Committee; Judiciary Committee and its Subcommittees (as of 108th Congress) on Administrative Oversight and the Courts, on Antitrust, Competition Policy and Consumer Rights, and on Constitution, Civil Rights and Property Rights (ranking member); Special Committee on Aging; Commission on Security and Cooperation in Europe.

Congressional membership: Democracy Policy Committee, Deputy Democratic Whip.

Telephones: Washington office: (202) 224-5323, TTY: (202) 224-1280; District offices: Green Bay: (920) 465-7508; La Crosse: (608) 782-5585; Middleton: (608) 828-1200, TTY: (608) 828-1215; Milwaukee: (414) 276-7282; Wausau: (715) 848-5660.

Internet address: http://feingold.senate.gov; E-mail address: Russ_Feingold@feingold.senate.gov

Voting address: Middleton 53562.

Mailing addresses: Washington office: 506 Hart Senate Office Building, Washington, D.C. 20510-4904; District offices: 1640 Main Street, Green Bay 54302; 425 State Street, Room 225, La Crosse 54601-3341; 1600 Aspen Commons, Room 100, Middleton 53562; 517 East Wisconsin Avenue, Room 408, Milwaukee 53202-4504; 401 5th Street, Room 410, Wausau 54403.

U.S. Representative
RYAN

U.S. Representative
BALDWIN

MEMBERS OF THE U.S. HOUSE OF REPRESENTATIVES

Paul Ryan (Rep.), 1st Congressional District

Born Janesville, 1970; married. Graduate Janesville Craig H.S.; B.A. in economics and political science Miami U. of Ohio 1992. Former aide to U.S. Senator Robert Kasten and employed at family construction business. Member: Janesville Bowmen, Inc.; Ducks Unlimited; St. Mary's Parish; Rock Co. Chapter of Junior Achievement (bd. of dir.).

Elected to U.S. House of Representatives 1998; reelected since 2000. Committee assignments: **109th Congress** — Ways and Means Committee and its Subcommittee on Social Security; Budget Committee (also 106th Congress); Joint Economic Committee (also 108th and 106th Congresses). **106th Congress** — Banking Committee; Government Reform Committee.

Telephones: Washington office: (202) 225-3031; District offices: Janesville: (608) 752-4050; Kenosha: (262) 654-1901; Racine: (262) 637-0510; Toll free: (888) 909-7926; Internet address: http://www.house.gov/ryan/

Voting address: Janesville 53547.

Mailing addresses: Washington office: 1113 Longworth House Office Building, Washington, D.C. 20515; District offices: 20 South Main Street, Suite 10, Janesville 53545; 5712 7th Avenue, Kenosha 53140; 304 6th Street, Racine 53403.

1st Congressional District: Kenosha, Milwaukee (part), Racine, Rock (part), Walworth, and Waukesha (part) Counties. (For detailed description, see Section 3.11, Wisconsin Statutes.)

Tammy Baldwin (Dem.), 2nd Congressional District

Born Madison, February 11, 1962. Graduate Madison West H.S.; B.A. in mathematics and government, Smith College (MA) 1984; J.D. UW-Madison 1989. Former practicing attorney, 1989-92. Member: American Civil Liberties Union of Wisconsin; Democratic Parties of Dane County and Wisconsin; Madison NAACP; State Bar of Wis. Madison City Council 1986; Dane Co. Board 1986-94.

State legislative service: Elected to Assembly 1992-96 (served until January 4, 1999).

Elected to U.S. House of Representatives 1998; reelected since 2000. Committee assignments: **109th Congress** — Energy and Commerce Committee.

Telephones: Washington office: (202) 225-2906; District offices: Beloit: (608) 362-2800; Madison: (608) 258-9800. Internet address: http://www.house.gov/baldwin/

Voting address: Madison 53703.

Mailing addresses: Washington office: 1022 Longworth House Office Building, Washington, D.C. 20515-4902; District offices: 400 E. Grand Avenue, Suite 402, Beloit 53511; 10 East Doty Street, Suite 405, Madison 53703.

2nd Congressional District: Columbia, Dane, Green, Jefferson (part), Rock (part), Sauk (part), and Walworth (part) Counties. (For detailed description, see Section 3.12, Wisconsin Statutes.)

U.S. Representative
KIND

U.S. Representative
MOORE

Ron Kind (Dem.), 3rd Congressional District

Born La Crosse, March 16, 1963; married; 2 children. Graduate Logan H.S.; B.A. Harvard U. 1985; M.A. London School of Economics (England); J.D. U. of Minnesota Law School 1990. Attorney. Former La Crosse County assistant district attorney and State of Wisconsin special prosecutor. Member: U.S. Supreme Court Bar; State Bar of Wis. and La Crosse Co. Bar Assn.; Assn. of State Prosecutors; Democratic Party; Wis. Harvard Club (bd. of dir.); Boys and Girls Club of La Crosse (bd. of dir.); Coulee Council on Alcohol and Other Drug Abuse (bd. of dir.); Moose Club; Optimist Club.

Elected to U.S. House of Representatives 1996; reelected since 1998. Committee assignments: **109th Congress** — Budget Committee (also 108th Congress); Education and the Workforce Committee (since 105th Congress); Resources Committee (since 105th Congress). Congressional memberships: New Democrat Coalition (co-chair); Upper Mississippi River Task Force (founder); Rural Health Care Coalition; Congressional Sportsmen's Caucus; Human Rights Caucus; Native American Caucus; Renewable Energy and Energy Efficiency Caucus. House Leadership: Chief Deputy Whip.

Telephones: Washington office: (202) 225-5506; District offices: Eau Claire: (715) 831-9214; La Crosse: (608) 782-2558; Toll free: (888) 442-8040; TTY: (888) 880-9180.

Internet address: http://www.house.gov/kind/

E-mail address: ron.kind@mail.house.gov

Voting address: La Crosse 54603.

Mailing addresses: Washington office: 1406 Longworth House Office Building, Washington, D.C. 20515-4906; District offices: 131 S. Barstow Street, Suite 301, Eau Claire 54701; 205 5th Avenue South, Suite 226, La Crosse 54601.

3rd Congressional District: Buffalo, Clark (part), Crawford, Dunn, Eau Claire, Grant, Iowa, Jackson, Juneau, La Crosse, Lafayette, Monroe, Pepin, Pierce, Richland, St. Croix, Sauk, Trempealeau, and Vernon Counties. (For detailed description, see Section 3.13, Wisconsin Statutes.)

Gwendolynne S. Moore (Dem.), 4th Congressional District

Born Racine, April 18, 1951; 3 children. Graduate North Division H.S. (Milwaukee); B.A. in political science, Marquette U. 1978; certification in credit union management, Milwaukee Area Technical College 1983. Former housing officer with Wisconsin Housing and Economic Development Authority; development specialist Milwaukee City Development; program and planning analyst with Wisconsin Departments of Employment Relations and Health and Social Services. Member: National Black Caucus of State Legislators; National Conference of State Legislatures' Host Committee, Milwaukee 1995; National Black Caucus of State Legislators – Host Committee (chair), 1997; Wisconsin Legislative Black and Hispanic Caucus (chair since 1997).

State legislative service: Elected to Assembly 1988 and 1990; elected to Senate 1992, 1996, and 2000. Senate President Pro Tempore 1997, 1995 (eff. 7/15/96).

Elected to U.S. House of Representatives 2004. Committee assignments: **109th Congress** — Financial Services Committee and its Subcommittees on Domestic and International Monetary Policy, Trade and Technology, on Financial Institutions and Consumer Credit, and on Oversight and Investigations.

Telephones: Washington office: (202) 225-4572; District office: Milwaukee: (414) 297-1140.

Internet address: www.house.gov/gwenmoore

Voting address: 4043 North 19th Place, Milwaukee 53209.

Mailing addresses: Washington office: 1408 Longworth House Office Building, Washington, D.C. 20515-4904; District office: 219 N. Milwaukee Street, Suite 3A, Milwaukee 53202-5818.

4th Congressional District: Milwaukee County (part): consisting of the Village of West Milwaukee; the Cities of Cudahy, Milwaukee, St. Francis, South Milwaukee, and West Allis (part). (For detailed description, see Section 3.14, Wisconsin Statutes.)

U.S. Representative
SENSENBRENNER

U.S. Representative
PETRI

F. James Sensenbrenner, Jr. (Rep.), 5th Congressional District

Born Chicago, June 14, 1943; married; 2 children. Graduate Milwaukee Country Day School 1961; A.B. Stanford U. 1965; J.D. UW-Madison Law School 1968. Attorney. Former assistant to State Senate Majority Leader Jerris Leonard and to U.S. Congressman Arthur Younger. Member: State Bar of Wis.; Friends of the Museum, Milwaukee County; Riveredge Nature Center; American Philatelic Society; Waukesha Co. Republican Party. Former member: Whitefish Bay Jaycees; Shorewood Men's Club.

State legislative service: Elected to Assembly 1968-74; elected to Senate in April 1975 special election and reelected 1976. Assistant Minority Leader 1977.

Elected to U.S. House of Representatives 1978; reelected since 1980. Committee assignments: **109th Congress** — Judiciary Committee (chp., also mbr. since 96th Congress). **106th Congress** — Science Committee (chp., also mbr. since 97th Congress). **103rd Congress** — House Select Committee on Narcotics Abuse and Control (since 100th Congress). **96th Congress** — Standards of Official Conduct Committee.

Telephones: Washington office: (202) 225-5101; District office: (262) 784-1111; Toll free: (800) 242-1119.

Internet address: http://www.house.gov/sensenbrenner/

E-mail address: sensenbrenner@mail.house.gov

Voting address: N76 W14726 North Point Drive, Menomonee Falls 53051-0186.

Mailing addresses: Washington office: 2449 Rayburn House Office Building, Washington, D.C. 20515-4905; District office: 120 Bishops Way, Room 154, Brookfield 53005-6294.

5th Congressional District: Jefferson (part), Ozaukee, Milwaukee (part) Counties: consisting of the Villages of Bayside (part), Brown Deer, Fox Point, River Hills, Shorewood, and Whitefish Bay; the Cities of Glendale, Wauwatosa, and West Allis (part); Washington and Waukesha (part) Counties. (For detailed description, see Section 3.15, Wisconsin Statutes.)

Thomas E. Petri (Rep.), 6th Congressional District

Born Marinette, May 28, 1940; married; 1 child. Graduate Goodrich H.S.; B.A. Harvard College 1962; J.D. Harvard Law School 1965. Attorney. Former Peace Corps volunteer; White House aide.

State legislative service: Elected to Senate 1972 and 1976.

Elected to U.S. House of Representatives in April 1979 special election; reelected since 1980. Committee assignments: **109th Congress** — Education and the Workforce Committee (vice chp., mbr. since 96th Congress) and its Subcommittee on 21st Century Competitiveness; Transportation and Infrastructure Committee (vice chp., mbr. since 98th Congress) and its Subcommittees on Highways, Transit and Pipelines (chp.); on Aviation; and on Railroads.

Telephones: Washington office: (202) 225-2476; District offices: Fond du Lac: (920) 922-1180; Oshkosh: (920) 231-6333; Toll free: (800) 242-4883.

Internet address: http://www.house.gov/petri/welcome.htm

Voting address: (Town of Empire) N5329 DeNeveu Lane, Fond du Lac 54935.

Mailing addresses: Washington office: 2462 Rayburn House Office Building, Washington, D.C. 20515-4906; District offices: 490 West Rolling Meadows Drive, Suite B, Fond du Lac 54937; 2390 State Road 44, Suite B, Oshkosh 54904.

6th Congressional District: Adams, Calumet (part), Dodge, Fond du Lac, Green Lake, Jefferson (part), Manitowoc, Marquette, Outagamie (part), Sheboygan, Waushara, and Winnebago Counties. (For detailed description, see Section 3.16, Wisconsin Statutes.)

U.S. Representative
OBEY

U.S. Representative
GREEN

David R. Obey (Dem.), 7th Congressional District

Born October 3, 1938; married. Graduate St. James Grade School; Wausau East H.S.; B.S. UW-Madison 1960; M.A. UW-Madison 1963. Former real estate broker; worker in family-owned supper club and motel.

State legislative service: Elected to Assembly 1962-68. Asst. Minority Leader 1967, 1969.

Elected to U.S. House of Representatives in April 1969 special election; reelected since 1970. Committee assignments: **109th Congress** — Appropriations Committee (ranking mbr., chp. 103rd Congress, mbr. since 91st Congress), *ex officio* mbr. of all its subcommittees including its Subcommittee on Labor, Health and Human Services, and Education (ranking mbr.).

Telephones: Washington office: (202) 225-3365; District offices: Superior: (715) 398-4426; Wausau: (715) 842-5606.

Voting address: 1212 Grand Avenue, No. 32, Wausau 54403.

Mailing addresses: Washington office: 2314 Rayburn House Office Building, Washington, D.C. 20515-4907; District offices: 1401 Tower Avenue, Suite 307, Superior 54880-1572; Federal Building, 401 Fifth Street, Suite 406A, Wausau 54403-5473.

7th Congressional District: Ashland, Barron, Bayfield, Burnett, Chippewa, Clark (part), Douglas, Iron, Langlade (part), Lincoln, Marathon, Oneida (part), Polk, Portage, Price, Rusk, Sawyer, Taylor, Washburn, and Wood Counties. (For detailed description, see Section 3.17, Wisconsin Statutes.)

Mark A. Green (Rep.), 8th Congressional District

Born Boston, Mass., June 1, 1960; married; 3 children. Graduate Abbot Pennings H.S., De Pere; B.A. UW-Eau Claire 1983; J.D. UW-Madison 1987. Attorney. Member: State Bar of Wis.; Brown Co. Junior Achievement Senior Advisory Bd.; Friends of the Wildlife Sanctuary; National Railroad Museum (hon.). Former member: Brown Co. Taxpayers Assn. (dir.); Heritage Hill Foundation (dir.); Downtown Green Bay Kiwanis; Green Bay School-Business Partnership Council; Packerland Optimist Club; St. Matthew's Parish Pastoral Council; Brown Co. Home Builders Assn.; World Teach Project (teacher in Kenya). Recipient: American Farm Bureau Federation *Friend of the Farm Bureau;* Americans for Tax Reform *Hero of the Taxpayer Award;* Citizens Against Government Waste *Taxpayer Hero;* Seniors Coalition *Senior Legislative Achievement Award;* National Federation of Independent Businesses *Guardian of Small Business Award;* Christian Coalition *Friend of the Family Award;* U.S. Chamber of Commerce *Spirit of Enterprise Award;* State Medical Society of Wis. *Health Leadership;* Independent Business Administration *Wisconsin Award;* National Rifle Assn. *Defender of Justice;* Wis. Counties Assn. *Outstanding Legislator;* Wis. Farm Bureau Volunteers for Agriculture *Friend of Agriculture;* Tavern League of Wis. *Legislator of the Year.*

State legislative service: Elected to Assembly 1992-96. Majority Caucus Chairperson 1994-98. Committee on Judiciary (chp., 1995-1998); American Legislative Exchange Council (state chm. 1995-96).

Elected to U.S. House of Representatives 1998; reelected since 2000. Assistant Majority Whip. Committee assignments: **109th Congress** — International Relations Committee and its Subcommittees on Africa, Global Human Rights and International Relations, and on Oversight and Investigations; Judiciary Committee and its Subcommittees on Commercial and Administrative Law, on Crime, Terrorism and Homeland Security, and on the Constitution. Congressional memberships: Missing and Exploited Children Caucus; Rural Caucus; Pro-Life Caucus; Sportsmen's Caucus; Privacy Caucus; Great Lakes Task Force; Cancer Caucus; Autism Caucus; Human Rights Caucus; Produce Caucus; Community Solutions and Initiatives Coalition.

Telephones: Washington office: (202) 225-5665; District offices: Green Bay: (920) 437-1954; Appleton: (920) 380-0061; Toll free: (800) 773-8579.

E-mail address: mark.green@mail.house.gov Internet address: http://www.house.gov/markgreen/

Voting address: Oneida 54155.

Mailing addresses: District offices: 700 East Walnut Street, Green Bay 54301; 609-A West College Avenue, Appleton 54911; Washington office: 1314 Longworth House Office Building, Washington, D.C. 20515-4908.

8th Congressional District: Brown, Calumet (part), Door, Florence, Forest, Kewaunee, Langlade (part), Marinette, Menominee, Oconto, Oneida (part), Outagamie (part), Shawano, Vilas, and Waupaca Counties. (For detailed description, see Section 3.18, Wisconsin Statutes.)

CONGRESSIONAL DISTRICTS
Enacted by 2001 Wisconsin Act 46

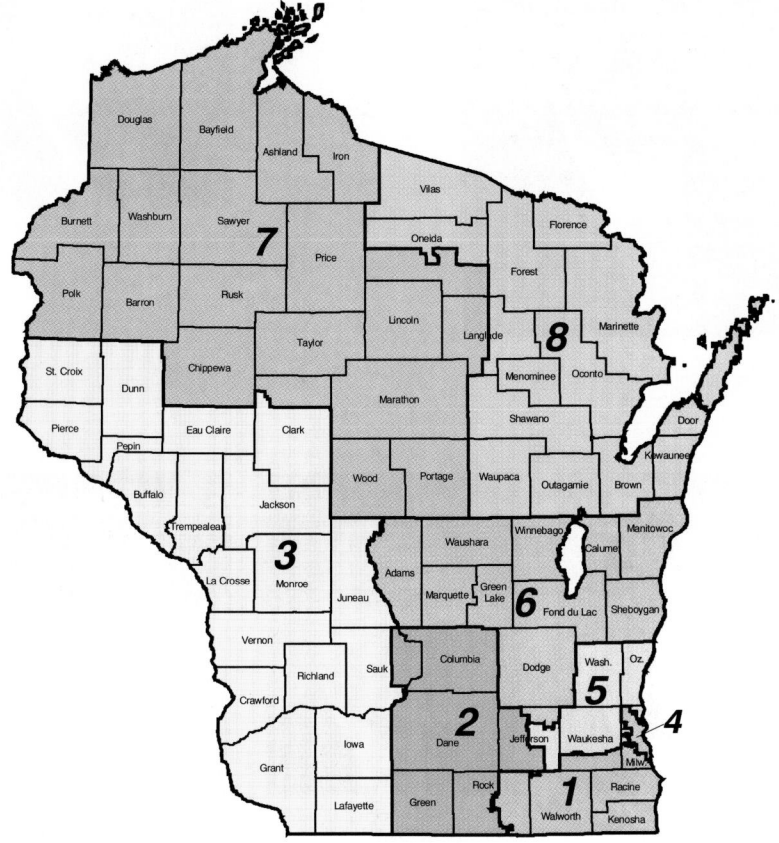

See Chapter 3, *2001-2002 Wisconsin Statutes,* for detail maps.

2000 POPULATION OF CONGRESSIONAL DISTRICTS

District	Population*	Deviation	Pct. Dev.	Minority Population Hispanic	Other
Cong. Dist. 1	670,458	−1	−0.00	37,888	46,517
Cong. Dist. 2	670,457	−2	−0.00	22,644	51,078
Cong. Dist. 3	670,462	3	0.00	6,193	19,916
Cong. Dist. 4	670,458	−1	−0.00	75,285	257,364
Cong. Dist. 5	670,458	−1	−0.00	14,906	25,632
Cong. Dist. 6	670,459	0	0.00	15,410	24,227
Cong. Dist. 7	670,462	3	0.00	5,823	27,102
Cong. Dist. 8	670,461	2	0.00	14,772	37,288
TOTAL	5,363,675			192,921	489,124

*Wisconsin's 8 congressional districts were established by 2001 Wisconsin Act 46, based on the 2000 U.S. Census of Population. The ideal size of each district is 670,459.

Source: U.S. Department of Commerce, Census Bureau, P.L. 94-171 Redistricting File, March 2001.

18

President
A. LASEE

President Pro Tempore
ZIEN

Majority Leader
SCHULTZ

Assistant Majority Leader
KEDZIE

Minority Leader
ROBSON

Assistant Minority Leader
HANSEN

Chief Clerk
MARCHANT

Sergeant at Arms
BLAZEL

2005 STATE ASSEMBLY OFFICERS

Speaker
GARD

Speaker Pro Tempore
FREESE

Majority Leader
HUEBSCH

Assistant Majority Leader
J. FITZGERALD

Minority Leader
KREUSER

Assistant Minority Leader
RICHARDS

Chief Clerk
FULLER

Sergeant at Arms
SKINDRUD

1st SENATE DISTRICT

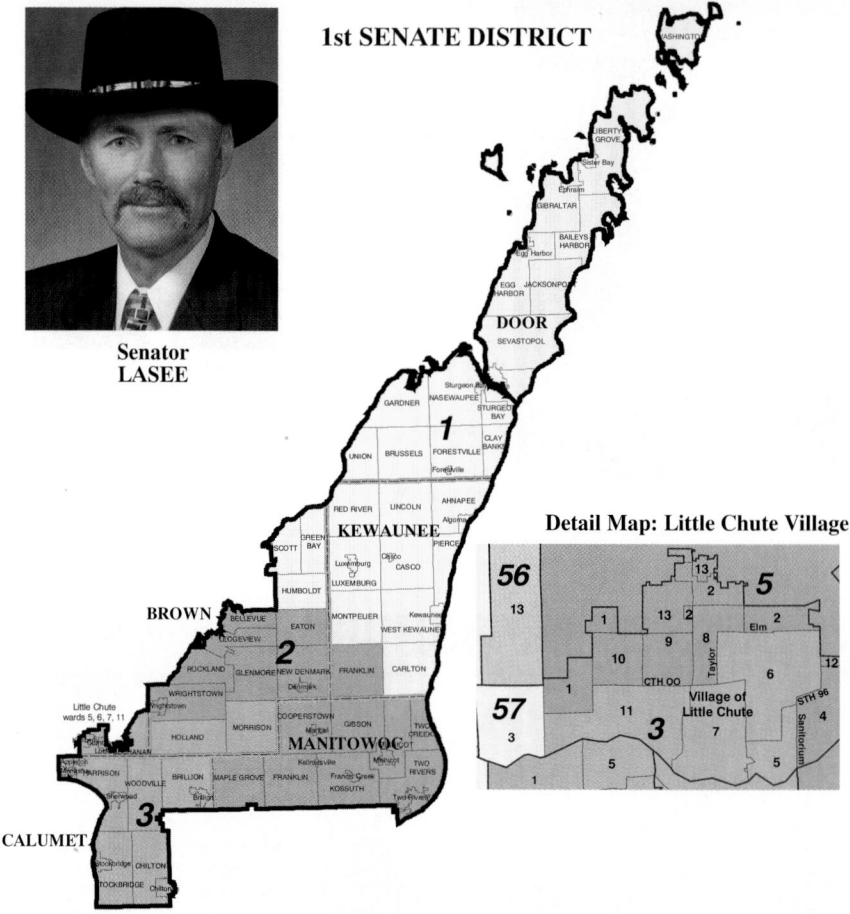

**Senator
LASEE**

Detail Map: Little Chute Village

Alan J. Lasee (Rep.), 1st Senate District

Born Town of Rockland, Brown County, July 30, 1937; married; 6 children. Attended St. Norbert H.S. Raises exotic animals including llamas, camels, miniature donkeys, and fainting goats. Former dairy farmer. Member: Brown Co. Farm Bureau (bd. of dir. 1972-75); Way-Morr Lions (pres. 1991-92, dir. 1976); Brown Co. Republican Party; Wisconsin Towns Assn. Former Brown Co. 4-H leader (licensed gun safety instructor). Town supervisor (1971-73); town chair. (1973-82, 1985-2000).

Elected to Assembly 1974. Elected to Senate in May 1977 special election; reelected since 1978. President of the Senate 2005, 2003. President Pro Tempore 1995 (eff. 1/5/95 to 6/13/96), 1993 (eff. 4/20/93). Minority Caucus Chairperson 1987, 1981, and 1979. Biennial committee assignments: **2005** — Campaign Finance Reform and Ethics; Organization (eff. 5/9/01); Jt. Com. on Employment Relations (co-chp. and mbr. since 2003); Jt. Com. on Legislative Organization (co-chp., mbr. since 5/9/01); Jt. Legis. Council (co-chp. and mbr. since 2003); State and Federal Relations; Disablility Bd.; Transportation Projects Commission (also 2003, 2001, 1997, vice chp. 1/93 to 6/96, mbr. 1987). **2001** — Insurance, Tourism, and Transportation; Labor and Agriculture. **1999** — Agriculture, Environmental Resources and Campaign Finance Reform; Insurance, Tourism, Transportation and Corrections. **1997** — Transportation, Agriculture and Rural Affairs (chp. eff. 4/21/98); State Government Operations and Corrections (eff. 4/21/98, also mbr. 1/95 to 6/96, also 1993); Agriculture and Environmental Resources (1/15/97 to 4/20/98); Human Resources, Labor, Tourism, Veterans and Military Affairs (eff. 4/21/98, also 1995, 1993); Council on Highway Safety (also 1995); Joint Legislative Council (eff. 4/21/98); Rustic Roads Bd. (eff. 4/21/98). **1995** — Agriculture, Transportation, Utilities and Financial Institutions; Transportation, Agriculture and Local Affairs (chp. 1/95 to 6/96); State Capitol and Executive Residence Bd. (mbr. since 1983); Legis. Coun. and its Com. on Federally Tax-Exempt Lands; Rustic Roads Bd. (also 1993). **1993** — Transportation, Agriculture, Local and Rural Affairs (mbr. and chp.); Jt. Com. on Audit (also 1991); Transportation, Agriculture, Tourism and Veterans Affairs (mbr. and vice chp.).

Telephone: Office: (608) 266-3512; District: (920) 336-8830.

E-mail address: Sen.Lasee@legis.state.wi.us

Voting address: (Town of Rockland) 2259 Lasee Road, De Pere 54115.

Mailing address: Office: Room 219 South, State Capitol, P.O. Box 7882, Madison 53707-7882.

**Representative
BIES**

**Representative
LASEE**

**Representative
OTT**

Garey Bies (Rep.), 1st Assembly District

Born Manitowoc, October 26, 1946; married; 4 children. Graduate Lincoln H.S., Manitowoc; Associate Degree Northeastern Technical College 1982. Full-time legislator. Former chief deputy sheriff, deputy sheriff, Door County Sheriff's Dept. 30 years, and project director for Door/Kewaunee Drug Task Force, 1990-2000. Navy veteran, 1964-69. Member: American Legion Post 527, 1970-present; Knights of Columbus, 1970-present; Northern Door Child Care (bd. dir.); St. Rosalia Catholic Church (former trustee and council member); Sturgeon Bay Rotary; volunteer guardian for disabled adults. Former member: Boy Scouts of America (cubmaster, scout master); Door/Kewaunee Selective Service Bd. (chp., also 2003); Door Co. Highway Safety Com.; Door Co. Local Emergency Planning Com.; Help of Door County (bd. dir.)

Elected to Assembly 2000; reelected since 2002. Biennial committee assignments: **2005** — Corrections and the Courts (chp., also 2003); Highway Safety (vice chp. since 2001); Natural Resources (also 2003); Veterans Affairs; Gov's Coun. on Highway Safety (since 2001); Wis. Sentencing Comn. (since 2003); Leg. Coun. Com. on State and Tribal Relations. **2003** — Tourism (vice chp.); Veterans and Military Affairs. **2001** — Agriculture; Children and Families; Criminal Justice; State Affairs; Tourism and Recreation.

Telephone: Office: (608) 266-5350; (888) 482-0001 (toll free); District: (920) 854-2811.

E-mail address: Rep.Bies@legis.state.wi.us

Voting address: 2520 Settlement Road, Sister Bay 54234.

Mailing address: Office: Room 125 West, State Capitol, P.O. Box 8952, Madison 53708.

Frank G. Lasee (Rep.), 2nd Assembly District

Born Oceanside, CA, December 11, 1961; 2 children. B.A. UW-Green Bay 1986. Small business owner. Member: Brown Co. Republican Party. Former member: Optimists (dir.); Rotary Club; Telecommunications Professionals of Wisconsin (dir.). Ledgeview Town Board (chair) 1993-97.

Elected to Assembly 1994; reelected since 1996. Biennial committee assignments: **2005** — Government Operations and Spending Limitations (chp. since 2003); Criminal Justice and Homeland Security. **2003** — Corrections and the Courts; Criminal Justice (since 1999); Insurance (mbr., chp. 1999); Ways and Means (mbr. since 1997). **2001** — Tax and Spending Limitations (chp. since 1995); Health (mbr. since 1995). **1999** — Legislative Council Committee on Dental Care Access. **1997** — Income Tax Review (chp.); Criminal Justice and Corrections; Insurance, Securities and Corporate Policy (also 1995); Legislative Council Committee on Telemedicine Issues. **1995** — Legislative Council Committee on Information Brokering, Computer Technology and Related Issues.

Telephone: Office: (608) 266-9870; (888) 534-0002 (toll free); District: (920) 406-9488.

E-mail address: Rep.Lasee@legis.state.wi.us

Voting address: 2380 Bluestone Place, Bellevue 54311.

Mailing address: Office: Room 105 West, State Capitol, P.O. Box 8952, Madison 53708.

Al Ott (Alvin R. Ott) (Rep.), 3rd Assembly District

Born Green Bay, June 19, 1949; married; 4 children. Graduate Brillion H.S.; UW-Madison Farm and Industry Short Course, 1968; 1st Class of Participants in WI Rural Leadership Program, 1986. Former agri-business salesman, owner/operator of independent agri-business, tenant dairy farmer, and cash crop farmer. Member: Forest-Ever Ready 4-H Club (adult leader); Republican Party of Wis.; Calumet Co. Agricultural Assn.; Calumet Co. Farm Progress 1993 Exec. Com. (chm.). Calumet Co. Board 1973-92 (vice chp.), chp. of its Ag/Extension Educ. Com. and vice chp. of its Land Conservation and Planning/Zoning Coms.; Wis. Land Conservation Bd. 1984-88 (secy.).

Elected to Assembly since 1986. Biennial committee assignments: **2005** — Agriculture (chp. since 1995, mbr. 1989, 1987); Natural Resources (mbr. since 1995); Rural Development (mbr. since 2003); Transportation (mbr. since 2003). **2001** — Energy and Utilities; Environment; World Dairy Center Auth. (also 1999). **1999** — Conservation and Land Use; Consumer Affairs (also 1997); Utilities. **1997** — Government Operations (also 1995); Legis. Coun. Com. on Utility Public Benefit Prog. **1995** — Environment and Utilities; Rural Affairs (also 1991); Legis. Coun. Com. on Recycling. **1993** — Agriculture, Forestry and Rural Affairs (ranking minority mbr.); Environmental Resources; Labor and Job Training; Legis. Coun. Com. on Protection of Rural Resources. **1991** — Agriculture, Aquaculture and Forestry.

Telephone: Office: (608) 266-5831; (888) 534-0003 (toll free); District: (920) 989-1240.

E-mail address: Rep.Ott@legis.state.wi.us

Voting address: (Town of Brillion) W2168 Campground Road, Forest Junction 54123-0112.

Mailing address: Office: Room 323 North, State Capitol, P.O. Box 8953, Madison 53708; District: P.O. Box 112, Forest Junction 54123-0112.

2nd SENATE DISTRICT

**Senator
COWLES**

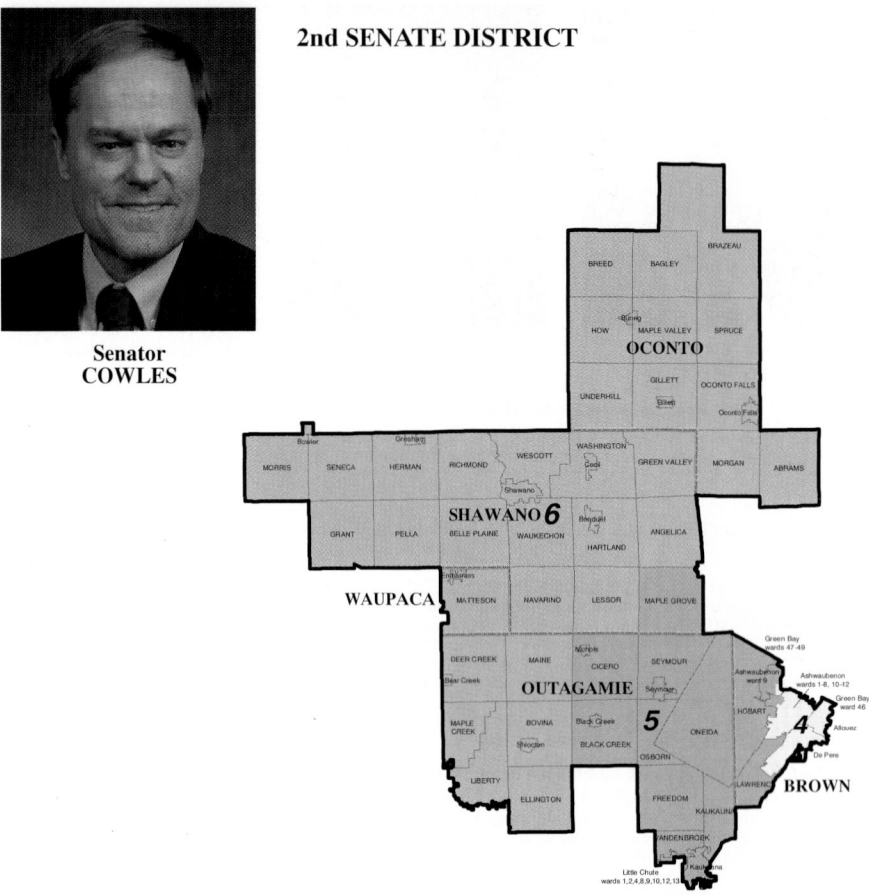

See Green Bay Area Detail Map on p. 96

Robert L. Cowles (Rep.), 2nd Senate District

Born Green Bay, July 31, 1950. B.S. UW-Green Bay 1975; graduate work UW-Green Bay. Full-time legislator. Former director of an alternative energy division for a communications construction company. Member: Allouez Kiwanis; Brown Co. Taxpayers Alliance; Prevent Blindness Wisconsin – NE Wis. Chapter; Friends of the Fox River Trail.

Elected to Assembly 1982-86 (resigned 4/21/87); elected to Senate in April 1987 special election; reelected since 1988. Biennial Senate committee assignments: **2005** — Energy, Utilities and Information Technology (chp.); Jt. Com. on Audit (also 1993, 2003); Jt. Com. on Finance (also 1993-99). **2003** — Energy and Utilities (chp.); Higher Education and Tourism; Building Comn. **2001** — Joint Com. for Review of Administrative Rules (also 1987 to 4/20/93); Review of Administrative Rules; Environmental Resources; Health, Utilities, Veterans and Military Affairs. **1999** — Jt. Survey Com. on Tax Exemptions; Joint Legislative Council (also 1997). **1997** — Environmental Education Bd. (since 1991). **1995** — Environment and Energy (chp. since 4/20/93). **1993** — Urban Affairs, Financial Institutions and Environmental Resources (mbr. and vice chp. to 4/20/93); Judiciary and Consumer Affairs (mbr. to 4/20/93); Legis. Coun. Com. on State Fire Programs (co-chp.). **1991** — Urban Affairs, Environmental Resources and Elections; Legis. Coun. Com. on Energy Resources; Gov.'s Council on Recycling. **1989** — Educational Financing, Higher Education and Tourism; Science, Technology, Communications and Energy; Legis. Coun. Com. on Nonpoint Source Pollution; Low-Level Radioactive Waste Council. **1987** — Economic Development, Financial Institutions and Fiscal Policies; Housing, Government Operations and Cultural Affairs. Assembly committee assignments: **1987** — Jt. Com. for Review of Administrative Rules (since 1983); Trade, Industry and Small Business. **1985** — Jt. Com. on Debt Management; Energy; Legis. Coun. Com. on Environmental Resource Management. **1983** — Energy and Utilities; Economic Development (eff. 10/25/83); Family and Economic Assistance; Revenue.

Telephone: Office: (608) 266-0484; (800) 334-1465 (toll free); District: (920) 448-5092; Fax: (920) 448-5093.

E-mail address: Sen.Cowles@legis.state.wi.us

Voting address: 300 West St. Joseph Street, Green Bay 54301.

Mailing address: Office: Room 122 South, State Capitol, P.O. Box 7882, Madison 53707-7882.

| Representative | Representative | Representative |
| MONTGOMERY | NELSON | AINSWORTH |

Phil Montgomery (Rep.), 4th Assembly District

Born Hammond, IN, July 7, 1957; married; 2 children. Graduate T.F. North H.S.; B.S. in Business and Commerce, U. of Houston-Downtown, Houston, TX 1988. Former systems engineer. Member: Green Bay Area Drug Alliance (Allocations Com.); Leadership Green Bay Alumni; Ashwaubenon Optimist Club; Waterfront Study Com. (past chp.); Junior Achievement; youth basketball coach.

Elected to Assembly 1998; reelected since 2000. Biennial committee assignments: **2005** — Energy and Utilities (chp., mbr. 2003); Jt. Survey Com. on Tax Exemptions (co-chp.); Housing; Insurance (mbr., chp. 2003); State-Federal Relations. **2003** — Financial Institutions (chp., vice chp. 2001, mbr. since 1999); Electronic Democracy and Government Reform; Health. **2001** — Jt. Com. on Information Policy and Technology; Information Policy and Technology; Personal Privacy (vice. chp.); Judiciary. **1999** — Campaigns and Elections; Family Law; Information Policy; Labor and Employment.

Telephone: Office: (608) 266-5840; District: (920) 496-5953; E-mail address: Rep.Montgomery@legis.state.wi.us

Voting address: 1305 Oak Crest Drive, Ashwaubenon 54313.

Mailing address: Office: Room 129 West, State Capitol, P.O. Box 8953, Madison 53708.

Tom Nelson (Dem.), 5th Assembly District

Born St. Paul, MN, March 3, 1976. Graduate Little Chute H.S. 1994; B.A. Carleton College (Northfield, MN) 1998; M.P.A. Princeton U. (Princeton, NJ) 2004. Full-time legislator. Member: Loaves and Fishes food pantry (bd. mbr.); Christ the King Lutheran Church, ELCA; Outagamie County Democratic Party.

Elected to Assembly 2004. Biennial committee assignments: **2005** — Health; Insurance; Rural Development; Transportation.

Telephone: Office: (608) 266-2418; (888) 534-0005 (toll free); District: (920) 759-7404.

E-mail address: Rep.Nelson@legis.state.wi.us

Voting address: 301 1/2 Fillmore, Kaukauna 54130.

Mailing address: Office: Room 418 North, State Capitol, P.O. Box 8953, Madison 53708.

John H. Ainsworth (Rep.), 6th Assembly District

Born Shawano Co., September 21, 1940; married; 4 children, 8 grandchildren. Graduate Shawano H.S. Dairy farmer. Member: Shawano Co. Republican Party; Farm Bureau Federation (dir. 1975-77, 1984-90); Midwest Livestock Producers Co-op. (dir. 1975-77, 1984-90); Shawano Co. Farm Bureau (pres. 1972-74); Wis. Beef Council (dir. 1987-89); Federal Land Bank Co-op. (dir. 1974-77); Shawano Co. Dairy Promotion (pres. 1982-84).

Elected to Assembly since 1990. Biennial committee assignments: **2005** — Transportation (chp. since 2001); Agriculture (mbr. since 1995); Forestry (vice chp. 2003); Highway Safety (since 2001); Jt. Legis. Coun. **2003** — Property Rights and Land Management; Rural Economic Development Bd. (since 1997); Legis. Coun. Com. on Recodification of Town Highway Statutes (co-chp.). **2001** — Rural Affairs and Forestry (chp. since 1999); Ways and Means (vice chp., mbr. 1999). **1999** — Conservation and Land Use; Legis. Coun. Coms. on Recodification of Operating While Intoxicated and Safety Laws Pertaining to Motor Vehicle, All-Terrain Vehicle, Boat or Snowmobile Operation, on State Tribal Relations. **1997** — Rural Affairs (chp., also 1995); Land Use (vice chp.); Children and Families; Education (also 1995); Leg. Coun. Com. on Conservation Laws Enforcement and American Indian Study Com. **1995** — Aging and Long-Term Care; Natural Resources (since 1991); Legis. Coun. Com. on the School Aid Formula. **1993** — Agriculture, Forestry and Rural Affairs; Trade, Science and Technology (ranking minority mbr.). **1991** — Agriculture, Aquaculture and Forestry; Public Health and Regulation; Small Business and Education or Training for Employment; Legis. Coun. Coms. on Private Forest Land Program (secy.), on Child Custody, Support and Visitation Laws.

Telephone: Office: (608) 266-3097; (888) 529-0006 (toll free); District: (715) 526-3810.

E-mail address: Rep.Ainsworth@legis.state.wi.us

Voting address: (Town of Waukechon) W6382 Waukechon Road, Shawano 54166.

Mailing address: Office: Room 309 North, State Capitol, P.O. Box 8952, Madison 53708.

3rd SENATE DISTRICT

Senator
CARPENTER

See Milwaukee County Detail Map on pp. 92 & 93

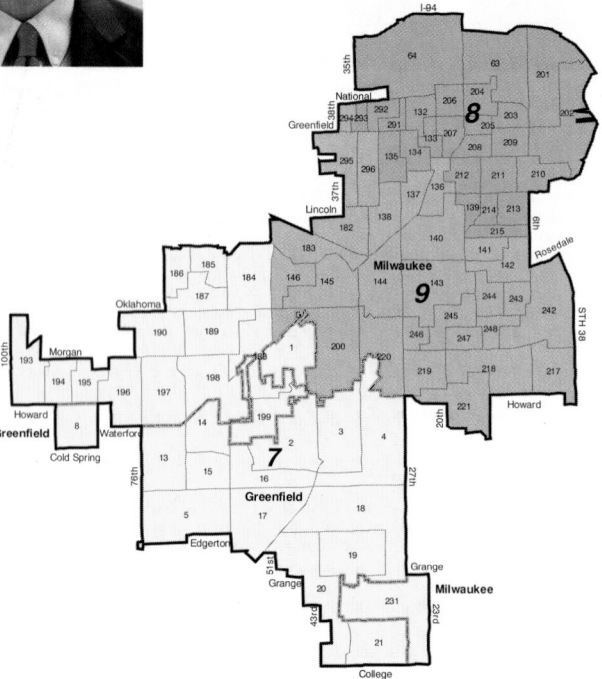

Tim Carpenter (Dem.), 3rd Senate District

Born Milwaukee. Graduate Pulaski H.S.; B.A. UW-Milwaukee; M.A. UW-Madison La Follette Institute. Member: Sierra Club; Jackson Park Neighborhood Assn. Recipient: Environmental Decade *Clean 16 Awards*; Shepherd Express *Legislator of the Year* 2003; Wis. Professional Fire Fighters *Legislator of the Year* 2002.

Elected to Assembly 1984-2000; elected to Senate 2002. Speaker Pro Tempore 1993. Biennial Senate committee assignments: **2005** — Health, Children, Families, Aging and Long-Term Care (also 2003); Labor and Election Process Reform; State and Federal Relations; Law Revision Com.; Council on Alcohol and Other Drug Abuse (also 2003). **2003** — Jt. Com. for Review of Administrative Rules (through 5/23/03); Administrative Rules (through 5/23/03); Judiciary, Corrections and Privacy; Council on Migrant Labor. Assembly committee assignments: **2001** — Aging and Long-Term Care (also 1997, 1995); Health (chp. 1991, mbr. since 1987); Public Health (also 1999); State and Local Finance. **1999** — Census and Redistricting; Urban and Local Affairs (also 1985). **1997** — Managed Care. **1995** — Legis. Coun. Com. to Review the Election Process. **1993** — Financial Institutions and Housing; Insurance, Securities and Corporate Policy; Joint Legislative Council and co-chp. of its Com. on Communication of Governmental Proceedings; Rules. **1991** — Elections and Constitutional Law (chp. 1989); Financial Institutions and Insurance (mbr. 1989, 1987, vice chp. 1985); Judiciary; Labor (since 1985); Public Health and Regulation; Special Com. on Reapportionment (vice chp.); Special Com. on Reform of Health Insurance; Legis. Coun. Com. on Campaign Financing. **1989** — Select Com. on the Census (co-chp.); Environmental Resources and Utilities; Legis. Coun. Coms. on Prenatal Care, on Privacy and Information Technology. **1987** — Elections (vice chp., also 1985); Housing and Securities; Legis. Coun. Com. on Solid Waste Management. **1985** — Economic Development; Transportation.

Telephone: Office: (608) 266-8535; (800) 249-8173 (toll free); Fax: (608) 267-0274; District: (414) 383-9161.

E-mail address: Sen.Carpenter@legis.state.wi.us

Voting address: 2957 South 38th Street, Milwaukee 53215.

Mailing address: Office: Room 126 South, State Capitol, P.O. Box 7882, Madison 53707-7882.

**Representative
KRUSICK**   **Representative
COLÓN**   **Representative
ZEPNICK**

Peggy Krusick (Dem.), 7th Assembly District

Born Milwaukee, Oct. 26, 1956; married; 1 daughter and 1 son. Grad. Milw. Hamilton H.S. 1974; B.A. in political science with honors, certificate in law studies, UW-Milwaukee 1978. Full-time legislator. Former Assembly legislative aide; staff mbr. Governor's Ombudsman Program for the Aging and Disabled. Member: Alliance for Attendance Truancy Abatement Task Force; Governor's State Call to Action Task Force to End Child Abuse and Neglect; Alzheimer's Assn.; Jackson Park Assn.; Wedgewood Park Assn.; Fairview Neighborhood Assn.; St. Gregory the Great Church. Recipient: *Wis. Council of Senior Citizens Award*, 2003; *Coalition of Wis. Aging Groups Award* 1998, 2001; Wis. Environmental Decade *Clean 16 Award* 1995-96; *Assn. of Wis. School Administrators Award* 1991; *Friends of Home Care Award* 1989; Milwaukee Police Assn. *Legislator of the Year Award* 1987.

Elected to Assembly in June 1983 special election; reelected since 1984. Author of 2004 Child Protection and Clergy Abuse Reporting Act; 2004 Child Support Collection Act; 2004 Comprehensive Background Checks for School Bus Drivers Act; 2002 Senior Care Prescription Drug Benefit Prog.; 1998 Caregiver Criminal Background Checks and Abuse Prevention Act; 1998 Nursing Home Resident Protection Act; 1998 Child Abuse Prosecution Act; 1998 Truancy Reform Act; 1996 Anti-Graffiti Act; 1994 Fair Prescription Drug Pricing Act; 1994 Truancy Driver's License Suspension Act; 1993 Welfare Fugitive Arrest Act; 1990 Stolen Goods Recovery Act; 1989 Elder Abuse Fund; 1987 Nursing Home Reform Act; 1985 Youth Suicide Prevention Act. Biennial committee assignments: **2005** — Aging and Long-Term Care (also 2001, 1993-97); Criminal Justice and Homeland Security; Family Law (since 1999).

Telephone: Office: (608) 266-1733; District: (414) 543-0017; E-mail address: Rep.Krusick@legis.state.wi.us

Voting address: 3426 South 69th Street, Milwaukee 53219.

Mailing address: Office: Room 128 North, State Capitol, P.O. Box 8952, Madison 53708.

Pedro Colón (Dem.), 8th Assembly District

Born Ponce, Puerto Rico, April 7, 1968; married; 2 daughters. Graduate Thomas More H.S. (Milwaukee); B.A. Marquette U. 1991; J.D. UW-Madison 1994. Attorney. Member: Wisconsin Hispanic Lawyers Assn.; State Bar of Wis.; National Association of Latino Elected Officials (NALEO).

Elected to Assembly 1998; reelected since 2000. Biennial committee assignments: **2005** — Jt. Com. on Finance; Highway Safety. **2003** — Budget Review (eff. 5/13/03); Corrections and the Courts (also 2001); Criminal Justice (since 1999); Health (also 2001); Ways and Means (resigned 5/13/03); Workforce Development; Migrant Labor Council (since 1999). **2001** — Judiciary. **1999** — Children and Families; Judiciary and Personal Privacy; Urban and Local Affairs.

Telephone: Office: (608) 267-7669; (888) 534-0008 (toll free); District: (414) 384-7522.

E-mail address: Rep.Colon@legis.state.wi.us

Voting address: 338 West Walker Street, Milwaukee 53204.

Mailing address: Office: Room 104 North, State Capitol, P.O. Box 8952, Madison 53708.

Josh Zepnick (Dem.), 9th Assembly District

Born Milwaukee, March 21, 1968; married. Graduate Rufus King H.S. (Milwaukee); B.A. UW-Madison 1990; M.A. Univ. of Minnesota 1998. Full-time legislator. Former project consultant, Milwaukee Jobs Initiative, Milwaukee Community Service Corps, and Urban Economic Development Association of Wisconsin; research associate, Center for Democracy and Citizenship; and aide to State Senator Bob Jauch and Congressman David R. Obey. Member: Jackson Park Neighborhood Assn.; Jackson Park Business Assn.; South Side Business Club. Former member: UFCW Local 1444.

Elected to Assembly 2002; reelected 2004. Biennial committee assignments: **2005** — Energy and Utilities; Financial Institutions (also 2003); Government Operations and Spending Limitations (also 2003); Southeast Wisconsin Freeways; State-Federal Relations. **2003** — Transportation; Workforce Development.

Telephone: Office: (608) 266-1707; (888) 534-0009 (toll free); Home: (414) 727-0841.

E-mail address: Rep.Zepnick@legis.state.wi.us

Voting address: 3173 South 49th Street, Milwaukee 53219

Mailing address: Office: Room 219 North, State Capitol, P.O. Box 8953, Madison 53708.

4th SENATE DISTRICT

Senator TAYLOR

See Milwaukee County Detail Map on pp. 92 & 93

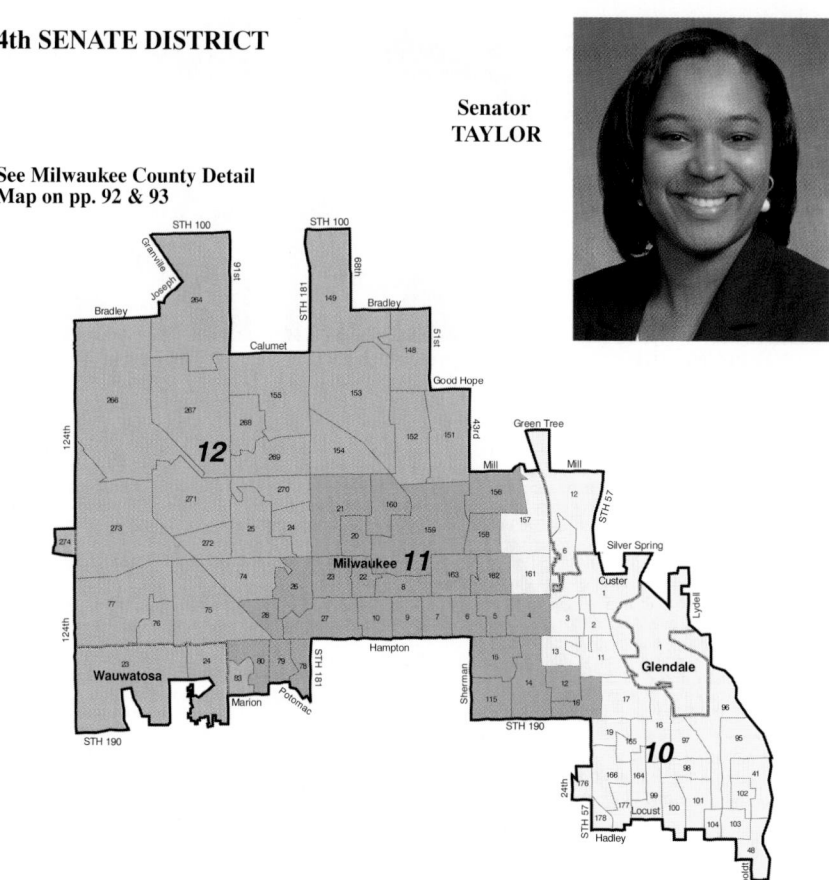

Lena C. Taylor (Dem.), 4th Senate District

Born Milwaukee, July 25, 1966; 1 child. Graduate Rufus King H.S. (Milwaukee) 1984; B.A. in English UW-Milwaukee 1990; J.D. SIU-Carbondale 1993. Attorney for Taylor & Assoc. Law Office and former attorney of Wis. State Public Defender's Office. Member: Democratic Party; NAACP (former exec. bd. mbr.); Alpha Kappa Alpha Sorority, Inc. (former Ivy Leaf rptr., former chair AKA Kids com.). Former member: Merrill Park Assoc.; Daystar (frm. bd. mbr.); West End Development Corp. (former bd. mbr., secy.). Recipient: Career Youth Development *Image Award;* AKA *Trailblazer Award;* Wisconsin Farm Bureau Federation *Friend of Agriculture Award;* Medical College of Wisconsin Award; Wisconsin Builders Association *Friend of the Housing Industry Award;* Milwaukee County Board of Supervisors Citation. Legislative Black and Hispanic Caucus (chp.).

Elected to Assembly in April 2003 special election; elected to Senate 2004. Biennial Senate committee assignments: **2005** — Jt. Com. on Finance; Judiciary, Corrections and Privacy; Wisconsin Housing and Economic Development Authority. Assembly committee assignments: **2003** — Criminal Justice; Economic Development; Financial Institutions; Tourism; Urban and Local Affairs.

Telephone: Office: (608) 266-5810; District: (414) 342-7176.

E-mail address: Sen.Taylor@legis.state.wi.us

Voting address: 4051 North 15th Street, Milwaukee 53209.

Mailing address: Office: Room 3 South, State Capitol, P.O. Box 7882, Madison 53707; District: 3407 West Highland Boulevard, Milwaukee 53208.

Representative
A. WILLIAMS

Representative
FIELDS

Representative
KESSLER

Annette P. Williams (Dem.), 10th Assembly District

Born Belzoni, MS, Jan. 10, 1937; 4 children. Grad. Milw. North Div. H.S.; attended Milw. Area Tech. College 1971-73; B.S. UW-Milwaukee 1975. Full-time legislator. Former mental health assistant, counselor, cashier/clerk, keypunch operator, typist. Lectured at Harvard, Yale, Marquette, Stanford, Johns Hopkins, and Minnesota Universities. Appeared on CBS's 60 Minutes, NBC's Today, ABC's World News, and PBS's MacNeil-Lehrer Report. First African American and first female candidate for Milwaukee County Exec. 1992. Awards: Education Week *Faces of the 20th Century;* UW-Milwaukee *Lifetime Achievement Award* 1998; New York Times – one of 13 innovators who changed education in the 20th century; UW-Milwaukee Alumni Assn.'s *Distinguished Alumnus* 1994; National Black Caucus of State Legislators *President's Award for Distinguished Service* 1990. Received presidential invitation to White House Conference on Parental Choice, January 1989. Auckland Inst. of Technology 1993 Visiting Fellow, Auckland, New Zealand; Scholar in Residence, National Alliance of Black School Educators 1996.

Elected to Assembly since 1980. Longest serving woman legislator in either house. Author of nation's first parents education choice legislation. Biennial committee assignments: **2005** — Education (since 2001); Education Reform (since 1999); Housing. **2003** — Financial Institutions. **2001** — Census and Redistricting (ranking minority mbr. eff. 5/16/01, also 1999). **1999** — State Affairs; Urban and Local Affairs (also 1997); Education Comn. of the States (since 1995).

Telephone: Office: (608) 266-0960; (888) 534-0010 (toll free); District: (414) 374-7474.

E-mail address: Rep.WilliamsA@legis.state.wi.us

Voting address: 3927 North 16th Street, Milwaukee 53206.

Mailing address: Office: Room 113 North, State Capitol, P.O. Box 8953, Madison 53708.

Jason M. Fields (Dem.), 11th Assembly District

Born Milwaukee, January 29, 1974, single. Graduate Milwaukee Lutheran H.S. 1992. Former stockbroker, financial advisor, banker. Member: Prince Hall Masonic Lodge No. 4; Alpha Phi Alpha Fraternity, Inc.; Milwaukee Urban League Young Professionals; National Association of Insurance and Financial Advisors; National Association of Black Accountants. Former member: Democratic Party of Wisconsin (Chairman of 4th Congressional District); Milwaukee County Democrats (2nd District vice chairman); YPM (Young Professionals of Milwaukee).

Elected to Assembly 2004. Biennial committee assignments: **2005** — Economic Development; Financial Institutions; Small Business; Urban and Local Affairs; Ways and Means.

Telephone: Office: (608) 266-3756; (888) 534-0011 (toll free); District: (414) 466-1660.

E-mail address: Rep.Fields@legis.state.wi.us

Voting address: 5686 North 60th Street, Milwaukee 53218

Mailing address: Office: Room 420 North, State Capitol, P.O. Box 8952, Madison 53708.

Frederick P. Kessler (Dem.), 12th Assembly District

Born Milwaukee, January 11, 1940; married; 2 children. Graduate Milwaukee Lutheran H.S. and Capitol Page School 1957; B.A. U. of Wisconsin-Madison 1962; L.L.B. U. of Wisconsin-Madison 1966. Labor arbitrator. Member: Goethe House (vice pres.; former pres.); Milwaukee Chapter ACLU (bd. mbr., former pres.); World Affairs Council of Milwaukee (bd. mbr.); Wis. Academy of Science, Arts & Letters (bd. mbr., secy.); Wis. Bar Assn. (bd. mbr. of ADR section); Industrial Relations Research Assn. (advisory com. mbr.); Democratic Party; DANK (German-American National Congress), Milwaukee chapter (former vice pres.); Milwaukee Donauschwaben; Amnesty International Group 107 (former chairman); Milwaukee Turners. County court judge (Milwaukee Co.) 1972-78; Circuit court judge (Milwaukee Co.) 1978-81, 1986-88.

Elected to Assembly 1960, 1964-70, 2004. Biennial committee assignments: **2005** — Campaigns and Elections; Criminal Justice and Homeland Security; Judiciary; State-Federal Relations. **1971** — Elections (chp., mbr. 1969, 1965); Judiciary (since 1965); Rules. **1961** — Education.

Telephone: Office: (608) 266-5813; (888) 534-0012 (toll free); District: (414) 362-0026.

E-mail address: Rep.Kessler@legis.state.wi.us

Voting address: 11221 West Sanctuary Drive, Milwaukee 53224.

Mailing address: Office: Room 109 North, State Capitol, P.O. Box 8952, Madison 53708.

5th SENATE DISTRICT

**Senator
REYNOLDS**

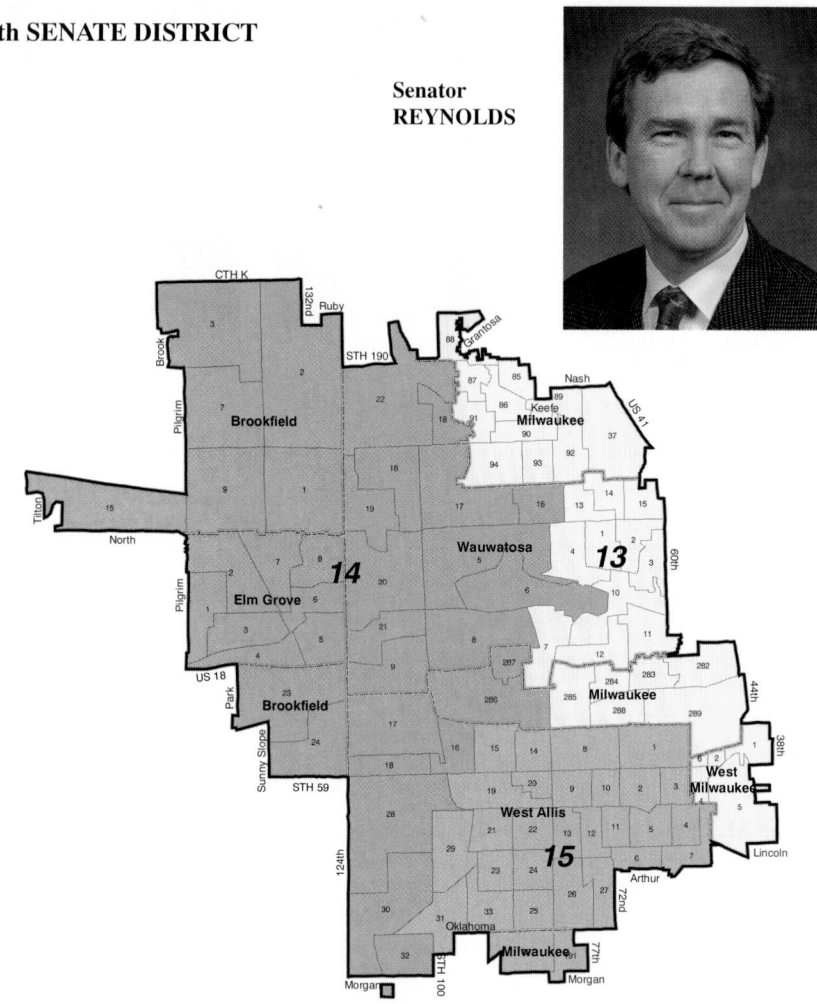

See Milwaukee County Detail Map on pp. 92 & 93

See Waukesha County Detail Map on pp. 94 & 95

Tom Reynolds (Rep.), 5th Senate District

Born Milwaukee, December 16, 1956; married; 5 children. Graduate Nathan Hale H.S. (West Allis) 1975. Self-employed owner of a printing business. Member: West Suburban Chamber of Commerce; Tosa United; Republican Party of Milwaukee County; Republican Party of Waukesha County; Wis. Council on Medical Education and Workforce; Minimum Wage Advisory Coun.; Consumer Protection Advisory Coun. Recipient: Republican Party of Milwaukee County *Tax Cutter of the Year* 2004, 2003; Pro-Life Wisconsin *Legislator of the Year Award* 2004; Wisconsin Grocers Assn. *Friend of Grocers* 2004; Wisconsin Farm Bureau Federation *Friend of Agriculture* 2003-2004; National Federation of Independent Businesses *Guardian of Small Business* 2003-2004.

Elected to Senate 2002. Biennial committee assignments: **2005** — Labor and Election Process Reform (chp.); Housing and Financial Institutions; Job Creation, Economic Development and Consumer Affairs; Jt. Com. for Review of Administrative Rules; State Fair Park Bd.; Legis. Council Spec. Com. on Adoption and Termination of Parental Rights Law. **2003** — Labor, Small Business Development and Consumer Affairs (chp.); Education, Ethics and Elections; Jt. Survey Com. on Retirement Systems; Law Revision Com.

Telephone: Office: (608) 266-2512; (866) 817-6061 (toll free); District: (414) 456-9230.

E-mail address: Sen.Reynolds@legis.state.wi.us

Voting address: 9430 West Schlinger Avenue, West Allis 53214.

Mailing address: Office: Room 306 South, State Capitol, P.O. Box 7882, Madison 53707-7882.

**Representative
CULLEN**

**Representative
VUKMIR**

**Representative
STASKUNAS**

David A. Cullen (Dem.), 13th Assembly District

Born Milwaukee, February 1, 1960; married; 2 children. Graduate John Marshall H.S.; B.S. in secondary ed. UW-Madison 1981; J.D. Marquette U. 1984. Attorney. Member: State Bar of Wis.; Forward Wisconsin, Inc. (bd. of dir.); Democratic Party of Wisconsin. Awards: Wis. Environmental Decade *Clean 16 Award* 2003-04, 1999-2000, 1993-96; Wis. Maternal and Child Health Coalition *Outstanding Elected Official* 1997. Milwaukee School Board 1983-90 (pres. 1987-90).

Elected to Assembly in May 1990 special election; reelected since November 1990. Biennial committee assignments: **2005** — Jt. Com. on Audit (since 1999); Family Law; Insurance (also 2003, 1999); Southeast Wisconsin Freeways. **2003** — Education Reform (since 1999); Judiciary (also mbr. 1995, 1993, vice chp. 1991). **2001** — Economic Development; Comn. on Uniform State Laws (also 1999). **1999** — Campaigns and Elections; Special Com. on the Renovation of Lambeau Field. **1997** — Campaign Finance Reform; Insurance, Securities and Corporate Policy (also 1995, vice chp. 1993); Law Revision Com. (also 1995); Legis. Coun. Com. on Discipline of Health Care Professionals.

Telephone: Office: (608) 267-9836; (888) 534-0013 (toll free); District: (414) 774-4115; Fax: (608) 282-3613.

E-mail address: Rep.Cullen@legis.state.wi.us

Voting address: 2845 North 68th Street, Milwaukee 53210.

Mailing address: Office: Room 216 North, State Capitol, P.O. Box 8952, Madison 53708.

Leah Vukmir (Rep.), 14th Assembly District

Born Milwaukee, April 26, 1958; 2 children. Graduate Brookfield East H.S. 1976; B.S. in nursing Marquette U. 1980; M.S. in nursing UW-Madison 1983. Registered nurse; nationally certified pediatric nurse practitioner. Former research fellow, Wisconsin Policy Research Institute; Past Pres. and Co-founder of Parents Raising Educational Standards in Schools (PRESS). Member: Republican Party of Milwaukee Co., Republican Party of Waukesha Co., Wauwatosa Republican Club; West Allis Speedskating Club (former ASU Speedskating Referee). Former member: Standards and Assessments Subcommittee of Gov. Thompson's Task Force on Education and Learning; English/Language Arts Task Force of Gov. Thompson's Council on Model Academic Standards. Nationally recognized authority and speaker on education issues and educational standards. Recipient: Center for Education Reform's *Unsung Hero Award* 1998; Brookfield East High School *Alumni Achievement Award* 2002.

Elected to Assembly 2002; reelected 2004. Biennial committee assignments: **2005** — Education Reform (chp., vice chp. 2003); Health (vice chp., mbr. 2003); Children and Families (since 2003); Criminal Justice and Homeland Security; Medicaid Reform. **2003** — Criminal Justice; Economic Development.

Telephone: Office: (608) 266-9180; District: (414) 453-0024; E-mail address: Rep.Vukmir@legis.state.wi.us

Voting address: 2544 North 93rd Street, Wauwatosa 53226.

Mailing address: Office: Room 307 North, State Capitol, P.O. Box 8953, Madison 53708.

Anthony J. Staskunas (Dem.), 15th Assembly District

Born West Allis, January 3, 1961; married; 3 children. Graduate West Allis Nathan Hale H.S.; B.A. *cum laude* UW-Milwaukee (Phi Beta Kappa) 1983; J.D. UW-Madison 1986. Legislator and attorney. Member: West Allis Chamber of Commerce (bd. of dir.); West Allis/West Milwaukee Community Alliance Against Drugs; volunteer attorney to West Allis/West Milwaukee Crimestoppers; Wisconsin Exposition Center (bd. dir.); volunteer West Allis Little League coach. Recipient: Wisconsin PTA *Friend of Education Award* 2004; West Allis/West Milwaukee Education Assn. *Friend of Education Award* 2000; Wisconsin Right to Life *Leadership Award* 2000; Independent Business Assn. of Wis. *Freshman of the Session Award* 1997-98 session; West Allis/West Milwaukee Alliance Against Drugs *Outstanding Community Involvement Award;* WMC *Working for Wisconsin Award* 2002, 2000; West Allis Chamber of Commerce *Distinguished Service Award.* Gov.'s Task Force on State and Local Govt. West Allis Board of Health (chm.). West Allis City Council 1988-97 (License and Health Com., chm.).

Elected to Assembly since 1996. Biennial committee assignments: **2005** — Energy and Utilities; Insurance; Judiciary (since 2001 and co-chp. of its 2001 Special Task Force on Identity Theft); Property Rights and Land Management; State Fair Park Bd. (since 2001). **2003** — Corrections and the Courts (also 1999); Criminal Justice (also 2001); Highway Safety; Transportation (also 2001). **2001** — Economic Development. **1999** — Family Law; Judiciary and Personal Privacy; Small Business and Economic Development (also 1997).

Telephone: Office: (608) 266-0620; (888) 534-0015 (toll free); District: (414) 541-9440.

E-mail address: Rep.Staskunas@legis.state.wi.us

Voting address: 2010 South 103rd Court, West Allis 53227.

Mailing address: Room 221 North, State Capitol, P.O. Box 8953, Madison 53708.

6th SENATE DISTRICT

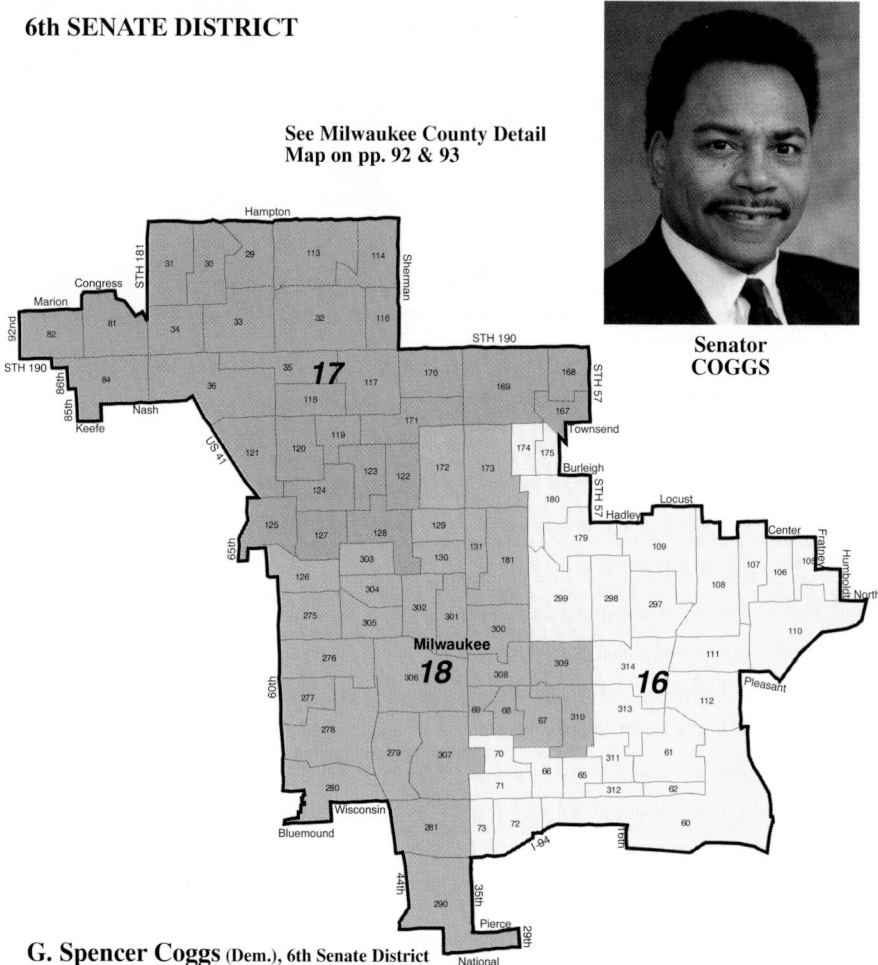

See Milwaukee County Detail
Map on pp. 92 & 93

Senator
COGGS

G. Spencer Coggs (Dem.), 6th Senate District

Born Milwaukee, August 6, 1949; married; 2 children. Graduate Riverside H.S.; A.A. MATC (Milw.) 1975; B.S. UW-Milwaukee 1976. Full-time legislator. Former City of Milwaukee health officer, postal worker, and industrial printer. Member: NAACP; National Labor Caucus of State Legislators (vice pres.); Natl. Conference of State Legislatures; Natl. Black Caucus of State Legislators (exec. com., labor com. chp); African American Male Natl. Council (exec. bd.); AFSCME Local 1091 (former chief steward). Former member: Fed. of Black City Empl. (pres.); Isaac Coggs and MLK Community Health Centers Bd. (bd. chair). Disadvantaged Business Enterprise (DBE) Advisory Committee to the Marquette Interchange Project (co-chp.); DBE Bus. Subcom. (chp.).

Elected to Assembly 1982-2002. Elected to Senate in November 2003 special election; reelected 2004. Majority Caucus Vice Chairperson 1989, 1987, 1985. Biennial Senate committee assignments: **2005** — Housing and Financial Institutions; Judiciary, Corrections and Privacy (res. 4/1/05, also 2003 eff. 12/1/03, res. 7/26/04); Jt. Com. for Review of Criminal Penalties (also 2003 eff. 12/1/03). **2003** — Jt. Com. for the Review of Administrative Rules; Select Com. on Control of Health Care Costs; Educational Communications Bd.; Jt. Legislative Council; Milwaukee Child Welfare Partnership Council. Assembly committee assignments: **2003** — Finance (also 2001); Jt. Com. on Finance (also 2001, 1993-97); Jt. Legislative Council; Workforce Development; Legis. Coun. Com. on State-Tribal Relations (also 1999, 1993, 1985-89). **2001** — Census and Redistricting; Children and Families (also 1999); Corrections and the Courts (also 1999); Public Health. **1999** — Government Operations. **1997** — Gang Violence Prevention Council. **1995** — Legis. Coun. Com. on Lead Poisoning Prevention and Control. **1993** — State Council on Alcohol and Other Drug Abuse; Speaker's Task Force on Gang Violence (chp., also 1991). **1991** — Urban and Local Affairs (chp. since 1985); Children and Human Services (since 1987); Colleges and Universities (since 1987); Urban Education (also 1989); Special Com. on Reapportionment. **1989** — Select Com. on the Census; State of Wis. Building Comn.

Telephone: Office: (608) 266-2500; (877) 474-2000 (toll free); District: (414) 442-6979.

E-mail address: Sen.Coggs@legis.state.wi.us

Voting address: 3732 North 40th Street, Milwaukee 53216.

Mailing address: Office: Room 22 South, State Capitol, P.O. Box 7882, Madison 53707.

Representative
YOUNG

Representative
TOLES

Representative
GRIGSBY

Leon D. Young (Dem.), 16th Assembly District

Born Los Angeles, July 4, 1967; single. Graduate Rufus King H.S.; attended UW-Milwaukee. Full-time legislator. Former police aide and police officer. Member: Democratic Party; Harambee Ombudsman Project; Milwaukee Police Association; League of Martin; House of Peace (Love Committee); NAACP; Urban League; Social Development Commission Minority Male Forum on Corrections; National Black Caucus of State Legislators' Task Force on African American Males; 100 Black Men; Milwaukee Metropolitan Fair Housing; Boy Scouts of America (Urban Emphasis Com.); Martin Luther King Community Center (Revitalization Com.).

Elected to Assembly since 1992. Biennial committee assignments: **2005** — Highway Safety (since 1999); Housing (also 1997); State Affairs (also 1995-2003, vice chp. 1993); Tourism (also 2003 eff. 2/14/03). **2003** — Criminal Justice (since 1999, resigned 5/13/03); Ways and Means (eff. 5/13/03). **2001** — Council on Alcohol and Other Drug Abuse (also 1999). **1999** — Transportation. **1997** — Government Operations; Highways and Transportation (also 1995). **1995** — Urban Education (also 1993). **1993** — Children and Human Services; Small Business and Economic Development; Urban and Local Affairs; Speaker's Task Force on African American Males; Legis. Coun. Com. on Educational Communications Technology.

Telephone: Office: (608) 266-3786; (888) 534-0016 (toll free); District: (414) 374-7414.

E-mail address: Rep.Young@legis.state.wi.us

Voting address: 2224 North 17th Street, Milwaukee 53205.

Mailing address: Office: Room 118 North, State Capitol, P.O. Box 8953, Madison 53708.

Barbara L. Toles (Dem.), 17th Assembly District

Born Milwaukee, July 31, 1956. Graduate West Division H.S. (Milwaukee) 1973. B.A. UW-Madison 1979. M.Ed. Marquette U. 1997. Full-time legislator. Adjunct faculty member, former community outreach coordinator and advisor, Milwaukee Area Technical College. Member: League of Women Voters of Milwaukee County (past pres.); Community Health Charities of Wisconsin (bd. mbr.); American Federation of Teachers Local 212 (ex. bd. mbr.); Milwaukee Forum (bd. mbr.); NAACP; Sigma Gamma Rho Sorority, Inc. Former member: American Association for Women in Community Colleges – MATC (pres.).

Elected to Assembly in January 2004 special election; reelected November 2004. Biennial committee assignments: **2005** — Economic Development; State Affairs; Ways and Means; Workforce Development (also 2003). **2003** — Children and Families; Health.

Telephone: Office: (608) 266-5580; (888) 534-0017 (toll free); District: (414) 444-3810.

E-mail address: Rep.Toles@legis.state.wi.us

Voting address: 3835 N. 56th Street, Milwaukee 53216.

Mailing address: Office: Room 124 North, State Capitol, P.O. Box 8953, Madison 53708.

Tamara D. Grigsby (Dem.), 18th Assembly District

Born Pullman, WA, November 19, 1974; single. Graduate Madison Memorial H.S. 1993; B.A. Howard U. (Washington, D.C.) 1997; M.S.W. UW-Madison 2000. Former social worker; adjunct professor, Carroll College, UW-Milwaukee; child advocate; family counselor. Member: NAACP; National Assn. of Social Workers; Martin Drive Neighborhood Assn.; Democratic Party of Wisconsin. Milwaukee County W-2 Monitoring Task Force.

Elected to Assembly 2004. Biennial committee assignments: **2005** — Children and Families; Criminal Justice and Homeland Security; Public Health; Tourism; Interstate Adult Offender Supervision Board; Milwaukee Child Welfare Partnership Council.

Telephone: Office: (608) 266-0645; (888) 534-0018 (toll free); District: (414) 931-0208.

E-mail address: Rep.Grigsby@legis.state.wi.us

Voting address: 1311 North 42nd Street, Milwaukee 53208.

Mailing address: Office: Room 122 North, State Capitol, P.O. Box 8952, Madison 53708.

7th SENATE DISTRICT

**Senator
PLALE**

**See Milwaukee County Detail Map on
pp. 92 & 93**

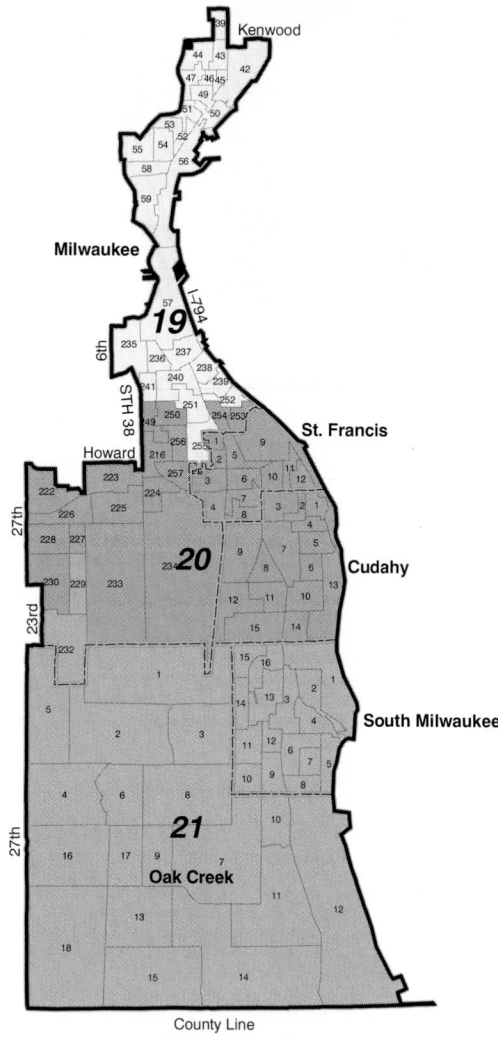

Jeffrey T. Plale

(Dem.), 7th Senate District

Born South Milwaukee, May 31, 1968; 2
children. Graduate South Milwaukee H.S.;
B.A. in communications and public relations
Marquette U. 1990; M.A. in communications and public relations Marquette U.
1992. Former investment agent. Member:
Boy Scouts of America Community Fund
Raising (former chp.); Marquette U. Alumni
Assn.; Ancient Order of Hibernians; Democratic Party of Wisconsin; Democratic Leadership Council; South Milwaukee Lions
Club; American Legislative Exchange
Council; Youth in Government (bd. of governors); Center for Policy Alternatives Flemming Fellowship. Recipient: WMC *Working
for Wisconsin Award* 2004, 2002, 2000,
1998; NFIB *Guardian of Small Business
Award* 1998. South Milwaukee City Council
1993-96.

Elected to Assembly in March 1996 special election; reelected November 1996-2002 (resigned eff. 5/9/03); elected
to Senate in April 2003 special election. Minority Caucus Chairperson 2005. Biennial Senate committee assignments:
2005 — Energy, Utilities and Information Technology; Higher Education and Tourism; Housing and Financial Institutions. **2003** — Jt. Com. on Audit; Economic Development, Job Creation and Housing. Assembly committee assignments: **2003** — Aging and Long-Term Care; Financial Institutions (since 1997); Tourism; Workforce Development.
2001 — Jt. Survey Com. on Retirement Systems; Energy and Utilities; Transportation; Forward Wisconsin, Inc. (since
1997); Building Comn. **1999** — Insurance; Utilities; Ways and Means; Speaker's Special Task Force on Abandoned
Children (co-chp.). **1997** — Government Operations; Insurance, Securities and Corporate Policy; Utilities Oversight;
Legis. Coun. Coms. on Historic Building Code, on Services for Visually Handicapped Students. **1995** — Jt. Com. for
Review of Administrative Rules; Urban and Local Affairs; Legis. Coun. Coms. on Adoption Laws, on Economics and
Health of the Tavern Industry.

Telephone: Office: (608) 266-7505; (800) 361-5487 (toll free); District: (414) 764-5292.

E-mail address: Sen.Plale@legis.state.wi.us

Voting address: 1404 18th Avenue, South Milwaukee 53172.

Mailing address: Office: Room 108 South, State Capitol, P.O. Box 7882, Madison 53707-7882.

Representative
RICHARDS

Representative
SINICKI

Representative
HONADEL

Jon Richards (Dem.), 19th Assembly District

Born Waukesha, September 5, 1963; married. Graduate Waukesha North H.S.; B.A. Lawrence U. 1986; J.D. UW-Madison (Law Review) 1994; attended Keio University (Tokyo). Attorney. Former English teacher in Japan and former volunteer with Mother Teresa, Calcutta, India. Member: Milwaukee River Revitalization Council; New Brady Street Area Association (bd. mbr.); Bay View Historical Society; Urban Ecology Center; Friends of Wisconsin State Parks; American Council of Young Political Leaders; National Caucus of Environmental Legislators; Water Tower Landmark Trust; Milwaukee Co. Democratic Party; Bay View Lions Club; Bay View Neighorhood Assn.; Wisconsin Assembly for Local Arts (bd. mbr.); Clean Wisconsin. Recipient: Environmental Decade *Clean 16 Award Winner;* Center for Policy Alternatives Flemming Fellow; Planned Parenthood of Wisconsin *Voice for Choice Award Winner;* Wis. Family Planning and Reproductive Health Assn. *Legislator of the Year.*

Elected to Assembly 1998; reelected since 2000. Assistant Minority Leader 2005, 2003. Biennial committee assignments: **2005** — Assembly Organization (also 2003); Financial Institutions (ranking min. mbr., also 2001, 2003); Jt. Com. on Legislative Organization (also 2003); Rules (also 2003). **2001** — Insurance; Tax and Spending Limitations; Transportation Projects Comn. **1999** — Colleges and Universities; Conservation and Land Use; Criminal Justice; Review of the Farmland Preservation Program.

Telephone: Office: (608) 266-0650; (888) 534-0019 (toll free); District: (414) 270-9898.
E-mail address: Rep.Richards@legis.state.wi.us
Internet address: www.legis.state.wi.us/assembly/asm19/asm19.html
Voting address: 1823 North Oakland Avenue, Milwaukee 53202.
Mailing address: Office: Room 107 North, State Capitol, P.O. Box 8953, Madison 53708.

Christine Sinicki (Dem.), 20th Assembly District

Born Milwaukee, March 28, 1960; married; 2 children. Graduate Bay View H.S. Full-time legislator. Former small business manager. Member: Delegate-U.S. Presidential Electoral College, 2000; Wisconsin Delegate to Democratic National Convention, Los Angeles; American Council of Young Political Leaders, Delegate to Israel and Palestine; Milwaukee Comn. on Domestic Violence and Sexual Assault; Healthier Communities Steering Com.; Wisconsin Civil Air Patrol, Major; Wisconsin Congress of Parents and Teachers (hon. lifelong mbr.); Milwaukee City Council Parents and Teachers Assn.; Bay View Historical Society; Bay View Lions Club; St. Francis/Cudahy Kiwanis; Fellow, Bowhay Institute, La Follette School, UW-Madison 2001; Founder, Conservatory of Lifelong Learning, Innovative School, Milwaukee Public School District; Flemming Fellow, Center for Policy Alternatives 2003. Awards: Wisconsin Environmental Decade *Clean 16* 2000; Wisconsin Ob/Gyn Physicians' *Legislator of the Year* 2000. Assembly Democratic Task Force on Working Families (chp.). State Assembly Milw. Caucus (chp. 2003). Milw. School Board 1991-98.

Elected to Assembly 1998; reelected since 2000. Minority Caucus Secretary 2001. Biennial committee assignments: **2005** — Agriculture; Children and Families (since 1999); Education Reform (since 1999); Labor (also 2003); Military Affairs. **2003** — Tourism; Veterans and Military Affairs. **2001** — Education; Personal Privacy (ranking minority mbr.); Wis. Housing and Economic Development Authority.

Telephone: Office: (608) 266-8588; (888) 534-0020 (toll free); District: (414) 481-7667.
E-mail address: Rep.Sinicki@legis.state.wi.us
Voting address: 3132 South Indiana Avenue, Milwaukee 53207.
Mailing address: Office: Room 321 West, State Capitol, P.O. Box 8953, Madison 53708.

Mark R. Honadel (Rep.), 21st Assembly District

Born Milwaukee, March 29, 1956; married; 3 children. Graduate Oak Creek H.S. 1974; attended Milwaukee Area Technical College and Marquette University. Independent businessman. Former professional metal fabricator, welding instructor, industrial manager. Member: South Milwaukee Street Scaping; Grant Park Garden Club; South Milwaukee Chamber of Commerce; South Milwaukee Lions. Former member: American Welding Society, V.I.C.A. welding judge.

Elected to Assembly in July 2003 special election; reelected 2004. Biennial committee assignments: **2005** — Southeast Wisconsin Freeways (chp); Small Business (vice chp.); Economic Development (also 2003 eff. 8/23/03); Energy and Utilities (also 2003 eff. 8/28/03). **2003** — Corrections and the Courts (eff. 8/28/03, res. 9/18/03); Insurance (eff. 9/18/03); Transportation (eff. 9/8/03).

Telephone: Office: (608) 266-0610; (888) 534-0021 (toll free); District: (414) 764-9921.
E-mail address: Rep.Honadel@legis.state.wi.us
Voting address: 1219 Manitoba Avenue, South Milwaukee 53172.
Mailing address: Office: Room 6 North, State Capitol, P.O. Box 8952, Madison 53708.

8th SENATE DISTRICT

See Milwaukee County Detail
Map on pp. 92 & 93

See Waukesha County Detail
Map on pp. 94 & 95

**Senator
DARLING**

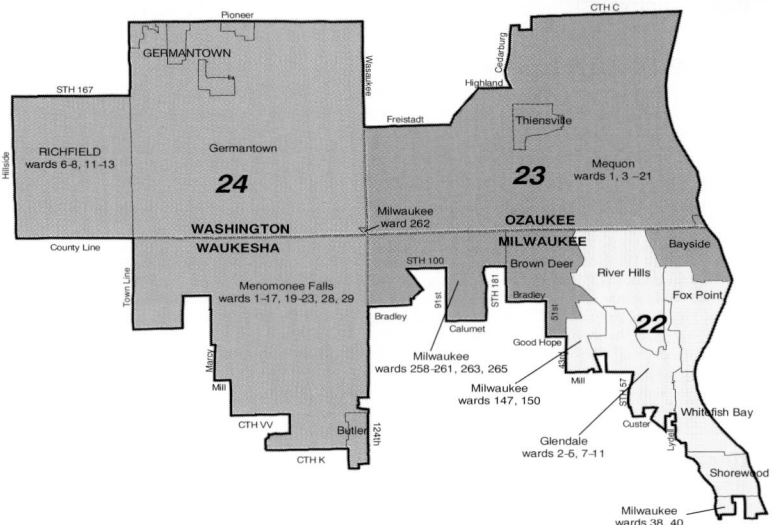

Alberta Darling (Rep.), 8th Senate District

Born Hammond, IN, April 28, 1944; married; 2 children. Graduate UW-Madison 1966; grad. work UW-Milwaukee 1972-74. Former teacher and marketing director. Member: North Shore Rotary; College Savings Program Bd. (EdVest) (chp.); Junior League of Milwaukee (former pres.); YMCA (bd. mbr.); Public Policy Forum. Former member: Next Door Foundation; Tempo Professional Women's Organization; Wis. Strategic Planning Council for Economic Development; Greater Milwaukee Com.; Goals for Greater Milwaukee 2000 Project (exec. com.); United Way (exec. com. dir.); Future Milwaukee (pres.); Milwaukee Forum; Children's Service Soc. of Wis. (bd. of dir.); American Red Cross of Wis. (exec. com., bd. of dir.); League of Women Voters; Today's Girls/Tomorrow's Women/Boys Girls Club (founder); NCSL Education Com. (chp.). Recipient: Fair Air Coalition *Friend of Education;* Metropolitan Milwaukee Assn. of Commerce *Champion of Commerce;* Wis. Head Start Directors Assn. *Award of Excellence;* National Assn. of Community Leadership *Leadership Award;* United Way *Gwen Jackson Leadership Award;* ESHAC *Governor's Service Award;* William Steiger *Award for Human Service;* St. Francis Children's Center *Children Service Award;* Riverwest *Effective State Leadership Award;* Milwaukee Civic Alliance *Community Leadership Award;* American Marketing Assn. *Marketer of the Year.*

Elected to Assembly in May 1990 special election; reelected November 1990; elected to Senate 1992; reelected since 1996. Biennial committee assignments: **2005** — Jt. Com. on Finance (co-chp. 2003, mbr. since 2001); Education; Health, Children, Families, Aging and Long-Term Care; Milwaukee Child Welfare Partnership Council (since 1995). **2003** — Jt. Com. on Audit; Jt. Com. on Employment Relations; Jt. Legislative Council (also 2001); Wis. Center District Board of Dir.; UW Hospitals and Clinics Authority Bd. **2001** — Education (also 1999, 1997, 1993). **1999** — Jt. Com. for Review of Administrative Rules (since 1993); Jt. Com. on Information Policy (also 1995); Judiciary and Consumer Affairs; Child Abuse and Neglect Prevention Bd. (since 1993). **1997** — Education and Financial Institutions (chp., eff. 4/21/98, also 1995); Business, Economic Development and Urban Affairs (eff. 4/21/98, also 1995); Judiciary (eff. 4/21/98, also 1995); Labor, Transportation and Financial Institutions; Education Comn. of the States (eff. 4/30/98, also 1995); Legis. Coun. Coms. on Faith-Based Approaches to Crime Prevention and Justice, on School Discipline and Safety (chp.).

Telephone: Office: (608) 266-5830; E-mail address: Sen.Darling@legis.state.wi.us

Voting address: 1325 West Dean Road, River Hills 53217.

Mailing address: Office: Room 316 South, State Capitol, P.O. Box 7882, Madison 53707-7882.

Representative
WASSERMAN

Representative
GIELOW

Representative
JESKEWITZ

Sheldon A. Wasserman (Dem.), 22nd Assembly District

Born Milwaukee, August 5, 1961; married; 3 children. Graduate Milwaukee John Marshall H.S. 1979; B.S. Phi Beta Kappa, UW-Milwaukee 1983; M.D. Medical College of Wisconsin 1987; Bethesda Hospital OB/GYN Residency 1987-91. Full-time legislator and practicing OB/GYN physician. Member: Shorewood Men's Club; Glendale Chamber of Commerce; Wis. Breast Cancer Coalition; American College of OB/GYNs (Fellow). Recipient: North Shore United Educators *Award of Excellence* 2004; Wisconsin Coalition Against Sexual Assault *Voices of Courage Award for Public Policy* 2002; Professional Fire Fighters of Wis. *Legislator of the Year* 2001; American Heart Assn. Wis. *Affiliate Heartsaver Award* 1999; Milwaukee Magazine *Best Legislator* 2003; K-8 Union High School Districts Coalition *Legislator of the Year* 1996; The Business Journal *40 Under 40 Award Winner* 1995.

Elected to Assembly since 1994. Biennial committee assignments: **2005** — Corrections and the Courts (since 2003); Health (since 1995); Medicaid Reform; Public Health (since 1999). **2003** — Government Operations and Spending Limitations. **2001** — Aging and Long-Term Care; Urban and Local Affairs (also 1995). **1999** — Government Operations; Insurance; Legis. Council Com. on Use of Prescription Drugs for Children. **1997** — Income Tax Review; Insurance, Securities and Corporate Policy. **1995** — Colleges and Universities.

Telephone: Office: (608) 266-7671; (888) 534-0022 (toll free); District: (414) 964-0663; Fax: (608) 282-3622.

E-mail address: Rep.Wasserman@legis.state.wi.us; Internet address: www.legis.state.wi.us/assembly/asm22/news/

Voting address: 3487 North Lake Drive, Milwaukee 53211.

Mailing address: Office: Room 214 North, State Capitol, P.O. Box 8953, Madison 53708.

Curt Gielow (Rep.), 23rd Assembly District

Born Evansville, IN, March 18, 1945; married; 2 sons. Graduate Red Bud (Illinois) H.S. 1963; B.S. in pharmacy, St. Louis Coll. of Pharmacy (St. Louis) 1968; M.H.A. Washington U. (St. Louis) 1973. Executive search consultant and businessman. Former hospital administrator, health care consultant, and entrepreneur. Member: St. John's Lutheran Church, Glendale (pres., fmr. elder); Lutheran Home Foundation (bd. mbr.). Former member: University of Wisconsin-Milwaukee Foundation (chm.); Historic Third Ward Assn. of Milw. (vice pres.); Sales and Marketing Executives of Milw. (vice pres.). Alderman, City of Mequon, 1997-2003 (Common Coun. Pres. 2001-02).

Elected to Assembly 2002; reelected 2004. Biennial committee assignments: **2005** — Medicaid Reform (chp.); Health (vice chp. 2003); Insurance (also 2003); Workforce Development (also 2003).

Telephone: Office: (608) 266-0486; District: (262) 242-2728; E-mail address: Rep.Gielow@legis.state.wi.us

Voting address: 3412 West Clubview Court, Mequon 53092.

Mailing address: Office: Room 316 North, State Capitol, P.O. Box 8952, Madison 53708.

Suzanne Jeskewitz (Rep.), 24th Assembly District

Born Galesville, February 21, 1942; married; 2 children, 3 grandchildren. Graduate Gale-Ettrick H.S. (Galesville); B.A. UW-La Crosse 1964. Former bank public relations representative, teacher, YMCA director, associate director of Menomonee Falls Chamber of Commerce, real estate broker. Member: Tri County YMCA Board of Managers (secy./treas.); Menomonee Falls Optimist Club; Menomonee Falls Chamber of Commerce (former chp. of Government Com. and Tourism Com.), Chamber Ambassador Committee; Menomonee Falls Intergovernmental Com.; Waukesha and Washington Co. Republican Parties. Menomonee Falls Planning Commission 1992-96; Waukesha Co. Board 1992-96.

Elected to Assembly 1996; reelected since 1998. Biennial committee assignments: **2005** — Audit (chp., also 2003); Jt. Com. on Audit (co-chp., also 2003); Children and Families (since 1999, vice chp. 1999); Colleges and Universities (since 2001); Criminal Justice and Homeland Security; Jt. Survey Com. on Retirement Systems (vice chp., mbr. 1997, 2003); Ways and Means (mbr. since 1997, vice chp. 1997). **2003** — Criminal Justice. **2001** — Financial Institutions (chp., also 1999); Criminal Justice (also 1999). **1999** — Consumer Affairs (chp. 1/99 to 5/99); Government Operations. **1997** — Mandates (vice chp.); Criminal Justice and Corrections; Wisconsin Works Oversight (vice chp.); Legis. Coun. Coms. on State Strategies for Economic Development, on Capture of Federal Resources.

Telephone: Office: (608) 266-3796; (888) 529-0024 (toll free); District: (262) 251-9595.

E-mail address: Rep.Jeskewitz@legis.state.wi.us

Voting address: N80 W15239 Hilltop Drive, Menomonee Falls 53051.

Mailing address: Office: Room 314 North, State Capitol, P.O. Box 8952, Madison 53708.

9th SENATE DISTRICT

**Senator
LEIBHAM**

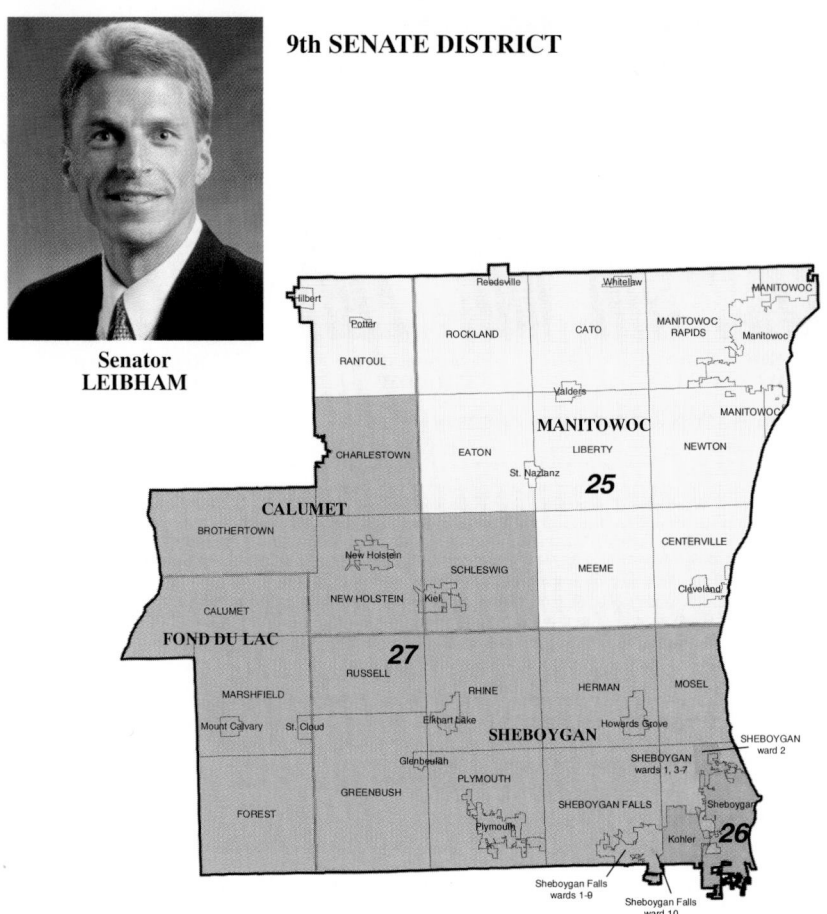

See Sheboygan Area Detail Map on p. 98

Joseph K. Leibham (Rep.), 9th Senate District

Born Sheboygan, June 6, 1969; married. Graduate Sheboygan Area Lutheran H.S.; B.A. UW-Madison 1991; attended UW-La Crosse 1987-89 and Ealing College (London, England) 1990. Former food service industry account executive and manager/membership development, Sheboygan County Chamber of Commerce. Member: Friends of Sheboygan Senior Center (vice pres.); Citizen's Police Academy (graduate); Boy Scouts of America (Eagle Scout); American Luther Assn.; Manitowoc County Vision 2011 Committee. Sheboygan City Council 1993-2000 (pres. 1995-96).

Elected to Assembly 1998-2000; elected to Senate 2002. Majority Caucus Vice Chairperson 2003. Biennial Senate committee assignments: **2005** — Jt. Com. for Review of Criminal Penalties (co-chp.); Jt. Com. on Finance; Energy, Utilities and Information Technologies. **2003** — Jt. Com. for Review of Adminstrative Rules (co-chp.); Administrative Rules (chp.); Transportation and Information Infrastructure (chp.); Energy and Utilities. Assembly committee assignments: **2001** — Jt. Com. on Audit (co-chp.); Audit (chp.); Census and Redistricting (vice chp., also 1999); Tax and Spending Limitations (vice chp.); Energy and Utilities; State and Local Finance; Transportation (also 1999). **1999** — Utilities (vice chp.); Small Business and Economic Development; State Affairs.

Telephone: Office: (608) 266-2056; (888) 295-8750 (toll free); District: (920) 457-7367.

E-mail address: Sen.Leibham@legis.state.wi.us

Internet address: leibhamsenate.com

Voting address: 3618 River Ridge Drive, Sheboygan 53083.

Mailing address: Office: Room 127 South, State Capitol, P.O. Box 7882, Madison 53707-7882.

Representative
ZIEGELBAUER

Representative
VAN AKKEREN

Representative
KESTELL

Bob Ziegelbauer (Dem.), 25th Assembly District

Born Manitowoc, August 26, 1951; single. Graduate Manitowoc Roncalli H.S.; B.B.A. U. of Notre Dame; M.B.A. U. of Pennsylvania, Wharton School. Small businessman; retail music store owner. Former City of Manitowoc finance director and part-time instructor at Silver Lake College. Member: Manitowoc Co. Local Emergency Planning Committee; Manitowoc-Two Rivers YMCA (dir. 1989-95). Manitowoc City Council 1981-84; Manitowoc Co. Board 1982-88; Lakeshore Technical College Bd. 1987-88; Manitowoc Public Utilities Comn. 1990-2000.

Elected to Assembly since 1992. Biennial committee assignments: **2005** — Agriculture; Education (since 1993); Government Operations and Spending Limitations; Tourism (also 2003); Ways and Means (since 1993). **2003** — Energy and Utilities (also member 2001 to 5/16/01); Rural Affairs. **2001** — State and Local Finance; Council on Workforce Excellence (also 1999). **1999** — Jt. Com. on Audit; Insurance; Utilities; Special Com. on the Renovation of Lambeau Field; Law Revision; Gov.'s Blue Ribbon Comn. on State-Local Partnerships for the 21st Century. **1997** — Government Operations; Income Tax Review; Insurance, Securities and Corporate Policy (also 1995); Mandates (also 1995). **1995** — Financial Institutions; Urban and Local Affairs; Forward Wisconsin, Inc.; Select Com. on Milwaukee Brewers Stadium; Legis. Coun. Coms. on Adoption Laws, on Economics and Health of the Tavern Industry, on Public School Open Enrollment.

Telephone: Office: (608) 266-0315; (888) 529-0025 (toll free); District: (920) 684-6783 (office); (920) 684-4362 (home); Fax: (608) 266-0316, (608) 282-3625, or (920) 684-6783.

E-mail address: Bob.Ziegelbauer@legis.state.wi.us

Internet address: www.bobziegelbauer.com

Voting address: 1213 South 8th Street, Manitowoc 54220.

Mailing address: Office: Room 207 North, State Capitol, P.O. Box 8953, Madison 53708; District: P.O. Box 325, Manitowoc 54221-0325.

Terry Van Akkeren (Dem.), 26th Assembly District

Born Sheboygan, March 10, 1954; widowed; 4 children. Graduate Sheboygan North H.S. 1972; Lakeshore Tech. College 1982. Engineering tech.; former tool and die maker. Sheboygan alderman 1986-2003; Sheboygan County Supervisor 1990-92.

Elected to Assembly 2002; reelected 2004. Biennial committee assignments: **2005** — Education (also 2003); Labor (also 2003); Natural Resources; Tourism (also 2003). **2003** — Economic Development.

Telephone: Office: (608) 266-0656; (888) 529-0026 (toll free); District: (920) 458-4398.

E-mail address: Rep.VanAkkeren@legis.state.wi.us

Voting address: 1719 North 13th Street, Sheboygan 53081.

Mailing address: Office: Room 220 North, State Capitol, P.O. Box 8953, Madison 53708.

Steve Kestell (Rep.), 27th Assembly District

Born Town of Lyndon, Sheboygan Co., June 15, 1955; married; 3 children. Graduate Plymouth H.S. Full-time legislator. Former retail manager and regional sales manager. Member: Sheboygan Co. Republican Party; Calumet Co. Republican Party; Family Resource Center of Sheboygan County (bd. mbr.). Former member: Gov.'s Council on Highway Safety; Howards Grove Jaycees; ADA Volunteer Firefighters; 4-H project leader; Junior Achievement instructor. Howards Grove School Bd. 1981-84, 1986-98 (pres. 1995-98).

Elected to Assembly 1998; reelected since 2000. Biennial committee assignments: **2005** — Children and Families (chp. since 2001, mbr. since 1999); Education (vice chp., mbr. since 1999); Family Law (vice chp. and mbr. since 2001); Rural Development (also 2003); Legis. Coun. Spec. Com. on Adoption and Termination of Parental Rights. **2003** — Agriculture (since 1999); Child Abuse and Neglect Prevention Bd. (since 4/7/2000). **2001** — Small Business and Consumer Affairs; Legis. Coun. Com. on Relative Caregivers (co-chp.). **1999** — Government Operations (vice chp.); Transportation; Legis. Coun. Spec. Com. on Navigable Waters Recodification.

Telephone: Office: (608) 266-8530; (888) 529-0027 (toll free); District: (920) 565-2044.

E-mail address: Rep.Kestell@legis.state.wi.us

Voting address: (Town of Herman) W3829 State Highway 32, Elkhart Lake 53020.

Mailing address: Office: Room 17 West, State Capitol, P.O. Box 8952, Madison 53708.

10th SENATE DISTRICT

**Senator
HARSDORF**

Detail Map: Somerset Town

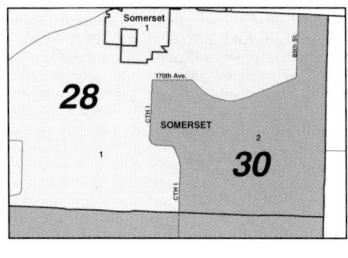

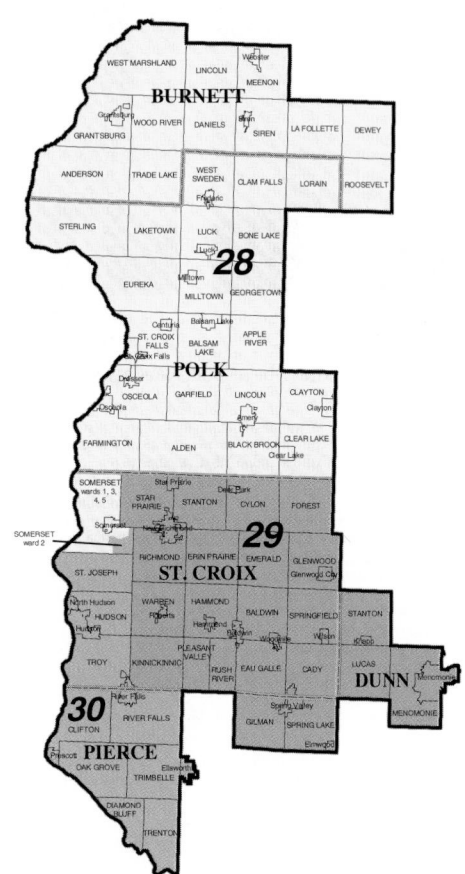

Sheila E. Harsdorf (Rep.), 10th Senate District

Born St. Paul, MN, July 25, 1956; 1 child. Graduate River Falls H.S.; B.S. in animal science, U. of Minnesota 1978; Wis. Rural Leadership Program, grad. of 1st class (1986). Legislator, dairy farmer, and former loan officer. Member: Pierce Co. Republican Party; Pierce Co. Farm Bureau (former dir. and treas.); Luther Memorial Church; Northern Edge Advisory Coun.; Passage Foundation Awards Com. Former member: Wis. State FFA Sponsors Bd. (chp.); Wis. Conservation Corps Bd. (secy.); Kinnickinnic River Land Trust Bd.; Pierce Co. Dairy Promotion Com. (past chm.); Wis. State ASCS Com.; Adv. Council on Small Business, Agriculture, Labor for Federal Reserve Bank of Minneapolis.

Elected to Assembly 1988-96; elected to Senate 2000; reelected 2004. Majority Caucus Sergeant at Arms 2005. Biennial Senate committee assignments: **2005** — Higher Education and Tourism (chp., also 2003); Jt. Survey Com. on Tax Exemptions (co-chp., mbr. 2003); Education (also 2001); Housing and Financial Institutions; World Dairy Center Authority (also 2003). **2003** — Jt. Com. on Finance; Finance; Jt. Legislative Council; Law Revision Com. (also 2001); Mississippi River Parkway Commission (also 2001). **2001** — Jt. Com. on Information Policy and Technology; Information Policy and Technology; 2001-2003 Biennial Budget; Labor and Agriculture; Environmental Education Bd.; Ad. Bd. for Midwest Center for Agricultural Research, Education, and Disease and Injury Prevention; Jt. Legis. Council Special Com. on the Public Health System's Response to Terrorism and Public Health Emergencies. Assembly committee assignments: **1997** — Jt. Com. on Finance (also 1995). **1995** — Legis. Coun. Com. on Land Use Policies. **1993** — Agriculture, Forestry and Rural Affairs; Colleges and Universities (ranking minority mbr. since 1991); Natural Resources (since 1989); Veterans and Military Affairs (eff. 4/26/93); Educational Communications Bd. (since 1989); Legis. Coun. Com. on University and State Economic Development. **1991** — Agriculture, Aquaculture and Forestry; State Affairs (also 1989); Legis. Coun. Com. on Farm Safety. **1989** — Agriculture and its Subcom. on Aquaculture; Special Com. on Bonding for Clean Water; Legis. Coun. Com. to Review Sexual Assault Laws.

Telephone: Office: (608) 266-7745; (800) 862-1092 (toll free); Fax: (608) 267-0369.

E-mail address: Sen.Harsdorf@legis.state.wi.us

Voting address: (Town of River Falls) N6627 County Road E, River Falls 54022.

Mailing address: Office: Room 131 South, P.O. Box 7882, Madison 53707-7882.

Representative PETTIS **Representative LAMB** **Representative RHOADES**

Mark L. Pettis (Rep.), 28th Assembly District

Born Osceola, December 18, 1950; married; 2 children, 5 grandchildren. Graduate Osceola H.S.; attended U.S. Navy school and Wis. Indianhead Technical College. Full-time legislator. Former small business owner and salesman. Vietnam Era veteran; served in U.S. Navy. Member: Fishbowl United Sportsmen Club (former pres.); NRA (life mbr.); Osceola Rod and Gun Club; Polk Co. Sportsmen Club; Wis. Right to Life; Burnett Co. Business and Recreation Council (former pres.); Am. Legion-Lund Brown Post (former cmdr. and former American Legion 12th Dist. vice cmdr.); 40/8 Voiture 236. Burnett Co. Board 1992-94.

Elected to Assembly 1998; reelected since 2000. Biennial committee assignments: **2005** — Tourism (chp., also 2003); Military Affairs (vice chp.); Aging and Long-Term Care (since 2001, vice chp. 2001); Natural Resources (since 2001); Legislative Council Committee on State-Tribal Relations (since 2001); Gov.'s Council on Tourism. **2003** — Veterans and Military Affairs (also 1999); Gov.'s Council on Tourism. **2001** — Jt. Com. on Information Policy and Technology (co-chp.); Information Policy and Technology (chp.); Insurance (vice chp.). **1999** — Tourism and Recreation.

Telephone: Office: (608) 267-2365; (888) 529-0028 (toll free); District: (715) 349-2206.

E-mail address: Mark.Pettis@legis.state.wi.us

Voting address: (Town of La Follette) 3984 State Road 70, Hertel 54845.

Mailing address: Office: Room 20 North, State Capitol, P.O. Box 8953, Madison 53708.

Andy Lamb (Rep.), 29th Assembly District

Born Dunn Co., September 7, 1973; married; 1 child. Graduate Spring Valley H.S. 1992; attended UW-Eau Claire. Farmer/consultant. Former auto general sales manager. Member Wilson Lutheran Church (council mbr.).

Elected to Assembly 2004. Biennial committee assignments: **2005** — Economic Development (vice chp.); Financial Institutions (vice chp.); Colleges and Universities; Transportation.

Telephone: Office: (608) 266-7683; (888) 529-0029 (toll free).

E-mail address: Rep.Lamb@legis.state.wi.us

Voting address: 1020 Elm Avenue West, Menomonie 54751.

Mailing address: Office: Room 9 West, State Capitol, P.O. Box 8952, Madison 53708.

Kitty Rhoades (Rep.), 30th Assembly District

Born St. Paul, MN, April 7, 1951; married; 3 children. Graduate Hudson H.S.; B.S. UW-River Falls 1973; M.A. Illinois State U. 1978. Consultant. Former educator, small business owner, and Chamber of Commerce pres. Member: St. Croix County Homemakers; Ducks Unlimited; St. Croix County Emergency Government Com.; Hudson Rotary (fmr. pres. and dist. officer). Former member: Chamber of Commerce Exec. Assn. (bd. of dir.); St. Croix River Regional Tourism Alliance (bd. of dir.); Governor's Council on Trails; Century College Pres. Adv. Council; UW-River Falls Alumni Foundation (bd. of dir.); Project Child Care (bd. of dir.).

Elected to Assembly 1998; reelected since 2000. Biennial committee assignments: **2005** — Finance (also 2003); Jt. Com. on Finance (also 2003). **2001** — Aging and Long-Term Care (chp.); Jt. Legislative Council (co-chp.); Colleges and Universities (vice chp. 1999); Education (also 1999); Financial Institutions (also 1999). **1999** — Conservation and Land Use; Rural Affairs and Forestry.

Telephone: Office: (608) 266-1526; (888) 529-0030 (toll free); District: (715) 386-0660.

E-mail address: Rep.Rhoades@legis.state.wi.us

Voting address: 708 4th Street, Hudson 54016.

Mailing address: Office: Room 320 East, State Capitol, P.O. Box 8953, Madison 53708.

11th SENATE DISTRICT

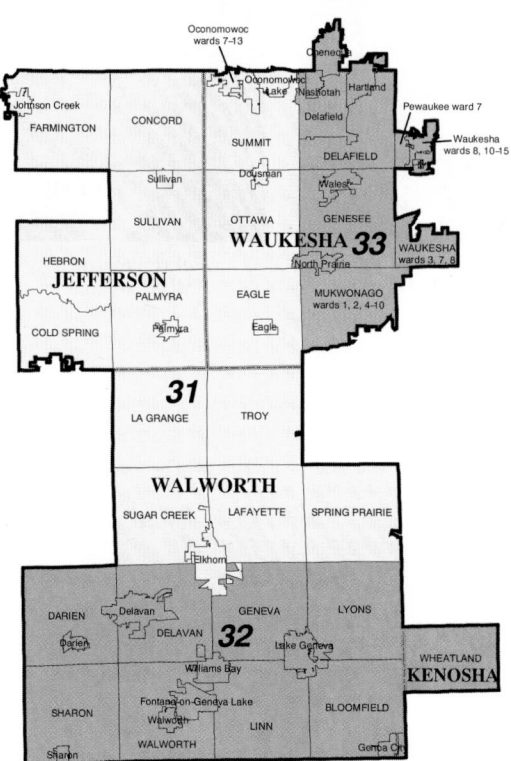

**Senator
KEDZIE**

**See Waukesha County Detail
Map on p. 94 & 95**

Neal J. Kedzie (Rep.), **11th Senate District**

Born Waukesha, January 27, 1956; married; 3 children. Graduate Oak Creek H.S.; B.S. UW-Whitewater 1978; graduate work UW-Whitewater 1985-present. Full-time legislator. Former government relations representative. Member: American Legislative Exchange Council; Civil Air Patrol (rank of major); National Assn. of Sportsmen Legislators; Walworth, Waukesha, and Jefferson Co. Republican Parties; Walworth Co. Farm Bureau; Boy Scouts USA; Walworth Co. Historical Society (*ex officio* mbr.). Former member: Lauderdale-La Grange Volunteer Fire Dept. (secy.). La Grange Town Board 1987-98 (chm. 1988-98); La Grange Planning and Zoning Comn. (chm.).

Elected to Assembly 1996-2000; elected to Senate 2002. Assistant Majority Leader 2005. Biennial Senate committee assignments: **2005** — Natural Resources and Transportation (chp.); Agriculture and Insurance; Campaign Finance Reform and Ethics; Higher Education and Tourism; Organization; Jt. Com. on Legislative Organization; Environmental Education Bd. (also 2003). **2003** — Environment and Natural Resources (chp.); Agriculture, Financial Institutions and Insurance; Labor, Small Business Development and Consumer Affairs; Transportation and Information Infrastructure. Assembly committee assignments: **2001** — Environment (chp., also 1999, mbr. 1997); Aging and Long-Term Care; Financial Institutions (since 1997); Natural Resources (also 1999); Jt. Survey Com. on Tax Exemptions; Environmental Education Bd. (also 1999). **1999** — Conservation and Land Use (vice chp.); Housing (vice chp. 1997); Urban and Local Affairs. **1997** — Rural Affairs (vice chp.); State-Federal Relations; Legis. Coun. Com. on Utility Public Benefit Programs.

Telephone: Office: (608) 266-2635; (800) 578-1457 (toll free); District: (262) 742-2025.

E-mail address: Sen.Kedzie@legis.state.wi.us

Voting address: (Town of La Grange) N7661 Highway 12, Elkhorn 53121.

Mailing address: Office: Room 313 South, State Capitol, P.O. Box 7882, Madison 53707-7882.

**Representative
NASS**

**Representative
LOTHIAN**

**Representative
VRAKAS**

Stephen L. Nass (Rep.), 31st Assembly District

Born Whitewater, October 7, 1952; single. Graduate Whitewater H.S.; B.S. UW-Whitewater 1978; M.S. Ed. in school business management, UW-Whitewater 1990. Former payroll benefits analyst and information analyst/negotiator. Member of Wis. Air National Guard, served in Middle East in Operations Desert Shield and Desert Storm. Member: American Legion; Veterans of Foreign Wars; National and Wis. Assns. of Parliamentarians; Kiwanis. Whitewater City Council 1977-81; UW-Whitewater Bd. of Visitors 1979-89.

Elected to Assembly since 1990. Biennial committee assignments: **2005** — Labor (chp. since 2003); Education Reform (vice chp., chp. 2001, mbr. since 1999); Property Rights and Land Management (vice chp.); Ways and Means (vice chp., mbr. 2003); Colleges and Universities (also 2003); Education (vice chp. 1995-2001, mbr. since 1991). **2001** — Labor and Workforce Development; Personal Privacy; Education Commission of the States (also 1999). **1999** — Government Operations; Labor and Employment (vice chp. 1997, mbr. 1995); Jt. Com. on Audit. **1997** — Mandates (chp.); Criminal Justice and Corrections; Rural Affairs; Legis. Coun. Com. on Services for Visually Handicapped Students.

Telephone: Office: (608) 266-5715; (888) 529-0031 (toll free); District: (262) 495-3424.

E-mail: Rep.Nass@legis.state.wi.us

Voting address: (Town of La Grange) N8330 Jackson Road, Whitewater 53190.

Mailing address: Office: Room 12 West, State Capitol, P.O. Box 8953, Madison 53708.

Thomas A. Lothian (Rep.), 32nd Assembly District

Born Cleveland, Ohio, December 14, 1928; married; 2 sons. Graduate Cleveland Heights H.S. 1947; B.A. in education Ohio State U. 1953; M.A. in chemistry Illinois Institute of Technology. Full-time legislator. Former assistant professor and administrator, U. of Illinois-Chicago. Member: Racine/Kenosha/Walworth Work Force Development Bd. (LEO); Geneva Lake Environmental Assn.; Geneva Lake Sailing School (fmr. treas.); Geneva Lake Assn.; Inland Lake Yacht Assn.; Skeeter Ice Boat Club (fmr. treas.); Wisconsin Counties Assn. (fmr. pres.); Walworth Co. Republican Party; National Republican Party; Williams Bay Master Plan Com.; Williams Bay Lions (fmr. pres.); Williams Bay United Church of Christ (trustee, deacon, fmr. moderator); Masonic Order (fmr. master); Shrine. Former member: Rock/Walworth Community Action, Inc. (dir.); American Chemical Society; U.S. Sailing; O'Hare Spacemen. Williams Bay village trustee 1974-82; Walworth Co. supervisor 1992-2003.

Elected to Assembly 2002; reelected 2004. Biennial committee assignments: **2005** — State-Federal Relations (chp.); Workforce Development (vice chp., also 2003); Economic Development (also 2003); Urban and Local Affairs (also 2003); Ways and Means (also 2003).

Telephone: Office: (608) 266-1190; (888) 529-0032 (toll free); District: (262) 245-5901.

E-mail address: Rep.Lothian@legis.state.wi.us

Voting address: 539 Park Ridge Road, Williams Bay 53191.

Mailing address: Office: Room 306 North, State Capitol, P.O. Box 8952, Madison 53708.

Daniel P. Vrakas (Rep.), 33rd Assembly District

Born Waukesha, October 31, 1955; 2 children. Graduate Waukesha H.S.; B.S. UW-Stevens Point 1979. Former restaurant owner. Member: U.P. Connection (bd. of dir.); Waukesha Co. Mediation Center (bd. of adv.); Waukesha Co. Republican Party; Hartland, Delafield, and Waukesha Chambers of Commerce; Lake Country Rotary Club; Executive Com. of the World Hellenic Parliament.

Elected to Assembly since 1990. Majority Caucus Chairperson since 1999; Majority Caucus Vice Chairperson 1997, 1995. Biennial committee assignments: **2005** — Jt. Survey Com. on Retirement Systems (co-chp. since 2001, mbr. since 1999); Labor (vice chp. since 2003); Assembly Organization (since 1999); Rules (since 1995); Workforce Development (since 2003); State of Wis. Building Commission (since 1999). **2003** — Electronic Democracy and Government Reform. **2001** — Labor and Workforce Development (vice chp.); Energy and Utilities; Environment (also 1999); Council on Workforce Investment (also 1999).

Telephone: Office: (608) 266-3007; (888) 529-0033 (toll free); District: (262) 367-5201.

E-mail address: Rep.Vrakas@legis.state.wi.us

Voting address: (City of Delafield) 1712 Bark River Drive, Hartland 53029.

Mailing address: Office: Room 119 West, State Capitol, P.O. Box 8953, Madison 53708.

12th SENATE DISTRICT

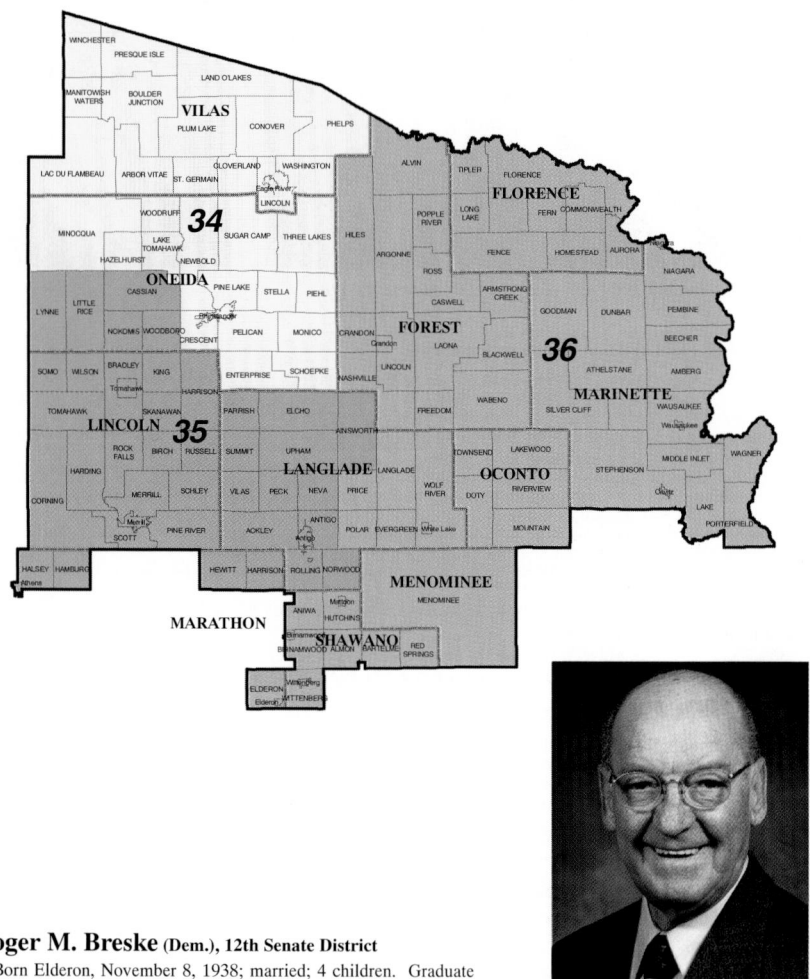

Roger M. Breske (Dem.), 12th Senate District

Born Elderon, November 8, 1938; married; 4 children. Graduate Wittenberg H.S. Full-time legislator. Former owner of bar and restaurant. Served in Army Reserve. Member: Wittenberg-Birnamwood FFA Alumni; Knights of Columbus.

**Senator
BRESKE**

Elected to Senate in November 1990 special election; reelected since 1992. Biennial committee assignments: **2005** — Higher Education and Tourism (also 2003); Natural Resources and Transportation; Veterans, Homeland Security, Military Affairs, Small Business and Government Reform. **2003** — Homeland Security, Veterans and Military Affairs and Government Reform; Transportation and Information Infrastructure; Council on Highway Safety (since 1999); Council on Tourism (since 1997); Transportation Projects Comn. (since 1993). **2001** — Insurance, Tourism and Transportation (chp.); Health, Utilities, Veterans and Military Affairs (also 1999); Jt. Survey Com. on Tax Exemptions (also 1999); Rustic Roads Bd. (also 1993). **1999** — Insurance, Tourism, Transportation and Corrections (chp.); Labor; Legis. Coun. Com. on State-Tribal Relations. **1997** — Insurance, Tourism and Rural Affairs (chp., eff. 1/15/97 to 4/20/98); Health, Human Services, Aging, Corrections, Veterans and Military Affairs (1/15/97 to 4/20/98); Human Services; Labor, Tourism, Veterans and Military Affairs (eff. 4/21/98); Insurance (eff. 4/21/98); Insurance, Tourism and Rural Affairs (chp. 1/15/97 to 4/20/98); Jt. Com. for Review of Administrative Rules (eff. 7/29/98). **1995** — Health, Human Services and Aging (also 1993); Human Resources, Labor, Tourism, Veterans and Military Affairs (also 1993); State Government Operations and Corrections. **1993** — Transportation, Agriculture, Tourism and Veterans Affairs (mbr. and chp. to 4/20/93); Health Care, Human Services and Corrections (mbr. to 4/20/93).

Telephone: Office: (608) 266-2509; (800) 334-8773 (toll free); District: (715) 454-6575.

E-mail address: Sen.Breske@legis.state.wi.us

Voting address: (Town of Elderon) 8800 State Highway 29, Eland 54427.

Mailing address: Office: Room 310 South, State Capitol, P.O. Box 7882, Madison 53707-7882.

Representative
MEYER

Representative
FRISKE

Representative
MURSAU

Dan Meyer (Rep.), 34th Assembly District

Born Neenah, January 1, 1949; married; 2 children. Graduate Neenah H.S.; B.B.A. UW-Oshkosh 1978. Full-time legislator. Former executive director of Eagle River Chamber of Commerce and Visitors Center. Vietnam Era veteran; served in U.S. Army. Member: Vilas County Republican Party; Amercian Legion Post 431. Mayor of Eagle River 1997 to April 2001.

Elected to Assembly 2000; reelected since 2002. Biennial committee assignments: **2005** — Finance (also 2003); Jt. Com. on Finance (also 2003). **2001**— Tourism and Recreation (vice chp.); Aging and Long-Term Care; Housing; Natural Resources; Small Business and Consumer Affairs; Urban and Local Affairs.

Telephone: Office: (608) 266-7141; (888) 534-0034 (toll free); District: (715) 479-6270.

E-mail address: Rep.Meyer@legis.state.wi.us

Voting address: 1013 Walnut Street, Eagle River 54521.

Mailing address: Office: Room 306 East, State Capitol, P.O. Box 8953, Madison 53708.

Donald Friske (Rep.), 35th Assembly District

Born Tomahawk, November 9, 1961; married; 3 children. Graduate Tomahawk H.S. Full-time legislator. Former deputy sheriff. Veteran; served in Army November 1979 to 1985. Member: Amvets; Optimist Club; NRA. Former member: American Legion.

Elected to Assembly 2000; reelected since 2002. Biennial committee assignments: **2005** — Forestry (chp., also 2003); Criminal Justice and Homeland Security (vice chp.); Jt. Com. for Review of Administrative Rules; Transportation (also 2003). **2003** — Criminal Justice (vice chp.); Energy and Utilities (mbr., vice chp. 2001); Family Law (also 2001). **2001** — Rural Affairs and Forestry (vice chp.); Corrections and the Courts; Small Business and Consumer Affairs; Tourism and Recreation.

Telephone: Office: (608) 266-7694; (888) 534-0035 (toll free); District: (715) 536-4515.

E-mail address: Rep.Friske@legis.state.wi.us

Voting address: N2998 Highway K, Merrill 54452.

Mailing address: Office: Room 312 North, State Capitol, P.O. Box 8952, Madison 53708.

Jeffrey L. Mursau (Rep.), 36th Assembly District

Born Oconto Falls, June 12, 1954; married; 4 children. Graduate Coleman H.S. 1972; attended UW-Oshkosh. Small business owner; electrical contractor and restaurant owner. Member: Crivitz Ski Cats waterski team (advisor, former pres.); Crivitz Lions Club; Crivitz, WI – Crivitz, Germany Sister City Organization (fmr. dir.); Wings over Wisconsin; St. Mary's Catholic Church. Recipient: Crivitz Business Association *Citizen of the Year* 1994. Crivitz Village President 1991-2004.

Elected to Assembly 2004. Biennial committee assignments: **2005** — Forestry (vice chp.); Tourism (vice chp.); Natural Resources; Rural Development; Small Business.

Telephone: Office: (608) 266-3780; (888) 534-0036 (toll free).

Voting address: 4 Oak Street, Crivitz 54114.

Mailing address: Office: Room 18 North, State Capitol, P.O. Box 8953, Madison 53708.

13th SENATE DISTRICT

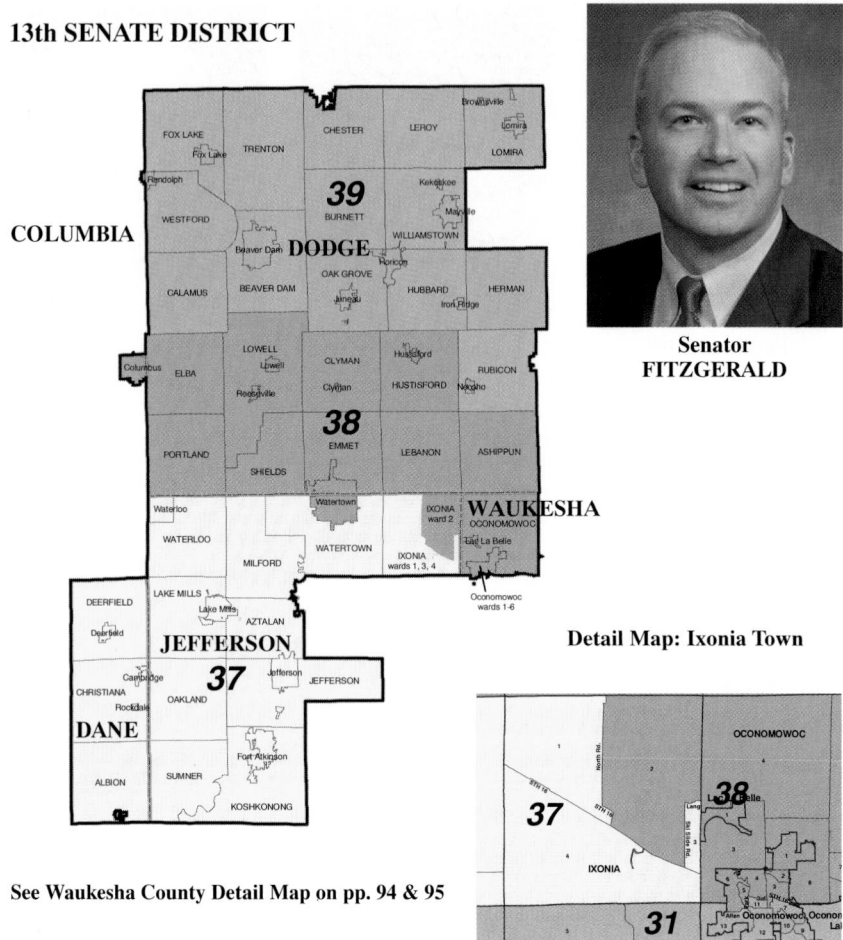

Senator FITZGERALD

Detail Map: Ixonia Town

See Waukesha County Detail Map on pp. 94 & 95

Scott L. Fitzgerald (Rep.), 13th Senate District

Born Chicago, IL, November 16, 1963; married; 3 children. Graduate Hustisford H.S. 1981; B.S. in journalism UW-Oshkosh 1985; U.S. Army Armor Officer Basic Course 1985; U.S. Army Command and General Staff College. Former associate newspaper publisher; member of the U.S. Army Reserve (rank of Lt. Colonel), Battalion CDR 1/274th 9th BDE, 100th Division. Member: Dodge Co. Republican Party (chm. 1992-94); Juneau Lions Club; Juneau Jaycees (former membership chp.); Reserve Officers Assn.; Knights of Columbus; Wisconsin Newspaper Assn. Former member: Forward Wisconsin, Inc.

Elected to Senate 1994; reelected since 1998. Majority Leader 9/17/04 to 11/10/04. Biennial committee assignments: **2005** — Jt. Com. on Finance (co-chp., mbr. since 2003); Jt. Com. on Audit; Jt. Com. on Employment Relations; Jt. Legislative Council. **2003** — Jt. Com. for Review of Criminal Penalties (co-chp.); Education, Ethics and Elections; Finance; Homeland Security, Veterans and Military Affairs and Government Reform; Judiciary, Corrections and Privacy; Claims Bd. (eff. 12/5/03). **2001** — Health, Utilities, Veterans and Military Affairs; Judiciary, Consumer Affairs, and Campaign Finance Reform; Privacy, Electronic Commerce and Financial Institutions (also 1999); Wis. Housing and Economic Development Authority. **1999** — Economic Development, Housing and Government Operations (member to 2/24/99, also 1997); Rural Economic Development Bd. (also 1997). **1997** — State Government Operations and Corrections (chp., eff. 4/21/98); Education (eff. 1/7/98); Health, Human Services, Aging, Corrections, Veterans and Military Affairs (1/15/97 to 4/20/98); Government Effectiveness (eff. 4/21/98, also 1995); Human Resources, Labor, Tourism, Veterans and Military Affairs (eff. 4/21/98); Jt. Com. on Information Policy (eff. 4/21/98, also 1995); Legis. Coun. Coms. on Local Government Spending (vice chp.), on the School Calendar. **1995** — Business, Economic Development and Urban Affairs (member to 6/96); Agriculture, Transportation, Utilities and Financial Institutions; Legis. Coun. Coms. on Americans with Disabilities Act (co-chp.), on Recodification of Fish and Game Laws.

Telephone: Office: (608) 266-5660; District: (920) 386-0260; E-mail address: Sen.Fitzgerald@legis.state.wi.us

Voting address: (Town of Clyman) N4692 Maple Road, Juneau 53039.

Mailing address: Office: Room 317 East, State Capitol, P.O. Box 7882, Madison 53707-7882.

**Representative
WARD**

**Representative
KLEEFISCH**

**Representative
FITZGERALD**

David W. Ward (Rep.), 37th Assembly District

Born Fort Atkinson, April 29, 1953; married; 1 child. Graduate Fort Atkinson H.S.; B.S. in agricultural economics, UW-Platteville 1976. President, family farm corporation. Member: Jefferson Co. Republican Party (former chp.); Jefferson Co. Farmco Cooperative (former vice pres.); Jefferson Co. Farm Bureau (former pres.); Wisconsin Farm Bureau Federation (former dir.). Former member: Wisconsin Milk Marketing Bd. (treas.). Recipient: Wisconsin Farm Bureau *Outstanding Young Farmer* 1983; UW-Platteville *Distinguished Alumni* 2001. Fort Atkinson School Board 1991-94.

Elected to Assembly since 1992. Biennial committee assignments: **2005** — Jt. Com. on Finance (vice chp., mbr. since 1999). **2003** — University of Wisconsin Hospitals and Clinics Authority. **1999** — Legis. Coun. Com. on Dental Care Access (co-chp.). **1997** — Financial Institutions (chp., mbr. since 1993); State Affairs (vice chp.); Agriculture (vice chp. 1995); Colleges and Universities; Education (since 1993); Wis. Housing and Economic Development Authority (also 1995). **1995** — Mandates (chp.); Spec. Com. on Gambling Oversight (also 1993); Legis. Coun. Com. on Adoption Laws (chp.). **1993** — Tourism and Recreation; Legis. Coun. Com. on Protection of Rural Resources.

Telephone: Office: (608) 266-3790; (888) 534-0037 (toll free); District: (920) 563-2769.

E-mail address: Rep.Ward@legis.state.wi.us

Internet address: www.legis.state.wi.us/assembly/asm37/news/

Voting address: (Town of Oakland) N3401 Highway G, Fort Atkinson 53538.

Mailing address: Office: Room 324 East, State Capitol, P.O. Box 8953, Madison 53708.

Joel Kleefisch (Rep.), 38th Assembly District

Born Waukesha, June 8, 1971; married; 1 child. Graduate Waukesha North H.S. 1989; B.A. Pepperdine U. 1993. Small business owner. Former investigative television news reporter for WISN-TV; legislative policy advisor and constituent director. Member: Watertown Elks Club; Watertown Moose Club; Okauchee Lions Club; Watertown Mentorship Program; Musky Mike's fishing pro-staff; Lakewatch Volunteer Organization (founder).

Elected to Assembly 2004. Biennial committee assignments: **2005** — State Affairs (vice chp.); Financial Institutions; Judiciary; State-Federal Relations.

Telephone: Office: (608) 266-8551; (888) 534-0038 (toll free).

E-mail address: Rep.Kleefisch@legis.state.wi.us

Voting address: W357 N6189 Spinnaker Drive, Oconomowoc 53066.

Mailing address: Office: Room 8 West, State Capitol, P.O. Box 8952, Madison 53708; District: P.O. Box 273, Okauchee 53069.

Jeff Fitzgerald (Rep.), 39th Assembly District

Born Chicago, IL; October 12, 1966; 1 son. Graduate Hustisford H.S.; B.S. UW-Oshkosh. Small business owner. Member: Dodge Co. Republican Party (former chm.); Beaver Dam Chamber of Commerce; Juneau Chamber of Commerce; Community Relations Board of Fox Lake Correctional Institution; American Legislative Exchange Council; Pheasants Forever; American Council of Young Political Leaders; State Legislative Leaders Foundation (bd. mbr.). Beaver Dam City Council 2000-July 2003.

Elected to Assembly 2000; reelected since 2002. Assistant Majority Leader 2005. Biennial committee assignments: **2005** — State Affairs (chp., also 2003); Assembly Organization; Financial Institutions (vice chp. 2003, mbr. since 2001); Labor (also 2003); Jt. Com. on Legislative Organization; Rules; State Building Comn. (also 2003). **2003** — Energy and Utilities. **2001** — Housing (vice chp.); Campaigns and Elections; Criminal Justice; Economic Development; Labor and Workforce Development; Speakers Task Force on Budget Review.

Telephone: Office: (608) 266-2540; District: (920) 485-0586.

E-mail: Rep.Fitzgerald@legis.state.wi.us

Voting address: 910 Sunset, Horicon 53032.

Mailing address: Office: Room 113 West, State Capitol, P.O. Box 8952, Madison 53708.

14th SENATE DISTRICT

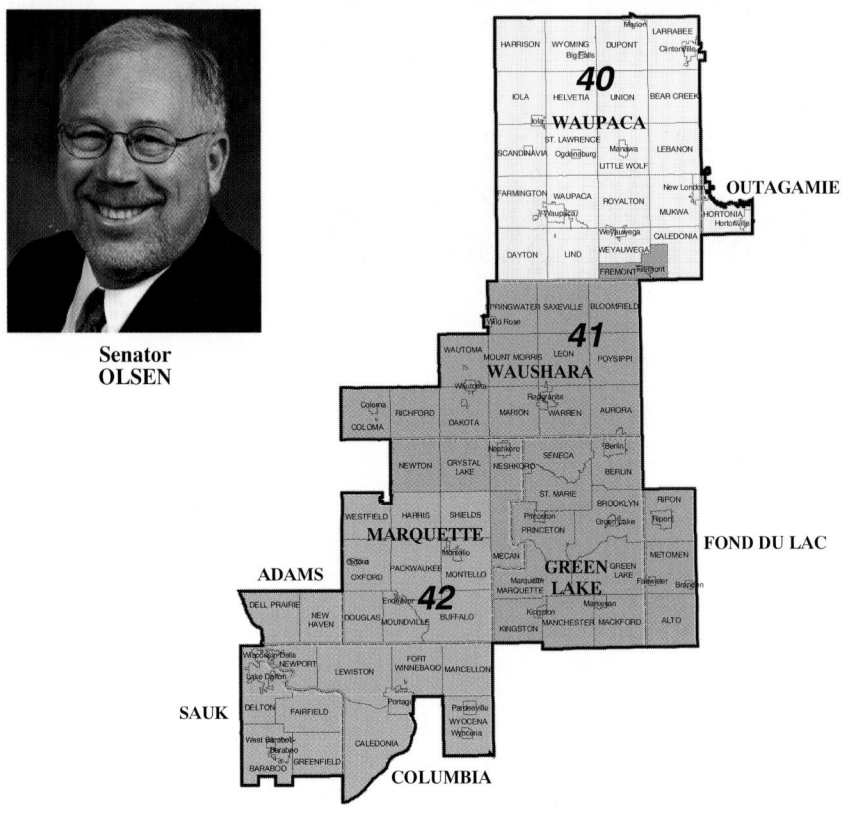

**Senator
OLSEN**

Luther S. Olsen (Rep.), 14th Senate District

Born Berlin, February 26, 1951; 6 children. Graduate Berlin H.S. 1969; B.S. UW-Madison 1973; Wis. Rural Leadership Program Group IV 1990-92. Feed, seed, and fertilizer dealer. Member: Green Lake Co. Republican Party; Waushara Co. Republican Party; Education Commission of the States Steering Committee; North Central Regional Education Laboratory (bd. of dir.). Former member: Waushara Co. Fair Bd. (dir.); Family Health/La Clinica director (1995-99); Berlin Area School Board 1976-97 (pres. 1986-95).

Elected to Assembly 1994-2002. Elected to Senate 2004. Biennial Senate committee assignments: **2005** — Education (chp.); Agriculture and Insurance; Finance; Jt. Com. on Finance; Child Abuse and Neglect Prevention Bd.; Educational Communications Board; University of Wisconsin Hospitals and Clinics Authority Bd. Assembly committee assignments: **2003** — Education (chp. since 1997, mbr. 1995); Education Reform (since 1999, vice chp. 2001); Health (since 1997); Housing; Rural Affairs; Workforce Development. **2001** — Ways and Means; Migrant Labor Council (since 1995). **1999** — Tourism and Recreation; Legis. Coun. Coms. on Dental Care Access, on Navigable Waters Recodification. **1997** — Colleges and Universities; State-Federal Relations; Gov.'s Council on Model Academic Standards; Legis. Coun. Coms. on Services for Visually Handicapped Students (chp.), on Children at Risk Program, on the School Calendar. **1995** — Government Operations (vice chp.); Jt. Com. for Review of Administrative Rules; Agriculture; Mandates; State Supported Programs Study and Adv. Com.; Legis. Coun. Coms. on Public Libraries, on Public School Open Enrollment, on the School Aid Formula.

Telephone: Office: (608) 266-0751; District: (920) 229-4141; E-mail address: Sen.Olsen@legis.state.wi.us

Voting address: 1023 Thomas Street, Ripon 54971.

Mailing address: Room 5 South, State Capitol, P.O. Box 7882, Madison 53707–7882.

**Representative
HUNDERTMARK**   **Representative
BALLWEG**   **Representative
HINES**

Jean L. Hundertmark (Rep.), 40th Assembly District

Born Milwaukee, February 25, 1954; married; 2 daughters. Graduate West Allis Central H.S.; graduate Bryant and Stratton College, Milwaukee 1973; Group VII–Wisconsin Rural Leadership Program 1996-98. Restaurant owner. Member: Waupaca and Outagamie Co. Republican Parties; Waupaca Co. Farm Bureau; Clintonville Area Historical Society; Leadership Waupaca County Steering Com.

Elected to Assembly 1998; reelected since 2000. Assistant Majority Leader 2003. Biennial committee assignments: **2005** — Financial Institutions (chp.); Education (since 1999); Health (also 2003, 1999); Labor (also 2003); Medicaid Reform; Veterans Affairs. **2003** — Aging and Long-Term Care (chp., also mbr. 2001); Assembly Organization; Jt. Com. on Legislative Organization; Rules; Veterans and Military Affairs (vice chp. since 1999). **2001** — Labor and Workforce Development (chp.); Tax and Spending Limitations. **1999** — Labor and Employment; Small Business and Economic Development; Legis. Coun. Com. on Labor Shortages (co-chp.).

Telephone: Office: (608) 266-3794; (888) 947-0040 (toll free); District: (715) 823-2241.

E-mail address: Rep.Hundertmark@legis.state.wi.us

Voting address: (Town of Larrabee) E8815 River Road, Clintonville 54929.

Mailing address: Office: Room 13 West, State Capitol, P.O. Box 8952, Madison 53708.

Joan Ballweg (Rep.), 41st Assembly District

Born Milwaukee, March 16, 1952; married; 3 children. Graduate Nathan Hale H.S. (West Allis) 1970; attended UW-Waukesha; B.A. Elementary Education, UW-Stevens Point 1974. Owner/manager of farm equipment business. Former 1st grade teacher. Member: Markesan Chamber of Commerce (former treas.); Waupun Chamber of Commerce; Green Lake County Farm Bureau; Waupun Memorial Hospital (bd. of dir., fmr. chp.); Agnesian HealthCare Enterprises, LLC management com. (fmr. secy.); volunteer, Markesan District Schools; Markesan PTA (fmr. pres.); Markesan AFS Chapter (hosting coordinator, pres., fmr. host family, liaison). Markesan District Education Assn. *Friend of Education Award* 1990. Markesan City Council 1987-91; Mayor of Markesan 1991-97.

Elected to Assembly 2004. Biennial committee assignments: **2005** — Colleges and Universities (vice chp.); Family Law; Insurance; Rural Affairs and Renewable Energy; Small Business.

Telephone: Office: (608) 266-8077; (888) 534-0041 (toll free); District: (920) 398-3708.

E-mail address: Rep.Ballweg@legis.state.wi.us

Voting address: 170 West Summit Street, Markesan 53946.

Mailing address: Office: Room 115 West, State Capitol, P.O. Box 8952, Madison 53708.

J.A. Hines (Rep.), 42nd Assembly District

Born West Salem, Ohio, May 1, 1927; married; 5 children. Graduate Homer Rural School, Homerville, Ohio; D.V.M. Ohio State University 1953. Full-time legislator. Veterinarian, beef farmer, bed and breakfast owner/operator. World War II veteran; served in Army, 1945-1947. Member: American Veterinary Medical Association (served on animal welfare committee); American Association of Bovine Practitioners (fmr. director of District 5); Wisconsin Hereford Association; Veterans of Foreign Wars Post 6003 (past commander); Oxford Lions Club; National Institute of Animal Agriculture (AABP liaison). Former member: Marquette Co. 4-H (board member and president); Board of Veterinary Examiners (chairman); Wisconsin Agri-business Council; Marquette Co. Farm Bureau. Westfield School Board 1969-81.

Elected to Assembly in November 2001 special election; reelected since 2002. Biennial committee assignments: **2005** — Public Health (chp. since 2003, mbr. since 2001); Aging and Long-Term Care (vice chp., mbr. since 2001); Agriculture (since 2001); Education (since 2001); Tourism (also 2003). **2001** — Tourism and Recreation.

Telephone: Office: (608) 266-7746; (888) 534-0042 (toll free); District: (608) 586-5999.

E-mail address: Rep.Hines@legis.state.wi.us

Fax number: Office: (608) 282-3642.

Voting address: W8632 County Road I, Oxford 53952.

Mailing address: Room 10 West, State Capitol, P.O. Box 8952, Madison 53708.

15th SENATE DISTRICT

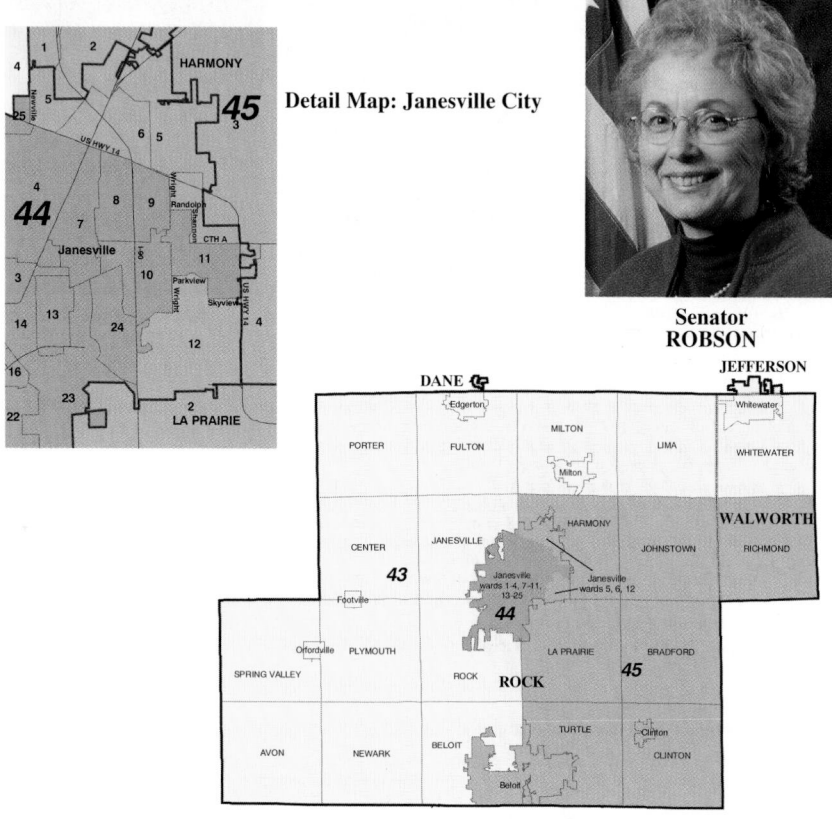

Detail Map: Janesville City

**Senator
ROBSON**

Judith Biros Robson (Dem.), 15th Senate District

Born Cleveland, OH; 3 children. B.S.N. St. John College; M.S. UW-Madison. Registered Nurse, associate degree nursing instructor at Blackhawk Technical College and geriatric nurse practitioner. Member: League of Women Voters (past vice president); Who's Who In American Nursing; Sigma Theta Tau Nursing Honor Society; Wis. Nurses Assn.; Wis. Public Health and Health Policy Institute (adv. bd.); Zonta International; AAUW; Beloit Bike and Ski Club.

Elected to Assembly in June 1987 special election; reelected 1988-96; elected to Senate 1998, 2002. Senate Minority Leader 2005; Senate Majority Caucus Chairperson 2001, 1999. Assembly: Minority Caucus Vice Chairperson 1995; Majority Caucus Vice Chairperson 1993; Majority Caucus Secretary 1991. Biennial Senate committee assignments: **2005** — Jt. Com. on Employment Relations; Jt. Com. on Legislative Organization; Organization; Jt. Legislative Council (also 2001, 1999). **2003** — Jt. Com. for Review of Administrative Rules (mbr., co-chp. 2001, 1999); Review of Administrative Rules (mbr., chp. 2001); Agriculture, Financial Institutions and Insurance (through 5/23/03); Education, Ethics and Elections; Health, Children, Families, Aging and Long Term Care. **2001** — Human Services and Aging (chp., also 1999); Jt. Com. on Audit (also 1999); Audit; Education (also 1999); Health, Utilities, Veterans and Military Affairs (also 1999); Jt. Legislative Council Special Com. on the Public Health System's Response to Terrorism and Public Health Emergencies (co-chp.); Jt. Legislative Council Special Com. on Improving Wisconsin's Fiscal Management. Migrant Labor Council. **1999** — Child Abuse and Neglect Prevention Bd.; Legis. Coun. Com. on Developmental Disabilities (co-chp.). Assembly committee assignments: **1997** — Environment; Health (chp. 1993, mbr. since 1987); Insurance, Securities and Corporate Policy (since 1993). **1995** — Environment and Utilities; Ways and Means (since 1989); Legis. Coun. Coms. on Prevention of Child Abuse and Neglect, on Teacher Preparation, Licensure and Regulation. **1993** — Environmental Resources; Rules; Trade, Science and Technology (eff. 4/26/93, also 1991); Legis. Coun. Com. on School Health Services. **1991** — Public Health and Regulation (chp.); Energy and Commerce (vice chp.); Task Force to Combat Controlled Substance Use by Pregnant Women and Women with Young Children (also 1989); Legis. Coun. Com. on Emergency Medical Services (chp.).

Telephone: Office: (608) 266-2253; (800) 334-1468 (toll free); District: (608) 365-6587.

E-mail address: Sen.Robson@legis.state.wi.us

Internet address: http://www.legis.state.wi.us/senate/sen15/sen15.html

Voting address: 2411 East Ridge Road, Beloit 53511.

Mailing address: Office: Room 202 South, State Capitol, P.O. Box 7882, Madison 53707-7882.

**Representative
TOWNS**

**Representative
SHERIDAN**

**Representative
BENEDICT**

Debi Towns (Rep.), 43rd Assembly District

Born Sycamore, IL, February 12, 1956; married; 4 children, 1 grandchild. Graduate Edgerton H.S. 1974; B.S.B.A. Cardinal Stritch Coll. (Milwaukee) 1996; M.S.E. UW-Whitewater 1999; attended UW-Oshkosh and UW-Madison. Owner, family dairy farm operation. Former business manager, Brodhead schools; financial consultant, Dept. of Public Instruction. Member: Wis. Assoc. of School Business Officials; Wis. Farm Bureau; Fulton Church. Recipient: School Administrator's Alliance *Legislator of the Year Award* 2004. Edgerton School Bd. 1985-91, 1994-96.

Elected to Assembly 2002; reelected 2004. Biennial committee assignments: **2005** — Education (chp., vice chp. 2003); Agriculture (also 2003); Colleges and Universities (also 2003); Education Reform (also 2003). **2003** — Financial Institutions.

Telephone: Office: (608) 266-9650; District: (608) 884-6681.

Voting address: 7930 North Eagle Road, Janesville 53548.

Mailing address: Office: Room 302 North, State Capitol, P.O. Box 8953, Madison 53708.

Michael J. Sheridan (Dem.), 44th Assembly District

Born Janesville, September 17, 1958; married; 3 children. Graduate Parker H.S. (Janesville) 1977; Associates degree, UW-Rock County (Janesville) 2004. UAW President. Former auto assembly worker; UAW vice president. Member: UAW; United Way (bd. mbr.); Janesville Performing Arts Center (bd. of dir.); Blackhawk Technical Coll. Foundation (bd. mbr.); Wisconsin UAW CAP (chp., fmr. area chp.); Leadership Development Academy (bd. of dir.); Rock Co. Labor Coalition; NAACP; LCLAA; Boy Scouts of America. Former member: Boys and Girls Club (bd. of dir.); Janesville School District ATODA (com. mbr.); UAW/GM Charity Raffle Organizing Com.; UAW Education Com.; Laborfest (treas.).

Elected to Assembly 2004. Biennial committee assignments: **2005** — Insurance; Labor; Small Business; Workforce Development.

Telephone: Office: (608) 266-7503; (888) 947-0044 (toll free); District: (608) 756-0788.

E-mail address: Rep.Sheridan@legis.state.wi.us

Voting address: 1032 Nantucket Drive, Janesville 53546.

Mailing address: Office: Room 412 North, State Capitol, P.O. Box 8953, Madison 53708.

Chuck Benedict (Dem.), 45th Assembly District

Born Norwalk, CT, August 13, 1946. Graduate New Canaan H.S. (Conn.) 1964; A.B. Dartmouth Coll. 1968; M.A. Princeton U. 1970; attended Duke U.; M.D. U. of Conn. Medical School 1979. Full-time legislator. Retired physician (neurologist); former high school math and science teacher. Member: Wisconsin Medical Society; American Academy of Neurology; American Assoc. for Advancement of Science; Beloit Mem. Hospital Ethics Com. (co-founder); League of Conservation Voters; Physicians for Social Responsibility.

Elected to Assembly 2004. Biennial committee assignments: **2005** — Health; Medicaid Reform; Public Health; Rural Affairs and Renewable Energy; State Affairs.

Telephone: Office: (608) 266-9967; District: (608) 362-7698.

Voting address: 1730 Morgan Terrace, Beloit 53511.

Mailing address: Office: Room 306 West, State Capitol, P.O. Box 8952, Madison 53708.

16th SENATE DISTRICT

**Senator
MILLER**

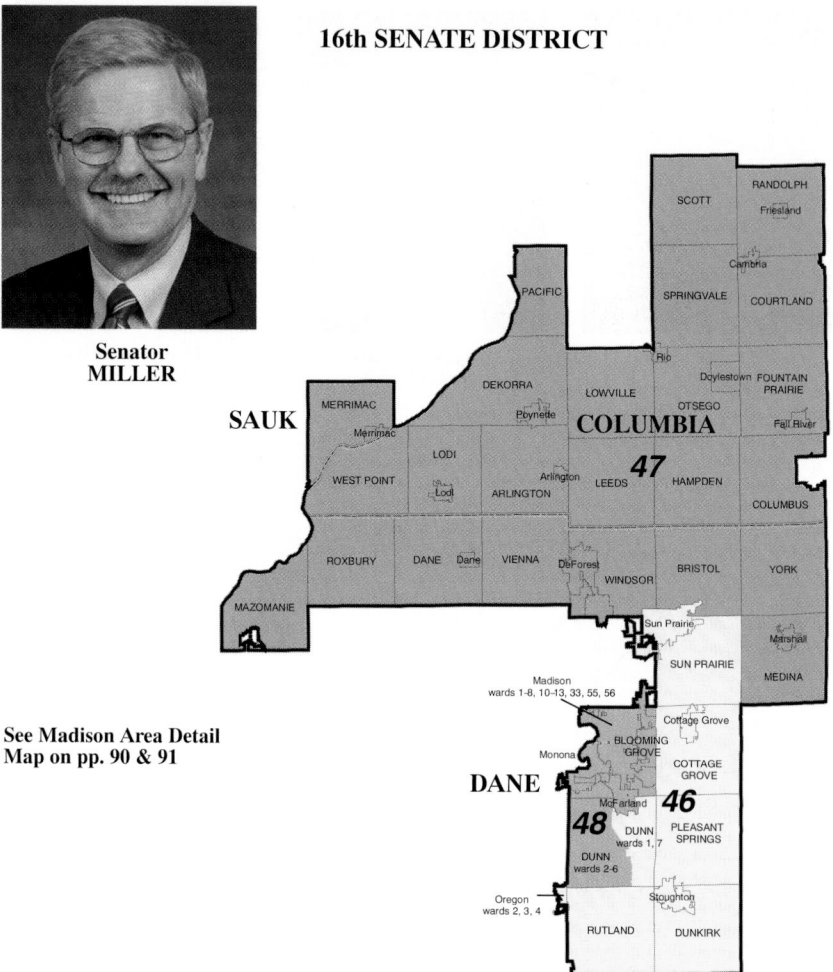

**See Madison Area Detail
Map on pp. 90 & 91**

Mark Miller (Dem.), 16th Senate District

Born Boston, MA, February 1, 1943; married; 3 children. Graduate Middleton H.S.; B.S. UW-Madison 1973; Bowhay Institute for Legislative Leadership Development 1999; Fleming Fellows Leadership Institute 2002. Former military pilot and real estate manager. Member: Midwest Progressive Elected Officials Network (co-chp.). Wis. Air National Guard, 1966-95 (ret. Lt. Colonel). Child Welfare Executive Steering Committee (since 2001); Research Education and Policy on Food Group (REAP) (founding mbr.); Environmental Action Teams (EnAct) (founding mbr.); Governor's Task Force to Improve Access to Oral Health 2005. Dane Co. Board of Supervisors 1996-2000.

Elected to Assembly 1998-2002; elected to Senate 2004. Minority Caucus Vice Chairperson 2005. Biennial Senate committee assignments: **2005** — Jt. Com. for Review of Administrative Rules; Agriculture and Insurance; Jt. Legislative Audit Com.; Campaign Finance Reform and Ethics; Jt. Legislative Council. Assembly committee assignments: **2003** — Aging and Long-Term Care (eff. 5/13/03); Budget Review; Children and Families (since 1999); Health (since 1999); Natural Resources (also 2001); Veterans and Military Affairs; Child Abuse and Neglect Prevention Bd.; Environmental Education Bd. (also 2001). **2001** — Environment. **1999** — Campaigns and Elections; Consumer Affairs; Public Health; Law Revision Committee.

Telephone: Office: (608) 266-9170; District: (608) 221-2701.

E-mail address: Sen.Miller@legis.state.wi.us

Voting address: 4903 Roigan Terrace, Monona 53716.

Mailing address: Office: Room 106 South, State Capitol, P.O. Box 7882, Madison 53707–7882.

**Representative
HEBL**

**Representative
HAHN**

**Representative
PARISI**

Gary Alan Hebl (Dem.), 46th Assembly District

Born Madison, May 15, 1951; married; 3 children. Graduate Sun Prairie H.S. 1969. B.A. Political Science UW-Madison 1973; Gonzaga U. Law School 1976. Attorney and owner of a title insurance company. Member: Dane Co. Bar Assn.; Wis. Bar Assn.; Sun Prairie Optimist Club (youth coordinator, fmr. pres.); Sun Prairie Chamber of Commerce (vice pres.); U.W. Flying Club (chm., bd. of dir.); Dane Co. Pilots Assn.; Aircraft Owners Assn.; Experimental Aircraft Assn.; Knights of Columbus (4th deg. mbr.); Sun Prairie Cable Access Bd.; Sun Prairie Telecommunications Bd.; YMCA (bd. of dir., fmr. pres.); Sun Prairie Public Library Bd. of Trustees (pres.); Sacred Heart Parish Council (fmr. trustee); Sun Prairie Quarterback Club (pres.). Recipient: Sun Prairie *Star* poll *Best Attorney in Sun Prairie* 2004, 2003, 2002; Madison Magazine *One of Madison's Best Real Estate Attorneys* 2002; Sun Prairie Exchange Club *Book of Golden Deeds Award* 2003; Chamber of Commerce *Judith Krivsky Business Person of the Year Award* 2002; Sun Prairie Business and Education Partnership *Outstanding Small Business of the Year* 2001.

Elected to Assembly 2004. Biennial committee assignments: **2005** — Natural Resources; Property Rights and Land Management; Small Business; Ways and Means.

Telephone: Office: (608) 266-7678.

E-mail address: Rep.Hebl@legis.state.wi.us

Voting address: 515 Scheuerell Lane, Sun Prairie 53590.

Mailing address: Office: Room 304 West, State Capitol, P.O. Box 8952, Madison 53708.

Eugene Hahn (Rep.), 47th Assembly District

Born Milwaukee, July 21, 1929; married; 4 children. Graduate Cambria H.S.; attended UW College of Agriculture 1947-48. Farmer. Member: Columbia Co. Farm Bureau; Church Elder; Friesland Community Men's Chorus; Friesland Band; Pardeeville Lodge 171 F. and A.M.; Columbia and Dane Co. Republican Parties; Scottish Rite Valley of Madison; Wis. Corn Growers Assn. Former member: Farmers Home Admin. (dir., chm.); Federal Land Bank (dir., chm.); Columbia Co. Environmental Protection League (chm.); Cambria Low Income Elderly Housing (dir., treas.); 1976 Farm Progress Show Com. (secy.); 4-H leader. Town assessor 1957-61; Columbia Co. Board 1972-91.

Elected to Assembly since 1990. Biennial committee assignments: **2005** — Rural Affairs and Renewable Energy (chp.); Jt. Survey Com. on Tax Exemptions (vice chp., co-chp. 2001, mbr. since 1999); Energy and Utilities; Transportation (since 1999, also 1993); Ways and Means (also 2003). **2003** — Rural Affairs (chp.); Economic Development; Education (since 1997). **2001** — Agriculture (vice chp., mbr. since 1995); Speaker's Railroad Crossing Task Force. **1999** — Consumer Affairs (eff. 4/27/99); Corrections and the Courts. **1997** — Tourism and Recreation (chp., also 1995, mbr. since 1991); Environment; Highways and Transportation (also 1995); Legis. Coun. Com. on Faith-Based Approaches to Crime Prevention and Justice. **1995** — Colleges and Universities; Judiciary (since 1991); Legis. Coun. Com. on Future of Recycling. **1993** — Highways; Legis. Coun. Com. on Remediation of Environmental Contamination.

Telephone: Office: (608) 266-3404; District: (920) 348-5765.

Voting address: (Town of Springvale) W3198 Old County Highway B, Cambria 53923.

Mailing address: Office: Room 15 West, State Capitol, P.O. Box 8952, Madison 53708.

Joseph T. Parisi (Dem.), 48th Assembly District

Born Madison, October 24, 1960; married; 1 child. Attended Middleton H.S.; B.A. in sociology, UW-Madison; attended Madison Area Technical College. Member: Operation Fresh Start (pres., bd. of dir.). Former member: Atwood Community Center (bd. of dir.). Dane County Clerk 1996-2004.

Elected to Assembly 2004. Biennial committee assignments: **2005** — Aging and Long-Term Care; Agriculture; Budget Review; Corrections and the Courts; Urban and Local Affairs.

Telephone: Office: (608) 266-5342; District: (608) 242-0575.

E-mail address: Rep.Parisi@legis.state.wi.us

Voting address: 3114 Oakridge Avenue, Madison 53704.

Mailing address: Office: Room 126 North, State Capitol, P.O. Box 8953, Madison 53708.

Dale W. Schultz (Rep.), 17th Senate District

Born Madison, June 12, 1953; married; 2 children. Graduate Madison West H.S.; B.B.A. UW-Madison 1975. Farm manager and real estate broker. Member: Sauk Co. Farm Bureau; Masons; Shrine; Lions; Hillpoint Rod and Gun Club; Taliesin Preservation, Inc. (bd. of dir.). Awards: Military Order of the Purple Heart *Legislator of the Year* 2002; National Wild Turkey Federation *Outstanding Legislator* 2001; National Farmers Organization of Wisconsin *Legislative Appreciation Award*; Wisconsin Wetlands Association and Sierra Club *Conservation Award* 2002; Deer and Elk Farmers Association *Legislator of the Year* 2002; WMC *Outstanding Legislator Award* 2001; Hazel Green Police Dept. *Honorary Police Officer* 2000; Tavern League of Wisconsin *Top Shelf Award* 2000; Neighborhood Housing Services *Legislative Leadership Award* 2000; *Excellence in Education Award* 2000; *Friend of Grocers Award* 2004; Trout Unlimited *Leadership Award* 1998; AFSCME Local 2748 *Appreciation Award* 1998; Wis. Sheriffs and Deputy Sheriffs Assn. *Commendation* 1997; Wis. Counties Assn. *Friend of County Government* 2004; Council of State Governments *Toll Fellow* 1996, 1995; Wis. Hospitals Assn. *Health Care Leadership Award* 2003; Wis. Farm Bureau Federation *Friend of Agriculture* 2004; Wis. Federation of Cooperatives *Friend of Cooperatives* 2003; Wis. Pharmacists Assn. *Outstanding Legislator*; Wis. Assn. of Health Underwriters *Insuring Freedom Award* 2004; Wis. Medical Society *Health Leadership Award* 2004.

Elected to Assembly 1982-91 (resigned 10/7/91); elected to Senate in September 1991 special election; reelected since 1994. Majority Leader 2005. Biennial committee assignments: **2005** — Organization (chp.); Jt. Com. on Employment Relations; Jt. Legis. Coun.; Jt. Com. on Legislative Organization; State and Federal Relations; Wis. Historical Soc. Bd. of Curators (since 2001); State Capitol and Executive Residence Bd. (since 1999). **2003** — Agriculture, Financial Institutions and Insurance (chp.); Jt. Survey Com. on Retirement Systems (co-chp.); Health, Children, Families, Aging and Long Term Care; Higher Education and Tourism; Transportation Projects Commission (also 2001).

Telephone: Office: (608) 266-0703; (800) 978-8008 (toll free); District: (608) 647-4614.

E-mail address: Sen.Schultz@legis.state.wi.us

Voting address: 515 North Central Avenue, Richland Center 53581.

Mailing address: Office: Room 211 South State Capitol, P.O. Box 7882, Madison 53707-7882.

Senator
SCHULTZ

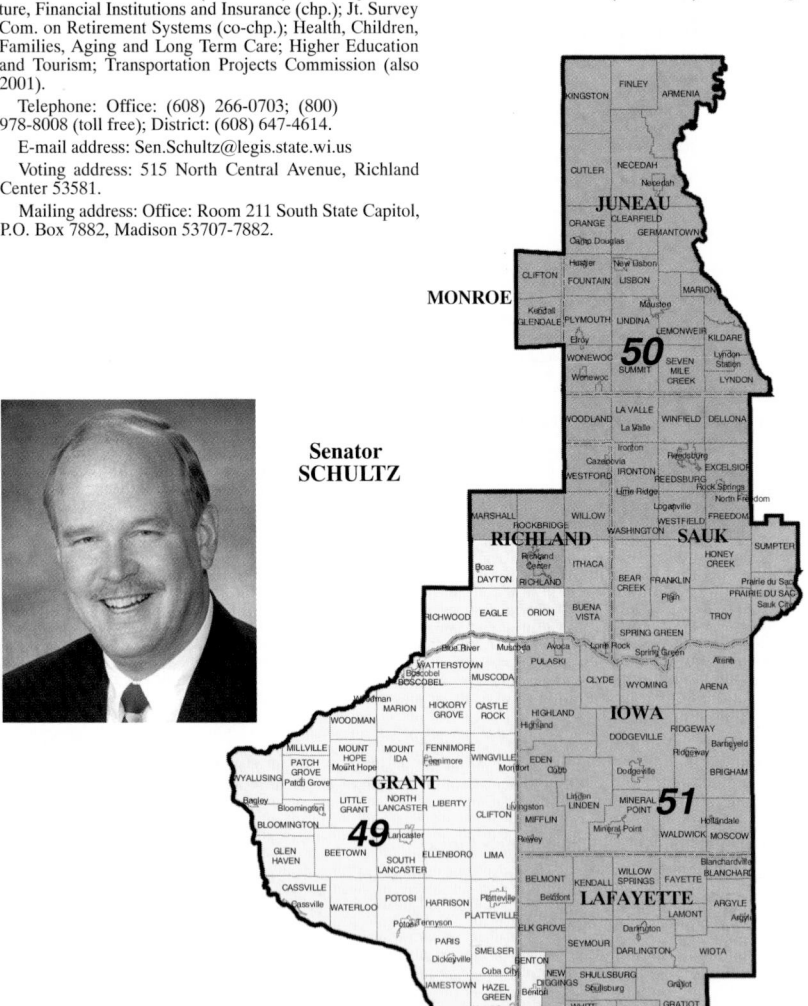

17th SENATE DISTRICT

Representative **Representative** **Representative**
LOEFFELHOLZ **ALBERS** **FREESE**

Gabe Loeffelholz (Rep.), 49th Assembly District

Born Town of Paris, Grant County, November 11, 1940; married; 2 children and 3 grandchildren. Graduate Platteville H.S. Farmer. Veteran; served in Wisconsin National Guard 1959-64. Member: Farm Bureau; NRA; D.A.V.; FFA Alumni; Dairyland Antique Tractor Club (president). Former member: Jaycees. Recipient: Wis. Towns Assn. *Legislative Friend of Towns Award* 2004; Wis. Farm Bureau Federation *Friend of Agriculture*; Wis. Builders Assn. *Friend of the Housing Industry.* Served on the Platteville School Board; Farm Service Agency; Conservation Board.

Elected to Assembly 2000; reelected since 2002. Biennial committee assignments: **2005** — Veterans Affairs (chp.); Agriculture (since 2001); Economic Development; Government Operations and Spending Limitations (also 2003); Military Affairs. **2003** — Rural Development (chp.); Education (also 2001); Veterans and Military Affairs. **2001** — Government Operations (vice chp.); Criminal Justice; Rural Affairs and Forestry; Transportation.

Telephone: Office: (608) 266-1170; (888) 872-0049 (toll free); E-mail address: Rep.Loeffelholz@legis.state.wi.us

Voting address: 1497 Airport Road, Platteville 53818-9599.

Mailing address: Office: Room 317 North, State Capitol, P.O. Box 8952, Madison 53708-8952.

Sheryl K. Albers (Rep.), 50th Assembly District

Born Baraboo, September 9, 1954; 1 son. Graduate Baraboo Senior H.S.; attended Carroll College 1972-74; B.A. Ripon College 1976; J.D. UW-Madison 2004. Graduate Group III, UW-Extension's Wisconsin Rural Leadership Program. Attorney in private practice, Hazelbaker & Assoc. S.C. Former Assembly Republican Caucus Policy Analyst. Member: Sauk Co. Farm Bureau (former treas.); Sauk Co. Republican Party (former chm.); American Council of Young Political Leaders.

Elected to Assembly in December 1991 special election; reelected since 1992. Biennial committee assignments: **2005** — Property Rights and Land Management (chp., also 2003); Budget Review; Children and Families (also 2003); Family Law; Judiciary (also 2003); Rural Affairs and Renewable Energy; Legis. Coun. Spec. Com. on Child Guardianship and Custody. **2003** — Jt. Com. for the Review of Criminal Penalties (co-chp.); Corrections and the Courts (vice chp.). **2001** — Jt. Com. on Finance (since 1997); Finance; Claims Bd. (since 1997). **1999** — Y2K Government Liability Task Force (chp.). **1997** — Legis. Coun. Com. on Conservation Laws Enforcement and American Indian Study Com. **1995** — Insurance, Securities and Corporate Policy (chp., mbr. 1993); Colleges and Universities (also 1993); Environment and Utilities; Natural Resources; Rural Affairs (also 1991); State of Wis. Building Comn.; Council on Child Labor (since 1991); Legis. Coun. Com. on Land Use Policies. **1993** — Environmental Resources; State Affairs (ranking minority mbr.). **1991** — Public Health and Regulation; Legislative Coun. Com. on Oversight of Community Mental Health Services (secy.).

Telephone: Office: (608) 266-8531; (877) 947-0050 (toll free); District: (608) 524-2529 or (608) 524-0022.

E-mail address: Rep.Albers@legis.state.wi.us

Voting address: 339 Golf Course Road, Reedsburg 53959.

Mailing address: Office: Room 15 North, State Capitol, P.O. Box 8952, Madison 53708.

Stephen J. Freese (Rep.), 51st Assembly District

Born Dubuque, IA, March 16, 1960; married; 2 children. Graduate Southwestern Community H.S. (Hazel Green); B.S. in political science, UW-Platteville 1982. Farm manager. Town of Jamestown supervisor 1980-94; Grant Co. Board 1982-92.

Elected to Assembly since 1990. Speaker Pro Tempore 2005, 2003, 2001, 1999, 1997, 1995; Minority Caucus Vice Chairperson 1993. Biennial committee assignments: **2005** — Campaigns and Elections (chp. since 1999); Assembly Organization (since 1995); Financial Institutions (also 2003); Public Health (since 1999); Rules (since 1993); Rural Affairs and Renewable Energy; Jt. Legislative Council (since 1995). **2003** — Electronic Democracy and Government Reform (vice chp.); Rural Affairs. **2001** — Census and Redistricting (also 1999); Rural Affairs and Forestry (also 1999); State Historical Society Bd. of Curators (since 1993); Mississippi River Parkway Comn. (also 1999). **1999** — Children and Families; Special Com. on The Renovation of Lambeau Field; Legis. Coun. Com. on Recodification of Operating While Intoxicated and Safety Laws Pertaining to Motor Vehicle, All-Terrain Vehicle, Boat or Snowmobile Operation. **1997** — Elections and Constitutional Law (also 1995); Judiciary (also 1995); Managed Care; Special Com. on Wis. Sesquicentennial (chp.); Wis. Sesquicentennial Comn.; Legis. Coun. Com. on Historic Building Code (vice chp.). **1995** — Aging and Long-Term Care; Health (since 1991); Labor and Employment.

Telephone: Office: (608) 266-7502; (888) 534-0051 (toll free); E-mail address: Rep.Freese@legis.state.wi.us

Voting address: 310 East North Street, Dodgeville 53533.

Mailing address: Office: Room 115 West, State Capitol, P.O. Box 8952, Madison 53708.

Carol A. Roessler (Rep.), 18th Senate District

Born Madison, January 16, 1948; married. Graduate Madison West H.S.; B.S. UW-Oshkosh 1972; preretirement education leadership training, U. of Michigan School of Gerontology. Full-time legislator. Former director Winnebago Co. nutrition program for older adults, instructor of preretirement education at Fox Valley Technical Institute. Member: NOVA Drug and Alcohol Treatment Services (bd. of dir.). Former member: Oshkosh Foundation (bd. of dir.); Oshkosh Com. on Aging; Oshkosh Big Brothers and Big Sisters (bd. of dir.); Boys and Girls Club of Oshkosh (bd. of dir.). Sampling of awards: Wis. Dental Assn. *Presidential Citation* 2002; Wis. Grocers Assoc. *Friend of Grocers* 2004, 2002; Wis. Manuf. and Commerce *Working for Wisconsin Award* 2002, 2000, 1998; Wis. Counties Assoc. *Outstanding Legislator* 2003-04, 2001-02, 1999-2000, 1997-98, 1995-96; Oshkosh Chamber of Commerce *Athena Award* 2001, 2000; Wis. Assoc. of Homes and Services for the Aging *Distinguished Service in Elder Advocacy Award* 2000; AFSCME Local 2748 *Friend of Probation and Parole Agents* 1998; Lutheran Soc. Serv. *Leadership Award* 1997; Boys and Girls Club of America *Service to Youth Award* 1997; Wis. State Council of Vietnam Veterans of America *Legislator of the Year* 1996; Wis. Hospital Assoc. *Health Care Advocate Award* 1996; Prof. Fire Fighters of Wis. *Legislator of the Year* 1996; Wis. Alliance of Cities *Certificate of Merit* 1996; Am. Cancer Soc. Am. Heart Assoc. and Am. Lung Assoc. *Legislative Leadership Award* 1995; Nat. Fed. of Ind. Business *Wisconsin Guardian of Small Business Award* 2004, 2003, 1995-96, 1989-90; Farm Bureau Volunteers for Agriculture *A Friend of Agriculture* 2003-04, 1995-96, 1993-94; Wis. Head Start Assoc. *Award of Excellence* 1993; Badger State Sheriffs Assoc. *Law and Order Award* 1993; Catholic War Veterans *Legislator of the Year* 1993; Wis. Assn. for Retarded Citizens *Elected Official Award* 1993, 1992, 1990; Coalition of Wis. Aging Groups and Wis. Coalition for Advocacy *Appreciation Award* 1993; Wis. Assn. of County Aging Unit Directors *Outstanding Service Award* 1992; Wis. Council on Aeronautics Aviation *Leadership Award* 1992; Fond du Lac Area Assn. of Commerce *Special Service Award* 1992; Wisconsin Community Action Program Assoc. *William Steiger Human Service Award* 1989; UW-Oshkosh *Outstanding Alumnus of the Year* 1988.

Elected to Assembly 1982-86 (resigned 4/20/87); elected to Senate in April 1987 special election; reelected since 1988. Biennial committee assignments: **2005** — Jt. Com. on Audit (co-chp., also 2003); Health, Children, Families, Aging and Long-Term Care (chp., also 2003); Judiciary, Corrections and Privacy; Council on Alcohol and Other Drug Abuse (vice chp., also 2003, 2001).

Telephone: Office: (608) 266-5300; (888) 736-8720 (toll free); District: (920) 233-6889.

E-mail address: Sen.Roessler@legis.state.wi.us

Voting address: 1506 Jackson Street, Oshkosh 54901.

Mailing address: Office: Room 8 South, State Capitol, P.O. Box 7882, Madison 53707-7882.

18th SENATE DISTRICT

Detail Map: Oshkosh Area

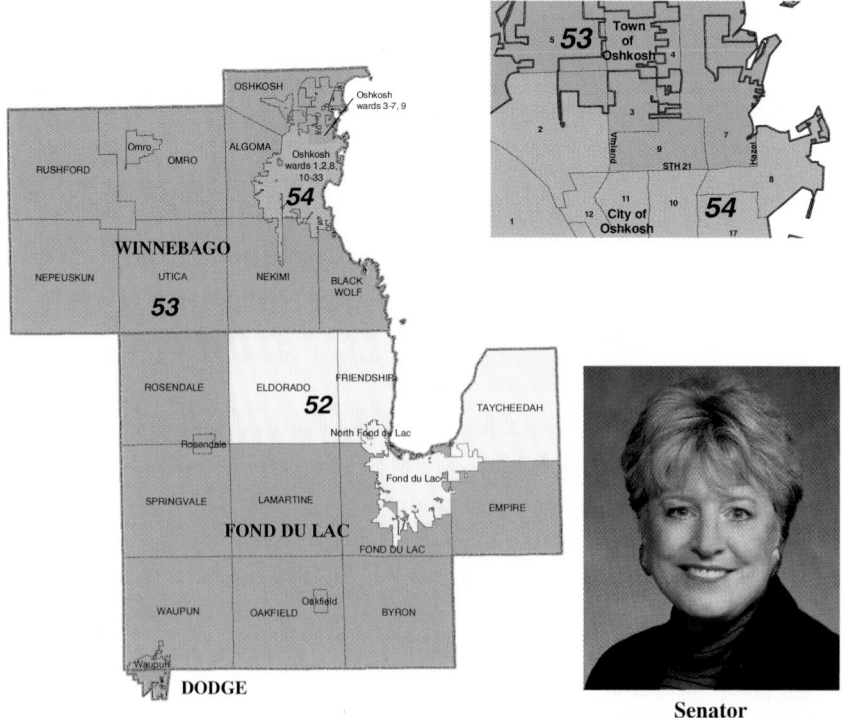

**Senator
ROESSLER**

Representative TOWNSEND   **Representative OWENS**   **Representative UNDERHEIM**

John F. Townsend (Rep.), 52nd Assembly District

Born St. Louis, MO, May 23, 1938; married; 2 children. Graduate Madison H.S. (Madison Heights, MI); B.S. Wayne State U. 1960; M.B.A. Wayne State U. 1967. Full-time legislator. Former partner in a small business and a corporate executive. Vietnam veteran; served in U.S. Navy and U.S. Naval Reserves; retired Captain U.S. Naval Reserves. Member: Fond du Lac Public Library Bd. (1992-98); Fond du Lac Salvation Army Adv. Bd.; Fond du Lac Noon Rotary (former programs chm.); Fond du Lac Redevelopment Authority (bd. mbr. 1996-98); Fond du Lac Adult Literacy (bd. mbr.); Wisconsin Literacy (bd. mbr.); Fond du Lac Arts Council (adv. bd.); Fond du Lac Visiting Nurses Assn. (bd. mbr.); VFW Post 1904; American Legion Post 0075. Fond du Lac County Economic Development Corp. (bd. mbr. 1992-96); Fond du Lac City Council 1992-98.

Elected to Assembly 1998; reelected since 2000. Biennial committee assignments: **2005** — Aging and Long-Term Care (chp.); Housing (vice chp., also 2003); Education (since 2001); Financial Institutions (also 2003); Military Affairs; Public Health (also 1999); Veterans Affairs. **2003** — Electronic Democracy and Government Reform (chp.); Veterans and Military Affairs (vice chp., mbr. 2001); Jt. Legislative Council. **2001** — Economic Development (chp.); Colleges and Universities (vice chp., mbr. 1999); Council on Alcohol and Other Drug Abuse; Migrant Labor Council.

Telephone: Office: (608) 266-3156; (888) 529-0052 (toll free); District: (920) 923-0935.
E-mail address: Rep.Townsend@legis.state.wi.us
Voting address: 297 Roosevelt Street, Fond du Lac 54935.
Mailing address: Office: Room 22 West, State Capitol, P.O. Box 8953, Madison 53708.

Carol Owens (Rep.), 53rd Assembly District

Born Wabeno, August 8, 1931; married; 4 children. Graduate Wabeno H.S.; attended Fox Valley and Moraine Park Technical Colleges. Former dairy farmer. Member: Wis. Towns Assn. (former dir.); Winnebago Co. Republicans; Fond du Lac County Women's Cancer Control Coalition; Waupun Community and Corrections Relations Bd. Former member: 4-H Golden Oak (leader-29 yrs.); Green Meadow PTA (program chm.). Recipient: Wis. Builders Assn. *Friend of the Housing Industry Award* 2003, 2002, 2001; Wis. Coalition Against Domestic Violence *DIVA Award* 2003; Pro-Life Wisconsin *Legislator of the Year Award* 2001; Wisconsin Council on Problem Gambling *Legislative Appreciation Award* 2002; National Federation of Independent Business *Guardian of Small Business Award* 2000; Wis. Counties Assn. *Outstanding Legislator Award* 1998; *Friends of Wisconsin Counties Award* 2001; Wis. Towns Assn. *Friend of Wis. Towns Award* 2001; Wis. Farm Bureau *Friend of Agriculture Award* 1996, 1994. Town of Nekimi Clerk 1977-93; Winnebago Co. Board 1982-93.

Elected to Assembly since 1992. Majority Caucus Secretary 2005, 2003, 2001, 1999. Biennial committee assignments: **2005** — Family Law (chp. since 2001, mbr. 1999); Corrections and the Courts (since 1999); Criminal Justice and Homeland Security; Rules (since 2001); State Capitol and Executive Residence Bd. (since 1997). **2003** — Criminal Justice (since 1999).

Telephone: Office: (608) 267-7990; (888) 534-0053 (toll free); District: (920) 589-4262; Fax: (608) 282-3653.
E-mail address: Rep.Owens@legis.state.wi.us
Voting address: (Town of Nekimi) 144 County Road C, Oshkosh 54904.
Mailing address: Office: Room 315 North, State Capitol, P.O. Box 8953, Madison 53708.

Gregg Underheim (Rep.), 54th Assembly District

Born La Crosse, August 22, 1950; single. Graduate La Crosse Central H.S.; B.S. UW-La Crosse 1972. Full-time legislator. Former high school English teacher, congressional aide to Congressman Thomas Petri, and small business owner. Member: Mid Morning Kiwanis Club; Kiwanis Club of Oshkosh (past pres.); YMCA; Winnebago Co. Republican Party; Oshkosh Choraliers.

Elected to Assembly in June 1987 special election; reelected since 1988. Biennial committee assignments: **2005** — Health (chp. since 1995, mbr. since 1989); Public Health (vice chp., also 2003, mbr. 1999); Colleges and Universities (since 1999, vice chp. 1997, mbr. 1987-91); Corrections and the Courts (since 2001); Insurance (also 2003, 1999). **2001** — State and Local Finance (chp.); Education Reform (also 1999). **1999** — Legis. Coun. Coms. on Arts Funding (co-chp.), on Use of Prescription Drugs for Children. **1997** — State-Federal Relations (chp.); Insurance, Securities and Corporate Policy (also 1993); State Affairs; Legis. Coun. Com. on School Discipline and Safety. **1995** — Ways and Means. **1993** — Spec. Com. on Health Care (ranking minority mbr.); Legis. Coun. Com. on Shared Governmental Services. **1991** — Financial Institutions and Insurance; Spec. Com. on Reform of Health Ins. (ranking minority mbr.).

Telephone: Office: (608) 266-2254; (888) 534-0054 (toll free); District: (920) 233-1082.
E-mail address: Rep.Underheim@legis.state.wi.us
Voting address: 1652 Beech Street, Oshkosh 54901.
Mailing address: Office: Room 11 North, State Capitol, P.O. Box 8953, Madison 53708.

19th SENATE DISTRICT

See Little Chute Village Map on p. 20
See Appleton Area Map on p. 98

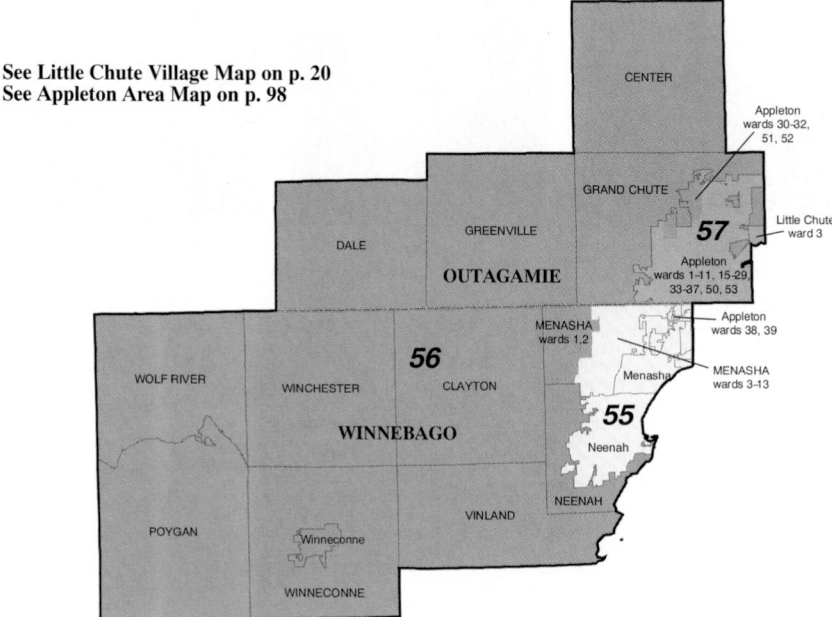

Michael G. Ellis (Rep.), 19th Senate District

Born Neenah, February 21, 1941; married. Graduate Neenah H.S.; B.S. in secondary education, UW-Oshkosh 1965. Legislator and farmer. Neenah City Council 1969-75.

Elected to Assembly 1970-80; elected to Senate since 1982. Minority Leader 1999 (resigned 1/25/00), 1997 (1/15/97 to 4/20/98), 1995 (eff. 6/96); Majority Leader 1997 (eff. 4/21/98), 1995 (eff. 1/95 to 6/96), 1993 (eff. 4/20/93); Assistant Minority Leader 1987, 1985. Biennial committee assignments: **2005** — Campaign Finance Reform and Ethics (chp.); State and Federal Relations (chp.). **2003** — Education, Ethics and Elections (chp.); Jt. Survey Com. on Tax Exemptions (co-chp., mbr. 2001). **2001** — Jt. Survey Com. on Retirement Systems (also 1999); Retirement Research Com. (also 1999); Universities, Housing, and Government Operations. **1999** — Jt. Com. on Employment Relations (resigned 1/25/00, mbr. since 1989); Jt. Com. on Legislative Organization (resigned 1/25/00, mbr. since 1985); Senate Organization (resigned 1/25/00, chp. 1997, eff. 4/21/98, also 1/95 to 6/96, 1993, mbr. since 1985); Disability Bd. (resigned 1/25/00, mbr. since 1989); Jt. Legislative Council (resigned 1/25/00, mbr. since 1989). **1995** — Jt. Com. on Information Policy (resigned 12/5/95); Spec. Com. on State and Federal Relations (vice chp. eff. 6/96, chp. 1/95 to 6/96); School Funding Commission. **1993** — Senate Rules (mbr. 1987 to 4/20/93). **1991** — Legis. Coun. Coms. on Drainage District Laws, on Issues Relating to Hunger Prevention, on Oversight of Community Mental Health Services, on Private Forest Land Programs. **1987** — Urban Affairs, Energy, Environmental Resources and Elections; Housing, Government Operations and Cultural Affairs (resigned 4/21/87); Legis. Coun. Com. on Natural and Recreational Resources. **1985** — Energy and Environmental Resources (also 1983); Tourism, Revenue, Financial Institutions and Forestry; Child Labor Coun. **1983** — Transportation; Legis. Coun. Peace Officer Study Com.

Telephone: Office: (608) 266-0718; District: (920) 751-4801.

Voting address: 1752 County Road GG, Neenah 54956.

Mailing address: Office: Room 118 South, State Capitol, P.O. Box 7882, Madison 53707-7882; District: 429 South Commercial Street, Neenah 54956.

**Senator
ELLIS**

**Representative
KAUFERT**

**Representative
McCORMICK**

**Representative
WIECKERT**

Dean R. Kaufert (Rep.), 55th Assembly District

Born Outagamie County, May 23, 1957; married; 2 children. Graduate Neenah H.S. Trophy and Awards store owner. Member: Winnebago Co. Republican Party; Neenah-Menasha Breakfast Optimists (former pres.); Fox Cities Chamber of Commerce. Neenah City Council 1985-91.

Elected to Assembly since 1990. Majority Caucus Sergeant at Arms 1997, 1995; Minority Caucus Sergeant at Arms 1993. Biennial committee assignments: **2005** — Jt. Com. on Finance (co-chp., also 2003, mbr. since 1997); Jt. Com. on Audit (vice chp., mbr. 2003); Jt. Com. on Employment Relations (also 2003); Jt. Legislative Council (also 2003). **1999** — Jt. Com. on Information Policy (also 1997). **1997** — Legis. Coun. Com. on Local Government Funding. **1995** — Financial Institutions (chp., mbr. 1993); Housing (vice chp., mbr. 1993, 1991); Criminal Justice and Corrections; Mandates; Small Business and Economic Development (also 1993); Spec. Com. on Gambling Oversight (vice chp.). **1993** — Criminal Justice and Public Safety (also 1991). **1991** — Environmental Resources, Utilities and Mining; Small Business and Education or Training for Employment; Legis. Coun. Com. on Energy Resources; Task Force on Regulatory Barriers to Affordable Housing.

Telephone: Office: (608) 266-5719; (888) 534-0055 (toll free); District: (920) 729-0521.
E-mail address: Rep.Kaufert@legis.state.wi.us
Voting address: 1360 Alpine Lane, Neenah 54956.
Mailing address: Office: Room 308 East, State Capitol, P.O. Box 8952, Madison 53708.

Terri McCormick (Rep.), 56th Assembly District

Born Waupun; 3 children. Graduate Lowell P. Goodrich H.S. (Fond du Lac); Assoc. Arts UW-Fond du Lac 1978; B.S. *magna cum laude* UW-Oshkosh 1980; post graduate work U. of Windsor 1982; Teacher Certificate Lawrence U. 1992; M.A. in Administrative Leadership, Marian College (Fond du Lac) 2000. Full-time legislator. Former education consultant. Member: American Legion Auxiliary; Winnebago and Outagamie County Republican Parties; Winnebago County Farm Bureau. Former member: Educational Services Inc. (past pres./founder); Education Consultants Ltd. (past pres./founder); Leadership Solutions Institute (past pres./founder); Dist. Citizen Adv. Counsel (chm.); Institute for Political Training/Fox Cities Chamber of Commerce (graduate); Task Force on Local Government Health Partnerships (chp.).

Elected to Assembly 2000; reelected since 2002. Biennial committee assignments: **2005** — Economic Development (chp., also 2003); Judiciary (vice chp. since 2001); Insurance (since 2001); Public Health (since 2001). **2003** — Education Reform (also 2001); Transportation. **2001** — Labor and Workforce Development; State and Local Finance.

Telephone: Office: (608) 266-7500; (888) 534-0056 (toll free); District: (920) 954-7515.
E-mail address: Rep.McCormick@legis.state.wi.us
Internet address: http://www.legis.state.wi.us/assembly/asm56/news/
Voting address: W6140 Long Court, Appleton 54914.
Mailing address: Office: Room 127 West, State Capitol, P.O. Box 8953, Madison 53708.

Steve Wieckert (Rep.), 57th Assembly District

Born Appleton, October 26, 1954; married. Graduate Appleton West H.S.; attended Philips Exeter Academy; B.A. in political science and M.A. in public administration from American University, Washington, D.C.; Congressional Research Service Graduate Institute. Legislator, Realtor, and CEO of Wieckert Real Estate. Former legislative asst. for Congressman Tom Petri, Washington, D.C. Author of "Cody's Law" promoting organ donation. Recipient: Independent Business Assoc. *Legislator of the Year Award* 1999; Wis. Urban Transit Assn. *Legislator of the Year* 2001; Wis. Builders Assn. *Friend of Housing* 2003, 2002, 2001; WMC *Working for Wisconsin Award* 2002, 2000, 1998; Wis. Paper Council *Champion of Paper* 2004; Wis. Realtors Assn. *Chairman's Award* 2004; Wis. Alliance of Cities *Representative of the Year* 2004; Wis. Council of Religious and Independent Schools *Friend of Religious and Independent Schools* 2004; NFIB *Guardian of Small Business* 2003-04; American Cancer Assn. *Certificate of Recognition* 2004. Member: Outagamie Co. Local Emergency Planning Com.; Fox Cities Chamber of Commerce; Fox Valley Homebuilder's Assn.; Realtors Assn. of Northeast Wis.; Rotary Club of Appleton; Outagamie Co. Republican Party (past chp.); ALEC; Farm Bureau; Coalition of Wis. Aging Groups; Wis. Nature Conservancy; Twin Cities Rod and Gun Club; Natl. Honor Soc. for Public Affairs and Administration; Participant, American Birkebeiner.

Elected to Assembly 1996; reelected since 1998. Biennial committee assignments: **2005** — Housing (chp.); Jt. Legis. Council (co-chp.); Insurance (vice chp.); Financial Institutions; Health; Labor; WHEDA Board.

Telephone: Office: (608) 266-3070; (888) 534-0057 (toll free); District: (920) 731-3000; Fax: (608) 282-3657.
E-mail address: Rep.Wieckert@legis.state.wi.us
Voting address: 1 Weatherstone Drive, Appleton 54914.
Mailing address: Office: Room 16 West, State Capitol, P.O. Box 8953, Madison 53708.

20th SENATE DISTRICT

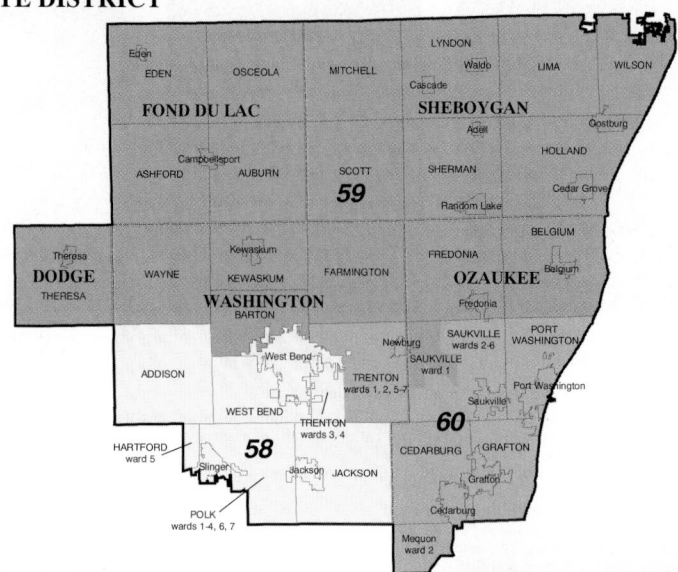

Detail Map: Trenton Town

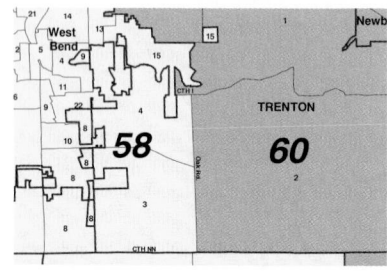

Senator
GROTHMAN

Glenn Grothman (Rep.), 20th Senate District

Born Milwaukee, July 3, 1955. Graduate Homestead H.S., Mequon; B.B.A.; J.D. UW-Madison. Former practicing attorney. Member: Kiwanis-West Bend Early Risers; Washington Co. Bar Assn.; Loyal Order of the Moose-West Bend; UW-Madison Alumni Assn. of Washington Co.; Kettle Moraine Symphony (bd. member). Recipient: Milwaukee Co. Rep. Party *Assembly Tax Cutter of the Year* 2002; Ind. Bus. Assn. *Legislator of the Year*; Wis. Counties Assn. *Outstanding Legislator Award*; Wis. Right to Life *Pro-Life Hero Award*; Pro-Life Wis. *Legislator of the Year*; Wis. Farm Bureau *Friend of Agriculture Award*; Apartment Assoc. *Legislator of the Year.*

Elected to Assembly in December 1993 special election; reelected 1994-2002; elected to Senate 2004. Majority Caucus Vice Chairperson 2003, 2001, 1999. Biennial Senate committee assignments: **2005** — Jt. Com. for Review of Administrative Rules (co-chp.); Jt. Survey Com. on Retirement Systems (co-chp.); Education; Judiciary, Corrections and Privacy; Jt. Legislative Council. Assembly committee assignments: **2003** — Administrative Rules (chp. since 2001); Jt. Com. for Review of Administrative Rules (co-chp. since 1995); Budget Review; Campaigns and Elections; Judiciary (vice chp. 1997, also 1995, mbr. 1993); Labor; Rules (since 1999); Law Revision Com. (co-chp. since 1997, mbr. 1995). **2001** — Children and Families (also 1999); Education Reform (also 1999). **1999** — Judiciary and Personal Privacy; Labor and Employment (since 1995); Legis. Coun. Com. on Use of Prescription Drugs for Children (co-chp.). **1997** — Income Tax Review; Legis. Coun. Coms. on Local Government Spending, on Programs for Prevention Services. **1993** — Spec. Com. on Welfare Reform; Legis. Coun. Com. on Americans with Disabilities Act.

Telephone: Office: (608) 266-7513; (800) 662-1227 (toll free); District: (262) 338-8061.

E-mail address: Sen.Grothman@legis.state.wi.us

Voting address: 111 South 6th Avenue, West Bend 53095.

Mailing address: Office: Room 20 South, State Capitol, P.O. Box 7882, Madison 53707-7882.

Representative STRACHOTA   **Representative LeMAHIEU**   **Representative GOTTLIEB**

Pat Strachota (Rep.), 58th Assembly District

Born Cuyahoga Co., Ohio, June 29, 1955; married; 4 children. Graduate Glen Oak/Gimour Academy 1973; B.A. Government, minor in American History, certificate in Urban Planning, St. Mary's College (Notre Dame, IN) 1977. Full-time legislator. Former personnel/safety analyst, Washington Co. Human Resource Dept. Member: West Bend Noon Rotary; Kettle Moraine YMCA (bd. mbr.); West Bend/Jackson Boys & Girls Club (bd. mbr.); West Bend Chamber of Commerce; Washington Co. Ag. and Industry Society; Washington Co. Historical Society; Friend of West Bend Art Gallery; St. Frances Cabrini Parish. Former member: West Bend Economic Development Corp. (bd. mbr.); Great Blue Heron Girl Scout Council (bd. mbr.). Washington Co. Board 1986-2002. Southeast Wisconsin Regional Planning Commission 1986-2002.

Elected to Assembly 2004. Biennial committee assignments: **2005** — Medicaid Reform (vice chp.); Aging and Long-Term Care; Health; Southeast Wisconsin Freeways; Ways and Means.

Telephone: Office: (608) 264-8486; District: (262) 338-3790.

E-mail address: Rep.Strachota@legis.state.wi.us

Voting address: 639 Ridge Road, West Bend 53095.

Mailing address: Office: Room 3 North, State Capitol, P.O. Box 8953, Madison 53708.

Daniel R. LeMahieu (Rep.), 59th Assembly District

Born Sheboygan, November 5, 1946; married; 3 children. Graduate Oostburg H.S. 1964; attended UW-Sheboygan and UW-Milwaukee. Former publisher of Lakeshore Weekly. Vietnam Era veteran; served in Army, 1969-71. Member: Oostburg Business Association (past pres.); Oostburg Kiwanis Club (past pres.). Recipient: *Friend of Agriculture Award* 2003-2004; Wis. Counties Assn. *Outstanding Legislator Award* 2003-2004; Wis. Grocers Assn. *Friend of Grocers Award* 2003-2004; *Friend of the Dairy Industry Award* 2003-2004. Sheboygan Co. Bd. 1988-Dec. 2002 (chm. 2000-Dec. 2002).

Elected to Assembly 2002; reelected 2004. Biennial committee assignments: **2005** — Urban and Local Affairs (chp., vice chp. 2003); Jt. Com. for Review of Administrative Rules (vice chp.); Aging and Long-Term Care (also 2003); Corrections and the Courts. **2003** — Rural Development; Small Business.

Telephone: Office: (608) 266-9175; (888) 534-0059 (toll free); District: (920) 564-3392.

E-mail address: Rep.LeMahieu@legis.state.wi.us

Voting address: 21 South 8th Street, Oostburg 53070.

Mailing address: Office: Room 17 North, State Capitol, P.O. Box 8952, Madison 53708; District: P.O. Box 700200, Oostburg 53070.

Mark Gottlieb (Rep.), 60th Assembly District

Born Milwaukee, December 11, 1956; married; 4 children. Graduate James Madison H.S. (Milwaukee) 1974; B.S. UW-Milwaukee 1981; M. Engr. UW-Milwaukee 1984. Civil engineer. Vietnam Era veteran, served in Navy, 1974-78. Member: American Legion Post 82; Ozaukee Co. Republican Party; Washington Co. Republican Party; Port Washington Chamber of Commerce; Grafton Chamber of Commerce. Recipient: Port Washington Chamber of Commerce *Citizen of the Year* 2002. City of Port Washington alderman 1991-97; Mayor of Port Washington 1997-2003.

Elected to Assembly 2002; reelected 2004. Majority Caucus Vice Chairperson 2005. Biennial committee assignments: **2005** — Review of Administrative Rules (chp.); Jt. Com. for Review of Administrative Rules (co-chp.); Southeast Wisconsin Freeways (vice chp.); Energy and Utilities (also 2003); Rules; Urban and Local Affairs (also 2003). **2003** — Colleges and Universities (vice chp.); Transportation; Veterans and Military Affairs.

Telephone: Office: (608) 267-2369; (888) 534-0060 (toll free); District: (262) 268-6998.

E-mail address: Rep.Gottlieb@legis.state.wi.us

Voting address: 1205 Noridge Trail, Port Washington 53074.

Mailing address: Office: Room 103 West, State Capitol, P.O. Box 8952, Madison 53708.

21st SENATE DISTRICT

**Senator
STEPP**

Detail Map: Racine Area

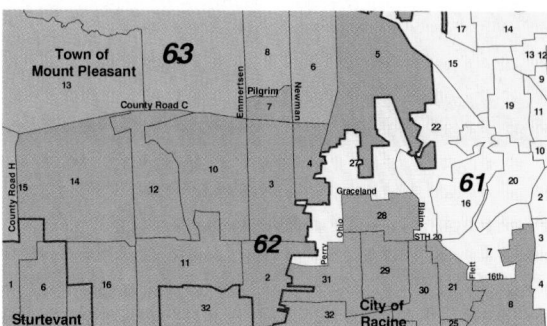

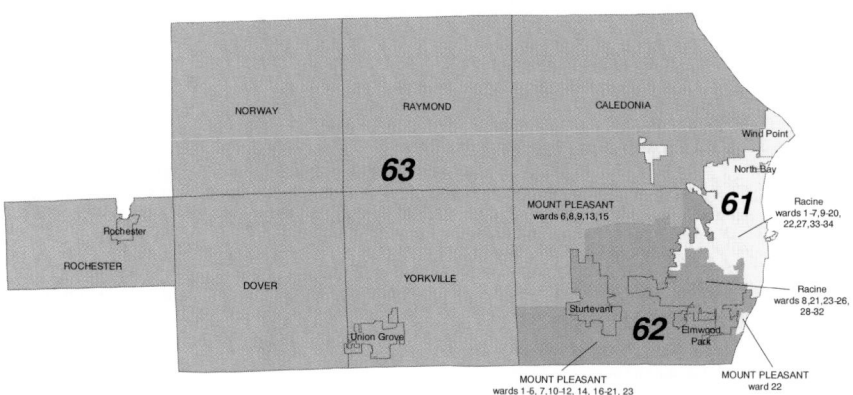

Cathy Stepp (Rep.), 21st Senate District

Born Kenosha, August 17, 1963; married; 2 children. Graduate Oak Creek H.S. 1981. Home builder. Member: Wisconsin Builders Assn. Bd.; National Assn. of Home Builders Bd.; Racine/Kenosha Builders Assn.; Metro. Builders Assn.; Racine Kiwanis. Former member: Natural Resources Bd.

Elected to Senate 2002. Majority Caucus Vice Chairperson 2005. Biennial committee assignments: **2005** — Housing and Financial Institutions (chp.); Natural Resources and Transportation; Jt. Com. for Review of Administrative Rules; Jt. Survey Com. on Retirement Systems. **2003** — Economic Development, Job Creation and Housing (chp.); Education, Ethics and Elections; Environment and Natural Resources; Judiciary, Corrections and Privacy; Wis. Housing and Economic Development Authority Bd.

Telephone: Office: (608) 266-1832; District: (262) 636-3617.

Internet address: www.legis.state.wi.us/senate/sen21/news/

Voting address: 14520 50th Road, Sturtevant 53177.

Mailing address: Office: Room 7 South, State Capitol, P.O. Box 7882, Madison 53707-7882.

Representative
TURNER

Representative
LEHMAN

Representative
VOS

Robert L. Turner (Dem.), 61st Assembly District

Born Columbus, MS, September 14, 1947; married; 3 children. Graduate R.E. Hunt H.S., Columbus, MS; attended Dominican College 1972; B.S. in business administration, UW-Parkside 1976. Vietnam veteran; served in Air Force 1967-70. Member: Big Brothers and Big Sisters (bd. of advisors); NAACP; American Legion; Vietnam Veterans of America (life mbr.); VFW Post 1391 (life mbr.); 33rd degree Mason; Urban League (bd. of dir., former pres.). Racine City Council 1976-2004; State Elections Board 1987-90 (chp. 1990).

Elected to Assembly since 1990. Minority Caucus Chairperson 2005, 2003; Minority Caucus Vice Chairperson 2001, 1999; Minority Caucus Sergeant at Arms 1997. Biennial committee assignments: **2005** — Assembly Organization (also 2003); Criminal Justice and Homeland Security; Judiciary; Rules (also 2003); Veterans Affairs. **2003** — Criminal Justice; State Affairs; Urban and Local Affairs (eff. 2/14/03). **2001** — Jt. Com. for Review of Administrative Rules; Labor and Workforce Development; Tax and Spending Limitations; Ways and Means (since 1991). **1999** — Financial Institutions (also 1995); Labor and Employment (since 1995); Transportation; State of Wis. Building Comn. (since 1991). **1997** — Highways and Transportation (also 1995). **1995** — Urban and Local Affairs; Governor's Clean Air Act Amendments Implementation Task Force (also 1993); Legis. Coun. Com. to Review the Election Process. **1993** — Transportation (chp.); Elections, Constitutional Law and Corrections; Excise and Fees (also 1991); Highways (also 1991); Legis. Coun. Com. on Emergency Government Services. **1991** — Elections and Constitutional Law (vice chp.); Trade, Science and Technology; Legis. Coun. Com. on Sexual Harassment.

Telephone: Office: (608) 266-0731; (888) 529-0061 (toll free); District: (262) 634-7371.
E-mail address: Rep.Turner@legis.state.wi.us
Voting address: 36 McKinley Avenue, Racine 53404.
Mailing address: Office: Room 212 North, State Capitol, P.O. Box 8953, Madison 53708.

John W. Lehman (Dem.), 62nd Assembly District

Born Rhinelander, August 2, 1945; married; 3 daughters. Graduate Washington Park H.S.; B.A. Luther College 1967; M.Ed. Carthage College 1979; attended UW-Parkside and UW-Madison. Full-time legislator. Former high school history and economics teacher. Member: Racine Co. Democratic Party; Praeder-Willi Syndrome Assn. of Wis.; Racine Heritage Museum; Friends of the Library, Racine Public Library; Clean Wisconsin; Sierra Club. Former member: Racine Public Library Bd. (former pres.); Racine Sister City Planning Council; Racine Bd. of Health; Racine Education Association. Racine City Council 1988-2000 (former pres.).

Elected to Assembly 1996; reelected since 1998. Biennial committee assignments: **2005** — Education (since 1997); Education Reform (since 2001); Insurance (also 2003); Workforce Development (also 2003). **2001** — Environment; Natural Resources (also 1999); Public Health (eff. 11/19/01); Small Business and Consumer Affairs; Legis. Coun. Spec. Com. on Mental Health Parity. **1999** — Family Law; Small Business and Economic Development (also 1997). **1997** — Urban and Local Affairs; Legis. Coun. Com. on the School Calendar.

Telephone: Office: (608) 266-0634; (888) 534-0062 (toll free); District: (262) 632-3330.
E-mail address: Rep.LehmanJ@legis.state.wi.us
Voting address: 708 Orchard Street, Racine 53405-2354.
Mailing address: Office: Room 303 West, State Capitol, P.O. Box 8952, Madison 53708.

Robin J. Vos (Rep.), 63rd Assembly District

Born Burlington, July 5, 1968; single. Graduate Burlington H.S. 1986; UW-Whitewater 1991. Small business owner. Former congressional district director; former legislative assistant. Member: Rotary Club (past pres.); Ducks Unlimited; Racine/Kenosha Farm Bureau; Racine Zoological Society; Knights of Columbus; Racine Co. Republican Party; Racine Area Manufacturers and Commerce; NFIB (leadership council mbr.); Union Grove Chamber of Commerce; Wind Lake Chamber of Commerce. UW Board of Regents 1989-91. Racine Co. Board 1994-2004 (former chp. of Finance and Personnel Com.).

Elected to Assembly 2004. Biennial committee assignments: **2005** — Children and Families (vice chp.); Campaigns and Elections; Financial Institutions; Government Operations and Spending Limitations; Labor; Medicaid Reform.

Telephone: Office: (608) 266-9171; (888) 534-0063 (toll free); Fax: (608) 282-3663; District: (262) 631-7871.
E-mail address: Rep.Vos@legis.state.wi.us
Voting address: 4710 Eastwood Ridge, Racine 53406.
Mailing address: Office: Room 304 North, State Capitol, P.O. Box 8953, Madison 53708.

22nd SENATE DISTRICT

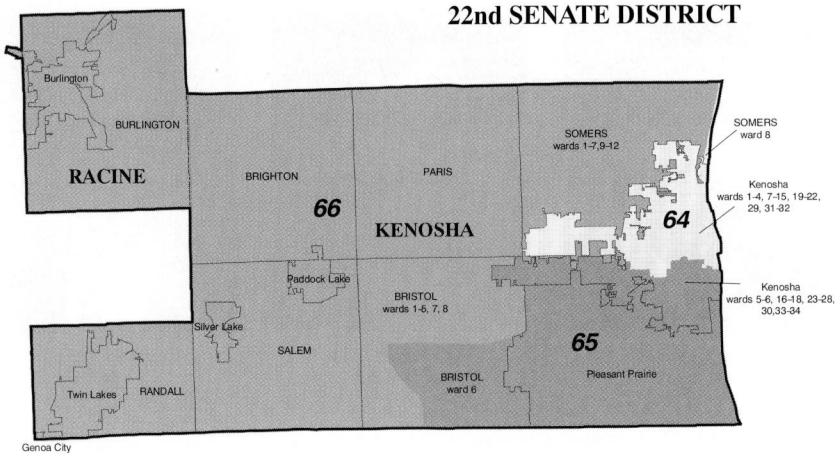

Detail Map: Kenosha City

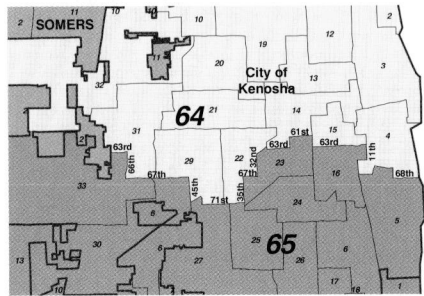

Senator
WIRCH

Robert W. Wirch (Dem.), 22nd Senate District

Born Kenosha, November 16, 1943; married; 2 children. Graduate Mary D. Bradford H.S.; B.A. UW-Parkside 1970. Full-time legislator. Former factory worker and liaison to JTPA programs. Served in Army Reserve 1965-71. Member: Polish Legion of American Veterans; Danish Brotherhood; Shalom Center Soup Kitchen Volunteer; Kenosha Sport Fishing and Conservation Assn.; Friends of the Museum; Kenosha Scout Leaders Rescue Squad Advisory Council; Senior Action Council; Kenosha Area Business Alliance; Democratic Party of Wis. Former member: Kenosha Boys and Girls Club (bd. of dir.). Kenosha County supervisor 1986-94 (served on Health and Human Services Com., Welfare Bd., and Developmental Disabilities Bd.).

Elected to Assembly 1992; reelected 1994; elected to Senate since 1996. Minority Caucus Chairperson 2003. Biennial committee assignments: **2005** — Energy, Utilities and Information Technology; Natural Resources and Transportation; Veterans, Homeland Security, Military Affairs, Small Business and Government Reform; Jt. Survey Com. on Retirement Systems (co-chp. 2001, 1999, mbr. since 1997); Retirement Research Com. (since 1997). **2003** — Energy and Utilities; Environment and Natural Resoures; Homeland Security, Veterans and Military Affairs and Government Reform. **2001** — Jt. Com. on Finance; Environmental Resources; Human Services and Aging (also 1999); Judiciary, Consumer Affairs, and Campaign Finance Reform. **1999** — Economic Development, Housing and Government Operations (chp.); Agriculture, Environmental Resources and Campaign Finance Reform; State of Wis. Building Comn.; Law Revision Com.; Transportation Projects Comn. **1997** — Jt. Com. on Audit (co-chp., eff. 1/15/97 to 4/20/98); Jt. Com. for Review of Administrative Rules (eff. 1/15/97 to 1/5/98, also 1995); Agriculture and Environmental Resources (eff. 1/15/97 to 4/20/98); Health, Family Services and Aging (eff. 4/21/98); Health, Human Services, Aging, Corrections, Veterans and Military Affairs (eff. 1/15/97 to 1/7/98); Judiciary, Campaign Finance Reform and Consumer Affairs (chp., eff. 1/5/98); Council on Workforce Excellence; Legis. Coun. Coms. on Conservation Laws Enforcement, on Disciplinary Procedures for Represented Police and Fire Personnel.

Telephone: Office: (608) 267-8979; District: (262) 694-7379; Office Hotline: (888) 769-4724.

E-mail address: Sen.Wirch@legis.state.wi.us

Voting address: 3007 Springbrook Road, Pleasant Prairie 53158.

Mailing address: Office: Room 415 South, State Capitol, P.O. Box 7882, Madison 53707-7882.

Representative
KREUSER

Representative
STEINBRINK

Representative
KERKMAN

James E. Kreuser (Dem.), 64th Assembly District

Born Kenosha, May 20, 1961; married; 2 sons. Graduate Tremper H.S. 1979; B.A. in political science, UW-Parkside 1983; M.P.A. UW-Parkside 1986. Full-time legislator. Former admin. assistant to Kenosha Co. Executive. Member: Unity Masonic Lodge No. 367; Senior Action Coun.; Kenosha Area Business Alliance; Dem. Party of Wis.; Danish Brotherhood; Polish Legion of Amer. Veterans; Ducks Unlimited; Kenosha Sport Fishing and Cons. Assn.; Urban League of Racine and Kenosha; Natl. Alliance of the Mentally Ill; Boys and Girls Club of Kenosha; AAUW; Dem. Leadership Council; Friends of the Kenosha Public Museum. Former member: Red Cross Exec. Bd.; UFCW No. 1444.

Elected to Assembly in August 1993 special election; reelected since 1994. Minority Leader 2005, 2003; Assistant Minority Leader 2001 (eff. 5/1/01). Biennial committee assignments: **2005** — Assembly Organization (since 2001); Jt. Com. on Employment Relations (also 2003); Jt. Com. on Legislative Organization (since 2001); Rules (since 2001); Jt. Legislative Council (also 2003). **2001** — Jt. Com. for Review of Admin. Rules (also 1999, 1997); Jt. Com. on Audit; Jt. Com. on Information Policy and Technology; Financial Institutions (also 1999); Veterans and Military Affairs (also 1999). **1999** — Jt. Com. on Information Policy; Transportation Projects Comn. (also 1997); Legis. Coun. Coms. on Navigable Waters Recodification, on State-Tribal Relations. **1997** — Elections and Constitutional Law (also 1995); Mandates (also 1995); Legis. Coun. Coms. on Health and Economics of the Tavern Industry, on Public School Open Enrollment. **1995** — Highways and Transportation.

Telephone: Office: (608) 266-5504; (888) 534-0064 (toll free); District: (262) 553-5555; Fax: (608) 282-3664.

E-mail address: Rep.Kreuser@legis.state.wi.us

Voting address: 3505 14th Place, Kenosha 53144.

Mailing address: Office: Room 201 West, State Capitol, P.O. Box 8952, Madison 53708.

John P. Steinbrink (Dem.), 65th Assembly District

Born Kenosha, April 17, 1949; married; 3 children. Graduate George Tremper H.S.; attended Carthage College and UW-Madison Farm and Industry Short Course. Grain farmer. Former dairy farmer. Member: Kenosha Co. Farm Bureau (former pres. and vice pres.); Danish Brotherhood; Senior Action Council; Wis. League of Municipalities; Moose Lodge No. 286; Italian-American Society; Kenosha Area Business Alliance. Former member: Wis. Electric Community Round Table; Conserv F.S.; Kenosha-Racine F.S.; Pleasant Prairie Police Auxiliary; Pleasant Prairie Planning Commission; Wisconsin Towns Assn. Pleasant Prairie Town Board 1985-89; Pleasant Prairie Village Board 1989-present (pres. 1995-present).

Elected to Assembly 1996; reelected since 1998. Biennial committee assignments: **2005** — Economic Development (also 2003); Energy and Utilities (also 2003); Natural Resources (since 1999); Transportation (ranking min. mbr., also 2003). **2003** — Agriculture (eff. 5/13/03); Budget Review; Governor's Coun. on Tourism. **2001** — Agriculture (since 1997); Government Operations (ranking minority mbr.); Tourism and Recreation (since 1997). **1997** — Highways and Transportation; Land Use.

Telephone: Office: (608) 266-0455; (888) 534-0065 (toll free); District: (262) 694-5863.

E-mail address: Rep.Steinbrink@legis.state.wi.us

Voting address: 8602 88th Avenue, Pleasant Prairie 53158.

Mailing address: Office: Room 307 West, State Capitol, P.O. Box 8953, Madison 53708.

Samantha Kerkman (Rep.), 66th Assembly District

Born Burlington, March 6, 1974; married. Graduate Wilmot H.S.; B.A. UW-Whitewater 1996. Full-time legislator. Former legislative aide. Member: Twin Lakes Chamber and Area Business Assn.; Twin Lakes American Legion Auxiliary Post 544; VFW Auxiliary Post 5830; Powers Lake Sportsmen Club.

Elected to Assembly 2000; reelected since 2002. Biennial committee assignments: **2005** — Budget Review (chp., also 2003); State-Federal Relations (vice chp.); Audit (vice chp. 2001); Jt. Com. on Audit (since 2001); Judiciary (since 2001); Southeast Wisconsin Freeways; Ways and Means (since 2001). **2003** — Financial Institutions (also 2001). **2001** — Urban and Local Affairs (vice chp.); Government Operations.

Telephone: Office: (608) 266-2530; (888) 534-0066 (toll free); District: (262) 279-1037.

E-mail address: Rep.Kerkman@legis.state.wi.us

Voting address: (Town of Randall) 8705 385th Avenue, Burlington 53105.

Mailing address: Office: Room 109 West, State Capitol, P.O. Box 8952, Madison 53708; District: P.O. Box 156, Powers Lake 53159.

23rd SENATE DISTRICT

See Eau Claire Area Detail Map on p. 97

**Senator
ZIEN**

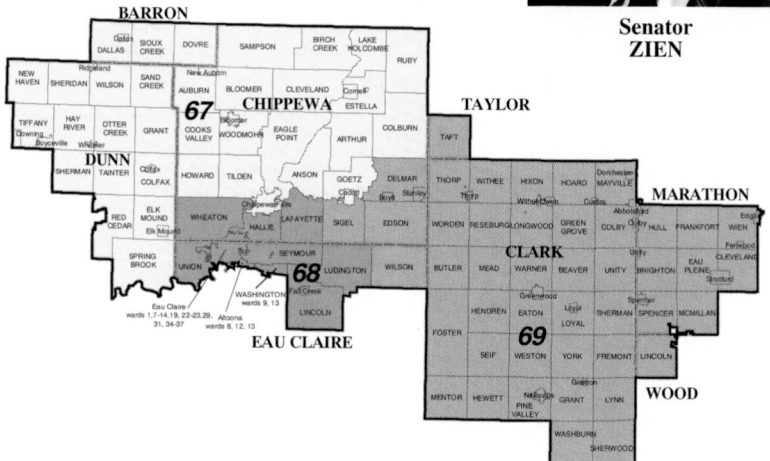

David A. Zien (Rep.), 23rd Senate District

Born Chippewa Falls, March 15, 1950; 4 children, 1 grandchild. Graduate Cadott H.S.; B.S. UW-Eau Claire 1974; M.S. UW-Stout; attended UW-Superior and UW-Madison. Full-time legislator. Former campus admin. at Northcentral Technical Coll.; employment, veteran's and welfare counselor; roofer, bouncer, farmhand, and longshoreman. Vietnam veteran; served in USMC 1968-70. Life Member: VFW; NRA; WRPA; Amer. Legion; WVV; VEC; VVA; WACVO; HOG; Grandma's Marathon. Member: Masons; Elks; Eagles; CMA; AMA; ABATE; MCMC; Eau Claire Peace Officers Pistol Club; Chippewa and Eau Claire Rod and Gun Clubs; Wis. Bear Hunters Assn.; Wis. Bowhunters Assn.; Wheaton Knight Riders; Chippewa Valley ATV; LEAA; Khe Sanh Vets; USMC League; Chippewa Falls, Stanley, Eau Claire, and Cadott Chambers of Commerce; Thorp, Cadott, Chippewa Valley, Stanley and Dunn Hist. Societies. Recipient: *Legislator of the Year:* Wis. Conservation Congress 2003, Wis. Fraternal Order of Police 2002, Prof. Firefighters of Wis. 2001, Wis. Troopers Assn. 2001, Wis. Fire Chiefs Assn. 2000, Wis. Bowhunters Assn. 2000, Wis. Builders Assn. 1998, Wis. DAV 1996, WACVO 1996 and 1993, Milw. Police Assn. 1995, VVA 1994, Amer. Legion 1993, VFW 1990, ABATE 1990; Wis. Alliance for Fire Safety *Outstanding Legislator* 2000; Natl. MC Hall of Fame *Inductee w/ Peter Fonda;* Iron Butt World HD Record *11 days, 11,233 miles;* Natl. Chiefs of Police and Amer. Fed. of Police Assns. *National Award* 1998; Wis. Grocers Assn. *Friend of Grocers* 2003-04, 1999-2000, 1997-98; NRA *Defender of Freedom Award by Charleton Heston* 1998; Cable 11 PACTV *Impact Award-Best Series by an Individual* 1997; Wis. Counties Assn. *Outstanding Legislator* 1995-96; Wis. Farm Bureau *Friend of Agriculture* 2003-04, 1995-96, 1993-94, 1991-92; NFIB *Guardian of Small Business* 1995-96, 1991-92; USMC League *Recruiter of the Year* 1995; Leader-Telegram *Readers' Choice Award: Most Popular Public Official* 1995; Hmong Stout Student Assn. *Outstanding Good Friend* 1993-94; Wis. Vietnam Veterans *Veteran of the Year* 1992; VEC *Damn Fine Legislator* 1992.

Elected to Assembly 1988-92 (resigned eff. 4/19/93); elected to Senate in April 1993 special election; reelected since 1994. President Pro Tempore 2005; Assistant Majority Leader 2003; Minority Caucus Chairperson 2001. Biennial committee assignments: **2005** — Judiciary, Corrections and Privacy (chp., also 2003); Job Creation, Economic Development and Consumer Affairs; Veterans, Homeland Security, Military Affairs, Small Business and Government Reform; Jt. Legis. Council; Judicial Coun. (since 2003); Sentencing Comn. (since 2003); Council on Tourism (since 1993). **2003** — Jt. Com. on Legislative Organization; Environment and Natural Resources; Homeland Security, Veterans and Military Affairs and Government Reform; Labor, Small Business Development and Consumer Affairs; Senate Organization.

Telephone: Office: (608) 266-7511; District: (715) 834-7723; E-mail address: Sen.Zien@legis.state.wi.us

Voting address: (Town of Wheaton, Chippewa County) 1716 63rd Street, Eau Claire 54703.

Mailing address: Office: Room 15 South, State Capitol, P.O. Box 7882, Madison 53707-7882.

Representative
WOOD

Representative
MOULTON

Representative
SUDER

Jeffrey Wood (Rep.), 67th Assembly District

Born Juneau Co., September 12, 1969; married; 2 children. Graduate Chippewa Falls Senior H.S. 1987; attended UW-Eau Claire. Full-time legislator. Former small business owner and local government reporter. Served in U.S. Navy and U.S. Naval Reserve 1986-94. Member: American Legion; Farm Bureau; Chamber of Commerce. Former member: Libertarian Party of the Chippewa Valley.

Elected to Assembly 2002; reelected 2004. Biennial committee assignments: **2005** — Ways and Means (chp., vice chp. 2003); Campaigns and Elections (also 2003); Education Reform (also 2003); Property Rights and Land Management (also 2003); Workforce Development (also 2003).

Telephone: Office: (608) 266-1194; (888) 534-0067 (toll free); District: (715) 726-9226.

E-mail address: Rep.WoodJ@legis.state.wi.us

Voting address: 1501 Miles Street, Chippewa Falls 54729.

Mailing address: Office: Room 7 North, State Capitol, P.O. Box 8953, Madison 53708.

Terry Moulton (Rep.), 68th Assembly District

Born Whitefish, MT, July 19, 1946; married; 2 children, 6 grandchildren. Graduate Chippewa Falls H.S. 1964; attended UW-Eau Claire. Sports store owner and fishing tackle manufacturer. Former hospital accountant and business office manager. Member: Chippewa Falls and Eau Claire Chambers of Commerce; Archery Range and Retailers Organization; Archery Trade Assn.; NRA; Muskies, Inc.; Chippewa Bowhunters; Chippewa Rod and Gun; Eau Claire Archers.

Elected to Assembly 2004. Biennial committee assignments: **2005** — Natural Resources (vice chp.); Health; Insurance; Tourism.

Telephone: Office: (608) 266-9172; (888) 534-0068 (toll free); District: (715) 552-1063.

E-mail address: Rep.Moulton@legis.state.wi.us

Voting address: 980 118th Street, Chippewa Falls 54729.

Mailing address: Office: Room 5 North, State Capitol, P.O. Box 8953, Madison 53708.

Scott Suder (Rep.), 69th Assembly District

Born Medford, September 28, 1968. Graduate Abbotsford H.S.; B.A. UW-Eau Claire 1991. Independent small businessman. Former legislative aide. Member of Wis. Air National Guard, 2003-present; veteran of Operation Iraqi Freedom. Member: Abbotsford Sportsman Club; Loyal Sportsman's Club; Rock Dam Rod and Gun Club; NRA (lifetime mbr.); Ducks Unlimited; NRA-ILA; Natl. Assn. of Sportsmen Legislators; Lublin Amer. Legion-Sons of the Amer. Legion; Wis. Farm Bureau; ALEC Criminal Justice Task Force (chm., 2002-04); ALEC Homeland Security Work Group (since 2004); Neillsville Amer. Legion; NWTF. Recipient: NWTF *Legislator of the Year* 2002; Amer. Police Hall of Fame *Distinguished Service Award*; NFIB *Guardian of Small Business Award*; *Friend of Wis. Grocers Award*; NRA *Defender of Freedom Award*; *Friend of Agriculture Award* 2000-04. Abbotsford City Coun. 1996-2001.

Elected to Assembly 1998; reelected since 2000. Biennial committee assignments: **2005** — Criminal Justice and Homeland Security (chp.); Rural Development (vice chp., also 2003); Agriculture (since 1999); Corrections and the Courts (vice chp. 1999-2001, mbr. 2003); Transportation (since 1999). **2003** — Criminal Justice (chp. and mbr. since 2001); Law Revision Com. (also 2001); Rural Economic Development Bd. **2001** — Census and Redistricting. **1999** — Campaigns and Elections (vice chp.); Highway Safety (eff. 10/12/99); Judiciary and Personal Privacy; Waste Cutters Task Force (chp.).

Telephone: Office: (608) 267-0280; (888) 534-0069 (toll free); District: (715) 223-6964.

E-mail address: Rep.Suder@legis.state.wi.us

Voting address: 102 South Fourth Avenue, Abbotsford 54405.

Mailing address: Office: Room 21 North, State Capitol, P.O. Box 8953, Madison 53708.

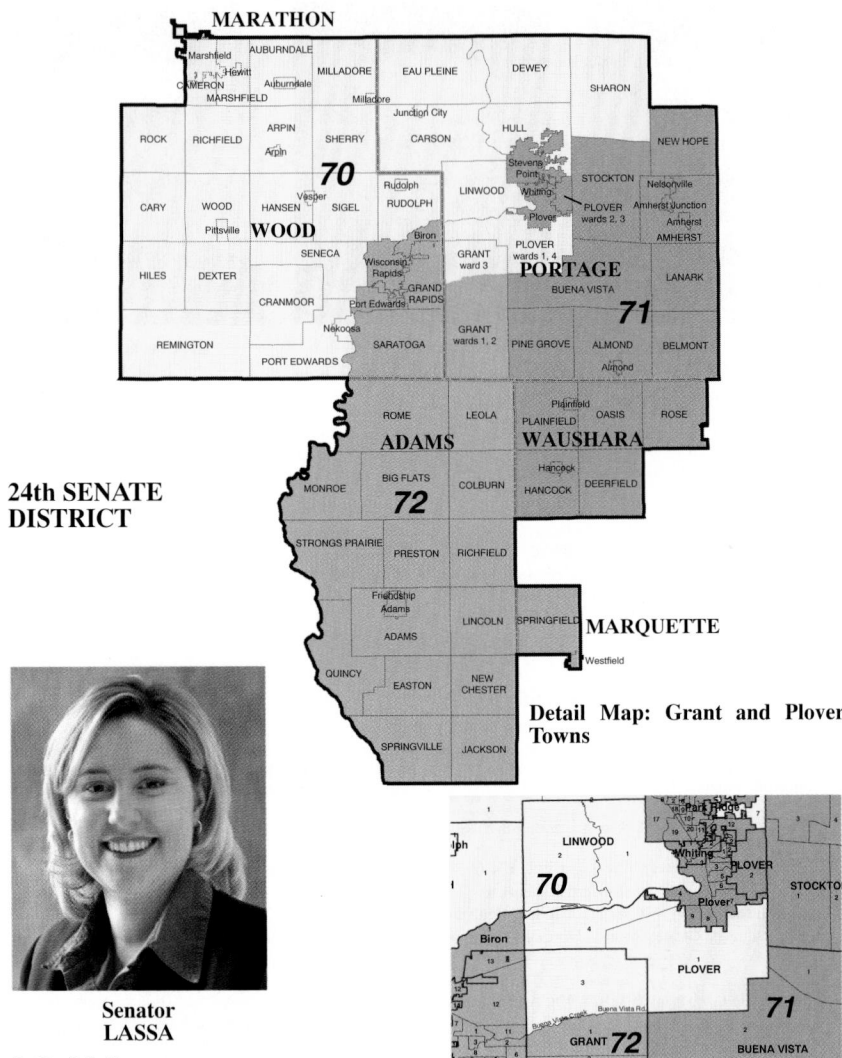

24th SENATE
DISTRICT

Detail Map: Grant and Plover
Towns

Senator
LASSA

Julie M. Lassa (Dem.), 24th Senate District

Born Stevens Point, October 21, 1970; married; 1 child. Graduate Stevens Point Area Senior H.S.; B.S. in political science and public administration, UW-Stevens Point 1993; UW-Madison La Follette Institute of Public Affairs graduate work. Full-time legislator. Former legislative aide and executive director, Plover Area Business Assn. Member: Heart of Wisconsin Business and Economic Alliance; Marshfield Area Chamber of Commerce and Industry; Business and Professional Women; Portage Co. Democratic Party (former chp.); Portage Co. Business Council. Dewey Town Board 1993-94.

Elected to Assembly 1998 to 2002 (resigned eff. 5/9/03); elected to Senate in April 2003 special election; reelected 2004. Minority Caucus Secretary 1999. Biennial Senate committee assignments: **2005** — Housing and Financial Institutions; Job Creation, Economic Development and Consumer Affairs (ranking min. mbr.); Jt. Legislative Audit Com. **2003** — Agriculture, Financial Institutions and Insurance; Jt. Com. for Review of Administrative Rules. Assembly committee assignments: **2003** — Agriculture (since 1999); Budget Review (ranking min. mbr.); Economic Development (ranking minority mbr., 2001); Financial Institutions; Rural Affairs; Child Abuse and Neglect Prevention Bd. (also 2001). **2001** — Colleges and Universities (also 1999); Labor and Workforce Development. **1999** — Small Business and Economic Development; Transportation; World Dairy Center Authority.

Telephone: Office: (608) 266-3123; (800) 925-7491 (toll free); District: (715) 342-0526.

E-mail address: Sen.Lassa@legis.state.wi.us

Voting address: 1900 Clark Street, Stevens Point 54481.

Mailing address: Office: Room 109 South, State Capitol, P.O. Box 7882, Madison 53707-7882.

**Representative
VRUWINK**

**Representative
MOLEPSKE**

**Representative
SCHNEIDER**

Amy Sue Vruwink (Dem.), 70th Assembly District

Born Wisconsin Rapids, May 22, 1975; married. Graduate Auburndale H.S. 1993; B.S. Marian College (Fond du Lac) 1997. Full-time legislator. Former legislative aide to U.S. Representative David R. Obey and Area Program Director for the Minnesota Farm Bureau. Member: Marshfield Business and Professional Women; Marshfield Area Chamber of Commerce and Industry; Coalition of Wisconsin Aging Groups; Wood County Farm Bureau; National Rifle Association; Wisconsin Bear Hunters; Central Wisconsin Fair Association; New Visions Art Gallery.

Elected to Assembly 2002; reelected 2004. Minority Caucus Secretary 2005, 2003. Biennial committee assignments: **2005** — Aging and Long-Term Care (also 2003); Agriculture (also 2003); Health (also 2003); Rural Affairs and Renewable Energy; Transportation (also 2003); Rural Economic Development Bd. **2003** — Transportation Projects Commission.

Telephone: Office: (608) 266-8366; (888) 534-0070 (toll free); District: (715) 652-2909.

E-mail address: Rep.Vruwink@legis.state.wi.us

Voting address: 9425 Flower Lane, Milladore 54454.

Mailing address: Office: Room 112 North, State Capitol, P.O. Box 8953, Madison 53708.

Louis John Molepske, Jr. (Dem.), 71st Assembly District

Born Stevens Point, January 6, 1974. Graduate Stevens Point Area H.S. 1993; B.A. Political science with an emphasis in Journalism UW-Madison 1997; J.D. Marquette 2001. Attorney. Former special prosecutor, Portage Co. D.A. office; assistant city attorney and mayoral assistant, City of Stevens Point. Member: Portage County Democratic Party; Portage County Bar Assn.; Wisconsin Bar Assn.; Knights of Columbus; Izaak Walton League (Bill Cook chapter); Portage County Big Brothers and Big Sisters; Wisconsin/Nicaragua Partners for the Americas; Lawyers Legislative Action Network; Wis. Bar Assn. Young Lawyers Div.; Wis. Bar Assn. Government Lawyers Division.

Elected to Assembly July 2003 special election; reelected 2004. Biennial committee assignments: **2005** — Agriculture (also 2003); Colleges and Universities; Financial Institutions (also 2003); Natural Resources; Transportation. **2003** — Education; Insurance; Rural Affairs; Workforce Development.

Telephone: Office: (608) 267-9649; (888) 534-0071 (toll free).

E-mail address: Rep.Molepske@legis.state.wi.us

Internet address: http://www.legis.state.wi.us/assembly/asm71/news

Voting address: 1557 Church Street, Stevens Point 54481.

Mailing address: Office: Room 111 North, State Capitol, P.O. Box 8953, Madison 53708.

Marlin D. Schneider (Dem.), 72nd Assembly District

Born La Crosse, Nov. 16, 1942; widowed; 2 children. Graduate Longfellow Elem. Sch.; La Crosse Central H.S. 1960; B.S. WSU-La Crosse 1965; M.S.T. UW-Stevens Point 1976; M.S. UW-Madison 1979; certificate from Madison Area Technical College Police Academy 1982. Full-time legislator.

Elected to Assembly since 1970. Longest serving member in the history of the Wisconsin Assembly. Assistant Minority Leader 1999, 1997, 1995; Assistant Majority Leader 1989; Majority Caucus Vice Chairperson 1973-81. Biennial committee assignments: **2005** — Administrative Rules; Jt. Com. for Review of Administrative Rules; Colleges and Universities (also 2003); Military Affairs; Rural Affairs and Renewable Energy; Jt. Legislative Council (also mbr. 1985-99, 2003, vice chp. 1993, chp. 1991); State Capitol and Executive Residence Bd.; Educational Communications Bd. **2003** — Veterans and Military Affairs (also 2001).

Telephone: Office: (608) 266-0215; (888) 529-0072 (toll free); Fax: (608) 282-3672 or (608) 266-8955; District: (715) 423-1223.

E-mail address: Rep.Schneider@legis.state.wi.us

Voting address: 3820 Southbrook Lane, Wisconsin Rapids 54494.

Mailing address: Office: Room 204 North, State Capitol, P.O. Box 8953, Madison 53708.

25th SENATE DISTRICT

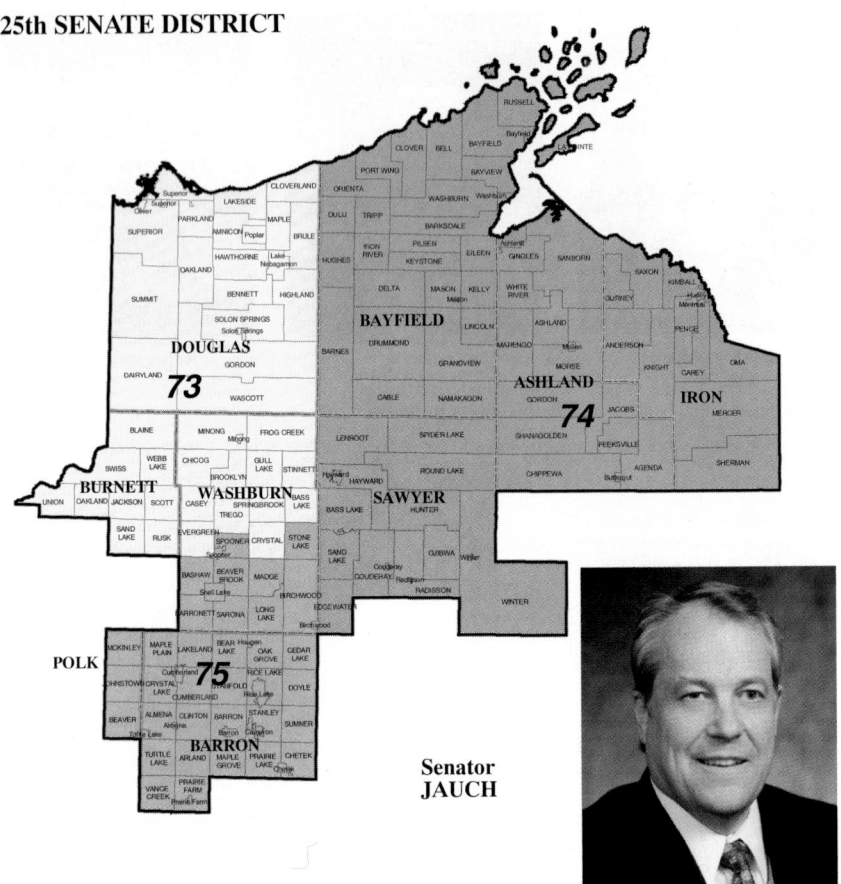

Senator
JAUCH

Robert Jauch (Dem.), 25th Senate District

Born Wheaton, IL, November 22, 1945; married; 2 children. Graduate Wheaton Central H.S.; attended UW-Eau Claire 1968-71, UW-Superior 1973. Full-time legislator. Former field rep. for Congressman David Obey. Veteran; served in Army 1964-68. Member: Hawthorne Lions; Vietnam Veterans of America; VFW; American Legion.

Elected to Assembly 1982, 1984; elected to Senate since 1986. Minority Leader 1995, 1993 (eff. 5/12/93). Biennial committee assignments: **2005** — Education (also 1993-2001); Jt. Com. for Review of Administrative Rules (also 1987-1993); Jt. Survey Com. on Tax Exemptions. **2003** — Education, Ethics and Elections; Health, Children, Families, Aging and Long Term Care. **2001** — Jt. Com. on Information Policy and Technology (co-chp.); 2001-03 Biennial Budget (chp.); Economic Development and Corrections (chp.); Privacy, Electronic Commerce and Financial Institutions (also 1999); Legis. Adv. Com. to the Minn.-Wis. Boundary Area Comn. (since 1997). **1999** — Jt. Com. on Information Policy (co-chp., also 1997, eff. 1/15/97 to 4/20/98, 1995); Jt. Com. on Finance (since 1991). **1997** — Education and Financial Institutions (eff. 4/21/98); Insurance, Tourism and Rural Affairs (eff. 1/15/97 to 4/20/98); Jt. Legislative Council (also 1995); Education Comn. of the States (also 1995); Submerged Cultural Resources Council (also 1995); Midwestern Higher Education Comn.; Legis. Coun. Coms. on Children at Risk Program, on School Discipline and Safety. **1995** — Jt. Com. on Employment Relations (resigned 10/17/95, also 1993); Jt. Com. on Legislative Organization (resigned 10/17/95, also 1993); Insurance (eff. 12/95-6/96); Insurance, Tourism, Veterans and Military Affairs (eff. 6/96); Senate Organization (resigned 10/17/95, also 1993); School Funding Comn.; Spec. Com. on State and Federal Relations (vice chp., resigned 10/17/95); Council on Alcohol and Other Drug Abuse; Disability Bd.; Legis. Coun. Com. on Lead Poisoning and Control. **1993** — Student Readiness Study Com.; Jt. Survey Com. for Retirement Systems (mbr. and co-chp. 1987 to 4/20/93); Retirement Research Com. (mbr. and co-chp. 1987-4/20/93); Legis. Coun. Coms. on AISC, on Children in Need of Protection or Services, on State Fire Programs.

Telephone: Office: (608) 266-3510; (800) 469-6562 (toll free); District: (715) 364-2438.

E-mail address: Sen.Jauch@legis.state.wi.us

Voting address: 5271 South Maple Drive, Poplar 54864-9126.

Mailing address: Office: Room 130 South, State Capitol, P.O. Box 7882, Madison 53707-7882.

Representative
BOYLE

Representative
SHERMAN

Representative
HUBLER

Frank Boyle (Dem.), 73rd Assembly District

Born Phillips, February 20, 1945; married; 2 children. Graduate Phillips H.S.; B.A. UW-Superior 1967; graduate work UW-Superior 1967-68; UW-Madison 1969-70. Full-time legislator. Former residential building contractor and construction worker. Member: Douglas Co. Democratic Party (past secy.); Intl. Laborers Union local; Tri-Lakes Civic Assn. (past pres. of the bd.); Summit Volunteer Fire Dept.; Adv. Committee to local REA; 7th Congressional Dist. Democratic Party; Amnicon-Dowling Lake Management 1978-present. Creator of annual Superior Days lobbying event. Douglas Co. Board 1984-87.

Elected to Assembly since 1986. Biennial committee assignments: **2005** — Colleges and Universities (also 1995-2001); Forestry (also 2003); Military Affairs. **2003** — Veterans and Military Affairs (also 2001, 1999, 1995); Legis. Coun. Com. on State-Tribal Relations (since 1999). **2001** — Criminal Justice; Tourism and Recreation; Legis. Adv. Com. to Minn.-Wis. Boundary Area Comn. (also 1999, 1989-95). **1999** — Natural Resources (also 1993-97, 1987-89). **1997** — State Affairs (chp. 1993, mbr. 1991); Legis. Coun. Com. on Local Government Funding and American Indian Study Com. (also 1995, co-chp. 1989-94). **1995** — Legis. Coun. Com. on Federally Tax-Exempt Lands. **1993** — Environmental Resources.

Telephone: Office: (608) 266-0640; (888) 534-0073 (toll free); District: (715) 399-2247; Fax: (608) 282-3673.

E-mail address: Rep.Boyle@legis.state.wi.us

Voting address: (Town of Summit) 4900 East Tri-Lakes Road, Superior 54880.

Mailing address: Office: Room 218 North, State Capitol, P.O. Box 8952, Madison 53708.

Gary E. Sherman (Dem.), 74th Assembly District

Born Chicago, May 5, 1949; 2 children. Graduate A.G. Lane Technical H.S. (Chicago); B.A. in history and American institutions, UW-Madison 1970; J.D. *cum laude* UW-Madison 1973. Attorney. Served in Air Force 1973. Member: State Bar of Wis. (former pres.); Port Wing Fire Dept. (former chief); American Law Institute; Ashland-Bayfield Counties Bar Assn. (former pres.); Port Wing Baseball Club (fish boil); American Legion Post 531; Amvets Post 1998 (LCO); Red Cliff Bar; Wis. Assn. of Criminal Defense Lawyers. State Superintendent's Advisory Council on Rural Schools, Libraries and Communities; Group Insurance Board.

Elected to Assembly 1998; reelected since 2000. Minority Caucus Vice Chairperson 2005, 2003. Biennial committee assignments: **2005** — Financial Institutions (also 2003); Rules; Transportation (since 1999); Veterans Affairs; Legis. Coun. Com. on State-Tribal Relations (since 1999). **2003** — Educ. Reform; Veterans and Military Affairs; Gov's Council on Highway Safety. **2001** — Criminal Justice; Education (also 1999); Highway Safety. **1999** — Campaigns and Elections; Judiciary and Personal Privacy; Rural Affairs and Forestry; Legis. Coun. Com. on Dental Care Access.

Telephone: Office: (608) 266-7690; (888) 534-0074 (toll free); District: (715) 774-3691; Fax: (608) 282-3674.

E-mail address: Rep.Sherman@legis.state.wi.us

Voting address: P.O. Box 157, Port Wing 54865.

Mailing address: Office: Room 320 West, State Capitol, P.O. Box 8953, Madison 53708.

Mary Hubler (Dem.), 75th Assembly District

Born July 31, 1952. Graduate Rice Lake H.S.; B.S. UW-Superior 1973; J.D. UW-Madison 1980. Full-time legislator. Attorney, former teacher. Member: Wisconsin Farmers Union; Barron Co. Farm Bureau; Barron Co. Historical Society; State Bar of Wis.; Ducks Unlimited; Women of the Moose, Chapter 725; Barron County Home and Community Education; Rice Lake Elks Lodge No. 1441.

Elected to Assembly since 1984. Biennial committee assignments: **2005** — Forestry (also 2003); Jt. Survey Com. on Retirement Systems (also 2003); Jt. Survey Com. on Tax Exemptions (also 2003); Veterans Affairs. **2003** — Rural Development; Veterans and Military Affairs. **2001** — Agriculture (vice chp. 1987, mbr. 1985); Rural Affairs and Forestry (also 1999); Small Business and Consumer Affairs. **1999** — Natural Resources. **1997** — Judiciary (also 1987, 1985); Tourism and Recreation (also 1995); Joint Legislative Council (also 1995) and its Com. on Conservation Laws Enforcement (secy.). **1995** — Com. on Uniform State Laws (also 1993); Governor's Council on Recycling (also 1993); Legis. Coun. Com. on Federally Tax-Exempt Lands. **1993** — Jt. Com. on Finance (since 1989); Legis. Coun. Coms. on Law Revision (co-chp., also 1989, mbr. 1987), on Child Custody, Support and Visitation Laws. **1989** — Select Com. on Health Care Financing; Legis. Coun. Com. on Marital Property Implementation (also 1987).

Telephone: Office: (608) 266-2519; (888) 534-0075 (toll free); District: (715) 234-7421.

E-mail address: Rep.Hubler@legis.state.wi.us

Voting address: 1966 21-7/8 Street (Hawthorne Lane), Rice Lake 54868.

Mailing address: Office: Room 119 North, State Capitol, P.O. Box 8952, Madison 53708.

26th SENATE DISTRICT

**Senator
RISSER**

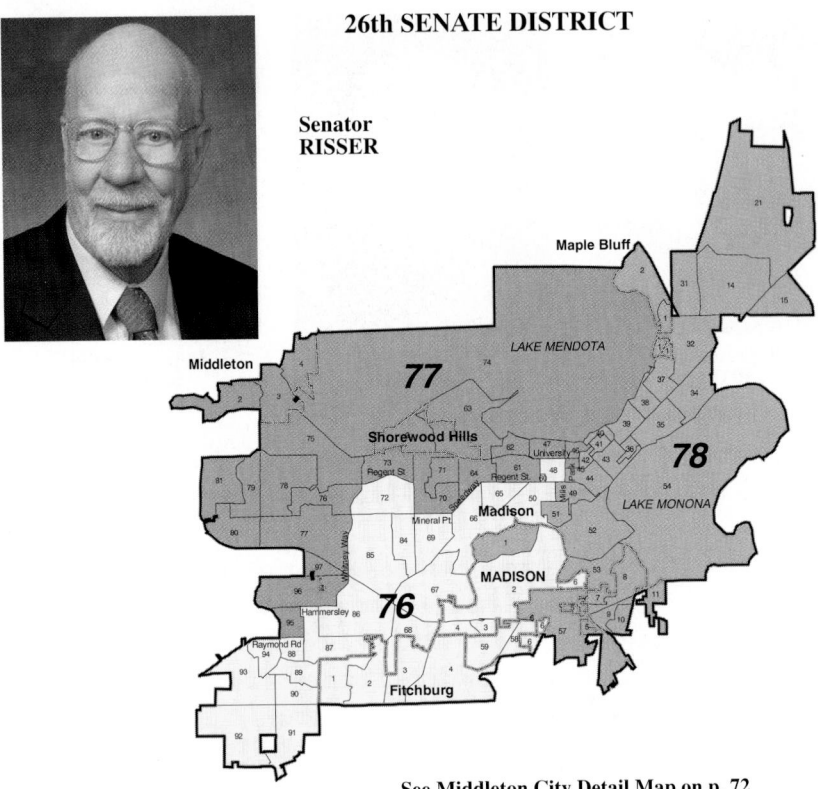

See Middleton City Detail Map on p. 72

See Madison Area Detail Map on pp. 90 & 91

Fred Risser (Dem.), 26th Senate District

Born Madison, May 5, 1927; married; 3 children. Attended Carleton College (MN), UW-Madison; B.A. U. of Oregon 1950; LL.B. U. of Oregon 1952. Attorney. World War II veteran; Navy. Member: State Bar of Wis. and Oregon and Dane Co. Bar Assns.; NCSL (past mbr. Natl. Exec. Com.); CSG (past mbr. Natl. Exec. Com., Midwestern Conf. chp. 1993, 1982).

Elected to Assembly 1956-60; elected to Senate in 1962 special election; reelected since 1964. Longest serving legislator in Wisconsin history. President of the Senate 2001, 1999, 1997 (eff. 1/15/97 to 4/20/98), 1995 (eff. 7/9/96), also 1979 to 4/20/93; Assistant Minority Leader 1995 (eff. 1/5/95 to 7/12/96), 1993 (eff. 4/20/93, also 1965); Sen. Pres. Pro Tempore 1977, 1975; Minority Ldr. 1967-73. Biennial committee assignments: **2005** — Campaign Finance Reform and Ethics; Judiciary, Corrections and Privacy (eff. 4/1/05); State and Federal Relations; Joint Legislative Council (co-chp. 2001, 1999, 1997, chp. 1987, 1983, 1971, mbr. since 1967); State of Wis. Building Comn. (vice chp., also 2001, 1999, 1971 to 5/19/93, mbr. since 1969); State Historical Society Bd. of Curators (since 1983); State Capitol and Executive Residence Bd. (chp. 2003, co-chp. 1989 to 4/20/98, mbr. since 1983). **2003** — Environment and Natural Resources. **2001** — Jt. Com. on Employment Relations (co-chp., also 1999, 1997, eff. 1/6/97 to 4/20/98, also 1995, eff. 7/9/96, also 1979 to 4/20/93, mbr. since 1973); Jt. Com. on Legislative Organization (co-chp., also 1999, 1997, eff. 1/15/97 to 4/20/98, also 1977 to 4/20/93, mbr. since 1967); Senate Organization (chp. 1987 to 4/20/98, also chp. 1977-1981, mbr. since 1967); Judiciary, Consumer Affairs, and Campaign Finance Reform; Disability Bd. (since 1997); Legis. Coun. Com. on Review of Fireworks Law (co-chp.). **1999** — Judiciary and Consumer Affairs. **1997** — Government Effectiveness (eff. 4/21/98); Judiciary (eff. 4/21/98); Judiciary, Campaign Finance Reform and Consumer Affairs (resigned 1/5/98, also 1995); Wis. Sesquicentennial Comn. (also 1995); Legis. Coun. Coms. on Discipline of Health Care Professionals (secy.), on Incentives for Resource Stewardship. **1993** — Judiciary and Insurance; Historic Sites Fdn., Inc. (vice pres. since 1989, mbr. since 1984); Senate Rules (since 1987). **1989** — Urban Affairs, Environmental Resources, Utilities and Elections (chp.); Jt. Com. on Debt Management (co-chp); Adv. Com. on the Capitol Master Plan (co-chp.). **1987** — Select Com. on the Regulation of Gambling; Com. on the Management of the Yahara Watershed; Legis. Coun. Coms. on Law Revision (co-chp. since 1979), on Surrogate Parenting (co-chp.), on Uniform Anatomical Gift Act (vice chp.). **1985** — Legis. Coun. Com. on Mental Health Issues (chp.). **1981** — Legis Coun. Coms. on Adoption Laws (vice chp.), on the Prosecutorial System (vice chp.), on Legis. Oversight (also 1979, 1977).

Telephone: Office: (608) 266-1627; District: (608) 238-5008; E-mail address: Sen.Risser@legis.state.wi.us

Voting address: 5008 Risser Road, Madison 53705.

Mailing address: Office: Room 123 South, State Capitol, P.O. Box 7882, Madison 53707-7882.

| Representative | Representative | Representative |
| BERCEAU | BLACK | POCAN |

Terese Berceau (Dem.), 76th Assembly District

Born Green Bay, August 23, 1950. Graduate Green Bay East H.S.; B.S. UW-Madison 1973; graduate studies in Urban and Regional Planning, UW-Madison. Staff, UW-Madison Robert M. La Follette School of Public Affairs; staff, Wis. Counties Assn.; real estate salesperson; substitute teacher. Member: Dane Co. Democratic Party; National Organization of Women; 1000 Friends of Wisconsin; Planned Parenthood Advocates of Wisconsin; Sierra Club. Former member: Monona Terrace Community and Convention Center Bd.; Greater Madison Convention and Visitors Bureau Bd. Recipient: Wis. Alliance of Cities *Urban Families Recognition* 2004; Wis. Community Action Program Assn. *Appreciation Award* 2004; Clean Wisconsin Action Fund *Clean Sixteen Award* 2003-2004; Domestic Abuse Intervention Services *Certificate of Recognition* 2004; Wis. Coalition Against Domestic Violence *"DV Diva" Award* 2003; Planned Parenthood of Wisconsin *Voice for Choice Award* 2000; Wisconsin Family Planning and Reproductive Health Assn. *Legislator of the Year* 2000; Domestic Abuse Intervention Service *Public Service Award* 2002; National Alliance for the Mentally Ill – Dane County *Community Action Citizen Award* 2003. City of Madison Community Development Authority (chp. 1989-92); Dane Co. Board of Supervisors 1992-2000.

Elected to Assembly 1998; reelected since 2000. Biennial committee assignments: **2005** — Budget Review; Insurance (also 2003); Urban and Local Affairs (since 1999); Ways and Means (also 2003); Historical Society of Wisconsin, Bd. of Curators (also 2001).

Telephone: Office: (608) 266-3784; District: (608) 204-9297; E-mail address: Rep.Berceau@legis.state.wi.us
Internet address: http://www.terese.org
Voting address: 4326 Somerset Lane, Madison 53711.
Mailing address: Office: Room 208 North, State Capitol, P.O. Box 8952, Madison 53708.

Spencer Black (Dem.), 77th Assembly District

Born May 25, 1950; married; 1 son. B.A. in economics and history, SUNY-Stony Brook 1972; M.S. in urban and regional planning UW-Madison 1980; M.A. in public policy and administration UW-Madison 1981. Former conservation representative, Sierra Club; curator of education, St. Historical Soc. of Wisconsin; high school teacher. Recipient: Wis. Federation of Teachers *Legislator of the Year* 1999; Clean Water Action Council *Environmental Advocate of the Year* 1993; Midwest Renewable Energy Association *Environmental Excellence Award* 1992; Izaak Walton League *Environmental Legislator of the Year* 1991; Wis. Community Action Programs Assn. *Gaylord Nelson Human Service Award* 1991; Audubon Soc. *Environmentalist of the Year Award* 1990; The Nature Conservancy *President's Public Service Award* 1989; Wis. Wildlife Fed. *Legislator of the Year Award* 1988; Common Cause *Leadership Award* 1985.

Elected to Assembly since 1984. Minority Leader 2001 (eff. 5/1/01); Assistant Minority Leader 2001 (1/3/01 to 5/1/01). Biennial committee assignments: **2005** — Adminstrative Rules (also 2003); Jt. Com. for Review of Administrative Rules (also 1999); Colleges and Universities (also 2003); Criminal Justice and Homeland Security; Natural Resources (also 2003, 1997, chp. 1987-93); Rural Development. **2003** — Electronic Democracy and Government Reform; Property Rights and Land Management. **2001** — Assembly Organization; Jt. Com. on Employment Relations (eff. 5/1/01); Jt. Com. on Legislative Organization; Rules; Jt. Legislative Council; Disability Bd. (eff. 5/1/01).

Telephone: Office: (608) 266-7521; District: (608) 233-0317; E-mail address: Rep.Black@legis.state.wi.us
Voting address: 5742 Elder Place, Madison 53705.
Mailing address: Office: Room 210 North, State Capitol, P.O. Box 8952, Madison 53708.

Mark Pocan (Dem.), 78th Assembly District

Born Kenosha, August 14, 1964. Graduate Mary D. Bradford H.S. (Kenosha); B.A. UW-Madison 1986. Small businessperson. Member: Midwest Progressive Elected Officials Network; Wisconsin Citizen Action (bd. mbr.); American Civil Liberties Union; Colombia Support Network/Apartadó Sister City Organization; 1000 Friends of Wisconsin; Wis. Environmental Decade; Painters and Allied Trades Union (AFL-CIO); Sierra Club; Action Wisconsin. Former member: Big Brothers-Big Sisters. Recipient: Wis. Environmental Decade *Clean 16 Award* 2004, 2002, 2000; ACLU *Special Recognition Award* 2001; Outreach, Inc. *Man of the Year* 1999; Wis. Federation of Teachers State Employees Council *Representative of the Year* 2003, 2002; Progressive Democratic Network *Rookie of the Year* 1999. Dane Co. Board 1991-96.

Elected to Assembly 1998; reelected since 2000. Biennial committee assignments: **2005** — Finance; Jt. Com. on Finance; Jt. Legislative Council. **2003** — Audit; Jt. Com. on Audit; Campaigns and Elections (also 2001); Colleges and Universities; Corrections and the Courts (since 1999); Criminal Justice. **2001** — Environment; Ways and Means. **1999** — Consumer Affairs; Education; Labor and Employment.

Telephone: Office: (608) 266-8570; District: (608) 256-6214; E-mail address: Rep.Pocan@legis.state.wi.us
Voting address: 309 North Baldwin Street, Madison 53703.
Mailing address: Office: Room 322 West, State Capitol, P.O. Box 8953, Madison 53708.

27th SENATE DISTRICT

**Senator
ERPENBACH**

Detail Map: Middleton City

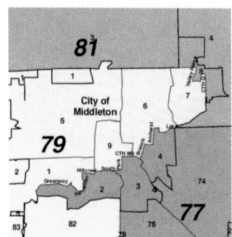

See Madison Area Detail Map on pp. 90 & 91

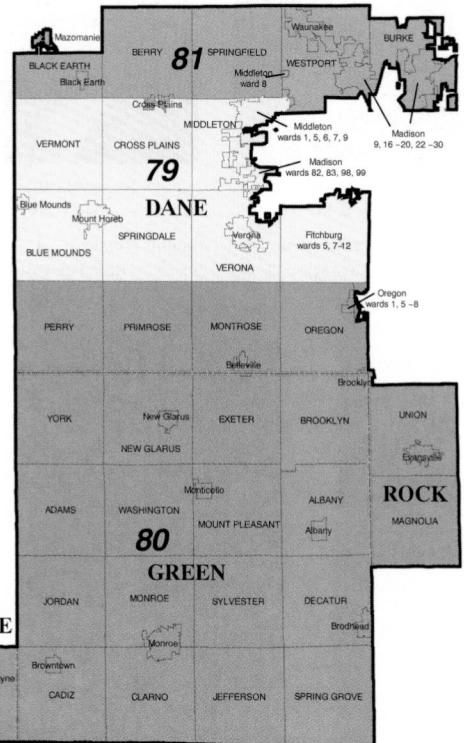

Jon B. Erpenbach (Dem.), 27th Senate District

Born Middleton, January 28, 1961; 2 children. Graduate Middleton H.S.; attended UW-Oshkosh 1979-81. Former communications director, legislative aide, radio personality, short order cook, meat packer, truck driver, and City of Middleton recreation instructor. Member: League of Women Voters; Environmental Decade of Wisconsin; NAACP; Wis. Farm Bureau; Wis. Hunting and Fishing Alliance.

Elected to Senate 1998, reelected 2002. Minority Leader 2003. Biennial committee assignments: **2005** — Agriculture and Insurance; Education (also 2001, 1999); Health, Children, Families, Aging and Long-Term Care. **2003** — Jt. Com. on Employment Relations; Jt. Com. on Legislative Organization; Senate Organization; Jt. Legis. Coun.; Disability Bd. Jt. Legis. Coun. Spec. Com. on Review of Open Records Law (co-chp. since 2001). **2001** — Privacy, Electronic Commerce and Financial Institutions (chp., also 1999); 2001-03 Biennial Budget; Health, Utilities, Veterans and Military Affairs (also 1999); Jt. Com. on Information Policy and Technology; Information and Policy Technology; Law Revision Committee (also 1999); Legis. Coun. Com. on Condominium Law Review (co-chp. since 1999). **1999** — Jt. Committee on Information Policy; Lambeau Field; Jt. Survey Committee on Retirement Systems; Joint Legislative Council; Census Education Bd.; Governor's Blue Ribbon Task Force on Passenger Rail; Democratic Leadership Institute (chp.).

Telephone: Office: (608) 266-6670; District: (888) 549-0027 (toll free).

E-mail address: Sen.Erpenbach@legis.state.wi.us

Voting address: 7781 Elmwood Avenue, No. 106, Middleton 53562.

Mailing address: Office: Room 19 South, State Capitol, P.O. Box 7882, Madison 53707-7882.

**Representative
POPE-ROBERTS**

**Representative
DAVIS**

**Representative
TRAVIS**

Sondy Pope-Roberts (Dem.), 79th Assembly District

Born Madison, April 27, 1950; widowed; one child. Graduate River Valley H.S. 1968; attended Madison Area Technical College and Edgewood College. Full-time legislator. Former Associate Director of the Foundation for Madison's Public Schools. Member: League of Women Voters; Black Hawk Council of Girl Scouts, Inc.; Wis. Council on Children and Families; Nature Conservancy; NARAL; Nat'l Caucus of Environmental Legislators; Midwest Progressive Elected Officials Network; Wis. Democracy Campaign; Sierra Club; Women's Leadership Network; Oakhill Correctional Institute Advisory Bd.

Elected to Assembly 2002; reelected 2004. Biennial committee assignments: **2005** — Aging and Long-Term Care (also 2003); Corrections and the Courts; Education (also 2003); Medicaid Reform. **2003** — Rural Affairs; Small Business.

Telephone: Office: (608) 266-3520; (888) 534-0079 (toll free); District: (608) 829-2750.

E-mail address: Rep.Pope-Roberts@legis.state.wi.us

Voting address: 3426 Valley Woods Drive, Verona 53593.

Mailing address: Office: Room 209 North, State Capitol, P.O. Box 8953, Madison 53708.

Brett H. Davis (Rep.), 80th Assembly District

Born Oshkosh, December 5, 1975; married; 1 child. Graduate Monroe H.S. 1994; B.A. in business marketing UW-Oshkosh 1999. Former legislative aide to State Rep. Mike Powers, State Sen. Joe Leibham, and former Governor and U.S. Health and Human Services Secretary Tommy Thompson. Member: Oregon-Brooklyn Lions Club; Farm Bureau; Riverfront Rock Community Advisory Bd.; Green, Rock, Dane Co. Republican Parties; Oregon Chamber of Commerce.

Elected to Assembly 2004. Biennial committee assignments: **2005** — Energy and Utilities (vice chp.); Education; Medicaid Reform; Transportation.

Telephone: Office: (608) 266-1192; (888) 534-0080 (toll free); District: (608) 835-0939.

E-mail address: Rep.Davis@legis.state.wi.us

Voting address: 1420 Ravenoaks Trail, Oregon 53575.

Mailing address: Office: Room 308 North, State Capitol, P.O. Box 8952, Madison 53708.

David M. Travis (Dem.), 81st Assembly District

Born September 21, 1948. B.A. UW-Milwaukee; M.A. La Follette Institute, UW-Madison; attended Madison Area Technical College and Bindl Flight School, Waunakee (private pilot's license). Instructor, Edgewood College; self-employed consultant; former instructor, UW-Milwaukee; private consultant to law firm, Senate Democratic Caucus staff director, policy analyst, administrative assistant, baker, grocery clerk, truck driver, factory worker, short-order cook, and busboy.

Elected to Assembly since 1978. Majority Leader 1993, 1991. Author of: child car seat law; computer and electronic transfer crime laws; personal harassment law; restrictions on possession of firearms in public buildings, in taverns, and by convicted felons; constitutional amendment against letter vetoes; handgun hotline law; local government code of ethics; violent juvenile offender act; domestic abuser firearm ban. Biennial committee assignments: **2005** — Audit; Jt. Legislative Audit; Campaigns and Elections (since 1999); Energy and Utilities (also 2003); Jt. Legislative Council; Rules (since 1991); Wisconsin Sentencing Commission (also 1995, fmr. chp.). **2003** — Aging and Long-Term Care (also 2001). **2001** — State Affairs. **1999** — Census and Redistricting; Corrections and the Courts. **1997** — Criminal Justice and Corrections (also 1995); Financial Institutions (also 1995); Legis. Coun. Com. on Faith-Based Approaches to Crime Prevention and Justice. **1995** — Elections and Constitutional Law; Ways and Means.

Telephone: Office: (608) 266-5340; E-mail address: Rep.Travis@legis.state.wi.us

Voting address: 5440 Willow Road, Waunakee 53597.

Mailing address: Office: Room 223 North, State Capitol, P.O. Box 8953, Madison 53708.

28th SENATE DISTRICT

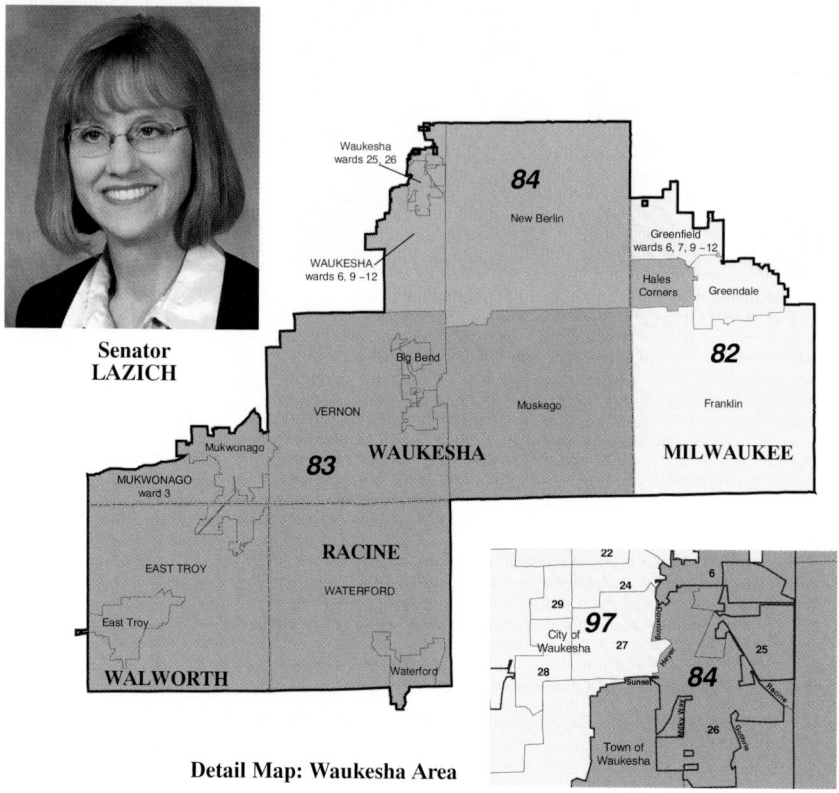

**Senator
LAZICH**

Detail Map: Waukesha Area

See Milwaukee County Detail
Map on pp. 92 & 93

See Waukesha County Detail Map
on pp. 94 & 95

Mary A. Lazich (Rep.), 28th Senate District

Born Loyal, October 3, 1952; married; 3 children. B.A. UW-Milwaukee, *summa cum laude.* Former county board supervisor and city council member. Member: Waukesha Co. Republican Party; Waukesha Co. Republican Women's Club; New Berlin Lioness; New Berlin Historical Society; Boy Scout Advisory Com., Potawatomi Area Council. Waukesha Co. Board supervisor 1990-93, and mbr. of its Legislative, Intergovernmental and Education Com., Health and Human Services Com., Transportation Com., and Community Development Block Grant Bd.; New Berlin City Council 1986-92 (former president, chm. of Finance Com., chm. of Board of Public Works, mbr. of Planning Commission and Crime Prevention Com.).

Elected to Assembly 1992-96 (resigned eff. 4/20/98); elected to Senate in April 1998 special election; reelected since 2000. Majority Caucus Chairperson 2003. Biennial Senate committee assignments: **2005** — Jt. Com. on Finance (also 2003); Finance (also 2003); Labor and Election Process Reform; Women's Council (also 1999, 1997).. **2003** — Jt. Com. on Administrative Rules; Administrative Rules; Energy and Utilities; Law Revision Com. (co-chp.). **2001** — Jt. Com. on Audit (also 1999, co-chp. 1998, eff. 4/21/98); Audit; Education (also 1999); Health, Utilities, Veterans and Military Affairs; Jt. Com. on Information Policy and Technology; Information Policy and Technology. **1999** — Council on Highway Safety **1997** — Education and Financial Institutions; State Government Operations and Corrections; Government Effectiveness; Forward Wisconsin, Inc. Assembly committee assignments: **1997** — Jt. Com. on Audit (co-chp., also 1995); Working Families (vice chp.); Financial Institutions; Health (since 1993); Labor and Employment (also 1995). **1995** — Insurance, Securities and Corporate Policy; Urban Education (also 1993); Welfare Reform; Legis. Coun. Com. on Health Care Information. **1993** — Excise and Fees; Judiciary; Transportation; Legis. Coun. Com. on Child Care Economics.

Telephone: Office: (608) 266-5400; (800) 334-1442 (toll free); District: (414) 425-9452.

E-mail address: Sen.Lazich@legis.state.wi.us

Voting address: 4405 South 129th Street, New Berlin 53151.

Mailing address: Office: Room 18 South, State Capitol, P.O. Box 7882, Madison 53707-7882.

**Representative
STONE**

**Representative
GUNDERSON**

**Representative
GUNDRUM**

Jeff Stone (Rep.), 82nd Assembly District

Born Topeka, KS, January 28, 1961; married. Graduate West Muskingum H.S. (Zanesville, OH); B.A. in political science and history, Washburn U. (Topeka) *magna cum laude* and Phi Kappa Phi 1983. Printing business owner. Member: Metro. Milw. Assn. of Commerce; Partners of Parks, Greenfield; Greenfield Chamber of Commerce (past secy.); Greendale Lions. Awards: Wis. Wholesale Beer Distributors Assn. *Legislator Award* 2001; Wis. Builders Assn. *Friend of the Housing Industry* 2001-05; Milwaukee Co. Republican Party *Taxcutter of the Year* 2001; *Legislative Leadership National Com. Against Drunk Driving Award* 2000; Wis. Manufacturers and Commerce *Working for Wisconsin* 2004, 2002, 2000, 1998; *Bowhay Institute for Legislative Leadership Development* 2000; NFIB *Guardian of Small Business* 1999-2000; Wis. Counties Assn. *Outstanding Legislator Award* 1999-2000. Greenfield City Council 1994-98.

Elected to Assembly in April 1998 special election; reelected since November 1998. Biennial committee assignments: **2005** — Jt. Com. on Finance (also 2003); Leg. Coun. Spec. Com. on Wisconsin's Transportation Network Infrastructure, on Sexually Violent Person Commitments; Milwaukee Child Welfare Partnership Council (since 1999, Subcom. on Adoption, 2002). **2003** — Governor's Airport Finance Com.; Local Government Health Partnership Task Force.

Telephone: Office: (608) 266-8590; (888) 534-0082 (toll free); District: (414) 529-1100.
E-mail address: Rep.Stone@legis.state.wi.us
Voting address: 5535 Grandview Drive, Greendale 53129.
Mailing address: Office: Room 304 East, State Capitol, P.O. Box 8953, Madison 53708.

Scott L. Gunderson (Rep.), 83rd Assembly District

Born Burlington, October 24, 1956; married; 3 children. Graduate Waterford H.S. 1974. Sports store owner and farmer. Member: Wind Lake Chamber of Commerce (past pres., vice pres.); Waterford Lions Club; Waterford FFA Alumni (past pres., vice pres.); St. Thomas Athletic Assn.; Wings Over Wis. (bd. mbr.); Ducks Unlimited; Pheasants Forever; Wis. Waterfowl Assn.; Racine Co. Farm Bureau; Racine Co. Fair (dir.). Former member: Waterford Chamber of Commerce (pres., vice pres.); Waterford Jaycees (pres., vice pres.); Waterford 4th of July Parade Com. Waterford Town Board 1991-95.

Elected to Assembly since 1994. Biennial committee assignments: **2005** — Natural Resources (chp., vice chp. 1999-2003, mbr. since 1995); Budget Review (vice chp., mbr. 2003); Tourism (also 2003); Urban and Local Affairs (chp. 1997-2003); State Fair Park Bd. (since 2001). **2003** — Jt. Com. for Review of Administrative Rules (since 1995); Review of Administrative Rules (also 2001). **2001** — Environment; Transportation; Wis. Coastal Management Council (since 1996). **1999** — Criminal Justice; Legis. Coun. Com. on Navigable Waters Recodification (co-chp.). **1997** — Criminal Justice and Corrections (also 1995); Legis. Coun. Coms. on Programs for Prevention Services (chp.), on Conservation Laws Enforcement.

Telephone: Office: (608) 266-3363; (888) 534-0083 (toll free); District: (262) 534-2616.
E-mail address: Rep.Gunderson@legis.state.wi.us
Voting address: Village of Waterford.
Mailing address: Office: Room 7 West, State Capitol, P.O. Box 8952, Madison 53708; District: P.O. Box 7, Waterford 53185.

Mark Gundrum (Rep.), 84th Assembly District

Born Milwaukee, March 20, 1970; married; 5 children. Graduate Waukesha Catholic Memorial H.S. 1988; B.A. in Economics and Political Science, graduated Phi Beta Kappa, UW-Madison 1992; J.D., Law Review, Moot Court, UW-Madison 1994. Attorney. Judicial intern for Fed. Court of Appeals (6th Circuit); prosecution intern for Outagamie Co. District Attorney's Office 1994; Staff attorney for Fed. District Judge, Eastern District of Wis. 1995-96; Army Officer Reserve Judge Advocate General Corps 2000-present. Member: State Bar of Wis.; Waukesha Co. Bar Assn.; New Berlin Teen Court Judge; Avery Task Force. Hales Corners Village Board 1995-99.

Elected to Assembly since 2000. Biennial committee assignments: **2005** — Judiciary (chp. since 2001); Campaigns and Elections (vice chp., also 2003); Corrections and the Courts (vice chp., mbr. 1999); Criminal Justice and Homeland Security; State Affairs (also 2003); Jt. Legis. Coun. Spec. Com. on Sexually Violent Person Commitments. **2003** — Criminal Justice (vice chp. 2001, mbr. since 1999); Jt. Legis. Coun. Spec. Com. on Review of the Open Records Law (co-chp.). **2001** — Education Reform (also 1999); Small Business and Consumer Affairs; Law Revision (also 1999); Uniform Law Comn. (also 1999); Identity Theft Task Force.

Telephone: Office: (608) 267-5158; District: (414) 425-2556; E-mail address: Rep.Gundrum@legis.state.wi.us
Internet address: www.legis.state.wi.us/assembly/asm84/news/
Voting address: 5239 South Guerin Pass, New Berlin 53151.
Mailing address: Office: Room 19 North, State Capitol, P.O. Box 8952, Madison 53708.

29th SENATE DISTRICT

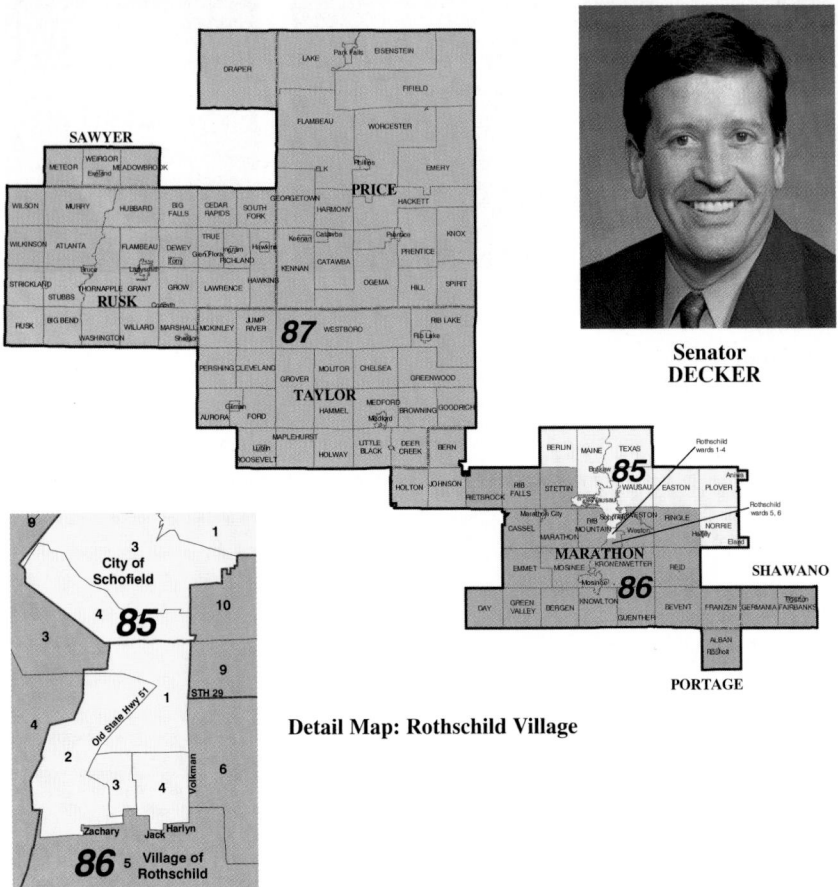

Senator
DECKER

Detail Map: Rothschild Village

Russell S. Decker (Dem.), **29th Senate District**

Born Athens, May 25, 1953; married; 2 children. Graduate Athens H.S.; bricklayer apprenticeship graduate, North-central Technical College 1980. Full-time legislator and journeyman bricklayer. Member: Bricklayers Intl. Union; Marathon Co. Democratic Party; National Rifle Association; Friends of Rib Mountain. Former member: Central Wisconsin Building Trades (pres.); Boy Scouts of America (assistant Cub master); Conservation Committee (secy./treas.); Bricklayers Joint Apprenticeship Committee.

Elected to Senate 1990; reelected since 1994. Biennial committee assignments: **2005** — Jt. Com. on Finance (since 1995); Job Creation, Economic Development and Consumer Affairs; Jt. Legislative Council. **2003** — Jt. Survey Com. on Tax Exemptions; Labor, Small Business Development and Consumer Affairs. **2001** — Labor and Agriculture; Rural Economic Development Bd. (since 1991). **1999** — Labor. **1997** — Labor, Transportation and Financial Institutions (eff. 1/15/97 to 4/20/98); Transportation, Agriculture and Rural Affairs (eff. 4/21/98); Human Resources, Labor, Tourism, Veterans and Military Affairs (eff. 4/21/98).

Telephone: Office: (608) 266-2502; (877) 496-0472 (toll free); District: (715) 359-8739.

Voting address: (Village of Weston) 6803 Lora Lee Lane, Schofield 54476.

Mailing address: Office: Room 323 South, State Capitol, P.O. Box 7882, Madison 53707-7882.

| Representative | Representative | Representative |
| SEIDEL | PETROWSKI | M. WILLIAMS |

Donna J. Seidel (Dem.), 85th Assembly District

Born Neenah, August 6, 1950; married; 1 daughter, 2 stepchildren. Graduate Neenah H.S.; B.S. UW-Stevens Point 1972. Full-time legislator. Former clerk of courts; investigator for district attorney's office; police officer. Member: Marathon County Democratic Party; Wausau Noon Optimists Club. Former member: North Central Technical College (bd. of trustees); Wis. Assn. of Clerks of Circuit Court (legislative com. chair, past pres.); United Way of Marathon Co. (bd. of dir.); The Womens' Community (bd. of dir., pres.); YMCA (bd. of dir.). Marathon Co. Clerk of Circuit Court 1989-2004.

Elected to Assembly 2004. Biennial committee assignments: **2005** — Children and Families; Corrections and the Courts; Tourism; Workforce Development.

Telephone: Office: (608) 266-0654; (888) 534-0085 (toll free); District: (715) 845-2988.

E-mail address: Rep.Seidel@legis.state.wi.us

Voting address: 807 South 20th Street, Wausau 54403.

Mailing address: Office: Room 409 North, State Capitol, P.O. Box 8953, Madison 53708.

Jerry Petrowski (Rep.), 86th Assembly District

Born Wausau, June 16, 1950; married; 4 children. Graduate Newman H.S. (Wausau); attended UW-Marathon County and Northcentral Technical College. Former ginseng, dairy, and beef farmer. Served in Army Reserve 1968-74. Member: Marathon Co. and 7th District Republican Parties; Farm Bureau; National Rifle Assn.; Wis. Rifle and Pistol Assn.; Friends of Rib Mountain; Marathon Lions. Former member: International Brotherhood of Electrical Workers Local #1791; Childcare Connection Bd.; Department of Transportation Law Enforcement Advisory Council. Recipient: Troopers Assn. *Legislator of the Year Award* 2003; Farm Bureau's *Friend of Agriculture Award* 2004; Wis. Vietnam Veterans' *Legislator of the Year Award* 2002.

Elected to Assembly 1998; reelected since 2000. Majority Caucus Sergeant at Arms 2005, 2003. Biennial committee assignments: **2005** — Highway Safety (chp. since 2001); Transportation (vice chp. since 2001, mbr. 1999); Agriculture (since 1999, vice chp. 1999); Military Affairs; Natural Resources; State Affairs (since 1999); Gov.'s Council on Highway Safety (also 2003). **2003** — Criminal Justice; Veterans and Military Affairs (since 1999). **1999** — Small Business and Economic Development.

Telephone: Office: (608) 266-1182; (888) 534-0086 (toll free); District: (715) 845-6193.

E-mail address: Rep.Petrowski@legis.state.wi.us

Voting address: (Town of Stettin) 720 North 136th Avenue, Marathon 54448-6193.

Mailing address: Office: Room 4 West, State Capitol, P.O. Box 8953, Madison 53708.

Mary Williams (Rep.), 87th Assembly District

Born Phillips, July 8, 1949; married; 3 children, 2 grandchildren. Graduate Phillips H.S. 1967; associate degree Taylor Co. Teachers Coll. 1969; B.S. Elementary Ed. UW-Stevens Point 1974. Restaurant owner. Former elementary teacher, Medford Area School Dist. Member: Farm Bureau; Dairy Promotion Com. (secy.); Dairy Breakfast Com.; Pri-Ru-Ta Resource Conservation and Development (pres.); Medford Area School Dist. Assets Com.; Taylor Co. Tobacco Coalition; Taylor Co. Safe & Stable Families; Wis. Restaurant Assn.; Nat'l Fed. of Independent Businesses; Chamber of Commerce; Friends of the Frances L. Simek Memorial Library; Whittlesey Whizzers Snowmobile Club; Taylor Co. Local Emergency Planning Com. Former member: Wis. Assn. of Resource Conservation and Development (pres.); Big Brothers/Big Sisters of Taylor Co. (pres.); Medford Public Library Bd. (pres. and secy.); Restorative Justice of Taylor Co. (pres.); International Trade, Business and Economic Development Council – Tourism Com. (chp.); Price Waterways Assn. (secy.); Cooperative Youth Fair (treas.); WEAC; NEA. Recipient: WCCO *Legislator of the Year* 2003; Nat'l MS Society *Outstanding Volunteer Advocate* 2003. Taylor Co. Tourism Council. Taylor Co. Bd. 1992-96.

Elected to Assembly 2002; reelected 2004. Biennial committee assignments: **2005** — Rural Development (chp.); Rural Affairs and Renewable Energy (vice chp.); Agriculture (vice chp. 2003); Forestry (also 2003); Natural Resources (also 2003); Small Business (also 2003). **2003** — Rural Affairs (vice chp.); Tourism.

Telephone: Office: (608) 266-7506; (888) 534-0087 (toll free); District: (715) 748-5980.

E-mail address: Rep.WilliamsM@legis.state.wi.us

Voting address: 542 Billings Avenue, Medford 54451.

Mailing address: Office: Room 18 West, State Capitol, P.O. Box 8953, Madison 53708.

30th SENATE DISTRICT

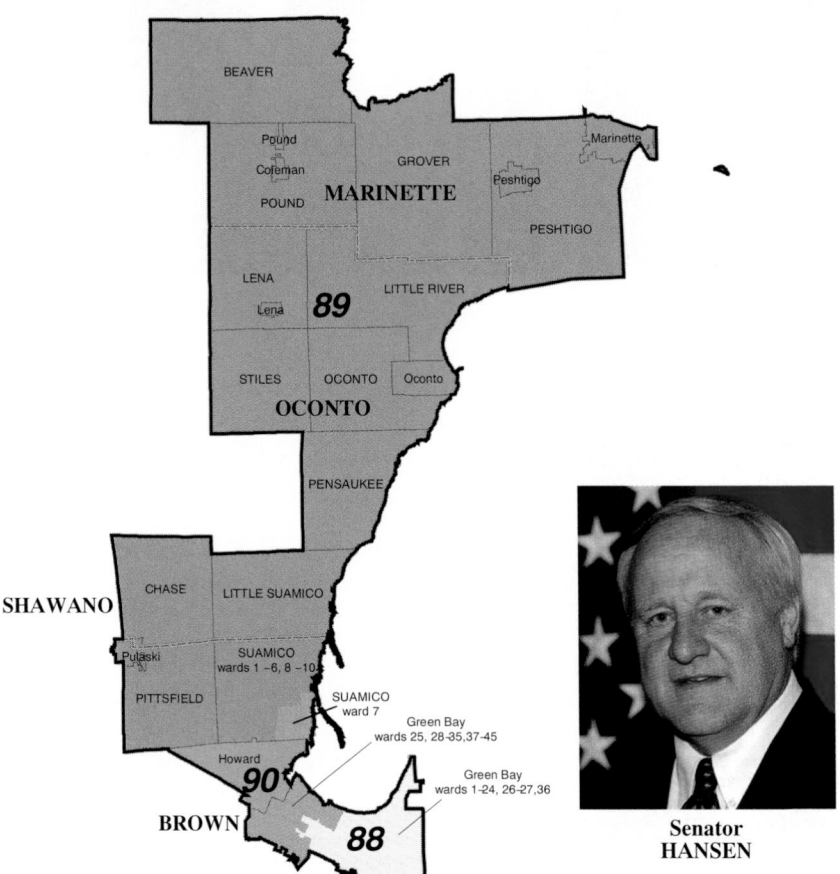

Senator
HANSEN

See Green Bay Area Detail Map on p. 96

Dave Hansen (Dem.), 30th Senate District

Born Green Bay, December 18, 1947; married; 3 children, 6 grandchildren. Graduate Green Bay West H.S.; B.S. UW-Green Bay 1971. Full-time legislator. Former teacher. Former truck driver for Green Bay Department of Public Works. Former Teamster's Union steward. Former member: Brown Co. Human Services Bd. (chp.); N.E.W. Zoo Advisory Bd.; Brown Co. Education and Recreation Com. (chp.). Brown Co. Bd. Supervisor 1996-2002.

Elected to Senate 2000; reelected 2004. Assistant Minority Leader 2005, 2003. Biennial committee assignments: **2005** — Agriculture and Insurance; Education; Labor and Election Process Reform; Jt. Com. on Legislative Organization (also 2003); Senate Organization (also 2003). **2003** — Jt. Com. on Audit (through 5/23/03); Audit (through 5/23/03); Agriculture, Financial Institutions and Insurance; Education, Ethics and Elections; Labor, Small Business Development and Consumer Affairs. **2001** — Labor and Agriculture (chp.); Committee for Review of Administrative Rules; Jt. Com. for Review of Administrative Rules; Environmental Resources; Human Services and Aging; Universities, Housing, and Government Operations; Transportation Projects Commission; Law Revision Committee; Unemployment Insurance Advisory Council (*ex officio* member).

Telephone: Office: (608) 266-5670; (866) 221-9395 (toll free); District: (920) 492-2200.

E-mail address: Sen.Hansen@legis.state.wi.us

Voting address: 920 Coppens Road, Green Bay 54303.

Mailing address: Office: Room 319 South, State Capitol, P.O. Box 7882, Madison 53707-7882.

Representative
KRAWCZYK

Representative
GARD

Representative
VAN ROY

Judy Krawczyk (Rep.), 88th Assembly District

Born Green Bay, January 24, 1939; married; 3 children, 7 grandchildren. Graduate St. Joseph's Academy H.S. 1957. Full-time legislator. Supper club owner. Member: N.E.W. Zoological Society Inc. of Brown Co. (pres.); Wis. Assn. of Women Highway Safety Leaders; American Business Women's Assn. (past pres.); Wis. Restaurant Assn.; Green Bay De Pere Antiquarian Society; Tavern League of Wis.; YWCA of Green Bay (past treas.); National Assn. of Sportsmen Legislators. Former member: St. Vincent's Auxiliary; Sky Ranch for Boys and Girls; 6th Dist. Rep. of National License Beverage Assn., received award for dedicated service 1981. Recipient: *Outstanding Restaurateur of the Year* 1999, 1984.

Elected to Assembly 2000; reelected since 2002. Biennial committee assignments: **2005** — Workforce Development (chp., also 2003); Health (since 2001); Natural Resources (since 2001); State Affairs (vice chp. 2001-2003). **2003** — Colleges and Universities (also 2001); Women's Council (also 2001). **2001** — Small Business and Consumer Affairs (vice chp.); Veterans and Military Affairs.

Telephone: Office: (608) 266-0485; (888) 534-0088 (toll free); District: (920) 469-4364.

E-mail address: Rep.Krawczyk@legis.state.wi.us

Voting address: 2495 Manitowoc Road, Green Bay 54311.

Mailing address: Office: Room 9 North, State Capitol, P.O. Box 8952, Madison 53708.

John Gard (Rep.), 89th Assembly District

Born Milwaukee, August 3, 1963; married; 1 daughter and 1 son. Graduate Lena H.S.; B.S. in political science and public administration UW-La Crosse 1986. Full-time legislator. Former legislative aide to Rep. David Prosser. Member: Lena Knights of Columbus; Muskies, Inc.; Peshtigo Lions; Harmony Sportsmen's Club.

Elected to Assembly in October 1987 special election; reelected since 1988. Speaker of the Assembly 2005, 2003. Biennial committee assignments: **2005** — Assembly Organization (chp., also 2003); Jt. Com. on Legislative Organization (co-chp., also 2003); Jt. Com. on Employment Relations (co-chp., also 2003, mbr. since 1997, eff. 11/4/97); Rules (vice chp., also 2003); Jt. Legislative Council (since 1997, eff. 11/4/97). **2001** — Jt. Com. on Finance (co-chp., also 1999, 1997, eff. 11/4/97); Jt. Com. on Audit (also 1999, 1997, eff. 11/4/97); Finance (chp.); Audit; Claims Bd. (also 1999); Transportation Projects Comn. (since 1993). **1999** — Special Com. on The Renovation of Lambeau Field (chp.). **1997** — Managed Care (chp.); Wisconsin Works Oversight (chp.); Aging and Long-Term Care (vice chp.); Mandates (also 1995); Tourism and Recreation (since 1993); Ways and Means (also 1995). **1995** — Welfare Reform (chp.); Legis. Coun. Com. on Federally Tax-Exempt Lands (chp.). **1993** — Jt. Com. for Review of Administrative Rules (also 1991); Special Com. on Welfare Reform (ranking minority mbr.). **1991** — Rural Affairs; Tourism and Recreation (ranking minority mbr.); Spec. Com. on Drug Enforcement, Education and Treatment; Council on Alcohol and Other Drug Abuse (also 1989); Special Com. on Welfare Review (ranking minority mbr.); Birth to Three Council. **1989** — Excise and Fees (ranking minority mbr.); Rural Development and Forestry; Small Business, Employment and Training; Citizen's Adv. Com. for the Community Services Block Grant.

Telephone: Office: (608) 266-3387; District: (715) 582-2923; E-mail address: Rep.Gard@legis.state.wi.us

Voting address: 481 Aubin Street, P.O. Box 119, Peshtigo 54157.

Mailing address: Office: Room 211 West, State Capitol, P.O. Box 8952, Madison 53708.

Karl Van Roy (Rep.), 90th Assembly District

Born Green Bay, December 1, 1938. Graduate Premontre H.S. (Green Bay) 1957; B.A. Economics, St. Norbert Coll. (De Pere) 1961. Full-time legislator. Former restaurateur. Served in U.S. Army 1962-64. Member: Wis. Restaurant Assn. (bd. of dir., past pres.); Howard-Suamico Optimist Club (past pres. and Optimist International life member); Brown Co. Republican Party; N.E.W. Zoo Board; YMCA Partners in Youth. Former member: Howard-Suamico Business Assn.; Green Bay Chamber of Commerce. Wis. Restaurant Assn. *Restaurateur of the Year* 1990.

Elected to Assembly 2002; reelected 2004. Biennial committee assignments: **2005** — Small Business (chp., vice chp. 2003); Highway Safety (also 2003); Insurance (also 2003); Tourism (also 2003); Transportation (also 2003).

Telephone: Office: (608) 266-0616; (888) 534-0090 (toll free); Fax: (608) 282-3690.

District: (920) 662-0804; Fax: (920) 662-0804.

E-mail address: Rep.VanRoy@legis.state.wi.us

Voting address: 805 Riverview Drive, Green Bay 54303.

Mailing address: Office: Room 123 West, State Capitol, P.O. Box 8953, Madison 53708. District: 2600 Tulip Lane, Green Bay 54313.

31st SENATE DISTRICT

See Eau Claire Area Detail Map on p. 97

Senator
BROWN

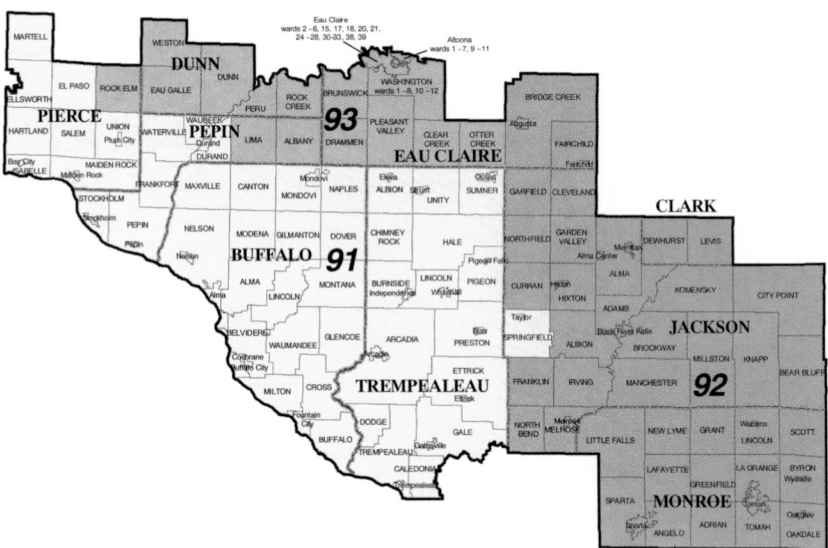

Ron Brown (Rep.), 31st Senate District

Born Marion, IN, September 18, 1946; married; 3 children. Graduate Central High (Ft. Wayne, IN) 1964; A.A.S. Purdue Ex.-Ft. Wayne 1981. Business owner. Former Fire Chief, City of Eau Claire and Fort Wayne, IN. Veteran; served in U.S. Air Force 1964-67. Member: American Legion Post 53; AMVETS; Vietnam Veterans of America; Mason F & AM Lodge 112 Eau Claire; United Way of Eau Claire (bd. mbr.); Eau Claire Co. Republican Party; Chambers of Commerce for Eau Claire, Black River Falls, Greater Tomah Area, Alma Area, Sparta Area, Arcadia Area, Trempealeau. Former member: Eau Claire Kiwanis; Great Lakes Division, International Assn. of Fire Chiefs (pres.); Wis. State Fire Chiefs Assn. (pres.); Eau Claire Co. Fire Chiefs Assn. (pres.); Chippewa Valley Technical College Advisory Com.

Elected to Senate 2002. Majority Caucus Chairperson 2005. Biennial committee assignments: **2005** — Veterans, Homeland Security, Military Affairs, Small Business and Government Reform (chp.); Agriculture and Insurance; Health, Children, Families, Aging and Long-Term Care (also 2003); Housing and Financial Institutions; Jt. Legislative Council (also 2003); Migrant Labor Council; Rural Economic Dev. Bd. (also 2003); Small Business Regulatory Review Bd. **2003** — Homeland Security, Veterans and Military Affairs and Government Reform (chp.); Agriculture, Financial Institutions and Insurance; Economic Development; Job Creation and Housing.

Telephone: Office: (608) 266-8546; (877) 763-6636 (toll free); District: (715) 834-7772.

E-mail address: Sen.Brown@legis.state.wi.us; Internet address: www.legis.state.wi.us/senate/sen31/sen31.html

Voting address: 1112 Violet Avenue, Eau Claire 54701.

Mailing address: Office: Room 409 South, State Capitol, P.O. Box 7882, Madison 53707-7882.

| Representative | Representative | Representative |
| GRONEMUS | MUSSER | KREIBICH |

Barbara Gronemus (Dem.), 91st Assembly District

Born Norwalk, November 21, 1931; 3 children, 5 grandchildren, 3 great-grandchildren. Graduate Ontario Public H.S. 1949. Full-time legislator. Former nursing home activity dir. and farmer/farmwife. Member: Wis. Women for Agriculture/Northwood Chapter; Wis. Farm Bureau; Wis. Farmers Union; Whitehall Lions Club; American Legion Aux.; Democratic Party of Wis. Major, Civil Air Patrol.

Elected to Assembly since 1982. Biennial committee assignments: **2005** — Agriculture (ranking minority mbr., also 2003-1995, 1987-89 1st woman chp., mbr. 1983-85); Natural Resources (since 1999); Rural Development; Transportation (also 2003). **2003** — Property Rights and Land Mgt. (ranking minority mbr.); Mississippi River Parkway Comn. (also 2001). **2001** — Rural Affairs and Forestry (ranking minority mbr., also 1999); Legis. Coun. Spec. Com. on Recodification of Town Highway Statutes; Legis. Adv. Com. to the Minn.-Wis. Boundary Area Comn.; Speaker's Task Force on Budget Review; Natural Resources Select Com. on Deer Mgt.; Agriculture Subcom. on Farm and Farm Safety. **1999** — Legis. Council Com. on Navigable Waters Recodification; Gov.'s Blue Ribbon Task Force on Aquaculture. **1993** — Agriculture, Forestry and Rural Affairs (chp.). **1991** — Agriculture, Aquaculture and Forestry (chp.).

Telephone: Office: (608) 266-7015; (888) 534-0091 (toll free); District: (715) 538-4130 or Fax: (715) 538-2119.

E-mail address: Rep.Gronemus@legis.state.wi.us

Voting address: 36301 West Street, Whitehall 54773.

Mailing address: Office: Room 114 North, State Capitol, P.O. Box 8952, Madison 53708; District: 36301 West Street, P.O. Box 676, Whitehall 54773-0676.

Terry M. Musser (Rep.), 92nd Assembly District

Born Black River Falls, November 15, 1947; married; 2 children, 3 grandchildren. Graduate Melrose H.S.; attended UW-La Crosse 1973-76. Farmer. Former driver license examiner. Vietnam veteran, 2 tours; paratrooper and Green Beret, 6th Special Forces, Fort Bragg, NC, 1965-68. Member: Wis. Vietnam Veterans Chapter 3 (life mbr.); Vietnam Veterans of America (life mbr.); American Legion (life mbr.); Veterans of Foreign Wars, Post 2112, Sparta (life mbr.); Disabled American Veterans, Black River Falls (life mbr.); AMVETS, Post 5494, Black River Falls (life mbr.); Monroe County 40 et 8; Wis. Farm Bureau Federation; Cataract Sportsman Club.

Elected to Assembly since 1984. Biennial committee assignments: **2005** — Military Affairs (chp.); Government Operations and Spending Limitations (vice chp., mbr. 2003); Veterans Affairs (vice chp.); Highway Safety (since 2001); Property Rights and Land Management (vice chp. 2003); State Affairs (also 2003, 1995). **2003** — Veterans and Military Affairs (chp. since 1995, ranking minority mbr. 1989 to 1995); Legis. Coun. Com. on State-Tribal Relations (chp., also 2001). **2001** — State and Local Finance (vice chp.); Tax and Spending Limitations; Urban and Local Affairs (also 1999).

Telephone: Office: (608) 266-7461; (888) 534-0092 (toll free); District: (608) 488-2955.

E-mail address: Rep.Musser@legis.state.wi.us

Voting address: (Town of Irving) W13550 Murray Road, Black River Falls 54615.

Mailing address: Office: Room 11 West, State Capitol, P.O. Box 8953, Madison 53708.

Robin G. Kreibich (Rep.), 93rd Assembly District

Born Wabasha, MN, June 4, 1959; 1 son, 2 daughters. Graduate River Falls H.S.; B.A. in journalism U. of Minnesota 1982; graduate Brown Institute (MN) 1981-82. Former WEAU-TV anchorman. Broadcast news awards: 1987 first place feature "God's Little Iron Man"; 1988 first place feature "Rubber Duck Race"; 1990 first place feature "Gorby's T-Shirt Man"; 1990 Best Series "New Richmond Band Russian Tour". Member: Masons; Elk's Club; Eau Claire Chamber of Commerce; Chippewa Valley Boy Scouts (bd. mbr.); Trinity Equestrian Center; Wis. Literacy Bd. Recipient: UW Alumni Assn. *Legislator of the Year* 2000; Wis. Technical College District Bds. Assn. *Legislator of the Year* 2000; Western Wis. Press Club *1st Place Award* 2000 (Mabel political ad); Chippewa Valley Tech. College *C.L. Greiber Award of Merit* 2001; Independent Colleges *Legislator of the Year* 2002; Dairy Business Assn. *Friend of the Dairy Industry Award* 2004. National Conference of State Legislature's "Blue Ribbon Legislative Comn." on higher education and fiscal policy 2005.

Elected to Assembly since 1992. Biennial committee assignments: **2005** — Colleges and Universities (chp. since 1995, mbr. 1993); Financial Institutions (since 1999); Housing (also 2003); Workforce Development. **2003** — Midwestern Higher Education Comn. (since 1995). **2001** — Insurance (also 1999). **1997** — Small Business and Economic Development (since 1993).

Telephone: Office: (608) 266-0660; (888) 534-0093 (toll free); District: (715) 839-1064.

E-mail address: Rep.Kreibich@legis.state.wi.us

Voting address: 3437 Nimitz Street, Eau Claire 54701.

Mailing address: Office: Room 107 West, State Capitol, P.O. Box 8952, Madison 53708.

32nd SENATE DISTRICT

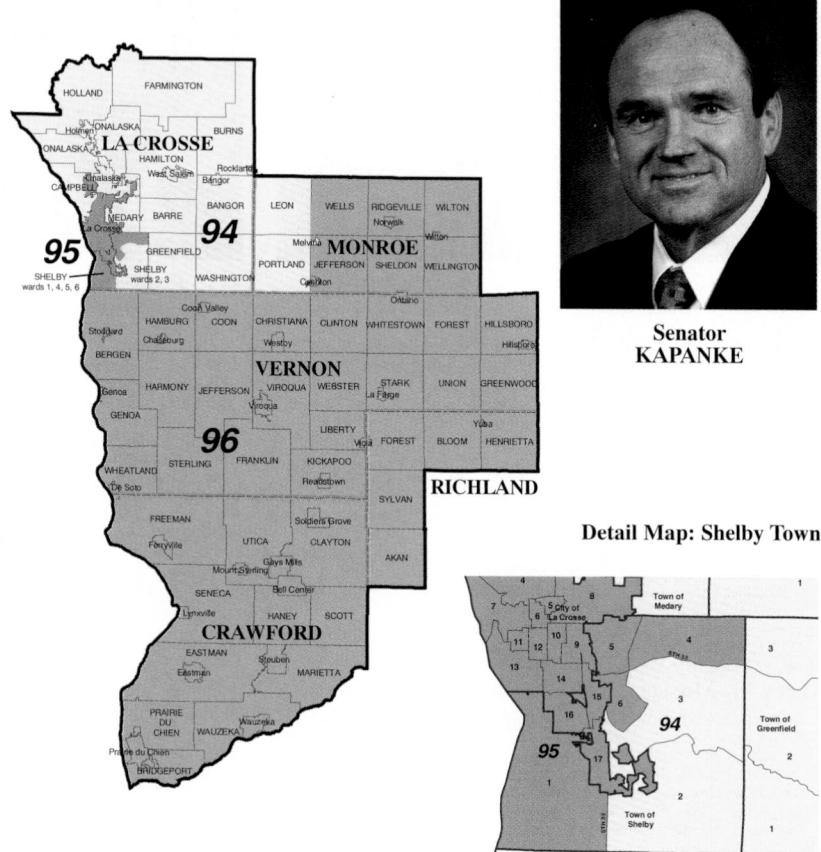

**Senator
KAPANKE**

Detail Map: Shelby Town

Daniel E. Kapanke (Rep.), 32nd Senate District

Born La Crosse, August 21, 1947; married; 4 children. Graduate Onalaska Luther H.S. 1965; B.S. UW-La Crosse 1975; M.E.P.D. UW-La Crosse 1987. Owner La Crosse Loggers baseball team. District sales manager Kaltenberg Seed Farms. Served in U.S. Marine Corps Reserve, 1967-72; Wisconsin National Guard 1971-72, 1991-92. Former member: La Crosse Area Development Corporation (bd. mbr.); La Crosse Area Convention and Visitors Bureau (bd. mbr.); La Crosse Area Planning Committee (bd. mbr.). Town of Campbell Board 1981-87, 1997-2004.

Elected to Senate 2004. Biennial committee assignments: **2005** — Agriculture and Insurance (chp.); Energy, Utilities and Information Technology; Higher Education and Tourism; Natural Resources and Transportation; Jt. Legislative Council.

Telephone: Office: (608) 266-5490; District: (608) 782-1871.

Voting address: 1610 Lakeshore Drive, La Crosse 54603.

Mailing address: Office: Room 104 South, State Capitol, P.O. Box 7882, Madison 53707-7882.

Representative
HUEBSCH

Representative
SHILLING

Representative
NERISON

Michael D. Huebsch (Rep.), 94th Assembly District

Born Milwaukee, July 19, 1964; married; 2 sons. Graduate Onalaska H.S. 1982; Oral Roberts U. 1982-87. Full-time legislator. Former marketing director and legislative assistant. Member: Onalaska Business Association; Family and Children's Center Community Board; Greater La Crosse Area Chamber of Commerce; La Crosse Co. Republican Party (past treas.); UW-La Crosse Chancellor's Community Council; Holmen Rod and Gun Club.

Elected to Assembly since 1994. Majority Leader 2005. Biennial committee assignments: **2005** — Rules (chp.); Assembly Organization (vice chp.); Jt. Com. on Employment Relations; Jt. Com. on Legislative Organization; Jt. Legislative Council. **2003** — Jt. Com. on Finance (since 2001); Finance (vice chp., mbr. since 2001). **2001** — Judicial Council (also 1999). **1999** — Judiciary and Personal Privacy (chp.); Family Law; Financial Institutions; Transportation; Ways and Means (since 1995); Special Com. on The Renovation of Lambeau Field; Child Abuse and Neglect Prevention Bd. (also 1997); Law Revision. **1997** — Children and Families (chp., mbr. 1995); Wis. Works Oversight (chp., eff. 12/19/97); Highways and Transportation; Legis. Adv. Com. to the Minn.-Wis. Boundary Area Comn. (also 1995). **1995** — Small Business and Economic Development; Welfare Reform.

Telephone: Office: (608) 266-2401; (888) 534-0094 (toll free); District: (608) 786-3512.

E-mail address: Rep.Huebsch@legis.state.wi.us

Voting address: 419 West Franklin, West Salem 54669.

Mailing address: Office: Room 215 West, State Capitol, P.O. Box 8952, Madison 53708.

Jennifer Shilling (Dem.), 95th Assembly District

Born Oshkosh, July 4, 1969; married. Graduate Buffalo Grove, IL H.S.; B.A. in political science and public administration, UW-La Crosse 1992. Full-time legislator. Former congressional aide and legislative aide. Member: UW-La Crosse Alumni Assn. (bd. mbr.); La Crosse Co. League of Women Voters; La Crosse Co. Democratic Party (former chp.); UW-La Crosse Chancellor's Community Council; Viterbo College Bd. of Advisors; Wis. Women in Government (bd. of dir.); Family and Children's Center Community Bd.; La Crosse Community Advisory Bd. La Crosse Co. Bd. 1990-92.

Elected to Assembly 2000; reelected since 2002. Minority Caucus Sergeant at Arms 2005. Biennial committee assignments: **2005** — Colleges and Universities (also 2003); Financial Institutions (since 2001); Health (also 2001); Highway Safety (also 2003); State of Wisconsin Building Commission. **2003** — Insurance (also 2001). **2001** — Personal Privacy; Legis. Adv. Com. to the Minn.-Wis. Boundary Area Comn.

Telephone: Office: (608) 266-5780; (888) 534-0095 (toll free); District: (608) 788-9854.

E-mail address: Rep.Shilling@legis.state.wi.us

Voting address: 2608 Main Street, La Crosse 54601.

Mailing address: Office: Room 120 North, State Capitol, P.O. Box 8953, Madison 53708.

Lee Nerison (Rep.), 96th Assembly District

Born La Crosse, July 31, 1952; married; 3 children. Graduate Viroqua H.S. 1970; UW-Madison Farm and Industry Short Course 1971. Farmer. Former dairy farmer. Member: Vernon Co-op Oil and Gas (bd. mbr., fmr. secretary); Coon Valley Lions (1st vice pres., fmr. 2nd vice pres., 3rd vice pres., secretary, treasurer). Former member: Viroqua FFA Alumni (reporter); Westby FFA Alumni; Church Council (vice pres., treasurer). Vernon Co. Board 1998-present (chairperson 2002-present).

Elected to Assembly 2004. Biennial committee assignments: **2005** — Agriculture (vice chp.); Energy and Utilities; Rural Affairs and Renewable Energy; Tourism.

Telephone: Office: (608) 266-3534; District: (608) 634-4562.

Voting address: S3035 CTH B, Westby 54667.

Mailing address: Office: Room 310 North, State Capitol, P.O. Box 8953, Madison 53708.

33rd SENATE DISTRICT

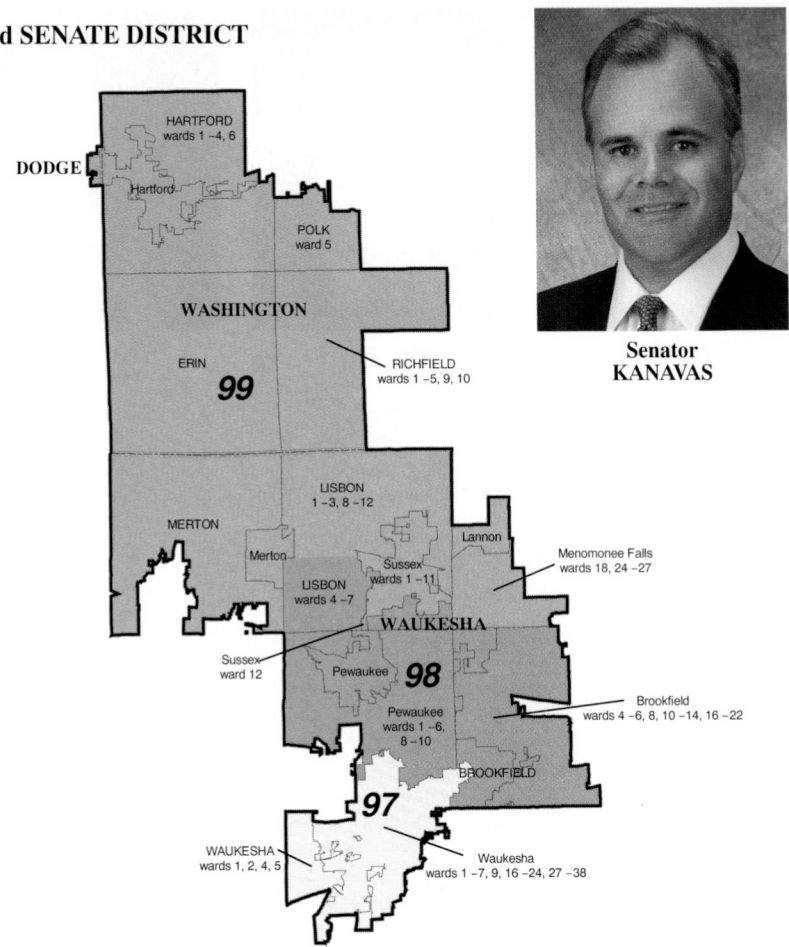

**Senator
KANAVAS**

See Waukesha County Detail Map on pp. 94 and 95

See Waukesha Area Detail Maps on pp. 74 & 97

Theodore J. Kanavas (Rep.), 33rd Senate District

Born April 29, 1961; married; 3 children. Graduate Brookfield East H.S.; BA Political Science, UW-Madison 1983; attended Pepperdine U. Law School. Co-founder, software company; senior software executive. Member: Waukesha Co. Republican Party (former membership dir.); Washington Co. Republican Party; Order of Ahepa, Chap. 43 (scholarship com.); Annunciation Greek Orthodox Church; Elmbrook Historical Society; Greater Brookfield Chamber of Commerce; Hartford Area Chamber of Commerce. Elmbrook School Board April 1999-2002.

Elected to Senate in July 2001 special election; reelected 2002. Biennial committee assignments: **2005** — Job Creation, Economic Development and Consumer Affairs (chp.); Labor and Election Process Reform; Jt. Survey Com. on Tax Exemptions; Veterans, Homeland Security, Military Affairs, Small Business and Government Reform; Wis. Housing and Economic Development Authority; Jt. Leg. Council Spec. Com. on Wisconsin's Transportation Infrastructure (chp.). **2003** — Jt. Com. on Finance; Finance; Health, Children, Families, Aging and Long Term Care (vice chp.); Transportation and Information Infrastructure (vice chp.); State Fair Park Bd.; Governor's Council on Highway Safety; Special Select Com. on Job Creation (co-chp.); Senate Select Com. on State and Local Government Relations; Statewide Multi-modal Improvement Program (proj. review com. mbr.). **2001** — Education; Privacy, Electronic Commerce and Financial Institutions; Human Services and Aging; Jt. Legislative Council Com. on Public and Private Broadband; Governor's Task Force on Financial Education; Governor's Council on Workforce Development.

Telephone: Office: (608) 266-9174; (800) 863-8883 (toll free); District: (262) 785-9187.

E-mail address: Sen.Kanavas@legis.state.wi.us

Voting address: 17570 Sierra Lane, Brookfield 53045.

Mailing address: Office: Room 10 South, State Capitol, P.O. Box 7882, Madison 53707-7882.

| Representative
NISCHKE | Representative
JENSEN | Representative
PRIDEMORE |

Ann Nischke (Rep.), 97th Assembly District

Born Milwaukee, January 19, 1951; married; 1 child. Graduate Cambria/Friesland H.S. 1968; B.S. Elementary Education, UW-Eau Claire 1977; attended UW-Oshkosh; graduate Leadership Milwaukee. Real estate associate. Former chamber of commerce and YMCA executive director; legislative aide; elementary school teacher. Member: Waukesha County Republican Party; Waukesha County Republican Women's Club; Rotary; Chamber of Commerce; TEMPO/Envision; Friends of Carroll College; Waukesha Symphony Orchestra; Trinity Ev. Lutheran Church.

Elected to Assembly 2002; reelected 2004. Biennial committee assignments: **2005** — Insurance (chp.); Aging and Long-Term Care (also 2003); Economic Development (vice chp. 2003); Education Reform (also 2003); Energy and Utilities (also 2003); Jt. Legislative Council. **2003** — Financial Institutions; Small Business.

Telephone: Office: (608) 266-8580; (888) 534-0097 (toll free); District: (262) 896-9620.

E-mail address: Rep.Nischke@legis.state.wi.us

Voting address: 202 West College Avenue, Waukesha 53186.

Mailing address: Office: Room 8 North, State Capitol, P.O. Box 8953, Madison 53708; District: P.O. Box 2005, Waukesha 53187-2005.

Scott R. Jensen (Rep.), 98th Assembly District

Born Waukesha, August 24, 1960; married; 3 children. Graduate Mukwonago H.S.; B.A. Drake University, Des Moines, IA 1982; M.P.P. Harvard U., Kennedy School of Government 1984. Public relations executive. Former chief of staff to Governor Tommy Thompson and former Assembly Republican caucus director.

Elected to Assembly in January 1992 special election; reelected since November 1992. Speaker of the Assembly 2001, 1999, and 1997 (eff. 11/4/97); Majority Leader 1995. Biennial committee assignments: **2005** — Jt. Com. on Finance (co-chp. 1/6/97–11/4/97). **2003** — Education Reform (chp.); Energy and Utilities (chp.); Family Law. **2001** — Jt. Com. on Employment Relations (co-chp., also 1999, 1997, eff. 11/4/97, mbr. 1995); Jt. Com. on Legislative Organization (co-chp., also 1999, 1997, eff. 11/4/97); Assembly Organization (chp., also 1999, 1997, eff. 11/4/97, vice chp. 1995); Rules (vice chp., also 1999, 1997, eff. 11/4/97, chp. 1995); Disability Bd. (since 1997); Retirement Research Com.; Jt. Legislative Council (since 1995). **1999** — Jt. Survey Com. on Retirement Systems. **1997** — Jt. Com. on Audit (resigned 11/4/97, also 1993); Campaign Finance Reform (resigned 12/19/97); Legis. Coun. Com. on Faith-Based Approaches to Crime Prevention and Justice (chp.). **1995** — Environment and Utilities and its Subcom. on Clean Air Act Implementation; Health; Jt. Com. on Information Policy.

Telephone: Office: (608) 264-6970; District: (262) 798-0650; E-mail address: Rep.Jensen@legis.state.wi.us

Voting address: 850 South Springdale Road, Waukesha 53186.

Mailing address: Office: Room 321 East, State Capitol, P.O. Box 8952, Madison 53708.

Don Pridemore (Rep.), 99th Assembly District

Born Milwaukee, October 20, 1946; married; 3 sons. Graduate Milwaukee Lutheran H.S. 1964; B.S.E.E. Marquette U. 1977. Full-time legislator. Former electronics research technician, electronics design engineer, and senior electronics project engineer. Vietnam Era veteran; served in U.S. Air Force 1965-69. Member: Hartford Area Taxpayers Assn. (com. mbr., fmr. pres.); Greater Hartford Optimists Club (charter bd. mbr.); Land-O-Hills Baseball League (commissioner); Erin Baseball Club (pres.); BSA Troop 741 (ASM); Washington and Waukesha Co. Republican Party; American Legion; VFW; NRA; Senior Friends (Hartford). Former member: IEEE; Wis. Citizens for Legal Reform (st. dir.). Erin Park Bd. 1995-present.

Elected to Assembly 2004. Biennial committee assignments: **2005** — Urban and Local Affairs (vice chp.); Budget Review; Education Reform; Ways and Means; Workforce Development.

Telephone: Office: (608) 267-2367; (888) 534-0099 (toll free); Fax: (608) 282-3699; District: (262) 670-0638.

E-mail address: Rep.Pridemore@legis.state.wi.us

Voting address: 2277 Highway K, Hartford 53027.

Mailing address: Office: Room 318 North, State Capitol, P.O. Box 8953, Madison 53708.

Robert J. Marchant: Senate Chief Clerk

Born Green Bay, April 1, 1971; married; 2 children. Graduate East De Pere H.S. 1989; B.S. UW-Madison 1994; J.D. UW-Madison 1997. Chief clerk and director of operations, Wisconsin Senate. Former attorney Wis. Legislative Reference Bureau; Bender, Levi and Marchant S.C. Member: American Society of Legislative Clerks and Secretaries (mbr. program com. and vice chp. technology and innovation com.); State Bar of Wisconsin.

Elected Senate Chief Clerk 1/20/04; reelected 2005.

Telephone: Office: (608) 266-2517.

Voting address: City of Watertown.

Mailing address: Office: Room 401, 17 West Main Street, Risser Justice Center, P.O. Box 7882, Madison 53707-7882.

Edward (Ted) A. Blazel: Senate Sergeant at Arms

Born Quincy, IL, June 14, 1972; married; 1 child. Graduate Quincy Senior H.S. 1990; B.A. St. Norbert College (De Pere) 1994; M.A. Marquette U. (Milwaukee) 1998; attended UW-Madison 1998-2002. Former legislative aide. Member: National Legislative Service and Security Assn. (Region 2 vice chair); Heritage Heights Community Assn. (bd. mbr.).

Elected Senate Sergeant at Arms 2003; reelected 2005.

Telephone: Office: (608) 266-1801.

Voting address: 5301 Knightsbridge Road, Madison 53714.

Mailing address: Office: Room B35 South, State Capitol, P.O. Box 7882, Madison 53707-7882.

Patrick E. Fuller: Assembly Chief Clerk

Born Toledo, OH, February 24, 1954; married; 1 child. Graduate St. Francis de Sales H.S. (Toledo) 1972; B.E. U. of Toledo 1980; M.B.A. Touro University International (Los Alamitos, CA) 2001. Former director Wisconsin Troops to Teachers Program, Wis. Dept. of Veterans Affairs 1998-2000. Vietnam Era and Operation Desert Storm veteran. Served in U.S. Marine Corps 1972-86; U.S. Army 1986-97. Member NRA; Second Marine Division Assn.; Veterans of Foreign Wars; Disabled Veterans of America; American Legion; American Hellenic Educational Progressive Assn.; Force Recon Association; 75th Ranger Regiment Association.

Elected Assembly Chief Clerk 2003; reelected 2005.

Telephone: Office: (608) 266-5811; E-mail address: Patrick.Fuller@legis.state.wi.us

Voting address: 214 Grove Street, Ridgeway 53582.

Mailing address: Office: Suite 208, 17 West Main Street, Madison 53708-8952.

Richard A. Skindrud: Assembly Sergeant at Arms

Born Mt. Horeb, September 15, 1944; married; 3 children. Former truck driver, farmer, county board supervisor, and state legislator. Vietnam veteran; served in Army as helicopter crew chief 1965-67. Member: Vietnam Veterans; American Legion; VFW; Sons of Norway. Town of Primrose Land Use Committee 1981-93; Dane Co. Board 1989-94 (chp. of its Land Conservation and UW Extension Coms., vice chp. of its Zoning and Natural Resources Coms. and mbr. of its Highway and Transportation Com.).

Elected to Assembly in June 1993 special election; reelected 1994-2000. Elected Assembly Sergeant at Arms 2003; reelected 2005. Majority Caucus Sergeant at Arms 2001, 1999. Biennial committee assignments: **2001** — State Affairs (chp. since 1997, vice chp. 1995, mbr. 1993); Tourism and Recreation (chp., mbr. since 1993); Corrections and the Courts; Small Business and Consumer Affairs; Governor's Council on Tourism (since 1997). **1999** — Consumer Affairs (vice chp., chp. 1995); Insurance; Review of Farmland Preservation Program (eff. 4/27/99).

Telephone: Office: (608) 267-9808.

E-mail address: Rick.Skindrud@legis.state.wi.us

Voting address: 9267 Skindrud Road, Mt. Horeb 53572.

Mailing address: Office: Room 411 West, State Capitol, P.O. Box 8953, Madison 53708.

SENATE DISTRICTS

Promulgated by the U.S. District Court for the Eastern District of Wisconsin May 30, 2002

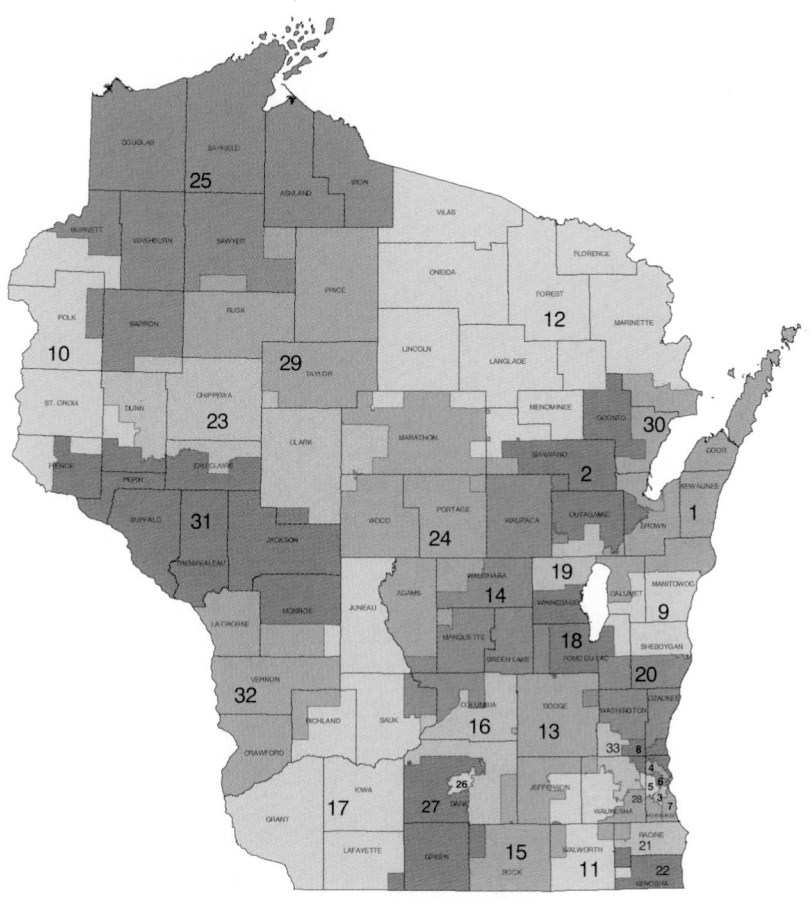

ASSEMBLY DISTRICTS

Promulgated by the U.S. District Court for the Eastern District of Wisconsin
May 30, 2002

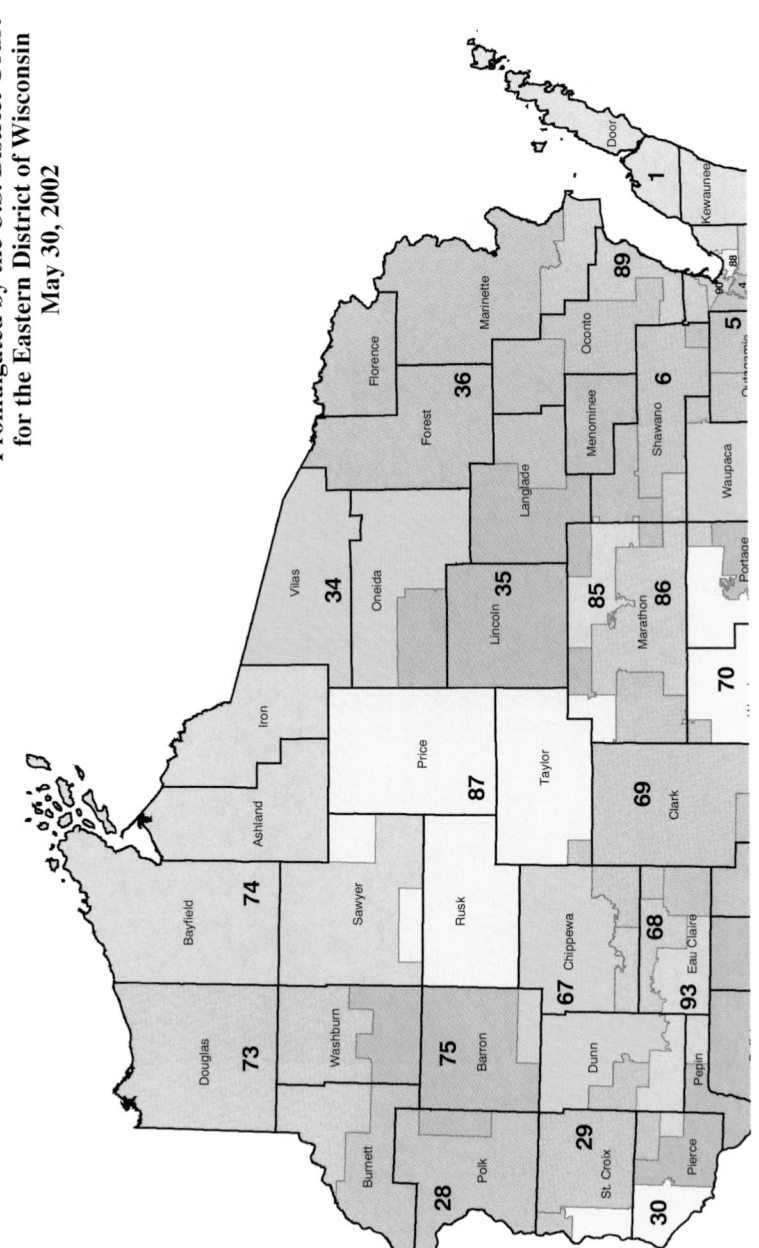

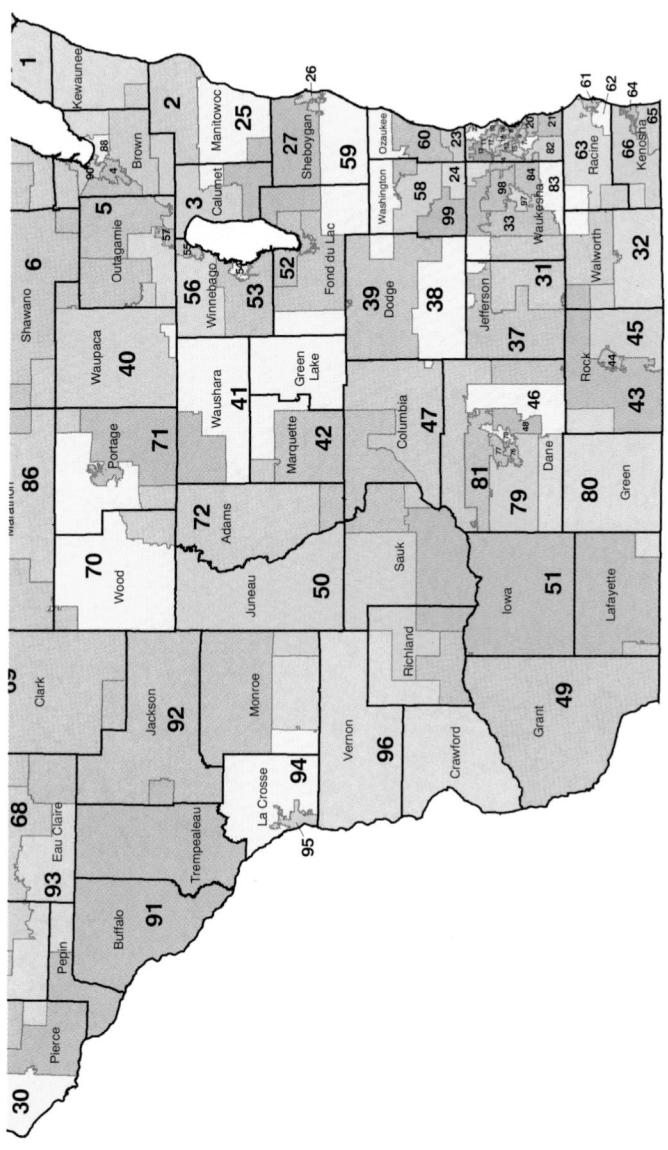

Detail Map: Madison Area

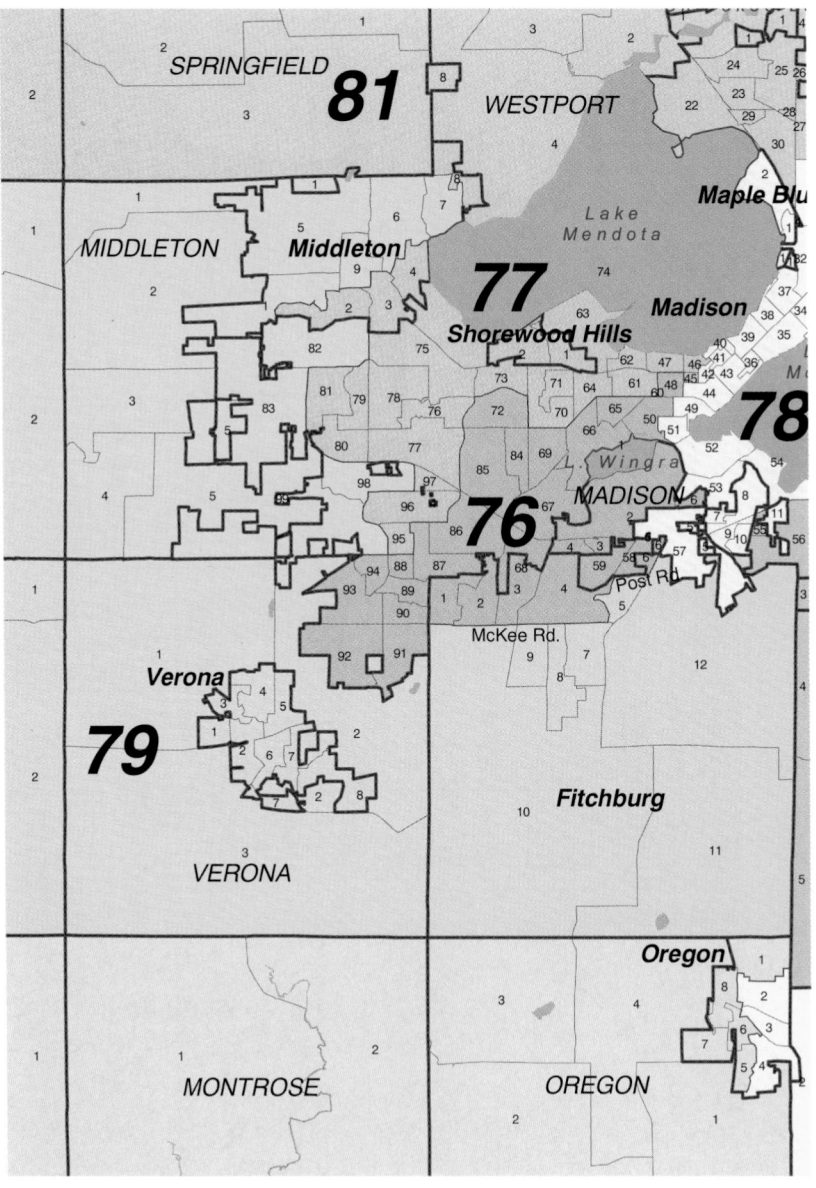

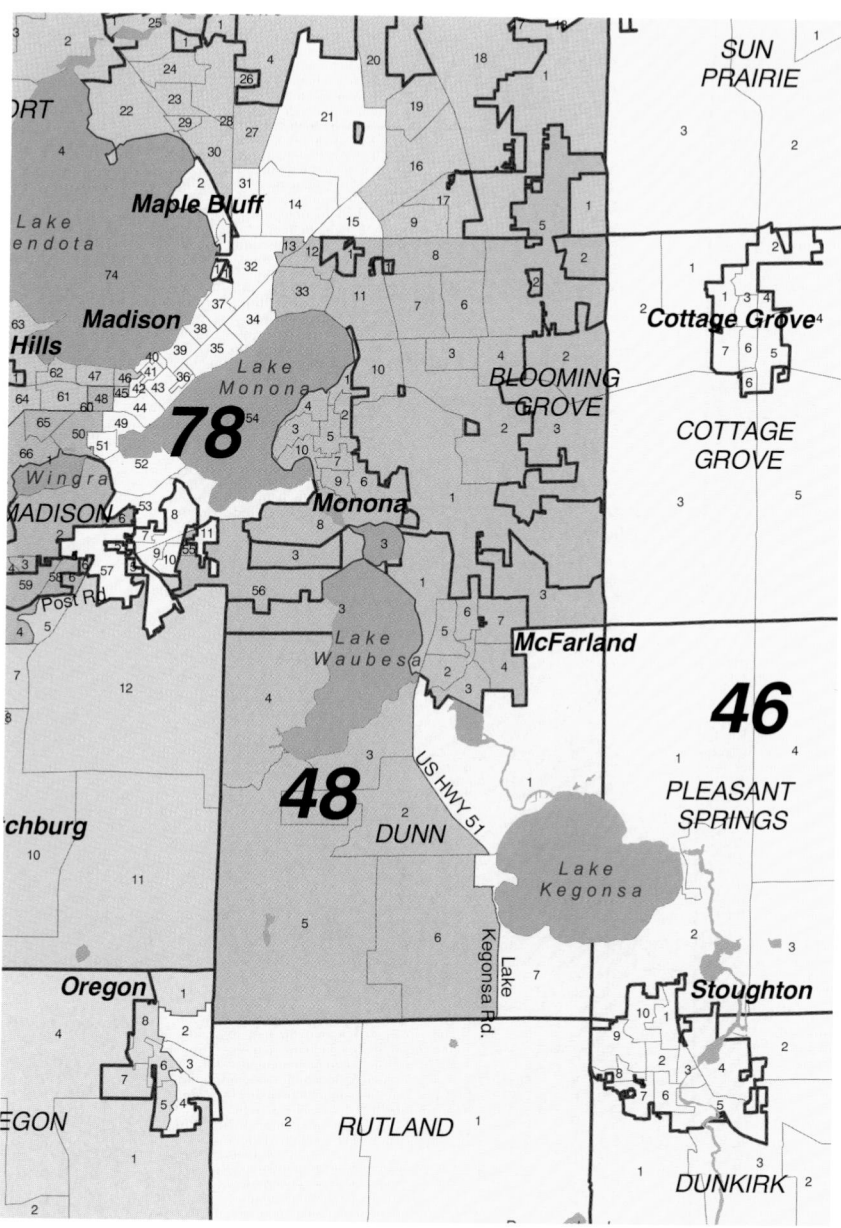

Detail Map: Milwaukee County (North)

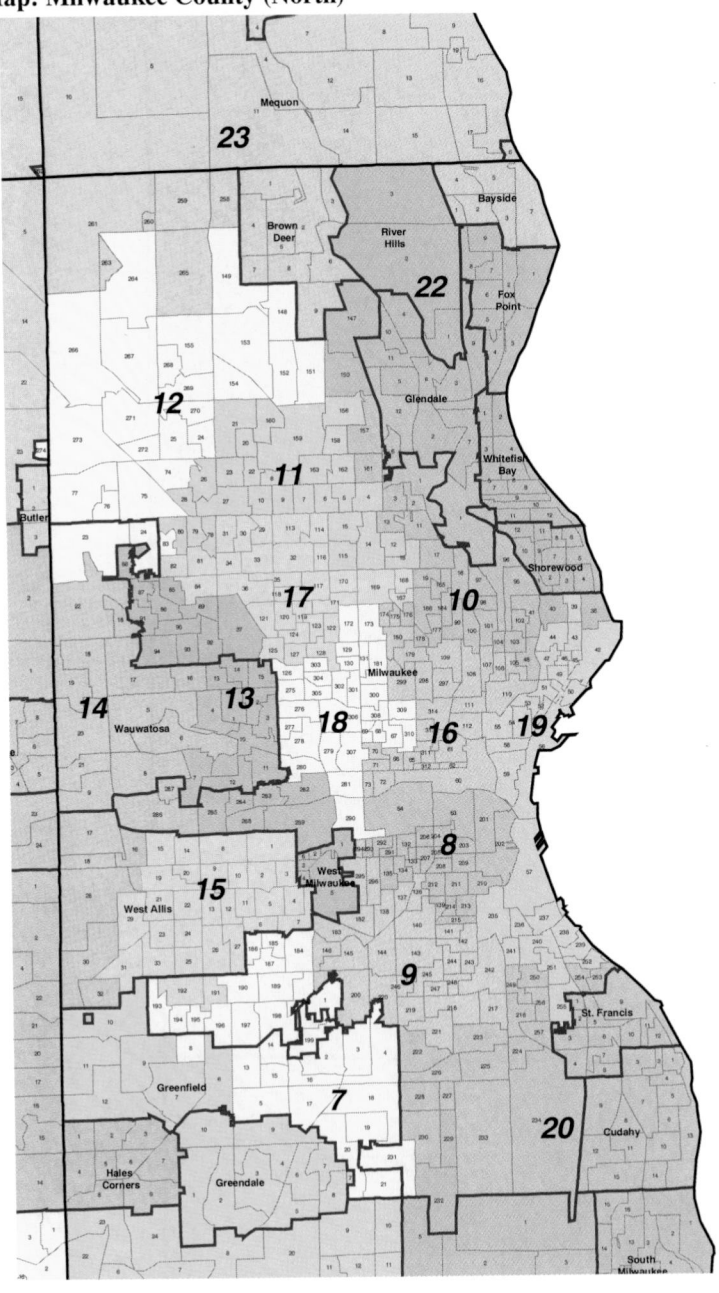

Detail Map: Milwaukee County (South)

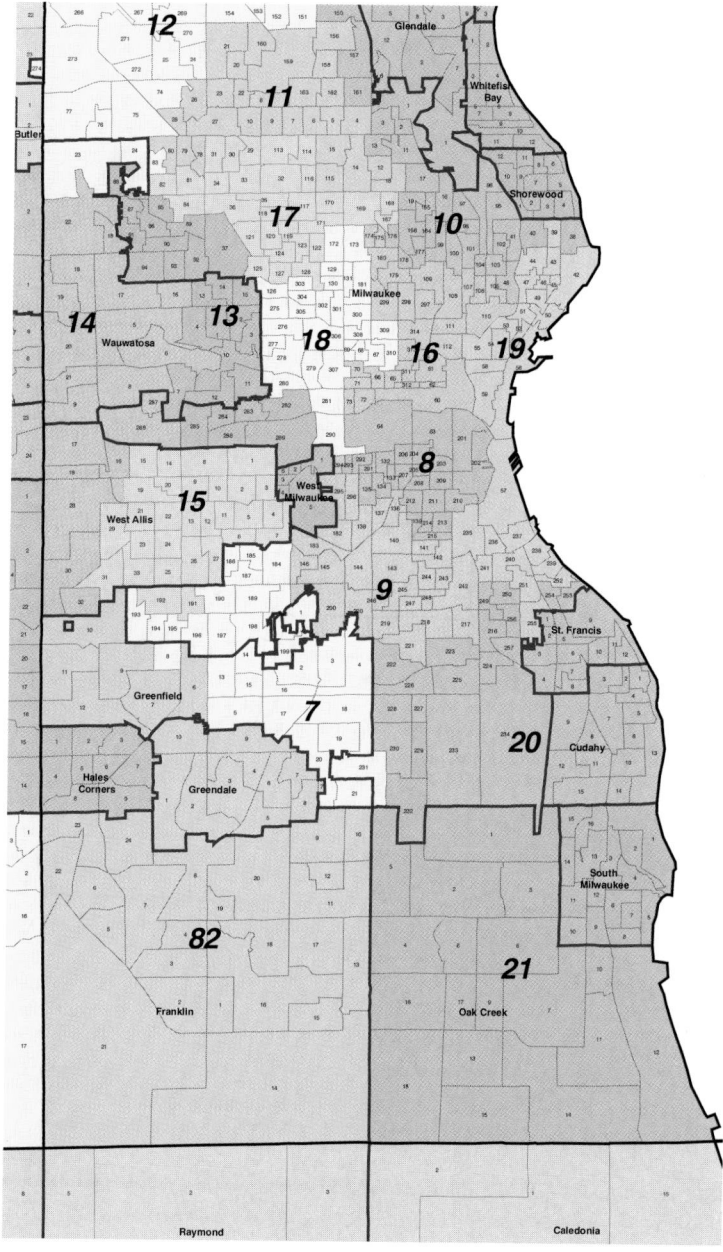

Detail Map: Waukesha County (West)

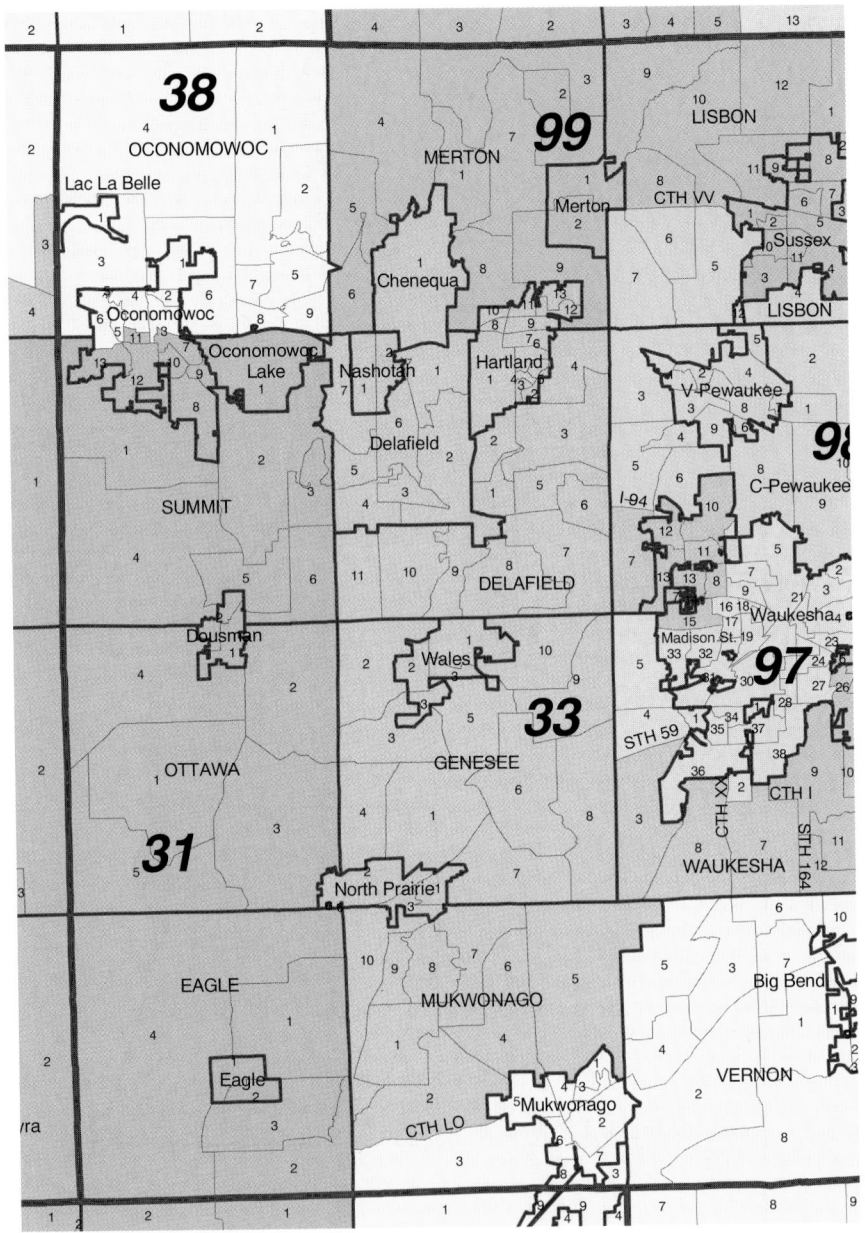

Detail Map: Waukesha County (East)

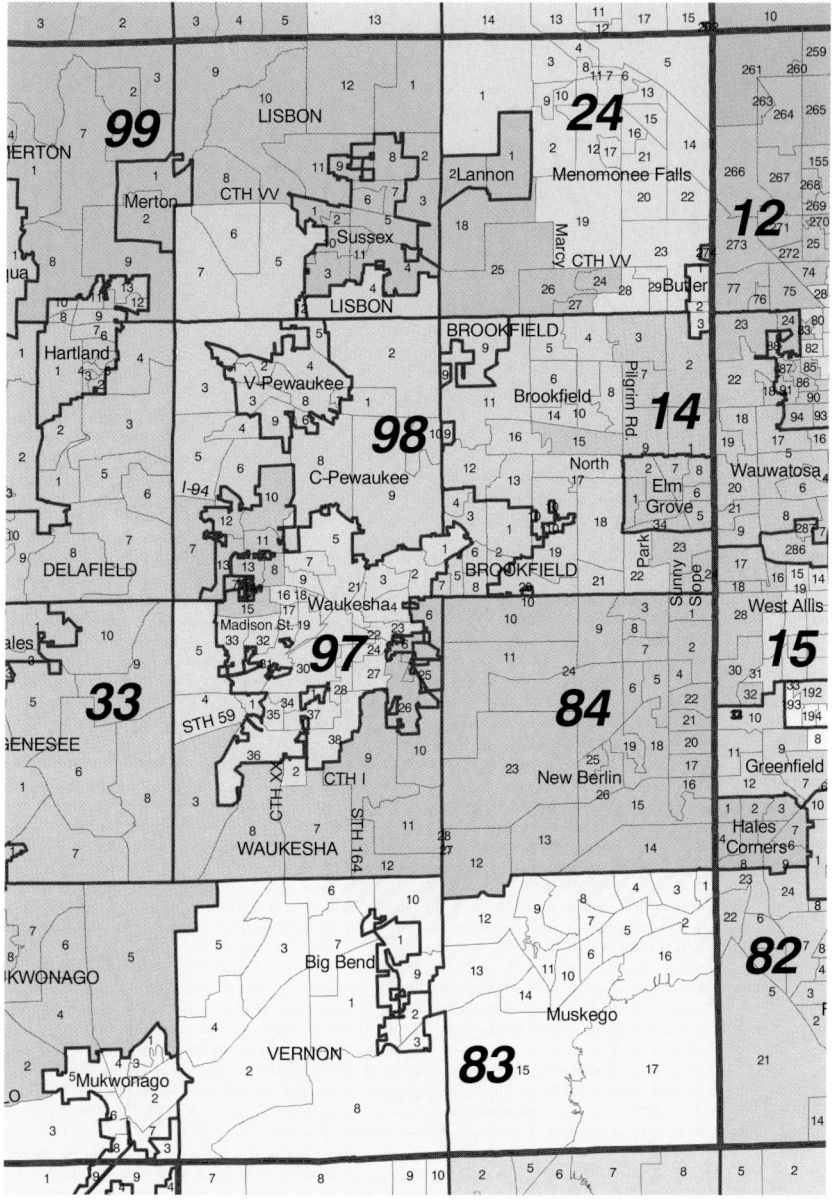

Detail Map: Green Bay Area

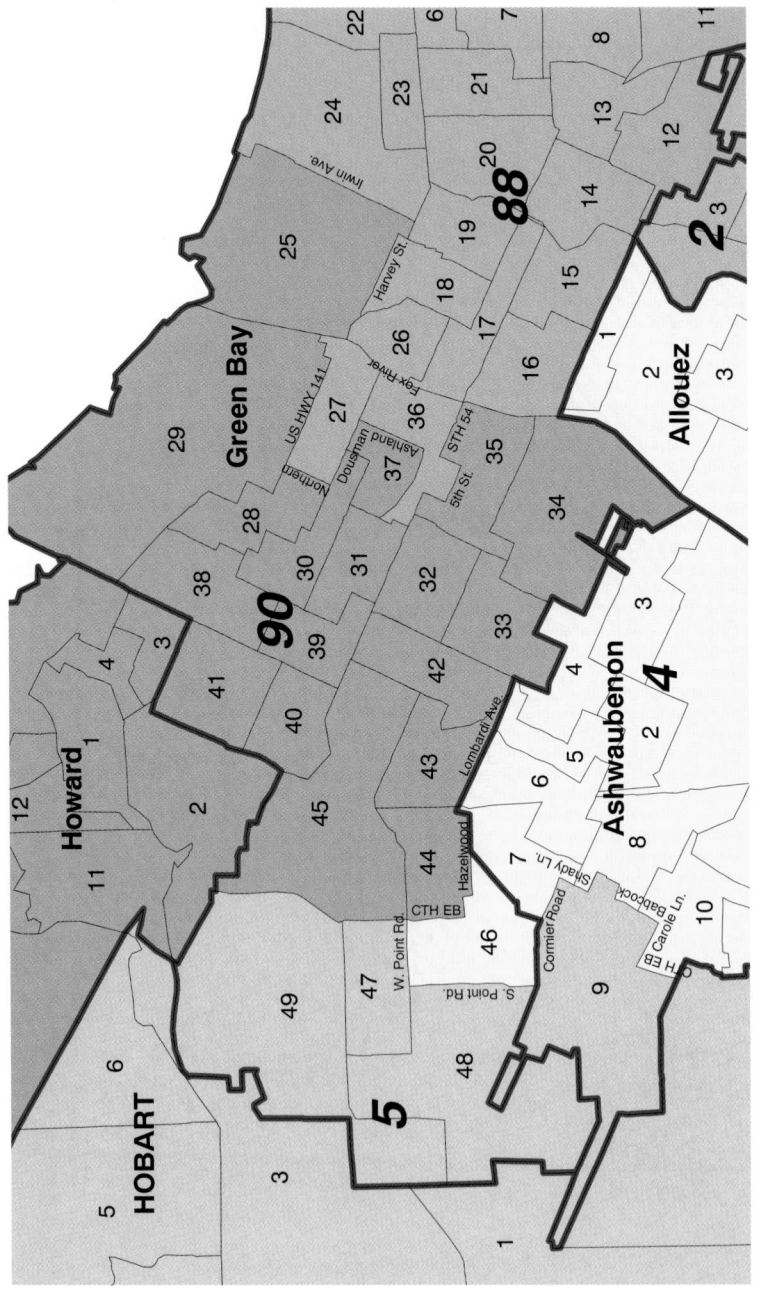

Detail Map: Eau Claire Area

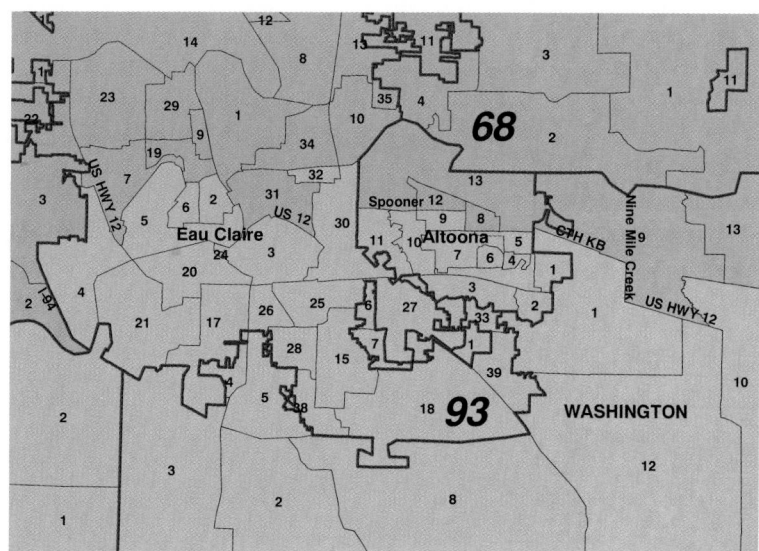

Detail Map: Waukesha Area

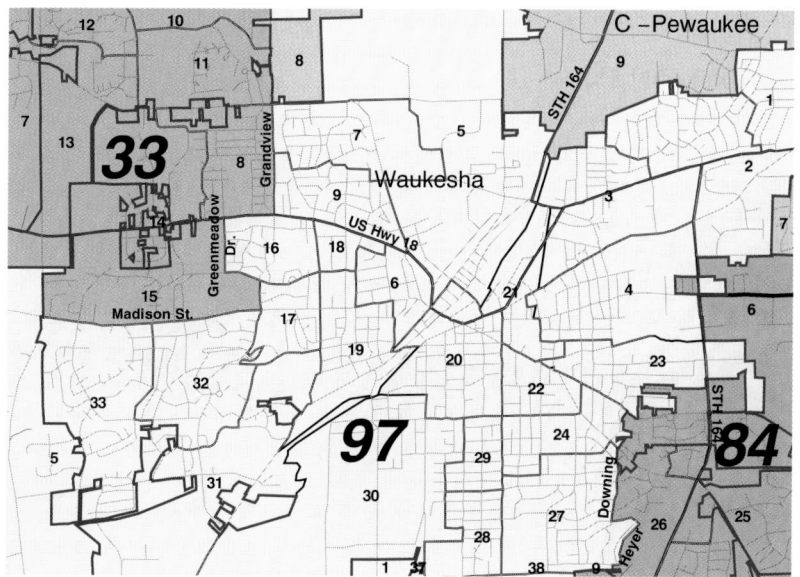

Detail Map: Sheboygan Area

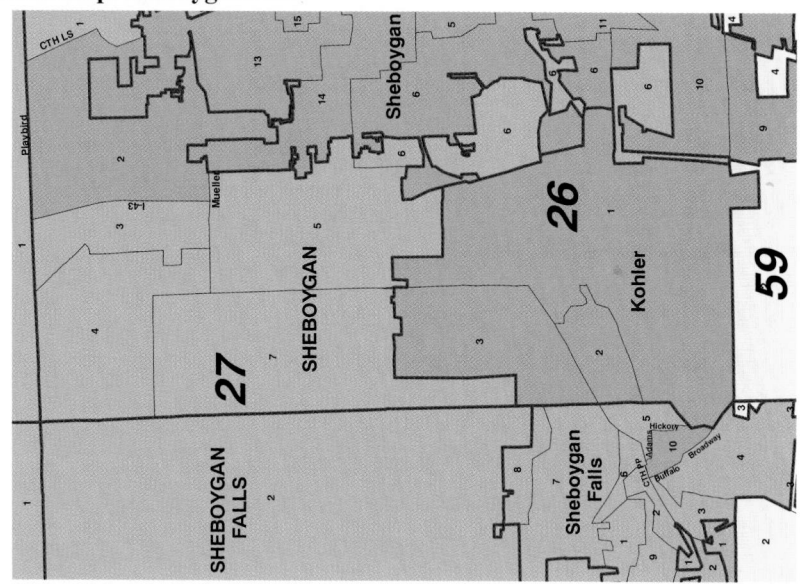

Detail Map: Appleton Area

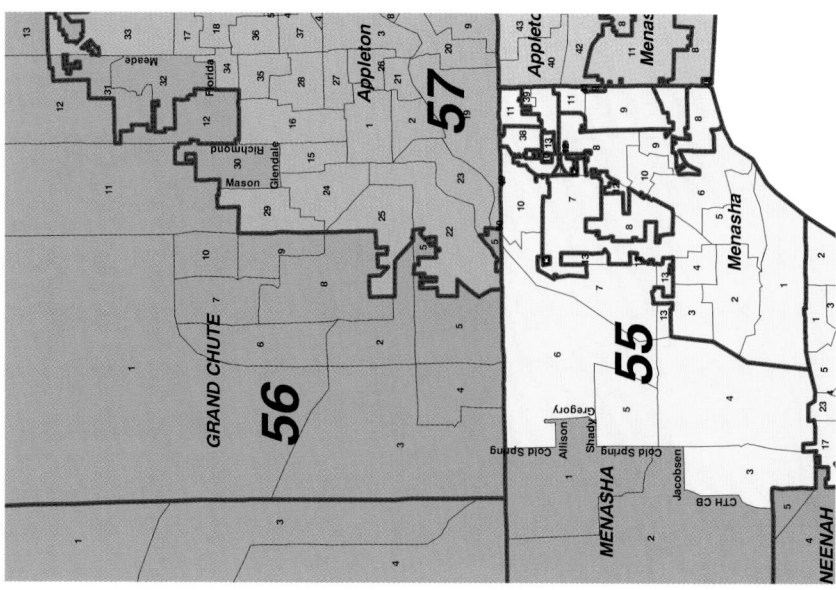

Feature
Article

The Wisconsin Court System: Demystifying the Judicial Branch

Vernon County Courthouse

L. Roger Turner

ᘐable of Contents

The Wisconsin Court System: Demystifying the Judicial Branch

By Robin Ryan, Legislative Attorney
Legislative Reference Bureau
Amanda Todd, Public Information Officer
Wisconsin Supreme Court

Graphics and Design by Kathleen Sitter, LRB

The court system has been called the least understood of the three branches of government. The executive branch, led by the governor, is highly visible and the work of its agencies is well-defined. The work of the legislative branch is similarly high profile. In contrast, the work of the third branch – the judicial branch, which is comprised of the state's 264 judges, 72 clerks of court, the Wisconsin State Law Library, and various agencies of the Supreme Court – is somewhat mysterious.

The differences between the judicial branch and the executive and legislative branches are apparent from the very beginning of the process: the selection of those who will serve. Wisconsin has elected its judges since statehood. Initially, these races were political affairs and the state's first Supreme Court justices ran on party tickets. But the state's founders sensed that the people would be best served by an independent judiciary, and took the first step by adding a directive to the 1848 constitution that judicial races not be held in conjunction with any general election for state or county officers or within 30 days either before or after such election. The 1878 election marked the first time that Wisconsin elected its judges on a nonpartisan basis, and that tradition continues today.

We elect our judges, but they do not carry out the wishes of the

Tiffany glass skylight in the Lafayette County Courthouse rotunda.
(Kathleen Sitter, LRB)

electorate or the electorate's representatives. In fact, judges sometimes make decisions that fly in the face of the majority sentiment on any given issue, for they do not – and must not – consider the wishes of the public in deciding individual cases. This independence is critical to preserving the democratic values that the people, and the people's elected representatives, hold dear. Chief Justice Shirley S. Abrahamson explains: "Most people who come to court would probably prefer a judge who would decide the case completely in their favor. But you can't guarantee that. So the next best thing is to get an impartial judge who's not in somebody's pocket."

Chief Justice Shirley S. Abrahamson was appointed to the Wisconsin Supreme Court on August 6, 1976. She was the first woman to serve on the state's highest court and the first woman to serve as chief justice. In 2006, "The Chief" will celebrate 30 years on the Supreme Court and 10 years as chief justice.

(Jay Salvo, Assembly Photographer)

Though they might work in relative obscurity, judges make decisions every day, in matters large and small, which affect many people. Most of us will come into contact with the judicial branch at some point in our lives. We might be serving on a jury, settling the estate of a deceased relative, adopting a child, divorcing, or disputing a traffic ticket. So there are practical reasons to understand the operation of the courts. But in a democracy there is a larger philosophical reason to improve public understanding of the judicial branch. Because the courts do not command armies or levy taxes, their authority depends upon the public's trust in them, and upon its willingness to abide by their decisions.

This article represents an effort to open the doors to the Wisconsin courts. Readers will learn about the function, structure, history, and funding of the three levels of state courts; the steps in a criminal and civil case; how judges are held accountable; how the practice of law is regulated; and initiatives to improve the justice system for people without lawyers. When she was sworn in as chief justice nearly a decade ago, Shirley Abrahamson vowed to make the "least-known" branch of government the "best-known." It is our hope that this article contributes in some small way to that lofty goal.

Circuit Courts

Circuit courts are the primary trial courts in Wisconsin. They hear and decide cases involving a wide variety of topics, including contracts, personal injury, family law, children in need of protection and/or services, juvenile delinquency, probate, traffic, small claims, landlord-tenant issues, and criminal law.

Power to decide cases

The circuit court may hear a case if the court has authority to decide the issues at stake in the case (subject matter jurisdiction) and if the court has authority to bring a defendant into court and enforce a judgment against the defendant (personal jurisdiction). The court's subject matter jurisdiction is conferred by the Wisconsin Constitution and is quite broad. The legislature may not by statute limit the nature or type of case that the courts may hear. In comparison, under the U.S. Constitution, Congress may limit the type of cases that federal trial courts may hear.

The court has personal jurisdiction in a civil case if the defendant is present in the state or has sufficient contacts with the state and if the pleadings are served on the defendant. State statutes spell out what constitutes sufficient contact, such as business dealings in the state, ownership of property in Wisconsin that is at issue in a case, and causing injury to another while in Wisconsin.

The determination of personal jurisdiction in a civil case is driven by several policy considerations. As a matter of fairness, a defendant should not have to defend him or herself against a suit in a state in which he or she has no associations and could not reasonably have anticipated the suit. In addition, a state court should not assert authority over matters that more appropriately belong in another state or in the federal courts.

The circuit court has personal jurisdiction over a defendant in a criminal case if the defendant violates a Wisconsin law while in Wisconsin. Wisconsin courts also have personal jurisdiction over a defendant who commits an act while out-of-state that contributes to a crime, the consequences of which occur in Wisconsin. The Wisconsin Supreme Court recently ruled that Wisconsin courts have personal jurisdiction over a

"Justice" as depicted in a mural decorating the Brown County Courthouse rotunda.

(Kathleen Sitter, LRB)

defendant who commits an act in Wisconsin manifesting an intent to kill, even though the murder takes place in another state (see *State v. Anderson,* published in May 2005 and described in the *Summary of Significant Decisions* section of this book).

Limits on exercise of power to decide cases

There are, however, limits on what cases the circuit courts will hear. They will not hear a case if the parties lack standing, or if the case is moot or is not ripe. Additionally, the circuit court will not hear a case in which it lacks competency. State law distinguishes between the court's jurisdiction (power to hear a case) and its competency (ability to arrive at a valid judgment in a case). A court lacks competency if certain statutory requirements are not satisfied, for example, time limits for filing suit, or requirements as to which circuit should decide a case.

Reasons a court will not decide a case

A court does not decide a case when the party bringing the case does not have **standing...**

A person must have a legal stake in a matter to bring the matter to court. In 2004, the U.S. Supreme Court declined to decide a case focusing on the Pledge of Allegiance upon finding that the plaintiff lacked standing. The plaintiff sued to prevent a school district in California from requiring his daughter to recite the Pledge of Allegiance, because it contains the words "under God." After hearing oral arguments in the case, *Elk Grove Unified School District v. Newdow,* the Supreme Court determined that the plaintiff did not have standing to assert his daughter's rights with respect to the Pledge because he did not have full custody of her. To find standing, courts generally require that a person suffered some actual or threatened injury and that the parties truly have adverse interests so that they may adequately represent the opposing sides of an issue.

When the issue is **moot...**

Courts only take cases in which a decision by the court will have an impact on the parties to the case. In other words, the court generally will not hear a case if the opportunity for the court to affect the outcome of the case has passed. However, the court may hear a case that is moot if: the issue in the case is of great public importance; the issue is likely to arise again and should be resolved to provide certainty; or if the question is capable and likely of repetition yet evades review because the judicial process (particularly the appellate court process) usually cannot be completed in time to have an effect on the parties. The U.S. Supreme Court took the landmark abortion case, *Roe v. Wade,* even though the plaintiff was no longer pregnant at the time of the appeal, finding that the question of whether a statutory ban on abortion is unconstitutional would reoccur, but could easily evade review because the time in which an abortion may be performed is shorter than the time it generally takes for a case to make it to the Supreme Court.

When the issue is not **ripe...**

Courts tend to dismiss a case for lack of ripeness if the facts of the case are not developed or if the action or events that the court is called upon to review are not final. Courts do not like to take hypothetical cases in part because it is difficult to make sound decisions of law on the basis of presumed scenarios and in part because courts prefer to devote their resources to cases of actual rather than presumed harm.

In addition, the courts are constrained from taking action that will encroach on the powers of the legislative or executive branches. Under the separation of powers doctrine, no branch of government may exercise a power of government assigned exclusively to another branch. The purpose of separating powers among the branches of government is to avoid concentration of governmental power in the hands of a few and to give the various branches the ability to check actions by the other branches.

In reviewing the validity of state laws, the courts are limited to determining whether the law violates any provision of the constitution. The courts may invalidate a law that violates individual rights, such as the right to equal protection or due process, or a law that is not enacted according to the process established in the constitution, for example, a bill that was not passed by a majority of the members of each house of the legislature. However, a court may not invalidate a law because the court finds that the legislature's method for addressing a problem was not the most efficient. Nor may the court substitute its determination of what is in the public interest for the determination of the legislature.

While the separation of powers doctrine limits the ability of the courts to act, it also protects the courts from encroachment by the legislature or governor. The Wisconsin Supreme Court established its judicial power in the three-branch system soon after Wisconsin became a state by deciding *Bashford v. Barstow* (1856), an election case that resulted in the ouster of an incumbent governor.

Representatives of the legislative, judicial, and executive branches work together to improve the justice system. Chief Justice Shirley S. Abrahamson moderates a discussion between Representative Mark Gundrum, chairperson of the Assembly Committee on the Judiciary, and Attorney General Peggy A. Lautenschlager on strategies to prevent wrongful convictions. (Kathleen Sitter, LRB)

Structure of the circuit courts

The circuit court system is composed of 69 circuits. Sixty-six of the circuits serve a single county and three circuits each serve two counties (Buffalo/Pepin, Florence/Forest, and Shawano/Menominee). Thirty-nine of the 69 circuits consist of more than one branch, for a total of 241 circuit court branches, each with one judge. The Milwaukee County circuit has the greatest number of branches, 47.

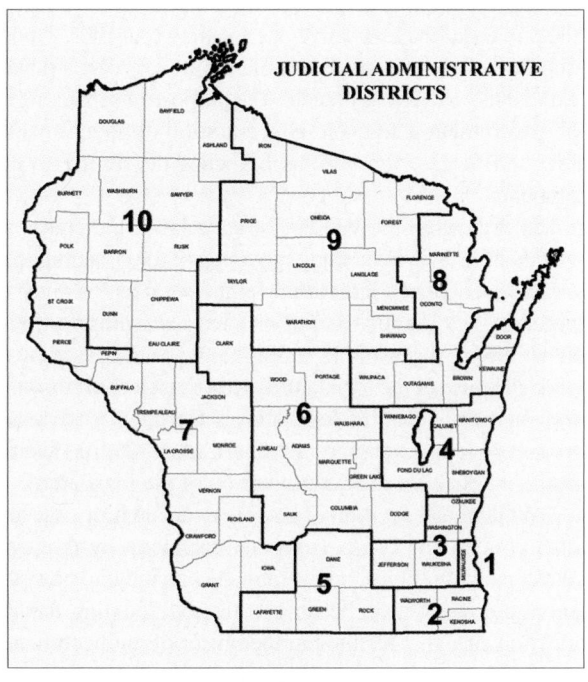

JUDICIAL ADMINISTRATIVE DISTRICTS

The circuit courts are organized into 10 geographical administrative districts, each led by a management team that includes a chief judge, selected by the Supreme Court from all the circuit court judges in the district, a deputy chief judge (appointed by the chief judge), and a district court administrator, who is a full-time professional. With the exception of Milwaukee County, where the chief judge is a full-time administrator, chief judges and their deputies maintain caseloads in addition to the administrative work. The management teams administer an increasingly complex system requiring the uniform application of justice while accommodating and respecting appropriate local variance. They assign judges and court reporters; equalize the flow of cases; establish policies, plans, and rules; supervise finances; work closely with county boards on security, facility, and staffing issues, and more. The chief judges and district court administrators meet regularly with the director of state courts to discuss current issues and to advise the Supreme Court and the director on matters of statewide concern.

Trial Court History

Wisconsin has not always had a unified statewide system of trial courts. Until the latter half of the 20th century, Wisconsin had multiple types of trial courts, many with overlapping jurisdictions. Furthermore, the types and organization of trial courts differed across the counties.

The Wisconsin Constitution, as adopted in 1848, mandated creation of a supreme court, circuit courts, courts of probate, and justice of the peace courts. The constitution also authorized the legislature to create municipal courts and other "inferior" courts, so-called because they had lesser authority than the circuit courts. Although probate courts were constitutionally mandated, the constitution permitted the legislature to forgo creation of probate courts as long as the legislature assigned authority over probate matters to inferior courts established in each county.

The first legislature created five regional circuit courts, each with one judge. Each of the circuit courts had the same broad civil and criminal jurisdiction. The first elections for circuit court judges were held in August 1848. The circuit court judges held court in each county within their districts at least once a year. Until 1852, the five circuit court judges sitting together also served as the state's supreme court, meeting twice a year. An independent supreme court was created in 1852, but the circuit courts continued to have appellate jurisdiction over all inferior trial courts, such as the justice of the peace, county, and municipal courts.

The first legislature also authorized justice of the peace, county, and municipal courts. Justice of the peace courts were created in villages and towns to handle civil disputes involving less than $100. In 1849, the legislature created county courts and gave them authority over probate matters, thus fulfilling the

Judge Roy H. Proctor presiding over Superior Court in the Dane County Courthouse, circa 1933. This Superior Court was one of many ad hoc trial courts created by the legislature prior to adoption of a uniform statewide system of trial courts. (State Historical Society, #WHi 26219)

constitutional requirement that a court in each county that was separate from the circuit courts handle probate matters. The legislature also granted county courts jurisdiction over civil matters involving less than $500. Initially, the county courts had uniform jurisdiction, but in 1854 the legislature began granting different authority to the various county courts.

The legislature increased the number of circuit courts as the population of the state, and hence caseloads, grew. However, the legislature was restricted in creating new circuit courts because the state constitution required that each circuit follow county borders and further permitted only one judge per circuit, so the legislature could not simply add a second circuit court branch in a county with a high caseload. (The one judge per circuit rule was modified by constitutional amendment in 1924). However, there were no such restrictions on the legislature's authority to create inferior courts. The legislature created additional inferior courts on an ad hoc basis, and specified the powers of each of these courts by statute. Although the circuit courts continued to have uniform jurisdiction, the number and variety of other trial courts meant that the trial court structure was different in every county.

Organized efforts to reform the judicial structure to reduce the number of courts, equalize caseloads, and provide uniformity across the state began in the early 1900s. After several failed attempts at reform, the legislature in 1959 abolished all the special statutory courts, authorized a single county court in each county, and assigned uniform jurisdiction to the county courts. The county court jurisdiction was very similar to the circuit court jurisdiction. The 1959 legislation also curtailed the jurisdiction of justice of the peace courts, and a 1966 constitutional amendment eliminated the constitutional provision requiring justice of the peace courts. A 1977 constitutional amendment abolished the requirement that a court other than the circuit court handle probate cases. This amendment cleared the way for the legislature to abolish county courts. In the same year the legislature passed a bill eliminating the county courts, creating 69 circuit courts with uniform jurisdiction, and restricting the authority of municipal courts to hearing ordinance violations. The unified system of trial courts resulting from the 1977 legislative session remains in place today.

Commencing a Civil Case

Civil cases start the same way regardless of the issues or parties involved and regardless of whether the case ultimately goes to trial. A case begins with pleadings, in which the parties state basic claims and responses. The parties then have an opportunity to investigate the claims and gather evidence through a process called discovery.

The court generally has little direct involvement in a case until shortly before trial, though the court is available to resolve preliminary matters and disputes.

Pleadings

The plaintiff starts a civil case by filing a summons, and generally a complaint, with the clerk of circuit court and paying a filing fee. A summons provides the defendant notice that a suit has been filed against him or her and notifies the defendant that he or she must answer the complaint. The complaint sets forth the plaintiff's allegations against the defendant. It must contain a short and plain statement of the plaintiff's claim, identify the events out of which the claim arises, and demand relief to satisfy the plaintiff's claim.

Garcia v. Mazda Motor of America

Adele Garcia bought a new car in February 2001. In the first eight months after her purchase, Garcia's car was in the repair shop four times for repairs to the transmission. The Wisconsin "Lemon Law" provides that if, within one year of purchase, a new vehicle requires repairs that are covered under warranty and if the vehicle is either out of service for at least 30 days or cannot be repaired after four attempts, the owner is entitled to a refund or a replacement vehicle.

On September 20, 2001, Garcia sent the car manufacturer a letter describing the history of the car's problems and repairs, stating her understanding that the Lemon Law entitled her to a refund or replacement.

The Lemon Law provides that a vehicle manufacturer must provide a refund or replacement within 30 days after a vehicle owner properly invokes the Lemon Law. As of November 21, 2001, Garcia did not have a replacement car and filed suit in the circuit court to enforce her rights under the Lemon Law.

The following pages contain sample documents from Garcia's case, which was eventually heard by the Wisconsin Supreme Court.

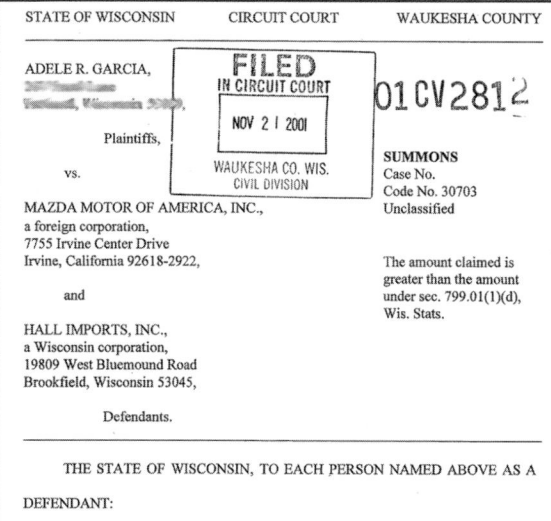

STATE OF WISCONSIN   CIRCUIT COURT   WAUKESHA COUNTY

ADELE R. GARCIA,

FILED
IN CIRCUIT COURT
NOV 2 1 2001
WAUKESHA CO. WIS.
CIVIL DIVISION

01 CV 2812

Plaintiffs,

vs.

SUMMONS
Case No.
Code No. 30703
Unclassified

MAZDA MOTOR OF AMERICA, INC.,
a foreign corporation,
7755 Irvine Center Drive
Irvine, California 92618-2922,

and

The amount claimed is greater than the amount under sec. 799.01(1)(d), Wis. Stats.

HALL IMPORTS, INC.,
a Wisconsin corporation,
19809 West Bluemound Road
Brookfield, Wisconsin 53045,

Defendants.

delivered to the Court, whose address
se, 515 West Moreland Boulevard,
arge, S.C., Plaintiff's attorneys, whose
1487, Waukesha, Wisconsin 53187.

THE STATE OF WISCONSIN, TO EACH PERSON NAMED ABOVE AS A

DEFENDANT:

n forty-five (45) days, the Court may

or other legal action requested in the

anything that is or may be incorrect in

YOU ARE HEREBY NOTIFIED that the Plaintiff named above has filed a lawsuit

or other legal action against you. The Complaint, which is attached, states the nature and

basis of the legal action.

Within forty-five (45) days of receiving this Summons, you must respond with a

written Answer, as that term is used in Chapter 802 of the Wisconsin Statutes, to the

Complaint. The Court may reject or disregard an Answer that does not follow the require-

vided by law. A judgment awarding

n now or in the future, and may also be

STROCH & LABARGE, S.C.,
orneys for Plaintiff

WILLIAM S. POCAN
State Bar No. 1007248
VINCENT P. MEGNA
State Bar No. 1013041

640 West Moreland Boulevard
P.O. Box 1487
Waukesha, WI 53187
(262) 547-2611

COMPLAINT
Case No.
Code No. 30703
Unclassified

NOW COMES the above-named Plaintiff, by her attorneys, Jastroch & LaBarge S.C., and as and for claims against the above-named defendants, alleges and shows Court as follows:

FIRST CLAIM

As and for a claim against the defendant, Mazda Motor of America, Inc., the Plaintiff alleges:

1. That the Plaintiff, Adele R. Garcia, is an adult and resides at [illegible] [illegible], Wisconsin [illegible]; that said Plaintiff is a "consumer," as that term is defined in sec. 218.0171(1)(b), Wis. Stats. and sec. 15 U.S.C. 2301(3).

2. That upon information and belief, the defendant, Mazda Motor of America, Inc., is a foreign corporation duly authorized and licensed to do business in the State of Wisconsin

• • •

4. That on or about February 23, 2001, the Plaintiff purchased from the defendant, Hall Imports, a new 2001 Mazda Tribute, vehicle identification [number] 4F2CU08101KM42278, as more fully set forth in copies of the Motor Vehicle Purchase

Contract and Wisconsin Title & License Plate Application which are attached hereto, incorporated by reference herein and collectively marked as Exhibit A; that the Plaintiff received delivery of said Mazda Tribute on or about February 23, 2001; that said Mazda Tribute is a "motor vehicle," as that term is defined in sec. 218.0171(1)(d), Wis. Stats., and a "consumer product," as that term is defined in sec. 15 U.S.C. 2301(1).

5. That upon information and belief, the full purchase price of said Mazda Tribute purchased by the Plaintiff from the defendant, Hall Imports, was $24,700.00, plus sales tax in the sum of $518.21, plus title, loan filing and license plate fees in the sum of $43.50, plus approximately $1,000.00 for an extended warranty, plus possible other charges; that upon information and belief, the Plaintiff received a trade-in allowance in the sum of $14,539.00 and financed the balance of said purchase price.

6. That a Mazda Motor of America, Inc. new vehicle manufacturer's warranty was provided by the defendant, Mazda Motor of America, Inc., to the Plaintiff at time of purchase; that as part of said purchase, said Mazda Tribute was warranted in writing to be free from mechanical and other defects.

7. That during the term of said warranty, and within the earlier of one year from the date of delivery or the expiration of said warranty, said Mazda Tribute was out of service for more than 30 days because of warranty nonconformities; that defects included, but were not necessarily limited to, problems with transmission, vehicle hard to come out of park, will not shift out of park, transmission would not move in reverse, no reverse gear, fluid very burnt, seized internally, vehicle revs on its own on highway, oil cooler, radiator, SES light on, stays on, paint, rattle from inside rear of vehicle and creaking noise.

The summons (previous page) and portions of the complaint filed in the Waukesha County Circuit Court on behalf of Adele Garcia asserting her right to a replacement car under the Wisconsin Lemon Law. In the complaint, Garcia alleges facts to show that her car is a "lemon".

WHEREFORE, the Plaintiff demands judgment against the defendants as follows:

(a) For a refund to the Plaintiff and any holder of a perfected security interest in said Mazda Tribute of the full purchase price of said Mazda Tribute, plus sales tax, title, loan filing and license plate fees, finance charges, all amounts paid at the point of sale, all collateral costs and all other amounts paid after sale for improvements/accessories, as applicable, less a reasonable allowance for use, and twice the amount of all pecuniary losses incurred heretofore or hereafter, as all these terms are [defined in ...] Wis. Stats.;

(b) For a refund/damages pursuant to 1[...]

(c) For rescission of the Purchase Agre[ement ...]

(d) For prejudgment interest on all liquidated sums as provided by law;

(e) For the Plaintiff's actual attorneys' fees;

(f) For the costs and disbursements incurred in this action; and

(g) For such other relief as the Court deems just and equitable.

Dated this _21st_ day of November, 2001.

JASTROCH & LaBARGE, S.C.
Attorneys for Plaintiff

By: _[signature]_
WILLIAM S. POCAN

The plaintiff must serve an authenticated copy of the summons and complaint on the defendant. The favored method for serving the defendant is to personally hand a copy of the summons to him or her. Alternatively, the server may hand the summons to another responsible adult at the defendant's residence or, in some cases, it is sufficient for the plaintiff to publish the summons in a newspaper and send it to the defendant's address. Any adult who is not a party to the lawsuit may serve the summons. The person who serves the summons must sign the summons at the time of service and note the date, time, place, and manner of service and upon whom the summons is served. The plaintiff then files proof of service with the court.

A plaintiff must commence a suit by serving the defendant with a summons within a certain time period established by a statute of limitation, or lose the right to sue. Statutes of limitation differ according to the type of suit. For example, a suit for breach of a sales contract must be commenced within six years; a suit for medical malpractice must be commenced within three years of the injury or within one year of discovery of the injury; and a suit to collect child support must be commenced within 20 years after the youngest child for whom support is due turns 18.

The defendant responds to the plaintiff's allegations in a document called an answer, in which the defendant must admit or deny an allegation or state that he or she does not know if the allegation is true, in which case the allegation is taken as denied. The defendant may also raise affirmative defenses (defenses that defeat the plaintiff's claims even if the plaintiff's allegations are true), for example, that the time period for filing the suit has expired, that the service of the summons and complaint was invalid, or that the complaint has already been settled in previous litigation. The defendant may also file a counterclaim against the plaintiff, or a cross-claim against a fellow defendant.

**DEFENDANT'S ANSWER TO PLAINTIFF'S COMPLAINT
AND AFFIRMATIVE DEFENSES**

Now comes the defendant, Hall Imports, Inc., by its attorneys, Hinshaw & Culbertson, and as and for its answer to the plaintiff's Complaint pleads as follows:

ANSWERING PLAINTIFF'S FIRST CLAIM

1. Answering paragraph 1, denies knowledge or information sufficient to form a belief as to the truth of the allegations contained therein.

2. Answering paragraph 2, admits that Mazda Motor of America, Inc. is a foreign corporation; admits that it is involved in the distribution of motor vehicles;

as to the truth of the allegations contained therein.

6. Answering paragraph 6, admits that a limited express written warranty accompanied the sale of the subject vehicle, but that said limited warranty was, and is, subject to all of the terms and conditions contained therein; further answering said paragraph, denies the remaining allegations contained therein.

Portions of the answer (here and following page) filed by Mazda in *Garcia v. Mazda Motor of America*, denying sufficient knowledge to answer most of Garcia's claims, and alleging several defenses.

AFFIRMATIVE DEFENSES

1. As and for a first affirmative defense alleges that plaintiff's claims against Hall Imports, Inc. fail to state a claim upon which relief can be granted.

2. As and for a second affirmative defense alleges that the plaintiff has failed to mitigate her damages.

3. As and for a third affirmative defense alleges upon information and belief that the defendant, Hall Imports, Inc., sustain no liability for the product in question as it was misused, abused and neglected by the plaintiff and/or other individuals, firms, organizations and/or entities.

4. As and for a fourth affirmative defense alleges upon information and belief that the plaintiff's cause of action and damage remedies are barred and/or limited by the express provisions of the written warranty which

5. As and for a fi by the plaintiff was solely and firms, organizations and/or ent

6. As and for a s claims against the defendant, H of said vehicle.

7. As and for a seventh affirmative defense, alleges that the defendant, Hall Imports, Inc., is entitled to a set-off for any amounts necessary to repair any damage and/or modifications to the subject vehicle.

8. As and for an eighth affirmative defense, alleges that the defendant, Hall Imports, Inc., provided no express or limited warranties to the plaintiff relating to the vehicle in question.

9. As and for a ninth affirmative defense, alleges that plaintiff's cause of action is barred due to the plaintiff having previously agreed to resolve this matter by the defendant, Mazda, providing a new vehicle selected by the plaintiff.

Wherefore, the defendant, Hall Imports, Inc., demands judgment dismissing the plaintiff's Complaint on its merits and for its costs and disbursements in this matter.

Dated this 4th day of January, 2002.

HINSHAW & CULBERTSON
Attorneys for Defendant,
Hall Imports, Inc.

By: _____
Jeffrey A. Fertl

The complaint and the answer together constitute the "pleadings" in a case. The purpose of the pleadings is to provide notice of the claims and defenses. The issues of the case generally are not narrowed until later in the proceedings.

What is venue?

Venue is the place where a case may be heard. In a civil case venue is generally in the county in which the claim arose, the county where property that is the subject of the claim is located, or the county in which the defendant lives or does substantial business. For example, a case arising out of an automobile accident may be heard in the county in which the accident occurred or the county in which the defendant lives. If none of these conditions applies, the plaintiff may choose the county of venue. In a criminal case, venue is in the county where the crime, or part of the crime, was committed. There are exceptions to these general venue rules. For example, cases in which the state is the sole defendant must be filed in Dane County. The purpose of guidelines for venue is to make court proceedings convenient for the parties and witnesses and to allocate caseload among the circuit courts.

Discovery

After an action is commenced, the parties begin discovery, which is intended to provide the parties mutual knowledge of facts relevant to a case before trial so that the trial is limited to resolving disputed facts and issues. Discovery also allows the parties to formulate and narrow the issues for trial and obtain and preserve evidence. A recipient of a discovery request generally must provide the information or material requested unless it is readily available from another source or is privileged. The scope of permitted discovery in a civil case is quite broad. A party may use discovery to obtain material that will be inadmissible as evidence at trial as long as the material is reasonably calculated to lead to admissible evidence. Methods of discovery include depositions (recorded interviews with witnesses under oath), interrogatories (written questions), requests for production of documents or things, medical examinations, and requests for admissions.

Ideally and usually, discovery takes place without direct involvement by the court. Except for medical examinations and inspection of medical records, discovery requests need not be authorized by the court. The recipient of a discovery request may seek a protective order denying certain discovery or limiting its scope if the discovery requested will cause annoyance, embarrassment, oppression, or undue burden or expense, or will inquire into privileged or irrelevant matters, and the party requesting discovery may request that the court intervene and order compliance.

Pretrial activities in court

After the pleadings are filed, the court may hold a scheduling conference with the parties and issue a scheduling order to manage the progress of the case. The scheduling order generally assigns dates for filing motions, amending pleadings, completing discovery, pretrial conferences between the judge and parties, and for trial. Some judges also use the scheduling conference to advise the parties to attempt to settle the case without going to trial.

In civil cases, parties often file a variety of pretrial motions with the court seeking court orders affecting the trial. For example, a defendant may seek dismissal of a whole case or certain issues in the case because the plaintiff has not stated a valid claim. Or, a party may seek an order compelling the opposing party to comply with a discovery request or a ruling on admissibility of certain pieces of evidence at trial. If the court requires additional information before ruling on a motion, the court may hold a hearing and may direct the parties to submit briefs, written materials that state the facts and present each side's position.

NOTICE OF MOTION AND MOTION FOR SUMMARY JUDGMENT

TO: *Adele R. Garcia*
c/o Attorney William S. Pocan
Jastroch & LaBarge, S.C.
640 W. Moreland Blvd.
Waukesha, WI 53187

Please take notice that the defendants, Mazda Motor of America, Inc. and Hall Imports, Inc.,

by their attorneys, Hinshaw & Culbertson, will move that branch of the Circuit Court of Waukesha

County presided over by the Honorable Lee S. Dreyfus, Jr., on the *17th* day of *June, 2002* at *10:30*

a.m., or as soon thereafter as counsel can be heard as follows:

      1.   For an order pursuant to §802.08, Wis. Stats. granting defendants summary judgment

on the grounds that there has previously been an accord and satisfaction of this matter insofar as the

plaintiff agreed to accept a replacement vehicle in full and complete settlement of the claims

advanced in her Complaint.

      2.   In the alternative, for an order pursuant to §802.08, Wis. Stats. granting the

defendants summary judgment on the grounds that the plaintiffs have failed to serve defendants with

a proper demand notice as required by §218.0171, Wis. Stats. prior to the commencement of suit.

**DEFENDANTS' BRIEF IN SUPPORT OF
MOTION FOR SUMMARY JUDGMENT AND TO ENFORCE SETTLEMENT**

    B.   **In The Alternative, This Action Should Be Dismissed
Since Plaintiffs Failed To Provide The Defendant With A
Proper Notice Before Commencing Her Lemon Law
Action.**

Defendants submit that this matter has previously been settled and the court should enforce

the settlement and dismiss this lawsuit. However, if the court finds that there is an issue of fact or

that a settlement was not reached, then this matter should be dismissed since the notice given by the

plaintiff was insufficient to trigger defendants' obligations under the lemon law.

    Section 218.0171, Wis. Stats. (Wisconsin lemon law) provides that if a nonconformity is not

repaired, the consumer's remedies under §218.0171(2) (b) are as follows:

        (b)(1) If after a reasonable attempt to repair the nonconformity is not
              repaired, the manufacturer shall carry out the requirement
              under subdivision (2) or (3), whichever is appropriate.

        (2)   *at the direction of the consumer* . . . do *one* of the following:

        (b)   accept return of the motor vehicle

Portions of a motion for summary judgment and a brief in support of motion filed by Mazda in *Garcia v. Mazda Motor of America*. Mazda asserts that Garcia is not entitled to relief because she allegedly failed to provide Mazda proper notice of her request for a replacement vehicle.

The statute goes on to indicate what the consumer must do to obtain relief under the statute:

(c) To receive a comparable new motor vehicle or a refund under par. (b)(1) or (2), the consumer described in sub. (1)(b)(1), (2) or (3), **shall offer to the manufacturer of the motor vehicle having the nonconformity to transfer title of that motor vehicle to that manufacturer.** No later than 30 days after that offer, the manufacturer shall provide the consumer with the comparable new motor vehicle or refund. When the manufacturer provides the new motor vehicle or refund, the

The second element required in the notice is an offer to transfer title of the vehicle to the manufacturer. Even if a remedy is elected, the notice fails if there is no offer to transfer title. (See trial court's decision in *Berends v. Mack Trucks*, Case No. 99-CV-665, Aff. of Jeffrey S. Fertl, ¶ 6). In this case, plaintiff's demand letter contains no offer to transfer title to the vehicle in conjunction with the requested relief, therefore, as a matter of law, it is invalid. Without a valid demand letter, plaintiff has failed to trigger defendant's obligation under the lemon law. Hence, in the alternative, defendants request that the court dismiss the plaintiff's lemon law claim, since plaintiff has failed to serve a proper notice which is a condition precedent to commencement of this action.

The courts resolve motions by order, often directing the prevailing party to prepare the order and submit it to the judge for his or her signature. The resolution of pretrial motions often dictates the future of a case. If a party wins a pretrial motion for summary judgment, the case is dismissed. Sometimes a party who loses important pretrial motions is more likely to agree to a settlement. A settlement must be accepted by a judge. Judges usually accept settlement agreements in civil cases with minimal review, although they look more closely at settlement agreements in divorce cases. If the parties do not settle, the case proceeds to trial.

JUDGMENT

The defendants, Mazda Motor of America, Inc. and Hall Imports, Inc., having moved the trial court for summary judgment dismissing plaintiff's Complaint; and the trial court having ordered that judgment be entered in favor of said defendants on July 9, 2002; *NOW, THEREFORE, IT IS ADJUDGED:*

1. That the Complaint of the plaintiff against the defendants, Mazda Motor of America, Inc. and Hall Imports, Inc., be dismissed without prejudice.

2. That defendants, Mazda Motor of America, Inc. and Hall Imports, Inc., be awarded costs as provided by law as against plaintiff, Adele Garcia, as taxed by the Circuit Court of Waukesha County in the amount of $ 266.86 —$5°° docket fee = $261.86

The circuit court agreed that Garcia had not provided Mazda with a proper request and dismissed Garcia's lawsuit.

Commencing a Criminal Case

Only the state may bring a criminal case. Generally a prosecutor starts a criminal case by filing a complaint. The court is directly involved in a criminal case from the beginning to protect the rights of the defendant. Parties have a right to discovery in a criminal case, but discovery is not as extensive in a criminal case as in a civil case because the state must have completed most of its investigation before bringing criminal charges.

The criminal complaint

Most criminal cases are started when a prosecutor, either a district attorney (who represents a county) or the attorney general (who represents the state), files a complaint with the court. The complaint states the crime charged, names the defendant, and gives the date, approximate time, and location of the crime. In a

A very simple complaint charging Munir Hamdan with carrying a concealed weapon. Hamdan was convicted in circuit court, but the Wisconsin Supreme Court ultimately overturned the conviction upon finding that a 1998 amendment to the Wisconsin Constitution afforded Mr. Hamdan the right to carry a concealed weapon in his store for security purposes. (See a description of Hamdan's case in the *Summary of Significant Decisions* section of this book.)

CIRCUIT COURT
STATE OF WISCONSIN   CRIMINAL DIVISION   MILWAUKEE COUNTY

STATE OF WISCONSIN, Plaintiff   **CRIMINAL COMPLAINT**

                                        CRIME
            v.   Carrying Concealed Weapon

HAMDAN Munir   STATUTE(S) VIOLATED
                                        941.23
Milwaukee, Wi.
(5/18/46 D.O.B.),   COMPLAINING WITNESS
            Defendant.   PO JOHN DREES

                                        CASE NUMBER
                                        F970115570

The above named complaining witness, being duly sworn, on information and belief states that the above named defendant, in the County of Milwaukee, State of Wisconsin, on 11-26-99 at 2483 W. Capitol Drive , City of Milwaukee , not being a peace officer, did go armed with a concealed and dangerous weapon, contrary to Wisconsin Statutes Section 941.23.

Upon conviction of this offense, a Class A Misdemeanor, the maximum possible penalty is a fine of not more than $10,000 or imprisonment for not more than 9 months, or both.

I am a City of Milwaukee police officer and base this complaint upon the statement of officer Ben Gojevic that on the above date, at the above place, s/he personally observed the above-named defendant in possession of a loaded .32 caliber pistol , which was located inside the DEFENDANT'S RIGHT FRONT TROUSER POCKET, wrapped in a sheet of plastic.

END OF COMPLAINT

Subscribed and sworn to before me and approved for filing this 2nd day of December ,199 9 .

_____   PO John G Drees
Assistant/Deputy-District Attorney   Complaining Witness

4639
ccw-03/07/97

EXHIBIT

2-1

complaint, the district attorney also presents sufficient facts to show why the defendant is being charged, identifies the source of the information contained in the complaint, and provides reasons why the source should be believed.

Prosecution of most crimes must be commenced within a certain time period that is established by a statute of limitation. The state generally has six years to commence prosecution of a felony (a crime for which a person may be sentenced to one year or more in prison) and three years for a misdemeanor (a crime for which the maximum penalty is a year in jail). However, there is no time limit for the prosecution of homicide. The main purpose of time limits is to ensure that criminal cases are tried while the evidence is still available and witnesses' memories are fresh. A case is commenced when a warrant, summons, or indictment is issued or an information is filed.

Pretrial court appearances

The defendant's first court date is called the initial appearance. The court informs the defendant of the charges filed against him or her and gives the defendant a copy of the complaint. The court also informs the defendant of his or her right to have an attorney and that if the defendant is indigent and requests counsel, the court will appoint an attorney. If the defendant is in custody, the court determines whether to release the defendant on bail, and if the defendant is released, imposes conditions for bail. In a misdemeanor case, the court may set the trial date at the initial appearance. The next court action in a misdemeanor case is the arraignment. Further steps are required in a felony case. At the initial appearance, the court informs a felony defendant that he or she is entitled to a preliminary examination before the criminal case may go forward.

The purpose of a preliminary examination is to determine in a felony case whether the district attorney can show probable cause to believe that the defendant committed a felony. If not, the court must dismiss the felony complaint. At the preliminary examination the district attorney and defendant may call witnesses and present evidence. If the court determines that the district attorney has shown probable cause or if the defendant waives his or her right to a preliminary examination, the case goes forward. The prosecutor files a pleading called an "information," which informs the court of the crime with which the defendant is charged and states the date and place of the crime.

An arraignment is held in both misdemeanor and felony cases. At the arraignment, the complaint or information is read out loud unless the defendant waives reading, and in a felony case the district attorney gives the defendant a copy of the information. The court then asks the defendant to submit a plea. The defendant may plead "guilty", "no contest", "not guilty", or "not guilty by reason of mental disease or defect". A plea of no contest has the same effect in a criminal case as a guilty plea, except it cannot be used as an admission of criminal action in a civil case. The defendant may not enter a plea of no contest without approval from the court. If the defendant pleads guilty or no contest, the court sentences the defendant or places the defendant on probation. If the defendant pleads not guilty or not guilty by reason of mental disease or defect, the case proceeds to trial.

Grand jury and John Doe proceedings

Although the vast majority of criminal cases in Wisconsin are begun by a district attorney filing a criminal complaint, some cases are commenced as the result of a grand jury or John Doe investigation. Grand jury and John Doe investigations are secret proceedings for which witnesses may be subpoenaed. Grand jury and John Doe proceedings are generally used when investigators need to take testimony under oath or compel a witness to testify in order to gather sufficient evidence to issue a criminal complaint.

A judge, usually upon the request of a district attorney, may assemble a grand jury to investigate suspected criminal activity. A grand jury consists of 17 people selected for jury service. The grand jury may request that the prosecutor subpoena and examine witnesses. Upon completing an investigation, a grand jury may by the vote of at least 14 members return an indictment, which is a written accusation that a person committed a crime. If the grand jury returns an indictment, the court issues a summons or warrant for the defendant.

A judge initiates a John Doe proceeding upon receiving a complaint about criminal activity from any person, including the district attorney. The judge must question the person who makes the complaint under oath and may subpoena and examine other witnesses (usually with the assistance of the district attorney). If the judge finds probable cause to believe that a person has committed a crime, a written complaint is filed and the judge issues a warrant for the arrest of the defendant named in the complaint.

Discovery

Discovery in a criminal case is generally less extensive than in a civil case. Discovery allows the parties to obtain certain information known by the opposing party. Upon request, the prosecution and defense must provide a list of witnesses it intends to call at trial, as well as statements of the witnesses, reports of expert witnesses, and any known criminal record of a witness. The parties must also disclose any physical evidence they intend to introduce at trial. A party may obtain a court order allowing scientific testing of evidence held by the opposing party. The prosecution must disclose statements made by the defendant that pertain to the crime or that the prosecution intends to introduce at trial. The prosecution is obligated to disclose exculpatory evidence (evidence that might weigh in the defendant's favor) to the defendant even if the defendant does not specifically request the information or material.

Pretrial motions and plea bargains

Parties in a criminal case often file pretrial motions. Common motions include motions to exclude physical evidence, a defendant's confession, or an eyewitness identification of the defendant. The court may require the attorneys to submit briefs on the motions, but briefing is less common on pretrial motions in criminal cases than civil cases.

Most criminal cases do not go to trial. Instead the prosecution and defense negotiate a settlement. The parties may agree upon the crimes to which a defendant will plead guilty and a sentence recommendation, or may only agree on the plea. The judge must review the agreement on the plea before accepting it to ensure that there is sufficient reason to believe that the defendant is guilty of the crime. If the parties agree on a sentence recommendation, the judge must review it to determine if it is appropriate. The judge is not bound by the sentence agreement.

Trial of a Civil or Criminal Case

The proceedings in a trial of a civil or criminal case are similar. Both may be to a jury or judge. Both start with opening statements, proceed to presentation of evidence followed by closing statements, and culminate with a decision. Depending on the result of the trial, a civil case may end with the awarding of damages and a criminal trial may end with sentencing. During the trial, the role of the judge is similar – determining the admissibility of evidence, guiding the jury, if there is one, and refereeing the actions of the attorneys.

Judge Sue E. Bischel is shown presiding over a jury trial in a products liability case. She is the second woman (retired Judge Vivi Dilweg was the first) to serve as a judge for the Brown County Circuit Court in Green Bay, and is one of a group of judges in the state who handle administrative duties such as budgeting and personnel issues in addition to their caseloads. She is deputy chief judge of the Eighth Judicial District, which encompasses Brown, Door, Kewaunee, Marinette, Oconto, Outagamie, and Waupaca counties. (Kathleen Sitter, LRB)

Jury or bench trial

A trial may be either to a jury and judge together, or to a judge alone (called a bench trial). In a civil case either party may request a jury, which usually consists of six jurors. In a criminal case, the defendant has a right to a jury. The defendant may waive the right to a jury, but the state does not have to accept the defendant's waiver, so the state may require that the case be tried to a jury. In a felony case the jury usually consists of 12 jurors and in a misdemeanor case, six jurors.

In a jury trial, after the jury is selected, the judge advises the jury of its role and the ground rules for the jury's participation in the trial. Once preliminary jury matters are settled, or at the beginning of a trial in a bench trial, each attorney has an opportunity to make an opening statement describing the case and what the attorney intends to prove.

Presentation of evidence

The heart of a trial is the presentation of evidence. Each side has an opportunity to present evidence; the plaintiff or prosecution goes first and must present sufficient evidence to prove his or her claims. Presentation of evidence is governed by the

A clerk swears in a witness in one of the state's circuit courts.

(Kathleen Sitter, LRB)

rules of evidence. A party may only present evidence that is relevant to the case. Certain types of evidence are not admissible even if relevant. Evidence obtained in the course of a privileged communication, such as between a doctor and patient, lawyer and client, or between spouses, is generally not admissible. Further, hearsay evidence, which is a statement by a witness reporting what the witness or another person said on a prior occasion, is generally not admissible. The judge is responsible for resolving questions of admissibility of evidence.

A party's presentation of evidence often consists of witness testimony, presentation of documents and perhaps of other tangible objects. Witnesses must testify under oath. The party that presents a witness has the first opportunity to ask questions of the witness under direct examination. The opposing party may then cross-examine the witness, asking questions on any matter that is relevant to any issue in the case. Any further questioning of a witness after the initial direct examination and cross-examination is generally limited to the issues raised on direct or cross-examination. Lay witnesses may only testify as to matters on which they have personal knowledge. However, an expert witness, a person who is demonstrated to have specialized knowledge, skill, experience, training, or education, may provide opinion testimony of a technical, scientific, or other specialized nature, if such expert testimony is useful.

Like witness testimony, documents and tangible objects must be relevant in order to be admissible as evidence at trial. To present tangible evidence such as written material, voice recordings, or other objects, the party presenting must first show that it is what it is purported to be; for example, a note written by a specified person, or a tape recording of the voice of a specified person, or a photograph of a particular place.

If a party believes that certain evidence should not be admitted, the party must object to admission of the evidence before it is admitted. The judge may give the parties an opportunity to argue for or against admission, generally out of the hearing range of the jurors, and then will rule on whether the evidence is admissible. If a party does not make a timely objection to admissibility of evidence, the party generally loses the right to contest admission of the evidence and to challenge any result that is based on the evidence.

How a judge makes decisions

In the course of a case, a judge will make decisions not just on evidence, but on many issues that arise. Some decisions he or she can make without delay by applying his or her knowledge of the law to the facts at hand. Other questions require research. A trial judge may read appellate court opinions dealing with questions similar to the one that he or she must answer. Even if no appellate court has written a decision dealing with exactly the same question, the opinions may cover similar scenarios or provide guidance. In addressing the broad range of questions that arise in the course of a case, judges often consult a reference manual called the *Wisconsin Benchbook*. There are *Benchbooks* for criminal, civil, family, juvenile, and probate cases – all revised on an annual basis by teams of judges and court commissioners. Judges use the *Benchbooks* to guide their research. If case law does not provide a clear answer to the questions, a judge may ask the parties to submit written arguments, called briefs, explaining why a question should be answered in their favor and citing case law to back up their arguments.

After the plaintiff or state finishes presenting evidence, the defendant may argue to the court that the case should be dismissed because the other side has not proven its case. If the court rejects the defendant's motion or delays ruling on it, the defense may present evidence in the case.

Jury instructions

In a jury trial, after both sides have presented their evidence, the judge confers with the attorneys and determines the wording of questions for the jury as well as the judge's instructions for the jury. The court may submit a single question to the jury, essentially asking which party should prevail, or may submit multiple questions, each addressing a determinative fact in the case. For example, in a civil negligence case, the judge may ask the jury whether the defendant used ordinary care; whether the defendant's actions caused the plaintiff's injury; and if the defendant did not use ordinary care and did cause the plaintiff's injury, what amount of damages the plaintiff should be awarded. In a criminal case, the judge asks the jury to determine whether the prosecution proved every element of a crime. For example, in a theft case, the judge asks the jury to determine whether the defendant

The jury box in the Lafayette County Courthouse awaits 12 citizens to exercise their role in the judicial process.
Opposite page: The "Sword of Justice" greets defendants and officers of the court.   (Kathleen Sitter, LRB)

intentionally took property of another; whether the owner of the property did not consent to this; whether the defendant knew that the owner did not consent; and whether the defendant intended to deprive the owner permanently of the property. The jury's answers to the series of questions determine in a civil case whether the plaintiff or defendant wins, and in a criminal case, whether the defendant is guilty or not guilty. A committee of legal experts in Wisconsin publishes guidebooks of suggested jury instructions for both civil and criminal cases. These model instructions, provided online to all judges, may be modified to fit a specific case.

In spoken and written instructions the judge advises the jurors of their responsibility to answer the questions and may give guidance on matters such as the burden of proof and determining the credibility of witnesses. The burden of proof includes both a burden of production (producing sufficient evidence that a jury or judge may find in the party's favor) and a burden of persuasion (the duty to convince the jury or judge of the party's view of the facts). The burden of production is generally on the plaintiff or state, except for certain defense claims, such as that a criminal defendant is not guilty by reason of mental disease or defect. The burden of persuasion in a civil case is generally by the preponderance of the evidence, and in a criminal case it is usually beyond a reasonable doubt.

The verdict and damages or sentencing

In a civil case, five-sixths of the jurors may return a verdict. In a criminal case, all the jurors must unanimously agree on the verdict in order to find the defendant guilty. In a trial before a judge without a jury, the judge determines which party prevails. Even in a trial to a jury, the judge may disregard the jury's finding (except a judge cannot disregard a jury's not guilty finding in a criminal case) and direct a verdict for one party, although this rarely occurs.

In a civil case, the jury or judge usually awards damages to a prevailing plaintiff. The judge may also direct the losing party to reimburse the prevailing party for costs incurred in connection with the trial.

In a criminal case, the judge determines the sentence for a defendant who has been convicted of a crime. The sentence may consist of a fine or imprisonment or both, or the judge may place a defendant on probation instead of imposing a sentence. If the defendant violates conditions of probation established by the judge, the judge may subsequently impose a sentence. Sentencing must accomplish several things. It must incapacitate the offender so that he or she cannot commit additional crimes, and also punish and rehabilitate the offender. Most judges believe that sentencing is the toughest part of the job because of the difficulty in structuring a sentence that will adequately serve these purposes. Without a crystal ball, it is impossible to know whether lengthy incarceration, probation, or something in between will best meet the needs of the defendant, the victim, and society.

Personnel in the courtroom

The court relies on a number of highly skilled assistants who perform a variety of jobs during trials. A clerk of court maintains a docket sheet recording the events in each case, is the custodian of the court's case file, and assists the judge in managing jurors and scheduling future court dates. The court reporter is a stenographer who makes a record of all the words spoken in open court. Wisconsin is currently facing a shortage of court reporters and the courts are working to increase the number of people entering this profession and exploring recording court proceedings by electronic means when court

reporters are unavailable. The bailiff is in charge of security and maintaining order in the courtroom. Some bailiffs are deputy sheriffs while others are civilians. In some cases an interpreter is needed to assist in communications with parties or witnesses who do not speak English well or who require sign-language interpretation.

Focus on the role of court interpreters

The increasing number of non-native-English speakers in Wisconsin has focused attention on the judicial system's need for a pool of qualified court interpreters. A good court interpreter must not only be fluent in English and the other language he or she is translating, but also must understand terminology used in court. In 1999, the director of state courts appointed a multidisciplinary committee to study the need for and use of interpreters in Wisconsin's courts and to recommend improvements.

When the Committee to Improve Interpreting in Wisconsin Courts commenced its work, the state's courts had no means of evaluating the skills of people providing language interpretation and no ability to hold these individuals to accepted professional standards. The interpreters' skills varied widely, and, in some cases, people who were providing interpretation had conflicts of interest. Consider the following stories – just a small sample – told to the committee:

- an interpreter confused "hat" and "gloves" until corrected by an observer in the gallery;
- a judge asked a woman to interpret for the woman's husband during their divorce trial;
- a judge asked an arresting officer to interpret for a prisoner;
- an interpreter asked the non-English-speaking person to pay him, even though he was already being paid by the county.

The Supreme Court has since implemented the committee's recommendations for improvement. The court adopted standards for interpreters, which were developed by the committee, in its Code of Ethics. The court has also engaged in an effort to educate judges, attorneys, and court staff on how to recognize when an interpreter is needed, how to properly use interpreters, and how to provide oversight of interpreter performance.

The most important change arising out of the committee's work is a rigorous testing and certification process for interpreters. Only those who speak English and another language at the level of a highly educated native speaker and can demonstrate a clear understanding of legal terminology will be certified. The process includes a two-day training program focusing on court process and ethics, a multipart written exam, and a lengthy oral exam. Of the first class of 34 Spanish language interpreters who reached the oral exam phase, eight passed. The 25 percent pass rate exceeds the average national rate of 12 percent. These interpreters – the first to be certified in Wisconsin – were sworn in at a ceremony in the Supreme Court Hearing Room in May 2004. Another class of Spanish interpreters was sworn in several months later, and the first class of Hmong interpreters is moving through the process. A roster of certified interpreters has been developed and distributed not only to judges and attorneys, but also to the law enforcement community to ensure accurate interpretation at every stage of the criminal justice process.

Dane County Court – Taking the Oath of Office for Court Interpreters: ". . . I will interpret truly, accurately, completely, and impartially, in accordance with the standards prescribed by law, the code of ethics for court interpreters, and Wisconsin guidelines for court interpreting . . ." (Kathleen Sitter, LRB)

Jury Service in Wisconsin

Managing the jury system is a delicate balancing act for a court. A successful system is attentive to both the efficiency of the process and the jurors' level of satisfaction. Those who manage the system must supply sufficient numbers of jurors to try all matters before the court without wasting court resources or the time and good will of the jurors.

Each year, across Wisconsin, about 70,000 people are summoned for jury duty. They are selected at random by the clerk of the circuit court for each county. Clerks primarily use lists provided by the state Department of Transportation (DOT) of individuals who hold driver's licenses or identification cards. Because the selection process must be random, no one may volunteer for jury duty. After the clerk determines how many jurors will be needed for a given period, a computer program randomly selects that number of names and juror questionnaires are sent out to those people. When the questionnaires are returned, they are reviewed to ensure that each potential juror is eligible under law to serve.

Jurors must be United States citizens, residents of Wisconsin, and residents of the circuit where they are summoned in order to serve. They must be at least 18 years of age and able to understand the English language.

When the people who have been summoned report to the local courthouse, they are checked in, provided with an orientation, and taken to the appropriate courtroom for the final selection process.

An American Sign Language interpreter signs for a juror at a jury orientation at the Milwaukee County Courthouse. People with disabilities regularly serve on Wisconsin juries and are accommodated in a variety of ways. At the podium is Jury Services Coordinator Lori Watson Schumann.   *(Kathleen Sitter, LRB)*

The final step in the selection process is called *voir dire*, which is a French phrase meaning "to speak the truth." This involves the judge and attorneys questioning the jurors, both as a group and as individuals, to try to develop a jury panel that both sides believe will be fair and impartial. The judge may ask prospective jurors whether they know any of the parties, attorneys, or witnesses in a case, and will explore whether the prospective jurors have any prejudice with respect to anyone they may know. The judge also will ask the prospective jurors if there are any reasons they cannot serve. After the judge concludes his or her questioning, the attorneys have an opportunity to question the prospective jurors.

Attorneys winnow the jury panel through the use of "for cause" and "peremptory" challenges. If an attorney challenges a juror for cause, he or she must provide a reason. There is no limit to the number of challenges made for cause. If an attorney claims a peremptory challenge, the juror is excused and the reason need not be given. Peremptory challenges may not be based upon race. There are a limited number of peremptory challenges allowed. After the jurors have been selected, the judge will instruct the members of the jury regarding the case and the rules of conduct.

These rules of conduct are very specific and important to the fairness of the process. Generally, they include prohibitions on discussing the case with anyone, including family, the court staff or other jurors (until it's time for deliberation), watching or reading news accounts of the trial, and conducting one's own investigation by looking at the Internet or going to places involved in the case, or consulting maps or calendars. All these rules are designed to ensure that the jurors reach a decision based only upon the law and the evidence presented in court.

Jury Diversity

In June 1996, the *Kenosha News* ran a story on a drug trial in that county's circuit court. The story began as follows:

A black defendant glanced at the white crowd from which a jury would be selected to decide her fate on a drug charge. She then asked her attorney, "Why aren't there any black people here?" [The attorney] scanned the 135 potential jurors filling the Kenosha Circuit courtroom and found no African-Americans.

Following her conviction, the woman based an appeal on Kenosha's jury selection system, but lost.

Efforts to ensure that Wisconsin juries reflect the racial and ethnic make-up of each county's population are many and varied – as are opinions on whether this is necessary. In that same *Kenosha News* story, criminal defense lawyers differed on the importance of a racially mixed jury. One lawyer said: "Diversity gives a sense of fairness to litigants. You wouldn't want, for example, only members of one occupation, political party or religion on a jury." But others opined that jurors' ability to understand testimony and arrive at a verdict based upon the facts and the law is all that matters. Another lawyer told the newspaper that he prefers white juries for his black clients, based upon conversations with blacks who have served as jurors. "Black jurors hold black defendants to a higher standard," the lawyer said. "Black jurors usually are in the middle class and see a black defendant as the bad apple."

While it is unreasonable to expect any one jury to represent the racial mix of a county, it is reasonable to expect that, over time, a county's jurors will be representative of the county population. In an effort to improve jury diversity, the legislature has given the courts the ability to tap different source lists in addition to the Department of Transportation list. Utility company customer lists, phone books, voter registration lists, lists of people receiving public assistance, and lists of high school graduates are among those acceptable for use by clerks who find that their DOT sampling has not provided an adequate representation of minorities. However, few Wisconsin counties actually use the supplemental lists, because they have not proven useful.

Jurors file into the jury box ready to hear the evidence presented in court. This jury was hearing a medical malpractice case in Brown County Circuit Court and gave permission for these photographs to be taken. The media are not permitted to photograph jurors during a case.

(Kathleen Sitter, LRB)

Alternatives to Traditional Civil and Criminal Procedure

Not all proceedings under the jurisdiction of the circuit courts follow formal civil or criminal procedures. Courts have developed less formal procedures to handle certain prevalent social problems such as family dysfunction, juvenile delinquency, and drug abuse. The courts also use less formal procedures for efficiency.

Improving how courts respond to family crisis

In cases affecting the family or in cases in which it appears that legal custody or physical placement of a child will be at issue, the circuit courts must refer the parties to mediation unless mediation would cause undue hardship or endanger the health and safety of one of the parties. Counties are required to appoint a director of family counseling services to provide such mediation. Parties referred to mediation by the court must participate in at least one mediation session unless the director of mediation services finds that mediation is not appropriate. Mediation is limited to the issues of child custody and physical placement and does not involve issues beyond the immediate interest of the child, such as property division and child support allocations, unless they directly bear on custody or placement. If the parties reach an agreement on custody and placement in mediation, the agreement is submitted for review by the judge. The judge will incorporate the agreement as part of the final judgment unless he or she finds that it is not in the best interests of the child. Successful mediation removes determinations regarding custody and placement from the adversarial forum of the courtroom. Of course, when mediation is not successful, custody and placement must be argued and decided under regular court procedures.[1]

Beyond custody issues, there are a variety of family problems that require court intervention. These problems constitute a large and growing portion of the work of Wisconsin courts, and the growing involvement of the courts in the lives of dysfunctional families has raised concern among those who work with families in crisis. The Wisconsin Supreme Court has been involved since 1995 in an effort to address this concern. This effort has sparked a number of projects.

Initiatives of the Wisconsin court system are improving how the courts respond to families in crisis with a number of projects...

In **Kenosha**, **Racine**, and **Waukesha** counties, a program to move children with special needs from foster care to permanent homes by linking key decision makers in the permanency process.

In **La Crosse** County, the Unified Family Court Project, which improves the handling of the complicated problems that one family may present – divorce, child abuse, juvenile delinquency, and more – by grouping all the cases involving an individual family in front of one judge to bring the full picture into clearer focus.

In **Milwaukee** County, an initiative to link the District Attorney's Office, Guardian *ad Litem*'s Office (which provides attorneys to represent the best interests of children who are involved in court proceedings), Termination of Parental Rights (TPR)/Adoption Unit and the Children's Court to one database to improve communication among agencies and create a "fast track" to permanent homes.

Beyond punishment: problem-solving courts

In the last decade, a new type of court known as the problem-solving court has appeared in jurisdictions around the U.S. These courts grew out of public concern and frustration over recidivism, also known as revolving-door syndrome. Problem-solving courts vary considerably in structure and operation, but in general they attempt to address the root causes of each defendant's offenses and depend upon a close collaboration between the courts and social services. Nationally, the most prominent problem-solving courts are drug court, mental health court, domestic violence court, community court, and teen court.[2] In general, community courts are found in large cities. Wisconsin does not have any community courts or mental health courts at this writing.

Problem-solving courts are not to be confused with another type of court that also recently has appeared on the landscape, the specialty court. Specialty courts follow the traditional, adversarial court model but handle only a specific type of case. For example, Milwaukee County has three courts dedicated to homicide and sexual assault cases, one court dedicated to gun violations, and three courts that handle drug offenses. These courts do not provide special treatment to offenders, but they do ensure that these offenses are handled in a prompt and uniform manner.

In Wisconsin, as of June 2004, there were 37 courts in 36 counties that were identified as problem-solving courts, also known as treatment courts. The vast

Mediating family disputes

It was, at first glance, a tragically unremarkable story: A 10-year-old boy showed up at school with bruises, his teacher made a report, police investigated, and the father was arrested and charged with felony child abuse.

In the normal course of events, the case would take about seven months to resolve and the father probably would have little or no contact with his son during that time. But this incident occurred in La Crosse County, where the court has institutionalized mediated child protection conferencing as the preferred method for handling child abuse/neglect cases. And that changed everything. The mediation brought together the family, attorneys, and social workers. They reached an agreement on a variety of conditions, which was submitted to and approved by the court. The father is now reenrolled in Alcoholics Anonymous, the child has a new doctor and a different medication, and a county social worker plugged the family into new services. The family stayed together, and the felony charge was ultimately dropped.

The program was implemented in La Crosse in October 1998 and mediators now handle about 50 cases per year (but never cases that involve an allegation of sexual assault, where it would be harmful to bring the victim and the accused together). An agreement is reached in mediation in 86 percent of cases. The judge sees each family every 60 days, which keeps them strongly connected, and the monitoring by social workers is often more stringent than would be possible under probation in a criminal child abuse case.

majority of these – 27, were teen courts, also known as peer or youth courts, which provide an alternative to the traditional juvenile justice system for first-time, nonviolent offenders. Teen courts focus on children between the ages of 11 and 18 who have committed relatively minor offenses such as vandalism or truancy and may be causing problems at school. Teen courts use teenagers as jurors, and sometimes as judges, attorneys, and court officers.

Teen court gives youth offenders a chance to clear their records and provides them with guidance, learning opportunities, and positive peer influence. In general, the defendants must be willing to admit guilt and must agree to abide by a "sentence" set by a panel of their peers. Often, these panels are comprised of former teen court defendants. Teen court dispositions generally focus on community service and may include letters of apology and essays about the impact of their misdeeds. Teen courts also provide a forum for adults and adolescents to work together to address community problems.

Many communities have chosen to begin a teen court because they sense that the traditional justice system does not have the resources to focus on first-time offenders. By reducing the docket of the juvenile court, teen courts – which often convene in the evening and operate on a shoestring with the help of volunteers – free up the court system to handle the more serious cases. And by addressing first offenses in a way that may reduce subsequent offenses, teen courts aim to redirect kids who might otherwise become defendants in those serious cases.

Circuit Court Judge Stuart A. Schwartz presides over a session of the Dane County Drug Court. Judge Schwartz sees participants frequently to review their progress and give support or impose sanctions as necessary.

(Kathleen Sitter, LRB)

Problem-solving courts for drug abusers, which are often called drug-treatment courts, are increasingly being used in Wisconsin. As of January 2005, three Wisconsin counties (Dane, La Crosse, and Monroe) had established treatment courts for adult drug abusers and three additional counties (Eau Claire, Pierce, and Wood) were running pilot programs to test the concept with a small number of offenders. Several other counties were in the planning stages, including Waukesha County where an alcohol-treatment court was under consideration. One county (Ashland) has a drug treatment court for juvenile offenders. Other counties have drug courts that function to improve the processing of cases rather than to provide treatment.

Drug-treatment courts focus on nonviolent felony drug offenders who are referred by the district attorney and who agree to participate in the program and receive drug treatment services instead of a sentence. The offenders appear regularly before the judge as a group. The judge reviews each case with the treatment providers and district attorney, and discusses each offender's progress directly with the offender in front of the group. The judge may order the treatment modified or may order sanctions for violating treatment requirements, for example, several days in jail. If an offender successfully completes treatment by staying off drugs, the court may expunge any record of conviction. However, if the offender does not succeed in treatment, he or she is returned to the regular criminal process for adjudication and sentencing.

Small claims and probate

Circuit courts also use streamlined procedures in the interests of efficiently managing workload. For example, Wisconsin law establishes less formal civil procedures for trying small claims actions, in which the vast majority of litigants represent themselves. Small claims include evictions, forfeitures, and other civil actions in which the amount claimed is less than $5,000.

An increasing number of Wisconsin counties have established local rules mandating that parties to a small claims action try mediation before a judge will hear the case. Generally, when parties appear for court, volunteer mediators are on hand to try to help them resolve their dispute before the judge steps in.

Probate is the legal process through which a court makes sure that a deceased person's property is distributed to his or her beneficiaries. Probate takes place in the court located in the county where the deceased person lived. Each county is required to appoint a register in probate. Parties to a probate action have the option of presenting the probate matter to the register to process under informal administration

A statement above the judge's bench in the Lafayette County Courthouse emphasizes the role of the people in their government. (Kathleen Sitter, LRB)

proceedings instead of filing the probate claim with the court. Determinations under informal administration are just as valid as probate actions taken into court.

Court of Appeals

The Court of Appeals hears appeals from the circuit court. The primary function of the court is to correct errors resulting from misapplication of well-settled law. However, the Court of Appeals also issues new rules of law.

Sixteen judges sit on the Court of Appeals, which is divided into four districts. District I serves Milwaukee County. District II is based in Waukesha, District III is based in Green Bay, and District IV is based in Madison. The 16 judges are apportioned unequally among the districts, reflecting differences in the caseload. Districts I and II each have 4 judges, District III has 3 judges, and District IV has 5 judges. Court of Appeals judges are elected in districtwide elections for 6-year terms and must reside in the district to be eligible for election. The Supreme Court appoints a chief judge from among the 16 judges to direct administrative matters for the Court of Appeals, and the chief judge appoints one judge in each district to serve as the presiding judge for the district.

Appeals in Wisconsin before 1978

Before 1978, when the Court of Appeals was created, parties had a right to appeal almost any kind of circuit court decision directly to the Supreme Court, which had to accept the appeals. By the late 1960s, the Supreme Court had accrued a persistent and growing backlog of cases. Parties in some cases had to wait several years for a Supreme Court decision. In 1977, the state adopted a constitutional amendment authorizing creation of an intermediate court of appeals. Creation of the Court of Appeals allowed the Supreme Court to focus on deciding important questions of law, rather than correcting errors made in the circuit court. The Court of Appeals originally had 12 judges and was projected to handle 1,200 appeals a year. At this writing, the court receives about 3,500 requests for review a year.

Appeal of a circuit court decision

The parties to a circuit court case have a right to appeal the circuit court's decision once the circuit court has entered a final judgment. Such appeals are called appeals of right. A party initiates an appeal by filing notice of appeal with the circuit court and submitting a copy of the notice to the clerk for the Court of Appeals. The Court of Appeals receives about 2,300 appeals of right each year and must review all of them.

The Wisconsin Court of Appeals, 2005. Back row, left to right: Judges Ralph Adam Fine, Harry G. Snyder, Paul B. Higginbotham, Charles P. Dykman, Daniel P. Anderson, David G. Deininger, Michael W. Hoover, Paul Lundsten, Margaret J. Vergeront. Front row, left to right: Judges Patricia S. Curley, Ted E. Wedemeyer, Jr., Gregory A. Peterson, Thomas Cane (chief judge), Neal P. Nettesheim (deputy chief judge), Richard S. Brown, Joan F. Kessler.

(Wisconsin Supreme Court)

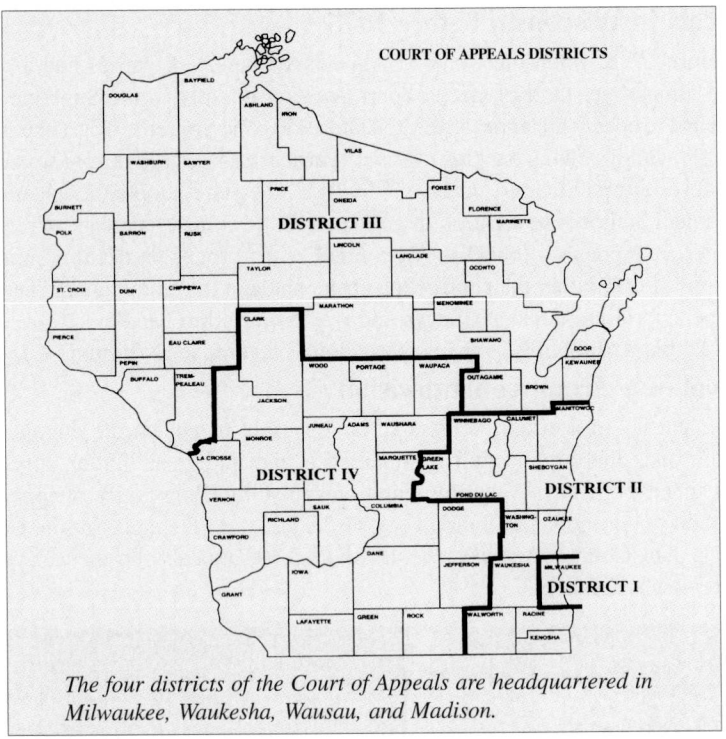

The four districts of the Court of Appeals are headquartered in Milwaukee, Waukesha, Wausau, and Madison.

The Court of Appeals may at its discretion also accept appeals from circuit court orders made in cases that are still pending in circuit court. The court generally does not accept such appeals for several reasons: a party's appeal may become unnecessary if the party wins the circuit court case; the circuit court is better equipped to gather the facts necessary to make initial decisions in a case; and it is more efficient for the Court of Appeals to allow the circuit court to conclude a case before getting involved. However, the Court of Appeals may accept an appeal in a pending circuit court case if reviewing the circuit court's order will provide significant assistance in deciding the circuit court case, clarify an issue of general importance, or protect a party from substantial or irreparable harm. For example, the Court of Appeals may accept an appeal of a decision that an insurance policy covers an injury, because if the Court of Appeals determines that the policy does not, the case may be concluded without addressing the issue of damages. A party seeking a discretionary appeal must petition the Court of Appeals. The court receives between 200 and 250 petitions for discretionary appeal a year and grants 40 to 50.

In an appeal, the petitioner (the party requesting review) submits specific questions for review. For example, the petitioner may ask the Court of Appeals to review the circuit court's interpretation of a particular statute or may ask for review of a circuit court decision to admit certain evidence. The appeals court generally

The Creation of the Court of Appeals: "It Was Tough Politics"

How did the District II Court of Appeals come to be headquartered in Waukesha, just down the road from District I in Milwaukee? In a word: politics.

After voters ratified a constitutional amendment on April 5, 1977, authorizing creation of the Wisconsin Court of Appeals, the legislature had to decide a key question: which four cities would be made headquarters for the appellate districts? Madison and Milwaukee, with their large populations and heavy caseloads were obvious choices. But Waukesha?

Frederick P. Kessler, who was a former state representative and a Milwaukee judge when the district lines were drawn (and who is now, again, a state representative) explained, "There was no logic. The logic should have been one (district) in Green Bay and Eau Claire, but...somebody said that to get Ed (Jackamonis, a Democrat and Speaker of the Assembly at the time) we have got to give him a building. And Ed represented the City of Waukesha. And so they said draw a district that makes Waukesha the logical place to put a Court of Appeals...and Ed went down from the floor of the speaker chambers and he pushed that bill through."

Kessler worked closely with then-Senate Majority Leader William A. Bablitch, to shepherd court reorganization through the legislature. Bablitch went on to serve as a justice of the Wisconsin Supreme Court from 1983-2003.

Kessler and Bablitch, along with Judges Thomas H. Barland of Eau Claire and James W. Rice of Monroe, provided a group interview on the subject of court reorganization for the Supreme Court's Oral History Project. In the interview, they recalled the art of the deal on both Waukesha and Wausau, which is home to the District III Court of Appeals.

"Stevens Point was my hometown, and I figured in any bill of this magnitude there must be something for Stevens Point," Bablitch recalled. "Now I didn't really want it in Stevens Point, but I just had that...instinct that someday that chip might be worth something.... I rounded up the votes (and) I had a majority to make Stevens Point – again, another relatively illogical choice – as the head of (District III).

"Well, Wausau just exploded because Wausau had been led to believe that this was theirs.... They had the building, they had everything there," he said.

Governor Martin J. Schreiber was facing an uphill battle (which he lost to Lee Sherman Dreyfus) for reelection at the time. Bablitch recalled that Schreiber called him into his office and there they laid the groundwork that gave Wausau the Court of Appeals headquarters and Stevens Point funds for the renovation of its downtown.

Everybody was happy, "except the western part of the state," Barland (also a former member of the state assembly) recalled.

does not review every facet of a circuit court decision, and rarely reviews a circuit court's determination of facts because the circuit court judge sees physical evidence and witnesses firsthand, and thus is in a better position to determine facts than an appellate judge, who only sees a written transcript of the trial.

Appellate briefs

Briefs are the heart of an appellate case. After filing a petition for appeal, the petitioner must submit a brief to the Court of Appeals and to the opposing party. The respondent (the party against whom an appeal is filed) must file a response brief, which may raise additional issues. The court may also direct the parties to address specific issues by brief. A brief must be clear and compelling because most Court of Appeals cases are decided on the basis of the briefs alone.

A brief contains certain standard sections. The brief starts with a statement of the issues presented. It contains a synopsis of the history of the case and of relevant facts. The most important part of the brief is the argument section, where a party lays out reasons for the court to rule in the party's favor and cites relevant statutes and prior court opinions that support the party's reasoning.

The Wisconsin State Law Library (WSSL) has copies of all briefs submitted in cases in which the Court of Appeals or Supreme Court issues a signed opinion. The briefs are posted on the WSSL Web site.

The Wisconsin State Law Library, the state's oldest public library, was established with the Wisconsin Territory in 1836 and funded with a $5,000 appropriation from Congress, which decided a frontier legislature would need law books. For many years, the State Law Library was housed in the State Capitol. Since 2002, it has occupied the second and third floors of the Risser Justice Center on the Capitol Square and continues to serve the needs of judges, lawyers, legislators, and members of the public. (Kathleen Sitter, LRB)

BRIEF OF PLAINTIFF-APPELLANT-CROSS-RESPONDENT, ADELE R. GARCIA

ON APPEAL FROM
CIRCUIT COURT FOR WAUKESHA COUNTY
THE HONORABLE LEE S. DREYFUS, JR. PRESIDING

ARGUMENT

THE WISCONSIN LEMON LAW DOES NOT REQUIRE A CONSUMER TO USE SPECIFIC STATUTORY TERMINOLOGY WHEN REQUESTING A COMPARABLE VEHICLE PURSUANT TO SEC. 218.0171(2)(c), WIS. STATS.

The Wisconsin Lemon Law was meant to be a self-enforcing consumer protection statute. In order to receive the remedies afforded by the Wisconsin Lemon Law, a consumer must comply with certain provisions, such as providing notice to the manufacturer and making a specific request for relief. A consumer is not, however, required to use specific statutory terminology or "magic words" in order to request a comparable new vehicle pursuant to sec. 218.0171(2)(c), Wis. Stats.

I.   A Consumer is not Required to Use "Magic Words" Regarding the Transfer of Title of the Lemon Vehicle to Trigger the Remedies of the Wisconsin Lemon Law.

The effect of the decision of the trial court in this matter to impose a requirement upon a consumer to use specific "magic words" in order to receive relief under the Wisconsin Lemon Law. According to the trial court:

Unless the vehicle is offered, meaning transfer of title is offered to the manufacturer, I'm satisfied it does not trigger the manufacturer's strict obligation under statute to provide the new vehicle or the refund in terms of whatever may be the selection of remedy. Now absent that occurring, as I said, it doesn't trigger the time period. (R. 33: 44; app. 163).

The trial court concluded that Ms. Garcia's notice to Mazda and Hall Imports, Inc. was insufficient merely because the specific words "offer to transfer title" did not appear in her written notice.

The trial court limited its determination to the first sentence of sec. 218.0171(2)(c), Wis. Stats., rather than reading the statute as a whole. The remaining language of the statute goes on to state that a consumer *shall* return the vehicle and provide the

Portions of the argument section from the petitioner's brief in *Garcia v. Mazda Motor of America* providing reasons why the court should find that Garcia properly invoked the Wisconsin Lemon Law in requesting a replacement vehicle.

The Wisconsin Lemon Law allows a consumer whose vehicle has a nonconformity that has been subject to a reasonable attempt to repair by a manufacturer to elect a comparable new vehicle or a refund in accordance with the provisions of the statute. In order to receive the elected remedy under the Wisconsin Lemon Law, a consumer must provide notice to the manufacturer of the lemon vehicle.

In relevant part, the Wisconsin Lemon Law states:

To receive a comparable new motor vehicle or a refund due under par. (b)1. or 2., a consumer described under sub. (1)(b)1., 2. or 3. shall offer to the manufacturer of the motor vehicle having the nonconformity to transfer title of that motor vehicle to that manufacturer. No later than 30 days after that offer, the manufacturer shall provide the consumer with the comparable new motor vehicle or refund. When the manufacturer provides the new motor vehicle or refund, the consumer shall return the motor vehicle having the nonconformity to the manufacturer and provide the manufacturer with the certificate of title and all endorsements necessary to transfer title to the manufacturer. Sec. 218.0171(2)(c), Wis. Stats.

A consumer is not required to do anything further to initiate a claim under the Wisconsin Lemon Law. The statute does not require that a consumer make an offer in a specific form, or even that it be in writing, nor does it require a consumer use specific language or "magic words".

Supervisory writs and no-merit reports

In addition to appeals, the Court of Appeals handles petitions for supervisory writs and no-merit reports. Petitions for supervisory writs are requests to the Court of Appeals to order the circuit court to fulfill its responsibilities. A supervisory writ is appropriate when the circuit court violates a clear duty to act or refrain from acting, causing grave or irreparable harm, and if an appeal will be an inadequate remedy. A supervisory writ may be requested to quash a subpoena or to require a judge to remove him or herself from a case. Many of the petitions for supervisory writ that the Court of Appeals receives are requests from prisoners to order the circuit court to hear pleas for postconviction relief. The court receives about 200 petitions for supervisory action a year and usually grants fewer than 10.

No-merit reports are reports by court-appointed attorneys explaining why pursuit of an appeal would be frivolous. (Court-appointed attorneys are generally representing indigent defendants.) If a court-appointed attorney finds that there are no substantive issues for appeal in a case, and the attorney cannot persuade the client to drop his or her appeal of right, the attorney must file a no-merit report, identifying any possible ground for appeal and discussing why an appeal would have no merit. The court then determines whether the appeal would be frivolous. The court receives about 600 no-merit reports a year.

Reviewing and deciding cases

Most Court of Appeals decisions are made by a 3-judge panel, which acts by majority vote. However, certain types of cases, including misdemeanors, child welfare, juvenile delinquency, and ordinance violations, are decided by a single judge unless a party requests otherwise and the court consents. In the districts with more than three judges, the judges form several 3-judge panels and the presiding judge distributes cases evenly among the panels without respect to the subject matter or the parties involved.

Panels meet several days a month. At their meetings, the judges generally reach a decision in the cases assigned, but they may decide to hear oral argument from the attorneys to gather further information or perspectives regarding issues presented in a case, or they may decide to certify a case to the Supreme Court. The Court of Appeals only hears oral argument in about 50 cases a year.

When making a decision in a case, the judges also determine the form in which they will issue their decision. The options are a judge-signed opinion, a per curiam opinion (an opinion that does not identify the author) for a case of lesser complexity or importance but still requiring an explanation, or summary disposition (a short order giving the decision and the reasons, but not engaging in analysis of the law). The court issues a judge-signed opinion for decisions that require significant explanation, develop new law, or if the judges do not all agree. A judge-signed opinion contains the facts of the case, the questions presented, and analysis of the relevant law, and identifies the author of the opinion as well as the other two judges who participated in the decision. Each judge on a panel is assigned an equal number

COURT OF APPEALS OF WISCONSIN
PUBLISHED OPINION

Case No.:   02-2260

†Petition for Review filed.

No.   02-2260(D)

¶16   LUNDSTEN, J. (*dissenting*). The majority concludes that Adele Garcia did not offer to transfer title to her vehicle to Mazda, within the meaning of Wisconsin's Lemon Law. I respectfully dissent because I believe Garcia gave Mazda clear notice that she was offering to transfer title under the Lemon Law.

¶17   As the majority explains, when certain criteria are met, Wisconsin's Lemon Law gives car owners a choice of two remedies and requires that the owners communicate their choice of remedy to the manufacturer. The applicable subsection provides in part:

> To receive a comparable new motor vehicle or a refund ... a consumer ... shall offer to the manufacturer of the motor vehicle having the nonconformity to transfer title of that motor vehicle to that manufacturer.

WIS. STAT. § 218.0171(2)(c). An offer under this subsection triggers a thirty-day time period for compliance by the manufacturer.

¶18   I agree with the majority that WIS. STAT. § 218.0171(2) unambiguously requires that a "lemon" owner communicate to the manufacturer the remedy the owner desires and offer to transfer title to their vehicle in exchange for a refund or a replacement vehicle. Under the statutory scheme, a manufacturer must receive clear notice of such a demand and offer so that the commencement date of the thirty-day time period for compliance is likewise clear.

cia wrote:

my understanding that the Lemon Law in the State of consin is that after a reasonable number of unsuccessful ir attempts by Mazda or its authorized dealers, or that vehicle has been out of service for a specific number of , that I'm entitled to either a comparable replacement cle or a refund of the purchase price. At this time the mobile has been out of service for a period of 16 days I would like to have a replacement.

cified that she was making her request for replacement under on Law and she specified that she wanted a replacement vehicle. s, in effect, "ah, but she did not actually offer to transfer title to en she gets the replacement." I do not understand this thinking.

re can be no doubt that Mazda understood that Garcia was t to a replacement vehicle under WIS. STAT. § 218.0171(2)(c) and communicating to the company that she would transfer the title to her "lemon" to Mazda. Indeed, she was statutorily obligated to transfer title when Mazda gave her a replacement:

> When the manufacturer provides the new motor vehicle ..., the consumer shall return the motor vehicle having the

¶23   Did Mazda think Garcia was trying to tri Garcia was asking for a replacement, but was not also c her current car, so that she would end up with two cars? Of course not. And, just as plainly, she could not succeed in such trickery because the statute requires that she transfer title upon receiving the replacement vehicle. To repeat, the only reasonable reading of Garcia's letter is that she was notifying Mazda that she wanted a replacement car and would, necessarily, give up her car, including title, when Mazda supplied a replacement.

¶24   Accordingly, I respectfully dissent.[1]

---

[1] Mazda and Hall cross-appeal, effectively supplying an alternative reason why they should prevail on appeal. I have reviewed this issue and would decide it against Mazda and Hall. However, because this is a dissent, I choose not to expend my limited resources writing on the topic.

Portions of Judge Lundsten's dissenting opinion in *Garcia v. Mazda Motor of America,* explaining that he reached a different conclusion than the other two judges deciding the case for the Court of Appeals.

Artwork and murals in the Brown County Courthouse in Green Bay capture the Beaux Arts style of architecture and design.

(Kathleen Sitter, LRB)

of opinions to write. The judges do not get to choose which opinions they write, although a judge who does not agree with a decision will not write the opinion. The author of the opinion circulates a draft opinion to the other judges on the panel. The other judges may sign off on the opinion or request changes. The author of the opinion may have to modify the opinion to arrive at a decision on which at least one of the two other judges agrees. The judge in the minority may file a dissenting opinion explaining why he or she disagrees. A judge may also file a concurring opinion explaining that he or she agrees with the outcome of the decision, but not with the reasoning. A decision is valid if the majority of judges on a panel agree on the outcome, even if they do not agree on the reasoning behind the decision. The court issues about 750 judge-signed opinions a year and about 450 to 500 per-curiam opinions a year.

Because the judges of the Court of Appeals work in separate districts, and on separate panels, they sometimes issue conflicting opinions, which are troublesome because the opinions issued in one district apply statewide. The court attempts to minimize conflicts by having a central staff attorney review all cases and alert judges of pending appeals that raise similar issues. The court may consolidate similar cases or review them together. Judges may also discuss pending cases with one another. If two panels or two judges do issue conflicting opinions, the Supreme Court may choose to review the cases to resolve the conflict.

Publication of opinions

The Court of Appeals publishes about one-quarter of its opinions to inform the public about important applications of the law and to serve as precedent, which means that attorneys and courts in future cases may cite the opinions as accurate descriptions of the law. Reasons for publishing an opinion include that the opinion states a new rule of law or modifies, clarifies, or criticizes an existing rule; the opinion applies an existing rule of law to a situation to which it had not been previously applied; the opinion resolves conflicts in prior decision; it provides a useful summary of existing law or lays out the legislative history for a law; or that the opinion covers a case that is of substantial interest to the public.

Opinions are published in bound volumes by two reporting services. *Callaghan's Wisconsin Reports* contains opinions of the Wisconsin Court of Appeals and the Wisconsin Supreme Court. The *North Western Reporter* also contains opinions

Wisconsin Supreme Court and Court of Appeals opinions are published in Callaghan's Wisconsin Reports *and in the* North Western Reporter. *(Kathleen Sitter, LRB)*

from the courts of several other Midwestern states. In addition, the text of the opinions may be found free of charge on several Web sites, including the Web sites of the Wisconsin Court System, the Wisconsin State Law Library, and the State Bar of Wisconsin.

After the appeal is decided

The Court of Appeals may affirm, reverse, or modify the lower-court order or judgment. Sometimes the lower court must take action in accordance with the Court of Appeals decision. For example, if the Court of Appeals finds error in a criminal sentence issued by a circuit court but does not determine a new sentence, the circuit court must impose a new sentence. Or the Court of Appeals may direct the circuit court to reconsider a prior decision in light of a new standard issued by the Court of Appeals.

The Court of Appeals affirms about 80 percent of the lower court rulings it reviews. The reversal rate differs between civil and criminal cases: about 75 percent of civil cases and 85 to 90 percent of criminal cases are affirmed.

Supreme Court

The Wisconsin Supreme Court has appellate jurisdiction to review cases decided by any of the lower courts. It has authority to hear original actions, which are cases that have not been decided by a lower court. The Supreme Court also has supervisory authority over the lower courts, general administrative responsibility for the court system, and regulatory authority over judges and lawyers.

The Court is composed of seven justices, elected in statewide elections to 10-year terms. In the event of a vacancy on the Supreme Court, the governor appoints a justice until an election may be held. The justice who has served the longest continuous term becomes the chief justice, unless he or she chooses not to serve as chief.

The Supreme Court meets in open session to discuss the administration of the state court system. Frequently on the agenda at these meetings are budget matters, petitions for new or amended court rules, and policy issues. The justices convene at the attorney table in the Supreme Court Hearing Room for these conferences. They are shown here meeting with members of the court staff. (Kathleen Sitter, LRB)

Jurisdiction

Unlike the Court of Appeals and circuit courts, the Supreme Court determines which cases it will hear. The Supreme Court receives over 1,000 requests for review a year and generally agrees to hear about 100 of them.

Cases come to the Supreme Court in four ways. The most common is a petition for review by a party who loses a case in the Court of Appeals. Alternatively, a party who loses in the circuit court and wishes to appeal directly to the Supreme Court without going through the Court of Appeals may petition the Supreme Court to allow the party to bypass the Court of Appeals. The Court of Appeals may certify a case that has been appealed and request that the Supreme Court decide it. (Even if the Court of Appeals does not certify a case to the Supreme Court, the Supreme Court has authority to preempt the Court of Appeals and decide the case.) And, finally, the Supreme Court may take original jurisdiction in a case, hearing arguments on a matter that has not been considered in the lower courts. The Supreme Court receives anywhere from 800 to 1,000 petitions for review of Court of Appeals decisions a year, 20-30 petitions for bypass, and a similar number of certifications. In addition to the approximately 100 petitions for review that the court accepts, it takes most of the certifications, few of the petitions for bypass, and a small number of the 10 or so petitions for original action received each year.

The court also receives requests to exercise its supervisory authority, generally 50 to 100 a year. Under its supervisory authority, the court may direct the lower courts to take or refrain from taking certain actions, for example, to quash a subpoena, dismiss a complaint, or require substitution of a judge. Most requests to the Supreme Court to exercise its supervisory authority concern actions in the Court of Appeals. Finally, the court also hears cases relating to regulation of attorneys and judges, which are discussed later in this article.

Determining which cases to hear

The general standard that the Supreme Court applies in determining whether to review a case "is not whether the matter was correctly decided or justice done in the lower court, but whether the matter is one which should trigger the institutional responsibilities of the Supreme Court."[3] The court is more likely to hear a case that presents a significant question of constitutional law or calls for a change in policy. The court favors cases that will have statewide impact over those that affect only a private interest, as well as cases that present a novel question or present a question that is likely to recur. It also accepts cases to resolve conflicts between current precedent; for example, a case in which a Court of Appeals opinion is in conflict with a controlling opinion of the U.S. Supreme Court, or a matter on which Court of Appeals districts have reached different conclusions.

The court applies additional criteria in determining whether to accept a case on bypass or certification from the Court of Appeals. Reasons for the court to accept a case on bypass or certification include that little (or conflicting) precedent exists governing the issues raised in the case, the justices foresee that they will ultimately choose to take the case regardless of how the Court of Appeals rules, and there is a need to hasten the appeals process.

The standard for taking a case on original jurisdiction is less defined. Generally, a case must be of great importance to the people of the state, must require relief that cannot adequately be provided by a lower court, and must require a speedy and

How a case comes to the Wisconsin Supreme Court

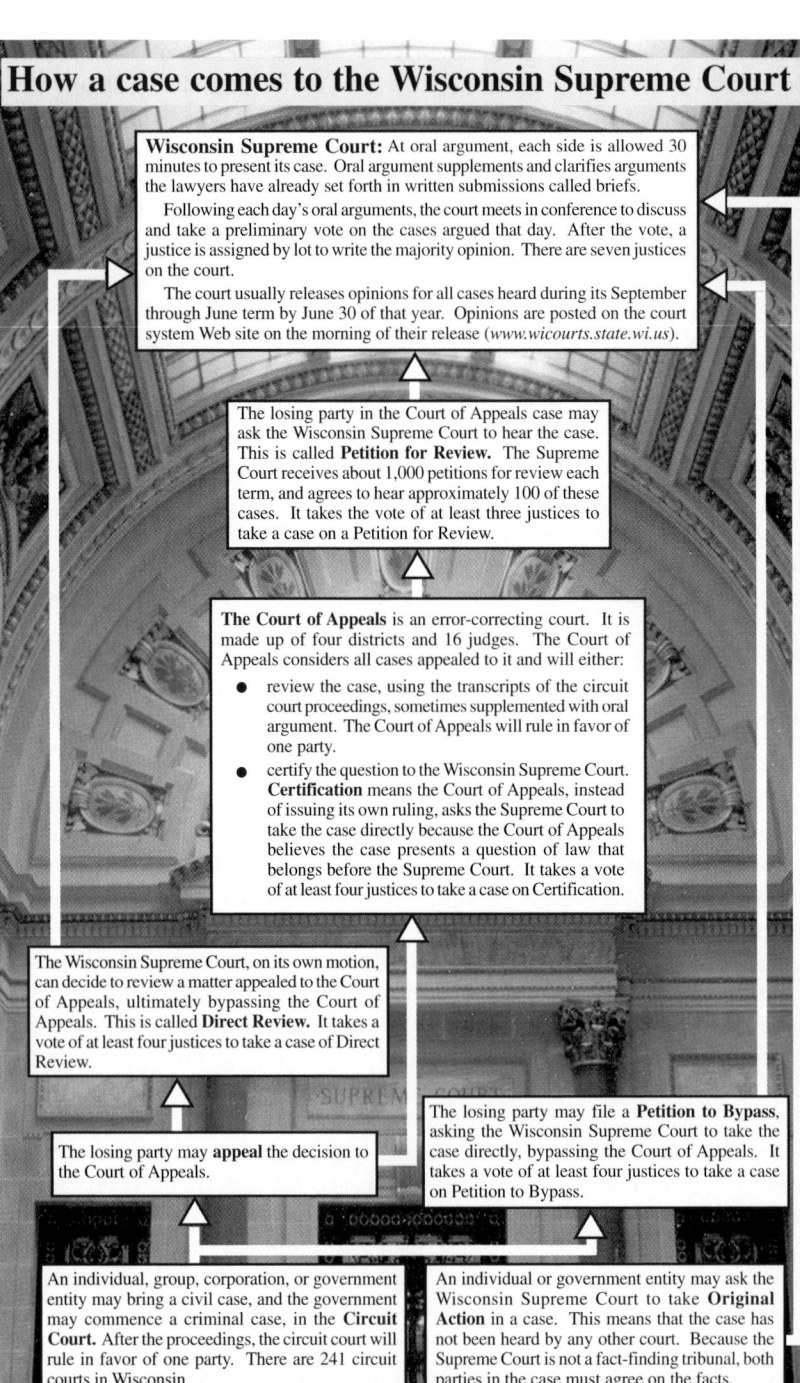

Wisconsin Supreme Court: At oral argument, each side is allowed 30 minutes to present its case. Oral argument supplements and clarifies arguments the lawyers have already set forth in written submissions called briefs.

Following each day's oral arguments, the court meets in conference to discuss and take a preliminary vote on the cases argued that day. After the vote, a justice is assigned by lot to write the majority opinion. There are seven justices on the court.

The court usually releases opinions for all cases heard during its September through June term by June 30 of that year. Opinions are posted on the court system Web site on the morning of their release (*www.wicourts.state.wi.us*).

The losing party in the Court of Appeals case may ask the Wisconsin Supreme Court to hear the case. This is called **Petition for Review.** The Supreme Court receives about 1,000 petitions for review each term, and agrees to hear approximately 100 of these cases. It takes the vote of at least three justices to take a case on a Petition for Review.

The Court of Appeals is an error-correcting court. It is made up of four districts and 16 judges. The Court of Appeals considers all cases appealed to it and will either:

● review the case, using the transcripts of the circuit court proceedings, sometimes supplemented with oral argument. The Court of Appeals will rule in favor of one party.

● certify the question to the Wisconsin Supreme Court. **Certification** means the Court of Appeals, instead of issuing its own ruling, asks the Supreme Court to take the case directly because the Court of Appeals believes the case presents a question of law that belongs before the Supreme Court. It takes a vote of at least four justices to take a case on Certification.

The Wisconsin Supreme Court, on its own motion, can decide to review a matter appealed to the Court of Appeals, ultimately bypassing the Court of Appeals. This is called **Direct Review.** It takes a vote of at least four justices to take a case of Direct Review.

The losing party may **appeal** the decision to the Court of Appeals.

The losing party may file a **Petition to Bypass**, asking the Wisconsin Supreme Court to take the case directly, bypassing the Court of Appeals. It takes a vote of at least four justices to take a case on Petition to Bypass.

An individual, group, corporation, or entity may bring a civil case, and the government may commence a criminal case, in the **Circuit Court.** After the proceedings, the circuit court will rule in favor of one party. There are 241 circuit courts in Wisconsin.

An individual or government entity may ask the Wisconsin Supreme Court to take **Original Action** in a case. This means that the case has not been heard by any other court. Because the Supreme Court is not a fact-finding tribunal, both parties in the case must agree on the facts.

authoritative determination. The court does not accept a case on original jurisdiction solely to expedite the judicial process, for the convenience of the parties, or to prevent multiple lawsuits. In recent years, the Supreme Court has exercised its original jurisdiction to determine whether the governor's use of the partial veto was constitutional, to determine whether changes to the Wisconsin Retirement System were constitutional, and whether Indian gaming agreements signed by the governor and Indian tribes were constitutional. (For the latter, see the description of *Panzer v. Doyle* in the *Summary of Significant Decisions* section of this book.)

Petitioning for review

A person seeking Supreme Court review must file a petition with the court stating the issues presented for review and providing reasons why the court should accept the case. The opposing party may file a response to the petition, but is generally not required to, except the court may require the opponent to respond to a petition for original jurisdiction. The court grants petitions to review a Court of Appeals decision by a vote of three justices. Four justices must consent for the court to accept a case on bypass or certification or to accept an original action.

Once the Supreme Court accepts a case, it generally establishes a schedule for parties to submit briefs. Like the Court of Appeals, the Supreme Court may limit the issues that it will decide. Parties write new briefs for the Supreme Court specific to the issues that the Supreme Court agrees to review. People who are not parties to the case may also request permission to file a brief, called an amicus curiae or "friend of the court" brief. In a case

The Consumer Law Litigation Clinic of the University of Wisconsin Law School filed an amicus curiae brief with the Supreme Court in *Garcia v. Mazda Motor of America*, supporting Garcia's argument that her request for a replacement vehicle adequately invoked the Wisconsin Lemon Law.

IN THE SUPREME COURT OF WISCONSIN

ADELE R. GARCIA,
   Plaintiff-Appellant-Cross-Respondent, Petitioner,

v.

Appeal No. 02-2260
Cir. Ct. No. 01-CV-2812

MAZDA MOTOR OF AMERICA, INC.,
a foreign corporation,
HALL IMPORTS, INC.,
a Wisconsin Corporation,
   Defendants-Respondents-Cross Appellants.

BRIEF AMICUS CURIAE IN SUPPORT OF PLAINTIFF-APPELLANT-CROSS RESPONDENT, PETITIONER SUBMITTED BY CONSUMER LAW LITIGATION CLINIC, UNIVERSITY OF WISCONSIN LAW SCHOOL

Judge Lee S. Dreyfus
Waukesha County Circuit Court
Case No. 01-CV-2812
Appeal No. 02-2260

Submitted by:

STEPHEN E. MEILI
State Bar ID No. 1018029
MARSHA M. MANSFIELD
State Bar ID No. 1006604
NELLE R. ROHLICH, Law Student

Consumer Law Litigation Clinic
University of Wisconsin Law School
975 Bascom Mall
Madison, WI 53706
(608) 263-6283

accepted on original jurisdiction, the court may also require the parties to submit stipulations of the relevant facts, because the Supreme Court does not decide facts. If necessary, the Supreme Court may refer a case to the circuit court for the limited purpose of determining the relevant facts.

The court generally hears oral arguments, but may choose to forgo oral argument if it appears that oral argument will not be sufficiently informative to justify expending the court's time and resources of the parties. If a party desires oral argument, the court will likely hear argument. Cases are assigned to a calendar for argument after the last brief is filed.

The Supreme Court seal embellishes the ceiling of the court's private conference room in the State Capitol.

(Kathleen Sitter, LRB)

The seal of the Supreme Court of Wisconsin is rich in symbolism. It shows a scale of justice, but it is not held by the blindfolded Greek goddess Themis, but by a human hand and arm. Thus, it recognizes that justice is in human hands. Above the scale is the ancient symbol of the all-seeing eye of deity. The seal was created sometime after August 12, 1848, when a joint resolution of the legislature provided that Edward H. Rudd be employed to engrave "a great seal for the state of Wisconsin and seals for the circuit courts and judges of probate of the several counties and supreme court of the state."

The Supreme Court in session

The court is in session from September through June. Before oral arguments, the justices meet in conference to discuss the cases to be heard. Each justice is randomly assigned to lead the discussion on several of the cases. In preargument conference, the justices identify issues that have not been adequately addressed in the briefs, determine what the attorneys should address during argument, and plan questions for the attorneys.

Oral arguments are a formal affair held once a month in the Supreme Court Chamber in the State Capitol. The petitioner and respondent are each given 30 minutes to speak (25 minutes for presentation and five minutes for rebuttal). The attorneys in the case speak from a podium facing the justices. Colored lights on the podium signal the attorney when to speak and stop. A green light signals an attorney

Attorneys arguing before the Wisconsin Supreme Court are held to stringent time limits that are tracked by the Supreme Court marshal (seated below). The attorney podium is equipped with red, yellow, and green lights to ensure that each side takes only its allotted 30 minutes. The yellow light is illuminated as a five-minute warning, and when the red light comes on, the attorney is expected to stop speaking.

(Kathleen Sitter, LRB)

to begin speaking. A yellow light is a five-minute warning. When the time expires, the marshal activates a red light, and the attorney must stop speaking. At any time during an attorney's presentation, the justices may, and usually do, interrupt with questions. All oral argument is open to the public and the schedules are posted on the court system Web site at *www.wicourts.gov.*

After an oral argument the justices meet again to take a preliminary vote. Once the justices make a decision in a case, one member of the majority is assigned at random to write the court's opinion. If the justice is not in the majority, another justice is chosen by lot. Law clerks for the justices generally write in-depth analyses of cases to prepare the justices to write and review opinions. The justice who writes the opinion circulates a draft to the other justices and then they meet to discuss it. Before meeting, other justices may submit comments on the draft opinion to the author. Any justice may also write a concurring or dissenting opinion. When the opinion and any concurring or dissenting opinions are completed, the court issues the decision. All Supreme Court opinions are published.

The seven justices convene in closed conference before and after oral argument to discuss the cases on the daily docket. The chief justice sits at the head of the table while justice number seven – the least senior justice – sits closest to the door. By tradition, the newest justice is the court's "gopher" during these conferences.

(Kathleen Sitter, LRB)

Administrative and regulatory authority

Under its administrative and supervisory authority, the Supreme Court makes rules governing pleading and practice, administration of the court system, and the practice of law.

Unlike the U.S. Supreme Court, where the chief justice handpicks the author for the majority opinion, the state Supreme Court chooses authors at random with the help of seven poker chips. The chips are blank on one side, and adorned with smiling faces and numbers one through seven on the other side. When the time comes to select an author for the majority opinion, the chief justice sets out the chips face-down and then the second most senior justice scrambles them and selects one. If the number corresponds to a justice in the majority, that justice will draft the opinion. If the number corresponds to a justice who plans to dissent, another chip is drawn.

(Kathleen Sitter, LRB)

The rules governing pleading, practice, and procedure in courts are incorporated in the state statutes. Generally, only the legislature may amend the statutes. However, because the state constitution grants the Supreme Court supervisory authority over the court system, the Supreme Court may by rule enact, amend, or repeal those portions of the statutes governing court practice. The

"Your job is to look at both sides and to listen to the advocacy on both sides, and then to come to a decision. A lot of times you can read the first set of briefs and you think, 'Well, boy, this certainly looks pretty simple. This case is going this way.' Then you read the second set of briefs, and you realize that, well, that isn't the way it ought to be going at all. And it's the same thing in oral argument. You have got to just be very careful that you are listening and reading both sides of every issue."
– Former Chief Justice Roland B. Day

legislature may also amend the pleading, practice, and procedure sections of the statutes, but should the legislature and court disagree on a provision concerning pleading, practice, or court procedure, the Supreme Court would have the final say.

Judicial Council

The Supreme Court receives advice on pleading, practice, and procedure from the Judicial Council. The Judicial Council is an independent body and can have significant influence on court activities. Its 21 members include a Supreme Court justice, a Court of Appeals judge, circuit and municipal court judges, the director of state courts, legislators, the attorney general, the deans of the University of Wisconsin and Marquette law schools, the state public defender, a district attorney, several representatives of the State Bar, and several citizen members. The council was created in part to give momentum to court reorganization efforts after reorganization legislation failed in the 1948 Legislature. The new council did in fact help usher through the court reorganization legislation of 1959.

The council's current charge is to advise the Supreme Court and the legislature on court jurisdiction, organization, and administration as well as pleading, practice, and procedure. The council studies issues at the request of the Supreme Court or the legislature, and also selects areas of study on its own. Examples of recent issues that the council has handled include clarification of the rules to be followed in small claims cases and standards for determining who may participate in an appellate case as an amicus curiae. The council may propose rule changes to the Supreme Court or bills to the legislature, and may also issue reports. The council has been less active in the last decade than in prior years, largely because its staff was eliminated in the 1995 biennial budget act. Since then, the council has been supported by the staff for the Judicial Commission, an agency primarily concerned with judicial discipline, which is discussed later in this article.

Attorney Marla J. Stephens of the State Public Defender's Office (left of the flag) chairs a meeting of the Judicial Council at the State Capitol.

(Kathleen Sitter, LRB)

The remainder of the Supreme Court rules are published as an appendix to the state statutes, but are solely a creation of the court and may not be affected by the legislature. The rules contain codes of professional conduct and ethics for attorneys and judges, provisions governing the use of jurors, requirements for training and education for attorneys and judges, and operating procedures for the courts. Recently, the Supreme Court has addressed several contentious issues by rule. In 2005, the court issued rules governing the conduct of judges and judge-candidates in judicial elections after several years of study, and also issued a rule imposing a $50 fee on attorneys to fund legal representation for low-income litigants in civil cases.

The Supreme Court is also responsible for activities that any head of an agency must perform. The Supreme Court justices must oversee a budget, develop long-term policy goals, and develop procedures for everyday activities. The director of state courts and his staff carry out these activities under the guidance of the Supreme Court.

Funding the Court System

 The Wisconsin court system is funded through a combination of state and county tax revenues, user fees, and grants. The Supreme Court and Court of Appeals are funded exclusively with state tax dollars, while the circuit court is supported in part by counties. Wisconsin's 72 counties are responsible for the cost of circuit court services not covered by the state. The state pays the salaries, fringe benefits, and travel expenses of judges and reserve judges (retired judges who hear cases when the need arises) and their court reporters. The counties pick up the remaining costs associated with circuit court operation – maintaining the courthouse, operating the Office of the Clerk of Circuit Court, ensuring that the building is safe and secure, providing videoconferencing, legal research tools, office supplies and equipment, funding the costs of court-appointed attorneys (other than attorneys from the Office of the State Public Defender) and witnesses, court-ordered medical and psychological exams, court interpreters, jurors, and more.

Like other organizations, the Wisconsin court system's major expenditures are for personnel. Nearly 70 percent of the courts' expenses are related to salaries and fringe benefits for the seven Supreme Court justices, 16 Court of Appeals judges, and 241 circuit court judges whose salaries, as set by the legislature, were as follows for 2004-2005:

Supreme Court Chief Justice	$131,877
Supreme Court Justice	$123,877
Court of Appeals Judge	$116,865
Circuit Court Judge	$110,250

Currently, the state makes payments to counties to cover some of the counties' court operating costs. In 2003, counties reported a total of $156.7 million in court costs; $24.1 million of this was offset through the state's financial assistance programs to counties, which include the circuit court support payment program, the guardian *ad litem* payment program, which provides reimbursement to counties for the cost of lawyers who are court-appointed to represent the best interests of children involved in legal disputes, and the interpreter services reimbursement program.

In the 2003-2004 state fiscal year, the Wisconsin court system spent $111,060,974. The court system's expenditures by program area are illustrated in Figure 1.

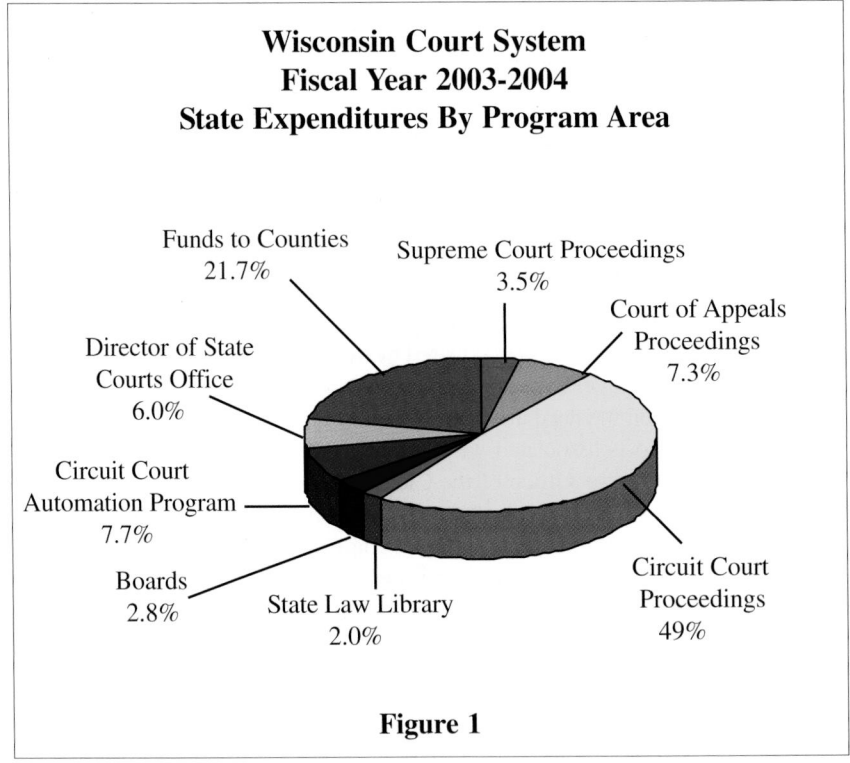

Wisconsin Court System
Fiscal Year 2003-2004
State Expenditures By Program Area

Funds to Counties 21.7%
Supreme Court Proceedings 3.5%
Court of Appeals Proceedings 7.3%
Director of State Courts Office 6.0%
Circuit Court Automation Program 7.7%
Boards 2.8%
State Law Library 2.0%
Circuit Court Proceedings 49%

Figure 1

As shown in Figure 2 (opposite page), the court system receives money from a variety of sources:
- general purpose revenue (state tax dollars), 87.8 percent;
- program revenue (fees or assessments), 11.9 percent; and
- other sources, 0.3 percent.

State tax dollars account for $97.5 million of the court system's budget. This is less than one percent of the total state tax dollars expended for all of state government.

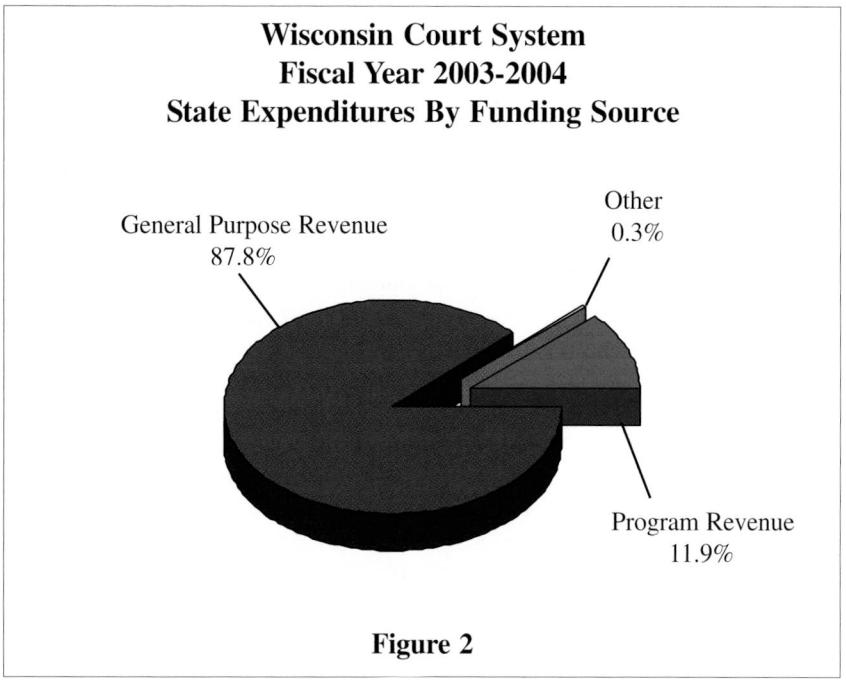

**Wisconsin Court System
Fiscal Year 2003-2004
State Expenditures By Funding Source**

General Purpose Revenue
87.8%

Other
0.3%

Program Revenue
11.9%

Figure 2

Several of the court system's programs use nontax funds to support their operations. For example, the Consolidated Court Automation Programs (CCAP) – the courts' computer system – is funded with fees that the courts collect each time a lawsuit is filed; the Office of Lawyer Regulation, the arm of the Supreme Court that regulates the practice of law and investigates and prosecutes complaints against attorneys, is funded with assessments on attorneys; the Board of Bar Examiners is funded with assessments on attorneys; and the Medical Mediation Panels, which provide mediation as a first step toward resolving medical malpractice claims, are funded from assessments on health care providers.

Other Courts Operating in Wisconsin

In addition to the state courts, several other courts have jurisdiction to operate in Wisconsin. Cities, towns, and villages may create municipal courts to hear ordinance violations. Although municipal courts are not state courts, they are connected to the state court system; all municipal court decisions may be appealed to the state courts, and the Wisconsin Supreme Court has supervisory jurisdiction over municipal judges. Unlike the municipal courts, federal courts and tribal courts are completely independent from the state court system. However, as described below, the federal, state, and tribal courts sometimes have overlapping jurisdiction.

Municipal courts

Wisconsin law allows municipalities (cities, towns, and villages) to establish trial courts to hear ordinance violations. If a municipality establishes a court, the court has exclusive jurisdiction over ordinance violations, which may include traffic, parking, first offense operating while intoxicated, truancy, minor drug possession, disorderly conduct, or animal control cases, among others. Ordinance violations are heard in circuit court if a municipality does not have a municipal court. At this writing, Wisconsin has 226 municipal courts, 13 of which serve more than one municipality. The state's only full-time municipal courts operate in Madison and Milwaukee. Municipal courts handle about 500,000 cases a year, which would otherwise flow through the circuit courts.

Most municipal court cases are begun with a citation, though they may also be initiated by summons and complaint as in circuit court. A defendant may simply pay the amount included on the citation and dispose of the case without appearing in court. Alternatively, the defendant may appear in court and either plead guilty or no contest or may plead not guilty and go to trial.

A trial in municipal court is before a judge. There is no right to a jury in municipal court. There is also no right to discovery. The rules of evidence do apply to municipal court trials. The standard of proof in a municipal court trial is by evidence that is clear, satisfactory, and convincing. Municipal courts may impose forfeitures (monetary fines) as penalties and order a defendant to pay restitution and court fees. If a defendant does not pay the forfeiture, restitution, or fees, the court may suspend the defendant's driving privileges. All municipal court judgments may be appealed to circuit court. Upon appeal, either party may request a jury trial. If neither party requests a new trial, the circuit court reviews the case on the basis of the written municipal court transcript.

Municipals judges are elected. Their terms may be two, three, or four years, as determined by the municipality. Unlike circuit and appeals court judges and Supreme Court justices, municipal court judges need not be licensed attorneys, although about half of them are. Municipal judges are governed by the Judicial Code of Conduct and are required to participate in continuing education programs. The salaries of municipal judges are set and paid by the municipality. Most municipal judgeships are not full-time positions.

Federal courts

The primary function of federal courts is to decide cases involving federal law, including the U.S. Constitution, federal statutes, and U.S. treaties. Federal courts also have jurisdiction over actions by a state against the citizens of another state, and the U.S. Supreme Court has exclusive jurisdiction over actions between states. Federal courts have authority to hear diversity of citizenship cases, which are cases involving citizens of different states, in which the amount in controversy is at least $75,000. Finally, the federal courts have jurisdiction over cases brought by an agency or officer of the U.S. government and cases affecting ambassadors or other public officials.

The grand atrium of the Milwaukee Federal Building and U.S. Courthouse, seat of the U.S. District Court for the Eastern District of Wisconsin, originally served as a post office workroom.

(Kathleen Sitter, LRB)

The federal courts are the final arbiters of federal law, and the state courts are the final arbiters of state law. However, cases frequently involve matters of both federal and state law, so federal courts routinely decide questions of state law and vice versa. When a federal court interprets state law, it follows state court readings of the law. Similarly, state courts follow federal court interpretations of federal law, and federal courts have authority to review state court interpretations of federal law. For example, in 1987, the Wisconsin Legislature adopted a hate crimes statute which increased the penalty for a crime if the defendant selected the victim in whole or in part because of the victim's race, religion, color, disability, sexual orientation, national origin, or ancestry. The Wisconsin Supreme Court found that the hate crimes statute violated the First Amendment to the U.S. Constitution. Because the Wisconsin decision was based on federal law, the U.S. Supreme Court had authority to review it. The U.S. Supreme Court in *State v. Mitchell* reversed the holding of the Wisconsin Supreme Court, allowing the Wisconsin hate crimes statute to stand.

The structure of the federal court system is similar to the structure of Wisconsin's state court system. The federal court system consists of trial courts, intermediate appellate courts, and a supreme court. The U.S. has 94 general trial courts, called district courts, two of which serve Wisconsin. The U.S. district court for the western district of Wisconsin is located in Madison. The U.S. district court for the eastern district of Wisconsin sits in Milwaukee and Green Bay. There are 12 federal appellate court circuits. The 7th circuit of the U.S. Court of Appeals serves Wisconsin, Illinois, and Indiana and is located in Chicago. As under the state court system, cases are generally initiated in district court, may be appealed to the circuit court of appeals, and ultimately may be appealed to the U.S. Supreme Court.

The Milwaukee Federal Building and U.S. Courthouse was completed in 1899. The judges of the U.S. District Court for the Eastern District of Wisconsin chose to keep the court in this building rather than moving to the new Henry S. Reuss Federal Plaza in 1983.

(Kathleen Sitter, LRB)

Tribal courts

Federally recognized Indian tribes are sovereign entities that have authority to govern the activities of Indians on tribal lands. As sovereigns, tribes may establish courts. Eleven federally recognized Indian tribes have land in Wisconsin, and each has established a court system. Tribal court jurisdiction is limited to deciding cases involving Indians or activities that take place on tribal lands. Tribal courts do not necessarily handle all the types of cases for which they have jurisdiction. The areas of law that tribal courts in Wisconsin commonly handle include child protection, domestic abuse, conservation, and housing.

Each of the tribes also determines the structure of its court system. All the tribes have a trial court. Appeals are handled in a variety of ways. Several of the tribes have their own supreme courts, including the Ho-Chunk and the Menominee. Others allow appeals to 3-judge panels consisting of judges from other tribes or from the tribal judges association. The Lac Courte Oreilles tribe allows appeals to the Tribal Governing Board. Tribes also use alternative dispute resolution processes such as youth courts and the Stockbridge-Munsee peacemaker system, under which trained community members help people resolve differences without court action.

The state and federal courts share with the tribal courts jurisdiction to decide cases involving Indians and events that occur on tribal lands. In 1953, the U.S. Congress passed legislation (Public Law 280) that granted six states broad civil and criminal jurisdiction over tribal lands. Wisconsin is one of the six states.

However, Public Law 280 does not apply to the Menominee reservation, so jurisdiction over the Menominee reservation is different from other Indian reservations in Wisconsin.

On tribal lands other than the Menominee reservation, state courts have broad criminal and civil jurisdiction. State criminal law applies on these tribal lands and may be enforced in state courts. However, tribal courts also have authority to act on violations of tribal criminal codes that take place on tribal lands. Jurisdiction over many types of civil claims is shared by the state and tribal courts, allowing a party to bring a case in either state or tribal court.

Judge Charles Cloud, a retired state court judge who has been selected to chair the Tribal Courts Council, a new committee of the American Bar Association Judicial Division, addresses the first meeting of the organizers for the inaugural national symposium on federal-state-tribal court relations. The planning group includes judges, lawyers, and court administrators from the three court systems; experts from Fox Valley Technical College's Criminal Justice Center for Innovation; and representatives of the U.S. Department of Justice, the National Center for State Courts, the National Judicial College, and the National Conference of Chief Justices. (Kathleen Sitter, LRB)

Allocating jurisdiction between state and tribal courts

Disagreements over which court system has jurisdiction in a case are not uncommon, and may result in hearings held in both the state and tribal courts on the same issues, leading to confusion and inefficiency. Several years ago, one such case was appealed to the Wisconsin Supreme Court – twice – giving the court an opportunity to offer guidance to the lower courts on allocating jurisdiction. The case, called *Teague v. Lake Superior Tribe of Chippewa,* involved a man named Jerry Teague who, between 1993 and 1995, managed the Bad River Casino, a business located on the Bad River Indian Reservation owned and operated by the Chippewa tribe. In 1996, after being terminated from his employment, Teague sued the tribe in Ashland County Circuit Court (the state court) on the ground that the tribe had breached its contract with him. The tribe moved to dismiss the lawsuit, arguing that it was a government entity acting under its constitution when it employed Teague and therefore was immune from being sued in state court in this matter. The judge denied the motion.

*The mural on the south wall of the Supreme Court depicts an early court proceeding
in Wisconsin history: the 1830 murder trial of Menominee Chief Oshkosh. This
early interaction of Indian law and courts established under the United States is
increasingly relevant as today's courts deal with issues of tribal sovereignty.*

(Kathleen Sitter, LRB)

Shortly after the state court denied the motion to dismiss, the tribe started a case
against Teague in tribal court. Each court was aware of the proceeding in the other
court, but the two did not communicate. They reached opposite results, with the
tribal court finding in favor of the tribe and the state court (following a jury trial)
finding for Teague. Both Teague and the tribe appealed, both seeking to enforce the
judgment in their favor.

The Supreme Court heard this case twice. The first time, the Supreme Court
criticized the "first-to-judgment" approach that the Court of Appeals had applied
to determine which verdict would stand. The Supreme Court said a decision should
not be based simply on which court issued a judgment first, but rather should be
reached through application of the doctrine of comity, which emphasizes recognition,
acceptance, and respect for differences in process. The court explained that the
lower courts should have applied comity early in the process to aid cooperation,
communication, and understanding between the two systems. The court then ordered,
on a 5-2 vote, that the circuit court case be dismissed and that the tribal court
judgment be given full faith and credit.

The spirit of cooperation, rather than competition, that the Supreme Court
emphasized in its decision is at the center of two initiatives currently underway in
Wisconsin. These initiatives both involve the development of protocols to guide
the state and tribal courts in deciding which court should handle any given case.
The first initiative was begun in the Tenth Judicial District, which is headquartered

in Eau Claire and covers 13 northwest Wisconsin counties. Representatives from the four Chippewa tribes in northern Wisconsin joined the chief judge of the Tenth Judicial District in December 2001 to sign and officially implement a new system – believed to be the first of its kind in the nation – for handling court cases in which the tribal and state courts share jurisdiction. The second initiative involves the implementation of similar protocols in the Ninth Judicial District, which is headquartered in Wausau and covers 12 counties in northcentral Wisconsin.

Under these protocols, state and tribal judges will temporarily stop actions that are filed in both courts and hold a joint hearing to determine which court should handle the case. If the judges cannot agree, a third judge will be summoned from a pool of state and tribal judges and the arguments will be reheard until a decision on jurisdiction is reached.

Judges

The judicial power of the courts rests in the hands of Wisconsin's 264 state judges and justices: 241 circuit court judges, 16 Court of Appeals judges, and seven Supreme Court justices. All are elected. In addition there are over 200 municipal judges in Wisconsin who generally serve in that capacity part-time. This section primarily pertains to state judges and justices.

Judicial selection

The legal requirements for becoming a judge or justice are few. A judge or justice must be a resident of the jurisdiction in which he or she serves and must have been licensed as an attorney in Wisconsin for the five years preceding election or appointment to judicial office. Once in judicial office, a judge or justice may not hold or campaign for any nonjudicial public office during the term for which he or she was elected or appointed, even if he or she resigns from judicial office.

Wisconsin used to have a mandatory retirement age for judges and justices. From 1955 to 1978, judges and justices had to retire at age 70. Since 1977, the Wisconsin Constitution has authorized the legislature to impose a maximum age of no less than 70, but the legislature has not done so.

Many of the requirements of state judges also apply to municipal judges, but others do not. Unlike state court judges, municipal judges need not be lawyers.

Judicial Selection Methods

A majority of states choose some or all of their judges by election. Thirteen of the states that elect their judges, including Wisconsin, hold nonpartisan elections. Others hold partisan elections for at least some of their judges. States that do not elect judges use systems that start with appointment and, with the exception of a handful, require the appointee to stand for a retention election in which there is no opponent. Appointive systems are often called "merit" systems. Most merit systems involve a permanent, nonpartisan commission that recruits, screens, and forwards prospective judges to the governor who fills vacancies from the list. In some merit systems, the governor or legislature has exclusive authority to make appointments.

Proponents of merit systems argue that they result in a better qualified and more independent judiciary. They further argue that judicial campaigns provide voters insufficient information about the candidates and that the rigors of campaigning and the need to raise campaign funds deter qualified people from running for judge, and take too much time away from a judge's official duties. Proponents of electing judges, on the other hand, argue that an appointive system is just as political because the judges are beholden to the executive who appointed them. Further, appointive systems do not result in a judiciary that is representative of the people of the state. Finally, elections are seen as providing legitimacy to the courts, placing them on a equal footing with the executive and legislative branches, whose members are also elected.

Terms of office

Judges on the circuit court and Court of Appeals serve 6-year terms and Supreme Court justices enjoy the longest term of any state elected official – 10 years. The terms are long in order to shield judges and justices from the winds of politics, to ensure that decisions are based upon the facts and the law, and are not swayed by popular opinion or political pressures. To further separate the nonpartisan judiciary from the other branches of government, judicial elections are held in the spring, and judicial terms begin on August 1. If a judge or justice resigns during his or her term, the governor appoints a replacement to serve until a successor may be elected.

About half of the judges currently sitting in Wisconsin initially obtained judicial office by appointment. Since the terms of judges and justices are relatively long, it is not uncommon for incumbents to leave during a term, affording the governor the opportunity to appoint a replacement. Four of the justices sitting on the Supreme Court as of this writing, Chief Justice Shirley S. Abrahamson and Justices Jon P. Wilcox, David Prosser, Jr., and Louis B. Butler, Jr., were

Judge Gerald C. Nichol served as a circuit court judge in Dane County for 16 years. He is now a reserve judge who fills in for active judges in different counties, which is a critical part of the court system and is especially vital to the small, rural counties that have only one judge. (Kathleen Sitter, LRB)

initially appointed to their positions. (Chief Justice Abrahamson and Justices Wilcox and Prosser subsequently won election to the court; Justice Butler will stand for election in 2008, the first year in which no other justice is running.) All told, six of the 14 justices who most recently joined the Supreme Court were initially appointed. On the Court of Appeals, six of the 16 current judges initially obtained office by appointment.

Three of the seven Supreme Court Justices, Ann Walsh Bradley, David T. Prosser, and Louis B. Butler, Jr. hear oral argument in a case before the Court. The justices sit according to seniority, with the most senior seated at the center of the bench. Justice Butler, the most junior member of the Court, poses a question to counsel for one of the parties. (Kathleen Sitter, LRB)

The length of an appointee's term is largely determined by luck. One appointee may serve for only a few months before he or she must run for election, while another may serve for several years before facing an election. To minimize the disruption to a court's business that may occur when justices or judges are running campaigns, the state constitution provides that only one Supreme Court justice may be elected in a year and only one Court of Appeals judge may be elected per Court of Appeals district in a year. This means that if the terms of other judges or justices on a court expire in the years immediately following an appointment, the appointee may have the opportunity to serve for several years without an election. For example, Governor Jim Doyle appointed Justice Butler to the Supreme Court in 2004 to succeed Justice Diane S. Sykes. The election to a new 10-year term for the seat currently held by Justice Butler will not be held until 2008 because the terms of three sitting justices are expiring, one each year, in 2005 (Justice Ann Walsh Bradley), 2006 (Justice N. Patrick Crooks), and 2007 (Justice Jon P. Wilcox). By contrast, Justice Sykes was appointed to the Supreme Court in 1999 and had to run for election in 2000.

Judicial campaigns

Judges and justices must be impartial. The impartiality requirement is difficult to reconcile with the demands of campaigning and persuading voters. To maintain impartiality, judges and candidates for judicial office are prohibited by the Code of Judicial Conduct from making a promise or commitment on any case, controversy, or issue that may come before the judge or judicial candidate if elected. Since the cases a court must decide may involve almost any political issue, such as sentencing of criminals or limitations on damages in personal injury cases, a judicial candidate may not take a public position on these issues. However, voters want to hear a candidate's views on these issues precisely because the courts do make decisions on them. How much a judicial candidate may say regarding political issues is an evolving discussion nationally. In 2002, the U.S. Supreme Court found in the case of *Republican Party of Minnesota v. White* that Minnesota's law prohibiting a judicial candidate from announcing his or her views on disputed legal or political issues violates the First Amendment right to free speech. While Wisconsin judges and judicial candidates are not subject to the same "announce" clause as Minnesota judges, they are prohibited from making promises. The U.S. Supreme Court did not address whether a rule barring candidates from promising how they would rule in specific cases violates the First Amendment.

What may a judge or judicial candidate discuss in a campaign? His or her experience, education, work ethic, and views on administrative and procedural issues concerning the judiciary are appropriate topics. A candidate also may obtain endorsements from interest groups. Given the limits on a candidate's discussion of political issues, the endorsements of interest groups may hold greater weight in judicial campaigns than in campaigns for other offices.

Judicial campaign activity is further restricted by the nonpartisan nature of the Wisconsin judiciary. Since statehood, Wisconsin has had an elected judiciary, but judges were not initially banned from participating in partisan activities. In fact, the political parties participated in nominating judicial candidates. Now, however, the Judicial Code of Conduct explicitly prohibits judges and candidates for judicial office from membership in a political party. Judges and candidates may not participate in party caucuses, writing party platforms, or other activities of a party. (The Judicial Code of Conduct does allow people who run for a judicial seat while holding a partisan office, such as legislators, to maintain party membership for the duration of the judicial campaign.)

The requirement for judicial impartiality also affects fundraising by judicial candidates. A candidate for judicial office may not solicit or accept campaign contributions directly from any person. Instead, a judge or judicial candidate must establish a campaign committee for this purpose. This rule is intended to limit any perceived pressure on people to contribute to a judicial campaign out of fear that a judge will rule against their interests if they do not make a contribution. Some have suggested that attorneys be banned from making political contributions since they arguably have much at stake in judicial selections. However, attorneys are also generally among those most informed about the qualifications of judicial candidates. Under current rules, lawyers may make contributions.

As is true for all elected offices, the reelection rate for incumbent judges and justices is high. An incumbent Supreme Court justice has not lost a race since 1967. Many judges, particularly on the Court of Appeals and in the circuit courts, run unopposed. Between 1990 and 1998, only 2 of the 26 elections for seats on the Court of Appeals were contested. During the same time, 296 of the 381 circuit court elections were uncontested. Of the 282 incumbent circuit court judges who ran for reelection, only 43 faced opposition.[4]

Interpreting statutes

Judges interpret several sources of law. They interpret statutes, the U.S. and Wisconsin Constitutions, and opinions written by higher courts. Wisconsin courts must follow the opinions of the Supreme Court when interpreting the U.S.

```
                III. WISCONSIN'S LEMON LAW

¶7. The issue in this case, whether Garcia's written demand for a
replacement vehicle under the Wisconsin Lemon Law complied with the
notice requirements of Wis. Stat. § 218.0171(2)(c), presents us with
a question of statutory interpretation. Statutory interpretation and
the application of a statute to specific facts are questions of law
that we review de novo. In re Commitment of Franklin, 2004 WI 38, ¶5,
___ Wis. 2d ___, 677 N.W.2d 276.

¶8. We begin the process of statutory interpretation by analyzing the
language of the statute. State ex rel. Kalal v. Circuit Court for
Dane County, 2004 WI 58, ¶¶44-45, ___ Wis. 2d ___, ___ N.W.2d ___. As
we have repeatedly stated, we construe remedial, consumer protection
statutes like the Wisconsin Lemon Law "with a view towards the social
problem which the legislature was addressing when enacting the law."
Dieter v. Chrysler Corp., 2000 WI 45, ¶19, 234 Wis. 2d 670, 610
N.W.2d 832 (citing Hughes v. Chrysler Motors Corp., 197 Wis. 2d 973,
982, 542 N.W.2d 148 (1996)). Put another way, we will liberally
construe remedial statutes to suppress the mischief and advance the
remedy that the legislature intended to afford. Hughes, 197 Wis. 2d
at 979 (citing Madison v. Hyland, Hall & Co., 73 Wis. 2d 364, 373,
243 N.W.2d 422 (1976)).

¶9. Wisconsin's Lemon Law, Wis. Stat. § 218.0171, became effective on
November 3, 1983. Like similar laws nationwide, the statute was
enacted to protect purchasers of new vehicles that turn out to be
defective (colloquially known as "lemons"). See, e.g., Hughes, 197
Wis. 2d at 978-80. Wisconsin's Lemon Law provides a remedy to the
```

```
                    IV. CONCLUSION

¶20. Our holding today resolves the issue we accepted for review, but
other factual issues remain for trial. We do not address the issues
of whether the parties reached a settlement,[6] whether Garcia's vehicle
actually was a lemon, or whether Mazda complied with the provisions
of the Wisconsin Lemon Law. These are factual issues properly before
the circuit court. Accordingly, we remand the case to the circuit
court for determination of these factual issues.

By the Court.-The decision of the court of appeals is reversed and
the cause is remanded to the circuit court.
```

Justice Prosser interprets the Wisconsin Lemon Law statute in the Supreme Court opinion in *Garcia v. Mazda Motor of America.*

Constitution and federal law. Wisconsin courts follow the Wisconsin Supreme Court in interpreting the Wisconsin Constitution and Wisconsin Statutes. Trial judges in Wisconsin must also follow the opinions of the Court of Appeals.

Although statutes are written to be clear, the legislature cannot always foresee all the different scenarios in which a statute will be applied or how a new law fits in context with other statutes. Further, parties deliberately search for ambiguity in a statute if it benefits their position. So judges are frequently called upon to resolve what a statute means and they apply a variety of historically developed techniques or rules to statutory interpretation.

The predominant method of statutory interpretation used by Wisconsin courts is the "plain meaning rule", under which judges look at the actual words of the statute to determine what it means. An alternative rule is the "mischief rule", under which judges look at what problem the statute was intended to solve and interpret the statute so as to solve the mischief. A third method is the "golden rule", under which judges aim to avoid absurd results. Judges disagree on whether, and to what extent, they should look beyond the text of the statute to determine its meaning, but the majority of the Wisconsin Supreme Court favors the plain meaning approach.

Agreeing on the proper method for interpreting a statute is only the first step. Two judges purporting to give a statute its plain meaning may say that the statute means two different things. There are numerous guides, called canons of interpretation, that judges apply in determining the plain meaning of a statute. Application of different canons often leads to different interpretations, though the canons do at least provide judges a common foundation. For example, one canon dictates that a judge should give effect to every word in a statute. Therefore if the statute calls for a "pattern of misconduct," the statute does not apply to one incident standing alone. A second canon provides that if the same word is used more than once in a statute, it has the same meaning each time it is used, but if a synonym is used, the synonym must have a different meaning. A third canon is that the specific overrides the general, so if there are two relevant statutes, the more specific prevails. Further, the canon *in pari material*, provides that the statutes must be interpreted as a whole and that judges should not interpret a sentence or phrase in isolation.

"Our decisions could not be result oriented, because we were establishing precedent to govern the citizens of this state for a substantial period of time. The rules of law had to be appropriate, not to change the result of any specific trial. No one wants to see a criminal who did a vicious act go free. That is not a desirable result. But when we are writing cases that are designed to protect citizens from unreasonable searches or to preserve the sanctity of the home from government invasion, you may be required to make decisions that have bad results in that case – but the principle of law, that is far more important."
– Former Court of Appeals Judge Gordon Myse

Group portrait of the Wisconsin Supreme Court in 1903, the year in which a constitutional amendment approved expansion of the court from five to seven justices. Seen here (left to right) are Justices Joshua E. Dodge, John B. Winslow, John B. Cassoday, Rouet D. Marshall, and Robert G. Siebecker. The portraits of former justices hang on the wall behind them. (State Historical Society, #WHi-23436)

Those judges who look beyond the text of a statute to interpret its meaning do so to different degrees. Some make this their starting point and others do so only to support an argument grounded in the plain meaning approach. Judges may look at several forms of legislative history to determine what the legislature was trying to accomplish in passing a bill or at least to support their interpretation of what the language of a statute means. In Wisconsin, the legislature maintains a file for each bill that is passed, which contains the instruction from the legislator who conceives the bill to the attorney who writes the text of the bill. The legislature also maintains the procedural history for every bill, which shows how the bill was altered by amendment as well as any failed amendments. Written testimony given at a hearing on the bill may be available, and the legislature's legal staff may have published memoranda describing what a bill does. If the governor partially vetoes a bill, the bill history includes a veto message explaining why, and perhaps explaining what the remaining text of the bill does. Sometimes the legislature passes legislation to change the law because legislators do not like the way the courts have interpreted the law. Court opinions then may become part of legislative history.

Interpreting the Constitution

In addition to interpreting statutes, the courts also interpret the U.S. and Wisconsin Constitutions. A constitution contains many broad principles and fewer specific requirements than statutes. A constitution is intended to stand for long periods of time without change. To amend the Wisconsin Constitution, the legislature must adopt the identical amendment in two successive biennial sessions of the legislature, and then the electorate must approve the amendment by a majority vote. Statutes, on the other hand may be changed as quickly as the two houses of the legislature can pass a bill and send it to the governor for approval. Given that a constitution cannot be frequently changed to adjust the law to societal changes, a constitution is designed to apply to a multitude of possible scenarios. The more general language of the constitutions often allows courts more latitude for interpretation than the statutes.

The Wisconsin Supreme Court has adopted a 3-part framework for interpreting the Wisconsin Constitution. First, the court looks at the plain meaning of the text of the constitution. Second, even if the text is arguably unambiguous, the court analyzes the debates between persons involved in writing the constitution as well as the practices in existence at the time it was written. Third, the court reviews the earliest legislative interpretations of the constitutional provision at issue. The court is much more willing to look at historical indicators of intent when interpreting the constitution than when interpreting the statutes.

Disqualification from a case

The very first decision a judge or justice must make is whether he or she can fairly and impartially hear the case. The Code of Judicial Conduct requires disqualification if presiding in the case presents a conflict of interest. Certain circumstances are presumed to create a conflict of interest, including that the judge or justice is related to a party or attorney, the judge is a party or witness in a case or

has a significant financial or personal interest in the outcome of the case, or that the judge or justice previously served as counsel to a party in the same action or case. If a judge removes him or herself from a case, the judge need not give a reason. Judges often choose to remain silent in this regard, especially when disclosing the reason for disqualification could have an impact on the other justices' ability to be impartial. A judge or justice need not disqualify him or herself if the parties are aware of the conflict and agree that the judge or

Detail of Lafayette County Courthouse window. (Kathleen Sitter, LRB)

justice may preside. If a circuit court or appeals court judge is disqualified, another judge serves in his or her place. If a justice disqualifies him or herself, the remaining members of the Supreme Court decide the case. Of course, disqualification of a justice leaves an even number of justices to decide the case and sometimes this results in a tie vote. In this situation, the lower court ruling stands. If there is no lower court ruling, the status quo prevails.

Discipline

The Code of Judicial Conduct, which is written by the Supreme Court, establishes standards for judges. The code imposes broad requirements such as impartiality and diligence, and specific rules such as a prohibition on unnecessary communication with parties to a case outside the courtroom, and a prohibition on using information learned in one's capacity as a judge for nonjudicial purposes.

Judges and justices are subject to investigation and discipline for misconduct. Misconduct includes violation of the Code of Judicial Conduct, failure to perform official duties, habitual use of alcohol or drugs which interferes with performance of judicial duties, or conviction of a felony.

Allegations of misconduct are investigated by the Judicial Commission. The Judicial Commission is comprised of nine members (one trial judge and one Court of Appeals judge, both appointed by the Supreme Court; two lawyers; and five people who are not lawyers and who are nominated by

Architectural detail, Milwaukee Federal Courthouse. (Kathleen Sitter, LRB)

the governor and appointed with the advice and consent of the senate). The Judicial Commission also investigates allegations that a judge or justice is impaired by a permanent disability from performing his or her official duties. After completing an investigation, the commission dismisses a complaint, resolves it informally, or files a formal action with the Supreme Court. The commission prosecutes complaints of misconduct or petitions of permanent disability before a panel of three Court of Appeals judges or before a jury. The panel or jury determines the facts of the case and makes recommendations for discipline. The Supreme Court reviews the findings and recommendations and determines the discipline. The Supreme Court may remove, reprimand, censure, or suspend a judge.

A judge or justice may also be removed by several other means. The legislature may remove a judge by a two-thirds vote of each house, or a judge or justice may be removed in a recall election.

Reserve judges and court commissioners

In addition to the full-time sitting judges, reserve judges and court commissioners may also perform judicial functions in Wisconsin. Any person who has served as a circuit court judge, Court of Appeals judge, or Supreme Court justice for at least six years may serve as a reserve judge. Reserve judges temporarily sit as circuit court or Court of Appeals judges as needed.

Circuit court judges may delegate a variety of judicial functions to court commissioners. Court commissioners must be attorneys licensed to practice in Wisconsin. Court commissioners may preside over various initial and uncontested proceedings, such as arraignments or preliminary hearings in a criminal case, uncontested probate matters, divorce proceedings, and paternity determinations. Court commissioners may not preside over a trial or jury selection. At the request of any party to an action, a circuit court judge reviews the decision of a court commissioner.

Attorneys

Most people are represented by an attorney when they go to court. Attorneys offer both substantive knowledge of the law and knowledge of court procedure. Attorneys work in a variety of settings. Some work as sole practitioners or as members of a firm. Firms range in size from just a few attorneys to dozens.

Other private sector attorneys work as counsel to a business or organization. Attorneys also work in the public sector. Prosecutors are all government employees and include district attorneys, attorneys employed by the state Department of Justice, and some counsel for counties or municipalities. The Office of the State Public Defender employs attorneys to represent indigent defendants. State agencies and local governments also employ attorneys to provide legal counsel.

About 21,500 people are licensed to practice law in Wisconsin. Almost half work as sole practitioners or for one of Wisconsin's 3,500 firms. Fourteen hundred attorneys work as in-house counsel for a business or organization and about 2,350 work in the public sector. A large proportion, almost 7,000, do not currently practice law, either because they are retired or working in a different

Madison Attorney Janet Kelly performs research at the Wisconsin State Law Library. (Kathleen Sitter, LRB)

profession or in the home. However, attorneys tend to maintain their licenses even if they are not practicing law so that they may have the option of practicing in the future. Of the 21,500, over 6,000 are residents of other states.

Eligibility requirements

The licensing requirements for attorneys are established by the Wisconsin Supreme Court and the licensing process is administered by the Board of Bar Examiners. The board consists of 11 members, all of whom are appointed by the Supreme Court. To obtain a license, an attorney must satisfy a legal competency requirement as well as a character and fitness requirement, and take an oath administered by a Supreme Court justice. Generally, about 700 to 800 attorneys are admitted to the Wisconsin bar each year. Overall, the number of licensed attorneys grows by a couple hundred each year. Twenty-eight percent of bar members in Wisconsin are women; this percentage is expected to rise over the next several decades, because 50 percent of law school graduates are women.

There are three ways to satisfy the legal competency requirement for admission to the bar.

- **Diploma privilege.** Any person who earns a law degree from a law school in Wisconsin (the University of Wisconsin Law School or the Marquette University Law School) satisfies the legal competency requirement. Wisconsin is currently the only state that allows bar membership based on the diploma privilege.

- **Bar exam.** A person may satisfy the competency requirement by passing the bar examination administered by the Board of Bar Examiners. The examination consists of the Multistate Bar Examination, which is given in all states, and an essay examination developed by the lawyer members of the Board of Bar Examiners. In order to take the bar examination, a person must have graduated from an American Bar Association-approved law school. About 75 percent of examination takers pass the examination.

- **Reciprocity.** An attorney who has practiced in another state for three of the preceding five years satisfies the competency requirement if the state in which the attorney is licensed accepts Wisconsin credentials as proof of competency to practice in that state. Wisconsin does not grant reciprocity to states that do not accept the Wisconsin diploma privilege as proof of competency.

All applicants for the Wisconsin bar must also establish that they are of good moral character and are fit to practice law. Reasons for denial of bar membership based on character or fitness include unlawful conduct, disciplinary action related to the practice of law, dishonesty, academic misconduct, or failure to pay child support. Applicants must report information relevant to character and fitness and provide references willing to vouch for the applicant. Every year several applicants who satisfy the competency requirement are denied bar admission on the basis of character and fitness.

One of the duties of the Wisconsin Supreme Court is to swear in new attorneys. Graduates of the law schools at Marquette and the UW take the oath in group ceremonies, and other new lawyers are sworn in by individual justices in small groups throughout the year. (Kathleen Sitter, LRB)

Attorney Oath

I will support the constitution of the United States and the constitution of the state of Wisconsin;

I will maintain the respect due to courts of justice and judicial officers;

I will not counsel or maintain any suit or proceeding which shall appear to me to be unjust, or any defense, except such as I believe to be honestly debatable under the law of the land;

I will employ, for the purpose of maintaining the causes confided to me, such means only as are consistent with truth and honor, and will never seek to mislead the judge or jury by any artifice or false statement of fact or law;

I will maintain the confidence and preserve inviolate the secrets of my client and will accept no compensation in connection with my client's business except from my client or with my client's knowledge and approval;

I will abstain from all offensive personality and advance no fact prejudicial to the honor or reputation of a party or witness, unless required by the justice of the cause with which I am charged;

I will never reject, from any consideration personal to myself, the cause of the defenseless or oppressed, or delay any person's cause for lucre or malice.

So help me God.

State Bar of Wisconsin

Every licensed attorney in Wisconsin must be a dues-paying member of the State Bar of Wisconsin. The State Bar provides continuing legal education courses, hosts education programs for the public and schools, staffs an attorney referral and information service, and lobbies. Today, the Supreme Court is in charge of the organization and governance of the State Bar, but the State Bar was initially founded in 1878 as an independent association of attorneys.

The Supreme Court did not make State Bar membership a requirement for attorneys until 1956. Since then, Wisconsin attorneys have twice challenged the mandatory bar membership requirement as a violation of the First Amendment. The U.S. Supreme Court resolved the first challenge in favor of mandatory bar membership in 1961 (*Lathrop v. Donohue*). The second round went to Wisconsin attorney Steven Levine, who persuaded a federal district court in 1988 that mandatory bar memberships did violate the First Amendment (*Levine v. Supreme Court of Wisconsin*). The Wisconsin Supreme Court temporarily suspended mandatory bar membership in response to the district court ruling. However, the U.S. Supreme Court again upheld mandatory bar membership in 1990 in response to a challenge in California, but did find that a state may not require attorneys to pay dues to support a bar association's political activities (*Keller v. State Bar of California*). The Wisconsin Supreme Court reinstituted mandatory bar membership in 1992, but now attorneys may deduct from their dues the amount used to support political activities of the State Bar. Steven Levine, the Wisconsin attorney who successfully challenged mandatory bar membership in 1988, was elected in 2005 to serve as president-elect of the State Bar starting in July 2005, and then as president for a year starting in July of 2006.

Regulation of attorneys

The Supreme Court is in charge of regulating attorneys. The court may discipline an attorney for misconduct or prohibit an attorney who is medically incapacitated from practicing law. Misconduct includes a violation of the rules of professional conduct for attorneys, a criminal act, dishonesty, fraud, misrepresentation, violation of a Supreme Court rule, and violation of the attorney's oath.

The Supreme Court established the Office of Lawyer Regulation (OLR) to investigate and prosecute cases of attorney misconduct and medical incapacity. OLR may file complaints of misconduct or incapacity with the court. A court-appointed attorney or reserve judge called a referee conducts a hearing on the complaint and recommends a determination, and if applicable, sanctions to the court. The court determines whether and how to discipline the attorney. The court may revoke or suspend an attorney's license, publicly or privately reprimand an attorney, impose monetary sanctions, or impose conditions on the attorney's practice of law. At the attorney's request, the court holds a hearing on the referee's report. The Supreme Court reviews between 20 and 40 attorney misconduct or incapacity cases each year.

An attorney whose license is suspended for a lesser violation may obtain reinstatement at the end of the suspension after fulfilling any conditions imposed by the Supreme Court. An attorney whose license is revoked or suspended for more than six months must petition for reinstatement and prove to a referee and to the Supreme Court that he or she is fit to practice law.

OLR received 2,225 inquiries and grievances in fiscal year 2003-2004. The most common grievances were lack of diligence by an attorney, lack of communication with the client, and misrepresentation or dishonesty. Approximately 16 percent of cases were forwarded for formal investigation, 3 percent were resolved through diversion programs, 11 percent were withdrawn, and the remaining 70 percent were closed for lack of sufficient information to support an allegation of misconduct. The Supreme Court and referees imposed public discipline on 66 attorneys, including six license revocations. The remaining public disciplines include suspensions or reprimands. In addition, 33 attorneys received private reprimands.

Navigating the Legal System

Litigants are not required to be represented by an attorney in court and a growing number are not. Some people choose not to be represented and some cannot afford to pay for legal representation. The state provides legal assistance to indigent defendants in criminal cases. Indigent litigants in civil cases generally must turn to private groups for legal assistance. Courts can provide some assistance to litigants who proceed without representation, but cannot assert a litigant's rights or strategize for a litigant as an attorney is likely to do.

Self-represented parties

Courts are seeing an increasing number of self-represented or *pro se* litigants navigating a legal system that is not designed to serve individuals without attorneys. These litigants fall into two categories: those who truly can't afford an attorney but are otherwise ineligible for any type of low-income legal assistance, and those who can afford an attorney but choose not to hire one.

Confusing language and complicated rules and procedures can alienate litigants representing themselves in court. The frustration experienced by a litigant is often shared by court staff, attorneys, and judges who must balance conflicting obligations to assist litigants, prioritize workload demands, and adhere to legal and ethical constraints concerning the unauthorized practice of law. Judges find

> *"Well over half of my original divorce and small claim filings are* pro se *(neither side has an attorney). Other counties in this district are close – some are a little higher and some a little lower."*
> *– Judge Gary Carlson, Taylor County Circuit Court*

The Waukesha County Family Court Self-Help Center provides both in-person and online assistance to court users who do not have attorneys. Litigants are increasingly representing themselves in court, and the legal profession is responding to this trend by providing a variety of new services.

(*Kathleen Sitter, LRB*)

themselves placed in the uneasy position of providing useful explanations of law and procedures without violating the judicial code. They are concerned about the appearance of impropriety if they intervene too much or too little, and the balancing act becomes all the more challenging in cases where one litigant is represented and the other is not.

A 1999 survey of 13 northwestern Wisconsin counties showed that more than half of family court cases involved at least one person who was not represented by an attorney. In Milwaukee County, the number of family court cases involving a self-represented litigant was more than 70 percent in 1999. Since then, "snapshot" surveys of case filings show the numbers have increased. In Dane County, a two-month snapshot of family court filings in 1999 revealed that in 48 percent of the cases, both litigants were self-represented; by 2002, in a similar two-month snapshot, that had number increased to 60 percent.

In 1999, Chief Justice Shirley S. Abrahamson appointed a *Pro Se* Working Group, comprised of judges, attorneys, law professors, advocates, and court staff, to study the problem and recommend solutions. The group's report, issued in December 2000, recommended simplifying court documents, establishing better referral systems to link people with legal help, and facilitating accurate and complete filing of paperwork. Since the report was issued, various initiatives have been undertaken to help *pro se* litigants navigate the court system.

In 2002, the Wisconsin Supreme Court adopted guidelines to help court staff to provide quality customer service while steering clear of the unauthorized practice of law. In 2003, the courts unveiled a new Self-Help Center on their Web site. In addition, counties across the state have developed their own court self-help centers to assist litigants with information, and have developed low-cost packets of forms with plain-English instructions for some of the most common court procedures and directories of local attorneys who might be willing to offer low-cost or "unbundled" legal services for those who need help only with specific items. In 2004, a statewide effort to provide understandable court forms that would be acceptable, but not mandatory, got underway. In 2005, this effort produced 34 plain-English forms and instructions for various actions related to divorce. Also in 2004, a group of central Wisconsin counties began work on a special plan to address the needs of self-represented litigants in rural areas where the small number of lawyers means more potential conflicts of interest for lawyers who volunteer their time to offer free legal advice. These lawyers, or their law firms, often discover that they represent the same banks and merchants whom the litigant is attempting to sue, meaning that they cannot ethically offer assistance to the *pro se* litigant. To address this conflict-of-interest problem, the rural counties are researching establishing a partnership with the University of Wisconsin-Extension that might allow videoconferencing to facilitate free legal advice from attorneys who practice in other parts of the state – essentially, virtual self-help centers.

The public defender system

The Sixth Amendment to the U.S. Constitution provides a criminal defendant the right to assistance of counsel. In the 1963 case *Gideon v. Wainwright*, the U.S. Supreme Court declared that if a criminal defendant cannot afford to pay for counsel, the state must provide counsel. It is up to the states to decide how counsel will be provided to indigent criminal defendants. In 1977, Wisconsin established a statewide public defender system, funded with state dollars, to provide legal representation to criminal defendants. Wisconsin's Office of the State Public Defender (SPD), provides legal representation to indigent adult defendants in criminal, commitment, and termination of parental rights cases. The SPD also provides legal representation to juveniles in delinquency cases and to children in certain child welfare cases, regardless of indigence.

The SPD represents indigent defendants at the trial level and also in appeals; it provided legal representation to 145,000 clients in 2004. The SPD employs attorneys to provide representation and also contracts with private attorneys to provide legal representation. In-house attorneys handle just over half of the cases. The SPD determines indigence according to statutory income and asset guidelines that were last modified in 1987.

Although Wisconsin's statewide public defender system is not unusual, it is also not typical of indigent defense across the 50 states. Some states leave it to the local government to provide counsel to indigent criminal defendants, allowing for inconsistency both in determinations as to who is indigent and in the quality of counsel provided. In jurisdictions without a public defender system, judges either appoint counsel from the private bar on a case-by-case basis, or the government contracts with private attorneys to take multiple indigent defense cases. The benefits to Wisconsin's statewide public defender system include that the attorneys assigned to provide indigent defense are generally experienced in criminal law and have been vetted, either through the hiring process for SPD employees or the certification

Howard B. Eisenberg (1946-2002), called "Wisconsin's Atticus Finch" (from Harper Lee's "To Kill a Mockingbird") by Chief Justice Shirley Abrahamson, wrote the statutes creating the state public defender system and was the first chief State Public Defender. Eisenberg, who later served as dean of Marquette Law School, continued to represent indigent defendants, free of charge, after leaving the Office of the State Public Defender.

(Andy Manis)

process for private bar attorneys. Wisconsin's system is uniform across the state. And, because the SPD makes indigence determinations, the intake process may start after defendants are charged, rather then waiting until the defendant makes his or her first appearance before a judge, avoiding the need to delay cases while counsel is appointed.

Representation for indigent litigants in civil cases

In civil cases, unlike criminal matters, litigants generally do not have a right to be provided counsel if they cannot afford to hire an attorney; however, the stakes in civil matters can be quite high. People faced with eviction from their homes, people who need restraining orders, people fighting for custody of their children are all involved in civil proceedings. Several legal aid organizations provide legal services to indigent clients in various parts of Wisconsin. They tend to represent clients in cases concerning eligibility for public benefits, family law (including divorce, custody, child support, and domestic violence), housing, education, employment, and consumer law.

Legal aid organizations are funded by a mix of public and private money. One source of funding is interest on lawyers' trust accounts (IOLTA). Wisconsin lawyers who receive funds that belong to a client must deposit the funds into a pooled interest-bearing account if the client's funds alone would not generate sufficient interest to cover the cost of maintaining a separate account. Interest on the pooled accounts is used to fund legal aid. Another source of funding is federal money distributed by the Legal Services Corporation (LSC), a private, nonprofit corporation created by the U.S. Congress. Organizations that receive LSC funding are subject to a number of restrictions, including that they may not provide representation in criminal cases, accept cases in which attorney's fees may be earned, challenge welfare reform laws, file class actions, lobby, litigate on behalf of prisoners, or represent clients in drug-related evictions from public housing.

In recent years, declining interest rates have taken a bite out of IOLTA, and a resulting toll on Wisconsin's ability to meet the civil legal service needs of low-income people. In 2004, the Wisconsin Trust Account Foundation (WisTAF), which operates the IOLTA program and distributes money to legal-services providers, took the unusual step of petitioning the Wisconsin Supreme Court to levy a $50 fee on all active members of the State Bar of Wisconsin in order to shore up the program. The court agreed that the situation was dire, and voted to impose the fee. In its order, the court made clear its concern that funding of legal services for the poor not fall exclusively on the shoulders of lawyers. "The legal profession, alone, cannot solve the problem of adequate civil legal representation for the poor, nor should it be expected to do so," the court wrote. "The very integrity of our justice system is compromised when legal representation for critical needs is available only to those with financial means. As such, this issue affects our entire community. Our entire community will need to participate if a long-term solution is to succeed."

Court Automation and Public Information

 The Wisconsin court system's Consolidated Court Automation Programs, better known as CCAP, represents one of the nation's first – and, as measured by its users, most successful – efforts to develop, implement, and maintain automated information systems for the courts and give the public Internet access to court information. CCAP's custom-developed software is in use in the courts' administrative offices as well as in courtrooms throughout the state.

As the Wisconsin court system moves toward electronic filing, visits to the clerk's office to file paperwork could become a thing of the past. Court automation is making the court system more efficient, improving government by facilitating the sharing of information among agencies, and making court information more accessible to the public.

(Kathleen Sitter, LRB)

A Capitol tour guide gives visitors an explanation of the four murals on the walls of the Supreme Court hearing room. The murals, along with the rest of the room, were the subject of significant restoration efforts from 1999-2001, as part of the Capitol restoration project. (Kathleen Sitter, LRB)

CCAP operates under the direction of the Director of State Courts and with guidance from the CCAP Steering Committee, which is comprised of judges, clerks of court, and court administrators from around the state.

Public access to court records and information

Public access to a variety of court information is available through the Wisconsin court system Web site at (*www.wicourts.gov*). One of the most popular sources of information within this site is Wisconsin Circuit Court Access (WCCA), which provides up-to-date information on action in circuit court cases across the state. WCCA receives about 2.3 million hits every day. Because easy public access to court records raises privacy concerns, the Director of State Courts Office in 2005 appointed the WCCA Oversight Committee, which will meet periodically to review WCCA and address concerns with an eye on maintaining access without unduly compromising individual privacy. A committee of the same name and with similar membership was convened in 1999 to develop guidelines for the site and was disbanded when this task was completed.

Named one of the nation's top 10 justice-related Web sites, WCCA is searchable statewide or county-by-county using various criteria including an individual's name or a case number. WCCA displays circuit court information such as party names, criminal charges, sentences, civil judgments, case schedules, and case events and is updated hourly. In addition to free individual inquiries, bulk information can be extracted from WCCA by subscribing to a fee-based service.

Supreme Court and Court of Appeals case information is also available on the Wisconsin court system Web site, free of charge. The information includes party names, attorney names and addresses, and case events.

In addition to case information, the Wisconsin court system Web site contains a wide variety of court information. Published opinions and calendars of the Supreme Court and Court of Appeals; downloadable court forms; budget information; historical facts; educational materials for children; press releases; court system telephone directories; and much more is available on this site.

To ensure that access is available to all, CCAP provides free, public-access computer terminals in every county courthouse.

Records automation

Court case, financial, and jury management applications within CCAP include features such as in-court processing, which provides litigants with the papers they need before they leave the courtroom; automated court calendars, which streamline the process for scheduling hearings; and bar code scanners to track files. Document imaging is used to help alleviate the physical storage requirements of large quantities of paper files, and pilot projects to develop an electronic-filing system are underway in several counties.

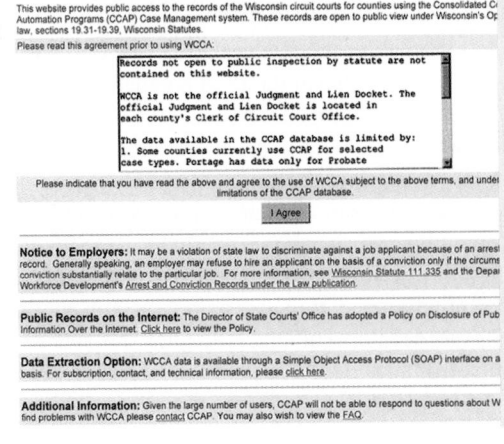

With 64 employees and a 2003-2005 budget of $20.8 million, CCAP replaces labor-intensive, paper-based court processes with state-of-the-art computer technology, saving time and valuable staff resources and helping the courts to run smoothly and efficiently. CCAP supports about 3,000 computers in 85 locations throughout the state, providing computer hardware, software, and a variety of technology services to the Wisconsin Supreme Court, the four districts of the Court of Appeals, the 72-county Circuit Court, and seven administrative departments.

While the court system may never be a "paperless" operation, building an infrastructure that will allow for electronic filing (e-filing) of documents in the Wisconsin courts is an important goal, for e-filing can save money, increase efficiency, and improve access to the courts. An electronic filing system is expected to save money in the long term for the courts, lawyers, and litigants by reducing the costs of printing, copying, mailing, courier services, travel, and storage of paper documents. E-filing also is expected to save time, increasing the speed with which documents can be sent to the court and to opposing counsel and eliminating hurdles for litigants who live far away from the courthouse. Further, e-filing will give the parties, lawyers, judges, and court staff the ability to electronically access and search court files and dockets from remote locations, 24 hours a day.

Progress toward e-filing began in 2000, when the director of state courts appointed a 20-person Electronic Filing Committee to examine the current system and make recommendations for change in order to accommodate e-filing. The committee was comprised of judges, clerks of court, court administrators, technology experts, and representatives from the state Department of Justice, as well as district attorneys, public defenders, and attorneys in private practice. The group tackled its job by working to identify possible barriers to e-filing in the law, policies, and court operations. This work involved identifying current court processes and flow of information through the court system and determining where workflow should be reengineered to create a more efficient system and to accommodate/facilitate electronic filing. Big picture concerns such as an integrated case management system and protection of privacy were considered alongside details such as how to clock filing times, collect fees, and verify signatures.

> Two recent projects are streamlining the court process for jurors and litigants. The **on-line juror qualification questionnaire**, which became available in 2004 at *www.wicourts.gov/services/juror/online.htm* allows potential jurors to provide their responses quickly and easily, and saves valuable court staff resources by reducing data entry. More than 13,000 people used the online jury questionnaire in the first eight months of this project.
>
> Electronic filing of court forms, better known as **e-filing**, is in the works for small claims and family cases. Attorneys or parties representing themselves will be able to fill out and file new cases or actions, respond to actions filed by other parties, print or reprint forms to be filed, and obtain information about electronically filing case information with the courts.

Sharing information with state and local agencies

Extensive data is shared between the courts and other justice business partners to facilitate the accurate and efficient administration of justice in Wisconsin. The following data interfaces are in production:

- **District Attorney to Circuit Courts** – District attorneys send criminal complaint/charging information electronically to the clerks of circuit court in 59 counties in the state. This information includes the name and address of the person being charged, the statutory citation, severity, and offense date of the violation.Plans are being made to expand this interface to remaining counties.

- **Circuit Courts with the Department of Transportation (DOT)** – Data are exchanged between the circuit courts and the Department of Transportation for the following initiatives: Citation filing (18 counties are now receiving citation filings electronically – 12 from weigh stations and 6 from the State Patrol); and Disposition Reporting (18 circuit courts are exporting forfeiture disposition data to the DOT for electronic citations). The electronic reporting of dispositions for nonelectronic citations is operating in two counties. Electronic reporting of suspensions and revocations to the DOT is currently in development.

- **Circuit Courts to the Crime Information Bureau (CIB)** – The dispositions and sentences for all circuit court criminal cases statewide are being reported to the Department of Justice's Crime Information Bureau. District attorneys, law enforcement, and others rely on this information when carrying out their duties.

- **Circuit Courts to the State Public Defender's Office** – The circuit court case, calendar, and disposition data for all circuit court criminal cases statewide are being reported to the State Public Defender's Office.

- **Circuit Courts to the Department of Revenue (DOR)** – 54 circuit courts are electronically intercepting the tax returns of people that have outstanding fines, fees, and forfeitures with the clerks of circuit court or registers in probate. In 2004, about $2.1 million was intercepted. Outstanding debt information is electronically sent to the DOR, which deducts the outstanding amounts from the specified tax returns. The funds are then sent to the clerks or registers to apply to the outstanding debts. Seventy-one counties are participating in the filing of electronic tax warrants from the DOR to the circuit courts. Satisfactions and releases are also electronically filed with the courts.

- **Future Interfaces with the Circuit Courts** – Numerous other data sharing projects are either being developed or planned in the upcoming year. The future interfaces with the circuit courts include Department of Workforce Development unemployment compensation warrant filings and judgment of conviction information exports to the Department of Corrections.

End notes

[1]See 1987 Wisconsin Act 355 for more explanation for creation of family counseling requirement (Judicial Council bill).

[2]Casey, Pamela and Rottman, David. *Problem-Solving Courts: Models and Trends.* National Center for State Courts, 2003.

[3]Supreme Court Internal Operating Procedures, II (intro.).

[4]Clausen, Charles D., "The Long and Winding Road: Political and Campaign Ethics Rules for Wisconsin Judges." *Marquette Law Review,* v.83, no.1, Fall 1999. See also "Wisconsin's Courts," *The Wisconsin Taxpayer.* The Wisconsin Taxpayer's Alliance, June 1999, v.67, no.6.

Court System Timeline

1836 Wisconsin territory created

The U.S. Congress established the territorial government of Wisconsin (covering present day Wisconsin, Iowa, and Minnesota) and created three judicial districts in the territory. The territorial Supreme Court, comprised of three district court judges appointed by President Andrew Jackson, convened for the first time on December 8, 1836, in Belmont. **Charles Dunn** was the first chief justice, and **David Irvin** and **William Frazer** were the two associate justices.

1848 Wisconsin became the nation's 30th state

The constitution of the new state granted the courts the power to hear and decide cases, and created five judicial circuits, allowing the voters of each district to choose a judge. The five circuit judges sat as the Supreme Court in Madison, reviewing their own cases. Chief Justice **Alexander Stow** of Fond du Lac and Associate Justices **Edward Whiton** of Janesville, **Levi Hubbell** of Milwaukee, **Mortimer Jackson** of Mineral Point, and **Charles Larrabee** of Horicon were elected to the court.

The 1848 Constitution gave the governor the authority to appoint a justice to the court when a vacancy occurs and provided that the appointee continue in the office until a successor is elected and qualified. This is still the system today.

1849 The Supreme Court expanded to six

The legislature created a sixth judicial circuit. Janesville lawyer **Wiram Knowlton** was elected judge, thus making six justices on the Supreme Court bench.

1850 County courts created

The legislature created county courts and gave them authority over probate matters and civil matters involving less than $500. Lawmakers also authorized justice of the peace and municipal courts to handle civil disputes involving less than $100.

1852 A new Supreme Court created

The constitution in 1848 had provided that the circuit court judges would sit as the Supreme Court for five years. The legislature took advantage of the five-year expiration to create a new, separate Supreme Court. For the first time, the members of the court provided an independent review of lower court rulings. The people of Wisconsin elected three men (in a September 1852 election) – Milwaukee lawyer **Abram D. Smith**, **Edward V. Whiton**, and Irish immigrant **Samuel Crawford** of Mineral Point – to serve as the first justices of the newly formed Wisconsin Supreme Court.

1853

The **first term** of the separate Wisconsin Supreme Court commenced on June 1, 1853. The justices' salary was $2,000 per year. The court's first case was *Winne v. Nickerson*, which involved a $10.40 debt and $14.36 in court costs. The dispute centered on a question of the reliability of an account book.

1858 Election day for judges set

The legislature enacted a law setting judicial elections for the first Tuesday in April, which continues to this day.

1870s

The **workload of the Supreme Court** greatly expanded. The court had no stenographers, typewriters, or even copyists, so each justice did his own clerical work. To keep up with the calendar, the justices voted to increase the number of cases on assignment to the court from 15 to 25. (Chief Justice **Edward Ryan** objected strenuously, accusing his fellow justices of attempting to kill him with labor.)

1874

After 15 years on the Supreme Court, Chief Justice **Luther Dixon**, a Portage resident who was saddled with financial problems, resigned and returned to private practice. The justices' annual salary was $2,500.

1877 More justices, longer terms

A constitutional amendment changed the number of justices from three to five and increased the term of service from six to 10 years to ensure that justices could issue rulings without constantly considering politics and reelection.

1878 **The Wisconsin Bar Association** was organized. The first membership roll was signed on January 9, 1878, by 265 state lawyers. **Moses M. Strong**, an attorney from Mineral Point, was elected as the bar's first president.

1881 The State Bar adopts its first **code of ethics**.

1889 The new State Bar surveyed the state and found 1,239 resident lawyers, many of whom were unqualified. **Reforming its admission standards** was one of the bar's first challenges.

1901 ## Selecting the chief justice

The people of Wisconsin amended the constitution to provide that the justice having the longest continuous service on the court shall be the chief justice; that is still the method today.

1903 ## ...And still more justices

A constitutional amendment established a court of **seven members**. That structure continues today.

1924 ## Nonpartisan elections

The legislature passed a law mandating that candidates for judicial office be nonpartisan, though nonpartisan judicial elections apparently date back to 1878 in Wisconsin.

The **annual salary** for Wisconsin Supreme Court justices is $12,000 a year.

1955 ## Job qualifications set

The people amended the constitution to provide that in order to become a Supreme Court justice or trial court judge, a person must be a qualified voter and licensed to practice law in Wisconsin for at least five years. The 1955 amendment also set a mandatory retirement age of 70 for justices. By 1977, this provision was removed.

1959 The legislature enacted a **reorganization of the court system**, abolishing municipal, district, superior, civil, and small claims courts. A uniform system of jurisdiction and procedure was established for county courts.

1961 The legislature created the post of administrative **director of the courts**. This position has since been redefined by the Supreme Court and renamed the director of state courts.

1966 The legislature ratified two constitutional amendments that **abolished the justice of the peace** courts and **permitted municipal courts**. Thus, the court system consisted of a Supreme Court, circuit courts, county courts, and municipal courts.

1976 **Shirley S. Abrahamson**, a UW Law School professor and Madison attorney was appointed to the Wisconsin Supreme Court by Governor Patrick J. Lucey. She was the **first woman on the court**.

1977 Wisconsin voters approved a constitutional amendment to **reorganize the court system**. The legislature eliminated county courts and created a single-level trial court (the circuit court). Lawmakers also authorized municipal courts, created the Court of Appeals, and provided for permissive review by the Wisconsin Supreme Court.

1999 **The Supreme Court Hearing Room** was shut down for renovation; court moved to temporary quarters until the hearing room was reopened in 2001.

2003 ## Majority female Supreme Court

In 2003, Justice **Patience Drake Roggensack** was elected to the Supreme Court, creating the first majority female Supreme Court along with Chief Justice **Shirley S. Abrahamson** and fellow Justices **Ann Walsh Bradley** and **Diane S. Sykes**. The female majority was temporary, ending when Justice Sykes was appointed to a federal judgeship in 2004.

2004 **Louis B. Butler, Jr.**, the first African-American Supreme Court justice in Wisconsin history, was appointed to the bench by Governor Jim Doyle.

SPECIAL ARTICLES IN PRIOR BLUE BOOKS, 1960 TO 2003

For 1919 to 1933 *Blue Books:* see 1954 *Blue Book,* pp. 177-182.
For 1935 to 1962 *Blue Books:* see 1964 *Blue Book,* pp. 227-232.

Commerce and Culture

The Indians of Wisconsin, by William H. Hodge, 1975 *Blue Book,* pp. 95-192.

The Population Resource of Wisconsin, by M.G. Toepel and H. Rupert Theobald, 1964 *Blue Book,* pp. 70-90.

Wisconsin Business and Industry, by James J. Brzycki, Paul E. Hassett, Joyce Munz Hach, Kenneth S. Kinney, and Robert H. Milbourne, 1987-1988 *Blue Book,* pp. 99-165.

Wisconsin Writers, by John O. [Jack] Stark, 1977 *Blue Book,* pp. 95-185.

Wisconsin's People: A Portrait of Wisconsin's Population on the Threshold of the 21st Century, by Paul R. Voss, Daniel L. Veroff, and David D. Long, 2003-2004 *Blue Book,* pp. 99-174.

Education

Conservation Education in Wisconsin, by Ingvald O. Hembre, 1964 *Blue Book,* pp. 212-225.

Education for Employment: 70 Years of Vocational, Technical and Adult Education in Wisconsin, by Kathleen A. Paris, 1981-1982 *Blue Book,* pp. 95-212.

The Wisconsin Idea: The University's Service to the State, by Jack Stark, 1995-1996 *Blue Book,* pp. 99-179.

The Wisconsin Idea for the 21st Century, by Alan B. Knox and Joe Corry, 1995-1996 *Blue Book,* pp. 180-192.

Environment

The Climate of Wisconsin, by Marvin W. Burley, 1964 *Blue Book,* pp. 143-148.

Exploring Wisconsin's Waterways, by Margaret Beattie Bogue, 1989-1990 *Blue Book,* pp. 99-297.

The Forest Resource of Wisconsin, by Louis A. Haertle, 1964 *Blue Book,* pp. 113-129.

The Landscape Resources of Wisconsin, by Philip H. Lewis, Jr., 1964 *Blue Book,* pp. 130-142.

The Mineral Resources of Wisconsin, by George F. Hanson, 1964 *Blue Book,* pp. 199-211.

The Natural Resources of Wisconsin, 1964 *Blue Book,* pp. 69-225.

The Physical Geography of Wisconsin, by Robert F. Black, 1964 *Blue Book,* pp. 171-177.

Protecting Wisconsin's Environment, by Selma Parker, 1973 *Blue Book,* pp. 97-161.

The Soils of Wisconsin, by Marvin T. Beatty, Ingvald O. Hembre, Francis D. Hole, Leonard R. Massie, and Arthur E. Peterson, 1964 *Blue Book,* pp. 149-170.

The Water Resources of Wisconsin, by C.L.R. Holt, Jr., Ken B. Young, and William H. Cartwright, 1964 *Blue Book,* pp. 178-198.

The Wildlife Resource of Wisconsin, by Ruth L. Hine, 1964 *Blue Book,* pp. 91-112.

Wisconsin's Troubled Waters, by Selma Parker, 1973 *Blue Book,* pp. 102-136.

Government

The Budget – State Fiscal Policy Document, by Dale Cattanach and Terry A. Rhodes, 1970 *Blue Book,* pp. 261-272.

The Changing World of Wisconsin Local Government, by Susan C. Paddock, 1997-1998 *Blue Book,* pp. 99-172.

Equal Representation: A Study of Legislative and Congressional Apportionment in Wisconsin, by H. Rupert Theobald, 1970 *Blue Book,* pp. 70-260.

In the People's Service: Wisconsin State Government and the Services It Provides for the People of Wisconsin, by H. Rupert Theobald, 1966 *Blue Book,* pp. 71-296.

The Legislative Process in Wisconsin, by Richard L. Roe, Pamela J. Kahler, Robin N. Kite, and Robert P. Nelson, 1993-1994 *Blue Book,* pp. 99-194.

Local Government in Wisconsin, by James R. Donoghue, 1979-1980 *Blue Book,* pp. 95-218.

Rules and Rulings: Parliamentary Procedure from the Wisconsin Perspective, by H. Rupert Theobald, 1985-1986 *Blue Book,* pp. 99-215.

Wisconsin's Military Establishment: Its Organization and Operation, 1962 *Blue Book,* pp. 69-265.

History

Capitals and Capitols in Early Wisconsin, by Stanley H. Cravens, 1983-1984 *Blue Book,* pp. 99-167.

A History of the Property Tax and Property Tax Relief in Wisconsin, by Jack Stark, 1991-1992 *Blue Book,* pp. 99-165.

Restoring the Vision: The First Century of Wisconsin's Capitol, by Michael J. Keane, 2001-2002 *Blue Book,* pp. 99-188.

Ten Events That Shaped Wisconsin's History, by Norman K. Risjord, 1999-2000 *Blue Book*, pp. 99-146.

Two Wisconsin Firsts, 1962 *Blue Book,* pp. 267-270.

Wisconsin at 150 Years, by Michael J. Keane and Daniel F. Ritsche, 1997-1998 *Blue Book,* color supplement.

Wisconsin Celebrates 150 Years of Statehood: A Photographic Review, 1999-2000 *Blue Book*, color supplement.

Wisconsin's Former Governors, 1848-1959, by M.G. Toepel, 1960 *Blue Book,* pp. 67-206.

Capitol Visitor's Guide

Hours: Building open daily 8 a.m. - 6 p.m. The Capitol closes at 4 p.m. weekends and holidays.

Information Desk: Located in the rotunda, ground floor.

Tours: Daily Monday - Saturday at 9, 10, and 11 a.m., 1, 2, and 3 p.m.; Sundays at 1, 2, and 3 p.m. A 4 p.m. tour is offered between Memorial Day and Labor Day. Tours start at the Information Desk in the rotunda and last 45 to 55 minutes. Reservations are required for groups of 10 or more. Call (608) 266-0382 7:30 a.m. - 5 p.m. Monday - Friday.

Observation Deck: 6th Floor, accessible from 4th floor via NW or W stairways. Open daily from Memorial Day to Labor Day. There is a small museum devoted to the Capitol at the entrance to the observation deck.

Souvenirs: Available at the Information Desk, include books, postcards, miniatures, and tour videos.

Capitol Police: Room B2 North.

Handicapped Entrances: At Martin Luther King Jr. Blvd., East Washington Avenue, Wisconsin Avenue, and West Washington Avenue.

Parking: Limited parking (meters) on the Capitol Square. Several public ramps are located within two blocks of the Capitol.

Food: Cafeteria, vending machines in rotunda basement.

Senate Chamber: South wing, 2nd floor; visitors gallery, 3rd floor.

Assembly Chamber: West wing, 2nd floor; visitors gallery, 3rd floor.

Supreme Court Hearing Room: East wing, 2nd floor.

Governor's Office and Conference Room: East wing, 1st floor.

Lieutenant Governor's Office: East wing, ground floor.

Attorney General's Office: East wing, 1st floor.

Legislative Offices: To find a specific office, check one of the Capitol Directories located in the rotunda and on the ground floor of each wing.

Hearings: Information about the time and location of public hearings is posted at the entrance to each legislative chamber.

Hearing Rooms: North Hearing Room, North wing, 2nd floor.

Grand Army of the Republic Hall, Room 417 North.

Joint Committee on Finance, Room 412 East.

Senate Hearing Room, Room 411 South.

Additional hearing rooms are located on the 2nd and 3rd floors of the Capitol.

Capitol Facts & Figures

Construction Chronology:
West wing: 1906 – 1909
East wing: 1908 – 1910
Central portion: 1910 – 1913
South wing: 1909 – 1913
North wing: 1914 – 1917
First meeting of legislature in building: 1909
Dedication: July 8, 1965
Renovation: 1990 – 2001

Statistics:
Height of each wing: 61 feet
Height of observation deck: 92 feet
Height of dome mural: 184 feet, 3 inches
Height of dome (to top of statue): 284 feet, 9 inches
Length of building from N to S & E to W: 483 feet, 9 inches
Floor space: 448,297 square feet
Volume: 8,369,665 cubic feet
Original cost: $7,203,826.35
(including grounds, furnishings, and
power plant)

The first of 453,200,000 Wisconsin state quarters was struck at the Denver Mint in October 2004. The design features a cow, a round of cheese, and an ear of corn and was selected by Wisconsin citizens in an

online poll. Interest in the coin surged in 2005 after varieties surfaced with apparent extra leaves on the corn stalk. The so-called "extra leaf" varieties were eagerly sought by collectors who paid a substantial premium over the 25 cent face value. (U.S. Mint)

The official release of the Wisconsin State Quarter took place at State Fair Park in West Allis on October 25, 2004. Among those in attendance were U.S. Mint Director Henrietta Holsman Fore (at the podium) and

Governor Jim Doyle and First Lady Jessica Doyle. They were joined by a large contingent of enthusiastic Wisconsin school children.
(Kathleen Sitter, LRB)

The S/V Denis Sullivan, *Wisconsin's Flagship, is a replica of a 19th century Great Lakes schooner. She was built in Milwaukee by more than 900 volunteers to serve as a floating classroom, focusing on water education and conservation programs, in addition to offering day and evening sails for the general public, and private receptions. The 137-foot sailing vessel is equipped with broadband interactive communications, including wireless and satellite feeds, which allow her to communicate directly with an interactive network of learners, educators and industry professions from the deck of the ship. The* Sullivan *travels south each winter to Florida, the Bahama Islands and the Dry Tortugas in the Gulf of Mexico to conduct an expeditionary learning program called, "Science Under Sail". Aboard ship, students and crew work together to bring the* Denis Sullivan *to life, studying marine life and learning navigation, math, and science.* (Chris Winters)

Wisconsin Constitution

3

Wisconsin Constitution: text as amended through June 2005 and votes on constitutional amendments and statewide referenda submitted to the people

Green County Courthouse

Kathleen Sitter, LRB

WISCONSIN CONSTITUTION

As amended through June 30, 2005 *

TABLE OF CONTENTS

WISCONSIN CONSTITUTION

As amended through June 30, 2005 *

Preamble

We, the people of Wisconsin, grateful to Almighty God for our freedom, in order to secure its blessings, form a more perfect government, insure domestic tranquility and promote the general welfare, do establish this constitution.

ARTICLE I.
DECLARATION OF RIGHTS

Equality; inherent rights. SECTION 1. [*As amended April 1986*] All people are born equally free and independent, and have certain inherent rights; among these are life, liberty and the pursuit of happiness; to secure these rights, governments are instituted, deriving their just powers from the consent of the governed. [*1983 AJR-9; 1985 AJR-9*]

Equality; inherent rights. SECTION 1. [*As amended November 1982*] All people are born equally free and independent, and have certain inherent rights; among these are life, liberty and the pursuit of happiness; to serve these rights, governments are instituted, deriving their just powers from the consent of the governed. [*1979 AJR-76; 1981 AJR-35; submit: May'82 Spec.Sess. AJR-1*]

Equality; inherent rights. SECTION 1. [*Original form*] All men are born equally free and independent, and have certain inherent rights; among these are life, liberty and the pursuit of happiness; to secure these rights, governments are instituted among men, deriving their just powers from the consent of the governed.

Slavery prohibited. SECTION 2. There shall be neither slavery, nor involuntary servitude in this state, otherwise than for the punishment of crime, whereof the party shall have been duly convicted.

Free speech; libel. SECTION 3. Every person may freely speak, write and publish his sentiments on all subjects, being responsible for the abuse of that right, and no laws shall be passed to restrain or abridge the liberty of speech or of the press. In all criminal prosecutions or indictments for libel, the truth may be given in evidence, and if it shall appear to the jury that the matter charged as libelous be true, and was published with good motives and for justifiable ends, the party shall be acquitted; and the jury shall have the right to determine the law and the fact.

Right to assemble and petition. SECTION 4. The right of the people peaceably to assemble, to consult for the common good, and to petition the government, or any department thereof, shall never be abridged.

Trial by jury; verdict in civil cases. SECTION 5. [*As amended November 1922*] The right of trial by jury shall remain inviolate, and shall extend to all cases at law without regard to the amount in controversy; but a jury trial may be waived by the parties in all cases in the manner prescribed by law. Provided, however, that the legislature may, from time to time, by statute provide that a valid verdict, in civil cases, may be based on the votes of a specified number of the jury, not less than five-sixths thereof. [*1919 AJR-26; 1921 AJR-14; 1921 c. 504*]

Trial by jury. SECTION 5. [*Original form*] The right of trial by jury shall remain inviolate; and shall extend to all cases at law, without regard to the amount in controversy; but a jury trial may be waived by the parties in all cases, in the manner prescribed by law.

Excessive bail; cruel punishments. SECTION 6. Excessive bail shall not be required, nor shall excessive fines be imposed, nor cruel and unusual punishments inflicted.

---

* Current provisions of the constitution are printed the full width of the page, and previous wordings (if any) follow each active provision in double-column format. Any section not indicated as having been amended and not followed by two-column text still exists as ratified by the people of Wisconsin when they adopted the Wisconsin Constitution on March 13, 1848.

Rights of accused. SECTION 7. In all criminal prosecutions the accused shall enjoy the right to be heard by himself and counsel; to demand the nature and cause of the accusation against him; to meet the witnesses face to face; to have compulsory process to compel the attendance of witnesses in his behalf; and in prosecutions by indictment, or information, to a speedy public trial by an impartial jury of the county or district wherein the offense shall have been committed; which county or district shall have been previously ascertained by law.

Prosecutions; double jeopardy; self-incrimination; bail; habeas corpus. SECTION 8. [*As amended per certification of the Board of State Canvassers dated April 7, 1982*] (1) No person may be held to answer for a criminal offense without due process of law, and no person for the same offense may be put twice in jeopardy of punishment, nor may be compelled in any criminal case to be a witness against himself or herself.

(2) All persons, before conviction, shall be eligible for release under reasonable conditions designed to assure their appearance in court, protect members of the community from serious bodily harm or prevent the intimidation of witnesses. Monetary conditions of release may be imposed at or after the initial appearance only upon a finding that there is a reasonable basis to believe that the conditions are necessary to assure appearance in court. The legislature may authorize, by law, courts to revoke a person's release for a violation of a condition of release.

(3) The legislature may by law authorize, but may not require, circuit courts to deny release for a period not to exceed 10 days prior to the hearing required under this subsection to a person who is accused of committing a murder punishable by life imprisonment or a sexual assault punishable by a maximum imprisonment of 20 years, or who is accused of committing or attempting to commit a felony involving serious bodily harm to another or the threat of serious bodily harm to another and who has a previous conviction for committing or attempting to commit a felony involving serious bodily harm to another or the threat of serious bodily harm to another. The legislature may authorize by law, but may not require, circuit courts to continue to deny release to those accused persons for an additional period not to exceed 60 days following the hearing required under this subsection, if there is a requirement that there be a finding by the court based on clear and convincing evidence presented at a hearing that the accused committed the felony and a requirement that there be a finding by the court that available conditions of release will not adequately protect members of the community from serious bodily harm or prevent intimidation of witnesses. Any law enacted under this subsection shall be specific, limited and reasonable. In determining the 10-day and 60-day periods, the court shall omit any period of time found by the court to result from a delay caused by the defendant or a continuance granted which was initiated by the defendant.

(4) The privilege of the writ of habeas corpus shall not be suspended unless, in cases of rebellion or invasion, the public safety requires it. [*June 1980 Spec.Sess. AJR-9; 1981 AJR-5*]

Prosecutions; second jeopardy; self-incrimination; bail; habeas corpus. SECTION 8. [*As amended November 1870*] No person shall be held to answer for a criminal offense without due process of law, and no person for the same offense shall be put twice in jeopardy of punishment, nor shall be compelled in any criminal case to be a witness against himself. All persons shall, before conviction, be bailable by sufficient sureties, except for capital offenses when the proof is evident or the presumption great; and the privilege of the writ of habeas corpus shall not be suspended unless when, in cases of rebellion or invasion, the public safety may require it. [*1869 AJR-6; 1870 SJR-3; 1870 c. 118*]

Criminal procedure. SECTION 8. [*Original form*] No person shall be held to answer for a criminal offense, unless on the presentment, or indictment of a grand jury, except in cases of impeachment, or in cases cognizable by justices of the peace, or arising in the army or navy, or in the militia when in actual service in time of war, or public danger; and no person for the same offence shall be put twice in jeopardy of punishment, nor shall be compelled in any criminal case to be a witness against himself; all persons shall, before conviction, be bailable by sufficient sureties except for capital offences when the proof is evident, or the presumption great; and the privilege of the writ of habeas corpus shall not be suspended unless when, in cases of rebellion, or invasion, the public safety may require.

Remedy for wrongs. SECTION 9. Every person is entitled to a certain remedy in the laws for all injuries, or wrongs which he may receive in his person, property, or character; he ought to obtain justice freely, and without being obliged to purchase it, completely and without denial, promptly and without delay, conformably to the laws.

Victims of crime. SECTION 9m. [*As created April 1993*] This state shall treat crime victims, as defined by law, with fairness, dignity and respect for their privacy. This state shall ensure that crime victims have all of the following privileges and protections as provided by law: timely disposition of the case; the opportunity to attend court proceedings unless the trial court finds sequestration is necessary to a fair trial for the defendant; reasonable protection from the accused throughout the criminal justice process; notification of court proceedings; the opportunity to confer with the prosecution; the opportunity to make a statement to the court at disposition; restitution; compensation; and information about the outcome of the case and the release of the accused. The legislature shall provide remedies for the violation of this section. Nothing in this section, or in any statute enacted pursuant to this section, shall limit any right of the accused which may be provided by law. [*1991 SJR-41; 1993 SJR-3*]

Treason. SECTION 10. Treason against the state shall consist only in levying war against the same, or in adhering to its enemies, giving them aid and comfort. No person shall be convicted of treason unless on the testimony of two witnesses to the same overt act, or on confession in open court.

Searches and seizures. SECTION 11. The right of the people to be secure in their persons, houses, papers, and effects against unreasonable searches and seizures shall not be violated; and no warrant shall issue but upon probable cause, supported by oath or affirmation, and particularly describing the place to be searched and the persons or things to be seized.

Attainder; ex post facto; contracts. SECTION 12. No bill of attainder, ex post facto law, nor any law impairing the obligation of contracts, shall ever be passed, and no conviction shall work corruption of blood or forfeiture of estate.

Private property for public use. SECTION 13. The property of no person shall be taken for public use without just compensation therefor.

Feudal tenures; leases; alienation. SECTION 14. All lands within the state are declared to be allodial, and feudal tenures are prohibited. Leases and grants of agricultural land for a longer term than fifteen years in which rent or service of any kind shall be reserved, and all fines and like restraints upon alienation reserved in any grant of land, hereafter made, are declared to be void.

Equal property rights for aliens and citizens. SECTION 15. No distinction shall ever be made by law between resident aliens and citizens, in reference to the possession, enjoyment or descent of property.

Imprisonment for debt. SECTION 16. No person shall be imprisoned for debt arising out of or founded on a contract, expressed or implied.

Exemption of property of debtors. SECTION 17. The privilege of the debtor to enjoy the necessary comforts of life shall be recognized by wholesome laws, exempting a reasonable amount of property from seizure or sale for the payment of any debt or liability hereafter contracted.

Freedom of worship; liberty of conscience; state religion; public funds. SECTION 18. [*As amended November 1982*] The right of every person to worship Almighty God according to the dictates of conscience shall never be infringed; nor shall any person be compelled to attend, erect or support any place of worship, or to maintain any ministry, without consent; nor shall any control of, or interference with, the rights of conscience be permitted, or any preference be given by law to any religious establishments or modes of worship; nor shall any money be drawn from the treasury for the benefit of religious societies, or religious or theological seminaries. [*1979 AJR-76; 1981 AJR-35; submit: May'82 Spec.Sess. AJR-1*]

Freedom of worship; liberty of conscience; state religion; public funds. SECTION 18. [*Original form*] The right of every man to worship Almighty God according to the dictates of his own conscience shall never be infringed; nor shall any man be compelled to attend, erect or support any place of worship, or to maintain any ministry, against his consent; nor shall any control of, or interference with, the rights of conscience be permitted, or any preference be given by law to any religious establishments or modes of worship; nor shall any money be drawn from the treasury for the benefit of religious societies, or religious or theological seminaries.

Religious tests prohibited. SECTION 19. No religious tests shall ever be required as a qualification for any office of public trust under the state, and no person shall be rendered incompetent to give evidence in any court of law or equity in consequence of his opinions on the subject of religion.

Military subordinate to civil power. SECTION 20. The military shall be in strict subordination to the civil power.

Rights of suitors. SECTION 21. [*As amended April 1977*] (1) Writs of error shall never be prohibited, and shall be issued by such courts as the legislature designates by law.

(2) In any court of this state, any suitor may prosecute or defend his suit either in his own proper person or by an attorney of the suitor's choice. [*1975 AJR-11; 1977 SJR-9*]

Writs of error. SECTION 21. [*Original form*] Writs of error shall never be prohibited by law.

Maintenance of free government. SECTION 22. The blessings of a free government can only be maintained by a firm adherence to justice, moderation, temperance, frugality and virtue, and by frequent recurrence to fundamental principles.

Transportation of school children. SECTION 23. [*As created April 1967*] Nothing in this constitution shall prohibit the legislature from providing for the safety and welfare of children by providing for the transportation of children to and from any parochial or private school or institution of learning. [*1965 AJR-70; 1967 AJR-7*]

Use of school buildings. SECTION 24. [*As created April 1972*] Nothing in this constitution shall prohibit the legislature from authorizing, by law, the use of public school buildings by civic, religious or charitable organizations during nonschool hours upon payment by the organization to the school district of reasonable compensation for such use. [*1969 AJR-74; 1971 AJR-10*]

Right to keep and bear arms. SECTION 25. [*As created November 1998*] The people have the right to keep and bear arms for security, defense, hunting, recreation or any other lawful purpose. [*1995 AJR-53; 1997 AJR-11*]

Right to fish, hunt, trap, and take game. SECTION 26. [*As created April 2003*] The people have the right to fish, hunt, trap, and take game subject only to reasonable restrictions as prescribed by law. [*2001 SJR-2; 2003 AJR-1*]

ARTICLE II.

BOUNDARIES

State boundary. SECTION 1. It is hereby ordained and declared that the state of Wisconsin doth consent and accept of the boundaries prescribed in the act of congress entitled "An act to enable the people of Wisconsin territory to form a constitution and state government, and for the admission of such state into the Union," approved August sixth, one thousand eight hundred and forty-six, to wit: Beginning at the northeast corner of the state of Illinois – that is to say, at a point in the center of Lake Michigan where the line of forty-two degrees and thirty minutes of north latitude crosses the same; thence running with the boundary line of the state of Michigan, through Lake Michigan, Green Bay, to the mouth of the Menominee river; thence up the channel of the said river to the Brule river; thence up said last-mentioned river to Lake Brule; thence along the southern shore of Lake Brule in a direct line to the center of the channel between Middle and South Islands, in the Lake of the Desert; thence in a direct line to the head waters of the Montreal river, as marked upon the survey made by Captain Cram; thence down the main channel of the Montreal river to the middle of Lake Superior; thence through the center of Lake Superior to the mouth of the St. Louis river; thence up the main channel of said river to the first rapids in the same, above the Indian village, according to Nicollet's map; thence due south to the main branch of the river St. Croix; thence down the main channel of said river to the Mississippi; thence down the center of the main channel of that river to the northwest corner of the state of Illinois; thence due east with the northern boundary of the state of Illinois to the place of beginning, as established by "An act to enable the people of the Illinois territory to form a constitution and state government, and for the admission of such state into the Union on an equal footing with the original states," approved April 18th, 1818.

Alternate boundary. [*An additional paragraph, adopted by the convention as part of Art. II, sec. 1, was rejected by the act which admitted Wisconsin into the Union (9 U.S. Stat. Ch. L, pp. 233-235)*]: Provided, however, that the following alteration of the foresaid boundary be, and hereby is proposed to the congress of the United States as the preference of the state of Wisconsin, and if the same shall be assented and agreed to by the congress of the United States, then the same shall be and forever remain obligatory on the state of Wisconsin, viz.: Leaving the aforesaid boundary line at the foot of the rapids of the St. Louis river; thence in a direct line, bearing south-westerly, to the mouth of the Iskodewabo, or Rum river, where the same empties into the Mississippi river, thence down the main channel of said Mississippi river as prescribed in the aforesaid boundary.

Enabling act accepted. SECTION 2. [*As amended April 1951*] The propositions contained in the act of congress are hereby accepted, ratified and confirmed, and shall remain irrevocable without the consent of the United States; and it is hereby ordained that this state shall never interfere with the primary disposal of the soil within the same by the United States, nor with any regulations congress may find necessary for securing the title in such soil to bona fide purchasers thereof; and in no case shall nonresident proprietors be taxed higher than residents. Provided, that nothing in this constitution, or in the act of congress aforesaid, shall in any manner prejudice or affect the right of the state of Wisconsin to 500,000 acres of land granted to said state, and to be hereafter selected and located by and under the act of congress entitled "An act to appropriate the proceeds of the sales of the public lands, and grant pre-emption rights," approved September fourth, one thousand eight hundred and forty-one. [*1949 AJR-64; 1951 AJR-7*]

Enabling act accepted. SECTION 2. [*Original form*] The propositions contained in the act of congress are hereby accepted, ratified and confirmed, and shall remain irrevocable without the consent of the United States; and it is hereby ordained that this state shall never interfere with the primary disposal of the soil within the same by the United States, nor with any regulations congress may find necessary for securing the title in such soil to bona fide purchasers thereof; and no tax shall be imposed on land the property of the United States; and in no case shall

nonresident proprietors be taxed higher than residents. Provided, that nothing in this constitution, or in the act of congress aforesaid, shall in any manner prejudice or affect the right of the state of Wisconsin to five hundred thousand acres of land granted to said state, and to be hereafter selected and located by and under the act of congress entitled "An act to appropriate the proceeds of the sales of the public lands, and grant pre-emption rights," approved September fourth, one thousand eight hundred and forty-one.

ARTICLE III.
SUFFRAGE

Electors. SECTION 1. [*As created April 1986*] Every United States citizen age 18 or older who is a resident of an election district in this state is a qualified elector of that district. [*1983 AJR-33; 1985 AJR-3*]

Implementation. SECTION 2. [*As created April 1986*] Laws may be enacted:

(1) Defining residency.

(2) Providing for registration of electors.

(3) Providing for absentee voting.

(4) Excluding from the right of suffrage persons:

(a) Convicted of a felony, unless restored to civil rights.

(b) Adjudged by a court to be incompetent or partially incompetent, unless the judgment specifies that the person is capable of understanding the objective of the elective process or the judgment is set aside.

(5) Subject to ratification by the people at a general election, extending the right of suffrage to additional classes. [*1983 AJR-33; 1985 AJR-3*]

Secret ballot. SECTION 3. [*As created April 1986*] All votes shall be by secret ballot. [*1983 AJR-33; 1985 AJR-3*]

Revision of Article III. The original 6 sections of Article III of the constitution were repealed in April 1986 when the wording of the article was reorganized into the 3 new sections shown above.

Electors. SECTION 1. [*As amended November 1934*] Every person, of the age of twenty-one years or upwards, belonging to either of the following classes, who shall have resided in the state for one year next preceding any election, and in the election district where he offers to vote such time as may be prescribed by the legislature, not exceeding thirty days, shall be deemed a qualified elector at such election: (1) Citizens of the United States.

(2) Persons of Indian blood, who have once been declared by law of congress to be citizens of the United States, any subsequent law of congress to the contrary notwithstanding.

(3) The legislature may at any time extend, by law, the right of suffrage to persons not herein enumerated; but no such law shall be in force until the same shall have been submitted to a vote of the people at a general election, and approved by a majority of all the votes cast on that question at such election; and provided further, that the legislature may provide for the registration of electors, and prescribe proper rules and regulations therefor. [*1931 AJR-52; 1933 SJR-74*]

Termination of voting by resident aliens. [*Subdivision 2 (of the text adopted in 1882), as amended November 1908*] 2. Persons of foreign birth who, prior to the first day of December, A.D. 1908, shall have declared their intentions to become citizens conformable to the laws of the United States on the subject of naturalization, provided that the rights hereby granted to such persons shall cease on the first day of December, A.D. 1912. [*1905 AJR-16; 1907 AJR-47; 1907 c. 661*]

Qualifications of electors. SECTION 1. [*As amended November 1882*] Every male person of the age of twenty-one years or upwards, belonging to either of the following classes, who shall have resided in the state for one year next preceding any election, and in the election district where he offers to vote such time as may be prescribed by the legislature not exceeding thirty days shall be deemed a qualified elector at such election. 1. Citizens of the United States. 2. Persons of foreign birth who shall have declared their intention to become citizens, conformably to the laws of the United States on the subject of naturalization. Persons of Indian blood who have once been declared by law of congress to be citizens of the United States, any subsequent law of congress to the contrary notwithstanding. 4. Civilized persons of Indian descent not members of any tribe; provided that the legislature may at any time extend, by law, the right of suffrage to persons not herein enumerated, but no such law shall be in force until the same shall have been submitted to a vote of the people at a general election, and approved by a majority of all the votes cast at such election; and provided further, that in incorporated cities and villages, the legislature may provide for the registration of electors and prescribe proper rules and regulations therefor. [*1881 AJR-26; 1882 SJR-18; 1882 c. 272*]

Equal suffrage to colored persons. In *Gillespie v. Palmer*, 20 Wis. (1866) 544, the Wisconsin Supreme Court ruled that Chapter 137, Laws of 1849, extending *equal suffrage to colored persons*, was approved by the voters on November 6, 1849.

Qualifications of electors. SECTION 1. [*Original form*] Every male person of the age of twenty-one years or upwards belonging to either of the following classes, who shall have resided in the state for one year next preceding any election, shall be deemed a qualified elector at such election:

[*First.*] White citizens of the United States.

[*Second.*] White persons of foreign birth who shall have declared their intention to become citizens, conformably to the laws of the United States on the subject of naturalization.

[*Third.*] Persons of Indian blood who have once been declared by law of congress to be citizens of the United States, any subsequent law of congress to the contrary notwithstanding.

[*Fourth.*] Civilized persons of Indian descent, not members of any tribe. Provided, that the legislature may at any time extend, by law, the right of suffrage to persons not herein enumerated, but no such law shall be in force until the same shall have been submitted to a vote of the people at a general election, and approved by a majority of all the votes cast at such election.

Who not electors. SECTION 2. [*Original form*] No person under guardianship, non compos mentis or insane shall be qualified to vote at any election; nor shall any person convicted of treason or felony be qualified to vote at any election unless restored to civil rights.

Votes to be by ballot. SECTION 3. [*Original form*] All votes shall be given by ballot except for such township officers as may by law be directed or allowed to be otherwise chosen.

Residence saved. SECTION 4. [*Original form*] No person shall be deemed to have lost his residence in this state by reason of his absence on business of the United States or of this state.

Military stationing does not confer residence. SECTION 5. [*Original form*] No soldier, seaman or marine in the army or navy of the United States shall be deemed a resident of this state in consequence of being stationed within the same.

Exclusion from suffrage. SECTION 6. [*Original form*] Laws may be passed excluding from the right of suffrage all persons who have been or may be convicted of bribery or larceny, or of any infamous crime, and depriving every person who shall make or become directly or indirectly interested in any bet or wager depending upon the result of any election from the right to vote at such election.

ARTICLE IV.
LEGISLATIVE

Legislative power. SECTION 1. The legislative power shall be vested in a senate and assembly.

Legislature, how constituted. SECTION 2. The number of the members of the assembly shall never be less than fifty-four nor more than one hundred. The senate shall consist of a number not more than one-third nor less than one-fourth of the number of the members of the assembly.

Apportionment. SECTION 3. [*As amended November 1982*] At its first session after each enumeration made by the authority of the United States, the legislature shall apportion and district anew the members of the senate and assembly, according to the number of inhabitants. [*1979 AJR-76; 1981 AJR-35; submit: May'82 Spec.Sess. AJR-1*]

Apportionment. SECTION 3. [*As amended November 1962*] At their first session after each enumeration made by the authority of the United States, the legislature shall apportion and district anew the members of the senate and assembly, according to the number of inhabitants, excluding soldiers, and officers of the United States army and navy. [*1959 SJR-12; 1961 SJR-11*]

Senate district area factor. SECTIONS 3, 4 and 5. [*Approved by voters April 1953*] An amendment to Art. IV, secs. 3, 4, 5, relating to senate apportionment based on area and population, was approved by 1951 SJR-50 and 1953 AJR-7. However, the Supreme Court held the amendment not validly submitted to the voters in *State ex rel. Thomson v. Zimmerman*, 264 W. 644, 60 NW (2d) 416.

Apportionment. SECTION 3. [*As amended November 1910*] At their first session after each enumeration made by the authority of the United States, the legislature shall apportion and district anew the members of the senate and assembly, according to the number of inhabitants, excluding Indians not taxed, soldiers, and officers of the United States army and navy. [*1907 SJR-18; 1909 SJR-35; 1909 c. 478*]

Census and apportionment. SECTION 3. [*Original form*] The legislature shall provide by law for an enumeration of the inhabitants of the state in the year one thousand eight hundred and fifty-five, and at the end of every ten years thereafter; and at their first session after such enumeration, and also after each enumeration made by the authority of the United States, the legislature shall apportion and district anew the members of the senate and assembly, according to the number of inhabitants, excluding Indians not taxed, and soldiers and officers of the United States army and navy.

Representatives to the assembly, how chosen. SECTION 4. [*As amended November 1982*] The members of the assembly shall be chosen biennially, by single districts, on the Tuesday succeeding the first Monday of November in even-numbered years, by the qualified electors of the several districts, such districts to be bounded by county, precinct, town or ward lines, to consist of contiguous territory and be in as compact form as practicable. [*1979 AJR-76; 1981 AJR-35; submit: May'82 Spec.Sess. AJR-1*]

Representatives to the assembly, how chosen. SECTION 4. [*As amended November 1881*] The members of the assembly shall be chosen biennially, by single districts, on the Tuesday succeeding the first Monday of November after the adoption of this amendment, by the qualified electors of the several districts, such districts to be bounded by county, precinct, town or ward lines, to consist of contiguous territory and be in as compact form as practicable. [*1880 SJR-9; 1881 AJR-7; 1881 c. 262*]

Assemblymen, how chosen. SECTION 4. [*Original form*] The members of the assembly shall be chosen annually by single districts, on the Tuesday succeeding the first Monday of November, by the qualified electors of the several districts. Such districts to be bounded by county, precinct, town, or ward lines, to consist of contiguous territory, and be in as compact form as practicable.

Senators, how chosen. SECTION 5. [*As amended November 1982*] The senators shall be elected by single districts of convenient contiguous territory, at the same time and in the same manner as members of the assembly are required to be chosen; and no assembly district shall be divided in the formation of a senate district. The senate districts shall be numbered in the regular series, and the senators shall be chosen alternately from the odd and even-numbered districts for the term of 4 years. [*1979 AJR-76; 1981 AJR-35; submit: May'82 Spec.Sess. AJR-1*]

Senators, how chosen. SECTION 5. [*As amended November 1881*] The senators shall be elected by single districts of convenient contiguous territory, at the same time and in the same manner as members of the assembly are required to be chosen, and no assembly district shall be divided in the formation of a senate district. The senate districts shall be numbered in the regular series, and the senators shall be chosen alternately from the odd and even-numbered districts. The senators elected or holding over at the time of the adoption of this amendment shall continue in office till their successors are duly elected and qualified; and after the adoption of this amendment all senators shall be chosen for the term of four years. [*1880 SJR-9; 1881 AJR-7; 1881 c. 262*]

Senators, how chosen. SECTION 5. [*Original form*] The senators shall be chosen by single districts of convenient contiguous territory, at the same time and in the same manner as members of the assembly are required to be chosen, and no assembly district shall be divided in the formation of a senate district. The senate districts shall be numbered in regular series, and the senators chosen by the odd-numbered districts shall go out of office at the expiration of the first year, and the senators chosen by the even-numbered districts shall go out of office at the expiration of the second year, and thereafter the senators shall be chosen for the term of two years.

Qualifications of legislators. SECTION 6. No person shall be eligible to the legislature who shall not have resided one year within the state, and be a qualified elector in the district which he may be chosen to represent.

Organization of legislature; quorum; compulsory attendance. SECTION 7. Each house shall be the judge of the elections, returns and qualifications of its own members; and a majority of each shall constitute a quorum to do business, but a smaller number may adjourn from day to day, and may compel the attendance of absent members in such manner and under such penalties as each house may provide.

Rules; contempts; expulsion. SECTION 8. Each house may determine the rules of its own proceedings, punish for contempt and disorderly behavior, and with the concurrence of two-thirds of all the members elected, expel a member; but no member shall be expelled a second time for the same cause.

Officers. SECTION 9. [*As amended April 1979*] Each house shall choose its presiding officers from its own members. [*1977 SJR-51; 1979 SJR-1*]

Officers. SECTION 9. [*Original form*] Each house shall choose its own officers, and the senate shall choose a temporary president when the lieutenant governor shall not attend as president, or shall act as governor.

Journals; open doors; adjournments. SECTION 10. Each house shall keep a journal of its proceedings and publish the same, except such parts as require secrecy. The doors of each house shall be kept open except when the public welfare shall require secrecy. Neither house shall, without consent of the other, adjourn for more than three days.

Meeting of legislature. SECTION 11. [*As amended April 1968*] The legislature shall meet at the seat of government at such time as shall be provided by law, unless convened by the governor in special session, and when so convened no business shall be transacted except as shall be necessary to accomplish the special purposes for which it was convened. [*1965 AJR-5; 1967 AJR-15*]

Meeting of legislature. SECTION 11. [*As amended November 1881*] The legislature shall meet at the seat of government at such time as shall be provided by law, once in two years, and no oftener, unless convened by the governor, in special session, and when so convened no business shall be transacted except as shall be necessary to accomplish the

special purposes for which it was convened. [*1880 SJR-9; 1881 AJR-7; 1881 c. 262*]

Place and time of meeting. SECTION 11. [*Original form*] The legislature shall meet at the seat of government, at such time as shall be provided by law, once in each year and not oftener, unless convened by the governor.

Ineligibility of legislators to office. SECTION 12. No member of the legislature shall, during the term for which he was elected, be appointed or elected to any civil office in the state, which shall have been created, or the emoluments of which shall have been increased, during the term for which he was elected.

Ineligibility of federal officers. SECTION 13. [*As amended April 1966*] No person being a member of congress, or holding any military or civil office under the United States, shall be eligible to a seat in the legislature; and if any person shall, after his election as a member of the legislature, be elected to congress, or be appointed to any office, civil or military, under the government of the United States, his acceptance thereof shall vacate his seat. This restriction shall not prohibit a legislator from accepting short periods of active duty as a member of the reserve or from serving in the armed forces during any emergency declared by the executive. [*1963 SJR-24; 1965 SJR-15*]

Ineligibility of federal officers. SECTION 13. [*Original form*] No person being a member of congress, or holding any military or civil office under the United States, shall be eligible to a seat in the legislature; and if any person shall, after his election as a member of the legislature, be elected to congress, or be appointed to any office, civil or military, under the government of the United States, his acceptance thereof shall vacate his seat.

Filling vacancies. SECTION 14. The governor shall issue writs of election to fill such vacancies as may occur in either house of the legislature.

Exemption from arrest and civil process. SECTION 15. Members of the legislature shall in all cases, except treason, felony and breach of the peace, be privileged from arrest; nor shall they be subject to any civil process, during the session of the legislature, nor for fifteen days next before the commencement and after the termination of each session.

Privilege in debate. SECTION 16. No member of the legislature shall be liable in any civil action, or criminal prosecution whatever, for words spoken in debate.

Enactment of laws. SECTION 17. [*As amended April 1977*] (1) The style of all laws of the state shall be "The people of the state of Wisconsin, represented in senate and assembly, do enact as follows:".

(2) No law shall be enacted except by bill. No law shall be in force until published.

(3) The legislature shall provide by law for the speedy publication of all laws. [*1975 AJR-11; 1977 SJR-9*]

Style of laws; bills. SECTION 17. [*Original form*] The style of the laws of the state shall be "The people of the state of Wisconsin, represented in senate and assembly, do enact as follows:" and no law shall be enacted except by bill.

Title of private bills. SECTION 18. No private or local bill which may be passed by the legislature shall embrace more than one subject, and that shall be expressed in the title.

Origin of bills. SECTION 19. Any bill may originate in either house of the legislature, and a bill passed by one house may be amended by the other.

Yeas and nays. SECTION 20. The yeas and nays of the members of either house on any question shall, at the request of one-sixth of those present, be entered on the journal.

SECTION 21. [*Repealed. 1927 SJR-61; 1929 SJR-7; vote April 1929*]

Compensation of members. SECTION 21. [*As amended November 1881*] Each member of the legislature shall receive for his services, for and during a regular session, the sum of five hundred dollars, and ten cents for every mile he shall travel in going to and returning from the place of meeting of the legislature on the most usual route. In case of an extra session of the legislature, no additional compensation shall be allowed to any member thereof, either directly or indirectly, except for mileage to be computed at the same rate as for a regular session. No stationery, newspapers, postage or other perquisite except the salary and mileage above provided, shall be received from the state by any member of the legislature for his services, or in any other manner as such member. [*1880 SJR-9; 1881 AJR-7; 1881 c. 262*]

Compensation of members. SECTION 21. [*As amended November 1867*] Each member of the legislature shall receive for his services three hundred and fifty dollars per annum and ten cents for every mile he shall travel in going to and returning from the place of the meeting of the legislature on the most usual route. In case of an extra session of the legislature no additional compensation shall be allowed to any member thereof either directly or indirectly. [*1865 SJR-26; 1866 SJR-16; 1867 c. 25*]

Compensation of members. SECTION 21. [*Original form*] Each member of the legislature shall receive for his services two dollars and fifty cents for each day's attendance during the session, and ten cents for every mile he shall travel in going to and returning from the place of the meeting of the legislature, on the most usual route.

Powers of county boards. SECTION 22. The legislature may confer upon the boards of supervisors of the several counties of the state such powers of a local, legislative and administrative character as they shall from time to time prescribe.

Town and county government. SECTION 23. [*As amended April 1972*] The legislature shall establish but one system of town government, which shall be as nearly uniform as practicable; but the legislature may provide for the election at large once in every 4 years of a chief executive officer in any county with such powers of an administrative character as they may from time to time prescribe in accordance with this section and shall establish one or more systems of county government. [*1969 SJR-58; 1971 SJR-4*]

Uniform town and county government. SECTION 23. [*As amended April 1969*] The legislature shall establish but one system of town and county government, which shall be as nearly uniform as practicable, except that the requirement of uniformity shall not apply to the administrative means of exercising powers of a local legislative character conferred by section 22 upon the boards of supervisors of the several counties; but the legislature may provide for the election at large once in every 4 years of a chief executive officer in any county with such powers of an administrative character as they may from time to time prescribe in accordance with this section. [*1967 AJR-18; 1969 SJR-8*]

Uniform town and county government. SECTION 23. [*As amended November 1962*] The legislature shall establish but one system of town and county government, which shall be as nearly uniform as practicable; but the legislature may provide for the election at large once in

every four years of a chief executive officer in any county having a population of five hundred thousand or more with such powers of an administrative character as they may from time to time prescribe in accordance with this section. [*1959 AJR-121; 1961 AJR-61*]

Uniform town and county government. SECTION 23. [*Original form*] The legislature shall establish but one system of town and county government, which shall be as nearly uniform as practicable.

Chief executive officer to approve or veto resolutions or ordinances; proceedings on veto. SECTION 23a. [*As amended April 1969*] Every resolution or ordinance passed by the county board in any county shall, before it becomes effective, be presented to the chief executive officer. If he approves, he shall sign it; if not, he shall return it with his objections, which objections shall be entered at large upon the journal and the board shall proceed to reconsider the matter. Appropriations may be approved in whole or in part by the chief executive officer and the part approved shall become law, and the part objected to shall be returned in the same manner as provided for in other resolutions or ordinances. If, after such reconsideration, two-thirds of the members-elect of the county board agree to pass the resolution or ordinance or the part of the resolution or ordinance objected to, it shall become effective on the date prescribed but not earlier than the date of passage following reconsideration. In all such cases, the votes of the members of the county board shall be determined by ayes and noes and the names of the members voting for or against the resolution or ordinance or the part thereof objected to shall be entered on the journal. If any resolution or ordinance is not returned by the chief executive officer to the county board at its first meeting occurring not less than 6 days, Sundays excepted, after it has been presented to him, it shall become effective unless the county board has recessed or adjourned for a period in excess of 60 days, in which case it shall not be effective without his approval. [*1967 AJR-18; 1969 SJR-8*]

Chief executive officer to approve or veto resolutions or ordinances; proceedings on veto. SECTION 23a. [*Created November 1962*] Every resolution or ordinance passed by the county board in any county having a population of five hundred thousand or more shall, before it becomes effective, be presented to the chief executive officer. If he approves, he shall sign it; if not, he shall return it with his objections, which objections shall be entered at large upon the journal and the board shall proceed to reconsider the matter. Appropriations may be approved in whole or in part by the chief executive officer and the part approved shall become law, and the part objected to shall be returned in the same manner as provided for in other resolutions or ordinances. If, after such reconsideration, two-thirds of the members-elect of the county board agree to

pass the resolution or ordinance or the part of the resolution or ordinance objected to, it shall become effective on the date prescribed but not earlier than the date of passage following reconsideration. In all such cases, the votes of members of the county board shall be determined by ayes and nays and the names of the members voting for or against the resolution or ordinance or the part thereof objected to shall be entered on the journal. If any resolution or ordinance is not returned by the chief executive officer to the county board at its first meeting occurring not less than six days, Sundays excepted, after it has been presented to him, it shall become effective unless the county board has recessed or adjourned for a period in excess of sixty days, in which case it shall not be effective without his approval. [*1959 AJR-121; 1961 AJR-61*]

Gambling. SECTION 24. [*As amended April 1993*] (1) Except as provided in this section, the legislature may not authorize gambling in any form.

(2) Except as otherwise provided by law, the following activities do not constitute consideration as an element of gambling:

(a) To listen to or watch a television or radio program.

(b) To fill out a coupon or entry blank, whether or not proof of purchase is required.

(c) To visit a mercantile establishment or other place without being required to make a purchase or pay an admittance fee.

(3) [*As amended April 1999*] The legislature may authorize the following bingo games licensed by the state, but all profits shall accrue to the licensed organization and no salaries, fees or profits may be paid to any other organization or person: bingo games operated by religious, charitable, service, fraternal or veterans' organizations or those to which contributions are deductible for federal or state income tax purposes. All moneys received by the state that are attributable to bingo games shall be used for property tax relief for residents of this state as provided by law. The distribution of moneys that are attributable to bingo games may not vary based on the income or age of the person provided the property tax relief. The distribution of moneys that are attributable to bingo games shall not be subject to the uniformity requirement of section 1 of article VIII. In this subsection, the distribution of all moneys attributable to bingo games shall include any earnings on the moneys received by the state that are attributable to bingo games, but shall not include any moneys used for the regulation of, and enforcement of law relating to, bingo games. [*1997 AJR-80; 1999 AJR-2*]

(3) The legislature may authorize the following bingo games licensed by the state, but all profits shall accrue to the licensed organization and no salaries, fees or profits may be paid to any other organization or person: bingo games operated by religious, charitable, service, fraternal or veterans' organizations or those to which contributions are deductible for federal or state income tax purposes.

(4) The legislature may authorize the following raffle games licensed by the state, but all profits shall accrue to the licensed local organization and no salaries, fees or profits may be paid to any other organization or person: raffle games operated by local religious, charitable, service, fraternal or veterans' organizations or those to which contributions are deductible for federal or state income tax purposes. The legislature shall limit the number of raffles conducted by any such organization.

(5) [*As amended April 1999*] This section shall not prohibit pari-mutuel on-track betting as provided by law. The state may not own or operate any facility or enterprise for pari-mutuel betting, or lease any state-owned land to any other owner or operator for such purposes. All moneys received by the state that are attributable to pari-mutuel on-track betting shall be used for property tax relief for residents of this state as provided by law. The distribution of moneys that are attributable to pari-mutuel on-track betting may not vary based on the income or age of the person provided the property tax relief. The distribution of moneys that are attributable to pari-mutuel on-track betting shall not be subject to the uniformity requirement of section 1 of article VIII. In this subsection, the distribution of all moneys attributable to pari-mutuel on-track betting shall include any earnings on the moneys received by the state that are attributable to pari-mutuel on-track betting, but shall not include any moneys used for the regulation of, and enforcement of law relating to, pari-mutuel on-track betting. [*1997 AJR-80; 1999 AJR-2*]

(5) This section shall not prohibit pari-mutuel on-track betting as provided by law. The state may not own or operate any facility or enterprise for pari-mutuel betting, or lease any state-owned land to any other owner or operator for such purposes.

(6) (a) [*As amended April 1999*] The legislature may authorize the creation of a lottery to be operated by the state as provided by law. The expenditure of public funds or of revenues derived from lottery operations to engage in promotional advertising of the Wisconsin state lottery is prohibited. Any advertising of the state lottery shall indicate the odds of a specific lottery ticket to be selected as the winning ticket for each prize amount offered. The net proceeds of the state lottery shall be deposited in the treasury of the state, to be used for property tax relief for residents of this state as provided by law. The distribution of the net proceeds of the state lottery may not vary based on the income or age of the person provided the property tax relief. The distribution of the net proceeds of the state lottery shall not be subject to the uniformity requirement of section 1 of article VIII. In this paragraph, the distribution of the net proceeds of the state lottery shall include any earnings on the net proceeds of the state lottery. [*1997 AJR-80; 1999 AJR-2*]

(6) (a) The legislature may authorize the creation of a lottery to be operated by the state as provided by law. The expenditure of public funds or of revenues derived from lottery operations to engage in promotional advertising of the Wisconsin state lottery is prohibited. Any advertising of the state lottery shall indicate the odds of a specific lottery ticket to be selected as the winning ticket for each prize amount offered. The net proceeds of the state lottery shall be deposited in the treasury of the state, to be used for property tax relief as provided by law.

(b) The lottery authorized under par. (a) shall be an enterprise that entitles the player, by purchasing a ticket, to participate in a game of chance if: 1) the winning tickets are randomly predetermined and the player reveals preprinted numbers or symbols from which it can be immediately determined whether the ticket is a winning ticket entitling the player to win a prize as prescribed in the features and procedures for the game, including an opportunity to win a prize in a secondary or subsequent chance drawing or game; or 2) the ticket is evidence of the numbers or symbols selected by the player or, at the player's option, selected by a computer, and the player becomes entitled to a prize as prescribed in the features and procedures for the game, including an opportunity to win a prize in a secondary or subsequent chance drawing or game if some or all of the player's symbols or numbers are selected in a chance drawing or game, if the player's ticket is randomly selected by the computer at the time of purchase or if the ticket is selected in a chance drawing.

(c) Notwithstanding the authorization of a state lottery under par. (a), the following games, or games simulating any of the following games, may not be conducted by the state as a lottery: 1) any game in which winners are selected based on the results of a race or sporting event; 2) any banking card game, including blackjack, baccarat or chemin de fer; 3) poker; 4) roulette; 5) craps or any other game that involves rolling dice; 6) keno; 7) bingo 21, bingo jack, bingolet or bingo craps; 8) any game of chance that is placed on a slot machine or any mechanical, electromechanical or electronic device that is generally available to be played at a gambling casino; 9) any game or device that is commonly known as a video game of chance or a video gaming machine or that is commonly considered to be a video gambling machine, unless such machine is a video device operated by the state in a game authorized under par. (a) to permit the sale of tickets through retail outlets under contract with the state and the device does not determine or indicate whether the player has won a prize, other than by verifying that the player's ticket or some or all of the player's symbols or numbers on the player's ticket have been selected in a chance drawing, or by verifying that the player's ticket has been randomly selected by a central system computer at the time of purchase; 10) any game that is similar to a game listed in this paragraph; or 11) any other game that is commonly considered to be a form of gambling and is not, or is not substantially similar to, a game conducted by the state under par. (a). No game conducted by the state under par. (a) may permit a player of the game to purchase a ticket, or to otherwise participate in the game, from a residence by using a computer, telephone or other form of electronic, telecommunication, video or technological aid. *[(1), (2)(intro.) amended; (6)(b), (c) created; June 1992 AJR-1; 1993 SJR-2]*

Lotteries and divorces. SECTION 24. [*As amended April 1987*] (1) Except as provided in this section, the legislature shall never authorize any lottery or grant any divorce.

(2) Except as otherwise provided by law, the following activities do not constitute consideration as an element of a lottery:

(a) To listen to or watch a television or radio program.

(b) To fill out a coupon or entry blank, whether or not proof of purchase is required.

(c) To visit a mercantile establishment or other place without being required to make a purchase or pay an admittance fee.

(3) The legislature may authorize the following bingo games licensed by the state, but all profits shall accrue to the licensed organization and no salaries, fees or profits may be paid to any other organization or person: bingo games operated by religious, charitable, service, fraternal or veterans' organizations or those to which contributions are deductible for federal or state income tax purposes.

(4) The legislature may authorize the following raffle games licensed by the state, but all profits shall accrue to the licensed local organization and no salaries, fees or profits may be paid to any other organization or person: raffle games operated by local religious, charitable, service, fraternal or veterans' organizations or those to which contributions are deductible for federal or state income tax purposes. The legislature shall limit the number of raffles conducted by any such organization.

(5) This section shall not prohibit pari-mutuel on-track betting as provided by law. The state may not own or operate any facility or enterprise for pari-mutuel betting, or lease any state-owned land to any other owner or operator for such purposes.

(6) The legislature may authorize the creation of a lottery to be operated by the state as provided by law. The expenditure of public funds or of revenues derived from lottery operations to engage in promotional advertising of the Wisconsin state lottery is prohibited. Any advertising of the state lottery shall indicate the odds of a specific lottery ticket to be selected as the winning ticket for each prize amount offered. The net proceeds of the state lottery shall be deposited in the treasury of the state, to be used for property tax relief as provided by law. *[Pari-mutuel: 1985 AJR-45; 1987 AJR-2. State lottery: 1985 SJR-1; 1987 AJR-3.]*

Lotteries and divorces. SECTION 24. [*As amended April 1977*] The legislature shall never authorize any lottery or grant any divorce. (1) The legislature may authorize bingo games licensed by the state, and operated by religious,

charitable, service, fraternal or veterans' organizations or those to which contributions are deductible for federal or state income tax purposes. All profits must inure to the licensed organization and no salaries, fees or profits shall be paid to any other organization or person. (2) The legislature may authorize raffle games licensed by the state, and operated by local religious, charitable, service, fraternal or veterans' organizations or those to which contributions are deductible for federal or state income tax purposes. The legislature shall limit the number of raffles conducted by any such organization. All profits must inure to the licensed local organization and no salaries, fees or profits shall be paid to any other organization or person. (3) Except as the legislature may provide otherwise, the following activities do not constitute consideration as an element of a lottery: (a) To listen to or watch a television or radio program. (b) To fill out a coupon or entry blank, whether or not proof of purchase is required. (c) To visit a mercantile establishment or other place without being required to make a purchase or pay an admittance fee. *[1975 AJR-43; 1977 AJR-10]*

Lotteries and divorces. SECTION 24. [*As amended April 1973*] The legislature shall never authorize any lottery, or grant any divorce, but may authorize bingo games licensed by the state, and operated by religious, charitable, service, fraternal or veterans' organizations or those to which contributions are deductible for federal or state income tax purposes. All profits must inure to the licensed organization and no salaries, fees or profits shall be paid to any other organization or person. Except as the legislature may provide otherwise, to listen to a television or radio program, to fill out a coupon or entry blank, whether or not proof of purchase is required, or to visit a mercantile establishment or other place without being required to make a purchase or pay an admittance fee does not constitute consideration as an element of a lottery. *[1971 SJR-13; 1973 AJR-6]*

Lotteries and divorces. SECTION 24. [*As amended April 1965*] The legislature shall never authorize any lottery, or grant any divorce. Except as the legislature may provide otherwise, to listen to or watch a television or radio program, to fill out a coupon or entry blank, whether or not proof of purchase is required, or to visit a mercantile establishment or other place without being required to make a purchase or pay an admittance fee does not constitute consideration as an element of a lottery. *[1963 SJR-42; 1965 SJR-13]*

Lotteries and divorces. SECTION 24. [*Original form*] The legislature shall never authorize any lottery, or grant any divorce.

Stationery and printing. SECTION 25. The legislature shall provide by law that all stationery required for the use of the state, and all printing authorized and required by them to be done for their use, or for the state, shall be let by contract to the lowest bidder, but the legislature may establish a maximum price; no member of the legislature or other state officer shall be interested, either directly or indirectly, in any such contract.

Extra compensation; salary change. SECTION 26. [*As amended April 1992*] (1) The legislature may not grant any extra compensation to a public officer, agent, servant or contractor after the services have been rendered or the contract has been entered into.

(2) Except as provided in this subsection, the compensation of a public officer may not be increased or diminished during the term of office:

(a) When any increase or decrease in the compensation of justices of the supreme court or judges of any court of record becomes effective as to any such justice or judge, it shall be effective from such date as to every such justice or judge.

(b) Any increase in the compensation of members of the legislature shall take effect, for all senators and representatives to the assembly, after the next general election beginning with the new assembly term.

(3) Subsection (1) shall not apply to increased benefits for persons who have been or shall be granted benefits of any kind under a retirement system when such increased benefits are provided by a legislative act passed on a call of ayes and noes by a three-fourths vote of all the members elected to both houses of the legislature and such act provides for sufficient state funds to cover the costs of the increased benefits. [*1989 AJR-47; 1991 AJR-16*]

Extra compensation; salary change. SECTION 26. [*As amended April 1977*] The legislature shall never grant any extra compensation to any public officer, agent, servant or contractor, after the services shall have been rendered or the contract entered into; nor shall the compensation of any public officer be increased or diminished during his term of office except that when any increase or decrease provided by the legislature in the compensation of the justices of the supreme court or judges of any court of record shall become effective as to any such justice or judge, it shall be effective from such date as to each of such justices or judges. This section shall not apply to increased benefits for persons who have been or shall be granted benefits of any kind under a retirement system when such increased benefits are provided by a legislative act passed on a call of ayes and noes by a three-fourths vote of all the members elected to both houses of the legislature, which act shall provide for sufficient state funds to cover the costs of the increased benefits. [*1975 AJR-11; 1977 SJR-9*]

Extra compensation; salary change. SECTION 26. [*As amended April 1974*] The legislature shall never grant any extra compensation to any public officer, agent, servant or contractor, after the services shall have been rendered or the contract entered into; nor shall the compensation of any public officer be increased or diminished during his term of office except that when any increase or decrease provided by the legislature in the compensation of the justices of the supreme court, or judges of the circuit court shall become effective as to any such justice or judge, it shall become effective from such date as to each of such justices or judges. This section shall not apply to increased benefits for persons who have been or shall be granted benefits of any kind under a retirement system when such increased benefits are provided by a legislative act passed on a call of yeas and nays by a three-fourths vote of all the members elected to both houses of the legislature, which act shall provide for sufficient state funds to cover the costs of the increased benefits. [*1971 SJR-3; 1973 SJR-15*]

Extra compensation; salary change. SECTION 26. [*As amended April 1967*] The legislature shall never grant any extra compensation to any public officer, agent, servant or contractor, after the services shall have been rendered or the contract entered into; nor shall the compensation of any public officer be increased or diminished during his term of office except that when any increase or decrease provided by the legislature in the compensation of the justices of the supreme court, or judges of the circuit court shall become effective as to any such justice or judge, it shall be effective from such date as to each of such justices or judges. This section shall not apply to increased benefits for teachers under a teachers' retirement system when such increased benefits are provided by a legislative act passed on a call of yeas and nays by a three-fourths vote of all the members elected to both houses of the legislature. [*1965 AJR-162; 1967 AJR-17*]

Extra compensation; salary change. SECTION 26. [*As amended April 1956*] The legislature shall never grant any extra compensation to any public officer, agent, servant or contractor, after the services shall have been rendered or the contract entered into; nor shall the compensation of any public officer be increased or diminished during his term of office. This section shall not apply to increased benefits for teachers under a teachers' retirement system when such increased benefits are provided by a legislative act passed on a call of yeas and nays by a three-fourths vote of all the members elected to both houses of the legislature. [*1953 SJR-21; 1955 SJR-8*]

Extra compensation; salary change. SECTION 26. [*Original form*] The legislature shall never grant any extra compensation to any public officer, agent, servant or contractor after the services shall have been rendered or the contract entered into; nor shall the compensation of any public officer be increased or diminished during his term of office.

Suits against state. SECTION 27. The legislature shall direct by law in what manner and in what courts suits may be brought against the state.

Oath of office. SECTION 28. Members of the legislature, and all officers, executive and judicial, except such inferior officers as may be by law exempted, shall before they enter upon the duties of their respective offices, take and subscribe an oath or affirmation to support the constitution of the United States and the constitution of the state of Wisconsin, and faithfully to discharge the duties of their respective offices to the best of their ability.

Militia. SECTION 29. The legislature shall determine what persons shall constitute the militia of the state, and may provide for organizing and disciplining the same in such manner as shall be prescribed by law.

Elections by legislature. SECTION 30. [*As amended November 1982*] All elections made by the legislature shall be by roll call vote entered in the journals. [*1979 AJR-76; 1981 AJR-35; submit: May'82 Spec.Sess. AJR-1*]

Elections by legislature. SECTION 30. [*Original form*] In all elections to be made by the legislature the members thereof shall vote viva voce, and their votes shall be entered on the journal.

Special and private laws prohibited. SECTION 31. [*As amended April 1993*] The legislature is prohibited from enacting any special or private laws in the following cases:

(1) For changing the names of persons, constituting one person the heir at law of another or granting any divorce.

(2) For laying out, opening or altering highways, except in cases of state roads extending into more than one county, and military roads to aid in the construction of which lands may be granted by congress.

(3) For authorizing persons to keep ferries across streams at points wholly within this state.

(4) For authorizing the sale or mortgage of real or personal property of minors or others under disability.

(5) For locating or changing any county seat.

(6) For assessment or collection of taxes or for extending the time for the collection thereof.

(7) For granting corporate powers or privileges, except to cities.

(8) For authorizing the apportionment of any part of the school fund.

(9) For incorporating any city, town or village, or to amend the charter thereof. [*(1) amended; June 1992 AJR-1; 1993 SJR-2*]

Special and private laws prohibited. SECTION 31. [*As amended November 1892*] The legislature is prohibited from enacting any special or private laws in the following cases:

1st. For changing the name of persons or constituting one person the heir at law of another.

2d. For laying out, opening or altering highways, except in cases of state roads extending into more than one county, and military roads to aid in the construction of which lands may be granted by congress.

3d. For authorizing persons to keep ferries across streams at points wholly within this state.

4th. For authorizing the sale or mortgage of real or personal property of minors or others under disability.

5th. For locating or changing any county seat.

6th. For assessment or collection of taxes or for extending the time for the collection thereof.

7th. For granting corporate powers or privileges, except to cities.

8th. For authorizing the apportionment of any part of the school fund.

9th. For incorporating any city, town or village, or to amend the charter thereof. [*1889 SJR-13; 1891 SJR-13; 1891 c. 362*]

Special or private laws. SECTION 31. [*Created November 1871*] The legislature is prohibited from enacting any special or private laws in the following cases:

1st. For changing the name of persons or constituting one person the heir at law of another.

2d. For laying out, opening or altering highways, except in cases of state roads extending into more than one county, and military roads to aid in the construction of which lands may be granted by congress.

3d. For authorizing persons to keep ferries across streams at points wholly within this state.

4th. For authorizing the sale or mortgage of real or personal property of minors or others under disability.

5th. For locating or changing any county seat.

6th. For assessment or collection of taxes or for extending the time for the collection thereof.

7th. For granting corporate powers or privileges, except to cities.

8th. For authorizing the apportionment of any part of the school fund.

9th. For incorporating any town or village or to amend the charter thereof. [*1870 SJR-14; 1871 AJR-29; 1871 c. 122*]

General laws on enumerated subjects. SECTION 32. [*As amended April 1993*] The legislature may provide by general law for the treatment of any subject for which lawmaking is prohibited by section 31 of this article. Subject to reasonable classifications, such laws shall be uniform in their operation throughout the state. [*June 1992 AJR-1; 1993 SJR-2*]

General laws on enumerated subjects. SECTION 32. [*Created November 1871*] The legislature shall provide general laws for the transaction of any business that may be prohibited by section thirty-one of this article, and all such laws shall be uniform in their operation throughout the state. [*1870 SJR-14; 1871 AJR-29; 1871 c. 122*]

Auditing of state accounts. SECTION 33. [*Created November 1946*] The legislature shall provide for the auditing of state accounts and may establish such offices and prescribe such duties for the same as it shall deem necessary. [*1943 SJR-35; 1945 SJR-24*]

Continuity of civil government. SECTION 34. [*Created April 1961*] The legislature, in order to ensure continuity of state and local governmental operations in periods of emergency resulting from enemy action in the form of an attack, shall (1) forthwith provide for prompt and temporary succession to the powers and duties of public offices, of whatever nature and whether filled by election or appointment, the incumbents of which may become unavailable for carrying on the powers and duties of such offices, and (2) adopt such other measures as may be necessary and proper for attaining the objectives of this section. [*1959 AJR-48; 1961 SJR-1*]

ARTICLE V.
EXECUTIVE

Governor; lieutenant governor; term. SECTION 1. [*As amended April 1979*] The executive power shall be vested in a governor who shall hold office for 4 years; a lieutenant governor shall be elected at the same time and for the same term. [*1977 SJR-51; 1979 SJR-1*]

Governor; lieutenant governor; term. SECTION 1. [*Original form*] The executive power shall be vested in a governor, who shall hold his office for two years; a

lieutenant governor shall be elected at the same time, and for the same term.

SECTION 1m. [*Repealed. 1977 SJR-51; 1979 SJR-1; vote April 1979*]

Governor; 4-year term. SECTION 1m. [*Created April 1967*] Notwithstanding section 1, beginning with the general election in 1970 and every four years thereafter,

there shall be elected a governor to hold office for a term of four years. [*1965 AJR-4; 1967 AJR-9 and SJR-12*]

SECTION 1n. [*Repealed. 1977 SJR-51; 1979 SJR-1; vote April 1979*]

Lieutenant governor; 4-year term. SECTION 1n. [*Created April 1967*] Notwithstanding section 1, beginning with the general election in 1970 and every four years

thereafter, there shall be elected a lieutenant governor to hold office for a term of four years. [*1965 AJR-4; 1967 AJR-9 and SJR-12*]

Eligibility. SECTION 2. No person except a citizen of the United States and a qualified elector of the state shall be eligible to the office of governor or lieutenant governor.

Election. SECTION 3. [*As amended April 1967*] The governor and lieutenant governor shall be elected by the qualified electors of the state at the times and places of choosing members of the legislature. They shall be chosen jointly, by the casting by each voter of a single vote applicable to both offices beginning with the general election in 1970. The persons respectively having the highest number of votes cast jointly for them for governor and lieutenant governor shall be elected; but in case two or more slates shall have an equal and the highest number of votes for governor and lieutenant governor, the two houses of the legislature, at its next annual session shall forthwith, by joint ballot, choose one of the slates so having an equal and the highest number of votes for governor and lieutenant governor. The returns of election for governor and lieutenant governor shall be made in such manner as shall be provided by law. [*1965 AJR-3; 1967 AJR-8 and SJR-11*]

Election. SECTION 3. [*Original form*] The governor and lieutenant governor shall be elected by the qualified electors of the state at the times and places of choosing members of the legislature. The persons respectively having the highest number of votes for governor and lieutenant governor shall be elected; but in case two or more shall have an equal and the highest number of votes for governor, or lieutenant

governor, the two houses of the legislature, at its next annual session shall forthwith, by joint ballot, choose one of the persons so having an equal and the highest number of votes for governor, or lieutenant governor. The returns of election for governor and lieutenant governor shall be made in such manner as shall be provided by law.

Powers and duties. SECTION 4. The governor shall be commander in chief of the military and naval forces of the state. He shall have power to convene the legislature on extraordinary occasions, and in case of invasion, or danger from the prevalence of contagious disease at the seat of government, he may convene them at any other suitable place within the state. He shall communicate to the legislature, at every session, the condition of the state, and recommend such matters to them for their consideration as he may deem expedient. He shall transact all necessary business with the officers of the government, civil and military. He shall expedite all such measures as may be resolved upon by the legislature, and shall take care that the laws be faithfully executed.

SECTION 5. [*Repealed. 1929 SJR-81; 1931 SJR-6; vote November 1932*]

Compensation of governor. SECTION 5. [*As amended November 1926*] The governor shall receive, during his continuance in office, an annual compensation of not less than five thousand dollars, to be fixed by law, which shall be in full for all traveling or other expenses incident to his duties. The compensation prescribed for governor immediately prior to the adoption of this amendment shall continue in force until changed by the legislature in a manner consistent with the other provisions of this constitution. [*1923 AJR-88; 1925 SJR-50; 1925 c. 413*]

Compensation of governor. SECTION 5. [*As amended November 1869*] The governor shall receive during his continuance in office, an annual compensation of five thousand dollars which shall be in full for all traveling or other expenses incident to his duties. [*1868 AJR-13; 1869 SJR-6; 1869 c. 186*]

Compensation of governor. SECTION 5. [*Original form*] The governor shall receive during his continuance in office, an annual compensation of one thousand two hundred and fifty dollars.

Pardoning power. SECTION 6. The governor shall have power to grant reprieves, commutations and pardons, after conviction, for all offenses, except treason and cases of impeachment, upon such conditions and with such restrictions and limitations as he may think proper, subject to such regulations as may be provided by law relative to the manner of applying for pardons. Upon conviction for treason he shall have the power to suspend the execution of the sentence until the case shall be reported to the legislature at its next meeting, when the legislature shall either pardon, or commute the sentence, direct the execution of the sentence, or grant a further reprieve. He shall annually communicate to the legislature each case of reprieve, commutation or pardon granted, stating the name of the convict, the crime of which he was convicted, the sentence and its date, and the date of the commutation, pardon or reprieve, with his reasons for granting the same.

Lieutenant governor, when governor. SECTION 7. [*As amended April 1979*] (1) Upon the governor's death, resignation or removal from office, the lieutenant governor shall become governor for the balance of the unexpired term.

(2) If the governor is absent from this state, impeached, or from mental or physical disease, becomes incapable of performing the duties of the office, the lieutenant governor shall serve as acting governor for the balance of the unexpired term or until the governor returns, the disability ceases or the impeachment is vacated. But when the governor, with the consent of the legislature, shall be out of this state in time of war at the head of the state's military force, the governor shall continue as commander in chief of the military force. [*1977 SJR-51; 1979 SJR-1*]

Lieutenant governor, when governor. SECTION 7. [*Original form*] In case of the impeachment of the governor, or his removal from office, death, inability from mental or physical disease, resignation, or absence from the state, the powers and duties of the office shall devolve upon the lieutenant governor for the residue of the term or until the governor, absent or impeached, shall have returned, or the disability shall cease. But when the governor shall, with the consent of the legislature, be out of the state in time of war, at the head of the military force thereof, he shall continue commander in chief of the military force of the state.

Secretary of state, when governor. SECTION 8. [*As amended April 1979*] (1) If there is a vacancy in the office of lieutenant governor and the governor dies, resigns or is removed from office, the secretary of state shall become governor for the balance of the unexpired term.

(2) If there is a vacancy in the office of lieutenant governor and the governor is absent from this state, impeached, or from mental or physical disease becomes incapable of performing the duties of the office, the secretary of state shall serve as acting governor for the balance of the unexpired term or until the governor returns, the disability ceases or the impeachment is vacated. [*1977 SJR-51; 1979 SJR-1*]

Lieutenant governor president of senate; when secretary of state to be governor. SECTION 8. [*Original form*] The lieutenant governor shall be president of the senate, but shall have only a casting vote therein. If, during a vacancy in the office of the governor, the lieutenant governor shall be impeached, displaced, resign, die, or from mental or physical disease become incapable of performing the duties of his office, or be absent from the state, the secretary of state shall act as governor until the vacancy shall be filled or the disability shall cease.

SECTION 9. [*Repealed. 1929 SJR-82; 1931 SJR-7; vote November 1932*]

Compensation of lieutenant governor. SECTION 9. [*As amended November 1869*] The lieutenant governor shall receive during his continuance in office an annual compensation of one thousand dollars. [*1868 AJR-13; 1869 SJR-6; 1869 c. 186*]

Compensation of lieutenant governor. SECTION 9. [*Original form*] The lieutenant governor shall receive double the per diem allowance of members of the senate, for every day's attendance as president of the senate, and the same mileage as shall be allowed to members of the legislature.

Governor to approve or veto bills; proceedings on veto. SECTION 10. [*As amended April 1990*] (1) (a) Every bill which shall have passed the legislature shall, before it becomes a law, be presented to the governor.

(b) If the governor approves and signs the bill, the bill shall become law. Appropriation bills may be approved in whole or in part by the governor, and the part approved shall become law.

(c) In approving an appropriation bill in part, the governor may not create a new word by rejecting individual letters in the words of the enrolled bill.

(2) (a) If the governor rejects the bill, the governor shall return the bill, together with the objections in writing, to the house in which the bill originated. The house of origin shall enter the objections at large upon the journal and proceed to reconsider the bill. If, after such reconsideration, two-thirds of the members present agree to pass the bill notwithstanding the objections of the governor, it shall be sent, together with the objections, to the other house, by which it shall likewise be reconsidered, and if approved by two-thirds of the members present it shall become law.

(b) The rejected part of an appropriation bill, together with the governor's objections in writing, shall be returned to the house in which the bill originated. The house of origin shall enter the objections at large upon the journal and proceed to reconsider the rejected part of the appropriation bill. If, after such reconsideration, two-thirds of the members present agree to approve the rejected part notwithstanding the objections of the governor, it shall be sent, together with the objections, to the other house, by which it shall likewise be reconsidered, and if approved by two-thirds of the members present the rejected part shall become law.

(c) In all such cases the votes of both houses shall be determined by ayes and noes, and the names of the members voting for or against passage of the bill or the rejected part of the bill notwithstanding the objections of the governor shall be entered on the journal of each house respectively.

(3) Any bill not returned by the governor within 6 days (Sundays excepted) after it shall have been presented to the governor shall be law unless the legislature, by final adjournment, prevents the bill's return, in which case it shall not be law. [*1987 AJR-71; 1989 SJR-11*]

Governor to approve or veto bills; proceedings on veto. SECTION 10. [*As amended November 1930*] Every bill which shall have passed the legislature shall, before it becomes a law, be presented to the governor; if he approve, he shall sign it, but if not, he shall return it, with his objections, to that house in which it shall have originated, who shall enter the objections at large upon the journal and proceed to reconsider it. Appropriation bills may be approved in whole or in part by the governor, and the part approved shall become law, and the part objected to shall be returned in the same manner as provided for other bills. If, after such reconsideration, two-thirds of the members present shall agree to pass the bill, or the part of the bill objected to, it shall be sent, together with the objections, to the other house, by which it shall likewise be reconsidered, and if approved by two-thirds of the members present it shall become a law. But in all such cases the votes of both houses shall be determined by yeas and nays, and the names of the members voting for or against the bill or the part of the bill objected to, shall be entered on the journal of each house respectively. If any bill shall not be returned by the governor within six days (Sundays excepted) after it shall have been presented to him, the same shall be a law unless the legislature shall, by their adjournment, prevent its return, in which case it shall not be a law. [*1927 SJR-35; 1929 SJR-40*]

Approval of bills. SECTION 10. [*As amended November 1908*] Every bill which shall have passed the legislature shall, before it becomes a law, be presented to the governor; if he approve, he shall sign it, but if not, he shall return it, with his objections, to that house in which it shall have originated, who shall enter the objections at large upon the journal and proceed to reconsider it. If, after such reconsideration, two-thirds of the members present shall

agree to pass the bill, it shall be sent, together with the objections to the other house, by which it shall likewise be reconsidered, and if approved by two-thirds of the members present it shall become a law. But in all such cases the votes of both houses shall be determined by yeas and nays, and the names of the members voting for or against the bill shall be entered on the journal of each house respectively. If any bill shall not be returned by the governor within six days (Sundays excepted) after it shall have been presented to him, the same shall be a law unless the legislature shall, by their adjournment, prevent its return, in which case it shall not be a law. [*1905 AJR-45; 1907 AJR-46; 1907 c. 661*]

Approval of bills. SECTION 10. [*Original form*] Every bill which shall have passed the legislature shall, before it becomes a law, be presented to the governor; if he approve, he shall sign it, but if not, he shall return it, with his objections, to that house in which it shall have originated, who shall enter the objections at large upon the journal, and proceed to reconsider it. If, after such reconsideration two-thirds of the members present shall agree to pass the bill, it shall be sent, together with the objections, to the other house, by which it shall likewise be reconsidered, and if approved by two-thirds of the members present, it shall become a law. But in all such cases the votes of both houses shall be determined by yeas and nays, and the names of the members voting for or against the bill, shall be entered on the journal of each house respectively. If any bill shall not be returned by the governor within three days (Sundays excepted) after it shall have been presented to him, the same shall be a law, unless the legislature shall, by their adjournment, prevent its return, in which case it shall not be a law.

ARTICLE VI.
ADMINISTRATIVE

Election of secretary of state, treasurer and attorney general; term. SECTION 1. [*As amended April 1979*] The qualified electors of this state, at the times and places of choosing the members of the legislature, shall in 1970 and every 4 years thereafter elect a secretary of state, treasurer and attorney general who shall hold their offices for 4 years. [*1977 SJR-51; 1979 SJR-1*]

Election of secretary of state, treasurer and attorney-general; term. SECTION 1. [*Original form*] There shall be chosen by the qualified electors of the state, at the times and places of choosing the members of the legislature, a secretary of state, treasurer and attorney-general, who shall severally hold their offices for the term of two years.

SECTION 1m. [*Repealed. 1977 SJR-51; 1979 SJR-1; vote April 1979*]

Secretary of state; 4-year term. SECTION 1m. [*Created April 1967*] Notwithstanding section 1, beginning with the general election in 1970 and every four years thereafter, there shall be chosen a secretary of state to hold office for a term of four years. [*1965 AJR-4; 1967 AJR-9 and SJR-12*]

SECTION 1n. [*Repealed. 1977 SJR-51; 1979 SJR-1; vote April 1979*]

Treasurer; 4-year term. SECTION 1n. [*Created April 1967*] Notwithstanding section 1, beginning with the general election in 1970 and every four years thereafter, there shall be chosen a treasurer to hold office for a term of four years. [*1965 AJR-4; 1967 AJR-9 and SJR-12*]

SECTION 1p. [*Repealed. 1977 SJR-51; 1979 SJR-1; vote April 1979*]

Attorney general; 4-year term. SECTION 1p. [*Created April 1967*] Notwithstanding section 1, beginning with the general election in 1970 and every four years thereafter, there shall be chosen an attorney general to hold office for a term of four years. [*1965 AJR-4; 1967 AJR-9 and SJR-12*]

Secretary of state; duties, compensation. SECTION 2. [*As amended November 1946*] The secretary of state shall keep a fair record of the official acts of the legislature and executive department of the state, and shall, when required, lay the same and all matters relative thereto before either branch of the legislature. He shall perform such other duties as shall be assigned him by law. He shall receive as a compensation for his services yearly such sum as shall be provided by law, and shall keep his office at the seat of government. [*1943 SJR-35; 1945 SJR-24*]

Secretary of state. SECTION 2. [*Original form*] The secretary of state shall keep a fair record of the official acts of the legislature and executive department of the state, and shall, when required, lay the same and all matters relative thereto, before either branch of the legislature. He shall be ex officio auditor, and shall perform such other duties as shall be assigned him by law. He shall receive as a compensation for his services yearly, such sum as shall be provided by law, and shall keep his office at the seat of government.

Treasurer and attorney general; duties, compensation. SECTION 3. The powers, duties and compensation of the treasurer and attorney general shall be prescribed by law.

County officers; election, terms, removal; vacancies. SECTION 4. [*As amended April 2005*] (1) (a) Except as provided in pars. (b) and (c) and sub. (2), coroners, registers of deeds, district attorneys, and all other elected county officers, except judicial officers, sheriffs, and chief executive officers, shall be chosen by the electors of the respective counties once in every 2 years.

(b) Beginning with the first general election at which the governor is elected which occurs after the ratification of this paragraph, sheriffs shall be chosen by the electors of the respective counties, or by the electors of all of the respective counties comprising each combination of counties combined by the legislature for that purpose, for the term of 4 years and coroners in counties in which there is a coroner shall be chosen by the electors of the respective counties, or by the electors of all of the respective counties comprising each combination of counties combined by the legislature for that purpose, for the term of 4 years.

(c) Beginning with the first general election at which the president is elected which occurs after the ratification of this paragraph, district attorneys, registers of deeds, county clerks, and treasurers shall be chosen by the electors of the respective counties, or by the electors of all of the respective counties comprising each combination of counties combined by the legislature for that purpose, for the term of 4 years and surveyors in counties in which the office of surveyor is filled by election shall be chosen by the electors of the respective counties, or by the electors of all of the respective counties comprising each combination of counties combined by the legislature for that purpose, for the term of 4 years.

(2) The offices of coroner and surveyor in counties having a population of 500,000 or more are abolished. Counties not having a population of 500,000 shall have the option of retaining the elective office of coroner or instituting a medical examiner system. Two or more counties may institute a joint medical examiner system.

(3) (a) Sheriffs may not hold any other partisan office.

(b) Sheriffs may be required by law to renew their security from time to time, and in default of giving such new security their office shall be deemed vacant.

(4) The governor may remove any elected county officer mentioned in this section except a county clerk, treasurer, or surveyor, giving to the officer a copy of the charges and an opportunity of being heard.

(5) All vacancies in the offices of coroner, register of deeds or district attorney shall be filled by appointment. The person appointed to fill a vacancy shall hold office only for the unexpired portion of the term to which appointed and until a successor shall be elected and qualified.

(6) When a vacancy occurs in the office of sheriff, the vacancy shall be filled by appointment of the governor, and the person appointed shall serve until his or her successor is elected and qualified. [*2003 AJR-10; 2005 SJR-2*]

County officers; election, terms, removal; vacancies. SECTION 4. [*As amended November 1998*] (1) Except as provided in sub. (2), coroners, registers of deeds, district attorneys, and all other elected county officers except judicial officers, sheriffs and chief executive officers, shall be chosen by the electors of the respective counties once in every 2 years.

(2) The offices of coroner and surveyor in counties having a population of 500,000 or more are abolished.

Counties not having a population of 500,000 shall have the option of retaining the elective office of coroner or instituting a medical examiner system. Two or more counties may institute a joint medical examiner system.

(3) (a) Sheriffs may not hold any other partisan office.

(b) Sheriffs may be required by law to renew their security from time to time, and in default of giving such new security their office shall be deemed vacant.

(c) Beginning with the first general election at which the governor is elected which occurs after the ratification of this paragraph, sheriffs shall be chosen by the electors of the respective counties once in every 4 years.

(4) The governor may remove any elected county officer mentioned in this section, giving to the officer a copy of the charges and an opportunity of being heard.

(5) All vacancies in the offices of coroner, register of deeds or district attorney shall be filled by appointment. The person appointed to fill a vacancy shall hold office only for the unexpired portion of the term to which appointed and until a successor shall be elected and qualified.

(6) When a vacancy occurs in the office of sheriff, the vacancy shall be filled by appointment of the governor, and the person appointed shall serve until his or her successor is elected and qualified. [*1995 AJR-37; 1997 SJR-43*]

County officers; election, terms, removal; vacancies. SECTION 4. [*As amended April 1982*]
(1) Sheriffs, coroners, registers of deeds, district attorneys, and all other elected county officers except judicial officers and chief executive officers, shall be chosen by the electors of the respective counties once in every 2 years.

(2) The offices of coroner and surveyor in counties having a population of 500,000 or more are abolished. Counties not having a population of 500,000 shall have the option of retaining the elective office of coroner or instituting a medical examiner system. Two or more counties may institute a joint medical examiner system.

(3) Sheriffs shall hold no other office. Sheriffs may be required by law to renew their security from time to time, and in default of giving such new security their office shall be deemed vacant.

(4) The governor may remove any elected county officer mentioned in this section, giving to the officer a copy of the charges and an opportunity of being heard.

(5) All vacancies in the offices of sheriff, coroner, register of deeds or district attorney shall be filled by appointment. The person appointed to fill a vacancy shall hold office only for the unexpired portion of the term to which appointed and until a successor shall be elected and qualified. [*1979 AJR-99; 1981 AJR-7*]

County officers; election, terms, removal; vacancies. SECTION 4. [*As amended April 1972*] Sheriffs, coroners, register of deeds, district attorneys, and all other county officers except judicial officers and chief executive officers, shall be chosen by the electors of the respective counties once in every two years. The offices of coroner and surveyor in counties having a population of 500,000 or more are abolished. Counties not having a population of 500,000 shall have the option of retaining the elective office of coroner or instituting a medical examiner system. Two or more counties may institute a joint medical examiner system. Sheriffs shall hold no other office; they may be required by law to renew their security from time to time, and in default of giving such new security their office shall be deemed vacant, but the county shall never be made responsible for the acts of the sheriff. The governor may remove any officer in this section mentioned, giving to such a copy of the charges against him and an opportunity of being heard in his defense. All vacancies shall be filled by appointment, and the person appointed to fill a vacancy shall hold only for the unexpired portion of the term to which he shall be appointed and until his successor shall be elected and qualified. [*1969 SJR-63; 1971 SJR-38*]

County officers; election, terms, removal; vacancies. SECTION 4. [*As amended April 1967*] Sheriffs, coroners, registers of deeds, district attorneys, and all other county officers except judicial officers and chief executive officers, shall be chosen by the electors of the respective counties once in every two years. The offices of coroner and

surveyor in counties having a population of 500,000 or more are abolished at the conclusion of the terms of office during which this amendment is adopted. Sheriffs shall hold no other office; they may be required by law to renew their security from time to time, and in default of giving such new security their office shall be deemed vacant, but the county shall never be made responsible for the acts of the sheriff. The governor may remove any officer in this section mentioned, giving to such a copy of the charges against him and an opportunity of being heard in his defense. All vacancies shall be filled by appointment, and the person appointed to fill a vacancy shall hold only for the unexpired portion of the term to which he shall be appointed and until his successor shall be elected and qualified. [*1965 AJR-72; 1967 SJR-7*]

County officers; election, terms, removal; vacancies. SECTION 4. [*As amended April 1965*] Sheriffs, coroners, register of deeds, district attorneys, and all other county officers except judicial officers and chief executive officers, shall be chosen by the electors of the respective counties once in every two years. The offices of coroner and surveyor in counties having a population of 500,000 or more are abolished at the conclusion of the terms of office during which this amendment is adopted. Sheriffs shall hold no other office, and shall not serve more than two terms or parts thereof in succession; they may be required by law to renew their security from time to time, and in default of giving such new security their office shall be deemed vacant, but the county shall never be made responsible for the acts of the sheriff. The governor may remove any officer in this section mentioned, giving to such a copy of the charges against him and an opportunity of being heard in his defense. All vacancies shall be filled by appointment, and the person appointed to fill a vacancy shall hold only for the unexpired portion of the term to which he shall be appointed and until his successor shall be elected and qualified. [*1963 AJR-14; 1965 SJR-17*]

County officers; election, terms, removal; vacancies. SECTION 4. [*As amended November 1962*] Sheriffs, coroners, registers of deeds, district attorneys, and all other county officers except judicial officers and chief executive officers, shall be chosen by the electors of the respective counties once in every two years. Sheriffs shall hold no other office, and shall not serve more than two terms or parts thereof in succession; they may be required by law to renew their security from time to time, and in default of giving such new security their office shall be deemed vacant, but the county shall never be made responsible for the acts of the sheriff. The governor may remove any officer in this section mentioned, giving to such a copy of the charges against him and an opportunity of being heard in his defense. All vacancies shall be filled by appointment, and the person appointed to fill a vacancy shall hold only for the unexpired portion of the term to which he shall be appointed and until his successor shall be elected and qualified. [*1959 AJR-121; 1961 AJR-61*]

County officers; election, terms, removal; vacancies. SECTION 4. [*As amended April 1929*] Sheriffs, coroners, registers of deeds, district attorneys, and all other county officers except judicial officers, shall be chosen by the electors of the respective counties once in every two years. Sheriffs shall hold no other office, and shall not serve more than two terms or parts thereof in succession; they may be required by law to renew their security from time to time, and in default of giving such new security their office shall be deemed vacant, but the county shall never be made responsible for the acts of the sheriff. The governor may remove any officer in this section mentioned, giving to such a copy of the charges against him and an opportunity of being heard in his defense. All vacancies shall be filled by appointment, and the person appointed to fill a vacancy shall hold only for the unexpired portion of the term to which he shall be appointed and until his successor shall be elected and qualified. [*1927 AJR-8; 1929 AJR-8*]

County officers. SECTION 4. [*As amended November 1882*] Sheriffs, coroners, registers of deeds, district attorneys, and all other county officers, except judicial officers shall be chosen by the electors of the respective counties, once in every two years. Sheriffs shall hold no other office and be ineligible for two years next succeeding the termination of their offices; they may be required by law to renew their security from time to time, and in default of giving such new security their office shall be deemed vacant, but the county shall never be made responsible for the acts of the sheriff. The governor may remove any officer in this section mentioned, giving to such a copy of the charges against him and an opportunity of being heard in his defense. All vacancies shall be filled by appointment and the person appointed to fill a vacancy shall hold only for the unexpired portion of the term to which he shall be appointed, and until his successor shall be elected and qualified. [*1881 AJR-16; 1882 SJR-20; 1882 c. 290*]

County officers. SECTION 4. [*Original form*] Sheriffs, coroners, registers of deeds and district attorneys shall be chosen by the electors of the respective counties, once in every two years, and as often as vacancies shall happen; sheriffs shall hold no other office, and be ineligible for two years next succeeding the termination of their offices. They may be required by law, to renew their security from time to time; and in default of giving such new security, their offices shall be deemed vacant. But the county shall never be made responsible for the acts of the sheriff. The governor may remove any officer in this section mentioned, giving to such officer a copy of the charges against him, and an opportunity of being heard in his defence.

ARTICLE VII.
JUDICIARY

Impeachment; trial. SECTION 1. [*As amended November 1932*] The court for the trial of impeachments shall be composed of the senate. The assembly shall have the power of impeaching all civil officers of this state for corrupt conduct in office, or for crimes and misdemeanors; but a majority of all the members elected shall concur in an impeachment. On the trial of an impeachment against the governor, the lieutenant governor shall not act as a member of the court. No judicial officer shall exercise his office, after he shall have been impeached, until his acquittal. Before the trial of an impeachment the members of the court shall take an oath or affirmation truly and impartially to try the impeachment according to evidence; and no person shall be convicted without the concurrence of two-thirds of the members present. Judgment in cases of impeachment shall not extend further than to removal from office, or removal from office and disqualification to hold any office of honor, profit or trust under the state; but the party impeached shall be liable to indictment, trial and punishment according to law. [*1929 SJR-103; 1931 SJR-8*]

Impeachments. SECTION 1. [*Original form*] The court for the trial of impeachments shall be composed of the senate. The house of representatives shall have the power of impeaching all civil officers of this state, for corrupt conduct in office, or for crimes and misdemeanors; but a majority of all the members elected shall concur in an impeachment. On the trial of an impeachment against the governor, the lieutenant governor shall not act as a member of the court. No judicial officer shall exercise his office, after he shall have been impeached, until his acquittal. Before the trial of an impeachment, the members of the court shall take an oath or affirmation, truly and impartially to try the impeachment according to evidence; and no person shall be convicted without the concurrence of two-thirds of the members present. Judgment in cases of impeachment shall not extend further than to removal from office, or removal from office and disqualification to hold any office of honor, profit or trust under the state; but the party impeached shall be liable to indictment, trial and punishment according to law.

Court system. SECTION 2. [*As amended April 1977*] The judicial power of this state shall be vested in a unified court system consisting of one supreme court, a court of appeals, a circuit court, such trial courts of general uniform statewide jurisdiction as the legislature may create by law, and a municipal court if authorized by the legislature under section 14. [*1975 AJR-11; 1977 SJR-9*]

Judicial power, where vested. SECTION 2. [*As amended April 1966*] The judicial power of this state, both as to matters of law and equity, shall be vested in a supreme court, circuit courts, and courts of probate. The legislature may also vest such jurisdiction as shall be deemed necessary in municipal courts, and may authorize the establishment of inferior courts in the several counties, cities, villages or towns, with limited civil and criminal jurisdiction. Provided, that the jurisdiction which may be vested in municipal courts shall not exceed in their respective municipalities that of circuit courts in their respective circuits as prescribed in this constitution; and that the legislature shall provide as well for the election of judges of the municipal courts as of the judges of inferior courts, by the qualified electors of the respective jurisdictions. The term of office of the judges of the said municipal and inferior courts shall not be longer than that of the judges of the circuit courts. [*1963 SJR-32; 1965 SJR-26*]

Judicial power, where vested. SECTION 2. [*Original form*] The judicial power of this state, both as to matters of law and equity, shall be vested in a supreme court, circuit courts, courts of probate, and in justices of the peace. The legislature may also vest such jurisdiction as shall be deemed necessary in municipal courts, and shall have power to establish inferior courts in the several counties, with limited civil and criminal jurisdiction. Provided, that the jurisdiction which may be vested in municipal courts shall not exceed in their respective municipalities that of circuit courts in their respective circuits as prescribed in this constitution; and that the legislature shall provide as well for the election of judges of the municipal courts as of the judges of inferior courts, by the qualified electors of the respective jurisdictions. The term of office of the judges of the said municipal and inferior courts shall not be longer than that of the judges of the circuit courts.

Supreme court: jurisdiction. SECTION 3. [*As amended April 1977*] (1) The supreme court shall have superintending and administrative authority over all courts.

(2) The supreme court has appellate jurisdiction over all courts and may hear original actions and proceedings. The supreme court may issue all writs necessary in aid of its jurisdiction.

(3) The supreme court may review judgments and orders of the court of appeals, may remove cases from the court of appeals and may accept cases on certification by the court of appeals. [*1975 AJR-11; 1977 SJR-9*]

Supreme court, jurisdiction. SECTION 3. [*Original form*] The supreme court, except in cases otherwise provided in this constitution, shall have appellate jurisdiction only, which shall be coextensive with the state; but in no case removed to the supreme court shall a trial by jury be allowed. The supreme court shall have a general superintending control over all inferior courts; it shall have power to issue writs of habeas corpus, mandamus, injunction, quo warranto, certiorari, and other original and remedial writs, and to hear and determine the same.

Supreme court: election, chief justice, court system administration. SECTION 4. [*As amended April 1977*] (1) The supreme court shall have 7 members who shall be known as justices of the supreme court. Justices shall be elected for 10-year terms of office commencing with the August 1 next succeeding the election. Only one justice may be elected in any year. Any 4 justices shall constitute a quorum for the conduct of the court's business.

(2) The justice having been longest a continuous member of said court, or in case 2 or more such justices shall have served for the same length of time, the justice whose term first expires, shall be the chief justice. The justice so designated as chief justice may, irrevocably, decline to serve as chief justice or resign as chief justice but continue to serve as a justice of the supreme court.

(3) The chief justice of the supreme court shall be the administrative head of the judicial system and shall exercise this administrative authority pursuant to procedures adopted by the supreme court. The chief justice may assign any judge of a court of record to aid in the proper disposition of judicial business in any court of record except the supreme court. [*1975 AJR-11; 1977 SJR-9*]

Supreme court justices; term; election; quorum. SECTION 1 [4]. [*As amended April 1903*] The chief justice and associate justices of the supreme court shall be severally known as the justices of said court, with the same terms of office of ten years respectively as now provided. The supreme court shall consist of seven justices, any four of whom shall be a quorum, to be elected as now provided, not more than one each year. The justice having been longest a continuous member of said court, or in case two or more such senior justices shall have served for the same length of time, then the one whose commission first expires shall be ex officio, the chief justice. [*1901 AJR-33; 1903 AJR-5; 1903 c. 10*]

Supreme court, how constituted. SECTION 1 [4]. [*As amended April 1889*] The chief justice and associate justices of the supreme court shall be severally known as justices of said court with the same terms of office, respectively, as now provided. The supreme court shall consist of five justices (any three of whom shall be a quorum), to be elected as now provided. The justice having been longest a continuous member of the court (or in case two or more of such senior justices having served for the same length of time, then the one whose commission first expires), shall be ex officio the chief justice. [*1887 SJR-19; 1889 AJR-7; 1889 c. 22*]

Supreme court, how constituted. SECTION 4. [*As amended November 1877*] The supreme court shall consist of one chief justice and four associate justices, to be elected by the qualified electors of the state. The legislature shall at its first session after the adoption of this amendment provide by law for the election of two associate justices of said court

to hold their offices respectively for terms ending two and four years respectively after the end of the term of the justice of the said court, then last to expire. And thereafter the chief justice and associate justices of the said court shall be elected and hold their offices respectively for the term of ten years. [*1876 SJR-16; 1877 SJR-2; 1877 c. 48*]

Supreme court, how constituted. SECTION 4. [*Original form*] For the term of five years, and thereafter until the legislature shall otherwise provide, the judges of the several circuit courts, shall be judges of the supreme court, four of whom shall constitute a quorum, and the concurrence of a majority of the judges present shall be necessary to a decision. The legislature shall have power, if they should think it expedient and necessary to provide by law, for the organization of a separate supreme court, with the jurisdiction and powers prescribed in this constitution, to consist of one chief justice, and two associate justices, to be elected by the qualified electors of the state, at such time and in such manner as the legislature may provide. The separate supreme court when so organized, shall not be changed or discontinued by the legislature; the judges thereof shall be so classified that but one of them shall go out of office at the same time; and their term of office shall be the same as is provided for the judges of the circuit court. And whenever the legislature may consider it necessary to establish a separate supreme court, they shall have power to reduce the number of circuit court judges to four, and subdivide the judicial circuits, but no such subdivision or reduction shall take effect until after the expiration of the term of some one of said judges, or till a vacancy occur by some other means.

SECTION 5. [*Repealed. 1975 AJR-11; 1977 SJR-9; vote April 1977*]

Judicial circuits. SECTION 5. [*Original form*] The state shall be divided into five judicial circuits, to be composed as follows: The first circuit shall comprise the counties of Racine, Walworth, Rock and Green; the second circuit, the counties of Milwaukee, Waukesha, Jefferson and Dane; the third circuit, the counties of Washington, Dodge, Columbia, Marquette, Sauk and Portage; the fourth circuit, the counties of Brown, Manitowoc, Sheboygan, Fond du Lac, Winnebago and Calumet; and the fifth circuit shall comprise the counties of Iowa, LaFayette, Grant, Crawford and St. Croix; and the county of Richland shall be attached to Iowa, the county of Chippewa to the county of Crawford, and the county of La Pointe to the county of St. Croix, for judicial purposes, until otherwise provided by the legislature.

Court of appeals. SECTION 5. [*Created April 1977*] (1) The legislature shall by law combine the judicial circuits of the state into one or more districts for the court of appeals and shall designate in each district the locations where the appeals court shall sit for the convenience of litigants.

(2) For each district of the appeals court there shall be chosen by the qualified electors of the district one or more appeals judges as prescribed by law, who shall sit as prescribed by law. Appeals judges shall be elected for 6-year terms and shall reside in the district from which elected. No alteration of district or circuit boundaries shall have the effect of removing an appeals judge from office during the judge's term. In case of an increase in the number of appeals judges, the first judge or judges shall be elected for full terms unless the legislature prescribes a shorter initial term for staggering of terms.

(3) The appeals court shall have such appellate jurisdiction in the district, including jurisdiction to review administrative proceedings, as the legislature may provide by law, but shall have no original jurisdiction other than by prerogative writ. The appeals court may issue all writs necessary in aid of its jurisdiction and shall have supervisory authority over all actions and proceedings in the courts in the district. [*1975 AJR-11; 1977 SJR-9*]

Circuit court: boundaries. SECTION 6. [*As amended April 1977*] The legislature shall prescribe by law the number of judicial circuits, making them as compact and convenient as practicable, and bounding them by county lines. No alteration of circuit boundaries shall have the effect of removing a circuit judge from office during the judge's term. In case of an increase of circuits, the first judge or judges shall be elected. [*1975 AJR-11; 1977 SJR-9*]

Alteration of circuits. SECTION 6. [*Original form*] The legislature may alter the limits or increase the number of circuits, making them as compact and convenient as practicable, and bounding them by county lines; but no such alteration or increase shall have the effect to remove a judge from office. In case of an increase of circuits, the judge or judges shall be elected as provided in this constitution and receive a salary of not less than that herein provided for judges of the circuit court.

Circuit court: election. SECTION 7. [*As amended April 1977*] For each circuit there shall be chosen by the qualified electors thereof one or more circuit judges as prescribed by law. Circuit judges shall be elected for 6-year terms and shall reside in the circuit from which elected. [*1975 AJR-11; 1977 SJR-9*]

Circuit judges; election, eligibility, term, salary. SECTION 7. [*As amended November 1924*] For each circuit there shall be chosen by the qualified electors thereof one circuit judge, except that in any circuit in which there is a county that had a population in excess of eighty-five thousand, according to the last state or United States census, the legislature may, from time to time, authorize additional circuit judges to be chosen. Every circuit judge shall reside in the circuit from which he is elected, and shall hold his office for such term and receive such compensation as the legislature shall prescribe. [*1921 SJR-24; 1923 SJR-27; 1923 c. 408*]

Circuit judges, election. SECTION 7. [*As amended April 1897*] For each circuit there shall be chosen by the qualified electors thereof, one circuit judge, except that in any circuit composed of one county only, which county shall contain a population, according to the last state or United States census, of one hundred thousand inhabitants or over, the legislature may from time to time authorize additional circuit judges to be chosen. Every circuit judge shall reside

in the circuit from which he is elected and shall hold his office for such term and receive such compensation as the legislature shall prescribe. [*1895 SJR-9; 1897 SJR-10; 1897 c. 69*]

Circuit judges, election. SECTION 7. [*Original form*] For each circuit there shall be a judge chosen by the qualified electors therein, who shall hold his office as is provided in this constitution, and until his successor shall be chosen and qualified; and after he shall have been elected, he shall reside in the circuit for which he was elected. One of said judges shall be designated as chief justice in such manner as the legislature shall provide. And the legislature shall at its first session provide by law as well for the election of, as for classifying the judges of the circuit court to be elected under this constitution, in such manner that one of said judges shall go out of office in two years, one in three years, one in four years, one in five years and one in six years, and thereafter the judge elected to fill the office shall hold the same for six years.

Circuit court: jurisdiction. SECTION 8. [*As amended April 1977*] Except as otherwise provided by law, the circuit court shall have original jurisdiction in all matters civil and criminal within this state and such appellate jurisdiction in the circuit as the legislature may prescribe by law. The circuit court may issue all writs necessary in aid of its jurisdiction. [*1975 AJR-11; 1977 SJR-9*]

Circuit court, jurisdiction. SECTION 8. [*Original form*] The circuit courts shall have original jurisdiction in all matters civil and criminal within this state, not excepted in this constitution, and not hereafter prohibited by law; and appellate jurisdiction from all inferior courts and tribunals, and a supervisory control over the same. They shall also

have the power to issue writs of habeas corpus, mandamus, injunction, quo warranto, certiorari, and all other writs necessary to carry into effect their orders, judgments and decrees, and give them a general control over inferior courts and jurisdictions.

Judicial elections, vacancies. SECTION 9. [*As amended April 1977*] When a vacancy occurs in the office of justice of the supreme court or judge of any court of record, the vacancy shall be filled by appointment by the governor, which shall continue until a successor is elected and qualified. There shall be no election for a justice or judge at the partisan general election for state or county officers, nor within 30 days either before or after such election. [*1975 AJR-11; 1977 SJR-9*]

Vacancies; judicial elections. SECTION 9. [*As amended April 1953*] When a vacancy shall happen in the office of judge of the supreme or circuit courts, such vacancy shall be filled by an appointment of the governor, which shall continue until a successor is elected and qualified; and a supreme circuit justice when so elected shall hold his office for a term of 10 years and a circuit judge when so elected shall hold his office for such term as the legislature prescribes for circuit judges elected under section seven of this article. There shall be no election for a judge or judges at any general election for state or county officers, nor within 30 days either before or after such election. [*1951 SJR-3; 1953 SJR-5*]

Vacancies; judicial elections. SECTION 9. [*Original form*] When a vacancy shall happen in the office of judge of the supreme or circuit courts, such vacancy shall be filled by an appointment of the governor, which shall continue until a successor is elected and qualified; and when elected such successor shall hold his office the residue of the unexpired term. There shall be no election for a judge or judges at any general election for state or county officers, nor within thirty days either before or after such election.

Judges: eligibility to office. SECTION 10. [*As amended April 1977*] (1) No justice of the supreme court or judge of any court of record shall hold any other office of public trust, except a judicial office, during the term for which elected. No person shall be eligible to the office of judge who shall not, at the time of election or appointment, be a qualified elector within the jurisdiction for which chosen.

(2) Justices of the supreme court and judges of the courts of record shall receive such compensation as the legislature may authorize by law, but may not receive fees of office. [*1975 AJR-11; 1977 SJR-9*]

Compensation and qualifications of judges. SECTION 10. [*As amended November 1912*] Each of the judges of the supreme and circuit courts shall receive a salary, payable at such time as the legislature shall fix, of not less than one thousand five hundred dollars annually; they shall receive no fees of office, or other compensation than their salary; they shall hold no office of public trust, except a judicial office, during the term for which they are respectively elected, and all votes for either of them for any office, except a judicial office, given by the legislature or the people, shall be void. No person shall be eligible to the office of judge who shall not, at the time of his election, be a citizen of the United States and have attained the age of twenty-five years, and be a qualified elector within the jurisdiction for which he may be chosen. [*1909 AJR-36; 1911 AJR-26; 1911 c.*

665]

Compensation and qualifications of judges. SECTION 10. [*Original form*] Each of the judges of the supreme and circuit courts shall receive a salary, payable quarterly, of not less than one thousand five hundred dollars annually; they shall receive no fees of office, or other compensation than their salaries; they shall hold no office of public trust, except a judicial office, during the term for which they are respectively elected, and all votes for either of them for any office, except a judicial office, given by the legislature or the people, shall be void. No person shall be eligible to the office of judge, who shall not, at the time of his election, be a citizen of the United States, and have attained the age of twenty-five years, and be a qualified elector within the jurisdiction for which he may be chosen.

SECTION 11. [*Repealed. 1975 AJR-11; 1977 SJR-9; vote April 1977*]

Terms of courts; change of judges. SECTION 11. [*Original form*] The supreme court shall hold at least one term annually, at the seat of government of the state, at such time as shall be provided by law. And the legislature may provide for holding other terms and at other places when they may deem it necessary. A circuit court shall be held at least twice in each year in each county of this state organized for judicial purposes. The judges of the circuit court may hold courts for each other, and shall do so when required by law.

Disciplinary proceedings. SECTION 11. [*Created April 1977*] Each justice or judge shall be subject to reprimand, censure, suspension, removal for cause or for disability, by the supreme court pursuant to procedures established by the legislature by law. No justice or judge removed for cause shall be eligible for reappointment or temporary service. This section is alternative to, and cumulative with, the methods of removal provided in sections 1 and 13 of this article and section 12 of article XIII. [*1975 AJR-11; 1977 SJR-9*]

Clerks of circuit and supreme courts. SECTION 12. [*As amended April 2005*] (1) There shall be a clerk of circuit court chosen in each county organized for judicial purposes by the qualified electors thereof, who, except as provided in sub. (2), shall hold office for two years, subject to removal as provided by law.

(2) Beginning with the first general election at which the governor is elected which occurs after the ratification of this subsection, a clerk of circuit court shall be chosen by the electors of each county, for the term of 4 years, subject to removal as provided by law.

(3) In case of a vacancy, the judge of the circuit court may appoint a clerk until the vacancy is filled by an election.

(4) The clerk of circuit court shall give such security as the legislature requires by law.

(5) The supreme court shall appoint its own clerk, and may appoint a clerk of circuit court to be the clerk of the supreme court. [*2003 AJR-10; 2005 SJR-2*]

Clerks of circuit and supreme courts. SECTION 12. [*As amended November 1882*] There shall be a clerk of the circuit court chosen in each county organized for judicial purposes by the qualified electors thereof, who shall hold his office for two years, subject to removal as shall be provided by law; in case of a vacancy, the judge of the circuit court shall have power to appoint a clerk until the vacancy shall be filled by an election; the clerk thus elected or appointed shall give such security as the legislature may require. The supreme court shall appoint its own clerk, and a clerk of the circuit court may be appointed a clerk of the supreme court. [*1881 AJR-16; 1882 SJR-20; 1882 c. 290*]

Clerks of courts. SECTION 12. [*Original form*] There shall be a clerk of the circuit court chosen in each county organized for judicial purposes, by the qualified electors thereof, who shall hold his office for two years, subject to removal, as shall be provided by law. In case of a vacancy, the judge of the circuit court shall have the power to appoint a clerk until the vacancy shall be filled by an election. The clerk thus elected or appointed shall give such security as the legislature may require; and when elected shall hold his office for a full term. The supreme court shall appoint its own clerk, and the clerk of a circuit court may be appointed clerk of the supreme court.

Justices and judges: removal by address. SECTION 13. [*As amended April 1977*] Any justice or judge may be removed from office by address of both houses of the legislature, if two-thirds of all the members elected to each house concur therein, but no removal shall be made by virtue of this section unless the justice or judge complained of is served with a copy of the charges, as the ground of address, and has had an opportunity of being heard. On the question of removal, the ayes and noes shall be entered on the journals. [*1975 AJR-11; 1977 SJR-9*]

Removal of judges. SECTION 13. [*As amended April 1974*] Any judge of the supreme, circuit, county or municipal court may be removed from office by address of both houses of the legislature, if two-thirds of all the members elected to each house concur therein, but no removal shall be made by virtue of this section unless the judge complained of shall have been served with a copy of the charges against him, as the ground of address, and shall have had an opportunity of being heard in his defense. On the question of removal, the ayes and noes shall be entered on the journals. [*1971 AJR-31; 1973 AJR-55*]

Removal of judges. SECTION 13. [*Original form*] Any judge of the supreme or circuit court may be removed from office by address of both houses of the legislature, if two-thirds of all the members elected to each house concur therein, but no removal shall be made by virtue of this section unless the judge complained of shall have been served with a copy of the charges against him, as the ground of address, and shall have had an opportunity of being heard in his defense. On the question of removal, the ayes and noes shall be entered on the journals.

Municipal court. SECTION 14. [*As amended April 1977*] The legislature by law may authorize each city, village and town to establish a municipal court. All municipal courts shall have uniform jurisdiction limited to actions and proceedings arising under ordinances of the municipality in which established. Judges of municipal courts may receive such compensation as provided by the municipality in which established, but may not receive fees of office. [*1975 AJR-11; 1977 SJR-9*]

Judges of probate. SECTION 14. [*Original form*] There shall be chosen in each county, by the qualified electors thereof, a judge of probate, who shall hold his office for two years and until his successor shall be elected and qualified, and whose jurisdiction, powers and duties shall be prescribed by law. Provided, however, that the legislature shall have power to abolish the office of judge of probate in any county, and to confer probate powers upon such inferior courts as may be established in said county.

SECTION 15. [*Repealed. 1963 SJR-32; 1965 SJR-26; vote April 1966*]

Justices of the peace. SECTION 15. [*As amended April 1945*] The electors of the several towns at their annual town meeting, and the electors of cities and villages at their charter elections except in cities of the first class, shall, in such manner as the legislature may direct, elect justices of the peace, whose term of office shall be for 2 years and until their successors in office shall be elected and qualified. In case of an election to fill a vacancy occurring before the expiration of a full term, the justice elected shall hold for the residue of the unexpired term.   Their number and classification shall be regulated by law. And the tenure of 2 years shall in no wise interfere with the classification in the first instance. The justices thus elected shall have such civil and criminal jurisdiction as shall be prescribed by law. [*1943 SJR-9; 1945 SJR-6*]

Justices of the peace. SECTION 15. [*Original form*] The electors of the several towns, at their annual town meeting, and the electors of cities and villages, at their charter elections, shall in such manner as the legislature may direct, elect justices of the peace, whose term of office shall be for two years, and until their successors in office shall be elected and qualified.   In case of an election to fill a vacancy, occurring before the expiration of a full term, the justice elected shall hold for the residue of the unexpired term. Their number and classification shall be regulated by law. And the tenure of two years shall in no wise interfere with the classification in the first instance. The justices, thus elected, shall have such civil and criminal jurisdiction as shall be prescribed by law.

SECTION 16. [*Repealed. 1975 AJR-11; 1977 SJR-9; vote April 1977*]

Tribunals of conciliation. SECTION 16. [*Original form*] The legislature shall pass laws for the regulation of tribunals of conciliation, defining their powers and duties. Such tribunals may be established in and for any township, and shall have power to render judgment to be obligatory on the parties when they shall voluntarily submit their matter in difference to arbitration, and agree to abide the judgment or assent thereto in writing.

SECTION 17. [*Repealed. 1975 AJR-11; 1977 SJR-9; vote April 1977*]

Style of writs; indictments. SECTION 17. [*Original form*] The style of all writs and process shall be, "The state of Wisconsin;" all criminal prosecutions shall be carried on in the name and by the authority of the same, and all indictments shall conclude against the peace and dignity of the state.

SECTION 18. [*Repealed. 1975 AJR-11; 1977 SJR-9; vote April 1977*]

Suit tax. SECTION 18. [*Original form*] The legislature shall impose a tax on all civil suits commenced or prosecuted in the municipal, inferior or circuit courts, which shall constitute a fund to be applied toward the payment of the salary of judges.

SECTION 19. [*Repealed. 1975 AJR-11; 1977 SJR-9; vote April 1977*]

Testimony in equity suits; master in chancery. SECTION 19. [*Original form*] The testimony in causes in equity shall be taken in like manner as in cases at law, and the office of master in chancery is hereby prohibited.

SECTION 20. [*Repealed. 1975 AJR-11; 1977 SJR-9; vote April 1977*] See Art. I, sec. 21.

Rights of suitors. SECTION 20. [*Original form*] Any suitor, in any court of this state, shall have the right to prosecute or defend his suit either in his own proper person, or by an attorney or agent of his choice.

SECTION 21. [*Repealed. 1975 AJR-11; 1977 SJR-9; vote April 1977*] See Art. IV, sec. 17.

Publication of laws and decisions. SECTION 21. [*Original form*] The legislature shall provide by law for the speedy publication of all statute laws, and of such judicial decisions, made within the state, as may be deemed expedient. And no general law shall be in force until published.

SECTION 22. [*Repealed. 1975 AJR-11; 1977 SJR-9; vote April 1977*]

Commissioners to revise code of practice. SECTION 22. [*Original form*] The legislature, at its first session after the adoption of this constitution, shall provide for the appointment of three commissioners, whose duty it shall be to inquire into, revise and simplify the rules of practice, pleadings, forms and proceedings, and arrange a system adapted to the courts of record of this state, and report the same to the legislature, subject to their modification and adoption; and such commission shall terminate upon the rendering of the report, unless otherwise provided by law.

SECTION 23. [*Repealed. 1975 AJR-11; 1977 SJR-9; vote April 1977*]

Court commissioners. SECTION 23. [*Original form*] The legislature may provide for the appointment of one or more persons in each organized county, and may vest in such persons such judicial powers as shall be prescribed by law. Provided, that said power shall not exceed that of a judge of a circuit court at chambers.

Justices and judges: eligibility for office; retirement. SECTION 24. [*As amended April 1977*]

(1) To be eligible for the office of supreme court justice or judge of any court of record, a person must be an attorney licensed to practice law in this state and have been so licensed for 5 years immediately prior to election or appointment.

(2) Unless assigned temporary service under subsection (3), no person may serve as a supreme court justice or judge of a court of record beyond the July 31 following the date on which such person attains that age, of not less than 70 years, which the legislature shall prescribe by law.

(3) A person who has served as a supreme court justice or judge of a court of record may, as provided by law, serve as a judge of any court of record except the supreme court on a temporary basis if assigned by the chief justice of the supreme court. [*1975 AJR-11; 1977 SJR-9*]

Retirement and eligibility for office of justices and circuit judges. SECTION 24. [*As amended April 1968*] No person seventy years of age or over may take office as a supreme court justice or circuit judge. No person may take or hold such office unless he is licensed to practice law in this state and has been licensed for five years immediately prior to his election or appointment. No supreme court justice or circuit judge may serve beyond the July 31 following the date on which he attains the age of seventy. A person who has served eight or more years as a supreme court justice or circuit judge may serve temporarily, on appointment by the chief justice of the supreme court or by any associate justice designated by the supreme court, as a judge of a circuit court, under such general laws as the legislature may enact. [*1965 SJR-36; 1967 SJR-96*]

Retirement and eligibility for office of justices and circuit judges. SECTION 24. [*Created April 1955*] No person seventy years of age or over may take office as a supreme court justice or circuit judge. No person may take or hold such office unless he is licensed to practice law in this state and has been so licensed for five years immediately prior to his election or appointment. No supreme court justice or circuit judge may serve beyond the end of the month in which he attains the age of seventy, but any such justice or judge may complete the term in which he is serving or to which he has been elected when this section takes effect. Any person retired under the provisions of this section may, at the request of the chief justice of the supreme court, serve temporarily as a circuit judge and shall be compensated as the legislature provides. This section shall take effect on July first following the referendum at which it is approved. [*1953 SJR-6; 1955 SJR-10*]

ARTICLE VIII.
FINANCE

Rule of taxation uniform; income, privilege and occupation taxes. SECTION 1. [*As amended April 1974*] The rule of taxation shall be uniform but the legislature may empower cities, villages or towns to collect and return taxes on real estate located therein by optional methods. Taxes shall be levied upon such property with such classifications as to forests and minerals including or separate or severed from the land, as the legislature shall prescribe. Taxation of agricultural land and undeveloped land, both as defined by law, need not be uniform with the taxation of each other nor with the taxation of other real property. Taxation of merchants' stock-in-trade, manufacturers' materials and finished products, and livestock need not be uniform with the taxation of real property and other personal property, but the taxation of all such merchants' stock-in-trade, manufacturers' materials and finished products and livestock shall be uniform, except that the legislature may provide that the value thereof shall be determined on an average basis. Taxes may also be imposed on incomes, privileges and occupations, which taxes may be graduated and progressive, and reasonable exemptions may be provided. [*1971 AJR-2; 1973 AJR-1*]

Rule of taxation uniform; income, privilege and occupation taxes. SECTION 1. [*As amended April 1961*] The rule of taxation shall be uniform but the legislature may empower cities, villages or towns to collect and return taxes on real estate located therein by optional methods. Taxes shall be levied upon such property with such classifications as to forests and minerals including or separate or severed from the land, as the legislature shall prescribe. Taxation of merchants' stock-in-trade, manufacturers' materials and finished products, and livestock need not be uniform with the taxation of real property and other personal property, but the taxation of all such merchants' stock-in-trade, manufacturers' materials and finished products and livestock shall be uniform, except that the legislature may provide that the value thereof shall be determined on an average basis. Taxes may also be imposed on incomes; privileges and occupations, which taxes may be graduated and progressive, and reasonable exemptions may be provided. [*1959 AJR-120; 1961 SJR-34*]

Rule of taxation uniform; income, privilege and occupation taxes. SECTION 1. [*As amended April 1941*]. The rule of taxation shall be uniform but the legislature may empower cities, villages or towns to collect and return taxes on real estate located therein by optional methods. Taxes shall be levied upon such property with such classifications as to forests and minerals including or separate or severed from the land, as the legislature shall prescribe. Taxes may also be imposed on incomes, privileges and occupations, which taxes may be graduated and progressive, and reasonable exemptions may be provided. [*1939 AJR-37; 1941 AJR-15*]

Rules of taxation; income taxes. SECTION 1. [*As amended April 1927*] The rule of taxation shall be uniform, and taxes shall be levied upon such property with such classifications as to forests and minerals, including or separate or severed from the land, as the legislature shall prescribe. Taxes may also be imposed on incomes, privileges and occupations, which taxes may be graduated and progressive, and reasonable exemptions may be provided. [*1925 AJR-51; 1927 AJR-3*]

Uniform rule of taxation; income tax. SECTION 1. [*As amended November 1908*] The rule of taxation shall be uniform, and taxes shall be levied upon such property as the legislature shall prescribe. Taxes may also be imposed on

incomes, privileges and occupations, which taxes may be graduated and progressive, and reasonable exemptions may be provided. [*1905 AJR-12; 1907 SJR-19; 1907 c. 661*]

Uniform rule of taxation. SECTION 1. [*Original form*] The rule of taxation shall be uniform, and taxes shall be levied upon such property as the legislature shall prescribe.

Appropriations; limitation. SECTION 2. [*As amended November 1877*] No money shall be paid out of the treasury except in pursuance of an appropriation by law. No appropriation shall be made for the payment of any claim against the state except claims of the United States and judgments, unless filed within six years after the claim accrued. [*1876 SJR-14; 1877 SJR-5; 1877 c. 158*]

Appropriations. SECTION 2. [*Original form*] No money shall be paid out of the treasury, except in pursuance of an appropriation by law.

Credit of state. SECTION 3. [*As amended April 1975*] Except as provided in s. 7 (2) (a), the credit of the state shall never be given, or loaned, in aid of any individual, association or corporation. [*1973 AJR-145; 1975 AJR-1*]

Credit of state. SECTION 3. [*Original form*] The credit of the state shall never be given, or loaned, in aid of any individual, association or corporation.

Contracting state debts. SECTION 4. The state shall never contract any public debt except in the cases and manner herein provided.

Annual tax levy to equal expenses. SECTION 5. The legislature shall provide for an annual tax sufficient to defray the estimated expenses of the state for each year; and whenever the expenses of any year shall exceed the income, the legislature shall provide for levying a tax for the ensuing year, sufficient, with other sources of income, to pay the deficiency as well as the estimated expenses of such ensuing year.

Public debt for extraordinary expense; taxation. SECTION 6. For the purpose of defraying extraordinary expenditures the state may contract public debts (but such debts shall never in the aggregate exceed one hundred thousand dollars). Every such debt shall be authorized by law, for some purpose or purposes to be distinctly specified therein; and the vote of a majority of all the members elected to each house, to be taken by yeas and nays, shall be necessary to the passage of such law; and every such law shall provide for levying an annual tax sufficient to pay the annual interest of such debt and the principal within five years from the passage of such law, and shall specially appropriate the proceeds of such taxes to the payment of such principal and interest; and such appropriation shall not be repealed, nor the taxes be postponed or diminished, until the principal and interest of such debt shall have been wholly paid.

Public debt for public defense; bonding for public purposes. SECTION 7. [*As amended April 1992*] (1) The legislature may also borrow money to repel invasion, suppress insurrection, or defend the state in time of war; but the money thus raised shall be applied exclusively to the object for which the loan was authorized, or to the repayment of the debt thereby created.

(2) Any other provision of this constitution to the contrary notwithstanding:

(a) The state may contract public debt and pledges to the payment thereof its full faith, credit and taxing power:

1. To acquire, construct, develop, extend, enlarge or improve land, waters, property, highways, railways, buildings, equipment or facilities for public purposes.

2. To make funds available for veterans' housing loans.

(b) The aggregate public debt contracted by the state in any calendar year pursuant to paragraph (a) shall not exceed an amount equal to the lesser of:

1. Three-fourths of one per centum of the aggregate value of all taxable property in the state; or

2. Five per centum of the aggregate value of all taxable property in the state less the sum of: a. the aggregate public debt of the state contracted pursuant to this section outstanding as of January 1 of such calendar year after subtracting therefrom the amount of sinking funds on hand on January 1 of such calendar year which are applicable exclusively to repayment of such outstanding public debt and, b. the outstanding indebtedness as of January 1 of such calendar year

of any entity of the type described in paragraph (d) to the extent that such indebtedness is supported by or payable from payments out of the treasury of the state.

(c) The state may contract public debt, without limit, to fund or refund the whole or any part of any public debt contracted pursuant to paragraph (a), including any premium payable with respect thereto and any interest to accrue thereon, or to fund or refund the whole or any part of any indebtedness incurred prior to January 1, 1972, by any entity of the type described in paragraph (d), including any premium payable with respect thereto and any interest to accrue thereon.

(d) No money shall be paid out of the treasury, with respect to any lease, sublease or other agreement entered into after January 1, 1971, to the Wisconsin State Agencies Building Corporation, Wisconsin State Colleges Building Corporation, Wisconsin State Public Building Corporation, Wisconsin University Building Corporation or any similar entity existing or operating for similar purposes pursuant to which such nonprofit corporation or such other entity undertakes to finance or provide a facility for use or occupancy by the state or an agency, department or instrumentality thereof.

(e) The legislature shall prescribe all matters relating to the contracting of public debt pursuant to paragraph (a), including: the public purposes for which public debt may be contracted; by vote of a majority of the members elected to each of the 2 houses of the legislature, the amount of public debt which may be contracted for any class of such purposes; the public debt or other indebtedness which may be funded or refunded; the kinds of notes, bonds or other evidence of public debt which may be issued by the state; and the manner in which the aggregate value of all taxable property in the state shall be determined.

(f) The full faith, credit and taxing power of the state are pledged to the payment of all public debt created on behalf of the state pursuant to this section and the legislature shall provide by appropriation for the payment of the interest upon and instalments of principal of all such public debt as the same falls due, but, in any event, suit may be brought against the state to compel such payment.

(g) At any time after January 1, 1972, by vote of a majority of the members elected to each of the 2 houses of the legislature, the legislature may declare that an emergency exists and submit to the people a proposal to authorize the state to contract a specific amount of public debt for a purpose specified in such proposal, without regard to the limit provided in paragraph (b). Any such authorization shall be effective if approved by a majority of the electors voting thereon. Public debt contracted pursuant to such authorization shall thereafter be deemed to have been contracted pursuant to paragraph (a), but neither such public debt nor any public debt contracted to fund or refund such public debt shall be considered in computing the debt limit provided in paragraph (b). Not more than one such authorization shall be thus made in any 2-year period. [*1989 SJR-76; 1991 SJR-30*]

Public debt for public defense; bonding for public purposes. SECTION 7. [*As amended April 1975*] (1) The legislature may also borrow money to repel invasion, suppress insurrection, or defend the state in time of war; but the money thus raised shall be applied exclusively to the object for which the loan was authorized, or to the repayment of the debt thereby created.

(2) Any other provision of this constitution to the contrary notwithstanding:

(a) The state may contract public debt and pledges to the payment thereof its full faith, credit and taxing power:

1. To acquire, construct, develop, extend, enlarge or improve land, waters, property, highways, buildings, equipment or facilities for public purposes.

2. To make funds available for veterans' housing loans.

(b) The aggregate public debt contracted by the state in any calendar year pursuant to paragraph (a) shall not exceed an amount equal to the lesser of:

1. Three-fourths of one per centum of the aggregate value of all taxable property in the state; or

2. Five per centum of the aggregate value of all taxable property in the state less the sum of: a. the aggregate public debt of the state contracted pursuant to this section outstanding as of January 1 of such calendar year after subtracting therefrom the amount of sinking funds on hand on January 1 of such calendar year which are applicable exclusively to repayment of such outstanding public debt and, b. the outstanding indebtedness as of January 1 of such calendar year of any entity of the type described in paragraph (d) to the extent that such indebtedness is supported by or payable from payments out of the treasury of the state.

(c) The state may contract public debt, without limit, to fund or refund the whole or any part of any public debt contracted pursuant to paragraph (a), including any premium payable with respect thereto and any interest to accrue thereon, or to fund or refund the whole or any part of any indebtedness incurred prior to January 1, 1972, by any entity of the type described in paragraph (d), including any premium payable with respect thereto and any interest to accrue thereon.

(d) No money shall be paid out of the treasury, with respect to any lease, sublease or other agreement entered into after January 1, 1971, to the Wisconsin State Agencies Building Corporation, Wisconsin State Colleges Building Corporation, Wisconsin State Public Building Corporation, Wisconsin University Building Corporation or any similar entity existing or operating for similar purposes pursuant to which such nonprofit corporation or such other entity undertakes to finance or provide a facility for use or occupancy by the state or an agency, department or instrumentality thereof.

(e) The legislature shall prescribe all matters relating to the contracting of public debt pursuant to paragraph (a), including: the public purposes for which public debt may be contracted; by vote of a majority of the members elected to each of the 2 houses of the legislature, the amount of public debt which may be contracted for any class of such purposes; the public debt or other indebtedness which may be funded or refunded; the kinds of notes, bonds or other evidence of public debt which may be issued by the state; and the manner in which the aggregate value of all taxable property in the state shall be determined.

(f) The full faith, credit and taxing power of the state are pledged to the payment of all public debt created on behalf of the state pursuant to this section and the legislature shall provide by appropriation for the payment of the interest upon and instalments of principal of all such public debt as the same falls due, but, in any event, suit may be brought against the state to compel such payment.

(g) At any time after January 1, 1972, by vote of a majority of the members elected to each of the 2 houses of the legislature, the legislature may declare that an emergency exists and submit to the people a proposal to authorize the state to contract a specific amount of public debt for a purpose specified in such proposal, without regard to the limit provided in paragraph (b). Any such authorization shall be effective if approved by a majority of the electors voting thereon. Public debt contracted pursuant to such authorization shall thereafter be deemed to have been contracted pursuant to paragraph (a), but neither such public debt nor any public debt contracted to fund or refund such public debt shall be considered in computing the debt limit provided in paragraph (b). Not more than one such authorization shall be thus made in any 2-year period. [*1973 AJR-145; 1975 AJR-1*]

Public debt for public defense; bonding for public purposes. SECTION 7. [*As amended April 1969*] (1) The legislature may also borrow money to repel invasion, suppress insurrection, or defend the state in time of war; but the money thus raised shall be applied exclusively to the object for which the loan was authorized, or to the repayment of the debt thereby created.

(2) Any other provision of this constitution to the contrary notwithstanding:

(a) The state may contract public debt and pledges to the payment thereof its full faith, credit and taxing power to acquire, construct, develop, extend, enlarge or improve land, waters, property, highways, buildings, equipment or facilities for public purposes.

(b) The aggregate public debt contracted by the state in any calendar year pursuant to paragraph (a) shall not exceed an amount equal to the lesser of:

1. Three-fourths of one per centum of the aggregate value of all taxable property in the state; or

2. Five per centum of the aggregate value of all taxable property in the state less the sum of: a. the aggregate public debt of the state contracted pursuant to this section outstanding as of January 1 of such calendar year after subtracting therefrom the amount of sinking funds on hand on January 1 of such calendar year which are applicable exclusively to repayment of such outstanding public debt and, b. the outstanding indebtedness as of January 1 of such calendar year of any entity of the type described in

paragraph (d) to the extent that such indebtedness is supported by or payable from payments out of the treasury of the state.

(c) The state may contract public debt, without limit, to fund or refund the whole or any part of any public debt contracted pursuant to paragraph (a), including any premium payable with respect thereto and any interest to accrue thereon, or to fund or refund the whole or any part of any indebtedness incurred prior to January 1, 1972, by any entity of the type described in paragraph (d), including any premium payable with respect thereto and any interest to accrue thereon.

(d) No money shall be paid out of the treasury, with respect to any lease, sublease or other agreement entered into after January 1, 1971, to the Wisconsin State Agencies Building Corporation, Wisconsin State Colleges Building Corporation, Wisconsin State Public Building Corporation, Wisconsin University Building Corporation or any similar entity existing or operating for similar purposes pursuant to which such nonprofit corporation or such other entity undertakes to finance or provide a facility for use or occupancy by the state or an agency, department or instrumentality thereof.

(e) The legislature shall prescribe all matters relating to the contracting of public debt pursuant to paragraph (a), including: the public purposes for which public debt may be contracted; by vote of a majority of the members elected to each of the 2 houses of the legislature, the amount of public debt which may be contracted for any class of such purposes; the public debt or other indebtedness which may be funded or refunded; the kinds of notes, bonds or other evidence of public debt which may be issued by the state; and the manner in which the aggregate value of all taxable property in the state shall be determined.

(f) The full faith, credit and taxing power of the state are pledged to the payment of all public debt created on behalf of the state pursuant to this section and the legislature shall provide by appropriation for the payment of the interest upon and instalments of principal of all such public debt as the same falls due, but, in any event, suit may be brought against the state to compel such payment.

(g) At any time after January 1, 1972, by vote of a majority of the members elected to each of the 2 houses of the legislature, the legislature may declare that an emergency exists and submit to the people a proposal to authorize the state to contract a specific amount of public debt for a purpose specified in such proposal, without regard to the limit provided in paragraph (b). Any such authorization shall be effective if approved by a majority of the electors voting thereon. Public debt contracted pursuant to such authorization shall thereafter be deemed to have been contracted pursuant to paragraph (a), but neither such public debt nor any public debt contracted to fund or refund such public debt shall be considered in computing the debt limit provided in paragraph (b). Not more than one such authorization shall be thus made in any 2-year period. [*1967 AJR-1; 1969 AJR-1*]

Public debt for public defense. SECTION 7. [*Original form*] The legislature may also borrow money to repel invasion, suppress insurrection, or defend the state in time of war; but the money thus raised shall be applied exclusively to the object for which the loan was authorized, or to the repayment of the debt thereby created.

Vote on fiscal bills; quorum. SECTION 8. On the passage in either house of the legislature of any law which imposes, continues or renews a tax, or creates a debt or charge, or makes, continues or renews an appropriation of public or trust money, or releases, discharges or commutes a claim or demand of the state, the question shall be taken by yeas and nays, which shall be duly entered on the journal; and three-fifths of all the members elected to such house shall in all such cases be required to constitute a quorum therein.

Evidences of public debt. SECTION 9. No scrip, certificate, or other evidence of state debt, whatsoever, shall be issued, except for such debts as are authorized by the sixth and seventh sections of this article.

Internal improvements. SECTION 10. [*As amended April 1992*] Except as further provided in this section, the state may never contract any debt for works of internal improvement, or be a party in carrying on such works.

(1) Whenever grants of land or other property shall have been made to the state, especially dedicated by the grant to particular works of internal improvement, the state may carry on such particular works and shall devote thereto the avails of such grants, and may pledge or appropriate the revenues derived from such works in aid of their completion.

(2) The state may appropriate money in the treasury or to be thereafter raised by taxation for:

(a) The construction or improvement of public highways.

(b) The development, improvement and construction of airports or other aeronautical projects.

(c) The acquisition, improvement or construction of veterans' housing.

(d) The improvement of port facilities.

(e) The acquisition, development, improvement or construction of railways and other railroad facilities.

(3) The state may appropriate moneys for the purpose of acquiring, preserving and developing the forests of the state. Of the moneys appropriated under the authority of this subsection in any one year an amount not to exceed two-tenths of one mill of the taxable property of the state as determined by the last preceding state assessment may be raised by a tax on property. [*1989 SJR-76; 1991 SJR-30*]

Internal improvements. SECTION 10. [*As amended April 1968*] The state shall never contract any debt for works of internal improvement, or be a party in carrying on such works; but whenever grants of land or other property shall have been made to the state, especially dedicated by the grant to particular works of internal improvement, the state may carry on such particular works and shall devote thereto the avails of such grants, and may pledge or appropriate the revenues derived from such works in aid of their completion. Provided, that the state may appropriate money in the treasury or to be thereafter raised by taxation for the construction or improvement of public highways or the development, improvement and construction of airports or other aeronautical projects or the acquisition, improvement or construction of veterans' housing or the improvement of port facilities. Provided, that the state may appropriate moneys for the purpose of acquiring, preserving and developing the forests of the state; but of the moneys appropriated under the authority of this section in any one year an amount not to exceed two-tenths of one mill of the taxable property of the state as determined by the last preceding state assessment may be raised by a tax on property. [*1965 SJR-28; 1967 SJR-18*]

Internal improvements. SECTION 10. [*As amended April 1960*] The state shall never contract any debt for works of internal improvement, or be a party in carrying on such works; but whenever grants of land or other property shall have been made to the state, especially dedicated by the grant to particular works of internal improvement, the state may carry on such particular works and shall devote thereto the avails of such grants, and may pledge or appropriate the revenues derived from such works in aid of their completion. Provided, that the state may appropriate money in the treasury or to be thereafter raised by taxation for the construction or improvement of public highways or the development, improvement and construction of airports or other aeronautical projects or the acquisition, improvement or construction of veterans' housing or the improvement of port facilities. Provided, that the state may appropriate moneys for the purpose of acquiring, preserving and developing the forests of the state; but there shall not be appropriated under the authority of this section in any one year an amount to exceed two-tenths of one mill of the taxable property of the state as determined by the last preceding state assessment. [*1957 AJR-39; 1959 SJR-20*]

Internal improvements. SECTION 10. [*As amended April 1949*] The state shall never contract any debt for works of internal improvement, or be a party in carrying on such works; but whenever grants of land or other property shall

have been made to the state, especially dedicated by the grant to particular works of internal improvement, the state may carry on such particular works and shall devote thereto the avails of such grants, and may pledge or appropriate the revenues derived from such works in aid of their completion. Provided, that the state may appropriate money in the treasury or to be thereafter raised by taxation for the construction or improvement of public highways or the development, improvement and construction of airports or other aeronautical projects or the acquisition, improvement or construction of veterans' housing. Provided, that the state may appropriate moneys for the purpose of acquiring, preserving and developing the forests of the state; but there shall not be appropriated under the authority of this section in any one year an amount to exceed two-tenths of one mill of the taxable property of the state as determined by the last preceding state assessment. [*1948 Spec.Sess. SJR-2; 1949 SJR-5*]

Internal improvements. SECTION 10. [*As amended April 1945*] The state shall never contract any debt for works of internal improvement, or be a party in carrying on such works; but whenever grants of land or other property shall have been made to the state, especially dedicated by the grant to particular works of internal improvement, the state may carry on such particular works, and shall devote thereto the avails of such grants, and may pledge or appropriate the revenues derived from such works in aid of their completion. Provided, that the state may appropriate money in the treasury or to be thereafter raised by taxation for the construction or improvement of public highways or the development, improvement and construction of airports or other aeronautical projects. Provided, that the state may appropriate moneys for the purpose of acquiring, preserving and developing the forests of the state; but there shall not be appropriated under the authority of this section in any one year an amount to exceed two-tenths of one mill of the taxable property of the state as determined by the last preceding state assessment. [*1943 SJR-16; 1945 SJR-7*]

Internal improvements. SECTION 10. [*As amended November 1924*] The state shall never contract any debt for works of internal improvement, or be a party in carrying on such works; but whenever grants of land or other property shall have been made to the state, especially dedicated by the grant to particular works of internal improvement, the state may carry on such particular works, and shall devote thereto the avails of such grants, and may pledge or appropriate the revenues derived from such works in aid of their completion. Provided, that the state may appropriate money in the treasury or to be thereafter raised by taxation for the construction or improvement of public highways. Provided, that the state may appropriate moneys for the purpose of acquiring, preserving and developing the forests of the state; but there shall not be appropriated under the authority of this section in any one year an amount to exceed two-tenths of one mill of the taxable property of the state as determined by the last preceding state assessment. [*1921 SJR-30; 1923 AJR-70; 1923 c. 289*]

Water power and forests. SECTION 10. [*Approved by voters November 1910*] An amendment to Art. VIII, sec. 10, authorizing a state property tax of two-tenths of one mill to finance appropriations for acquisition and development of water power and forests was approved by 1907 SJR-43. There was no "second consideration" resolution but 1909 SB\553 enacted the proposal into law as Chap. 514, Laws of 1909. The procedure was declared invalid by the Supreme Court in *State ex rel. Owen v. Donald*, 160 W 21, 151 NW

331.

Public highways. [*As amended November 1908, a new sentence was added at the end of the section*] Provided, that the state may appropriate money in the treasury or to be thereafter raised by taxation for the construction or improvement of public highways. [1905 SJR-14; 1907 SJR-22; 1907 c. 238]

Internal improvements. SECTION 10. [*Original form*] The state shall never contract any debt for works of internal improvement, or be a party in carrying on such works, but whenever grants of land or other property shall have been made to the state, especially dedicated by the grant to particular works of internal improvements, the state may carry on such particular works, and shall devote thereto the avails of such grants, and may pledge or appropriate the revenues derived from such works in aid of their completion.

ARTICLE IX.
EMINENT DOMAIN AND PROPERTY OF THE STATE

Jurisdiction on rivers and lakes; navigable waters. SECTION 1. The state shall have concurrent jurisdiction on all rivers and lakes bordering on this state so far as such rivers or lakes shall form a common boundary to the state and any other state or territory now or hereafter to be formed, and bounded by the same; and the river Mississippi and the navigable waters leading into the Mississippi and St. Lawrence, and the carrying places between the same, shall be common highways and forever free, as well to the inhabitants of the state as to the citizens of the United States, without any tax, impost or duty therefor.

Territorial property. SECTION 2. The title to all lands and other property which have accrued to the territory of Wisconsin by grant, gift, purchase, forfeiture, escheat or otherwise shall vest in the state of Wisconsin.

Ultimate property in lands; escheats. SECTION 3. The people of the state, in their right of sovereignty, are declared to possess the ultimate property, in and to all lands within the jurisdiction of the state; and all lands the title to which shall fail from a defect of heirs shall revert or escheat to the people.

ARTICLE X.
EDUCATION

Superintendent of public instruction. SECTION 1. [*As amended November 1982*] The supervision of public instruction shall be vested in a state superintendent and such other officers as the legislature shall direct; and their qualifications, powers, duties and compensation shall be prescribed by law. The state superintendent shall be chosen by the qualified electors of the state at the same time and in the same manner as members of the supreme court, and shall hold office for 4 years from the succeeding first Monday in July. The term of office, time and manner of electing or appointing all other officers of supervision of public instruction shall be fixed by law. [*1979 AJR-76; 1981 AJR-35; submit: May'82 Spec.Sess. AJR-1*]

Superintendent of public instruction. SECTION 1 [*As amended November 1902*] The supervision of public instruction shall be vested in a state superintendent and such other officers as the legislature shall direct; and their qualifications, powers, duties and compensation shall be prescribed by law. The state superintendent shall be chosen by the qualified electors of the state at the same time and in the same manner as members of the supreme court, and shall hold his office for four years from the succeeding first Monday in July. The state superintendent chosen at the general election in November, 1902, shall hold and continue in his office until the first Monday in July, 1905, and his successor shall be chosen at the time of the judicial election

in April, 1905. The term of office, time and manner of electing or appointing all other officers of supervision of public instruction shall be fixed by law. [*1899 SJR-21; 1901 SJR-24; 1901 c. 258*]

Superintendent of public instruction. SECTION 1. [*Original form*] The supervision of public instruction shall be vested in a state superintendent, and such other officers as the legislature shall direct. The state superintendent shall be chosen by the qualified electors of the state, in such manner as the legislature shall provide; his powers, duties and compensation shall be prescribed by law. Provided, that his compensation shall not exceed the sum of twelve hundred dollars annually.

School fund created; income applied. SECTION 2. [*As amended November 1982*] The proceeds of all lands that have been or hereafter may be granted by the United States to this state for educational purposes (except the lands heretofore granted for the purposes of a university) and all moneys and the clear proceeds of all property that may accrue to the state by forfeiture or escheat; and the clear proceeds of all fines collected in the several counties for any breach of the penal laws, and all moneys arising from any grant to the state where the purposes of such grant are not specified, and the 500,000 acres of land to which the state is entitled by the provisions of an act of congress, entitled "An act to appropriate the proceeds of the sales of the public lands and to grant pre-emption rights," approved September 4, 1841; and also the 5 percent of the net proceeds of the public lands to which the state shall become entitled on admission into the union (if congress shall consent to such appropriation of the 2 grants last mentioned) shall be set apart as a separate fund to be called "the school fund," the interest of which and all other revenues derived from the school lands shall be exclusively applied to the following objects, to wit:

(1) To the support and maintenance of common schools, in each school district, and the purchase of suitable libraries and apparatus therefor.

(2) The residue shall be appropriated to the support and maintenance of academies and normal schools, and suitable libraries and apparatus therefor. [1979 AJR-76; 1981 AJR-35; submit: May'82 Spec.Sess. AJR-1]

School fund created; income applied. SECTION 2. [*Original form*] The proceeds of all lands that have been or hereafter may be granted by the United States to this state for educational purposes (except the lands heretofore granted for the purpose of a university) and all moneys and the clear proceeds of all property that may accrue to the state by forfeiture or escheat, and all moneys which may be paid as an equivalent for exemption from military duty; and the clear proceeds of all fines collected in the several counties for any breach of the penal laws, and all moneys arising from any grant to the state where the purposes of such grant are not specified, and the five hundred thousand acres of land to which the state is entitled by the provisions of an act of congress, entitled "An act to appropriate the proceeds of the sales of the public lands and to grant pre-emption

rights," approved the fourth day of September, one thousand eight hundred and forty-one; and also the five per centum of the net proceeds of the public lands to which the state shall become entitled on her admission into the union (if congress shall consent to such appropriation of the two grants last mentioned) shall be set apart as a separate fund to be called "the school fund," the interest of which and all other revenues derived from the school lands shall be exclusively applied to the following objects, to wit:

1. To the support and maintenance of common schools, in each school district, and the purchase of suitable libraries and apparatus therefor.

2. The residue shall be appropriated to the support and maintenance of academies and normal schools, and suitable libraries and apparatus therefor.

District schools; tuition; sectarian instruction; released time. SECTION 3. [*As amended April 1972*] The legislature shall provide by law for the establishment of district schools, which shall be as nearly uniform as practicable; and such schools shall be free and without charge for tuition to all children between the ages of 4 and 20 years; and no sectarian instruction shall be allowed therein; but the legislature by law may, for the purpose of religious instruction outside the district schools, authorize the release of students during regular school hours. [1969 AJR-41; 1971 AJR-17]

District schools; tuition; sectarian instruction. SECTION 3. [*Original form*] The legislature shall provide by law for the establishment of district schools, which shall be as nearly uniform as practicable; and such schools shall be

free and without charge for tuition to all children between the ages of four and twenty years; and no sectarian instruction shall be allowed therein.

Annual school tax. SECTION 4. Each town and city shall be required to raise by tax, annually, for the support of common schools therein, a sum not less than one-half the amount received by such town or city respectively for school purposes from the income of the school fund.

Income of school fund. SECTION 5. Provision shall be made by law for the distribution of the income of the school fund among the several towns and cities of the state for the support of common schools therein, in some just proportion to the number of children and youth resident therein between the ages of four and twenty years, and no appropriation shall be made from the school fund to any city or town for the year in which said city or town shall fail to raise such tax; nor to any school district for the year in which a school shall not be maintained at least three months.

State university; support. SECTION 6. Provision shall be made by law for the establishment of a state university at or near the seat of state government, and for connecting with the same, from time to time, such colleges in different parts of the state as the interests of education may require. The proceeds of all lands that have been or may hereafter be granted by the United States to the state for the support of a university shall be and remain a perpetual fund to be called "the university fund," the interest of which shall be appropriated to the support of the state university, and no sectarian instruction shall be allowed in such university.

Commissioners of public lands. SECTION 7. The secretary of state, treasurer and attorney general, shall constitute a board of commissioners for the sale of the school and university lands and for the investment of the funds arising therefrom. Any two of said commissioners shall be a quorum for the transaction of all business pertaining to the duties of their office.

Sale of public lands. SECTION 8. Provision shall be made by law for the sale of all school and university lands after they shall have been appraised; and when any portion of such lands shall be sold and the purchase money shall not be paid at the time of the sale, the commissioners shall take security by mortgage upon the lands sold for the sum remaining unpaid, with seven per cent interest thereon, payable annually at the office of the treasurer. The commissioners shall be authorized to execute a good and sufficient conveyance to all purchasers of such lands, and to discharge any mortgages taken as security, when the sum due thereon shall have been paid. The commissioners shall have power to withhold from sale any portion of such lands when they shall deem it expedient, and shall invest all moneys arising from the sale of such lands, as well as all other university and school funds, in such manner as the legislature shall provide, and shall give such security for the faithful performance of their duties as may be required by law.

ARTICLE XI.
CORPORATIONS

Corporations; how formed. SECTION 1. [*As amended April 1981*] Corporations without banking powers or privileges may be formed under general laws, but shall not be created by special act, except for municipal purposes. All general laws or special acts enacted under the provisions of this section may be altered or repealed by the legislature at any time after their passage. [*1979 AJR-53; 1981 AJR-13*]

Corporations; how formed. SECTION 1. [*Original form*] Corporations without banking powers or privileges may be formed under general laws, but shall not be created by special act, except for municipal purposes, and in cases where, in the judgment of the legislature, the objects of the corporation cannot be attained under general laws. All general laws or special acts enacted under the provisions of this section may be altered or repealed by the legislature at any time after their passage.

Property taken by municipality. SECTION 2. [*As amended April 1961*] No municipal corporation shall take private property for public use, against the consent of the owner, without the necessity thereof being first established in the manner prescribed by the legislature. [*1959 AJR-22; 1961 SJR-8*]

Property taken by municipality. SECTION 2. [*Original form*] No municipal corporation shall take private property for public use, against the consent of the owner, without the necessity thereof being first established by the verdict of a jury.

Municipal home rule; debt limit; tax to pay debt. SECTION 3. [*As amended April 1981*] (1) Cities and villages organized pursuant to state law may determine their local affairs and government, subject only to this constitution and to such enactments of the legislature of statewide concern as with uniformity shall affect every city or every village. The method of such determination shall be prescribed by the legislature.

(2) No county, city, town, village, school district, sewerage district or other municipal corporation may become indebted in an amount that exceeds an allowable percentage of the taxable property located therein equalized for state purposes as provided by the legislature. In all cases the allowable percentage shall be 5 percent except as specified in pars. (a) and (b):

(a) For any city authorized to issue bonds for school purposes, an additional 10 percent shall be permitted for school purposes only, and in such cases the territory attached to the city for school purposes shall be included in the total taxable property supporting the bonds issued for school purposes.

(b) For any school district which offers no less than grades one to 12 and which at the time of incurring such debt is eligible for the highest level of school aids, 10 percent shall be permitted.

(3) Any county, city, town, village, school district, sewerage district or other municipal corporation incurring any indebtedness under sub. (2) shall, before or at the time of doing so, provide for the collection of a direct annual tax sufficient to pay the interest on such debt as it falls due, and also to pay and discharge the principal thereof within 20 years from the time of contracting the same.

(4) When indebtedness under sub. (2) is incurred in the acquisition of lands by cities, or by counties or sewerage districts having a population of 150,000 or over, for public, municipal purposes, or for the permanent improvement thereof, or to purchase, acquire, construct, extend,

add to or improve a sewage collection or treatment system which services all or a part of such city or county, the city, county or sewerage district incurring the indebtedness shall, before or at the time of so doing, provide for the collection of a direct annual tax sufficient to pay the interest on such debt as it falls due, and also to pay and discharge the principal thereof within a period not exceeding 50 years from the time of contracting the same.

(5) An indebtedness created for the purpose of purchasing, acquiring, leasing, constructing, extending, adding to, improving, conducting, controlling, operating or managing a public utility of a town, village, city or special district, and secured solely by the property or income of such public utility, and whereby no municipal liability is created, shall not be considered an indebtedness of such town, village, city or special district, and shall not be included in arriving at the debt limitation under sub. (2). [*1979 SJR-28; 1981 SJR-5*]

Municipal home rule; debt limit; tax to pay debt.
SECTION 3. [*As amended April 1966*] Cities and villages organized pursuant to state law are hereby empowered, to determine their local affairs and government, subject only to this constitution and to such enactments of the legislature of state-wide concern as shall with uniformity affect every city or every village. The method of such determination shall be prescribed by the legislature. No county, city, town, village, school district or other municipal corporation may become indebted in an amount that exceeds an allowable percentage of the taxable property located therein equalized for state purposes as provided by the legislature. In all cases the allowable percentage shall be five per centum except as follows: (a) For any city authorized to issue bonds for school purposes, an additional ten per centum shall be permitted for school purposes only, and in such cases the territory attached to the city for school purposes shall be included in the total taxable property supporting the bonds issued for school purposes. (b) For any school district which offers no less than grades one to twelve and which at the time of incurring such debt is eligible for the highest level of school aids, ten per centum shall be permitted. Any county, city, town, village, school district, or other municipal corporation incurring any indebtedness as aforesaid, shall before or at the time of doing so, provide for the collection of a direct annual tax sufficient to pay the interest on such debt as it falls due, and also to pay and discharge the principal thereof within twenty years from the time of contracting the same; except that when such indebtedness is incurred in the acquisition of lands by cities, or by counties having a population of one hundred fifty thousand or over, for public, municipal purposes, or for the permanent improvement thereof, the city or county incurring the same shall, before or at the time of so doing, provide for the collection of a direct annual tax sufficient to pay the interest on such debt as it falls due, and also to pay and discharge the principal thereof within a period not exceeding fifty years from the time of contracting the same. An indebtedness created for the purpose of purchasing, acquiring, leasing, constructing, extending, adding to, improving, conducting, controlling, operating or managing a public utility of a town, village, city or special district, and secured solely by the property or income of such public utility, and whereby no municipal liability is created, shall not be considered an indebtedness of such town, village, city or special district, and shall not be included in arriving at such debt limitation. [*1963 SJR-59; 1965 AJR-10*]

Municipal home rule; debt limit; tax to pay debt.
SECTION 3. [*As amended April 1963*] Cities and villages organized pursuant to state law are hereby empowered, to determine their local affairs and government, subject only to this constitution and to such enactments of the legislature of state-wide concern as shall with uniformity affect every city or every village. The method of such determination shall be prescribed by the legislature. No county, city, town, village, school district or other municipal corporation may become indebted in an amount that exceeds an allowable percentage of the taxable property located therein equalized for state purposes as provided by the legislature. In all cases the allowable percentage shall be five per centum except as follows: (a) For any city authorized to issue bonds for school purposes, an additional ten per centum shall be permitted for school purposes only, and in such cases the territory attached to the city for school purposes shall be included in

the total taxable property supporting the bonds issued for school purposes. (b) For any school district which offers no less than grades one to twelve and which at the time of incurring such debt is eligible for the highest level of school aids, ten per centum shall be permitted. Any county, city, town, village, school district, or other municipal corporation incurring any indebtedness as aforesaid, shall before or at the time of doing so, provide for the collection of a direct annual tax sufficient to pay the interest on such debt as it falls due, and also to pay and discharge the principal thereof within twenty years from the time of contracting the same; except that when such indebtedness is incurred in the acquisition of lands by cities, or by counties having a population of one hundred fifty thousand or over, for public, municipal purposes, or for the permanent improvement thereof, the city or county incurring the same shall, before or at the time of so doing, provide for the collection of a direct annual tax sufficient to pay the interest on such debt as it falls due, and also to pay and discharge the principal thereof within a period not exceeding fifty years from the time of contracting the same. An indebtedness created for the purpose of purchasing, acquiring, leasing, constructing, extending, adding to, improving, conducting, controlling, operating or managing a public utility of a town, village or city, and secured solely by the property or income of such public utility, and whereby no municipal liability is created, shall not be considered an indebtedness of such town, village or city, and shall not be included in arriving at such five or eight per cent debt limitation. [*1961 AJR-92; 1963 AJR-19*]

Municipal home rule; debt limit; tax to pay debt.
SECTION 3. [*As amended April 1961*] Cities and villages organized pursuant to state law are hereby empowered, to determine their local affairs and government, subject only to this constitution and to such enactments of the legislature of state-wide concern as shall with uniformity affect every city or every village. The method of such determination shall be prescribed by the legislature. No county, city, town, village, school district, or other municipal corporation shall be allowed to become indebted in any manner or for any purpose to any amount, including existing indebtedness, in the aggregate exceeding five per centum on the value of the taxable property therein, to be ascertained, other than for school districts and counties having a population of 500,000 or over, by the last assessment for state and county taxes previous to the incurring of such indebtedness and for school districts and counties having a population of 500,000 or over by the value of such property as equalized for state purposes; except that for any city which is authorized to issue bonds for school purposes the total indebtedness of such city shall not exceed in the aggregate eight per centum of the value of such property as equalized for state purposes and except that for any school district offering no less than grades one to twelve and which is at the time of incurring such debt eligible for the highest level of school aids, the total indebtedness of such school district shall not exceed ten per centum of the value of such property as equalized for state purposes; the manner and method of determining such equalization for state purposes to be provided by the legislature. Any county, city, town, village, school district, or other municipal corporation incurring any indebtedness as aforesaid, shall, before or at the time of doing so, provide for the collection of a direct annual tax sufficient to pay the interest on such debt as it falls due, and also to pay and

discharge the principal thereof within twenty years from the time of contracting the same; except that when such indebtedness is incurred in the acquisition of lands by cities, or by counties having a population of one hundred fifty thousand or over, for public, municipal purposes, or for the permanent improvement thereof, the city or county incurring the same shall, before or at the time of so doing, provide for the collection of a direct annual tax sufficient to pay the interest on such debt as it falls due, and also to pay and discharge the principal thereof within a period not exceeding fifty years from the time of contracting the same. An indebtedness created for the purpose of purchasing, acquiring, leasing, constructing, extending, adding to, improving, conducting, controlling, operating or managing a public utility of a town, village or city, and secured solely by the property or income of such public utility, and whereby no municipal liability is created, shall not be considered an indebtedness of such town, village or city, and shall not be included in arriving at such five or eight per centum debt limitation. [*1959 SJR-6; 1961 AJR-1*]

Municipal home rule; debt limit; tax to pay debt.
SECTION 3. [*As amended November 1960*] Cities and villages organized pursuant to state law are hereby empowered, to determine their local affairs and government, subject only to this constitution and to such enactments of the legislature of state-wide concern as shall with uniformity affect every city or every village. The method of such determination shall be prescribed by the legislature. No county, city, town, village, school district, or other municipal corporation shall be allowed to become indebted in any manner or for any purpose to any amount, including existing indebtedness, in the aggregate exceeding five per centum on the value of the taxable property therein, to be ascertained, other than for school districts and counties having a population of 500,000 or over, by the last assessment for state and county taxes previous to the incurring of such indebtedness and for school districts and counties having a population of 500,000 or over by the value of such property as equalized for state purposes; except that for any city which is authorized to issue bonds for school purposes the total indebtedness of such city shall not exceed in the aggregate eight per centum of the value of such property as equalized for state purposes; the manner and method of determining such equalization for state purposes to be provided by the legislature. Any county, city, town, village, school district, or other municipal corporation incurring any indebtedness as aforesaid, shall, before or at the time of doing so, provide for the collection of a direct annual tax sufficient to pay the interest on such debt as it falls due, and also to pay and discharge the principal thereof within twenty years from the time of contracting the same; except that when such indebtedness is incurred in the acquisition of lands by cities, or by counties having a population of one hundred fifty thousand or over, for public, municipal purposes, or for the permanent improvement thereof, the city or county incurring the same shall, before or at the time of so doing, provide for the collection of a direct annual tax sufficient to pay the interest on such debt as it falls due, and also to pay and discharge the principal thereof within a period not exceeding fifty years from the time of contracting the same. Providing, that an indebtedness created for the purpose of purchasing, acquiring, leasing, constructing, extending, adding to, improving, conducting, controlling, operating or managing a public utility of a town, village or city, and secured solely by the property or income of such public utility, and whereby no municipal liability is created, shall not be considered an indebtedness of such town, village or city, and shall not be included in arriving at such five or eight per centum debt limitation. [*1957 SJR-47; 1959 SJR-53*]

Municipal home rule; debt limit; tax to pay debt.
SECTION 3. [*As amended April 1955*] Cities and villages organized pursuant to state law are hereby empowered, to determine their local affairs and government, subject only to this constitution and to such enactments of the legislature of state-wide concern as shall with uniformity affect every city or every village. The method of such determination shall be prescribed by the legislature. No county, city, town, village, school district, or other municipal corporation shall be allowed to become indebted in any manner or for any purpose to any amount, including existing indebtedness, in

the aggregate exceeding five per centum on the value of the taxable property therein, to be ascertained, other than for school district, by the last assessment for state and county taxes previous to the incurring of such indebtedness and for school districts by the value of such property as equalized for state purposes; except that for any city which is authorized to issue bonds for school purposes the total indebtedness of such city shall not exceed in the aggregate eight per centum of the value of such property as equalized for state purposes; the manner and method of determining such equalization for state purposes to be provided by the legislature. Any county, city, town, village, school district, or other municipal corporation incurring any indebtedness as aforesaid, shall, before or at the time of doing so, provide for the collection of a direct annual tax sufficient to pay the interest on such debt as it falls due, and also to pay and discharge the principal thereof within twenty years from the time of contracting the same; except that when such indebtedness is incurred in the acquisition of lands by cities, or by counties having a population of one hundred fifty thousand or over, for public, municipal purposes, or for the permanent improvement thereof, the city or county incurring the same shall, before or at the time of so doing, provide for the collection of a direct annual tax sufficient to pay the interest on such debt as it falls due, and also to pay and discharge the principal thereof within a period not exceeding fifty years from the time of contracting the same. Providing, that an indebtedness created for the purpose of purchasing, acquiring, leasing, constructing, extending, adding to, improving, conducting, con- trolling, operating or managing a public utility of a town, village or city, and secured solely by the property or income of such public utility, and whereby no municipal liability is created, shall not be considered an indebtedness of such town, village or city, and shall not be included in arriving at such five or eight per centum debt limitation. [*1953 SJR-17; 1955 AJR-18*]

Municipal home rule; debt limit; tax to pay debt.
SECTION 3. [*As amended April 1951*] Cities and villages organized pursuant to state law are hereby empowered, to determine their local affairs and government, subject only to this constitution and to such enactments of the legislature of state-wide concern as shall with uniformity affect every city or every village. The method of such determination shall be prescribed by the legislature. No county, city, town, village, school district, or other municipal corporation shall be allowed to become indebted in any manner or for any purpose to any amount, including existing indebtedness, in the aggregate exceeding 5 per centum on the value of the taxable property therein, to be ascertained by the last assessment for state and county taxes previous to the incurring of such indebtedness; except that for any city which is authorized to issue bonds for school purposes the total indebtedness of such city shall not exceed in the aggregate 8 per centum of the value of such property. Any county, city, town, village, school district, or other municipal corporation incurring any indebtedness as aforesaid, shall, before or at the time of doing so, provide for the collection of a direct annual tax sufficient to pay the interest on such debt as it falls due, and also to pay and discharge the principal thereof within 20 years from the time of contracting the same; except that when such indebtedness is incurred in the acquisition of lands by cities, or by counties having a population of 150,000 or over, for public, municipal purposes, or for the permanent improvement thereof, the city or county incurring the same shall, before or at the time of so doing, provide for the collection of a direct annual tax sufficient to pay the interest on such debt as it falls due, and also to pay and discharge the principal thereof within a period not exceeding 50 years from the time of contracting the same. Providing, that an indebtedness created for the purpose of purchasing, acquiring, leasing, constructing, extending, adding to, improving, conducting, controlling, operating or managing a public utility of a town, village or city, and secured solely by the property or income of such public utility, and whereby no municipal liability is created, shall not be considered an indebtedness of such town, village or city, and shall not be included in arriving at such 5 or 8 per centum debt limitation. [*1949 SJR-11; 1951 SJR-9*]

Municipal home rule; debt limit; tax to pay debt.
SECTION 3. [*As amended November 1932*] Cities and

villages organized pursuant to state law are hereby empowered, to determine their local affairs and government, subject only to this constitution and to such enactments of the legislature of state-wide concern as shall with uniformity affect every city or every village. The method of such determination shall be prescribed by the legislature. No county, city, town, village, school district, or other municipal corporation shall be allowed to become indebted in any manner or for any purpose to any amount, including existing indebtedness, in the aggregate exceeding five per centum on the value of the taxable property therein, to be ascertained by the last assessment for state and county taxes previous to the incurring of such indebtedness. Any county, city, town, village, school district, or other municipal corporation incurring any indebtedness as aforesaid, shall, before or at the time of doing so, provide for the collection of a direct annual tax sufficient to pay the interest on such debt as it falls due, and also to pay and discharge the principal thereof within twenty years from the time of contracting the same; except that when such indebtedness is incurred in the acquisition of lands by cities, or by counties having a population of one hundred fifty thousand or over, for public, municipal purposes, or for the permanent improvement thereof, the city or county incurring the same shall, before or at the time of so doing, provide for the collection of a direct annual tax sufficient to pay the interest on such debt as it falls due, and also to pay and discharge the principal thereof within a period not exceeding fifty years from the time of contracting the same. Providing, that an indebtedness created for the purpose of purchasing, acquiring, leasing, constructing, extending, adding to, improving, conducting, controlling, operating or managing a public utility of a town, village or city, and secured solely by the property or income of such public utility, and whereby no municipal liability is created, shall not be considered an indebtedness of such town, village or city, and shall not be included in arriving at such five per centum debt limitation. [*1929 AJR-61; 1931 AJR-14*]

Municipal home rule; debt limit; tax to pay debt. SECTION 3. [*As amended November 1924*] Cities and villages organized pursuant to state law are hereby empowered, to determine their local affairs and government, subject only to this constitution and to such enactments of the legislature of state-wide concern as shall with uniformity affect every city or every village. The method of such determination shall be prescribed by the legislature. No county, city, town, village, school district, or other municipal corporation shall be allowed to become indebted in any manner or for any purpose to any amount, including existing indebtedness, in the aggregate exceeding five per centum on the value of the taxable property therein, to be ascertained by the last assessment for state and county taxes previous to the incurring of such indebtedness. Any county, city, town, village, school district, or other municipal corporation incurring any indebtedness as aforesaid, shall, before or at the time of doing so, provide for the collection of a direct annual tax sufficient to pay the interest on such debt as it falls due, and also to pay and discharge the principal thereof within twenty years from the time of contracting the same; except that when such indebtedness is incurred in the acquisition of lands by cities, or by counties having a population of one hundred fifty thousand or over, for public, municipal purposes, or for the permanent improvement thereof, the city or

incurring the same shall, before or at the time of so doing, provide for the collection of a direct annual tax sufficient to pay the interest on such debt as it falls due, and also to pay and discharge the principal thereof within a period not exceeding fifty years from the time of contracting the same. [*1921 SJR-5; 1923 SJR-18; 1923 c. 203*]

Organization of cities and villages. SECTION 3. [*As amended November 1912*] It shall be the duty of the legislature, and they are hereby empowered to provide for the organization of cities and incorporated villages, and to restrict their power of taxation, assessment, borrowing money, contracting debts, and loaning their credit, so as to prevent abuses in assessments and taxation, and in contracting debts by such municipal corporations. No county, city, town, village, school district, or other municipal corporation shall be allowed to become indebted in any manner or for any purpose to any amount, including existing indebtedness, in the aggregate exceeding five per centum on the value of the taxable property therein, to be ascertained by the last assessment for state and county taxes previous to the incurring of such indebtedness. Any county, city, town, village, school district, or other municipal corporation incurring any indebtedness as aforesaid, shall, before or at the time of doing so, provide for the collection of a direct annual tax sufficient to pay the interest on such debt as it falls due, and also to pay and discharge the principal thereof within twenty years from the time of contracting the same; except that when such indebtedness is incurred in the acquisition of lands by cities, or by counties having a population of one hundred fifty thousand or over, for public, municipal purposes, or for the permanent improvement thereof, the city or county incurring the same shall, before or at the time of so doing, provide for the collection of a direct annual tax sufficient to pay the interest on such debt as it falls due, and also to pay and discharge the principal thereof within a period not exceeding fifty years from the time of contracting the same. [*1909 SJR-32; 1911 SJR-26; 1911 c. 665*]

Municipal debt limit. [*An amendment approved by the voters in November 1874 added two new paragraphs at the end of the section*] No county, city, town, village, school district, or other municipal corporation shall be allowed to become indebted in any manner or for any purpose to any amount including existing indebtedness, in the aggregate exceeding five per centum on the value of the taxable property therein to be ascertained by the last assessment for state and county taxes previous to the incurring of such indebtedness. Any county, city, town, village, school district or other municipal corporation incurring any indebtedness as aforesaid, shall, before or at the time of doing so provide for the collection of a direct annual tax sufficient to pay the interest on said debt as it falls due, and also to pay and discharge the principal thereof within twenty years from the time of contracting the same. [1872 AJR-17; 1873 SJR-6; 1874 c. 3]

Organization of cities and villages. SECTION 3. [*Original form*] It shall be the duty of the legislature, and they are hereby empowered, to provide for the organization of cities and incorporated villages, and to restrict their power of taxation, assessment, borrowing money, contracting debts and loaning their credit, so as to prevent abuses in assessments and taxation, and in contracting debts by such municipal corporations.

Acquisition of lands by state and subdivisions; sale of excess. SECTION 3a. [*As amended April 3, 1956*] The state or any of its counties, cities, towns or villages may acquire by gift, dedication, purchase, or condemnation lands for establishing, laying out, widening, enlarging, extending, and maintaining memorial grounds, streets, highways, squares, parkways, boulevards, parks, playgrounds, sites for public buildings, and reservations in and about and along and leading to any or all of the same; and after the establishment, layout, and completion of such improvements, may convey any such real estate thus acquired and not necessary for such improvements, with reservations concerning the future use and occupation of such real estate, so as to protect such public works and improvements, and their environs, and to preserve the view, appearance, light, air, and usefulness of such public works. If the governing body of a county, city, town or village elects to accept a gift or dedication of land made on condition that the land be devoted to a special purpose and the condition subsequently becomes impossible or

impracticable, such governing body may by resolution or ordinance enacted by a two-thirds vote of its members elect either to grant the land back to the donor or dedicator or his heirs or accept from the donor or dedicator or his heirs a grant relieving the county, city, town or village of the condition; however, if the donor or dedicator or his heirs are unknown or cannot be found, such resolution or ordinance may provide for the commencement of proceedings in the manner and in the courts as the legislature shall designate for the purpose of relieving the county, city, town or village from the condition of the gift or dedication. [*1953 SJR-29; 1955 SJR-9*]

Acquisition of lands by state and cities; sale of excess. SECTION 3a. [*Created November 1912*] The state or any of its cities may acquire by gift, purchase, or condemnation lands for establishing, laying out, widening, enlarging, extending, and maintaining memorial grounds, streets, squares, parkways, boulevards, parks, playgrounds, sites for public buildings, and reservations in and about and along and leading to any or all of the same; and after the establishment, layout, and completion of such improvements, may convey any such real estate thus acquired and not necessary for such improvements, with reservations concerning the future use and occupation of such real estate, so as to protect such public works and improvements, and their environs, and to preserve the view, appearance, light, air, and usefulness of such public works. [*1909 SJR-63; 1911 SJR-25; 1911 c. 665*]

General banking law. SECTION 4. [*As amended April 1981*] The legislature may enact a general banking law for the creation of banks, and for the regulation and supervision of the banking business. [*1979 AJR-53; 1981 AJR-13*]

General banking law. SECTION 4. [*Created November 1902. This section was adopted to replace original sections 4 and 5 of this article*] The legislature shall have power to enact a general banking law for the creation of banks, and for the regulation and supervision of the banking business, provided that the vote of two-thirds of all the members elected to each house, to be taken by yeas and nays, be in favor of the passage of such law. [*P1899 AJR-16; 1901 SJR-25; 1901 c. 73*]

Legislature prohibited from incorporating banks. SECTION 4. [*Original form, repealed November 1902. 1899 AJR-16; 1901 SJR-25; 1901 c. 73*] The legislature shall not have power to create, authorize or incorporate, by any general, or special law, any bank, or banking power or privilege, or any institution or corporation having any banking power or privilege whatever, except as provided in this article.

Referendum on banking laws. SECTION 5. [*Original form, repealed November 1902. 1899 AJR-16; 1901 SJR-25; 1901 c. 73*] The legislature may submit to the voters, at any general election, the question of "bank," or "no bank," and if at any such election a number of votes equal to a majority of all the votes cast at such election on that subject shall be in favor of banks, then the legislature shall have power to grant bank charters, or to pass a general banking law, with such restrictions and under such regulations as they may deem expedient and proper for the security of the bill holders. Provided, that no such grant or law shall have any force or effect until the same shall have been submitted to a vote of the electors of the state, at some general election, and been approved by a majority of the votes cast on that subject at such election.

ARTICLE XII.
AMENDMENTS

Constitutional amendments. SECTION 1. Any amendment or amendments to this constitution may be proposed in either house of the legislature, and if the same shall be agreed to by a majority of the members elected to each of the two houses, such proposed amendment or amendments shall be entered on their journals, with the yeas and nays taken thereon, and referred to the legislature to be chosen at the next general election, and shall be published for three months previous to the time of holding such election; and if, in the legislature so next chosen, such proposed amendment or amendments shall be agreed to by a majority of all the members elected to each house, then it shall be the duty of the legislature to submit such proposed amendment or amendments to the people in such manner and at such time as the legislature shall prescribe; and if the people shall approve and ratify such amendment or amendments by a majority of the electors voting thereon, such amendment or amendments shall become part of the constitution; provided, that if more than one amendment be submitted, they shall be submitted in such manner that the people may vote for or against such amendments separately.

Constitutional conventions. SECTION 2. If at any time a majority of the senate and assembly shall deem it necessary to call a convention to revise or change this constitution, they shall recommend to the electors to vote for or against a convention at the next election for members of the legislature. And if it shall appear that a majority of the electors voting thereon have voted for a convention, the legislature shall, at its next session, provide for calling such convention.

ARTICLE XIII.
MISCELLANEOUS PROVISIONS

Political year; elections. SECTION 1. [*As amended April 1986*] The political year for this state shall commence on the first Monday of January in each year, and the general election shall be held on the Tuesday next succeeding the first Monday of November in even-numbered years. [*1983 AJR-33; 1985 AJR-3*]

Political year; elections. SECTION 1. [*As amended November 1884*] The political year for the state of Wisconsin shall commence on the first Monday in January in each year, and the general election shall be holden on the Tuesday next succeeding the first Monday in November. The first general election for all state and county officers, except judicial officers, after the adoption of this amendment, shall be holden in the year A.D. 1884, and thereafter the general election shall be held biennially. All state, county or other officers elected at the general election

in the year 1881, and whose term of office would otherwise expire on the first Monday of January in the year 1884, shall hold and continue in such offices respectively until the first Monday in January in the year 1885. [*1881 AJR-16; 1882 SJR-20; 1882 c. 290*]

Political year; general election. SECTION 1. [*Original form*] The political year for the state of Wisconsin shall commence on the first Monday in January in each year, and the general election shall be holden on the Tuesday succeeding the first Monday in November in each year.

SECTION 2. [*Repealed. 1973 SJR-6; 1975 SJR-4; vote April 1975*]

Dueling. SECTION 2. [*Original form*] Any inhabitant of this state who may hereafter be engaged, either directly or indirectly, in a duel, either as principal or accessory, shall forever be disqualified as an elector, and from holding any

office under the constitution and laws of this state, and may be punished in such other manner as shall be prescribed by law.

Eligibility to office. SECTION 3. [*As amended November 1996*] (1) No member of congress and no person holding any office of profit or trust under the United States except postmaster, or under any foreign power, shall be eligible to any office of trust, profit or honor in this state.

(2) No person convicted of a felony, in any court within the United States, no person convicted in federal court of a crime designated, at the time of commission, under federal law as a misdemeanor involving a violation of public trust and no person convicted, in a court of a state, of a crime designated, at the time of commission, under the law of the state as a misdemeanor involving a violation of public trust shall be eligible to any office of trust, profit or honor in this state unless pardoned of the conviction.

(3) No person may seek to have placed on any ballot for a state or local elective office in this state the name of a person convicted of a felony, in any court within the United States, the name of a person convicted in federal court of a crime designated, at the time of commission, under federal law as a misdemeanor involving a violation of public trust or the name of a person convicted, in a court of a state, of a crime designated, at the time of commission, under the law of the state as a misdemeanor involving a violation of public trust, unless the person named for the ballot has been pardoned of the conviction. [*1993 AJR-3; 1995 AJR-16*]

Eligibility to office. SECTION 3. [*Original form*] No member of congress, nor any person holding any office of profit or trust under the United States (postmasters excepted) or under any foreign power; no person convicted of any infamous crime in any court within the United States;

and no person being a defaulter to the United States or to this state, or to any county or town therein, or to any state or territory within the United States, shall be eligible to any office of trust, profit or honor in this state.

Great seal. SECTION 4. It shall be the duty of the legislature to provide a great seal for the state, which shall be kept by the secretary of state, and all official acts of the governor, his approbation of the laws excepted, shall be thereby authenticated.

SECTION 5. [*Repealed. 1983 AJR-33; 1985 SJR-3; vote April 1986*]

Residents on Indian lands, where to vote. SECTION 5. [*Original form*] All persons residing upon Indian lands, within any county of the state, and qualified to exercise the right of suffrage under the constitution, shall be entitled to

vote at the polls which may be held nearest their residence, for state, United States or county officers. Provided, that no person shall vote for county officers out of the county in which he resides.

Legislative officers. SECTION 6. The elective officers of the legislature, other than the presiding officers, shall be a chief clerk and a sergeant at arms, to be elected by each house.

Division of counties. SECTION 7. No county with an area of nine hundred square miles or less shall be divided or have any part stricken therefrom, without submitting the question to a vote of the people of the county, nor unless a majority of all the legal voters of the county voting on the question shall vote for the same.

Removal of county seats. SECTION 8. No county seat shall be removed until the point to which it is proposed to be removed shall be fixed by law, and a majority of the voters of the county voting on the question shall have voted in favor of its removal to such point.

Election or appointment of statutory officers. SECTION 9. All county officers whose election or appointment is not provided for by this constitution shall be elected by the electors of the respective counties, or appointed by the boards of supervisors, or other county authorities, as the legislature shall direct. All city, town and village officers whose election or appointment is not provided for by this constitution shall be elected by the electors of such cities, towns and villages, or of some division thereof, or appointed by such authorities thereof as the legislature shall designate for that purpose. All other officers whose election or appointment is not provided for by this constitution, and all officers whose offices may hereafter be created by law, shall be elected by the people or appointed, as the legislature may direct.

Vacancies in office. SECTION 10. [*As amended April 1979*] (1) The legislature may declare the cases in which any office shall be deemed vacant, and also the manner of filling the vacancy, where no provision is made for that purpose in this constitution.

(2) Whenever there is a vacancy in the office of lieutenant governor, the governor shall nominate a successor to serve for the balance of the unexpired term, who shall take office after confirmation by the senate and by the assembly. [*1977 SJR-51; 1979 SJR-1*]

Vacancies in office. SECTION 10. [*Original form*] The legislature may declare the cases in which any office shall be deemed vacant, and also the manner of filling the vacancy, where no provision is made for that purpose in this constitution.

Passes, franks and privileges. SECTION 11. [*As amended November 1936*] No person, association, copartnership, or corporation, shall promise, offer or give, for any purpose, to any political committee, or any member or employe thereof, to any candidate for, or incumbent of any office or position under the constitution or laws, or under any ordinance of any town or municipality, of this state, or to any person at the request or for the advantage of all or any of them, any free pass or frank, or any privilege withheld from any person, for the traveling accommodation or transportation of any person or property, or the transmission of any message or communication.

No political committee, and no member or employe thereof, no candidate for and no incumbent of any office or position under the constitution or laws, or under any ordinance of any town or municipality of this state, shall ask for, or accept, from any person, association, copartnership, or corporation, or use, in any manner, or for any purpose, any free pass or frank, or any privilege withheld from any person, for the traveling accommodation or transportation of any person or property, or the transmission of any message or communication.

Any violation of any of the above provisions shall be bribery and punished as provided by law, and if any officer or any member of the legislature be guilty thereof, his office shall become vacant.

No person within the purview of this act shall be privileged from testifying in relation to anything therein prohibited; and no person having so testified shall be liable to any prosecution or punishment for any offense concerning which he was required to give his testimony or produce any documentary evidence.

Notaries public and regular employes of a railroad or other public utilities who are candidates for or hold public offices for which the annual compensation is not more than three hundred dollars to whom no passes or privileges are extended beyond those which are extended to other regular employes of such corporations are excepted from the provisions of this section. [*1933 AJR-50; 1935 AJR-67*]

Free passes forbidden. SECTION 11. [*Created November 1902*] No person, association, co-partnership, or corporation, shall promise, offer or give, for any purpose, to any political committee, or any member or employee thereof, to any candidate for, or incumbent of any office or position under the constitution or laws, or under any ordinance of any town or municipality, of this state, or to any person at the request or for the advantage of all or any of them, any free pass or frank, or any privilege withheld from any person, for the traveling accommodation or transportation of any person or property, or the transmission of any message or communication.

No political committee, and no member or employee thereof, no candidate for and no incumbent of any office or position under the constitution or laws, or under any ordinance of any town or municipality of this state, shall ask for, or accept, from any person, association, co-partnership, or corporation, or use, in any manner, or for any purpose,

any free pass or frank, or any privilege withheld from any person, for the traveling accommodation or transportation of any person or property, or the transmission of any message or communication.

Any violation of any of the above provisions shall be bribery and punished as provided by law, and if any officer or any member of the legislature be guilty thereof, his office shall become vacant.

No person within the purview of this act shall be privileged from testifying in relation to anything therein prohibited; and no person having so testified shall be liable to any prosecution or punishment for any offense concerning which he was required to give his testimony or produce any documentary evidence.

The railroad commissioner and his deputy in the discharge of duty are excepted from the provisions of this amendment. [*1899 SJR-12; 1901 AJR-8; 1901 c. 437*]

Recall of elective officers. SECTION 12. [*As amended April 1981*] The qualified electors of the state, of any congressional, judicial or legislative district or of any county may petition for the recall of any incumbent elective officer after the first year of the term for which the incumbent was elected, by filing a petition with the filing officer with whom the nomination petition to the office in the primary is filed, demanding the recall of the incumbent.

(1) The recall petition shall be signed by electors equaling at least twenty-five percent of the vote cast for the office of governor at the last preceding election, in the state, county or district which the incumbent represents.

(2) The filing officer with whom the recall petition is filed shall call a recall election for the Tuesday of the 6th week after the date of filing the petition or, if that Tuesday is a legal holiday, on the first day after that Tuesday which is not a legal holiday.

(3) The incumbent shall continue to perform the duties of the office until the recall election results are officially declared.

(4) Unless the incumbent declines within 10 days after the filing of the petition, the incumbent shall without filing be deemed to have filed for the recall election. Other candidates may file for the office in the manner provided by law for special elections. For the purpose of conducting elections under this section:

(a) When more than 2 persons compete for a nonpartisan office, a recall primary shall be held. The 2 persons receiving the highest number of votes in the recall primary shall be the 2 candidates in the recall election, except that if any candidate receives a majority of the total number of votes cast in the recall primary, that candidate shall assume the office for the remainder of the term and a recall election shall not be held.

(b) For any partisan office, a recall primary shall be held for each political party which is by law entitled to a separate ballot and from which more than one candidate competes for the party's nomination in the recall election. The person receiving the highest number of votes in the recall primary for each political party shall be that party's candidate in the recall election. Independent candidates and candidates representing political parties not entitled by law to a separate ballot shall be shown on the ballot for the recall election only.

(c) When a recall primary is required, the date specified under sub. (2) shall be the date of the recall primary and the recall election shall be held on the Tuesday of the 4th week after the recall primary or, if that Tuesday is a legal holiday, on the first day after that Tuesday which is not a legal holiday.

(5) The person who receives the highest number of votes in the recall election shall be elected for the remainder of the term.

(6) After one such petition and recall election, no further recall petition shall be filed against the same officer during the term for which he was elected.

(7) This section shall be self-executing and mandatory. Laws may be enacted to facilitate its operation but no law shall be enacted to hamper, restrict or impair the right of recall. [*1979 SJR-5; 1981 SJR-2*]

Recall of elective officers. SECTION 12. [*Created November 1926*] The qualified electors of the state or of any county or of any congressional, judicial or legislative district may petition for the recall of any elective officer after the first year of the term for which he was elected, by filing a petition with the officer with whom the petition for nomination to such office in the primary election is filed, demanding the recall of such officer. Such petition shall be signed by electors equal in number to at least twenty-five per cent of the vote cast for the office of governor at the last preceding election, in the state, county or district from which such officer is to be recalled. The officer with whom such petition is filed shall call a special election to be held not less than forty nor more than forty-five days from the filing of such petition. The officer against whom such petition has been filed shall continue to perform the duties of his office until the result of such special election shall have been officially declared. Other candidates for such office may be nominated in the manner as is provided by law in primary elections. The candidate who shall receive the highest number of votes shall be deemed elected for the remainder of the term. The name of the candidate against whom the recall petition is filed shall go on the ticket unless he resigns within ten days after the filing of the petition. After one such petition and special election, no further recall petition shall be filed against the same officer during the term for which he was elected. This article shall be self-executing and all of its provisions shall be treated as mandatory. Laws may be enacted to facilitate its operation, but no law shall be enacted to hamper, restrict or impair the right of recall. [*1923 SJR-39; 1925 SJR-12; 1925 c. 270*]

ARTICLE XIV.

SCHEDULE

Effect of change from territory to state. SECTION 1. That no inconvenience may arise by reason of a change from a territorial to a permanent state government, it is declared that all rights, actions, prosecutions, judgments, claims and contracts, as well of individuals as of bodies corporate, shall continue as if no such change had taken place; and all process which may be issued under the authority of the territory of Wisconsin previous to its admission into the union of the United States shall be as valid as if issued in the name of the state.

Territorial laws continued. SECTION 2. All laws now in force in the territory of Wisconsin which are not repugnant to this constitution shall remain in force until they expire by their own limitation or be altered or repealed by the legislature.

SECTION 3. [*Repealed. 1979 AJR-76; 1981 AJR-35; submit: May'82 Spec.Sess. AJR-1; vote November 1982*]

Territorial fines accrue to state. SECTION 3. [*Original form*] All fines, penalties, or forfeitures accruing to the territory of Wisconsin shall enure to the use of the state.

SECTION 4. [*Repealed. 1979 AJR-76; 1981 AJR-35; submit: May'82 Spec.Sess. AJR-1; vote November 1982*]

Rights of action and prosecution saved. SECTION 4. [*Original form*] All recognizances heretofore taken, or which may be taken before the change from territorial to a permanent state government, shall remain valid, and shall pass to and may be prosecuted in the name of the state; and all bonds executed to the governor of the territory, or to any other officer or court in his or their official capacity, shall pass to the governor or state authority and their successors in office, for the uses therein respectively expressed, and may be sued for and recovered accordingly; and all the estate, or property, real, personal or mixed, and all judgments, bonds, specialties, choses in action and claims or debts of whatsoever description of the territory of Wisconsin, shall enure to and vest in the state of Wisconsin, and may be sued for and recovered in the same manner and to the same extent by the state of Wisconsin as the same could have been by the territory of Wisconsin. All criminal prosecutions and penal actions which may have arisen, or which may arise before the change from a territorial to a state government, and which shall then be pending, shall be prosecuted to judgment and execution in the name of the state. All offenses committed against the laws of the territory of Wisconsin before the change from a territorial to a state government, and which shall not be prosecuted before such change, may be prosecuted in the name and by the authority of the state of Wisconsin with like effect as though such change had not taken place; and all penalties incurred shall remain the same as if this constitution had not been adopted. All actions at law and suits in equity which may be pending in any of the courts of the territory of Wisconsin at the time of the change from a territorial to a state government may be continued and transferred to any court of the state which shall have jurisdiction of the subject matter thereof.

SECTION 5. [*Repealed. 1979 AJR-76; 1981 AJR-35; submit: May'82 Spec.Sess. AJR-1; vote November 1982*]

Existing officers hold over. SECTION 5. [*Original form*] All officers, civil and military, now holding their offices under the authority of the United States or of the territory of Wisconsin shall continue to hold and exercise their respective offices until they shall be superseded by the authority of the state.

SECTION 6. [*Repealed. 1979 AJR-76; 1981 AJR-35; submit: May'82 Spec.Sess. AJR-1; vote November 1982*]

Seat of government. SECTION 6. [*Original form*] The first session of the legislature of the state of Wisconsin shall commence on the first Monday in June next, and shall be held at the village of Madison, which shall be and remain the seat of government until otherwise provided by law.

SECTION 7. [*Repealed. 1979 AJR-76; 1981 AJR-35; submit: May'82 Spec.Sess. AJR-1; vote November 1982*]

Local officers hold over. SECTION 7. [*Original form*] All county, precinct, and township officers shall continue to hold their respective offices, unless removed by the competent authority, until the legislature shall, in conformity with the provisions of this constitution, provide for the holding of elections to fill such offices respectively.

SECTION 8. [*Repealed. 1979 AJR-76; 1981 AJR-35; submit: May'82 Spec.Sess. AJR-1; vote November 1982*]

Copy of constitution for president. SECTION 8. [*Original form*] The president of this convention shall, immediately after its adjournment, cause a fair copy of this constitution, together with a copy of the act of the legislature of this territory, entitled "An act in relation to the formation of a state government in Wisconsin, and to change the time of holding the annual session of the legislature," approved October 27, 1847, providing for the calling of this convention, and also a copy of so much of the last census of this territory as exhibits the number of its inhabitants, to be forwarded to the president of the United States to be laid before the congress of the United States at its present session.

SECTION 9. [*Repealed. 1979 AJR-76; 1981 AJR-35; submit: May'82 Spec.Sess. AJR-1; vote November 1982*]

Ratification of constitution; election of officers. SECTION 9. [*Original form*] This constitution shall be submitted at an election to be held on the second Monday in March next, for ratification or rejection, to all white male persons of the age of twenty-one years or upwards, who shall then be residents of this territory and citizens of the United States, or shall have declared their intention to become such in conformity with the laws of congress on the subject of naturalization; and all persons having such qualifications shall be entitled to vote for or against the adoption of this constitution, and for all officers first elected under it. And if the constitution be ratified by the said electors it shall become the constitution of the state of Wisconsin. On such of the ballots as are for the constitution shall be written or printed the word "yes," and on such as are against the constitution the word "no." The election shall be conducted in the manner now prescribed by law, and the returns made by the clerks of the boards of supervisors or county commissioners (as the case may be) to the governor of the territory at any time before the tenth day of April next. And in the event of the ratification of this constitution by a majority of all the votes given, it shall be the duty of the governor of this territory to make proclamation of the same, and to transmit a digest of the returns to the senate and assembly of the state on the first day of their session. An election shall be held for governor, lieutenant governor, treasurer, attorney-general, members of the state legislature, and members of congress, on the second Monday of May

SECTION 10. *[Repealed. 1979 AJR-76; 1981 AJR-35; submit: May'82 Spec.Sess. AJR-1; vote November 1982]*

Congressional apportionment. SECTION 10. *[Original form]* Two members of congress shall also be elected on the second Monday of May next; and until otherwise provided by law, the counties of Milwaukee, Waukesha, Jefferson, Racine, Walworth, Rock and Green, shall constitute the first congressional district, and elect one member; and the

next; and no other for further notice of such election shall be required.

counties of Washington, Sheboygan, Manitowoc, Calumet, Brown, Winnebago, Fond du Lac, Marquette, Sauk, Portage, Columbia, Dodge, Dane, Iowa, LaFayette, Grant, Richland, Crawford, Chippewa, St. Croix and La Pointe, shall constitute the second congressional district, and shall elect one member.

SECTION 11. *[Repealed. 1979 AJR-76; 1981 AJR-35; submit: May'82 Spec.Sess. AJR-1; vote November 1982]*

First elections. SECTION 11. *[Original form]* The several elections provided for in this article shall be conducted according to the existing laws of the territory; provided, that no elector shall be entitled to vote except in the town, ward or precinct where he resides. The returns of election for senators and members of assembly shall be transmitted to the clerk of the board of supervisors or county commissioners, as the case may be; and the votes shall be canvassed and certificates of election issued as now provided by law. In the first senatorial district the returns of the election for senator shall be made to the proper officer in the county of Brown; in the second senatorial district to the proper officer in the county of Columbia; in the third senatorial district to the proper officer in the county of Crawford; in the fourth senatorial district to the proper

officer in the county of Fond du Lac; and in the fifth senatorial district to the proper officer in the county of Iowa. The returns of election for state officers and members of congress shall be certified and transmitted to the speaker of the assembly, at the seat of government, in the same manner as the vote for delegate to congress are required to be certified and returned by the laws of the territory of Wisconsin, to the secretary of said territory, and in such time that they may be received on the first Monday in June next; and as soon as the legislature shall be organized the speaker of the assembly and the president of the senate shall, in the presence of both houses, examine the returns and declare who are duly elected to fill the several offices hereinbefore mentioned, and give to each of the persons elected a certificate of his election.

SECTION 12. *[Repealed. 1979 AJR-76; 1981 AJR-35; submit: May'82 Spec.Sess. AJR-1; vote November 1982]*

Legislative apportionment. SECTION 12. *[Original form]* Until there shall be a new apportionment, the senators and members of the assembly shall be apportioned among the several districts, as hereinafter mentioned, and each

district shall be entitled to elect one senator or member of the assembly, as the case may be. *[Enumeration of districts omitted as obsolete: see R.S. 1849 pp. 40-43; R.S. 1858 pp. 49-53]*

Common law continued in force. SECTION 13. Such parts of the common law as are now in force in the territory of Wisconsin, not inconsistent with this constitution, shall be and continue part of the law of this state until altered or suspended by the legislature.

SECTION 14. *[Repealed. 1979 AJR-76; 1981 AJR-35; submit: May'82 Spec.Sess. AJR-1; vote November 1982]*

Officers, when to enter on duties. SECTION 14. *[Original form]* The senators first elected in the even-numbered senate districts, the governor, lieutenant governor and other state officers first elected under this constitution, shall enter upon the duties of their respective offices on the first Monday of June next, and shall continue

in office for one year from the first Monday of January next; the senators first elected in the odd-numbered senate districts, and the members of the assembly first elected, shall enter upon their duties respectively on the first Monday of June next, and shall continue in office until the first Monday in January next.

SECTION 15. *[Repealed. 1979 AJR-76; 1981 AJR-35; submit: May'82 Spec.Sess. AJR-1; vote November 1982]*

Oath of office. SECTION 15. *[Original form]* The oath of office may be administered by any judge or justice of the peace until the legislature shall otherwise direct.

Implementing revised structure of judicial branch. SECTION 16. *[As affected November 1982]* (1), (2), (3) and (5) *[Repealed]*

(4) *[Amended]* The terms of office of justices of the supreme court serving on August 1, 1978, shall expire on the July 31 next preceding the first Monday in January on which such terms would otherwise have expired, but such advancement of the date of term expiration shall not impair any retirement rights vested in any such justice if the term had expired on the first Monday in January. *[1979 AJR-76; 1981 AJR-35; submit: May'82 Spec.Sess. AJR-1]*

Implementing revised structure of judicial branch. SECTION 16. *[Created April 1977]* (1) The 1975/1977 amendment relating to a revised structure of the judicial branch shall take effect on August 1 of the year following the year of ratification by the voters.

(2) All county courts and the branches thereof in existence on the effective date of this amendment shall, as trial courts of general uniform statewide jurisdiction, continue after such effective date with the same jurisdiction, powers and duties conferred by law upon such courts and the branches and judges thereof until the legislature by law

alters or abolishes such county courts and their jurisdiction, powers and duties.

(3) Subject to the jurisdiction established in section 14 of article VII, municipal courts and municipal court judges shall continue after the effective date of this amendment with the same jurisdiction, powers and duties as conferred upon such courts and judges on the effective date until the legislature acts under sections 2 and 14 of article VII to alter or abolish such municipal courts and their jurisdiction, powers and duties.

(4) The terms of office of justices of the supreme court serving on the effective date shall expire on the July 31 next preceding the first Monday in January on which such terms would otherwise have expired, but such advancement of the date of term expiration shall not impair any retirement rights vested in any such justice if the term had expired on the first Monday in January.

(5) Prior to the effective date of this amendment the legislature shall by law establish one or more appeals court districts, provide for the election of appeals judges in such districts, and determine the jurisdiction of the court of appeals under section 21 of article I and section 5 of article VII as affected by this amendment, so that the court of appeals shall become operative on the effective date. [*1975 AJR-11; 1977 SJR-9*]

Note: Attached resolutions and signatures appear at the end of the constitution as printed in the *Revised Statutes* of 1849 and 1858.

HISTORY OF CONSTITUTIONAL AMENDMENTS
April 5, 2005

Art.	Sec.	Subject	First Approval	Second Approval	Submission to People	Date of Election	Vote For	Vote Against	Total Vote for Governor
IV	4	Assemblymen, 2-year terms	Ch.95 1853	Ch.89 1854	Ch.89 1854	Nov. 1854	6,549	11,580	——[1]
IV	5	Senators, 4-year terms	"	"	"	"	6,348	11,885	"
IV	11	Biennial legislative sessions	"	"	"	"	6,752	11,589	——[1]
V	5	Governor's salary, changed from $1,250 to $2,500 a year	SJR 35 JR 4 1861	SJR 15 JR 6 1862	Ch.202 1862	Nov. 1862	14,519	32,612	"
IV	21	*Change legislators' pay to $350 a year	SJR 26 JR 9 1865	SJR 16 JR 3 1866	Ch.25 1867	Nov. 1867	58,363	24,418	142,522
V	5	*Change governor's salary from $1,250 to $5,000 a year	AJR 13 JR 9 1868	SJR 6 JR 2 1869	Ch.186 1869	Nov. 1869	47,353	41,764	130,781
V	9	*Change lieutenant governor's salary to $1,000 a year	"	"	"	"	"	"	"
I	8	*Grand jury system modified	AJR 6 JR 7 1869	SJR 3 JR 3 1870	Ch.118 1870	Nov. 1870	48,894	18,606	146,953[2]
IV	31,32	*Private and local laws, prohibited on 9 subjects	SJR 14 JR 13 1870	AJR 29 JR 1 1871	Ch.122 1871	Nov. 1871	54,087	3,675	147,274
VII	4	Supreme court, 1 chief and 4 associate justices	SJR 12 JR 2 1871	AJR 16 JR 8 1871	Ch.111 1872	Nov. 1872	16,272	29,755	——[1]
XI	3	*Indebtedness of municipalities limited to 5%	AJR 17 JR 11 1872	SJR 6 JR 4 1873	Ch.37 1874	Nov. 1874	66,061	1,509	"
VII	4	*Supreme court, 1 chief and 4 associate justices	SJR 16 JR 10 1876	SJR 5 JR 1 1877	Ch.48 1877	Nov. 1877	79,140	16,763	178,122
VIII	2	*Claims against state, 6-year limit	SJR 14 JR 7 1876	AJR 7 none[3] 1877	Ch.158 1877	"	33,046	3,371	"
IV	4,5,1	Biennial sessions; assemblymen 2-year, senators 4-year terms	SJR 9 none[3] 1880	SJR 18 JR 5 1881	Ch.262 1881	Nov. 1881	53,532	13,936	171,856
IV	21	*Change legislators' pay to $500 a year	none[3]	SJR 20 JR 3 1881	"	"	"	"	"
III	1	*Voting residence 30 days; in municipalities voter registration	AJR 26 1881	AJR 2 JR 4 1882	Ch.272 1882	Nov. 1882	36,223	5,347	——[1]
VI	4	*County officers except judicial, vacancies filled by appointment	AJR 16 1881	AJR 7 JR 3 1882	Ch.290 1882	"	60,091	8,089	"
VII	12	*Clerk of court, full term election	"	"	"	"	"	"	"
XIII	1	*Political year; biennial elections	"	"	"	"	"	"	"
X	1	State superintendent, qualifications and pay fixed by legislature	AJR 16 JR 34 1885	SJR 13 JR 4 1887	Ch.357 1887	Nov. 1888	12,967	18,342	354,714
VII	4	*Supreme court, composed of 5 justices of supreme court	SJR 19 JR 5 1887	SJR 7 JR 2 1889	Ch.22 1889	Apr. 1889	125,759	14,712	211,111[4]
IV	31	*Cities incorporated by general law	SJR 13 JR 4 1889	SJR 10 JR 9 1891	Ch.362 1891	Nov. 1892	15,718	9,015	371,559
X	1	State superintendent, pay fixed by law	AJR 15 JR 10 1893	SJR 24 JR 3 1895	Ch.177 1895	Nov. 1896	38,752	56,506	444,110
VIII	7	*Circuit judges, additional in populous counties	SJR 9 JR 8 1895	SJR 25 JR 2 1897	Ch.69 1897	Apr. 1897	45,823	41,513	119,572[4]
IV	1	*State superintendent, nonpartisan 4-year term, pay fixed by law	SJR 21 JR 16 1899	AJR 8 JR 9 1901	Ch.258 1901	Nov. 1902	71,550	57,411	365,676
XI	4	*General banking law authorized	AJR 16 JR 13 1899	AJR 5 JR 7 1901	Ch.73 1901	"	64,836	44,620	"
XI	5	*Banking law referenda requirement repealed	"	"	"	"	"	"	"
XIII	11	*Free passes prohibited	SJR 12 JR 8 1899	AJR 47 JR 25 1901	Ch.437 1901	Apr. 1903	67,781	40,697	114,468[4]
VII	4	*Supreme court, 7 justices, 10-year terms	AJR 33 JR 8 1901	AJR 46 JR 13 1903	Ch.10 1903	Nov. 1908	51,377	39,857	449,656
III	1	*Suffrage for full citizens only	AJR 16 JR 15 1905	SJR 19 JR 29 1907	Ch.661 1907	"	85,838	36,733	"
V	10	*Governor's approval of bills in 6 days	AJR 45 JR 14 1905	SJR 22 JR 18 1907	"	"	85,958	27,270	"
VIII	1	*Income tax	AJR 12 JR 12 1905	SJR 35 JR 55 1907	"	"	85,696	37,729	"
VIII	10	*Highways, appropriations for	SJR 14 JR 11 1905	AJR 33 JR 7 1907	Ch.238 1907	Nov. 1910	116,421	46,739	319,522
IV	3	*Apportionment after each federal census	SJR 18 JR 30 1907		Ch.478 1909	"	54,932	52,634	"
IV	21	*Change legislators' pay to $1,000 a year	AJR 8 JR 35 1907		Ch.508 1909	"	44,153	76,278	"
VIII	10	Water power and forests, appropriations for[5]	SJR 43 JR 31 1907	Ch.514 1909	Ch.514 1909	"	62,468[5]	45,924[5]	"
VII	10	*Judges' salaries, time of payment	AJR 36 JR 34 1909	AJR 26 JR 24 1911	Ch.665 1911	Nov. 1912	44,855	34,865	393,849

HISTORY OF CONSTITUTIONAL AMENDMENTS
April 5, 2005–Continued

Art.	Sec.	Subject	First Approval			Second Approval			Submission to People		Date of Election	For	Against	Total Vote for Governor
XI	3	*City or county debt for lands, discharge within 50 years	SJR 32	JR 44	1909	SJR 26	JR 42	1911	"	"	"	46,369	34,975	"
XI	3a	*Public parks, playgrounds, etc.	SJR 63	JR 38	1909	SJR 25	JR 48	1911	"	"	"	48,424	33,931	"
IV	1	Initiative and referendum	AJR 36	JR 74	1911	AJR 4	JR 22	1913	Ch.770	1913	Nov. 1914	84,934	148,536	325,430
IV	21	Change legislators' pay to $600 a year, 2 cents a mile for additional round trips	AJR 78	JR 66	1911	AJR 8	JR 24	1913	"	"	"	68,907	157,202	"
VII	6,7	Judicial circuits, decreased number, additional judges	AJR 134	JR 67	1911	AJR 11	JR 26	1913	Ch.770	1913	Nov. 1914	63,311	154,827	"
VIII	new	State annuity insurance	SJR 72	JR 65	1911	AJR 38	JR 35	1913	"	"	"	59,909	170,338	325,430
VIII	new	State insurance	AJR 119	JR 56	1911	AJR 9	JR 12	1913	"	"	"	58,490	165,966	"
XI	new	Home rule of cities and villages	SJR 31	JR 73	1911	SJR 19	JR 21	1913	"	"	"	86,020	141,472	"
XI	new	Municipal power of condemnation	AJR 104	JR 37	1911	AJR 10	JR 25	1913	"	"	"	61,122	154,945	"
XII	1	Constitutional amendments, submission after 3/5 approval by one legislature	SJR 57	JR 71	1911	SJR 22	JR 17	1913	"	"	"	71,734	160,761	"
XII	new	Constitution amended upon petition	AJR 36	JR 74	1911	AJR 4	JR 22	1913	"	"	"	68,435	150,215	"
XIII	new	Recall of civil officers	SJR 9	JR 41	1911	SJR 18	JR 15	1913	"	"	"	81,628	144,386	"
IV	21	Legislators' pay fixed by law	AJR 16	JR 23	1917	AJR 13	JR 37	1919	Ch.480	1919	Apr. 1920	126,243	132,258	—1
VII	6,7	Judicial circuits, decreased number, additional judges	AJR 74	JR 20	1917	SJR 100	JR 92	1919	Ch.604	1919	Nov. 1922	113,786	116,436	481,828
I	5	*Jury verdict, 5/6 in civil cases	AJR 26	JR 58	1919	AJR 14	JR 17	1921	Ch.504	1921	"	171,433	156,820	"
VII	4	Sheriffs, no limit on successive terms	AJR 22	JR 38	1919	AJR 39	JR 36	1921	Ch.437	1921	"	161,832	207,594	"
VI	new	Municipal indebtedness for public utilities	AJR 21	JR 54	1919	AJR 16	JR 37	1921	Ch.566	1921	"	105,234	219,639	"
XI	21	Change legislators' pay to $750 a year	SJR 8	JR 28	1921	SJR 18	JR 18	1923	Ch.241	1923	Apr. 1924	189,635	250,236	344,137[4]
IV	7	*Circuit judges, additional in populous counties	SJR 24	JR 24	1921	SJR 27	JR 64	1923	Ch.408	1923	Nov. 1924	240,207	226,562	796,432
VII	10	*Forestry, appropriations for	SJR 30	JR 29	1921	AJR 70	JR 57	1923	Ch.289	1923	"	336,360	173,563	"
VIII	3	*Home rule for cities and villages	SJR 5	JR 39	1921	SJR 18	JR 34	1923	Ch.203	1923	"	299,792	190,165	"
XI	5	*Governor's salary fixed by law	AJR 88	JR 79	1923	AJR 50	JR 52	1925	Ch.413	1925	Nov. 1926	202,156	188,302	552,912
XIII	12	*Recall of elective officials	SJR 39	JR 39	1923	SJR 12	JR 16	1925	Ch.270	1925	"	205,868	201,125	"

Note: JR 41 of 1925, which became Joint Rule 16 of the Wisconsin Legislature, established a new procedure to incorporate the "submission to the people" clause into the proposal at second approval.

Art.	Sec.	Subject	First Approval			Second Approval			Date of Election	For	Against	Total Vote for Governor
IV	21	Change legislators' pay to $1,000 for session	AJR 16	JR 33	1925	AJR 2	JR 12	1927	Apr. 1927	151,786	199,260	308,885[4]
VIII		*Severance tax: forests, minerals	AJR 51	JR 61	1925	AJR 3	JR 13	1927	"	179,217	141,888	"
IV	21	*Legislators' salary repealed; to be fixed by law	SJR 61	JR 57	1927	SJR 7	JR 6	1929	Apr. 1929	237,250	212,846	397,912[2]
VI	4	*Sheriffs succeeding themselves for 2 terms	AJR 8	JR 24	1927	AJR 8	JR 13	1929	"	259,881	210,964	"
V	10	*Item veto on appropriation bills	SJR 35	JR 37	1927	SJR 40	JR 43	1929	Nov. 1930	252,655	153,703	606,825
V	5	*Governor's salary provision repealed; fixed by law	SJR 81	JR 69	1929	SJR 6	JR 52	1931	Nov. 1932	452,605	275,175	1,124,502
V	9	*Lieutenant governor's salary repealed; fixed by law	SJR 82	JR 70	1929	SJR 7	JR 53	1931	"	427,768	267,120	"
VII	1	*Wording of section corrected	SJR 103	JR 72	1929	SJR 8	JR 58	1931	"	436,113	221,563	"
XI	3	*Municipal indebtedness for public utilities	AJR 61	JR 74	1929	AJR 14	JR 71	1931	"	401,194	279,631	"
III	1	*Women's suffrage	AJR 52	JR 91	1931	SJR 74	JR 76	1933	Nov. 1934	411,088	166,745	953,797

Art.	Sec.	Subject	First Approval		Second Approval		Date of Election	Vote		Total Vote for Governor
								For	Against	
XIII	11	*Free passes, permitted as specified	AJR 50 JR 63	1933	AJR 67 JR 98	1935	Nov. 1936	365,971	361,799	1,237,095
VIII	1	Installment payment of real estate taxes	AJR 37 JR 88	1939	AJR 15 JR 18	1941	Apr. 1941	330,971	134,808	547,213[2]
VII	15	*Justice of peace, abolish office in first class cities	SJR 9 JR 27	1943	SJR 6 JR 2	1945	Apr. 1945	160,965	113,408	381,192[4]
VIII	10	*Aeronautical program	SJR 16 JR 37	1943	SJR 7 JR 3	1945	"	187,111	101,169	"
VI	4	*Sheriffs, no limit on successive terms	AJR 6 JR 36	1943	AJR 10 JR 47	1945	Apr. 1946	121,144	170,131	306,354[4]
IV	33	*Auditing of state accounts	SJR 35 JR 60	1943	SJR 24 JR 73	1945	Nov. 1946	480,938	308,072	1,040,444
X	2	*Auditing (part of same proposal)	SJR 35 JR 60	1943	SJR 24 JR 73	1945	"			"
XI	3	Public transportation of school children to any school	SJR 48 JR 73	1943	SJR 19 JR 78	1945	Nov. 1948	437,817	545,475	1,266,139
II	2	Repeal; relating to exercise of eminent domain by municipalities	SJR 30 JR 89	1945	SJR 15 JR 48	1947	"	210,086	807,318	"
VIII	10	Prohibition on taxing federal lands repealed	AJR 26 JR 33	1947	SJR 6 JR 2	1949	Apr. 1949	245,412	297,237	633,606[4]
II	2	*Allow internal improvement debt for veterans' housing	SJR 2 JR 1	SS'48	SJR 5 JR 1	1949	"	311,576	290,736	"
XI	3	*Prohibition on taxing federal lands repealed	AJR 64 JR 11	1949	AJR 7 JR 7	1951	Apr. 1951	305,612	186,284	515,822[4]
IV	3,4,5	*City debt limit 8% for combined city and school purposes	SJR 11 JR 12	1949	SJR 9 JR 8	1951	Apr. 1951	313,739	191,897	515,822[4]
VII	9	Apportionment based on area and population[6]	SJR 50 JR 59	1951	AJR 7 JR 9	1951	Apr. 1953	433,043[6]	406,133[6]	735,860[4]
VII	24	*Judicial elections to full terms	SJR 3 JR 41	1951	SJR 5 JR 12	1953	"	386,972	345,094	"
XI	3	*Judges: qualifications, retirement	SJR 6 JR 46	1953	SJR 10 JR 14	1955	Apr. 1955	380,214	177,929	520,554[4]
IV	26	*School debt limit, equalized value	SJR 17 JR 47	1953	AJR 18 JR 12	1955	"	320,376	228,641	"
XI	3a	*Teachers' retirement benefits	SJR 21 JR 41	1953	SJR 8 JR 17	1955	Apr. 1956	365,560	255,284	740,411[4]
VI	11	Sheriffs, no limit on successive terms	AJR 13 JR 23	1953	AJR 22 JR 53	1955	"	269,722	328,603	"
XI	10	*Municipal acquisition of land for public purposes	SJR 29 JR 35	1953	SJR 9 JR 36	1955	"	376,692	193,544	"
XIII	3	Free passes, not for public use	AJR 12 JR 61	1953	AJR 47 JR 54	1955	"	188,715	380,207	"
VIII	26	*Port development	AJR 39 JR 58	1957	SJR 20 JR 15	1959	Apr. 1960	472,177	451,045	1,182,160[7]
XI	34	*Debt limit in populous counties, 5% of equalized valuation	SJR 47 JR 59	1957	SJR 53 JR 32	1959	Nov. 1960	686,104	529,467	1,728,009
IV	4	Salary increases during term for various public officers	SJR 21 JR 29	1959	SJR 6 JR 11	1961	Apr. 1961	297,066	307,575	765,807[4]
IV	1	*Continuity of civil government	AJR 48 JR 50	1959	SJR 1 JR 10	1961	"	498,869	132,728	"
VI	2	Sheriffs, no limit on successive terms	AJR 31 JR 48	1959	AJR 7 JR 9	1961	"	283,495	388,238	"
VIII	1	*Personal property classified for tax purposes	AJR 120 JR 77	1959	SJR 34 JR 13	1961	"	381,881	220,434	"
XI	3	*Municipal eminent domain, abolished jury verdict of necessity	AJR 22 JR 47	1959	SJR 8 JR 12	1961	"	348,406	259,566	"
XI	3	*Debt limit 10% of equalized valuation for integrated aid school district	SJR 6 JR 35	1959	AJR 1 JR 8	1961	"	409,963	224,783	"
IV	3	*"Indians not taxed" exclusion removed from apportionment formula	SJR 12 JR 30	1959	SJR 11 JR 32	1961	Nov. 1962	631,296	259,577	1,265,900
IV	23	*County executive: 4-year term	AJR 121 JR 68	1959	AJR 61 JR 64	1961	"	527,075	331,393	"
IV	23a	*County executive: 2-year terms	"		"		"	524,240	319,378	"
VI	23a	*County executive veto power	"		"		"			
IV	3	Time for apportionment of seats in the state legislature	AJR 162 JR 96	1961	AJR 23 JR 9	1963	Apr. 1963	232,851	277,014	635,510[4]
IV	26	Salary increases during term for justices and judges	SJR 76 JR 68	1961	SJR 4 JR 7	1963	"	216,205	335,774	"
VIII	10	*Equalized value debt limit	AJR 92 JR 71	1961	AJR 19 JR 8	1963	"	285,296	231,702	"
VIII	10	Maximum state appropriation for forestry increased	AJR 133 JR 90	1961	AJR 73 JR 32	1963	Apr. 1964	440,978	536,724	1,046,801[4]
XI	3	Property valuation for debt limit adjusted	AJR 134 JR 91	1961	AJR 74 JR 33	1963	"	336,994	572,276	"
XII	1	Constitutional amendments, submission of related items in a single proposition	SJR 15 JR 30	1961	SJR 1 JR 1	SS'63	"	317,676	582,045	"

HISTORY OF CONSTITUTIONAL AMENDMENTS
April 5, 2005–Continued

Art.	Sec.	Subject	First Approval	Second Approval	Date of Election	Vote For	Vote Against	Total Vote for Governor
VI	4	*Coroner and surveyor abolished in counties of 500,000	AJR 14, JR 30, 1963	SJR 17, JR 5, 1965	Apr. 1965	380,059	215,169	738,831[4]
IV	24	*Lotteries, definition revised	SJR 42, JR 35, 1963	SJR 13, JR 2, 1965	"	454,390	194,327	"
IV	13	*Legislators on active duty in armed forces	SJR 24, JR 34, 1963	SJR 15, JR 14, 1965	Apr. 1966	362,935	189,641	564,132[4]
VII	2	*Establishment of inferior courts	SJR 32, JR 48, 1963	SJR 26, JR 50, 1965	"	321,434	216,341	"
VII	15	*Justices of the peace abolished	"	"	"	"	"	"
XI	3	*Special district public utility debt limit	SJR 59, JR 44, 1963	SJR 11, JR 51, 1965	"	307,502	199,919	"
I	23	*Transportation of children to private schools	AJR 70, JR 46, 1965	AJR 7, JR 13, 1967	Apr. 1967	494,236	377,107	856,650[4]
IV	26	*Judicial salary increased during term	AJR 162, JR 96, 1965	AJR 17, JR 17, 1967	"	489,989	328,292	"
IV	1m,1n	*4-year term for governor and lieutenant governor	AJR 4, JR 80, 1965	SJR 12, JR 10, 1967	"	534,368	310,478	"
V	3	*Joint election of governor and lieutenant governor	AJR 3, JR 45, 1965	SJR 12, JR 10, 1967	"	507,339	312,267	"
VI	1m	*4-year term for secretary of state	AJR 4, JR 80, 1965	SJR 12, JR 10, 1967	"	520,326	311,974	"
VI	1n	*4-year term for state treasurer	AJR 4, JR 80, 1965	SJR 12, JR 10, 1967	"	514,280	314,873	"
VI	1p	*4-year term for attorney general	AJR 4, JR 80, 1965	SJR 12, JR 10, 1967	"	515,962	311,603	"
VI	4	*Sheriffs, no limit on successive terms	AJR 72, JR 61, 1965	SJR 11, JR 11, 1967	"	508,242	324,544	"
IV	11	*Legislative sessions, more than one permitted in biennium	AJR 5, JR 57, 1965	AJR 8, JR 14, 1967	Apr. 1967	670,757	267,997	856,650[4]
IV	24	*Uniform retirement date for justices and circuit judges	SJR 36, JR 101, 1965	AJR 15, JR 48, 1967	Apr. 1968	734,046	215,455	884,996[4]
VII	24	*Temporary appointment of justices and circuit judges	SJR 36, JR 101, 1965	SJR 96, JR 56, 1967	"	678,249	245,807	"
VII	10	*Forestry appropriation from sources other than property tax	SJR 28, JR 43, 1965	SJR 18, JR 25, 1967	"	652,705	286,512	"
VII	23	*Uniform county government modified	AJR 18, JR 49, 1967	SJR 8, JR 2, 1969	Apr. 1969	326,445	321,851	706,324[2]
IV	23a	*County executive to have veto power	"	AJR 1, JR 3, 1969	"	411,062	258,366	"
VIII	7	*State public debt for specified purposes allowed	AJR 1, JR 58, 1969	AJR 10, JR 27, 1971	Apr. 1972	871,707	298,016	—[1]
I	24	*Private use of school buildings	AJR 74, JR 38, 1969	SJR 4, JR 13, 1971	"	571,285	515,255	"
IV	23	*County government systems authorized	SJR 58, JR 32, 1969	SJR 38, JR 21, 1971	"	795,497	323,930	"
VI	4	*Coroner/medical examiner option	SJR 63, JR 33, 1969	AJR 17, JR 28, 1971	"	595,075	585,511	"
X	3	*Released time for religious instruction	AJR 41, JR 37, 1971	AJR 21, JR 5, 1973	Apr. 1973	447,240	520,936	1,008,553[2]
I	25	*Equality of the sexes	AJR 140, JR 44, 1971	AJR 6, JR 3, 1973	"	645,544	391,499	"
IV	24	*Charitable bingo authorized	SJR 13, JR 31, 1971	SJR 15, JR 15, 1973	Apr. 1974	396,051	315,545	758,587[4]
IV	26	*Increased benefits for retired public employes	SJR 3, JR 12, 1971	AJR 55, JR 25, 1973	"	493,496	193,867	"
VII	13	*Removal of judges by 2/3 vote of legislature for cause	AJR 31, JR 30, 1971	AJR 1, JR 29, 1973	"	353,377	340,518	"
I	1	*Taxation of agricultural lands	AJR 1, JR 39, 1971	AJR 1, JR 3, 1975	Apr. 1975	385,915	300,232	699,043[4]
VIII	3,7	*Public debt for veterans' housing	AJR 145, JR 38, 1973	AJR 1, JR 3, 1975	"	342,396[8]	341,291[8]	"
VIII	7,10	Internal improvements for transportation facilities[8]	AJR 133, JR 37, 1973	AJR 2, JR 2, 1975	"	310,434	337,925	"
XI	3	Exclusion of certain debt from municipal debt limit	SJR 44, JR 32, 1973	SJR 55, JR 133, 1975	"	395,616	282,726	"
XIII	2	*Dueling; repeal of disenfranchisement	SJR 6, JR 10, 1973	SJR 4, JR 4, 1975	"	"	"	"
XI	3	Municipal indebtedness increased up to 10% of equalized valuation[8]	AJR 58, JR 35, 1973	AJR 6, JR 6, 1975	Apr. 1976	328,097	715,420	1,168,606[4]
VIII	7(2)(a),10	Internal improvements for transportation facilities[8]	AJR 133, JR 37, 1973	AJR 2, JR 2, 1975	Nov. 1976[8]	722,658	935,152	1,332,220[7]

Art.	Sec.	Subject	First Approval		Second Approval		Date of Election	Vote For	Vote Against	Total Vote for Governor
IV	24	*Charitable raffle games authorized	AJR 43 JR 19	1975	AJR 10 JR 6	1977	Apr. 1977	483,518	300,473	775,490[4]
VII	2	*Unified court system [also changed I-21; IV-17 and 26; VII-3 to 11, 14, 16 to 23; XIV-16(1) to (4)]	AJR 11 JR 13	1975	SJR 9 JR 7	1977	"	490,437	215,939	"
VII	5	*Court of appeals created [also changed I-21(1); VII-2 and 3(3); XIV-16(5)]	"	"	"	"	"	455,350	229,316	"
VII	11,13	*Court system disciplinary proceedings	"	"	"	"	"	565,087	151,418	
VII	24	*Retirement age for justices and judges set by law	AJR 22 JR 15	1975	AJR 20 JR 18	1977	Apr. 1978	506,207	244,170	
IV	23	*Town government uniformity	SJR 51 JR 32	1977	SJR 1 JR 3	1979	Apr. 1979	179,011	383,395	
V	7,8	*Gubernatorial succession	"	"	"	"	"	538,959	187,440	840,166[4]
XIII	10	*Lieutenant governor vacancy	"	"	"	"	"	540,186	181,497	"
IV	9	*Senate presiding officer [also changed 5-8]	"	"	"	"	"	372,734	327,008	"
V	1	*4-year constitutional officer terms (improved wording) [also changed V-1m and 1n; VI-1, 1m, 1n and 1p]	"	"	"	"	"	533,620	164,768	"
I	8	*Right to bail[9]	AJR 9 JR 76	SS'80	AJR 5 JR 8	1981	Apr. 1981	505,092[9]	185,405[9]	
XI	1,4	*Obsolete corporation and banking provisions	AJR 53 JR 21	1979	AJR 13 JR 9	1981	"	418,997	186,898	
XI	3	*Indebtedness period for sewage collection or treatment systems	SJR 28 JR 43	1979	SJR 5 JR 7	1981	"	386,792	250,866	
XIII	12	*Primaries in recall elections	SJR 5 JR 41	1979	SJR 2 JR 6	1981	"	366,635	259,820	
VI	4	*Counties responsible for acts of sheriff	AJR 99 JR 38	1979	AJR 7 JR 15	1981	Apr. 1982	316,156	219,752	
I	1,18	*Gender-neutral wording (also changed X-1 and 2)	AJR 76 JR 36	1979	AJR 35 JR 29	1981	Nov. 1982	771,267	479,053	1,580,344
IV	3	*Military personnel treatment in redistricting	"	"	"	"	"	834,188	321,331	
IV	4,5	*Obsolete 1881 amendment reference	AJR 76 JR 36	1979	AJR 35 JR 29	1981	Nov. 1982	919,349	238,884	1,580,340
IV	30	*Elections by legislature	"	"	"	"	"	977,438	193,679	
X	1	*Obsolete reference to election and term of superintendent of public instruction	AJR 76 JR 36	1979	AJR 35 JR 29	1981	Nov. 1982	934,236	215,961	
X	2	*Obsolete reference to military draft exemption purchase	"	"	"	"	"	887,488	295,693	
XIV	3	*Obsolete transition from territory to statehood (also changed XIV-4 to 12; XIV-14, 15)	"	"	"	"	"	926,875	223,213	
XIV	16(1)	*Obsolete transitional provisions of 1977 court reorganization [also changed XIV-16(2), (3), (5)]	"	"	"	"	"	882,091	237,698	"
XIV	16(4)	*Terms on supreme court effective date provision	"	"	"	"	"	960,540	190,366	
I	1	*Rewording to parallel Declaration of Independence	AJR 9 JR 40	1983	AJR 9 JR 21	1985	Apr. 1986	419,699	65,418	461,118[4]
III	1-6	*Revision of suffrage defined by general law	AJR 33 JR 30	1983	AJR 3 JR 14	1985	"	401,911	83,183	"
XIII	1	*Modernizing constitutional text	"	"	"	"	"	404,273	82,512	"
XIII	5	*Obsolete suffrage right on Indian land	"	"	"	"	"	381,339	102,090	"
IV	24(5)	*Permitting pari-mutuel on-track betting	AJR 45 JR 36	1985	AJR 2 JR 3	1987	Apr. 1987	580,089	529,729	837,747[4]
IV	24(6)	*Authorizing the creation of a state lottery	SJR 1 JR 35	1985	AJR 3 JR 4	1987	Apr. 1987	739,181	391,942	"
VIII	1	Authorizing income tax credits or refunds for property or sales taxes	AJR 117 JR 74	1987	SJR 9 JR 2	1989	Apr. 1989	405,765	406,863	882,784[4]
V	10	*Redefining the partial veto power of the governor	SJR 71 JR 76	1987	SJR 11 JR 39	1989	Apr. 1990	387,068	252,481	685,878[4]
VIII	10	Providing housing for persons of low or moderate income	AJR 101 JR 55	1989	AJR 7 JR 2	1991	Apr. 1991	295,823	402,921	
VIII	7(2)(a)1	*Railways and other railroad facilities (also created VIII-10)	SJR76 JR 52	1989	SIR 30 JR 9	1991	Apr.1992	650,592	457,690	—1

HISTORY OF CONSTITUTIONAL AMENDMENTS
April 5, 2005–Continued

Art.	Sec.	Subject	First Approval	Second Approval	Date of Election	Vote For	Vote Against	Total Vote for Governor
IV	26	*Legislative and judiciary compensation, effective date	AJR 47 · JRS4 · 1989	AJR 16 · JR 13 · 1991	''	736,832	348,645	2,531,114[7]
VIII	1	Residential property tax reduction	AJR 81 · JR76 · 1989	SJR 12 · JR 14 · 1991	Nov. 1992	675,876	1,536,975	1,075,386[2]
I	9m	*Crime victims	SJR 41 · JR 17 · 1991	SJR 3 · JR 2 · 1993	Apr. 1993	861,405	163,087	''
IV	24	*Gambling, limiting "lottery"; divorce under general law (also amended IV-31,32)	AJR 1 · JR 27 · SS'92	SJR 2 · JR 3 · 1993	''	623,987	435,180	939,676[4]
I	3	Removal of unnecessary references to masculine gender [also amended I-3, 7, 9, 19, 21(2); IV-6, 12, 13, 23a; V-4, 6; VI-2; VII-1, 12; XI-3a; XIII-4, 11, 12(6)]	AJR 121 · JR 21 · 1993	AJR 12 · JR 3 · 1995	Apr. 1995	412,032	498,801	''
IV	24(6)(a)	Authorizing sports lottery dedicated to athletic facilities	SJR 49 · JR 27 · 1993	SJR 3 · JR 2 · 1995	Apr. 1995	348,818	618,377	''
VII	10(1)	Removal of restriction on judges holding nonjudicial public office after resignation during the judicial term	AJR 81 · JR 20 · 1993	AJR 15 · JR 4 · 1995	Apr. 1995	390,744	503,239	''
XIII	3	*Eligibility to seek or hold public office if convicted of a felony or a misdemeanor involving violation of a public trust	AJR 3 · JR 19 · 1993	AJR 16 · JR 28 · 1995	Nov. 1996	1,292,934	543,516	2,196,169[7]
I	25	*Guaranteeing the right to keep and bear arms	AJR 53 · JR 27 · 1995	AJR 11 · JR 21 · 1997	Nov. 1998	1,205,873	425,052	1,756,014
VI	4(1)(3) (5)(6)	*4-year term for sheriff; sheriffs permitted to hold nonpartisan office; allowed legislature to provide for election to fill vacancy during term	AJR 37 · JR 23 · 1995	SJR 43 · JR 18 · 1997	Nov. 1998	1,161,942	412,508	''
IV	24(3) (5)(6)	*Distributing state lottery, bingo and pari-mutuel proceeds for property tax	AJR 80 · JR 19 · 1997	AJR 2 · JR 2 · 1999	Apr. 1999	648,903	105,976	758,965[4]
I	(26)	*Right to fish, hunt, trap, and take game	SJR 2 · JR 16 · 2001	AJR 1 · JR 8 · 2003	Apr. 2003	668,459	146,182	800,785[4]
VI	4(1)(3) (4)	*4-year term for county clerks, treasurers, clerks of circuit court, district attorneys, coroners, elected surveyors, and registers of deeds (also amended VII–12)	AJR 10 · JR 12 · 2003	SJR 2 · JR 2 · 2005	Apr. 2005	534,742	177,037	552,790[4]

*Ratified.

[1] No election for statewide office. [2] Total vote for State Superintendent. [3] No number assigned to joint resolution. [4] Total vote for Justice of Supreme Court. [5] Ratified but declared invalid by Supreme Court in *State ex rel. Owen v. Donald*, 160 Wis. 21 (1915). [6] Ratified but declared invalid by Supreme Court in *State ex rel. Thomson v. Zimmerman*, 264 Wis. 644 (1953). [7] Total vote for presidential delegate election. [8] Recount resulted in rejection (342,132 to 342,309). However, the Dane County Circuit Court ruled the recount invalid due to election irregularities and required that the referendum be resubmitted to the electorate. Resubmitted to the electorate November 1976 by the 1975 Wisconsin Legislature by Ch. 224, s.145, Laws of 1975. [9] As a result of a Dane County Circuit Court injunction, vote totals were certified April 7, 1982, by the Board of State Canvassers.

Sources: Official records of the State Elections Board; *Laws of Wisconsin 2003* and previous volumes.

SUMMARY – CHANGING THE WISCONSIN CONSTITUTION

To amend the Wisconsin Constitution, it is necessary for two consecutive Wisconsin Legislatures to adopt an identical amendment (known as "first consideration" and "second consideration") and for a majority of the electorate to ratify the amendment at a subsequent election. See Art. XII, Sec. 1.

Since the adoption of the Wisconsin Constitution in 1848, the electorate has voted 140 out of 190 times to amend a total of 124 sections of the constitution (excluding the same vote for more than one item but including a vote that was later resubmitted by the legislature and two votes declared invalid by the courts). The Wisconsin Legislature adopted 154 acts or joint resolutions to submit these changes to the electorate.

STATEWIDE REFERENDA ELECTIONS OTHER THAN CONSTITUTIONAL AMENDMENTS

Question	Law Submitting		Date of Election	Vote For	Against
Territorial					
*Formation of a state government	Territorial Laws 1846, page 5 (Jan.31)		Apr. 1846	12,334	2,487
Ratification of first constitution	Art. XIX, Sec. 9 of 1846 Constitution		Apr. 1847	14,119	20,231
Extend suffrage to colored persons[1]	Supl. resolution to 1846 Constitution		Apr. 1847	7,664	14,615
*Ratification of second constitution	Art. XIV, Sec. 9 of 1848 Constitution		Mar. 1848	16,799	6,384
State					
*Extend suffrage to colored persons[2]	Ch.137	1849	Nov. 1849	5,265	4,075
*State banks; advisory referendum	Ch.143	1851	Nov. 1851	31,289	9,126
*General banking law	Ch.479	1852	Nov. 1852	32,826	8,711
*Liquor prohibition; advisory referendum	Ch.101	1853	Nov. 1853	27,519	24,109
Extend suffrage to colored persons	Ch.44	1857	Nov. 1857	28,235	41,345
*Amend general banking law; redemption of bank notes	Ch.98	1858	Nov. 1858	27,267	2,837
*Amend general banking law; circulation of bank notes	Ch.242	1861	Nov. 1861	57,646	2,515
*Amend general banking law; interest rate 7% per year	Ch.203	1862	Nov. 1862	46,269	7,794
Extend suffrage to colored persons[2]	Ch.414	1865	Nov. 1865	46,588	55,591
*Amend general banking law; taxing shareholders	Ch.102	1866	Nov. 1866	49,714	19,151
*Abolish office of bank comptroller	JR12	1867			
*Incorporation of savings banks and savings societies	Ch.28	1868	Nov. 1868	15,499	1,948
*Women's suffrage upon school matters	Ch.384	1876	Nov. 1876	4,029	3,069
Revise 1897 banking law; banking department under commission	Ch.211	1885	Nov. 1886	43,581	38,998
*Primary election law	Ch.303	1897	Nov. 1898	86,872	92,607
Pocket ballots and coupon voting systems	Ch.451	1903	Nov. 1904	130,366	80,102
Women's suffrage	Ch.522	1905	Apr. 1906	45,958	111,139
*Soldiers' bonus financed by 3-mill property tax and income tax	Ch.227	1911	Nov. 1912	135,545	227,024
*Wisconsin prohibition enforcement act	Ch.667	1919	Sept. 1919	165,762	57,324
*U.S. prohibition act (Volstead Act); memorializing Congress to amend	Ch.556	1919	Nov. 1920	419,309	199,876
*Repeal of Wisconsin prohibition enforcement act; advisory referendum	SJR42	1925	Nov. 1926	349,443	177,603
*Modification of Wisconsin prohibition enforcement act; advisory referendum	"	"	"	350,337	196,402
County distribution of auto licenses; advisory referendum	SJR14	1929	Apr. 1929	321,688	200,545
*Sunday blue law repeal; advisory referendum	SJR26	1931	Apr. 1931	183,716	368,674
Old-age pensions; advisory referendum	AJR116	1931	Apr. 1932	396,436	271,786
*Teacher tenure law repeal; advisory referendum	AJR42	SS'33	Apr. 1934	531,915	154,729
Property tax levy for high school aid; 2 mills of assessed valuation	AJR67	1939	Apr. 1940	403,782	372,524
Daylight saving time; advisory referendum	Ch.525	1943	Apr. 1944	131,004	410,315
*3% retail sales tax for veterans bonus; advisory referendum	SJR24	1947	Apr. 1947	313,091	379,740
	SJR58	1947	Nov. 1948	258,497	825,990

STATEWIDE REFERENDA ELECTIONS OTHER THAN CONSTITUTIONAL AMENDMENTS–Continued

Question	Law Submitting			Date of Election	Vote For	Vote Against
4-year term for constitutional officers; advisory referendum	SJR11	JR13	1951	Apr. 1951	210,821	328,613
Apportionment of legislature by area and population; advisory referendum		Ch.728	1951	Nov. 1952	689,615	753,092
*New residents entitled to vote for president and vice president		Ch.76	1953	Nov. 1954	550,056	414,680
Statewide educational television tax-supported; advisory referendum	AJR74	JR66	1953	Nov. 1954	308,385	697,262
*Daylight saving time		Ch.6	1957	Apr. 1957	578,661	480,656
*Ex-residents entitled to vote for president and vice president		Ch.512	1961	Nov. 1962	627,279	229,375
Gasoline tax increase for highway construction; advisory referendum	AJR3	JR3	SS'63	Apr. 1964	150,769	889,364
*New residents entitled to vote after 6 months		Chs.88,89	1965	Nov. 1966	582,389	256,246
*Recreational lands bonding; advisory referendum	AJR12	JR4	1969	Apr. 1969	292,560	409,789
State control and funding of vocational education; advisory referendum	AJR17	JR5	1969	Apr. 1969	361,630	322,882
Water pollution abatement bonding			"	"	446,763	246,968
*New residents entitled to vote after 10 days		Ch.85	1975	Nov. 1976	1,017,887	660,875
*Presidential voting revised		Ch.394	1977	Nov. 1978	782,181	424,386
*Overseas voting revised			"	"	658,289	524,029
*Public inland lake protection and rehabilitation districts		Ch.299	1979	Nov. 1980	1,210,452	355,024
Nuclear weapons moratorium and reduction; advisory referendum	AJR99	JR38	1981	Sept. 1982	641,514	205,018
*Nuclear waste site locating; advisory referendum	AJR5	JR5	1983	Apr. 1983	78,327	628,414
Gambling casinos on excursion vessels; advisory referendum		WisAct 321	1991	Apr. 1993	465,432	604,289
Gambling casino restrictions; advisory referendum			"	"	646,827	416,722
*Video poker and other forms of video gambling allowed; advisory referendum			"	"	358,045	702,864
*Pari-mutuel on-track betting continuation; advisory referendum			"	"	548,580	507,403
*State-operated lottery continuation; advisory referendum			"	"	773,306	287,585
*Extended suffrage in federal elections to adult children of U.S. citizens living abroad		WisAct 182	1999	Nov. 2000	1,293,458	792,975

*Ratified.

[1]For text of resolution, see Wisconsin State Historical Society, Constitutional Series, Volume II, *The Convention of 1846*, edited by Milo M. Quaife, p. 755.

[2]In *Gillespie v. Palmer*, 20 Wis. 544 (1866), the Wisconsin Supreme Court ruled that Chapter 137, Laws of 1849, extending suffrage to colored persons, was ratified November 6, 1849.

Sources: Official records of the State Elections Board; *Laws of Wisconsin*, 2003 and previous volumes.

SUMMARY – STATEWIDE REFERENDA ELECTIONS

Statewide referendum questions are submitted to the electorate by the Wisconsin Legislature: 1) to ratify a law extending the right of suffrage (as required by the state constitution); 2) to ratify a law that has passed contingent on voter approval; or 3) to seek voter opinion through an advisory referendum. Since 1848, the Wisconsin Legislature has presented 52 referendum questions to the Wisconsin electorate. Two of these passed: one to ratify the state constitution and one to allow the formation of a state government. During territorial times, the territorial legislature sent 4 questions to the electorate.

Framework of Government

4

The framework of Wisconsin government: an overall view of Wisconsin government, a chart of its organization, and a map of state agencies

Milwaukee County Courthouse

Kathleen Sitter, LRB

LOCATION OF STATE AGENCIES IN MADISON
June 15, 2005

State Agency	Street Address	Map Locator Number
Administration, Department of	101 E. Wilson St.	14
Agriculture, Trade and Consumer Protection, Department of	2811 Agriculture Dr.	—
Attorney General, Office of the	State Capitol, Rm. 114 East	1
Commerce, Department of	201 W. Washington Ave.	17
Corrections, Department of	3099 E. Washington Ave.	—
Educational Approval Board	30 W. Mifflin St., 9th Floor	9
Educational Communications Board	3319 W. Beltline Hwy.	—
Elections Board	17 W. Main St., Suite 310	6
Emergency Management, Wisconsin	2400 Wright St.	—
Employee Trust Funds, Department of	801 W. Badger Rd.	—
Ethics Board	44 E. Mifflin St., Suite 601	3
Financial Institutions, Department of	345 W. Washington Ave.	18
Governor, Office of the	State Capitol, Rm. 115 East	1
Health and Family Services, Department of	1 W. Wilson St.	15
Higher Educational Aids Board	131 W. Wilson St., Suite 902	16
Housing and Economic Development Authority	201 W. Washington Ave	17
Insurance, Commissioner of	125 S. Webster St.	12
Investment Board	121 E. Wilson St.	13
Justice, Department of	17 W. Main St.	6
Legislative Audit Bureau	22 E. Mifflin St.	2
Legislative Council	1 E. Main St., Suite 401	5
Legislative Fiscal Bureau	1 E. Main St., Suite 301	5
Legislative Reference Bureau	1 E. Main St., Suite 200	5
Legislative Technology Services Bureau	17 S. Fairchild St., Suite 400	7
Lieutenant Governor, Office of the	State Capitol, Rm. 19 East	1
Military Affairs, Department of	2400 Wright St.	—
Natural Resources, Department of	101 S. Webster St.	11
Public Instruction, Department of	125 S. Webster St.	12
Public Service Commission	610 N. Whitney Way	—
Railroads, Office of the Commissioner	610 N. Whitney Way	—
Regulation and Licensing, Department of	1400 E. Washington Ave., Rm. 173	—
Revenue, Department of	2135 Rimrock Rd.	—
Revisor of Statutes Bureau	131 W. Wilson St., Suite 800	16
Secretary of State, Office of the	30 W. Mifflin St., 10th Floor	9
State Courts, Director of	State Capitol, Rm. 16 East	1
State Employment Relations, Office of	101 E. Wilson St.	14
State Law Library	120 Martin Luther King, Jr. Blvd	6
State Historical Society Museum	30 N. Carroll St.	8
State Historical Society of Wisconsin	816 State St.	19
State Public Defender, Office of the	17 S. Fairchild St., 2nd Floor	7
State Treasurer, Office of the	1 S. Pinckney St., Suite 550	4
Supreme Court	State Capitol, Rm. 16 East	1
Technical College System	345 W. Washington Ave., 2nd Floor	18
Tourism, Department of	201 W. Washington Ave.	17
Transportation, Department of	4802 Sheboygan Ave.	—
University of Wisconsin System	1220 Linden Dr.	—
Veterans Affairs, Department of	30 W. Mifflin St.	9
Wisconsin Veterans Museum	30 W. Mifflin St.	9
Workforce Development, Department of	201 E. Washington Ave.	10

Sources: Wisconsin Department of Administration, *State of Wisconsin Governmental Directory,* June 2004; List of State Agencies at: http://www.wisconsin.gov/state/core/agency_index.html [June 7, 2005].

CENTRAL MADISON LOCATOR MAP

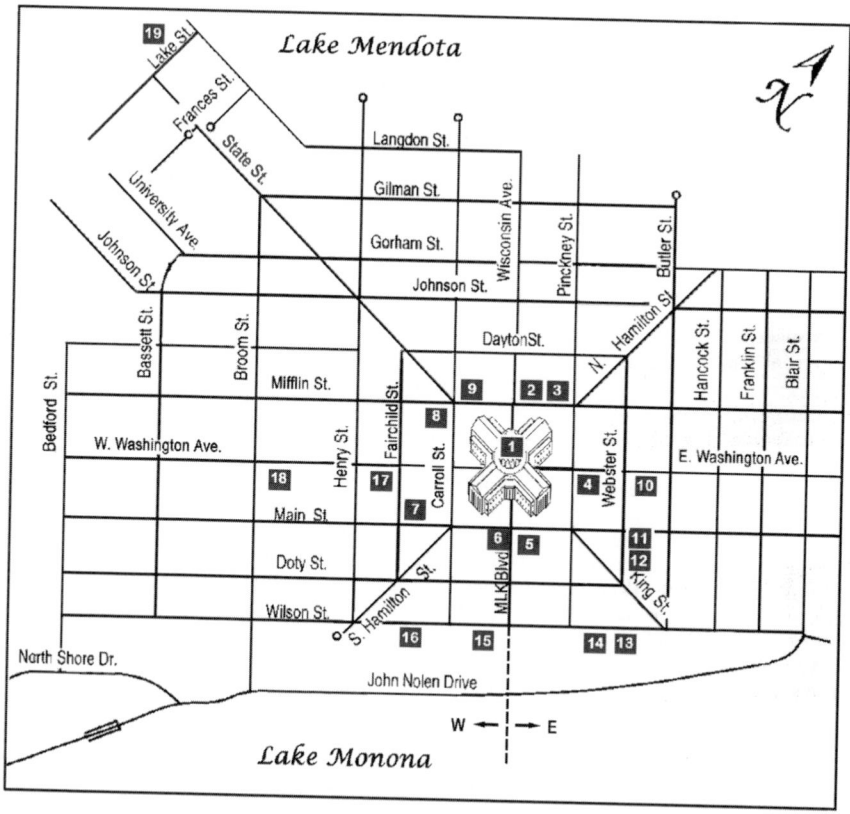

Base map: City of Madison, Engineering Division, July 2000.

THE FRAMEWORK OF WISCONSIN GOVERNMENT

Government at a Glance

Wisconsin state government is divided into three branches: legislative, executive, and judicial. The legislative branch includes the Wisconsin Legislature, which is composed of the senate and the assembly, and the service agencies and staff that assist the legislators. The executive branch, headed by the governor, includes five other elected constitutional officers, as well as 17 departments and 12 independent agencies created by statute. The judicial branch consists of the Wisconsin Supreme Court, the Court of Appeals, circuit courts, and municipal courts, as well as the staff and advisory groups that assist the courts. Each of the three branches is described in detail in its respective section of the *Blue Book*. In addition, the feature article in this edition focuses on the judicial branch.

Local units of government in Wisconsin include 72 counties, 190 cities, 400 villages, 1,260 towns, and several hundred special districts.

Origins of the 30th State

Wisconsin's original residents were Native American hunters who arrived here about 14,000 years ago. The territory's first farmers appear to have been the Hopewell people who raised corn, squash, and pumpkins in this area about 2,000 years ago. They also were hunters and fishers, and their trade routes stretched to the Atlantic Coast and the Gulf of Mexico. Later arrivals included the Chippewa, Ho-Chunk (Winnebago), Mahican/Munsee, Menominee, Oneida, Potawatomi, and Sioux.

From Wilderness to Statehood. The first Europeans to reach Wisconsin were French explorers, fur trappers, and missionaries. Wisconsin was included in the French sphere of influence from the 1630s until the signing of the 1763 Treaty of Paris, which concluded the French and Indian War and ceded the land encompassing Wisconsin to Great Britain. At the end of the Revolutionary War, 20 years later, the British ceded the vast, unsettled territory west of the Appalachian Mountains to the new United States of America. (Actual British control of the area did not end, however, until 1814 at the conclusion of the War of 1812.)

As a U.S. territory, Wisconsin was initially governed by the Northwest Ordinance of 1787, and then sequentially by the laws of the Indiana Territory, the Illinois Territory, the Michigan Territory and, finally in 1836, the Wisconsin Territory.

On August 6, 1846, the Congress of the United States authorized the people living in what was then called the Territory of Wisconsin "to form a constitution and State government, for the purpose of being admitted into the Union". Based on this enabling act, the people of the territory called a constitutional convention in Madison to draft a fundamental law for governing the new state. The first proposal for a constitution was drafted in 1846 and submitted to the people on April 6, 1847, but the voters rejected it on a 20,231-to-14,119 vote because of several controversial provisions involving banking, voting rights, property rights of married women, and homesteading.

On March 13, 1848, a second convention submitted its draft, which was ratified by a vote of 16,799 to 6,384. The constitution then adopted remains in force to this day although it has been amended on numerous occasions.

On May 29, 1848, Wisconsin became the 30th state admitted to the Union.

State Powers and Prohibitions. The enabling act passed by the U.S. Congress in 1846 declared that the Territory of Wisconsin was authorized to form a constitution and state government "on an equal footing with the original States in all respects whatsoever". From the moment of its birth, like the original states, the State of Wisconsin, its people, its lawmaking bodies, its administrative machinery, and its courts were subject to the U.S. Constitution.

In ratifying the U.S. Constitution, the 13 original states specifically delegated a number of powers to the U.S. Congress. Wisconsin agreed to this delegation when joining the Union. Congress is given the authority to regulate interstate and foreign commerce, maintain armed forces, declare war, coin money, establish a postal system, and grant patents and copyrights. Congress also has power to "make all laws which shall be necessary and proper" for carrying out its responsibilities.

The Tenth Amendment to the U.S. Constitution specifies: "The powers not delegated to the United States by the constitution, nor prohibited by it to the States, are reserved to the States, respectively, or to the people." Although the powers delegated to the federal government and the powers reserved to the states might appear to be neatly delineated, government responsibilities and activities have not been that clear-cut. In fact, many powers are exercised concurrently by the federal government and the states. Through judicial interpretation and laws enacted in response to changing societal needs, the powers exercised by Congress have been greatly expanded to include many activities once considered reserved to the states, as well as new authority not even imagined by the drafters, such as regulation of television and radio or development of a space exploration program. Likewise, the states have broadened their functions as society and technology have evolved.

The Many Sources of State Law

On April 20, 1836, the U.S. Congress passed the Organic Law establishing the Wisconsin Territory, as of July 3, 1836. It prescribed that the existing laws of the Territory of Michigan, to which Wisconsin had belonged, were to be "extended over the said territory . . . subject, nevertheless, to be altered, modified or repealed, by the governor and legislative assembly".

The Wisconsin Constitution continued the laws of the Territory of Wisconsin, by providing in Section 2 of Article XIV: "All laws now in force in the territory of Wisconsin which are not repugnant to this constitution shall remain in force until they expire by their own limitation or be altered or repealed by the legislature."

In addition to the provisions of the U.S. and Wisconsin Constitutions, the citizens of this state are governed by the wide-ranging laws contained in more than 6,000 pages of the Wisconsin Statutes. Even this body of law is not detailed enough. The Wisconsin Legislature has found that some areas are so technically complex that implementation of legislative policy must be left to certain state agencies with the power to issue administrative rules that have the effect of state law.

Notwithstanding the detailed wording of statutory law and administrative rules, there will still be specific provisions that are subject to various interpretations. In these cases, formal law is further defined by courts or administrative commissions authorized to interpret state law.

Making State Government Work

According to the general division of state government powers, the legislative branch enacts the laws; the executive branch carries them out (or executes them); and the judicial branch interprets them. This very simple description of state government tells only part of the story. Actually, all three branches play a part in establishing public policy, determining the meaning of the law, and ensuring that the laws are faithfully administered.

When most people think of "the law", they tend to regard it as something restrictive – a rule prohibiting certain actions. Although this may be one outcome, the real reason for the existence of law in a democratic system is to give the greatest benefit to the greatest number of people while protecting the individual rights prescribed by the federal and state constitutions. The only manner in which this can be achieved is by establishing a specific set of rules that attempt to prescribe for all citizens the limits of their rights and obligations.

Developing Public Policy. Policy cannot become law without legislative action. Each member of the legislature may introduce bills proposing new laws, joint resolutions proposing constitutional amendments, or simple and joint resolutions dealing with other matters, and each may offer amendments to proposals introduced by other members.

The governor also plays a major role in the development of formal public policy. The Wisconsin Constitution requires the governor to "communicate to the legislature, at every session, the condition of the state, and recommend such matters . . . for their consideration as he may deem expedient." This is done in the state of the state message, the budget message, and in special messages focusing on particular matters. In cases where a specific problem needs immediate legislative attention, the governor may call the legislature into a special session focusing on the matter. Before a bill becomes law, it must be passed by the legislature and signed by the governor. If the governor vetoes the bill instead of signing it, it can only become law if it is approved a second time by a two-thirds vote in each house of the legislature. In the case of appropriation bills that authorize spending, such as a budget, the governor can use the "partial veto" and veto only parts of the bill rather than the whole proposal. The veto power gives the governor a great deal of control over the content of any new law.

Once a new proposal is enacted, the governor, as the chief executive officer of the state, takes an active part in implementing the policy through oversight of the agencies involved in day-to-day administration of the law. According to the constitution, the governor "shall expedite all such measures as may be resolved upon by the legislature, and shall take care that the laws be faithfully executed."

The judicial branch also has an official role to play in the development of public policy. Although courts are not involved in the enactment of new laws, they do resolve conflicts about existing law – that is, they interpret the law. A court decision may occasionally result in an interpretation of a law that has quite a different effect from what the legislature originally intended. The legislature can redraft and clarify that law if it disagrees with the interpretation.

The opinions and concerns voiced by citizens of Wisconsin constitute the major source of ideas for new legislation. New policy proposals often result from everyday situations citizens encounter in their own communities. If they think that greater property tax relief is needed or that health insurance is unaffordable or that the business climate could be improved, they may determine "there ought to be a law". An individual may decide to write a letter to the editor of a newspaper, contact a legislator, or tell the governor about it. An association to which the person belongs may hire a spokesperson, called a "lobbyist", to recommend legislation or appear at legislative hearings.

State agencies are another primary source of public policy ideas. While administering current programs, departments are in a natural position to see how policies are working and whether they need to be changed, expanded, or abolished. Department heads have opportunities to discuss their problems with the governor, especially during development of the biennial budget, and they may be invited to contribute expert testimony at legislative hearings.

Increasing Services. In 1848, when Wisconsin became a state, government services were relatively simple. In his annual report of 1849, the secretary of state reported payments to only 14 people within the state's executive branch, and that included the constitutional officers. In 2004, full- and part-time state employees totaled 77,258.

This growth is primarily the result of the increasing size and complexity of today's society. At one time, many Wisconsin residents had little opportunity for formal schooling; in 2004, the University of Wisconsin System enrolled 173,058 students and in 2003, public elementary and secondary enrollments totaled 880,031. In 2002, the Technical College System served 429,355 students. Once, the wooden Watertown Plank Road constituted an unequaled technological advancement over the muddy wagon trails of the day; by 2004, Wisconsin had 113,269 miles of highways and streets, almost 80% of them paved, and 99 publicly owned airports. In 1900, the average U.S. life expectancy at birth was 47.3 years; by 2001, it had reached 77.2 years (74.4 for males and 79.8 for females). As Wisconsin's population increases in numbers and lives longer, the state faces many challenges, including improving education, renovating mature industries, developing the economy, protecting the environment, and improving transportation and health care.

Local Units of Government

In order to carry out its numerous responsibilities, every state has created subordinate units of local government. In most cases, these are legal, rather than constitutional, creations. This means the legislature may abolish them, change them, or give them increased or decreased powers and duties, as it chooses. In Wisconsin, the local units of government consist of counties, cities, villages, towns, and school districts. Special districts may be formed to handle regional concerns. Within the limits of statutory law, each unit has the power to tax and to make legally binding rules governing its own affairs.

Counties. Wisconsin has 72 counties. Together, they cover the entire territory of the state. The government offices for each county are located in a municipality within the county designated as the "county seat". The governing body of the county is the board of supervisors. The number of supervisors may vary from county to county, but within a particular county each supervisor must represent, as nearly as practicable, an equal number of inhabitants. County supervisors are elected in the spring nonpartisan elections for 2-year terms, with the exception of the members of the Milwaukee County Board of Supervisors who serve 4-year terms. Other county officials, all of whom are elected in the fall partisan elections, include the sheriff, who is elected for a 4-year term, and other administrative officers serving 2-year terms, such as the district attorney, clerk, treasurer, coroner, register of deeds, and clerk of circuit courts. Reflecting a constitutional amendment ratified on April 5, 2005, by 2008 all county officers will serve 4-year terms. As permitted by law, counties may employ a registered land surveyor in lieu of electing a surveyor, and the majority do. An appointed county medical examiner system may be substituted for an elected coroner. (Milwaukee County must appoint a medical examiner and a registered land surveyor.)

Since January 1, 1987, counties have been required to have a central administrative officer. They may choose to have an elected "county executive", who is chosen for a 4-year term in the spring nonpartisan elections, or a "county administrator" appointed by the county board. If the county has neither an executive nor an administrator, the board must designate an elected or appointed official to serve as "administrative coordinator" for the county. The county board chairperson often is chosen for this post. There are 10 counties with elected executives; 10 have appointed administrators; and 48 have an appointed administrative coordinator.

Cities and Villages. Wisconsin's 190 cities and 400 villages are incorporated under general law. Based on a constitutional amendment ratified in 1924, they have "home rule" powers to determine their local affairs. In general, minimum population for incorporation as a village is 150 residents for an isolated village and 2,500 for a metropolitan village located in a more densely populated area. For cities, the minimums are 1,000 and 5,000, respectively, but an existing village that exceeds 1,000 population may opt for city status. Depending on population, a city may be assigned to one of four classes, but the city must initiate the change from one class to another when its population changes. For example, Milwaukee currently is the only "first class" city. Although Madison meets the population requirements to change from "second class" to "first class", it has not chosen to do so.

Wisconsin cities currently use two forms of executive organization. The vast majority elect a mayor and a city common council, but 10 operate under a council-manager system, in which the elected council selects the manager to serve as chief executive. In those cities with the mayor-council form of government, 82 have also appointed full- or part-time city administrators. City alderpersons are elected for 2-year terms in the spring nonpartisan elections, except in Milwaukee, where alderpersons serve 4-year terms.

In most villages, executive power is vested in the village president, who presides over the village board of trustees and votes as an *ex officio* trustee, but 11 villages use a village manager form of government with the manager chosen by the elected board. An additional 83 have created full- or part-time village administrators. Village trustees are elected for 2-year terms in the spring nonpartisan elections.

Towns. Town governments govern those areas of Wisconsin that are not included inside the corporate boundaries of either a city or a village. Wisconsin has 1,260 towns, including the entire County of Menominee, which is designated as a town. Towns have only those powers granted by the Wisconsin Statutes. In addition to their traditional responsibility for local road maintenance, town governments carry out a variety of functions and, in some instances, even undertake urban-type services. The town board is usually composed of 3 supervisors, but if a board is authorized to exercise village powers or if the town population is 2,500 or more it may have up to 5 members. (Menominee County has 7 town board members, who also serve as the county board of supervisors.) Town supervisors are elected for 2-year terms in the spring nonpartisan election. They perform a number of administrative functions, and the town board chairperson has certain executive powers and duties. A town board may also create the position of town administrator.

Supervisors are expected to carry out the policies set at the annual town meeting. The annual meeting is held on the second Tuesday of April (or another date set by the electors), and during the meeting all qualified voters of the town are entitled to discuss and vote on matters specified by state law.

School Districts. There are 426 school districts in Wisconsin. These are special units of government organized to carry out a single function, the operation of the public schools. Each district is run by an elected school board, which appoints the district administrators.

WISCONSIN STATE GOVE

January

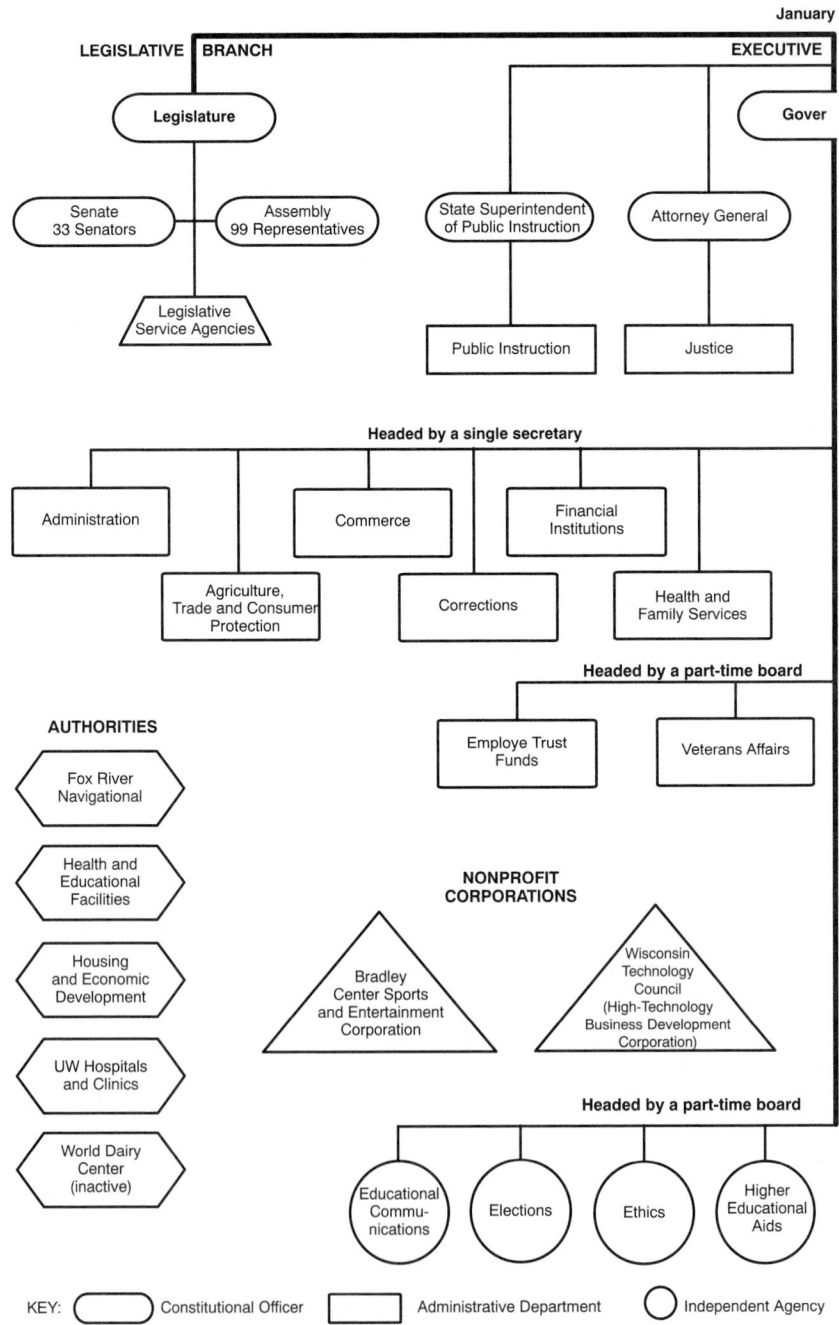

LEGISLATIVE | **BRANCH**　　　　　　　　　　　　　　　　　　**EXECUTIVE**

Legislature　　　　　　　　　　　　　　　　　　　　　Gover

| Senate 33 Senators | Assembly 99 Representatives | State Superintendent of Public Instruction | Attorney General |

Legislative Service Agencies

Public Instruction　　　　Justice

Headed by a single secretary

| Administration | Commerce | Financial Institutions |

Agriculture, Trade and Consumer Protection　　　Corrections　　　Health and Family Services

Headed by a part-time board

AUTHORITIES

Fox River Navigational

Employe Trust Funds　　　Veterans Affairs

Health and Educational Facilities

Housing and Economic Development

NONPROFIT CORPORATIONS

Bradley Center Sports and Entertainment Corporation

Wisconsin Technology Council (High-Technology Business Development Corporation)

UW Hospitals and Clinics

World Dairy Center (inactive)

Headed by a part-time board

Educational Commu-nications　　　Elections　　　Ethics　　　Higher Educational Aids

KEY:　　⬭ Constitutional Officer　　▭ Administrative Department　　◯ Independent Agency

Units of state government not shown on the chart are listed on following page.

RNMENT ORGANIZATION

2005

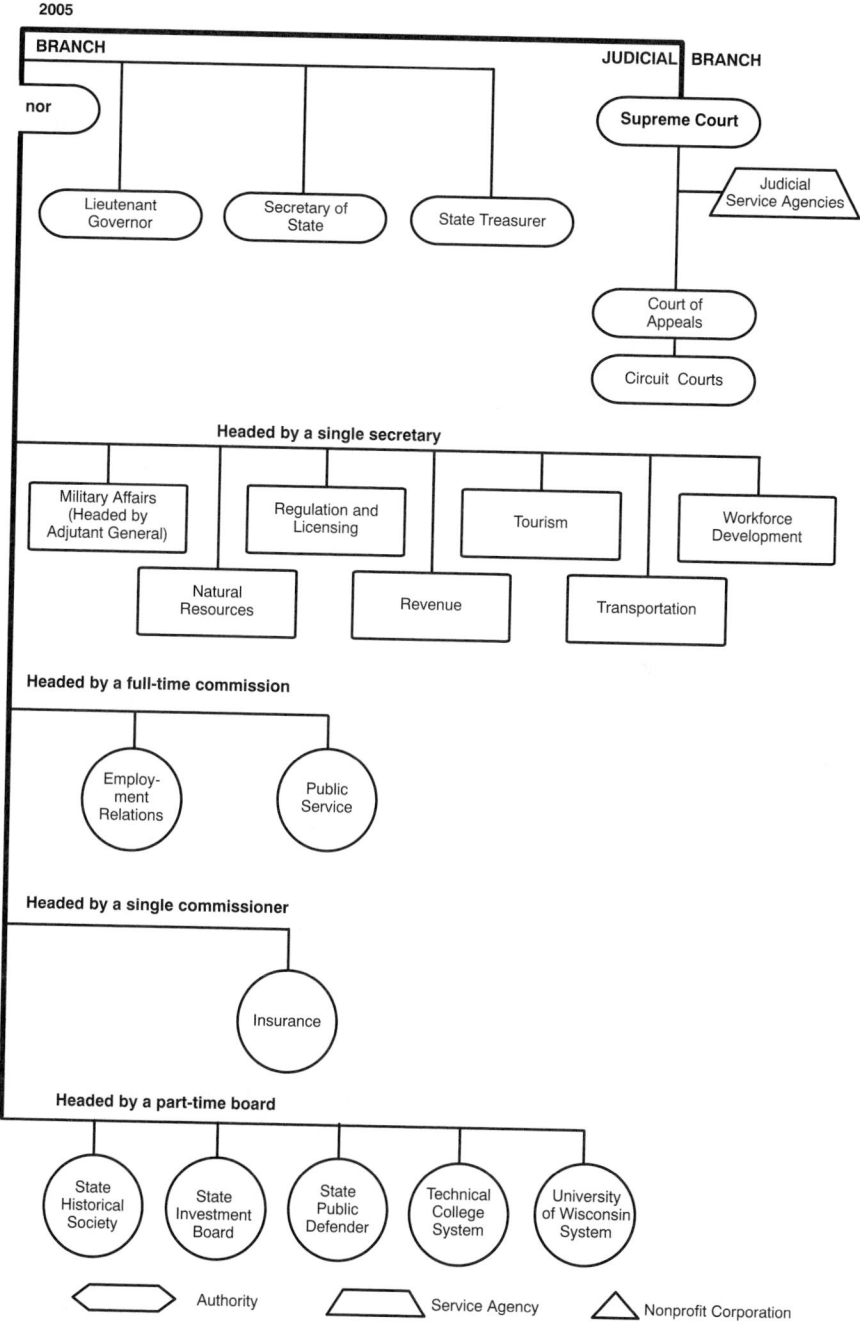

BRANCH

JUDICIAL BRANCH

nor

Supreme Court

Judicial Service Agencies

Lieutenant Governor

Secretary of State

State Treasurer

Court of Appeals

Circuit Courts

Headed by a single secretary

Military Affairs (Headed by Adjutant General)

Regulation and Licensing

Tourism

Workforce Development

Natural Resources

Revenue

Transportation

Headed by a full-time commission

Employ-ment Relations

Public Service

Headed by a single commissioner

Insurance

Headed by a part-time board

State Historical Society

State Investment Board

State Public Defender

Technical College System

University of Wisconsin System

Authority   Service Agency   Nonprofit Corporation

Units of State Government Not Shown on Organization Chart

The following units of state government are independent entities, which are attached to the agencies indicated for administrative purposes under Section 15.03 of the statutes.

Boards

Board on Aging and Long-Term Care (DOA)

Arts Board (Tourism)

Burial Sites Preservation Board (State Historical Society)

Child Abuse and Neglect Prevention Board (DHFS)

Claims Board (DOA)

College Savings Program Board (Treasurer)

Crime Victims Rights Board (DOJ)

Depository Selection Board (DOA)

Development Finance Board (Commerce)

Disability Board (Governor)

Educational Approval Board (Veterans Affairs)

Emergency Medical Services Board (DHFS)

Environmental Education Board (UW)

Board on Health Care Information (DHFS)

Historic Preservation Review Board (State Historical Society)

Incorporation Review Board (DOA)

Independent Review Board (DHFS)

Information Technology Management Board (DOA)

Interstate Adult Offender Supervision Board (DOC)

Investment and Local Impact Fund Board (DOR)

Kickapoo Reserve Management Board (Tourism)

Lake Michigan Commercial Fishing Board (DNR)

Lake Superior Commercial Fishing Board (DNR)

Land and Water Conservation Board (DATCP)

Law Enforcement Standards Board (DOJ)

Livestock Facility Siting Review Board (DATCP)

Lower Wisconsin State Riverway Board (Tourism)

Minority Business Development Board (Commerce)

National and Community Service Board (DOA)

Prison Industries Board (DOC)

Public Records Board (DOA)

Rural Economic Development Board (Commerce)

Small Business Regulatory Review Board (Commerce)

State Capitol and Executive Residence Board (DOA)

State Fair Park Board (Tourism)

State Use Board (DOA)

Veterinary Diagnostic Laboratory Board (UW)

Volunteer Fire Fighter and Emergency Medical Technician Service Award Board (DOA)

Waste Facility Siting Board (DOA)

Governor's Work-Based Learning Board (DWD)

Commissions

Labor and Industry Review Commission (DWD)

Sentencing Commission (DOA)

Tax Appeals Commission (DOA)

Wisconsin Waterways Commission (DNR)

Councils

Council on Developmental Disabilities (DHFS)

Groundwater Coordinating Council (DNR)

Invasive Species Council (DNR)

Milwaukee Child Welfare Partnership Council (DHFS)

Council on Physical Disabilities (DHFS)

Council on Recycling (DNR)

Council on Utility Public Benefits (DOA)

Wisconsin Land Council (DOA)

Women's Council (DOA)

Divisions

Division of Hearings and Appeals (DOA)

Division of Trust Lands and Investments (DOA)

Offices

Office of Credit Unions (DFI)

Office of Justice Assistance (DOA)

Office of the Commissioner of Railroads (PSC)

Office of State Employment Relations (DOA)

Legislative Branch

5

The legislative branch: profile of the legislative branch, description of the legislative process, summary of 2003-04 legislation, and description of legislative committees and service agencies

Grant County Courthouse

Kathleen Sitter, LRB

OFFICERS OF THE 2005 LEGISLATURE

SENATE

President . . . . Senator Alan J. Lasee
President pro tempore . . . . Senator David A. Zien
Chief clerk . . . . Honorable Robert J. Marchant
Sergeant at arms . . . . Honorable Edward Blazel

Majority Party Officers		Minority Party Officers
Leader	Senator Dale W. Schultz	Senator Judith Biros Robson
Assistant leader	Senator Neal J. Kedzie	Senator Dave Hansen
Caucus chairperson	Senator Ron Brown	Senator Jeffrey T. Plale
Caucus vice chairperson .	Senator Cathy Stepp	Senator Mark Miller
Caucus sergeant at arms	Senator Sheila E. Harsdorf	None

Chief Clerk: Mailing Address: P.O. Box 7882, Madison 53707-7882; Location: 17 West Main Street, Suite 401; Telephone: (608) 266-2517.

Sergeant at Arms: Mailing Address: P.O. Box 7882, Madison 53707-7882; Location: B35 South, State Capitol; Telephone: (608) 266-1801.

ASSEMBLY

Speaker . . . . Representative John G. Gard
Speaker pro tempore . . . . Representative Stephen J. Freese
Chief clerk . . . . Honorable Patrick E. Fuller
Sergeant at arms . . . . Honorable Richard A. Skindrud

Majority Party Officers		Minority Party Officers
Leader	Representative Michael D. Huebsch	Representative James E. Kreuser
Assistant leader	Representative Jeff Fitzgerald	Representative Jon Richards
Caucus chairperson	Representative Daniel P. Vrakas	Representative Robert L. Turner
Caucus vice chairperson .	Representative Mark Gottlieb	Representative Gary E. Sherman
Caucus secretary	Representative Carol Owens	Representative Amy Sue Vruwink
Caucus sergeant at arms .	Representative Jerry Petrowski	Representative Jennifer Shilling

Chief Clerk: Mailing Address: P.O. Box 8952, Madison 53708-8952; Location: 17 West Main Street, Suite 208; Telephone: (608) 266-1501.

Sergeant at Arms: Mailing Address: P.O. Box 8952, Madison 53708-8952; Location: 411 West, State Capitol; Telephone: (608) 267-9808.

LEGISLATIVE HOTLINE: Monday-Friday, 8:15 a.m.-4:45 p.m.; Telephone: Madison Area: 266-9960; Outside Madison Area: (800) 362-9472; TTY: (800) 228-2115.

LEGISLATIVE INTERNET ADDRESS: http://www.legis.state.wi.us

LEGISLATIVE BRANCH

A PROFILE OF THE LEGISLATIVE BRANCH

The legislative branch consists of the bicameral Wisconsin Legislature, made up of the senate with 33 members and the assembly with 99 members, together with the service agencies created by the legislature and the staff employed by each house. The legislature's main responsibility is to make policy by enacting state laws. Its service agencies assist it by performing fiscal analysis, research, bill drafting, auditing, statute editing, and information technology functions.

A new legislature is sworn into office in January of each odd-numbered year, and it meets in continuous biennial session until its successor is sworn in. The 2005 Legislature is the 97th Wisconsin Legislature. It convened on January 3, 2005, and will continue until January 3, 2007.

U.S. and Wisconsin Constitutions Grant Broad Legislative Powers. The power to determine the state's policies and programs lies primarily in the legislative branch of state government. According to the Wisconsin Constitution: "The legislative power shall be vested in a senate and assembly." This power is quite extensive, but certain limitations are imposed by the U.S. Constitution and the Wisconsin Constitution. In addition, the legislature's power is restricted by the governor's authority to veto legislation, but a veto may be overridden by a two-thirds vote in both houses of the legislature.

All actions taken by the legislature must conform with the U.S. Constitution. For example, the U.S. Congress has exclusive powers to regulate foreign affairs and coin money, and states are denied the power to make treaties with foreign countries. In addition, state legislation may not abridge the rights guaranteed in the U.S. Bill of Rights. Powers that are not granted exclusively to the U.S. Congress or denied the states are considered to be reserved for the individual states.

In addition to the boundaries set by the U.S. Constitution, the legislature's authority is also limited by the state constitution. For instance, the Wisconsin Constitution requires the legislature to establish as uniform a system of town government as practicable, prevents it from enacting private or special laws on certain subjects, and prohibits laws that would infringe on the rights of Wisconsin citizens, as protected by the Declaration of Rights of the Wisconsin Constitution.

Biennial Sessions: 4-Year Senate Terms; 2-Year Assembly Terms. Originally, members of the assembly served for one year, while senators served for 2 years. An 1881 constitutional amendment doubled the respective terms to the current 2 and 4 years and converted the legislature from annual to biennial sessions.

Since its adoption on March 13, 1848, the Wisconsin Constitution has provided that the membership of the assembly shall be not less than 54 nor more than 100, and the membership of the senate shall consist of not more than one-third nor less than one-fourth of the number of assembly members. The first legislature had 85 members – 19 senators and 66 assemblymen. (Assembly members were renamed "representatives to the assembly" in 1969.) The number increased several times until the legislature became a 133-member body in 1862, with the constitutionally permitted maximums of 33 in the senate and 100 in the assembly. Over a century later, membership dropped to 132 in the 1973 Legislature, when the number of representatives was reduced to 99 so that each of the 33 senate districts would encompass 3 assembly districts. This is the current number and structure.

THE WISCONSIN LEGISLATURE

Number of Positions 2005 Legislature: Senate: 33 members, 219 employees; Assembly: 99 members, 329 employees.

Total Budget 2003-05: $124,948,100 (including service agencies).

Constitutional Reference: Article IV.

Statutory Reference: Chapter 13, Subchapter I.

Election of Legislators. All members of the legislature are elected from single-member districts. At the general election on the first Tuesday after the first Monday in November of even-numbered years, the voters of Wisconsin elect all members of the assembly and approximately one-half of the senators. These legislators-elect assume office in January of the following odd-numbered year when they convene to open the new legislative session at the State Capitol, together with the "holdover" senators who still have 2 years remaining of their 4-year terms. When a midterm vacancy occurs in any legislative office, it is filled through a special election called by the governor.

The 33 senators are elected for 4-year terms from districts numbered 1 through 33. The 16 senators representing even-numbered districts are elected in the years in which a presidential election occurs. The 17 senators who represent odd-numbered districts are elected in the years in which a gubernatorial election is held.

Since statehood in 1848, the Wisconsin Constitution has required the legislature, after each U.S. decennial census, to redraw the districts for both houses "according to the number of inhabitants". Thus, Wisconsin was following this practice long before the U.S. Supreme Court decided in 1962 that all states must redistrict according to the "one person, one vote" principle.

Under the campaign finance reporting law enacted by the 1973 Legislature, candidates for the legislature, as well as for other public offices, are required to make full, detailed disclosure of their campaign contributions and expenditures to the Elections Board, which was created by the same law. Limits are placed on the amounts of contributions received from individuals and various committees. State law also requires legislators and candidates for legislative office to file a statement of their economic interests with the state Ethics Board. A 1977 law authorized candidates for legislative office and statewide executive and judicial offices to receive public campaign funding from state revenues, funded by a $1 check-off on state individual income tax returns.

Political Parties in the Legislative Process. Partisan political organizations play an important role in the Wisconsin legislative process. Since 1949, virtually all legislators have been affiliated with either the Democratic Party or the Republican Party. The strongest representation of other parties was between 1911 and 1937, when there were one or more Socialists in the legislature, and between 1933 and 1947, when the Progressives maintained an independent party. In fact, in 1937 the Progressive Party had a plurality in both houses.

Party organization in the legislature is based on the party group called the "caucus". In each house, all members of a particular political party form that party's caucus. Thus, there are four caucuses related to the party divisions in the two houses. The primary purpose of a caucus is to help party members maintain a unified position on critical issues. Party leaders, however, do not expect to secure party uniformity on every measure under consideration.

Caucus meetings may be held at regular intervals or whenever convened by party leaders, and occasionally the senate and assembly caucuses of the same party meet in joint caucus. A caucus meeting is scheduled shortly after the general election and before the opening of the session to select candidates for the various leadership positions in each house. Although each party caucus nominates a slate of officers, the positions are usually won by the nominees of the majority party when a vote is taken in the full house.

Legislative Officers and Leadership. The Wisconsin Constitution originally required the lieutenant governor to serve as president of the senate. As a result of an April 1979 constitutional amendment, the senate now selects its own president from among its members. When the president of the senate is absent or unable to preside, the president pro tempore, elected from the membership, may preside as substitute president.

The presiding officer of the assembly is the speaker, who is elected by majority vote of the assembly membership. The speaker supervises all other officers of the chamber and appoints

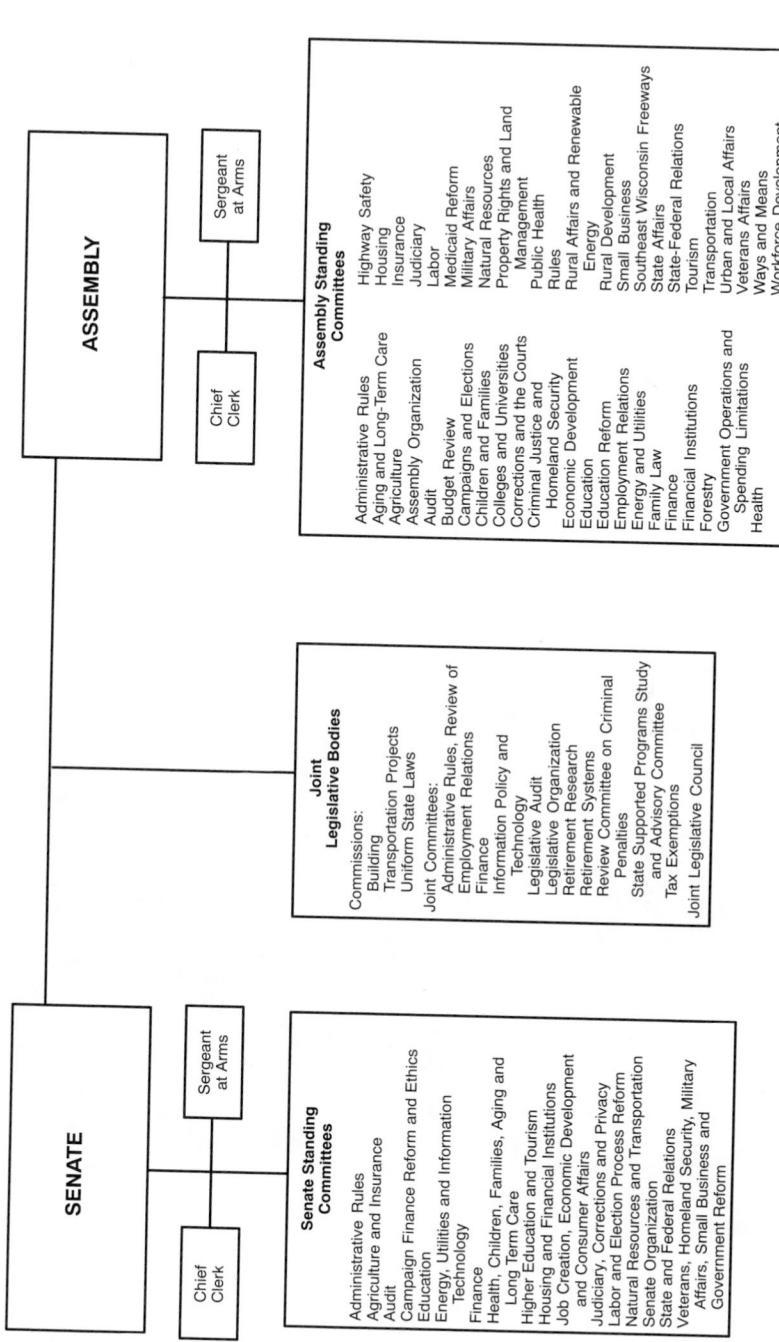

WISCONSIN LEGISLATURE

SENATE

Chief Clerk

Sergeant at Arms

Senate Standing Committees

Administrative Rules
Agriculture and Insurance
Audit
Campaign Finance Reform and Ethics
Education
Energy, Utilities and Information Technology
Finance
Health, Children, Families, Aging and Long Term Care
Higher Education and Tourism
Housing and Financial Institutions
Job Creation, Economic Development and Consumer Affairs
Judiciary, Corrections and Privacy
Labor and Election Process Reform
Natural Resources and Transportation
Senate Organization
State and Federal Relations
Veterans, Homeland Security, Military Affairs, Small Business and Government Reform

Joint Legislative Bodies

Commissions:
Building
Transportation Projects
Uniform State Laws

Joint Committees:
Administrative Rules, Review of
Employment Relations
Finance
Information Policy and Technology
Legislative Audit
Legislative Organization
Retirement Research
Retirement Systems
Review Committee on Criminal Penalties
State Supported Programs Study and Advisory Committee
Tax Exemptions

Joint Legislative Council

ASSEMBLY

Chief Clerk

Sergeant at Arms

Assembly Standing Committees

Administrative Rules
Aging and Long-Term Care
Agriculture
Assembly Organization
Audit
Budget Review
Campaigns and Elections
Children and Families
Colleges and Universities
Corrections and the Courts
Criminal Justice and Homeland Security
Economic Development
Education
Education Reform
Employment Relations
Energy and Utilities
Family Law
Finance
Financial Institutions
Forestry
Government Operations and Spending Limitations
Health
Highway Safety
Housing
Insurance
Judiciary
Labor
Medicaid Reform
Military Affairs
Natural Resources
Property Rights and Land Management
Public Health
Rules
Rural Affairs and Renewable Energy
Rural Development
Small Business
Southeast Wisconsin Freeways
State Affairs
State-Federal Relations
Tourism
Transportation
Urban and Local Affairs
Veterans Affairs
Ways and Means
Workforce Development

LEGISLATURE

committees. When the speaker is absent or unable to preside, the speaker pro tempore, who is also elected from the membership, may substitute.

Each party in each house elects floor leaders, respectively known as the majority leader and assistant majority leader and the minority leader and assistant minority leader. To varying degrees, these party officers play powerful roles in directing and coordinating legislative activities.

Each house has a chief clerk and a sergeant at arms, who are elected by, but are not themselves members of, the legislature. The chief clerk serves as the clerk of the house when it is in session and supervises the preparation of legislative records. In conjunction with the presiding officers, the chief clerks supervise personnel and administrative functions for their respective houses. The sergeants at arms maintain order in and about the chambers and supervise the messengers.

Legislative Compensation. When the 2005 Legislature convened on January 3, 2005, all members were eligible for a salary of $45,569 per year. The process for setting legislative salaries requires the Director of the Office of State Employment Relations to submit proposed changes as part of the state compensation plan to the legislature's Joint Committee on Employment Relations. If the committee approves the plan, the new salary goes into effect for all legislators at the next inauguration. The committee also sets the salaries of the chief clerks and the sergeants at arms of the two houses within a range established under civil service procedures.

Members of the legislature, the chief clerks, and the sergeants at arms are entitled to an allowance not to exceed $88 per day ("per diem") for living expenses for each day spent in Madison on legislative business if they certify by affidavit that they have established temporary residence at the state capital. Those who choose not to establish temporary residence are entitled to half that amount. All members are reimbursed for one weekly round trip from the capital to their homes. They also are reimbursed for expenses incurred while serving as legislative members of a state or interstate agency or when specifically authorized to attend meetings of such agencies as nonmembers. The Speaker of the Assembly also receives a stipend, currently $25 per month.

Inauguration day is usually an occasion of ceremony and good fellowship. Since Senators serve 4-year terms, only half the members must take the oath at the start of each session. In 2005, members from even-numbered districts were sworn in. Here, newly elected Senator Glenn Grothman is welcomed by Senator Carol Roessler, beginning her 5th full term. (Richard G. B. Hanson II, Senate Photographer)

2005-2006 SESSION SCHEDULE

January 3, 2005	2005 Inauguration
January 12, 2005	Floorperiod
January 25-27, 2005	Floorperiod
February 8, 2005	Floorperiod
February 15-24, 2005	Floorperiod
March 8-17, 2005	Floorperiod
April 5-14, 2005	Floorperiod
April 28, 2005	Deadline for sending bills to governor
May 3-12, 2005	Floorperiod
May 31-July 1, 2005 (or until passage of budget)	Floorperiod
August 11, 2005	Deadline for sending nonbudget bills to governor*
September 20-29, 2005	Floorperiod
October 25-November 10, 2005	Floorperiod
December 6-15, 2005	Floorperiod
January 5, 2006	Deadline for sending bills to governor
January 17-February 2, 2006	Floorperiod
February 21-March 9, 2006	Floorperiod
April 13, 2006	Deadline for sending bills to governor
April 25-May 4, 2006	Last general-business floorperiod
May 16-18, 2006	Limited-business floorperiod
May 23, 2006	Deadline for sending bills to governor
May 30 and 31, 2006	Veto review floorperiod
June 14, 2006	Deadline for sending bills to governor
June 1, 2006-January 3, 2007	Interim committee work
December 27 and 28, 2006	Limited-business floorperiod
December 29, 2006	Deadline for sending bills to governor
January 3, 2007	2007 Inauguration

Any floorperiod may be convened earlier or extended beyond its scheduled dates by majority action of the membership or the organization committees of the two houses. The Committee on Senate Organization may schedule sessions outside floorperiods for senate action on gubernatorial nominations, but the assembly does not have to hold skeleton sessions during these appointment reviews. The legislature may call itself into extraordinary session or the governor may call a special session during a floorperiod or on any intervening day.

*Deadline for budget bill will depend on bill's passage.

Source: 2005 Senate Joint Resolution 1.

Legislators receive allowances for their office and mailing expenses while attending legislative sessions. If the legislature is in session three or fewer days in a particular month, legislative leadership may authorize an interim expense allowance to cover postage and clerical assistance ($25 for representatives and $75 for senators).

Legislative Sessions. Members of each new legislature convene in the State Capitol at 2 p.m. on the first Monday in January of each odd-numbered year to take the oath of office, select officers, and organize for business. The initial meeting occurs on January 3 if the first Monday falls on January 1 or 2. The previous legislature usually holds its adjournment meeting on the same day, just prior to the convening of the new legislature. Thus, there is almost no interim between the two.

Originally, the constitution required the legislature to meet once during each annual session. An 1881 amendment restricted the body to one meeting in the two years comprising the biennial session. As a result, the legislature scheduled its meetings in a continuing biennial session with periodic recesses. It would meet in regular session from January through June of the odd-numbered year and then recess after completing the major portion of its work. It then reconvened from time to time in the remainder of the biennium, as needed. When a legislature had completed its work for the biennium, it adjourned *sine die,* meaning it did not set a date to reconvene. At that point, the 2-year session was over, and the legislature could not return unless called into special session by the governor.

In 1968, the state constitution was amended to permit the legislature to determine its own meeting schedule for the biennium. Beginning with the 1971 Legislature, annual sessions were formally initiated by law with the requirement that regular sessions begin in January of each year. Early in each biennium, the Joint Committee on Legislative Organization develops a work schedule for the 2-year period and submits it to the legislature in the form of a joint resolution. The 2005-2006 session schedule, for example, is structured around 17 floorperiods, with periods of committee work interspersed throughout the biennium.

Meetings of the respective houses of the legislature are held in the senate and assembly chambers in the State Capitol. Usually, the legislature meets Tuesday through Thursday of each week. Toward the end of many floorperiods, however, the houses may meet continuously during the day Tuesday through Friday and hold evening sessions. Unless otherwise ordered, daily sessions begin at 10 a.m. for the senate and 9 a.m. for the assembly (10 a.m. on the first legislative day of the week). Daily sessions usually extend beyond noon, especially later in the legislative session. If business permits, afternoons may be devoted to committee hearings or a combination of hearings and late afternoon sessions.

As illustrated in the foregoing description, the word "session" has several meanings. The "legislative session" usually refers to the 2-year period that comprises a particular legislature. If the legislature is "not in session", that may mean it is in an interim period between floorperiods. Saying that either the senate or assembly is "not in session", however, may mean that the house has adjourned for the day or that it has recessed until a later hour of the same day.

Extraordinary and Special Sessions. Beginning in 1962, the legislature adopted procedures that would permit it to reassemble through a petition signed by a majority of the members of each house. An amendment to the 1977 Joint Rules codified this procedure by allowing the legislature to call itself into an "extraordinary session". The legislature may convene in extraordinary session or extend a floorperiod at the direction of the majority of the members of the organization committee in each house, by passage of a joint resolution, or by a joint petition signed by the majority of members of each house.

In addition, the governor has the authority to call a "special session", in which the legislature can act only upon matters specifically mentioned in the governor's call. As of the adjournment of the 2003 Legislature, there had been 78 special sessions since Wisconsin became a state in 1848. It is possible for a regular session and a special session to be scheduled at different times during a week or even on the same day. Because special sessions may occur at any time during the legislative biennium, enactments resulting from a special session are now numbered within the regular sequence of biennial laws.

Session Records. Each house of the legislature keeps a record of its actions known as the daily journal. This record differs from the federal *Congressional Record* in that it does not provide a transcript or abbreviated account of speeches made on the floor. It is, instead, an outline record of the business before the house, including procedural actions taken on all measures considered on that particular day, roll call votes, communications received from the governor or the other house, special committee reports, and miscellaneous items.

The *Bulletin of the Proceedings of the Wisconsin Legislature* is generally issued weekly during floorperiods and less often during committee work periods. Each issue contains a cumulative record of actions taken on bills, joint resolutions, and resolutions by both houses, listed by bill or resolution number. It includes a subject and author index to legislation; a subject index to the legislative journals; a subject index to new laws and enrolled bills and joint resolutions; a numeric listing of statute sections affected by these laws; changes made to statutory court rules by supreme court orders; and the complete text of constitutional amendments ratified since the most recent publication of the *Wisconsin Statutes*. Another part indexes and reports action on administrative rule changes. The *Bulletin* also includes a directory of lobbying organizations, licensed lobbyists, and legislative liaisons from state agencies.

Each week during the session, the chief clerks jointly issue a *Weekly Schedule of Committee Activities,* listing the business scheduled by the various committees for the coming week, together with the time and place of each hearing and advanced notices on hearings deemed to be of special interest. Each house also issues a daily calendar indicating the business to be taken up on the floor that day.

Complete texts of bills, amendments, and resolutions; bill histories; a subject index to legislation; hearing notices and calendars; and other information on the legislature are available on the Internet at www.legis.state.wi.us. Reference copies of all these legislative documents are available at the Legislative Reference Bureau, and numerous libraries throughout the state also receive

The President of the Senate is the highest ranking official in the Senate and presides over floor sessions. Here President Alan Lasee (left) confers with Senator Michael Ellis. The two are the longest serving Republicans in the Senate. (Richard G. B. Hanson II, Senate Photographer)

them. Individuals and organizations may subscribe to receive printed versions of legislative documents. (See the table on Legislative Service in this section for fees and details.)

Standing Committees. To a large extent, the legislature does its work in committees. In the 2005 Legislature, the senate has 17 standing committees, the assembly 45, and there are 11 joint standing committees, composed of members from both houses. Joint standing committees are created in the statutes and membership is determined by law. Regular standing committees are created under the rules of their respective houses.

The standing committees in the individual houses consist of legislators only and operate throughout the biennium. Each committee is concerned with one or more broad subject areas related to government functions. It may hold public hearings on measures introduced in the legislature, conduct studies and investigations, and generally review matters within its area of concern. Legislative committees may also appoint subcommittees or study groups.

Senate rules require that each senator serve on at least one standing committee, and the Committee on Senate Organization sets the number of members on each committee. Usually the two major political parties are represented on the committees in proportion to their membership in the senate. The chairperson of the organization committee, who is also the majority leader, makes the appointments to committees. Committee nominations for individual members of the minority party are proposed by that party. An exception to the general method of appointment is the Committee on Senate Organization. It is an *ex officio* committee, consisting of members in leadership positions: the president, the majority and minority leaders, and the assistant leaders.

In the assembly, the speaker determines the number of members of each committee and the division of membership between the majority and minority parties. Under assembly rules, the speaker appoints majority party committee members directly and minority party committee members upon nomination by the assembly minority leader. Customarily, every member serves on at least one committee, although the rules are silent on the distribution of committee assignments. The speaker may appoint himself or herself to one or more standing committees and is a nonvoting member of all others. By rule, the Committee on Assembly Organization is composed of the speaker, the speaker pro tempore, the majority and minority leaders, the assistant leaders, and the caucus chairpersons. The Committee on Rules includes all members of the organization committee plus one majority and one minority party member appointed by the speaker.

Temporary Special Committees. In addition to the standing committees, special committees may be appointed during a legislative session to study specific problems or conduct designated investigations and report to the legislature before the conclusion of the session.

Prior to 1947, the legislature created interim committees to investigate particular subjects. They functioned between legislative sessions and reported their findings and recommendations to the next legislature. Since 1947, almost all interim studies have been referred to the Joint Legislative Council, which coordinates a program of study and investigation after deciding which topics it will consider. The council usually appoints separate committees to study specific matters, and these committees include nonlegislative members.

Employees of the Legislature. Each house of the legislature provides staff services, which are managed by the respective chief clerk and sergeant at arms under the supervision of the Committee on Senate Organization or the speaker of the assembly. Although senate and assembly employees are not part of the classified service, they are paid in accordance with the compensation and classification plan established for employees in the classified service and within pay ranges approved by the Joint Committee on Legislative Organization.

The legislature employs six service agencies to provide financial and program audits, fiscal information and analysis, bill drafting, research services, legal counsel and policy assistance, computer and telecommunications services, and statutory revision.

The press plays an important role in the legislative process: it both informs the public about legislative activity, and allows members to express their concerns to the public. Senator Tom Reynolds addresses the press, flanked by (from left) Senator Leibham and Representatives Vos, Gundrum, and Ott. (Richard G. B. Hanson II, Senate Photographer)

THE LEGISLATURE ON THE INTERNET

Legislative Information

The Wisconsin Legislature's Internet home page at **http://www.legis.state.wi.us** provides extensive information regarding the legislature and the legislative process. Follow the links under **Legislative Activity** to access bills, acts, statutes, calendars, and other legislative activity during current and past sessions. Full text documents, including the Wisconsin Constitution, are also available online. The **Spotlight** link reports on-going legislative activity. In addition, the legislative **service agencies** have individual home pages where their publications can be downloaded.

The **Folio** search engine enables users to search for specific acts, bills, or statutes from 1995 to date. Folio may be accessed through the legislature's home page or at **http://folio.legis.state.wi.us**.

The legislature's home page links to individual legislator's home pages, which include information such as e-mail addresses, district maps, committee assignments, and biographical information. Some legislators also provide brief audio clips and personally designed pages to communicate with their constituents.

Live Video and Audio

The legislature offers a live audio service for those who want to track floor debate as it happens. Separate **InSession** links on the legislature's home page provide detailed directions for listening to discussions in the assembly and senate during floor sessions. The links include the calendars for their respective houses. The assembly also provides a live video stream of the floor session under the **Assembly Chamber Video** link. Some committees, including the Joint Committee on Finance, provide audio links for their hearings.

Legislative Notification Service

This service allows citizens to track legislation by creating a profile of items of interest. Profiles may include specific proposals identified by author, committee, or subject matter and may specify activity occurring at various stages of the legislative process. After a profile is filed on the Web site **http://notify.legis.state.wi.us**, users will receive daily or weekly e-mails of relevant activities.

NEWS MEDIA CORRESPONDENTS
ACCREDITED TO THE 2005 LEGISLATURE
April 2005

Organization	Correspondents	Telephone
Newspaper and Wire Services		
Appleton Post-Crescent	Ben Jones	255-9256
Associated Press	Ryan Foley, Todd Richmond, J.R. Ross	255-3679
Badger Herald	Ryan Masse, Chris Werner	257-4712
Capital Times	Dave Callender, Matt Pommer, Anita Weier	252-6475/252-6429
Capitol News Service	Stan Milam	335-8585
Green Bay Press-Gazette	Karen Lincoln Michel	255-9254
Isthmus	Bill Lueders	251-5627
Lee Newspapers/WSJ	Tom Sheehan	252-6198/(800) 362-8333, ext. 6198
Milwaukee Journal Sentinel	Stacy Forster, Patrick Marley, Steve Walters	258-2262/258-2274
Wheeler News Service	Thom Gerresten	(715) 389-2373
Wheeler Reports	George Coburn, Gwyn Guenther, Dick Wheeler	287-0130
Wisconsin Catholic Newspapers	John Huebscher	257-0004
Wisconsin State Journal	Phil Brinkman, Pat Simms	252-6145/252-6129
Radio and Television		
WIBA-AM and FM (Madison)	John Colbert	251-1978/274-2995
WISC-TV (Madison)	Colin Benedict	277-5246
WKOW-TV (Madison)	Steve Jandacek	273-2727
WMTV-TV (Madison)	Ryan Lobenstein	274-1500
WNWC-FM (Madison)	Christie McKittrick, Mike Powers	271-1025
WOLX-FM (Madison)	Adam Elliot	826-0077
WTDY-AM (Madison)	Robin Colbert, Tim Morrissey, Rich Schuh	271-1301
Wisconsin Public Radio	Shawn Johnson, Shamane Mills, Connie Walker	265-4358/263-7985
Wisconsin Radio Network	Andrew Beckett, Dale Forbis, Bob Hague, Jackie Johnson	251-3900
Wisconsin Public Television	Kathy Bissen, Frederica Freyberg, Art Hackett, Andy Moore	263-2121/263-8496/ 263-8585/263-5628/ 265-6646
Internet News Service		
Wisconsin Eye (wiseye.org)	Jeff Roberts	255-1000
Wispolitics.com	Greg Bump, Jeff Mayers, Mike Schramm	441-8418

Sources: Assembly Sergeant at Arms and information from various news organizations.

HOW A BILL BECOMES A LAW

The legislature decides policy by passing bills. A bill must pass both houses of the legislature and be signed by the governor before it becomes law. Other proposals introduced in the legislature also support the body's policy making function. Joint resolutions, which must pass both houses, may propose constitutional amendments, develop a session schedule, or modify the rules that govern both houses. They do not require the governor's signature. Simple resolutions, which are adopted by only one house, may organize the house at the beginning of the session, propose changes to house rules, or ask the attorney general for a legal opinion on a bill.

Introducing a Bill. A bill that proposes to make a change in current law will amend, create, repeal, renumber, renumber and amend, or repeal and recreate one or more sections of the *Wisconsin Statutes*. After the Legislative Reference Bureau drafts a bill, it is ready for introduction in one of the legislative houses. Each measure must go through regular procedures and be passed by the house of origin before it can go to the other house, where the process is repeated.

No one but individual legislators or legislative committees may introduce a bill. However, the statutes direct the Joint Committee on Finance to introduce the governor's executive budget bill without change. The legislator who introduces a bill is its "author"; others in the house of origin who support the bill may sign on as "coauthors". The measure may also list "cosponsors" from the second house.

When passing laws, legislators act as the representatives of the people. Therefore, the constitution requires that every bill introduced in the legislature begin with the words: "The people of the state of Wisconsin, represented in senate and assembly, do enact as follows:".

Fiscal Estimates and Bill Analyses. Fiscal estimates put a price tag on legislation. In 1953, Wisconsin pioneered fiscal estimates, often called "fiscal notes", and many other states have copied this important legislative tool. Every measure that increases or decreases state or general local government revenues or expenditures must be accompanied by a reliable estimate of its short-range and long-range fiscal effects. Agencies that would ultimately administer the proposed program or be affected by the measure, should it be enacted, prepare most fiscal notes. In the highly technical area of public retirement systems, the Joint Survey Committee on Retirement Systems prepares fiscal estimates with the assistance of research staff. In these cases, the note must evaluate not only the fiscal effect of a proposal but also its legality under state and federal law and its desirability as a matter of public policy.

Since 1967, the Legislative Reference Bureau has prepared an analysis of each bill introduced in the legislature, explaining in plain language the existing law and how it will change if the bill becomes law. The analysis is printed in the bill immediately following the title. As a general rule, analyses are not updated to reflect amendments approved during the legislative process, so they usually describe only the content of the bill at introduction.

Introduction, First Reading, and Referral to Committee. A bill is introduced when the chief clerk of the author's house assigns it a number and records the introduction for the house journal. Traditionally, the "first reading" took place when the clerk read that part of the proposal's title known as the "relating clause" – the clause that briefly describes the subject matter of the bill, e.g., "relating to the powers and duties of state traffic patrol officers and motor vehicle inspectors" when the house was meeting. In recent times, the clerk usually distributes a report showing the numbers and relating clauses of proposals offered for introduction which takes the place of an actual reading. After first reading, the presiding officer usually refers the proposal to the appropriate standing committee for review. Generally bills that appropriate money, provide for revenue, or relate to taxation are referred to the Joint Committee on Finance before they can be enacted into law.

Committee Hearings. All committee proceedings are open to the general public. Neither assembly nor senate rules require a chairperson to schedule a hearing. If a hearing is held, anyone may speak to the committee to support or oppose a measure or merely to present information to the committee without taking a position. Persons may also register for or against a proposal or submit written comments or petitions without making an oral presentation.

Committees do not keep verbatim transcripts of their hearings, but they do maintain appearance records listing persons who testify or register at the hearing, together with any printed information

Representative Tamara Grigsby, who began her first term in the Assembly in 2005, addresses her colleagues. (Brent Nicastro, Assembly Photographer)

those parties submit relative to bills and resolutions before the committee. Records for the current legislative session are filed in the office of the committee chairperson. Copies of appearance records for prior sessions, beginning with the 1951 session, are filed in the Legislative Reference Bureau.

The chairperson of a committee decides whether or not to take action on a particular proposal. If the decision is to act, the chairperson will call an "executive session" of the committee. In the session, committee members discuss the bill and may ask questions of persons in attendance, but no further public testimony is taken. At the close of the executive session, the committee decides whether to recommend passage of the bill as originally introduced, passage with amendments, or rejection. If the result is a tie vote, the committee can report the bill without recommendation. A committee's decision is contained in a brief report to the house. (Bills that receive a negative recommendation are almost never reported to the floor.)

The following is an example of a committee report to the senate from the *Senate Journal,* May 18, 2005:

The Committee on **Veterans, Homeland Security, Military Affairs, Small Business and Government Reform** reports and recommends:

Senate Bill 126

Relating to: changing the requirements for the publication of city and village ordinances.

Introduction of Senate Amendment 1 to Senate Substitute Amendment 1.

Ayes, 4 – Senators Brown, Zien, Kanavas and Breske.

Noes, 1 – Senator Wirch.

Adoption of Senate Amendment 1 to Senate Substitute Amendment 1.

Ayes, 4 – Senators Brown, Zien, Kanavas and Breske.

Noes, 1 – Senator Wirch.

Adoption of Senate Substitute Amendment 1.

Ayes, 3 – Senators Brown, Zien and Kanavas.

Noes, 2 – Senators Breske and Wirch.

Passage as amended.

Ayes, 3 – Senators Brown, Zien and Kanavas.

Noes, 2 – Senators Breske and Wirch.

Ronald Brown

Chairperson

Committee chairpersons determine the scheduling of committee hearings. A committee is allowed a reasonable period of time to consider matters referred to it. A majority of the members of the assembly may withdraw a bill not reported by an assembly committee 21 days after the date of referral by motion or petition. In the senate, a majority may vote to withdraw a bill from a committee at any time but not during the 7 days preceding any scheduled committee hearing nor the 7 days following the date on which the hearing was held. In both houses, when an attempt is unsuccessful, all subsequent motions to withdraw the same proposal require at least a two-thirds vote of the members. In practice, bills are very rarely withdrawn from committees without a committee report.

Scheduling Debate. Both the senate and assembly make use of a daily calendar to schedule proposals for consideration. In the 2005 Legislature, all proposals reported by senate standing committees are referred to the Committee on Senate Organization; in the assembly, they are referred to the Committee on Rules. These committees schedule business for floor debate.

Parliamentary Procedure. The rules of parliamentary procedure, which are guides for each house, facilitate the legislative process and are printed in pamphlets, titled "Senate Rules" and "Assembly Rules". Each house may create new rules and amend or repeal its current rules by passage of a simple resolution. "Joint Rules" deal with the relations between the houses and with administrative proceedings common to both. Changes in joint rules require the passage of a joint resolution.

Parliamentary process may seem unduly cumbersome to the onlooker, but it helps the houses operate in an organized fashion. The process is designed to protect the minority in its right to be

Representative Jean Hundertmark exchanges views with colleague Representative Dan Meyer on the floor of the Assembly. (Jay Salvo, Assembly Photographer)

heard and to promote careful deliberation and orderly consideration of all legislation. For particularly difficult procedural questions, the presiding officer of each house has access to such standard sources as *Mason's Manual of Legislative Procedure, Jefferson's Manual,* and *Rulings of the Chair.*

Second Reading. Once a bill is scheduled for house action, the clerk gives it a second reading by title. The purpose of a second reading is to consider amendments. An amendment may be a "simple" amendment, which makes changes within the bill, or a "substitute amendment", which completely replaces the original bill. Members may offer, debate, and vote upon amendments at any time prior to a vote to "engross" the measure and read it a third time. Engrossment of a bill incorporates all adopted amendments and all approved technical corrections into a proposal in its house of origin. The rules of both houses require a formal delay after the proposal is engrossed, which gives legislators time to reconsider the issues raised by the bill. In many cases, however, the rules are suspended by unanimous consent or a two-thirds vote so that second and third readings can occur on the same legislative day.

Third Reading. The purpose of the third reading is to make a final decision on a proposal itself. After a third reading, the proposal is put to the house for a vote with the following questions: "This bill having been read 3 separate times, the question is, 'Shall the bill pass?'" (for the senate) or "Shall the bill be passed?" (for the assembly). Members can debate the bill's contents at this point, but it is not subject to amendment. When all members finish speaking they vote. A bill may pass on a voice vote, unless a roll call vote is required by the state constitution, by law or legislative rule, or by request of a prescribed number of members.

Action in the Second House. If the bill passes, it is "messaged" (sent) to the other house, where it goes through substantially the same procedure as in the first house. In the second house, however, the bill may be referred directly to the daily calendar without referral to a standing committee. When the second house concurs in the bill, whether with or without additional amendments, the measure is messaged back to the house of origin.

If the second house amends the bill before concurring, the house of origin must vote upon those amendments. If the original house rejects amendments or further amends the bill, the resulting proposal may be sent back to the second house or to a conference committee made up of members representing both houses, where attempts are made to iron out the differences between the 2 versions. The compromise version, drawn up by the conference committee, cannot be amended in either house when it is brought to a vote. When both houses have agreed on identical wording of a bill, the Legislative Reference Bureau "enrolls" it in its final form, incorporating any amendments and corrections approved by both houses, and the measure is forwarded for the governor's signature.

On average about 1,600 bills were introduced in each of the past 10 legislatures, but only about 20% of those passed. Bills fail for many reasons: the house of origin may vote to "indefinitely postpone" or "table" a bill and then never take it up again; the second house may vote to "nonconcur" or may concur but with amendments unacceptable to the house of origin; or the proposal may "die in committee" and never be reported back to the house. An unsuccessful proposal does not carry over to the following legislature. A member must reintroduce it as a new bill.

Action of the Governor. The governor has 6 days (excluding Sundays) in which to act on the bill by: 1) signing it, in which case it becomes law; 2) vetoing it in whole or, if an appropriation bill, in part; or 3) failing to sign it within 6 days, in which case it becomes law without the governor's signature. Partial veto of words or numbers within a bill is permitted in the case of bills which contain an appropriation. If the governor signs the bill but vetoes part of it, the portion not vetoed becomes law.

Bills are not sent to the office of the governor immediately following passage but are presented when the governor calls for them. The legislative session schedule, however, provides deadlines after each floorperiod when all bills not yet called for must be sent to the governor. It also provides a specific floorperiod for final legislative review of the governor's vetoes.

If the governor vetoes a bill, in whole or part, the vetoed parts must be returned to the house of origin with the governor's written objections. A vetoed bill or part of a bill can become law despite the governor's objections, but it requires a two-thirds vote in each house to override the veto. If either house fails to muster the sufficient number of votes, the governor's veto is sustained, and the vetoed bill or portion dies.

Session Laws. Each new law is numbered as a Wisconsin Act, based on the year of the legislative session and its order of enactment, e.g., 2005 Wisconsin Act 1. The date of enactment is the date the governor approves the act, the date it becomes a law without the governor's signature, or the date the legislature votes to override the governor's veto. The secretary of state assigns the new law a date of publication. On or before that date, copies of the act in pamphlet form, called a "slip law", must be available for public distribution. The secretary of state must publish the act's number, title, and original bill number within 10 working days after the date of enactment in the newspaper designated as the official state paper for publication of legal notices (currently the *Wisconsin State Journal*). The notice contains the date of enactment and date of publication and states the act is available for public distribution. The act takes effect the day after its assigned publication date, unless another effective date is specified in the law itself.

Ultimately, the Legislative Reference Bureau combines all the laws enacted during the biennium into bound volumes, called "Wisconsin Session Laws". The Revisor of Statutes Bureau incorporates any portions of these laws that make changes in the statutes into the edition of the "Wisconsin Statutes" dated for that legislative biennium. Thus, the edition identified as the *2003-2004 Wisconsin Statutes* includes all statutory changes resulting from laws enacted by the 2003 Legislature.

The Budget Bill. The budget bill is the longest and most complex bill of the session. Because Wisconsin's budget covers a 2-year period from July 1 of one odd-numbered year through June 30 of the next, its development involves a chain of events stretching over almost a year. In the fall of every even-numbered year, state agencies must submit funding requests to the Department of Administration. Their funding requests include estimates of the cost of existing services over the next 2 years and may propose changes they hope are made in their programs. The Department of Administration's state budget office then compiles the data for review by the governor or governor-elect. While developing the budget, the governor may hold a hearing on any department's budget request to get additional input.

State law requires the governor to deliver the budget message to the new legislature on or before the last Tuesday in January, although the legislature may extend the deadline at the governor's request. The state budget report and the biennial executive budget bill or bills accompany the message.

In the legislature, the Joint Committee on Finance holds hearings on the departmental requests and governor's program initiatives. When these are completed, it reports the budget bill to the house of the legislature in which it was introduced. The committee's report takes the form of a substitute amendment. The bill then follows the normal legislative procedure through both houses of the legislature and is submitted for the governor's approval. The governor may sign the budget bill, veto it in its entirety (which would be unlikely), or use partial vetoes, as is usually the case. To meet the state's budgetary cycle, the new budget law should be effective by July 1 of the odd-numbered year, but there sometimes is a delay of several days, or even weeks or months, during which state agencies continue to operate at their levels of appropriation from the preceding budget.

Further Reading. The preceding section has provided a brief description of how a bill becomes a law in Wisconsin. In practice, legislative procedure is more complex than explained here. The feature article from the *1993-1994 Wisconsin Blue Book* contains a more detailed description and uses a case study approach to further illustrate the legislative process. It may be accessed via the *Wisconsin Blue Book* link on the Legislative Reference Bureau's Web site: www.legis.state.wi.us/lrb/pubs

EXECUTIVE VETOES, 1931 – 2003 SESSIONS

| Session | Bills Vetoed in Entirety | | | Bills Partially Vetoed | | | Partial Vetoes Contained in Biennial Budget Bills | |
	Number Vetoed	Vetoes Sustained	Vetoes Overridden	Number Partially Vetoed	All Partial Vetoes Sustained	One or More Partial Vetoes Overridden	Number of Partial Vetoes[1]	Vetoes Overridden
1931	38	38	—	2	2	—	12	0
1933	15	15	—	1	1	—	12	0
1935	27	27	—	4	4	—	0	0
1937	10	10	—	1	1	—	0	0
1939	22[2]	22	—	4	4	—	1	0
1941	17	17	—	1	1	—	1	0
1943	39	19	20	1	—	1	0	0
1945	31	26	5	2	1	1	1	0
1947	10	9	1	1	1	—	4	0
1949	17	15	2	2	1	1	0	0
1951	18	18	—	—	—	—	0	0
1953	31	28	3	4[3]	4	—	2	0
1955	38	38	—	—	—	—	0	0
1957	35	34	1	3	3	—	2	0
1959	36	32	4	1	1	—	0	0
1961	69	67	2	3	3	—	2	0
1963	72	68	4	1	1	—	0	0
1965	24	23	1	4	4	—	1	0
1967	18	18	—	5	5	—	0	0
1969	34	33	1	11	11	—	27	0
1971	32	29	3	8	8	—	12	0
1973	13	13	—	18	15	3	38	2
1975	37	31	6	22	18	4	42	5
1977	21	17	4	16	13	3	67	21
1979	19	16	3	9	7	2	45	1
1981	11	9	2	11	10	1	121[4]	0
1983	3	3	—	11	10	1	70	6
1985	7	7	—	7	6	1	78	2
1987	38	38	—	20	20	—	290	0
1989	35	35	—	28	28	—	203	0
1991	33	33	—	13	13	—	457	0
1993	8	8	—	24	24	—	78	0
1995	4	4	—	21	21	—	112	0
1997	3	3	—	8	8	—	152	0
1999	5	5	—	9	9	—	255	0
2001	—	—	—	3	3	—	315	0
2003	54	54	—	10	10	--	131	0

Note: The legislature is not required to act on vetoes. Any veto not acted upon is counted as sustained, including pocket vetoes. "Vetoes sustained" includes the following pocket vetoes: 1937 (5); 1941 (13); 1943 (4); 1951 (14); 1955 (10); 1957 (1); 1973 (1). A "pocket veto" resulted if the governor took no action on a bill after the legislature had adjourned *sine die*. (*Sine die*, from the Latin for "without a day", means the legislature adjourns without setting a date to reconvene.) With this type of adjournment, the legislature concluded all its business for the biennium, and there was no opportunity for it to sustain or override the veto (see Article V, Section 10, *Wisconsin Constitution*). Under current legislative session schedules, in which the legislature usually adjourns on the final day of its existence, just hours before the newly elected legislature is seated, the pocket veto is unlikely.

[1]As listed in each veto message by the governor.

[2]Attorney general ruled veto of 1939 SB-43 was void and it became law (see Vol. 28, *Opinions of the Attorney General*, p. 423).

[3]1953 AB-141, partially vetoed in two separate sections by separate veto messages, is counted as one.

[4]Attorney general ruled several vetoes "ineffective" because the governor failed to express his objections (see Vol. 70, *Opinions of the Attorney General*, p. 189).

Source: Compiled by Wisconsin Legislative Reference Bureau from the *Bulletin of the Proceedings of the Wisconsin Legislature* and the Assembly and Senate *Journals*.

2005-2006 LEGISLATIVE SERVICE

The complete 2005-2006 Legislative Service consists of 6 parts, which may be ordered by subscription from the Document Sales office:

Bills, resolutions, and amendments (complete text of each as introduced).

Acts are the laws enacted in bill form by the legislature and signed by the governor or passed over the governor's veto. The acts are distributed separately as "slip laws".

Journals are a daily record of the business conducted in each house, but they are not verbatim accounts. The service provides preliminary editions of the journals (published on the morning after the legislative day on yellow paper for senate journals and green paper for assembly journals) and the final corrected editions (printed on white paper and distributed two or three weeks later).

The **Bulletin of Proceedings** contains a numerical listing of all bills and other measures introduced in each house of the legislature and a cumulative record of actions taken on each. It includes a subject index to all measures introduced and to all acts, a list of proposals introduced by each legislator, and a numerical listing of statutory sections affected by acts and enrolled bills. It is issued as needed during the biennial session.

The **Weekly Schedule of Committee Activities** lists the time and place of legislative committee hearings for the coming week and advanced notices for hearings on issues of special interest.

Administrative Rules lists the administrative rules submitted by executive branch agencies by clearinghouse rule number. It includes a subject index, a list of agency contacts, and a cumulative record of actions taken on each proposal.

To obtain all or part of the legislative service, contact Document Sales, Wisconsin Department of Administration, 202 S. Thornton Avenue, P.O. Box 7840, Madison 53707-7840 or call (608) 266-3358, TTY (608) 264-8499, or (800) 362-7253 for an order form. Any part may be ordered separately. Prepayment is required on all orders. Faxed orders are accepted at (608) 281-8150 when paying with a credit card. Subscribers receive their documents through the mail. All subscriptions to the 2005-2006 Legislative Service will expire on December 31, 2006.

SERVICE	Interdepartmental Delivery*	United Parcel Service (UPS) and U.S. Postal Service*
Complete service, including daily calendars	$500	$845
Bills, resolutions, and amendments	160	335
Acts (slip laws)	20	85
Journals	55	145
Bulletin of Proceedings	200	350
Weekly Schedule of Committee Activities . . .	15	85
Administrative Rules	65	95

*All sales are subject to the 5% state sales tax, 0.5% county sales tax, and 0.1% stadium tax, where applicable.

Assistant Minority Leader Jon Richards (left) discusses the upcoming Assembly floor session with Majority Caucus Chairperson Dan Vrakas. (Jay Salvo, Assembly Photographer)

POLITICAL COMPOSITION OF THE WISCONSIN LEGISLATURE 1885 – 2005

Legislative Session[1]	Senate							Assembly						
	D	R	P	S	SD	M[3]	Vacant	D	R	P	S	SD	M[4]	Vacant
1885	13	20	—	—	—	—	—	39	61	—	—	—	—	—
1887	6	25	—	—	—	2	—	30	57	—	—	—	13	—
1889	6	24	—	—	—	3	—	29	71	—	—	—	—	—
1891	19	14	—	—	—	—	—	66	33	—	—	—	1	—
1893	26	7	—	—	—	—	—	56	44	—	—	—	—	—
1895	13	20	—	—	—	—	—	19	81	—	—	—	—	—
1897	4	29	—	—	—	—	—	8	91	—	—	—	1	—
1899	2	31	—	—	—	—	—	19	81	—	—	—	—	—
1901	2	31	—	—	—	—	—	18	82	—	—	—	—	—
1903	3	30	—	—	—	—	—	25	75	—	—	—	—	—
1905	4	28	—	—	1	—	—	11	85	—	—	4	—	—
1907	5	27	—	—	1	—	—	19	76	—	—	5	—	—
1909	4	28	—	—	1	—	—	17	80	—	—	3	—	—
1911	4	27	—	—	2	—	—	29	59	—	—	12	—	—
1913	9	23	—	—	1	—	—	37	57	—	—	6	—	—
1915	11	21	—	—	1	—	—	29	63	—	—	8	—	—
1917	6	24	—	3	—	—	—	14	79	—	7	—	—	—
1919	2	27	—	4	—	—	—	5	79	—	16	—	—	—
1921	2	27	—	4	—	—	—	2	92	—	6	—	—	—
1923	—	30	—	3	—	—	—	1	89	—	10	—	—	—
1925	—	30	—	3	—	—	—	1	92	—	7	—	—	—
1927	—	31	—	2	—	—	—	3	89	—	8	—	—	—
1929	—	31	—	2	—	—	—	6	90	—	3	—	1	—
1931	1	30	—	2	—	—	—	2	89	—	9	—	—	—
1933	9	23	—	1	—	—	—	59	13	24	3	—	1	—
1935	13	6	14	—	—	—	—	35	17	45	3	—	—	—
1937	9	8	16	—	—	—	—	31	21	46	2	—	—	—
1939	6	16	11	—	—	—	—	15	53	32	—	—	—	—
1941	3	24	6	—	—	—	—	15	60	25	—	—	—	—
1943	4	23	6	—	—	—	—	14	73	13	—	—	—	—
1945	6	22	5	—	—	—	—	19	75	6	—	—	—	—
1947	5	27	1	—	—	—	—	11	88	—	—	—	—	1
1949	3	27	—	—	—	—	3	26	74	—	—	—	—	—
1951	7	26	—	—	—	—	—	24	75	—	—	—	—	1
1953	7	26	—	—	—	—	—	25	75	—	—	—	—	—
1955	8	24	—	—	—	1	—	36	64	—	—	—	—	—
1957	10	23	—	—	—	—	—	33	67	—	—	—	—	—
1959	12	20	—	—	—	1	—	55	45	—	—	—	—	—
1961	13	20	—	—	—	—	—	45	55	—	—	—	—	—
1963	11	22	—	—	—	—	—	46	53	—	—	—	—	1
1965	12	20	—	—	—	1	—	52	48	—	—	—	—	—
1967	12	21	—	—	—	—	—	47	53	—	—	—	—	—
1969	10	23	—	—	—	—	—	48	52	—	—	—	—	—
1971	12	20	—	—	—	—	1	67	33	—	—	—	—	—
1973	15	18	—	—	—	—	—	62	37	—	—	—	—	—
1975	18	13	—	—	—	—	2	63	36	—	—	—	—	—
1977	23	10	—	—	—	—	—	66	33	—	—	—	—	—
1979	21	10	—	—	—	—	2	60	39	—	—	—	—	—
1981	19	14	—	—	—	—	—	59	39	—	—	—	—	1
1983	17	14	—	—	—	—	2	59	40	—	—	—	—	—
1985	19	14	—	—	—	—	—	52	47	—	—	—	—	—
1987	19	11	—	—	—	—	3	54	45	—	—	—	—	—
1989	20	13	—	—	—	—	—	56	43	—	—	—	—	—
1991	19	14	—	—	—	—	—	58	41	—	—	—	—	—
1993[2] ...	15	15	—	—	—	—	3	52	47	—	—	—	—	—
1995[2] ...	16	17	—	—	—	—	—	48	51	—	—	—	—	—
1997[2] ...	17	16	—	—	—	—	—	47	52	—	—	—	—	—
1999	17	16	—	—	—	—	—	44	55	—	—	—	—	—
2001	18	15	—	—	—	—	—	43	56	—	—	—	—	—
2003	15	18	—	—	—	—	—	41	58	—	—	—	—	—
2005	14	19	—	—	—	—	—	39	60	—	—	—	—	—

Note: The number of assembly districts was reduced from 100 to 99 beginning in 1973.

Key: Democrat (D); Progressive (P); Republican (R); Socialist (S); Social Democrat (SD); Miscellaneous (M).

[1]Political composition at inauguration.

[2]In the 1993, 1995, and 1997 Legislatures, majority control of the senate shifted during the session. On 4/20/93, vacancies were filled resulting in a total of 16 Democrats and 17 Republicans; on 6/16/96, there were 17 Democrats and 16 Republicans; and on 4/19/98, there were 16 Democrats and 17 Republicans.

[3]Miscellaneous = one Independent and one People's (1887); one Independent and 2 Union Labor (1889).

[4]Miscellaneous = 3 Independent, 4 Independent Democrat, and 6 People's (1887); one Union Labor (1891); one Fusion (1897); one Independent (1929); one Independent Republican (1933).

Sources: Pre-1943 data is taken from the Secretary of State, *Officers of Wisconsin: U.S., State, Judicial, Congressional, Legislative and County Officers,* 1943 and earlier editions, and the *Wisconsin Blue Book,* various editions. Later data compiled from Wisconsin Legislative Reference Bureau sources.

Senator Fred Risser and Representative Marlin Schneider have served a combined 82 years in the Wisconsin Legislature. Senator Risser was first elected in 1956 and is the longest serving legislator in Wisconsin history. Representative Schneider, first elected in 1970, is the longest serving member of the Wisconsin Assembly in state history. (Brent Nicastro, Assembly Photographer)

STATUTES, SESSION LAWS, AND ADMINISTRATIVE CODE

Printed Materials

The printed state documents listed below are available from Document Sales, 202 S. Thornton Avenue, P.O. Box 7840, Madison 53707-7840; telephone (608) 266-3358; TTY (608) 264-8499.

Prices listed do not reflect 5% state sales tax and, where applicable, 0.5% county sales tax and/or 0.1% stadium tax. Taxes must be included with payment. Prepayment is required for all orders. Make check or money order payable to Wisconsin Department of Administration. For MasterCard or Visa orders, call (608) 264-9419 or (800) 362-7253.

Wisconsin Statutes 2003-2004:

Hardcover 5-volume set – $146 (picked up); $152 (shipped)

Softcover 5-volume set – $124 (picked up); $130 (shipped)

2003 Laws of Wisconsin: Hardcover 2-volume set – $32.30 (picked up); $35.75 (shipped)

Wisconsin Administrative Code, including loose-leaf *Administrative Register.* Subscriptions are available for the entire code or individual code books. Contact Document Sales at (608) 266-3358 for current pricing information.

Machine-Readable Data

WisLaw, the computer-searchable CD-ROM, contains the Wisconsin Statutes and Annotations, plus the Wisconsin and U.S. Constitutions, Supreme Court Rules, Wisconsin Acts, recent Opinions of the Attorney General, the Administrative Code and Register, executive orders, town law forms, and the Wisconsin Code of Military Justice.

WisLaw is continuously updated and is available only by annual subscription. (The number of CD updates released in any 12-month period may vary.) The CD will only be delivered upon receipt of a signed end-user license, subscription form, and full payment. Subscription forms and *WisLaw* end-user license are available at Document Sales (see address above) or through the Revisor of Statutes Bureau home page at **http://www.legis.state.wi.us/rsb/**

Sources: Wisconsin Department of Administration, Document Sales, and Revisor of Statutes Bureau.

STANDING COMMITTEES
OF THE 2005 WISCONSIN LEGISLATURE

All standing committees of the 2005 Wisconsin Legislature are described in this section. The standing committees of the senate are created by the Committee on Senate Organization while standing committees of the assembly are enumerated in Assembly Rule 9. In the case of each standing committee listed below, the names of committee officers are followed by those of the majority party and minority party, separated by a semicolon. An * indicates the ranking minority member.

SENATE STANDING COMMITTEES

Administrative Rules — GROTHMAN, *chairperson;* STEPP, REYNOLDS; JAUCH*, MILLER.

Agriculture and Insurance — KAPANKE, *chairperson;* KEDZIE, BROWN, OLSEN; ERPENBACH*, HANSEN, MILLER.

Audit — ROESSLER, *chairperson;* COWLES, S. FITZGERALD; MILLER*, LASSA.

Campaign Finance Reform and Ethics — ELLIS, *chairperson;* LASEE, KEDZIE; RISSER*, MILLER.

Education — OLSEN, *chairperson;* DARLING, HARSDORF, GROTHMAN; JAUCH*, ERPENBACH, HANSEN.

Energy, Utilities, and Information Technology — COWLES, *chairperson;* LEIBHAM, KAPANKE; PLALE*, WIRCH.

Finance — S. FITZGERALD, *chairperson;* LAZICH, COWLES, DARLING, LEIBHAM, OLSEN; DECKER*, TAYLOR.

Health, Children, Families, Aging and Long Term Care — ROESSLER, *chairperson;* DARLING, BROWN; ERPENBACH*, CARPENTER.

Higher Education and Tourism — HARSDORF, *chairperson;* KEDZIE, KAPANKE; BRESKE*, PLALE.

Housing and Financial Institutions — STEPP, *chairperson;* HARSDORF, BROWN, REYNOLDS; PLALE*, LASSA, COGGS.

Job Creation, Economic Development and Consumer Affairs — KANAVAS, *chairperson;* ZIEN, REYNOLDS; LASSA*, DECKER.

Judiciary, Corrections and Privacy — ZIEN, *chairperson;* ROESSLER, GROTHMAN; COGGS* (resigned 4/1/05), RISSER* (appointed 4/1/05), TAYLOR.

Labor and Election Process Reform — REYNOLDS, *chairperson;* LAZICH, KANAVAS; HANSEN*, CARPENTER.

Natural Resources and Transportation — KEDZIE, *chairperson;* STEPP, KAPANKE; WIRCH*, BRESKE.

Senate Organization — SCHULTZ, *chairperson;* A. LASEE, KEDZIE; ROBSON*, HANSEN.

State and Federal Relations — ELLIS, *chairperson;* A. LASEE, SCHULTZ; RISSER*, CARPENTER.

Veterans, Homeland Security, Military Affairs, Small Business and Government Reform — BROWN, *chairperson;* ZIEN, KANAVAS; BRESKE*, WIRCH.

ASSEMBLY STANDING COMMITTEES

Administrative Rules — GOTTLIEB, *chairperson;* LeMAHIEU, *vice chairperson;* FRISKE; SCHNEIDER*, BLACK.

Aging and Long-Term Care — TOWNSEND, *chairperson;* HINES, *vice chairperson;* PETTIS, LeMAHIEU, NISCHKE, STRACHOTA; KRUSICK*, VRUWINK, POPE-ROBERTS, PARISI.

Agriculture — OTT, *chairperson;* NERISON, *vice chairperson;* AINSWORTH, PETROWSKI, KESTELL (resigned 1/28/05), HINES (appointed 1/28/05), SUDER, M. WILLIAMS, LOEFFELHOLZ, TOWNS; GRONEMUS*, VRUWINK, ZIEGELBAUER, SINICKI, MOLEPSKI, PARISI.

Assembly Organization — GARD, *chairperson;* HUEBSCH, *vice chairperson;* FREESE, J. FITZGERALD, VRAKAS; KREUSER*, RICHARDS, TURNER.

Audit — JESKEWITZ, *chairperson;* KAUFERT, *vice chairperson;* KERKMAN; TRAVIS*, CULLEN.

Budget Review — KERKMAN, *chairperson;* GUNDERSON, *vice chairperson;* ALBERS, PRIDEMORE; PARISI*, BERCEAU.

Campaigns and Elections — FREESE, *chairperson;* GUNDRUM, *vice chairperson;* WOOD, VOS; TRAVIS*, KESSLER.

Children and Families — KESTELL, *chairperson;* VOS, *vice chairperson;* ALBERS, JESKEWITZ, VUKMIR; GRIGSBY*, SINICKI, SEIDEL.

Colleges and Universities — KREIBICH, *chairperson;* BALLWEG, *vice chairperson;* UNDERHEIM, NASS, JESKEWITZ, TOWNS, LAMB; SHILLING*, SCHNEIDER, BLACK, BOYLE, MOLEPSKE.

Corrections and the Courts — BIES, *chairperson;* GUNDRUM, *vice chairperson;* UNDERHEIM, OWENS, SUDER, LeMAHIEU; POPE-ROBERTS*, WASSERMAN, SEIDEL, PARISI.

Criminal Justice and Homeland Security — SUDER, *chairperson;* FRISKE, *vice chairperson;* OWENS, F. LASEE, JESKEWITZ, GUNDRUM, VUKMIR; TURNER*, KRUSICK, BLACK, KESSLER, GRIGSBY.

Economic Development — MCCORMICK, *chairperson;* LAMB, *vice chairperson;* LOEFFELHOLZ, NISCHKE, LOTHIAN, HONADEL; FIELDS*, STEINBRINK, TOLES.

Education — TOWNS, *chairperson;* KESTELL, *vice chairperson;* NASS, HUNDERTMARK, TOWNSEND, HINES, DAVIS; LEHMAN*, A. WILLIAMS, ZIEGELBAUER, POPE-ROBERTS, VAN AKKEREN.

Education Reform — VUKMIR, *chairperson;* NASS, *vice chairperson;* TOWNS, WOOD, NISCHKE, PRIDEMORE; SINICKI*, A. WILLIAMS, LEHMAN.

Employment Relations — GARD (speaker), *chairperson;* HUEBSCH (majority leader), KAUFERT (cochair, Joint Committee on Finance), KREUSER* (minority leader).

Energy and Utilities — MONTGOMERY, *chairperson;* DAVIS, *vice chairperson;* HAHN, GOTTLIEB, NISCHKE, HONADEL, NERISON; TRAVIS*, STASKUNAS, STEINBRINK, ZEPNICK.

Family Law — OWENS, *chairperson;* KESTELL, *vice chairperson;* ALBERS, BALLWEG; CULLEN*, KRUSICK.

Representative Sheldon Wasserman, one of two physicians in the legislature, testifies on behalf of his bill to create enhanced licensing requirements for drivers over the age of 75. (Brent Nicastro, Assembly Photographer)

Finance — KAUFERT, *chairperson;* WARD, *vice chairperson;* JENSEN, STONE, RHOADES, MEYER; COLÓN*, POCAN.

Financial Institutions — HUNDERTMARK, *chairperson;* LAMB, *vice chairperson;* FREESE, KREIBICH, WIECKERT, TOWNSEND, J. FITZGERALD, VOS, KLEEFISCH; RICHARDS*, SHERMAN, SHILLING, ZEPNICK, MOLEPSKE, FIELDS.

Forestry — FRISKE, *chairperson;* MURSAU, *vice chairperson;* AINSWORTH, M. WILLIAMS; HUBLER*, BOYLE.

Government Operations and Spending Limitations — F. LASEE, *chairperson;* MUSSER, *vice chairperson;* LOEFFELHOLZ, VOS; ZEPNICK*, ZIEGELBAUER.

Health — UNDERHEIM, *chairperson;* VUKMIR, *vice chairperson;* GIELOW, WIECKERT, KRAWCZYK, HUNDERTMARK, STRACHOTA, MOULTON; WASSERMAN*, SHILLING, VRUWINK, BENEDICT, NELSON.

Highway Safety — PETROWSKI, *chairperson;* BIES, *vice chairperson;* AINSWORTH, VAN ROY, MUSSER; YOUNG*, SHILLING, COLÓN.

Housing — WIECKERT, *chairperson;* TOWNSEND, *vice chairperson;* KREIBICH, MONTGOMERY; A. WILLIAMS*, YOUNG.

Insurance — NISCHKE, *chairperson;* WIECKERT, *vice chairperson;* UNDERHEIM, MONTGOMERY, MCCORMICK, GIELOW, VAN ROY, BALLWEG, MOULTON; CULLEN*, LEHMAN, STASKUNAS, BERCEAU, NELSON, SHERIDAN.

Judiciary — GUNDRUM, *chairperson;* MCCORMICK, *vice chairperson;* ALBERS, KERKMAN, KLEEFISCH; STASKUNAS*, TURNER, KESSLER.

Labor — NASS, *chairperson;* VRAKAS, *vice chairperson;* J. FITZGERALD, WIECKERT, HUNDERTMARK, VOS; VAN AKKEREN*, SINICKI, SHERIDAN.

Medicaid Reform — GIELOW, *chairperson;* STRACHOTA, *vice chairperson;* HUNDERTMARK, VUKMIR, DAVIS, VOS; BENEDICT*, WASSERMAN, POPE-ROBERTS.

Military Affairs — MUSSER, *chairperson;* PETTIS, *vice chairperson;* PETROWSKI, TOWNSEND, LOEFFELHOLZ; SCHNEIDER*, BOYLE, SINICKI.

Natural Resources — GUNDERSON, *chairperson;* MOULTON, *vice chairperson;* OTT, PETTIS, BIES, KRAWCZYK, M. WILLIAMS, PETROWSKI, MURSAU; BLACK*, GRONEMUS, STEINBRINK, VAN AKKEREN, MOLEPSKE, HEBL.

Property Rights and Land Management — ALBERS, *chairperson;* NASS, *vice chairperson;* MUSSER, WOOD; HEBL*, STASKUNAS.

Public Health — HINES, *chairperson;* UNDERHEIM, *vice chairperson;* TOWNSEND, FREESE, MCCORMICK; WASSERMAN*, GRIGSBY, BENEDICT.

Rules — HUEBSCH, *chairperson;* GARD, *vice chairperson;* FREESE, J. FITZGERALD, VRAKAS, GOTTLIEB, OWENS; TRAVIS*, TURNER, KREUSER, RICHARDS, SHERMAN.

Rural Affairs and Renewable Energy — HAHN, *chairperson;* M. WILLIAMS, *vice chairperson;* NERISON, FREESE, ALBERS, BALLWEG; VRUWINK*, SCHNEIDER, BENEDICT.

Rural Development — M. WILLIAMS, *chairperson;* SUDER, *vice chairperson;* OTT, KESTELL, MURSAU; NELSON*, GRONEMUS, BLACK.

Small Business — VAN ROY, *chairperson;* HONADEL, *vice chairperson;* M. WILLIAMS, BALLWEG, MURSAU; SHERIDAN*, FIELDS, HEBL.

Southeast Wisconsin Freeways — HONADEL, *chairperson;* GOTTLIEB, *vice chairperson;* KERKMAN, STRACHOTA; ZEPNICK*, CULLEN.

State Affairs — J. FITZGERALD, *chairperson;* KLEEFISCH, *vice chairperson;* MUSSER, GUNDRUM, KRAWCZYK, PETROWSKI; TOLES*, YOUNG, BENEDICT.

State-Federal Relations — LOTHIAN, *chairperson;* KERKMAN, *vice chairperson;* MONTGOMERY, KLEEFISCH; KESSLER*, ZEPNICK.

Tourism — PETTIS, *chairperson;* MURSAU, *vice chairperson;* GUNDERSON, HINES, VAN ROY, MOULTON, NERISON; ZIEGELBAUER*, YOUNG, VAN AKKEREN, SEIDEL, GRIGSBY.

Transportation — AINSWORTH, *chairperson;* PETROWSKI, *vice chairperson;* HAHN, SUDER, FRISKE, OTT, LAMB, VAN ROY, DAVIS; STEINBRINK*, GRONEMUS, SHERMAN, VRUWINK, MOLEPSKE, NELSON.

When a bill is considered by a committee, the authors typically appear to explain the need for the legislation. Representatives Terry Moulton (left) and Dean Kaufert testified before the Committee on Insurance about their bill on health savings accounts in January 2005. (Jay Salvo, Assembly Photographer)

Urban and Local Affairs — LeMAHIEU, *chairperson;* PRIDEMORE, *vice chairperson;* GUNDERSON, LOTHIAN, GOTTLIEB; BERCEAU*, FIELDS, PARISI.

Veterans Affairs — LOEFFELHOLZ, *chairperson;* MUSSER, *vice chairperson;* TOWNSEND, HUNDERTMARK, BIES; SHERMAN*, TURNER, HUBLER.

Ways and Means — WOOD, *chairperson;* NASS, *vice chairperson;* HAHN, JESKEWITZ, KERKMAN, LOTHIAN, STRACHOTA, PRIDEMORE; BERCEAU*, ZIEGELBAUER, TOLES, HEBL, FIELDS.

Workforce Development — KRAWCZYK, *chairperson;* LOTHIAN, *vice chairperson;* VRAKAS, KREIBICH, WOOD, GIELOW, PRIDEMORE; SEIDEL*, LEHMAN, TOLES, SHERIDAN.

PERSONAL DATA ON WISCONSIN LEGISLATORS
1995 – 2005 Sessions

	1995 Sen.	1995 Rep.	1997 Sen.	1997 Rep.	1999 Sen.	1999 Rep.	2001 Sen.	2001 Rep.	2003 Sen.	2003 Rep.	2005 Sen.	2005 Rep.
Party affiliation												
Democrat	16	48	17	47	17	44	18	43	15	41	14	39
Republican	17	51	16	52	16	55	15	56	18	58	19	60
Number with previous legislative service												
In senate	32	0	32	0	30	0	30	0	27	0	28	0
In assembly	21	87	23	89	23	78	24	89	22	84	23	81
Highest number of prior sessions in same house	16	12	17	13	18	14	19	15	20	16	21	17
Occupations												
Full-time legislator	12	40	14	38	14	38	15	40	13	39	11	39
Attorney	6	10	6	11	5	10	5	10	3	8	2	11
Farmer	1	14	0	15	1	12	1	13	3	9	3	10
Other	14	35	13	35	13	39	13	33	15	45	17	41
Education												
High school only	2	15	2	15	2	12	2	13	4	12	4	9
Beyond high school	31	84	31	84	31	87	31	86	29	87	29	90
Bachelor's or associate degree	27	66	28	66	26	67	28	67	25	65	26	70
Advanced degree	8	26	9	30	8	29	8	31	8	32	8	34
Number with experience on local governing body												
County board	2	22	3	21	4	19	4	18	4	19	4	18
Municipal board	8	24	6	29	6	31	5	36	8	35	10	28
Age												
Oldest	67	69	69	71	71	69	73	71	75	75	77	77
Youngest	31	26	33	28	35	27	37	26	33	27	34	28
Average	48	45	48	46	50	46	52	47	51	49	52	50
Veterans	6	14	5	14	4	14	4	15	4	12	4	14
Marital status												
Single	5	28	4	25	6	23	5	23	5	17	10	25
Married	28	70	29	73	27	74	29	76	28	80	23	70
Widowed	0	1	0	1	0	2	0	0	0	2	0	4
Number of women	8	24	9	22	11	19	11	22	8	27	8	26

Sen. – Senators; Rep. – Representatives.

Note: Most data are recorded as of the date on which the legislature first convened; ages are determined as of January 1.

Sources: *Wisconsin Blue Book*, various issues, and data collected by the Wisconsin Legislative Reference Bureau, January 2005.

Legislators use committee hearings as a way to gain a deeper understanding of pending legislation. Here Senator Spencer Coggs poses a question to a witness. (Richard G. B. Hanson II, Senate Photographer)

JOINT LEGISLATIVE COMMITTEES AND COMMISSIONS

Joint committees and commissions are created by statute and include members from both houses. Two joint committees include nonlegislative members. Names of committee officers are followed by those of the majority and minority party, separated by a semicolon. The ranking minority member is indicated by an *. Commissions also include gubernatorial appointees and, in 2 cases, the governor. All telephone numbers that do not include an area code are Madison numbers, area code 608.

Joint Committee for Review of
ADMINISTRATIVE RULES

Members: SENATOR GROTHMAN, REPRESENTATIVE GOTTLIEB, *cochairpersons;* SENATORS STEPP, REYNOLDS; JAUCH*, MILLER; REPRESENTATIVES LeMAHIEU, FRISKE; SCHNEIDER*, BLACK.

Mailing Addresses: Senator Grothman, Room 20 South, State Capitol, P.O. Box 7882, Madison 53707-7882; Representative Gottlieb, Room 103 West, State Capitol, P.O. Box 8952, Madison 53708-8952.

Telephones: Senator Grothman, 266-7513; Representative Gottlieb, 267-2369.

E-mail: sen.grothman@legis.state.wi.us; rep.gottlieb@legis.state.wi.us

Statutory References: Sections 13.56, 227.19, 227.24, and 227.26.

Agency Responsibility: The Joint Committee for Review of Administrative Rules must review proposed rules when standing committees object to them. It also may suspend rules that have been promulgated; suspend or extend the effective period of all or part of emergency rules; and order an agency to put unwritten policies in rule form.

When a standing committee objects to a proposed rule or portion of a rule, it must be referred to the joint committee. The joint committee then has 30 days to review the rule, but that period may be extended for an additional 30 days. The joint committee may uphold or reverse the standing committee's action. If it concurs with the objection, it introduces bills concurrently in both houses to prevent promulgation of the rule. If either bill is enacted, the agency may not adopt the rule unless specifically authorized to do so by subsequent legislative action. If the joint committee disagrees with the objection, it may overrule the standing committee and allow the agency to adopt the rule or it may request the agency to modify the rule.

The joint committee may suspend a rule after holding a public hearing, but suspension must be based on one or more of the following reasons: absence of statutory authority; an emergency related to public health or welfare; failure to comply with legislative intent; conflict with existing state law; a change in circumstances since passage of the law that authorized the rule; or a rule that is arbitrary or capricious or imposes undue hardship. Within 30 days following the suspension, the committee must introduce bills concurrently in both houses to repeal the suspended rule. If either bill is enacted, the rule is repealed and the agency may not promulgate it again unless authorized by the legislature. If both bills fail to pass, the rule remains in effect and may not be suspended again.

The joint committee receives notice of any action in the circuit court of Dane County for declaratory judgments about the validity of a rule and may intervene in the action with the consent of the Joint Committee on Legislative Organization.

Organization: The joint committee consists of 5 senators and 5 representatives, and the membership from each house must include representatives of both the majority and minority parties.

History: The Joint Committee for Review of Administrative Rules was one of the first of its kind in the country, and it has served as a model widely copied by other states. Chapter 221, Laws of 1955, revised administrative rules procedures and created the committee with "advisory powers only". It could investigate complaints about rules and recommend changes to rule-making agencies but could not directly affect the rule-making process. In 1966, the committee received authority to suspend a rule based on testimony at a public hearing. With enactment of Chapter 34, Laws of 1979, the joint committee acquired the power to review proposed rules based on the objections of a legislative standing committee. Further modifications occurred when 1985 Wisconsin Act 182 authorized the joint committee to extend its 30-day review period and allowed it to negotiate with agencies to modify existing rules.

State of Wisconsin
BUILDING COMMISSION

Members: GOVERNOR DOYLE, *chairperson;* SENATORS ROESSLER, ZIEN; RISSER; REPRESENTATIVES J. FITZGERALD, VRAKAS; SHILLING; TERRY MCGUIRE (citizen member appointed by governor). Nonvoting advisory members from Department of Administration: MARC MAROTTA (departmental secretary), ADEL TABRIZI (chief engineer), DAVID HALEY (chief architect).

Secretary: ROBERT G. CRAMER, *administrator,* Division of Facilities Development, Department of Administration.

Mailing Address: P.O. Box 7866, Madison 53707-7866.

Location: 101 East Wilson Street, 7th Floor, Madison.

Telephone: 266-1855.

Fax: 267-2710.

Total Budget 2003-05: $20,479,100*.

*Total budget includes bond revenues, building trust fund expenditures, and debt service payments for state office buildings, the State Capitol, and the Executive Residence.

Statutory Reference: Section 13.48.

Agency Responsibility: The State of Wisconsin Building Commission coordinates the state building program and establishes long-range plans for development of the state's physical plant. The commission determines the projects to be incorporated into the long-range program and recommends a biennial building program to the legislature, including the amount to be appropriated in the biennial budget. It oversees all state construction, except highway development. In addition, the commission may authorize expenditures from the State Building Trust Fund for construction, remodeling, maintenance, and planning of future development. The commission is the only state body that can authorize the contracting of state debt. All transactions for the sale of instruments that result in a state debt liability must be approved by official resolution of the commission.

Organization: The 11-member commission includes 6 legislators. One legislator from each house must be a member of the legislature's State Supported Programs Study and Advisory Committee, and both the majority and minority parties in each house must be represented. Terms of legislative members expire on the second Wednesday in January of odd-numbered years. The citizen member serves at the pleasure of the governor.

History: The State of Wisconsin Building Commission was created by Chapter 563, Laws of 1949, to establish a long-range public building program. Another 1949 law (Chapter 604) gave the commission authority to organize the quasi-public Wisconsin State Public Building Corporation. This legal device, familiarly known as a "dummy building corporation", was used to finance public buildings to house state agencies because the Wisconsin Constitution prevented direct borrowing by the state for such projects. The quasi-public corporation was first used in 1925, when the University Building Corporation was developed to permit construction of revenue-producing facilities on the Madison campus, including dormitories and athletic buildings. The State Agencies Building Corporation, a similar entity, was formed in 1958 (Chapter 593, Laws of 1957) to finance nonrevenue-producing buildings, such as classroom facilities, and Chapter 267, Laws of 1961, extended the corporation's authority to the financing of public welfare buildings.

In 1969, voters amended the constitution, and the legislature passed Chapter 259, which provided for direct state borrowing and ended the use of the various building corporations. The law enlarged the powers of the commission to finance capital facilities for all state agencies.

A separate State Bond Board, including 4 members of the Building Commission, was established by Chapter 259 to supervise the contracting of state debt. Chapter 90, Laws of 1973, abolished the bond board and returned its duties and responsibilities to the Building Commission.

Joint Review Committee on
CRIMINAL PENALTIES

Members: SENATOR LEIBHAM, *chairperson;* SENATOR COGGS; 2 vacancies (representatives); PEGGY A. LAUTENSCHLAGER (attorney general); MATTHEW J. FRANK (secretary of corrections); NICHOLAS CHIARKAS (state public defender); DENNIS D. CONWAY, ROBERT PEKOWSKI (reserve judges appointed by supreme court); BRADLEY GEHRING, ALLAN KEHL (public members appointed by governor).

Mailing Address: Senator Leibham, Room 127 South, State Capitol, P.O. Box 7882, Madison 53707-7882.

Telephone: Senator Leibham, 266-2056.

E-mail: sen.leibham@legis.state.wi.us

Statutory Reference: Section 13.525.

Agency Responsibility: The Joint Review Committee on Criminal Penalties, created by 2001 Wisconsin Act 109, reviews any bill that creates a new crime or revises a penalty for an existing crime when requested to do so by a chairperson of a standing committee in the house of origin to which the bill was referred. The presiding officer in the house of origin may also request a report from the joint committee if the bill is not referred to a standing committee.

Committee reports on bills submitted for its review concern the costs or savings to public agencies; the consistency of proposed penalties with existing penalties; whether alternative language is needed to conform the proposed penalties to existing penalties; and whether any acts prohibited by the bill are already prohibited under existing law.

Once a report is requested for a bill, a standing committee may not vote on the bill and the house of origin may not pass the bill before the joint committee submits its report or before the 30th day after the request is made, whichever is earlier.

Once an Assembly committee reports favorably on a bill, the Assembly Rules Committee determines when or if it will go before the full Assembly. Traditionally, the Majority Leader chairs the committee – in this case, Representative Michael Huebsch. (Jay Salvo, Assembly Photographer)

Organization: Legislative members include one majority and one minority party member from each house. One reserve judge must reside somewhere within judicial administrative districts one through 5, and the other in districts 6 through 10. Public members must include an individual with law enforcement experience and one who is an elected county official.

Joint Committee on
EMPLOYMENT RELATIONS

Members: SENATOR A. LASEE (senate president), REPRESENTATIVE GARD (assembly speaker), *cochairpersons;* SENATORS SCHULTZ (majority leader), ROBSON (minority leader); REPRESENTATIVES HUEBSCH (majority leader), KREUSER (minority leader); SENATOR S. FITZGERALD, REPRESENTATIVE KAUFERT (joint finance committee cochairpersons).

Mailing Address: Legislative Council Staff, P.O. Box 2536, Madison 53701-2536.

Location: 1 East Main Street, Suite 401, Madison.

Telephone: 266-1304.

Statutory References: Sections 13.111, 20.923, and 230.12; Chapter 111, Subchapter V.

Agency Responsibility: The Joint Committee on Employment Relations approves all changes to the collective bargaining agreements that cover state employees represented by unions and the compensation plans for nonrepresented state employees. These plans and agreements include pay adjustments; fringe benefits; performance awards; pay equity adjustments; and other items related to wages, hours, and conditions of employment. The committee also approves the assignment of unclassified positions to the executive salary group ranges.

In the case of unionized employees, the Office of State Employment Relations submits tentative agreements negotiated between it and certified labor organizations to the committee. If the committee disapproves an agreement, it is returned to the bargaining parties for renegotiation.

The Office of State Employment Relations also submits the compensation plans for nonrepresented employees to the committee. One plan covers all nonrepresented classified employees and certain officials outside the classified service, including legislators, justices of the supreme court, court of appeals judges, circuit court judges, constitutional officers, district attorneys, heads of executive agencies, division administrators, and others designated by law. The faculty and academic staff of the UW System are covered by a separate pay plan, which is based on recommendations made by the UW Board of Regents.

After public hearings on the nonrepresented employee plans, the committee may modify the office's recommendations, but the committee's modifications are subject to the governor's veto. A veto may be overridden by the vote of 6 committee members.

When the committee approves an agreement for unionized employees, it introduces those portions requiring legislative approval in bill form and recommends passage without change. If the legislature fails to adopt the bill, the agreement is returned to the bargaining parties for renegotiation.

Organization: The committee, which was established by Chapter 270, Laws of 1971, is a permanent joint legislative committee comprised of 8 *ex officio* members. It is assisted in its work by the Legislative Council Staff and the Legislative Fiscal Bureau.

Joint Committee on
FINANCE

Members: SENATOR S. FITZGERALD, REPRESENTATIVE KAUFERT, *cochairpersons;* SENATORS LAZICH, DARLING, COWLES, LEIBHAM, OLSEN; DECKER*, TAYLOR; REPRESENTATIVES WARD, STONE, JENSEN, RHOADES, MEYER; POCAN*, COLÓN.

Mailing Addresses: Senator S. Fitzgerald, Room 317 East, State Capitol, P.O. Box 7882, Madison 53707-7882; Representative Kaufert, Room 308 East, State Capitol, P.O. Box 8952, Madison 53708-8952.

The Speaker is the highest ranking officer in the Assembly. As the leader of the majority party, he wields great influence over the procedural and policy agenda of the body. Speaker John Gard, who currently holds the position, presides over a floor session. (Jay Salvo, Assembly Photographer)

Telephones: Senator S. Fitzgerald, 266-5660; Representative Kaufert, 266-5719.

E-mail: sen.fitzgerald@legis.state.wi.us; rep.kaufert@legis.state.wi.us

Statutory References: Sections 13.09-13.11, 16.505, 16.515, and 20.865 (4).

Agency Responsibility: The Joint Committee on Finance examines all legislation that deals with state income and spending. It also gives final approval to a wide variety of state payments and assessments. Any bill introduced in the legislature that appropriates money, provides for revenue, or relates to taxation must be referred to the joint committee.

The joint committee introduces the biennial budget as recommended by the governor. After holding a series of public hearings and executive sessions, it submits its own version of the budget as a substitute amendment to the governor's budget bill for consideration by the legislature.

At regularly scheduled quarterly meetings, the joint committee considers agency requests to adjust their budgets. It may approve a request for emergency funds if it finds that the legislature has authorized the activities for which the appropriation is sought. It may also transfer funds between existing appropriations and change the number of positions authorized to an agency in the budget process.

When required, the joint committee introduces legislation to pay claims against the state, resolve shortages in funds, and restore capital reserve funds of the Wisconsin Housing and Economic Development Authority to the required level. As an emergency measure, it may reduce certain state agency appropriations when there is a decrease in state revenues.

The joint committee gives final approval for a variety of fiscal operations including: disposition of federal block grant funds and private gifts, grants, and bequests; changes in supplemental security income payment levels if approved by the governor; plans to deal with shortfalls in state agency fund accounts; disposition of oil overcharge funds; and expenditure plans for federal low-income assistance funds. In addition, the committee may inquire into the operations of any state agency for the purpose of improving agency efficiency.

Organization: The committee is a joint standing committee composed of the 8 senators on the Senate Finance Committee and the 8 representatives on the Assembly Finance Committee. It generally includes members of the majority and minority party in each house. Cochairpersons of the joint committee are appointed in the same manner as are standing committees of their respective houses.

History: The use of a joint standing committee to consider appropriation bills dates back to 1857 when the legislature created the Joint Committee on Claims. In 1911 (Chapter 6), the Joint Committee on Finance replaced the claims committee and was given the responsibility to consider all bills related to revenue and taxation. Chapter 609, Laws of 1915, authorized the governor, secretary of state, and state treasurer to approve emergency appropriations when the legislature was not in session to permit departments with insufficient funds to carry out their normal duties. Chapter 97, Laws of 1929, transferred this function to a new Emergency Board, which consisted of the governor and the cochairpersons of the joint finance committee. The power to approve supplemental appropriations, transfer funds between appropriations, and handle other interim fiscal matters was given to a joint legislative committee called the Board on Government Operations (BOGO) by Chapter 228, Laws of 1959. BOGO's functions were transferred to the Joint Committee on Finance by Chapter 39, Laws of 1975.

Joint Committee on
INFORMATION POLICY AND TECHNOLOGY

Members: Inactive.

Statutory Reference: Section 13.58.

Agency Responsibility: The Joint Committee on Information Policy and Technology reviews information management practices of state and local units of government to ensure economic and efficient service, maintain data security and integrity, and protect the privacy of individuals who are subjects of the databases. It studies the effects of proposals by the state to expand existing information technology or implement new technologies. With concurrence of the Joint Committee on Finance, it may direct the Department of Administration to report on any information technology system project that could cost $1 million or more in the current or succeeding biennium. The committee may direct the Department of Administration to prepare reports or conduct studies and may make recommendations to the governor, the legislature, state agencies, or local governments based on this information. The committee is composed of 3 majority and 2 minority party members from each house of the legislature. It was created by 1991 Wisconsin Act 317 and its membership was revised by 1999 Wisconsin Act 9.

Joint
LEGISLATIVE AUDIT COMMITTEE

Members: SENATOR ROESSLER, REPRESENTATIVE JESKEWITZ, *cochairpersons;* SENATOR S. FITZGERALD, REPRESENTATIVE KAUFERT (joint finance committee cochairpersons); SENATORS COWLES; MILLER*, LASSA; REPRESENTATIVES KERKMAN; TRAVIS*, CULLEN.

Mailing Addresses: Senator Roessler, Room 8 South, State Capitol, P.O. Box 7882, Madison 53707-7882; Representative Jeskewitz, Room 314 North, State Capitol, P.O. Box 8952, Madison 53708-8952.

Telephones: Senator Roessler, 266-5300; Representative Jeskewitz, 266-3796.

E-mail: sen.roessler@legis.state.wi.us; rep.jeskewitz@legis.state.wi.us

Statutory Reference: Section 13.53.

Agency Responsibility: The Joint Legislative Audit Committee, which was created by Chapter 224, Laws of 1975, advises the Legislative Audit Bureau, subject to general supervision of the Joint Committee on Legislative Organization. Its members include the cochairpersons of the Joint Committee on Finance, plus 2 majority and 2 minority party members from each house of the legislature. The committee evaluates candidates for the office of state auditor and makes recommendations to the Joint Committee on Legislative Organization, which selects the auditor.

The committee may direct the state auditor to undertake specific audits and review requests for special audits from individual legislators or standing committees, but no legislator or standing committee may interfere with the auditor in the conduct of an audit.

The committee reviews each report of the Legislative Audit Bureau and then confers with the state auditor, other legislative committees, and the audited agencies on the report's findings. It may propose corrective action and direct that followup reports be submitted to it.

The committee may hold hearings on audit reports, ask the Joint Committee on Legislative Organization to investigate any matter within the scope of the audit, and request investigation of any matter relative to the fiscal and performance responsibilities of a state agency. If an audit report cites financial deficiencies, the head of the agency must report to the Joint Legislative Audit Committee on remedial actions taken. Should the agency head fail to report, the committee may refer the matter to the Joint Committee on Legislative Organization and the appropriate standing committees.

When the committee determines that legislative action is needed, it may refer the necessary information to the legislature or a standing committee. It can also request information from a committee on action taken or seek advice of a standing committee on program portions of an audit. The committee may introduce legislation to address issues covered in audit reports.

Members of the Legislature sometimes invite outside experts to inform them on a particular issue. In this photo, members of the Senate Republican leadership hear from a Colorado authority discussing TABOR, the taxpayer bill of rights. (Richard G. B. Hanson II, Senate Photographer)

JOINT LEGISLATIVE COUNCIL

Members: SENATOR A. LASEE (senate president), REPRESENTATIVE WIECKERT (designated by assembly speaker), *cochairpersons;* SENATORS ZIEN (president pro tempore), SCHULTZ (majority leader), ROBSON (minority leader), S. FITZGERALD (cochairperson, Joint Committee on Finance), DECKER (ranking minority member, Joint Committee on Finance), BROWN, GROTHMAN, KAPANKE, MILLER, RISSER; REPRESENTATIVES GARD (assembly speaker), FREESE (speaker pro tempore), HUEBSCH (majority leader), KREUSER (minority leader), KAUFERT (cochairperson, Joint Committee on Finance), POCAN (ranking minority member, Joint Committee on Finance), AINSWORTH, NISCHKE, SCHNEIDER, TRAVIS. (Members designated by title serve *ex officio.*)

Director of Legislative Council Staff: TERRY C. ANDERSON, terry.anderson@legis.state.wi.us

Deputy Director: LAURA D. ROSE, laura.rose@legis.state.wi.us

Legislative Council Rules Clearinghouse: RONALD SKLANSKY, *director,* ronald.sklansky@legis.state.wi.us; RICHARD SWEET, *assistant director,* richard.sweet@legis.state.wi.us

Mailing Address: P.O. Box 2536, Madison 53701-2536.

Location: 1 East Main Street, Suite 401, Madison.

Telephone: 266-1304.

Fax: 266-3830.

Internet Address: http://www.legis.state.wi.us/lc

Publications: General Report of the Joint Legislative Council to the Legislature; State Agency Staff Members With Responsibilities Related to the Legislature; Wisconsin Legislator Briefing Book; Directory of Joint Legislative Council Committees; rules clearinghouse reports; staff briefs; information memoranda on substantive issues considered by council committees; staff memoranda; amendment and act memoranda.

Number of Employees: 35.17.

Total Budget 2003-05: $6,945,000.

Statutory References: Sections 13.81-13.83, 13.91, and 227.15.

Agency Responsibility: The Joint Legislative Council creates special committees made up of legislators and interested citizens to study various problems of state and local government. Study topics are selected from requests presented to the council by law, joint resolution, individual legislators, and others. After research and public hearings, the study committees draft proposals and submit them to the council, which must approve those drafts it wants introduced in the legislature as council bills.

The council is assisted in its work by the Legislative Council Staff, a bureau created in Section 13.91, Wisconsin Statutes. The staff also provides legal counsel and scientific and policy research assistance to all of the legislature's substantive standing committees and joint statutory committees (except the Joint Committee on Finance) and assists individual legislators on request. The staff operates the rules clearinghouse to review proposed administrative rules and assists standing committees in their oversight of rulemaking.

By law, the Legislative Council Staff must be "strictly nonpartisan" and must observe the confidential nature of the research and drafting requests received by it. The law requires that state agencies and local governmental units cooperate fully with the council staff in its carrying out of its statutory duties.

Organization: The council consists of 22 legislators. The majority of them serve *ex officio*, and the remainder are appointed as are members of standing committees. The president of the senate and the speaker of the assembly serve as cochairpersons of the council, but each may designate another member to assume that office. The council operates two permanent statutory committees and various special committees appointed to study selected subjects. The Legislative Council Staff director is appointed from outside the classified service by the Joint Committee on Legislative Organization, and the director makes staff appointments from outside the service.

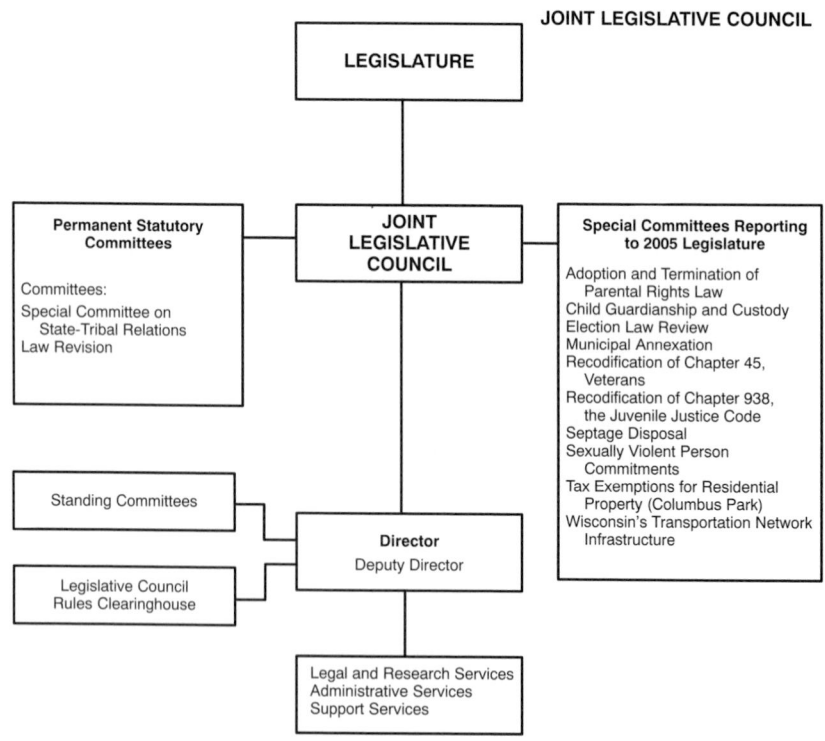

JOINT LEGISLATIVE COUNCIL

LEGISLATURE

JOINT LEGISLATIVE COUNCIL

Permanent Statutory Committees

Committees:
Special Committee on
    State-Tribal Relations
Law Revision

Special Committees Reporting to 2005 Legislature

Adoption and Termination of
    Parental Rights Law
Child Guardianship and Custody
Election Law Review
Municipal Annexation
Recodification of Chapter 45,
    Veterans
Recodification of Chapter 938,
    the Juvenile Justice Code
Septage Disposal
Sexually Violent Person
    Commitments
Tax Exemptions for Residential
    Property (Columbus Park)
Wisconsin's Transportation Network
    Infrastructure

Standing Committees

Director
Deputy Director

Legislative Council
Rules Clearinghouse

Legal and Research Services
Administrative Services
Support Services

History: Chapter 444, Laws of 1947, created the council to conduct interim studies on subjects affecting the general welfare of the state. The first council was organized later that year with 12 members. In 1967, the council began to appoint staff members to provide legal counsel and technical assistance to legislative standing committees. The 1979 executive budget (Chapter 34) assigned the administrative rules clearinghouse function to the council. 1993 Wisconsin Act 52 made a number of reorganizational changes. The act renamed the council the Joint Legislative Council and designated the president of the senate and the speaker of the assembly (or their designees) cochairpersons. Under Act 52, the council was directed to reorganize at the beginning of the biennial session, instead of May 1 of the odd-numbered year, and its support agency was officially named the Legislative Council Staff.

PERMANENT STATUTORY COMMITTEES

Special Committee on State-Tribal Relations

Members: REPRESENTATIVE MUSSER, *chairperson;* SENATORS BROWN, COGGS, ZIEN; REPRESENTATIVES BIES, McCORMICK, PETTIS, SHERMAN; DONNA LYNK (Bad River Band of Lake Superior Tribe of Chippewa Indians), LOUIS TAYLOR (Lac Courte Oreilles Band of Lake Superior Chippewa Indians), CAROL BROWN (Lac du Flambeau Band of Lake Superior Chippewa Indians), MARK MONTANO (Red Cliff Band of Lake Superior Chippewas), HOWARD J. BICHLER (St. Croix Band of Chippewa Indians), JON F. GREENDEER (Ho-Chunk Nation), GARY BESAW (Menominee Indian Tribe of Wisconsin), VINCE DELA ROSA (Oneida Tribe of Indians of Wisconsin), JOHN ALLOWAY (Forest County Potawatomi Community), DOUGLAS HUCK (Stockbridge-Munsee Community, Mohican Nation).

The Special Committee on State-Tribal Relations is appointed by the Joint Legislative Council each biennium to study issues related to American Indians and the Indian tribes and bands in this state and develop specific recommendations and legislative proposals relating to such issues. Legislative membership includes not fewer than 6 nor more than 12 members with at least one member of the majority and the minority party from each house. The council appoints no fewer than 6 and no more than 11 members from names submitted by federally recognized Wisconsin Indian tribes or bands or the Great Lakes Inter-Tribal Council. The council may not appoint more than one member recommended by any one tribe or band or the Great Lakes Inter-Tribal Council. Chapter 39, Laws of 1975, created the committee as the American Indian Study Committee, and 1999 Wisconsin Act 60 renamed it and revised the membership. The committee's composition and duties are prescribed in Section 13.83 (3) of the statutes.

. . .Technical Advisory Committee

Members: JIM WEBER (Department of Health and Family Services), MAURA WHELAN (Department of Justice), MICHAEL LUTZ (Department of Natural Resources), J.P. LEARY (Department of Public Instruction), TOM OURADA (Department of Revenue), REGGIE NEWSON (Department of Transportation), RACHELLE ASHLEY (Department of Workforce Development).

Under Section 13.83 (3) (f), Wisconsin Statutes, as created by Chapter 39, Laws of 1975, the Technical Advisory Committee, consisting of representatives of 7 major executive agencies, assists the Special Committee on State-Tribal Relations.

Law Revision Committee

Members: SENATOR GROTHMAN, REPRESENTATIVE SUDER, *cochairpersons;* SENATORS CARPENTER, KEDZIE, RISSER; REPRESENTATIVE HUBLER.

The Law Revision Committee is appointed each biennium by the Joint Legislative Council. The membership of the committee is not specified, but it must include majority and minority party representation from each house. The committee reviews minor nonsubstantive remedial changes to the statutes as proposed by state agencies, in attorney general's opinions, or in court decisions declaring a Wisconsin statute unconstitutional, ambiguous, or otherwise in need of revision. It considers proposals by the Revisor of Statutes to correct statutory language and session laws that conflict or need revision, and it may submit recommendations for major law revision projects to the Joint Legislative Council. It serves as the repository for interstate compacts and agreements and makes recommendations to the legislature regarding revision of such agreements. The committee was created by Chapter 204, Laws of 1979, and its composition and duties are prescribed in Section 13.83 (1) of the statutes.

SPECIAL COMMITTEES REPORTING IN 2005

Special Committee on Adoption and Termination of Parental Rights Law

Members: REPRESENTATIVE JESKEWITZ, *chairperson;* SENATORS PLALE, REYNOLDS; REPRESENTATIVES KESTELL, SINICKI; SUSAN DREYFUS, JOSEPH EHMANN, CHRISTOPHER R. FOLEY, STEPHEN W. HAYES, PATRICK KENNEY, MARY JANE PROFT, JODI TIMMERMAN.

The special committee is directed to study current law relating to adoption and termination of parental rights (TPR) to determine whether modifications should be made to encourage adoptions in Wisconsin and to make the adoption and TPR processes more efficient and more cost effective. The committee shall consider creating a state tax credit for adoption expenses. The committee shall also study TPR and adoption in the context of the child welfare system to ensure compliance with federal law and to ensure that permanency is achieved for children as quickly as possible.

Special Committee on Child Guardianship and Custody

Members: SENATOR A. LASEE, *chairperson;* SENATOR JAUCH; REPRESENTATIVES ALBERS, NASS, NISCHKE, WOOD, ZIEGELBAUER; ROSEMARY ALBRECHT, THOMAS P. DONEGAN, SANDRA CARDO GORSUCH, MARY KASPAREK, BETTY KLUG, PATTI SEGER.

The special committee is directed to examine current state laws regarding guardianship of minors, the rights and responsibilities of guardians, and to develop proposed legislation to clarify and improve current guardianship laws. The committee will also review the provisions of the Uniform Child Custody Jurisdiction and Enforcement Act which has been proposed by the National Conference of Commissioners on Uniform State Laws, and determine whether the state should replace the 1968 Uniform Child Custody Jurisdiction Act with the Uniform Child Custody Jurisdiction and Enforcement Act.

Representatives Mark Gundrum (left) and Mark Pettis offer testimony on pending legislation before a committee. (Jay Salvo, Assembly Photographer)

Special Committee on Election Law Review

Members: SENATOR LEIBHAM, *chairperson;* SENATOR ERPENBACH; REPRESENTATIVES FREESE, SCHNEIDER, WIECKERT; MARILYN K. BHEND, JOYCE BUECHEL, JANICE DUNN, CINDI HESSE, KEVIN J. KENNEDY, KATHY NICKOLAUS, JAMES TROUPIS, MIKE WITTENWYLER.

The special committee is directed to examine the election process and the administration of elections in the state, other than campaign financing law. The special committee shall specifically examine the implementation of the federal Help America Vote Act of 2002, state oversight of elections in Wisconsin, and the recount process. The special committee may also examine other election-related issues such as voter registration and identification, new technologies for voting, the adequacy of staffing at polling places, and the adequacy of training received by poll workers.

Special Committee on Municipal Annexation

Members: SENATOR A. LASEE, *chairperson;* SENATOR BROWN; REPRESENTATIVES GOTTLIEB, KAUFERT, KERKMAN, ZEPNICK; ROGER W. CLARK, GERALD DERR, CHRISTINE JONES, PAT KASTER, WARREN P. KRAFT, J. MICHAEL MOONEY, MIKE PARMENTIER.

The special committee is directed to review conflicts that arise under current annexation law and practice and the consequences of those conflicts, including costs to taxpayers and other affected parties; and to determine if there is consensus on the means to reduce annexation disputes and encourage more boundary cooperation between towns and cities or villages, and to make related recommendations.

Special Committee on Recodification of Chapter 45, Veterans

Members: REPRESENTATIVE TOWNSEND, *chairperson;* SENATORS BRESKE, BROWN, S. FITZGERALD; REPRESENTATIVES KRAWCZYK, LOEFFELHOLZ, MUSSER, SCHNEIDER; KENNETH BROWN, ANTHONY HARDIE, JOHN O'BRIEN, LARRY OLSON, TIM THIERS, KENNETH WENDT.

The special committee is directed to conduct a recodification of Chapter 45, Wisconsin Statutes, relating to veterans, to include reorganizing the chapter in a logical manner, renumbering and retitling sections, consolidating related provisions, modernizing language, resolving ambiguities in language, making other necessary organizational changes, and making minor substantive changes.

Special Committee on Recodification of Chapter 938, the Juvenile Justice Code

Members: REPRESENTATIVE SUDER, *chairperson;* SENATORS JAUCH, ZIEN; REPRESENTATIVES BIES, KERKMAN, OWENS, SCHNEIDER; DAVID L. BOROWSKI, DON GARBER, GINA PRUSKI, TOM SCHLEITWILER.

The special committee is directed to conduct a study of the recodification of Chapter 938, Wisconsin Statutes, relating to the Juvenile Justice Code, to include a study of the possible reorganization of certain parts of the chapter to fit in a logical manner with the rest of the chapter, renumbering and retitling of certain sections and subsections, consolidating related provisions, modernizing language, resolving ambiguities in language, codifying court decisions, and making minor substantive changes.

Special Committee on Septage Disposal

Members: REPRESENTATIVE AINSWORTH, *chairperson;* SENATORS JAUCH, KEDZIE; REPRESENTATIVES OTT, STEINBRINK; SANDRA BEGALKE, BERNARD DEFLORIAN, RANDY RENON, WALLY THOM.

The special committee is directed to examine the current capacity and future need for disposal of septage that is pumped from septic tanks and holding tanks, to review the laws related to this subject, and to develop proposed legislation that will assure protection of public health and the environment, as well as the availability of disposal options for future population and business growth.

Floor debate is one point in the legislative process when the minority party can make its viewpoint known. Here Assistant Minority Leader Dave Hansen (seated) discusses strategy with Senator Jon Erpenbach. (Richard G. B. Hanson II, Senate Photographer)

Special Committee on Sexually Violent Person Commitments

Members: SENATOR DARLING, *chairperson;* SENATORS LAZICH, PLALE; REPRESENTATIVES GUNDRUM, STASKUNAS, STONE; REBECCA DALLET, MIKE NOFZINGER, RICHARD J. SANKOVITZ, SALLY TESS.

The special committee is directed to study current law relating to the commitment, periodic reexamination, supervised release, and discharge of sexually violent persons.

Special Committee on Tax Exemptions for Residential Property (Columbus Park)

Members: REPRESENTATIVE J. FITZGERALD, *chairperson;* SENATORS LASSA, STEPP; REPRESENTATIVES BERCEAU, GOTTLIEB, NISCHKE, VUKMIR; GREGG HAGOPIAN, PAUL HOFFMAN, ROBERT JONES, FREDERIC E. MOHS, TIMOTHY J. RADELET, MARY REAVEY, FRITZ RUF, JOHN SAUER, EARL R. THAYER.

The special committee is directed to study issues surrounding the property tax exemption for property leased as residential housing, including: 1) the impact of *Columbus Park Housing v. City of Kenosha*, 267 Wis. 2d 59 (2003), on the exemption; 2) the effect of the exemption on municipalities, property taxpayers, residents of tax-exempt housing, the availability of financing for development of low-income housing, and benevolent activities of tax-exempt organizations; and 3) any other issues the committee considers relevant. The committee shall develop and recommend legislation relating to these issues as it finds appropriate.

Special Committee on Wisconsin's Transportation Network Infrastructure

Members: SENATOR KANAVAS, *chairperson;* SENATORS LEIBHAM, RISSER; REPRESENTATIVES LEMAHIEU, STONE, TOWNSEND, VAN ROY, ZEPNICK; BOB COOK, GEOFF CROWLEY, GEORGE GROSSARDT, JOHN KREILKAMP, PAUL OLSEN, JEROME THIELE, PETER J. THILLMAN, TOM WALKER.

The special committee is directed to examine Wisconsin's transportation network infrastructure, especially the infrastructure for the transportation modes of railroads, seaports, and air, to determine ways to improve these facilities; to encourage intermodal forms of transportation; and to encourage regional cooperation among Midwestern states in improving freight and passenger transportation to increase efficiency and to alleviate highway congestion.

Joint Committee on
LEGISLATIVE ORGANIZATION

Members: SENATOR A. LASEE (senate president), REPRESENTATIVE GARD (assembly speaker), *cochairpersons;* SENATORS SCHULTZ (majority leader), ROBSON (minority leader), KEDZIE (assistant majority leader), HANSEN (assistant minority leader); REPRESENTATIVES HUEBSCH (majority leader), KREUSER (minority leader), J. FITZGERALD (assistant majority leader), RICHARDS (assistant minority leader).

Mailing Address: Legislative Council Staff, P.O. Box 2536, Madison 53701-2536.

Location: 1 East Main Street, Suite 401, Madison.

Telephone: 266-1304.

Statutory References: Sections 13.80 and 13.90.

Agency Responsibility: The Joint Committee on Legislative Organization is the policy-making body for the legislative service bureaus: the Legislative Audit Bureau, the Legislative Fiscal Bureau, the Legislative Reference Bureau, the Legislative Technology Services Bureau, and the Revisor of Statutes Bureau. In this capacity, it assigns tasks to each bureau, approves bureau budgets, and sets the salary of bureau heads. The joint committee selects the five bureau heads, but it acts on the recommendation of the Joint Legislative Audit Committee when appointing the state auditor. The joint committee also selects the director of the Legislative Council Staff.

The committee may inquire into misconduct by members and employees of the legislature. It oversees a variety of operations, including computer use, space allocation for legislative offices and legislative service agencies, parking on the State Capitol Park grounds, and sale and distribution of legislative documents. The joint committee recommends which newspaper should serve as the official state newspaper for publication of state legal notices. It advises the Ethics Board on its operations and, upon recommendation of the Joint Legislative Audit Committee, may investigate any problems the Legislative Audit Bureau finds during its audits. The committee may employ outside consultants to study ways to improve legislative staff services and organization.

Organization: The 10-member joint committee is a permanent body, consisting of the presiding officers and party leadership of both houses. The committee has established a Subcommittee on Legislative Services to advise it on text processing and other matters. The Legislative Council Staff provides staff assistance to the committee.

History: The joint committee was created by Chapter 149, Laws of 1963, as part of a legislative reorganization proposed by the Committee on Legislative Organization and Procedure under the authority of Chapter 686, Laws of 1961. The 1963 law also transferred the Legislative Reference

Bureau and the Statutory Revision Bureau to the legislative branch and placed them under the supervision of the joint committee. The three other service agencies were placed under the committee's authority by later legislation: the Legislative Audit Bureau in Chapter 659, Laws of 1965; the Legislative Fiscal Bureau in Chapter 215, Laws of 1971; and the Legislative Technology Services Bureau in 1997 Wisconsin Act 27.

In 1966, the joint committee was empowered to investigate misconduct by legislators and legislative staff. Actions by subsequent legislatures expanded the joint committee's supervision of legislative operations to include legislative office space, legislative computer operations, and publication of notices and documents.

Joint Survey Committee on
RETIREMENT SYSTEMS

Members: SENATOR GROTHMAN, REPRESENTATIVE VRAKAS, *cochairpersons;* SENATORS STEPP; WIRCH; REPRESENTATIVES JESKEWITZ; HUBLER; JANE HAMBLEN (assistant attorney general appointed by attorney general), *secretary;* DAVID STELLA (designated by secretary of employee trust funds), JORGE GOMEZ (insurance commissioner); MICHAEL R. LUTTIG (public member appointed by governor).

Research Director: vacancy.

Mailing Address: Risser Justice Center, P.O. Box 8952, Madison 53708-8952.

Telephone: 267-0507.

Publications: A summary compilation of the committee's reports is issued at the end of each legislative session.

Number of Employees: 3.00.

Total Budget 2003-05: $365,200.

Statutory Reference: Section 13.50.

Agency Responsibility: The Joint Survey Committee on Retirement Systems makes recommendations on all legislation that affects retirement and pension plans for public officers and employees, and its recommendations must be attached as an appendix to each retirement bill. Neither house of the legislature may consider such a bill until the joint survey committee submits a written report that describes the proposal's purpose, probable costs, actuarial effect, and desirability as a matter of public policy.

Organization: The 10-member joint survey committee includes majority and minority party representation from each legislative house. An experienced actuary from the Office of the Commissioner of Insurance may be designated to serve in the commissioner's place on the committee. The public member cannot be a participant in any public retirement system in the state and is expected to "represent the interests of the taxpayers". Appointed members serve 4-year terms unless they lose the status upon which the appointment was based. The joint survey committee is authorized to employ a research director and staff under the classified service to assist it in developing its reports.

RETIREMENT RESEARCH COMMITTEE

Members: All members of the Joint Survey Committee on Retirement Systems including the same officers; vacancy (designated by director of the office of state human resources management); vacancy (representing state, county, and municipal employees); vacancy (representing State Teachers Retirement System); vacancy (representing Milwaukee Teachers Annuity and Retirement Fund); 3 vacancies (public members); vacancy (chief executive or member of governing body of a participating local government); vacancy (annuitant member serving on the Employee Trust Funds Board). (All, except *ex officio* members, are appointed by governor.)

Mailing Address: Risser Justice Center, P.O. Box 8952, Madison 53708-8952.

Telephone: 267-0507.

Publications: *Staff Report 83: 2000 Comparative Study of Major Public Employee Retirement Systems.*

Statutory Reference: Section 13.51.

Agency Responsibility: The Retirement Research Committee, originally named the Retirement Research Council, was created as a permanent study group by Chapter 375, Laws of 1959. The principal duty of the 19-member committee is to conduct an ongoing review of state retirement benefits and retirement programs. All administrators of public employee pension or retirement plans to which the state contributes must submit financial reports to the committee. The committee investigates and reports to the legislature on the status of public employee retirement systems. It also maintains a library of public employee pension and retirement plans from throughout the United States.

Organization: The officers and staff of the Joint Survey Committee on Retirement Systems serve the same functions for the Retirement Research Committee. Employee/employer representatives and public members are appointed for 4-year terms, unless they lose the status upon which the appointment is based.

Joint Legislative
STATE SUPPORTED PROGRAMS
STUDY AND ADVISORY COMMITTEE

Members: Inactive.

Statutory Reference: Section 13.47.

Agency Responsibility: Members of the Joint Legislative State Supported Programs Study and Advisory Committee visit and inspect the State Capitol and all institutions and office buildings

Senate Majority Leader Dale Schultz (left) and Speaker pro tempore of the Assembly Stephen Freese (right) hosted Minister President Roland Koch of the German state of Hessen in May 2005. (Jay Salvo, Assembly Photographer)

President pro tempore of the Senate David Zien (right) works with Senator Tim Carpenter in the Senate Chamber. (Richard G. B. Hanson II, Senate Photographer)

owned or leased by the state. They are granted free and full access to all parts of the buildings, the surrounding grounds, and all persons associated with the buildings. The committee may also examine any institution, program, or organization that receives direct or indirect state financial support.

Organization: The committee consists of 5 senators and 6 representatives. Members appointed from each house must represent the two major political parties, and one legislator from each house must also be a member of the State of Wisconsin Building Commission. Assistance to the committee is provided by the Legislative Council Staff.

History: The use of a legislative committee to visit and supervise the use of state institutions and property dates back to 1881. The current joint committee was created by Chapter 266, Laws of 1973. It replaced the Committee to Visit State Properties, which had combined the functions of the Committee to Visit State Institutions, created in 1947 to inspect state property and state institutions, and the Committee on Physical Plant Maintenance, created in 1957 to manage the State Capitol and the single state office building then in existence.

Joint Survey Committee on
TAX EXEMPTIONS

Members: SENATOR HARSDORF, REPRESENTATIVE MONTGOMERY, *cochairpersons;* SENATORS KANAVAS, JAUCH*; REPRESENTATIVES HAHN, HUBLER*; MICHAEL MORGAN (secretary of revenue); F. THOMAS CREERON (Department of Justice representative appointed by attorney general); KATHRYN DUNN (public member appointed by governor).

Mailing Address: Legislative Council Staff, P.O. Box 2536, Madison 53701-2536.

Telephone: 266-1304.

Statutory Reference: Section 13.52.

Agency Responsibility: The Joint Survey Committee on Tax Exemptions, created by Chapter 153, Laws of 1963, considers all legislation related to the exemption of persons or property from state or local taxes. It is assisted by the Legislative Council Staff.

Any legislative proposal that affects tax exemptions must be referred to the committee immediately upon introduction. Budget bills containing tax exemptions are referred simultaneously to the joint survey committee and the Joint Committee on Finance. The joint survey committee must report within 60 days on the tax exemptions contained within a budget bill. Neither house of the legislature may consider tax exemption proposals until the joint survey committee has issued its report, attached as an appendix to the bill, describing the proposal's legality, desirability as public policy, and fiscal effect. In the course of its review, the committee is authorized to conduct investigations, hold hearings, and subpoena witnesses.

Organization: The 9-member committee includes representation from each house of the legislature with 2 members from the majority party and one from the minority party. The public member must be familiar with the tax problems of local government. Members' terms expire on January 15 of odd-numbered years.

TRANSPORTATION PROJECTS COMMISSION

Members: GOVERNOR DOYLE, *chairperson;* SENATORS KEDZIE, A. LASEE, LEIBHAM, BRESKE, vacancy; REPRESENTATIVES AINSWORTH, MONTGOMERY, VRUWINK, 2 vacancies; LEE MEYERHOFER, MICHAEL RYAN, LEONARD SOBCZAK (citizen members appointed by governor). Nonvoting member: FRANK BUSALACCHI (secretary of transportation).

Commission Secretary: BARBARA JUREWICZ, barbara.jurewicz@dot.state.wi.us

Mailing Address: P.O. Box 7913, Madison 53707-7913.

Location: Hill Farms State Transportation Building, 4802 Sheboygan Avenue, Room 901, Madison.

Telephone: 266-5408.

Fax: 267-1856.

Statutory Reference: Section 13.489.

Agency Responsibility: The Transportation Projects Commission, created by 1983 Wisconsin Act 27, includes representation from each house of the legislature with 3 members from the majority party and 2 from the minority party. The commission reviews Department of Transportation recommendations for major highway projects. The department must report its recommendations to the commission by September 15 of each even-numbered year, and the commission, in turn, reports its recommendations to the governor or governor-elect, the legislature, and the Joint Committee on Finance before December 15 of each even-numbered year. The department must also provide the commission with a status report on major transportation projects every 6 months. The commission also approves the preparation of environmental impact or assessment statements for potential major highway projects.

Commission on
UNIFORM STATE LAWS

Members: JOANNE HUELSMAN, *chairperson;* REPRESENTATIVE CULLEN, *vice chairperson;* BRUCE MUNSON (revisor of statutes), *secretary;* SENATOR RISSER; REPRESENTATIVE GUNDRUM; PETER J. DYKMAN (designated by chief, Legislative Reference Bureau); vacancy (designated by director, Legislative Council Staff); ANN WALSH BRADLEY, WALTER KELLY (public members appointed by governor).

Mailing Address: 131 West Wilson Street, Suite 800, Madison 53703-3261.

Telephone: 266-2011.

Fax: 264-6978.

Statutory Reference: Section 13.55.

Agency Responsibility: The Commission on Uniform State Laws advises the legislature on uniform laws and model laws. It examines subjects on which interstate uniformity is desirable and the best methods for achieving it, cooperates with the National Conference of Commissioners on Uniform State Laws in preparing uniform acts, and prepares bills adapting the uniform acts to Wisconsin. The commission reports biennially to the Law Revision Committee of the Joint Legislative Council.

Organization: The commission consists of 9 members, including 2 public members appointed by the governor for 4-year terms. Legislative members serve 2-year terms, must represent the 2 major political parties, and must be state bar association members. A legislative seat that cannot be filled by a bar member may be filled by a former legislator.

History: The commission was originally created by Chapter 83, Laws of 1893, which authorized the governor to appoint 3 members to serve as the Commissioners for the Promotion of Uniformity of Legislation in the United States. In 1931, Chapter 67 designated the Revisor of Statutes as the sole Wisconsin commissioner. Chapter 173, Laws of 1941, added the chief of the Legislative Reference Library as a commissioner. The commission was created in its present form by Chapter 312, Laws of 1957, and its membership was expanded to include 2 members of the State Bar appointed by the governor. Chapter 135, Laws of 1959, added the director (then called the executive secretary) of the Legislative Council Staff as a member. Chapter 294, Laws of 1979, added 4 legislative members and deleted the requirement that public members appointed by the governor be members of the State Bar. 2003 Wisconsin Act 2 added a requirement that legislative members must be state bar association members.

LEGISLATIVE SERVICE AGENCIES

LEGISLATIVE AUDIT BUREAU

State Auditor: JANICE L. MUELLER, janice.mueller@

Deputy State Auditor: JACOB KLAM, jacob.klam@

Special Assistant to the State Auditor: JOE CHRISMAN, james.chrisman@

Audit Directors: DIANN L. ALLSEN, diann.allsen@; DON BEZRUKI, don.bezruki@; JULIE GORDON, julie.gordon@; BRYAN NAAB, bryan.naab@; PAUL STUIBER, paul.stuiber@; KATE WADE, kate.wade@

Mailing Address: 22 East Mifflin Street, Suite 500, Madison 53703-2512.

Telephone: 266-2818.

Fax: 267-0410.

Internet Address: http://www.legis.state.wi.us/lab

E-mail Address: Leg.Audit.Info@legis.state.wi.us

Address e-mail by combining the user ID and the state extender: userid@**legis.state.wi.us**

Publications: Audit reports of individual state agencies and programs; biennial reports.

Number of Employees: 86.80.

Total Budget 2003-05: $13,036,900.

Statutory Reference: Section 13.94.

Agency Responsibility: The Legislative Audit Bureau is responsible for conducting financial and program audits to assist the legislature in its oversight function. The bureau performs financial audits to determine whether agencies have conducted and reported their financial transactions legally and properly. It undertakes program audits to analyze whether agencies have managed their programs efficiently and effectively and have carried out the policies prescribed by law.

The bureau's authority extends to executive, legislative, and judicial agencies; authorities created by the legislature; special districts or zones; and certain service providers that receive state funds. The bureau may audit any county, city, village, town, or school district at the request of the Joint Legislative Audit Committee.

The bureau audits and reports on the financial transactions and records of every state agency at least once every 5 years. Agencies or funds audited more frequently include the State of Wisconsin Investment Board, the Department of Employee Trust Funds, State Fair Park, the state lottery, and various state insurance funds. In addition, the bureau provides an annual audit opinion on the state's comprehensive financial statements, which are prepared by the Department of Administration.

Typically, the bureau's program audits are conducted at the request of the Joint Legislative Audit Committee, initiated by bureau staff, or required by legislation. The reports are reviewed by the Joint Legislative Audit Committee, which may hold hearings on them and may introduce legislation in response to audit recommendations.

Organization: The director of the bureau is the State Auditor, who is appointed by the Joint Committee on Legislative Organization upon the recommendation of the Joint Legislative Audit Committee. Both the State Auditor and the bureau's staff are appointed from outside the classified service.

History: The bureau was created as a legislative service agency under the jurisdiction of the Joint Committee on Legislative Organization by Chapter 659, Laws of 1965. It replaced the Department of State Audit, which was created by Chapter 9, Laws of 1947, as an executive agency.

For many students, their first interest in government is awakened by a class trip to the Capitol. These trips often include a visit with a legislator representing their district, in this case Senator Robert Cowles, to provide a deeper understanding of the workings of state government, and the citizen's role in it. (Richard G. B. Hanson II, Senate Photographer)

Statutory Advisory Council

Municipal Best Practices Reviews Advisory Council: CRAIG KNUTSON, MORT MCBAIN (representing the Wisconsin Counties Association); DANIEL ELSASS (representing the League of Wisconsin Municipalities); EDWARD HUCK (representing the Wisconsin Alliance of Cities); vacancy (representing the Wisconsin Towns Association). (All are appointed by the State Auditor.)

The 5-member Municipal Best Practices Reviews Advisory Council advises the State Auditor on the selection of county and municipal service delivery practices to be reviewed by the State Auditor. The auditor is required to conduct periodic reviews of procedures and practices used by local governments in the delivery of governmental services; identify variations in costs and effectiveness of such services between counties and municipalities; and recommend practices to save money or provide more effective service delivery. Council members are chosen from candidates submitted by the organizations represented. The council was created by 1999 Wisconsin Act 9 in Section 13.94 (8), Wisconsin Statutes, and succeeds the council created by 1995 Wisconsin Act 27.

LEGISLATIVE COUNCIL STAFF, see pp. 285-87

LEGISLATIVE FISCAL BUREAU

Director: ROBERT WM. LANG.

Assistant Director: TERRY A. RHODES.

Program Supervisors: FRED AMMERMAN, JERE BAUER, DARYL HINZ, DAVID LOPPNOW, TONY MASON, CHARLES MORGAN, ROB REINHARDT.

Administrative Assistant: VICKI HOLTEN.

Mailing Address: 1 East Main Street, Suite 301, Madison 53703.

Telephone: 266-3847.

Fax: 267-6873.

Internet Address: www.legis.state.wi.us/lfb

E-mail Address: fiscal.bureau@legis.state.wi.us

Publications: Biennial budget and budget adjustment: summaries of state agency budget requests; cumulative and comparative summaries of the governor's proposals, Joint Committee on Finance provisions and legislative amendments, and separate summaries of legislative amendments when necessary; summary of governor's partial vetoes. Informational reports, budget issue papers on various state programs, and revenue estimates. (Reports and papers available on the Internet or upon request.)

Number of Employees: 35.00.

Total Budget 2003-05: $6,883,000.

Statutory Reference: Section 13.95.

Agency Responsibility: The Legislative Fiscal Bureau develops fiscal information for the legislature, and its services must be impartial and nonpartisan. One of the bureau's principal duties is to staff the Joint Committee on Finance and assist its members. As part of this responsibility, the bureau studies the state budget and its long-range implications, reviews state revenues and expenditures, and suggests alternatives to the committee and the legislature. In addition, the bureau provides information on all other bills before the joint committee and analyzes agency requests for new positions and appropriation supplements outside of the budget process.

The bureau provides fiscal information to any legislative committee or legislator upon request. On its own initiative, or at legislative direction, the bureau may conduct studies of any financial issue affecting the state. To aid the bureau in performing its duties, the director or designated employees are granted access, with or without notice, to all state departments and to any records maintained by the agencies relating to their expenditures, revenues, operations, and structure.

The Legislature depends on legislative service agencies to provide its members with expert assistance. Bob Lang, Director of the Legislative Fiscal Bureau, explains the fiscal implications of a proposal to Representative Dean Kaufert, cochairperson of the Joint Committee on Finance, and Speaker John Gard. (Jay Salvo, Assembly Photographer)

Organization: The Joint Committee on Legislative Organization is the policy-making body for the Legislative Fiscal Bureau, and it selects the bureau's director. The director is assisted by an assistant director and program supervisors responsible for broadly defined subject areas of government budgeting and fiscal operations. The director and all bureau staff are chosen outside the classified service.

History: The bureau was created by Chapter 154, Laws of 1969. It evolved from the legislative improvement study that was initiated by Chapter 686, Laws of 1961, using a Ford Foundation grant and state funding. Through the improvement program, the legislature developed its own fiscal staff, known as the Legislative Budget Staff, under the supervision of the Legislative Programs Study Committee. In February 1968, the study committee renamed the budget staff the Legislative Fiscal Bureau and specified its functions. Chapter 215, Laws of 1971, transferred responsibility for the bureau's supervision to the Joint Committee on Legislative Organization.

LEGISLATIVE REFERENCE BUREAU

Chief: STEPHEN R. MILLER, 267-2175, steve.miller@legis.state.wi.us

General Counsel: PETER J. DYKMAN, 266-7098, peter.dykman@legis.state.wi.us

Administrative Services: CATHLENE HANAMAN, *manager,* 267-9810, cathlene.hanaman@legis.state.wi.us

Information and Research Services: LAWRENCE S. BARISH, *research manager,* 266-0344, larry.barish@legis.state.wi.us

Legal Services: PETER R. GRANT, DEBORA A. KENNEDY, JEFFREY T. KUESEL, REBECCA C. TRADEWELL, *managing attorneys.*

Library Services: MARIAN G. ROGERS, *managing librarian,* 266-2824, marian.rogers@legis.state.wi.us

Mailing Address: P.O. Box 2037, Madison 53701-2037.

Location: 1 East Main Street, Suite 200.

Telephones: Legal: 266-3561; Research: 266-0341; Library Circulation: 266-7040.

Fax: Legal: 264-6948; Research and Library: 266-5648.

Internet Address: http://www.legis.state.wi.us/lrb

Publications: *Wisconsin Blue Book;* informational reports on various subjects; *Selective List of Recent Acquisitions*; various sections of the *Bulletin of the Proceedings of the Wisconsin Legislature.* (All informational reports and the *Blue Book* are also available on the Internet.)

Number of Employees: 58.00.

Total Budget 2003-05: $10,607,600.

Statutory Reference: Section 13.92.

Agency Responsibility: The Legislative Reference Bureau provides nonpartisan, professional, confidential bill drafting, research, and library services to the legislature. Although it is primarily a legislative service agency, the bureau also serves public officials, students of government, and citizens.

By statute, the bureau is responsible for drafting all legislative proposals and amendments for introduction in the legislature. Legislative attorneys also prepare plain language analyses that are printed with all bills and most resolutions. A significant portion of the work of the legislative attorneys involves the drafting of the state's biennial budget.

The bureau enrolls the final text of all bills that have passed both houses prior to their submission for the governor's action. The bureau is also responsible for publishing each act, and, in consultation with the Revisor of Statutes, produces the bound volumes of all session laws enacted during the biennial legislative session.

The reference and library sections collect and make available a broad range of information to aid legislators and other government officials in the performance of their duties. The reference section publishes reports on subjects of legislative concern and, in the odd-numbered years, it publishes the 1,000-page *Wisconsin Blue Book,* the official almanac of Wisconsin government. The reference desk responds to inquiries about the work of the legislature and state government in general. The bureau also offers seminars on legislative procedure to students and civic groups.

LEGISLATIVE SERVICE AGENCIES

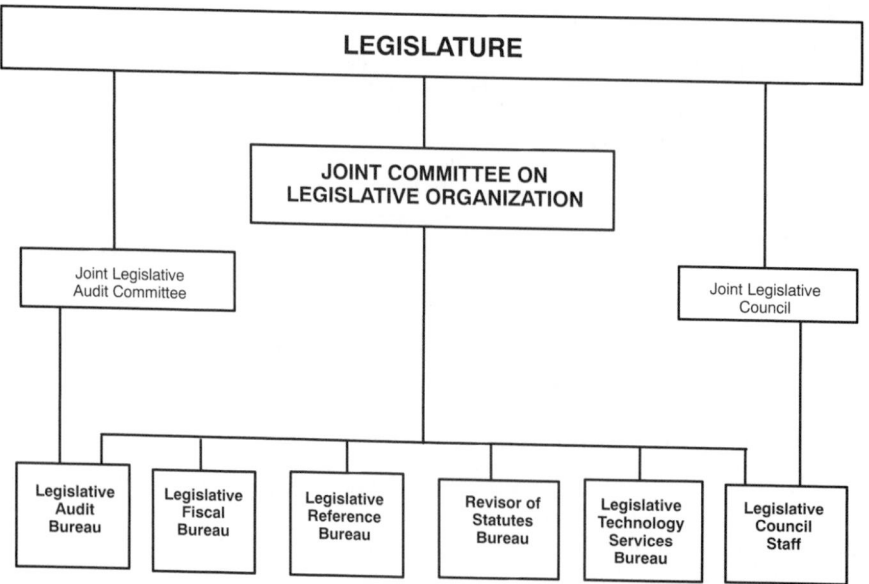

Representative Jennifer Shilling addresses her colleagues from the floor of the Assembly. In keeping with the Assembly's "paperless" policy, members access documents being debated with laptop computers. (Jay Salvo, Assembly Photographer)

The Dr. H. Rupert Theobald Legislative Library contains the bureau's extensive collection of material pertaining to government and public policy issues. The library staff prepares the *Index to the Bulletin of the Proceedings of the Wisconsin Legislature* which includes a subject index to legislation, authors indexes, and subject indexes to legislative journals, administrative rules, and Wisconsin acts.

State law requires the bureau to maintain the drafting records of all legislation introduced and to use those records to provide information on legislative intent. Drafting records, beginning with the 1927 session, are available to the public as part of the bureau's noncirculating reference collection.

Organization: The Joint Committee on Legislative Organization is the policy-making body for the bureau, and it selects the bureau chief. The bureau chief and staff members are appointed from outside the classified service.

History: The bureau was created in 1901 by Chapter 168 as the Legislative Reference Library under the governance of the Free Library Commission. It represented the first organized effort in the nation to provide a state legislature with professional staff assistance. Bill drafting responsibilities were officially assigned in 1907 by Chapter 508, although this service actually had been performed earlier. Editing of the *Wisconsin Blue Book* was added to the agency's duties in 1929 (Chapter 194). Chapter 149, Laws of 1963, renamed the agency the Legislative Reference Bureau and placed it under the direction of the Joint Committee on Legislative Organization.

LEGISLATIVE TECHNOLOGY SERVICES BUREAU

Director: MARSHA HENFER.

Mailing Address: 17 South Fairchild Street, Suite 400, Madison 53703-3219.

Telephone: 264-8582.

Fax: 267-6763.

Internet Address: http://www.legis.state.wi.us/ltsb

Publications: *Wisconsin Legislative Strategic Technology Plan.*

Number of Employees: 43.00.

Total Budget 2003-05: $6,776,800.

Statutory Reference: Section 13.96.

Agency Responsibility: The Legislative Technology Services Bureau is responsible for providing information technology support to both legislators and legislative agencies. It also coordinates the planning and execution of electronic information programs and services as needed. The bureau's services must be nonpartisan, and it must protect the confidentiality of the information originated, maintained, and processed by the electronic equipment it supports.

The bureau develops and supports the specialized programs used for bill drafting, production of the *Wisconsin Statutes* and *Administrative Code,* and publication of the *Wisconsin Blue Book.* In addition, it supports the publication of legislative documents including bills and amendments, house journals, daily calendars, and the Bulletin of the Proceedings. It maintains and implements improvements in the computer networks that allow legislative offices and service agencies to exchange information electronically and work together. The bureau inventories the legislature's computer hardware and software and oversees technology replacement schedules. It also provides mapping and redistricting services following each decennial U.S. Census, develops database services that allow legislators to serve their constituents more efficiently, delivers audio and video services, session support, manages the technology for the legislature's Internet site, and offers training services for legislators and staff in the use of information technology. The bureau's duties include maintenance of the legislature's payroll and accounting system, consultation on equipment and procedures for legislative administration, legislative office management, and on-line publication and communication.

Organization: The Joint Committee on Legislative Organization is the policy-making body for the bureau. It selects the director and is specifically responsible for reviewing and approving all information technology proposals. The director appoints bureau staff. Both the director and the staff serve outside the classified service.

History: The bureau was statutorily created by 1997 Wisconsin Act 27 as the Integrated Legislative Information Staff and was renamed by 1997 Wisconsin Act 237.

REVISOR OF STATUTES BUREAU

Revisor of Statutes: BRUCE MUNSON, 267-3536, bruce.munson@legis.state.wi.us

Deputy Revisor and Assistant Revisor, Statutes: BRUCE J. HOESLY, 266-7590, bruce.hoesly@legis.state.wi.us

Assistant Revisor, Administrative Code: GARY L. POULSON, 266-7275, gary.poulson@legis.state.wi.us

Mailing Address: 131 West Wilson Street, Suite 800, Madison 53703-3261.

Telephone: 266-2011.

Fax: 264-6978.

Internet Address: http://www.legis.state.wi.us/rsb

Publications: Wisconsin Statutes and Annotations; Wisconsin Administrative Code and Register; Wisconsin Town Law Forms; *WisLaw*® on CD-ROM.

Number of Employees: 10.00.

Total Budget 2003-05: $1,681,200.

Statutory Reference: Section 13.93.

Agency Responsibility: The Revisor of Statutes Bureau edits, annotates, and publishes the Wisconsin Statutes and Annotations, prepares revision and corrections bills, edits and publishes the Wisconsin Administrative Code and Register, and performs related law publishing and advisory functions.

The bureau incorporates newly enacted laws into the existing statutes, thereby updating the state's statutory code. The statutes are published every two years when the legislature completes its session. The bureau also releases quarterly updated versions of the statutes on *WisLaw®*, its CD-ROM periodical, and on its Internet site.

The bureau prepares revisor's corrections bills to correct errors or resolve conflicts arising from the enactment of laws. It reviews attorney general's opinions, federal district and appellate court decisions, and state appellate or supreme court decisions that declare a Wisconsin statute or session law to be ambiguous, in conflict with other laws, anachronistic, unconstitutional, or otherwise in need of revision. These findings are reported to the Joint Legislative Council's Law Revision Committee. The revisor also systematically examines the statutes and session laws for similar defects and proposes revision bills to the Law Revision Committee.

The bureau edits and publishes the Wisconsin Administrative Code and the semimonthly Wisconsin Administrative Register, which contains rule hearing and publication notices and summaries of emergency rules. It also prepares the Wisconsin Town Law Forms distributed to town officials to aid them in administering town government. These publications are also published on *WisLaw®* and the bureau's Internet site.

Organization: The Joint Committee on Legislative Organization is the policy-making body for the bureau and appoints the revisor. The revisor and all bureau staff are members of the classified service.

History: Wisconsin was the first state to adopt a plan for continuous revision of its statutes when Chapter 546, Laws of 1909, provided for a Revisor of Statutes to be appointed by the trustees of the state library. The editing and distribution of the Wisconsin Administrative Code and Register were added to the revisor's duties in 1955, but the responsibility for sale and distribution of these documents was transferred in 1963 to the Department of Administration. Chapter 149, Laws of 1963, moved the revisor to the legislative branch by creating the Statutory Revision Bureau under the supervision of the Joint Committee on Legislative Organization. A 1965 law renamed the bureau the Revisor of Statutes Bureau.

Senator Dale Schultz meets with the press informally at the rostrum of the Assembly Chamber immediately following a joint session featuring an address by the governor. (Richard G. B. Hanson II, Senate Photographer)

Ray DePerry, President of the Great Lakes Inter-Tribal Council, delivered an historic Tribal State of the State address in the Assembly Chamber on March 8, 2005. The speech was preceded by an Indian Color Guard and a prayer (above) offered by Leon Vallierre-Ozaawaagosh of the Lac du Flambeau Ojibwe Language Program. (Richard G. B. Hanson II, Senate Photographer)

SUMMARY OF SIGNIFICANT LEGISLATION
ENACTED BY THE 2003 LEGISLATURE

This section highlights significant legislation enacted by the 2003 Wisconsin Legislature in the biennial session that began January 6, 2003, and concluded January 3, 2005. The legislation summarized here is categorized by subject matter. In some cases, an individual act is described under a single subject heading, but when an act affects more than one area of state law, such as 2003 Wisconsin Act 33 (the budget act), significant provisions are separately described under the appropriate subject headings. The section concludes with a summary of major proposals that failed to be enacted or adopted.

The regular session of the 2003 Legislature was organized into the following floorperiods:

January 6, 2003	April 29-May 8, 2003	January 20-February 5, 2004
January 28-30, 2003	May 28-June 27, 2003	February 24-March 11, 2004
February 18-20, 3003	September 23-October 2, 2003	April 27-29, 2004
March 11-20, 2003	November 4-13, 2003	May 11-12, 2004

The following table summarizes activity in recent legislative sessions:

	Legislative Session				
	1995-96	1997-98	1999-2000	2001-02	2003-04
Total Drafting Requests	13,631	11,908	9,774	10,192	9,560
Bills Introduced	1,781	1,521	1,503	1,440	1,568
Assembly Bills	1,103	979	973	941	998
Senate Bills	678	542	530	499	570
Acts	469	338	198	109	327
Percentage of Bills Enacted	26.3%	22.2%	13.2%	7.6%	20.9%
Bills Totally Vetoed	4	3	5	0	54
Bills Partially Vetoed	21	8	10	3	10

SIGNIFICANT 2003-2004 LEGISLATION

Administrative Law

Act 118 *(AB-655)* makes various changes relating to administrative rules.

The act:

- Allows five or more persons, a municipality, or an association that represents a farm, labor, business, or professional group, to petition the Department of Administration (DOA) to require the Department of Agriculture, Trade and Consumer Protection (DATCP), the Department of Natural Resources (DNR), the Department of Transportation (DOT), the Department of Workforce Development (DWD), or the Department of Commerce, to prepare an economic impact report regarding proposed rules from their agencies.

- Requires an agency to prepare an economic impact report if a proposed rule will cost $20 million during the first five years or would adversely affect the economy, productivity, competition, jobs, environment, public health or safety, or government.

- Requires an economic impact report to include the effect of a proposed rule on businesses and the state economy, an analysis of the problem the proposed rule is intended to solve, and costs and benefits of the proposed rule.

- Requires DOA to ensure that an economic impact report complies with state law.

- Requires the analysis of a proposed rule to include a summary and comparison of any federal regulation of the same activity, data and findings used to support the proposed rule, documentation supporting its effect on small businesses, and compliance costs incurred by the private sector.

- Requires the report that is currently sent to the legislature to include the public comments and the agency's response to those comments.
- Allows a hearing examiner to award costs and attorney fees if an administrative hearing claim or defense is frivolous.
- Requires an administrative hearing involving a petitioner who is not a Wisconsin resident to be held in the county where the property involved is located or in the county where the dispute arose.

Legislative bodies elect leaders from among their membership to facilitate smooth operation and communication. On the left is John Gard, the Speaker of the Assembly, who controls the agenda on behalf of the majority party. On the right is Jim Kreuser, the Minority Leader, who is the voice of the minority party. In the center is Stephen Freese, the Speaker pro tempore of the Assembly, who often presides over floor sessions. (Brent Nicastro, Assembly Photographer)

Agriculture

Act 235 (*AB-868*) regulates the siting and expansion of livestock facilities by generally allowing local governments to disapprove a proposal to site or expand a livestock facility only if:

- The site is zoned and the zoning prohibits the proposed livestock facility.
- The livestock facility violates one of the standards that DATCP adopts under the act and either will have more than 500 animal units (500 beef cattle or other livestock that produces animal waste approximately equivalent to that produced by 500 beef cattle) or will be of a size for which the local government required a conditional use permit before the act took effect.
- The livestock facility will have more than 500 animal units or will be of a size requiring a conditional use permit, and the livestock facility will violate a local ordinance that is more stringent than DATCP's standards and that is necessary to protect public health or safety.

The act also prohibits a local government from restricting the size of livestock facilities in an agricultural zoning district unless it also has a zoning district permitting livestock facilities without regard to size and requires a local government to demonstrate that any ban of livestock facilities in an agricultural zoning district is necessary to protect public health or safety.

The act generally requires a political subdivision to approve or disapprove a proposal for siting or expanding a livestock facility within 90 days and creates the Livestock Facility Siting Review Board to review certain decisions on siting or expansion.

Children

Act 279 (*SB-207*) requires a member of the clergy who has a reasonable belief that a child seen in the course of professional duties has been sexually abused or threatened with sexual abuse or that a member of the clergy has sexually abused a child or threatened a child with sexual abuse to report that abuse, unless the information was obtained in a confidential setting.

Courts and Civil Actions

Act 279 (*SB-207*):

- Requires a member of the clergy to report to the proper authorities if he or she reasonably believes that a child seen in the course of professional duties has been sexually abused or threatened with sexual abuse or that another member of the clergy has sexually abused or threatened to sexually abuse a child, unless the information was obtained in a confidential setting.
- Allows a person who is injured because of sexual contact with a member of the clergy when the person is less than 18 years of age to bring an action against that member of the clergy and to bring an action against the religious organization that employed the member of the clergy if the clergy member's supervisor knew or should have known that the member of the clergy previously had sexual contact with a person under the age of 18, failed to report that sexual contact, and failed to exercise ordinary care to prevent similar incidents.
- Prohibits any settlement of a claim for sexual abuse of a child by a member of the clergy that limits the rights of an injured person to disclose the sexual contact to certain persons, including the district attorney and a therapist.
- Allows a person to bring an action for damages resulting from sexual contact while the person was under the age of 18 at any time before the injured party reaches the age of 35 years.

Crime and Criminal Procedure

Act 36 (*AB-288*) changes the crime of identity theft by:

- Making the offense applicable to more types of personal identification documents and personal identifying information.
- Applying the prohibition on identity theft to documents or information relating to a deceased individual.
- Expanding the scope of the prohibition to cover harm to the reputation, property, or person of the victim; harm to a deceased person's estate; and efforts to avoid delivery of a court paper or penalty.
- Allowing the deception element to be proven with evidence that the defendant falsely represented that the document or information involved was his or her own.
- Treating the unauthorized use of a private or government entity's identifying documents or information the same way as the unauthorized use of an individual's identifying documents or information.
- Specifying that a person may be prosecuted and punished for identity theft, regardless of where the crime occurred, if the victim is a Wisconsin resident or is located in Wisconsin, and allowing an identity theft case to be brought in the county in which the victim resides.
- Making it a crime for a person to engage in certain deceptive activities relating to the person's identity in connection with a transaction with a financial institution.
- Permitting more frequent use of hearsay and telephonic or televised testimony at preliminary hearings in identity theft cases.

Discrimination

Act 23 (*SB-24*) provides an exception to the public accommodations law to permit a fitness center to limit the use of its facilities and services to persons of the same sex.

Domestic Relations

Act 130 (*AB-279*) creates a rebuttable presumption in a custody proceeding against awarding legal custody of a child to a parent who engaged in domestic abuse. This presumption supersedes the presumption that joint legal custody is in the child's best interest. The presumption created by this act may be rebutted only by a preponderance of evidence that the parent has successfully completed a certified treatment program for batterers and that it is in the child's best interest for the parent to be awarded legal custody. If the court awards periods of physical placement with a child to a parent who has engaged in domestic abuse, the court must provide for the safety of the child and the victim of the abuse by imposing specified conditions. The act also requires that a guardian ad litem in a custody proceeding investigate whether either parent engaged in domestic abuse, that any required mediation intake form ask whether either parent engaged in domestic abuse, and that both guardians ad litem and mediators have training on domestic violence.

Education

Act 33 (*SB-44*) makes the following changes to the laws governing primary and secondary education:

- Eliminates the requirement that the state pay two-thirds of school district costs.
- Eliminates the requirement that the Department of Public Instruction (DPI) develop, and that school boards and charter schools adopt and administer, a high school graduation test.

Act 155 (*AB-847*) requires each private school participating in the Milwaukee Parental Choice Program (MPCP) to submit to DPI evidence of sound fiscal practices and of financial viability, a copy of the school's certificate of occupancy, and proof that the private school's administrator has participated in a fiscal management training program. The act also authorizes DPI to bar a private school from continuing to participate in the program if the school misrepresents required information, violates various notice requirements, fails to refund overpayments to the state, or fails to meet certain standards. DPI may also ban participation if it finds that conditions at the school present an imminent threat to the health or safety of pupils.

Act 207 (*AB-169*) requires a public library, upon request, to disclose to the custodial parent or guardian of a child under the age of 16 all library records relating to the child's use of the library's materials or services.

Elections

Act 24 (*AB-112*) changes the date of the presidential preference primary to the third Tuesday in February.

Employment

Act 63 (*AB-2*) grants a wage claim lien (which gives an employee to whom unpaid wages are owed, or DWD on behalf of the employee, a claim on the employer's property for those unpaid wages) priority over a prior lien of a commercial lending institution as to the first $3,000 of unpaid wages covered under the lien that were earned within the six months preceding the date on which the employee filed the wage claim. The act also excludes from coverage under the wage claim lien law independent contractors; managerial, executive, and commissioned sales employees; and employees who are privy to confidential matters involving the employer-employee relationship.

Environment

Act 118 (*AB-655*) makes the following changes in the laws related to air quality management:

- Requires DNR, before DNR may adopt an emission standard for a hazardous air contaminant, to find that residents are exposed to unsafe levels of the contaminant or will be so exposed unless an emission standard is adopted and that DNR's proposed method for compliance with the emission standard is the most cost-effective method practicable.

- Provides for legislative committee review of proposed federal Clean Air Act implementation plans and designations of areas that do not comply with federal air quality requirements.
- Requires DNR to adopt administrative requirements that are consistent with federal Environmental Protection Agency (EPA) administrative requirements when EPA adopts a new source performance standard or an emission standard for a hazardous air contaminant.
- Requires DNR to simplify and expedite the process under which it authorizes the construction, operation, or both, of sources of air pollution with low emissions of air pollutants.
- Requires DNR to authorize the start of construction of a source of air pollution before issuance of a construction permit to avoid undue hardship.
- Requires DNR to exempt minor sources of air pollution from the requirement to obtain air pollution permits if emissions from the sources do not present a significant hazard to public health, safety, or welfare or to the environment.
- Limits the time within which DNR must act on applications for air pollution permits, requires DNR to refund application fees when its action is not timely, and requires reports concerning the reasons for delays in issuing permits and how future delays will be avoided.

Act 310 (*AB-926*) increases the regulation of high capacity wells, which are wells that have the capacity to withdraw more than 100,000 gallons a day. Under the act, DNR may only grant permits for certain high capacity wells if the permits contain conditions to ensure that the wells will not cause significant environmental impacts. Wells that are subject to this provision are those located near trout streams and wild and scenic rivers, those that may have a significant impact on a spring that usually has a flow of at least one cubic foot per second, and those with a water loss of more than 95 percent. The act also requires DNR to administer a program to mitigate the effects of preexisting wells that are located near trout streams and wild and scenic rivers.

Under Act 310, DNR must designate two groundwater management areas, one in and around Brown County and one in and around Waukesha County, where groundwater levels in wells have

Minority Leader Judith Biros Robson confers with Senator Fred Risser on the Senate floor. (*Richard G. B. Hanson II, Senate Photographer*)

been reduced by 150 feet or more. The act requires DNR to assist local governments in groundwater management areas by providing advice, incentives, and funding for research and planning related to groundwater management.

Financial Institutions

Act 63 (*AB-2*) relaxes eligibility requirements for membership in a credit union; expands the ability of credit unions to invest in credit union service organizations; expands a credit union's authority to act as a trustee, custodian, or depository of funds; permits credit unions to sell insurance products; expands the authority of a Wisconsin credit union to establish branch offices inside or outside of Wisconsin and of a non-Wisconsin credit union to establish branch offices in Wisconsin; removes certain limitations on mergers and acquisitions of credit unions; includes confidentiality requirements for certain regulators of credit unions; authorizes certain actions by credit union boards of directors without a meeting; changes certain requirements relating to credit union reserve accounts and credit union examinations; and exempts credit unions from certain statutory provisions from which other financial institutions are exempt.

The act also allows a state savings bank, state savings and loan association, or state bank to become certified by the Department of Financial Institutions as a universal bank. A universal bank retains its status as a savings and loan association, savings bank, or state bank and generally remains subject to existing regulatory and supervisory requirements, but has additional powers as a universal bank. The act allows a universal bank to engage in any activity authorized for any state savings bank, state savings and loan association, or state bank. The act also generally permits a universal bank to exercise all powers that may be exercised directly by certain federal financial institutions; to exercise lending powers similar to those of state banks; to purchase, sell, and underwrite certain investment securities and equity securities and to invest in certain properties and projects; to pledge its assets as security for deposits; to exercise the same trust powers that trust company banks may exercise; to securitize its assets for sale to the public; to exercise all powers necessary or convenient to effect the purposes for which the universal bank is organized or to further the businesses in which the universal bank is lawfully engaged; and to engage in activities that are reasonably related to the purposes of the universal bank.

Finally, the act provides that subordinate liens held by a state or local government unit (such as tax liens) no longer have priority over other subordinate security interests and liens and may be discharged by the disposition of the collateral to the same extent as other subordinate liens.

Act 294 (*AB-755*) enacts the Uniform Electronic Transactions Act (UETA) in Wisconsin. Generally, UETA facilitates certain electronic transactions by validating the provision and use of electronic records and electronic signatures. Under former law, a combination of state and federal laws (most significantly, the federal law commonly known as "E-Sign") governed the use of electronic records, transactions, and signatures in Wisconsin. The act:

- Specifies that if the parties to a transaction agree to conduct the transaction electronically a document or signature may not be denied legal effect solely because it is electronic.

- Provides that if the parties to a transaction agree to conduct the transaction electronically and if a law requires a party to provide information in writing to another person, a party may generally satisfy the requirement by providing the information in an electronic document.

- Permits electronic notarization or verification of a signature or document relating to a transaction if the notary's or verifier's electronic signature is accompanied by all other information required by law.

- Validates contracts formed in automated transactions by the interaction of automated agents of the parties or by the interaction of one party's automated agent and an individual.

- Generally permits a person to satisfy any law that requires retention of a document by retaining an electronic document, if the retained information satisfies certain requirements relating to accuracy and accessibility.

- Permits a person to submit in electronic format, if the governmental unit consents, any document that is required by law to be submitted in writing to a governmental unit and that requires a written signature.
- Provides that a document or signature may not be excluded as evidence solely because it is in electronic form.

The act does not cover certain types of electronic transactions, records, and notices, such as those relating to wills and trusts, cancellation of health insurance, product recalls, and hazardous material transportation.

Local Law

Act 31 (*AB-378*) modifies public utility aid payments so that, for production plants that begin operation after December 31, 2003, counties and municipalities receive public utility aid payments based on the megawatt capacity of the production plants located in the county or municipality, rather than on the production plant's net book value, as determined by the Public Service Commission (PSC).

Natural Resources

Act 118 (*AB-655*) makes the following changes to the laws under which DNR regulates navigable waters such as the placement of piers and bridges and the removal of material from river and lake beds. The act:

- Requires DNR to issue statewide general permits as legislative rules for certain structures and activities that required individual permits under prior law. An individual permit is one that authorizes one specific structure or activity and every application for such a permit is subject to the public notice and hearing requirements described below. A general permit is one that applies to a class of structures or activities but a person seeking to act under a general permit must notify DNR. The general permitting process is exempt from the notice and hearing requirements.
- Restricts the types of conditions that DNR may impose on general permits to construction and design requirements, location requirements to ensure that navigation is not interfered with and riparian rights of adjacent riparian owners are not adversely affected, and restrictions to protect areas that have special natural resource interest. Under prior law, DNR could impose conditions that were reasonably necessary to prevent pollution or to protect public or riparian rights in navigable waters.
- Exempts certain structures and activities from the permitting process.
- Allows persons to seek a determination from DNR as to whether a proposed structure or activity is exempt. If DNR does not act within 15 days of the request for the determination, the structure or activity is generally exempt from the permitting process.
- Allows DNR to require compliance with individual or general permitting requirements for a structure or activity that would otherwise be exempt if the structure or activity will cause pollution, will adversely impact public rights and interests, or will cause material injury to riparian rights.
- Gives DNR specific inspection authority for exemption determinations and approvals to proceed under general permits.
- Requires DNR to issue a statewide general permit for the grading and removal of topsoil from areas of less than 10,000 square feet from a bank of a navigable water. Under prior law, an individual permit was required.
- Expands the types of structures and activities in navigable waters that the legislature may directly authorize. If not directly authorized by the legislature, a person must comply with the DNR permitting process.
- Revises the application, public notice, and hearing procedures for obtaining an individual permit from DNR and the procedure for obtaining administrative review of permit decisions issued by DNR.

- Expands the exemption for placement of boathouses to include certain boathouses that are used exclusively for commercial purposes.

Act 240 (*AB-519*) regulates the feeding of deer by:

- Prohibiting the feeding of deer in a county if any of the county is a chronic wasting disease control zone, if a positive test for chronic wasting disease or bovine tuberculosis has been confirmed after December 31, 1997, in the county, or if a portion of the county is within a 10-mile radius of a location of an animal that was positive for chronic wasting disease or bovine tuberculosis.
- Allowing a person to feed deer for viewing purposes in other counties if the feeding site is within 50 yards of the person's home or public business, is not closer than 100 yards to a roadway with a speed limit of 45 miles per hour or more, contains no more than two gallons of material, and if the feeding material does not contain animal parts or by-products.
- Allowing a person to feed deer for hunting during any deer hunting season in counties or parts of counties not subject to chronic wasting disease control and if no more than two gallons of material are at a site, sites are at least 100 yards apart, no more than two gallons of material are placed in any area comprising 40 acres or less, and the feeding material does not contain animal parts or by-products.

Occupational Regulation

Act 150 (*AB-403*) adopts the Uniform Athlete Agents Act, which requires agents for student athletes to register with the Department of Regulation and Licensing and regulates contracts and other aspects of the relationship between agents and student athletes. The act also allows a civil action against an agent who damages the educational institution when violating the act.

Public Utilities

Act 48 (*AB-61*) requires the PSC to reimburse wireless telecommunications providers and local governments for certain costs related to providing wireless 911 telephone service. The reimbursements, which are funded by a surcharge paid by wireless customers, are limited to reimbursing wireless providers for costs incurred in complying with Federal Communications Commission orders that require wireless providers to identify the location of callers who make wireless 911 calls. Only one wireless 911 emergency system in each county may be reimbursed.

Act 89 (*SB-300*) changes the requirements for approving proposals for electric transmission lines, electric generating facilities, and natural gas pipelines by, among other things, creating procedures for the PSC and DNR to coordinate review of such proposals; simplifying the procedure for the PSC to review proposed electric transmission lines that use existing transmission corridors; requiring the PSC, DNR, and DOT to rank the types of transmission corridors that may be used for siting new electric transmission lines; requiring the PSC to consider whether a proposal will use abandoned, idle, or underused commercial or industrial sites; and allowing local governments that receive distributions funded by environmental impact fees for new electric transmission lines to use the distributions for any purpose approved by the PSC.

Act 152 (*AB-843*) allows natural gas and electric utilities to finance pollution control costs for existing facilities by issuing bonds that will be repaid from customers' utility fees. The utility may assign the right to collect the fees to a third party, which would repay the bonds so that the debt associated with bonds is not the debt of the utility. The act protects the third party's interest in the fees if the utility becomes bankrupt or insolvent.

Act 278 (*SB-272*) generally restricts a municipality that offers cable television, telecommunications, or broadband Internet service from offering the service unless it performs a cost-benefit analysis and holds a public hearing on the ordinance or resolution authorizing the service. These requirements do not apply to certain municipalities that the PSC previously has certified as alternative telecommunications utilities. Such municipalities may offer the service if the voters of the municipality approve an advisory referendum that supports the service. In addition, the requirements do not apply to a municipality that was providing cable television service on March 1, 2004. Also, the requirements do not apply to the following: 1) broadband Internet service offered in an area if the municipality determines that the area has no current or planned broadband Internet ser-

The majority and minority leaders have the primary responsibility for carrying out their party's agenda on the floor. Majority Leader Michael Huebsch (left) and Minority Leader James Kreuser meet in the Assembly Chamber. (Jay Salvo, Assembly Photographer)

vice available; and 2) wholesale broadband Internet service if the municipality does not compete with more than one other provider of such service. Finally, the act generally prohibits municipalities that provide cable television service from requiring nonsubscribers to pay for the service, and the act generally requires municipal telecommunications utilities to set rates based on certain costs that apply to private sector telecommunications utilities.

Taxation

Act 37 (*SB-197*) requires a corporation that does business both inside and outside Wisconsin to apportion its income, for income tax and franchise tax purposes, using an apportionment fraction composed of a single sales factor, rather than an apportionment fraction composed of a sales factor representing 50 percent of the fraction and a property factor and payroll factor each representing 25 percent of the fraction.

Act 255 (*SB-261*) creates income and franchise tax credits for investments in businesses that have their headquarters and the majority of their employees in Wisconsin, that have been operating for fewer than seven years, and that are engaged in manufacturing, agriculture, or processing products or developing new products or processes.

Transportation

Blood Alcohol Levels

Act 30 (*AB-88*) changes the prohibited alcohol concentration for a person who operates a motor vehicle, all-terrain vehicle, snowmobile, or a boat, from 0.1 to 0.08. A first-time violator who has an alcohol concentration between 0.08 and 0.1 does not have to pay certain court costs or submit to an alcohol assessment and may have his or her record purged of the conviction after 10 years, if he or she does not reoffend within that time.

Driving Privileges

Act 33 (*SB-44*) implements parts of the federal USA Patriot Act of 2001 by imposing certain requirements on DOT's issuance of commercial driver license (CDL) "H" endorsements, which authorize the operation of vehicles transporting hazardous materials for which federal law requires placarding, or any quantity of a material listed as a select agent or toxin under federal law. Under the act, DOT may not issue or renew an "H" endorsement unless the applicant has submitted documentary proof of the applicant's U.S. citizenship or legal presence in the U.S. and the federal Transportation Security Administration (TSA) in the Department of Homeland Security has notified DOT that the applicant does not pose a security threat. An "H" endorsement is valid for four years, after which it may be renewed if the licensee passes a security threat screening by the TSA. DOT must obtain certain information on the application form for an "H" endorsement, including the applicant's criminal history, and forward it to the TSA. A licensee holding an "H" endorsement must notify DOT within 24 hours if he or she is convicted of certain criminal offenses.

Act 280 (*SB-350*) requires DOT to conduct a background investigation, including a criminal history search, of each applicant for issuance or renewal of a school bus endorsement to a driver's license and to record the date on which DOT finished the investigation. DOT must also make a good-faith effort to obtain out-of-state criminal history information for an applicant who has not resided in Wisconsin within the past two years. The act expands the list of crimes that disqualify a person from obtaining or renewing a school bus endorsement, changes disqualification periods, and allows disqualification for adjudication of delinquency as well as conviction. The act also authorizes DOT to specify additional disqualifying crimes and offenses and the time period during which the disqualification applies. Under the act, DOT also may not issue or renew a school bus endorsement to someone who identifies himself or herself as a person listed on the abuse registry maintained by the Department of Health and Family Services. Although a school bus endorsement continues to be renewed every eight years, DOT must conduct a criminal history search every four years and, if appropriate, cancel the endorsement. The act also requires similar criminal background checks of residents of Iowa, Illinois, Michigan, or Minnesota who are licensed to drive a school bus in those states if they drive a school bus in Wisconsin without a DOT school bus endorsement.

Funding

Act 33 (*SB-44*) allows DOT to use general obligation bonds to finance certain highway projects. Under former law, major highway projects, southeast Wisconsin freeway rehabilitation projects, and state highway rehabilitation projects could be funded with general obligation bond proceeds only if DOT's estimates of federal highway funding were at least 5 percent below the anticipated levels and the Joint Committee on Finance approved a DOT plan for using the proceeds. The act allows general obligation bond proceeds to be used to fund, and allocates general obligation bond proceeds for expenditure obligations for, southeast Wisconsin freeway rehabilitation projects and state highway rehabilitation projects, without regard to federal funding levels. The act also increases from $140 million to $1 billion the amount of general obligation bond debt that may be incurred to fund these highway projects.

Act 33 (*SB-44*) transfers $175 million from the transportation fund to the general fund.

Act 64 (*AB-602*) decreases the authorized limit on general obligation bonds that may be issued for major highway projects, southeast Wisconsin freeway rehabilitation projects, and state highway rehabilitation projects from $1 billion to $565,480,400. The act also requires that, beginning on July 1, 2005, debt service on these bonds be paid from the general fund rather than the transportation fund.

MAJOR PROPOSALS THAT FAILED ENACTMENT OR ADOPTION

Beverages

Assembly Bill 335 would have allowed an underage person to possess, consume, or be provided alcohol beverages while accompanied by a parent, guardian, or spouse of legal drinking age only if the underage person is at least 18 years of age.

Business and Consumer Law

Assembly Bill 898 and *Senate Bill 486* would have regulated rental-purchase transactions.

Constitutional Amendments

Assembly Joint Resolution 55 and *Senate Joint Resolution 56* would have required voter approval for certain state and local taxing, spending, and bonding decisions; limited use of emergency taxes by the state; and required budget reserves, refund of amounts in excess of approved amounts, and the reduction of tax rates to reflect the excess of revenues over expenditures.

Crime and Criminal Procedure

Assembly Bills 40 and 444 and *Senate Bill 214* would have permitted persons to carry concealed weapons under certain circumstances.

Discrimination

Assembly Bill 41 and *Senate Bill 58* would have permitted an educational agency to refuse to employ or to terminate from employment an unpardoned felon, whether or not the circumstances of the felony substantially relate to the circumstances of the particular job.

Assembly Bill 67 would have expanded the definition of employment discrimination based on creed to include discriminating against an employee for refusing to participate in certain acts, such as sterilizations; abortions; certain procedures involving in vitro human embryos or fetal tissue; withholding or withdrawing nutrition or hydration under specified circumstances; or euthanasia.

Domestic Relations

Assembly Bill 475 would have defined marriage as a civil contract between one man and one woman, creating the legal status of husband and wife.

Education

Assembly Bill 126 would have directed the Legislative Audit Bureau to study the Milwaukee Parental Choice Program.

Assembly Bills 259, 260, and 472 and *Senate Bills 219 and 221* would have extended the Milwaukee Parental Choice Program to additional pupils or private schools.

Assembly Bills 261, 503, and 746 and *Senate Bills 220, 253, and 382* would have expanded eligibility to attend independent charter schools or authorized additional independent charter schools.

Assembly Bills 836 and 847 and *Senate Bills 363 and 406* would have required criminal background checks of persons employed by private schools participating in the Milwaukee Parental Choice Program.

Assembly Bill 466 would have established levy limits for technical college districts.

Assembly Bill 830 would have authorized funds for engineering instruction at the University of Wisconsin-Rock County campus.

Elections

Assembly Bill 111 would have required most voters to provide identification to vote in elections.

Senate Bill 12 would have made extensive changes to campaign finance and related laws.

Employment

Assembly Bill 633 would have prohibited a county, city, village, or town from enacting a local minimum wage ordinance that does not strictly conform to the state minimum wage law.

Gambling

Assembly Bill 144 and *Senate Bill 41* would have limited the governor's power to enter into Indian gaming compacts without legislative approval.

Local Law

Assembly Bill 466 would have created levy limits that applied to cities, villages, towns, and counties.

Occupational Regulation

Assembly Bill 67 would have prohibited the Board of Nursing, the Medical Examining Board, and the Pharmacy Examining Board from disciplining health care practitioners for refusing to participate in certain acts, such as sterilizations; abortions; certain procedures involving in vitro human embryos or fetal tissue; and withholding or withdrawing nutrition or hydration or euthanasia. The bill also would have created immunity from civil liability for damages caused by such refusals.

Assembly Bill 559 would have created requirements for the cremation and disposal of human remains.

Public Utilities

Senate Bill 8 would have created an exception to the open records law to allow security system plans of public utilities to be withheld from public inspection.

Senate Bill 302 would have exempted broadband Internet service from PSC and local government regulation.

Assembly Bill 529 would have created remedies for persons damaged by electric current caused by electric utilities and cooperatives.

Assembly Bill 555 would have subjected nuclear power plants to the same requirements for PSC approval that apply to other types of power plants.

Assembly Bill 958 would have prohibited former PSC commissioners from utility-related employment for a period of time after they served as commissioners.

Taxation

Assembly Bill 547 and *Senate Bill 267* would have changed state and local sales and use taxes to conform to the multistate streamlined sales and use tax agreement.

Transportation

Assembly Bills 58, 462, 464, and 465 would have limited the use of a cellular telephone while operating a motor vehicle.

Assembly Bill 748 would have generally allowed owners of certain outdoor advertising signs along state trunk highways and owners of businesses advertised on these signs to remove obstructing trees or other vegetation located in the highway right-of-way if the trees or other vegetation would have prevented a driver traveling at the posted speed limit from seeing the sign for six uninterrupted seconds.

Senator Russell Decker congratulates Gwen Moore, who left the Senate in January to become Wisconsin's first black representative in Congress. (Richard G. B. Hanson II, Senate Photographer)

Executive Branch

6

The executive branch: profile of the executive branch and descriptions of constitutional offices, departments, independent agencies, state authorities, regional agencies, and interstate agencies and compacts

Langlade County Courthouse

Dave Tice, UW-Extension, Langlade County

ELECTIVE CONSTITUTIONAL EXECUTIVE STATE OFFICERS

Office	Officer/Party	Residence[1]	Term Expires	Annual Salary[2]
Governor	Jim Doyle (Democrat)	Madison	January 1, 2007	$131,768
Lieutenant Governor	Barbara Lawton (Democrat)	Green Bay	January 1, 2007	69,579
Secretary of State	Douglas J. La Follette (Democrat)	Kenosha	January 1, 2007	62,549
State Treasurer	Jack C. Voight (Republican)	Appleton	January 1, 2007	62,549
Attorney General	Peggy A. Lautenschlager (Democrat)	Fond du Lac	January 1, 2007	127,868
Superintendent of Public Instruction	Elizabeth Burmaster (nonpartisan office)	Madison	July 4, 2005	109,587

[1]Residence when originally elected.

[2]Annual salary as established for term of office by the Wisconsin Legislature.

Sources: 2003-2004 Wisconsin Statutes; Wisconsin Legislative Reference Bureau, Wisconsin Brief 04-20, *Salaries of State Elected Officials*, December 2004.

The State Capitol dominates a 13.5 acre park on Madison's isthmus. (Kathleen Sitter, LRB)

EXECUTIVE BRANCH

A PROFILE OF THE EXECUTIVE BRANCH

Structure of the Executive Branch

The structure of Wisconsin state government is based on a separation of powers among the legislative, executive, and judicial branches. The legislative branch sets broad policy objectives and establishes the general structures and regulations for carrying them out. The executive branch supervises the day-to-day administration of the programs and policies, while the judicial branch is responsible for adjudicating any conflicts that may arise from the interpretation or application of the laws.

Constitutional Officers. The executive branch includes the state's six constitutional officers – the governor, lieutenant governor, secretary of state, state treasurer, attorney general, and state superintendent of public instruction. Originally, the term of office for all constitutional officers was two years, but since the 1970 elections, their terms have been four years. All, except the state superintendent, are elected on partisan ballots in the fall elections of the even-numbered years at the midpoint between presidential elections. Though originally a partisan officer, the superintendent is now elected on a nonpartisan ballot in the April election.

The governor, as head of the executive branch, is constitutionally required to "take care that the laws be faithfully executed". In Article V of the state constitution, as ratified in 1848, the people of Wisconsin provided for the election of a governor and a lieutenant governor who would become "acting governor" in the event of a vacancy in the governor's office. Originally, the lieutenant governor was also the presiding officer of the senate. (By subsequent amendments, the lieutenant governor was relieved of senate duties and now assumes the full title of "governor" if the office is vacated.)

In Article VI, the constitution provided for three additional elected officers to assist in administering the laws of the new state. The first session of the legislature in 1848 authorized the secretary of state to keep official records, including enrolled laws and various state papers, and to act as state auditor by examining the treasurer's books and preparing budget projections for the legislature. The state treasurer was given responsibility for receiving all money and tax collections and paying out only those amounts authorized by the legislature for the operation of state government. The attorney general was to provide legal advice to the legislature and other constitutional officers and represent the state in legal matters tried in the courts of this state, other states, and the federal government.

The sixth officer, created by Article X of the constitution, was the state superintendent of public instruction. The first legislature gave the superintendent very specific duties, including the mandate to travel throughout the state inspecting common schools and advocating good public schools. The superintendent was to recommend texts, take a census of school age children, collect statistics on existing schools, and determine the apportionment of school aids.

The simplicity of administering state government in the early years is illustrated by the fact that total expenditures for 1848 government operations were only $13,472, which included the expenses of the legislature and circuit courts. As prescribed by the constitution and state law, the salaries of all six constitutional officers totaled $5,050 that year. (The lieutenant governor did not receive a salary, but he was given a double legislative per diem.) The state's annual budget totaled $24.3 billion in 2004-2005, and many of the duties first assigned to the constitutional officers are now carried out by specialized state agencies.

1967 Reorganization. Over a century later, the Wisconsin Committee on the Reorganization of the Executive Branch, in its report to the 1967 Legislature, concluded that state government could no longer be neatly divided into precise legislative, executive, and judicial domains. In many instances the subjects of legislation had become so technically complex that the legislature found it necessary to grant rule-making authority to the administrative agencies. The courts had also encountered a staggering load of technical detail and had come to depend on administrative agencies to use their quasi-judicial powers to assist the judicial branch.

Although the Wisconsin Constitution delegated ultimate responsibility for state administration to the governor, the proliferation of agencies over the years had made it increasingly difficult for one official to exercise effective executive control. The committee identified 85 state agencies within the executive branch of Wisconsin state government, many of which had no direct relationship to the governor. Chapter 75, Laws of 1967, attempted to integrate agencies by function and make them responsive to the elected chief executive, by drastically reducing the number of executive agencies from 85 to 32. Like everything else, state government does not remain static, however. Since the 1967 reorganization, the legislature has created new state agencies, while abolishing or consolidating others. The following sections describe the current organization of the executive branch.

Departments. The term "department" is used to designate a principal administrative agency within the executive branch. Within a department, the major subunit is the division, which is headed by an administrator. Each division, in turn, is divided into bureaus, headed by directors. Bureaus may include sections, headed by chiefs, and smaller units, headed by supervisors. There currently are 17 departments in the executive branch.

Wisconsin Administrative Departments

Administration	Natural Resources
Agriculture, Trade and Consumer Protection	Public Instruction
Commerce	Regulation and Licensing
Corrections	Revenue
Employee Trust Funds	
Financial Institutions	Tourism
Health and Family Services	Transportation
Justice	Veterans Affairs
Military Affairs	Workforce Development

In the majority of cases, the departments are headed by a secretary appointed by the governor with the advice and consent of the senate. Only the Department of Employee Trust Funds and the Department of Veterans Affairs are headed by boards that select the secretary. When administrators are personally chosen by and serve at the pleasure of the governor, they usually work in close cooperation with the chief executive.

Debate about whether the governor should directly appoint department heads continues. Public administration theory has long held that a governor can be the chief executive only if he or she has the authority to hold department heads directly accountable. On the other hand, the original purpose of a board was to insulate a department from politics, thereby enabling its head and staff to develop expertise and a sense of professionalism.

Independent Agencies. In addition to constitutional offices and administrative departments, there are 12 units of the executive branch that have been specifically designated as independent agencies.

Independent Executive Agencies

Educational Communications Board	Public Service Commission
Elections Board	State Historical Society of Wisconsin
Employment Relations Commission	State Investment Board
Ethics Board	State Public Defender Board
Higher Educational Aids Board	Technical College System
Office of the Commissioner of Insurance	University of Wisconsin System

Although the independent agencies are usually headed by part-time boards or multiple commissioners, the governor appoints most of these officials, with advice and consent of the senate, which serves to strengthen executive control of these units.

Authorities. In some instances, the legislature has decided to create corporate public bodies, known as "authorities", to handle specific functions. Although they are agencies of the state, the authorities operate outside the regular government structure and are intended to be financially self-sufficient. Currently, there are four authorities operating in Wisconsin – the Wisconsin Health and Educational Facilities Authority (WHEFA), the Wisconsin Housing and Economic Development Authority (WHEDA), the University of Wisconsin Hospitals and Clinics Authority, and the Fox River Navigational System Authority. (A fifth, the World Dairy Center Authority is currently inactive.) WHEDA, WHEFA, and UW Hospitals and Clinics Authority are authorized to issue bonds to finance their respective activities. Most authority members are appointed by the governor with advice and consent of the senate, but some are chosen from the legislature or serve as *ex officio* members.

Nonprofit Corporations. In 1985, the legislature created the Bradley Center Sports and Entertainment Corporation, a public, nonprofit corporation, which operates the Bradley Center in Milwaukee, the home of the Milwaukee Bucks, the Milwaukee Admirals hockey team, and the Marquette University basketball team. The corporation is headed by a board of directors appointed by the governor.

1999 Wisconsin Act 105 created the Wisconsin Technology Council, referenced in the statutes as the High-Technology Business Development Corporation. It supports the creation, development, and retention of science-based and technology-based businesses in the state.

The Wisconsin Artistic Endowment Foundation, created in 2001 Wisconsin Act 16, supports the arts by converting donated property and art objects into cash and distributing these and other moneys to the arts board that provide operating support to arts organizations.

Special Districts. The legislature may create special districts that serve "a statewide public purpose." These districts oversee the management of facilities for exposition centers, sports teams, and the cultural arts. Members of the governing boards are appointed by public officials. Currently, the Wisconsin Center, Miller Park, Lambeau Field, and the Madison Overture Center operate as special districts.

Boards, Councils, and Committees. Many departments and agencies have subordinate part-time boards, councils, and committees that carry out specific tasks or act in an advisory capacity. Boards may function as policy-making units, and some are granted policy-making or quasi-judicial powers. Examining boards set the standards of professional competence and conduct for the professions they supervise, and they are authorized to examine new practitioners, grant licenses, and investigate complaints of alleged unprofessional conduct. Councils function on a continuing basis to study and recommend solutions for problems arising in a specified functional area of state government. Committees usually are short-term bodies, appointed to study a specific problem and to recommend solutions or policy alternatives.

Boards are always created by statute. Councils are usually created by statute, but committees, because of their temporary nature, are created by session law rather than being written into the statutes. In addition, agency heads may create and appoint their own councils or committees as needed. The *Blue Book* describes only those units created by statute.

Attached Units. Under the 1967 reorganization, certain boards, commissions, and councils were attached to departments or independent agencies for administrative purposes only. These units are sometimes referred to as "15.03 units" because of the statutory section number that defines them. The larger agencies are expected to provide various services, such as budgeting and program coordination, but the 15.03 units exercise their statutory powers independently of the department or agency to which they are attached.

Government Employment

Classified Service. An important feature of Wisconsin state government employment is the merit system. Wisconsin's civil service, which is called "classified service", is designed to ensure that the most qualified person is hired for the job, based on test results and experience, rather than political affiliation. In 1905, Wisconsin was one of the first states to adopt such a system, and the Wisconsin classified service was considered one of the strongest because it encompassed the major portion of state personnel.

Since the 1967 reorganization of the executive branch, the trend has been to make top agency positions, including deputy secretaries, executive assistants, and division administrators, unclassified appointments. Despite this change at the top levels, most state employees, with the principal exception of legislative staff and the University of Wisconsin faculty and academic appointments, are hired and promoted through the classified service on the basis of merit.

Salaries. All positions in the classified service are categorized so that those involving similar duties, responsibilities, and qualifications are paid on the same basis. The Office of State Employment Relations (OSER) is directed to apply the principle of equal pay for equivalent skills and responsibilities when assigning a classification to a pay range.

State employees may join labor unions and engage in collective bargaining, but they are prohibited by state law from striking. Collective bargaining agreements, negotiated between OSER and labor organizations, are submitted to the Joint Committee on Employment Relations. The committee forwards its recommendations to the legislature in bill form for approval of salaries, fringe benefits, and other changes in the law. If the committee or legislature does not approve the proposed agreement, it is returned for renegotiation.

Each biennium, OSER establishes the compensation plan of classifications and related salary ranges for those classified employees not covered by collective bargaining agreements, subject to modification by the Joint Committee on Employment Relations. The governor may veto the committee's actions, although the vote of six committee members can override a veto. Some provisions of the compensation plan, as approved by the committee, may require changes in existing law, in which case they must be presented in bill form to the legislature for enactment.

Number of State Employees. The increasing size and complexity of state government is reflected in the number of employees. To illustrate this, a total of 1,924 people worked for Wisconsin state government in 1906. By contrast, in 2004, full and part-time state employees totaled 77,258. According the the Legislative Fiscal Bureau, this corresponds to 68,074 full-time equivalent employees.

Housing State Government

The first capitol in Madison was built during the Wisconsin Territory days at a cost of more than $60,000. Construction began in 1837 but was not completed until 1845. The building, which served as the first state capitol, was demolished in 1863 to make way for a larger second capitol, which was completed in 1866. When the second state capitol was extensively damaged by fire in 1904, construction of the current capitol began. The present capitol, which was completed in 1917 for $7,203,826.35, has recently undergone extensive restoration and renovation, costing more than $140 million, to prepare it for the 21st century.

Today, the agencies of state government in Madison are housed in the capitol and various state-owned office buildings, with additional space leased from private landlords. There are also state office buildings in Eau Claire, Green Bay, La Crosse, Milwaukee, Waukesha, and Wisconsin Rapids, plus district offices maintained throughout the state for the field units of many of the operating departments.

Besides its office buildings, the state owns or maintains a variety of educational, correctional, and mental health institutions across Wisconsin. The University of Wisconsin System operates 13 degree-granting institutions and 13 two-year colleges that feature freshman-sophomore instruction.

The state's adult corrections program, under the direction of the Department of Corrections, currently operates 5 maximum security prisons, 11 medium security prisons, 2 minimum security institutions, a prison for women, and 16 correctional centers. The department's juvenile corrections program operates Ethan Allen School at Wales and Lincoln Hills School at Irma for male juveniles and Southern Oaks Girls School at Union Grove, along with the Mendota Juvenile Treatment Center, an inpatient mental health treatment center.

Through the Department of Health and Family Services, the state operates 4 mental health institutions at Madison, Oshkosh, and Mauston, and 3 centers for the developmentally disabled at Madison, Chippewa Falls, and Union Grove.

The Department of Public Instruction maintains a school that offers special training for blind and visually impaired students at Janesville and a similar school for the deaf and hard-of-hearing at Delavan. The Wisconsin Veterans Homes at King in Waupaca County and Union Grove in Racine County are operated by the state to serve eligible Wisconsin veterans and qualifying spouses.

Functions of the Executive Branch

Governor and Lieutenant Governor. The governor, as Wisconsin's chief executive officer, represents all the people of the state. Because of this, the Office of the Governor is the focal point for receiving suggestions and complaints about state affairs. Administratively, the governor exercises authority through the power of appointment, consultation with department heads, and execution of the executive budget after its enactment by the legislature. The governor plays a key role in the legislative process through drafting the initial version of the biennial budget, which is submitted to the legislature in the form of a bill. Other opportunities to influence legislative action arise in the chief executive's state of the state message and special messages to the legislature about topics of concern. The governor also shapes the legislative process through the power to veto bills, call special sessions of the legislature, and appoint committees or task forces to study state problems and make recommendations for changes in the law.

Based on a 1979 amendment, the constitution provides that if the incumbent governor dies, resigns, or is removed from office, the lieutenant governor becomes governor for the unexpired term. The lieutenant governor serves temporarily as "acting governor" when the governor is impeached, incapacitated, or absent from the state.

Commerce. While the U.S. Constitution specifically delegates to Congress the regulation of interstate commerce, each state regulates intrastate commerce within its borders. The definitions of interstate and intrastate commerce overlap at times, and over the years the U.S. Supreme Court has greatly broadened the meaning of the "commerce clause" in the federal constitution. Despite this broad interpretation, the states continue to exercise considerable authority over commerce.

Commerce involves goods, services, and commercial documents, as well as transportation and communication, so the state's involvement in regulating commerce is broad. The state's primary objective is to protect the public as consumers and as participants in financial transactions. Wisconsin state government is also interested in maintaining a stable, orderly market for carrying out commercial activities and for promoting the state's economic development.

One aspect of consumer protection is the inspection of farm products and the conditions under which they are produced. The state inspects cattle for infectious diseases, conducts research in animal and plant diseases, regulates the use of pesticides, grades fruits and vegetables for marketing, and sets standards for processed food. Explicit standards are set by law or in the administrative rules promulgated by the Department of Agriculture, Trade and Consumer Protection. The department is concerned not only with the conditions of growing and processing food but also with fair trade practices in its sale.

Another important aspect of consumer protection is the licensing of various trades and professions. Individuals working in certain professions must achieve state-mandated levels of training and proficiency before they can offer their services to the public. Examples include professions affecting public health, such as doctors and nurses, or public safety, such as architects and engineers. The Department of Regulation and Licensing assists a variety of examining boards associated with various trades and professions and directly regulates certain types of professional activity.

The state protects consumers by maintaining an orderly market in which the public can conduct business. State activities include specifying methods of fair competition, regulating rates for public utilities, setting standards for the operation of financial institutions, regulating gambling, and regulating the sale of securities and insurance. The Department of Financial Institutions regulates banks, savings institutions, credit unions, and the sale of securities. It also registers trademarks, corporations, and other organizations and files Uniform Commercial Code documents. The Office of the Commissioner of Insurance regulates the sale of insurance. The Public Service Commission regulates public utility rates and services. The Gaming Division in the Department of

Administration regulates racing and charitable gambling and oversees gaming compacts between Indian tribes and the state. The Department of Revenue administers the Wisconsin Lottery.

The state is concerned with promoting economic development. The Department of Commerce provides assistance to communities and small businesses, promotes international trade, and recommends private and public sector programs to further long-term growth. Through the Wisconsin Development Fund, it awards grants or loans to fund technical research, labor training programs, and other major economic development projects that promise to create jobs and increase capital investment. The Department of Tourism promotes travel to Wisconsin's scenic, historic, artistic, educational, and recreational sites. It stimulates the development of private commercial tourist facilities and encourages local tourist-related businesses.

In the interests of public safety and welfare, the state enforces laws that regulate public and private buildings. The Department of Commerce enforces dwelling codes, reviews construction plans for new buildings, inspects subsystems that serve buildings, and performs training and consulting services for the building industry.

Education. Wisconsin officially recognized the importance of education within a democratic society at statehood in 1848 when it provided for the establishment of local schools in the state constitution and required that education be free to all children. The constitution further directed the legislature to establish a state university at Madison and colleges throughout the state as needed.

Wisconsin's public educational institutions now enroll over one million students each year. In fall 2003, there were 880,031 pupils in the public elementary and secondary schools and 173,058 students enrolled in the University of Wisconsin System in the fall of 2004. The Technical College System enrolled 113,253 students in its associate degree programs in the fall of 2002 and 316,102 in its vocational, technical diploma, and college transfer classes.

Wisconsin relies on 426 local school districts to administer its elementary and secondary programs. Twelve cooperative educational service agencies (CESAs) furnish support activities to the local districts on a regional basis, and the Department of Public Instruction, headed by the State Superintendent of Public Instruction, a nonpartisan constitutional officer, provides supervision and consultation for the districts.

In 1970 the state was divided into 16 vocational, technical, and adult education districts. These districts, renamed technical college districts, are each supervised by a district board that has taxing power. At the state level, the Technical College System Board supervises the districts.

At the collegiate level, all state-financed institutions of higher education are integrated into a single University of Wisconsin System. The system's two largest campuses at Madison and Milwaukee offer programs leading to doctoral degrees. Eleven other degree-granting institutions provide 4-year courses of baccalaureate study, and 13 UW Colleges provide 2-year courses of college-level study. State funding also supports Wisconsin residents enrolled at the Medical College of Wisconsin, Inc.

Three other state agencies perform educational functions. The Higher Educational Aids Board administers federal and state student financial assistance programs. The Educational Communications Board operates the state's networks for educational radio and educational television. The State Historical Society of Wisconsin maintains the state historical library, museum, and various historic sites.

Environmental Resources and Transportation. From a wilderness inhabited by 305,391 people in 1850, the state has evolved into a complex society with an estimated 2005 population of 5,563,896. Most of Wisconsin is not densely populated, and the state has a comparatively large amount of open space. However, population growth, higher levels of consumption, and industrial development have increased environmental pollution.

Once pioneers could come to a wilderness, cut the forests, clear the land, and hunt and fish with little thought of damage to the soil, streams, or wildlife. Now these resources must be protected from destruction, depletion, or extinction. The Department of Natural Resources administers numerous programs that control water quality, air pollution, and solid waste disposal. Under state regulations, municipalities and industries cannot dump untreated sewage or industrial wastes into surface waters; smokestacks and automobiles must meet air pollution limits; farmers are encouraged to preserve soil and groundwater quality; and solid waste disposal facilities must meet construction and operation standards. The department regulates hunting and fishing to protect fish and wildlife resources and manages other programs designed to conserve and restore endangered and threatened species. It also promotes recreational and educational opportunities through state parks, forests, trails, and natural areas.

The Department of Transportation administers a variety of programs related to environmental resources. The highways that crisscross the state have a major impact on land use and people's lifestyles. Urban freeways and interstate highways greatly affect the use and development of surrounding land. They determine where people live, work, and play. When state government plans the location and financing of highways and roads, it must carefully consider both short- and long-range consequences.

The state's highway system consists of interstate highways, state highways, county trunk highways, town roads, city and village streets, and park and forest roads. The state is concerned not only with building and maintaining adequate roads to meet demands, but also with providing for the safety of travelers using those roads. In 2005, more than 5 million vehicles were registered in Wisconsin, and more than 3.8 million residents were licensed to drive. With 836 traffic fatalities in 2003, and 784 in 2004, traffic safety is a constant concern.

The department must ensure that licensed drivers know the laws, are physically fit to drive, and have the required driving skills. It keeps track of drivers' records and can suspend the licenses of those who prove hazardous to themselves or others. It oversees highway construction and maintenance, highway patrol, and enforcement of driver and vehicle standards. The department is also involved in developing aviation and airports in Wisconsin and with promoting mass transit and passenger rail transportation.

Human Relations and Resources. Besides protecting the environment, the state must also protect its citizens directly. Population growth that affects the quality of land, water, and air resources has an increasingly complex effect on people themselves and their relationships to each other and their government. The inhabitants of a state are its prime resource, and government must ensure their general welfare. Records of birth, marriage, divorce, and death are collected and used to identify trends and potential problems.

In the state's early days, public health was primarily concerned with preventing the spread of communicable diseases. Today, the work of the Department of Health and Family Services includes protection from biological terrorist attacks, disease prevention and detection, health education programs, and maintenance of institutions for the care and treatment of the mentally handicapped or mentally ill. The department is also responsible for a broad range of social services for the aged, the handicapped, and children.

A wide range of work-related issues are subject to state regulation. Minimum wages and maximum hours are set by law. If a worker is injured on the job, state worker's compensation may be available; unemployment compensation helps many workers faced with loss of a job. If a worker is seeking a job, the state (in partnership with the federal government) provides a job service to help the individual find work or to acquire the skills necessary for employment. If a worker suspects job discrimination because of age, race, creed, color, handicap, marital status, sex, national origin, ancestry, sexual orientation, or arrest or conviction record, the state may investigate the matter. The Department of Workforce Development is responsible for protecting and assisting workers. The department also provides training and other services to help welfare recipients join the labor market under the state's Wisconsin Works (W-2) program and provides employment and assistance to rehabilitate the handicapped. The Employment Relations Commission mediates or arbitrates labor disputes between workers and their employers.

The Department of Veterans Affairs has grant and loan programs to help eligible veterans acquire a home, business, or education, and it provides personal and medical care for eligible elderly veterans and their spouses at the Wisconsin Veterans Homes at King and Union Grove.

The state also protects its citizens from society's lawless elements by maintaining stability and order. Law enforcement is largely a local matter, but the Department of Corrections is responsible for segregating convicted adult and juvenile offenders in its penal institutions and rehabilitating them for eventual return to society. The Office of the State Public Defender represents indigents in trial and postconviction legal proceedings. The Department of Justice furnishes legal services to state agencies and technical assistance and training to local law enforcement agencies. It also enforces state laws against gambling, arson, child pornography, and narcotic drugs.

The state maintains an armed military force, the Wisconsin National Guard, to protect the populace in times of state or national emergency, whether natural or human caused, and to supplement the federal armed forces in time of war. These activities come under the jurisdiction of the Department of Military Affairs.

General Executive Functions. The services described so far are direct services to the public. In order for the state to perform these functions, it must also perform certain "staff" functions. The state requires general departments that oversee the hiring of agency personnel and provide space, equipment, salaries, and a retirement system for them. It must levy and collect taxes to support its activities, manage these state funds, and ensure that they are spent according to law. It also evaluates agency operations to assure that the various departments are performing their assigned tasks and preparing for future needs.

Some agencies are designed to perform staff functions almost exclusively. The Department of Administration, for example, is called the state's "housekeeping" department. Its duties include state budgeting, preauditing, engineering and facilities management, state planning, and data processing. The Office of State Employment Relations operates the state's classified service system. The Department of Revenue collects taxes levied by state law, distributes part of that revenue to local units of government, and calculates the equalized value of the property that has been assessed by local government.

The Department of Employee Trust Funds manages the state's retirement systems and the employee insurance programs that cover state and local government workers. At any one time, the state must have large sums of money in its employee trust funds to meet its obligations. The Investment Board invests these funds in stocks, bonds, and real estate in order to earn the maximum amount of interest possible until the funds are needed. The Office of the State Treasurer processes the receipt and disbursement of these and other state moneys.

The Office of the Secretary of State handles general executive duties, such as keeping various state records and affixing the state seal on certain records. The Elections Board oversees the state's election processes, monitors campaign expenditures, and keeps election records. The Ethics Board administers a code of ethics for state public officials and regulates lobbyists and their employers.

This introduction illustrates how state government both benefits and regulates dozens of aspects of life in Wisconsin. The following sections describe in detail the agencies that make up the executive branch of state government and the numerous services they perform each day.

Total Budget, under each agency's entry, reflects the dollars budgeted through the 2003-2005 legislative session.

Number of Employees are the number of full-time equivalent positions in each agency's "adjusted base", which is the set of figures each agency uses to begin budgeting for the next biennium. It fully reflects the effects of 2003 Wisconsin Act 33.

Telephone numbers listed without an area code are Madison numbers in area code 608.

OFFICE OF THE GOVERNOR

Governor: JAMES E. DOYLE.

Chief of Staff: SUSAN GOODWIN.

Deputy Chief of Staff: RANDY ROMANSKI.

Chief Legal Counsel: AMY KASPER.

Communications Director: DAN LEISTIKOW.

Press Secretary: MELANIE FONDER.

Policy Director: KIRK BROWN.

Agency Affairs Director: TIM CASPER.

Agency Liaisons: LIAM GOLDRICK, KATE MAWDSLEY, TIM WELLNITZ, DONNA WONG.

Legislative Director: PATRICK HENDERSON.

Legislative Liaison: ANDREW MOYER.

External Relations Director: TED OSTHELDER.

Appointments Director: MINDY WALKER.

Director of Constituent Services: RICH WEST.

Correspondence Administrator: DONNA O'CONNELL.

Scheduling Director: SARAH KLEIN.

Director of Milwaukee Office: RAY HARMON, 819 North 6th Street, Room 560, Milwaukee 53203, (414) 227-4344.

Director of Northern Office: BRYCE LUCHTERHAND, 400 4th Avenue South, Park Falls 54552, (715) 762-5900.

Director of Wisconsin Office in Washington, D.C.: AMY JOHNSON, 444 North Capitol Street, No. 613, Washington, D.C. 20001, (202) 624-5870.

Mailing Address: P.O. Box 7863, Madison 53707-7863.

Location: 115 East, State Capitol, Madison.

Telephone: 266-1212.

Office E-mail: governor@wisconsin.gov

Fax: General: 267-8983; Press office: 266-3970; Policy: 261-6804.

Internet Address: http://www.wisgov.state.wi.us/

Number of Employees: 39.75.

Total Budget 2003-05: $7,608,000.

Constitutional Reference: Article V.

Statutory Reference: Chapter 14, Subchapter I.

Agency Responsibility: As the state's chief executive, the governor represents all the people and is responsible for safeguarding the public interest. The constitution sets certain limits on the governor's powers, but the increased size and complexity of state government have given the governor's office many more responsibilities than it originally had.

The governor gives policy direction to the state and plays an important role in the legislative process. Through the biennial budget, developed and administered in conjunction with the Department of Administration and various agency heads, the governor ultimately reviews and directs the activities of all administrative agencies. Major policy changes are highlighted in the governor's annual state of the state message and other special messages to the legislature.

The governor has other specialized powers related to the legislative process. The chief executive may call a special legislative session to deal with specific legislation, may veto an entire bill, or may veto parts of appropriation bills. In the case of either whole or partial vetoes, a two-thirds vote of the members present in each house of the legislature is required to override the governor's action.

Although various administrators direct the day-to-day operations of state agencies, the governor is considered the head of the executive branch. For the most part, the individuals, commissions, or part-time boards that head the major administrative departments are appointed by, and serve at the pleasure of, the governor, although many of these appointments require senate confirmation.

As the state's chief administrative officer, the governor must approve federal aid expenditures; state land purchases; highway and airport construction; land or building leases for state use; and numerous state contracts, including compacts negotiated with Indian gaming authorities. The governor may request the attorney general to protect the public interest in various legal actions.

The statutes authorize the governor to create special advisory committees or task forces to conduct studies and make recommendations. These committees frequently attract experienced citizens from many fields, who donate their time and expertise as a public service. The governor also appoints over 1,000 persons to various councils and boards, which are created by law to advise and serve state government, and personally serves on selected bodies, such as the State of Wisconsin Building Commission.

If a vacancy occurs in the state senate or assembly, state law directs the governor to call a special election. Vacancies in elective county offices and judicial positions can be filled by gubernatorial appointment for the unexpired terms or until a successor is elected. The governor may dismiss sheriffs, district attorneys, coroners, or registers of deeds for proven malfeasance.

The governor serves as commander in chief of the Wisconsin National Guard when it is called into state service during emergencies, such as natural disasters and civil disturbances. (When National Guard units perform national service, they are under command of the U.S. President.)

The chief executive has sole power to extradite a person charged with a criminal offense and to exercise executive clemency by granting a pardon, reprieve, or sentence commutation to a convicted criminal offender. The nonstatutory Pardon Advisory Board, which was created by execu-

Governor Jim Doyle accepted a report from his Homeland Security Advisor, Major General Al Wilkening, which details ongoing state efforts to increase homeland security in Wisconsin. In his remarks, the Governor highlighted significant progress, but also noted the state's need to remain vigilant and continue efforts to improve security. (Office of the Governor)

tive order in 1980 to expedite the pardon process, reviews applications for executive clemency and makes recommendations to the governor.

History: Before Wisconsin entered the Union, the U.S. President appointed the territorial governor, but the state constitution, adopted in 1848, gave executive powers to an elected governor. Debate during the constitutional conventions revealed reluctance to change the duties traditionally performed by the chief executive. Questions regarding the post of governor concentrated instead on the amount of salary, length of term, location of residence and, above all, veto power. An effort to divest the governor of veto power failed, as did attempts to vest pardoning power in the legislature and to deny the governor power to remove county officials from office for cause.

There have been several constitutional amendments adopted over the years affecting the authority of the governor. A 1967 amendment lengthened the governor's term from 2 to 4 years, effective 1971. A constitutional amendment, ratified in 1930, empowered the governor to approve appropriation bills in part, thereby creating the partial veto. Another amendment, ratified in 1990, restricted the partial veto power by forbidding the governor to create new words by striking individual letters within words.

Statutory Councils

State Council on Alcohol and Other Drug Abuse: DONNA WONG (designated to represent governor), SENATORS ROESSLER, CARPENTER; REPRESENTATIVES TOWNSEND, PARISI; MICHAEL MYSZEWSKI (attorney general designee), STEVE FERNAN (superintendent of public instruction designee), HELENE NELSON (secretary of health and family services), EILEEN MALLOW (commissioner of insurance designee), SALLY TESS (secretary of transportation designee), DAVE COLLINS (secretary of corrections designee), CHARLOTTE RASMUSSEN (chairperson of Pharmacy Examining Board designee), DOUG ENGLEBERT (Controlled Substances Board representative), vacancy (Governor's Commission on Law Enforcement and Crime representative), MICHAEL WAUPOOSE (service provider representative), MARK SEIDL (nominated by Wisconsin County Human Service Association, Inc.); MARK A. COOK, SANDY HARDIE, LINDA MAYFIELD, ANN R. NAVERA, JOYCE O'DONNELL, JAN VISTE. (All except *ex officio* members or their designees are appointed by governor.)

The State Council on Alcohol and Other Drug Abuse recommends, coordinates, and reviews the efforts of state agencies to control and prevent alcohol and drug abuse. It evaluates program effectiveness, recommends improved programming, issues reports to educate people about the dangers of drug abuse, and allocates responsibility for various alcohol and drug abuse programs among state agencies. The council also recommends legislation, cooperates with federal agencies, and receives federal funds.

The 22-member council includes 6 members with a professional, research, or personal interest in alcohol and other drug abuse problems, appointed for 4-year terms, and one of them must be a consumer representing the public. It was created by Chapter 384, Laws of 1969, as the Drug Abuse Control Commission. Chapter 219, Laws of 1971, changed its name to the Council on Drug Abuse and placed the council in the executive office. It was renamed the Council on Alcohol and Other Drug Abuse by Chapter 370, Laws of 1975, and the State Council on Alcohol and Other Drug Abuse by Chapter 221, Laws of 1979. Its composition and duties are prescribed in Sections 14.017 (2) and 14.24 of the statutes.

Standards Development Council: Inactive.

The 7-member Standards Development Council, created by 1997 Wisconsin Act 27, was directed to submit to the governor, by November 14, 1997, recommendations relating to pupil academic standards in mathematics, science, reading and writing, geography, and history. The act provided that if the governor approved the standards, he or she was authorized to issue them as an executive order. The council is directed to periodically review the standards and recommend changes to the governor. The composition and duties of the council are prescribed in Sections 14.017 (3) and 14.23 of the statutes.

INDEPENDENT UNIT ATTACHED FOR BUDGETING, PROGRAM COORDINATION, AND RELATED MANAGEMENT FUNCTIONS BY SECTION 15.03 OF THE STATUTES

DISABILITY BOARD

Disability Board: GOVERNOR JAMES E. DOYLE, CHIEF JUSTICE SHIRLEY ABRAHAMSON, SENATOR LASEE (senate president), SENATOR ROBSON (senate minority leader), REPRESENTATIVE GARD (assembly speaker), REPRESENTATIVE KREUSER (assembly minority leader), PHILIP FARRELL (dean, UW Medical School).

Statutory References: Sections 14.015 (1) and 17.025.

Agency Responsibility: The Disability Board is authorized by law to determine when a temporary disability exists in any of the constitutional offices because the incumbent is incapacitated due to illness or injury, and it may fill a temporary vacancy. The board, which was created by Chapter 422, Laws of 1969, originally had similar powers for supreme court justices and circuit court judges, but these were repealed by Chapter 449, Laws of 1977, and Chapter 332, Laws of 1975, respectively.

Governor Jim Doyle threw out the ceremonial first pitch at the Madison Mallards home opener. The Madison Mallards are part of the Northwoods League, a summer baseball league with teams composed of collegiate players. Wisconsin is also represented by teams in Eau Claire, La Crosse, and Wausau. (Office of the Governor)

GOVERNOR'S APPOINTMENTS TO MISCELLANEOUS COMMITTEES AND ORGANIZATIONS

Groundwater Advisory Committee

Members: DuWayne Johnsrud (gubernatorial appointee/agricultural representative), Ron Kuehn (legislative appointee/agricultural representative), *cochairpersons;* Gubernatorial appointees: Jodi Habush Sinykin (environmental representative), Keith Meyers (well drillers representative); Legislative appointees: Mike Carter (agricultural representative); Andrew Graham, Stuart Gross (environmental representatives); Doug Hahn, David Holdener, M. Carol McCartney (industrial representatives); Dan Duchniak, Lawrie Kobza, Robert Nauta (municipal representatives); DNR appointee: Todd L. Ambs (secretary of natural resources designee).

Contact person: Jill Jonas.

Address: Department of Natural Resources, 101 South Webster Street, P.O. Box 7921, Madison 53707.

Telephone: (608) 267-7545; Fax: (608) 267-7650.

Internet Address: http://dnr.wi.gov/org/water/dwg/gac/index.htm

The committee, created by 2003 Wisconsin Act 310, shall recommend a coordinated strategy for addressing groundwater management issues by affected local governmental units and regional planning commissions, with the assistance of the department of natural resources and other state agencies. The committee will issue its recommendations through two reports to the legislature's environmental standing committees, one by December 31, 2006, and one by December 31, 2007. The committee will terminate on December 31, 2007.

Wisconsin Humanities Council

Members: Gubernatorial appointees: Grady J. Frenchick, Beverly Jambois, Mary C. Knapp, Connie Loden, Leotha A. Stanley, Bobbi A. Webster. (The governor appoints 6 members to the council. Other members are elected by the council.)

Executive Director: Dean Bakopoulos.

Address: 222 South Bedford Street, Suite F, Madison 53703-3688.

Telephone: (608) 262-0706; Fax: (608) 263-7970.

E-mail Address: contact@wisconsinhumanities.org

Internet Address: http://www.wisconsinhumanities.org

Publications: Grant guidelines, speakers bureau catalogs, and a newsletter, *Perspectives.*

The Wisconsin Humanities Council, an independent, nonprofit organization, was established in 1972 under the provisions of federal Public Law 89-209. Members of the council include civic leaders; representatives of business, government, labor, professional, cultural, and educational institutions; and scholars and teachers in the humanities. The council receives annual funding from the National Endowment for the Humanities, the State of Wisconsin, and other sources. It makes grants to support projects that promote the use, understanding, and appreciation of the humanities among Wisconsin citizens. Any nonprofit organization or institution may apply to the council for project support. In planning and presenting public programs, applicant organizations must ordinarily involve scholars with graduate degrees in the humanities.

The Medical College of Wisconsin, Inc.

Board of Trustees: Gubernatorial appointees: Curt S. Culver, Don H. Davis, Jr., Timothy T. Flaherty, Jon D. Hammes, Timothy E. Hoeksema, Jeffrey A. Joerres, Natalie Black Kohler, Sheldon B. Lubar, Linda T. Mellowes, Ulice Payne, Jr., Edward J. Zore. (The governor appoints one-third of the board with senate consent.)

President: T. Michael Bolger.

Mailing Address: 8701 Watertown Plank Road, P.O. Box 26509, Milwaukee 53226-0509.

As part of his "Capital for the Day" visit in Pierce, Polk, and St. Croix counties, Governor Doyle dedicated the purchase of the 2,780-acre Straight Lake parcel of land near Luck in Polk County. The State of Wisconsin is contributing $8.8 million through the Knowles-Nelson Stewardship Fund to the $10.6 million project. The purchase will preserve rare wetlands, a 100-year old hardwood forest, and savannah-like grasslands. (Office of the Governor)

Telephone: (414) 456-8225; Fax: (414) 456-6560.

State Appropriation 2003-05: $12,337,600.

Publications: *Alumni News,* annual reports, directory of physician consultants, *Facts, Medical College of Wisconsin News, World.*

Statutory Reference: Sections 13.106, 39.15, and 39.155.

The Medical College of Wisconsin, Inc., is a private nonprofit educational corporation located in Milwaukee. The college receives a specified sum under the "student capitation" program for each Wisconsin resident it enrolls. The Higher Educational Aids Board determines whether applicants qualify as state residents. The college also receives state funds for its family medicine residency program.

The governor appoints one-third of the college's board of trustees for 6-year terms. The college is required to fulfill certain reporting requirements, and the Legislative Audit Bureau conducts biennial postaudits of expenditures made under state appropriations.

In September 1967, Marquette University terminated its sponsorship of the college, then known as the Marquette School of Medicine, Inc. To increase the supply of physicians in Wisconsin, the legislature enacted Chapter 3, Laws of 1969, which appropriated funds to the school provided Wisconsin residents received first preference for admission. The legislature made a token appropriation to test the law's constitutionality, and the Wisconsin Supreme Court ruled the law constitutional in *State ex rel. Warren v. Rueter,* 44 Wis. 2d 201 (1969). Chapter 185, Laws of 1969, fully funded state support for the college. In 1970, the college's name was changed to The Medical College of Wisconsin, Inc.

GOVERNOR'S SPECIAL COMMITTEES
June 30, 2005

The committees described in this section include those Governor Jim Doyle created or continued. Most of the committees were created under Section 14.019, Wisconsin Statutes, which provides that "the governor may, by executive order, create nonstatutory committees in such number and with such membership as desired, to conduct such studies and to advise the governor in such matters as directed." Committee members serve at the pleasure of the governor.

Unless terminated sooner, a special committee expires automatically on the fourth Monday of January of the year in which a new gubernatorial term begins. The governor may, however, provide for its continued existence by executive order. In that event, existing members continue to serve unless they resign or until the governor replaces them. Some of the following committees date back more than 40 years.

The law also provides that the governor may designate an employee of the Office of the Governor or of the Department of Administration to coordinate the activities of nonstatutory committees. In some cases, the governor has ordered other state agencies to staff and financially support committees.

When a new gubernatorial term begins, each committee is required to submit a final report to the governor or governor-elect prior to the new term. Copies of each final report and any other report a special committee prepared must be submitted to the Reference and Loan Library in the Department of Public Instruction and distributed under Section 35.83 (3), Wisconsin Statutes.

Section 20.505 (3) (a), Wisconsin Statutes, provides for the expenses of special committees created by executive order. In addition, certain committees receive specific state appropriations, and some receive federal funds because they are established in response to federal program requirements.

The special committees are listed in alphabetical order by the key word in each committee name.

Autism Advisory Council

Members: NISSAN BAR-LEV, HEATHER BOYD, TERRI ENTERS, VIVIAN HAZELL, ROSALIA HELMS, JOAN KETTERMAN, DEBRA MANDARINO, MILANA MILLAN, PAULA PETIT, PAUL REUTEMAN, GLEN SALLOWS, PAM STOIKA, MICHAEL WILLIAMS.

Contact person: DONNA WONG.

Address: Office of the Governor, Room 115 East, State Capitol, Madison 53707.

Telephone: 266-1212.

Fax: 261-6804.

Governor Jim Doyle created the council in Executive Order 94, April 5, 2005, to meet quarterly and advise the Department of Health and Family Services on strategies for implementing statewide supports and services for children with autism. Of the maximum 15 members appointed by the governor to the council, at least a majority must be parents of children with autism. The remaining members may be providers of services to autistic children, local government officials, persons who are knowledgeable of autism issues, or simply members of the general public.

Bicycle Coordinating Council

Members: SENATOR COWLES (appointed by senate majority leader), SENATOR ROBSON (appointed by senate minority leader); REPRESENTATIVE WARD (appointed by assembly speaker), REPRESENTATIVE BLACK (appointed by assembly minority leader); LISA MARSHALL (designated by secretary of tourism); DOUG DALTON (designated by secretary of transportation), LARRY CORSI (designated by director, Department of Transportation, Bureau of Transportation Safety), BRIGIT BROWN (designated by secretary of natural resources); DOUGLAS WHITE (designated by state superintendent of public instruction); JON MORGAN (designated by secretary of health and family services); PETER A. FLUCKE, CHRISTOPHER S. FORTUNE, CRAIG A. HEYWOOD, VIRGINIA L. HICKS, BRENDA MAXWELL, MARJORIE S. WARD, MAURICE WILLIAMS, JR. (public members).

Contact person: TOM HUBER, thomas.huber@dot.state.wi.us
Address: Department of Transportation, P.O. Box 7913, Madison 53707-7913.
Telephone: 267-7757.
Fax: 267-0294.

Governor Tommy G. Thompson created the council in Executive Order 122, June 24, 1991, and Governor Doyle recreated it in Executive Order 60, June 17, 2004. A similar council was originally created by Governor Patrick J. Lucey in June 1977 under Executive Order 43, and it has been recreated several times since. The council consists of not more than 17 members. The council considers all matters relating to: efforts of state agencies to encourage the use of the bicycle as an alternative means of transportation; promoting bicycle safety and education; promoting bicycling as a recreational and tourist activity; and disseminating information on state and federal funding for bicycle programs. The council also reviews the bicycle programs of state agencies, issues reports to the governor and the legislature, and makes recommendations concerning pertinent legislation.

Biobased Industry Consortium

Members: JAN ALF, ERIC APFELBACH, SUE BEITLICH, BILL BRUINS, BRUCE BULLAMORE, CHAD COOGEN, EARL GUSTAFSON, CRAIG HARMES, CHARLES HILL, JOHN IMES, JOHN LAWSON, SUE LEVAN, JOHN MALCHINE, MATT REBOLI, THOMAS SCHARFF, ROBERT SHERMAN, MICHAEL SUSSMAN, SCOT WALL, HOLLY YOUNGBEAR-TIBBETTS, KIM ZUHLKE.
Contact person: BARBARA KNAPP.
Address: Department of Agriculture, Trade and Consumer Protection, 2811 Agriculture Drive, Madison 53718.
Telephone: 224-4746.
Fax: 224-5045.

Governor Jim Doyle created the consortium in Executive Order 101, May 27, 2005. The goal of the consortium is to promote economic growth through the development and use of biobased products and bioenergy in an environmentally sound manner. The intent is to invest in research and new technologies that convert agriculture and forest products into sources of energy and/or substitutes for petro-chemicals in manufactured products. The consortium will assess Wisconsin's strengths and recommend areas for future investment. The consortium has up to 20 members, including representatives from the farm, forestry, chemical manufacturing, and other businesses; energy companies; electric utilities; environmental organizations; the university research community; and other critical sectors. Upon submitting its final report to the governor, the consortium will dissolve.

State of Wisconsin Citizen Corps Council

Members: WILLIAM MCREYNOLDS, *chairperson;* JENNIFER WARMKE (emergency management professional), *vice chairperson;* STEVE HERMAN, BRIAN O'KEEFE, NEIL STROBEL (local law enforcement representatives); TERRY DRYDEN, TOM HINZ (sheriff representatives); KEITH TVEIT (fire chief representative); JOHNNY WINSTON, SHANNON YOUNG (firefighter representatives); CARRIE EBNER, CAROL POOL (emergency medical services representatives); TERRI LEECE, DOREEN MARTINEZ (charitable organization representatives); AUGUST ERDMANN, BRYAN ROESSLER, ROGER WEBER, BETSY WILCOX, YA YANG (nongovernmental representatives); RICK CORNELIUS (tribal representative).
Contact person: DAVE STEINGRABER.
Address: Office of Justice Assistance, 131 West Wilson Street, Suite 610, Madison 53702-0001.
Telephone: 266-3323.
Fax: 266-6676.

Governor Jim Doyle created the council in Executive Order 67, September 8, 2004, to act as a statewide advisory council to encourage community participation in domestic preparedness through public education, training, and volunteer service. The council provides information and recommendations to the governor, the legislature, and the public regarding the operation, program priorities, and allocation of funds for the Wisconsin Citizen Corps initiative. Members of the council, which consists of up to 20 members, are appointed by the governor, including chairperson and vice chairperson. Membership consists of at least one representative from local law enforcement, a county sheriff, a local fire chief, a local firefighter, a local emergency medical services professional, an emergency management professional, representatives from charitable organizations with a focus on disaster readiness and volunteer mobilization, a member from an existing local or county Citizens Corps Council, and nongovernmental citizen members.

Wisconsin Coastal Management Council

Members: GARY E. BECKER, *chairperson;* vacancy, *vice chairperson;* SENATOR WIRCH; REPRESENTATIVE VAN AKKEREN; JAMES P. HURLEY (UW System representative), GARY DILWEG (designated by secretary of administration), TODD L. AMBS (designated by secretary of natural resources), LAWRENCE KIECK (designated by secretary of transportation); vacancy (tribal government representative); ROBERT D. BROWNE, SHARON COOK, KENNETH L. LEINBACH, LARRY J. MACDONALD, DOUGLAS T. OITZINGER, WILLIAM SCHUSTER.

Contact person: MIKE FRIIS.

Address: Wisconsin Coastal Management Program, Department of Administration, 101 East Wilson Street, 10th Floor, P.O. Box 8944, Madison 53708-8944.

Telephone: 267-7982.

Fax: 267-6917.

Internet: http://coastal.wisconsin.gov

Acting Governor Martin J. Schreiber established the council in Executive Order 49, October 7, 1977. It has been recreated or revised several times, and was continued most recently by Governor Doyle in Executive Order 1, January 27, 2003. It succeeded the Coastal Coordinating and Advisory Council appointed by Governor Lucey in 1974. The 1977 council was created to comply with provisions of the federal Coastal Zone Management Act of 1972 and to implement Wisconsin's official Great Lakes Management Program, which received federal approval on May 22, 1978. The council advises the governor on issues pertaining to the Great Lakes coasts and assists in providing policy direction for Wisconsin's coastal management efforts. Members represent the legislature, state agencies, units of local government, tribal governments, and citizens. To provide opportunities for full participation in the program, the governor encouraged the council to establish citizens' committees to advise the council on key issues affecting the coasts. The council endorsed "Wisconsin Coastal Management Program: Needs Assessment and Multi-Year Strategy, 2002-2006" in April 2001.

Governor's Committee for People With Disabilities

Members: JOHN W. OLSON (at-large member), *chairperson;* JORJAN BOLIN (Council on Physical Disabilities); MARTHA RASMUS (Council on Mental Health); JACKIE WENKMAN (Council on Developmental Disabilities); ALEX H. SLAPPEY (Council for Deaf and Hard of Hearing); ED WEISS (Council on Blindness); JAN VISTE (State Council on Alcohol and Other Drug Abuse); WAYNE COREY, THOMAS FELL, DANIEL LAATSCH, NANCY LEIPZIG, JOSEPH MIELCZAREK, JR., SANDRA POPP (at-large members). Nonvoting *ex officio* member: LT. GOVERNOR LAWTON.

Contact person: MALIKA MONGER.

Address: 1 West Wilson Street, Room 1150, Madison 53703-7851.

Telephone: 261-8880.

Fax: 266-3386.

The Wisconsin Governor's Committee for People with Disabilities in its present form was established in March of 1976 by Governor Patrick Lucey, and has been reauthorized through executive order by every governor since that time. The original executive order provided initial guidance for the committee to advise the governor's office on a broad range of issues affecting people with disabilities. The committee's mission, "to enhance the health and general well-being of disabled citizens in Wisconsin", was created out of a realization that state government lacked a process of systematically communicating the needs of people with disabilities to responsible state and local officials. In an effort to enhance the value of the committee, the executive order was rewritten in 2004 to support a focus on issues, policies, and programs that will encourage involvement in the workforce.

The committee consists of the Lieutenant Governor as a nonvoting, *ex officio* member, and not more than 20 members, appointed by the governor to serve at his pleasure. The committee as a whole includes Wisconsin residents with disabilities and individuals that have demonstrated interest in the concerns of all disability groups. All serve as unpaid volunteers. Six of the committee members represent specific disability constituencies: 1) Council on Blindness; 2) Wisconsin Council for the Deaf and Hard of Hearing; 3) Wisconsin Council on Developmental Disabilities; 4) Wisconsin Council on Mental Health; 5) State Council on Alcohol and Other Drug Abuse; and 6) Council on Physical Disabilities.

The committee meets quarterly, usually in March, June, September, and December. In addition to the Executive Committee, the Governor's Committee also has two subcommittees: the Business Leadership Network Subcommittee and the Youth Leadership Forum Subcommittee.

Early Intervention Interagency Coordinating Council

Members: SANDRA L. BUTTS, *chairperson;* vacancy, *vice chairperson;* vacancy (state legislator); RANDY BLUMER (designated by commissioner of insurance), LINDA HUFFER (Department of Health and Family Services, Division of Disability and Elder Services designee), SHARON FLEISCHFRESSER (Department of Health and Family Services, Division of Public Health designee), LAURA SATERFIELD (State Office of Child Care designee), JILL HAGLUND (Department of Public Instruction designee); SUE A. CHAPMAN, NICOLE R. BOWMAN FARRELL, DIANE FETT, CYNTHIA S. FLAUGER, PENNY NANGLE, ANDREW PAULSON, SAMANTHA L. PLATKOWSKI, LINDA TUCHMAN, TERRI VINCENT, NORMA J. VRIEZE, ANNETTA L. WRIGHT.

Contact person: SUSAN ABBEY, abbeysk@dhfs.state.wi.us

Address: Department of Health and Family Services, 1 West Wilson Street, Room 518, P.O. Box 7851, Madison 53707-7851.

Telephone: 267-3270.

Fax: 261-6752.

Governor Tommy G. Thompson first established the council in Executive Order 17, June 26, 1987, and recreated it in Executive Order 334, May 21, 1998. Governor Doyle continued it in Executive Order 1, January 27, 2003. Often called the "Birth to Three" Council, it was created to comply with the federal Individuals With Disabilities Education Act of 1986 and recreated to comply with the federal Individuals With Disabilities Education Act of 1997. The council advises and assists the Department of Health and Family Services in the development and administration of early intervention services for infants and toddlers with developmental delays and their families. It consists of at least 15 members and is directed by the governor to include at least 4 parents of infants, toddlers, or children aged 12 or younger with disabilities; at least 4 private or public providers of early intervention services; at least one state legislator; at least one member involved in personnel training; at least one representative of a Head Start agency or program; and other members representing state agencies that provide services or payment for early intervention services to infants and toddlers and their families. Members, other than those serving *ex officio*, serve 3-year terms. The governor directed that the council be attached to the Department of Health and Family Services for administrative and support purposes. The council issues an annual report for each federal fiscal year, most recently for October 1, 2003-September 30, 2004.

Governor's Economic Growth Council

Members: THOMAS HEFTY, JOHN NOEL, *cochairpersons;* LYLE BALISTRERI, THOMAS BOLDT, MICHAEL BOLGER, MICHAEL BROWN, ELIZABETH BURMASTER, JOHN BYRNES, PAUL CARBONNE, ROBERT CERVENKA, DAN CLANCY, ANN CRUMP, LARRY FERGUSON, JAMES HANEY, MARY JURMAIN, RALPH KAUTEN, TIMOTHY KEANE, THOMAS LYON, PAUL MIRABELLA, DAVID NEWBY, DONALD NICHOLS, HARVEY PIERCE, KEVIN REILLY, JOEL ROGERS, TIMOTHY SHEEHY, ARTHUR SMITH, THOMAS STILL, JOHN TORINUS, LARRY WEYERS.

Governor Jim Doyle announced the formation of the council in a press release dated June 25, 2003. The governor directed the council to review information collected from 12 growth round-tables from around the state and 8 cabinet level working groups established to focus on economic growth issues. Further, the governor requested the council to identify any gaps or oversights in the roundtable and working group information, set priorities among the various issues and initia-tives, and offer recommendations on implementing growth initiatives.

Governor's Task Force on Educational Excellence

Members: MICHAEL SPECTOR, *chairperson;* KATHLEEN ADEE, WILLIAM ANDREKOPOULOS, BARBARA ARNOLD, DEBRA BROWN, MARK BUGHER, JUDITH CRAIN, TIM CULLEN, JERRY DESCHANE, JOHN DREW, NEIL DURESKY, JIM FORBES, LOIS GLOVER, ANDREW GOKEE, KIM LENTZ GRAU, THOMAS HALL, MARK C. HANNA, DAVID HASE, PAM JOHNSON, WILLIE JUDE, THAI LEE, BRUCE MEREDITH, CECILIA MILLARD, DEAN RYERSON, TIMOTHY SCOBIE, REGINA SIEGEL, JAY SMITH, JEFFREY E. SMITH, RITA TENORIO.

Governor Jim Doyle created the task force in Executive Order 22, August 22, 2003, to examine the current state of education in Wisconsin and identify measures to remove educational barriers and positively reform the system, including the costs structures (such as teacher development, special education funding, and early investments in education) and sources of revenue (such as state and local taxes). The task force dissolved on June 30, 2004, when a final report was issued.

Governor's Task Force on Energy Efficiency and Renewables

Members: LEE CULLEN, *chairperson;* NINO AMATO, SPENCER BLACK, JAMES BOULLION, FORREST CEEL, ROBERT COWLES, GEORGE EDGAR, KRISTINE EUCLIDE, DAVID HELBACH, CHARLES HIGLEY, SCOTT JENSEN, DOUGLAS JOHNSON, CHARLES MCGINNIS, THOMAS MEINZ, SR., DONALD RECK, KEITH REOPELLE, FRED RISSER, BRIAN RUDE, LARRY SALUSTRO, RANDY SCHNEIDER, DANIEL SCHOOFF, DAVID SIMON, ROY THILLY, MICHAEL VICKERMAN, MARK WILLIAMSON.

Governor Jim Doyle created the task force in Executive Order 25, September 30, 2003, to advise the governor on policy options and business initiatives to reduce Wisconsin's dependence on out-of-state energy, while helping to save ratepayers money. The task force, comprised of lead-ers from the energy sector, disbanded when it submitted its final report to the governor in October 2004.

Governor's Council on Financial Literacy

Members: JESSICA DOYLE, *honorary chairperson;* LORRIE KEATING HEINEMANN, *chairperson;* WILLIAM WILCOX, *vice chairperson;* RICHARD ACKLEY, WENDY BAUMANN, DEBORAH BLANKS, JEREMIAH BOYLE, ELIZABETH BURMASTER, ROBERTA GASSMAN, JORGE GOMEZ, DAVID HACKWORTHY, KATHRYN MARCZAK, MERIDEE MAYNARD, KEVIN MCKINLEY, MICHAEL MORGAN, ANN PEGGS, ANTONIO RILEY, MARK SCHUG, CATHERINE TIERNEY, DOUG TIMMERMAN.

Contact person: DAVID MANCL, *executive director.*

Address: 345 West Washington Avenue, Fourth Floor, Madison 53708.

Telephone: 261-9540.

Fax: 264-7979.

Governor Jim Doyle created the council in Executive Order 92, March 30, 2005, to work with existing state agencies, private entities, and nonprofit associations in improving the financial liter-acy of Wisconsin citizens. The council was directed to develop a unified strategy, establish benchmarks, promote best practices, catalog existing materials, and create a financial literacy Web site. The council has not more than 20 members, with an honorary chairperson, chairperson, and vice chairperson selected from within the group. The Secretary of the Department of Financial Institutions will submit semiannual progress reports to the governor, starting on December 31, 2005.

Glass Ceiling Commission

Members: Appointments pending.

Contact person: JOANNA RICHARD.

Address: Department of Workforce Development, 201 East Washington Avenue, P.O. Box 7946, Madison 53707-7946.

Telephone: 266-7552.

Governor Tommy G. Thompson created the commission in Executive Order 223, June 23, 1994, and Governor Doyle continued it most recently in Executive Order 1, January 27, 2003, to implement the recommendations of the Governor's Task Force on the Glass Ceiling Initiative. The governor directed the commission to develop a Wisconsin Employer Compact Program to encourage state businesses and organizations to voluntarily eliminate barriers and promote advancement of women and minorities to upper ranks of management; develop a Governor's Glass Ceiling Award Program to recognize state businesses and organizations that advance women and minorities to top executive and management positions; develop the capacity to inform employers on glass ceiling issues and programs that have eliminated barriers to promoting women and minorities to upper management positions; identify businesses and industries that provide better than average opportunities for women and minorities to advance to upper management and promote the expansion of such industries in Wisconsin; and promote the appointment of qualified women and minorities to public and private boards of directors. Members of the commission are selected from the private and public sectors and serve 3-year terms. The secretary of workforce development serves as chairperson.

Wisconsin Encourages Healthy Lifestyles Council

Members: Inactive

Governor Scott McCallum created the council in Executive Order 48, June 24, 2002, and Governor Doyle continued it in Executive Order 1, January 27, 2003. The governor directed the council to design a plan to promote the overall health and well-being of state employees relying on core principles developed in *Healthiest Wisconsin 2010*; study successful public and private employer health promotion plans; encourage all state agencies to establish a healthy lifestyles council; identify incentives to promote participation by state employees in the program; and encourage healthy eating habits and participation in physical activity 30 minutes per day.

State Historical Records Advisory Board

Members: SKIP H. BELSTNER, MATTHEW BLESSING, PATRICIA A. BOGE, ANITA T. DOERING, PETER GOTTLIEB, MENZI L. BEHRND KLODT, LAURA MCCOY, JANE M. PEDERSON, RICK PIFER, KENNETH J. WIRTH.

Coordinator: PETER GOTTLIEB, pgottlieb@whs.wisc.edu

Address: 816 State Street, Madison 53706.

Telephone: 264-6480.

Governor Patrick Lucey created the advisory board on April 4, 1977. It was most recently continued by Governor Doyle in Executive Order 1, January 27, 2003. That action enables the state to participate in the grants program of the National Historical Publications and Records Commission, which coordinates the preservation of historic records in the United States and approves federal grants to the state advisory board. The board promotes the availability and use of historical records as keys to improved understanding of our cultural heritage. Members serve staggered 3-year terms.

Governor's Homeland Security Council

Members: MAJOR GENERAL ALBERT WILKENING, *chairperson;* DAVID COLLINS, SHERI JOHNSON, MARC SCHMIDT, JOHNNIE SMITH, DAVID STEINGRABER, JAMES WARREN.

Contact person: RANDI MILSAP, randi.milsap@dma.state.wi.us
Address: 2400 Wright Street, P.O. Box 14587, Madison 53708.
Telephone: 242-3072.

Governor Jim Doyle created the council in Executive Order 7, March 18, 2003, to advise the governor and coordinate the state's homeland security preparedness efforts to deter, prevent, respond, and recover from possible terrorist attacks. The council works with federal, state, and local agencies, nonprofit organizations, and private industry to prevent and respond to any threat of terrorism, to promote personal preparedness, and to make recommendations to the governor on additional steps to further enhance Wisconsin's homeland security.

Governor's Inter-Agency Council on Homelessness

Members: JUDITH WILCOX, *chairperson;* BERNARDINE JUNO, *vice chairperson;* LEE CARROLL, THEOLA CARTER, JESSICA CLARK, BOB COCROFT, RICK DeMOYA, WILLIAM GRAHN, CHRIS GUNST, MARK MOODY, SINIKKA SANTALA, RON SCHNYDER, PHILIP WELLS, JANICE WILBERG.
Contact person: DONNA WONG.
Address: Office of the Governor, Room 115 East, State Capitol, Madison 53707.
Telephone: 266-1212.
Fax: 261-6804.

Governor Jim Doyle created the council in Executive Order 66, August 9, 2004, to provide recommendations, outcome based performance standards, and agency responsibilities and timelines for preventing and ending the occurrence of homelessness in Wisconsin. The council consists of not more than 15 members appointed by the governor, of which 2 members are designated as chairperson and vice chairperson. The council will dissolve when the governor accepts its final report of findings and recommendations.

Governor's Task Force to Improve Access to Oral Health Care

Members: BLANE CHRISTMAN, *chairperson;* ERENDIRA ALMANZA, LORI BARBEAU, BILL BAZAN, STEPHANIE BURRELL, DAVID CAROLL, CARL EISENBERG, CURT GIELOW, MONICA HEBL, WENDY MACDOUGALL, MARK MILLER, MAUREEN OOSTDIK-HURD, MIDGE PFEFFER, CARRIE STEMPSKI, GRACIELA VILLADONIGA.
Contact person: DONNA WONG.
Address: Office of the Governor, Room 115 East, State Capitol, Madison 53707.
Telephone: 266-1212.
Fax: 261-6804.

Governor Jim Doyle created the task force as part of the KidsFirst Initiative, September 3, 2004, to develop strategies and policy recommendations on educating, recruiting, and retaining dental health professionals, while improving access to dental care for all children, particularly those in Medicaid and BadgerCare. The task force is also directed to analyze dental health issues, such as the most effective ways to spend Medicaid dollars on preventive dental care, and to offer solutions to the governor, the secretary of health and family services, and the secretary of regulation and licensing.

Statewide Independent Living Council

Members: LEONILA VEGA, *chairperson;* JOHN NOUSAINE (director of a center for independent living); STEPHEN J. WEST (representative of the directors of Native American Vocational Rehabilitation programs), CHARLES A. BENNER, CYNTHIA D. BENTLEY, DAVID BRODY, CHRISTINE M. MEISENHEIMER, AUDREY NELSON, MARENA PAMANET, ROXAN PEREZ, JANEAL L. QUINNELL, EVELYN SAYLOR, TIM J. SHEEHAN, LISLE SUZAWITH. Nonvoting members: CHARLENE DWYER (representing Department of Workforce Development, Division of Vocational Rehabilitation), SINIKKA SANTALA (representing Department of Health and Family Services), DIANE POOLE (representing Department of Transportation), MARY FRANCES TROUDT (representing Department of Commerce).

Contact person: Roxan Perez.

Address: 1 West Wilson Street, Room 1150, P.O. Box 7850, Madison 53707-7850.

Telephone: 266-7797.

Fax: 264-7742.

Governor Tommy G. Thompson created the council in Executive Order 212, February 10, 1994, to comply with the 1992 amendments to the federal Rehabilitation Act of 1973. Governor Doyle recreated the council in Executive Order 65, August 6, 2004. In coordination with the Division of Vocational Rehabilitation, the council has the responsibility to develop and submit the state plan for independent living services for the severely disabled to state and federal agencies; monitor, review, and evaluate the state plan; and submit reports to the U.S. Commissioner of the Rehabilitation Services Administration as requested.

The council consists of 14 voting members and 4 *ex officio* members representing the Department of Workforce Development, the Department of Health and Family Services, the Department of Transportation, and the Department of Commerce. The majority of members must be persons with disabilities who do not work for a center for independent living or the State of Wisconsin. At least one member must be a director of a center for independent living chosen by centers for independent living, and at least one representative of the directors of Native American vocational rehabilitation programs. Voting members of the council serve staggered 3-year terms and may serve no more than two consecutive terms.

International Trade Council

Members: Lon Sprecher, *chairperson;* Roger Axtell, David D. Baskerville, Bob Brown, Mary P. Burke, Dan Clancy, Criss Davis, Jane Dauffenbach, Jack L. Fischer, Heide Forman, Jon T. Geenen, Thomas P. Gehl, James Hall, James S. Haney, Joe Heil, Paul Hsu, Pauline Klaffenboeck, Cora B. Marrett, Richard Martens, Rick Mickschl, Susan Huber Miller, Frederick Monique, Rod Nilsestuen, Tom O'Heron, Jerome Okarma, E. Marty Payne, Kailas Rao, John S. Skilton, Kathi P. Seifert, Bill Stephen, Steve Wasser, Rolf Wegenke.

Contact person: Mary Regel.

Address: Division of International and Export Development, Department of Commerce, 201 West Washington Avenue, Madison 53702.

Telephone: 266-1767.

Governor Tommy G. Thompson created the council in Executive Order 301, November 19, 1996, as amended in Executive Order 319, October 28, 1997, and Governor Doyle continued it in Executive Order 1, January 27, 2003, to advise the governor and the secretaries for the Department of Commerce and the Department of Agriculture, Trade and Consumer Protection on the state's role in the development of international trade. The council is directed to study the impact of national policies on Wisconsin business; state policies that could increase incentives for international trade; and trade services that are now provided and those that need to be further developed. The governor instructed the council to: develop procedures to integrate public and private export services into a system that is easy to use; develop an annual International Trade Development Plan that would include specific benchmarks and evaluation criteria for trade development services; target markets for trade development; and encourage public and private cooperative trade services and programs. The council is directed to develop educational programs on international trade for all levels of schooling and is required to create grant programs to support expansion of foreign trade by Wisconsin businesses. The council consists of not more than 35 members, and the governor appoints the chair from the voting membership. The chair may designate individuals with specialized knowledge in international trade to serve as nonvoting associate members of the council.

State Interoperability Executive Council

Members: David Steingraber (executive director of the Office of Justice Assistance), *chairperson;* Sue Riseling (chief of police representative), *vice chairperson;* Albert Wilkening (adjutant general); SCOTT HASSETT (department of natural resources secretary); FRANK BUSALACCHI (department of transportation secretary); MATT MISZEWSKI (administrator, Department of Administration, Division of Enterprise Technology); THOMAS CZAJA, DAVID SPENNER (chief of police representatives); KURT HEUER, ANN HRAYCHUCK (sheriff representatives); NEIL CAMERON (fire chief representative); MELINDA ALLEN, BEN SCHLIESMAN (local emergency management professionals); vacancy (tribal official); DOUGLAS OITZINGER.

Contact person: DAVID STEINGRABER.

Address: Office of Justice Assistance, 131 West Wilson Street, Suite 610, Madison 53702-0001.

Telephone: 266-3323.

Fax: 266-6676.

Governor Jim Doyle created the council in Executive Order 87, February 2, 2005, to develop goals, standards, strategies, and short- and long-term recommendations for statewide public safety radio interoperability. Of the 15 council members, 10 are designated according to the executive order, which requires the minimum following individuals: Executive Director of the Office of Justice Assistance (or designee), the Adjutant General (or designee), Secretary of the Department of Natural Resource (or designee), Secretary of the Department of Transportation (or designee), Administrator of the Division of Enterprise Technology in the Department of Administration (or designee), a chief of police, a sheriff, a fire chief, a local emergency management professional, and a tribal official.

Governor's Advisory Council on Judicial Selection

Members: SUSAN STEINGASS, *chairperson;* MICHELLE BEHNKE, FRANK DAILY, STAN DAVIS, JON FURLOW, LUTECIA GONZALEZ, ROBERT JAMBOIS, ED MANYDEEDS, MATTHEW ROBBINS.

Contact person: AMY KASPER, *governor's legal counsel.*

Address: Office of the Governor, Room 115 East, State Capitol, P.O. Box 7863, Madison 53707-7863.

Telephone: 266-1212.

Governor Anthony Earl established the council in Executive Order 1, January 6, 1983. Governor Thompson recreated and restructured the council in Executive Order 2, January 28, 1987, and Governor McCallum recreated and restructured it in Executive Order 6, April 27, 2001. Governor Doyle continued the council in Executive Order 1, January 27, 2003. The council makes recommendations to the governor on filling vacancies in the state court system. It is expected to provide the governor with a list of at least 3, but not more than 5, qualified persons, no later than 6 weeks after notification that the vacancy exists. The council consists of permanent members and up to 2 temporary members, who are selected according to the particular type of vacancy and serve only until the council makes its recommendations. For a supreme court vacancy, the governor appoints up to 2 temporary members. For a court of appeals vacancy, the governor appoints up to 2 temporary members who must reside in the district in which the vacancy occurs. In the case of circuit courts, the chairperson appoints up to 2 temporary members who must reside in the circuit.

Governor's Juvenile Justice Commission

Members: DEIRDRE WILSON GARTON, *chairperson;* JERRY JANSEN, *vice chairperson;* JENNIFER BIAS, ANDREW P. BISSONNETTE, PATRICIA DAVENPORT, GUS DOYLE, TERRANCE C. ERICKSON, CHRISTOPHER FOLEY, BARBARA FRANKS, MARC HAMMER, KAREN HARDEN, SHEQUALAH R. HATCHETT, ANNETTE HETHERINGTON, TASHA JENKINS, EDDIE M. JACKSON, KENN JOHNSON, JIM MOESER, JEANETTA ROBINSON, RONALD ROCHON, CAVELL L. SAMUELS, JOHN SWEENEY, CHARLES A. TUBBS, POLLY WOLNER, JOE BEE XIONG.

Contact person: DAVID STEINGRABER.

Address: Office of Justice Assistance, 131 West Wilson Street, Suite 610, Madison 53702-0001.

Telephone: 266-3323.

Fax: 266-6676.

Governor Tommy G. Thompson created the commission as the Juvenile Justice Advisory Group in Executive Order 55, January 30, 1989, repealed and recreated it as the Governor's Juvenile Justice Commission in Executive Order 110, February 6, 1991, and Governor Doyle continued it most recently in Executive Order 1, January 27, 2003. The commission awards funds received by the state under the federal Juvenile Justice and Delinquency Prevention Act, the Juvenile Accountability Block Grant, and other state and federal programs. It also advises the governor and the legislature on juvenile justice issues. The Office of Justice Assistance provides staff and pays the expenses of the commission.

Governor's Commission on Law Enforcement and Crime

Members: Appointments pending.

Contact person: DAVID STEINGRABER.

Address: Office of Justice Assistance, 131 West Wilson Street, Suite 610, Madison 53702-0001.

Telephone: 266-3323.

Fax: 266-6676.

Governor Tommy G. Thompson created the commission in Executive Order 31, November 25, 1987, and Governor Doyle continued it most recently in Executive Order 1, January 27, 2003. The governor designated the commission to serve as the primary body for law enforcement planning and policy development. The Office of Justice Assistance provides staffing and pays the expenses of the commission.

Governor's Council on Natural Resources in Northern Wisconsin

Members: Inactive.

Governor Tommy G. Thompson established the council in Executive Order 100, July 2, 1990, and Governor Doyle continued it most recently in Executive Order 1, January 27, 2003. The governor directed the council to study policies to manage and use natural resources in northern Wisconsin and to recommend programs to ensure the availability of these resources.

Pardon Advisory Board

Members: AMY KASPER (governor's legal counsel), *chairperson;* MICHAEL LEW (representing secretary of corrections); DANIEL J. O'BRIEN (representing attorney general); JENNIFER L. BIAS, SEAN DUFFY, C.H. McCLELLAND, SHANNON YOUNG.

Address: Office of the Governor, Room 115 East, State Capitol, P.O. Box 7863, Madison 53707-7863.

Telephone: 266-7603.

Governor Lee Sherman Dreyfus originally created the Pardon Advisory Board in Executive Order 39, March 6, 1980. Governor Thompson recreated and restructured the board in Executive Order 121, June 3, 1991, and Governor McCallum recreated the board in Executive Order 24, September 12, 2001, as amended by Executive Order 50, July 18, 2002. Governor Doyle continued it in Executive Order 1, January 27, 2003. The board consists of 7 members appointed by the governor and specifies the application process. One member represents the secretary of corrections and another represents the attorney general. The governor's legal counsel or his/her designee is a voting member and chairs the board. Four members constitute a quorum for executive action by the board. The board reviews applications for executive clemency and makes recommendations to the governor on each request. As part of its review procedure, it may hold a public hearing on each qualifying application and hear from the applicant. After a hearing is concluded, the board makes a recommendation to grant, deny, or defer each application. The factors the board considers in making its decision include, but are not limited to, the severity of the offense, time passed since discharge or conviction, the applicant's need for clemency, and the applicant's activities and conduct since committing the offense.

Governor's Council on Physical Fitness and Health

Members: ALEXANDRA K. ADAMS, SUSAN BIETILA, GREGORY D. BRETTHAUER, LARRY CAIN, ERIN CARLIN, AARON L. CARREL, PAUL COSTANZO, TERRY ERICKSON, WALLY GRAFFEN, LAURA J.

GRANEY, YVENNE D. GREER, MARILYN HURT, RAYMOND D. MARTINEZ, CHARLES MCCAULEY, KAREN ORDINANS, LARRY REED, VIRGILIO RODRIGUEZ, MARY J. TUCKWELL, MICHAEL J. WOODZICKA.

Contact person: NICOLE HUDZINSKI.

Address: Office of the Governor, Room 115 East, State Capitol, P.O. Box 7863, Madison 53707-7863.

Telephone: 266-7424.

Governor Anthony Earl established the council in Executive Order 10, April 19, 1983, and Governor Doyle most recently continued it in Executive Order 1, January 27, 2003. The council makes recommendations to the governor concerning programs and policy development related to fitness and health. It develops cooperative relationships among state agencies, educational institutions, businesses, associations, and foundations in order to improve the availability of fitness and health activities to all citizens.

Governor's Poet Laureate Commission

Members: CATHRYN ANNE COFELL-MUTSCHLER, *chairperson;* DAVID C. BROSTROM, JANE HAMBLEN, BARBARA C. HOUGHTON, MARILYN L. TAYLOR, LINDA WARE, vacancy.

Contact person: CATHRYN ANNE COFELL-MUTSCHLER.

Address: 736 West Prospect Avenue, Appleton 54914.

Telephone: (920) 738-1824.

Poet Laureate: DENISE SWEET.

Governor Tommy G. Thompson created the commission in Executive Order 404, July 31, 2000, to recommend candidates for the poet laureate of Wisconsin and Governor Doyle continued it in Executive Order 1, January 27, 2003. The 7 members are appointed to 4-year terms. Each of 5 organizations recommended one person for membership: the Council for Wisconsin Writers, the Wisconsin Fellowship of Poets, the Wisconsin Regional Writers Association, the Wisconsin Humanities Council, and the Wisconsin Arts Board. The governor directed the commission to recommend three candidates; assign responsibilities to the poet laureate; and assist that individual in performing official duties. The poet laureate is required to choose and lead one project that will contribute to the growth of poetry in this state subject to commission approval; plan and attend at least four statewide literary events each year; and perform in at least four government, state, and civil events as requested by the governor's office, school systems, and literary organizations. Governor Doyle appointed Denise Sweet, of Green Bay, to a four-year term in September 2004.

State Rehabilitation Council

Members: LINDA VEGOE (client assistance programs), *chairperson;* PAULETTE BARTELT (disability advocacy groups), *vice chairperson;* CRAIG WEHNER (community rehabilitation program service provider), *secretary/treasurer;* JANEAL QUINNELL (Statewide Independent Living Council); PATRICE M. COLETTI, GAIL KOLVENBACH (parent training and information center); LYNDA KRAUSE (vocational rehabilitation counselor); PETER G. LUCAS (vocational rehabilitation recipient); JOHN W. LUI, DEBBIE ROY, vacancy (business, industry and labor); ROBERT BUETTNER, CHRISTOPHER MARSCHMAN, DELORIS TRUHN, TED M. URIBE (disability advocacy groups); GERALD CYWINSKI, KAREN B. FUNKHOUSER, KEVIN KLUEVER (vocational rehabilitation recipients); THOMAS DRAGHI (American Indian vocational rehabilitation); STEVEN GILLES (Department of Public Instruction). Nonvoting member: CHARLENE DWYER (administrator, Division of Vocational Rehabilitation Services).

Contact person: PATRICIA SEVERT.

Address: Division of Vocational Rehabilitation, 201 East Washington Avenue, P.O. Box 7852, Madison 53707-7852.

Telephone: 261-0090.

Governor Tommy G. Thompson created the council in Executive Order 363, January 30, 1999, to advise the Department of Workforce Development on the statewide vocational rehabilitation plan for disabled individuals required under 29 U.S. Code Section 720, *et seq.* Governor Doyle continued the council in Executive Order 1, January 27, 2003. The council is similar to one established in Executive Order 196, July 1, 1993, as the State Rehabilitation Advisory Council. Council members serve 3-year terms. A majority must be individuals with disabilities not employed by the Department of Workforce Development, Division of Vocational Rehabilitation Services. The administrator of that division is a nonvoting *ex officio* member of the council. The council issued "Annual Report" in 2004.

Telecommunications Relay Service Council

Members: THOMAS E. HARBISON, *chairperson;* RONALD E. BYINGTON, JILL COLLINS, CHERI FRENCH, DAVID FRIGEN, LORI ANN FULLER, KAREN E. JORGENSEN, JACK HATHWAY, HELEN RUTH KOPPES, TOM MEITNER.

Contact person: JACK R. CASSELL, jack.cassell@doa.state.wi.us

Address: Bureau of Telecommunications Management, Department of Administration, 101 East Wilson Street, 8th Floor, P.O. Box 7844, Madison 53707-7844.

Telephones: 267-0613; call relay: 1-800-947-6644; TTY: 267-6934.

Fax: 266-2164.

Governor Tommy G. Thompson created the council in Executive Order 95, June 19, 1990, recreated it in Executive Order 131, October 2, 1991, and Governor Doyle continued it most recently in Executive Order 1, January 27, 2003. The council was directed to advise the Bureau of Telecommunications Management in the Department of Administration on the feasibility or desirability of: establishing requirements and procedures for a telecommunications relay service; requiring the service to be available 24 hours a day, 7 days a week; requiring users to pay rates that are no greater than rates for functionally equivalent voice telecommunications service; prohibiting relay service operators from refusing or limiting the length of calls; prohibiting relay service operators from disclosing the contents of calls, keeping records of their contents beyond the duration of the calls, and intentionally altering the content of a call; requiring relay service operators to take training on the problems faced by hearing-impaired and speech-impaired persons using the service; and authorizing the establishment by contract of a statewide telecommunications relay service. The council consists of not more than 11 members, 4 of whom must use a telecommunications relay service. These must include one speech-impaired person, one hearing-impaired person, one speech- and hearing-impaired person, and one person not having a speech or hearing impairment. Five of the members must include one representative each from the Wisconsin Association of the Deaf, Wisconsin Telecommunications, Inc., Wisconsin State Telephone Association, a local exchange telecommunications utility, and an interexchange telecommunications utility doing business in this state.

Governor's Commission on the United Nations

Members: WOLFGANG SCHMIDT, *chairperson;* CAROL EDLER BAUMANN, LOU ANN BOHN, ROBERT CHASE, JOSEPH W. ELDER, TAMERIN HAYWARD, KATHERINE P. MARRS, THAO N. NUON, JOAN ROBERTSON, PREM SHARMA, JOHN SMART.

Contact person: GARETH A. SHELLMAN, *assistant director.*

Address: UWM Institute of World Affairs, P.O. Box 413, Milwaukee 53201.

Telephone: (414) 229-3228.

Fax: (414) 229-3626.

Originally created in 1959, the commission was continued most recently by Governor Doyle in Executive Order 1, January 27, 2003. The commission is responsible for sponsoring statewide educational programs about the United Nations, coordinating Wisconsin's official participation in the annual observance of United Nations Day, expressing its views on issues affecting the UN, and communicating its views to public officials and the news media. The membership of the commission is drawn from various civic, religious, labor, business, and educational organizations. The commission issued "Executive Summary Report" for the years 2000-2002 in December 2002.

Governor's Task Force on Waste Materials, Recovery and Disposal

Members: RICHARD BISHOP, BRIAN BOROFKA, GEORGE DRECKMANN, FRANKLYN ERICSON, LOREEN FERGUSON, JEFFREY FIELKOW, PAUL JENKS, MELEESA JOHNSON, BRIAN JONGETJES, JENNIFER KUNDE, CHARLES LARSCHEID, MICHAEL MICHELS, LYNN MORGAN, JOHN RIENDL, ARTHUR VOGEL.
Contact person: CYNTHIA MOORE.

Address: Department of Natural Resources, 101 South Webster Street, Madison 53707.
Telephone: 276-7550.

Fax: 267-2768.

Governor Jim Doyle created the task force in Executive Order 106, June 14, 2005, to study and make recommendations on the economics of landfilling and recycling solid wastes, maximizing the productive use of waste materials, and minimizing both the generation of waste materials and the environmental impacts of toxic and nontoxic solid wastes, now and for future generations. The task force shall consist of no more than 20 members, all appointed by the governor, with one member serving as the chairperson. The task force will provide ongoing reports to the secretary of natural resources and will disband when the governor accepts its final report in December 2006.

Governor's Council on Workforce Investment

Members: LYLE BALISTRERI, PHILLIP L. NEUENFELDT, MARK REIHL (labor representatives); JAMES SCHRAMM (local government representative); LEE RASCH, JOEL ROGERS, JOAN WILK (public education representatives); THOMAS L. BURSE, RODNEY J. COPES, JEWEL CURRIE, KATHLEEN DRENGLER, BARBARA FLEISNER, JOSEPH GILLES, JAMES S. HANEY, SUSAN H. HATCH, JOHN HEYER, JAMES P. HILL, ELLEN HOLT, JERRY JOHNSON, CELESTINE KOEHN, DONALD W. LAYDEN, JR., PAUL A. LINZMEYER, XIONG LO, DOUGLAS L. MOQUIN, A. KENT OLSON, SALLY PELTZ, DONALD J. ROUSE, CHRISTOPHER A. RUUD, PATRICK J. SCHILLINGER, GEORGANN STINSON, JULIA TAYLOR, NORMA TIRADO-KELLENBERGER, DAVID VIERTHALER, DEAN WELCH (private sector representatives). MARY P. BURKE, ELIZABETH BURMASTER, DANIEL CLANCY, TERRANCE CRANEY, GOVERNOR JIM DOYLE, MATTHEW J. FRANK, ROBERTA GASSMAN, HELENE NELSON, JOHN A. SCOCOS (state agency representatives); SENATORS HANSEN, LEIBHAM, REPRESENTATIVE ZEPNICK (state legislative representatives).
Contact person: SUE GLEASON.

Address: Department of Workforce Development, P.O. Box 7972, Madison 53707-7972.
Telephone: 266-0522.

Governor Tommy G. Thompson created the council in Executive Order 385, November 17, 1999, and Governor Doyle most recently continued it in Executive Order 88, February 2, 2005, to qualify the state to receive federal funds allotted under the Workforce Investment Act of 1998. The council consists of members appointed in accordance with federal law and additional members the governor may designate. As specified by law, the majority of members are from the private sector. The governor directed the council to carry out the duties and functions prescribed in WIA, Public Law 105-220; to advise the governor on workforce development strategy and policy, and undertake research and other activities to assist the governor in enhancing the operation and performance of workforce programs in the state; and to provide direction and guidance for the Wisconsin Forward Award to advance high performance workplaces, and advance other initiatives to support a skilled workforce. The governor further directed that all appropriate state agencies work together on the council and at the local level to develop a strong, skilled workforce for Wisconsin's future.

STATE OFFICERS APPOINTED BY THE GOVERNOR
AS REQUIRED BY STATUTE
June 30, 2005

Officers[1]	Name	Home Address[2]	Term Expires[3]	Salary or Per Diem[4]
*Accounting Examining	Joann Noe Cross	Oshkosh	July 1, 2004	$25 per day
Board	Frederick Franklin	Milwaukee	July 1, 2004	$25 per day
Secs. 15.08, 15.405 (1)	Roman M. Jungers II	Waupaca	July 1, 2005	$25 per day
	Karen J. Bindl	Sun Prairie	July 1, 2006	$25 per day
	Norbert J. Johnson	Milton	July 1, 2006	$25 per day
	Lucretia Mattson	Eau Claire	July 1, 2007	$25 per day
	Steve Corbeille	Crivitz	July 1, 2009	$25 per day
	Thomas J. Kilkenny[5]	Brookfield	July 1, 2009	$25 per day
Adjutant General	Maj. Gen. Albert Wilkening	Brooklyn	Sept. 1, 2007	Group 4
Sec. 15.31				
*Administration, Dept. of, Secy.	Marc Marotta	Mequon	Pleasure of Gov.	Group 8
Secs. 15.05 (1) (a), 15.10				
Adult Offender Supervision	Ann M. Gustafson	Hudson	May 1, 2007	None
Board, Interstate	Amy Kasper	Madison	May 1, 2007	None
Sec. 15.145 (3)	Gregory Potter	Wisconsin Rapids	May 1, 2009	None
	Tamara Grigsby	Milwaukee	May 1, 2007	None
	William Rankin	Janesville	May 1, 2009	None
Adult Offender Supervision	William Rankin	Janesville	Pleas. of Gov.	None
Board, Interstate				None
Compact Administrator				None
Sec. 304.16 (2)(d)				None
Affirmative Action,	Tracy M. Han	Middleton	July 1, 2005	None
Council on	Laura A. Millot	Rhinelander	July 1, 2005	None
Secs. 15.09 (1)(a), 15.177	Sandra L. Ryan	Sun Prairie	July 1, 2005	None
	Roland W. Wetley	West Allis	July 1, 2005	None
	Yolanda Santos Adams	Kenosha	July 1, 2006	None
	Alicia Herrera	Milwaukee	July 1, 2006	None
	Janice K. Hughes	Madison	July 1, 2006	None
	James R. Parker	La Crosse	July 1, 2006	None
	Meredith Reitman	Whitefish Bay	July 1, 2006	None
	Lakshmi Bharadwaj	Shorewood	July 1, 2007	None
	Blong Moua	Schofield	July 1, 2008	None
	Santiago Rosas	Madison	July 1, 2008	None
*Aging and Long-Term Care,	Margaret F. Tollaksen	West Allis	May 1, 2006	None
Board on	Ava Arnold	Beloit	May 1, 2007	None
Secs. 15.07 (1)(b) 9,	Patricia A. Finder-Stone	De Pere	May 1, 2007	None
15.105 (10)	Eugene Lehrmann	Madison	May 1, 2007	None
	Tanya L. Meyer	Gleason	May 1, 2007	None
	Rose Boron	Mosinee	May 1, 2009	None
*Agriculture, Trade and	Cynthia Brown	Menomonie	May 1, 2007	Not exc. $35 per day nor $1,000 per yr.
Consumer Protection, Board of	Enrique Figueroa	Milwaukee	May 1, 2007	Not exc. $35 per day nor $1,000 per yr.
Secs. 15.07 (1)(a), 15.07 (5)(d),15.13	Margaret Krome	Madison	May 1, 2007	Not exc. $35 per day nor $1,000 per yr.
	Richard L. Cates	Spring Green	May 1, 2009	Not exc. $35 per day nor $1,000 per yr.
	Michael Dummer	Holmen	May 1, 2009	Not exc. $35 per day nor $1,000 per yr.
	Shelly A. Mayer	Slinger	May 1, 2009	Not exc. $35 per day nor $1,000 per yr.
	Andrew Diercks	Coloma	May 1, 2011	Not exc. $35 per day nor $1,000 per yr.
	Michael Krutza	Wausau	May 1, 2011	Not exc. $35 per day nor $1,000 per yr.
	Brian Rude	Coon Valley	May 1, 2011	Not exc. $35 per day nor $1,000 per yr.

Officers[1]	Name	Home Address[2]	Term Expires[3]	Salary or Per Diem[4]
*Agriculture, Trade and Consumer Protection, Dept. of, Secy. Secs. 15.05 (1)(d), 15.07 (1)	Rod Nilsestuen	DeForest	Pleas. of Gov.	Group 6
Alcohol and Other Drug Abuse, State Council on Secs. 14.017 (2), 15.09	Lisa M. Hardt	Madison	Pleas. of Gov.	None
	James W. Koleas	Milwaukee	Pleas. of Gov.	None
	Mark C. Seidl	Algoma	Pleas. of Gov.	None
	Michael Waupoose	Madison	Pleas. of Gov.	None
	Mark A. Cook	Cambridge	July 1, 2005	None
	Ann R. Navera	Burlington	July 1, 2005	None
	Joyce O'Donnell	West Allis	July 1, 2005	None
	Sandy Hardie	Eden	July 1, 2007	None
	Linda Mayfield	Milwaukee	July 1, 2007	None
	Jan S. Viste	Oshkosh	July 1, 2007	None
*Architects, Landscape Architects, Professional Engineers, Designers and Land Surveyors, Board of Secs. 15.08, 15.405 (2)	John Fernholz	Holmen	July 1, 2004	$25 per day
	Ruth G. Johnson	Madison	July 1, 2004	$25 per day
	Arno Wm. Haering	Wausau	July 1, 2004	$25 per day
	Martin J. Hanson	Eau Claire	July 1, 2005	$25 per day
	Robert G. Hoskins	Franklin	July 1, 2005	$25 per day
	Michael Ohberg	Waukesha	July 1, 2005	$25 per day
	James G. Otto	Hubertus	July 1, 2005	$25 per day
	Rick Van Goethem	Green Bay	July 1, 2005	$25 per day
	Lynda Farrar	Oregon	July 1, 2006	$25 per day
	James E. Rusch	New Richmond	July 1, 2006	$25 per day
	Nancy L. Sobczak	Racine	July 1, 2006	$25 per day
	Walter L. Wilson	Milwaukee	July 1, 2006	$25 per day
	Scott B. Berg	Appleton	July 1, 2007	$25 per day
	Gary A. Gust	Menomonie	July 1, 2007	$25 per day
	Matthew J. Janiak	Mondovi	July 1, 2007	$25 per day
	Wayne G. Tlusty	Rib Lake	July 1, 2007	$25 per day
	Charles Kopplin[5]	Milwaukee	July 1, 2009	$25 per day
	Rosheen Styczinski[5]	Milwaukee	July 1, 2009	$25 per day
	7 vacancies			
*Artistic Endowment Foundation Chap. 247	Donald W. Baumgartner[5]	Milwaukee	May 1, 2007	None
	Judy Nagel[5]	De Pere	May 1, 2007	None
	Ginger Alden[5]	Wausau	May 1, 2009	None
	Marvin Fishman[5]	Milwaukee	May 1, 2009	None
	Suzette Renwick	La Crosse	May 1, 2010	None
Arts Board Sec. 15.445 (1)	Julilly Kohler	Milwaukee	May 1, 2006	None
	Michael Reyes	Brown Deer	May 1, 2006	None
	Robert A. Wagner	Milwaukee	May 1, 2006	None
	Linda L. Ware	Wausau	May 1, 2006	None
	Jerry Hembd	Superior	May 1, 2007	None
	Gerald Kember	La Crosse	May 1, 2007	None
	Barbara Lawton	Madison	May 1, 2007	None
	Sharon Stewart	Washburn	May 1, 2007	None
	Linda Grunau	Elm Grove	May 1, 2008	None
	Paul Meinke	Green Bay	May 1, 2008	None
	Barbara Munson	Mosinee	May 1, 2008	None
	Glenda Noel-Ney	Madison	May 1, 2008	None
	Matthew Wahl	Eau Claire	May 1, 2008	None
Athletic Trainers Affiliated Credentialing Board Sec. 15.406 (4)	Kathleen A. O'Connell	Stevens Point	July 1, 2003	$25 per day
	Heidi J. Gutschow	Green Bay	May 1, 2004	$25 per day
	William H. Bartlett	Madison	July 1, 2004	$25 per day
	Russell D. DeLap	Brookfield	July 1, 2006	$25 per day
	John Sybeldon	Wausau	July 1, 2006	$25 per day
	Ryan Berry[5]	Madison	July 1, 2009	$25 per day
*Auctioneer Board Sec. 15.504 (3)	Mark E. Shain	Greenwood	May 1, 2003	$25 per day
	Marie M. Skic	Merrill	May 1, 2003	$25 per day
	Jay N. Clarke	Ripon	May 1, 2006	$25 per day
	Patrick J. McNamara	Lancaster	May 1, 2006	$25 per day
	Timothy Sweeny[5]	Ripon	May 1, 2008	$25 per day
	Carl Theorin[5]	Wausau	May 1, 2008	$25 per day
	Alan S. Hager[5]	Lena	May 1, 2009	$25 per day

Officers[1]	Name	Home Address[2]	Term Expires[3]	Salary or Per Diem[4]
*Banking Review Board Secs. 15.07 (1)(b) 1, 15.07 (5)(b), 15.555 (1)	Thomas E. Spitz .... DeForest		May 1, 2006	$25 per day, not exc. $1,500 per yr.
	Douglas L. Farmer[5] .... La Crosse		May 1, 2007	$25 per day, not exc. $1,500 per yr.
	Christine A. Neuman .... Green Bay		May 1, 2008	$25 per day, not exc. $1,500 per yr.
	Debra R. Lins .... Prairie du Sac		May 1, 2009	$25 per day, not exc. $1,500 per yr.
	Ralph Tenuta[5] .... Kenosha		May 1, 2010	$25 per day, not exc. $1,500 per yr.
*Barbering and Cosmetology Examining Board Secs. 15.08, 15.405 (17)	Leon G. Lauer .... Green Bay		July 1, 2004	$25 per day
	Jeannie M. Bush .... La Crosse		July 1, 2006	$25 per day
	Nancy Paggao[5] .... Appleton		July 1, 2006	$25 per day
	Mary B. Blake .... Green Bay		July 1, 2007	$25 per day
	Janice M. Boeck .... Racine		July 1, 2007	$25 per day
	Eugene Gottfredsen .... Beloit		July 1, 2007	$25 per day
	Vera Harris[5] .... Madison		July 1, 2007	$25 per day
	Jeffrey Patterson .... Madison		July 1, 2008	$25 per day
	vacancy			
*Bradley Center Sports and Entertainment Corporation, Bd. of Directors of the Sec. 232.03	Douglas G. Kiel .... Wauwatosa		July 1, 2006	None
	Gail A. Lione .... Milwaukee		July 1, 2006	None
	Rolen Womack .... Brown Deer		July 1, 2006	None
	Virgis W. Colbert .... Mequon		July 1, 2009	None
	Ulice Payne, Jr. .... Greenfield		July 1, 2009	None
	Gary Sweeney .... Fox Point		July 1, 2009	None
	Ned Bechthold .... Elm Grove		July 1, 2011	None
	James L. Forbes .... River Hills		July 1, 2011	None
	Michael F. Hart .... Mequon		July 1, 2011	None
Building Commission Sec. 13.48 (2)	Terry McGuire .... Beloit		Pleas. of Gov.	None
*Burial Sites Preservation Board Secs. 15.07 (5)(o), 15.705 (1)	Roseanne M. Meer .... Madison		July 1, 2006	$25 per day
	Robert Powless .... Odanah		July 1, 2006	$25 per day
	Kathryn C. Egan-Bruhy .... Minocqua		July 1, 2007	$25 per day
	Clarice M. Ritchie .... Crandon		July 1, 2007	$25 per day
	Robert Boszhardt .... La Crosse		July 1, 2008	$25 per day
	David Grignon .... Keshena		July 1, 2008	$25 per day
Child Abuse and Neglect Prevention Board Secs. 15.07 (1)(a), 15.195 (4)	Michael J. Lien .... Two Rivers		May 1, 2005	None
	Reginald Bicha .... River Falls		May 1, 2006	None
	Robert Jambois .... Kenosha		May 1, 2006	None
	Sandra J. McCormick .... La Crosse		May 1, 2006	None
	Cyrus Behroozi .... Hartford		May 1, 2007	None
	Bruce Pamperin .... Menomonie		May 1, 2007	None
	Anne Arnesen .... Madison		May 1, 2008	None
	Jordan Greenbaum .... Milwaukee		May 1, 2008	None
	Donna Wong .... Madison		Pleas. of Gov.	None
*Chiropractic Examining Board Secs. 15.08, 15.405 (5)	Susan Feith .... Wisconsin Rapids		May 1, 2005	$25 per day
	Steven R. Conway .... Athens		July 1, 2005	$25 per day
	James W. Weber .... Rice Lake		July 1, 2005	$25 per day
	Wendy M. Henrichs .... Rhinelander		July 1, 2007	$25 per day
	Steven Silverman .... Merrill		July 1, 2007	$25 per day
	Char Glocke .... Onalaska		July 1, 2008	$25 per day
Circus World Museum Foundation Secs. 44.16 (2)	Wayne McGown .... Madison		Pleas. of Gov.	None
Claims Board Secs. 15.07 (2)(e), 15.105 (2)	Amy Kasper .... Madison		Pleas. of Gov.	None
*College Savings Program Board Sec. 14.57	Michael D. Wolff .... Madison		May 1, 2003	None
	William Oemichen .... New Glarus		May 1, 2007	None
	Jeff Plale .... South Milwaukee		May 1, 2007	None
	Paul Adamski[5] .... Stevens Point		May 1, 2009	None
	Alberta Darling[5] .... River Hills		May 1, 2009	None
	vacancy			
*Commerce, Dept. of, Secy. Secs. 15.05 (1)(a), 15.15	Mary Burke[5] .... Madison		Pleas. of Gov.	Group 6
Contractor Financial Responsibility Council Secs. 15.09 (1)(a), 15.157 (4)	Bruce D. McMiller .... Wisconsin Rapids		July 1, 2003	None
	Lawrence E. Schauder .... Janesville		July 1, 2003	None
	Mary L. Schroeder .... Brookfield		July 1, 2003	None
	James E. Cauley .... Elm Gove		July 1, 2004	None
	Kenneth L. Lepak .... Stevens Point		July 1, 2004	None

Officers[1]	Name	Home Address[2]	Term Expires[3]	Salary or Per Diem[4]
Controlled Substances Board Sec. 15.405 (5g)	Cecilia Hillard	Milwaukee	July 1, 2007	None
	Darold Treffert	Fond du Lac	July 1, 2007	None
*Corrections, Dept. of, Secy. Secs. 15.05 (1)(a), 15.14	Matthew Frank	Middleton	Pleas. of Gov.	Group 6
*Credit Union Review Board Secs. 15.07 (1)(b) 3, 15.07 (5)(s), 15.185 (7)(b)	Dennis L. Lombard	Manitowoc	May 1, 2006	$25 per day, not exc. $1,500 per yr.
	Lisa M. Greco	Brookfield	May 1, 2007	$25 per day, not exc. $1,500 per yr.
	Quirin E. Braam	New Berlin	May 1, 2008	$25 per day, not exc $1,500 per yr.
	Dennis Degenhardt	Fitchburg	May 1, 2009	$25 per day, not exc. $1,500 per yr.
	Carla Altepeter	Oshkosh	May 1, 2010	$25 per day, not exc. $1,500 per yr.
*Credit Unions, Office of, Director Sec. 15.185 (7)(a)	Suzanne T. Cowan	Oregon	Pleas. of Gov.	Group 3
Crime Victims Rights Bd. Sec. 15.255 (2)	Angela Sutkiewicz	Sheboygan	May 1, 2007	None
Criminal Penalties, Joint Review Committee on Sec. 13.525 (1)	Bradley Gehring	Appleton	Pleas. of Gov.	None
	Allen Kehl	Kenosha	Pleas. of Gov.	None
Deaf and Hard of Hearing, Council for the Secs. 15.09 (1)(a), 15.197 (8)	John J. Boyer	Madison	July 1, 2005	None
	Kathryn Dunn	Milwaukee	July 1, 2005	None
	Diane Abbott	Manitowoc	July 1, 2007	None
	Brian W. Fruits	Madison	July 1, 2007	None
	Janice Lichter	Glendale	July 1, 2007	None
	Diane C. McMahon	Manitowoc	July 1, 2007	None
	Liz Baish	Wauwatosa	July 1, 2009	None
	Harry W. Mauldin, Jr.	Madison	July 1, 2009	None
	Julie A. Springer	Menomonie	July 1, 2009	None
*Deferred Compensation Board Secs. 15.07 (1)(b) 14, 15.07 (5)(f), 15.165 (4)	Martin Beil	Mazomanie	July 1, 2005	None
	Jon R. Traver	Monona	July 1, 2006	None
	Michael H. Drury	Merrill	July 1, 2007	None
	2 vacancies			
*Dentistry Examining Board Secs. 15.08, 15.405 (6)	Judith E. Ficks	Mequon	July 1, 2002	$25 per day
	Bruce J. Barrette	Peshtigo	July 1, 2005	$25 per day
	Keith Clemence	Hales Corners	July 1, 2005	$25 per day
	Karen M. Jahimiak	Brookfield	July 1, 2005	$25 per day
	Lori R. Barbeau[5]	New Berlin	July 1, 2006	$25 per day
	David T. Carroll	Schofield	Dec. 31, 2006	$25 per day
	Nanette Kosydar Dreves	La Crosse	Dec. 31, 2006	$25 per day
	William R. Skarie[5]	Weston	July 1, 2007	$25 per day
	Linda Bohecek[5]	Eau Claire	July 1, 2008	$25 per day
	Anne N. Taylor[5]	Milwaukee	July 1, 2008	$25 per day
Development Finance Board Secs. 15.07 (1) (cm), 15.155 (1)	Darian Luckett	Milwaukee	May 1, 2005	None
	Antonio Riley	Milwaukee	May 1, 2005	None
	R.J. Twilegar	Madison	May 1, 2005	None
	Mickey Judkins	Eau Claire	May 1, 2006	None
	Mark Reihl	Madison	May 1, 2006	None
	Cheryl R. Weston	Madison	May 1, 2006	None
	Ralph Kauten	Fitchburg	May 1, 2007	None

Officers[1]	Name	Home Address[2]	Term Expires[3]	Salary or Per Diem[4]
Developmental Disabilities, Council on Secs. 15.09 (1)(a), 15.197 (11n)	Sandra L. Butts	Milwaukee	July 1, 2005	None
	Mari K. Frederick	Wautoma	July 1, 2005	None
	Catharine Krieps	West Bend	July 1, 2005	None
	Maureen Arcand	Madison	July 1, 2006	None
	Cynthia D. Bentley	Milwaukee	July 1, 2006	None
	Gerald A. Born	Madison	July 1, 2006	None
	Deanna L. Clevett-Yost	Washburn	July 1, 2006	None
	Kristin C. Tomek	Eau Claire	July 1, 2006	None
	Jacquelyn E. Wenkman	Jefferson	July 1, 2006	None
	Craig R. Feidler	Neenah	July 1, 2007	None
	Denise R. Konicki	Madison	July 1, 2007	None
	Susan Kay Nutter	La Crosse	July 1, 2007	None
	Raymond J. Pavelko	West Salem	July 1, 2007	None
	Roxanne M. Price	La Crosse	July 1, 2007	None
	Cindy Zellner-Ehlers	Sturgeon Bay	July 1, 2007	None
	Jonathan Donnelly	Madison	July 1, 2008	None
	Ruth Gullerud	Eau Claire	July 1, 2008	None
	Daniel Remick	Madison	July 1, 2008	None
	Linda Rodriguez	Racine	July 1, 2008	None
	Shu Cheng	Eau Claire	July 1, 2009	None
	Barbara Katz	Madison	July 1, 2009	None
*Dietitians Affiliated Credentialing Board Sec. 15.406 (2)	Dolores A. Price	Boyd	July 1, 2005	$25 per day
	Diane L. Johnson	Hazelhurst	July 1, 2006	$25 per day
	Virginia Jordan	Eau Claire	July 1, 2007	$25 per day
	Susan Nitzke	Cottage Grove	July 1, 2007	$25 per day
*Domestic Abuse, Council on Secs. 15.09 (1)(a), 15.197 (16)	Arline Daily Hillestad	Stevens Point	July 1, 2003	None
	Timothy Carpenter	Milwaukee	July 1, 2005	None
	Mariana Rodriguez	Milwaukee	July 1, 2005	None
	Carol Roessler	Oshkosh	July 1, 2005	None
	Ann E. Stoffel[5]	West Bend	July 1, 2005	None
	Gene Redhail	Green Bay	July 1, 2006	None
	Kathie Stolpman	Milwaukee	July 1, 2006	None
	Geri A. Heinz	Wausau	July 1, 2007	None
	Dean Kaufert	Madison	July 1, 2007	None
	Rachel Rodriguez[5]	Madison	July 1, 2007	None
	Mai Zong Vue[5]	Madison	July 1, 2007	None
	Stormy M. Walker[5]	Milwaukee	July 1, 2007	None
	L. Kevin Hamberger[5]	Franklin	July 1, 2008	None
	vacancy			
Dry Cleaner Environmental Response Council Sec. 15.347 (2)	Jill C. Fitzgerald	Muskego	July 1, 2002	None
	Steven F. Plater	Cedarburg	July 1, 2003	None
	Jeanne M. Tarvin	Milwaukee	July 1, 2003	None
	Jim S. Fitzgerald	Mequon	July 1, 2004	None
	Richard W. Klinke	Cottage Grove	July 1, 2004	None
	James Cherwinka	Wausau	July 1, 2005	None
Dwelling Code Council Secs. 15.09 (1)(a), 15.157 (3)	Jeffrey D. Bechard	Eau Claire	July 1, 2005	None
	Harold F. Last	Waupaca	July 1, 2005	None
	Dennis J. O'Loughlin	DeForest	July 1, 2005	None
	Randolph J. Thelen	Elkhorn	July 1, 2005	None
	Brian E. Walter	Neenah	July 1, 2006	None
	Kenneth M. Dentice	La Crosse	July 1, 2006	None
	Steven Levine	Madison	July 1, 2006	None
	Frank Opatik	Wausau	July 1, 2006	None
	Gary Ruhl	Oshkosh	July 1, 2006	None
	Mary L. Schroeder	Brookfield	July 1, 2007	None
	Allan Bachmann	Madison	July 1, 2007	None
	Daniel A. Nowak	Waukesha	July 1, 2007	None
	Thomas Palecek	Marshfield	July 1, 2007	None
	William J. Roehr	Germantown	July 1, 2007	None
	William Turner	Hayward	July 1, 2007	None
	John Vande Castle	Fond du Lac	July 1, 2007	None
	Michael Wallace	New Richmond	July 1, 2007	None
	Paul M. Welnak	Mukwonago	July 1, 2007	None
Education Commission of the States Sec. 39.76	Jessica Doyle	Madison	Pleas. of Gov.	None
	Douglas Hastad	La Crosse	Pleas. of Gov.	None
	Bette Lang	Beloit	Pleas. of Gov.	None

Officers[1]	Name	Home Address[2]	Term Expires[3]	Salary or Per Diem[4]
Educational Approval Board Sec. 15.675 (1)	Christy L. Brown	Bayside	Pleas. of Gov.	None
	Michael J. Cooney	Oshkosh	Pleas. of Gov.	None
	Terrance L. Craney	Baraboo	Pleas. of Gov.	None
	Joe Heim	La Crosse	Pleas. of Gov.	None
	Richard F. Raemisch	Waunakee	Pleas. of Gov.	None
	John Scocos	Fitchburg	Pleas. of Gov.	None
	Monica Williams	Appleton	Pleas. of Gov.	None
*Educational Communications Board Secs. 15.07 (1)(a) 5, 15.57	June Anderson	Oshkosh	May 1, 2007	None
	Rolf Wegenke	Madison	May 1, 2007	None
	Thomas Basting	Madison	May 1, 2009	None
	Eileen Littig[5]	Green Bay	May 1, 2009	None
	Diane Everson[5]	Edgerton	Pleas. of Gov.	None
Elections Board Secs. 15.07 (1)(a) 2, 15.07 (5)(n), 15.61	Donald Goldberg	Bayside	May 1, 2005	$25 per day
	David Halbrooks	Milwaukee	May 1, 2005	$25 per day
	David Anstaett	Madison	May 1, 2007	$25 per day
	Kirby Brant	Madison	May 1, 2007	$25 per day
	Shane Falk	Madison	May 1, 2007	$25 per day
	Patrick J. Hodan	Milwaukee	May 1, 2007	$25 per day
	Carl Holborn	Milwaukee	May 1, 2007	$25 per day
	Robert Kasieta	Verona	May 1, 2007	$25 per day
	John P. Savage	Milwaukee	May 1, 2007	$25 per day
	John C. Schober	New Berlin	May 1, 2007	$25 per day
*Emergency Management Div., Administrator of Sec. 15.313 (1)	Johnnie Smith	Sun Prairie	Pleas. of Gov.	Group 1
Emergency Medical Services Board Sec. 15.195 (8)	Steven D. Bane	West Allis	May 1, 2006	None
	Kenneth Johnson	Greenleaf	May 1, 2006	None
	Travis Teesch	Kaukauna	May 1, 2006	None
	Tracy A. Aldrich	Plover	May 1, 2007	None
	Joe Covelli	River Falls	May 1, 2007	None
	Brenda Fellenz	Marshfield	May 1, 2007	None
	Troy W. Haase	Fond du Lac	May 1, 2007	None
	Mark Fredrickson	Menasha	May 1, 2008	None
	Cal Lintz	Green Bay	May 1, 2008	None
	Gloria Murawsky	Milwaukee	May 1, 2008	None
	Keith Wesley	Eau Claire	May 1, 2008	None
*Employee Trust Funds Board Secs. 15.07 (1)(a) 3, 15.07 (5)(f), 15.16 (1) (c)	Cynthia A. Van Bogaert[5]	Brooklyn	May 1, 2009	$25 per day
*Employment Relations, Office of, Dir. Sec. 15.105 (29)	Karen Timberlake[5]	Madison	Pleas. of Gov.	Group 7
*Employment Relations Comn. Secs. 15.06 (1), 15.58	Judith M. Neumann	Madison	March 1, 2007	Group 5
	Paul P. Gordon	Chippewa Falls	March 1, 2009	Group 5
	Susan Bauman[5]	Madison	March 1, 2011	Group 5
*Ethics Board Secs. 15.07 (1) (a)(cm), 15.07 (5)(k), 15.62	Paul M. Holzem	Madison	May 1, 2000	$25 per day
	James R. Morgan	Madison	May 1, 2001	$25 per day
	Dorothy C. Johnson	Appleton	May 1, 2004	$25 per day
	David L. McRoberts	Madison	May 1, 2005	$25 per day
	Richard Warch	Ellison Bay	May 1, 2008	$25 per day
	Courtney Hunt[5]	Milwaukee	May 1, 2009	$25 per day
Federal-State Relations Office, Director Sec. 16.548 (1)	Sarah Neimeyer	Washington, D.C.	Pleas. of Gov.	Group 3
*Financial Institutions, Dept. of Secy. of Secs. 15.05 (1)(a), 15.18	Lorrie Keating Heinemann	Oshkosh	Pleas. of Gov.	Group 6

Officers[1]	Name	Home Address[2]	Term Expires[3]	Salary or Per Diem[4]
Forestry, Council on Sec. 15.347 (19)	Dennis G. Brown	Rhinelander	Pleas. of Gov.	None
	Troy Brown	Antigo	Pleas. of Gov.	None
	Roger Breske	Eland	Pleas. of Gov.	None
	Leon A. Church	Appleton	Pleas. of Gov.	None
	Fred A. Clark	Baraboo	Pleas. of Gov.	None
	Russ Decker	Schofield	Pleas. of Gov.	None
	Paul J. DeLong	Madison	Pleas. of Gov.	None
	Donald Friske	Merrill	Pleas. of Gov.	None
	Jon T. Geenen	Kaukauna	Pleas. of Gov.	None
	James Heerey	New Auburn	Pleas. of Gov.	None
	William J. Horvath	Stevens Point	Pleas. of Gov.	None
	Mary Hubler	Rice Lake	Pleas. of Gov.	None
	Mary J. Huston	Madison	Pleas. of Gov.	None
	Kenneth A. Ottman	Milwaukee	Pleas. of Gov.	None
	Robert Rogers	Custer	Pleas. of Gov.	None
	Frederic J. Souba, Jr.	Wisconsin Rapids	Pleas. of Gov.	None
	Jeffrey C. Stier	Madison	Pleas. of Gov.	None
	William C. Ward	Green Bay	Pleas. of Gov.	None
*Fox River Navigational System Authority Sec. 237.02	Bill R. Willis	Green Bay	July 1, 2005	None
	Elwyn Nelson[5]	Oshkosh	July 1, 2007	None
	Will C. Stark[5]	De Pere	July 1, 2007	None
	William Raaths[5]	Menasha	July 1, 2008	None
	Robert Stark[5]	Appleton	July 1, 2008	None
	Ron Van De Hey	Kaukauna	July 1, 2008	None
*Funeral Directors Examining Board Secs. 15.08, 15.405 (16)	Bonnie Gift	Fennimore	July 1, 2004	$25 per day
	Rick D. Unbehaun	Richland Center	July 1, 2005	$25 per day
	J.C. Frazier	Milwaukee	July 1, 2006	$25 per day
	Connie C. Ryan	Madison	July 1, 2006	$25 per day
	David E. Olsen	Jefferson	July 1, 2007	$25 per day
	Rosalie Murphy[5]	Lena	July 1, 2009	$25 per day
*Geologists, Hydrologists and Soil Scientists, Examining Board of Professional Secs. 15.08, 15.405 (2m)	Joan E. Underwood	Plymouth	July 1, 2004	$25 per day
	Robert J. Karnauskas	Pewaukee	July 1, 2005	$25 per day
	Stephen V. Donohue	De Pere	July 1, 2006	$25 per day
	Thomas J. Evans	Madison	July 1, 2006	$25 per day
	Jon H. Gumtow	Random Lake	July 1, 2006	$25 per day
	Ruth G. Johnson	Madison	July 1, 2007	$25 per day
	John Hahn[5]	Elm Grove	July 1, 2008	$25 per day
	Randall Hunt[5]	Cross Plains	July 1, 2008	$25 per day
	Frederick Madison[5]	Lodi	July 1, 2009	$25 per day
	Sue Bridson[5]	Madison	July 1, 2009	$25 per day
	William Mode[5]	Neenah	July 1, 2009	$25 per day
	Patricia Trochlell[5]	Blue Mounds	July 1, 2009	$25 per day
Great Lakes Compact Comn. Sec. 14.78 (1)	Fred P. Schnook	Ashland	July 1, 2008	None
	Todd Ambs	Madison	July 1, 2009	None
	Dave Hansen	Green Bay	July 1, 2009	None
	Nathaniel E. Robinson	Madison	Pleas. of Gov.	None
Great Lakes Protection Fund Sec. 14.84	Patrick J. Osborne	Madison	Oct. 11, 2003	None
	Todd Ambs	Madison	Oct. 11, 2005	None
	Alan Fish	Madison	Oct. 11, 2006	None
Groundwater Coordinating Council Secs. 15.09 (5)(f), 15.347 (13)	George Kraft	Amherst	July 1, 2007	None
Group Insurance Board Secs. 15.07 (1)(b), 15.07 (5)(f), 15.165 (2)	Martin Beil	Madison	May 1, 2005	None
	Robert Baird	Waukesha	May 1, 2007	$25 per day
	Janis Doleschal	Milwaukee	May 1, 2007	$25 per day
	Stephen Frankel	Mequon	May 1, 2007	$25 per day
	Esther M. Olson	Stoughton	May 1, 2007	$25 per day
	Gary Sherman	Port Wing	Pleas. of Gov.	None
*Health and Educational Facilities Authority, Wis. Sec. 231.02 (1)	Edward M. Aprahamian	Mequon	June 30, 2005	None
	Paul B. Luber	Whitefish Bay	June 30, 2006	None
	Paul J. Senty	Middleton	June 30, 2007	None
	Linda C. Bruce	Superior	June 30, 2008	None
	Tonit Calaway	Milwaukee	June 30, 2010	None
	John Noreiko	Madison	June 30, 2010	None
	Tim K. Size	Sauk City	July 1, 2011	None

Officers[1]	Name	Home Address[2]	Term Expires[3]	Salary or Per Diem[4]
*Health and Family Services, Dept. of, Secy. Secs. 15.05 (1)(a), 15.19	Helene Nelson	Madison	Pleas. of Gov.	Group 9
Health Care Information, Board on Sec. 15.07 (2)(b), 15.195 (6)	Glen E. Grady	Neillsville	May 1, 2005	None
	Pamela Grady	Racine	May 1, 2005	None
	Jerry Popowski	Sun Prairie	May 1, 2005	None
	Cynthia M. Chicker	Richland Center	May 1, 2006	None
	Ronald L. Harms	Hortonville	May 1, 2006	None
	Sherri Hauser	West Bend	May 1, 2006	None
	Christopher J. Queram	Middleton	May 1, 2006	None
	Kevin Hayden	Madison	May 1, 2007	None
	Susan L. Turney	Marshfield	May 1, 2007	None
	Gregory Britton	Beloit	May 1, 2008	None
	David Kindig	Madison	May 1, 2008	None
Health Care Liability Insurance Plan/Injured Patients and Families Compensation Fund Bd. of Governors Sec. 619.04 (3), 655.27 (2)	Barbara Kuhl	Neillsville	May 1, 2003	None
	Kermit L. Newcomer	La Crosse	May 1, 2004	None
	Mark H. Femal	Waunakee	May 1, 2005	None
	Joan T. Schmit	Madison	May 1, 2005	None
*Hearing and Speech Examining Board Secs. 15.08, 15.405 (6m)	Steven A. Harvey	Brookfield	July 1, 2005	$25 per day
	Joseph M. Hulwi	Eleva	July 1, 2005	$25 per day
	Gerard L. Kupperman	Oconomowoc	July 1, 2005	$25 per day
	Michael K. Thelen	Appleton	July 1, 2005	$25 per day
	Alma Peters	Mequon	July 1, 2006	$25 per day
	Terrence M. Greenleaf	Whitewater	July 1, 2007	$25 per day
	Katie Lepak[5]	Milwaukee	July 1, 2007	$25 per day
	Marilyn S. Workinger	Marshfield	July 1, 2007	$25 per day
	Brice Baier	Brown Deer	July 1, 2008	$25 per day
	Thomas E. Fisher	Wausau	July 1, 2008	$25 per day
Higher Educational Aids Board Secs. 15.07 (1)(a) 1, 15.67 (1)	Gregory L. Gracz	Milwaukee	May 1, 2005	None
	Mary Q. Cuene	Green Bay	May 1, 2006	None
	Mary Jo Green	Nekoosa	May 1, 2006	None
	Betty Womack	Wales	May 1, 2006	None
	Colleen Bunner	Kenosha	May 1, 2007	None
	Khalaf Khalaf	Kenosha	May 1, 2007	None
	Debra E. McKinney	Fond du Lac	May 1, 2007	None
	Thomas Shields	Kaukauna	May 1, 2007	None
	Elizabeth Tucker	Platteville	May 1, 2007	None
	B. Ann Neviaser	Madison	May 1, 2008	None
Higher Educational Aids Board, Exec. Secy. Sec. 39.29	Connie Hutchison	McFarland	Pleas. of Gov.	Group 3
Highway Safety, Council on Secs. 15.09 (1)(a), 15.467 (3)	Rodney W. Kreunen	Madison	July 1, 2004	None
	Randy Thiel	Sheboygan	July 1, 2005	None
	Sherrick Anderson	Beloit	July 1, 2006	None
	John Corbin	Brookfield	July 1, 2006	None
	Dave Collins	Madison	July 1, 2006	None
	Kari K. Kinnard	Appleton	July 1, 2006	None
	Kate Mawdlsey	Madison	July 1, 2006	None
	Dennis Kocken	Green Bay	July 1, 2007	None
	Katherine Siegler	Ashland	July 1, 2007	None
	LaVerne E. Hermann	Milwaukee	July 1, 2008	None
Historic Preservation Review Board Sec. 15.705 (2)	Dan J. Joyce	Kenosha	July 1, 2005	None
	Diane A. Kealty	Whitefish Bay	July 1, 2005	None
	Valentine J. Schute, Jr.	La Crosse	July 1, 2005	None
	Diane Al Shihabi	Middleton	July 1, 2005	None
	Daniel J. Stephans	Madison	July 1, 2005	None
	Shawn K. Graff	Slinger	July 1, 2006	None
	Carol A. Johnson	Spring Green	July 1, 2006	None
	William G. Laatsch	Sturgeon Bay	July 1, 2006	None
	David V. Mollenhoff	Madison	July 1, 2006	None
	Robert J. Salzer	Beloit	July 1, 2006	None
	Anne E. Biebel	Madison	July 1, 2007	None
	Bruce T. Block	Bayside	July 1, 2007	None
	Robert Gough	Eau Claire	July 1, 2007	None
	Kelly Jackson	Lac du Flambeau	July 1, 2007	None
	Kubet Luchterhand	Ellison Bay	July 1, 2007	None

Officers[1]	Name	Home Address[2]	Term Expires[3]	Salary or Per Diem[4]
Historical Society Endowment Fund Council Secs. 15.09 (1)(a), 15.707 (3)	Inactive			
*Housing and Economic Development Authority, Wis. Sec. 234.02 (1)	Perry Armstrong	Waunakee	Jan. 1, 2006	None
	Geoffrey Hurtado	Milwaukee	Jan. 1, 2006	None
	David W. Kruger	Madison	Jan. 1, 2007	None
	Daniel Lee[5]	Waunakee	Jan. 1, 2007	None
	Cheryll A. Olson-Collins	DeForest	Jan. 1, 2008	None
	Linda Stewart[5]	Milwaukee	Jan. 1, 2008	None
*Housing and Economic Development Authority, Wis., Executive Director Sec. 234.02 (3)	Antonio Riley	Milwaukee	Feb. 1, 2007	Group 6
Independent Review Board Sec. 15.195 (9)	Jay Gold	Madison	May 1, 2003	None
	Paul J. Millea	Milwaukee	May 1, 2003	None
	Jerry Popowski	Sun Prairie	May 1, 2005	None
	David R. Zimmerman	Madison	May 1, 2005	None
Information Technology Management Board Sec. 15.215 (1)	Mitchell Habib	Mequon	May 1, 2003	None
	Ray Fischer	West Bend	May 1, 2005	None
	2 vacancies			
*Insurance, Commissioner of Secs. 15.06 (1) (b), (3)(a) 1, 15.06 (3)(b), 15.73	Jorge A. Gomez	Fox Point	Pleas. of Gov.	Group 5
Interagency Coordinating Council Secs. 15.09 (1)(a), 15.107 (7)	Sandra L. K. Breitborde	Monona	July 1, 2003	None
	Sandra Kreul	Madison	July 1, 2003	None
	Eileen K. Mallow	Madison	July 1, 2003	None
	David R. Zimmerman	Madison	July 1, 2003	None
	Priscilla A Boroniec	Madison	July 1, 2005	None
	Sandra Mahkorn	Milwaukee	July 1, 2005	None
Interstate Compact for, Supervision of Probationers and Parolees, Administrator of Sec. 304.13 (1m)(e)	William Rankin	Madison	Pleas. of Gov.	None
Interstate Compact on Juveniles, Administrator of Sec. 48.993	Silvia R. Jackson	Madison	Pleas. of Gov.	None
Interstate Compact on the Placement of Children, Administrator of Sec. 48.988 (7)	Burnie Bridge	Madison	Pleas. of Gov.	None
Invasive Species Council Sec. 15.347 (18)	Charles Henriksen	Baileys Harbor	July 1, 2007	None
	Gregory Long	New Berlin	July 1, 2007	None
	Peter T. Murray	Madison	July 1, 2007	None
	Dennis L. Seevers	Arpin	July 1, 2007	None
	Kenneth F. Raffa	Madison	July 1, 2008	None
	Rick Yedica	Luxemburg	July 1, 2008	None
	Rebecca Sapper	Ashland	July 1, 2009	None
	James Reinartz	Saukville	July 1, 2010	None
Investment and Local Impact Fund Board Sec. 15.435	Richard L. Gurnoe	Bayfield	May 1, 2001	None
	Sidney Bjorkman	Amery	May 1, 2003	None
	Erhard Huettl	Wabeno	May 1, 2003	None
	Daniel B. Merriam	Ladysmith	May 1, 2003	None
	Roger O. Day, Jr.	Rhinelander	May 1, 2004	None
	Elizabeth M. Sorensen	Bruce	May 1, 2004	None
	Michael S. Brandner	Medford	May 1, 2005	None
	Ronald E. Henkel	Laona	May 1, 2006	None
	vacancy			
*Investment Board, State of Wis. Secs. 15.07 (1)(a) 4, 15.07 (2)(a), 15.07 (5)(a), 15.76	Thomas Boldt	Appleton	May 1, 2009	$50 per day
	William H. Levit, Jr.	Milwaukee	May 1, 2009	$50 per day
	Deloris Sims	Milwaukee	May 1, 2009	$50 per day
	Stephen Bablitch	Whitefish Bay	May 1, 2011	$50 per day
	David M. Geertsen	Racine	May 1, 2011	$50 per day
	James Senty[5]	La Crosse	May 1, 2011	$50 per day
*Judicial Commission Sec. 757.83	Michael R. Miller	West Bend	Aug. 1, 2005	$25 per day
	Bill Vander Loop	Kaukauna	Aug. 1, 2006	$25 per day
	Dallas Neville[5]	Eau Claire	Aug. 1, 2007	$25 per day
	James M. Haney[5]	Plover	Aug. 1, 2008	$25 per day
	vacancy			

Officers[1]	Name	Home Address[2]	Term Expires[3]	Salary or Per Diem[4]
Judicial Council Secs. 15.09 (1)(a), 758.13 (1)	Al Foeckler	Oak Creek	July 1, 2006	None
	Michael Christopher	Madison	July 1, 2007	None
	Kenneth Kratz	Appleton	Pleas. of Gov.	None
Justice Assistance, Office of Exec. Staff Director Sec. 15.105 (19)	David Steingraber	Oregon	Pleas. of Gov.	Group 2
*Kickapoo Reserve Management Board Secs. 15.07 (1) (b) 20, 15.07 (5) (y), 15.445 (2)	Senn R. Brown	Madison	May 1, 2006	$25 per day
	George E. Nettum[5]	Viroqua	May 1, 2006	$25 per day
	Richard Wallin	Viroqua	May 1, 2006	$25 per day
	Rebecca E. Zahm[5]	La Farge	May 1, 2006	$25 per day
	Susan C. Cushing	La Farge	May 1, 2007	$25 per day
	Jo Deen B. Lowe	Kendall	May 1, 2007	$25 per day
	Jack H. Robinson	Ontario	May 1, 2007	$25 per day
	Katie Thomson	La Crosse	May 1, 2007	$25 per day
	Ronald Johnson	La Farge	May 1, 2008	$25 per day
	William Quackenbush[5]	Black River Falls	May 1, 2008	$25 per day
	vacancy			
*Labor and Industry Review Commission Secs. 15.06 (2)(a), 15.225 (1)	David B. Falstad[5]	Oconomowoc	March 1, 2007	Group 5
	Robert Glaser	Brown Deer	March 1, 2009	Group 5
	James Flynn[5]	Madison	March 1, 2011	Group 5
Labor and Management Council Secs. 15.09 (1)(a), 15.227 (17)	James Newell	Eau Claire	July 1, 2001	None
	Jonathan T. Swain	Mequon	July 1, 2002	None
	Phil Albert	Madison	July 1, 2003	None
	James S. Haney	Madison	July 1, 2003	None
	Jay G. Kopplin	Greendale	July 1, 2003	None
	Candice M. Owley	Milwaukee	July 1, 2003	None
	Ronald E. Sweet	Wauwatosa	July 1, 2003	None
	Peter Fox	Madison	July 1, 2004	None
	Bradley C. Fulton	Sun Prairie	July 1, 2004	None
	David R. Newby	Madison	July 1, 2004	None
	Jennifer Reinert	Madison	July 1, 2004	None
	Lyle A. Balistreri	Wauwatosa	July 1, 2005	None
	Charles D. Evans	Horicon	July 1, 2005	None
	Thomas J. Leinenkugel	Chippewa Falls	May 1, 2005	None
	Thomas N. Lesch	Oak Creek	May 1, 2005	None
	Martin Beil	Mazomanie	July 1, 2006	None
	James C. Englebert	Menasha	July 1, 2006	None
	Mary L. Lund	La Crosse	July 1, 2006	None
	3 vacancies			
Laboratory of Hygiene Bd. Sec. 15.915 (2)	Michael E. Russell	Arena	May 1, 2006	None
	David S. Taylor	Verona	May 1, 2006	None
	David Berwanger	Baraboo	May 1, 2007	None
	George Million	Wausau	May 1, 2007	None
	John Stanley	DeForest	May 1, 2007	None
	Deborah L. Turski	Madison	May 1, 2007	None
	Robert Bagley	Racine	May 1, 2008	None
Lake Michigan Commercial Fishing Board Sec. 15.345 (3)	Charles W. Henriksen	Baileys Harbor	Pleas. of Gov.	None
	Richard R. Johnson	Ellison Bay	Pleas. of Gov.	None
	Michael Le Clair	Two Rivers	Pleas. of Gov.	None
	Mark Maricque	Green Bay	Pleas. of Gov.	None
	Dan Pawlitzke	Two Rivers	Pleas. of Gov.	None
	Neil A. Schwarz	Sheboygan	Pleas. of Gov.	None
	Dean Swaer	Oconto	Pleas. of Gov.	None
Lake States Wood Utilization Consortium Sec. 26.37 (1)	Inactive			
Lake Superior Commercial Fishing Board Sec. 15.345 (2)	Jeff Bodin	Bayfield	Pleas. of Gov.	None
	Bill Damberg	Bayfield	Pleas. of Gov.	None
	Maurine Halvorson	Bayfield	Pleas. of Gov.	None
	Craig Hoopman	Bayfield	Pleas. of Gov.	None
	vacancy			
Land and Water Conservation Bd. Secs. 15.07 (1)(b) 10, 15.07 (1)(cm), 15.07 (5)(h), 15.135 (4)(am)	Dennis M. Caneff	Verona	May 1, 2006	$25 per day
	Harvey Stower	Amery	May 1, 2006	$25 per day
	Sandi M. Cihlar	Mosinee	May 1, 2007	$25 per day
	Mark Cupp[5]	Muscoda	May 1, 2008	$25 per day
	William Elman[5]	Appleton	May 1, 2009	$25 per day

Officers[1]	Name	Home Address[2]	Term Expires[3]	Salary or Per Diem[4]
Law Enforcement Standards Board Sec. 15.255 (1)	Susan Armagost	Madison	May 1, 2006	None
	Edward Baumann	Pewaukee	May 1, 2006	None
	Steven J. Lelinski	Milwaukee	May 1, 2006	None
	Donnie Snow	Racine	May 1, 2006	None
	William Brandimore	Wausau	May 1, 2007	None
	Michael J. Serpe	Kenosha	May 1, 2007	None
	Roberta E. Sindelar	Friendship	May 1, 2007	None
	Patricia Seger	Madison	May 1, 2008	None
	Timothy Baxter	Wauzeka	May 1, 2009	None
	Scott Pedley	Darlington	May 1, 2009	None
Library and Network Development, Council on Secs. 15.09 (1)(a), 15.377 (6)	Mary M. Bayorgeon	Appleton	July 1, 2005	None
	Bob Koechley	Fitchburg	July 1, 2005	None
	A. Eugene Neyhart	Sussex	July 1, 2005	None
	John C. Reid	West Bend	July 1, 2005	None
	Barbara Arnold	Madison	July 1, 2006	None
	Donald Bulley	South Milwaukee	July 1, 2006	None
	Catherine Hansen	Glendale	July 1, 2006	None
	Lisa Jewell	Superior	July 1, 2006	None
	C. Patricia LaViolette	Green Bay	July 1, 2006	None
	Douglas H. Lay	Mosinee	July 1, 2006	None
	Cal Potter	Sheboygan	July 1, 2007	None
	Michael Bahr	Germantown	July 1, 2007	None
	John Nichols	Oshkosh	July 1, 2007	None
	Kathy L. Pletcher	Green Bay	July 1, 2007	None
	Linda Stelter	Eau Claire	July 1, 2007	None
	Kristine Wendt	Rhinelander	July 1, 2007	None
	Kristi A. Williams	Cottage Grove	July 1, 2007	None
	Miriam Erickson	Fish Creek	July 1, 2008	None
	Lisa Solverson	Viroqua	July 1, 2008	None
*Lower Wisconsin State Riverway Board Secs. 15.07 (1)(b) 15, 15.07 (5)(w), 15.445 (3)	Ritchie J. Brown	Black River Falls	May 1, 2006	$25 per day
	Melody K. Moore	Mazomanie	May 1, 2006	$25 per day
	L.B. Nice	Boscobel	May 1, 2006	$25 per day
	Gerald Dorscheid	Arena	May 1, 2007	$25 per day
	Greg Greenheck	Lone Rock	May 1, 2007	$25 per day
	Frederick Madison[5]	Lodi	May 1, 2008	$25 per day
	Don Greenwood	Spring Green	May 1, 2008	$25 per day
	Ronald Leys	Gays Mills	May 1, 2008	$25 per day
	William Lundberg[5]	Wisconsin Rapids	May 1, 2008	$25 per day
Madison Cultural Arts District Board Secs. 71.05 (1) (c) 6, 229.842	Tino Balio	Madison	July 1, 2004	None
	George F. Lightbourn	Madison	July 1, 2005	None
	Sue Ann Thompson	Madison	July 1, 2006	None
	Deirdre Wilson Garton	Madison	Pleas. of Gov.	None
Main Street Programs, Council on Secs. 15.09 (1)(a), 15.157 (7)	Dennis W. Leong	Middleton	July 1, 2005	None
	Terrence W. Martin	Waupaca	July 1, 2005	None
	William R. Neureuther	Hubertus	July 1, 2005	None
	Penney L. Van Vleet	Pewaukee	July 1, 2005	None
	Dick Best	Menomonie	July 1, 2006	None
	Ben Cress	Manitowoc	July 1, 2006	None
	Ann Eaves	Madison	July 1, 2006	None
	John Gardner	Stevens Point	July 1, 2006	None
	Shawn Graff	Slinger	July 1, 2006	None
	Lisa Kotter	Clintonville	July 1, 2006	None
	Timothy L. Anderson	Madison	July 1, 2007	None
	Virginia Haske	Algoma	July 1, 2007	None
	Judith Wall	Prairie du Chien	July 1, 2007	None
*Marriage and Family Therapy, Professional Counseling, and Social Work, Examining Board of Secs. 15.08 (7), 15.405 (7c)	George J. Kamps	Green Bay	July 1, 2005	$25 per day
	Ada Williams Parr	Brown Deer	July 1, 2006	$25 per day
	Evelyn Pumphrey	Milwaukee	July 1, 2006	$25 per day
	Ann Marie Starr[5]	Shorewood	July 1, 2006	$25 per day
	LaMarr J. Franklin	Glendale	July 1, 2007	$25 per day
	Bruce Kuehl	Menomonie	July 1, 2007	$25 per day
	Susan M. Putra	Watertown	July 1, 2007	$25 per day
	Mary Jo Walsh	Mukwonago	July 1, 2007	$25 per day
	Eric M. Alvin	Madison	July 1, 2008	$25 per day
	Linda Schwallie	Green Bay	July 1, 2008	$25 per day
	Leslie Mirkin[5]	Madison	July 1, 2009	$25 per day
	Abe Rabinowitz	Middleton	July 1, 2009	$25 per day
	vacancy			

Officers[1]	Name	Home Address[2]	Term Expires[3]	Salary or Per Diem[4]
Massage Therapy and Body Work Council Sec. 15.407 (7)	Amy Remillard	Waukesha	July 1, 2006	None
	Carie Martin	Eau Claire	July 1, 2007	None
	Mary Ellen Martin	Mosinee	July 1, 2007	None
	Claude J. Gagnon	Milwaukee	July 1, 2008	None
	Xiping Zhou	Madison	July 1, 2008	None
	Lillian Pounds	Milwaukee	July 1, 2009	None
*Medical College of Wis., Inc., Board of Trustees of the Sec. 39.15	Jon D. Hammes	Mequon	May 1, 2006	None
	Don H. Davis, Jr.	Whitefish Bay	May 1, 2007	None
	Timothy E. Hoeksema	Chenequa	May 1, 2007	None
	Jeffrey E. Joerres	Milwaukee	May 1, 2008	None
	Ulice Payne, Jr.	Milwaukee	May 1, 2008	None
	Edward Zore	Milwaukee	May 1, 2008	None
	Timothy Flaherty	Neenah	May 1, 2009	None
	Natalie Black Kohler	Kohler	May 1, 2009	None
	Linda Mellowes	Milwaukee	May 1, 2009	None
	Curt S. Culver	Nashotah	May 1, 2010	None
	Sheldon Lubar[5]	Milwaukee	May 1, 2011	None
Medical Education Review Committee Sec. 39.16	Inactive (7 members)			
*Medical Examining Board Secs. 15.08, 15.405 (7)	Ronald E. Grossman	Mequon	July 1, 2004	$25 per day
	Virginia Heinemann	Wausau	July 1, 2004	$25 per day
	Karen A. Kalishek	Shawano	July 1, 2004	$25 per day
	Lief W. Erickson, Jr.	Burlington	July 1, 2005	$25 per day
	Mary R. Cook	Madison	July 1, 2006	$25 per day
	Alfred L. Franger	Brookfield	July 1, 2006	$25 per day
	Daniel J. Miota	Wauwatosa	July 1, 2006	$25 per day
	Jon E. Gudeman	Milwaukee	July 1, 2007	$25 per day
	Ian Munro	Green Bay	July 1, 2007	$25 per day
	Sujatha Kailas	Fond du Lac	July 1, 2008	$25 per day
	Sandra Osborn	Verona	July 1, 2008	$25 per day
	Bhupinder Saini	Cudahy	July 1, 2008	$25 per day
	Jack M. Lockhart[5]	La Crosse	July 1, 2009	$25 per day
	Gene Musser[5]	Middleton	July 1, 2009	$25 per day
Mental Health, Council on Secs. 15.09 (1)(a), 15.197 (1)	John A. Quaal	Pewaukee	July 1, 2004	None
	Carmen Cerna	Mindoro	July 1, 2005	None
	Robert A. Harms	Ashland	July 1, 2005	None
	Sinikka Santala	Waunakee	July 1, 2005	None
	Michael J. Bachhuber	Madison	July 1, 2006	None
	Jackie M. Baldwin	St. Germain	July 1, 2006	None
	Gail McCelland	Milwaukee	July 1, 2006	None
	Martha S. Rasmus	Milwaukee	July 1, 2006	None
	Tim H. Steller	Wausau	July 1, 2006	None
	Ramona L. Williams	Milwaukee	July 1, 2006	None
	Virginia Fobart	Kenosha	July 1, 2007	None
	John Humphries	Mount Horeb	July 1, 2007	None
	Judith Wicox	Madison	July 1, 2007	None
	Rose Borntrager	Cadott	July 1, 2008	None
	Algernon Felice	Madison	July 1, 2008	None
	Pamela Pauloski	Chaseburg	July 1, 2008	None
*Merit Recruitment and Selection Administrator, Division of (OSER) Sec. 15.173 (1) (b)	Patricia M. Almond	Madison	March 26, 2004	Group 3
*Midwest Interstate Low-Level Radioactive Waste Comn., Wis. Commissioner Sec. 14.81 (1)	Stanley York	Middleton	Pleas. of Gov.	None
Midwestern Higher Educ. Comn. Sec. 14.90 (1)	Jesus Salas	Milwaukee	July 1, 2006	None
	Rolf Wegenke	Sun Prairie	July 1, 2006	None
	John E. Kerrigan	Dubuque, IA	Pleas. of Gov.	None

Officers[1]	Name	Home Address[2]	Term Expires[3]	Salary or Per Diem[4]
Migrant Labor, Council on	Richard W. Okray	Plover	July 1, 2003	None
Secs. 15.09 (1)(a), 15.227 (8)	John F. Ebbott	Milwaukee	July 1, 2004	None
	Darrell L. Krause	Hudson	July 1, 2004	None
	John I. Bauknecht	Cross Plains	July 1, 2005	None
	Rosa M. Dominguez	Milwaukee	July 1, 2005	None
	Kimberly J. Myers	Eau Claire	July 1, 2005	None
	James Kern	Mondovi	July 1, 2006	None
	Lupe Martinez	New Berlin	July 1, 2006	None
	Silvia N. Perez	Milwaukee	July 1, 2006	None
	Doris P. Slesinger	Madison	July 1, 2007	None
	Steve Ziobro	Reeseville	July 1, 2007	None
	vacancy			
Milwaukee Child Welfare	Celestine Koehn	Menomonee Falls	July 1, 2004	None
Partnership Council	Linda Davis	Mequon	July 1, 2006	None
Secs. 15.09 (1)(a), 15.197 (24)	David L. Huffman	Milwaukee	July 1, 2006	None
	Peggy West	Milwaukee	July 1, 2006	None
	Earnestine Willis	Milwaukee	July 1, 2006	None
	Julius Agara	Milwaukee	July 1, 2007	None
	Willie Johnson, Jr.	Milwaukee	July 1, 2007	None
	Archie L. Ivy	Milwaukee	July 1, 2007	None
	Michael Skwierawski	Milwaukee	July 1, 2007	None
	Elisa Castellon	Shorewood	July 1, 2008	None
	Toni Clark	Milwaukee	July 1, 2008	None
	Thomas Donegan	Milwaukee	July 1, 2008	None
	Mary Howard Johnstone	Milwaukee	July 1, 2008	None
	Wanda Montgomery	Milwaukee	July 1, 2008	None
	Leonor Rosas	Milwaukee	July 1, 2008	None
	vacancy			
Milwaukee River Revitalization	James N. Heiligenstein	West Bend	July 1, 2005	None
Council	Alfred L. Schlecht	Grafton	July 1, 2005	None
Secs. 15.09 (1)(a), 15.347 (15)	Gary Ahrens	Milwaukee	July 1, 2006	None
	Jon Richards	Milwaukee	July 1, 2006	None
	Dan Small	Belgium	July 1, 2006	None
	Christopher Svoboda	Milwaukee	July 1, 2006	None
	Cheryl Brickman	Mequon	July 1, 2007	None
	Ray Krueger	Whiefish Bay	July 1, 2007	None
	Christine Nuernberg	Mequon	July 1, 2008	None
	Nancy Frank	Elkhorn	July 1, 2008	None
	Ronald Stadler	Fredonia		
Minority Business Development	John Cadotte	Hayward	May 1, 2007	None
Board	Willie Johnson, Jr.	Milwaukee	May 1, 2007	None
Sec. 15.155 (3)	Winnifred Thomas	Seymour	May 1, 2007	None
	Charles V. Vang	Milwaukee	May 1, 2007	None
	2 vacancies			
Mississippi River Parkway	Barbara Gronemus	Whitehall	Feb. 1, 2004	None
Commission	Sheila Harsdorf	River Falls	Feb. 1, 2004	None
Sec. 14.85 (1)(a)	Norman M. Murray	Pepin	Jan. 20, 2008	None
	Frank Fiorenza	Potosi	Feb. 1, 2008	None
	Michael A. Hunter	Prescott	Feb. 1, 2008	None
	Chester H. Lee	Viroqua	Feb. 1, 2008	None
	Alan L. Lorenz	La Crosse	Feb. 1, 2008	None
	Robert Miller	Alma	Feb. 1, 2008	None
	Lee Nerison	Westby	Feb. 1, 2008	None
	Mary Ann Stemper	Prairie du Chien	Feb. 1, 2008	None
	Russell Stevens	Trempealeau	Feb. 1, 2009	None
Multifamily Dwelling Code	Bruce A. Fuerbringer	Eau Claire	July 1, 2005	None
Council	Edward R. Gray	Kenosha	July 1, 2005	None
Secs. 15.09 (1)(a), 15.157 (12)	Harry R. Macco	De Pere	July 1, 2005	None
	Richard P. Paur	Milwaukee	July 1, 2005	None
	Fred Stier	Waukesha	July 1, 2005	None
	Jeffery Brohmer	La Crosse	July 1, 2006	None
	Beth A. Gonnering	Kenosha	July 1, 2006	None
	David A. Nitz	Berlin	July 1, 2006	None
	William J. Roehr	Germantown	July 1, 2006	None
	Emory Budzinski	Mosinee	July 1, 2007	None
	James Klett	Whitefish Bay	July 1, 2007	None
	Korinne Schneider	Milwaukee	July 1, 2007	None
	Keviin Wipperfurth	McFarland	July 1, 2007	None
	Greta Hansen	Edgerton	July 1, 2008	None

Officers[1]	Name	Home Address[2]	Term Expires[3]	Salary or Per Diem[4]
National and Community Service Board Sec. 15.105 (24)	V. Thomas Metcalfe	Monona	May 1, 2005	None
	Harold Reckleberg	Casco	May 1, 2005	None
	Robert Guenther	Sheboygan	May 1, 2006	None
	Kathleen D. Groat	Appleton	May 1, 2006	None
	Joel M. Haubrich	Milwaukee	May 1, 2006	None
	Jeanan Yasiri	Madison	May 1, 2006	None
	Adrian O. Adekola	Madison	May 1, 2007	None
	Cameron Dary	Waupun	May 1, 2007	None
	Lance A. Hanson	Eau Claire	May 1, 2007	None
	Karen Peck Katz	Milwaukee	May 1, 2007	None
	Walter H. Kraemer	Menomonee Falls	May 1, 2007	None
	Yia Thao	Green Bay	May 1, 2007	None
	Albert H. Wilkening	Madison	May 1, 2007	None
	Micabil Diaz-Martinez	Madison	May 1, 2008	None
	Larry Kleinsteiber	Madison	May 1, 2008	None
	Mark Mueller	Cottage Grove	May 1, 2008	None
	Marilynn Pelky	Racine	May 1, 2008	None
*Natural Resources, Dept. of, Secy. Sec. 15.05 (1)(c)	Scott Hassett	Madison	Pleas. of Gov.	Group 7
*Natural Resources Board Secs. 15.07 (1)(a), 15.34	Jonathan Ela	Madison	May 1, 2005	None
	Gerald M. O'Brien	Stevens Point	May 1, 2005	None
	Herbert F. Behnke	Shawano	May 1, 2007	None
	Howard Poulson	Palmyra	May 1, 2007	None
	Christine Thomas	Plover	May 1, 2009	None
	Jane Wiley	Wausau	May 1, 2009	None
	John W. Welter[5]	Eau Claire	May 1, 2011	None
*Nursing, Board of Secs. 15.01 (6), 15.08, 15.405 (7g)	Marie Kohlbeck	Whitelaw	July 1, 2005	$25 per day
	June A. Bahr	Fond du Lac	July 1, 2006	$25 per day
	Jacqueline A. Johnsrud	Eastman	July 1, 2006	$25 per day
	Marilyn A Kaufmann	Cleveland	July 1, 2006	$25 per day
	Blaine J. Ropson	Milwaukee	July 1, 2007	$25 per day
	Kathleen L. Sullivan	Madison	July 1, 2007	$25 per day
	Terrie Garcia	Waukesha	July 1, 2008	$25 per day
	Margaret Heine	Janesville	July 1, 2009	$25 per day
	vacancy			
*Nursing Home Administrator Examining Board Secs. 15.08, 15.405 (7m)	Robert A. Kessler	Pewaukee	July 1, 2005	$25 per day
	Kenneth D. Arneson	Oshkosh	July 1, 2006	$25 per day
	Patricia A. Schultz[5]	Elroy	July 1, 2006	$25 per day
	Jerry J. Shallock[5]	Rhinelander	July 1, 2006	$25 per day
	David Eagan	Kenosha	July 1, 2007	$25 per day
	Mary K. Lease	Oregon	July 1, 2007	$25 per day
	Mary Pike	Middleton	July 1, 2007	$25 per day
	Mary Ann Clark[5]	Cumberland	July 1, 2009	$25 per day
	vacancy			
*Occupational Therapists Affiliated Credentialing Board Sec. 15.406 (5)	Judith E. Ficks	Mequon	July 1, 2005	$25 per day
	Cindy F. Plamann	Appleton	July 1, 2005	$25 per day
	Mylinda Barisas-Matula[5]	Sheboygan	July 1, 2006	$25 per day
	Deborah McKernan-Ace[5]	Stoughton	July 1, 2006	$25 per day
	Dorothy Olson	Appleton	July 1, 2007	$25 per day
	Gail C. Slaughter	Two Rivers	July 1, 2007	$25 per day
	2 vacancies			
*Optometry Examining Bd. Secs. 15.08, 15.405 (8)	Leon D. Griffin[5]	Madison	July 1, 2005	$25 per day
	Swaminat Balachandran	Verona	July 1, 2006	$25 per day
	Kerry L. Griebenow	New London	July 1, 2006	$25 per day
	Richard Wright	Sun Prairie	July 1, 2007	$25 per day
	Raymond Heiser	Wausau	July 1, 2008	$25 per day
	Kathi Leach	Junction City	July 1, 2008	$25 per day
	Gregory Foster[5]	Neillsville	July 1, 2009	$25 per day
*Parole Commission Chairperson Sec. 15.145 (1)	Lenard Wells	Milwaukee	March 1, 2007	Group 2
*Petroleum Storage Environmental Cleanup Council Secs. 15.09 (1)(a), 15.157 (11)	5 vacancies			

Officers[1]	Name	Home Address[2]	Term Expires[3]	Salary or Per Diem[4]
*Pharmacy Examining Board	Michael J. Bettiga	Green Bay	July 1, 2003	$25 per day
Secs. 15.08, 15.405 (9)	Georgina Forbes	Madison	July 1, 2004	$25 per day
	John P. Bohlman	Boscobel	July 1, 2005	$25 per day
	Susan L. Sutter	Horicon	July 1, 2005	$25 per day
	Pamela J. Phillips[5]	Green Bay	July 1, 2006	$25 per day
	Danny Trotter[5]	Edgerton	July 1, 2006	$25 per day
	Mark A. Zwaska[5]	Oconomowoc	July 1, 2006	$25 per day
	Fredric E. Moskol[5]	Madison	July 1, 2008	$25 per day
Physical Disabilities,	Marge Liberski	Green Bay	July 1, 2003	None
Council on	John Meissner	Little Chute	July 1, 2003	None
Secs. 15.09 (1)(a), 15.197 (4)	JorJan Borlin	Dodgeville	July 1, 2004	None
	Linda Rowley	Mineral Point	July 1, 2004	None
	Jacqueline S. Stenberg	Superior	July 1, 2004	None
	Pamela A. Wilson	Madison	July 1, 2004	None
	Joanne Zimmerman	Bayside	July 1, 2004	None
	Denise E. Gilchrist	Eau Claire	July 1, 2004	None
	Christine R. Duranceau	Rothschild	July 1, 2005	None
	Jeffrey J. Fox	Gordon	July 1, 2005	None
	Virginia I. Lukken	Mount Horeb	July 1, 2005	None
	Karen E. Secor	Montreal	July 1, 2005	None
	Jon A. Baltmanis	Waupaca	July 1, 2006	None
	Patricia Lerch	Lac du Flambeau	July 1, 2007	None
	Lewis Tyler	Brookfield	July 1, 2007	None
*Physical Therapists	Barbara Anne Flaherty	Oshkosh	July 1, 2004	$25 per day
Affiliated Credentialing Bd.	Laurie B. Kontney	Muskego	July 1, 2005	$25 per day
Sec. 15.406 (1)	Enid Mistele[5]	Sparta	July 1, 2006	$25 per day
	Otto Cordero[5]	Sauk City	July 1, 2007	$25 per day
	Jane Stroede[5]	Wisconsin Dells	July 1, 2009	$25 per day
Physician's Assistants,	Mary Pangman Schmitt[5]	Waterford	July 1, 2006	None
Council on				
Secs. 15.08, 15.407 (2)				
*Podiatrists Affiliated	P. Michael Jacobs	Onalaska	July 1, 2004	$25 per day
Credentialing Board	Ian C. Furness	Fond du Lac	July 1, 2005	$25 per day
Secs. 15.08, 15.406 (3)	Debra S. Truckey[5]	Racine	July 1, 2006	$25 per day
	Lisa Reinicke	Janesville	July 1, 2007	$25 per day
*Prison Industries Board	Carol Vollmer Pope	Brookfield	May 1, 2004	None
Secs. 15.07 (1)(b) 12,	Jose Carrillo	Janesville	May 1, 2006	None
15.145 (2)	Corey F. Odom	Milwaukee	May 1, 2006	None
	Pat Farley[5]	Sun Prairie	May 1, 2007	None
	Debra M. Pickett[5]	Darlington	May 1, 2007	None
	Bill G. Smith	Madison	May 1, 2007	None
	Lyle Balistreri[5]	Wauwatosa	May 1, 2008	None
	Matthew J. Frank[5]	Madison	May 1, 2008	None
	James E. Moore[5]	Kaukauna	May 1, 2008	None
*Private Employer Health Care	James G. Krogstad	Madison	May 1, 2002	None
Coverage Board	DeWayne G. Bierman	Sparta	May 1, 2003	None
Sec. 15.165 (5)	Kenneth W. Conger	Kohler	May 1, 2003	None
	Gary A. Meier	Racine	May 1, 2003	None
	Tim Size	Madison	May 1, 2003	None
	Gina Erickson	Janesville	May 1, 2004	None
	James R. Janes	Butte des Morts	May 1, 2004	None
	Christopher J. Queram	Middleton	May 1, 2004	None
	3 vacancies			
*Psychology Examining	B. Ann Neviaser	Madison	July 1, 2004	$25 per day
Board	Don L. Crowder	Lake Geneva	July 1, 2005	$25 per day
Secs. 15.08, 15.405 (10m)	Timothy P. Melchert	Milwaukee	July 1, 2006	$25 per day
	Barbara Seldin	Neenah	July 1, 2006	$25 per day
	McArthur Weddle	Milwaukee	July 1, 2006	$25 per day
	vacancy			
*Public Defender Board	John Hogan	Rhinelander	May 1, 2006	None
Secs. 15.07 (1)(a), 15.78	Joe Morales	Racine	May 1, 2006	None
	Pamela Pepper	Shorewood	May 1, 2006	None
	Mai Neng Xiong	Wausau	May 1, 2006	None
	James M. Brennan	Milwaukee	May 1, 2007	None
	Ellen Thorn	West Salem	May 1, 2007	None
	Daniel Berkos	Mauston	May 1, 2008	None
	Nancy Wettersten	Madison	May 1, 2008	None
	vacancy			

Officers[1]	Name	Home Address[2]	Term Expires[3]	Salary or Per Diem[4]
Public Health Council Sec. 15.197(13)	Jose Avila	Milwaukee	July 1, 2006	None
	Bevan Baker	Milwaukee	July 1, 2006	None
	John Bartkowski	Milwaukee	July 1, 2006	None
	Stephen Hargarten	Milwaukee	July 1, 2006	None
	Terri Kramolis	Ashland	July 1, 2006	None
	Charles LaRoque	Spooner	July 1, 2006	None
	June Munro	Green Bay	July 1, 2006	None
	Douglas Nelson	Milwaukee	July 1, 2006	None
	Richard Perry	Beloit	July 1, 2006	None
	Thai Vue	La Crosse	July 1, 2006	None
	Sandy Anderson	Baraboo	July 1, 2007	None
	Jayne Bielecki	Stanley	July 1, 2007	None
	Corazon Loteyro	Mercer	July 1, 2007	None
	Elizabeth Raduege	Hayward	July 1, 2007	None
	Kurt Reed	Marshfield	July 1, 2007	None
	JoAnn Weidmann	Pewaukee	July 1, 2007	None
	Christopher Fischer	Appleton	July 1, 2008	None
	Catherine Frey	Madison	July 1, 2008	None
	Gary Gilmore	La Crosse	July 1, 2008	None
	Loren Leshan	Milwaukee	July 1, 2008	None
	Ayaz Samadani	Beaver Dam	July 1, 2008	None
	Julie Willems Van Dijk	Wausau	July 1, 2008	None
	Jeanan Yasiri	Madison	July 1, 2008	None
Public Records Board Sec. 15.105 (4)	Carol Hemersbach	Greenwood	Pleas. of Gov.	None
	Michael A. Keever	Appleton	Pleas. of Gov.	None
	Rita K. Kidd	Richland Center	Pleas. of Gov.	None
	Carolyn Smith	Ridgeway	Pleas. of Gov.	None
*Public Service Commission Secs. 15.06 (1), 15.79	Robert Garvin	Madison	March 1, 2007	Group 5
	Dan Ebert[5]	Madison	March 1, 2009	Group 5
	Mark Meyer	La Crosse	March 1, 2011	Group 5
*Railroads, Commissioner of Secs. 15.06 (1)(ar), 15.795 (1)	Rodney W. Kreunen	Madison	March 1, 2005	Group 5
*Real Estate Appraisers Board Secs. 15.07 (1)(b) 17, 15.07 (1)(cm), 15.07 (5)(x), 15.405 (10r)	Mark P. Kowbel	Racine	May 1, 2003	$25 per day
	Roger D. Roslansky	La Crosse	May 1, 2004	$25 per day
	LaMarr J. Franklin	Glendale	May 1, 2005	$25 per day
	Sharon R. Fiedler	Neenah	May 1, 2006	$25 per day
	Karen Scott	Madison	May 1, 2006	$25 per day
	Marla Britton	Westby	May 1, 2007	$25 per day
	vacancy			
*Real Estate Board Secs. 15.07 (1)(b) 8, 15.07 (1)(cm), 15.07 (5)(r), 15.405 (11)	Rebecca J. Dysland	Milwaukee	July 1, 2005	$25 per day
	Maria E. Watts	Waukesha	July 1, 2005	$25 per day
	Richard A. Kollmansberger	Oconomowoc	July 1, 2006	$25 per day
	Peter Sveum	Stoughton	July 1, 2006	$25 per day
	Lloyd Levin	Milwaukee	July 1, 2007	$25 per day
	Lisabeth Weirich	Middleton	July 1, 2007	$25 per day
	vacancy			
Real Estate Curriculum and Examinations, Council on Secs. 15.09 (1)(a), 15.407 (5)	Susan E. Hamer	Green Bay	July 1, 2004	None
	Lawrence Sager	Madison	July 1, 2004	None
	Paul G. Hoffman	Waukesha	July 1, 2006	None
	Barbara McGill	Brookfield	July 1, 2006	None
	Peter Sveum	Stoughton	July 1, 2006	None
	Richard Hinsman	Racine	July 1, 2007	None
	Peggy Lovejoy	West Salem	July 1, 2007	None
Recycling, Council on Secs. 15.09 (1)(b), 15.347 (17)	Jeffrey A. Fielkow	Milwaukee	Jan. 7, 2007	None
	Neil N. Peters-Michaud	Middleton	Jan. 7, 2007	None
	John S. Piotrowski	Tomahawk	Jan. 7, 2007	None
	John Reindl	Madison	Jan. 7, 2007	None
	Cecilia A. Stencil	Weyerhaeuser	Jan. 7, 2007	None
	William R. Swift	Germantown	Jan. 7, 2007	None
	Charlotte R. Zieve	Elkhart Lake	Jan. 7, 2007	None
*Regional Transportation Authority Sec. 59.966 (2)	Inactive			
*Regulation and Licensing, Dept. of, Secy. Secs. 15.05 (1)(a), 15.40	Celia McCraney Jackson[5]	Milwaukee	Pleas. of Gov.	Group 4
Respiratory Care Practitioners Examining Council Secs. 15.08, 15.407 (1)(d)	vacancy			

Officers[1]	Name	Home Address[2]	Term Expires[3]	Salary or Per Diem[4]
Retirement Board, Wis. Secs. 15.07 (1)(a), 15.165 (3)(b)	Marilyn J. Wigdahl	La Crosse	May 1, 1999	None
	Richard Gale	West Allis	May 1, 2006	$25 per day
	Herbert Stinski	Milton	May 1, 2007	$25 per day
	John David	Watertown	May 1, 2008	$25 per day
	Nan Kottke	Wausau	May 1, 2008	$25 per day
	Mary Von Ruden	Sparta	May 1, 2008	$25 per day
	Wayne E. Koessl	Kenosha	May 1, 2009	$25 per day
	Dennis McBride	Milwaukee	May 1, 2010	$25 per day
Retirement Research Com. Sec. 13.51 (2)	7 vacancies			
Retirement Systems, Jt. Survey Com. on Sec. 13.50 (1)(c)	Michael R. Luttig	Madison	July 1, 2003	None
*Revenue, Dept. of, Secy. Secs. 15.05 (1)(a), 15.43	Michael Morgan	Milwaukee	Pleas. of Gov.	Group 7
Rural Economic Development Board Secs. 15.155 (4)(a) 5	Michael Krutza	Wausau	May 1, 2006	None
	Richard Martin	Oakfield	May 1, 2007	None
	vacancy			None
*Rural Health Development Council Secs. 15.09 (1)(a), 15.157 (8)	Kenneth M. Viste, Jr.	Oshkosh	July 1, 2005	None
	Scot A. Wall	Cashton	July 1, 2005	None
	Alan K. David	Cedarburg	July 1, 2006	None
	Craig W.C. Schmidt	Berlin	July 1, 2006	None
	Blane Christman	Ladysmith	July 1, 2007	None
	Byron J. Crouse	Fitchburg	July 1, 2007	None
	Janet K. Recore	Wautoma	July 1, 2007	None
	Tim K. Size	Sauk City	July 1, 2008	None
	BeckySue Wolf[5]	Abrams	July 1, 2008	None
	Linda L. McFarlin	Friendship	July 1, 2009	None
	2 vacancies			
*Savings Institutions Review Board Sec. 15.185 (3)	Paul C. Adamski	Stevens Point	May 1, 2007	$10 per day
	Douglas J. Timmerman	Madison	May 1, 2007	$10 per day
	George E. Gary	Milwaukee	May 1, 2009	$10 per day
	Robert Holmes	Tomah	May 1, 2009	$10 per day
	James K. Olson	Appleton	May 1, 2009	$10 per day
Sentencing Commission Sec. 15.105 (27)	Ronald K. Malone	Oak Creek	Jan. 1, 2006	None
	Peter Naze	Green Bay	Jan. 1, 2006	None
	Gerald Mowris	Madison	Jan. 1, 2007	None
	Marshall Murray	Milwaukee	Jan. 1, 2007	None
	Ann Hraychuck	Balsam Lake	Jan. 1, 2008	None
	Richard Myers	Appleton	Jan. 1, 2008	None
	Susan Steingass	Madison	Jan. 1, 2008	None
Small Business Environmental Council Secs. 15.09 (1)(a), 15.157 (10)	Peter J. Van Horn	Pewaukee	July 1, 2004	None
	J. Robert Nicholson	Waunakee	July 1, 2005	None
	Michael Simpson	Milwaukee	July 1, 2006	None
Small Business Regulatory Review Board Sec. 15.155 (5)	Minoo Seifoddini	Lake Geneva	May 1, 2006	None
	Karen Vernal	Wauwatosa	May 1, 2006	None
	Bernard Ziegeweid	Arcadia	May 1, 2006	None
	James Bohren	Sheboygan	May 1, 2008	None
	Randy Meffert	Waunakee	May 1, 2008	None
	Rick Petershack	Madison	May 1, 2008	None
*Snowmobile Recreational Council Secs. 15.09 (1)(a), 15.347 (7)	Kathleen Rasmussen	Cable	July 1, 2005	None
	Thomas Chwala	Lake Mills	July 1, 2006	None
	Larry D. Erickson	Hurley	July 1, 2006	None
	Richard Steimel	Dane	July 1, 2006	None
	Donna Jean White	Cambria	July 1, 2007	None
	Nick Berens	Antigo	July 1, 2007	None
	Karen Carlson	Frederic	July 1, 2007	None
	Mike J. Cerny	Sharon	July 1, 2007	None
	Beverly Dittmar	Eagle River	July 1, 2007	None
	John Schweitzer	Black River Falls	July 1, 2007	None
	Michael Willman	Merrill	July 1, 2007	None
	Jerry Green[5]	Black River Falls	July 1, 2008	None
	Samuel Landes[5]	Dane	July 1, 2008	None
	Andrew F. Malecki[5]	Green Bay	July 1, 2008	None
	Thomas J. Thornton[5]	Grand View	July 1, 2008	None

Officers[1]	Name	Home Address[2]	Term Expires[3]	Salary or Per Diem[4]
Southeast Wis. Professional Baseball Park Dist. Board Sec. 229.66 (2)	Greg Borca	Mequon	July 1, 2005	None
	Michael Lehman	Hartford	July 1, 2007	None
	Lisa Neubauer	Racine	July 1, 2007	None
	David Spano	Elm Grove	July 1, 2007	None
	Gregory M. Wesley	Milwaukee	July 1, 2007	None
	Jay Williams	Mequon	July 1, 2007	None
Speech-Language Pathology and Audiology, Council on Secs. 15.08, 15.407 (4)	Lynn L. Reinemann	Racine	July 1, 2004	None
	Michael Collins	Middleton	July 1, 2006	None
	Debra McLauchlin	Milwaukee	July 1, 2006	None
	John Knox	New Berlin	July 1, 2008	None
	Gregory Wiersema	Fond du Lac	July 1, 2008	None
State Capitol and Executive Residence Board Sec. 15.105 (5)	Eugene Potente, Jr.	Pleasant Prairie	May 1, 2005	None
	Robert Lewcock	Oconomowoc	May 1, 2007	None
	Anthony A. Puttnam	Madison	May 1, 2007	None
	Debra A. Woodward	Madison	May 1, 2007	None
	John J. Fernholz	Holmen	May 1, 2009	None
	Arlan K. Kay	Madison	May 1, 2009	None
	Sally Basting	Madison	May 1, 2011	None
State Employees Suggestion Board Sec. 15.175 (1)	James Behrend	Delafield	May 1, 2005	None
	David M. Vriezen	Madison	May 1, 2007	None
	Sandy Drew	Madison	May 1, 2009	None
*State Fair Park Board Secs. 15.07 (1)(b), 15 15.07 (5)(j), 15.445 (4)	Scott Gunderson	Union Grove	Jan. 3, 2005	None
	Timothy R. Sheehy	Fox Point	May 1, 2006	$10 per day, not exc. $600 per year
	Jeff Plale	South Milwaukee	Jan. 7, 2007	None
	Thomas Reynolds	West Allis	Jan. 7, 2007	None
	Anthony Staskunas	West Allis	Jan. 7, 2007	None
	Martin Greenberg	Milwaukee	May 1, 2007	$10 per day, not exc. $600 per year
	Sue Crane[5]	Burlington	May 1, 2008	$10 per day not exc. $600 per year
	Richard Gale	West Allis	May 1, 2009	$10 per day, not exc. $600 per year
	Bennie Joyner	Milwaukee	May 1, 2009	$10 per day, not exc. $600 per year
	Michelle Nettles[5]	Milwaukee	May 1, 2010	$10 per day, not exc. $600 per year
	Scott Soldon	Shorewood	May 1, 2010	$10 per day, not exc. $600 per year
*State Historical Society of Wisconsin Board of Curators Sec. 15.70	Linda Clifford	Madison	July 1, 2006	None
	Elizabeth Adelman	Mukwonago	July 1, 2007	None
	Victor Ferrall[5]	Orfordville	July 1, 2008	None
	Helen Laird	Marshfield	Pleas. of Gov.	None
State Trails Council Secs. 15.09 (1)(a), 15.347 (16)	Connie Loden	Hurley	July 1, 2005	None
	Ken L. Carpenter	Cambridge	July 1, 2007	None
	Randy Harden	Sheboygan	July 1, 2007	None
	Thomas Huber	Madison	July 1, 2007	None
	Ramsey A.R. Lee	Whitewater	July 1, 2007	None
	Thomas J. Thornton	Grand View	July 1, 2007	None
	Alison Dwyer	Madison	July 1, 2009	None
	Michael P. McFadzen	Plymouth	July 1, 2009	None
	David Phillips	Madison	July 1, 2009	None
State Use Board Secs. 15.07 (1)(b), 15.105 (22)	Nickolas C. George, Jr.	Madison	May 1, 2003	None
	Bill G. Smith	Middleton	May 1, 2003	None
	David M. Dumke	Brule	May 1, 2005	None
	Cleo Ann Eliason	McFarland	May 1, 2005	None
	Pat Farley	Sun Prairie	May 1, 2005	None
	Michael Casey	Bloomington	May 1, 2007	None
	Jean A. Vogt	Hubertus	May 1, 2007	None
	Thomas Swant	Madison	May 1, 2009	None
*Tax Appeals Commission Secs. 15.01 (2), 15.06 (1)(a), 15.06 (3)(a) 2, 15.105 (1)	Diane Norman	McFarland	March 1, 2007	Group 4
	Jennifer W. Nashold	Madison	March 1, 2009	Group 4
	David Swanson[5]	Milwaukee	March 1, 2011	Group 4
Tax Exemptions, Jt. Survey Com. on Sec. 13.52 (1) (d)	Kathryn Dunn	Greendale	Jan. 15, 2007	None
Teachers Retirement Board Secs. 15.07 (5)(f), 15.165 (3)(a)	Theodore Bratanow	Grafton	May 1, 2007	$25 per day
	Daniel A. Nerad	Green Bay	May 1, 2008	$25 per day
	Roberta Rasmus	Chippewa Falls	May 1, 2008	$25 per day
	Robert Shaw	Eau Claire	May 1, 2009	None

Officers[1]	Name	Home Address[2]	Term Expires[3]	Salary or Per Diem[4]
*Technical College System Board Secs. 15.07 (1)(a), 15.07 (5)(e), 15.94	A.J. Amato	Madison	May 1, 2005	$100 per year
	Annie T. Vang	Madison	May 1, 2005	$100 per year
	Mary Cuene	Green Bay	May 1, 2007	$100 per year
	Phillip L. Neuenfeldt	Milwaukee	May 1, 2007	$100 per year
	L. Anne Reid	West Bend	May 1, 2007	$100 per year
	Lorraine Carter	Milwaukee	May 1, 2009	$100 per year
	Ann Greenheck	Lone Rock	May 1, 2009	$100 per year
	Jose Vasquez	Wauwatosa	May 1, 2009	$100 per year
	Allan Kehl[5]	Kenosha	May 1, 2011	$100 per year
	Brent Smith[5]	La Crosse	May 1, 2011	$100 per year
Tourism, Council on Secs. 15.09 (1)(a), 15.447 (1)	Peter J. Chapman	Oshkosh	July 1, 2005	None
	Deborah T. Archer	Madison	July 1, 2006	None
	Cristina Danforth	Oneida	July 1, 2006	None
	Doug A. Neilson	Milwaukee	July 1, 2006	None
	Patricia M. Thornton	Grand View	July 1, 2006	None
	Tom Tourville	La Crosse	July 1, 2006	None
	Linda John	Brown Deer	July 1, 2007	None
	David Olsen	Jefferson	July 1, 2007	None
	Karen Raymore	Sturgeon Bay	July 1, 2007	None
	Lola L. Roeh	Elkhart Lake	July 1, 2007	None
	William J. Slater	Delavan	July 1, 2008	None
	Gloria Cobb	Lac du Flambeau	July 1, 2008	None
	Romy Snyder	Sun Prairie	July 1, 2008	None
	Kari Johnson Zambon	Rhinelander	July 1, 2008	None
*Tourism, Dept. of, Secy. Secs. 15.05 (1)(a), 15.44	Jim Holperin	Eagle River	Pleas. of Gov.	Group 6
*Transportation, Dept. of, Secy. Secs. 15.05 (1)(a), 15.46	Frank Busalacchi	Brookfield	Pleas. of Gov.	Group 7
Transportation Projects Commission Sec. 13.489 (1)	Lee Meyerhofer	Kaukauna	Pleas. of Gov.	None
	Michael R. Ryan	Waunakee	Pleas. of Gov.	None
	Leonard Sobczak	Racine	Pleas. of Gov.	None
Uniform State Laws, Commission on Sec. 13.55 (1)	Ann Walsh Bradley	Madison	May 1, 2007	None
	Walter Kelly	Shorewood	May 1, 2009	None
*Univ. of Wis. Hospitals and Clinics Authority Sec. 15.96, 233.02	Carol L. Booth-Parks	Madison	Pleas. of Gov.	None
	Richard W. Choudoir	Columbus	Pleas. of Gov.	None
	Dian Palmer	Brookfield	July 1, 2006	None
	Kenneth Viste	Oshkosh	July 1, 2007	None
	Patrick Boyle[5]	Madison	July 1, 2008	None
*Univ. of Wis. System, Bd. of Regents of the Secs. 15.07 (1)(a), 15.91	Roger E. Axtell	Janesville	May 1, 2006	None
	Gregory L. Gracz	Milwaukee	May 1, 2006	None
	Mark Bradley	Wausau	May 1, 2007	None
	Peggy Rosenzweig	Wauwatosa	May 1, 2007	None
	Christopher Semenas[5]	Kenosha	May 1, 2008	None
	Danae D. Davis	Milwaukee	May 1, 2008	None
	Michael Falbo[5]	Franklin	May 1, 2008	None
	David Walsh	Madison	May 1, 2008	None
	Chuck Pruitt	Shorewood	May 1, 2009	None
	Jesus Salas	Milwaukee	May 1, 2009	None
	Eileen Connolly-Keesler	Neenah	May 1, 2010	None
	Thomas Loftus[5]	Sun Prairie	May 1, 2011	None
	Milton L. McPike[5]	Mazomanie	May 1, 2011	None
	Judith VanderMeulen Crain[5]	Green Bay	May 1, 2012	None
	Michael Spector[5]	Shorewood	May 1, 2012	None
Utility Public Benefits Council on Sec. 15.107 (17)	Thelma A. Sias	Milwaukee	July 1, 2004	None
	James Boullion	Madison	July 1, 2008	None
*Veterans Affairs, Board of Secs. 15.07 (1)(a), 15.49	Donald L. Heiliger	Stoughton	May 1, 2005	None
	Mack E. Hughes	Milwaukee	May 1, 2007	None
	Walter M. Stenavich	Racine	May 1, 2007	None
	Kenneth C. Wendt	Sturgeon Bay	May 1, 2007	None
	Marvin J. Freedman[5]	Middleton	May 1, 2009	None
	Peter J. Moran	Superior	May 1, 2009	None
	Rodney Moen[5]	Whitehall	May 1, 2011	None

Officers[1]	Name	Home Address[2]	Term Expires[3]	Salary or Per Diem[4]
Veterinary Diagnostic Laboratory Board Sec. 15.915 (1)	Tod R. Fleming	Baraboo	May 1, 2006	None
	Mark E. Riechers	Darlington	May 1, 2006	None
	Berwyn Cadman	Ridgeland	May 1, 2007	None
	Lloyd Sorenson	La Crosse	May 1, 2007	None
	Linda Hodorff	Eden	May 1, 2008	None
*Veterinary Examining Bd. Secs. 15.08, 15.405 (12)	James R. Johnson	Waukesha	July 1, 2005	$25 per day
	JoAnn Kleman	Mosinee	July 1, 2006	$25 per day
	Larry D. Mahr	Oregon	July 1, 2006	$25 per day
	Joan Wywialowski	Phillips	July 1, 2006	$25 per day
	Marthina L. Greer[5]	Lomira	July 1, 2007	$25 per day
	Donald J. Peterson[5]	Barron	July 1, 2008	$25 per day
	Theresa L. Waage[5]	Argyle	July 1, 2008	$25 per day
	Robert R. Spencer[5]	La Crosse	July 1, 2009	$25 per day
Volunteer Fire Fighter and Emergency Medical Technician Service Award Board Sec.15.105 (26)	Robert H. Seitz	Monticello	May 1, 2005	None
	Kenneth A. Bartz	Mount Horeb	May 1, 2006	None
	Gregorio Montoto	Mukwonago	May 1, 2006	None
	Allen R. Schraeder	Ripon	May 1, 2006	None
	Melinda R. Allen	Juda	May 1, 2007	None
	Brad R. Cook	Pardeeville	May 1, 2007	None
	Carl Stolte	Reedsburg	May 1, 2007	None
*Waste Facility Siting Board Secs. 15.07 (1)(b) 11, 15.07 (5)(t), 15.105 (12)	Michael A. Marsden	Grand Chute	May 1, 2003	$35 per day
	James Schuerman[5]	Wisconsin Rapids	May 1, 2007	$35 per day
	Dale R. Shaver[5]	Waukesha	May 1, 2008	$35 per day
*Waterways Commission, Wis. Secs. 15.01 (2), 15.06 (1)(ag), 15.06 (3)(a) 3, 15.345 (1)	Patrick T. Zielke	La Crosse	March 1, 1999	None
	Kenneth Genisot[5]	Gile	March 1, 2006	None
	Roger E. Walsh[5]	Wauwatosa	March 1, 2008	None
	James F. Rooney[5]	Racine	March 1, 2009	None
	Kurt Koeppler[5]	Oshkosh	March 1, 2010	None
Wisconsin Center District Board of Directors Sec. 229.42 (4)(e)	Franklyn M. Gimbel	Milwaukee	May 1, 2006	None
	Marc Marotta	Mequon	May 1, 2006	None
	Stephen H. Marcus	Milwaukee	May 1, 2007	None
	Jacob Weissgerber	Hartland	May 1, 2007	None
Wisconsin Land Council Sec. 15.107 (16)	Timothy M. Hanna	Appleton	July 1, 2005	None
	Jane Licht	McFarland	July 1, 2005	None
	Richard Stadelman	Shawano	July 1, 2005	None
	Jerry J. Doyle	Sheboygan	July 1, 2006	None
	Robert T. Gottschalk	Madison	July 1, 2006	None
	Brian W. Ohm	Madison	July 1, 2006	None
	Willard J. Beitlich	Stoddard	July 1, 2007	None
	Jennifer D. Hill-Kelley	Green Bay	July 1, 2007	None
	Sean P. Phelan	Wauwatosa	July 1, 2007	None
Women's Council Secs. 15.09 (1)(a), 15.107 (11)	Nicole Bowman-Farrell	Shawano	July 1, 2006	None
	Kris Martinsek	Milwaukee	July 1, 2006	None
	Ann Peggs	Green Bay	July 1, 2006	None
	Renee Boldt	Appleton	July 1, 2007	None
	Jane D. Clark	Madison	July 1, 2007	None
	Joan M. Prince	Milwaukee	July 1, 2007	None
	Arlene C. Siss	Platteville	July 1, 2007	None
Work-Based Learning Board, Governor's Sec. 15.225 (3)	Sally A. Henzl	Racine	Pleas. of Gov.	None
	Charles E. Sambs	Roberts	Pleas. of Gov.	None
	Dean T. Schultz	Eau Claire	Pleas. of Gov.	None
	Kate L. Shaffer	Weston	Pleas. of Gov.	None
	Willie Sinclair	Milwaukee	Pleas. of Gov.	None
	Patrick VanLieshout	Green Bay	Pleas. of Gov.	None
	Dorothy Walker	Milwaukee	Pleas. of Gov.	None
	Judith F. Warmuth	Belleville	Pleas. of Gov.	None
Work-Based Learning Board, Governor's, Exec. Dir. Sec. 15.225 (3)	Terry Craney	Baraboo	Pleas. of Gov.	Group 3
Worker's Compensation Rating Committee Sec. 626.31 (1)(b)	Edward J. Hayden	Hartland	Pleas. of Gov.	None
	John C Metcalf	Madison	Pleas. of Gov.	None

Officers[1]	Name	Home Address[2]	Term Expires[3]	Salary or Per Diem[4]
*Workforce Development, Dept. of, Secy. Secs. 15.05 (1)(a), 15.22	Roberta Gassman	Madison	Pleas. of Gov.	Group 6
World Dairy Center Authority Sec. 235.02	Inactive			

*Nominated by the governor and appointed with the advice and consent of the senate. Senate confirmation is required for secretaries of departments, members of commissions and commissioners, governing boards, examining boards, and other boards as designated by statute.

[1]List includes *only* appointments made by the governor. Additional members frequently serve *ex officio* or are appointed by other means. The governor also appoints members of intrastate regional agencies and nonstatutory committees and makes temporary appointments under statute Chapter 17 to elected state and county offices when vacancies occur. For complete membership list of unit, including officers, see full description elsewhere in the *Blue Book*. Section numbers under each entry refer to statute sections authorizing appointment by the governor. Statute Section 21.18 provides for the governor's military staff.

[2]Home address is the municipality from which the officer was appointed to a full-time office or the current address of part-time officials.

[3]Terms are specified by the following statute sections or as otherwise provided by law: Sec. 15.05 (1) – secretaries; Sec. 15.06 (1) – commissioners; Sec. 15.07 (1) – governing boards and attached boards; Sec. 15.08 (1) – examining boards and councils; Sec. 15.09 (1) – councils.

[4]Members of boards and councils are reimbursed for actual and necessary expenses incurred in performing their duties. In addition, examining board members receive $25 per day for days worked, and members of certain other boards under statute Section 15.07 (5) receive a per diem as noted in the table. Statute Section 20.923 places state officials in one of 10 executive salary groups for which salary ranges have been established. Group salary ranges, as proposed by the Office of State Employment Relations on May 4, 2005, to the Joint Committee on Employment Relations in the proposed *2005-2007 Compensation Plan* for the period June 26, 2005 through June 24, 2006, are: Group 1: $55,286-$85,694; Group 2: $59,711-$92,553; Group 3: $64,488-$99,957; Group 4: $69,647-$107,954; Group 5: $75,220-$116,592; Group 6: $81,238-$125-921; Group 7: $87,738-$135,994; Group 8: $94,758-$146,876; Group 9: $102,339-$158,627; Group 10: $110,528-$171,320.
Group salary ranges proposed for the period June 25, 2006 through March 31, 2007, are: Group 1: $56,393-$87,410; Group 2: $60,905-$94,403; Group 3: $65,778-$101,957; Group 4: $71,042-$110,117; Group 5: $76,726-$118,926; Group 6: $82,864-$128,441; Group 7: $89,494-$138,716; Group 8: $96,654-$149,814; Group 9: $104,387-$161,801; Group 10: $112,739-$174,747.
Group salary ranges proposed for the period April 1, 2007 through June 23, 2007, are: Group 1: $56,959-$88,287; Group 2: $61,517-$95,353; Group 3: $66,438-$102,980; Group 4: $71,754-$111,219; Group 5: $77,496-$120,121; Group 6: $83,697-$129,732; Group 7: $90,394-$140,111; Group 8: $97,627-$151,322; Group 9: $105,438-$163,430; Group 10: $113,873-$176,505.

[5]Nominated by governor but not yet confirmed by senate.

Source: Appointment lists maintained by governor's office and received by the Legislative Reference Bureau on or before June 30, 2005.

Lieutenant Governor Barbara Lawton greets students at Spring Valley Elementary School, Spring Valley. (Office of the Lieutenant Governor)

OFFICE OF THE LIEUTENANT GOVERNOR

Lieutenant Governor: BARBARA LAWTON.
Chief of Staff: BRIAN MATAKIS.
Policy Director: EMILY CURTIS.
Director of Operations: JOHN LEASE.
Mailing Address: P.O. Box 2043, Madison 53702-2043.
Location: Room 19 East, State Capitol, Madison.
Telephone: 266-3516.
Fax: 267-3571.
Agency E-mail Address: ltgov@ltgov.state.wi.us
Internet Address: www.ltgov.state.wi.us
Number of Employees: 4.00.
Total Budget 2003-05: $694,400.
Constitutional References: Article V, Sections 1, 2, 3, 7, and 8; Article XIII, Section 10.
Statutory Reference: Chapter 14, Subchapter II.

Agency Responsibility: The lieutenant governor is the state's second-ranking executive officer, a position comparable to that of the Vice President of the United States. If the incumbent governor dies, resigns, or is removed from office, the lieutenant governor becomes governor for the balance of the unexpired term. (Prior to a constitutional amendment in April 1979, the lieutenant governor was considered only "acting governor" in those circumstances.) The lieutenant governor serves as acting governor when the governor is temporarily unable to perform the duties of the office due to impeachment, incapacitation, or absence from the state. If the lieutenant governor becomes governor, he or she must nominate a new lieutenant governor and the successor must be confirmed by the senate and the assembly.

The governor may designate the lieutenant governor to represent the governor's office on any statutory board, commission, or committee on which the governor is entitled to membership. Under such designation, the lieutenant governor has all the authority and responsibility granted by law to the governor. The governor may also designate the lieutenant governor to represent the chief executive's office on any nonstatutory committee or intergovernmental body created to maintain relationships with federal, state, and local governments or regional agencies. The lieutenant governor participates in national organizations of lieutenant governors and may be asked by the governor to coordinate specific state services and programs.

Organization: From 1848 until 1970, the lieutenant governor was elected for a 2-year term on a separate ballot in the November general election of even-numbered years. Since 1970, following amendment of the Wisconsin Constitution, voters have elected the governor and lieutenant governor on a joint ballot to a 4-year term. Candidates are nominated independently in the September primary, but voters cast a combined ballot for the two offices in the November election.

History: The Territory of Wisconsin had no lieutenant governor, but the secretary of the territory was authorized to act as governor in the event of the governor's death or absence. The Wisconsin Constitution of 1848 provided for the post of lieutenant governor after considerable debate. Some delegates to the convention argued that the president of the senate, chosen from the membership of that body, should succeed the governor, with the secretary of state second in line of succession. The convention delegates who objected to a person's becoming governor without being elected on a statewide basis prevailed, however, and the post of lieutenant governor was included in the constitution.

Originally, the lieutenant governor was also the president of the senate and could cast a deciding vote in case of a tie. In 1979, the voters ratified a constitutional amendment enabling the senate to choose its own presiding officer from among its members, beginning in 1981.

Department of
ADMINISTRATION

Secretary of Administration: MARC MAROTTA, 266-1741, marc.marotta@

Deputy Secretary: GINA FRANK-REECE, 266-1741, gina.frank-reece@

Executive Assistant: SEAN DILWEG, 266-1741, sean.dilweg@

Legal Counsel: JOHN ROTHSCHILD, 267-0202, john.rothschild@

Mailing Address: P.O. Box 7864, Madison 53707-7864.

Location: State Administration Building, 101 East Wilson Street, Madison.

Telephone: (608) 266-1741.

Fax: (608) 267-3842.

Internet Address: http://www.doa.state.wi.us

Number of Employees: 902.08.

Total Budget 2003-05: $912,855,700.

Statutory References: Sections 15.10 and 15.103; Chapter 16.

Address e-mail by combining the user ID and the state extender: userid@**doa.state.wi.us**

Administrative Services, Division of: GAIL RIEDASCH, *administrator,* 267-3836, gail.riedasch@; TOM HERMAN, *deputy administrator,* 266-0239, tom.herman@; Fax: 264-9500; P.O. Box 7869, Madison 53707-7869.

> *Financial Management, Bureau of:* MARTHA KERNER, *director,* 266-1359, martha.kerner@
>
> *Personnel, Bureau of:* PETER OLSON, *director,* 266-2308, peter.olson@
>
> *State Prosecutors Office:* STUART MORSE, *director,* 267-2700, stuart.morse@

Capitol Police, Division of: DAVID HEINLE, *acting police chief and adminstrator,* 266-7546, david.heinle@; Fax: 267-9343; B2N State Capitol, Madison, 53702.

Energy, Division of: KIMBERLY WALKER, *administrator,* 261-6357, kimberly.walker@; STEVEN K. TRYON, *assistant to the administrator,* 266-2035, steven.tryon@; Fax: 267-6931; P.O. Box 7868, Madison 53707-7868.

> *Energy Assistance, Bureau of:* vacancy, *director,* 266-7601.
>
> *Energy Efficiency, Bureau of:* GARY GORLEN, *director,* 266-8870, gary.gorlen@

Enterprise Operations, Division of: PATRICK J. FARLEY, *administrator,* 266-0779, patrick.farley@; JAMES M. LANGDON, *deputy administrator,* 267-2715, james.langdon@; Fax: 267-0600; P.O. Box 7867, Madison 53707-7867.

> *Enterprise Fleet, Bureau of;* JOHN MARX, *director,* 267-7693, john.marx@
>
> *Procurement, Bureau of:* HELEN MCCAIN, *director,* 267-9634, helen.mccain@
>
> *State Risk Management, Bureau of:* ROLLIE BOEDING, *director,* 266-1866, rollie.boeding@; Fax: 264-1866.
>
> *State Minority Business Program:* GODWIN AMEGASHIE, *director,* 267-7806, godwin.amegashie@

Enterprise Technology, Division of: MATTHEW MISZEWSKI, *administrator,* 264-9502, matthew.miszewski@; DAVID HINRICHS, *deputy administrator,* 267-0614, dave.hinrichs@; Fax: 267-0626; P.O. Box 7844, Madison 53707-7844.

> *Customer Relations and Business Management, Bureau of:* JEAN GREENE, *director,* 264-6198, jean.greene@
>
> *Development and Operations, Bureau of:* JIM SCHMOLESKY, *director,* 266-1952, jim.schmolesky@
>
> *Infrastructure and Networks, Bureau of:* ROBERT STUESSY, *director,* 264-6186, robert.stuessy@

Executive Budget and Finance, Division of: DAVID SCHMIEDICKE, *administrator,* 266-1035, david.schmiedicke@; JENNIFER KRAUS, *deputy administrator,* 266-2214, jennifer.kraus@; Fax: 267-0372; P.O. Box 7864, Madison 53707-7864.

ADMINISTRATION

DEPARTMENT OF ADMINISTRATION

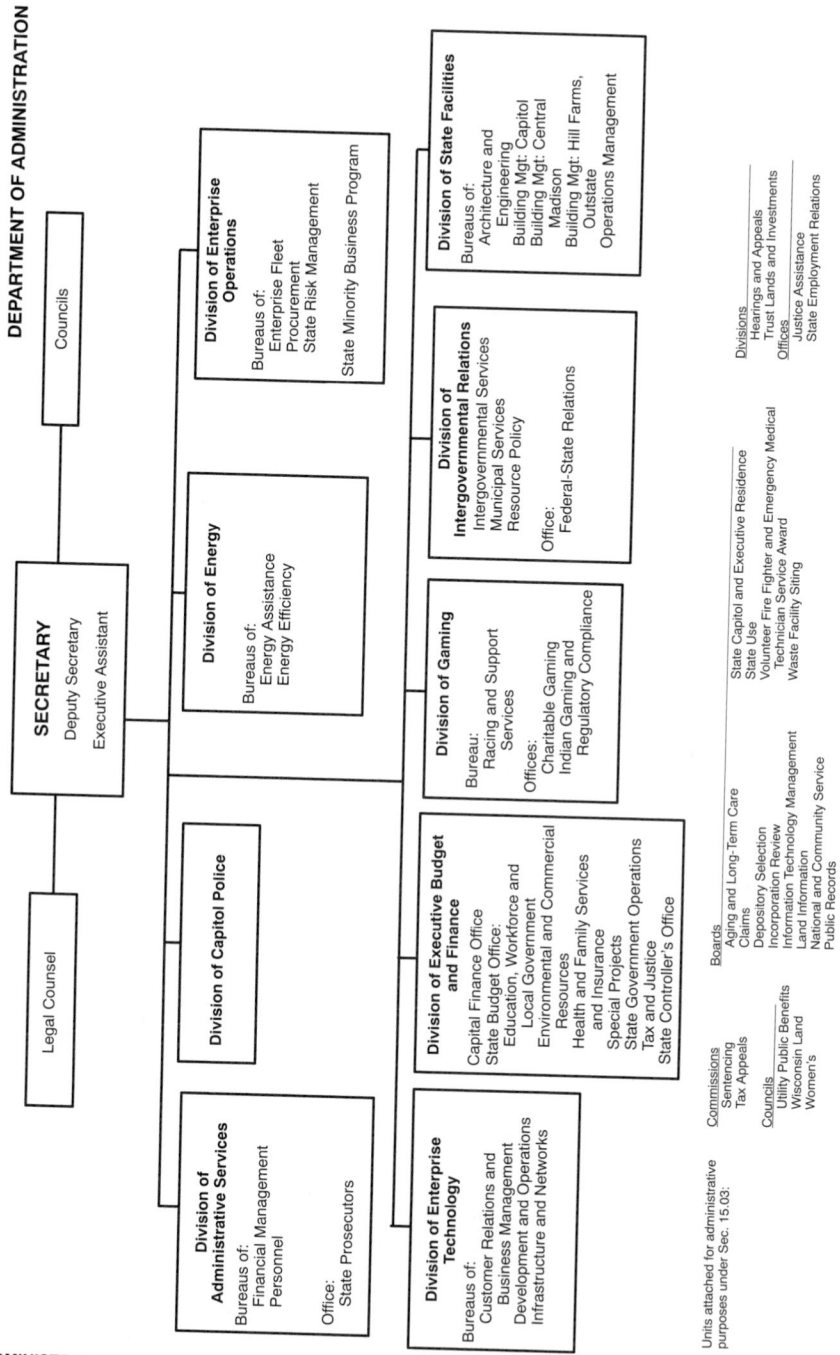

SECRETARY
Deputy Secretary
Executive Assistant

Legal Counsel

Councils

Division of Administrative Services
Bureaus of:
Financial Management
Personnel

Office:
State Prosecutors

Division of Capitol Police

Division of Enterprise Technology
Bureaus of:
Customer Relations and Business Management
Development and Operations
Infrastructure and Networks

Division of Executive Budget and Finance
Capital Finance Office
State Budget Office:
Education, Workforce and Local Government
Environmental and Commercial Resources
Health and Family Services and Insurance
Special Projects
State Government Operations
Tax and Justice
State Controller's Office

Division of Gaming
Bureau:
Racing and Support Services
Offices:
Charitable Gaming
Indian Gaming and Regulatory Compliance

Division of Energy
Bureaus of:
Energy Assistance
Energy Efficiency

Division of Enterprise Operations
Bureaus of:
Enterprise Fleet
Procurement
State Risk Management

State Minority Business Program

Division of Intergovernmental Relations
Intergovernmental Services
Municipal Services
Resource Policy
Office:
Federal-State Relations

Division of State Facilities
Bureaus of:
Architecture and Engineering
Building Mgt: Capitol
Building Mgt: Central Madison
Building Mgt: Hill Farms, Outstate
Operations Management

Units attached for administrative purposes under Sec. 15.03:

Commissions
Sentencing
Tax Appeals

Councils
Utility Public Benefits
Wisconsin Land
Women's

Boards
Aging and Long-Term Care
Claims
Depository Selection
Incorporation Review
Information Technology Management
Land Information
National and Community Service
Public Records

State Capitol and Executive Residence
State Use
Volunteer Fire Fighter and Emergency Medical Technician Service Award
Waste Facility Siting

Divisions
Hearings and Appeals
Trust Lands and Investments
Offices
Justice Assistance
State Employment Relations

Capital Finance Office: FRANK HOADLEY, *director,* 266-2305, frank.hoadley@

State Budget Office:

  Education, Workforce and Local Government: ROBERT HANLE, *team leader,* 266-1037, bob.hanle@

  Environmental and Commercial Resources: KIRSTEN GRINDE, *team leader,* 266-1040, kirsten.grinde@

  Health and Family Services and Insurance: JAMES JOHNSTON, *team leader,* 266-3420, james.johnston@

  Special Projects: vacancy.

  State Government Operations: DAN CAUCUTT, *team leader,* 266-0777, dan.caucutt@

  Tax and Justice: JOHN KOSKINEN, *team leader,* 266-2081, john.koskinen@

State Controller's Office: WILLIAM J. RAFTERY, *state controller,* 266-1694, bill.raftery@; P.O. Box 7932, Madison 53707-7932.

Gaming, Division of: vacancy, *administrator,* 270-2534; Fax: 270-2564; 2005 West Beltline Highway, Suite 201, P.O. Box 8979, Madison 53708-8979; Internet Address: http://www.doa.state.wi.us/gaming

  Charitable Gaming, Office of: BRIAN WHITTOW, *director,* 270-2545, brian.whittow@

  Indian Gaming and Regulatory Compliance, Office of: LINDA MINASH, *director,* 270-2534, linda.minash@

  Racing and Support Services, Bureau of: RICHARD PEDERSEN, *director,* 270-2546, richard.pedersen@

Intergovernmental Relations, Division of: LAURA E. ARBUCKLE, *administrator,* 267-1824, laura.arbuckle@; HARALD JORDAHL, *deputy administrator,* 261-7520, harald.jordahl@; Fax: 267-6917; P.O. Box 8944, Madison 53708-8944; Internet Address: http://www.doa.state.wi.us/dhir

  Intergovernmental Services: vacancy.

  Municipal Services: DONALD R. HARRIER, JR., *director,* 267-2705, don.harrier@

  Resource Policy: MIKE FRIIS, 267-7982, *director,* mike.friis@

  Federal-State Relations, Office of: vacancy, *director,* 444 North Capitol Street, Suite 613, N.W., Washington, D.C. 20001, (202) 624-5870; Fax: (202) 624-5871.

State Facilities, Division of: ROBERT G. CRAMER, *administrator,* 266-1031, robert.cramer@; MARILYN PIERCE, *deputy administrator,* 266-7066, marilyn.pierce@; RONALD W. KROHN, *assistant to the administrator,* 266-8874, ronald.krohn@; Fax: 267-2710; P.O. Box 7866, Madison 53707-7866; Internet Address: http://www.doa.state.wi.us/dsf/dsfmain.asp

  Architecture and Engineering, Bureau of: ADEL TABRIZI, *director and state chief engineer,* 266-3850, adel.tabrizi@

  Building Management: Capitol, Bureau of: MICHAEL STARK, *director,* 266-1173, michael.stark@

  Building Management: Central Madison, Bureau of: JOHN WALKER, *director,* 266-1097, john.walker@

  Building Management: Hill Farms, Outstate, Bureau of: LOUIS SILLER, JR., *director,* 266-2119, louis.siller@

  Operations Management, Bureau of: GILBERT T. FUNK, *director,* 266-2645, gil.funk@

Publications: Agency Budget Requests and Revenue Estimates; Annual Fiscal Report; Biennial Report; Budget in Brief; Budget Message; Capitol Budget Recommendations; Comprehensive Annual Financial Report; Continuing Disclosure Annual Report; Decisions of Tax Appeals Commission; Executive Budget; Summary of Tax Exemption Devices; Wisconsin Energy Statistics; Wisconsin Population Estimates.

Agency Responsibility: One of the chief duties of the Department of Administration is to provide the governor with fiscal management information and the policy alternatives required for preparation of Wisconsin's biennial budget. It analyzes administrative and fiscal issues facing the state and recommends solutions. The department also coordinates telecommunications, energy, and land use planning. It regulates racing, charitable gaming, and Indian gaming. It is responsible for providing a wide range of support services to other state agencies and manages the state's buildings and leased office space. The department maintains a federal-state relations office in Washington, D.C.

Organization: The department is administered by a secretary appointed by the governor with the advice and consent of the senate. The secretary must be appointed "on the basis of recognized interest, administrative and executive ability, training and experience in and knowledge of problems and needs in the field of administration." The secretary appoints the department's division administrators from outside the classified service.

Unit Functions: The *Division of Administrative Services* provides numerous support services to the department and agencies attached for administrative support, including personnel, records and forms, space and property management, financial management, mail, business recovery, and management planning. Other major functions are to prepare and administer the departmental budget, advise the secretary on policies and procedures, and perform internal audits. It pays the salaries and any associated fringe benefits for all district attorneys and their staff attorneys. It also reviews and pays the compensation of special prosecutors for the 71 district attorneys' offices. (Menominee and Shawano Counties share a district attorney.)

The *Division of Capitol Police* uses officers working in Madison, Milwaukee, and West Allis (at the State Fair Park), to provide a wide range of investigative, security, and related public safety services to state agencies, employees, and others. It protects state facilities; conducts criminal investigations, including the use of sophisticated surveillance and alarm devices used to detect criminal activity; and provides protective services to the governor and visiting dignitaries. The division's uniformed patrol officers detect and complete preliminary investigations of crimes, traffic accidents, and traffic violations. They also protect lives and property in department-managed facilities. The Capitol Police are also responsible for monitoring and managing other potential safety threats, such as hazardous material spills, injury accidents, and other situations impacting the safety of employees and visitors. The division also maintains bike and horse patrols to enhance public contact with officers and to meet other needs.

The *Division of Energy* advises the department and the governor on state and regional energy policies as well as contributes to the development of energy legislation. It also administers federal programs encouraging energy efficiency and use of renewable energy besides petroleum violation escrow funds. The division is responsible for administering the Wisconsin Focus on Energy Program and it develops energy efficiency and renewable energy programs.

The division also administers the Home Energy Plus Programs, which include the federally funded Low-Income Home Energy Assistance Program (LIHEAP), the Low-Income Home Weatherization Program, the State Public Benefits Weatherization and Bill Payment Assistance programs, and the Lead Hazard Reduction Program. These programs provide energy conservation services and assistance to help offset the cost of home energy.

In consultation with the Council on Utility Public Benefits, the division administers energy conservation grants for programs that promote energy efficiency, renewable resources, electric reliability, and environmental protection.

The *Division of Enterprise Operations* manages state government contracts and purchasing and is responsible for interdepartmental mail services, auto and air fleet transportation, risk management, records management, sale and distribution of state agency documents, and minority business contracting. In addition, the division handles municipal cooperative purchasing, contracting with work centers, federal and state surplus property disposition, and recycling and waste reduction programs for state agencies. The division manages the state's self-funded programs for state liability and property insurance and worker's compensation protection, and it assists agencies in controlling and reducing losses.

The *Division of Enterprise Technology* manages the state's information-technology (IT) assets and uses technology to improve government efficiency. It provides computer services to state agencies and some local governments. It also operates the statewide voice, data, and video telecommunications network. In consultation with business and IT managers from state agencies and local governments, the division develops strategies, policies, and standards for "enterprise use" (cross-agency and multijurisdictional use of IT resources). The division provides training, research, and print and mail services to other state agencies. It is also responsible for providing statewide computer systems for district attorneys and coordinating electronic information sharing among the courts, district attorneys, and justice agencies at the state and local levels. The division provides consultation on geographic information systems (GIS) to government and nonprofit groups.

The *Division of Executive Budget and Finance* provides fiscal and policy analysis to the governor for development of executive budget proposals and assists agencies in the technical preparation of budget requests. It reviews legislation and coordinates the fiscal estimates that accompany all expenditure bills. It also advises the State of Wisconsin Building Commission and the governor on the issuance of state debt and administers finances for the clean water revolving loan fund program. The division maintains the management information system for authorized state employee positions. It establishes accounting policies and procedures, maintains the state's central payroll and accounting systems, monitors agency internal control procedures, and produces the state's annual fiscal and financial reports.

The *Division of Gaming* regulates racing, pari-mutuel on-track wagering and simulcasting, bingo, raffles, crane games, and Class III Indian gaming pursuant to tribal-state gaming compacts. The division licenses and performs compliance audits of racetrack operations and bingo games and raffles conducted by nonprofit, charitable, religious, fraternal, and service organizations. Supervision of racetrack operations includes animal drug testing, monitoring and collection of taxes, and ensuring humane treatment of animals. The division sponsors the "Adopt-a-Greyhound" program. The division conducts tribal gaming compliance audits and certifies vendors to conduct gaming business in accordance to state/tribal compacts and federal law.

The *Division of Intergovernmental Relations* advises the department and the governor on state, local, and tribal relationships and coordinates the state's federal agenda by reviewing federal legislation and directing state lobbying efforts at the federal level (through the Office of Federal-State Relations in Washington, D.C.). Other duties include managing the Coastal Management Program, which focuses on environmental and economic issues related to Lakes Michigan and Superior and adjoining counties. The division provides annual population estimates for both state and municipal use, prepares population projections, develops demographic research on the state's changing population, and is responsible for coordinating and distributing census information.

The division administers the Wisconsin Land Information program. It oversees the Municipal Boundary Review Program, which examines changes in local government boundaries, and issues advisory opinions on municipal annexations. It administers the Plat Review Program, which coordinates state agency and county planning agency subdivision plat review, and examines land subdivision plats and assessors' plats to ensure compliance with state surveying, mapping, and minimum layout standards. The division also administers comprehensive planning grants to local governmental units.

The *Division of State Facilities* develops and administers the state building program under the direction of the State of Wisconsin Building Commission. Its functions include statewide facilities planning and evaluation, real estate acquisition, architectural and engineering design, technology, consultation, management and supervision of construction projects, energy conservation, power plant fuel management, fuels procurement, administration of state building contracts, and ensuring access for people with disabilities to state buildings. The division operates and maintains 32 major buildings in 7 cities through the state. These include the State Capitol, the Executive Residence, and state office buildings in Madison. The division is responsible for all state real estate leasing, planning of office space, and building engineering services.

History: The legislature created the Department of Administration in Chapter 228, Laws of 1959, and authorized it to provide centralized staff services to the governor, to assume common administrative functions for other executive agencies, and to coordinate the state's business affairs. Chapter 228 also abolished the Bureaus of Engineering, Personnel, and Purchases; the Department of Budget and Accounts; and the Division of Departmental Research in the Office of the Governor. Their functions and personnel were transferred to the new department.

Since its creation, the department has assumed additional duties. State comprehensive planning responsibilities and population estimation were added in 1967 and 1972, respectively. 1976

Executive Order 36 moved the Office of Emergency Energy Assistance from the Office of the Governor to the department's State Planning Office and broadened its responsibilities to include energy policy planning and program management. The 1989 executive budget created the Division of Housing (subsequently repealed in 2003) and gave the department responsibility for grant and loan programs for low- and moderate-income housing. The 1991 executive budget created the Division of Information Technology Services to consolidate and manage the state's computer and telecommunications resources.

Other functions assigned to the department have included the Coastal Management Program (1981), low-income weatherization assistance (1991), low-income energy assistance (1995), a college tuition prepayment program (1995) (later transferred to the Office of the State Treasurer by 1999 Wisconsin Act 9), municipal boundary and plat review (1997), and the Wisconsin Fresh Start Program (1998).

Over the years, legislation has transferred various functions out of the department. Chapter 645, Laws of 1961, created a separate Personnel Board to review departmental decisions. Chapter 196, Laws of 1977, transferred the administration of civil service, collective bargaining, and classification and compensation to the newly created Department of Employment Relations. The Division of Emergency Government, which became part of the department in 1979, was moved to the Department of Military Affairs by 1989 Wisconsin Act 31. Regulation of mobile home dealers and mobile parks was transferred to the Department of Commerce by 1999 Wisconsin Act 9. With the repeal of the Division of Housing, 2003 Wisconsin Act 33 transferred grant and loan programs for low- and moderate-income housing to the Department of Commerce.

Gaming Regulation. 1997 Wisconsin Act 27 repealed the Wisconsin Gaming Board and created the Division of Gaming in the department to monitor gaming on Indian lands and regulate pari-mutuel wagering, racing, and charitable gaming.

Originally, the Wisconsin Constitution stated: "The legislature shall never authorize any lottery." This provision was interpreted as prohibiting all forms of gambling. Following a 1973 constitutional amendment to allow charitable bingo, the legislature enacted Chapter 156, Laws of 1973, to permit bingo games and create the Bingo Control Board in the Department of Regulation and Licensing. Charitable raffles were permitted by a 1977 constitutional amendment, and the legislature assigned their regulation to the Bingo Control Board in Chapter 426, Laws of 1977.

Pari-mutuel on-track wagering and the state lottery were permitted by constitutional amendments in 1987. The legislature created the Racing Board to regulate the sport in 1987 Wisconsin Act 354. The Wisconsin Lottery, originally operated by the Lottery Board, was created by 1987 Wisconsin Act 119.

The Wisconsin Gaming Commission, created by 1991 Wisconsin Act 269, replaced the Lottery Board and the Racing Board and also assumed responsibility for Indian gaming, charitable gaming (bingo and raffles), and crane games. The Wisconsin Gaming Board, created by 1995 Wisconsin Act 27, replaced the Gaming Commission. (That act also transferred responsibility for management of the Wisconsin Lottery to the Department of Revenue.) 1997 Wisconsin Act 27 transferred gaming duties, except for lottery regulation, to the Department of Administration.

Statutory Councils

Acid Deposition Research Council: Inactive.

The 7-member Acid Deposition Research Council makes recommendations on types and levels of funding for acid deposition research and reviews "acid rain" research. The council was created by 1985 Wisconsin Act 296, and its composition and duties are prescribed in Sections 15.107 (5) and 16.02 of the statutes.

Certification Standards Review Council: PAUL JUNIO (commercial laboratory representative), *chairperson;* KURT KNUTH (large municipal wastewater plant representative); RANDY HERWIG (small municipal wastewater plant representative); JAMES KINSCHER (industrial laboratory representative); KATIE EDGINGTON (public water utility representative); vacancy (solid and hazardous waste disposal facility representative); MARCIA KUEHL (demonstrated interest in laboratory certification); vacancy (livestock farmer); GEORGE BOWMAN (appointed by UW-Madison chancellor to represent Laboratory of Hygiene). (Unless otherwise designated, all are appointed by secretary of administration.)

The 9-member Certification Standards Review Council reviews the Department of Natural Resources laboratory certification and registration program and makes recommendations to the department about its programs for testing water, wastewater, waste material, soil, and hazardous waste. The council's members serve 3-year terms, and no member may serve more than two consecutive terms. The council was created by 1983 Wisconsin Act 410, and its composition and duties are prescribed in Sections 15.107 (12) and 299.11 (3) of the statutes.

Interagency Coordinating Council: PRISCILLA BORONIEC (representing Medical Assistance program, Department of Health and Family Services), *chairperson;* TOM KORPADY (secretary of employee trust funds designee); SANDRA MAHKORN (representative, health statistics unit, Department of Health and Family Services), SANDRA L.K. BREITBORDE (representative, health care information unit, Department of Health and Family Services), DAVID R. ZIMMERMAN (representative, health statistics research analysis, UW System), DAVID HINRICHS (representative, Department of Administration), EILEEN K. MALLOW (representative, Office of the Commissioner of Insurance). (All but secretary of employee trust funds or designee are appointed by governor.)

The 7-member Interagency Coordinating Council advises and assists state agencies in coordinating the collection and dissemination of health care data, including agency budgets for data collection programs. It also establishes criteria for analyzing complaints filed against health care plans and grievances filed with health maintenance organizations. The council reports on its activities at least twice a year to the Board on Health Care Information in the Department of Health and Family Services. The six representative members serve 4-year terms. The council was created by 1995 Wisconsin Act 433, and its composition and duties are prescribed in Sections 15.107 (7) and 16.03 of the statutes.

Small Business, Veteran-Owned Business and Minority Business Opportunities, Council on: AUGISTINE MURRAY, *chairperson;* TRINA S. DENNIS, *vice chairperson;* E. AGGO AKYEA, CRAIG A. ANDERSON, MOHAMMED HASHIM, WILLIAM F. LORENZ, JUAN C. LANDA, SEYOUM MENGESHA, BRIAN A. MITCHELL, DENISE D. POMMER, ALLEN R. SCHRAEDER, LENI M. SIKER. (All are appointed by secretary of administration.) Nonvoting secretary: PATRICK J. FARLEY (Department of Administration employee designated by the departmental secretary).

The 13-member Council on Small Business, Veteran-Owned Business and Minority Business Opportunities advises the department on the participation of its constituent groups in state purchasing. Its members are appointed for 3-year terms and may not serve more than two consecutive full terms. The law prescribes minimum membership numbers for the types of businesses represented on the council: racial minority-owned (2); owned by handicapped person (1); nonprofit for rehabilitation of disabled (1); and veteran-owned (2). At least one member must represent the Department of Commerce and one the consumers. The council was created by Chapter 419, Laws of 1977, and its name and membership were amended by 1991 Wisconsin Act 170 to include veteran-owned business. Its composition and duties are prescribed in Sections 15.107 (2) and 16.755 of the statutes.

INDEPENDENT UNITS ATTACHED FOR BUDGETING, PROGRAM COORDINATION, AND RELATED MANAGEMENT FUNCTIONS BY SECTION 15.03 OF THE STATUTES

BOARD ON AGING AND LONG-TERM CARE

Members: EVA ARNOLD, ROSE BORON, PATRICIA A. FINDER-STONE, EUGENE I. LEHRMANN, TANYA L. MEYER, MARGARET F. TOLLAKSEN, vacancy (appointed by governor with senate consent).

Executive Director: GEORGE F. POTARACKE, (608) 246-7013, george.potaracke@ltc.state.wi.us

Mailing Address: 1402 Pankratz Street, Suite 111, Madison 53704.

Telephones: (608) 246-7013; Ombudsman Program: (800) 815-0015; Medigap Helpline: (800) 242-1060.

Fax: (608) 246-7001.

E-mail Address: boaltc@ltc.state.wi.us

Publications: Biennial Report.

Number of Employees: 25.00.

Total Budget 2003-05: $3,310,000.

Statutory References: Sections 15.07 (1)(b) 9., 15.105 (10), and 16.009.

Agency Responsibility: The 7-member Board on Aging and Long-Term Care reports biennially to the governor and the legislature on long-term care for the aged and disabled; state involvement in long-term care; program recommendations; and actions taken by state agencies to carry out the board's recommendations. The board monitors the development and implementation of federal, state, and local laws and regulations related to long-term care facilities. The board's ombudsman service investigates complaints from persons receiving long-term care concerning improper treatment or noncompliance with federal or state law and serves as mediator or advocate to resolve disputes between patients and institutions.

The board operates the Medigap Helpline, which provides information and counseling on various types of insurance, including health, hospital indemnity, cancer, nursing home, and long-term care and nursing home policies designed to supplement Medicare. Helpline information also covers the Health Insurance Risk-Sharing Plan (HIRSP), group insurance continuation and conversion rights, and health maintenance organization plans for Medicare beneficiaries.

The board members, who serve staggered 5-year terms, must have demonstrated a continuing interest in the problems of providing long-term care for the aged and disabled. At least four must be public members with no interest in or affiliation with any nursing home. The board appoints the executive director from the classified service.

The board was created by Chapter 20, Laws of 1981, which merged the Board on Aging and the Governor's Ombudsman Program for the Aging and Disabled, as the result of a legislative study. Predecessor agencies included the State Commission on Aging, created by Chapter 581, Laws of 1961, followed in 1967 (Chapters 75 and 327) by the Council on Aging in the Department of Health and Social Services, which was subsequently renamed the Board on Aging in Chapter 332, Laws of 1971.

CLAIMS BOARD

Members: ROBERT HUNTER (Department of Justice representative designated by attorney general), *chairperson;* JOHN ROTHSCHILD (Department of Administration representative designated by secretary of administration), *secretary;* SENATOR LAZICH (designated by chairperson, Senate Committee on Finance), REPRESENTATIVE MEYER (designated by chairperson, Assembly Committee on Finance); AMY KASPER (representative of the Office of the Governor designated by governor).

Secretary: JOHN ROTHSCHILD.

Mailing Address: P.O. Box 7864, Madison 53707-7864.

Location: State Administration Building, 101 East Wilson Street, 10th Floor, Madison.

Telephone: (608) 264-9595.

Fax: (608) 267-3842.

E-mail Address: patricia.reardon@doa.state.wi.us

Number of Employees: 0.00.

Total Budget 2003-05: $65,000.

Statutory References: Sections 15.07 (2)(e), 15.105 (2), and 16.007.

Agency Responsibility: The 5-member Claims Board investigates and pays, denies, or makes recommendations on all money claims against the state of $10 or more, when such claims are referred to it by the Department of Administration. The findings and recommendations of the board are reported to the legislature together with appropriate legislative proposals. No claim may be considered by the legislature until the board has made its recommendation.

Originally, the statutory procedure for making claims against the state was to file the claim with the Director of Budget and Accounts or to have a legislator introduce it as a bill. The legislature created the Claims Commission in Chapter 669, Laws of 1955, to handle these matters. Under the 1967 executive branch reorganization, the commission was renamed the Claims Board, and it absorbed the Commission for the Relief of Innocent Persons and the Judgment Debtor Relief Commission.

DEPOSITORY SELECTION BOARD

Members: JACK C. VOIGHT (state treasurer), MARC MAROTTA (secretary of administration), MICHAEL MORGAN (secretary of revenue).

Statutory References: Sections 15.105 (3) and 34.045.

Agency Responsibility: The 3-member Depository Selection Board, as created by Chapter 418, Laws of 1977, establishes procedures to be used by state agencies in the selection of depositories for public funds and in contracting for their banking services. The board's *ex officio* members may designate others to serve in their place. The secretary of revenue replaced the executive director of the investment board as a member as a result of 2001 Wisconsin Act 16.

DIVISION OF HEARINGS AND APPEALS

Administrator: DAVID H. SCHWARZ, david.schwarz@dha.state.wi.us

Mailing Address: 5005 University Avenue, Suite 201, Madison 53705-5400.

Telephone: (608) 266-8007.

Fax: Madison: (608) 264-9885; Milwaukee: (414) 227-3818; Eau Claire: (715) 831-3235.

E-mail Address: dha.mail@dha.state.wi.us

Internet Address: http://dha.state.wi.us

Number of Employees: 50.80.

Total Budget 2003-05: $9,023,400.

Statutory References: Sections 15.103 (1), 50.04 (4)(e), 227.43, 301.035, and 949.11.

Publications: Probation and Parole Digest.

Agency Responsibility: The Division of Hearings and Appeals conducts quasi-judicial hearings for several state agencies. It must decide contested administrative proceedings for the Department of Natural Resources, cases arising under the Department of Justice's Crime Victim Compensation Program, and appeals related to actions of the Department of Health and Family Services. It also hears appeals from the Department of Transportation, including those related to motor vehicle dealer licenses, highway signs, motor carrier regulation, and disputes arising between motor vehicle dealers and manufacturers. The division conducts hearings for the Department of Corrections on adult probation and parole revocation and juvenile aftercare supervision. It also handles contested cases for the Division of Economic Support in the Department of Workforce Development, the Department of Public Instruction, the Department of Employee Trust Funds, and the Low-Income Home Energy Assistance Program of the Department of Administration. Other agencies may contract with the division for hearing services.

The secretary of administration appoints the division's administrator from the classified service. By law, the division operates independently of the department except for certain budgeting and management functions. 1983 Wisconsin Act 27 created the division by combining the Division of Natural Resources Hearings and the Division of Nursing Home Forfeiture Appeals, both originating with the 1977 Legislature. In 1986, the division received jurisdiction over crime victim compensation hearings and cases involving protection of human burial sites. With the creation of the Department of Corrections in 1990, the legislature transferred a portion of the Office of Administrative Hearings from the Department of Health and Social Services to the division, making the division responsible for parole, probation, and juvenile aftercare revocation. When the Office of the Commissioner of Transportation was abolished in 1993, the legislature transferred many Department of Transportation hearing functions to the division. Contested administrative hearings for the Department of Health and Family Services and the Department of Workforce Development were transferred to the division by 1995 Wisconsin Act 370.

INCORPORATION REVIEW BOARD

Members: LAURA ARBUCKLE (designated by secretary of administration), *chairperson*; TERRENCE J. MCMAHON, LONNIE MULLER (appointed by Wisconsin Towns Association); PAUL FISK (appointed by League of Wisconsin Municipalities); MIKE HUGGINS (appointed by Wisconsin Alliance of Cities).

Contact person: ERICH SCHMIDTKE, Planning Analyst, Division of Intergovernmental Relations.

Mailing Address: 101 East Wilson Street, 10th Floor, Madison 53702.

Telephone: (608) 264-6102.

Statutory References: Sections 15.07 (2)(m), 15.105 (23), 16.53 (4), 66.0203, and 66.0207.

The 5-member Incorporation Review Board reviews petitions to incorporate territory as a city or village to determine whether the petition meets certain public interest statutory standards. These standards may include characteristics of the proposed municipality's territory, that part of the territory beyond its most densely populated core, its ability to provide services and generate revenue, and its impact on neighboring jurisdictions. The board is also charged with prescribing and collecting an incorporation review fee. The board must present its findings within 180 days after receipt of referral from a circuit court unless the court sets a different time limit or all parties agree to a stay to allow time for an alternative dispute resolution of any disagreements. Any board member who owns property in, or resides in the town that is the subject of the incorporation petition, or a contiguous city or village, must be replaced for purposes of reviewing that petition. Members serve at the pleasure of the appointing authority and, with the exception of the DOA representative, serve only in an advisory capacity.

INFORMATION TECHNOLOGY MANAGEMENT BOARD

Members: Inactive.

Statutory References: Sections 15.105 (28).

Agency Responsibility: The Information Technology Management Board advises the Department of Administration on strategic information technology plans submitted by state agencies, the management of the state's information technology assets, and progress made on agency projects. The board may review the department's decisions on appeal from other state agencies. The board's membership includes the governor, the cochairpersons of the legislature's Joint Committee on Information Policy and Technology or their designees, a member of the minority party from the senate and the assembly, the secretary of administration or designee, 2 heads of departments or independent agencies appointed by the governor, and two other members appointed by the governor to 4-year terms. The board was created by 2001 Wisconsin Act 16 and attached to the Department of Administration by 2003 Wisconsin Act 33.

OFFICE OF JUSTICE ASSISTANCE

Executive Director: DAVID STEINGRABER.

Mailing Address: 131 West Wilson Street, Suite 610, Madison 53702.

Telephone: (608) 266-3323.

Fax: (608) 266-6676.

Publications: Anti-Drug Abuse Strategy; Crime and Arrests in Wisconsin; Drug Arrests in Wisconsin; Drug Data Trends; Jail Population Trends; Juvenile Justice Improvement Plan; Sexual Assaults in Wisconsin; Violence Against Women Plan; Wisconsin Homeland Security Strategic Plan.

Number of Employees: 36.00.

Total Budget 2003-05: $60,544,500.

Statutory References: Sections 15.105 (19) and 16.964.

Agency Responsibility: The Office of Justice Assistance administers a variety of public safety programs including federal grants related to criminal justice and homeland security. Specific grant programs include the Juvenile Justice and Delinquency Prevention Act, the Anti-Drug Abuse Act, the Local Law Enforcement Block Grant Program, the Edward Bryne Memorial State and Local Law Enforcement Assistance Program, the Justice Assistance Grant (new program including both the Bryne and LLEGB programs), the Juvenile Accountability Incentive Block

Grant Program, Police Corps, the Violence Against Women Act, and Homeland Security funding which includes Local Law Enforcement Terrorism Prevention Programs, Citizen Corps, and the Urban Area Security Initiative. The governor appoints its executive director.

The office also manages the Statistical Analysis Center, which adminsters the State Uniform Crime Reporting System, oversees the implementation of the law enforcement Incident Based Reporting System, and provides justice agencies with statistical reports and analysis and the Wisconsin Justice Information Sharing (WIJIS) initiative. The office supports the Governor's Juvenile Justice Commission, the Wisconsin State Citizen Corps Council, the WIJIS Policy Advisory Group, the State Interoperability Executive Council, and numerous other advisory groups related to program responsibilities.

The Office of Justice Assistance originally was the Wisconsin Council on Criminal Justice, created by executive order in 1969 in the Department of Justice as the state planning body required by the federal Law Enforcement Assistance Administration. In 1971, the council was transferred by executive order to the governor's office. Chapter 418, Laws of 1977, created the council as a statutory agency in the governor's office. 1983 Wisconsin Act 27 created the council as an independent statutory body and attached it to the Department of Administration. The council was repealed and recreated under its current name by 1987 Wisconsin Act 27.

WISCONSIN LAND COUNCIL

Members: Timothy M. Hanna (city representative), *chairperson;* Laura Arbuckle (designated by secretary of administration), Judy Ziewacz (secretary of agriculture, trade and consumer protection designee), Jim O'Keefe (secretary of commerce designee), Dreax Watermolen (secretary of natural resources designee), Michael Lehman (secretary of revenue designee), Tanace Matthiesen (designated by secretary of transportation), Ted W. Koch (state cartographer); Jane Licht (county representative), Richard Stadelman (town representative), Jerry J. Doyle (local government representative), Brian W. Ohm (UW System representative); Willard J. Beitlich, Robert T. Gottschalk, Jennifer D. Hill-Kelley, Sean Phelan (public members). (All except *ex officio* members or their designees are appointed by governor.)

Executive Director: Harald Jordahl, harald.jordahl@doa.state.wi.us

Mailing Address: 101 East Wilson Street, 10th Floor, Madison 53702-0001.

Telephone: (608) 267-3369.

Fax: (608) 267-6917.

Internet Address: http://www.doa.state.wi.us/olis/

Number of Employees: 0.00.

Total Budget 2003-05: $59,300.

Statutory References: Sections 15.107 (16), 16.023, and 66.1001.

Publications: Intergovernmental Cooperation – A Guide to Preparing the Intergovernmental Cooperation Element of a Comprehensive Plan; How to Hire a Planning Consultant. Others available at: http://www.doa.state.wi.us.

Agency Responsibility: The 16-member Wisconsin Land Council identifies the state's land use goals and priorities and studies current land use laws in order to recommend legislation to the governor. Studies cover coordination and conflict within state land use law, conflict between state land use law and county and municipal ordinances, and county and municipal land use ordinances that conflict with one another. The council studies local government policies and the activities of the federal government and American Indian governments that have an impact on Wisconsin's land use goals and laws. The council established technical working groups: State Agency Resource Working Group (SARWG) and State Local-Private Working Group. It also represents selected state agencies, to discuss, analyze, and address state land use issues. The council approves planning grants to local governmental units under the Comprehensive Planning Law.

The council, which was created by 1997 Wisconsin Act 27, is scheduled to sunset on August 31, 2005. In a report submitted in August 2004, the council recommended that its functions and those of the Land Information Board be assigned to the SARWG.

AmeriCorps members in La Crosse paint a house as a service project for their community's annual Neighbor's Day. AmeriCorps is one of the community service programs coordinated by the National and Community Service Board. In addition to a living allowance, participants who complete a year of service receive money which may be used for higher education tuition or to repay student loans. (Department of Administration)

NATIONAL AND COMMUNITY SERVICE BOARD

Members: KAREN PECK KATZ (youth education and training representative); MARGUITA FOX (older adult volunteer representative); KATHLEEN GROAT (private, nonprofit organization representative); RICHARD GROBSCHMIDT (superintendent of public instruction designee); GAIL RIEDASCH (secretary of administration designee); ANTHONY HALLMAN (local government representative); WALTER KRAEMER (organized labor representative); JOEL HAUBRICH, JEANAN YASIRI (business representatives); CAMERON DARY (national service youth representative); MARILYNN PELKY (national service program representative); ADRIAN ADEKOLA, ROBERT GUENTHER, LANCE HANSON, HAROLD RECKELBERG, YIA THAO (public members). Nonvoting members: LINDA SUNDE (Corporation for National and Community Service); LARRY KLEINSTEIBER, AMY MCDOWELL, MICABIL DÍAZ MARTÍNEZ, LARRY OLSON. (All except *ex officio* members are appointed by governor.)

Executive Director: THOMAS H. DEVINE, devinth@dhfs.state.wi.us

Mailing Address: P.O. Box 8916, Madison 53708-8916.

Location: 1 West Wilson Street, Room 456, Madison.

Telephones: (608) 261-6716; (800) 620-8307 (toll free).

Fax: (608) 266-9313.

Internet Address: www.servewisconsin.org

Number of Employees: 6.00.

Total Budget 2003-05: $7,658,400.

Statutory References: Sections 15.105 (24) and 16.22.

Agency Responsibility: The National and Community Service Board, created by 1993 Wisconsin Act 437, in accordance with the federal National and Community Trust Act of 1993, oversees the planning and implementation of community service programs in Wisconsin that meet previously unmet human, public safety, educational, environmental, and homeland security needs. The board is authorized to receive and distribute funds from governmental and private sources, and it acts as an intermediary between the Corporation for National and Community Service (CNCS) and local agencies providing funding for AmeriCorps State programs.

The board's voting members, who must number at least 16, are appointed to serve 3-year terms. No more than 4 of them may be state officers and employees, and no more than 9 may be members from the same political party. To the extent practicable, membership should be diverse in terms of race, national origin, age, sex, and disability. Nonvoting members appointed by the governor must include the state representative of the CNCS and may include representatives of state agencies providing community social services.

BOARD OF COMMISSIONERS OF PUBLIC LANDS

Commissioners: DOUGLAS J. LA FOLLETTE (secretary of state), JACK C. VOIGHT (state treasurer), PEGGY A. LAUTENSCHLAGER (attorney general). (All serve as *ex officio* members.)

DIVISION OF TRUST LANDS AND INVESTMENTS

Executive Secretary: TIA NELSON, 266-8369, tia.nelson@bcpl.state.wi.us; TOM GERMAN, *deputy secretary,* 267-2233, tom.german@bcpl.state.wi.us

Mailing Address: P.O. Box 8943, Madison 53708-8943.

Location: 125 South Webster Street, Suite 200, Madison.

Telephone: (608) 266-1370.

Fax: (608) 267-2787.

Internet Address: http://bcpl.state.wi.us

District Office: MICHAEL PAUS, *administrator,* michael.paus@bcpl.state.wi.us, P.O. Box 277, 7271 Main Street, Lake Tomahawk 54539-0277, (715) 277-3366; Fax: (715) 277-3363.

Publications: Biennial Report, State Trust Fund Loan Program Brochure.

Number of Employees: 7.50.

Total Budget 2003-05: $2,915,800.

Constitutional Reference: Article X, Sections 2, 7, and 8.

Statutory References: Section 15.103 (4) and Chapter 24.

Agency Responsibility: The Board of Commissioners of Public Lands manages the state's remaining trust lands, administers trust funds to support public education, and maintains the state's original 19th century land survey and land sales records. During the 1800s, the federal government granted approximately 10 million acres of land to Wisconsin to encourage the state's development. Lands were granted to aid in the construction of wagon roads, canals, railroads, and the first State Capitol. Trust lands were granted to support public education. Although most of these lands have been sold, nearly 78,000 acres remain in the board's ownership. These lands are managed for sustained yield forestry and are available for public recreation.

The proceeds from trust land sales became trust funds, with the principal invested in loans to Wisconsin school districts and municipalities, and government bonds. The largest trust fund, the Common School Fund, is derived from land sales and supplemented by penal fines, civil forfeitures and penalties, and unclaimed property. Earnings from this fund are distributed annually by the Department of Public Instruction to public school libraries. Smaller funds provide support for the University of Wisconsin System and the state's general fund.

The board appoints an executive secretary to administer the Division of Trust Lands and Investments, which serves as the board's operating agency.

Article X, Section 7 of the Wisconsin Constitution established "a board of commissioners for the sale of school and university lands and for the investment of funds arising therefrom" consisting of the Secretary of State, State Treasurer, and Attorney General. The Revised Statutes of 1849 created the Board of Commissioners of the School and University Lands. The board was renamed the Board of Commissioners of Public Lands in the Revised Statutes of 1878. Chapter 75, Laws of 1967, created the Division of Trust Lands and Investments, under the supervision of the Board of Commissioners of Public Lands and attached the division to the Department of Natural Resources. Since then, the legislature has successively attached the division to the Department of Justice (Chapter 34, Laws of 1979), the Department of Administration (1993 Wisconsin Act 16), the Office of the State Treasurer (1995 Wisconsin Act 27), and the Department of Administration (1997 Wisconsin Act 27).

PUBLIC RECORDS BOARD

Members: PETER GOTTLIEB (representing the director, state historical society), *chairperson;* MAUREEN MCGLYNN FLANAGAN (representing the attorney general), *vice chairperson;* CAROL HEMERSBACH (public member), *secretary;* CAROLYN SMITH (representing the governor), BRYAN NAAB (representing the state auditor), RUSSELL WHITESEL (representing the joint legislative council staff director), MICHAEL A. KEEVER (small business representative), RITA K. KIDD (representative of school board or governing body of a municipality). (Representatives are appointed by the respective officers or the governor.)

Executive Secretary: STEVEN B. HIRSCH, steve.hirsch@doa.state.wi.us

Mailing Address: 4622 University Avenue, Room 10A, Madison 53702.

Telephone: (608) 266-2996.

Fax: (608) 266-5050.

Internet Address: http://www.doa.state.wi.us (use Public Records Board link under "Business in DOA").

Publications: Biennial Report; General Schedules for Records Common to State Agencies and Local Units of Government; Records Inventory, Analysis and Scheduling Manual; Registry of State Agency Record Series Containing Personally Identifiable Information.

Statutory References: Sections 15.105 (4) and 16.61.

Agency Responsibility: The Public Records Board is responsible for the preservation of important state records, the cost-effective management of records by state agencies, and the orderly disposition of state records that have become obsolete. State agencies must have written approval from the board to dispose of records they generate or receive.

1991 Wisconsin Acts 39 and 269 directed the board to create a registry of those record series that contain personally identifiable information and made it the repository for general information about state computer matching programs.

Originally created by Chapter 316, Laws of 1947, as the Committee on Public Records and placed under the State Historical Society, the agency was transferred to the governor's office by Chapter 547, Laws of 1957. The committee was renamed the Public Records Board and attached to the Department of Administration by Chapter 75, Laws of 1967. Chapter 350, Laws of 1981, changed the board's name to the Public Records and Forms Board and added forms management to its duties. In 1995, Wisconsin Act 27 designated the board's current name and removed its forms management duties.

SENTENCING COMMISSION

Members: SUSAN STEINGASS (appointed by governor), *chairperson*; PEGGY A. LAUTENSCHLAGER (attorney general); NICHOLAS L. CHIARKAS (state public defender); SENATORS COGGS, ZIEN; REPRESENTATIVES BIES, TRAVIS; PATRICK FIEDLER, ELSA LAMELAS (circuit court judges appointed by supreme court); PATTI SEGER (crime victims representative appointed by attorney general); WILLIAM LENNON (prosecutor appointed by attorney general); JOHN BIRDSALL (attorney appointed by criminal law section, State Bar of Wisconsin); ANN HRAYCHUCK, RONALD K. MALONE, GERALD MOWRIS, MARSHALL MURRAY, RICHARD MYERS, PETER NAZE (appointed by governor). Nonvoting members: MATTHEW FRANK (secretary of corrections); LENARD WELLS (chairperson, parole commission); JOHN VOELKER (director of state courts).

Number of Employees: 2.00.

Total Budget 2003-05: $471,200.

Statutory Reference: Sections 15.01 (2), 15.105 (27), and 973.30.

Agency Responsibility: The 18-member Sentencing Commission monitors and compiles data on sentencing practices; provides information on costs of sentencing practices to the legislature, state agencies, and the public; provides information to judges and lawyers on sentencing guidelines; distributes an annual report that includes current sentencing guidelines and changes in those guidelines to all circuit court judges; reports on whether race is a basis for imposing sentences; assists the legislature in determining the cost of additions or revisions to the criminal code that affect sentencing; and compiles and reports statistics semiannually on criminal sentences in this state.

All but *ex officio* and legislative members serve 3-year terms. Terms of circuit court judges and prosecutors, however, end immediately when they leave office. Two of the members the governor appoints must not be public employees. The commission, which was created by 2001 Wisconsin Act 109, is scheduled to sunset on December 31, 2007.

STATE CAPITOL AND EXECUTIVE RESIDENCE BOARD

Members: SENATORS LEIBHAM, RISSER, SCHULTZ; REPRESENTATIVES LADWIG, OWENS, SCHNEIDER; ROBERT CRAMER (designated by secretary of administration); JAMES SEWELL (designated by director, state historical society); DAVID HALEY (engineer employed by the Department of Administration and appointed by secretary); JOHN J. FERNHOLZ (landscape architect); ARLAN K. KAY, ANTHONY PUTTNAM (architects); ROBERT E. LEWCOCK, EUGENE POTENTE, JR., DEBRA A. WOODWARD (interior designers); SALLY C. BASTING (citizen member). (All except *ex officio* members and their designees are appointed by governor.)

Statutory References: Sections 15.105 (5) and 16.83.

Agency Responsibility: The 16-member State Capitol and Executive Residence Board, created by Chapter 183, Laws of 1967, includes 7 citizen members with specified expertise, appointed by the governor to serve staggered 6-year terms. The board sets standards for design, composition, and appropriateness of repairs, replacements, and additions to the State Capitol and Executive Residence.

Office of State
EMPLOYMENT RELATIONS

Director: KAREN E. TIMBERLAKE, 266-9820, karen.timberlake@

Executive Assistant: SUSAN CRAWFORD, 266-9672, susan.crawford@

Legal Counsel: DAVID J. VERGERONT, 266-0047, david.vergeront@

State Employee Suggestion Program: ROBERT TOOMEY, *coordinator,* (608) 266-0664, robert.toomey@; Program e-mail: suggest@, Program Internet address: http://suggest.state.wi.us

Affirmative Action, Division of: DEMETRI FISHER, *administrator,* 266-3017, demetri.fisher@

Compensation and Labor Relations, Division of: JAMES A. PANKRATZ, *administrator,* 266-1860, jim.pankratz@

   Compensation, Bureau of: PAUL HANKES, *director,* 266-1729, paul.hankes@

   Labor Relations, Bureau of: MARK WILD, *director,* 266-9564, mark.wild@

Merit Recruitment and Selection, Division of: PATRICIA M. ALMOND, *administrator,* 266-1499, patricia.almond@

   Agency Services, Bureau of: LEEAN WHITE, *director,* 267-0344, leean.white@

   Outreach Services, Bureau of: JENNIFER GEBERT, *director,* 267-2155, jennifer.gebert@

Address e-mail by combining the user ID and the state extender: userid**@oser.state.wi.us**

Mailing Address: P.O. Box 7855, Madison 53707-7855.

Location: 101 East Wilson Street, 4th Floor.

Telephones: General: (608) 266-9820, TTY: (608) 267-1004; State job information: (608) 266-1731, TTY: (608) 266-1498.

Fax: (608) 267-1020.

Internet Address: http://oser.state.wi.us

Publications: Affirmative Action Recruitment Resource Directory; Council on Affirmative Action Report; Current Employment Opportunities Bulletin; State Employment Options Program Annual Report; A Study Guide for Employment Examinations with Wisconsin State Government; Summer Affirmative Action Report; Veterans Employment Report; W-2 Hiring Report; Wisconsin Civil Service Job Information; Written Hiring Reasons Report.

Number of Employees: 58.50.

Total Budget 2003-05: $11,555,600.

Statutory References: Sections 15.105(29); Chapter 111, Subchapter V, and Chapter 230.

Agency Responsibility: The Office of State Employment Relations is responsible for personnel and employment relations policies and programs for state government employees. The office administers the state's classified service, which is designed to staff state governmental agencies with employees chosen on the basis of merit. It evaluates job categories, determines employee performance and training needs, and assists managers in their supervisory duties. The office sets standards for and ensures compliance with affirmative action plans. It represents the executive branch in its role as an employer under the state's employment relations statutes.

A director, who is appointed by the governor, administers the office. The director appoints the administrators of the Division of Affirmative Action and the Division of Compensation and Labor Relations from outside the classified service. The governor appoints the administrator of the Division of Merit Recruitment and Selection to a 5-year term, with the advice and consent of the senate, based on a competitive examination. The governor may appoint the administrator for subsequent 5-year terms with the senate's consent.

Unit Functions: The *Division of Affirmative Action* administers the state's equal employment opportunity/affirmative action program and reports annually to the governor and legislature about the affirmative action accomplishments of state agencies. It develops standards for executive agencies, the UW System, and legislative service agencies and provides staff support to the Council on Affirmative Action. The division provides technical assistance to agencies in the development and implementation of affirmative action plans, trains new supervisors, and monitors agency programs.

The *Division of Compensation and Labor Relations* administers the state's compensation plan and leave statutes and policies. It also assists in state agency compliance with the federal and state family and medical leave acts. The division represents the state as employer in negotiating wages, benefits, and working conditions with the 19 labor unions that represent state employees, but the legislature must ratify all contracts. The division also serves the state in arbitration proceedings, conducts labor relations training programs for state management representatives, and coordinates the Labor-Management Cooperation Program.

The *Division of Merit Recruitment and Selection,* created in Section 15.105 (29)(b) in 2003 Wisconsin Act 33, administers the state's civil service system by coordinating the recruiting, testing, evaluating, and hiring of applicants. The division administers layoffs, transfers, and reinstatements of nonrepresented classified employees. The division also allocates positions to classifications, assigns nonrepresented classifications to pay ranges, and assigns represented classifications to pay ranges as part of the collective bargaining process. It administers the state's performance evaluation program and assists in state agency compliance with protective occupation determinations and the federal Fair Labor Standards Act. It also administers programs that assist Wisconsin Works (W-2) clients and food stamp recipients in obtaining state employment. In addition, it operates Wisconsin Personnel Partners, which provides personnel services to local government units on a fee basis. The division also oversees the administration of employee assistance programs in all state agencies, under which state employees and their families receive assistance with personal or work-related problems.

History: An office that administers state employment procedures dates back to the creation of a State Civil Service Commission in Chapter 363, Laws of 1905. The law declared that appointments to and promotions in the civil service would be made only according to merit. Chapter 456, Laws of 1929, reconstituted the commission as the Personnel Board within the newly created

Bureau of Personnel. This structure continued for 30 years until the legislature placed the board and bureau in the new Department of Administration, created in Chapter 228, Laws of 1959.

In 1972, Governor Patrick Lucey issued an executive order creating an affirmative action unit in the Bureau of Personnel. The order also directed the head of every state agency to encourage women and minorities to apply for promotions and to designate an affirmative action officer responsible for developing an affirmative action plan.

Chapter 196, Laws of 1977, created the Department of Employment Relations and transferred to it from the Department of Administration the organizational units and functions of the Employee Relations Division, including affirmative action, personnel, collective bargaining, and human resources services.

The legislature reorganized personnel functions in 1983 Wisconsin Act 27 by assigning classification and compensation responsibility to the secretary and recruitment and examination responsibility to a statutorily created Division of Merit Recruitment and Selection. The same law created the Personnel Board as an independent agency to review civil service rules and investigate and report on their impact. 1989 Wisconsin Act 31 abolished the Personnel Board and transferred its functions to the department. The 2003-05 biennial budget, Act 33, abolished the department and created the Office of State Employment Relations attached to the Department of Administration.

Statutory Council and Board

Affirmative Action, Council on: LAURA A. MILLOT (appointed by governor), *chairperson;* vacancy (appointed by senate president), *vice chairperson;* ROGER V. PULLIAM (appointed by assembly speaker), *secretary;* HUGO HENRY (appointed by senate minority leader), ADELENE ROBINSON (appointed by assembly minority leader); YOLANDA SANTOS ADAMS, AMOS C. ANDERSON, LAKSHMI BHARADWAT, ALICE HERRERA, JANICE K. HUGHES, JAMES R. PARKER, SANDRA RYAN, ROLAND W. WETLEY, 2 vacancies (appointed by governor).

Contact person: DEMETRI FISHER, *administrator,* Division of Affirmative Action, 266-3017.

The 15-member Council on Affirmative Action advises the director of state employment relations, evaluates affirmative action programs throughout the classified service, seeks compliance with state and federal regulations, and recommends improvements in the state's affirmative action efforts. The council must report annually to the legislature and governor. It may recommend legislation, consult with agency personnel and other interested groups, and conduct hearings. Council members serve 3-year terms. A majority of them must be public members, and a majority must represent minority persons, women, and people with disabilities. The council was created by Chapter 196, Laws of 1977, in the Department of Employment Relations and is located in the Office of State Employment Relations (2003 Wisconsin Act 33). Its composition and duties are prescribed in Sections 15.105 (29)(d) and 230.46 of the statutes.

State Employees Suggestion Board: JIM BEHREND, SANDY DREW, DAVID M. VRIEZEN (all appointed by governor).

The 3-member State Employees Suggestion Board administers an awards program to encourage unusual and meritorious suggestions and accomplishments by state employees that promote economy and efficiency in government services. Board members are appointed for 4-year terms, and at least one of them must be a state officer or employee. The board was created by Chapter 278, Laws of 1953, as the Wisconsin State Employees Merit Award Board and renamed in 1987 Wisconsin Act 142. It has been successively located in the Bureau of Personnel, the Department of Administration, in the Department of Employment Relations (1989 Wisconsin Act 31), and the Office of State Employment Relations (2003 Wisconsin Act 33). Its composition and duties are prescribed in Sections 15.105 (29)(c) and 230.48 of the statutes.

STATE USE BOARD

Members: DAVID M. DUMKE (public member), *chairperson;* PATRICK J. FARLEY (Department of Administration representative); THOMAS J. SWANT (mental health representative, Department of Health and Family Services); CLEO ANN ELIASON (vocational rehabilitation representative, Department of Workforce Development); BILL G. SMITH (small business representative);

NICKOLAS C. GEORGE, JR. (private business representative); JEAN A. VOGT (work center representative); MICHAEL CASEY (public member). (All are appointed by governor.)

Mailing Address: Bureau of Procurement, Division of Enterprise Operations, P.O. Box 7867, Madison 53707-7867.

Telephone: (608) 266-5462.

Fax: (608) 267-0600.

Publication: Annual Report to the Secretary.

Number of Employees: 1.50.

Total Budget 2003-05: $200,000.

Statutory References: Sections 15.105 (22) and 16.752.

Agency Responsibility: The 8-member State Use Board was created by 1989 Wisconsin Act 345. Its members, who serve 4-year terms, oversee state purchases from work centers certified by the board. To be certified, centers must meet certain conditions: 1) the work center must make a product or provide a service the state needs; 2) it must offer these goods or services at a fair market price; and 3) it must employ individuals with severe disabilities for at least 75% of the direct labor used in providing the goods or services.

TAX APPEALS COMMISSION

Members: JENNIFER E. NASHOLD, *chairperson;* DIANE E. NORMAN, DAVID C. SWANSON (appointed by governor with senate consent).

Legal Assistant: EVIE J. SCHWARTZLOW, 266-1391, evie.schwartzlow@tac.state.wi.us

Mailing Address: 5005 University Avenue, Suite 110, Madison 53705.

Telephone: (608) 266-1391.

Fax: (608) 261-7060.

Number of Employees: 5.00.

Total Budget 2003-05: $861,900.

Statutory References: Sections 15.01 (2), 15.06 (1), 15.105 (1), and 73.01.

Publications: Decisions are at: http://www.wisbar.org (under Legal Research).

Agency Responsibility: The 3-member Tax Appeals Commission hears and decides disputes between persons or entities and the Department of Revenue involving all major, state-imposed taxes. The commission hears appeals arising under the homestead and farmland preservation tax credit programs and decides appeals of state assessments of manufacturing property or penalties for late filing. It conducts appeals hearings on real estate transfer fees, license fees for telephones and electric cooperatives, county sales and use taxes, and relative property values within taxation units. The commission may also decide disputes between persons or entities and the Department of Transportation, regarding certain motor vehicle taxes and fees.

The *Small Claims Division,* created in Section 15.105 (1), Wisconsin Statutes, by 1985 Wisconsin Act 29, may determine tax matters in which the amount in controversy is less than $2,500 unless the commission decides that the matter should not be heard as a small claims case or the Department of Revenue concludes that the case has statewide significance.

The tax appeals commissioners serve staggered 6-year terms and must be experienced in tax matters. The chairperson, who is designated by the governor to serve a 2-year term, must not serve on or under any committee of a political party. Employees of the commission are appointed by the chairperson from the classified service.

The Tax Appeals Commission was created as the Board of Tax Appeals by Chapter 412, Laws of 1939. Before 1939, individuals took appeals of income and property taxes to the local county board of review with appeal permitted to the state Tax Commission. Corporations took their appeals to the Commissioner of Taxation with appeal to the circuit court. The board was renamed the Tax Appeals Commission by Chapter 75, Laws of 1967.

COUNCIL ON UTILITY PUBLIC BENEFITS

Members: DAN SCHOOFF (appointed by secretary of administration), *chairperson;* JAMES BOULLION, THELMA A. SIAS (appointed by governor); 2 vacancies (appointed by senate majority leader); vacancy (appointed by senate minority leader); THOMAS MEINZ, DON RECK (appointed by assembly speaker); FORREST CEEL (appointed by assembly minority leader); ALLEN K. SHEA (appointed by secretary of natural resources); DAN EBERT (appointed by public service commission chairperson).

Mailing Address: Division of Energy, P.O. Box 7868, Madison 53707-7868.

Telephone: (608) 266-9770.

Statutory References: Sections 15.107 (17) and 16.957.

The 11-member Council on Utility Public Benefits advises the Department of Administration on issues related to energy efficiency, conservation programs, and energy assistance to low-income households, including weatherization, payment of energy bills, and early identification and prevention of energy crises. Services are provided through community action agencies, nonprofit corporations, or local governments. Grants are also awarded to nonprofit corporations for energy conservation and efficiency services, renewable resources in the least competitive sectors of the energy conservation market, and programs that promote environmental protection, electric system reliability, or rural economic development. The council was created by 1999 Wisconsin Act 9, and its members are appointed for 3-year terms.

VOLUNTEER FIRE FIGHTER AND EMERGENCY MEDICAL TECHNICIAN SERVICE AWARD BOARD

Members: MARC MAROTTA (secretary of administration); ROBERT H. SEITZ (fire chiefs statewide organization representative); KENNETH A. BARTZ (volunteer fire fighters statewide organization representative); MELINDA R. ALLEN (volunteer emergency medical service technician); GREGORIO MONTOTO, ALLEN R. SCHRAEDER, CARL STOLTE (representatives of municipalities using volunteer fire fighters), BRAD R. COOK (individual experienced in financial planning). (All but *ex officio* members are appointed by governor.)

Contact person: TERRI LENZ, 261-2298.

Mailing Address: 101 East Wilson Street, 6th Floor, Madison 53702.

Telephone: (608) 261-6580.

Number of Employees: 0.00.

Total Budget 2003-05: $1,970,400.

Statutory References: Sections 15.105 (26) and 16.25.

The 8-member Volunteer Fire Fighter and Emergency Medical Technical Service Award Board establishes administrative rules for the operation of a service awards program designed to provide monetary rewards for volunteer fire fighters and emergency medical service technicians based on their length of service to a community. The board contracts with qualified private individuals or organizations to provide investment plans and administrative services to municipalities that choose to participate in the service awards program, but the communities make their payments directly to the plan provider. The board must establish procedures for appeal of decisions by the Department of Administration or the plan providers when the decisions substantially affect the interests of individual participants. In appointing the board members, who serve 3-year terms, the governor must seek representatives from different regions of the state and from municipalities of different sizes. Representatives of the fire chiefs and volunteer fire fighters organizations must be volunteer fire fighters themselves. The board was created by 1999 Wisconsin Act 105.

WASTE FACILITY SITING BOARD

Members: MICHAEL A. MARSDEN (town official), *chairperson;* PATRICIA TRAINER (designated by secretary of transportation), *secretary;* DAVID JELINSKI (designated by secretary of agriculture, trade and consumer protection), DAVID K. STOREY (designated by secretary of commerce); JAMES SCHUERMAN (town official); DALE SHAVER (county official). (Town and county officials are appointed by governor with senate consent.)

Executive Director: DAVID H. SCHWARZ.

Mailing Address: 5005 University Avenue, Suite 201, Madison 53705-5400.

Telephone: (608) 266-7709.
Fax: (608) 264-9885
Publications: Opinions of the Waste Facility Siting Board; Standard Notice.
Statutory References: Sections 15.07 (1)(b) 11., 15.105 (12), 289.33, and 289.64.

Agency Responsibility: The 6-member Waste Facility Siting Board supervises a mandated negotiation-arbitration procedure between applicants for new or expanded solid or hazardous waste facility licenses and local committees composed of representatives from the municipalities affected by proposed facilities. It is authorized to make final awards in arbitration hearings and can enforce legal deadlines and other obligations of applicants and local committees during the process.

Town and county officials serve staggered 3-year terms, and the governor, when making these appointments, must consider timely recommendations of the Wisconsin Towns Association and the Wisconsin Counties Association. The board appoints an executive director who is authorized to request assistance from any state agency in helping the board fulfill its duties. The board is funded by a fee on each ton of waste disposed of in a licensed solid or hazardous waste facility. The board was created by Chapter 374, Laws of 1981, and is the first such agency established in the nation.

WOMEN'S COUNCIL

Members: KRISTINE MARTINSEK (public member appointed by governor), *chairperson;* 2 vacancies (senators appointed by senate majority leader); REPRESENTATIVES KERKMAN, KRAWCZYK (appointed by assembly speaker); JOAN M. PRINCE (designated by governor); MARY JO BAAS, HEATHER SMITH (public members appointed by senate president); DEB JORDAHL, AMY POLASKY (public members appointed by assembly speaker); RENEE BOLDT, NICOLE BOWMAN-FARRELL, JANE D. CLARK, ANN PEGGS, ARLENE C. SISS (public members appointed by governor).
Executive Director: CHRISTINE LIDBURY.
Mailing Address: 101 East Wilson Street, 8th Floor, Madison 53702.
Telephone: (608) 266-2219.
Fax: (608) 267-0626.
Internet Address: http://womenscouncil.wi.gov
Publications: Numerous publications related to the council's mission.
Number of Employees: 1.00.
Total Budget 2003-05: $214,200.
Statutory References: Sections 15.107 (11) and 16.01.

Agency Responsibility: The 15-member Women's Council is charged with identifying barriers that prevent women in Wisconsin from participating fully and equally in all aspects of life. The council promotes public and private sector initiatives that empower women through educational opportunity; provides a clearinghouse for information relating to women's issues; works in cooperation with related groups and organizations; and promotes opportunities for partnerships with various organizations to address issues affecting Wisconsin women. The council advises state agencies about the impact upon women of current and emerging state policies, laws, and rules; recommends changes to the public and private sectors and initiates legislation to further women's economic and social equality and improve this state's tax base and economy; and disseminates information on the status of women in this state.

The governor or governor's designee serves a 4-year term on the council; all other members serve 2-year terms. The governor appoints 6 public members, one of whom the governor designates as chairperson. The Women's Council was created by 1983 Wisconsin Act 27. It was preceded by a nonstatutory commission, the Governor's Commission on the Status of Women, which was created in 1964 and abolished in 1979.

Department of
AGRICULTURE, TRADE AND CONSUMER PROTECTION

Board of Agriculture, Trade and Consumer Protection: CYNTHIA BROWN, RICHARD CATES, ANDREW DIERCKS, MICHAEL DUMMER, ENRIQUE FIGUEROA, MICHAEL KRUTZA, SHELLY MAYER (agricultural representatives); MARGARET KROME, BRIAN RUDE (consumer representatives) (appointed by governor with senate consent).

Secretary of Agriculture, Trade and Consumer Protection: RODNEY J. NILSESTUEN, 224-5015.

Deputy Secretary: JUDY K. ZIEWACZ, 224-5001.

Executive Assistant: MARTIN M. HENERT, 224-5035.

Wisconsin Agricultural Statistics Service: ROBERT J. BATTAGLIA, *state agricultural statistician,* 224-4848, robert.battaglia@

Administrative Law Judge: CHERYL F. DANIELS, 224-5026, cheryl.daniels@

Legal Counsel, Office of: JAMES K. MATSON, *chief counsel,* 224-5023, james.matson@

Budget Director: BARBARA H. KNAPP, 224-4746, barb.knapp@

For e-mail combine the user ID and the state extender: **userid@datcp.state.wi.us**

Mailing Address: P.O. Box 8911, Madison 53708-8911.

Location: 2811 Agriculture Drive, Madison.

Telephones: Consumer Protection Hotline: (800) 422-7128; Farmers Assistance Hotline: (800) 942-2474; Wisconsin Telemarketing No-Call List sign-up: (866) 966-2255.

Fax: Office of the Secretary: 224-5045; Division of Agricultural Development: 224-5110; Division of Agricultural Resource Management: 224-4656; Division of Animal Health: 224-4871; Division of Food Safety: 224-4710; Division of Management Services: 224-4737; Division of Trade and Consumer Protection: 224-4939.

Internet Address: http://www.datcp.state.wi.us

Departmental E-mail Address: datcp_web@datcp.state.wi.us

Agricultural Development, Division of: WILL H. HUGHES, *administrator,* 224-5142, will.hughes@

  Agricultural Business Development Group: PERRY L. BROWN, *supervisor,* 224-5114, perry.brown@

  Agricultural Market Development Group: LORA J. KLENKE, *supervisor,* 224-5119, lora.klenke@

  Farm Services Group: DAVID D. HANSEN, *supervisor,* 224-5055, david.hansen@

Agricultural Resource Management, Division of: KATHY F. PIELSTICKER, *administrator,* 224-4567, kathy.pielsticker@

  Agrichemical Management, Bureau of: vacancy, *director,* 224-4550.

  Land and Water Resources, Bureau of: J. DAVID JELINSKI, *director,* 224-4621, dave.jelinski@

  Plant Industry, Bureau of: vacancy, *director and assistant division administrator,* 224-4590.

Animal Health, Division of: ROBERT G. EHLENFELDT, *state veterinarian, administrator,* 224-4880, robert.ehlenfeldt@

  Administrative Services, Bureau of: SHEILA M. GRAHAM, *director and assistant division administrator,* 224-4885, sheila.graham@

  Animal Disease Control, Bureau of: PAUL J. MCGRAW, *assistant state veterinarian, director,* 224-4884, paul.mcgraw@

  State Humane Officer: YVONNE M. BELLAY, 224-4888, yvonne.bellay@

Food Safety, Division of: STEVEN B. STEINHOFF, *administrator,* 224-4701, steve.steinhoff@

  Food Safety and Inspection, Bureau of: CHARLES T. LEITZKE, *director,* 224-4711, tom.leitzke@

  Meat Safety and Inspection, Bureau of: TERRY L. BURKHARDT, *director,* 224-4725, terry.burkhardt@

DEPARTMENT OF AGRICULTURE, TRADE AND CONSUMER PROTECTION

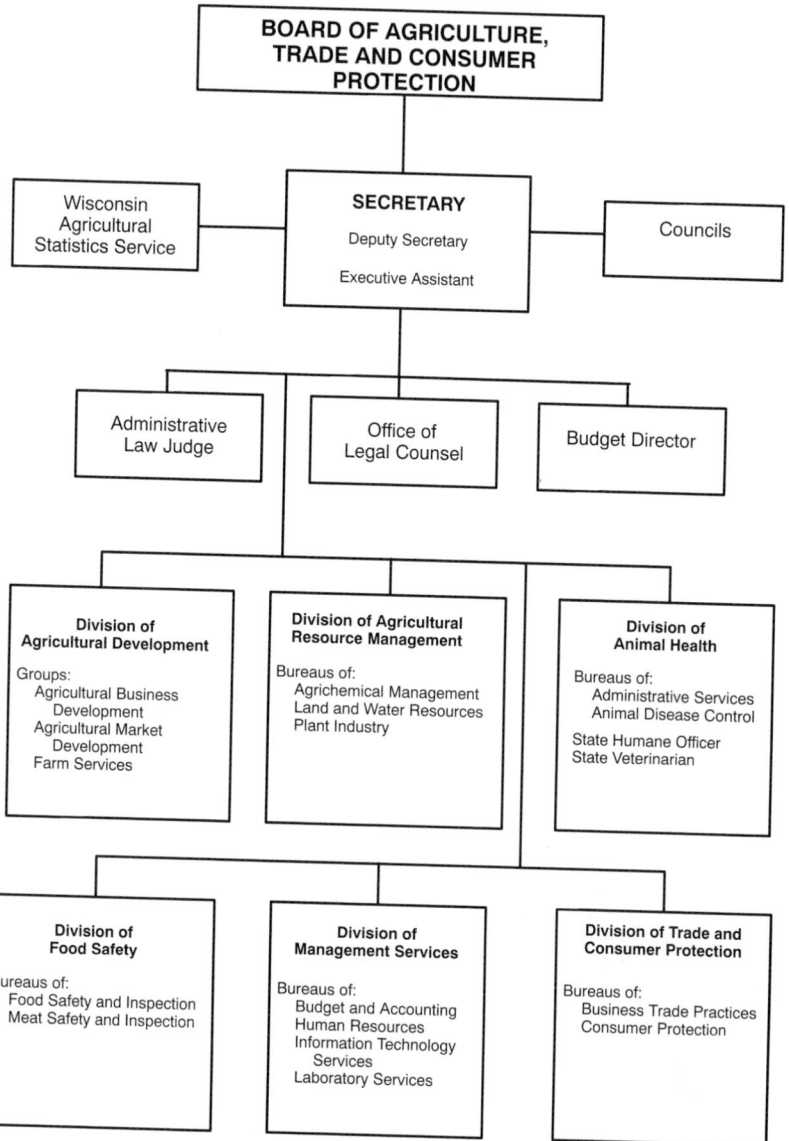

Units attached for administrative purposes under Sec. 15.03: Land and Water Conservation Board
Livestock Facility Siting Review Board

Management Services, Division of: Susan J. Buroker, *administrator,* 224-4740, susan.buroker@
　Budget and Accounting, Bureau of: Karen Van Schoonhoven, *director,* 224-4800,
　karen.vanschoonhoven@
　Human Resources, Bureau of: Georgia J. Pedracine, *director and assistant division admin-istrator,* 224-4761, georgia.pedracine@
　Information Technology Services, Bureau of: Susan J. Buroker, *acting director,* 224-4777,
　susan.buroker@
　Laboratory Services, Bureau of: Steven M. Sobek, *director,* 267-3503, steve.sobek@
Trade and Consumer Protection, Division of: Janet A. Jenkins, *administrator,* 224-4929,
　janet.jenkins@
　Business Trade Practices, Bureau of: Jeremy S. McPherson, *director,* 224-4922,
　jeremy.mcpherson@
　Consumer Protection, Bureau of: Jim L. Rabbitt, *director and assistant division administra-tor,* 224-4965, jim.rabbitt@

Publications: Agricultural Land Sales; *Chloroacetanilide Herbicide Metabolites in Wisconsin Groundwater; Complaint Guide for the Wisconsin Consumer;* Farm Transfers in Wisconsin – A Guide for Farmers; *Groundwater Protection: An Evaluation of Wisconsin's Atrazine Rule; Groundwater Quality – Agricultural Chemicals in Wisconsin Groundwater May 2002;* Guide to Wisconsin Cheese Factory Outlets and Tours; *Landlord and Tenants: The Wisconsin Way; Livestock Guidance: Local Planning for Livestock Operations in Wisconsin; Planning for Agri-culture in Wisconsin: A Guide for Communities; Preventing Senior Citizen Rip-offs;* Wisconsin Agricultural Statistics; Wisconsin Dairy Plant Directory; Wisconsin Nursery Directory; Wis-consin Pest Bulletin.

Number of Employees: 603.94.

Total Budget 2003-05: $145,956,400.

Statutory References: Sections 15.13, 15.135, and 15.137; Chapters 88, 91-100, 127, and 136.

　Agency Responsibility: The Department of Agriculture, Trade and Consumer Protection regu-lates agriculture, trade, and commercial activity in Wisconsin for the protection of the state's citi-zens. It enforces the state's primary consumer protection laws, including those relating to decep-tive advertising, unfair business practices, and consumer product safety. The department oversees enforcement of Wisconsin's animal health and disease control laws and conducts a variety of pro-grams to conserve and protect the state's vital land, water, and plant resources.

　The department administers financial security programs to protect agricultural producers, facil-itates the marketing of Wisconsin agricultural products in interstate and international markets, and promotes agricultural development and diversification.

　Organization: The 9 members of the Board of Agriculture, Trade and Consumer Protection serve staggered 6-year terms. Of the board members, 2 must be consumer representatives and 7 must have an agricultural background. Appointments to the board must be made "without regard to party affiliation, residence or interest in any special organized group". The board directs and supervises the department, which is administered by a secretary appointed by the governor with the advice and consent of the senate. The secretary appoints the division administrators from out-side the classified service.

　Unit Functions: The *Division of Agricultural Development* provides services to assist produc-ers, agribusinesses, and organizations to develop national and international markets for Wiscon-sin agricultural products and to foster agricultural development and diversification in the state. It also provides counseling and mediation services to farmers, administers a rural electric power service program with the Public Service Commission, and oversees the operation of producer-elected marketing boards that assess fees within their respective groups for promotion, research, and education related to their commodities. The division also administers Agricultural Develop-ment and Diversification grants, a federal-state market news program, the "Something Special From Wisconsin" and Alice in Dairyland marketing programs, as well as the state aid programs for county and district fairs, the Livestock Breeders Association, and World Dairy Expo.

　The *Division of Agricultural Resource Management* administers programs designed to protect the state's agricultural resources, as well as public health and the environment. It works to prevent agricultural practices that contaminate surface water and groundwater and jointly administers a nonpoint source pollution control program with the Department of Natural Resources. It directs programs related to farmland preservation and soil and land conservation, agricultural chemical cleanup, drainage districts, and agricultural impact statements. It regulates the sale and use of pesticides, animal feed, fertilizers, seed, and soil and plant additives and conducts programs to prevent and control plant pests, such as the gypsy moth.

The *Division of Animal Health* works closely with agricultural producers and veterinarians to diagnose, prevent, and control serious domestic animal diseases that threaten public health and the food chain. It licenses and inspects animal dealers and markets, regulates the import and export of animals across state lines, acts to prevent the spread of animal diseases, and assists in the enforcement of state humane laws. Through the Premises Identification Program, it registers persons who keep livestock and assigns an identification code to each place at which livestock are kept to facilitate animal disease control. It also regulates emerging industries, such as aquaculture and farm-raised deer.

The *Division of Food Safety* protects the state's food supply. From production through processing, packaging, distribution, and retail sale, the division works to ensure safe and wholesome food and to prevent fraud and misbranding in food sales. It licenses and inspects dairy plants, food and beverage processing establishments, meat slaughter and processing facilities, food warehouses, grocery stores, and other food establishments. The division inspects all dairy farms; inspects and samples food products; oversees food grading; and regulates the advertising, packaging, and labeling of food products.

The *Division of Management Services* provides administrative services to the department, including budget and accounting; facilities and fleet management; shipping, mailing, and printing; human resource management; and information technology services. The division also operates a general laboratory that provides analytical support to departmental inspection and sampling programs.

The *Division of Trade and Consumer Protection* enforces a wide range of consumer protection laws and handles nearly 200,000 consumer complaints and inquiries annually. It promulgates and enforces rules pertaining to deceptive advertising, consumer fraud, consumer product safety, landlord-tenant practices, home improvement, telecommunications, telemarketing, motor vehicle repair, fair packaging and labeling, weights and measures, and many other aspects of marketing. To promote fair and open competition in the marketplace, the division investigates and regulates unfair and anticompetitive business practices. It monitors the financial condition and business practices of dairy plants, grain warehouses, food processing plants, and public storage warehouses in order to protect agricultural producers and depositors. It also administers the state's Telemarketing No-Call List.

History: The present form of the Department of Agriculture, Trade and Consumer Protection is largely the result of the consolidation of several related agencies in 1929, but the department traces its lineage and responsibilities back to pre-statehood days.

From its beginnings, Wisconsin has been concerned with agriculture; food quality, safety, and labeling; plant and animal health; unfair business and trade practices; and consumer protection, and has taken steps to protect the public. The 1839 territorial legislature provided for the inspection of certain food and other products and established a program to regulate weights and measures. County inspectors were responsible for certifying the grade, wholesomeness, quantity, and proper packaging of food and distilled spirits, with county treasurers charged with enforcing the weights and measures standards. The 1867 Legislature, in Chapter 176, authorized the governor to appoint a treasury agent to enforce the laws relating to itinerant sales by "hawkers and peddlers". The 1889 Legislature, in Chapter 452, created the Office of the Dairy and Food Commissioner to enforce food safety, food labeling, and weights and measures laws. Other legislation over the years created various related functions such as the State Veterinarian, the State Board of Agriculture, the Inspector of Apiaries, the State Orchard and Nursery Inspector, the State Supervisor of Illuminating Oils, and the State Humane Agent.

The Department of Agriculture was created by Chapter 413, Laws of 1915, which combined the functions of several prior entities including the Board of Agriculture, Livestock Sanitary Board, State Veterinarian, Inspector of Apiaries, and Orchard and Nursery Inspector. Under the control and supervision of a Commissioner of Agriculture appointed by the governor with senate consent, the department had the responsibility to promote the interests of agriculture, dairying, horticulture, manufactures, and the domestic arts. It collected and published farm crop, livestock, and other statistics relating to state resources and regulated the practice of veterinary medicine. Through its own informational publications and paid advertisements in print media both inside the country and in foreign lands, it also sought to further the "development and enrichment" of the state by attracting "desirable immigrants" and "capital seeking profitable investment". These efforts were intended to promote the advantages and opportunities offered by the state "to the farmer, the merchant, the manufacturer, the home seeker, and the summer visitor".

The Division of Markets was created within the Department of Agriculture by Chapter 670, Laws of 1919. The duty of the division was to promote, in the interest of the producer, distributor, and consuming public, the economical and efficient distribution of farm products. Responsibilities included devising systems for marketing, grading, standardization, and storage of farm products; preventing deceptive practices; maintaining a market news service for collecting and reporting information on the supply, demand, prices, and commercial movement of farm products; and designing copyrighted trademarks, labels, and brands for Wisconsin farm products. A separate

Wisconsin is a national leader in preparing for rapid, effective responses to animal disease outbreaks. It was the first state to enact a Livestock Premises Registration Law (2003 Wisconsin Act 229) which requires that, by January 2006, all keepers of livestock register with the department. Premises registration is the first step in a national animal identification system. Pictured are some of the Department of Agriculture, Trade and Consumer Protection staff who have made key contributions to statewide animal health efforts: Melissa Mace, State Veterinarian Bob Ehlenfeldt, Sue Buroker, Brian Shah, and attorney Dennis Fay. (Department of Agriculture, Trade and Consumer Protection)

Department of Markets was created by Chapter 571, Laws of 1921, under the direction of a commissioner of markets appointed by the governor with senate consent. The department retained most of the duties of the former division, but was allowed to give assistance to cooperative associations and was specifically charged with regulating unfair methods of competition in business and unfair trade practices.

The modern department had its inception when Chapter 479, Laws of 1929, created the Department of Agriculture and Markets by consolidation of the Department of Agriculture, the Department of Markets, the Dairy and Food Commissioner, the State Treasury Agent, the State Supervisor of Inspectors of Illuminating Oils, and the State Humane Agent. The department, which was under the control of three commissioners appointed by the governor with senate consent, assumed all duties performed by the component agencies. The department was reorganized and renamed the Department of Agriculture by Chapter 85, Laws of 1939, but its basic mission and authority was not changed. The department was overseen by a 7-member State Board of Agriculture, whose members, appointed by the governor with senate consent, in turn appointed the department's director. All members of the board were required to be persons experienced in farming.

The department's name was changed to the current Department of Agriculture, Trade and Consumer Protection by Chapter 29, Laws of 1977. This law also specified that one of the 7 board members must be a consumer representative.

1995 Wisconsin Act 27 directed the governor, rather than the board, to appoint the department secretary with senate consent, and expanded the board's membership to 8, including 2 consumer representatives. The board continues to set policy for the agency. Act 27 also consolidated the administration of most consumer protection activities within the department by transferring some staff and functions from the Department of Justice. However, the Department of Justice cooperates in the enforcement of consumer protection laws by providing legal services such as civil litigation. 1997 Wisconsin Act 95 added a ninth board member to represent agriculture.

In recent decades, the legislature has expanded the department's responsibilities related to land and water resources, including the areas of soil conservation, drainage districts, groundwater protection, nonpoint source pollution abatement, pesticides, animal disease control, and agricultural chemical storage and cleanup. It has allowed the department to create marketing boards for agricultural commodities, to promote agricultural development and diversification, and promote the state's agricultural products in interstate and international markets. The department also conducts programs for protecting producers against catastrophic financial defaults, farmland preservation, and farm mediation.

Statutory Councils

Agricultural Producer Security Council: RON STATZ (National Farmer's Organization, Inc., representative), *chairperson;* JOHN PETTY (Wisconsin Agri-Service Association, Inc., representative), *vice chairperson;* MIKE CARTER (Wisconsin Potato and Vegetable Growers Association, Inc., representative), DAVE DANIELS (Wisconsin Farm Bureau Federation representative), JOHN D. EXNER (Midwest Food Processor's Association, Inc., representative), RICHARD KELLER (Farmer's Educational and Cooperative Union of America, Wisconsin Division, representative), JOHN MANSKE (Wisconsin Federation of Cooperatives representative), JOHN UMHOEFER (Wisconsin Cheese Makers Association representative), JIM ZIMMERMAN (representative of both the Wisconsin Corn Growers Association, Inc. and the Wisconsin Soybean Association, Inc.), vacancy (Wisconsin Dairy Products Association, Inc., representative) (appointed by the Secretary of Agriculture, Trade and Consumer Protection).

The 10-member Agricultural Producer Security Council advises the Department of Agriculture, Trade and Consumer Protection (DATCP) on the administration and enforcement of agricultural producer security programs. All members are appointed by the secretary of DATCP for 3-year terms. The council was created by 2001 Wisconsin Act 16 and its composition and duties are prescribed in Sections 15.137 (1) and 126.90 of the statutes.

Fertilizer Research Council: Voting members: RICHARD MORRIS (crop producing farmer representative), *chairperson;* FRANK MASTERS (industry representative nominated by fertilizer industry), *vice chairperson;* JOHN CULLEN, MIKE MILEZIVA (industry representatives nominated by fertilizer industry); DARRELL REIGEL, JEFF SOMMERS (crop producing farmer representatives); PATRICK SORGE (water quality expert appointed by secretary of natural resources). (All except the water quality expert are appointed jointly by secretary of agriculture, trade and consumer protection and dean of UW-Madison College of Agricultural and Life Sciences.) Nonvoting members: KATHY PIELSTICKER (designated by secretary of agriculture, trade and consumer protection), BONNER KARGER (designated by secretary of natural resources), STEVE VENTURA (designated by dean, UW-Madison College of Agricultural and Life Sciences).

Mailing Address: P.O. Box 8911, Madison 53708-8911.

Telephone: 224-4614.

The 10-member Fertilizer Research Council meets annually to review and recommend projects involving research on soil management, soil fertility, plant nutrition, and for research on surface and groundwater problems related to fertilizer use. The Agriculture, Trade and Consumer Protection secretary grants final approval for project funding. These research projects are granted to the UW System and are financed through funds generated from the sale of fertilizer and soil or plant additives in Wisconsin. The council's voting members are appointed for 3-year terms and may not serve more than 2 consecutive terms. The council was created by Chapter 418, Laws of 1977, and its composition and duties are prescribed in Sections 15.137 (5) and 94.64 (8m) of the statutes.

INDEPENDENT UNITS ATTACHED FOR BUDGETING, PROGRAM COORDINATION, AND RELATED MANAGEMENT FUNCTIONS BY SECTION 15.03 OF THE STATUTES

LAND AND WATER CONSERVATION BOARD

Members: WILLIAM R. ELMAN (resident of city of 50,000 or more), *chairperson*; KIRSTEN GRINDE (designated by secretary of administration), SCOTT HASSETT (secretary of natural resources), JUDY ZIEWACZ (designated by secretary of agriculture, trade and consumer protection); PATRICK LAUGHRIN, THOMAS RUDOLPH, KATHERINE ZOWIN (county land conservation committee members); MARK E. CUPP (representing governmental unit involved in river management); SANDI M. CIHLAR (farmer); DENNIS M. CANEFF (representing charitable natural resources organization); HARVEY STOWER (public member). (All except *ex officio* members or designees are appointed by governor with senate consent.)

Advisory Members: PATRICIA LEAVENWORTH (U.S. Department of Agriculture, Natural Resources Conservation Service); BEN BRANCEL (U.S. Department of Agriculture, Farm Service Agency); FRED MADISON (designated by dean of the UW-Madison College of Agricultural and Life Sciences); ROBIN SHEPARD (appointed by director of UW-Extension); DALE OLSON (designated by staff of county land conservation committees).

Statutory References: Sections 15.135 (4), 91.06, and 92.04.

Agency Responsibility: The 11-member Land and Water Conservation Board advises the secretary and department regarding soil and water conservation, animal waste management, and farmland preservation. As part of its farmland preservation duties, the board certifies agricultural preservation plans and zoning ordinances. It reviews and makes recommendations to the department on county land and water resource plans, local livestock regulations, agricultural shoreland management ordinances, and funding allocations to county land conservation committees. The board also advises the UW System annually about needed research and education programs related to soil and water conservation. In addition, it assists the Department of Natural Resources with issues related to runoff from agriculture and other rural sources of pollution.

The board's 3 county land conservation committee members are chosen by the Wisconsin Land and Water Conservation Association, Inc., to serve 2-year terms. The 4 members who must fulfill statutorily defined categories serve staggered 4-year terms. The undesignated member serves a 2-year term. In addition, the board must invite the appointment of advisory members from agencies or organizations specified by statute.

The board was originally created as the Land Conservation Board by Chapter 346, Laws of 1981, which also abolished the Agricultural Lands Preservation Board and transferred its functions to the new board. Chapter 346 also transferred administration of the state's soil and water conservation program from the UW System to the department but continued the university's responsibility for soil and water conservation research and educational programs. 1993 Wisconsin Act 16 changed the name of the board to the Land and Water Conservation Board.

LIVESTOCK FACILITY SITING REVIEW BOARD

Members: Members are nominated by the Secretary of Agriculture, Trade and Consumer Protection and appointed by the governor with senate consent. Of the seven members, three are public members, and one each represents towns, counties, environmental interests, and livestock farming interests.

Telephone: 224-4500.

The 7-member Livestock Facility Siting Review Board may review certain decisions made by political subdivisions relating to the siting or expansion of livestock facilities, such as feedlots. An aggrieved person may challenge the decision of a city, village, town, or county government approving or disapproving the siting or expansion of a livestock facility by requesting the board to review the decision. If the board determines that a challenge is valid, it shall reverse the decision of the governmental body. The decision of the board is binding, but either party may appeal the board's decision in circuit court. Members are appointed for 5-year terms. The four members representing specific interests are selected from lists submitted by the Wisconsin Towns Association, Wisconsin Counties Association, environmental organizations, and statewide agricultural organizations, respectively. The board was created by 2003 Wisconsin Act 235 and its composition and duties are prescribed in Sections 15.135 (1) and 93.90 of the statutes.

The huge titan arum or "corpse flower", so-named because of its malodorous aroma, is native to the rain forests of Sumatra. Botanists at the UW-Madison have been successful in cultivating flowering plants from seeds harvested from native plants. Visitors flocked to the UW-Madison's Botany Greenhouse in June 2005 to view the latest titan arum blossom. "Titan IV" reached a height of 98 inches and was the fourth corpse flower to bloom at the UW-Madison in the last five years. (UW-Madison)

Department of
COMMERCE

Secretary of Commerce: MARY P. BURKE, 266-7088.
Deputy Secretary: DAVID K. STOREY, 266-8976.
Executive Assistant: AARON D. OLVER, 266-8976.
General Counsel: JOSEPH THOMAS, 261-5402, jthomas@
Office of Communications: TONY HOZENY, *director,* 267-9661, thozeny@
Mailing Address: P.O. Box 7970, Madison 53707-7970.
Location: 201 West Washington Avenue, Madison.
Telephones: 266-1018; Business hotline: (800) 435-7287.
Fax: Business: 267-2829; Eau Claire: (715) 836-2510; Green Bay: (920) 498-6313; Milwaukee: (414) 382-1754; Milwaukee Center-City Initiative: (414) 227-4064; Stevens Point: (715) 346-4277.
Publications: A variety of reports are available upon request.
Internet Address: http://commerce.wi.gov
Number of Employees: 445.50.
Total Budget 2003-05: $447,831,300.
Statutory References: Section 15.15; Chapter 560.

For e-mail combine the user ID and the state extender: userid@**commerce.state.wi.us**

Forward Wisconsin, Inc. (public-private economic development partnership):
Internet Address: http://forwardwisconsin.com/
Telephone: (800) 669-1190 (toll free).
E-mail Address: info@forwardWI.com

Administrative Services, Division of: vacancy, *administrator,* 266-3494; Division Fax: 266-0182.
Fiscal Services and Procurement, Bureau of: COLLEEN HOLTAN, *director,* 267-7200, choltan@
Human Resources, Facilities and Safety, Bureau of: BARRY WANNER, *director,* 264-7836, bwanner@
Information Technology, Bureau of: JIM WILSON, *director,* 266-7404, jwilson@
Policy and Budget Development, Bureau of: LOUIS CORNELIUS, *director,* 266-8629, lcornelius@
Business Development, Division of: TODD KEARNEY, *acting administrator,* 266-5576, tkearney@; Division Fax: 267-2829.
Business Development, Bureau of: JOHN STRICKER, *director,* 261-7710, jstricker@
Entrepreneurship, Bureau of: PAM CHRISTENSON, *director,* 267-9834, pchristenson@
Minority Business Development, Bureau of: vacancy, *director,* 266-8380; Fax: 267-9550.
Community Development, Division of: JIM O'KEEFE, *administrator,* 264-7837, jokeefe@; Division Fax: 266-8969.
Community Finance, Bureau of: JAMES FRYMARK, *director,* 266-2742, jfrymark@
Downtown Development, Bureau of: JAMES ENGLE, *director,* 267-0766, jengle@
Housing, Bureau of: MARTY EVANSON, *director,* 267-2713, mevanson@
Environmental and Regulatory Services, Division of: BERNICE A. MATTSSON, *administrator,* 266-9403, bmattssno@; P.O. Box 14427, Madison 53708-4207, Division Fax: 267-1381.
Petroleum Environmental Cleanup Fund Administration (PECFA) Bureau: OSCAR HERRERA, *director,* 266-7605, oherra@; Claim Review: P.O. Box 7838, Madison 53707-7838, 267-7642; Site Review: P.O. Box 8044, Madison 53708-8044, 261-7732.
Petroleum Products and Tanks, Bureau of: PHILIP EDW. ALBERT, *director,* 266-8076, palbert@; P.O. Box 7839, Madison 53707-7839.

DEPARTMENT OF COMMERCE

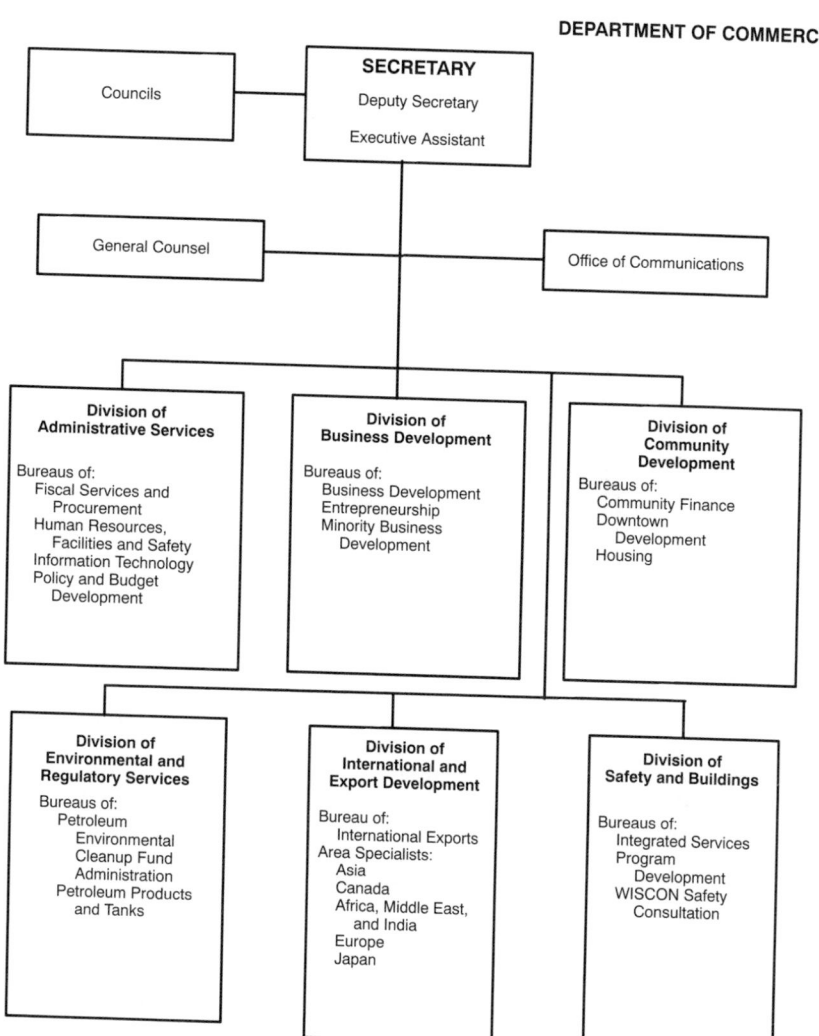

SECRETARY
Deputy Secretary
Executive Assistant

Councils

General Counsel

Office of Communications

Division of Administrative Services

Bureaus of:
Fiscal Services and Procurement
Human Resources, Facilities and Safety
Information Technology
Policy and Budget Development

Division of Business Development

Bureaus of:
Business Development
Entrepreneurship
Minority Business Development

Division of Community Development

Bureaus of:
Community Finance
Downtown Development
Housing

Division of Environmental and Regulatory Services

Bureaus of:
Petroleum Environmental Cleanup Fund Administration
Petroleum Products and Tanks

Division of International and Export Development

Bureau of:
International Exports
Area Specialists:
Asia
Canada
Africa, Middle East, and India
Europe
Japan

Division of Safety and Buildings

Bureaus of:
Integrated Services Program Development
WISCON Safety Consultation

Units attached for administrative purposes under Sec. 15.03:
Development Finance Board
Minority Business Development Board
Rural Economic Development Board
Small Business Regulatory Review Board

International and Export Development, Division of: MARY REGEL, *acting administrator,* 266-1767, mregel@; Division Fax: 266-5551; Regional Outreach Consultants: JOHN KONKEL, Eau Claire: (715) 833-6441; BRAD SCHNEIDER, Oshkosh: (920) 303-9353; SUSAN DRAGOTTA, Waukesha: (262) 691-5147; LOU JANOWSKI, Madison: 266-0393, ljanowski@.

International Exports, Bureau of: MARY REGEL, *director,* 266-1767, mregel@
Area Specialists: Asia: BENG YEAP, 266-1480, byeap@; *Canada:* STANLEY PFRANG, 267-0639, spfrang@; *Africa, Middle East, and India:* LOU JANOWSKI, 266-0393, ljanowski@; *Europe:* BRAD SCHNEIDER, (920) 420-1796, bschneider@; *Japan:* TAKAHIRO HAGISAKO, 266-9487, thagisako@

Safety and Buildings, Division of: vacancy, *administrator,* 266-1816; RONALD L. BUCHHOLZ, *deputy administrator,* 266-1817, rbuchholz@; Division Fax: 267-9566; Regional Fax: Chippewa Falls: (715) 726-2549; Green Bay: (920) 492-5604; Hayward: (715) 634-5150; La Crosse: (608) 785-9330; Shawano: (715) 524-3633; Stevens Point: (715) 345-5269; Waukesha: (262) 548-8614.

Integrated Services, Bureau of: RANDALL V. BALDWIN, *director,* 267-9152, rbaldwin@
Program Development, Bureau of: ROBERT G. DuPONT, *director,* 266-8984, rdupont@
WISCON Safety Consultation, Bureau of: HAMPTON ROTHWELL, *director,* 267-0313, hrothwell@

Agency Responsibility: The Department of Commerce administers the state's economic development programs and policies. It provides consultation, technical assistance, and other services for industrial and commercial expansion. The department promotes the development or relocation of new businesses within the state and the retention of existing firms, especially small or minority-owned enterprises. In addition, it encourages job creation, particularly in economically depressed areas, and helps communities draw up development plans. The agency administers federal economic assistance programs that affect local governments and businesses. It also provides financial assistance for foreign trade development and reports on state economic trends, business aid programs, and long-term development strategies. Businesses and communities may use the department's information clearinghouse for help in dealing with other state and federal agencies. The department administers and enforces laws to assure safe and sanitary conditions in public and private buildings. It also administers the relocation assistance program and regulates petroleum products and petroleum storage tank systems. The agency provides housing assistance to benefit low- and moderate-income households.

Organization: The department is directed by a secretary, who is appointed by the governor with the advice and consent of the senate. The secretary appoints the division administrators from outside the classified service.

Unit Functions: The *Office of the Secretary* coordinates economic development programs in conjunction with other state agencies, private corporations, and Forward Wisconsin, Inc., a public-private partnership that promotes Wisconsin businesses and is supported by private donations and state funding. The secretary advises the governor and legislature on state economic growth and community development.

The *Division of Administrative Services* provides internal management services to the department in the areas of information technology, telecommunications, personnel, payroll, employee development, affirmative action, policy and budget development, procurement and printing, fiscal management, health and safety, property and space management, and mail services.

The *Division of Business Development* administers statewide business economic development programs and provides a wide array of technical assistance to local municipalities and businesses interested in starting or expanding operations in Wisconsin. The division also administers many of the state's economic development financing programs, including Customized Labor Training, the Early Planning Grant Program, the Major Economic Development Program, the Minority Business Development Program, the Rural Economic Development Program, the Technology Development Fund, the Gaming Economic Development Diversification Program, the economic development component of the federally funded Community Development Block Grant Program for small cities, the tax credit programs, the Industrial Revenue Bond Program, and the Technology Commercialization Grant and Loan Program. The Development Zone Program encourages private sector investment in economically depressed areas by providing tax incentives to develop employment opportunities for the unemployed and persons facing barriers to employment, and also encourages investment related to agricultural businesses. Under the Technology Zone Program, the division certifies new or expanding businesses located in 8 designated areas of the state that qualify as "high-technology" operations for tax credits to the Department of Revenue. The Industrial Revenue Bond Program provides low-cost, long-term financing for eligible facilities.

The division promotes the state's business climate, publicizes business developments, and provides information on the state's economy to assist expanding or relocating businesses. It provides information on resources for business start-ups, public and private financing programs, and government permits. The division helps small businesses understand and comply in a cost-effective manner with clean air regulations through the Small Business Clean Air Assistance Program and advocates the interests of small businesses through its Small Business Ombudsman Program.

The *Division of Community Development* administers a variety of programs to help Wisconsin communities be desirable places for families to live and businesses to thrive. The Main Street Program assists communities in revitalizing their downtown areas. Other programs provide assistance in management, marketing, and financial analysis to entrepreneurs and small businesses in smaller communities. The Community-Based Economic Development Program provides funding to assist communities and community-based organizations with economic development planning, business incubator development, and business assistance services. The Brownfields Initiative provides assistance and funding to persons, businesses, development organizations, and municipalities for redevelopment and environmental remediation activities for contaminated sites where the owner cannot be located or cannot meet the cleanup costs. Through its educational loan repayment programs, the division helps medically underserved communities in both rural and urban areas recruit and retain physicians, dentists, and other primary health care providers. The division also administers programs that provide financial assistance to communities for infrastructure improvements, blight elimination, and community facilities through the public facilities portion of the federally funded Community Development Block Grant Program for small cities. In addition, it provides technical assistance and approves relocation payment plans and assistance service plans under the state's eminent domain law.

To provide housing assistance to low- and moderate-income households, the division administers funding through the Local Housing Organization Grant Program for local organizations that offer housing opportunities and services. It awards grants under the Fresh Start Program that helps young people obtain housing and provides construction work experience particularly for high school dropouts and other young people-at-risk. The division channels federal funding to local organizations through various programs, including the Home Investment Partnerships and Community Block Grant Programs. It administers state and federal funds to provide immediate shelter for the homeless and support transitional and permanent housing, as well. To meet federal and state requirements, the division prepares the state consolidated housing plan that addresses housing and community development needs.

The *Division of Environmental and Regulatory Services,* created in Section 15.153 (3), Wisconsin Statutes, by 1995 Wisconsin Act 27, is responsible for sampling and testing petroleum products. It inspects existing tank systems at terminals, bulk plants, and retail and nonretail sites. It registers, reviews plans, and issues permits for new underground and aboveground storage tank systems. The division also cooperates with the Department of Natural Resources in administering the state's Petroleum Storage Environmental Cleanup Fund Act (PECFA) program for sites environmentally damaged through petroleum contamination and supervises the remediation of low and medium priority sites.

The *Division of International and Export Development,* created in Section 15.153 (4), Wisconsin Statutes, by 1995 Wisconsin Act 27, provides counseling and technical assistance to state businesses interested in increasing sales to foreign markets. It coordinates participation in international trade shows and organizes trade missions. Wisconsin currently maintains trade offices jointly with other states or organizations or has contract trade representatives in Brazil, Canada, Europe, Mexico, and China.

The *Division of Safety and Buildings* promotes public safety, health, and welfare by administering state laws pertaining to commercial buildings, dwellings, structures, amusement rides, ski lifts, mines, and the subsystems that serve buildings, such as plumbing, boilers, private sewage, electrical service, fire sprinklers, heating, and elevators. It oversees the housing design and construction requirements of the Fair Housing Law. The division develops and enforces health and safety-related administrative rules, reviews plans for proposed construction, makes initial and follow-up inspections, issues credentials, and provides training and consulting services. It also assesses business safety practices and offers recommendations through the Safety Consultation Program. Finally, the division administers the Fire Dues Program. The program provides support and direction for municipal fire protection and is funded by dues paid to the Office of the Commissioner of Insurance by insurers providing fire coverage.

History: The state's promotion of business and economic development originated with the Division of Industrial Development, established in the governor's office by Chapter 271, Laws of 1955. The division was transferred to the newly created Department of Resource Development in 1959 and renamed the Division of Economic Development. Chapter 614, Laws of 1965, returned it to the governor's office. While in the executive office, it absorbed the Office of Economic Opportunity (1966), which had been created in the Department of Resource Development to administer the federal antipoverty programs enacted in 1964. Under the 1967 executive branch reorganization, the division became part of the Department of Local Affairs and Development, and local and regional planning functions were integrated into it.

Chapter 125, Laws of 1971, elevated the division to departmental status as the Department of Business Development. The department absorbed the Division of Tourism from the Department of Natural Resources in 1975. Under Chapter 361, Laws of 1979, the Department of Business Development was reunited with the Department of Local Affairs and Development to form the

Commerce Secretary Mary Burke announces a $250,000 Technology Development Loan to EraGen Biosciences, Inc., of Madison. The loan is to fund facility upgrades designed to help the company maintain its leading position in the genetic testing industry. (Department of Commerce)

Department of Development, subsequently renamed the Department of Commerce by 1995 Wisconsin Act 27.

The department's responsibility for state tourism promotion ended with creation of the Department of Tourism by 1995 Wisconsin Act 27. Act 27 also transferred the PECFA program and the safety and buildings functions from the Department of Industry, Labor and Human Relations to the Department of Commerce. In 2003, Wisconsin Act 33 transferred housing programs to the department from the Department of Administration.

Wisconsin was a pioneer in the use of administrative law for safety and building regulation. The 1911 Legislature created the Industrial Commission in Chapter 485 to set standards for a safe place of employment. This "safe place" statute was extended in Chapter 588, Laws of 1913, to include public buildings, defined as "any structure used in whole or in part as a place of resort, assemblage, lodging, trade, traffic, occupancy, or use by the public, or by three or more tenants." The commission adopted its first building code in 1914. Programs added over the years include plumbing, heating, ventilation, air conditioning, energy conservation, private on-site waste treatment systems, accessibility for people with disabilities, and electrical inspection and certification.

Other programs absorbed by the department, as a result of 1995 Wisconsin Act 27, include plat review from the Department of Agriculture, Trade and Consumer Protection; municipal boundary review from the Department of Administration; and relocation assistance under eminent domain law from the Department of Industry, Labor and Human Relations. Plat review and municipal boundary review were transferred to the Department of Administration in 1997 Wisconsin Act 27.

Statutory Councils

Automatic Fire Sprinkler System Contractors and Journeymen Council: JAMES SMITH (department employee), *secretary;* JEFF BATEMAN, GREG HINTZ (representing licensed automatic fire sprinkler contractors); DAN DRIEBEL, CHRIS SCHOENBECK (licensed journeymen automatic fire sprinkler fitters) (all appointed by secretary of commerce).

Mailing Address: P.O. Box 2689, Madison 53701-2689.

Telephone: 266-0251.

The 5-member Automatic Fire Sprinkler System Contractors and Journeymen Council reviews the content of examinations and advises the department on related matters. Journeymen and contractor members serve staggered 4-year terms. The council was created as an examining council in the Department of Health and Social Services by Chapter 255, Laws of 1971; transferred to the Department of Industry, Labor and Human Relations by Chapter 221, Laws of 1979; and transferred to the Department of Commerce by 1995 Wisconsin Act 27. The council's duties and composition are prescribed in Sections 15.157 (9) and 145.17 (2) of the statutes.

Contractor Financial Responsibility Council: KENNETH L. LEPAK, LAWRENCE E. SCHAUDER, MARY L. SCHROEDER (on-site contractors of one- and 2-family housing); BRUCE D. McMILLER (certified building inspector employed by local government); JAMES E. CAULEY (all appointed by governor).

Mailing Address: P.O. Box 2689, Madison 53701-2689.

Telephone: 266-9292.

The 5-member Contractor Financial Responsibility Council recommends rules for promulgation by the department for certification of contractors' financial responsibility. Council members serve staggered 3-year terms. One member cannot be a building contractor or inspector. The council was created by 1993 Wisconsin Act 126 in the Department of Industry, Labor and Human Relations and transferred to the Department of Commerce by 1995 Wisconsin Act 27. Its composition and duties are prescribed in Sections 15.157 (4) and 101.625 of the statutes.

Dwelling Code Council: JEFFREY D. BECHARD, WILLIAM J. ROEHR, GARY RUHL, PAUL M. WELNAK (building trade labor organization representatives); KENNETH M. DENTICE, DANIEL A. NOWAK, MICHAEL WALLACE, BRIAN E. WALTER (certified building inspectors employed by local government); MARY L. SCHROEDER, RANDOLPH J. THELEN (representatives of on-site housing contractors); FRANK OPATIK, THOMAS PALECEK (manufactured housing representatives); HAROLD F. LAST (architect, engineer, or designer); WILLIAM TURNER, JOHN E. VANDE CASTLE (construction material supply representatives); ALLAN BACHMANN (one- and 2-family house remodeling contractor); STEVEN LEVINE, DENNIS J. O'LAUGHLIN (public members) (all appointed by governor). Nonvoting secretary: LARRY SWAZIEK (department employee appointed by secretary of commerce).

Mailing Address: P.O. Box 2689, Madison 53701-2689.

Telephone: 267-7701.

The 18-member Dwelling Code Council reviews the rules and standards for one- and 2-family dwellings and manufactured housing. Members are appointed to 3-year terms. One public member must represent persons with disabilities. The council was created by Chapter 404, Laws of 1975, in the Department of Industry, Labor and Human Relations and transferred to the Department of Commerce by 1995 Wisconsin Act 27. Its composition and duties are prescribed in Sections 15.157 (3), 101.62, and 101.72 of the statutes.

Main Street Programs, Council on: DAVID K. STOREY (designated by secretary of commerce), *chairperson;* BRIAN MCCORMICK (designated by director, state historical society); TIMOTHY L. ANDERSON (Wisconsin Downtown Action Council representative); DICK BEST (local chamber of commerce representative); SHAWN K. GRAFF (Wisconsin Trust for Historic Preservation representative); VIRGINIA HASKE (city, village, or town representative); JOHN GARDNER (planning profession representative); TERRANCE W. MARTIN (architectural profession); WILLIAM R. NEUREUTHER (financial community); BEN CRESS, PENNY L. VANVLEET (business community); ANN B. EAVES, LISA KOTTER, DENNIS W. LEONG, JUDITH WALL (members with expertise in downtown revitalization). (All except *ex officio* members or their designees are appointed by governor.) Nonvoting secretary: JAMES ENGLE (department employee designated by secretary of commerce).

The 15-member Council on Main Street Programs helps develop the state's Main Street Program for revitalization of business areas, reviews the program's effectiveness, and recommends municipalities for participation. Members are appointed for 3-year terms, and representative members must provide geographic diversity. At least 3 members must own or operate a business in a business area that has requested services under the Main Street Program. At least 5 members must have experience in business area revitalization combined with historical preservation. The council was created by 1987 Wisconsin Act 109, and its composition and duties are prescribed in Sections 15.157 (7), 560.081, and 560.082 of the statutes.

Multifamily Dwelling Code Council: EDWARD R. GRAY, WILLIAM J. ROEHR (skilled building trades labor representatives); DAVID A. NITZ (municipal inspector from county less than 50,000 population); RICHARD P. PAUR (municipal inspector from county over 50,000 population); JEFFREY BROHMER, BRUCE A. FUERBRINGER (fire service workers); BETH A. GONNERING, HARRY R. MACCO (multifamily dwelling contractors and developers); EMORY BUDZINSKI, FRED STIER, KEVIN WIPPERFURTH (materials manufacturers and finished product suppliers); JAMES R. KLETT (representing architects, engineers, and designers of multifamily housing); GRETA HANSEN, KORINNE SCHNEIDER (public members) (all appointed by governor). Nonvoting secretary: JAMES QUAST (department employee member).

Mailing Address: P.O. Box 2689, Madison 53701-2689.

Telephone: 266-9292.

The 14-member Multifamily Dwelling Code Council advises the department on rules for multifamily dwelling construction. Members are appointed to 3-year terms. Those representing designated businesses and professions must be actively engaged in their work. At least one of the fire services representatives must be a fire chief. At least one of the public members must be a fair housing advocate. The council was created by 1991 Wisconsin Act 39 in the Department of Industry, Labor and Human Relations and transferred to the Department of Commerce by 1995 Wisconsin Act 27. Its composition and duties are prescribed in Sections 15.157 (12) and 101.972 of the statutes.

Petroleum Storage Environmental Cleanup Council: SCOTT HASSETT (secretary of natural resources), MARY P. BURKE (secretary of commerce); 5 vacancies. (All other members are nominated by the two secretaries and appointed by governor.)

Mailing Address: P.O. Box 7838, Madison 53707-7838.

Telephone: 266-3723.

The 7-member Petroleum Storage Environmental Cleanup Council advises the Department of Commerce and the Department of Natural Resources on issues related to petroleum spills, cleanup, and claims for awards. Five members are appointed for 4-year terms by the governor from nominations by the secretaries of commerce and natural resources, who must consider representatives from petroleum product transporters, manufacturers, suppliers, retailers and wholesalers, professional geologists, hydrologists and soil scientists, and environmental scientists, consultants, contractors, and engineers. The council was created by 1987 Wisconsin Act 399 in the Department of Industry, Labor and Human Relations and transferred to the Department of Commerce by 1995 Wisconsin Act 27. Its composition and duties are prescribed in Sections 15.157 (11) and 101.143 (8) of the statutes.

Plumbers Council: LYNITA DOCKEN (department employee), *secretary;* DAVE JONES (master plumber), DON WIEDOFF (journeyman plumber) (all appointed by secretary of commerce).

Mailing Address: 4003 North Kinney Coulee Road, La Crosse 54650.

Telephone: (608) 785-9349.

The 3-member Plumbers Council advises the department about the testing and licensing of plumbers. The 2 plumber members are appointed for 2-year terms. The council was created by Chapter 327, Laws of 1967, as an examining council in the Department of Health and Social Services; renamed and moved to the Department of Industry, Labor and Human Relations by Chapter 221, Laws of 1979; and transferred to the Department of Commerce by 1995 Wisconsin Act 27. Its composition and duties are prescribed in Sections 15.157 (6) and 145.02 (4) of the statutes.

Rural Health Development Council: JIM O'KEEFE (designated by secretary of commerce), MEG TAYLOR (designated by secretary of health and family services); BYRON J. CROUSE (UW Medical School); ALAN K. DAVID (Medical College of Wisconsin, Inc.); TIMOTHY J. SIZE (Wisconsin Health and Educational Facilities Authority); vacancy (Farmers Home Administration); 2 vacancies (private rural lender representatives); CRAIG W.C. SCHMIDT, vacancy (rural health care facility representatives); KENNETH M. VISTE, JR. (physician practicing in rural area); BLANE CHRISTMAN (dentist practicing in rural area); BECKY SUE WOLF (nurse practicing in rural area); JANET K. RECORE (dental hygienist practicing in rural area); LINDA L. MCFARLIN (public health services representative). (All except *ex officio* members or their designees are appointed by governor with senate consent.)

The 15-member Rural Health Development Council advises the department regarding administration of the health professions loan assistance program, delivery of health care and improvement of facilities in rural areas, and coordination of state and federal programs available to assist rural health facilities. Appointed members serve 5-year terms. The council was created by 1989 Wisconsin Act 317, and its composition and duties are prescribed in Sections 15.157 (8) and 560.185 of the statutes.

Small Business Environmental Council: JAMES REYNOLDS (appointed by senate president); CARL KOMMSA (appointed by senate minority leader); JAY MEILI (appointed by assembly speaker); PATRICIA HASKINS (appointed by assembly minority leader); BERNICE A. MATTSSON (appointed by secretary of commerce); MARK W. MCDERMID (appointed by secretary of natural resources); J. ROBERT NICHOLSON, MICHAEL H. SIMPSON, PETER J. VAN HORN (representing general public and appointed by governor).

The 9-member Small Business Environmental Council advises the Department of Natural Resources on the effectiveness of assistance programs to small businesses that enable them to comply with the federal Clean Air Act. It also advises on the fairness and effectiveness of air pollution rules promulgated by the Department of Natural Resources and the U.S. Environmental Protection Agency regarding the impact on small businesses. Members are appointed to 3-year terms. The 4 members appointed by legislative officers must own or represent owners of small business stationary air pollution sources. The 3 members appointed by the governor may not own or represent small business stationary sources. The council was created by 1991 Wisconsin Act 302, and its composition and duties are prescribed in Sections 15.157 (10) and 560.11 of the statutes.

INDEPENDENT UNITS ATTACHED FOR BUDGETING, PROGRAM COORDINATION, AND RELATED MANAGEMENT FUNCTIONS BY SECTION 15.03 OF THE STATUTES

DEVELOPMENT FINANCE BOARD

Members: DAVID K. STOREY (designated by secretary of commerce), SUE GLEASON (designated by secretary of workforce development), KATHLEEN CULLEN (designated by director, Technical College System Board); RALPH KAUTEN (scientific community); vacancy (technical community); MARK REIHL (labor community); MICHEY JUDKINS (small business community); CHERYL R. WESTON (minority business community); DARIAN LUCKETT (financial community). (All except *ex officio* members are appointed by governor.)

Statutory References: Section 15.155 (1); Chapter 560, Subchapter V.

Agency Responsibility: The 9-member Development Finance Board awards grants and loans from the Wisconsin Development Fund. Its 6 appointed members serve 2-year terms. The board may make technology grants or loans to consortiums to support research to develop new products or improve existing products or processes. Businesses may obtain customized labor training grants or loans to provide state residents with job training in new technology and industrial skills if the training is not available through existing federal, state, or local resources. Funds are available for major economic development projects that cannot secure other financing and for activities that do not fit into existing programs. Through Employee Ownership Assistance Loans, the board approves funding for feasibility studies by employee groups considering the purchase of existing businesses as an alternative to plant closings. The board was created by 1987 Wisconsin Act 27.

MINORITY BUSINESS DEVELOPMENT BOARD

Members: JOHN W. CADOTTE, WILLIE JOHNSON, JR., RAVI KALLA, DINA C. KNIBBS, DAVID K. STOREY, WINNIFRED THOMAS, CHARLES V. VANG (all appointed by governor).

Statutory References: Section 15.155 (3); Chapter 560, Subchapter VII.

Agency Responsibility: The Minority Business Development Board may award grants or loans to minority group members, minority businesses, or local development corporations for projects to plan a new business (early planning projects) or projects to start a new business or expand an existing business (development projects). Recipients must finance a portion of the project's cost from private funds. Department of Commerce rules governing the administration of the programs are subject to board review. Board members serve 2-year terms; the number and qualifications of members are not specified by law. The board was created by 1989 Wisconsin Act 31.

RURAL ECONOMIC DEVELOPMENT BOARD

Members: WILL HUGHES (designated by secretary of agriculture, trade and consumer protection), DAVID K. STOREY (designated by secretary of commerce); SENATORS BROWN, DECKER; REPRESENTATIVES SUDER, VRUWINK; MICHAEL R. KRUTZA, RICHARD MARTIN, TIMOTHY MCGETTIGAN. (All except *ex officio* members or designees are appointed by governor.)

Statutory References: Sections 15.155 (4) and 560.17.

Agency Responsibility: The 9-member Rural Economic Development Board awards grants or loans to rural businesses with fewer than 50 employees to assist in starting or expanding their operations. The board includes 4 legislative members who represent the majority and minority parties in each house and must be from rural districts. The 3 members appointed by the governor serve 3-year terms. Each of them must have experience operating a business located in a rural municipality, and at least one must have operated a cooperative. The board was created by 1989 Wisconsin Act 31.

SMALL BUSINESS REGULATORY REVIEW BOARD

Members: Pat Farley (Department of Administration representative), Dennis Fay (Department of Agriculture, Trade and Consumer Protection representative), David K. Storey (Department of Commerce representative), Sue Reinardy (Department of Health and Family Services representative), Al Shea (Department of Natural Resources representative), Chris Klein (Department of Regulation and Licensing representative), Laura Engan (Department of Revenue representative), Hal Bergan (Department of Workforce Development representative), Senator Brown (senate small business committee chairperson), Representative Honadel (assembly small business committee chairperson); James Bohren, Richard Petershack, Minoo Selfoddini, Bernard Ziegewald, 2 vacancies (appointed by governor).

Statutory References: Sections 15.07 (1)(b), 15.155 (5), 227.24 (3), and 227.30.

Agency Responsibility: The 16-member Small Business Regulatory Review Board may determine that a newly filed emergency rule would have a significant fiscal impact on small businesses, defined as ones that employ 25 or fewer full-time employees or have gross annual sales of less than $5 million. The board may further determine whether the issuing agency has complied with statutory provisions that seek to reduce the impact of rules on small businesses and whether the data used to propose a rule is accurate. If the board finds an agency has not complied with the law, it may request compliance from that agency, and, in addition, suggest changes to the proposed rule. The board may also review state agency rules and guidelines to determine whether they place an unnecessary burden on small businesses. If the board determines a rule or guidelines does place an undue burden on small businesses, it submits a report and recommendations to the Joint Committee for Review of Administrative Rules.

The department secretaries appoint department representatives. The 6 members the governor appoints represent small business and serve 3-year terms. The senate majority leader and assembly speaker each appoint one chairperson from standing committees concerned with small business. The board was created by 2003 Wisconsin Act 145.

The increasing number of farmer's markets in Wisconsin offer greater opportunities for small-scale growers to market their products directly to consumers. (Department of Tourism)

Department of
CORRECTIONS

Secretary of Corrections: MATTHEW J. FRANK, 240-5055, matthew.frank@
Deputy Secretary: RICK RAEMISCH, 240-5055, rick.raemisch@
Executive Assistant: JESSICA CLARK, 240-5055, jessica.clark@
Office of Legal Counsel: KEVIN POTTER, *chief,* 240-5035, kevin.potter@
Legislative Liaison: ROBERT MARGOLIES, 240-5056, robert.margolies@
Public Information Director: JOHN DIPKO, 240-5060, john.dipko@
Detention Facilities, Office of: MARTIN J. ORDINANS, *director,* 240-5052, martin.ordinans@;
Milwaukee: (414) 227-5199.
Victim Services, Office of: COLLEEN JO WINSTON, *director,* 240-5888, colleen.winston@
Mailing Address: P.O. Box 7925, Madison 53707-7925.
Location: 3099 East Washington Avenue, Madison 53704.
Telephone: 240-5000.
Fax: 240-3305.
Internet Address: http://www.wi-doc.com
Number of Employees: 10,419.33.
Total Budget 2003-05: $1,950,361,500.
Statutory References: Section 15.14; Chapter 301.

Address e-mail by combining the user ID and the state extender: userid@**doc.state.wi.us**

Adult Institutions, Division of: STEVEN B. CASPERSON, *administrator,* 240-5100,
steven.casperson@; DENISE SYMDON, *assistant administrator,* 240-5103, denise.symdon@;
JOHN BETT, *assistant administrator,* 240-5102, john.bett@; Division Fax: 240-3310.
   Correctional Enterprises, Bureau of: vacancy, *director,* 3099 East Washington Avenue, Madison 53704, 240-5200; Fax: 240-3320.
   Health Services, Bureau of: JAMES GREER, *director,* 240-5122, james.greer@
   Offender Classification and Movement, Bureau of: DICK VERHAGEN, *director,* 240-5810, dick.verhagen@

PRISONS

Maximum Security:
   Columbia Correctional Institution: GREG GRAMS, *warden,* P.O. Box 950, Portage 53901-0950, (608) 742-9100; Fax: (608) 742-9111.
   Dodge Correctional Institution: CATHY JESS, *warden,* P.O. Box 661, Waupun 53963-0661, (920) 324-5577; Fax: (920) 324-6354.
   Green Bay Correctional Institution: WILLIAM POLLARD, *warden,* P.O. Box 19033, Green Bay 54307-9033, (920) 432-4877; Fax: (920) 432-5388.
   Waupun Correctional Institution: PHIL KINGSTON, *warden,* P.O. Box 351, Waupun 53963-0351, (920) 324-5571; Fax: (920) 324-7250.
   Wisconsin Secure Program Facility: RICHARD SCHNEITER, *warden,* P.O. Box 1000, Boscobel 53805-1000, (608) 375-5656; Fax: (608) 375-5595.

Medium Security:
   Fox Lake Correctional Institution: JODINE DEPPISCH, *warden,* P.O. Box 147, Fox Lake 53933-0147, (920) 928-3151; Fax: (920) 928-6929.
   Jackson Correctional Institution: RANDY HEPP, *warden,* P.O. Box 232, Black River Falls 54615-0232, (715) 284-4550; Fax: (715) 284-7335.
   Kettle Moraine Correctional Institution: LARRY JENKINS, *warden,* P.O. Box 31, Plymouth 53073-0031, (920) 526-3244; Fax: (920) 526-3989.
   Milwaukee Secure Detention Facility: JOHN HUSZ, *superintendent,* 1015 North 10th Street, P.O. Box 05740, Milwaukee 53205-0740, (414) 212-3535; Fax: (414) 212-6811.

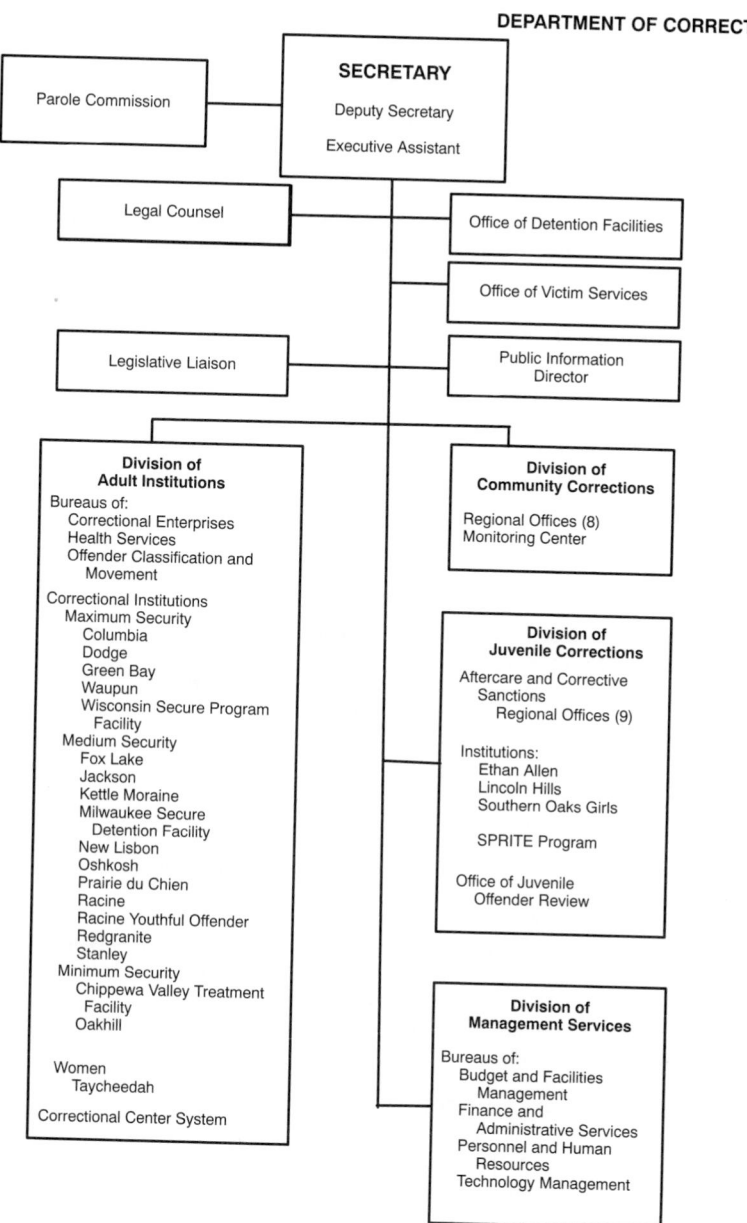

DEPARTMENT OF CORRECTIONS

Parole Commission

SECRETARY

Deputy Secretary

Executive Assistant

Legal Counsel

Office of Detention Facilities

Office of Victim Services

Legislative Liaison

Public Information Director

**Division of
Adult Institutions**

Bureaus of:
 Correctional Enterprises
 Health Services
 Offender Classification and
  Movement

Correctional Institutions
 Maximum Security
  Columbia
  Dodge
  Green Bay
  Waupun
  Wisconsin Secure Program
   Facility
 Medium Security
  Fox Lake
  Jackson
  Kettle Moraine
  Milwaukee Secure
   Detention Facility
  New Lisbon
  Oshkosh
  Prairie du Chien
  Racine
  Racine Youthful Offender
  Redgranite
  Stanley
 Minimum Security
  Chippewa Valley Treatment
   Facility
  Oakhill

 Women
  Taycheedah

Correctional Center System

**Division of
Community Corrections**

Regional Offices (8)
Monitoring Center

**Division of
Juvenile Corrections**

Aftercare and Corrective
 Sanctions
  Regional Offices (9)

Institutions:
 Ethan Allen
 Lincoln Hills
 Southern Oaks Girls

SPRITE Program

Office of Juvenile
 Offender Review

**Division of
Management Services**

Bureaus of:
 Budget and Facilities
  Management
 Finance and
  Administrative Services
 Personnel and Human
  Resources
 Technology Management

Units attached for administrative purposes under Sec. 15.03: Interstate Adult Offender Supervision Board
Prison Industries Board

New Lisbon Correctional Institution: CATHY FARREY, *warden,* 2000 Progress Road, New Lisbon 53950, (608) 562-6400.

Oshkosh Correctional Institution: JUDY SMITH, *warden,* P.O. Box 3530, Oshkosh 54903-3530, (920) 231-4010; Fax: (920) 236-2615/2626.

Prairie du Chien Correctional Facility: RICHARD SCHNEITER, *superintendent,* P.O. Box 9900, Prairie du Chien 53821-9900, (608) 326-7828; Fax: (608) 326-7736.

Racine Correctional Institution: QUALA CHAMPAGNE, *warden,* 2019 Wisconsin Street, Sturtevant 53177, (262) 886-3214; Fax: (262) 886-3514.

Racine Youthful Offender Correctional Institution: DAN A. BUCHLER, *warden,* P.O. Box 2200, Racine 53401-2200, (262) 638-1999; Fax: (262) 638-1777.

Redgranite Correctional Institution: JEFFREY ENDICOTT, *warden,* 1006 County Road EE, Redgranite 54970, (920) 566-2600; Fax: (920) 566-2610.

Stanley Correctional Institution: DAN BENIK, *warden,* 100 Corrections Drive, Stanley 54768-6500, (715) 644-2960; Fax (715) 644-2966.

Minimum Security:

Chippewa Valley Correctional Treatment Facility: DAN BENIK, *warden,* East Park Avenue, Chippewa Falls 54729, (715) 720-2850; Fax (715) 644-2966.

Oakhill Correctional Institution: DEIRDRE MORGAN, *warden,* P.O. Box 938, Oregon 53575-0938, (608) 835-3101; Fax: (608) 835-9196.

Women:

Taycheedah Correctional Institution: ANA BOATWRIGHT, *warden,* 751 County Road K, Fond du Lac 54935-2946, (920) 929-3800; Fax: (920) 929-2946.

CENTER SYSTEM

MICKEY THOMPSON, *warden, Wisconsin Correctional Center System,* 5140 Highway M, P.O. Box 25, Oregon 53575-0025, (608) 835-5711; Fax: (608) 835-3175.

Black River Correctional Center: TIM NELSON, *superintendent,* W6898 East Staffon Road, Route #5, P.O. Box 433 C, Black River Falls 54615-0433, (715) 333-5681; Fax: (715) 333-2708.

John C. Burke Correctional Center: SUSAN ROSS, *superintendent,* 900 South Madison Street, P.O. Box 900, Waupun 53963-0900, (920) 324-3460; Fax: (920) 324-4575.

Felmers Chaney Correctional Center: TOM VANDEN BOOM, *superintendent,* 2825 North 30th Street, Milwaukee 53210, (414) 874-1600; Fax: (414) 874-1695.

Drug Abuse Correctional Center: SHERYL L. GRAEBER, *superintendent,* Kempster Hall/Winnebago Mental Health Institute, 1305 North Drive, P.O. Box 36, Winnebago 54985-0036, (920) 236-2700; Fax: (920) 426-5601.

Robert E. Ellsworth Correctional Center: LARRY MAHONEY, *superintendent,* 21425-A Spring Street, Union Grove 53182-9408, (262) 878-6000; Fax: (262) 878-6015.

Flambeau Correctional Center: JOHN CLARK, *superintendent,* N671 County Road M, Hawkins 54530-9400, (715) 585-6394; Fax: (715) 585-6563.

Gordon Correctional Center: JOHN CLARK, *superintendent,* 10401 East County Road G, Gordon 54838, (715) 376-2680; Fax: (715) 376-4361.

Kenosha Correctional Center: DAVE ANDRASKA, *superintendent,* 6353 14th Avenue, Kenosha 53143, (262) 653-7099; Fax: (262) 653-7241.

McNaughton Correctional Center: DAVID BURTON, *superintendent,* 8500 Rainbow Road, Lake Tomahawk 54539-9558, (715) 277-2484; Fax: (715) 277-2293.

Milwaukee Women's Correctional Center: DIANE WILLIAMS, *superintendent,* 615 West Keefe Avenue, Milwaukee 53212, (414) 267-6101; Fax: (414) 267-6130.

Oregon Correctional Center: JANE DIER-ZIMMEL, *superintendent,* 5140 Highway M, P.O. Box 25, Oregon 53575-0025, (608) 835-3233; Fax: (608) 835-3175.

Sanger B. Powers Correctional Center: JAMES NAGLE, *superintendent,* N8375 County Line Road, Oneida 54155-9300, (920) 869-1095; Fax: (920) 869-2650.

St. Croix Correctional Center: JO SKALSKI, *superintendent,* 1859 North 4th Street, P.O. Box 36, New Richmond 54017-0036, (715) 246-6971; Fax: (715) 246-3680.

Marshall E. Sherrer Correctional Center: TOM VANDEN BOOM, *superintendent,* 1318 North 14th Street, Milwaukee 53205-2596, (414) 343-5000; Fax: (414) 343-5039.

Thompson Correctional Center: JANE DIER-ZIMMEL, *superintendent,* 434 State Farm Road, Deerfield 53531-9562, (608) 423-3415; Fax: (608) 423-9852.

Winnebago Correctional Center: JAMES NAGLE, *superintendent,* 4300 Sherman Road, P.O. Box 128, Winnebago 54985-0128, (920) 424-0402; Fax: (920) 424-0430.

Community Corrections, Division of: vacancy, *administrator,* 240-5300; WILLIAM J. GROSSHANS, *assistant administrator, business and records*; Fax: 240-3330.

Region 1: ART THURMER, *chief,* 2445 Darwin Road, Suite 102, Madison 53704, 246-1960; Fax: 246-1900.

Region 2: TERI LEE DANNER, *chief,* 9531 Rayne Road, Suite 11, Sturtevant 53177-1833, (262) 884-3780; Fax: (262) 884-3799.

Region 3: JAN CUMMINGS, *chief,* 819 North 6th Street, Room 121, Milwaukee 53203-1675, (414) 227-4195; Fax: (414) 227-5043.

Region 4: JAMES MILLER, *chief,* 1360 American Drive, Neenah 54956, (920) 751-4623; Fax: (920) 751-4601.

Region 5: LARRY LIEGEL, *chief,* 718 West Clairemont Avenue, P.O. Box 780, Eau Claire 54701-6143, (715) 836-5508; Fax: (715) 836-2331.

Region 6: ROBERT GRUSNICK, *chief,* 56-A South Brown Street, P.O. Box 497, Rhinelander 54501-0497, (715) 365-2587; Fax: (715) 369-5255.

Region 7: SALLY TESS, *chief,* 141 Northwest Barstow Street, Room 129, Waukesha 53188-3756, (262) 521-5157; Fax: (262) 548-8697.

Region 8: BARBARA SUTTON, *chief,* 427 East Tower Drive, Wautoma 54982-5589, (920) 787-5555; Fax: (920) 787-5589.

Monitoring Center: DOUGLAS MILSAP, *director,* 5706 Odana Road, Madison 53719, 273-5767, douglas.milsap@

Juvenile Corrections, Division of: CHARLES A. TUBBS, *administrator,* 240-5901, charles.tubbs@; SILVIA R. JACKSON, *assistant administrator,* 240-5902, silvia.jackson@; P.O. Box 8930, Madison 53708-8930; Division Fax: 240-3370.

Aftercare and Corrective Sanctions:

Eau Claire: 718 West Clairemont Avenue, Room 140, Eau Claire 54701-6143, (715) 836-6683.

Green Bay: 200 North Jefferson Street, Suite 134, Green Bay 54301, (920) 448-6548.

Madison: 2909 Landmark Place, Suite 104, Madison 53713, 288-3350.

Milwaukee: 4200 North Holton Street, Suite 120, Milwaukee 53212, (414) 229-0701.

Neenah: 1356 American Drive, Neenah 54956, (920) 729-3900.

Schofield: 1699 Schofield Avenue, Suite 120, Schofield 54476-1021, (715) 241-8890.

Spooner: 802 Northland Drive, Spooner 54801, (715) 635-5902.

Sturtevant: 9531 Rayne Road, Suite 3, Sturtevant 53177-1833, (262) 884-3748.

Wisconsin Rapids: 131 24th Street South, Wisconsin Rapids 54494-6281, (715) 422-5279.

Institutions:

Ethan Allen School: KYLE K. DAVIDSON, *superintendent,* P.O. Box 900, Wales 53183-0900, (262) 646-3341; Fax: (262) 646-3761, kyle.davidson@

Lincoln Hills School: PAUL J. WESTERHAUS, *superintendent,* W4380 Copper Lake Road, Irma 54442-9720, (715) 536-8386; Fax (715) 536-8236, paul.westerhaus@

Southern Oaks Girls School: PATRICIA J. OGREN, *superintendent,* 21425B Spring Street, Union Grove 53182-9707, (262) 878-6500; Fax: (262) 878-6520, patricia.ogren@

SPRITE Program: MICHAEL KASS, *program director,* 2909 Landmark Place, Suite 104, Madison 53713, 288-3356; Fax: 288-3378, michael.kass@

Juvenile Offender Review, Office of: JUDITH L. HEINE, *director,* 240-5918; Fax: 240-3370, judith.heine@

Management Services, Division of: EARL FISCHER, *administrator,* 240-5400, earl.fischer@; Division Fax: 240-3340.

   Budget and Facilities Management, Bureau of: ROBERT NIKOLAY, *director,* 240-5405, robert.nikolay@

   Finance and Administrative Services, Bureau of: JERRY SALVO, *director,* 240-5420, jerry.salvo@

   Personnel and Human Resources, Bureau of: JEAN NICHOLS, *director,* 240-5496, jean.nichols@

   Technology Management, Bureau of: vacancy, *director,* 240-5646.

Agency Responsibility: The Department of Corrections administers Wisconsin's state prisons, community correctional centers, and juvenile corrections programs. It supervises the custody and discipline of all prisoners in order to protect the public and seeks to rehabilitate offenders and reintegrate them into society. The department currently operates 19 correctional facilities and 16 community correctional centers for adults, and 3 facilities for juveniles. It also supervises prisoners on probation and parole; monitors compliance with deferred prosecution programs; and may make recommendations for pardons or commutations of sentence when requested by the governor. The department maintains a register of sex offenders who are required to report by law.

Organization: The department is administered by a secretary who is appointed by the governor with the advice and consent of the senate. The secretary appoints the division administrators from outside the classified service.

Unit Functions: The *Office of Detention Facilities,* in the office of the secretary, is responsible for the inspection and evaluation of all local detention facilities, including jails, houses of correction, secure juvenile detention centers, and municipal lockups. It provides technical assistance and training on various detention issues.

   The *Division of Adult Institutions* supervises adult inmates in a variety of correctional settings. It assigns inmates to one of 6 security classifications, based on their records, backgrounds, and the risk they may pose to the public, correctional officers, and other inmates.

   Security classifications include 2 levels each of maximum, medium, and minimum security. These levels determine how closely inmates are guarded, how restricted their movements are within the institution, and the programs in which they may participate. Although prisons are classified by the highest level of security for which the facility is built and administered, an individual facility may contain several security levels.

   The prison program is designed to offer offenders opportunities to develop skills necessary to lead law-abiding lives upon release. Services include evaluation of an offender's background and needs and the provision of programs to meet those needs. Programs include academic and vocational education, alcohol and other drug abuse treatment, other clinical treatment, work, and religious observance. The division offers job training for inmates through Badger State Industries, which produces various items, including furniture, textiles and linens, license plates, and signs, and performs such services as printing and data entry.

   The division also administers 16 minimum security correctional centers across the state. Center staff work closely with probation and parole agents to assist the transition of inmates back into the community. Center programming includes basic education, alcohol and drug counseling, work experience, and work release. The division operates the Milwaukee Secure Detention Facility, which confines offenders who have violated conditions of community supervision as well as those participating in alcohol and other drug abuse inpatient programs.

   The *Division of Community Corrections* supervises persons released on parole or sentenced to probation or extended supervision. The supervision is community-based to strengthen family and community ties, encourage lawful behavior, and provide local treatment programs. Probation and parole agents hold offenders accountable for their behavior, provide direct services, and refer their clients to community service agencies. They also provide investigative services to the courts, the Division of Adult Institutions, and the Parole Commission to aid in sentencing, institutional programming, and parole planning. Under limited circumstances, agents supervise juveniles released to aftercare programs and persons conditionally released from mental health facilities.

The *Division of Juvenile Corrections,* created in Section 301.025, Wisconsin Statutes, by 1995 Wisconsin Act 27, administers programs to treat and rehabilitate delinquent youth and protect the public. It operates the state's juvenile corrections institutions and community corrections programs. Through its Juvenile Offender Review Program, the division determines whether offenders in the institutions are eligible for release, oversees the aftercare services of those who are released, and selects the participants for intensive surveillance under the Corrective Sanctions Program. The division also administers the Community Youth and Family Aids Program, which offers financial incentives to counties to divert juveniles from state institutions and into less restrictive community rehabilitation programs, and it awards grants to counties that participate in the Intensive Aftercare Program, which offers a wide range of social, educational, and employment assistance.

The *Division of Management Services* provides budgeting, data processing, personnel, and telecommunications services and oversees accounting, procurement, and facilities management.

History: In Chapter 288, Laws of 1851, the legislature established a commission to locate and supervise the building and administration of a state prison. The commissioners chose Waupun as the site, and the facility was opened in 1852. Waupun housed both male and female offenders until 1933 when the Wisconsin Prison for Women opened in Taycheedah.

From 1853 to 1874 an elected state prison commissioner ran the prison. Beginning in 1874, the governor appointed three state prison commissioners to hire a warden and direct state prison operation. In 1881, prisons and other public welfare functions were placed under the supervision of the State Board of Supervision of Wisconsin Charitable, Reformatory and Penal Institutions, subsequently renamed the State Board of Control of the Wisconsin Reformatory, Charitable and Penal Institutions in 1891. Both adult and juvenile facilities came under the board's control.

By 1939, the Division of Corrections within the newly created Department of Public Welfare had assumed supervision of prisons, juvenile institutions, and parole and probation. Under the 1967 executive branch reorganization, the division became part of the Department of Health and Social Services. The division was reorganized as a separate Department of Corrections in 1989 Wisconsin Act 31, but responsibility for juvenile offenders remained with the Department of Health and Social Services until 1995 Wisconsin Act 27 transferred juvenile corrections and related services to the Department of Corrections.

Waupun was the state's only prison until 1898, when the Wisconsin State Reformatory for prisoners from 16 to 30 years-of-age opened at Green Bay. The age limitation was repealed in 1966 and the facility was renamed the Green Bay Correctional Institution in 1978. A separate facility for women, the Industrial Home for Women, began operations in Taycheedah in 1921. The Wisconsin Prison for Women at Taycheedah opened in 1933. Fox Lake Correctional Institution opened in 1962. Further expansion of the state prison system occurred when Kettle Moraine Boys School was converted to an adult institution in 1975, followed by the conversion of Oregon School for Girls to a minimum security prison (Oakhill) in 1977. The Dodge Correctional Institution, which serves as reception and evaluation center for all adult male felons sentenced by Wisconsin courts, opened in 1978. Rapid growth of the prison population led to the opening of the Columbia and the Oshkosh Correctional Institutions in 1986, the Racine Correctional Institution in 1991, the Jackson Correctional Institution in 1996, a super maximum security prison, located in Boscobel, in 1999, the Redgranite Correctional Institution in 2001, the Stanley Correctional Institution in 2003, and the New Lisbon Correctional Institution in 2004. The department opened a minimum security facility to serve the needs of inmates with alcohol and other drug abuse problems in Chippewa Falls in 2004.

While the capacity of Wisconsin prisons had grown considerably since 1986, the number of prisoners confined to adult institutions grew from just over 6,000 in 1989 to more than 15,000 in 1995. As a result, 1995 Wisconsin Act 344 authorized the department to contract with other states to house Wisconsin prisoners. 1997 Wisconsin Act 27 authorized housing state prisoners in private prisons in other states. By the end of 2002, out-of-state prisons housed more than 3,400 Wisconsin inmates. Near the end of 2004, fewer than 300 inmates were located out-of-state, due to new institutions, an increased number of beds at existing prisons, expanded contracting with county sheriffs to house inmates in county jails, and expanded noninstitutionalization options created in 2003 Wisconsin Act 33.

Wisconsin's first juvenile institution for boys opened in 1860 at Waukesha and was replaced by Kettle Moraine at Plymouth in 1963. A second facility, Wisconsin School for Boys, which was subsequently renamed the Ethan Allen School, opened at Wales in 1959. Lincoln Hills School for Boys began operations in 1970. (It was opened to girls in 1976 and the school was renamed.) The first juvenile institution for girls was established in 1875 in Milwaukee as a private agency that received state aid. The Wisconsin School for Girls, later renamed the Oregon School for Girls, opened in 1931 and closed in 1976. Girls were then sent to Lincoln Hills. In response to concerns about overcrowding at Lincoln Hills and the need for treatment programs for girls, the legislature authorized a separate facility, which opened as Southern Oaks Girls School at Union Grove in 1994. Another juvenile facility was opened in Prairie du Chien in 1997, but it has been converted into a medium security adult prison.

Probation and parole were unknown in the early years of statehood. Criminal sentences were for definite periods of time and to be fully served. Until 1860, executive pardons were the only means for early release. Chapter 324, Laws of 1860, established early releases for good behavior, known as "good time". Calculations of good time ended with the adoption of mandatory release dates for crimes committed after May 31, 1984. Parole was first enacted in 1889, but was apparently invalidated by the Wisconsin Supreme Court. New parole provisions were enacted in 1897 for the Green Bay Reformatory and for the Waupun State Prison in Chapter 110, Laws of 1907. That law allowed the State Board of Control to parole prisoners with the governor's approval, but the approval requirement was removed in 1947. The State Board of Control was also given supervisory responsibility for prisoners placed on probation in 1909. Currently, the Parole Commission, created in 1989, has final authority in granting discretionary paroles. Under 1997 Wisconsin Act 283, a person who is convicted of a felony committed on or after December 31, 1999, and sentenced to prison must serve a specified time in prison followed by a specified period of "extended supervision" in the community. Persons given this "bifurcated sentence" are not eligible for parole.

Statutory Commission

Parole Commission: LENARD WELLS (appointed by governor with senate consent), *chairperson*; JAYNE HACKBARTH, JAMES HART, M. JEANNE HUIBREGTSE, STEVEN LANDREMAN, FRANCES PAUL, SHARON WILLIAMS, vacancy (appointed by chairperson from classified service).

Address: 3099 East Wasshington Avenue, P.O. Box 7960, Madison 53707-7960.

Telephone: 240-7280.

Fax: 240-7299.

E-mail Address: parole.commission@doc.state.wi.us

The 8-member Parole Commission is the final authority for granting discretionary paroles for prisoners who committed felonies before December 31, 1999. (Parole is not an option in the case of felonies committed on or after that date.) The commission conducts regularly scheduled interviews to consider the parole of inmates confined in a state correctional institution, a contracted facility, or a county house of corrections or inmates transferred to mental health institutions. The governor appoints the commission's chairperson for a 2-year term.

The commission's statutory predecessor, the Parole Board, was created by Chapter 221, Laws of 1979, to advise the secretary of health and social services, and its members were appointed by the secretary. The commission was created by 1989 Wisconsin Act 107. Its composition and duties are prescribed in Sections 15.145 (1) and 304.01 of the statutes.

INDEPENDENT UNITS ATTACHED FOR BUDGETING, PROGRAM COORDINATION, AND RELATED MANAGEMENT FUNCTIONS BY SECTION 15.03 OF THE STATUTES

INTERSTATE ADULT OFFENDER SUPERVISION BOARD

Members: WILLIAM RANKIN (compact administrator); TAMARA GRIGSBY (legislative branch representative); GREGORY J. POTTER (judicial branch representative); AMY KASPER (executive branch representative); ANN GUSTAFSON (victims' group representative) (appointed by governor).

Statutory References: Sections 15.145 (3) and 304.16 (4).

Agency Responsibility: The 5-member Interstate Adult Offender Supervision Board officially appoints the Wisconsin representative to the national commission. The board advises the department on its participation in the compact and on the operation of the compact within this state. The representatives serve 4-year terms while the compact administrator serves at the pleasure of the governor.

PRISON INDUSTRIES BOARD

Members: DEBRA M. PICKETT, CAROL VOLLMER POPE, BILL G. SMITH (private business and industry representatives); LYLE A. BALISTRIERI, J.C. HILL, JAMES E. MOORE (private labor organization representatives); COREY F. ODOM (Technical College System representative); MATTHEW J. FRANK (Department of Corrections representative); PATRICK FARLEY (Department of Administration representative). (All are appointed by governor.)

Statutory References: Sections 15.145 (2) and 303.015.

Agency Responsibility: The 9-member Prison Industries Board advises Prison Industries. It develops a plan for the manufacturing and marketing of prison industry products, the provision of prison industry services, and research and development activities. No prison industry may be established or permanently closed without board approval. The board reviews the department's budget request for Prison Industries and may make recommendations to the governor for changes. The board gives prior approval for Prison Industries purchases exceeding $250,000. Members are appointed for 4-year terms. It was created by 1983 Wisconsin Act 27.

EDUCATIONAL COMMUNICATIONS BOARD

Board Members: ROLF WEGENKE (private schools representative), *chairperson;* ELIZABETH BURMASTER (superintendent of public instruction), *vice chairperson;* SENATORS COGGS, OLSEN; REPRESENTATIVES NISCHKE, SCHNEIDER; MARC MAROTTA (secretary of administration), KEVIN P. REILLY (president, UW System), DAN CLANCY (director, Technical College System), THOMAS J. BASTING, SR., EILEEN LITTIG (public members); DARYLANN WHITEMARSH (public schools representative), EILEEN CONNOLLY-KESSLER (appointed by UW System Board of Regents), BERNARD KUBALE (president, Wisconsin Public Radio Association), DIANE EVERSON (educational TV coverage area representative), DARNELL COLE (appointed by Technical College System Board). (Public members and representatives of public and private schools are appointed by governor.)

Executive Director: WENDY WINK, 264-9676, wwink@ecb.state.wi.us

Deputy Director: PHIL CORRIVEAU, 263-4199, corriveau@wpr.org

Education, Division of: JOHN ASHLEY, *administrator,* 264-9689, Fax: 264-9685, jashley@ecb.state.wi.us

Engineering Services, Division of: DENNIS BEHR, *administrator,* 264-9746, Fax: 264-9664, dbehr@ecb.state.wi.us

Public Radio, Division of: PHIL CORRIVEAU, *director,* 821 University Avenue, Madison 53706, 263-4199, Fax: 263-9763, corriveau@wpr.org

Public Television, Division of: MALCOLM BRETT, *director,* 821 University Avenue, Madison 53706, 263-9598, Fax: 263-9763, brett@wpt.org

Mailing Address: 3319 West Beltline Highway, Madison 53713-4296.

Telephone: (608) 264-9600.

Fax: (608) 264-9664.

Internet Address: http://www.ecb.org

Publications: Biennial report; Interconnect Newsletter; Parade of Programs (ITV schedule for elementary/secondary schools); Telelink Newsletter; Television Program Guide; teachers' manuals and guides for instructional television programs.

Number of Employees: 71.00.

Total Budget 2003-05: $32,432,700.

Statutory References: Section 15.57; Chapter 39, Subchapter I.

Agency Responsibility: The Educational Communications Board oversees statewide instructional telecommunications programming, a public broadcasting system, and public service media for the cultural and educational needs of the state's citizens. The board plans, constructs, and operates the state's public radio and television networks, and it is the licensee for the state's 16 public radio stations and 5 public television stations. The board operates the Emergency Weather System and the Amber Alert System. The board shares responsibility for public broadcasting with the University of Wisconsin Board of Regents. Programming is produced through UW facilities or acquired from national, regional, state, and local sources. The board also is affiliated with public television stations licensed to Milwaukee Area Technical College, television station WSDE in Duluth, and several public radio stations.

Educational services include selection, acquisition or production, implementation, and evaluation of instructional programming and accompanying multimedia materials (CD-ROMs, manuals, and software) in cooperation with teachers in public and private schools, the Cooperative Educational Service Agencies, the Department of Public Instruction, the Technical College System, and the UW System. The board administers a telecommunication operations center, satellite facilities, and an intructional television fixed service system (ITFS).

Organization: The board includes 16 members. Those appointed by the governor, the UW Board of Regents, and the Technical College System Board serve 4-year terms. Legislative members must represent the majority and minority party in each house. The board appoints an executive director from outside the classified service. Division administrators are appointed by the executive director and may be from outside the classified service.

Unit Functions: The *Division of Education* provides public service media, instructional television and multimedia programming along with field services, online assistance, and other instructional services for public and private PK-12 schools and higher education. It offers professional development opportunities for professional educators through the use of distance learning technologies.

The *Division of Engineering Services* develops, operates, and maintains the statewide telecommunication systems used to receive and deliver instructional, educational, and cultural programming. It coordinates broadcasting from the Emergency Alert System, the National Weather Service, and the Amber Alert System.

The *Division of Public Radio* operates the statewide Wisconsin Public Radio service in partnership with UW-Extension. Wisconsin Public Radio service includes two networks: 1) National Public Radio News Network and 2) Classical Music Network and the Wisconsin Ideas Network – both of which offer national, regional, and local programming.

The *Division of Public Television* operates the statewide Wisconsin Public Television service in partnership with UW-Extension. Daytime broadcast hours are devoted to children's and instructional programming and evening hours to cultural, informational, and entertainment programs. Wisconsin Public Television delivers national programming from the Public Broadcasting Service and produces programs on topics of regional and state interest.

History: Wisconsin's history in educational broadcasting dates back to the oldest public radio station in the nation. The University of Wisconsin's research in "wireless" communication led to the beginning of scheduled radio broadcasting in 1919 on Station 9XM, which was renamed WHA-AM in 1922. Wisconsin made a commitment to statewide educational broadcasting in 1945. Chapter 570, Laws of 1945, created the State Radio Council to plan, produce, and transmit educational, cultural, and service programs over a statewide FM radio network. Over the next two decades, the council constructed and activated 10 radio transmitters. In Chapter 360, Laws of 1953, the council also assumed responsibility for research in educational television.

Recognizing that good reading skills are key to academic success, Into the Book – *a production of the Educational Communications Board – develops powerful comprehension strategies for students in kindergarten through third grade. The content of* Into the Book *is based on learning strategies developed in collaboration with Wisconsin educators. Video programs and interactive online activities designed for students, as well as lesson plans and professional development materials for teachers, combine to make learning to read a dynamic endeavor.* (Jim Gill, *Educational Communications Board*)

The 1967 executive branch reorganization renamed the council the Educational Broadcasting Board, created the Educational Broadcasting Division under its supervision, and attached the board and the division to the Coordinating Council for Higher Education. The name was changed to the Educational Communications Board in Chapter 276, Laws of 1969. With the demise of the Coordinating Council, the Educational Communications Board became an independent agency in Chapter 100, Laws of 1971. In 1971, the board began to extend educational television to the entire state, and it had constructed 5 UHF television stations by 1977. Signal translator facilities erected in the 1980s extended service to areas of the state beyond the reach of regular transmitters. By 1994, the board completed construction of 17 instructional television fixed service systems, which are licensed with the Federal Communications Commission (FCC). Most recently, the Educational Communications Board has completed the statewide transition to digital broadcasting, in accordance with the FCC mandate to convert to the digital format.

ELECTIONS BOARD

Elections Board: DONALD R. GOLDBERG (designated by governor)*;* DAVID ANSTAETT (designated by chief justice of supreme court); PATRICK J. HODAN (designated by assembly speaker); JOHN C. SCHOBER (designated by senate majority leader); SHANE FALK (designated by senate minority leader); CARL HOLBORN (designated by assembly minority leader); ROBERT KASIETA (designated by chairperson Wisconsin Democratic Party); KIRBY BRANT (designated by chairperson Wisconsin Libertarian Party); JOHN P. SAVAGE (designated by chairperson Wisconsin Republican Party) (all appointed by governor).

Executive Director: KEVIN J. KENNEDY, 266-8087, kevin.kennedy@seb.state.wi.us

Legal Counsel: GEORGE A. DUNST, 266-0136, george.dunst@seb.state.wi.us

Statewide Voter Registration System Project Director: BARBARA A. HANSEN, 267-0714, barbara.hansen@seb.state.wi.us

Campaign Finance and Agency Operations Director: SHARRIE HAUGE, 266-0404, sharrie.hauge@seb.state.wi.us

Lead Elections Specialist: DIANE LOWE, 266-3276, diane.lowe@seb.state.wi.us

Lead Campaign Auditor: RICHARD BOHRINGER, 267-7735, richard.bohringer@seb.state.wi.us

Mailing Address: P.O. Box 2973, Madison 53701-2973.

Location: 17 West Main Street, Suite 310, Madison.

Telephones: General office: (608) 266-8005; Election services: 266-3276; Campaign finance services: 267-7735.

Internet Address: http://elections.state.wi.us

Fax: (608) 267-0500.

Publications: Absentee Voting in Wisconsin Nursing Homes; biennial report; calendar of election events; various guides and checklists for candidates, political committees, election officials, and clerks.

Number of Employees: 11.00.

Total Budget 2003-05: $2,759,600.

Statutory References: Section 15.61; Chapters 5-12.

Agency Responsibility: The Elections Board administers the state's election and campaign laws, investigates alleged violations of those laws, and brings civil actions to collect forfeitures. It may subpoena alleged violators or their records and notify the district attorney or attorney general of any grounds for civil or criminal prosecution. The board also has compliance review authority over local election officials' actions relating to ballot preparation, candidate nomination, voter qualifications, and election administration. The board issues formal opinions upon request, promulgates administrative rules, and holds information and training meetings with local election officials to promote uniform election procedures. The board is responsible for the training and certification of all chief election inspectors in the state.

The board administers the campaign finance registration and reporting system, which limits and requires full disclosure of contributions and disbursements made on behalf of every candidate for public office. The statutes specify which candidates, individuals, political parties, and groups must register and file detailed financial statements. Registration and reporting are required for nonresident committees that make contributions and for all individuals who make independent disbursements. The board administers the electronic filing of campaign finance reports of all registrants that receive contributions in excess of $20,000 in a campaign period for candidate committees or in excess of $20,000 in a biennium for other registrants.

The board also administers the Wisconsin Election Campaign Fund, created by Chapter 107, Laws of 1977, to provide publicly funded grants to eligible candidates for statewide and legislative office. Candidates who apply for the grants must, with some exceptions, agree to abide by spending limits. Funding for the grants is provided from a $1 checkoff on the state income tax form that does not affect the taxpayer's liability.

The board administers the federal Help America Vote Act of 2002 that establishes certain election requirements regarding the conduct of federal elections in the state. One of the requirements is to implement a computerized, centralized statewide voter registration system.

Organization: The governor appoints the Elections Board members to serve 2-year terms. The number of members may vary because, in addition to the 6 members designated by specified officials, it must include the chief officer of each political party whose candidate for governor received at least 10% of the vote in the most recent gubernatorial election. The board employs an executive director from outside the classified service to act as the chief election officer of the state. Administrative and support services are provided by the Department of Administration.

History: The Elections Board was created as an independent agency by Chapter 334, Laws of 1973. This law transferred administration of the state's election laws from the secretary of state to the board and created the campaign finance registration and reporting system.

Statutory Council

Election Administration Council: (appointed by the executive director of the Elections Board). The Election Administration Council assists the Elections Board in preparing and revising as necessary a state plan that meets the requirements of Public Law 107-252, the federal "Help America Vote Act of 2002", which will enable participation by the state in federal financial assistance programs authorized under that law. The members of the council are appointed by the executive director of the Elections Board. The membership must include the clerk or executive director of the board of election commissioners of the two counties or municipalities having the largest population, one or more election officials of other counties or municipalities, representatives of organizations that advocate for the interests of the voting public, and other electors of Wisconsin. The council was created by 2003 Wisconsin Act 265, and its composition and duties are prescribed in Sections 5.05 (10) and 15.617 (1) of the statutes.

Department of
EMPLOYEE TRUST FUNDS

Employee Trust Funds Board: MARILYN J. WIGDAHL (Wisconsin Retirement Board member), *chairperson;* WAYNE E. KOESSL (Wisconsin Retirement Board member), *vice chairperson;* ROBERT M. NIENDORF (Wisconsin Retirement Board member), *secretary;* GARY E. SHERMAN (governor's designee on Group Insurance Board); KAREN TIMBERLAKE (Director of the Office of State Employment Relations); IRENA MACEK, WAYNE D. MCCAFFERY, NANCY L. THOMPSON (Teachers Retirement Board members); JOHN L. BROWN, RICK GALE (Wisconsin Retirement Board members); CYNTHIA A. VAN BOGAERT (appointed by governor to represent taxpayers), THERON FISHER (annuitant, elected by annuitants), KATHLEEN KREUL (Technical College or educational support personnel employee). (Board representatives are appointed by their respective boards; the technical college or public school educational support employee is elected by the constituency groups.)

Secretary of Employee Trust Funds: ERIC O. STANCHFIELD, 266-0301, eric.stanchfield@

Deputy Secretary: DAVID A. STELLA, 266-3641, dave.stella@

Executive Assistant: RHONDA L. DUNN, 266-9854, rhonda.dunn@

Internal Audit, Office of: ROBERT J. SCHAEFER, *director,* 266-3951, robert.schaefer@

Legislation, Communications and Planning, Office of: VICKI POOLE, *director,* 261-7940, vicki.poole@

Legal Services, Office of: ROBERT F. WEBER, *chief counsel,* 266-5804, rob.weber@

Information Technology, Division of: JOANNE CULLEN, *administrator,* 266-3960, joanne.cullen@

Insurance Services, Division of: THOMAS C. KORPADY, *administrator,* 266-0207, tom.korpady@

Management Services, Division of: PAMELA S. HENNING, *administrator,* 267-2929, pamela.henning@

Retirement Services, Division of: SARI KING, *administrator,* 266-0222, sari.king@

Trust Finance and Employer Services, Division of: JOHN VINCENT, *administrator,* 261-7942,
john.vincent@

Address e-mail by combining the user ID and the state extender: userid@**etf.state.wi.us**

Mailing Address: P.O. Box 7931, Madison 53707-7931.

Location: 801 West Badger Road, Madison.

Milwaukee Branch Office: 819 North 6th Street, Room 550, Milwaukee 53203,
(414) 227-4294.

Telephones: Member services: 266-3285 (Madison) or (877) 533-5020; Appointments (608)
266-5717; Telephone message center: (800) 991-5540; Self-service line: (877) 383-1888; TTY:
267-0676.

Internet Address: http://etf.wi.gov (includes e-mail inquiry form).

Publications: Comprehensive Annual Financial Report; *Employer Bulletin; It's Your Benefit;
Trust Fund News;* and various employer manuals and employee brochures on the Wisconsin
Retirement System, the group insurance plans, the deferred compensation program, and the
employee reimbursement account program.

Number of Employees: 198.35.

Total Budget 2003-05: $44,041,800.

Statutory References: Sections 15.16 and Chapter 40.

Agency Responsibility: The Department of Employee Trust Funds administers various
employee benefit programs, including the retirement, group insurance, disability, and deferred
compensation programs and employee reimbursement and commuter benefits accounts. It serves
all state employees and teachers and most municipal employees.

Organization: The 13-member Employee Trust Funds Board provides direction and supervision to the department and the Wisconsin Retirement System (WRS). Board membership
includes 2 *ex officio* members and 11 members who are appointed or elected for 4-year terms to
represent employers, employees, taxpayers, and annuitants. The member appointed by the governor to represent taxpayers must have specific professional experience and cannot be a WRS participant. The board approves all administrative rules; authorizes payment of all retirement annuities, except those for disability; and hears appeals of benefit determinations. It appoints the
secretary from outside the classified service, and the secretary selects the deputy from outside the
service. Division and office heads are appointed from within the classified service by the secretary.

Unit Functions: The *Division of Information Technology* develops and implements the department's information technology systems, coordinates technological resources, and provides technical services to the department.

The *Division of Insurance Services* is responsible for policy development and implementation
of health, life, disability, and long-term care insurance; accumulated sick leave conversion credit;
employee reimbursement and commuter benefits accounts; and the Private Employer Health Care
Purchasing Alliance.

The *Division of Management Services* provides support services for human resources, payroll,
facility management, capital budget and inventory, records management, document design, mail
and supplies, word processing, library, and telecommunications. It also oversees quality assurance functions and provides ombudsperson services for members' complaints.

The *Division of Retirement Services* develops and implements retirement policies and services
for the members of the retirement system, including calculation and payment of retirement and
related benefits. The division monitors and interprets related state and federal legislation.

The *Division of Trust Finance and Employer Services* develops and implements the necessary
policies, training, and support for employers participating in the benefit programs. It collects and
reconciles data on all active members of the retirement system and provides annual statements
to those who are not receiving benefits.

History: The 1891 Legislature initiated pension coverage for local government employees
when it required Milwaukee to create a pension fund for retired and disabled police and fire fight-

ers in Chapter 287. Sixteen years later, the legislature extended pension coverage to protective service employees of smaller cities through Chapter 671, Laws of 1907. The 1909 Legislature authorized a pension system for City of Milwaukee teachers in Chapter 510; and Chapter 323, Laws of 1911, created a retirement system for those school districts throughout the rest of the state that wished to enroll their teachers. With enactment of Chapter 459, Laws of 1921, Wisconsin established a mandatory, joint contributory, statewide teachers' pension system, covering virtually all teachers in public schools (outside of Milwaukee), normal schools, and the University of Wisconsin.

The legislature first provided retirement plans for general municipal employees outside of Milwaukee in Chapter 175, Laws of 1943. In the same session, a retirement system was created for general employees by Chapter 176, Laws of 1943. Local fire and police pension funds were closed to new members by Chapter 206, Laws of 1947, and these employees have since been covered with the general employees. Chapter 60, Laws of 1951, created the Public Employees Social Security Fund, making Wisconsin the first state in the nation to permit some state and local government employees to be covered by Social Security.

Chapter 211, Laws of 1959, created group life and group health insurance programs for state employees, a group life insurance program for municipal employees, and the Group Insurance Board to monitor the administration of the programs. The 1967 executive branch reorganization created the Department of Employee Trust Funds to administer the various retirement funds, and the Group Insurance Board was attached to it.

Chapter 280, Laws of 1975, initiated the merger of the existing, separate retirement funds that covered all publicly employed teachers in the state and all state and local public employees, except employees of the City of Milwaukee and Milwaukee County who have their own systems. The legislature transferred local police and fire pension funds to the overall general employee system in Chapter 182, Laws of 1977. The implementation of the merged Wisconsin Retirement System was completed, effective January 1, 1982, by Chapter 96, Laws of 1981.

Statutory Boards

Deferred Compensation Board: MARTIN BEIL, MICHAEL DRURY, EDWARD D. MAIN, JOHN F. NELSON, JON TRAVER (appointed by governor with senate consent).
The 5-member Deferred Compensation Board establishes rules for offering deferred compensation plans to state and local employees and contracts with deferred compensation plan providers. Its members are appointed for 4-year terms. The board was created by 1989 Wisconsin Act 31, and its composition and duties are prescribed in Sections 15.165 (4) and 40.80 of the statutes.

Group Insurance Board: STEPHEN FRANKEL (public member), *chairperson;* RANDY A. BLUMER (designated by commissioner of insurance), *vice chairperson;* vacancy (designated by governor); ROBERT BAIRD (WRS-insured local government participant); JANE HAMBLEN (designated by attorney general); DAVID SCHMIEDICKE (designated by secretary of administration); KAREN TIMBERLAKE (Director of the Office of State Employment Relations); MARTIN BEIL (WRS-insured nonteacher participant); ESTHER M. OLSON (WRS-insured teacher participant); JANIS DOLESCHAL (retired WRS-insured participant). (All except *ex officio* members are appointed by governor.)
The 10-member Group Insurance Board oversees the group health, life, income continuation, and other insurance programs offered to state employees, covered local employees, and retirees. The board's 5 appointed members serve 2-year terms. The board was created by Chapter 211, Laws of 1959, and its composition and duties are prescribed in Sections 15.165 (2) and 40.03 (6) of the statutes.

Private Employer Health Care Coverage Board: TIM SIZE (hospitals), JAMES KROGSTAD (insurance agents), vacancy (health maintenance organizations); GINA ERICKSON, vacancy (employees eligible to receive coverage from an employer who employs 50 employees or less); DEWAYNE G. BIERMAN (insurers); JAMES JANES, CHRISTOPHER QUERAM (eligible employer who employs 50 employees or less); vacancy (physician); GARY MEIER, vacancy (representing the public interest) (all appointed by governor with senate consent). *Nonvoting members:* ERIC O.

STANCHFIELD (secretary of employee trust funds); HELENE NELSON (secretary of health and family services).

Mailing Address: P.O. 7931, Madison 53707-7931.

Telephone: 261-0731.

Fax: 261-0142.

Statutory References: 15.07 (1) (b) 22. and 15.165 (5).

Agency Responsibility: The 13-member Private Employer Health Care Coverage Board was created by 1999 Wisconsin Act 9 to oversee the Private Employer Health Care Purchasing Alliance Program. Appointed members serve 3-year terms. The board sets the criteria for administrative contracts of the program's health care coverage plans, establishes enrollment periods, and sets the commission rates that may be paid to insurance agents selling coverage. The board must submit a report no later than January 1, 2008, recommending whether the Department of Employee Trust Funds should continue its involvement with the program. The board is scheduled to sunset on January 1, 2010.

Teachers Retirement Board: ROBERTA RASMUS (school board member appointed by governor), SUZANNE M. DOEMEL, WAYNE D. MCCAFFERY, DENNIS PANICUCCI, JAMES R. TRIPP, DAVID WILTGEN, vacancy (public school teachers); R. THOMAS PEDERSEN (technical college teacher); DAN NERAD (public school administrator appointed by governor); THEODORE BRATANOW, ROBERT SHAW (UW System representatives appointed by governor); LON L. MISHLER (teacher annuitant); IRENA MACEK (Milwaukee teacher). (Members not appointed by governor are elected by their constituent groups.)

The 13-member Teachers Retirement Board advises the Employee Trust Funds Board about retirement matters related to teachers, recommends and approves or rejects administrative rules, authorizes payment of disability annuities for teachers, and hears appeals of staff determinations of disability. Board members serve staggered 5-year terms; the 2 UW System representatives may not be from the same campus. The board was created by Chapter 204, Laws of 1953, and its composition and duties are prescribed in Sections 15.165 (3) (a) and 40.03 (7) of the statutes.

Wisconsin Retirement Board: MARILYN J. WIGDAHL (participating state employee), NANETTE R. KOTTKE (county clerk or deputy), DENNIS R. MCBRIDE (nonparticipant representing taxpayers), JOHN DAVID (city or village chief executive or governing board member); HERBERT STINSKI (participating city or village finance officer); RICK GALE (participating city or village employee); WAYNE E. KOESSL (county or town governing body member); MARY VON RUDEN (participating employee of local employer other than city or village); JORGE GOMEZ (commissioner of insurance). (All, except insurance commissioner or designee, are appointed by governor.)

The 9-member Wisconsin Retirement Board advises the Employee Trust Funds Board about retirement matters related to state and local general and protective employees and performs the same functions for these employees as the Teachers Retirement Board does for teachers. The board's appointed members serve staggered 5-year terms, and the municipal official and county board member are nominated by their respective statewide associations. The board was created by Chapter 96, Laws of 1981, and its composition and duties are prescribed in Sections 15.165 (3) (b) and 40.03 (8) of the statutes.

EMPLOYMENT RELATIONS COMMISSION

Commissioners: JUDITH M. NEUMANN, *chairperson,* 266-0166, judy.neumann@; PAUL GORDON, paul.gordon@; SUSAN J.M. BAUMAN, susan.bauman@ (appointed by governor with senate consent).

General Counsel: PETER G. DAVIS, 266-2993, peter.davis@

Team Leaders: MARSHALL L. GRATZ, (414) 963-4695, marshall.gratz@; WILLIAM C. HOULIHAN, 266-0147, william.houlihan@; GEORGANN KRAMER, 266-9287, georgann.kramer@

Mailing Address: P.O. Box 7870, Madison 53707-7870.

Location: 18 South Thornton Avenue, Madison.

Telephone: (608) 266-1381.

Fax: (608) 266-6930.

Agency E-mail Address: werc@werc.state.wi.us

Internet Address: http://werc.wi.gov

Address e-mail by combining the user ID and the agency extender: userid@**werc.state.wi.us**

Publications: Biennial reports; complaint procedures manual; agency decisions.

Number of Employees: 23.50.

Total Budget 2003-05: $5,245,400.

Statutory References: Sections 15.58, 230.44, and 230.45; Chapter 111.

Agency Responsibility: The Employment Relations Commission promotes collective bargaining and peaceful labor relations in the private and public sectors. It processes various types of labor relations cases, including elections, bargaining unit clarifications, union security referenda, mediations, interest arbitrations, grievance arbitrations, prohibited or unfair labor practices, and declaratory rulings. The commission also issues decisions arising from state employee civil service appeals, including appeals relating to certain classification, examination, and appointment issues, disciplinary actions, hazardous employment injury benefits, and noncontractual grievances. The commission's decisions are subject to review in state court. In addition to mediating labor disputes, the commission provides training and assistance to parties interested in labor/management cooperation and a consensus approach to resolving labor relations issues.

Organization: The 3 full-time commissioners are chosen for staggered 6-year terms, and the governor designates one commissioner to serve as chairperson for a 2-year term. The chairperson functions as the agency administrator and is assisted by supervisors who head teams of attorney/ mediators and their support staff. The general counsel reviews all complaint appeals and declaratory ruling records; prepares draft decisions for commission consideration; and serves as liaison to the legislature and to the attorney general, who represents the commission in court.

History: Chapter 51, Laws of 1937, created the Wisconsin Labor Relations Board as an independent agency in the executive branch. Chapter 57, Laws of 1939, replaced the board with the Employment Relations Board and amended state laws governing labor relations. The 1967 Legislature renamed the board the Employment Relations Commission and continued it as an independent agency.

Over the years, the legislature has expanded the rights of public employees and the duties of the commission in the area of public employment labor relations. Chapter 509, Laws of 1959, authorized municipal employees to organize and be represented by labor organizations in negotiating wages, hours, and conditions of employment. Chapter 124, Laws of 1971, gave municipal employees the right to bargain collectively and made a municipal employer's refusal to bargain a prohibited practice. Chapters 246 and 247, Laws of 1971, established compulsory interest arbitration for police and firefighters in Milwaukee and other municipalities. Chapter 270, Laws of 1971, gave state employees the right to bargain collectively. 2003 Wisconsin Act 33 abolished the Personnel Commission and transferred to the Employment Relations Commission responsibility for various appeals related to state employment.

ETHICS BOARD

Members: JAMES R. MORGAN, *chairperson;* PAUL M. HOLZEM, *vice chairperson;* DAVID L. MCROBERTS, *secretary;* COURTNEY L. HUNT, DOROTHY JOHNSON, RICHARD WARCH (appointed by governor with senate consent).
Executive Director: R. ROTH JUDD.
Mailing Address: 44 East Mifflin Street, Suite 601, Madison 53703.
Telephone: (608) 266-8123.
Fax: (608) 264-9319.
Internet Address: http://ethics.state.wi.us
Agency E-mail: ethics@ethics.state.wi.us
Publications: Annual Report; Digest of Opinions of the Ethics Board; guidelines on standards of conduct for state and local officials; informational guides on the lobby law; directories of licensed lobbyists and registered lobbying organizations.
Number of Employees: 5.75.
Total Budget 2003-05: $1,219,600.
Statutory References: Sections 15.07 (1) (c) and 15.62; Chapter 13, Subchapter III; and Chapter 19, Subchapter III.

Agency Responsibility: The Ethics Board administers the Code of Ethics for State Public Officials and Wisconsin's lobbying law. The intent of the Ethics Code is to forbid a state official from using a public position to obtain anything of value for the personal benefit of the official, the official's family, or the official's private business. Wisconsin's lobbying law prohibits lobbyists and the organizations that employ them from furnishing anything of value to a state official or employee except in a limited number of well-defined circumstances. The Ethics Board renders advisory opinions to officials, local governments, and others asking about their own conduct; collects and makes available information about the financial interests of state officials, candidates, and nominees; and compiles and disseminates on its Web site information about organizations' efforts to influence legislation and administrative rules as well as the time and money spent by those organizations in lobbying activities. The Ethics Board also investigates and prosecutes violations of the Ethics Code and lobbying law.

Organization: The six board members serve staggered 6-year terms and must be U.S. citizens and state residents. While serving on the board and for one year prior to appointment, no member may be or have been a member of a political party or a partisan political organization or be or have been a candidate for partisan elective public office. No member may concurrently hold a local or state office or be employed by state or local government. The board appoints an executive director.

History: ETHICS REGULATION. Chapter 90, Laws of 1973, created the Ethics Board to administer the ethics code created by the act. Originally, the standards of conduct and reporting requirements in what is currently titled the "Code of Ethics Public Officials and Employees" applied only to key state officials in the executive and legislative branches. Chapters 223 and 277, Laws of 1977, extended the code's application to judges and many state employees. Chapter 277, a major revision of the ethics code, strengthened the required standards of conduct and required officials to report additional information about their personal financial interests. Chapter 120, Laws of 1979, enhanced the ability of local governments to enforce codes of conduct for local officials. The 1981 Legislature applied the ethics code to board members and key employees of what are currently termed technical college districts (Chapter 269) and employees of the Wisconsin Housing and Economic Development Authority (Chapter 349). The code was extended to municipal judges by 1983 Wisconsin Act 27. 1987 Wisconsin Act 365 applied the code to division administrators in the classified service, increased the penalties for code violations, and lessened the standard of proof in enforcement actions from "beyond a reasonable doubt" to "clear and convincing evidence." 1991 Wisconsin Act 39 created an ethics code applicable to local public officials of counties, cities, villages, towns, school boards, and other governmental units, with enforcement authority vested in the district attorney of each county.

LOBBYING REGULATION. Lobbying in Wisconsin has been a regulated activity since Chapter 145, Laws of 1858, prohibited giving or accepting compensation for employment as a lobbyist contingent on the success or failure of legislation and required all lobbyists to identify themselves and their employers to legislators. Chapter 243, Laws of 1899, established a lobbying registry to further identify the subjects of lobbying efforts and regularly report lobbying expenses. Chapter 247, Laws of 1905, prohibited personal, direct attempts by paid lobbyists to influence legislators, other than through appearing at committee meetings, public addresses, or broadly disseminated writings. These prohibitions continued until 1947. Chapter 609, Laws of 1947, required lobbyists to obtain licenses and prohibited attempting to influence votes by promises of support or opposition at future elections or engaging in any practice which might reflect discredit on the practice of lobbying or the legislature. Registration, licensing, reporting, and lobbying practice regulations were further revised by Chapter 659, Laws of 1965 and Chapter 278, Laws of 1977, which also made the Secretary of State responsible for enforcement of lobbying law. 1989 Wisconsin Act 338 transferred regulation of the lobbying law to the Ethics Board. Act 338 also broadened the definition of lobbying activity and expanded expenditure reporting requirements.

1997 Wisconsin Act 186 deleted the requirement that a lobbying principal (a person or organization employing a lobbyist) report semiannually to the Ethics Board the subject matter and specific issues addressed in each legislative proposal or administrative rule on which the principal has attempted to influence legislative or administrative action. Instead, Act 186 substitutes the requirement for a principal to identify to the board the bills and proposed rules on which they have made a lobbying communication within 15 days of the first communication. The act also established reporting requirements regarding the time and expenses associated with certain lobbying activities. 1999 Wisconsin Act 9 extended these reporting requirements to subjects of lobbying not yet assigned a bill or rule number.

Department of
FINANCIAL INSTITUTIONS

Secretary of Financial Institutions: LORRIE KEATING HEINEMANN, 264-7800, Fax: 261-4334.

Deputy Secretary: JOHN COLLINS, 264-7800.

Executive Assistant: KATHRYN B. CARLSON, 267-1719, kathryn.carlson@

Financial Literacy, Office of: DAVID D. MANCL, *director,* 261-9540, david.mancl@; P.O. Box 8041, Madison 53708-8041; Fax: 264-7968.

Consumer Affairs, Office of: PAUL EGIDE, *director,* 267-3518, paul.egide@; Consumer Act inquiries: 264-7969, (800) 452-3328 in Wisconsin, P.O. Box 8041, Madison 53708-8041.

General Counsel: CHRISTOPHER GREEN, 266-7968, chris.green@; Fax: 264-7818.

Mailing Address: P.O. Box 8861, Madison 53708-8861.

Location: 345 West Washington Avenue, 5th Floor, Madison.

Telephones: 261-9555; TDY: 266-8818.

Fax: 261-7200.

Internet Address: http://www.wdfi.org

Number of Employees: 134.00.

Total Budget 2003-05: $26,991,000.

Statutory References: Sections 15.18 and 182.01; Chapters 224, Subchapter II, and 421-427.

Address e-mail by combining the user ID and the state extender: userid@**dfi.state.wi.us**

Administrative Services and Technology, Division of: WILLIAM J. MORRISSEY, *administrator,* 267-1707, william.morrissey@; P.O. Box 7876, Madison 53707-7876; Division Fax: 261-7200.

DEPARTMENT OF FINANCIAL INSTITUTIONS

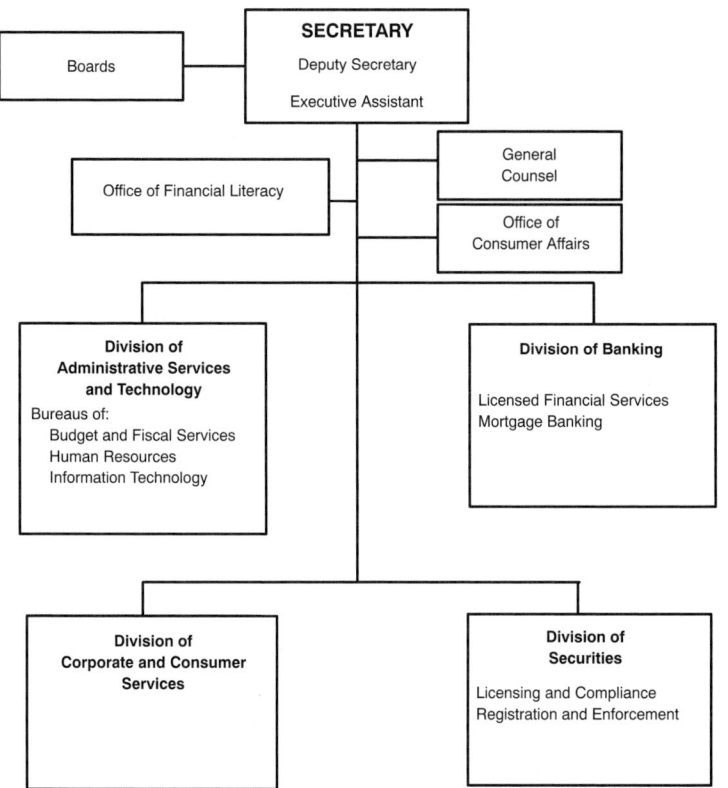

Unit attached for administrative purposes under Sec. 15.03: Office of Credit Unions

Budget and Fiscal Services, Bureau of: SUSAN J. DIETZEL, *director,* 267-0399, susan.dietzel@

Human Resources, Bureau of: LEE ISAACSON, *director,* 261-2303, lee.isaacson@

Information Technology, Bureau of: JOHN AMUNDSON, *director,* 267-1714, john.amundson@

Banking, Division of: MICHAEL MACH, *administrator,* 266-0451; P.O. Box 7876, Madison 53707-7876; Division Fax: 267-6889.

    Licensed Financial Service Bureau: JEAN PLALE, *director,* 266-0447, jean.plale@

    Mortgage Banking Bureau: JEAN PLALE, *director,* 266-0447, jean.plale@

Corporate and Consumer Services, Division of: RAY ALLEN, *deputy administrator,* 264-7952, ray.allen@; P.O. Box 7846, Madison 53707-7846; Division Fax: 267-6813.

Securities, Division of: PATRICIA D. STRUCK, *administrator,* 266-3432, patricia.struck@; P.O. Box 1768, Madison 53701-1768; Division Fax: 256-1259.

    Legal Counsel: RANDALL E. SCHUMANN, 266-3414, randall.schumann@

    Licensing and Compliance: KENNETH L. HOJNACKI, *director,* 266-7824, kenneth.hojnacki@

    Registration and Enforcement: DAVID COHEN, *supervising attorney,* 266-2801, david.cohen@

Publications: Annual Report; Annual Report on Condition of Wisconsin Banks; Annual Report on Condition of Wisconsin Savings and Loan Associations and Savings Banks; Quarterly Report on Condition of Wisconsin Banks; Securities Bulletin; brochures and pamphlets on credit and consumer protection; industry bulletins, newsletters, and online forms.

Agency Responsibility: The Department of Financial Institutions regulates state-chartered banks, savings and loans associations, and savings banks, as well as various operations of the securities industry. It examines and files charters and other documents of businesses and organizations and registers and regulates the mortgage banking industry and other financial service providers. It oversees Uniform Commercial Code filings. It also administers the Wisconsin Consumer Act and registers merchants who extend credit. The department is self-supporting through program revenue derived from fees and assessments paid by regulated entities and individuals.

Organization: The department is administered by a secretary, who is appointed by the governor with the advice and consent of the senate. The secretary appoints the administrators for 3 of the 4 divisions from outside the classified service and the administrator of the Division of Administrative Services and Technology from the classified service.

Unit Functions: The *Office of Financial Literacy* in the office of the secretary provides information to the public on matters of personal finance and investor protection, with an emphasis on the financial and economic literacy of Wisconsin's youth.

The *Office of Consumer Affairs*, also in the office of the secretary, administers the Wisconsin Consumer Act, which resolves consumer complaints and advises consumers and lenders regarding their rights and responsibilities under consumer law.

The *Division of Administrative Services and Technology* provides support services to the department through its administration of the agency's budget, personnel, procurement, and information technology services.

The *Division of Banking,* created in Section 15.183 (1), Wisconsin Statutes, by 1995 Wisconsin Act 27, is advised by the Banking Review Board. It regulates and supervises state-chartered banks and consumer financial service industries under statutory Chapters 220 through 224. In addition to chartering and regularly examining state banks, the division licenses loan companies, mortgage bankers, mortgage brokers, loan originators, collection agencies, community currency exchanges, sales finance companies, adjustment service companies, sellers of checks, insurance premium finance companies, and credit services organizations. It also regulates auto dealers' installment sales contracts. The division investigates applications for expanded banking powers, new financial products, and interstate bank acquisitions and mergers. It may conduct joint examinations with Federal Reserve System examiners and with the Federal Deposit Insurance Corporation. With Banking Review Board approval, the administrator may establish uniform rules for savings programs and fiduciary operations.

The division supervises state-chartered savings and loan associations and savings banks and enforces the laws governing them under statutory Chapters 214 and 215 with the advice of the Savings Institutions Review Board. It works to resolve consumer complaints and reviews and approves applications for acquisitions, new branches and other offices, and the organization of mutual holding companies. It may rule on interstate mergers or acquisitions. It also conducts joint examinations of associations with the federal Office of Thrift Institutions and may examine savings banks with the Federal Deposit Insurance Corporation.

The *Division of Corporate and Consumer Services* is responsible for examining and filing business records for corporations and other organizations. It examines charters, documents that affect mergers, consolidations, and dissolutions, and reviews the annual reports of various businesses, including partnerships, corporations, limited liability companies, cooperatives, and foreign corporations. It also examines and files documents under the Uniform Commercial Code, including statements of business indebtedness, consignments, terminations, and financing statements and maintains the statewide Uniform Commercial Code lien system. The division prepares certified copies of the records in its custody and responds to inquiries about corporations and other business entities and organizations for which it has records.

The *Division of Securities,* created in Section 15.183 (3), Wisconsin Statutes, by 1995 Wisconsin Act 27, regulates the sale of investment securities and franchises under statutory Chapters 551, 552, and 553. It examines and registers the offerings and may bar them from registration in this

Department of Financial Institutions employee Charlotte Rucks helps a customer file a corporate annual report. The Department's Division of Corporate and Consumer Services reviews and maintains charters, annual reports, and other documents that are required to be submitted by various businesses including partnerships, corporations, limited liability companies, cooperatives, and foreign corporations. (Department of Financial Institutions)

state. The division licenses and monitors the activities of broker-dealers, securities agents, investment advisers, and investment adviser representatives. It conducts field audits and investigates complaints. When violations are detected, it initiates the appropriate administrative, injunctive, or criminal action. The division also regulates corporate takeovers.

History: The Department of Financial Institutions was created in 1995 Wisconsin Act 27. The act reorganized formerly independent offices of the commissioners of banking, savings and loan, and securities as divisions and transferred them to the department. In addition, Act 27 transferred the responsibility for business organization filings and the Uniform Commercial Code lien information filings to the department from the Office of the Secretary of State. The same act transferred the regulation of mortgage bankers and loan originators and solicitors to the department from the Department of Regulation and Licensing.

Banking. For the first five years of statehood, no regular commercial banks existed in Wisconsin. Prior to amendment in 1902, Article XI of the Wisconsin Constitution required that any banking law must be approved in a statewide referendum. Bank regulation began when the legislature created the Office of Bank Comptroller in Chapter 479, Laws of 1852, and the voters approved the law in 1853. That law allowed any group meeting state requirements to go into the banking business. It was designed primarily to regulate the issuance of bank notes. Bank supervision was transferred to the state treasurer in 1868 and remained with that office until 1903.

The 1902 constitutional amendment gave the legislature the power to enact general banking laws without a referendum. In Chapter 234, Laws of 1903, the legislature created the State Banking Department. The department also supervised savings and loan associations until 1947 and credit unions until 1972. Under the 1967 executive branch reorganization, the department continued as an independent agency and was renamed the Office of the Commissioner of Banking. 1995

Wisconsin Act 27 reorganized the agency as the Division of Banking and transferred it to the Department of Financial Institutions.

Savings Institutions. Attempts to register and examine savings and loan associations date back to the 1850s in Wisconsin, but there are no records of any associations incorporating under these laws. In 1876, the legislature passed Chapter 384 to require that savings banks and savings societies register with the county registers of deeds and the secretary of state. Voters approved the law in November 1876. Several associations incorporated shortly afterward. Beginning with Chapter 368, Laws of 1897, building and loan associations were regulated by the bank examiner in the state treasurer's office.

In 1903, responsibility for regulating savings and loan associations was transferred to the State Banking Department. Chapter 411, Laws of 1947, moved regulation from that department to the newly created Savings and Loan Association Department. The law also created the forerunner of the current Savings Institutions Review Board. In 1967, the executive branch reorganization act renamed the department the Office of the Commissioner of Savings and Loan. In 1991 Wisconsin Act 221, the office assumed responsibility for chartering, regulating, and examining savings banks. The same law created the Savings Bank Review Board. 1995 Wisconsin Act 27 reorganized the agency as the Division of Savings and Loan and transferred it to the Department of Financial Institutions. It was renamed the Division of Savings Institutions in 1999 and repealed in 2003 Wisconsin Act 33. Its duties were transferred to the Division of Banking.

Securities. Laws enacted by states to protect the public against securities fraud are commonly referred to as "blue sky" laws. (The term "blue sky" is believed to have originated when a judge ruled that a particular stock had about the same value as a patch of blue sky.) Wisconsin's first "blue sky" law was Chapter 756, Laws of 1913. This law was revised successively in 1919, 1933, 1941, and 1969. The current Wisconsin Uniform Securities Law was enacted as Chapter 71, Laws of 1969, and it is based upon the model Uniform Securities Act, which has been adopted in most states. From 1913 until 1939, the regulation of securities came under the jurisdiction first of the Railroad Commission (and its successor the Public Service Commission) and later the State Banking Department. The Department of Securities was created by Chapter 68, Laws of 1939, to regulate the sale of stocks, bonds, and other forms of business ownership or debt. It was renamed the Office of the Commissioner of Securities by Chapter 75, Laws of 1967. 1995 Wisconsin Act 27, reorganized the agency as the Division of Securities and transferred it to the Department of Financial Institutions.

Statutory Boards and Council

Banking Review Board: DOUGLAS L. FARMER, DEBRA R. LINS, CHRISTINE A. NEUMANN, THOMAS E. SPITZ, RALPH J. TENUTA (appointed by governor with senate consent).

The 5-member Banking Review Board advises the Division of Banking regarding the banking industry in Wisconsin and reviews the division's administrative actions. Members are appointed for staggered 5-year terms, and at least 3 of them must each have at least 5 years' banking experience. No member may act in any matter involving a bank of which the member is an officer, director, or stockholder or to which that person is indebted. The board was created by Chapter 10, Laws of Special Session 1931-32, under the State Banking Department (renamed the Office of the Commissioner of Banking in 1967), and transferred to the Department of Financial Institutions by 1995 Wisconsin Act 27. Its composition and duties are prescribed in Sections 15.185 (1) and 220.035 of the statutes.

Loan Originator Review Council: BRIAN FAUST, STEVE JACOBSON, RICHARD PARINS (loan originators); DIRK TODD (mortgage broker agent); MARIE JONES (mortgage banker agent); vacancy (loan solicitor) (all appointed by secretary of financial institutions); KATHRYN CARLSON (designated by secretary of financial institutions).

The 7-member Loan Originator Review Council approves examination standards in the law of mortgage banking and brokering proposed by the Division of Banking for applicants who either register or renew a certificate of registration as loan originators and loan solicitors. The council also approves the standards of curriculum for required course work taken by loan originators and loan solicitors that covers primary and subordinate mortgage finance transactions. The appointed members serve 4-year terms. The council was created in 2003 Wisconsin Act 260 and its composition and duties are prescribed in Sections 15.187 (1), 224.72 (3)(b), (7)(d), and 224.79 of the statutes.

Savings Institutions Review Board: PAUL C. ADAMSKI, GEORGE E. GARY, ROBERT W. HOLMES, JAMES OLSON, DOUGLAS J. TIMMERMAN (appointed by governor with senate consent).

The 5-member Savings Institutions Review Board advises the Division of Banking on matters impacting savings and loan associations and savings banks in Wisconsin. It reviews division orders and determinations, hears appeals on certain actions taken by the division, and may act on any matter submitted by the division. Members serve 5-year terms. At least 3 of them must each have a minimum of 5 years' experience in the savings and loan or savings bank business in this state. Chapter 441, Laws of 1974, created the board as the Savings and Loan Review Board in the Savings and Loan Association Department (renamed the Office of the Commissioner of Savings and Loan in 1967) and 1995 Wisconsin Act 27 transferred it to the Department of Financial Institutions. In 2003, Act 33 renamed the board and eliminated the Savings Bank Review Board. Its composition and duties are prescribed in Sections 15.185 (3) and 215.04 of the statutes.

INDEPENDENT UNIT ATTACHED FOR BUDGETING, PROGRAM COORDINATION, AND RELATED MANAGEMENT FUNCTIONS BY SECTION 15.03 OF THE STATUTES

OFFICE OF CREDIT UNIONS

Director: SUZANNE COWAN, 267-2609, Fax: 267-0479.

Mailing Address: P.O. Box 14137, Madison 53708-0137.

Location: 345 West Washington Avenue, 3rd Floor, Madison.

Telephone: 261-9543.

Fax: 267-0479.

Internet Address: http://www.wdfi.org

Publications: Annual Report on Condition of Credit Unions, Financial Information Bulletin (semiannual).

Number of Employees: 20.00.

Total Budget 2003-05: $3,615,500.

Statutory References: Section 15.185 (7) (a); Chapter 186.

Agency Responsibility: The Office of Credit Unions regulates credit unions chartered to do business in Wisconsin. It charters new credit unions, examines credit union records and assets, consents to consolidation of credit unions within the state and, in cooperation with similar agencies in neighboring states, approves interstate mergers. If a credit union is not in compliance with state law, the office may remove its officers, suspend operations, or take possession of the credit union's business. The director is appointed by the governor and must have at least 3 years' experience either in the operation of a credit union or in a credit union supervisory agency or a combination of both. All personnel and budget requests by the office must be processed and forwarded without change by the department, unless the office requests or concurs in a change.

History: Regulation of credit unions began in 1913 (Chapter 733) when the legislature passed a law that required "cooperative credit associations" to obtain their charters from the State Banking Department. That law was repealed by Chapter 334, Laws of 1923, which required the department to charter and regulate "credit unions". The Office of the Commissioner of Credit Unions was created in Chapter 193, Laws of 1971, as a separate agency by removing the credit union division and its advisory board from the Office of the Commissioner of Banking and giving it expanded powers. 1995 Wisconsin Act 27 created the Office of Credit Unions and attached it to the Department of Financial Institutions under Section 15.03, Wisconsin Statutes.

Statutory Board

Credit Union Review Board: CARLA L. ALTEPETER, QUIRIN E. BRAAM, DENNIS DEGENHARDT, LISA M. GRECO, DENNIS L. LOMBARD (appointed by governor with senate consent).

The 5-member Credit Union Review Board advises the Office of Credit Unions regarding credit unions in Wisconsin. It reviews rules and regulations issued by the office, acts as an appeals board for persons aggrieved by any act of the office, and may require the office to submit its actions for approval. Members serve staggered 5-year terms and each must have at least 5 years' experience in credit union operations. The board was created within the State Banking Department by Chapter 411, Laws of 1947, then transferred to the Office of the Commissioner of Credit Unions in 1971, and later made part of the Office of Credit Unions in 1995 Wisconsin Act 27. Its composition and duties are prescribed in Sections 15.185 (7) (b) and 186.015 of the statutes.

Department of
HEALTH AND FAMILY SERVICES

Secretary of Health and Family Services: HELENE NELSON, 266-9622.

Deputy Secretary: ROBERTA HARRIS, 266-9622, harrira@

Executive Assistant: JASON HELGERSON, 266-9622, helgeja@

Chief Legal Counsel: DIANE WELSH, 266-8428, welshdm@

Legislative Liaison: RON HERMES, 266-9622, hermer@

Public Information: STEPHANIE MARQUIS, 266-9622, marquis@

Strategic Finance, Office of: FREDI ELLEN BOVE, *director,* 266-2907, bovefe@; Fax: 267-0358.

   Area Administration Section: DIANE WALLER, *director,* 267-8929, wallejd@

   Budget Section: ANDREW FORSAITH, *director,* 266-7684, forsaac@

   Program Evaluation Section: PATRICK W. COOPER, *director,* 267-2846, coopepw@

   Tribal Affairs Section: JAMES WEBER, *director,* 267-5068, weberja@

Mailing Address: P.O. Box 7850, Madison 53707-7850.

Location: Wilson Street State Human Services Building, 1 West Wilson Street, Madison.

Telephone: 266-9622.

Internet Address: http://www.dhfs.state.wi.us or http://dhfs.wisconsin.gov

Publications: Annual fiscal reports; Biennial reports; Reports and informational brochures (available through divisions).

Number of Employees: 6,210.85.

Total Budget 2003-05: $12,435,439,500.

Statutory References: Section 15.19; Chapter 46.

Address e-mail by combining the user ID and the state extender: userid@dhfs.state.wi.us

Children and Family Services, Division of: BURNEATTA BRIDGE, *administrator,* 267-3905, bridgB@; WILLIAM FISS, *deputy administrator,* 266-3728, fisswr@; P.O. Box 8916, Madison 53708-8916, Fax: 266-6836.

   Milwaukee Child Welfare, Bureau of: DENISE REVELS-ROBINSON, *director,* (414) 220-7029, reveldr@

   Program Evaluation and Planning, Bureau of: JOHN TUOHY, *director,* 267-3832, tuohyjo@

   Programs and Policies, Bureau of: MARK CAMPBELL, *director,* 266-6799, campbmd@

   Regulation and Licensing, Bureau of: JILL CHASE, *director,* 267-7933, chasejd@

Disability and Elder Services, Division of: SINIKKA SANTALA, *administrator,* 266-0554, santass@

   Client Rights Office: JIM YEADON, *director,* 266-5525, yeadojd@

   Operations, Office of: RITA PRIGIONI, *director,* 266-8472, prigire@

   Quality Assurance, Bureau of: CRIS ROS DUKLER, *director,* 267-7185, rosducs@; Milwaukee office: 819 North Sixth Street, 53203, (414) 227-5000.

DEPARTMENT OF HEALTH AND FAMILY SERVICES

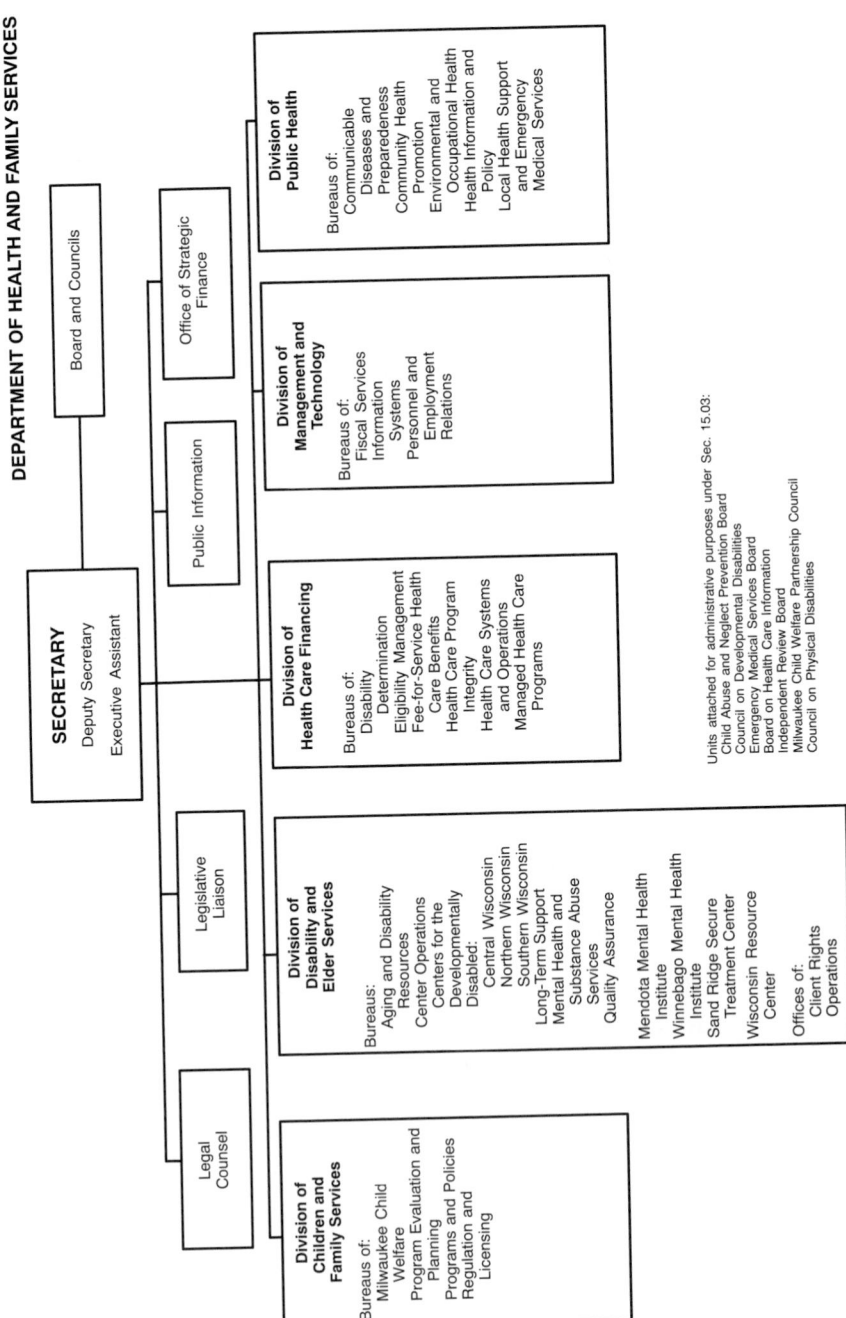

SECRETARY
Deputy Secretary
Executive Assistant

Board and Councils

Office of Strategic Finance

Public Information

Legislative Liaison

Legal Counsel

Division of Public Health

Bureaus of:
Communicable Diseases and Preparedeness
Community Health Promotion
Environmental and Occupational Health
Health Information and Policy
Local Health Support and Emergency Medical Services

Division of Management and Technology

Bureaus of:
Fiscal Services
Information Systems
Personnel and Employment Relations

Division of Health Care Financing

Bureaus of:
Disability Determination
Eligibility Management
Fee-for-Service Health Care Benefits
Health Care Program Integrity
Health Care Systems and Operations
Managed Health Care Programs

Division of Disability and Elder Services

Bureaus:
Aging and Disability Resources
Center Operations
Centers for the Developmentally Disabled:
Central Wisconsin
Northern Wisconsin
Southern Wisconsin
Long-Term Support
Mental Health and Substance Abuse Services
Quality Assurance

Mendota Mental Health Institute
Winnebago Mental Health Institute
Sand Ridge Secure Treatment Center
Wisconsin Resource Center

Offices of:
Client Rights
Operations

Division of Children and Family Services

Bureaus of:
Milwaukee Child Welfare
Program Evaluation and Planning
Programs and Policies
Regulation and Licensing

Units attached for administrative purposes under Sec. 15.03:
Child Abuse and Neglect Prevention Board
Council on Developmental Disabilities
Emergency Medical Services Board
Board on Health Care Information
Independent Review Board
Milwaukee Child Welfare Partnership Council
Council on Physical Disabilities

Long-Term Support: associate division administrator for: JUDITH FRYE, 266-5156, fryeje@

Supplemental Security Income: KATHLEEN LUEDTKE, 266-6890, luedtka@

Aging and Disability Resources, Bureau of: DONNA McDOWELL, *director,* 266-3840, mcdowdb@

Blind and Visually Impaired, Office of: LINDA HUFFER, *director,* 266-5651, huffell@

Deaf and Hard of Hearing, Office of: MICHAEL NELIPOVICH, *director,* 266-3109, nelipmi@

Center Operations, Bureau of: THEODORE BUNCK, *director,* 301-9200, buncktj@

Central Wisconsin Center for the Developmentally Disabled: THEODORE BUNCK, *director,* 317 Knutson Drive, Madison 53704-1197, 301-9200, Fax: 301-1390, buncktj@

Northern Wisconsin Center for the Developmentally Disabled: JACQUELINE RUEDEN, *interim director,* 2820 East Park Avenue, P.O. Box 340, Chippewa Falls 54729-0340, (715) 723-5542, Fax: (715) 723-5841, ruedejt@

Southern Wisconsin Center for the Developmentally Disabled: JAMES HUTCHINSON, *director,* 2415 Spring Street, P.O. Box 100, Union Grove 53182-0100, (262) 878-2411, Fax: (262) 878-2922, hutchje@

Long-Term Support, Bureau of: CHUCK WILHELM, *director,* 266-8402, wilheca@

Mental Health and Substance Abuse Services, associate division administrator for: JOHN EASTERDAY, 267-9391, eastejt@

Mental Health and Substance Abuse Services, Bureau of: JOYCE ALLEN, *director,* 266-1351, allenj@

Mendota Mental Health Institute: GREGORY VAN RYBROEK, *director,* 301 Troy Drive, Madison 53704-1599, 301-1000, Fax: 301-1390, vanrygj@

Winnebago Mental Health Institute: JOANN O'CONNOR, *director,* P.O. Box 9, Winnebago 54985-0009, (920) 235-4910, Fax: (920) 237-2043, oconnjb@

Sand Ridge Secure Treatment Center: STEVEN WATTERS, *director,* 1111 North Road, Mauston 53948, (608) 847-4438, Fax: (608) 847-1790, wattesj@

Wisconsin Resource Center: BYRAN BARTOW, *director,* 1505 North Street, P.O. Box 16, Winnebago 54985-0016, (920) 426-4310, Fax: (920) 231-6353, bartobd@

Health Care Financing, Division of: MARK B. MOODY, *administrator,* 266-8922, moodymb@; CHERYL McILQUHAM, *deputy administrator,* 266-8922, mcilqcj@; P.O. Box 309, Madison 53701-0309, Fax: 266-6786.

Disability Determination, Bureau of: JUDITH FRYBACK, *director,* 266-1981, frybajc@

Eligibility Managment, Bureau of: vacancy, *director,* 261-6877.

Fee-for-Service Health Care Benefits, Bureau of: JAMES VAVRA, *director,* 261-7838, vavrajj@

Health Care Program Integrity, Bureau of: ALAN WHITE, *director,* 266-7436, whiteas@

Health Care Systems and Operations, Bureau of: KEN DYBEVIK, *director,* 267-7118, dybevkk@

Managed Health Care Programs, Bureau of: ANGELA DOMBROWICKI, *director,* 266-1935, dombra@

Management and Technology, Division of: SUSAN REINARDY, *administrator,* 267-7142, reinasj@; P.O. Box 7850, Madison 53707-7850; Fax: 267-6749.

Fiscal Services, Bureau of: DONALD N. WARNKE, *director,* 266-5869, warnkdn@

Information Systems, Bureau of: DENISE WEBB, *director,* 266-0123, webbdb@

Personnel and Employment Relations, Bureau of: CHERYL L. ANDERSON, *director,* 266-9862, andercl@

Public Health, Division of: SHERI JOHNSON, *administrator and State Health Officer,* 267-7828, johnssl@; HERB BOSTROM, *deputy administrator,* 266-9780, bostrhh@; P.O. Box 2659, Madison 53701-2659, Fax: 267-2832, TTY: 266-1511.

Communicable Diseases and Preparedness, Bureau of: AKAN UKOENINN, *director,* 267-9003, ukoena@

Community Health Promotion, Bureau of: MILLIE JONES, *director,* 266-2684, jonesmj@

Environmental and Occupational Health, Bureau of: THOMAS SIEGER, *director,* 264-9880, siegetl@

Health Information and Policy, Bureau of: SUSAN S. WOOD, *director,* 261-4958, woodss@

Local Health Support and Emergency Medical Services, Bureau of: MARGARET TAYLOR, *director,* 266-8154, taylome@

Agency Responsibility: The Department of Health and Family Services administers a wide range of services to clients in the community and at state institutions, regulates certain care providers, and supervises and consults with local public and voluntary agencies. Its responsibilities span public health, mental health, substance abuse, long-term care, services to people who have a disability, medical assistance, and children's services.

Organization: The department is administered by a secretary who is appointed by the governor with the advice and consent of the senate. The secretary appoints the division administrators from outside the classified service.

Unit Functions: The *Office of Strategic Finance*, located within the secretary's office, provides departmental planning, budgeting, and evaluation services. It oversees the department's regional offices. It is also responsible for administration of department contracts and oversight of county and Native American tribal human service programs. The director of strategic finance is appointed by the secretary from the classified service.

The *Division of Children and Family Services* administers programs to preserve and strengthen families, and prevent child abuse and neglect, domestic abuse, substance abuse, and teen pregnancy. It provides statewide oversight of county child welfare services and regulates and licenses child welfare institutions, as well as individuals and organizations providing foster care and day care. In 1998, it assumed responsibility for operating Milwaukee County's child welfare system. It searches for homes for special needs adoptions and hard to place children and is responsible for the state adoption records search program. The division administers hunger prevention programs.

The *Division of Disability and Elder Services* administers a variety of programs that provide long-term support for the elderly and people with disabilities, and mental health and substance abuse treatment. It oversees adult day care programs, and licenses and regulates hospitals, nursing homes, home health agencies, and community-based residential facilities. It performs caregiver background checks and investigations. The division is responsible for client rights reviews and investigations at the institutions and in the community. It also administers the state's institutional programs for persons whose mental and physical needs cannot be met in a community setting. The institutions provide medical, psychological, social, and rehabilitative services. The two mental health institutes provide treatment for persons with mental health problems who are in need of hospitalization. Mendota Mental Health Institute houses a secure correctional facility to meet the mental health needs of male adolescents from Department of Corrections juvenile institutions. The division operates the Wisconsin Resource Center as a medium security facility for mentally ill prison inmates whose treatment needs cannot be met in the Department of Corrections. It also provides treatment at the Sand Ridge Secure Treatment Center for individuals civilly committed under the sexually violent persons law, and persons placed on supervised release and community notification. The division provides staff services to the Council on Developmental Disabilities and the Statewide Independent Living Council.

The *Division of Health Care Financing* administers programs that provide assistance to persons who are impoverished, aged, or disabled, including Medical Assistance and food stamps. It performs disability determinations for Supplemental Security Income (SSI), Social Security disability benefits, and Medical Assistance. It administers BadgerCare, which provides health insurance to low-income working families, SeniorCare, which is a prescription drug assistance program for seniors, and the Health Insurance Risk-Sharing Plan (HIRSP), which is designed to offer affordable health insurance to persons whose coverage has been cancelled, rejected, or substantially reduced or who have had a sizeable increase in premiums. It oversees managed health care programs and the purchase of health care for individuals who are impoverished and without insurance.

The *Division of Management and Technology* oversees financial management, information systems and technology, personnel and employment relations, affirmative action and civil rights compliance, purchasing, facilities management, and other administrative services. It handles billing and collection of client debts and bills Medical Assistance and Medicare claims to the federal government.

The *Division of Public Health* promotes and protects public health in Wisconsin through various services and regulations. It administers programs for chronic and communicable disease prevention and control, environmental and occupational health, emergency medical services, and programs relating to maternal and child health, including the Women, Infants and Children (WIC) Supplemental Food Program. It licenses emergency medical service providers and technicians and approves and supervises their training. The division is also responsible for inspecting restaurants, hotels and motels, bed and breakfast establishments, camps and campgrounds, food vending, and swimming pools. The division performs vital record keeping functions that include providing birth, death, marriage, and divorce certificates and gathering and publishing vital statistics. It also is responsible for the collection, analysis, and dissemination of public health care information.

History: The Department of Health and Family Services combines supervision of many state and local functions that had developed separately in the 1800s. For more than two decades after statehood, Wisconsin created separate governing boards and institutions for the care of prisoners; juveniles; and blind, deaf, and mentally ill persons. By 1871, there were six such institutions. The first attempt to institute overall supervision of these services came when the legislature passed Chapter 136, Laws of 1871, creating the State Board of Charities and Reform. Its duties included examination of the operations of state institutions and their boards and investigation of practices in local asylums, jails, and schools for the blind and deaf.

In Chapter 298, Laws of 1881, the legislature abolished the separate institutional boards and combined their functions under the State Board of Supervision of Wisconsin Charitable, Reformatory and Penal Institutions. The State Board of Charities and Reform continued to operate until 1891. In that year, the two boards were combined as the State Board of Control of the Wisconsin Reformatory, Charitable and Penal Institutions in Chapter 221, Laws of 1891, thus completing the consolidation of public welfare activities.

In the early days of statehood, public health was primarily a function of local governments. In Chapter 366, Laws of 1876, the legislature established the State Board of Health to "study the vital statistics of this state, and endeavor to make intelligent and profitable use of the collected records of death and sickness among the people." The board was directed to "make sanitary investigations and inquiries respecting the causes of disease, and especially of epidemics; the causes of mortality, and the effects of localities, employments, conditions, ingesta, habits and circumstances on the health of the people." This directive defines much of the work still done in public health. Later legislation required the board to take responsibility for tuberculosis care (1905), to direct its efforts toward preventing blindness in infants (1909), and to inspect water and sewerage systems to prevent typhoid and dysentery (1919). In addition, at various times, the board licensed restaurants, health facilities, barbers, embalmers, and funeral directors.

By the time the federal government entered the field of public welfare during the Great Depression of the 1930s, Wisconsin had already pioneered a number of programs, including aid to children and pensions for the elderly (enacted in 1931). The Wisconsin Children's Code, enacted by Chapter 439, Laws of 1929, was one of the most comprehensive in the nation. The state's initial response to federal funding was to establish separate departments to administer social security funds and other public welfare programs. After several attempts at reorganization and a series of studies, the legislature established the State Department of Public Welfare in Chapter 435, Laws of 1939, to provide unified administration of all existing welfare functions. Public health and care for the aged were delegated to separate agencies.

The executive branch reorganization act of 1967 created the Department of Health and Social Services. The Board of Health and Social Services, appointed by the governor, directed the new department and appointed the departmental secretary to administer the agency. In addition to combining public welfare, public health, and care for the aged in the reorganization act, the 1967 Legislature added the Division of Vocational Rehabilitation in Chapter 43. In Chapter 39, Laws of 1975, the legislature abolished the board and replaced it with a secretary appointed by the governor with the advice and consent of the senate. That same law called for a reorganization of the department, which was completed by July 1977. The Department of Health and Social Services was renamed the Department of Health and Family Services (DHFS), effective July 1, 1996.

The decades of the 1960s and 1970s saw an expansion of public welfare and health services at both the federal and state levels. Especially notable were programs for medical care for the needy and aged (Medical Assistance and Medicare), drug treatment programs, food stamps, Aid to Families with Dependent Children Program (AFDC), and increased regulation of hospitals and nursing homes.

While continuing to administer its established programs, the department was assigned additional duties during the 1980s in the areas of child support, child abuse and neglect, programs for the handicapped, and welfare reform. However, 1989 Wisconsin Acts 31 and 107 created a separate Department of Corrections to administer adult corrections institutions and programs, and 1995 Wisconsin Act 27 transferred responsibility for juvenile offenders to that department.

1995 Wisconsin Act 27 revised AFDC and transferred it and other income support programs including Medical Assistance eligibility and food stamps to the Department of Workforce Development (DWD). (Wisconsin Works, known as W-2, replaced AFDC in 1995 Wisconsin Act 289.) Existing welfare reform programs, including Job Opportunities and Basic Skills (JOBS), Learnfare, Parental Responsibility, and Work-Not-Welfare, were also transferred to DWD, along with child and spousal support, the Children First Program, Older American Community Service Employment, refugee assistance programs, and vocational rehabilitation functions. Health care facilities plan review was transferred from the Department of Industry, Labor and Human Relations to DHFS by 1995 Wisconsin Act 27. Act 27 also transferred laboratory certification to the Department of Agriculture, Trade and Consumer Protection and low-income energy assistance to the Department of Administration.

As a result of 1995 Wisconsin Act 303, the department assumed responsibility for direct administration and operation of Milwaukee County child welfare services. Primary responsibility for the Health Insurance Risk-Sharing Program (HIRSP) was transferred to the department from the Office of the Commissioner of Insurance by 1997 Wisconsin Act 27. 2001 Wisconsin Act 16 transferred the Medical Assistance Eligibility Program and the Food Stamp Program to DHFS from the Department of Workforce Development.

Three century-old rail tunnels are highlights of a bicycle journey along the Elroy-Sparta Trail, the nation's first rails-to-trails conversion. (Department of Tourism)

Statutory Board and Councils

Birth Defect Prevention and Surveillance, Council on: RICHARD PAULI (UW Medical School representative), WILLIAM RHEAD (Medical College of Wisconsin representative), EVELYN BROWN (pediatric nurse representative), PEGGY HELM-QUEST (children with special health care needs program representative), MORGAN GROVES (early intervention services program representative), SANDRA PARK (bureau of health information and policy representative), PHILIP GIAMPIETRO (State Medical Society representative), BARBARA PINEKENSTEIN (Wisconsin Health and Hospital Association representative), NELLEEN NOACK (Wisconsin Chapter, American Academy of Pediatrics representative), RAYMOND KESSEL (Council on Developmental Disabilities representative), JOHNNA SCOTT (nonprofit organization representative), LINDA ROWLEY (parent/guardian of children with birth defect), DEBBIE STEIN (local health department representative). (All appointed by secretary of health and family services.)

The Council on Birth Defect Prevention and Surveillance makes recommendations to the department regarding the adminstration of the Wisconsin Birth Defects Registry. The registry documents diagnoses and counts the number of birth defects for children up to age two. The council advises what birth defects are to be reported; the content, format, and procedures for reporting; and the contents of the aggregated reports. Members are appointed to 4-year terms. The UW Medical School and Medical College of Wisconsin, Inc. representatives must have expertise in birth defects epidemiology. Nurse representatives must specialize in pediatrics or have expertise in birth defects. The program representatives are from the appropriate subunits in the department. The nonprofit representative must be from an organization whose primary purpose is birth defect prevention and which does not promote abortion as a method of prevention. The council was created by 1999 Wisconsin Act 114. Its duties and composition are prescribed in Sections 15.197 (12) and 253.12 (4) of the statutes.

Blindness, Council on: RHONDA STAATS, *chairperson;* EDWARD WEISS, *vice chairperson;* WILLIAM HYDE, *secretary;* JEAN BRENAMAN, MICHAEL DUKIN, MARY GLINIECKI, V.K. HANSEN, PHILIP TAUGHER, REBECCA WILLIAMS (appointed by secretary of health and family services).

The 9-member Council on Blindness makes recommendations to the department and other state agencies on policies, procedures, services, programs, and research that affect blind or visually impaired people. Members are appointed by the secretary for staggered 3-year terms, and 7 of them must be blind or visually impaired. Originally, the council was created by Chapter 305, Laws of 1947, as the Advisory Committee of the Blind to advise the Board of Public Welfare and the State Superintendent of Public Instruction. The current council was created in the Department of Health and Social Services by Chapter 366, Laws of 1969. Its composition and duties are prescribed in Sections 15.197 (2) and 47.03 (9) of the statutes.

Deaf and Hard of Hearing, Council for the: JANICE LICHTER, *chairperson;* DIANE MCMAHON, *vice chairperson;* KATHRYN DUNN, BRIAN FRUITS, BILLY MAULDIN, ALEX SLAPPEY, JULIE SPRINGER, 2 vacancies (appointed by governor).

The 9-member Council for the Deaf and Hard of Hearing advises the department on the provision of effective services to deaf, hard-of-hearing, late-deafened, and deaf-blind people. Members are appointed for staggered 4-year terms. The council was created by Chapter 34, Laws of 1979, as the Council for the Hearing Impaired and renamed by 1995 Wisconsin Act 27. Its duties and composition are prescribed in Sections 15.09 (5) and 15.197 (8) of the statutes.

Domestic Abuse, Council on: L. KEVIN HAMBERGER (public member), ARLINE HILLESTAD (designated by senate minority leader), *cochairpersons;* LISA STEWART-BOETTCHER (designated by assembly speaker), STORMY WALKER (designated by assembly minority leader), vacancy (designated by senate majority leader); GERI HEINZ, DEAN KAUFERT, GENE REDHAIL, MARIANA RODRIGUEZ, RACHEL RODRIGUEZ, KATHIE STOLPMAN, MAI ZONG VUE, GERALD WILKIE. (All are appointed by governor, but those not designated by legislative leadership require senate consent.)

The 13-member Council on Domestic Abuse makes recommendations to the secretary on domestic abuse, reviews grant applications, advises the department and legislature on domestic abuse policy, and, in conjunction with the Judicial Conference, develops forms for filing petitions for domestic abuse restraining orders and injunctions. Members are appointed for staggered

3-year terms. Members designated by legislative leadership do not have to be legislators. The council was created by Chapter 111, Laws of 1979, and its composition and duties are prescribed in Sections 15.197 (16) and 46.95 (3) of the statutes.

Health Insurance Risk-Sharing Plan, Board of Governors of the: MARK MOODY (health and family services secretary designee), *chairperson;* EILEEN MALLOW (insurance commissioner designee); CLAIRE JOHNSON, vacancy (participating nonprofit insurer representatives); JAY FULKERSON, LARRY ZANONI (other participating insurers); MICHELE BACHHUBER (State Medical Society of Wisconsin representative); JOE KACHELSKI (Wisconsin Hospital Association representative); PAUL NANNIS (integrated multidisciplinary health system representative); DIANNE GREENLEY, BILL SMITH, ANNETTE STEBBINS, vacancy (public members). (All, except *ex officio* members, are appointed by the secretary of health and family services.)

The 13-member Board of Governors of the Health Insurance Risk-Sharing Plan approves the program budget and approves contracts with the plan administrator, establishes grievance procedures for HIRSP plan applicants and participants; collects assessments from all insurers; develops and implements a program to publicize the plan; establishes a payment rate for covered expenses; and advises the department on choices for coverage for eligible individuals. The board may also prepare and distribute certificate of eligibility and enrollment instruction forms and may provide for reinsurance of risks incurred by the plan.

The 11 appointed members serve staggered 3-year terms. The secretary of health and family services or a designee serves as chairperson. The 4 public members include one small business representative and one individual who has coverage under the plan. The board was created by Chapter 313, Laws of 1979, in the Office of the Commissioner of Insurance, and was transferred to the Department of Health and Family Services, with modifications in its duties and membership, by 1997 Wisconsin Act 27. Its composition and duties are prescribed in Section 149.15 of the statutes.

Mental Health, Council on: GINGER FOBART, *chairperson;* MICHAEL BACHHUBER, JACKIE BALDWIN, ROSE BORNTRAGER, PAMELA PAULOSKI, JOHN QUAAL (consumers and family members of mental health services); CARMEN CERNA, GAIL McCELLAND, MARTHA RASMUS (representing private organizations or groups concerned with mental health services); ALGERNON FELICE (provider of mental health services); JOHN HUMPHRIES, SINIKKA SANTALA, TIM STELLER, JUDY WILCOX (state and county agencies concerned with mental health services or facilities); vacancy (nominated by secretary of health and family services); RICK HALL, KEVIN KALLAS, LAWRENCE SCHOMER (appointed by secretary of health and family services)

The Council on Mental Health is composed of 15 members required by statutes and an additional 3 nonstatutory members appointed by the secretary of health and family services to comply with federal requirements. The council advises the department, governor, and legislature on mental health programs; provides recommendations on the expenditure of federal mental health block grants; reviews the department's plans for mental health services; and serves as an advocate for the mentally ill. Members are appointed for staggered 3-year terms and must have demonstrated knowledge of mental health problems. At least half of the members must be consumers of mental health services or persons who are not service providers. The council also must include representation from service providers, state and county agencies that provide services, and private organizations interested in mental health. The council was created by 1983 Wisconsin Act 439, and its composition and duties are prescribed in Sections 15.197 (1) and 51.02 of the statutes.

Public Health Council: JOHN BARTKOWSKI, CATHERINE FREY, CORAZON LOTEYRO, DOUGLAS NELSON, THAI VUE, JEANAN YASIRI (consumer representatives); SANDY ANDERSON, LOREN LESHAN, JUNE MUNRO, RICHARD PERRY, ELIZABETH RADUEGE, KURT REED, AYAZ SAMADANI (provider representatives); JOSE AVILA, JAYNE BIELECKI, GARY GILMORE (health professionals educator representatives); BEVAN BAKER, TERRI KRAMOLIS, JULIE WILLEMS VAN DIJK, JOANN WEIDMANN (local health representatives); CHARLES LAROQUE (tribal representative); CHRISTOPHER FISCHER, STEPHEN HARGARTEN (public safety representatives) (nominated by secretary of health and family services and appointed by governor).

The 23-member Public Health Council advises the Department of Health and Family Services, the governor, the legislature, and the public on progress made in the implementation of the department's 10-year public health plan and coordination of responses to public health emergencies.

Members serve 3-year terms and must include representatives of health care consumers, health care providers, health professions educators, local health departments and boards, federally recognized American Indian tribes or bands in this state, public safety agencies, and, if established by the secretary of health and family services, the Public Health Advisory Committee. 2003 Wisconsin Act 186 created the council and its composition and duties are prescribed in Sections 15.197 (13) and 250.07 (1m) of the statutes.

Trauma Advisory Council: RANDOLPH SZLABICK (physician), *chairperson;* STEVE STROMAN (physician), *vice chairperson;* RAYMOND GEORGEN, AIMEN SHAABAN (physicians); CECILE D'HUYVETTER, JOHN FOLSTAD (registered nurses); JAMES AUSTAD (EMS municipal representative); EDWARD MISHEFSKE (EMS); MERRILEE CARLSON, BARBARA LARSON (rural hospital representatives); KAREN BRASEL, JEFF GRIMM (urban hospital representatives); STEVE BANE (EMS Board representative (appointed by secretary of health and family services).

State Trauma Care System Coordinator: MARIANNE PECK, 266-0601, peckme@dhfs.state.wi.us

The 13-member Trauma Advisory Council advises the department on developing and implementing a statewide trauma care system. Membership must include physicians, registered nurses, prehospital emergency medical service providers, urban and rural hospital personnel, and the medical services board. They must represent "all geographical areas of the state". Physician appointees must represent urban and rural areas, and one of the prehospital emergency medical service providers must represent a municipality. The council was created by 1997 Wisconsin Act 154 and its composition and duties are prescribed in Sections 15.197 (25) and 146.56 (1) of the statutes.

INDEPENDENT UNITS ATTACHED FOR BUDGETING, PROGRAM COORDINATION, AND RELATED MANAGEMENT FUNCTIONS BY SECTION 15.03 OF THE STATUTES

CHILD ABUSE AND NEGLECT PREVENTION BOARD

Members: NIC DIBBLE (designated by superintendent of public instruction), *chairperson;* SENATOR ROESSLER (appointed by senate president), SENATOR WIRCH (appointed by senate minority leader); REPRESENTATIVE KESTELL (appointed by assembly speaker), REPRESENTATIVE MILLER (appointed by assembly minority leader); ALYSSA WHITNEY (designated by governor) NANCY J. NUSBAUM (designated by attorney general), KITTY KOCOL (designated by secretary of health and family services); ANNE ARNESON, REGINALD BICHA, ANNETTE M. CRUZ, JORDAN GREENBAUM, ROBERT JAMBOIS, MICHAEL J. LIEN, SANDRA J. MCCORMICK, BRUCE F. PAMPERIN (public members appointed by governor).

Executive Director: MARY ANNE SNYDER, maryanne.snyder@ctf.state.wi.us

Mailing Address: 110 East Main Street, Suite 614, Madison 53703-3316.

Telephone: 266-6871; (866) 640-3936 (toll free).

Fax: 266-3792.

Internet Address: http://wctf.state.wi.us

Publications: Positive Parenting: Tips on Discipline; Child Sexual Abuse Prevention: Tips for Parents; Positive Parenting: Tips on Fathering; Never Shake a Baby!; 2004 Blue Ribbons for KIDS Campaign and Beyond the Blue Ribbon Award; and the Positive Parenting Kit.

Number of Employees: 4.00.

Total Budget 2003-05: $5,452,000.

Statutory References: Sections 15.195 (4) and 48.982.

Agency Responsibility: The 16-member Child Abuse and Neglect Prevention Board administers the Children's Trust Fund and awards grants to community-based programs and family resource centers that prevent child abuse and neglect by strengthening families. The board provides education on prevention and positive parenting through printed materials and informational seminars. It recommends policies to the legislature, governor, and state agencies to protect children and support prevention activities. Funding is derived through charges on duplicate birth certificates, the sale of the "Celebrate Children" special license plate, federal matching funds, and private contributions. In 2001, the board created a nonprofit corporation to raise additional money for the trust fund.

The board's 8 public members serve staggered 3-year terms. The board appoints the executive director and staff from the classified service. It was created by 1983 Wisconsin Act 27.

COUNCIL ON DEVELOPMENTAL DISABILITIES

Members: GERALD BORN (appointed by governor), *chairperson;* vacancy (designated by secretary of workforce development), SINIKKA SANTALA (designated by secretary of health and family services), CAROLYN STANFORD TAYLOR (designated by superintendent of public instruction), DANIEL BIER (designated by UW Waisman Center Director); JEFFREY SPITZER-RESNICK (designated by Wisconsin Coalition for Advocacy); MAUREEN ARCAND, CYNTHIA BENTLEY, KRISTIN BERG, SHU-CHUAN CHENG, JONATHAN DONNELLY, CRAIG FEIDLER, MARI FREDERICK, PATRICIA GOUGÉ, RUTH GULLERUD, BARBARA KATZ, CATHARINE KRIEPS, DENISE MEITNER, SUSAN KAY NUTTER, RAYMOND PAVELKO, ROXANNE PRICE, DANIEL REMICK, LINDA RODRIGUEZ, JACQUELYN WENKMAN, DEANNA YOST, CINDY ZELLNER-EHLERS, vacancy (appointed by governor).

Executive Director: JENNIFER ONDREJKA, ondrejm@dhfs.state.wi.us

Mailing Address and Location: 201 West Washington Avenue, Suite 110, Madison 53703-2796.

Telephone: 266-7826; TTY: 266-6660.

Fax: 267-3906.

Internet Address: http://www.wcdd.org

E-mail Address: help@wcdd.org

Statutory References: Sections 15.09 (1)(a), 15.197 (11n), and 51.437 (14r).

Agency Responsibility: The Council on Developmental Disabilities advises the Department of Health and Family Services, other state agencies, the legislature, and the governor on matters related to developmental disabilities. The statutes do not specify the number of council members, but all who serve are appointed for staggered 4-year terms, must be state residents, represent all geographic areas of the state, and the state's diversity with respect to race and ethnicity. The public members appointed by the governor must include representatives of public and private nonprofit agencies that provide direct services at the local level to persons with developmental disabilities. At least 60% of the council's members must be persons who have developmental disabilities or are the parents or guardians of such individuals, but these members may not be associated with public or private agencies that receive federal funding. The council was created within the department by Chapter 322, Laws of 1971, and made an independent unit by Chapter 29, Laws of 1977.

EMERGENCY MEDICAL SERVICES BOARD

Members: STEVEN D. BANE, *chairperson;* TRACY A. ALDRICH, BRENDA FELLENZ, TROY HAASE, DONALD R. HUNJADI, KENNETH JOHNSON, CAL LINTZ, GLORIA ANN MURAWSKY, TRAVIS TEESCH, GLORIA WALL, vacancy (voting members appointed by governor). *Ex officio* nonvoting members: MARGARET TAYLOR (designated by secretary of health and family services), DONALD HAGEN (designated by secretary of transportation), STEVE TEALE (designated by state director, Technical College System Board), BRUCE GORDON (state medical director for emergency medical services).

Mailing Address: P.O. Box 309, Madison 53701-0309.

Telephone: 261-9437.

Statutory References: Sections 15.195 (8) and 146.55 (3).

Agency Responsibility: The 15-member Emergency Medical Services Board appoints an advisory committee of physicians to advise the department on the selection of the state medical director for emergency medical services and to review that person's performance. It also advises the director on medical issues; reviews emergency medical service statutes and rules concerning the transportation of patients; and recommends changes to the Department of Health and Family Services and the Department of Transportation. The board includes personnel from the appropriate state agencies and related emergency services in its deliberations.

The board includes 11 voting members, appointed for 3-year terms, who must "represent the various geographical areas of the state" and various types of emergency medical service providers. The board, which was created by 1993 Wisconsin Act 16, replaced the Emergency Medical Services Assistance Board, created by 1989 Wisconsin Act 102.

BOARD ON HEALTH CARE INFORMATION

Members: KEVIN HAYDEN (public member), *chairperson;* CRISTOPHER J. QUERAM (public member), *vice chairperson;* CYNTHIA M. CHICKER (medical records administrator), *secretary;* SHERRI HAUSER, vacancy (employer purchasers of health care); PAMELA GRADY (registered nurse), SUSAN L. TURNEY (physician), RONALD L. HARMS (physician nominated by State Medical Society), GLEN E. GRADY, GREGORY BRITTON (hospital representatives); DAVID A. KINDIE (public member). (All are appointed by governor.)

Mailing Address: P.O. Box 309, Madison 53701-0309.

Location: 1 West Wilson Street, Room 372, Madison.

Telephone: 261-4958.

Statutory References: Sections 15.195 (6) and 153.07.

Agency Responsibility: The 11-member Board on Health Care Information advises the Department of Health and Family Services on the collection, analysis, and dissemination of health data. It also approves administrative rules proposed by the department on the subject of health care information.

Members are appointed to 4-year terms. The records administrator must be registered by the American Medical Record Association. The board was created in the Department of Health and Social Services by 1987 Wisconsin Act 399, transferred to the Office of the Commissioner of Insurance by 1993 Wisconsin Act 16, and to the Department of Health and Family Services by 1997 Wisconsin Act 27.

INDEPENDENT REVIEW BOARD

Members: JAY GOLD (privacy expert), *chairperson;* PAUL J. MILLEA (medical ethicist), *vice chairperson;* EILEEN MALLOW (insurance commissioner designee), DAVID R. ZIMMERMAN (statistician/researcher), vacancy (health care purchaser) (all but insurance commissioner or designee appointed by governor).

Mailing Address: P.O. Box 309, Madison 53701-0309.

Telephone: 261-4958.

Statutory References: Sections 15.195 (9) and 153.67.

Agency Responsibility: The 5-member Independent Review Board examines requests for patient data originating with health care providers that are not hospitals or ambulatory surgery centers. Information from these health care providers is released only with board approval unless it is already available from public use files. The department may promulgate rules that specify circumstances under which the board does not have to review data requests. The 4 appointed members serve 4-year terms. The medical ethicist must be from the UW System or the Medical College of Wisconsin, Inc. The board may not include an employee of the Department of Health and Family Services. It was created by 1999 Wisconsin Act 9.

MILWAUKEE CHILD WELFARE PARTNERSHIP COUNCIL

Members: ARCHIE L. IVY, *chairperson;* SENATOR DARLING (appointed by senate president); SENATOR COGGS (appointed by senate minority leader); REPRESENTATIVE STONE (appointed by assembly speaker); REPRESENTATIVE GRIGSBY (appointed by assembly minority leader); TONI CLARK, WILLIE JOHNSON, JR., PEGGY WEST (Milwaukee County board members nominated by Milwaukee County Executive); WANDA MONTGOMERY, vacancy (children's services network nominees); ELISA CASTELLON, LINDA DAVIS, THOMAS DONEGAN, DAVID L. HOFFMAN, MARY HOWARD JOHNSTONE, LEONOR ROSAS, MICHAEL SKWIERAWSKI, ERNESTINE WILLIS, vacancy. (All but legislators are appointed by governor.)

Contact Person: DENISE REVELS-ROBINSON.

Mailing Address: 1555 North Rivercenter Drive, Suite 220, Milwaukee 53212.

Telephone: (414) 220-7029.

Statutory References: Sections 15.197 (24) and 46.023 (2).

Agency Responsibility: The 19-member Milwaukee Child Welfare Partnership Council makes recommendations to the Department of Health and Family Services and the legislature regarding policies and plans to improve the child welfare system in Milwaukee County, including a neighborhood-based system for delivery of services. It may also recommend funding priorities and identify innovative public and private funding opportunities. The 15 nonlegislative members are appointed to 3-year terms, and the governor designates one of the public members as chairperson. At least 6 public members must be residents of Milwaukee County. The council was created by 1995 Wisconsin Act 303.

COUNCIL ON PHYSICAL DISABILITIES

Members: JOR JAN BORLIN, *chairperson;* JEFF FOX, *vice chairperson;* JOANNE ZIMMERMAN, *secretary;* DONNA WONG (designated by governor), MARGE LIBERSKI AZNOE, JON BALTMANIS, CHRISTINE DURANCEAU, PATRICIA LERCH, VIRGINIA LUKKEN, JOHN MEISSNER, KAREN SECOR, JACQUELINE STENBERG, LEWIS TYLER, PAMELA WILSON (all members are appointed by governor).

Contact Person: DAN JOHNSON.

Mailing Address: P.O. Box 7851, Madison 53707-7851.

Location: 1 West Wilson Street, Room 1150, Madison.

Telephones: 266-9582; TTY 267-9880.

Fax: 267-3208.

E-mail Address: johnsdc@dhfs.state.wi.us

Number of Employees: 0.00.

Total Budget 2003-05: $22,100.

Statutory References: Sections 15.197 (4) and 46.29.

Agency Responsibility: The 14-member Council on Physical Disabilities develops and modifies the state plan for services to persons with physical disabilities. It advises the secretary of health and family services, recommends legislation, encourages public understanding of the needs of persons with physical disabilities, and promotes programs to prevent physical disability. The 13 appointed members serve 3-year terms and must be state residents. At least 6 members must be persons with physical disabilities; 2 may be parents, guardians, or relatives of persons with physical disabilities; and at least one must be a service provider. The council must include equitable representation for sex, race, and urban and rural areas. The council was created by 1989 Wisconsin Act 202.

HIGHER EDUCATIONAL AIDS BOARD

Members: STEVEN E. VAN ESS (UW System financial aids administrator), *chairperson;* ANN NEVIASER (independent colleges and universities representative), *vice chairperson;* MARY JO GREEN (Technical College System financial aids administrator), *secretary;* KEVIN INGRAM (designated by superintendent of public instruction); GREGORY GRACZ (UW System Board of Regents member); MARY CUENE (Technical College System Board member); LUKE NAEGELE (UW System student representative); COLLEEN BUNNER (Technical College System student representative); DEBRA E. MCKINNEY (independent colleges and universities financial aid administrator); KHALAF KHALAF (independent colleges and universities student representative); BETTY WOMACK (public member). (All members, except *ex officio* member, are appointed by governor.)

Executive Secretary: CONNIE HUTCHISON, (608) 264-6181, connie.hutchison@heab.state.wi.us

Mailing Address: P.O. Box 7885, Madison 53707-7885.

Location: Suite 902, 131 West Wilson Street, Madison.

Telephone: (608) 267-2206.

Fax: (608) 267-2808.

Agency E-mail: HEABmail@heab.state.wi.us

Internet Address: http://heab.wi.gov

Publications: Biennial report; Report on Financial Aid Programs; various board reports.

Number of Employees: 11.00.

Total Budget 2003-05: $171,026,500.

Statutory References: Section 15.67; Chapter 39, Subchapter III.

Agency Responsibility: The Higher Educational Aids Board is responsible for the management and oversight of the state's student financial aid system for Wisconsin residents attending institutions of higher education. It also enters into interstate agreements and performs student loan collection services.

The board establishes policies for the state's student financial aid programs, including academic excellence scholarships, Wisconsin tuition grants, Wisconsin higher education grants, talent incentive grants, handicapped student grants, Indian student grants, minority student grants (private sector and Technical College System), teacher education loans, minority teacher loans, nursing loans, and interstate reciprocity. It administers the contracts for medical and dental education services and the Wisconsin Health Education Loan Program and approves the participants in the Medical College of Wisconsin, Inc., per capita grant program.

Organization: The 11-member board includes the superintendent of public instruction or designee, 7 members who serve 3-year terms, and 3 student members who serve 2-year terms. The students must be at least 18 years old, residents of this state, enrolled at least half-time, and in good academic standing. The UW and private nonprofit institution students must be undergraduates. The governor appoints the board's executive secretary.

History: The Higher Educational Aids Board originated as the State Commission for Academic Facilities. It was created by Chapter 573, Laws of 1963, to administer Title I of the Federal Higher Education Facilities Act of 1963, which funded grants for university and college building programs in Wisconsin. Chapter 264, Laws of 1965, gave the commission student financial aid responsibilities and changed its name to the State Commission for Higher Educational Aids. Chapter 313, Laws of 1967, authorized the commission to organize the Wisconsin Higher Education Corporation to administer the federal Guaranteed Student Loan Program. The corporation was given an independent board of directors as a private nonstock corporation in 1984. Chapter 276, Laws of 1969, renamed the commission the Higher Educational Aids Board. The Higher Educational Aids Board was inadvertently repealed by 1995 Wisconsin Act 27, but was continued as the Higher Educational Aids Council by Executive Order 283. The legislature recreated the board in 1997 Wisconsin Act 27.

STATE HISTORICAL SOCIETY OF WISCONSIN

Board of Curators: MARK J. GAJEWSKI, *president;* JUDITH NAGEL, *president-elect;* CRAIG C. CULVER, *treasurer;* HELEN LAIRD (designated by governor); REPRESENTATIVE FREESE (designated by assembly speaker); SENATOR SCHULTZ (designated by senate president), SENATOR RISSER, REPRESENTATIVE BERCEAU (minority party members); ELIZABETH ADELMAN, LINDA CLIFFORD, VICTOR E. FERRALL (appointed by governor with senate consent); BETTE AREY, RUTH BARKER, THOMAS H. BARLAND, MURRAY D. BECKFORD, BRUCE T. BLOCK, PATRICIA A. BOGE, MARY F. BUESTRIN, THOMAS CAESTECKER, KENNETH CONGER, WILLIAM J. CRONON, LAURIE DAVIDSON, NESS FLORES, BEVERLY A. HARRINGTON, JOHN O. HOLZHUETER, JOHN E. KERRIGAN, ELLEN D. LANGILL, CORA B. MARRETT, GENEVIEVE G. MCBRIDE, JERRY PHILLIPS, JANICE M. RICE, JOHN M. RUSSELL, JOHN SCHROEDER, KATHLEEN SWEENEY, ANNE WEST, CARLYLE H. WHIPPLE. (Unless otherwise indicated, curators are elected by the membership of the state historical society or serve *ex officio.*)

Board Secretary: ELLSWORTH H. BROWN

Director: ELLSWORTH H. BROWN, 264-6440, ehbrown@

Associate Director: ROBERT B. THOMASGARD, JR., 264-6442, rbthomasgard@

Special Assistant: BETSY B. TRANE, 264-6589, bbtrane@

Public Information: ROBERT L. GRANFLATEN, *coordinator,* 264-6586, rlgranflaten@

| For e-mail combine the user ID and the state extender: userid@**whs.wisc.edu** |

Administrative Services, Division of: DAVID H. SELIGMAN, *administrator,* 264-6434, dhseligman@

   Facility Maintenance: THOMAS F. TODD, *coordinator,* 264-6431, tftodd@

   Financial Services: DAVID H. SELIGMAN, 264-6434, dhseligman@

   Human Resources: ALICE L. JACKSON, *coordinator,* 264-6448, aljackson@

   Information Technology: PAUL E. HEDGES, *coordinator,* 264-6451, pehedges@

Historic Preservation – Public History, Division of: MICHAEL E. STEVENS, *administrator and State Historic Preservation Officer,* 264-6464, mestevens@

   Historic Preservation Section: JAMES R. DRAEGER, *section chief,* 264-6511, jrdraeger@; *state archaeologist:* JOHN H. BROIHAHN, 264-6496, jhbroihahn@

   School and Local Assistance Section: vacancy, *section chief; burial sites preservation coordinator:* LESLIE E. EISENBERG, 264-6503, leeisenberg@

   Society Press: KATHRYN BORKOWSKI, *editorial director and state historian,* 264-6461, klborkowski@

Historic Sites, Division of: ALICIA L. GOEHRING, *administrator,* 264-6515, algoehring@; GREG T. PARKINSON, *deputy administrator,* 264-6581, gtparkinson@

   First Capitol: Highway G, Belmont 53510. Contact: ALLEN L. SCHROEDER, (608) 987-2122, alschroeder@

   H.H. Bennett Studio and History Center: DALE B. WILLIAMS, *site director,* (608) 253-3523; · 215 Broadway, P.O. Box 147, Wisconsin Dells 53965; dbwilliams@

   Madeline Island Historical Museum: La Pointe 54850. Contact: STEVE R. COTHERMAN, *site director,* (715) 747-2415, srcotherman@

   Old Wade House: JEFFREY R. SCHULTZ, *site director,* (920) 526-3271; P.O. Box 34, Greenbush 53026; jrschultz@

   Old World Wisconsin: PETER S. ARNOLD, *site director,* (262) 594-6300; S103 W37890 Highway 67, Eagle 53119; psarnold@

   Pendarvis: ALLEN L. SCHROEDER, *site director,* (608) 987-2122; 114 Shake Rag Street, Mineral Point 53565; alschroeder@

   Stonefield Village: ALLEN L. SCHROEDER, *site director,* (608) 725-5210; P.O. Box 125, Cassville 53806; alschroeder@

   Villa Louis: MICHAEL P. DOUGLASS, *site director,* (608) 326-2721; P.O. Box 65, Prairie du Chien 53821; mpdouglass@

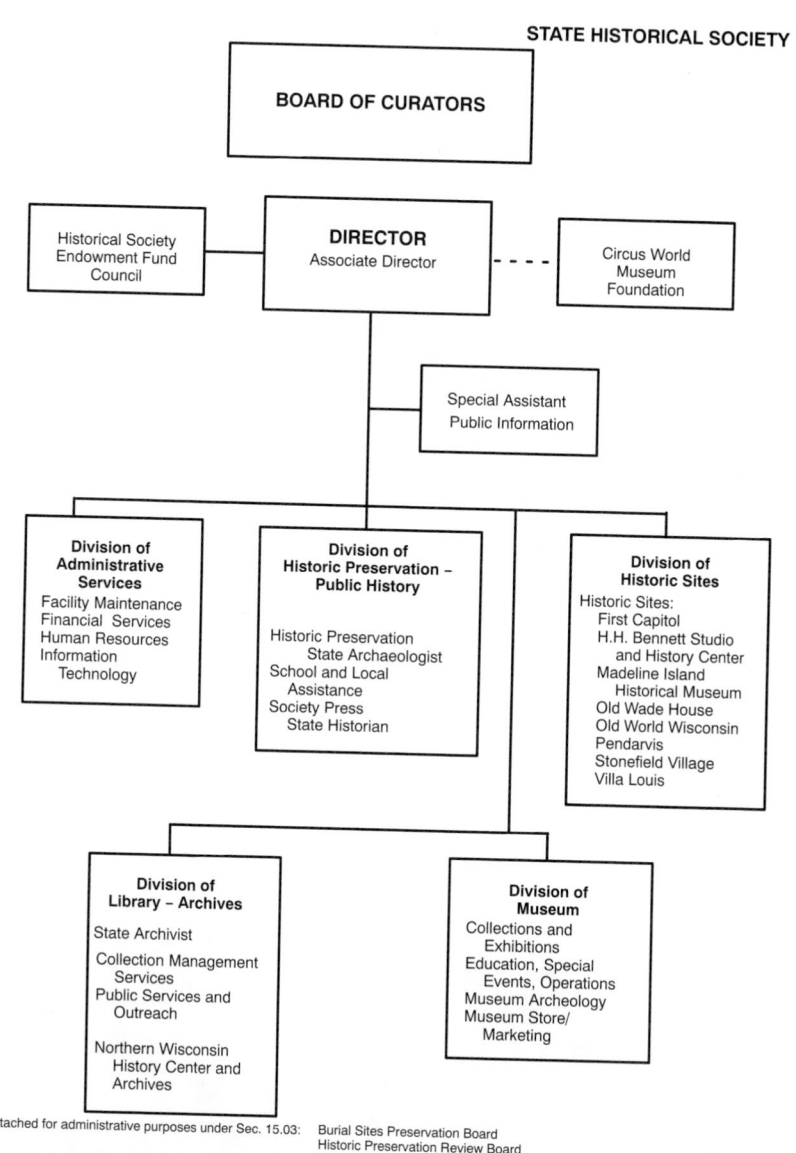

STATE HISTORICAL SOCIETY

BOARD OF CURATORS

Historical Society Endowment Fund Council

DIRECTOR
Associate Director

Circus World Museum Foundation

Special Assistant
Public Information

Division of Administrative Services
Facility Maintenance
Financial Services
Human Resources
Information
Technology

Division of Historic Preservation – Public History

Historic Preservation
State Archaeologist
School and Local
Assistance
Society Press
State Historian

Division of Historic Sites
Historic Sites:
First Capitol
H.H. Bennett Studio
and History Center
Madeline Island
Historical Museum
Old Wade House
Old World Wisconsin
Pendarvis
Stonefield Village
Villa Louis

Division of Library – Archives
State Archivist
Collection Management
Services
Public Services and
Outreach
Northern Wisconsin
History Center and
Archives

Division of Museum
Collections and
Exhibitions
Education, Special
Events, Operations
Museum Archeology
Museum Store/
Marketing

Units attached for administrative purposes under Sec. 15.03: Burial Sites Preservation Board
Historic Preservation Review Board

Library – Archives, Division of: PETER GOTTLIEB, *state archivist,* 264-6480, pgottlieb@; MICHAEL I. EDMONDS, *deputy administrator,* 264-6538, miedmonds@
  Collection Management Services: vacancy, *coordinator,* 264-6456.
  Public Services and Outreach: RICHARD L. PIFER, *coordinator,* 264-6477, rlpifer@
  Northern Wisconsin History Center and Archives at the Northern Great Lakes Visitor Center: LINDA L. MITTLESTADT, *archivist,* (715) 685-9983; 29270 County Highway G, Ashland 54806; llmittlestad@

Museum, Division of: ANN L. KOSKI, *administrator,* 261-9359, alkoski@; JENNIFER L. KOLB, *deputy administrator,* 261-2461, jlkolb@

Collections and Exhibitions: PAUL G. BOURCIER, *chief curator,* 264-6573, pgbourcier@
Education, Special Events, Operations: JENNIFER L. KOLB, *deputy administrator,* 261-2461, jlkolb@
Museum Archeology: KELLY E. HAMILTON, *coordinator,* 264-6560, kehamilton@
Museum Store/Marketing: JOHN W. LEMKE, *store manager,* 264-6550, jwlemke@

Main Information Desk: (608) 264-6400.

Mailing Address: 816 State Street, Madison 53706-1482.

Archives and Library Location: 816 State Street, Madison.

Archives Telephone: 264-6460; Archives Fax: 264-6486; Library Telephone: 264-6534; Library Fax: 264-6520.

Museum Location: 30 North Carroll Street, Madison 53703-2707.

Museum Information: 264-6555; Museum Tours: 264-6557; Museum Fax: 264-6575.

Internet Address: http://www.wisconsinhistory.org

Publications: *Badger History Bulletin; Columns; Exchange; Wisconsin Magazine of History.* The society also publishes books, research guides, and miscellaneous brochures. Recent publications include *Native People of Wisconsin; Wisconsin History Highlights;* and *Third Down and a War to Go: The All-American 1942 Wisconsin Badger.*

Number of Employees: 142.79.

Total Budget 2003-05: $35,834,100.

Statutory References: Section 15.70; Chapter 44, Subchapters I and II.

Agency Responsibility: The mission of the State Historical Society of Wisconsin, known informally as the Wisconsin Historical Society, is to connect people to the past. The society has a statutory duty to collect and preserve historical and cultural resources related to Wisconsin and to make them available to the public. To meet these objectives, the society maintains a major history research collection in Madison and in 14 area research centers; operates a museum, eight his-

Some 350 middle and high school students gathered at the Historical Society's headquarters in Madison to take part in the state finals of National History Day – a year-long program engaging students in a wide range of historical research projects. Forty-five finalists from Wisconsin went on to compete in the national finals at College Park, Maryland. (State Historical Society)

toric sites, an office at the Northern Great Lakes Visitor Center, and statewide school services programs. It owns Circus World Museum, which is managed by Circus World Museum Foundation. It provides public history programming such as National History Day and collaborates with other agencies such as Wisconsin Public Television to deliver history programming to the public. It provides technical services and advice to about 350 affiliated local historical societies throughout the state. It conducts, publishes, and disseminates research on Wisconsin and U.S. history, serves as the state's historic preservation office, which regulates the designation of historic structures and archeological sites by administering the state and national registers of historic places. The society is also responsible for regulation of the state's Burial Sites Preservation Law.

Organization: The state historical society is both a state agency and a membership organization. The society's Board of Curators includes 8 statutory appointments and up to 30 members who are elected according to the society's constitution and bylaws. The 3 members appointed by the governor with senate consent serve staggered 3-year terms. The board selects the society's director, who serves as administrative head and as secretary to the board.

Unit Functions: The *Division of Administrative Services* provides management and program support in the areas of financial services, budgeting, information technology, human resources, purchasing, and facility maintenance of the society's headquarters building.

The *Division of Historic Preservation – Public History* helps make the history of Wisconsin more accessible to state residents and awards historic designations to places of historic value. It administers Wisconsin's portion of the National Register of Historic Places in partnership with the National Park Service and manages the State Register of Historic Places. It nominates places of architectural, historic, and archeological significance to the registers. It reviews federal, state, and local projects for their effect on historic and archeological properties. The division certifies historic building rehabilitation projects for state and federal income tax credits, archeological sites for property tax exemptions, and historic buildings as eligible for the state historic building code. The division administers the historical markers program, identifies and promotes underwater archeological sites, and administers the state's burial sites preservation program. The division edits and publishes most of the materials issued by the society, including books, a bimonthly membership newsletter and a quarterly magazine of history. The division offers instructional materials and programs to schools and teachers to assist them in teaching the history of Wisconsin, coordinates the state's National History Day program, and aids local affiliated historical societies by providing technical assistance.

The *Division of Historic Sites* operates 8 historic sites and outdoor museums: First Capitol, H.H. Bennett Studio and History Center, Madeline Island Historical Museum, Old Wade House, Old World Wisconsin, Pendarvis, Stonefield Village, and Villa Louis. These sites contain historic structures and service buildings that reflect major themes of Wisconsin history, such as ethnic pioneer settlement, mining, farming, fur trade, exploration, transportation, rural life, and town development.

The society owns an additional historic site in Baraboo, Circus World Museum, which is operated independently by the Circus World Museum Foundation. This museum offers an extensive collection of circus memorabilia, unique circus wagons, and it operates a circus in Baraboo during the summer months.

The *Division of Library – Archives* maintains notable collections in Wisconsin and North American history including areas such as genealogy; labor; business and industry; social action, including civil rights, antiwar movements, and reproductive rights issues; mass communications; and dramatic arts, including theater, motion pictures, and television. The library and archives serve as the North American history research collection for the UW-Madison. The library acts as regional depository for U.S. government publications and official depository for Wisconsin state government publications. The archives program acquires, catalogs, preserves, and makes available primary source materials, including manuscripts, maps, newspapers, photographs, sound recordings, films, videos, and other records pertaining to Wisconsin history and selected fields of U.S. history. It serves as the state archives, collecting and providing access to permanent records of state and local government. In partnership with several other institutions, the archives operates 14 Area Research Centers throughout Wisconsin to bring its archival holdings on regional history closer to the public. It also makes available the collections of the Wisconsin Center for Film and Theater Research, which is administered jointly by the society and the UW-Madison.

The *Division of Museum* collects and preserves the material culture of Wisconsin and interprets the state's history and prehistory for the public. It operates the State Historical Museum, supervises the preservation and development of artifact collections, and operates an archeology program under a cooperative agreement with the Department of Transportation and the Department of Natural Resources. The division fulfills its educational role through exhibitions, tours, and a variety of public programs conducted at the museum in Madison and other venues throughout the state.

History: The State Historical Society of Wisconsin was originally founded in 1846 as a private association. It was chartered by the Wisconsin Legislature in Chapter 17, Laws of 1853, which made the society responsible for the preservation and care of all records, articles, and other materials of historic interest to the state. The society has received state funding since 1854 (Chapter 16) – longer than any other state historical society in the nation.

The legislature expanded the state's historic preservation program in Chapter 29, Laws of 1977, by making the society responsible for preservation activities associated with the designation, restoration, and repair of historic properties. Chapter 341, Laws of 1981, provided statutory support for local ordinances designed to preserve historic buildings. It set up a framework for a state historic building code with alternative standards for the preservation or restoration of historic structures. 1987 Wisconsin Act 395 strengthened the state's historic preservation laws by creating the State Register of Historic Places to protect historic and prehistoric properties. This law and 1987 Wisconsin Act 399 provided state tax credits and exemptions for owners of certain historic and archeological properties.

1985 Wisconsin Act 29 formalized the practice of allowing the historical society to enter into a lease agreement with a nonprofit corporation, now called the Circus World Museum Foundation, for the purpose of operating the Circus World Museum.

While in Madison on a book promotion tour, longtime Public Broadcasting System news anchor Robert MacNeil visited the Wisconsin Historical Society archives to review some of his papers, which are included in the Society's mass communications history collections. (State Historical Society)

Statutory Council

Historical Society Endowment Fund Council: Inactive.

The Historical Society Endowment Fund Council advises the state historical society regarding the raising and disbursement of funds used to support the society's historical and cultural preservation services and educational activities. The 10-member council must include representation from the Wisconsin Arts Board, the State Historical Society of Wisconsin, the Wisconsin Academy of Science, Arts and Letters, the Wisconsin Humanities Council, Wisconsin Public Radio and Wisconsin Public Television, and 4 public members, all appointed by the governor. The council was created by 1997 Wisconsin Act 27 and its composition and duties are prescribed in Section 15.707 (3) of the statutes.

INDEPENDENT UNITS ATTACHED FOR BUDGETING, PROGRAM COORDINATION, AND RELATED MANAGEMENT FUNCTIONS BY SECTION 15.03 OF THE STATUTES

BURIAL SITES PRESERVATION BOARD

Burial Sites Preservation Board: ELLSWORTH H. BROWN (state historical society director); ROBERT F. BOSZHARDT, KATHERINE C. EGAN-BRUHY, ROSANNE M. MEER (nominated by Wisconsin Archaeological Survey); DAVID J. GRIGNON, ROBERT D. POWLESS, SR., CLARICE M. RITCHIE (nominated by the Great Lakes Inter-Tribal Council, Inc., and the Menominee Tribe). Nonvoting members: MICHAEL E. STEVENS (state historic preservation officer), JOHN H. BROIHAHN (state archeologist). (All except *ex officio* members are appointed by governor.)

Burial Sites Preservation Program Coordinator: LESLIE E. EISENBERG.

Mailing Address: 816 State Street, Madison 53706-1482.

Telephones: (608) 264-6503; (800) 342-7834 (within Wisconsin).

Statutory References: Section 15.705 (1); Chapter 157, Subchapter III.

Agency Responsibility: The Burial Sites Preservation Board was created to protect all the interests related to human burial sites and to ensure equal treatment and respect for all human burials, regardless of ethnic origin, cultural background, or religious affiliation. The board develops detailed policies to implement the burial sites preservation program; reviews decisions of the director or the administrative hearing examiner concerning applications for permits to disturb cataloged burial sites; and reviews the director's decisions regarding the disposition of human remains and burial objects removed from a burial site. This program was created by 1985 Wisconsin Act 316.

Organization: The 9-member board includes 3 members with professional qualifications in archeology, physical anthropology, or history and 3 members of federally recognized Indian nations in Wisconsin who have a knowledge of tribal preservation planning, history, or archeology or who serve as elders, traditional persons, or spiritual leaders of a tribe. The 6 appointed members serve 3-year terms.

HISTORIC PRESERVATION REVIEW BOARD

Historic Preservation Review Board: DIANE AL SHIHABI, ANNE E. BIEBEL, BRUCE T. BLOCK, ROBERT J. GOUGH, SHAWN K. GRAFF, KELLY S. JACKSON, CAROL McCHESNEY JOHNSON, DAN J. JOYCE, DIANE KEALTY, WILLIAM G. LAATSCH, KUBET LUCHTERHAND, DAVID V. MOLLENHOFF, ROBERT J. SALZER, VALENTINE J. SCHUTE, JR., DANIEL J. STEPHANS (all appointed by governor).

State Historic Preservation Officer: MICHAEL E. STEVENS, 264-6464.

Mailing Address: 816 State Street, Madison 53706-1482.

Telephone: (608) 264-6498.

Statutory References: Section 15.705 (2); Chapter 44, Subchapter II.

Agency Responsibility: The Historic Preservation Review Board approves nominations to the Wisconsin State Register of Historic Places and the National Register of Historic Places upon recommendation of the State Historic Preservation Officer. (By statute, the director of the State Historical Society serves as the state officer or designates someone to do so.) The board approves

A unique photo album from 1912 documenting the construction of noted architect Frank Lloyd Wright's home and studio, Taliesin in Spring Green, was displayed at the State Capitol. In an effort spearheaded by former Historical Society staff editor and current member of the board Jack Holzheuter (seated at left), the historical images were purchased in an online auction earlier that month with over $22,000 in hurriedly raised donations. Also pictured are former Society Visual Materials Archivist George Talbot (center) and Wisconsin Public Television producer Art Hackett. (State Historical Society)

the distribution of federal grants-in-aid for preservation; advises the state historical society; and requests comments from planning departments of affected municipalities, local landmark commissions, and local historical societies regarding properties being considered for nomination to the state and national registers. The board was created by Chapter 29, Laws of 1977.

Organization: The board consists of 15 members appointed by the governor to staggered 3-year terms. At least 9 must be professionally qualified in the areas of architecture, archeology, art history, and history. Up to 6 members may be qualified in related fields, such as landscape architecture, urban and regional planning, law, or real estate.

Office of the Commissioner of
INSURANCE

Commissioner: JORGE GOMEZ, 267-3782, jorge.gomez@

Deputy Commissioner: CLARE STAPLETON CONCORD, 267-1233, clare.stapleton-concord@

Insurance Administrator: EILEEN K. MALLOW, 266-7843, eileen.mallow@

Legal Counsel: FRED NEPPLE, 266-7726, fred.nepple@

Administrative Services, Division of: vacancy, *administrator,* 266-5673; JOHN MONTGOMERY, *deputy administrator,* 264-8113, john.montgomery@

Regulation and Enforcement, Division of: RANDY A. BLUMER, *administrator,* 267-9460, randy.blumer@

 Financial Analysis and Examinations, Bureau of: ROGER PETERSON, *director,* 267-4384, roger.peterson@

 Market Regulation, Bureau of: SUSAN EZALARAB, *director,* 266-8885, sue.ezalarab@

Address e-mail by combining the user ID and the state extender: **userid@oci.state.wi.us**

Mailing Address: P.O. Box 7873, Madison 53707-7873.

Location: 125 South Webster Street, Madison 53702.

Telephones: General: 266-3585; Agent licensing: 266-8699; Insurance complaint hotline: (800) 236-8517; Local Government Property Insurance Fund: (877) 229-0009 (Wisconsin only); State Life Insurance Fund: (800) 562-5558.

Fax: 266-9935.

Internet Address: http://oci.wi.gov

Publications: Annual reports; *Wisconsin Insurance News;* various pamphlets and materials for consumers, insurance companies, and agents. (Contact the Office of the Commissioner of Insurance.)

Number of Employees: 131.00.

Total Budget 2003-05: $203,461,400.

Statutory References: Section 15.73; Chapter 601.

Agency Responsibility: The Office of the Commissioner of Insurance supervises insurance industry practices in Wisconsin. The office examines industry financial practices and market conduct, licenses agents, reviews policy forms for compliance with state legislation, investigates consumer complaints, and provides consumer information. Its goals are to ensure the financial soundness of insurers doing business in Wisconsin; secure fair treatment for policyholders, claimants, and insurers; encourage industry self-regulation; emphasize loss prevention as part of good insurance practice; and educate the public on insurance issues.

The office administers two segregated insurance funds. The State Life Insurance Fund offers up to $10,000 of low-cost life insurance protection to any Wisconsin resident who meets prescribed risk standards. The Local Government Property Insurance Fund provides mandatory coverage for local governments against fire loss, as well as optional coverage for certain property damage or liabilities they may incur.

The agency oversees activities of the Health Care Liability Insurance Plan, which provides liability coverage for hospitals, physicians, and other health care providers in Wisconsin, and the Injured Patients and Families Compensation Fund, which provides medical malpractice coverage for qualified health care providers on claims in excess of a provider's underlying coverage.

Organization: The commissioner of insurance is appointed by the governor with the advice and consent of the senate. The commissioner cannot be a candidate for public office and there are stringent restrictions on the commissioner's political activities. The commissioner appoints the deputy commissioner from outside the classified service and the division administrators from the classified service.

Unit Functions: The *Division of Administrative Services* provides strategic and contingency planning, information technology, budget, human resources, accounting, contracting and procurement, and other support services for the agency.

The *Division of Regulation and Enforcement* conducts field reviews of insurer underwriting, rating, claim handling, and marketing practices. It investigates insurance agent activities, prepares enforcement proceedings, and prosecutes offenders. It helps consumers resolve problems with insurers and agents and carries out the agency's consumer education program. Other duties include review of rates, forms, and contracts filed with the office to ensure their compliance with state law; examination of insurer advertising files; and licensing and testing of insurance intermediaries.

The division conducts field examinations of the financial condition of insurers domiciled in this state and monitors the financial condition of insurers doing business in this state. It oversees insurer rehabilitation and liquidation, and audits and collects insurer taxes and fees. It also administers the fire department dues program in cooperation with the Department of Commerce and the state treasurer, whereby dues paid by insurers who provide fire coverage are disbursed to municipalities for fire protection and the fire fighters' pension and disability funds.

History: State regulation of insurance dates back to 1870 when Chapter 56 created a Department of Insurance in the secretary of state's office to license agents and, upon complaint, examine the books of fire and inland navigation insurance companies. In 1878 (Chapter 214), the legislature created a separate Department of Insurance, headed by a commissioner appointed by the governor, to perform these functions. From 1881 to 1911, based on Chapter 300, Laws of 1881, an elected commissioner administered the insurance department. With the enactment of Chapter 484, Laws of 1911, the insurance commissioner was again made an appointee. The 1967 executive branch reorganization act renamed the department the Office of the Commissioner of Insurance and continued it as an independent regulatory agency.

Other highlights include the development of the standard fire insurance contract in Chapter 195, Laws of 1891, and stricter regulation of the life insurance industry in 1907 to prevent fraud and misrepresentation. In 1911 and 1913, Wisconsin added coverage of local governments' property and buildings under the State Insurance Fund.

Wisconsin became the only state to establish a state life insurance fund for its residents under Chapter 577, Laws of 1911, which authorized the Department of Insurance to issue life insurance and annuity contracts. Since 1947 (Chapters 487 and 521), the office's responsibilities have included the review of all insurance policy forms and the filing of most premium rates. Wisconsin's current insurance laws are largely the result of a recodification developed between 1967 and 1979 by the Legislative Council and they have served as a basis for the model acts adopted by the National Association of Insurance Commissioners (an association of state insurance regulators).

Statutory Boards and Council

Insurance Security Fund, Board of Directors of the: JAMES P. THOMAS (insurer representative appointed by commissioner), *chairperson;* JORGE GOMEZ (insurance commissioner), PEGGY A. LAUTENSCHALGER (attorney general), JACK C. VOIGHT (state treasurer); MARK V. AFABLE, MARK J. BACKE, JOHN F. CLEARY, JAMES E. CRIST, DAVID G. DIERCKS, PETER C. FARROW, J. STANLEY HOFFERT, WILLIAM M. O'REILLY, JAMES P. THOMAS, TOD J. ZACHARIAS (insurance industry representatives appointed by commissioner).

The Board of Directors of the Insurance Security Fund administers a fund that protects certain insurance policyholders and claimants from excessive delay and loss in the event of insurer liquidation. The fund consists of life, allocated annuity, health, HMO, property and casualty, and administrative accounts. The fund supports continuation of coverage under many life, annuity, and health policies. It is financed by assessments paid by most insurers in this state. The board may consist of 7 to 14 members but must include the attorney general, state treasurer, and insurance commissioner or their designees. The industry members must be chosen from representatives of insurers who are subject to the security fund law, and one member must be a representative of a service insurance corporation. The commissioner may provide that specific insurers or associations of insurers will be considered board members and may act through their authorized representatives. The board's advice and recommendations to the commissioner are not subject to the state's open records law. The board was originally created in Chapter 144, Laws of 1969, with substantial revisions in Chapter 109, Laws of 1979, and its composition and duties are prescribed in Sections 646.12 and 646.13 of the statutes.

Injured Patients and Families Compensation Fund/Wisconsin Health Care Liability Insurance Plan, Board of Governors of the: JORGE GOMEZ (insurance commissioner), *chairperson;* DAVID MAURER, PAUL MESTELLE, CHRISTOPHER S. SPENCER (insurance industry representatives appointed by commissioner); DONALD TAITELMAN (named by State Bar of Wisconsin); JAMES JANSEN (named by Wisconsin Academy of Trial Lawyers); SUSAN TURNEY, vacancy (named by State Medical Society of Wisconsin); GEORGE QUINN (named by Wisconsin Hospital Association); MARK H. FEMAL, BARBARA KUHL, KERMIT L. NEWCOMER, JOAN T. SCHMIT (public members appointed by governor).

The 13-member Board of Governors of the Injured Patients and Families Compensation Fund/Wisconsin Health Care Liability Insurance Plan oversees the health care liability plans for licensed physicians and nurse anesthetists, medical partnerships and corporations, cooperative sickness care associations, ambulatory surgery centers, hospitals, some nursing homes, and certain other health care providers. The board also supervises the Injured Patients and Families Compensation Fund, which pays medical malpractice claims in excess of a provider's underlying coverage. The 4 public members serve staggered 3-year terms, and at least 2 of them must not be attorneys or physicians nor be professionally affiliated with any hospital or insurance company. The insurance commissioner or the commissioner's designee, who must be an employee of the office of the commissioner, serves as chairperson. The board was created by the medical malpractice law, Chapter 37, Laws of 1975, and its composition and duties are prescribed in Sections 619.04 (3) and 655.27 of the statutes.

Injured Patients and Families Compensation Fund Peer Review Council: JOHN KELLY, *chairperson;* MICHAEL GILMAN, SANDRA OSBORN (physicians); TOM KIRSCHBAUM, vacancy (public members).

The 5-member Injured Patients and Families Compensation Fund Peer Review Council reviews within one year of the first payment on a claim each claim for damages arising out of medical care provided by a health care provider or provider's employee, if the claim is paid by any of the following: the Patients Compensation Fund, a mandatory health care risk-sharing plan, a private health care liability insurer, or a self-insurer. The council can recommend adjustments in fees paid to the Injured Patients and Families Compensation Fund and the Wisconsin Health Care Liability Insurance Plan or premiums paid to private insurers, if requested by the insurer. The Board of Governors of the Injured Patients and Families Compensation Fund/Wisconsin Health Care Liability Insurance Plan appoints the council and designates its officers and the terms of the members. Not more than 3 members may be physicians. The chairperson must be a physician, who also serves as an *ex officio* nonvoting member of the Medical Examining Board. The council was created by 1985 Wisconsin Act 340, and its composition and duties are prescribed in Section 655.275 of the statutes.

State of Wisconsin
INVESTMENT BOARD

Members: JAMES A. SENTY, *chairperson;* THOMAS BOLDT, *vice chairperson;* ERIC O. STANCHFIELD (nonteacher participant appointed by Wisconsin Retirement Board), *secretary;* LAURA ENGAN (designated by the secretary of administration); DAVID GEERTSEN (representing Local Government Pooled-Investment Fund participants); WAYNE D. MCCAFFERY (teacher participant appointed by Teachers Retirement Board); STEPHEN E. BABLITCH, WILLIAM H. LEVIT, JR., DELORIS SIMS. (Except as noted, the governor appoints the members with senate consent.)

Executive Director: DAVID C. MILLS, 266-9451.

Deputy/Assisant Executive Director: GAIL HANSON, 261-0187.

Chief Investment Officer – Public Equities: JEAN LEDFORD, 261-0188.

Chief Investment Officer – Private Markets: ROBERT SEVERANCE, 266-7111.

Head – Public Fixed Income: ALAIN HUNG, 267-2257.

Administrative Services: KEN JOHNSON, *chief operating officer,* 267-0221.

Internal Audit: BRANDON DUCK, *internal auditor,* 261-2417.

Legal Services: KEITH L. JOHNSON, *chief legal officer,* 266-8824.

Public Information Officer: VICKI HEARING, 261-2415.

Legislative and Beneficiary Liaison: SANDY DREW, 261-0182.

Mailing Address: P.O. Box 7842, Madison 53707-7842.

Location: 121 East Wilson Street, Madison.

Telephone: (608) 266-2381; Toll-Free Beneficiary Hotline: (800) 424-7942.

Fax: (608) 266-2436.

Internet Address: http://www.swib.state.wi.us

Agency E-mail Address: info@swib.state.wi.us

Publication: Annual Report.

Number of Employees: 104.50.

Total Budget 2003-05: $35,441,000.

Statutory References: Section 15.76; Chapter 25.

Agency Responsibility: The State of Wisconsin Investment Board is responsible for investing the assets of the Wisconsin Retirement System, the State Life Insurance Fund, the Local Government Property Insurance Fund, the State Historical Society of Wisconsin Endowment Trust Fund, the Injured Patients and Families Compensation Fund, the Tuition Trust Fund, EdVest, and the State Investment Fund.

For purposes of investment, the retirement system's assets are divided into two funds. The Fixed Retirement Investment Trust is a broadly diversified portfolio of domestic and international common stocks, corporate and government bonds, corporate loans, and private markets that include real estate holdings and private debt and equity. The Variable Retirement Investment Trust is invested primarily in common stocks. On December 31, 2004, Wisconsin Retirement System trust funds constituted 92% (approximately $64.6 billion) of the $70 billion managed by the Investment Board.

The State Investment Fund invests the commingled cash balances of various state and local government funds in short-term investments with earnings and losses distributed on a pro rata basis to the individual component funds. The fund encompasses the cash balance of the state's general fund and over 50 separate state funds, including the Children's Trust Fund, the Lottery Fund, the Recycling Fund, the Tuition Trust Fund, and the Wisconsin Election Campaign Fund, as well as various state agency accounts. Authorized local governments may participate by depositing moneys in the Local Government Pooled-Investment Fund, which is a separate fund within the State Investment Fund.

Organization: Appointments to the 9-member board, which is a corporate body with power to sue and be sued, are for 6-year terms. At least 4 out of 5 of the general members must have had a minimum of 10 years investment experience, and none may have a financial interest in or be employed by a dealer or broker in securities, mortgages, or real estate investments. The sixth member appointed by the governor must have 10 years of financial experience and be an employee of a government that participates in the Local Government Pooled-Investment Fund.

The board appoints the executive director and the director of internal audit from outside the classified service. The executive director, with the participation of the board, appoints the assistant executive director, chief investment officers, and the investment directors from outside the classified service. All other professional employees are appointed by the executive director from outside the classified service. Board employees may not have any direct or indirect financial interest in any firm engaged in the sale or marketing of real estate or investments nor give paid investment advice to others.

Unit Functions: *Administrative Services* is responsible for administration of the agency's budget, legislative liaison, policy analysis, human resources, information technology, financial operations and accounting, communications, and general administrative services.

The *Chief Investment Officers and the Head of Fixed Income,* operating under the supervision of the executive director, monitor and direct the activities of the investment directors for compliance with board investment policies, guidelines, and reporting procedures. The position of chief investment officer was created by 1995 Wisconsin Act 174.

The *Internal Audit* unit, directed by the internal auditor, may review any activity of the board and has access to records of the board and any external party under contract with the board. The auditor plans and conducts audits under the direction of the board; assists with external audits and reviews of the board; and monitors the board's contractual agreements with financial institutions, investment advisers, and any other external party providing investment services. The internal audit function was created by 1995 Wisconsin Act 274.

History: Chapter 459, Laws of 1921, created a mandatory pension system for teachers and three separate boards to invest the annuity funds of public school, normal school, and university teachers. The 1929 Legislature created the State Annuity and Investment Board and made it responsible for investing the assets of the teachers' pension funds and other state funds, except the school funds that remained under control of the Commissioners of Public Lands (Chapter 491). The board also assumed oversight and asset management of funds for the newly created state employee pension system as the result of Chapter 176, Laws of 1943.

Chapter 511, Laws of 1951, replaced the three teacher retirement boards and the Annuity and Investment Board with State Teachers Retirement Board and the State Investment Board, which was responsible for investing the assets of all non-Milwaukee teachers. Chapter 511 also granted the State Investment Board authority to invest the assets of the nonteaching, non-Milwaukee public employees who were covered under the Wisconsin Retirement Fund. Chapter 430, Laws of 1957, brought the funds of the Milwaukee teachers under the control of the State Investment Board. Chapter 96, Laws of 1981, consolidated all public employee retirement plans, with the exception of the City and County of Milwaukee, into the Wisconsin Retirement System (WRS), and the State Investment Board has continued to invest the funds for the WRS.

Chapter 449, Laws of 1925, created a State Board of Deposits to insure state funds on deposit in state banks through a deposit fund, managed by the state treasurer under the direction of the board. The board's duties were to designate the banks in which state funds could be deposited and to specify the maximum amount of state funds each could receive. Participating banks paid into the deposit fund, which was designed to reimburse any losses incurred through bank failure.

Chapter 511, Laws of 1951, authorized the State Investment Board to invest the state's operating funds and directed it to carry out the investment functions of the State Board of Deposits. Although state funds had been invested since 1911, the 1951 reorganization increased the types of investments the board could consider for the funds under its supervision. Previously, the state's operating funds had been placed in noninterest bearing accounts. In 1957, the legislature created the State Investment Fund, which merged all state funds except for a handful that are reported separately. The Local Government Pooled-Investment Fund, created in 1976, allows local government to invest their idle cash at competitive rates of return and withdraw it on a two-day notice with no penalty.

Department of
JUSTICE

Attorney General: PEGGY A. LAUTENSCHLAGER, 266-1221.

Deputy Attorney General: DANIEL P. BACH, 266-1221.

Mailing Address: P.O. Box 7857, Madison 53707-7857.

Location: Attorney General's Office, 114 East, State Capitol; Department of Justice, 17 West Main Street, Madison.

Telephones: General: 266-1221; Arson Tip Line: (800) 362-3005; Office of Crime Victims Services: (800) 446-6564; Drug Tip Helpline: (800) 622-DRUG (622-3784); Amber Alert Hotline: (866) 65AMBER.

Fax: 267-2779.

Internet Address: http://www.doj.state.wi.us

Number of Employees: 550.18.

Total Budget 2003-05: $143,278,800.

Constitutional References: Article VI, Sections 1 and 3.

Statutory References: Section 15.25; Chapter 165.

Criminal Investigation, Division of: JAMES R. WARREN, *administrator,* 266-1671; JOELL E. SCHIGUR, *administrative officer,* 266-1671; Fax: 267-2777.

 Administrative Services Bureau: ROBBIE LOWERY, *director,* 266-1671.

 Arson and Special Assignments Bureau: CAROLYN S. KELLY, *director,* 266-1671.

 Gaming Bureau and Financial Crimes Unit: ROBERT W. SLOEY, *director,* 266-1671.

 Investigative Services Bureau: CRAIG S. KLYVE, *director,* 266-1671.

 Narcotics Bureau: MICHAEL G. MYSZEWSKI, *director,* 266-1671.

 Public Integrity Unit: DEAN NICKEL, *special agent in charge,* 266-0328.

Law Enforcement Services, Division of: MICHAEL A. ROBERTS, *administrator,* 266-7052; Fax: 266-1656.

 Crime Information Bureau: GERRY COLEMAN, *director,* 266-7314.

 Crime Laboratory Bureau-Madison: JEROME A. GEURTS, *director,* 266-2031, 4706 University Avenue, Madison 53705-2174.

 Crime Laboratory Bureau-Milwaukee: MICHAEL J. CAMP, *director,* (414) 382-7500, 1578 South 11th Street, Milwaukee 53204-2860.

 Crime Laboratory Bureau-Wausau: MICHAEL A. HAAS, *director,* (715) 845-8626, 7100 West Stewart Avenue, Wausau 54401.

 Training and Standards Bureau: DENNIS E. HANSON, *director,* 266-7864.

Legal Services, Division of: MICHAEL R. BAUER, *administrator,* 266-0332; Fax: 266-1656.

 Civil Litigation and Employment Unit: COREY FINKELMEYER, *director,* 266-7906.

 Criminal Appeals Unit: GREGORY WEBER, *director,* 266-3935.

 Criminal Litigation, Antitrust, Consumer Protection, and Public Integrity Unit: STEVEN TINKER, *director,* 266-1447.

 Environmental Protection Unit: THOMAS DAWSON, *director,* 266-8912.

 Medicaid Fraud Control Unit: WILLIAM HANRAHAN, *director,* 266-9222.

 State Programs, Administration, and Revenue Unit: SANDY TARVER, *director,* 266-7630.

Management Services, Division of: CINDY O'DONNELL, *administrator,* 267-1300; Fax: 266-1656.

 Budget and Finance, Bureau of: JACK R. BENJAMIN, *director,* 267-6714.

 Computing Services, Bureau of: FRANK ACE, *director,* 266-7076.

 Human Resources, Bureau of: GARY MARTINELLI, *director,* 266-0461.

 Communications, Office of: BRIAN RIESELMAN, 266-1221.

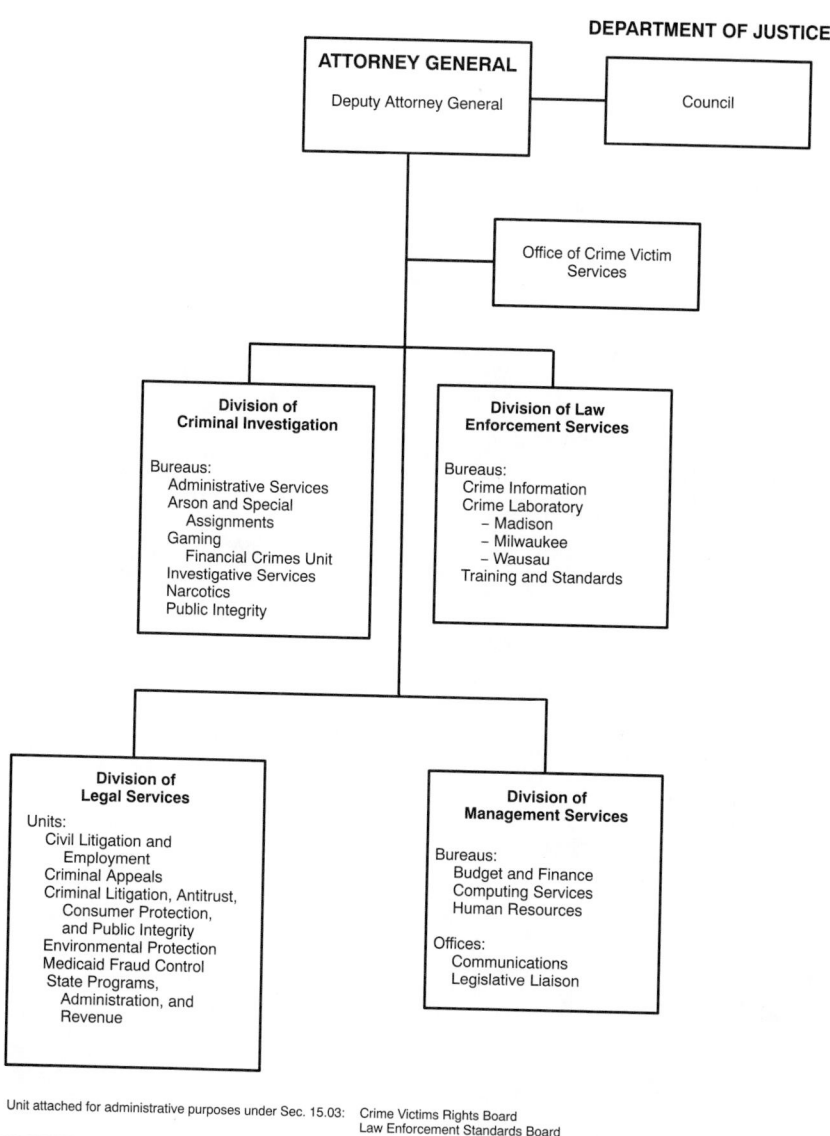

DEPARTMENT OF JUSTICE

ATTORNEY GENERAL

Deputy Attorney General

Council

Office of Crime Victim Services

Division of Criminal Investigation

Bureaus:
Administrative Services
Arson and Special Assignments
Gaming
Financial Crimes Unit
Investigative Services
Narcotics
Public Integrity

Division of Law Enforcement Services

Bureaus:
Crime Information
Crime Laboratory
– Madison
– Milwaukee
– Wausau
Training and Standards

Division of Legal Services

Units:
Civil Litigation and Employment
Criminal Appeals
Criminal Litigation, Antitrust, Consumer Protection, and Public Integrity
Environmental Protection
Medicaid Fraud Control
State Programs, Administration, and Revenue

Division of Management Services

Bureaus:
Budget and Finance
Computing Services
Human Resources

Offices:
Communications
Legislative Liaison

Unit attached for administrative purposes under Sec. 15.03: Crime Victims Rights Board
Law Enforcement Standards Board

Legislative Liaison, Office of: MARK RINEHART, 266-1221.

Crime Victims Services, Office of: NANCY J. NUSBAUM, *director,* 266-0109, P.O. Box 7951, Madison 53707-7951.

Publications: Opinions of the Attorney General; Annual Report; Criminal Investigation and Physical Evidence Handbook; Domestic Abuse Incident Report; Law Enforcement Bulletin; *When Crime Strikes: Injured Victims Can Get Help;* Wisconsin Law Enforcement Film Catalog; *Wisconsin Open Meetings Law: A Citizen's Guide; Wisconsin Open Meetings Law: A Compliance Guide;* Wisconsin Prosecutor's Newsletter.

Agency Responsibility: The Department of Justice provides legal advice and representation, criminal investigation, and various law enforcement services for the state. It represents the state in civil cases and handles criminal cases that reach the Wisconsin Court of Appeals or the Wisconsin Supreme Court. It also represents the state in criminal cases on appeal in federal courts and participates with other states in federal cases that are important to Wisconsin. The department provides legal representation in lower courts when expressly authorized by law or requested by the governor, either house of the legislature, or a state agency head. It also represents state agencies in court reviews of their administrative decisions.

Organization: The Department of Justice is directed by the attorney general, a constitutional officer who is elected on a partisan ballot to a 4-year term. The attorney general selects the department's division administrators, with the exception of the administrator of the Division of Criminal Investigation, which is a classified position.

State Crime Laboratory forensic scientist Robert Block extracts residue of controlled substances from a $100 bill. The Wisconsin Department of Justice's crime laboratories help law enforcement officers analyze physical evidence. (Department of Justice)

Unit Functions: The *Division of Criminal Investigation,* created in Section 15.253 (2), Wisconsin Statutes, by 1991 Wisconsin Act 269, investigates crimes that are statewide in nature. Special agents work closely with local law enforcement officials and prosecuting attorneys to investigate and prosecute arson, explosions of suspected criminal origin, high level drug trafficking, illegal gaming, pornography, antitrust violations, organized crime, financial crimes, and public corruption. Upon request, the division assists local law enforcement agencies on cases, such as murders and multijurisdictional theft or fraud.

The *Division of Law Enforcement Services* provides advanced technical services, information, and training to state and local law enforcement agencies and jails. It maintains central fingerprint identification records and computerized criminal history information, operates the Handgun Hotline, and provides criminal history background check services. The statewide telecommunications system links Wisconsin police agencies to national, state, and local crime files, and three crime laboratories help law enforcement officers analyze physical evidence.

The division ensures that all officers at the municipal, county, and state levels meet the mandatory recruitment and training qualifications established by the Law Enforcement Standards Board. Regional academies are certified by the board to offer basic training for law enforcement recruits, jail officers, or security detention officers or to provide the annual recertification classes required for all officers. Training resources and instructors are also provided to local law enforcement organizations.

The *Division of Legal Services* provides legal representation and advice to the governor, legislature, other state officers and agencies, district attorneys, and county corporation counsels. It enforces state environmental, antitrust, employment, consumer protection, and Medicaid fraud laws. It also prosecutes economic crimes and represents the state in all felony appeals and litigation brought by prison inmates. At the request of district attorneys, the division provides special prosecutors in complex homicide, drug, and white collar cases. It defends the state in civil lawsuits filed against the state or its officers and employees and handles matters related to public records, Indian law, and fair housing.

The *Division of Management Services* prepares the agency budget; manages agency personnel, finances, and facilities; and provides information technology services.

The *Office of Crime Victims Services* administers state and federal programs that assist victims of crime. Three programs receive funding from surcharges assessed against convicted criminals: the Crime Victim Compensation Program reimburses victims and their dependents for out-of-pocket medical and other expenses; the Sexual Assault Victim Services Program provides grants to nonprofit organizations that offer services to sexual assault victims; and the Victim/Witness Assistance Program partially reimburses counties for their costs of providing services. Federal funding supports two departmental programs: the Wisconsin Victim Resource Center, which mediates victims claims, and the Elder Advocacy Program, which provides technical assistance and training to citizens and professionals in the area of financial abuse of the elderly, including consumer fraud and financial abuse by family members and caregivers.

History: When Wisconsin became a territory in 1836, the U.S. President appointed the attorney general. In 1839, a territorial act gave the governor the power to appoint the attorney general with the consent of the Legislative Council (the upper house of the territorial legislature) to a term of 3 years. The Wisconsin Constitution, as adopted in 1848, provided for an elected attorney general with a 2-year term. A constitutional amendment ratified in 1967 increased the term to 4 years, effective in 1971.

Chapter 75, Laws of 1967, named the agency headed by the attorney general the Department of Justice and transferred to its control the State Crime Laboratory, the arson investigation program from the Commissioner of Insurance, and the criminal investigation functions of the Beverage and Cigarette Tax Division of the Department of Revenue. The 1975 Legislature returned alcohol and tobacco tax enforcement to the Department of Revenue.

The 1969 Legislature added enforcement of certain laws related to dangerous drugs, narcotics, and organized crime to the duties of the department and created the public intervenor to intervene in or initiate proceedings to protect public rights in water and other natural resources. In Chapter 189, Laws of 1979, the legislature transferred the crime victims program from the Department of Industry, Labor and Human Relations to the Department of Justice. 1995 Wisconsin Act 27 transferred the public intervenor to the Department of Natural Resources and consumer protection functions to the Department of Agriculture, Trade and Consumer Protection.

Statutory Council

Crime Victims Council: BETH TABOR, MARY VAN DYKE (victim services representatives); ANN GOLLNER (law enforcement representative); MARTIN LIPSKE (district attorney representative); BARBARA H. KEY (judicial representative); JENNY BELICH, JULIA BURNEY-WITHERSPOON, QUALA CHAMPAGNE, KATHY CONNOLLY, NORM GAHN, MELINDA HUGHES, MARION MORGAN, JEN SENICK-CELMER, RICHARD SICCHIO, JOAN TERRY (citizen members). (All are appointed by attorney general.)

The 15-member Crime Victims Council provides advice and recommendations on victims' rights issues and legislation. Members are appointed for staggered 3-year terms, and the 10 citizen members must have demonstrated sensitivity and concern for crime victims. The council was created by Chapter 189, Laws of 1979, as the Crime Victims Compensation Council. It was renamed in Chapter 20, Laws of 1981, and its duties and composition are prescribed in Sections 15.09 (5) and 15.257 (2) of the statutes.

INDEPENDENT UNITS ATTACHED FOR BUDGETING, PROGRAM COORDINATION, AND RELATED MANAGEMENT FUNCTIONS BY SECTION 15.03 OF THE STATUTES

CRIME VICTIMS RIGHTS BOARD

Members: KEN KRATZ (district attorney appointed by Wisconsin District Attorneys' Association); CHARLES MCGEE (local law enforcement representative appointed by the attorney general); TRISHA ANDERSON (county provider of victim and witness services appointed by attorney general); CHRISTINE NOLAN (citizen member appointed by the Crime Victims Council); ANGELA SUTKIEWICZ (citizen member appointed by governor).

Statutory References: Sections 15.255 (2) and 950.09.

The 5-member Crime Victims Rights Board may review complaints made to the Department of Justice regarding the rights of a crime victim in cases where there is probable cause to believe a crime victim's rights have been violated, but the board cannot act until the department has completed its actions on the complaint.

Actions of the board are not subject to approval or review by the attorney general. The board may issue a private or public reprimand against a public officer or agency that violates a crime victim's rights; refer a possible violation of a victim's rights by a judge to the judicial commission; seek appropriate relief on behalf of a crime victim necessary to protect that person's rights; or bring a civil action against a public officer or agency for intentional violations. In a criminal case, the board may not seek to appeal, reverse, or modify a conviction or sentence. Civil actions brought by the board may result in a forfeiture of not more than $1,000.

Members serve 4-year terms. The 2 citizen members may not be employed in law enforcement, by a district attorney, or by a county board to provide crime victim's services. The board was created by 1997 Wisconsin Act 181.

LAW ENFORCEMENT STANDARDS BOARD

Members: EDWARD BAUMANN (law enforcement representative), *chairperson;* SCOTT E. PEDLEY (law enforcement representative), *vice chairperson;* WILLIAM BRANDIMORE, STEVEN J. LELINSKI, ROBERTA E. SINDELAR, vacancy (law enforcement representatives); TIMOTHY C. BAXTER (district attorney); MICHAEL J. SERPE, vacancy (local government representatives); JACK ROBINSON (public member); DAVID COLLINS (designated by secretary of transportation), PEGGY A. LAUTENSCHLAGER (attorney general), DAVID O. STEINGRABER (executive director, Office of Justice Assistance), RANDY STARK (designated by secretary of natural resources). Nonvoting member: DAVID WILLIAMS (special agent in charge, Milwaukee FBI Office). (All except *ex officio* members are appointed by governor.)

Secretary: MICHAEL A. ROBERTS, *administrator,* Division of Law Enforcement Services, P.O. Box 7857, Madison 53707-7857.

Statutory References: Sections 15.255 and 165.85.

Agency Responsibility: The 15-member Law Enforcement Standards Board sets minimum employment, education, and training standards for law enforcement, tribal law enforcement, and jail and secure detention officers. It certifies persons who meet the standards as qualified to be officers. The board consults with other government agencies regarding the development of training schools and courses, conducts research to improve law enforcement and jail administration and performance, and evaluates governmental units' compliance with standards. Its appointed members serve staggered 4-year terms. The law enforcement representatives must include at least one sheriff and one chief of police. The public member cannot be employed in law enforcement. Chapter 466, Laws of 1969, created the board.

Curriculum Advisory Committee: RONALD CRAMER (sheriff), CHARLES MCGEE (police chief), *cochairpersons;* TONY BARTHULY, JOSEPH COUGHLIN, MICHAEL KING, STEVEN LINTON, DANIEL VERGIN (police chiefs); DARRELL BERGLIN, DAVID GRAVES, EVERETT MUHLHAUSEN, ROBERT SCHMIDT, TERRY VOGEL (sheriffs); DARREN PRICE (training director, Wisconsin State Patrol) (appointed by Law Enforcement Standards Board).

The 13-member Curriculum Advisory Committee advises the Law Enforcement Standards Board on the establishment of curriculum requirements for training of law enforcement and jail and secure detention officers. The board may appoint no more than one sheriff and one police chief from any one of the state's 8 administrative districts. The statutes do not stipulate length of terms. Chapter 466, Laws of 1969, created the committee and its composition and duties are prescribed in Section 165.85 (3) (d) of the statutes.

Department of
MILITARY AFFAIRS

Commander in Chief: GOVERNOR JIM DOYLE.

Adjutant General: **MAJOR GENERAL ALBERT H. WILKENING,** 242-3001,
al.wilkening@wi.ngb.army.mil

Deputy Adjutant General for Army: BRIG. GEN. KERRY G. DENSON, 242-3010,
kerry.denson@wi.ngb.army.mil

Deputy Adjutant General for Air: MAJ. GEN. FRED R. SLOAN, 242-3020,
fred.sloan@wimadi.ang.af.mil

Division of Emergency Management: JOHNNIE L. SMITH, *administrator,* 242-3210,
johnnie.smith@dma.state.wi.us

Executive Assistant: LARRY L. OLSON, 242-3009, larry.olson@wi.ngb.army.mil

Mailing Address: P.O. Box 8111, Madison 53708-8111.

Location: 2400 Wright Street, Madison 53704-2572.

Telephones: General: 242-3000; Division of Emergency Management: 242-3232; 24-hour hotline for emergencies and hazardous materials spills: (800) 943-0003.

Fax: 242-3111; Division of Emergency Management: 242-3247.

Internet Address: Department of Military Affairs and Wisconsin National Guard:
http://dma.wi.gov; Wisconsin Emergency Management:
http://emergencymanagement.wi.gov; Wisconsin Homeland Security:
http://homelandsecurity.wi.gov

Number of State Employees: 385.16.

Total State Budget 2003-05: $112,677,600.

Total Federal Budget: Approximately $259.8 million annually.

Constitutional References: Article IV, Section 29; Article V, Section 4.

Statutory References: Sections 15.31 and 15.313; Chapters 21 and 166.

Adjutant General Staff:

  Assistant Adjutant General: BRIG. GEN. BRUCE D. SCHRIMPF,
  bruce.schrimpf@wi.ngb.army.mil

  U.S. Property and Fiscal Officer: COL. ROBERT G. TRELAND, Camp Williams, Camp Douglas,
  (608) 427-7266, bob.treland@wi.ngb.army.mil; COL. PETER E. SEAHOLM, *Director of
  Resource Management,* (608) 427-7212, peter.seaholm@wi.ngb.army.mil

  Inspector General: COL. JOAN ARNOLD, 242-3086, joan.arnold@wi.ngb.army.mil

  Director of Public Affairs: LT. COL. TIMOTHY D. DONOVAN, 242-3050,
  tim.donovan@wi.ngb.army.mil

  Staff Judge Advocate: COL. TERENCE J. MCARDLE, 242-3077,
  terence.mcardle@wi.ngb.army.mil

  Legal Counsel: RANDI WIND MILSAP, 242-3072, randi.milsap@dma.state.wi.us

  State Budget and Finance Officer: BRETT COOMBER, 242-3155,
  brett.coomber@dma.state.wi.us

  State Human Resources Officer: LYNN E. BOODRY, 242-3163,
  lynn.boodry@dma.state.wi.us

  Wisconsin National Guard Challenge Academy (Fort McCoy): COL. (RET.) M.G. MACLAREN,
  director, (608) 269-9000, director@challenge.dma.state.wi.us

Joint Staff:

  Chief of Staff, Joint Staff: COL. SCOTT LEGWOLD, 242-3006, scott.legwold@wi.ngb.army.mil

  Human Resources (J1), Director of Manpower and Personnel: COL. JOHN MCCOY, 242-3700,
  john.mccoy@wi.ngb.army.mil

  Intelligence (J2), Director of Security and Intelligence: COL. TIMOTHY PFRANG, 242-3038,
  tim.pfrang@wi.ngb.army.mil

  Operations (J3/J7), Director of Operations: LT. COL. PAUL RUSSELL, 242-3540,
  paul.russell@wi.ngb.army.mil

  Facilities (J4), Director of Installation Management: COL. JEFFREY J. LIETHEN, 242-3365,
  jeff.liethen@dma.state.wi.us

  Strategic Plans (J5), Director of Strategic Plans and Policy: LT. COL. LUANNE SLEGER,
  242-3028, luanne.sleger@wi.ngb.army.mil

  Information Systems (J6), Director of Information Systems for C4: COL. MARK MATHWIG,
  242-3650, mark.mathwig@wi.ngb.army.mil

  Resources Management (J8), Director of Resource Management: LT. COL. JIM BARDEEN,
  (608) 427-7280, james.bardeen@wi.ngb.army.mil

Wisconsin Army National Guard: BRIG. GEN. KERRY G. DENSON, *commander,* 242-3010,
kerry.denson@wi.ngb.army.mil

  Senior Enlisted Advisor: COMMAND SGT. MAJ. JOHN HAUSCHILDT, 242-3012,
  john.hauschildt@wi.ngb.army.mil

  Army National Guard Staff:

    Chief of Staff, Army Staff: COL. ROBERT H. RONGE, 242-3030,
    robert.ronge@wi.ngb.army.mil

    Deputy Chief of Staff for Personnel (G1): COL. MARK BRUNS, 242-3444,
    mark.bruns@wi.ngb.army.mil

    Deputy Chief of Staff for Operations (G3): COL. KEVIN GREENWOOD, 242-3500,
    kevin.greenwood@wi.ngb.army.mil

    Deputy Chief of Staff for Logistics (G4): COL. DENNIS SIMONS, 242-3552,
    dennis.simons@wi.ngb.army.mil

    Deputy Chief of Staff for Aviation and Safety: COL. JEFFREY D. PAULSON, 242-3140,
    jeffrey.paulson@wi.ngb.army.mil

    Recruiting and Retention Command: LT. COL. TIMOTHY LAWSON, 242-3804,
    tim.lawson@wi.ngb.army.mil

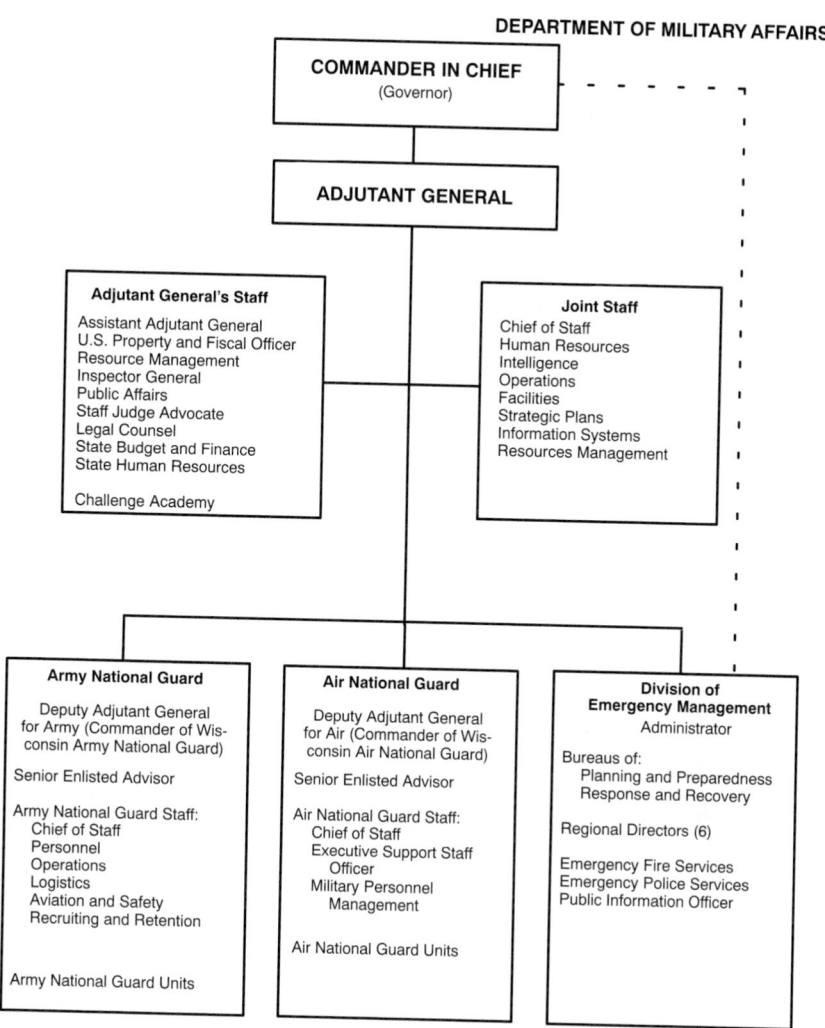

DEPARTMENT OF MILITARY AFFAIRS

COMMANDER IN CHIEF
(Governor)

ADJUTANT GENERAL

Adjutant General's Staff
Assistant Adjutant General
U.S. Property and Fiscal Officer
Resource Management
Inspector General
Public Affairs
Staff Judge Advocate
Legal Counsel
State Budget and Finance
State Human Resources

Challenge Academy

Joint Staff
Chief of Staff
Human Resources
Intelligence
Operations
Facilities
Strategic Plans
Information Systems
Resources Management

Army National Guard
Deputy Adjutant General for Army (Commander of Wisconsin Army National Guard)

Senior Enlisted Advisor

Army National Guard Staff:
Chief of Staff
Personnel
Operations
Logistics
Aviation and Safety
Recruiting and Retention

Army National Guard Units

Air National Guard
Deputy Adjutant General for Air (Commander of Wisconsin Air National Guard)

Senior Enlisted Advisor

Air National Guard Staff:
Chief of Staff
Executive Support Staff
Officer
Military Personnel
Management

Air National Guard Units

Division of Emergency Management
Administrator

Bureaus of:
Planning and Preparedness
Response and Recovery

Regional Directors (6)

Emergency Fire Services
Emergency Police Services
Public Information Officer

Army National Guard Units (major commands):

32nd (Separate) Infantry Brigade (Light) (Camp Douglas): BRIG. GEN. JAMES A. KRUECK, *commander,* (608) 427-7357, james.krueck@wi.ngb.army.mil; LT. COL. MARK R. GREENWOOD, *administrative officer,* (608) 427-7349, mark.greenwood@wi.ngb.army.mil

57th Field Artillery Brigade (Milwaukee): COL. DOMINIC A. CARIELLO, *commander,* LT. COL. JOHN SCHROEDER, *administrative officer,* (414) 961-8605, john.schroeder@wi.ngb.army.mil

64th Troop Command (Madison): COL. WILLIAM KASTEN, *commander;* LT. COL. JULIE GERETY, *administrative officer,* 242-3840, julie.gerety@wi.ngb.army.mil

264th Engineer Group (Chippewa Falls): COL. MARK MICHIE, *commander;* LT. COL. JAMES LEWIS, *administrative officer,* (715) 720-3403, james.lewis@wi.ngb.army.mil

426th Regiment (Wisconsin Military Academy) (Fort McCoy): COL. DALE POMMERENING, commander; MAJ. JEFF KURKA, *administrative officer,* (608) 388-9990, jeff.kurka@wi.ngb.army.mil

Wisconsin Air National Guard: MAJ. GEN. FRED R. SLOAN, *commander,* 242-3020, fred.sloan@wimadi.ang.af.mil

Senior Enlisted Advisor: vacancy.

Air National Guard Staff:

Chief of Staff, Air Staff: BRIG. GEN. STEVEN E. FOSTER.

Executive Support Staff Officer: COL. GERALD C. OLESEN, 242-3120, gerald.olesen@wimadi.ang.af.mil

Military Personnel Management Officer: CHIEF MASTER SGT. JANET GAEDKE, 242-3122, janet.gaedke@wimadi.ang.af.mil

Air National Guard Units (major commands):

115th Fighter Wing (Madison): COL. JOSEPH BRANDEMUEHL, *commander,* 245-4501, joe.brandemuehl@wimadi.ang.af.mil

128th Air Refueling Wing (Milwaukee): COL. DONALD DUNBAR, *commander,* (414) 944-8405, donald.dunbar@wimilw.ang.af.mil

Volk Field Combat Readiness Training Center (Camp Douglas): COL. GUNTHER H. NEUMANN, *commander,* (608) 427-1200, gunther.neumann@wicrtc.ang.af.mil

128th Air Control Squadron (Volk Field): LT. COL. HERBERT T. DANNENBERG, *commander,* (608) 427-1295, herb.dannenberg@wicrtc.ang.af.mil

Emergency Management, Division of: JOHNNIE L. SMITH, *administrator,* 242-3210, johnnie.smith@dma.state.wi.us

Planning and Preparedness, Bureau of: STEVE PETERSON, *director,* 242-3206, steve.peterson@dma.state.wi.us

Response and Recovery, Bureau of: ROB RUDE, *director,* 242-3203, rob.rude@dma.state.wi.us

Public Information Officer: LORI GETTER, 242-3239, lori.getter@dma.state.wi.us

Southwest Regional Office (Madison): LARRY REED, *director and response section supervisor,* 242-3336, larry.reed@dma.state.wi.us

East Central Regional Office (Fond du Lac): DAN DAHLKE, *director,* (920) 929-3730, dan.dahlke@dma.state.wi.us

Northeast Regional Office (Wausau): ERIK LOWMAN, *director,* (715) 845-9517, erik.lowman@dma.state.wi.us

Northwest Regional Office (Spooner): RHONDA REYNOLDS, *director,* (715) 635-8704, rhonda.reynolds@dma.state.wi.us

Southeast Regional Office (Waukesha): PATRICK O'CONNOR, *director,* (262) 782-1515, pat.oconnor@dma.state.wi.us

West Central Regional Office (Eau Claire): LOIS RISTOW, *director,* (715) 839-3825, wemwco@discover-net.net

Emergency Fire Services: vacancy.

Emergency Police Services: vacancy.

Publications: *At Ease;* Biennial Report; Wisconsin Emergency Management *Digest.*

Agency Responsibility: The Department of Military Affairs provides an armed military force through the Wisconsin National Guard, which is organized, trained, equipped, and available for deployment under official orders in state and national emergencies. The federal mission of the National Guard is to provide trained units to the U.S. Army and U.S. Air Force in time of war or national emergency. Its state mission is to help civil authorities protect life and property and preserve peace, order, and public safety in times of natural or human-caused emergencies.

The *Division of Emergency Management* is headed by a division administrator appointed by the governor with the advice and consent of the senate. It coordinates the development and imple-

Soldiers of Company A, 1st Battalion, 128th Infantry, Wisconsin Army National Guard, share a moment with Iraqi children, while elders in traditional garb look on. (U.S. Army, 1st Battalion, 128th Infantry)

mentation of the state emergency operations plan; provides assistance to local jurisdictions in the development of their programs and plans; administers private and federal disaster and emergency relief funds; and maintains the state's 24-hour duty officer reporting and response system. The division also conducts training programs in emergency planning for businesses and state and local officials, as well as educational programs for the general public. Under Title III of the federal 1986 Superfund Amendments and Reauthorization Act and 1987 Wisconsin Act 342, the division requires public and private entities that possess hazardous substances to file reports on these substances. It establishes local emergency response committees and oversees implementation of their plans and corresponding state plans. The division administers emergency planning performance grants that assist local emergency planning committees in complying with state and federal law. In addition, the division contracts with regional hazardous materials response teams which respond to the most dangerous levels of hazardous substance releases. It also coordinates planning and training for off-site radiological emergencies at nuclear power plants in and near Wisconsin. The Emergency Police Services (EPS) program provides support to law enforcement in times of crisis. The program coordinates state law enforcement response to emergencies, including coordination of mutual aid for law enforcement assistance in natural disasters, prison disturbances, and other emergencies.

A key resource within Wisconsin Emergency Management (WEM) is its system of 6 regional offices located throughout the state. The regional offices are co-located with the Wisconsin State Patrol district headquarters in Waukesha, Fond du Lac, Eau Claire, Spooner, and Wausau and at WEM's central office in Madison. Each office is assigned to work with a group of surrounding counties ranging in number from 8 to 14. Regional Directors are knowledgeable in each of the division's programs, and support both municipal and county programs in planning, training, exercising, response and recovery activities, as well as the coordination of administrative activities between the division and local governments. When disasters and emergencies strike, they are the division's initial responders, serving as field liaisons for the State Emergency Operations Center.

Organization: The Wisconsin Constitution designates the governor as the commander in chief of the Wisconsin National Guard. The department is directed by the adjutant general, who is appointed by the governor for a 5-year term and may serve successive terms. The adjutant general must be an officer actively serving in the Army or Air National Guard of Wisconsin who has attained at least the rank of lieutenant colonel with a minimum of 5 years of continuous, federally recognized commissioned service in the National Guard immediately preceding the date of appointment.

In addition to state support, the Wisconsin National Guard is also funded and maintained by the federal government, and when it is called up in an active federal duty status, the President of the United States becomes its commander in chief. The federal government provides arms and ammunition, equipment and uniforms, major outdoor training facilities, pay for military and support personnel, and training and supervision. The state provides personnel; conducts training as required under the National Defense Act; and shares the cost of constructing, maintaining, and operating armories and other military facilities. The composition of Wisconsin Army and Air National Guard units is authorized by the U.S. Secretary of Defense through the National Guard Bureau. All officers and enlisted personnel must meet the same physical, education, and other eligibility requirements as members of the active-duty U.S. Army or U.S. Air Force.

History: Until the 20th century, the United States relied heavily on military units organized by the states to fight its wars. Known as "minutemen" in the American Revolution, state militias, which could be called up on brief notice, provided soldiers for the Revolutionary War, the Mexican War, the Civil War, and the Spanish-American War.

In 1792, the U.S. Congress passed a law that required all able-bodied men between 18 and 45 years of age to serve in local militia units, a provision that was incorporated into the territorial statutes of Wisconsin. The Wisconsin Constitution, as adopted in 1848, authorized the legislature to determine the composition, organization, and discipline of the state militia.

The 1849 Wisconsin Statutes specified the procedure for the organization of locally controlled "uniform companies". Each uniform company included 30 men who had to equip themselves with arms and uniforms.

By 1858 (Chapter 87), the legislature provided for the organization of the State Militia, which ultimately replaced the uniform companies. As commander in chief of the militia, the governor appointed the adjutant general and the general officers and issued commissions to the elected officers of uniform companies. The governor could provide arms for the officers, but they were required to supply their own uniforms and horses. Not until 1873 (Chapter 202) was money appropriated from the general fund to help support militia companies. Chapter 208, Laws of 1879, changed the militia's name to the Wisconsin National Guard.

Federal supervision of and financial responsibility for the National Guard came with Congressional passage of the Dick Act in 1903. Congress passed the law in response to the lack of uniformity among state units, which became evident during the Spanish-American War and subsequent occupation of the Philippines. The act set standards for Guard units, granted federal aid, and provided for inspections by regular U.S. Army officers.

The National Defense Act of 1933 formally created the National Guard of the United States, a reserve component of the active U.S. Army. The act allowed the mobilization of intact National Guard units through their simultaneous dual enlistment as state and federal military forces. This permitted Guard personnel to mobilize for federal duty directly from state status in event of a federal emergency, rather than being discharged to enlist in the federal forces, as was done in World War I. A 1990 U.S. Supreme Court case upheld the authority of the U.S. Congress to send Army National Guard units (under U.S. Army command) out of the country to train for their federal mission.

Wisconsin National Guard troops fought in the Civil War, the Spanish-American War, World War I, and World War II. Wisconsin troops from the "Iron Brigade" gained national recognition in the Civil War, and the 32nd "Red Arrow" Infantry Division won fame for its combat record in both World Wars. The Wisconsin Air National Guard became a separate service in 1947, and members of the Wisconsin Air Guard served in the Korean War. Over the past 50 years, Wisconsin units have been called to active federal service on numerous occasions. In 1961, the 32nd Division was activated during the Berlin Crisis. More than 1,400 Guard members from Wisconsin

In Iraq, soldiers of Company A, 1st Battalion, 128th Infantry, Wisconsin Army National Guard, train soldiers of the Iraqi National Army. (U.S. Army, 1st Battalion, 128th Infantry)

were sent to the Persian Gulf to participate in Operations Desert Shield and Desert Storm in 1990-91. Beginning in 1996, units were called to support peacekeeping efforts in the Balkans. Wisconsin Air National Guard units were deployed to enforce U.N. no-fly zones in Southwest Asia in the 1990s, and two units were called to support Operation Allied Force, the NATO air operations over Kosovo in 1999.

Within hours of the September 11, 2001, terrorist attacks on America, the Wisconsin National Guard began yet another period of extensive support to U.S. military operations. Air National Guard units in Wisconsin have provided fighter aircraft to patrol the skies over major U.S. cities and critical national infrastructure, tanker aircraft to refuel patrolling fighters and U.S. military aircraft overseas, and critical radar support to North American Aerospace Defense Command and the Federal Aviation Administration. Wisconsin Army Guard soldiers enhanced security at nine of Wisconsin's commercial airports until the federal Transportation Security Agency could establish a new security system. Wisconsin Army National Guard units began mobilizing into active federal service in December 2001, and unit mobilizations have continued in support of military efforts in Afghanistan (Operation Enduring Freedom) and Iraq (Operation Iraqi Freedom), as well as Operation Noble Eagle homeland defense missions in the United States. By June 6, 2005, more than 5,500 members of the Wisconsin Army and Air National Guard had been mobilized to serve on active duty since September 11, 2001.

The 1967 executive branch reorganization created the Department of Military Affairs to assume the state's responsibilities for the Wisconsin National Guard and the functions of the Wisconsin State Armory Board that had been created in 1943 to construct or acquire armories to house and train the National Guard.

The **Division of Emergency Management** originated as the Office of Civil Defense, which was developed to administer emergency programs in case of enemy attack and was located in the governor's office under Chapter 443, Laws of 1951. Its predecessors include the Wisconsin Council of Defense, organized by executive order of Governor Julius P. Heil in 1940, and the State Council on Civil Defense, created in the governor's office by Chapter 9, Laws of 1943. The 1943 council was abolished in 1945 and its functions transferred to the adjutant general, who was appointed director of the Office of Civil Defense by the governor, as permitted in the 1951 law.

Chapter 628, Laws of 1959, renamed the office the Bureau of Civil Defense and added responsibilities for natural and human-caused disasters. The 1967 executive branch reorganization transferred the bureau to the Department of Local Affairs and Development as the Division of Emergency Government. In Chapter 361, Laws of 1979, the division was transferred to the Department of Administration. The division became part of the Department of Military Affairs in 1989 Wisconsin Act 31 and was renamed by 1995 Wisconsin Act 247. When 1997 Wisconsin Act 27 abolished the State Emergency Response Board, the division assumed the board's responsibilities pertaining to hazardous chemical substances and spills and the contracts with regional hazardous materials response teams. Since 1997, Wisconsin Emergency Management has coordinated the state's terrorism preparedness efforts, by working to deter, prevent, respond to, and recover from terrorist attacks. In March 2003 (Executive Order 7), Governor Doyle created the Governor's Homeland Security Council to advise the governor and coordinate the efforts of state and local officials regarding the prevention of, and response to, potential threats to the homeland security of the state. The council works with federal, state, and local agencies, nonprofit organizations, and private industry to prevent and respond to any threat of terrorism, to promote personal preparedness and to make recommendations to the governor on what additional steps are needed to further enhance Wisconsin's homeland security.

Major General Al Wilkening, the adjutant general of Wisconsin, talks with soldiers of the 829th Engineer Detachment deployed at a base in southern Kuwait in support of Operation Iraqi Freedom.
(Wisconsin Army National Guard, 829th Engineer Detachment)

Department of
NATURAL RESOURCES

Natural Resources Board: GERALD M. O'BRIEN (member-at-large), *chairperson;* HOWARD D. POULSON (southern member), *vice chairperson;* JONATHAN P. ELA (southern member), *secretary;* HERBERT F. BEHNKE, JOHN W. WELTER, STEPHEN D. WILLETT (northern members); CHRISTINE L. THOMAS (southern member). (All are appointed by governor with senate consent.)

Secretary of Natural Resources: SCOTT HASSETT, 266-2121, scott.hassett@

Deputy Secretary: WILLIAM H. SMITH, 264-6133, william.h.smith@

Executive Assistant: MARY SCHLAEFER, 264-6266, mary.schlaefer@

Legal Services, Bureau of: RICHARD L. PROSISE, *director,* 266-0060, richard.prosise@

Management and Budget, Bureau of: JOSEPH P. POLASEK, JR., *director,* 266-2794, joseph.polasekjr@

Diversity Affairs, Office of: TERESA J. SCOLLON, *director,* 266-5833, teresa.scollon@

Mailing Address: P.O. Box 7921, Madison 53707-7921.

Location: State Natural Resources Building (GEF 2), 101 South Webster Street, Madison.

Telephones: General: (608) 266-2621; Violation Hotline (to report poaching or other violations of natural resources laws): (800) TIP-WDNR (847-9367) or #367 by cellular phone; Spill Line: (800) 943-0003; Outdoor Report (recorded message): (608) 266-2277; TDD: (608) 267-6897.

Fax: (608) 267-3579.

Internet Address: www.dnr.wi.gov

Address e-mail by combining the user ID and the state extender: userid**@dnr.state.wi.us**

Air and Waste, Division of: ALLEN K. SHEA, *administrator,* 266-5896, allen.shea@; MARY JO KOPECKY, *deputy administrator,* 261-8448, maryjo.kopecky@

Air Management, Bureau of: LLOYD L. EAGAN, *director,* 266-0603, lloyd.eagan@

Cooperative Environmental Assistance, Bureau of: MARK MCDERMID, *director,* 267-3125, mark.mcdermid@

Remediation and Redevelopment, Bureau of: MARK F. GIESFELDT, *director,* 267-7562, mark.giesfeldt@

Waste Management, Bureau of: SUZANNE A. BANGERT, *director,* 266-0014, suzanne.bangert@

Customer and Employee Services, Division of: VANCE RAYBURN, *administrator,* 266-2241, vance.rayburn@

Communication and Education, Bureau of: LAUREL J. STEFFES, *director,* 266-8109, laurel.steffes@

Community Financial Assistance, Bureau of: MICHELE A. YOUNG, *director,* 266-7566, michele.young@

Customer Service and Licensing, Bureau of: DIANE L. BROOKBANK, *director,* 267-7799, diane.brookbank@

Finance, Bureau of: BLANCA E. RIVERA, *director,* 266-2951, blanca.rivera@

Human Resources, Bureau of: DEBRA K. MARTINELLI, *director,* 266-2048, debra.martinelli@

Technology Services, Bureau of: ARTHUR K. PRZYBYL, *director,* 266-7547, arthur.przybyl@

Enforcement and Science, Division of: AMY SMITH, *administrator,* 266-0015, amy.smith@

Integrated Science Services, Bureau of: JOHN R. SULLIVAN, *director,* 267-9753, john.r.sullivan@

Law Enforcement, Bureau of: RANDALL J. STARK, *director,* 266-1115, randall.stark@

Forestry, Division of: PAUL DELONG, *administrator and State Forester,* 264-9224, paul.delong@

Forest Management, Bureau of: ROBERT J. MATHER, *director,* 266-1727, robert.mather@

Forest Protection, Bureau of: TRENT L. MARTY, *director,* 266-7978, trent.marty@

Forestry Services, Bureau of: WENDY M. MCCOWN, *director,* 266-7510, wendy.mccown@

Forestry Sciences, Office of: DARRELL E. ZASTROW, *director,* 266-0290, darrell.zastrow@

DEPARTMENT OF NATURAL RESOURCES

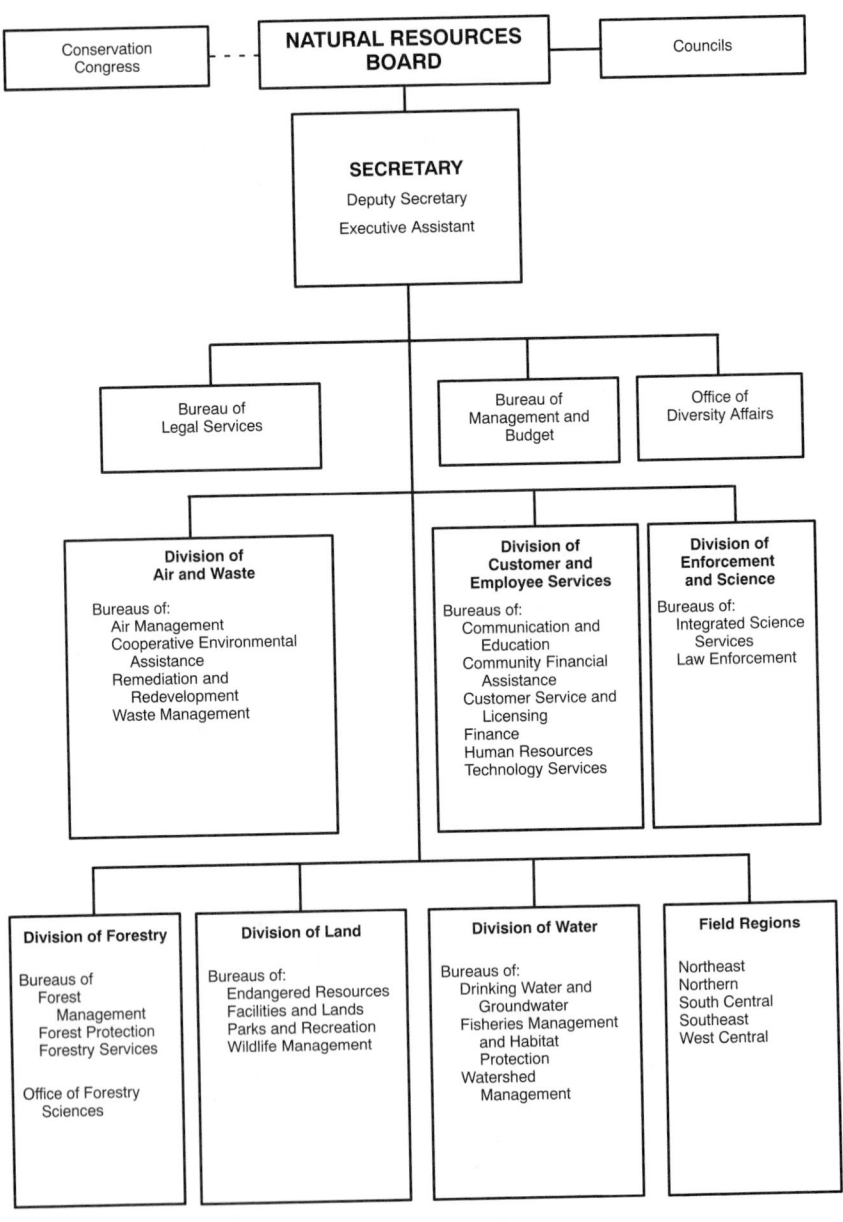

Conservation Congress — NATURAL RESOURCES BOARD — Councils

SECRETARY
Deputy Secretary
Executive Assistant

Bureau of Legal Services

Bureau of Management and Budget

Office of Diversity Affairs

Division of Air and Waste
Bureaus of:
Air Management
Cooperative Environmental Assistance
Remediation and Redevelopment
Waste Management

Division of Customer and Employee Services
Bureaus of:
Communication and Education
Community Financial Assistance
Customer Service and Licensing
Finance
Human Resources
Technology Services

Division of Enforcement and Science
Bureaus of:
Integrated Science Services
Law Enforcement

Division of Forestry
Bureaus of
Forest Management
Forest Protection
Forestry Services

Office of Forestry Sciences

Division of Land
Bureaus of:
Endangered Resources
Facilities and Lands
Parks and Recreation
Wildlife Management

Division of Water
Bureaus of:
Drinking Water and Groundwater
Fisheries Management and Habitat Protection
Watershed Management

Field Regions
Northeast
Northern
South Central
Southeast
West Central

Units attached for administrative purposes under Sec. 15.03:
Groundwater Coordinating Council
Invasive Species Council
Lake Michigan Commercial Fishing Board
Lake Superior Commercial Fishing Board
Council on Recycling
Wisconsin Waterways Commission

School children help Department of Natural Resources Secretary Scott Hassett plant an oak tree at the State Capitol in honor of the Year of Wisconsin Forestry. *(Department of Natural Resources)*

Land, Division of: LAURIE OSTERNDORF, *administrator,* 267-7552, laurie.osterndorf@; SARAH S. HURLEY, *deputy administrator,* 267-7472, sarah.hurley@

    Endangered Resources, Bureau of: SIGNE L. HOLTZ, *director,* 264-9210, signe.holtz@

    Facilities and Lands, Bureau of: STEVEN W. MILLER, *director,* 266-5782, steven.miller@

    Parks and Recreation, Bureau of: WILLIAM MORRISSEY, *director,* 266-2185, bill.morrissey@

    Wildlife Management, Bureau of: THOMAS M. HAUGE, *director,* 266-2193, thomas.hauge@

Water, Division of: TODD L. AMBS, *administrator,* 264-6278, todd.ambs@; BRUCE J. BAKER, *deputy administrator,* 266-1902, bruce.baker@

    Drinking Water and Groundwater, Bureau of: JILL D. JONAS, *director,* 267-7545, jill.jonas@

    Fisheries Management and Habitat Protection, Bureau of: MICHAEL D. STAGGS, *director,* 267-0796, michael.staggs@

    Watershed Management, Bureau of: RUSSELL A. RASMUSSEN, *director,* 267-7651, russell.rasmussen@

Field Regions:

    Northeast: RONALD KAZMIERCZAK, *director,* (920) 492-5815, 1125 North Military Avenue, P.O. Box 10448, Green Bay 54307-0448, ronald.kazmierczak@

Northern: JOHN F. GOZDZIALSKI, *director,* (715) 635-4010, Highway 70 West, P.O. Box 309, Spooner 54801; Co-regional office: (715) 369-8901, 107 Sutliff Avenue, P.O. Box 818, Rhinelander 54501, john.gozdzialski@

South Central: RUTHE BADGER, *director,* (608) 275-3260, 3911 Fish Hatchery Road, Fitchburg 53711, ruthe.badger@

Southeast: GLORIA L. MCCUTCHEON, *director,* (414) 263-8510, 2300 North Dr. Martin Luther King Jr. Drive, P.O. Box 12436, Milwaukee 53212, gloria.mccutcheon@

West Central: SCOTT HUMRICKHOUSE, *director,* (715) 839-3712, 1300 W. Clairemont Avenue, P.O. Box 4001, Eau Claire 54702-4001, scott.humrickhouse@

Publications: *Wisconsin Natural Resources* (bimonthly magazine by subscription – call (608) 267-7410 or (800) 678-9472); *Wisconsin State Parks – Explore and Enjoy;* parks newspapers and visitor guides; hunting, fishing, trapping, snowmobiling, ATV, and boating regulations; various brochures, fact sheets, and reports (lists available). Teachers may write to the Bureau of Communication and Education for a list of publications.

Number of Employees: 2,823.75.

Total Budget 2003-05: $912,056,700.

Statutory References: Sections 15.05 (1) (c), 15.34, and 15.343; Chapters 23, 26-33, 87, 88, and 160.

Agency Responsibility: The Department of Natural Resources (DNR) is responsible for implementing state and federal laws that protect and enhance Wisconsin's natural resources, including its air, land, water, forests, wildlife, fish, and plants. It coordinates the many state-administered programs that protect the environment and provides a full range of outdoor recreational opportunities for Wisconsin residents and visitors.

Organization: The 7 members of the Natural Resources Board serve staggered 6-year terms. At least 3 of them must be from the northern part of the state and at least 3 from the southern part. Board members are subject to restrictions on holding DNR permits or depending on permit holders for a significant portion of their income. The board directs and supervises the department and acts as a formal point of contact for citizens.

The department is administered by a secretary appointed by the governor with the advice and consent of the senate. The secretary appoints the department's division administrators from outside the classified service. The regional directors, who are appointed from the classified service, manage all of the agency's field operations for their respective areas and report directly to the secretary.

Unit Functions: The *Division of Air and Waste* protects the state's air quality and general environmental health through air pollution control and solid and hazardous waste management in cooperation with the federal Environmental Protection Agency, international agencies, local governments, private industry, and citizens. It develops air quality implementation plans, monitors air quality, conducts inspections, operates a permit program, and initiates compliance actions in accordance with state and federal requirements. The division's waste management program oversees plan review, licensing, inspection, and compliance actions, relating to the generation, transportation, treatment, storage, reuse, and disposal of solid and hazardous waste materials. It reviews and approves local recycling programs and provides technical and marketing assistance and public outreach in support of recycling efforts and expertise for businesses regarding pollution prevention and waste reduction. It also regulates metallic mining activities and oversees the statewide implementation of county and local nonmetallic mining reclamation programs. The division's remediation and redevelopment program is responsible for the cleanup of contaminated sites that fall under the following legislation: the hazardous substances spills law, the environmental repair law, the abandoned container law, the federal Superfund law, the state land recycling law, and the Resource Conservation and Recovery Act.

The *Division of Customer and Employee Services* provides a variety of customer services including the sale of hunting and fishing licenses, boat, ATV, and snowmobile registration, environmental education programs and public information. It oversees distribution of financial aids for environmental programs that benefit local governments and nonprofit conservation organizations, such as the Clean Water Fund and the Stewardship Fund, and acts as liaison to federal and state agencies. The division also provides a variety of management services for the department, including budgetary and financial services, personnel and human resource management, computer and information technology support, affirmative action, employee assistance, training, and telecommunication services.

The *Division of Enforcement and Science* is responsible for enforcing the state's conservation, hunting, fishing, environmental, and safety laws and for conducting research on natural resource issues. Its game wardens and environmental staff promote compliance with the law through educational outreach programs, such as classes in hunting, boating, snowmobile, and all-terrain vehicle safety. The division reviews major public and private proposals under the federal and state Environmental Policy Acts, certifies laboratories and operators of wastewater treatment systems, water supply systems, incinerators, sanitary landfills, and septage services. The division is also responsible for provision of agency laboratory services (analytical chemistry and biological) through the Wisconsin State Laboratory of Hygiene and other private contract laboratories as necessary. The division also conducts biological and social science research, provides technical writing, editing, and publication of research results, and it provides expertise to assist other divisions and guide the department in policy formation. The Office of Energy is also housed in the division, and is responsible for improving and increasing the coordination of transmission construction project reviews between the Public Service Commission and the department. The Office of Energy is responsible for coordinating the regulatory review for siting utility projects and serves all DNR programs by developing guidance and information on natural resources issues as they relate to the broader planning and infrastructure development efforts for Wisconsin's energy future.

The *Division of Forestry,* created by 1999 Wisconsin Act 9, is responsible for the administration and implementation of programs that protect and manage the state's forest resources in a sustainable manner so as to provide economic, ecological, social, recreational, and cultural benefits. The division is involved with the management of about 16 million acres of public and private forest land and millions of urban trees in the state. All of the 490,000 acres of state forest land were certified in 2004 as sustainably managed by third party auditors from the Forest Stewardship Council and Sustainable Forestry Initiative. Foresters provide assistance to private woodlot owners; offer expertise in urban forestry; manage and monitor forest insects and diseases; operate three tree nurseries; provide public education and awareness activities; and work in partnership with county foresters, the timber industry, and environmental groups. The division administers grants and loans to county forests, urban forestry grants to communities, forest landowner grants to woodland owners, and forest fire protection grants to fire departments. The fire management program is responsible for forest fire protection on 18 million acres of forest, brush, and grassland and coordinates with local fire departments to prevent and control forest fires.

The *Division of Land* has major responsibility for protecting and conserving state wildlife; state lands, parks, trails, southern forests, and recreation areas; rare and endangered animal and plant species, and natural communities; and outdoor recreational resources. The division operates educational programs and helps private landowners manage their lands for the benefit of wildlife and rare resources. It manages wildlife and habitats on about 1.5 million acres of land owned or leased by the state and works with federal, county, and other local government authorities to protect and manage the resources on an additional 3.6 million acres of public lands, including national and county forests. The wildlife program manages populations such as deer, bear, furbearers, waterfowl and birds, and maintains and restores habitats such as wetlands, grasslands, and prairies. The endangered resources program works to restore and maintain the endangered populations of Wisconsin's native plant and animal species, supported primarily by funds derived from voluntary contributions designated by taxpayers on their state income tax returns and through the Endangered Resources license plate. Parks personnel manage the state's extensive parks, southern forests, recreation areas, and trails systems, which are designed for the conservation of natural resources and a wide variety of recreational activities including biking, hiking, snowmobiling, and camping. The division is also responsible for land acquisition and the development of public use facilities on state lands, and it coordinates the Stewardship Program, which provides grants for the purchase of lands for natural and recreational areas, wildlife habitats, urban green spaces, local parks, trails, and riverways.

The *Division of Water* works with many partners to protect public health and safety, and the quality and quantity of Wisconsin's groundwater, surface water, and aquatic ecosystems. The division is responsible for implementing the Clean Water Act in order to achieve the goal of fishable and swimmable waters throughout Wisconsin. Division staff work to prevent or regulate water pollution from industries, municipal sewage treatment facilities, construction sites, farms, and urban areas. The division monitors compliance, sets water quality standards, and provides financial and technical assistance. Division programs protect drinking water and groundwater resources for both human and ecosystem health, and ensure the safety and security of the state's drinking water systems and private wells. The division strives to enhance and restore outstanding fisheries in Wisconsin's waters. It regulates sport and commercial fishing through licensing and provides fish hatchery services, fish stocking and surveying, aquatic habit improvement, angler education, and public access programs. The division helps protect the waters of the state that are held in trust for all the people of the state through the Public Trust Doctrine. Division staff oversee the placement of structures in state waters, wetland management and restoration, shoreland zoning, and floodplain management. The division helps local government units to protect lives and property through floodplain management and dam safety inspections. The division cooperates with many states and Canada to protect the water quality, quantity, and ecosystems of the Mississippi River and Great Lakes basins.

The *Field Regions* enable the department to make its programs accessible to the general public. Each of the 5 regions is divided into 4 to 6 geographic management units whose boundaries are principally based on major river basins. Most DNR field staff work within these units, although some, such as conservation wardens, are assigned to counties within units. This structure combines employees with different types of expertise into interdisciplinary teams responsible for assessing natural resource and environmental needs from a broader perspective.

History: Today, the Department of Natural Resources has dual responsibility for both traditional conservation duties and environmental protection. Its history and structure reflect more than a century of government and citizen involvement with these concerns. Wisconsin's earliest conservation legislation focused on fish, game, and forests. Chapter 253, Laws of 1874, created a Board of Fish Commissioners charged with hatching fish eggs received from the federal government and distributing the fry to Wisconsin waters. The governor was authorized in 1885 by Chapter 455 to appoint 3 fish wardens to enforce fishing regulations and collect statistics from commercial fishermen. Chapter 456, Laws of 1887, directed the governor to appoint 4 game wardens to enforce all laws protecting fish and game.

Chapter 229, Laws of 1897, established a 3-member commission to develop legislation creating a forestry department. The commission was directed to devise ways to use the state's forest resources without harming the climate or water supplies and to preserve forest resources without retarding the state's economic development. The report of this commission led to Chapter 450, Laws of 1903, which established a Department of State Forestry with a superintendent appointed by the Board of State Forest Commissioners. Chapter 495, Laws of 1907, created a State Park Board with authority to acquire and manage land for park purposes.

Chapter 406, Laws of 1915, consolidated all park and conservation functions under a 3-member Conservation Commission of Wisconsin, appointed by the governor with senate approval. From then until 1995, the management and conservation of Wisconsin's natural resources was directed by a part-time commission or board, except for the period 1923 to 1927, when a single full-time commissioner was created by Chapter 118, Laws of 1923, to head the Department of Conservation. Since the enactment of 1995 Wisconsin Act 27, which provided that the secretary would be appointed by the governor with senate consent rather than appointed by the board, the current board's role has been an advisory one.

The 1960s saw major changes in conservation legislation. Chapter 427, Laws of 1961, created a committee charged with developing a long-range plan for acquiring and improving outdoor recreation areas. It initiated the Outdoor Recreation Act Program (ORAP) to fund land acquisitions. In 1969, Chapter 353 expanded ORAP and authorized the state to incur debt up to $56 million between 1969 and 1981 for the purpose of providing outdoor recreation opportunities. With enactment of 1989 Wisconsin Act 31, the legislature created the Stewardship Program, which

State park naturalists guide hikes, chat with campers around campfires, and answer questions from school children. Visitors to Wisconsin state parks, such as Kohler-Andrae State Park pictured here, enjoy a wide range of interpretive programs including guided or self-guided nature hikes, displays and exhibits, evening programs, and the Junior Ranger/Wisconsin Explorer Program. (Robert Queen, Department of Natural Resources)

authorized up to $250 million in state debt to acquire and develop land for recreational uses, wild-life habitats, fisheries, and natural areas.

Wisconsin's antipollution efforts date back to Chapter 412, Laws of 1911, when the legislature gave the State Board of Health investigative powers in water pollution cases. Prior to that, such investigations were primarily the responsibility of local government. In Chapter 264, Laws of 1927, the legislature created a committee to supervise the water pollution control activities carried out by several state agencies, including the Conservation Commission. The Department of Resource Development, which had been created by Chapter 442, Laws of 1959, assumed water pollution control duties under Chapter 614, Laws of 1965, and statewide air pollution regulation with Chapter 83, Laws of 1967.

In the 1967 executive branch reorganization, the legislature created the Department of Natural Resources by combining the Department of Conservation and the Department of Resource Development. The new department was given authority to regulate air and water quality, as well as solid waste disposal, and directed to develop an integrated program to protect air, land, and water resources.

Chapter 274, Laws of 1971, required all state agencies to report on the environmental impacts of proposed actions that could significantly affect environmental quality. Chapter 275, Laws of 1971, provided for state protection of endangered fish and wildlife, and Chapter 370, Laws of 1977, placed nongame species and endangered wild plants under state protection. A program protecting surface waters from nonpoint source pollution was created by Chapter 418, Laws of 1977, and a groundwater protection program, based on numerical standards for polluting substances, was created by 1983 Wisconsin Act 410. In Wisconsin Act 335, the 1989 Legislature made major changes in the laws governing recycling, source reduction, and disposal of solid wastes.

Statutory Councils

Dry Cleaner Environmental Response Council: JILL C. FITZGERALD (small dry cleaning operation); RICHARD W. KLINKE, STEVEN PLATER (large dry cleaning operation); JAMES E. CHERWINKA (wholesale distributor of dry cleaning solvent); JEANNE TARVIN (engineer, professional geologist, hydrologist, or soil scientist); JIM FITZGERALD (manufacturer or seller of dry cleaning equipment) (appointed by governor).

The 6-member Dry Cleaner Environmental Response Council advises the department on matters related to the Dry Cleaner Environmental Response Program, which is administered by DNR and provides awards to dry cleaning establishments for assistance in the investigation and cleanup of environmental contamination. Council members are appointed for staggered 3-year terms. The council, which is scheduled to sunset on June 30, 2032, was created by 1997 Wisconsin Act 27, as amended by 1997 Wisconsin Act 300. Its composition and duties are prescribed in Sections 15.347 (2) and 292.65 (13) of the statutes.

Council on Forestry: PAUL DELONG (chief state forester); SENATORS BRESKE, DECKER; REPRESENTATIVES FRISKE, HUBLER; FREDERIC SOUBA, JR. (forest products company which owns and manages large forest land tracts representative); WILLIAM HORVATH (owners of nonindustrial, private forest land representative); vacancy (counties containing county forests representative); WILLIAM WARD (paper and pulp industry representative); TROY BROWN (lumber industry representative); MARY HUSTON (nonprofit conservation organization representative); FRED CLARK (forester who provides consultation services); JEFFREY STIER (school of forestry representative); JAMES HEEREY (conservation education representative); JON GEENEN (forestry-affiliated labor union representative); KENNETH OTTMAN (urban and community forestry representative); ROBERT ROGERS (Society of American Foresters representative); DENNIS BROWN (timber producer organization representative); LEON CHURCH (secondary wood industry representative).

The 19-member Council on Forestry advises the governor, the legislature, the Departments of Natural Resources and Commerce, and other state agencies on topics relating to forestry in Wisconsin including: protection from fire, insects, and disease; sustainable forestry; reforestation and forestry genetics; management and protection of urban forests; increasing the public's knowledge and awareness of forestry issues; forestry research; economic development and marketing of forestry products; legislation affecting forestry; and staff and funding needs for forestry programs. The council shall submit a biennial report on the status of the state's forestry resources and industry to the governor and the appropriate standing committees of the legislature by June 1 of each odd-numbered year. All members are appointed by the governor. Lengths of terms are not specified by law. The council was created by 2001 Wisconsin Act 109. Its composition and duties are prescribed in Sections 15.347 (19) and 26.02 of the statutes.

Metallic Mining Council: Inactive.

The 9-member Metallic Mining Council advises the department on matters relating to the reclamation of mined land. Its members are appointed by the secretary of natural resources for staggered 3-year terms, and they are expected to represent "a variety and balance of economic, scientific, and environmental viewpoints." The council was created by Chapter 377, Laws of 1977, and its composition and duties are prescribed in Sections 15.347 (12) and 144.448 of the statutes.

Milwaukee River Revitalization Council: SHARON GAYAN (designated by secretary of natural resources), KIT SORENSON (designated by secretary of tourism); GARY A. AHRENS, JOHN D. BUECHEL, PETER J. GUNNLAUGSSON, JAMES HEILIGENSTEIN, RAYMOND R. KRUEGER, PATRICK T. MARCHESE, MARY ANN PETERSON, ALFRED L. SCHLECHT, 3 vacancies. (All except *ex officio* members are appointed by governor.)

The 13-member Milwaukee River Revitalization Council advises the legislature, governor, and department on matters related to environmental, recreational, and economic revitalization of the Milwaukee River Basin, and it assists local governments in planning and implementing projects. It is also responsible for developing and implementing a plan that encourages multiple recreational, entrepreneurial, and cultural activities along the streams of the Milwaukee River Basin. Its 11 appointed members serve 3-year terms. Each of the priority watersheds in the basin must be represented by at least one council member. The council was created by 1987 Wisconsin Act 399, and its composition and duties are prescribed in Sections 15.347 (15) and 23.18 of the statutes.

Natural Areas Preservation Council: SUSAN SULLIVAN BORKIN (MPM employee appointed by Milwaukee Public Museum board of directors), *chairperson;* PATRICIA MARINAC (DPI employee appointed by superintendent of public instruction), *vice chairperson;* SIGNE HOLTZ (DNR employee appointed by Natural Resources Board), *secretary;* CRAIG THOMPSON (DNR employee appointed by Natural Resources Board); JOHN W. ATTIG, TIMOTHY J. EHLINGER, DENNIS H. YOCKERS, JOY B. ZEDLER (UW employees appointed by UW System Board of Regents); EVELYN A. HOWELL, SUSAN E. LEWIS, CHARLES LUTHIN (appointed by council of the Wisconsin Academy of Sciences, Arts and Letters).

The 11-member Natural Areas Preservation Council advises the department on matters pertaining to the protection of natural areas that contain native biotic communities and habitats for rare species. It also makes recommendations about gifts or purchases for the state natural areas system. The council was created by Chapter 566, Laws of 1951, as the State Board for Preservation of Scientific Areas. It was renamed the Scientific Areas Preservation Council in Chapter 327, Laws of 1961, and given its current name in 1985 Wisconsin Act 29. One of the appointments from the Wisconsin Academy of Sciences, Arts and Letters must represent private colleges in the state. Its composition and duties are prescribed in Sections 15.347 (4) and 23.26 of the statutes.

Snowmobile Recreational Council: NICHOLAS BERENS, KAREN CARLSON, THOMAS CHWALA, BEVERLY ANN DITTMAR, LARRY ERICKSON, ANDY MALECKI, KATHLEEN RASMUSSEN, THOMAS THORNTON, MICHAEL WILLMAN (northern representatives); MICHAEL J. CERNY, JERRY GREEN, SAM LANDES, JON SCHWEITZER, RICHARD J. STEIMEL, DONNA JEAN WHITE (southern representatives). (All are appointed by governor with senate consent.)

The 15-member Snowmobile Recreational Council carries out studies and makes recommendations to the governor, the legislature, and the Department of Natural Resources and the Department of Transportation regarding all matters affecting snowmobiling. Council members are appointed for staggered 3-year terms. At least 5 must represent the northern part of the state, and at least 5 must represent the southern part. The council was created by Chapter 277, Laws of 1971, and its composition and duties are prescribed in Sections 15.347 (7) and 350.14 of the statutes.

State Trails Council: KEN L. CARPENTER, THOMAS HUBER, CHRISTOPHER KEGEL, DONALD M. KIRN, RAMSEY A.R. LEE, CONNIE LODEN, MICHAEL MCFADZEN, DAVID PHILLIPS, THOMAS J. THORNTON (appointed by governor).

The 9-member State Trails Council advises the department about the planning, acquisition, development, and management of state trails. Its members are appointed for 4-year terms. It was created by 1989 Wisconsin Act 31, and its composition and duties are prescribed in Sections 15.347 (16) and 23.175 (2) (c) of the statutes.

Independent Organization — Conservation Congress

Conservation Congress Executive Council: STEVEN OESTREICHER (District 3), *chairperson;* EDGAR HARVEY, JR. (District 8), *vice chairperson;* ALLEN OPALL (District 3), *secretary-treasurer;* RALEIGH FOX, RICHARD KIRCHMEYER (District 1); MICHAEL REITER, RAYMOND SMITH (District 2); JERRY AULIK, ROBERT ELLINGSON, JR. (District 4); RUSSELL HITZ, MARC SCHULTZ (District 5); MERLIN LINDOW, DAVID PUHL (District 6); DICK KOERNER, DALE MAAS (District 7); LARRY BONDE (District 8); DAVID LADD, MICHAEL ROGERS (District 9); JOE CAPUTO, KENNETH RISLEY (District 10); PAUL MADDEN, DAVID POFF (District 11); THEODORE LIND, EDWARD REWOLINSKI (District 12).

The Conservation Congress is a private citizens group, and its 24-member executive council advises the Natural Resources Board on all matters under the board's jurisdiction. The Conservation Congress is organized into 12 districts statewide. Each district elects 2 members to one-year terms on the executive council. The congress originated in 1934 and received statutory recognition in Chapter 179, Laws of 1971. Its duties are prescribed in Section 15.348 of the statutes.

INDEPENDENT UNITS ATTACHED FOR BUDGETING, PROGRAM COORDINATION, AND RELATED MANAGEMENT FUNCTIONS BY SECTION 15.03 OF THE STATUTES

GROUNDWATER COORDINATING COUNCIL

Groundwater Coordinating Council: TODD AMBS (designated by secretary of natural resources), BERNI MATTSSON (designated by secretary of commerce), NICHOLAS J. NEHER (designated by secretary of agriculture, trade and consumer protection), HENRY ANDERSON (designated by secretary of health and family services), DAN SCUDDER (designated by secretary of transportation), FRANCES GARB (designated by president, UW System), JAMES ROBERTSON (state geologist), vacancy (representing governor).

Statutory References: Sections 15.347 (13) and 160.50.

Agency Responsibility: The 8-member Groundwater Coordinating Council advises state agencies on the coordination of nonregulatory programs related to groundwater management. Member agencies exchange information regarding groundwater monitoring, budgets for groundwater programs, data management, public information efforts, laboratory analyses, research, and state appropriations for research. The council reports annually to the legislature, governor, and agencies represented regarding the council's activities and recommendations and its assessment of the current state of groundwater resources and related management programs. Persons designated to serve on behalf of their agency heads must be agency employees with "sufficient authority to deploy agency resources and directly influence agency decision making." The governor's representative serves a 4-year term. The council was created by 1983 Wisconsin Act 410.

INVASIVE SPECIES COUNCIL

Invasive Species Council: LAURIE OSTERNDORF (DNR secretary designee); LAURA ARBUCKLE (DOA secretary designee); ESTHER CHAPMAN (DATCP secretary designee); BERNICE MATTSSON (Commerce secretary designee); WILL CHRISTIANSON (Tourism secretary designee); RICHARD STARK (DOT secretary designee); CHARLES HENRIKSEN, GREGORY LONG, PETER MURRAY, KENNETH RAFFA, JAMES REINARTZ, REBECCA SAPPER, DENNIS SEEVERS (appointed by governor).

The 13-member Invasive Species Council conducts studies related to controlling invasive species and makes recommendations to the Department of Natural Resources regarding a system for classifying invasive species under the department's statewide invasive species control program and procedures for awarding grants to public and private agencies engaged in projects to control invasive species. All except *ex officio* members or their designees are appointed by the governor to 5-year terms to represent public and private interests affected by the presence of invasive species in the state. The council was created by 2001 Wisconsin Act 109. Its composition and duties are prescribed in Sections 15.347 (18) and 23.22 of the statutes.

LAKE MICHIGAN COMMERCIAL FISHING BOARD

Lake Michigan Commercial Fishing Board: CHARLES W. HENRIKSEN, RICHARD R. JOHNSON, MICHAEL LECLAIR, MARK MARICQUE, DEAN SWAER (licensed, active commercial fishers); NEIL A. SCHWARZ (licensed, active wholesale fish dealer); DAN PAWLITZKE (state citizen). (All are appointed by governor.)

Statutory References: Sections 15.345 (3) and 29.33 (7).

Agency Responsibility: The 7-member Lake Michigan Commercial Fishing Board was created by Chapter 418, Laws of 1977. Its members must live in counties contiguous to Lake Michigan. The 5 commercial fishers must represent fisheries in specific geographic areas. The board reviews applications for transfers of commercial fishing licenses between individuals, establishes criteria for allotting catch quotas to individual licensees, assigns catch quotas when the department establishes special harvest limits, and assists the department in establishing criteria for identifying inactive license holders.

LAKE SUPERIOR COMMERCIAL FISHING BOARD

Lake Superior Commercial Fishing Board: MAURINE HALVORSON, CRAIG HOOPMAN, ERIC JOHNSON (licensed, active commercial fishers); JEFF BODIN (licensed, active wholesale fish dealer); BILL DAMBERG (state citizen). (All are appointed by governor.)

Statutory References: Sections 15.345 (2) and 29.33 (7).

Agency Responsibility: The 5-member Lake Superior Commercial Fishing Board was created by Chapter 418, Laws of 1977. Its members must live in counties contiguous to Lake Superior. The board reviews applications for transfers of commercial fishing licenses between individuals, establishes criteria for allotting catch quotas to individual licensees, assigns catch quotas when

Department of Natural Resources fisheries biologists remove scales from a walleye before releasing it back into White Sand Lake in Vilas County. Sampling scales from fish reveals age and growth patterns within the population, and environmental conditions of the lake. (Robert Queen, Department of Natural Resources)

the department establishes special harvest limits, and assists the department in establishing criteria for identifying inactive license holders.

COUNCIL ON RECYCLING

Council on Recycling: JEFFREY A. FIELKOW, NEIL PETERS-MICHAUD, JOHN S. PIOTROWSKI, JOHN REINDL, CECELIA A. STENCIL, WILLIAM R. SWIFT, CHARLOTTE R. ZIEVE (appointed by governor).

Statutory References: Sections 15.347 (17) and 159.22.

Agency Responsibility: The 7 members of the Council on Recycling are appointed to 4-year terms that coincide with that of the governor. The council, which was created by 1989 Wisconsin Act 335, promotes implementation of the state's solid waste reduction, recovery, and recycling programs; helps public agencies coordinate programs and exchange information; advises state agencies about creating administrative rules and establishing priorities for market development; and advises the DNR and the UW System about education and research related to solid waste recycling. The council also promotes a regional and interstate marketing system for recycled materials and reports to the legislature about market development and research to encourage recycling. The council advises the department about statewide public information activities and advises the governor and the legislature.

WISCONSIN WATERWAYS COMMISSION

Wisconsin Waterways Commission: JAMES F. ROONEY (Lake Michigan area), *chairperson;* KENNETH GENISOT (Lake Superior area), MAUREEN KINNEY (Mississippi River area), KURT KOEPPLER (Lake Winnebago watershed), ROGER WALSH (inland area). (All are appointed by governor with senate consent.)

Mailing Address: P.O. Box 7921, Madison 53707.

Location: State Natural Resources Building (GEF 2), 101 South Webster Street, Madison.

Telephone: (608) 266-5897.

Statutory References: Sections 15.345 (1) and 30.92.

Agency Responsibility: The 5-member Wisconsin Waterways Commission was created by Chapter 274, Laws of 1977. Its members serve staggered 5-year terms, and each must represent a specific geographic area and be knowledgeable about that area's recreational water use problems. The commission may have studies conducted to determine the need for recreational boating facilities; approve financial aid to local governments for development of recreational boating projects, including the acquisition of weed harvesters; and recommend administrative rules for the recreational facilities boating program.

Office of the
STATE PUBLIC DEFENDER

Public Defender Board: DANIEL M. BERKOS, *chairperson;* STELLA A. YOUNG (public member), *secretary;* JAMES M. BRENNAN, JOHN HOGAN, PAMELA PEPPER, ELLEN THORN, NANCY C. WETTERSTEN (State Bar members); JOSEPH G. MORALES, MAI NENG XIONG (public members). (Except as indicated, all are state bar members. All are appointed by governor with senate consent.)

State Public Defender: NICHOLAS L. CHIARKAS, 266-0087, chiarkasn@

Deputy State Public Defender: KELLI THOMPSON, 266-5480, thompsonk@

Executive Assistant/Legislative Liaison: KRISTA GINGER, 264-8572, gingerk@

Legal Counsel: KELLIE KRAKE, 267-0299, krakek@

Public Information Officer: RANDY KRAFT, 267-3587, kraftr@

Chief Information Officer: GAIL ZAUCHA, 261-0621, zauchag@

Administrative Services Division: ARLENE F. BANOUL, *director,* 266-9447, banoula@
Appellate Division: MARLA J. STEPHENS, *director,* Madison: 264-8573; Milwaukee: (414) 227-4891; stephensm@
Assigned Counsel Division: DEBORAH M. SMITH, *director,* 261-8856, smithd@
Trial Division: MICHAEL TOBIN, *director,* 266-8259, tobinm@
Deputy Trial Division Director/Affirmative Action Officer: JENNIFER BIAS, 261-7981, biasj@

For e-mail combine the user ID and the state extender: userid@**mail.opd.state.wi.us**

Mailing Address: P.O. Box 7923, Madison 53707-7923.
Location: 315 North Henry Street, 2nd Floor, Madison.
Telephone: 266-0087.
Fax: 267-0584.
Internet Address: http://www.wisspd.org
Number of Employees: 527.55.
Total Budget 2003-05: $140,930,600.
Statutory References: Section 15.78; Chapter 977.

Agency Responsibility: The Office of the State Public Defender makes determinations of indigence and provides legal representation for specified defendants who are unable to afford a private attorney. The state public defender, who must be a member of the state bar, serves at the pleasure of the Public Defender Board.

Organization: The 9-member Public Defender Board appoints the state public defender, promulgates rules for determining indigence, and establishes procedures for certifying lists of private attorneys who can be assigned as counsel. Board members are appointed for staggered 3-year terms, and at least 5 of these must be members of the State Bar of Wisconsin. Members may not be or be employed by a judicial or law enforcement officer, a district attorney, a corporation counsel, or the state public defender.

Unit Functions: The *Administrative Services Division* oversees purchasing, personnel and payroll services, budget preparation, case management, and fiscal analysis.

The *Appellate Division* uses both program staff and private attorneys to provide appellate assistance to indigents in all counties. It represents indigents involved in post-conviction or post-commitment proceedings in certain state and federal courts. It also acts upon certain cases relating to persons confined to state correctional and mental health institutions.

The *Assigned Counsel Division* oversees a variety of functions related to appointment of private attorneys to represent indigent clients in cases not handled by staff, including certification and training, logistical support, and payment of fees.

The *Trial Division* provides legal representation at the trial level to indigent persons who have been charged with adult felony crimes or misdemeanors punishable by imprisonment. It also represents minors charged with juvenile offenses, persons petitioned mentally ill, or individuals involved in family disputes, including paternity actions and termination of parental rights.

History: Both the United States Constitution (Sixth and Fourteenth Amendments) and the Wisconsin Constitution (Article I, Section 7), as interpreted by the U.S. and Wisconsin Supreme Courts, guarantee the right to publicly-provided counsel for poor people charged with crimes or facing potential deprivations of liberty. In 1859, the Wisconsin Supreme Court ruled, in *Carpenter and Sprague vs. the County of Dane* (9 Wis. 274), that a county is liable to pay for an attorney provided by the court in a criminal case to represent an indigent defendant who cannot otherwise afford representation.

The position of state public defender was created in 1966 by Chapter 479, Laws of 1965, under the supervision of the Wisconsin Supreme Court and funded, in part, by a private grant from the Ford Foundation. The duties of the office were originally confined to appellate defense, and its mission was to pursue post-conviction appeals for indigents before the appropriate court, including the U.S. Supreme Court. Defense of indigents at the trial court level remained a county responsibility, dependent upon court-appointed private counsel paid by the county or privately funded public defender services.

Chapter 29, Laws of 1977, transferred the state public defender from the judicial branch to the executive branch as an independent agency under the Public Defender Board, which was authorized to appoint the defender to a 5-year renewable term with removal only for cause. (Chapter 356, Laws of 1979, later provided that the public defender serve at the pleasure of the board.) Chapter 29 also transferred the responsibility for defense of indigents at the trial level from the counties to the public defender's office, but representation by the defender's staff was limited, based on funding and statutory criteria. Trial duties were, and continue to be, divided between state attorneys and private counsel paid by the state.

Chapter 29, Laws of 1977, directed the public defender to determine the percentage of cases that private counsel would handle in each county. Chapter 356, Laws of 1979, established those percentages by law with the public defender staff assuming various portions of the caseloads in 47 counties and private counsel responsible for all cases in the remaining 25 counties. 1985 Wisconsin Act 29 expanded the use of public defender staff attorneys to all 72 counties and repealed the sunset provision enacted in 1979, which would have abolished the agency, effective November 15, 1985.

1995 Wisconsin Act 27 directed the public defender to enter into annual fixed fee contracts with private counsel and limited the number of trial-level cases assigned to private attorneys to one-third of all cases handled. It also eliminated public defender representation in some cases, including certain matters related to prison and jail conditions, sentence modifications, probation and parole revocations, child support, and parents of children in need of protection or services (CHIPS).

Department of
PUBLIC INSTRUCTION

State Superintendent: ELIZABETH BURMASTER, 266-1771, elizabeth.burmaster@

Deputy State Superintendent: ANTHONY EVERS, 266-1771, anthony.evers@

Chief of Staff/Executive Assistant to State Superintendent: TRICIA YATES, 266-1771, tricia.yates@

Special Assistant: SUE GRADY, 266-1771, sue.grady@

Policy Initiatives Advisor: MICHAEL THOMPSON, 266-3584, michael.thompson@

Legal Services, Office of: vacancy, *chief legal counsel,* 266-9353.

Education Information Services: JOHN JOHNSON, *director,* 266-1098, john.johnson@

Mailing Address: P.O. Box 7841, Madison 53707-7841.

Location: State Education Building (GEF 3), 125 South Webster Street, Madison.

Telephones: 266-3390; (800) 441-4563; TDD: 267-2427.

Fax: 267-1052.

Internet Addresses: Departmental: http://www.dpi.state.wi.us
BadgerLink: http://www.badgerlink.net

Address e-mail by combining the user ID and the state extender: userid@**dpi.state.wi.us**

Number of Employees: 637.14.

Total Budget 2003-05: $11,118,309,600.

Constitutional Reference: Article X, Section 1.

Statutory References: Section 15.37; Chapters 43 and 115-121.

Academic Excellence, Division for: DEBORAH MAHAFFEY, *assistant superintendent,* 266-3361, deborah.mahaffey@; Division Fax: 267-9275.

Career and Technical Education: MARGARET ELLIBEE, *director,* 267-9251, margaret.ellibee@

Content and Learning: MICHAEL G. GEORGE, *director,* 266-2364, michael.george@

Teacher Education, Professional Development, and Licensing: KATHRYN M. LIND, *director,* 266-1788, kathryn.lind@

Finance and Management, Division for: BRIAN PAHNKE, *assistant superintendent,* 267-9124, brian.pahnke@; Division Fax: 266-3644.

Community Nutrition: DAVID C. DEES, *director,* 267-9123, david.dees@

Human Resources: KATHERINE J. KNUDSON, *director,* 267-9200, katherine.knudson@

Management Services: SUZANNE LINTON, *director,* 266-3320, suzanne.linton@

Policy and Budget: MICHAEL BORMETT, *director,* 266-2804, michael.bormett@

School Financial Services: DAVID R. CARLSON, *director,* 266-6968, david.carlson@

School Management Services: ROBERT A. SOLDNER, *director,* 266-7475, robert.soldner@

School Nutrition: RICHARD A. MORTENSEN, *director,* 267-9121, richard.mortensen@

Learning Support: Equity and Advocacy, Division for: CAROLYN STANFORD TAYLOR, *assistant superintendent,* 266-1649, carolyn.stanford.taylor@; Division Fax: 267-3746, Division TTY: 267-2427.

Special Education: STEPHANIE PETSKA, *director,* 266-1781, stephanie.petska@

Student Services, Prevention and Wellness: DOUGLAS WHITE, *director,* 266-3584, douglas.white@

Statewide Vision and Hearing Services: SUE ENOCH, *director,* 266-9849, sue.enoch@

Wisconsin Center for the Blind and Visually Impaired: 1700 West State Street, Janesville 53546-5399, (608) 758-6100, (800) 832-9784, Fax: (608) 758-6161.

Wisconsin Educational Services Program for the Deaf and Hard of Hearing: ALEX SLAPPEY, *director,* 309 West Walworth Avenue, Delavan 53115-1099, (262) 740-2066, voice: (877) 973-3323, TTY: (877) 973-3324, Fax: (262) 728-7160, alex.slappey@

Libraries, Technology, and Community Learning, Division for: RICHARD GROBSCHMIDT, *assistant superintendent,* 266-2205, richard.grobschmidt@

Division Internet Address: http://www.dpi.state.wi.us/dpi/dltcl

Applications Development: TIFFANY BOYD, *supervisor,* 266-6947, tiffany.boyd@

Bright Beginnings/Family-School-Community Involvement: JANE L. GRINDE, *director,* 266-9356, jane.grinde@

Information Technology: BRIAN WILMOT, *director,* 266-7049, brian.wilmot@

Instructional Media and Technology: vacancy, *director,* 266-3856.

Library and Statistical Information: KAY IHLENFELDT, 266-3108, kay.ihlenfeldt@

Public Library Development: MICHAEL CROSS, *director,* 267-9225, michael.cross@

Reference and Loan Library: SALLY DREW, *director,* 224-6161, sally.drew@

Reading and Student Achievement, Division for: MARGARET PLANNER, *assistant superintendent,* 266-5450, margaret.planner@

Educational Accountability: JAMES M. WALL, *director,* 267-1072, james.wall@

Successful Schools and Student Achievement: JAMES M. WALL, *director,* 267-1072, james.wall@

Wisconsin Educational Opportunity Programs and Urban Education: KEVIN INGRAM, (414) 227-4413, kevin.ingram@

Publications: Biennial Report; *Channel;* Directory of Wisconsin Public/Private Schools; various curriculum, instruction, library and student services publications and research studies. SEA-change, School Performance Report, Wisconsin Information Network for Successful Schools (WINSS), and electronic publications are available at the department's Internet site.

Agency Responsibility: The Department of Public Instruction provides direction and technical assistance for public elementary and secondary education in Wisconsin. The department offers a broad range of programs and professional services to local school administrators and staff. It distributes state school aids and administers federal aids to supplement local tax resources, improves curriculum and school operations, ensures education for children with disabilities, offers professional guidance and counseling, and develops school and public library resources.

Organization: The department is headed by the State Superintendent of Public Instruction, a constitutional officer who is elected on the nonpartisan spring ballot for a term of 4 years. The

DEPARTMENT OF PUBLIC INSTRUCTION

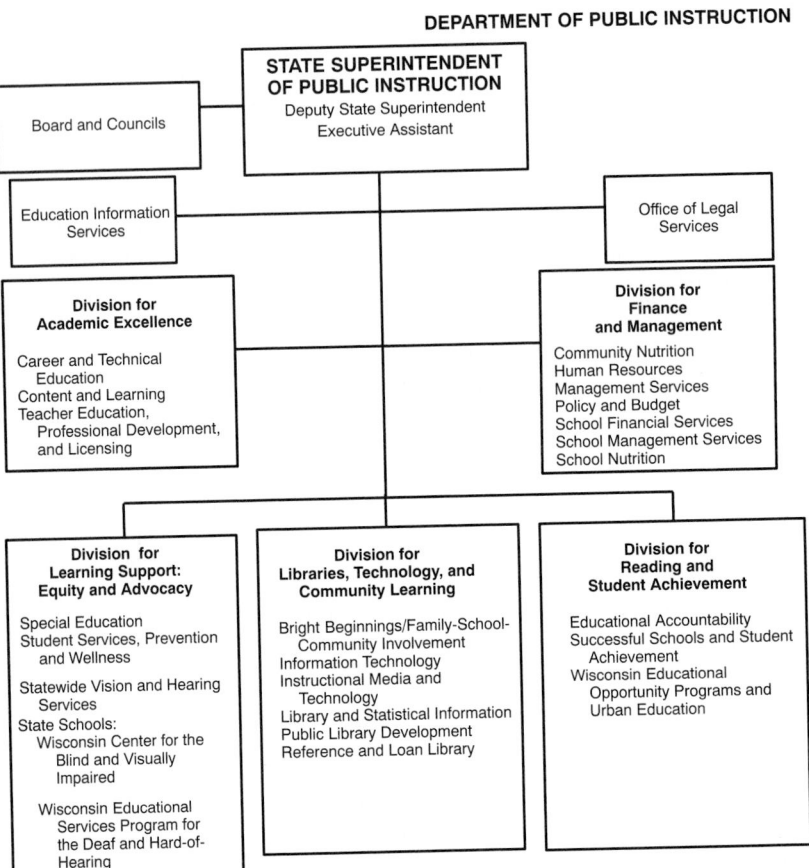

state superintendent appoints a deputy state superintendent and assistant state superintendents from outside the classified service. The assistant superintendents are responsible for administering the operating divisions of the department. The superintendent also appoints the director of the Office of Educational Accountability, which was created in Section 15.374 (1), Wisconsin Statutes, by 1993 Wisconsin Act 16.

Unit Functions: The *Division for Academic Excellence* offers assistance with curriculum development, developing and implementing academic and technical skills standards, instructional methods and strategies, educational opportunity programs, "virtual" schools and other online education programs, and professional development. The division reviews college and university teacher and administrator training programs and licenses public school teachers, pupil services personnel, administrators, and library professionals, as well as private school teachers and administrators who request and qualify for a license. It monitors school district and vocational education compliance with state nondiscrimination laws and rules.

The division administers a variety of programs that provide assistance, scholarships, and grants to public school students and teachers on the basis of merit and need. These programs include presidential awards for mathematics and science teachers, U.S. Senate youth, talent search and talent incentive grants, the federal Robert C. Byrd Honors Scholarships, and international exchanges with Germany and Japan. It conducts youth options and technical preparation programs, and the high school equivalency/general educational development (HSED/GED) program for state residents who have not completed high school. It administers federal programs that provide grants under Blue Ribbon Schools, foreign language assistance, student advanced placement, and alternate education. The division also administers funds for school districts under the Carl D. Perkins Vocational and Technical Education Act of 1998 to enhance and improve vocational and technical educational programs. It administers part of the state and federally funded Bilingual/English as a Second Language Program.

The *Division for Finance and Management* distributes state and federal school aids and grants; administers school district revenue limits; monitors the Milwaukee Parental Choice Program and the interdistrict open enrollment program; prescribes school financial accounting methods; consults with school districts on their budgets; and collects, analyzes, and publishes school finance data. Consulting services are provided to assist districts and charter schools with management and planning, school district reorganization, pupil transportation, private school relations, school board elections and duties, and finance and asset management. The division is responsible for both state and federally funded school food and nutrition services, nonschool child care food services, and elderly nutrition programs. It also provides support services to the department for financial management, human resources, budget preparation, educational policy and administrative rule development, and legislative analysis.

The *Division for Learning Support: Equity and Advocacy*, created in Section 15.373 (1), Wisconsin Statutes, as the Division for Handicapped Children by Chapter 327, Laws of 1967, and most recently renamed in 1993 Wisconsin Act 335, provides technical assistance, leadership, advocacy, staff development, training, and education to help meet the diverse cultural, emotional, social, health, and educational needs of Wisconsin's youth. The mission is met through collaboration with federal, state, and local groups. The division, through the state schools, Wisconsin Educational Services Program for the Deaf and Hard of Hearing and Wisconsin Center for the Blind and Visually Impaired, provides direct instruction to students and technical assistance through outreach to local educational agencies, communities, and families statewide. The division manages state and federal resources, monitors and evaluates programs and practices, and facilitates school-district and community efforts to meet specific needs of students. The division administers programs involving school nursing, social work, and psychological services; guidance and counseling services; alcohol, tobacco, and other drug abuse; suicide prevention; alcohol and traffic safety; school-age parents; school violence; prevention of HIV and other sexually transmitted diseases; pregnancy prevention; character education; health education; physical activity; comprehensive school health programs; compulsory school attendance; and after-school programs.

The division offers technical assistance and financial aid to help school districts provide a better education for children with disabilities, combat educational discrimination, and train professional staff. It is responsible for special educational programs and services for children with disabilities. It must ensure that all children with disabilities are identified, evaluated, and given appropriate education and services. It supervises all special education programs and checks their compliance with departmental standards and state and federal law. The division provides consultation for and supervision of the Pupil Nondiscrimination Program and Gender Equity Program.

The division administers the Wisconsin Educational Services Program for the Deaf and Hard of Hearing and the Wisconsin Center for the Blind and Visually Impaired (WCBVI). Each program operates a residential school for state residents who are ages 3 to 20, impaired, and in need of individualized instruction free of charge. Both schools provide academic and vocational education on site. Both programs also offer instructional and technical assistance, teaching materials, and evaluations of pupils to local school districts and other agencies. WCBVI also provides summer programs for students and adults and administers the Federal Quota Funds for student materials.

The *Division for Libraries, Technology, and Community Learning*, created as the Division for Library Services in Section 15.373 (2), Wisconsin Statutes, by Chapter 327, Laws of 1967, and most recently renamed in 2001 Wisconsin Act 48, provides assistance for the development and improvement of public and school libraries; fosters interlibrary cooperation and resource sharing; and promotes information and instructional technology in libraries. The division administers the state aid program for Wisconsin's 17 public library systems. It also administers the federal Library Services and Technology Act, the federal Educational Technology Grants, and the federal Learn and Serve America Program. Electronic content is provided through WINSS (Wisconsin

Information Network for Successful Schools), and other department resources. The division provides interlibrary loan and reference services to the state's libraries, maintains an electronic union catalog of statewide library holdings, and administers BadgerLink, the statewide full-text database project that allows access to thousands of magazines, newsletters, newspapers, pamphlets, and historical documents (www.badgerlink.net). It operates a professional library for department staff, state educators, and librarians. The division directs the public librarian certification program, the summer library reading program, and programs that foster family and community involvement and quality early childhood programs (including kindergarten) in schools, libraries, and communities. With grants from the Corporation for National and Community Service, the division oversees VISTA (Volunteers In Service To America) and AmeriCorps members who work around the state to promote learning and partnerships to close the achievement gap. Other grants enable the division to develop and enhance early childhood collaboration and civic learning. It also administers the department's data processing, information technology support, and school and library data collections.

The *Division for Reading and Student Achievement* is responsible for ensuring that all children attain proficiency in meeting the Wisconsin Model Academic Standards. The three teams in this division, Educational Accountability, Successful Schools and Student Achievement, and Wisconsin Educational Opportunity Programs and Urban Education, have as a major focus closing the achievement gap that exists among children of color, the economically disadvantaged, and their peers.

The Successful Schools and Student Achievement Team provides assessment results through statewide tests that measure student proficiency related to the Wisconsin Model Academic Standards. These data assist district and school personnel in evaluating and making decisions related to educational planning and programming. This team provides accountability outcomes related to state and federal legislation and gives technical assistance in evaluating results and developing improvement plans to schools and districts. Resources provided to districts and schools include a number of programs under the federal Elementary and Secondary Education Act of 1965 and the No Child Left Behind Act of 2001, including programs under Title I-Part A, Reading First, Even Start Family Literacy, Migrant Education, Neglected and Delinquent Youth, Comprehensive School Reform, Innovative Programs, McKinney-Vento Homeless Assistance Act, and the state class size reduction program Students Achievement Guarantee in Education (SAGE).

The Wisconsin Educational Opportunity Programs and Urban Education Team focuses on improving high school graduation rates, reducing dropouts and encourages non-traditional, minority, disadvantaged, and low-income students with college potential to pursue postsecondary education. Programs to achieve team objectives include state and federal Talent Search, Talent Incentive Program, Early Identification Program, Minority Pre-College Scholarship Program, Gear Up, and Upward Bound. The Urban Education program was established in 1995 to provide services to urban areas including Beloit, Kenosha, Milwaukee, and Racine to facilitate cooperative efforts to address the challenges and equity needs facing families, children, and educators in an urban setting. The Preschool to Grade 5 (P-5) program was created to provide for the special needs of this population.

History: The Wisconsin Constitution, as adopted in 1848, required the state legislature to provide by law for the establishment of district schools that would be free to all children between the ages of 4 and 20 years. It also created a State Superintendent of Public Instruction to supervise public education. Under the 1849 Wisconsin Statutes, the superintendent was ordered to visit schools in all the counties, recommend textbooks and courses of instruction, and distribute state money for public schools to the counties.

Originally, the superintendent was elected to a 2-year term at the partisan general election in November. With the adoption of a constitutional amendment in 1902, the superintendent was placed on the nonpartisan April ballot and given a 4-year term of office.

In the early years of statehood, the hiring of teachers was entirely a local matter. In 1861, the legislature created county superintendents of schools with the power to license teachers beginning in 1862. The state superintendent was also given licensing authority in 1868 (Chapter 169). Local districts and county superintendents continued to license teachers until 1939, when the legislature gave that power exclusively to the Department of Public Instruction.

State Superintendent of Public Instruction Elizabeth Burmaster reads to early childhood students. Beginning with the nation's first kindergarten in 1856, Wisconsin has been a leader in providing learning opportunities to younger students. (Department of Public Instruction)

For a number of years, state support of public education consisted of money derived principally from the sale of public lands that the federal government had granted to the state. In Chapter 287, Laws of 1885, the legislature levied a one-mill (one-tenth of a cent) state property tax to be collected by the state and distributed to counties for school support. The state's first attempt to equalize tax support for schools in property-poor districts was the Wisconsin Elementary Equalization Law of 1927 (Chapter 536). It was promoted by State Superintendent John Callahan, who also urged a 40% level of state support for local school costs – a figure not reached until after 1970. The 1995 Legislature enacted a law to ensure that state aids and school levy tax credits would cover two-thirds of local school revenues, but subsequently repealed that requirement in 2003.

Originally, Wisconsin only required tax support for elementary schools. Individual cities, such as Racine and Kenosha, funded their own high schools. The legislature enacted public support for high schools in 1875 (Chapter 323). Kindergarten originated in 1856 when Margarethe Schurz started a German-speaking program for children 2 through 5 years of age in Watertown, Wisconsin. The first public school kindergarten opened in Manitowoc in 1873 for 4- and 5-year-old children. The program continued to spread until, in 1973, the legislature required school districts to provide a 5-year-old kindergarten. In the 1990s, an increasing number of school districts offered full-day programs for 5-year-old children and kindergarten programs for 4-year-olds.

Although state law had contained some curriculum requirements as early as 1849, the legislature did not establish high school graduation requirements until 1983. In 1985, it prescribed a detailed set of standards local districts must meet to be eligible for state aid. The 1997 Legislature mandated that school boards adopt pupil academic standards in certain subjects, a series of examinations to measure pupil achievement in 4th, 8th, and 10th grades, and a high school graduation examination. The 2003 Legislature eliminated the high school graduation examination.

State concern for special education began with the establishment of the Wisconsin Institute for Education of the Blind in Janesville in 1850 and a school for the deaf in Delavan in 1852. These schools were administered by public welfare agencies until transferred to the Department of Public Instruction in 1947. The 1927 Legislature enacted laws to provide aid for special classes for "crippled children" and increased aid for districts to educate mentally handicapped children. Funding for education of all handicapped children was enacted in 1973 to comply with federal law.

While state administration of school libraries fell under the jurisdiction of the superintendent, the Free Library Commission set standards for public libraries. In 1965, the legislature transferred this function to the department.

Statutory Board and Councils

Alcohol and Other Drug Abuse Programs, Council on: HOLLY HART, *chairperson;* JEAN CRUIKSHANK, DOROTHY CRUST, PAT DEMOS, CLAUDE GILMORE, JOHN GREENWOOD, LISA HESCH, BARBARA HICKMAN, TASHA JENKINS, BOB KOVAR, PAT NEUDECKER, EVAN NORRIS, BARBARA PARISI, CINDY RINDFLEISCH, ROBERT RYKAL, GEORGE THATTAKARA, DENIS TUCKER, ROBERT ULLMAN (appointed by state superintendent).

The Council on Alcohol and Other Drug Abuse Programs advises the state superintendent about programs to prevent or reduce alcohol, tobacco, and other drug abuse by minors. The council consists of 18 members (by administrative rule) who serve at the pleasure of the state superintendent. The council was created by Chapter 331, Laws of 1979, and its duties are prescribed in Section 115.36 of the statutes.

Blind and Visual Impairment Education Council: NISSAN BAR-LEV (special education director), *chairperson;* AMY JONES, KAREN SMITH, TRUDY SWENSON (parents of visually impaired children); KAY GLODOWSKI, CHERYL ORGAS, RICHARD POMO (members of organizations affiliated with visually impaired); SUSAN KOKKO, DAWN SOTO (licensed teachers of visually impaired); JULIE HAPEMAN (licensed teacher of orientation and mobility); vacancy (licensed general education teacher); NANCY THOMPSON (school board member); RON DAYTON (school district administrator); FRED WOLLENBURG (CESA representative); LYN AYER (higher education representative); MARY ANN DAMM (Braille transcriber); ERICA WEISE (visually impaired representative) (all appointed by superintendent).

The 17-member Blind and Visual Impairment Education Council advises the state superintendent on statewide activities that will benefit visually impaired pupils; makes recommendations for improvements in services provided by the Wisconsin Center for the Blind and Visually Impaired; and proposes ways to improve the preparation of teachers and staff and coordination between the department and other agencies that offer services to the visually impaired. Members serve 3-year terms. At least one must be certified by the Library of Congress as a Braille transcriber. The higher education representative must either have experience as an educator of the visually impaired or an educator of teachers of the visually impaired. At least one of the three remaining members must be visually impaired. The council was created as the Council on the Blind by Chapter 276, Laws of 1969, renamed as the Council on the Education of the Blind in

Chapter 292, Laws of 1971, and renamed and substantially revised by 1999 Wisconsin Act 9. Its composition and duties are prescribed in Sections 15.377 (1) and 115.37 of the statutes.

Deaf and Hard-of-Hearing Education Council: CORA CORAZON-HOLLOWAY, CHRISTIANNE MURN (parents of hearing impaired children); POLLY ANN WILLIAMS-SLAPPEY (teacher of hearing impaired pupils); MARY GUIDO (licensed speech-language pathologist); JOHN WALDRON (school district special education director); JOANNE COLUMBO (licensed audiologist with expertise in educational audiology); AMY OTIS-WILBORN (educator of hearing impaired teachers); SUZETTE GARAY (technical college interpreter training instructor); SANDRA TONEY COOLEY (educational interpreter); ROBIN BARNES, KEVIN MCDONOUGH, ALICE SYKORA (other members) (all appointed by state superintendent).

The Deaf and Hard-of-Hearing Education Council advises the state superintendent on issues related to pupils who are hearing impaired. It informs the superintendent on services, programs, and research that could benefit those students. The council makes recommendations for improving services provided by the Wisconsin Educational Services Program for the Deaf and Hard of Hearing; reviews and makes recommendations on the level of quality and services available to hearing-impaired pupils; proposes ways to improve the preparation of teachers and other staff who provide services to the hearing impaired; and proposes ways to improve coordination between the department and providers of services to the hearing impaired. The council's 12 members serve 3-year terms. It was created by 2001 Wisconsin Act 57, and its composition and duties are prescribed in Sections 15.377 (2) and 115.372 of the statutes.

Library and Network Development, Council on: JOHN C. REID (public member), *chairperson;* A. EUGENE NEYHART (public member), *vice chairperson;* BARBARA ARNOLD (professional member), *secretary;* MARY M. BAYORGEON, CATHERINE HANSEN, LISA JEWELL, C. PATRICIA LAVIOLETTE, JOHN NICHOLS, KATHY PLETCHER, LISA SOLVERSON, LINDA STELTER, KRISTINE WENDT (professional members); MICHAEL BAHR, DONALD BULLEY, MIRIAM ERICKSON, ROBERT KOECHLEY, DOUGLAS H. LAY, CALVIN POTTER, KRISTI A. WILLIAMS (public members) (appointed by governor).

The 19-member Council on Library and Network Development advises the state superintendent and the administrator of the Division for Libraries, Technology, and Community Learning on the performance of their duties regarding library service. Members serve 3-year terms. The professional members represent various types of libraries and information services. The public members must demonstrate an interest in libraries and other types of information services. The council was created by Chapter 347, Laws of 1979, and its composition and duties are prescribed in Sections 15.377 (6) and 43.07 of the statutes.

Professional Standards Council for Teachers: LINDA HELF (public school teacher), *chairperson;* RYAN CHAMPEAU (public school principal), *vice chairperson;* REBECCA VAIL (public school district adminstrator), *secretary;* MARLENE OTT, TERRY SCHOESSOW, MURIEL SMITH-GROSS, MARY ZIMMERMAN, LYNN ZINDL (public school teachers); ANN CATTAU, LEAH JERABEK (public school pupil service professionals); DIANE OPPERMAN (public school special education teacher); GLORIA GOSS (private school teacher); JEFFREY BARNETT, CONNIE FOSTER (UW System educational faculty members); HILARY POLLACK (private college education faculty member); RUSS KAESKE, vacancy (public school board members); PAT LEWNO (parent of public school child); vacancy (student enrolled in teacher preparatory program) (appointed by state superintendent with senate consent).

The 19-member Professional Standards Council for Teachers advises the state superintendent regarding licensing and evaluating teachers; evaluation and approval of teacher education programs; the status of teaching in Wisconsin; school board practices to develop effective teaching; peer mentoring; evaluation systems; and alternative dismissal procedures.

Members serve 3-year terms, except the student member, who serves for 2 years. Public school teachers and pupil service professionals are recommended by the largest statewide labor organization representing teachers. The private school teacher is recommended by the Wisconsin Council of Religious and Independent Schools. The public school administrator and principal are recommended by their statewide organizations. Faculty members are recommended by the UW System president and the Wisconsin Association of Independent Colleges and Universities. The council was created by 1997 Wisconsin Act 298, and its composition and duties are prescribed in Sections 15.377 (8) and 115.245 of the statutes.

School District Boundary Appeal Board: ELIZABETH BURMASTER (superintendent of public instruction); DON BRIC, JAMES CRANDALL, DENNIS KAVANAUGH, MARY MALONEY, MARIAN MIEDEN, SUE NANNINGA, MICHAEL PIERCE, JUDITH REMINGTON, PATTI SILVER, MARY THURMAIER, THERESE TRAVIA, WALTER WETZEL (appointed by state superintendent).

The 13-member School District Boundary Appeal Board hears appeals from persons aggrieved by actions taken under Chapter 117, Wisconsin Statutes, providing for school district reorganization. The appointed members include 4 each from large, medium, and small district school boards, who are appointed for staggered 2-year terms. No two members may live within the boundaries of the same CESA. The board was created by 1983 Wisconsin Act 27, and its composition and duties are prescribed in Sections 15.375 (2) and 117.05 of the statutes.

Special Education, Council on: PATRICIA YAHLE, *chairperson;* BASIMAH ABDULLAH, BRIAN ANDERSON, EVELYN AZBELL, JUDI BECKER, GERALD FULTS, REBECCA GROVES, CYNTHIA HIRSCH, MARY HOPKINS-BEST, GLEN LAMPING, KIRBY LENTZ, MONICA LOPEZ, MANUEL LUGO, CHARLOTTE PRICE, TONIA SMITH, CYNTHIA SQUIRE, BETH WROBLEWSKI (appointed by state superintendent).

The Council on Special Education advises the state superintendent on programs for children with disabilities. It assists in developing evaluations, and reporting data to the U.S. Department of Education, developing policies, and advising the state superintendent regarding the needs of children with disabilities. The number of council members is unspecified, but the following categories must be represented: regular and special education teachers; institutions of higher education that train special education personnel; state and local education officials; administrators of programs for children with disabilities; agencies involved in financing or delivery of related services; private schools and charter schools; a vocational, community, or business organization that provides transitional services; the Department of Corrections; parents of children with disabilities; and individuals with disabilities. Council members are appointed for 3-year terms, and the majority must be individuals with disabilities or parents of children with disabilities. The council was created as the Council on Exceptional Education by Chapter 89, Laws of 1973, and renamed and revised by 1997 Wisconsin Act 164. Its composition and duties are prescribed in Section 15.377 (4) of the statutes.

PUBLIC SERVICE COMMISSION

Commissioners: DANIEL EBERT, 267-7897, daniel.ebert@, *chairperson;* ROBERT M. GARVIN, 267-7899, robert.garvin@; MARK MEYER, 267-7898, mark.meyer@ (appointed by governor with senate consent).

Executive Assistant to the Chairperson: DAN SCHOOFF, 266-1261, dan.schooff@

Secretary to the Commission: CHRISTY ZEHNER, 266-1247, christy.zehner@

Administrative Law Judge, Office of: DAVID C. WHITCOMB, 261-8522, david.whitcomb@

Governmental and Public Affairs, Office of: LINDA BARTH, *director,* 267-0912, linda.barth@

General Counsel: DAVID J. GILLES, 266-1264, dave.gilles@

Legislative Liaison: MATTHEW PAGEL, 266-1383, matthew.pagel@

Administrative Services, Division of: GORDON GRANT, *acting administrator,* 267-9086, gordon.grant@

Gas and Energy Division: ROBERT NORCROSS, *administrator,* 266-0699, robert.norcross@

Telecommunications Division: GARY EVENSON, *administrator,* 267-6744, gary.evenson@

Water, Compliance and Consumer Affairs, Division of: AMELIA RAMIREZ, *administrator,* 267-7829, amelia.ramirez@

Address e-mail by combining the user ID and the state extender: userid@**psc.state.wi.us**

Mailing Address: P.O. Box 7854, Madison 53707-7854.

Location: Public Service Commission Building, 610 North Whitney Way, Madison.

Telephones: 266-5481; Consumer affairs: (800) 225-7729 (in-state only) or 266-2001; TTY: (800) 251-8345 (in-state only) or 267-1479.

Fax: 266-3957.

E-mail Address: pscrecs@psc.state.wi.us

Internet Address: http://psc.wi.gov

Publications: Biennial report; various statistics on electric utilities, gas utilities, and telephone companies and guides for utility customers.

Number of Employees: 173.50.

Total Budget 2003-05: $45,024,100.

Statutory References: Sections 15.06 and 15.79; Chapter 196.

Agency Responsibility: The Public Service Commission (PSC) is responsible for regulating Wisconsin's public utilities and ensuring that utility services are provided to customers at prices reasonable to both ratepayers and utility owners. The commission regulates the rates and services of electric, gas distribution, heating, telephone, water, and combined water and sewer utilities. In most instances, its jurisdiction does not extend to the activities of electric cooperatives.

Responsibilities of the commission include setting utility rates, determining levels for adequate and safe service, and approving utility bond sales and stock offerings. It confirms or rejects utility applications for major construction projects, such as power plants. In addition to ensuring utility compliance with statutes, administrative codes, and record-keeping requirements, the commission's staff investigates and mediates thousands of consumer complaints annually. During the complaint process, commission staff reviews all pertinent information to make certain that the utility's handling of the complaint is in compliance with the applicable rules. The commission also rules on proposed mergers between utility companies.

Organization: The governor appoints the 3 full-time commissioners, with senate approval, to serve staggered 6-year terms, but an individual commissioner holds office until a successor is appointed and qualified. No commissioner may have a financial interest in a railroad or public utility or serve on or under a political party committee. The governor designates a chairperson who, in turn, may appoint division administrators from outside the classified service.

Unit Functions: The *Division of Administrative Services* provides personnel and business management services to the commission and maintains central records.

The *Gas and Energy Division* is responsible for all major aspects of state regulation of electric and natural gas utilities. It regulates rates charged by these utilities and their terms and conditions of service, and reviews their planning and construction activity. It oversees transmission line construction and natural gas pipeline operations. In addition, the division examines environmental impacts and energy use and conservation issues. The division also addresses stray voltage issues on farms and implements programs to increase competition in the electric utility industry. The division intervenes in actions that are pending before federal regulatory agencies and may affect Wisconsin ratepayers.

The *Telecommunications Division* is responsible for overseeing the telecommunication industry in Wisconsin and regulating those services that are subject to PSC jurisdiction within the mandates and direction of state law and related requirements of the Federal Telecommunications Act of 1996. Tasks of the division include: promoting competition and ensuring access to modern and affordable telecommunications, monitoring service quality and the deployment of advanced infrastructure, overseeing the Wireless 911 Fund that supports county and wireless emergency response systems, and assisting with administration of the Universal Service Fund Program. It also oversees the providers of retail and wholesale telecommunications services in the state by: administering price regulation plans and alternative forms of regulation; reviewing earnings and rate levels of companies subject to rate jurisdiction; reviewing tariffs, contracts, and agreements to prevent unfair cross-subsidies and other anticompetitive activities; certifying new providers in the state; arbitrating interconnection agreements between providers and approving negotiated agreements; and resolving interconnection disputes between service providers.

The *Division of Water, Compliance and Consumer Affairs* is responsible for the regulation of water and combined water and sewer utilities. It audits all utility records for compliance with commission directives and the Uniform System of Accounts and offers assistance to utilities to help them comply with state laws and rules. In addition to ensuring utility compliance with statutes, administrative codes, and record-keeping requirements, the commission's staff investigates and mediates thousands of consumer complaints annually.

History: Public utility regulation in Wisconsin followed and was closely related to railroad regulation. Railroads were the first modern enterprise to have their rates regulated, and Wisconsin became one of the first states to pass such laws. Chapter 273, Laws of 1874, established a railroad rate structure and provided for 3 appointed railroad commissioners to supervise rail freight operations. Two years later in Chapter 57, Laws of 1876, the legislature repealed much of the 1874 law and established a single appointed commissioner of railroads. The commissioner was made an elected official in 1881 (Chapter 300).

The forerunner of today's commission dates from Chapter 362, Laws of 1905, which created an appointed 3-member Railroad Commission to supervise rail operations, appraise railroad property, and set rates. With the enactment of Chapter 499, Laws of 1907, which extended the powers of the Railroad Commission, Wisconsin became the first state to regulate all public utilities.

Chapter 183, Laws of 1931, renamed the agency the Public Service Commission of Wisconsin and made it responsible for comprehensive motor carrier regulation in 1933 (Chapter 488). The 1967 executive branch reorganization continued the commission as an independent agency. Chapter 29, Laws of 1977, transferred the commission's railroad and motor carrier regulatory functions to the Transportation Commission (recreated in 1982 as the now defunct Office of the Commissioner of Transportation). Railroad regulation was assigned to the newly created Office of the Commissioner of Railroads by 1993 Wisconsin Act 123.

Laws passed in 1985 provided for a partial deregulation of public utility holding companies and telecommunications service, and 1993 Wisconsin Act 496 established a new regulatory framework for telecommunications utilities, which authorizes the commission to regulate the prices utilities charge rather than limiting their total earnings.

Statutory Councils

Telecommunications Privacy Council: NEIL TRILLING, *chairperson;* CHERYL BARNES, MIKE CAUBLE, DAVID J. GILLES, LEONARD P. LEVINE, PAUL NELSON, SUE MCALLAN ROSKA, MARLIN SCHNEIDER, LOUISE TRUBEK, PAUL VERHOEVEN, ROBERT WELLS, HENRY CLAY WHITE (appointed by Public Service Commission).

The Telecommunications Privacy Council advises the commission on guidelines designed to protect the privacy of users of telecommunications services. The number of members on the council is not specified, but all must represent telecommunications providers or consumers. The council was created by 1993 Wisconsin Act 496 and its composition and duties are prescribed in Section 196.209 of the statutes.

Universal Service Fund Council: RICHARD SCHLIMM, *chairperson;* JEFF BECK, JILL COLLINS, TOM FRAZIER, PAUL FUGLIE, HELEN GEE, WILL HUGHES, GWEN JACKSON, JEAN PAUK, GARY RADLOFF, PAMELA SHERWOOD, FRED WEIER, PAM YOUNG-HOLMES (appointed by Public Service Commission).

Universal Services Manager: ANITA SPRENGER, Public Service Commission, P.O. Box 7854, Madison 53707-7854; Telephone: 266-3843; Fax: 266-3957; TTY: (800) 251-8345 (in-state only) or 267-1479; anita.sprenger@

The Universal Service Fund Council advises the commission on the administration of the Universal Service Fund, which assists low-income customers, disabled customers, and customers in areas where telecommunication service costs are relatively high, in obtaining affordable access to basic telecommunication services. The Universal Service Fund manager acts as liaison between the commission and the council. The number of members on the council is not specified. All must represent telecommunication service providers or consumers, but the majority of members must be consumers. The council was created by 1993 Wisconsin Act 496 and its composition and duties are prescribed in Section 196.218 (6) of the statutes.

INDEPENDENT UNIT ATTACHED FOR BUDGETING, PROGRAM COORDINATION, AND RELATED MANAGEMENT FUNCTIONS BY SECTION 15.03 OF THE STATUTES

OFFICE OF THE COMMISSIONER OF RAILROADS

Commissioner of Railroads: RODNEY W. KREUNEN, 266-3182, rodney.kreunen@psc.state.wi.us
Legal Counsel: DOUGLAS S. WOOD, 266-9536, woodd@psc.state.wi.us
Mailing Address: P.O. Box 8968, Madison 53708-8968.
Location: 610 North Whitney Way, Suite 110, Madison.
Telephone: 261-8221.
Fax: 261-8220.
Number of Employees: 7.00.
Total Budget 2003-05: $1,172,200.
Statutory References: Sections 15.06 (1) (a) and 15.795 (1); Chapters 189-192 and 195.

Agency Responsibility: The Office of the Commissioner of Railroads enforces regulations related to railway safety and determines the safety of highway crossings including the adequacy of railroad warning devices. The office is funded by assessments on railroads.

The governor appoints the commissioner with senate consent to a 6-year term and holds office until a successor is appointed. The commissioner may not have a financial interest in railroads and may not serve on or under any committee of a political party. The office was created by 1993 Wisconsin Act 123 as an independent regulatory agency to assume the functions relating to railroad regulation that 1993 Wisconsin Act 16 had transferred to the Public Service Commission when the Office of the Commissioner of Transportation was eliminated.

A train arrives at the Milwaukee Airport Rail Station (MARS). The station, which opened in January 2005, was constructed using a combination of federal and state funds. MARS is one of just four Amtrak stations serving airports nationally. The facility, which is adjacent to General Billy Mitchell International Airport, also includes a 300-car parking lot. (Department of Transportation)

Department of
REGULATION AND LICENSING

Secretary of Regulation and Licensing: CELIA M. JACKSON, 266-1352, drlsecretary@drl.state.wi.us

Deputy Secretary: SANDRA M. ROWE, 267-2435, sandra.rowe@drl.state.wi.us

Executive Assistant and Legislative Liaison: LARRY J. MARTIN, 266-8608, larry.martin@drl.state.wi.us

Legal Services, Office of: STEVE GLOE, *General Counsel,* 266-0011, steve.gloe@drl.state.wi.us

Mailing Address: P.O. Box 8935, Madison 53708-8935.

Location: 1400 East Washington Avenue, Room 173, Madison.

Telephones: 266-2112 (for operator, select menu option "6"); TTY: 267-2416.

Internet Address: http://drl.wi.gov

Fax: 267-0644.

Number of Employees: 126.00

Total Budget 2003-05: $22,261,600.

Statutory References: Sections 15.08, 15.085, 15.40, and 15.405-15.407; Chapters 440-459, 470, and 480.

Enforcement, Division of: ERIC CALLISTO, *administrator,* 266-3445, eric.callisto@drl.state.wi.us

Management Services, Division of: ROBBI MURPHY, *administrator,* 261-2392, robbi.murphy@drl.state.wi.us.

Professional Credential Processing, Division of: CATHY POND, *administrator,* 266-0557, cathy.pond@drl.state.wi.us

Board Services, Division of: KIMBERLY NANIA, *administrator,* 261-2393, kimberly.nania@drl.state.wi.us

Education, Office of: BARBARA SHOWERS, *director,* 266-7703, barbara.showers@drl.state.wi.us

Business and Design Professions, Bureau of: vacancy, *director,* 261-4486.

   Accounting Examining Board (266-2112): NORBERT J. JOHNSON, *chairperson;* THOMAS J. KILKENNY, *vice chairperson;* FREDERICK W. FRANKLIN, *secretary;* KAREN J. BINDL, LUCRETIA MATTSON, ROMAN M. JUNGERS II*, vacancy*.

   Architects, Landscape Architects, Professional Engineers, Designers and Land Surveyors, Examining Board of (266-2112).

   The 5 professional sections listed below comprise the examining board for a total of 15 professional members and 10 public members. Examining board officers: JAY FERNHOLZ, *chairperson;* RICK A. VAN GOETHEM, *vice chairperson;* RUTH G. JOHNSON*, *secretary.*

   Architect Section: JAMES G. OTTO, *chairperson;* WALTER L. WILSON, *vice chairperson;* GARY A. GUST, *secretary;* ARNO W. HAERING*, vacancy*.

   Landscape Architect Section: JAY FERNHOLZ, *chairperson;* WAYNE G. TLUSTY, *vice chairperson;* RUTH G. JOHNSON*, *secretary;* ROSHEEN STYCZINSKI, BERNIE A. ABRAHAMSON*.

   Engineer Section: LYNDA F. FARRAR*, *chairperson;* NANCY L. SOBCZAK, *vice chairperson;* MARTIN J. HANSON, *secretary;* DALE R. PACZKOWSKI, vacancy*.

   Designer Section: JAMES W. DORN, *chairperson;* SCOTT B. BERG, *vice chairperson;* DONNA M. ROZAR*, *secretary;* MICHAEL J. OHBERG, vacancy*.

   Land Surveyor Section: RICK A. VAN GOETHEM, *chairperson;* JAMES E. RUSCH, *vice chairperson;* ROBERT HOSKINS*, *secretary;* MATTHEW J. JANIAK, vacancy*.

   Auctioneer Board (266-2112): MARK SHAIN*, *chairperson;* MARIE SKIC*, *vice chairperson;* CARL THEORIN, *secretary;* JAY CLARKE, PATRICK J. MCNAMARA, TIMOTHY SWEENEY, ALAN S. HAGER*.

---

*Asterisk indicates public member. Other members represent the profession regulated, unless otherwise noted. The governor appoints all examining board and council members with the advice and consent of the senate, unless otherwise indicated.

Barbering and Cosmetology Examining Board (266-2112): LEON G. LAUER, *chairperson;* JEANNIE M. BUSH (electrologist), *vice chairperson;* JEFFREY A. PATTERSON, *secretary;* MARY B. BLAKE, E. ROD GOTTFREDSEN; NANCY PAGGAO (representing a private school of barbering or cosmetology), JANICE M. BOECK (representing a public school of barbering or cosmetology), LEE MARTINEZ*, vacancy*.

Funeral Directors Examining Board (266-2112): RICK D. UNBEHAUN, *chairperson;* J.C. FRAZIER, *vice chairperson;* BONNIE GIFT*, *secretary;* DAVID E. OLSEN, CONNIE C. RYAN, ROSALIE A. MURPHY*.

Nursing Home Administrator Examining Board (266-2112): JERRY SCHALLOCK, *chairperson;* DAVID M. EGAN, *vice chairperson;* PATRICIA A. SCHULZ, *secretary;* KENNETH D. ARNESON, MARY ANN CLARK, ROBERT A. KESSLER (physician), MARY K. LEASE (registered nurse), MARY F. PIKE*, vacancy*. Nonvoting member: PATRICIA BENESH (designee of secretary of health and family services).

Professional Geologists, Hydrologists and Soil Scientists, Examining Board of: (266-2112). The 3 professional sections listed below comprise the examining board for a total of 9 professional members and 3 public members. Examining board officers: STEPHEN V. DONOHUE, *chairperson;* TRACY C. BENZEL, *vice chairperson;* JOAN UNDERWOOD FALLON, *secretary.*

Geologist Section: THOMAS J. EVANS, *chairperson;* JOAN UNDERWOOD FALLON, *vice chairperson;* DAVID M. MICKELSON, *secretary;* vacancy*.

Hydrologist Section: STEPHEN V. DONOHUE, *chairperson;* ROBERT J. KARNAUSKAS, *vice chairperson;* vacancy, RUTH G. JOHNSON*.

Soil Scientist Section: TRACY C. BENZEL, *chairperson;* ROBERT C. WENDT, *vice chairperson;* JON H. GUMTOW, *secretary;* vacancy*.

Real Estate Appraisers Board (266-2112): MARK KOWBEL (licensed appraiser), *chairperson;* SHARON FIEDLER (certified residential appraiser), *vice chairperson;* ROGER ROSLANSKY*, *secretary;* KAREN SCOTT (certified general appraiser), vacancy (assessor), LAMARR J. FRANKLIN*, vacancy*.

Direct Licensing and Real Estate, Bureau of: ROXANNE PETERSON, *director,* 266-5521, roxanne.peterson@drl.state.wi.us

Real Estate Board (266-2112): RICHARD A. KOLLMANSBERGER, *chairperson;* PETER A. SVEUM, *vice chairperson;* MARIA E. WATTS*, *secretary;* LLOYD P. LEVIN, LISABETH WEIRICH, REBECCA J. DYSLAND*, vacancy*.

Real Estate Curriculum and Examinations, Council on (266-2112): PETER SVEUM (member of Real Estate Board designated by board), *chairperson;* SUSAN E. HAMER, RICHARD HINSMAN, PEGGY LOVEJOY, BARBARA MCGILL, PAUL G. HOFFMAN*, LAWRENCE SAGER*.

Health Professions, Bureau of: TOM RYAN, *director,* 266-8098, thomas.ryan@drl.state.wi.us

Controlled Substances Board (266-2112): CYNTHIA BENNING (designated by Pharmacy Examining Board), *chairperson;* DAROLD A. TREFFERT (psychiatrist), *vice chairperson;* YVONNE M. BELLAY (designated by secretary of agriculture, trade and consumer protection), *secretary;* ROBERT BLOCK (designated by attorney general), DOUG ENGLEBERT (designated by secretary of health and family services); CECILIA J. HILLARD (pharmacologist).

Dentistry Examining Board (266-2112): BRUCE BARRETTE (dentist), *chairperson;* RICHARD J. STRAND (dentist), *vice chairperson;* NANETTE KOSYDAR DREVES (dental hygienist), *secretary;* LORI R. BARBEAU, KEITH D. CLEMENCE, WILBER G. GILL, KAREN M. JAHIMIAK (dentists); DAVID T. CARROLL, CATHERINE E. SCHLEIS (dental hygienists); JUDITH E. FICKS*, ANNE N. TAYLOR*.

---

*Asterisk indicates public member. Other members represent the profession regulated, unless otherwise noted. The governor appoints all examining board and council members with the advice and consent of the senate, unless otherwise indicated.

Boards and Councils within the Department of Regulation and Licensing

Unit	Statutory Citation	Session Laws Creating or Amending	Duties Specified in Wisconsin Statutes
Accounting Examining Board	S. 15.405 (1)	Ch. 337, L. 1913; Ch. 327, L. 1967.	Ch. 442
Architects, Landscape Architects, Professional Engineers, Designers and Land Surveyors, Examining Board of	S. 15.405 (2)	Ch. 644, L. 1917; Ch. 486, L. 1931; Ch. 547, L. 1955; Ch. 446, L. 1969; 1993 WisActs 463 and 465, 1997 WisAct 300.	Ch. 443
Auctioneer Board	S. 15.405 (3)	1993 WisAct 102.	Ch. 480
Barbering and Cosmetology Examining Board	S. 15.405 (17)	Ch. 221, L. 1915 (Committee of Examiners in Barbering); Ch. 431, L. 1939 (Board of Examiners in Cosmetology); 1987 WisAct 265 (combined the 2).	Ch. 454
Chiropractic Examining Board	S. 15.405 (5)	Ch. 408, L. 1925.	Ch. 446
Controlled Substances Board	S. 15.405 (5g)	Ch. 384, L. 1969; Ch. 219, L. 1971; 1995 WisAct 305.	Ch. 961
Dentistry Examining Board	S. 15.405 (6)	Ch. 129, L. 1885; 1997 WisAct 96	Ch. 447
Funeral Directors Examining Board	S. 15.405 (16)	Ch. 420, L. 1905; Ch. 39, L. 1975 and 1983 WisAct 485.	Ch. 445
Hearing and Speech Examining Board	S. 15.405 (6m)	Ch. 300, L. 1969; 1989 WisAct 316.	Ch. 459
Council on Speech-Language Pathology and Audiology	S. 15.407 (4)	1989 WisAct 316.	S. 459.23 and 459.44
Marriage and Family Therapy, Professional Counseling and Social Work Examining Board	S. 15.405 (7c)	1991 WisAct 160, 2001 WisAct 80.	S. 457.03
Massage Therapy and Bodywork Council	S. 15.407 (7)	2001 WisAct 74	Ch. 460
Medical Examining Board	S. 15.405 (7)	Ch. 264, L. 1897.	Ch. 448, Subchap.II
Athletic Trainers Affiliated Credentialing Board	S. 15.406 (4)	1999 WisAct 9.	Ch. 448, Subchap.VI
Dietitians Affiliated Credentialing Board	S. 15.406 (2)	1993 WisAct 443; 1997 WisAct 75	S. 448.74
Occupational Therapists Affiliated Credentialing Board	S. 15.406 (5)	1999 WisAct 180.	Ch. 448, Subchap.VII
Perfusionists Examining Council	S. 15.407 (2m)	2001 WisAct 89	S. 448.40 (2)
Physical Therapists Affiliated Credentialing Board	S. 15.406 (1)	Ch. 327, L. 1967; 1993 WisAct 107, 2001 WisAct 70.	S. 440.035
Physician Assistants, Council on	S. 15.407 (2)	Ch. 149, L. 1973.	S. 448.20
Podiatrists Affiliated Credentialing Board	S. 15.406 (3)	1997 WisAct 175.	Ch. 448, Subchap. IV
Respiratory Care Practitioners Examining Council	S. 15.407 (1m)	1989 WisAct 229.	S. 15.407 (1)
Nursing, Board of	S. 15.405 (7g)	Ch. 346, L. 1911.	S. 441.01
Registered Nurses, Examining Council on	S. 15.407 (3)(a)	Ch. 365, L. 1921.	S. 441.05
Licensed Practical Nurses, Examining Council on	S. 15.407 (3)(b)	Ch. 402, L. 1949.	S. 441.10
Nursing Home Administrator Examining Board	S. 15.405 (7m)	Ch. 478, L. 1969.	Ch. 456
Optometry Examining Board	S. 15.405 (8)	Ch. 488, L. 1915.	Ch. 449
Pharmacy Examining Board	S. 15.405 (9)	Ch. 167, L. 1882.	Ch. 450
Pharmacist Advisory Council	S. 15.407 (6)	1997 WisAct 68.	S. 450.025
Professional Geologists, Hydrologists and Soil Scientists, Examining Board of	S. 15.405 (2m)	1997 WisAct 300.	Ch. 470
Psychology Examining Board	S. 15.405 (10m)	Ch. 290, L. 1969.	Ch. 455
Real Estate Appraisers Board	S. 15.405 (10r)	1989 WisAct 340.	S. 458.03
Real Estate Board	S. 15.405 (11)	Ch. 656, L. 1919; Ch. 94, L. 1981.	Ch. 452
Real Estate Curriculum and Examinations, Council on	S. 15.407 (5)	1989 WisAct 341; 1989 WisAct 359.	S. 452.06 (2)
Veterinary Examining Board	S. 15.405 (12)	Ch. 294, L. 1961.	Ch. 453

Hearing and Speech Examining Board (266-2112): GERARD L. KUPPERMAN (hearing instrument specialist), *chairperson;* ALMA PETERS (speech-language pathologist), *vice chairperson;* TERRENCE M. GREENLEAF (hearing instrument specialist), *secretary;* THOMAS E. FISHER (audiologist), STEVEN A. HARVEY (otolaryngologist), JOSEPH M. HULWI (hearing instrument specialist), MICHAEL K. THELEN (audiologist), MARLIYN S. WORKINGER (speech-language pathologist); KATIE LEPAK* (hearing aid user), BRUCE BAIER*.

Speech-Language Pathology and Audiology, Council on (266-2112): MICHAEL J. COLLINS, DEBRA K. MC LAUCHLIN, LYNN L. REINEMANN (speech-language pathologists), JOHN G. KNOX, GREGORY N. WIERSEMA (audiologists).

Medical Examining Board (266-2112): ALFRED L. FRANGER, *chairperson;* BHUPINDER S. SAINI, *vice chairperson;* LIEF W. ERICKSON, JR., *secretary;* JON E. GUDEMAN, SUJATHA KAILAS, JACK M. LOCKART, DANIEL J. MIOTA (DO), IAN MUNRO, GENE MUSSER, SANDRA L. OSBORN; MARY R. COOK*, VIRGINIA S. HEINEMANN*, vacancy*. Nonvoting member: vacancy (Patients Compensation Fund Peer Review Council).

Athletic Trainers Affiliated Credentialing Board (266-2112): BRADLEY J. SHERMAN, *chairperson;* RUSSELL D. DELAP, *vice chairperson;* WILLIAM H. BARTLETT (MD), *secretary*; HEIDI J. GUTSCHOW, KATHLEEN A. O'CONNELL; JOHN SYBELDON*.

Dietitians Affiliated Credentialing Board (266-2112): SUSAN A. NITZKE, *chairperson;* VIRGINIA JORDAN, *vice chairperson;* DIANE L. JOHNSON, *secretary;* DELORES A. PRICE*.

Occupational Therapists Affiliated Credentialing Board (266-2112): CINDY ERB, *chairperson;* GAIL C. SLAUGHTER, *vice chairperson;* JUDITH E. FICKS*, *secretary;* MYLINDA BARISAS-MATULA, DEBORAH MCKERNAN-ACE, DOROTHY J. OLSON (occupational therapy assistants), vacancy*.

Perfusionists Examining Council (266-2112): GARY HAWKINS, JR., DAVID B. HELLENBRAND, MATTHEW J. HIETPAS, W. DUDLEY JOHNSON (physician); vacancy*. (Medical Examining Board appoints all except the public member.)

Physical Therapists Affiliated Credentialing Board (266-2112): LAURIE B. KONTNEY, *chairperson;* OTTO A. CORDERO, *vice chairperson;* BARBARA A. FLAHERTY, *secretary;* vacancy (physical therapist assistant); vacancy*.

Physician Assistants, Council on (266-2112): DANIEL S. BARRY, *chairperson;* RICHARD L. FAUST, *vice chairperson;* JERRY NOACK (designee of vice chancellor for health sciences, UW-Madison), *secretary;* vacancy; MARY PANGMAN SCHMITT*. (Medical Examining Board appoints the physician assistant members.)

Podiatrists Affiliated Credentialing Board (266-2112): LISA REINICKE, *chairperson;* P. MICHAEL JACOBS, *vice chairperson;* IAN FURNESS, *secretary;* DEBRA S. TRUCKEY*.

Respiratory Care Practitioners Examining Council (266-2112): SUSAN EVANS, *chairperson;* ANN M. JOHNSON, ANN M. MEICHER, EDWARD WINGA (MD); vacancy*. (Medical Examining Board appoints all except public member.)

Pharmacy Examining Board (266-2112): MICHAEL BETTIGA, *chairperson;* SUSAN SUTTER, *vice chairperson;* CHARLOTTE L. RASMUSSEN*, *secretary;* CYNTHIA A. BENNING, JOHN P. BOHLMAN, FREDERIC E. MOSKOL; GEORGINA FORBES*.

Pharmacist Advisory Council (Inactive).

Veterinary Examining Board (266-2112): LARRY D. MAHR, *chairperson;* JAMES R. JOHNSON, *vice chairperson;* JOANN KLEMAN (veterinary technician), *secretary;* MARTHINA L. GREER, DONALD J. PETERSON, ROBERT R. SPENCER; SARAH KAMKE*, THERESA L. WAAGE*.

---

*Asterisk indicates public member. Other members represent the profession regulated, unless otherwise noted. The governor appoints all examining board and council members with the advice and consent of the senate, unless otherwise indicated.

DEPARTMENT OF REGULATION AND LICENSING

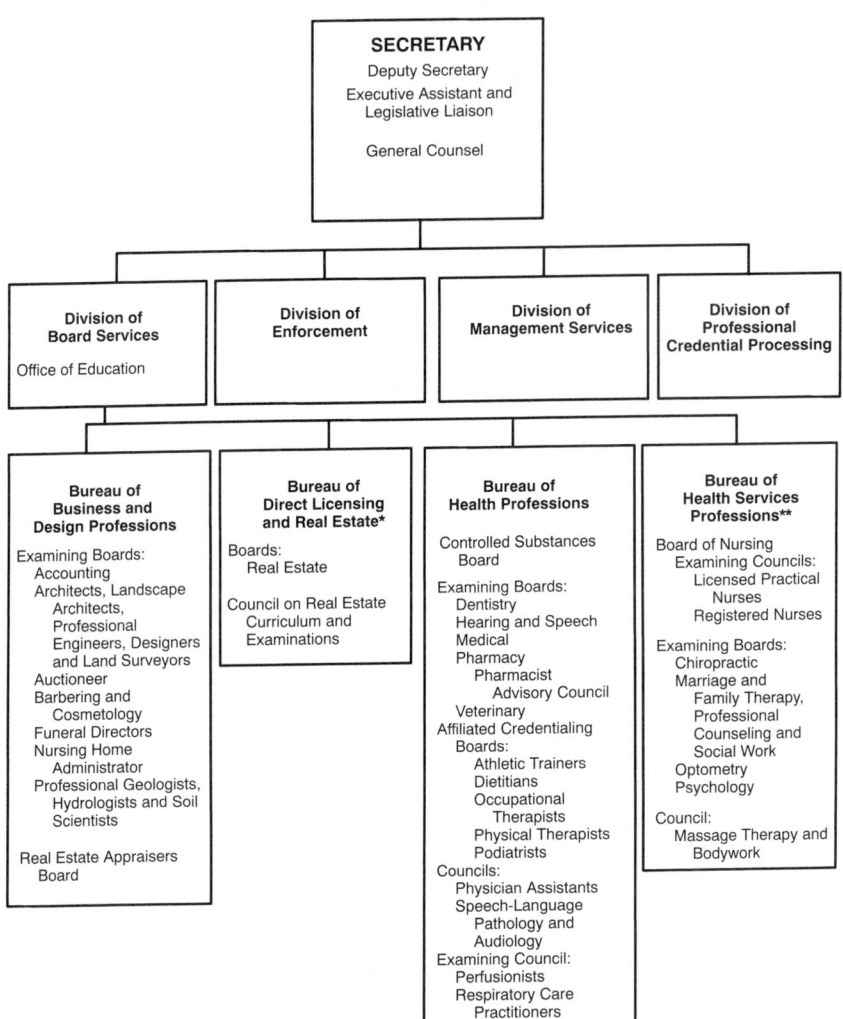

*The Bureau of Direct Licensing and Real Estate has direct licensing responsibilities for auctioneers; real estate brokers and salespersons; time-share salespersons; interior designers; charitable organizations; professional fund-raisers and fund-raising counsels; cemetery authorities, salespersons, and preneed sellers; private detectives, private detective agencies, and private security persons; home inspectors; and boxing.

**The Bureau of Health Services Professions conducts the direct licensing responsibilities for the certification of acupuncturists and direct registration for music, art, and dance therapists.

Health Services Professions, Bureau of: JEFF SCANLAN, *director,* 267-7223, jeff.scanlan@drl.state.wi.us

Nursing, Board of (266-2112): KIMBERLY NANIA, *director;* JACQUELINE A. JOHNSRUD (RN), *chairperson;* JUNE A. BAHR (LPN), *vice chairperson;* KATHLEEN L. SULLIVAN (RN), *secretary;* TERRIE T. GARCIA (RN), MARGARET HEINE (LPN), MARILYN A. KAUFMANN (RN), BLAINE J. ROPSON (RN), MARIE KOHLBECK*, vacancy*.

Registered Nurses, Examining Council on: (Inactive).

Licensed Practical Nurses, Examining Council on: (Inactive).

Chiropractic Examining Board (266-2112): JAMES W. WEBER, *chairperson;* WENDY M. HENRICHS, *vice chairperson;* STEVEN J. SILVERMAN, *secretary;* STEVEN R. CONWAY, SUSAN FEITH*, CHAR D. GLOCKE*.

Marriage and Family Therapy, Professional Counseling and Social Work Examining Board (266-2112). The following 3 sections comprise the examining board, for a total of 10 professional members and 3 public members. Examining board officers: LINDA SCHWALLIE, *chairperson;* GEORGE J. KAMPS, *vice chairperson;* EVELYN PUMPHREY, *secretary.*

Marriage and Family Therapist Section: LINDA SCHWALLIE, *chairperson;* ANN MARIE STARR, *vice chairperson;* BRUCE P. KUEHL, *secreatary;* ABE RABINOWITZ*.

Professional Counseling Section: SUSAN M. PUTRA, *chairperson;* LAMARR J. FRANKLIN*, *vice chairperson;* EVELYN PUMPHREY, *secretary;* LESLIE D. MIRKIN.

Social Work Section: GEORGE J. KAMPS (clinical social worker), *chairperson;* MARY JO WALSH (advanced practice social worker), *vice chairperson;* ERIC M. ALVIN (government social worker), *secretary;* ADA WILLIAMS PARR (independent social worker), vacancy*.

Optometry Examining Board (266-2112): KERRY L. GRIEBENOW, *chairperson;* LEON D. GRIFFIN, JR., *vice chairperson;* KATHI LEACH, *secretary;* GREGORY A. FOSTER, RICHARD T. WRIGHT, SWAMINAT BALACHANDRAN*, RAYMOND W. HEISER*.

Psychology Examining Board (266-2112): DON J. CROWDER, *chairperson;* TIMOTHY P. MELCHERT, *vice chairperson;* MCARTHUR WEDDLE*, *secretary;* BARBARA SELDIN, vacancy, B. ANN NEVIASER*.

Massage Therapy and Bodywork Council: CLAUDE GAGNON, *chairperson;* CARIE MARTIN, *vice chairperson;* LILLIAN C. POUNDS, *secretary;* MARY ELLEN MARTIN, AMY REMILLARD, VLAD THOMAS, XIPING ZHOU.

Publications: Biennial reports; Consumer Complaints: Other Resources; The Impaired Professionals Procedure; Information About Your Hearing; *Regulation: In Partnership with the Consumer;* Wisconsin Directory of Accredited Schools of Nursing; plus informational bulletins for credential holders, regulatory digests, monthly disciplinary reports, and statute/rules code-books.

Agency Responsibility: The Department of Regulation and Licensing is responsible for credentialing and regulating various professions and occupations in the state. It provides administrative services to the state occupational regulatory authorities responsible for regulation of occupations and offers policy assistance in such areas as evaluating and establishing new professional licensing programs, creating routine procedures for legal proceedings, and adjusting policies in response to public needs. Currently, the department and regulatory authorities are responsible for regulating about 314,000 credential holders and 109 types of credentials.

The department investigates and prosecutes complaints against credential holders and assists with drafting statutes and administrative rules. Through the Office of Impaired Professional Procedures, it enforces participation agreements with credential holders who are chemically impaired, allowing them to retain their professional credentials if they comply with requirements, including treatment for chemical dependency.

---

*Asterisk indicates public member. Other members represent the profession regulated, unless otherwise noted. The governor appoints all examining board and council members with the advice and consent of the senate, unless otherwise indicated.

The department provides direct regulation and licensing of certain occupations and activities and also regulates schools of barbering and cosmetology; aesthetics; electrology; and manicuring. It is assisted by the Controlled Substances Board, which promulgates rules regulating the use of substances that have a potential for abuse.

Numerous boards and regulatory authorities attached to the department have independent responsibility for the regulation of specific professions in the public interest. Within statutory limits, they determine the education and experience required for credentialing, develop and evaluate examinations, and establish standards for professional conduct. These standards are set by administrative rule and enforced through legal action upon complaints from the public. The regulatory authorities may reprimand a credential holder; limit, suspend, or revoke the credential of a practitioner who violates laws or board rules; and, in some cases, impose forfeitures.

Regulatory authority members must be state residents, and they cannot serve more than two consecutive terms. No member may be an officer, director, or employee of a private organization that promotes or furthers the profession or occupation regulated by that board.

Organization: The governor appoints the secretary of the department with the advice and consent of the senate. The secretary appoints a deputy secretary, an executive assistant, and the heads of various subunits from outside the classified service.

The boards and councils attached to the department consist primarily of members of the professions and occupations they regulate. In 1975, the legislature mandated that at least one public member serve on each board. In 1984, it required an additional public member on most boards. Public members are prohibited from having ties to the profession they regulate. In most cases, the governor appoints all members of the licensing and regulatory boards with the advice and consent of the senate. However, in some cases, council members are appointed by the governor without senate confirmation, by the secretary of the department, or by their related examining boards.

Unit Functions: The *Division of Board Services* provides professional support to the department's regulatory boards and committees, including legal services, technical and policy support, and consultation services for continuing education and examination requirements.

The *Division of Enforcement* investigates complaints against credential holders and initiates formal disciplinary actions, where appropriate. The division also inspects business establishments of credential holders and has authority to audit specific trust accounts and financial records.

The *Division of Management Services* provides adminstrative and technical support assistance to the department and boards, including human resources, information technology, budget and fiscal, and administrative support services.

The *Division of Professional Credential Processing* receives applications for licenses and permits, creates applicant records, and determines whether credential criteria have been met.

History: Chapter 75, Laws of 1967, created the Department of Regulation and Licensing and attached to it 14 separate examining boards that had been independent agencies. The 1967 reorganization also transferred to the department some direct licensing and registration functions not handled by boards, including those for private detectives and detective agencies, charitable organizations, and professional fund-raisers and solicitors.

The department's responsibilities have changed significantly since its creation. Initially, it performed routine housekeeping functions for the examining boards, which continued to function as independent agencies. Subsequently, a series of laws required the department to assume various substantive administrative functions previously performed by the boards and to provide direct regulation of several professions.

Department of
REVENUE

Secretary of Revenue: MICHAEL L. MORGAN, 266-6466, michael.morgan@; Fax: 266-5718.

Deputy Secretary: LAURA J. ENGAN, 266-6466, laura.engan@; Fax: 266-5718.

Executive Assistant/Information Director: AUDRA BRENNAN, 266-6466, audra.brennan@; Fax: 266-5718.

General Counsel, Office of: LILI BEST CRANE, *chief counsel,* 266-3974, lili.crane@; Fax: 266-9949.

Technology Services, Office of: OSKAR ANDERSON, *director,* 266-0218, oanderson@; Fax: 263-9923.

Legislative Liaison: SHERRIE GATES-HENDRIX, 267-1262, sgateshe@

Communications Director: EVA ROBELIA, 261-2271, eva.robelia@; Fax: 266-5718.

Address e-mail by combining the user ID and the state extender: userid@**dor.state.wi.us**

Enterprise Services Division: KIRBIE G. MACK, *administrator,* 264-8175, kirbie.mack@

> *Budget and Strategic Services Bureau:* PAT LASHORE, *director,* 266-3347, plashore@

> *Financial and Management Services Bureau:* ANTHONY TIMMONS, *director,* 266-8469, anthony.timmons@

> *Human Resource Services Bureau:* PAT JACKSON-WARD, *assistant director,* 266-3842, patricia.jackson-ward@

Income, Sales and Excise Tax Division: DIANE L. HARDT, *administrator,* 266-2772, dhardt@; LILI BEST CRANE, *deputy administrator,* 266-2772, lili.crane@; Division Fax: 261-6240.

> *Audit Bureau:* VICKI GIBBONS, *director,* 266-2772, vgibbons@

> *Compliance Bureau:* VICKI R. SIEKERT, *director,* 266-9635, vsiekert@

Lottery Division: MICHAEL J. EDMONDS, *administrator,* 267-4500, michael.edmonds@; SAVERIO MAGLIO, *deputy administrator,* 267-4817, saverio.maglio@; Division Fax: 264-6644.

> *Operations Bureau:* ANDREW BOHAGE, *director,* 264-6644, abohage@

> *Product Development Bureau:* SAVERIO MAGLIO, *director,* 267-4817, saverio.maglio@

> *Retailer Relations Bureau:* BOB HAYD, *director,* 267-7180, rhayd@

Processing and Customer Service Division: PAT LASHORE, *administrator,* 266-2772, plashore@; Division Fax: 266-9829.

> *Customer Service and Education Bureau:* CATHERINE BINK, *director,* 266-2772, cbink@

> *Processing Bureau:* CHERYL SULLIVAN, *director,* 266-2772, cheryl.sullivan@

Research and Policy Division: vacancy, *administrator,* 267-8973; Division Fax: 266-8704.

> *Income Tax Policy and Economic Team:* REBECCA BOLDT, *team leader,* 266-6785, rboldt@

> *Sales and Property Tax Policy Team:* PAUL ZIEGLER, *team leader,* 266-5773, paul.ziegler@

State and Local Finance Division: MICHAEL LEHMAN, *administrator,* 266-0939, michael.lehman@; JEAN GERSTNER, *deputy assistant administrator,* 266-9759, jgerstne@; Division Fax: 264-6887.

> *Assessment Practices Bureau:* FRANK HUMPHREY, *director,* 261-5364, fhumphre@

> *Property Tax Bureau:* DANIEL DAVIS, *director,* 261-5350, ddavis@

Mailing Address: P.O. Box 8933, Madison 53713-8933.

Locations: 2135 Rimrock Road, Madison, and district and branch offices throughout the state.

Telephone: (608) 266-2772.

Fax: (608) 267-0834.

Internet Address: http://www.dor.state.wi.us

Publications: *Agricultural Assessment Guide;* biennial report; *County and Municipal Revenues and Expenditures;* A Guide for Property Owners; *Quarterly Economic Outlook;* Summary of

DEPARTMENT OF REVENUE

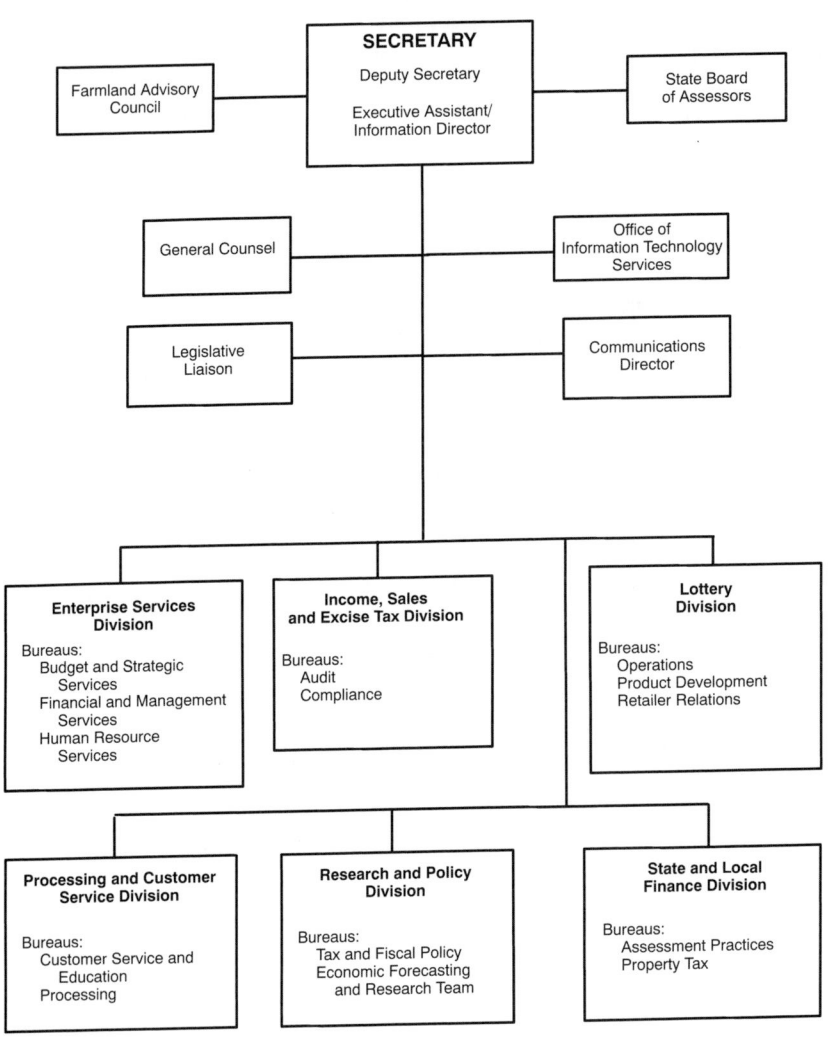

Unit attached for administrative purposes under Sec. 15.03: Investment and Local Impact Fund Board

Tax Exemption Devices; *Town, Village, and City Taxes; Wisconsin Tax Bulletin;* and various brochures on specific issues.

Number of Employees: 1,195.85.

Total Budget 2003-05: $320,333,100.

Statutory References: Sections 15.43 and 15.435; Chapters 70-79, 125, and 139.

Agency Responsibility: The Department of Revenue administers all major state tax laws (except the insurance premiums tax) and enforces the state's alcohol beverage and tobacco laws. It estimates state revenues, forecasts state economic activity, helps formulate tax policy, and administers the Wisconsin Lottery. It also determines equalized value of taxable property and assesses manufacturing property. It administers local financial assistance programs and assists local governments in their property assessments and financial management.

Organization: The department is administered by a secretary who is appointed by the governor with the advice and consent of the senate. The secretary appoints the administrators of the Income, Sales and Excise Tax Division and the Processing and Customer Service Division from the classified service and the other division administrators from outside the classified service.

Unit Functions: The *Office of General Counsel* provides legal counsel and opinions; drafts and reviews tax legislation and administrative rules; represents the department in all cases brought before the Tax Appeals Commission; and represents the department in nontax cases before administrative agencies. It also is responsible for providing a prompt and impartial review of all assessments appealed by individuals, partnerships, trusts, and corporations relating to income, franchise, sales, use, withholding, and gift taxes and the homestead tax credit.

The *Enterprise Services Division* establishes policies and provides centralized support services in the areas of personnel, employee development, equal employment, employment relations, fiscal management, budget and management analysis, procurement, and other management services.

The *Income, Sales and Excise Tax Division* administers and collects taxes under the state income, sales, estate, and excise tax laws. It also administers the earned income tax credit, farmland tax relief credit, and farmland preservation credit programs.

The *Lottery Division* administers the Wisconsin Lottery. It manages the design, distribution, and sale of lottery products; conducts lottery game drawings; handles media relations; assists retailers with marketing lottery products; and answers players' questions.

The *Processing and Customer Service Division* processes tax returns and administers the homestead tax credit, promotes electronic filing opportunities, answers customer inquiries, and informs taxpayers about state tax laws and taxpayer assistance programs.

The *Research and Policy Division* provides detailed analyses of fiscal and economic policies to the departmental secretary, the governor, and other state officials. It assesses the impact of current and proposed tax laws, prepares official general fund tax collection estimates, issues quarterly forecasts of the state's economy, and develops statistical reports.

The *State and Local Finance Division* assists local units of government by supervising administration of the general property tax, establishing equalized values, and providing financial management assistance. It assesses all manufacturing property and administers the state's utility, pipeline, railroad, and airline taxes. It also administers the state shared revenue program, various tax credit programs, and the general purpose financial reporting requirements for counties and municipalities.

History: The antecedents of the Department of Revenue date back at least to Chapter 130, Laws of 1868, which created a State Board of Assessors, composed of the secretary of state and the entire state senate, to perform the state's taxing functions. At that time, the property tax was the state's primary source of revenue.

Chapter 235, Laws of 1873, changed the board's composition to the secretary of state, state treasurer, and attorney general. The 1899 Legislature created the Office of Tax Commissioner (Chapter 206) to supervise the state's taxation system and made the commissioner a member and presiding officer of the State Board of Assessors.

The composition of the State Board of Assessors was changed again in Chapter 237, Laws of 1901, when the legislature replaced the constitutional officers with two assistant commissioners. The 1905 Legislature abolished the State Board of Assessors (Chapter 380) and assigned its functions to a 3-member Tax Commission, appointed by the governor with the advice and consent of the senate. This structure lasted until Chapter 412, Laws of 1939, created the Department of Taxation, headed by a single commissioner. Chapter 75, Laws of 1967, renamed the agency the Department of Revenue and the commissioner became the secretary.

Throughout the years, certain tax-related functions have been moved from one agency or level of government to another. For example, local officials originally assessed manufacturing property, but the 1973 Legislature gave the department responsibility for assessing all manufacturing property in the state.

Department of Revenue employees Bhaheetharan Sathasivam and Andrea Priboth staff a Volunteer Tax Assistance (VITA) site. The VITA program is a cooperative effort by the Internal Revenue Service and individual states in which trained volunteers provide free income tax help to low-income, elderly, disabled, and other needy individuals. Approximately 40,000 persons are helped each year at about 40 locations around the state. (Department of Revenue)

Similarly, the 1939 Legislature made the Department of Taxation responsible for performing audits upon the request of local governmental units. After assignment to several other agencies, the legislature returned this function to the Department of Revenue in 1971. In 1983, the legislature repealed the department's mandatory municipal audit functions but left intact its discretionary oversight of municipal accounting.

The department currently is responsible for administration of the Wisconsin State Lottery. The lottery was originally created by 1987 Wisconsin Act 119 and administered by the Lottery Board. It was later managed by the Wisconsin Gaming Commission. 1995 Wisconsin Act 27, which transferred the State Lottery to the Department of Revenue, also repealed the commission and created the Gaming Board. The Gaming Board was repealed in 1997 Wisconsin Act 27.

Statutory Board and Council

State Board of Assessors: WILLIAM B. WARDWELL, *chairperson;* LINDA ADLER, THOMAS HYLAND, STEVE LARRABEE, JULIE MATHES, DANIEL STORM, MARK A. WEBER (Department of Revenue employees appointed by secretary).

The State Board of Assessors investigates objections to the amount, valuation, or taxability of real or personal manufacturing property, as well as objections to the penalties issued for late filing or nonfiling of required manufacturing property report forms. The number of board members is determined by the secretary, but all must be department employees. The board was created by Chapter 90, Laws of 1973, and its composition and duties are prescribed in Section 70.995 (8) of the statutes.

Farmland Advisory Council: MICHAEL L. MORGAN (secretary of revenue), *chairperson;* JOHN MALCHINE (agribusiness), CARL AXNESS (knowledgeable about agricultural lending practices), BRUCE JONES (UW System agricultural economist), TIM HANNA (mayor of a city of 40,000 or more population), LINDA BOCHERT (environmental expert), vacancy (representing nonagricultural business), STEVE HINTZ (urban studies professor), HERB TAUCHEN (farmer) (all appointed by secretary of revenue); MELVIN RAATZ (assessor) (appointed by secretary of revenue as an advisor to council).

Contact: MICHAEL L. MORGAN, 266-6466.

Agency Responsibility: The 9-member Farmland Advisory Council advises the Department of Revenue on implementing use-value assessment of agricultural land and reducing urban sprawl. It is required to report annually to the legislature on the usefulness of use-value assessment as a way to preserve farmland, discourage urban sprawl, and reduce the conversion of farmland to other uses. It also recommends changes to the shared revenue formula to compensate local governments adversely affected by use-value assessment. In carrying out its duties, it cooperates with the Wisconsin Strategic Growth Task Force of the State Interagency Land Use Council. The council was created by 1995 Wisconsin Act 27, and its composition and duties are prescribed in Section 73.03 (49) of the statutes.

INDEPENDENT BOARD ATTACHED FOR BUDGETING, PROGRAM COORDINATION, AND RELATED MANAGEMENT FUNCTIONS BY SECTION 15.03 OF THE STATUTES

INVESTMENT AND LOCAL IMPACT FUND BOARD ("THE MINING BOARD")

Investment and Local Impact Fund Board: ROGER O. DAY, JR. (public member), *chairperson;* MARY P. BURKE (secretary of commerce), MICHAEL L. MORGAN (secretary of revenue); RONALD E. HENKEL, DANIEL B. MERRIAM (public members); MICHAEL BRANDNER, ELIZABETH SORENSEN (municipal officials); ERHARD HUETTL, vacancy (county officials); SIDNEY BJORKMAN (school board member); RICHARD L. GURNOE (Native American member). (All except *ex officio* members or their designees are appointed by governor with senate consent.)

Contact: BLAIR P. KRUGER, (608) 266-1310.

Mailing Address: P.O. Box 8933, Madison 53708-8933.

Location: State Revenue Building, 2135 Rimrock Road, Madison.

Statutory References: Sections 15.435 (1) and 70.395 (2).

Agency Responsibility: The 11-member Investment and Local Impact Fund Board administers the Investment and Local Impact Fund, created by the same law to help municipalities alleviate costs associated with social, educational, environmental, and economic impacts of metalliferous mineral mining. The board certifies to the Department of Administration the amount of the payments to be distributed to municipalities from the fund. It also provides guidance and funding to local governments throughout the development of a mining project.

The board's 9 appointed members serve staggered 4-year terms, including the 5 local officials recommended by: the League of Wisconsin Municipalities (1), the Wisconsin Towns Association (1), the Wisconsin Association of School Boards (1), and the Wisconsin Counties Association (2). A Native American member is recommended by the Great Lakes Inter-Tribal Council, Inc. Certain board members must meet qualifications based on residence in or adjacent to a county or municipality with a metallic minerals ore body or mineral development. The board was created by Chapter 31, Laws of 1977.

Currently, there are no operating or proposed mines in the state, and the board is inactive.

Office of the
SECRETARY OF STATE

Secretary of State: DOUGLAS La FOLLETTE, 266-8888.

Deputy Secretary of State: SUSAN CHURCHILL, 266-3470.

Administrative Services Division: MARLENE KOPLIN, *administrator,* 267-6810.

Government Records Division: MARJORIE H. EHLE, *administrator,* 266-1437.

Mailing Address: P.O. Box 7848, Madison 53707-7848.

Location: 30 West Mifflin Street, 10th Floor, Madison 53703.

Telephone: (608) 266-8888.

Fax: (608) 266-3159.

Internet Address: www.sos.state.wi.us

Publications: Notary Public Information Brochure.

Number of Employees: 8.50.

Total Budget 2003-05: $1,318,300.

Constitutional References: Article VI, Sections 1 and 2.

Statutory Reference: Chapter 14, Subchapter III.

Agency Responsibility: The Office of the Secretary of State performs a variety of services for state government and Wisconsin municipalities. Wisconsin's Constitution requires the secretary of state to maintain the official acts of the legislature and governor, and to keep the Great Seal of the State of Wisconsin and affix it to all official acts of the governor.

Organization: The secretary of state, a constitutional officer elected on a partisan ballot in the November general election, heads the Office of the Secretary of State.

Unit Functions: The *Administrative Services Division* maintains revenue and expenditure accounting systems and provides administrative support for the agency.

The *Government Records Division* keeps the Great Seal of the State of Wisconsin and affixes it to all official acts of the governor, issues notary public commissions, registers trade names and trademarks, coordinates the publication of state laws with the Legislative Reference Bureau, records official acts of the legislature and the governor, and files oaths of office. It also files deeds for state lands and buildings, issues notary authentications and apostilles (a form of international authentication of notaries public), preserves the original copies of all enrolled laws and resolutions, and files annexations, charter ordinances, and incorporation papers for villages and cities.

History: The 1836 congressional act that organized the Territory of Wisconsin provided for a secretary of the territory to be appointed by the President of the United States. This office was the forerunner of the post of secretary of state created by the Wisconsin Constitution. Delegates to the constitutional conventions of 1846 and 1848 determined that the secretary of state would be a constitutional officer. From the beginning of statehood until 1970, the secretary of state was elected for a 2-year term. Pursuant to a constitutional amendment ratified in 1967 and effective since the 1970 election, the term was extended to 4 years.

In the early days of statehood, the secretary of state personally performed a broad range of duties that are now delegated to the specialized departments of the executive branch. Chapter 276, Laws of 1969, created the Office of the Secretary of State to assist the secretary.

Office of the
STATE TREASURER

State Treasurer: JACK C. VOIGHT, 266-1714, jack.voight@ost.state.wi.us

Deputy State Treasurer: JOHN W. RADER, 266-7982, john.rader@ost.state.wi.us

Executive Assistant: SHANE T. SAWALL, 266-3712, shane.sawall@ost.state.wi.us

Mailing Address: P.O. Box 7871, Madison 53707-7871.

Location: One South Pinckney Street, Suite 550, Madison.

Telephones: (608) 266-1714, Toll-free (800) 462-2814; Unclaimed property: (608) 267-7977, Toll-free (877) 699-9211; EdVest College Savings Program: (888) 338-3789.

Fax: (608) 266-2647.

Internet Address: http://www.ost.state.wi.us

Publications: Monthly report on the Local Government Investment Pool (LGIP); periodic newsletter for local clerks and treasurers; semiannual classified listing of unclaimed property owners; and reports to investors in the EdVest program.

Number of Employees: 11.00.

Total Budget 2003-05: $4,417,900.

Constitutional References: Article VI, Sections 1 and 3.

Statutory Reference: Chapter 14, Subchapter IV.

Agency Responsibility: The Office of the State Treasurer serves citizens and local government by providing for receipt, custody, oversight, and disbursement of moneys deposited by law with the state, as well as unclaimed property reported to the state. The office also adminsters the state's Section 529 college savings program.

Organization: The state treasurer, a constitutional officer elected for a 4-year term by partisan ballot in the November general election, heads the Office of the State Treasurer and is the fiscal trustee for the State of Wisconsin.

Functions: The state treasurer administers the Local Government Pooled-Investment Fund. The office makes a daily determination of funds available for investment by the State of Wisconsin Investment Board. The state treasurer serves as custodian of unclaimed and escheated property that is transferred to the state when owners and heirs cannot be found and runs outreach programs to locate rightful owners. The state treasurer also administers EdVest, the state's $1.3 billion Section 529 college savings program.

History: The territorial treasurer, an office created in 1839, was appointed by the governor, but the Wisconsin Constitution, adopted in 1848, made the office an elective partisan position. From 1848 through 1968, the state treasurer was elected to a 2-year term in the November general election. Since 1970, following ratification of a constitutional amendment in April 1967, the state treasurer has been elected to a 4-year term. Chapter 276, Laws of 1969, created the Office of the State Treasurer to assist the treasurer.

INDEPENDENT UNIT ATTACHED FOR BUDGETING, PROGRAM COORDINATION, AND RELATED MANAGEMENT FUNCTIONS BY SECTION 15.03 OF THE STATUTES

COLLEGE SAVINGS PROGRAM BOARD

Members: ALBERTA DARLING, *chairperson;* JACK C. VOIGHT (state treasurer), *vice chairperson;* TOBY MARCOVICH (UW Board of Regents president); ROLF WEGENKE (president of the Wisconsin Association of Independent Colleges and Universities); JAMES A. SENTY (designated by the chairperson of the Investment Board); L. ANN REID (president of the Technical College System Board); PAUL C. ADAMSKI, MICHAEL CLUMPNER, WILLIAM OEMICHEN, JEFF PLALE, MICHAEL D. WOLFF. (All except *ex officio* members are appointed by the governor with senate consent.)

Mailing Address: P.O. Box 7871, Madison 53707-7871.

Telephone: 264-7886.

Fax: 266-2647.

E-mail Address: marty.olle@ost.state.wi.us

Internet Address: http://www.edvest.state.wi.us

Statutory References: Sections 14.57, 14.64, and 15.07 (1) (b) 2.

Agency Responsibility: The 11-member College Savings Program Board was created by 1999 Wisconsin Act 44 and its members serve 4-year terms. It administers the EdVest college savings program that provides for tax-sheltered investment accounts held in a trust fund to cover future higher education expenses.

Sarah Vance, in the Office of the State Treasurer, assists a client in receiving his unclaimed property. The office serves as custodian of property when owners and heirs cannot be found and runs outreach programs to locate rightful owners. Unclaimed property includes dormant bank accounts and abandoned safe deposit boxes, lost paychecks, stocks, and uncashed business vendor checks. (Office of the State Treasurer)

TECHNICAL COLLEGE SYSTEM

Technical College System Board: BRENT SMITH (public member), *president;* MARY QUINETTE CUENE (public member), *vice president;* ROBERTA GASSMAN (secretary of workforce development), *secretary;* ELIZABETH BURMASTER (superintendent of public instruction), PEGGY ROSENZWEIG (designated by UW System Board of Regents President); ALLEN KEHL (employer member); PHILLIP L. NEUENFELDT (employee member); ANN GREENHECK (farmer member); ANNIE K. VANG (student member); A.J. AMATO, LORRAINE CARTER, L. ANNE REID, JOSE VASQUEZ (public members). (All except *ex officio* members are appointed by governor.)

President and State Director: DANIEL CLANCY, 266-7983, daniel.clancy@

Executive Assistant: MORNA FOY, 266-2449, morna.foy@

Finance and Policy, Division of: GREG WAGNER, *vice president,* 266-2947, greg.wagner@

   Financial and Administrative Services, Office of: vacancy, *assistant vice president.*

   Internal Operations, Office of: NORMAN KENNEY, *assistant vice president,* 266-1766, norman.kenney@

     Policy and Government Relations, Office of: JANET WASHBON, *assistant vice president,* 266-2017, janet.washbon@

     Legal Counsel: vacancy.

Instruction, Student Services, and Economic Development, Division of: KATHLEEN CULLEN, *vice president,* 266-9399, kathleen.cullen@

   Instruction, Office of: vacancy, *assistant vice president.*

   Student Support and Assessment, Office of: JAYSON CHUNG, *assistant vice president,* 266-5517, jayson.chung@

Address e-mail by combining the user ID and the state extender: userid@**wtcsystem.edu**

Mailing Address: P.O. Box 7874, Madison 53707-7874.

Location: 345 West Washington Avenue, Madison.

Telephone: 266-1207.

Fax: 266-1690.

Internet Address: http://www.wtcsystem.edu

Publications: *Wisconsin Technical Colleges;* Technical College Facts; annual and biennial reports; annual evaluation reports of technical college offerings and services; cost allocation summaries; employer satisfaction reports; graduate follow-up reports.

Number of Employees: 74.50.

Total Budget 2003-05: $354,699,400.

Statutory References: Section 15.94; Chapter 38.

Agency Responsibility: The Technical College System Board is the coordinating agency for the Technical College System. The board establishes statewide policies and standards for the educational programs and services provided by the 16 technical college districts that cover the state. The district boards, in turn, are responsible for the direct operation of their respective schools and programs. They are empowered to levy property taxes, provide for facilities and equipment, employ staff, and contract for services. The districts set academic and grading standards, appoint the district directors, hire instructional and other staff, and manage the district budget.

The system board supervises district operations through reporting and audit requirements and consultation, coordination, and support services. It sets standards for building new schools and adding to current facilities. It also provides assistance to districts in meeting the needs of target groups, including services for the disadvantaged, the disabled, women, dislocated workers, the incarcerated, and minorities.

The board administers state and federal aids. It works with the Department of Public Instruction to coordinate secondary and postsecondary vocational and technical programs. It also cooperates with the University of Wisconsin System to establish coordinated programming to make the services of the two agencies fully available to state residents. The board cooperates with the Department of Workforce Development to provide training for apprentices.

Organization: The 13-member Technical College System Board includes 9 members appointed by the governor to serve staggered 6-year terms and a technical college student appointed for a 2-year term. The student must be 18 years of age and a state resident who is enrolled at least half-time and in good academic standing. The governor may not appoint a student member from the same technical college in any two consecutive terms. No person may serve as board president for more than two successive annual terms. A 1971 opinion of the attorney general held that a member of a technical college district board could not serve concurrently on the state board (60 *OAG* 178). The board appoints a director from outside the classified service to serve at its pleasure, and the director selects the executive assistant and division administrators from outside the classified service.

The 16 technical college districts encompass 47 campuses. Each district is headed by a board of 9 members who serve staggered 3-year terms. District boards include 2 employers, 2 employees, a school district administrator, a state or local elected official, and 3 additional members as defined by statute. A district appointment committee, composed of county board chairpersons or school board presidents, appoints the board members, subject to approval of the state system board.

Unit Functions: The *Division of Finance and Policy* develops and coordinates budgeting, planning, and policy analysis. It is responsible for facilities development; research; labor market information; legislative analysis; management information; government relations; and oversight of district budgets, enrollments, and policies. The division also provides accounting, data processing, purchasing, and personnel services.

The *Division of Instruction, Student Services, and Economic Development* has responsibility for program definition, approval, evaluation, and review. It focuses on programs in agriculture, office services, marketing, home economics (including family and consumer education), health occupations, trade and industry (including apprenticeship, fire service, law enforcement, safety, and technical and vocational training), general education, adult basic education, and environmental education.

The division is responsible for personnel certification, student financial aid, federal projects for the disabled and disadvantaged, adult and continuing education outreach, and Job Training Partnership Act projects. It serves as liaison to business, industry, and secondary schools.

History: Laws passed in 1907 permitted cities to operate trade schools for persons age 16 or older as part of the public school system (Chapter 122), and allowed them to establish technical schools or colleges, under the control of either the school board or a special board (Chapter 344). In Chapter 616, Laws of 1911, Wisconsin was the first state to establish a system of state aid and support for industrial education. The law required every community with a population of 5,000 or more to establish an industrial education board, which was authorized to levy a property tax. It created the State Board of Industrial Education and an assistant for industrial education in the office of the State Superintendent of Public Instruction.

In the Laws of 1911, Wisconsin was the first state to set up apprenticeship agreements (Chapter 347) and require employers to release 14- to 16-year-olds for part-time attendance in continuation schools for apprentices, if such schooling was available (Chapter 505). Hours in class were to count as part of the total paid work hours. The schools, established through the work of Charles McCarthy, first director of the present-day Legislative Reference Bureau, emphasized general cultural and vocational education, as well as trade skills.

Due in part to the efforts of McCarthy, the U.S. Congress passed the Smith-Hughes Act in 1917, the first federal legislation specifically designed to promote vocational education, which it modeled on Wisconsin's vocational training programs. The act offered financial aid to states to help pay teachers' and administrators' salaries and provided funds for teacher training.

Chapter 494, Laws of 1917, changed the name of the State Board of Industrial Education to the State Board of Vocational Education, authorized it to employ a state director, and designated it as the sole agency to work with the newly created federal board.

During the Great Depression, Wisconsin tightened its compulsory school attendance laws, which resulted in more 14- to 18-year-olds attending vocational school. The demand for adult education also increased, as recognized by Chapter 349, Laws of 1937, which renamed the board the State Board of Vocational and Adult Education. During that same period, the vocational school in Milwaukee began to offer college transfer courses.

Events of the 1960s transformed the Wisconsin vocational-technical system into the postsecondary system of today. Federal vocational school legislation affected business education and emphasized training for the unemployed. The federal Vocational Education Act, passed in 1963, helped the local boards build new facilities. Chapter 51, Laws of 1961, authorized the state board to offer associate degrees for 2-year technical courses. The 1965 Legislature passed Chapter 292, which required a system of vocational, technical and adult education (VTAE) districts covering the entire state by 1970 and changed the board's name to the State Board of Vocational, Technical and Adult Education. (Chapter 327, Laws of 1967, dropped "State" from the name.) College transfer programs were authorized in Madison, Milwaukee, and Rhinelander.

As a result of federal and state legislative changes in the 1960s, VTAE enrollments more than doubled to 466,000 between 1967 and 1982. The 1970s also saw significant increases in the number of associate degree programs. Other major statutory changes included the requirement that VTAE schools charge tuition and that they improve cooperation and coordination with the University of Wisconsin System. More recently, a greater emphasis has been placed on services to 16- to 18-year-old students.

In the past two decades, the system has increased its focus on lifelong learning; education for economic development; and services for groups that formerly had less access to education, including people in rural areas, women, and minorities. The system has placed special emphasis on assisting the unemployed, displaced homemakers, and those with literacy problems.

1993 Wisconsin Act 399 renamed the VTAE system, changing it to the Technical College System, and designated the state board as the Technical College System Board. District VTAE schools became "technical colleges".

Department of
TOURISM

Secretary of Tourism: JIM HOLPERIN, 266-2345, jholperin@
Deputy Secretary: GENYNE L. EDWARDS, 266-8773, gedwards@
Mailing Address: P.O. Box 8690, Madison 53708-8690.
Location: 201 West Washington Avenue, 2nd Floor, Madison.
Telephone: 266-7621; Personalized trip planning and publications: (800) 432-8747; Travel Information M-F 8:00 a.m.-4:30 p.m.: (800) 372-2737.
Fax: 266-3403.
Agency Internet Address: http://agency.travelwisconsin.com
Tourism Information Internet Address: http://travelwisconsin.com

| For e-mail combine the user ID and the state extender: userid@**travelwisconsin.com** |

Administrative Services, Bureau of: JUDY MARTI, *director,* 261-8770, jmarti@
Communications and Industry Services, Bureau of: JERRY HUFFMAN, *director,* 261-8195, jhuffman@
Customer and Technology Services, Bureau of: RENEA G. DETTMAN, *director,* 267-7176, rdettman@
Marketing Services, Bureau of: SARAH M. KLAVAS, *director,* 266-3750, sklavas@; Fax: 261-8213.
Number of Employees: 50.45.
Total Budget 2003-05: $26,017,200.
Statutory References: Section 15.44; Chapter 41.
Publications: *Wisconsin Travel Guide*; *Rustic Roads*; guides for biking and seasonal events and recreation; *Wisconsin Heritage Traveler;* Wisconsin State Parks Visitor Guide; Wisconsin Snowmobile Guide.

Agency Responsibility: The Department of Tourism promotes travel to Wisconsin's scenic, historic, artistic, educational, and recreational sites. Travel sectors targeted by the department include leisure, meetings and conventions, sports, group tour, and international. Through planning, research, and assistance it provides guidance to the tourism and recreation industry to aid in the development of facilities. It also assists cooperative projects between profit and nonprofit tourist ventures. The department encourages local tourist development through the Joint Effort Marketing Program.

Organization: The governor appoints the secretary with the advice and consent of the senate to direct the department. The secretary appoints the bureau directors from the classified service.

Unit Functions: The *Bureau of Administrative Services* is responsible for the internal operations of the department, including policy planning and analysis, accounting, human resources, payroll, facility management, and purchasing services.

The *Bureau of Communications and Industry Services* is responsible for the department's community and public relations, as well as economic development and heritage tourism projects. The bureau works with private business to promote and develop commercial tourist facilities. It also provides assistance for cooperative projects between profit and nonprofit tourist ventures and encourages local tourism efforts.

The *Bureau of Customer and Technology Services* maintains and operates Wisconsin's 10 travel information centers, which are located at points of entry on the state's borders. It produces a consumer show program that provides information at exhibitions focusing on hunting, fishing, boating, golf, sports, and other outdoor activities. It also handles travel information requests for the agency. The bureau also manages electronic distribution of information, Internet application development, the department's e-marketing and e-communications efforts, and Web sites for the agency.

The *Bureau of Marketing Services* promotes and advertises Wisconsin as "the Midwest's premiere travel destination". Through market research, coordinated advertising, promotional campaigns and programs, a grant program, and publications targeted to travelers' interests, the bureau is charged with attracting in-state and out-of-state tourists and associated travel dollars. It also assists in the production of commercials, advertisements, and educational materials.

History: State tourism promotion originated in the Department of Natural Resources to encourage travel to state parks and commercial recreational sites. Chapter 39, Laws of 1975, transferred tourism functions to the Department of Business Development and created the Division of Tourism as a statutory entity within the department. Chapter 361, Laws of 1979, created the Department of Development, which absorbed the division, through a merger of the Department of Business Development and the Department of Local Affairs and Development. 1995 Wisconsin Act 27 reorganized the division as the Department of Tourism, effective January 1, 1996.

Statutory Council

Tourism, Council on: DEBORAH T. ARCHER, *chairperson;* LINDA ADLER, PETER J. CHAPMAN, GLORIA L. COBB, CRISTINA DANFORTH, DOUG A. NEILSON, DAVID OLSEN, KAREN RAYMORE, LOLA L. ROEH, WILLIAM J. SLATER, ROMY SNYDER, GREGORY B. SWANBERG, PATRICIA M. THORNTON, TOM TOURVILLE; JIM HOLPERIN (secretary of tourism); SENATORS BRESKE, ZIEN; REPRESENTATIVES PETTIS, STEINBRINK; GEORGE TZOUGROS (executive director, Arts Board); ELLSWORTH BROWN (director, state historical society). (All except *ex officio* members are appointed by governor.)

The 21-member Council on Tourism advises the secretary about tourism and encourages Wisconsin private companies to promote the state in their advertisements. The 14 appointed members serve 3-year terms and assist the secretary in formulating a statewide marketing plan. Nominations for public member appointments must be sought from (but are not limited to) multicounty regional associations engaged in promoting tourism; statewide associations of businesses related to tourism; area visitor and convention bureaus; arts organizations; the Great Lakes Inter-Tribal Council, Inc., and other agencies with knowledge of American Indian tourism; and persons engaged in businesses catering to tourists. Nominees must have experience in marketing and promotion strategy and must represent the different geographical areas of the state and the diversity of the tourism industry. The council was created by 1987 Wisconsin Act 1 in the Department of Development and transferred to the Department of Tourism by 1995 Wisconsin Act 27. Its composition and duties are prescribed in Sections 15.447 (1) and 41.12 of the statutes.

INDEPENDENT UNITS ATTACHED FOR BUDGETING, PROGRAM COORDINATION, AND RELATED MANAGEMENT FUNCTIONS BY SECTION 15.03 OF THE STATUTES

ARTS BOARD

Members: BARBARA LAWTON, *chairperson;* LINDA L. WARE, *vice chairperson;* PAUL MEINKE, *secretary;* BRUCE BERNBERG, FERNE YANGYETIE CAULKER, LINDA GRUNAU, GERALD KEMBER, JULILLY KOHLER, BARBARA E. MUNSON, GLENDA P. NOEL-NEY, MICHAEL REYES, SHARON STEWART, ROBERT A. WAGNER, MATTHEW WAHL, vacancy (appointed by governor).
Executive Director: GEORGE TZOUGROS, 267-2006, george.tzougros@arts.state.wi.us
Mailing Address: State Administration Building, 101 East Wilson Street, 1st Floor, Madison 53702.
Telephone: 266-0190; TTY: 267-9629.
Fax: 267-0380.
E-mail Address: artsboard@arts.state.wi.us
Internet Address: http://www.arts.state.wi.us
Publications: Print and Internet: Basic Record Keeping Procedures Handbook for Grant Applications; Wisconsin Art and Craft Fairs Directory; Wisconsin Art Museums and Gallery Guide; Wisconsin Performing Arts Presenters Network Guide; Wisconsin Touring and Arts in Education Artist Directory. Internet only: Annual Report; Guide to Programs and Services; Statewide Arts Service Organization Directory; grant applications (all programs).
Number of Employees: 11.00.
Total Budget 2003-05: $6,924,600.
Statutory References: Section 15.445 (1); Chapter 44, Subchapter III.
 Agency Responsibility: The legislature directs the 15-member Arts Board to study and assist artistic and cultural activities in the state, assist communities in developing their own arts programs, and plan and implement funding programs for groups or individuals engaged in the arts.
 As a funding agency, the board assists arts organizations and individual artists through a variety of programs designed to provide broad public access to the arts, strengthen the state's artistic resources, and create opportunities for individuals of exceptional talent. Financial support programs for individuals and organizations include apprenticeships, artists-in-education programs, challenge grants, community activities, fellowships, opportunity grants, program assistance and support, and programs for presenters. The board also provides matching grants to local arts agencies and municipalities through the Wisconsin Regranting Program.
 The board aids Wisconsin's artistic community through an information program that includes workshops, conferences, research projects, and publications. The board regularly produces and distributes materials on local, state, and national arts activities for both the arts community and the general public. It arranges for the governor's official portrait, and it selects the artwork placed in state buildings as required by law.
 Board members serve staggered 3-year terms and must be state residents with a concern for the arts. Each geographic quadrant of the state must be represented by at least 2 members. The board selects the executive director from outside the classified service. Chapter 90, Laws of 1973, created the board and attached it to the Department of Administration to succeed the Governor's Council on the Arts, which Governor Gaylord Nelson had established in 1963. 1995 Wisconsin Act 27 attached the board to the Department of Tourism.

KICKAPOO RESERVE MANAGEMENT BOARD

Members: SUSAN C. CUSHING, RONALD M. JOHNSON, JACK H. ROBINSON, REBECCA E. ZAHM (residents of specified municipalities and school districts); GEORGE E. NETTUM, RICHARD WALLIN (watershed residents outside specified units); vacancy (watershed resident nominated by Ho-

Chunk Nation); Jo Deen B. Lowe (member with knowledge of watershed's cultural resources, nominated by Ho-Chunk Nation); Senn R. Brown (education representative), Katie Thompson (recreation and tourism representative), William L. Quackenbush (environmental advocate) (nonresidents of watershed appointed by governor with senate consent).

Executive Director: Marcy West, marcy.west@krm.state.wi.us

Mailing Address: S 3661 State Highway 131, La Farge 54639.

Telephone: (608) 625-2960.

Fax: (608) 625-2962.

E-mail Address: kickapoo.reserve@krm.state.wi.us

Internet Address: http://kvr.state.wi.us

Publications: Kickapoo Valley Reserve Visitors' Guide.

Number of Employees: 3.00.

Total Budget 2003-05: $1,254,000.

Statutory References: Sections 15.07 (1) (b) 20., 15.445 (2), 41.40, and 41.41.

Agency Responsibility: The 11-member Kickapoo Reserve Management Board manages 8,569 acres in the Kickapoo Valley Reserve to preserve and enhance the area's environmental, scenic, and cultural features; provides facilities for the use and enjoyment of visitors; and promotes the reserve as a destination for vacationing and recreation. Subject to the approval of the governor, the board may purchase land for inclusion in the reserve and trade land in the reserve under certain conditions. The Kickapoo Valley Reserve Visitor Center offers meeting and classrooms, interactive exhibits, and tourist information.

The board also may lease land for purposes consistent with the management of the reserve or for agricultural purposes; authorize, license, regulate, and collect and spend revenue from private concessions in the reserve; accept gifts, grants, and bequests; and cooperate with and provide matching funds to nonprofit groups organized to provide assistance to the reserve.

The board may not authorize mining in the reserve or on any land acquired by the board and may not sell land that is in the reserve. It has authority to promulgate rules about use of the waters, land, and facilities under its jurisdiction, and the Department of Tourism is responsible for enforcement of state laws and rules relating to the reserve.

The governor appoints board members for staggered 3-year terms. Four members must be residents of villages, towns, and school districts in the immediate vicinity of the reserve; 2 must be residents of the Kickapoo River watershed outside of the immediate vicinity of the reserve; and 3 members who are not residents of the watershed are appointed by the governor to represent education, environment, and tourism issues. In addition, 2 members are nominated by the Ho-Chunk Nation, one of whom is a resident of the watershed, and the other must have an interest in and knowledge of the cultural resources within the watershed. Various state agencies must appoint nonmember liaisons to the board, and the board may request that any federally recognized American Indian tribe or band in this state, other than the Ho-Chunk Nation, appoint a nonmember liaison. The board appoints the executive director from outside the classified service. The board was created as the Kickapoo Valley Governing Board by 1993 Wisconsin Act 349 and attached to the Department of Administration. 1995 Wisconsin Act 27 attached the board to the Department of Tourism, and it was renamed by 1995 Wisconsin Act 216.

LOWER WISCONSIN STATE RIVERWAY BOARD

Members: William Lundberg (recreational user group representative), *chairperson;* Melody K. Moore (Dane County), *vice chairperson;* Lloyd B. Nice (Grant County), *secretary;* Gerald Dorscheid (Iowa County), Greg Greenheck (Richland County), Donald Greenwood (Sauk County), Ronald Leys (Crawford County). (County representatives are nominated by respective county boards and appointed by governor.) Ritchie J. Brown, Fred Madison (recreational use groups' representative appointed by governor with senate consent).

Executive Director: Mark E. Cupp, 202 North Wisconsin Avenue, P.O. Box 187, Muscoda 53573-0187, mark.cupp@lwr.state.wi.us

With more state parks (5), lighthouses (10), and miles of shoreline (250) than any other county in the country, Door County enchants visitors from around the world. Here, sea kayakers enjoy the scenic coastline. (Department of Tourism)

Telephone: (608) 739-3188; (800) 221-3792.

Fax: (608) 739-4263.

Internet Address: http://lwr.state.wi.us

Publications: Summary of regulations, Strategic Plan, Biennial Report.

Number of Employees: 2.00.

Total Budget 2003-05: $303,600.

Statutory References: Section 15.445 (3); Chapter 30, Subchapter IV.

Agency Responsibility: The 9-member Lower Wisconsin State Riverway Board is responsible for protecting and preserving the scenic beauty and natural character of the riverway. The board reviews permit applications for buildings, walkways, timber harvests, utility facilities, bridges, and other structures in the riverway and issues permits for activities that meet established standards.

Board members serve staggered 3-year terms. Each of the 6 county representatives must be either an elected official or a resident of a city or village that abuts the Lower Wisconsin State Riverway or of a town located at least in part in the riverway. The 3 members representing recreational user groups may not reside in any of the 6 specified counties. The board was created by 1989 Wisconsin Act 31 and attached to the Department of Natural Resources. 1995 Wisconsin Act 27 attached the board to the Department of Tourism.

STATE FAIR PARK BOARD

Members: MARTIN GREENBERG (business experience), *chairperson;* SENATORS REYNOLDS, PLALE; REPRESENTATIVES GUNDERSON, STASKUNAS (legislative members recommended by party leadership and appointed by governor); MICHELLE NETTLES, TIMOTHY R. SHEEHY (general business experience); SUE CRANE (business agricultural experience); BENNIE JOYNER, JR. (business technology experience); RICHARD GALE (West Allis resident); SCOTT SOLDON (state resident); ROD NILSESTUEN (secretary of agriculture, trade and consumer protection); JIM HOLPERIN (secretary of tourism). (All are appointed by governor with senate consent.)

Executive Director: RANDY PRASSE, (414) 266-7021.

Executive Assistant: MARIAN SANTIAGO-LLOYD, (414) 266-7021.

Mailing Address: 640 South 84th Street, West Allis 53214.

Telephone: (414) 266-7000; (414) 266-7100 (ticket office); (800) 884-FAIR (recorded announcement of events).

Fax: (414) 266-7007.

E-mail Address: wsfp@sfp.state.wi.us

Internet Address: http://www.wsfp.state.wi.us

Publications: *A Brief History of the Wisconsin State Fair;* WSFP Update (semi-annual); cook book (semi-annual); annual non-fair events schedule; monthly non-fair events schedule; fair brochures, daily events schedule, and premium books.

Number of Employees: 30.20.

Total Budget 2003-05: $35,605,200.

Statutory References: Section 15.445 (4); Chapter 42.

Agency Responsibility: The State Fair Park Board manages the State Fair Park and supervises its use for fairs, exhibits, or promotional events for agricultural, commercial, educational, and recreational purposes and leases or licenses the property at reasonable rates for other uses when not needed for public purposes. The board is also directed to develop new facilities at State Fair Park and to provide a permanent location for an annual Wisconsin State Fair, major sports events, agricultural and industrial expositions, and other programs of civic interest.

Organization: The State Fair Park Board consists of 13 members. Legislative members, who represent the majority and minority parties, are nominated by party leadership and appointed by the governor. The 7 citizen members serve staggered 5-year terms. The board appoints the park director from outside the classified service.

History: Beginning with the first Wisconsin State Fair at Janesville in October 1851, the event has served as a showcase for Wisconsin agriculture and commerce. The State Agricultural Society, which sponsored the first fair, continued to operate it through 1897. In that year, Chapter 301 created the Wisconsin State Board of Agriculture and placed operation of the fair under its control. When the Department of Agriculture was created in 1915, the state fair became part of the new department.

In Chapter 149, Laws of 1961, the independent Wisconsin Exposition Department, headed by a 7-member board, was created to manage the fair and the park's year-round operation. Under the 1967 executive branch reorganization, the Exposition Department became the Wisconsin Exposition Council in the Department of Local Affairs and Development.

Chapter 125, Laws of 1971, created a 3-member State Fair Park Board, appointed by the governor and attached to the Department of Agriculture for administrative purposes. In 1985 Wisconsin Act 20, the legislature increased board membership to 5, specified 5-year terms of service, and required senate confirmation of the governor's nominees.

In 1990, as provided by 1989 Wisconsin Act 219, the State Fair Park Board became an independent body. 1995 Wisconsin Act 27 attached the board to the Department of Tourism, and 1999 Wisconsin Act 197 revised and increased board membership.

Over the years, the location of the state fair was debated and even its continued existence was in doubt. At various times between 1851 and 1885, Fond du Lac, Janesville, Madison, Milwaukee, and Watertown hosted the fair. Milwaukee was chosen as the state fair site from 1886 through 1891, and the fairs held there were so successful that a permanent site was purchased in what is now West Allis, a Milwaukee suburb. That site, first used for the 1892 fair, is included in the state fair's location today.

Several studies published during the 1960s recommended that the fair be moved to a larger site in the Milwaukee area. Chapter 125, Laws of 1971, decided the fair would remain at its site (partially in West Allis, partially in Milwaukee), with updated or new facilities being funded through self-amortizing state bonds. Fair operations have been self-financed since 1935. 1999 Wisconsin Act 9 provided funding for substantial construction and renovation of park facilities. 1999 Wisconsin Act 197 authorized the board to create a nonprofit corporation to raise funds and provide support and contract with that same corporation for operation and development of the park. Act

197 also authorized the park board to permit private individuals to construct facilities on fair grounds under a lease agreement with the board.

Today, State Fair Park draws more than 2 million visitors to its events and activities each year, and the Wisconsin State Fair, with attendance of more than 900,000, remains the state's oldest and largest annual event.

Scenic vistas throughout the state offer spectacular views like this one at Devil's Lake State Park near Baraboo. (Department of Tourism)

Department of
TRANSPORTATION

Secretary of Transportation: FRANK BUSALACCHI, 266-1114, frank.busalacchi@

Deputy Secretary: RUBEN ANTHONY, JR., 266-1114, ruben.anthony-jr@

Executive Assistant: CHRISTOPHER P. KLEIN, 266-1114, christopher.klein@

General Counsel, Office of: vacancy, *director,* 266-8810.

Policy, Budget and Finance, Office of: KENNETH NEWMAN, *director,* 267-9618, kenneth.newman@

Public Affairs, Office of: PEG SCHMITT, *director,* 266-7744, peg.schmitt@, Fax: 266-7186.

Mailing Address: P.O. Box 7910, Madison 53707-7910.

Location: Hill Farms State Transportation Building, 4802 Sheboygan Avenue, Madison.

Internet Address: http://www.dot.state.wi.us

Number of Employees: 3,645.83.

Total Budget 2003-05: $3,738,281,800.

Statutory References: Sections 15.46, 15.465, and 15.467; Chapters 80, 84-86, 110, 114, and 340-351.

Address e-mail by combining the user ID and the state extender: userid@**dot.state.wi.us**

Business Management, Division of: BRENDA BROWN, *administrator,* 266-2090, brenda.brown@

Business Services, Bureau of: JAMES D. MCDONNELL, *director,* 264-7700, james.mcdonnell@

Human Resource Services, Bureau of: SUSAN CHRISTOPHER, *director,* 266-7460, susan.christopher@; TTY: 267-0259 (for affirmative action/equal employment opportunity).

Information Technology Services, Bureau of: JOYCE S. GELDERMAN, *director,* 266-0033, joyce.gelderman@

Motor Vehicles, Division of: LYNNE B. JUDD, *administrator,* 266-7079, lynne.judd@; GARY PRIDEAUX-WENTZ, *operations manager,* 266-9890, gary.prideaux-wentz@

Driver Services, Bureau of: PATRICK FERNAN, *director,* 261-8605, patrick.fernan@

Field Services, Bureau of: GARY GUENTHER, *director,* 266-2743, gary.guenther@

Vehicle Services, Bureau of: JANE ZARADA, *director,* 267-5121, jane.zarada@

Vehicle Emission Testing (Southeast Wisconsin): (800) 242-7510.

Motor Vehicle District Managers:

Southwest Region: DAVE COADY, (608) 246-7540, 2001 Bartillon Drive, Madison 53704-2614, dave.coady@; DONALD REINCKE, (608) 789-4630, 9477 Highway 16 East, Onalaska 54650-8527, donald.reincke@

North Central Region: JILL HJELSAND, (920) 929-3720, 833 South Rolling Meadows Drive, Fond du Lac 54936-2067, jill.hjelsand@

Northwest Region: RICHARD GIETZEL, (715) 234-3773, 113 North Main Street, Rice Lake 54868, richard.gietzel@

Northeast Region: LINDA LEWIS, (920) 492-5731, 942 Vanderperren Way, Green Bay 54304-5344, linda.lewis@

Southeast Region: MARY LUTHER, (262) 785-7155, 2115 E. Moreland Boulevard, Suite D, Waukesha 53186-2985, mary.luther@; SANDRA BRISCO, (414) 266-1109, 1150 North Alois Street, #614, Milwaukee 53208, sandra.brisco@; HAZEL WILLS, (414) 227-4890, 819 North 6th Street, Milwaukee 53203-1606, hazel.wills@

State Patrol, Division of: DAVID L. COLLINS, *Superintendent,* 267-7102, david.collins@; COLONEL BENJAMIN H. MENDEZ, 266-3908, benjamin.mendez@
Division Mailing Address: P.O. Box 7912, Madison 53707-7912.
Telephones: General: (608) 266-3212; Road Condition Reports: Madison: (608) 246-7580; Milwaukee: (414) 785-7140; elsewhere in Wisconsin: (800) 762-3947.
Fax: 267-4495.
Communications, Bureau of: DAVID A. HEWITT, *director,* 266-0184, david.hewitt@
Field Operations, Bureau of: MAJOR SANDRA K. HUXTABLE, 267-9522, sandra.huxtable@

DEPARTMENT OF TRANSPORTATION

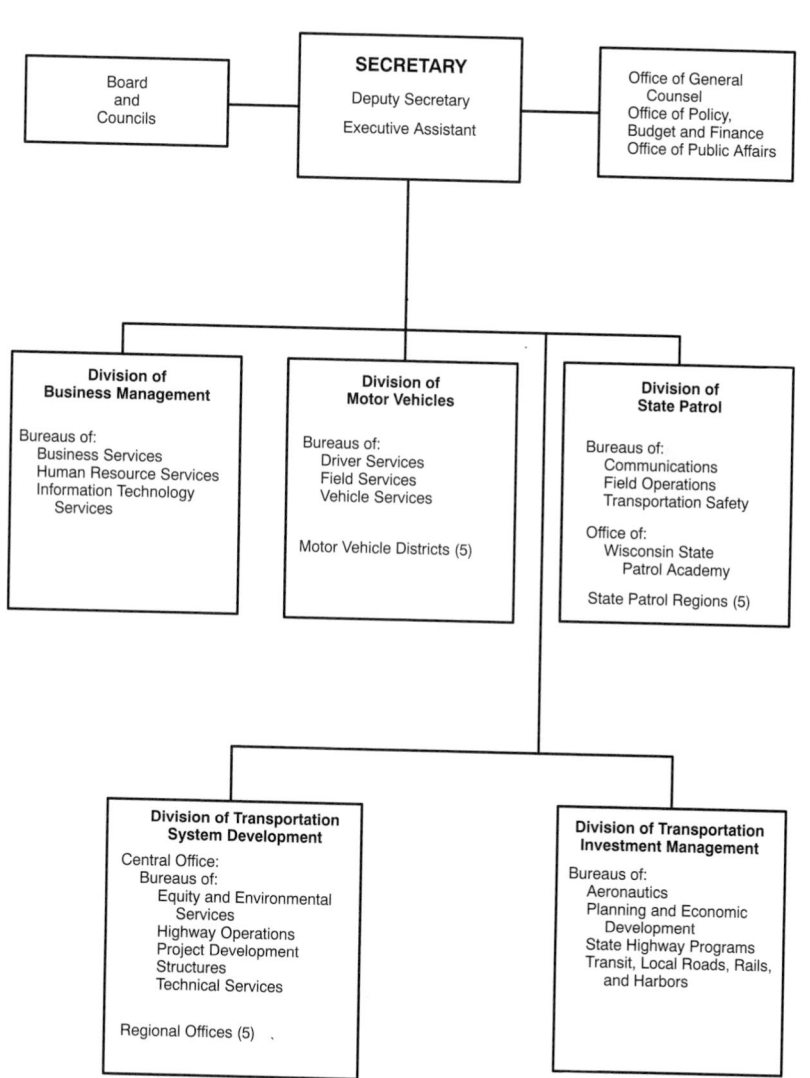

Wisconsin State Patrol Academy, Office of: MAJOR DARREN C. PRICE, *director of training,* (608) 269-2500, darren.price@; Fax: (608) 269-5681; 95 South 10th Avenue, Fort McCoy 54656-5168.

State Patrol Region Captains/Executive Officers:

Southwest Region:

DeForest Post: DAVID C. HEINLE, *captain,* (608) 846-8500, david.heinle@; RUTH M. FERG, *executive officer,* (608) 846-8500, ruth.ferg@; Fax: (608) 846-8536; 911 West North Street, P.O. Box 610, DeForest 53532-0610.

Tomah Post: GREGORY M. SCHAUB, *executive officer,* (608) 374-0513, gregory.schaub@; Fax: (608) 374-0599; 23928 Lester McMullin Drive, P.O. Box 604, Tomah 54660-0604.

Southeast Region:

Waukesha Post: VARLA J. BISHOP, *captain,* (262) 785-4700, varla.bishop@; TED MEAGHER, *executive officer,* (262) 785-4700, ted.meagher@; Fax: (262) 785-4722; 21115 Highway 18, Waukesha 53186-2985.

Northeast Region:

Fond du Lac Post: DAVID J. PICHETTE, *captain,* (920) 929-3700, david.pichette@; NICHOLAS SCORCIO, JR., *executive officer,* (920) 929-3700, nicholas.scorcio@; Fax: (920) 929-7666; 851 South Rolling Meadows Drive, P.O. Box 984, Fond du Lac 54936-0984.

North Central Region:

Wausau Post: JEFFREY J. FRENETTE, *captain,* (715) 845-1143, jeffrey.frenette@; TIMOTHY L. CARNAHAN, *executive officer,* (715) 845-1143, timothy.carnahan@; Fax: (715) 848-9255; 2805 Martin Avenue, Wausau 54401-7172.

Northwest Region:

Eau Claire Post: DOUGLAS M. NOTBOHM, *captain,* (715) 839-3800, douglas.notbohm@; Fax: (715) 839-3841; NICHOLAS R. WANINK, *executive officer,* (715) 839-3800, nicholas.wanink@; Fax: (715) 839-3873; 5005 Highway 53 South, Eau Claire 54701-8846.

Spooner Post: LEE F. MCMENAMIN, *executive officer,* (715) 635-2141, lee.mcmenamin@; Fax: (715) 635-6373; W7102 Green Valley Road, Spooner 54801.

Transportation Safety, Bureau of: MAJOR DANIEL W. LONSDORF, *director,* 266-3048, daniel.lonsdorf@

Transportation System Development, Division of: KEVIN CHESNIK, *administrator,* 267-7111, kevin.chesnik@; Division Fax: 264-6667.

Division Mailing Address: 4802 Sheboygan Avenue, Room 451, P.O. Box 7965, Madison 53707-7965.

Division E-mail Address: division-office.dtid@dot.state.wi.us

Statewide Bureaus Operations Director: PAUL TROMBINO, 264-6677, paul.trombino@; Fax: 264-6667.

Equity and Environmental Services, Bureau of: EUGENE S. JOHNSON, *director,* 267-9527, eugene.johnson@; Fax: 266-7818.

Highway Operations, Bureau of: DAVID I. VIETH, *director,* 267-8999, david.vieth@; Fax: 267-7856; JOHN M. CORBIN, *State Traffic Engineer,* 266-0459, john.corbin@; Fax: 261-6295.

Project Development, Bureau of: DONALD J. MILLER, *director,* 266-3707, donald.miller@; Fax: 266-8459.

Structures, Bureau of: vacancy, *director,* 266-0075; Fax: 261-6277.

Technical Services, Bureau of: DANIEL K. MCGUIRE, *director,* 246-5399, daniel.mcguire@; Fax: 267-0307.

Budget and Planning, Office of: LINDA SEAQUIST, *chief,* 266-2836, linda.seaquist@

Regional Operation Director: RORY L. RHINESMITH, 266-2392, rory.rhinesmith@; Fax: 264-6667.

Southwest Region, La Crosse: JOSEPH OLSON, *director,* (608) 785-9022, joseph.olson@; Fax: (608) 785-9969; TTY: (608) 789-7862; 3550 Mormon Coulee Road, La Crosse 54601-6767; ROSE PHETTEPLACE, *operations manager,* (608) 246-3801, rose.phetteplace@; Fax: (608) 246-7996; TTY: (608) 246-5385; 2101 Wright Street, Madison 53704-2583.

Southeast Region, Waukesha: DEWAYNE JOHNSON, *director,* (262) 548-5884, dewayne.johnson@; Fax: (414) 548-5662; TTY: (414) 548-8801; 141 Northwest Barstow Street, Waukesha 53187-0798; vacancy, *operations manager.*

Northeast Region, Green Bay: MICHAEL BERG, *director,* (715) 421-8300, michael.berg@; WILL DORSEY, *operations manager,* (920) 492-5643, will.dorsey@; Fax: (920) 492-5640; TTY: (920) 492-5673; 944 Vanderperren Way, P.O. Box 28080, Green Bay 54324-0080.

North Central Region, Rhinelander: DANIEL GRASSER, *director,* (715) 365-3490, daniel.grasser@; Fax: (715) 365-5780; TTY: (715) 365-5719; 510 Hanson Lake Road, P.O. Box 777, Rhinelander 54501-0777; JERALD MENTZEL, *operations manager,* (715) 421-8300, jerald.mentzel@; Fax: (715) 423-0334; 2610 Industrial Street, P.O. Box 8021, Wisconsin Rapids 54495-8021.

Northwest Region, Eau Claire: DONALD GUTKOWSKI, *director,* (715) 836-2891, donald.gutkowski@; Fax: (715) 836-2807; TTY: (715) 836-6578; 718 West Clairemont Avenue, Eau Claire 54701-5108; JERALD MENTZEL, *operations manager,* (715) 392-7925, jerald.mentzel@; Fax: (715) 392-7863; TTY Relay Service: (800) 947-3529; 1701 North Fourth Street, Superior 54880-1068.

Transportation Investment Management, Division of: MARK WOLFGRAM, *administrator,* 266-5791, mark.wolfgram@; Fax: 266-0686; P.O. Box 7913, Madison 53707-7913.

Aeronautics, Bureau of: DAVID GREENE, *director,* 266-2480, david.greene@

Planning and Economic Development, Bureau of: SANDRA BEAUPRÉ, *director,* 266-7575, sandra.beaupre@

The Merrimac Ferry, which crosses the Wisconsin River between Sauk and Columbia Counties, is Wisconsin's only free ferry. Operated by the Wisconsin Department of Transportation, it shuttles Wisconsin Highway 113 traffic between Okee on the east bank and Merrimac on the west bank. It holds up to 15 cars, plus bicycles and pedestrians, and operates 24 hours a day, 7 days a week, normally from April 15 through November 30. (Department of Transportation)

State Highway Programs, Bureau of: ROBERT ST. CLAIR, *director,* 266-9495, robert.st.clair@

Transit, Local Roads, Rails, and Harbors, Bureau of: ROD CLARK, *director,* 266-2963, rod.clark@

Publications: Biennial Report; Five-Year Airport Improvement Program (annual); Motorcyclist Handbook for Wisconsin; *Rustic Roads;* Six-Year Highway Improvement Program; Traffic Safety Reporter; *Trucking Wisconsin Style;* Wisconsin Aeronautical Chart (annual); Wisconsin Airport Directory (odd-numbered years); Wisconsin Alcohol Traffic Facts; Wisconsin Aviation Bulletin (quarterly); Wisconsin Commercial Drivers' Manual; Wisconsin Drivers' Book; Wisconsin Highway Map; Wisconsin Motorists' Handbook and Study Guide; Wisconsin Traffic Crash Facts (annual), State Highway Plan 2020; Wisconsin Motorcycle Crash Facts.

Agency Responsibility: The Department of Transportation is responsible for the planning, promotion, and protection of all transportation systems in the state. Its major responsibilities involve highways, motor vehicles, motor carriers, traffic law enforcement, railroads, waterways, mass transit, and aeronautics.

The department works with several federal agencies in the administration of federal transportation aids. It also cooperates with departments at the state level in travel promotion, consumer protection, environmental analysis, and transportation services for elderly and handicapped persons.

Organization: The secretary is appointed by the governor with the advice and consent of the senate and has overall management responsibility for the department. The secretary appoints the deputy secretary, executive assistant, and all division administrators from outside the classified service.

Unit Functions: The *Division of Business Management* plans and administers the department's programs for accounting and auditing, information technology, human resources, purchasing, vehicle fleet, facilities, and management services.

The *Division of Motor Vehicles* issues vehicle titles and registrations, individual identification cards, and handicapped parking permits; examines and licenses drivers, commercial driving instructors, and vehicle salespersons; certifies commercial driver examiners; licenses motor carriers, commercial driving schools, vehicle dealers, manufacturers, and distributors; and investigates consumer complaints about vehicle sales and trade practices. It keeps the records of drivers' traffic violations and demerit points. It is responsible for the vehicle emissions inspection program, and it administers reciprocal trucking agreements with other states and the Canadian provinces and provides traffic accident data to law enforcement officials, highway engineers, and traffic safety and media representatives. The division operates 5 district offices and over 100 customer service centers to support the state's approximately 3.8 million licensed drivers and over 5 million registered vehicles.

The *Division of State Patrol* promotes highway safety by enforcing state traffic laws regarding motor vehicles and motor carriers. The State Patrol also has criminal law enforcement powers and can assist local law enforcement agencies by providing emergency police services. It operates the statewide mobile data communications network, which is available to local law enforcement agencies, and it makes annual inspections of Wisconsin's school buses and ambulances. The division oversees 5 district offices and a law enforcement training academy open to all federal, state, county, local, and tribal law enforcement officers.

The *Division of Transportation System Development* ensures the efficient delivery, maintenance, and operations of the State Trunk Highway (STH) system. The division is split into two basic areas: Statewide Bureaus and Regional Operations. It provides uniform direction in planning, design, and construction phases of project delivery as well as improving the safety and efficiency of the STH system. The division also provides leadership in the protection of public interests and resources through public and local interactions.

The five state statewide bureaus include: 1) Equity and Environmental Services, 2) Highway Operations, 3) Project Development, 4) Structures, and 5) Technical Services. These statewide bureaus advise the regional offices as well as other divisions regarding engineering, economic, environmental, and social standards and practices. It also monitors the quality and efficiency of the department's various programs and assures compliance with federal and state laws and regulations. The five regional offices manage the operation and development of state highways and participate in the development, management, and implementation of local road and non-highway transportation projects. They also maintain working relationships with local units of government, represent the department in local and regional planning efforts, and represent local and regional needs in departmental processes.

The *Division of Transportation Investment Management* performs statewide planning for highways, railroads, harbors, airports, and mass transit and promotes a multimodal transportation system to best serve state citizens and businesses. The division directs data collection; provides service to local governments and planning agencies; and manages state road aids, highway finance, and other transportation assistance programs. The division is responsible for uniform statewide direction in the planning, design, construction, maintenance, and operation of Wisconsin's airports, harbors, highways, and railroads. The division is involved with the state's 134 public use airports, 3,660 miles of railroad tracks, 15 commercial water ports, and the approximately 12,000 miles of roads and streets in the STH system, including 640 miles of Interstate highways within the state. The division administers all state and federal funding for airport, railroad, and harbor development projects in Wisconsin.

History: The history of the Department of Transportation mirrors the evolution of twentieth century transportation. The Highway Commission was created when Chapter 337, Laws of 1911, authorized state aid for public highways. Later, Chapter 410, Laws of 1939, consolidated registration, licensing, inspection, enforcement, and highway safety promotion in the Motor Vehicle Department. The legislature established the Aeronautics Commission in Chapter 513, Laws of 1945, and directed it to cooperate with the federal government and other states to "prepare for the generally expected extensive expansion of aviation following the termination of World War II."

The Department of Transportation was created by Chapter 75, Laws of 1967, which merged the Highway Commission, the Aeronautics Commission, and the Motor Vehicle Department. Chapter 500, Laws of 1969, required three divisions within the department: aeronautics, highways, and motor vehicles. The department was strengthened by Chapter 29, Laws of 1977, which vested accountability at the departmental, instead of divisional, level and gave the secretary, rather than the governor, the authority to appoint division heads. The secretary was also allowed to reorganize the department with the governor's approval.

Statutory Board and Councils

Highway Safety, Council on: JOHN M. SYBELDON (citizen member), *chairperson;* ROBERT W. CHRISTIAN (citizen member), *vice chairperson;* RANDY THIEL (state officer), *secretary;* SENATORS BRESKE, KANAVAS; REPRESENTATIVES BIES, PETROWSKI, SHERMAN; DAVID COLLINS, JOHN CORBIN, RODNEY W. KREUNEN, vacancy (state officers); JOAN FERNAN, LAVERNE E. HERMANN, ARNOLD C. WIDDES (citizen members). (All except legislators are appointed by governor.)

The 15-member Council on Highway Safety advises the secretary about highway safety matters. The council includes 2 senators and 3 assembly representatives who serve on standing committees that deal with transportation matters. The other 10 members, who serve staggered 3-year terms, include 5 state officers with transportation and highway safety duties and 5 citizen members. The council was originally created in the Office of the Governor by Chapter 276, Laws of 1969, and was moved to the Department of Transportation by Chapter 34, Laws of 1979. Its composition and duties are prescribed in Sections 15.467 (3) and 85.07 (2) of the statutes.

Rustic Roads Board: THOMAS P. SOLHEIM, *chairperson;* MARION FLOOD, *vice chairperson;* SENATOR KEDZIE; REPRESENTATIVE AINSWORTH; RAYMOND DEHAHN, DANIEL FEDDERLY, ROBERT HANSEN, BRUCE LINDGREN, ALAN LORENZ, CHARLES RAYALA. (Nonlegislative members are appointed by secretary of transportation.)

The 10-member Rustic Roads Board oversees the application and selection process of locally-nominated county highways and local roads for inclusion in the Rustic Roads network. Established in 1973, the Rustic Roads Program is a partnership between local officials and state government to showcase some of Wisconsin's most picturesque and lightly-traveled roadways for the leisurely enjoyment of hikers, bikers, and motorists. The board includes the chairpersons of the senate and assembly committees with jurisdiction over transportation matters. Its 8 nonlegislative members serve staggered 4-year terms, and at least 4 of them must be nominees of the Wisconsin

The Sixth Street Viaduct, which links downtown Milwaukee to the city's South Side, opened in September 2002. The Wisconsin Department of Transportation managed 75% of the project's $49.7 million cost. The .7 mile structure, which includes sidewalks and bicycle lanes, improves access to the Menomonee River Valley, and will serve as a key alternate route during the reconstruction of the Marquette Interchange on Interstate Highway 94. (Department of Transportation)

Counties Association. The board was created by Chapter 142, Laws of 1973, and its composition and duties are prescribed in Sections 15.465 (2) and 83.42 of the statutes.

Uniformity of Traffic Citations and Complaints, Council on: vacancy (designated by secretary of transportation), *chairperson;* WILLIAM HARLEY (Department of Transportation law enforcement member); MILTON MARQUARDT (designated by Wisconsin Sheriffs and Deputy Sheriffs Association); LT. JOHN CRAM (designated by County Traffic Patrol Association); LT. JOE DUESTER (designated by Chiefs of Police Association); GERALD MOWRIS (designated by State Bar of Wisconsin); BRIAN ROESSLER (designated by Wisconsin Council of Safety); SANDY WILLIAMS (designated by Wisconsin District Attorneys Association); TODD MEURER (designated by Judicial Conference); GARY L. CARLSON (designated by Director of State Courts).

The 10-member Council on Uniformity of Traffic Citations and Complaints recommends forms used for traffic violations. The council was created by Chapter 292, Laws of 1967, as the Uniform Traffic Citation and Complaint Committee and renamed by 1985 Wisconsin Act 145. Its composition and duties are prescribed in Sections 15.467 (4) and 345.11 of the statutes.

UNIVERSITY OF WISCONSIN SYSTEM

Board of Regents: DAVID G. WALSH, *president;* MARK J. BRADLEY, *vice president;* ELIZABETH A. BURMASTER (superintendent of public instruction), BRENT SMITH (president, Technical College System Board); ROGER E. AXTELL, EILEEN CONNOLLY-KEESLER, JUDITH VANDERMUELEN CRAIN, DANAE D. DAVIS, GREGORY L. GRACZ, THOMAS LOFTUS, MILTON MCPIKE, CHARLES PRUITT, GERARD A. RANDALL, JR., PEGGY ROSENZWEIG, JESUS SALAS, MICHAEL J. SPECTOR; CHRIS SEMENAS (student). (All except *ex officio* members are appointed by governor with senate consent.)

Secretary to the Board: JUDITH A. TEMBY, 1860 Van Hise Hall, 1220 Linden Drive, Madison 53706-1557, (608) 262-2324.

Mailing Address: Central administrative offices for the UW System and the UW Colleges are located in Madison. Individual universities and 2-year UW Colleges can be reached by contacting them directly. Administrative offices for UW-Extension are in Madison; Extension representatives are located at each county seat.

Publications: administrative directory; biennial and annual reports; *Fact Book; Introduction to the University of Wisconsin System;* unit bulletins, catalogs, reports, circulars; periodicals and books.

Number of Employees: 30,391.05.

Total Budget 2003-05: $7,005,199,100.

Constitutional Reference: Article X, Section 6.

Statutory References: Section 15.91; Chapter 36.

System Administration
1220 Linden Drive, Madison 53706-1559
General Telephone: (608) 262-2321
Internet Address: http://www.wisconsin.edu

President of the University of Wisconsin System: KEVIN P. REILLY, 1720 Van Hise Hall, 1220 Linden Drive, Madison 53706-1559, (608) 262-2321.

Senior Executive Vice President for Administration and Chief Operating Officer: DONALD J. MASH, 1730 Van Hise Hall, 262-4048.

Senior Vice President for Academic Affairs: CORA B. MARRETT, 1624 Van Hise Hall, 262-3826.

Vice President for Finance: DEBORAH A. DURCAN, 1752 Van Hise Hall, 262-1311.

General Counsel: PATRICIA A. BRADY, 1856 Van Hise Hall, 262-6497.

UW-Madison
161 Bascom Hall, 500 Lincoln Drive, Madison 53706
General Telephone: (608) 262-1234
Internet Address: http://www.wisc.edu

Chancellor: JOHN WILEY, 161 Bascom Hall, 500 Lincoln Drive, Madison 53706, 262-9946.

Provost and Vice Chancellor for Academic Affairs: PETER SPEAR, 150 Bascom Hall, 262-1304.

Vice Chancellor for Administration: DARRELL BAZZELL, 100 Bascom Hall, 263-2467.

Vice Chancellor for Legal and Executive Affairs: MELANY STINSON NEWBY, 361 Bascom Hall, 263-7400.

Vice Chancellor for Medical Affairs: PHILIP M. FARRELL, 4129 Health Sciences Learning Center, 750 Highland Avenue, 263-4910.

Dean of Agricultural and Life Sciences: ELTON ABERLE, 140 Agricultural Hall, 262-4930.

Dean of Business: MICHAEL KNETTER, 5110 Grainger Hall, 262-1758.

Dean of Education: W. CHARLES READ, 123 Education Building, 262-6137.

Dean of Engineering: PAUL PEERCY, 2610 Engineering Hall, 262-3482.

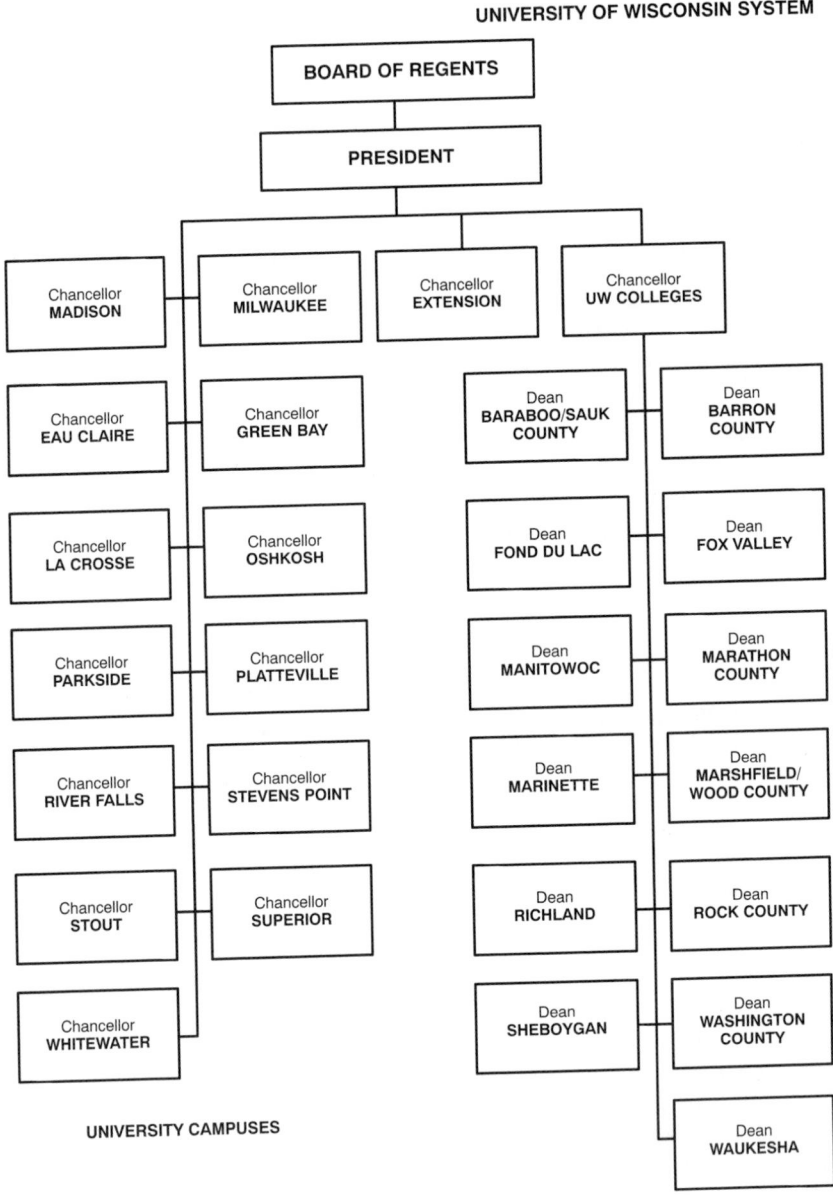

UNIVERSITY OF WISCONSIN SYSTEM

BOARD OF REGENTS

PRESIDENT

| Chancellor MADISON | Chancellor MILWAUKEE | Chancellor EXTENSION | Chancellor UW COLLEGES |

Chancellor EAU CLAIRE — Chancellor GREEN BAY

Chancellor LA CROSSE — Chancellor OSHKOSH

Chancellor PARKSIDE — Chancellor PLATTEVILLE

Chancellor RIVER FALLS — Chancellor STEVENS POINT

Chancellor STOUT — Chancellor SUPERIOR

Chancellor WHITEWATER

UNIVERSITY CAMPUSES

Dean BARABOO/SAUK COUNTY — Dean BARRON COUNTY

Dean FOND DU LAC — Dean FOX VALLEY

Dean MANITOWOC — Dean MARATHON COUNTY

Dean MARINETTE — Dean MARSHFIELD/WOOD COUNTY

Dean RICHLAND — Dean ROCK COUNTY

Dean SHEBOYGAN — Dean WASHINGTON COUNTY

Dean WAUKESHA

TWO-YEAR COLLEGES

Units attached for administrative purposes under Sec. 15.03:
Environmental Education Board
Veterinary Diagnostic Laboratory Board

Dean of the Graduate School: MARTIN CADWALLADER, 333 Bascom Hall, 262-1044.

Dean of Human Ecology: ROBIN DOUTHITT, 141 Human Ecology Building, 262-4847.

Dean of International Studies and Programs: GILLES BOUSQUET, 268 Bascom Hall, 262-9833.

Dean of Law: KENNETH DAVIS, JR., 5211 Law Building, 262-0618.

Dean of Letters and Science: GARY D. SANDEFUR, 105 South Hall, 263-2303.

Director of Libraries: KENNETH FRAZIER, 372 Memorial Library, 262-2600.

Dean of Medical School: PHILIP M. FARRELL, 4129 Health Sciences Learning Center, 750 Highland Avenue, 263-4910.

Dean of Nursing: KATHARYN A. MAY, BX2455 Clinical Science Center-Module K6, 263-5155.

Dean of Pharmacy: JEANETTE C. ROBERTS, 1126B Rennebohm Hall, 262-1414.

Dean of Veterinary Medicine: DARYL BUSS, 2015 Linden Drive West, 263-6716.

Interim Dean of Students: LORI BERQUAM, 75 Bascom Hall, 263-5702.

Dean of Continuing Studies: HOWARD MARTIN, Room 203, 905 University Avenue, 262-5821.

Chair of the Academic Staff Executive Committee: BRUCE D. BECK, 170B Bascom Hall, 263-4240.

Chair of the University Committee: MURRAY K. CLAYTON, 380 Russell Laboratories, 1630 Linden Drive, 262-0530.

Secretary of the Faculty: DAVID MUSOLF, 133 Bascom Hall, 262-3956.

Director of Admissions: ROBERT SELTZER, 360 Armory and Gymnasium, 262-0464.

Registrar: JOANNE BERG, 130C Peterson Building, 262-0102.

UW-Milwaukee

P.O. Box 413, Milwaukee 53201-0413
General Telephone: (414) 229-1122
Internet Address: http://www.uwm.edu

Chancellor: CARLOS E. SANTIAGO, 202 Chapman Hall, P.O. Box 413, Milwaukee 53201, 229-4331.

Provost/Vice Chancellor: RITA CHENG, 215 Chapman Hall, 229-4501.

Interim Vice Chancellor, Administrative Affairs: vacancy, 310 Chapman Hall, 229-4461.

Vice Chancellor for Research and Dean of the Graduate School: ABBAS OURMAZE, 247 Mitchell Hall, 229-5483.

Interim Vice Chancellor for Student Affairs: MARY ROGGEMAN, 132 Chapman Hall, 229-4038.

Vice Chancellor, University Relations: THOMAS LULJAK, 180A Chapman Hall, 229-4035.

Dean, College of Engineering and Applied Science: WILLIAM GREGORY, 524 Engineering and Mathematical Sciences Building, 229-4126.

Dean, College of Letters and Science: G. RICHARD MEADOWS, 218A Holton Hall, 229-5895.

Dean, School of Allied Health Professions: RANDALL S. LAMBRECHT, 897 Enderis Hall, 229-4712.

Dean, School of Architecture and Urban Planning: ROBERT C. GREENSTREET, 241 Architecture and Urban Planning Building, 229-4016.

Dean, School of the Arts: WILLIAM ROBERT BUCKER, 284 Arts Building, 229-4762.

Dean, School of Business Administration: KANTI PRASAD, N425 Business Administration Building, 229-6256.

Dean, School of Education: ALFONZO THURMAN, 595 Enderis Hall, 229-4181.

Dean, School of Library and Information Science: JOHANNES BRITZ, 1193 Enderis Hall, 229-4709.

Dean, School of Nursing: SALLY LUNDEEN, 767B Cunningham Hall, 229-4189.

Dean, School of Social Welfare: STAN STOJKOVIC, 1095 Enderis Hall, 229-4400.

Interim Dean, Outreach and Continuing Education Extension: MARK KRUEGER, 161 West Wisconsin Avenue, 53203, 227-3326.

Director of Admissions: BETH L. WECKMUELLER, 222 Mellencamp Hall, 229-6164.

Interim Secretary of the University: RANDALL RYDER, 225 Mitchell Hall, 229-5989.

UW-Eau Claire
Schofield Hall, Park and Garfield Avenues, P.O. Box 4004, Eau Claire 54702-4004
General Telephone: (715) 836-2637
Internet Address: http://www.uwec.edu

Interim Chancellor: VICKI LORD LARSON, 836-2327.
Provost and Vice Chancellor, Academic Affairs: RONALD N. SATZ, 836-2320.
Vice Chancellor, Business and Student Services: ANDREW SOLL, 836-5182.
Dean, College of Arts and Sciences: DONALD P. CHRISTIAN, 836-2542.
Dean, College of Education and Human Sciences: KATHERINE RHOADES, 836-3671.
Dean, College of Business: V. THOMAS DOCK, 836-5509.
Dean, College of Nursing and Health Sciences: L. ELAINE WENDT, 836-5287.
Associate Vice Chancellor, Student Development and Diversity: KIMBERLY BARRETT, 836-5992.
Executive Director, Enrollment Services and Admissions: KRISTINA ANDERSON, 836-5415.
Registrar: SUE E. MOORE, 836-3887.

UW-Green Bay
2420 Nicolet Drive, Green Bay 54311-7001
General Telephone: (920) 465-2000
Internet Address: http://www.uwgb.edu

Chancellor: W. BRUCE SHEPARD, 465-2207.
Provost and Vice Chancellor for Academic Affairs: SUE K. HAMMERSMITH, 465-2334.
Associate Provost for Student Services/Dean of Students: SUE KEIHN, 465-2152.
Vice Chancellor, Business and Finance: THOMAS MAKI, 465-2210.
Assistant Chancellor, Planning and Budget: DEAN RODEHEAVER, 465-2039.
Assistant Chancellor for University Advancement: STEVE SWAN, 465-2074.
Interim Dean, Liberal Arts and Sciences: FERGUS HUGHES, 465-2336.
Dean, Professional and Graduate Studies: FRITZ ERICKSON, 465-2050.
Communications Director: CHRISTOPHER SAMPSON, 465-2527.
Marketing and Media Relations Director: SCOTT HILDEBRAND, 465-2526.
Registrar: MICHAEL HERRITY, 465-2155.

UW-La Crosse
1725 State Street, La Crosse 54601-9959
General Telephone: (608) 785-8000
Internet Address: http://www.uwlax.edu

Chancellor: DOUGLAS N. HASTAD, 785-8004.
Provost/Vice Chancellor: ELIZABETH J. HITCH, 785-8007.
Vice Chancellor, Administration and Finance: RONALD LOSTETTER, 785-8021.
Vice Chancellor, Advancement and External Relations: KENNA L. CHRISTIANS, 785-8492.
Assistant to the Chancellor for Affirmative Action and Diversity: ALFRED S. THOMPSON, JR., 785-8541.
Associate Vice Chancellor for Academic Affairs: VIJENDRA AGARWAL, 785-8007.
Executive Director, Human Resources: JENNIFER WILSON, 785-8013.
Director, Campus Planning: MATTHEW N. LEWIS, 785-8019
Chief Information Officer: JOHN P. TILLMAN, 785-8662.
Dean of Students and Academic Services: vacancy, 785-8151.

Dean, College of Business Administration: WILLIAM G. COLCLOUGH III, 785-8095.

Interim Dean, College of Education, Exercise Science, Health and Recreation: RICK MIKAT, 785-8156.

Dean, College of Liberal Studies: JOHN B. MASON, 785-8116.

Dean, College of Science and Allied Health: MICHAEL E. NELSON, 785-8218.

Interim Director, Admissions: KATHY KIEFER, 785-8939.

Director, University Relations: CARY R. HEYER, 785-8492.

Registrar: DIANE L. SCHUMACHER, 785-8953.

UW-Oshkosh
800 Algoma Boulevard, Oshkosh 54901-8617
General Telephone: (920) 424-1234
Internet Address: http://www.uwosh.edu

Chancellor: RICHARD H. WELLS, 424-0200.

Chancellor's Leadership Fellow: SUSAN NUERNBERG, 424-0424.

Provost/Vice Chancellor: LANE EARNS, 424-0300.

Vice Chancellor, Student Affairs: PETRA M. ROTER, 424-4000.

Assistant Vice Chancellor, Academic Support: MURIEL A. HAWKINS, 424-3080.

Interim Assistant Vice Chancellor, Graduate Studies: MARSHA D. ROSSITER, 424-1223.

Associate Vice Chancellor, Enrollment and Information Services: JOHN F. BERENS, 424-3334.

Vice Chancellor, Administrative Services: THOMAS G. SONNLEITNER, 424-3030.

Dean, College of Business Administration: E. ALAN HARTMAN, 424-1424.

Dean, College of Education and Human Services: FREDERICK L. YEO, 424-3322.

Dean, College of Letters and Science: MICHAEL ZIMMERMAN, 424-1210.

Interim Dean, College of Nursing: ROSEMARY SMITH, 424-3089.

Dean of Students: JAMES M. CHITWOOD, 424-3100.

Director, Admissions: JILL M. ENDRIES, 424-0228.

Director of Budgets: LORI WORM, 424-3033.

Registrar: LISA M. DANIELSON, 424-3007.

UW-Parkside
P.O. Box 2000, Kenosha 53141-2000
General Telephone: (262) 595-2345
Internet Address: http://www.uwp.edu

Chancellor: JOHN P. KEATING, 595-2211.

Provost/Vice Chancellor: REBECCA MARTIN, 595-2261.

Associate Provost: GERALD GREENFIELD, 595-2144.

Vice Chancellor, Administrative and Fiscal Affairs: WILLIAM W. STREETER, 595-2141.

Associate Vice Chancellor for Student Services/Dean of Students: STEPHEN MCLAUGHLIN, 595-2598.

Assistant Vice Chancellor for University Relations and Advancement: LENNY KLAVER, 595-2591.

Dean, College of Arts and Sciences: DONALD CRESS, 595-2188.

Interim Dean, School of Business and Technology: JAYAVEL SOUNDERPANDIAN, 595-2243.

Interim Assistant Vice Chancellor for Enrollment Management and Director of Admissions: MATTHEW JENSEN, 595-2784 or 595-2355.

Registrar: vacancy, 595-2237.

UW-Platteville
1 University Plaza, Platteville 53818-3099
General Telephone: (608) 342-1491
Internet Address: http://www.uwplatt.edu

Chancellor: DAVID J. MARKEE, 342-1234.
Provost and Vice Chancellor for Academic Affairs: CAROL SUE BUTTS, 342-1261.
Associate Vice Chancellor: DAVID VAN BUREN, 342-1262.
Vice Chancellor for Administrative Services: STEPHEN ZIELKE, 342-1226.
Assistant Chancellor for Student Affairs: MICHAEL VINEY, 342-1854.
Director of Admissions and Enrollment Services: ANGELA UDELHOFEN, 342-1125.
Dean, College of Business, Industry, Life Science and Agriculture: DUANE M. FORD, 342-1547.
Dean, College of Engineering, Mathematics and Science: RICHARD SHULTZ, 342-1561.
Dean, College of Liberal Arts and Education: MITTIE J. NIMOCKS, 342-1151.
Dean, School of Graduate Studies: DAVID VAN BUREN, 342-1262.
Registrar: EDWARD DENEEN, 342-1321.

UW-River Falls
410 South Third Street, River Falls 54022-5001
General Telephone: (715) 425-3911
Internet Address: http://www.uwrf.edu

Chancellor: DON BETZ, 425-3201.
Provost/Vice Chancellor: VIRGINIA M. COOMBS, 425-3700.
Vice Chancellor, Administration and Finance: MARY HALADA, 425-3737.
Dean, College of Agriculture, Food and Environmental Sciences: STEPHEN C. RIDLEY, 425-3841.
Interim Dean, College of Arts and Sciences: TERRY BROWN, 425-3777.
Dean, College of Education and Graduate Studies: CONNIE D. FOSTER, 425-3774.
Dean, College of Business and Economics: BARBARA H. NEMECEK, 425-3335.
Dean, Outreach and Graduate Studies: vacancy, 425-3350.
Dean for Student Development and Campus Diversity: ROGER A. BALLOU, 425-3711.
Director of Admissions: ALAN TUCHTENHAGEN, 425-3500.
Registrar: JUDY GEORGE, 425-3342.

UW-Stevens Point
Room 213 Old Main, 2100 Main Street, Stevens Point 54481-3897
General Telephone: (715) 346-0123
Internet Address: http://www.uwsp.edu

Chancellor: LINDA BUNNELL, 346-2123.
Provost/Vice Chancellor: VIRGINIA HELM, 346-4686.
Assistant Chancellor, Business Affairs: GREGORY DIEMER, 346-2641.
Assistant Chancellor, Student Affairs: ROBERT TOMLINSON, 346-2481.
Associate Vice Chancellor, Personnel and Budget: NANCY BAYNE, 346-3710.
Associate Vice Chancellor, Teaching, Learning and Academic Programs: STEVE BONDESON, 346-3668.
Chief Information Officer, Information Technology: DAVID DUMKE, 346-3612.
Executive Director, University Extension: JOAN SOSALLA, 898-9472.
Dean, College of Fine Arts and Communication: JEFFREY MORIN, 346-4920.

Dean, College of Letters and Science: LANCE GRAHN, 346-4224.

Dean, College of Natural Resources: CHRISTINE THOMAS, 346-4185.

Dean, College of Professional Studies: JOAN NORTH, 346-3169.

Director, Admissions and High School Relations/Registrar: CATHY GLENNON, 346-2441; Registration and Records: 346-4301.

Director of International Programs: DAVID STASZAK, 346-3693.

UW-Stout
P.O. Box 790, Menomonie 54751-0790
General Telephone: (715) 232-1431
Internet Address: http://www.uwstout.edu

Chancellor: CHARLES W. SORENSEN, 232-2441.

Provost/Vice Chancellor, Academic and Student Affairs: ROBERT SEDLAK, 232-2421.

Vice Chancellor, Administrative and Student Life Services: DIANE MOEN, 232-1683.

Assistant Vice Chancellor, Academic and Student Affairs: CLAUDIA SMITH, 232-2421.

Dean, College of Arts and Sciences: JOHN MURPHY, 232-2596.

Dean, College of Human Development: JOHN WESOLEK, 232-2687.

Dean, College of Technology, Engineering and Management: ROBERT MEYER, 232-1251.

Dean of Students: PINCKNEY HALL, 232-1181.

Director of Admissions and School Relations: CYNTHIA GILBERTS, 232-2639.

Registrar: JEFF KIRSCHLING, 232-2121.

UW-Superior
Belknap and Catlin Streets, P.O. Box 2000, Old Main Room 212, Superior 54880-4500
General Telephone: (715) 394-8101
Internet Address: http://www.uwsuper.edu

Chancellor: JULIUS E. ERLENBACH, 394-8221.

Provost: DAVID J. PRIOR, 394-8449.

Director of Admissions: JAMES MILLER, 394-8396.

Dean of Faculties: DAVID J. PRIOR, 394-8449.

Registrar: BARBARA A. ERICKSON, 394-8218.

UW-Whitewater
Hyer Hall, 800 West Main Street, Whitewater 53190-1790
General Telephone: (262) 472-1234
Internet Address: http://www.uww.edu

Chancellor: MARTHA DUNAGIN SAUNDERS, 472-1918.

Provost/Vice Chancellor for Academic Affairs: RICHARD J. TELFER, 472-1672.

Vice Chancellor, Administrative Affairs: JAMES W. FREER, 472-1922.

Assistant Chancellor for Student Affairs: BARBARA C. JONES, 472-1051.

Associate Vice Chancellor for Academic Affairs: BARBARA S. MONFILS, 472-1055.

Dean, College of Arts and Communication: JOHN H. HEYER, 472-1221.

Dean, College of Business and Economics: CHRISTINE L. CLEMENTS, 472-1343.

Dean, College of Education: JEFFREY C. BARNETT, 472-1101.

Dean, College of Letters and Sciences: HOWARD L. ROSS, 472-1711.

Dean, Graduate School, Continuing Education and Summer Session: LEE JONES, 472-1100.

Director of Admissions: STEPHEN MCKELLIPS, 472-1512.

Registrar: DANIEL EDLEBECK, 472-1570.

An aerial view of the University of Wisconsin-Stout campus in Menomonie, centered on the Bowman Hall Clock Tower. The school was founded in 1891 by James Huff Stout, a member of the family which controlled the lumbering firm of Knapp, Stout and Company. Originally called the Stout Manual Training School, its early focus on education in industrial trades and domestic science is reflected in today's curriculum. (University of Wisconsin-Stout)

UW Colleges
780 Regent Street, P.O. Box 8680, Madison 53708-8680
Internet Address: http://www.uwc.edu/

Interim Chancellor: MARGARET CLEEK, (608) 262-1783.

Interim Provost/Vice Chancellor: GREG LAMPE, (608) 263-1794.

Vice Chancellor, Administrative Services: STEVEN WILDECK, (608) 265-3040.

Associate Vice Chancellor for Academic Affairs: WAVA HANEY, (608) 263-7217.

Assistant Vice Chancellor for Instructional Technology: RICHARD CLEEK, (608) 265-5764.

Registrar: DAN VANDE YACHT, (608) 262-9652.

Baraboo/Sauk County: 1006 Connie Road, Baraboo 53913-1098, (608) 356-8351,
http://www.baraboo.uwc.edu
Dean: MICHAEL BROPHY.

Barron County: 1800 College Drive, Rice Lake 54868-2497, (715) 234-8176,
http://www.barron.uwc.edu
Dean: PAUL CHASE.

Fond du Lac: 400 University Drive, Fond du Lac 54935-2998, (920) 929-3600,
http://www.fdl.uwc.edu
Dean: DANIEL BLANKENSHIP.

Fox Valley: 1478 Midway Road, Menasha 54952-1297, (920) 832-2600,
http://www.fox.uwc.edu
Dean: JAMES PERRY.

Manitowoc: 705 Viebahn Street, Manitowoc 54220-6699, (920) 683-4700,
http://www.manitowoc.uwc.edu
Interim Dean: MARY BETH EMMERICHS.

Marathon County: 518 South 7th Avenue, Wausau 54401-5396, (715) 261-6100,
http://www.uwmc.uwc.edu
Dean: JAMES VENINGA.

Marinette: 750 West Bay Shore Street, Marinette 54143-4299, (715) 735-4300,
http://www.marinette.uwc.edu
Dean: PAULA LANGTEAU.

Marshfield/Wood County: 2000 West 5th Street, Marshfield 54449-0150, (715) 389-6500,
http://www.marshfield.uwc.edu
Dean: ANDREW KEOGH.

Richland: 1200 Highway 14 West, Richland Center 53581-1399, (608) 647-6186,
http://www.richland.uwc.edu
Dean: DEBORAH CURETON.

Rock County: 2909 Kellogg Avenue, Janesville 53546-5699, (608) 758-6565,
http://www.rock.uwc.edu
Interim Dean: DIANE PILLARD.

Sheboygan: One University Drive, Sheboygan 53081-4789, (920) 459-6600,
http://www.sheboygan.uwc.edu
Dean: RAYMOND HERNANDEZ.

Washington County: 400 University Drive, West Bend 53095-3699, (262) 335-5200,
http://www.washington.uwc.edu
Dean: DAVID NIXON.

Waukesha: 1500 University Drive, Waukesha 53188-2799, (262) 521-5200,
http://www.waukesha.uwc.edu
Interim Dean: JANE CRISLER.

UW-Extension
432 North Lake Street, Madison 53706-1498
General Telephone: (608) 262-3980
Internet Address: http://www.uwex.edu

Interim Chancellor: MARV VAN KEKERIX, 262-3786.
Interim Vice Chancellor/Provost: ELLEN FITZSIMMONS, 262-6151.
Assistant to the Chancellor: BARB SANDRIDGE, 265-2653.
Interim Dean,Outreach and E-Learning Extension: LEE ZABOROWSKI, 262-1034.
Dean and Director, Cooperative Extension: ARLEN LEHOLM, 263-2775.
Interim Vice Chancellor for Administrative and Financial Services: SUE SCHYMANSKI, 263-6470.
Director, Broadcasting and Media Innovations: BYRON KNIGHT, 263-2129.
Director, Business and Manufacturing Extension: ERICA KAUTEN, 263-7794.
Director, Information Systems: RON KRAEMER, 263-6012.
Secretary of the Faculty/Academic Staff: vacancy, 262-4387.

Officers and Units Required by Statute

State Cartographer: THEODORE KOCH, (608) 262-6852, 384 Science Hall, 550 North Park Street, Madison 53706-1491.

State Geologist: JAMES ROBERTSON, (608) 263-7384, Geological and Natural History Survey, 3817 Mineral Point Road, Madison 53705-5100.

Agricultural Safety and Health Center: CHERYL SKJOLAAS, *director,* (608) 265-0568, 230 Agricultural Engineering Building, 460 Henry Mall, Madison 53706.

Center for Environmental Education: RANDY CHAMPEAU, *director,* (715) 346-4973, 110 College of Natural Resources, 403 Learning Resources Center, Stevens Point 54481.

Geological and Natural History Survey: JAMES ROBERTSON, *state geologist,* (608) 262-1705, 3817 Mineral Point Road, Madison 53705-5100.

Area Health Education Center: NANCY SUGDEN, *director,* (608) 263-4927, 203 Bradley Memorial, 1300 University Avenue, Madison 53706.

Wisconsin State Herbarium: PAUL E. BERRY, *director,* (608) 262-2792, Department of Botany, Room 160, Birge Hall, Madison 53706-1381.

Psychiatric Research Institute: NED KALIN, *director,* (608) 263-6079, 6001 Research Park Boulevard, Madison 53719.

Robert M. La Follette Institute of Public Affairs: DONALD A. NICHOLS, *director,* (608) 262-3581, 1225 Observatory Drive, Madison 53706.

State Soils and Plant Analysis Laboratory: JOHN PETERS, *director,* (608) 262-4364, 8452 Mineral Point Road, Madison 53705.

Institute for Excellence in Urban Education: WANDA BLANCHETT, *associate dean for academic affairs,* (414) 229-4675 or (414) 229-4181, School of Education, P.O. Box 413, UW-Milwaukee, Milwaukee 53201.

Center for Urban Land Economics Research: KERRY VANDELL, *director,* (608) 262-5800, 975 University Avenue, Room 5262, Grainger Hall, Madison 53706.

School of Veterinary Medicine: DARYL BUSS, *dean,* (608) 263-6716, 2015 Linden Drive West, Madison 53706-1102.

Agency Responsibility: The prime responsibilities of the University of Wisconsin System are teaching, public service, and research. The system provides postsecondary academic education for more than 160,000 students, including 120,000 full-time equivalent undergraduates.

Organization: The UW System consists of 13 degree-granting universities, 13 two-year colleges, and statewide extension programs. UW-Madison and UW-Milwaukee offer bachelor's, master's, doctoral, and professional degrees. Eleven other universities in the UW System offer associate, bachelor's, and master's degree programs: UW-Eau Claire, UW-Green Bay, UW-La Crosse, UW-Oshkosh, UW-Parkside, UW-Platteville, UW-River Falls, UW-Stevens Point, UW-Stout, UW-Superior, and UW-Whitewater.

The two-year UW Colleges serve local and commuter students by providing freshman-sophomore university course work that is transferable to degree-granting campuses. In addition, the colleges offer general education associate degrees. While college faculty and staff are employed by the UW System, municipalities and/or counties own the campuses and buildings in which the UW Colleges are located.

UW-Extension provides noncredit and for-credit classroom and distance learning courses, as well as continuing education and a wide range of public service programs.

The 17-member Board of Regents of the University of Wisconsin System establishes policies to govern the system and plans for the future of public higher education in Wisconsin. Two members serve *ex officio;* the student member serves a 2-year term; and the other 14 members serve staggered 7-year terms. The governor may not appoint a student member from the same institution in any 2 consecutive terms.

The board appoints the president of the UW System, the chancellors of the 13 universities, the chancellor of UW-Extension and the UW Colleges, and the deans of the 13 UW Colleges. All appointees serve at the pleasure of the board. The board also sets admission standards, reviews and approves university budgets, and establishes the regulatory framework within which the individual units operate.

Unit Functions: The president of the University of Wisconsin System has full executive responsibility for system operation and management. This officer carries out the duties prescribed by statute; implements the policies established by the Board of Regents; manages and coordinates the system's administrative offices; and exercises fiscal control through budget development, management-planning programs, and coordination and evaluation of the academic programs on all campuses.

Each chancellor serves as executive head of a particular campus or program, administers board policies under the direction of the system's president, and is accountable to the board of regents. Subject to board policy, the chancellors, in consultation with their faculties, design curricula and set degree requirements; determine academic standards and establish grading systems; define and administer institutional standards for faculty peer evaluation; screen candidates for appointment, promotion, and tenure; administer auxiliary services; and control all funds allocated to or generated by their respective programs.

History: Today's UW System is the product of the 1971 merger of two existing university boards – the Board of Regents of the University of Wisconsin and the Board of Regents of the State Universities – and the institutions they governed.

From earliest times, Wisconsin lawmakers recognized the need for a tax-supported university. The territorial legislature passed laws in 1836, 1838, and 1839 regarding establishment and location of a university, and Article X, Section 6, of the state constitution ratified in 1848, provided for a state university at or near the seat of state government. Chapter 20, Laws of 1848, which implemented the constitutional provision, delegated university administration to a board of regents and classes began in 1849. Critical to the university's early development was Chapter 114, Laws of 1866, which reorganized the board of regents, expanded its authority, and authorized the governor to appoint the regents. The 1866 reorganization provided for instruction in agriculture on the Madison campus and an experimental farm, thereby making the university eligible, as Wisconsin's land grant institution, to receive the proceeds derived from sale of lands granted by the federal government to support agricultural education and research.

The State Universities originated with Chapter 82, Laws of 1857, which provided funds for a system of 2-year normal schools to train teachers and created the Board of Regents of Normal Schools. The first normal school opened at Platteville in 1866 and the ninth 50 years later at Eau Claire. In 1929, the 9 normal schools became "state teachers colleges" and were authorized to offer baccalaureate degree programs. They were renamed state colleges in 1951 and state universities in 1964. Chapter 75, Laws of 1967, renamed the governing body, designating it the Board of Regents of State Universities.

A group of students meets with Professor Hal Bertilson in front of the historic Old Main building on the University of Wisconsin-Superior campus. Founded in 1893, the school is now known as "Wisconsin's Public Liberal Arts College". *(University of Wisconsin-Superior)*

Chapter 100, Laws of 1971, mandated the merger of Wisconsin's two systems of public higher education to form the University of Wisconsin System. Chapter 335, Laws of 1973, recreated Chapter 36 of the statutes and provided a single statutory charter to govern public higher education in Wisconsin. The University of Wisconsin Colleges, which were previously called UW Centers, were renamed by 1997 Wisconsin Act 237.

ORGANIZATION CREATED BY STATUTE
WITHIN THE UNIVERSITY OF WISCONSIN SYSTEM

LABORATORY OF HYGIENE

Laboratory of Hygiene Board: DARRELL BAZZELL (designated by president of UW System), HERB BOSTROM (designated by secretary of health and family services), MARY JO KOPECKY (designated by secretary of natural resources), SUSAN BUROKER (designated by secretary of agriculture, trade and consumer protection); ROBERT BAGLEY (local health department representative);

DEBORAH TURSKI (physician representing clinical laboratories); DAVID BERWANGER (representing private environmental testing laboratories); MICHAEL RUSSELL (representing occupational health laboratories); JOHN STANLEY (medical examiner or coroner); GEORGE MILLION, DAVID TAYLOR (public members). Nonvoting member: RONALD H. LAESSIG (director, Laboratory of Hygiene). (All except *ex officio* officers or designees are appointed by governor.)

Director: RONALD H. LAESSIG.

Medical Director: DANIEL F. KURTYCZ.

Associate Director: PEGGY HINTZMAN.

Mailing Address: 465 Henry Mall, Madison 53706-1578; 2601 Agriculture Drive, Madison 53707-7996 (Environmental Health Division).

Telephones: (608) 262-1293; Customer service: (800) 442-4618; Administrative office: (608) 262-3911; Wisconsin Occupational Health Laboratory: (608) 224-6210, (800) 446-0403; Proficiency Testing Program: (608) 265-1100, (800) 462-5261; Environmental Health Division: (608) 224-6202.

Internet Address: http://www.slh.wisc.edu

Division Fax: (608) 262-3257; Environmental Health Division Fax: (608) 224-6213.

Publications: Newborn Screening Newsletter; Occupational Health Newsletter; *Results*; reference manual; State Lab Examiner (annual report); assorted special publications.

Number of Employees: 294.25.

Total Budget 2003-05: $54,993,600.

Statutory References: Sections 15.07 (1), 15.915 (2), and 36.25 (11).

Agency Responsibility: The Laboratory of Hygiene, headed by a director appointed by the UW Board of Regents, provides complete laboratory services for appropriate state agencies and local health departments in the areas of water quality, air quality, public health, and contagious diseases. It performs laboratory tests and consultation for physicians, health officers, local agencies, private citizens, and resource management officials to prevent and control diseases and environmental hazards. As part of the UW-Madison, the laboratory provides facilities for teaching and research in the fields of public health and environmental protection.

The laboratory operates under the direction and supervision of the Laboratory of Hygiene Board, composed of 11 members, 7 of whom are appointed by the governor to serve 3-year terms.

History: Chapter 344, Laws of 1903, created the Laboratory of Hygiene at the University of Wisconsin to examine water supplies, investigate contagious and infectious diseases, and function as the official laboratory of the State Board of Health. The executive branch reorganization act of 1967 extended the laboratory's services to the Department of Natural Resources.

INDEPENDENT UNITS ATTACHED FOR BUDGETING, PROGRAM COORDINATION, AND RELATED MANAGEMENT FUNCTIONS BY SECTION 15.03 OF THE STATUTES

ENVIRONMENTAL EDUCATION BOARD

Environmental Education Board: PATRICIA A. MARINAC (K-12 environmental educators' representative), *chairperson;* SENATORS KEDZIE, RISSER; REPRESENTATIVES FRISKE, MOLEPSKE; SHELLEY LEE (designated by superintendent of public instruction), VANCE RAYBURN (designated by secretary of natural resources), ROBIN HARRIS (designated by president, UW System), JAMES GIBSON (designated by president, Technical College System Board); GAIL GILSON PIERCE (nature centers, museums, zoos), MIKE KRYSIAK (business and industry representative), WILLIAM NEUHAUS (labor representative), GERRY MICH (forestry representative), STEVE SANDSTROM (higher education institutions faculty representative), JANET BRANDT (energy industry representative), DAVID D. WISNEFSKE (conservation and environmental organizations representative), ALICIA ADAMS (agricultural representative). (Unless otherwise designated, members are appointed by president of UW System.)

Mailing Address: 110B College of Natural Resources, UW-Stevens Point, Stevens Point 54481.

Telephone: (715) 346-3805.

Internet Address: http://www.uwsp.edu/cnr/weeb

Statutory References: Sections 15.915 (6) and 115.375.

Agency Responsibility: The Environmental Education Board awards matching grants to public agencies and nonprofit corporations to develop and distribute environmental education programs. The board consults with the state's educational agencies, the Department of Natural Resources and other state agencies to identify needs and establish priorities for environmental education. Its 17 members include 9 representatives of educational institutions and nongovernmental interest groups who are appointed to serve 3-year terms. The senate and assembly members must represent the majority and the minority parties in their respective houses. The board was created by 1989 Wisconsin Act 299 and was transferred from the Department of Public Instruction to the UW System by 1997 Wisconsin Act 27.

VETERINARY DIAGNOSTIC LABORATORY BOARD

Veterinary Diagnostic Laboratory Board: TOD FLEMING (animal agriculture industry representative), *chairperson;* ROBERT EHLENFELDT (designated by secretary of agriculture, trade and consumer protection), DARRELL BAZZELL (designated by chancellor of UW-Madison), DARYL BUSS (dean of the UW-Madison School of Veterinary Medicine), LINN WILBUR (veterinarian employed by the federal government); BERWYN CADMAN, LLOYD SORENSON (veterinarians); LINDA HODORFF, MARK RIECHERS (livestock producers); ROBERT SHULL (laboratory director) (nonvoting member). (All except *ex officio* members are appointed by governor.)

Mailing Address: 6101 Mineral Point Road, Madison 53705-4494.

Telephone: (608) 262-5432.

Fax: (608) 262-5005.

Statutory References: Sections 15.915 (1) and 36.58.

Agency Responsibility: The Veterinary Diagnostic Laboratory Board oversees the Veterinary Diagnostic Laboratory, which provides animal health testing and diagnostic services on a statewide basis for all types of animals. The board has 10 members, 6 of whom are appointed by the governor to serve staggered 3-year terms. The board prescribes policies for the laboratory's operation, develops its biennial budget, and sets fees for laboratory services. It also consults with the UW-Madison chancellor on the appointment of the laboratory director.

History: Both the board and the laboratory were created by 1999 Wisconsin Act 107, which transferred the laboratory's facilities and employees from the Department of Agriculture, Trade and Consumer Protection to the University of Wisconsin System, effective July 1, 2000.

Department of
VETERANS AFFAIRS

Board of Veterans Affairs: KENNETH C. WENDT, *chairperson;* MACK E. HUGHES, *vice chairperson;* MARVIN FREEDMAN, DONALD L. HEILIGER, RODNEY MOEN, PETER MORAN, WALTER M. STENAVICH. (All are veterans appointed by governor with senate consent.)

Secretary of Veterans Affairs: JOHN A. SCOCOS, 266-1315, john.scocos@

Deputy Secretary: WILLIAM J. KLOSTER, 266-1315, william.kloster@

Executive Assistant: ANTHONY HARDIE, 266-1315, anthony.hardie@

Legal Counsel: JOHN ROSINSKI, 266-7916, john.rosinski@

Policy, Planning and Budget, Office of: KEN ABRAHAMSEN, *director,* 266-0117, ken.abrahamsen@

Public Affairs, Office of: ANDREW M. SCHUSTER, *director,* 267-1797, andrew.schuster@

Mailing Address: P.O. Box 7843, Madison 53707-7843.

Location: 30 West Mifflin Street, Madison.

Telephone: (608) 266-1311, toll free: 1-800-WIS-VETS (800-947-8387).

Fax: (608) 264-7616.

Internet Address: www.dva.state.wi.us

Address e-mail by combining the user ID and the state extender: userid@**dva.state.wi.us**

Number of Employees: 975.60.

Total Budget 2003-05: $339,005,700.

Statutory References: Section 15.49; Chapter 45.

Administration, Division of: SETH PERELMAN, *administrator,* 266-3081, seth.perelman@; Fax: 264-6089.

   Administrative Services, Bureau of: BRADLEY CZEBOTAR, *director,* 266-3344, brad.czebotar@; Fax (608) 266-5414.

   Fiscal Services, Bureau of: RANDALL L. KRUEGER, *director,* 267-1789, randy.krueger@

   Information Systems, Bureau of: ANTHONY J. CAPPOZZO, *director,* 267-7207, tony.cappozzo@

Veterans Benefits, Division of: KENNETH BLACK, *administrator,* 266-0644, kenneth.black@; Fax: (608) 267-0403.

   Veterans Benefits, Bureau of: LAWRENCE E. DEWANE, *director,* 266-1309, larry.dewane@

   Veterans Cemeteries, Bureau of: KENNETH G. GRANT, *director,* 261-0179, ken.grant@

      Military Funeral Honors Program: (877) 944-6667, Fax: (866) 454-0356.

Veterans Homes, Division of: THOMAS M. RHATICAN, *administrator,* (608) 264-7619, tom.rhatican@

   Wisconsin Veterans Home, King 54946-0600, Fax: (715) 258-5736; JOHN WILLIAM CROWLEY, *commandant,* bill.crowley@; CHRIS WROLSTAD, *deputy commandant,* (715) 258-4251 chris.wrolstad@; CURT KIESSLING, *adjutant,* (715) 258-4249, curt.kiessling@; *Public Information/Volunteer Coordinator:* RICH CALCUT, (715) 258-4247, rich.calcut@

   Activities Services, Bureau of: CATHY LEAVERTON, (715) 258-1486, cathy.leaverton@

   Admissions and Discharges, Bureau of: MARIAN BOUSHLEY, (715) 258-4252, marian.boushley@

   Dietary Services, Bureau of: JACKIE MOORE, (715) 258-1679, jackie.moore@

   Engineering/Physical Plant, Bureau of: DOUG TYNDALL, (715) 258-4253, doug.tyndall@

   Financial Services, Bureau of: MARK MCCARTY, (715) 258-4248, mark.mccarty@

   Materials Management, Bureau of: NANCY J. O'CONNELL, (715) 258-4242, nancy.oconnell@

   Medical Services, Bureau of: PAUL DRINKA, (715) 258-4240, paul.drinka@

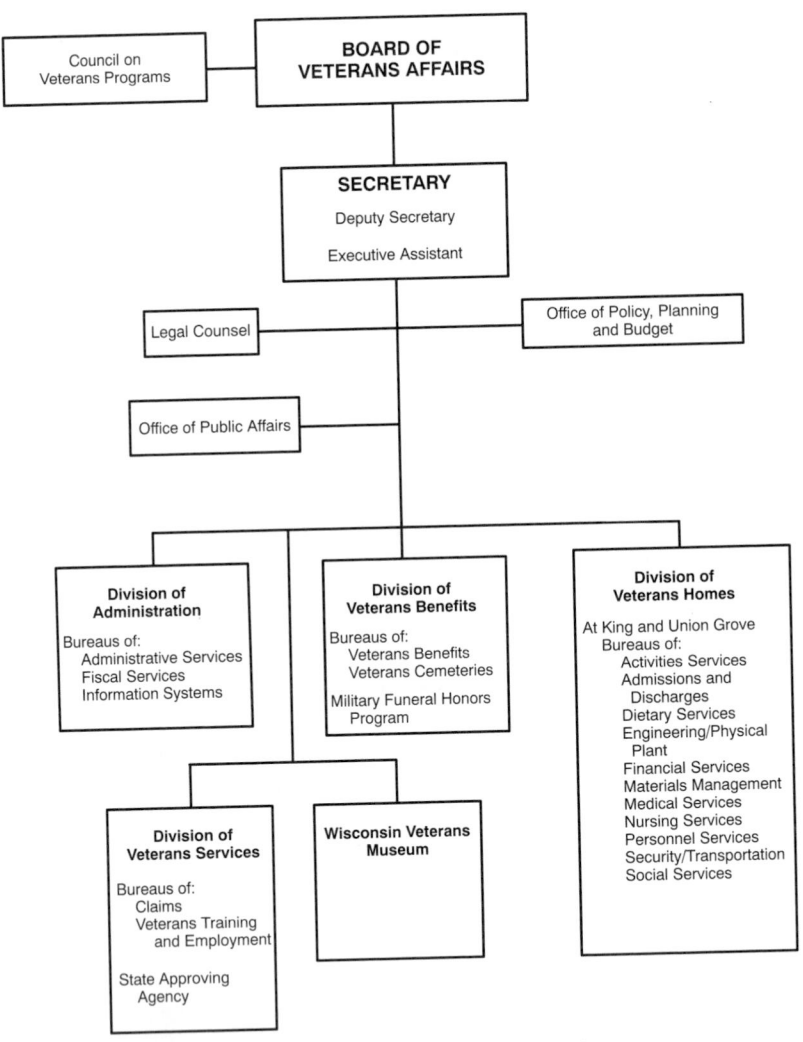

DEPARTMENT OF VETERANS AFFAIRS

Unit attached for administrative purposes under Sec. 15.03: Educational Approval Board

Nursing Services, Bureau of: DONNA WARZYNSKI, (715) 258-5586, donna.warzynski@

Personnel Services, Bureau of: NEAL SPRANGER, (715) 258-4244, neal.spranger@

Security/Transportation, Bureau of: RON WOODS, (715) 258-1485, ron.woods@

Social Services, Bureau of: SHERRY KELLEY, (715) 258-1660, sherry.kelley@

Wisconsin Veterans Home, Union Grove, 21425D Spring Street, Union Grove 53182; GLEN J. BROWER, *commandant,* (262) 878-6752, glen.brower@; STEVEN STEAD, *deputy commandant,* (262) 878-5668, steve.stead@

Human Resources: GARY WISTROM, *director,* (262) 878-6770, gary.wistrom@

Food Service: BRENDA PHILLIPS, *director,* (262) 878-5263, brenda.phillips@

Social Services: JOAN CLARK, *director,* (262) 878-6749, joan.clark@

Veterans Services, Division of: RICHARD G. DEMOYA, *administrator,* 266-1378, rick.demoya@; Fax: 267-0403.

Claims, Bureau of: MARK RUTBERG, *director,* VA Regional Office, 5400 West National Avenue, BM 157, Milwaukee 53214, (414) 902-5763, mark.rutberg@; Fax: (414) 902-9421.

Veterans Training and Employment, Bureau of: vacancy.

State Approving Agency: RICHARD G. DEMOYA, *manager,* 266-1378, rick.demoya@

Wisconsin Veterans Museum: RICHARD H. ZEITLIN, *director,* 266-1009, richard.zeitlin@

Publications: *The Bugle; The Courier; Old Abe the War Eagle; USS Wisconsin; WDVA Update; Wisconsin in the Civil War; Wisconsin's Warriors;* brochures on the state veterans' programs and services for Wisconsin veterans, Wisconsin Veterans Museum (Madison), the Wisconsin Veterans Home (King), the Wisconsin Veterans Home (Union Grove), and Wisconsin's veterans memorial cemeteries.

Agency Responsibility: The Department of Veterans Affairs provides educational and economic assistance to eligible veterans of the U.S. Armed Forces and their dependents through loan and grant programs. It also operates the Wisconsin veterans homes at King and Union Grove, the Wisconsin Veterans Museum in Madison, the Southern Wisconsin Veterans Memorial Cemetery at Union Grove, the Northern Wisconsin Veterans Memorial Cemetery near Spooner, and the Central Wisconsin Veterans Memorial Cemetery at King.

Senator Robert Cowles greets the family of Army Specialist Michelle Witmer in the Senate Parlor after the Senate passed a resolution honoring the life of Spc. Witmer, who was killed in action in Iraq in April 2004. Pictured are Michelle's sisters, Rachel and Charity, who were also serving in Iraq at the time of her death. Spc. Witmer was the first member of the Wisconsin National Guard to be killed in action since World War II, and was the first female National Guard soldier from any state to be killed in action. (Richard G. B. Hanson II, Senate Photographer)

The department currently serves an estimated 470,000 veterans living in Wisconsin, including approximately 76,200 veterans of the World War II era, 65,200 from the Korean War era, 150,000 from the Vietnam War era, and 66,000 from the Gulf War era.

Organization: The department is headed by a board of 7 members who serve staggered 6-year terms. All board members must be veterans, as defined by statute, and at least 2 must be Vietnam War veterans. Administrative powers and duties are exercised by the department secretary, who is appointed by the board.

Unit Functions: The *Division of Administration* administers data processing and fiscal management, systems analysis, human resources, personnel benefits and training, procurement, and verification and processing of veterans' eligibility applications.

The *Division of Veterans Benefits* administers loan and emergency grant programs offered by the state, state veteran cemeteries, and the state military funeral honors program.

The department offers 30-year fixed rate home loans for veterans primary residence and home improvement loans for the veterans principal residence. These loan programs are funded through self-amortizing general obligation bonds. The division's property management section maintains properties reclaimed by foreclosure due to loan defaults and arranges to sell them at fair market value to recoup loan expenses.

The department also offers through the division of veterans benefits, personal loans to qualified veterans. These loans can be used for any purpose. Personal loans under this program are funded through the veterans trust fund. Revenue from these loans fund veteran benefits and department operating costs.

Emergency grants are available to qualified veterans to provide subsistence aid for veterans who have experienced a loss of income due to illness or disability, and veterans who require health care that cannot be obtained through other means. These grants have strict income and asset limits.

The division provides administration for the veterans memorial cemeteries. These cemeteries provide burial space for veterans, their spouses, and eligible family members. Veterans can be buried free of charge; non-veteran spouses and family members are charged a burial fee.

The division administers the military funeral honors program, coordinating the efforts of veterans service organizations, the active duty military and reserve forces, as well as the Wisconsin National Guard. The division provides training of veteran organizations and military units who provide military funeral honors requested by the family. The division has limited capability to provide military funeral honors teams with departmental staff.

The *Division of Veterans Homes* administers the state's facilities for eligible veterans who are permanently incapacitated from performing any substantially gainful employment due to age or physical disability and who may be admitted if they meet service and residency criteria. Applicants must apply their income and resources to the cost of their care as required by Medicaid eligibility standards. The spouses of eligible veterans may also be admitted.

The Wisconsin Veterans Home at King serves approximately 740 members. It includes licensed skilled nursing care buildings, cottages for married couples, and the Central Wisconsin Veterans Memorial Cemetery. Residents receive complete medical and nursing care, along with therapeutic treatments and social services. Veterans and spouses or surviving spouses may be admitted at King.

The Wisconsin Veterans Home at Union Grove provides community-based residential facilities to serve veterans and their spouses who do not require skilled nursing home care but do need assisted-living services. Construction of a 120-bed skilled nursing care facility, scheduled for completion by November 2005, will allow for a full continuum of long-term care similar to that currently available at King.

The *Division of Veterans Services* administers education and employment services programs, claims services, and transition assistance programs.

The Bureau of Claims assists Wisconsin veterans with processing federal claims for compensation, pension, education, back pay, or any other problems arising from military service. The bureau, which provides mobile services to supplement the main office located at the U.S. Department of Veterans Affairs Regional Office in Milwaukee, also provides grants to veterans service organizations involved with claim efforts.

As part of the Bureau of Veterans Training and Employment, the Veterans Assistance Program operates veterans assistance centers in Tomah, King, and Union Grove. Through the centers, homeless veterans and veterans at risk of becoming homeless receive education, job training, and rehabilitative services to enable them to obtain steady employment and affordable housing. The program is a joint effort with the U.S. Department of Veterans Affairs and community-based agencies and is supplemented by service delivery support and outreach to veterans service organizations, veterans health care facilities, and correctional institutions. The bureau also provides an array of employment and educational services to include transition assistance, grants, job referrals, academic credit for military experience programs, and assistance in obtaining teaching credentials through the Troops to Teachers Program.

The State Approving Agency coordinates programs and approves schools to assist veterans to effectively use their GI Bill benefits.

The *Wisconsin Veterans Museum* in Madison is dedicated to Wisconsin veterans of all wars. It houses and exhibits artifacts related to Wisconsin's participation in U.S. military actions from the Civil War to the present and offers programs to the public on the history of Wisconsin's war efforts. It also houses exhibits and archives documenting the history of the Wisconsin National Guard and operates the Wisconsin National Guard Museum at Camp Douglas.

History: Legislation to benefit Wisconsin veterans dates back to the post-Civil War era. Most of the enactments between the Civil War and World War I were concerned with providing relief for destitute veterans and their families. In 1887, the Grand Army of the Republic (GAR), the prominent Civil War veterans' organization, founded the Grand Army Home at King, supported by private donations and federal and state subsidies. Now called the Wisconsin Veterans Home, the institution was first operated by the GAR and later by a state board and the adjutant general's office. Further recognition of Civil War veterans came in 1901, when the legislature established a Grand Army of the Republic headquarters and museum in the State Capitol. In 1993, the state opened the Wisconsin Veterans Museum in a separate building on the Capitol Square. The Southern Wisconsin Veterans Home at Union Grove, authorized in 1999 Wisconsin Act 9, opened in 2001.

After World War I, the 1919 Legislature granted a cash bonus, or alternatively an education bonus, to soldiers who fought in the war. It also created a fund for the relief of sick, wounded, or disabled veterans, administered by the Service Recognition Board and later its successor, the Soldiers' Rehabilitation Board. Other legislation between World Wars I and II provided funds for hospitalization, memorials, and free courses through the University of Wisconsin-Extension.

Chapter 443, Laws of 1943, created the Veterans Recognition Board to provide medical, hospital, educational, and economic assistance to returning Wisconsin veterans of World War II and their dependents.

The creation of the Department of Veterans Affairs by Chapter 580, Laws of 1945, brought all veterans programs under a single agency. The department absorbed the Grand Army Home, the GAR Memorial Hall, the veterans claim services, and the Soldiers' Rehabilitation Board. The department was assigned the economic aid, hospital care, and education grants programs. It also took over three segregated veterans funds that were combined into the Veterans Trust Fund in 1961.

Two major new programs relating to housing and education were implemented after World War II. Beginning with legislation in 1947, programs were established to help veterans finance home loans through a trust fund. The state supreme court declared earmarking liquor tax moneys for the fund unconstitutional under the internal improvements clause, but a constitutional amendment, approved by the voters in 1949, resolved the problem. Chapter 627, Laws of 1949, authorized loans to qualified veterans for a portion of the value of their housing. The legislature converted this program to a second mortgage home loan program in 1973, when it established the Primary Home Loan Program that is financed with general obligation bonds. The state's use of general obligation bonding to offer home loans to veterans raised constitutional concerns. The legislature responded by proposing an amendment to the Wisconsin Constitution, which the voters ratified in April 1975.

1997 Wisconsin Act 27 expanded eligibility for state veterans benefits to any person who has served on active duty in the U.S. armed forces for two continuous years or the full period of the individual's initial service obligation, whichever is less, regardless of when or where the service occurred, including during peacetime. Previously, to be considered a "veteran" for the purposes of state benefits, a person must generally have performed active service for 90 days or more during a designated war period or a period of duty during specified conflicts or peacekeeping operations.

1999 Wisconsin Act 136 required the department to administer a program to coordinate the provision of military funeral honors to eligible deceased veterans. 2003 Wisconsin Act 102 authorized the department to develop and operate residential, treatment, and nursing care facilities in northwestern Wisconsin, on surplus land located at the Northern Wisconsin Center for the Developmentally Disabled in Chippewa Falls.

Governor Jim Doyle, Wisconsin Department of Veterans Affairs Secretary John A. Scocos, and department commanders of Wisconsin veterans service organizations lead over 40 color guard marching units onto the field at Camp Randall Stadium in Madison during the University of Wisconsin Badger Football Salute to Wisconsin Veterans. (Department of Veterans Affairs)

Statutory Council

Council on Veterans Programs: RUSS ALSTEEN (Navy Club of the U.S.A.), *chairperson;* JESSE HARO (Catholic War Veterans of the U.S.A.), BUD MAUTZ (American Legion), KEN KUEHNL (Disabled American Veterans), ITALO BENSONI (Veterans of Foreign Wars), PAUL A. BIALK (Marine Corps League), TIMOTHY E. THIERS (AMVETS), vacancy (Veterans of World War I of the U.S.A., Inc.), MARVIN ROSLANSKY (American Ex-Prisoners of War), vacancy (Vietnam Veterans Against the War), STEVE HOUSE (Vietnam Veterans of America), PAUL WEPRINSKY (Jewish War Veterans of the U.S.A.), JERRY RABETSKY (Polish Legion of American Veterans), WILLIAM SIMS (National Association for Black Veterans, Inc.), PAUL FINE (Army and Navy Union of the United States of America), CLIFTON SORENSON (Wisconsin Association of

Concerned Veterans Organizations), PHYLLIS PERK (United Women Veterans, Inc.), ROBERT MCFAUL (U.S. Submarine Veterans of World War II), vacancy (Federation of Minority Veterans, Inc.), WILLIAM HUSTAD (Wisconsin Vietnam Veterans, Inc.), RICK CHERONE (Military Order of the Purple Heart), vacancy (American Red Cross), RICK GATES (County Veterans Service Officers Association), JACK STONE (Wisconsin chapter of the Paralyzed Veterans of America). (All are appointed by their respective organizations.)

The Council on Veterans Programs studies and presents policy alternatives and recommendations to the Board of Veterans Affairs. It is comprised of representatives appointed for one-year terms by organizations that have a direct interest in veterans' affairs. The council was created by Chapter 443, Laws of 1943, and its composition and duties are prescribed in Sections 15.497 and 45.35 (3d) of the statutes.

INDEPENDENT BOARD ATTACHED FOR BUDGETING, PROGRAM COORDINATION, AND RELATED MANAGEMENT FUNCTIONS BY SECTION 15.03 OF THE STATUTES

EDUCATIONAL APPROVAL BOARD

Members: TERRANCE L. CRANEY, *chairperson;* CHRISTY L. BROWN, MICHAEL GOONEY, JOSEPH HEIM, RICHARD F. RAEMISCH, JOHN A. SCOCOS, MONICA WILLIAMS (appointed by governor).
Executive Secretary: DAVID C. DIES, 267-7733.
Mailing Address: 30 West Mifflin Street, Madison 53703.
Telephone: (608) 266-1996.
Fax: (608) 264-8477.
Publications: EAB Quarterly; A Guide to the EAB; School and Program Approval Guide; Wisconsin Directory of Private Postsecondary Schools.
Number of Employees: 5.00.
Total Budget 2003-05: $987,500.
Statutory References: Sections 15.495 and 45.54.

Agency Responsibility: The Educational Approval Board is an independent state agency responsible for protecting Wisconsin's consumers, by regulating and monitoring for-profit postsecondary business, trade, or distance learning schools; out-of-state, nonprofit colleges and universities; and in-state, nonprofit institutions incorporated after 1991. The board currently oversees more than 130 schools serving more than 30,000 adults in degree and nondegree programs.

The board consists of not more than 7 members who serve at the pleasure of the governor and represent state agencies and others interested in educational programs. It employs the executive secretary and other staff from the classified service. Originally formed by order of the governor in 1944, the legislature created the agency in Chapter 137, Laws of 1953, as the Governor's Educational Advisory Committee to approve and supervise schools and educational courses that trained veterans under various federal laws. A 1957 law (Chapter 438) directed the committee to certify those private vocational schools that offered adequate courses and to prevent fraud and misrepresentation. Chapter 568, Laws of 1963, gave the committee responsibility for licensing agents of private vocational schools, and Chapter 595, Laws of 1965, renamed it the Educational Approval Council. It was renamed the Educational Approval Board and attached to the Department of Public Instruction by Chapter 214, Laws of 1967. The board was attached to the Board of Vocational, Technical and Adult Education by Chapter 125, Laws of 1971.

The Educational Approval Board was repealed by 1995 Wisconsin Act 27, as part of an initiative to create a state Department of Education. The Wisconsin Supreme Court ruled the measure unconstitutional and the agency's functions were continued under Executive Orders 283 and 287 which created the Educational Approval Council. The legislature recreated the board in 1997 Wisconsin Act 27 and attached it to the Higher Educational Aids Board. In 1999 Wisconsin Act 9, the board was attached to the Department of Veterans Affairs. 2001 Wisconsin Act 16 repealed statutory language which specifically made the board responsible for approving schools and courses of instruction for veterans and war orphans.

Department of
WORKFORCE DEVELOPMENT

Secretary of Workforce Development: ROBERTA GASSMAN, 267-1410,
roberta.gassman@

Deputy Secretary: MICABIL DÍAZ-MARTÍNEZ, 266-2284, micabil.diaz-martinez@

Executive Assistant: JOANNA RICHARD, 267-3200, joanna.richard@

Legal Counsel: HOWARD BERNSTEIN, 266-9427, howard.bernstein@

Chief Information Officer (information technology): ELLEN VOGEL, 266-5683, ellen.vogel@

Communications Director: ROSE LYNCH, 266-6753, rose.lynch@

Office of Economic Advisors: TERRY LUDEMAN, 267-3262, terry.ludeman@

Mailing Address: P.O. Box 7946, Madison 53707-7946.

Location: 201 East Washington Avenue, Madison.

Telephone: (608) 266-3131.

Fax: (608) 266-1784.

Internet Address: http://www.dwd.state.wi.us

Publications: Contact individual divisions for publications.

Number of Employees: 2,179.75.

Total Budget 2003-05: $2,143,828,100.

Statutory References: Sections 15.22, 15.223, 15.225, and 15.227; Chapters 49, 102-106, 108, 109, and 111.

Address e-mail by combining the user ID and the state extender: userid@**dwd.state.wi.us**

Administrative Services Division: LARRY STUDESVILLE, *administrator,* 261-4599,
larry.studesville@; GREGORY R. SMITH, *assistant administrator,* 261-2138, gregory.r.smith@

    Budget and Planning, Bureau of: THOMAS K. SMITH, *director,* 266-7895, thomas.smith@

    Finance, Bureau of: KIPP SONNENTAG, *director and controller,* 266-7272, kipp.sonnentag@

    General Services, Bureau of: JEANNE FREY, *director,* 266-1777, jeanne.frey@

    Human Resource Services, Bureau of: WILLIAM F. KOMAREK, *director,* 266-6496,
bill.komarek@

    Information Technology Services, Bureau of: VINNIE THOUSAND, *director,* 266-5588,
vinnie.thousand@

Equal Rights Division: LUCIA NUÑEZ, *administrator,* 266-0946, lucia.nunez@;
Division TTY: 264-8752.

    Civil Rights, Bureau of: LEANNA WARE, *director,* 266-1997, leanna.ware@

    Labor Standards, Bureau of: ROBERT ANDERSON, *director,* 266-3345, bob.anderson@

    Support Services, Office of: LYNN HENDRICKSON, *manager,* 266-7560, lynn.hendrickson@

Unemployment Insurance, Division of: HAL BERGAN, *administrator,* 266-8533, hal.bergan@;
ROBERT WHITAKER, *deputy administrator,* 267-7743, bob.whitaker@

    Benefit Operations, Bureau of: LUTFI SHAHRANI, *director,* 267-9543, lutfi.shahrani@

    Legal Affairs, Bureau of: DANIEL J. LAROCQUE, *director,* 267-1406, daniel.larocque@

    Tax and Accounting, Bureau of: ANDREA REID, *director,* 266-3177, andrea.reid@

    Benefit Centers:

        Madison: Initial claims: (608) 232-0678; Employee inquiries: (608) 232-0824; Employer inquiries: (608) 232-0633.

        Milwaukee: Initial claims: (414) 438-7700; Employee inquiries: (414) 438-7713; Employer inquiries: (414) 438-7705.

        Statewide: Initial claims: (800) 822-5246; Employee inquiries: (800) 494-4944; Employer inquiries: (800) 247-1744.

DEPARTMENT OF WORKFORCE DEVELOPMENT

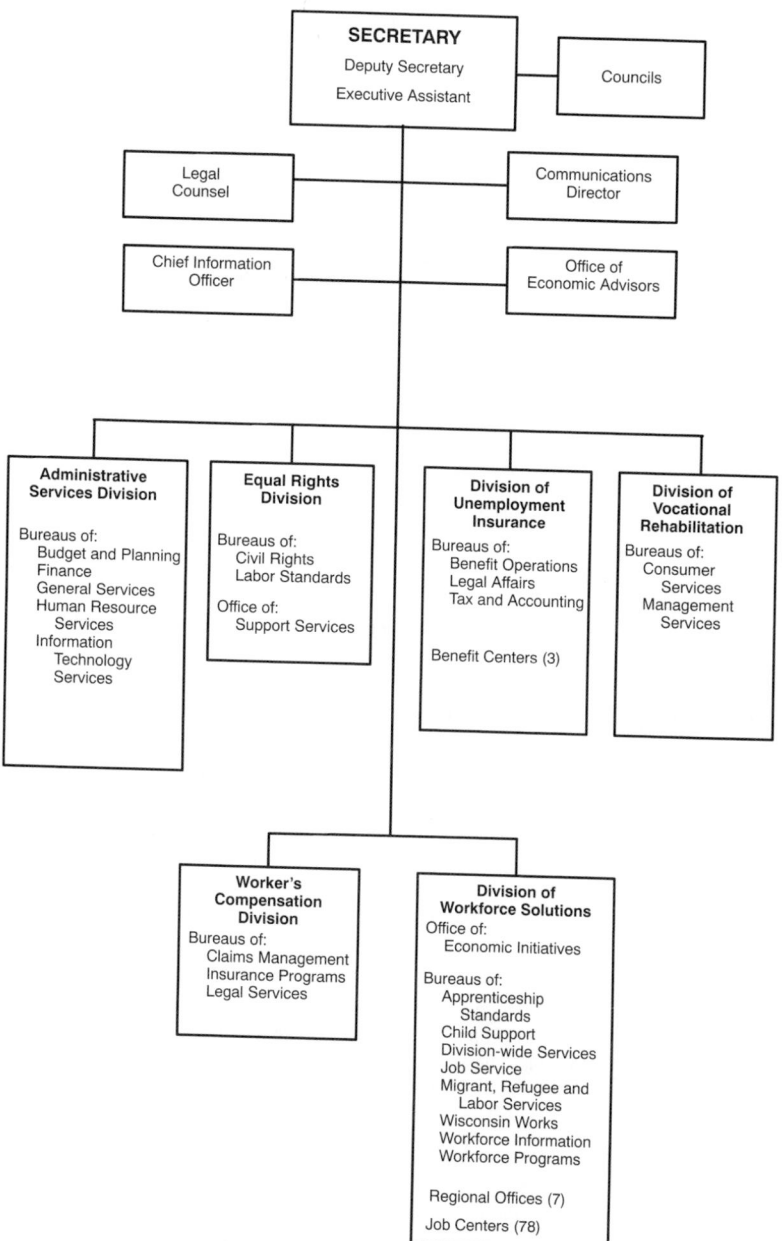

SECRETARY
Deputy Secretary
Executive Assistant

Councils

Legal
Counsel

Communications
Director

Chief Information
Officer

Office of
Economic Advisors

**Administrative
Services Division**

Bureaus of:
  Budget and Planning
  Finance
  General Services
  Human Resource
    Services
  Information
    Technology
    Services

**Equal Rights
Division**

Bureaus of:
  Civil Rights
  Labor Standards

Office of:
  Support Services

**Division of
Unemployment
Insurance**

Bureaus of:
  Benefit Operations
  Legal Affairs
  Tax and Accounting

Benefit Centers (3)

**Division of
Vocational
Rehabilitation**

Bureaus of:
  Consumer
    Services
  Management
    Services

**Worker's
Compensation
Division**

Bureaus of:
  Claims Management
  Insurance Programs
  Legal Services

**Division of
Workforce Solutions**

Office of:
  Economic Initiatives

Bureaus of:
  Apprenticeship
    Standards
  Child Support
  Division-wide Services
  Job Service
  Migrant, Refugee and
    Labor Services
  Wisconsin Works
  Workforce Information
  Workforce Programs

Regional Offices (7)

Job Centers (78)

Units attached for administrative purposes under Sec. 15.03:   Labor and Industry Review Commission
Governor's Work-Based Learning Board

Vocational Rehabilitation, Division of: CHARLENE DWYER, *administrator,* (608) 261-2126, charlene.dwyer@, 201 East Washington Avenue, Suite A100, Madison 53707-7852; MANUEL LUGO, *acting deputy administrator,* (608) 261-4576, manuel.lugo@; Division TTY: (608) 243-5601.

   Consumer Services, Bureau of: MANUEL LUGO, *director,* 261-0074, manuel.lugo@

   Management Services, Bureau of: GERALD GUENTHER, *director,* 261-0064, jerry.guenther@

   Local Offices: To contact a local DVR office, call (800) 442-3477 or visit
   http://dwd.wisconsin.gov/dvr/locations/default.htm

Worker's Compensation Division: FRANCES HUNTLEY-COOPER, *administrator,* 266-6841, frances.huntley-cooper@; JOHN CONWAY, *deputy administrator,* 266-0337, john.conway@

   Claims Management, Bureau of: LEE SHOREY, *director,* 267-9407, lee.shorey@

   Insurance Programs, Bureau of: BRIAN KRUEGER, *director,* 267-4415, brian.krueger@

   Legal Services, Bureau of: JIM O'MALLEY, *director,* 267-6704, jim.o'malley@

Workforce Solutions, Division of: BILL CLINGAN, *administrator,* 266-6824, william.clingan@; RONALD HUNT, *deputy adminstrator,* 266-2687, ron.hunt@

   Economic Initiatives, Office of: SUSAN GLEASON, *acting director,* 266-0522, susan.gleason@

   Apprenticeship Standards, Bureau of: KAREN P. MORGAN, *director,* 266-3133,
   karen.morgan@

   Child Support, Bureau of: SUSAN PFEIFFER, *director,* 267-4337, susan.pfeiffer@

   Division-wide Services, Bureau of: JOAN LARSON, *director,* 266-6721, joan.larson@

   Job Service, Bureau of: BRIAN SOLOMON, *director,* 267-7514, brian.solomon@

   Migrant, Refugee and Labor Services, Bureau of: MATEO CADENA, *director,* 266-0002, mateo.cadena@

   Wisconsin Works, Bureau of: NANCY BUCKWALTER, *director,* 266-7160, nancy.buckwalter@

   Workforce Information, Bureau of: SANDY BREITBORDE, *director,* 266-8212,
   sandy.breitborde@

   Workforce Programs, Bureau of: CONNIE COLUSSY, *director,* 267-9704, connie.colussy@

   Regional Offices:

     Ashland: 411 Ellis Avenue, P.O. Box 72, Ashland 54806-0072, (715) 682-7285.

     Eau Claire: 221 West Madison Street, Suite 218, Eau Claire 54703-4404, (715) 836-2177.

     Green Bay: 200 North Jefferson Street, Suite 428, Green Bay 54301, (920) 448-5305.

     Madison: 3319 West Beltline Highway, Room E234, Madison 53713-2834, (608) 243-2404.

     Milwaukee: 819 North 6th Street, 8th Floor, Milwaukee 53203-1697, (414) 227-4836.

     Rhinelander: P.O. Box 697, 100 West Keenan Street, Rhinelander 54501, (715) 365-2568.

     Waukesha: 141 NW Barstow Street, Room 157, Waukesha 53188-3789, (262) 521-5303.

   Agency Responsibility: The Department of Workforce Development conducts a variety of work-related programs designed to connect people with employment opportunities in Wisconsin. It has major responsibility for the state's employment and training services, including Wisconsin Works (W-2), which is designed to move welfare recipients into the labor force; job centers; job training and placement services provided in cooperation with private sector employers; apprenticeship programs; and employment-related services for people with disabilities. It oversees the unemployment insurance and worker's compensation programs and is also responsible for adjudicating cases involving employment discrimination, housing discrimination, and labor law.

   Organization: The department is administered by a secretary who is appointed by the governor with the advice and consent of the senate. The secretary appoints the division administrators from outside the classified service.

   Unit Functions: The *Administrative Services Division* provides management and program support to the other divisions, including budget, facilities, finance, human resources, and information technology services.

The *Equal Rights Division,* created by Chapter 327, Laws of 1967, enforces state laws that protect citizens from discrimination in employment, housing, and public accommodations. It also administers the enforcement of family and medical leave laws and the labor laws relating to hours, conditions of work, minimum wage standards, and timely payment of wages. It determines prevailing wage rates and enforces them for state and municipal public works projects not including highway projects. The division also enforces child labor laws and plant closing laws.

The *Division of Unemployment Insurance* administers programs to pay benefits to unemployed workers, collect employer taxes, resolve contested benefit claims and employer tax issues, detect unemployment insurance fraud, and collect unemployment insurance overpayments and delinquent taxes. The division also collects wage information for national and Wisconsin New Hire Directory databases.

The *Division of Vocational Rehabilitation* provides employment services to individuals who have significant physical and mental disabilities that create barriers in obtaining, maintaining, or improving employment. Each person is counseled and may receive medical, psychological, and vocational evaluations and training services. Employment programs, which are supported through state and federal funding, include vocational rehabilitation for eligible persons with disabilities; supported employment, including job coaching for individuals with severe disabilities; and the Business Enterprise Program, which establishes business or vending stand locations for individuals who are legally blind.

The *Worker's Compensation Division* administers programs designed to ensure that injured workers receive required benefits from insurers or self-insured employers; encourage rehabilitation and reemployment for injured workers; and promote the reduction of work-related injuries, illnesses, and deaths.

The *Division of Workforce Solutions* oversees all workforce services administered by the department, including Wisconsin Works (W-2) and the Wisconsin Shares child care subsidy. It manages the child support program and the state labor exchange system; analyzes and distributes labor market information; monitors migrant worker services; and operates the state apprenticeship program. The division also administers a comprehensive interdepartmental employment and training system through public-private partnerships and a statewide network of 78 job centers.

History: In response to the state's industrialization, which began in the 1880s, Wisconsin took the lead nationally in adjusting labor laws to modern industrial conditions. Based on European models, the legislature adopted social insurance, whereby the costs of correcting labor problems, such as worker injuries and unemployment, were imposed on employers as an inducement to prevent the problems.

Wisconsin's laws, enacted during the early part of the 20th century, dealt with minimum wages, conditions of employment for women and children, worker's compensation, free public employment offices, apprenticeship standards, and job safety regulations. Many of these programs served as models for legislation in other states. Wisconsin's original worker's compensation act (Chapter 50, Laws of 1911) was the first state law of its kind in the nation. In the 1930s, Wisconsin led in developing the unemployment compensation system (Chapter 20, Laws of Special Session 1931) and issued the first benefit check in the nation in 1936.

Since World War II, Wisconsin has enacted legislation prohibiting discrimination in employment on the basis of race, sex, creed, national origin, marital status, ancestry, arrest or conviction record, off-duty use of lawful products, membership in military reserve, sexual orientation, age, and disability. Similar laws now protect access to housing and public accommodations.

Early in the 20th century, the state delegated labor law administration to a politically independent body of experts, the State Industrial Commission, and its advisory committees. The commission was encouraged to solve problems through administrative decisionmaking and the development of administrative rules to supplement the laws. A close tie between state government and the University of Wisconsin enabled the governor and legislature to translate reforms conceived in the academic arena into law. This cooperative meshing of academic research and government action came to be known as "The Wisconsin Idea".

The Department of Workforce Development evolved from the Wisconsin Bureau of Labor Statistics, which was created in 1883. The bureau was succeeded by the State Industrial Commission

First Lady Jessica Doyle and Department of Workforce Development (DWD) Secretary Roberta Gassman present an Early Childhood Excellence grant for $397,000 to the Penfield Children's Center in Milwaukee, a recognized leader in early childhood education. The award from DWD is to support the center's services to low-income and special needs children. (Department of Workforce Development)

in 1911. Following the 1967 executive branch reorganization, the commission directed the new Department of Industry, Labor and Human Relations (DILHR) and was renamed the Industry, Labor and Human Relations Commission by Chapter 276, Laws of 1969. The commission was replaced by a secretary in Chapter 29, Laws of 1977.

Effective July 1, 1996, the Department of Industry, Labor and Human Relations was renamed the Department of Industry, Labor and Job Development by 1995 Wisconsin Act 29, but the department was given the option of using the name Department of Workforce Development in 1995 Wisconsin Act 289. It formally chose to exercise that option beginning July 1, 1996, and the legislature officially recognized the name choice in 1997 Wisconsin Act 3.

The department was significantly altered by 1995 Wisconsin Act 27. It assumed many duties formerly performed by other agencies, in particular supervision of welfare and income mainte-nance programs and vocational rehabilitation services, which were transferred from the former Department of Health and Social Services. At the same time, the Division of Safety and Buildings was transferred out of the department to the new Department of Commerce. 1997 Wisconsin Act 191 assigned the department primary responsibility for establishing and operating a statewide sys-tem for enforcing child, family, and spousal support obligations, including expanded authority to deny, revoke, or suspend various licenses, permits, and credentials of delinquent payors.

The statutes provide that the minimum wage is set through the administrative rules process, which includes legislative review. In January 2004, the secretary established the Minimum Wage Advisory Council to recommend an appropriate increase in the minimum wage. The council was comprised of representatives from business, labor organizations, the university system, and the legislature, and issued its final report on May 1, 2004.

Statutory Councils

Wisconsin Apprenticeship Council: KENNETH CURRY, RONALD STEINER, *cochairpersons;* WAYNE BELANGER, JULIE BROLIN, EARL BUFORD, MARGARET ELLIBEE, GERT GROHMANN, TERRY HAYDEN, BERNARD KURZAWA, MIKE LEWIN, MARCIE MARQUARDT, JOHN METCALF, JAMES MOORE, DAVID NEWBY, JOHN A. PEETERS, ROBERT RIBERICH, THOMAS SCHOENBERGER, LETHA SLOAN, RON SPLAN, MARJORIE WOOD. (All are appointed by the Labor and Industry Review Commission.)

Mailing Address: P.O. Box 7972, Madison 53707-7972.

Telephone: (608) 266-3133.

The Wisconsin Apprenticeship Council advises the department on matters pertaining to Wisconsin's apprenticeship system. The statutes do not stipulate the number of council members. The council was created by Chapter 29, Laws of 1977, and its duties and composition are prescribed in Sections 15.09 (5) and 15.227 (13) of the statutes.

Labor and Management Council: Inactive.

Mailing Address: P.O. Box 7972, Madison 53707-7972.

Telephone: (608) 266-5138.

The 21-member Labor and Management Council provides a forum for labor, management, and public sector representatives to discuss issues that affect the state's economy and to foster positive labor-management relations in the workplace. Council members serve 5-year terms. The council was created by 1987 Wisconsin Act 27, and its composition and duties are prescribed in Section 15.227 (17) of the statutes.

Migrant Labor, Council on: REPRESENTATIVE COLÓN, *chairperson;* SENATORS BROWN, WIRCH; REPRESENTATIVE TOWNSEND; JAMES KERN, DARRELL L. KRAUSE, KIMBERLY J. MYERS, RICHARD W. OKRAY, STEVE ZIOBRO (employers of migrant workers); JOHN I. BAUKNECHT, ROSA M. DOMINGUEZ, JOHN F. EBBOTT, LUPE MARTINEZ, SILVIA N. PEREZ, DORIS P. SLESINGER, vacancy (migrant workers' representatives). (All except legislative members are appointed by governor.)

Mailing Address: P.O. Box 7903, Madison 53707-7903.

Telephone: (608) 261-4425.

The 16-member Council on Migrant Labor advises the department and other state officials about matters affecting migrant workers. The council's 4 legislator members represent the two major political parties and are appointed "to act as representatives of the public". The nonlegislative members serve 3-year terms. The council was created by Chapter 17, Laws of 1977, and its composition and duties are prescribed in Sections 15.227 (8), 103.967, and 103.968 of the statutes.

Self-Insurers Council: JOHN WITTRY, *chairperson;* BURMA L. HUDSON, JILL E. JOSWIAK, RICK KANTE, DAWN NEUMAN (appointed by secretary of workforce development).

Mailing Address: P.O. Box 7901, Madison 53707-7901.

Telephone: (608) 266-8327.

The 5-member Self-Insurers Council advises the department about matters related to companies that cover their own worker's compensation losses rather than insuring them with an insurance carrier. Members are appointed for 3-year terms by the secretary of the department. The council was created by Chapter 29, Laws of 1977, and its duties and composition are prescribed in Sections 15.09 (5) and 15.227 (11) of the statutes.

Unemployment Insurance, Council on: GREGORY A. FRIGO (permanent classified employee of department) (nonvoting member), *chairperson;* JAMES BUCHEN, EARL GUSTAFSON, ROBERT OYLER, DANIEL PETERSON (employer representatives); ED LUMP (employer representative, small business owner or representing small business association); MICHAEL BOLTON, ROBERT W. LYONS, PHIL NEUENFELDT, DENNIS PENKALSKI, RED PLATZ (employee representatives). (All are appointed by secretary of workforce development.)

Mailing Address: P.O. Box 8942, Madison 53708-8942.

Telephone: (608) 266-3189.

The 11-member Council on Unemployment Insurance advises the legislature and the department about unemployment compensation matters. It includes 5 employers and 5 labor representatives who are appointed for 6-year terms, plus a permanent, classified employee of the department who acts as the council's nonvoting chairperson. In making council appointments, the secretary must consider "balanced representation of the industrial, commercial, construction, nonprofit and public sectors of the state's economy." One employer representative must be a small business owner or represent a small business association. The council was created as the Council on Unemployment Compensation by Chapter 327, Laws of 1967. Its name was changed by 1997 Wisconsin Act 39. Its composition and duties are prescribed in Sections 15.227 (3) and 108.14 (5) of the statutes.

Worker's Compensation, Council on: FRANCES HUNTLEY-COOPER (department employee), *chairperson;* MICHELLE K. BEAN, JEFFREY J. BEIRIGER, JEFFREY BRAND, JAMES A. BUCHEN, SCOTT SHAVER (employer representatives); JAMES FURLEY, RON KENT, DAVID NEWBY, CAROL VETTER, PAUL WELNAK (employee representatives); JODIE CONNOR, DON GORDON, BRUCE OLSON (nonvoting insurance company representatives). (All are appointed by secretary of workforce development.)

Mailing Address: P.O. Box 7901, Madison 53707-7901.

Telephone: (608) 266-6841.

The 14-member Council on Worker's Compensation is appointed by the secretary of the department to advise the legislature and the department about worker's compensation and related matters. The council was created by Chapter 281, Laws of 1963, as the Advisory Committee on Workmen's Compensation, appointed by the Industrial Commission. It was given its current name and located in the Department of Industry, Labor and Human Relations by Chapter 327, Laws of 1967. The council includes three nonvoting representatives of insurers authorized to do worker's compensation insurance business in Wisconsin and a department employee acting as chairperson. The council's composition and duties are prescribed in Sections 15.227 (4) and 102.14 (2) of the statutes.

INDEPENDENT UNITS ATTACHED FOR PROGRAM COORDINATION AND RELATED MANAGEMENT FUNCTIONS BY SECTION 15.03 OF THE STATUTES

LABOR AND INDUSTRY REVIEW COMMISSION

Labor and Industry Review Commission: JAMES T. FLYNN, *chairperson;* DAVID B. FALSTAD, ROBERT GLASER (appointed by governor with senate consent).

General Counsel: JAMES L. PFLASTERER, james.pflasterer@dwd.state.wi.us

Mailing Address: P.O. Box 8126, Madison 53708-8126.

Location: Public Broadcasting Building, 3319 West Beltline Highway, Madison.

Telephone: (608) 266-9850.

Fax: (608) 267-4409.

E-mail Address: dwdlirc@dwd.state.wi.us

Internet Address: www.dwd.state.wi.us/lirc

Publications: Informational brochure.

Number of Employees: 25.93.

Total Budget 2003-05: $5,510,700.

Statutory References: Sections 15.225, 15.227, and 103.04.

Agency Responsibility: The 3-member Labor and Industry Review Commission is a quasi-judicial body, created by Chapter 29, Laws of 1977, which handles petitions seeking review of the decisions of the Department of Workforce Development related to unemployment insurance, worker's compensation, fair employment, and public accommodations. It also hears appeals about discrimination in postsecondary education involving a person's physical condition or developmental disability. Commission decisions may be appealed to the circuit court. Commission decisions are enforced by the Department of Justice or the commission's legal staff. Commission members serve full-time for staggered 6-year terms, and they select a chairperson from their membership to serve for a 2-year period. By law, the commission's budget must be transmitted to the governor by the department without modification, unless the commission agrees to the change.

GOVERNOR'S WORK-BASED LEARNING BOARD

Governor's Work-Based Learning Board: Gov. JAMES DOYLE, *chairperson;* ELIZABETH BURMASTER (State Superintendent of Public Instruction); BRENT SMITH (president, Technical College System Board), DANIEL CLANCY (director, Technical College System Board); ROBERTA GASSMAN (secretary of workforce development); BILL CLINGAN (division administrator, Department of Workforce Development); 2 vacancies (representing organized labor and appointed by assembly speaker and senate majority leader, respectively); 2 vacancies (representing business and industry and appointed by assembly speaker and senate majority leader, respectively); KATE L. SHAFFER, WILLIE SINCLAIR (representing organized labor); DEAN T. SCHULTZ, JUDITH WARMUTH (representing business and industry); CHARLES SAMBS, PATRICK VAN GIESHOUT (representing secondary vocational education and work-based learning); SALLY A. HENZL (representing public interest). (All but *ex officio* members and those appointed by legislature are appointed by governor.)

Executive Director: TERRY CRANEY.

Mailing Address: 131 West Wilson Street, Suite 1001, P.O. Box 7891, Madison 53707-7891.

Telephone: (608) 266-0223.

Fax: (608) 261-4862.

Internet Address: http//:www.dwd.state.wi.us/gwblb

Number of Employees: 10.00.

Total Budget 2003-05: $5,369,400.

Statutory References: 15.07 (2) (k), 15.225 (3), 106.12, and 118.34 (4)

   Agency Responsibility: The 17-member Governor's Work-Based Learning Board, created by 1999 Wisconsin Act 9, plans and implements the Youth Apprenticeship, School-to-Work, and Work-Based Learning Programs and any such other employment and education programs assigned by the governor to the board. By statute, the governor serves as chairperson of the board and must appoint the executive director from outside the classified service.

STATE AUTHORITIES

Authorities are public, corporate bodies created for specific purposes.

FOX RIVER NAVIGATIONAL SYSTEM AUTHORITY

Board of Directors: RON VAN DE HEY (Outagamie County representative), *chairperson;* ROBERT J. STARK (Outagamie County representative), *vice chairperson;* BILL RAATHS (Winnebago County representative), *secretary;* BILLY WILLIS (Brown County representative), *treasurer;* WILL STARK (Brown County representative); JACK NELSON (Winnebago County representative); CHARLES VERHOEVEN (designated by secretary of natural resources); WILL DORSEY (designated by secretary of transportation); JIM DRAEGER (designated by director, state historical society) (county residents are appointed by the governor).

Executive Director: HARLAN P. KIESOW.

Telephone: (920) 759-9833.

Number of Employees: 7.00 (not state funded).

Total Budget 2003-05: $61,400.

Statutory References: Chapter 237.

Agency Responsibility: The Fox River Navigational System Authority will rehabilitate, repair, and manage the navigation system on or near the Fox River in 3 counties, once the federal government transfers the ownership of the navigational system to the State of Wisconsin and the authority enters into a lease agreement with the Department of Administration (DOA). The authority may enter into contracts with third parties to replace, repair, rehabilitate, and operate the system. It may not sublease all or any part of the navigational system without DOA approval. It may enter into contracts with nonprofit organizations to raise funds. The authority may charge fees for services provided to watercraft owners and users of navigational facilities. While the authority may contract debt, it may not issue bonds. It must submit a management plan to DOA that addresses the costs of operating the navigational system and how it will manage its funds. In addition it must submit an audited financial statement annually.

Organization: The Fox River Navigational System Authority is a public corporation consisting of 9 members. The 6 members the governor appoints serve 3-year terms. At least one member from each of the 3 counties must be a resident of a city, village, or town in which a navigational system lock is located. The board appoints the executive director to serve at its pleasure. The board receives staff support from the East Central Wisconsin Regional Planning Commission.

The authority was created by 2001 Wisconsin Act 16.

UNIVERSITY OF WISCONSIN HOSPITALS AND CLINICS AUTHORITY

Board of Directors: PATRICK G. BOYLE (appointed by governor with senate consent), *chairperson;* ROGER E. AXTELL (UW Board of Regents member appointed by board president), *vice chairperson;* SENATOR OLSEN (designated by senate cochairperson, Joint Committee on Finance), REPRESENTATIVE WARD (designated by assembly cochairperson, Joint Committee on Finance); DIAN PALMER, KENNETH M. VISTE (appointed by governor with senate consent); CHARLES PRUITT, PEGGY ROSENZWEIG (UW Board of Regents members appointed by board president); JOHN WILEY (chancellor, UW-Madison); PHILIP M. FARRELL (dean, UW-Madison Medical School); LAYTON G. RIKKERS (departmental chairperson, UW-Madison Medical School, appointed by UW-Madison chancellor), KATHARYN MAY (UW health professions faculty, other than UW Medical School, appointed by UW-Madison chancellor); MARC MAROTTA (secretary of administration). Nonvoting members: CAROL L. BOOTH, RICHARD W. CHOUDOIR (labor representatives appointed by governor).

President and Chief Executive Officer: DONNA K. SOLLENBERGER.

Mailing Address: 600 Highland Avenue, Room H4/810, Madison 53792-8350.

Location: 600 Highland Avenue, Madison.

Telephone: (608) 263-8025.

Fax: (608) 263-9830.

Publications: *Health Bound; HealthLink; Kids Connections; Level One; Medical Directions.*

Number of Employees: 6,643 (not state funded).

Total Budget 2004-05: $663,105,000 (not state funded).

Statutory References: Section 15.96; Chapter 233.

Agency Responsibility: The University of Wisconsin Hospitals and Clinics Authority operates the UW Hospital and Clinics, including the UW Children's Hospital. Through the UW Hospital and Clinics and its other programs it delivers health care, including care for the indigent; provides an environment for instruction of physicians, nurses, and other health-related disciplines; sponsors and supports health care research; and assists health care programs and personnel throughout the state. Subject to approval by its board of directors, the Authority may issue bonds to support its operations and may seek financing from the Wisconsin Health and Educational Facilities Authority.

A parallel state agency named the University of Wisconsin Hospitals and Clinics Board was created by Section 15.96, Wisconsin Statutes, to employ some of the hospital's employees. The employees of this state agency are included in the 6,643 hospital employees. The governing body of this state agency has the same composition as the board of directors of the Authority. The Authority is responsible for the payroll of this state agency.

The Med Flight helicopters operated by the University of Wisconsin Hospitals and Clinics Authority (UWHC) make more than 1,300 flights per year, providing care and transport to critically ill or injured patients within a 225-mile radius of Madison. The UWHC, a nonprofit, self-financing entity established under state law, has over 6,600 employees who deliver a full range of health care services to patients, including the indigent, as well as conducting research and the training of physicians, nurses, and other health-related disciplines. (University of Wisconsin Hospitals and Clinics Authority)

Organization: The Authority is a public corporation, which is self-financing. It derives much of its income from charges for clinical and hospital services. The 15-member board of directors includes 2 nonvoting members from two separate bargaining units that represent Authority employees. The governor's appointees serve 3-year terms. The board elects a chairperson annually and appoints the chief executive officer for the Authority. The Authority was created by 1995 Wisconsin Act 27, which separated UW Hospital and Clinics and their related services from the UW System, effective July 1, 1996.

WISCONSIN HEALTH AND EDUCATIONAL FACILITIES AUTHORITY

Members: JOHN A. NOREIKA, *chairperson;* TIMOTHY K. SIZE, *vice chairperson;* EDWARD M. APRAHAMIAN, LINDA C. BRUCE, TONIT M. CALAWAY, PAUL B. LUBER, PAUL J. SENTY (appointed by governor with senate consent).

Executive Director: LAWRENCE R. NINES.

Mailing Address: 18000 West Sarah Lane, Suite 140, Brookfield 53045-5841.

Telephone: (262) 792-0466.

Fax: (262) 792-0649.

Agency E-mail Address: info@whefa.com

Internet Address: http://www.whefa.com

Publications: Annual Report; WHEFA Capital Comments Newsletter.

Number of Employees: 4.00 (not state funded).

Statutory Reference: Chapter 231.

Agency Responsibility: The Wisconsin Health and Educational Facilities Authority (WHEFA) issues bonds on behalf of tax-exempt health care and educational facilities to help them finance their capital costs. Since interest earned on the bonds is exempt from federal income taxation, they can be marketed at lower interest rates, which reduces the cost of borrowing. The Authority has no taxing power and receives no general appropriations from the state; it supports its operations by imposing fees on participating institutions. WHEFA's bonds and notes are funded solely through loan repayments from the borrowing institution or sponsor. Technically, they are not a debt, liability, or obligation of the State of Wisconsin or any of its subdivisions.

WHEFA may issue bonds to finance any qualifying capital project, including new construction, remodeling, and renovation; expansion of current facilities; and purchase of new equipment or furnishings. Some projects require prior approval from the Department of Health and Family Services (DHFS). Upon completion of a project, the Authority may collect rents and revenues to cover the principal and interest on the bonds and administrative expenses. WHEFA may establish rules for the use of a project and appoint the institution or unit administering the facility as its agent.

WHEFA may also issue bonds to refinance outstanding debt of qualifying health care and educational institutions. Health care institutions qualify only when DHFS certifies that refinancing will lead to rate reductions.

Organization: WHEFA is a public corporation. Its 7 members are appointed for staggered 7-year terms, and no more than 4 may be members of the same political party. Each member's appointment remains in effect until a successor is appointed. The governor annually appoints one member as chairperson, and the Authority appoints the executive director. The executive director and staff are employed outside the classified service and are not paid by state funds.

History: The agency was created as the Wisconsin Health Facilities Authority by Chapter 304, Laws of 1973. Operations began in September 1979, after the Wisconsin Supreme Court found the law constitutional in *State ex rel. Wisconsin Health Facilities Authority v. Lindner,* 91 Wis. 2d 145 (1979), when it ruled that assistance to a religiously affiliated hospital does not advance religion or foster unnecessary entanglement between church and state. The Authority issued its first debt in December 1979.

1987 Wisconsin Act 27 expanded the scope of the agency to include assistance to educational facilities and continuing care retirement communities and changed its name to reflect the broader responsibilities. 1993 Wisconsin Act 438 added not-for-profit institutions that have health education as their primary purpose. 2003 Wisconsin Act 109 further expanded the scope of the agency to include the issuance of bonds for the benefit of private, tax-exempt elementary or secondary educational institutions.

WISCONSIN HOUSING AND
ECONOMIC DEVELOPMENT AUTHORITY

Members: PERRY ARMSTRONG, *chairperson;* DAVID W. KRUGER, *vice chairperson;* DANIEL F. LEE, *secretary;* GEOFFREY HURTADO, *treasurer;* SENATORS KANAVAS, TAYLOR; REPRESENTATIVES WIECKERT, YOUNG; MARY BURKE (secretary of commerce), MARC MAROTTA (secretary of administration); CHERYLL A. OLSON-COLLINS, LINDA STEWART. (All except legislative and *ex officio* members are appointed by governor with senate consent.)

Executive Director: ANTONIO RILEY, 266-2893, antonio.riley@

Deputy Executive Director: NELSON FLYNN, 266-2748, nelson.flynn@

Executive Assistant: CHRIS GUNST, 261-5930, chris.gunst@

Executive Secretary: MAUREEN BRUNKER, 266-7354, maureen.brunker@

Mailing Address: P.O. Box 1728, Madison 53701-1728; Milwaukee Office: Suite 100, 101 West Pleasant Street, Milwaukee 53212.

Location: Suite 700, 201 West Washington Avenue, Madison.

Telephones: Madison: (608) 266-7884; Milwaukee: (414) 227-4039; Hotline: (800) 334-6873.

Fax: Madison: (608) 267-1099; Milwaukee: (414) 227-4704.

Internet Address: http://www.wheda.com

Address e-mail by combining the user ID and the state extender: userid@**wheda.com**

Asset Management: RAE ELLEN PACKARD, *director,* 266-6622, rae_ellen.packard@

Community Development: JOHN SCHULTZ, *director,* (414) 227-2292, john.schultz@

Credit: MARY C. ZINS, *director,* 266-2184, mary.zins@

Economic Development: vacancy, *director,* 266-2027.

Financial Services: LAURA B. MORRIS, *chief financial officer,* 266-1640, laura.morris@

General Counsel: NELSON FLYNN, 266-2748, nelson.flynn@

Human Resources and Administration: FLOYD DEBOW, *director,* 267-2921, floyd.debow@

Information Technology: JAMES SIEBERS, *director,* 266-3183, jim.siebers@

Publications: Annual Report; Dividends for Wisconsin; Inventory of Federally Assisted Rental Housing – State of Wisconsin; Wisconsin Housing Authorities Directory.

Number of Employees: 172.00 (not state funded).

Total Budget 2003-05: (not state funded).

Statutory Reference: Chapter 234.

Agency Responsibility: The Wisconsin Housing and Economic Development Authority (WHEDA) provides loans for low- and moderate-income housing, as well as small business and agricultural development projects. The Authority finances most of its programs through the sale of bonds that technically are not an obligation of the State of Wisconsin. Since interest earned on the bonds is exempt from federal income taxation, they can be marketed at lower interest rates, which reduces the cost of borrowing.

WHEDA's single family housing programs include the Home Ownership Mortgage (HOME) Program and the Home Improvement Loan Program. The HOME program provides first mortgage loans to qualified Wisconsin low- and moderate-income families who are purchasing a first home or buying housing in a designated target area. Home improvement loans are provided to low- and moderate-income households at below-market rates to assist them in repairing or improving the energy efficiency of their homes. Other single family programs include a lease-purchase program and assistance program for closing costs. The Authority also administers the property tax deferral loan program for low-income elderly homeowners to enable them to pay property taxes and special assessments on their homes.

Both federally taxable and tax-exempt bonds are used to finance multifamily housing programs, which include homeless and special needs housing initiatives and loans to help with predevelopment of rental housing projects. In addition, the Authority administers the federal Affordable Housing Tax Credit Program for developers of affordable rental housing.

WHEDA acts for the state in administering federally funded housing programs in coordination with the U.S. Department of Housing and Urban Development. Foremost among these are the Section 8 programs of the federal Housing and Community Development Act of 1979, which fund construction and rehabilitation of rental housing through rent subsidies to owners.

A companion organization, the WHEDA Foundation, makes grants to nonprofit organizations and local governments for housing projects that benefit persons-in-crisis. Grants are made to acquire and/or rehabilitate existing housing or construct new housing. The foundation also receives grant money on behalf of WHEDA.

WHEDA administers several economic development programs that encourage job creation and economic growth. These include the Credit Relief Outreach Program (CROP), a loan guarantee program for Wisconsin farmers, and the Linked Deposit Loan Program, which provides an interest rate subsidy for loans to businesses owned and controlled by women and minorities.

The Authority administers a variety of loan guarantee programs: the Agribusiness Fund for businesses that utilize Wisconsin agricultural commodities; the Farm Assets Reinvestment Management Loan Program that assists qualified farmers in acquiring equipment, facilities, land, or livestock or improving facilities or land; and the WHEDA Small Business Guarantee for the expansion of businesses with 50 or fewer employees. It administers the Beginning Farmer Bond Program to help new farmers finance their first farm through tax-exempt bonds.

Organization: WHEDA is a public corporation consisting of 12 members. In addition to the secretary of administration and the secretary of commerce, or their designees, there are 4 legislative members who must represent the majority and minority party in each house. The 6 public members serve staggered 4-year terms, and the governor selects one to serve as chairperson for a one-year term. The governor appoints WHEDA's executive director with the advice and consent of the senate for a 2-year term. Staff members are employed outside the classified service and are not paid from state funds.

History: WHEDA was created as the Wisconsin Housing Finance Authority by Chapter 287, Laws of 1971. Program operations began in July 1973, after the Wisconsin Supreme Court declared the Housing Finance Authority constitutional in *State ex rel. Warren v. Nusbaum*, 59 Wis. 2d 391 (1973). The Authority issued its first debt instruments in March 1974. In 1983, Wisconsin Act 81 broadened the Authority's mission to include financing for economic development projects and changed the name to the Wisconsin Housing and Economic Development Authority. In 1985 Wisconsin Acts 9 and 153 and 1987 Wisconsin Act 421, the legislature expanded WHEDA's powers to include the insuring and subsidizing of farm operating loans, drought assistance loan guarantees, and interest rate reductions. The legislature added loan guarantee programs for agricultural development and small businesses (1989 Wisconsin Act 31), recycling (1989 Wisconsin Act 335), tourism businesses (1989 Wisconsin Act 336), and businesses located in targeted areas of the state (1991 Wisconsin Act 39). 1993 Wisconsin Act 16 transferred the property tax deferral loan program to WHEDA from the Department of Administration.

WORLD DAIRY CENTER AUTHORITY

Members: Inactive.

Statutory Reference: Chapter 235.

Agency Responsibility: The World Dairy Center Authority is directed to establish a center for the development of dairying in Wisconsin, the United States, and the world. The Authority, which is supported by private funding, analyzes worldwide trends in the dairy industry and recommends actions to be taken by Wisconsin to compete in the global dairy market. It coordinates access to commercial, technical, and general dairy information; promotes Wisconsin and U.S. dairy cattle, technology, products, and services in the global dairy market; and develops new markets for dairy and dairy-related products in cooperation with the Department of Agriculture, Trade and Consumer Protection.

Organization: The Authority is a public corporation consisting of 23 members, including 12 who are appointed by the governor to serve 4-year terms. The governor also appoints an additional public member to serve as chairperson for one year and the executive director to serve a 2-year term.

History: The Authority was created by 1991 Wisconsin Act 39.

Wisconsin's title of "America's Dairyland" is exemplified by this pastoral scene near Darlington.
(Kathleen Sitter, LRB)

NONPROFIT CORPORATIONS

A public nonprofit corporation is created by the legislature for a specific purpose.

BRADLEY CENTER SPORTS AND ENTERTAINMENT CORPORATION

Board of Directors: ULICE PAYNE, JR. (appointed by governor with senate consent), *chairperson;* VIRGIS W. COLBERT, JAMES L. FORBES, GAIL A. LIONE (nominated by Bradley Family Foundation); NED W. BECHTHOLD, MICHAEL F. HART, DOUGLAS G. KIEL, GARY SWEENEY, ROLEN L. WOMACK, JR. (All are appointed by governor; the 6 members not nominated by the foundation require senate consent.)

Mailing Address: 1001 North Fourth Street, Milwaukee 53203-1314.

Telephone: (414) 227-0400.

Fax: (414) 227-0497.

E-mail Address: email@bcsec.com

Internet Address: http://www.bradleycenter.com

Statutory Reference: Section 232.03.

Agency Responsibility: The Bradley Center Sports and Entertainment Corporation is a public nonprofit corporation, created by 1985 Wisconsin Act 26 to receive the donation of the Bradley Center, a sports and entertainment facility located in Milwaukee County, from the Bradley Center Corporation. Its responsibility is to own and operate the center for the economic and recreational benefit of the citizens of Wisconsin. The center is the home of the Milwaukee Bucks basketball team, the Milwaukee Admirals hockey team, and the Marquette University men's basketball team. Other tenants are family entertainment shows and concerts. The state and its political subdivisions are not liable for any debt or obligation of the corporation. The corporation may not divest itself of the center, nor may it dissolve unless the legislature directs it to do so by law. If the corporation is dissolved, all of its assets become state property.

State law exempts the corporation from most open records and open meeting laws applicable to state agencies, but the board must submit an annual financial statement to the governor and the legislature.

Organization: The 9 directors of the corporation's board serve staggered 7-year terms, and the board selects its chairperson annually. The 6 members who require senate consent are to "represent the diverse interests of the people of this state" and must be state residents, while 3 of them must have executive and managerial business experience, and no director may be an elected public official.

WISCONSIN ARTISTIC ENDOWMENT FOUNDATION

Board of Directors: BARBARA LAWTON (chairperson of the arts board); SENATOR GROTHMAN (designated by senate majority leader); SENATOR WIRCH (designated by senate minority leader); vacancy (designated by assembly speaker); REPRESENTATIVE BERCEAU (designated by assembly minority leader); GINGER ALDEN, JEFFREY B. BARTELL, DONALD W. BAUMGARTNER, MARVIN FISHMAN, JUDY NAGEL, SUZETTE RENWICK, 2 vacancies (appointed by governor). Nonvoting member: GEORGE TZOUGROS (executive secretary of the arts board).

Executive Director: GEORGE TZOUGROS.

Mailing Address: Wisconsin Arts Board, 101 East Wilson Street, 1st Floor, Madison, 53702.

Telephone: 266-0190.

Fax: 267-0380.

Internet Address: http://arts.state.wi.us

Statutory Reference: Chapter 247.

Agency Responsibility: The Wisconsin Artistic Endowment Foundation is a nonprofit corporation that supports the arts by converting donated property and art objects into cash and distributing these and other moneys to the arts board for programs that provide operating support to arts organizations. The foundation also directly funds various arts programs, which are reviewed biennially with the advice of the arts board and statewide arts organizations.

Of the 14 board members, 2 come from the arts board, the chairperson of the arts board (or designee) and the executive secretary of the arts board (nonvoting member), while 4 are appointed by legislative officers: majority leader of the senate, minority leader of the senate, speaker of the assembly, and minority leader of the assembly. The governor appoints the remaining 8 nominees for 7-year terms, but they must represent diverse artistic interests and each of the geographic regions of the state, with one member knowledgeable in marketing and fundraising. The foundation was created by 2001 Wisconsin Act 16 and can only be dissolved by the legislature.

WISCONSIN TECHNOLOGY COUNCIL (HIGH-TECHNOLOGY BUSINESS DEVELOPMENT CORPORATION)

Directors: MARK D. BUGHER, *chairperson;* MARY BURKE (secretary of commerce); ERICA KAUTEN (designated by president, UW System); DAN CLANCY (state director, Technical College System Board); ROLF WEGENKE (executive director, Wisconsin Association of Independent Colleges and Universities); ALOZIE AGUWA, RICHARD ATKIN, IAN BIGGS, ROBERT W. BRENNAN, PAUL J. CARBONE, ROBERT. CARLSON, ROBERT F. CERVENKA, SUJEET CHAND, DAN COLLINS, CARLOS DE LA HUERGA, TREVOR D'SOUZA, JAN EDDY, MICHAEL FLANAGAN, WILLIAM D. GREGORY, TERRY GROSENHEIDER, CARL E. GULBRANDSEN, JAMES HANEY, E. KELLY HANSEN, TOM HEFTY, JOE HILL, AL JACOBS, JERRY JOHNSON, STAN JOHNSON, ANDERSON LANIYONU III, TOD P. LINSTROTH, WILLIAM LINTON, JAMES MAUER, JOHN P. NEIS, PAUL S. PEERCY, ALEXANDER T. PENDLETON, CHERYL PERKINS, FREDERICK T. RIKKERS, EUGENE SARAGNESE, DALE SCHULTZ, TONI SIKES, MICHAEL R. SUSSMAN, DAVID G. WALSH, ED WOJCIECHOWSKI (all except *ex officio* members are appointed by corporation).

President: TOM STILL, tstill@wisconsintechnologycouncil.com

Telephone: (608) 442-7557.

Fax: (608) 231-6877.

Internet Address: http://www.wisconsintechnologycouncil.com

Statutory Reference: Section 560.27.

Agency Responsibility: The Wisconsin Technology Council, referenced in the statutes as the High-Technology Business Development Corporation, supports the creation, development, and retention of science-based and technology-based businesses in Wisconsin. Created in 1999 Wisconsin Act 106, the corporation is a nonstock, nonprofit entity under Chapter 181, Wisconsin Statutes. The Department of Commerce may make core annual grants to the corporation if the corporation: 1) submits an expenditure plan that the secretary of commerce approves; 2) provides 50% of the funding for the project from other sources; 3) provides information requested by the department related to funds received from private sources; and 4) enters into a written agreement with the department related to the use of grants. Core department grants may not exceed $200,000 in fiscal year 2000-01 and $250,000 in any fiscal year thereafter. In addition, the corporation may accept funding grants from other public or private sources. The state does not guarantee any obligations of the corporation. The corporation is required to submit an annual report on its activities to the governor and the legislature.

The board of directors consists of 4 *ex officio* members and at least 11 other members who are appointed by the board of directors. The appointed members must include one or more individuals from each of the following categories: entrepreneurs, high-technology businesses, venture capital industry, investment banking industry, local governments, business development community, and professionals who provide services to those in the other categories. Members are appointed to 5-year terms. Some of the initial appointments were made by the governor and legislative leadership. Wisconsin Act 106 provided that the corporation must specify in its bylaws the method for electing new board members and for filling vacancies.

Designed by world-renowned architect Santiago Calatrava, the Quadracci Pavillion at the Milwaukee Art Museum has captured the hearts and imaginations of visitors. (Department of Tourism)

REGIONAL AGENCIES

The following agencies were created by state law to function in one specific area of the state, usually an area composed of more than one county.

REGIONAL PLANNING COMMISSIONS

Regional planning commissions advise local units of government on the planning and delivery of public services to the citizens of a defined region, and they prepare and adopt master plans for the physical development of the region they serve. Regional planning provides a way to address problems that transcend local government boundaries, and offers joint solutions for intergovernmental cooperation.

The commissions may conduct research studies; make and adopt plans for the physical, social, and economic development of the region; assist in grant writing for financial assistance; provide advisory services to local governmental units and other public and private agencies; and coordinate local programs that relate to their objectives. Many commissions serve as a one-stop source of statistical information for the local governments of their area.

Currently, there are eight regional planning commissions, serving all but six of the state's 72 counties. Their boundaries are based on such considerations as common topographical and geographical features; the extent of urban development; existence of special or acute agricultural, forestry, or other rural problems; or regional physical, social, and economic characteristics.

Among the many categories of projects developed or assisted by regional planning commissions are rail and air transportation, waste disposal and recycling, highways, air and water quality, farmland preservation and zoning, outdoor recreation, parking and lakefront studies, and land records modernization.

Chapter 466, Laws of 1955, created the statute that governs the state's regional planning commissions (Section 66.0309, Wisconsin Statutes) and authorized the governor (or a state agency designated by the governor) to create a regional planning commission upon petition by the local governing bodies. Chapter 596, Laws of 1959, amended the law to require a public hearing on a petition to form a planning commission unless the governing bodies of all the local governmental units in the proposed region join in the petition. The 1959 law also made the governor's power to create a commission contingent upon the consent of the governing bodies of local units that in combination include more than 50% of the region's population and equalized assessed valuation of property.

Membership of regional planning commissions varies according to conditions defined by statute. Unless otherwise specified by a region's local governments, the term of office for a commissioner is six years. The commissions are funded through state and federal planning grants, contracts with local governments for special planning services, and a statutorily authorized levy of up to .003% of equalized real estate value charged to each local governmental unit.

As authorized by state law, Wisconsin's regional planning commissions have established the Wisconsin Council of Regional Planning Organizations. The council's purposes include assisting the study of common problems and serving as an information clearinghouse.

Bay-Lake Regional Planning Commission

Region: Brown, Door, Florence, Kewaunee, Manitowoc, Marinette, Oconto, and Sheboygan Counties.

Members: JAMES E. GILLIGAN (Sheboygan), *chairperson;* CHERYL R. MAXWELL (Marinette), *vice chairperson;* LOIS L. TREVER (Oconto), *secretary-treasurer;* PAUL JADIN, CHRIS SWAN, CHRISTOPHER ZABEL (Brown); JAIME FOREST, 2 vacancies (Door); EDWIN A. KELLEY, YVONNE VAN PEMBROOK, JOHN ZOELLER (Florence); MARY HANRAHAN, BRIAN PAPLHAM, CHARLES R. WAGNER (Kewaunee); KEVIN M. CRAWFORD, DONALD C. MARKWARDT, SCHAW VANG (Manitowoc); FLORENCE I. MAGNUSON, MARY G. MEYER (Marinette); DONALD A. GLYNN, THOMAS D. KUSSOW (Oconto); FLOSSIE MEYER, JAMES R. SCHRAMM (Sheboygan).

Executive Director: MARK A. WALTER, mwalter@baylakerpc.org
Mailing Address: Old Fort Square, 211 North Broadway, Suite 211, Green Bay 54303-2757.
Telephone: (920) 448-2820; Fax: (920) 448-2823.
Internet Address: http://www.baylakerpc.org

East Central Wisconsin Regional Planning Commission

Region: Calumet, Fond du Lac, Green Lake, Marquette, Menominee, Outagamie, Shawano, Waupaca, Waushara, and Winnebago Counties.

Members: ERNIE BELLIN (Winnebago), *chairperson;* MERLIN GENTZ (Calumet), *vice chairperson;* WILMA SPRINGER, CLARENCE WOLF (Calumet); WALTER M. CACIC, DON WILSON, HOWARD ZELLMER (Marquette); BRIAN KOWALKOWSKI, RANDY REITER, RUTH M. WINTER (Menominee); LARRY CAIN, MARVIN FOX, DONALD GRISSMAN, TIM HANNA, ROBERT PALTZER, CLIFFORD SANDERFOOT (Outagamie); MARSHALL GIESE, ARLYN TOBER, M. EUGENE ZEUSKE (Shawano); DUANE BROWN, ROBERT DANIELSON, DICK KOEPPEN, BRIAN SMITH (Waupaca); YVONNE FEAVEL, NEAL STREHLOW, NORMAN WEISS (Waushara); DAVID ALBRECHT, WILLIAM CASTLE, MARK HARRIS, ARDEN SCHROEDER, PHILLIPS SCOVILLE (RICHARD WOLLANGK, alternate) (Winnebago).

Executive Director: ERIC W. FOWLE, efowle@eastcentralrpc.org
Mailing Address: 132 Main Street, Menasha 54952-3100.
Telephone: (920) 751-4770; Fax: (920) 751-4771.
Internet Address: http://www.eastcentralrpc.org

Mississippi River Regional Planning Commission

Region: Buffalo, Crawford, Jackson, La Crosse, Monroe, Pepin, Pierce, Trempealeau, and Vernon Counties.

Members: RICHARD WILHELM (Pierce), *chairperson;* EUGENE SAVAGE (Jackson), *vice chairperson;* JAN KEIL (La Crosse), *secretary-treasurer;* BERGIE RITSCHER, JAMES SCHOLMEIER, KATHLEEN VINEHOUT (Buffalo); VIRGIL BUTTERIS, GERALD F. KRACHEY, ROBERT ZINKLE (Crawford); JAMES E. CHRISTENSON, RON CARNEY (Jackson); VICKI BURKE, JAMES E. EHRSAM (La Crosse); GEORGE BAKER, JAMES KUHN, CEDRIC A. SCHNITZLER (Monroe); GEORGE T. DUPRE, NORMAN MURRAY, DAVID SMITH (Pepin); RICHARD E. PURDY, WILLIAM SCHROEDER (Pierce); MARGARET M. BAECKER, JOHN KILLIAN, JEROLD O. NYSVEN (Trempealeau); GEORGE NETTUM, JO ANN NICKELATTI, ELDON D. WARREN (Vernon).

Executive Director: GREGORY D. FLOGSTAD.
Mailing Address: 1707 Main Street, Suite 240, La Crosse 54601-3227.
Telephone: (608) 785-9396; Fax: (608) 785-9394.
E-mail Address: plan@mrrpc.com
Internet Address: http://www.mrrpc.com

North Central Wisconsin Regional Planning Commission

Region: Adams, Forest, Juneau, Langlade, Lincoln, Marathon, Oneida, Portage, Vilas, and Wood Counties.

Members: ERHARD HUETTL (Forest), *chairperson;* VIRGINIA HEINEMANN (Marathon), *vice chairperson;* MAURICE MATHEWS (Wood), *secretary-treasurer;* WILBUR FRITZ, DONALD E. KRAHN, HERBERT RIECKMANN, JR. (Adams); DONALD KLINE, PAUL MILLAN (Forest); ROBERT HAYWARD, HELMI MEHUS, SUSAN NOBLE (Juneau); GEORGE BORNEMANN, ROBERT CURRAN, FRANK TRIMMEL (Langlade); TOM RICK, E. RICHARD SIMON, DOUGLAS WILLIAMS (Lincoln); BRADLEY M. KARGER, BETTYE NALL (Marathon); BEVERLY J. LONG, WILBUR PETROSKEY, THOMAS RUDOLPH (Oneida); 3 vacancies (Portage); 3 vacancies (Vilas); FRED CAMACHO, vacancy (Wood).

Executive Director: DENNIS L. LAWRENCE.
Mailing Address: 210 McClellan Street, Suite 210, Wausau 54403.

Telephone: (715) 849-5510; Fax: (715) 849-5110.
E-Mail Address: staff@ncwrpc.org
Internet Address: http://www.ncwrpc.org

Northwest Regional Planning Commission

Region: Ashland, Bayfield, Burnett, Douglas, Iron, Price, Rusk, Sawyer, Taylor, and Washburn Counties.

Members: DOUGLAS FINN (Douglas), *chairperson;* JOHN BLAHNIK (Bayfield), *vice chairperson;* HAROLD HELWIG (Sawyer), *secretary-treasurer;* PEG KURILLA, RONALD NYE, FRED SCHNOOK (Ashland); WILLIAM KACVINSKY, vacancy (Bayfield); PHILIP LINDEMAN, CLIFFORD MAIN (Burnett); BILL ECKMAN, DAVID ROSS, JOHN SHEPARD (Douglas); JIM KICHAK, GUS KRONE (Iron); LYMAN CODDINGTON, NEIL HAGMANN, DANIEL RACETTE (Price); DAN GUDIS, ELDON SKOGEN, RANDY TATUR (Rusk); JEAN LAIER (Sawyer); ALLEN BEADLES, RON DECHATELETS, JIM METZ, GEORGE SOUTHWORTH (Taylor); PETER HUBIN, LOUIS VILLELLA, ROBERT WASHKUHN (Washburn); DONALD MOORE (Bad River Tribal Council); HENRY ST. GERMAINE (Lac du Flambeau Tribal Council); RAY DEPERRY (Red Cliff Tribal Council); LOUIS TAYLOR (Lac Courte Oreilles Tribal Council); DAVID MERRILL (St. Croix Tribal Council).
Executive Director: MYRON SCHUSTER.
Mailing Address: 1400 South River Street, Spooner 54801-1390.
Telephone: (715) 635-2197; Fax: (715) 635-7262.
E-mail Address: mschuster@nwrpc.com
Internet Address: http://www.nwrpc.com

Southeastern Wisconsin Regional Planning Commission

Region: Kenosha, Milwaukee, Ozaukee, Racine, Walworth, Washington, and Waukesha Counties.

Members: THOMAS H. BUESTRIN (Ozaukee), *chairperson;* WILLIAM R. DREW (Milwaukee), *vice chairperson;* GUSTAV W. WIRTH (Ozaukee), *secretary;* RICHARD A. HANSEN (Racine), *treasurer;* LEON F. DREGER, LEONARD R. JOHNSON, ADELENE ROBINSON (Kenosha); LEE HOLLOWAY, LINDA J. SEEMEYER (Milwaukee); ROBERT A. BROOKS (Ozaukee); MICHAEL J. MIKLASEVICH, JAMES E. MOYER (Racine); ANTHONY F. BALESTRIERI, GREGORY L. HOLDEN, ALLEN L. MORRISON (Walworth); KENNETH F. MILLER, DANIEL S. SCHMIDT, DAVID L. STROIK (Washington); KENNETH C. HERRO, ANSELMO VILLARREAL, PAUL G. VRAKAS (Waukesha).
Executive Director: PHILIP C. EVENSON.
Mailing Address: W239 N1812 Rockwood Drive, P.O. Box 1607, Waukesha 53187-1607.
Telephone: (262) 547-6721; Fax: (262) 547-1103.
E-mail Address: sewrpc@sewrpc.org
Internet Address: http://www.sewrpc.org

Southwestern Wisconsin Regional Planning Commission

Region: Grant, Green, Iowa, Lafayette, and Richland Counties.

Members: ANN GREENHECK (Richland), *chairperson;* TOM DALY (Green), *vice chairperson;* COLETTA WEGMANN (Grant), *secretary-treasurer;* EUGENE BARTELS, EILEEN NICKELS (Grant); DONNA DOUGLAS, NATHAN KLASSY (Green); RON DENTINGER, RICHARD GORDER, ROBERT REGAN (Iowa); LAWRENCE L. CHERREY, TIMOTHY MCGETTIGAN, JACK SAUER (Lafayette); GERALD W. COOK, ROBERT SMITH (Richland).
Executive Director: LAWRENCE T. WARD.
Mailing Address: Room 719 Pioneer Tower, 1 University Plaza, UW-Platteville, Platteville 53818.
Telephone: (608) 342-1214; Fax: (608) 342-1220.

E-mail Address: wardla@uwplatt.edu

Internet Address: http://www.swwrpc.org

West Central Wisconsin Regional Planning Commission

Region: Barron, Chippewa, Clark, Dunn, Eau Claire, Polk, and St. Croix Counties.

Members: ARTHUR JACOBSON (St. Croix), *chairperson;* ROGER HAHN (Eau Claire), *vice chairperson;* RICHARD CREASER (Dunn), *secretary-treasurer;* ARNOLD L.G. ELLISON, JESS MILLER, OLE SEVERUD (Barron); LAVERNE LUDWIGSON, EUGENE RINECK, DOUG SANDVICK (Chippewa); ERLIN DAHL, DON KIRN, ROBERT ROGSTAD (Clark); CALVIN CHRISTIANSON, RICHARD H. JOHNSON (Dunn); JOHN L. FRANK, GORDON STEINHAUER (Eau Claire); THOMAS NILSSEN, GENE SOLLMAN, GAIL TESSMAN (Polk); LEON BERENSCHOT, LINDA LUCKEY (St. Croix).

Director: JERRY L. CHASTEEN.

Mailing Address: 800 Wisconsin Street, Mail Box 9, Eau Claire 54703-3606.

Telephone: (715) 836-2918; Fax: (715) 836-2886.

E-mail Address: wcwrpc@wcwrpc.org

Internet Address: http://www.wcwrpc.org

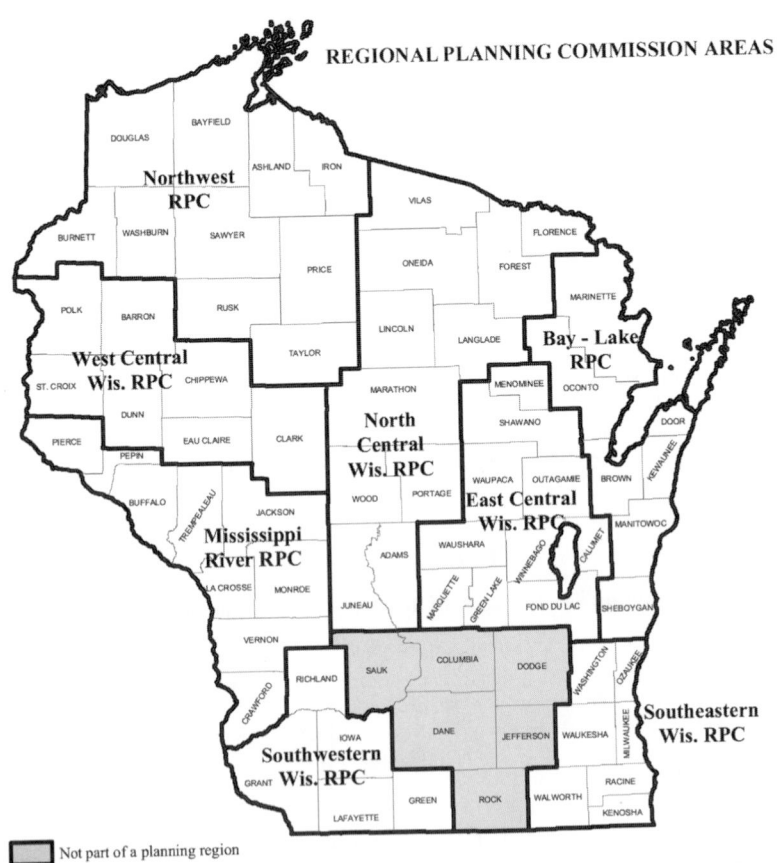

REGIONAL PLANNING COMMISSION AREAS

☐ Not part of a planning region

Map produced by Wisconsin Legislative Technology Services Bureau.

MADISON CULTURAL ARTS DISTRICT BOARD

District Board Members: CAROL T. TOUSSAINT (appointed by City of Madison Mayor), *chairperson;* LAMARR Q. BILLUPS (designated by Dane County Executive), *vice chairperson;* LINDA BALDWIN (appointed by City of Madison Mayor), *secretary;* TINO T. BALIO (UW Board of Regents nominee appointed by governor), *treasurer;* DEIRDRE GARTON (designated by governor); DANA CHABOT (designated by City of Madison Mayor); GEORGE LIGHTBOURN, SUE ANN THOMPSON (appointed by governor); WILLIAM C. KEYS (Madison School Board nominee appointed by City of Madison Mayor); WARREN E. ONKEN, JAMES K. RUHLY, MICHAEL E. VERVEER (appointed by City of Madison Mayor); MICHAEL SKINDRUD (appointed by Dane County Executive).

Staff: ROBERT D'ANGELO.

Mailing Address: 201 State Street, Madison 53703.

Telephone: 258-4177.

Internet Address: http://www.ci.madison.wi.us/mayor/301650.html

Statutory Reference: Chapter 229, Subchapter V.

Agency Responsibility: The Madison Cultural Arts District Board manages the Overture Center for the Arts, which is owned by the Overture Development Corporation. The center is organized for the performance of cultural arts, the development of resident arts organizations, and the dissemination of the arts throughout the community. The Madison Board is organized as a local cultural arts district. Arts districts are public corporations that may acquire, construct, operate, and manage cultural arts facilities. A local district may issue revenue bonds, invest funds, set standards for the use of facilities, and establish and collect fees for usage.

The 10 appointed members serve staggered 4-year terms. At least one of the governor's appointees must demonstrate an interest in the cultural arts. The Madison Common Council must approve the 6 members appointed by the mayor. At least 2 members appointed by the mayor must exhibit an interest in the cultural arts and not more than 3 may be elected public officials. The member appointed by the Dane County Executive may not be a county official. Local arts districts were created by 1999 Wisconsin Act 65.

REGIONAL TRANSPORTATION AUTHORITY

Members: Inactive.

Region: Kenosha, Milwaukee, Ozaukee, Racine, Walworth, Washington, and Waukesha Counties.

Statutory Reference: Section 59.58 (6)

The Regional Transportation Authority was designed to coordinate highway and transit programs in a 7-county region in southeastern Wisconsin. The 11-member authority was created by 1991 Wisconsin Act 39.

SOUTHEAST WISCONSIN PROFESSIONAL
BASEBALL PARK DISTRICT

District Board Members: JAY B. WILLIAMS (at-large member appointed by governor), *chairperson;* MICHAEL LEHMAN (Washington County), *vice chairperson;* GREGORY BORCA (Ozaukee County), DAVID SPANO (Waukesha County), LISA NEUBAUER (Racine County), GREGORY WESLEY (Milwaukee County) (county members appointed by governor); DANIEL McKEITHAN, JR., PERFECTO RIVERA (Milwaukee County), KAREN MAKOUTZ (Ozaukee County), DOUGLAS STANSIL (Racine County), FREDERICK GIERACH (Washington County), SUSAN DREYFUS (Waukesha County) (members appointed by county's chief executive officer); MARK THOMSEN (City of Milwaukee representative appointed by mayor).

Executive Director: MICHAEL R. DUCKETT.

Mailing Address: Miller Park, One Brewers Way, Milwaukee 53214.

Telephone: (414) 902-4040.

Fax: (414) 902-4033.

Statutory Reference: Chapter 229, Subchapter III.

Agency Responsibility: The Southeast Wisconsin Professional Baseball Park District is majority owner of Miller Park, the home of the Milwaukee Brewers baseball club. It is a public corporation that may acquire, construct, maintain, improve, operate, and manage baseball park facilities which include parking lots, garages, restaurants, parks, concession facilities, entertainment facilities, and other related structures. The district may impose a sales tax and a use tax at a rate not to exceed 0.1%.

The district is also authorized to issue bonds for certain purposes related to baseball park facilities. A city or county within the district's jurisdiction may make loans or grants to the district, expend funds to subsidize the district, borrow money for baseball park facilities, or grant property to the state dedicated for use by a professional baseball park.

The district, which was created by 1995 Wisconsin Act 56, includes Milwaukee, Ozaukee, Racine, Washington, and Waukesha Counties. The district board consists of 13 members, 6 appointed by the governor, 6 appointed by the chief executive officers of each county in the district, and one appointed by the mayor of Milwaukee. The governor appoints the chairperson. Members appointed by the governor must be confirmed by the senate. Members appointed by county executive officers or the mayor of Milwaukee must be confirmed by their respective county boards or the city council.

PROFESSIONAL FOOTBALL STADIUM DISTRICT

Board Members: JOHN ROGERS, *chairperson;* ANN PATTESON, *vice chairperson;* RON ANTONNEAU, *secretary;* TED PAMPERIN, *treasurer;* MARGARET JENSEN, THOMAS KOEHLER, GILES TASSOUL.

Statutory Reference: Chapter 229, Subchapter IV.

Agency Responsibility: The Professional Football Stadium District is responsible for the renovation of Lambeau Field, the designated home of the Green Bay Packers football team. It is a public corporation that may acquire, construct, equip, maintain, improve, operate, and manage football stadium facilities or hire others to do the same. The district issued bonds for the redevelopment of Lambeau Field, which was substantially completed on July 31, 2003. Maintenance and operation of the stadium is governed by provisions of the Lambeau Field Lease Agreement by and among the district, Green Bay Packers, Inc., and the City of Green Bay. The district currently imposes a 0.5% sales and use tax approved by Brown County voters in a referendum. Proceeds from the tax must first be used to pay current debt service on the district's bonds. Remaining amounts can be used for district administrative expenses, maintenance, and operating costs of stadium facilities and related purposes consistent with statutory limitations and Lease provisions. The district was created by 1999 Wisconsin Act 167.

WISCONSIN CENTER DISTRICT

Board of Directors: FRANKLYN M. GIMBEL (private sector representative appointed by governor), chairperson; JACOB WEISSBERGER (private sector representative appointed by governor), vice chairperson; WILLIE L. HINES, JR. (Milwaukee Common Council President), *secretary;* W. MARTIN MORICS (City of Milwaukee comptroller), *treasurer;* SENATOR DARLING (designated by senate cochairperson, Joint Committee on Finance), REPRESENTATIVE KAUFERT (assembly cochairperson, Joint Committee on Finance); MARC MAROTTA (secretary of administration); STEPHEN H. MARCUS (private sector representative appointed by governor); JOHN J. BURKE, JR., RICK GALE (private sector representatives appointed by Milwaukee County Executive); THERESA M. ESTNESS (mayor of city that contributes room taxes appointed by Milwaukee County Executive); ALDERMEN D'AMATO, MURPHY (public sector representatives appointed by Milwaukee Common Council President); JAMES C. KAMINSKI, CAROL SKORNICKA (private sector representatives appointed by Mayor of City of Milwaukee).

President: RICHARD A. GEYER, (414) 908-6050, rgeyer@wcd.org

Mailing Address: 400 West Wisconsin Avenue, Milwaukee 53203.

Telephone: (414) 908-6000.

Fax: (414) 908-6010.

Internet Addresses: http://www.wcd.org, http://www.midwestairlinescenter.com, http://milwaukeetheatre.org, http://www.uscellulararena.com

Statutory Reference: Chapter 229, Subchapter II.

Agency Responsibility: The Wisconsin Center District (WCD) owns and operates the U.S. Cellular Arena, the Milwaukee Theatre, and the Midwest Airlines Center. The district is not supported by property taxes or state subsidies. It is funded by operating revenue and special sales taxes on hotel rooms, restaurant food and beverages, and car rentals within its taxing boundaries (Milwaukee County). The WCD is classified by law as a local exposition district that may acquire, construct, and operate an exposition center and related facilities; enter into contracts and grant concessions; mortgage district property and issue bonds; and invest funds as the district board considers appropriate. Local exposition districts are public corporations. Interest income on exposition district bonds is tax-exempt, and the district is exempt from state income and franchise taxes.

The board has 15 members, 13 of whom serve 3-year terms. Legislative members serve for terms concurrent with their term of office. Public officials can no longer serve after their term of office expires. Public sector representatives appointed by the Milwaukee Common Council President must be city residents. The 2 private sector representatives the Mayor of Milwaukee appoints must reside in the city. The private sector representatives the county executive appoints must live outside the City of Milwaukee. Of the 4 gubernatorial appointees, 2 must live in Milwaukee County but not in the City of Milwaukee. The governor's appointees must include the secretary of the state Department of Administration (or designee) and a member who has significant involvement with the lodging industry. Local exposition districts were created by 1993 Wisconsin Act 263.

INTERSTATE AGENCIES AND COMPACTS

Wisconsin is party to a variety of interstate compacts. These agreements are binding on two or more states, and they establish uniform guidelines or procedures for agencies within the signatory states. The following section lists agencies created by enactment of enabling legislation in all of the participating states or by interstate agreement of their respective governors. It also describes interstate compacts that are expressly ratified in the Wisconsin Statutes but do not require appointment of delegates.

EDUCATION COMMISSION OF THE STATES

Wisconsin Delegates: GOVERNOR DOYLE, *chairperson;* ELIZABETH BURMASTER (superintendent of public instruction); SENATORS ELLIS, OLSEN; 3 vacancies (public members appointed by governor).

Mailing Addresses: Wisconsin delegation: Secretary of the Department of Administration, 101 East Wilson Street, P.O. Box 7864, Madison 53707-7864. National commission: Education Commission of the States, 700 Broadway, Suite 1200, Denver, Colorado 80203.

Telephones: Wisconsin: 266-1741; National Commission: (303) 299-3600.

Internet Address: http://www.ecs.org

Statutory References: Sections 39.75 and 39.76.

Agency Responsibility: The Education Commission of the States was established to develop national cooperation among executive, legislative, educational, and lay leaders of the various states. It offers a forum for discussing policy alternatives in the education field; provides an information clearinghouse about educational problems and their various solutions throughout the nation; and facilitates the improvement of state and local educational systems. The governor designates the chairperson of the 7-member delegation, and the Department of Administration provides staff services. Wisconsin's participation in the commission originated in Chapter 641, Laws of 1965, which established an interstate compact for education and specified the composition of the Wisconsin delegation.

WISCONSIN GREAT LAKES COMPACT COMMISSION

Wisconsin Members: TODD L. AMBS (state officer member), *secretary;* DAVE HANSEN, FRED SCHNOOK (all appointed by governor).

Mailing Addresses: Wisconsin Great Lakes Compact Commission: Wisconsin Department of Natural Resources, P.O. Box 7921, Madison 53707-7921. Great Lakes Commission: Thomas Crane, *acting executive director,* The Argus II Building, 400 Fourth Street, Ann Arbor, Michigan 48103-4816.

Telephones: Wisconsin Great Lakes Compact Commission: (608) 264-6278; Great Lakes Commission: (734) 665-9135.

Commission Fax: (734) 665-4370.

Internet Address: http://www.glc.org

Publications of the Great Lakes Commission: *Advisor; ANS Update;* annual reports; special reports.

Statutory Reference: Section 14.78.

Agency Responsibility: The Wisconsin Great Lakes Compact Commission represents Wisconsin on the 8-state Great Lakes Commission. The interstate commission promotes orderly development of the water resources of the Great Lakes Basin; offers advice on balancing industrial, commercial, agricultural, water supply, and residential and recreational uses of the lakes' water resources; and enables basin residents to benefit from public works, such as navigational aids.

Commissioners from the states of Illinois, Indiana, Michigan, Minnesota, New York, Ohio, Pennsylvania, and Wisconsin share information and coordinate state positions on issues of regional concern.

Organization: Members of the Wisconsin Great Lakes Compact Commission serve as Wisconsin's delegates to the Great Lakes Commission. The governor appoints Wisconsin's 3 members on the basis of their knowledge of and interest in Great Lakes Basin problems. One commissioner, who must be a state officer or employee, is appointed to an indefinite term and serves as secretary of Wisconsin's compact commission and as a member of the executive committee of the interstate commission. Wisconsin's other commissioners serve 4-year terms.

History: The Great Lakes Commission was established in 1955 following enactment of enabling legislation by a majority of the Great Lakes states. It replaced the Deep Waterways Commission, established to promote the St. Lawrence Seaway project. With enactment of Chapter 275, Laws of 1955, Wisconsin ratified the Great Lakes Basin Compact and created the Wisconsin Great Lakes Compact Commission. Congress recognized the Great Lakes Basin Compact in P.L. 90-419 on July 24, 1968.

GREAT LAKES PROTECTION FUND

Wisconsin Representatives: TODD L. AMBS, ALAN FISH (appointed by governor with senate consent).

Mailing Addresses and Telephones: 101 South Webster Street, Madison 53703, (608) 264-6278; 610 Walnut Street, Madison 53726. Great Lakes Protection Fund: Russ Van Herick, *executive director,* 1560 Sherman Avenue, Suite 880, Evanston, Illinois 60201, (847) 425-8150, Fax: (847) 424-9832.

Statutory Reference: Section 14.84.

Agency Responsibility: The Great Lakes Protection Fund was created by the Council of Great Lakes Governors to finance projects for the protection and cleanup of the Great Lakes. Priorities include the prevention of toxic pollution, the identification of effective clean-up approaches, the demonstration of natural resource stewardship, and the classification of health effects of toxic pollution.

In 1989, the governors of Illinois, Michigan, Minnesota, New York, Ohio, Pennsylvania, and Wisconsin signed the formal agreement creating the Great Lakes Protection Fund, and the Wisconsin Legislature approved the state's participation in 1989 Wisconsin Act 31. The fund was incorporated as a not-for-profit corporation, managed by a board of directors composed of 2 representatives from each member state. Each state's contribution to the original $100 million endowment was determined by estimating its proportion of Great Lakes water consumption. Wisconsin's share was $12 million.

LOWER ST. CROIX MANAGEMENT COMMISSION

Wisconsin Member: SCOTT HUMRICKHOUSE (designated by secretary of natural resources).

Telephone and Mailing Address: Department of Natural Resources, West Central Region, P.O. Box 4001, Eau Claire 54702-4001, (715) 839-3700.

Agency Responsibility: The Lower St. Croix Management Commission was created to provide a forum for discussion of problems and programs associated with the Lower St. Croix National Scenic Riverway. It coordinates planning, development, protection, and management of the riverway for Wisconsin, Minnesota, and the U.S. government.

The commission was created by a cooperative agreement signed in 1973 by the National Park Service and the governors of Wisconsin and Minnesota. It consists of one member each from the National Park Service and the natural resources departments of the two states.

MIDWEST INTERSTATE LOW-LEVEL RADIOACTIVE WASTE COMMISSION

Wisconsin Member: STANLEY YORK (appointed by governor with senate consent).

Mailing Addresses: Chair and Executive Director Stanley York, Midwest Interstate Low-Level Radioactive Waste Commission, P.O. Box 309, Madison 53701-0309.

Telephones: Wisconsin member: 831-5434; Commission: 267-4793.

Fax: Wisconsin member: 831-1375; Commission: 267-4799.

Statutory References: Sections 14.81 and 16.11.

Agency Responsibility: The Midwest Interstate Low-Level Radioactive Waste Commission is responsible for the disposal of low-level radioactive wastes. Based on the Midwest Interstate Low-Level Radioactive Waste Compact, it may negotiate agreements for disposal of waste at facilities within or outside the region; appear as an intervenor before any court, board, or commission in any matter related to waste management; and review the emergency closure of a regional facility. The commission is directed to settle disputes between party states regarding the compact and adopt a regional management plan designating host states for the establishment of needed regional facilities.

Wisconsin's commission member must promote Wisconsin's interest in an equitable distribution of responsibilities among compact member states, encourage public access and participation in the commission's proceedings, and notify the governor and legislature if the commission proposes to designate a disposal facility site in this state.

Organization: The commission represents Indiana, Iowa, Minnesota, Missouri, Ohio, and Wisconsin, each of which has one voting member.

History: 1983 Wisconsin Act 393 ratified the Midwest Interstate Low-Level Radioactive Waste Compact, which provided for formation of the Midwest Low-Level Radioactive Waste Commission, and 1995 Wisconsin Act 115 ratified amendments to the compact. The U.S. Congress encouraged the development of such compacts by enacting the Low-Level Radioactive Waste Policy Act in 1980, as amended by the Low-Level Radioactive Waste Policy Amendments Act of 1985.

MIDWESTERN HIGHER EDUCATION COMMISSION

Wisconsin Members: JOHN KERRIGAN (designated by governor); SENATOR HARSDORF (appointed by senate president); REPRESENTATIVE KREIBICH (appointed by assembly speaker); JESUS SALAS, ROLF WEGENKE (appointed by governor).

Mailing Address: 1300 South Second Street, Suite 130, Minneapolis, Minnesota 55454-1079.

Telephone: (612) 626-8288.

Statutory Reference: Sections 14.90 and 39.80.

Agency Responsibility: The Midwestern Higher Education Commission was organized to further higher educational opportunities for residents of compact states. The commission may enter into agreements with member and nonmember states, or their universities and colleges, to provide programs and services for students, including student exchanges and improved access. The commission also studies the effects of the Midwestern Higher Education Compact on higher education and the needs and resources for programs in member states. The compact's three core functions are cost-savings initiatives, student access, and policy research and analysis.

Organization: The commission, composed of eligible states that have ratified the Midwestern Higher Education Compact, currently includes Illinois, Indiana, Kansas, Michigan, Minnesota, Missouri, Nebraska, North Dakota, Ohio, and Wisconsin. Each state appoints 5 members to the commission, including the governor (or governor's designee) and 2 legislators, who serve 2-year terms. The 2 at-large members appointed by the governor serve 4-year terms, and must be selected from the field of higher education. Any member state may withdraw from the compact 2 years after the passage of a law authorizing withdrawal.

History: Wisconsin ratified the Midwestern Higher Education Compact in 1993 Wisconsin Act 358, effective July 1, 1994.

MISSISSIPPI RIVER PARKWAY COMMISSION

Wisconsin Commissioners: ALAN L. LORENZ (La Crosse County), *chairperson;* ROBERT MILLER (Buffalo County), *vice chairperson;* SENATOR HARSDORF, vacancy; REPRESENTATIVES GRONEMUS, NERISON; MARY ANNE STEMPER (Crawford County); FRANK FIORENZA (Grant County); NORMAN M. MURRAY (Pepin County); MICHAEL A. HUNTER (Pierce County); RUSSELL H. STEVENS (Trempealeau County); CHESTER H. LEE (Vernon County). (Legislators are nominated by presiding officer and appointed by governor. County representatives are appointed by governor.) Nonvoting members: MARY BURKE (secretary of commerce), SCOTT HASSETT (secretary of natural resources), FRANK BUSALACCHI (secretary of transportation), ELLWORTH BROWN (director, state historical society), JAMES HOLPERIN (secretary of tourism).

Contact: ALAN L. LORENZ, lorenzall@msn.com

Mailing Address: W4927 Hoeth Street, La Crosse 54601.

Telephone: (608) 788-8264.

Statutory Reference: Section 14.85.

Agency Responsibility: The Mississippi River Parkway Commission coordinates development and preservation of Wisconsin's portion of the Great River Road corridor along the Mississippi River. It assists and advises state and local agencies about maintaining and enhancing the scenic, historic, economic, and recreational assets within the corridor and cooperates with similar commissions in other Mississippi River states and the Province of Ontario. On June 15, 2000, the U.S. Secretary of Transportation designated the entire 250-mile length of the Wisconsin Great River Road as a National Scenic Byway, thereby recognizing it as an outstanding example of America's scenic beauty.

Organization: The 17-member Wisconsin commission includes 12 voting members, appointed to 4-year terms, and 5 nonvoting *ex officio* members. The 4 legislative members must represent the two major political parties in each house.

The commission selects its own chairperson who is Wisconsin's sole voting representative at national meetings of the Mississippi River Parkway Commission.

History: The Wisconsin commission is part of the Mississippi River Parkway Commission, which was given statutory recognition by Chapter 482, Laws of 1961. It dates back to 1939 when Wisconsin Governor Julius P. Heil appointed a 10-member committee to cooperate with agencies from other Mississippi River states in planning the Great River Road. This scenic route extends from the Gulf of Mexico to the Mississippi River's headwaters at Lake Itasca, Minnesota. North of Lake Itasca, the route connects with the Trans-Canada Highway and terminates at Minaki, Ontario.

The Federal Highway Aid Acts of 1973, 1976, and 1978 provided Wisconsin approximately $21 million in Great River Road funding. While categorical funding is no longer available, the Wisconsin Department of Transportation has continued improvements to Wisconsin's portion of the Great River Road, including pedestrian and bicycle trails, landscaping, preservation of historic sites, and other programs. Wisconsin has also received nearly $3.0 million in discretionary grants from the National Scenic Byways Program from 2000 through 2004. These grants were matched with 20% state and local government funds.

UPPER MISSISSIPPI RIVER BASIN ASSOCIATION

Wisconsin Representative: TODD L. AMBS (appointed by governor).

Mailing Addresses: Wisconsin representative: 101 South Webster Street, Madison 53703. Upper Mississippi River Basin Association: Holly Stoerker, Executive Director, 415 Hamm Building, 408 St. Peter Street, St. Paul, Minnesota 55102.

Madison Location: 115 East, State Capitol, Madison.

Telephones: Wisconsin: 264-6278; Minnesota: (612) 224-2880.

Agency Responsibility: The Upper Mississippi River Basin Association is a nonprofit organization created by Illinois, Iowa, Minnesota, Missouri, and Wisconsin to facilitate cooperative action regarding the basin's water and related land resources. It sponsors studies of river-related issues, cooperative planning for use of the region's resources, and an information exchange. It also enables the member states to develop regional positions on resource issues and to advocate the basin states' collective interests before the U.S. Congress and federal agencies. The association has placed major emphasis on its Environmental Management Program, a partnership among the U.S. Army Corps of Engineers, the U.S. Fish and Wildlife Service, and the five states. This program, which was approved by the federal Water Resources Development Act of 1986, authorized habitat rehabilitation projects, resource inventory and analysis, recreation projects, and river traffic monitoring.

Organization: The association consists of one representative from each member state. The members annually elect one of their number to serve as chairperson. Five federal agencies with major water resources responsibilities serve as advisory members: the Environmental Protection Agency and the U.S. Departments of Agriculture, Army, Interior, and Transportation.

History: The Upper Mississippi River Basin Association was formed on December 2, 1981, when the articles of association were signed by representatives of the member states. In late 1983 and early 1984, executive orders were issued by four of the five governors reaffirming membership in the association.

INTERSTATE COMPACTS

Interstate Compact on Adoption and Medical Assistance

The compact authorizes the Department of Health and Family Services to enter into agreements with other states that have adoption assistance programs for children with special needs. In these agreements, other states must provide Medical Assistance (MA) benefits to children who were adopted as residents of Wisconsin, and Wisconsin must provide the same benefits to children who were adopted as residents of other states. Any interstate agreement is revocable upon written notice to the other state but remains in effect for one year after the date of the notice. Benefits already granted continue even if the agreement is revoked. The compact has been adopted by 48 states and the District of Columbia. (1985 Wisconsin Act 302)

Statutory Reference: Section 48.9985.

Administrator: Department of Health and Family Services.

Interstate Compact for Adult Offender Supervision

The compact creates cooperative procedures for individuals placed on parole, probation, or extended supervision in one state to be supervised in another state if certain conditions are met. The compact has been adopted by 49 states, the District of Columbia, and Puerto Rico. (2001 Wisconsin Act 96)

Statutory Reference: Section 304.16.

Administrator: William Rankin, Department of Corrections (appointed by governor).

Corrections Compact

The compact allows Wisconsin to enter into contracts with states that are party to the compact to confine Wisconsin's inmates in the other state's correctional facilities or receive inmates from other states. The contract provides for inmate upkeep and special services. The compact has been adopted by 40 states and the District of Columbia. (Chapter 20, Laws of 1981)

Statutory Reference: Sections 302.25 and 302.26.

Administrator: Department of Corrections.

Agreement on Detainers

The agreement is designed to clear up indictments or complaints that serve as a basis for a detainer lodged against a prisoner incarcerated in one jurisdiction and wanted in another. The agreement allows the state making the request to obtain temporary custody of the prisoner to conduct a trial on outstanding charges. The agreement has been adopted by 48 states and the District of Columbia. (Chapter 255, Laws of 1969)

Statutory Reference: Sections 976.05 and 976.06.

Emergency Management Assistance Compact

The compact authorizes states that are members to provide mutual assistance to other member states in an emergency or disaster declared by the governor of the affected state. Under the compact, member states cooperate in emergency-related training and formulate plans for interstate cooperation in responding to a disaster. The compact has been adopted by all of the states, except California and Hawaii. (1999 Wisconsin Act 26)

Statutory Reference: Section 166.30.

Administrator: Division of Emergency Management, Department of Military Affairs.

Interstate Compact on Juveniles

The compact sets up cooperative procedures for out-of-state supervision of juveniles. It applies to cooperative supervision of delinquent juveniles on probation, extended supervision, or parole; the return of delinquent juveniles who have escaped or absconded; the return of nondelinquent juveniles who have run away from home; and additional measures for the protection of juveniles and the public. A revised compact is in the process of being ratified by all states. (Chapter 300, Laws of 1955)

Statutory Reference: Sections 938.991-938.998.

Administrator: Silvia R. Jackson, Department of Corrections (appointed by governor).

Interstate Compact on Mental Health

The compact facilitates the proper and expeditious treatment of persons with mental illness or mental retardation by the cooperative action of the party states, to the benefit of the person, their families, and society. The compact (and enacting laws) provides for this to be done irrespective of the legal residence and citizenship status of the person. The compact has been adopted in 45 states and the District of Columbia. (Chapter 611, Laws of 1965)

Statutory Reference: Sections 51.75-51.80.

Administrator: Department of Health and Family Services.

Nurse Licensure Compact

The compact allows a nurse licensed by a party state to practice nursing in any other party state without obtaining a license. It requires each party state to participate in a database of all licensed nurses. The compact has been adopted by Arizona, Arkansas, Delaware, Idaho, Iowa, Maine, Maryland, Mississippi, Nebraska, New Mexico, North Carolina, North Dakota, South Dakota, Tennessee, Texas, Utah, Virginia, and Wisconsin. (1999 Wisconsin Act 22)

Statutory Reference: Section 441.50.

Administrator: Department of Regulation and Licensing.

Interstate Compact on Placement of Children

The compact provides a legal framework to administer child placement activities among the party states to ensure protection and services when a child is in one state and the most suitable placement is in a different state. It requires notice and proof of suitability before a placement is made; allocates legal and administrative responsibilities during the continuance of the placement; provides a basis for enforcement of rights; and authorizes joint actions to improve operations and services. All states have adopted the compact. (Chapter 354, Laws of 1977)

Statutory Reference: Sections 48.988 and 48.989.

Administrator: Burnie Bridge, Department of Health and Family Services (appointed by governor).

Interstate Agreement on Qualification of Educational Personnel

The agreement authorizes the State Superintendent of Public Instruction to enter into contracts with party states to accept their educational personnel. These agreements allow Wisconsin to offer initial licenses to teachers from contracting states and allows other states to accept Wisconsin-trained teachers on the same basis. The agreement has been adopted by 34 states and the District of Columbia. (Chapter 42, Laws of 1969)

Statutory Reference: Sections 115.46-115.48.

Administrator: State Superintendent of Public Instruction.

Interstate Compact for Supervision of Parolees and Probationers

The compact creates cooperative procedures for individuals placed on parole or probation in one state to be supervised in another state if certain conditions are met. All states have adopted the compact. (Chapter 345, Laws of 1939)

Statutory Reference: Sections 304.13 and 304.135.

Administrator: William Rankin, Department of Corrections (appointed by governor).

Judicial
Branch

7

The judicial branch: profile of the judicial branch, summary of recent significant supreme court decisions, and descriptions of the supreme court, court system, and judicial service agencies

Brown County Courthouse

Kathleen Sitter, LRB

WISCONSIN SUPREME COURT

Justice	First Assumed Office	Began First Elected Term	Current Term Expires July 31
Shirley S. Abrahamson, Chief Justice	1976*	August 1979	2009
Jon P. Wilcox	1992*	August 1997	2007
Ann Walsh Bradley	1995	August 1995	2005
N. Patrick Crooks	1996	August 1996	2006
David T. Prosser, Jr.	1998*	August 2001	2011
Patience D. Roggensack	2003	August 2003	2013
Louis B. Butler, Jr.**	2004*	–––	2008

*Initially appointed by the governor.
**Appointed to Supreme Court on August 25, 2004, to fill a vacancy created by the resignation of Justice Diane S. Sykes.
Sources: *2003-2004 Wisconsin Statutes;* Director of State Courts, departmental data, March 2005.

The Supreme Court's chamber in the East Wing of the State Capitol provides the setting for the court's formal portrait. Pictured from left to right are Justice Patience D. Roggensack, Justice N. Patrick Crooks, Justice Jon P. Wilcox, Chief Justice Shirley S. Abrahamson, Justice Ann Walsh Bradley, Justice David T. Prosser, Jr., and Justice Louis B. Butler, Jr. (Wisconsin Supreme Court)

JUDICIAL BRANCH

A PROFILE OF THE JUDICIAL BRANCH

Introducing the Court System. The judicial branch and its system of various courts may appear very complex to the nonlawyer. It is well-known that the courts are required to try persons accused of violating criminal law and that conviction in the trial court may result in punishment by fine or imprisonment or both. The courts also decide civil matters between private citizens, ranging from landlord-tenant disputes to adjudication of corporate liability involving many millions of dollars and months of costly litigation. In addition, the courts act as referees between citizens and their government by determining the permissible limits of governmental power and the extent of an individual's rights and responsibilities.

A court system that strives for fairness and justice must settle disputes on the basis of appropriate rules of law. These rules are derived from a variety of sources, including the state and federal constitutions, legislative acts and administrative rules, as well as the "common law", which reflects society's customs and experience as expressed in previous court decisions. This body of law is constantly changing to meet the needs of an increasingly complex world. The courts have the task of seeking the delicate balance between the flexibility and the stability needed to protect the fundamental principles of the constitutional system of the United States.

The Supreme Court. The judicial branch is headed by the Wisconsin Supreme Court of 7 justices, each elected statewide to a 10-year term. The supreme court is primarily an appellate court and serves as Wisconsin's "court of last resort". It also exercises original jurisdiction in a small number of cases of statewide concern. There are no appeals to the supreme court as a matter of right. Instead, the court has discretion to determine which appeals it will hear.

In addition to hearing cases on appeal from the court of appeals, there also are three instances in which the supreme court, at its discretion, may decide to bypass the appeals court. First, the supreme court may review a case on its own initiative. Second, it may decide to review a matter without an appellate decision based on a petition by one of the parties. Finally, the supreme court may take jurisdiction in a case if the appeals court finds it needs guidance on a legal question and requests supreme court review under a procedure known as "certification".

The Court of Appeals. The Court of Appeals, created August 1, 1978, is divided into 4 appellate districts covering the state, and there are 16 appellate judges, each elected to a 6-year term. The "court chambers", or principal offices for the districts, are located in Madison (5 judges), Milwaukee (4 judges), Waukesha (4 judges), and Wausau (3 judges).

In the appeals court, 3-judge panels hear all cases, except small claims actions, municipal ordinance violations, traffic violations, and mental health, juvenile, and misdemeanor cases. These exceptions may be heard by a single judge unless a panel is requested.

Circuit Courts. Following a 1977-78 reorganization of the Wisconsin court system, the circuit court became the "single level" trial court for the state. Circuit court boundaries were revised so that, except for 3 combined-county circuits (Buffalo-Pepin, Forest-Florence, and Shawano-Menominee), each county became a circuit, resulting in a total of 69 circuits.

In the more populous counties, a circuit may have several branches with one judge assigned to each branch. As of June 30, 2005, Wisconsin had a combined total of 241 circuits or circuit branches and the same number of circuit judgeships, with each judge elected to a 6-year term. For administrative purposes, the circuit court system is divided into 10 judicial administrative districts, each headed by a chief judge appointed by the supreme court. The circuit courts are funded with a combination of state and county money. For example, state funds are used to pay the salaries of judges, and counties are responsible for most court operating costs.

A final judgment by the circuit court can be appealed to the Wisconsin Court of Appeals, but a decision by the appeals court can be reviewed only if the Wisconsin Supreme Court grants a petition for review.

Municipal Courts. Individually or jointly, cities, villages, and towns may create municipal courts with jurisdiction over municipal ordinance violations that have monetary penalties. Over 200 municipalities have done so. These courts are not courts of record, and they have limited jurisdiction. Usually, municipal judgeships are not full-time positions.

Selection and Qualification of Judges. In Wisconsin, all justices and judges are elected on a nonpartisan ballot in April. The Wisconsin Constitution provides that supreme court justices and appellate and circuit judges must have been licensed to practice law in Wisconsin for at least 5 years prior to election or appointment. While state law does not require that municipal judges be attorneys, municipalities may impose such a qualification in their jurisdictions.

Supreme court justices are elected on a statewide basis; appeals court and circuit court judges are elected in their respective districts. The governor may make an appointment to fill a vacancy in the office of justice or judge to serve until a successor is elected. When the election is held, the candidate elected assumes the office for a full term.

Since 1955, Wisconsin has permitted retired justices and judges to serve as "reserve" judges. At the request of the chief justice of the supreme court, reserve judges fill vacancies temporarily or help to relieve congested calendars. They exercise all the powers of the court to which they are assigned.

Judicial Agencies Assisting the Courts. Numerous state agencies assist the courts. The Wisconsin Supreme Court appoints the Director of State Courts, the State Law Librarian and staff, the Board of Bar Examiners, the director of the Office of Lawyer Regulation, and the Judicial Education Committee. Other agencies that assist the judicial branch include the Judicial Commission, Judicial Council, and the State Bar of Wisconsin.

The shared concern of these agencies is to improve the organization, operation, administration, and procedures of the state judicial system. They also function to promote professional standards, judicial ethics, and legal research and reform.

Court Process in Wisconsin. Both state and federal courts have jurisdiction over Wisconsin citizens. State courts generally adjudicate cases pertaining to state laws, but the federal government may give state courts jurisdiction over specified federal questions. Courts handle two types of cases – civil and criminal.

Civil Cases. Generally, civil actions involve individual claims in which a person seeks a remedy for some wrong done by another. For example, if a person has been injured in an automobile accident, the complaining party (plaintiff) may sue the offending party (defendant) to compel payment for the injuries.

In a typical civil case, the plaintiff brings an action by filing a summons and a complaint with the circuit court. The defendant is served with copies of these documents, and the summons directs the defendant to respond to the plaintiff's attorney. Various pretrial proceedings, such as pleadings, motions, pretrial conferences, and discovery, may be required. If no settlement is reached, the matter goes to trial. The U.S. and Wisconsin Constitutions guarantee trial by jury, but if both parties consent, the trial may be conducted by the court without a jury. The jury in a civil case consists of 6 persons unless a greater number, not to exceed 12, is requested. Five-sixths of the jurors must agree on the verdict. Based on the verdict, the court enters a judgment for the plaintiff or defendant.

Wisconsin law provides for small claims actions that are streamlined and informal. These actions typically involve the collection of small personal or commercial debts and are limited to questions of $5,000 or less. Small claims cases are decided by the circuit court judge, unless a jury trial is requested. Attorneys commonly are not used.

Criminal Cases. Under Wisconsin law, criminal conduct is an act prohibited by state law and punishable by a fine or imprisonment or both. There are two types of crime – felonies and misdemeanors. A felony is punishable by confinement in a state prison for one year or more; all other crimes are misdemeanors punishable by imprisonment in a county jail. Misdemeanors have a maximum sentence of 12 months unless the violator is a "repeater" as defined in the statutes.

Because a crime is an offense against the state, the state, rather than the crime victim, brings action against the defendant. A typical criminal action begins when the district attorney, an elected county official who acts as an agent of the state in prosecuting the case, files a criminal complaint in the circuit court stating the essential facts concerning the offense charged. The defendant may or may not be arrested at that time. If the defendant has not yet been arrested, the judge or a court commissioner then issues an "arrest warrant" in the case of a felony or a "summons" in the case of a misdemeanor. A law enforcement officer then must serve a copy of the warrant or summons on an individual and make an arrest.

Once in custody, the defendant is taken before a circuit judge or court commissioner, informed of the charges, and given the opportunity to be represented by a lawyer at public expense if he or she cannot afford to hire one. Bail may be set at this time or later. In the case of a misdemeanor, a trial date is set. In felony cases, the defendant has a right to a preliminary examination, which is a hearing before the court to determine whether the state has probable cause to charge the individual. If the defendant does not waive the preliminary examination, the judge or court commissioner transfers the action to a circuit court for a formal hearing, called an "arraignment". If probable cause is found, the person is bound over for trial.

If the preliminary examination is waived, or if it is held and probable cause found, the district attorney files an information (a sworn accusation on which the indictment is based) with the court. The arraignment is then held before the circuit court judge, and the defendant enters a plea ("guilty", "not guilty", "no contest subject to the approval of the court", or "not guilty by reason of mental disease or defect").

The case next proceeds to trial in circuit court. Criminal cases are tried by a jury of 12, unless the defendant waives a jury trial or there is agreement for fewer jurors. The jury considers the evidence presented at the trial, determines the facts and renders a verdict of guilty or not guilty based on instructions given by the circuit judge. If the jury issues a verdict of guilty, a judgment of conviction is entered and the court determines the sentence. The court may order a presentence investigation before pronouncing sentence.

In a criminal case, the jury's verdict must be unanimous. If not, the defendant is acquitted (cleared of the charge). Once acquitted, a person cannot be tried again in criminal court for the same charge, based on provisions in both the federal and state constitutions that prevent double jeopardy. Aggrieved parties may, however, bring a civil action against the individual for damages, based on the incident.

History of the Court System. The basic powers and framework of the court system in Wisconsin were established by Article VII of the Wisconsin Constitution when Wisconsin became a state in 1848. At that time, judicial power was vested in a supreme court, circuit courts, courts of probate, and justices of the peace. Subject to certain limitations, the legislature was granted power to establish inferior courts and municipal courts and determine their jurisdiction.

The constitution originally divided the state into five judicial circuit districts. The five judges who presided over those circuit courts were to meet at least once a year at Madison as a "Supreme Court" until the legislature established a separate court. The Wisconsin Supreme Court was instituted in 1853 with 3 members chosen in statewide elections – one was elected as chief justice and the other 2 as associate justices. In 1877, a constitutional amendment increased the number of associate justices to 4. An 1889 amendment prescribed the current practice under which all court members are elected as justices. The justice with the longest continuous service presides as chief justice, unless that person declines, in which case the office passes to the next justice in terms of seniority. Since 1903, the constitution has required a court of 7 members.

Over the years, the legislature created a large number of courts with varying types of jurisdiction. As a result of numerous special laws, there was no uniformity among the counties. Different types of courts in a single county had overlapping jurisdiction, and procedure in the various courts was not the same. A number of special courts sprang up in heavily urbanized areas, such as Milwaukee County, where the judicial burden was the greatest. In addition, many municipalities established police justice courts for enforcement of local ordinances, and there were some 1,800 justices of the peace.

The 1959 Legislature enacted Chapter 315, effective January 1, 1962, which provided for the initial reorganization of the court system. The most significant feature of the reorganization was the abolition of special statutory courts (municipal, district, superior, civil, and small claims). In addition, a uniform system of jurisdiction and procedure was established for all county courts.

The 1959 law also created the machinery for smoother administration of the court system. One problem under the old system was the imbalance of caseloads from one jurisdiction to another. In some cases, the workload was not evenly distributed among the judges within the same jurisdiction. To correct this, the chief justice of the supreme court was authorized to assign circuit and county judges to serve temporarily as needed in either type of court. The 1961 Legislature took another step to assist the chief justice in these assignments by creating the post of Administrative Director of Courts. This position has since been redefined by the supreme court and renamed the Director of State Courts. In recent years, the director has been given added administrative duties and increased staff to perform them.

The last step in the 1959 reorganization effort was the April 1966 ratification of two constitutional amendments that abolished the justices of the peace and permitted municipal courts. At this point the Wisconsin system of courts consisted of the supreme court, circuit courts, county courts, and municipal courts.

In April 1977, the court of appeals was authorized when the voters ratified an amendment to Article VII, Section 2, of the Wisconsin Constitution, which outlined the current structure of the state courts:

The judicial power of this state shall be vested in a unified court system consisting of one supreme court, a court of appeals, a circuit court, such trial courts of general uniform statewide jurisdiction as the legislature may create by law, and a municipal court if authorized by the legislature under section 14.

In June 1978, the legislature implemented the constitutional amendment by enacting Chapter 449, Laws of 1977, which added the court of appeals to the system and eliminated county courts.

General Douglas MacArthur began his military career with an appointment to West Point by Milwaukee Congressman Theobald Otjen in 1899. His Milwaukee connection is commemorated by this statue in MacArthur Square at the entrance to the Milwaukee County Courthouse. (Kathleen Sitter, LRB)

SUPREME COURT

Chief Justice: SHIRLEY S. ABRAHAMSON
Justices: JON P. WILCOX
ANN WALSH BRADLEY
N. PATRICK CROOKS
DAVID T. PROSSER, JR.
PATIENCE D. ROGGENSACK
LOUIS B. BUTLER, JR.

Mailing Address: Supreme Court and Clerk: P.O. Box 1688, Madison 53701-1688.

Locations: Supreme Court: Room 16 East, State Capitol, Madison; Clerk: 110 East Main Street, Madison.

Telephone: 266-1298.

Fax: 261-8299.

Internet Address: http://www.wicourts.gov

Clerk of Supreme Court: CORNELIA G. CLARK, 266-1880, Fax: 267-0640.

Court Commissioners: COLEEN KENNEDY, NANCY KOPP, JULIE RICH, DAVID RUNKE; 266-7442.

Number of Positions: 38.50.

Total Budget 2003-05: $8,522,400.

Constitutional References: Article VII, Sections 2-4, 9-11, and 13.

Statutory Reference: Chapter 751.

Responsibility: The Wisconsin Supreme Court is the final authority on matters pertaining to the Wisconsin Constitution and the highest tribunal for all actions begun in the state, except those involving federal issues appealable to the U.S. Supreme Court. The court decides which cases it will hear, usually on the basis of whether the questions raised are of statewide importance. It exercises "appellate jurisdiction" if 3 or more justices grant a petition to review a decision of a lower court. It exercises "original jurisdiction" as the first court to hear a case if 4 or more justices approve a petition requesting it to do so. Although the majority of cases advance from the circuit court to the court of appeals before reaching the supreme court, the high court may decide to bypass the court of appeals. The supreme court can do this on its own motion or at the request of the parties; in addition, the court of appeals may certify a case to the supreme court, asking the high court to take the case directly from the circuit court.

The supreme court does not take testimony. Instead, it decides cases on the basis of written briefs and oral argument. It is required by statute to deliver its decisions in writing, and it may publish them in the *Wisconsin Reports* as it deems appropriate.

The supreme court sets procedural rules for all courts in the state, and the chief justice serves as administrative head of the state's judicial system. With the assistance of the director of state courts, the chief justice monitors the status of judicial business in Wisconsin's courts. When a calendar is congested or a vacancy occurs in a circuit or appellate court, the chief justice may assign an active judge or reserve judge to serve temporarily as a judge of either type of court.

Organization: The supreme court consists of 7 justices elected to 10-year terms. They are chosen in statewide elections on the nonpartisan April ballot and take office on the following August 1. The Wisconsin Constitution provides that only one justice can be elected in any single year, so supreme court vacancies are sometimes filled by gubernatorial appointees who serve until a successor can be elected. The authorized salary for supreme court justices for fiscal year 2004-05 is $123,876. The chief justice receives $131,876.

The justice with the most seniority on the court serves as chief justice unless he or she declines the position. In that event, the justice with the next longest seniority serves as chief justice. Any 4 justices constitute a quorum for conducting court business.

The court staff is appointed from outside the classified service. It includes the director of state courts who assists the court in its administrative functions; 4 commissioners who are attorneys and assist the court in its judicial functions; a clerk who keeps the court's records; and a marshal who performs a variety of duties. Each justice has a secretary and one law clerk.

WISCONSIN COURT SYSTEM – ADMINISTRATIVE STRUCTURE

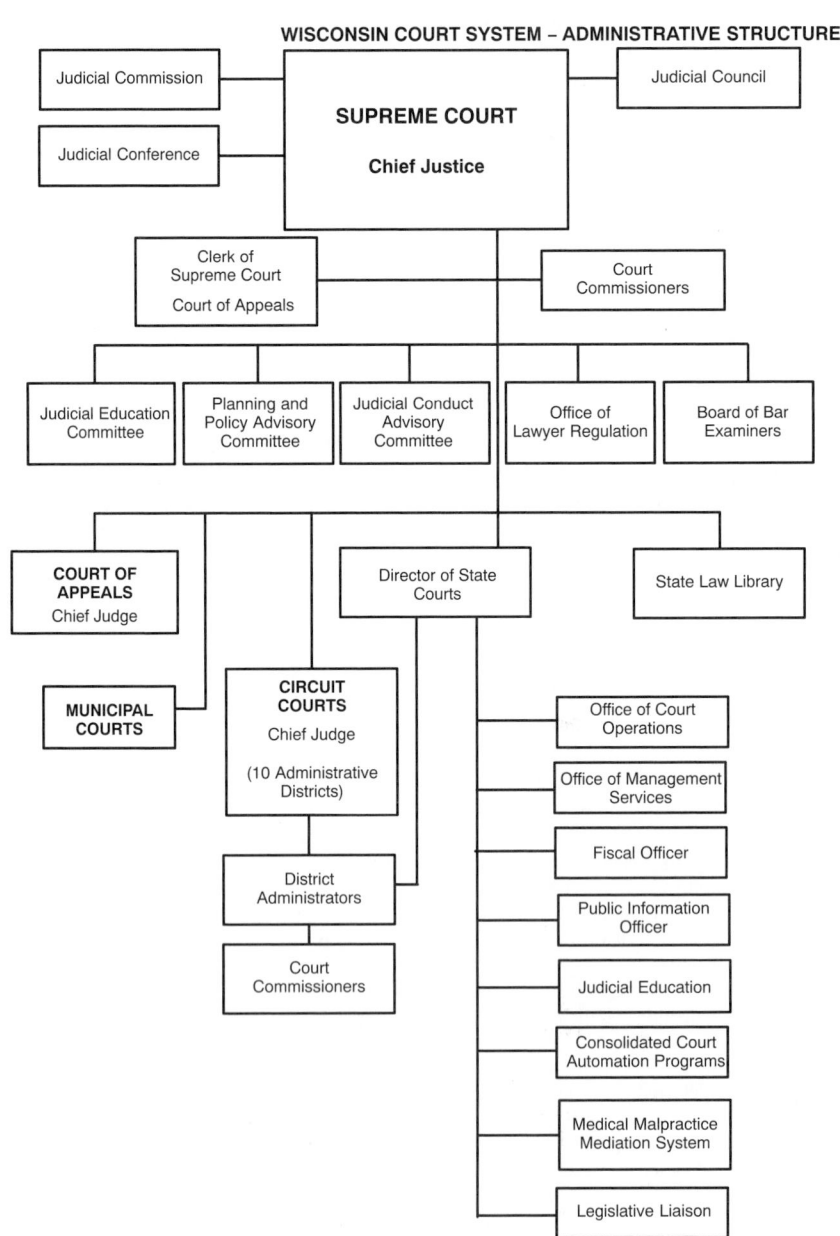

Associated Unit: State Bar of Wisconsin

COURT OF APPEALS

Judges: District I:	Patricia S. Curley (2008)
	Ralph Adam Fine (2006)
	Joan F. Kessler (2010)
	Ted E. Wedemeyer, Jr.* (2009)
District II:	Daniel P. Anderson* (2007)
	Richard S. Brown (2006)
	Neal P. Nettesheim (2008)
	Harry G. Snyder (2010)
District III:	R. Thomas Cane** (2007)
	Michael W. Hoover* (2009)
	Gregory Peterson (2011)
District IV:	David G. Deininger* (2009)
	Charles P. Dykman (2010)
	Paul B. Higginbotham (2011)
	Paul Lundsten (2007)
	Margaret J. Vergeront (2006)

Note: *indicates the presiding judge of the district. **indicates chief judge of the Court of Appeals. The judges' current terms expire on July 31 of the year shown.

Court of Appeals Clerk: Cornelia G. Clark, P.O. Box 1688, Madison 53701-1688; Location: 110 East Main Street, Suite 215, Madison, 266-1880, Fax: 267-0640.

Staff Attorneys: 10 East Doty Street, 7th Floor, Madison 53703, 266-9320.

Internet Address: http://www.wicourts.gov/appeals

Number of Positions: 75.50.

Total Budget 2003-05: $16,434,200.

Constitutional Reference: Article VII, Section 5.

Statutory Reference: Chapter 752.

Organization: A constitutional amendment ratified on April 5, 1977, mandated the Court of Appeals, and Chapter 187, Laws of 1977, implemented the amendment. The court consists of 16 judges serving in 4 districts (4 judges each in Districts I and II, 3 judges in District III, and 5 judges in District IV). The Wisconsin Supreme Court appoints a chief judge of the Court of Appeals to serve as administrative head of the court for a 3-year term, and the clerk of the supreme court serves as the clerk for the court.

Appellate judges are elected for 6-year terms in the nonpartisan April election and begin their terms of office on the following August 1. They must reside in the district from which they are chosen. Only one Court of Appeals judge may be elected in a district in any one year. The authorized salary for appeals court judges for fiscal year 2004-05 is $116,865.

Functions: The Court of Appeals has both appellate and supervisory jurisdiction, as well as original jurisdiction to issue prerogative writs. The final judgments and orders of a circuit court may be appealed to the Court of Appeals as a matter of right. Other judgments or orders may be appealed upon leave of the appellate court.

The court usually sits as a 3-judge panel to dispose of cases on their merits. However, a single judge may decide certain categories of cases, including juvenile cases; small claims; municipal ordinance and traffic violations; and mental health and misdemeanor cases. No testimony is taken in the appellate court. The court relies on the trial court record and written briefs in deciding a case, and it prescreens all cases to determine whether oral argument is needed. Both oral argument and "briefs only" cases are placed on a regularly issued calendar. The court gives criminal cases preference on the calendar when it is possible to do so without undue delay of civil cases. Staff attorneys, secretaries, and law clerks assist the judges.

Decisions of the appellate court are delivered in writing, and the court's publication committee determines which decisions will be published in the *Wisconsin Reports*. Only published opinions have precedential value and may be cited as controlling law in Wisconsin.

District I: 633 West Wisconsin Avenue, Suite 1400, Milwaukee 53203-1908. Telephone: (414) 227-4680.

District II: 2727 North Grandview Boulevard, Suite 300, Waukesha 53188-1672. Telephone: (262) 521-5230.

District III: 2100 Stewart Avenue, Suite 310, Wausau 54401. Telephone: (715) 848-1421.

District IV: 10 East Doty Street, Suite 700, Madison 53703-3397. Telephone: (608) 266-9250.

CIRCUIT COURTS

District 1: Milwaukee County Courthouse, 901 North 9th Street, Room 609, Milwaukee 53233-1425. Telephone: (414) 278-5113; Fax: (414) 223-1264.

Chief Judge: MICHAEL P. SULLIVAN[1].

Administrator: BRUCE HARVEY.

District 2: Racine County Courthouse, 730 Wisconsin Avenue, Racine 53403-1274. Telephone: (262) 636-3133; Fax: (262) 636-3437.

Chief Judge: GERALD P. PTACEK.

Administrator: KERRY CONNELLY.

District 3: Waukesha County Courthouse, 515 West Moreland Boulevard, Room 359, Waukesha 53188-2428. Telephone: (262) 548-7209; Fax: (262) 548-7815.

Chief Judge: KATHRYN W. FOSTER.

Administrator: MICHAEL NEIMON.

District 4: 315 Algoma Boulevard, Suite 102, Oshkosh 54901-4773. Telephone: (920) 424-0028; Fax: (920) 424-0096.

Chief Judge: L. EDWARD STENGEL.

Administrator: JERRY LANG.

District 5: City-County Building, Room 319, Madison 53709-0001. Telephone: 267-8820; Fax: 267-4151.

Chief Judge: MICHAEL N. NOWAKOWSKI.

Administrator: GAIL RICHARDSON.

District 6: 2957 Church Street, Suite B, Stevens Point 54481-5210. Telephone: (715) 345-5295; Fax: (715) 345-5297.

Chief Judge: JAMES EVENSON.

Administrator: STEVE SEMMANN.

District 7: La Crosse County Law Enforcement Center, 333 Vine Street, Room 3504, La Crosse 54601-3296. Telephone: (608) 785-9546; Fax: (608) 785-5530.

Chief Judge: MICHAEL J. ROSBOROUGH.

Administrator: PATRICK BRUMMOND.

District 8: 414 East Walnut Street, Suite 221, Green Bay 54301-5020. Telephone: (920) 448-4281; Fax: (920) 448-4336.

Chief Judge: JOSEPH M. TROY.

Administrator: KATHLEEN MURPHY.

District 9: 2100 Stewart Avenue, Suite 310, Wausau 54401. Telephone: (715) 842-3872; Fax: (715) 845-4523.

Chief Judge: DOROTHY BAIN.

Administrator: SCOTT JOHNSON.

District 10: 405 South Barstow Street, Suite C, Eau Claire 54701-3606.
Telephone: (715) 839-4826; Fax: (715) 839-4891.
 Chief Judge: EDWARD BRUNNER[2].
 Administrator: GREGG MOORE.
Internet Address: http://www.wicourts.gov/circuit
State-Funded Positions: 511.00.
Total Budget 2003-05: $156,955,500.
Constitutional References: Article VII, Sections 2, 6-11, and 13.
Statutory Reference: Chapter 753.

---

[1]Kitty Brennan designated by the supreme court to become chief judge on August 1, 2005.
[2]Benjamin Proctor designated by the supreme court to become chief judge on August 1, 2005.

Responsibility: The circuit court is the trial court of general jurisdiction in Wisconsin. It has original jurisdiction in both civil and criminal matters unless exclusive jurisdiction is given to another court. It also reviews state agency decisions and hears appeals from municipal courts. Jury trials are conducted only in circuit courts.

The constitution requires that a circuit be bounded by county lines. As a result, each circuit consists of a single county, except for 3 two-county circuits (Buffalo-Pepin, Florence-Forest, and Menominee-Shawano). Where judicial caseloads are heavy, a circuit may have several branches, each with an elected judge. Statewide, 39 of the state's 69 judicial circuits had multiple branches as of June 30, 2005, for a total of 241 circuit judgeships.

Organization: Circuit judges, who serve 6-year terms, are elected on a nonpartisan basis in the county in which they serve in the April election and take office the following August 1. The governor may fill circuit court vacancies by appointment, and the appointees serve until a successor is elected. The authorized salary for circuit court judges for fiscal year 2004-05 is $110,250. The state pays the salaries of circuit judges and court reporters. It also covers some of the expenses for interpreters, guardians ad litem, judicial assistants, court-appointed witnesses, and jury per diems. Counties bear the remaining expenses for operating the circuit courts.

 Administrative Districts. Circuit courts are divided into 10 administrative districts, each supervised by a chief judge, appointed by the supreme court from the district's circuit judges. A judge usually cannot serve more than 3 successive 2-year terms as chief judge. The chief judge has authority to assign judges, manage caseflow, supervise personnel, and conduct financial planning.

The chief judge in each district appoints a district court administrator from a list of candidates supplied by the director of state courts. The administrator manages the nonjudicial business of the district at the direction of the chief judge.

 Circuit Court Commissioners are appointed by the circuit court to assist the court, and they must be attorneys licensed to practice law in Wisconsin. They may be authorized by the court to conduct various civil, criminal, family, small claims, juvenile, and probate court proceedings. Their duties include issuing summonses, arrest warrants, or search warrants; conducting initial appearances; setting bail; conducting preliminary examinations and arraignments; imposing monetary penalties in certain traffic cases; conducting certain family, juvenile, and small claims court proceedings; hearing petitions for mental commitments; and conducting uncontested probate proceedings. On their own authority, court commissioners may perform marriages, administer oaths, take depositions, and issue subpoenas and certain writs.

The statutes require Milwaukee County to have full-time family, small claims, and probate court commissioners. All other counties must have a family court commissioner, and they may employ other full- or part-time court commissioners as deemed necessary.

JUDGES OF CIRCUIT COURT
June 30, 2005

Circuits[1]	Court Location	Judges	Term Expires July 31
Adams	Friendship	Charles A. Pollex	2009
Ashland	Ashland	Robert E. Eaton	2006
Barron			
Branch 1	Barron	James C. Babler	2010
Branch 2	Barron	Edward R. Brunner	2006
Bayfield	Washburn	John P. Anderson	2009
Brown			2009
Branch 1	Green Bay	Donald R. Zuidmulder	2006
Branch 2	Green Bay	Mark Warpinski	2010
Branch 3	Green Bay	Susan Bischel	2008
Branch 4	Green Bay	Kendall M. Kelley	2005
Branch 5	Green Bay	Peter J. Naze[2]	2009
Branch 6	Green Bay	John D. McKay	2007
Branch 7	Green Bay	Richard J. Dietz	2009
Branch 8	Green Bay	William M. Atkinson	2006
Buffalo-Pepin	Alma	James Duvall[9]	2009
Burnett	Siren	Michael J. Gableman	2010
Calumet	Chilton	Donald A. Poppy	
Chippewa			2008
Branch 1	Chippewa Falls	Roderick A. Cameron	2007
Branch 2	Chippewa Falls	Thomas J. Sazama	2006
Clark	Neillsville	Jon M. Counsell	
Columbia			2009
Branch 1	Portage	Daniel S. George	2005
Branch 2	Portage	James O. Miller[2]	2009
Branch 3	Portage	Richard L. Rehm	2007
Crawford	Prairie du Chien	Michael T. Kirchman	
Dane			2005
Branch 1	Madison	Robert A. DeChambeau[2]	2005
Branch 2	Madison	Maryann Sumi[2]	2006
Branch 3	Madison	John C. Albert	2010
Branch 4	Madison	Steven D. Ebert	2007
Branch 5	Madison	Diane M. Nicks	2009
Branch 6	Madison	Shelley J. Gaylord	2009
Branch 7	Madison	Moria G. Krueger	2006
Branch 8	Madison	Patrick J. Fiedler	2005
Branch 9	Madison	Richard Niess[2]	2009
Branch 10	Madison	Angela B. Bartell	2009
Branch 11	Madison	Daniel R. Moeser	2006
Branch 12	Madison	David T. Flanagan	2009
Branch 13	Madison	Michael W. Nowakowski	2010
Branch 14	Madison	C. William Foust	2010
Branch 15	Madison	Stuart A. Schwartz	2010
Branch 16	Madison	Sarah B. O'Brien	2010
Branch 17	Madison	James L. Martin	
Dodge			2008
Branch 1	Juneau	Daniel W. Klossner	2007
Branch 2	Juneau	John R. Storck	2007
Branch 3	Juneau	Andrew P. Bissonnette	
Door			2006
Branch 1	Sturgeon Bay	D. Todd Ehlers	2006
Branch 2	Sturgeon Bay	Peter C. Diltz	
Douglas			2009
Branch 1	Superior	Michael T. Lucci	2007
Branch 2	Superior	George L. Glonek	
Dunn			2010
Branch 1	Menomonie	William C. Stewart, Jr.	2009
Branch 2	Menomonie	Rod Smeltzer	
Eau Claire			2006
Branch 1	Eau Claire	Lisa Stark	2005
Branch 2	Eau Claire	Eric J. Wahl[2]	2006
Branch 3	Eau Claire	William M. Gabler	2006
Branch 4	Eau Claire	Benjamin D. Proctor	2006
Branch 5	Eau Claire	Paul J. Lenz	
Florence (see *Forest-Florence*)			
Fond du Lac			2008
Branch 1	Fond du Lac	Dale L. English	2010
Branch 2	Fond du Lac	Peter L. Grimm	2009
Branch 3	Fond du Lac	Richard J. Nuss	2010
Branch 4	Fond du Lac	Steven W. Weinke	2005
Branch 5	Fond du Lac	Robert J. Wirtz[2]	2008
Forest-Florence	Crandon	Robert A. Kennedy, Jr.	
Grant			2005
Branch 1	Lancaster	Robert P. VandeHey[2]	2009
Branch 2	Lancaster	George S. Curry	2009
Green	Monroe	James R. Beer	2005
Green Lake	Green Lake	William M. McMonigal[2]	2010
Iowa	Dodgeville	William D. Dyke	2005
Iron	Hurley	Patrick John Madden[2]	2008
Jackson	Black River Falls	Gerald W. Laabs	

JUDGES OF CIRCUIT COURT
June 30, 2005–Continued

Circuits[1]	Court Location	Judges	Term Expires July 31
Jefferson			
Branch 1	Jefferson	John M. Ullsvik	2009
Branch 2	Jefferson	William F. Hue	2007
Branch 3	Jefferson	Jacqueline R. Erwin	2009
Branch 4	Jefferson	Randy R. Koschnick[2]	2005
Juneau	Mauston	John Pier Roemer	2010
Kenosha			
Branch 1	Kenosha	David Mark Bastianelli	2009
Branch 2	Kenosha	Barbara A. Kluka	2007
Branch 3	Kenosha	Bruce E. Schroeder	2008
Branch 4	Kenosha	Michael S. Fisher[3]	2005
Branch 5	Kenosha	Wilbur W. Warren III	2009
Branch 6	Kenosha	Mary K. Wagner	2009
Branch 7	Kenosha	S. Michael Wilk	2006
Kewaunee	Kewaunee	Dennis J. Mleziva	2010
La Crosse			
Branch 1	La Crosse	Ramona A. Gonzalez	2007
Branch 2	La Crosse	Michael J. Mulroy	2007
Branch 3	La Crosse	Dennis G. Montabon	2009
Branch 4	La Crosse	John J. Perlich	2009
Branch 5	La Crosse	Dale T. Pasell[2]	2005
Lafayette	Darlington	William D. Johnston	2009
Langlade	Antigo	James P. Jansen[4]	2005
Lincoln			
Branch 1	Merrill	Jay R. Tlusty	2010
Branch 2	Merrill	Glenn H. Hartley[2]	2005
Manitowoc			
Branch 1	Manitowoc	Patrick L. Willis	2010
Branch 2	Manitowoc	Darryl W. Deets	2007
Branch 3	Manitowoc	Fred H. Hazlewood[5]	2005
Marathon			
Branch 1	Wausau	Dorothy L. Bain	2010
Branch 2	Wausau	Gregory Huber	2010
Branch 3	Wausau	Vincent K. Howard	2008
Branch 4	Wausau	Gregory Grau	2007
Branch 5	Wausau	Patrick Brady[2]	2005
Marinette			
Branch 1	Marinette	David G. Miron	2008
Branch 2	Marinette	Tim A. Duket	2008
Marquette	Montello	Richard O. Wright	2007
Menominee (see *Shawano-Menominee*)			
Milwaukee			
Branch 1	Milwaukee	Maxine Aldridge White[2]	2005
Branch 2	Milwaukee	M. Joseph Donald	2009
Branch 3	Milwaukee	Clare L. Fiorenza	2009
Branch 4	Milwaukee	Mel Flanagan	2006
Branch 5	Milwaukee	Mary Kuhnmuench	2010
Branch 6	Milwaukee	Kitty K. Brennan	2006
Branch 7	Milwaukee	Jean W. DiMotto	2009
Branch 8	Milwaukee	William Sosnay	2006
Branch 9	Milwaukee	Paul R. Van Grunsven[2]	2005
Branch 10	Milwaukee	Timothy G. Dugan[2]	2005
Branch 11	Milwaukee	Dominic S. Amato	2007
Branch 12	Milwaukee	David L. Borowski	2009
Branch 13	Milwaukee	Mary Triggiano[2]	2005
Branch 14	Milwaukee	Christopher R. Foley	2010
Branch 15	Milwaukee	Michael B. Brennan	2007
Branch 16	Milwaukee	Michael J. Dwyer	2009
Branch 17	Milwaukee	Francis Wasielewski	2008
Branch 18	Milwaukee	Patricia D. McMahon[2]	2005
Branch 19	Milwaukee	John E. McCormick[6]	2005
Branch 20	Milwaukee	Dennis P. Moroney	2006
Branch 21	Milwaukee	William Brash	2008
Branch 22	Milwaukee	Timothy M. Witkowiak	2009
Branch 23	Milwaukee	Elsa C. Lamelas	2006
Branch 24	Milwaukee	Charles F. Kahn	2010
Branch 25	Milwaukee	John A. Franke[2]	2005
Branch 26	Milwaukee	Michael P. Sullivan	2008
Branch 27	Milwaukee	Kevin E. Martens	2008
Branch 28	Milwaukee	Thomas R. Cooper	2006
Branch 29	Milwaukee	Richard J. Sankovitz	2009
Branch 30	Milwaukee	Jeffrey A. Conen	2009
Branch 31	Milwaukee	Daniel A. Noonan	2008
Branch 32	Milwaukee	Michael D. Guolee	2008
Branch 33	Milwaukee	Carl Ashley[2]	2005
Branch 34	Milwaukee	Glen H. Yamahiro	2010
Branch 35	Milwaukee	Frederick C. Rosa[2]	2005
Branch 36	Milwaukee	Jeffrey A. Kremers[2]	2005
Branch 37	Milwaukee	Karen Christenson	2010
Branch 38	Milwaukee	Jeffrey A. Wagner	2006
Branch 39	Milwaukee	Michael G. Malmstadt	2006
Branch 40	Milwaukee	Joseph R. Wall	2007

JUDGES OF CIRCUIT COURT
June 30, 2005–Continued

Circuits[1]	Court Location	Judges	Term Expires July 31
Milwaukee (continued)			
Branch 41	Milwaukee	John J. DiMotto	2008
Branch 42	Milwaukee	David A. Hansher	2009
Branch 43	Milwaukee	Marshall Murray	2006
Branch 44	Milwaukee	Daniel L. Konkol	2010
Branch 45	Milwaukee	Thomas P. Donegan	2010
Branch 46	Milwaukee	Bonnie L. Gordon	2006
Branch 47	Milwaukee	John Siefert[2]	2005
Monroe			
Branch 1	Sparta	Steven L. Abbott	2007
Branch 2	Sparta	Michael J. McAlpine	2010
Oconto			
Branch 1	Oconto	Larry L. Jeske[7]	2005
Branch 2	Oconto	Richard D. Delforge	2010
Oneida			
Branch 1	Rhinelander	Robert E. Kinney	2008
Branch 2	Rhinelander	Mark A. Mangerson	2006
Outagamie			
Branch 1	Appleton	Brad Priebe[8,9]	2005
Branch 2	Appleton	Dennis C. Luebke	2009
Branch 3	Appleton	Joseph M. Troy[2]	2005
Branch 4	Appleton	Harold V. Froehlich	2006
Branch 5	Appleton	Michael W. Gage	2009
Branch 6	Appleton	Dee R. Dyer	2006
Branch 7	Appleton	John A. Des Jardins	2006
Ozaukee			
Branch 1	Port Washington	Paul V. Malloy	2009
Branch 2	Port Washington	Thomas R. Wolfgram	2007
Branch 3	Port Washington	Joseph D. McCormack	2009
Pepin (see *Buffalo-Pepin*)			
Pierce	Ellsworth	Robert W. Wing	2010
Polk			
Branch 1	Balsam Lake	Molly E. GaleWyrick	2008
Branch 2	Balsam Lake	Robert H. Rasmussen	2009
Portage			
Branch 1	Stevens Point	Frederic W. Fleishauer[2]	2005
Branch 2	Stevens Point	John V. Finn	2007
Branch 3	Stevens Point	Thomas T. Flugaur	2006
Price	Phillips	Douglas T. Fox	2008
Racine			
Branch 1	Racine	Gerald P. Ptacek	2007
Branch 2	Racine	Stephen A. Simanek	2010
Branch 3	Racine	Emily S. Mueller[2]	2005
Branch 4	Racine	John S. Jude	2010
Branch 5	Racine	Dennis J. Barry[2]	2005
Branch 6	Racine	Wayne J. Marik	2009
Branch 7	Racine	Charles H. Constantine	2008
Branch 8	Racine	Faye M. Flancher	2009
Branch 9	Racine	Allan "Pat" B. Torhorst	2009
Branch 10	Racine	Richard J. Kreul	2006
Richland	Richland Center	Edward E. Leineweber	2009
Rock			
Branch 1	Janesville	James P. Daley	2008
Branch 2	Janesville	R. Alan Bates	2010
Branch 3	Janesville	Michael J. Byron	2010
Branch 4	Beloit	Daniel Dillon	2007
Branch 5	Beloit	John W. Roethe	2009
Branch 6	Janesville	Richard T. Werner	2009
Branch 7	Beloit	James E. Welker	2006
Rusk	Ladysmith	Frederick A. Henderson	2010
St. Croix			
Branch 1	Hudson	Eric J. Lundell	2008
Branch 2	Hudson	Edward F. Vlack	2007
Branch 3	Hudson	Scott R. Needham	2006
Sauk			
Branch 1	Baraboo	Patrick J. Taggart	2006
Branch 2	Baraboo	James Evenson	2010
Branch 3	Baraboo	Guy Reynolds	2006
Sawyer	Hayward	Norman L. Yackel	2009
Shawano-Menominee			
Branch 1	Shawano	James R. Habeck	2008
Branch 2	Shawano	Thomas G. Grover	2007
Sheboygan			
Branch 1	Sheboygan	L. Edward Stengel	2009
Branch 2	Sheboygan	Timothy M. Van Akkeren	2007
Branch 3	Sheboygan	Gary J. Langhoff[2]	2005
Branch 4	Sheboygan	Terence T. Bourke	2009
Branch 5	Sheboygan	James J. Bolgert	2006
Taylor	Medford	Gary Lee Carlson	2010
Trempealeau	Whitehall	John A. Damon	2007
Vernon	Viroqua	Michael J. Rosborough[2]	2005
Vilas	Eagle River	Neal A. Nielsen	2010

JUDGES OF CIRCUIT COURT
June 30, 2005–Continued

Circuits[1]	Court Location	Judges	Term Expires July 31
Walworth			
Branch 1	Elkhorn	Robert J. Kennedy	
Branch 2	Elkhorn	James L. Carlson	2006
Branch 3	Elkhorn	John R. Race	2010
Branch 4	Elkhorn	Michael S. Gibbs	2009
Washburn	Shell Lake	Eugene D. Harrington	2010
Washington			2009
Branch 1	West Bend	Patrick J. Faragher	
Branch 2	West Bend	Annette Kingsland Ziegler	2007
Branch 3	West Bend	David C. Resheske	2009
Branch 4	West Bend	Andrew Gonring	2006
Waukesha			2006
Branch 1	Waukesha	Michael D. Bohren	
Branch 2	Waukesha	Mark S. Gempeler	2007
Branch 3	Waukesha	Ralph M. Ramirez[2]	2008
Branch 4	Waukesha	Paul F. Reilly	2005
Branch 5	Waukesha	Lee Sherman Dreyfus, Jr.	2009
Branch 6	Waukesha	Patrick C. Haughney	2008
Branch 7	Waukesha	J. Mac Davis	2008
Branch 8	Waukesha	James R. Kieffer	2009
Branch 9	Waukesha	Donald J. Hassin, Jr.	2009
Branch 10	Waukesha	Linda Van De Water	2009
Branch 11	Waukesha	Robert G. Mawdsley	2009
Branch 12	Waukesha	Kathryn W. Foster	2006
Waupaca			2006
Branch 1	Waupaca	Philip M. Kirk[2]	
Branch 2	Waupaca	John P. Hoffmann	2005
Branch 3	Waupaca	Raymond Huber	2010
Waushara	Wautoma	Lewis R. Murach[10]	2006
Winnebago			2005
Branch 1	Oshkosh	Thomas J. Gritton	
Branch 2	Oshkosh	Scott C. Woldt[2,9]	2006
Branch 3	Oshkosh	Barbara Hart Key	2005
Branch 4	Oshkosh	Robert A. Hawley	2010
Branch 5	Oshkosh	William H. Carver	2006
Branch 6	Oshkosh	Bruce K. Schmidt	2010
Wood			2009
Branch 1	Wisconsin Rapids	Gregory J. Potter	
Branch 2	Wisconsin Rapids	James M. Mason	2008
Branch 3	Wisconsin Rapids	Edward F. Zappen, Jr.	2010
			2009

[1]Circuits are comprised of one county each, except for Buffalo-Pepin, Forest-Florence, and Shawano-Menominee. The current annual salary for all circuit court judges is $110,040. Salaries could change as of August 1, 2005, when the circuit court judges commence new terms.

[2]Reelected on April 1, 2005, for a 6-year term to commence on August 1, 2005.
[3]Anthony Milisauskas was newly elected on April 1, 2005, for a 6-year term to commence on August 1, 2005.
[4]Fred W. Kawalski was newly elected on April 1, 2005, for a 6-year term to commence on August 1, 2005.
[5]Jerome L. Fox was newly elected on April 1, 2005, for a 6-year term to commence on August 1, 2005.
[6]Dennis R. Cimpl was newly elected on April 1, 2005, for a 6-year term to commence on August 1, 2005.
[7]Michael T. Judge was newly elected on April 1, 2005, for a 6-year term to commence on August 1, 2005.
[8]Mark McGinnis was newly elected on April 1, 2005, for a 6-year term to commence on August 1, 2005.
[9]Appointed by governor.
[10]Guy Dutcher was newly elected on April 1, 2005, for a 6-year term to commence on August 1, 2005.
Sources: *2003-2004 Wisconsin Statutes;* State Elections Board, departmental data, May 2005; Director of State Courts, departmental data, April 2005; governor's appointment notices.

MUNICIPAL COURTS

Constitutional References: Article VII, Sections 2 and 14.

Statutory References: Chapters 755 and 800.

Internet Address: http://www.wicourts.gov/municipal

Responsibility: The Wisconsin Legislature authorizes cities, villages, and towns to establish municipal courts to exercise jurisdiction over municipal ordinance violations that have monetary penalties. In addition, the Wisconsin Supreme Court ruled in 1991 (*City of Milwaukee v. Wroten,* 160 Wis. 2d 107) that municipal courts have authority to rule on the constitutionality of municipal ordinances.

As of May 1, 2005, there were 238 municipal courts with 240 municipal judges. Courts may have multiple branches; the City of Milwaukee's municipal court, for example, has 3 branches. (Milwaukee County, which is the only county authorized to appoint municipal court commissioners, had 4 part-time commissioners as of May 2005.) Two or more municipalities may agree to form a joint court, and there are 30 joint courts, serving up to 10 municipalities each. Besides Milwaukee, Madison is the only city with a full-time municipal court.

Upon convicting a defendant, the municipal court may order payment of a forfeiture plus costs and assessments, or, if the defendant agrees, it may require community service in lieu of a forfeiture. In general, municipal courts may also order restitution up to $4,000. Where local ordinances conform to state drunk driving laws, a municipal judge may suspend or revoke a driver's license.

If a defendant fails to pay a forfeiture or make restitution, the municipal court may suspend the driver's license or commit the defendant to jail. Municipal court decisions may be appealed to the circuit court of the county where the offense occurred.

Organization: Municipal judges are elected at the nonpartisan April election and take office May 1. The local governing body fixes the term of office at 2 to 4 years and determines the position's salary. There is no state requirement that the office be filled by an attorney, but a municipality may enact such a qualification by ordinance.

If a municipal judge is ill, disqualified, or unavailable, the chief judge of the judicial administrative district containing the municipality may transfer the case to another municipal judge in the district. If none is available, the case will be heard in circuit court.

History: Chapter 276, Laws of 1967, authorized cities, villages, and towns to establish municipal courts after the forerunner of municipal courts (the office of the justice of the peace) was eliminated by a constitutional amendment, ratified in April 1966. A constitutional amendment ratified in April 1977, which reorganized the state's court system, officially granted the legislature the power to authorize municipal courts.

STATEWIDE JUDICIAL AGENCIES

A number of statewide administrative and support agencies have been created by supreme court order or legislative enactment to assist the Wisconsin Supreme Court in its supervision of the Wisconsin judicial system.

DIRECTOR OF STATE COURTS

Director of State Courts: A. JOHN VOELKER, 266-6828, john.voelker@

Deputy Director for Court Operations: SHERYL GERVASI, 266-3121, sheryl.gervasi@

Deputy Director for Management Services: PAM RADLOFF, 266-8914, pam.radloff@

Consolidated Court Automation Programs: JEAN BOUSQUET, *director,* 267-0678, jean.bousquet@

Fiscal Officer: BRIAN LAMPRECH, 266-6865, brian.lamprech@

Judicial Education: DAVID H. HASS, *director,* 266-7807, david.hass@

Medical Malpractice Mediation System: RANDY SPROULE, *director,* 266-7711, randy.sproule@

Public Information Officer: AMANDA TODD, 264-6256, amanda.todd@

Legislative Liaison: NANCY ROTTIER, 267-9733, nancy.rottier@

Address e-mail by combining the user ID and the state extender: userid**@wicourts.gov**

Mailing Address: Director of State Courts: P.O. Box 1688, Madison 53701-1688; Staff: 110 East Main Street, Madison 53703.

Location: Director of State Courts: Room 16 East, State Capitol, Madison; Staff: 110 East Main Street, Madison.

Fax: 267-0980.

Internet Address: http://www.wicourts.gov

Number of Employees: 124.25.

Total Budget 2003-05: $30,572,800.

References: Wisconsin Statutes, Chapter 655, Subchapter VI, and Section 758.19; Supreme Court Rules 70.01-70.08.

Responsibility: The Director of State Courts administers the nonjudicial business of the Wisconsin court system and informs the chief justice and the supreme court about the status of judicial business. The director is responsible for supervising state-level court personnel; developing the court system's budget; and directing the courts' work on legislation, public information, and information systems. This office also controls expenditures; allocates space and equipment; supervises judicial education, interdistrict assignment of active and reserve judges, and planning and research; and administers the medical malpractice mediation system.

The director is appointed by the supreme court from outside the classified service. The position was created by the supreme court in orders, dated October 30, 1978, and February 19, 1979. It replaced the administrative director of courts, which had been created by Chapter 261, Laws of 1961.

STATE LAW LIBRARY

State Law Librarian: JANE COLWIN, 261-2340, jane.colwin@wicourts.gov

Deputy Law Librarian: JULIE TESSMER, 261-7557, julie.tessmer@wicourts.gov

Mailing Address: P.O. Box 7881, Madison 53707-7881.

Location: 120 Martin Luther King, Jr. Blvd., 2nd Floor, Madison 53703.

Telephones: General Information and Circulation: 266-1600; Reference Assistance: 267-9696; Toll-free: (800) 322-9755.

Fax: 267-2319.

Internet Address: http://wsll.state.wi.us
Reference E-mail Address: wsll.ref@wicourts.gov
Publications: *WSLL @ Your Service* (e-newsletter) at http://wsll.state.wi.us/news.html
Number of Employees: 16.50.
Total Budget 2003-05: $5,172,600.
References: Wisconsin Statutes, Section 758.01; Supreme Court Rule 82.01.

Responsibility: The State Law Library is a public library open to all citizens of Wisconsin. It serves as the primary legal resource center for the Wisconsin Supreme Court and Court of Appeals, the Department of Justice, the Wisconsin Legislature, the Office of the Governor, executive agencies, and members of the State Bar of Wisconsin. The library is administered by the supreme court, which appoints the library staff and determines the rules governing library use. The library acts as a consultant and resource for county law libraries throughout the state. Milwaukee County and Dane County contract with the State Law Library for management and operation of their courthouse libraries (the Milwaukee Legal Resource Center and the Dane County Law Library).

The library's 150,000-volume collection features session laws, statutory codes, court reports, administrative rules, legal indexes, and case law digests of the U.S. government, all 50 states and U.S. territories. It also includes selected documents of the federal government, legal and bar periodicals, legal treatises, and legal encyclopedias. The library also offers reference, basic legal research, and document delivery services. The collection circulates to judges, attorneys, legislators, and government personnel.

OFFICE OF LAWYER REGULATION

Board of Administrative Oversight: W.H. LEVIT, JR. (lawyer), *chairperson;* ANN USTAD SMITH (lawyer), *vice chairperson;* JAMES W. MOHR, JR., SCOTT ROBERTS, THOMAS S. SLEIK, DEBORAH M. SMITH, TERRY ROSE, vacancy (lawyers); CLAIRE FOWLER, KRISTA L. GINGER, T. JAMES KENNEDY, MICHAEL J. O'NEILL (nonlawyers). (All members are appointed by the supreme court.)

Preliminary Review Committee: JAMES D. WICKHEM (lawyer), *chairperson;* JAMES D. FRIEDMAN (lawyer), *vice chairperson;* MICHAEL ANDERSON, WAYNE A. ARNOLD, THOMAS W. BERTZ, JOHN R. DAWSON, KARRI L. FRITZ-KLAUS, BERNARD T. McCARTAN, FRANK D. REMINGTON (lawyers); MICHAEL S. ARIENS, STEVEN K. GJERDE, JOAN GREENDEER-LEE, M. TAMBURA OMOIELE, THOMAS RADMER (nonlawyers). (All members are appointed by the supreme court.)

Special Preliminary Review Panel: KARA M. BURGOS, LORI S. KORNBLUM, JAMES G. POUROS, JANE C. SCHLICHT (lawyers); DENNIS B. GORDER, DEAN HELSTAD, DARLO WENTZ (nonlawyers). (All members are appointed by the supreme court.)

Sixteen District Committees (all members are appointed by the supreme court):

District 1 Committee (serves Jefferson, Kenosha, and Walworth Counties): FREDERICK ZIEVERS (lawyer), *chairperson;* MICHAEL D. BRENNAN, ROBERT I. DUMEZ, PAUL GAGLIARDI, JOHN P. HIGGINS, CHRISTOPHER W. ROSE, MATTHEW S. VIGNALI (lawyers); PAUL G. ALDIGE, JOHN G. BRAIG, CHERYL FRIEDL, GAIL GENTZ (nonlawyers).

District 2 Committee (serves Milwaukee County): NANCY M. KENNEDY (lawyer), *chairperson;* MICHAEL STEINLE (lawyer), *vice chairperson;* KATHRYN BACH, PATRICIA KLING BALLMAN, EMILE BANKS, THOMAS A. CABUSH, DAN CONLEY, MARGARDETTE M. DEMET, JOHN DeSTEFANIS, ROBIN DORMAN, IRVING D. GAINES, LORI GENDELMAN, JOHN GERMANOTTA, MARIO GONZALES, JAMES W. GREER, EDWARD A. HANNAN, THEODORE HODAN, LAWRENCE P. KAHN, KENAN J. KERSTEN, R. JEFFREY KRILL, CATHERINE LaFLEUR, ANN LAMPIRIS, CLAYTON L. RIDDLE, SHERYL A. ST. ORES, JO SWAMP, TIMOTHY S. TRECEK, KATHERINE WILLIAMS (lawyers); J. STEPHEN ANDERSON, NEILAND COHEN, DONALD G. DORO, PATRICK DOYLE, SHEL GENDELMAN, JEFFREY HANEWALL, JOHN HANLON, BARBARA J.

JANUSIAK, PETER J. MARIK, JOAN PRINCE, RICHARD SILBERMAN, VICTORIA L. TOLIVER, WILLIAM WARD (nonlawyers).

District 3 Committee (serves Fond du Lac, Green Lake, and Winnebago Counties): ALYSON ZIERDT (lawyer), *chairperson;* F. DAVID KRIZENESKY, DAVID J. SCHULTZ, JOHN B. SELSING, MARK T. SLATE, WILLIAM R. SLATE, STEVEN R. SORENSON, ALEXANDER L. ULLENBERG, JOHN S. ZARBANO (lawyers); RONALD A. DETJEN, JOHN FAIRHURST, SHARON MIKKELSEN, KAREN SCHNEIDER, ELLEN C. SORENSEN (nonlawyers).

District 4 Committee (serves Calumet, Door, Kewaunee, Manitowoc, and Sheboygan Counties): GARY BENDIX (lawyer), *chairperson;* THOMAS S. BURKE, RICHARD R. CRAMER, DAVID GASS, RALPH F. HERLACHE, MARK JINKINS, RANDALL J. NESBITT, JAMES UNGRODT (lawyers); ROBERT A. DOBBS, SUSAN M. MCANINCH, DENNIS MCINTOSH (nonlawyers).

District 5 Committee (serves Buffalo, Clark, Crawford, Jackson, La Crosse, Monroe, Pepin, Richland, Trempealeau, and Vernon Counties): JAMES G. CURTIS (lawyer), *chairperson;* MICHAEL C. ABLAN, JAMES P. CZAJKOWSKI, MARVIN H. DAVID, GLORIA L. DOYLE, RALPH OSBORNE, JR., GEORGE PARKE III, RICHARD A. RADCLIFFE, J. DAVID RICE, JON D. SEIFERT, FRANK R. VAZQUEZ (lawyers); KEITH A. JOHNSON, JACQUELINE A. JOHNSRUD, PAUL R. LORENZ, JOHN PARKYN, LINDA LEE SONDREAL (nonlawyers).

District 6 Committee (serves Waukesha County): GARY KUPHALL (lawyer), *chairperson;* MARK P. ANDRINGA, CHERYL A. GEMIGNANI, LANCE S. GRADY, ANTHONY J. MENTING, ROD W. ROGAHN, ROBYN A. SCHUCHARDT, WILLIAM A. SWENDSON (lawyers); DENNIS R. BLASIUS, JULIE DEYOUNG, CARLA FRIEDRICH, ROBERT V. PURTOCK, DENNIS M. WALLER (nonlawyers).

District 7 Committee (serves Adams, Columbia, Juneau, Marquette, Portage, Sauk, Waupaca, Waushara, and Wood Counties): MARC A. BICKFORD (lawyer), *chairperson;* GARY KRYSHAK, JEROME P. MERCER, JAMES J. NATWICK, LEON SCHMIDT, JR., JOHN E. SHANNON, JR. (lawyers); ELLEN M. DAHL, DOROTHY E. MANSAVAGE, DONALD STEIN, JAMES E. STRASSER (nonlawyers).

District 8 Committee (serves Dunn, Eau Claire, Pierce, and St. Croix Counties): DOUGLAS M. JOHNSON (lawyer), *chairperson;* TERRENCE GHERTY (lawyer), *vice chairperson;* ROBERT L. LOBERG, JANE E. LOKKEN, KEITH RODLI, JAMES D. RYBERG, BEVERLY WICKSTROM (lawyers); VIRGINIA COOMBS, DAVID CRONK, JOHN H. SCHULTE, KURT W. WOOD, JANE SMANDA ZELLER (nonlawyers).

District 9 Committee (serves Dane County): AMY R. SMITH (lawyer), *chairperson;* LEE R. ATTERBURY, WILLIAM F. BAUER, JANICE N. BENSKY, MARK F. BORNS, ANDREW CLARKOWSKI, BRUCE F. EHLKE, MAUREEN MCGLYNN FLANAGAN, PETER E. HANS, RICHARD B. JACOBSON, JAMES R. JANSEN, KAREN JULIAN, MARSHA MANSFIELD, RICH J. MUNDT, WILLIAM F. MUNDT, LAURI ROMAN, MEREDITH J. ROSS, BRUCE AL. SCHULTZ, THOMAS W. SHELLANDER, TODD G. SMITH, ALISON TENBRUGGENCATE (lawyers); NINA PETROVICH BARTELL, CHARLES A. BUNGE, DAVID CHARLES DIES, PAUL M. DOWNEY, R.C. HECHT, ROBERT C. HODGE, JUDITH A. MILLER, ELLEN PRITZKOW, RODNEY TAPP, DAVID G. UTLEY (nonlawyers).

District 10 Committee (serves Marinette, Menominee, Oconto, Outagamie, and Shawano Counties): JAMES N. MIRON (lawyer), *chairperson;* RICHARD THOMAS ELROD, GALE MATTISON, LAURA C. SMYTHE (lawyers); RAYMOND ZAGORASKI (nonlawyer).

District 11 Committee (serves Ashland, Barron, Bayfield, Burnett, Chippewa, Douglas, Iron, Polk, Price, Rusk, Sawyer, Taylor, and Washburn Counties): JOHN C. GRINDELL (lawyer), *chairperson;* JOSEPH CRAWFORD, GUY T. LUDVIGSON, FORREST O. MAKI, DANIEL F. SNYDER, KATHERINE M. STEWART (lawyers); JAMES CRANDELL, DIANE FJELSTAD, MARY ANN KING, MARGARET KOLBEK (nonlawyers).

District 12 Committee (serves Grant, Green, Iowa, Lafayette, and Rock Counties): MARGERY MEBANE TIBBETTS (lawyer), *chairperson;* CRAIG DAY, DAVID B. FEINGOLD, THOMAS H. GEYER, DERRICK A. GRUBB, WILLIAM T. HENDERSON, RAY JABLONSKI, GAYLE BRANAUGH JEBBIA, PETER KELLY, PATRICK K. MCDONALD, ERIC D. REINICKE (lawyers); DALE E. ANDERSON, RHONDA L. HARTWIG, DONALD C. HOLLOWAY, MICHAEL F. METZ, THERON E. PARSONS IV, GERALD PELISHEK, KATHLEEN J. ROELLI, JOHN SIMONSON, CLINTON A. WRUCK (nonlawyers).

District 13 Committee (serves Dodge, Ozaukee, and Washington Counties): GARY R. SCHMAUS (lawyer), *chairperson;* WILLIAM BUCHHOLZ (lawyer), *vice chairperson;* GERALD H. ANTOINE, PAUL DIMICK (lawyers); DEBORAH L. LUKOVICH, ALAN MARTENS, JOHN C. RALSTON (nonlawyers).

District 14 Committee (serves Brown County): SANDRA L. HUPFER (lawyer), *chairperson;* CYNTHIA CAINE TRELEVEN (lawyer), *vice chairperson;* LAURA J. BECK, TERRY GERBERS, MARK A. PENNOW, BETH RAHMIG PLESS, SUSAN J. REIGEL, FRANK S. WOCHOS (lawyers); GREGORY L. GRAF, GEORGE KREMPIN, GERALD C. LORITZ, KIM E. NIELSEN (nonlawyers).

District 15 Committee (serves Racine County): JOSEPH J. MURATORE, JR. (lawyer), *chairperson;* JOHN BARRY STUTT (lawyer), *vice chairperson;* TIMOTHY D. BOYLE, THOMAS M. DEVINE, SCOTT W. FRENCH, SALLY HOELZEL, MICHAEL J. KELLY, MARK LUKOFF, MARK F. NIELSEN (lawyers); GILBERT G. BAUMANN, JOHN P. CRIMMINGS, CONNIE CROWDER, RAYMOND G. FEEST (nonlawyers).

District 16 Committee (serves Forest, Florence, Langlade, Lincoln, Marathon, Oneida, and Vilas Counties): JOHN DANNER (lawyer), *chairperson;* SARAH L. RUFFI (lawyer), *vice chairperson;* DAVID J. CONDON, DAWN R. LEMKE, WILLIAM D. MANSELL, CHRISTINE R.H. OLSEN, JEROME TLUSTY, ROBERT W. ZIMMERMAN (lawyers); THOMAS E. BURG, JUDY A. FRYMARK, GERALD GIBSON, ARNO WM. HAERING, MICHAEL LAMBRECHT, TOM LONSDORF (nonlawyers).

Office of Lawyer Regulation: KEITH L. SELLEN, *director,* Keith.Sellen@wicourts.gov; JOHN O'CONNELL, *deputy director,* John.O'Connell@wicourts.gov; ELIZABETH ESTES, *deputy director,* Elizabeth.Estes@wicourts.gov

Telephone: 267-7274; Central Intake toll-free (877) 315-6941.

Fax: 267-1959.

Mailing Address: 110 East Main Street, Suite 315, Madison 53703-3383.

Number of Employees: 26.50.

Total Budget 2003-05: $4,024,600.

References: Supreme Court Rules, Chapters 21 and 22.

Responsibility: The Office of Lawyer Regulation was created by order of the supreme court, effective October 1, 2000, to assist the court in fulfilling its constitutional responsibility to supervise the practice of law and protect the public from professional misconduct by members of the State Bar of Wisconsin. This agency assumed the attorney disciplinary functions that had previously been performed by the Board of Attorneys Professional Responsibility and, prior to January 1, 1978, by the Board of State Bar Commissioners.

The director of the Office of Lawyer Regulation is appointed by the supreme court and must be admitted to the practice of law in Wisconsin no later than six months following appointment. The Board of Administrative Oversight and the Preliminary Review Committee perform oversight and adjudicative responsibilities under the supervision of the supreme court.

The Board of Administrative Oversight consists of 12 members, eight lawyers and four public members. Board members are appointed by the supreme court to staggered 3-year terms and may not serve more than two consecutive terms. The board monitors the overall system for regulating lawyers but does not handle actions regarding individual complaints or grievances. It reviews the "fairness, productivity, effectiveness and efficiency" of the system and reports its findings to the supreme court. After consultation with the director, it proposes the annual budget for the agency to the supreme court.

The Office of Lawyer Regulation receives and evaluates all complaints, inquiries, and grievances related to attorney misconduct or medical incapacity. The director is required to investigate any grievance that appears to support an allegation of possible attorney misconduct, and the attorney in question must cooperate with the investigation. District investigative committees are appointed in the 16 State Bar districts by the supreme court to aid the director in disciplinary investigations, forward matters to the director for review, and provide assistance when grievances can be settled at the district level.

After investigation, the director decides whether the matter should be forwarded to a panel of the Preliminary Review Committee, be dismissed, or be diverted for alternative action. This

14-member committee consists of nine lawyers and five public members, who are appointed by the supreme court to staggered 3-year terms and may not serve more than two consecutive terms.

If a panel of the Preliminary Review Committee determines there is cause to proceed, the director may seek disciplinary action, ranging from private reprimand to filing a formal complaint with the supreme court that requests public reprimand, license suspension or revocation, monetary payment, or imposing conditions on the continued practice of law. An attorney may be offered alternatives to formal disciplinary action, including mediation, fee arbitration, law office management assistance, evaluation and treatment for alcohol and other substance abuse, psychological evaluation and treatment, monitoring of the attorney's practice or trust account procedures, continuing legal education, ethics school, or the multistate professional responsibility examination.

Formal disciplinary actions for attorney misconduct are filed by the director with the supreme court, which appoints a referee from a permanent panel of attorneys and reserve judges to hear discipline cases, make disciplinary recommendations to the court, and to approve the issuance of certain private and public reprimands. Referees conduct hearings on complaints of attorney misconduct, petitions alleging attorney medical incapacity, and petitions for reinstatement. They make findings, conclusions, and recommendations and submit them to the supreme court for review and appropriate action. Only the supreme court has the authority to suspend or revoke a lawyer's license to practice law in the State of Wisconsin.

BOARD OF BAR EXAMINERS

Board of Bar Examiners: JOHN O. OLSON (State Bar member), *chairperson;* JOSEPH D. KEARNEY (Marquette University Law School faculty), *vice chairperson;* GLENN E. CARR, MARY BETH KEPPEL, JAMES A. MORRISON, CATHERINE M. ROTTIER (State Bar members); CHARLES H. CONSTANTINE (circuit court judge); KEVIN M. KELLY (UW Law School faculty); MARK J. BAKER, DENNIS DANNER, CAROLYN MILANES DEJOIE (public members). (All members are appointed by the supreme court.)

Director: GENE R. RANKIN, 266-9760; Fax: 266-1196.

Mailing Address: 110 East Main Street, Room 715, Madison 53703.

E-mail Address: bbe@wicourts.gov

Internet Address: http://www.wicourts.gov/bbe

Number of Employees: 8.00.

Total Budget 2003-05: $1,243,800.

References: Supreme Court Rules, Chapters 30, 31, and 40.

Responsibility: The 11-member Board of Bar Examiners manages all bar admissions by examination or by reciprocity; conducts character and fitness investigations of all candidates for admission to the bar, including diploma privilege graduates; and administers the Wisconsin mandatory continuing legal education requirement for attorneys.

The board originated as the Board of Continuing Legal Education, created in 1975 by rule of the Wisconsin Supreme Court. It became the Board of Attorneys Professional Competence in 1978 and was renamed the Board of Bar Examiners, effective January 1, 1991. Members are appointed for staggered 3-year terms, but no member may serve more than two consecutive full terms. The number of public members was increased from one to 3 by a supreme court order, effective January 1, 2001.

JUDICIAL COMMISSION

Members: HANNAH C. DUGAN (State Bar member), *chairperson;* JAMES M. HANEY, MICHAEL R. MILLER, DALLAS S. NEVILLE, ILEEN SIKOWSKI, WILLIAM VANDER LOOP (nonlawyers); DAVID HANSHER (circuit court judge); GREGORY S. PETERSON (appeals court judge); DONALD LEO BACH (State Bar member). (Judges and State Bar members appointed by supreme court. Nonlawyers are appointed by governor with senate consent.)

Executive Director: JAMES C. ALEXANDER.

Administrative Assistant: LAURY BUSSAN.

Mailing Address: 110 East Main Street, Suite 606, Madison 53703-3328.

Telephone: 266-7637.

Fax: 266-8647.

Agency E-mail: judcmm@wicourts.gov

Publication: Annual Report.

Number of Employees: 2.00.

Total Budget 2003-05: $434,600.

Statutory References: Sections 757.001, 757.81-757.99.

Responsibility: The 9-member Judicial Commission conducts investigations for review and action by the supreme court regarding allegations of misconduct or permanent disability of a judge or court commissioner. Members are appointed for 3-year terms but cannot serve more than two consecutive full terms.

The commission's investigations are confidential. If an investigation results in a finding of probable cause that a judge or court commissioner has engaged in misconduct or is disabled, the commission must file a formal complaint of misconduct or a petition regarding disability with the supreme court. Prior to filing a complaint or petition, the commission may request a jury hearing of its findings before a single appellate judge. If it does not request a jury hearing, the chief judge of the court of appeals selects a 3-judge panel to hear the complaint or petition.

The commission is responsible for prosecution of a case. After the case is heard by a jury or panel, the supreme court reviews the findings of fact, conclusions of law, and recommended disposition. It has ultimate responsibility for determining appropriate discipline in cases of misconduct or appropriate action in cases of permanent disability.

History: In 1972, the Wisconsin Supreme Court created a 9-member commission to implement the Code of Judicial Ethics it had adopted. The code enumerated standards of personal and official conduct and identified conduct that would result in disciplinary action. Subject to supreme court review, the commission had authority to reprimand or censure a judge.

A constitutional amendment approved by the voters in 1977 empowered the supreme court, using procedures developed by the legislature, to reprimand, censure, suspend, or remove any judge for misconduct or disability. With enactment of Chapter 449, Laws of 1977, the legislature created the Judicial Commission and prescribed its procedures. The supreme court abolished its own commission in 1978.

JUDICIAL CONDUCT ADVISORY COMMITTEE

Judicial Conduct Advisory Committee: GEORGE S. CURRY (circuit court or reserve judge serving in a rural area), *chairperson;* JAMES EVENSON (judicial administrative district chief judge); PAUL LUNDSTEN (court of appeals judge); DENNIS P. MORONEY (circuit court or reserve judge serving in an urban area); BRUCE GOODNOUGH (municipal court judge); ROBERT RADCLIFFE (reserve judge); DAVID FLESCH (circuit court commissioner); FRANK R. TERSCHAN (State Bar member); LAURA P. DEGOLIER (public member). (All members are selected by the supreme court.)

Mailing Address: P.O. Box 1688, Madison 53701-1688.

Internet Address: http://www.wicourts.gov/supreme/sc_judcond.asp

Telephone: 266-6828.

Fax: 267-0980.

Reference: Supreme Court Rules, Chapter 60, Appendix.

Responsibility: The Wisconsin Supreme Court established the Judicial Conduct Advisory Committee as part of its 1997 update to the Code of Judicial Conduct. The 9-member committee gives formal advisory opinions and informal advice regarding whether actions judges are contemplating comply with the code. It also makes recommendations to the supreme court for amendment to the Code of Judicial Conduct or the rules governing the committee.

JUDICIAL CONFERENCE

Members: All supreme court justices, court of appeals judges, circuit court judges, reserve judges, 3 municipal court judges (designated by the Wisconsin Municipal Judges Association), 3 judicial representatives of tribal courts (designated by the Wisconsin Tribal Judges Association), one circuit court commissioner designated by the Family Court Commissioner Association, and one circuit court commissioner designated by the Judicial Court Commissioner Association.

References: Section 758.171, Wisconsin Statutes; Supreme Court Rule 70.15.

Responsibility: The Judicial Conference, which was created by the Wisconsin Supreme Court, meets at least once a year to recommend improvements in administration of the justice system, conduct educational programs for its members, and adopt forms necessary for the administration of certain court proceedings. Since its initial meeting in January 1979, the conference has devoted sessions to family and children's law, probate, mental health, appellate practice and procedures, civil law, criminal law, and traffic law. It also maintains a standing committee on legislation.

JUDICIAL COUNCIL

Members: DAVID T. PROSSER, JR. (justice designated by supreme court); TED E. WEDEMEYER (judge designated by court of appeals); A. JOHN VOELKER (director of state courts); MARK S. GEMPELER, EDWARD E. LEINEWEBER, JAMES MASON, EARL W. SCHMIDT (circuit court judges designated by Judicial Conference); SENATOR ZIEN (chairperson, senate judicial committee); REPRESENTATIVE GUNDRUM (chairperson, assembly judicial committee); PEG LAUTENSCHLAGER (attorney general); BRUCE MUNSON (revisor of statutes); DAVID E. SCHULTZ (faculty member, UW Law School, designated by dean); JAY GRENIG (dean, Marquette University Law School); MARLA L. STEPHENS (designated by state public defender); SUSAN L. COLLINS (member of the Board of Governors, State Bar, designated by president-elect); BETH E. HANAN, JAMES L. MARTIN, D.J. WEIS (State Bar members selected by State Bar); KENNETH E. KRATZ(district attorney appointed by governor); 2 vacancies (public members appointed by governor).

Mailing Address: 110 East Main Street, Suite 606, Madison 53703.

Telephone: 266-7637.

Fax: 266-8647.

Statutory References: Sections 757.83 (4) and 758.13.

Responsibility: The Judicial Council, created by Chapter 392, Laws of 1951, assumed the functions of the Advisory Committee on Rules of Pleading, Practice and Procedure, created by the 1929 Legislature. The 21-member council is authorized to advise the supreme court and the legislature on any matter affecting the administration of justice in Wisconsin, and it may recommend legislation to change the procedure, jurisdiction, or organization of the courts. The council studies the rules of pleading, practice, and procedure and advises the supreme court about changes that will simplify procedure and promote a speedy disposition of litigation.

Several council members serve at the pleasure of their appointing authorities. The 4 circuit judges selected by the Judicial Conference serve 4-year terms. The 3 members selected by the

State Bar and the 2 citizen members appointed by the governor serve 3-year terms. The executive director of the Judicial Commission provides staff services to the council.

JUDICIAL EDUCATION COMMITTEE

Judicial Education Committee: SHIRLEY S. ABRAHAMSON (supreme court chief justice); MARGARET J. VERGERONT (designated by appeals court chief judge); A. JOHN VOELKER (director of state courts); JAMES J. BOLGERT, DARRYL W. DEETS, FAYE M. FLANCHER, MOLLY E. GALEWYRICK, MICHAEL S. GIBBS, WILLIAM F. HUE, DAVID G. MIRON, FREDERICK C. ROSA (circuit court judges appointed by supreme court); EDWARD REISNER (designated by dean, UW Law School); THOMAS HAMMER (designated by dean, Marquette University Law School); ROBERT G. MAWDSLEY (dean, Wisconsin Judicial College).

Office of Judicial Education: DAVID H. HASS, *director,* david.hass@wicourts.gov

Mailing Address: Office of Judicial Education, 110 East Main Street, Room 200, Madison 53703.

Telephone: 266-7807.

Fax: 261-6650.

E-mail Address: JED@wicourts.gov

Internet Address: http://www.wicourts.gov/education

Reference: Supreme Court Rules 32-33, 75.05.

Responsibility: The 14-member Judicial Education Committee approves educational programs for judges and court personnel. The 8 circuit court judges on the committee serve staggered 2-year terms and may not serve more than two consecutive terms. The dean of the Wisconsin Judicial College is an *ex officio* member of the committee and has voting privileges.

In 1976, the supreme court issued Chapter 32 of the Supreme Court Rules, which established a mandatory program of continuing education for the Wisconsin judiciary, effective January 1, 1977. This program applies to all supreme court justices and commissioners, appeals court judges and staff attorneys, circuit court judges, and reserve judges. Each person subject to the rule must obtain a specified number of credit hours of continuing education within a 6-year period. The Office of Judicial Education, which the supreme court established in 1971, administers the program. It also sponsors initial and continuing educational programs for municipal judges and circuit court clerks.

PLANNING AND POLICY ADVISORY COMMITTEE

Planning and Policy Advisory Committee: SHIRLEY S. ABRAHAMSON (supreme court chief justice), *chairperson;* WILLIAM M. MCMONIGAL, *vice chairperson;* RICHARD BROWN (appeals court judge selected by court); CARL ASHLEY, JEFFREY CONEN, BONNIE GORDON, ALLAN TORHORST, MICHAEL BOHREN, RICHARD NUSS, DAVID FLANAGAN, DIANE NICKS, EDWARD LEINEWEBER, PAT MADDEN, J.D. MCKAY, WILLIAM STEWART (circuit court judges elected by judicial administrative districts); DAVID NISPEL (municipal judge elected by Wisconsin Municipal Judges Association); HANNAH DUGAN, JOHN WALSH (selected by State Bar Board of Governors); JAMES DWYER (nonlawyer, elected county official); OSCAR BOLDT, JOHN KAMINSKI (nonlawyers); MICHAEL TOBIN (public defender); SCOTT JOHNSON (court administrator); JOHN ZAKOWSKI (prosecutor); KRIS DEISS (circuit court clerk); DARCY MCMANUS (circuit court commissioner). (Unless indicated otherwise, members are appointed by the chief justice.)

Planning Subcommittee: MARGARET VERGERONT (appeals court judge); RODERICK CAMERON, BARBARA KLUKA, MICHAEL NOWAKOWSKI, RICHARD J. SANKOVITZ (circuit court judges); SCOTT JOHNSON (court administrator); CAROLYN OLSON (circuit court clerk); DARCY MCMANUS (circuit court commissioner). *Ex-officio* members: SHIRLEY S. ABRAHAMSON (supreme court chief justice), WILLIAM M. McMONIGAL (circuit court judge, vice chairperson of Planning and Policy Advisory Committee), A. JOHN VOELKER (director of state courts).

Staff Policy Analyst: ERIN SLATTENGREN, erin.slattengren@wicourts.gov

Mailing Address: 110 East Main Street, Room 410, Madison 53703.

Telephone: 266-8861.

Fax: 267-0911.

Internet Address: http://www.wicourts.gov/about/committees/ppac.htm

Reference: Supreme Court Rule 70.14.

Responsibility: The 26-member Planning and Policy Advisory Committee advises the Wisconsin Supreme Court and the Director of State Courts on planning and policy and assists in a continuing evaluation of the administrative structure of the court system. It participates in the budget process of the Wisconsin judiciary and appoints a subcommittee to review the budget of the court system. The committee meets at least quarterly, and the supreme court meets with the committee annually. The Director of State Courts participates in committee deliberations, with full floor and advocacy privileges, but is not a member of the committee and does not have a vote.

This committee was created in 1978 as the Administrative Committee of the Courts and renamed the Planning and Policy Advisory Committee in December 1990.

WISCONSIN JUDICIAL SYSTEM — ASSOCIATED UNIT
STATE BAR OF WISCONSIN

Board of Governors (effective July 1, 2005): *Officers:* D. MICHAEL GUERIN, *president;* STEVEN A. LEVINE, *president-elect;* MICHELLE A. BEHNKE, *past president;* GRETCHEN G. VINEY, *secretary;* MARK A. PENNOW, *treasurer;* KENT I. CARNELL, *chair of the board. District members:* LISA M. ARENT, ROBERT J. ASTI, DANIEL P. BACH, THOMAS W. BERTZ, GRANT E. BIRTCH, JAMES C. BOLL, JR., BARBARA L. BURBACH, JOSEPH M. CARDAMONE III, JOHN L. CATES, ANDREW J. CHEVREZ, JAMES E. COLLIS, GWENDOLYN G. CONNOLLY, WILLIAM J. DOMINA, REX A. EWALD, THOMAS L. FRENN, EUGENE A. GASIORKIEWICZ, C. MICHAEL HAUSMAN, JOHN W. HEIN, GREGG M. HERMAN, MARGARET WRENN HICKEY, KENNETH A. KNUDSON, CATHERINE A. LA FLEUR, GRANT F. LANGLEY, ROBERT JOHN LIGHTFOOT II, JOHN P. MACY, PEGGY L. MILLER, PAUL R. NORMAN, JOHN F. O'MELIA, JR., J. DAVID RICE, ELIZABETH G. RICH, DANIEL L. SHNEIDMAN, DEBORAH M. SMITH, R. MICHAEL WATERMAN, vacancy. *Young Lawyers Division:* LYNNE SOLOMON. *Government Lawyers Division:* JAMES G. GODLEWSKI. *Nonresident Lawyers Division:* JOEL HIRSCHHORN, DANIEL F. RINZEL, ALBERT E. WEHDE. *Senior Lawyers Division:* MYRON E. LAROWE. *Nonlawyer members:* YVONNE D. FEAVEL, CORWIN VANDER ARK, vacancy.

Executive Director: GEORGE C. BROWN.

Mailing Address: P.O. Box 7158, Madison 53708-7158.

Location: 5302 Eastpark Boulevard, Madison.

Internet Address: http://www.wisbar.org; Consumer site: http://www.legalexplorer.com

Telephones: General: 257-3838; Lawyer Referral and Information Service: (800) 362-9082.

Agency E-mail: drossmiller@wisbar.org

Publications: *A Gift to Your Family: Planning Ahead for Future Health Care Needs; Wisconsin Lawyer Directory; Wisconsin Lawyer Magazine;Wisconsin News Reporter's Legal Handbook;* Consumer Pamphlet Series (19 titles); various brochures, pamphlets, videotapes, and DVDs.

References: Supreme Court Rules, Chapters 10 and 11.

Responsibility: The State Bar of Wisconsin is an association of persons authorized to practice law in Wisconsin. It works to raise professional standards, improve the administration of justice and the delivery of legal services, and provide continuing legal education to lawyers. The State Bar conducts legal research in substantive law, practice, and procedure and develops related reports and recommendations. It also maintains the roll of attorneys, collects mandatory assessments imposed by the supreme court for supreme court boards and to fund civil legal services for the poor, and performs other administrative services for the judicial system.

Attorneys may be admitted to the State Bar by the full Wisconsin Supreme Court or by a single justice. Members are subject to the rules of ethical conduct prescribed by the supreme court, whether they practice before a court, an administrative body, or in consultation with clients whose interests do not require court appearances.

Organization: Subject to rules prescribed by the Wisconsin Supreme Court, the State Bar is governed by a board of governors, of not fewer than 49 members, consisting of the board's 6 officers, not fewer than 34 members selected by State Bar members from the association's 16 districts, 6 selected by divisions of the State Bar, and 3 nonlawyers appointed by the supreme court. The board of governors selects the executive director and the president of the board.

History: In 1956, the Wisconsin Supreme Court ordered the organization of the State Bar of Wisconsin, effective January 1, 1957, to replace the formerly voluntary Wisconsin Bar Association, organized in 1877. All judges and attorneys entitled to practice before Wisconsin courts were required to join the State Bar. Beginning July 1, 1988, the Wisconsin Supreme Court suspended its mandatory membership rule, and the State Bar temporarily became a voluntary membership association, pending the disposition of a lawsuit in the U.S. Supreme Court. The Supreme Court ruled in *Keller v. State Bar of California*, 496 U.S. 1 (1990) that it is permissible to mandate membership provided certain restrictions are placed on the political activities of the mandatory State Bar. Effective July 1, 1992, the Wisconsin Supreme Court reinstated the mandatory membership rule upon petition from the State Bar Board of Governors.

Detail from the Martin Luther King Jr. Boulevard entrance to the Risser Justice Center in Madison, the home of the State Law Library. (Kathleen Sitter, LRB)

SUMMARY OF SIGNIFICANT DECISIONS OF THE WISCONSIN SUPREME COURT AND COURT OF APPEALS

October 2002 – June 2005

Robert Nelson and Mike Dsida
Legislative Reference Bureau

CONSTITUTIONAL LAW

Governor's Power Regarding Indian Gaming Compacts

In *Panzer v. Doyle*, 2004 WI 52, 271 Wis. 2d 295, 680 N.W. 2d 666 (2004), the supreme court took original jurisdiction at the request of legislative leaders to determine the limit on the governor's power to negotiate Indian gaming compacts. The court discussed the long and complicated history of legalized gambling in Wisconsin, involving state and federal statutes and constitutions, and tribal sovereignty. The court concluded that if a state regulates, rather than prohibits, gambling, then the state may not restrict gambling on tribal reservations if such activities are permitted for any purpose by any person.

In 1992, based on a state law that allowed the governor to negotiate compacts, the governor signed agreements with all 11 federally recognized tribes and bands in the state regarding the operation of slot machines, blackjack, and pull-tabs. In 1993, an amendment to the state constitution was approved by the voters that clarified what was meant by a lottery and prohibited the state from conducting casino-style games. In 2003, the newly elected governor and the tribes agreed to new compacts that allowed casino-style games such as roulette. The compacts would be in effect until terminated by mutual agreement of both parties. The compacts also waived state and tribal sovereign immunity.

The court held that the governor did not violate the separation of powers by negotiating these contracts because the power delegated to the governor by state statute, although quite broad, is "...an expedient solution to the quandary of who should act on behalf of the state in gaming negotiations." (p. 339) The court said, however, that upholding the constitutionality of the statutory delegation does not automatically validate every compact term. The court held that the governor did not have the authority to commit the state to a compact that runs until both parties agree to terminate it because that agreement gave away power delegated to the governor that the legislature cannot take back, circumventing the procedural safeguards that ensure that the delegated power could be reclaimed by future legislatures.

The court then discussed the expansion in the types of games allowed by the compact and held that the constitutional amendment limiting the types of games that were allowed precluded the governor and the legislature from agreeing to any games other than those allowed under the original gaming compacts. Finally, the court reviewed the arguments regarding the waiver of state sovereign immunity and determined that it violated the legislature's fundamental authority to waive sovereign immunity.

Chief Justice Shirley Abrahamson issued a long and detailed dissent, saying that the majority was right about the constitutionality of the statute granting the governor authority to negotiate the gaming compacts, but was wrong on all of the other issues in the case.

CRIMINAL LAW

The Right To Bear (Concealed) Arms

In two separate cases, the supreme court considered whether the state's statutory prohibition on the carrying of concealed weapons became unconstitutional with the adoption of an amendment to the Wisconsin Constitution establishing the "right to keep and bear arms" (Article I, Section 25). In *State v. Cole*, 2003 WI 112, 264 Wis. 2d 520, the court ruled that the statute is not unconstitutional in all cases; however, in *State v. Hamdan*, 2003 WI 113, 264 Wis. 2d 433, the court ruled that the statute was unconstitutional under the circumstances of that case.

In the former case, the defendant, Phillip Cole, was a passenger in an automobile that the police pulled over. The police searched Cole and the vehicle and found marijuana in Cole's pocket and loaded pistols in the glove compartment and under the driver's seat. Cole acknowledged that he carried the pistol in the glove compartment for protection. He was ultimately charged with, and pled guilty to, carrying a concealed weapon. Cole then requested that the conviction be vacated, arguing that the concealed weapons statute was, on its face, an unconstitutional infringement of the right to bear arms. The trial court rejected Cole's argument, and the case was ultimately appealed to the supreme court.

In a unanimous decision, the supreme court upheld Cole's conviction. The court began by determining that the statute should be presumed constitutional. The court then found that the right to bear arms was a fundamental constitutional right and that the applicable test for determining the constitutionality of the concealed weapons statute was whether it was a reasonable exercise of the state's police power – thereby rejecting Cole's argument that the statute should be subject to greater scrutiny.

Next, the court turned to Cole's substantive arguments that the statute, which predated the amendment, was effectively repealed by it and that the statute was too broad to constitute a reasonable exercise of the state's power. First, the court examined the language of the amendment. The court began by rejecting the argument that the statute and the amendment are incompatible, supporting its conclusion with similar rulings from courts in other states. It also used out-of-state cases to support its conclusion that the concealed weapons statute was narrow enough to constitute a reasonable exercise of the state's power. The court then examined the history of the amendment, which indicated that the amendment's proponents intended to preserve existing gun control regulations. The court also noted that the legislature, after the amendment was ratified, unsuccessfully attempted to modify the concealed weapons statute. The court indicated that the legislature would not have undertaken such efforts unless it believed that the concealed weapons statute was still valid. Finally, the court noted that public opinion polls taken at the time the amendment was ratified indicated that 80% of Wisconsinites opposed legalizing the carrying of concealed weapons. According to the court, that information supported its conclusion that the amendment and the statute are compatible.

The court also rejected Cole's argument that the concealed weapons statute was unconstitutional when applied to him. First, the court determined that Cole had waived that argument by pleading guilty. Second, the court stated that Cole had not presented any evidence of an imminent threat which might have justified his carrying of a concealed weapon. The court also indicated that the constitutional right to bear arms "is clearly not rendered illusory by prohibiting an individual from keeping a loaded weapon hidden either in the glove compartment or under the front seat in a vehicle."

Chief Justice Abrahamson concurred but argued: 1) that a statute that predates a constitutional amendment with which it may conflict should not be presumed constitutional; and 2) that the test used by the majority opinion (whether the statute was a reasonable exercise of police power) did not differ from the "rational basis" test that the majority rejected. Justice N. Patrick Crooks wrote a separate concurring opinion. He asserted that the statute is unconstitutional but that Cole's conviction should stand because he did not make his constitutional argument on time. Justice David Prosser also wrote a concurring opinion, in which he contended that the majority opinion did not adequately address the history of the amendment. Justice Prosser argued that the history indicated that the right to bear arms is not a "fundamental right" and is subject to reasonable regulation.

In *State v. Hamdan*, the court came to a very different conclusion. Munir Hamdan, the defendant, owned and operated a grocery and liquor store that was located in a high-crime neighborhood in Milwaukee and had been the target of four armed robberies and the site of two fatal shootings in the 1990s. With the knowledge of local law enforcement officers, Hamdan kept a handgun under the store's front counter, in an area that was not accessible to the public. One night, as the time came to close the store, Hamdan brought the handgun, which was wrapped in a plastic bag, to the back room for storage. Two police officers then entered the store to conduct a license check. When summoned by his son, Hamdan placed the wrapped gun in his pants pocket and returned to the main part of the store. When asked by one of the officers if he kept a gun in the store, Hamdan pulled the wrapped gun out of his pocket. The officers confiscated the gun but did not charge him with any offense. Six days later, however, he was charged with unlawfully carrying a concealed weapon.

Hamdan filed a motion to dismiss the charge, arguing that the concealed weapons statute is unconstitutional. The trial court denied the motion. Hamdan was convicted and fined $1.

On appeal, the supreme court reversed Hamdan's conviction. First, the court rejected Hamdan's argument that the "going armed" requirement of the concealed weapons statute should be reconstrued so that it would not apply in his case. Among other things, the court noted that it "would certainly have no problem finding that a customer was 'going armed' if the *customer* moved around Hamdan's store with a pistol concealed in his trousers." It also explained that the statute provided no way to distinguish "going armed" within a person's own home or business from "going armed" elsewhere. Second, the court rejected Hamdan's claim that he acted out of necessity or self-defense (either of which would have been a defense to prosecution). With respect to Hamdan's necessity claim, the court stated that there was no "natural physical force" that necessitated his carrying a concealed weapon. The court then explained that, notwithstanding the neighborhood's crime rate or Hamdan's own victimization, there was no specific or imminent threat to Hamdan, to others, or to anyone's property.

Turning to Hamdan's constitutional argument, the court stated that the constitutional right to bear arms was subject to reasonable regulations on weapons and that the general prohibition on the carrying of concealed weapons is constitutional. But the court also noted that the state may not apply such regulations in a way that nullifies the constitutional right. To determine whether the right remains meaningful in the face of the regulation, the court must assess whether the individual's need for carrying a concealed weapon substantially outweighs the public benefit associated with the regulation.

In conducting that analysis, the court first explained that Wisconsin law is "anomalous" in that it completely bans the carrying of concealed weapons "while simultaneously recognizing the right of individuals to own, possess, and carry firearms for lawful purposes." It then explained that the concealed weapons law "serves many valuable purposes in promoting public safety," including discouraging people from acting violently on impulse, and helping people know when a dangerous weapon is present. The court, however, stated that these rationales are not particularly compelling when applied to a person operating his or her own business. At the same time, "a citizen's desire to exercise the right to keep and bear arms for purposes of security is at its apex when undertaken to secure one's home or privately owned business." Moreover, according to the court, Wisconsin law provides no other reasonable way for a person to exercise his or her constitutional right in his or her own home or business; requiring the person to carry the weapon openly is "simply not reasonable." The court added, however, that a person who carries a concealed weapon may do so only for a lawful purpose.

Applying those principles to the case before it, the court acknowledged that Hamdan's conduct was prohibited under the concealed weapons statute. Nevertheless, under the particular circumstances of his case, "Hamdan's interests in maintaining a concealed weapon in his store and carrying it personally during an unexpected encounter with visitors substantially outweighed the State's interest in enforcing the concealed weapons statute." In addition, "Hamdan had no reasonable means of keeping and handling the weapon in his store except to conceal it." Therefore, the court found that the concealed weapons statute was unconstitutional as applied to Hamdan and reversed his conviction. The court concluded by: 1) urging the legislature to clarify the concealed weapons law and consider the possibility of developing a licensing or permit system for concealed weapons; and 2) specifying the method by which courts are to consider a right-to-bear-arms defense in future cases.

Justice William Bablitch, in a concurring opinion, stressed what he perceived to be the reasonableness of the majority opinion (in comparison to the chief justice's dissent) and asserted that courts will handle future concealed weapons cases, under the framework outlined by the majority, in much the same way that they handle search and seizure cases. Justice Ann Walsh Bradley also concurred, but specified that she did not join in the majority opinion on how courts should consider right-to-bear-arms defenses in future cases. Justice Crooks concurred in part and dissented in part. He agreed that Hamdan's conviction was improper, but he argued that the majority opinion was creating an exception to the concealed weapons prohibition that was not justified by the language of the statute. Instead, he argued, the court should have struck down the statute as a whole. Chief Justice Abrahamson dissented. She stated that the majority opinion improperly based its decision on its own determination about what appropriate policy is with respect to concealed weapons in a private business. She also challenged the majority opinion's division of responsibility between the judge and jury for certain issues that will arise in future concealed weapons cases, and questioned whether a valid prohibition on the carrying of concealed weapons was possible under the majority opinion.

Truth-in-Sentencing and Sentence Modification

In a series of cases, the supreme court considered the circumstances under which a court can modify the sentence of a person convicted of a crime under the "truth-in-sentencing" (TIS) law. TIS was enacted in two stages. First, with TIS-I, the legislature eliminated parole, required that all prison sentences be served in their entirety, and significantly increased the maximum sentence length for all felonies (other than those punishable by life imprisonment). Three years later, TIS-II took effect. TIS-II reduced the maximum sentence length for most crimes and classified nearly all felonies using a Class A to I classification scheme. (Previously, many felonies were unclassified, while others were classified as Class A, B, BC, C, D, or E felonies.) TIS-II also provided a new procedure, set forth in section 973.195 of the statutes, for a prisoner who has served a specified percentage of the confinement that was ordered by the court and who is not a Class A or B felon to petition the court to convert the rest of the confinement into community supervision.

State v. Gallion, 2004 WI 42, 270 Wis. 2d 535, provided the supreme court its first opportunity to address how sentences can be modified in light of these changes. Most of the court's opinion was an effort to reinvigorate long-standing rules for judges to follow when initially imposing a sentence. But along the way, the court also rejected Gallion's argument that his 21-year term of confinement, imposed under TIS-I for homicide by intoxicated use of a motor vehicle, was "harsh and excessive," in light of the fact that the maximum term of confinement for that crime under TIS-II dropped to 15 years. The court stated that TIS-II simply did not apply to him. It also suggested that the legislature, by barring Class B felons from proceeding under section 973.195, did not intend for TIS-II changes to be used in the manner proposed by Gallion, whose offense was a Class B felony.

Justice Jon Wilcox concurred, but noted his concerns that the majority opinion's discussion of sentencing rules invited excessive scrutiny of sentences by appellate courts.

In *State v. Crochiere*, 2004 WI 78, 273 Wis. 2d 57, the court considered other long-standing rules relating to criminal sentences in the context of TIS: those allowing for a sentence to be modified based on a "new factor." Under the "new factor" cases, a court can modify a sentence only if there are facts that are highly relevant to sentencing that were not known to the trial judge at sentencing, either because they were not then in existence or because they were unknowingly overlooked by all of the parties. Crochiere sought to invoke this rule with respect to his sentence for reckless endangerment. After serving about half of that sentence, Crochiere asked the court to modify it, arguing that his rehabilitation (which was not considered a "new factor" before TIS but could have been considered in parole decisions) must now be a "new factor" under the TIS sentencing system, given that that system has no place for parole. The court rejected Crochiere's argument and reaffirmed the "new factor" line of cases. It stated that to do otherwise would result in prisoners serving less than their full sentences and would "undercut the clear intent of the legislature in enacting TIS."

The court's third case on this topic was *State v. Trujillo*, 2005 WI 45, __ Wis. 2d __ (to be published). In that case the defendant was convicted of burglary under TIS-I and was sentenced to eight years of confinement – six months more than the maximum for burglary under TIS-II. Trujillo brought a motion to modify his sentence, contending that the changes made by TIS-II were a "new factor". The supreme court rejected Trujillo's argument, relying on *State v. Hegwood*, 113 Wis. 2d 544 (1983), which had rebuffed a similar sentence modification motion. The court also justified its conclusion by noting that the legislature did not make any of the TIS-II penalties apply retroactively, even though it could have done so. It also indicated that the sentence modification procedure in section 973.195 of the statutes (which Trujillo could not yet use because he had not served the requisite of his sentence) provided a prisoner an adequate opportunity to argue for modifying a sentence based on a change in the law. Moreover, the court asserted that Trujillo's argument was inconsistent with the legislature's goal in enacting TIS – certainty in sentencing – and that, if adopted, it would open the floodgates to sentence modification motions by prisoners sentenced under TIS-I.

Chief Justice Abrahamson dissented. She argued that the legislature had never intended for the higher TIS-I penalties to take effect and that the elimination of parole – which, before TIS, could effectively reduce the amount of time spent in prison by an inmate – made *Hegwood* irrelevant. Justice Louis Butler, Jr. also dissented, asserting that *Hegwood* should be overruled and that trial courts should be free to decide, on a case-by-case basis, whether a change in the law justified modifying a sentence.

On the same day that it decided *Trujillo*, the court issued its opinion in *State v. Tucker*, 2005 WI 46, __ Wis. 2d __ (to be published). Relying on its opinion in *Trujillo*, the court rejected Tucker's request to modify his two sentences, a request based on the fact that the terms of confinement imposed for his TIS-I crimes were longer than they could have been had he committed them after TIS-II took effect. But with both the state and Tucker arguing that section 973.195 applies only to a person sentenced under TIS-II, the court went on to examine that issue and concluded that the statute applies to TIS-I cases as well. Initially, the court noted that the language of the statute could be construed either as consistent or inconsistent with the parties' arguments about the reach of section 973.195. Thus, the court turned to other sources of information to interpret the statute. First, the court noted that the legislature provided that other procedures established when TIS-II was enacted apply only to TIS-II sentences. The court stated that this supported the conclusion that section 973.195 applies to TIS-I sentences, since the legislature clearly could have specified otherwise. A Legislative Reference Bureau analysis of the bill and other commentary also supported that conclusion. The court also stressed that one of the four grounds on which a petition can be filed under section 973.195 is that the law has changed in a way that would have decreased the petitioner's time in prison if the change had applied to him or her. Since the legislative act that created section 973.195 made those kinds of changes in the law, the court reasoned that the legislature intended for section 973.195 to cover a person sentenced under TIS-I.

After reaching its conclusion that section 973.195 applies to TIS-I sentences, the court also discussed *how* it would apply in those cases. The court stated that, if a person was sentenced to a state prison for a crime under TIS-I, the amount of prison time that the person would need to serve before filing a petition under section 973.195 would be the same as the amount of time that a person convicted of the same crime under TIS-II would need to serve.

Chief Justice Abrahamson and Justice Butler wrote brief dissenting opinions, with each of them simply referring to their respective dissenting opinions in *Trujillo*.

In its last sentence modification case of the term, *State v. Stenklyft*, 2005 WI 71, __ Wis. 2d __ (to be published), the supreme court considered the constitutionality of section 973.195. In that case Stenklyft was convicted in November 2000 of causing great bodily harm by operating a motor vehicle while under the influence of an intoxicant. In March 2003, after serving more than 75% of his 30-month term of confinement, Stenklyft asked the trial court to modify his sentence, based on his conduct in prison. The district attorney objected to Stenklyft's request and asserted that, under the statute, the court could not grant the petition over the state's objection. The trial court disagreed and granted the petition.

On appeal, the supreme court, in two majority opinions, one authored by Chief Justice Abrahamson and one by Justice Crooks, agreed with the trial court that the district attorney cannot prevent a trial court from considering a petition filed under section 973.195. The two opinions focused on the relevant language of the statute, which states that "the court shall deny the inmate's petition" if the district attorney objects to it. Both opinions stated that the statute would be unconstitutional if the word "shall" gave the district attorney the absolute right to prevent the court from modifying a sentence. As the chief justice stated, it would authorize the district attorney to invade the "exclusive core constitutional power of the judiciary to impose a penalty", which includes the power to modify a previously imposed penalty. The chief justice also asserted that section 973.195 "interferes with the impartial administration of justice by delegating judicial power to one of the parties in the litigation." Justice Crooks added that the statute can be interpreted in a way that avoids the constitutional problem. Specifically, the word "shall" can be construed so that it provides direction to the court without imposing a mandatory requirement. Thus, the court would have the "discretion to accept or reject the objection of the district attorney."

Nevertheless, Justice Crooks concluded that the trial court's decision must be reversed. Justice Crooks stated that, based on the record of the case, the court did not adequately consider all of the factors, including the "nature of the crime, character of the defendant, protection of the public, positions of the State and of the victim, and other relevant factors such as the inmate's conduct", that it needed to examine in deciding whether to modify the sentence. Thus, the case was returned to the circuit court for a full consideration of those factors.

Justice Wilcox dissented. He argued that section 973.195 does not relate to the court's inherent power to modify sentences. Instead, it created a new power, shared among all three branches, that is subject to reasonable regulations imposed by the legislature.

Where Does the State's Jurisdiction End?

In *State v. Anderson*, 2005 WI 54, __ Wis. 2d __ (to be published), a first-degree intentional homicide case, the supreme court considered the question of where a criminal prosecution can take place, if at all, when there is no definitive evidence regarding where the relevant criminal acts occurred. In that case the court ruled that the trial could proceed based on evidence that the defendant, Derek Anderson, probably formed the intent to kill his father, Allen Krnak, while Anderson was in Wisconsin. The court also determined that the case could be tried in Jefferson County.

Allen and Donna Krnak and their younger son Thomas disappeared in July 1998. The Krnaks, who lived in Jefferson County, had planned a trip to their cabin in Waushara County for the Independence Day weekend. Apparently, they never made it there. A year and a half later, ten miles from the North Carolina college that Anderson once attended, a hunter found the skeletal remains of a man who was ultimately identified as Allen Krnak. Medical examiners determined that Krnak died as a result of blows to the head and face. Donna and Thomas Krnak were never found.

Anderson was indicted in North Carolina in 2001 for murdering his father. Two years later, however, the local district attorney concluded that there was not enough evidence to prove that the crime occurred there. Thus, in August 2003, the district attorney for Jefferson County filed a criminal complaint against Anderson, charging him with first-degree intentional homicide.

At the preliminary hearing, the court heard evidence regarding the events leading up to the Krnaks' disappearance and the investigation that followed. According to the testimony, Allen Krnak received a phone call at work on the afternoon of Thursday, July 2, 1998, that greatly upset him. After the call, Krnak told a co-worker, "I have to fly out of here" and "we may have to go to a funeral." Anderson initially told police that he did not remember calling his father that day. He later told his aunt, however, that he had called his father from the family home that afternoon but that he was only asking about where to find a tool.

Anderson also told investigators that his parents and brother left the house Thursday afternoon but did not return as scheduled on Sunday. Anderson waited until Monday evening to contact the sheriff. Four days later, Anderson called a conservation warden in Sauk County and informed him that his parents may have been in the area. Within 90 minutes, the warden was able to find the family's empty pickup truck in the Dell Creek Wildlife Area. Eleven days later, a detective learned that the truck's odometer indicated that it had been driven 2,600 miles more than what was indicated on detailed mileage logs Krnak had kept. (The site in North Carolina where Krnak's body was found was 780 miles from the family's home.) Anderson attempted to explain the discrepancy by saying that he had been driving the vehicle. Additional testimony at the preliminary hearing indicated that Anderson had been nonchalant about his family's disappearance. Finally, a map that had been drawn for Krnak by a co-worker was found, with Anderson's fingerprint on it, in the glove compartment of Donna Krnak's sedan – a car that Anderson was using after his parents and brother disappeared.

At the end of the hearing, the circuit court concluded that there was evidence that Anderson formed the intent to kill his father in Jefferson County and that, as a result, the state had jurisdiction over the case. The court also ruled that the case could be tried in Jefferson County. Anderson then appealed.

The supreme court upheld the circuit court's decision. In looking at whether the state had jurisdiction over the case, the court first determined that the intent to kill is a separate element of first-degree intentional homicide. It then rejected Anderson's argument that, for the purpose of the state's jurisdiction statute, the intent to kill element cannot take place apart from the act causing the victim's death. In doing so, the court relied extensively on its conclusion that the legislature had intended to expand parts of the state's jurisdictional statute in 1955. The court added that the jurisdictional requirement can be met when the defendant acts in a way that manifests the intent to kill. The court then stated that the evidence from the preliminary hearing created a reasonable inference that Anderson probably called Krnak at work to lure him home early in order to kill him – which the court stated manifested an intent, formed in Wisconsin, to commit the crime.

The court then stated that testimony that had been improperly excluded at the preliminary hearing, when combined with other evidence, created a reasonable inference that Krnak was killed in Jefferson County, thus providing the basis for venue (that is, for trying the case) in that county. The excluded testimony, relating Krnak's story about how Anderson had once threatened him and had tried to "club him", was hearsay; but according to the court it was admissible under one of the exceptions to the ban on hearsay.

In a footnote, the court stated that its decisions regarding jurisdiction and venue applied only to the preliminary hearing. The court noted that, at the trial, the state would need to meet the "beyond a reasonable doubt" standard when trying to establish jurisdiction and venue.

In a concurring opinion, Justice Bradley stated that she agreed with the majority opinion regarding territorial jurisdiction and venue but not regarding the admissibility of the excluded testimony, which she argued was not needed to resolve those issues. In a separate concurrence, Justice Butler joined the majority opinion regarding jurisdiction and the excluded testimony, but not regarding venue. He argued that there was no evidence indicating that Anderson was any more likely to have committed the crime in Jefferson County than in other possible locations. In such a case, he stated, the case may be heard in the county in which the defendant was last seen alive.

You Have the Right to Remain Silent... But Not the Right To Lie

A person who commits a crime may not lie about it to a law enforcement officer. If a person does so, that constitutes a new crime: obstructing an officer. That was the conclusion of the supreme court in *State v. Reed*, 2005 WI 53, __ Wis. 2d __ (to be published).

Brent Reed's criminal case began when a highway patrol officer saw a person sitting in the driver's seat of a car that was parked alongside the highway. The officer turned back to investigate and found the same person, Reed, sitting in the passenger's seat. After approaching the car, the officer smelled alcohol. Reed identified himself and immediately stated that he was not driving because he knew that he had had too much to drink. Reed stated that a "Mr. Triller" was driving but that, after an argument, Triller pulled the car over and walked away. Reed, however, could not tell the officer which way Triller walked or provide Triller's phone number. After refusing to perform sobriety tests, Reed was arrested.

After Reed's arrest, a backup officer drove five miles up the highway in an unsuccessful effort to find Triller. Eventually, an officer was able to contact Triller by phone. Triller told the officer that he had not been with Reed. As a result, the state charged Reed with obstructing an officer, in addition to drunk driving.

Reed asked the trial court to dismiss the obstruction charge, arguing that he could not be prosecuted for making an "exculpatory denial" – a statement denying involvement in a crime by a person who committed it. When the court denied his motion, Reed appealed. Like the trial court, the court of appeals concluded that Reed had done more than simply deny committing the crime. He had also provided false information relating to the crime, "frustrating the police function." Therefore, the court concluded that he could be charged with obstruction.

The supreme court agreed that Reed's conduct, as described in the complaint, constituted obstruction. But the court took a different route to reach that conclusion. It broadened the circumstances under which a person can be prosecuted, so that even the simplest of false denials can be treated as obstruction.

The court began by rejecting three arguments made by Reed in support of allowing exculpatory denials. First, the court stated that it did not matter what affect saying "I didn't do it" had on the police. What mattered, according to the court, was the person's intent. Specifically, did the person intend to mislead or deceive a law enforcement officer? If the answer is "yes," the person is guilty of obstruction. Second, the court rejected Reed's arguments that, without an exculpatory denial exception, a person who commits a crime, when asked about it by an officer, will be forced to: 1) admit guilt; 2) deny guilt and thereby commit obstruction; or 3) remain silent and have that pre–arrest silence used against the person. The court stated that the problems a defendant faces by remaining silent cannot justify a lie. Third, the court rejected Reed's claims that, without an exculpatory denial exception, police and prosecutors would use the obstruction statute to "pile on" offenses. Among other things, the court stated that Reed's argument was "entirely speculative." The court concluded its opinion by explicitly overruling *State v. Espinoza*, 2002 WI App 51, 250 Wis. 2d 804, the court of appeals case that had established the exculpatory denial exception.

Chief Justice Abrahamson concurred with the result but disagreed with the majority's reasoning. She explained that overruling *State v. Espinoza* was unnecessary, since Reed's statement, which contained false information, was not merely an exculpatory denial. She also argued that overruling *Espinoza* is unwise, because doing so conflicts with other court opinions and the intent of the legislature and because, without *Espinoza*, the obstruction statute can be used improperly to manufacture crimes by inducing false denials. Justice Prosser also concurred, but criticized the majority for its "literal, inflexible interpretation of the statute" and the chief justice for "authorizing deception."

The Criminal Consequences of Legislative Misconduct

In two separate cases, the Wisconsin Supreme Court permitted state legislators to be criminally prosecuted for misconduct in public office. Affirming the decisions of the court of appeals, the court paved the way for criminal trials of former Senate Majority Leader Chuck Chvala (in *State v. Chvala*, 2005 WI 30, __ Wis. 2d __) (to be published) and former Speaker of the Assembly Scott Jensen, former Assembly Majority Leader Steve Foti, and Sherry Schultz, a member of Foti's staff (in *State v. Jensen*, 2005 WI 31, __ Wis. 2d __) (to be published).

The criminal case against Chvala and the criminal case against Jensen, Foti, and Schultz (which also involved misdemeanor charges against former Assistant Majority Leader Bonnie Ladwig) proceeded on separate but similar tracks. Both arose out of secret "John Doe" investigations. In the former case, prosecutors charged Chvala with seven felony counts of misconduct in public office. The charges were based on his alleged use of state employees of the Senate Democratic Caucus (SDC) for various Democratic political campaigns while those employees were on state time or using state resources. Prosecutors also charged Chvala with 13 additional felony counts of extortion and campaign finance law violations. In the other case, prosecutors charged Jensen with three felony counts of misconduct in public office and one misdemeanor count of intentional misuse of a public position for private benefit. Foti was charged with one felony count of misconduct in public office. Schultz was charged with one felony count of misconduct in public office. The felony counts against Foti and Schultz and one of the felony counts against Jensen were based on the same alleged conduct: Schultz's work, at the direction of Jensen and Foti, on political campaigns while she was on state time or while she was using state resources. The other felony counts against Jensen were based on his alleged use of two state employees, while they were on state time or using state resources, to recruit and assist Republican candidates for political office, and on his alleged use of state employees to work for Taxpayers for Jensen, a political campaign committee.

In both cases, the defendants asked the trial court to dismiss the complaint. When the trial court denied their motions, they asked for, and received, permission to appeal. Chvala's petition, however, was granted only with respect to four of the misconduct charges. The court denied the petition with respect to the other counts of the complaint.

The court of appeals issued its opinion in Chvala's case first (*State v. Chvala*, 2004, WI App 53, 271 Wis. 2d 115). The court began its analysis by rejecting Chvala's claims that the misconduct in public office statute is unconstitutionally vague. Relying on the Senate Policy Manual, guidelines issued by the Senate Chief Clerk, and other statutes, the court explained that Chvala's duties as a legislator were clear enough for a reasonable person to know that using SDC staff to work on political campaigns with state resources conflicted with those duties. The court added that the misconduct statute may be applied to those duties without reliance on any person's standards. The court then determined that the statute is not unconstitutionally overbroad, since it does not interfere with legitimate political activity. Next, the court rejected Chvala's argument that he was immune from prosecution under the constitution's Speech and Debate Clause. According to the court, the use of state employees for political campaigns is not integral to the legislative process. Therefore, the Speech and Debate Clause does not apply. Finally, the court considered Chvala's argument that the State's prosecution violated the separation of powers doctrine. According to Chvala, the legislature alone has the authority to regulate the conduct of its members. Chvala also argued that deciding whether an activity is "legislative" or "political" is not a proper subject for the judiciary to resolve. The court, however, concluded that using senate documents to determine the scope of Chvala's duties did not improperly intrude upon the legislature's powers. The court also stated that, with limited exceptions, the allegations in the complaint relating to the misconduct counts described "political campaign activity of the most basic type" and that the court would not need to speculate about whether it constituted legitimate legislative activity. Therefore, those counts could be properly resolved by the courts.

Two months later, the court of appeals issued a similar ruling in the case against Jensen, Foti, and Schultz (*State v. Jensen*, 2004 WI App 89, 272 Wis. 2d 707). Relying in part on its opinion in *State v. Chvala*, the court ruled again that the misconduct in public office statute was not unconstitutionally vague or overbroad and that, given the allegations in the complaint, the case did not require the court to address a "political question." The court of appeals also rejected the *Jensen* defendants' argument that the allegations of the complaint did not describe a violation of the misconduct statute. The court stated that the complaint provided sufficient information to describe the offenses involved.

Chvala and the *Jensen* defendants appealed, but in abbreviated opinions issued on the same day, the Wisconsin Supreme Court upheld the court of appeals' decisions. Only four justices participated in the case (three had excused themselves), but those justices were unanimous in ruling that the misconduct statute is not unconstitutionally overbroad, that prosecution of the case would not involve a violation of the separation of powers doctrine, and that the charges were proper matters for courts to consider. In the *Chvala* case, the court also unanimously ruled that the criminal charges did not conflict with the Speech and Debate Clause. However, the court split on the vagueness issue in both cases; two justices voted to uphold the court of appeals' decision, and two voted to reverse it. Given that split, the court of appeals' decisions remained in force in both cases. The cases were then returned to the circuit court for trial.

What Are the Rights of Crime Victims Under the Constitution?

In *State v. Schilling*, 2005 WI 17, 278 Wis. 2d 216, the supreme court decided that crime victims do not have enforceable rights under the first sentence of Article I, Section 9m of the Wisconsin Constitution which states: "This state should treat crime victims ... with fairness, dignity and respect for their privacy". Instead, the court ruled that the sentence merely articulates the state's policies regarding the treatment of crime victims.

Daniel Marinko murdered his ex-wife, Jennifer Hansen Marinko, in Price County in October 1999. He was ultimately convicted of first-degree intentional homicide and armed burglary. At the sentencing hearing in April 2001, Patrick Schilling, the prosecuting attorney, played part of the tape of the 911 telephone call that the victim's son had made to the police after discovering his mother's body. Schilling had made sure that the victim's children would not be present at the sentencing hearing, but he did not inform other family members that he was going to play the tape or give them an opportunity to leave the courtroom before he played it. Schilling turned off the tape when he realized the effect that it was having on them.

In July 2001, five of the victim's family members filed a complaint against Schilling with the Crime Victims Rights Board. After conducting a hearing, the board found that Schilling had violated the rights of those family members "to be treated with fairness, dignity, respect, courtesy and sensitivity" when he played the 911 tape. As a remedy, the board ordered a private reprimand of Schilling. Schilling then asked the Dane County Circuit Court to review the board's decision. When that court reversed the decision, the board appealed.

In a unanimous opinion, the supreme court upheld the circuit court's decision and ruled that the first sentence of Article I, Section 9m does not create independent, enforceable rights. In reaching that conclusion, the court explained that the broad language of that sentence provides only a statement of policy or a general guide to the more specific rights contained in the rest of that section. The court also relied on the legislature's rejection of other versions of the amendment that would have listed fairness, dignity, and privacy in the same way as other rights. In addition, it noted that the amendment's structure is parallel to the structure of statutes relating to victims' rights that were in effect when the amendment was adopted: a general provision (described in the statutes as "Legislative intent") was followed by a more specific list of rights. Finally, the court stated that legislative activity occurring after the adoption of the amendment confirms that the legislature did not intend for the first sentence of Article I, Section 9m to create enforceable rights. First, the legislature enacted a new statutory provision entitled "Rights of Victims" but did not include a right to fairness, dignity, or respect for privacy in that provision. Second, in summarizing that legislation, the Legislative Reference Bureau did not list the right to fairness, dignity, or respect for privacy as among the rights conferred by the Constitution. Thus, the court concluded that Article I, Section 9m does not create an enforceable right to fairness, dignity, or respect for privacy.

CIVIL LAW

Easement from Landlocked Property

In *McCormick v. Schubring*, 2003 WI 149, 267 WI 2d 122, 672 N.W. 2d 63 (2003), the supreme court was asked if an easement granted by the circuit court to an owner of landlocked property should be approved. The county took 40 acres from the original owner of three 40-acre parcels of land for failure to pay taxes, with the result that the remaining 80 acres did not have access to a public road. The 40-acre parcel owned by the county included a gravel road that was used by the landlocked owner of the 80-acre parcel. The county 40-acre parcel was sold to a person who was unaware of the existence of the gravel road or of any possible easement. Later, the original owner of the 120 acres sold the remaining 80 acres to a person who used the gravel road to access the property. The owner of the 40-acre parcel eventually denied that use. The owner of the 80 landlocked acres brought this action to obtain an easement of necessity over the 40-acre parcel.

An easement of necessity, said the court, may be provided when property is landlocked and the owner needs access to that property from a public highway. To obtain an easement of necessity, the court said the petitioner must prove that there was common ownership of the properties at the time of the severance that created the landlocked condition and that the landlocked property did not have access to a public road after it was severed from the original property. The court held that finding these two requirements does not create an easement of necessity as a matter of law. Rather, the court must look at the conditions that gave rise to the severance and the equities involved in creating an easement of necessity.

In the present case, the original property was not landlocked and when severed the landlocked parcel came into existence, thus meeting the minimum requirements for the creation of an easement of necessity. The court noted that the current owner of the landlocked parcel purchased the property with the knowledge that a private road existed to gain access to the public road. The landlocked owner did not produce the severance that resulted in the landlocked condition, and because of the wild condition of the property, there would be limited use of the landlocked property without access. But the owner of the landlocked property knew there was no easement when they purchased that property. The other property owner tried diligently to find out if there was any easement on the property before purchasing the property, and the creation of the easement would reduce the value of the property and make the building of a home less desirable.

The supreme court determined that the circuit court balanced the benefits and burdens resulting from creating an easement of necessity and upheld the circuit court decision because it was not an erroneous exercise of discretion.

Limits on Medical Malpractice Wrongful Death Actions

This case, *Maurin v. Hall*, 2004 WI 100, 274 Wis. 2d 28, 682 N.W. 2d 866 (2004), resulted from the misdiagnosis of a five-year old girl's diabetic condition. The child became ill, was misdiagnosed by a physician's assistant as having an ear infection, was misdiagnosed the next day by a doctor, and the next day was correctly diagnosed as diabetic by another doctor. Nevertheless, the child died. The jury awarded the girl's estate damages for her predeath pain and suffering in excess of the statutory medical malpractice maximum and her parents damages for the loss of society and companionship as the result of the wrongful death in excess of the wrongful death statute maximum. The circuit court reduced the pain and suffering award but found that the statutory cap on damages in wrongful death actions was unconstitutional because it deprived the plaintiffs of the right to a jury trial, violated the due process and equal protection clauses of the constitution, and usurped judicial power. While this case was on appeal, the supreme court decided in another case that the statutory maximum damage award in medical malpractice cases was constitutional.

The doctor argued that the total recovery by the estate and parents for all pain and suffering and wrongful death was limited to the maximum amount set forth in the medical malpractice statute. The parents argued that the child's estate may recover the maximum allowed in the medical malpractice statute while they could recover the maximum amount allowed under the wrongful death statute. The supreme court reviewed the current statutes and legislative history and held that the language that set a cap on the total noneconomic damages for bodily injury or death for each occurrence of medical malpractice created a single cap for the damages in this case. The court said that since this case involved the death of a child as the result of medical malpractice, the cap on noneconomic damages in the wrongful death statute applies. This cap, said the court, applies to each person who suffers the noneconomic damages as a result of the wrongful death, so in this case each parent may be awarded an amount up to the statutory limit.

The supreme court then reviewed the constitutionality of the wrongful death damage limit and determined that the because right to a jury was not directly infringed by the legislature's limit on damages, the limit was constitutional.

Chief Justice Abrahamson concurred in the reversal and remand to the circuit court, but argued that the decision should not have been based on an interpretation not briefed or discussed by any of the parties. She also argued that the majority failed to recognize the difference between an action by the estate for the pain and suffering incurred by the child before her death and an action brought by the parents for the loss of society and companionship of their child. These are two separate actions and should not have been lumped together, said the concurrence.

Justice Wilcox concurred in the majority opinion but wrote to disagree with the Abrahamson discussion of the issue of remitter, while Justice Bradley wrote a concurring opinion saying that the discussion in the majority opinion of the constitutionality of the statute was premature and should not have proceeded until the arguments were fully developed and briefed.

Necessary Elements for a Waiver of Liability Provision to be Effective

Many recreational facilities, including ski resorts, horse riding stables, and exercise clubs, require a person who wants to use the facility to sign a form that purports to waive any liability of the owner of the facility for any injury to the person while using the facility (an exculpatory provision). This case, *Atkins v. Swimwest*, 2005 WI 4, _____, 690 N.W. 2d 835 (2005), required the supreme court to review such a provision to determine if it should be enforced. The case involved a wrongful death action by the son of a woman who died while swimming in a pool. When the woman came to the pool to swim, she was required to pay a fee and fill out a card with her name and address. The card included a provision stating that she agreed to assume all liability for herself without regard to fault and to hold harmless Swimwest and its employees for any conditions or injury while at the facility. A few minutes after she entered the pool she was found motionless near the bottom of the four-foot deep lap pool.

The supreme court noted that, generally, exculpatory provisions are analyzed on principals of contract law and that the court strictly construes them against the party seeking to rely on them. The court said that such provisions are subject to a review on public policy grounds because of the tension between allowing parties to contract freely and ensuring that tort law is considered, which requires persons to be responsible for their negligent acts. The court noted that recent cases required the waiver of liability to be clear and unambiguous and alert the signer to the nature and significance of what is being signed. Those cases, said the court, require that the waiver provision be separate and distinct, and prohibit a waiver of liability for intentional or reckless conduct. In addition, one of the cases suggested that there must be an opportunity for the person to negotiate or bargain about the provision.

The court held that the liability waiver used by Swimwest violated public policy for a number of reasons. The waiver, said the court, was overly broad and one-sided because it used the phrase "...without regard to fault...," which is not clear and could be interpreted to include intentional or reckless conduct, not just negligence. The waiver, said the court, did not provide the signer with adequate notice of the waiver's nature and significance, in part because the waiver provision was on a form that served two purposes, to register as a guest and to waive liability. The waiver itself, said the court, was not a conspicuous part of the form; rather, the entire form was of the same color and in capital letters, with only one signature for both purposes. Finally, the court said the waiver is against public policy because the signer was not given an opportunity to bargain over the contents of the waiver.

Justice Patience Roggensack concurred with the opinion but believed that the court put too much emphasis on the inability to negotiate the terms of the waiver, saying that factor should not be a separate reason for finding that an exculpatory provision violated public policy.

Justice Wilcox dissented, saying that the form was very short and clear on its face. To add additional legal language to the form, or to separate it from the registration form, would only cause confusion on the part of the signer. He also disagreed with the requirement that the signer have the ability to bargain,saying that requirement impractical, especially since the court set no standards.

The Application of the "Odd-Lot" Doctrine in Employment Cases

The facts in this case, *Beecher v. LIRC*, 2004 WI 88, 273 Wis 2d. 136, 682 N.W. 2d 29 (2004), are fairly simple. The plaintiff, after working 29 years in a strenuous metal-working job and after two back surgeries, sought a determination that he was permanently disabled. Expert testimony was presented for both sides and the administrative law judge found that the employee was permanently disabled. The Labor and Industry Review Commission (LIRC) reversed the decision, in part because the employee had failed to make enough of an effort to find other work, and this failure meant that the employee did not meet the criteria for being covered under the odd-lot doctrine. That doctrine provides that if an employee shows that he or she is unable to obtain gainful employment because of the work-related impairment and other factors, such as age, training, and education, then the employee has made a prima facie case of permanent and total disability and the burden shifts to the employer to show that the employee could obtain gainful employment. The doctrine says that the prima facie case applies even if the employee can find occasional, part-time employment (an odd-lot job) even with the impairment. The circuit court upheld LIRC and the court of appeals reversed the circuit court decision, saying LIRC improperly applied the odd-lot doctrine.

The supreme court first had to decide what standard it would use to review the LIRC decision. The court held that the court of appeals incorrectly gave LIRC's decision great weight because the odd-lot doctrine is not based on a statute, but rather was created by the courts, and the court retains the power to explain and modify its own precedents without deferring to an agency interpretation of those precedents. The court found that the numerous factors cited by LIRC in its decision should have been considered only in evaluating loss of earnings; they were not part of an evidentiary rule and did not impose a burden of proof on the employee. The odd-lot doctrine, in contrast, was created by the court as an exception to the general rule that permanent total disability awards are based on proof of total disability. Under that doctrine, the court held, the burden of proof shifts to the employer to show employability if the injured employee can show that because of the injury, age, education, and capacity, he or she is unable to secure gainful employment, even if the employee has some residual, insignificant earning capacity. Because LIRC incorrectly interpreted the odd-lot doctrine, the court returned the case to LIRC to redetermine if the employee was permanently and totally disabled.

Chief Justice Abrahamson concurred, but disagreed with the majority opinion that the odd-lot doctrine was created by the court; she argued that the court had been interpreting a statute, not making its own policy.

Justice Bradley concurred, but said the majority should not have decided that the courts created the odd-lot doctrine as judge-made common law without the benefit of briefs and oral argument.

Reasonable Accommodation for Employment of a Person with a Disability

The supreme court was asked in two cases to decide the type of accommodation that an employer must provide for a disabled employee. In *Crystal Lake Cheese Factory v. LIRC*, 2003 WI 106, 264 Wis. 2d 200, 664 N.W. 2d 651 (2003), an employee was severely injured in an auto accident that was unrelated to her employment and required the use of a wheelchair. The employee wanted to return to her position as head of a department that weighted, cut, packed, labeled, and prepared cheese for shipment. All four of the people in the department were trained to assist the other department employees. The employer's consultant determined that the employer could not create reasonable accommodations that would allow the employee to do the job she had before the accident. The employee's consultant disagreed and the employee filed a charge of discrimination on the basis of disability when the employer refused to reinstate her. The administrative law judge determined that no reasonable accommodations could be made without imposing a hardship on the employer. The Labor and Industry Review Commission (LIRC) reversed the hearing decision, requiring the employer to modify the duties of the employee as part of the accommodation for the employee's disability, and its decision was upheld by the circuit court and court of appeals.

The supreme court gave great weight to LIRC's decision and said that it should be set aside only if LIRC's action depended on findings of fact that were not supported by substantial evidence. The court noted that once a disability is proved, the burden shifts to the employer to show that even if reasonable accommodations were provided, the employee would not be able to perform the duties of the job, or that the necessary accommodations to allow the employee to perform the duties of the job would create a hardship on the employer.

The court upheld LIRC's decision, finding that the employer discriminated by not modifying the duties of the employee as part of the accommodation for her disability. The court also found that the employer could have accommodated the employee without hardship, because there was credible testimony that coworkers could do the duties the employee could not and because the employee infrequently performed the duties which she was now unable to perform.

Justice Prosser dissented, saying that the majority misinterpreted the statute and used the wrong standard of review because LIRC had been inconsistent regarding its interpretation of this issue.

The second case, *Hutchinson Technology, Inc. v. LIRC*, 2004 WI 90, 273 Wis 2d 394, 682 N.W. 2d 717 (2004), expanded on the discussion of the type of accommodation that an employer must make for a person with a disability. The employee in this case had lower back pain that allowed her to work only eight of the full 12-hour shifts that the employer required. The employer terminated her when she could not return to 12-hour shifts that all other employees worked. The administrative law judge, LIRC, the circuit court and the court of appeals found for the employee.

As in the Crystal Lake case, the court had to decide if the employer could accommodate the employee's disability so that the injured employee could continue at the job without creating a hardship for the employer. Again, the court found that the employer did not meet its burden of proving that no reasonable accommodation could be made since the employee was willing and able to work eight-hour shifts and the employer did not present any evidence as to how this would create a hardship.

Justice Diane Sykes concurred, saying this case was controlled by the earlier court decision, which she argued was incorrect.

Justice Roggensack dissented, saying that the employer had the right to use 12-hour shifts as an efficient method of manufacturing and the employee in this case cannot be accommodated because she cannot work the required 12 hours. Requiring an employer to adjust its work shifts to accommodate an employee with a disability is a sea change in the law, said Roggensack.

Standard for Board of Adjustment Zoning Variance Decision

The supreme court, in *State ex rel Ziervogel v. Board of Adjustment*, 2004 WI 23, 269 Wis. 2d 546, 676 N.W. 2d 401 (2004), overturned an earlier supreme court case that held that all requests for zoning variances must meet the burden of proving that without the variance, the property owner would have no reasonable use of the property. In this case, the owners of lake property requested a variance from the county zoning ordinance to expand their home with a vertical addition. The variance was denied because they had a home on the property, so they could not meet the no reasonable use burden.

The supreme court noted that state law authorizes boards of adjustment to grant variances to allow some flexibility, avoid the taking of a person's property, balance the public interest of zoning compliance with the private interest of individuals, and allow relief from the strict enforcement of zoning where individual injustice may otherwise occur. The statute gives boards discretion to consider the conditions that are unique to the property, not to the property owner.

After reviewing the difference between an area variance and a use variance, where the property owner wants to use the property in a way that is inconsistent with the type of zoning allowed, the court overruled its previous decision as it applied to an area variance. The court said, "Application of the 'no reasonable use' standard to area variances overwhelms all other considerations in the analysis, rendering irrelevant any inquiry into the uniqueness of the property, the purpose of the ordinance, and the effect of the variance on the public interest." (p. 567)

The court held that in area variance cases, the standard is unnecessary hardship, which depends on the purpose of the zoning ordinance in question, the effect of the zoning ordinance on the particular property involved, and the effect of the variance on the neighborhood and public interest. The court said that the hardship must be unique to the property and not created by the owner, and that the burden of proving the hardship rests with the property owner.

In *State v. Waushara County Board of Adjustment*, 2004 WI 56, 271 Wis. 2d 530, 679 N.W. 2d 514 (2004), another variance case involving an addition to lake property, the supreme court clarified the standard that the board of adjustment must use to determine whether to grant a variance. The court held that the board must focus on the purpose of the ordinance that established the zoning and grant a variance if enforcement would unreasonably prevent an owner from using the property for a permitted purpose. The court concluded that the facts of each case should be analyzed in light of the ordinance's purpose and the board should have flexibility to determine if strict compliance with the ordinance would create unnecessary hardship.

Justice Bradley dissented, saying that the *Waushara* decision sacrifices the constitutionally protected public trust rights that all citizens have in the navigable waters of the state.

Subpoena of Legislative Electronic Data

This case discusses the extent to which a John Doe criminal investigation can gain access to the electronic records of the legislature. This is one of those rare cases where a state agency, the Legislative Technology Services Bureau (LTSB), petitioned the supreme court for a supervisory writ against a John Doe judge. The case, *In the matter of a John Doe Proceeding v. Wisconsin*, 2004 WI 65, 272 Wis. 2d 208, 680 N.W. 2d 792 (2004), involved a subpoena issued by the judge in the John Doe proceeding seeking access to all of the electronic data of the legislature in the custody of LTSB as part of an investigation into alleged criminal conduct involving the legislative political caucuses. The court first reviewed the powers and duties of a judge in a John Doe proceeding, noting that the judge has the power to issue subpoenas but does not have the power to grant immunity or to "...ferret out crime wherever he or she thinks it might exist." (p.   )

The court was presented with a number of arguments on behalf of LTSB for refusing to provide the data. The court held that merely because LTSB is required to maintain the confidential nature of the data does not create a privilege and does not excuse it from complying with a valid subpoena for documents to investigate a crime. The court was also urged to deny the subpoena because to allow it would violate the constitutional provision prohibiting liability in any civil or criminal action for words spoken by legislators in debate. The court stated that it could not determine from the record if the allegations involved the duties that legislators were elected to perform. Even if the allegations did involve those duties, said the court, that immunity applies only to the use of the information for prosecution, not to maintaining the secrecy of the communication. The court recognized that this constitutional immunity applies to all of the duties of a legislator, not just speech on the floor of the house, but stated that it does not provide a "...safe haven for a legislator who has committed a criminal or an unconstitutional act...". (p.   )

In response to the argument that the data should not be disclosed because to do so would violate the separation of powers, the court noted that the subpoena did not attempt to change the way the legislature functioned, only to determine if a crime had been committed. The employees of the legislature are not immune from criminal prosecution; to do so would usurp the role of the executive branch in executing the law and prosecuting crime. The court also held that the courts will not decide whether the legislature adhered to its internal rules of governance because the legislature is free to repeal any of its rules at any time, and failure to obey one of its own rules is an ad hoc repeal of that rule. But the court held that the provision giving LTSB authority to maintain the confidential nature of legislative electronic data has nothing to do with the process of legislation or how it determines the qualifications of its members. In addition, said the court, the confidential nature of the communication will be maintained until the legislator or staff member is heard by the judge on the merits of any claim regarding the nature of a specific communication.

The court ultimately denied the subpoena because it was overbroad and in violation of the Fourth Amendment to the U.S. Constitution, which prohibits unreasonable searches. The court noted that the subpoena was much like the general warrant that is prohibited by the Fourth Amendment, because it asked for all data in the custody of LTSB without any limit as to time or nature. This could amount, said the court, to the equivalent of millions of pages of documents. Based on these findings, the court held that the request for all electronic data of an entire branch of government for an unlimited period, without specifying the topics or types of documents in which evidence of a crime could be found, was overly broad.

Chief Justice Abrahamson concurred in the opinion but was concerned that the majority opinion failed to give significant guidance to litigants and the John Doe judge. In addition, the chief justice said that the discussion of the Fourth Amendment was unnecessary and was not based on any arguments briefed by the parties.

What is a Trial?

This case, *City of Pewaukee v. Carter*, 2004 WI 136, 271 Wis 2d 108 (2004), required the supreme court to determine when a trial occurs. As the court said, "Defining the word 'trial' would not seem to present a particularly difficult task, and in the abstract, it is not difficult." But this case ended up in the Wisconsin Supreme Court because there was no agreed-upon definition of its meaning.

The case involved a traffic accident resulting from the defendant operating a motor vehicle while intoxicated. In municipal court, the city presented three witnesses and documentary evidence regarding the violation but was not able to use the defendant's blood test because the officer who had taken the blood was not available to testify. The city rested its case and the defendant, instead of presenting any evidence, moved to dismiss the action on the ground that the city had failed to meet its burden of proof. The motion was granted and the city requested a new trial in circuit court under a statute that allows either party to request a new trial.

Both the circuit court and the court of appeals denied the city's request, saying that there could not be a new trial because there had not been a trial at the municipal court. The supreme court reviewed extrinsic sources, including Black's Law Dictionary and cases from other states, to determine if a trial had been held, and concluded that the court of appeals had incorrectly decided that a trial had not been held. The court held that to determine if there has been a trial, the courts should focus on the substance of the proceeding and on indicators of a trial, including whether the proceeding began with pleadings, whether it took place in court before a judge, whether the parties were present, whether evidence was introduced, and whether a decision was rendered on the evidence.

An earlier case relied upon by the defendant, said the court, did not involve a trial at the municipal court because a motion to dismiss the case was made before the introduction of any evidence or the swearing in of any witnesses. This case, in contrast, included the presentation of witnesses, cross examination, and the introduction of documentary evidence. The defendant, said the court, had the opportunity to present evidence, rest his case, or move for dismissal. Based on the evidence presented, the municipal court issued a dismissal.

The supreme court specifically withdrew the language in the earlier-cited decision that required that a case be "fully litigated" or that there be a "full trial" at the municipal court before allowing another trial at the circuit court. The legislative history, said the court, does not support the position that "...allowing a new trial in circuit court when a municipality fails to meet its burden of proof in municipal court defeats the legislative objective of limiting new trials in circuit court." (p.) The court concluded that there was a trial at the municipal court so the city had the right to a new trial at the circuit court.

When is an Agent Really an Agent for the Service of a Summons

This case presents a dilemma for those persons who attempt to serve a person in a civil action by serving the agent of that person. In *Mared v. Mansfield*, 2005 WI 5,_____, 690 N.W. 2d 835 (2005), a process server attempted to serve a summons on Mansfield at his place of business.

The receptionist referred the process server to another employee, who said he was authorized to accept the service of the summons. Upon asking again to serve Mansfield, the employee insisted that he was authorized to accept service, so the process server left the summons with that employee. Later, when attempting to reopen the default judgment in the action, Mansfield stated that his employee did not have authority to accept service. The circuit court reopened the default judgment, and after finding that the service was not made on Mansfield or on a competent person at his abode, dismissed the action for lack of personal jurisdiction on Mansfield because of ineffective service. The court of appeals reversed.

The supreme court reviewed the statute, which said that service may be effective by serving the summons upon the defendant or upon an agent authorized by appointment or by law to accept service. Thus, the question was whether the service was on an agent authorized to accept service. The service of the summons is a condition necessary to obtain personal jurisdiction and must be done correctly to ensure that the person is aware that an action is being started.

The court of appeals determined that only the apparent authority of the agent to accept service is necessary, not actual authority; otherwise, a process server could never be sure that service was effective if a person said he or she was a person's agent. The supreme court rejected this argument, citing other statutes that allow service on a person who is "apparently in charge." If the legislature wanted to allow an apparent agent to accept service, the court said, the legislature would have included that language.

The court went on to conclude that in this case, although the process server had a reasonable belief that the person was an agent, that belief was insufficient. Service of process creates personal jurisdiction and subjects a person to the decision of a court, so actual authority to accept service is necessary. The principal, said the court, must have established an explicit agency agreement, which was not true in this case. The court noted that this case illustrated how risky it is to attempt to serve a defendant's agent.

Statistics

8

Statistical information on Wisconsin: agriculture, associations, commerce and industry, conservation and recreation, education, employment and income, geography and climate, history, local and state government, military and veterans affairs, news media, population and vital statistics, post offices, social services, state and local finance, and transportation

Lafayette County Courthouse

Kathleen Sitter, LRB

WISCONSIN STATE DOCUMENT DEPOSITORY LIBRARIES

Most of the data presented in the statistical section of the *Wisconsin Blue Book* are based on publications issued by the federal government and Wisconsin state agencies. Persons wishing to consult the original sources for further information may find them at one of following depository libraries or may borrow many of them from libraries throughout the state on interlibrary loan. State depository libraries are designated to receive copies of all collected publications. Regional depository libraries receive approximately three-quarters of all collected publications, and limited depository libraries receive two-thirds.

City	Library	Street Address
STATE LEVEL DEPOSITORY		
Madison	Dr. H. Rupert Theobald Library, Legislative Reference Bureau	1 E. Main Street, Suite 200
Madison	State Historical Society of Wisconsin	816 State Street
Madison	Reference and Loan Library, Department of Public Instruction	2109 S. Stoughton Road
REGIONAL DEPOSITORY		
Eau Claire	William D. McIntyre Library, UW-Eau Claire	105 Garfield Avenue
Fond du Lac	Fond du Lac Public Library	32 Sheboygan Street
Green Bay	Cofrin Library, UW-Green Bay	2420 Nicolet Drive
La Crosse	La Crosse Public Library	800 Main Street
Milwaukee	Milwaukee Public Library	814 W. Wisconsin Avenue
Platteville	Elton S. Karrmann Library, UW-Platteville	1 University Plaza
Racine	Racine Public Library	75 Seventh Street
River Falls	Chalmer Davee Library, UW-River Falls	410 S. Third Street
Stevens Point	UW-Stevens Point Library	900 Reserve Street
Superior	Superior Public Library	1530 Tower Avenue
LIMITED DEPOSITORY		
Appleton	Appleton Public Library	225 N. Oneida Street
Appleton	Seeley G. Mudd Library, Lawrence University	113 S. Lawe Street
Baraboo	T.N. Savides Library, UW College-Baraboo/Sauk County	1006 Connie Road
Beaver Dam	Beaver Dam Community Library	311 N. Spring Street
Beloit	Morse Library, Beloit College Library	731 College Street
Eau Claire	L.E. Phillips Memorial Public Library	400 Eau Claire Street
Green Bay	Brown County Library	515 Pine Street
Hayward	Lac Courte Oreilles Ojibwa College Community Library	13466 W. Trepania Road
Janesville	Gary J. Lenox Library, UW College-Rock County	2909 Kellogg Avenue
Janesville	Hedberg Public Library	316 S. Main Street
Kenosha	UW-Parkside Library	900 Wood Road
La Crosse	Murphy Library, UW-La Crosse	1631 Pine Street
Madison	Madison Public Library	201 W. Mifflin Street
Manitowoc	Manitowoc Public Library	707 Quay Street
Marshfield	UW College-Marshfield/Wood County Library	2000 W. Fifth Street
Menomonie	Library Learning Center, UW-Stout Library	315-Tenth Avenue
Milwaukee	Alverno College Library	3401 S. Thirty-ninth Street
Milwaukee	Golda Meir Library, UW-Milwaukee	2311 E. Hartford Avenue
Milwaukee	Marquette University Raynor Memorial Libraries	1355 W. Wisconsin Avenue
Oshkosh	Forrest R. Polk Library, UW-Oshkosh	800 Algoma Boulevard
Oshkosh	Oshkosh Public Library	106 Washington Avenue
Portage	Portage Public Library	253 W. Edgewater Street
Rhinelander	Richard J. Brown Library, Nicolet Area Technical College	County Highway G
Rice Lake	UW College-Barron County Library	1800 College Drive
Ripon	Lane Library, Ripon College	300 Seward Street
Shawano	Shawano City-County Library	128 S. Sawyer Street
Superior	Jim Dan Hill Library, UW-Superior	Belknap and Catlin Streets
Two Rivers	Lester Public Library	1001 Adams Street
Waukesha	UW College-Waukesha County Library	1500 University Drive
Waukesha	Waukesha Public Library	321 Wisconsin Avenue
Wausau	Marathon County Public Library	300 N. First Street
Wauwatosa	Wauwatosa Public Library	7635 W. North Avenue
West Bend	UW College-Washington County Library	400 University Drive
Whitewater	Harold G. Andersen Library, UW-Whitewater	800 W. Main Street
Wisconsin Rapids	McMillan Memorial Library	490 E. Grand Avenue

Source: Wisconsin Department of Public Instruction, Reference and Loan Library at:
http://www.dpi.state.wi.us/dpi/dltcl/rll/liblist.html [February 4, 2005].

HIGHLIGHTS OF AGRICULTURE IN WISCONSIN

Farm Production — In 2003, Wisconsin ranked first nationally in the production of cheese (including 68% of domestic Muenster and Brick production and 100% of Limburger production) and dry whey products and second (to California) in the production of milk and butter. In crop production, it ranked first in cranberries, corn for silage, and snap beans for processing. It was among the top five producers of oats, potatoes, tart cherries, carrots, maple syrup, mint for oil, sweet corn for processing, green peas for processing, and cucumbers for pickles. Wisconsin is also the leading producer of mink pelts. As befits the state known as "America's Dairyland", Wisconsin had more milk cows than any other state in the nation except California, with almost 1.25 million head, about 14% of the nation's total.

Cash Receipts and Income — Total net Wisconsin farm income was $1.625 billion in 2003, an increase of $482 million from 2001. Wisconsin ranked 11th nationally in total net income in 2003, up from 17th in 2001. California led the nation in farm income for 2003 with $8.5 billion, while Rhode Island, with $9.8 million, ranked last.

Total cash receipts for Wisconsin farm products marketed in 2003 amounted to almost $5.9 billion. California led the nation that year in total cash receipts from farm marketings at $27.8 billion, while Wisconsin ranked 10th. Dairy products accounted for 48.3% of Wisconsin's cash receipts from farm marketings in 2003, with food grains and feed and oil crops providing 16.8% and meat animals 14%.

Number and Size of Farms — From 1999 to 2004, the number of farms in the nation declined by 73,810 to 2,113,470; in Wisconsin, the number dropped from about 78,000 to 76,500. Until the 1990s, the number of Wisconsin's farms had decreased fairly steadily from a peak of 199,877 in 1935, but the decline has slowed in recent years. Wisconsin farmland decreased from 23.5 million acres to 15.6 million acres between 1935 and 2004, and the average farm size increased from 117 acres to 204 acres over the same period.

Marathon and Dane Counties had the largest number of farms in Wisconsin in 2002. Marathon County had 2,898 farms, 332 fewer than in 1998, and Dane County had 2,887 farms, a loss of 243. Grant County had the most farmland in 2002 with 606,000 acres. Adams County had the largest average farm size at 298 acres. Smallest were the Milwaukee County farms, averaging 72 acres.

Value of Farms and Farmland — Land and buildings on Wisconsin farms were valued at about $35.9 billion in 2003, an increase of $5.07 billion or 16.5% from 2001. The average value per farm increased from $400,130 in 2001 to $469,020 in 2003. The average value per acre in 2003 was $2,300, an increase of $350 over 2001.

The average price for agricultural land sold in Wisconsin during 2003 was $3,268 per acre, a $447 increase from the $2,821 average selling price in 2002. Land continuing in agricultural use after sale sold for a statewide average of $2,480 per acre in 2003; agricultural land that sold for other uses was purchased for an average price of $5,500 per acre.

Farm Assets and Debts — Wisconsin farms recorded total assets of $43.4 billion in 2003 and total farm debt of $6.7 billion for a debt-to-asset ratio of 15.4%, making it 18th highest in the nation, and topping the national average of 14.4%; Arizona had the lowest debt ratio at 3.5%. California's total farm debt of $20 billion was the highest among the 50 states. Texas led the nation both in total farm assets ($111.6 billion) and in equity ($98.3 billion).

Farm Ownership — According to the 2002 Census of Agriculture, about 68% of the farms in Wisconsin were operated by full owners, and about 27% were operated by part owners. Only about 4.6% of Wisconsin farms were run by tenants. The vast majority of Wisconsin farms (89%) were individually run or operated by family organizations or partnerships, while only a small number were organized as family or nonfamily corporations.

The following tables present selected data. Consult footnoted sources for more detailed information on agriculture.

WISCONSIN'S RANK IN AGRICULTURE, 2003

Commodity	Unit	United States (000s)	Wisconsin (000s)	Wisconsin Percent of U.S.	Rank in U.S.	Leading State in U.S.
CASH RECEIPTS						
ALL COMMODITIES		$211,646,849	5,876,052	2.8%	10	California
Livestock and livestock products		105,470,948	4,093,706	3.9	7	Texas
Crops		106,175,901	1,782,346	1.7	20	California
PRODUCTION						
DAIRY						
Milk production	Lbs	170,312,000	22,266,000	13.1%	2	California
Butter	Lbs	1,242,358	309,264	24.9	2	California
Cheese (excluding cottage cheese)	Lbs	8,597,976	2,276,648	26.5	1	Wisconsin
American	Lbs	3,669,509	828,438	22.6	1	Wisconsin
Swiss	Lbs	264,807	35,776	13.5	2	Ohio
Limburger	Lbs	712	712	100.0	1	Wisconsin
Brick and Muenster	Lbs	89,290	60,330	67.6	1	Wisconsin
Mozzarella	Lbs	2,806,099	776,996	27.7	2	California
Italian	Lbs	3,522,049	1,031,859	29.3	1	Wisconsin
Cottage cheese						
4 or more milkfat	Lbs	385,176	9,455	2.5	10	New York
Less than 4 milkfat	Lbs	380,033	11,809	3.1	6	New York
Whey products						
Dry whey	Lbs	1,086,343	326,670	30.1	1	Wisconsin
Lactose	Lbs	588,455	119,412	20.3	NA	NA
LIVESTOCK AND POULTRY						
Cattle and calves, all[1]	Head	94,882	3,350	3.5	9	Texas
Milk cows[1]	Head	8,991	1,245	13.8	2	California
Hogs and pigs, all[2]	Head	60,040	490	0.8	16	Iowa
Sheep[1]	Head	6,090	83	1.4	19[5]	Texas
Equine[3]	Head	5,317	120	2.3	22[6]	Texas
Chickens[2]	Head	448,748	5,500	1.2	21	Iowa
Broilers	Head	8,266,500	34,400	0.4	19	Georgia
Trout, sold 12" or longer	Lbs	50,716	441	0.9	8	Idaho
Mink pelts	Pelts	2,549	706	27.7	1	Wisconsin
Honey	Lbs	181,096	5,698	3.1	8	California
Eggs	Eggs	87,196,000	1,137,000	1.3	19	Iowa
CROPS						
Corn for grain	Bu	10,113,887	367,650	3.6	8	Iowa
Corn for silage	Tons	105,864	14,080	13.3	1	Wisconsin
Oats	Bu	144,649	15,410	10.7	4	North Dakota
Soybeans	Bu	2,453,665	46,760	1.9	15	Illinois
Wheat, all	Bu	2,336,526	12,300	0.5	23	Kansas
Barley	Bu	276,087	1,925	0.7	16	North Dakota
Hay (dry only), all	Tons	157,123	4,380	2.8	15	Texas
Potatoes, all	Cwt	457,814	32,800	7.2	3	Idaho
Tobacco	Lbs	802,654	4,255	0.5	11	North Carolina
Dry edible beans	Cwt	22,515	124	0.6	16	North Dakota
Cherries, tart	Lbs	226,500	13,300	5.9	4	Michigan
Apples	Lbs	8,613,300	68,000	0.8	12	Washington
Strawberries	Cwt	20,811	45	0.2	10	California
Maple syrup[4]	Gals	1,507	100	6.6	4	Vermont
Cranberries	Bbl	6,183	3,607	58.3	1	Wisconsin
Mint for oil	Lbs	8,702	241	2.8	5	Washington
Carrots, all	Tons	445	96	21.6	3	Washington
Onions	Cwt	69,695	690	1.0	12	California
Cabbage for fresh market	Cwt	22,364	989	4.4	9	California
Sweet corn for fresh market	Cwt	28,982	629	2.2	12	Florida
Sweet corn for processing	Tons	3,266	681	20.9	3	Minnesota
Green peas for processing	Tons	468	84	18.0	3	Minnesota
Snap beans for processing	Tons	728	271	37.2	1	Wisconsin
Cucumbers for pickles	Tons	648	36	5.6	2	Michigan

Abbreviations: Bbl = barrels, Bu = bushels, Cwt = hundredweight, Gals = gallons, Lbs = pounds, NA = not available.

Note: Wisconsin is also a leading state in the production of turkeys, ducks, ginseng, and forage; Wisconsin's rank is not available for these commodities.

[1]January 1, 2004 inventory. [2]December 1, 2003 inventory. [3]January 1, 1999 inventory. [4]Data for 2004. [5]Tied with Michigan. [6]Tied with Oregon.

Sources: U.S. Department of Agriculture, National Agricultural Statistics Service, "Wisconsin's Rank in the Nation's Agriculture, 2003", October 25, 2004, at: http://www.nass.usda.gov/wi/rankwi.pdf; U.S. Department of Agriculture, Economic Research Service, "Ranking of 25 Top Producing States in 25 Leading Commodities, 2003", August 24, 2004, and "Cash Receipts and 4 Leading Commodities for the 50 States, 2003", September 16, 2004, at: http://www.ers.usda.gov/Data/FarmIncome/firkdmu.htm; Wisconsin Agricultural Statistics Service, departmental data, December 2004.

WISCONSIN CASH RECEIPTS FROM FARM MARKETINGS
By Commodity, 1999 – 2003 (In Thousands)

Commodity	1999	2000	2001	2002	2003
ALL COMMODITIES	**$5,556,488**	**$5,366,655**	**$5,931,499**	**$5,520,802**	**$5,876,052**
LIVESTOCK, DAIRY, AND POULTRY	**4,193,688**	**3,869,650**	**4,519,941**	**3,792,248**	**4,093,706**
Meat animals	**701,021**	**816,715**	**839,680**	**716,622**	**823,624**
Cattle and calves	600,175	700,966	707,049	627,622	711,340
Hogs	96,133	110,089	127,958	83,915	105,936
Sheep and lambs	4,713	5,660	4,673	5,085	6,348
Milk, wholesale	**3,146,262**	**2,688,309**	**3,244,752**	**2,662,650**	**2,838,258**
Poultry and eggs	**229,454**	**236,189**	**256,750**	**227,521**	**249,351**
Broilers	57,204	50,184	53,703	43,590	54,180
Chicken eggs	35,741	48,898	51,458	49,312	55,618
Other poultry	43,249	44,229	51,200	51,415	51,475
Miscellaneous livestock	**116,951**	**128,437**	**178,759**	**185,455**	**182,473**
Honey	4,080	5,141	4,450	8,911	8,205
Wool	90	62	50	72	120
Trout	1,689	1,732	1,833	1,760	1,677
Other livestock	111,092	118,602	167,126	169,332	167,071
Mink pelts	19,852	24,658	23,123	22,512	20,961
All other livestock*	91,240	93,944	144,003	146,820	146,110
CROPS	**1,362,800**	**1,497,006**	**1,411,558**	**1,728,553**	**1,782,346**
Food grains	**18,931**	**20,891**	**28,550**	**38,047**	**39,123**
Rye	18,103	20,373	NR	NR	NR
Wheat	828	610	NR	NR	NR
Feed crops	**566,366**	**619,045**	**510,619**	**682,807**	**717,576**
Barley	1,385	1,350	852	869	996
Corn	516,274	565,828	451,899	611,702	643,653
Hay	39,534	46,647	51,861	60,533	65,319
Oats	9,173	5,221	6,007	9,702	7,608
Tobacco	**6,335**	**4,198**	**3,496**	**5,971**	**6,680**
Oil crops	**169,020**	**205,624**	**153,716**	**244,565**	**230,787**
Soybeans	168,257	204,917	153,340	244,247	230,397
Vegetables	**342,122**	**393,583**	**382,586**	**378,344**	**380,751**
Beans, dry	3,066	2,822	2,547	2,107	2,868
Potatoes, fall	142,240	189,028	186,466	194,340	179,774
Beans, snap, processing	32,882	34,802	28,008	35,872	30,389
Beets, processing	2,187	2,850	2,146	NA	NA
Cabbage	11,322	12,587	9,711	7,020	9,593
Carrots	6,324	6,759	5,025	6,681	6,300
Corn, sweet	48,637	48,127	54,687	43,831	56,938
Cucumbers, processing	5,643	7,305	5,870	5,366	6,422
Onions, storage	5,523	4,621	3,515	4,755	6,228
Peas, green, processing	19,366	21,464	16,249	13,505	17,373
Miscellaneous vegetables	61,900	61,460	64,050	63,500	63,500
Fruits and nuts	**83,223**	**70,720**	**83,037**	**124,037**	**152,615**
Apples	8,916	17,151	15,235	13,856	18,838
Cherries, tart	1,561	2,211	2,654	2,048	5,481
Cranberries	66,118	45,192	58,428	101,615	121,381
Strawberries, spring	5,148	4,576	5,060	4,988	5,265
Other berries	1,350	1,460	1,260	1,100	1,200
All other crops	**176,804**	**182,945**	**249,553**	**254,781**	**254,814**
Maple product	1,778	1,800	1,986	2,315	2,212
Mint (peppermint and spearmint)	6,361	5,090	4,903	4,334	2,396
Greenhouse/nursery	165,360	172,001	228,084	234,459	237,827
Floriculture	65,315	65,156	74,584	79,359	82,327
Christmas trees	32,500	37,500	29,000	29,300	29,500

Note: Bold figures indicate category totals of the commodities immediately following and indicate categories included in next higher level of aggregation. Category totals may include amounts for specific commodities not listed separately or that are not listed to provide confidentiality to large producers in concentrated industries.
NA – not available. NR – not for release.
*Horses and mules are included in "all other livestock".
Source: U.S. Department of Agriculture, Economic Research Service, "Farm Cash Receipts, 1997-2003", July 29, 2004 at: http://www.ers.usda.gov/Data/FarmIncome/FinFidMu.htm

2003 WISCONSIN CASH RECEIPTS FROM FARM MARKETINGS
(Percent of All Commodities)

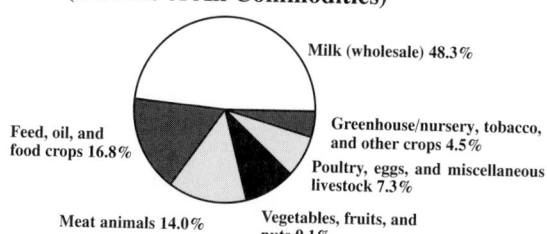

Milk (wholesale) 48.3%

Feed, oil, and food crops 16.8%

Greenhouse/nursery, tobacco, and other crops 4.5%

Poultry, eggs, and miscellaneous livestock 7.3%

Meat animals 14.0%

Vegetables, fruits, and nuts 9.1%

WISCONSIN FARM INCOME AND DEBT, 1999-2003

	1999	2000	2001	2002	2003
Number of farms	78,000	77,500	77,000	77,000	76,500
Average net farm income per farm (dollars)	$17,125	$9,757	$14,859	$13,086	$21,255
		Income (in thousands)			
Value of crop production	$1,487,582	$1,362,228	$1,417,892	$1,816,884	$1,688,685
Value of livestock production	4,194,759	3,831,296	4,470,012	3,845,161	4,094,337
Revenues from services and forestry	821,982	875,927	1,009,787	938,710	972,685
VALUE OF AGRICULTURAL SECTOR OUTPUT[1]	$6,504,322	$6,069,452	$6,897,691	$6,600,756	$6,755,707
Less: Purchased inputs[2]	3,219,514	3,306,528	3,584,302	3,384,871	3,164,223
Less: Motor vehicle registration and licensing	13,436	12,518	14,455	12,038	7,192
Less: Property taxes	338,174	347,087	337,741	304,052	309,990
Plus: Direct Government payments	503,046	603,213	415,110	330,604	484,302
GROSS VALUE ADDED	$3,436,244	$3,006,532	$3,376,303	$3,230,399	$3,758,604
Less: Capital consumption (depreciation)	866,794	920,646	959,886	969,854	965,153
NET VALUE ADDED[3]	$2,569,450	$2,085,886	$2,416,417	$2,260,545	$2,793,451
Less: Factor payments[4]	1,233,669	1,329,722	1,272,277	1,252,902	1,167,470
NET FARM INCOME[5]	$1,335,781	$756,164	$1,144,140	$1,007,643	$1,625,981
		Debt (in thousands)			
Farm assets	$32,405,516	$36,065,214	$38,305,768	$40,780,320	$43,380,461
Farm debt	5,645,763	5,982,824	6,288,468	6,531,705	6,699,068
Equity	$26,759,754	$30,082,390	$32,017,300	$34,248,614	$36,681,393
Ratio:					
Debt/equity	21.1	19.9	19.6	19.1	18.3
Debt/assets	17.4	16.6	16.4	16.0	15.4

[1]Value of agricultural sector output is the gross value of the commodities and services produced within a year.
[2]Includes purchases of feed, livestock, poultry, and seed; outlays for fertilizers and lime, pesticides, fuel and electricity; capital repair and maintenance; and marketing, storage, transportation, contract labor, and other expenses.
[3]Net value added is the sector's contribution to the national economy and is the sum of the income from production earned by all factors of production, regardless of ownership.
[4]Includes compensation for hired labor, net rent received by nonoperator landlords, and interest payments.
[5]Net farm income is the farm operators' share of income from the sector's production activities.
Sources: U.S. Department of Agriculture, Economic Research Service, "Value added to the U.S. economy by the agricultural sector via the production of goods and services, 1990-2003, Wisconsin", September 4, 2004, at: http://www.ers.usda.gov/data/FarmIncome/finfidmu.htm and "Farm business balance sheet, December 31, 1990-2003", October 27, 2004, at: http://www.ers.usda.gov/Data/FarmBalanceSheet/fbsdmu.htm. Average net farm income calculated by Wisconsin Legislative Reference Bureau. Prior year's numbers have been revised to reflect updated source data.

NUMBER, SIZE AND VALUE OF FARMS IN WISCONSIN, 1935 – 2003

Year	Number of Farms	Land in Farms (acres)	Average Size of Farm (acres)	Value of Land and Buildings Total (in millions)	Value of Land and Buildings Average per Farm	Value of Land and Buildings Average per Acre
1935	200,000	23,500,000	117	$1,246	$6,228	$53
1940	187,000	22,900,000	123	1,191	6,368	52
1945	178,000	23,600,000	133	1,440	8,088	61
1950	174,000	23,600,000	136	2,100	12,071	89
1955	155,000	23,200,000	150	2,343	15,117	101
1960	138,000	22,200,000	161	2,953	21,396	133
1965	124,000	21,400,000	173	3,317	26,750	155
1970	110,000	20,100,000	183	4,663	42,393	232
1975	100,000	19,300,000	193	8,376	83,762	434
1980	93,000	18,600,000	200	18,674	200,800	1,004
1985	83,000	17,900,000	216	16,898	203,586	944
1990	80,000	17,600,000	220	14,098	176,220	801
1995	80,000	16,800,000	210	17,472	218,400	1,040
1996	79,000	16,600,000	210	18,758	237,443	1,130
1997	79,000	16,500,000	209	19,305	244,367	1,170
1998	78,000	16,300,000	209	20,212	259,128	1,240
1999	78,000	16,200,000	208	23,490	301,154	1,450
2000	77,500	16,000,000	206	27,200	350,968	1,700
2001	77,000	15,800,000	205	30,810	400,130	1,950
2002	77,000	15,700,000	204	33,755	438,377	2,150
2003	76,500	15,600,000	204	35,880	469,020	2,300

Note: "Farm" is defined as a place that sells, or would normally sell, at least $1,000 of agricultural products during the year. The actual number of farms in Wisconsin peaked at 199,877 in 1935. "Average Size of Farm", "Value Average per Farm", and "Total" figures calculated by the Wisconsin Legislative Reference Bureau. Prior years' data have been revised to reflect updated source data.
Sources: U.S. Department of Agriculture, National Agricultural Statistics Service, "Farms and Land in Farms", February 2004; "Farm Numbers and Land in Farms: Final Estimates 1998-2002", February 2004; "Agricultural Land Values and Cash Rents – Final Estimates, 1999-2003", March 2004.

CASH RECEIPTS AND INCOME FROM FARMING
By State, 2003
(In Thousands)

State	Cash Receipts Livestock and Products	Crops	Total	Government Payments[1]	Income Gross	Net	Rank[2]
Alabama	$2,739,169	$676,129	$3,415,298	$220,086	$4,127,619	$1,604,440	12
Alaska	27,580	23,316	50,896	2,021	56,713	10,060	49
Arizona	1,258,603	1,327,419	2,586,023	134,663	3,028,539	1,077,743	24
Arkansas	3,215,107	2,083,102	5,298,209	843,675	5,952,183	1,914,275	7
California	6,992,958	20,811,838	27,804,796	653,657	29,377,486	8,474,761	1
Colorado	3,675,669	1,288,642	4,964,311	319,967	5,562,475	1,171,639	21
Connecticut	164,657	320,175	484,832	8,200	560,519	92,894	44
Delaware	592,662	167,557	760,219	18,533	859,125	155,678	39
Florida	1,205,816	5,243,767	6,449,583	134,597	6,832,939	1,831,021	8
Georgia	3,221,872	2,024,456	5,246,328	552,356	6,194,824	2,971,056	4
Hawaii	85,814	463,539	549,353	1,448	599,650	121,933	41
Idaho	2,177,350	1,775,893	3,953,243	152,231	4,439,955	1,217,690	20
ILLINOIS	1,799,851	6,490,106	8,289,958	865,813	9,288,826	1,657,021	9
Indiana	1,798,954	3,362,656	5,161,609	446,374	5,956,758	1,327,733	17
IOWA	6,073,014	6,560,188	12,633,200	1,050,621	13,121,662	2,022,623	6
Kansas	6,178,600	2,867,497	9,046,096	807,739	10,365,146	1,386,902	16
Kentucky	2,225,703	1,243,300	3,469,002	146,890	4,298,866	863,702	25
Louisiana	697,345	1,296,021	1,993,366	441,947	2,272,333	710,944	27
Maine	271,878	226,887	498,765	11,553	562,589	84,415	45
Maryland	846,612	619,888	1,466,500	66,667	1,756,964	326,809	37
Massachusetts	87,122	297,624	384,746	14,185	468,569	40,117	46
MICHIGAN	1,399,301	2,421,523	3,820,824	254,973	4,403,193	444,496	35
MINNESOTA	4,072,171	4,515,789	8,587,959	787,441	9,248,577	1,568,401	13
Mississippi	2,164,558	1,246,445	3,411,004	475,825	3,933,735	1,148,406	22
Missouri	2,628,329	2,344,432	4,972,761	512,358	5,727,626	1,538,969	14
Montana	1,105,266	786,878	1,892,144	355,806	2,381,953	575,983	31
Nebraska	6,867,368	3,753,907	10,621,275	725,799	11,960,387	3,227,861	3
Nevada	254,327	141,474	395,801	11,931	460,456	111,278	42
New Hampshire	62,206	87,642	149,848	5,978	180,547	16,508	47
New Jersey	187,852	658,034	845,886	12,095	962,505	127,327	40
New Mexico	1,596,800	542,790	2,139,590	92,478	2,274,749	715,637	26
New York	1,914,618	1,224,758	3,139,376	160,965	3,581,349	597,202	30
North Carolina	4,157,845	2,758,504	6,916,349	361,886	8,839,977	1,628,756	10
North Dakota	870,197	2,907,322	3,777,519	651,968	4,377,411	1,315,316	19
Ohio	1,809,452	2,852,781	4,662,233	398,754	6,011,539	1,470,336	15
Oklahoma	3,504,006	1,022,107	4,526,113	357,988	5,040,851	2,036,673	5
Oregon	804,856	2,478,876	3,283,732	111,140	3,990,226	493,216	33
Pennsylvania	2,859,177	1,407,089	4,266,265	182,865	5,034,263	1,106,794	23
Rhode Island	8,669	48,555	57,224	1,084	65,712	9,789	50
South Carolina	890,001	754,455	1,644,455	129,078	1,959,377	680,602	28
South Dakota	2,119,214	1,898,701	4,017,915	548,510	4,786,611	1,320,900	18
Tennessee	1,070,850	1,267,803	2,338,653	175,661	2,952,786	480,152	34
Texas	10,311,440	5,030,521	15,341,961	1,666,040	17,966,065	5,939,216	2
Utah	879,733	258,421	1,138,154	56,400	1,384,942	367,873	36
Vermont	402,722	78,928	481,650	28,454	561,560	102,266	43
Virginia	1,532,161	695,131	2,227,292	176,953	2,760,737	528,624	32
Washington	1,527,072	3,818,220	5,345,292	265,089	5,921,210	680,392	29
West Virginia	316,990	72,550	389,540	13,155	503,209	14,830	48
WISCONSIN	4,093,706	1,782,346	5,876,052	484,302	6,755,707	1,625,981	11
Wyoming	723,726	149,920	873,645	51,206	1,203,854	291,448	38
UNITED STATES[3]	$105,470,948	$106,175,899	$211,646,847	$15,949,402	$240,914,848	$59,228,677	

[1]Includes both cash payments and payments-in-kind (PIK).

[2]Ranking of net income calculated by Wisconsin Legislative Reference Bureau.

[3]Detail may not add due to rounding.

Source: U.S. Department of Agriculture, Economic Research Service at:
http://www.ers.usda.gov/Data/FarmIncome/receipts/rankings/misc/rk50stat.wk1, August 4, 2004
http://www.ers.usda.gov/Data/FarmIncome/govt_pay/GP2003st.wk1, July 29, 2004
http://www.ers.usda.gov/Data/FarmIncome/50State/50stmenu.htm, September 2, 2004.

NUMBER AND SIZE OF FARMS IN WISCONSIN
By County, 1998 and 2002

County	1998				2002			
	No. of Farms	Avg. Size of Farms in Acres	Land in Farms Acres (in thousands)	Rank	No. of Farms	Avg. Size of Farms in Acres	Land in Farms Acres (in thousands)	Rank
Adams	420	317	133	52[1]	414	298	124	52[1]
Ashland	230	226	52	64[1]	227	259	59	64
Barron	1,680	216	363	15	1,647	214	352	12[1]
Bayfield	380	247	94	58	468	239	112	54
Brown	1,280	170	218	36	1,117	176	197	37
Buffalo	1,170	291	341	19	1,128	280	316	18
Burnett	410	210	86	61	451	218	98	58[1]
Calumet	840	190	160	45	733	205	150	45
Chippewa	1,750	234	410	6	1,621	231	374	8
Clark	2,230	206	460	4	2,200	210	461	4
Columbia	1,640	220	360	17	1,526	228	348	14
Crawford	1,100	232	255	30	1,278	199	255	30
Dane	3,130	181	568	2	2,887	179	515	3
Dodge	2,150	199	428	5	1,968	205	404	5
Door	840	160	134	51	877	154	135	50
Douglas	310	245	76	62[1]	391	217	85	62
Dunn	1,680	241	405	7	1,683	237	399	6
Eau Claire	1,110	190	211	37	1,174	174	204	36
Florence	100	200	20	68	121	177	21	68
Fond du Lac	1,790	202	361	16	1,634	211	344	15[1]
Forest	130	223	29	67	164	205	34	67
Grant	2,630	254	667	1	2,490	243	606	1
Green	1,550	215	333	20	1,490	206	307	20
Green Lake	680	221	150	46	670	221	148	47
Iowa	1,610	249	401	8	1,686	218	367	10
Iron	50	200	10	69	62	206	13	69
Jackson	920	289	266	27	914	282	258	26[1]
Jefferson	1,480	180	267	26	1,421	174	248	31
Juneau	770	245	189	39	805	224	180	40
Kenosha	460	202	93	59	466	190	89	61
Kewaunee	970	181	176	43[1]	915	190	174	41[1]
La Crosse	920	203	187	41	868	201	174	41[1]
Lafayette	1,360	274	373	12	1,205	284	343	17
Langlade	540	246	133	52[1]	542	260	141	49
Lincoln	510	180	92	60	593	166	98	58[1]
Manitowoc	1,440	184	265	28[1]	1,469	175	257	28[1]
Marathon	3,230	175	565	3	2,898	183	531	2
Marinette	650	229	149	47	729	204	149	46
Marquette	530	257	136	49	624	233	146	48
Menominee*	—	—	—	—	4	89	354[3]	72
Milwaukee	100	80	8	70[1]	78	72	6	71
Monroe	1,880	194	365	14	1,938	182	352	12[1]
Oconto	1,110	199	221	35	1,132	193	219	35
Oneida	140	286	40	66	183	279	51	66
Outagamie	1,560	179	279	25	1,430	184	263	25
Ozaukee	500	152	76	62[1]	533	142	75	63
Pepin	510	224	114	54	501	222	111	55
Pierce	1,520	196	298	22[1]	1,510	177	267	24
Polk	1,540	194	299	21	1,659	177	293	21
Portage	1,090	271	295	24	1,197	244	292	22
Price	430	235	101	57	477	218	104	57
Racine	650	209	136	49	631	197	124	52[1]
Richland	1,230	215	265	28[1]	1,358	190	258	26[1]
Rock	1,550	248	384	9	1,529	225	344	15[1]
Rusk	690	255	176	43[1]	715	242	173	43
St. Croix	1,820	188	342	18	1,864	166	310	19
Sauk	1,730	214	370	13	1,673	211	353	11
Sawyer	220	236	52	64[1]	230	235	54	65
Shawano	1,570	190	298	22[1]	1,465	185	271	23
Sheboygan	1,170	174	204	38	1,116	175	195	38
Taylor	1,030	235	242	32	1,056	244	257	28[1]
Trempealeau	1,670	228	381	10	1,744	211	368	9
Vernon	2,240	169	379	11	2,230	171	382	7
Vilas	50	160	8	70[1]	71	137	10	70
Walworth	1,020	230	235	34	988	222	220	34
Washburn	420	248	104	56	471	224	105	56
Washington	920	151	139	48	844	154	130	51
Waukesha	750	151	113	55	762	129	98	58[1]
Waupaca	1,320	189	249	31	1,398	177	247	32
Waushara	740	254	188	40	717	269	193	39
Winnebago	1,010	181	183	42	963	177	170	44
Wood	1,150	209	240	33	1,108	206	228	33
STATE[2]	78,000	210	16,400		77,131	204	15,742	

Note: "Farm" is defined as a place that sells, or would normally sell, at least $1,000 of agricultural products during the year. USDA Census of Agriculture data may differ from USDA estimates in other tables.

*Menominee County did not report separately in 1998.

[1]Tied. [2]State totals as recorded by source document. [3]354 total acres of farmland reported. Number is not in thousands.

Sources: U.S. Department of Agriculture, National Agricultural Statistics Service, "Number of Farms, Average Size, and Land in Farms: by Counties, Wisconsin, 1997-98" at: http://www.nass.usda.gov/wi/farmno.htm [March 19,1999], and "2002 Census of Agriculture Volume 1 Chapter 2: Wisconsin County Level Data", June 2004 at: http://www.nass.usda.gov/census/census02/volume1/wi/st55_2_001_001.pdf. Rank calculated by Wisconsin Legislative Reference Bureau.

NUMBER AND ACREAGE OF FARMS
By State, 1999 and 2004

State	Number of Farms 1999	Number of Farms 2004	Farm Acreage (in thousands) 1999	Farm Acreage (in thousands) 2004	Average Farm Size (acres) 1999	Average Farm Size (acres) 2004
Alabama	48,000	44,000	9,200	8,700	192	198
Alaska	580	620	910	900	1,569	1,452
Arizona*	10,900	10,200	27,000	26,400	2,474	2,588
Arkansas	48,500	47,500	14,650	14,400	302	303
California	85,000	77,000	28,100	26,700	330	347
Colorado	30,000	30,900	31,900	30,900	1,063	1,000
Connecticut	4,250	4,200	370	360	87	86
Delaware	2,600	2,300	570	530	219	230
Florida	45,000	43,000	10,500	10,100	234	235
Georgia	49,000	49,000	11,000	10,700	224	218
Hawaii	5,500	5,500	1,420	1,300	258	236
Idaho	24,500	25,000	11,900	11,800	486	472
ILLINOIS	79,000	73,000	27,600	27,500	349	377
Indiana	64,800	59,300	15,400	15,000	237	253
IOWA	95,000	89,700	32,800	31,700	345	353
Kansas	65,000	64,500	47,500	47,200	731	732
Kentucky	91,000	85,000	13,600	13,800	149	162
Louisiana	30,000	27,200	8,130	7,850	271	289
Maine	7,100	7,200	1,320	1,370	186	190
Maryland	12,600	12,100	2,160	2,050	171	169
Massachusetts	6,100	6,100	540	520	89	85
MICHIGAN	53,000	53,200	10,190	10,100	192	190
MINNESOTA	81,000	79,800	28,200	27,600	348	346
Mississippi	42,000	42,200	11,220	11,050	267	262
Missouri	110,000	106,000	30,200	30,100	275	284
Montana	27,800	28,000	59,200	60,100	2,129	2,146
Nebraska	54,000	48,300	46,300	45,900	857	950
Nevada	3,150	3,000	6,400	6,300	2,032	2,100
New Hampshire	3,300	3,400	440	450	133	132
New Jersey	9,600	9,900	830	820	86	83
New Mexico*	18,000	17,500	45,100	44,700	2,506	2,554
New York	37,500	36,000	7,710	7,600	208	211
North Carolina	58,000	52,000	9,300	9,000	160	173
North Dakota	31,000	30,300	39,400	39,400	1,271	1,300
Ohio	79,000	77,300	14,850	14,600	188	189
Oklahoma	84,000	83,500	33,900	33,700	404	404
Oregon	40,000	40,000	17,300	17,200	433	430
Pennsylvania	59,300	58,200	7,670	7,700	129	132
Rhode Island	800	850	60	60	75	71
South Carolina	25,000	24,400	4,940	4,850	198	199
South Dakota	32,500	31,600	44,000	43,800	1,354	1,386
Tennessee	89,000	85,000	11,900	11,600	134	136
Texas	227,500	229,000	131,100	130,000	576	568
Utah	15,500	15,300	11,600	11,600	748	758
Vermont	6,700	6,400	1,300	1,250	194	195
Virginia	49,000	47,500	8,730	8,600	178	181
Washington	38,000	35,000	15,650	15,200	412	434
West Virginia	21,000	20,800	3,600	3,600	171	173
WISCONSIN	78,000	76,500	16,200	15,500	208	203
Wyoming	9,200	9,200	34,600	34,440	3,755	3,743
UNITED STATES	2,187,280	2,113,470	948,460	936,600	434	443

Note: "Farm" is defined as a place that sells, or would normally sell, at least $1,000 of agricultural products during the year.

*Includes individual farms on reservation land.

Sources: U.S. Department of Agriculture, National Agricultural Statistics Service, "Farm Numbers and Land in Farms, Final Estimates 1998-2002", February 2004, and "Farms, Land in Farms and Livestock, Summary 2004", January 2005.

WISCONSIN FARM OPERATORS
By County, 2002

County	Total Farms	Full Owners	Part Owners	Tenants	Individual or Family	Partnership	Family-held Corporation	Other than Family-held	Other*
Adams	414	303	97	14	350	40	20	2	2
Ashland	227	153	73	1	213	10	4	--	--
Barron	1,647	1,086	500	61	1,514	67	63	--	3
Bayfield	468	313	142	13	420	24	20	--	4
Brown	1,117	726	324	67	983	95	37	1	1
Buffalo	1,128	792	291	45	996	88	37	5	2
Burnett	451	302	136	13	418	22	7	1	3
Calumet	733	408	289	36	640	47	41	4	1
Chippewa	1,621	1,106	466	49	1,500	84	33	3	1
Clark	2,200	1,407	697	96	2,070	97	32	--	1
Columbia	1,526	1,009	437	80	1,348	126	39	4	9
Crawford	1,278	939	284	55	1,136	115	22	--	5
Dane	2,887	1,971	719	197	2,470	283	95	15	24
Dodge	1,968	1,247	612	109	1,721	152	83	8	4
Door	877	625	231	21	795	52	25	2	3
Douglas	391	273	107	11	372	8	6	4	1
Dunn	1,683	1,212	417	54	1,536	98	43	2	4
Eau Claire	1,174	896	248	30	1,096	55	17	2	4
Florence	121	81	36	4	108	9	4	--	--
Fond du Lac	1,634	1,006	541	87	1,415	133	66	10	10
Forest	164	119	43	2	151	11	--	--	2
Grant	2,490	1,726	601	163	2,185	234	46	5	20
Green	1,490	1,035	346	109	1,300	137	45	2	6
Green Lake	670	450	199	21	572	64	25	3	6
Iowa	1,686	1,237	355	94	1,462	174	39	4	7
Iron	62	43	17	2	57	2	3	--	--
Jackson	914	663	224	27	808	60	41	3	2
Jefferson	1,421	960	383	78	1,274	94	43	6	4
Juneau	805	589	192	24	726	62	13	2	2
Kenosha	466	300	128	38	371	40	49	3	3
Kewaunee	915	606	301	8	827	62	22	3	1
La Crosse	868	607	224	37	782	66	16	--	4
Lafayette	1,205	804	299	102	1,065	112	18	7	3
Langlade	542	360	160	22	456	41	42	1	2
Lincoln	593	375	186	32	526	41	24	--	2
Manitowoc	1,469	928	492	49	1,338	90	36	2	3
Marathon	2,898	1,896	857	145	2,614	162	116	3	3
Marinette	729	505	203	21	661	44	16	2	6
Marquette	624	456	159	9	563	40	13	1	7
Menominee	4	3	--	1	3	1	--	--	--
Milwaukee	78	51	18	9	67	1	8	--	2
Monroe	1,938	1,427	440	71	1,744	127	58	4	5
Oconto	1,132	749	332	51	1,050	61	20	--	1
Oneida	183	150	32	1	155	10	9	5	4
Outagamie	1,430	906	448	76	1,264	104	52	6	4
Ozaukee	533	341	143	49	456	34	36	4	3
Pepin	501	343	146	12	431	53	13	2	2
Pierce	1,510	1,082	379	49	1,355	72	66	3	14
Polk	1,659	1,194	420	45	1,542	72	36	2	7
Portage	1,197	779	358	60	1,057	81	52	5	2
Price	477	304	163	10	452	18	6	--	1
Racine	631	396	187	48	540	53	37	--	1
Richland	1,358	1,029	290	39	1,201	116	31	1	9
Rock	1,529	1,013	401	115	1,347	100	66	3	13
Rusk	715	444	251	20	650	42	22	1	-
St. Croix	1,864	1,412	377	75	1,672	109	64	3	16
Sauk	1,673	1,169	429	75	1,411	165	80	7	10
Sawyer	230	148	71	11	211	5	11	1	2
Shawano	1,465	922	515	28	1,325	92	44	3	1
Sheboygan	1,116	636	414	66	984	74	50	3	3
Taylor	1,056	676	348	32	991	39	22	3	1
Trempealeau	1,744	1,312	377	55	1,567	133	31	4	9
Vernon	2,230	1,565	569	96	2,054	136	24	4	12
Vilas	71	52	11	8	51	3	14	1	2
Walworth	988	597	259	132	782	83	96	7	20
Washburn	471	324	137	10	434	17	12	3	5
Washington	844	508	273	63	722	75	43	4	--
Waukesha	762	536	166	60	662	55	38	3	4
Waupaca	1,398	921	441	36	1,277	78	41	1	1
Waushara	717	497	195	25	606	62	38	1	10
Winnebago	963	623	285	55	829	77	47	2	5
Wood	1,108	747	314	47	988	58	51	2	4
STATE	77,131	52,370	21,205	3,556	68,719	5,347	2,519	207	339

*Includes cooperative, estate or trust, institutional, etc.

Source: U.S. Department of Agriculture, National Agricultural Statistics Service, *2002 Census of Agriculture*, Volume I, Chapter 2: Wisconsin County Level Data, June 2004 at: http://www.nass.usda.gov/census/census02/volume1/wi/st55_2_040_040.pdf.

WISCONSIN TOTAL AGRICULTURAL LAND SALES
By County, 2002 and 2003

| County[1] | Total Agricultural Land Sales[2] | | | | Land Continuing in Agricultural Use | | Agricultural Land Diverted to Other Uses | |
| | Number | | Dollar Avg. per Acre | | Dollar Avg. per Acre | | Dollar Avg. per Acre | |
	2002	2003	2002	2003	2002	2003	2002	2003
Adams	18	20	$1,787	$2,195	$1,802	$2,318	$1,690	$2,037
Ashland	10	16	741	1,254	808	702	489	1,635
Barron	85	93	1,423	1,681	1,347	1,724	1,948	1,518
Bayfield	24	30	766	1,629	618	1,332	988	2,190
Brown	16	26	5,564	17,569	2,400	3,302	7,546	21,584
Buffalo	57	58	1,594	1,627	1,503	1,534	1,782	1,748
Burnett	41	32	1,357	1,821	1,395	1,735	1,147	1,927
Calumet	26	26	4,074	2,875	2,124	2,844	11,558	4,103
Chippewa	86	84	1,732	1,598	1,627	1,460	1,889	2,284
Clark	107	112	1,493	1,382	1,501	1,361	1,368	1,618
Columbia	61	64	3,063	3,447	2,730	3,149	3,560	4,310
Crawford	60	38	1,593	1,771	1,468	1,502	1,865	2,032
Dane	84	72	7,458	8,747	5,336	5,403	12,249	16,073
Dodge	55	85	2,863	3,257	2,665	3,135	3,804	4,167
Door	17	22	2,601	3,138	2,528	2,404	2,670	3,936
Douglas	15	17	738	1,753	751	1,250	711	2,573
Dunn	69	95	1,773	2,238	1,725	1,885	1,844	2,815
Eau Claire	57	47	1,905	2,430	1,959	2,297	1,656	2,890
Florence	11	8	1,956	1,670	1,837	1,867	2,337	1,313
Fond du Lac	50	48	2,936	3,314	2,474	2,843	6,520	6,111
Forest	3	3	1,506	2,823	1,506	--	--	2,823
Grant	71	82	1,834	2,155	1,807	2,010	2,043	2,757
Green	47	55	2,073	2,804	1,860	2,557	2,476	2,890
Green Lake	26	17	2,703	2,732	2,643	2,732	3,447	--
Iowa	72	81	2,356	2,563	2,280	2,527	2,495	4,403
Iron	5	1	752	900	681	--	802	900
Jackson	47	48	1,186	1,622	1,187	1,407	1,129	2,092
Jefferson	29	46	3,371	4,757	3,251	4,313	3,932	9,214
Juneau	34	29	1,562	1,780	1,493	1,609	1,844	2,133
Kenosha	15	13	10,328	17,407	8,687	8,206	18,282	27,244
Kewaunee	21	21	2,292	2,284	2,010	2,298	3,942	1,963
La Crosse	22	33	2,389	3,816	1,919	2,930	2,727	3,980
Lafayette	82	59	2,156	2,287	2,157	2,285	2,150	2,600
Langlade	35	31	1,608	1,623	1,418	1,182	2,772	2,309
Lincoln	25	28	1,065	2,123	1,125	1,213	951	2,585
Manitowoc	45	24	2,526	2,280	2,227	1,996	3,740	3,560
Marathon	111	112	1,855	2,023	1,593	1,831	2,912	2,639
Marinette	30	21	1,989	2,411	2,099	2,348	1,628	2,555
Marquette	27	20	2,347	2,422	2,088	2,139	3,628	7,259
Milwaukee	1	3	17,925	31,675	--	--	17,925	31,675
Monroe	70	58	1,799	2,152	1,740	2,005	1,990	2,544
Oconto	38	27	2,128	2,037	2,118	1,554	2,169	3,050
Oneida	8	7	1,705	1,049	1,811	998	1,024	1,453
Outagamie	43	41	3,961	7,969	2,356	4,038	6,259	9,748
Ozaukee	23	10	8,681	13,518	7,857	4,253	11,886	24,196
Pepin	13	19	2,033	2,029	2,062	1,917	1,991	2,370
Pierce	42	39	2,791	3,396	2,366	2,514	3,689	4,855
Polk	79	84	2,276	3,055	2,120	3,092	2,700	2,954
Portage	43	44	1,770	1,960	1,831	1,880	1,658	2,340
Price	40	29	983	1,244	987	667	966	1,423
Racine	21	21	7,372	6,720	5,680	5,564	9,959	9,638
Richland	53	57	1,802	2,147	1,944	2,025	1,421	2,303
Rock	45	41	2,980	3,400	2,796	3,339	3,587	3,950
Rusk	39	59	1,027	1,316	1,066	1,374	969	1,236
St. Croix	68	83	6,281	5,322	2,956	4,034	7,929	6,637
Sauk	54	84	2,134	3,145	2,044	2,668	2,426	12,506
Sawyer	22	16	4,332	2,050	4,394	2,555	3,936	1,939
Shawano	76	61	1,949	2,170	2,030	2,240	1,346	2,058
Sheboygan	34	38	3,693	4,436	2,882	3,377	5,972	6,785
Taylor	67	88	1,018	1,314	1,043	1,319	948	1,301
Trempealeau	63	54	1,525	1,710	1,514	1,725	1,571	1,688
Vernon	92	85	1,748	1,988	1,712	1,903	1,931	2,247
Vilas	1	1	1,000	1,463	--	--	1,000	1,463
Walworth	41	44	4,685	6,338	3,879	5,255	7,072	11,797
Washburn	35	18	1,485	1,531	1,482	1,566	1,490	1,487
Washington	39	30	7,743	9,248	6,459	6,481	8,647	10,567
Waukesha	30	26	13,285	17,647	4,902	17,320	18,372	17,689
Waupaca	40	38	2,624	2,313	2,394	2,137	3,713	3,739
Waushara	26	29	1,969	2,421	1,780	2,176	2,915	6,587
Winnebago	27	24	5,638	5,964	4,568	3,719	7,178	13,913
Wood	34	30	1,519	1,736	1,469	1,581	1,683	2,078
STATE	3,003	3,005	$2,821	$3,268	$2,251	$2,480	$4,514	$5,500

[1]Menominee County had no agricultural sales in years shown.
[2]Includes land with and without buildings and other improvements.
Source: U.S. Department of Agriculture, National Agricultural Statistics Service, "Agricultural Land Sales: Total Agricultural Land, Wisconsin, 2002" at: http://www.nass.usda.gov/wi/landsales/total02.pdf and "Agricultural Land Sales: Total Agricultural Land, Wisconsin, 2003" at: http://www.nass.usda.gov/wi/landsales/total03.pdf.

FARM ASSETS AND DEBT
By State, 2003

State	Number of Farms[1]	Total Farm Assets[2]	Total Farm Debt[2]	Total Farm Equity[2]	Debt as Percentage of Assets
		(in thousands)			
Alabama	45,000	$18,902,697	$2,360,894	$16,541,803	12.5%
Alaska	610	689,891	25,579	664,313	3.7
Arizona	10,300	44,563,325	1,574,549	42,988,776	3.5
Arkansas	47,500	25,970,336	4,883,911	21,086,425	18.8
California	78,500	96,474,966	19,955,205	76,519,760	20.7
Colorado	31,400	27,348,304	4,143,010	23,205,294	15.2
Connecticut	4,200	2,844,396	337,822	2,506,573	11.9
Delaware	2,300	1,941,015	433,220	1,507,795	22.3
Florida	44,000	34,336,453	5,371,732	28,964,720	15.6
Georgia	49,300	30,027,371	4,114,917	25,912,455	13.7
Hawaii	5,500	4,435,495	282,687	4,152,809	6.4
Idaho	25,000	18,978,686	3,289,403	15,689,283	17.3
ILLINOIS	73,000	87,252,034	10,479,532	76,772,502	12.0
Indiana	59,500	46,121,413	6,390,681	39,730,732	13.9
IOWA	90,000	83,633,920	14,433,584	69,200,336	17.3
Kansas	64,500	38,766,242	7,819,804	30,946,438	20.2
Kentucky	87,000	29,972,936	3,906,624	26,066,312	13.0
Louisiana	27,200	12,769,068	1,976,353	10,792,715	15.5
Maine	7,200	2,222,561	423,054	1,799,507	19.0
Maryland	12,100	9,222,160	1,283,283	7,938,877	13.9
Massachusetts	6,100	4,275,529	444,723	3,830,805	10.4
MICHIGAN	53,300	30,380,255	3,513,463	26,866,791	11.6
MINNESOTA	80,000	56,051,737	9,982,317	46,069,420	17.8
Mississippi	42,800	16,959,592	3,201,558	13,758,035	18.9
Missouri	106,000	53,947,099	6,725,191	47,221,908	12.5
Montana	28,000	27,045,575	2,899,686	24,145,889	10.7
Nebraska	48,500	48,175,692	10,085,285	38,090,407	20.9
Nevada	3,000	3,611,740	302,635	3,309,105	8.4
New Hampshire	3,400	1,150,647	123,039	1,027,607	10.7
New Jersey	9,900	7,241,490	538,626	6,702,864	7.4
New Mexico	17,500	12,318,563	1,612,220	10,706,343	13.1
New York	37,000	16,408,819	2,808,312	13,600,506	17.1
North Carolina	53,500	30,897,491	4,235,354	26,662,137	13.7
North Dakota	30,300	25,925,517	4,356,822	21,568,695	16.8
Ohio	77,600	44,588,994	4,898,469	39,690,525	11.0
Oklahoma	83,500	30,188,488	4,717,099	25,471,389	15.6
Oregon	40,000	20,973,710	2,763,202	18,210,508	13.2
Pennsylvania	58,200	26,551,730	3,230,000	23,321,730	12.2
Rhode Island	850	469,401	45,931	423,470	9.8
South Carolina	24,400	9,726,996	1,330,489	8,396,507	13.7
South Dakota	31,600	28,648,075	4,478,554	24,169,521	15.6
Tennessee	87,000	30,989,554	3,013,393	27,976,162	9.7
Texas	229,000	111,624,300	13,286,228	98,338,072	11.9
Utah	15,300	13,299,893	951,097	12,348,796	7.2
Vermont	6,500	3,216,821	435,239	2,781,582	13.5
Virginia	47,500	24,594,227	2,441,010	22,153,218	9.9
Washington	35,500	22,291,709	3,788,155	18,503,555	17.0
West Virginia	20,800	5,438,532	455,584	4,982,947	8.4
WISCONSIN	76,500	43,380,461	6,699,068	36,681,393	15.4
Wyoming	9,200	11,911,347	1,149,582	10,761,765	9.7
UNITED STATES[3]	2,126,860	$1,378,757,252	$197,998,175	$1,180,759,076	14.4%

[1]"Farm" is defined as a place that sells, or would normally sell, at least $1,000 of agricultural products during the year.

[2]Dollar amounts represent farm businesses, excluding household assets and debts.

[3]Detail may not add to total due to rounding.

Sources: U.S. Department of Agriculture, National Agricultural Statistics Service, "Farms and Land in Farms, February 2004" at: http://usda.mannlib.cornell.edu/reports/nassr/other/zfl–bb/fmno0204.pdf, U.S. Department of Agriculture, Economic Research Service reports on value of total farm assets, debt, equity and ratio of debt/assets at: http://www.ers.usda.gov/Data/FarmBalanceSheet/50stbsht.htm.

STATEWIDE ASSOCIATIONS OF WISCONSIN
Listed by Key Word

AAA Wisconsin, Inc.
Ted R. Gambill, Pres. and COO
P.O. Box 33, Madison 53701-0033
(608) 836-6555

Academic Staff Public Representative Org.
Bill Steffenhagen, Pres.
44 E. Mifflin St., Suite 101, Madison 53703
(608) 286-9599 aspro@aspro.net

Academy of Sciences, Arts and Letters, Wis.
Michael Strigel, Exec. Dir.
1922 University Ave., Madison 53705-4013
(608) 263-1692 mstrigel@wisconsinacademy.org

Accountants, Wis. Inst. of Certified Public
LeRoy Schmidt, Exec. Dir.
P.O. Box 1010, Brookfield 53008-1010
(262) 785-0445 leroy@wicpa.org

Activity Professionals, Wis. Representatives of (WRAP)
Jean Curtis, Pres.
2100 E. 6th St., Merrill 54452
(715) 536-0355 jcurtis@lincoln.co.wi.us.com

AFL-CIO Women's Committee, Wis. State
Paula Dorsey, Chairperson
6333 Bluemound Rd. West, Milwaukee 53213
(414) 771-0700 solidarity@wisaflcio.org

AFSCME, AFL-CIO, Wis. Legis. Council No. 11
Sandra L. Bloomfield, Exec. Dir.
8033 Excelsior Dr., Suite A, Madison 53717-1903
(608) 836-6666

AFT - Wisconsin (Federation of Teachers)
Bob Beglinger, Pres.
1334 Applegate Rd., Madison 53713
(608) 277-7700 beglinger@aft-wisconsin.org

Aging Groups, Coalition of Wis. - Elder Law Center
Helen Marks Dicks
2850 Dairy Dr., Suite 100, Madison 53718
(608) 224-0606 hmdicks@cwag.org

Agribusiness Council, Wis.
Farron Havens
211 Canal Rd., Waterloo 53594
(920) 478-4943 fhavenswac@mhtc.net

Agricultural Educators, Wis. Assn. of
Richard F. Aide, Exec. Dir.
N10496 Buckhorn Rd., Fox Lake 53933-9765
(920) 324-8787 dick@waae.com

Agricultural Students, Postsecondary (PAS)
Paul Cutting
Southwestern Technical College,1800 Bronson Blvd.
Fennimore 53809
(800) 362-3322 ext. 2505 pcutting@swtc.edu

Agriculture, Wis. Women for
Victoria Coughlin, Pres.
N 901 Welsh Rd., Watertown 53098
(920) 261-1777

Agri-Service Assn., Inc., Wis.
John Petty, Exec. Dir.
6000 Gisholt Dr., Suite 208, Madison 53713-4816
(608) 223-1111 info@wasa.org

Agronomy, Amer. Soc. of
Ellen Bergseld, Exec. Vice Pres.
677 S. Segoe Rd., Madison 53711
(608) 273-8080

AIA Wisconsin
William Babcock, Exec. Dir.
321 S. Hamilton St., Madison 53703-4000
(608) 257-8477 aiaw@aiaw.org

Air/Vac Assn., Inc., National
Maxine D. O'Brien, Exec. Dir.
P.O. Box 620830, Middleton 53562-0830
(608) 836-3851 navamax@aol.com

Alcohol Problems Council of Wis.
Francis H. Hanson, Treas.
P.O. Box 8022, Madison 53708
(608) 222-3483

American Fed. of State, County and Municipal Employees,
AFL-CIO
Area Field Serv. Dir.
8033 Excelsior Dr., Suite A, Madison 53717-1903
(608) 836-6666

American Legion Aux. (Dept. of Wis.)
Kathy Wollmer, Secy./Treas.
2930 American Legion Drive, P.O. Box 140
Portage 53901-0124
(608) 745-0124 alawi@amlegionauxwi.org

American Legion, Dept. of Wis.
William West, State Adj.
P.O. Box 388, Portage 53901
(608) 745-1090 info@wilegion.org

Amusement and Music Operators, Wis.
Maxine D. O'Brien, Exec. Dir.
P.O. Box 620830, Middleton 53562-0830
(608) 836-6090 wamomax@aol.com

Amvets (Dept. of Wis.)
Michael H. Mahoney, Exec. Dir.
War Memorial Center, 750 Lincoln Memorial Dr., Rm. 306
Milwaukee 53202
(414) 273-5288 amvetswi@wi.net

Amvets Ladies Aux., Dept. of Wis.
Kathleen A. Hawkins, Exec. Secy.
2630 Iris Ct., Racine 53402-1440
(414) 681-0237 kathleen.hawkins@marquette.edu

Anesthesiologists, Wis. Soc. of
Stuart Sykes, B.M., Secy.
1005 Columbia Rd., Madison 53705-2105
(608) 233-2764 wssykes5@aol.com

Anesthetists, Wis. Assn. of Nurse, Inc.
Thomas Hilbert, Pres.
1034 Chapel Street, Marshfield 54449
(715) 389-2956 hilberttr@hotmail.com

Animals, Alliance for
Lori Nitzel, Exec. Dir.
122 State St., Suite 406, Madison 53703-2500
(608) 257-6333 Alliance@AllAnimals.org

Animals, Citizens United for
Hannelore Schilling Zarse, Pres.
P.O. Box 07176, Milwaukee 53207
(414) 545-3145 animalrights@bdmail.com

Annuitants, Wis. Coalition of
Edwin Kehl, Pres.
318 Karen Ct., Madison 53705
(608) 233-6737 wcoaemk@chorus.net

Apartment Assn., Wis.
Karen Miskimen, Admin.
402 E. Washington Ave., Madison 53703
(608) 227-1024 admin@waaonline.org

Apple Growers Assn., Wis.
Anna M. Maenner, Exec. Dir.
211 Canal Rd., Waterloo 53594
(920) 478-4277 acminc@gdinet.com

Aquaculture Assn., Wis.
Bill West, Pres.
N5811 Twelve Corners Rd., Black Creek 54106
(920) 730-0684 blueiris@famvid.com

Arborist Assn., Wis.
Scott Nelson, Pres.
Madison Gas and Electric, P.O. Box 1231, Madison 53701
(608) 252-7186 snelson@mge.com

Arc - Wisconsin, Disability Assoc. Inc., The
James Hoegemeier, Exec. Dir.
600 Williamson St., Suite J, Madison 53703
(608) 251-9272 arcwjim@chorus.net

Arthritis Foundation, Wis. Chapter
Judy Haugsland, Pres/CEO
8556 W. National Ave., West Allis 53227-1736
(414) 321-3933, (800) 242-9945 info.wi@arthritis.org

Artists Assn., Wis. Regional
Leslee Nelson, Advisor
723 Lowell Center, 610 Langdon St., Madison 53703-1195
(608) 263-7814 lnelson@dcs.wisc.edu

Asphalt Pavement Assn., Wis., Inc.
Patrick Goss, Exec. Vice Pres.
4600 American Parkway, Suite 206, Madison 53718
(608) 255-3114 info@wispave.org

Auctioneers Assn., Inc., Wis.
Maxine O'Brien, Exec. Dir.
P.O. Box 620830, Middleton 53562-0830
(608) 836-6542 waamaxine@aol.com

Automatic Merchandising Council, Wis.
David Kwarciany, Jr., Govt. Affairs Chm.
16300 W. Silver Spring Dr., Menomonee Falls 53051
(262) 781-8507

Automobile and Truck Dealers Assn., Inc., Wis.
Gary D. Williams, Pres.
150 E. Gilman St., Suite A, Madison 53703-1441
(608) 251-5577

Automobile Clubs in Assn., Inc., Wis.
Ray Schirmer, Newsletter Editor
2805 E. Wausau Ave., Wausau 54403-3178
(715) 845-1398

Automotive Aftermarket Association, Wis.
Gary Manke, Exec. Dir.
5330 Wall Street, Suite 100, Madison 53718-7929
(608) 240-2065 gmanke@medaassn.com

Automotive Historians, Soc. of (Wis. Ch.)
Kenneth E. Nimocks, Jr.
3765 Spring Green Rd., Green Bay 54313-7565
(920) 865-4004 knimocks@netnet.net

Automotive Parts Assn., Inc., Wis.
Gary W. Manke, CAE, Exec. Dir.
5330 Wall Street, Suite 100, Madison 53718-7929
(608) 240-2066 gmanke@medaassn.com

Bandmasters' Assn., Inc., Wis.
Donna Wirth, Exec. Secy.
14544 Squire Ln., Kiel 53042
(920) 894-3991 wbasec@dotnet.com

Bankers Assn., Wis.
Kurt R. Bauer, Pres/CEO
P.O. Box 8880, Madison 53708
(608) 441-1200 bauer@wisbank.com

Bankers Assn., Wis. Mortgage
James E. Hough, Exec. Dir.
P.O. Box 1606, Madison 53701-1606
(800) 532-1091 hough@hamilton-consulting.com

Bankers of Wis., Community
Daryll J. Lund, Pres. & CEO
455 Cty Road M., Suite 101, Madison 53719
(608) 833-4229 daryll@communitybankers.org

Beef Council, Inc., Wis.
John W. Freitag, Exec. Dir.
680 Grand Canyon Dr., Madison 53719
(608) 833-7177 jwf@beeftips.com

Beer Distributors Assn., Inc., Wis.
Eric Jensen, Exec. Dir.
16 N. Carroll Street, Suite 950, Madison 53703
(608) 255-6464 ericj@chorus.net

Berry Growers Assn., Wis.
Anna Maenner, Exec. Dir.
211 Canal Rd., Waterloo 53594
(920) 478-3852 acminc@gdinet.com

Bike Wisconsin Education and Action Coalition
William E. Hauda, Exec. Dir.
P.O. Box 310, Spring Green 53588
(888) 575-3640 wisbike@mhtc.net

Biomedical Research and Education, Wis. Assn. for
Gale Davy, Exec. Dir.
2947 N. 56 St., Milwaukee 53210
(414) 899-9246 wabre@execpc.com

Blind and Visually Impaired, Inc., Badger Assn. of the
Patrick Brown, Exec. Dir.
912 N. Hawley Rd., Milwaukee 53213-3292
(414) 615-0108 pbrown@badgerassoc.org

Blind, Inc., Wis. Council of the
Richard Pomo, Exec. Dir.
754 Williamson St., Madison 53703
(608) 255-1166

Botanical Club of Wis.
Lynn White, Pres.
N2280 Acorn Rd., Clintonville 54929
(920) 799-1960 mtclimberdave@frontiernet.net

Bowhunters Assn., Wis., Inc.
Wright Allen, Pres.
P.O. Box 240, Clintonville 54929
(715) 823-4670 wbh@frontiernet.net

Bowling Assn., Wis. State
Phillip A. LaPorte, Exec. Secy/Treas.
N104 W16275 Hedge Way, Germantown 53022
(262) 532-0623 plaporte@wibowl.com

Bowling Proprietors Assn. of Wis.
Gary Hartel, Exec. Dir.
N35 W21140 Capitol Drive, Suite 5, Pewaukee 53072
(414) 783-4292

Brain Injury Assn. of Wis., Inc.
Caroline Feller, Exec. Dir.
2900 N. 117 St., Suite 100, Wauwatosa 53222
(414) 778-4144 biaw@execpc.com

Breeders Assn., Wis. Brown Swiss
Barbara Muenzenberger, Secy.-Treas.
W561 Muenzenberger Rd., Coon Valley 54623
(608) 486-2297 bovalleyswiss@aol.com

Breeders Assn., Wis. Draft Horse
Mrs. Richard Lee, Secy.
W5072 Faro Springs Rd., Hilbert 54129
(920) 989-1131

Breeders Assn., Wis. Guernsey
Debbie Lakey, Secy.-Treas.
W23375 11th St., Trempealeau 54661
(608) 534-6010 wigba@msn.com

Breeders' Assn., Wis. Livestock
Marv Espenscheid, Exec. Dir.
P.O. Box 296, Argyle 53504-0296
(608) 543-3778 wlbaosf@mhtc.net

Breeder's Assn., Wis. Shorthorn
Ann Jennings, Secy.
W3876 Old B Rd., Rio 53960-9767
(920) 992-5515

Brewers Assn., Wis. State
Martin J. Schreiber
2700 S. Shore Drive, Suite A, Milwaukee 53207-2300
(414) 482-1214 martin@martinschreiber.com

Broadcasters Assn., Wis.
John Laabs, Pres.
44 E. Mifflin St., Suite 900, Madison 53703-2800
(608) 255-2600 jlaabs@aol.com

Buck and Bear Club, Inc., Wis.
Steve Ashley, Dir. of Records
335 Edgewood Dr., Hudson 54016
(800) 273-6408 sashley@wi-buck-bear.org

Builders and Contractors of Wis., Inc., Associated
Stephen L. Stone, Pres.
5330 Wall St., Madison 53718
(608) 244-5883 sstone@abcwi.org

Builders Assn., Wis.
Bill Wendle, Exec. Vice Pres.
4868 High Crossing Blvd., Madison 53704-7403
(608) 242-5151 info@wisbuild.org

Builders Assn. of Wis., Master
Edward J. Hayden
17100 W. Bluemound Rd., Suite 102, Brookfield 53005
(262) 785-1430 ed@buildacea.org

Burial Vault Assn., Wis.
Mark Lipscomb, Jr., Exec. Dir.
522 N. Water St., Milwaukee 53202
(414) 276-5763 marklipscombjr@sbcglobal.net

Business Assn. of Wis., Independent
Steven E. Sobiek, Exec. Dir.
1400 E. Washington Ave., Suite 282, Madison 53703-3041
(608) 251-5546

Business, Natl. Federation of Independent (Wis. Ch.)
Bill G. Smith, State Director
10 E. Doty, Suite 201, Madison 53703
(608) 255-6083 Bill.Smith@nfib.org

Businesses, Inc., Wis. Independent
Thomas Dohm, Pres.
P.O. Box 2135, Madison 53701-2135
(608) 255-0373 tdohm@wibiz.org

Cable Communications Assn., Wis.
Thomas Hanson, Exec. Dir.
22 E. Mifflin Street, Suite 1010, Madison 53703
(608) 256-1683

Camp Assn., American, Wis.
Katherine S. Mace, Exec.
3217 Sandwood Way, Madison 53713
(608) 663-0051 acawisconsin@charter.net

Campground Owners, Inc., Wis. Assn. of
Lori Severson, Exec. Dir.
17630 N. Main St., P.O. Box 130, Galesville 54630
(608) 582-2092 or (800) 843-1821
director@wisconsincampgrounds.com

Cancer Soc., Amer. (Midwest Div.)
Russ Hinz, COO Mission Delivery
P.O. Box 902, Pewaukee 53072
(262) 523-5516 russ.hinz@cancer.org

Carpenters, Wis. State Council of
Mark S. Reihl, Exec. Dir.
115 W. Main St., Madison 53703
(608) 256-1206 mreihl@tds.com

Carwash Assn., Inc., Badger State
Maxine D. O'Brien, Exec. Dir.
P.O. Box 620830, Middleton 53562-0830
(608) 836-3851

Cast Metals Assn., Wis.
Brian L. Mitchell, Exec. Dir.
P.O. Box 247, Oconomowoc 53066
(262) 244-0045 blm@mitchellgov.com

Cattlemen's Assn., Wis.
Dick Hauser, Legislative Com. Chair
31877 Dog Hollow Rd., Richland Center 53581
(608) 585-4848 wbia@tds.net

CattleWomen's Council, Wis.
Nancy Thomas, Chm.
P.O. Box 236, Cobb 53526
(608) 623-2544

Cemetery Assn., Wisconsin
Christine Toson Hentges, Pres.
c/o Tribute Companies, 352 Cottonwood Ave., Suite D
Hartland 53029
(262) 367-9991 christieh@tributeinc.com

Cemetery Soc., Wis. State Old
Beverly Silldorff, Pres.
12116 N. Briarhill Rd., Mequon 53097
(262) 242-3290 dondorf@execpc.com

Charter Schools Assn., Wis.
Senn Brown, Secy.
P.O. Box 628243, Middleton 53562
(608) 238-7491 sennb@charter.net

Children and Families, Inc., Wis. Council on
Charity Eleson, Exec. Dir.
16 N. Carroll St., Suite 600, Madison 53703
(608) 284-0580

Children of the American Revolution, Wis. St. Soc.
Mrs. Ivan Niedling, Honorary Sr. State Pres.
700 3rd St., Plover 54467
(715) 341-1996

Children with Behavioral Disorders, Inc., Wis. Assn. for
Debbie Brent, Prog. Chair
P.O. Box 1993, Waukesha 53187-1993
(262) 691-7435 brentde@wauwatosa.k12.wi.us

Children's Service Soc. of Wis.
Kenneth Munson, CEO
1212 S. 70th St., Milwaukee 53214
(414) 453-1400

Chiropractic Assn., Wis.
Russell A. Leonard, Exec. Dir.
521 E. Washington Ave., Madison 53703
(608) 256-7023 rleonard@aol.com

Christmas Tree Producers Assn., Inc., Wis.
Cheryl Nicholson, Exec. Secy.
W9833 Hogan Road, Portage 53901-9279
(608) 742-8663

Churches, Wis. Council of
Rev. Scott Anderson, Exec. Dir.
750 Windsor St., Suite 301, Sun Prairie 53590-2149
(608) 837-3108 sanderson@wichurches.org

Cities, Wis. Alliance of
Ed Huck, Exec. Dir.
14 W. Mifflin St., Madison 53703
(608) 257-5881 ed@wiscities.org

Citizens for Global Solutions
William Frayer, Pres.
2339 Meachem St., Racine 53403
(262) 633-7887 wfrayer@execpc.com

City/County Management Assn., Wis.
Ed Henschel, Exec. Dir.
115 South 84th St., Milwaukee 53214
(414) 777-5382 ehenschel@virchowkrause.com

Civil Air Patrol, Wis. Wing
Col. Clair Jowett, Commander
2400 Wright St., Madison 53704
(608) 242-3067 terry.norby@dma.state.wi.us

Civil Trial Counsel of Wis.
Jane A. Svinicki, Exec. Dir.
1123 N. Water Street, Milwaukee 53202
(414) 276-1881 ctcw@ctcw.org

Clerks of Circuit Court Assn., Wis.
Jeffrey Schmidt, Pres.
1201 S. Spring St., Port Washington 53074
(920) 284-8410 jeffrey.schmidt@wicourts.gov

Coalition for Advocacy, Inc., Wis.
Lynn Breedlove, Exec. Dir.
16 N. Carroll St., Suite 400, Madison 53703-2716
(608) 267-0214 lynnb@w-c-a.org

Collectors Assn., Inc., Wis.
Nancy J. Borgen, Exec. Secy.
P.O. Box 2288, La Crosse 54602
(608) 791-2114 wcai@cbdlax.com

Colleges and Universities, Wis. Assn. of Independent
Dr. Rolf Wegenke, Pres.
122 W. Washington Ave., Suite 700, Madison 53703-2718
(608) 256-7761 mail@waicuweb.org

Colleges, Inc., Wis. Foundation for Independent
Mark E. Torinus, Pres.
735 N. Water St., Suite 600, Milwaukee 53202
(414) 273-5980 wfic@wficweb.org

Colonial Wars in the State of Wis., Society of
Jerry P. Hill, Gov.
5677 N. Consaul Pl., Milwaukee 53217-4818
(414) 332-9479 jerryp@execpc.com

Common Cause in Wis.
Jay Heck, Exec. Dir.
P.O. Box 2597, Madison 53701-2597
(608) 256-2686 ccwisjwh@itis.com

Communication, International Training in
Priscilla W. Bartoloth, Chair
8728 Jackson Park Blvd., Wauwatosa 53226-2710
(414) 774-6812 pbartoloth@netzero.com

Community Action Program Assn., Wis.
Richard Schlimm, Exec. Dir.
1310 Mendota St., Suite 107, Madison 53714-1039
(608) 244-4422 rschlimm@charterinternet.com

Concrete Assn., Wis. Precast
Patrick Essie, Exec. Dir.
16 N. Carroll St., Suite 900, Madison 53703
(608) 256-7701 aditscheit@essieconsulting.com

Concrete Assn., Wis. Ready Mixed
Patrick Essie, Exec. Dir.
16 N. Carroll St., Suite 925, Madison 53703
(608) 250-6304 info@wrmca.com

Concrete Masonry Assn., Wis.
Jane Svinicki, Exec. Dir.
1123 N. Water St., Milwaukee 53202
(414) 276-0667 jane@svinicki.com

Concrete Pavement Assn., Wis.
Kevin McMullen, Pres.
2434 American Lane, Suite 1, Madison 53704
(608) 240-1020 kmcmullen@tds.net

Construction Employers Assn., Inc., Allied
Edward J. Hayden, Exec. Vice Pres.
17100 W. Bluemound Rd., Suite 102, Brookfield 53005
(262) 785-1430 ed@buildacea.org

Contractors Assn. of Wis., Mechanical
Jeffrey Beiriger, Exec. Dir.
10427 W. Lincoln Ave., Suite 1600, Milwaukee 53227-1201
(414) 543-7622 jeff@pmsmca.com

Contractors Assn., Inc., Wis. Underground
Richard W. Wanta, Exec. Dir.
2835 N. Mayfair Rd., Suite 35, Milwaukee 53222-4405
(414) 778-1050 rwanta@wuca.org

Cooperatives, Wis. Fed. of
William Oemichen, Pres/CEO
131 W. Wilson St., Suite 400, Madison 53703-3269
(608) 258-4400 bill.oemichen@wfcmac.coop

Corn Promotion Board, Inc., Wis.
Bob Oleson, Exec. Dir.
W1360 Hwy 106, Palmyra 53156
(262) 495-2232 wicorn@idcnet.com

Counties Assn., Wis.
Mark D. O'Connell, Exec. Dir.
22 E. Mifflin St., Suite 900, Madison 53703
(608) 663-7188

Counties Mineral Resources Assn., Inc., Wis.
Erhard Huettl, Chm.
6116 Evergreen Lane, Wabeno 54566-9631
(715) 473-5314

Counties Utility Tax Assn., Wis.
Michael R. Vaughan, Exec. Dir.
P.O. Box 2038, Madison 53701-2038
(608) 257-7181

County Agricultural Agents, Wis. Assn.
Jerry Clark, Pres.
711 N. Bridge St., Room 13, Chippewa Falls 54729
(715) 726-7950 jerome.clark@ces.uwex.edu

County and Municipal Employees,
    Wis. Council 40 AFSCME, AFL-CIO
Robert Chybowski, Exec. Dir.
8033 Excelsior Dr., Suite B, Madison 53717-1903
(608) 836-4040

County Clerk's Assn., Wis.
Marge Bostelmann, Pres.
492 Hill St., Green Lake 54941
(920) 294-4005 mbostel@co.green-lake.wi.us

County Code Administrators, Wis.
330 Court Street, Eagle River 54521

County Constitutional Officers Assn., Inc., Wis.
Jay Zahn, State Pres.
Door County Clerk of Courts, P.O. Box 670
Sturgeon Bay 54235
(920) 746-2286

County Executives and Administrators Assn., Wis.
Allen Buechel, Pres.
160 S. Macy St., Fond du Lac 54935
(920) 929-3155 executive@co.fond-du-lac.wi.us

County Forests Assn., Wis.
Colette J. Matthews, Exec. Dir.
518 W. Somo Ave., Tomahawk 54487
(715) 453-6741 wcfa@newnorth.net

County Officers, Wis. Assn. of
Donna Hanson, Treas.
Administrative Center, 400 4th St. N., Rm. 1290
La Crosse 54601-3200
(608) 785-9712 hanson.donna@co.la-crosse.wi.us

County Personnel Directors, Wis. Assn. of
Michael Collard, Pres.
508 New York Ave., Rm. 336, Sheboygan 53081
(920) 459-3105 collamjc@co.sheboygan.wi.us

County Planning Directors Assn., Wis.
Phil Blazkowski, Planning Dir.
Rock County Courthouse, 51 S. Main St., Janesville 53545
(608) 757-5587 phil@co.rock.wi.us

County Police Assn. Ltd., Wis.
Bob Wierenga, Pres.
P.O. Box 764, Delavan 53115
(262) 728-2233 info@wcpawi.com

County Surveyors Assn., Inc., Wis.
William C. Jung, Pres.
N5416 Abbey Rd., Onalaska 54650
(608) 783-1929

County Treasurers Assn., Wis.
Mary Ann Kropp, Treas.
224 S. Second St., Medford 54451
(715) 748-1466

County Veterans Service Officers Assn. of Wis.
Mark Baldwin, Jr., Secy.-Treas.
432 E. Washington St., West Bend 53095
(262) 335-4457 amanda.kadow@co.washington.wi.us

Court Reporters Assn., Wis.
Ron Kuehn, Lobbyist
DeWitt Ross and Stevens, 2 E. Mifflin St., Suite 600
Madison 53703
(608) 252-9325

Credit Union, Education Assn., Wis.
Mark Schrimpf, Pres.
P.O. Box 8003, Madison 53708-8003
(608) 274-9828

Credit Union League, Wis.
Tom Liebe, Dir. of Gov. Affairs
N25 W23131 Paul Rd., Pewaukee 53072
(262) 549-0200 tliebe@wcul.org

Crop Improvement Assn., Wis.
Bradley Biddick, Secy.-Treas.
554 Moore Hall, UW-Madison, 1575 Linden Dr.
Madison 53706-1597
(608) 262-1341 wcia@mhub.agronomy.wisc.edu

Crop Science Society of America
Ellen Bergfeld, Exec. Vice Pres.
677 S. Segoe Rd., Madison 53711-1086
(608) 273-8080

Dahlia Soc., Badger State
Monique Volden, Secy.
1167 State Road 78, Mt. Horeb 53572
(608) 437-6846

Dairy Products Assn., Inc., Wis.
Brad Legreid, Exec. Dir.
8383 Greenway Blvd., Middleton 53562-3506
(608) 836-3336

Dairy Technology Soc., Wis.
Robert L. Bradley, Secy.
UW-Madison, A203A Babcock Hall,1605 Linden Dr.
Madison 53706
(608) 263-2007 rbradley@wisc.edu

Dance Council, Wis.
Lowell Center, 610 Langdon St., Rm. 735
Madison 53703
(608) 262-7392

Democratic Party of Wis.
Linda Honold, Chair
222 West Washington Ave., Suite 150
Madison 53703
(608) 255-5172 party@wisdems.org

Diabetes Assn., Amer. (Wis. Area)
Nancy K. Bill, Exec. Dir.
2323 N. Mayfair Rd., Suite 502, Wauwatosa 53226
(800) 342-2383 nbill@diabetes.org

Dietetic Assn., Inc., Wis.
Lynn Edwards, Exec. Coor.
1411 W. Montgomery St., Sparta 54656
(608) 269-0042 wda@centurytel.net

Domestic Violence, Wis. Coalition Against
Mary R. Lauby, Exec. Dir.
307 S. Paterson St., Suite 1, Madison 53703
(608) 255-0539 maryl@wcadv.org

Driver and Traffic Safety Education Assn., Wis.
Kevin Kirby, Pres.
534 S. Eastern Avenue, Rhinelander 54501
(715) 362-4772 kirbykev@rhinelander.k12.wi.us

Eagle Forum-Wis.
Doris R. Moore, Pres.
3500 Studio Ct., Brookfield 53045-1934
(262) 781-2918

Easter Seals Wis., Inc.
Christine Fessler, Pres/CEO
101 Nob Hill Rd., Suite 301, Madison 53713-3969
(608) 277-8288 info@wi.easterseals.com

Economic Development Assn., Wis.
Daniel J. Schwartzer, Exec. Dir.
4600 American Parkway, Suite 208, Madison 53718
(608) 255-5666 weda@weda.org

Economic Education, Inc., Wis. Council on
James R. Guenther, Pres.
161 W. Wisconsin Ave., Suite 3143, Milwaukee 53203
(414) 221-9400 wicnclee@ameritech.net

Education Assn., Council, Wis.
Bob Burke, Dir. Gov. Rel.
P.O. Box 8003, Madison 53708-8003
(608) 276-7711

Education Association, Creation
Eugene A. Sattler, Dir.
W2228 Badger Ave., Pine River 54965-9640
(920) 987-5979

Educators' Assn., Inc., Wis. Retired
Jane Elmer, Exec. Dir.
2564 Branch St., Middleton 53562
(608) 831-5115 jelmer@wrea.net

Egg Producers Assn., Wis.
Scott Schneider, Pres.
N6680 Hwy O, Marshall 53559
(920) 648-3530 sljc@charter.net

Electric Cooperative Assn., Wis.
David Jenkins, Mgr.
131 W. Wilson St., Suite 400, Madison 53703-3269
(608) 258-4400 david.jenkins@wfcmac.coop

Electric Utilities of Wis., Municipal
Lary H. Bocock, Secy.-Treas.
P.O. Box 867, Sun Prairie 53590-0385
(608) 837-5500 lbocock@wppisys.org

Electrical Contractors Assn., Inc., National (Wis. Chap.)
Mark Thomas, Exec. Vice-Pres.
2200 Kilgust Rd., Madison 53713
(608) 221-4650 mark@wisneca.com

Electronic Service Assn., Wis.
Jeff Paschke, Pres.
316 N. Koeller St., Oshkosh 54902
(920) 426-5556 jeffp@athenet.net

EMS Assn., Wis.
Don Hunjadi, Exec. Dir.
21332 W. 7 Mile Rd., Franksville 53126-9769
(800) 793-6820 WEMSA@wisconsinems.com

Engineering Assn., State
Mark Klipstein, Pres.
4510 Regent St., Madison 53705-4963
(608) 233-4696 wisea@wisea.org

Engineering Companies of Wis., Amer. Coun. of
Carol Godiksen, Exec. Dir.
3 S. Pinckney St., Suite 800, Madison 53703
(608) 257-9223 acecwi@acecwi.org

Environment Wis., Inc.
Jeffrey Swiggum, Treas.
222 S. Hamilton St., No. 1, Madison 53703-3201
(608) 256-0565 weathergeek@tds.net

Environmental Education, Inc., Wis. Assn. for
Carol Weston, Admin. Asst.
08 Nelson Hall, UW-Stevens Point, Stevens Point 54481
(715) 346-2796 waee@uwsp.edu

Environmental Science and Public Policy, Midwest
Center for
Jeffery Foran, Pres.
1845 N. Farwell Avenue, Suite 100, Milwaukee 53202
(414) 271-7280 mcespp@mcespp.org

Environmental Technologists, Federation of, Inc.
Triese Haase, Admin.
P.O. Box 624, Slinger 53086
(262) 644-0070 info@fetinc.org

Equipment Dealers Assn., Midwest
Gary W. Manke, CAE, CEO
5330 Wall Street, Suite 100, Madison 53718-7929
(608) 240-4700 gmanke@medaassn.com

Ex-POWS, American
Shirley Wittenberg, Adj.
1329 Lauderdale Pl., Onalaska 54650
(608) 783-2127

Fabricare Institute, Wis.
Brian Swingle, Exec. Dir.
12342 W. Layton Ave., Greenfield 53228
(414) 529-4707 bswingle@toriphillips.com

Fairs, Wis. Assn. of
Jane L. Grabarski, Secy.-Treas.
985 Cty Rd. A, Grand Marsh 53936-9509
(608) 584-5327

Families Against Mandatory Minimums (Wis. Chap.)
Carla Widener, Wis. Coord.
6828 W. Wisconsin Ave., Wauwatosa 53213-3816
(414) 476-4599

Family and Children's Agencies, Wis. Assn. of
John Grace, Exec. Dir.
131 W. Wilson St., Suite 901, Madison 53703
(608) 257-5939 jgrace@wafca.org

Family Court Commissioners Assn., Wis.
Michael Bruch, Exec. Secy.
Room 707, Milwaukee County Courthouse, 901 N. 9th St.
Milwaukee 53233
(414) 278-5288 michael.bruch@wicourts.gov

Family Research Institute of Wis., Inc.
Julaine K. Appling, Exec. Dir.
P.O. Box 2075, Madison 53701-2075
(608) 256-3228 fri@fri-wi.org

Family Ties, Inc., Wis.
Hugh Davis, Exec. Dir.
16 N. Carroll St., Suite 640, Madison 53703
(608) 267-6888 info@wifamilyties.org

Farm Bureau Federation, Cooperative, Wis.
Roger Cliff, Corp. Secy.
1212 Deming Way, P.O. Box 5550
Madison 53705-0550
(608) 828-5703

Farm Bureau Service Cooperative, Wis.
Debbi Raemisch, Manager
P.O. Box 5550, Madison 53705-0550
(608) 828-5712 draemisch.fbcenter@wfbf.com

Farmers Educational and Cooperative Union of America,
Wis. Div. (Wisconsin Farmers Union)
Sue Saeger, Pres.
117 W. Spring St., Chippewa Falls 54729-2359
(800) 272-5531 wfusueb@charter.net

Fathers for Children and Families, Wis.
Jan Raz, Pres.
P.O. Box 1742, Madison 53701-1742
(608) 255-3237

Fertilizer and Chemical Assn., Wis.
Mike Turner, Exec. Dir.
2317 International Ln., Suite 102, Madison 53704
(608) 249-4070 wfca@choiceonemail.com

FFA, Wis. Assn. of
Dean P. Gagnon, State Advisor
P.O. Box 7841, Madison 53707-7841
(608) 267-9255 dean.gagnon@dpi.state.wi.us

Financial Services Assn., Wis.
Thomas Hanson, Exec. Dir.
22 E. Mifflin Street, Suite 1010, Madison 53703
(608) 256-6413

Fire Fighters of Wis., Inc., Professional
Rick Gale, State Pres.
7 N. Pinckney St., Suite 135, Madison 53703-2840
(608) 251-5832 pffwpres@aol.com

Firefighters Assn., Inc., Wis. State
Larry Plumer, Pres.
P.O. Box 126, Durand 54736-0126
(800) 588-2989 wsfa@wi-state-firefighters.org

Food Processors Assn., Inc., Midwest
John D. Exner, CAE, Pres.
P.O. Box 1297, Madison 53701-1297
(608) 255-9946 info@mwfpa.org

Food Protection, Wis. Assn. For
Randall Daggs, Secy.
P.O. Box 329, Sun Prairie 53590-0329
(608) 837-2087 rdaggs@juno.com

Forest History Association of Wis., Inc.
Miles Benson, Pres.
2511 Lovewood Dr., Wisconsin Rapids 54494

Forest Industry Safety and Training Alliance, Inc.
Barb Henderson, Exec. Dir.
3243 Golf Course Rd., Rhinelander 54501
(800) 551-2656 fista@newnorth.net

Foresters, Inc., Assn. of Consulting, Wis. Chap.
Keith Krajewski, Chm.
S7051 County Rd. B, Eau Claire 54701
(715) 833-9594 akforestry@earthlink.net

Fresh Market Vegetable Growers Assn., Wis.
Anna Maenner, Exec. Dir.
211 Canal Rd., Waterloo 53594
(920) 478-3852 office@wisconsinfreshproduce.org

Funeral Directors Assn., Wis.
Mark Paget, Exec. Dir.
2300 N. Mayfair Rd., Suite 595, Wauwatosa 53226-1508
(414) 453-3060 info@wfda.org

Funeral Service Alliance of Wis.
Patrick Essie, Exec. Dir.
16 N. Carroll St., Suite 900, Madison 53703
(608) 251-8044

Genealogical Society, Inc., Wis. State
Gary L. Haas, Pres.
P.O. Box 5106, Madison 53705
(608) 833-4327 wsgs@chorus.net

Golf Assn., Inc., Wis. State
Thomas J. Schmidt, Exec. Dir.
333 Bishops Way, Suite 104, Brookfield 53005
(262) 786-4301 info@wsga.org

Golf Course Supts. Assn., Inc., Wis.
Marc Davison, Pres.
2400 Klondike Rd., Green Bay 54311
(920) 339-4640 mdavison@usexchange.net

Grandparents Rights of Wis., Inc.
Sherry Galonski, Pres.
P.O. Box 341015, Milwaukee 53234
(414) 535-1218 or (920) 989-1869

Grange, Wis. State
Alan Arner, Master
25 S. Martin Rd., Janesville 53545-2658
(608) 756-0545 wisgrange@charter.net

Green Industry Federation, Wis.
Brian Swingle, Exec. Dir.
12342 W. Layton Ave., Greenfield 53228
(414) 529-4705 bswingle@toriphillips.com

Grocers Assn., Inc., Wis.
Brandon Scholz, Pres.
1 South Pinckney, Suite 504, Madison 53703
(608) 244-7150 brandon@wisconsingrocers.com

Grounds Management Assn. of Wis.
Lou Wierichs, Past Pres.
1635 W. Haskel St., Appleton 54914
(920) 734-5615

Hatcheries Assn., Wis.
Louis Arrington
Animal Science Dept., UW-Madison, 1675 Observatory Dr.
Madison 53706
(608) 262-1774 lcarring@ansci.wis.edu

Hazardous Materials Responders, Inc., Wis. Assn.
Edward A. Kassing, Treas.
3114 Catur Lane, Eau Claire 54701
(715) 835-4263 kassinge@charter.net

Head Start Assn., Wis.
Shelley Cousin, Exec. Dir.
122 E. Olin Ave., Suite 110, Madison 53713
(608) 442-6879 cousin@whsaonline.org

Health Care Assn., Wis.
James McGinn, Dir. of Govt. Rel.
121 S. Pinckney St., Suite 500, Madison 53703
(608) 257-0125 jim@whca.com

Health Care Assn., Wis. Primary
Sarah V. Lewis, Exec. Dir.
49 Kessel Court, Suite 210, Madison 53711
(608) 277-7477 wphca@wphca.org

Health Charities of Wis., Community
Jane Wood, Pres.
611 N. Broadway, Suite 400, Milwaukee 53202
(414) 933-4216 or (800) 783-0242 janew@chcwi.org

Health Information Management Assn., Wis.
Cassandra Bissen, Exec. Dir.
2350 South Ave., Suite 107, La Crosse 54601-6272
(608) 787-0168 whima@execpc.com

Health Plans, Wis. Assn. of
Nancy J. Wenzel, Exec. Dir.
10 E. Doty St., Suite 503, Madison 53703
(608) 255-8599

Health, Physical Education, Recreation and Dance, Wis.
    Assn. for
Keith Bakken, Exec. Dir.
24 Mitchell Hall, UW-La Crosse, 1725 State St.
La Crosse 54601
(608) 785-8175 wahperd@uwlax.edu

Health, Wis. Initiative on Smoking and (WISH)
Jack E. Lohman, Dir.
266 E. Nob Hill Dr., Colgate 53017
(414) 541-9474 jlohman@execpc.com

Hearing Professionals, Wis. Alliance of
Doug Johnson, Exec. Dir. -Gen'l Counsel
1 E. Main St., Suite 305, Madison 53703-2558
(608) 257-3541 dqj@supranet.net

Heart Assn., American (Greater Midwest Affiliate)
Jeffrey G. Ranous, Senior Adv. Dir.
2850 Dairy Dr., #300, Madison 53708
(608) 221-8866 jeffrey.ranous@heart.org

Hereford Assn., Wis. Polled
Ruth Espenscheid, Secy.
P.O. Box 299, Argyle 53504-0299
(608) 543-3788 wlbaosf@mhtc.net

Highway Users Conference, Wis.
Ernest W. Stetenfeld, Chm.
10 E. Doty St., Suite 517, Madison 53703
(608) 828-2486 estetenfeld@aaawisconsin.com

History, Wis. Council for Local
Thomas McKay, Exec. Secy.
816 State St., Madison 53706
(608) 264-6583

Holstein Assn., Wis.
Christianne Williams, Dir. of Operations
P.O. Box 10, Baraboo 53913-0010
(800) 223-4269 chrisw@wisholsteins.com

Home Health United/VNS, Inc.
Tom Brown, Pres/CEO
4801 Hayes Rd., Madison 53704
(608) 242-1516

Homecare Organization, Wis.
Russell King, Exec. Dir.
5610 Medical Circle, Suite 33, Madison 53719
(608) 278-1115 wishomecare@earthlink.net

Horse Club, Inc., Wis. Morgan
Debbie Fairbanks, Secy.
N 7655 County Rd. J, Monticello 53570
(608) 527-6064 minglwd@tds.net

Horse Council, Wis. State, Inc.
Amy Bourne, Adm. Asst.
132A S. Ludington St., Columbus 53925
(920) 623-0393 info@wisconsinstatehorsecouncil.org

Horse Trail Assn., Inc., Glacial Drumlin
Ken Carpenter, Pres.
P.O. Box 82, Deerfield 53531-0082
(608) 576-4104 nails21@charter.net

Hospice Organization and Palliative Experts of Wis. (HOPE)
Melanie G. Ramey, Exec. Dir.
3240 University Ave., Suite 2, Madison 53705-3570
(608) 233-7166 MELR217@aol.com

Hospital Assn., Inc., Wis.
Steve Brenton, Pres.
P.O. Box 259038, Madison 53725-9038
(608) 274-1820

Housing Alliance, Wis.
Ross Kinzler, Exec. Dir.
202 State St., Suite 200, Madison 53703-2215
(608) 255-3131 ross@housingalliance.us

Humane Societies, Inc., Wis. Federated
Sally Krause, Pres.
P.O. Box 508, Delavan 53115
(262) 728-6822 flgscnor@pensys.com

Humanities Council, Wis.
Dean Bakopoulos, Exec. Dir.
222 S. Bedford St., Suite F, Madison 53703-3688
(608) 262-0706 contact@wisconsinhumanities.org

Innkeepers Assn., Wis.
Trisha A. Pugal, Pres., CEO
1025 S. Moorland Rd., Suite 200, Brookfield 53005
(262) 782-2851 pugal@lodging-wi.com

Insulation Contractors Assn., Inc., Wis.
Deborah Wanta, Exec. Secy.
P.O. Box 26797, Milwaukee 53226-0797
(414) 778-1050 debbiewanta@hotmail.com

Insurance Agents of Wis., Inc., Professional
Ronald Von Haden, Exec. Vice-Pres.
6401 Odana Rd., Madison 53719-1126
(608) 274-8188 rvonhaden@piaw.org

Insurance Agents of Wisconsin, Independent
Robert C. Jaritz, Exec. Vice-Pres.
725 John Nolen Dr., Madison 53713-1421
(608) 256-4429 iiaw@aol.com

Insurance Alliance, Wis.
Eric Englund, Pres.
44 E. Mifflin St., Suite 201, Madison 53703
(608) 255-1749 wial@tds.net

Insurance Companies, Wis. Assn. of Mutual
Gerald R. Mueller, Pres.
P.O. Box 14106, Madison 53708-0106
(608) 246-2552 wamic@chorus.net

International Institute of Wis., Inc.
Alexander P. Durtka, Jr., Pres.
1110 N. Old World 3rd St., Milwaukee 53203-1117
(414) 225-6220 iiw@execpc.com

Interscholastic Athletic Assn., Wis.
Douglas E. Chickering, Exec. Dir.
P.O. Box 267, Stevens Point 54481
(715) 344-8580 dchickering@wiaawi.org

Japan-America Soc. of Wis., Inc.
Alexander P. Durtka, Jr., Pres.
1110 W. 3rd St., Suite 420, Milwaukee 53203-1117
(414) 225-6220 jasw@execpc.com

Jaycees, Inc., Wis.
Steve Moddie, Exec. Vice Pres.
P.O. Box 1547, Appleton 54912-1547
(920) 731-7681 evp@wijaycees.org

Jewish Learning, Inc., Wis. Soc. for
Sharie Berliant, Gwen Ellen Rivkin, Co-Pres.
5225 N. Ironwood Rd., Suite 120, Milwaukee 53217-4909
(414) 963-4135 wsjl@execpc.com

Judges Assn. Ldt., Wis. Municipal
Ronald J. Wambach, Secy.-Treas.
10150 W. National Ave., Suite 390, West Allis 53227-2041
(414) 541-6800 wmja@execpc.com

Kidney Foundation of Wis., Inc., Natl.
Cynthia A. Huber, CEO
16655 W. Bluemound Road, Suite 240
Brookfield 53005-5935
(262) 821-0705 or (800) 543-6393 nkfw@kidneywi.org

Labor and Employment Relations Assn. (Wis. Ch.)
Cary Silverstein, Secy
1615 E. Dean Rd., Fox Point 53217
(414) 352-5140 csilve1013@aol.com

Labor History Society, Wis.
Ken Germanson, Pres.
6333 W. Blue Mound Rd., Milwaukee 53213
(414) 483-1754 advoken@execpc.com

Laborers' Dist. Council, Wis.
Michael R. Ryan, Pres. and Bus. Mgr.
4633 Liuna Way, Suite 101, DeForest 53532
(608) 846-8242 mryan@wilaborers.org

Lakes, Inc., Wis. Assn. of
Peter T. Murray, Exec. Dir.
One Point Place, Suite 101, Madison 53719-2809
(608) 662-0923 wal@wisconsinlakes.org

Land and Water Conservation Assn., Inc., Wis.
Rebecca Baumann, Exec. Dir.
One Point Place, Suite 101, Madison 53719
(608) 833-1833 rebeccabaumann@wlwca.org

Language Teachers, Wis. Assn. for (WAFLT)
Jaci Collins, Pres.
Manitowoc School District,1433 S. 8th St.
Manitowoc 54220
(920) 683-4861 ext. 6176 collinsj@mpsd.k12.wi.us

Law Librarians Assn. of Wis., Inc.
Beverly Butula, Pres.
Davis and Kuelthau, 111 E. Kilbourn, Suite 1400
Milwaukee 53202
(414) 225-1721 bbutlula@dkattorneys.com

Lawyers Assistance Program, Wis.
Shell Goar
(800) 543-2625 sgoar@wisbar.org

Lawyers, Assn. for Women
Catherine M. Priebe Hertzberg, Pres.
11609 Elmhurst Pkwy., Wauwatosa 53226
(414) 985-5300 danarobb@bizwi.rr.com

Lawyers, Wis. Academy of Trial
Jane E. Garrott
44 E. Mifflin St., Suite 103, Madison 53703-2897
(608) 257-5741 exec@watl.org

League of Women Voters of Wis., Inc.
Andrea Kaminski, Exec. Dir.
122 State St., Suite 405, Madison 53703-2500
(608) 256-0827 lwvwisconsin@lwvwi.org

Learning Disabilities Assn. of Wis.
Linda Lehmann, Pres.
13035 W. Bluemound Rd., Suite 100, Brookfield 53005
(414) 299-9002 ldawisconsin@hotmail.com

Legal Assn. for Women
Theresa Roetter, Pres.
P.O. Box 3006, Madison 53704-0006
(608) 244-1354 troetter@hill-law-firm.com

Leukemia and Lymphoma Soc. (Wis. Chap.)
Bede Barth, Exec. Dir.
4125 N. 124th St., Unit A, Brookfield 53005
(262) 790-4701

Libertarian Party of Wisconsin
Ed Thompson, Chair
P.O. Box 20815, Greenfield 53220-0815
(800) 236-9236 lpwichair@aol.com

Libraries, Inc., Friends of Wis.
Sister Mary Ellen Paulson, Pres.
2367 S. 84th St., West Allis 53227-2501
(414) 327-4713 paulsom@mail.milwaukee.k12.wi.us

Lions Clubs Internatl. (Multiple Dist. 27 – Wis.)
Dwaine A. Habrat, State Exec. Secy.
2817 B Post Rd., Stevens Point 54481-6416
(715) 341-2277 lionstat@coredcs.com

Liquid Waste Carriers Assn., Wis.
Ann Ditscheit
16 N. Carroll St., Suite 900, Madison 53703
(608) 255-2770 aditscheit@essieconsulting.com

Livestock and Meat Council, Wis.
Daniel Vogel, Marketing Division
2811 Agriculture Dr., Madison 53704-6777
(608) 224-5113 dan.vogel@datcp.state.wi.us

Lobbyists, Inc., Assn. of Wis.
Mary Kaja, Exec. Dir.
1 E. Main St., Suite 305, Madison 53703
(608) 257-3541 awl@supranet.net

Loggers Assn., Wis. Professional
Gene Francisco, Exec. Dir.
P.O. Box 326, Tomahawk 54487
(877) 819-9908 wpla@klinktech.net

LSLA Education, Inc.
Tim Kassis, Pres.
P.O. Box 160, Antigo 54409
(715) 623-5410 lsla@lakestateslumber.com

Lumber Assoc., Inc., Wis. Retail
David L. Rosenmeier
W175 N11086 Stonewood Dr., Germantown 53022
(262) 250-1835 wrla@wrlamsi.com

Lung Assn. of Wis., Amer.
Margaret MacLeod Brahm, Pres.
13100 W. Lisbon Rd., Suite 700, Brookfield 53005
(262) 703-4200 amlung@lungwisconsin.org

Lupus Foundation of Amer., Inc., Wis. Chap.
Sue Hartt, Foundation Mgr.
1109 N. Mayfair Road, Suite 208, Milwaukee 53225
(414) 443-6400 lupuswi@hotmail.com

Make-A-Wish Foundation of Wis.
Patti Gorsky, Pres.
13195 W. Hampton Ave., Butler 53007
(262) 781-4445 info@wisconsin.wish.org

Manufacturers' Agents, Inc., Wis. Assn. of
C.J. Bluem, Exec. Dir.
1504 N. 68th St., Milwaukee 53213-2806
(414) 778-0640 wama@wama.org

Manufacturers and Commerce, Wis.
James S. Haney, Pres., P.O. Box 352
Madison 53701-0352
(608) 258-3400 wmc@wmc.org

Map Society, Ltd., Wis.
Virginia Schwartz, Secy.-Treas.
c/o Milwaukee Public Library, 814 W. Wisconsin Ave.
Milwaukee 53233-2387
(414) 286-3216 vschwa@mpl.org

Maple Syrup Producers Assoc., Wis.
Gretchen Grape, Exec. Dir.
33186 Cty Hwy W, Holcombe 54745
(715) 447-5758 gretchen_grape@yahoo.com

Marine Corps League, Dept. of Wis.
Timothy Baranzyk, Commandant
3560 S. 81st St., Milwaukee 53220-1020
(414) 604-2366 tbaranzyk@wi.rr.com

Marine Corps League Auxiliary
Diane Solberg, Pres.
1415 Ohio St., Racine 53405-3119
(262) 633-4070

Marketing and Management Assn., Wis.
Mae Laatsch, State Dir.
130 Keyes, P.O. Box 85, Lake Mills 53551
(920) 648-5965 mlaatsch@matcmadison.edu

Matchcover Club, Badger State
Marilyn Reese, Editor
3201 S. 72nd St., Milwaukee 53219-3969

Mayflower Descendants in the State of Wis., Soc. of
Mrs. Robert R. Pekowsky, Historian
77 Oak Creek Trail, Madison 53717-1509
(608) 833-3625 martell135@aol.com

Meat Processors, Inc., Wis. Assn. of
Ken Bisarek, Exec. Secy.
Box 505, Bloomington 53804
(608) 994-3173 kbisarek@hotmail.com

Medical Society of Wis., State
Susan Turney, Exec. Vice-Pres/CEO
P.O. Box 1109, Madison 53701-1109
(608) 442-3800

Mining Impact Coalition of Wis., Inc.
David Blouin, Coord.
P.O. Box 55372, Madison 53705
(608) 233-8455 burroak15@aol.com

Mortgage Brokers, Wis. Assn. of
Patrick Essie, Exec. Dir.
16 N. Carroll St., Suite 900, Madison 53703
(608) 259-9262

Mothers Against Drunk Driving (MADD)
Kari Kinnard, Exec. Dir.
P.O. Box 536, Appleton 54912-0536
(920) 831-6540 maddwi@tds.net

Motor Carriers Assn., Wis.
Thomas Howells, Pres.
562 Grand Canyon Dr., Madison 53719-1033
(608) 833-8200 thowells@witruck.org

Movers Assn., Wis.
Cherie Tuhus, Division Admin.
562 Grand Canyon Dr., Madison 53719-1033
(608) 833-8200 ctuhus@witruck.org

MRA - The Management Assn., Inc.
Susan M. Fronk, Pres.
N19 W24400 Riverwood Dr., Waukesha 53188
(262) 523-9090

Muck Farmers Assn., Wis.
Rod Gumz, Pres.
N570 6th Court, Endeavor 53930
(608) 981-2488

Multiple Sclerosis Soc., Natl. (Wis. Chap.)
Colleen G. Kalt, Pres.
1120 James Drive, Suite A, Hartland 53029
(262) 369-4400 colleen.kalt@wisms.org

Municipalities, League of Wis.
Dan Thompson, Exec. Dir.
202 State St., Suite 300, Madison 53703
(608) 267-2380 league@lwm-info.org

Music Educators Assn., Inc., Wis.
Eric Runestad, Exec. Dir.
1102 Stephenson Lane, Waunakee 53597
(608) 850-3566 erunestad@wsmamusic.org

Music Heritage Soc., Inc., Wis.
Howard Kanetzke
6333 Masthead Dr., Madison 53705-4325
(608) 238-6567

Myasthenia Gravis Foundation of Amer. (Wis. Chapter)
Kristine Laufer, Chp.
2474 S. 96th St., West Allis 53227
(262) 938-9800 wiscmg@yahoo.com

NAIFA Wisconsin
Susan K. Linck, Exec. Vice Pres.
2702 International Lane, No. 207, Madison 53704
(608) 244-3131

NAMI Wisconsin, Inc.
Donna M. Wrenn, Exec. Dir.
4233 W. Beltline Hwy, Madison 53711
(608) 268-6000 namiwisc@choiceonemail.com

National Farmers Organization, Wis.
Don Hamm, State Pres.
955 17th Street, Prairie du Sac 53578
(608) 643-3341 ext. 222 dhamm@nfo.org

National Guard Assn., Inc., Wis.
Ronald R. Wagner, Exec. Dir.
2400 Wright St., Rm. 208, Madison 53704-2572
(608) 242-3114 wingainc@terracom.net

National Guard Enlisted Assn., Inc., Wis.
Bonnie Moser, Exec. Dir.
2400 Wright St., Madison 53704-2572
(608) 242-3112 wngea@yahoo.com

Natural Food Associates, Inc., Wis.
Michael Hittner, Pres.
910 W. Grand Ave, Wisconsin Rapids 54495
(715) 421-2061

Nature Conservancy, Wis. Chap.
Mary Jean Huston, State Dir.
633 W. Main St., Madison 53703
(608) 251-8140

Navy Club of USA
Ralph Sura, Cmdr.
6219 Douglas Ave., Racine 53402-5206
(262) 752-4093

Newspaper Assn., Inc., Wis.
Peter D. Fox, Exec. Dir.
P.O. Box 5580, Madison 53705
(608) 238-7171 pfox@wnanews.com

Nursery Assn., Wis.
Brian Swingle, Exec. Dir.
12342 W. Layton Ave., Greenfield 53228
(414) 529-4705 bswingle@toriphillips.com

Nurses Assn., Wis.
Gina Dennik-Champion, Exec. Dir.
6117 Monona Dr., Madison 53716-3995
(608) 221-0383 info@wisconsinnurses.org

Nurses, Wis. Assn. of Licensed Practical
Thomas Hanson, Exec. Dir.
22 E. Mifflin Street, Suite 1010, Madison 53703
(608) 256-5299

Nursing Home Social Workers Assn., Wis.
Jeff McCabe, Pres.
c/o Brewster Village, 3300 W. Brewster St.
Appleton 54914
(920) 225-1985 mccabeja@co.outagamie.wi.us

Nursing, Inc., Wis. League for
Mary Ann Tanner, Admin. Secy.
2121 E. Newport Ave., Milwaukee 53211
(414) 332-6271

Obstetrics and Gynecology, Wis. Soc. of, Wis.
  Section/ACOG
Dawn M. Maerker, Exec. Dir.
N44 W25940 Lindsay Rd., P.O. Box 636
Pewaukee 53072-0636
(262) 695-7411 dmman@wi.rr.com

Occupational Therapy Assn., Inc., Wis.
Linda Anderson, Pres.
122 E. Olin Ave., Suite 165, Madison 53713
(608) 287-1606 wota@execpc.com

Ophthalmology, Wis. Academy of
Richard H. Paul, Exec. Dir.
10 W. Phillip Rd., Suite 120
Vernon Hills, IL 60061-1730
(800) 780-4312 eyeorg@aol.com

Orchid Soc., Wis.
Bruce Efflandt
c/o Bernie's Floral Studio, 1559 W. Forest Home Ave.
Milwaukee 53204
(414) 645-0292 berniesfloral@mail.com

Ornithology, Inc., Wis. Soc. for
Christine Reel, Treas.
2022 Sherryl Lane, Waukesha 53188-3142
(262) 547-6128 dcreel@execpc.com

Orthodontists, Wis. Soc. of
Dr. Mark Lenz, Pres.
1558 S. Green Bay Rd., Racine 53406
(262) 634-6900 mlenzortho@aol.com

Otolaryngology - Head and Neck Surgery, Wis Soc. of
Timothy L. Smith, Secy.-Treas.
MCW Clinic at Froedtert Hospital, Dept. of Otolaryngology
9200 W. Wisconsin Ave., Milwaukee 53226
(414) 805-5581 tlsmith@mcw.edu

Outdoor Advertising Assoc. of Wis.
Janet Swandby, Exec. Dir.
44 E. Mifflin St., Suite 101, Madison 53703
(608) 286-0764 swandby@swandby.com

Paper Council, Wis.
Patrick J. Schillinger, Pres.
250 N. Green Bay Rd., P.O. Box 718, Neenah 54957-0718
(920) 722-1500 schillinger@wipapercouncil.org

Parents and Teachers Inc., Wis. Congress of
Cynthia DiCamelli, Pres.
4797 Hayes Rd., Suite 2, Madison 53704-3288
(608) 244-1455

Park and Recreation Assn., Inc., Wis.
Steven J. Thompson, Exec. Vice Pres.
6601-C Northway, Greendale 53129
(414) 423-1210 wpra@execpc.com

Pathologists, Wis. Soc. of
Dawn M. Maerker, Exec. Secy.
P.O. Box 636, N44 W25940 Lindsay Rd.
Pewaukee 53072
(262) 695-7411 dmman@wi.rr.com

Pay Telephone Assn., Wis.
Cindy Denman
16 N. Carroll St., Suite 900, Madison 53703
(608) 846-1128 cdenman@patrickessie.com

Peace and Justice, Wis. Network for
Judy Miner, Off. Coor., 122 State Street, No. 402
Madison 53703-2500
(608) 250-9240 info@wnpj.org

Pediatric Dentists, Wis. Soc. of
Dennis M. Connolly, DDS, Pres.
2901 35th St., Kenosha 53140
(262) 658-3488 dconnoll@wi.net

Perinatal Care, Wis. Assn. for
Ann E. Conway, Exec. Dir.
McConnell Hall, 1010 Mound St., Madison 53715
(608) 267-6060 wapc@perinatalweb.org

Perinatal Foundation
Ann E. Conway, Exec. Dir.
McConnell Hall, 1010 Mound St., Madison 53715
(608) 267-6200 foundation@perinatalweb.org

Petroleum Council, Wis. (Div. of Amer. Petroleum Institute)
Erin T. Roth, Exec. Dir.
10 E. Doty St., Suite 517, Madison 53703
rothe@api.org

Petroleum Marketers Assn. of Wis./Wis. Assn. of
  Convenience Stores
Robert J. Bartlett, Pres.
121 S. Pinckney St., Suite 300, Madison 53703
(608) 256-7555 bbartlett@pmawwacs.org

Pharmacy Soc. of Wis.
Christopher Decker, Exec. Vice Pres.
701 Heartland Tr., Madison 53717
(608) 827-9200 cdecker@pswi.org

PHCC/Master Plumbers - Wis. Assn.
Martin B. Tirado
1123 N. Water Street, Milwaukee 53202
(800) 369-7422 tirado@svinicki.com

Phenological Soc., Wis.
Mark Schwartz, Pres.
Department of Geography, UW-Milwaukee, P.O. Box 413
Milwaukee 53201
(414) 229-3740 mds@uwm.edu

Physical Medicine and Rehabilitation, Wis. Soc. of
Frank J. Salvi, Pres.
6630 University Avenue, Madison 53562
(608) 263-8640

Physical Therapy Assn., Wis.
Karen Oshman, Exec. Dir.
802 W. Broadway, Suite 208, Madison 53713
(608) 221-9191 wpta@wpta.org

Physician Assistants, Wis. Academy of
Jeff Nicholson
P.O. Box 1109, Madison 53701-1109
(800) 762-8965 wapa@wismed.org

Physicians, Inc., Am. College of Emergency (Wis. Ch.)
Richard H. Paul, Exec. Dir.
10 W. Phillip Rd., Suite 120, Vernon Hills, IL 60061-1330
(800) 798-4911 wacep@aol.com

Physicians, Wis. Academy of Family
Larry Pheifer, Exec. Dir.
142 N. Main Street, Thiensville 53092
(262) 512-0606 academy@wafp.org

Pipe Welding Bureau, Natl. Certified (Wis. Chap.)
Marcie M. Marquardt, Chap. Exec.
5940 Seminole Centre Ct., Suite 102, Madison 53711
(608) 288-1414 OrganServ@aol.com

Podiatric Medicine, Wis. Soc. of
Dr. Kevin Kortsch, Exec. Secy.
2802 N. 71st St., Milwaukee 53210-1157
(414) 476-4223 kpkmke@juno.com

Police Assn., Wis. Chiefs of
Donald Thaves, Exec. Dir.
River Ridge - 1141 South Main St., Shawano 54166
(715) 524-8283 dthaves@frontiernet.net

Police Assn., Wis. Professional
Thomas W. Bahr, Exec. Dir.
340 Coyier Ln., Madison 53713
(608) 273-3840

Polygraph Assn., Wis.
Anthony O'Neill, Pres.
346 S. Emery St., Peshtigo 54157
(715) 923-8381 wispoly@new.rr.com

Pork Assn., Wis. Cooperative
Keri Retallick, Exec. Vice Pres.
9185 Old Potosi Rd., Lancaster 53813-0327
(608) 723-7551 wppa@wppa.org

Postal History Soc., Wis.
Frank Moertl, Pres.
N95 W32259 County Line Rd., Hartland 53029-9735
(262) 966-7096 frankann@ticon.net

Potato and Vegetable Growers Assn., Wis.
Jim Bacon, Pres.
P.O. Box 327, Antigo 54409-0327
(715) 623-7683

Potato Growers Aux., Inc., Wis.
Deb Bacon, Pres.
P.O. Box 327, Antigo 54409-0327
(715) 623-7683

Potato Improvement Assn., Wis. Seed
John Hein, Pres.
P.O. Box 173, Antigo 54409-0173
(715) 623-7683

Powersports Dealers Assn., Inc., Wis.
Randy Harden, Dir.
5531B N. Hwy 42, Sheboygan 53083
(920) 565-7522 ext.1 randy.harden@nohvis.com

Prevent Blindness Wis., Inc.
Donna Brady, Exec. Dir.
759 N. Milwaukee St., Milwaukee 53202-3714
(414) 765-0505

Preventive Medicine, Wis., Soc. for
Henry A. Anderson, M.D., Pres.
200 Lakewood Blvd., Madison 53704-5916
(608) 266-1253 anderha@dhfs.state.wi.us

Printing Industries of Wis., Inc.
N. Niall Power, Pres
P.O. Box 126, Elm Grove 53122-0126
(262) 785-7040 info@piw.org

Psychological Assn., Wis.
Sarah Bowen, Exec. Dir.
121 S. Hancock, Madison 53703
(608) 251-1450 wispsych@execpc.com

Quality, Amer. Soc. for
Paul E. Borawski, Exec. Dir.
600 N. Plankinton Ave., Milwaukee 53203
(414) 272-8575 cs@asq.org

Radiologic Technologists, Wis. Soc. of
Sheryl Smith, Pres.
927 Amy Drive, Holmen 54636
(608) 526-4249 rosh927@aol.com

Radiological Soc., Wis.
Michael J. Herzog, Exec. Dir.
P.O. Box 757, Pewaukee 53072-0757
(262) 650-6772 medassn@aol.com

Railroad Passengers, Wis. Assn. of
Mark Weitenbeck, Treas.
3385 S. 119th St., West Allis 53227-3943
(414) 541-1112 wisarp@hotmail.com

Reading Assn., Wis. State
Sue Bradley, Admin. Asst.
N7902 E. Friesland Rd., Randolph 53956
(920) 326-6280 wsra@centurytel.net

Real Property Listers Assn., Wis.
Lori J. Scully, Pres.
220 E. State St., Room 110, Mauston 53948
(608) 847-9311 propspec@co.juneau.wi.us

Register of Deeds Assn., Wis.
Jodi Helgeson, Pres.
P.O. Box 219, Friendship 53934
(608) 339-4206 jhelgeson@co.adams.wi.us

Rehabilitation for Wisconsin, Inc.
Michael G. Kirby, Exec. Dir.
1302 Mendota St., Suite 200, Madison 53714
(608) 244-5310 mkirby@rfw.org

Republican Party of Wis.
Darrin Schmitz, Exec. Dir.
P.O. Box 31, Madison 53701-0031
(608) 257-4765 gop@wisgop.org

Reserve Officers Assn. of the U.S. (Dept. of Wis.)
LTC Timothy Lubinsky, Exec. Secy.
728 Newbury St., Ripon 54971
(920) 748-2308 lubintw@dhfs.state.wi.us

Residential Services Association of Wis.
Jane Svinicki, Exec. Dir.
1123 N. Water Street, Milwaukee 53202-6634
(414) 276-9273 info@rsawisconsin.org

Restaurant Assn., Wis.
Edward J. Lump, Pres/CEO
2801 Fish Hatchery Rd., Madison 53713
(608) 270-9950 elump@wirestaurant.org

Retarded, Inc., Wis. Parents Coalition for the
Kevin Underwood, Pres.
669 McCarthy Dr. North, Hartford 53027
(920) 474-4129

RID (Remove Intoxicated Drivers)
Mardy Meacham, Coord.
122 Eagle Lake Ave., Mukwonago 53149-1107
(262) 363-5554 christysmom1@cs.com

Right to Life, Inc., Wis.
Barbara L. Lyons, Exec. Dir.
10625 W. North Ave., LL, Milwaukee 53226-2331
(877) 855-5007 admin@wrtl.org

Runaway Services, Wis. Assn. for
Patricia Balke, Exec. Dir.
2318 E. Dayton St., Madison 53704-4949
(608) 241-2649 pbalke@sbcglobal.net

Saddlebred Assn. of Wis., Amer.
Shelagh Roell, Pres.
2745 Chadwick Ct., Brookfield 53045
(262) 784-3554

Safety Belt Coalition, Wis.
Ernest W. Stetenfeld, Chm.
P.O. Box 33, Madison 53701-0033
(608) 828-2486 estetenfeld@aaawisconsin.com

Safety Patrols Inc., Wis.
Nan Delaney, Exec. Dir.
8401 Excelsior Drive, Madison 53717
(608) 828-2491 addelaney@aaawisconsin.com

St. Francis Children's Center, Inc.
Gerald Coon, Exec. Dir.
6700 N. Port Washington Rd.
Milwaukee 53217-3919
(414) 351-0450 gcoon@sfcckids.org

Sanitary Engineering, Amer. Soc. of (Wis. Chap.)
Ervin Mirr, Secy.
4610 Raven Ct., Brookfield 53005-1242
(262) 781-4725

School Administrators, Assn. of Wis.
Thomas Beattie, Exec. Dir.
4797 Hayes Rd., Suite 103, Madison 53704-3288
(608) 241-0300 tbeattie@awsa.org

School Attorneys Assn., Wis.
Ken Cole, Secy.
122 W. Washington Ave., Suite 400, Madison 53703
(608) 257-2622 kcole@wasb.org

School Boards, Inc., Wis. Assn. of
Ken Cole, Exec. Dir.
122 W. Washington Ave., Suite 400, Madison 53703
(608) 257-2622 kcole@wasb.org

School Bus Assn., Wis.
Robert W. Christian, Exec. Dir.
P.O. Box 168, Sheboygan 53082-0168
(920) 457-7008 dirbob@dirwsba.com

School Music Assn., Inc., Wis.
Eric Runestad, Exec. Dir.
1102 Stephenson Lane, Waunakee 53597
(608) 850-3566 erunestad@wsmamusic.org

School Music, Wis. Foundation for
Eric Runestad, Exec. Dir.
1102 Stephenson Lane, Waunakee 53597
(608) 850-3566 erunestad@wsmamusic.org

Schools Accreditation, Religious and Independent, Wis.
Beatrice Weiland, Exec. Dir.
26538 Richard Dr., Wind Lake 53185
(262) 895-3679 wrisa@wrisa.net

Schools, Wis. Assn. of Christian
Matt Williams, Exec. Dir.
W10085 Pike Plains Rd., Dunbar 54119
(715) 324-6900 ext. 1650 mwilliams@nbbc.edu

Seasonal Residents Assn.
Nick Kaufmann
P.O. Box 46108, Madison 53744
(800) 880-9944 info@wisra.org

Seniors of Wis., Inc., United
Dorothy Seeley, Pres.
4515 W. Forest Home Ave., Milwaukee 53219-4837
(414) 321-0220

Sexual Assault, Wis. Coalition Against
Linda Morrison, Exec. Dir
600 Williamson St., Suite N-2, Madison 53703
(608) 257-1516 wcasa@wcasa.org

Sheet Metal and Air Conditioning Contractors Assn. of Wis, Inc.
Peter Lentz, Exec. Vice Pres.
10427 W. Lincoln Ave., Suite 1600, Milwaukee 53227
(414) 543-7622

Sheriffs and Deputy Sheriffs Assn., Wis.
James Cardinal, Exec. Dir.
P.O. Box 145, Chippewa Falls 54729-0145
(715) 723-7173 jcardinal@wsdsa.org

Sheriff's Assn., Badger State
Sheriff Scott Pedley, Pres.
P.O. Box 148, 138 West Catherine St.
Darlington 53530-0148
(608) 776-4870 scott.pedley@lafayettecountywi.org

Shiitake Growers Assn. of Wis., Inc.
Mary Ellen Kozak, Pres.
N3296 Kozuzek Rd., Peshtigo 54157
(715) 582-4997 fieldandforest@centurytel.net

Sign Assn., Wis.
Christopher Ruditys, Exec. Dir.
223 N. Water St., Suite 300, Milwaukee 53202
(414) 271-9277 ruditys@wamllc.net

Sister Relationships, Inc., Wis.
Alexander P. Durtka, Jr., Pres.
1110 N. Old World Third St., Milwaukee 53203-1102
(414) 732-4192 wisci@execpc.com

Skills USA-VICA (Post Secondary)
Paul Morschauser, State Mgr.
3550 Anderson Street, Madison 53704
(608) 246-6829 pmorschauser@matcmadison.edu

Soccer Assn., Inc., Wis.
John Janasik, Pres.
10708 W. Hayes Ave., West Allis 53227
(414) 545-7227 janasik@execpc.com

Social Workers, Inc., Natl. Assn. of (Wis. Chap.)
Marc Herstand, Exec. Dir.
16 N. Carroll St., Suite 220, Madison 53703
(608) 257-6334 naswwi@tds.net

Socialist Party of Wis.
Paul J. Cigler, State Chm.
1001 E. Keefe Ave., Milwaukee 53212
(414) 332-0654

Sod Producers Assn., Wis.
Gina Halter, Exec. Secy.
22920 Hanson Rd., Union Grove 53182
(262) 895-6820

Soft Drink Assn., Wis.
Martin Schreiber, Secy.-Treas.
2700 S. Shore Dr., Suite A, Milwaukee 53207-2300
(414) 482-1214 martin@martinschreiber.com

Soil Science Soc. of America
Ellen Bergseld, Exec. Vice Pres.
677 S. Segoe Rd., Madison 53711
(608) 273-8080

Sons of the Amer. Revolution, Wis. Soc. of the
John W. Plummer, Pres.
268 Hayler Ct., Oregon 53575-1108
(608) 835-3351 wispres@linkus.net

Soybean Assn., Wis.
R. Karls, Exec. Dir.
2976 Triverton Pike Dr., Madison 53711-5840

Specialized Medical Vehicle Association of Wisconsin
Jason Pape, Pres.
P.O. Box 209, New Richmond 54017
(800) 236-4650

Speech-Language Pathology and Audiology Assn., Wis.
Kathy Erdman, Pres.
P.O. Box 1109, Madison 53701-1109
(800) 545-0640 wsha@wismed.org

Stamp Clubs, Inc., Wis. Federation of
Karen L. Weigt, Secy.
4184 Rose Ct., Middleton 53562-4339
(608) 836-1509 karenweigt@earthlink.net

State Employees Union, Wis. (AFSCME Council 24,
AFL-CIO)
Marty Beil, Exec. Dir.
8033 Excelsior Dr., Suite C, Madison 53717-1903
(608) 836-0024 mbeil@wseu-24.org

Student Financial Aid Administrators, Wis. Assn. of
Steve Schuetz, Pres.
Ripon College, 300 Seward St., Ripon 54971
(920) 748-8101 schuetzs@ripon.edu

Students, Inc., United Council of UW
Stephanie Hilton, Pres.
14 W. Mifflin St., Suite 212, Madison 53703
(608) 263-3422 president@unitedcouncil.net

Surgeons, Wis. Soc. of Oral and Maxillofacial
Dr. Mark Jackson
P.O. Box 1109, Madison 53701
(608) 283-5402

Surgeons, Wis. Soc. of Plastic
Phil Sonderman, Pres.
2300 N. Mayfair Rd., Suite 795, Milwaukee 53226
(414) 479-3500

Surveyors, Inc., Wis. Soc. of Land
Harold S. Charlier, Exec. Dir.
2935 Coventry Ln., Waukesha 53188-1350
(262) 549-1533 hscwsls@aol.com

Taxicab Owners, Wis. Assn. of
Jason Pape, Secy.-Treas.
P.O. Box 92, New Richmond 54017
(800) 236-4650

Taxpayer Organizations, Inc., Federation of Wis.
Donald J. Kristopeit, Pres.
228 14th Ave., South Milwaukee 53172-1111
(414) 762-3321

Taxpayers Alliance, Wis.
Todd A. Berry, Pres.
401 North Lawn Ave., Madison 53704-5033
(608) 241-9789 wistax@wistax.org

Taxpayers Assn., Inc., Wis. Property
Thomas Dohm, Pres.
P.O. Box 1493, Madison 53701-1493
(608) 255-7473

Teachers, American Assn. of Physics (Wis. Section)
Erik Hendrickson, Secy.-Treas.
Dept. of Physics and Astronomy, UW-Eau Claire
Eau Claire 54702-4004
(715) 836-5834 hendrije@uwec.edu

Teamsters Joint Council No.39, Wis.
Paul G. Lovinus, Secy.-Treas.
10020 W. Greenfield Ave., Milwaukee 53214
(414) 258-4545

Telecommunications Assn., Wis. State
William C. Esbeck, Exec. Dir.
6602 Normandy Ln., Madison 53719-1035
(608) 833-8866 bill.esbeck@wsta.info

Telemedia Council, Inc., Natl.
Marieli Rowe, Exec. Dir.
1922 University Ave., Madison 53726
(608) 218-1182 ntelemedia@aol.com

Telephone Assn., Wis. Locally Owned
Robert Squires, Secy.
P.O. Box 263, Manawa 54949
(920) 596-1709

Textile Services, Wis. Assn. of
Brian Swingle, Exec. Dir.
12342 W. Layton Ave., Greenfield 53228
(414) 529-4703 bswingle@toriphillips.com

Theatre Owners of Wis., Natl. Assn. of
Paul J. Rogers, Pres.
P.O. Box 146, Sussex 53089
(715) 387-3060

Timber Producers Assn., Inc., Michigan-Wisconsin
Alan Hastreiter, Pres.
P.O. Box 1278, Rhinelander 54501-1278
(715) 282-5828

Title Assn., Inc., Wis. Land
Karen E. Gilster, Exec. Off.
P.O. Box 873, West Salem 54669
(800) 589-9582 kgilster@wlta.org

Tool Die and Machining Association of Wis.
Rebecca Fisher, Exec. Secy
W175 N11117 Stonewood Dr., Suite 204
Germantown 53022
(262) 532-2440 toolmakr@tdmaw.org

Tourism Federation, Wis.
Janet R. Swandby
44 E. Mifflin St., Suite 101, Madison 53703
(608) 286-9599 swandby@swandby.com

Towing Assoc., Wis.
Mike DeHaan
562 Grand Canyon Dr., Madison 53719-1033
(608) 833-8200 mdehaan@witrucking.org

Towns Assn., Wis.
Richard J. Stadelman, Exec. Dir.
W7686 County Road MMM, Shawano 54166-6086
(715) 526-3157 wtowns@frontiernet.net

Translators and Interpreters Guild, AFL-CIO (Wis. Chap.)
Rick Kissell
P.O. Box 1101, Milwaukee 53201-1101
(414) 643-8039 rick@kissell.org

Transportation Builders Assn., Wis.
Tom Walker, Exec. Dir.
1 South Pinckney St., Suite 818, Madison 53703
(608) 256-6891 twalker@wtba.org

Transportation Development Assn. of Wis., Inc.
Robert Cook, Exec. Dir.
131 W. Wilson Street, Suite 302, Madison 53703
(608) 256-7044 bob.cook@tdawisconsin.org

Transportation Union, United
Thomas P. Dwyer II, State Dir.
7 N. Pinckney St., Suite 50C, Madison 53703-2840
(608) 251-4120

Tree Farm Com., Wis. State
Tom Jacobs, Chm.
P.O. Box 285, Stevens Point 54481
(715) 582-4340 wtfc@athenet.net

Trees For Tomorrow, Inc.
Gail Gilson Pierce, Exec. Dir.
P.O. Box 609, Eagle River 54521-0609
(800) 838-9472 learning@treesfortomorrow.com

United Nations Reform, Campaign for
Everett Refior, State Coordinator
435 W. Starin Rd., Apt. 118AA, Whitewater 53190
(262) 473-5209 refiore@uww.edu

United Professionals for Quality Care/SEIU District 1199W
Dian Palmer, Pres.
2001 W. Beltline Hwy, Suite 201, Madison 53713
(608) 277-1199 info@1199wup.org

University of Wis. Foundation
Andrew A. Wilcox, Pres.
1848 University Ave., Madison 53726
(608) 263-4545

Utilities Assn., Wis.
William R. Skewes, Exec. Dir.
P.O. Box 2117, Madison 53701-2117
(608) 257-3151 kwilcox@wisconsinutilities.com

Utility Investors, Inc., Wis.
Kenyon C. Kies, Exec. Dir.
10 E. Doty St., Suite 500, Madison 53703-3397
(608) 663-5813 contact@wuiinc.org

Utility Tax Assn., Wis.
Marge Pearce, Rec. Secy.
4809 Moenning Rd.. Sheboygan 53081
(920) 458-2000 margep@powercom.net

Vegetable Council, Inc., Wis.-Minn. Canned
Robert Goeres, Coord.
307 Nestles Ave., P.O. Box 303, Lodi 53555
(608) 592-4236

Veteran Organizations, Wis. Assn. of Concerned
Matthew M. Stevenson, Contact Person
P.O. Box 8073, Green Bay 54308-8073
(920) 437-9709 boom@netnet.net

Veterans Against the War, Vietnam
John Zutz, Coord.
2922 N. Booth St., Milwaukee 53212-2537

Veterans Assn., WAC (Women's Army Corps)
Naomi Horwitz, Pres.
7921 West Congress, No. 1, Milwaukee 53218-4526
(414) 464-2765

Veterans of America, Wis. Paralyzed
Donald Fell, Exec. Dir.
2311 S. 108th St., West Allis 53227-1901
(414) 328-8910 info@wisconsinpva.org

Veterans of Foreign Wars (Dept. of Wis.)
Michael L. Furgal, Adj/Qm
P.O. Box 1623, Madison 53701-1623
(608) 255-6655 wivfw@tds.net

Veterans of World War I (Aux.)
Carla Kleinheinz, Pres.
8088 136th St., Chippewa Falls 54729
(715) 723-2183

Veterans, Catholic War
Ray Wozniak, Dept. Cmdr.
418 Forest Ave., Fond du Lac 54935
(920) 922-3636

Veterans, Catholic War, Ladies Aux. (Wis. Dept.)
Susan Jane Schwartz, Pres.
645 W. Scott St., #102, Fond du Lac 54937

Veterans, Disabled Amer. (Dept. of Wis.)
Maurice Jackson, Adj.
130 Dauphin St., Green Bay 54301
(920) 406-0620 gbdav@tds.net

Veterans, Disabled Amer., Aux. (Dept. of Wis.)
Sharon Cornell, Comdr.
2631 S. Carpenter St., Appleton 54915
(920) 734-3474

Veterans, Foreign War (Auxiliary)
Geri Dorow, Pres.
4273 W. Granada St., Greenfield 53221
(414) 282-2499 gadorow04@aol.com

Veterans, Jewish War
Leonard C. Brody, Cmdr.
7933 W. Denver Ave., Milwaukee 53223
(414) 353-2092 minnette@core.com

Veterans, Natl. Assoc. for Black (Wis. Chap.)
Robert A. Cocroft, Chair
P.O. Box 11432, Milwaukee 53211-0432
(800) 842-4597 nabvets@nabvets.com

Veterans, Polish Legion of American
Joseph Soulak, Cmdr.
723 Milwaukee Ave., South Milwaukee 53172
(414) 762-2520

Veterans, Polish Legion of American, Ladies Aux.
   (Dept. of Wis.)
Debbie Lamb, St. Pres.
2619 Roosevelt Rd., Kenosha 53143
(262) 652-1499 dlamb@wi.rr.com

Veterans, U.S. Submarine of WWII
Owen Williams, St. Cmdr.
309 Gibson St., Apt. L, Mukwonago 53149-1354
(262) 363-7330

Veterans, United Spanish War, Aux.
Peggy Schaefer, Pres.
7300 W. Dean Rd., No. 338, Milwaukee 53223-2600

Veterans, Wis. Vietnam
William F. Hustad, Pres.
W4489 Exeter Crossing Rd., Monticello 53570
(608) 527-2942 wfhus1@tds.net

Veterinary Medical Assn., Wis.
Leslie G. Grendahl, Exec. Dir.
301 N. Broom St., Madison 53703
(608) 257-3665 wvma@wvma.org

Wetlands Assn., Wis.
Becky Abel, Exec. Dir.
222 S. Hamilton St., Suite 1, Madison 53703
(608) 250-9971 info@wiscwetlands.org

Wildlife Society, Wis. Chapter
Tim Van Deelen, Pres.
P.O. Box 863, Madison 53701
(608) 265-3280 trvandeelen@wisc.edu

Wine and Spirit Inst., Wis.
Eric J. Petersen, Exec. Dir.
22 N. Carroll St., Suite 200, Madison 53703-2724
(608) 256-5223 eric.petersen@capitolconsultants.net

Wisconsin AIRS, Inc.
Susan Richards, Pres.
1820 Appleton Road, Menasha 54952
(920) 954-7200 susan.richards@unitedwayfoxcities.org

Wisconsin Information Network (WIN)
Dottie Feder, Pres.
17305 Oak Park Row, Brookfield 53045
(262) 786-6200 dfeder@execpc.com

Wisconsin Intercollegiate Athletic Conference
Gary F. Karner, Commissioner
780 Regent Street, Madison 53715
(608) 263-4402 gkarner@uwsa.edu

Women Business Owners, Wis., Inc.,Natl. Assn. of
Dana Kader Robb, Pres.
P.O. Box 259900, Madison 53725-9900
(414) 778-0602 danarobb@bizwi.rr.com

Women Highway Safety Leaders, Inc., Wis. Assn. of
LaVerne Hoerig, National Rep.
1321 Clara Ave., Sheboygan 53081-5261
(920) 452-0905

Women Veterans, United
Vera Roddy, Pres.
2256 N. 60th St., Milwaukee 53208
(414) 443-6453 vroddy@milwol.com

Women, Wis. National Organization for
Robyn Klinge, Exec. Dir.
122 State Street, Suite 403, Madison 53703
(608) 255-3911 admin@winow.org

Women's Network, Wis.
Administrator
122 State St., Suite 404, Madison 53703-2500
(608) 255-9809 wiwomen@execpc.com
Woodland Owners Assn., Inc., Wis.
Nancy C. Bozek, Exec. Dir.
P.O. Box 285, Stevens Point 54481-0285
(715) 346-4798 nbozek@uwsp.edu
Writers, Inc., Council for Wis.
Ted Hertel, Treas.
10535 North Port Washington Rd., Suite 204
Mequon 53092
thertel@execpc.com

WWOA Foundation, Inc. (Wisconsin Woodland
Owners Assn)
Charles Haubrich, Pres.
3606 Dyer Lake Rd.. Burlington 53105
(262) 534-5116 senocenter@senocenter.org

Youth Development Initiative, Inc., Wis. Positive
Susan Allen, Exec. Dir.
314 S. Thomas St., P.O. Box 10, Westfield 53964
(608) 296-9960 wipyd@maqs.net

Source: This list was compiled from a questionnaire mailed to known statewide associations in Fall 2004.

NOTE

If you know of any additional PERMANENT, STATEWIDE, NONPROFIT associations – other than religious or fraternal – please send the information to the Blue Book Editor, Legislative Reference Bureau, P.O. Box 2037, Madison, Wisconsin 53701-2037. New associations which meet the stated criteria will be included in the next edition of the *Wisconsin Blue Book*.

HIGHLIGHTS OF COMMERCE AND INDUSTRY IN WISCONSIN

Manufacturing — Value added by manufacture in Wisconsin totaled $65.4 billion in 2003, an increase of $4.2 billion since 1999. The industry groups with the highest value added in 2003 were transportation equipment, $11.8 billion; food, $7.7 billion; paper, $7.1 billion; machinery, $6.3 billion; and fabricated metal products, $5.9 billion.

Wisconsin ranked 10th among the states in value added by manufacture in 2003. Leaders in this category were California, $197.5 billion; Texas, $123.8 billion; and Ohio, $109.3 billion. The national total for value added was $1.910 trillion in 2003, a decrease of $53 billion since 1999.

Energy Consumption — In 2003, Wisconsin's total energy use per capita reached 328 million Btu, about 15.9% higher than the usage rate in 1990 and more than 26.2% higher than in 1970. Seen from a national perspective, Wisconsin has gone from consuming energy at about 85% of the U.S. average in 1970 to about 5% more than the national average in 2003. Compared to various national averages, Wisconsin places a much heavier reliance on coal for its energy usage, but uses less petroleum, natural gas, nuclear power, and renewable energy. As energy consumption has increased, Wisconsin, which was an exporter of electricity in the 1970s, has increasingly become a net importer. Of the petroleum consumed in Wisconsin in 2003, the largest portion, about 83%, was used for transportation, followed by residential (8%) and industrial (4%) usage.

Gasoline Usage and Tax — In 2002, each automobile in Wisconsin was driven an average of 13,545 miles. This is 1,342 miles, or about 11%, more than the national average of 12,203 miles per year. Wisconsin automobiles averaged 22.2 miles per gallon of gasoline, nearly the same as the national average of 22.1 mpg. These mileage and fuel economy statistics pertain to standard passenger cars and do not include data for minivans, pickup trucks, or "sport utility vehicles" (SUVs). The state motor fuel tax, which is indexed to account for the effects of inflation, increased 0.8 of a cent on April 1, 2005, to a total of 29.9 cents per gallon. (The federal government's gasoline tax on that date was 18.4 cents per gallon for a total of 48.3 cents per gallon in federal and state taxes.) Since indexing began on April 1, 1985, the average adjustment in state tax has usually been between 0.4 and 0.8 cents.

Exports and Markets — In 2004, Wisconsin's leading exports were industrial machinery and computers, $4.5 billion; scientific and medical instruments, $1.6 billion; and electric machinery, $1.3 billion. The leading market for Wisconsin exports in 2004 was Canada ($4.9 billion), followed by Mexico ($1.1 billion), and Japan ($624.6 million). The total of all exports from Wisconsin to all markets in 2004 was $12.7 trillion.

Financial Institutions — The number of banks operating in Wisconsin has decreased from the post-Depression high of 647 in 1982 to 280 in 2004. Over the same period, deposits increased from $22.5 billion to $79.4 billion. In 2004, Wisconsin's 42 state and federally chartered savings institutions had total deposits of $16.7 billion.

In 2004, Wisconsin had 287 state-chartered credit unions with nearly 2 million members and $13.7 billion in assets.

Corporations — In 2004, a total of 2,566 foreign corporations were licensed in Wisconsin, an 82.2% increase from 1,408 in 1990. Incorporation and licensing fees collected by the state in 2004 totaled almost $16.5 million.

The following tables present selected data. Consult footnoted sources for more detailed information about commerce and industry.

WISCONSIN USE OF PETROLEUM 1970 – 2003
(In Trillions of Btu)

Year	Total[1]	Transportation	Residential	Industrial	Agricultural	Commercial	Electric Utility
1970	457.7	271.2	107.9	21.1	18.1	31.5	7.9
1975	475.0	314.0	87.6	19.3	18.8	27.5	7.8
1980	454.4	329.2	71.2	13.2	21.4	14.6	4.8
1985	412.0	314.3	51.7	9.4	19.2	16.0	1.4
1986	433.8	322.9	47.7	22.2	18.6	20.9	1.5
1987	423.8	328.7	42.6	21.0	15.7	14.8	1.0
1988	447.3	344.0	48.7	22.4	14.5	16.5	1.2
1989	453.6	346.4	50.2	22.7	16.5	16.8	1.0
1990	444.4	347.7	42.6	22.1	16.0	15.0	1.0
1991	441.9	350.0	42.8	18.1	15.6	14.4	1.0
1992	449.4	360.8	41.9	15.7	16.0	14.0	1.0
1993	462.8	372.1	42.0	18.2	15.4	14.1	1.0
1994	471.0	379.1	40.1	21.8	15.8	13.2	1.0
1995	473.3	384.2	40.8	18.5	15.6	13.4	0.8
1996	488.6	393.2	43.5	20.9	15.9	14.2	0.9
1997	492.7	401.5	40.5	20.8	15.3	13.1	1.5
1998	491.4	411.3	33.9	19.1	14.5	10.8	1.8
1999	508.6	422.2	36.6	21.2	15.0	11.6	2.0
2000	503.4	416.0	38.8	20.5	14.4	12.1	1.6
2001	506.0	417.5	36.7	25.0	14.0	11.5	1.3
2002	515.6	430.1	38.0	19.2	14.4	11.8	2.1
2003[2]	519.0	430.8	39.6	19.1	14.6	12.2	2.7

[1]Detail may not add to total due to rounding.

[2]Preliminary estimates.

Source: Wisconsin Department of Administration, Division of Energy, *Wisconsin Energy Statistics – 2004*, "Wisconsin Petroleum Use, by Economic Sector, 1970-2003", 2004.

WISCONSIN AND U.S. ENERGY CONSUMPTION BY RESOURCE 1970 – 2003
In Millions of Btu per Capita

Energy Resource	1970	1975	1980	1985	1990	1995	1998	1999	2000	2001	2002	2003[1]
Petroleum												
U.S.	127	133	128	113	114	112	113	115	116	115	113	114
Wisconsin	104	104	97	87	91	92	93	96	94	94	94	94
Wisconsin as % of U.S. per capita	82%	78	75	77	80	82	82	83	81	82	83	83
Natural Gas												
U.S.	106	93	90	75	77	86	83	82	85	80	82	77
Wisconsin	75	80	73	64	63	74	68	71	73	67	70	71
Wisconsin as % of U.S. per capita	70%	86	82	86	81	87	82	86	86	83	86	92
Coal												
U.S.	60	59	68	74	76	75	79	77	80	77	77	78
Wisconsin	80	57	69	78	83	91	98	100	102	102	99	102
Wisconsin as % of U.S. per capita	123%	90	99	105	120	141	148	151	148	159	158	158
Nuclear												
U.S.	1	9	12	17	25	27	26	27	28	28	28	28
Wisconsin	0	24	23	25	25	23	19	23	23	23	25	24
Wisconsin as % of U.S. per capita	33%	276	189	143	100	87	75	86	83	82	88	87
Renewable[2]												
U.S.	13	13	17	19	17	18	17	17	16	14	15	16
Wisconsin	7	8	12	14	13	13	13	13	14	14	15	15
Wisconsin as % of U.S. per capita	55%	59	70	72	75	75	76	80	90	101	96	94
Electric Imports[3]												
Wisconsin	-6	-4	-1	0	8	15	18	17	16	20	23	22
Total Resource Use												
U.S.	307	307	315	298	309	318	317	319	325	314	316	313
Wisconsin	260	269	272	268	283	309	310	320	323	319	326	328
Wisconsin as % of U.S. per capita	84%	88	86	90	91	97	98	100	99	102	103	105

[1]Preliminary data.

[2]Includes wood, waste, alcohol, and other biomass energy; hydroelectric; geothermal; solar; and wind.

[3]Import of electricity reflects estimated resource energy used in other states or Canada to produce electricity imported into Wisconsin. This resource energy is estimated assuming 11,300 Btu per kWh imported into Wisconsin. A negative number indicates energy used in Wisconsin to produce electricity exported out of state.

Source: Wisconsin Department of Administration, Division of Energy, *Wisconsin Energy Statistics – 2004*, November 2004. Percentages calculated by Division of Energy.

AUTOMOBILE USAGE AND GASOLINE MILEAGE
Wisconsin and United States, 1980 - 2002

Year	Average Miles Driven Per Auto		Average Auto Miles Per Gallon of Gasoline	
	Wisconsin	U.S.	Wisconsin	U.S.
1980	9,782	8,813	16.1	16.0
1985	10,455	9,419	17.6	17.5
1990	11,659	10,504	20.3	20.2
1991	11,734	10,571	21.2	21.1
1992	12,051	10,857	21.1	21.0
1993	11,992	10,804	20.6	20.5
1994	12,201	10,992	20.8	20.7
1995	12,435	11,203	21.2	21.1
1996	12,576	11,330	21.3	21.2
1997	12,855	11,581	21.6	21.5
1998	13,047	11,754	21.7	21.6
1999	13,151	11,848	21.5	21.4
2000	13.293	11,976	22.0	21.9
2001	13,132	11,831	22.2	22.1
2002*	13,545	12,203	22.2	22.1

Note: This table does not include data for minivans, pickup trucks, or sport utility vehicles. Wisconsin and U.S. figures are derived from different sources and may not be strictly comparable.

*Preliminary data.

Source: Wisconsin Department of Administration, Division of Energy, *Wisconsin Energy Statistics - 2004*, November 2004.

WISCONSIN MOTOR VEHICLE FUEL TAX, 1925 - 2005

Date of Change	Gasoline Tax Per Gallon[1]	Change Amount	Change Percent
April 1, 1925	2.0¢	2.0¢	---
April 1, 1931	4.0	2.0	100.0%
July 1, 1955	6.0	2.0	50.0
July 1, 1966	7.0	1.0	16.7
May 1, 1980	9.0	2.0	28.6
August 1, 1981	13.0	4.0	44.4
August 1, 1983	15.0	2.0	15.4
July 1, 1984	16.0	1.0	6.7
April 1, 1985[2]	16.5	0.5	3.1
April 1, 1986	17.5	1.0	6.1
April 1, 1987	18.0	0.5	2.9
August 1, 1987[3]	20.0	2.0	11.1
April 1, 1988	20.9	0.9	4.5
April 1, 1989	20.8	(0.1)	(0.5)
April 1, 1990	21.5	0.7	3.4
April 1, 1991	22.2	0.7	3.3
April 1, 1993[4]	23.2	1.0	4.5
April 1, 1994	23.1	(0.1)	(0.4)
April 1, 1995[5]	23.4	0.3	1.3
April 1, 1996[5]	23.7	0.3	1.3
April 1, 1997	23.8	0.1	0.4
November 1, 1997[6]	24.8	1.0	4.2
April 1, 1998	25.4	0.6	2.4
April 1, 1999	25.8	0.4	1.6
April 1, 2000	26.4	0.6	2.3
April 1, 2001	27.3	0.9	3.4
April 1, 2002	28.1	0.8	2.9
April 1, 2003	28.5	0.4	1.4
April 1, 2004	29.1	0.6	2.1
April 1, 2005	29.9	0.8	2.7

[1]Tax rates for some alternate fuels are based on energy density. The rates effective April 1, 2005, are 21.9 cents for LPG (liquified petroleum gas) and 23.9 cents for CNG (compressed natural gas). E85 (85% fuel ethanol) is taxed at the same rate as gasoline.

[2]Beginning in April 1985, the state motor fuel tax was indexed (1983 Wisconsin Act 27) to take into account fuel consumption and inflation. By law, the tax increase or decrease is automatically calculated annually, based on the inflation rate from the National Highway Maintenance and Operations Cost Index and the percentage change in motor fuel consumption. (The federal gasoline tax has been 18.4 cents per gallon since October 1, 1993.)

[3]Statutory adjustment (1987 Wisconsin Act 27).

[4]1991 Wisconsin Act 119 postponed further fuel tax indexing until April 1, 1993.

[5]1993 Wisconsin Act 16 set aside the calculation of the consumption factor for 1995 and 1996 and provided fixed consumption factors for each year.

[6]1997 Wisconsin Act 27 increased the motor fuel tax rate and modified the indexing formula to take into account only the change to the cost index.

Sources: Session laws of the Wisconsin Legislature; Wisconsin Department of Revenue, *Motor Vehicle Fuel Tax Information*, April 2005 and previous years, and departmental data.

VALUE ADDED BY MANUFACTURING
By State, 1999 and 2003
(In Thousands)

State	Value Added 1999	Value Added 2003	2003 State Rank	State	Value Added 1999	Value Added 2003	2003 State Rank
Alabama	$30,182,798	$29,768,242	24	Montana	$1,791,616	$1,793,537	47
Alaska	1,110,863	1,413,087	49	Nebraska	11,814,683	11,843,831	35
Arizona	33,166,079	29,016,543	25	Nevada	3,827,177	5,040,107	42
Arkansas	20,873,095	22,729,668	28	New Hampshire	9,952,585	8,908,698	36
California	218,179,285	197,547,397	1	New Jersey	51,501,791	51,979,452	12
Colorado	19,407,467	17,242,913	32	New Mexico	13,548,803	6,149,934	40
Connecticut	27,074,960	25,771,357	26	New York	80,439,706	80,198,578	9
Delaware	6,070,193	4,606,503	44	North Carolina	90,441,717	89,016,793	7
District of Columbia	142,062	195,804	51	North Dakota	2,263,526	2,519,555	46
Florida	41,962,588	42,391,298	17	Ohio	118,177,947	109,282,204	3
Georgia	62,639,804	58,683,253	11	Oklahoma	17,995,474	17,685,839	31
Hawaii	1,311,128	1,224,485	50	Oregon	24,593,372	25,109,453	27
Idaho	7,308,868	7,701,444	38	Pennsylvania	89,385,735	93,776,840	5
ILLINOIS	96,828,988	93,534,022	6	Rhode Island	5,810,543	6,039,219	41
Indiana	77,905,886	80,988,082	8	South Carolina	35,286,553	39,228,391	19
IOWA	28,434,173	32,738,826	22	South Dakota	6,988,337	3,775,635	45
Kansas	22,123,510	20,428,603	29	Tennessee	47,601,973	51,129,897	13
Kentucky	40,555,360	35,562,332	21	Texas	131,145,638	123,845,909	2
Louisiana	26,607,281	30,604,577	23	Utah	11,845,305	12,719,678	34
Maine	7,591,824	7,377,409	39	Vermont	4,919,446	4,971,665	43
Maryland	19,143,585	18,490,466	30	Virginia	49,193,934	46,848,691	14
Massachusetts	45,753,436	46,265,933	15	Washington	36,923,564	38,896,066	20
MICHIGAN	101,569,673	97,552,030	4	West Virginia	9,190,096	8,204,573	37
MINNESOTA	40,301,585	41,451,418	18	WISCONSIN	61,160,365	65,354,715	10
Mississippi	23,789,526	17,168,991	33	Wyoming	1,253,583	1,721,791	48
Missouri	45,556,108	43,120,239	16	UNITED STATES*	$1,962,643,592	$1,909,615,972	

*State amounts may not sum to United States total due to rounding.

Source: U.S. Census Bureau, *1999 Annual Survey of Manufactures, Geographic Area Statistics*, April 2001, and *2003 Annual Survey of Manufactures, Geographic Area Statistics*, May 2005.

VALUE ADDED BY MANUFACTURING IN WISCONSIN
By Industry Group, 1997 – 2003
(In Thousands)

Industry Group	1997	1999	2001	2003
Transportation equipment	$5,519,239	$6,880,115	$6,542,830	$11,846,678
Food	6,498,229	7,014,187	7,719,549	7,696,824
Paper	5,934,172	6,188,819	6,557,174	7,089,579
Machinery	8,355,559	8,383,993	7,948,123	6,307,282
Fabricated metal products	5,884,507	6,218,405	5,855,127	5,937,123
Electrical equipment, appliances, and components	3,677,350	3,941,286	3,842,816	3,947,480
Chemicals	2,888,523	3,164,288	3,332,319	3,657,681
Printing and related support activities	2,476,608	2,771,862	2,880,064	3,115,369
Plastics and rubber products	2,539,184	2,866,286	2,906,664	2,822,125
Computer and electronic products	2,470,629	2,856,499	2,638,805	2,541,190
Primary metal industries	2,297,730	2,281,855	2,026,112	2,179,272
Wood products	2,227,905	2,702,649	2,800,862	2,082,629
Miscellaneous manufacturing	1,304,871	1,374,898	1,597,683	1,997,699
Nonmetallic mineral products	1,209,486	1,311,022	1,485,568	1,634,848
Furniture and related products	1,008,655	1,114,757	1,151,689	1,307,566
Beverage and tobacco products	557,570	476,854	450,313	601,729
Leather and allied products	387,568	327,769	271,111	166,253
Textile mills	199,394	157,027	155,066	161,892
Textile products	88,280	119,786	105,703	95,195
Apparel	97,458	98,555	89,642	79,317
TOTAL*	$54,974,219	$59,586,713	$59,584,740	$65,354,715

*Total may not add due to rounding.

Source: U.S. Census Bureau, *2003 Annual Survey of Manufactures, Geographic Area Statistics*, May 2005, and previous editions.

WISCONSIN EXPORTS
By Leading Export, 2000 – 2004 (In Millions)

Export*	2004	2003	2002	2001	2000
Industrial machinery and computers ...	$4,462,483	$3,889,425	$3,606,692	$3,424,236	$3,598,994
Scientific and medical instruments	1,633,554	1,607,719	1,590,408	1,535,977	1,393,827
Electric machinery	1,288,475	900,443	782,912	903,753	864,886
Vehicles, equipment, and parts	967,982	964,485	829,433	777,623	860,697
Paper and paper products	686,630	584,602	556,145	525,188	554,692
Plastics and plastic products	496,808	471,171	425,445	427,570	399,986
Cereals	216,597	219,204	238,005	200,875	192,126
Iron or steel articles	171,304	145,501	144,670	152,464	155,375
Printed books and newspapers	169,694	152,459	145,599	162,711	167,344
Furniture, fixtures, and bedding	134,065	97,522	88,452	86,386	90,974
Miscellaneous chemical products	126,980	122,026	122,199	108,497	108,148
Wood, charcoal, and articles of wood ..	102,720	93,947	85,840	80,187	82,402
Bakery cereal, flour, starch, and milk ..	98,654	97,634	87,159	78,645	49,552
Raw hides, skins, and leather	98,052	116,028	119,021	130,762	89,135
Oil seeds	90,074	129,003	167,737	138,370	163,428
Soaps and waxes	84,991	73,224	71,447	59,310	51,195
Base metal articles	84,498	71,455	74,031	79,371	80,095
Miscellaneous edible preparations	84,060	73,916	65,641	61,884	52,543
Aircraft, spacecraft, and parts	83,706	105,475	76,287	95,618	63,008
Beverages, spirits, and vinegar	77,956	61,604	33,511	27,189	18,970
Total of leading exports	$11,159,282	$9,976,843	$9,310,635	$9,056,618	$9,037,377
Total of all exports	$12,706,343	$11,509,835	$10,684,271	$10,488,671	$10,508,413

*Export categories based on U.S. Census Bureau, Foreign Trade Division, 2004 Schedule B commodity codes.
Source: Wisconsin Department of Commerce, Wisconsin Export Data by Product, February 11, 2005, at: http://commerce.wi.gov/ IE/IE–WIExportsByProduct.xls. Detail may not add to total due to rounding.

WISCONSIN EXPORTS
By Leading Market, 2000 – 2004 (In Millions)

Market	2004	2003	2002	2001	2000
Canada	$4,856,674	$4,349,326	$3,923,197	$3,771,344	$4,136,405
Mexico	1,064,414	788,033	716,951	670,109	673,710
Japan	624,627	816,690	957,658	733,008	748,914
China (Mainland)	583,303	548,228	359,024	319,570	177,383
United Kingdom	517,304	493,976	417,230	448,025	497,021
Germany	460,588	448,464	425,131	376,260	377,960
France..........................	364,565	371,093	340,097	366,144	332,209
Belgium	330,803	262,653	256,065	223,887	196,283
Australia	325,525	279,937	255,158	241,564	207,506
Korea, Republic of	273,018	258,387	214,924	220,859	235,320
Italy	229,446	231,869	237,425	254,191	209,990
Netherlands	228,291	241,869	283,223	312,267	267,048
Hong Kong	193,697	161,818	154,983	163,013	182,165
China (Taiwan)	188,689	152,878	139,835	153,301	165,275
Brazil	158,117	105,569	131,500	169,377	158,389
Chile	147,010	84,866	72,791	80,884	120,176
Singapore	141,566	125,834	102,962	112,063	120,981
India	115,344	93,572	124,552	82,216	56,837
Spain	95,129	105,276	80,272	72,070	82,452
Saudia Arabia	91,955	90,656	90,556	98,224	56,994
Total of Leading Markets	$10,990,065	$10,010,993	$9,283,534	$8,868,375	$9,003,017
Total of All Markets*	$12,706,343	$11,509,835	$10,684,271	$10,488,671	$10,508,413

*Includes markets not identified by country.
Source: Wisconsin Department of Commerce, Wisconsin Export Data by Destination, February 11, 2005, at: http://commerce.wi.gov/IE/IE–WIExportsByCountry.xls. Detail may not add to totals due to rounding.

BASIC DATA ON WISCONSIN CORPORATIONS
1905 – 2004

	Transactions[1]			Fees			
	Domestic						
Year[2] Calendar	Articles of Incorporation Filed[3]	Amdts. and Restated Articles	Foreign Corporations Licensed[3]	Fees for Articles of Incorporation	Fees for Foreign Corporation[4]	Other Corporation Fees[5]	Total Fees Collected
1905	98	---	95	---	---	---	
1915	1,043	382	112	$28,287	$3,743	$89,695	$69,312
1925	1,438	896	198	57,614	11,139	78,153	121,725
1935	1,272	439	176	30,839	8,956	41,631	146,906
1945	1,120	680	131	31,823	4,826	113,963	81,426
1955	2,537	874	287	89,951	31,146	175,973	150,612
1965	4,063	1,320	401	344,906	120,506	193,844	297,070
Fiscal							659,256
1975	5,976	1,483	663	361,013	386,061	594,498	1,341,572
1980	7,334	1,978	753	373,220	753,461	788,204	1,914,885
1985	7,605	2,359	1,018	485,835	1,142,129	1,371,476	2,999,440
1990	8,387	2,525	1,408	546,550	2,368,900	1,491,104	4,406,554
1995	10,031	2,716	1,507	829,555	4,208,178	2,538,521	7,576,254
1996	10,196	2,592	1,476	843,645	3,707,643	2,735,822	7,287,110
1997	14,599	2,616	1,950	1,446,285	3,928,923	3,137,473	8,512,681
1998	15,352	2,761	2,218	1,581,395	4,621,261	3,644,146	9,846,802
1999	18,641	3,082	2,358	1,943,935	4,830,592	3,524,182	10,298,709
2000	21,133	3,088	2,464	2,265,455	6,403,447	3,548,264	12,217,166
2001	20,461	3,064	2,394	2,631,375	6,901,290	3,257,622	12,790,287
2002	22,734	3,145	2,314	2,735,390	6,330,109	3,408,267	12,473,766
2003	26,629	3,057	2,436	3,223,455	7,379,300	5,262,635	15,865,390
2004	31,440	3,644	2,566	3,820,735	6,253,800	6,406,280	16,480,815

[1]Includes only those corporate entities for which the reporting agency is the office of record.
[2]Since 1974, data is computed on a fiscal year basis, ending June 30 of year shown.
[3]Beginning in 1997, includes limited liability companies.
[4]Since 1974, totals include fees for foreign corporation annual reports.
[5]Includes fees for filing annual reports and corporation charter documents other than articles of incorporation.
Sources: Wisconsin Department of Financial Institutions, departmental data for 1997-2002, April 2003; and 2003-2004, March 2005; previous data from the Office of the Wisconsin Secretary of State.

FINANCIAL INSTITUTIONS OPERATING IN WISCONSIN
Number and Deposits, 1900 – 2004

Year*	Number	Total Deposits (in thousands)	Year*	Number	Total Deposits (in thousands)
1900	349	$124,892	1995	449	59,918,000
1910	630	268,766	1996	428	62,735,000
1920	976	767,534	1997	416	65,663,000
1930	936	935,006	1998	400	69,261,000
1940	574	993,155	1999	390	72,446,000
1950	556	2,965,580	2000	365	75,379,000
1960	561	4,385,838	2001	337	78,567,000
1970	602	8,750,823	2002	328	83,602,000
1980	634	24,763,910	2003	319	95,909,000
1990	504	37,588,879	2004	322	96,111,000

*Data for 1994 and later include federal charter savings associations and state-chartered savings associations, supervised by the U.S. Office of Thrift Supervision, and institutions operating in Wisconsin but headquartered outside the state. Deposits for these years are rounded to nearest thousands of dollars.

Sources: **1950 and earlier:** Board of Governors of the Federal Reserve System, *All-Bank Statistics, U.S.,* 1959; **1960:** Wisconsin Commissioner of Banks, agency data, December 1965; **1970:** Federal Deposit Insurance Corporation, *Assets and Liabilities – Commercial and Mutual Savings Banks,* June 1971; **1980:** Federal Deposit Insurance Corporation, corporate data; **1981-93:** Federal Deposit Insurance Corporation, *Data Book: Operating Banks and Branches,* Book 3, June 30, 1993, and previous issues; **1994 to date:** *Federal Deposit Insurance Corporation, Summary of Deposits.* "State Totals by Charter Class for All Institution Deposits, Deposits of All FDIC-Insured Institutions Operating in Wisconsin", June 30, 2004, and previous issues.

WISCONSIN FINANCIAL INSTITUTIONS
December 31, 2004

Type of Institution or Branch	Total	Insured Commercial Banks and Trust Companies				Insured Savings Institutions	
		National Charter	State Charter / Federal Reserve System			Federal Charter	State Charter
			Member	Nonmember			
Institutions without branches	81	8	8	54		6	5
Institutions operating branches	227	32	19	149		14	13
Total institutions	308	40	27	203		20	18
Total branches	1,971	657	382	522		350	60
TOTAL OFFICES	2,279	697	409	725		370	78

Source: Federal Deposit Insurance Corporation, *Statistics on Banking, Fourth Quarter, 2004*, "Table 103: Number of Offices of FDIC-Insured Depository Institutions, December 31, 2004", at: http://www2.fdic.gov/sdi/sob/0412/all103.asp [March 30, 2005].

WISCONSIN STATE-CHARTERED CREDIT UNIONS
Number, Members, and Assets
1930 – 2004

Year	Credit Unions	Membership		Assets	
		Total Members	Annual % Increase	Total Assets (in millions)	Annual % Increase
1930	22	4,659	--	$0.5	--
1935	383	57,847	--	2.9	--
1940	592	153,849	--	11.2	--
1945	536	144,524	--	19.1	--
1950	542	193,296	--	42.9	--
1955	696	292,552	--	120.6	--
1960	733	363,444	--	206.4	--
1965	781	493,399	--	346.6	--
1970	766	628,543	--	480.4	--
1975	673	805,123	--	875.5	--
1980	618	1,060,292	--	1,403.8	--
1985	550	1,261,407	--	2,831.4	--
1986	528	1,294,117	2.6%	3,208.3	13.3%
1987	506	1,350,111	4.3	3,428.5	6.9
1988	483	1,392,846	3.2	3,619.5	5.6
1989	457	1,424,415	2.3	3,819.3	5.5
1990	440	1,485,109	4.3	4,148.8	8.6
1991	427	1,596,547	7.5	4,495.6	8.4
1992	418	1,608,412	0.7	4,991.5	11.0
1993	406	1,646,847	2.4	5,360.1	7.4
1994	394	1,714,182	4.1	5,755.1	7.4
1995	384	1,744,696	1.8	6,179.2	7.4
1996	375	1,773,611	1.7	6,569.9	6.3
1997	369	1,803,529	1.7	7,175.4	9.2
1998	358	1,834,944	1.7	8,192.4	14.2
1999	350	1,887,429	2.9	8,737.3	6.7
2000	340	1,918,729	1.7	9,425.9	7.9
2001	326	1,883,387	-1.8	10,439.4	10.8
2002	308	1,937,867	2.9	11,665.6	11.7
2003	298	1,966,929	1.5	12,772.5	9.5
2004	287	1,992,238	1.3	13,684.4	7.1

Note: Annual percentage increase not available for years preceding 1986.

Source: Wisconsin Department of Financial Institutions, Office of Credit Unions, *Year-End 2004 Bulletin* [March 2005] and previous years' annual reports. Percentages calculated by Wisconsin Legislative Reference Bureau.

FDIC-INSURED INSTITUTIONS OPERATING IN WISCONSIN
By County, June 30, 2004

County	Commercial Banks			Savings Institutions		
	Number of		Deposits	Number of		Deposits
	Institutions	Offices	(in millions)	Institutions	Offices	(in millions)
Adams	4	5	$156	1	1	$15
Ashland	4	9	236	0	0	0
Barron	10	19	672	3	4	98
Bayfield	5	11	169	0	0	0
Brown	17	65	3,808	5	21	560
Buffalo	6	10	231	1	1	6
Burnett	3	8	175	0	0	0
Calumet	7	11	326	2	3	57
Chippewa	8	18	516	4	8	112
Clark	8	20	413	1	1	26
Columbia	11	28	777	2	2	68
Crawford	5	11	274	2	2	87
Dane	31	110	6,333	7	56	2,860
Dodge	17	32	764	5	8	162
Door	4	16	588	2	4	105
Douglas	7	12	462	1	2	46
Dunn	10	25	303	1	2	36
Eau Claire	12	24	929	3	14	277
Florence	2	3	58	0	0	0
Fond du Lac	12	32	1,093	5	5	239
Forest	3	6	123	0	0	0
Grant	12	34	858	1	3	103
Green	10	17	585	2	3	108
Green Lake	9	12	390	2	2	37
Iowa	7	13	269	1	1	33
Iron	1	2	59	0	0	0
Jackson	3	9	214	1	1	1
Jefferson	14	27	919	1	1	31
Juneau	7	12	272	1	3	33
Kenosha	11	35	1,567	3	4	50
Kewaunee	5	13	302	1	1	28
La Crosse	14	35	1,240	1	6	414
Lafayette	10	16	279	0	0	0
Langlade	6	7	137	0	0	0
Lincoln	5	11	276	2	2	78
Manitowoc	12	27	1,057	3	3	76
Marathon	18	41	1,781	3	9	260
Marinette	10	17	528	1	4	106
Marquette	6	10	188	0	0	0
Milwaukee	21	195	22,767	16	92	5,208
Monroe	10	18	444	1	2	73
Oconto	7	16	300	0	0	0
Oneida	9	19	616	0	0	0
Outagamie	18	41	1,818	8	24	673
Ozaukee	12	35	1,425	4	10	205
Pepin	3	3	174	0	0	0
Pierce	8	16	441	2	3	51
Polk	9	21	583	1	1	11
Portage	13	22	773	1	1	116
Price	5	8	135	1	1	77
Racine	13	54	2,166	5	13	296
Richland	6	7	170	2	2	71
Rock	15	37	1,330	4	9	269
Rusk	5	8	148	1	1	26
St. Croix	12	25	678	3	5	106
Sauk	13	35	1,111	1	1	1
Sawyer	6	10	329	1	1	22
Shawano	10	16	415	1	1	42
Sheboygan	13	36	1,611	4	6	71
Taylor	4	8	261	1	1	105
Trempealeau	11	18	430	0	0	0
Vernon	8	15	336	2	2	47
Vilas	8	14	360	0	0	0
Walworth	15	38	1,195	4	5	102
Washburn	5	9	201	1	1	17
Washington	10	28	1,130	5	24	680
Waukesha	27	132	5,595	14	44	1,451
Waupaca	9	25	756	3	3	54
Waushara	11	16	253	1	1	16
Winnebago	10	29	1,178	6	17	403
Wood	11	29	947	5	9	404
TOTAL*	280	1,796	$79,403	42	458	$16,708

*Total number of institutions is an unduplicated total for institutions operating in more than one county. Deposit figures do not add to state totals due to rounding.

Note: Menominee County did not report separately.

Source: Federal Deposit Insurance Corporation, "Deposits of all FDIC-Insured Institutions Operating in Wisconsin: State Totals by County, as of June 30, 2004" at: http://www2.fdic.gov/sod/index.asp [November 22, 2004].

HIGHLIGHTS OF CONSERVATION AND RECREATION IN WISCONSIN

Recreation — Wisconsin's recreational assets include more than 14,000 lakes, 2,000 miles of trout streams, almost 6,000 state-owned campsites, and 6 million acres of hunting land. Wisconsin currently operates 44 state parks, 12 state forests, and 5 recreation areas. The parks range in size from Devil's Lake with 9,117 acres to Copper Culture with 42 acres. The largest single state recreational facility is the Northern Highland-American Legion Forest with 223,283 acres. A total of 25 state trails are open to the public, covering more than 750 miles.

Visitors to Wisconsin's state parks, forests, trails, and recreation areas numbered nearly 16.1 million in 2004.

Hunting and fishing are major recreational activities. Recently, approximately 22 million fish and 1 million game animals of various species have been taken annually. Over 657,000 resident annual fishing licenses were sold in 2003. In addition, resident husband and wife fishing licenses totaled over 215,000, and nonresident annual and family annual fishing licenses totaled approximately 171,000. Nearly 611,000 boats were registered in 2003, and 184,806 annual and 168,915 daily vehicle admission stickers were sold at the parks that year.

Land Acquisition — Three land acquisition programs have been established to acquire land for recreational purposes. From 1961 through 1992, the Outdoor Recreation Act Program (ORAP) acquired 555,816 acres for the state's conservation and recreation programs at a cost of almost $172 million. From 1989, when the legislature created the current Warren Knowles-Gaylord Nelson Stewardship Program, through 1999-2000, the stewardship fund has spent over $144 million to acquire an additional 172,000 acres. From 2000-01 through 2003-04, the Stewardship 2000 Fund acquired over 58,000 acres and spent over $102 million.

Natural Resources Funding and Expenditures — The Department of Natural Resources spent almost $434 million on conservation and recreation programs in fiscal year 2003-04, down from $517 million in fiscal year 2002-03. Funding comes from the state's general fund and segregated funds, including registration and licensing fees, park stickers, and federal aids.

The following tables present selected data. Consult footnoted sources for more detailed information about conservation and recreation.

FISH AND GAME HARVESTED AND STOCKED

Catch and Harvest Data for Wisconsin Fish, 2003-2004[1]

	Catch	Harvest		Catch	Harvest
Panfish (bluegill, perch, crappie, sunfishes)	52,308,375	20,782,536	Walleye	1,139,240	244,445
Bass (largemouth and smallmouth)	2,062,107	63,734	Muskellunge	84,959	2,736
Northern Pike	1,016,862	178,549	Great Lakes trout	---	96,209
			Great Lakes salmon	---	367,619

Harvest Indicators, 2003-2004

Wild turkey	55,524	Raccoon (2003)	341,435
Pheasant[2]	216,039	Red fox (2003)	15,510
Ruffed grouse[2]	320,130	Gray fox (2003)	42,573
Gray partridge[2]	1,161	Coyotes (2003)	54,885
Bobwhite quail[2]	1,169	Deer (with guns)	388,344
Woodcock[2]	51,242	Deer (with bows)	95,607
Squirrels[2]	578,395	Bear	2,905
Cottontail rabbit[2]	271,923	Ducks[3]	677,400
Snowshoe hare[2]	34,370	Canada geese	73,838

Furbearer Harvest, 2003

Muskrats	313,627	Bobcat	371
Mink	25,972	Opossum	38,878
Beaver	62,126	Skunk	8,943
River otter	1,588	Fisher	1,126

Total value of all pelts purchased by licensed Wisconsin fur buyers $2,224,078

Fish and Wildlife Stocked

Wild pheasants (Iowa strain) released at 3 sites (2003)	823
Game farm pheasants released (2003)	34,956
Warmwater fish, produced and distributed (annual average)	3,321,503
Warmwater fish fry, produced and distributed (annual average)	20,456,890
Coldwater fish (annual average)	6,211,547

[1]Harvest is the actual number of fish caught and kept; catch is the estimate of all fish caught, including those released.
[2]Estimates based on hunter surveys.
[3]Harvest data from U.S. Fish and Wildlife Service, Division of Migratory Bird Management.

Source: Wisconsin Department of Natural Resources, departmental data, March 2005.

FISH AND GAME LICENSES AND RECREATION PERMITS
Number Issued, 1998 – 2003

	1998	1999	2000	2001	2002	2003
Boats registered	559,321	564,312	573,919	575,920	619,124	610,800
Snowmobiles registered	205,772	214,611	223,665	214,331	209,128	220,652
All terrain vehicles registered	89,580	97,420	113,622	160,511	176,146	200,515
Annual park admission stickers for motor vehicles	176,951	174,371	175,893	175,354	185,371	184,806
Daily park admission for motor vehicles	271,147	294,617	335,060	321,974	168,076	168,915
Deer hunting and license tags including nonresident	522,522	528,760	525,023	521,135	462,022	491,403
Small game hunting license tags including nonresident	150,990	152,777	142,369	135,733	132,000	139,109
Resident annual fishing licenses	518,583	511,912	616,802	626,712	637,288	657,997
Resident husband and wife fishing licenses	117,782	104,494	110,636	109,720	211,835	215,260
Resident senior/junior fishing licenses	75,275	88,885	NA	NA	NA	NA
Nonresident annual fishing licenses	99,525	101,755	105,078	104,549	106,324	107,617
Nonresident family annual fishing licenses	31,224	31,017	31,300	30,634	63,726	63,286
15-day nonresident family fishing licenses	19,645	20,808	19,689	19,502	33,049	32,158
15-day nonresident fishing licenses	34,977	32,179	32,934	33,093	42,061	40,245
4-day nonresident fishing licenses	129,230	120,884	119,232	118,807	118,551	118,419
Resident sports licenses	91,135	94,062	92,014	86,130	75,123	72,541
Nonresident sports licenses	14	131	232	279	277	313
2-day Great Lakes fishing licenses	41,223	27,585	24,380	38,554	31,021	31,667
Resident archer's licenses	179,760	177,661	171,978	169,821	138,011	158,650
Nonresident archer's licenses	6,666	7,573	8,581	8,460	6,691	7,449
Guide licenses (resident only)	1,515	858	1,333	1,434	1,511	1,492
Conservation patron licenses	53,874	67,167	77,415	81,315	81,896	81,074
Nonresident patron licenses	1	21	28	25	38	38

NA – Not available. Included in annual fishing license total.
Source: Wisconsin Department of Natural Resources, departmental data, April 2005.

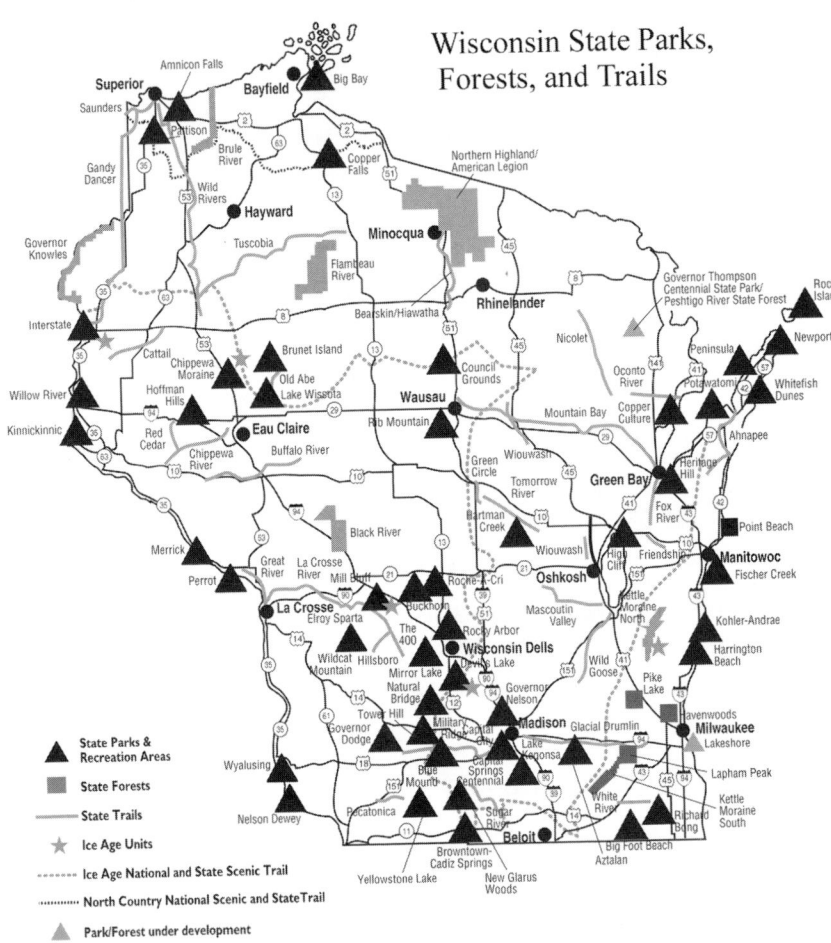

Wisconsin State Parks, Forests, and Trails

Legend:
- ▲ State Parks & Recreation Areas
- ■ State Forests
- —— State Trails
- ★ Ice Age Units
- -------- Ice Age National and State Scenic Trail
- ·········· North Country National Scenic and State Trail
- ▲ Park/Forest under development

Source: Wisconsin Department of Natural Resources, March 2005.

WISCONSIN STATE FORESTS, PARKS, TRAILS, AND RECREATION AREAS

Name	Location	Dominant Features	Established	Acres	Number of visitors[1]				
					1990	1995	2000	2003	2004
NORTHERN FORESTS									
Black River	SE of Black River Falls US 12, STH 27 & 54	Abundance of wildlife and scenery	1957	67,070	238,311	195,579	97,576	64,226	56,620
Brule River	S of Brule, STH 27	Excellent fishing and canoeing	1907	40,882	141,113	125,339	174,351	107,719	102,810
Flambeau River	23 mi. W of Phillips CTH W	Outstanding canoeing river	1931	90,147	154,685	162,665	177,241	126,926	126,926
Governor Knowles	1 mi. W of Grantsburg STH 70	River scenery	1970	19,753	73,755	89,714	121,092	101,830	112,135
Northern Highland-American Legion	SE Iron, WC Vilas, NC Oneida Counties	Scenic lakes and forests	1925	223,283	1,796,734	2,050,151	2,024,498	1,920,027	1,920,027
Peshtigo River	5 mi. W of Crivitz, N of CTH W	Diverse natural communities, rivers	2001	9,200	NA	NA	NA	NA	NA
TOTAL				450,335	2,404,598	2,623,448	2,594,758	2,320,728	2,318,518
SOUTHERN FORESTS									
Havenwoods	Milwaukee, N. Hopkins St.	A nature preserve in the city	1978	237	55,961	60,461	49,581	50,222	38,376
Kettle Moraine North	N of Kewaskum, STH 45, 23 & 67	Glacial formations	1936	29,268	613,657	921,634	620,903	723,654	678,389
Kettle Moraine South	Whitewater US 12, STH 59/67	Glacial topography	1936	22,300	1,270,800	1,225,384	1,230,519	1,106,117	2,508,233
Lapham Peak	S of Delafield, CTH C	Highest point in co., glacial formations	1985	1,006	NA	200,033	232,911	181,102	179,609
Loew Lake	10 mi. W of Menomonee Falls CTH Q	Kettle lake, glacial valley	1987	1,086	NA	NA	NA	NA	NA
Pike Lake	2 mi. E of Hartford STH 60	Glacial lake	1960	678	187,804	154,890	156,325	189,585	143,123
Point Beach	4 mi. N of Two Rivers STH 42	Sand beach, natural history	1938	2,903	242,615	360,119	366,500		386,300
TOTAL				57,478	2,370,837	2,922,521	2,697,305	2,617,180	3,934,030
STATE PARKS									
Amnicon Falls	10 mi. SE of Superior US 2	Scenic waterfalls, covered bridge	1961	825	47,495	74,389	84,773	86,927	87,916
Aztalan	4 mi. E of Lake Mills CTH Q	Ancient Native American village	1947	172	15,935	49,150	60,565	58,534	65,940
Big Bay	On Madeline Island in Lake Superior	Sand beach, natural history	1963	2,418	72,053	125,772	108,365	137,798	128,436
Big Foot Beach	1 mi. S of Lake Geneva STH 12 & 120	A beach park	1949	271	172,679	161,457	177,963	218,254	NA
Blue Mound	1 mi. NW of Blue Mounds STH 18 & 151	Highest point in southern Wisconsin	1959	1,153	163,283	157,349	154,128	130,025	137,160
Brunet Island	1 mi. NW of Cornell	River island park	1936	1,225	216,619	244,720	178,962	174,313	152,846
Buckhorn	13 mi. N of Mauston STH 58, CTH G	River scenery	1971	6,990	58,517	84,549	107,590	115,123	94,682
Copper Culture[2]	W of Oconto STH 22	Archaeological site	1959	42	NA	NA	NA	NA	NA
Copper Falls	4 mi. N of Mellen STH 13 & 169	River gorge, waterfalls	1929	2,676	120,038	140,773	125,080	113,475	146,161
Council Grounds	1 mi. NW of Merrill STH 107	River scenery	1938	509	207,720	205,806	213,411	212,858	218,412
Devil's Lake	3 mi. S of Baraboo STH 123	Bluffs, mountain scenery	1911	9,117	1,118,901	1,117,887	1,317,275	1,159,408	1,159,099
Gov. Dodge	3 mi. N of Dodgeville STH 23	Rocky promontories	1948	5,270	336,889	417,934	407,629	456,636	444,879
Gov. Nelson	5 mi. E of Middleton CTH M	Wooded lakeshore, Indian effigy mounds	1975	422	146,451	183,830	218,017	236,817	153,791
Gov. Thompson Centennial	15 mi. NW of Crivitz near Ranch and Parkway Rds	Caldron Falls Reservoir	2000	2,187			NA	NA	NA
Harrington Beach	10 mi. N of Port Washington I 43, CTH D	Lake Michigan shoreline	1966	637	95,094	115,064	114,912	94,773	NA
Hartman Creek	6 mi. NW of Waupaca STH 54	Lake scenery, pine plantation	1962	1,417	222,928	224,388	239,539	179,781	175,715
Heritage Hill	S Green Bay STH 57	Restored early American buildings	1973	48	55,813	36,546	NA	NA	NA
High Cliff	9 mi. E of Menasha STH 114	Wooded bluffs, Lake Winnebago	1954	1,147	602,217	687,235	820,560	819,900	833,500
Interstate	St. Croix Falls US 8	River gorge, rocky bluffs, glacial features	1900	1,330	230,215	320,649	354,715	280,242	264,811
Kinnickinnic	6 mi. W of River Falls CTH F	River scenery	1972	1,239	101,265	211,800	207,900	239,500	174,700
Kohler-Andrae	4 mi. S of Sheboygan STH 141	Lake Michigan sand dunes	1928	988	298,858	330,471	378,483	413,467	387,398
Lake Kegonsa	3 mi. N of Stoughton CTH N	Prairie and lakeshore	1962	343	262,141	180,218	187,782	196,244	145,995
Lake Wissota	5 mi. NE of Chippewa Falls STH 29 CTH K & O	Lake scenery	1962	1,062	122,246	118,707	108,222	107,262	99,914

WISCONSIN STATE FORESTS, PARKS, TRAILS, AND RECREATION AREAS–Continued

Name	Location	Dominant Features	Established	Acres	Number of visitors[1]				
					1990	1995	2000	2003	2004
Merrick	1mi. N of Fountain City STH 35	Mississippi River, birds	1932	320	93,212	81,024	101,609	124,150	101,044
Mill Bluff	4 mi. W of Camp Douglas US 12 & 16	Rocky bluffs	1936	1,258	22,259	30,350	49,541	53,300	53,200
Mirror Lake	1 mi. S of Lake Delton	Lake scenery	1962	2,179	231,167	260,113	341,452	320,851	305,293
Natural Bridge	15 mi. NW of Sauk City CTH C	Natural rock bridge	1973	530	15,373	27,314	57,454	40,983	32,339
Nelson Dewey	1 mi. N of Cassville CTH VV	Home of first governor, river bluffs	1935	756	66,177	43,722	102,581	140,934	140,495
New Glarus Woods	1 mi. S of New Glarus STH 69 & CTH NN	Wooded valleys, natural oak woods	1934	411	8,698	27,711	48,276	54,659	55,581
Newport	2 mi. SE of Gill's Rock STH 42	Lake scenery, forests	1964	2,373	142,217	204,466	177,194	142,333	139,387
Pattison	10 mi. S of Superior STH 35	Highest waterfall in Wisconsin	1920	1,476	137,066	140,583	167,221	181,362	177,027
Peninsula	N of Fish Creek STH 42	Green Bay, limestone bluffs	1910	3,776	839,437	944,655	1,105,651	1,110,280	1,064,166
Perrot	1 mi. N of Trempealeau STH 35	River scenery, wooded bluffs	1918	1,270	328,243	309,449	208,537	266,862	248,083
Potawatomi	2 mi. NW of Sturgeon Bay STH 42	Limestone bluffs	1928	1,225	192,928	233,139	228,909	210,055	206,059
Rib Mountain	4 mi. SW of Wausau CTH N	State's third highest location, views	1927	1,172	157,602	214,205	208,670	265,063	226,632
Roche-A-Cri	2 mi. N of Friendship STH 13	Woodlands, 300-ft.-high rock outcropping	1948	604	38,668	93,569	72,232	77,169	60,863
Rock Island[3]	Ferry (no vehicles) from Washington Island	Island scenery, historic stone buildings	1965	912	12,946	16,201	16,998	16,521	16,178
Rocky Arbor	1 mi. NW of Wisconsin Dells US 12	Rocky ledges, wooded valleys	1932	225	55,528	61,492	57,545	84,269	44,047
Tower Hill	3 mi. S of Spring Green STH 23 & CTH C	Historic shot tower, panoramic views	1922	77	49,114	61,117	51,031	38,058	33,082
Whitefish Dunes	10 mi. NE of Sturgeon Bay STH 57	Lake Michigan, sand dunes	1967	863	157,532	264,523	189,778	164,013	156,283
Wildcat Mountain	3 mi. S of Ontario STH 33	Bluff lands, Kickapoo River	1948	3,643	130,800	150,200	173,100	163,106	187,150
Willow River	NE of Hudson CTH A	River scenery, waterfalls, lake	1967	2,891	293,559	231,118	354,470	304,146	310,977
Wyalusing	12 mi. S of Prairie du Chien US 18 & CTH C&X	Jct. of Wisconsin and Mississippi Rivers	1917	2,628	185,102	184,116	173,439	190,324	202,031
Yellowstone Lake	7 mi. NW of Argyle CTH N	Lake scenery, wooded valleys	1970	968	255,614	228,551	270,981	268,439	272,125
TOTAL				71,045	8,080,599	8,964,766	9,749,086	9,648,214	8,903,397

STATE TRAILS[3]

Name	Location	Dominant Features	Established	Acres	1990	1995	2000	2003	2004
"400"	Reedsburg STH 23/33 to Elroy STH 80/82	23 miles of trail, bluffs	1988	413	NA	24,494	35,125	37,585	40,605
Ahnapee[2]	Sturgeon Bay STH42/57 to E of Luxemburg CTH A	18.6 miles of trail, river scenery	1970	353	3,896	NA	NA	NA	NA
Bearskin-Hiawatha	Minocqua to CH K & Heafford Jct. to Tomahawk	24.6 miles of trail, forests	1973	516	30,840	39,835	6,950	100,200	123,250
Buffalo River	Fairchild to Mondovi, US 10	36.4 miles of trail, rural scenery	1976	424	31,580	28,960	39,280	NA	38,307
Chippewa River	Eau Claire SW to Red Cedar Trail, STH 85	20 miles of trail, river scenery	1990	273	NA	NA	334,607	113,280	120,570
Elroy-Sparta	Elroy STH 80/82 to Sparta STH 71	32.5 miles of trail, hills, valleys, tunnels	1965	639	46,500	59,250	60,075	56,490	57,450
Gandy Dancer[2]	St. Croix Falls US 8 to S of Superior CTH C	66 miles of trail, forests, connects to MN	1989	809	39,626	109,239	157,569	205,406	NA
Glacial Drumlin[2]	Waukesha CTH X to Cottage Grove CTH N	49 miles of trail, Ice Age features, views	1984	651	40,000	23,200	65,572	64,778	200,581
Great River[2]	Onalaska US53 to NW Trempealeau STH35/54	24 miles of trail, river and bluffs	1986	256	NA	NA	NA	NA	58,965
Green Circle[2]	Circles Stevens Point area	Rivery scenery	1986	66	66	NA	NA	NA	NA
Hillsboro[2]	Union Center to Hillsboro, STH 33/80/82	4.3 miles of trail, rural scenery	1992	NA	NA	NA	NA	NA	NA
Ice Age[4]	Sturgeon Bay to St. Croix Falls	Moraines and other glacial features	1988	360	20,000	27,750	37,150	39,985	NA
La Crosse River	Sparta STH 16 to NE of La Crosse	24.5 miles of trail, broad river valley	1988	515	41,447	60,073	67,224	108,484	42,685
Military Ridge	Verona US 18/151 to Dodgeville STH 23	39.9 miles of trail, most on crest of ridge	1978	1,062	NA	NA	NA	NA	60,468
Mountain-Bay[2]	Wausau CTH SS to Green Bay CTH HS	80.5 miles of trail, varied landscape	1981	255	NA	NA	NA	NA	NA
Old Abe	NE of Chippewa Falls CTH S – Cornell STH27/64	17 miles of trail, Chippewa River	1993	212	NA	NA	NA	NA	NA
Pecatonica[2]	Belmont E to Calamine, CTH G	10 miles of trail, stream	1990	427	24,545	38,490	47,760	48,990	NA
Red Cedar	Menomonie STH 29 S to Chippewa River Trail	14.5 miles of trail, river, and bluffs	1974	207	NA	NA	NA	NA	55,990
Saunders[2]	S of Superior CTH C SW to MN border	8.4 miles of trail, wet woods	1991	265	NA	NA	NA	NA	NA
Sugar River	New Glarus STH 39/69 to Brodhead STH 11	23.5 miles of trail, farms, prairies, woods	1972	265	36,050	42,275	45,362	47,708	67,451

WISCONSIN STATE FORESTS, PARKS, TRAILS, AND RECREATION AREAS–Continued

Name	Location	Dominant Features	Established	Acres	Number of visitors[1]				
					1990	1995	2000	2003	2004
Tomorrow River[2]	Plover to Portage-Waupaca County line	15 miles of trail, glacial terrain	1996	211	NA	NA	NA	NA	NA
Tuscobia[2]	Park Falls CTH B to Rice Lake CTH SS	74 miles of trail, forests	1966	836	19,150	45,250	44,150	44,100	NA
Wild Goose[2]	Fond du Lac US 41/151 to STH 60 S of Juneau	32 miles of trail, Horicon Marsh	1986	411	NA	NA	NA	NA	NA
Wild Rivers[2]	Solon Springs CTH A to Rice Lake	63.5 miles of trail, woods	1993	789	---	NA	NA	NA	NA
Wiouwash[2]	Oshkosh-Hortonville, Split Rock-Aniwa	51.6 miles of trail, prairies, and woods	1992	228	---	NA	NA	NA	NA
TOTAL				10,178	292,187	670,715	875,252	904,332	866,322
RECREATION AREAS									
Richard Bong	8 mi. SE of Burlington STH 142	Small lakes, open space, varied recreation	1963	4,515	278,264	544,090	462,274	432,187	NA
Browntown-Cadiz Springs	6 mi. W of Monroe STH 11	Spring-fed lakes	1970	644	51,637	97,379	99,191	117,002	59,928
Chippewa Moraine	6 mi. E of New Auburn CTH M	Kettle lakes, other glacial features	1974	3,063	NA	12,125	17,737	23,949	27,035
Fischer Creek[2]	12 mi. N of Two Rivers STH 42	Lake Michigan shoreline	1991	124	NA	NA	NA	NA	NA
Hoffman Hills	8 mi. NE of Menomonie CTH B or E	Wooded hills	1980	707	18,275	23,330	32,460	30,620	34,150
TOTAL				9,053	348,176	676,924	611,662	603,758	121,113

Abbreviations: US – U.S. highway; STH – state trunk highway; CTH – county trunk highway; NA – not available.
[1]State forest and park estimates derived by multiplying the number of cars by 3.5 (average number of persons per car).
[2]Operated locally or by county; no attendance information available.
[3]Not accessible by vehicle.
[4]Various owners and operators (National Scenic Trail).
Source: Wisconsin Department of Natural Resources, Bureau of Parks and Recreation, departmental data, April 2005.

DEPARTMENT OF NATURAL RESOURCES SOURCES OF FUNDING
Fiscal Years 1999-2000 – 2003-04 (In Thousands)

Source of Funding	1999-2000	2000-01	2001-02	2002-03	2003-04
Segregated funds					
All-terrain vehicle registration fees	$816	$1,031	$1,676	$1,721	$1,739
Boat registration fees	4,599	4,988	5,596	5,287	5,114
Dry cleaner fund	105	1,226	755	1,414	707
Endangered resources voluntary payments	1,269	1,365	1,474	1,633	1,896
Environmental improvement fund	1,241	1,690	1,796	1,915	1,951
Environmental management account	13,935	14,698	15,972	16,532	13,920
Federal aids	27,236	33,815	30,545	37,784	34,058
Fishing, hunting licenses and permits	54,624	59,454	64,281	70,051	59,730
Forestry mill tax	59,969	64,278	70,135	76,076	79,182
Gifts and donations	105	93	115	68	126
Great Lakes trout stamp	1,490	1,559	1,270	1,211	1,142
Heritage State Parks and Forests Trust Fund	114	0	61	34	32
Motorcycle account	97	81	118	82	98
Nonpoint source account	5,733	3,709	4,039	3,885	4,108
Park stickers and fees	10,864	12,083	11,962	11,430	10,748
Petroleum storage environmental cleanup fund . . .	4,225	4,175	4,507	4,341	4,310
Pheasant restoration fund	350	369	381	398	334
Program revenue	20,466	20,054	24,366	20,337	17,750
Recycling fund	32,531	32,885	21,462	33,545	28,229
Snowmobile registration fees	3,281	3,342	4,173	3,421	3,295
Trout stamp	1,131	1,465	1,304	1,370	1,348
Waste management fund	58	0	110	5	14
Water resources account	12,548	10,365	11,028	12,676	11,685
Waterfowl stamp	368	278	340	361	350
Wild turkey restoration fund	316	439	532	513	703
Wisconsin Natural Resources Magazine	1,456	1,048	981	866	848
TOTAL	$258,928	$274,490	$278,979	$306,956	$283,417
General funds					
General purpose revenue	$169,765	$168,768	$122,758	$149,529	$91,894
Program revenues	18,473	20,050	19,691	21,106	21,012
Program revenue – services	10,629	11,064	13,142	13,407	11,013
Federal aids	22,160	23,624	27,189	25,942	26,309
TOTAL	$221,027	$223,506	$182,780	$209,984	$150,228
GRAND TOTAL	$479,995	$497,996	$461,759	$516,940	$433,645

Source: Wisconsin Department of Natural Resources, departmental data, March 2005.

DEPARTMENT OF NATURAL RESOURCES EXPENDITURES
Fiscal Years 1999-2000 – 2003-04
(In Thousands)

Program	1999-2000	2000-01	2001-02	2002-03	2003-04
Land Management	**$76,349***	**$84,186***	**$88,988***	**$90,947***	**$91,975***
Wildlife management	14,096	15,063	15,217	16,272	15,358
Forestry	30,758	34,749	38,070	42,117	44,393
Southern Forests	3,947	4,507	4,486	4,617	4,831
Parks	13,862	15,191	15,810	15,951	15,598
Endangered resources	2,542	2,763	2,879	3,028	3,290
Facilities and lands	6,755	7,152	7,844	8,035	8,038
Lands program management	4,390	4,761	4,682	928	466
Air and Waste Management	**$36,791***	**$37,971***	**$36,868***	**$37,981***	**$36,134***
Air management	13,586	14,742	15,587	15,947	15,632
Remediation and redevelopment	15,325	14,769	12,450	12,786	11,618
Waste management	7,186	7,756	8,014	8,407	7,885
Air/waste program management	694	704	817	842	998
Enforcement and Science	**$33,205**	**$37,339***	**$36,630***	**$36,425***	**$34,706***
Law enforcement	---	25,833	24,662	24,968	23,490
Integrated science services	---	10,832	11,279	10,877	10,550
Enforcement/science program management	---	674	689	579	666
Water Management	**$59,580***	**$64,083***	**$65,346***	**$63,428***	**$62,381***
Fisheries management and habitat protection	24,585	26,554	27,337	27,856	27,102
Watershed management	20,128	21,430	22,315	21,635	22,594
Drinking and groundwater	9,250	10,196	11,167	10,180	9,071
Water integration team	691	638	453	265	---
Mississippi/Lower St. Croix team	1,134	1,143	---	---	---
Water program management	3,790	4,122	4,074	3,492	3,614
Conservation Aids	**$34,921***	**$30,358***	**$36,289***	**$41,653***	**$33,751***
Fish and wildlife aids	763	1,189	1,233	760	856
Forestry aids	10,457	8,813	10,512	9,802	8,407
Recreational aids	16,257	11,634	13,558	14,633	11,930
Aids in lieu of taxes	3,618	4,438	6,217	6,583	6,126
Enforcement aids	1,383	1,350	1,866	1,723	1,722
Wildlife damage aids	2,442	2,934	2,903	8,153	4,709
Environmental Aids	**$45,110***	**$41,597***	**$29,452***	**$42,966***	**$35,980***
Water quality aids	10,521	7,128	5,146	3,946	3,408
Solid and hazard waste aids	32,374	33,748	22,132	35,020	28,410
Environmental aids	1,763	282	225	74	603
Environmental planning aids	452	439	529	380	381
Nonpoint aids	---	---	1,420	3,547	3,179
Debt Service	**$116,944***	**$117,413***	**$82,412***	**$114,518***	**$62,169***
Resource	21,894	24,595	24,975	27,927	19,038
Environmental	1,499	1,873	1,722	2,093	1,601
Water quality	91,810	89,052	53,802	82,401	39,731
Administrative facility	1,741	1,893	1,913	2,097	1,799
Acquisition and Development	**$7,017***	**$10,071***	**$8,870***	**$14,983***	**$10,205***
Wildlife	439	638	1,176	1,180	575
Fish	922	1,305	1,384	1,765	1,233
Forestry	487	1,681	1,090	5,572	1,044
Southern Forests	173	374	711	863	474
Parks	1,141	3,709	2,070	2,744	3,389
Endangered resources	-260	1,512	508	1,123	1,422
Facilities and lands	3,812	530	1,615	1,511	2,051
CAER (Customer Assistance and External Relations)	277	292	315	173	18
Law enforcement	---	15	1	52	---
Mississippi/Lower St. Croix	26	15	---	---	---
Administration and Technology	**$47,777***	**$52,487***	**$53,947***	**$50,731***	**$42,730***
Administration	1,396	1,564	1,555	1,207	1,144
Administrative and field services	6,887	7,428	6,754	6,760	5,816
Enterprise and technology	12,550	13,325	13,144	13,980	9,752
Finance	6,416	7,216	6,752	6,627	6,337
Personnel and human services	2,329	2,484	2,397	2,436	2,413
Legal services	2,520	2,737	2,525	2,588	2,553
Management and budget	691	845	806	881	841
Facility rental	5,550	6,194	6,815	6,938	5,774
Non-budget accounts	9,438	10,694	13,199	9,313	8,101
Customer Assistance and External Relations (CAER)	**$22,261***	**$22,491***	**$22,957***	**$23,308***	**$23,611***
Communication and education strategy	3,768	3,854	3,807	3,855	3,672
Community financial assistance	4,002	4,450	4,448	4,802	5,782
Cooperative environmental assistance	1,377	1,066	1,097	1,192	1,240
Customer service and licensing	11,331	11,225	11,841	11,855	11,103
CAER program management	1,783	1,886	1,764	1,604	1,815
TOTAL	**$479,955**	**$497,996**	**$461,759**	**$516,940**	**$433,643**

*Total of detail immediately following. Totals do not add due to rounding.

Source: Wisconsin Department of Natural Resources, departmental data, March 2005.

NATURAL RESOURCES LAND ACQUISITIONS
Fiscal Years 1984-1985 – 2003-04

Fiscal Year	Fisheries Mgmnt.	Northern Forests	Parks	Natural Areas	Southern Forests	Wildlife Mgmnt.	Rivers and Resource Areas	Others	Total
			ACRES ACQUIRED						
		OUTDOOR RECREATION ACT PROGRAM (ORAP)					456	—	14,876
1984-85	3,237	4,275	857	321	614	5,116	456	—	14,876
1985-86	2,692	3,030	1,050	505	290	4,717	104	297	12,685
1986-87	2,195	874	713	1,968	523	2,940	184	1	9,399
1987-88	1,328	918	439	1,543	727	1,932	37	69	6,993
1988-89	1,734	979	7,675	796	61	8,556	967	80	20,848
1989-90	2,137	972	724	901	283	4,269	2,501	—	11,787
1990-91	278	245	4,038	2,926	272	773	560	—	9,091
1991-92	51	—	—	280	—	—	39	—	370
TOTAL*	70,456	105,829	67,617	17,971	24,132	235,697	29,539	4,575	555,816
		WARREN KNOWLES-GAYLORD NELSON STEWARDSHIP FUND							
1990-91	999	684	1,407	1,569	1,295	5,257	7,262	52	18,524
1991-92	1,563	791	373	2,095	156	3,912	15,195	164	24,250
1992-93	1,240	721	624	2,502	298	4,635	4,307	189	14,517
1993-94	2,440	355	1,754	1,477	306	2,752	2,965	434	12,483
1994-95	7,891	371	284	1,901	370	4,288	762	377	16,246
1995-96	2,070	915	1,206	5,150	395	2,980	1,675	375	14,766
1996-97	1,230	213	880	140	160	2,180	2,025	125	6,953
1997-98	925	275	108	1,080	80	3,740	9,770	245	16,223
1998-99	495	815	636	1,872	512	1,897	533	40	6,800
1999-2000	2,409	495	3,088	3,320	108	14,682	17,396	21	41,519
TOTAL	21,262	5,635	10,360	21,106	3,680	46,323	61,890	2,022	172,281
		STEWARDSHIP 2000 FUND							
2000-01	2,210	149	4,300	923	164	4,826	2,468	11	15,051
2001-02	1,196	5,918	1,344	1,609	208	4,553	525	703	15,673
2002-03	1,545	208	1,960	1,256	0	3,347	2,133	7	10,456
2003-04	1,031	3,607	2,126	1,280	151	6,941	1,809	12	16,957
TOTAL	5,982	9,882	9,730	5,068	523	19,667	6,935	733	58,137
			COST TO ACQUIRE (in thousands)						
		OUTDOOR RECREATION ACT PROGRAM (ORAP)					$470	—	$9,968
1984-85	$2,032	$1,766	$1,076	$187	$1,548	$2,888	$470	—	$9,968
1985-86	1,788	1,878	1,680	291	924	2,790	132	$16	9,500
1986-87	1,472	645	830	1,215	580	1,526	253	3	6,524
1987-88	917	489	689	642	1,412	666	34	—	4,849
1988-89	1,005	405	7,901	554	87	1,485	388	123	11,947
1989-90	1,810	405	735	610	490	1,880	2,208	—	8,138
1990-91	112	97	1,890	656	222	338	317	—	3,632
1991-92	17	—	1	336	—	—	24	—	377
TOTAL*	$28,894	$24,833	$42,839	$8,268	$14,233	$42,619	$9,093	$401	$171,180
		WARREN KNOWLES-GAYLORD NELSON STEWARDSHIP FUND							
1990-91	$1,157	$288	$369	$1,477	$1,453	$2,688	$3,982	$1,550	$12,964
1991-92	1,301	416	467	845	398	2,829	5,569	—	11,825
1992-93	1,066	547	566	1,473	249	1,616	1,972	5	7,494
1993-94	1,847	178	898	725	793	2,035	1,718	—	8,194
1994-95	3,328	640	764	3,422	1,315	3,655	1,138	1	14,263
1995-96	2,337	542	2,758	3,100	1,035	2,594	1,290	42	13,698
1996-97	1,490	377	1,160	588	617	1,994	1,439	14	7,679
1997-98	1,127	136	362	2,067	293	4,136	11,021	1,162	20,304
1998-99	1,175	942	1,548	1,005	1,170	3,154	468	3,400	12,862
1999-2000	2,176	549	2,578	3,465	402	12,453	13,712	—	35,335
TOTAL	$17,004	$4,615	$11,470	$18,167	$7,725	$37,154	$42,309	$6,174	$144,618
		STEWARDSHIP 2000 FUND							
2000-01	$4,429	$533	$8,605	$1,946	$727	$4,091	$546	$355	$21,232
2001-02	3,692	13,594	3,035	2,976	1,105	5,101	931	3,618	32,141
2002-03	3,627	436	4,171	3,383	0	3,528	3,683	40	18,868
2003-04	2,745	6,975	4,880	2,578	567	7,951	4,418	0	30,012
TOTAL	$14,493	$21,538	$20,691	$10,781	$2,399	$20,671	$9,578	$4,013	$102,253

Note: In addition, easements for 99,975 acres have been acquired since 1961 at a cost of $26,284,534. Easements on 41,044 acres were acquired in 2002-03 at a cost of $8,486,714. Easements on 2,526 acres were acquired in 2003-04 at a cost of $3,095,281.

*Total reflects all transactions since 1961. Data represented is historical acquisition data. Acres and dollars may have changed in later years due to sales, exchanges, and redesignating properties to different acquisition functions.

Source: Wisconsin Department of Natural Resources, Bureau of Facilities and Lands, departmental data, March 2005.

CONSERVATION AND RECREATION LAND IN WISCONSIN
Acres By Ownership, June 30, 2004

County[1]	Wisconsin Department of Natural Resources					County Parks and Forests[3]	Total
	Federal Government[2]	Forests and Wild Rivers	Natural and Park Areas	Fisheries and Wildlife	Total DNR		
Adams	344	--	5,089	8,741	13,830	813	14,987
Ashland	216,763	756	5,107	6,784	12,647	43,041	272,451
Barron	--	60	338	6,200	6,598	16,468	23,066
Bayfield	278,059	49	9,774	10,347	20,170	169,353	467,582
Brown	--	--	609	2,396	3,005	5,807	8,812
Buffalo	9,374	--	814	12,649	13,463	535	23,372
Burnett	--	15,157	229	54,420	69,806	108,918	178,724
Calumet	--	--	1,199	10,592	11,791	1,131	12,922
Chippewa	--	--	6,574	3,651	10,225	33,416	43,641
Clark	--	224	--	266	490	133,660	134,150
Columbia	2,846	19	548	20,371	20,938	815	24,599
Crawford	15,269	6,074	2,341	4,064	12,480	579	28,328
Dane	1,442	4,147	2,543	14,270	20,960	3,205	25,607
Dodge	20,918	--	216	23,331	23,548	1,131	45,597
Door	29	--	9,980	3,526	13,505	1,281	14,815
Douglas	--	40,953	3,850	7,598	52,401	270,813	323,214
Dunn	1,022	--	2,169	11,495	13,663	1,183	15,868
Eau Claire	--	--	140	2,468	2,608	54,714	57,322
Florence	85,028	5,630	4,980	42	10,653	39,973	135,654
Fond du Lac	1,706	10,696	507	13,500	24,703	1,691	28,100
Forest	344,008	25	454	3,532	4,011	30,877	378,896
Grant	6,469	13,629	3,638	534	17,801	1,070	25,340
Green	--	--	1,457	3,696	5,154	487	5,641
Green Lake	--	--	343	17,949	18,292	747	19,039
Iowa	--	8,661	6,694	4,150	19,505	381	19,886
Iron	--	61,569	2,186	11,660	75,414	182,015	257,429
Jackson	1,697	67,565	518	7,509	75,592	122,868	200,157
Jefferson	250	3,553	511	14,136	18,200	661	19,111
Juneau	79,831	--	4,517	5,763	10,280	16,240	106,351
Kenosha	--	--	4,838	1,942	6,780	2,700	9,480
Kewaunee	--	--	396	2,428	2,823	273	3,096
La Crosse	12,192	2,972	368	3,805	7,145	3,096	22,433
Lafayette	--	--	1,530	4,048	5,577	278	5,855
Langlade	32,727	3	307	16,093	16,403	131,654	180,784
Lincoln	--	1,881	2,797	7,206	11,884	102,664	114,548
Manitowoc	120	2,903	334	6,255	9,492	1,052	10,664
Marathon	--	356	1,695	23,830	25,881	34,149	60,030
Marinette	--	11,951	4,372	10,053	26,376	238,730	265,106
Marquette	1,185	--	832	10,537	11,369	359	12,913
Milwaukee	--	237	--	--	237	16,359	16,596
Monroe	15,529	--	1,547	3,602	5,149	7,317	27,995
Oconto	141,498	472	817	5,178	6,466	44,974	192,938
Oneida	11,184	74,361	2,856	8,385	85,602	105,227	202,013
Outagamie	35	--	1,224	7,807	9,031	2,631	11,697
Ozaukee	536	--	2,294	237	2,531	1,243	4,310
Pepin	--	--	1,426	3,506	4,932	243	5,175
Pierce	--	--	1,626	1,433	3,059	1,223	4,282
Polk	1,085	4,984	2,090	13,198	20,272	21,799	43,156
Portage	--	--	1,044	28,412	29,456	3,349	32,805
Price	151,317	9,066	259	9,892	19,217	103,403	273,937
Racine	--	--	99	3,087	3,187	5,484	8,671
Richland	--	6,170	--	1,598	7,768	98	7,866
Rock	297	--	91	7,127	7,218	3,188	10,703
Rusk	--	15,202	--	3,273	18,475	91,382	109,857
St. Croix	302	--	2,955	6,758	9,713	8,688	18,703
Sauk	4,954	4,620	13,701	4,190	22,511	1,498	28,963
Sawyer	--	71,828	452	9,095	81,374	2,534	83,908
Shawano	126,686	--	1,024	13,857	14,881	117,927	259,494
Sheboygan	108	15,794	924	3,960	20,678	1,159	21,945
Taylor	123,952	--	249	8,014	8,263	18,534	150,749
Trempealeau	4,207	58	1,618	4,869	6,545	362	11,114
Vernon	6,863	52	3,957	1,573	5,583	1,538	13,984
Vilas	54,536	139,470	726	7,710	147,905	49,054	251,495
Walworth	--	6,835	1,269	5,866	13,970	766	14,736
Washburn	--	155	745	5,653	6,554	149,585	156,139
Washington	--	4,548	285	6,737	11,569	1,524	13,093
Waukesha	--	11,612	606	5,008	17,225	9,905	27,130
Waupaca	--	--	1,927	7,552	9,479	1,080	10,559
Waushara	232	--	622	17,411	18,034	1,990	20,256
Winnebago	2,118	--	5	9,198	9,203	1,784	13,105
Wood	2,312	173	14	14,955	15,142	59,949	77,403
STATE	1,759,030	624,469	141,246	600,976	1,366,691	2,594,625	5,720,346

[1] Land in Menominee County that is not privately owned is held by the Menominee Nation.

[2] Federal lands include national parks, national forests, and lands controlled by the U.S. Fish and Wildlife Service as of June 30, 2002.

[3] Includes lands designated as public areas and trust lands not listed separately as of June 30, 2002.

Source: Wisconsin Department of Natural Resources, departmental data, March 2005.

HIGHLIGHTS OF EDUCATION IN WISCONSIN

Universities and Colleges — A total of 173,058 students enrolled in the University of Wisconsin System for the 2004 fall semester. The system's 2003 summer school enrollment was 45,690, and the enrollments in UW-Extension's credit outreach enrolled 37,492 in 2003-04.

Wisconsin's private institutions of higher education encompass a broad range of schools, including 3 universities, 16 colleges, 4 technical and professional schools, and 5 theological seminaries. Over the past five years, enrollments in private institutions have grown from 52,195 in 1998-99 to approximately 55,999 in 2004-05.

Two Native American tribes in Wisconsin have established public community colleges supported solely by local funding. The Lac Courte Oreilles Ojibwa Community College was founded in 1982 by the tribal council at Hayward. For Fall 2002, it reported a total undergraduate enrollment of 550. The College of the Menominee Nation, which opened in 1993 at Keshena, operates through a cooperative program with the UW-Stevens Point and UW College-Marathon County. For Fall 2002, it reported a total undergraduate full- and part-time enrollment of 530.

Technical Colleges — Wisconsin's Technical College System had a total enrollment of 429,355 students in 2002-03. Enrollments for individual institutions that year ranged from 10,611 at Nicolet Technical College in Rhinelander to 56,862 at Milwaukee Area Technical College.

Elementary and Secondary Schools — Following a peak enrollment of 999,921 in 1971-72, public school registrations declined to a low of 767,542 in 1984-85. In the last five years enrollments have remained midway between those levels, with a total of 880,031 in 2003-04.

In the 2004-05 school year, 136,792 students, or 13.6% of Wisconsin's more than 1 million elementary and secondary pupils, were enrolled in private schools. Like their public counterparts, private schools experienced fairly level enrollments over the past five years.

Teachers — Of Wisconsin's 61,038 public school teachers employed in the 2003-04 school year, 42,182 taught in elementary grades and 18,856 were secondary teachers. In the 2003-04 school year, Wisconsin's average salary for all teachers was $43,382. Nationally, Wisconsin ranked 23rd for the 2002-03 school year. California had the highest average salary that year at an estimated $56,283. South Dakota's average salary was the lowest at $32,416.

Educational Alternatives — In the past 10 years, reported enrollment in Wisconsin home-based private education programs increased from 8,690 in 1992-93 to 21,034 in 2003-04. In September 2003, Wisconsin charter school enrollments totaled 21,368 students and 134 charter schools are currently operating in 46 counties.

Educational Expenditures — State and local expenditures for education in Wisconsin for 2003-04 totaled $12.9 billion, or $2,367 per capita, based on Wisconsin's estimated population. Wisconsin ranked 13th in the nation at total expenditures per pupil of $8,634 for 2001-02, while New Jersey was first ($11,793) and Utah was 50th ($4,900). In 2004-05, school costs in Wisconsin totaled $9.6 billion ($4.9 billion in state school aid and $3.6 billion from the gross school levy). The 2004-05 cost per pupil was $11,050.

Educational Attainment — In 2001-02, Wisconsin ranked 18th among the states in doctoral degrees conferred, 22nd in master's degrees awarded, and 15th in bachelor's degrees earned. In 2002-03, it ranked 13th in public high school diplomas.

The following tables present selected data. Consult footnoted sources for more detailed information about education.

UNIVERSITY OF WISCONSIN SYSTEM
Fall Enrollment 1999 – 2004

Institution	Total Full and Part-Time On Campus Enrollment						2004-05 Detail	
	1999-00	2000-01	2001-02	2002-03	2003-04	2004-05	Female	Male
Universities*	**145,083**	**146,344**	**147,056**	**148,182**	**160,703**	**160,797**	**88,677**	**72,120**
Eau Claire	10,402	10,553	10,643	10,862	10,599	10,541	6,290	4,251
Green Bay	5,442	5,479	5,558	5,378	5,448	5,455	3,616	1,839
La Crosse	9,295	9,133	9,092	8,750	8,746	8,501	5,091	3,410
Madison*	40,740	41,219	41,552	41,507	41,588	41,169	21,631	19,538
Undergraduate*	28,270	28,476	28,788	28,677	28,583	28,217	14,988	13,229
Agricultural and Life Sciences	2,099	2,106	2,152	2,190	2,238	2,253	1,267	986
Business	1,534	1,614	1,481	1,332	1,301	1,282	532	750
Education	2,505	2,487	2,420	2,371	2,317	2,254	1,709	545
Engineering	3,482	3,544	3,651	3,601	3,475	3,355	641	2,714
Human Ecology	835	863	949	1,005	988	907	762	145
Letters and Science	17,127	17,179	17,520	17,495	17,528	17,366	9,383	7,983
Medicine	219	213	207	222	202	227	176	51
Nursing	411	440	392	446	514	549	504	45
Pharmacy	58	30	16	15	20	24	14	10
University Special†	1,704	1,749	1,680	1,628	1,651	1,549	846	703
Graduate	8,620	8,620	8,744	8,822	8,924	8,943	4,387	4,556
Law	853	887	839	849	851	870	397	473
Medical	609	694	687	687	711	746	420	326
Pharmacy	366	474	500	529	551	529	353	176
Veterinary Medicine	318	319	314	315	317	315	240	75
Milwaukee*	22,964	23,202	23,828	24,344	24,890	26,084	14,292	11,792
Undergraduate*	17,113	1,779	18,404	18,877	19,672	20,743	11,152	9,591
Allied Health Professions	879	812	734	828	1,105	1,267	954	313
Architecture and Urban Planning	623	637	656	626	821	865	290	575
Business Administration	3,193	3,207	3,312	3,285	3,899	4,028	1,691	2,337
Education	1,493	1,579	1,689	1,730	2,849	2,705	1,990	715
Engineering and Applied Science	1,477	1,610	1,660	1,621	1,863	1,869	220	1,649
Fine Arts	1,393	1,470	1,526	1,575	1,764	1,847	1,015	832
Letters and Science	6,492	6,826	7,135	5,980	8,850	9,433	5,200	4,233
Library and Information Science	51	105	156	165	299	299	163	136
Nursing	734	782	836	1,081	1,567	1,729	1,527	202
Social Welfare	778	751	700	694	1,070	1,160	803	357
Special Programs	1,112	932	979	2,083	803	882	439	443
University Special†	1,580	1,324	1,392	1,226	1,127	1,170	665	505
Graduate	4,271	4,099	4,032	4,241	4,091	4,171	2,475	1,696
Oshkosh	10,783	10,777	10,929	11,245	11,013	11,059	6,662	4,397
Parkside	4,951	4,965	5,016	4,972	5,072	5,074	2,879	2,195
Platteville	5,340	5,494	5,511	5,939	6,134	6,182	2,442	3,740
River Falls	5,711	5,835	5,822	5,647	5,799	5,837	3,590	2,247
Stevens Point	8,544	8,608	8,735	8,667	8,750	8,711	4,839	3,872
Stout	7,517	7,696	7,780	7,901	7,708	7,547	3,831	3,716
Superior	2,741	2,843	2,787	2,861	2,832	2,804	1,657	1,147
Whitewater	10,653	10,540	10,471	10,758	10,548	10,489	5,596	4,893
Colleges*	**10,910**	**11,382**	**12,377**	**12,453**	**12,410**	**12,261**	**6,795**	**5,466**
Baraboo/Sauk County	676	752	653	644	648	637	314	323
Barron County	534	540	570	612	519	497	285	212
Fond du Lac	558	570	684	735	698	672	386	286
Fox Valley	1,510	1,678	1,776	1,787	1,732	1,689	909	780
Manitowoc	505	603	647	624	636	654	367	287
Marathon County	1,167	1,224	1,292	1,305	1,298	1,326	721	605
Marinette	546	518	535	547	510	471	274	197
Marshfield/Wood County	595	561	643	632	630	667	410	257
Richland	434	419	496	523	521	515	286	229
Rock County	823	853	981	933	910	885	501	384
Sheboygan	749	744	768	805	780	721	379	342
Washington County	857	913	939	932	958	983	519	464
Waukesha	1,956	2,007	2,245	2,142	2,204	2,020	1,049	971
SYSTEM TOTAL	155,993	157,726	159,433	160,635	173,113	173,058	95,472	77,586

*Total of subsequent detail. University totals for 2003-04 and 2004-05 were taken directly from the source.

†"University Special" designates students at UW-Madison and UW-Milwaukee who are allowed to take courses without having to qualify as degree candidates.

Sources: University of Wisconsin System, *Factbook 2002-03*, October 2002 and previous issues; University of Wisconsin-Madison, *Enrollment Facts at a Glance, Fall 2004-2005*, October 2004, and previous issues; University of Wisconsin-Milwaukee, *Fact Book, 2001-02*, 2002-03 and previous issues; University of Wisconsin-Milwaukee, *Enrollment Report Fall Semester 2003-04*, 2004-05; University of Wisconsin System, Office of Policy Analysis and Research, "Single-Year Headcount Reports", at: http://www.uwsa.edu/opar/ssb/single_year_hc.htm [June 2005].

UNIVERSITY OF WISCONSIN SYSTEM
Summer Session Enrollment 1999 – 2003

	Total Enrollment					2003 Detail	
Institution	1999[2]	2000	2001	2002	2003	Female	Male
Universities[1]	**39,372**	**40,338**	**40,793**	**41,207**	**41,493**	**25,035**	**16,458**
Eau Claire	2,511	2,489	2,550	2,682	2,592	1,775	817
Green Bay	855	932	943	1,046	946	686	260
La Crosse	2,509	2,434	2,448	2,200	2,171	1,377	794
Madison (by college)[1]	11,433	12,796	12,701	13,032	13,053	7,053	6,000
Agricultural and Life Sciences	1,058	1,099	1,087	1,259	1,365	763	602
Business	622	771	738	688	583	260	323
Continuing Studies	1,652	1,860	1,882	1,712	1,996	1,268	728
Education	1,141	1,165	1,151	1,164	1,123	819	304
Engineering	1,376	1,518	1,535	1,609	1,701	375	1,326
Human Ecology	348	359	377	417	418	316	102
Institute for Environmental Studies	57	57	73	76	68	43	25
Law	203	226	229	218	241	101	140
Letters and Science	4,240	4,836	4,725	4,934	5,233	2,796	2,437
Medicine	337	427	450	453	481	278	203
Nursing	189	197	165	181	181	173	8
Pharmacy	104	159	156	179	210	135	75
Veterinary Medicine	106	122	128	127	127	83	44
Summer Session Specials	—	1,881	1,933	1,740	2,024	1,281	743
Milwaukee	8,140	8,006	8,204	8,212	8,542	5,257	3,285
Oshkosh	1,929	1,842	2,072	1,879	1,748	1,245	503
Parkside	1,602	1,384	1,352	1,351	1,311	830	481
Platteville	1,283	1,321	1,289	1,375	1,513	793	720
River Falls	1,649	1,640	1,617	1,568	1,441	957	484
Stevens Point	1,985	1,991	1,909	1,993	2,066	1,322	744
Stout	2,384	2,340	2,528	2,662	2,575	1,471	1,104
Superior	855	766	817	807	661	441	220
Whitewater	2,237	2,397	2,711	2,803	2,874	1,828	1,046
Colleges[1]	**3,032**	**3,099**	**3,644**	**4,076**	**4,197**	**2,792**	**1,405**
Baraboo/Sauk County	100	150	184	108	142	88	54
Barron	72	80	107	73	80	64	16
Fond du Lac	169	102	156	315	329	229	100
Fox Valley	440	413	485	514	586	349	237
Manitowoc	180	194	227	218	182	117	65
Marathon County	265	254	307	356	339	212	127
Marinette	127	123	130	136	127	83	44
Marshfield/Wood County	159	136	139	119	171	135	36
Richland	72	34	80	87	90	58	32
Rock County	252	271	309	342	347	238	109
Sheboygan	234	241	280	292	252	161	91
Washington County	142	171	186	191	183	125	58
Waukesha	820	930	1,054	1,100	1,045	692	353
Online Courses	—	—	—	225	324	241	83
SYSTEM TOTAL	**42,404**	**43,437**	**44,437**	**45,283**	**45,690**	**27,827**	**17,863**

[1]Total of detail immediately following. UW-Madison college subtotals vary slightly from campus total because they are derived from a different source.

[2]Statistics for the UW-Madison campus in 1999 reflect a database that uses a different timeframe from other years. The UW registrar's office reports resulting numbers are lower than normally expected.

Sources: University of Wisconsin-Madison, Office of the Registrar, *University of Wisconsin-Madison, Enrollment Report for Summer Sessions, 2003*, and previous issues; University of Wisconsin System, *2004 Fact Book*, January 2005.

UNIVERSITY OF WISCONSIN – EXTENSION PROGRAMS 1999-2000 – 2003-04

Program type	1999-2000	2000-01	2001-02	2002-03	2003-04
Cooperative Education Extension Teaching Contacts[1]					
Agriculture/Agribusiness	408,137	177,112	233,696	345,918	108,796
Community, Natural Resources and Economic Development . . .	205,498	147,220	143,221	115,947	114,747
Family Living Programs	346,791	461,024	395,049	426,298	418,082
4-H and Youth Development	306,733	99,299	250,825	238,789	244,690
Wisconsin Geological and Natural History Survey	9,860	15,802	16,615	21,680	22,330
Continuing Education Extension and					
Business and Manufacturing Extension					
Number of programs	5,802	6,737	5,977	---	---
Number of enrollments	161,987	181,251	176,795	---	---
Business AnswerLine-assisted clients	---	---	---	2,438	3,254
Student contact hours	---	---	---	103,867	---
Credit Outreach (off-campus UW credit courses)					
Online courses	---	---	---	198	244
Online certificate and degree programs	---	---	---	15	16
Noncredit programs	---	---	---	6,225	5,729
Number of credits	66,064	74,694	25,020	---	---
Number of enrollments	23,931	25,999	25,020	30,157[6]	37,492[6]
Online enrollments	---	---	---	3,857	4,359
Noncredit enrollments	---	---	---	182,074	167,284
UW HELP contacts	---	---	---	29,389	32,001
Learner Support Services contacts	---	---	---	73,463	65,026
Online applications to UW System campuses	---	---	---	85,287	104,738
Independent Learning enrollments					
University credit	3,693	3,196	3,398	---	---
Continuing education	1,113	709	625	---	---
High school credit	940	782	553	---	---
Wisconsin Technical College System credit	100	66	54	---	---
Total Independent Learning enrollments	---	---	---	3,849	3,247
Small Business Development Center					
Counseling clients	2,295	1,982	1,690	2,081	2,384
Hours of counseling	15,013	19,628	19,446	21,290	22,331
Wisconsin Innovation Service Center clients	240	251	271	---	---
Training programs	---	606	605	535	515
Training programs attendees[2]	---	10,664	11,988	11,208	10,587
Distance Education[3]					
Educational Teleconference Network (ETN) sessions	873	859	679	---	---
WISLINE[4] teleconference programming hours	76,536	80,876	88,089	---	---
WisView Audiographics	---	---	---	---	---
Compressed video sessions	2,205	1,142	2,996	---	---
Satellite videoconference programs	146	151	99	---	---
Public Radio/Television Audience[5]					
Wisconsin Public Radio (listeners per week)	344,300	374,700	381,100	399,600	414,600
Wisconsin Public Television (viewers per week)	601,000	575,000	826,700	571,000	574,000
Wisconsin Public Television telecourses (enrollments)	2,189	3,571	3,633	3,651	3,711
Interactive conferencing hours	---	---	---	154,676	159,298

[1]Cooperative Extension data are for the calendar year. In addition, its faculty and staff offer contacts through publications, telephone, mass media, and the World Wide Web.

[2]Small Business Development Center training programs are also included in Continuing Education Extension/Business and Manufacturing totals.

[3]Enrollment figures included under Distance Education are included in other division/unit enrollment/contacts.

[4]WISLINE is a centralized teleconferencing network available through regular telephone connections.

[5]Wisconsin Public Radio and Wisconsin Public Television are cooperative services of the University of Wisconsin-Extension and the Wisconsin Educational Communications Board.

[6]Undergraduate and graduate enrollments combined.

Source: University of Wisconsin-Extension, *2004 Annual Report*, at: http://www1.uwex.edu/annualreport/index.cfm [February 22, 2005] and previous editions.

ENROLLMENT IN WISCONSIN TECHNICAL COLLEGE SYSTEM

Annual Enrollment Summary, 1994-95 – 2002-03

School Year	Total[1]	College Parallel	Associate Degree	Technical Diploma	Vocational Adult	Non-Post Secondary[2]	Community Services
1994-95	434,780	17,826	100,593	98,639	258,024	—	20,214
1995-96	431,405	16,937	98,572	97,853	257,567	—	18,259
1996-97	434,885	16,199	100,341	97,839	260,324	—	17,150
1997-98	439,068	17,012	100,787	34,609	257,441	76,562	15,421
1998-99	442,274	17,218	102,590	35,658	253,764	80,256	15,619
1999-2000	453,668	16,850	104,262	34,878	264,320	79,258	16,011
2000-01	439,934	16,760	106,248	35,631	248,976	80,032	14,870
2001-02	451,271	17,953	108,921	38,038	255,888	82,993	14,675
2002-03	429,355	19,064	113,253	40,098	232,766	81,860	13,277

[1]Unduplicated student headcount. [2]Includes basic education, the hearing impaired program, and the visually impaired program.
Source: Wisconsin Technical College System, *WTCS Facts*, March 2004 and previous issues.

Annual Enrollment Summary, By Technical College – 2002-03

Technical College	Total[1]	College Parallel	Associate Degree[2]	Technical Diploma	Vocational Adult	Non-Post Secondary[3]	Community Services
Blackhawk	13,913	—	2,821	1,528	8,491	2,565	274
Chippewa Valley	20,498	—	5,922	2,417	11,746	3,758	—
Fox Valley	50,227	—	10,819	3,636	33,952	5,332	1,493
Gateway	28,524	—	8,935	2,933	13,032	8,097	—
Lakeshore	16,118	—	3,429	1,464	9,632	3,242	—
Madison Area	48,626	7,073	12,784	4,633	21,872	6,050	4,260
Mid-State	13,696	—	4,531	1,547	7,357	2,050	482
Milwaukee Area	56,862	10,998	20,134	3,983	16,744	25,812	189
Moraine Park	23,184	—	8,875	3,017	10,447	4,141	127
Nicolet	10,611	993	1,621	671	6,625	871	1,774
Northcentral	19,281	—	4,753	1,597	10,496	5,043	—
Northeast	39,223	—	10,080	3,928	25,320	3,817	843
Southwest	10,436	—	2,307	1,163	7,237	1,254	—
Waukesha	32,263	—	6,874	3,642	18,664	4,613	2,784
Western	20,700	—	5,375	1,755	12,445	3,482	501
Wisconsin Indianhead	25,193	—	3,993	2,184	18,706	1,733	550
TOTAL	429,355	19,064	113,253	40,098	232,766	81,860	13,277

[1]Unduplicated student headcount. [2]Includes both collegiate and noncollegiate students. [3]Includes basic education, the hearing impaired program, and the visually impaired program.
Source: Wisconsin Technical College System, *WTCS Facts*, March 2004 and previous issues.

WISCONSIN PRIVATE INSTITUTIONS OF HIGHER EDUCATION
Fall Enrollment, 2000-01 – 2004-05

Institution (Location)	Total College-Credit Enrollments				
	2000-01	2001-02	2002-03	2003-04	2004-05
Universities and Colleges					
Alverno College (Milwaukee)	1,933	1,952	2,000	2,000	2,160
Beloit College (Beloit)	1,254	1,273	1,175	1,175	1,235
Cardinal Stritch College (Milwaukee)	5,994	5,855	6,312	6,954	6,832
Carroll College (Waukesha)	2,902	2,897	3,020	2,968	2,062
Carthage College (Kenosha)	2,222	2,345	2,473	2,200	2,200
Concordia University Wisconsin (Mequon)	4,268	4,810	4,541	4,900	5,200
Edgewood College (Madison)	2,077	2,110	2,000	2,300	2,413
Immanuel Lutheran College (Eau Claire)	44	NA	NA	NA	NA
Lakeland College (Sheboygan)	3,410	3,588	3,586	3,586	4,019
Lawrence University (Appleton)	1,285	1,323	1,325	1,325	1,350
Marian College of Fond du Lac (Fond du Lac)	2,514	2,558	2,672	2,672	2,777
Marquette University (Milwaukee)	10,892	10,832	11,000	11,042	11,000
Mount Mary College (Milwaukee)	1,246	1,216	1,401	1,400	1,600
Mount Senario College (Ladysmith)*	829	425	NA	NA	NA
Northland College (Ashland)	774	794	750	800	750
Ripon College (Ripon)	862	906	987	987	1,001
St. Norbert College (De Pere)	2,132	2,131	2,196	2,133	2,164
Silver Lake College (Manitowoc)	938	920	1,030	1,030	1,104
Viterbo College (La Crosse)	2,154	2,623	2,200	2,300	2,500
Wisconsin Lutheran College (Milwaukee)	634	716	634	669	706
Technical and Professional					
Bellin College of Nursing (Green Bay)	151	160	176	206	207
Medical College of Wisconsin, Inc. (Milwaukee)	1,189	1,235	1,224	1,259	1,359
Milwaukee Institute of Art and Design (Milwaukee)	646	650	650	636	630
Milwaukee School of Engineering (Milwaukee)	2,620	2,563	2,586	2,383	2,363
Theological Seminaries					
Immanuel Lutheran Seminary (Eau Claire)	4	NA	NA	NA	NA
Nashotah House (Nashotah)	0	46	NA	49	NA
Sacred Heart School of Theology (Hales Corners)	119	154	137	71	155
St. Francis Seminary (Milwaukee)	86	104	101	69	68
Wisconsin Lutheran Seminary (Mequon)	149	165	182	128	144
TOTAL	53,328	54,351	54,358	55,242	55,999

*Mount Senario College closed effective August 31, 2002.

NA – Not available.

Sources: For 2000-01 and previous years, Wisconsin Association of Collegiate Registrars and Admissions Officers, *Opening Fall Enrollment in Wisconsin Institutions of Higher Education for the Academic Year 2000-2001*, April 2001, and previous issues; for 2001-02 and later, Wisconsin Association of Independent Colleges and Universities, *Wisconsin's Private Colleges and Universities*, 2004 and 2005, *Guide to Admissions and Financial Aid*, 2004 and 2005 and previous issues; National Center for Education Statistics, *Integrated Postsecondary Education Data System*, at: http://nces.ed.gov/ipeds [April 21, 3003]; and individual registrar offices.

DIPLOMAS AND EARNED DEGREES
By State

State	High School Diplomas Private 2000-01[1]	Public 2002-03[2]	Associate Degree	Bachelor's Degree	Master's Degree	Doctorate Degree (Ph.D., Ed.D., etc.)	First Professional Degree (M.D., J.D., etc.)
Alabama	4,234	36,850	7,927	20,314	8,284	527	1,066
Alaska	247	7,160	906	1,377	432	19	0
Arizona	2,079	47,610	13,008	22,014	11,248	809	713
Arkansas	1,236	27,410	4,213	10,078	2,470	165	490
California	30,285	331,730	84,209	131,152	47,699	5,531	8,056
Colorado	2,418	41,650	8,076	22,275	8,565	721	845
Connecticut	5,126	32,980	4,413	14,647	7,510	593	992
Delaware	1,534	6,770	1,163	4,936	1,549	158	291
District of Columbia	1,555	2,560	612	8,591	7,364	541	2,681
Florida	14,038	120,340	48,952	56,351	20,294	2,283	3,217
Georgia	6,622	67,100	9,061	29,999	12,052	1,162	2,326
Hawaii	3,388	10,000	3,309	4,901	1,543	130	131
Idaho	461	15,940	4,583	4,913	1,241	91	132
ILLINOIS	15,621	120,570	25,924	57,430	28,529	2,535	4,501
Indiana	4,593	56,460	11,891	33,947	9,089	1,022	1,611
IOWA	2,667	34,290	9,939	19,388	3,878	579	1,580
Kansas	1,903	29,850	7,209	14,787	5,055	416	701
Kentucky	3,654	34,360	7,305	16,401	4,914	382	1,004
Louisiana	8,398	37,710	5,370	20,312	5,855	537	1,510
Maine	2,045	12,950	1,975	5,793	1,319	39	184
Maryland	7,666	51,520	7,750	22,330	11,591	972	1,129
Massachusetts	9,686	55,250	14,251	43,097	25,884	2,287	3,912
MICHIGAN	9,226	110,610	18,768	47,929	22,069	1,497	2,440
MINNESOTA	4,563	59,980	11,842	24,706	8,377	873	1,521
Mississippi	3,452	23,380	7,602	11,899	3,386	334	541
Missouri	6,883	54,890	10,948	32,082	13,914	953	2,420
Montana	543	10,740	1,528	5,277	990	73	121
Nebraska	2,375	20,250	4,206	10,639	3,211	333	795
Nevada	605	12,940	2,392	4,489	1,501	107	152
New Hampshire	2,189	12,950	2,923	7,249	2,378	123	166
New Jersey	12,345	82,320	12,643	28,376	10,330	980	1,540
New Mexico	1,362	17,650	3,757	6,432	2,616	280	286
New York	26,601	146,030	51,148	98,332	50,921	3,464	8,477
North Carolina	4,299	68,310	14,739	36,071	9,377	1,114	1,831
North Dakota	374	8,030	1,884	4,810	913	54	181
Ohio	13,869	113,610	19,888	52,748	18,076	1,921	3,282
Oklahoma	1,581	36,280	7,250	16,232	5,225	439	1,025
Oregon	2,517	31,630	6,518	14,450	4,905	418	1,020
Pennsylvania	18,092	118,980	23,826	68,999	23,201	2,307	4,438
Rhode Island	1,616	9,080	3,557	8,845	2,079	242	249
South Carolina	2,923	33,140	7,132	16,886	4,155	449	777
South Dakota	510	8,800	1,856	4,365	943	73	163
Tennessee	5,462	43,580	8,085	23,480	7,971	781	1,435
Texas	10,500	228,510	31,831	79,595	25,416	2,560	5,110
Utah	820	30,280	9,160	18,188	3,666	350	393
Vermont	1,342	6,820	1,515	4,673	1,380	57	261
Virginia	5,470	71,620	12,255	32,948	10,689	1,167	2,213
Washington	3,526	58,490	20,035	24,462	7,551	654	1,196
West Virginia	827	17,230	2,926	9,022	2,245	146	407
WISCONSIN	5,387	61,730	10,450	28,783	7,823	857	1,064
Wyoming	54	6,000	2,423	1,655	445	55	122
UNITED STATES[3]	278,773	2,684,920	595,133	1,291,900	482,118	44,160	80,698

[1]Private high school diploma detail may not add to total due to rounding.

[2]Estimated.

[3]Higher Education totals include U.S. Service schools.

Sources: U.S. Department of Education, Office of Educational Research and Improvement, National Center for Education Statistics, *Digest of Education Statistics, 2003*, at: http://nces.ed.gov [March 25, 2005]; U.S. Department of Education, National Center for Education Statistics, *Private School Universe Survey, 2001-2002*.

WISCONSIN SCHOOL DISTRICT FINANCIAL DATA
1980-81 – 2004-05

Fiscal Year	State School Aid Amount[2]	Percent Change	Gross School Levy Amount[2]	Percent Change	Total School Costs[1] Amount[2]	Percent Change	Student Enrollment Number	Percent Change	Cost Per Pupil Amount	Percent Change
1980-81	$848.5	---	$1,219.9	---	$2,317.1	---	830,247	---	$2,791	---
1981-82	907.2	7.0%	1,319.5	8.2%	2,458.8	6.1%	804,262	-3.1%	3,057	9.5%
1982-83	1,018.8	12.3	1,373.5	4.1	2,579.7	4.9	784,830	-2.4	3,287	7.5
1983-84	1,053.5	3.4	1,482.1	7.9	2,722.7	5.5	774,646	-1.3	3,515	6.9
1984-85	1,117.2	6.0	1,566.0	5.7	2,918.2	7.2	767,542	-0.9	3,802	8.2
1985-86	1,299.2	16.3	1,583.3	1.1	3,154.5	8.1	768,234	1.0	4,106	8.0
1986-87	1,358.1	4.5	1,709.5	8.0	3,344.9	6.0	767,819	-0.1	4,356	6.1
1987-88	1,481.6	9.1	1,840.4	7.7	3,590.9	7.4	772,363	0.6	4,649	6.7
1988-89	1,572.4	6.1	1,989.9	8.1	3,848.4	7.2	774,859	0.3	4,967	6.8
1989-90	1,693.2	7.7	2,158.5	8.5	4,142.1	7.6	782,905	1.0	5,291	6.5
1990-91	1,857.4	19.7	2,356.4	9.2	4,555.7	10.0	797,621	1.9	5,712	8.0
1991-92	1,950.4	5.0	2,568.0	9.0	4,877.1	7.1	814,671	2.1	5,987	4.8
1992-93	2,046.0	4.9	2,843.8	10.7	5,287.9	8.4	829,415	1.8	6,375	6.5
1993-94	2,186.6	6.9	2,988.1	5.1	5,527.1	4.5	844,001	1.8	6,549	2.7
1994-95	2,462.0	12.6	2,995.7	0.3	5,848.2	5.8	860,581	2.0	6,796	3.8
1995-96	2,705.2	9.9	3,023.6	.9	6,150.2	5.2	870,175	1.1	7,068	4.0
1996-97	3,566.1	31.8	2,528.1	-16.4	6,546.8	6.4	879,149	1.0	7,447	5.4
1997-98	3,804.7	6.7	2,590.4	2.5	6,939.0	6.0	881,248	0.2	7,874	5.7
1998-99	3,989.4	4.9	2,735.8	5.6	7,250.7	4.5	879,537	-0.2	8,244	4.7
1999-2000	4,226.3	5.9	2,795.2	2.2	7,546.9	4.1	877,852	-0.2	8,597	4.3
2000-01	4,463.3	5.6	2,927.8	4.7	7,899.5	4.8	879,476	0.2	8,982	4.6
2001-02	4,602.4	3.1	3,071.8	4.9	8,347.5	5.7	879,361	0.0	9,493	5.7
2002-03	4,775.2	3.8	3,192.0	3.9	8,749.9	4.8	881,231	0.2	10,023	4.7
2003-04	4,806.4	0.7	3,367.6	5.5	9,187.4[3]	5.0	880,031	-0.1	10,524[3]	5.0
2004-05	4,858.0	1.1	3,610.7	7.2	9,646.8[3]	5.0	NA	NA	11,050[3]	5.0

NA – Not available.

[1]Includes the gross costs of general operations, special projects, debt service, and food service; the net cost of capital projects; and the costs of CESA and County Children with Disabilities Education Board operations.

[2]In millions of dollars; 1996-97 through 2004-05 are appropriated amounts.

[3]Preliminary.

Source: Wisconsin Department of Public Instruction, School Financial Services Team, departmental data, March 2005.

WISCONSIN SCHOOL DISTRICTS
Districts Ranked by Total Enrollments, 1998-99 – 2003-04

Enrollment Level*	Number of Districts 1998-99	1999-2000	2000-01	2001-02	2002-03	2003-04
1-499	86	86	86	93	98	101
500-999	126	128	134	132	129	128
1,000-1,999	111	111	109	109	109	106
2,000-2,999	42	42	42	40	44	42
3,000-3,999	22	22	22	24	22	24
4,000-4,999	14	12	13	13	13	13
5,000-9,999	14	16	16	16	16	17
10,000 and above	11	11	11	11	11	11
TOTAL	426	428	433	438	442	442

*Enrollment for 1999-2000 and later includes data for nondistrict-sponsored charter schools.

Districts Ranked by 9-12 Enrollments, 1998-99 – 2003-04

Enrollment Level[1]	Number of Districts 1998-99	1999-2000	2000-01	2001-02	2002-03	2003-04
0[2]	47	49	52	54	58	58
1-299	138	138	144	148	147	152
300-499	89	88	83	80	83	79
500-999	87	84	85	86	81	80
1,000-1,999	44	48	48	48	81	80
2,000 and above	21	21	21	22	22	22
TOTAL	426	428	433	438	442	442

[1]Enrollment for 1999-2000 and later includes data for nondistrict-sponsored charter schools.

[2]This group includes the K-8 districts, which do not have secondary level students.

Sources: Wisconsin Department of Public Instruction, *Basic Facts About Wisconsin's Elementary and Secondary Schools, 2003-2004*, and previous issues; departmental data, April 2005.

ENROLLMENT IN WISCONSIN PUBLIC AND PRIVATE ELEMENTARY AND SECONDARY SCHOOLS

Public Schools, 1994-95 – 2003-04

Grade Level	1994-95	1995-96	1996-97	1997-98	1998-99	1999-2000	2000-01	2001-02	2002-03	2003-04
Pre-kindergarten	18,531	18,045	19,790	19,627	20,090	20,814	23,751	24,673	26,092	26,668
Kindergarten	61,898	62,859	62,455	60,932	59,610	58,536	56,507	57,469	57,670	59,372
1	64,040	64,574	64,925	64,115	62,656	61,413	59,962	58,174	58,538	58,368
2	64,247	63,141	63,921	64,297	63,501	62,260	61,205	61,655	58,628	58,877
3	65,127	64,541	63,286	64,032	64,312	63,680	62,810	63,509	60,819	59,196
4	65,996	65,427	64,670	63,662	64,255	64,914	64,455	65,101	62,436	61,744
5	64,380	66,577	65,943	65,120	63,969	64,950	65,570	65,762	64,213	62,970
6	65,362	65,289	67,317	66,746	65,786	64,977	66,163	67,208	66,925	65,762
7	65,844	66,723	66,527	68,581	67,996	67,107	66,367	67,398	68,631	68,192
8	65,790	65,788	66,488	66,601	68,475	67,880	67,950	66,558	67,751	68,663
9	73,063	74,700	75,089	75,863	76,664	78,953	78,140	77,802	77,508	77,798
10	67,229	70,262	71,315	71,522	71,277	70,913	73,796	73,512	73,022	72,043
11	61,667	64,458	66,983	67,503	67,148	67,301	67,605	70,297	70,284	70,989
12	57,407	57,791	60,440	63,119	63,725	64,015	65,195	65,946	68,714	69,389
Ungraded Elementary and Secondary	—	—	—	—	—	—	—	—	—	—
TOTAL	860,581	870,175	879,149	881,720	879,464	877,713	879,476	879,361	881,231	880,031

Private Schools, 1994-95 – 2004-05

Grade Level	1994-95	1995-96	1996-97	1997-98	1998-99	1999-2000	2000-01	2001-02	2002-03	2003-04	2004-05
Pre-kindergarten	9,877	11,653	11,482	11,617	12,114	12,728	12,901	12,866	13,487	13,604	14,434
Kindergarten	13,593	13,355	13,214	12,930	12,866	12,660	13,012	12,625	11,736	11,191	11,517
1	13,553	13,619	14,028	12,936	13,118	12,896	12,694	12,468	12,021	11,201	10,950
2	13,282	13,078	13,452	13,153	12,847	12,797	12,696	12,337	11,888	11,460	10,970
3	13,163	12,940	13,109	12,899	13,000	12,705	12,605	12,467	11,807	11,412	11,187
4	13,212	12,739	12,647	12,471	12,599	12,922	12,478	12,369	11,896	11,304	11,114
5	12,549	12,910	12,513	12,252	12,255	12,513	12,655	12,201	11,865	11,309	11,047
6	12,550	12,082	12,447	11,866	11,921	12,078	12,042	12,116	11,286	10,994	10,824
7	11,509	11,406	11,194	11,389	10,963	11,332	11,185	11,192	11,193	10,408	10,420
8	11,210	11,070	11,019	10,769	11,052	10,858	10,959	10,938	10,682	10,683	10,247
9	6,798	6,735	6,277	6,409	6,105	6,747	6,574	6,372	6,414	6,112	6,332
10	5,893	6,375	6,299	6,070	6,054	6,062	6,461	6,273	6,076	6,214	5,950
11	5,504	5,619	5,855	5,807	5,637	5,873	5,698	6,005	5,949	5,880	5,925
12	5,309	5,359	5,116	5,587	5,497	5,426	5,450	5,397	6,073	5,750	5,665
Ungraded Elementary and Secondary	—*	—*	1,593	1,010	1,125	769	926	519	246	330	210
TOTAL	148,002	148,940	150,245	147,165	147,153	148,366	148,336	146,145	142,619	137,852	136,792

Note: Discrepancies between these statistics and those shown in earlier *Blue Books* reflect revised data in the source.

*Ungraded enrollment not reported by department for 1993-94 through 1995-96.

Sources: Wisconsin Department of Public Instruction, *Basic Facts About Wisconsin's Elementary and Secondary Schools, 2003-2004*, and previous issues; departmental data, April, 2005.

PUBLIC SCHOOL STUDENT DROPOUTS
By County, 1998-99 – 2002-03

County	Number of Dropouts – Grades 9-12[1]					Annual Dropout Rate[2]				
	1998-99	1999-2000	2000-01	2001-02	2002-03	1998-99	1999-2000	2000-01	2001-02	2002-03
Adams	16	--	11	7	14	2.56%	--	1.69%	1.05%	2.13%
Ashland	12	--	1	11	10	1.03	--	0.09	1.03	0.93
Barron	35	26	39	30	21	1.16	0.86%	1.31	1.03	0.74
Bayfield	7	16	12	7	9	0.93	2.20	1.61	0.96	1.24
Brown	184	268	230	135	192	2.22	2.25	1.89	1.09	1.51
Buffalo	9	15	8	12	2	1.08	1.85	0.94	1.44	0.24
Burnett	12	7	16	29	10	1.59	0.94	2.15	4.08	2.55
Calumet	9	9	6	6	10	0.52	0.53	0.36	0.36	0.60
Chippewa	55	37	62	48	23	1.77	1.20	1.97	1.56	0.77
Clark	25	18	13	15	46	1.13	0.86	0.64	0.75	1.21
Columbia	27	35	28	21	26	0.85	1.11	0.90	0.66	0.82
Crawford	8	5	14	8	7	0.77	0.48	1.39	0.84	0.75
Dane	418	419	360	328	384	2.21	2.18	1.80	1.60	1.85
Dodge	18	8	32	16	9	0.59	0.26	1.05	0.51	0.31
Door	19	13	18	6	8	1.23	0.87	1.19	0.40	0.53
Douglas	17	86	75	49	92	0.72	3.78	3.48	2.29	4.08
Dunn	26	20	38	17	24	1.28	0.98	1.89	0.84	1.17
Eau Claire	16	38	31	34	14	0.35	0.81	0.66	0.76	0.33
Florence	3	1	1	1	2	1.01	0.35	0.34	0.34	0.75
Fond du Lac	88	80	66	101	52	1.71	1.55	1.28	2.03	1.02
Forest	6	5	19	11	20	0.95	0.79	3.11	1.90	3.36
Grant	25	20	18	16	8	0.81	0.65	0.59	0.53	0.27
Green	31	23	21	16	20	1.71	1.23	1.10	0.84	1.08
Green Lake	8	4	5	1	8	0.53	0.28	0.36	0.08	0.63
Iowa	3	6	1	7	11	0.24	0.48	0.08	0.55	0.89
Iron	2	2	2	1	3	0.59	0.58	0.61	0.32	0.91
Jackson	33	14	18	10	8	3.24	1.37	1.79	0.95	0.75
Jefferson	103	64	60	65	86	2.37	1.46	1.37	1.48	1.99
Juneau	18	33	43	39	42	1.20	2.25	2.88	2.67	2.00
Kenosha	279	279	140	223	126	3.73	3.67	1.78	2.79	1.51
Kewaunee	9	12	9	4	6	0.64	0.86	0.64	0.28	0.44
La Crosse	81	36	54	57	44	1.58	0.70	1.08	1.14	0.87
Lafayette	4	8	4	7	5	0.32	0.62	0.32	0.59	0.44
Langlade	26	16	15	19	10	1.85	1.18	1.06	1.35	0.81
Lincoln	10	8	24	40	37	0.55	0.42	1.29	2.17	2.08
Manitowoc	75	91	82	80	53	1.77	2.12	1.93	1.89	1.27
Marathon	63	65	36	73	61	0.94	0.97	0.72	1.09	0.91
Marinette	18	29	24	20	19	0.69	1.15	0.94	0.78	0.77
Marquette	10	7	14	10	15	1.24	0.90	1.82	1.34	1.91
Menominee	14	28	35	14	3	4.44	8.31	10.87	3.98	0.21
Milwaukee	3,106	2,661	2,165	1,787	2,611	7.54	6.41	5.48	4.44	6.10
Monroe	31	18	25	23	21	1.27	0.73	1.00	0.94	0.86
Oconto	43	37	23	18	19	2.56	2.17	1.34	1.03	1.11
Oneida	70	52	63	82	69	3.02	0.31	2.54	3.35	2.84
Outagamie	50	88	73	68	47	0.53	0.92	0.73	0.67	0.46
Ozaukee	21	21	35	19	4	0.47	0.46	0.75	0.40	0.28
Pepin	7	10	2	5	0	1.00	1.48	0.31	0.81	0.00
Pierce	10	11	13	14	10	0.39	0.42	0.51	0.55	0.40
Polk	14	5	14	11	17	0.52	0.19	0.51	0.41	0.55
Portage	58	80	59	60	34	1.64	2.25	1.69	1.70	1.02
Price	5	4	5	7	2	0.51	0.41	0.52	0.76	0.22
Racine	319	508	338	378	332	3.42	5.52	3.64	3.92	3.35
Richland	11	15	2	6	7	1.48	2.01	0.30	0.86	1.01
Rock	222	234	211	159	147	2.70	2.87	2.50	1.86	1.72
Rusk	2	--	7	6	10	0.21	--	0.75	0.66	1.13
St. Croix	14	26	13	22	10	0.41	0.75	0.37	0.61	0.33
Sauk	54	71	99	56	59	1.42	1.79	2.43	1.38	1.21
Sawyer	20	18	16	16	13	2.51	2.30	2.12	2.03	1.67
Shawano	34	36	29	18	101	1.56	1.67	1.34	0.81	1.66
Sheboygan	80	148	149	87	12	1.22	2.27	2.29	1.33	0.37
Taylor	4	--	5	15	8	0.30	--	0.39	1.23	0.66
Trempealeau	21	14	19	10	20	1.11	0.73	1.00	0.53	1.07
Vernon	10	17	15	11	16	0.62	1.05	0.99	0.72	1.18
Vilas	7	4	7	8	11	1.12	0.63	1.11	1.26	1.75
Walworth	64	59	93	83	61	1.43	1.27	1.92	1.68	1.20
Washburn	8	5	14	6	16	0.74	0.45	1.27	0.57	1.53
Washington	78	97	94	77	92	1.12	1.40	1.35	1.10	1.30
Waukesha	86	56	66	76	72	0.45	0.28	0.33	0.38	0.35
Waupaca	49	61	28	40	36	1.36	1.69	0.79	0.87	0.99
Waushara	4	12	5	2	2	0.40	1.14	0.48	0.19	0.57
Winnebago	112	132	123	149	132	1.52	1.76	1.61	1.92	1.71
Wood	97	90	41	23	27	2.00	1.84	0.85	0.47	0.56
STATE	6,533	6,441	5,536	4,936	5,562	2.35%	2.29%	1.98%	1.75%	1.93%

[1]Dropouts do not include alternative and charter schools.

[2]Rate for entire school year determined by dividing the number of dropouts by total enrollment. Rates calculated by Wisconsin Legislative Reference Bureau.

Source: Wisconsin Department of Public Instruction at: http://www.dpi.state.wi.us/dpi/spr/xls/drpout03.xls [May 9, 2005].

WISCONSIN PUBLIC SCHOOL SALARIES
Instructional Staff and Salaries, 2002-03 (Revised) and 2003-04

	2002-03		2003-04	
Classification	Number	Average Salary	Number	Average Salary (est.)
Total Instructional Staff	66,941	$46,046	67,595	$46,593
Principals	2,618	NA	2,597	NA
Nonsupervisory	4,053	NA	3,960	NA
All Teachers	60,270	42,775	61,038	43,382
Secondary	18,745	43,172	18,856	43,382
Men	9,165	NA	9,109	NA
Women	9,580	NA	9,747	NA
Elementary	41,525	42,597	42,182	43,382
Men	8,047	NA	8,007	NA
Women	33,478	NA	34,175	NA

NA – Not available
Source: National Education Association, *Rankings and Estimates: Rankings of the States 2003 and Estimates of School Statistics 2004*, May 2004, and previous issues.

Average Teacher Salaries, 1985-86 – 2003-04

Year	All Teachers[1]	Elementary	Secondary[2]	Middle School (grades 6-8)	Junior High (grades 7-9)	Senior High
1985-86	$26,347	$25,449	—	$26,760	$27,329	$27,133
1990-91	33,077	31,761	—	33,491	34,229	34,681
1991-92	35,227	34,313	$36,983	—	—	—
1992-93	35,926	34,181	36,442	—	—	—
1993-94	36,644	34,865	37,171	—	—	—
1994-95	37,746	37,180	39,104	—	—	—
1995-96	38,182	37,740	39,136	—	—	—
1996-97	39,057	38,690	39,850	—	—	—
1997-98	39,899	39,524	40,709	—	—	—
1998-99	40,657	40,423	NA	—	—	—
1999-2000	41,153	40,913	41,675	—	—	—
2000-01	41,646	41,403	42,175	—	—	—
2001-02	42,232	41,982	42,787	—	—	—
2002-03	42,775	42,597	43,172	—	—	—
2003-04 (estimated)	43,382	43,382	43,382	—	—	—

NA – Not available
[1]Includes base salaries for full-time teachers only. Districts with unsettled contracts are not included.
[2]Source no longer includes a breakdown of secondary teachers (middle, junior high, senior high) after 1990-91.
Sources: Wisconsin Department of Public Instruction, departmental data for 1985-91; National Education Association, *Rankings and Estimates: Rankings of the States 2003 and Estimates of School Statistics 2004*, May 2004, and previous issues.

AVERAGE ANNUAL SALARIES OF PUBLIC SCHOOL TEACHERS
By State, 2002-03

State	Average Salary	State Rank	State	Average Salary	State Rank
Alabama	$38,246	40	Montana	$35,754	47
Alaska	49,685	12	Nebraska	37,896	41
Arizona	40,894*	28	Nevada	41,795*	26
Arkansas	37,753*	43	New Hampshire	41,909	25
California	56,283*	1	New Jersey	54,158	3
Colorado	42,679	24	New Mexico	36,965	46
Connecticut	55,367	2	New York	53,017	5
Delaware	50,772	10	North Carolina	43,076	22
District of Columbia	50,763	11	North Dakota	33,869	50
Florida	40,281	30	Ohio	45,490	16
Georgia	45,533	15	Oklahoma	34,877	48
Hawaii	44,464	20	Oregon	47,600	14
Idaho	40,148	31	Pennsylvania	51,428	7
ILLINOIS	51,475	6	Rhode Island	51,076*	8
Indiana	44,966	17	South Carolina	40,362	29
IOWA	39,059	34	South Dakota	32,416	51
Kansas	37,795	42	Tennessee	39,677	33
Kentucky	38,981	35	Texas	39,974	32
Louisiana	37,166	45	Utah	38,268	39
Maine	38,518	37	Vermont	41,491	27
Maryland	49,677	13	Virginia	43,152	21
Massachusetts	50,819	9	Washington	44,958	18
MICHIGAN	53,563*	4	West Virginia	38,481	38
MINNESOTA	44,745	19	**WISCONSIN**	42,775	23
Mississippi	34,555*	49	Wyoming	38,838	36
Missouri	37,655	44	UNITED STATES	$45,891*	

*Data estimated.

Source: National Education Association, *Rankings and Estimates: Rankings of the States 2003 and Estimates of School Statistics 2004*, at: http://www.nea.org/edstats/images/04rankings.pdf [May 2004].

STATE AND LOCAL EDUCATION PAYROLLS
Instructional Employees, By State, March 2003

State	Kindergarten-12				Higher Education			
	FTE Employees*		Payroll		FTE Employees*		Payroll	
	Number	Rank	(in thousands)	Rank	Number	Rank	(in thousands)	Rank
Alabama	67,549	25	$195,177	26	11,927	22	$62,739	18
Alaska	12,252	47	46,912	44	1,136	50	7,010	50
Arizona	67,888	24	224,422	22	12,142	21	53,748	24
Arkansas	44,082	32	123,004	32	6,685	32	33,786	33
California	441,964	1	2,077,482	1	62,655	1	379,608	1
Colorado	68,628	23	220,475	23	15,060	14	74,181	16
Connecticut	60,142	27	265,477	20	5,983	33	35,334	32
Delaware	10,353	50	42,197	47	2,654	41	13,270	39
Florida	190,516	5	623,908	8	28,768	3	153,576	3
Georgia	153,537	9	500,476	10	16,165	12	83,148	13
Hawaii	21,683	42	67,088	42	2,628	42	13,717	38
Idaho	22,538	40	64,849	43	3,364	38	12,894	41
ILLINOIS	192,882	4	716,286	5	24,819	7	119,725	8
Indiana	90,382	15	317,070	16	21,457	10	92,550	11
IOWA	52,820	29	152,082	29	10,782	25	54,356	20
Kansas	52,623	30	150,302	30	8,501	30	42,444	29
Kentucky	62,385	26	177,614	27	9,690	28	47,692	28
Louisiana	73,801	20	204,494	25	9,929	26	50,023	26
Maine	27,898	37	80,426	41	1,589	48	7,449	49
Maryland	81,367	19	357,793	14	14,854	15	81,308	15
Massachusetts	113,375	13	449,163	11	9,863	27	47,736	27
MICHIGAN	145,312	10	603,923	9	26,342	5	143,068	5
MINNESOTA	88,303	16	299,916	17	12,757	19	61,155	19
Mississippi	49,284	31	116,527	33	8,913	29	40,517	30
Missouri	87,780	17	266,313	19	12,844	18	54,132	21
Montana	16,413	45	44,940	46	2,137	44	10,350	44
Nebraska	31,396	36	94,327	36	4,398	36	19,810	36
Nevada	21,688	41	80,973	40	2,743	40	13,140	40
New Hampshire	26,474	38	82,277	39	1,761	46	9,263	46
New Jersey	161,526	8	775,270	4	13,339	17	83,296	12
New Mexico	33,435	35	96,238	35	5,884	34	21,347	35
New York	338,567	3	1,490,119	2	28,560	4	145,440	4
North Carolina	132,778	11	437,935	12	23,893	8	113,797	9
North Dakota	10,873	49	36,997	49	3,084	39	12,331	42
Ohio	171,449	6	653,748	7	25,199	6	120,196	7
Oklahoma	55,444	28	158,489	28	8,028	31	38,054	31
Oregon	43,688	33	148,384	31	12,326	20	54,077	22
Pennsylvania	164,345	7	672,767	6	22,761	9	130,861	6
Rhode Island	19,602	43	86,786	38	2,566	43	10,758	43
South Carolina	69,896	22	205,183	24	11,439	24	50,876	25
South Dakota	14,349	46	37,786	48	2,065	45	9,406	45
Tennessee	83,873	18	260,336	21	11,863	23	54,027	23
Texas	423,969	2	1,270,957	3	41,576	2	226,011	2
Utah	33,579	34	98,299	34	5,158	35	30,844	34
Vermont	16,425	44	46,354	45	1,436	49	7,883	47
Virginia	129,593	12	421,935	13	17,854	11	95,252	10
Washington	72,251	21	293,408	18	14,302	16	71,123	17
West Virginia	24,659	39	87,554	37	3,898	37	19,112	37
WISCONSIN	90,907	14	325,999	15	15,737	13	83,019	14
Wyoming	10,895	48	32,146	50	1,752	47	7,469	48
UNITED STATES	4,484,166		$16,313,673		625,652		$3,205,019	

*FTE – Full-time equivalent employees.

Source: U.S. Department of Commerce, Bureau of the Census, *State and Local Government Employment and Payroll, March 2003*, at: http://www.census.gov/govs/www/apesstl03.html [March 8, 2005]. Rank calculated by Wisconsin Legislative Reference Bureau.

STATE AND LOCAL EXPENDITURES FOR PUBLIC EDUCATION IN WISCONSIN
1999-2000 – 2003-04
(In Millions)

Agency/Program	1999-2000	2000-01	2001-02	2002-03	2003-04
Public elementary and secondary schools[1]	$7,535.4	$7,899.8	$8,349.0	$8,749.9	$9,187.4[4]
Department of Public Instruction	67.2	71.7	77.5	81.0	82.9
University of Wisconsin System	2,853.5	3,163.4	3,226.3	3,439.3	3,647.9
Higher Educational Aids Board	54.8	68.1	67.7	73.5	80.7
Medical College of Wisconsin, Inc. (state funding)	7.6	8.0	7.6	7.6	5.5
Public libraries (local expenditures)[2]	153.7	165.4	174.3	182.7	189.8
Wisconsin Technical College System Board	162.2	174.6	179.3	177.7	175.8
TEACH Wisconsin Initiative[3]	51.1	63.6	53.9	66.5	–––[5]
Educational Communications Board	14.5	14.9	14.4	14.4	13.2
State Historical Society	17.6	19.6	18.8	18.1	16.9
Arts Board (Department of Administration)	3.5	3.5	3.5	3.3	3.1
TOTAL	$10,921.0	$11,652.6	$12,172.3	$12,814.0	$12,998.4
Per capita expenditures based on total state population	$2,070	$2,172	$2,254	$2,350	$2,367

[1]Includes the gross costs of general operations, special projects, debt service, and food service; the net cost of capital projects; and the costs of CESA and County Children with Disabilities Education Board operations.

[2]Expenditures are for calendar year ending in the fiscal year shown. Total expenditures are reduced by amount of federal and state aid received because these amounts are reflected in DPI expenditures for the overlapping fiscal year.

[3]Educational technology program expenditures.

[4]Preliminary.

[5]The TEACH Wisconsin Initiative was moved to the Department of Administration by 2003 Wisconsin Act 33 (the executive budget) effective 8/10/03.

Sources: Wisconsin Department of Administration, *Annual Fiscal Report, Appendix (Budgetary Basis) 2002*, 2003 and previous issues; Wisconsin Department of Administration, Demographic Services Center, *Official Population Estimates, November 25, 2003* and previous issues; Wisconsin Legislative Fiscal Bureau, Informational Paper #27, *Elementary and Secondary School Aids*, January, 2005; Wisconsin Department of Public Instruction, Library Service Data, 2003; Wisconsin Department of Public Instruction, School Financial Services Team, departmental data, March 2005. Per capita data calculated by Wisconsin Legislative Reference Bureau.

EDUCATION EXPENDITURES
BY STATE AND LOCAL GOVERNMENTS
By State, Fiscal Year 2001-02
(In Millions)

State	Total Expenditures*	Higher Education	Local Schools
Alabama – State	$3,231	$2,720	---
Local	5,089	---	$5,089
Alaska – State	882	475	287
Local	1,225	13	1,212
Arizona – State	2,212	1,889	---
Local	6,584	814	5,770
Arkansas – State	1,832	1,438	---
Local	2,951	---	2,951
California – State	17,289	13,869	171
Local	59,538	6,506	53,032
Colorado – State	3,009	2,731	74
Local	6,002	126	5,876
Connecticut – State	2,218	1,555	326
Local	5,634	---	5,634
Delaware – State	733	629	---
Local	1,204	---	1,204
Florida – State	5,105	3,719	---
Local	20,690	2,073	18,617
Georgia – State	5,011	3,858	---
Local	12,355	33	12,322
Hawaii – State	2,257	792	1,442
Local	0+	---	0+
Idaho – State	704	604	---
Local	1,719	88	1,631
ILLINOIS – State	6,128	4,622	---
Local	19,825	1,884	17,940
Indiana – State	4,146	3,556	---
Local	8,046	58	7,988
IOWA – State	2,140	1,804	---
Local	4,328	524	3,804
Kansas – State	1,578	1,302	---
Local	3,923	469	3,454
Kentucky – State	2,981	2,403	---
Local	3,896	---	3,896
Louisiana – State	2,771	2,092	---
Local	5,223	---	5,223
Maine – State	699	559	11
Local	1,792	---	1,792
Maryland – State	3,414	2,796	3
Local	8,728	736	7,992
Massachusetts – State	3,188	2,515	7
Local	10,255	2	10,254
MICHIGAN – State	6,590	6,126	---
Local	17,155	1,170	15,985
MINNESOTA – State	3,496	2,947	---
Local	7,770	---	7,770
Mississippi – State	1,698	1,391	---
Local	3,403	450	2,953
Missouri – State	2,556	2,033	---
Local	8,000	612	7,388

State	Total Expenditures*	Higher Education	Local Schools
Montana – State	637	484	---
Local	1,155	22	1,132
Nebraska – State	1,116	990	---
Local	2,681	202	2,479
Nevada – State	904	810	---
Local	2,775	---	2,775
New Hampshire – State	630	561	---
Local	1,809	---	1,809
New Jersey – State	4,558	3,198	854
Local	15,985	830	15,155
New Mexico – State	1,468	1,261	---
Local	2,708	201	2,507
New York – State	7,619	6,163	---
Local	40,104	1,820	38,284
North Carolina – State	4,602	4,054	34
Local	10,660	1,093	9,566
North Dakota – State	563	510	---
Local	749	---	749
Ohio – State	6,515	5,220	---
Local	17,108	614	16,495
Oklahoma – State	2,520	2,228	1
Local	4,383	---	4,383
Oregon – State	2,040	1,842	---
Local	5,503	696	4,807
Pennsylvania – State	7,304	5,155	75
Local	16,992	615	16,377
Rhode Island – State	672	480	66
Local	1,509	---	1,509
South Carolina – State	2,763	2,130	140
Local	5,616	0+	5,616
South Dakota – State	377	320	---
Local	983	42	941
Tennessee – State	3,315	2,958	---
Local	6,152	---	6,152
Texas – State	11,558	9,955	453
Local	34,145	2,526	31,618
Utah – State	2,351	2,131	---
Local	2,845	---	2,845
Vermont – State	524	429	---
Local	937	---	937
Virginia – State	4,657	4,018	45
Local	10,492	136	10,356
Washington – State	4,825	3,982	150
Local	8,041	---	8,041
West Virginia – State	1,181	941	---
Local	2,338	59	2,279
WISCONSIN – State	3,197	2,808	---
Local	9,367	902	8,465
Wyoming – State	287	226	---
Local	991	134	857
U.S. TOTAL – State	$162,054	$131,282	$4,065
Local	$432,537	$25,529	$407,008

Note: State payments to local governments for education aids appear as local government expenditures.

*"Total expenditures" includes "other education" expenditures not reported separately. Figures may not add to total due to rounding.

Source: U.S. Department of Commerce, Bureau of the Census, "State and Local Government Finances by Level of Government and by State: 2001-02", at: http://www.census.gov/govs/www/estimate02.html [March 1, 2005].

STATE AND LOCAL PER CAPITA EDUCATION EXPENDITURES
By State, Fiscal Year 1999-2000

State	All Education Amount	All Education Rank	Elementary and Secondary Amount	Elementary and Secondary Rank	Higher Education Amount	Higher Education Rank	Other Education[1] Amount	Other Education[1] Rank
Alabama	$1,747	35[2]	$1,116	39	$534	21	$98	15[2]
Alaska	2,808	1	2,129	1	598	12	82	26
Arizona	1,534	46	997	47	481	30	56	40
Arkansas	1,570	45	975	49	464	32	131	4
California	1,876	22	1,273	21	532	22	71	33[2]
Colorado	1,838	24	1,205	28	584	15	48	48
Connecticut	1,974	12	1,532	4	351	46	91	20
Delaware	2,188	5	1,282	19	707	4	199	1
District of Columbia	1,695	---	1,554	---	141	---	---	---
Florida	1,428	50	1,052	44	317	50	59	39
Georgia	1,804	29	1,294	16	411	39	99	13[2]
Hawaii	1,530	47	945	50	569	16	16	50
Idaho	1,648	41	1,086	41	487	28	75	30
ILLINOIS	1,830	25	1,326	13	407	41	98	15[2]
Indiana	1,883	20	1,209	26[2]	595	14	79	28
IOWA	2,038	10	1,238	23	694	5	106	9
Kansas	1,817	27	1,146	36	620	9	51	45[2]
Kentucky	1,577	44	977	48	503	26	97	17
Louisiana	1,608	43	1,057	43	439	35	112	7
Maine	1,747	35[2]	1,310	14	363	45	74	31
Maryland	1,899	16	1,269	22	546	20	84	23[2]
Massachusetts	1,803	30	1,372	10	331	47	99	13[2]
MICHIGAN	2,262	3	1,519	6	689	6	54	41[2]
MINNESOTA	2,090	9	1,456	7	531	23[2]	103	11[2]
Mississippi	1,694	37	1,033	45	549	19	111	8
Missouri	1,649	40	1,157	32	408	40	84	23[2]
Montana	1,819	26	1,150	35	531	23[2]	138	3
Nebraska	1,909	15	1,209	26[2]	632	7	68	36[2]
Nevada	1,512	48	1,156	33[2]	329	48	27	49
New Hampshire	1,666	39	1,236	24	376	44	54	41[2]
New Jersey	2,233	4	1,766	2	414	38	52	44
New Mexico	2,032	11	1,173	31	774	1	85	22
New York	2,141	7	1,752	3	321	49	68	36[2]
North Carolina	1,760	33	1,130	38	558	18	71	33[2]
North Dakota	1,954	14	1,156	33[2]	718	3	80	27
Ohio	1,816	28	1,277	20	447	34	92	19
Oklahoma	1,691	38	1,105	40	516	25	70	35
Oregon	1,885	19	1,235	25	596	13	54	41[2]
Pennsylvania	1,894	18	1,332	12	416	37	146	2
Rhode Island	1,772	32	1,285	18	383	43	104	10
South Carolina	1,776	31	1,204	29	484	29	88	21
South Dakota	1,613	42	1,142	37	404	42	68	36[2]
Tennessee	1,471	49	1,002	46	418	36	51	45[2]
Texas	1,881	21	1,362	11	470	31	49	47
Utah	1,896	17	1,081	42	731	2	84	23[2]
Vermont	2,185	6	1,448	9	610	10	128	5
Virginia	1,855	23	1,287	17	495	27	73	32
Washington	1,962	13	1,301	15	566	17	96	18
West Virginia	1,754	34	1,188	30	463	33	103	11[2]
WISCONSIN	2,130	8	1,453	8	602	11	76	29
Wyoming	2,277	2	1,530	5	628	8	119	6
UNITED STATES	$1,854		$1,298		$477		$78	

[1]Includes state educational administration and services, tuition grants, fellowships, aid to private schools, and special programs.

[2]Tied.

Source: U.S. Department of Education, Office of Educational Research and Development, National Center for Education Statistics, *Digest of Education Statistics, 2003*, at: http://nces.ed.gov [January 2005]. Rank calculated by Wisconsin Legislative Reference Bureau.

EXPENDITURES PER PUPIL
By State and Source
1989-90, 1999-2000, 2000-01, and 2001-02

State	1989-90	1999-2000	2000-01	2001-02	2001-02 State Rank	Federal	State	Local
		Expenditures per Pupil				Revenue Sources for 2001-02 Pupil Expenditure		
Alabama	$3,327	$5,638	$5,885[1]	$6,029[1]	45	10.4%	58.7%	30.9%
Alaska	8,431	8,806	9,216	9,563	7	16.8	56.6	26.6
Arizona	4,053	4,999	5,278	5,964	47	10.3	49.7	40.0
Arkansas	3,485	5,277	5,568	6,276	41	10.7	55.5	33.7
California	4,391	6,314	6,987[1]	7,434[1]	24	9.3	59.4	31.3
Colorado	4,720	6,215	6,567	6,941	33	6.0	42.2	51.8
Connecticut	7,601	9,753	10,127	10,577	3	4.6	42.7	52.7
Delaware	5,694	8,310	8,958	9,284	8	8.6	64.3	27.1
District of Columbia	8,850	10,107	12,046	12,102	—	13.0	—	87.0
Florida	4,997	5,831	6,170	6,213	43	10.0	45.3	44.6
Georgia	4,187	6,437	6,929	7,380	25	7.2	49.2	43.7
Hawaii	4,448	6,530	6,596	7,306	28	9.1	89.1	1.9
Idaho	3,078	5,315	5,725	6,011	46	8.8	61.1	30.1
ILLINOIS	5,118	7,133	7,643	7,956	16	7.7	33.9	58.4
Indiana	4,549	7,192	7,630	7,734	21	6.1	50.9	43.1
IOWA	4,453	6,564	6,930	7,338	27	7.0	48.0	45.0
Kansas	4,752	6,294	6,925	7,339	26	7.9	57.8	34.3
Kentucky	3,675	5,921	6,079	6,523	38	10.5	59.6	29.8
Louisiana	3,855	5,804	6,037	6,567	37	12.5	49.2	38.3
Maine	5,373	7,667	8,232	8,818	9	8.2	44.2	47.7
Maryland	6,196	7,731	8,256	8,692	10	6.4	37.2	56.4
Massachusetts	6,237	8,761	9,509	10,232	4	5.5	43.2	51.4
MICHIGAN	5,546	8,110	8,278[1]	8,653[1]	11	7.3	64.6	28.1
MINNESOTA	4,971	7,190	7,645	7,736	20	5.5	61.4	33.1
Mississippi	3,094	5,014	5,175	5,354	49	15.0	54.1	30.9
Missouri	4,507	6,187	6,657	7,135[2]	29	7.6	36.3	56.2
Montana	4,736	6,314	6,726	7,062	30	13.2	47.9	38.9
Nebraska	4,842	6,683	7,223	7,741	19	7.8	35.5	56.6
Nevada	4,117	5,760	5,807	6,079	44	6.1	31.5	62.4
New Hampshire	5,304	6,860	7,286	7,935	17	4.7	51.8	43.4
New Jersey	7,983	10,337	11,248	11,793	1	4.2	42.9	52.9
New Mexico	3,515	5,825	6,313	6,882	34	14.2	72.0	13.8
New York	8,062	9,846	10,716	11,218	2	6.3	48.2	45.5
North Carolina	4,236	6,045	6,346	6,501	39	8.5	64.5	27.1
North Dakota	4,189	5,667	6,125	6,709	36	14.0	38.2	47.8
Ohio	5,045	7,065	7,571	8,069	15	5.9	45.6	48.5
Oklahoma	3,508	5,395	6,019	6,229	42	11.9	56.7	31.5
Oregon	5,474	7,149	7,528	7,642	22	8.3	55.9	35.7
Pennsylvania	6,228	7,772	8,210	8,537	14	7.0	37.8	55.2
Rhode Island	6,249	8,904	9,315	9,703	6	6.2	42.1	51.8
South Carolina	4,081	6,130	6,631	7,017	32	9.1	51.0	39.9
South Dakota	3,731	5,632	6,191	6,424	40	14.1	36.4	49.5
Tennessee	3,664	5,383	5,687[1]	5,959[1]	48	9.5	43.6	46.9
Texas	4,150	6,288	6,539	6,771	35	9.3	40.8	49.8
Utah	2,764	4,378	4,674	4,900	50	8.3	59.0	32.7
Vermont	6,227	8,323	9,153	9,806	5	6.3	69.5	24.2
Virginia	4,612	6,841	7,281	7,496	23	6.3	40.9	52.9
Washington	4,703	6,376	6,750[2]	7,039[2]	31	8.5	62.4	29.1
West Virginia	4,361	7,152	7,534	7,844	18	10.5	60.9	28.5
WISCONSIN	5,524	7,806	8,243	8,634	13	5.6	53.7	40.8
Wyoming	5,577	7,425	7,835	8,645	12	8.3	48.8	42.8
UNITED STATES	$4,962	$6,911	$7,376[1,2]	$7,734[1]		7.9%	49.3%	42.8%

[1]Prekindergarten students imputed, affecting total student count and per pupil expenditure calculation.

[2]Value affected by redistribution of reported expenditure values to correct for missing data items.

Source: U.S. National Center for Education Statistics, *National Public Education Financial Survey*, 2000-01 and 2001-02 at: http://nces.ed.gov/quicktables [January 2005]. Rank calculated by Wisconsin Legislative Reference Bureau. Detail may not add due to rounding.

WISCONSIN HOME-BASED PRIVATE EDUCATIONAL PROGRAMS
1994-95 to 2003-04 Enrollments

Grade Level	1994-95	1995-96	1996-97	1997-98	1998-99	1999-2000	2000-01	2001-02	2002-03	2003-04
1	1,020	1,127	1,237	1,342	1,372	1,424	1,481	1,524	1,473	1,403
2	1,024	1,125	1,244	1,334	1,404	1,450	1,377	1,446	1,489	1,377
3	1,010	1,121	1,200	1,275	1,414	1,428	1,453	1,414	1,514	1,522
4	1,028	1,148	1,222	1,279	1,297	1,446	1,410	1,496	1,408	1,453
5	911	1,084	1,184	1,266	1,292	1,382	1,468	1,395	1,503	1,427
6	908	1,011	1,138	1,274	1,331	1,421	1,396	1,549	1,452	1,457
7	949	1,112	1,123	1,290	1,609	1,445	1,438	1,423	1,528	1,487
8	968	1,062	1,161	1,229	1,335	1,496	1,487	1,466	1,511	1,512
9	1,019	1,215	1,299	1,475	1,482	1,589	1,683	1,710	1,532	1,488
10	1,055	1,309	1,397	1,604	1,596	1,726	1,678	1,792	1,729	1,616
11	921	1,216	1,279	1,419	1,564	1,681	1,637	1,699	1,657	1,592
12	571	638	799	881	1,016	1,150	1,188	1,154	1,245	1,241
Ungraded	1,096	1,371	1,519	1,791	1,791	2,199	2,686	2,945	3,247	3,459
TOTAL	12,480	14,539	15,802	17,459	18,503	19,837	20,382	21,013	21,288	21,034

Note: A home-based private educational program is a program of educational instruction provided to a child by a child's parent or guardian or by a person designated by the parent or guardian. These programs must provide at least 875 hours of instruction each school year and must offer a sequentially progressive curriculum of fundamental instruction in reading, language arts, mathematics, social studies, science, and health.

Source: Wisconsin Department of Public Instruction, "Home-Based Private Educational Program Enrollment Trends: 1984-85 through 2003-04, Enrollments by Grades and Totals" at: http://www.dpi.state.wi.us/dfm/sms/hbstats.html [January 18, 2005].

WISCONSIN CHARTER SCHOOL ENROLLMENT
By County and Race, September 2003

County*	Total Students Total	Female	Male	White	Black	Hispanic	Asian	American Indian
Barron	44	23	21	43	--	--	--	1
Bayfield	13	4	9	13	--	--	--	--
Brown	8	3	5	7	--	--	--	1
Clark	15	4	11	14	--	--	--	1
Columbia	71	34	37	70	--	--	--	1
Crawford	50	22	28	48	--	--	1	1
Dane	873	442	431	600	161	62	37	13
Dodge	120	45	75	114	--	6	--	--
Door	27	9	18	26	--	--	--	1
Douglas	8	2	6	7	--	1	--	--
Dunn	48	19	29	41	--	3	4	--
Eau Claire	371	87	284	317	7	7	32	8
Fond du Lac	24	6	18	22	1	1	--	--
Forest	34	15	19	14	--	--	--	20
Green	69	34	35	63	2	--	4	--
Green Lake	5	5	--	4	1	--	--	--
Iron	7	2	5	6	--	--	--	1
Jefferson	8	7	1	7	--	1	--	--
Juneau	26	11	15	25	--	--	--	1
Kenosha	410	224	186	332	22	38	15	3
Kewaunee	16	7	9	16	--	--	--	--
La Crosse	378	181	197	311	17	12	32	6
Lafayette	4	--	4	4	--	--	--	--
Manitowoc	4	2	2	4	--	--	--	--
Marathon	290	127	163	220	6	4	55	5
Milwaukee	12,834	6,225	6,609	2,252	7,677	2,443	345	117
Monroe	178	69	109	168	1	7	2	--
Oconto	40	19	21	38	--	1	1	--
Outagamie	1,207	571	636	1,105	23	22	39	18
Ozaukee	450	232	218	450	--	--	--	--
Pierce	119	41	78	107	3	2	4	3
Portage	1,263	609	654	1,032	15	45	169	2
Racine	1,495	753	742	909	377	197	10	2
Richland	17	8	9	16	--	--	--	--
Rock	109	59	50	94	9	2	4	--
Rusk	50	23	27	48	1	1	--	--
St. Croix	10	6	4	10	--	--	--	--
Sauk	17	5	12	16	--	--	--	1
Sawyer	34	14	20	14	--	--	--	20
Taylor	2	1	1	--	--	--	2	--
Vernon	22	12	10	22	--	--	--	--
Walworth	107	50	57	102	--	2	--	3
Waukesha	122	73	49	93	5	24	--	--
Waupaca	22	4	18	20	--	1	--	1
Winnebago	265	140	125	248	--	8	9	--
Wood	82	29	53	73	1	4	1	3
TOTAL	21,368	10,258	11,110	9,145	8,330	2,896	764	233

*A total of 134 charter schools operated in 46 counties under Section 118.40, Wisconsin Statutes.

Source: Wisconsin Department of Public Instruction, departmental data, September 2003.

WISCONSIN PUBLIC LIBRARY SYSTEMS, 2003

Library System	Resource Library	Address	Counties or Cities Served	2003 Total Service Population	2003 Circulation	State Aid for 2003 Fiscal Year
Arrowhead	Hedberg Public Library (608) 758-6600	316 S. Main Street Janesville 53545-3912	Rock	154,599	1,775,439	$449,504
Eastern Shores	Mead Public Library (920) 459-3400 Ext. 3414	710 N. 8th Street Sheboygan 53081-4563	Ozaukee, Sheboygan	199,014	2,289,826	553,829
Indianhead Federated	L.E. Phillips Memorial Public Library (715) 839-5001	400 Eau Claire Street Eau Claire 54701	Barron, Chippewa, Dunn, Eau Claire, Pepin, Pierce, Polk, Price, Rusk, St. Croix	430,636	4,174,110	1,269,052
Kenosha County	Kenosha Public Library (262) 564-6324	812 56th Street P.O. Box 1414 Kenosha 53141-1414	Kenosha	154,234	1,194,037	501,266
Lakeshores	Racine Public Library (262) 636-9248	75th Seventh Street Racine 53403-1200	Racine, Walworth	275,547	1,930,750	812,152
Manitowoc-Calumet	Manitowoc Public Library (920) 683-4863 Ext. 337	707 Quay Street Manitowoc 54220	Calumet, Manitowoc	115,340	1,215,482	472,880
Mid-Wisconsin Federated	West Bend Community Memorial Library (262) 335-5151	630 Poplar Street West Bend 53095-3246	Dodge, Jefferson, Washington, City of Whitewater	302,315	2,987,675	1,204,742
Milwaukee County Federated	Milwaukee Public Library (414) 286-3020	814 W. Wisconsin Avenue Milwaukee 53233-2385	Milwaukee	941,408	8,136,055	3,506,411
Nicolet Federated	Brown County Library (920) 448-4400 Ext. 351	515 Pine Street Green Bay 54301-5194	Brown, Door, Florence, Kewaunee, Marinette, Menominee, Oconto, Shawano	418,441	3,525,981	1,043,702
Northern Waters Library Service	Superior Public Library (715) 394-8860	1530 Tower Avenue Superior 54880-2563	Ashland, Bayfield, Burnett, Douglas, Iron, Sawyer, Vilas, Washburn	153,903	1,188,338	557,078
Outagamie Waupaca	Appleton Public Library (920) 832-6170	225 N. Oneida Street Appleton 54911	Outagamie, Waupaca	230,601	2,535,402	577,590
South Central	Madison Public Library (608) 266-6363	201 W. Mifflin Street Madison 53703	Adams, Columbia, Dane, Green, Portage, Sauk, Wood	758,237	10,435,250	1,921,499
Southwest Wisconsin	Platteville Public Library (608) 348-7441	65 S. Elm Street Platteville 53818-3139	Crawford, Grant, Iowa, Lafayette, Richland	125,418	847,495	349,967
Waukesha County Federated	Waukesha Public Library (262) 524-3681	321 Wisconsin Avenue Waukesha 53186-4786	Waukesha	371,242	4,413,469	906,506
Winding Rivers	La Crosse Public Library (608) 789-7123	800 Main Street La Crosse 54601-4122	Buffalo, Jackson, Juneau, La Crosse, Monroe, Trempealeau, Vernon	265,838	2,190,383	749,499
Winnefox	Oshkosh Public Library (920) 236-5210	106 Washington Avenue Oshkosh 54901-4985	Fond du Lac, Green Lake, Marquette, Waushara, Winnebago	315,013	3,708,118	1,113,082
Wisconsin Valley Library Service	Marathon County Public Library (715) 261-7211	300 N. First Street Wausau 54403-5405	Clark, Forest, Langlade, Lincoln, Marathon, Oneida, Taylor	278,932	2,175,918	960,315
TOTAL				5,490,718	54,723,728	$16,949,074

Sources: Wisconsin Department of Public Instruction, Public Library Statistics, "Statistics at the State and System Level, 2003: 2003 Wisconsin Public Library Service Data: State Totals" at:
http://www.dpi.state.wi.us/dpi/dltcl/pld/lib_stat.html, and *Wisconsin Public Library Directory, 2004*, August 2004.

HIGHLIGHTS OF EMPLOYMENT AND INCOME IN WISCONSIN

Labor Force — An average of about 2,919,200 workers were employed in Wisconsin in 2004. Another 152,000 were part of the available work force but were unemployed, resulting in an average unemployment rate of 4.9% for 2004. Since 1970, Wisconsin's labor force has increased by over 1.1 million workers from 1,941,700 to 3,071,200 in 2004. Based on January figures, the state's highest unemployment rate for that period occurred in 1983 when it reached 11.7%.

Employment by Industry — An average of 2.8 million Wisconsin workers were engaged in nonfarm employment in 2004. The greatest number worked in service enterprises (almost 2.2 million); trade, transportation, and utilities (539,500); and manufacturing (501,800).

Nationally, 129.9 million were employed in nonfarm work in 2003. Trade, transportations, and utilities, with 25.3 million workers; and government, with 21.6 million, were the largest segments.

In March 2002, manufacturing and retail trade together accounted for more than one-third of the number of employees in Wisconsin. The vast majority (85%) of the more than 142,000 business establishments in the state had fewer than 20 employees in March 2002. Manufacturing accounted for the greatest number of large-sized firms, 409 out of 1,104 establishments with 250 or more employees.

Income by Industry — Earned income, which consists of wages and salaries, labor income, and proprietor's income, totaled $136.3 billion in Wisconsin in 2004. In 2004, service industries provided the greatest percentage of Wisconsin's earned income, about 28.6%, with manufacturing at 22.7%. Government (all levels) and government enterprises were a distant third at 14.4%. Nonetheless, Wisconsin ranks third nationally in percentage of earned income from manufacturing, behind Indiana and Michigan.

Personal Income — Personal income in Wisconsin totaled $177.2 billion in 2004. Wisconsin's per capita personal income of $32,157 lags behind the national average of $32,937, ranking Wisconsin 22nd among the states. Connecticut had the highest per capita personal income ($45,398 in 2004, or about 138% of the national average). Mississippi had the lowest per capita personal income in 2004 at $24,650, about 75% of the national average.

Wisconsin's total adjusted gross income (total income reported for tax purposes) in 2003 was about $115.4 billion, or $21,020 per capita. Per capita income increased 4.5% over four years from $20,116 in 1999 to $21,020 in 2003. Ozaukee County had the highest per capita AGI in 2003 with $36,196, followed by Waukesha County with $31,411. Eau Claire County is third ($31,021), and Dane County is fourth ($25,233). Rusk County ($12,518), Forest County ($11,351), and Menominee County ($4,180) had the lowest per capita adjusted gross incomes.

Unemployment Benefits — In an average month in 2004, Wisconsin reported that 78,800 persons (about 51% of the 153,500 unemployed) received unemployment compensation. Nationally, almost 3 million workers, or 36.8% of those unemployed, received benefits during an average month. The average weekly benefit in Wisconsin was $251, less than the national average of $263. The highest average weekly benefit of $351 was paid in Massachusetts, followed by New Jersey ($331), Rhode Island ($324), and Hawaii ($323). Lowest in the nation were Mississippi ($172), Alabama ($177), Arizona ($177), and Alaska ($194).

The following tables present selected data. Consult footnoted sources for more detailed information about employment and income.

EMPLOYMENT IN WISCONSIN, BY INDUSTRY
Annual Average, 2000 – 2004
(In Thousands)

	2000	2001	2002	2003	2004
Civilian Labor Force	2,992.3	3,032.1	3,037.9	3,068.7	3,071.2
Unemployed	101.0	133.2	160.9	172.1	152.0
Percentage of labor force unemployed	3.4%	4.4%	5.3%	5.6%	4.9%
Employed	2,891.2	2,898.9	2,877.0	2,896.7	2,919.2
Total nonfarm	2,833.8	2,813.9	2,782.4	2,775.3	2,803.2
Goods producing	723.0	689.5	656.2	631.9	631.8
Manufacturing	594.1	560.3	528.3	504.0	501.8
Construction	124.8	125.4	124.1	124.1	126.3
Natural resources and mining	4.0	3.9	3.8	3.8	3.8
Service producing	2,110.8	2,124.3	2,126.1	2,143.4	2,171.4
Trade, transportation, and utilities	552.9	547.7	536.7	536.3	539.5
Educational and health services	339.6	349.6	357.2	364.6	376.3
Local government	275.0	283.0	285.2	282.8	281.2
Professional and business services	247.0	238.5	239.8	244.3	250.9
Leisure and hospitality	236.7	238.6	240.4	245.5	249.9
Financial activities	149.1	151.8	153.8	156.9	157.6
Other services, except public services	126.3	131.3	132.2	132.7	135.1
State government	97.9	100.7	99.7	100.2	101.4
Information	53.6	53.3	51.2	50.3	49.9
Federal government	32.6	30.1	29.9	29.8	29.5

Note: Industry classifications in this table are defined by the North American Industry Classification System (NAICS), and are not directly comparable to the Standard Industrial Classification (SIC) codes used previously.

Sources: Wisconsin Department of Workforce Development, Bureau of Workforce Information, Labor Market Information, "Local Area Unemployment Statistics (LAUS) Program Data, 2000-2004", at: http://worknet.wisconsin.gov/worknet/dalaus.aspx?menuselection=da [March 28, 2005], and "Current Employment Statistics (CES) Program Data, 2004 and previous years", at: http://worknet.wisconsin.gov/worknet/daces.aspx?menuselection=da [March 28, 2005].

MANUFACTURING EMPLOYMENT IN WISCONSIN
By Industry Group, 1999 – 2003

Industry Group	Number of Employees for week including March 12				
	1999	2000	2001	2002	2003
Machinery	85,462	83,401	77,784	67,314	61,301
Fabricated metal products	77,130	76,075	72,537	66,302	61,620
Food	58,198	60,872	60,833	62,140	58,103
Transportation equipment	43,498	44,050	40,601	34,498	37,022
Paper	43,319	42,378	38,865	37,436	35,406
Printing and related support activities	40,418	38,662	38,231	35,057	35,041
Plastics and rubber products	35,676	36,887	35,480	30,297	29,751
Electrical equipment, appliances, and components	32,487	32,509	30,028	26,701	27,043
Wood products	29,318	29,858	29,024	28,714	29,230
Primary metal industries	26,142	26,440	24,511	22,229	22,323
Computer and electronic products	25,504	24,210	22,931	20,516	16,234
Furniture and related products	17,851	18,393	18,321	17,036	15,796
Miscellaneous manufacturing	19,295	19,173	17,742	16,697	20,199
Chemicals	13,082	14,353	13,806	13,147	12,150
Nonmetallic mineral products	10,666	10,623	10,006	9,971	10,346
Leather and allied products	4,475	3,850	2,957	2,176	2,117
Beverage and tobacco products	2,893	2,528	2,497	---[1]	2,873
Apparel	2,829	2,505	2,382	---[2]	1,318
Textile products	2,310	2,505	2,359	2,057	1,810
Textile mills	2,385	2,376	2,214	2,202	1,694
Petroleum and coal products	415	412	422	---[3]	---[4]
TOTAL	573,353	572,060	543,531	499,518	481,862

Note: Some industries have reported number of employees as an employment-size class rather than a specific number.
[1]2,500 to 4,999 employment-size class.
[2]1,000 to 2,499 employment-size class.
[3]250 to 499 employment-size class.
[4]Industries with fewer than 950 employees not reported in 2003.
Source: U.S. Census Bureau, *2002 County Business Patterns – Wisconsin*, November 2004, and prior years; U.S. Census Bureau, *2003 Annual Survey of Manufactures, Geographic Area Statistics*, May 2005.

EMPLOYMENT TRENDS IN WISCONSIN
January 1990 – January 2005
(In Thousands)

Month and Year	Civilian Labor Force*	Employed	Unemployed	Unemployment Rate	Total Nonfarm Employment	Service Providing	Goods Producing	Manufacturing	Trade, Transportation, and Utilities
Jan. 1990	2,567.2	2,437.8	129.4	5.0	2,206.7	1,615.2	591.5	513.7	448.0
Jan. 1991	2,592.1	2,441.7	150.4	5.8	2,232.9	1,650.1	582.8	505.9	454.4
Jan. 1992	2,621.2	2,476.4	144.8	5.5	2,269.0	1,684.2	584.8	504.0	456.2
Jan. 1993	2,677.2	2,536.6	140.7	5.3	2,324.9	1,726.8	598.1	513.5	459.8
Jan. 1994	2,777.1	2,630.0	147.1	5.3	2,383.8	1,772.9	610.9	523.1	473.4
Jan. 1995	2,830.6	2,711.3	119.3	4.2	2,476.9	1,828.9	648.0	556.5	489.7
Jan. 1996	2,862.5	2,736.8	125.7	4.4	2,523.8	1,873.7	650.1	555.9	500.2
Jan. 1997	2,909.8	2,785.2	124.6	4.3	2,559.9	1,900.6	659.3	559.9	504.2
Jan. 1998	2,937.8	2,825.9	111.9	3.8	2,625.2	1,941.6	683.6	583.2	512.5
Jan. 1999	2,951.4	2,839.3	112.1	3.8	2,686.4	1,993.0	693.4	586.5	526.7
Jan. 2000	2,960.9	2,856.6	104.3	3.5	2,748.9	2,047.6	701.3	590.2	541.4
Jan. 2001	3,003.3	2,877.0	126.2	4.2	2,770.7	2,081.2	689.5	577.0	549.2
Jan. 2002	3,009.8	2,832.0	177.8	5.9	2,719.4	2,075.9	643.5	531.6	533.0
Jan. 2003	3,038.7	2,851.4	187.3	6.2	2,721.3	2,092.2	629.1	520.6	529.4
Jan. 2004	3,050.4	2,871.9	178.5	5.9	2,718.1	2,111.1	607.0	493.5	529.5
Feb. 2004	3,060.4	2,872.4	188.0	6.1	2,727.3	2,123.9	603.4	492.6	522.5
Mar. 2004	3,060.2	2,869.5	190.7	6.2	2,744.3	2,135.6	608.7	494.5	524.7
Apr. 2004	3,046.0	2,887.9	158.1	5.2	2,783.7	2,160.5	623.2	497.3	529.4
May 2004	3,049.6	2,902.9	146.7	4.8	2,817.5	2,183.5	634.0	500.4	537.4
June 2004	3,117.2	2,956.0	161.2	5.2	2,848.0	2,201.9	646.1	506.6	543.6
July 2004	3,115.6	2,965.1	150.6	4.8	2,824.2	2,172.4	651.8	508.7	539.9
Aug. 2004	3,093.0	2,952.4	140.5	4.5	2,832.7	2,177.4	655.3	512.1	543.2
Sept. 2004	3,060.0	2,935.2	124.8	4.1	2,833.6	2,188.7	644.9	506.5	542.8
Oct. 2004	3,068.0	2,944.3	123.7	4.0	2,843.3	2,201.0	642.3	504.3	546.7
Nov. 2004	3,069.9	2,941.4	128.5	4.2	2,843.6	2,205.8	637.8	503.6	557.5
Dec. 2004	3,063.9	2,931.4	132.4	4.3	2,822.4	2,194.8	627.6	501.1	557.1
Jan. 2005	3,047.4	2,882.8	164.5	5.4	2,749.7	2,138.6	611.1	496.3	533.3

Note: Data are estimates that are revised monthly and annually and are seasonally unadjusted. Industry classifications in this table are defined by the North American Industrial Classification System (NAICS), and are not directly comparable to the Standard Industrial Classification (SIC) codes used previously.

*Civilian labor force includes both employed and unemployed persons, age 16 and over, and excludes current military personnel and other institutionalized individuals.

Sources: Wisconsin Department of Workforce Development, Wisconsin Worknet, "Current Employment Statistics (CES)" 1998-2004 monthly reports at: http://worknet.wisconsin.gov/worknet/downloads.aspx?menuselection=da&pgm=CES [March 25, 2005] and Wisconsin Department of Workforce Development, Wisconsin Worknet, "Local Area Unemployment Statistics (LAUS)" 1998-2004 reports at: http://worknet.wisconsin.gov/worknet/dalaus.aspx?menuselection=da [March 25, 2005].

WISCONSIN PERSONAL EARNED INCOME
By Source, 2001 – 2003, (In Millions)

Industry	2001	2002	2003
Services*	$32,864	$34,743	$36,634
Manufacturing	28,312	28,705	29,567
Government and government enterprises	17,171	17,924	18,881
Retail trade	8,215	8,589	8,727
Real estate, rental, and leasing	1,555	1,606	1,792
Finance and insurance	7,419	7,864	8,430
Construction	7,518	7,647	7,984
Utilities	976	1,000	1,034
Transportation and warehousing	4,382	4,418	4,578
Wholesale trade	6,094	6,339	6,492
Agricultural services, forestry, and fishing	409	425	430
Farm earnings	923	805	1,119
Mining	212	213	222
TOTAL	$116,050	$120,278	$125,890

Note: Industry classifications in this table are defined by the North American Industry Classification System (NAICS), and are not directly comparable to the Standard Industrial Classification (SIC) codes used previously.

*Services includes the following NAICS classification categories: Professional and technical services; Management of companies and enterprises; Administrative and waste services; Educational services; Health care and social assistance; Arts, entertainment, and recreation; Accommodation and food services; and Other services except public administration.

Source: U.S. Department of Commerce, Bureau of Economic Analysis, Income and employment tables by NAICS industry, 2001-2003, Table SA05N: *Personal Income by Major Source and Earnings by Industry – Wisconsin*, at: http://www.bea.doc/bea/regional/spi/default.cfm [March 28, 2005].

DISTRIBUTION OF WISCONSIN BUSINESS ESTABLISHMENTS
By Number of Employees and Establishments, March 2002

Industry[1]	Total Employees[2]	Number of Establishments by Employment Size						
		Total	1 to 19	20 to 49	50 to 99	100 to 249	250 to 499	500 or more
Forestry, fishing, hunting and agricultural support	3,411	621	601	12	3	4	0	1
Mining	2,298	168	137	23	3	5	0	0
Utilities	16,262	294	182	51	24	24	8	5
Construction	117,141	16,368	15,278	799	191	69	21	10
Manufacturing	499,518	9,771	6,060	1,651	922	729	257	152
Food, beverage, and tobacco products[3]	62,140	1,031	566	203	114	88	39	21
Textiles, textile products, apparel and leather and allied products[4]	6,435	338	250	51	17	14	5	1
Wood products	28,714	659	422	118	61	40	9	9
Paper	37,436	249	66	44	50	46	26	17
Printing and related support activities	35,057	969	710	123	63	49	13	11
Chemicals	13,147	322	189	74	35	17	2	5
Plastics and rubber products	30,297	465	189	114	79	54	26	3
Nonmetallic mineral products	9,971	380	280	66	16	10	6	2
Primary metal	22,229	218	90	37	27	42	13	9
Fabricated metal products	66,302	1,988	1,318	357	147	135	20	11
Machinery	67,314	1,187	690	210	146	88	32	21
Computer and electronic products	20,516	299	148	56	42	37	11	5
Electrical equipment, appliances, and components	26,701	198	86	29	22	24	22	15
Transportation equipment	34,498	275	157	30	24	28	20	16
Furniture and related products	17,036	564	428	66	36	24	8	2
Miscellaneous manufacturing	16,697	609	457	69	42	32	5	4
Wholesale trade	117,202	7,801	6,475	879	263	138	34	12
Durable goods	69,643	5,297	4,460	595	151	70	17	4
Nondurable goods	47,559	2,504	2,015	284	112	68	17	8
Retail trade	309,173	21,366	18,209	1,927	660	503	60	7
Motor vehicles and parts	40,402	2,702	2,187	312	155	45	2	1
Furniture and home furnishings	10,241	1,225	1,115	92	13	5	0	0
Electronics and appliances	8,657	893	822	40	12	18	1	0
Building materials and garden supplies	31,362	2,299	1,925	255	58	61	0	0
Food and beverages	57,799	2,366	1,737	259	206	153	11	0
Health and personal care	16,936	1,382	1,083	256	39	4	0	0
Gasoline stations	22,795	2,551	2,403	133	11	4	0	0
Clothing and clothing accessories	19,803	2,324	2,129	162	30	3	0	0
Sporting goods, hobbies, books and music	12,837	1,440	1,299	109	26	6	0	0
General merchandise	54,316	706	321	61	86	194	43	1
Miscellaneous retail	16,524	2,513	2,322	180	11	0	0	0
Nonstore retailers (including online)	17,501	965	866	68	13	10	3	5
Transportation and warehousing	77,746	5,288	4,488	527	168	81	14	10
Information	49,517	2,065	1,575	275	121	61	24	9
Publishing	17,001	611	459	82	38	20	9	3
Broadcasting and telecommunications	20,095	904	691	116	55	30	10	2
Information and data processing	8,681	283	221	30	16	7	5	4
Finance and insurance	136,673	8,822	7,871	616	183	91	28	33
Real estate and rental and leasing	27,368	4,743	4,516	166	42	15	4	0
Professional, scientific, and technical services	90,826	11,278	10,369	636	170	84	15	4
Management of companies and enterprises	57,989	883	571	123	76	55	37	21
Administrative support and waste management	111,379	6,229	5,123	579	290	169	53	15
Educational services	45,069	1,310	952	234	60	44	4	16
Health care and social services	331,180	13,332	11,065	1,236	427	405	106	93
Ambulatory health care	109,194	7,580	6,676	569	181	101	30	23
Hospitals	99,034	163	12	0	10	48	36	57
Nursing and residential care	69,728	2,157	1,568	229	141	185	25	9
Social assistance	53,224	3,432	2,809	438	95	71	15	4
Arts, entertainment, and recreation	33,143	2,458	2,080	252	66	51	7	2
Accomodations and food services	198,215	13,229	9,891	2,553	678	95	8	4
Accomodations	25,582	1,553	1,227	223	60	33	6	4
Food services and drinking places	172,633	11,676	8,664	2,330	618	62	2	0
Other services (except public administration)	115,101	15,365	14,362	765	158	63	14	3
Repair and maintenance	25,077	4,647	4,476	139	22	9	1	0
Personal and laundry services	26,377	4,238	4,077	120	26	14	1	0
Religious, grantmaking, civic, professional, and like organizations	63,647	6,480	5,809	506	110	40	12	3
Auxiliaries[5]	16,366	273	158	55	25	22	3	10
Unclassified establishments	239	422	422	0	0	0	0	0
TOTAL	2,355,816	142,086	120,385	13,359	4,530	2,708	697	407

[1] Industry categories and the total include subcategories not reported separately.

[2] Number of employees for the week including March 12, 2002. Excludes most government and railroad employees and self-employed persons.

[3] Beverage and tobacco product manufacturers report number of employees using employment-size class of 2,500 to 4,999, which is not included in industry group total.

[4] Apparel manufacturers report number of employees using employment-size class of 1,000 to 2,499, which is not included in industry group total.

[5] Auxiliaries primarily provide support services for enterprises that have multiple establishments under common ownership. Does not include corporate, subsidiary and regional management, which are listed separately under "Management of companies and enterprises".

Source: U.S. Census Bureau, *2002 County Business Patterns – Wisconsin*, November 2004.

EMPLOYEES IN NONAGRICULTURAL
(In

State	Total[1]	Construction	Manufacturing	Trade, Transportation, and Utilities	Information	Finance, Insurance, and Real Estate
Alabama	1,875	99	294	371	32	97
Alaska	300	17	12	61	7	14
Arizona	2,289	177	174	445	49	159
Arkansas	1,144	51	206	240	20	50
California	14,410	789	1,545	2,722	471	887
Colorado	2,150	150	156	404	85	154
Connecticut	1,643	61	200	305	40	143
Delaware	414	24	36	78	7	46
Florida	7,286	446	389	1,462	172	484
Georgia	3,860	195	452	823	127	217
Hawaii	567	28	15	108	10	28
Idaho	572	37	62	116	9	27
ILLINOIS	5,818	277	718	1,187	135	403
Indiana	2,897	145	573	573	41	141
IOWA	1,440	65	220	303	34	95
Kansas	1,312	63	172	262	47	70
Kentucky	1,783	83	266	371	30	86
Louisiana	1,906	119	156	381	29	101
Maine	606	30	64	123	11	35
Maryland	2,483	168	148	462	50	156
Massachusetts	3,186	137	326	573	92	224
MICHIGAN	4,412	190	727	815	71	219
MINNESOTA	2,651	125	344	522	63	176
Mississippi	1,117	51	178	219	15	46
Missouri	2,676	134	313	533	67	163
Montana	400	23	19	84	8	20
Nebraska	904	46	102	194	22	62
Nevada	1,087	100	44	195	16	59
New Hampshire	617	29	80	139	12	37
New Jersey	3,980	159	352	878	102	277
New Mexico	776	47	36	136	16	34
New York	8,404	319	615	1,473	277	697
North Carolina	3,803	212	604	721	76	192
North Dakota	333	16	23	72	8	18
Ohio	5,391	230	844	1,045	97	312
Oklahoma	1,451	63	143	277	32	83
Oregon	1,562	77	196	314	34	98
Pennsylvania	5,602	245	716	1,115	123	338
Rhode Island	484	21	59	81	11	34
South Carolina	1,813	112	277	347	27	91
South Dakota	378	19	38	77	7	28
Tennessee	2,668	116	414	580	52	139
Texas	9,373	551	901	1,928	235	585
Utah	1,074	67	112	214	30	65
Vermont	299	15	38	58	7	13
Virginia	3,500	218	305	635	101	187
Washington	2,659	156	267	510	92	153
West Virginia	726	33	65	135	13	31
WISCONSIN	2,779	124	506	538	50	158
Wyoming	250	20	9	48	4	10
UNITED STATES[2]	129,931	6,722	14,525	25,275	3,198	7,974

[1]Includes mining, not shown separately. Mining is included with construction for Delaware and Hawaii.

[2]State totals do not sum to U.S. totals because of differing methodologies.

Source: U.S. Department of Commerce, Bureau of the Census, *Statistical Abstract of the United States: 2004-2005*, October 2004.

ESTABLISHMENTS, BY STATE – 2003
Thousands)

Professional and Business Services	Education and Health Services	Leisure and Hospitality	Other Services	Government	State
186	187	154	84	359	.... Alabama
23	33	30	11	82	.... Alaska
320	246	232	86	394	.... Arizona
103	140	88	41	198	.... Arkansas
2,108	1,536	1,398	506	2,427	.... California
287	214	246	86	357	.... Colorado
196	263	125	62	246	.... Connecticut
59	50	38	18	57	.... Delaware
1,258	886	809	318	1,056	.... Florida
494	387	350	172	633	.... Georgia
70	65	100	24	119	.... Hawaii
70	63	54	18	113	.... Idaho
766	718	499	251	856	.... ILLINOIS
255	362	273	106	423	.... Indiana
105	190	126	56	245	.... IOWA
124	157	109	53	250	.... Kansas
154	228	157	77	312	.... Kentucky
179	245	198	71	380	.... Louisiana
51	107	58	21	104	.... Maine
361	339	219	116	463	.... Maryland
437	575	288	117	417	.... Massachusetts
587	544	398	171	681	.... MICHIGAN
295	367	233	119	402	.... MINNESOTA
79	115	123	37	244	.... Mississippi
304	352	262	118	428	.... Missouri
33	53	52	16	86	.... Montana
91	113	78	35	160	.... Nebraska
121	76	304	30	135	.... Nevada
54	93	62	20	90	.... New Hampshire
574	539	321	152	624	.... New Jersey
89	99	81	29	195	.... New Mexico
1,041	1,496	645	349	1,486	.... New York
421	428	335	162	645	.... North Carolina
24	48	30	15	76	.... North Dakota
607	727	488	227	802	.... Ohio
156	175	126	74	292	.... Oklahoma
170	188	151	57	268	.... Oregon
598	978	469	260	743	.... Pennsylvania
49	91	49	23	67	.... Rhode Island
187	178	194	65	329	.... South Carolina
24	55	40	16	74	.... South Dakota
287	313	247	103	412	.... Tennessee
1,044	1,119	858	358	1,648	.... Texas
132	118	100	33	197	.... Utah
20	52	33	10	52	.... Vermont
549	369	307	181	639	.... Virginia
292	312	248	99	521	.... Washington
56	108	66	55	142	.... West Virginia
245	367	245	131	412	.... **WISCONSIN**
16	21	31	10	64	.... Wyoming
15,997	16,577	12,125	5,393	21,575	.... UNITED STATES[2]

UNEMPLOYMENT, UNEMPLOYMENT RATES, AND UNEMPLOYMENT INSURANCE BENEFITS
By State, 2004

| | | Unemployment | | | Unemployment Insurance Benefits | |
| | | Persons (in thousands) | | Insured as | Average | Total Paid |
State	Rate[1]	Total	Insured[2]	% of Total[3]	Weekly	(in thousands)
Alabama	5.6%	122.1	32.2	26.4%	$176.64	$246,257
Alaska	7.5	25.3	13.7	54.2	193.71	130,380
Arizona	5.0	131.6	38.4	29.2	176.95	274,244
Arkansas	5.7	73.2	30.1	41.1	228.16	256,934
California	6.2	1,079.6	434.0	40.2	260.27	4,999,608
Colorado	5.5	128.4	32.0	24.9	298.04	382,888
Connecticut	4.9	83.5	44.0	52.7	284.04	602,708
Delaware	4.1	16.2	9.2	56.8	246.63	109,130
District of Columbia	8.2	23.0	5.9	25.7	257.35	86,414
Florida	4.8	386.2	111.6	28.9	223.15	1,014,086
Georgia	4.6	180.0	59.5	33.1	242.02	586,537
Hawaii	3.3	21.1	8.5	40.3	323.32	114,767
Idaho	4.7	33.7	15.8	46.9	229.00	144,351
ILLINOIS	6.2	390.4	157.2	40.3	279.12	2,066,127
Indiana	5.2	163.2	56.9	34.9	266.88	651,022
IOWA	4.8	71.6	26.8	37.4	261.08	312,493
Kansas	5.5	69.4	24.0	34.6	271.76	294,451
Kentucky	5.3	102.2	34.4	33.7	257.38	415,986
Louisiana	5.7	117.5	34.6	29.4	194.78	280,286
Maine	4.6	31.7	11.5	36.3	235.33	115,692
Maryland	4.2	119.1	41.3	34.7	253.70	430,777
Massachusetts	5.1	171.9	93.7	54.5	351.35	1,509,933
MICHIGAN	7.1	341.8	145.6	42.6	289.15	1,895,894
MINNESOTA	4.7	132.8	50.2	37.8	317.67	700,551
Mississippi	6.2	75.6	22.7	30.0	171.87	153,128
Missouri	5.7	161.1	60.1	37.3	205.05	515,176
Montana	4.4	21.7	8.7	40.1	197.32	67,388
Nebraska	3.8	35.6	13.0	36.5	219.51	117,741
Nevada	4.3	48.8	22.8	46.7	244.83	238,912
New Hampshire	3.8	27.3	7.5	27.5	250.69	78,560
New Jersey	4.8	216.5	124.9	57.7	330.90	1,976,635
New Mexico	5.7	49.3	13.9	28.2	220.41	125,412
New York	5.8	544.0	206.5	38.0	270.53	2,466,994
North Carolina	5.5	221.7	84.6	38.2	255.66	909,178
North Dakota	3.4	11.1	3.8	34.2	226.39	36,177
Ohio	6.1	354.5	111.0	31.3	251.97	1,216,934
Oklahoma	4.8	78.7	22.5	28.6	218.55	207,177
Oregon	7.4	132.1	53.6	40.6	251.61	586,651
Pennsylvania	5.5	337.1	186.0	55.2	293.61	2,330,993
Rhode Island	5.2	29.7	13.5	45.5	324.34	201,528
South Carolina	6.8	134.2	41.4	30.8	210.66	348,103
South Dakota	3.5	13.8	3.2	23.2	205.31	25,713
Tennessee	5.4	144.9	47.7	32.9	209.26	465,971
Texas	6.1	642.9	159.0	24.7	259.34	1,712,777
Utah	5.2	56.6	14.1	24.9	265.71	154,217
Vermont	3.7	12.3	6.6	53.7	256.36	80,556
Virginia	3.7	132.5	37.7	28.5	240.28	376,194
Washington	6.2	193.8	78.6	40.6	309.76	1,064,300
West Virginia	5.3	41.6	15.7	37.7	219.07	141,667
WISCONSIN	4.9	153.5	78.8	51.3	250.67	851,618
Wyoming	3.9	10.2	3.5	34.3	238.36	40,696
UNITED STATES[4]	5.5%	8,149.0	2,995.3	36.8%	$262.50	$34,307,856

Note: Unemployment and unemployment insurance data include Puerto Rico and U.S. Virgin Islands, not listed separately.

[1]Total unemployed as a percentage of civilian workforce in the state.

[2]Insured unemployed are unemployed persons receiving unemployment benefits.

[3]Percentage calculated by Wisconsin Legislative Reference Bureau.

[4]Because of separate processing and weighting procedures, U.S. totals may differ from the sum of state data.

Sources: U.S. Department of Labor, Employment and Training Administration, "State Financial Data – 4th Quarter 2004", at: http://workforcesecurity.doleta.gov/unemploy/content/data_stats/datasum04/4thqtr/finance.asp [May 19, 2005], and "State Benefits Data – 4th Quarter 2004", at: http://workforcesecurity.doleta.gov/unemploy/content/data_stats/datasum04/4thqtr/benefits.asp [May 18, 2005]; U.S. Department of Labor, Bureau of Labor Statistics, "2004 Local Area Unemployment Statistics", at: http://www.bls.gov/lau/lastrk04.htm [March 10, 2005].

WISCONSIN ADJUSTED GROSS INCOME
By County, 1999 – 2003

County	2003 AGI[1]	Per Capita AGI					2003 Rank
		1999	2000	2001	2002	2003	
Adams	$256,312,113	$12,179	$13,170	$12,192	$12,088	$12,532	69
Ashland	219,611,391	12,187	12,667	12,969	12,661	12,980	68
Barron	735,334,916	15,359	15,823	15,995	16,047	16,026	45
Bayfield	237,459,005	14,481	15,061	14,942	14,895	15,436	48
Brown	5,141,736,321	21,512	22,545	21,841	21,959	21,911	8
Buffalo	219,083,609	14,446	14,974	15,014	14,787	15,677	46
Burnett	228,471,964	13,097	14,550	13,243	12,943	14,164	59
Calumet	930,354,929	20,078	21,217	20,713	20,663	21,333	9
Chippewa	955,038,942	15,461	16,178	16,555	16,372	16,650	40
Clark	442,712,605	12,949	12,864	13,057	13,279	13,033	67
Columbia	1,088,515,822	19,195	20,072	19,292	19,567	20,209	15
Crawford	232,957,652	13,018	13,420	12,666	13,014	13,385	65
Dane	11,235,241,397	23,713	25,136	24,750	24,395	25,233	4
Dodge	1,571,628,187	17,294	18,344	18,075	17,907	17,941	30
Door	551,343,995	19,648	20,367	19,116	18,508	19,131	24
Douglas	702,378,919	14,343	15,217	15,509	15,370	16,119	43
Dunn	624,238,772	14,081	15,161	14,954	14,798	15,110	49
Eau Claire	2,975,034,549	17,288	18,408	18,065	17,344	31,021	3
Florence	74,302,611	12,774	13,786	13,996	13,661	14,314	57
Fond du Lac	1,901,796,867	18,664	19,419	18,946	18,849	19,170	22
Forest	115,266,199	11,244	11,795	12,067	11,230	11,351	71
Grant	716,334,195	13,630	14,052	14,291	13,608	14,258	58
Green	646,409,692	18,554	18,930	18,349	18,080	18,644	37
Green Lake	331,337,750	16,082	16,651	17,016	16,777	17,212	27
Iowa	434,005,604	16,347	17,332	17,902	18,645	18,600	28
Iron	92,590,407	13,158	14,204	12,888	12,684	13,349	66
Jackson	275,048,664	13,936	13,862	13,351	13,619	14,078	60
Jefferson	1,468,398,547	18,395	19,089	18,618	18,427	18,871	25
Juneau	377,040,376	14,396	15,432	14,423	14,167	14,886	51
Kenosha	2,961,320,833	18,861	19,944	18,803	18,759	19,200	21
Kewaunee	364,197,009	17,021	17,929	17,824	17,112	17,638	33
La Crosse	2,221,962,952	18,015	19,171	18,536	18,634	20,423	14
Lafayette	234,400,199	13,431	13,843	14,116	13,991	14,429	56
Langlade	307,912,199	14,027	14,871	14,625	14,293	14,610	55
Lincoln	515,962,226	16,601	17,074	16,289	16,544	17,188	38
Manitowoc	1,516,867,305	17,767	18,110	18,016	17,742	18,054	29
Marathon	2,618,253,377	19,221	19,283	19,582	19,325	20,474	13
Marinette	653,836,213	14,309	14,878	14,590	14,564	14,872	52
Marquette	239,086,009	15,155	16,083	15,568	16,020	16,059	44
Menominee	19,197,501	3,973	4,240	4,524	5,417	4,180	72
Milwaukee	16,849,028,608	17,400	18,067	18,083	17,492	17,900	31
Monroe	626,762,165	14,149	14,579	14,060	13,464	14,904	50
Oconto	629,188,503	16,301	16,970	16,405	16,451	16,878	39
Oneida	701,684,825	18,469	19,762	18,417	18,524	18,733	26
Outagamie	3,678,747,004	21,118	22,422	22,287	21,646	21,970	7
Ozaukee	3,059,162,918	36,488	38,948	36,096	34,992	36,196	1
Pepin	123,753,774	15,068	15,609	16,116	15,508	16,496	41
Pierce	764,832,324	18,072	19,595	18,795	19,053	20,062	16
Polk	755,303,057	19,763	18,645	16,836	16,635	17,482	36
Portage	1,227,569,604	16,582	17,350	18,139	17,310	17,875	32
Price	216,543,522	14,365	14,091	14,242	13,999	13,629	64
Racine	4,001,092,088	20,206	20,464	20,504	20,476	20,939	10
Richland	264,258,426	14,373	14,335	14,447	14,289	14,634	54
Rock	3,029,875,460	18,373	18,921	18,281	18,372	19,600	20
Rusk	192,023,911	11,879	12,377	12,278	12,180	12,518	70
St. Croix	1,764,440,000	23,921	25,281	25,003	23,973	25,163	5
Sauk	1,131,637,753	18,989	19,847	18,810	18,761	19,662	18
Sawyer	234,983,079	13,086	14,249	14,215	13,563	14,041	61
Shawano	613,998,903	14,953	15,408	14,984	14,465	14,812	53
Sheboygan	2,348,928,310	20,202	20,284	20,077	19,765	20,480	12
Taylor	318,111,798	15,248	15,409	15,037	15,556	16,126	42
Trempealeau	550,982,990	16,580	17,211	17,577	18,565	19,964	17
Vernon	392,252,946	13,305	13,598	13,138	12,897	13,685	63
Vilas	379,456,078	16,710	18,010	16,584	16,751	17,520	35
Walworth	1,875,091,373	19,961	20,920	19,017	19,275	19,608	19
Washburn	257,773,700	15,029	17,023	15,065	15,914	15,561	47
Washington	3,033,587,210	24,438	24,958	24,468	24,003	24,880	6
Waukesha	11,660,155,574	31,472	32,484	31,354	30,868	31,411	2
Waupaca	925,944,004	17,697	17,615	17,156	17,022	17,523	34
Waushara	339,822,170	14,841	15,680	13,991	13,584	13,783	62
Winnebago	3,291,832,557	19,811	21,032	20,599	20,488	20,551	11
Wood	1,453,168,039	18,041	19,631	19,045	18,566	19,133	23
STATE[2]	**$115,392,447,489**	**$20,116**	**$20,878**	**$20,453**	**$20,135**	**$21,020**	

[1]"Wisconsin adjusted gross income" (AGI) is Wisconsin income as reported to the Wisconsin Department of Revenue for income tax purposes and is based on the federal income tax definition of gross income as modified by certain additions and subtractions required by state law.

[2]State totals and state per capita figures include amounts not allocated to a particular county.

Sources: Wisconsin Department of Revenue, "Wisconsin Adjusted Gross Income by County, Amount and Rank for 2002 and 2003" [January 2005] and earlier volumes, and "Wisconsin Municipal Per Return Income Report for 2003" at: http://www.dor.state.wi.us/ra/munagi04.html [January 2005] and previous reports. Per capita AGI rank calculated by Wisconsin Legislative Reference Bureau.

PERCENT OF EARNED INCOME

State	Total Earned Income (in millions)[1]	Rank per Capita[2]	Farm Earnings	Agricultural Services, Forestry Fishing and Other[3]	Mining	Construction	Manufacturing	Utilities
Alabama	$92,113	42	1.65%	0.72%	0.77%	6.31%	17.53%	1.63%
Alaska	18,920	9	0.07	1.47	6.18	8.30	3.91	1.09
Arizona	124,463	38	0.73	0.38	0.57	8.77	10.33	0.90
Arkansas	52,617	48	3.64	1.02	0.74	5.06	17.59	1.09
California	999,569	11	0.89	0.59	0.29	6.55	12.18	1.01
Colorado	134,989	7	0.55	0.18	2.02	8.14	8.25	0.80
Connecticut	124,032	2	0.14	0.06	0.13	5.63	14.11	1.27
Delaware	25,262	6	0.83	0.09	0.11	6.36	11.02	0.97
District of Columbia	60,960	1	0.00	2.21	0.01	1.31	0.45	0.44
Florida	372,979	39	0.41	0.48	0.12	7.30	6.27	0.79
Georgia	215,700	25	1.08	0.34	0.25	5.88	11.85	1.35
Hawaii	32,619	17	0.67	0.20	0.16	6.78	2.67	0.86
Idaho	27,965	44	3.51	1.53	0.48	8.20	12.79	1.15
ILLINOIS	346,122	13	0.59	0.10	0.46	5.87	13.80	0.89
Indiana	143,792	34	0.70	0.14	0.39	6.36	27.21	1.11
IOWA	68,887	33	5.20	0.35	0.21	6.07	18.62	1.27
Kansas	64,913	30	1.16	0.34	1.26	5.47	17.23	1.10
Kentucky	86,038	40	0.81	0.42	1.76	5.68	19.21	0.61
Louisiana	91,513	43	0.70	0.62	4.58	6.64	11.83	1.07
Maine	24,436	49	0.23	1.29	0.03	6.85	13.00	1.06
Maryland	152,683	12	0.21	0.09	0.08	7.73	7.00	1.66
Massachusetts	216,453	3	0.04	0.21	0.17	5.68	12.16	0.66
MICHIGAN	254,588	18	0.30	0.14	0.30	5.56	23.32	1.12
MINNESOTA	148,221	8	1.47	0.25	0.30	6.20	15.48	1.00
Mississippi	49,610	51	2.72	1.13	1.03	5.02	16.51	1.25
Missouri	134,750	32	0.61	0.30	0.31	6.70	14.28	0.85
Montana	18,371	46	1.49	1.12	2.96	7.80	5.85	1.54
Nebraska	43,137	24	3.72	0.35	0.33	6.22	11.81	1.22
Nevada	61,143	16	0.14	0.06	1.39	11.59	4.58	0.99
New Hampshire	34,868	15	0.10	0.38	0.13	7.07	16.12	1.21
New Jersey	266,452	5	0.09	0.05	0.08	5.43	11.01	0.86
New Mexico	37,294	47	1.95	0.37	3.55	6.70	6.03	0.88
New York	599,752	4	0.15	0.22	0.20	4.05	7.28	1.01
North Carolina	194,291	35	0.90	0.35	0.14	6.46	17.30	0.73
North Dakota	15,852	20	8.82	0.61	1.84	6.09	8.35	2.32
Ohio	273,354	29	0.43	0.11	0.38	5.45	20.30	0.78
Oklahoma	72,957	41	1.67	0.25	5.18	4.74	14.96	1.61
Oregon	84,406	31	1.05	1.79	0.16	6.51	15.55	0.93
Pennsylvania	307,024	21	0.38	0.18	0.57	5.79	15.14	1.20
Rhode Island	26,113	26	0.08	0.23	0.08	5.74	12.50	1.07
South Carolina	84,041	45	0.40	0.46	0.12	7.09	18.26	1.30
South Dakota	17,407	36	7.48	0.53	0.36	5.97	10.70	0.99
Tennessee	141,176	27	0.13	0.26	0.20	5.84	17.65	0.24
Texas	563,140	19	0.66	0.26	4.24	6.24	12.66	1.78
Utah	52,588	37	0.48	0.10	1.13	7.61	12.17	0.73
Vermont	14,846	28	1.19	0.58	0.37	7.38	15.78	1.54
Virginia	210,440	10	0.18	0.16	0.36	6.62	8.40	0.77
Washington	167,849	14	0.96	1.18	0.18	6.64	11.90	0.37
West Virginia	31,635	50	−0.26	0.47	6.07	6.02	12.53	1.74
WISCONSIN	136,285	22	1.11	0.33	0.18	6.21	22.73	0.83
Wyoming	12,521	23	1.19	0.39	14.56	8.19	5.06	1.62
UNITED STATES	$7,535,137		0.73%	0.37%	0.84%	6.16%	13.06%	1.04%

[1]Includes wages and salaries, other labor income, and proprietor's income

[2]Per capita rank calculated by the Wisconsin Legislative Reference Bureau.

[3]"Other" consists of income of U.S. residents employed by international organizations and foreign embassies and consulates in the United States.

[4]"Services" consists of the following NAICS industry categories: Professional and technical services; Management of companies and enterprises; Administrative and waste services; Educational services; Health care and social assistance; Arts, entertainment and recreation; Accommodation and food services; and Other services except public administration.

Source: U.S. Department of Commerce, Bureau of Economic Analysis, Table 4 of "State Personal Income for the Fourth Quarter of 2004 and State Per Capita Personal Income for 2004", *Survey of Current Business*, April 2005.

BY INDUSTRY, BY STATE – 2004

Transportation	Wholesale Trade	Retail Trade	Information	Finance and Insurance	Real Estate and Rentals	Services[4]	Government and Government Enterprises	State
3.06%	4.88%	7.48%	2.04%	4.99%	1.83%	27.38%	19.74%	.... Alabama
6.71	1.89	6.80	2.42	3.08	1.78	25.37	30.93	.... Alaska
3.08	5.22	8.23	2.51	6.76	3.62	32.19	16.71	.... Arizona
5.57	4.77	6.81	3.39	4.03	1.50	27.26	17.51	.... Arkansas
2.71	4.71	6.77	5.75	7.20	3.34	31.97	15.22	.... California
2.76	4.87	6.25	8.25	6.78	3.88	31.97	15.30	.... Colorado
1.78	4.72	6.30	3.15	16.05	1.98	32.79	11.90	..... Connecticut
2.21	4.58	6.53	2.13	15.25	1.67	34.35	13.92	...... Delaware
0.62	0.69	1.02	4.49	4.14	1.59	42.96	40.05	District of Columbia
3.07	5.51	8.05	3.44	7.04	3.12	38.20	16.19	.... Florida
4.47	6.75	6.52	5.93	6.24	2.65	30.09	16.59	.... Georgia
3.95	2.94	6.82	2.45	3.95	2.46	35.66	30.42	.... Hawaii
3.00	4.36	8.27	1.75	4.03	2.21	29.92	18.80	.... Idaho
3.89	6.32	5.73	3.19	9.42	2.55	33.77	13.41	...... ILLINOIS
3.77	4.84	6.48	1.73	4.67	2.02	27.16	13.41	.... Indiana
3.78	5.12	7.18	2.57	7.91	1.48	24.31	15.93	.... IOWA
3.78	5.50	6.73	5.47	5.68	1.86	26.16	18.28	.... Kansas
5.54	5.10	7.09	1.79	4.88	1.39	27.58	18.12	.... Kentucky
4.53	4.41	6.94	2.22	4.06	2.43	30.53	19.44	.... Louisiana
2.54	4.27	9.14	2.36	6.15	1.77	32.62	18.72	.... Maine
2.35	4.39	6.59	2.96	6.38	3.02	35.59	21.96	.... Maryland
1.80	5.30	5.78	3.92	11.74	2.23	39.09	11.23	.... Massachusetts
2.72	4.73	6.26	1.92	4.82	3.08	32.51	13.22	..... MICHIGAN
3.42	6.43	6.29	2.95	8.28	2.00	32.47	13.44	.... MINNESOTA
3.72	3.81	7.74	1.77	3.76	1.44	26.73	23.37	...... Mississippi
3.82	5.43	6.96	3.90	6.01	1.95	33.51	15.38	.... Missouri
3.83	4.05	9.03	2.26	4.56	4.02	29.23	22.27	.... Montana
6.72	5.31	6.80	2.93	7.14	1.47	28.39	17.60	.... Nebraska
3.08	3.74	7.59	1.87	6.31	2.95	41.14	14.57	.... Nevada
1.79	6.23	9.82	2.74	7.02	2.52	33.14	11.74	... New Hampshire
3.46	7.21	6.89	4.35	9.00	2.61	34.56	14.41	..... New Jersey
2.71	3.15	7.87	2.09	3.77	1.87	30.77	28.28	.... New Mexico
2.03	4.65	5.06	5.97	17.08	2.81	35.19	14.27	..... New York
2.94	5.34	6.88	2.68	6.01	2.19	29.16	18.92	... North Carolina
3.76	5.74	7.05	2.66	5.02	1.23	25.25	21.27	.... North Dakota
3.28	5.36	6.77	2.27	6.29	2.02	31.70	14.84	.... Ohio
3.71	3.94	7.10	3.03	4.44	1.98	26.34	21.05	.... Oklahoma
3.22	6.25	7.33	2.80	5.08	2.36	30.28	16.68	.... Oregon
3.61	5.05	6.77	3.00	7.19	2.26	35.87	12.98	..... Pennsylvania
1.70	4.32	6.70	3.67	7.95	1.78	37.10	17.08	..... Rhode Island
2.81	4.45	8.04	2.02	4.79	2.25	27.53	20.46	... South Carolina
2.95	4.76	7.82	2.12	7.11	2.06	28.24	18.93	.... South Dakota
5.63	5.67	7.85	2.16	6.20	2.27	32.16	13.73	.... Tennessee
4.41	5.98	6.60	3.78	6.64	3.21	28.65	14.90	.... Texas
4.31	4.50	7.85	3.18	6.01	2.27	31.08	18.59	.... Utah
2.22	3.98	8.54	2.34	4.82	1.63	32.10	17.53	.... Vermont
2.67	3.84	5.96	4.60	5.79	2.67	35.03	22.94	.... Virginia
3.17	5.01	6.91	6.82	6.03	2.48	29.63	18.73	..... Washington
3.50	3.84	7.60	1.94	3.50	1.21	29.71	22.15	... West Virginia
3.51	5.07	6.57	2.36	6.57	1.49	28.64	14.41	... WISCONSIN
5.06	3.37	6.93	1.45	3.14	2.95	22.55	23.53	.... Wyoming
3.25%	5.14%	6.64%	3.90%	7.70%	2.61%	32.50%	16.07%	UNITED STATES

PERSONAL INCOME IN WISCONSIN
1929 – 2004

| | | | | | | Per Capita Personal Income | | | | |
| | Wisconsin | Wisconsin | | | | United States | | | | |
Year	Personal Income (in millions)[1]	Per Capita Amount	Annual % Change	State Rank	As % of National Average	Per Capita Amount	High[2]	State	Low	State
1929	$1,975	$673	---	18	96%	$700	$1,152	New York	$271	S.C.
1930	1,733	588	---	18	95	620	1,035	New York	202	Miss.
1935	1,416	461	---	19	97	474	722	Delaware	177	Miss.
1940	1,720	547	---	21	92	595	1,027	New York	215	Miss.
1945	3,499	1,182	---	22	96	1,237	1,644	Delaware	629	Miss.
1950	5,178	1,506	---	24	100	1,510	2,075	Nevada	770	Miss.
1955	6,899	1,875	---	21	98	1,911	2,527	Conn.	1,045	Miss.
1960	8,948	2,258	---	20	99	2,276	2,926	Conn.	1,237	Miss.
1965	11,803	2,789	---	22	98	2,859	3,583	Conn.	1,688	Miss.
1970	17,609	3,979	---	21	97	4,085	5,263	Alaska	2,617	Miss.
1975	27,810	6,086	---	25	99	6,172	10,683	Alaska	4,203	Miss.
1980	47,623	10,107	---	20	100	10,114	14,866	Alaska	7,007	Miss.
1985	65,709	13,840	---	28	94	14,758	20,321	Alaska	9,892	Miss.
1990	88,635	18,072	---	24	93	19,477	26,504	Conn.	13,089	Miss.
1991	92,124	18,557	2.7%	25	93	19,892	26,512	Conn.	13,702	Miss.
1992	98,917	19,683	6.1	24	94	20,854	28,362	Conn.	14,559	Miss.
1993	103,379	20,331	3.3	23	95	21,346	28,975	Conn.	15,290	Miss.
1994	109,927	21,413	5.3	23	97	22,172	29,693	Conn.	16,291	Miss.
1995	115,180	22,215	3.7	24	96	23,076	31,045	Conn.	16,885	Miss.
1996	121,718	23,273	4.8	25	96	24,175	32,424	Conn.	17,702	Miss.
1997	129,099	24,514	5.3	22	97	25,334	34,375	Conn.	18,550	Miss.
1998	138,667	26,175	6.8	20	97	26,883	36,822	Conn.	19,545	Miss.
1999	144,702	27,135	3.7	20	97	27,939	38,332	Conn.	20,053	Miss.
2000	153,548	28,570	5.3	20	96	29,845	41,489	Conn.	21,005	Miss.
2001	158,888	29,392	2.9	21	96	30,575	42,920	Conn.	21,950	Miss.
2002	162,866	29,937	1.9	21	97	30,804	42,521	Conn.	22,511	Miss.
2003	167,979	30,685	2.5	22	97	31,472	42,972	Conn.	23,466	Miss.
2004	177,154	32,157	4.8	22	98	32,937	45,398	Conn.	24,650	Miss.

Note: Alaska and Hawaii were not included in U.S. totals before 1950. Numbers after 1970 have been updated based on revised U.S. Department of Commerce data. 2004 data are preliminary and may change after publication.

[1]Personal income includes all forms of income received by persons from business establishments; federal, state, and local governments; households and institutions; and foreign countries. Allowance is made for "in kind" income not received as cash.

[2]High shown is for the 50 states. In the following years, jurisdictions other than states had higher per capita personal income: 1950: Alaska (prestatehood) – $2,400, District of Columbia – $2,228; 1991: District of Columbia – $27,567; 1992: District of Columbia – $28,916; 1993: District of Columbia – $29,996; 1994: District of Columbia – $30,835; 1995: District of Columbia – $31,266; 1996: District of Columbia – $32,786; 1997: District of Columbia – $34,488; 2001: District of Columbia – $44,827; 2002: District of Columbia – $46,407; 2003: District of Columbia – $48,446; 2004: District of Columbia – $51,803.

Source: U.S. Department of Commerce, Bureau of Economic Analysis, Regional Accounts Data, *Annual State Personal Income*, at: http://www.bea.doc.gov/bea/regional/spi/#download [March 28, 2005].

HIGHLIGHTS OF GEOGRAPHY AND CLIMATE IN WISCONSIN

Land and Water Area — Wisconsin encompasses 34.8 million acres, not including those parts of the Mississippi River and Great Lakes located within the boundaries of the state. Its inland lakes, covering more than 982,000 acres, make up almost 3% of the state's total surface area. Based on land area, the largest county in the state is Marathon with 988,744 acres; the smallest is Ozaukee with 148,448 acres. The geographic center of the state is located in Wood County about 9 miles southeast of Marshfield.

Lakes — The largest lake in Wisconsin is Lake Winnebago (137,708 acres), which covers parts of three counties; the deepest natural lake is Green Lake in Green Lake County with a maximum depth of 236 feet. Most of Wisconsin's largest lakes are concentrated in the northern two-thirds of the state, and they include artificial bodies of water created by dams. Wisconsin has 15,057 lakes (6,040 named). Green County has only five lakes while Vilas County has 1,318.

High Points — The state's highest recorded elevation is Timms Hill in Price County, at 1,952 feet. There are also other recorded elevations of at least 1,900 feet in Forest, Langlade, Lincoln, and Marathon Counties.

Temperature — In 2003, the annual statewide average temperature was 43.2° Fahrenheit. Across the state, normal regional temperatures vary from 40.4° in the north central area to 46.5° in the southeast. Normal temperatures are the averages for the period 1971-2000, based on computations by the Wisconsin Climatology Office.

Precipitation — In 2003, the total statewide average rainfall was 28.39 inches. Regional precipitation averages varied from a high of 30.75 inches in the south central to a low of 25.55 inches in the west central. Normal precipitation correspond to the averages for the period 1971-2000, according to the State Climatology Office.

The following tables present selected data. Consult footnoted sources for more detailed information about geography and climate.

WISCONSIN'S LARGEST WATER AREAS

Name	County[1]	Area in Acres
Lake Winnebago	Winnebago (also Calumet and Fond du Lac)	137,708
Lake Pepin[2]	Pepin	---
Lake Petenwell	Juneau (also Adams and Wood)	23,040
Lake Chippewa (Chippewa Flowage)	Sawyer	15,300
Poygan Lake	Winnebago (also Waushara)	14,102
Castle Rock Lake	Juneau (also Adams)	13,955
Turtle-Flambeau Flowage	Iron	13,545
Lake Koshkonong	Rock (also Dane and Jefferson)	10,460
Lake Mendota	Dane	9,842
Lake Wisconsin	Sauk (also Columbia)	9,000
Lake Butte des Morts	Winnebago	8,857
Lake Onalaska	La Crosse	7,688
Green Lake (Big Green Lake)[3]	Green Lake	7,346
Big Eau Pleine Reservoir	Marathon	6,830
Lake Du Bay	Portage (also Marathon)	6,700
Beaver Dam Lake	Dodge	6,542
Willow Flowage	Oneida	6,306
Lake Wissota	Chippewa	6,300
Shawano Lake	Shawano	6,063
Geneva Lake	Walworth	5,262
Lake Winneskiek	Crawford	5,250
Puckaway Lake	Green Lake (also Marquette)	5,039
Lac Courte Oreilles	Sawyer	5,039
Lake St. Croix	St. Croix (also Pierce)	4,668
Lake Winneconne	Winnebago	4,507
Holcombe Flowage	Chippewa (also Rusk)	3,890
Trout Lake	Vilas	3,816
Pelican Lake	Oneida	3,585
Fence Lake	Vilas	3,555
Tomahawk Lake	Oneida	3,392
Gile Flowage	Iron	3,384
Long Lake	Washburn	3,290
Lake Monona	Dane	3,274
Namekagon Lake	Bayfield	3,227
Lake Kegonsa	Dane	3,209

[1]County listed first contains the water's source of origin. Other counties covered by the water area are shown in parentheses.
[2]Lake Pepin is part of Mississippi River backwaters. Definite area cannot be determined because of fluctuations, but past DNR estimates have ranged over 27,000 acres.
[3]Green Lake, at a maximum depth of 236 feet, is Wisconsin's deepest natural lake.
Sources: Wisconsin Department of Natural Resources, *Wisconsin Lakes, 2001*, and DNR department data at: http://www.dnr.state.wi.us [October 22, 2004].

LAND AND INLAND LAKE AREA OF WISCONSIN COUNTIES

County	Total Land Area Acres	Inland Lakes Number	Inland Lakes Acres	County	Total Land Area Acres	Inland Lakes Number	Inland Lakes Acres
Adams	414,554	47	2,309	Marinette	897,126	442	13,735
Ashland	668,045	157	5,936	Marquette	291,514	93	5,736
Barron	552,218	369	17,748	Menominee	229,094	128	4,044
Bayfield	944,800	962	22,629	Milwaukee	154,598	41	197
Brown	338,355	22	170	Monroe	576,493	120	3,437
Buffalo	438,061	8	196	Oconto	638,701	378	11,053
Burnett	525,773	509	31,258	Oneida	719,680	1,129	68,447
Calumet	204,698	8	98	Outagamie	409,818	33	213
Chippewa	646,675	449	20,027	Ozaukee	148,448	39	709
Clark	778,010	32	1,076	Pepin	148,659	29	278
Columbia	495,226	56	3,095	Pierce	368,954	38	6,016
Crawford	366,522	77	6,243	Polk	587,053	437	20,900
Dane	769,210	36	21,520	Portage	516,038	136	12,203
Dodge	564,659	29	13,246	Price	801,638	389	15,129
Door	308,941	25	3,254	Racine	213,184	21	3,919
Douglas	837,843	431	14,113	Richland	375,168	9	251
Dunn	545,299	21	3,963	Rock	461,101	76	11,174
Eau Claire	408,090	20	2,838	Rusk	584,403	250	7,854
Florence	312,339	259	7,259	St. Croix	461,965	64	3,667
Fond du Lac	462,662	42	1,655	Sauk	536,083	28	11,004
Forest	648,992	824	22,531	Sawyer	804,109	496	56,183
Grant	734,624	33	1,569	Shawano	571,206	134	8,912
Green	373,754	5	350	Sheboygan	328,723	72	2,111
Green Lake	226,739	36	17,120	Taylor	623,910	284	6,183
Iowa	488,109	15	685	Trempealeau	469,811	26	409
Iron	484,627	494	29,368	Vernon	508,717	57	256
Jackson	631,885	135	5,004	Vilas	559,181	1,318	93,689
Jefferson	356,486	35	3,770	Walworth	355,398	37	12,798
Juneau	491,270	57	45,950	Washburn	518,195	964	31,265
Kenosha	174,611	33	3,674	Washington	275,725	54	3,080
Kewaunee	219,290	15	251	Waukesha	355,571	118	15,156
La Crosse	289,754	19	8,568	Waupaca	480,698	240	7,169
Lafayette	405,485	8	565	Waushara	400,659	138	4,623
Langlade	558,509	841	9,122	Winnebago	280,691	30	169,755
Lincoln	565,312	727	15,741	Wood	507,379	78	6,245
Manitowoc	378,579	101	1,492	STATE	34,758,464	15,057	982,155
Marathon	988,774	194	19,762				

Note: Land area statistics from the U.S. Bureau of the Census; lake statistics from Wisconsin Department of Natural Resources. Lake Superior and Lake Michigan are not included in totals.

Sources: Wisconsin Department of Natural Resources, *Wisconsin Lakes, 2001*; U.S. Department of Commerce, Census Bureau, 2000 Census of Population and Housing, *Summary Population and Housing Characteristics, Wisconsin*, Table 16.

SELECTED HIGH POINTS IN WISCONSIN*

Site	County	Location by Section, Township, Range	Elevation in Feet
Timms Hill	Price	N. 11, T. 34N., R. 2E.	1,952
Sugarbush Hill	Forest	SW. 36, T. 36N., R. 13E.	1,939
Rib Mountain	Marathon	SE. 8, T. 28N., R. 7E.	1,924
Lookout Mountain	Lincoln	SW. 27, T. 34N., R. 8E.	1,920
Kent Tower Hill	Langlade	NW. 21, T. 32N., R. 13E.	1,903
Mt. Whittlesey	Ashland	SE. 9, T. 44N., R. 2W.	1,872
Penokee Range	Iron	NE. 6, T. 44N., R. 1W.	1,860
Meteor Hill	Sawyer	SW. 17, T. 37N., R. 8W.	1,801
Carter Hills	Oconto	NW. 6, T. 33N., R. 15E.	1,781
Blue Hills	Rusk	27, T. 35N., R. 9W.	1,750
West Blue Mound	Iowa	NW. 1, T. 6N., R. 5E.	1,719
Mount Telemark	Bayfield	NW. 28, T. 43N., R. 7W.	1,700
McCaslin Mountain	Marinette	S. 29, T. 34N., R. 17E.	1,650
Blue Hills	Barron	W. 25, T. 35N., R. 10W.	1,593
Sauk Point	Sauk	SW. 15, T. 11N., R. 7E.	1,530
Flambeau Ridge	Chippewa	SE. 3, T. 32N., R. 7W.	1,489
East Blue Mound	Dane	5,6, T. 6N., R. 6E.	1,481
Powers Bluff	Wood	SE. 30, T. 24N., R. 4E.	1,480
Baraboo Range	Columbia	SE. 6, T. 11N., R. 8E.	1,450
Greenfield Hill	Monroe	SW. 9, T. 18N., R. 2W.	1,440
North Platte Mound	Lafayette	SE. 31, T. 4N., R. 1E.	1,410
Frederic Tower Hill	Polk	NW. 1, T. 36N., R. 17W.	1,409
Saddle Mound	Jackson	NE. 33, T. 22N., R. 1W.	1,400
Wadels Hill	La Crosse	NE. 24, SE. 14, T. 18N., R. 5W.	1,380
Johnson Hill	Juneau	NW. 11, T. 15N., R. 2E.	1,369
Summit Hill	Douglas	21, T. 45N., R. 14W.	1,360
Montana Ridge	Buffalo	2,3,11, T. 22 N., R. 10W.	1,360
Irish Ridge	Vernon	2-4, 11-12, T. 14N., R. 3W.	1,354
Dunnewa Hill	Dunn	NE. 24, T. 30N., R. 11W.	1,332
Holy Hill	Washington	SW. 14, T. 9N., R. 18E.	1,322
Rising Sun Ridge	Crawford	NW. 22, T. 11N., R. 5W.	1,312
Parnell Hill	Sheboygan	NE. 10, T. 14N., R. 20E.	1,300
Rohrscheib Hill	Pepin	SW. 22, T. 25N., R. 11W.	1,300
Pleasant Ridge	Richland	NE. 19, T. 12N., R. 1W.	1,290
Friendship Mound	Adams	SW. 32, T. 18N., R. 6E.	1,270
Kettle Moraine	Fond du Lac	SE. 2, T. 14N., R. 18E.	1,240
Military Ridge	Grant	31, T. 7N., R. 2W.	1,230
Lapham Peak	Waukesha	SE. 29, T. 7N., R. 18E.	1,062
Kettle Moraine	Jefferson	NE. 26, T. 5N., R. 16E.	1,020
Morrison Hill	Brown	NW. 24, T. 21 N., R. 20E.	1,020
Cherneyville Hill	Kewaunee	NE. 32, T. 23N., R. 23E.	

*This list is based on data compiled by the State Cartographer's Office and includes the highest named point in each county having an elevation of at least 1,020 feet. The listing should not be construed as a ranking of all of the highest points in the state because 1) it includes only named features; 2) it includes only one high point per county; and 3) there may be others of comparable height that are unrecorded. Many elevations are approximations.

Source: Wisconsin State Cartographer's Office, *Individual High Points for WI Counties,* at:
http://www.sco.wisc.edu/maps/cntyelevation.php [October 22, 2004].

WISCONSIN TEMPERATURES AND PRECIPITATION,
By Region and Month, 2003

	Jan.	Feb.	Mar.	Apr.	May	June	July	Aug.	Sept.	Oct.	Nov.	Dec.	Annual[1]
Statewide													
2003 Temperature (°F) ...	14.0	13.9	29.1	42.4	53.4	62.8	68.5	70.1	59.3	46.4	33.1	25.7	43.2
Normal Temperature[2]	13.2	19.0	30.1	43.2	55.5	64.5	69.1	66.9	58.1	46.6	32.4	19.0	43.1
2003 Precipitation (inches)	0.38	0.66	1.89	2.77	4.78	3.32	3.39	2.07	3.18	1.39	3.18	1.38	28.39
Normal Precipitation[2] ...	1.22	1.00	1.96	2.86	3.37	4.02	4.07	4.27	3.74	2.50	2.29	1.35	32.64
Regions[3]													
Northwest													
2003 Temperature	11.2	10.7	25.9	40.8	52.4	61.5	67.4	69.0	58.3	45.1	29.5	22.8	41.2
Normal Temperature	9.5	16.2	28.0	41.7	54.4	63.1	68.1	65.9	56.6	45.1	29.8	15.4	41.2
2003 Precipitation	0.17	0.47	1.93	2.53	5.02	4.30	3.79	1.40	3.18	1.63	1.53	0.99	26.94
Normal Precipitation	1.12	0.83	1.78	2.39	3.29	4.19	4.29	4.44	3.89	2.57	2.16	1.09	32.04
North Central													
2003 Temperature	10.7	9.7	25.7	39.0	51.2	60.7	66.0	67.6	57.4	43.7	29.5	23.1	40.4
Normal Temperature	10.3	16.0	26.8	40.4	53.2	61.8	66.4	64.2	55.3	44.0	29.8	16.1	40.4
2003 Precipitation	0.45	0.92	2.10	3.77	4.73	3.14	2.95	2.17	2.87	1.62	2.13	1.36	28.21
Normal Precipitation	1.25	0.92	1.78	2.40	3.31	4.01	4.06	4.36	4.03	2.73	2.27	1.32	32.44
Northeast													
2003 Temperature	13.0	11.7	26.9	39.3	51.4	60.9	66.9	67.5	57.4	44.5	32.1	25.2	41.4
Normal Temperature	12.5	17.5	28.1	41.3	53.6	62.5	67.0	64.8	56.0	44.8	31.3	18.4	41.5
2003 Precipitation	0.38	1.09	2.27	3.76	3.16	3.10	3.31	3.49	4.50	1.19	2.50	1.52	30.27
Normal Precipitation	1.31	0.98	1.98	2.65	3.29	3.69	3.70	3.81	3.74	2.52	2.33	1.47	31.47
West Central													
2003 Temperature	14.7	15.1	30.9	45.5	55.7	65.3	70.2	72.1	60.8	48.1	33.6	25.4	44.8
Normal Temperature	12.7	19.3	31.2	45.2	57.4	66.4	70.8	68.3	59.3	47.6	32.3	18.5	44.1
2003 Precipitation	0.33	0.67	2.04	3.08	5.23	3.34	2.83	1.42	2.53	0.98	2.16	0.94	25.55
Normal Precipitation	1.06	0.87	1.93	3.05	3.69	4.24	4.45	4.54	3.82	2.36	2.19	1.14	33.34
Central													
2003 Temperature	15.0	14.8	31.0	43.8	55.0	64.2	69.3	70.9	60.1	46.9	34.3	26.7	44.3
Normal Temperature	14.5	20.2	31.2	44.5	56.7	65.8	70.2	67.7	59.0	47.5	33.2	20.1	44.2
2003 Precipitation	0.56	0.64	1.76	2.12	4.84	3.55	3.14	2.63	3.45	1.18	1.61	1.31	28.81
Normal Precipitation	1.15	1.01	2.07	3.02	3.52	3.88	4.13	4.22	3.72	2.36	2.29	1.31	32.68
East Central													
2003 Temperature	16.6	16.2	30.1	41.5	52.0	62.0	68.6	70.0	59.9	47.5	36.4	29.5	44.2
Normal Temperature	17.0	21.4	31.2	42.8	54.6	64.1	69.5	67.9	59.8	48.3	35.2	22.8	44.6
2003 Precipitation	0.45	0.66	1.89	2.38	4.08	3.00	4.29	2.84	3.13	1.40	4.72	1.52	30.36
Normal Precipitation	1.44	1.14	2.09	2.81	2.95	3.51	3.38	3.86	3.42	2.43	2.38	1.60	31.01
Southwest													
2003 Temperature	16.7	17.4	32.4	46.1	56.0	65.2	70.7	72.7	60.6	48.6	35.8	27.8	45.8
Normal Temperature	15.7	21.9	33.4	46.1	57.9	67.2	71.4	69.0	60.5	48.9	34.5	21.5	45.7
2003 Precipitation	0.55	0.47	1.44	2.08	5.19	3.32	3.31	1.78	3.40	1.24	4.99	1.42	29.19
Normal Precipitation	1.07	1.08	2.09	3.55	3.60	4.35	4.33	4.46	3.42	2.34	2.34	1.29	33.92
South Central													
2003 Temperature	17.3	19.0	32.9	45.6	55.5	65.0	71.1	72.7	61.5	48.9	37.3	28.3	46.3
Normal Temperature	16.8	22.3	33.5	45.8	57.8	67.2	71.3	68.9	60.6	49.0	35.4	22.5	45.9
2003 Precipitation	0.30	0.35	1.49	1.92	5.66	2.78	3.98	1.41	3.21	1.54	6.04	2.07	30.75
Normal Precipitation	1.28	1.25	2.20	3.47	3.40	4.19	4.07	4.24	3.51	2.48	2.41	1.61	34.11
Southeast													
2003 Temperature	18.6	20.7	33.8	44.6	53.8	63.4	69.9	71.9	61.5	49.0	38.9	30.2	46.4
Normal Temperature	18.9	24.0	34.0	45.0	56.3	66.0	71.2	69.4	61.4	49.9	37.0	24.7	46.5
2003 Precipitation	0.29	0.36	1.64	1.81	5.25	2.03	3.27	1.93	2.00	1.69	4.91	2.12	27.30
Normal Precipitation	1.56	1.32	2.19	3.48	3.13	3.76	3.82	4.22	3.48	2.51	2.55	1.91	33.93

[1]Annual temperature reflects the average of the monthly figures; annual precipitation is the total for the year.
[2]Normal temperatures and normal precipitation are the averages for the period 1971-2000, based on data computed by the State Climatology Office.
[3]The counties in each region are:
Northwest — Barron, Bayfield, Burnett, Chippewa, Douglas, Polk, Rusk, Sawyer, and Washburn.
North Central — Ashland, Clark, Iron, Lincoln, Marathon, Oneida, Price, Taylor, and Vilas.
Northeast — Florence, Forest, Langlade, Marinette, Menominee, Oconto, and Shawano.
West Central — Buffalo, Dunn, Eau Claire, Jackson, La Crosse, Monroe, Pepin, Pierce, St. Croix, and Trempealeau.
Central — Adams, Green Lake, Juneau, Marquette, Portage, Waupaca, Waushara, and Wood.
East Central — Brown, Calumet, Door, Fond du Lac, Kewaunee, Manitowoc, Outagamie, Sheboygan, and Winnebago.
Southwest — Crawford, Grant, Iowa, Lafayette, Richland, Sauk, and Vernon.
South Central — Columbia, Dane, Dodge, Green, Jefferson, and Rock.
Southeast — Kenosha, Milwaukee, Ozaukee, Racine, Walworth, Washington, and Waukesha.
Source: Wisconsin Agricultural Statistics Service, *Wisconsin 2004 Agricultural Statistics*, at: http://www.nass.usda.gov/wi/rlsetoc.htm.

HIGHLIGHTS OF HISTORY IN WISCONSIN

History — On May 29, 1848, Wisconsin became the 30th state in the Union, but the state's written history dates back more than 300 years to the time when the French first encountered the diverse Native Americans who lived here. In 1634, the French explorer Jean Nicolet landed at Green Bay, reportedly becoming the first European to visit Wisconsin. The French ceded the area to Great Britain in 1763, and it became part of the United States in 1783. First organized under the Northwest Ordinance, the area was part of various territories until creation of the Wisconsin Territory in 1836.

Since statehood, Wisconsin has been a wheat farming area, a lumbering frontier, and a preeminent dairy state. Tourism has grown in importance, and industry has concentrated in the eastern and southeastern part of the state.

Politically, the state has enjoyed a reputation for honest, efficient government. It is known as the birthplace of the Republican Party and the home of Robert M. La Follette, Sr., founder of the progressive movement.

Political Balance — After being primarily a one-party state for most of its existence, with the Republican and Progressive Parties dominating during portions of the state's first century, Wisconsin has become a politically competitive state in recent decades. The Republicans gained majority control in both houses in the 1995 Legislature, an advantage they last held during the 1969 session. Since then, control of the senate has changed several times. Republicans have controlled both houses since the 2003 session.

Governor Jim Doyle is only the second Democrat to serve since 1979. In the last 50 years, Wisconsin's two main urban areas – Milwaukee and Madison – have provided over half of the state's constitutional officers. During this period, nine women have served as constitutional officers: two as lieutenant governor, one as attorney general, two as secretary of state, two as state treasurer, and two as superintendent of public instruction.

National Office — Although the Democratic candidate has carried Wisconsin five times in a row, presidential elections in the state tend to be close. In fact, no candidate has received a majority of votes cast since Michael Dukakis in 1988. This has resulted in Wisconsin being regarded as a hotly contested "swing state" in recent presidential elections.

Wisconsin voters tend to retain their U.S. Senators in office for long periods of time. Five senators in this century have served three terms or more, topped by Senator William Proxmire's 30 years in office. Democrats have held both of Wisconsin's U.S. Senate seats over the past 40 years, except for the 12 years served by Republican Senator Robert W. Kasten, Jr.

Currently, four Democrats and four Republicans represent Wisconsin in the U.S. House of Representatives, and four of the current members have been elected nine or more times in regular elections. Democrats held the majority of offices from 1973 to 1991. The Republicans took the majority in 1993 and 1995 but lost it to the Democrats in 1997. Certain congressional districts have traditionally been represented by one party or the other with little relationship to statewide politics.

Voter Turnout — Turnout in presidential and gubernatorial elections may vary as much as a half million votes from election to election. Although individual elections have been up and down, the trend has been upward. Nearly 3 million votes were cast in the 2004 presidential election, by far the most in state history.

Supreme Court — Although justices of the Wisconsin Supreme Court are elected officials, they frequently are first named to the court by gubernatorial appointment to fill a vacancy. Subsequently, the appointees must be elected to the office if they wish to stay on the court; most have been successful. Among the current seven justices, four came to the court by the appointment route. The first woman justice to serve the court, Shirley S. Abrahamson, was appointed in 1976. She was elected in 1979 and became chief justice in 1996.

SIGNIFICANT EVENTS IN WISCONSIN HISTORY

Under the Flag of France

Although American Indians lived in the area of present-day Wisconsin for several thousand years before the arrival of the French – numbering about 20,000 when the French arrived – the written history of the state began with the accounts of French explorers. The French explored the state, named places and established trading posts, but left relatively little mark on it. They were interested in the fur trade, rather than agricultural settlement, and were never present in large numbers.

1634 — Jean Nicolet: First known European to reach Wisconsin. Sought Northwest Passage.

1654-59 — Pierre Esprit Radisson and Medart Chouart des Groseilliers: First of the fur traders in Wisconsin.

1661 — Father Rene Menard: First missionary to Wisconsin Indians.

1665 — Father Claude Allouez founded mission at La Pointe.

1666 — Nicholas Perrot opened fur trade with Wisconsin Indians.

1672 — Father Allouez and Father Louis Andre built St. Francois Xavier mission at De Pere.

1673 — Louis Jolliet and Father Jacques Marquette discovered Mississippi River.

1678 — Daniel Greysolon Sieur du Lhut (Duluth) explored western end of Lake Superior.

1685 — Perrot made Commandant of the West.

1690 — Perrot discovered lead mines in Wisconsin and Iowa.

1701-38 — Fox Indian Wars.

1755 — Wisconsin Indians, under Charles Langlade, helped defeat British General Braddock.

1763 — Treaty of Paris. Wisconsin became part of British colonial territory.

Under the Flag of England

Wisconsin experienced few changes under British control. It remained the western edge of European penetration into the American continent, important only because of the fur trade. French traders worked in the state and British and colonial traders began to appear, but Europeans continued to be visitors rather than settlers.

1761 — Fort at Green Bay accepted by English.

1763 — Conspiracy of Pontiac. Two Englishmen killed by Indians at Muscoda.

1764 — Charles Langlade settled at Green Bay. First permanent settlement.

1766 — Jonathan Carver visited Wisconsin seeking Northwest Passage.

1774 — Quebec Act made Wisconsin a part of Province of Quebec.

1781 — Traditional date of settlement at Prairie du Chien.

1783 — Second Treaty of Paris. Wisconsin became United States territory.

Achieving Territorial Status

In spite of the Treaty of Paris, Wisconsin remained British in all but title until after the War of 1812. In 1815, the American army established control. Gradually, Indian title to the southeastern half of the state was extinguished. Lead mining brought the first heavy influx of settlers and ended the dominance of the fur trade in the economy of the area. The lead mining period ran from about 1824 to 1861. Almost half of the 11,683 people who lived in the territory in 1836 were residents of the lead mining district in the southwestern corner of the state.

1787 — Under the Northwest Ordinance of 1787, Wisconsin was made part of the Northwest Territory. The governing units for the Wisconsin area prior to statehood were:

1787-1800 — Northwest Territory.

1800-1809 — Indiana Territory.

1809-1818 — Illinois Territory.

1818-1836 — Michigan Territory.

1836-1848 — Wisconsin Territory.

1795 — Jacques Vieau established trading posts at Kewaunee, Manitowoc, and Sheboygan. Made headquarters at Milwaukee.

1804 — William Henry Harrison's treaty with Indians at St. Louis. United States extinguished Indian title to lead region (a cause of Black Hawk War).

1814 — Fort Shelby built at Prairie du Chien. Captured by English and name changed to Fort McKay.

1815 — War with England concluded. Fort McKay abandoned by British.

1816 — Fort Shelby rebuilt at Prairie du Chien (renamed Fort Crawford). Astor's American Fur Company began operations in Wisconsin.

1818 — Solomon Juneau bought trading post of Jacques Vieau at Milwaukee.

1820 — Rev. Jedediah Morse preached first Protestant sermon in Wisconsin at Fort Howard (Green Bay) July 9. Henry Schoolcraft, James Duane Doty, Lewis Cass made exploration trip through Wisconsin.

1822 — New York Indians (Oneida, Stockbridge, Munsee, and Brothertown) moved to Wisconsin. First mining leases in southwest Wisconsin.

1825 — Indian Treaty established tribal boundaries.

1826-27 — Winnebago Indian War. Surrender of Chief Red Bird.

1828 — Fort Winnebago begun at Portage.

1832 — Black Hawk War.

1833 — Land treaty with Indians cleared southern Wisconsin land titles. First news-paper, *Green Bay Intelligencer*, established.

1834 — Land offices established at Green Bay and Mineral Point. First public road laid out.

1835 — First steamboat arrived at Milwaukee. First bank in Wisconsin opened at Green Bay.

1836 — Act creating Territory of Wisconsin signed April 20 by President Andrew Jackson. (Provisions of Ordinance of 1787 made part of the act.)

Wisconsin Territory

Wisconsin's population reached 305,000 by 1850. About half of the new immigrants were from New York and New England. The rest were principally from England, Scotland, Ireland, Germany, and Scandinavia. New York's Erie Canal gave Wisconsin a water outlet to the Atlantic Ocean and a route for new settlers. Wheat was the primary cash crop for most of the newcomers.

State politics revolved around factions headed by James Doty and Henry Dodge. As political parties developed, the Democrats proved dominant throughout the period.

Peshtigo fire as depicted in Harper's Weekly, *1871.* (State Historical Society, #WHi 1781)

1836 — Capital located at Belmont – Henry Dodge appointed governor, July 4, by President Andrew Jackson. First session of legislature. Madison chosen as permanent capital.

1837 — Madison surveyed and platted. First Capitol begun. Panic of 1837 – all territorial banks failed. Winnebago Indians ceded all claims to land in Wisconsin. Imprisonment for debt abolished.

1838 — Territorial legislature met in Madison. Milwaukee and Rock River Canal Company chartered.

1840 — First school taxes authorized and levied.

1841 — James D. Doty appointed governor by President John Tyler.

1842 — C.C. Arndt shot and killed in legislature by James R. Vineyard.

1844 — Nathaniel P. Tallmadge appointed governor. Wisconsin Phalanx (a utopian colony) established at Ceresco (Ripon).

1845 — Dodge reappointed governor. Mormon settlement at Voree (Burlington). Swiss colony came to New Glarus.

1846 — Congress passed enabling act for admission of Wisconsin as state. First Constitutional Convention met in Madison.

1847 — Census population 210,546. First Constitution rejected by people. Second Constitutional Convention.

1848 — Second Constitution adopted. President James K. Polk signed bill on May 29 making Wisconsin a state.

Early Statehood

Heavy immigration continued after statehood. The state remained largely agricultural with wheat the primary crop. Slavery, banking laws, and temperance were the major issues of the period. Despite the number of foreign immigrants and a shift from Democratic control to Republican control, most political leaders continued to have ties to the northeastern United States. New York state laws and institutions provided models for much of the activity of the early legislative sessions.

1848 — Legislature met June 5. Governor Nelson Dewey inaugurated June 7. State university incorporated. First telegram

reached Milwaukee. Large scale German immigration began.

1849 — School code adopted. First free, tax-supported, graded school with high school at Kenosha.

1850 — Bond Law for controlling sale of liquor passed. State opened the Wisconsin Institute for Education of the Blind at Janesville.

1851 — First railroad train – Milwaukee to Waukesha. First state fair at Janesville.

1852 — School for deaf opened at Delavan. Prison construction begun at Waupun.

1853 — Impeachment of Judge Levi Hubbell. Capital punishment abolished (third state to take action).

1854 — Republican Party named at a meeting in Ripon. First class graduated at state university. Joshua Glover, fugitive slave, arrested in Racine, and the Wisconsin Supreme Court, in related matter, declared Fugitive Slave Law of 1850 unconstitutional. Milwaukee and Mississippi Railroad reached Madison.

1856 — Bashford-Barstow election scandal. Legislative report on maladministration of school funds.

1857 — Railroad completed to Prairie du Chien. First high school class graduated at Racine. Industrial School for Boys opened at Waukesha.

1858 — Legislative investigation of bribery in 1856 Legislature.

1859 — Abraham Lincoln spoke at state fair in Milwaukee.

1861 — Beginning of Civil War. Governor called for volunteers for military service. Bank riot in Milwaukee. Office of county superintendent of schools created.

1862 — Governor Louis P. Harvey drowned. Draft riots. Edward G. Ryan's address at Democratic Convention criticized Lincoln's conduct of war.

1864 — Cheese factory started at Ladoga, Fond du Lac County, by Chester Hazen.

1865 — 96,000 Wisconsin soldiers served in Civil War; losses were 12,216.

The Maturing Commonwealth

After the Civil War Wisconsin matured into a modern political and economic entity. Heavy immigration continued throughout the period. The mix of immigrants remained similar to that prior to the Civil War until the end of the century, when Poles began to appear in large numbers.

The Republican Party remained in control of state government throughout the period, but was challenged by Grangers, Populists, Socialists, and Temperance candidates in addition to the Democratic Party and dissidents within the Republican Party. Temperance, the use of foreign languages in schools, railroad regulation, and currency reform were major issues in the state throughout the period.

Wheat culture gradually declined in importance in Wisconsin as more fertile wheatlands were opened to cultivation in the north and west. In the 1880s and 1890s, dairying gradually became the primary agricultural pursuit in the state. The agricultural school at the university developed into a national leader in the field of dairy science. From the 1870s through the 1890s, lumbering prospered in the northern half of the state. At its peak from 1888 to 1893, it accounted for one-fourth of all wages paid in the state. By the end of the period, Milwaukee and the southeastern half of the state had developed a thriving heavy machinery industry. The paper industry was established in the Fox River Valley by the end of the century. The tanning and the brewing industries were also prominent.

1866 — First state normal school opened at Platteville. Agricultural College at university reorganized under Morrill Act.

1871 — Peshtigo fire burned over much of 6 counties in northeast Wisconsin, resulting in over 1,000 deaths.

1872 — Wisconsin Dairymen's Association organized at Watertown.

1873 — Invention of typewriter by C. Latham Sholes. The Patrons of Husbandry, an agricultural organization nicknamed the Grangers, elected Governor William R. Taylor.

1874 — Potter Law limiting railroad rates passed.

1875 — Free high school law passed; women eligible for election to school boards. State Industrial School for Girls established at Milwaukee. Republicans defeated Grangers. Oshkosh almost destroyed by fire.

1876 — Potter Law repealed. Hazel Green cyclone.

1877 — John T. Appleby patented knotter for twine binders.

1882 — Constitution amended to make legislative sessions biennial. First hydroelectric plant established at Appleton.

1883 — Major hotel fire at the Newhall House in Milwaukee killed 71. South wing of Capitol extension collapsed; 7 killed. Agricultural Experiment Station established at university.

1885 — Gogebic iron range discoveries made Ashland a major shipping port.

1886 — Strikes related to the 8-hour work day movement at Milwaukee culminate in confrontation with militia at Bay View; 5 killed. Agricultural Short Course established at university.

1887 — Marshfield almost destroyed by fire.

1889 — Bennett Law, requiring classroom instruction in English, passed. Wisconsin Supreme Court in the "Edgerton Bible case", prohibited reading and prayers from the King James Bible in public schools. Arbor Day authorized. Former Governor Jeremiah Rusk became first U.S. Secretary of Agriculture.

1890 — Stephen M. Babcock invented quick, easy, accurate test for milk butterfat content.

1891 — Bennett Law repealed after bitter opposition from German Protestants and Catholics.

1893 — Wisconsin Supreme Court ordered state treasurer to refund to the state interest on state deposits, which had customarily been retained by treasurers.

1894 — Forest fires in northern and central Wisconsin.

1897 — Corrupt practice act passed.

1898 — Wisconsin sent 5,469 men to fight in Spanish-American War; losses were 134.

1899 — Antipass law prohibited railroads from giving public officials free rides. Tax commission created. New Richmond tornado.

The Progressive Era

The state's prominent role in the reform movements which swept the country at the beginning of the century gave Wisconsin national fame and its first presidential candidate. Republicans dominated the state legislature, but Progressive and Stalwart factions fought continually for control of the party. Milwaukee consistently returned a strong Socialist contingent to the legislature.

Large-scale European immigration ended during this period, but ethnic groups retained strong individual identities and remained a significant force in the politics and culture of the state. Important social issues were reflected in the calendar of progressive legislation enacted during the period. The 2 world wars caused great stress because of the large German population of the state.

Heavy machinery manufacturing, paper products and dairying consolidated their position as the leading economic activities. As the last virgin forests in the northern half of the state were cut over, lumbering faded in importance. Brewing temporarily disappeared with the advent of Prohibition.

1900 — Wisconsin's first state park, Inter-

state near St. Croix Falls, established.

1901 — First Wisconsin-born Governor, Robert M. La Follette, inaugurated. Teaching of agriculture introduced into rural schools. Legislative Reference Library, which served as a model for other states and the Library of Congress, established – later renamed the Legislative Reference Bureau.

1904 — Primary election law approved by referendum vote. State Capitol burned.

1905 — State civil service established; auto license law passed; tuberculosis sanitoria authorized. Forestry Board created. Railroad Commission, regulating railroads and subsequently utilities, created.

1907 — Current Capitol begun.

1908 — Income tax amendment adopted.

1910 — Milwaukee elected Emil Seidel first Socialist mayor. Eau Claire first Wisconsin city to adopt commission form of government.

William Jennings Bryan addresses a rally in Columbus during his 1900 presidential campaign. (State Historical Society, #WHi 32826)

1911 — First income tax law; teachers' pension act; vocational schools authorized; Industrial and Highway Commissions created; workmen's compensation act enacted.

1913 — Direct election of Wisconsin's U.S. senators approved.

1915 — Conservation Commission, State Board of Agriculture, and State Board of Education created.

1917 — Capitol completed, cost $7,258,763. 120,000 Wisconsin soldiers served in World War I; losses were 3,932. Wisconsin first state to meet draft requirements; 584,559 registrations.

1919 — Eighteenth Amendment (Prohibition) ratified.

The Dry Era in Wisconsin. (State Historical Society, #WHi 32825)

1920 — Nineteenth Amendment (women's suffrage) ratified; first state to deliver ratification to Washington.

1921 — Equal rights for women and prohibition laws enacted.

1923 — Military training made optional at university.

1924 — La Follette won Wisconsin's vote for president as Progressive Party candidate. Reforestation amendment to state constitution adopted.

1925 — Senator La Follette died on June 18.

1929 — Professor Harry Steenbock of University of Wisconsin patented radiation of Vitamin D. Legislature repealed all Wisconsin laws for state enforcement of Prohibition.

1932 — Forest Products Laboratory erected at Madison.

1933 — Dairy farmers undertook milk strike to protest low prices. Wisconsin voted for repeal of 18th Amendment (Prohibition) to U.S. Constitution.

1934 — Wisconsin Progressive Party formed.

1942 — Governor-elect Loomis died; Supreme Court decided Lieutenant Governor Goodland to serve as acting governor.

1941-45 — Wisconsin enrolled 375,000 for World War II; casualties 7,980.

1946 — Wisconsin Progressive Party dissolved and rejoined Republican Party.

The Middle Years of the Twentieth Century

After the demise of the Progressives, the Democratic Party began a gradual resurgence and, by the late 1950s, became strongly competitive for the first time in over a century. With the decline in foreign immigration, the traditional ethnic differences became muted, but significant numbers of blacks appeared in the urban areas of the state for the first time. Discrimination in housing and employment became matters of concern. Other important issues included the growth in the size of state government, radicalism on the university campuses, welfare programs and environmental questions. Tourism emerged as a major industry during this period.

1948 — Centennial Year.

1949 — Legislature enacted new formula for distribution of state educational aids and classified school districts for this purpose.

1950 — Wisconsin enrolled 132,000 for the Korean Conflict; 800 casualties.

1951 — First major legislative reapportionment since 1892.

1957 — Legislation prohibited lobbyists from giving anything of value to a state employee.

1958 — Professor Joshua Lederberg, UW geneticist, Nobel prize winner in medicine.

1959 — Gaylord Nelson, first Democratic governor since 1933, inaugurated. Circus

World Museum established at Baraboo. Frank Lloyd Wright, architect, died.

1960 — Mrs. Dena Smith elected state treasurer, first woman elected to statewide office in Wisconsin.

1961 — Legislation enacted to initiate long-range program of acquisition and improvement of state recreation facilities (ORAP program). Federal supervision of Menominee Indian tribe terminated on April 29; reservation became 72nd county.

1962 — Selective sales tax and income tax withholding enacted. Kohler Company strike, which began in 1954, settled.

1963 — John Gronouski, state tax commissioner, appointed U.S. Postmaster General. State expenditures from all funds for 1963-64 fiscal year top $1 billion for first time.

1964 — Wisconsin Supreme Court redistricted legislature after legislature and governor failed to agree on a plan. Two National Farmers Organization members killed in demonstration at Bonduel stockyard. Legislature enacted property tax relief for aged. The office of county superintendent of schools abolished, but Cooperative Educational Service Agencies (CESAs) created to provide regional services.

1965 — School compulsory attendance age raised to 18. All parts of state placed into vocational school districts. County boards reapportioned on population basis. State law prevented discrimination in housing. The State Capitol, in use since 1917, officially dedicated, after extensive remodeling and cleaning.

1966 — 1965 Legislature held first full even-year regular session since 1882. Governor Warren P. Knowles called out National Guard to keep order during civil rights demonstrations in Wauwatosa. Wisconsin Supreme Court upheld Milwaukee Braves baseball team move to Atlanta. Grand jury investigation of illegal lobbying activities in the legislature resulted in 13 indictments.

1967 — Executive branch reorganized along functional lines. Ban on colored oleomargarine repealed. Racial rioting in Milwaukee in July-August. Marathon marches demonstrate for Milwaukee open housing ordinance. Antiwar protests at the University of Wisconsin in Madison culminate in riot with injuries.

1968 — Constitutional amendment permitted the legislature to meet as provided by law rather than once a biennium, resulting in annual sessions. Ninety black students expelled from Wisconsin State University-Oshkosh when December demonstration damaged the administration building. Wisconsin's first heart transplant performed at St. Luke's Hospital in Milwaukee; first successful bone marrow transplant performed by team of scientists and surgeons at the University of Wisconsin in Madison.

1969 — Selective sales tax became general sales tax. On opening day of special legislative session on welfare and urban aids, welfare mothers and UW-Madison students, led by Father James Groppi, took over the Assembly Chamber; National Guard called to protect Capitol. Groppi cited for contempt and jailed; contempt charge upheld by Wisconsin Supreme Court. Student strikes at UW in Madison demanded Black studies department; National Guard activated to restore order. Congressman Melvin R. Laird appointed U.S. Secretary of Defense. Wisconsin's portion of Interstate Highway System completed.

Fr. James Groppi occupies the Assembly Chamber, 1969. (State Historical Society, #WHi 4934)

1970 — Army Mathematics Research Building at the UW in Madison bombed by anti-war protestors, resulting in one death. "Old Main" at Wisconsin State University-Whitewater burned down in apparent arson. First elections to 4-year terms in Wisconsin history for all constitutional officers, based on constitutional amendment ratified in 1967. UW scientists, headed by Dr. Har Gobind Khorana, succeeded in the first total synthesis of a gene.

1971 — The legislature, now meeting in regular session throughout the biennium, enacted major shared tax redistribution, merger of University of Wisconsin and State University systems, revision of municipal employee relations laws.

1972 — Legislature enacted comprehensive consumer protection act, lowered the age of majority from 21 to 18, required environmental impact statement for all legislation affecting the environment, repealed railroad full crew law, and ratified the unsuccessful "equal rights" amendment to U.S. Constitution. Record highway death toll, 1,168.

1973 — State constitutional amendment permitting bingo adopted. Barbara Thompson first woman to hold the elective office of State Superintendent of Public Instruction. The 1954 Menominee Termination Act repealed by Congress. Legislature enacted state ethics code, repealed oleomargarine tax, funded programs for the education of all handicapped children, and established procedures for informal probate of simple estates.

1974 — Legislature enacted comprehensive campaign finance act and strengthened open meetings law. Democrats swept all constitutional offices and gained control of both houses of the 1975 Legislature for first time since 1893. Kathryn Morrison first woman elected to the state senate. Striking teachers fired in Hortonville.

1964-1975 — 165,400 Wisconsinites served in Vietnam; 1,239 were killed.

Recent History

Democrats lost control of the senate in 1993 for the first time since 1974, and in 1995 they lost control of the assembly for the first

time since 1970. Control of the senate has changed several times since then. Women began to be widely represented in the legislature for the first time in the 90s.

Health care reform, restructuring welfare, the business climate in the state, taxation, education, and prisons were the chief concerns of policymakers in the 90s.

California challenged Wisconsin's dominance of the dairy industry. After an economic downturn in the 80s, the 90s saw a robust economy throughout most of the state with Madison leading the entire country in employment for several months. The farm sector and brewing industry continued to experience difficulties, however.

Litigation and demonstrations over off-reservation resource rights of the Chippewa Indians continued throughout the 80s to be replaced by controversy over Indian gaming in the 90s and into the new century.

1975 — Menominee Indians occupied Alexian Brothers Novitiate. Legislature made voter registration easier, established property tax levy limits on local governments, and eliminated statutory distinctions based on sex. UW-Madison scientist, Dr. Howard Temin, shared 1975 Nobel Prize in physiology-medicine.

1976 — U.S. District Court ordered integration of Milwaukee public schools. Ice storm damage reached $50.4 million. Wisconsin Legislature established a system for compensating crime victims. Exxon discovered sulfide zinc and copper deposits in Forest County. Shirley S. Abrahamson was appointed first woman on the Wisconsin Supreme Court. Wisconsin Supreme Court declared negative school aids law unconstitutional.

1977 — Governor Patrick J. Lucey appointed Ambassador to Mexico, and Lieutenant Governor Martin Schreiber became "acting governor". First state employees union strike lasted 15 days; National Guard ran prisons. Constitutional amendments authorized raffle games and revised the structure of the court system by creating a Court of Appeals. Legislation enacted included public support of elections campaigns, no-fault divorce, and implied consent law for drunk driving.

1978 — Wisconsin Supreme Court allowed cameras in state courtrooms. Vel Phillips elected secretary of state, first black constitutional officer. Laws enacted included a hazardous waste management program.

1979 — Constitutional amendment removed lieutenant governor from serving as president of the senate. Moratorium on tax collections gave state taxpayers a 3-month "vacation" from taxes. Shirley S. Abrahamson, became the first woman elected to Wisconsin Supreme Court after serving by appointment for 3 years. Legislature established school of veterinary medicine at the UW-Madison.

1980 — Eric Heiden of Madison won five Olympic gold medals for ice speed skating, named winner of the Sullivan Award as best amateur athlete in the country. 15,000 Cuban refugees housed for the summer at Fort McCoy. Former Governor Lucey ran as independent candidate for U.S. Vice President. State revenue shortfall led to 4.4 percent cuts in state spending. Laws enacted included specific rights for victims and witnesses of crimes, and mental patient commitment revisions.

1981 — U.S. Supreme Court ruled against Wisconsin's historic open primary. Laws enacted included stronger penalties for drunk driving and changes in mining taxes.

1982 — State unemployment hit highest levels since the Great Depression. Voters endorsed first statewide referendum in nation calling for a freeze on nuclear weapons. Laws enacted included extensions in the fair employment law, an "employees' right-to-know" law pertaining to toxic substances in the workplace, a new public records law, and a historic preservation law. Jos. Schlitz Brewing Co. acquired by Stroh Brewing Co. of Detroit, all Milwaukee operations closed.

1983 — Continued recession forced adoption of budget including a 10 percent tax surcharge and a pay freeze for state employees. Law raising minimum drinking age to 19 passed (effective 7/1/85). In one-day uprising, inmates at Waupun State Prison took 15 hostages, but released them uninjured. Laws enacted included a "lemon law" on motor vehicle warranties, changes in child support collection procedures and levels. UW-Madison School of Veterinary Medicine enrolled its first class.

1984 — Most powerful U.S. tornado of 1984 destroyed Barneveld; 9 dead. Democratic

party chose presidential convention delegates in caucuses rather than by presidential preference primary as a result of the Democratic National Committee rules changes. Indian treaty rights to fish and hunt caused controversy. First liver transplants in Wisconsin conducted at UW Hospital. Laws enacted included a marital property reform act, groundwater protection act, establishment of high school graduation requirements, a "right-to-die" act, prohibition of smoking in public areas. Economic conditions began to improve from the low-point of the previous 2 years.

1985 — Milwaukee air crash killed 31. Major consolidation of state banks by large holding companies. Laws enacted included authorization for public utilities to form holding companies, comparable worth, and teen pregnancy prevention measures. First state tax amnesty program.

1986 — Farm land values dropped across the state. Exxon dropped plans to develop copper mine near Crandon. Laws enacted allowed regional banking, set sulfur dioxide emission limits, raised the drinking age to 21, and limited damages payable in malpractice actions.

1987 — Voters approved constitutional amendments allowing pari-mutuel betting and a state lottery. Laws enacted included a mandatory seatbelt law, antitakeover legislation, gradual end to the inheritance and gift taxes, and a "learnfare" program designed to keep in school the children of families receiving Aid to Families With Dependent Children (AFDC). G. Heileman Brewing Company taken over by Alan Bond.

1988 — Driest summer since the 1930s. The first state lottery games began. Chrysler Corporation's automobile assembly plant in Kenosha, the nation's oldest car plant, closed. Laws enacted included mandatory family leave for employees.

1989 — Laws enacted included creation of Department of Corrections, the Lower Wisconsin State Riverway, and a statewide land stewardship program.

1990 — More than 1,400 Wisconsin National Guard and Reserve soldiers were called to active duty in Persian Gulf crisis, 11 casualties. The number of Milwaukee murders set a new record, raising demands for crime and drug controls. Laws enacted included a major recycling law and Milwaukee Parental Choice voucher program for public and nonsectarian private schools.

1991 — The price of raw milk hit lowest point since 1978. First Indian gambling compacts signed. Governor Tommy G. Thompson vetoed a record 457 items in the state budget.

1992 — Train derailment caused major spill of toxic chemicals and evacuation of over 22,000 people in Superior. Thousands of opponents, including children, staged protests at 6 abortion clinics in Milwaukee throughout the summer. Laws enacted included parental consent for abortion, health care reform, and creation of a 3-member Gaming Commission.

1993 — Wisconsin Congressman Les Aspin and UW-Madison President Donna Shalala named President Bill Clinton's Secretary of Defense and Secretary of Health and Human Services, respectively. Thousands in Milwaukee became ill as a result of cryptosporidium in the water supply. California passed Wisconsin in milk production. Republicans won control of state senate for the first time since 1974. Laws enacted included a 1999 sunset for traditional welfare programs, a cap on school spending, and permission to organize limited liability companies.

1994 — Laws enacted included removal of about $1 billion in public school operating taxes from property tax by 1997, a new regulatory framework for Public Service Commission regulation of telecommunication utilities, and granting towns most of the same powers exercised by cities and villages.

1995 — Republicans won control of state assembly for the first time since 1970. Elk reintroduced in northern Wisconsin. July heat wave contributed to 172 deaths.

1996 — Governor Thompson's new welfare reform plan, known as Wisconsin Works (W-2), received national attention. Train derailment forced evacuation of Weyauwega. Pabst Brewing closed 152-year-old brewery in Milwaukee. Senator George Petak was removed from office in the first successful legislative recall election in state history.

1997 — Groundbreaking for controversial new Miller Park, future home of the Milwaukee Brewers baseball team.

After 47 years as home to the Milwaukee Braves, Green Bay Packers, and Milwaukee Brewers, County Stadium was torn down in 2001. (Milwaukee Brewers Baseball Club)

1998 — Tammy Baldwin became first Wisconsin woman elected to the U.S. Congress. U.S. Supreme Court upheld constitutionality of extension of Milwaukee Parental Choice school vouchers to religious schools. Second state tax amnesty program. Laws enacted included a mining moratorium, new penalties for failure to pay child support, truth-in-sentencing, and protection of fetuses.

1999 — Governor Tommy Thompson began record fourth term. Laws enacted included "smart growth", graduated drivers licensing, a sales tax rebate. Supermax, the state's high security prison, opened at Boscobel. Record low unemployment.

2000 — Legislature approved a local sales tax and revenue bonds for renovation of Lambeau Field, home of the Green Bay Packers.

2001 — Governor Thompson ended a record 14 years in office and assumed post of U.S. Secretary of Health and Human Services. Lt. Governor Scott McCallum became governor and appointed State Senator Margaret Farrow as the first woman to serve as lieutenant governor. Chronic Wasting Disease discovered in the state's deer herd. Extensive Mississippi River flooding. Miller Park opened. Laws enacted included telemarketing "no call" list, wetland protection, and the "senior care" prescription drug assistance plan.

2002 — Barbara Lawton became the first woman elected lieutenant governor and Peggy A. Lautenschlager became first woman elected attorney general. Deadliest single traffic accident in state history killed 10 and injured 40 near Sheboygan. Investigation into legislative caucus staffs resulted in criminal charges against five legislators. Seven Milwaukee County board members recalled over pension scandal.

2003 — Jim Doyle became first Democratic governor in 16 years. The Crandon mine issue was apparently resolved when local Indian tribes purchased the ore deposits. The renovated Lambeau Field opened. Senator Gary George became the second legislator in Wisconsin history to be recalled. A number of Wisconsin Guard and Reserve units were activated for ser-

vice in the Iraq war. Wisconsin held its first mourning dove hunt.

2004 — Louis Butler, Jr., became the first black member of the Wisconsin Supreme Court. State government began to reduce its automobile fleet after allegations of misuse. Significant legislation included a livestock facility siting law and revision to clean air and water laws intended to spur job creation. Voter turnout in the fall election was 73%, the highest in many years.

2005 — The state minimum wage was increased. Election process reform was a major issue before the legislature.

Sources: State Historical Society, *The Thirtieth Star, 1948; The 1958 Compton Yearbook* and succeeding editions; *The Americana Annual – 1967;* Robert C. Nesbit, *Wisconsin, A History;* Wisconsin Legislative Reference Bureau, *Clippings: Wisconsin History.*

On August 24, 2004, Louis B. Butler, Jr., was sworn in as the first black Supreme Court Justice in Wisconsin history. (Jay Salvo, Assembly Photographer)

FAMOUS CITIZENS OF WISCONSIN

Edward P. Allis (1824-1889), industrialist — developed the steel rolling mill.

Don Ameche* (1908-1993), actor — began career in radio, appeared in 56 movies; won Academy Award for *Cocoon*.

Roy Chapman Andrews* (1884-1960), explorer — found first dinosaur egg in the Gobi Desert.

Les Aspin* (1938-1995), political leader — President Clinton's first secretary of defense, January 1993 – December 1993; served 22 years in the U.S. Congress.

Stephen M. Babcock (1843-1931), chemist — devised butterfat content test.

John Bardeen* (1908-1991), physicist — twice winner of the Nobel Prize for development of the transistor and for the theory of superconductivity.

John Bascom (1827-1911), educator — president, University of Wisconsin 1874-1887; leader in upgrading the university to a nationally recognized institution.

Aaron Bohrod (1907-1992), painter — twice winner of the Guggenheim Fellowship; artist-in-residence at the University of Wisconsin-Madison.

Richard Ira "Dick" Bong* (1920-1945), aviator — leading World War II pilot; shot down 40 enemy planes to become America's "all time ace"; awarded Congressional Medal of Honor.

Olympia Brown (1835-1926), minister and publisher — first ordained woman minister in U.S.; key figure in women's rights movement.

Jerome I. Case (1819-1891), manufacturer — leader in mechanization of agriculture.

Carrie Chapman Catt* (1859-1947), suffragist — President of the National American Woman Suffrage Association, which she reorganized as the League of Women Voters with 2 million members after passage of the 19th amendment guaranteed women the vote.

Bernard J. Cigrand* (1866-1932), activist — leader in the movement to celebrate Flag Day.

Laurel Blair Salton Clark* (1961-2003), astronaut and naval flight surgeon — mission specialist died in crash of space shuttle Columbia.

John R. Commons (1862-1945), economist — drafted Wisconsin civil service law.

Seymour Cray* (1925-1996), computer scientist — called the "father of the supercomputer".

Leo T. Crowley (1889-1972), banker — structured the Federal Deposit Insurance Corporation as its chairperson, 1934-1945.

Patrick Cudahy (1849-1919), businessman — founder of a leading meat-packing company.

August Derleth* (1909-1971), author — noted for many contributions to literature about Wisconsin.

Ole Evinrude (1877-1934), inventor — developed the first outboard motor designed for mass production.

Edna Ferber (1885-1968), author — received 1925 Pulitzer Prize for the novel, *So Big.*

Lynn Fontanne (1887-1983) and **Alfred Lunt***, acting couple — appeared in theater, motion pictures, and television; jointly awarded Presidential Medal of Freedom in 1964.

Zona Gale* (1874-1938), author — recipient of 1921 Pulitzer Prize in drama for the play, *Miss Lulu Bett.*

Hamlin Garland* (1860-1940), author — received 1922 Pulitzer Prize for the novel, *A Daughter of the Middle Border.*

Ezekiel Gillespie (1818-1892), activist — plaintiff in 1866 Wisconsin Supreme Court case which resulted in extension of suffrage to Wisconsin Blacks; one of the founders of the first African Methodist Episcopal church in Wisconsin.

William T. Green (1863-1911), activist — first Black attorney in Wisconsin; active in securing the 1895 passage of the first civil rights law in the state.

Owen J. Gromme* (1896-1991), painter — wildlife artist, author of *Birds of Wisconsin,* and painter of the 1945 federal duck stamp.

John A. Gronouski* (1919-1996), political leader — postmaster general under Presidents Kennedy and Johnson; one of the architects of the modern Democratic Party in Wisconsin.

Mildred Fish Harnack* (1902-1943), war hero — while instructor at the University of Berlin, organized resistance group and transmitted intelligence to Allies; executed by Nazis.

Cordelia Harvey (1824-1895), humanitarian — instrumental in establishing military hospitals in the North during the Civil War.

Woodrow Charles "Woody" Herman (1913-1987), musician — jazz clarinetist and one of the outstanding "big band" leaders.

William Dempster Hoard (1836-1918), farmer and governor — introduced the French version of the silo and the subearth vault for curing cheese.

Harry Houdini (1874-1926), magician — world-renowned escape artist.

J. Willard Hurst (1911-1997), legal scholar — University of Wisconsin-Madison professor of law; nationally recognized expert in legal history.

Samuel C. Johnson (1833-1919), industrialist — founded wax products firm.

George F. Kennan* (1904-2005), diplomat, scholar and statesman — architect of Cold War "containment policy".

Walter J. Kohler, Sr.* (1875-1940), industrialist and governor — founded plumbing equipment company.

Julius Frank Anthony "Pee Wee King" Kuczynski* (1914-2000), musician — member of the Country Music Hall of Fame; author of over 400 songs including "Tennessee Waltz", one of the state songs of the State of Tennessee.

Belle Case La Follette* (1859-1931), lawyer and editor — first woman to graduate from the University of Wisconsin Law School; leader in support of the rights of women and African Americans.

Robert M. La Follette, Sr.* (1855-1925), political leader — progressive reformer as governor and U.S. Senator.

Carl Laemmle (1867-1939), business executive — major figure in the growth of the motion picture industry; built Universal City Studios.

Earl L. "Curly" Lambeau (1898-1965), professional football coach — founder and coach of the Green Bay Packers; instrumental in establishing the National Football League.

Mary Lasker* (1901-1994), philanthropist — her financial donations and influence supported vast expansion of cancer research; awarded Presidential Medal of Freedom in 1969.

William D. Leahy* (1875-1959), fleet admiral U.S. Navy — Chief of Naval Operations and President Roosevelt's chief of staff during World War II; the only Wisconsinite to wear the 5 stars of fleet admiral.

Aldo Leopold (1887-1948), teacher and author — University of Wisconsin professor and prominent ecologist; wrote *Sand County Almanac*.

Wladziu Valentino Liberace* (1919-1986), musician — world famous pianist-singer; known for his showmanship.

Vince Lombardi (1913-1970), professional football coach — 1959-1968 coach of the Green Bay Packers, the first NFL team to win 3 consecutive championships.

Alfred Lunt* (1893-1977) and **Lynn Fontanne**, acting couple — appeared in theater, motion pictures, and television; jointly awarded Presidential Medal of Freedom in 1964.

Douglas A. MacArthur (1880-1964), general — served in World Wars I and II, noted for his Philippine campaign, led post-war occupation of Japan, commander of UN forces in Korea.

Frederic March* (1897-1975), actor — won Academy Awards for *Dr. Jekyll and Mr. Hyde* and *Best Years of Our Lives*.

Helen Farnsworth Mears* (1872-1916), sculptor — created the Frances Willard statue in Statuary Hall of the U.S. Capitol and "The Genius of Wisconsin" in the Wisconsin Capitol.

Charles McCarthy (1873-1921), government innovator — established and directed first legislative reference library in the nation (forerunner of the Legislative Reference Bureau); wrote *The Wisconsin Idea*; advocate of vocational schools.

Golda Meir (1898-1978), political leader — prime minister of Israel (1969-1974); was educated and taught school in Milwaukee.

William "Billy" Mitchell (1879-1936), brigadier general, U.S. Army — fervent advocate of a strong air force.

John Muir (1838-1914), naturalist — promoted the national parks system.

Gaylord Nelson* (1916-2005), state legislator, governor, and U.S. senator — founder of Earth Day.

Lorine Niedecker* (1903-1970), poet — author of several books of poetry; featured in most anthologies of 20th century American poetry.

Albert Ochsner* (1858-1925), surgeon — pioneer in radium cancer treatment.

Georgia O'Keeffe* (1887-1986), artist — innovative painter of flowers and landscapes, awarded Presidential Medal of Freedom in 1977.

George C. Poage (1880-1962), athlete — first Black athlete to compete in the modern Olympics; won bronze medals in the 200 and 400 meter hurdles in the 1904 Olympics at St. Louis.

Mitchel Red Cloud, Jr.* (1925-1950), Winnebago war hero — posthumously awarded Congressional Medal of Honor for service in Korea; first member of a Wisconsin tribe so honored.

Albert Ringling (1852-1916), circus promoter — merged Ringling Brothers Circus with Barnum and Bailey Circus to become the "Greatest Show On Earth".

Jeremiah Rusk (1830-1893), soldier, governor, and congressman — brigadier general in Union army, first U.S. Secretary of Agriculture.

Carl Schurz (1829-1906), political activist — German immigrant to Wisconsin and national supporter of German-American interests; served as brigadier general in Union army, U.S. Secretary of the Interior, U.S. Senator from Missouri, ambassador to Spain, newspaper owner, and writer.

Margaretha Meyer Schurz (1833-1876), educator — opened the first U.S. kindergarten in Watertown in 1856, married to Carl Schurz.

C. Latham Sholes (1819-1890), inventor and journalist — developed first practical typewriter.

Donald Kent "Deke" Slayton* (1924-1993), astronaut — flew the first joint U.S.-Soviet space mission; awarded NASA Distinguished Service Medal in 1965.

Walter W. "Red" Smith* (1905-1982), sports columnist and commentator — first sportswriter to receive the Pulitzer Prize (1976) for distinguished criticism as a reporter with the *New York Times*.

Harry Steenbock* (1886-1967), biochemist — produced Vitamin D in food by irradiation with ultraviolet light.

Brooks Stevens* (1911-1995), industrial designer — one of the founders of the Industrial Designers Society of America; designer of many notable automobiles and other items including trains, motorcycles, and appliances.

Howard Temin (1934-1994), scientist — winner of 1975 Nobel Prize in physiology for work on the relationship between viruses and cancer.

Spencer Tracy* (1900-1967), actor — won Academy Award for *Boys Town* and *Captains Courageous*.

Frederick Jackson Turner* (1861-1932), historian — developed noted theories regarding the American frontier; won 1933 Pulitzer Prize for history.

Charles Van Hise* (1857-1929), educator — president, University of Wisconsin 1903-1918; promoted the expansion of the university into many new fields, influenced the organization of graduate study as a separate division, and saw university enrollment double.

Thorstein Veblen* (1857-1929), economist — wrote *The Theory of the Leisure Class.*

William Vilas (1840-1908), political leader — served as U.S. Postmaster General, Secretary of Interior, and U.S. Senator; organized the Rural Free Delivery (RFD) mail system.

Cadwallader C. Washburn (1818-1882), multimillionaire businessman, congressman, and governor — had extensive flour, rail, and lumber business interests.

Orson Welles* (1915-1986), actor and director — performed in theater, radio, television, and motion pictures; directed and starred in the highly acclaimed movie, *Citizen Kane.*

Laura Ingalls Wilder* (1867-1957), author of children's books — wrote a series of books, including *Little House on the Prairie*, based on her life growing up in the Midwest.

Thornton N. Wilder* (1897-1975), playwright and novelist — received Pulitzer Prize for the novel *The Bridge of San Luis Rey* (1928) and the plays *Our Town* (1938) and *The Skin of Our Teeth* (1942).

Frances Willard (1839-1898), social reformer — organized the Woman's Christian Temperance Union.

Daniel Hale Williams (1856-1931), doctor — first physician to perform open heart surgery; only African American fellow in the original American College of Surgeons; began study of medicine in Janesville.

Laura Ross Wolcott (1834-1915), physician and suffragist — first woman physician in Wisconsin; active in organizing and first president of the Wisconsin Woman's Suffrage Association.

Frank Lloyd Wright* (1867-1959), architect — internationally known innovative designer.

Note: Only deceased Wisconsin citizens are included in this list.
*Born in Wisconsin.
Sources: Encyclopedias, books, newspaper, and periodical accounts.

Former U.S. Vice President Walter F. Mondale speaks of his former U.S. Senate colleague, Gaylord Nelson, at a memorial service at the Wisconsin State Capitol on July 13, 2005. Nelson, who died on July 3, 2005, served in the Wisconsin Senate (1949-59), as Governor (1959-63), and U.S. Senator (1963-81) and was known as an impassioned defender of the environment and the founder of Earth Day. The United States Congress designated a 33,500 acre Gaylord Nelson Wilderness area within Wisconsin's Apostle Islands National Lakeshore in 2004. (Robert Paolino, LRB)

HISTORIC SITES IN WISCONSIN

		Attendance[1]				2003-04
Site	Location	2000-01	2001-02	2002-03	2003-04	Revenue[2]
Bennett Studio	Wisconsin Dells	4,418	3,565	3,995	5,853	$58,666
Madeline Island	La Pointe	13,222	12,563	12,618	11,955	102,540
Old Wade House	Greenbush	13,963	16,475	15,423	15,487	145,560
Old World Wisconsin	Eagle	70,283	69,043	57,112	54,092	1,004,107
Pendarvis	Mineral Point	6,704	5,860	5,856	5,268	63,347
Stonefield	Cassville	6,163	6,258	4,510	4,516	35,561
Villa Louis	Prairie du Chien	16,152	14,211	16,114	16,062	166,144
TOTAL		130,905	127,975	115,628	113,233	$1,575,925
Circus World Museum[3]	Baraboo	125,585	111,330	68,150	54,610	$1,082,886

[1]Sites are generally open from May to October, with the exception of Circus World, which is open all year. For current information: http://www.wisconsinhistory.org/sitesmuseum.asp

[2]Revenue from admissions and inside sales (such as gift shop sales, restaurant sales, and tram rides).

[3]Statistics are for calendar year. Owned by the State Historical Society of Wisconsin, but operated by a private, nonprofit foundation.

Source: State Historical Society of Wisconsin, departmental data, April 2005.

OFFICIAL HISTORICAL MARKERS IN WISCONSIN
June 2005

County	Location/Nearest Community	Subject
Adams	At the Park, Hwy 13, 3 miles north of Friendship	Roche-a-Cri State Park
Adams	S. Arkdale Cemetery, 1801 Cypress Ave., Town of	Site of First Norwegian Evangelical
	Strongs Prairie	Lutheran Church of Roche-a-Cri
Ashland	Bay View Park, Hwy 2, Ashland	Fleet Admiral William D. Leahy
Ashland	Northland College campus, Ellis Avenue, Ashland	Northland College
Ashland	In park on Hwy 2 at western limits of Ashland	Radisson-Groseilliers Fort
Ashland	La Pointe, Madeline Island	Madeline Island
Ashland	Hwy 13, 10 miles south of Mellen	Great Divide
Ashland	Hwy 2, Odanah	The Bad River
Barron	Rest Area #34, westbound Hwy 53, 2 mi. south of Chetek ..	Pine Was King (Pineries)
Barron	2411-23 Street, Rice Lake	Our Lady of Lourdes Catholic Church
Bayfield	Hwy 13, 0.5 mile east of Cornucopia	Tragedy of the Siskiwit
Bayfield	Hwy 13, Port Wing	School Consolidation
Bayfield	Hwy 13, 2.3 miles north of Washburn	Madeline Island
Brown	Denmark War Memorial Pk., Wisconsin Ave. (CTH KB) ...	Denmark
Brown	In park at corner of Broadway and George Sts., De Pere ...	Marquette-Jolliet Expedition
Brown	In Voyageur Park, De Pere	Rapides des Peres – Voyageur Park
Brown	403 North Broadway, De Pere	White Pillars
Brown	222 South Baird Street, Green Bay	Cnesses Israel Synagogue
Brown	Outside Packer Hall of Fame, Green Bay	Green Bay Packers
Brown	1008 South Monroe Avenue, Green Bay	Hazelwood
Brown	2640 South Webster Avenue, Green Bay	Heritage Hill State Park
Brown	Hwy 57, 5 miles northeast of Green Bay	Red Banks
Buffalo	Hwy 35, 0.5 mile north of Alma	Beef Slough
Burnett	Crex Meadows Wildlife Area, off Hwy F, N. of Grantsburg .	Crex Meadows
Calumet	Wayside #4, intersection of Hwys 55 and 151, Brothertown	
	Town	Brothertown Indians of Wisconsin
Calumet	City Hall, 2110 Washington Street, New Holstein	New Holstein
Calumet	Stockbridge Harbor, CTH E, Village of Stockbridge	Stockbridge Harbor
Chippewa	Hwy 124, 3 miles north of Chippewa Falls	Nation's First Cooperative Generating
		Station
Chippewa	2820 East Park Avenue, Chippewa Falls	Northern WI Center for the Developmentally
		Disabled
Chippewa	Fairgrounds, 308 Jefferson Ave., Chippewa Falls	Northern Wisconsin State Fair
Chippewa	Cornell Mill Yard Park and Bridge St., Cornell	Cornell Pulpwood Stacker
Chippewa	West side of Hwy 178, near Hwy T	Cobban Bridge
Chippewa	Hwy 178, 0.5 mile north of Jim Falls..................	Old Abe, the War Eagle
Clark	2 blocks west of Hwy 13, Colby	Colby Cheese
Columbia	Rest Area #12, westbound I90-94, E. of WI River	The Circus
Columbia	711 West James Street, Columbus	Governor James Taylor Lewis
Columbia	Hwy 113 at Wisconsin River crossing	Merrimac Ferry
Columbia	120 N. Main Street, Pardeeville	Historic Pardeeville
Columbia	Hwy 33, 0.5 mile east of Portage	Fort Winnebago
Columbia	West Wisconsin and Crook Streets, Portage	Frederick Jackson Turner
Columbia	Hwy 33, 0.5 mile east of Portage	Marquette
Columbia	Hwy CM, 5 miles northeast of Portage	Potters' Emigration Society
Columbia	Museum at The Portage, 804 MacFarlane Rd., Portage	Society Hill Historic District
Columbia	Across from sheriff's office, Cook Street, Portage	Ketchum's Point
Columbia	Rest Area #11, eastbound I90-94, 0.5 mi. E. of WI River ...	Rest Areas on the I-Roads
Columbia	Hwy 51, 0.5 mile south of Poynette	John Muir View
Columbia	Hwy 16, 4 miles east of Wisconsin Dells	Kingsley Bend Indian Mounds
Columbia	314 Broadway, Wisconsin Dells	Stroud Bank
Columbia	Village Park, 150 Lovers Lane, Wyocena	Major Elbert Dickason/Dickason's "Hotel"

OFFICIAL HISTORICAL MARKERS IN WISCONSIN
June 2005–Continued

County	Location/Nearest Community	Subject
Crawford	Hwy 171, 0.5 mile east of Gays Mills	Gays Mills Apple Orchards
Crawford	Hwy 35, 1.2 miles south of Lynxville	Rafting on the Mississippi
Crawford	Cornelius Family Park, 211 S. Main St., Prairie du Chien	Black Hawk's Surrender
Crawford	Fort Crawford Museum, 717 S. Beaumont Rd., Prairie du Chien	Fort Crawford
Crawford	Mississippi River Bridge, Prairie du Chien	Pere Marquette and Sieur Jolliet
Crawford	Beaumont and Rice Streets, Prairie du Chien	Museum of Medical Progress
Crawford	Mississippi River Bridge, Prairie du Chien	Prairie du Chien
Crawford	At entrance, Villa Louis Road, Prairie du Chien	Villa Louis
Crawford	521 N. Villa Road, Prairie du Chien	Villa Louis
Crawford	In lawn west of the Villa, Villa Louis, Prairie du Chien	War of 1812
Crawford	Hwy 61, 0.5 mile south of Soldiers Grove	James Davidson
Crawford	Soldiers Grove Park, Mill and Main Sts., Soldiers Grove	Soldiers Grove Origin
Dane	In park off Hwy A, Albion	Albion Academy
Dane	8770 Ridge Drive, Belleville	Primrose Lutheran Church
Dane	1 mile northeast of Blue Mounds, Hwy F	Brigham Park
Dane	Quivey's Grove, 6261 Nesbitt Road, Fitchburg	Mann House
Dane	2915 Syene Rd., Fitchburg	McCoy House
Dane	Camp Randall Memorial Park, UW-Madison campus	Camp Randall
Dane	8-12 N. Blount St., Madison	Ceramic Art Studio of Madison
Dane	4718 Monona Dr., Madison	Nathaniel Dean, Dean House
Dane	Vilas Communication Hall, UW-Madison campus	9XM-WHA
Dane	Bascom Hill, UW-Madison campus	North Hall
Dane	GEF III, 125 S. Webster St., Madison	Peck Cabin
Dane	Resurrection Cemetery, 2705 Regent St., Madison	Site of Former Greenbush Cemetery Burials
Dane	Olbrich Park, 3330 Atwood Ave., Madison	Third Lake Passage
Dane	415 E. Wilson St., Madison	Tragedy of War
Dane	816 State Street, Madison	State Historical Society
Dane	501 South Thornton Avenue, Madison	Yahara River Parkway
Dane	Indian Lake County Park, Hwy 19, 1 mi. E. of Marxville	Indian Lake Passage
Dane	Village Park, 39 Brodhead Street, Mazomanie	Historic Mazomanie
Dane	Branch Creek Conservancy Pk, Pleasant Branch Rd., Middleton	Pheasant Branch Encampment
Dane	Indian Mound Pk., 6200 Bl. of Ridgewood Ave., Monona	Outlet Mound
Dane	Entrance to Prairie Mound Cemetery, CTH M, Vil. of Oregon	Revolutionary War Veteran
Dane	Hwy 51, east shore of Lake Waubesa	Stephen Moulton Babcock (1843-1931)
Dane	Yahara River Bridge, W. Main St., 381 E. Main St., Stoughton	Main Street Historic District
Dane	La Follette County Park, 3 miles north of Stoughton	Robert Marion La Follette, Sr. (1855-1925)
Dane	300 E. Main Street, Sun Prairie	Georgia O'Keeffe
Dodge	214-216 Front St., Beaver Dam	Frederick Douglas
Dodge	Adams Spring Park, Spring Street, Fox Lake	Bernard "Bunny" Berrigan (1908-1942)
Dodge	Addie Joss Park, Juneau	Adrian "Addie" Joss
Dodge	105 N. River St., Lowell	Lowell Women Firefighters
Dodge	Rest Area #64, northbound Hwy 41	World War II
Dodge	Hwys 28 and 67, on Main Street, Mayville	Wisconsin's First Iron Smelter
Dodge	Hwy 175, Theresa	Solomon Juneau House
Dodge	Jct. Hwys 26 and 67, Waupun	Auto Race – Green Bay to Madison
Door	12171 Garrett Bay Rd., Ellison Bay	The Clearing
Door	Noble Square, 4167 Main Street, Fish Creek	The Alexander Noble House
Door	Namur, Hwy 57	Belgian Settlement in Wisconsin
Door	6145 Cave Point Drive, Town of Jacksonport	Jacksonport United Methodist Church
Door	Olde Stone Quarry Park, CTH B, Town of Sevastopol	Leathem and Smith Quarry
Door	Hwy 42, 0.5 mile north of junction with Hwy 57	The Orchards of Door County
Douglas	Hwy 2, Brule	Brule River
Douglas	Hwys F and B, Lake Nebagamon	Evergreen Park Cottage Sanatorium
Douglas	Hwy 2, Poplar	Major "Dick" Bong
Douglas	Hwy 53, 1.5 miles south of Solon Springs	Brule-St. Croix Portage
Douglas	Allouez (Superior), along Hwys 2, 13, and 53	Burlington Northern Ore Docks
Douglas	Rest Area #23, Hwys 2 & 53, southern limits of Superior	Northwest Portal of Wisconsin
Douglas	Memorial Park, Superior	Old Stockade Site
Douglas	Whaleback Museum, Barker's Island, Superior	S.S. Meteor, last of the Whalebacks
Douglas	Superior Central High School, 1015 Belknap St., Superior	Summer White House – 1928
Douglas	Harbor Entry, Wisconsin Point Road, Superior	The Superior Entry
Douglas	Between McCaskill and Holden Bldgs., UW-Superior	University of Wisconsin-Superior
Douglas	Tourist Information Center, City Park, Hwy 2, Superior	Wartime Shipbuilding
Dunn	Caddie Woodlawn Park, Hwy 25, Menomonie	Caddie Woodlawn
Dunn	Rest Area #61, eastbound I94, Menomonie	Chippewa Valley White Pine
Dunn	205 Main Street, Menomonie	Mabel Tainter Memorial
Dunn	Rest Area #62, I94	World War I
Eau Claire	Wayside #4, Hwy 85, 0.5 mi. west of Hwy 37, Eau Claire	Silver Mine Ski Jump
Fond du Lac	Fond du Lac Co. Park, W11413 CTH TC, Brandon	The Raube Road Site
Fond du Lac	Hwy 151, 6 miles north of Fond du Lac	Edward S. Bragg
Fond du Lac	Rolling Meadows Golf Course, 560 W. Rolling Meadows Dr., Fond du Lac	County Home Cemetery Fond du Lac
Fond du Lac	Main Street and Forest Avenue, Fond du Lac	Military Road
Fond du Lac	30 East 2nd Street, Fond du Lac	Wisconsin Progressive Party
Fond du Lac	St. John the Baptist Church, Hwy W, Johnsburg	Father Caspar Rehrl
Fond du Lac	Southeast corner of Blackburn and Blossom Sts., Ripon	Birthplace of Republican Party

OFFICIAL HISTORICAL MARKERS IN WISCONSIN
June 2005–Continued

County	Location/Nearest Community	Subject
Fond du Lac	Pedrick Wayside, Hwy 23, Ripon	Carrie Chapman Catt
Fond du Lac	In park on Union Street, 1 block south of Hwy 23, Ripon	Ceresco
Fond du Lac	Ripon College campus, Ripon	Ripon College
Fond du Lac	Taycheedah Correctional Institution, Tn. of Taycheedah	Home of Governor James Duane Doty
Fond du Lac	Hwy 49, 4 miles east of Waupun	Horicon Marsh
Forest	Hwy 8, 1.8 miles east of Crandon	Northern Highland
Forest	Hwy 32, 1 mile south of Laona	Laona School Forest
Forest	Hwy 55, 0.5 mile north of Mole Lake	Battle of Mole Lake
Grant	Hwy 61, 0.3 miles south of Boscobel	The Gideons
Grant	117 East Front Street, Cassville	Old Denniston House
Grant	620 Lincoln Avenue, Fennimore	The "Dinky"
Grant	Hwy 80 at the WI-IL state line, south of Hazel Green	Point of Beginning (Survey Point)
Grant	Cemetery, 1 block west of Hwys 61, 35, and 81, Lancaster	Nelson Dewey
Grant	Highway 35 and Slabtown Rd., 5 miles west of Lancaster	Pleasant Ridge
Grant	Rountree Hall, UW-Platteville	First State Normal School
Grant	114-108 South Main St., Potosi	Village of Potosi
Green	Monticello Monument Wayside, Hwy 69, Monticello	Nickolaus Gerber
Green	Village Park, 300 Blk of 2nd St., Hwy O, New Glarus	Herbert Kubly
Green	Hwy 69, New Glarus	New Glarus
Green Lake	Nathan Strong Park, East Huron St. (Hwy 116), Berlin	Lucy Smith Morris
Green Lake	Riverside Park, Berlin	Upper Fox River
Iowa	Hwy 14, 3 miles east of Arena	Village of Dover
Iowa	CTH Y, 3 mi. S. of Dodgeville	Dodge's Grove and Fort Union
Iowa	Courthouse lawn, Hwy 151, Dodgeville	Iowa County Courthouse
Iowa	Hwy YZ, 4 miles east of Dodgeville	Old Military Road
Iowa	Water Tower Park, Hwy 151, Mineral Point	Historic Mineral Point
Iowa	Iowa Co. Fairgrounds, 900 Fair St., Mineral Point	Laurence F. Graber, "Mr. Alfalfa"
Iowa	114 Shake Rag Street, Mineral Point	Shake Rag
Iowa	Library Park, Mineral Point	Wisconsin Territory
Iowa	9 Fountain St., Mineral Point	Site of Fort Jackson
Iowa	Frank Lloyd Wright Visitor Ctr., CTH C, Spring Green	Military River Crossing
Iowa	Hwy 14, east of Wisconsin River, near Spring Green	Frank Lloyd Wright
Iowa	Tower Hill State Park, Hwy C, south of Hwy 14	Shot Tower
Iron	Hwy 2, 10 miles west of Hurley	Gogebic Iron Range
Iron	Wayside WI Info. Ctr., Hwy 51, 1 mile north of Hurley	Iron Mining in Wisconsin
Jackson	Hwys 121 and 95, 1.5 mile west of Alma Center	Silver Mound
Jackson	Bell Mound Scenic Overlook, 5 mi. S. of Black River Falls	Black River Valley Scenic Outlook
Jackson	Hwy 54, 5 miles east of Black River Falls	Mitchell Red Cloud, Jr. (1925-1950)
Jackson	Rest Area #8, westbound I94, 15 mi. SE Black River Falls	The Passenger Pigeon
Jackson	Rest Area #7, eastbound I94, 15 mi. SE Black River Falls	Sphagnum Moss
Jackson	Rest Area #6, westbound I94	Highground Veterans Memorial
Jackson	Hwy 27, 6 miles south of Black River Falls	Martin W. Torkelson
Jefferson	In park, north off Hwy 12, just east of Cambridge	Lake Ripley – Ole Evinrude
Jefferson	Burnt Village Co. Park, Hwy N, 2 mi. SE of Ft. Atkinson	Black Hawk War Encampment "Burnt Village"
Jefferson	400 block of Milwaukee Avenue East, Fort Atkinson	Fort Koshkonong
Jefferson	Koshkonong Mounds Road, near Fort Atkinson	Lake Koshkonong Effigy Mounds
Jefferson	Blackhawk Island Road, Town of Sumner	Lorine Niedecker
Jefferson	Hwy 106, western city limits of Fort Atkinson	Panther Intaglio
Jefferson	Rest Area #14, westbound I94	In Service to Their Country
Jefferson	3 miles east of Lake Mills on Hwy B, south on Hwy Q	Aztalan State Park
Jefferson	Rest Area #13, eastbound I94, 1 mile east of Lake Mills	Drumlins
Jefferson	Bald Bluff Overlook, CTH H, 1 1/2 mi. S. of Palmyra	Black Hawk War Encampment
Jefferson	919 Charles St., Watertown	First Kindergarten
Jefferson	7 miles southeast of Watertown, Hwy 16	Highway Marking
Jefferson	919 Charles Street, Watertown	Octagon House
Jefferson	One Main St. (at bridge), Watertown	Trail Discovery
Juneau	Hwy C, 0.5 mile east of Camp Douglas	Castle Rock
Juneau	Camp Williams, off I94	Wisconsin Military Reservation
Juneau	On the trail at the western edge of Elroy	Elroy-Sparta State Trail
Juneau	In village park, Hwy HH, Lyndon Station	Hop Raising
Juneau	Rest Area #10, westbound I90-94	The Sand Counties – Aldo Leopold Territory
Juneau	Rest Area #9, eastbound I90-94, near Mauston	The Wisconsin River
Juneau	Rest Area #9, eastbound I90-94, near Mauston	The Iron Brigade
Kenosha	Rest Area #126, I94	Cordelia A.P. Harvey
Kenosha	24th Ave. & 56th St., Kenosha	Auto Production in Kenosha
Kenosha	Hwy 31 eastbound at 95th St., Kenosha	Green Bay Ethnic Trail
Kenosha	Green Ridge Cemetery, 6604 7th Ave., Kenosha	John McCaffery Burial Site
Kenosha	6501 3rd Avenue, Kenosha	Kemper Hall
Kenosha	5117 – 4th Ave., Kenosha	Kenosha (Southport) Lighthouse
Kenosha	Library Park, Kenosha	Reuben Deming
Kenosha	15620 12th St., Kenosha	Schaefer Mammoth Site
Kenosha	Hwy 32 at the southern edge of Kenosha	32nd Division Memorial Highway
Kenosha	Rest Area-Tourist Info. Ctr. #26, westbound I94, N of I11	The Name "Wisconsin"
Kewaunee	Ferry yard, Kewaunee	Car-Ferry Service
La Crosse	Rest Area #15, eastbound I90	The Driftless Area
La Crosse	McGilvray Rd. Overlook, Van Loon State Wildlife Area	The McGilvray "Seven Bridges Road"
La Crosse	Halfway Creek Lutheran Church, 2.5 mi. E. of Holmen	Luther College
La Crosse	Bishop's View Overlook, Hwy 33, 5 mi. E. of La Crosse	The Coulee Region
La Crosse	Rest Area #31, I94, French Island, La Crosse	Major General C.C. Washburn

OFFICIAL HISTORICAL MARKERS IN WISCONSIN
June 2005–Continued

County	Location/Nearest Community	Subject
La Crosse	La Crosse	Red Cloud Park
La Crosse	Corner of Front and State Streets, La Crosse	Spence Park
La Crosse	Rest Area-Tourist Info. Ctr. #31, 190, La Crosse	Upper Mississippi
La Crosse	Hwy 16 Valley View Mall entrance, just N. of Medary	Valley View Site
La Crosse	Neshonoc Cemetery, West Salem	Hamlin Garland
La Crosse	Swarthout Lakeside Park, Hwy 16, West Salem	Village of Neshonoc
Lafayette	First Capitol State Park, Hwy G, 4 mi. northwest of Belmont	Belmont-Wisconsin Territory 1836
Lafayette	First Capitol State Park, Hwy G, 4 mi. northwest of Belmont	Gov. Tommy G. Thompson's 1998 Address at Wisconsin's First Capitol
Lafayette	First Capitol State Park, Hwy G, 4 mi. northwest of Belmont	1998 Wisconsin Assembly (Sesquicentennial Marker)
Lafayette	Hwy 11, 1 mile west of Benton	Father Samuel Mazzuchelli
Lafayette	Intersection of Hwys F, 78, & Madison St., Blanchardville	Zarahemia – Predecessor of Blanchardville
Lafayette	101 S. Main St., Blanchardville	Zenas Gurley
Lafayette	Hwy 23, 5 miles south of Mineral Point	Fort Defiance
Lafayette	Hwy 11, 1 mile west of Shullsburg	Wisconsin Lead Region
Langlade	Hwy 52, near junction with Hwy 64	Antigo Silt Loam, State Soil of Wisconsin
Langlade	Wayside, Hwy 45, 3 miles south of Antigo	Langlade County Forest, Wisconsin's First County Forest
Langlade	Junction of Hwys 55 and 64, Langlade	De Langlade
Langlade	Hwy 55, 3.5 miles north of Lily at Wolf River	Old Military Road
Lincoln	715 E. 2nd St., Merrill	Merrill City Hall
Lincoln	Hwy 64 over the Prairie River – 200 W. First St., Merrill	Three Arch Stone Bridge
Manitowoc	CTH R, 1/2 mile N. of Schley Rd.	Rock Mill
Manitowoc	Rest Area #51, southbound I43, S. of Brown County line	Wisconsin's Dairy Industry
Manitowoc	Rest Area #52, northbound I43, S. of Brown County line	Wisconsin's Maritime Industries
Manitowoc	Lake Michigan Carferry Dock, 700 S. Lakeview Dr., Manitowoc	S. S. Badger/Manitowoc and the Car Ferries
Manitowoc	Mariner's Park, S. 8th St., at the Manitowoc River	Manitowoc's Maritime Heritage
Manitowoc	Manitowoc Maritime Museum, 75 Maritime Drive	Manitowoc Submarines
Manitowoc	Silver Lake Park, Hwy 151, west of Manitowoc	Winnebago Trail
Manitowoc	924 Pinecrest Lane, Manitowoc Rapids	Collins Road Bridge Span
Manitowoc	Pioneer Rd. and CTH XX, Meeme	Meeme Poll House
Manitowoc	St. Nazianz Village Hall, 228 W. Main St., St. Nazianz	George Washington School
Manitowoc	108 W. Birch, St. Nazianz	St. Nazianz
Manitowoc	Central Park, Two Rivers	Ice Cream Sundae
Manitowoc	Point Beach State Park, N. of Two Rivers on County O	Rawley Point Lighthouse
Manitowoc	Valders Memorial Park, Hwy J, Valders	Thorstein Veblen
Marathon	Rothschild Pk., Grand Ave., Park & Kort Sts., Rothschild	Wisconsin's 1st Home-Built Flying Machine
Marathon	UW-Marathon County campus, Wausau	The First Teachers' Training School in Wisconsin
Marathon	Wayside, northbound Hwy 51, 1 mile south of Hwy 153	First Workers Compensation Policy
Marinette	Peshtigo Cemetery, Oconto Avenue, Peshtigo	Peshtigo Fire Cemetery
Marinette	N2155 USH 141, Town of Pound	Lena Road Schoolhouse
Marinette	W2349 County JJ, Wausaukee	McAllister State Graded School
Marquette	Hwy 22, 8 miles south of Montello	John Muir Country
Marquette	Rest Area #82, Hwy 51, 4 miles north of Westfield	Korean War
Marquette	Westfield Town Hall, W 7703 Ember Ave. at 4th	Russell Flats
Menominee	Hwys 47 and 55, 5 miles north of Shawano	Menominee Reservation
Menominee	Hwy, 55, 2.5 miles north of Keshena	Spirit Rock
Milwaukee	8801 West Grange Avenue, Greendale	Wisconsin's Lime Industry
Milwaukee	8685 West Grange Avenue, Greendale	Jeremiah Curtin House
Milwaukee	6500 Northway, Greendale	Village of Greendale
Milwaukee	92nd and Forest Home Ave., Greenfield	Janesville Plank Road
Milwaukee	7325 West Forest Home Ave., Greenfield	Town of Greenfield
Milwaukee	Zillman Park, S. Kinnickinnic Ave., Milwaukee	Bay View's Immigrants
Milwaukee	South Superior Street and East Russell Ave., Milwaukee	Bay View's Rolling Mill
Milwaukee	2000 West Wisconsin Avenue, Milwaukee	Captain Frederick Pabst
Milwaukee	Zeidler Park, 300 block of West Michigan St., Milwaukee	Carl Frederick Zeidler
Milwaukee	East Hartford & North Maryland Aves., UW-Milwaukee	Carl Sandburg Hall
Milwaukee	1756 North Prospect Avenue, Milwaukee	Civil War Camp
Milwaukee	Lobby, 700 West Virginia Street, Milwaukee	The Cream City
Milwaukee	Grounds of VA Hospital, Wood (Milwaukee)	Erastus B. Wolcott, M.D.
Milwaukee	Fourth Street and Kilbourn Avenue, Milwaukee	First African-American Church Built in Wisconsin
Milwaukee	Foot of East Michigan Street, Milwaukee	First Milwaukee Cargo Pier
Milwaukee	Layton Avenue, Milwaukee	General Mitchell Field
Milwaukee	Golda Meir Library on UW-Milwaukee campus	Golda Meir
Milwaukee	4th and State Streets, Milwaukee	Invention of the Typewriter
Milwaukee	Marquette Law School, 1103 W. WI Ave., Milwaukee	Mabel Wanda Raimey
Milwaukee	Civic Center, Milwaukee	MacArthur Square
Milwaukee	Merrill Park, 461 North 35th St., Milwaukee	Merrill Park
Milwaukee	Currie Park, Wauwatosa	Milwaukee County's First Airport
Milwaukee	East Hartford and North Downer Avenues, Milwaukee	Milwaukee-Downer College
Milwaukee	231 West Michigan Street, Milwaukee	Milwaukee Interurban Terminal, 1905-1951
Milwaukee	Zablocki VA Medical Center, Hwy 59	National Soldiers Home
Milwaukee	At the lighthouse in Lake Park, Milwaukee	North Point Lighthouse
Milwaukee	East North Avenue, Milwaukee	Old North Point Water Tower
Milwaukee	Wells and Edison Streets, Milwaukee	Oneida Street Station, T.M.E.R. and L. Co.
Milwaukee	144 East Wells Street, Milwaukee	Pabst Theater

OFFICIAL HISTORICAL MARKERS IN WISCONSIN
June 2005–Continued

County	Location/Nearest Community	Subject
Milwaukee	Cathedral Square Park, northeast corner, Milwaukee	Rescue of Joshua Glover
Milwaukee	North Avenue and Lake Drive, Milwaukee	Saint John's Infirmary
Milwaukee	North Lake Drive, Milwaukee	St. Mary's School of Nursing
Milwaukee	North Water and East Erie Streets, Milwaukee	Sinking of the *Lady Elgin*
Milwaukee	200 North Broadway, Milwaukee	Third Ward Fire
Milwaukee	Mitchell Hall, UW-Milwaukee, North Downer Avenue	The University of Wisconsin-Milwaukee
Milwaukee	Miller Brewing Company, Milwaukee	Watertown Plank Road
Milwaukee	100 East Wisconsin Avenue, Milwaukee	Wisconsin's Oldest Newspaper: The Milwaukee Sentinel
Milwaukee	3500 block on N. Oakland Ave., Shorewood	Lueddeman's On-the-River
Milwaukee	4145 N. Oakland Ave., Shorewood	Shorewood Armory
Milwaukee	1701 E. Capitol Drive, Shorewood	Shorewood High School
Milwaukee	3930 N. Murray Ave., Shorewood	Shorewood Village Hall
Milwaukee	909 Menomonee Ave., South Milwaukee	Lawson Airplane Company
Milwaukee	State Fair Park, Main Gate, West Allis	Camp Harvey
Milwaukee	In triangle at 57th, Hayes, and Fillmore, West Allis	Meadowmere
Milwaukee	State Fair Park, Main Gate, West Allis	Wisconsin State Fair Park
Monroe	Hwy 12, 4 miles west of Camp Douglas	Mesas and Buttes
Monroe	Rest Area #16, westbound I90, 5 miles east of Bangor	Coulee Country
Monroe	At the Kendall Depot, North Railroad Street, Kendall	Elroy-Sparta State Trail
Monroe	200 West Main Street, Sparta	Masonic Lodge
Monroe	112 South Court Street, Sparta	Monroe County Courthouse
Monroe	124 West Main Street, Sparta	Sparta Free Library
Monroe	123 West Main Street, Sparta	U.S. Post Office
Monroe	In park on Hwy 12, Tomah	Tomah
Oconto	Hwy F, 1.5 miles east of Lakewood	The Holt and Balcom Logging Camp No. 1
Oconto	Chicago and Main Streets, Oconto	First Church of Christ Scientist
Oconto	On Oconto River at Brazeau Avenue, Oconto	Mission of St. Francois Xavier
Oconto	Copper Culture State Park, Oconto	Old Copper Culture Cemetery
Oneida	Oneida County Courthouse grounds, Rhinelander	First Rural Zoning Ordinance
Oneida	Hodag Park, Rhinelander	The Hodag
Oneida	W. edge of National Forest, off Hwy 32 E. of Three Lakes	Nicolet National Forest
Outagamie	807 South Oneida Street, Appleton	First Electric Street Railway
Outagamie	600 Vulcan Street, Appleton	World's First Hydroelectric Central Station
Outagamie	North of jct. Hwys BB and 45, 4 miles west of Appleton	South Greenville Grange No. 225
Outagamie	Thelen Park, Kaukauna	Revolutionary War Veterans
Outagamie	Hwy 96, 0.1 mile west of Little Chute	Treaty of the Cedars
Outagamie	Beacon Avenue and Division Street, New London	Birthplace of the American Water Spaniel
Ozaukee	Intersection of CTHs R & C, Belgium	Wisconsin's Luxembourgers
Ozaukee	Columbia Rd. and Mequon Ave., Cedarburg	Cedar Creek
Ozaukee	City Hall, Washington Avenue, Cedarburg	Historic Cedarburg
Ozaukee	W62 N646 Washington Ave., Cedarburg	Interurban Bridge
Ozaukee	Doctor's Park, Washington Ave. and Mill St., Cedarburg	Washington Avenue Historic District
Ozaukee	Covered Bridge Road, 1 mile north of Five Corners	Last Covered Bridge
Ozaukee	Mequon City Hall, 11333 North Cedarburg Rd., Mequon	Wisconsin's German Settlers
Ozaukee	108 N. Lake St., Port Washington	The Wisconsin Chair Company Fire
Ozaukee	Triangle Park and Green Bay Rd., Saukville	The Saukville Trails
Ozaukee	Entrance Wall, 250 S. Main St., Thiensville	Historic Thiensville
Ozaukee	Junction of Hwys F and M, 3 miles west of Thiensville	The Oldest Lutheran Church in Wisconsin
Ozaukee	Hwy I, 0.5 mile east of Waubeka	Birthplace of Flag Day
Pepin	Hwy 35, 1 mile north of Stockholm	Maiden Rock
Pepin	Hwy 35, Pepin Park	Laura Ingalls Wilder
Pepin	Hwy 35, 3 miles northwest of Pepin	Site of Fort St. Antoine
Pierce	Hwy 35, 1 mile south of Hwy 63, southeast of Hager City	"Bow and Arrow"
Pierce	Hwy 35, 3 miles west of Maiden Rock	Lake Pepin
Pierce	Spring Pond Park, East Mill Rd., Plum City	Historic Plum City
Pierce	Hwy 65, 3 miles south of I94	Edgar Wilson Nye
Polk	Hwy 35, Luck	Danish Cooperative Company
Polk	City Park, St. Croix Falls	The Battle of St. Croix Falls
Polk	Interstate Park, Hwy 8, St. Croix Falls	State Park Movement in Wisconsin
Polk	Overlook Park, N. Washington (Main) St., St. Croix Falls	Where Are the Falls of the St. Croix?
Portage	County W, Buena Vista Marsh Wildlife Area	Wisconsin's Greater Prairie Chicken
Portage	Portage County Park, Hwy E, 3 miles south of Knowlton	Du Bay Trading Post
Portage	1700 block of Monroe St., Stevens Point	The Historic Southside Railroad Complex of Stevens Point
Price	Movrich Park, Willow Avenue, Town of Fifield	Historic Fifield
Price	Hwy 13, Phillips City Park, Phillips	Phillips Fire
Racine	Weimhoff-Jucker Park, Burlington	Mormons in Early Wisconsin
Racine	Hwy 31 at 5 Mile Rd., Town of Caledonia	Bohemian School House
Racine	Zoological Gardens, 2131 N. Main St., Racine	Northside Historic District of Cream Brick Cottages
Racine	Graceland and Mound Cemeteries, 1147 West Blvd., Racine	Soldiers of the American Revolution
Racine	Simonsen Park, Main & Fourteenth Sts., Racine	Southside Historic District
Racine	Hwy 11, western limits of Racine	The Spark
Racine	Racine Village Park, 4725 Lighthouse Dr., Racine	The Wind Point Lighthouse
Racine	1407 71st Drive, Union Grove	Revolutionary War Veteran
Racine	Heg Park Road, Waterford	Old Muskego
Richland	Boaz Park, Hwy 171, Boaz	Ocooch Mountains
Richland	Boaz Park, Hwy 171, Boaz	Richard M. Brewer
Richland	Wayside, Hwy 14, 1 mi. E. Gotham, Town of Buena Vista	The Pursuit West

OFFICIAL HISTORICAL MARKERS IN WISCONSIN
June 2005–Continued

County	Location/Nearest Community	Subject
Richland	Krouskop Park, 400 W. 6th St. (Hwy 14), Richland Center	Ada James
Richland	Krouskop Park, 400 W. 6th St. (Hwy 14), Richland Center	Birthplace of General Telephone and Electronics Corporation (GTE)
Richland	Hwy 14, 5 miles west of Richland Center	Boaz Mastodon
Richland	Pier County Park, Hwy 80, Rockbridge	Rockbridge
Richland	5 miles west of Richland Center on Hwy 14	Rural Electrification
Richland	Pier Co. Park, Hwy 80, Rockbridge	Troop Encampment
Rock	Beloit College campus, Beloit	Beloit College
Rock	Rock River Heritage Wky., Public Ave. & State St., Beloit	Black Hawk at Turtle Village
Rock	Tourist Info. Ctr. #22, westbound I90, south of Beloit	Black Hawk War
Rock	Rest Area-Tourist Information Center, westbound I90	Medal of Honor
Rock	I43 at I90, Beloit	Wisconsin's First Aviator
Rock	Hwy 140, 4 miles south of Clinton	Jefferson Prairie Settlement
Rock	11204 N. Church St., Cooksville	Historic Cooksville/Historic Waucoma
Rock	Mt. Philip Cemetery, west of Darien	Soldier of the American Revolution
Rock	Hwy 51, 0.5 miles south of Edgerton	Wisconsin's Tobacco Land
Rock	Blackhawk Golf Course Clubhouse, 2100 Palmer, Janesville	The Black Hawk War/Black Hawk's Grove
Rock	NW corner of Delavan Dr. and Beloit Ave., Janesville	Burr Robins Circus
Rock	In Courthouse Park on S. Atwood Ave., Janesville	First State Fair, October 1-2, 1851
Rock	Rock County Historical Society, 10 S. High St., Janesville	Janesville Tank Company
Rock	Rest Area #17, eastbound I90	Rock River Industry
Rock	Hwy 51, 3.8 miles south of Janesville	Route of Abraham Lincoln 1832 and 1859
Rock	18 South Janesville Street, Hwy 26, Milton	Milton House
Rock	On southwest bank of Storr's Lake, off Hwy 26, Milton	Storr's Lake, Milton
Rock	Beckman Mill Co. Park, Co. Rd. H, Town of Newark	How-Beckman Mill
Rock	Hwy J, Shopiere	Home of Governor Harvey
Rusk	Appolonia Cong. Church, Hwy 8 & Cemetery Rd., Bruce	Appolonia
Rusk	Hwy 8, Weyerhauser	Chippewa River and Menomonie Railway
St. Croix	Rest Area-Tourist Info. Ctr. #25, I94 east of Hudson	Brule-St. Croix Waterway
St. Croix	Hwy 35, 4.7 miles north of Hudson	St. Croix River
St. Croix	Campus Drive, Outlot #3, New Richmond	New Richmond Cyclone
Sauk	Devil's Lake State Park, S5975 Park Rd., Baraboo	Civilian Conservation Corps
Sauk	Hwy 33 at County U, 5 miles east of Baraboo	Lower Narrows
Sauk	Hwy 12, 1.5 miles south of Baraboo	Ringling Brothers Circus
Sauk	E8948 Diamond Hill Rd., North Freedom	Mid-Continent Railway Historical Society
Sauk	Reedsburg Area Historical Park, 3 mi. E. of Reedsburg	Clare A. Briggs, Cartoonist
Sauk	State Hwy 136, 0.75 mi. N of STH 154, Rock Springs	Van Hise Rock
Sauk	Derleth Park, Water Street, Sauk City	August W. Derleth
Sauk	Hwy 12, 5 miles northwest of Sauk City	The Baraboo Range
Sauk	Lower WI Riverway, Hwy 78, 2 mi. N. of Sauk City	Battle of Wisconsin Heights
Sauk	Lower WI Riverway, Hwy 60, 2 mi. E. of Spring Green	Western Escape
Sauk	Hwy A, 1.5 miles south of Wisconsin Dells	Dawn Manor – Site of Lost City of Newport
Sauk	Hwy 16, 0.1 mile west of Wisconsin Dells	Wisconsin Dells
Sawyer	Hwys 70 and 27, Couderay	Court Oreilles
Sawyer	Hwys 27 and 70, 7 miles west of Couderay	Radisson-Groseilliers
Sawyer	Hermans Landing, Cty Rd CC, at bridge, Hayward	The Chippewa Flowage
Sawyer	Lac Courte Oreilles Reservation, 13891 W. Mission Rd.	St. Francis Solanus Indian Mission
Sawyer	Hwy 27, 5.5 miles south of Hayward	Namekagon-Court Oreilles Portage
Sawyer	Hwy W, 6.75 miles southeast of Winter	John Deitz, "Battle of Cameron Dam"
Shawano	Hwy 22, 3.5 miles east of Shawano	Shawano
Shawano	Hwy 45 at city limits of Wittenberg	Homme Homes
Sheboygan ...	50 South Main Street, Cedar Grove	Early Dutch Settlers in Wisconsin
Sheboygan ...	Hwy 23, in the Park at Greenbush, 6 mi. W. of Plymouth	Old Wade House State Park
Sheboygan ...	Memorial Park, Cedar Grove, 3 miles south of Oostburg	Dutch Settlement
Sheboygan ...	Heritage House Triangle Pk., Ctr. & N. 10th Sts., Oostburg	Historic Oostburg
Sheboygan ...	Sheboygan North Point Park, North Point Dr., Sheboygan	The Phoenix Tragedy
Sheboygan ...	Center Avenue and North Water Street, Sheboygan	Seils-Sterling Circus
Sheboygan ...	9th Street and Panther Avenue, Sheboygan	Sheboygan Indian Mound Park
Sheboygan ...	Rochester Inn, 504 Water St., Sheboygan Falls	Cole Historic District
Sheboygan ...	Sheboygan River Dam, Broadway St., Sheboygan Falls	Downtown Sheboygan Falls Historic District
Taylor	Hwy 102, Rib Lake	Rib Lake Lumber Company
Taylor	Hwy 102, 5 miles northeast of Rib Lake	Rustic Road
Trempealeau ..	Hwy 53, 1.5 miles southeast of Galesville	Decorah Peak
Trempealeau ..	Rest Area #5, eastbound I94, 2 miles southeast of Osseo	Winnebago Indians
Trempealeau ..	Great River State Tr., Hwy 35, 0.5 mi. E. of Trempealeau	The Mississippi River Parkway: First Project
Trempealeau ..	Perrot State Park	Brady's Bluff
Trempealeau ..	Perrot State Park, off Hwy 93	Perrot's Post
Vernon	Hwy 14, 0.5 mile north of Coon Valley	Nation's First Watershed Project
Vernon	Hwy 35, 2.5 miles north of De Soto	Battle of Bad Axe
Vernon	Hwy 35, 2 miles north of De Soto	Chief Win-no-shik, the Elder
Vernon	Hwy 35, Genoa	Dams on the Mississippi
Vernon	In power plant parking lot, west side of Hwy 35, Genoa	Wisconsin's First Nuclear-Fueled Generating Station
Vernon	Hwy 33, 0.1 mile west of Hillsboro	Admiral Marc A. Mitscher
Vernon	Hillsboro Lake Park, 300 Water Ave. at Hwys 80, 82, 33, Hillsboro	African American Settlers of the Cheyenne Valley
Vernon	Hwy 14, 0.5 mile north of Viroqua	Governor Rusk
Vernon	City Hall, 202 N. Main St., Viroqua	Viroqua's First Settler
Vilas	Hwy M, 6 miles south of Boulder Junction	First Forest Patrol Flight
Vilas	Trout Lake Nursery, Hwy M	Forest Restoration – The Beginning

OFFICIAL HISTORICAL MARKERS IN WISCONSIN
June 2005-Continued

County	Location/Nearest Community	Subject
Vilas	Hwy 47, Flambeau Lake	Lac du Flambeau
Vilas	Lac Vieux Desert Park, West Shore Dr. near Land O'Lakes	Lac Vieux Desert
Vilas	Hwys 32 and 45, 0.5 mile south of Land O'Lakes	32nd Division Memorial Highway
Vilas	Hwy 45, 1.5 miles south of Land O'Lakes	Wisconsin River Headwaters
Vilas	Sayner Park, Sayner	Snowmobile
Walworth	Village Park, Allen Grove, on Hwy X, 3 mi. SW of Darien	Allen Family
Walworth	City of Delavan Parking Lot, 218 South 7th St., Delavan	Birthplace of "The Greatest Show on Earth"
Walworth	Horton Park, Hwy 11 in Delavan	Delavan's Circus Colony
Walworth	Tower Park, Walworth Ave., Delavan	Delavan's Historic Brick Street
Walworth	Grounds of State School for the Deaf, Hwy 11, Delavan	Wisconsin's First School for Deaf
Walworth	300 Church Street, East Troy	East Troy Railroad
Walworth	Veterans Memorial Park, Hwy 12, Genoa City	First Swedish Settlers in Wisconsin
Walworth	Hwy BB, 3.5 miles south of Lake Geneva	Wisconsin's First 4-H Club
Washburn	Hwy 70, 0.5 mile east of Spooner	Yellow River
Washburn	Junction of Hwys 53 and 63, Trego	Namekagon River
Washington	Dheinsville Park, Holy Hill Rd., Germantown	Dheinsville Settlement
Washington	Hwy 83, Hartford	"Kissel"
Washington	South side of Hwy 33, 550 feet west of jct. with Hwy 144	Great Divide
Washington	At the park, Hwy A, E. of Hwy 114, NW of West Bend	Lizard Mound County Park
Waukesha	408 Main St., Delafield	Delafield Fish Hatchery
Waukesha	Southern Kettle Moraine State Forest, County C, Delafield	Lapham Peak
Waukesha	Mission Road at Mill Road, west of Delafield	Nashotah Mission
Waukesha	1101 North Genesee Street, Delafield	St. John's Northwestern Military Academy
Waukesha	Hwy 18, near Dousman	Masonic Home
Waukesha	Main Street, Lannon	Lannon Stone
Waukesha	N51 W34922 Wisconsin Ave., Okauchee	Historic Okauchee
Waukesha	Carroll College campus, Waukesha	Carroll College
Waupaca	Municipal Airport, Clintonville	Birthplace of an Airline
Waupaca	Walter Olen Park, Clintonville	Four-Wheel Drive
Waupaca	Marden Memorial Center, WI Veterans Home, King	General Charles King
Waupaca	Marden Memorial Center, WI Veterans Home, King	Grand Army Home
Waupaca	Triangle Park, Jct. of Hwy 22 with 110 and Hwy B, Manawa	Melvin O. Handrich – Medal of Honor Recipient
Waupaca	Hwy 110, 3.5 miles south of Marion	Chief Waupaca
Waushara	County J, 2 miles south of Almond	Sir Henry Wellcome
Waushara	State Hwy 49, Auroraville	The Auroraville Fountain
Waushara	6th Ave., Town of Hancock	Whistler Mound Group and Enclosure
Winnebago	9088 Clayton Avenue, Town of Menasha	Fox-Irish Cemetery
Winnebago	Menasha Hotel, Main and Mills Streets, Menasha	Wisconsin Central Railroad
Winnebago	Fritsie Park, Menasha	Butte des Morts
Winnebago	Interior walkway, 135 W. Wisconsin Ave., Neenah	Wisconsin Avenue Commercial Historic District
Winnebago	Scott Park, 515 E. Main St., Omro	Historic Omro
Winnebago	1619 Oshkosh Avenue, Oshkosh	Coles Bashford House
Winnebago	Oshkosh Public Museum, 1331 Algoma Blvd., Oshkosh	Edgar Sawyer House
Winnebago	Rainbow Park, Oshkosh	Knaggs Ferry
Winnebago	Wittman Field Airport, 20th Street Road, Oshkosh	S.J. Wittman
Winnebago	UW-Oshkosh campus, Oshkosh	University of Wisconsin-Oshkosh
Winnebago	Town of Winchester Cemetery, 1 mi. SW of Winchester	Samuel N. Rogers, Sr., American Revolutionary Soldier
Winnebago	Hwy B, west of Winneconne	Poygan Paygrounds
Wood	Wayside #4, junction of Hwys 10 and 13	Prisoners of War
Wood	West 100 Block of North Central Ave., Marshfield	Founder's Square
Wood	Riverside Park, Hwys 54 and 73, Nekoosa	Point Basse
Wood	Hwy 54, 5 miles west of Port Edwards	Cranberry Culture
Wood	Hwys 54 and 73, southern city limits of Wisconsin Rapids	Centralia Pulp and Paper Mill

Sources: State Historical Society of Wisconsin, Historical Markers Council, *A Guide to Wisconsin Historical Markers*, 1982; Division of Historic Preservation, departmental data, June 2005.

WISCONSIN VOTE IN PRESIDENTIAL ELECTIONS
1848 – 2004

Key:
A – American (Know Nothing)	LF – Labor-Farm/Laborista-Agrario	SL – Socialist Labor
AFC – America First Coalition	Lib – Libertarian	Soc – Socialist
Cit – Citizens	LR – Liberal Republican	SoD – Southern Democrat
Com – Communist	NA – New Alliance	SPW – Socialist Party of Wis.
Con – Constitution	Nat – National	SW – Socialist Worker
CU – Constitutional Union	ND – National Democrat	Tax – U.S. Taxpayers
D – Democrat	NER – National Economic Recovery	TBL – The Better Life
ER – Independents for Economic Recovery	NL – Natural Law	3rd – Third Party
FS – Free Soil	People's – People's (Populist)	U – Union
G – Greenback	Pop – Populist	UL – Union Labor
Gr – Grassroots	PP – People's Progressive	USL – U.S. Labor
Ind – Independent	Prog – Progressive	W – Whig
IP – Ind. Progressive	Proh – Prohibition	WG – Wisconsin Greens
IS – Ind. Socialist	R – Republican	WIA – Wis. Independent Alliance
ISL – Ind. Socialist Labor	Rfm – Reform	Workers – Workers
ISW – Ind. Socialist Worker	SD – Social Democrat	WW – Worker's World

Note: The party designation listed for a candidate is taken from the Congressional Quarterly *Guide to U.S. Elections*. A candidate whose party did not receive 1% of the vote for a statewide office in the previous election or who failed to meet the alternative requirement of Section 5.62, Wisconsin Statutes, must be listed on the Wisconsin ballot as "independent". In this listing, candidates whose party affiliations appear as "Ind", followed by a party designation, were identified on the ballot simply as "independent" although they also provided a party designation or statement of principle.

Under the Electoral College system, each state is entitled to electoral votes equal in number to its total congressional delegation of U.S. Senators and U.S. Representatives.

1848 (4 electoral votes)	
Lewis Cass (D)	15,001
Zachary Taylor (W)	13,747
Martin Van Buren (FS)	10,418
TOTAL	39,166

1852 (5 electoral votes)	
Franklin Pierce (D)	33,658
Winfield Scott (W)	22,210
John P. Hale (FS)	8,814
TOTAL	64,682

1856 (5 electoral votes)	
John C. Fremont (R)	66,090
James Buchanan (D)	52,843
Millard Fillmore (A)	579
TOTAL	119,512

1860 (5 electoral votes)	
Abraham Lincoln (R)	86,113
Stephen A. Douglas (D)	65,021
John C. Breckinridge (SoD)	888
John Bell (CU)	161
TOTAL	152,183

1864 (8 electoral votes)	
Abraham Lincoln (R)	83,458
George B. McClellan (D)	65,884
TOTAL	149,342

1868 (8 electoral votes)	
Ulysses S. Grant (R)	108,857
Horatio Seymour (D)	84,707
TOTAL	193,564

1872 (10 electoral votes)	
Ulysses S. Grant (R)	104,994
Horace Greeley (D & LR)	86,477
Charles O'Conor (D)	834
TOTAL	192,305

1876 (10 electoral votes)	
Rutherford B. Hayes (R)	130,668
Samuel J. Tilden (D)	123,927
Peter Cooper (G)	1,509
Green Clay Smith (Proh)	27
TOTAL	256,131

1880 (10 electoral votes)	
James A. Garfield (R)	144,398
Winfield S. Hancock (D)	114,644
James B. Weaver (G)	7,986
John W. Phelps (A)	91
Neal Dow (Proh)	68
TOTAL	267,187

1884 (11 electoral votes)	
James G. Blaine (R)	161,157
Grover Cleveland (D)	146,477
John P. St. John (Proh)	7,656
Benjamin F. Butler (G)	4,598
TOTAL	319,888

1888 (11 electoral votes)	
Benjamin Harrison (R)	176,553
Grover Cleveland (D)	155,232
Clinton B. Fisk (Proh)	14,277
Alson J. Streeter (UL)	8,552
TOTAL	354,614

1892 (12 electoral votes)	
Grover Cleveland (D)	177,325
Benjamin Harrison (R)	171,101
John Bidwell (Proh)	13,136
James B. Weaver (People's)	10,019
TOTAL	371,581

1896 (12 electoral votes)	
William McKinley (R)	268,135
William J. Bryan (D)	165,523
Joshua Levering (Proh)	7,507
John M. Palmer (ND)	4,584
Charles H. Matchett (SL)	1,314
Charles E. Bentley (Nat)	346
TOTAL	447,409

1900 (12 electoral votes)	
William McKinley (R)	265,760
William J. Bryan (D)	159,163
John G. Wooley (Proh)	10,027
Eugene V. Debs (SD)	7,048
Joseph F. Malloney (SL)	503
TOTAL	442,501

1904 (13 electoral votes)	
Theodore Roosevelt (R)	280,164
Alton B. Parker (D)	124,107
Eugene V. Debs (SD)	28,220
Silas C. Swallow (Proh)	9,770
Thomas E. Watson (People's)	530
Charles H. Corregan (SL)	223
TOTAL	443,014

WISCONSIN VOTE IN PRESIDENTIAL ELECTIONS
1848 – 2004–Continued

1908 (13 electoral votes)
William H. Taft (R)	
William J. Bryan (D)	247,747
Eugene V. Debs (SD)	166,632
Eugene W. Chafin (Proh)	28,164
August Gillhaus (SL)	11,564
	314
TOTAL	454,421

1912 (13 electoral votes)
Woodrow Wilson (D)	164,230
William H. Taft (R)	130,596
Theodore Roosevelt (Prog)	62,448
Eugene V. Debs (SD)	33,476
Eugene W. Chafin (Proh)	8,584
Arthur E. Reimer (SL)	632
TOTAL	399,966

1916 (13 electoral votes)
Charles E. Hughes (R)	220,822
Woodrow Wilson (D)	191,363
Allan Benson (Soc)	27,631
J. Frank Hanly (Proh)	7,318
TOTAL	447,134

1920 (13 electoral votes)
Warren G. Harding (R)	498,576
James M. Cox (D)	113,422
Eugene V. Debs (Soc)	80,635
Aaron S. Watkins (Proh)	8,647
TOTAL	701,280

1924 (13 electoral votes)
Robert M. La Follette (Prog)	453,678
Calvin Coolidge (R)	311,614
John W. Davis (D)	68,096
William Z. Foster (Workers)	3,834
Herman P. Faris (Proh)	2,918
TOTAL	840,140

1928 (13 electoral votes)
Herbert Hoover (R)	544,205
Alfred E. Smith (D)	450,259
Norman Thomas (Soc)	18,213
William F. Varney (Proh)	2,245
William Z. Foster (Workers)	1,528
Verne L. Reynolds (SL)	381
TOTAL	1,016,831

1932 (12 electoral votes)
Franklin D. Roosevelt (D)	707,410
Herbert Hoover (R)	347,741
Norman Thomas (Soc)	53,379
William Z. Foster (Com)	3,112
William D. Upshaw (Proh)	2,672
Verne L. Reynolds (SL)	494
TOTAL	1,114,808

1936 (12 electoral votes)
Franklin D. Roosevelt (D)	802,984
Alfred M. Landon (R)	380,828
William Lemke (U)	60,297
Norman Thomas (Soc)	10,626
Earl Browder (Com)	2,197
David L. Calvin (Proh)	1,071
John W. Aiken (SL)	557
TOTAL	1,258,560

1940 (12 electoral votes)
Franklin D. Roosevelt (D)	704,821
Wendell Willkie (R)	679,206
Norman Thomas (Soc)	15,071

Earl Browder (Com)	2,394
Roger Babson (Proh)	2,148
John W. Aiken (SL)	1,882
TOTAL	1,405,522

1944 (12 electoral votes)
Thomas Dewey (R)	674,532
Franklin D. Roosevelt (D)	650,413
Norman Thomas (Soc)	13,205
Edward Teichert (Ind)	1,002
TOTAL	1,339,152

1948 (12 electoral votes)
Harry S Truman (D)	647,310
Thomas Dewey (R)	590,959
Henry Wallace (PP)	25,282
Norman Thomas (Soc)	12,547
Edward Teichert (Ind)	399
Farrell Dobbs (ISW)	303
TOTAL	1,276,800

1952 (12 electoral votes)
Dwight D. Eisenhower (R)	979,744
Adlai E. Stevenson (D)	622,175
Vincent Hallinan (IP)	2,174
Farrell Dobbs (ISW)	1,350
Darlington Hoopes (IS)	1,157
Eric Hass (ISL)	770
TOTAL	1,607,370

1956 (12 electoral votes)
Dwight D. Eisenhower (R)	954,844
Adlai E. Stevenson (D)	586,768
T. Coleman Andrews (Ind Con)	6,918
Darlington Hoopes (Ind Soc)	754
Eric Hass (Ind SL)	710
Farrell Dobbs (Ind SW)	564
TOTAL	1,550,558

1960 (12 electoral votes)
Richard M. Nixon (R)	895,175
John F. Kennedy (D)	830,805
Farrell Dobbs (Ind SW)	1,792
Eric Hass (Ind SL)	1,310
TOTAL	1,729,082

1964 (12 electoral votes)
Lyndon B. Johnson (D)	1,050,424
Barry M. Goldwater (R)	638,495
Clifton DeBerry (Ind SW)	1,692
Eric Hass (Ind SL)	1,204
TOTAL	1,691,815

1968 (12 electoral votes)
Richard M. Nixon (R)	809,997
Hubert H. Humphrey (D)	748,804
George C. Wallace (Ind A)	127,835
Henning A. Blomen (Ind SL)	1,338
Frederick W. Halstead (Ind SW)	1,222
TOTAL	1,689,196

1972 (11 electoral votes)
Richard M. Nixon (R)	989,430
George S. McGovern (D)	810,174
John G. Schmitz (A)	47,525
Benjamin M. Spock (Ind Pop)	2,701
Louis Fisher (Ind SL)	998
Gus Hall (Ind Com)	663
Evelyn Reed (Ind SW)	506
TOTAL	1,851,997

WISCONSIN VOTE IN PRESIDENTIAL ELECTIONS
1848 – 2004–Continued

1976 (11 electoral votes)
Jimmy Carter (D) 1,040,232
Gerald R. Ford (R) 1,004,987
Eugene J. McCarthy (Ind) 34,943
Lester Maddox (A) 8,552
Frank P. Zeidler (Ind Soc) 4,298
Roger L. MacBride (Ind Lib) 3,814
Peter Camejo (Ind SW) 1,691
Margaret Wright (Ind Pop) 943
Gus Hall (Ind Com) 749
Lyndon H. LaRouche, Jr. (Ind USL) 738
Jules Levin (Ind SL) 389
TOTAL 2,104,175

1980 (11 electoral votes)
Ronald Reagan (R) 1,088,845
Jimmy Carter (D) 981,584
John Anderson (Ind) 160,657
Ed Clark (Ind Lib) 29,135
Barry Commoner (Ind Cit) 7,767
John Rarick (Ind Con) 1,519
David McReynolds (Ind Soc) 808
Gus Hall (Ind Com) 772
Deidre Griswold (Ind WW) 414
Clifton DeBerry (Ind SW) 383
TOTAL 2,273,221

1984 (11 electoral votes)
Ronald Reagan (R) 1,198,800
Walter F. Mondale (D) 995,847
David Bergland (Lib) 4,884
Bob Richards (Con) 3,864
Lyndon H. LaRouche, Jr. (Ind) 3,791
Sonia Johnson (Ind Cit) 1,456
Dennis L. Serrette (Ind WIA) 1,007
Larry Holmes (Ind WW) 619
Gus Hall (Ind Com) 597
Melvin T. Mason (Ind SW) 445
TOTAL 2,212,018

1988 (11 electoral votes)
Michael S. Dukakis (D) 1,126,794
George Bush (R) 1,047,499
Ronald Paul (Ind Lib) 5,157
David E. Duke (Ind Pop) 3,056
James Warren (Ind SW) 2,574
Lyndon H. LaRouche, Jr. (Ind NER) 2,302
Lenora B. Fulani (Ind NA) 1,953
TOTAL 2,191,612

1992 (11 electoral votes)
Bill Clinton (D) 1,041,066
George Bush (R) 930,855
Ross Perot (Ind) 544,479
Andre Marrou (Lib) 2,877
James Gritz (Ind AFC) 2,311
Ron Daniels (LF) 1,883
Howard Phillips (Ind Tax) 1,772
J. Quinn Brisben (Ind Soc) 1,211
John Hagelin (NL) 1,070
Lenora B. Fulani (Ind NA) 654
Lyndon H. LaRouche, Jr. (Ind ER) 633
Jack Herer (Ind Gr) 547
Eugene A. Hem (3rd) 405
James Warren (Ind SW) 390
TOTAL 2,531,114

1996 (11 electoral votes)
Bill Clinton (D) 1,071,971
Bob Dole (R) 845,029
Ross Perot (Rfm) 227,339
Ralph Nader (Ind WG) 28,723
Howard Phillips (Tax) 8,811
Harry Browne (Lib) 7,929
John Hagelin (Ind NL) 1,379
Monica Mooerhead (Ind WW) 1,333
Mary Cal Hollis (Ind Soc) 848
James E. Harris (Ind SW) 483
TOTAL 2,196,169

2000 (11 electoral votes)
Al Gore (D) 1,242,987
George W. Bush (R) 1,237,279
Ralph Nader (WG) 94,070
Pat Buchanan (Ind Rfm) 11,446
Harry Browne (Lib) 6,640
Howard Phillips (Con) 2,042
Monica G. Moorehead (Ind WW) 1,063
John Hagelin (Ind Rfm) 878
James Harris (Ind SW) 306
TOTAL 2,598,607

2004 (10 electoral votes)
John F. Kerry (D) 1,489,504
George W. Bush (R) 1,478,120
Ralph Nader (Ind WG) 16,390
Michael Badnarik (Lib) 6,464
David Cobb (WG) 2,661
Walter F. Brown (Ind SPW) 471
James Harris (Ind SW) 411
TOTAL 2,997,007

Note: Some totals include scattered votes for other candidates.

Sources: Official records of the Elections Board and Congressional Quarterly, *Guide to U.S. Elections*, 1994.

VOTE FOR GOVERNOR IN GENERAL ELECTIONS
1848 – 2002

Key:
A – American
C – Conservative
Com – Communist
Con – Constitution
D – Democrat
DS – Democratic Socialist
G – Greenback
Ind – Independent
IC – Independent Communist
ID – Independent Democrat
IL – Independent Labor
IP – Independent Prohibition

IPR – Independent Prohibition Republic
ISL – Independent Socialist Labor
ISW – Independent Socialist Worker
IW – Independent Worker
L – Labor
LF – Labor–Farm/Laborista–Agrario
Lib – Libertarian
Nat – National
NR – National Republic
People's – People's (Populist)
PLS – Progressive Labor Socialist
PP – People's Progressive

Prog – Progressive
Proh – Prohibition
R – Republican
Soc – Socialist
SD – Social Democrat
SDA – Social Democrat of America
SL – Socialist Labor
SW – Socialist Worker
Tax – U.S. Taxpayers
U – Union
UL – Union Labor
W – Whig
WG – Wisconsin Greens

Note: Candidates whose party did not receive 1% of the vote for a statewide office in the previous election or who failed to meet the alternative requirement of Section 5.62, Wisconsin Statutes, are listed on the Wisconsin ballot as "independent". When a candidate's party affiliation is listed as "independent" and a party designation is shown in italics, "independent" was the official ballot listing, but a party designation was found by the Wisconsin Legislative Reference Bureau in newspaper reports.

1848
Nelson Dewey (D)[1]	19,875
John Hubbard Tweedy (W)[1]	14,621
Charles Durkee (Ind)[1]	1,134
TOTAL	35,309

1849
Nelson Dewey (D)	16,649
Alexander L. Collins (W)	11,317
Warren Chase (Ind)	3,761
TOTAL	31,759

1851
Leonard James Farwell (W)	22,319
Don Alonzo Joshua Upham (D)	21,812
TOTAL	44,190

1853
William Augustus Barstow (D)	30,405
Edward Dwight Holton (R)	21,886
Henry Samuel Baird (W)	3,304
TOTAL	55,683

1855
William Augustus Barstow (D)[2]	36,355
Coles Bashford (R)	36,198
TOTAL	72,598

1857
Alexander William Randall (R)	44,693
James B. Cross (D)	44,239
TOTAL	90,058

1859
Alexander William Randall (R)	59,999
Harrison Carroll Hobart (D)	52,539
TOTAL	112,755

1861
Louis Powell Harvey (R)	53,777
Benjamin Ferguson (D)	45,456
TOTAL	99,258

1863
James Taylor Lewis (R)	72,717
Henry L. Palmer (D)	49,053
TOTAL	122,029

1865
Lucius Fairchild (R)	58,332
Harrison Carroll Hobart (D)	48,330
TOTAL	106,674

1867
Lucius Fairchild (R)	73,637
John J. Tallmadge (D)	68,873
TOTAL	142,522

1869
Lucius Fairchild (R)	69,502
Charles D. Robinson (D)	61,239
TOTAL	130,781

1871
Cadwallader Colden Washburn (R)	78,301
James Rood Doolittle (D)	68,910
TOTAL	147,274

1873
William Robert Taylor (D)	81,599
Cadwallader Colden Washburn (R)	66,224
TOTAL	147,856

1875
Harrison Ludington (R)	85,155
William Robert Taylor (D)	84,314
TOTAL	170,070

1877
William E. Smith (R)	78,759
James A. Mallory (D)	70,486
Edward Phelps Allis (G)	26,216
Collin M. Campbell (Soc)	2,176
TOTAL	178,122

1879
William E. Smith (R)	100,535
James G. Jenkins (D)	75,030
Reuben May (G)	12,996
TOTAL	189,005

1881
Jeremiah McLain Rusk (R)	81,754
N.D. Fratt (D)	69,797
T.D. Kanouse (Proh)	13,225
Edward Phelps Allis (G)	7,002
TOTAL	171,856

1884
Jeremiah McLain Rusk (R)	163,214
N.D. Fratt (D)	143,945
Samuel Dexter Hastings (Proh)	8,545
William L. Utley (G)	4,274
TOTAL	319,997

1886
Jeremiah McLain Rusk (R)	133,247
Gilbert Motier Woodward (D)	114,529
John Cochrane (People's)	21,467
John Myers Olin (Proh)	17,089
TOTAL	286,368

1888
William Dempster Hoard (R)	175,696
James Morgan (D)	155,423
E.G. Durant (Proh)	14,373
D. Frank Powell (L)	9,196
TOTAL	354,714

1890
George Wilbur Peck (D)	160,388
William Dempster Hoard (R)	132,068
Charles Alexander (Proh)	11,246
Reuben May (UL)	5,447
TOTAL	309,254

1892
George Wilbur Peck (D)	178,095
John Coit Spooner (R)	170,497
Thomas C. Richmond (Proh)	13,185
C.M. Butt (People's)	9,638
TOTAL	371,559

1894
William H. Upham (R)	196,150
George Wilbur Peck (D)	142,250
D. Frank Powell (People's)	25,604
John F. Cleghorn (Proh)	11,240
TOTAL	375,449

1896
Edward Scofield (R)	264,981
Willis C. Silverthorn (D)	169,257
Joshua H. Berkey (Proh)	8,140
Christ Tuttrop (SL)	1,306
Robert Henderson (Nat)	407
TOTAL	444,110

VOTE FOR GOVERNOR IN GENERAL ELECTIONS
1848 – 2002–Continued

1898

Edward Scofield (R)	173,137
Hiram Wilson Sawyer (D)	135,353
Albinus A. Worsley (People's)	8,518
Eugene Wilder Chafin (Proh)	8,078
Howard Tuttle (SDA)	2,544
Henry Riese (SL)	1,473
TOTAL	329,430

1900

Robert Marion La Follette (R)	264,419
Louis G. Bomrich (D)	160,674
J. Burritt Smith (Proh)	9,707
Howard Tuttle (SD)	6,590
Frank R. Wilke (SL)	509
TOTAL	441,900

1902

Robert Marion La Follette (R)	193,417
David Stuart Rose (D)	145,818
Emil Seidel (SD)	15,970
Edwin W. Drake (Proh)	9,647
Henry E.D. Puck (SL)	791
TOTAL	365,676

1904

Robert Marion La Follette (R)	227,253
George Wilbur Peck (D)	176,301
William A. Arnold (SD)	24,857
Edward Scofield (NR)	12,136
William H. Clark (Proh)	8,764
Charles M. Minkley (SL)	249
TOTAL	449,570

1906

James O. Davidson (R)	183,558
John A. Aylward (D)	103,311
Winfield R. Gaylord (SD)	24,437
Ephraim L. Eaton (Proh)	8,211
Ole T. Rosaas (SL)	455
TOTAL	320,003

1908

James O. Davidson (R)	242,935
John A. Aylward (D)	165,977
H.D. Brown (SD)	28,583
Winfred D. Cox (Proh)	11,760
Herman Bottema (SL)	393
TOTAL	449,656

1910

Francis Edward McGovern (R)	161,619
Adolph H. Schmitz (D)	110,442
William A. Jacobs (SD)	39,547
Byron E. Van Keuren (Proh)	7,450
Fred G. Kremer (SL)	430
TOTAL	319,522

1912

Francis Edward McGovern (R)	179,360
John C. Karel (D)	167,316
Carl D. Thompson (SD)	34,468
Charles Lewis Hill (Proh)	9,433
William H. Curtis (SL)	3,253
TOTAL	393,849

1914

Emanuel Lorenz Philipp (R)	140,787
John C. Karel (D)	119,509
John James Blaine (Ind)	32,560
Oscar Ameringer (SD)	25,917
David W. Emerson (Proh)	6,279
John Vierthaler (Ind)	352
TOTAL	325,430

1916

Emanuel Lorenz Philipp (R)	229,889
Burt Williams (D)	164,555
Rae Weaver (Soc)	30,649
George McKerrow (Proh)	9,193
TOTAL	434,340

1918

Emanuel Lorenz Philipp (R)	155,799
Henry A. Moehlenpah (D)	112,576
Emil Seidel (SD)	57,523
William C. Dean (Proh)	5,296
TOTAL	331,582

1920

John James Blaine (R)	366,247
Robert McCoy (D)	247,746
William Coleman (Soc)	71,126
Henry H. Tubbs (Proh)	6,047
TOTAL	691,294

1922

John James Blaine (R)	367,929
Arthur A. Bentley (D)	51,061
Louis A. Arnold (Soc)	39,570
M.L. Welles (Proh)	21,438
Arthur A. Dietrich (ISL)	1,444
TOTAL	481,828

1924

John James Blaine (R)	412,255
Martin L. Lueck (D)	317,550
William F. Quick (Soc)	45,268
Adolph R. Bucknam (Proh)	11,516
Severi Alanne (IW)	4,107
Farrand K. Shuttleworth (IPR)	4,079
Jose Snover (SL)	1,452
TOTAL	796,432

1926

Fred R. Zimmerman (R)	350,927
Charles Perry (Ind)	76,507
Virgil H. Cady (D)	72,627
Herman O. Kent (Soc)	40,293
David W. Emerson (Proh)	7,333
Alex Gorden (SL)	4,593
TOTAL	552,912

1928

Walter Jodok Kohler, Sr. (R)	547,738
Albert George Schmedeman (D)	394,368
Otto R. Hauser (Soc)	36,924
Adolph R. Bucknam (Proh)	6,477
Joseph Ehrhardt (IL)	1,938
Alvar J. Hayes (IW)	1,420
TOTAL	989,143

1930

Philip Fox La Follette (R)	392,958
Charles E. Hammersley (D)	170,020
Frank B. Metcalfe (Soc)	25,607
Alfred B. Taynton (Proh)	14,818
Fred Bassett Blair (IC)	2,998
TOTAL	606,825

1932

Albert George Schmedeman (D)	590,114
Walter Jodok Kohler, Sr. (R)	470,805
Frank B. Metcalfe (Soc)	56,965
William C. Dean (Proh)	3,148
Fred Bassett Blair (Com)	2,926
Joe Ehrhardt (SL)	398
TOTAL	1,124,502

1934

Philip Fox La Follette (Prog)	373,093
Albert George Schmedeman (D)	359,467
Howard Greene (R)	172,980
George A. Nelson (Soc)	44,589
Morris Childs (IC)	2,454
Thomas W. North (PR)	857
Joe Ehrhardt (ISL)	332
TOTAL	953,797

1936

Philip Fox La Follette (Prog)	573,724
Alexander Wiley (R)	363,973
Arthur W. Lueck (D)	268,530
Joseph F. Walsh (U)	27,934
Joseph Ehrhardt (SL)	1,738
August F. Fehlandt (Proh)	1,008
TOTAL	1,237,095

1938

Julius Peter Heil (R)	543,675
Philip Fox La Follette (Prog)	353,381
Harry Wilbur Bolens (D)	78,446
Frank W. Smith (U)	4,564
John Schleier, Jr. (ISL)	1,459
TOTAL	981,560

1940

Julius Peter Heil (R)	558,678
Orland Steen Loomis (Prog)	546,436
Francis Edward McGovern (D)	264,985
Fred Bassett Blair (Com)	2,340
Louis Fisher (SL)	1,158
TOTAL	1,373,754

1942

Orland Steen Loomis (Prog)	397,664
Julius Peter Heil (R)	291,945
William C. Sullivan (D)	98,153
Frank P. Zeidler (Soc)	11,295
Fred Bassett Blair (IC)	1,092
Georgia Cozzini (ISL)	490
TOTAL	800,985

VOTE FOR GOVERNOR IN GENERAL ELECTIONS
1848 – 2002–Continued

1944

Walter Samuel Goodland (R)	697,740
Daniel O. Hoan (D)	536,357
Alexander O. Benz (Prog)	76,028
George A. Nelson (Soc)	9,183
Georgia Cozzini (Ind–ISL)	1,122
TOTAL	1,320,483

1946

Walter Samuel Goodland (R)	621,970
Daniel W. Hoan (D)	406,499
Walter H. Uphoff (Soc)	8,996
Sigmund G. Eisenscher (IC)	1,857
Jerry R. Kenyon (ISL)	959
TOTAL	1,040,444

1948

Oscar Rennebohm (R)	684,839
Carl W. Thompson (D)	558,497
Henry J. Berquist (PP)	12,928
Walter H. Uphoff (Soc)	9,149
James E. Boulton (ISW)	356
Georgia Cozzini (ISL)	328
TOTAL	1,266,139

1950

Walter Jodok Kohler, Jr. (R)	605,649
Carl W. Thompson (D)	525,319
M. Michael Essin (PP)	3,735
William O. Hart (Soc)	3,384
TOTAL	1,138,148

1952

Walter Jodok Kohler, Jr. (R)	1,009,171
William Proxmire (D)	601,844
M. Michael Essin (Ind)	3,706
TOTAL	1,615,214

1954

Walter Jodok Kohler, Jr. (R)	596,158
William Proxmire (D)	560,747
Arthur Wepfer (Ind)	1,722
TOTAL	1,158,666

1956

Vernon W. Thomson (R)	808,273
William Proxmire (D)	749,421
TOTAL	1,557,788

1958

Gaylord Anton Nelson (D)	644,296
Vernon W. Thomson (R)	556,391
Wayne Leverenz (Ind)	1,485
TOTAL	1,202,219

1960

Gaylord Anton Nelson (D)	890,868
Philip G. Kuehn (R)	837,123
TOTAL	1,728,009

1962

John W. Reynolds (D)	637,491
Philip G. Kuehn (R)	625,536
Adolf Wiggert (Ind)	2,477
TOTAL	1,265,900

1964

Warren P. Knowles (R)	856,779
John W. Reynolds (D)	837,901
TOTAL	1,694,887

1966

Warren P. Knowles (R)	626,041
Patrick J. Lucey (D)	539,258
Adolf Wiggert (Ind)	4,745
TOTAL	1,170,173

1968

Warren P. Knowles (R)	893,463
Bronson C. La Follette (D)	791,100
Adolf Wiggert (Ind)	3,225
Robert Wilkinson (Ind)	1,813
TOTAL	1,689,738

1970

Patrick J. Lucey (D)	728,403
Jack B. Olson (R)	602,617
Leo James McDonald (A)	9,035
Georgia Cozzini (Ind–SL)	1,287
Samuel K. Hunt (Ind–SW)	888
Myrtle Kastner (Ind–PLS)	628
TOTAL	1,343,160

1974

Patrick J. Lucey (D)	628,639
William D. Dyke (R)	497,189
William H. Upham (A)	33,528
Crazy Jim[3] (Ind)	12,107
William Hart (Ind–DS)	5,113
Fred Blair (Ind–C)	3,617
Georgia Cozzini (Ind–SL)	1,492
TOTAL	1,181,685

1978

Lee Sherman Dreyfus (R)	816,056
Martin J. Schreiber (D)	673,813
Eugene R. Zimmerman (C)	6,355
John C. Doherty (Ind)	2,183
Adrienne Kaplan (Ind–SW)	1,548
Henry A. Ochsner (Ind–SL)	849
TOTAL	1,500,996

1982

Anthony S. Earl (D)	896,872
Terry J. Kohler (R)	662,738
Larry Smiley (Lib)	9,734
James P. Wickstrom (Con)	7,721
Peter Seidman (Ind–SW)	3,025
TOTAL	1,580,344

1986

Tommy G. Thompson (R)	805,090
Anthony S. Earl (D)	705,578
Kathryn A. Christensen (LF)	10,323
Darold E. Wall (Ind)	3,913
Sanford Knapp (Ind)	1,668
TOTAL	1,526,573

1990

Tommy G. Thompson (R)	802,321
Thomas A. Loftus (D)	576,280
TOTAL	1,379,727

1994

Tommy G. Thompson (R)	1,051,326
Charles J. Chvala (D)	482,850
David S. Harmon (Lib)	11,639
Edward J. Frami (Tax)	9,188
Michael J. Mangan (Ind)	8,150
TOTAL	1,563,835

1998

Tommy G. Thompson (R)	1,047,716
Ed Garvey (D)	679,553
Jim Mueller (Ind)	11,071
Edward J. Frami (Tax)	10,269
Mike Mangan (Ind)	4,985
A-Ja-mu Muhammad (Ind)	1,604
Jeffrey L. Smith (WG)	14
TOTAL	1,756,014

2002

Jim Doyle (D)	800,515
Scott McCallum (R)	734,779
Ed Thompson (Lib)	185,455
Jim Young (WG)	44,111
Alan D. Eisenberg (Ind)	2,847
Ty A. Bollerud (Ind)	2,637
Mike Mangan (Ind)	1,710
Aneb Jah Rasta Sensas-Utcha Nefer-I (Ind)	929
TOTAL	1,775,349

[1] Votes for Dewey and Tweedy are from *1874 Blue Book;* Durkee vote is based on county returns, as filed in the Office of the Secretary of State, but returns from Manitowoc and Winnebago Counties were missing. Without these 2 counties, Dewey had 19,605 votes and Tweedy had 14,514 votes.

[2] Barstow's plurality was set aside in *Atty. Gen. ex rel. Bashford v. Barstow,* 4 Wis. 567 (1855) because of irregularities in the election returns.

[3] Legal name.

Source: Elections Board records. Totals include scattered votes for other candidates.

WISCONSIN GOVERNORS SINCE 1848

Governor[1]	Political Party	Service As Governor[2]		Born	Birthplace	Died	Burial Place
		Began	Ended				
1 Nelson Dewey	Democrat	6-7-1848	1-5-1852	12-19-1813	Lebanon, Conn.	7-21-1889	Lancaster, Wis.
2 Leonard James Farwell	Whig	1-5-1852	1-2-1854	1-5-1819	Watertown, N.Y.	4-11-1889	Grant City, Mo.
3 William Augustus Barstow	Democrat	1-2-1854	3-21-1856	9-13-1813	Plainfield, Conn.	12-13-1865	Cleveland, Ohio
4 Arthur MacArthur[3]	Democrat	3-21-1856	3-25-1856	1-26-1815	Glasgow, Scotland	8-26-1896	Washington, D.C.
5 Coles Bashford	Republican	3-25-1856	1-4-1858	1-24-1816	Putnam Co., N.Y.	4-25-1878	Oakland, Cal.
6 Alexander William Randall	Republican	1-4-1858	1-6-1862	10-31-1819	Ames, N.Y.	7-26-1872	Elmira, N.Y.
7 Louis Powell Harvey[4]	Republican	1-6-1862	4-19-1862	7-22-1820	East Haddam, Conn.	4-19-1862	Madison, Wis.
8 Edward Salomon[4]	Republican	4-19-1862	1-4-1864	8-11-1828	Stroebeck, Prussia	4-21-1909	Frankfurt, Germany
9 James Taylor Lewis	Republican	1-4-1864	1-1-1866	10-30-1819	Clarendon, N.Y.	8-4-1904	Columbus, Wis.
10 Lucius Fairchild	Republican	1-1-1866	1-1-1872	12-27-1831	Kent, Ohio	5-23-1896	Madison, Wis.
11 Cadwallader Colden Washburn	Republican	1-1-1872	1-5-1874	4-22-1818	Livermore, Me.	5-14-1882	La Crosse, Wis.
12 William Robert Taylor	Democrat	1-5-1874	1-3-1876	7-10-1820	Woodbury, Conn.	3-17-1909	Madison, Wis.
13 Harrison Ludington	Republican	1-3-1876	1-7-1878	7-30-1812	Ludingtonville, N.Y.	6-17-1891	Milwaukee, Wis.
14 William E. Smith	Republican	1-7-1878	1-2-1882	6-18-1824	Near Inverness, Scotland	2-13-1883	Milwaukee, Wis.
15 Jeremiah McLain Rusk	Republican	1-2-1882	1-7-1889	6-17-1830	Morgan Co., Ohio	11-21-1893	Viroqua, Wis.
16 William Dempster Hoard	Republican	1-7-1889	1-5-1891	10-10-1836	Stockbridge, N.Y.	11-22-1918	Ft. Atkinson, Wis.
17 George Wilbur Peck	Democrat	1-5-1891	1-7-1895	9-28-1840	Henderson, N.Y.	4-16-1916	Milwaukee, Wis.
18 William Henry Upham	Republican	1-7-1895	1-4-1897	5-3-1841	Westminster, Mass.	7-2-1924	Marshfield, Wis.
19 Edward Scofield	Republican	1-4-1897	1-7-1901	3-28-1842	Clearfield, Pa.	2-3-1925	Oconto, Wis.
20 Robert Marion La Follette, Sr.[5]	Republican	1-7-1901	1-1-1906	6-14-1855	Primrose, Dane Co., Wis.	6-18-1925	Madison, Wis.
21 James O. Davidson[5]	Republican	1-1-1906	1-2-1911	2-10-1854	Sogn, Norway	12-16-1922	Madison, Wis.
22 Francis Edward McGovern	Republican	1-2-1911	1-4-1915	1-21-1866	Elkhart Lake, Wis.	5-16-1946	Milwaukee, Wis.
23 Emanuel Lorenz Philipp	Republican	1-4-1915	1-3-1921	3-25-1861	Honey Creek, Sauk Co., Wis.	6-15-1925	Milwaukee, Wis.
24 John James Blaine	Republican	1-3-1921	1-3-1927	5-4-1875	Wingville, Grant Co., Wis.	4-18-1934	Boscobel, Wis.
25 Fred R. Zimmerman	Republican	1-3-1927	1-7-1929	11-20-1880	Milwaukee, Wis.	12-14-1954	Milwaukee, Wis.
26 Walter Jodok Kohler, Sr.	Republican	1-7-1929	1-5-1931	3-3-1875	Sheboygan, Wis.	4-21-1940	Kohler, Wis.
27 Philip Fox La Follette	Republican	1-5-1931	1-2-1933	5-8-1897	Madison, Wis.	8-18-1965	Madison, Wis.
28 Albert George Schmedeman	Democrat	1-2-1933	1-7-1935	11-25-1864	Madison, Wis.	11-26-1946	Madison, Wis.
29 Philip Fox La Follette	Progressive	1-7-1935	1-2-1939	5-8-1897	Madison, Wis.	8-18-1965	Madison, Wis.
30 Julius Peter Heil	Progressive	1-2-1939	1-4-1943	7-24-1876	Duesmond, Germany	11-30-1949	Milwaukee, Wis.
— Orland Steen Loomis[6,7]	Republican	Died prior to inauguration		11-2-1893	Mauston, Wis.	12-7-1942	Mauston, Wis.
31 Walter Samuel Goodland[6,7]	Republican	1-4-1943	3-12-1947	12-22-1862	Sharon, Wis.	3-12-1947	Racine, Wis.
32 Oscar Rennebohm[7]	Republican	3-12-1947	1-1-1951	5-25-1889	Leeds, Columbia Co., Wis.	10-15-1968	Madison, Wis.
33 Walter Jodok Kohler, Jr.	Republican	1-1-1951	1-7-1957	4-4-1904	Sheboygan, Wis.	3-10-1976	Kohler, Wis.
34 Vernon Wallace Thomson	Republican	1-7-1957	1-5-1959	11-5-1905	Richland Center, Wis.	4-2-1988	Richland Center, Wis.
35 Gaylord Anton Nelson	Democrat	1-5-1959	1-7-1963	6-4-1916	Clear Lake, Wis.	7-3-2005	Clear Lake, Wis.
36 John W. Reynolds	Republican	1-7-1963	1-4-1965	4-4-1921	Green Bay, Wis.	1-6-2002	Door County, Wis.
37 Warren Perley Knowles	Democrat	1-4-1965	1-4-1971	8-19-1908	River Falls, Wis.	4-1-1993	River Falls, Wis.
38 Patrick Joseph Lucey[8]	Democrat	1-4-1971	7-6-1977	3-21-1918	La Crosse, Wis.	-----	-----
39 Martin James Schreiber[8]	Republican	7-6-1977	1-1-1979	4-8-1939	Milwaukee, Wis.	-----	-----
40 Lee Sherman Dreyfus	Democrat	1-1-1979	1-3-1983	6-20-1926	Milwaukee, Wis.	-----	-----
41 Anthony Scully Earl	Democrat	1-3-1983	1-5-1987	4-12-1936	Lansing, Mich.	-----	-----
42 Tommy George Thompson[9]	Republican	1-5-1987	2-1-2001	11-19-1941	Elroy, Wis.	-----	-----
43 Scott McCallum[9]	Democrat	2-1-2001	1-6-2003	5-2-1950	Fond du Lac, Wis.	-----	-----
44 James E. Doyle	Democrat	1-6-2003	-----	11-23-1945	Madison, Wis.	-----	-----

[1] Includes those serving as acting governor when office is vacated. Administrations are numbered.

[2] Article XIII, Section 1 of the Wisconsin Constitution was amended in November 1884 so that the term of office of all state and county officers began in January of odd-numbered years, rather than January of even-numbered years.

[3] Served as acting governor during dispute over who won gubernatorial election.

[4] Salomon became acting governor on death of Harvey on 4/19/62.

[5] Davidson served as acting governor from La Follette's resignation until beginning the terms to which he was elected on 1/7/07.

[6] Goodland became acting governor on death of Governor-elect Loomis and served entire 1943-44 term.

[7] Rennebohm became acting governor on the death of Goodland on 3/12/47.

[8] Schreiber became acting governor when Lucey resigned to become U.S. ambassador to Mexico.

[9] McCallum became governor when Thompson resigned to become U.S. Secretary of Health and Human Services.

Sources: "Wisconsin's Former Governors", 1960 Wisconsin Blue Book, pp. 69-206; Blue Book biographies.

WISCONSIN CONSTITUTIONAL OFFICERS, 1848 – 2005

Name	Term[1]	Residence
Governor		
(See separate table)		
Lieutenant Governors		
John E. Holmes (D)	1848-1850	Jefferson
Samuel W. Beall (D)	1850-1852	Taycheedah
Timothy Burns (D)	1852-1854	La Crosse
James T. Lewis (R)	1854-1856	Columbus
Arthur McArthur (D)[2]	1856-1858	Milwaukee
Erasmus D. Campbell (D)	1858-1860	La Crosse
Butler G. Noble (R)	1860-1862	Whitewater
Edward Salomon (R)[3]	1862-1864	Milwaukee
Wyman Spooner (R)	1864-1870	Elkhorn
Thaddeus C. Pound (R)	1870-1872	Chippewa Falls
Milton H. Pettit (R)[4]	1872-3/23/73	Kenosha
Charles D. Parker (D)	1874-1878	Pleasant Valley
James M. Bingham (R)	1878-1882	Chippewa Falls
Sam S. Fifield (R)	1882-1887	Ashland
George W. Ryland (R)	1887-1891	Lancaster
Charles Jonas (D)	1891-1895	Racine
Emil Baensch (R)	1895-1899	Manitowoc
Jesse Stone (R)	1899-1903	Watertown
James O. Davidson (R)[5]	1903-1907	Soldiers Grove
William D. Connor (R)	1907-1909	Marshfield
John Strange (R)	1909-1911	Oshkosh
Thomas Morris (R)	1911-1915	La Crosse
Edward F. Dithmar (R)	1915-1921	Baraboo
George F. Comings (R)	1921-1925	Eau Claire
Henry A. Huber (R)	1925-1933	Stoughton
Thomas J. O'Malley (D)	1933-1937	Milwaukee
Henry A. Gunderson (Prog)[6]	1937-10/16/37	Portage
Herman L. Ekern (Prog)[6]	5/16/1938-1939	Madison
Walter S. Goodland (R)[7]	1939-1945	Racine
Oscar Rennebohm (R)[8]	1945-1949	Madison
George M. Smith (R)	1949-1955	Milwaukee
Warren P. Knowles (R)	1955-1959	New Richmond
Philleo Nash (D)	1959-1961	Wisconsin Rapids
Warren P. Knowles (R)	1961-1963	New Richmond
Jack Olson (R)	1963-1965	Wisconsin Dells
Patrick J. Lucey (D)	1965-1967	Madison
Jack Olson (R)	1967-1971	Wisconsin Dells
Martin J. Schreiber (D)[9]	1971-1979	Milwaukee
Russell A. Olson (R)	1979-1983	Randall
James T. Flynn (D)	1983-1987	West Allis
Scott McCallum (R)[10]	1987-2001	Fond du Lac
Margaret A. Farrow (R)[10]	2001-2003	Pewaukee
Barbara Lawton (D)	2003-	Green Bay
Secretaries of State		
Thomas McHugh (D)	1848-1850	Delavan
William A. Barstow (D)	1850-1852	Waukesha
Charles D. Robinson (D)	1852-1854	Green Bay
Alexander T. Gray (D)	1854-1856	Janesville
David W. Jones (D)	1856-1860	Belmont
Lewis P. Harvey (R)	1860-1862	Shopiere
James T. Lewis (R)	1862-1864	Columbus
Lucius Fairchild (R)	1864-1866	Madison
Thomas S. Allen (R)	1866-1870	Mineral Point
Llywelyn Breese (R)	1870-1874	Portage
Peter Doyle (D)	1874-1878	Prairie du Chien
Hans B. Warner (R)	1878-1882	Ellsworth
Ernst G. Timme (R)	1882-1891	Kenosha
Thomas J. Cunningham (D)	1891-1895	Chippewa Falls
Henry Casson (R)	1895-1899	Viroqua
William H. Froehlich (R)	1899-1903	Jackson
Walter L. Houser (R)	1903-1907	Mondovi
James A. Frear (R)	1907-1913	Hudson
John S. Donald (R)	1913-1917	Mt. Horeb
Merlin Hull (R)	1917-1921	Black River Falls
Elmer S. Hall (R)	1921-1923	Green Bay
Fred R. Zimmerman (R)	1923-1927	Milwaukee
Theodore Dammann (R)	1927-1935	Milwaukee
Theodore Dammann (Prog)	1935-1939	Milwaukee
Fred R. Zimmerman (R)[11]	1939-12/14/54	Milwaukee

WISCONSIN CONSTITUTIONAL OFFICERS, 1848 – 2005–Continued

Name	Term[1]	Residence
Louis Allis (R)[11]	12/16/54-1/3/55	Milwaukee
Mrs. Glenn M. Wise (R)[11]	1/3/55-1957	Madison
Robert C. Zimmerman (R)	1957-1975	Madison
Douglas J. La Follette (D)	1975-1979	Kenosha
Mrs. Vel R. Phillips (D)	1979-1983	Milwaukee
Douglas J. La Follette (D)	1983-	Madison

State Treasurers

Jarius C. Fairchild (D)	1848-1852	Madison
Edward H. Janssen (D)	1852-1856	Cedarburg
Charles Kuehn (D)	1856-1858	Manitowoc
Samuel D. Hastings (R)	1858-1866	Trempealeau
William E. Smith (R)	1866-1870	Fox Lake
Henry Baetz (R)	1870-1874	Manitowoc
Ferdinand Kuehn (D)	1874-1878	Milwaukee
Richard Guenther (R)	1878-1882	Oshkosh
Edward C. McFetridge (R)	1882-1887	Beaver Dam
Henry B. Harshaw (R)	1887-1891	Oshkosh
John Hunner (D)	1891-1895	Eau Claire
Sewell A. Peterson (R)	1895-1899	Rice Lake
James O. Davidson (R)	1899-1903	Soldiers Grove
John J. Kempf (R)[12]	1903-7/30/04	Milwaukee
Thomas M. Purtell (R)[12]	7/30/04-1905	Cumberland
John J. Kempf (R)	1905-1907	Milwaukee
Andrew H. Dahl (R)	1907-1913	Westby
Henry Johnson (R)	1913-1923	Suring
Solomon Levitan (R)	1923-1933	Madison
Robert K. Henry (D)	1933-1937	Jefferson
Solomon Levitan (Prog)	1937-1939	Madison
John M. Smith (R)[4]	1939-8/17/47	Shell Lake
John L. Sonderegger (R)[13]	8/19/47-9/30/48	Madison
Clyde M. Johnston (appointed from staff)[13]	10/1/48-1949	Madison
Warren R. Smith (R)[4]	1949-12/4/57	Milwaukee
Mrs. Dena A. Smith (R)[13]	12/5/57-1959	Milwaukee
Eugene M. Lamb (D)	1959-1961	Milwaukee
Mrs. Dena A. Smith (R)[4]	1961-2/20/68	Milwaukee
Harold W. Clemens (R)[13]	2/21/68-1971	Oconomowoc
Charles P. Smith (D)	1971-1991	Madison
Cathy S. Zeuske (R)	1991-1995	Shawano
Jack C. Voight (R)	1995-	Appleton

Attorneys General

James S. Brown (D)	1848-1850	Milwaukee
S. Park Coon (D)	1850-1852	Milwaukee
Experience Estabrook (D)	1852-1854	Geneva
George B. Smith (D)	1854-1856	Madison
William R. Smith (D)	1856-1858	Mineral Point
Gabriel Bouck (D)	1858-1860	Oshkosh
James H. Howe (R)[14]	1860-1862	Green Bay
Winfield Smith (R)[14]	1862-1866	Milwaukee
Charles R. Gill (R)	1866-1870	Watertown
Stephen Steele Barlow (R)	1870-1874	Dellona
Andrew Scott Sloan (R)	1874-1878	Beaver Dam
Alexander Wilson (R)	1878-1882	Mineral Point
Leander F. Frisby (R)	1882-1887	West Bend
Charles E. Estabrook (R)	1887-1891	Manitowoc
James L. O'Connor (D)	1891-1895	Madison
William H. Mylrea (R)	1895-1899	Wausau
Emmett R. Hicks (R)	1899-1903	Oshkosh
Lafayette M. Sturdevant (R)	1903-1907	Neillsville
Frank L. Gilbert (R)	1907-1911	Madison
Levi H. Bancroft (R)	1911-1913	Richland Center
Walter C. Owen (R)[15]	1913-1918	Maiden Rock
Spencer Haven (R)[15]	1918-1919	Hudson
John J. Blaine (R)	1919-1921	Boscobel
William J. Morgan (R)	1921-1923	Milwaukee
Herman L. Ekern (R)	1923-1927	Madison
John W. Reynolds (R)	1927-1933	Green Bay
James E. Finnegan (D)	1933-1937	Milwaukee
Orlando S. Loomis (Prog)	1937-1939	Mauston
John E. Martin (R)[16]	1939-6/1/48	Madison
Grover L. Broadfoot (R)[16]	6/5/48-1 1/12/48	Mondovi
Thomas E. Fairchild (D)[16]	11/12/48-1951	Verona
Vernon W. Thomson (R)	1951-1957	Richland Center

WISCONSIN CONSTITUTIONAL OFFICERS, 1848 – 2005–Continued

Name	Term[1]	Residence
Stewart G. Honeck (R)	1957-1959	Madison
John W. Reynolds (D)	1959-1963	Green Bay
George Thompson (R)	1963-1965	Madison
Bronson C. La Follette (D)	1965-1969	Madison
Robert W. Warren (R)[17]	1969-10/8/74	Green Bay
Victor A. Miller (D)[17]	10/8/74-1 1/25/74	St. Nazianz
Bronson C. La Follette (D)[17]	11/25/74-1987	Madison
Donald J. Hanaway (R)	1987-1991	Green Bay
James E. Doyle (D)	1991-2003	Madison
Peggy A. Lautenschlager (D)	2003-	Fond du Lac

Superintendents of Public Instruction[18]

Eleazer Root	1849-1852	Waukesha
Azel P. Ladd	1852-1854	Shullsburg
Hiram A. Wright	1854-1855	Prairie du Chien
A. Constantine Barry	1855-1858	Racine
Lyman C. Draper	1858-1860	Madison
Josiah L. Pickard	1860-1864	Platteville
John G. McMynn	1864-1868	Racine
Alexander J. Craig	1868-1870	Madison
Samuel Fallows	1870-1874	Milwaukee
Edward Searing	1874-1878	Milton
William Clarke Whitford	1878-1882	Milton
Robert Graham	1882-1887	Oshkosh
Jesse B. Thayer	1887-1891	River Falls
Oliver Elwin Wells	1891-1895	Appleton
John Q. Emery	1895-1899	Albion
Lorenzo D. Harvey	1899-1903	Milwaukee
Charles P. Cary	1903-1921	Delavan
John Callahan	1921-1949	Madison
George Earl Watson	1949-1961	Wauwatosa
Angus B. Rothwell[19]	1961-7/1/66	Manitowoc
William C. Kahl[19]	7/1/66-1973	Madison
Barbara Thompson	1973-1981	Madison
Herbert J. Grover[20]	1981-4/9/93	Cottage Grove
John T. Benson	1993-2001	Marshall
Elizabeth Burmaster	2001-	Madison

[1]Article XIII, Section 1 of the Wisconsin Constitution was amended in 1884, to provide the terms for all partisan state officers would begin in odd-numbered, rather than even-numbered, years. The section was further amended in 1968 to change the term from 2-years to 4-years, effective with the November 1970 elections.

[2]Served as acting governor 3/21/1856 to 3/25/1856 during dispute over outcome of gubernatorial election.

[3]Became acting governor on the death of Governor Louis P. Harvey on 4/19/1862.

[4]Died in office.

[5]Became acting governor on 1/1/1906 when Robert M. La Follette, Sr., resigned to become U.S. Senator.

[6]Resigned to accept appointment to the State Tax Commission. Ekern appointed by Governor Philip La Follette to fill the unexpired term. Appointment ruled valid in State ex rel. Martin v. Ekern, 228 Wis. 645 (1937).

[7]Goodland reelected lieutenant governor, November 1942; became acting governor on 1/1/1943 for the term of deceased Governor-elect Orlando Loomis.

[8]Became acting governor on the death of Goodland on 3/12/1947.

[9]Became acting governor when Lucey resigned on 7/6/1977 to accept appointment as U.S. ambassador to Mexico.

[10]McCallum became governor on 2/1/2001 when Governor Tommy Thompson resigned to become U.S. Secretary of Health and Social Services. Farrow was appointed lieutenant governor on 5/9/2001.

[11]Died 12/14/1954 after being elected to a new 2-year term. Allis was appointed to fill the unexpired term. Wise was appointed to fill the full 2-year term.

[12]Appointed 7/30/1904 to fill a vacancy caused by the failure of Kempf to give the required bond.

[13]Appointed.

[14]Resigned in October 1862 to join the Union Army. Smith was appointed 10/7/1862 to replace him.

[15]Resigned 1/7/1918 after being elected to the Wisconsin Supreme Court. Haven was appointed to fill the unexpired term.

[16]Resigned to accept appointment to the Wisconsin Supreme Court. Broadfoot was appointed to fill the unexpired term. Broadfoot resigned to accept appointment to the Wisconsin Supreme Court, and Attorney General-elect Fairchild was appointed to fill the unexpired term.

[17]Resigned to accept appointment as U.S. District Judge for the Eastern District of Wisconsin. Miller appointed to fill the unexpired term. Bronson La Follette was elected to a full term and Miller resigned so that La Follette could be appointed to fill the rest of Warren's unexpired term.

[18]Prior to 1902, the state superintendent was elected on a partisan ballot in November, and the term began the first Monday in January. A constitutional amendment moved the election to the nonpartisan April ballot and the beginning of the term to the first Monday in July beginning in July 1905.

[19]Resigned to accept appointment to the Coordinating Committee for Higher Education. Kahl was appointed to fill the unexpired term.

[20]Resigned 4/9/1993. Lee Sherman Dreyfus was appointed to serve as "interim superintendent" for remainder of the unexpired term but did not officially become superintendent.

Source: Wisconsin Legislative Reference Bureau, Wisconsin Blue Books, various editions, and bureau records.

JUSTICES OF THE SUPREME COURT
1836 – 2005

Name	Term	Residence[1]
	Judges During the Territorial Period	
Charles Dunn (Chief Justice)[2]	1836-1848	
William C. Frazier	1836-1838	
David Irvin	1836-1838	
Andrew G. Miller	1836-1848	
	Circuit Judges Who Served as Justices 1848-53[3]	
Alexander W. Stow	1848-1851 (C.J.)	Fond du Lac
Levi Hubbell	1848-1853 (C.J. 1851)	Milwaukee
Edward V. Whiton	1848-1853 (C.J. 1852-53)	Janesville
Charles H. Larrabee	1848-1853	Horicon
Mortimer M. Jackson	1848-1853	Mineral Point
Wiram Knowlton	1850-1853	Prairie du Chien
Timothy O. Howe	1851-1853	Green Bay
	Justices Since 1853	
Edward V. Whiton	1853-1859 (C.J.)	Janesville
Samuel Crawford	1853-1855	New Diggings
Abram D. Smith	1853-1859	Milwaukee
Orsamus Cole	1855-1892 (C.J. 1880-92)	Potosi
Luther S. Dixon[4]	1859-1874 (C.J.)	Portage
Byron Paine[4]	1859-1864, 1867-71	Milwaukee
Jason Downer[4]	1864-1867	Milwaukee
William P. Lyon[4]	1871-1894 (C.J. 1892-94)	Racine
Edward G. Ryan[4]	1874-1880 (C.J.)	Racine
David Taylor	1878-1891	Sheboygan
Harlow S. Orton	1878-1895 (C.J. 1894-95)	Madison
John B. Cassoday[4]	1880-1907 (C.J. 1895-07)	Janesville
John B. Winslow[4]	1891-1920 (C.J. 1907-20)	Racine
Silas U. Pinney	1892-1898	Madison
Alfred W. Newman	1894-1898	Trempealeau
Roujet D. Marshall[4]	1895-1918	Chippewa Falls
Charles V. Bardeen[4]	1898-1903	Wausau
Joshua Eric Dodge[4]	1898-1910	Milwaukee
Robert G. Siebecker[5]	1903-1922 (C.J. 1920-22)	Madison
James C. Kerwin	1905-1921	Neenah
William H. Timlin	1907-1916	Milwaukee
Robert M. Bashford[4]	Jan.-June 1908	Madison
John Barnes	1908-1916	Rhinelander
Aad J. Vinje[4]	1910-1929 (C.J. 1922-29)	Superior
Marvin B. Rosenberry[4]	1916-1950 (C.J. 1929-50)	Wausau
Franz C. Eschweiler[4]	1916-1929	Milwaukee
Walter C. Owen	1918-1934	Maiden Rock
Burr W. Jones[4]	1920-1926	Madison
Christian Doerfler[4]	1921-1929	Milwaukee
Charles H. Crownhart[4]	1922-1930	Madison
E. Ray Stevens	1926-1930	Madison
Chester A. Fowler[4]	1929-1948	Fond du Lac
Oscar M. Fritz[4]	1929-1954 (C.J. 1950-54)	Milwaukee
Edward T. Fairchild[4]	1929-1957 (C.J. 1954-57)	Milwaukee
John D. Wickhem[4]	1930-1949	Madison
George B. Nelson[4]	1930-1942	Stevens Point
Theodore G. Lewis[4]	Nov. 15-Dec. 5, 1934	Madison
Joseph Martin[4]	1934-1946	Green Bay
Elmer E. Barlow[4]	1942-1948	Arcadia
James Ward Rector[4]	1946-1947	Madison
Henry P. Hughes	1948-1951	Oshkosh
John E. Martin[4]	1948-1962 (C.J. 1957-62)	Green Bay
Grover L. Broadfoot[4]	1948-1962 (C.J. Jan.-May 1962)	Mondovi
Timothy Brown[4]	1949-1964 (C.J. 1962-64)	Madison
Edward J. Gehl	1950-1956	Hartford
George R. Currie[4]	1951-1968 (C.J. 1964-68)	Sheboygan
Roland J. Steinle[4]	1954-1958	Milwaukee
Emmert L. Wingert[4]	1956-1959	Madison
Thomas E. Fairchild	1957-1966	Verona
E. Harold Hallows[4]	1958-1974 (C.J. 1968-74)	Milwaukee
William H. Dieterich	1959-1964	Milwaukee
Myron L. Gordon	1962-1967	Milwaukee
Horace W. Wilkie[4]	1962-1976 (C.J. 1974-76)	Madison
Bruce F. Beilfuss	1964-1983 (C.J. 1976-83)	Neillsville
Nathan S. Heffernan[4]	1964-1995 (C.J. 1983-95)	Sheboygan
Leo B. Hanley[4]	1966-1978	Milwaukee
Connor T. Hansen[4]	1967-1980	Eau Claire
Robert W. Hansen	1968-1978	Milwaukee
Roland B. Day[4]	1974-1996 (C.J. 1995-96)	Madison

JUSTICES OF THE SUPREME COURT
1836 – 2005–Continued

Name	Term		Residence[1]
Shirley S. Abrahamson[4]	1976-	(C.J. 1996-)	Madison
William G. Callow	1978-1992		Waukesha
John L. Coffey	1978-1982		Milwaukee
Donald W. Steinmetz	1980-1999		Milwaukee
Louis J. Ceci[4]	1982-1993		Milwaukee
William A. Bablitch	1983-2003		Stevens Point
Jon P. Wilcox[4]	1992-		Wautoma
Janine P. Geske[4]	1993-1998		Milwaukee
Ann Walsh Bradley	1995-		Wausau
N. Patrick Crooks	1996-		Green Bay
David T. Prosser, Jr.[4]	1998-		Appleton
Diane S. Sykes[4]	1999-2004		Milwaukee
Patience D. Roggensack	2003-		Madison
Louis B. Butler, Jr.[4]	2004-		Milwaukee

Note: The structure of the Wisconsin Supreme Court has varied. There were 3 justices during the territorial period. From 1848 to 1853, circuit judges acted as supreme court judges (5 from 1848 to 1850 and 6 from 1850 to 1853). From 1853 to 1877, there were 3 elected justices. The number was increased to 5 by constitutional amendment in 1877. In 1903 the constitution was amended to raise the number to 7.

[1]Home address is the municipality from which the justice was originally appointed or elected.

[2]As a result of a constitutional amendment adopted in April 1889, the most senior justice serves as chief justice. Previously, the chief justice was elected or appointed to that position.

[3]Circuit judges acted as Supreme Court justices 1848-1853.

[4]Initially appointed to the court.

[5]Siebecker was elected April 7, 1903, but prior to inauguration for his elected term was appointed April 9, 1903, to fill the vacancy caused by the death of Justice Bardeen.

Sources: Wisconsin Legislative Reference Bureau, *Wisconsin Blue Books,* 1935, 1944, 1977; Elections Board records; Wisconsin Supreme Court, *Wisconsin Reports,* various volumes.

SENATE PRESIDENTS PRO TEMPORE, SENATE PRESIDENTS AND ASSEMBLY SPEAKERS, 1848 – 2005

Legislative Session	Senate Presidents Pro Tempore or Presidents[1]	Residence	Assembly Speakers	Residence
1848	No permanent president pro tempore	---	Ninian E. Whiteside (D)	Lafayette County
1849	No permanent president pro tempore	---	Harrison C. Hobart (D)	Sheboygan
1850	No record	---	Moses M. Strong (D)	Mineral Point
1851	No record	---	Frederick W. Horn (D)	Cedarburg
1852	E.B. Dean, Jr.	Madison	James M. Shafter (W)	Sheboygan
1853	Duncan C. Reed	Milwaukee	Henry L. Palmer (D)	Milwaukee
1854	Benjamin Allen	Hudson	Frederick W. Horn (D)	Cedarburg
1855	Eleazor Wakeley	Whitewater	Charles C. Sholes (R)	Kenosha
1856	Louis Powell Harvey (R)	Southport	William Hull (D)	Grant County
1857	No permanent president pro tempore	---	Wyman Spooner (R)	Elkhorn
1858	Hiram H. Giles	Stoughton	Frederick S. Lovell (R)	Kenosha County
1859	Dennison Worthington (R)	Summit	William P. Lyon (R)	Racine
1860	Moses M. Davis (R)	Portage	William P. Lyon (R)	Racine
1861	Alden I. Bennett (R)	Beloit	Amasa Cobb (R)	Mineral Point
1862	Frederick O. Thorp (D)	West Bend	James W. Beardsley (UD)	Prescott
1863	Wyman Spooner (R)	Elkhorn	J. Allen Barber (R)	Lancaster
1864	Smith S. Wilkinson (R)	Prairie du Sac	William W. Field (U)	Fennimore
1865	Willard H. Chandler (U)	Windsor	William W. Field (U)	Fennimore
1866	Willard H. Chandler (U)	Windsor	Henry D. Barron (U)	St. Croix Falls
1867	George F. Wheeler (U)	Nanuapa	Angus Cameron (U)	La Crosse
1868	Newton M. Littlejohn (R)	Whitewater	Alexander M. Thomson (R)	Janesville
1869	George C. Hazelton (R)	Boscobel	Alexander M. Thomson (R)	Janesville
1870	David Taylor (R)	Sheboygan	James M. Bingham (R)	Palmyra
1871	Charles G. Williams (R)	Janesville	William E. Smith (R)	Fox Lake
1872	Charles G. Williams (R)	Janesville	Daniel Hall (R)	Watertown
1873	Henry L. Eaton (R)	Lone Rock	Henry D. Barron (R)	St. Croix Falls
1874	John C. Holloway (R)	Lancaster	Gabriel Bouck (D)	Oshkosh
1875	Henry D. Barron (R)	St. Croix Falls	Frederick W. Horn (R)	Cedarburg
1876	Robert L.D. Potter (R)	Wautoma	Sam S. Fifield (R)	Ashland
1877	William H. Hiner (R)	Fond du Lac	John B. Cassoday (U)	Janesville
1878	Levi W. Barden (R)	Portage	Augustus R. Barrows (GB)	Chippewa Falls
1879	William T. Price (R)	Black River Falls	David M. Kelly (R)	Green Bay
1880	Thomas B. Scott (R)	Grand Rapids	Alexander A. Arnold (R)	Galesville
1881	Thomas B. Scott (R)	Grand Rapids	Ira B. Bradford (R)	Augusta
1882	George B. Burrows (R)	Madison	Franklin L. Gilson (R)	Ellsworth
1883	George W. Ryland (R)	Lancaster	Earl P. Finch (D)	Oshkosh
1885	Edward S. Minor (R)	Sturgeon Bay	Hiram O. Fairchild (R)	Marinette
1887	Charles K. Erwin (R)	Tomah	Thomas B. Mills (R)	Millston
1889	Thomas A. Dyson (R)	La Crosse	Thomas B. Mills (R)	Millston
1891	Frederick W. Horn (D)	Cedarburg	James J. Hogan (D)	La Crosse
1893	Robert J. MacBride (R)	Neillsville	Edward Keogh (D)	Milwaukee
1895	Thompson D. Weeks (R)	Whitewater	George B. Burrows (R)	Madison
1897	Lyman W. Thayer (R)	Ripon	George A. Buckstaff (R)	Oshkosh
1899	Lyman W. Thayer (R)	Ripon	George H. Ray (R)	La Crosse
1901	James J. McGillivray (R)	Black River Falls	George H. Ray (R)	La Crosse
1903-05	James J. McGillivray (R)	Black River Falls	Irvine L. Lenroot (R)	West Superior
1907	James H. Stout (R)	Menomonie	Herman L. Ekern (R)	Whitehall
1909	James H. Stout (R)	Menomonie	Levi H. Bancroft (R)	Richland Center
1911	Harry C. Martin (R)	Darlington	C.A. Ingram (R)	Durand
1913	Harry C. Martin (R)	Darlington	Merlin Hull (R)	Black River Falls
1915	Edward T. Fairchild (R)	Milwaukee	Lawrence C. Whittet (R)	Edgerton
1917	Timothy Burke (R)	Green Bay	Lawrence C. Whittet (R)	Edgerton
1919	Willard T. Stevens (R)	Rhinelander	Riley S. Young (R)	Darien
1921	Timothy Burke (R)	Green Bay	Riley S. Young (R)	Darien
1923	Henry A. Huber (R)	Stoughton	John L. Dahl (R)	Rice Lake
1925	Howard Teasdale (R)	Sparta	Herman Sachtjen (R)[2]	Madison
	Howard Teasdale (R)	Sparta	George A. Nelson (R)[2]	Milltown
1927	William L. Smith (R)	Neillsville	John W. Eber (R)	Milwaukee
1929	Oscar H. Morris (R)	Milwaukee	Charles B. Perry (R)	Wauwatosa
1931	Herman J. Severson (P)	Iola	Charles B. Perry (R)	Wauwatosa
1933	Orland S. Loomis (R)	Mauston	Cornelius T. Young (D)	Milwaukee
1935	Harry W. Bolens (D)	Port Washington	Jorge W. Carow (P)	Ladysmith
1937	Walter J. Rush (R)	Neillsville	Paul R. Alfonsi (P)	Pence
1939	Edward J. Roethe (R)	Fennimore	Vernon W. Thomson (R)	Richland Center
1941-43	Conrad Shearer (R)	Kenosha	Vernon W. Thomson (R)	Richland Center
1945	Conrad Shearer (R)	Kenosha	Donald C. McDowell (R)	Soldiers Grove

SENATE PRESIDENTS PRO TEMPORE, SENATE PRESIDENTS AND ASSEMBLY SPEAKERS, 1848 – 2005–Continued

Legislative Session	Senate Presidents Pro Tempore or Presidents[1]	Residence	Assembly Speakers	Residence
1947	Frank E. Panzer (R)	Brownsville	Donald C. McDowell (R)	Soldiers Grove
1949	Frank E. Panzer (R)	Brownsville	Alex L. Nicol (R)	Sparta
1951-53	Frank E. Panzer (R)	Brownsville	Ora R. Rice (R)	Delavan
1955	Frank E. Panzer (R)	Brownsville	Mark Catlin, Jr. (R)	Appleton
1957	Frank E. Panzer (R)	Brownsville	Robert G. Marotz (R)	Shawano
1959	Frank E. Panzer (R)	Brownsville	George Molinaro (D)	Kenosha
1961	Frank E. Panzer (R)	Brownsville	David J. Blanchard (R)	Edgerton
1963	Frank E. Panzer (R)	Brownsville	Robert D. Haase (R)	Marinette
1965	Frank E. Panzer (R)	Brownsville	Robert T. Huber (D)	West Allis
1967-69	Robert P. Knowles (R)	New Richmond	Harold V. Froehlich (R)	Appleton
1971	Robert P. Knowles (R)	New Richmond	Robert T. Huber (D)[3]	West Allis
	Robert P. Knowles (R)	New Richmond	Norman C. Anderson (D)[3]	Madison
1973	Robert P. Knowles (R)	New Richmond	Norman C. Anderson (D)	Madison
1975	Fred A. Risser (D)	Madison	Norman C. Anderson (D)	Madison
1977-81	Fred A. Risser (D)[1]	Madison	Edward G. Jackamonis (D)	Waukesha
1983-89	Fred A. Risser (D)	Madison	Thomas A. Loftus (D)	Sun Prairie
1991	Fred A. Risser (D)	Madison	Walter J. Kunicki (D)	Milwaukee
1993	Fred A. Risser (D)[4]	Madison	Walter J. Kunicki (D)	Milwaukee
	Brian D. Rude (R)[4]	Coon Valley	Walter J. Kunicki (D)	Milwaukee
1995	Brian D. Rude (R)[5]	Coon Valley	David T. Prosser, Jr. (R)	Appleton
	Fred A. Risser (D)[5]	Madison	David T. Prosser, Jr. (R)	Appleton
1997	Fred A. Risser (D)[6]	Madison	Ben Brancel (R)[7]	Endeavor
	Brian D. Rude (R)[6]	Coon Valley	Scott R. Jensen (R)[7]	Waukesha
1999	Fred A. Risser (D)	Madison	Scott R. Jensen (R)	Waukesha
2001	Fred A. Risser (D)	Madison	Scott R. Jensen (R)	Waukesha
2003-05	Alan J. Lasee (R)	De Pere	John Gard (R)	Peshtigo

Note: Political party indicated is for session elected and is obtained from newspaper accounts for some early legislators.

Key: D-Democrat; GB-Greenback; P-Progressive; R-Republican; U-Union; UD-Union Democrat; W-Whig.

[1]Table lists the ranking legislator in each house, not the presiding officer. The "president pro tempore" is listed until May 1, 1979; "president of the senate" is listed after that date when the lieutenant governor's function as president was eliminated by a constitutional amendment adopted in April 1979. See separate table for a list of lieutenant governors.

[2]George A. Nelson (R), Polk County, was elected to serve at special session, 4/15/26 to 4/16/26, following the resignation of Herman Sachtjen after the regular session to accept circuit judge appointment.

[3]Anderson was elected speaker 1/18/72 to succeed Huber who resigned 12/12/71 to accept appointment as chairman of the Highway Commission.

[4]A new president was elected on 4/20/94 after a change in party control following two special elections.

[5]A new president was elected on 7/9/96 after a change in party control following a recall election.

[6]A new president was elected on 4/21/98 after a change in party control following a special election.

[7]Jensen was elected speaker 11/4/97 to succeed Brancel who resigned to become Wisconsin Secretary of Agriculture, Trade and Consumer Protection.

Source: Wisconsin Legislative Reference Bureau records.

MAJORITY AND MINORITY LEADERS OF THE
WISCONSIN SENATE AND ASSEMBLY, 1937 – 2005

	Senate		Assembly	
Session	Majority	Minority	Majority	Minority
1937	Maurice P. Coakley (R)	NA	NA	NA
1939	Maurice P. Coakley (R)	Philip E. Nelson (P)	NA	Paul R. Alfonsi (P)
1941	Maurice P. Coakley (R)	Cornelius T. Young (D)	Mark S. Catlin, Jr. (R)	Andrew J. Biemiller (P)
				Robert E. Tehan (D)
1943	Warren P. Knowles (R)[1]	NA	Mark S. Catlin, Jr. (R)	Elmer L. Genzmer (D)
	John W. Byrnes (R)[1]			Lyall T. Beggs (P)
1945	Warren P. Knowles (R)	Anthony P. Gawronski (D)	Vernon W. Thomson (R)	Lyall T. Beggs (P)
				Leland S. McParland (D)
1947	Warren P. Knowles (R)	Robert E. Tehan (D)	Vernon W. Thomson (R)	Leland S. McParland (D)
1949	Warren P. Knowles (R)	NA	Vernon W. Thomson (R)	Leland S. McParland (D)
1951	Warren P. Knowles (R)	Gaylord Nelson (D)	Arthur O. Mockrud (R)	George Molinaro (D)
1953	Warren P. Knowles (R)	Henry W. Maier (D)	Mark S. Catlin, Jr. (R)	George Molinaro (D)
1955	Paul J. Rogan (R)	Henry W. Maier (D)	Robert G. Marotz (R)	Robert T. Huber (D)
1957	Robert Travis (R)	Henry W. Maier (D)	Warren A. Grady (R)	Robert T. Huber (D)
1959	Robert Travis (R)	Henry W. Maier (D)	Keith Hardie (D)	David J. Blanchard (R)
1961	Robert Travis (R)	William R. Moser (D)	Robert D. Haase (R)	Robert T. Huber (D)
1963	Robert P. Knowles (R)	Richard J. Zaborski (D)	Paul R. Alfonsi (R)	Robert T. Huber (D)
1965	Robert P. Knowles (R)	Richard J. Zaborski (D)	Frank L. Nikolay (D)	Robert D. Haase (R)[2]
				Paul J. Alfonsi (R)[2]
1967	Jerris Leonard (R)	Fred A. Risser (D)	J. Curtis McKay (R)	Robert T. Huber (D)
1969	Ernest C. Keppler (R)	Fred A. Risser (D)	Paul R. Alfonsi (R)	Robert T. Huber (D)
1971	Ernest C. Keppler (R)	Fred A. Risser (D)	Norman C. Anderson (D)[3]	Harold V. Froehlich (R)
			Anthony S. Earl (D)[3]	
1973	Raymond C. Johnson (R)	Fred A. Risser (D)	Anthony S. Earl (D)	John C. Shabaz (R)
1975	Wayne F. Whittow (D)	Cilfford W. Krueger (R)	Terry A. Willkom (D)	John C. Shabaz (R)
1977	William A. Bablitch (D)	Cilfford W. Krueger (R)	James W. Wahner (D)	John C. Shabaz (R)
1979	William A. Bablitch (D)	Cilfford W. Krueger (R)	James W. Wahner (D)	John C. Shabaz (R)
1981	William A. Bablitch (D)	Walter J. Chilsen (R)	Thomas A. Loftus (D)	John C. Shabaz (R)
1983	Timothy F. Cullen (D)	James E. Harsdorf (R)	Gary K. Johnson (D)	Tommy G. Thompson (R)
1985	Timothy F. Cullen (D)	Susan S. Engeleiter (R)	Dismas Becker (D)	Tommy G. Thompson (R)
1987	Joseph A. Strohl (D)	Susan S. Engeleiter (R)	Thomas A. Hauke (D)	Betty Jo Nelsen (R)
1989	Joseph A. Strohl (D)	Michael G. Ellis (R)	Thomas A. Hauke (D)	David T. Prosser (R)
1991	David W. Helbach (D)	Michael G. Ellis (R)	David M. Travis (D)	David T. Prosser (R)
1993	David W. Helbach (D)[4]	Michael G. Ellis (R)[4]	David M. Travis (D)	David T. Prosser (R)
	Michael G. Ellis (R)[4]	David W. Helbach (D)[4,5]		
		Robert Jauch (D)[5]		
1995	Michael G. Ellis (R)[6]	Robert Jauch (D)[6]	Scott R. Jensen (R)	Walter J. Kunicki (D)
		Charles Chvala (D)[6,7]		
	Charles Chvala (D)[7]	Michael G. Ellis (R)[7]		
1997	Charles Chvala (D)[8]	Michael G. Ellis (R)[8]	Steven M. Foti (R)	Walter J. Kunicki (D)[9]
	Michael G. Ellis (R)[8]	Charles Chvala (D)[8]		Shirley Krug (D)[9]
1999	Charles Chvala (D)	Michael G. Ellis (R)[10]	Steven M. Foti (R)	Shirley Krug (D)
		Mary E. Panzer (R)[10]		
2001	Charles Chvala (D)	Mary E. Panzer (R)	Steven M. Foti (R)	Shirley Krug (D)[12]
	Russell Decker (D)[11]			Spencer Black (D)[12]
	Fred A. Risser (D)[11]			
	Jon B. Erpenbach (D)[11]			
2003	Mary E. Panzer (R)[13]	Jon B. Erpenbach (D)	Steven M. Foti (R)	James E. Kreuser (D)
	Scott Fitzgerald (R)[13]			
	Dale W. Schultz (R)[14]			
2005	Dale W. Schultz (R)	Judith Biros Robson (D)	Michael D. Huebsch (R)	James E. Kreuser (D)

Note: Majority and minority leaders, who are chosen by the party caucuses in each house, were first recognized officially in the senate and assembly rules in 1963. Prior to the 1977 session, these positions were also referred to as "floor leader".

Key: (D) – Democrat; (P) – Progressive; (R) – Republican.

NA – Not available.

[1]Knowles granted leave of absence to return to active duty in U.S. Navy; Byrnes chosen to succeed him on 4/30/1943.

[2]Haase resigned 9/15/1965; Alfonsi elected 10/4/1965.

[3]Earl elected 1/18/1972 to succeed Anderson who became Assembly Speaker when Huber resigned.

[4]Democrats controlled senate from 1/4/1993 to 4/20/1993 when Republicans assumed control after a special election.

[5]Helbach resigned 5/12/1993; Jauch elected 5/12/1993.

[6]Jauch resigned 10/17/1995; Chvala elected 10/24/1995.

[7]Republicans controlled senate from 1/5/1995 to 6/13/1996 when Democrats assumed control after a recall election.

[8]Democrats controlled the senate from 1/6/1997 to 4/21/1998 when Republicans assumed control after a special election.

[9]Kunicki resigned 6/3/1998; Krug elected 6/3/1998.

[10]Ellis resigned 1/25/2000; Panzer elected 1/25/2000.

[11]Decker and Risser elected co-leaders 11/22/2002. Erpenbach elected leader 12/4/2002.

[12]Black elected 5/1/2001.

[13]Panzer resigned 9/17/2004; Fitzgerald elected 9/17/2004.

[14]Schultz elected 11/9/2004.

Sources: *Wisconsin Blue Book*, various editions; newspaper accounts.

SENATE AND ASSEMBLY CHIEF CLERKS AND SERGEANTS AT ARMS, 1848 – 2005

Legislative Session	Senate Chief Clerk	Senate Sergeant at Arms	Assembly Chief Clerk	Assembly Sergeant at Arms
1848	Henry G. Abbey	Lyman H. Seaver	Daniel N. Johnson	John Mullanphy
1849	William R. Smith	F. W. Shollner	Robert L. Ream	Felix McLinden
1850	William R. Smith	James Hanrahan	Alex T. Gray	E. R. Hugunin
1851	William Hull	E. D. Masters	Alex T. Gray	C. M. Kingsbury
1852	John K. Williams	Patrick Cosgrove	Alex T. Gray	Elisha Starr
1853	John K. Williams	Thomas Hood	Thomas McHugh	Richard F. Wilson
1854	Samuel G. Bugh	J. M. Sherwood	Thomas McHugh	William H. Gleason
1855	Samuel G. Bugh	William H. Gleason	David Atwood	William Blake
1856	Byron Paine	Joseph Baker	James Armstrong	Egbert Mosely
1857	William Henry Brisbane	Alanson Filer	William C. Webb	William C. Rogers
1858	John L. V. Thomas	Nathaniel L. Stout	L. H. D. Crane	Francis Massing
1859	Hiram Bowen	Asa Kinney	L. H. D. Crane	Emmanual Munk
1860	J. H. Warren	Asa Kinney	L. H. D. Crane	Joseph Gates
1861	J. H. Warren	J. A. Hadley	L. H. D. Crane	Craig B. Peebe
1862	J. H. Warren	B. U. Caswell	John S. Dean	A. A. Huntington
1863	Frank M. Stewart	Luther Bashford	John S. Dean	A. M. Thompson
1864	Frank M. Stewart	Nelson Williams	John S. Dean	A. M. Thompson
1865	Frank M. Stewart	Nelson Williams	John S. Dean	Alonzo Wilcox
1866	Frank M. Stewart	Nelson Williams	E. W. Young	L. M. Hammond
1867	Leander B. Hills	Asa Kinney	E. W. Young	Daniel Webster
1868	Leander B. Hills	W. H. Hamilton	E. W. Young	C. L. Harris
1869	Leander B. Hills	W. H. Hamilton	E. W. Young	Rolin C. Kelly
1870	Leander B. Hills	E. M. Rogers	E. W. Young	Ole C. Johnson
1871	O. R. Smith	W. W. Baker	E. W. Young	Sam S. Fifield
1872	J. H. Waggoner	W. D. Hoard	E. W. Young	Sam S. Fifield
1873	J. H. Waggoner	Albert Emonson	E. W. Young	O. C. Bissel
1874	J. H. Waggoner	O. U. Aiken	George W. Peck	Joseph Deuster
1875	Fred A. Dennett	O. U. Aiken	R. M. Strong	J. W. Brackett
1876	A. J. Turner	E. T. Gardner	R. M. Strong	Elisha Starr
1877	A. J. Turner	C. E. Bullard	W. A. Nowell	Thomas B. Reid
1878	A. J. Turner[1] Charles E. Bross[1]	L. J. Brayton	Jabez R. Hunter	Anton Klaus
1879	Charles E. Bross	Chalmers Ingersoll	John E. Eldred	Miletus Knight
1880	Charles E. Bross	Chalmers Ingersoll	John E. Eldred	D. H. Pulcifer
1881	Charles E. Bross	W. W. Baker	John E. Eldred	G. W. Church
1882	Charles E. Bross	A. T. Glaze	E. D. Coe	D. E. Welch
1883	Charles E. Bross	A. D. Thorp	I. T. Carr	Thomas Kennedy
1885	Charles E. Bross	Hubert Wolcott	E. D. Coe	John M. Ewing
1887	Charles E. Bross	T. J. George	E. D. Coe	William A. Adamson
1889	Charles E. Bross	T .J. George	E. D. Coe	F. E. Parsons
1891	J. P. Hume	John A. Barney	George W. Porth	Patrick Whelan
1893	Sam J. Shafer	John B. Becker	George W. Porth	Theodore Knapstein
1895	Walter L. Houser	Charles Pettibone	W. A. Nowell	B. F. Millard
1897	Walter L. Houser	Charles Pettibone	W. A. Nowell	C. M. Hambright
1889	Walter L. Houser	Charles Pettibone	W. A. Nowell	James H. Agen
1901	Walter L. Houser	Charles Pettibone	W. A. Nowell	A. M. Anderson
1903	Theodore W. Goldin	Sanfield McDonald	C. O. Marsh	A. M. Anderson
1905	L .K. Eaton	R. C. Falconer	C. O. Marsh	Nicholas Streveler
1907	A. R. Emerson	R. C. Falconer	C. E. Shaffer	W. S. Irvine
1909	F. E. Andrews	R. C. Falconer	C. E. Shaffer	W. S. Irvine
1911-13	F. M. Wylie	C. A. Leicht	C. E. Shaffer	W. S. Irvine
1915	O. G. Munson	F. E. Andrews	C. E. Shaffer	W. S. Irvine
1917	O. G. Munson	F. E. Andrews	C. E. Shaffer	T. G. Cretney
1919	O. G. Munson	John Turner	C. E. Shaffer	T. G. Cretney
1921	O. G. Munson	Vincent Kielpinski	C. E. Shaffer	T. G. Cretney
1923	F. W. Schoenfeld	C. A. Leicht	C. E. Shaffer	T. W. Bartingale
1925	F. W. Schoenfeld	C. A. Leicht	C. E. Shaffer	C. E. Hanson
1927-29	O. G. Munson	George W. Rickeman	C. E. Shaffer	C. F. Moulton
1931	R. A. Cobban	Emil A. Hartman	C. E. Shaffer	Gustave Rheingans
1933	R. A. Cobban	Emil A. Hartman	John J. Slocum	George C. Faust
1935-37	Lawrence R. Larsen	Emil A. Hartman	Lester R. Johnson	Gustave Rheingans
1939	Lawrence R. Larsen	Emil A. Hartman	John J. Slocum	Robert A. Merrill
1941-43	Lawrence R. Larsen	Emil A. Hartman	Arthur L. May	Norris J. Kellman
1945	Lawrence R. Larsen	Harold E. Damon	Arthur L. May	Norris J. Kellman
1947-53	Thomas M. Donahue	Harold E. Damon	Arthur L. May	Norris J. Kellman
1955-57	Lawrence R. Larsen	Harold E. Damon	Arthur L. May	Norris J. Kellman
1959	Lawrence R. Larsen	Harold E. Damon	Norman C. Anderson	Thomas H. Browne
1961	Lawrence R. Larsen	Harold E. Damon	Robert G. Marotz	Norris J. Kellman
1963	Lawrence R. Larsen	Harold E. Damon	Kenneth E. Priebe	Norris J. Kellman
1965	Lawrence R. Larsen[2] William P. Nugent[2]	Harold E. Damon	James P. Buckley	Thomas H. Browne
1967	William P. Nugent	Harry O. Levander	Arnold W. F. Langner[3] Wilmer H. Struebing[3]	Louis C. Romell
1969	William P. Nugent	Kenneth Nicholson	Wilmer H. Struebing	Louis C. Romell
1971	William P. Nugent	Kenneth Nicholson	Thomas P. Fox	William F. Quick
1973	William P. Nugent	Kenneth Nicholson	Thomas S. Hanson	William F. Quick
1975	Glenn E. Bultman	Robert M. Thompson	Everett E. Bolle	Raymond J. Tobiasz
1977	Donald J. Schneider	Robert M. Thompson	Everett E. Bolle	Joseph E. Jones

SENATE AND ASSEMBLY CHIEF CLERKS
AND SERGEANTS AT ARMS, 1848 – 2005–Continued

Legislative	Senate		Assembly	
Session	Chief Clerk	Sergeant at Arms	Chief Clerk	Sergeant at Arms
1979	Donald J. Schneider	Daniel B. Fields	Marcel Dandeneau	Joseph E. Jones
1981	Donald J. Schneider	Daniel B. Fields	David R. Kedrowski	Lewis T. Mittness
1983	Donald J. Schneider	Daniel B. Fields	Joanne M. Duren	Lewis T. Mittness
1985	Donald J. Schneider	Daniel B. Fields	Joanne M. Duren	Patrick Essie
1987	Donald J. Schneider	Daniel B. Fields	Thomas T. Melvin	Patrick Essie
1989-91	Donald J. Schneider	Daniel B. Fields	Thomas T. Melvin	Robert G. Johnston
1993	Donald J. Schneider	Daniel B. Fields[4]	Thomas T. Melvin	Robert G. Johnston
		Jon H. Hochkammer[4]		
1995	Donald J. Schneider	Jon H. Hochkammer	Thomas T. Melvin[5]	John A. Scocos
			Charles R. Sanders[5]	
1997	Donald J. Schneider	Jon H. Hochkammer	Charles R. Sanders	John A. Scocos[6]
				Denise L. Solie[6]
1999	Donald J. Schneider	Jon H. Hochkammer	Charles R. Sanders	Denise L. Solie
2001	Donald J. Schneider	Jon H. Hochkammer[7]	John A. Scocos[7]	Denise L. Solie
2003	Donald J. Schneider[8]	Edward A. Blazel	Patrick E. Fuller	Richard A. Skindrud
	Robert J. Marchant[8]			
2005	Robert J. Marchant	Edward A. Blazel	Patrick E. Fuller	Richard A. Skindrud

[1]Bross appointed 2/6/78; Turner resigned 2/7/78.

[2]Larsen died 3/2/65; Nugent appointed 3/31/65.

[3]Langner resigned 5/2/67; Struebing appointed 5/16/67.

[4]Fields served until 8/2/93. Randall Radtke served as Acting Sergeant from 8/3/93 to 11/3/93. Hochkammer was elected 1/25/94.

[5]Melvin retired 1/31/95; Sanders elected 5/24/95.

[6]Scocos resigned 9/25/97; Solie elected 1/15/98.

[7]Scocos resigned 2/25/02. Hochkammer resigned 9/2/02. No replacement was named for either.

[8]Schneider resigned 7/4/03; Marchant elected 1/20/04.

Sources: Wisconsin Legislative Reference Bureau, *Wisconsin Blue Book,* various editions; journals and organizing resolutions of each house.

MEMBERS OF THE WISCONSIN LEGISLATURE, 1848 – 1999
See the Legislative Reference Bureau webpage at
http://www.legis.state.wi.us/lrb/pubs/ib/99ib1.pdf

WISCONSIN LEGISLATIVE SESSIONS, 1848 – 2003

Session	Opening and Adjournment Dates	Length of Session			Measures Introduced			Vetoes[1]		
		Calendar Days[2]	Meeting Days[3] (S)	(A)	Bills	Jt. Res.	Res.	Bills Vetoed	Over-ridden	Laws Enacted
1848	6/5-8/21	78	58	59	217	0	0	0	0	155
1849	1/10-4/2	83	69	65	428	0	0	1	1	220
1850	1/9-2/11	34	29	29	438	0	0	1	0	284
1851	1/8-3/17	69	59	59	707	0	0	9	0	407
1852	1/14-4/19	97	78	78	813	0	0	2	1	504
1853	1/12-4/4; 6/6-7/13	153	100	104	1,145	0	0	3	0	521
1854	1/11-4/3	83	66	66	880	0	0	2	0	437
1855	1/10-4/2	83	79	79	955	0	0	6	0	500
1856	1/9-3/31; 9/3-10/14	125	94	103	1,242	0	0	1	0	688
1857	1/14-3/9	55	46	46	895	0	0	0	0	517
1858	1/13-3/31; 4/10-5/17	116	95	97	1,364	157	342	28	0	436
1859	1/12-3/21	69	58	57	986	113	143	9	0	680
1860	1/11-4/2	83	66	67	1,024	69	246	2	0	489
1861	1/9-4/17	99	81	80	857	100	235	2	0	387
1861SS[4]	5/15-5/27	13	11	11	28	24	34	0	0	15
1862	1/8-4/7; 6/3-6/17	105	86	88	1,008	125	207	27	8	514
1862SS	9/10-9/26	17	15	15	43	25	37	0	0	17
1863	1/14-4/2	79	65	67	895	101	157	7	1	383
1864	1/13-4/4	83	68	69	835	66	141	0	0	509
1865	1/11-4/10	90	73	72	1,132	82	190	2	0	565
1866	1/10-4/2	83	75	74	1,107	64	208	5	0	733
1867	1/9-4/11	93	71	72	1,161	97	161	2	0	790
1868	1/8-3/6	59	46	45	987	73	119	2	0	692
1869	1/13-3/11	58	40	43	887	52	81	12	1	657
1870	1/12-3/17	65	51	51	1,043	54	89	2	0	666
1871	1/11-3/25	74	58	60	1,066	55	82	4	0	671
1872	1/10-3/26	77	61	60	709	79	124	2	0	322
1873	1/8-3/20	72	49	55	611	62	122	4	0	308
1874	1/14-3/12	58	50	49	688	91	111	2	0	349
1875	1/13-3/6	53	44	42	637	39	93	2	0	344
1876	1/12-3/14	63	50	50	715	57	115	2	0	415
1877	1/10-3/8	58	41	41	720	59	95	4	0	384
1878	1/9-3/21	72	55	55	735	79	134	2	0	342
1878SS	6/4-6/7	4	4	4	6	14	10	0	0	5
1879	1/8-3/5	57	43	43	610	49	105	0	0	256
1880	1/14-3/17	64	50	49	669	58	93	3	0	323
1881	1/12-4/14	93	63	64	780	104	100	3	0	334
1882	1/11-3/31	80	57	57	728	57	90	6	0	330
1883	1/10-4/4	85	57	67	705	75	100	2	0	360
1885	1/14-4/13	90	65	66	963	97	108	8	0	471
1887	1/12-4/15	94	69	68	1,293	114	60	10	0	553
1889	1/9-4/19	101	64	64	1,355	136	82	5	1	529
1891	1/14-4/25	102	68	69	1,216	137	91	8	1	483
1892SS	6/28-7/1	4	4	4	4	7	16	0	0	1
1892SS	10/17-10/27	11	9	9	8	6	14	0	0	2
1893	1/11-4/21	101	62	62	1,124	135	86	6	0	312
1895	1/9-4/20	102	70	70	1,154	139	88	0	0	387
1896SS	2/18-2/28	11	8	8	3	11	15	0	0	1
1897	1/13-4/21; 8/17-8/20	103	75	76	1,077	155	39	11	0	381
1899	1/11-5/4	114	78	77	910	113	40	4	0	357
1901	1/9-5/15	127	89	89	1,091	81	39	22	0	470
1903	1/14-5/23	130	87	89	1,115	65	81	23	0	451
1905	1/11-6/21	162	114	117	1,357	134	101	19	0	523
1905SS	12/4-12/19	16	12	14	24	15	26	0	0	17
1907	1/9-7/16	189	114	123	1,685	205	84	26	1	677
1909	1/13-6/18	157	100	101	1,567	213	49	24	0	550
1911	1/11-7/15	186	137	138	1,710	267	37	15	0	665
1912SS	4/30-5/6	7	6	6	41	7	6	0	0	22
1913	1/8-8/9	214	138	147	1,847	175	79	23	0	778
1915	1/13-8/24	224	147	148	1,560	220	79	15	0	637
1916SS	10/10-10/11	2	2	2	2	8	4	0	0	2
1917	1/10-7/16	188	130	133	1,439	229	115	18	0	679
1918SS	2/19-3/9	19	14	14	27	22	28	2	0	16
1918SS	9/24-9/25	2	2	2	2	6	9	0	0	2
1919	1/8-7/30	204	107	106	1,350	268	100	40	0	703

WISCONSIN LEGISLATIVE SESSIONS, 1848 – 2003–Continued

Session	Opening and Adjournment Dates	Length of Session			Measures Introduced			Vetoes[1]		
		Calendar Days[2]	Meeting Days[3] (S)	(A)	Bills	Jt. Res.	Res.	Bills Vetoed	Over-ridden	Laws Enacted
1919SS	9/4-9/8	5	4	3	7	4	6	0	0	7
1920SS	5/25-6/4	11	7	7	46	10	22	2	0	32
1921	1/12-7/14	184	116	116	1,199	207	93	41	1	591
1922SS	3/22-3/28	7	4	4	10	7	12	1	0	4
1923	1/10-7/14	186	114	120	1,247	215	93	52	0	449
1925	1/14-6/29	167	103	107	1,144	200	115	73	0	454
1926SS	4/15-4/16	2	2	2	1	8	12	0	0	1
1927	1/12-8/13	214	121	128	1,341	235	167	88	2	542
1928SS	1/24-2/4	12	9	8	20	35	23	0	0	5
1928SS	3/6-3/13	8	6	6	13	9	17	0	0	2
1929	1/9-9/20	255	137	135	1,366	278	185	44	0	530
1931	1/14-6/27	165	98	104	1,429	291	160	36	0	487
1931SS	11/24/31-2/5/32	74	48	42	99	93	83	2	0	31
1933	1/11-7/25	196	111	121	1,411	324	157	15	0	496
1933SS	12/11/33-2/3/34	55	30	34	45	160	53	0	0	20
1935	1/9-9/27	262	153	156	1,662	346	190	27	0	556
1937	1/13-7/2	171	97	114	1,404	228	127	10	0	432
1937SS	9/15-10/16	32	23	23	28	18	23	0	0	15
1939	1/11-10/6	269	154	154	1,559	268	133	22	0	535
1941	1/8-6/6	150	90	93	1,368	160	109	17	0	333
1943	1/13-8/3; (1944: 1/12-1/22)	375	105	104	1,153	202	136	39	20	577
1945	1/10-6/20; 9/5-9/6	240	97	93	1,156	208	109	31	5	590
1946SS	7/29-7/30	2	2	2	2	6	14	0	0	2
1947	1/8-7/19; 9/9-9/11	247	114	114	1,220	195	97	10	1	615
1948SS	7/19-7/20	2	2	2	0	5	11	0	0	0
1949	1/12-7/9; 9/12-9/13	245	105	106	1,432	188	86	17	2	643
1951	1/10-6/14	156	91	90	1,559	157	73	18	0	735
1953	1/14-6/12; 10/26-11/6	297	97	98	1,593	175	70	31	3	687
1955	1/12-6/24; 10/3-10/21	283	111	114	1,503	256	74	38	0	696
1957	1/9-6/28; 9/23-9/27	262	107	108	1,512	246	71	39	1	706
1958SS	6/11-6/13	3	3	3	3	7	13	0	0	3
1959	1/14/59-5/27/60 (1959: 1/14-7/25, 11/3-12/23; 1960: 1/6-1/22, 5/16-5/27)	500	159	163	1,769	272	84	36	4	696
1961	1/11/61-1/9/63 (1961: 1/11-8/12, 10/30-12/22; 1962: 1/8-1/12, 6/18-7/31, 12/27-12/29; 1963: 1/9)	729	184	185	1,592	295	68	73	2	689
1963	1/9/63-1/13/65 (1963: 1/9-8/6, 11/4-11/21; 1964: 4/13-4/29, 11/9-11/11; 1965: 1/13)	736	150	142	1,619	241	110	72	4	580
1963SS	12/10-12/12	3	3	3	9	10	10	0	0	3
1965[5]	1/13/65-1/2/67 (1965: 1/13-7/30, 10/4-11/4; 1966: 5/2-6/10; 1967: 1/2)	720	161	157	1,818	293	86	24	1	666
1967	1/11/67-1/6/69 (1967: 1/11-3/9, 4/4-7/28, 10/17-11/16, 12/5-12/16; 1968: none; 1969: 1/6)	727	122	126	1,700	215	61	18	0	355
1969	1/6/69-1/4/71 (1969: 1/6, 1/21-11/15; 1970: 1/5-1/16; 1971: 1/4)	729	165	165	2,014	232	101	34	1	501
1969SS[6]	9/29/69-1/17/70	111	28	18	5	5	8	0	0	1
1970SS	12/22/70	1	1	1	0	1	5	0	0	0
1971	1/4/71-1/1/73 (1971: 1/4, 1/19-10/28; 1972: 1/18-3/10, 7/13-7/15; 1973: 1/1)	729	179	180	2,568	291	121	32	3	336
1972SS	4/19-4/28	10	5	6	9	4	4	0	0	6

WISCONSIN LEGISLATIVE SESSIONS, 1848 – 2003–Continued

Session	Opening and Adjournment Dates	Length of Session — Calendar Days[2]	Length of Session — Meeting Days[3] (S)	Length of Session — Meeting Days[3] (A)	Measures Introduced — Bills	Measures Introduced — Jt. Res.	Measures Introduced — Res.	Vetoes[1] — Bills Vetoed	Vetoes[1] — Over-ridden	Laws Enacted
1973 .... 1/1/73-1/6/75		736	150	150	2,501	277	126	13	0	341
(1973: 1/1, 1/16-2/15, 3/13-7/26, 10/2-10/26; 1974: 1/29-3/29, 11/19-11/20; 1975: 1/6)										
1973SS 12/17-12/21		5	5	5	3	2	6	0	0	2
1974SS 4/29-6/13		46	17	21	12	1	4	0	0	6
1974SS[7] 11/19-11/20		2	2	1	2	0	0	0	0	1
1975 .... 1/6/75-1/3/77		729	124	125	2,325	169	88	36	6	414
(1975: 1/6, 1/1-2/20, 4/1-7/16, 9/2-9/26; 1976: 1/28-3/26, 6/15-6/17; 1977: 1/3)										
1975SS 12/9-12/11		3	3	3	13	1	2	1	0	7
1976SS 5/18		1	1	1	2	2	3	0	0	1
1976SS[7] 6/15-6/17		3	3	3	13	4	3	0	0	8
1976SS 9/8		1	1	1	4	1	1	0	0	2
1977 .... 1/3/77-1/1/79		729	84	112	2,053	182	48	21	4	442
(1977: 1/3, 1/11-2/18, 3/29-7/1, 9/6-9/30; 1978: 1/24-26, 1/31-3/31, 6/13-6/15; 1979: 1/1)										
1977SS 6/30		1	1	1	0	1	2	0	0	0
1977SS 11/7-11/11		5	5	5	6	4	2	0	0	5
1978SS[7] 6/13-6/15		3	3	3	2	5	2	0	0	2
1978SS 12/20		1	1	1	2	4	2	0	0	2
1979 .... 1/3/79-1/5/81		734	85	99	1,920	203	40	19	3	350
(1979: 1/3, 1/9, 1/23-3/2, 4/17-6/29, 10/2-11/2; 1980: 1/29-4/2, 5/28-5/30; 1981: 1/5)										
1979SS 9/5		1	1	1	10	3	2	0	0	5
1980SS[8] 1/22-1/25		4	2	4	8	3	2	0	0	0
1980SS 6/3- 7/3		31	13	12	20	14	2	0	0	7
1981 .... 1/5/81-1/3/83		729	121	130	1,987	176	70	10	2	381
(1981: 1/5, 1/13, 1/27-2/20, 4/7-7/17, 9/30-10/30, 12/15-12/17; 1982: 1/20-6/14; 1983: 1/3)										
1981SS[9] 11/4-11/17		14	8	7	6	3	2	0	0	3
1982SS[9] 4/6-4/30, 5/5-5/20		45	18	21	4	2	2	1	0	1
1982SS[10] 5/26-5/28		3	3	3	13	7	2	0	0	9
1983 .... 1/3/83-1/7/85		736	72	80	1,902	173	50	3	0	521
(1983: 1/3, 1/25-1/28, 2/8-2/18, 4/12-6/30, 10/4-10/28; 1984: 1/31-4/6, 5/22-5/24; 1985: 1/7)										
1983SS 1/4-1/6		3	3	1	2	2	1	0	0	2
1983SS 4/12-4/14		3	3	3	1	1	0	0	0	1
1983SS 7/11-7/14		4	4	4	5	3	1	0	0	4
1983SS 10/18-10/28		11	8	7	12	1	0	0	0	11
1984SS 2/2-4/4		63	18	13	2	1	0	0	0	0
1984SS 5/22-5/24		3	3	2	12	5	1	0	0	11
1985 .... 1/7/85-1/7/87		331	68	66	1,624	171	41	7	0	293
(1985: 1/7, 1/15, 1/29-2/8, 3/19-3/21, 4/23-6/29, 9/24-10/18; 1986: 1/28-3/26, 5/20-5/22; 1987: 1/7)										
1985SS 3/19-3/21		3	2	2	6	1	0	0	0	3
1985SS 9/24-10/19		26	11	7	21	1	0	0	0	17
1985SS 10/31		1	1	1	1	3	0	0	0	1
1985SS 11/20		1	1	1	24	2	0	0	0	12
1986SS 1/27-5/30		124	34	27	1	4	0	0	0	1
1986SS 3/24-3/26		3	3	3	1	1	0	0	0	1
1986SS 5/20-5/29		10	6	4	44	3	0	0	0	12
1986SS 7/15		1	1	1	3	1	0	0	0	2

WISCONSIN LEGISLATIVE SESSIONS, 1848 – 2003–Continued

Session	Opening and Adjournment Dates	Length of Session			Measures Introduced			Vetoes[1]		
		Calendar Days[2]	Meeting Days[3]		Bills	Jt. Res.	Res.	Bills Vetoed	Over-ridden	Laws Enacted
			(S)	(A)						
1987[10]	1/5/87-1/3/89	730	60	73	1,628	199	21	35	0	412
	(1987: 1/5, 1/13, 1/27-2/6, 3/17-3/19, 4/21-7/2, 10/6-10/30; 1988: 1/26-3/25, 5/17-5/19; 1989: 1/3)									
1987SS	9/15-9/16	2	2	2	2	1	0	0	0	2
1987SS	11/18/87-6/7/88	203	9	11	19	3	0	3	0	5
1988SS	6/30	1	1	1	5	1	3	0	0	3
1989	1/3/89-1/7/91	735	68	70	1,557	244	45	35	0	361
	(1989: 1/3, 1/4-1/9, 1/10, 1/11-1/23, 1/24-2/3, 2/6-3/13, 3/14-3/16, 3/17-4/24, 4/25-4/27, 4/28-5/15, 5/16-6/30, 10/3-11/10, 11/13-12/31; 1990: 1/1-1/22, 1/23-3/23, 3/26-5/14, 5/15-5/17, 5/18-12/31; 1991: 1/1-1/4, 1/7)									
1989SS	10/10/89-3/22/90	164	52	49	52	6	0	0	0	7
1990SS	5/15/90	1	1	1	7	1	0	0	0	0
1991	1/7/91-1/4/93	729	102	100	1,676	244	32	33	0	318
	(1991: 1/7, 1/15, 1/29-3/14, 4/16-5/16, 6/4-7/3, 10/1-11/8; 1992: 1/28-3/27, 5/19-5/21; 1993: 1/4)									
1991SS	1/29/-7/4	157	49	52	16	1	0	0	0	2
1991SS	10/15/91-5/21/92	220	50	47	9	2	0	0	0	1
1992SS[8]	4/14-6/4	52	20	17	7	1	2	0	0	2
1992SS	6/1	1	1	1	0	2	0	0	0	0
1992SS	8/25-9/15	22	7	7	1	1	2	0	0	1
1993	1/4/93-1/3/95	730	88	85	2,147	207	47	8	0	491
	(1993: 1/7,1/26-3/11, 4/20-7/16, 10/5-10/28; 1994: 1/25-3/25, 5/17-5/19; 1995: 1/3)									
1994SS	5/18-5/19	2	2	2	6	1	0	0	0	3
1994SS[11]	6/7-6/23	17	8	8	3	4	0	0	0	3
1995	1/3/95-1/6/97	735	76	87	1,779	163	38	4	0	467
	(1995: 1/3-5,1/17-2/2, 2/14-3/9,4/4-6,5/16-6/1, 6/13-6/29,9/19-10/5,11/7-16; 1996: 1/9-2/1,3/5-28,5/7-17,7/9-11; 1997: 1/6)									
1995SS	1/4	1	1	1	1	1	0	0	0	1
1995SS	9/5-10/10	36	11	11	1	1	0	0	0	1
1997	1/6/97-1/4/99	729	87	90	1,508	183	30	3	0	333
	(1997: 1/6,1/14,1/28-30,2/12,2/25-26, 3/4-20,5/13-29,6/10-9/29,11/4-6, 11/18-20; 1998: 1/13-22,2/3-12,3/10-26,4/21-5/21; 1999: 1/4)									
1998SS[12]	4/21-5/21	31	11	11	13	2	2	0	0	5
1999[13]	1/4/99-1/3/01	731	97	101	1,498	168	52	5	0	196
	(1999: 1/4,1/14,1/26-28,2/16-18, 3/2-4,3/16-25,5/11-10/6,10/26-11/11; 2000: 1/25-2/10,3/7-30,5/2-4,5/23-24; 2001: 1/3)									
1999SS[7]	10/27-11/11	16	7	8	3	1	0	0	0	1
2000SS	5/4-5/9	8	3	3	2	2	1	0	0	1

WISCONSIN LEGISLATIVE SESSIONS, 1848 – 2003–Continued

Session	Opening and Adjournment Dates	Length of Session Calendar Days[2]	Meeting Days[3] (S)	(A)	Measures Introduced Bills	Jt. Res.	Res.	Vetoes[1] Bills Vetoed	Over- ridden	Laws Enacted
2001	1/3/01-1/6/03	734	62	63	1,436	174	75	0	0	106
	(2001: 1/3,1/30-2/1,2/13-15,3/6-22,5/1-10, 6/5-7/26,10/2-4,10/16-11/8; 2002: 1/22-2/7,2/26-3/14,4/30-5/2, 5/14-15; 2003: 1/6)									
2001SS[7]	5/1-5/3	3	1	2	1	0	0	0	0	1
2002SS[7]	1/22-7/8	168	59	52	1	2	7	0	0	1
2002SS[7]	5/13-5/15	3	3	2	2	0	0	0	0	1
2003[14]	1/3/03-1/3/05	729	104	94	1,567	164	78	54	0	326
	(2003: 1/6-1/7, 1/28-1/30, 2/18-2/20, 3/3-3/20, 4/29-5/8, 5/28-6/25, 9/23-10/2, 10/28-11/13; 2004: 1/20-2/5, 2/24-3/11, 4/27, 5/11-5/13; 2005: 1/3)									
2003SS	1/30-2/20	22	7	7	1	0	0	0	0	1

Note: For 1836-1847 territorial sessions, see *1873 Blue Book*, p. 205.

[1]Partial vetoes not included. See Executive Vetoes table. [2]Number of calendar days from session opening date to final adjournment. [3]Number of days senate or assembly met, including "skeleton sessions" (those days on which the senate or assembly leadership calls the house in session *in absentia* to fulfill a procedural requirement). [4]SS denotes special session. Regular and special sessions may run concurrently with meetings held on the same day. Each is counted as a separate meeting day. [5]Although 1965 Legislature adjourned to 1/11/67, terms automatically expired on 1/2/67. [6]Senate adjourned the special session 11/15/69; assembly, 1/17/70. [7]Special session met concurrently with regular session. [8]1979 Legislature met concurrently in extraordinary and special session, 1/22/80 - 1/25/80. [9]Legislature met concurrently in special session and extended floorperiod. [10]Extraordinary sessions held in September 1987, and April, May and June 1988. May 1988 extraordinary session ran concurrently with May 1988 veto review period and also with June 1988 extraordinary session. [11]Extraordinary session held, 6/15/94 - 6/23/94. [12]Extraordinary session held in April 1998. [13]Extraordinary session held in April and May 2000. [14]Extraordinary sessions held in February, July, and August 2003; December 2003-February 2004; March 2004; May 2004; and July 2004.

Sources: *Bulletin of the Proceedings of the Wisconsin Legislature*, various editions; and senate and assembly journals.

WISCONSIN MEMBERS, U.S. HOUSE OF REPRESENTATIVES
1848 – 2005

Name	Party	Residence	District	Term
Adams, Henry C	Rep.	Madison	2	1903-1906
Amlie, Thomas R	Rep., Prog.	Elkhorn	1	1931-1933; 1935-1939
Aspin, Les	Dem.	East Troy	1	1971-1993
Atwood, David	Rep.	Madison	2	1870-1871
Babbitt, Clinton	Dem.	Beloit	1	1891-1893
Babcock, Joseph W	Rep.	Necedah	3	1893-1907
Baldus, Alvin	Dem.	Menomonie	3	1975-1981
Baldwin, Tammy	Dem.	Madison	2	1999-
Barber, J. Allen	Rep.	Lancaster	3	1871-1875
Barca, Peter W	Dem.	Kenosha	1	1993-1995
Barnes, Lyman E	Dem.	Appleton	8	1893-1895
Barney, Samuel S	Rep.	West Bend	5	1895-1903
Barrett, Thomas M	Dem.	Milwaukee	5	1993-2003
Barwig, Charles	Dem.	Mayville	2	1889-1895
Beck, Joseph D	Rep.	Viroqua	7	1921-1929
Berger, Victor L	Soc.	Milwaukee	5	1911-1913; 1919; 1923-1929
Biemiller, Andrew J	Dem.	Milwaukee	5	1945-1947; 1949-1951
Billinghurst, Charles	Rep.	Juneau	3	1855-1859
Blanchard, George W	Rep.	Edgerton	1	1933-1935
Boileau, Gerald J	Rep., Prog.	Wausau	8,7	1931-1939
Bolles, Stephen	Rep.	Janesville	1	1939-1941
Bouck, Gabriel	Dem.	Oshkosh	6	1877-1881
Bragg, Edward S	Dem.	Fond du Lac	5,2	1877-1883; 1885-1887
Brickner, George H	Dem.	Sheboygan Falls	5	1889-1895
Brophy, John C	Rep.	Milwaukee	4	1947-1949
Brown, James S	Dem.	Milwaukee	1	1863-1865
Brown, Webster E	Rep.	Rhinelander	9,10	1901-1907
Browne, Edward E	Rep.	Waupaca	8	1913-1931
Burchard, Samuel D	Dem.	Beaver Dam	5	1875-1877
Burke, Michael E	Dem.	Beaver Dam	6,2	1911-1917
Bushnell, Allen R	Dem.	Madison	3	1891-1893
Byrnes, John W	Rep.	Green Bay	8	1945-1973
Cannon, Raymond J	Dem.	Milwaukee	4	1933-1939
Cary, William J	Rep.	Milwaukee	4	1907-1919
Caswell, Lucien B	Rep.	Fort Atkinson	2,1	1875-1883; 1885-1891
Cate, George W	Reform	Stevens Point	8	1875-1877
Clark, Charles B	Rep.	Neenah	6	1887-1891
Classon, David G	Rep.	Oconto	9	1917-1923
Cobb, Amasa	Rep.	Mineral Point	3	1863-1871
Coburn, Frank P	Dem.	West Salem	7	1891-1893
Cole, Orasmus	Whig	Potosi	2	1849-1851
Cook, Samuel A	Rep.	Neenah	6	1895-1897
Cooper, Henry Allen	Rep.	Racine	1	1893-1919; 1921-1931
Cornell, Robert J	Dem.	De Pere	8	1975-1979
Dahle, Herman B	Rep.	Mount Horeb	2	1899-1903
Darling, Mason C	Dem.	Fond du Lac	2	1848-1849
Davidson, James H	Rep.	Oshkosh	6,8	1897-1913; 1917-1918
Davis, Glenn R	Rep.	Waukesha	2,9	1947-1957; 1965-1975
Deuster, Peter V	Dem.	Milwaukee	4	1879-1885
Dilweg, La Vern R	Dem.	Green Bay	8	1943-1945
Doty, James D	Dem.	Neenah	3	1849-1853
Durkee, Charles	Free Soil	Kenosha	1	1849-1853
Eastman, Ben C	Dem.	Platteville	2	1851-1855
Eldridge, Charles A	Dem.	Fond du Lac	4,5	1863-1875
Esch, John Jacob	Rep.	La Crosse	7	1899-1921
Flynn, Gerald T	Dem.	Racine	1	1959-1961
Frear, James A	Rep.	Hudson	10,9	1913-1935
Froehlich, Harold V	Rep.	Appleton	8	1973-1975
Gehrmann, Bernard J	Prog.	Mellen	10	1935-1943
Green, Mark A.	Rep.	Green Bay	8	1999-
Griffin, Michael	Rep.	Eau Claire	7	1894-1899
Griswold, Harry W	Rep.	West Salem	3	1939-1941
Guenther, Richard W	Rep.	Oshkosh	6,2	1881-1889
Gunderson, Steven	Rep.	Osseo	3	1981-1997
Hanchett, Luther	Rep.	Plover	2	1861-1862
Haugen, Nils P	Rep.	Black River Falls	8,10	1887-1895
Hawkes, Charles, Jr	Rep.	Horicon	2	1939-1941
Hazelton, George C	Rep.	Boscobel	3	1877-1883
Hazelton, Gerry W	Rep.	Columbus	2	1871-1875
Henney, Charles W	Dem.	Portage	2	1933-1935
Henry, Robert K	Rep.	Jefferson	2	1945-1947
Hopkins, Benjamin F	Rep.	Madison	2	1867-1870
Hudd, Thomas R	Dem.	Green Bay	5	1886-1889
Hughes, James	Dem.	De Pere	8	1933-1935
Hull, Merlin	Prog.	Black River Falls	7,9	1929-1931; 1935-1953
Humphrey, Herman L	Rep.	Hudson	7	1877-1883
Jenkins, John J	Rep.	Chippewa Falls	10,11	1895-1909
Johns, Joshua L	Rep.	Appleton	8	1939-1943
Johnson, Jay	Dem.	New Franken	8	1997-1999
Johnson, Lester R	Dem.	Black River Falls	9	1953-1965
Jones, Burr W	Dem.	Madison	3	1883-1885
Kading, Charles A	Rep.	Watertown	2	1927-1933
Kasten, Robert W., Jr	Rep.	Waukesha	9	1975-1979
Kastenmeier, Robert W	Dem.	Sun Prairie	2	1959-1991
Keefe, Frank B	Rep.	Oshkosh	6	1939-1951
Kersten, Charles J	Rep.	Whitefish Bay	5	1947-1949; 1951-1955
Kimball, Alanson M	Rep.	Waushara	6	1875-1877
Kind, Ron	Dem.	La Crosse	3	1997-
Kleczka, Gerald D	Dem.	Milwaukee	4	1984-2005
Kleczka, John C	Rep.	Milwaukee	4	1919-1923
Klug, Scott L	Rep.	Madison	2	1991-1999

WISCONSIN MEMBERS, U.S. HOUSE OF REPRESENTATIVES
1848 – 2005–Continued

Name	Party	Residence	District	Term
Konop, Thomas F	Dem.	Kewaunee	9	1911-1917
Kopp, Arthur W	Rep.	Platteville	3	1909-1913
Kustermann, Gustav	Rep.	Green Bay	9	1907-1911
La Follette, Robert M., Sr	Rep.	Madison	3	1885-1891
Laird, Melvin R	Rep.	Marshfield	7	1953-1969
Lampert, Florian	Rep.	Oshkosh	6	1918-1930
Larrabee, Charles H	Dem.	Horicon	3	1859-1861
Lenroot, Irvine L	Rep.	Superior	11	1909-1918
Lynch, Thomas	Dem.	Antigo	9	1891-1895
Lynde, William Pitt	Dem.	Milwaukee	1,4	1848-1849; 1875-1879
Macy, John B	Dem.	Fond du Lac	3	1853-1855
Magoon, Henry S	Rep.	Darlington	3	1875-1877
McCord, Myron H	Rep.	Merrill	9	1889-1891
McDill, Alexander S	Rep.	Plover	8	1873-1875
McIndoe, Walter D	Rep.	Wausau	6	1863-1867
McMurray, Howard J	Dem.	Milwaukee	5	1943-1945
Miller, Lucas M	Dem.	Oshkosh	6	1891-1893
Minor, Edward S	Rep.	Sturgeon Bay	8,9	1895-1907
Mitchell, Alexander	Dem.	Milwaukee	1,4	1871-1875
Mitchell, John L	Dem.	Milwaukee	4	1891-1893
Monahan, James G	Rep.	Darlington	3	1919-1921
Moody, James P	Dem.	Milwaukee	5	1983-1993
Moore, Gwen	Dem.	Milwaukee	4	2005-
Morse, Elmer A	Rep.	Antigo	10	1907-1913
Murphy, James W	Dem.	Platteville	3	1907-1909
Murray, Reid F	Rep.	Ogdensburg	7	1939-1953
Nelson, Adolphus P	Rep.	Grantsburg	11	1918-1923
Nelson, John Mandt	Rep.	Madison	2,3	1906-1919; 1921-1933
Neumann, Mark W	Rep.	Janesville	1	1995-1999
Obey, David R	Dem.	Wausau	7	1969-
O'Konski, Alvin E	Rep.	Mercer	10	1943-1973
O'Malley, Thomas D. P	Dem.	Milwaukee	5	1933-1939
Otjen, Theobald	Rep.	Milwaukee	4	1895-1907
Paine, Halbert E	Rep.	Milwaukee	1	1865-1871
Peavey, Hubert H	Rep.	Washburn	11,10	1923-1935
Petri, Thomas E	Rep.	Fond du Lac	6	1979-
Potter, John F	Rep.	East Troy	1	1857-1863
Pound, Thaddeus C	Rep.	Chippewa Falls	8	1877-1883
Price, Hugh H	Rep.	Black River Falls	8	1887
Price, William T	Rep.	Black River Falls	8	1883-1886
Race, John A	Dem.	Fond du Lac	6	1965-1967
Randall, Clifford E	Rep.	Kenosha	1	1919-1921
Rankin, Joseph	Dem.	Manitowoc	5	1883-1886
Reilly, Michael K	Dem.	Fond du Lac	6	1913-1917; 1930-1939
Reuss, Henry S	Dem.	Milwaukee	5	1955-1983
Roth, Toby	Rep.	Appleton	8	1979-1997
Rusk, Jeremiah M	Rep.	Viroqua	6,7	1871-1877
Ryan, Paul	Rep.	Janesville	1	1999-
Sauerhering, Edward	Rep.	Mayville	2	1895-1899
Sauthoff, Harry	Prog.	Madison	2	1935-1939; 1941-1945
Sawyer, Philetus	Rep.	Oshkosh	5,6	1865-1875
Schadeberg, Henry C	Rep.	Burlington	1	1961-1965; 1967-1971
Schafer, John C	Rep.	Milwaukee	4	1923-1933; 1939-1941
Schneider, George J	Rep., Prog.	Appleton	9,8	1923-1933; 1935-1939
Sensenbrenner, F. James, Jr	Rep.	Menomonee Falls	9,5	1979-
Shaw, George B	Rep.	Eau Claire	7	1893-1894
Sloan, A. Scott	Rep.	Beaver Dam	3	1861-1863
Sloan, Ithamar C	Rep.	Janesville	2	1863-1867
Smith, Henry	Union Labor	Milwaukee	4	1887-1889
Smith, Lawrence H	Rep.	Racine	1	1941-1959
Somers, Peter J	Dem.	Milwaukee	4	1893-1895
Stafford, William H	Rep.	Milwaukee	5	1903-1911; 1913-1919; 1921-1923; 1929-1933
Stalbaum, Lynn E	Dem.	Racine	1	1965-1967
Steiger, William A	Rep.	Oshkosh	6	1967-1978
Stephenson, Isaac	Rep.	Marinette	9	1883-1889
Stevenson, William H	Rep.	La Crosse	3	1941-1949
Stewart, Alexander	Rep.	Wausau	9	1895-1901
Sumner, Daniel H	Dem.	Waukesha	2	1883-1885
Tewes, Donald E	Rep.	Waukesha	2	1957-1959
Thill, Lewis D	Rep.	Milwaukee	5	1939-1943
Thomas, Ormsby B	Rep.	Prairie du Chien	7	1885-1891
Thomson, Vernon W	Rep.	Richland Center	3	1961-1975
Van Pelt, William K	Rep.	Fond du Lac	6	1951-1963
Van Schaick, Isaac W	Rep.	Milwaukee	4	1885-1887; 1889-1891
Voigt, Edward	Rep.	Sheboygan	2	1917-1927
Washburn, Cadwallader C	Rep.	Mineral Point, La Crosse	2	1855-1861; 1867-1871
Wasielewski, Thaddeus F	Dem.	Milwaukee	4	1941-1947
Weisse, Charles H	Dem.	Sheboygan Falls	6	1903-1911
Wells, Daniel, Jr	Dem.	Milwaukee	1	1853-1857
Wells, Owen A	Dem.	Fond du Lac	6	1893-1895
Wheeler, Ezra	Dem.	Berlin	5	1863-1865
Williams, Charles G	Rep.	Janesville	1	1873-1883
Winans, John	Dem.	Janesville	1	1883-1885
Withrow, Gardner R	Rep., Prog.	La Crosse	3	1931-1939; 1949-1961
Woodward, Gilbert M	Dem.	La Crosse	7,3	1883-1885
Zablocki, Clement J	Dem.	Milwaukee	4	1949-1983

Sources: Wisconsin Legislative Reference Bureau, *Wisconsin Blue Book*, various editions; Congressional Quarterly, *Guide to U.S. Elections*, 1985; and official election records.

WISCONSIN MEMBERS, U.S. HOUSE OF REPRESENTATIVES
By District, 1943 – 2005

District	Name	Service	Party	Residence	Alphabetical Listing	
1st	Lawrence H. Smith	1941-59	Rep.	Racine	Aspin	1st
	Gerald T. Flynn	1959-61	Dem.	Racine	Baldus	3rd
	Henry C. Schadeberg	1961-65; 1967-71	Rep.	Burlington	Baldwin	2nd
	Lynn E. Stalbaum	1965-67	Dem.	Racine	Barca	1st
	Les Aspin[1]	1971-93	Dem.	East Troy	Barrett	5th
	Peter W. Barca[1]	1993-95	Dem.	Kenosha	Biemiller	5th
	Mark W. Neumann	1995-99	Rep.	Janesville	Brophy	4th
	Paul Ryan	1999-	Rep.	Janesville	Byrnes	8th
					Cornell	8th
2nd	Harry Sauthoff	1941-45	Prog.	Madison	Davis	2nd, 9th
	Robert K. Henry	1945-47	Rep.	Jefferson	Dilweg	8th
	Glenn R. Davis	1947-57	Rep.	Waukesha	Flynn	1st
	Donald E. Tewes	1957-59	Rep.	Waukesha	Froehlich	8th
	Robert W. Kastenmeier	1959-91	Dem.	Sun Prairie	Green	8th
	Scott L. Klug	1991-99	Rep.	Madison	Gunderson	3rd
	Tammy Baldwin	1999-	Dem.	Madison	Henry	2nd
					Hull	9th
3rd	William H. Stevenson	1941-49	Rep.	La Crosse	Johnson, J.	8th
	Gardner R. Withrow	1949-61	Rep.	La Crosse	Johnson, L.	9th
	Vernon W. Thomson	1961-75	Rep.	Richland Center	Kasten	9th
	Alvin Baldus	1975-81	Dem.	Menomonie	Kastenmeier	2nd
	Steven Gunderson	1981-97	Rep.	Osseo	Keefe	6th
	Ron Kind	1997-	Dem.	La Crosse	Kersten	5th
					Kind	3rd
4th	Thaddeus F. Wasielewski	1941-47	Dem.	Milwaukee	Kleczka	4th
	John C. Brophy	1947-49	Rep.	Milwaukee	Klug	2nd
	Clement J. Zablocki[2]	1949-83	Dem.	Milwaukee	Laird	7th
	Gerald D. Kleczka[2]	1984-2005	Dem.	Milwaukee	McMurray	5th
	Gwen Moore	2005-	Dem.	Milwaukee	Moody	5th
					Moore	4th
5th[3]	Howard J. McMurray	1943-45	Dem.	Milwaukee	Murray	7th
	Andrew J. Biemiller	1945-47; 1949-51	Dem.	Milwaukee	Neumann	1st
	Charles J. Kersten	1947-49; 1951-55	Rep.	Whitefish Bay	Obey	7th
	Henry S. Reuss	1955-83	Dem.	Milwaukee	O'Konski	10th
	James P. Moody	1983-93	Dem.	Milwaukee	Petri	6th
	Thomas M. Barrett	1993-2003	Dem.	Milwaukee	Race	6th
	F. James Sensenbrenner, Jr.	2003-	Rep.	Menomonee Falls	Reuss	5th
					Roth	8th
6th	Frank B. Keefe	1939-51	Rep.	Oshkosh	Ryan	1st
	William K. Van Pelt	1951-65	Rep.	Fond du Lac	Sauthoff	2nd
	John A. Race	1965-67	Dem.	Fond du Lac	Schadeberg	1st
	William A. Steiger[4]	1967-78	Rep.	Oshkosh	Sensenbrenner	9th, 5th
	Thomas E. Petri[4]	1979-	Rep.	Fond du Lac	Smith	1st
					Stalbaum	1st
7th	Reid F. Murray	1939-53	Rep.	Ogdensburg	Steiger	6th
	Melvin R. Laird[5]	1953-69	Rep.	Marshfield	Stevenson	3rd
	David R. Obey[5]	1969-	Dem.	Wausau	Tewes	2nd
					Thomson	3rd
8th	La Vern R. Dilweg	1943-45	Dem.	Green Bay	Van Pelt	6th
	John R. Byrnes	1945-73	Rep.	Green Bay	Wasielewski	4th
	Harold V. Froehlich	1973-75	Rep.	Appleton	Withrow	3rd
	Robert J. Cornell	1975-79	Dem.	De Pere	Zablocki	4th
	Toby Roth	1979-97	Rep.	Appleton		
	Jay Johnson	1997-99	Dem.	New Franken		
	Mark A. Green	1999-	Rep.	Green Bay		
9th[3,6]	Merlin Hull	1935-53	Prog.	Black River Falls		
	Lester R. Johnson	1953-65	Dem.	Black River Falls		
	Glenn R. Davis	1965-75	Rep.	Waukesha		
	Robert W. Kasten	1975-79	Rep.	Thiensville		
	F. James Sensenbrenner, Jr.	1979-2003	Rep.	Menomonee Falls		
10th[7]	Alvin E. O'Konski	1943-73	Rep.	Rhinelander		

[1]Aspin resigned 1/20/1993, to become U.S. Secretary of Defense. Barca was elected in a special election, 5/4/1993.
[2]Zablocki died 12/3/1983. Kleczka was elected in a special election, 4/3/1984.
[3]In the congressional reapportionment following the 2000 Census, Wisconsin's delegation was reduced from 9 to 8 members. The previous 4th, 5th, and 9th were reconfigured into the new 4th and 5th.
[4]Steiger died 12/4/1978, following his November 1978 election. Petri was elected in a special election, 4/3/1979.
[5]Laird resigned 1/21/1969, to become U.S. Secretary of Defense. Obey was elected in a special election, 4/1/1969.
[6]In the congressional redistricting based on the results of the 1960 Census of Population, the previous 9th District in western Wisconsin ceased to exist and a new 9th District was created in the Waukesha-Milwaukee metropolitan area.
[7]In the congressional reapportionment based on the results of the 1970 Census of Population, Wisconsin's delegation was reduced from 10 members to 9 members.
Sources: *1944 Wisconsin Blue Book* and Wisconsin Legislative Reference Bureau data.

U.S. SENATORS FROM WISCONSIN, 1848 – 2005

Class 1		Class 3	
Name	Service	Name	Service
Henry Dodge (D)	1848-1857	Isaac P. Walker (D)	1848-1855
James R. Doolittle (R)	1857-1869	Charles Durkee (UR)	1855-1861
Matthew H. Carpenter (R)	1869-1875	Timothy O. Howe (UR)	1861-1879
Angus Cameron (R)[1]	1875-1881	Matthew H. Carpenter (R)	1879-1881
Philetus Sawyer (R)	1881-1893	Angus Cameron (R)[1]	1881-1885
John Lendrum Mitchell (D)	1893-1899	John C. Spooner (R)	1885-1891
Joseph Very Quarles (R)	1899-1905	William F. Vilas (D)	1891-1897
Robert M. La Follette, Sr. (R)[2]	1906-1925	John C. Spooner (R)	1897-1907
Robert M. La Follette, Jr. (R)[3]	1925-1935	Isaac Stephenson (R)[5]	1907-1915
(P)	1935-1947	Paul O. Husting (D)	1915-1917
Joseph R. McCarthy (R)	1947-1957	Irvine L. Lenroot (R)[6]	1918-1927
William Proxmire (D)[4]	1957-1989	John J. Blaine (R)	1927-1933
Herbert H. Kohl (D)	1989-	F. Ryan Duffy (D)	1933-1939
		Alexander Wiley (R)	1939-1963
		Gaylord A. Nelson (D)	1963-1981
		Robert W. Kasten, Jr. (R)	1981-1993
		Russell D. Feingold (D)	1993-

Note: Each state has two U.S. Senators, and each serves a 6-year term. They were elected by their respective state legislatures until passage of the 17th Amendment to the U.S. Constitution on April 8, 1913, which provided for popular election. Article I, Section 3, Clause 2, of the U.S. Constitution divides senators into three classes so that one-third of the senate is elected every two years. Wisconsin's seats were assigned to Class 1 and Class 3 at statehood.

Key: Democrat (D); Progressive (P); Republican (R); Union Republican (UR)

[1] Not a candidate for reelection to Class 1 seat, but elected 3/10/1881 to fill vacancy caused by death of Class 3 Senator Carpenter on 2/24/1881.

[2] Elected 1/25/1905 but continued to serve as governor until 1/1/1906.

[3] Elected 9/29/1925 to fill vacancy caused by death of Robert La Follette, Sr., on 6/18/1925.

[4] Elected 8/27/1957 to fill vacancy caused by death of McCarthy on 5/2/1957.

[5] Elected 5/17/1907 to fill vacancy caused by resignation of Spooner on 4/30/1907.

[6] Elected 5/2/1918 to fill vacancy caused by death of Husting on 10/21/1917.

Source: Wisconsin Legislative Reference Bureau records.

HIGHLIGHTS OF LOCAL AND STATE GOVERNMENT IN WISCONSIN

Employment and Earnings — In March 2003, Wisconsin ranked 18th among the states in full-time equivalent (FTE) state and local government employees with 288,044. The State of Wisconsin employed 71,040, while local government employed 217,004.

In March 2003, Wisconsin ranked 17th in average total payroll for state and local government employees with $1,007,280,196. California ranked first with a payroll of $7,996,219,320 and South Dakota ranked 50th with $115,117,829.

Units of Local Government — As of January 1, 2005, Wisconsin had 1,922 general units of local government – 72 counties, 190 cities, 400 villages, and 1,260 towns.

Counties varied in 2004 population from Milwaukee at 939,358 to Menominee with 4,616. These two counties were also highest and lowest in 2003 full value property assessments at $47.3 billion and $220.5 million, respectively. As determined by the U.S. Bureau of the Census in 2000, Marathon County is the largest in land area with 1,545 square miles and Ozaukee County the smallest with 232 square miles.

Based on the 2000 census, Wisconsin's city residents totaled 2,994,433 in 2000, a 5.2% increase from the 1990 census; village population was 687,007, a 19.7% increase; and town population was 1,668,306, a 13.3% increase. As of January 1, 2004, a total of 80 Wisconsin municipalities had populations of 10,000 or more. The City of Milwaukee ranked first at 593,920, and the Village of Waunakee, with 10,002 residents, was smallest in the group.

Administration — Wisconsin cities may adopt a mayor, manager, or commission form of government. Of 190 cities, 10 have a city manager and 180 have a mayor. Currently, no city uses the commission form of government. Villages may use a president or manager form of government. Of 400 villages, only 11 have an appointed manager. Currently, 82 cities and 83 villages employ an administrator in a full-time or combined position.

Each county board is headed by a chairperson chosen by the board. In addition, 10 counties have an elected county executive, 14 have an appointed county administrator, and 48 have an appointed administrative coordinator.

The following tables present selected data. Consult footnoted sources for more detailed information about local and state government.

WISCONSIN STATE GOVERNMENT EMPLOYEES
By Status and Funding, 1994 – 2004

Employee Status[1]	1994	1999	2004	Type of Funding for Authorized Positions[3]	1994	1999	2004
Classified	40,255	38,377	40,633	State appropriations . . .	32,060	33,312	35,535
Unclassified	16,069	20,625	22,592	User fees	17,410	17,093	17,785
Limited Term	8,691	8,219	6,729	Federal appropriations .	8,208	8,298	9,327
Project	788	666	585	Segregated funds	5,478	5,366	5,427
Seasonal	171	154	90	TOTAL[4]	63,157	64,069	68,074
Other[2]	4,185	5,869	6,629				
TOTAL[4]	70,159	73,910	77,258				

[1]Headcount of employees working on a full- or part-time basis as of June 30.
[2]Includes UW System graduate assistants.
[3]Full-time equivalent positions authorized by legislature, as of June 30.
[4]Detail may not add to total due to rounding.
Sources: Wisconsin Department of Administration, Division of Executive Budget and Finance, *State Employment Report*, November 2000 and previous issues, and departmental data, April 2005.

WISCONSIN STATE CLASSIFIED SERVICE PROFILE
1994 – 2004

Category	1994 Number	1994 Percent of Work Force	1999 Number	1999 Percent of Work Force	2004 Number	2004 Percent of Work Force
Permanent Classified Employees	40,416	100.0%	38,732	100.0%	40,475	100.0%
Persons with Disabilities	3,627	9.0	3,517	9.1	2,771	6.8
Persons with Severe Disabilities . .	286	0.7	510	1.3	379	0.9
Women	21,153	52.3	19,902	51.4	20,703	51.2
Racial/ethnic minorities	2,505	6.2	2,971	7.7	3,573	8.8
Black	1,292	3.2	1,607	4.1	1,818	4.5
Hispanic	497	1.2	569	1.5	801	2.0
Asian	370	0.9	474	1.2	641	1.6
American Indian	346	0.9	321	0.8	313	0.8

Source: Wisconsin State Office of Employment Relations, *Affirmative Action Report for Wisconsin State Government July 2004 to June 2005*, and Wisconsin Department of Employment Relations for previous issues.

WISCONSIN STATE AND LOCAL GOVERNMENT
EMPLOYMENT AND PAYROLLS

Employees and Payrolls by Function, March 2003

	Total	Full-Time Equivalent Employees Per 10,000 Population	Total Payroll (in thousands)
Education	167,941	309	$585,155
Elementary and secondary	(119,525)	(219.7)	(394,062)
Higher education institutions	(44,280)	(81.4)	(179,299)
Libraries (local)	(2,957)	(5.4)	(7,369)
Other	(1,179)	(2.2)	(4,425)
Government administration (including courts)	18,620	34	69,384
Police protection	16,304	30	64,704
Public welfare and social insurance administration	15,795	29	46,537
Health and hospitals	12,631	23	40,922
Streets and highways	11,081	20	39,816
Corrections	12,945	24	41,946
Fire protection	4,898	9	20,976
Natural resources	3,154	6	10,811
Parks and recreation	3,605	7	11,062
Sewerage (local)	2,003	4	7,571
Transit	2,630	5	10,102
Utilities (electric and water supply)	2,539	5	9,792
Housing and community development	1,221	2	3,615
Solid waste management (local)	1,501	3	5,087
Other	11,176	21	39,800
TOTAL	288,044	530	$1,007,280

Source: U.S. Department of Commerce, Bureau of the Census, *Public Employment Data:* March 2003, at: http:ftp2.census.gov/ govs/apes/03stlwi.txt [December 16, 2004].

Employment and Payrolls, 1990 – 2003

Year	Employees (full-time equivalents) State	Employees (full-time equivalents) Local	Employees (full-time equivalents) Total	Monthly Payroll (in thousands)[1] State	Monthly Payroll (in thousands)[1] Local	Monthly Payroll (in thousands)[1] Total
1990	66,541	183,318	249,859	$152,660	$409,907	$562,567
1993	69,577	189,886	259,463	192,481	480,703	673,184
1994	68,688	200,179	268,867	194,641	528,605	723,246
1995	64,664	201,123	265,787	197,252	547,852	745,104
1996[2]	—	—	—	—	—	—
1997	64,709	201,633	266,342	204,267	569,193	773,460
1998	64,703	211,790	276,493	207,996	625,686	833,681
1999	63,185	207,587	270,772	214,684	628,043	842,727
2000	63,697	219,793	283,490	230,570	662,358	892,928
2001	69,428	218,824	288,252	257,605	676,935	934,540
2002	70,962	218,982	288,543	261,095	719,434	977,410
2003	71,040	217,004	288,044	268,249	739,031	1,007,280

[1]Prior to 1997, annual data reflected October payrolls. Beginning with the 1997 Annual Survey of Government Employment and Payroll, data reflects March payrolls.
[2]There was no survey in 1996.

Source: U.S. Department of Commerce, Bureau of the Census, *Government Employment: March 2003* and previous issues, at: http://ftp2.census.gov/govs/apes/03stlwi.txt [December 17, 2004].

STATE AND LOCAL GOVERNMENT EMPLOYEES
Number and Earnings by State, March 2003 Payroll

State	Full-time Equivalent Employees Number Total	State	Local	Earnings March Payroll Total	State	Local
Alabama	269,674	85,518	184,156	$758,999,242	$278,925,140	$480,074,102
Alaska	51,102	24,837	26,265	197,563,784	98,227,470	99,336,314
Arizona	261,492	65,372	196,120	856,632,408	210,725,321	645,907,087
Arkansas	153,382	54,087	99,295	394,037,314	159,143,111	234,894,203
California	1,805,446	389,345	1,416,101	7,996,219,320	1,826,238,182	6,169,981,138
Colorado	256,018	67,406	188,612	887,996,182	269,918,650	618,077,532
Connecticut	176,369	59,967	116,402	725,918,233	264,424,813	461,493,420
Delaware	45,947	24,455	21,492	160,656,568	85,027,143	75,629,425
District of Columbia	44,271	—	44,271	204,226,620	—	204,226,620
Florida	806,682	186,861	619,821	2,590,947,421	604,299,660	1,986,647,761
Georgia	484,515	121,255	363,260	1,413,734,297	383,623,897	1,030,110,400
Hawaii	71,764	57,458	14,306	238,674,782	186,679,580	51,995,202
Idaho	78,548	23,320	55,228	217,151,389	68,972,280	148,179,109
ILLINOIS	641,248	133,916	507,332	2,253,948,185	485,669,666	1,768,278,519
Indiana	332,380	90,788	241,592	976,009,951	277,481,891	698,528,060
IOWA	179,633	52,795	126,838	552,733,473	204,201,682	348,531,791
Kansas	178,042	43,908	134,134	504,879,558	143,049,710	361,829,848
Kentucky	227,902	78,828	149,074	621,162,006	250,966,072	370,195,934
Louisiana	279,087	90,189	188,898	746,906,863	278,224,661	468,682,202
Maine	75,041	21,830	53,211	215,831,708	73,465,780	142,365,928
Maryland	287,513	91,762	195,751	1,096,158,924	343,447,084	752,711,840
Massachusetts	320,372	91,064	229,308	1,242,413,118	371,706,682	870,706,436
MICHIGAN	512,026	137,062	374,964	1,862,175,130	524,838,115	1,337,337,015
MINNESOTA	283,691	75,220	208,471	1,013,609,731	310,579,660	703,030,071
Mississippi	186,130	56,269	129,861	451,697,979	158,046,258	293,651,721
Missouri	311,972	90,912	221,060	871,959,633	251,331,577	620,628,056
Montana	52,886	18,700	34,186	145,969,214	57,945,604	88,023,610
Nebraska	113,703	33,500	80,203	332,386,423	92,943,948	239,442,475
Nevada	92,655	24,716	67,939	360,932,268	89,706,641	271,225,627
New Hampshire	68,192	20,359	47,833	212,384,317	67,157,613	145,226,704
New Jersey	489,448	146,698	342,750	2,088,686,795	647,503,984	1,441,182,811
New Mexico	122,040	46,325	75,715	335,000,910	134,636,776	200,364,134
New York	1,193,262	248,150	945,112	5,215,580,288	1,067,276,735	4,148,303,553
North Carolina	469,942	131,265	338,677	1,429,597,844	425,797,626	1,003,800,218
North Dakota	41,178	18,009	23,169	119,309,670	51,324,315	67,985,355
Ohio	619,869	136,871	482,998	2,054,318,446	483,289,081	1,571,029,365
Oklahoma	201,632	65,511	136,121	540,749,912	195,870,586	344,879,326
Oregon	181,607	57,022	124,585	627,664,640	205,132,544	422,532,096
Pennsylvania	569,356	159,463	409,893	2,004,086,862	594,664,189	1,409,422,673
Rhode Island	54,944	20,080	35,864	222,892,539	80,680,094	142,212,445
South Carolina	242,222	77,275	164,947	674,042,342	225,639,013	448,403,329
South Dakota	43,445	13,062	30,383	115,117,829	38,923,584	76,194,245
Tennessee	311,601	83,495	228,106	880,713,325	246,425,477	634,287,848
Texas	1,253,022	265,748	987,274	3,682,580,373	881,915,911	2,800,664,462
Utah	122,209	47,674	74,535	369,581,819	153,141,165	216,440,654
Vermont	38,660	13,538	25,122	117,470,815	48,080,833	69,389,982
Virginia	411,100	115,818	295,282	1,297,376,491	390,976,240	906,400,251
Washington	321,153	112,606	208,547	1,246,767,866	414,377,121	832,390,745
West Virginia	93,383	37,215	56,168	265,731,032	108,291,522	157,439,510
WISCONSIN	288,044	71,040	217,004	1,007,280,196	268,248,950	739,031,246
Wyoming	43,651	12,103	31,548	123,553,044	37,243,004	86,310,040
UNITED STATES	15,760,451	4,190,667	11,569,784	$54,522,019,079	$15,116,406,641	$39,405,612,438

Source: U.S. Department of Commerce, Bureau of the Census, 2003 public employment data at:
http://www.census.gov/govs/www/apestl03.html [December 21, 2004]
http://www.census.gov/govs/www/apesst03.html [December 21, 2004]
http://www.census.gov/govs/www/apesloc03.html [December 21, 2004]

LOCAL UNITS OF GOVERNMENT BY STATE AND TYPE – 2002
See *2003-2004 Wisconsin Blue Book*, p. 735

BASIC DATA ON WISCONSIN COUNTIES

County (year created)[1]	County Seat	Full Value 2003 Assessment (in millions)[2]	Population 2004 Estimate	Pct. Change[3]	2004 Rank	Land Area in Sq. Miles[4]	2004 Density per Sq. Mile[5]
Adams (1848)	Friendship	$1,660,724	20,707	3.95%	52	647.7	32.0
Ashland (1860)	Ashland	908,069	16,969	0.61	59	1,043.8	16.3
Barron (1859)	Barron	2,839,238	46,540	3.51	29	862.8	53.9
Bayfield (1845)	Washburn	1,771,672	15,575	3.74	64	1,476.3	10.6
Brown (1818)	Green Bay	14,465,487	237,841	4.93	4	528.7	449.9
Buffalo (1853)	Alma	705,963	14,033	1.66	67	684.5	20.5
Burnett (1856)	Meenon[6]	2,026,826	16,398	4.62	61	821.5	20.0
Calumet (1836)	Chilton	2,396,792	44,361	9.18	30	319.8	138.7
Chippewa (1845) ...	Chippewa Falls	3,239,644	59,466	7.74	24	1,010.4	58.9
Clark (1853)	Neillsville	1,359,767	34,373	2.43	41	1,215.6	28.3
Columbia (1846) ...	Portage	3,587,812	54,596	4.06	26	773.8	70.6
Crawford (1818) ...	Prairie du Chien	777,456	17,501	1.50	57	572.7	30.6
Dane (1836)	Madison	34,696,825	450,730	5.67	2	1,201.9	375.0
Dodge (1836)	Juneau	4,508,050	88,285	2.78	17	882.3	100.1
Door (1851)	Sturgeon Bay	5,579,066	29,114	4.12	43	482.7	60.3
Douglas (1854)	Superior	2,397,987	43,708	0.97	33	1,309.1	33.4
Dunn (1854)	Menomonie	2,143,904	41,737	4.71	36	852.0	49.0
Eau Claire (1856) ..	Eau Claire	5,177,369	96,214	3.30	16	637.6	150.9
Florence (1881)	Florence	409,010	5,214	2.48	71	488.0	10.7
Fond du Lac (1836) .	Fond du Lac	5,298,866	99,608	2.38	14	722.9	137.8
Forest (1885)	Crandon	831,263	10,198	1.74	68	1,014.1	10.1
Grant (1836)	Lancaster	1,863,897	50,552	1.93	28	1,147.9	44.0
Green (1836)	Monroe	1,851,534	35,163	4.51	40	584.0	60.2
Green Lake (1858) ..	Green Lake	1,672,012	19,344	1.25	55	354.3	54.6
Iowa (1829)	Dodgeville	1,406,278	23,639	3.77	48	762.7	31.0
Iron (1893)	Hurley	647,410	6,948	1.27	70	757.2	9.2
Jackson (1853)	Black River Falls	977,313	19,677	3.02	54	987.3	19.9
Jefferson (1836)	Jefferson	4,725,683	78,342	3.40	20	557.0	140.6
Juneau (1856)	Mauston	1,365,455	25,470	4.75	46	767.6	33.2
Kenosha (1850)	Kenosha	10,106,677	156,082	4.35	8	272.8	572.1
Kewaunee (1852) ...	Kewaunee	1,132,916	20,860	3.33	51	342.6	60.9
La Crosse (1851) ...	La Crosse	5,620,718	109,616	2.33	13	452.7	242.1
Lafayette (1846)	Darlington	659,123	16,311	1.08	62	633.6	25.7
Langlade (1879)	Antigo	1,328,310	21,227	2.35	50	872.7	24.3
Lincoln (1874)	Merrill	1,887,116	30,271	2.13	42	883.3	34.3
Manitowoc (1836) ..	Manitowoc	4,321,880	84,264	1.65	19	591.5	142.5
Marathon (1850) ...	Wausau	7,152,373	129,962	3.28	10	1,545.0	84.1
Marinette (1879) ...	Marinette	2,815,418	44,204	1.89	31	1,401.8	31.5
Marquette (1836) ...	Montello	1,193,081	15,051	3.41	66	455.5	33.0
Menominee (1961) ..	Keshena	220,446	4,616	1.18	72	358.0	12.9
Milwaukee (1834) ..	Milwaukee	47,266,665	939,358	−0.09	1	241.6	3,888.7
Monroe (1854)	Sparta	1,788,049	42,626	4.23	34	900.8	47.3
Oconto (1851)	Oconto	2,741,652	37,679	5.69	39	998.0	37.8
Oneida (1885)	Rhinelander	4,853,443	37,726	2.58	38	1,124.5	33.5
Outagamie (1851) ..	Appleton	9,937,346	168,840	4.81	6	640.3	263.7
Ozaukee (1853)	Port Washington	8,453,949	85,160	3.45	18	232.0	367.1
Pepin (1858)	Durand	400,377	7,568	4.92	69	232.3	32.6
Pierce (1853)	Ellsworth	2,380,732	38,615	4.92	37	576.5	67.0
Polk (1853)	Balsam Lake	3,438,520	43,870	6.17	32	917.3	47.8
Portage (1836)	Stevens Point	3,730,748	68,935	2.61	23	806.3	85.5
Price (1879)	Phillips	1,145,016	15,954	0.83	63	1,252.6	12.7
Racine (1836)	Racine	10,965,781	191,853	1.60	5	333.1	576.0
Richland (1842)	Richland Center	807,713	18,098	0.97	56	586.2	30.9
Rock (1836)	Janesville	7,722,415	155,536	2.12	9	720.5	215.9
Rusk (1901)	Ladysmith	847,324	15,512	1.08	65	913.1	17.0
St. Croix (1840)	Hudson	5,936,959	72,522	14.83	22	721.8	100.5
Sauk (1840)	Baraboo	4,617,519	58,595	6.10	25	837.6	70.0
Sawyer (1883)	Hayward	2,524,237	17,027	5.13	58	1,256.4	13.6
Shawano (1853)	Shawano	2,257,869	41,944	3.15	35	892.5	47.0
Sheboygan (1836) ..	Sheboygan	6,665,404	115,447	2.48	12	513.6	224.8
Taylor (1875)	Medford	1,039,309	19,872	0.98	53	974.9	20.4
Trempealeau (1854) .	Whitehall	1,173,678	27,765	2.80	45	734.1	37.8
Vernon (1851)	Viroqua	1,146,907	28,928	3.11	44	794.9	36.4
Vilas (1893)	Eagle River	4,920,933	21,966	4.44	49	873.7	25.1
Walworth (1836) ...	Elkhorn	9,478,615	97,052	5.48	15	555.3	174.8
Washburn (1883) ...	Shell Lake	1,750,202	16,762	4.53	60	809.7	20.7
Washington (1836) ..	West Bend	9,759,743	123,587	5.18	11	430.8	286.9
Waukesha (1846) ...	Waukesha	37,450,170	373,339	3.48	3	555.6	672.0
Waupaca (1851)	Waupaca	2,943,136	53,148	2.55	27	751.1	70.8
Waushara (1851) ...	Wautoma	1,953,939	24,806	7.54	47	626.0	39.6
Winnebago (1840) ..	Oshkosh	9,225,241	161,863	3.25	7	438.6	369.1
Wood (1856)	Wisconsin Rapids	3,657,194	76,235	0.90	21	792.8	96.2
State Total		$360,710,211	5,532,955	3.16%		54,310.1	101.9

[1]Counties are created by legislative act. Depending on the date, Wisconsin counties were created by the Michigan Territorial Legislature (1818-1836), the Wisconsin Territorial Legislature (1836-1848), or the Wisconsin State Legislature (after 1848). [2]Reflects actual market value of all taxable general property, including personal property and real estate, as determined by the Wisconsin Department of Revenue. [3]Change from 2000 U.S. Census. [4]Determined by U.S. Census Bureau. [5]2004 density and population rank calculated by Wisconsin Legislative Reference Bureau. [6]Town of Siren is used as a mailing address for county offices.

Sources: Wisconsin Department of Revenue, Division of State and Local Finance, *Town, Village, and City Taxes 2003: Taxes Levied 2003 − Collected 2004,* 2004; Wisconsin Department of Administration, *Population and Housing Estimates,* October 2004.

COUNTY OFFICERS IN WISCONSIN
June 30, 2005

County	County Board Number of Supervisors	Chairperson	Administrator, Executive, or Administrative Coordinator[1]
Adams	20	Alfred Sebastiani	Alfred Sebastiani (AC)
Ashland	21	Peg Kurilla	Thomas Kieweg (CA)
Barron	29	Ole Severude	Duane Hebert (CA)
Bayfield	13	William D. Kacvinsky	Mark Abeles-Allison (CA)
Brown	26	Patrick Moynihan, Jr.	Carol L. Kelso (CE)
Buffalo	16	Del D. Twidt	Bruce Cornish (AC)
Burnett	21	Clifford L. Main	Candace Fitzgerald (CA)
Calumet	21	Merlin Gentz	William P. Craig (CA)
Chippewa	29	Michael J. Murphy	Michael J. Murphy (AC)
Clark	29	Wayne Hendrickson	Wayne Hendrickson (AC)
Columbia	31	Susan Martin	Jeanne Miller (AC)
Crawford	17	Robert G. Dillman	Robert G. Dillman (AC)
Dane	37	Kevin Kesterson	Kathleen Falk (CE)
Dodge	37	Russell Kottke	Russell Kottke (AC)
Door	21	Charlie Most, Jr.	Judith Genereaux (CA)
Douglas	28	Douglas G. Finn	Steve Koszarek (CA)
Dunn	29	B. Jane Hoyt	Eugene C. Smith (AC)
Eau Claire	29	Bruce Willett	J. Thomas McCarty (CA)
Florence	12	Gary Lindow	Geraldine L. Meyer (AC)
Fond du Lac	36	Brenna Garrison-Bruden	Allen J. Buechel (CE)
Forest	21	Erhard E. Huettl, Sr.	Erhard E. Huettl, Sr. (AC)
Grant	31	Eugene Bartels	Eugene Bartels (AC)
Green	31	Thomas Daly	Michael J. Doyle (AC)
Green Lake	21	Orrin W. Helmer	Margaret R. Bostelmann (AC)
Iowa	21	Robert Regan	Robert Regan (AC)
Iron	15	Gustaf R. Krone	Jodie Bednar-Clemens (AC)
Jackson	19	Steven Dickinsen	Steven Dickinsen (AC)
Jefferson	30	Sharon Schmeling	Willard D. Hausen (CA)
Juneau	21	James C. Barrett	James C. Barrett (AC)
Kenosha	28	Dennis Elverman	Allan K. Kehl (CE)
Kewaunee	20	Robert A. Weidner	Edward J. Dorner (CA)
La Crosse	35	Steven P. Doyle	Steve O'Malley (CA)
Lafayette	16	Jack Sauer	Jack Sauer (AC)
Langlade	21	Michael Klimoski	Michael Klimoski (AC)
Lincoln	22	E. Richard Simon	John Mulder (CA)
Manitowoc	25	Paul B. Hansen	Daniel R. Fischer (CE)
Marathon	38	Keith Langenhahn	Mort McBain (CA)
Marinette	30	George A. Bousley	Steve A. Corbeille (CA)
Marquette	17	Howard Zellmer	Brent Miller (AC)
Menominee	7	Randolph H. Reiter	Ronald Corn, Sr. (AC)
Milwaukee	25	Lee Holloway	Scott Walker (CE)
Monroe	24	Dennis Hubbard	Dennis Hubbard (AC)
Oconto	31	Leland T. Rymer	Kevin Hamann (AC)
Oneida	21	Andrew Smith	Andrew Smith (AC)
Outagamie	36	Clifford Sanderfoot	Robert N. Paltzer, Jr. (CE)
Ozaukee	31	Robert A. Brooks	ThomasW. Meaux (CA)
Pepin	12	Peter Adler	Larry Krcmar (AC)
Pierce	17	Ronald O. Anderson	Mark Schroeder (AC)
Polk	23	Robert Blake	Vacancy (AC)
Portage	29	O. Philip Idsvoog	O. Philip Idsvoog (AC)
Price	21	Daniel Racette	Daniel Racette (AC)
Racine	23	Kenneth Vetrovec	William McReynolds (CE)
Richland	21	Ann M. Greenheck	Victor V. Vlasak (AC)
Rock	29	Richard K. Ott	Craig Knutson (CA)
Rusk	21	Randy Tatur	Denise Nelson (AC)
St. Croix	31	Clarence Malick	Charles Whiting (AC)
Sauk	31	William F. Wenzel	Gene M. Wiegand (AC)
Sawyer	15	Hal Helwig	Hal Helwig (AC)
Shawano	30	Marshal Giese	Frank Pascarella (AC)
Sheboygan	34	William C. Goehring	Adam N. Payne (AC)
Taylor	17	Jim Metz	Jim Metz (AC)
Trempealeau	17	Barbara Semb	Barbara Semb (AC)
Vernon	29	Lee Nerison	Vacancy (AC)
Vilas	21	Charles Rayala, Jr.	Charles Rayala, Jr. (AC)
Walworth	25	Ann Lohrmann	David A. Bretl (CA)
Washburn	21	Peter J. Hubin	Michael D. Miller (AC)
Washington	30	Kenneth F. Miller	Douglas Johnson (AC)
Waukesha	35	James T. Dwyer	Daniel M. Finley (CE)
Waupaca	27	Dick Koeppen	Mary A. Robbins (AC)
Waushara	21	Norman Weiss	Debra Behringer (AC)
Winnebago	38	David Albrecht	Mark L. Harris (CE)
Wood	38	Charles Gurtler	Charles Gurtler (AC)

COUNTY OFFICERS IN WISCONSIN
June 30, 2005–Continued

County	Clerk	County Clerk Office Address
Adams	Cindy Phillippi (D)	P.O. Box 278, 400 N. Main St., Friendship 53934
Ashland	Patricia Somppi (D)	201 W. Main St., Rm. 202, Ashland 54806
Barron	Dee Ann Cook (R)	330 E. LaSalle Av. Rm. 210, Barron 54812
Bayfield	Scott S. Fibert (D)	P.O. Box 878, 117 E. 6th St., Washburn 54891
Brown	Darlene K. Marcelle (R)	P.O. Box 23600, Green Bay 54305-3600
Buffalo	Roxann M. Halverson (D)	P.O. Box 58, 407 South 2nd St., Alma 54610-0058
Burnett	Wanda Hinrichs (D)	7410 County Road K, Rm. 105, Siren 54872
Calumet	Beth A. Hauser (R)	206 Court St., Chilton 53014
Chippewa	Kathleen M. Bernier (R)	711 N. Bridge St., Rm. 109, Chippewa Falls 54729
Clark	Christina M. Jensen (R)	517 Court St., Rm. 301, Neillsville 54456
Columbia	Jeanne Miller (R)	P.O. Box 177, Portage 53901
Crawford	Janet L. Geisler (R)	220 N. Beaumont Rd., Prairie du Chien 53821
Dane	Robert Ohlsen (D)	210 Martin Luther King Jr. Blvd., Rm. 112, Madison 53703
Dodge	Karen J. Gibson (R)	127 E. Oak St., Juneau 53039
Door	Nancy A. Bemmann (R)	P.O. Box 670, Sturgeon Bay 54235
Douglas	Susan T. Sandvick (D)	1313 Belknap St., Rm. 101, Superior 54880
Dunn	Lorraine Hartung (D)	800 Wilson Av., Menomonie 54751
Eau Claire	Janet K. Loomis (D)	721 Oxford Av., Eau Claire 54703
Florence	Geraldine L. Meyer (R)	P.O. Box 410, Florence 54121
Fond du Lac	Joyce A. Buechel (R)	P.O. Box 1557, Fond du Lac 54936-1557
Forest	Sandra L. Neddo (D)	200 E. Madison St., Crandon 54520
Grant	Chris Carl (R)	P.O. Box 529, 111 S. Jefferson St., Lancaster 53813
Green	Michael J. Doyle (R)	1016 16th Av., Monroe 53566
Green Lake	Margaret R. Bostelmann (R)	P.O. Box 3188, Green Lake 54941-3188
Iowa	Greg Klusendorf (R)	222 N. Iowa St., Dodgeville 53533
Iron	Michael J. Saari (D)	300 Taconite St., Suite 101, Hurley 54534
Jackson	Kyle Deno (D)	307 Main St., Black River Falls 54615
Jefferson	Barbara A. Frank (R)	320 S. Main St., Rm. 109, Jefferson 53549
Juneau	Kathleen Kobylski (R)	220 E. State St., Mauston 53948
Kenosha	Edna R. Highland (D)	1010 56th St., Kenosha 53140
Kewaunee	Linda J. Teske (D)	613 Dodge St., Kewaunee 54216
La Crosse	Marion I. Naegle (R)	400 N. 4th St., Rm. 1210, La Crosse 54601
Lafayette	Linda L. Bawden (R)	P.O. Box 40, 626 Main St., Darlington 53530
Langlade	Kathryn Jacob (D)	800 Clermont St., Antigo 54409
Lincoln	Robert D. Kunkel (R)	1110 E. Main St., Merrill 54452
Manitowoc	Charlene M. Peterson (D)	1010 S. 8th St., Ste. 115, Manitowoc 54220
Marathon	Nan Kottke (D)	500 Forest St., Wausau 54403
Marinette	Kathy Brandt (R)	1926 Hall Av., Marinette 54143-1717
Marquette	James R. Thalacker (R)	P.O. Box 186, Montello 53949
Menominee	Ruth Waupoose (D)	P.O. Box 279, Keshena 54135-0279
Milwaukee	Mark Ryan (D)	901 N. 9th St., Rm. 105, Milwaukee 53233
Monroe	Susan A. Matson (R)	202 South K St., Rm. 1, Sparta 54656
Oconto	Rose Stellmacher (R)	301 Washington St., Oconto 54153-1699
Oneida	Robert Bruso (D)	P.O. Box 400, Rhinelander 54501-0400
Outagamie	Nancy J. Christensen (R)	410 S. Walnut St., Appleton 54911
Ozaukee	Mary S. Marchese (R)	P.O. Box 994, 121 W. Main St., Port Washington 53074-0994
Pepin	Marcia Bauer (D)	P.O. Box 39, 740 7th Av. W., Durand 54736
Pierce	Jamie R. Feuerhelm (D)	P.O. Box 119, 414 W. Main St., Ellsworth 54011
Polk	Catherine Albrecht (R)	100 Polk County Plaza, Ste. 110, Balsam Lake 54810
Portage	Roger Wrycza (D)	1516 Church St., Stevens Point 54481
Price	Jean Gottwald (D)	126 Cherry St., Rm. 106, Phillips 54555
Racine	Joan C. Rennert (D)	730 Wisconsin Av., Racine 53403
Richland	Victor V. Vlasak (R)	P.O. Box 310, Richland Center 53581
Rock	Kay S. O'Connell (D)	51 S. Main St., Janesville 53545
Rusk	Denise Nelson (D)	311 Miner Av. E., Ste. C150, Ladysmith 54848
St. Croix	Cindy Campbell (D)	1101 Carmichael Rd., Hudson 54016
Sauk	Beverly J. Mielke (R)	505 Broadway, Rm. 144, Baraboo 53913
Sawyer	Kris Mayberry (R)	P.O. Box 836, Hayward 54843
Shawano	Rosemary Bohm (R)	311 N. Main St., Shawano 54166
Sheboygan	Julie Glancey (D)	508 New York Av., Sheboygan 53081-4126
Taylor	Bruce P. Strama (D)	224 S. 2nd St., Medford 54451
Trempealeau	Paul L. Syverson (D)	P.O. Box 67, 36245 Main St., Whitehall 54773
Vernon	Ron Hoff (R)	Courthouse Annex, Rm. 108, Viroqua 54665
Vilas	James A. Sanborn (R)	330 Court St., Eagle River 54521
Walworth	Kimberly S. Bushey (R)	P.O. Box 1001, Elkhorn 53121
Washburn	John L. Brown (R)	P.O. Box 639, 10 4th Av., Shell Lake 54871
Washington	Brenda Jaszewski (R)	P.O. Box 1986, 432 E. Washington St., West Bend 53095-7986
Waukesha	Kathy Nickolaus (R)	1320 Pewaukee Rd., Rm. 120, Waukesha 53188
Waupaca	Mary A. Robbins (R)	811 Harding St., Waupaca 54981
Waushara	John C. Benz (R)	P.O. Box 488, Wautoma 54982-0488
Winnebago	Susan T. Ertmer (R)	P.O. Box 2808, Oshkosh 54901-2808
Wood	Cynthia Meyers (D)	P.O. Box 8095, 440 Market St., Wisconsin Rapids 54495-8095

COUNTY OFFICERS IN WISCONSIN
June 30, 2005–Continued

County	Treasurer	Register of Deeds	Clerk of Circuit Court
Adams	Mary Ann Bays (R)	Jodi Helgeson (R)	Dianna Helmrick (D)
Ashland	Tracey A. Hoglund (R)	Karen M. Miller (D)	Kathleen R. Colgrove (R)
Barron	Yvonne K. Ritchie (R)	Shawn M. Hanson (R)	Judith Wells Espeseth (R)
Bayfield	Daniel R. Anderson (D)	Patricia A. Olson (D)	Kay L. Cederberg (D)
Brown	Kerry M. Blaney (D)	Cathy A. Williquette (D)	Paul G. Janquart (D)
Buffalo	Marilynn Sheahan (R)	Donna J. Carothers (R)	Roselle M. Urness (R)
Burnett	Joanne Pahl (D)	Jeanine Chell (D)	Trudy Schmidt (D)
Calumet	Michael V. Schlaak (R)	Debra Tasch (A)	Barbara Van Akkeren (R)
Chippewa	Arlene M. Zwiefelhofer (D)	Marge L. Geissler (D)	Karen J. Hepfler (D)
Clark	Kathryn M. Brugger (D)	Lois Hagedorn (D)	Gail Walker (D)
Columbia	Deborah A. Raimer (R)	Lisa Walker (R)	Susan Raimer (R)
Crawford	Martin E. Sprosty (D)	Melissa Mezera (A)	Donna M. Steiner (D)
Dane	David Gawenda (D)	Jane Licht (D)	Judith Coleman (D)
Dodge	Patti Hilker (R)	Chris Planasch (R)	Lynn M. Hron (R)
Door	Jay Zahn (R)	Carey Petersilka (R)	Nancy Robillard (R)
Douglas	Sandy J. Petzold (D)	Kathy F. Hanson (D)	Joan Osty (D)
Dunn	Mary D. Erpenbach (R)	James M. Mrdutt (D)	Clara D. Minor (D)
Eau Claire	Larry C. Lokken (D)	Mary L. Kaiser (D)	Diana J. Miller (D)
Florence	JoAnne Friberg (R)	Pattie Gehlhoff (R)	Paula Coraggio (R)
Fond du Lac	Judeen V. Damm (R)	Patricia Kraus (R)	Mary L. Karst (R)
Forest	Amy T. Krause (D)	Paul Aschenbrenner (D)	Thomas A. Kalkofen (D)
Grant	Louise Ketterer (R)	Marilyn Pierce (R)	Diane Perkins (R)
Green	Sherri Hawkins (R)	Cynthia A. Meudt (R)	Carol K. Thompson (R)
Green Lake	Kathleen A. Morris (R)	Leone Seaman (R)	Susan J. Krueger (R)
Iowa	Jolene Millard (R)	Dixie Edge (R)	Carolyn K. Olson (R)
Iron	Mark Beaupré (D)	Robert Traczyk (D)	Karen Ransanici (D)
Jackson	Carol Bue (D)	Shari Marg (D)	Claudia Singleton (D)
Jefferson	John E. Jensen (R)	Larry D. Eckert (R)	Kenneth M. Schopen (R)
Juneau	Ann Marie Vinopal (R)	Christie L. Bender (R)	Louise Schulz (R)
Kenosha	Teri A. Jacobson (D)	Louise I. Principe (D)	Gail Gentz (D)
Kewaunee	Annette A. Teske (R)	Marilyn G. Mueller (D)	Lorraine Riemer (R)
La Crosse	Donna M. Hanson (R)	Deborah J. Flock (R)	Pamela Radtke (R)
Lafayette	Rebecca Taylor (R)	Joseph Boll (R)	Catherine McGowan (R)
Langlade	Janice Burkhart (D)	Sandra M. Fischer (D)	Victoria Adamski (D)
Lincoln	Jan Lemmer (D)	Jolene C. Callahan (R)	Cindy L. Kimmon (R)
Manitowoc	Edwin P. Brey (D)	Preston F. Jones (D)	Lynn Zigmunt (D)
Marathon	Lorraine I. Beyersdorff (R)	Michael J. Sydow (D)	Diane L. Sennholz (D)
Marinette	Cris J. Faucett (R)	Melanie I. Huempfner (R)	Linda L. Dumke-Marquardt (R)
Marquette	Diana Campbell (R)	Bernice M. Wegner (R)	Mary Lou Schmidt (R)
Menominee	Barbara Frechette-Kelley (D)	Pamela J. Waukau (D)	Pamela J. Waukau (D)
Milwaukee	Daniel Diliberti (D)	John LaFave (D)	John W. Barrett (D)
Monroe	Annette M. Erickson (R)	John D. Burke (R)	Carol Thorsen (R)
Oconto	Victoria Coopman (R)	Loralee Lasley (R)	Michael C. Hodkiewicz (R)
Oneida	Jennie Huber (R)	Thomas H. Leighton (R)	Kenneth J. Gardner (R)
Outagamie	Dina Mumford (R)	Janice Flenz (R)	Lonnie Wolf (R)
Ozaukee	Karen L. Makoutz (R)	Ronald A. Voigt (R)	Jeffrey S. Schmidt (R)
Pepin	Nancy M. Richardson (R)	Rita M. Conlin (R)	Rosemary E. Carlisle (R)
Pierce	P. Leland Skog (R)	Vicki J. Nelson (R)	Peg Feuerhelm (D)
Polk	Amanda C. Nissen (D)	Laurie Anderson (D)	Lois Hoff (R)
Portage	Stephanie Stokes (D)	Cynthia A. Wisinski (D)	Bernadette A. Flatoff (D)
Price	Lynn M. Neeck (D)	Judith L. Chizek (D)	Chris Cress (D)
Racine	Elizabeth A. Majeski (R)	James Ladwig (R)	Taraesa L. Wheary (R)
Richland	Julie Keller (R)	Susan Triggs (R)	Ann Robinson (R)
Rock	Vicki Brown (D)	Randy Leyes (R)	Eldred Mielke (D)
Rusk	Joanne Phetteplace (R)	Linda Ann Effertz (D)	Renae R. Baxter (D)
St. Croix	Cheryl A. Slind (R)	Kathleen H. Walsh (D)	Lori N. Meyer (R)
Sauk	Patricia L. Carignan (R)	Brent Bailey (R)	Donna Mueller (R)
Sawyer	Dianne M. Ince (R)	Paula Chisser (R)	Ricki Briggs (R)
Shawano	Kay Schroeder (R)	Amy Dillenburg (R)	Susan M. Krueger (R)
Sheboygan	Laura Henning-Lorenz (D)	Darlene I. Navis (D)	Nan G. Todd (D)
Taylor	Mary Ann Kropp (R)	Marvel A. Lemke (R)	Yvonne B. Bauer (R)
Trempealeau	Laurie Halama (D)	Rose Ottum (D)	Angeline J. Sylla (R)
Vernon	Sandra Vold-Brudos (R)	Konna Spaeth (R)	Kathy Buros (R)
Vilas	Jerri Radtke (R)	Joan E. Hansen (R)	Jean Numrich (R)
Walworth	Kathy M. DuBois (R)	Connie J. Woolever (R)	Sheila T. Reiff (R)
Washburn	Janet L. Ullom (R)	Diane M. Poach (R)	DeeAnn C. McLellan (D)
Washington	Janice Gettelman (R)	Sharon Martin (R)	Kristine M. Deiss (R)
Waukesha	Pamela Reeves (R)	Michael J. Hasslinger (R)	Carolyn T. Evenson (R)
Waupaca	James W. Goeser (R)	George E. Jorgensen (R)	Terrie J. Tews (R)
Waushara	Elaine Wedell (R)	Gary Schindler (R)	Jane Putskey (R)
Winnebago	Mary Krueger (R)	Julie Pagel (R)	Diane Fremgen (D)
Wood	Karen J. Kubisiak (D)	René L. Krause (D)	Cindy L. Joosten (R)

COUNTY OFFICERS IN WISCONSIN
June 30, 2005–Continued

County	District Attorney	Sheriff	Coroner/Medical Examiner
Adams	Mark Thibodeau (D)	Roberta Sindelar (D)	George J. Coulter (R)
Ashland	Sean Duffy (R)	John Kovach (D)	Barbara Beeksma (D)
Barron	Angela L. Holmstrom (D)	Thomas J. Richie (D)	Thomas Aydt (ME)
Bayfield	Craig Haukaas (R)	Robert K. Follis (D)	Gary Victorson (D)
Brown	John P. Zakowski (R)	Dennis N. Kocken (R)	Alan G. Klimek (ME)
Buffalo	Thomas Clark (A)	Bernard Brunkow (A)	Peter A. Samb (R)
Burnett	Kenneth L. Kutz (D)	Dean W. Roland (R)	Patrick Taylor (ME)
Calumet	Kenneth R. Kratz (R)	Gerald A. Pagel (R)	Michael Klaeser (ME)
Chippewa	Jon M. Theisen (R)	Douglas J. Ellis (D)	Katherine Gerrits (D)
Clark	Darwin Zwieg (D)	Louis Rosandich (R)	Richard Schleifer (R)
Columbia	Jane E. Kohlwey (R)	Steven R. Rowe (R)	Marc T. Playman (R)
Crawford	Timothy C. Baxter (D)	Robert L. Ostrander (D)	Camille Smith (D)
Dane	Brian Blanchard (D)	Gary Hamblin (R)	John E. Stanley (D)
Dodge	Steven Bauer (R)	Todd M. Nehls (R)	John Burgbacher (ME)
Door	Raymond Pelrine (R)	Terry Vogel (R)	Vacancy (ME)
Douglas	Daniel Blank (D)	Tom Dalbec (D)	Darrell Witt (ME)
Dunn	James M. Peterson (R)	Dennis Smith (D)	Chris Kruse (ME)
Eau Claire	G. Richard White (R)	Ronald Cramer (R)	Thomas Thelen (ME)
Florence	Douglas J. Drexler (R)	Jeffery Rickaby (R)	Mary T. Johnson (R)
Fond du Lac	Thomas L. Storm (R)	Gary M. Pucker (R)	Jeffrey Jentzen (ME)
Forest	Leon Stenz (R)	Roger W. Wilson (D)	Peter G. Meisinger (ME)
Grant	Lisa Riniker (R)	Keith Govier (R)	Ronald Sturmer (R)
Green	Gary L. Luhman (R)	Randy Roderick (R)	Janet S. Perry (R)
Green Lake	James W. Camp (R)	Michael M. Handel (R)	Darlene Strey (R)
Iowa	Erik Peterson (R)	Steve Michek (R)	Bill Finley (D)
Iron	Martin Lipske (D)	Robert Bruneau (D)	Paul Samardich (D)
Jackson	Anna L. Becker (D)	Richard Young (R)	Ruth Garbers (D)
Jefferson	David J. Wambach (R)	Paul Milbrath (R)	Patrick J. Theder (R)
Juneau	Tracey Braun (R)	Brent H. Oleson (R)	Howard T. Fischer (R)
Kenosha	Robert J. Jambois (D)	David G. Beth (R)	Vacancy (ME)
Kewaunee	Andrew Naze (D)	John Cmeyla (D)	David Hudson (R)
La Crosse	Scott L. Horne (R)	Michael J. Weissenberger (R)	John Steers (ME)
Lafayette	Charlotte Doherty (D)	Scott Pedley (R)	A. Virginia Douglas (D)
Langlade	Ralph M. Uttke (R)	David C. Steger (R)	Larry E. Shadick (R)
Lincoln	Don Dunphy (R)	Tom Koth (R)	David Haskins (D)
Manitowoc	Mark Rohrer (D)	Ken Petersen (D)	Debra J. Kakatsch (D)
Marathon	Jill N. Falstad (D)	Randy Hoenisch (D)	John Larson (ME)
Marinette	Joseph J. Klumb (R)	Michael D. Kessler (R)	George F. Smith (R)
Marquette	Richard Dufour (R)	Ray Fullmer (R)	Thomas G. Wastart II (R)
Menominee	Gary R. Bruno (R)[2]	Bryan S. Lepscier, Sr. (D)	Robert J. Webster (D)
Milwaukee	E. Michael McCann (D)	David A. Clarke, Jr. (D)	Jeffrey M. Jentzen (ME)
Monroe	Dan Cary (R)	Peter Quinn (A)	Toni Eddy-Ballman (ME)
Oconto	Jay Conley (R)	Michael Jansen (R)	Laurie Parisey (R)
Oneida	Patrick F. O'Melia (R)	Jeff Hoffman (A)	Ronald Koth (ME)
Outagamie	Carrie A. Schneider (R)	Bradley G. Gehring (R)	Ruth Ann Wulgaert (R)
Ozaukee	Sandy A. Williams (R)	Maury A. Straub (R)	John R. Holicek (R)
Pepin	Jon D. Seifert (D)	John C. Andrews (D)	Duane A. Sinz (I)
Pierce	John M. O'Boyle (D)	Everett Muhlhausen (R)	Sue Dzubay (R)
Polk	Karen R. Olson (D)	Ann Hraychuck (D)	Jonn B. Dinnies (ME)
Portage	Thomas B. Eagon (D)	John Charewicz (D)	Scott W. Rifleman (R)
Price	Mark Fuhr (D)	Wallace C. Krenzke (D)	James Dalbesio III (D)
Racine	Michael Nieskes (R)	Robert Carlson (D)	Thomas A. Terry (ME)
Richland	Wm. Andrew Sharp (R)	Darrell Berglin (R)	Ralph W. Shireman (R)
Rock	David J. O'Leary (D)	Eric A. Runaas (D)	Jenifer Keach (A)
Rusk	Kathleen A. Pakes (D)	David Kaminski (D)	Annette Grotzinger (I)
St. Croix	Eric G. Johnson (R)	Dennis D. Hillstead (R)	Cynthia Litzell (ME)
Sauk	Patricia A. Barrett (R)	Randy M. Stammen (R)	Betty A. Hinze (R)
Sawyer	Thomas Van Roy (R)	James Meier (R)	Dean Pearson (R)
Shawano	Gary R. Bruno (R)[2]	Robert A. Schmidt (R)	Marcus Jesse (R)
Sheboygan	Joe DeCecco (D)	Michael Helmke (D)	David J. Leffin (D)
Taylor	Karl J. Kelz (R)	Jack Kay (D)	Scott Perrin (ME)
Trempealeau	Jeri Marsolek (D)	Randy Niederkorn (D)	Bonnie Kindschy (D)
Vernon	Timothy Gaskell (D)	Gene Cary (R)	Janet L. Reed (R)
Vilas	Albert Moustakis (R)	John A. Niebuhr (R)	Paul Tirpe (R)
Walworth	Phillip A. Koss (R)	David Graves (R)	John T. Griebel (R)
Washburn	J. Michael Bitney (R)	Terrence C. Dryden (R)	Karen L. Baker (R)
Washington	Todd K. Martens (R)	Brian Rahm (D)	Pamela A. Monroe (ME)
Waukesha	Paul E. Bucher (R)	Dan Trawicki (R)	Lynda Biedrzycki (ME)
Waupaca	John P. Snider (R)	Steve Liebe (R)	Barry Tomaras (R)
Waushara	Michelle Pennewell (A)[3]	David R. Peterson (R)	Roland Handel (R)
Winnebago	William Lennon (R)	Michael Brooks (R)	Barry L. Busby (R)
Wood	Todd P. Wolf (R)	Thomas Reichert (A)	Garry R. Kronstedt (R)

COUNTY OFFICERS IN WISCONSIN
June 30, 2005–Continued

County	Surveyor[4]	County	Surveyor[4]
Adams	Gregory Rhinehart	Marathon	Chester Nowaczyk
Ashland	David Carlson	Marinette	Jerome A. Pillath
Barron	Mark Netterland	Marquette	Jerol Smart
Bayfield	Robert Mick	Menominee	Mike Miller
Brown	Vacancy	Milwaukee	None
Buffalo	Joseph P. Nelson	Monroe	Garold A. Sime (R)
Burnett	Kathleen E. Swingle	Oconto	Mark Teuteberg
Calumet	Patrick Worden	Oneida	Michael J. Romportl[5]
Chippewa	Steven J. Johnson	Outagamie	James Hebert
Clark	Wade Pettit	Ozaukee	Mark Banton
Columbia	James Grothman	Pepin	Ron Jasperson
Crawford	Richard Marx	Pierce	Robert Lannan
Dane	Vacancy	Polk	Steve Geiger
Dodge	Jerry Thomasen	Portage	Joseph S. Glodowski (D)
Door	None	Price	Alfred Schneider
Douglas	Norbert Rehder	Racine	Dennis Stephan
Dunn	Leon Herrick	Richland	Michael Goebel
Eau Claire	Matt Janiak	Rock	Donald Barnes
Florence	None	Rusk	David Kaiser
Fond du Lac	Norman G. Hakala	St. Croix	Brian Halling
Forest	None	Sauk	Patrick Dederich (D)
Grant	Larry Austin	Sawyer	Dan Ploeger
Green	None	Shawano	Robert W. Nordin
Green Lake	Al Shute	Sheboygan	Edgar Harvey, Jr.
Iowa	Bruce Bowden (R)	Taylor	Robert Meyer
Iron	None	Trempealeau	None
Jackson	John Ellingson	Vernon	Curtis Cummer
Jefferson	Thomas R. Wollin	Vilas	Thomas Boettcher (R)
Juneau	Bryan Meyer	Walworth	Lee Kreblin
Kenosha	None	Washburn	Steven J. Waak
Kewaunee	None	Washington	Scott Schmidt
La Crosse	William Jung	Waukesha	Vacancy
Lafayette	Larry Schmidt	Waupaca	Joseph Glodowski
Langlade	David Tlusty	Waushara	Michael Moe
Lincoln	Anthony Dallman	Winnebago	None
Manitowoc	None	Wood	Wayne O. Basler (R)

Key: A – Appointed without party designation; AC – Administrative Coordinator; CA – County Administrator; CE – County Executive; D – Democrat; I – Independent; R – Republican; ME – Medical Examiner.

Note: All officers are elected countywide with the exception of the county board chairperson, county administrator, administrative coordinator, and medical examiner, who are elected or appointed by the county board. Elected county officers serve 2-year terms, except county executives who serve 4-year terms. Beginning 2003, sheriffs serve 4-year terms per constitutional amendment ratified 11/3/98. Reflecting a constitutional amendment ratified 4/5/2005, beginning 2006, clerks of circuit court and coroners will serve 4-year terms; beginning 2008, all remaining county officers will serve 4-year terms.

[1]Counties with a population of 500,000 or more are statutorily required to establish the office of county executive. Smaller counties may establish the office of county executive or name a county administrator. In counties without a county executive or county administrator, the county board must designate an elected or appointed official to serve as administrative coordinator.

[2]Menominee and Shawano Counties have a joint district attorney's office located in Shawano County.

[3]Appointed by governor for a term to commence on August 1, 2005.

[4]County boards are permitted to designate any registered land surveyor to perform the duties of the county surveyor. Surveyors are appointed unless party designation is shown.

[5]Land information director.

Source: Data collected from county clerks by Wisconsin Legislative Reference Bureau, November 2004, and governor's appointment notices.

WISCONSIN CITIES
January 1, 2005

City (Year Incorporated)[1]	County	2000 Census	2004 Estimate	Percent Change	2000 Nonwhite[4]	2000 Hispanic
First Class Cities (150,000 or more) — 1 City						
Milwaukee (1846)	Milwaukee, Washington, Waukesha .	596,974	593,920	−0.51%	254,339	71,646
Second Class Cities (39,000 to 149,999) — 15 Cities						
Appleton (1857)	Calumet, Outagamie, Winnebago ...	70,087	71,895	2.58	5,063	1,775
Brookfield (1954)	Waukesha	38,649	39,607	2.48	2,145	453
Eau Claire (1872)[3]	Chippewa, Eau Claire	61,704	63,897	3.55	3,777	619
Fond du Lac (1852)[3]	Fond du Lac	42,203	42,865	1.57	2,065	1,232
Green Bay (1854)	Brown	102,767	103,653	0.86	9,885	7,294
Janesville (1853)[3]	Rock	60,200	61,310	1.84	2,089	1,569
Kenosha (1850)[2]	Kenosha	90,352	92,808	2.72	9,663	9,003
La Crosse (1856)	La Crosse	51,818	51,507	−0.60	4,068	592
Madison (1856)	Dane	208,054	217,935	4.75	29,033	8,512
Oshkosh (1853)[3]	Winnebago	62,916	65,095	3.46	4,105	1,062
Racine (1848)[2]	Racine	81,855	80,806	−1.28	18,471	11,422
Sheboygan (1853)	Sheboygan	50,792	50,672	−0.24	4,569	3,034
Superior (1858)	Douglas	27,368	27,221	−0.54	1,465	226
Wauwatosa (1897)[2]	Milwaukee	47,271	46,511	−1.61	2,523	813
West Allis (1906)[2]	Milwaukee	61,254	60,607	−1.06	2,667	2,155
Third Class Cities (10,000 to 38,999) — 29 Cities						
Baraboo (1882)[2]	Sauk	10,711	11,188	4.45	243	168
Beloit (1857)[3]	Rock	35,775	36,058	0.79	6,786	3,257
Chippewa Falls (1869) ...	Chippewa	12,925	13,155	1.78	264	82
Cudahy (1906)	Milwaukee	18,429	18,315	−0.62	743	872
De Pere (1883)[2]	Brown	20,559	22,038	7.19	619	202
Franklin (1956)[2]	Milwaukee	29,494	31,804	7.83	2,427	780
Glendale (1950)[2]	Milwaukee	13,367	13,024	−2.57	1,672	236
Greenfield (1957)	Milwaukee	35,476	36,059	1.64	1,588	1,376
Hartford (1883)[2]	Dodge, Washington	10,905	12,068	10.66	188	326
Kaukauna (1885)	Outagamie	12,983	13,926	7.26	537	103
Manitowoc (1870)	Manitowoc	34,053	34,612	1.64	1,941	859
Marinette (1887)	Marinette	11,741	11,638	−0.94	252	123
Marshfield (1883)[2]	Marathon, Wood	18,800	19,012	1.13	496	146
Menasha (1874)	Calumet, Winnebago	16,331	16,779	2.74	570	590
Middleton (1963)[2]	Dane	15,770	16,446	4.29	1,018	444
Muskego (1964)	Waukesha	21,397	22,203	3.77	306	281
Neenah (1873)	Winnebago	24,507	25,193	2.80	717	495
New Berlin (1959)	Waukesha	38,220	38,896	1.77	1,360	595
Oconomowoc (1875)[2] ...	Waukesha	12,382	13,194	6.56	203	204
Pewaukee (1999)[2]	Waukesha	11,783	12,425	5.45	261	153
River Falls (1875)[2]	Pierce, St. Croix	12,560	13,067	4.04	378	119
Stevens Point (1858)	Portage	24,551	25,094	2.21	1,677	395
Sun Prairie (1958)[2]	Dane	20,369	23,226	14.03	1,243	555
Two Rivers (1878)[3]	Manitowoc	12,639	12,599	−0.32	458	170
Watertown (1853)	Dodge, Jefferson	21,598	22,732	5.25	409	1,067
Waukesha (1895)[2]	Waukesha	64,825	66,816	3.07	3,071	5,563
Wausau (1872)	Marathon	38,426	38,912	1.26	5,226	398
West Bend (1885)[2]	Washington	28,152	29,204	3.74	554	519
Wisconsin Rapids (1869) .	Wood	18,435	18,410	−0.14	998	242
Fourth Class Cities (under 10,000) — 145 Cities						
Abbotsford (1965)	Clark, Marathon	1,956	2,001	3.41	15	39
Adams (1926)[2]	Adams	1,831	1,843	0.66	30	37
Algoma (1879)[2]	Kewaunee	3,357	3,322	−1.04	29	33
Alma (1885)	Buffalo	942	937	−0.53	26	8
Altoona (1887)[2]	Eau Claire	6,698	6,719	0.31	245	49
Amery (1919)[2]	Polk	2,845	2,902	2.00	49	27
Antigo (1885)[2]	Langlade	8,560	8,586	0.30	203	103
Arcadia (1925)	Trempealeau	2,402	2,373	−1.21	21	74
Ashland (1887)[2]	Ashland, Bayfield	8,620	8,577	−0.50	779	118
Augusta (1885)	Eau Claire	1,460	1,463	0.21	46	19
Barron (1887)	Barron	3,248	3,319	2.19	60	61
Bayfield (1913)	Bayfield	611	616	0.82	139	3
Beaver Dam (1856)	Dodge	15,169	15,366	1.30	292	640
Berlin (1857)[2]	Green Lake, Waushara	5,305	5,326	0.40	95	242
Black River Falls (1883) .	Jackson	3,618	3,627	0.25	214	42
Blair (1949)	Trempealeau	1,273	1,296	1.81	9	17
Bloomer (1920)	Chippewa	3,347	3,446	2.96	29	11

WISCONSIN CITIES
January 1, 2005–Continued

City (Year Incorporated)[1]	County	Population[4]				
		2000 Census	2004 Estimate	Percent Change	2000 Nonwhite[4]	2000 Hispanic
Boscobel (1873)[2]	Grant	3,047	3,403	11.68	146	36
Brillion (1944)[2]	Calumet	2,937	2,969	1.09	34	15
Brodhead (1891)	Green, Rock	3,180	3,181	0.03	44	31
Buffalo (1859)	Buffalo	1,040	1,059	1.83	14	6
Burlington (1900)[2]	Racine, Walworth	9,936	10,183	2.49	177	462
Cedarburg (1885)[2]	Ozaukee	11,102	11,331	2.06	185	94
Chetek (1891)	Barron	2,180	2,242	2.84	24	21
Chilton (1877)	Calumet	3,708	3,760	1.40	46	32
Clintonville (1887)[2]	Waupaca	4,736	4,675	-1.29	82	102
Colby (1891)	Clark, Marathon	1,616	1,706	5.57	25	62
Columbus (1874)[2]	Columbia, Dodge	4,479	4,704	5.02	63	44
Cornell (1956)[2]	Chippewa	1,466	1,447	-1.30	20	5
Crandon (1898)	Forest	1,961	1,962	0.05	165	18
Cuba City (1925)	Grant, Lafayette	2,156	2,155	-0.05	10	2
Cumberland (1885)	Barron	2,280	2,341	2.68	53	17
Darlington (1877)	Lafayette	2,418	2,416	-0.08	15	27
Delafield (1959)[2]	Waukesha	6,472	6,720	3.83	109	95
Delavan (1897)[2]	Walworth	7,956	8,158	2.54	271	1,690
Dodgeville (1889)	Iowa	4,220	4,479	6.14	75	18
Durand (1887)	Pepin	1,968	1,976	0.41	19	4
Eagle River (1937)[2]	Vilas	1,443	1,481	2.63	55	12
Edgerton (1883)[2]	Dane, Rock	4,898	5,017	2.43	104	188
Elkhorn (1897)[2]	Walworth	7,305	8,191	12.13	140	448
Elroy (1885)[2]	Juneau	1,578	1,558	-1.27	16	20
Evansville (1896)[2]	Rock	4,039	4,409	9.16	62	72
Fennimore (1919)	Grant	2,387	2,388	0.04	12	18
Fitchburg (1983)[2]	Dane	20,501	22,030	7.46	2,863	1,329
Fort Atkinson (1878)[3]	Jefferson	11,621	11,943	2.77	209	508
Fountain City (1889)	Buffalo	983	1,000	1.73	5	1
Fox Lake (1938)[2]	Dodge	1,454	1,477	1.58	24	51
Galesville (1942)	Trempealeau	1,427	1,445	1.26	12	6
Gillett (1944)	Oconto	1,262	1,256	-0.48	34	11
Glenwood City (1895)	St. Croix	1,183	1,231	4.06	11	2
Green Lake (1962)	Green Lake	1,100	1,135	3.18	9	10
Greenwood (1891)	Clark	1,079	1,087	0.74	5	12
Hayward (1915)	Sawyer	2,129	2,230	4.74	216	18
Hillsboro (1885)[2]	Vernon	1,302	1,299	-0.23	8	9
Horicon (1897)	Dodge	3,775	3,747	-0.74	49	79
Hudson (1857)[2]	St. Croix	8,775	10,561	20.35	151	91
Hurley (1918)	Iron	1,818	1,805	-0.72	42	16
Independence (1942)	Trempealeau	1,244	1,262	1.45	7	20
Jefferson (1878)[2]	Jefferson	7,208	7,458	3.47	154	498
Juneau (1887)	Dodge	2,485	2,656	6.88	19	63
Kewaunee (1883)[2]	Kewaunee	2,806	2,892	3.06	43	16
Kiel (1920)[2]	Calumet, Manitowoc	3,450	3,538	2.55	37	25
Ladysmith (1905)[2]	Rusk	3,932	3,760	-4.37	135	30
Lake Geneva (1883)[2]	Walworth	7,148	7,276	1.79	186	1,054
Lake Mills (1905)[3]	Jefferson	4,843	4,971	2.64	83	113
Lancaster (1878)[2]	Grant	4,070	4,042	-0.69	27	17
Lodi (1941)	Columbia	2,882	2,949	2.32	32	29
Loyal (1948)	Clark	1,308	1,309	0.08	14	10
Manawa (1954)	Waupaca	1,330	1,349	1.43	12	18
Marion (1898)	Shawano, Waupaca	1,297	1,302	0.39	8	1
Markesan (1959)	Green Lake	1,396	1,373	-1.65	6	44
Mauston (1883)[2]	Juneau	3,740	4,133	10.51	100	79
Mayville (1885)	Dodge	4,902	5,164	5.34	40	71
Medford (1889)[2]	Taylor	4,350	4,311	-0.90	55	25
Mellen (1907)	Ashland	845	834	-1.30	24	8
Menomonie (1882)[2]	Dunn	14,937	15,247	2.08	828	170
Mequon (1957)[2]	Ozaukee	22,643	23,416	3.41	1,202	261

WISCONSIN CITIES
January 1, 2005–Continued

City (Year Incorporated)[1]	County	2000 Census	2004 Estimate	Percent Change	2000 Nonwhite[4]	2000 Hispanic
				Population[4]		
Merrill (1883)	Lincoln	10,146	10,144	-0.02	173	104
Milton (1969)[2]	Rock	5,132	5,419	5.59	64	47
Mineral Point (1857)	Iowa	2,617	2,636	0.73	24	11
Mondovi (1889)[2]	Buffalo	2,634	2,688	2.05	33	12
Monona (1969)[2]	Dane	8,018	7,965	-0.66	384	256
Monroe (1882)	Green	10,843	10,973	1.20	168	158
Montello (1938)	Marquette	1,397	1,447	3.58	34	33
Montreal (1924)	Iron	838	834	-0.48	10	6
Mosinee (1931)[2]	Marathon	4,063	4,162	2.44	35	28
Neillsville (1882)	Clark	2,731	2,716	-0.55	81	26
Nekoosa (1926)	Wood	2,590	2,593	0.12	52	47
New Holstein (1926)	Calumet	3,301	3,313	0.36	38	19
New Lisbon (1889)	Juneau	1,436	1,429	-0.49	28	20
New London (1877)[2]	Outagamie, Waupaca	7,085	7,232	2.07	135	174
New Richmond (1885)[2]	St. Croix	6,310	7,244	14.80	93	49
Niagara (1992)[2]	Marinette	1,880	1,858	-1.17	9	14
Oak Creek (1955)[2]	Milwaukee	28,456	31,029	9.04	1,675	1,267
Oconto (1869)	Oconto	4,708	4,711	0.06	89	37
Oconto Falls (1919)[2]	Oconto	2,843	2,883	1.41	49	12
Omro (1944)[2]	Winnebago	3,177	3,312	4.25	32	88
Onalaska (1887)	La Crosse	14,839	15,782	6.35	658	141
Osseo (1941)	Trempealeau	1,669	1,669	0.00	12	6
Owen (1925)	Clark	936	931	-0.53	12	4
Park Falls (1912)	Price	2,793	2,689	-3.72	53	30
Peshtigo (1903)	Marinette	3,474	3,499	0.72	61	25
Phillips (1891)	Price	1,675	1,676	0.06	49	6
Pittsville (1887)	Wood	866	885	2.19	8	2
Platteville (1876)[3]	Grant	9,989	10,109	1.20	348	88
Plymouth (1877)	Sheboygan	7,781	8,080	3.84	95	86
Port Washington (1882)[2]	Ozaukee	10,467	10,683	2.06	243	168
Portage (1854)	Columbia	9,728	9,966	2.45	575	330
Prairie du Chien (1872)[2]	Crawford	6,018	6,053	0.58	287	53
Prescott (1857)[2]	Pierce	3,764	3,873	2.90	56	46
Princeton (1920)	Green Lake	1,504	1,476	-1.86	16	12
Reedsburg (1887)[2]	Sauk	7,827	8,573	9.53	135	124
Rhinelander (1894)	Oneida	7,735	8,041	3.96	215	56
Rice Lake (1887)[2]	Barron	8,312	8,490	2.14	187	125
Richland Center (1887)	Richland	5,114	5,151	0.72	72	47
Ripon (1858)[2]	Fond du Lac	7,450	7,619	2.27	88	151
St. Croix Falls (1958)	Polk	2,033	2,102	3.39	19	27
St. Francis (1951)[2]	Milwaukee	8,662	8,728	0.76	356	392
Schofield (1951)	Marathon	2,117	2,250	6.28	76	28
Seymour (1879)	Outagamie	3,335	3,400	1.95	126	40
Shawano (1874)[2]	Shawano	8,298	8,425	1.53	818	134
Sheboygan Falls (1913)	Sheboygan	6,772	7,139	5.42	108	58
Shell Lake (1961)[2]	Washburn	1,309	1,338	2.22	16	13
Shullsburg (1889)	Lafayette	1,246	1,228	-1.44	6	0
South Milwaukee (1897)	Milwaukee	21,256	21,360	0.49	722	852
Sparta (1883)[2]	Monroe	8,648	8,994	4.00	196	157
Spooner (1909)[2]	Washburn	2,653	2,705	1.96	85	32
Stanley (1898)	Chippewa, Clark	1,898	3,378	77.98	16	24
Stoughton (1882)	Dane	12,354	12,654	2.43	347	153
Sturgeon Bay (1883)[2]	Door	9,437	9,696	2.74	195	121
Thorp (1948)	Clark	1,536	1,569	2.15	7	9
Tomah (1883)[2]	Monroe	8,419	8,648	2.72	368	119
Tomahawk (1891)	Lincoln	3,770	3,789	0.50	67	29
Verona (1977)[2]	Dane	7,052	8,888	26.04	161	50
Viroqua (1885)[2]	Vernon	4,335	4,362	0.62	48	30
Washburn (1904)[2]	Bayfield	2,280	2,284	0.18	176	15
Waterloo (1962)	Jefferson	3,259	3,310	1.56	50	240
Waupaca (1875)[2]	Waupaca	5,676	5,821	2.55	113	194
Waupun (1878)[2]	Dodge, Fond du Lac	10,718	10,670	-0.45	1,427	304
Wautoma (1901)	Waushara	1,998	2,115	5.86	58	144

WISCONSIN CITIES
January 1, 2005–Continued

		Population[4]				
City (Year Incorporated)[1]	County	2000 Census	2004 Estimate	Percent Change	2000 Nonwhite[4]	2000 Hispanic
Westby (1920)	Vernon	2,045	2,113	3.33	6	19
Weyauwega (1939)[2]	Waupaca	1,806	1,896	4.98	31	17
Whitehall (1941)[2]	Trempealeau	1,651	1,666	0.91	5	5
Whitewater (1885)[3]	Jefferson, Walworth	13,437	13,996	4.16	632	873
Wisconsin Dells (1925) ..	Adams, Columbia, Sauk	2,418	2,457	1.61	47	41

Note: A city is not automatically reclassified based on changes in population but must take action to initiate a reclassification. Under Section 62.05(2), Wisconsin Statutes, to change from one class to another a city must: 1) meet the required population size according to the last federal census; 2) fulfill required governmental changes; and 3) publish a mayoral proclamation.

[1]There are 190 cities in Wisconsin as of January 1, 2005.

[2]One of 82 cities with a city administrator holding a full-time or combined position.

[3]One of 10 cities with a city manager.

[4]Population totals include corrections made by the U.S. Census Bureau through 8/28/2002. Race and ethnicity data have not been adjusted. Population estimates are based on the corrected totals.

[5]In the 2000 U.S. Census, respondents were allowed to choose more than one race. The column "nonwhite" includes all who chose at least one race other than white.

Sources: Wisconsin Department of Administration, Division of Intergovernmental Relations, Demographic Services Center, *Official Population Estimate of Wisconsin Municipalities*, January 1, 2004; League of Wisconsin Municipalities, *Directory of Wisconsin City and Village Officials*, August 2004; and data collected by Wisconsin Legislative Reference Bureau.

WISCONSIN VILLAGES
January 1, 2005

		Population				
Village (Year Incorporated)[1]	County	2000 Census	2004 Estimate	Percent Change	2000 Nonwhite	2000 Hispanic
Adell (1918)	Sheboygan	517	519	0.39%	11	12
Albany (1883)	Green	1,191	1,180	−0.92	12	14
Allouez (1986)[2]	Brown	15,443	15,494	0.33	1,105	199
Alma Center (1902)	Jackson	446	458	2.69	5	7
Almena (1945)	Barron	720	750	4.17	15	11
Almond (1905)	Portage	459	451	−1.74	2	33
Amherst (1899)	Portage	964	1,027	6.54	8	5
Amherst Junction (1912)	Portage	305	328	7.54	0	0
Aniwa (1899)	Shawano	272	269	−1.10	8	3
Arena (1923)	Iowa	685	764	11.53	10	5
Argyle (1903)	Lafayette	823	817	−0.73	1	6
Arlington (1945)[2]	Columbia	484	547	13.02	2	3
Arpin (1978)	Wood	337	337	0.00	4	4
Ashwaubenon (1977)[2]	Brown	17,634	17,661	0.15	763	202
Athens (1901)	Marathon	1,095	1,111	1.46	8	23
Auburndale (1881)	Wood	738	763	3.39	0	0
Avoca (1870)	Iowa	608	623	2.47	10	3
Bagley (1919)	Grant	339	340	0.29	9	5
Baldwin (1875)[2]	St. Croix	2,667	3,253	21.97	38	11
Balsam Lake (1905)	Polk	950	1,012	6.53	37	4
Bangor (1899)	La Crosse	1,400	1,394	−0.43	25	9
Barneveld (1906)	Iowa	1,088	1,153	5.97	14	1
Bay City (1909)	Pierce	491	503	2.44	4	0
Bayside (1953)[3]	Milwaukee, Ozaukee	4,518	4,286	−5.14	241	77
Bear Creek (1902)	Outagamie	415	422	1.69	4	45
Belgium (1922)	Ozaukee	1,678	1,887	12.46	31	69
Bell Center (1901)	Crawford	116	116	0.00	1	0
Belleville (1892)	Dane, Green	1,908	2,030	6.39	27	15
Bellevue (2003)[2,4]	Brown	11,828	13,836	16.98	374	310
Belmont (1894)	Lafayette	871	898	3.10	3	1
Benton (1892)	Lafayette	976	998	2.25	16	0
Big Bend (1928)	Waukesha	1,278	1,286	0.63	26	23
Big Falls (1925)	Waupaca	85	84	−1.18	1	0
Birchwood (1921)	Washburn	518	533	2.90	15	12
Birnamwood (1895)	Marathon, Shawano	795	812	2.14	19	1
Biron (1910)	Wood	915	897	−1.97	18	16
Black Creek (1904)	Outagamie	1,192	1,218	2.18	20	13
Black Earth (1901)	Dane	1,320	1,313	−0.53	33	16
Blanchardville (1890)	Iowa, Lafayette	806	804	−0.25	5	3
Bloomington (1880)	Grant	701	697	−0.57	2	0
Blue Mounds (1912)	Dane	708	733	3.53	12	7
Blue River (1916)	Grant	429	427	−0.47	1	1
Boaz (1939)	Richland	137	136	−0.73	1	0
Bonduel (1916)	Shawano	1,416	1,442	1.84	25	27
Bowler (1923)	Shawano	343	344	0.29	75	0
Boyceville (1922)	Dunn	1,043	1,075	3.07	15	4
Boyd (1891)	Chippewa	680	677	−0.44	2	1

WISCONSIN VILLAGES
January 1, 2005–Continued

Village (Year Incorporated)[1]	County	2000 Census	2004 Estimate	Percent Change	2000 Nonwhite	2000 Hispanic
Brandon (1881)	Fond du Lac	912	914	0.22	1	7
Brokaw (1903)	Marathon	107	137	28.04	1	2
Brooklyn (1905)	Dane, Green	916	1,046	14.19	12	13
Brown Deer (1955)[3]	Milwaukee	12,170	11,845	-2.67	2,088	260
Brownsville (1952)	Dodge	570	567	-0.53	3	2
Browntown (1890)	Green	252	261	3.57	0	6
Bruce (1901)	Rusk	787	785	-0.25	7	2
Butler (1913)[2]	Waukesha	1,881	1,855	-1.38	48	16
Butternut (1903)	Ashland	407	396	-2.70	7	1
Cadott (1895)	Chippewa	1,345	1,356	0.82	15	2
Cambria (1866)	Columbia	792	785	-0.88	10	51
Cambridge (1891)[2]	Dane, Jefferson	1,101	1,175	6.72	10	11
Cameron (1894)	Barron	1,546	1,681	8.73	28	28
Camp Douglas (1893)	Juneau	592	569	-3.89	10	10
Campbellsport (1902)	Fond du Lac	1,913	1,938	1.31	20	8
Cascade (1914)	Sheboygan	681	698	2.50	8	11
Casco (1920)	Kewaunee	572	583	1.92	9	5
Cashton (1901)	Monroe	1,005	1,043	3.78	6	16
Cassville (1882)	Grant	1,085	1,068	-1.57	8	4
Catawba (1922)	Price	149	141	-5.37	1	0
Cazenovia (1902)	Richland, Sauk	326	351	7.67	2	1
Cecil (1905)	Shawano	466	515	10.52	21	3
Cedar Grove (1899)	Sheboygan	1,887	1,977	4.77	24	50
Centuria (1904)	Polk	865	957	10.64	25	13
Chaseburg (1922)	Vernon	306	291	-4.90	0	0
Chenequa (1928)[2]	Waukesha	583	590	1.20	13	5
Clayton (1909)	Polk	507	540	6.51	11	0
Clear Lake (1894)	Polk	1,051	1,080	2.76	5	33
Cleveland (1958)	Manitowoc	1,361	1,409	3.53	16	20
Clinton (1882)	Rock	2,162	2,235	3.38	38	69
Clyman (1924)	Dodge	388	385	-0.77	10	18
Cobb (1902)	Iowa	442	447	1.13	3	2
Cochrane (1910)	Buffalo	435	421	-3.22	2	4
Coleman (1903)	Marinette	716	719	0.42	3	2
Colfax (1904)	Dunn	1,136	1,154	1.58	9	15
Coloma (1939)	Waushara	461	467	1.30	1	14
Combined Locks (1920)[2]	Outagamie	2,422	2,659	9.79	29	30
Conrath (1915)	Rusk	98	110	12.24	3	0
Coon Valley (1907)	Vernon	714	717	0.42	3	2
Cottage Grove (1924)[2]	Dane	4,059	4,559	12.32	150	73
Couderay (1922)	Sawyer	96	93	-3.13	19	1
Crivitz (1974)	Marinette	998	1,024	2.61	21	11
Cross Plains (1920)[2]	Dane	3,084	3,342	8.37	31	13
Curtiss (1917)	Clark	198	215	8.59	3	68
Dallas (1903)	Barron	356	356	0.00	8	5
Dane (1899)	Dane	799	857	7.26	29	15
Darien (1951)	Walworth	1,572	1,595	1.46	27	222
DeForest (1903)[2]	Dane	7,368	8,061	9.41	272	161
De Soto (1886)	Crawford, Vernon	366	432	18.03	17	6
Deer Park (1913)	St. Croix	227	230	1.32	0	0
Deerfield (1891)[2]	Dane	1,971	2,041	3.55	87	43
Denmark (1915)[2]	Brown	1,958	2,017	3.01	41	6
Dickeyville (1947)	Grant	1,043	1,056	1.25	5	3
Dorchester (1901)	Clark, Marathon	827	854	3.26	8	19
Dousman (1917)	Waukesha	1,584	1,757	10.92	32	37
Downing (1909)	Dunn	257	260	1.17	4	3
Doylestown (1907)	Columbia	328	337	2.74	3	14
Dresser (1919)	Polk	732	789	7.79	12	4
Eagle (1899)	Waukesha	1,707	1,737	1.76	26	52
East Troy (1900)[2]	Walworth	3,564	3,850	8.02	55	105
Eastman (1909)	Crawford	437	448	2.52	4	8
Eden (1912)	Fond du Lac	687	733	6.70	1	29
Edgar (1898)[2]	Marathon	1,386	1,431	3.25	13	2
Egg Harbor (1964)[2]	Door	250	261	4.40	3	0
Eland (1905)	Shawano	251	245	-2.39	17	3
Elderon (1917)	Marathon	189	180	-4.76	0	9
Eleva (1902)	Trempealeau	635	657	3.46	10	0
Elk Mound (1905)	Dunn	785	822	4.71	26	5
Elkhart Lake (1894)	Sheboygan	1,021	1,056	3.43	4	11
Ellsworth (1887)	Pierce	2,909	3,056	5.05	28	33
Elm Grove (1955)[3]	Waukesha	6,249	6,250	0.02	153	75
Elmwood (1905)	Pierce	841	825	-1.90	6	12
Elmwood Park (1960)	Racine	474	464	-2.11	16	6
Embarrass (1895)	Waupaca	487	483	-0.82	0	3
Endeavor (1946)	Marquette	440	449	2.05	11	3
Ephraim (1919)[2]	Door	353	356	0.85	3	1
Ettrick (1948)	Trempealeau	521	532	2.11	7	0
Exeland (1920)	Sawyer	212	206	-2.83	23	3

WISCONSIN VILLAGES
January 1, 2005–Continued

Village (Year Incorporated)[1]	County	2000 Census	2004 Estimate	Percent Change	2000 Nonwhite	2000 Hispanic
				Population		
Fairchild (1880)	Eau Claire	564	518	-8.16	8	10
Fairwater (1921)	Fond du Lac	350	357	2.00	2	0
Fall Creek (1906)	Eau Claire	1,236	1,284	3.88	16	0
Fall River (1903)	Columbia	1,097	1,232	12.31	15	6
Fenwood (1904)	Marathon	174	163	-6.32	0	0
Ferryville (1912)	Crawford	174	182	4.60	2	0
Fontana-on-Geneva Lake (1924)[2]	Walworth	1,754	1,842	5.02	23	19
Footville (1918)	Rock	788	776	-1.52	12	1
Forestville (1960)	Door	429	427	-0.47	4	0
Fox Point (1926)[3]	Milwaukee	7,012	6,886	-1.80	297	74
Francis Creek (1960)	Manitowoc	681	700	2.79	0	6
Frederic (1903)[2]	Polk	1,262	1,244	-1.43	26	5
Fredonia (1922)	Ozaukee	1,934	2,111	9.15	48	27
Fremont (1882)	Waupaca	666	695	4.35	7	7
Friendship (1907)	Adams	781	773	-1.02	36	8
Friesland (1946)	Columbia	298	303	1.68	2	3
Gays Mills (1900)[2]	Crawford	625	627	0.32	2	3
Genoa (1935)	Vernon	263	259	-1.52	5	0
Genoa City (1901)	Kenosha, Walworth	1,949	2,466	26.53	38	63
Germantown (1927)[2]	Washington	18,260	19,001	4.06	680	205
Gilman (1914)	Taylor	474	468	-1.27	3	8
Glen Flora (1915)	Rusk	93	95	2.15	4	0
Glenbeulah (1913)	Sheboygan	378	406	7.41	1	2
Grafton (1896)[2]	Ozaukee	10,464	11,160	6.65	193	165
Granton (1916)	Clark	406	397	-2.22	8	1
Grantsburg (1887)	Burnett	1,369	1,438	5.04	39	16
Gratiot (1891)	Lafayette	252	247	-1.98	2	0
Greendale (1939)[3]	Milwaukee	14,405	14,128	-1.92	458	340
Gresham (1908)[3]	Shawano	575	597	3.83	169	12
Hales Corners (1952)[2]	Milwaukee	7,765	7,682	-1.07	162	162
Hammond (1880)	St. Croix	1,153	1,636	41.89	14	3
Hancock (1902)	Waushara	463	460	-0.65	15	40
Hartland (1891)[2]	Waukesha	7,905	8,267	4.58	132	119
Hatley (1912)	Marathon	476	500	5.04	12	0
Haugen (1918)	Barron	287	288	0.35	0	2
Hawkins (1922)	Rusk	317	349	10.09	6	0
Hazel Green (1867)	Grant, Lafayette	1,183	1,178	-0.42	5	4
Hewitt (1973)	Wood	670	708	5.67	2	2
Highland (1873)	Iowa	855	868	1.52	0	3
Hilbert (1898)	Calumet	1,089	1,106	1.56	11	16
Hixton (1920)	Jackson	446	444	-0.45	6	1
Hobart (2003)[2,5]	Brown	5,090	5,486	7.78	956	44
Hollandale (1910)	Iowa	283	284	0.35	1	1
Holmen (1946)[2]	La Crosse	6,200	6,984	12.65	265	56
Hortonville (1894)[2]	Outagamie	2,357	2,503	6.19	66	15
Howard (1959)[2]	Brown, Outagamie	13,546	15,208	12.27	461	147
Howards Grove (1967)	Sheboygan	2,792	2,926	4.80	24	21
Hustisford (1870)	Dodge	1,135	1,149	1.23	5	14
Hustler (1914)	Juneau	113	118	4.42	0	0
Ingram (1907)	Rusk	76	78	2.63	0	0
Iola (1892)	Waupaca	1,298	1,303	0.39	17	17
Iron Ridge (1913)	Dodge	998	1,003	0.50	5	10
Ironton (1914)	Sauk	250	250	0.00	6	4
Jackson (1912)[2]	Washington	4,938	5,678	14.99	51	61
Johnson Creek (1903)[2]	Jefferson	1,581	1,744	10.31	30	63
Junction City (1911)	Portage	440	432	-1.82	12	19
Kekoskee (1958)	Dodge	169	171	1.18	9	3
Kellnersville (1971)	Manitowoc	374	367	-1.87	5	0
Kendall (1894)	Monroe	482	478	-0.83	1	3
Kennan (1903)	Price	171	166	-2.92	0	3
Kewaskum (1895)[2]	Fond du Lac, Washington	3,277	3,557	8.54	52	30
Kimberly (1910)[2]	Outagamie	6,146	6,362	3.51	138	46
Kingston (1923)	Green Lake	288	296	2.78	4	1
Knapp (1905)	Dunn	421	454	7.84	4	4
Kohler (1912)	Sheboygan	1,926	2,010	4.36	47	16
Kronenwetter (2002)[2,6]	Marathon	5,369	5,791	7.86	—	—
La Farge (1899)	Vernon	775	777	0.26	16	5
La Valle (1883)	Sauk	326	324	-0.61	1	7
Lac La Belle (1931)[7]	Jefferson, Waukesha	329	340	3.34	0	1
Lake Delton (1954)	Sauk	1,982	2,599	31.13	79	33
Lake Hallie (2003)[8]	Chippewa	0	5,345	—	—	—
Lake Nebagamon (1907)	Douglas	1,015	1,017	0.20	13	8
Lannon (1930)	Waukesha	1,009	962	-4.66	18	16
Lena (1921)	Oconto	529	520	-1.70	3	5

WISCONSIN VILLAGES
January 1, 2005–Continued

Village (Year Incorporated)[1]	County	Population 2000 Census	2004 Estimate	Percent Change	2000 Nonwhite	2000 Hispanic
Lime Ridge (1910)	Sauk	169	161	-4.73	0	1
Linden (1900)	Iowa	615	615	0.00	6	0
Little Chute (1899)[2]	Outagamie	10,476	10,775	2.85	203	175
Livingston (1914)	Grant, Iowa	597	589	-1.34	0	2
Loganville (1917)	Sauk	276	274	-0.72	0	1
Lohrville (1910)	Waushara	408	414	1.47	8	9
Lomira (1899)	Dodge	2,233	2,378	6.49	21	57
Lone Rock (1886)	Richland	929	905	-2.58	12	14
Lowell (1894)	Dodge	366	374	2.19	8	12
Lublin (1915)	Taylor	110	102	-7.27	0	0
Luck (1905)	Polk	1,210	1,221	0.91	20	12
Luxemburg (1908)	Kewaunee	1,935	2,147	10.96	19	9
Lyndon Station (1903)	Juneau	458	460	0.44	17	7
Lynxville (1899)	Crawford	176	181	2.84	2	3
Maiden Rock (1887)	Pierce	121	120	-0.83	1	1
Maple Bluff (1930)[3]	Dane	1,358	1,350	-0.59	31	9
Marathon City (1884)[2]	Marathon	1,640	1,618	-1.34	24	5
Maribel (1963)	Manitowoc	284	287	1.06	9	1
Marquette (1958)	Green Lake	169	175	3.55	1	1
Marshall (1905)	Dane	3,432	3,563	3.82	83	138
Mason (1925)	Bayfield	72	79	9.72	9	0
Mattoon (1901)	Shawano	466	461	-1.07	21	2
Mazomanie (1885)	Dane	1,485	1,543	3.91	35	29
McFarland (1920)[2]	Dane	6,416	7,051	9.90	143	73
Melrose (1914)	Jackson	529	519	-1.89	5	4
Melvina (1922)	Monroe	93	89	-4.30	2	0
Menomonee Falls (1892)[3]	Waukesha	32,647	33,660	3.10	1,045	377
Merrillan (1881)	Jackson	585	582	-0.51	24	4
Merrimac (1899)[2]	Sauk	416	423	1.68	8	6
Merton (1922)[2]	Waukesha	1,926	2,185	13.45	25	14
Milladore (1933)	Portage, Wood	268	273	1.87	3	0
Milltown (1910)	Polk	888	904	1.80	18	7
Minong (1915)	Washburn	531	545	2.64	14	4
Mishicot (1950)	Manitowoc	1,422	1,439	1.20	13	4
Montfort (1893)	Grant, Iowa	663	666	0.45	5	0
Monticello (1891)	Green	1,146	1,147	0.09	8	12
Mount Calvary (1962)	Fond du Lac	956	953	-0.31	79	80
Mount Hope (1919)	Grant	186	183	-1.61	0	3
Mount Horeb (1899)[2]	Dane	5,860	6,244	6.55	81	34
Mount Pleasant (2003)[2]	Racine	23,142	24,347	5.21	1,989	1,149
Mount Sterling (1936)	Crawford	215	207	-3.72	2	0
Mukwonago (1905)[2]	Walworth, Waukesha	6,162	6,428	4.32	83	117
Muscoda (1894)	Grant, Iowa	1,453	1,429	-1.65	14	19
Nashotah (1957)	Waukesha	1,266	1,379	8.93	14	13
Necedah (1870)[2]	Juneau	888	896	0.90	15	6
Nelson (1978)	Buffalo	395	399	1.01	3	1
Nelsonville (1913)	Portage	191	186	-2.62	5	0
Neosho (1902)	Dodge	593	592	-0.17	6	3
Neshkoro (1906)	Marquette	453	458	1.10	3	3
New Auburn (1902)	Barron, Chippewa	562	577	2.67	4	2
New Glarus (1901)[2]	Green	2,111	2,104	-0.33	23	27
Newburg (1973)	Ozaukee, Washington	1,119	1,154	3.13	26	20
Nichols (1967)	Outagamie	307	298	-2.93	23	4
North Bay (1951)	Racine	260	260	0.00	17	15
North Fond du Lac (1903)[2]	Fond du Lac	4,557	4,729	3.77	76	52
North Freedom (1893)	Sauk	649	642	-1.08	11	7
North Hudson (1912)	St. Croix	3,463	3,649	5.37	94	17
North Prairie (1919)	Waukesha	1,571	1,815	15.53	12	17
Norwalk (1894)	Monroe	653	640	-1.99	4	209
Oakdale (1988)	Monroe	297	317	6.73	4	1
Oakfield (1903)	Fond du Lac	1,012	1,022	0.99	9	29
Oconomowoc Lake (1959)[2]	Waukesha	564	645	14.36	8	4
Ogdensburg (1912)	Waupaca	224	218	-2.68	0	0
Oliver (1917)	Douglas	358	391	9.22	10	0
Ontario (1890)	Vernon	476	475	-0.21	6	23
Oostburg (1909)	Sheboygan	2,660	2,773	4.25	18	33
Oregon (1883)[2]	Dane	7,514	7,976	6.15	162	50
Orfordville (1900)	Rock	1,272	1,325	4.17	17	29
Osceola (1886)[2]	Polk	2,421	2,597	7.27	53	22
Oxford (1912)	Marquette	536	536	0.00	16	10
Paddock Lake (1960)	Kenosha	3,012	3,106	3.12	62	135
Palmyra (1866)[2]	Jefferson	1,766	1,779	0.74	24	115
Pardeeville (1894)[2]	Columbia	1,982	2,051	3.48	28	43
Park Ridge (1938)	Portage	488	470	-3.69	11	4
Patch Grove (1921)	Grant	166	160	-3.61	0	3
Pepin (1860)	Pepin	878	925	5.35	15	0
Pewaukee (1876)[2]	Waukesha	8,170	8,864	8.49	284	99

WISCONSIN VILLAGES
January 1, 2005–Continued

				Population		
Village (Year Incorporated)[1]	County	2000 Census	2004 Estimate	Percent Change	2000 Nonwhite	2000 Hispanic
Pigeon Falls (1956)	Trempealeau	388	395	1.80	4	0
Plain (1912)	Sauk	792	793	0.13	8	7
Plainfield (1882)	Waushara	899	894	−0.56	14	161
Pleasant Prairie (1989)[2]	Kenosha	16,136	18,122	12.31	730	544
Plover (1971)[2]	Portage	10,520	11,074	5.27	274	142
Plum City (1909)	Pierce	574	607	5.75	1	1
Poplar (1917)	Douglas	552	572	3.62	9	2
Port Edwards (1902)[2]	Wood	1,944	1,915	−1.49	122	18
Potosi (1887)	Grant	711	722	1.55	6	7
Potter (1980)	Calumet	252	251	−0.40	6	0
Pound (1914)	Marinette	355	351	−1.13	2	0
Poynette (1892)[2]	Columbia	2,266	2,461	8.61	39	33
Prairie du Sac (1885)[2]	Sauk	3,231	3,463	7.18	42	66
Prairie Farm (1901)	Barron	508	531	4.53	3	16
Prentice (1899)	Price	626	640	2.24	10	13
Pulaski (1910)[2]	Brown, Oconto, Shawano	3,060	3,334	8.95	67	29
Radisson (1953)	Sawyer	222	223	0.45	21	6
Randolph (1870)	Columbia, Dodge	1,869	1,847	−1.18	17	27
Random Lake (1907)	Sheboygan	1,551	1,599	3.09	27	25
Readstown (1898)	Vernon	395	394	−0.25	0	0
Redgranite (1904)	Waushara	1,040	2,019	94.13	44	32
Reedsville (1892)	Manitowoc	1,187	1,182	−0.42	19	10
Reeseville (1899)	Dodge	703	712	1.28	7	8
Rewey (1902)	Iowa	311	307	−1.29	11	1
Rib Lake (1902)	Taylor	878	870	−0.91	8	3
Ridgeland (1921)	Dunn	265	263	−0.75	1	1
Ridgeway (1902)	Iowa	689	696	1.02	12	0
Rio (1887)	Columbia	938	981	4.58	15	16
River Hills (1930)[3]	Milwaukee	1,631	1,625	−0.37	229	34
Roberts (1945)	St. Croix	969	1,275	31.58	17	9
Rochester (1912)	Racine	1,149	1,134	−1.31	17	40
Rock Springs (1894)	Sauk	425	421	−0.94	3	5
Rockdale (1914)	Dane	1,700	1,738	2.24	1	1
Rockland (1919)	La Crosse	625	639	2.24	10	1
Rosendale (1915)	Fond du Lac	923	969	4.98	3	3
Rosholt (1907)	Portage	518	512	−1.16	3	11
Rothschild (1917)	Marathon	4,970	5,071	2.03	187	14
Rudolph (1960)	Wood	423	426	0.71	21	6
St. Cloud (1909)	Fond du Lac	497	501	0.80	2	4
St. Nazianz (1956)	Manitowoc	749	740	−1.20	16	17
Sauk City (1854)[2]	Sauk	3,109	3,211	3.28	41	117
Saukville (1915)[2]	Ozaukee	4,068	4,167	2.43	83	89
Scandinavia (1894)	Waupaca	349	375	7.45	5	0
Sharon (1892)	Walworth	1,549	1,548	−0.06	44	113
Sheldon (1917)	Rusk	256	249	−2.73	1	0
Sherwood (1968)[2]	Calumet	1,550	2,059	32.84	22	15
Shiocton (1903)	Outagamie	954	956	0.21	4	64
Shorewood (1900)[3]	Milwaukee	13,763	13,535	−1.66	1,053	345
Shorewood Hills (1927)[2]	Dane	1,530	1,675	9.48	112	55
Silver Lake (1926)	Kenosha	2,341	2,435	4.02	38	72
Siren (1948)[2]	Burnett	988	999	1.11	40	1
Sister Bay (1912)[2]	Door	886	914	3.16	10	6
Slinger (1869)[2]	Washington	3,901	4,143	6.20	57	54
Soldiers Grove (1888)	Crawford	653	629	−3.68	6	3
Solon Springs (1920)	Douglas	576	583	1.22	30	3
Somerset (1915)	St. Croix	1,556	2,014	29.43	39	18
South Wayne (1911)	Lafayette	484	485	0.21	2	0
Spencer (1902)	Marathon	1,932	1,947	0.78	11	18
Spring Green (1869)[2]	Sauk	1,444	1,463	1.32	10	2
Spring Valley (1895)[2]	Pierce, St. Croix	1,189	1,263	6.22	10	7
Star Prairie (1900)	St. Croix	574	642	11.85	13	1
Stetsonville (1949)	Taylor	563	560	−0.53	6	4
Steuben (1900)	Crawford	177	167	−5.65	1	1
Stockbridge (1908)	Calumet	649	681	4.93	7	0
Stockholm (1903)	Pepin	97	99	2.06	0	0
Stoddard (1911)[2]	Vernon	815	805	−1.23	7	1
Stratford (1910)	Marathon	1,523	1,559	2.36	27	15
Strum (1948)	Trempealeau	1,001	1,020	1.90	5	14
Sturtevant (1907)[2]	Racine	5,287	5,451	3.10	959	303
Suamico (2003)[2]	Brown	8,686	10,067	15.90	155	54
Sullivan (1915)	Jefferson	688	691	0.44	6	1
Superior (1949)	Douglas	500	550	10.00	15	1
Suring (1914)	Oconto	605	586	−3.14	11	1
Sussex (1924)[2]	Waukesha	8,828	9,576	8.47	220	147
Taylor (1919)	Jackson	513	514	0.19	14	0
Tennyson (1940)	Grant	370	368	−0.54	0	2
Theresa (1898)	Dodge	1,252	1,300	3.83	12	24
Thiensville (1910)[2]	Ozaukee	3,254	3,278	0.74	100	34

WISCONSIN VILLAGES
January 1, 2005–Continued

Village (Year Incorporated)[1]	County	2000 Census	2004 Estimate	Percent Change	2000 Nonwhite	2000 Hispanic
				Population		
Tigerton (1896)	Shawano	764	741	−3.01	20	8
Tony (1911)	Rusk	105	100	−4.76	0	1
Trempealeau (1867)[2]	Trempealeau	1,319	1,435	8.79	17	8
Turtle Lake (1898)[2]	Barron, Polk	1,065	1,089	2.25	60	11
Twin Lakes (1937)[2]	Kenosha	5,124	5,388	5.15	95	127
Union Center (1913)	Juneau	214	217	1.40	1	3
Union Grove (1893)[2]	Racine	4,322	4,459	3.17	86	102
Unity (1903)	Clark, Marathon	368	365	−0.82	0	2
Valders (1919)	Manitowoc	948	1,001	5.59	6	5
Vesper (1948)	Wood	541	540	−0.18	6	4
Viola (1899)[2]	Richland, Vernon	667	704	5.55	6	8
Waldo (1922)	Sheboygan	450	455	1.11	11	0
Wales (1922)	Waukesha	2,523	2,547	0.95	27	26
Walworth (1901)	Walworth	2,304	2,476	7.47	37	165
Warrens (1973)	Monroe	286	285	−0.35	8	2
Waterford (1906)[2]	Racine	4,048	4,399	8.67	57	76
Waunakee (1893)[2]	Dane	8,995	10,002	11.20	140	86
Wausaukee (1924)	Marinette	572	562	−1.75	17	5
Wauzeka (1890)	Crawford	768	784	2.08	14	5
Webster (1916)	Burnett	653	675	3.37	60	2
West Baraboo (1956)	Sauk	1,248	1,272	1.92	42	20
West Milwaukee (1906)[2]	Milwaukee	4,201	4,142	−1.40	384	504
West Salem (1893)[2]	La Crosse	4,738	4,809	1.50	84	27
Westfield (1902)	Marquette	1,217	1,229	0.99	24	43
Weston (1996)[2]	Marathon	12,079	13,003	7.65	793	84
Weyerhaeuser (1906)	Rusk	353	344	−2.55	2	1
Wheeler (1922)	Dunn	317	320	0.95	2	3
White Lake (1926)	Langlade	329	350	6.38	5	7
Whitefish Bay (1892)[3]	Milwaukee	14,163	13,979	−1.30	656	221
Whitelaw (1958)	Manitowoc	730	741	1.51	5	4
Whiting (1947)	Portage	1,760	1,724	−2.05	72	20
Wild Rose (1904)	Waushara	765	758	−0.92	11	17
Williams Bay (1919)[2]	Walworth	2,415	2,566	6.25	25	90
Wilson (1911)	St. Croix	176	189	7.39	8	2
Wilton (1890)	Monroe	519	532	2.50	6	44
Wind Point (1954)	Racine	1,853	1,834	−1.03	93	24
Winneconne (1887)[2]	Winnebago	2,401	2,501	4.16	22	15
Winter (1973)	Sawyer	344	351	2.03	9	5
Withee (1901)	Clark	508	501	−1.38	6	2
Wittenberg (1893)	Shawano	1,177	1,169	−0.68	40	3
Wonewoc (1878)	Juneau	834	826	−0.96	9	3
Woodman (1917)	Grant	96	95	−1.04	0	0
Woodville (1911)	St. Croix	1,104	1,232	11.59	18	8
Wrightstown (1901)[9]	Brown, Outagamie	1,934	2,267	17.22	41	34
Wyeville (1923)	Monroe	146	143	−2.05	5	4
Wyocena (1909)	Columbia	668	702	5.09	13	8
Yuba (1935)	Richland	92	92	0.00	0	0

[1]There are 400 villages in Wisconsin as of January 1, 2005.

[2]One of 83 villages with an administrator, holding either a full-time or combination position.

[3]One of 11 villages operating under the manager form of government.

[4]The Town of Bellevue became a village on 2/14/2003.

[5]The Town of Hobart became a village on 5/13/2002.

[6]Part of the Town of Kronenwetter became the Village of Kronenwetter on 11/20/2002.

[7]Part of the Town of Ixonia became the Village of Lac La Belle on 3/28/2002.

[8]Part of the Town of Hallie became the Village of Lake Hallie on 2/18/2003.

[9]Part of the Town of Kaukauna was annexed by the Village of Wrightstown on 2/28/2002.

Sources: Wisconsin Department of Administration, Division of Intergovernmental Relations, Demographic Services Center, *Official Population Estimate of Wisconsin Municipalities, January 1, 2004;* League of Wisconsin Municipalities, *Directory of Wisconsin City and Village Officials,* July 2004.

WISCONSIN CITIES AND VILLAGES OVER 10,000 POPULATION

City or Village (County)	2000 Census	2004 Estimate	Percent Change	Rank	2000 Nonwhite[2]	2000 Hispanic
Cities						
Appleton (Calumet, Outagamie, Winnebago)	70,087	71,895	2.58%	6	5,063	1,775
Baraboo (Sauk)	10,711	11,188	4.45	69	243	168
Beaver Dam (Dodge)	15,169	15,366	2.06	47	292	640
Beloit (Rock)	35,775	36,058	0.79	20	6,786	3,257
Brookfield (Waukesha)	38,649	39,607	2.48	16	2,145	453
Burlington (Racine, Walworth)	9,936	10,183	26.04	77	177	462
Cedarburg (Ozaukee)	11,102	11,331	0.76	68	185	94
Chippewa Falls (Chippewa)	12,925	13,155	1.78	57	264	82
Cudahy (Milwaukee)	18,429	18,315	-0.62	40	743	872
De Pere (Brown)	20,559	22,038	7.19	34	619	202
Eau Claire (Chippewa, Eau Claire)	61,704	63,897	3.55	9	3,777	619
Fitchburg (Dane)	20,501	22,030	2.55	35	2,863	1,329
Fond du Lac (Fond du Lac)	42,203	42,865	1.57	15	2,065	1,232
Fort Atkinson (Jefferson)	11,621	11,943	5.59	65	209	508
Franklin (Milwaukee)	29,494	31,804	7.83	23	2,427	780
Glendale (Milwaukee)	13,367	13,024	-2.57	59	1,672	236
Green Bay (Brown)	102,767	103,653	0.86	3	9,885	7,294
Greenfield (Milwaukee)	35,476	36,059	1.64	19	1,588	1,376
Hartford (Dodge, Washington)	10,905	12,068	10.66	64	188	326
Hudson (St. Croix)	8,775	10,561	9.16	76	151	91
Janesville (Rock)	60,200	61,310	1.84	10	2,089	1,569
Kaukauna (Outagamie)	12,983	13,926	7.26	53	537	103
Kenosha (Kenosha)	90,352	92,808	2.72	4	9,663	9,003
La Crosse (La Crosse)	51,818	51,507	-0.60	12	4,068	592
Madison (Dane)	208,054	217,935	4.75	2	29,033	8,512
Manitowoc (Manitowoc)	34,053	34,612	1.64	21	1,941	859
Marinette (Marinette)	11,749	11,638	-0.94	67	252	123
Marshfield (Marathon, Wood)	18,800	19,012	1.13	37	496	146
Menasha (Calumet, Winnebago)	16,331	16,779	2.74	43	570	590
Menomonie (Dunn)	14,937	15,247	4.25	48	828	170
Mequon (Ozaukee)	22,643	23,416	1.56	30	1,202	261
Merrill (Lincoln)	10,146	10,144	-0.02	78	173	104
Middleton (Dane)	15,770	16,446	4.29	44	1,018	444
Milwaukee (Milwaukee, Washington, Waukesha)	596,974	593,920	-0.51	1	254,339	71,646
Monroe (Green)	10,843	10,973	1.41	72	168	158
Muskego (Waukesha)	21,397	22,203	3.77	33	306	281
Neenah (Winnebago)	24,507	25,193	2.80	27	717	495
New Berlin (Waukesha)	38,220	38,896	1.77	18	1,360	595
Oak Creek (Milwaukee)	28,456	31,029	9.04	24	1,675	1,267
Oconomowoc (Waukesha)	12,382	13,194	1.60	56	203	204
Onalaska (La Crosse)	14,839	15,782	2.84	45	658	141
Oshkosh (Winnebago)	62,916	65,095	3.46	8	4,105	1,062
Pewaukee (Waukesha)	11,783	12,425	5.45	63	261	153
Platteville (Grant)	9,989	10,109	0.05	79	348	88
Port Washington (Ozaukee)	10,467	10,683	4.98	74	243	168
Racine (Racine)	81,855	80,806	-1.28	5	18,471	11,422
River Falls (Pierce, St. Croix)	12,560	13,067	4.04	58	378	119
Sheboygan (Sheboygan)	50,792	50,672	-0.24	13	4,569	3,034
South Milwaukee (Milwaukee)	21,256	21,360	0.49	36	722	852
Stevens Point (Portage)	24,551	25,094	2.21	28	1677	395
Stoughton (Dane)	12,354	12,654	2.43	61	347	153
Sun Prairie (Dane)	20,369	23,226	14.03	31	1243	555
Superior (Douglas)	27,368	27,221	-0.54	26	1,465	226
Two Rivers (Manitowoc)	12,639	12,599	-0.32	62	458	170
Watertown (Dodge, Jefferson)	21,598	22,732	5.25	32	409	1,067
Waukesha (Waukesha)	64,825	66,816	3.07	7	3,071	5,563
Waupun (Dodge, Fond du Lac)	10,718	10,670	-0.45	75	1,427	304
Wausau (Marathon)	38,426	38,912	1.26	17	5,226	398
Wauwatosa (Milwaukee)	47,271	46,511	-1.61	14	2,523	813
West Allis (Milwaukee)	61,254	60,607	-1.06	11	2,667	2,155
West Bend (Washington)	28,152	29,204	3.74	25	554	519
Whitewater (Jefferson, Walworth)	13,437	13,996	4.16	51	632	873
Wisconsin Rapids (Wood)	18,435	18,410	-0.14	39	998	242
Villages						
Allouez (Brown)	15,443	15,494	0.33	46	1,105	199
Ashwaubenon (Brown)	17,634	17,661	0.15	42	763	202
Bellevue (Brown)	11,828	13,836	16.98	54	374	310
Brown Deer (Milwaukee)	12,170	11,845	-2.67	66	2,088	260
Germantown (Washington)	18,260	19,001	4.06	38	680	205
Grafton (Ozaukee)	10,464	11,160	6.65	70	193	165
Greendale (Milwaukee)	14,405	14,128	-1.92	50	458	340
Howard (Brown)	13,546	15,208	12.27	49	461	147
Little Chute (Outagamie)	10,476	10,775	2.85	73	203	175
Menomonee Falls (Waukesha)	32,647	33,660	3.10	22	1,045	377
Mount Pleasant (Racine)	23,142	24,347	5.21	29	1,989	1,149
Pleasant Prairie (Kenosha)	16,136	18,122	12.31	41	730	544
Plover (Portage)	10,520	11,074	5.27	71	274	142
Shorewood (Milwaukee)	13,763	13,535	-1.66	55	1,053	345
Suamico (Brown)	8,686	10,067	15.90	80	155	54
Waunakee (Dane)	8,995	10,002	11.20	81	140	86
Weston (Marathon)	12,079	13,003	7.65	60	793	84
Whitefish Bay (Milwaukee)	14,163	13,979	-1.30	52	656	221

[1]Population totals include corrections made by the U.S. Census Bureau through 8/28/2002. Race and ethnicity data have not been adjusted. Population estimates are based on the corrected totals.

[2]In the 2000 U.S. Census, respondents were allowed to choose more than one race. The column "nonwhite" includes all who chose at least one race other than white.

Source: Wisconsin Department of Administration, Division of Intergovernmental Relations, Demographic Services Center, *Official Population Estimates, January 1, 2004*, July 2004.

WISCONSIN TOWNS OVER 2,500 POPULATION
2000 U.S. Census and 2004 Estimate

Town (County)	2000 Census*	2004 Estimate	Percent Change
Addison (Washington)	3,341	3,505	4.91%
Alden (Polk)	2,615	2,806	7.30
Algoma (Winnebago)	5,702	6,024	5.65
Arbor Vitae (Vilas)	3,153	3,261	3.43
Barton (Washington)	2,546	2,587	1.61
Beaver Dam (Dodge)	3,440	3,665	6.54
Beloit (Rock)	7,038	7,293	3.62
Bloomfield (Walworth)	5,537	6,039	9.07
Bradley (Lincoln)	2,573	2,671	3.81
Bristol (Dane)	2,698	3,134	16.16
Bristol (Kenosha)	4,538	4,692	3.39
Brockway (Jackson)	2,580	2,692	4.34
Brookfield (Waukesha)	6,390	6,418	0.44
Buchanan (Outagamie)	5,827	6,715	15.24
Burke (Dane)	2,990	3,081	3.04
Burlington (Racine)	6,384	6,511	1.99
Caledonia (Racine)	23,614	24,452	3.55
Campbell (La Crosse)	4,410	4,417	0.16
Cedarburg (Ozaukee)	5,550	5,720	3.06
Center (Outagamie)	3,163	3,328	5.22
Chase (Oconto)	2,082	2,503	20.22
Clayton (Winnebago)	2,974	3,301	11.00
Cottage Grove (Dane)	3,839	3,904	1.69
Dayton (Waupaca)	2,734	2,853	4.35
Delafield (Waukesha)	7,820	8,210	4.99
Delavan (Walworth)	4,559	4,767	4.56
Dover (Racine)	3,908	4,021	2.89
Dunn (Dane)	5,270	5,280	0.19
Eagle (Waukesha)	3,117	3,444	10.49
Eagle Point (Chippewa)	3,049	3,290	7.90
East Troy (Walworth)	3,830	3,888	1.51
Ellington (Outagamie)	2,535	2,700	6.51
Empire (Fond du Lac)	2,620	2,736	4.43
Erin (Washington)	3,664	3,802	3.77
Farmington (Washington)	3,239	3,433	5.99
Farmington (Waupaca)	4,148	4,247	2.39
Fox Lake (Dodge)	2,402	2,632	9.58
Freedom (Outagamie)	5,241	5,466	4.29
Fulton (Rock)	3,158	3,220	1.96
Genesee (Waukesha)	7,284	7,502	2.99
Geneva (Walworth)	4,642	4,858	4.65
Grafton (Ozaukee)	3,980	4,078	2.46
Grand Chute (Outagamie)	18,392	19,723	7.24
Grand Rapids (Wood)	7,801	7,960	2.04
Greenbush (Sheboygan)	2,619	2,599	-0.76
Greenville (Outagamie)	6,844	7,634	11.54
Harrison (Calumet)	5,756	7,917	37.54
Hartford (Washington)	4,031	4,023	-0.20
Hayward (Sawyer)	3,279	3,440	4.91
Holland (La Crosse)	3,042	3,168	4.14
Hudson (St. Croix)	6,213	7,214	16.11
Hull (Portage)	5,493	5,544	0.93
Ixonia (Jefferson)	2,902	3,190	9.92
Jackson (Washington)	3,516	3,637	3.44
Janesville (Rock)	3,048	3,264	7.09
Koshkonong (Jefferson)	3,395	3,514	3.51
Lac du Flambeau (Vilas)	3,004	3,136	4.39
Lafayette (Chippewa)	5,199	5,662	8.91
Ledgeview (Brown)	3,363	4,241	26.11
Lima (Sheboygan)	2,948	2,909	-1.32
Lincoln (Vilas)	2,579	2,708	5.00
Lisbon (Waukesha)	9,359	9,630	2.90
Little Suamico (Oconto)	3,877	4,381	13.00
Lodi (Columbia)	2,791	3,084	10.50
Lyons (Walworth)	3,440	3,704	7.67
Madison (Dane)	7,005	6,936	-0.99
Manitowoc Rapids (Manitowoc)	2,520	2,538	0.71
Menasha (Winnebago)	15,858	16,695	5.28
Menominee (Menominee)	4,562	4,616	1.18
Menomonie (Dunn)	3,174	3,354	5.67%
Merrill (Lincoln)	2,979	3,076	3.26
Merton (Waukesha)	7,988	8,220	2.90
Middleton (Dane)	4,594	5,230	13.84
Milton (Rock)	2,844	2,948	3.66
Minocqua (Oneida)	4,859	5,128	5.54
Mukwa (Waupaca)	2,773	2,906	4.80
Mukwonago (Waukesha)	6,868	7,391	7.62
Neenah (Winnebago)	2,657	2,745	3.31
Newbold (Oneida)	2,710	2,830	4.43
Norway (Racine)	7,600	7,860	3.42
Oakland (Jefferson)	3,135	3,252	3.73
Oconomowoc (Waukesha)	7,451	7,646	2.62
Onalaska (La Crosse)	5,210	5,406	3.76
Oneida (Outagamie)	4,147	4,298	3.64
Oregon (Dane)	3,148	3,276	4.07
Osceola (Polk)	2,085	2,578	23.65
Oshkosh (Winnebago)	3,234	2,808	-13.17
Ottawa (Waukesha)	3,758	3,822	1.70
Pacific (Columbia)	2,518	2,651	5.28
Pelican (Oneida)	2,902	2,602	-10.34
Peshtigo (Marinette)	3,702	3,903	5.43
Pine Lake (Oneida)	2,720	2,827	3.93
Pittsfield (Brown)	2,433	2,547	4.69
Pleasant Springs (Dane)	3,053	3,143	2.95
Pleasant Valley (Eau Claire)	2,681	2,932	9.36
Plymouth (Sheboygan)	3,115	3,274	5.10
Polk (Washington)	3,938	4,011	1.85
Randall (Kenosha)	2,929	3,098	5.77
Raymond (Racine)	3,516	3,639	3.50
Rib Mountain (Marathon)	7,556	7,635	1.05
Rice Lake (Barron)	3,026	3,130	3.44
Richfield (Washington)	10,373	11,195	7.92
Rock (Rock)	3,338	3,340	0.06
Rome (Adams)	2,656	2,888	8.73
St. Joseph (St. Croix)	3,436	3,642	6.00
Salem (Kenosha)	9,871	10,767	9.08
Saratoga (Wood)	5,383	5,457	1.37
Scott (Brown)	3,138	3,519	12.14
Sevastopol (Door)	2,667	2,790	4.61
Seymour (Eau Claire)	2,978	3,099	4.06
Sheboygan (Sheboygan)	5,874	7,013	19.39
Shelby (La Crosse)	4,687	4,772	1.81
Somers (Kenosha)	9,059	9,294	2.59
Somerset (St. Croix)	2,644	3,044	15.13
Sparta (Monroe)	2,753	2,953	7.26
Springdale (Dane)	2,762	2,802	1.45
Springfield (Dane)	12,354	12,654	2.43
Star Prairie (St. Croix)	2,944	3,306	12.30
Stephenson (Marinette)	3,065	3,225	5.22
Stockton (Portage)	2,896	2,974	2.69
Sugar Creek (Walworth)	3,331	3,624	8.80
Summit (Waukesha)	4,999	5,068	1.38
Taycheedah (Fond du Lac)	3,666	3,810	3.93
Trenton (Washington)	4,440	4,595	3.49
Troy (St. Croix)	3,661	4,308	17.67
Union (Eau Claire)	2,402	2,514	4.66
Vernon (Waukesha)	7,227	7,358	1.81
Washington (Eau Claire)	6,995	7,227	3.32
Waterford (Racine)	5,938	6,281	5.78
Waukesha (Waukesha)	8,596	8,659	0.73
Wescott (Shawano)	3,653	3,765	3.07
West Bend (Washington)	4,834	4,835	0.02
Westport (Dane)	3,586	3,761	4.88
Wheatland (Kenosha)	3,292	3,354	1.88
Wilson (Sheboygan)	3,227	3,356	4.00
Windsor (Dane)	5,286	5,607	6.07
Woodmohr (Chippewa)	2,366	2,537	7.23
Yorkville (Racine)	3,291	3,310	0.58

*Population totals include corrections made by the U.S. Census Bureau through 8/28/2002. Population estimates are based on the corrected totals.

Source: Wisconsin Department of Administration, Division of Intergovernmental Relations, Demographic Services Center, *Official Population Estimates, January 1, 2004,* October 2004.

WISCONSIN POPULATION
BY COUNTY AND MUNICIPALITY
April 1, 2000 and January 1, 2004

County and Municipality	2000 Census[1]	2004 Estimate	Percent Change	County and Municipality	2000 Census[1]	2004 Estimate	Percent Change
ADAMS COUNTY	19,920	20,707	3.95%	Prairie Farm, town	603	609	1.00
Adams, city	1,831	1,843	0.66	Prairie Farm, village	508	531	4.53
Adams, town	1,267	1,288	1.66	Prairie Lake, town	1,369	1,466	7.09
Big Flats, town	946	1,016	7.40	Rice Lake, city	8,312	8,490	2.14
Colburn, town	181	185	2.21	Rice Lake, town	3,026	3,130	3.44
Dell Prairie, town	1,415	1,480	4.59	Sioux Creek, town	689	723	4.93
Easton, town	1,194	1,260	5.53	Stanfold, town	669	693	3.59
Friendship, village	781	773	−1.02	Stanley, town	2,237	2,405	7.51
Jackson, town	926	969	4.64	Sumner, town	598	648	8.36
Leola, town	265	275	3.77	Turtle Lake, town	622	643	3.38
Lincoln, town	311	321	3.22	Turtle Lake (part), village	1,000	1,008	0.80
Monroe, town	363	411	13.22	Vance Creek, town	747	781	4.55
New Chester, town	2,141	2,081	−2.80				
New Haven, town	657	680	3.50	BAYFIELD COUNTY	15,013	15,575	3.74
Preston, town	1,360	1,429	5.07	Ashland (part), city	0	0	0.00
Quincy, town	1,181	1,283	8.64	Barksdale, town	801	826	3.12
Richfield, town	144	148	2.78	Barnes, town	610	647	6.07
Rome, town	2,656	2,888	8.73	Bayfield, city	611	616	0.82
Springville, town	1,167	1,235	5.83	Bayfield, town	625	713	14.08
Strongs Prairie, town	1,115	1,137	1.97	Bayview, town	491	517	5.30
Wisconsin Dells (part), city	19	5	−.2	Bell, town	230	242	5.22
				Cable, town	836	844	0.96
				Clover, town	211	223	5.69
ASHLAND COUNTY	16,866	16,969	0.61	Delta, town	235	251	6.81
Agenda, town	513	507	−1.17	Drummond, town	541	546	0.92
Ashland (part), city	8,620	8,577	−0.50	Eileen, town	640	648	1.25
Ashland, town	603	604	0.17	Grand View, town	483	531	9.94
Butternut, village	407	396	−2.70	Hughes, town	408	419	2.70
Chippewa, town	433	438	1.15	Iron River, town	1,059	1,101	3.97
Gingles, town	640	710	10.94	Kelly, town	377	402	6.63
Gordon, town	357	369	3.36	Keystone, town	369	371	0.54
Jacobs, town	835	826	−1.08	Lincoln, town	293	304	3.75
La Pointe, town	246	275	11.79	Mason, town	326	329	0.92
Marengo, town	362	372	2.76	Mason, village	72	79	9.72
Mellen, city	845	834	−1.30	Namakagon, town	285	295	3.51
Morse, town	515	538	4.47	Orienta, town	101	103	1.98
Peeksville, town	176	176	0.00	Oulu, town	540	540	0.00
Sanborn, town	1,272	1,272	0.00	Pilsen, town	203	224	10.34
Shanagolden, town	150	148	−1.33	Port Wing, town	420	419	−0.24
White River, town	892	927	3.92	Russell, town	1,216	1,329	9.29
				Tripp, town	209	217	3.83
BARRON COUNTY	44,963	46,540	3.51	Washburn, city	2,280	2,284	0.18
Almena, town	910	949	4.29	Washburn, town	541	555	2.59
Almena, village	720	750	4.17				
Arland, town	670	687	2.54	BROWN COUNTY	226,658	237,841	4.93
Barron, city	3,248	3,319	2.19	Allouez, village	15,443	15,494	0.33
Barron, town	1,014	993	−2.07	Ashwaubenon, village	17,634	17,661	0.15
Bear Lake, town	587	633	7.84	[3]Bellevue, village	11,828	13,836	16.98
Cameron, village	1,546	1,681	8.73	De Pere, city	20,559	22,038	7.19
Cedar Lake, town	944	996	5.51	Denmark, village	1,958	2,017	3.01
Chetek, city	2,180	2,242	2.84	Eaton, town	1,414	1,510	6.79
Chetek, town	1,686	1,740	3.20	Glenmore, town	1,187	1,235	4.04
Clinton, town	920	966	5.00	Green Bay, city	102,767	103,653	0.86
Crystal Lake, town	778	814	4.63	Green Bay, town	1,772	1,889	6.60
Cumberland, city	2,280	2,341	2.68	[4]Hobart, village	5,090	5,486	7.78
Cumberland, town	942	956	1.49	Holland, town	1,339	1,431	6.87
Dallas, town	604	605	0.17	Howard (part), village	13,546	15,208	12.27
Dallas, village	356	356	0.00	Humboldt, town	1,338	1,413	5.61
Dovre, town	680	738	8.53	Lawrence, town	1,548	2,096	35.40
Doyle, town	498	519	4.22	Ledgeview, town	3,363	4,241	26.11
Haugen, village	287	288	0.35	Morrison, town	1,651	1,700	2.97
Lakeland, town	963	1,017	5.61	New Denmark, town	1,482	1,526	2.97
Maple Grove, town	968	976	0.83	Pittsfield, town	2,433	2,547	4.69
Maple Plain, town	876	897	2.40	Pulaski (part), village	3,013	3,221	6.90
New Auburn (part), village	15	23	53.33	Rockland, town	1,522	1,642	7.88
Oak Grove, town	911	927	1.76	Scott, town	3,138	3,519	12.14
				Suamico, town	8,686	10,067	15.90

WISCONSIN POPULATION
BY COUNTY AND MUNICIPALITY
April 1, 2000 and January 1, 2004–Continued

County and Municipality	2000 Census[1]	2004 Estimate	Percent Change	County and Municipality	2000 Census[1]	2004 Estimate	Percent Change
Wrightstown, town	2,013	2,181	8.35	New Holstein, city	3,301	3,313	0.36
Wrightstown (part),				New Holstein, town	1,457	1,512	3.77
village	1,934	2,230	15.31	Potter, village	252	251	−0.40
				Rantoul, town	812	826	1.72
BUFFALO COUNTY	13,804	14,033	1.66	Sherwood, village	1,550	2,059	32.84
Alma, city	942	937	−0.53	Stockbridge, town	1,383	1,433	3.62
Alma, town	377	384	1.86	Stockbridge, village	649	681	4.93
Belvidere, town	442	443	0.23	Woodville, town	993	967	−2.62
Buffalo, city	1,040	1,059	1.83				
Buffalo, town	667	696	4.35	CHIPPEWA COUNTY	55,195	59,466	7.74
Canton, town	304	312	2.63	Anson, town	1,881	1,983	5.42
Cochrane, village	435	421	−3.22	Arthur, town	710	733	3.24
Cross, town	366	390	6.56	Auburn, town	580	636	9.66
Dover, town	484	489	1.03	Birch Creek, town	520	533	2.50
Fountain City, city	983	1,000	1.73	Bloomer, city	3,347	3,446	2.96
Gilmanton, town	470	467	−0.64	Bloomer, town	926	972	4.97
Glencoe, town	478	483	1.05	Boyd, village	680	677	−0.44
Lincoln, town	187	184	−1.60	Cadott, village	1,345	1,356	0.82
Maxville, town	325	332	2.15	Chippewa Falls, city	12,925	13,155	1.78
Milton, town	517	525	1.55	Cleveland, town	900	957	6.33
Modena, town	318	312	−1.89	Colburn, town	727	777	6.88
Mondovi, city	2,634	2,688	2.05	Cooks Valley, town	632	672	6.33
Mondovi, town	449	468	4.23	Cornell, city	1,466	1,447	−1.30
Montana, town	306	311	1.63	Delmar, town	941	972	3.29
Naples, town	584	612	4.79	Eagle Point, town	3,049	3,290	7.90
Nelson, town	586	592	1.02	Eau Claire (part), city . . .	1,910	1,985	3.93
Nelson, village	395	399	1.01	Edson, town	966	1,014	4.97
Waumandee, town	515	529	2.72	Estella, town	469	487	3.84
				Goetz, town	695	740	6.47
BURNETT COUNTY	15,674	16,398	4.62	[5]Hallie, town	4,703	149	−96.83
Anderson, town	372	402	8.06	Howard, town	648	686	5.86
Blaine, town	224	224	0.00	Lafayette, town	5,199	5,662	8.91
Daniels, town	665	682	2.56	[5]Lake Hallie, village	0	5,345	---[2]
Dewey, town	565	593	4.96	Lake Holcombe, town . .	1,010	1,061	5.05
Grantsburg, town	967	1,067	10.34	New Auburn (part),			
Grantsburg, village	1,369	1,438	5.04	village	547	554	1.28
Jackson, town	765	805	5.23	Ruby, town	446	454	1.79
La Follette, town	511	514	0.59	Sampson, town	816	861	5.51
Lincoln, town	286	300	4.90	Sigel, town	825	842	2.06
Meenon, town	1,172	1,229	4.86	Stanley (part), city	1,898	3,378	77.98
Oakland, town	778	856	10.03	Tilden, town	1,185	1,246	5.15
Roosevelt, town	197	206	4.57	Wheaton, town	2,366	2,537	7.23
Rusk, town	420	421	0.24	Woodmohr, town	883	859	−2.72
Sand Lake, town	556	559	0.54				
Scott, town	590	630	6.78	CLARK COUNTY	33,557	34,373	2.43
Siren, town	873	881	0.92	Abbotsford (part), city . .	1,412	1,402	−0.71
Siren, village	988	999	1.11	Beaver, town	854	904	5.85
Swiss, town	815	851	4.42	Butler, town	88	87	−1.14
Trade Lake, town	871	923	5.97	Colby (part), city	1,156	1,240	7.27
Union, town	351	353	0.57	Colby, town	908	935	2.97
Webb Lake, town	381	412	8.14	Curtiss, village	198	215	8.59
Webster, village	653	675	3.37	Dewhurst, town	321	359	11.84
West Marshland, town . .	331	361	9.06	Dorchester (part), village	823	850	3.28
Wood River, town	974	1,017	4.41	Eaton, town	665	677	1.80
				Foster, town	95	96	1.05
CALUMET COUNTY	40,631	44,361	9.18	Fremont, town	1,190	1,251	5.13
Appleton (part), city	10,974	11,241	2.43	Grant, town	920	948	3.04
Brillion, city	2,937	2,969	1.09	Granton, village	406	397	−2.22
Brillion, town	1,438	1,529	6.33	Green Grove, town	675	685	1.48
Brothertown, town	1,404	1,425	1.50	Greenwood, city	1,079	1,087	0.74
Charlestown, town	789	782	−0.89	Hendren, town	513	512	−0.19
Chilton, city	3,708	3,760	1.40	Hewett, town	314	316	0.64
Chilton, town	1,130	1,146	1.42	Hixon, town	740	754	1.89
Harrison, town	5,756	7,917	37.54	Hoard, town	821	842	2.56
Hilbert, village	1,089	1,106	1.56	Levis, town	504	527	4.56
Kiel (part), city	321	320	−0.31	Longwood, town	698	710	1.72
Menasha (part), city	688	1,124	63.37	Loyal, city	1,308	1,309	0.08

WISCONSIN POPULATION
BY COUNTY AND MUNICIPALITY
April 1, 2000 and January 1, 2004–Continued

County and Municipality	2000 Census[1]	2004 Estimate	Percent Change	County and Municipality	2000 Census[1]	2004 Estimate	Percent Change
Loyal, town	787	799	1.52	De Soto (part), village	118	183	55.08
Lynn, town	834	833	-0.12	Eastman, town	790	804	1.77
Mayville, town	919	948	3.16	Eastman, village	437	448	2.52
Mead, town	290	298	2.76	Ferryville, village	174	182	4.60
Mentor, town	570	579	1.58	Freeman, town	719	736	2.36
Neillsville, city	2,731	2,716	-0.55	Gays Mills, village	625	627	0.32
Owen, city	936	931	-0.53	Haney, town	330	338	2.42
Pine Valley, town	1,121	1,224	9.19	Lynxville, village	176	181	2.84
Reseburg, town	740	751	1.49	Marietta, town	510	525	2.94
Seif, town	212	209	-1.42	Mount Sterling, village	215	207	-3.72
Sherman, town	831	873	5.05	Prairie du Chien, city	6,018	6,053	0.58
Sherwood, town	252	278	10.32	Prairie du Chien, town	1,076	1,108	2.97
Stanley (part), city	0	0	0.00	Scott, town	503	521	3.58
Thorp, city	1,536	1,569	2.15	Seneca, town	893	917	2.69
Thorp, town	730	748	2.47	Soldiers Grove, village	653	629	-3.68
Unity, town	745	778	4.43	Steuben, village	177	167	-5.65
Unity (part), village	163	164	0.61	Utica, town	674	679	0.74
Warner, town	627	645	2.87	Wauzeka, town	369	360	-2.44
Washburn, town	304	304	0.00	Wauzeka, village	768	784	2.08
Weston, town	638	657	2.98				
Withee, town	885	911	2.94	DANE COUNTY	426,526	450,730	5.67
Withee, village	508	501	-1.38	Albion, town	1,858	1,885	1.45
Worden, town	657	683	3.96	Belleville (part), village	1,795	1,891	5.35
York, town	853	871	2.11	Berry, town	1,084	1,133	4.52
				Black Earth, town	449	488	8.69
COLUMBIA COUNTY	52,468	54,596	4.06	Black Earth, village	1,320	1,313	-0.53
Arlington, town	848	883	4.13	Blooming Grove, town	1,768	1,744	-1.36
Arlington, village	484	547	13.02	Blue Mounds, town	842	877	4.16
Caledonia, town	1,171	1,223	4.44	Blue Mounds, village	708	733	3.53
Cambria, village	792	785	-0.88	Bristol, town	2,698	3,134	16.16
Columbus (part), city	4,443	4,704	5.87	Brooklyn (part), village	502	586	16.73
Columbus, town	711	704	-0.98	Burke, town	2,990	3,081	3.04
Courtland, town	463	477	3.02	Cambridge (part), village	1,014	1,086	7.10
Dekorra, town	2,350	2,406	2.38	Christiana, town	1,313	1,332	1.45
Doylestown, village	328	337	2.74	Cottage Grove, town	3,839	3,904	1.69
Fall River, village	1,097	1,232	12.31	Cottage Grove, village	4,059	4,559	12.32
Fort Winnebago, town	855	855	0.00	Cross Plains, town	1,419	1,470	3.59
Fountain Prairie, town	810	825	1.85	Cross Plains, village	3,084	3,342	8.37
Friesland, village	298	303	1.68	Dane, town	968	989	2.17
Hampden, town	563	567	0.71	Dane, village	799	857	7.26
Leeds, town	813	826	1.60	DeForest, village	7,368	8,061	9.41
Lewiston, town	1,187	1,221	2.86	Deerfield, town	1,470	1,509	2.65
Lodi, city	2,882	2,949	2.32	Deerfield, village	1,971	2,041	3.55
Lodi, town	2,791	3,084	10.50	Dunkirk, town	2,053	2,048	-0.24
Lowville, town	987	1,026	3.95	Dunn, town	5,270	5,280	0.19
Marcellon, town	1,024	1,054	2.93	Edgerton (part), city	7	11	57.14
Newport, town	681	685	0.59	Fitchburg, city	20,501	22,030	7.46
Otsego, town	757	767	1.32	Madison, city	208,054	217,935	4.75
Pacific, town	2,518	2,651	5.28	Madison, town	7,005	6,936	-0.99
Pardeeville, village	1,982	2,051	3.48	Maple Bluff, village	1,358	1,350	-0.59
Portage, city	9,728	9,966	2.45	Marshall, village	3,432	3,563	3.82
Poynette, village	2,266	2,461	8.61	Mazomanie, town	1,185	1,198	1.10
Randolph, town	699	736	5.29	Mazomanie, village	1,485	1,543	3.91
Randolph (part), village	523	513	-1.91	McFarland, village	6,416	7,051	9.90
Rio, village	938	981	4.58	Medina, town	1,235	1,278	3.48
Scott, town	791	823	4.05	Middleton, city	15,770	16,446	4.29
Springvale, town	550	555	0.91	Middleton, town	4,594	5,230	13.84
West Point, town	1,634	1,750	7.10	Monona, city	8,018	7,965	-0.66
Wisconsin Dells (part), city	2,293	2,345	2.27	Montrose, town	1,134	1,158	2.12
Wyocena, town	1,543	1,602	3.82	Mount Horeb, village	5,860	6,244	6.55
Wyocena, village	668	702	5.09	Oregon, town	3,148	3,276	4.07
				Oregon, village	7,514	7,976	6.15
				Perry, town	670	692	3.28
CRAWFORD COUNTY	17,243	17,501	1.50	Pleasant Springs, town	3,053	3,143	2.95
Bell Center, village	116	116	0.00	Primrose, town	682	719	5.43
Bridgeport, town	946	986	4.23	Rockdale, village	214	210	-1.87
Clayton, town	956	950	-0.63	Roxbury, town	1,700	1,738	2.24

WISCONSIN POPULATION
BY COUNTY AND MUNICIPALITY
April 1, 2000 and January 1, 2004–Continued

County and Municipality	2000 Census[1]	2004 Estimate	Percent Change	County and Municipality	2000 Census[1]	2004 Estimate	Percent Change
Rutland, town	1,887	1,973	4.56	Egg Harbor, village	250	261	4.40
Shorewood Hills, village	1,732	1,724	–0.46	Ephraim, village	353	356	0.85
Springdale, town	1,530	1,675	9.48	Forestville, town	1,086	1,157	6.54
Springfield, town	2,762	2,802	1.45	Forestville, village	429	427	–0.47
Stoughton, city	12,354	12,654	2.43	Gardner, town	1,197	1,234	3.09
Sun Prairie, city	20,369	23,226	14.03	Gibraltar, town	1,063	1,156	8.75
Sun Prairie, town	2,308	2,345	1.60	Jacksonport, town	738	759	2.85
Vermont, town	839	866	3.22	Liberty Grove, town	1,858	1,958	5.38
Verona, city	7,052	8,888	26.04	Nasewaupee, town	1,873	1,949	4.06
Verona, town	2,153	2,150	–0.14	Sevastopol, town	2,667	2,790	4.61
Vienna, town	1,294	1,307	1.00	Sister Bay, village	886	914	3.16
Waunakee, village	8,995	10,002	11.20	Sturgeon Bay, city	9,437	9,696	2.74
Westport, town	3,586	3,761	4.88	Sturgeon Bay, town	865	895	3.47
Windsor, town	5,286	5,607	6.07	Union, town	880	901	2.39
York, town	703	715	1.71	Washington, town	660	698	5.76
DODGE COUNTY	85,897	88,285	2.78	**DOUGLAS COUNTY**	43,287	43,708	0.97
Ashippun, town	2,308	2,383	3.25	Amnicon, town	1,074	1,105	2.89
Beaver Dam, city	15,169	15,366	1.30	Bennett, town	622	631	1.45
Beaver Dam, town	3,440	3,665	6.54	Brule, town	591	614	3.89
Brownsville, village	570	567	–0.53	Cloverland, town	247	246	–0.40
Burnett, town	919	935	1.74	Dairyland, town	186	191	2.69
Calamus, town	1,005	1,034	2.89	Gordon, town	645	688	6.67
Chester, town	960	954	–0.63	Hawthorne, town	1,045	1,064	1.82
Clyman, town	849	865	1.88	Highland, town	245	261	6.53
Clyman, village	388	385	–0.77	Lake Nebagamon, village	1,015	1,017	0.20
Columbus (part), city . . .	36	0	--²	Lakeside, town	609	619	1.64
Elba, town	1,086	1,110	2.21	Maple, town	649	665	2.47
Emmet, town	1,221	1,303	6.72	Oakland, town	1,144	1,193	4.28
Fox Lake, city	1,454	1,477	1.58	Oliver, village	358	391	9.22
Fox Lake, town	2,402	2,632	9.58	Parkland, town	1,240	1,265	2.02
Hartford (part), city	10	4	–60.00	Poplar, town	552	572	3.62
Herman, town	1,207	1,221	1.16	Solon Springs, town	807	859	6.44
Horicon, city	3,775	3,747	–0.74	Solon Springs, village . .	576	583	1.22
Hubbard, town	1,643	1,737	5.72	Summit, town	1,042	1,043	0.10
Hustisford, town	1,379	1,416	2.68	Superior, city	27,368	27,221	–0.54
Hustisford, village	1,135	1,149	1.23	Superior, town	2,058	2,165	5.20
Iron Ridge, village	998	1,003	0.50	Superior, village	500	550	10.00
Juneau, city	2,485	2,656	6.88	Wascott, town	714	765	7.14
Kekoskee, village	169	171	1.18				
Lebanon, town	1,664	1,726	3.73	**DUNN COUNTY**	39,858	41,737	4.71
Leroy, town	1,116	1,116	0.00	Boyceville, village	1,043	1,075	3.07
Lomira, town	1,228	1,250	1.79	Colfax, town	909	992	9.13
Lomira, village	2,233	2,378	6.49	Colfax, village	1,136	1,154	1.58
Lowell, town	1,169	1,182	1.11	Downing, village	257	260	1.17
Lowell, village	366	374	2.19	Dunn, town	1,492	1,551	3.95
Mayville, city	4,902	5,164	5.34	Eau Galle, town	797	801	0.50
Neosho, village	593	592	–0.17	Elk Mound, town	1,121	1,272	13.47
Oak Grove, town	1,126	1,131	0.44	Elk Mound, village	785	822	4.71
Portland, town	1,106	1,138	2.89	Grant, town	426	443	3.99
Randolph (part), village .	1,346	1,334	–0.89	Hay River, town	546	589	7.88
Reeseville, village	703	712	1.28	Knapp, village	421	454	7.84
Rubicon, town	2,005	2,187	9.08	Lucas, town	658	697	5.93
Shields, town	554	563	1.62	Menomonie, city	14,937	15,247	2.08
Theresa, town	1,080	1,110	2.78	Menomonie, town	3,174	3,354	5.67
Theresa, village	1,252	1,300	3.83	New Haven, town	656	683	4.12
Trenton, town	1,301	1,298	–0.23	Otter Creek, town	474	523	10.34
Watertown (part), city . .	8,063	8,515	5.61	Peru, town	247	257	4.05
Waupun (part), city	7,436	7,347	–1.20	Red Cedar, town	1,673	1,851	10.64
Westford, town	1,400	1,433	2.36	Ridgeland, village	265	263	–0.75
Williamstown, town	646	655	1.39	Rock Creek, town	793	850	7.19
				Sand Creek, town	586	616	5.12
DOOR COUNTY	27,961	29,114	4.12	Sheridan, town	483	505	4.55
Baileys Harbor, town . . .	1,003	1,080	7.68	Sherman, town	748	777	3.88
Brussels, town	1,112	1,142	2.70	Spring Brook, town	1,320	1,484	12.42
Clay Banks, town	410	418	1.95	Stanton, town	715	800	11.89
Egg Harbor, town	1,194	1,323	10.80	Tainter, town	2,116	2,308	9.07

WISCONSIN POPULATION
BY COUNTY AND MUNICIPALITY
April 1, 2000 and January 1, 2004–Continued

County and Municipality	2000 Census[1]	2004 Estimate	Percent Change	County and Municipality	2000 Census[1]	2004 Estimate	Percent Change
Tiffany, town	633	660	4.27	Springvale, town	727	733	0.83
Weston, town	630	626	–0.63	Taycheedah, town	3,666	3,810	3.93
Wheeler, village	317	320	0.95	Waupun (part), city	3,282	3,323	1.25
Wilson, town	500	503	0.60	Waupun, town	1,385	1,418	2.38
EAU CLAIRE COUNTY	93,142	96,214	3.30	FOREST COUNTY	10,024	10,198	1.74
Altoona, city	6,698	6,719	0.31	Alvin, town	186	195	4.84
Augusta, city	1,460	1,463	0.21	Argonne, town	532	545	2.44
Bridge Creek, town	1,844	1,845	0.05	Armstrong Creek, town	463	469	1.30
Brunswick, town	1,598	1,638	2.50	Blackwell, town	347	354	2.02
Clear Creek, town	712	734	3.09	Caswell, town	102	102	0.00
Drammen, town	800	815	1.88	Crandon, city	1,961	1,962	0.05
Eau Claire (part), city	59,794	61,912	3.54	Crandon, town	614	638	3.91
Fairchild, town	351	372	5.98	Freedom, town	376	378	0.53
Fairchild, village	564	518	–8.16	Hiles, town	404	421	4.21
Fall Creek, village	1,236	1,284	3.88	Laona, town	1,367	1,376	0.66
Lincoln, town	1,080	1,121	3.80	Lincoln, town	1,005	1,021	1.59
Ludington, town	998	1,057	5.91	Nashville, town	1,157	1,182	2.16
Otter Creek, town	531	532	0.19	Popple River, town	79	90	13.92
Pleasant Valley, town	2,681	2,932	9.36	Ross, town	167	170	1.80
Seymour, town	2,978	3,099	4.06	Wabeno, town	1,264	1,295	2.45
Union, town	2,402	2,514	4.66				
Washington, town	6,995	7,227	3.32	GRANT COUNTY	49,597	50,552	1.93
Wilson, town	420	432	2.86	Bagley, village	339	340	0.29
				Beetown, town	734	759	3.41
FLORENCE COUNTY	5,088	5,214	2.48	Bloomington, town	399	397	–0.50
Aurora, town	1,186	1,222	3.04	Bloomington, village	701	697	–0.57
Commonwealth, town	419	425	1.43	Blue River, village	429	427	–0.47
Fence, town	231	234	1.30	Boscobel, city	3,047	3,403	11.68
Fern, town	153	158	3.27	Boscobel, town	433	431	–0.46
Florence, town	2,319	2,365	1.98	Cassville, town	487	491	0.82
Homestead, town	378	388	2.65	Cassville, village	1,085	1,068	–1.57
Long Lake, town	197	204	3.55	Castle Rock, town	314	330	5.10
Tipler, town	205	218	6.34	Clifton, town	304	316	3.95
				Cuba City (part), city	1,945	1,942	–0.15
FOND DU LAC COUNTY	97,296	99,608	2.38	Dickeyville, village	1,043	1,056	1.25
Alto, town	1,103	1,109	0.54	Ellenboro, town	608	612	0.66
Ashford, town	1,773	1,838	3.67	Fennimore, city	2,387	2,388	0.04
Auburn, town	2,075	2,187	5.40	Fennimore, town	599	609	1.67
Brandon, village	912	914	0.22	Glen Haven, town	490	478	–2.45
Byron, town	1,550	1,596	2.97	Harrison, town	497	512	3.02
Calumet, town	1,514	1,526	0.79	Hazel Green, town	1,043	1,149	10.16
Campbellsport, village	1,913	1,938	1.31	Hazel Green (part),			
Eden, town	979	983	0.41	village	1,171	1,163	–0.68
Eden, village	687	733	6.70	Hickory Grove, town	443	472	6.55
Eldorado, town	1,447	1,487	2.76	Jamestown, town	2,077	2,106	1.40
Empire, town	2,620	2,736	4.43	Lancaster, city	4,070	4,042	–0.69
Fairwater, village	350	357	2.00	Liberty, town	552	568	2.90
Fond du Lac, city	42,203	42,865	1.57	Lima, town	721	757	4.99
Fond du Lac, town	2,027	2,306	13.76	Little Grant, town	257	255	–0.78
Forest, town	1,108	1,137	2.62	Livingston (part), village	584	580	–0.68
Friendship, town	2,406	2,484	3.24	Marion, town	517	560	8.32
Kewaskum (part), village	0	0	0.00	Millville, town	147	149	1.36
Lamartine, town	1,616	1,667	3.16	Montfort (part), village	603	609	1.00
Marshfield, town	1,118	1,125	0.63	Mount Hope, town	225	232	3.11
Metomen, town	709	723	1.97	Mount Hope, village	186	183	–1.61
Mount Calvary, village	956	953	–0.31	Mount Ida, town	523	539	3.06
North Fond du Lac,				Muscoda, town	674	718	6.53
village	4,557	4,729	3.77	Muscoda (part), village	1,357	1,348	–0.66
Oakfield, town	767	772	0.65	North Lancaster, town	515	530	2.91
Oakfield, village	1,012	1,022	0.99	Paris, town	754	761	0.93
Osceola, town	1,802	1,850	2.66	Patch Grove, town	390	393	0.77
Ripon, city	7,450	7,619	2.27	Patch Grove, village	166	160	–3.61
Ripon, town	1,379	1,407	2.03	Platteville, city	9,989	10,109	1.20
Rosendale, town	783	791	1.02	Platteville, town	1,343	1,380	2.76
Rosendale, village	923	969	4.98	Potosi, town	831	818	–1.56
St. Cloud, village	497	501	0.80	Potosi, village	711	722	1.55

WISCONSIN POPULATION
BY COUNTY AND MUNICIPALITY
April 1, 2000 and January 1, 2004–Continued

County and Municipality	2000 Census[1]	2004 Estimate	Percent Change
Smelser, town	756	773	2.25
South Lancaster, town	808	824	1.98
Tennyson, village	370	368	-0.54
Waterloo, town	557	582	4.49
Watterstown, town	362	368	1.66
Wingville, town	394	405	2.79
Woodman, town	194	199	2.58
Woodman, village	96	95	-1.04
Wyalusing, town	370	379	2.43
GREEN COUNTY	33,647	35,163	4.51
Adams, town	464	490	5.60
Albany, town	775	891	14.97
Albany, village	1,191	1,180	-0.92
Belleville (part), village	113	139	23.01
Brodhead (part), city	3,180	3,181	0.03
Brooklyn, town	944	992	5.08
Brooklyn (part), village	414	460	11.11
Browntown, village	252	261	3.57
Cadiz, town	863	865	0.23
Clarno, town	1,079	1,098	1.76
Decatur, town	1,688	1,849	9.54
Exeter, town	1,261	1,527	21.09
Jefferson, town	1,212	1,231	1.57
Jordon, town	577	610	5.72
Monroe, city	10,843	10,973	1.20
Monroe, town	1,142	1,229	7.62
Monticello, village	1,146	1,147	0.09
Mount Pleasant, town	547	573	4.75
New Glarus, town	943	1,189	26.09
New Glarus, village	2,111	2,104	-0.33
Spring Grove, town	861	884	2.67
Sylvester, town	809	866	7.05
Washington, town	627	722	15.15
York, town	605	702	16.03
GREEN LAKE COUNTY	19,105	19,344	1.25
Berlin (part), city	5,222	5,242	0.38
Berlin, town	1,145	1,188	3.76
Brooklyn, town	1,904	1,950	2.42
Green Lake, city	1,100	1,135	3.18
Green Lake, town	1,258	1,273	1.19
Kingston, town	900	916	1.78
Kingston, village	288	296	2.78
Mackford, town	585	587	0.34
Manchester, town	848	867	2.24
Markesan, city	1,396	1,373	-1.65
Marquette, town	481	494	2.70
Marquette, village	169	175	3.55
Princeton, city	1,504	1,476	-1.86
Princeton, town	1,540	1,592	3.38
St. Marie, town	341	349	2.35
Seneca, town	424	431	1.65
IOWA COUNTY	22,780	23,639	3.77
Arena, town	1,444	1,479	2.42
Arena, village	685	764	11.53
Avoca, village	608	623	2.47
Barneveld, village	1,088	1,153	5.97
Blanchardville (part), village	146	148	1.37
Brigham, town	908	959	5.62
Clyde, town	322	326	1.24
Cobb, village	442	447	1.13
Dodgeville, city	4,220	4,479	6.14
Dodgeville, town	1,407	1,594	13.29
Eden, town	397	406	2.27

County and Municipality	2000 Census[1]	2004 Estimate	Percent Change
Highland, town	797	808	1.38
Highland, village	855	868	1.52
Hollandale, village	283	284	0.35
Linden, town	873	868	-0.57
Linden, village	615	615	0.00
Livingston (part), village	13	9	-30.77
Mifflin, town	617	640	3.73
Mineral Point, city	2,617	2,636	0.73
Mineral Point, town	867	891	2.77
Montfort (part), village	60	57	-5.00
Moscow, town	594	619	4.21
Muscoda (part), village	96	81	-15.63
Pulaski, town	381	382	0.26
Rewey, village	311	307	-1.29
Ridgeway, town	581	614	5.68
Ridgeway, village	689	696	1.02
Waldwick, town	500	504	0.80
Wyoming, town	364	382	4.95
IRON COUNTY	6,861	6,948	1.27
Anderson, town	61	61	0.00
Carey, town	191	191	0.00
Gurney, town	158	158	0.00
Hurley, city	1,818	1,805	-0.72
Kimball, town	540	536	-0.74
Knight, town	284	284	0.00
Mercer, town	1,732	1,809	4.45
Montreal, city	838	834	-0.48
Oma, town	355	383	7.89
Pence, town	198	193	-2.53
Saxon, town	350	349	-0.29
Sherman, town	336	345	2.68
JACKSON COUNTY	19,100	19,677	3.02
Adams, town	1,208	1,302	7.78
Albion, town	1,093	1,133	3.66
Alma, town	983	1,038	5.60
Alma Center, village	446	458	2.69
Bear Bluff, town	128	119	-7.03
Black River Falls, city	3,618	3,627	0.25
Brockway, town	2,580	2,692	4.34
City Point, town	189	184	-2.65
Cleveland, town	438	466	6.39
Curran, town	366	387	5.74
Franklin, town	325	337	3.69
Garden Valley, town	406	407	0.25
Garfield, town	529	607	14.74
Hixton, town	611	629	2.95
Hixton, village	446	444	-0.45
Irving, town	602	659	9.47
Knapp, town	275	297	8.00
Komensky, town	462	416	-9.96
Manchester, town	680	716	5.29
Melrose, town	402	420	4.48
Melrose, village	529	519	-1.89
Merrillan, village	585	582	-0.51
Millston, town	136	142	4.41
North Bend, town	397	405	2.02
Northfield, town	586	569	-2.90
Springfield, town	567	608	7.23
Taylor, village	513	514	0.19
JEFFERSON COUNTY	75,767	78,342	3.40
Aztalan, town	1,447	1,467	1.38
Cambridge (part), village	87	89	2.30
Cold Spring, town	766	774	1.04
Concord, town	2,023	2,056	1.63

WISCONSIN POPULATION
BY COUNTY AND MUNICIPALITY
April 1, 2000 and January 1, 2004–Continued

County and Municipality	2000 Census[1]	2004 Estimate	Percent Change	County and Municipality	2000 Census[1]	2004 Estimate	Percent Change
Farmington, town	1,498	1,522	1.60	Twin Lakes, village	5,124	5,388	5.15
Fort Atkinson, city	11,621	11,943	2.77	Wheatland, town	3,292	3,354	1.88
Hebron, town	1,135	1,143	0.70				
[6]Ixonia, town	2,902	3,190	9.92	KEWAUNEE COUNTY	20,187	20,860	3.33
Jefferson, city	7,208	7,458	3.47	Ahnapee, town	977	992	1.54
Jefferson, town	2,395	2,252	–5.97	Algoma, city	3,357	3,322	–1.04
Johnson Creek, village	1,581	1,744	10.31	Carlton, town	1,000	1,032	3.20
Koshkonong, town	3,395	3,514	3.51	Casco, town	1,153	1,207	4.68
Lac La Belle (part),				Casco, village	572	583	1.92
village	0	2	0.00	Franklin, town	997	1,053	5.62
Lake Mills, city	4,843	4,971	2.64	Kewaunee, city	2,806	2,892	3.06
Lake Mills, town	1,936	2,008	3.72	Lincoln, town	957	994	3.87
Milford, town	1,055	1,062	0.66	Luxemburg, town	1,402	1,465	4.49
Oakland, town	3,135	3,252	3.73	Luxemburg, village	1,935	2,147	10.96
Palmyra, town	1,145	1,163	1.57	Montpelier, town	1,371	1,412	2.99
Palmyra, village	1,766	1,779	0.74	Pierce, town	897	910	1.45
Sullivan, town	2,124	2,234	5.18	Red River, town	1,476	1,524	3.25
Sullivan, village	688	691	0.44	West Kewaunee, town	1,287	1,327	3.11
Sumner, town	904	902	–0.22				
Waterloo, city	3,259	3,310	1.56	LA CROSSE COUNTY	107,120	109,616	2.33
Waterloo, town	832	877	5.41	Bangor, town	583	596	2.23
Watertown (part), city	13,535	14,217	5.04	Bangor, village	1,400	1,394	–0.43
Watertown, town	1,876	1,914	2.03	Barre, town	1,014	1,107	9.17
Whitewater (part), city	2,611	2,808	7.55	Burns, town	979	980	0.10
				Campbell, town	4,410	4,417	0.16
JUNEAU COUNTY	24,316	25,470	4.75	Farmington, town	1,733	1,843	6.35
Armenia, town	707	768	8.63	Greenfield, town	1,538	1,688	9.75
Camp Douglas, village	592	569	–3.89	Hamilton, town	2,103	2,292	8.99
Clearfield, town	737	767	4.07	Holland, town	3,042	3,168	4.14
Cutler, town	282	290	2.84	Holmen, village	6,200	6,984	12.65
Elroy, city	1,578	1,558	–1.27	La Crosse, city	51,818	51,507	–0.60
Finley, town	84	86	2.38	Medary, town	1,463	1,478	1.03
Fountain, town	582	599	2.92	Onalaska, city	14,839	15,782	6.35
Germantown, town	1,174	1,317	12.18	Onalaska, town	5,210	5,406	3.76
Hustler, village	113	118	4.42	Rockland, village	625	639	2.24
Kildare, town	557	615	10.41	Shelby, town	4,687	4,772	1.81
Kingston, town	58	56	–3.45	Washington, town	738	754	2.17
Lemonweir, town	1,763	1,802	2.21	West Salem, village	4,738	4,809	1.50
Lindina, town	730	733	0.41				
Lisbon, town	1,020	1,038	1.76	LAFAYETTE COUNTY	16,137	16,311	1.08
Lyndon, town	1,217	1,328	9.12	Argyle, town	479	481	0.42
Lyndon Station, village	458	460	0.44	Argyle, village	823	817	–0.73
Marion, town	433	455	5.08	Belmont, town	676	717	6.07
Mauston, city	3,740	4,133	10.51	Belmont, village	871	898	3.10
Necedah, town	2,156	2,349	8.95	Benton, town	469	492	4.90
Necedah, village	888	896	0.90	Benton, village	976	998	2.25
New Lisbon, city	1,436	1,429	–0.49	Blanchard, town	261	278	6.51
Orange, town	549	566	3.10	Blanchardville (part),			
Plymouth, town	639	655	2.50	village	660	656	–0.61
Seven Mile Creek, town	369	375	1.63	Cuba City (part), city	211	213	0.95
Summit, town	623	662	6.26	Darlington, city	2,418	2,416	–0.08
Union Center, village	214	217	1.40	Darlington, town	757	772	1.98
Wonewoc, town	783	803	2.55	Elk Grove, town	463	476	2.81
Wonewoc, village	834	826	–0.96	Fayette, town	366	373	1.91
				Gratiot, town	653	642	–1.68
KENOSHA COUNTY	149,577	156,082	4.35	Gratiot, village	252	247	–1.98
Brighton, town	1,450	1,504	3.72	Hazel Green (part),			
Bristol, town	4,538	4,692	3.39	village	12	15	25.00
Genoa City (part), village	0	0	0.00	Kendall, town	320	317	–0.94
Kenosha, city	90,352	92,808	2.72	Lamont, town	267	282	5.62
Paddock Lake, village	3,012	3,106	3.12	Monticello, town	148	139	–6.08
Paris, town	1,473	1,514	2.78	New Diggings, town	473	473	0.00
Pleasant Prairie, village	16,136	18,122	12.31	Seymour, town	363	380	4.68
Randall, town	2,929	3,098	5.77	Shullsburg, city	1,246	1,228	–1.44
Salem, town	9,871	10,767	9.08	Shullsburg, town	364	357	–1.92
Silver Lake, village	2,341	2,435	4.02	South Wayne, village	484	485	0.21
Somers, town	9,059	9,294	2.59	Wayne, town	496	485	–2.22

WISCONSIN POPULATION
BY COUNTY AND MUNICIPALITY
April 1, 2000 and January 1, 2004–Continued

County and Municipality	2000 Census[1]	2004 Estimate	Percent Change	County and Municipality	2000 Census[1]	2004 Estimate	Percent Change
White Oak Springs, town	97	100	3.09	Reedsville, village	1,187	1,182	−0.42
Willow Springs, town	632	676	6.96	Rockland, town	896	935	4.35
Wiota, town	900	898	−0.22	St. Nazianz, village	749	740	−1.20
				Schleswig, town	1,900	1,995	5.00
LANGLADE COUNTY	20,740	21,227	2.35	Two Creeks, town	551	557	1.09
Ackley, town	510	530	3.92	Two Rivers, city	12,639	12,599	−0.32
Ainsworth, town	571	596	4.38	Two Rivers, town	1,912	1,921	0.47
Antigo, city	8,560	8,586	0.30	Valders, village	948	1,001	5.59
Antigo, town	1,487	1,525	2.56	Whitelaw, village	730	741	1.51
Elcho, town	1,317	1,353	2.73				
Evergreen, town	468	501	7.05	MARATHON COUNTY	125,834	129,962	3.28
Langlade, town	472	490	3.81	Abbotsford (part), city	544	599	10.11
Neva, town	994	1,027	3.32	Athens, village	1,095	1,111	1.46
Norwood, town	918	972	5.88	Bergen, town	615	639	3.90
Parrish, town	108	126	16.67	Berlin, town	887	939	5.86
Peck, town	354	361	1.98	Bern, town	562	580	3.20
Polar, town	995	988	−0.70	Bevent, town	1,126	1,172	4.09
Price, town	243	249	2.47	Birnamwood (part), village	10	16	60.00
Rolling, town	1,452	1,527	5.17	Brighton, town	611	613	0.33
Summit, town	168	161	−4.17	Brokaw, village	107	137	28.04
Upham, town	689	708	2.76	Cassel, town	847	879	3.78
Vilas, town	249	250	0.40	Cleveland, town	1,160	1,284	10.69
White Lake, village	329	350	6.38	Colby (part), city	460	466	1.30
Wolf River, town	856	927	8.29	Day, town	1,023	1,049	2.54
				Dorchester (part), village	4	4	0.00
LINCOLN COUNTY	29,641	30,271	2.13	Easton, town	1,062	1,079	1.60
Birch, town	801	773	−3.50	Eau Pleine, town	750	764	1.87
Bradley, town	2,573	2,671	3.81	Edgar, village	1,386	1,431	3.25
Corning, town	826	848	2.66	Elderon, town	567	581	2.47
Harding, town	334	345	3.29	Elderon, village	189	180	−4.76
Harrison, town	793	844	6.43	Emmet, town	842	911	8.19
King, town	842	869	3.21	Fenwood, village	174	163	−6.32
Merrill, city	10,146	10,144	−0.02	Frankfort, town	651	668	2.61
Merrill, town	2,979	3,076	3.26	Franzen, town	505	515	1.98
Pine River, town	1,877	1,955	4.16	Green Valley, town	514	541	5.25
Rock Falls, town	598	644	7.69	Guenther, town	302	327	8.28
Russell, town	693	723	4.33	Halsey, town	645	662	2.64
Schley, town	909	938	3.19	Hamburg, town	910	935	2.75
Scott, town	1,287	1,355	5.28	Harrison, town	418	439	5.02
Skanawan, town	354	381	7.63	Hatley, village	476	500	5.04
Somo, town	121	138	14.05	Hewitt, town	545	572	4.95
Tomahawk, city	3,770	3,789	0.50	Holton, town	907	916	0.99
Tomahawk, town	439	465	5.92	Hull, town	773	776	0.39
Wilson, town	299	313	4.68	Johnson, town	993	1,014	2.11
				Knowlton, town	1,688	1,780	5.45
MANITOWOC COUNTY	82,893	84,264	1.65	[7]Kronenwetter, village	5,369	5,791	7.86
Cato, town	1,616	1,663	2.91	Maine, town	2,407	2,419	0.50
Centerville, town	713	722	1.26	Marathon, town	1,085	1,106	1.94
Cleveland, village	1,361	1,409	3.53	Marathon City, village	1,640	1,618	−1.34
Cooperstown, town	1,389	1,403	1.01	Marshfield (part), city	417	484	16.07
Eaton, town	761	786	3.29	McMillan, town	1,790	1,889	5.53
Francis Creek, village	681	700	2.79	Mosinee, city	4,063	4,162	2.44
Franklin, town	1,293	1,324	2.40	Mosinee, town	2,146	2,253	4.99
Gibson, town	1,352	1,419	4.96	Norrie, town	967	1,030	6.51
Kellnersville, village	374	367	−1.87	Plover, town	686	709	3.35
Kiel (part), city	3,129	3,218	2.84	Reid, town	1,191	1,228	3.11
Kossuth, town	2,033	2,095	3.05	Rib Falls, town	907	968	6.73
Liberty, town	1,287	1,320	2.56	Rib Mountain, town	7,556	7,635	1.05
Manitowoc, city	34,053	34,612	1.64	Rietbrock, town	927	980	5.72
Manitowoc, town	1,073	1,127	5.03	Ringle, town	1,408	1,482	5.26
Manitowoc Rapids, town	2,520	2,538	0.71	Rothschild, village	4,970	5,071	2.03
Maple Grove, town	852	867	1.76	Schofield, city	2,117	2,250	6.28
Maribel, village	284	287	1.06	Spencer, town	1,341	1,464	9.17
Meeme, town	1,538	1,543	0.33	Spencer, village	1,932	1,947	0.78
Mishicot, town	1,409	1,435	1.85	Stettin, town	2,191	2,243	2.37
Mishicot, village	1,422	1,439	1.20	Stratford, village	1,523	1,559	2.36
Newton, town	2,241	2,319	3.48				

WISCONSIN POPULATION
BY COUNTY AND MUNICIPALITY
April 1, 2000 and January 1, 2004–Continued

County and Municipality	2000 Census[1]	2004 Estimate	Percent Change	County and Municipality	2000 Census[1]	2004 Estimate	Percent Change
Texas, town	1,703	1,754	2.99	Greenfield, city	35,476	36,059	1.64
Unity (part), village	205	201	−1.95	Hales Corners, village	7,765	7,682	−1.07
Wausau, city	38,426	38,912	1.26	Milwaukee (part), city	596,974	593,920	−0.51
Wausau, town	2,214	2,257	1.94	Oak Creek, city	28,456	31,029	9.04
Weston, town	514	567	10.31	River Hills, village	1,631	1,625	−0.37
Weston, village	12,079	13,003	7.65	St. Francis, city	8,662	8,728	0.76
Wien, town	712	738	3.65	Shorewood, village	13,763	13,535	−1.66
				South Milwaukee, city	21,256	21,360	0.49
MARINETTE COUNTY	43,384	44,204	1.89	Wauwatosa, city	47,271	46,511	−1.61
Amberg, town	854	855	0.12	West Allis, city	61,254	60,607	−1.06
Athelstane, town	601	609	1.33	West Milwaukee, village	4,201	4,142	−1.40
Beaver, town	1,123	1,158	3.12	Whitefish Bay, village	14,163	13,979	−1.30
Beecher, town	783	801	2.30				
Coleman, village	716	719	0.42	MONROE COUNTY	40,896	42,626	4.23
Crivitz, village	998	1,024	2.61	Adrian, town	682	738	8.21
Dunbar, town	1,303	1,230	−5.60	Angelo, town	1,268	1,303	2.76
Goodman, town	820	843	2.80	Byron, town	1,394	1,465	5.09
Grover, town	1,729	1,815	4.97	Cashton, village	1,005	1,043	3.78
Lake, town	1,064	1,101	3.48	Clifton, town	693	722	4.18
Marinette, city	11,749	11,638	−0.94	Glendale, town	563	604	7.28
Middle Inlet, town	831	880	5.90	Grant, town	483	500	3.52
Niagara, city	1,880	1,858	−1.17	Greenfield, town	626	653	4.31
Niagara, town	924	943	2.06	Jefferson, town	800	823	2.88
Pembine, town	1,036	1,093	5.50	Kendall, village	482	478	−0.83
Peshtigo, city	3,474	3,499	0.72	Lafayette, town	318	329	3.46
Peshtigo, town	3,702	3,903	5.43	La Grange town	1,761	1,837	4.32
Porterfield, town	1,991	2,071	4.02	Leon, town	858	943	9.91
Pound, town	1,367	1,397	2.19	Lincoln, town	827	871	5.32
Pound, village	355	351	−1.13	Little Falls, town	1,334	1,436	7.65
Silver Cliff, town	529	568	7.37	Melvina, village	93	89	−4.30
Stephenson, town	3,065	3,225	5.22	New Lyme, town	141	148	4.96
Wagner, town	722	773	7.06	Norwalk, village	653	640	−1.99
Wausaukee, town	1,196	1,288	7.69	Oakdale, town	679	736	8.39
Wausaukee, village	572	562	−1.75	Oakdale, village	297	317	6.73
				Portland, town	686	684	−0.29
MARQUETTE COUNTY	14,555	15,051	3.41	Ridgeville, town	491	542	10.39
Buffalo, town	1,085	1,151	6.08	Scott, town	117	118	0.85
Crystal Lake, town	513	525	2.34	Sheldon, town	682	695	1.91
Douglas, town	768	794	3.39	Sparta, city	8,648	8,994	4.00
Endeavor, village	440	449	2.05	Sparta, town	2,753	2,953	7.26
Harris, town	729	749	2.74	Tomah, city	8,419	8,648	2.72
Mecan, town	726	745	2.62	Tomah, town	1,194	1,261	5.61
Montello, city	1,397	1,447	3.58	Warrens, village	286	285	−0.35
Montello, town	1,043	1,058	1.44	Wellington, town	544	571	4.96
Moundville, town	574	587	2.26	Wells, town	529	559	5.67
Neshkoro, town	595	607	2.02	Wilton, town	925	966	4.43
Neshkoro, village	453	458	1.10	Wilton, village	519	532	2.50
Newton, town	550	565	2.73	Wyeville, village	146	143	−2.05
Oxford, town	859	931	8.38				
Oxford, village	536	536	0.00	OCONTO COUNTY	35,652	37,679	5.69
Packwaukee, town	1,297	1,296	−0.08	Abrams, town	1,757	1,924	9.50
Shields, town	456	487	6.80	Bagley, town	333	342	2.70
Springfield, town	628	678	7.96	Brazeau, town	1,408	1,448	2.84
Westfield, town	689	759	10.16	Breed, town	657	721	9.74
Westfield, village	1,217	1,229	0.99	Chase, town	2,082	2,503	20.22
				Doty, town	249	268	7.63
MENOMINEE COUNTY	4,562	4,616	1.18	Gillett, city	1,262	1,256	−0.48
Menominee, town	4,562	4,616	1.18	Gillett, town	1,090	1,107	1.56
				How, town	563	576	2.31
MILWAUKEE COUNTY	940,164	939,358	−0.09	Lakewood, town	875	916	4.69
Bayside (part), village	4,415	4,179	−5.35	Lena, town	757	758	0.13
Brown Deer, village	12,170	11,845	−2.67	Lena, village	529	520	−1.70
Cudahy, city	18,429	18,315	−0.62	Little River, town	1,065	1,087	2.07
Fox Point, village	7,012	6,886	−1.80	Little Suamico, town	3,877	4,381	13.00
Franklin, city	29,494	31,804	7.83	Maple Valley, town	670	697	4.03
Glendale, city	13,367	13,024	−2.57	Morgan, town	882	973	10.32
Greendale, village	14,405	14,128	−1.92	Mountain, town	860	873	1.51

WISCONSIN POPULATION
BY COUNTY AND MUNICIPALITY
April 1, 2000 and January 1, 2004–Continued

County and Municipality	2000 Census[1]	2004 Estimate	Percent Change	County and Municipality	2000 Census[1]	2004 Estimate	Percent Change
Oconto, city	4,708	4,711	0.06	Seymour, town	1,216	1,246	2.47
Oconto, town	1,251	1,375	9.91	Shiocton, village	954	956	0.21
Oconto Falls, city	2,843	2,883	1.41	Vandenbroek, town	1,351	1,317	-2.52
Oconto Falls, town	1,139	1,206	5.88	Wrightstown (part),			
Pensaukee, town	1,214	1,313	8.15	village	0	37	0.00
Pulaski (part), village	2	0	--[2]				
Riverview, town	829	869	4.83	OZAUKEE COUNTY	82,317	85,160	3.45
Spruce, town	871	913	4.82	Bayside (part), village	103	107	3.88
Stiles, town	1,465	1,560	6.48	Belgium, town	1,513	1,558	2.97
Suring, village	605	586	-3.14	Belgium, village	1,678	1,887	12.46
Townsend, town	963	1,033	7.27	Cedarburg, city	11,102	11,331	2.06
Underhill, town	846	880	4.02	Cedarburg, town	5,550	5,720	3.06
				Fredonia, town	2,083	2,126	2.06
ONEIDA COUNTY	36,776	37,726	2.58	Fredonia, village	1,934	2,111	9.15
Cassian, town	962	1,008	4.78	Grafton, town	3,980	4,078	2.46
Crescent, town	2,071	2,099	1.35	Grafton, village	10,464	11,160	6.65
Enterprise, town	274	275	0.36	Mequon, city	22,643	23,416	3.41
Hazelhurst, town	1,267	1,320	4.18	Newburg (part), village	92	88	-4.35
Lake Tomahawk, town	1,160	1,186	2.24	Port Washington, city	10,467	10,683	2.06
Little Rice, town	314	314	0.00	Port Washington, town	1,631	1,664	2.02
Lynne, town	210	209	-0.48	Saukville, town	1,755	1,786	1.77
Minocqua, town	4,859	5,128	5.54	Saukville, village	4,068	4,167	2.43
Monico, town	364	378	3.85	Thiensville, village	3,254	3,278	0.74
Newbold, town	2,710	2,830	4.43				
Nokomis, town	1,363	1,417	3.96	PEPIN COUNTY	7,213	7,568	4.92
Pelican, town	2,902	2,602	-10.34	Albany, town	620	702	13.23
Piehl, town	93	94	1.08	Durand, city	1,968	1,976	0.41
Pine Lake, town	2,720	2,827	3.93	Durand, town	694	706	1.73
Rhinelander, city	7,735	8,041	3.96	Frankfort, town	362	364	0.55
Schoepke, town	352	353	0.28	Lima, town	716	731	2.09
Stella, town	633	670	5.85	Pepin, town	580	627	8.10
Sugar Camp, town	1,781	1,846	3.65	Pepin, village	878	925	5.35
Three Lakes, town	2,339	2,388	2.09	Stockholm, town	75	170	126.67
Woodboro, town	685	692	1.02	Stockholm, village	97	99	2.06
Woodruff, town	1,982	2,049	3.38	Waterville, town	859	872	1.51
				Waubeek, town	364	396	8.79
OUTAGAMIE COUNTY	161,091	168,840	4.81				
Appleton (part), city	58,301	59,738	2.46	PIERCE COUNTY	36,804	38,615	4.92
Bear Creek, village	415	422	1.69	Bay City, village	491	503	2.44
Black Creek, town	1,268	1,291	1.81	Clifton, town	1,657	1,853	11.83
Black Creek, village	1,192	1,218	2.18	Diamond Bluff, town	479	508	6.05
Bovina, town	1,130	1,208	6.90	El Paso, town	690	737	6.81
Buchanan, town	5,827	6,715	15.24	Ellsworth, town	1,064	1,115	4.79
Center, town	3,163	3,328	5.22	Ellsworth, village	2,909	3,056	5.05
Cicero, town	1,092	1,111	1.74	Elmwood, village	841	825	-1.90
Combined Locks, village	2,422	2,659	9.79	Gilman, town	772	838	8.55
Dale, town	2,288	2,483	8.52	Hartland, town	814	850	4.42
Deer Creek, town	682	685	0.44	Isabelle, town	289	282	-2.42
Ellington, town	2,535	2,700	6.51	Maiden Rock, town	589	610	3.57
Freedom, town	5,241	5,466	4.29	Maiden Rock, village	121	120	-0.83
Grand Chute, town	18,392	19,723	7.24	Martell, town	1,070	1,137	6.26
Greenville, town	6,844	7,634	11.54	Oak Grove, town	1,522	1,770	16.29
Hortonia, town	1,063	1,072	0.85	Plum City, village	574	607	5.75
Hortonville, village	2,357	2,503	6.19	Prescott, city	3,764	3,873	2.90
Howard (part), village	0	0	0.00	River Falls (part), city	10,242	10,678	4.26
Kaukauna, city	12,983	13,926	7.26	River Falls, town	2,304	2,379	3.26
[8]Kaukauna, town	1,116	1,202	7.71	Rock Elm, town	504	526	4.37
Kimberly, village	6,146	6,362	3.51	Salem, town	505	517	2.38
Liberty, town	834	874	4.80	Spring Lake, town	550	582	5.82
Little Chute, village	10,476	10,775	2.85	Spring Valley (part),			
Maine, town	831	898	8.06	village	1,187	1,263	6.40
Maple Creek, town	687	684	-0.44	Trenton, town	1,737	1,806	3.97
New London (part), city	1,467	1,515	3.27	Trimbelle, town	1,511	1,544	2.18
Nichols, village	307	298	-2.93	Union, town	618	636	2.91
Oneida, town	4,147	4,298	3.64				
Osborn, town	1,029	1,096	6.51	POLK COUNTY	41,319	43,870	6.17
Seymour, city	3,335	3,400	1.95	Alden, town	2,615	2,806	7.30

WISCONSIN POPULATION
BY COUNTY AND MUNICIPALITY
April 1, 2000 and January 1, 2004–Continued

County and Municipality	2000 Census[1]	2004 Estimate	Percent Change	County and Municipality	2000 Census[1]	2004 Estimate	Percent Change
Amery, city	2,845	2,902	2.00	Catawba, town	283	294	3.89
Apple River, town	1,067	1,138	6.65	Catawba, village	149	141	−5.37
Balsam Lake, town	1,384	1,456	5.20	Eisenstein, town	669	678	1.35
Balsam Lake, village . . .	950	1,012	6.53	Elk, town	1,183	1,199	1.35
Beaver, town	753	829	10.09	Emery, town	325	324	−0.31
Black Brook, town	1,208	1,350	11.75	Fifield, town	989	999	1.01
Bone Lake, town	710	757	6.62	Flambeau, town	535	574	7.29
Centuria, village	865	957	10.64	Georgetown, town	164	161	−1.83
Clam Falls, town	547	556	1.65	Hackett, town	202	205	1.49
Clayton, town	912	966	5.92	Harmony, town	211	221	4.74
Clayton, village	507	540	6.51	Hill, town	364	382	4.95
Clear Lake, town	800	831	3.88	Kennan, town	378	380	0.53
Clear Lake, village	1,051	1,080	2.76	Kennan, village	171	166	−2.92
Dresser, village	732	789	7.79	Knox, town	399	408	2.26
Eureka, town	1,338	1,468	9.72	Lake, town	1,319	1,367	3.64
Farmington, town	1,625	1,745	7.38	Ogema, town	882	897	1.70
Frederic, village	1,262	1,244	−1.43	Park Falls, city	2,793	2,689	−3.72
Garfield, town	1,443	1,550	7.42	Phillips, city	1,675	1,676	0.06
Georgetown, town	1,004	1,068	6.37	Prentice, town	479	478	−0.21
Johnstown, town	520	552	6.15	Prentice, village	626	640	2.24
Laketown, town	918	927	0.98	Spirit, town	315	332	5.40
Lincoln, town	2,304	2,406	4.43	Worcester, town	1,711	1,743	1.87
Lorain, town	328	333	1.52				
Luck, town	881	880	−0.11	**RACINE COUNTY**	188,831	191,853	1.60
Luck, village	1,210	1,221	0.91	Burlington (part), city . . .	9,936	10,183	2.49
McKinley, town	328	335	2.13	Burlington, town	6,384	6,511	1.99
Milltown, town	1,146	1,225	6.89	Caledonia, town	23,614	24,452	3.55
Milltown, village	888	904	1.80	Dover, town	3,908	4,021	2.89
Osceola, town	2,085	2,578	23.65	Elmwood Park, village . .	474	464	−2.11
Osceola, village	2,421	2,597	7.27	Mount Pleasant, village .	23,142	24,347	5.21
St. Croix Falls, city	2,033	2,102	3.39	North Bay, village	260	260	0.00
St. Croix Falls, town	1,119	1,186	5.99	Norway, town	7,600	7,860	3.42
Sterling, town	724	736	1.66	Racine, city	81,855	80,806	−1.28
Turtle Lake (part), village	65	81	24.62	Raymond, town	3,516	3,639	3.50
West Sweden, town	731	763	4.38	Rochester, town	2,254	2,442	8.34
				Rochester, village	1,149	1,134	−1.31
PORTAGE COUNTY	67,182	68,935	2.61	Sturtevant, village	5,287	5,451	3.10
Alban, town	897	911	1.56	Union Grove, village . . .	4,322	4,459	3.17
Almond, town	679	699	2.95	Waterford, town	5,938	6,281	5.78
Almond, village	459	451	−1.74	Waterford, village	4,048	4,399	8.67
Amherst, town	1,435	1,464	2.02	Wind Point, village	1,853	1,834	−1.03
Amherst, village	964	1,027	6.54	Yorkville, town	3,291	3,310	0.58
Amherst Junction, village	305	328	7.54				
Belmont, town	623	644	3.37	**RICHLAND COUNTY** . . .	17,924	18,098	0.97
Buena Vista, town	1,187	1,235	4.04	Akan, town	444	453	2.03
Carson, town	1,299	1,343	3.39	Bloom, town	487	497	2.05
Dewey, town	975	1,019	4.51	Boaz, village	137	136	−0.73
Eau Pleine, town	931	941	1.07	Buena Vista, town	1,575	1,608	2.10
Grant, town	2,020	2,078	2.87	Cazenovia (part), village	326	327	0.31
Hull, town	5,493	5,544	0.93	Dayton, town	723	734	1.52
Junction City, village . . .	440	432	−1.82	Eagle, town	593	595	0.34
Lanark, town	1,449	1,527	5.38	Forest, town	390	406	4.10
Linwood, town	1,111	1,125	1.26	Henrietta, town	479	471	−1.67
Milladore (part), village .	0	13	—[2]	Ithaca, town	648	669	3.24
Nelsonville, village	191	186	−2.62	Lone Rock, village	929	905	−2.58
New Hope, town	736	750	1.90	Marshall, town	600	594	−1.00
Park Ridge, village	488	470	−3.69	Orion, town	628	646	2.87
Pine Grove, town	904	926	2.43	Richland, town	1,364	1,372	0.59
Plover, town	2,415	2,447	1.33	Richland Center, city . . .	5,114	5,151	0.72
Plover, village	10,520	11,074	5.27	Richwood, town	618	627	1.46
Rosholt, village	518	512	−1.16	Rockbridge, town	721	748	3.74
Sharon, town	1,936	1,997	3.15	Sylvan, town	547	551	0.73
Stevens Point, city	24,551	25,094	2.21	Viola (part), village	422	420	−0.47
Stockton, town	2,896	2,974	2.69	Westford, town	594	603	1.52
Whiting, village	1,760	1,724	−2.05	Willow, town	493	493	0.00
				Yuba, village	92	92	0.00
PRICE COUNTY	15,822	15,954	0.83				

WISCONSIN POPULATION
BY COUNTY AND MUNICIPALITY
April 1, 2000 and January 1, 2004–Continued

County and Municipality	2000 Census[1]	2004 Estimate	Percent Change	County and Municipality	2000 Census[1]	2004 Estimate	Percent Change
ROCK COUNTY	152,307	155,536	2.12	Baldwin, town	903	938	3.88
Avon, town	586	594	1.37	Baldwin, village	2,667	3,253	21.97
Beloit, city	35,775	36,058	0.79	Cady, town	710	774	9.01
Beloit, town	7,038	7,293	3.62	Cylon, town	629	649	3.18
Bradford, town	1,007	1,020	1.29	Deer Park, village	227	230	1.32
Brodhead (part), city ...	0	0	0.00	Eau Galle, town	882	965	9.41
Center, town	1,005	1,042	3.68	Emerald, town	691	761	10.13
Clinton, town	893	904	1.23	Erin Prairie, town	658	662	0.61
Clinton, village	2,162	2,235	3.38	Forest, town	590	614	4.07
Edgerton (part), city	4,891	5,006	2.35	Glenwood, town	755	823	9.01
Evansville, city	4,039	4,409	9.16	Glenwood City, city	1,183	1,231	4.06
Footville, village	788	776	–1.52	Hammond, town	947	1,287	35.90
Fulton, town	3,158	3,220	1.96	Hammond, village	1,153	1,636	41.89
Harmony, town	2,351	2,440	3.79	Hudson, city	8,775	10,561	20.35
Janesville, city	60,200	61,310	1.84	Hudson, town	6,213	7,214	16.11
Janesville, town	3,048	3,264	7.09	Kinnickinnic, town	1,400	1,585	13.21
Johnstown, town	802	795	–0.87	New Richmond, city	6,310	7,244	14.80
La Prairie, town	929	913	–1.72	North Hudson, village ..	3,463	3,649	5.37
Lima, town	1,312	1,321	0.69	Pleasant Valley, town ...	430	473	10.00
Magnolia, town	854	868	1.64	Richmond, town	1,556	2,004	28.79
Milton, city	5,132	5,419	5.59	River Falls (part), city ..	2,318	2,389	3.06
Milton, town	2,844	2,948	3.66	Roberts, village	969	1,275	31.58
Newark, town	1,571	1,585	0.89	Rush River, town	498	527	5.82
Orfordville, village	1,272	1,325	4.17	St. Joseph, town	3,436	3,642	6.00
Plymouth, town	1,270	1,279	0.71	Somerset, town	2,644	3,044	15.13
Porter, town	925	959	3.68	Somerset, village	1,556	2,014	29.43
Rock, town	3,338	3,340	0.06	Spring Valley (part),			
Spring Valley, town	813	814	0.12	village	2	0	–_2
Turtle, town	2,444	2,423	–0.86	Springfield, town	808	885	9.53
Union, town	1,860	1,976	6.24	Stanton, town	1,003	1,015	1.20
				Star Prairie, town	2,944	3,306	12.30
RUSK COUNTY	15,347	15,512	1.08	Star Prairie, village	574	642	11.85
Atlanta, town	627	654	4.31	Troy, town	3,661	4,308	17.67
Big Bend, town	402	412	2.49	Warren, town	1,320	1,501	13.71
Big Falls, town	107	109	1.87	Wilson, village	176	189	7.39
Bruce, village	787	785	–0.25	Woodville, village	1,104	1,232	11.59
Cedar Rapids, town	37	36	–2.70				
Conrath, village	98	110	12.24	SAUK COUNTY	55,225	58,595	6.10
Dewey, town	523	554	5.93	Baraboo, city	10,711	11,188	4.45
Flambeau, town	1,067	1,104	3.47	Baraboo, town	1,828	1,902	4.05
Glen Flora, village	93	95	2.15	Bear Creek, town	497	540	8.65
Grant, town	767	787	2.61	Cazenovia (part), village	0	24	0.00
Grow, town	473	469	–0.85	Dellona, town	1,199	1,392	16.10
Hawkins, town	170	169	–0.59	Delton, town	2,024	2,145	5.98
Hawkins, village	317	349	10.09	Excelsior, town	1,410	1,499	6.31
Hubbard, town	168	168	0.00	Fairfield, town	1,023	1,070	4.59
Ingram, village	76	78	2.63	Franklin, town	696	696	0.00
Ladysmith, city	3,932	3,760	–4.37	Freedom, town	416	427	2.64
Lawrence, town	240	269	12.08	Greenfield, town	911	943	3.51
Marshall, town	683	703	2.93	Honey Creek, town	736	744	1.09
Murry, town	275	272	–1.09	Ironton, town	650	670	3.08
Richland, town	206	215	4.37	Ironton, village	250	250	0.00
Rusk, town	475	491	3.37	La Valle, town	1,203	1,296	7.73
Sheldon, village	256	249	–2.73	La Valle, village	326	324	–0.61
South Fork, town	120	122	1.67	Lake Delton, village ...	1,982	2,599	31.13
Strickland, town	300	310	3.33	Lime Ridge, village	169	161	–4.73
Stubbs, town	587	614	4.60	Loganville, village	276	274	–0.72
Thornapple, town	811	826	1.85	Merrimac, town	868	899	3.57
Tony, village	105	100	–4.76	Merrimac, village	416	423	1.68
True, town	291	283	–2.75	North Freedom, village .	649	642	–1.08
Washington, town	312	334	7.05	Plain, village	792	793	0.13
Weyerhaeuser, village ...	353	344	–2.55	Prairie du Sac, town	1,138	1,157	1.67
Wilkinson, town	66	69	4.55	Prairie du Sac, village ...	3,231	3,463	7.18
Willard, town	539	586	8.72	Reedsburg, city	7,827	8,573	9.53
Wilson, town	84	86	2.38	Reedsburg, town	1,236	1,260	1.94
				Rock Springs, village ...	425	421	–0.94
ST. CROIX COUNTY	63,155	72,522	14.83	Sauk City, village	3,109	3,211	3.28

WISCONSIN POPULATION
BY COUNTY AND MUNICIPALITY
April 1, 2000 and January 1, 2004–Continued

County and Municipality	2000 Census[1]	2004 Estimate	Percent Change	County and Municipality	2000 Census[1]	2004 Estimate	Percent Change
Spring Green, town	1,585	1,719	8.45	Seneca, town	567	583	2.82
Spring Green, village ...	1,444	1,463	1.32	Shawano, city	8,298	8,425	1.53
Sumpter, town	1,021	1,054	3.23	Tigerton, village	764	741	−3.01
Troy, town	773	775	0.26	Washington, town	1,903	1,967	3.36
Washington, town	904	941	4.09	Waukechon, town	928	1,000	7.76
West Baraboo, village ..	1,248	1,272	1.92	Wescott, town	3,653	3,765	3.07
Westfield, town	611	611	0.00	Wittenberg, town	894	922	3.13
Winfield, town	752	783	4.12	Wittenberg, village	1,177	1,169	−0.68
Wisconsin Dells (part), city	106	107	0.94	SHEBOYGAN COUNTY .	112,656	115,447	2.48
Woodland, town	783	884	12.90	Adell, village	517	519	0.39
				Cascade, village	681	698	2.50
SAWYER COUNTY	16,196	17,027	5.13	Cedar Grove, village ...	1,887	1,977	4.77
Bass Lake, town	2,244	2,340	4.28	Elkhart Lake, village ...	1,021	1,056	3.43
Couderay, town	469	468	−0.21	Glenbeulah, village	378	406	7.41
Couderay, village	96	93	−3.13	Greenbush, town	2,619	2,599	−0.76
Draper, town	171	181	5.85	Herman, town	2,044	2,164	5.87
Edgewater, town	586	596	1.71	Holland, town	2,360	2,372	0.51
Exeland, village	212	206	−2.83	Howards Grove, village .	2,792	2,926	4.80
Hayward, city	2,129	2,230	4.74	Kohler, village	1,926	2,010	4.36
Hayward, town	3,279	3,440	4.91	Lima, town	2,948	2,909	−1.32
Hunter, town	765	826	7.97	Lyndon, town	1,463	1,504	2.80
Lenroot, town	1,165	1,248	7.12	Mitchell, town	1,286	1,328	3.27
Meadowbrook, town ...	146	149	2.05	Mosel, town	839	815	−2.86
Meteor, town	170	175	2.94	Oostburg, village	2,660	2,773	4.25
Ojibwa, town	267	280	4.87	Plymouth, city	7,781	8,080	3.84
Radisson, town	465	480	3.23	Plymouth, town	3,115	3,274	5.10
Radisson, village	222	223	0.45	Random Lake, village ..	1,551	1,599	3.09
Round Lake, town	962	1,040	8.11	Rhine, town	2,244	2,299	2.45
Sand Lake, town	774	825	6.59	Russell, town	399	405	1.50
Spider Lake, town	391	415	6.14	Scott, town	1,804	1,858	2.99
Weirgor, town	370	401	8.38	Sheboygan, city	50,792	50,672	−0.24
Winter, town	969	1,060	9.39	Sheboygan, town	5,874	7,013	19.39
Winter, village	344	351	2.03	Sheboygan Falls, city ...	6,772	7,139	5.42
				Sheboygan Falls, town ..	1,706	1,712	0.35
SHAWANO COUNTY	40,664	41,944	3.15	Sherman, town	1,520	1,529	0.59
Almon, town	591	593	0.34	Waldo, village	450	455	1.11
Angelica, town	1,635	1,737	6.24	Wilson, town	3,227	3,356	4.00
Aniwa, town	586	609	3.92				
Aniwa, village	272	269	−1.10	TAYLOR COUNTY	19,680	19,872	0.98
Bartelme, town	700	780	11.43	Aurora, town	386	380	−1.55
Belle Plaine, town	1,867	1,911	2.36	Browning, town	850	887	4.35
Birnamwood, town	711	747	5.06	Chelsea, town	719	743	3.34
Birnamwood (part), village	785	796	1.40	Cleveland, town	262	273	4.20
Bonduel, village	1,416	1,442	1.84	Deer Creek, town	733	751	2.46
Bowler, village	343	344	0.29	Ford, town	276	275	−0.36
Cecil, village	466	515	10.52	Gilman, village	474	468	−1.27
Eland, village	251	245	−2.39	Goodrich, town	487	487	0.00
Fairbanks, town	687	706	2.77	Greenwood, town	642	663	3.27
Germania, town	339	350	3.24	Grover, town	233	243	4.29
Grant, town...........	974	986	1.23	Hammel, town	735	746	1.50
Green Valley, town	1,024	1,031	0.68	Holway, town	854	866	1.41
Gresham, village	575	597	3.83	Jump River, town	311	304	−2.25
Hartland, town	825	874	5.94	Little Black, town	1,148	1,189	3.57
Herman, town	741	761	2.70	Lublin, village	110	102	−7.27
Hutchins, town	539	558	3.53	Maplehurst, town	359	363	1.11
Lessor, town	1,112	1,219	9.62	McKinley, town	418	437	4.55
Maple Grove, town	1,045	1,032	−1.24	Medford, city	4,350	4,311	−0.90
Marion (part), city	1	11	--[2]	Medford, town	2,216	2,224	0.36
Mattoon, village	466	461	−1.07	Molitor, town	263	271	3.04
Morris, town	485	497	2.47	Pershing, town	180	174	−3.33
Navarino, town	422	415	−1.66	Rib Lake, town	768	778	1.30
Pella, town	877	906	3.31	Rib Lake, village	878	870	−0.91
Pulaski (part), village ...	45	113	151.11	Roosevelt, town	444	441	−0.68
Red Springs, town	981	1,023	4.28	Stetsonville, village	563	560	−0.53
Richmond, town	1,719	1,844	7.27	Taft, town	361	374	3.60
				Westboro, town	660	692	4.85

WISCONSIN POPULATION
BY COUNTY AND MUNICIPALITY
April 1, 2000 and January 1, 2004–Continued

County and Municipality	2000 Census[1]	2004 Estimate	Percent Change	County and Municipality	2000 Census[1]	2004 Estimate	Percent Change
TREMPEALEAU COUNTY	27,010	27,765	2.80	Cloverland, town	919	984	7.07
Albion, town	595	627	5.38	Conover, town	1,137	1,183	4.05
Arcadia, city	2,402	2,373	-1.21	Eagle River, city	1,443	1,481	2.63
Arcadia, town	1,555	1,621	4.24	Lac du Flambeau, town	3,004	3,136	4.39
Blair, city	1,273	1,296	1.81	Land O'Lakes, town	882	918	4.08
Burnside, town	529	529	0.00	Lincoln, town	2,579	2,708	5.00
Caledonia, town	759	837	10.28	Manitowish Waters, town	646	669	3.56
Chimney Rock, town	276	288	4.35	Phelps, town	1,350	1,438	6.52
Dodge, town	414	425	2.66	Plum Lake, town	486	509	4.73
Eleva, village	635	657	3.46	Presque Isle, town	513	552	7.60
Ettrick, town	1,284	1,307	1.79	St. Germain, town	1,932	2,031	5.12
Ettrick, village	521	532	2.11	Washington, town	1,577	1,624	2.98
Gale, town	1,425	1,477	3.58	Winchester, town	454	487	7.27
Galesville, city	1,427	1,445	1.26				
Hale, town	988	1,044	5.67	WALWORTH COUNTY	92,013	97,052	5.48
Independence, city	1,244	1,262	1.45	Bloomfield, town	5,537	6,039	9.07
Lincoln, town	829	824	-0.60	Burlington (part), city	0	0	0.00
Osseo, city	1,669	1,669	0.00	Darien, town	1,747	1,851	5.95
Pigeon, town	894	940	5.15	Darien, village	1,572	1,595	1.46
Pigeon Falls, village	388	395	1.80	Delavan, city	7,956	8,158	2.54
Preston, town	951	966	1.58	Delavan, town	4,559	4,767	4.56
Strum, village	1,001	1,020	1.90	East Troy, town	3,830	3,888	1.51
Sumner, town	806	849	5.33	East Troy, village	3,564	3,850	8.02
Trempealeau, town	1,618	1,731	6.98	Elkhorn, city	7,305	8,191	12.13
Trempealeau, village	1,319	1,435	8.79	Fontana on Geneva Lake,			
Unity, town	556	550	-1.08	village	1,754	1,842	5.02
Whitehall, city	1,651	1,666	0.91	Geneva, town	4,642	4,858	4.65
				Genoa City (part), village	1,949	2,466	26.53
VERNON COUNTY	28,056	28,928	3.11	Lafayette, town	1,708	1,797	5.21
Bergen, town	1,317	1,385	5.16	La Grange, town	2,444	2,495	2.09
Chaseburg, village	306	291	-4.90	Lake Geneva, city	7,148	7,276	1.79
Christiana, town	871	881	1.15	Linn, town	2,194	2,288	4.28
Clinton, town	1,354	1,425	5.24	Lyons, town	3,440	3,704	7.67
Coon, town	683	708	3.66	Mukwonago (part),			
Coon Valley, village	714	717	0.42	village	0	31	0.00
De Soto (part), village	248	249	0.40	Richmond, town	1,835	1,899	3.49
Forest, town	583	604	3.60	Sharon, town	912	916	0.44
Franklin, town	923	958	3.79	Sharon, village	1,549	1,548	-0.06
Genoa, town	705	718	1.84	Spring Prairie, town	2,089	2,177	4.21
Genoa, village	263	259	-1.52	Sugar Creek, town	3,331	3,624	8.80
Greenwood, town	770	837	8.70	Troy, town	2,328	2,367	1.68
Hamburg, town	848	916	8.02	Walworth, town	1,676	1,749	4.36
Harmony, town	739	810	9.61	Walworth, village	2,304	2,476	7.47
Hillsboro, city	1,302	1,299	-0.23	Whitewater (part), city	10,826	11,188	3.34
Hillsboro, town	766	780	1.83	Whitewater, town	1,399	1,446	3.36
Jefferson, town	974	1,017	4.41	Williams Bay, village	2,415	2,566	6.25
Kickapoo, town	566	583	3.00				
La Farge, village	775	777	0.26	WASHBURN COUNTY	16,036	16,762	4.53
Liberty, town	167	206	23.35	Barronett, town	405	422	4.20
Ontario, village	476	475	-0.21	Bashaw, town	921	1,012	9.88
Readstown, village	395	394	-0.25	Bass Lake, town	535	597	11.59
Stark, town	349	363	4.01	Beaver Brook, town	643	692	7.62
Sterling, town	713	708	-0.70	Birchwood, town	453	510	12.58
Stoddard, village	815	805	-1.23	Birchwood, village	518	533	2.90
Union, town	531	560	5.46	Brooklyn, town	281	293	4.27
Viola (part), village	245	284	15.92	Casey, town	466	472	1.29
Viroqua, city	4,335	4,362	0.62	Chicog, town	268	265	-1.12
Viroqua, town	1,560	1,629	4.42	Crystal, town	323	339	4.95
Webster, town	676	715	5.77	Evergreen, town	1,076	1,094	1.67
Westby, city	2,045	2,113	3.33	Frog Creek, town	160	164	2.50
Wheatland, town	533	577	8.26	Gull Lake, town	158	175	10.76
Whitestown, town	509	523	2.75	Long Lake, town	737	757	2.71
				Madge, town	454	474	4.41
VILAS COUNTY	21,033	21,966	4.44	Minong, town	858	922	7.46
Arbor Vitae, town	3,153	3,261	3.43	Minong, village	531	545	2.64
Boulder Junction, town	958	985	2.82	Sarona, town	382	412	7.85
				Shell Lake, city	1,309	1,338	2.22

WISCONSIN POPULATION
BY COUNTY AND MUNICIPALITY
April 1, 2000 and January 1, 2004–Continued

County and Municipality	2000 Census[1]	2004 Estimate	Percent Change
Spooner, city	2,653	2,705	1.96
Spooner, town	677	714	5.47
Springbrook, town	536	548	2.24
Stinnett, town	263	272	3.42
Stone Lake, town	544	569	4.60
Trego, town	885	938	5.99
WASHINGTON COUNTY	117,496	123,587	5.18
Addison, town	3,341	3,505	4.91
Barton, town	2,546	2,587	1.61
Erin, town	3,664	3,802	3.77
Farmington, town	3,239	3,433	5.99
Germantown, town	278	269	–3.24
Germantown, village	18,260	19,001	4.06
Hartford (part), city	10,895	12,064	10.73
Hartford, town	4,031	4,023	–0.20
Jackson, town	3,516	3,637	3.44
Jackson, village	4,938	5,678	14.99
Kewaskum, town	1,119	1,138	1.70
Kewaskum, (part) village	3,277	3,557	8.54
Milwaukee (part), city	0	0	0.00
Newburg (part), village	1,027	1,066	3.80
Polk, town	3,938	4,011	1.85
Richfield, town	10,373	11,195	7.92
Slinger, village	3,901	4,143	6.20
Trenton, town	4,440	4,595	3.49
Wayne, town	1,727	1,844	6.77
West Bend, city	28,152	29,204	3.74
West Bend, town	4,834	4,835	0.02
WAUKESHA COUNTY	360,767	373,339	3.48
Big Bend, village	1,278	1,286	0.63
Brookfield, city	38,649	39,607	2.48
Brookfield, town	6,390	6,418	0.44
Butler, village	1,881	1,855	–1.38
Chenequa, village	583	590	1.20
Delafield, city	6,472	6,720	3.83
Delafield, town	7,820	8,210	4.99
Dousman, village	1,584	1,757	10.92
Eagle, town	3,117	3,444	10.49
Eagle, village	1,707	1,737	1.76
Elm Grove, village	6,249	6,250	0.02
Genesee, town	7,284	7,502	2.99
Hartland, village	7,905	8,267	4.58
Lac La Belle, (part) village	329	338	2.74
Lannon, village	1,009	962	–4.66
Lisbon, town	9,359	9,630	2.90
Menomonee Falls, village	32,647	33,660	3.10
Merton, town	7,988	8,220	2.90
Merton, village	1,926	2,185	13.45
Milwaukee (part), city	0	0	0.00
Mukwanago, town	6,868	7,391	7.62
Mukwonago (part), village	6,162	6,397	3.81
Muskego, city	21,397	22,203	3.77
Nashotah, village	1,266	1,379	8.93
New Berlin, city	38,220	38,896	1.77
North Prairie, village	1,571	1,815	15.53
Oconomowoc, city	12,382	13,194	6.56
Oconomowoc, town	7,451	7,646	2.62
Oconomowoc Lake, village	564	645	14.36
Ottawa, town	3,758	3,822	1.70
Pewaukee, city	11,783	12,425	5.45
Pewaukee, village	8,170	8,864	8.49
Summit, town	4,999	5,068	1.38

County and Municipality	2000 Census[1]	2004 Estimate	Percent Change
Sussex, village	8,828	9,576	8.47
Vernon, town	7,227	7,358	1.81
Wales, village	2,523	2,547	0.95
Waukesha, city	64,825	66,816	3.07
Waukesha, town	8,596	8,659	0.73
WAUPACA COUNTY	51,825	53,148	2.55
Bear Creek, town	838	875	4.42
Big Falls, village	85	84	–1.18
Caledonia, town	1,466	1,507	2.80
Clintonville, city	4,736	4,675	–1.29
Dayton, town	2,734	2,853	4.35
Dupont, town	741	770	3.91
Embarrass, village	487	483	–0.82
Farmington, town	4,148	4,247	2.39
Fremont, town	632	653	3.32
Fremont, village	666	695	4.35
Harrison, town	509	516	1.38
Helvetia, town	649	670	3.24
Iola, town	818	874	6.85
Iola, village	1,298	1,303	0.39
Larrabee, town	1,301	1,369	5.23
Lebanon, town	1,648	1,722	4.49
Lind, town	1,381	1,454	5.29
Little Wolf, town	1,430	1,508	5.45
Manawa, city	1,330	1,349	1.43
Marion (part), city	1,296	1,291	–0.39
Matteson, town	956	996	4.18
Mukwa, town	2,773	2,906	4.80
New London (part), city	5,618	5,717	1.76
Ogdensburg, village	224	218	–2.68
Royalton, town	1,544	1,496	–3.11
St. Lawrence, town	740	748	1.08
Scandinavia, town	1,075	1,117	3.91
Scandinavia, village	349	375	7.45
Union, town	804	820	1.99
Waupaca, city	5,676	5,821	2.55
Waupaca, town	1,155	1,205	4.33
Weyauwega, city	1,806	1,896	4.98
Weyauwega, town	627	637	1.59
Wyoming, town	285	298	4.56
WAUSHARA COUNTY	23,066	24,806	7.54
Aurora, town	971	1,061	9.27
Berlin (part), city	83	84	1.20
Bloomfield, town	1,018	1,045	2.65
Coloma, town	660	722	9.39
Coloma, village	461	467	1.30
Dakota, town	1,259	1,265	0.48
Deerfield, town	629	653	3.82
Hancock, town	531	560	5.46
Hancock, village	463	460	–0.65
Leon, town	1,281	1,389	8.43
Lohrville, village	408	414	1.47
Marion, town	2,065	2,163	4.75
Mount Morris, town	1,092	1,121	2.66
Oasis, town	405	396	–2.22
Plainfield, town	533	549	3.00
Plainfield, village	899	894	–0.56
Poysippi, town	972	974	0.21
Redgranite, village	1,040	2,019	94.13
Richford, town	588	608	3.40
Rose, town	595	611	2.69
Saxeville, town	974	999	2.57
Springwater, town	1,389	1,420	2.23
Warren, town	675	712	5.48
Wautoma, city	1,998	2,115	5.86

WISCONSIN POPULATION
BY COUNTY AND MUNICIPALITY
April 1, 2000 and January 1, 2004–Continued

County and Municipality	2000 Census[1]	2004 Estimate	Percent Change	County and Municipality	2000 Census[1]	2004 Estimate	Percent Change
Wautoma, town	1,312	1,347	2.67	Aurburndale, village	738	763	3.39
Wild Rose, village	765	758	−0.92	Biron, village	915	897	−1.97
				Cameron, town	510	518	1.57
WINNEBAGO COUNTY	156,763	161,863	3.25	Cary, town	398	424	6.53
Algoma, town	5,702	6,024	5.65	Cranmoor, town	175	175	0.00
Appleton (part), city	812	916	12.81	Dexter, town	379	400	5.54
Black Wolf, town	2,330	2,423	3.99	Grand Rapids, town	7,801	7,960	2.04
Clayton, town	2,974	3,301	11.00	Hansen, town	707	724	2.40
Menasha (part), city	15,643	15,655	0.08	Hewitt, village	670	708	5.67
Menasha, town	15,858	16,695	5.28	Hiles, town	188	186	−1.06
Neenah, city	24,507	25,193	2.80	Lincoln, town	1,554	1,590	2.32
Neenah, town	2,657	2,745	3.31	Marshfield (part), city	18,383	18,528	0.79
Nekimi, town	1,419	1,448	2.04	Marshfield, town	811	826	1.85
Nepeuskun, town	689	720	4.50	Milladore, town	706	717	1.56
Omro, city	3,177	3,312	4.25	Milladore (part), village	268	260	−2.99
Omro, town	1,875	2,011	7.25	Nekoosa, city	2,590	2,593	0.12
Oshkosh, city	62,916	65,095	3.46	Pittsville, city	866	885	2.19
Oshkosh, town	3,234	2,808	−13.17	Port Edwards, town	1,446	1,477	2.14
Poygan, town	1,037	1,120	8.00	Port Edwards, village	1,944	1,915	−1.49
Rushford, town	1,471	1,535	4.35	Remington, town	305	304	−0.33
Utica, town	1,168	1,225	4.88	Richfield, town	1,523	1,613	5.91
Vinland, town	1,849	1,904	2.97	Rock, town	856	877	2.45
Winchester, town	1,676	1,724	2.86	Rudolph, town	1,161	1,161	0.00
Winneconne, town	2,145	2,252	4.99	Rudolph, village	423	426	0.71
Winneconne, village	2,401	2,501	4.16	Saratoga, town	5,383	5,457	1.37
Wolf River, town	1,223	1,256	2.70	Seneca, town	1,202	1,163	−3.24
				Sherry, town	809	819	1.24
WOOD COUNTY	75,555	76,235	0.90	Sigel, town	1,130	1,145	1.33
Arpin, town	786	807	2.67	Vesper, village	541	540	−0.18
Arpin, village	337	337	0.00	Wisconsin Rapids, city	18,435	18,410	−0.14
Auburndale, town	829	836	0.84	Wood, town	786	794	1.02

[1]Population totals include corrections made by the U.S. Census Bureau through 8/28/2002. Population estimates are based on the corrected totals.

[2]Because of data limitations, percentage is not relevant.

[3]The Town of Bellevue became a village on 2/14/2003.

[4]The Town of Hobart became a village on 5/13/2002.

[5]Part of the Town of Hallie became the Village of Lake Hallie on 2/18/2003.

[6]Part of the Town of Ixonia became the Village of Lac La Belle on 3/28/2002.

[7]Part of the Town of Kronenwetter became the Village of Kronenwetter on 11/20/2002.

[8]Part of the Town of Kaukauna was annexed by the Village of Wrightstown on 2/28/2002.

Source: Wisconsin Department of Administration, Demographic Services Center, *Official Population Estimates, January 1, 2004,* October 2004.

HIGHLIGHTS OF MILITARY AND VETERANS AFFAIRS IN WISCONSIN

Military Service — More Wisconsinites served in World War II than in any other conflict, with Vietnam ranking second, but fatalities were heaviest in the Civil War. From the Civil War through the operations in Iraq and Afghanistan, about 26,700 Wisconsinites have lost their lives performing military service during times of conflict. As of mid-2005, more than 6,700 members of the Wisconsin Army and Air National Guard had been mobilized to serve on active duty since September 11, 2001.

As of June 2005, almost 9,800 citizen-soldiers and airmen were serving in Army and Air National Guard units at military facilities located in 67 communities throughout the state.

Veterans' Programs — Since the end of World War II, more than 573,000 grants and loans totaling over $3 billion have been provided to Wisconsin veterans. Historically, most of the grants have been for educational purposes, while the overwhelming number of loans were for housing. The grants have also covered subsistence and emergency health care assistance for needy veterans. Veterans may qualify for low-interest home mortgage and home improvement loans. In addition, eligible veterans and, in some instances, spouses and dependent children of deceased veterans may qualify for personal loans to finance expenses, such as education, business start-ups or purchases, medical bills, debt consolidation, and mobile home purchases.

In 2003, Wisconsin veterans and their families received more than $26.8 million in federal educational assistance. The largest portion ($20.1 million) went to 5,760 veterans participating in a program popularly known as the "Montgomery GI Bill". A total of 47,213 disabled Wisconsin veterans received over $390 million in benefits through the compensation and pension programs, and 6,489 beneficiaries of deceased veterans received over $56 million in benefits.

The Wisconsin Veterans Homes at King and Union Grove had 798 members at the end of 2004. In general, to be eligible for residence, a veteran must have completed certain military service requirements and be a Wisconsin resident on the date of admission to a veterans home. In addition, he or she must have been a resident of Wisconsin at the time of entry into service or a resident of the state for any 5-year period after service and prior to application for admission. Depending on availability of space, spouses and surviving spouses or parents of qualifying veterans may also be admitted.

The following tables present selected data. Consult the footnoted sources for more detailed information about military and veterans affairs.

WISCONSIN'S MILITARY SERVICE

Military Action	Number Served	Number Killed
Civil War	91,379[1]	12,216
Spanish-American War	5,469	134[2]
Mexican Border Service	4,168	NA
World War I	122,215	3,932
World War II	332,200[3]	8,390
Korean Conflict	132,000[3]	729
Vietnam	165,400[4]	1,239[5]
Lebanon/Grenada	400[6]	1
Panama	520[7]	1
Operations Desert Shield/Desert Storm	10,400[8]	11
Somalia	426[9]	2
Bosnia/Kosovo	678[10]	NA
Afghanistan	NA[11]	1
Iraq	NA[12]	40

Note: Includes Wisconsin residents who served on active duty during declared wars and officially designated periods of hostilities. NA – Not available.

[1]Total includes some who enlisted more than once. The net number of soldiers recruited in Wisconsin was about 80,000.

[2]Casualties only from Wisconsin 1st, 2nd, 3rd and 4th Regiments. No details available for Wisconsin residents serving in federal units.

[3]U.S. Veterans Administration letter, October 17, 1961.

[4]U.S. Veterans Administration report, March 31, 1990.

[5]Total includes 1,131 from U.S. Department of Defense and 108 additional names from Wisconsin Department of Veterans Affairs.

[6]Based on statistics developed for legislation to extend state benefits to veterans who served on active duty in Lebanon or its territorial waters between August 1, 1982, and August 1, 1984, or in Grenada between October 23, 1983, and November 21, 1983.

[7]U.S. Department of Defense statistics on troop involvement.

[8]Based on Wisconsin Department of Veterans Affairs formula for determining number of state residents on active duty who served in the Middle East/Persian Gulf area (beginning August 1990) and Guard and Reserve troops activated for duty in support of Desert Shield/Desert Storm.

[9]Based on Wisconsin Department of Veterans Affairs formula for determining the number of state residents who served during Operation Restore Hope, beginning December 9, 1992.

[10]Based on Wisconsin Department of Veterans Affairs formula for determining the number of state residents who served in Operation Joint Endeavor, Operation Joint Guard, and Operation Joint Forge from November 1995 to present.

[11]The number of state residents who served in Operation Enduring Freedom (from October 2001 to present) is not available.

[12]The number of state residents who served in Operation Iraqi Freedom (from March 2003 to present) is not available.

Source: Wisconsin Department of Veterans Affairs, departmental data, June 2005.

DIRECT STATE BENEFITS TO WISCONSIN WAR VETERANS
1943 – 1961

Fiscal Year	Number of Grants and Loans	Total Benefits	Rehabilitation Trust Funds	Housing Fund
8/1/43-1946	6,359	$975,173	$975,173	---
1947	10,701	2,207,914	2,207,914	---
1948	9,578	3,511,527	3,511,527	---
1949	6,086	2,512,517	2,512,517	---
1950	5,867	3,463,058	2,040,658	$1,422,400
1951	6,137	5,178,106	2,104,550	3,073,556
1952	10,442	22,362,081	1,995,116	20,366,965
1953	5,099	8,842,780	1,331,140	7,511,640
1954	4,507	4,420,030	1,502,748	2,917,282
1955	3,482	4,236,298	1,112,173	3,124,125
1956	3,639	5,389,187	787,861	4,601,326
1957	2,890	4,246,004	730,452	3,515,552
1958	2,779	4,912,233	660,994	4,251,239
1959	2,954	5,419,609	670,262	4,749,347
1960	3,345	7,341,922	591,272	6,750,650
1961	3,081	6,654,189	584,426	6,069,763

Note: The 1961 Legislature merged all veterans' funds into the Veterans Trust Fund.

Source: Wisconsin Department of Veterans Affairs, departmental data, March 1995.

VETERANS BENEFITS, 1962 – 2004

Fiscal Year	Number of Grants and Loans	Total Benefits	Grants: Economic	Grants: Educational	Full-Time Educational Grants	Economic Assistance	Personal Loan Program	Loans: Second Mortgage Housing	Loans: Revenue Bond Housing Loans	Loans: Gen. Obligation Bond Housing Loans
1962	3,073	$6,681,585	$53,891	$2,100	--	$515,008	--	$6,110,586	--	--
1963	2,835	6,118,117	64,152	3,654	--	416,836	--	5,633,475	--	--
1964	2,514	4,609,470	79,702	8,540	--	422,850	--	4,098,378	--	--
1965	2,384	3,737,259	100,751	13,654	--	359,705	--	3,263,149	--	--
1966	3,272	5,160,560	113,710	36,294	--	677,311	--	4,333,245	--	--
1967	6,366	7,903,147	112,526	164,921	--	1,450,836	--	6,174,864	--	--
1968	7,117	9,520,005	128,691	191,355	--	2,393,521	--	6,806,438	--	--
1969	7,258	7,979,372	150,793	262,126	--	2,603,989	--	4,962,464	--	--
1970	8,296	9,265,183	193,044	289,743	--	3,605,092	--	5,177,305	--	--
1971	9,087	10,634,778	248,906	283,652	--	3,851,973	--	6,250,247	--	--
1972	9,846	13,207,891	290,603	332,319	--	4,005,623	--	8,570,346	--	--
1973	16,275	24,534,161	434,170	608,959	$407,069	6,733,164	--	16,350,799	--	--
1974	29,106	25,448,547	549,417	1,021,859	1,834,337	7,704,081	--	14,338,853	--	--
1975	32,898	69,554,865	607,279	1,240,917	1,836,207	9,098,837	--	10,076,963	$46,694,662	--
1976	40,229	216,478,556	536,855	1,245,312	1,861,901	9,537,622	--	4,371,839	6,333,640	$192,591,387
1977	37,807	257,778,554	658,110	1,360,835	1,682,805	9,198,256	--	760,546	--	243,804,763
1978	34,106	208,941,251	496,715	1,232,768	1,196,114	9,819,842	--	1,073,815	--	195,435,266
1979	29,670	229,493,527	455,621	1,217,333	901,368	8,907,225	--	809,132	--	217,202,848
1980	25,670	197,668,743	362,556	1,099,266	731,672	6,735,632	--	843,433	--	187,896,184
1981	16,926	90,183,867	424,041	1,092,510	479,232	4,323,114	--	1,345,430	67,130,619	15,388,921
1982	13,333	16,221,058	378,614	1,159,025	469,347	3,656,939	--	1,062,015	8,400,780	1,094,338
1983	11,516	56,700,920	591,351	986,106	391,542	3,073,217	--	762,930	--	50,895,774
1984	11,522	58,137,350	469,314	1,227,239	328,036	3,116,789	--	782,463	--	52,213,509
1985	10,326	47,689,638	453,502	1,483,693	225,043	2,737,544	--	552,106	--	42,237,750
1986	9,648	19,297,133	378,999	1,255,252	157,379	3,678,759	--	243,147	--	13,583,597
1987	7,690	18,883,716	529,634	807,253	127,789	2,802,819	--	141,370	--	14,474,851
1988	6,643	28,134,558	426,595	696,352	91,392	2,405,642	--	289,606	--	24,224,971
1989	6,614	35,412,289	533,929	698,946	77,787	2,459,813	--	832,436	--	30,809,378
1990	6,150	44,837,433	636,434	683,355	62,025	2,776,835	--	327,819	--	40,350,965
1991	6,279	48,562,575	398,706	743,351	50,993	3,945,614	--	62,960	--	43,360,951
1992	4,871	35,155,551	381,312	526,215	137,799	4,192,505	--	18,799	--	29,898,921
1993	4,314	22,446,997	472,302	512,770	167,838	2,673,585	--	--	--	18,620,502
1994	5,314	58,337,813¹	451,666	716,858	667	2,567,053	--	--	--	33,157,403
1995	6,080	126,009,594¹	552,893	754,052	--	2,544,584	--	--	--	111,133,109
1996	7,483	80,581,789	601,030	1,609,350	--	3,189,625	--	--	--	75,181,784
1997	7,231	99,984,937	937,294	1,797,649	--	2,401,548	--	--	--	94,848,446
1998	7,767	160,760,389	783,664	1,680,881	--	666,575²	$10,215,928²	--	--	147,413,341
1999	6,493	139,857,465	2,263,317	1,447,882	--	--	11,837,974	--	--	124,908,352
2000	5,912	143,192,551	3,226,128	1,786,205	--	--	10,802,068	--	--	127,378,150
2001	5,020	73,390,596	1,205,846	1,768,452	--	--	9,034,356	--	--	61,381,942
2002	5,951	88,227,531	1,925,094	2,822,134	--	--	15,780,270	--	--	67,700,033
2003	6,255	83,866,773	1,752,733	2,909,812	--	--	19,792,680	--	--	59,411,548
2004	5,628	95,593,212	1,296,310	4,384,642	--	--	11,808,566	--	--	78,103,694

Note: The 1961 Legislature merged all veterans' funds into the Veterans Trust Fund.
¹Includes $21,444,166 (FY94) and $11,024,956 (FY95) in consumer loans under the Veterans Trust Fund stabilization provision of 1993 Wisconsin Act 16.
²Personal loan program replaced economic assistance loans.
Source: Wisconsin Department of Veterans Affairs, departmental data, June 2005.

FEDERAL EXPENDITURES FOR VETERANS BENEFITS
By State, Federal Fiscal Year 2003

State	Number of Veterans	Educational Benefits Total Assistance[2] ($000s)	Montgomery GI Bill Amount ($000s)	Veterans	Compensation and Pension[1] Benefits to Living Veterans Amount ($000s)	Veterans	Benefits to Beneficiaries of Deceased Veterans Amount ($000s)	Veterans
Alabama	426,343	$41,566	$27,461	6,522	$527,229	64,014	$139,213	18,286
Alaska	66,044	7,457	5,649	1,115	97,422	11,365	6,485	597
Arizona	560,181	64,072	50,643	16,653	538,253	60,781	99,439	8,939
Arkansas	271,820	22,198	13,313	3,812	388,834	37,680	81,581	9,508
California	2,260,708	228,027	192,219	38,472	1,886,387	238,796	399,116	40,018
Colorado	428,916	54,169	42,080	8,276	407,237	50,933	71,646	6,773
Connecticut	271,417	23,136	8,437	2,524	165,032	22,174	28,692	3,460
Delaware	80,316	4,621	3,375	945	58,816	7,888	12,094	1,329
District of Columbia	37,973	6,876	1,811	843	47,395	5,562	10,911	1,243
Florida	1,811,225	157,211	117,057	25,511	1,702,283	224,361	357,849	36,813
Georgia	738,822	112,620	79,743	15,227	743,227	96,101	185,825	22,035
Hawaii	113,234	15,939	11,078	2,918	119,724	13,987	19,787	1,757
Idaho	136,038	12,664	9,772	2,181	137,972	15,784	19,618	1,888
ILLINOIS	898,883	73,449	64,354	15,927	508,161	69,036	88,048	11,444
Indiana	544,752	30,724	23,448	6,190	349,485	46,899	63,163	7,320
IOWA	271,738	14,619	11,584	4,055	182,889	22,855	32,996	4,254
Kansas	248,849	23,085	18,478	4,213	206,388	26,291	40,331	4,432
Kentucky	361,841	30,207	21,424	4,840	398,428	45,125	82,320	10,518
Louisiana	368,553	35,796	26,490	7,546	413,057	46,723	95,664	13,500
Maine	142,741	12,926	5,572	1,350	239,818	21,441	28,377	3,117
Maryland	473,716	41,499	31,421	9,299	376,336	50,281	80,340	8,335
Massachusetts	495,619	26,837	15,981	4,199	489,406	60,507	92,387	9,386
MICHIGAN	826,533	44,270	35,664	8,683	495,172	69,937	89,424	11,116
MINNESOTA	431,221	27,084	17,855	5,728	364,245	44,172	55,373	7,090
Mississippi	241,682	18,744	13,904	3,964	292,349	32,340	74,253	10,435
Missouri	553,049	44,629	31,910	7,563	455,572	54,907	91,979	10,650
Montana	104,004	8,485	6,372	1,490	123,515	13,707	14,633	1,596
Nebraska	162,537	16,518	11,683	3,325	202,321	22,185	28,223	3,061
Nevada	241,458	18,210	14,833	3,025	216,373	26,914	33,488	3,169
New Hampshire	128,396	8,972	4,631	984	128,335	15,254	19,849	1,874
New Jersey	592,307	30,496	17,562	4,385	397,455	52,794	80,902	8,587
New Mexico	183,428	23,320	16,401	3,385	299,585	27,396	42,114	4,324
New York	1,171,030	88,849	45,922	11,095	938,579	121,393	176,110	23,562
North Carolina	765,896	92,920	69,021	12,219	885,455	100,828	186,254	22,171
North Dakota	57,112	6,343	4,418	1,693	59,375	7,503	8,208	1,113
Ohio	1,039,597	63,112	49,970	12,966	718,810	97,279	136,810	17,196
Oklahoma	356,049	45,944	29,171	7,452	599,155	55,177	107,317	11,039
Oregon	364,559	31,630	24,143	4,947	397,645	40,786	56,644	5,698
Pennsylvania	1,150,351	59,224	41,787	10,580	847,100	105,027	170,580	21,151
Rhode Island	91,429	5,094	3,173	920	96,793	10,834	17,824	1,802
South Carolina	408,480	40,530	27,828	6,134	440,194	52,484	103,712	12,453
South Dakota	75,966	7,716	4,488	1,656	94,138	10,861	14,541	1,895
Tennessee	539,411	44,407	32,701	6,805	546,663	64,137	126,471	15,970
Texas	1,657,311	212,444	166,406	32,873	2,001,463	229,885	419,508	45,267
Utah	156,803	15,103	10,919	3,452	121,248	15,072	19,121	1,906
Vermont	58,320	9,398	1,655	430	54,464	5,839	9,564	991
Virginia	746,836	92,462	73,796	16,528	699,194	97,133	168,699	17,601
Washington	632,034	74,276	57,801	10,467	732,539	83,731	115,132	10,432
West Virginia	189,475	42,083	7,928	2,831	265,578	25,807	45,147	5,542
WISCONSIN	477,990	26,844	20,176	5,760	390,544	47,213	56,288	6,489
Wyoming	56,493	4,849	3,966	984	49,855	6,280	6,914	674
UNITED STATES	24,469,484	$2,243,652	$1,627,474	374,942	$22,897,495	2,775,459	$4,510,963	509,806

[1]The Disability Compensation Program provides payments to veterans for service-related disability, to surviving spouses and dependent children, and to dependent parents of veterans who died as a result of service-connected disability. The Pension Program provides payments to needy veterans who are permanently disabled as a result of nonservice-connected disability; survivors may be included in the program.

[2]Includes educational programs not listed separately, such as educational benefits to dependents and spouses and vocational rehabilitation programs designed to aid disabled veterans.

Source: U.S. Department of Veterans Affairs, Office of Planning and Analysis, "Veteran Data and Information: Program Statistics, Table 22: Estimated Selected Expenditures by State, FY 2003", and departmental data, May 2005.

WISCONSIN NATIONAL GUARD

JOINT UNITS

Joint Force Headquarters Wisconsin
Joint Force Headquarters Detachment – Madison
   54th Civil Support Team (WMD) – Madison

ARMY UNITS

Joint Force Headquarters Separate Units
   Recruiting and Retention Command – Madison
   Det. 52, OSA Command – Madison
   13th Medical Dental Detachment – Madison
   13th Medical Dental Detachment – Marshfield
32nd (Separate) Infantry Brigade (Light)
Headquarters and Headquarters Co. (–) – Camp Douglas
   Det. 1, HHC 32nd Infantry Brigade – Wausau
   Troop E (–), 105th Calvary – Merrill
   Det. 1, Troop E – Antigo
   32nd Engineer Company – Onalaska
   232nd Military Intelligence Company – Madison
2nd Battalion, 127th Infantry
Headquarters and Headquarters Co. – Appleton
   Company A (–) – Waupun
   Det. 1, Co. A – Ripon
   Company B – Green Bay
   Company C – Fond du Lac
   Company D – Marinette
1st Battalion, 128th Infantry
Headquarters and Headquarters Co. (–) – Eau Claire
   Det. 1, Headquarters Co. – Abbotsford
   Company A – Menomonie
   Company B (–) – New Richmond
   Det. 1, Co. B – Rice Lake
   Company C (–) – Arcadia
   Det. 1, Co. C (–) – Neillsville
   Company D – River Falls
2nd Battalion, 128th Infantry
Headquarters and Headquarters Co. – Madison
   Company A (–) – Fort Atkinson
   Det. 1, Co. A – Elkhorn
   Company B (–) – Oconomowoc
   Det. 1, Co. B – Hartford
   Company C (–) – Baraboo
   Det. 1, Co. C – Reedsburg
   Company D – Watertown
1st Battalion, 120th Field Artillery
Headquarters and Headquarters Service Btry. (–) –
   Wisconsin Rapids
   Det. 1, HHS – Mosinee
   Battery A – Marshfield
   Battery B – Clintonville
   Battery C – Stevens Point
132nd Support Battalion
Headquarters and Headquarters Co. (–) – Portage
   Det. 1, HHC (Bde. Material Mgt. Ofc.) – Madison
   Company A (–) – Janesville
   Det. 1, Co. A (NORFAST) – Eau Claire
   Det. 2, Co. A (CENFAST) – Waupaca
   Company B (–) – Mauston

   Det. 1, Co. B – Onalaska
   Company C (Med.) – Milwaukee
64th Troop Command
Headquarters and Headquarters Det. – Madison
   HHC 332nd Support Center (Corps RAOC) – Berlin
   64th Support Detachment (ROC ASG) – Monroe
641st Troop Command Battalion
Headquarters and Headquarters Det. – Madison
   32nd Military Police Company (–) – Milwaukee
   Det. 1, 32nd MP Company – Madison
   Co. B, 118th Medical Battalion – Waukesha
   832nd Medical Co. (Air Ambulance) – West Bend
   Det. 1, Co. D, 109th AVIM – West Bend
   Det. 1, 139th Mobile Public Affairs Det. – Madison
   132 Army Band – Madison
   232nd Personnel Services Company – Madison
732nd Maintenance Battalion
Headquarters and Headquarters Det. – Tomah
   107th Maintenance Co. (–) – Sparta
   Det. 1, 107th Maintenance Co. – Viroqua
   Det. 2, 107th Maintenance Co. – Sussex
   1157th Transportation Co. – Oshkosh
   1158th Transportation Co. (–) – Tomah
   Det. 1, 1158th Trans. Co. – Beloit
   Det. 2, 1158th Trans. Co. – Black River Falls
1st Battalion, 147th Command Aviation
Headquarters and Headquarters Co. – Madison
   Company A – Madison
   Company C – Madison
   Company D – Madison
57th Field Artillery Brigade
Headquarters and Headquarters Btry. (–) – Milwaukee
   Det. 1, Hq. Btry. – Two Rivers
1st Battalion, 121st Field Artillery (MLRS)
Headquarters and Headquarters Service Btry. – Milwaukee
   Battery A – Milwaukee
   Battery B (–) – Plymouth
   Det. 1, Btry. B – Two Rivers
   Battery C – Sussex
1st Battalion, 126th Field Artillery
Headquarters and Headquarters Btry. – Kenosha
   Battery A – Whitewater
   Battery B – Oak Creek
   Battery C – Racine
   Service Battery – Burlington
264th Engineer Group
Headquarters and Headquarters Co. – Chippewa Falls
   229th Engineer Co. (CSE) (–) – Prairie du Chien
   Det. 1, 229th Engineer Co. (CSE) – Platteville
   829th Engineer Detachment (Utilities) – Richland Center
   106th Engineer Detachment (Quarry) – Ashland
724th Engineer Battalion

Headquarters and Headquarters Co. (–) – Hayward
Det. 1, Headquarters and Headquarters Co. – Superior
Company A (–) – Medford
Det. 1, Co. A – Chippewa Falls
Company B (–) – Spooner
Det. 1, Co. B – Superior
Company C (–) – Tomahawk
Det. 1, Co. C – Rhinelander

426th Leadership Regiment (Wisconsin Military Academy)
Headquarters and Headquarters Det. – Fort McCoy
Training Site Command – Fort McCoy
1st Battalion, 426th Rgt. (FA) – Fort McCoy
2nd Battalion, 426th Rgt. (GS) – Fort McCoy

AIR UNITS

Headquarters, Wisconsin Air National Guard – Madison
115th Fighter Wing – Truax Field, Madison
115th Operations Group
176th Fighter Squadron
115th Operations Support Flight
115th Maintenance Group
115th Aircraft Maintenance Squadron
115th Maintenance Squadron
115th Maintenance Operations Flight
115th Mission Support Group
115th Logistics Readiness Squadron
115th Security Forces Squadron
115th Mission Support Flight
115th Services Flight
115th Civil Engineer Squadron
115th Communications Flight
115th Medical Group

128th Air Refueling Wing – Mitchell Field, Milwaukee
128th Operations Group
126th Air Refueling Squadron
128th Operations Support Flight
126th Weather Flight
128th Maintenance Group
128th Aircraft Maintenance Squadron
128th Maintenance Squadron
128th Maintenance Operations Flight
128th Mission Support Group
128th Logistics Readiness Squadron
128th Security Forces Squadron
128th Mission Support Flight
128th Services Flight
128th Civil Engineer Squadron
128th Communications Flight
128th Medical Group
Volk Field Combat Readiness Training Center – Camp Douglas
128th Air Control Squadron – Volk Field CRTC, Camp Douglas

Bold Face – Major Command
(–) – Headquarters of a split unit
Abbreviations:
ASG – Area Support Group
AVIM – Aviation Intermediate Maintenance
Bde. – Brigade
Btry. – Battery
CENFAST – Forward Area Support Team (Central)
Co. – Company
CSE – Combat Support Equipment
CRTC – Combat Readiness Training Center
Det. – Detachment
FA – Field Artillery
GS – General Studies

HHC – Headquarters and Headquarters Company
HHS – Headquarters and Headquarters Services
HHSB – Headquarters and Headquarters Service Battery
HQ – Headquarters
Med. – Medical
MLRS – Multiple Launch Rocket System
MP – Military Police
NORFAST – Forward Area Support Team (North)
OSA – Operational Support Airlift
RAOC – Rear Area Operations Center
Rgt. – Regiment
ROC – Rear Operations Center
WMD – Weapons of Mass Destruction

Source: Wisconsin Department of Military Affairs, departmental data, January 2005.

MEMBERSHIP, WISCONSIN VETERANS HOMES
1888 – 2004

	Civil and Indian Wars	Spanish-American	World War I		World War II		Korean Conflict		Total
			Men	Women	Men	Women	Men	Women	
1888	72	---	---	---	---	---	---	---	72
1890	139	---	---	---	---	---	---	---	139
1900	680	---	---	---	---	---	---	---	680
1910	699	---	---	---	---	---	---	---	699
1920	532	---	---	---	---	---	---	---	532
1930	254	108	10	14	---	---	---	---	386
1940	89	196	101	130	---	---	---	---	516
1950	27	156	189	93	5	1	---	---	471
1960	4	74	203	94	40	5	---	---	450
1961	3	66	221	88	39	8	---	---	427
1962	3	66	223	82	52	9	---	---	431
1963	3	67	235	87	57	10	---	---	459
1964	3	63	237	105	61	16	---	---	485
1965	2	62	247	112	77	16	---	---	516
1966	1	56	258	112	86	21	---	---	534
1967	1	46	272	120	93	20	---	---	555
1968	1	48	253	123	93	16	---	---	534
1969	1	43	253	145	101	14	---	---	560
1970	1	35	279	146	153	20	1	0	635
1971	1	39	316	160	184	31	2	0	723
1972	0	28	279	155	199	39	2	0	702
1973	0	25	285	108	199	37	0	1	715
1974	0	21	279	175	185	37	0	2	699

	Spanish-American		World War I		World War II		Korean Conflict		Vietnam		Other Eras*		Total
	Vets.	Deps.	Vets.	Deps.	Vets.	Deps.	Vets.	Deps.	Vets.	Deps.	Vets.	Deps.	
1975	1	18	272	171	198	40	3	2	0	0	0	0	705
1976	1	14	254	167	209	40	2	2	0	0	0	0	689
1977	1	13	270	164	205	41	4	2	0	0	0	0	700
1978	1	11	261	158	218	38	3	2	0	0	0	0	692
1979	1	11	244	146	227	37	4	1	0	0	0	0	672
1980	1	8	242	144	241	36	5	1	0	0	0	0	678
1981	0	8	224	139	264	40	8	2	0	0	0	0	685
1982	0	7	189	124	282	43	11	2	0	0	0	0	658
1983	0	5	171	111	297	42	14	2	1	0	0	0	643
1984	0	4	144	97	316	47	21	2	3	0	0	0	634
1985	0	4	129	102	329	54	28	0	5	0	0	0	651
1986	0	4	117	92	348	56	35	5	7	0	0	0	664
1987	0	2	108	84	384	60	36	4	8	0	0	0	686
1988	0	1	84	76	395	55	45	7	8	0	0	0	671
1989	0	2	62	75	399	67	50	7	9	1	0	0	672
1990	0	2	49	65	431	76	62	8	10	1	3	0	707
1991	0	2	43	57	440	74	69	10	10	2	3	0	710
1992	0	1	33	44	442	77	82	10	12	1	2	0	704
1993	0	1	23	41	463	73	94	9	11	1	2	0	718
1994	0	1	14	33	488	83	99	11	12	2	1	0	744
1995	0	1	8	31	484	84	99	12	16	2	1	0	738
1996	0	1	4	24	489	79	103	12	25	1	1	0	739
1997	0	1	3	20	479	82	107	11	38	1	3	0	744
1998	0	0	1	17	460	83	123	12	39	1	9	0	745
1999	0	0	0	12	445	87	128	11	41	3	13	1	741
2000	0	0	0	10	423	94	132	12	47	4	21	2	745
2001	0	0	0	9	414	95	133	10	51	3	25	2	742
2002	0	0	0	8	404	103	130	11	54	3	29	2	744
2003	0	0	0	7	433	105	140	13	67	3	35	2	805
2004	0	0	0	3	416	99	148	15	72	3	40	2	798

Deps. – Dependents.

*Other periods of hostilities for which expeditionary medals were awarded.

Source: Wisconsin Department of Veterans Affairs, departmental data, June 2005.

WISCONSIN NEWSPAPERS
Daily Newspapers

Municipality	Newspaper[1]	Publisher
Antigo 54409, 612 Superior St.	Antigo Daily Journal	Marie Berner
Appleton 54911, 306 W. Washington St., P.O. Box 59	The Post-Crescent	Ellen Leifeld
Ashland 54806, 122 W. Third St., P.O. Box 313	The Daily Press	Gary Pennington
Baraboo 53913, 219 First St., P.O. Box 9	News Republic	Russell Cunningham
Beaver Dam 53916-0558, 805 Park Ave., P.O. Box 558	Daily Citizen	Jim Kelsh
Beloit 53511, 149 State St.	Beloit Daily News	Kent Eymann
Chippewa Falls 54729, 321 Frenette Dr., P.O. Box 69	The Chippewa Herald	Mark Baker
Eau Claire 54702, 701 S. Farwell St., P.O. Box 570	Leader-Telegram	Pieter Graaskamp
Fond du Lac 54936, 33 W. Second St., P.O. Box 630	The Reporter	Genia Lovett
Fort Atkinson 53538, 28 W. Milwaukee Ave., P.O. Box 801	Daily Jefferson County Union	Brian Knox
Green Bay 54306, 133 S. Monroe Ave., P.O. Box 2467	The Green Bay News-Chronicle	Frank A. Wood
Green Bay 54305-3430, P.O. Box 23430	Green Bay Press-Gazette	William T. Nusbaum
Janesville 53545, One S. Parker Dr., P.O. Box 5001	The Janesville Gazette	Skip Bliss
Kenosha 53140, 5800 7th Ave., P.O. Box 190	Kenosha News	Kenneth Dowdell
La Crosse 54601, 401 N. Third St., P.O. Box 865	La Crosse Tribune	Mike Jameson
Madison 53708, 1901 Fish Hatchery Rd., P.O. Box 8060	The Capital Times	Clayton Frink
Madison 53708, 1901 Fish Hatchery Rd., P.O. Box 8058	Wisconsin State Journal	James Hopson
Manitowoc 54220, 902 Franklin St., P.O. Box 790	Herald Times Reporter	Bill Nusbaum
Marinette 54143, 1809 Dunlap Ave., P.O. Box 77	EagleHerald	Dennis Colling
Marshfield 54449, 111 W. Third St., P.O. Box 70	Marshfield News-Herald	Helen Jungwirth
Milwaukee 53203, 225 E. Michigan St., Suite 540, P.O. Box 514033	The Daily Reporter	Mark Stodder
Milwaukee 53201, 333 W. State St., P.O. Box 661	Milwaukee Journal Sentinel	Keith Spore
Monroe 53566, 1065 Fourth Ave., West, P.O. Box 230	Monroe Times	Carl C. Hearing
Oshkosh 54901, 224 State St., P.O. Box 2926	The Oshkosh Northwestern	Kevin Doyle
Portage 53901, 309 DeWitt St., P.O. Box 470	Daily Register	Russell Cunningham
Racine 53403, 212 Fourth St., P.O. Box 786	The Journal Times	Richard Johnston
Rhinelander 54501, 314 Courtney St., P.O. Box 778	The Daily News	Jay Anderle
Shawano 54166, 1464 E. Green Bay St., P.O. Box 416	Shawano Leader	Rod Christensen
Sheboygan 53081, 632 Center Ave., P.O. Box 358	The Sheboygan Press	Richard Roesgen
Stevens Point 54481, 1200 Third Ct.	Stevens Point Journal	Bob Robbins
Superior 54880, 1226 Ogden Ave.	The Daily Telegram	Todd Keute
Watertown 53094, 115 W. Main St., P.O. Box 140	Watertown Daily Times	James Clifford
Waukesha 53187, 801 N. Barstow St., P.O. Box 7	Waukesha Freeman	Jeff Hovind
Wausau 54402, 800 Scott St., P.O. Box 1286	Wausau Daily Herald	Bob Robbins
West Bend 53095, 100 S. Sixth Ave., P.O. Box 478	West Bend Daily News	Steve Ciccantelli
Wisconsin Rapids 54495, 220 First Ave. South	The Daily Tribune	Helen Jungwirth

Other Newspapers

Municipality	Newspaper	Published	Publisher
Abbotsford 54405	The Tribune Phonograph	Wed.	Carol O'Leary
Adams 53910	Adams County Times	Wed.	Richard A. Hannagan
Albany 53502	Albany Vision	Wed.	Hilary Bauman
Algoma 54201	Algoma Record-Herald	Thurs.	Frank Wood
Alma (Cochrane 54622)	Buffalo County Journal	Thurs.	Michael, Gary, Daniel Stumpf
Amery 54001	Amery Free Press	Tues.	Palmer H. Sondreal
Arcadia 54612	The Arcadia News-Leader	Thurs.	Charles Blaschko
Argyle 53504	Pecatonica Valley Leader	Thurs.	Patrick and Michael Reilly
Ashwaubenon (Green Bay 54304)	The Ashwaubenon Press	Fri.	Michael Aubinger
Augusta 54722	Augusta Area Times	Thurs.	Chad Nyseth
Baldwin 54002	The Baldwin Bulletin	Tues.	Thomas Hawley
Balsam Lake 54810	County Ledger Press	Thurs.	Tom Miller
Barron 54812	Barron News-Shield	Wed.	James Bell
Bayview[2]	The Bayviewer	Thurs.	Cristy Garcia-Thomas
Belleville 53508	Belleville Recorder	Tues.	Stuart Shapiro
Beloit 53511	The Chronicle	Sat.	Eugene Relerford
Berlin 54923	The Berlin Journal	Thurs.	Ty Gonyo
Black Earth 53515	News-Sickle-Arrow	Thurs.	Dan & Mark Witte
Black River Falls 54615	Banner Journal	Wed.	Dan & Mark Witte
Blair 54616	The Blair Press	Thurs.	Lee Henschel
Bloomer 54724	Bloomer Advance	Wed.	Mary Ann Sarno
Boscobel 53805-1531	Boscobel Dial	Thurs.	John Ingebritsen
Brillion 54110	The Brillion News	Thurs.	Zane & Noel Zander
Brodhead 53520-0255	The Independent Register	Wed.	Kim Markham
Brookfield[2]	Brookfield News	Thurs.	Cristy Garcia-Thomas
Brown Deer[2]	Brown Deer Herald	Thurs.	Cristy Garcia-Thomas
Burlington 53105	Burlington Standard Press	Thurs.	Jack Cruger[4]
Cadott 54727	The Cadott Sentinel	Thurs.	Trygg Hansen
Cambridge 53523	The Cambridge News	Thurs.	Brian Knox
Campbellsport 53010	Campbellsport News	Thurs.	James Ninnemann

WISCONSIN NEWSPAPERS
Other Newspapers–Continued

Municipality	Newspaper	Published	Publisher
Cashton 54619	Cashton Record	Wed.	Paul Fanning
Cedarburg 53012	Ozaukee County News Graphic	Mon. & Thurs.	Philip Paige
Chetek 54728	The Chetek Alert	Thurs.	Melodee Eckerman
Chilton 53014	Chilton Times-Journal	Thurs.	James Moran
Clinton 53525	The Clinton Topper	Thurs.	Jack Cruger
Clintonville 54929	Clintonville Tribune-Gazette	Thurs.	Jeff Hoffman
Cochrane 54622	Cochrane-Fountain City Recorder	Thurs.	Michael, Gary, Daniel Stumpf
Colfax 54730	The Colfax Messenger	Wed.	Carlton DeWitt
Columbus 53925	Columbus Journal	Sat.	James Kelsh
Cornell 54732	Cornell/Lake Holcombe Courier	Thurs.	Trygg Hansen
Cottage Grove 53527-9632	The Herald-Independent	Thurs.	Brian Knox
Crandon 54520	The Forest Republican	Wed.	Jay Anderle
Cuba City 53807	Tri-County Press	Thurs.	John Ingebritsen
Cudahy[2]	Cudahy Reminder Enterprise	Thurs.	Cristy Garcia-Thomas
Cumberland 54829	Cumberland Advocate	Wed.	Sharon & Craig Bucher
Darlington 53530	Republican-Journal	Thurs.	Brian Lund
Deerfield 53531	The Independent	Thurs.	Brian Knox
DeForest 53532	DeForest Times-Tribune	Thurs.	Art Drake
Delavan 53115-0366	The Delavan Enterprise	Thurs.	John Halverson[4]
Denmark 54208	The Denmark Press	Thurs.	Frank Wood
De Pere 54115-5066	De Pere Journal	Thurs.	Frank Wood
Dodgeville 53533	The Dodgeville Chronicle	Thurs.	Patrick & Michael Reilly
Dousman (Hartland 53029)	The Kettle Moraine Index	Thurs.	Gary Jasiek
Durand 54736	The Courier-Wedge	Thurs.	Gary, Michael Stumpf
Eagle River 54521	Vilas County News-Review	Wed.	Byron McNuttt
East Troy 53120	East Troy News	Thurs.	Jack Cruger
East Troy 53120	East Troy Times	Wed.	Katie Matteson
Eau Claire 54702	The Country Today	Wed.	Pieter Graaskamp
Edgar (Abbotsford 54405)	The Record Review	Wed.	Carol O'Leary
Edgerton 53534	The Edgerton Reporter	Wed.	Diane and Helen Everson
Elkhorn 53121	Elkhorn Independent	Thurs.	Jack Cruger
Ellsworth 54011-4117	Pierce County Herald	Wed.	Steve Dzubay
Elm Grove[2]	Elm Grove Elm Leaves	Thurs.	Cristy Garica-Thomas
Elmwood (Spring Valley 54767)	The Elmwood Argus	Wed.	Duane DeYoung
Elroy 53929	Trail Communities Messenger	Thurs.	Bill Smith
Evansville 53536	Evansville Review	Wed.	Stan Gildner
Fennimore 53809	The Fennimore Times	Thurs.	John Ingebritsen
Fitchburg 53711	Fitchburg Star	Thurs.	Don Gimberline
Florence 54121	The Florence Mining News	Wed.	Julie Giddings
Fox Lake[3]	The Representative	Thurs.	Ty Gonyo
Fox Point[2]	Fox Point/Bayside/River Hills Herald	Thurs.	Cristy Garcia-Thomas
Franklin[2]	Franklin Hub	Thurs.	Cristy Garcia-Thomas
Frederic 54837	Inter-County Leader	Wed.	Doug Panek
Friendship (Adams 53910)	Friendship Reporter	Wed.	Richard A. Hannagan
Galesville 54630	Galesville Republican	Thurs.	John Ph Graf
Gays Mills 54631	Crawford County Independent	Thurs.	John Ingebritsen
Germantown[2]	Germantown Banner Press	Wed.	Cristy Garcia-Thomas
Glendale[2]	Glendale Herald	Thurs.	Cristy Garcia-Thomas
Glenwood City 54013	The Tribune Press Reporter	Wed.	Carlton DeWitt
Glidden 54527	The Glidden Enterprise	Wed.	Robert Hart
Grantsburg 54840	Burnett County Sentinel	Wed.	Byron Higgin
Green Lake[3]	Green Lake County Reporter	Thurs.	Ty Gonyo
Greendale[2]	Greendale Village Life	Thurs.	Cristy Garcia-Thomas
Greenfield[2]	Greenfield Observer	Thurs.	Cristy Garcia-Thomas
Hales Corners[2]	Hales Corners Village Hub	Thurs	Cristy Garcia-Thomas
Hammond 54015	Central St. Croix News	Wed.	Art Groth
Hartford 53027	Hartford Times Press	Thurs.	Phil Hermann[5]
Hartland 53029	Lake Country Reporter	Mon. & Thurs.	Gary Jasiek
Hayward 54843	Sawyer County Record	Wed.	Wanda Moeller
Hillsboro 54634	Hillsboro Sentry-Enterprise	Thurs.	Jack Knowles
Holmen 54636	Holmen Courier	Fri.	Chris Hardie
Horicon 53032	Horicon Reporter	Thurs.	Andrew Johnson
Hudson 54016	Hudson Star-Observer	Thurs.	Steve Dzubay
Hurley 54534	Iron County Miner	Thurs.	Ernest Moore[5]
Iola 54945	The Iola Herald	Thurs.	Trey Foerster
Juneau 53039	Dodge County Independent News	Thurs.	James Clifford
Kaukauna 54130	Times Villager	Wed. & Sat.	Glenn Hansen
Kewaskum 53040	The Statesman	Thurs.	Lana Kuehl
Kewaunee 54216-0086	The Kewaunee Enterprise	Thurs.	Frank Wood
Kiel 53042	Tri-County News	Thurs.	Mike Mathes
Ladysmith 54848	Ladysmith News	Thurs.	Thomas Bell
La Farge (Viola 54664)	Epitaph-News	Thurs.	Bonnie Howell-Sherman
Lake Geneva 53147	Lake Geneva Regional News	Thurs.	Howard Brown
Lake Mills 53551	The Lake Mills Leader	Thurs.	Brian Knox
Lancaster 53813	Grant County Herald Independent	Thurs.	John Ingebritsen
Lodi 53555	The Lodi Enterprise	Thurs.	Brian Knox
Loyal 54446	Tribune Record Gleaner	Wed.	Dean Lesar

WISCONSIN NEWSPAPERS
Other Newspapers–Continued

Municipality	Newspaper	Published	Publisher
Luck 54853	Enterprise Press	Thurs.	Tom Miller
Luxemburg 54217	Luxemburg News	Thurs.	Frank Wood
Madison 53703	Isthmus	Thurs.	Vincent P. O'Hern
Madison 53703	The Madison Times	Thurs.	David Hammonds
Manawa (Iola 54945)	The Manawa Advocate	Thurs.	Trey Foerster
Marion 54950	The Marion Advertiser	Thurs.	Daniel S. Brandenburg
Markesan 53946	Markesan Regional Reporter	Thurs.	Ty Gonyo
Mauston 53948	Juneau County Star Times	Wed. & Sat.	Russell Cunningham
Mayville 53050	The Mayville News	Thurs.	Andrew Johnson
McFarland 53558-9204	McFarland Thistle/Community Life	Thurs.	Brian Knox
Medford 54451	The Star News	Thurs.	Carol O'Leary
Mellen 54546	The Mellen Weekly-Record	Wed.	James Christl
Melrose 54642	The Chronicle	Wed.	Chris Hardie
Menomonee Falls[2]	Menomonee Falls News	Wed.	Cristy Garcia-Thomas
Menomonie 54751	The Dunn County News	Sun. & Wed.	Steven Jahn
Mequon[2]	Mequon-Thiensville Courant	Thurs.	Cristy Garcia-Thomas
Middleton 53562	Middleton Times-Tribune	Thurs.	Dan & Mark Witte
Milton 53563	Milton Courier	Thurs.	Brian Knox
Milwaukee 53204	The Business Journal	Fri.	Mark Sabljak
Milwaukee 53212	Milwaukee Community Journal	Wed. & Fri.	Patricia O'Flynn Pattillo
Milwaukee 53206	Milwaukee Courier	Fri.	Faithe Colas
Milwaukee 53206	Milwaukee Star	Thurs.	Faithe Colas
Milwaukee 53212	The Milwaukee Times	Thurs.	Linda Jackson
Milwaukee 53202	Shepherd Express Metro	Thurs.	Louis Fortis
Mineral Point 53565	The Democrat Tribune	Thurs.	Patrick & Michael Reilly
Minocqua 54548	Lakeland Times	Tues. & Fri.	Don Walker
Mondovi 54755	Mondovi Herald-News	Thurs.	Perry Nyseth
Montello 53949	The Marquette County Tribune	Thurs.	Dan & Mark Witte
Mosinee 54455	The Mosinee Times	Thurs.	John Durst & James Kress
Mount Horeb 53572	Mount Horeb Mail	Thurs.	Dan & Mark Witte
Mukwonago 53149	Mukwonago Chief	Wed.	Susan Hall
Muscoda 53573	The Progressive	Thurs.	Wendell Smith
Muskego[2]	Muskego Sun	Thurs.	Cristy Garcia-Thomas
Neillsville 54456	The Clark County Press	Wed.	Dan Witte
New Berlin 53151[2]	New Berlin Citizen	Thurs.	Cristy Garcia-Thomas
New Glarus 53574	Post Messenger	Wed.	Dan & Mark Witte
New London 54961	Press-Star	Fri.	Bill Melendes
New Richmond 54017-0338	New Richmond News	Thurs.	Steve Dzubay
Niagara 54151	The Niagara Journal	Wed.	Nancy Gomez & Margie Yadro
Oak Creek[2]	Oak Creek Pictorial	Thurs.	Cristy Garcia-Thomas
Oconomowoc 53066	Oconomowoc Enterprise	Thurs.	Kevin Passon
Oconomowoc (Hartland 53029)	Oconomowoc Focus	Mon. & Thurs.	Gary Jasiek
Oconto 54153	Oconto County Reporter	Wed.	Frank Wood
Oconto Falls 54154	Oconto County Times-Herald	Wed.	Roger F. Shellman
Omro 54963	Omro Herald	Thurs.	Ty Gonyo
Onalaska 54650	Onalaska Community Life	Fri.	Chris Hardie
Ontario 54651	The County Line	Thurs.	Karen Parker
Oregon 53575	The Oregon Observer	Thurs.	Don Gimberline
Orfordville 53576	Orfordville Journal & Footville News	Wed.	George Stewart
Osceola 54020	The Sun	Wed.	Carter Johnson
Osseo 54758	The Tri-County News	Wed.	Chad Nyseth
Palmyra 53156	The Enterprise	Fri.	Pat Bogumil
Park Falls 54552	The Park Falls Herald	Thurs.	Ken Dischler
Peshtigo 54157	Peshtigo Times	Wed.	Mary Ann Gardon
Phillips 54555	The-Bee	Thurs.	Trish Kempkes
Platteville 53818	The Platteville Journal	Tues.	John Ingebritsen
Plymouth 53073	The Review	Tues. & Thurs.	Barry & Christie Johanson
Port Washington 53074	Ozaukee Press	Thurs.	William Schanen III
Poynette 53955	Poynette Press	Wed.	Art Drake
Prairie du Chien 53821	Courier-Press	Mon. & Wed.	William H. Howe
Prescott 54021	Prescott Journal	Thurs.	Gary B. Rawn
Princeton 54968	Princeton Times-Republic	Thurs.	Ty Gonyo
Random Lake 53075	The Sounder	Thurs.	Gary Feider
Reedsburg 53959	Reedsburg Independent	Thurs.	Dan & Mark Witte
Reedsburg 53959	Reedsburg Times Press	Wed. & Sat.	Russell Cunningham
Rice Lake 54868	Rice Lake Chronotype	Wed.	Warren Dorrance
Richland Center 53581	The Richland Observer	Thurs.	Erik Olson
Ripon 54971	The Ripon Commonwealth Press	Thurs.	Tim Lyke
River Falls 54022	River Falls Journal	Thurs.	Steve Dzubay
St. Croix Falls 54024	Standard-Press	Thurs.	Tom Miller
St. Francis[2]	St. Francis Reminder-Enteprise	Thurs.	Cristy Garcia-Thomas
Sauk City 53583	The Sauk Prairie Eagle	Wed.	Rusty Cunningham
Sauk City 53583	The Sauk Prairie Star	Thurs.	Dan & Mark Witte
Seymour 54165	Times-Press	Thurs.	Criag Lane
Sharon (Walworth 53189)	The Sharon Reporter	Thurs.	Mabel Jackson[4]
Sheboygan Falls (Plymouth 53073)	The Sheboygan Falls News	Wed.	Barry & Christie Johanson

WISCONSIN NEWSPAPERS
Other Newspapers–Continued

Municipality	Newspaper	Published	Publisher
Shell Lake 54871	Washburn County Register	Thurs.	Valdemar Jensen
Shorewood[2]	Shorewood Herald	Thurs.	Cristy Garcia-Thomas
South Milwaukee[2]	South Milwaukee Voice Graphic	Thurs.	Cristy Garcia-Thomas
Sparta 54656	Monroe Co. Democrat	Thurs.	William Gleiss
Sparta 54656	Sparta Herald	Mon.	Ted Radde
Spooner 54801	Spooner Advocate	Thurs.	Janet Krokson
Spring Green 53588	Home News	Wed.	Jim & Linda Schwanke
Spring Valley 54767	The Spring Valley Sun	Wed.	Duane DeYoung
Stanley 54768	The Stanley Republican	Thurs.	B.J. Fazendin
Stevens Point 54481	Portage County Gazette	Fri.	Pete Leahy
Stoughton 53589	The Stoughton Courier Hub	Thurs.	Don Gimberline
Sturgeon Bay 54235	Door County Advocate	Tues. Thurs, & Sat.	Patrick & Chris Wood
Sun Prairie 53590	The Star	Thurs.	Brian Knox
Sussex (Hartland 53029)	Sussex Sun	Tues.	Gary Jasiek
Thorp 54771	The Thorp Courier	Wed.	Mark LaGasse
Three Lakes (Eagle River 54521)	The Three Lakes News	Wed.	Byron McNutt
Tomah 54660	The Tomah Journal	Thurs.	Chris Hardie
Tomah 54660	Tomah Monitor-Herald	Mon.	Chris Hardie
Tomahawk 54487	Tomahawk Leader	Tues.	Larry & Kathy Tobin
Turtle Lake 54889	The Times	Thurs.	David Slack
Twin Lakes 53181	Westosha Report	Sat.	Jack Cruger
Union Grove 53182	Westine Report	Thurs.	Jack Cruger
Valders 54245	The Valders Journal	Thurs.	Brian Thomsen
Verona 53593	The Verona Press	Thurs.	Don Gimberline
Viroqua 54665	Vernon County Broadcaster	Thurs.	Chris Hardie
Walworth 53184	The Times	Thurs.	Jack Cruger
Washburn 54891	The County Journal	Thurs.	Gary Pennington
Washington Island 54246	Washington Island Observer	Thurs.	Gail Larson Toerpe
Waterford 53185	The Waterford Post	Fri.	Jack Cruger
Waterloo 53594	The Courier	Thurs.	Brian Knox
Waunakee 53597	The Waunakee Tribune	Thurs.	Art Drake
Waupaca 54981	Waupaca County Post	Thurs.	Scott Turner
Waupun 53963	Neighbors	Sat.	James Kelsh
Wausau 54402	City Pages	Thurs.	Tammy Stezenski
Wautoma 54982	The Waushara Argus	Wed.	Mary Kunasch
Wauwatosa[2]	Wauwatosa News Times	Thurs.	Cristy Garcia-Thomas
West Allis[2]	West Allis Star	Thurs.	Cristy Garcia-Thomas
West Salem 54669	The Coulee News	Thurs.	Chris Hardie
Westby 54667	The Times	Thurs.	Chris Hardie
Weyauwega 54983	The Chronicle	Thurs.	Scott Turner
Whitefish Bay[2]	Whitefish Bay Herald	Wed.	Cristy Garcia-Thomas
Whitehall 54773	Whitehall Times	Thurs.	Charles A. Gauger
Whitewater 53190	The Whitewater Register	Wed.	Jack Cruger
Winneconne 54986	The Winneconne News	Wed.	John Rogers
Winter 54896	Sawyer County Gazette	Wed.	Meredith Rickert
Wisconsin Dells 53965	Wisconsin Dells Events	Wed. & Sat.	Russell Cunningham
Withee 54498	O-W Enterprise	Wed.	Mark Gorke & Mark Renderman[5]
Wittenberg 54499	The Wittenberg Enterprise	Thurs.	Gordon Boldig[5]
Woodville 54028	The Woodville Leader	Wed.	Duane DeYoung

[1]A "newspaper" is defined by Section 985.03 (1) (c), Wisconsin Statutes, as follows: "A newspaper, under this chapter, is a publication appearing at regular intervals and at least once a week, containing reports of happenings of recent occurrence of a varied character, such as political, social, moral and religious subjects, designed to inform the general reader ...".

[2]Combined editorial office in New Berlin 53151.

[3]Combined editorial office in Berlin 54923.

[4]General manager.

[5]Editor.

Source: *2004 Directory,* Wisconsin Newspaper Association; data compiled by Wisconsin Legislative Reference Bureau.

WISCONSIN PERIODICALS

Name	Issued	Publishers
AAA Living	Bimonthly	AAA Wisconsin, P.O. Box 33, Madison 53701-0033
Action Tracks	1 per year	Byron McNutt, P.O. Box 1929, Eagle River 54521-1929
AFSCME Reports	Monthly	AFSCME Int'l Area Office, 8033 Excelsior Dr., Suite A, Madison 53717-1903
Agri-View	Weekly	Matt Meyers, 2001 Fish Hatchery Rd., Madison 53708
Agronomy Journal	Bimonthly	American Society of Agronomy, 677 S. Segoe Rd., Madison 53711-1048
Airwaves	Monthly	Wisconsin Public Television, R. 1076 Vilas Hall, 821 University Ave., Madison 53706
Akiing	Monthly	Paul DeMain, 8558N County Road K, Hayward 54843
American Bowler	Quarterly	American Bowling Congress, 5301 S. 76th St., Greendale 53129-1128
American Orthoptic Journal	1 per year	UW Press, 1930 Monroe St., 3rd Floor, Madison 53711-2059
Antique & Collectables Monthly Newmagazine	Monthly	Krause Publications, Inc., 700 E. State St., Iola 54990-0001
Antique Review	Monthly	Krause Publications, Inc., 700 E. State St., Iola 54990-0001
Antique Trader Weekly	Weekly	Krause Publications, Inc., 700 E. State St., Iola 54990-0001
Arctic Anthropology	2 per year	UW Press, 1930 Monroe St., 3rd Floor, Madison 53711-2059
Astronomy	Monthly	Kalmbach Publishing Co., P.O. Box 1612, Waukesha 53187-1612
At Ease	Quarterly	Wisconson National Guard, 2400 Wright St., Madison 53704
Badger Common 'Tater	Monthly	Wis. Potato and Vegetable Growers Assn., Inc., P.O. Box 327, Antigo 54409-0327
Badger Herald	Daily (M-F)	Marc Molik, 326 W. Gorham St., Madison 53703
Badger Legionnaire	Monthly	Wisconsin American Legion, 2930 American Legion Dr., P.O. Box 388, Portage 53901
Badger Rails	6 per year	Wis. Assn. of Railroad Passengers, 408 Fremont, Lake Mills 53551
Badger Sportsman	Monthly	James Moran and James Bellin, P.O. Box 125, Redgranite 54970
Bank Note Reporter	Monthly	Krause Publications, Inc., 700 E. State St., Iola 54990-0001
Beloit College Magazine	3 per year	Beloit College, Office of Public Affairs, 700 College St., Beloit 53511-5595
Beloit Fiction Journal	1 per year	Heather Skyler, Beloit College, Box 11700, College St., Beloit 53511
Benefits & Compensation Digest	Monthly	International Foundation of Employee Benefits Plans, P.O. Box 69, Brookfield 53008-0069
Benefits Quarterly	4 per year	International Soc. of Certified Employee Benefit Specialists, P.O. Box 209, Brookfield 53008-0209
Big Reel	Monthly	Krause Publications, Inc., 700 E. State St., Iola 54990-0001
Birds & Blooms	6 per year	Reiman Publications, 5400 South 60th St., Greendale 53129
Blade	Monthly	Krause Publications, Inc., 700 E. State St., Iola 54990-0001
Business Journal, The	Weekly	Mark J. Sabljak, 600 W. Virginia St., Suite 500, Milwaukee 53204
Card Trade	Monthly	Krause Publications, Inc., 700 E. State St., Iola 54990-0001

WISCONSIN PERIODICALS–Continued

Name	Issued	Publishers
Catholic Knight	3 per year	Catholic Knights, P.O. Box 05900, Milwaukee 53205-0900
Cessna Owner Magazine	Monthly	Jones Publishing, Inc., N7450 Aanstad Rd., Iola 54945-5000
Chain O'Lakes Picture Post	Weekly (15 summer weeks)	Scott B. Turner, P.O. Box 152, Waupaca 54981-0152
Cheese Reporter	Weekly	Dick Groves, 2810 Crossroads Dr., Suite 3000, Madison 53718
Child Welfare Report	Monthly	Impact Publications, P.O. Box 322, Waupaca 54981
Classic Toy Trains	9 per year	Kalmbach Publishing Co., P.O. Box 1612, Waukesha 53187-1612
C N A	Monthly	Krause Publications, Inc., 700 E. State St., Iola 54990-0001
Coin Prices	Bimonthly	Krause Publications, Inc., 700 E. State St., Iola 54990-0001
Coins	Monthly	Krause Publications, Inc., 700 E. State St., Iola 54990-0001
Collector Magazine & Price Guide	Monthly	Krause Publications, Inc., 700 E. State St., Iola 54990-0001
Columns	Bimonthly	State Historical Society of Wis., 816 State St., Madison 53706-1482
Comics & Games Retailer	Monthly	F & W Publications, Inc., 700 E. State St., Iola 54990-0001
Comics Buyer's Guide	Weekly	F & W Publications, Inc., 700 E. State St., Iola 54990-0001
Connection, The	Monthly	Barbara Gardner, 4590 State Highway 13, Port Wing 54865
Contemporary Literature	Quarterly	UW Press, 1930 Monroe St., 3rd Floor, Madison 53711-2059
Corporate Report Wisconsin	Monthly	Scott Klug, 1131 Mills St., P.O. Box 317, Black Earth 53151
Cotton & Quail Antique Gazette	Monthly	Krause Publications, Inc., 700 E. State St., Iola 54990-0001
Courier, The	Monthly	Wisconsin Veterans Home, Wisconsin Veterans Home, N2665 County Rd. QQ, King 54946
Credit Union Executive	Semimonthly	Roger Napiwocki, Credit Union National Assn., 5710 Mineral Point Rd., Madison 53705
Credit Union Magazine	Monthly	Jill Tomalin, Credit Union National Assn., P.O. Box 431, Madison 53701-0431
Crop Science	Bimonthly	Crop Science Soc. of Amer., 677 S. Segoe Rd., Madison 53711-1048
Crop Weather	Weekly (Apr.-Nov.)	Dept. of Agriculture, Trade and Consumer Protection, P.O. Box 8934, Madison 53708-8934
Daily Cardinal	Daily (M-F)	Daily Cardinal Media Corp., 821 University Ave., Madison 53706-1497
Deer and Deer Hunting	9 per year	Krause Publications, Inc., 700 E. State St., Iola 54990-0001
Director, The	Monthly	NFDA Services, Inc., 13625 Bishops Dr., Brookfield 53005
Discoveries	Monthly	F & W Publications, Inc., 700 E. State St., Iola 54990-0001
Doll Costuming	6 per year	Jones Publishing, Inc., N7450 Aanstad Rd., Iola 54945-9704
Doll Crafter	Monthly	Jones Publishing, Inc., N7450 Aanstad Rd., Iola 54945-9704
Drum Corps World	18 per year	Sights and Sounds, Inc., P.O. Box 8052, Madison 53708-8052
EAA Sport Aviation	Monthly	Experimental Aircraft Association, EAA Aviation Center, P.O. Box 3086, Oshkosh 54903-3086

WISCONSIN PERIODICALS–Continued

Name	Issued	Publishers
EAA Sport Pilot	Monthly	Experimental Aircraft Association, EAA Aviation Center, P.O. Box 3086, Oshkosh 54903-3086
Easter Seals Network News	2 per year	Easter Seals Wisconsin, Inc., 101 Nob Hill Rd., Suite 301, Madison 53713-3969
Ecological Restoration	Quarterly	UW Press, 1930 Monroe St., 3rd Floor, Madison 53711-2059
Equipment Today	Monthly	Cygnus Publishing, 1233 Janesville Ave., Fort Atkinson 53538
ESM news.mke	Quarterly	Engineers and Scientists of Milwaukee, 700 W. State St., Room T200, Milwaukee 53233
Exponent	Weekly	UW-Platteville, 317 Pioneer Tower, 1 University Plz., Platteville 53818-3012
Fantasy Sports	Quarterly	Krause Publications, Inc., 700 E. State St., Iola 54490-0001
Feminist Collections: A Quarterly of Women's Studies Resources	Quarterly	Phyllis Holman Weisbard, UW System Women's Studies Librarian, 430 Memorial Library, 728 State St., Madison 53706
Feminist Periodicals: A Current Listing of Contents	Quarterly	Phyllis Holman Weisbard, UW System Women's Studies Librarian, 430 Memorial Library, 728 State St., Madison 53706
FineScale Modeler	10 per year	Kalmbach Publishing, 21027 Crossroads Cir., Waukesha 53186-4055
Fired Arts and Crafts	Monthly	Jones Publishing, Inc., N7450 Aanstad Rd., Iola 54945-9704
Focus	28 per year	Wis. Taxpayers Alliance, 401 North Lawn Ave., Madison 53704-5033
Forward	4 per year	League of Women Voters of Wis., 122 State St., Suite 405, Madison 53703-2500
Forward in Christ	Monthly	Wis. Evangelical Lutheran Synod, 2929 N. Mayfair Rd., Milwaukee 53222-4398
Foto News	Weekly	Tim Schreiber, 807 E. First St., Merrill 54452
Frame Building News	5 per year	Krause Publications, Inc., 700 E. State St., Iola 54990-0001
Freethought Today	10 per year	Freedom From Religion Foundation, Inc., P.O. Box 750, Madison 53701-0750
FYI Northwoods	Biweekly	Joan McDonald, P.O. Box 93, Presque Isle 54557
Gargoyle, The	2 per year	Wis. Law Alumni Assn., UW Law School, 975 Bascom Mall, Madison 53706
GFWC Wis. Clubwoman	Quarterly	Sue Gallagher, 7907 East County Road X, Clinton 53525
Goldmine	Biweekly	F & W Publications, Inc., 700 E. State St., Iola 54990-0001
Guide, The	Quarterly	Equitable Reserve Assn., P.O. Box 448, Neenah 54957-0448
Gun and Knife Show Calendar	Quarterly	Krause Publications, Inc., 700 E. State St., Iola 54990-0001
Gun List	Biweekly	Krause Publications, Inc., 700 E. State St., Iola 54990-0001
Gwiazda Polarna Polish Biweekly Newspaper	Biweekly	Point Publications, Inc., 2804 Post Rd., Stevens Point 54481-6452
Harmonizer, The	Bimonthly	SPEBSQSA (Barbershop Harmony Society), 7930 Sheridan Rd., Kenosha 53143
Hoard's Dairyman	Semimonthly	W.D. Hoard and Sons Co., 28 Milwaukee Ave., W., Fort Atkinson 53538-2018
Home & Family Finance	Quarterly	Credit Union National Assn., P.O. Box 431, Madison 53701-0431

WISCONSIN PERIODICALS–Continued

Name	Issued	Publishers
Hummingbird: Magazine of the Short Poem	Quarterly	Phyllis Walsh, P.O. Box 96, Richland Center 53581
Impact Magazine	Quarterly	Wis. Park and Recreation Assn., 6601-C Northway, Greendale 53129
In Business	Monthly	Jody Glynn Patrick, 200 River Place, #250, Madison 53716
Inscriptions	3 per year	Dan Buckman, 3334 W. Grant St., Milwaukee 53215
Journal of Environmental Quality	Bimonthly	American Society of Agronomy, 677 S. Segoe Rd., Madison 53711-1048
Journal of Human Resources	Quarterly	UW Press, 1930 Monroe St., 3rd Floor, Madison 53711-2059
Journal of Natural Resources and Life Sciences Education	1 per year	American Society of Agronomy, 677 S. Segoe Rd., Madison 53711-1048
Journal of the Pharmacy Soc. of Wisconsin	6 per year	Pharmacy Society of Wisconsin, 701 Heartland Trail, Madison 53717
Kalhwisaks	Biweekly	Oneida Nation of Wisconsin, P.O. Box 365, Oneida 54155
La Crosse Union Herald	Monthly	Union Herald, Inc., 1920 Ward Ave., Suite 12, La Crosse 54601-6761
Labor Press	Monthly	AFL-CIO Milwaukee, 633 S. Hawley Rd., #110, Milwaukee 53214
Land Economics	Quarterly	UW Press, 1930 Monroe St., 3rd Floor, Madison 53711-2059
Landscape Journal	2 per year	UW Press, 1930 Monroe St., 3rd Floor, Madison 53711-2059
Legal-Legislative Reporter	Monthly	International Foundation of Employee Benefit Plans, P.O. Box 69, Brookfield 53008-0069
Living Church, The	Weekly	The Living Church Foundation, Inc., P.O. Box 514036, Milwaukee 53203-3436
Luso-Brazilian Review	2 per year	UW Press, 1930 Monroe St., 3rd Floor, Madison 53711-2059
Madison Magazine	Monthly	Jenifer Winiger, 7025 Raymond Rd., Madison 53719
Marketplace Magazine	4 weeks	Brian Rasmussen, 1486 Kenwood Center, Menasha 54952
Marquette Law Review	Quarterly	Students and Faculty of Marquette Law School, 1103 W. Wisconsin Ave., Milwaukee 53233
Marquette Magazine	Quarterly	Marquette University, P.O. Box 1881, Milwaukee 53201-1881
Maturity Times	Monthly	Action Publications, N6637 Rolling Meadows Dr., Fond du Lac 54937-9471
Metal Roofing	Bimonthly	Krause Publications, Inc., 700 E. State St., Iola 54990-0001
Midwest Flyer Magazine	Bimonthly	Dave Weiman, P.O. Box 199, Oregon 53575-0199
Midwest Racing News	36 per year	Hometown Publications, Inc., W130 N10437 Washington Dr., Germantown 53022
Military Trader	Monthly	Krause Publications, Inc., 700 E. State St., Iola 54990-0001
Milk & Liquid Food Transporter	Monthly	Glen Street Publications, Inc., W4652 Glen St., Appleton 54913-9563
Milwaukee History	Quarterly	Milwaukee County Historical Society, 910 N. Old World 3rd St., Milwaukee 53203-1591
Milwaukee Magazine	Monthly	Betty Quadracci, 417 E. Chicago St., Milwaukee 53202
Model Railroader	Monthly	Kalmbach Publishing Co., 21027 Crossroads Cir., Waukesha 53186-4055
Monatshefte	Quarterly	UW Press, 1930 Monroe St., 3rd Floor, Madison 53711-2059
N (Nude and Natural)	4 per year	The Naturists, LLC, P.O. Box 132, Oshkosh 54903-0132

WISCONSIN PERIODICALS–Continued

Name	Issued	Publishers
New Books on Women and Feminism	2 per year	Phyllis Holman Weisbard, UW System Women's Studies Librarian, 430 Memorial Library, 728 State St., Madison 53706
News from Indian Country	Biweekly	Paul DeMain, 8558N County Road K, Hayward 54843
North Woods Trader	2 per week	Byron McNutt, P.O. Box 1929, Eagle River 54521-1929
Northbound	Quarterly	Trees For Tomorrow, Natural Resources Education Center, 519 Sheridan East, P.O. Box 609, Eagle River 54521
Numismatic News	Weekly	Krause Publications, Inc., 700 E. State St., Iola 54990-0001
Old Cars Price Guide	Bimonthly	Krause Publications, Inc., 700 E. State St., Iola 54990-0001
Old Cars Weekly	Weekly	Krause Publications, Inc., 700 E. State St., Iola 54990-0001
On Premise	Bimonthly	Pete Madland, 2817 Fish Hatchery Rd., Madison 53713
On WEAC In Print	Monthly (Exc. July, Aug., & Dec.)	Wis. Education Assn. Council, 33 Nob Hill Dr., Madison 53713-2199
On Wisconsin	Quarterly	Wis. Alumni Assn., 650 N. Lake St., Madison 53706-1476
Paper Collectors' Marketplace	Monthly	Doug Watson, 470 N. Main St., P.O. Box 128, Scandinavia 54977-0128
Passenger Pigeon, The	Quarterly	Wisconsin Society for Ornithology, 810 Ganser Dr., Waunakee 53597-1930
Pharmacy in History	Quarterly	Amer. Institute of the History of Pharmacy, 777 Highland Ave., Madison 53705-2222
PhotoDaily	Daily	Rohn Engh, PhotoSource Internatl., Pine Lake Farm, 1910 35th Rd., Osceola 54020-5602
PhotoLetter	Weekly	Rohn Engh, PhotoSource Internatl., Pine Lake Farm, 1910 35th Rd., Osceola 54020-5602
PhotoStockNOTES	Weekly (on-line)	Rohn Engh, PhotoSource Internatl., Pine Lake Farm, 1910 35th Rd., Osceola 54020-5602
Pipers Magazine	Monthly	Jones Publishing, Inc., N7450 Aanstad Rd., Iola 54945-9704
Popular Ceramics Magazine	6 per year	Jones Publishing, Inc., N7450 Aanstad Rd., Iola 54945-9704
Postcard Collector	Monthly	Krause Publications, Inc., 700 E. State St., Iola 54990-0001
Professional, The	5 per year	AFT-Wisconsin, 1334 Applegate Rd., Madison 53713
Progressive, The	Monthly	Matthew Rothschild, 409 E. Main St., Madison 53703-2863
Quality Progress	Monthly	American Society for Quality, P.O. Box 3005, Milwaukee 53201-3005
Quarterly, The	Quarterly	College of Agricultural and Life Sciences, 440 Henry Mall, Madison 53706
Renascence: Essays on Values in Literature .	Quarterly	Marquette University, Raynor Memorial Libraries, M-164, P.O. Box 1881, Milwaukee 53201-1881
Research Profile	2 per year	Graduate School, UW-Milwaukee, P.O. Box 340, Milwaukee 53201
Rethinking Schools	Quarterly	Rethinking Schools, Ltd., 1001 E. Keefe Ave., Milwaukee 53212
Ripon College Magazine	4 per year	Ripon College, P.O. Box 248, Ripon 54971
Royal Purple	Weekly (during semester)	UW-Whitewater, 62 E University Center, Whitewater 53190

WISCONSIN PERIODICALS–Continued

Name	Issued	Publishers
Rural Builder	7 per year	Krause Publications, Inc., 700 E. State St., Iola 54990-0001
Sabbath Recorder, The	Monthly	American Sabbath Tract and Comm. Council, P.O. Box 1678, Janesville 53547
SCRYE	Monthly	F & W Publications, Inc., 700 E. State St., Iola 54990-0001
Searching Together	Quarterly	Word of Life Church, P.O. Box 548, St. Croix Falls 54024-0548
Sheep!	Bimonthly	Dave Belanger, W11564 Hwy 64, Withee 54498
Silent Sports	Monthly	Scott B. Turner, P.O. Box 152, Waupaca 54981-0152
Soil Science Society of America Journal	Bimonthly	Soil Science Society of America, 677 S. Segoe Rd., Madison 53711-1048
Soo, The	Quarterly	Soo Line Historical and Technical Society, 3410 Kasten Ct., Middleton 53562-1026
Southeastern Wisconsin Regional Planning Commission Newsletter	Quarterly	Southeastern Wis. Regional Planning Comn., P.O. Box 1607, Waukesha 53187-1607
Spanish Journal	Weekly	Rhonda Welch, 719 South 6th St., Milwaukee 53204
Spectator	Biweekly	UW-Eau Claire, 108 Hibbard Hall, Eau Claire 54701
Sports Collectors Digest	Weekly	Krause Publications, Inc., 700 E. State St., Iola 54990-0001
Substance	3 per year	UW Press, 1930 Monroe St., 3rd Floor, Madison 53711-2059
Timber Producer, The	Monthly	Mich.-Wis. Timber Producers Assn., P.O. Box 1278, Rhinelander 54501
Today's Dads	Monthly	Wisconsin Fathers for Children and Families, P.O. Box 1742, Madison 53701-1742
Toy Cars & Models	Monthly	F & W Publications, Inc., 700 E. State St., Iola 54990-0001
Toy Shop	Biweekly	F & W Publications, Inc., 700 E. State St., Iola 54990-0001
Trains Magazine	Monthly	Kalmbach Publishing Co., 21027 Crossroads Cir., P.O. Box 1612, Waukesha 53187-1612
Trapper and Predator Caller	10 per year	Krause Publications, Inc., 700 E. State St., Iola 54990-0001
Travel Wisconsin News (E-Newsletter)	6 per year	Jerry Huffman, Wis. Dept. of Tourism, P.O. Box 8690, Madison 53708
Tuff Stuff	Monthly	Krause Publications, Inc., 700 E. State St., Iola 54990-0001
Turkey & Turkey Hunting	6 per year	Krause Publications, Inc., 700 E. State St., Iola 54990-0001
Union Labor News	Monthly	Union Labor News Publishers, Ltd., 1602 S. Park St., Madison 53715-2159
Update	2 per year	UW-Madison School of Business, 975 University Ave., Madison 53706-1323
Vacation Week	Weekly (June-Aug.)	Byron McNutt, P.O. Box 1929, Eagle River 54521-1929
Voyageur: NE Wisconsin's Historical Review	2 per year	Brown County Historical Society, P.O. Box 8085, Green Bay 54308-8085
Western Builder	Weekly	Reed Construction Data, 440 S. Executive Dr., Suite 220, Brookfield 53005
WFU News	10 per year	Wis. Farmers Union, 117 W. Spring St., Chippewa Falls 54729-2359
Wisconservation	Monthly	Wisconsin Wildlife Federation, P.O. Box 68, Prescott 54021-0068

WISCONSIN PERIODICALS–Continued

Name	Issued	Publishers
Wis. Academy Review	Quarterly	Joan Fischer, Editor, Wis. Academy of Sciences, Arts and Letters, 1922 University Ave., Madison 53726
Wis. Agriculturist	12 per year	Farm Progress Companies, 102 E. Jefferson St., Brandon 53919
Wis. Archeologist	Semiannual	Wis. Archeological Society, 215 Sabin Hall, UW-Milwaukee, 3413 N. Downer Ave., Milwaukee 53211
Wis. Counties	Monthly	Wis. Counties Assn., 22 E. Mifflin St., Suite 900, Madison 53703
Wis. Economic Indicators	Monthly	Wis. Dept. of Workforce Development, P.O. Box 7944, Madison 53707-7944
Wis. Energy Cooperative News	Monthly	Wis. Federation of Cooperatives, 131 W. Wilson St., Suite 400, Madison 53703
Wis. Farm Reporter	Semimonthly	Dept. of Agriculture, Trade and Consumer Protection, P.O. Box 8934, Madison 53708-8934
Wis. Horsemen's News	Monthly	Scott B. Turner, P.O. Box 152, Waupaca 54981-0152
Wis. International Law Journal	3 per year	UW Law School, 975 Bascom Mall, Madison 53706
Wis. Jaycee Journal	Quarterly	Jaycees of Wis. Foundation, Inc., P.O. Box 1547, Appleton 54912
Wis. Law Journal	Weekly	Ann Richmond, 225 E. Michigan St., Milwaukee 53203-3433
Wis. Law Review	Bimonthly	UW Law School, 2347 Law Building, 975 Bascom Mall, Madison 53706-1399
Wis. Lawyer	Monthly	State Bar of Wisconsin, P.O. Box 7158, Madison 53707-7158
Wis. Lion	6 per year	Barbara Theisen, 2817 B Post Rd., Stevens Point 54481
Wis. Magazine of History	Quarterly	State Historical Society of Wis., 816 State St., Madison 53706-1488
Wis. Mapping Bulletin	6 per year/ electronic	State Cartographer's Office, 384 Science Hall, UW-Madison, 550 N. Park St., Madison 53706
Wis. Medical Journal	8 per year	Wisconsin Medical Society, P.O. Box 1109, Madison 53701-1109
Wis. Natural Resources	Bimonthly	Wisconsin Department of Natural Resources, P.O. Box 7921, Madison 53707-7921
Wis. Outdoor Journal	8 per year	Krause Publications, Inc., 700 E. State St., Iola 54990-0001
Wis. Police Journal	Quarterly	Wis. Professional Police Assn., 340 Coyier Ln., Madison 53713
Wis. Professional Agent	Monthly	PIA of Wisconsin, 6401 Odana Rd., Madison 53719-1126
Wis. Realtor	Monthly	William E. Malkasian, 4801 Forest Run Rd., Suite 201, Madison 53704
Wis. Report	Weekly	Wisconsin Report Publishing Co., 18310 Benington Dr., Brookfield 53045-5419
Wis. Restaurateur	Bimonthly	Wis. Restaurant Assn., 2801 Fish Hatchery Rd., Madison 53713-3120
Wis. Safety & Health News	Quarterly	Wis. Council of Safety Div., Wis. Manufacturers & Commerce, 501 E. Washington Ave., Madison 53703-2914
Wis. School Musician	Quarterly	Eric Runestad, 1102 Stephenson Lane, Waunakee 53597
Wis. School News	Monthly	Wis. Assn. of School Boards, Inc., 122 W. Washington Ave., Madison 53703-2718
Wis. State Farmer	Weekly	Scott B. Turner, P.O. Box 152, Waupaca 54981-0152
Wis. State Genealogical Society Newsletter	Quarterly	Wis. State Genealogical Soc., P.O. Box 5106, Madison 53705-0106

WISCONSIN PERIODICALS–Continued

Name	Issued	Publishers
Wis. Taxpayer, The	Monthly	Wis. Taxpayers Alliance, 401 North Lawn Ave., Madison 53704-5033
Wis. Trails	Bimonthly	Scott Klug, 1131 Mills St., P.O. Box 317, Black Earth 53515
Wis. Waterfowl	2 per year	Bast and Durbin and Associates, 614 W. Capitol Dr., Hartland 53029
Wisconsin Week	Biweekly (during school year)	University Communications, 19 Bascom Hall, 500 Lincoln Dr., Madison 53706-1380
Women in Higher Education	Monthly	The Wenniger Company, 5376 Farmco Drive, Madison 53704
Woodland Management	Quarterly	Wisconsin Woodland Owners Assn., Inc., P.O. Box 285, Stevens Point 54481-0285
World Airshow News	Bimonthly	Jeffrey Parnall, P.O. Box 975, East Troy 53120-2324
World Coin News	Monthly	Krause Publications, Inc., 700 E. State St., Iola 54990-0001
Xpress	4 per year	American Bowling Congress, 5301 S. 76th St., Greendale 53129

NOTE

If you know of any additional permanent Wisconsin publications that are published at periodic intervals, please send the information to the Blue Book Editor, Legislative Reference Bureau, P.O. Box 2037, Madison, Wisconsin 53701-2037.

BROADCASTING STATIONS IN WISCONSIN

City	Station	Channel/Frequency	City	Station	Channel/Frequency
\multicolumn{6}{c}{**Commercial Television Stations**}					
Appleton	WACY	32	Madison	WMSN-TV	47
Chippewa Falls	WEUX	48	Madison	WMTV	15
Eagle River	WYOW	34	Mayville	WWRS-TV	52
Eau Claire	WEAU-TV	13	Milwaukee	WCGV-TV	24
Eau Claire	WQOW-TV	18	Milwaukee	WDJT-TV	58
Fond du Lac	WMMF-TV	68	Milwaukee	WISN-TV	12
Green Bay	WBAY-TV	2	Milwaukee	WITI	6
Green Bay	WFRV-TV	5	Milwaukee	WTMJ-TV	4
Green Bay	WGBA	26	Milwaukee	WVCY-DT*	22
Green Bay	WLUK-TV	11	Milwaukee	WVCY-TV	30
Janesville	WBUW-TV	57	Milwaukee	WVTV	18
Kenosha	WPXE	55	Racine	WJJA	49
La Crosse	WKBT	8	Rhinelander	WJFW-TV	12
La Crosse	WLAX	25	Suring	WIWB	14
La Crosse	WXOW-TV	19	Wausau	WAOW-TV	9
Madison	WISC-TV	3	Wausau	WSAW-TV	7
Madison	WKOW-DT*	26	Wittenberg	WFXS	55
Madison	WKOW-TV	27			

City	Station	Channel/Frequency	City	Station	Channel/Frequency
\multicolumn{6}{c}{**Educational Television Stations**}					
Green Bay	WPNE[1]	38	Milwaukee	WMVS[3]	10
La Crosse	WHLA-TV[1]	31	Milwaukee	WMVT[3]	36
Madison	WHA-TV[2]	21	Park Falls	WLEF-TV[1]	36
Menomonie	WHWC-TV[1]	28	Wausau	WHRM-TV[1]	20

*DT – Digital television station.

City	Station	Channel/Frequency	City	Station	Channel/Frequency
\multicolumn{6}{c}{**Commercial Radio Stations**}					
Adams	WDKM-FM	106.1	Eau Claire	WBIZ	1400
Algoma	WBDK-FM	96.7	Eau Claire	WBIZ-FM	100.7
Algoma	WRLU-FM	104.1	Eau Claire	WIAL-FM	94.1
Allouez	WJLW-FM	106.7	Elk Mound	WECL-FM	92.9
Altoona	WISM-FM	98.1	Elm Grove	WGLB	1560
Amery	WXCE	1260	Evansville	WKPO-FM	105.9
Antigo	WACD-FM	106.1	Fond du Lac	KFIZ	1450
Antigo	WATK	900	Fond du Lac	KFIZ-FM	107.1
Antigo	WRLO-FM	105.3	Fond du Lac	WFDL-FM	97.7
Appleton	WAPL-FM	105.7	Fond du Lac	WRPN	1600
Appleton	WSCO	1570	Fond du Lac	WTCX-FM	96.1
Ashland	WATW	1400	Forestville	WRKU-FM	102.1
Ashland	WBSZ-FM	93.3	Fort Atkinson	WFAW	940
Ashland	WJJH-FM	96.7	Fort Atkinson	WKCH-FM	106.5
Balsam Lake	WLMX-FM	104.9	Fort Atkinson	WSJY-FM	107.3
Baraboo	WRPQ	740	Green Bay	WDUZ	1400
Beaver Dam	WBEV	1430	Green Bay	WTAQ	1360
Beaver Dam	WXRO-FM	95.3	Green Bay	WIXX-FM	101.1
Beloit	WGEZ	1490	Green Bay	WKSZ-FM	95.9
Beloit	WTJK	1380	Green Bay	WNFL	1440
Berlin	WBJZ-FM	104.7	Green Bay	WQLH-FM	98.5
Berlin	WISS	1090	Hallie	WOGO	680
Black River Falls	WWIS	1260	Hallie	WWIB-FM	103.7
Black River Falls	WWIS-FM	99.7	Hartford	WTKM	1540
Bloomer	WQRB-FM	95.1	Hartford	WTKM-FM	104.9
Brillion	WXWX-FM	107.5	Hayward	WHSM	910
Brookfield	WFMR-FM	106.9	Hayward	WHSM-FM	101.1
Chetek	WATQ-FM	106.7	Hayward	WRLS-FM	92.3
Chilton	WMBE	1530	Holmen	WKBH	1570
Chippewa Falls	WCFW-FM	105.7	Hudson	WMIN	740
Chippewa Falls	WEAQ	1150	Hurley	WHRY	1450
Cleveland	WLKN-FM	98.1	Iron River	WNXR-FM	107.3
Clintonville	WFCL	1380	Jackson	WRRD	540
Clintonville	WJMQ-FM	92.3	Janesville	WCLO	1230
Columbus	WTLX-FM	100.5	Janesville	WJVL-FM	99.9
Denmark	WPCK-FM	104.9	Kaukauna	WJOK	1050
Dodgeville	WDMP	810	Kaukauna	WOGB-FM	103.1
Dodgeville	WDMP-FM	99.3	Kenosha	WIIL-FM	95.1
Durand	WJRV-FM	95.9	Kenosha	WLIP	1050
Durand	WRDN	1430	Kewaunee	WAUN-FM	92.7
Eagle River	WERL	950	Kimberly	WHBY	1150
Eagle River	WRJO-FM	94.5	La Crosse	KQEG-FM	102.7
Eau Claire	WAXX-FM	104.5	La Crosse	WIZM	1410
Eau Claire	WAYY	790	La Crosse	WIZM-FM	93.3

BROADCASTING STATIONS IN WISCONSIN–Continued

City	Station	Channel/Frequency	City	Station	Channel/Frequency
La Crosse	WKBH-FM	100.1	Oshkosh	WOSH	1490
La Crosse	WKTY	580	Oshkosh	WPKR-FM	99.5
La Crosse	WLFN	1490	Oshkosh	WVBO-FM	103.9
La Crosse	WLXR-FM	104.9	Oshkosh	WWWX-FM	96.9
La Crosse	WQCC-FM	106.3	Park Falls	WCQM-FM	98.3
La Crosse	WRQT-FM	95.7	Park Falls	WNBI	980
Ladysmith	WJBL-FM	93.1	Peshtigo	WSFQ-FM	96.3
Ladysmith	WLDY	1340	Platteville	WPLV	1590
Lake Geneva	WLKG-FM	96.1	Platteville	WPLV-FM	107.1
Lake Geneva	WZRK	1550	Plymouth	WJUB	1420
Lancaster	WGLR	1280	Plymouth	WXER-FM	104.5
Lancaster	WGLR-FM	97.7	Port Washington	WPJP-FM	100.1
Madison	WCJZ-FM	96.3	Portage	WBKY-FM	95.9
Madison	WIBA	1310	Portage	WDDC-FM	100.1
Madison	WIBA-FM	101.5	Portage	WPDR	1350
Madison	WLMV	1480	Poynette	WHFA	1240
Madison	WMGN-FM	98.1	Prairie du Chien	WPRE	980
Madison	WOLX-FM	94.9	Prairie du Chien	WQPC-FM	94.3
Madison	WTDY	1670	Racine	WBJX	1460
Madison	WTSO	1070	Racine	WEZY-FM	92.1
Madison	WTUX	1550	Racine	WKKV-FM	100.7
Madison	WZEE-FM	104.1	Racine	WRJN	1400
Manitowoc	WCUB	980	Reedsburg	WBDL-FM	102.9
Manitowoc	WLTU-FM	92.1	Reedsburg	WNFM-FM	104.9
Manitowoc	WOMT	1240	Reedsburg	WRDB	1400
Manitowoc	WQTC-FM	102.3	Rhinelander	WHDG-FM	97.5
Marathon	WKQH-FM	104.9	Rhinelander	WOBT	1240
Marinette	WLST-FM	95.1	Rhinelander	WRHN-FM	100.1
Marinette	WMAM	570	Rice Lake	WAQE	1090
Marshfield	WDLB	1450	Rice Lake	WJMC	1240
Marshfield	WLJY-FM	106.5	Rice Lake	WJMC-FM	96.1
Mauston	WRJC	1270	Rice Lake	WKFX-FM	99.1
Mauston	WRJC-FM	92.1	Richland Center	WRCO	1450
Mayville	WMDC-FM	98.7	Richland Center	WRCO-FM	100.9
Medford	WIGM	1490	River Falls	WEVR	1550
Medford	WKEB-FM	99.3	River Falls	WEVR-FM	106.3
Menomonee Falls	WJMR-FM	98.3	Rudolph	WIZD-FM	99.9
Menomonie	WMEQ	880	Schofield	WRIG	1390
Menomonie	WMEQ-FM	92.1	Seymour	WECB-FM	104.3
Merrill	WJMT	730	Shawano	WOWN-FM	99.3
Merrill	WMZK-FM	104.1	Shawano	WTCH	960
Middleton	WWQM-FM	106.3	Sheboygan	WBFM-FM	93.7
Milwaukee	WEMP	1250	Sheboygan	WCLB	950
Milwaukee	WISN	1130	Sheboygan	WHBL	1330
Milwaukee	WJYI	1340	Sheboygan Falls	WHBZ-FM	106.5
Milwaukee	WJZI-FM	93.3	Shell Lake	WCSW	940
Milwaukee	WKLH-FM	96.5	Shell Lake	WGMO-FM	95.3
Milwaukee	WKTI-FM	94.5	Sparta	WCOW-FM	97.1
Milwaukee	WLTQ-FM	97.3	Sparta	WKLJ	1290
Milwaukee	WLUM-FM	102.1	Spencer	WOSQ-FM	92.3
Milwaukee	WLZR-FM	102.9	Stevens Point	WSPT	1010
Milwaukee	WMCS	1290	Stevens Point	WSPT-FM	97.9
Milwaukee	WMYX-FM	99.1	Sturgeon Bay	WDOR	910
Milwaukee	WNOV	860	Sturgeon Bay	WDOR-FM	93.9
Milwaukee	WOKY	920	Sturgeon Bay	WLYD-FM	99.7
Milwaukee	WRIT-FM	95.7	Sturgeon Bay	WSRG-FM	97.7
Milwaukee	WTMJ	620	Sturtevant	WEXT-FM	104.7
Milwaukee	WVCY-FM	107.7	Sun Prairie	WMAD-FM	92.1
Minocqua	WLKD	1570	Sun Prairie	WNWC	1190
Minocqua	WMQA-FM	95.9	Superior	KRBR-FM	102.5
Mishicot	WZOR-FM	94.7	Superior	WDSM	710
Monroe	WEKZ	1260	Superior	WGEE	970
Monroe	WEKZ-FM	93.7	Suring	WRVM-FM	102.7
Mosinee	WOFM-FM	94.7	Sussex	WKSH	1640
Mukwonago	WFZH-FM	105.3	Three Lakes	WLSL-FM	93.7
Neenah-Menasha	WNAM	1280	Tomah	WBOG-FM	94.5
Neenah-Menasha	WNCY-FM	100.3	Tomah	WTMB	1460
Neenah-Menasha	WROE-FM	94.3	Tomah	WXYM-FM	96.1
Neillsville	WCCN	1370	Tomah	WVCX-FM	98.9
Neillsville	WCCN-FM	107.5	Tomahawk	WJJQ	810
Neillsville	WPKG-FM	92.7	Tomahawk	WJJQ-FM	92.5
Nekoosa	WMMA-FM	93.9	Trempealeau	WFBZ-FM	105.5
New London	WOZZ-FM	93.5	Two Rivers	WTRW	1590
Oconto	WOCO	1260	Verona	WMMM-FM	105.5
Oconto	WOCO-FM	107.1	Viroqua	WVRQ	1360

BROADCASTING STATIONS IN WISCONSIN–Continued

City	Station	Channel/Frequency	City	Station	Channel/Frequency
Viroqua	WVRQ-FM	102.3	Wausau	WXCO	1230
Washburn	WEGZ-FM	105.9	Wautoma	WAUH-FM	102.3
Watertown	WJJO-FM	94.1	Wauwatosa	WXSS-FM	103.7
Watertown	WTTN	1580	West Bend	WBKV	1470
Waukesha	WAUK	1510	West Bend	WBWI-FM	92.5
Waukesha	WMIL-FM	106.1	Whitehall	WHTL-FM	102.3
Waunakee	WBZU-FM	105.1	Whitewater	WKCH-FM	106.5
Waupaca	WDUX	800	Whitewater	WSLD-FM	104.5
Waupaca	WDUX-FM	92.7	Whiting	WYTE-FM	96.7
Waupun	WFDL	1170	Wisconsin Dells	WIBU	900
Wausau	WDEZ-FM	101.9	Wisconsin Dells	WNNO-FM	106.9
Wausau	WIFC-FM	95.5	Wisconsin Rapids	WFHR	1320
Wausau	WSAU	550	Wisconsin Rapids	WGLX-FM	103.3

Noncommercial Radio Stations

City	Station	Channel/Frequency	City	Station	Channel/Frequency
Appleton	WEMI-FM	91.9	Menomonie	WVSS-FM[2]	90.7
Appleton	WLFM-FM	91.1	Milladore	WGNV-FM	88.5
(Lawrence University)			Milwaukee	WMSE-FM	91.7
Auburndale	WLBL[1]	930	(Milwaukee School of Engineering)		
Beloit	WBCR-FM	90.3	Milwaukee	WMWK-FM	88.1
(Beloit College)			Milwaukee	WUWM-FM[2]	89.7
Brule	WHSA-FM[1]	89.9	Milwaukee	WYMS-FM	88.9
Burlington	WBSD-FM	89.1	(Milw. Board of Education)		
(Burlington Area School District)			Oshkosh	WRST-FM[2]	90.3
Delafield	WHAD-FM[1]	90.7	Oshkosh	WVCY	690
Eau Claire	WDVM	1050	Park Falls	WHBM-FM	90.3
Eau Claire	WHEM-FM	91.3	Platteville	WSUP-FM[2]	90.5
Eau Claire	WUEC-FM[2]	89.7	Reserve	WOJB-FM	88.9
Eau Claire	WVCF-FM	90.5	Rhinelander	WXPR-FM	91.7
Goodman	WMVM-FM	91.3	Ripon	WRPN-FM	90.1
Green Bay	WEMY-FM	91.5	(Ripon College)		
Green Bay	WHID-FM[2]	88.1	River Falls	WRFW-FM[2]	88.7
Green Bay	WORQ-FM	90.1	Sheboygan	WSHS-FM	91.7
Green Bay	WPNE-FM[1]	89.3	(Sheboygan Area School District)		
Highland	WHHI-FM[1]	91.3	Sister Bay	WHND-FM[1]	89.7
Kenosha	WGTD-FM	91.1	Stevens Point	WWSP-FM[2]	89.9
(Gateway Technical College)			Sturgeon Bay	WPFF-FM	90.5
La Crosse	WHLA-FM[1]	90.3	Sturgeon Bay	WRGX-FM	88.5
La Crosse	WLSU-FM[2]	88.9	Superior	KUWS-FM[2]	91.3
Lancaster	WJTY-FM	88.1	Waukesha	WCCX-FM	104.5
Madison	WERN-FM[1]	88.7	(Carroll College)		
Madison	WHA[2]	970	Wausau	WCLQ-FM	89.5
Madison	WNWC-FM	102.5	Wausau	WHRM-FM[1]	90.9
(Northwestern College)			Wausau	WLBL-FM[1]	91.9
Madison	WORT-FM	89.9	Wausau	WXPW-FM	91.9
Menomonie	WHWC-FM[1]	88.3	Whitewater	WSUW-FM[2]	91.7

[1]Licensed to the Wisconsin Educational Communications Board.
[2]Licensed to the University of Wisconsin System Board of Regents.
[3]Operated by the Milwaukee Area Technical College Board.
Source: *Broadcasting and Cable Yearbook 2003-2004.*

HIGHLIGHTS OF POPULATION AND VITAL STATISTICS IN WISCONSIN

State and County Population — Wisconsin's 2004 population was officially estimated to be 5,532,955, a 0.7% increase over the 2000 U.S. Census count of 5,363,715. The state grew 9.6% in the 1990s. By contrast, the growth in the preceding decade from 1980 to 1990 was less than 4% and represented the smallest increase in decennial census counts in state history. The greatest increase occurred between 1840 and 1850, the decade in which Wisconsin became a state, when population jumped 886.9% from 30,945 to 305,391.

Between 1990 and 2000, population increased over 20% in Marquette, St. Croix, Walworth, and Washington Counties. Since 2000, St. Croix County has been the fastest growing county with a population increase of 7.3%, followed by Waushara and Calumet Counties. Dane County had the largest absolute growth, adding an estimated 12,355 people. Waukesha County grew by 7,310 people.

Population by Race and Age — In responding to the 2000 U.S. Census of Population, for the first time individuals were given the opportunity to identify themselves as being of more than one race. About 1.2% of Wisconsin's population selected multiple races. As a result, comparisons between the 2000 Census and earlier censuses must be made with caution. It is not clear whether someone who selected Asian and white, for example, for the 2000 Census would have selected Asian or white in 1990. Only those who selected a single race are used in the following comparisons. Between 1890 and 2000, the nonwhite population in Wisconsin increased from 0.7% to over 11.0%. Indians were the largest minority group from 1890 until 1950; Blacks have been the largest since 1950. In 2000, Milwaukee County had the largest Black population at 231,157, followed by Racine County with 19,777, Dane County with 17,069, Kenosha County with 7,600, and Rock County with 7,048. For the first time, more than half of the population of the City of Milwaukee was nonwhite. Wisconsin's Hispanic population more than doubled from 1990 to 2000, reaching 192,921. The Asian population almost doubled to 90,393.

The 2000 Wisconsin Indian population was 47,228, an increase of 21.1% over the 1990 population of 38,986. Wisconsin has 11 Indian reservations.

According to the 2004 estimates, Wisconsin had a voting age population of 4,119,320 or 74.5% of the total population.

Vital Statistics — In 2003, Wisconsin recorded 34,220 marriages and 17,150 divorces and annulments. Both the marriage and divorce rates in Wisconsin have been lower than the national rate for more than 75 years. Total deaths in 2003 numbered 46,040 (8.4 per 1,000 population).

The following tables present selected data. Consult footnoted sources for more detailed information about population and vital statistics.

WISCONSIN POPULATION, 1840 – 2004

Year	Population	Increase	Percent Increase	Rural	Urban	Percent Urban	Density[1]
1840	30,945	---	---	30,945	---	---	0.6
1850	305,391	274,446	886.9%	276,768	28,623	9.4%	5.6
1860	775,881	470,490	154.1	664,007	111,874	14.4	14.1
1870	1,054,670	278,789	35.9	847,471	207,099	19.6	19.2
1880	1,315,497	260,827	24.7	998,293	317,204	24.1	24.0
1890	1,693,330	377,833	28.7	1,131,044	562,286	33.2	30.9
1900	2,069,042	375,712	22.2	1,278,829	790,213	38.2	37.4
1910	2,333,860	264,818	12.8	1,329,540	1,004,320	43.0	42.6
1920	2,632,067	298,207	12.8	1,387,209	1,244,858	47.3	47.6
1930	2,939,006	306,939	11.7	1,385,163	1,553,843	52.9	53.0
1940	3,137,587	198,581	6.7	1,458,443	1,679,144	53.5	57.3
1950	3,434,575	296,988	9.5	1,446,687[2]	1,987,888[2]	57.9	62.7
1960	3,951,777	517,202	15.1	1,429,598	2,522,179	63.8	72.2
1970	4,417,821	466,044	11.8	1,507,313	2,910,418	65.9	81.3
1980	4,602,299	184,478	6.5	1,685,035	3,020,732	64.2	86.6
1990	4,891,769	289,470	4.0	1,679,813	3,211,956	65.7	90.1
2000	5,363,715	471,906	9.6	1,700,032	3,663,643	68.3	98.8
2001	5,400,449	36,774	0.7	NA	NA	NA	NA
2002	5,453,896	53,447	1.7	NA	NA	NA	NA
2003	5,490,718	36,822	0.7	NA	NA	NA	NA
2004	5,532,955	42,237	0.7	NA	NA	NA	NA

NA – Not available.

[1]Population per square mile of land area.

[2]The "urban" definition was revised beginning with the 1950 census.

Sources: 2000 Census of Population, *Wisconsin Summary Population Characteristics*, November 2002; Wisconsin Department of Administration, Demographic Services Center, *Official Population Estimates*, January 1, 2002, October 2002, and previous issues; Wisconsin Department of Administration, Demographic Services Center, *Time Series of the Final Official Population Estimates and Census Counts for Wisconsin Counties: 1970-2003*; Wisconsin Department of Administration, Demographic Services Center, *Final Population Estimates for Wisconsin Counties*, January 1, 2004.

WISCONSIN POPULATION – 2000 CENSUS
By Sex, Race, and Hispanic Origin

County	Total Population	Male	Female	White	Black	Indian, Eskimo, Aleut	Asian, Pacific Islander	Other	2 or More*	Hispanic Origin (of any race)
Adams	18,643	9,456	9,187	18,201	50	110	65	62	155	268
Ashland ...	16,866	8,307	8,559	14,690	36	1,745	61	49	285	188
Barron	44,963	22,274	22,689	43,924	63	363	163	142	308	430
Bayfield ...	15,013	7,590	7,423	13,280	20	1,409	42	39	223	91
Brown	226,778	112,763	114,015	206,688	2,641	5,191	4,999	4,300	2,959	8,698
Buffalo ...	13,804	6,926	6,878	13,623	16	42	48	11	64	85
Burnett	15,674	7,897	7,777	14,616	56	698	48	33	223	120
Calumet ...	40,631	20,311	20,320	39,282	124	139	632	154	300	435
Chippewa ..	55,195	27,468	27,727	54,006	89	176	500	93	331	289
Clark	33,557	16,819	16,738	32,904	43	161	104	188	157	404
Columbia ..	52,468	26,448	26,020	50,990	460	185	187	232	414	827
Crawford ..	17,243	8,717	8,526	16,780	233	37	47	29	117	129
Dane	426,526	211,020	215,506	379,447	17,069	1,404	14,868	6,118	7,620	14,387
Dodge	85,897	44,942	40,955	81,843	2,142	345	321	744	502	2,188
Door	27,961	13,773	14,188	27,356	53	183	84	91	194	267
Douglas ...	43,287	21,332	21,955	41,273	246	786	285	85	612	315
Dunn	39,858	20,094	19,764	38,294	135	107	854	148	320	335
Eau Claire ..	93,142	45,093	48,049	88,443	482	500	2,375	305	1,037	879
Florence ...	5,088	2,597	2,491	4,995	8	22	15	7	41	23
Fond du Lac	97,296	47,477	49,819	93,562	876	371	873	814	800	1,987
Forest	10,024	5,016	5,008	8,607	118	1,133	21	23	122	108
Grant	49,597	25,164	24,433	48,719	259	64	234	71	250	280
Green	33,647	16,558	17,089	33,021	86	70	97	120	253	327
Green Lake .	19,105	9,407	9,698	18,687	29	38	66	170	115	393
Iowa	22,780	11,350	11,430	22,484	38	25	81	26	126	75
Iron	6,861	3,362	3,499	6,743	6	41	12	4	55	45
Jackson	19,100	10,198	8,902	17,109	433	1,176	39	193	150	357
Jefferson ...	74,021	36,712	37,309	71,309	210	249	347	1,220	686	3,031
Juneau	24,316	12,162	12,154	23,491	81	316	110	138	180	347
Kenosha ...	149,577	74,149	75,428	132,193	7,600	564	1,438	4,924	2,858	10,757
Kewaunee ..	20,187	10,126	10,061	19,897	31	55	28	61	115	153
La Crosse ..	107,120	51,926	55,194	100,883	1,016	440	3,397	286	1,098	990
Lafayette ..	16,137	8,060	8,077	15,980	17	18	42	23	57	92
Langlade ...	20,740	10,291	10,449	20,311	31	113	62	42	181	171
Lincoln ...	29,641	14,810	14,831	28,977	123	130	124	86	201	243
Manitowoc .	82,887	41,060	41,827	79,485	245	356	1,678	494	629	1,343
Marathon ..	125,834	62,774	63,060	118,079	347	435	5,741	324	908	979
Marinette ..	43,384	21,415	21,969	42,550	100	215	128	91	300	325
Marquette ..	15,832	8,600	7,232	14,828	545	165	58	60	176	421
Menominee	4,562	2,250	2,312	528	3	3,981	1	15	34	122
Milwaukee .	940,164	450,574	489,590	616,973	231,157	6,794	24,567	39,931	20,742	82,406
Monroe	40,899	20,605	20,294	39,474	188	376	210	347	304	740
Oconto	35,634	17,935	17,699	34,836	48	277	77	84	312	240
Oneida ...	36,776	18,310	18,466	35,934	121	242	126	77	276	244
Outagamie .	160,971	80,285	80,686	151,101	867	2,471	3,651	1,311	1,570	3,207
Ozaukee ..	82,317	40,592	41,725	79,621	765	162	896	276	597	1,073
Pepin	7,213	3,626	3,587	7,134	6	14	18	6	35	25
Pierce	36,804	18,151	18,653	36,071	91	105	168	104	265	301
Polk	41,319	20,650	20,669	40,342	63	436	118	82	278	329
Portage ...	67,182	33,490	33,692	64,316	215	242	1,540	288	581	967
Price	15,822	7,949	7,873	15,541	16	95	52	23	95	116
Racine ...	188,831	93,457	95,374	156,796	19,777	687	1,440	6,972	3,159	14,990
Richland ...	17,924	8,882	9,042	17,636	27	46	43	51	121	167
Rock	152,307	74,980	77,327	138,610	7,048	422	1,252	2,691	2,284	5,953
Rusk	15,347	7,614	7,733	14,992	79	65	55	54	102	116
St. Croix ...	63,155	31,608	31,547	61,796	177	159	403	141	479	483
Sauk	55,225	27,292	27,933	53,775	142	479	153	324	352	938
Sawyer	16,196	8,169	8,027	13,236	51	2,603	51	56	199	145
Shawano ...	40,664	20,311	20,353	37,251	91	2,545	154	128	495	407
Sheboygan .	112,646	56,503	56,143	104,438	1,224	409	3,726	1,642	1,207	3,789
Taylor	19,680	9,966	9,714	19,427	17	37	46	37	116	127
Trempealeau	27,010	13,526	13,484	26,688	35	45	39	77	126	240
Vernon	28,056	13,867	14,189	27,723	18	42	62	75	136	186
Vilas	21,033	10,469	10,564	18,865	43	1,909	40	39	137	181
Walworth ..	93,759	46,626	47,133	88,597	790	219	636	2,452	1,065	6,136
Washburn ..	16,036	8,071	7,965	15,599	27	162	34	19	195	143
Washington	117,493	58,608	58,885	114,778	465	296	709	474	771	1,529
Waukesha ..	360,767	177,484	183,283	345,506	2,646	788	5,468	3,128	3,231	9,503
Waupaca ...	51,731	25,899	25,832	50,660	87	217	146	280	341	714
Waushara ..	23,154	11,669	11,485	22,413	62	72	87	314	206	848
Winnebago .	156,763	78,149	78,614	148,795	1,756	726	2,924	1,121	1,441	3,065
Wood	75,555	37,030	38,525	72,855	201	528	1,227	223	521	709
STATE ..	5,363,675	2,649,041	2,714,634	4,769,857	304,460	47,228	90,393	84,842	66,895	192,921

*For the first time in the 2000 Census, individuals were allowed to select more than one race.

Source: U.S. Department of Commerce, U.S. Census Bureau, *Profile of General Demographic Characteristics, 2000 Census of Population and Housing, Wisconsin,* May 2001.

POPULATION CHANGES BY COUNTY, 2000-2004
State Increase: +3.16%

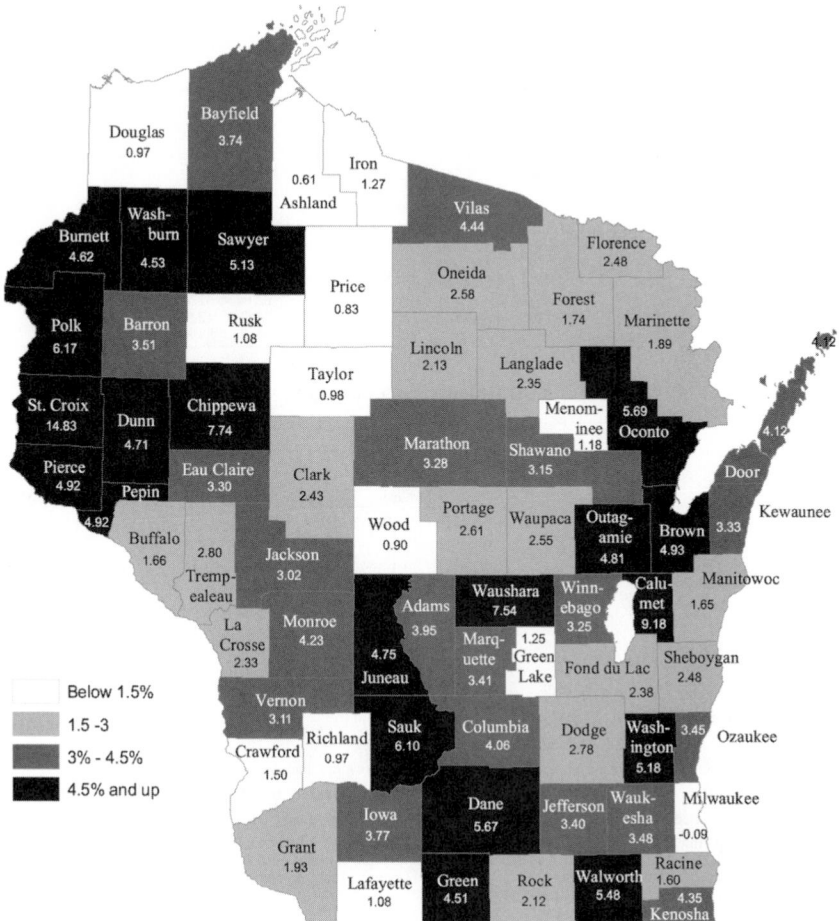

Below 1.5%
1.5 - 3
3% - 4.5%
4.5% and up

Douglas 0.97
Bayfield 3.74
Iron 1.27
0.61
Ashland
Vilas 4.44
Wash-burn 4.53
Burnett 4.62
Sawyer 5.13
Florence 2.48
Price 0.83
Oneida 2.58
Forest 1.74
Marinette 1.89
Polk 6.17
Barron 3.51
Rusk 1.08
Lincoln 2.13
Langlade 2.35
St. Croix 14.83
Dunn 4.71
Taylor 0.98
Menom-inee 1.18
5.69
Oconto 4.12
Chippewa 7.74
Marathon 3.28
Shawano 3.15
Door
Pierce 4.92
Eau Claire 3.30
Clark 2.43
Pepin 4.92
Buffalo 1.66
2.80
Jackson 3.02
Wood 0.90
Portage 2.61
Waupaca 2.55
Outag-amie 4.81
Brown 4.93
3.33
Kewaunee
Tremp-ealeau
Waushara 7.54
Winn-ebago 3.25
Calu-met 9.18
1.65
Manitowoc
La Crosse 2.33
Monroe 4.23
Adams 3.95
Marq-uette 3.41
1.25
Green Lake
Fond du Lac 2.38
Sheboygan 2.48
Juneau 4.75
Vernon 3.11
Sauk 6.10
Columbia 4.06
Dodge 2.78
Wash-ington 5.18
3.45
Ozaukee
Crawford 1.50
Richland 0.97
Dane 5.67
Jefferson 3.40
Wauk-esha 3.48
Milwaukee -0.09
Grant 1.93
Iowa 3.77
Lafayette 1.08
Green 4.51
Rock 2.12
Walworth 5.48
Racine 1.60
4.35
Kenosha

Source: Wisconsin Department of Administration, Demographic Services Center, *Official Population Estimates, January 1, 2004,* October 2004. Map produced by Wisconsin Legislative Technology Services Bureau.

WISCONSIN POPULATION, BY RACE, 1890 – 2000
Population Totals

U.S. Census Year	Total Population	White	Black	American Indian[1]	Asian[2]	Other Races	2 or More[3]	Hispanic Origin (of any race)[4]
1890	1,693,330	1,680,828	2,444	9,930	128	---	---	---
1900	2,069,042	2,057,911	2,542	8,372	217	---	---	---
1910	2,333,860	2,320,555	2,900	10,142	260	3	---	---
1920	2,632,067	2,616,938	5,201	9,611	314	3	---	---
1930	2,939,006	2,916,255	10,739	11,548	451	13	---	---
1940	3,137,587	3,112,752	12,158	12,265	388	24	---	---
1950	3,434,575	3,392,690	28,182	12,196	1,119	388	---	---
1960	3,951,777	3,858,903	74,546	14,297	2,836	1,195	---	---
1970[5]	4,417,933	4,258,959	128,224	18,924	6,557	5,067	---	62,875
1980[5]	4,705,642	4,443,035	182,592	29,320	22,043	41,788	---	62,782
1990	4,891,769	4,512,523	244,539	39,387	53,583	42,538	---	93,194
2000	5,363,675	4,769,857	304,460	47,228	90,393	84,842	66,895	192,921

Population Percentages

U.S. Census Year	White	Black	American Indian[1]	Asian[2]	Other Races	2 or More[3]	Hispanic Origin (of any race)[4]
1890	99.3%	0.1%	0.6%	---	---	---	---
1900	99.5	0.1	0.4	---	---	---	---
1910	99.4	0.1	0.4	---	---	---	---
1920	99.4	0.2	0.4	---	---	---	---
1930	99.2	0.4	0.4	---	---	---	---
1940	99.2	0.4	0.4	---	---	---	---
1950	98.8	0.8	0.4	---	---	---	---
1960	97.6	1.9	0.4	0.1%	---	---	---
1970	96.4	2.9	0.4	0.2	0.1%	---	1.4%
1980	94.4	3.9	0.6	0.3	0.9	---	1.3
1990	92.2	5.0	0.8	1.2	0.9	---	1.9
2000	88.9	5.7	0.9	1.7	1.6	1.2%	3.6

[1]Aleut and Eskimo populations included beginning in 1960.

[2]Native Hawaiian and Other Pacific Islanders are grouped with Asian.

[3]For the first time in the 2000 Census, individuals were allowed to select more than one race.

[4]The 1990 data on Hispanic/Spanish origin are generally comparable with those for the 1980 census, but not the 1970 census.

[5]Total has been corrected by the U.S. Census Bureau. Details not adjusted to revised total.

Sources: U.S. Department of Commerce, Bureau of the Census, 1970 Census of Population, *Characteristics of Population, Wisconsin;* 1980 Census of Population, *Characteristics of Population, General Social and Economic Characteristics;* 1990 Census of Population, *General Population Characteristics, Wisconsin,* Table 3, June 1992; *Profile of General Demographic Characteristics, 2000 Census of Population and Housing, Wisconsin,* May 2001.

WISCONSIN POPULATION BY RACE AND HISPANIC ORIGIN
2000 Census

Total Wisconsin Population: 5,363,675

Race	Total	Percent	Race	Total	Percent
One race	5,296,780	98.8%	**Two or more races**	66,895	1.2%
White	4,769,857	88.9			
Black or African American	304,460	5.7	**Race as selected alone or in**		
American Indian and Alaska Native	47,228	0.9	**combination with other race(s)[3]**		
Asian	88,763	1.7	White	4,827,514	90.0
Asian Indian	12,665	0.2	Black or African American	326,506	6.1
Chinese	11,184	0.2	American Indian and		
Filipino	5,158	0.1	Alaska Native	69,386	1.3
Japanese	2,868	0.1	Asian	102,768	1.9
Korean	6,800	0.1	Native Hawaiian and Other		
Vietnamese	3,891	0.1	Pacific Islander	4,310	0.1
Other Asian[1]	46,197	0.9	Other race	104,662	2.0
Native Hawaiian and Other					
Pacific Islander	1,630	--	**Hispanic or Latino and Race**		
Native Hawaiian	458	--	Hispanic or Latino (of any race)	192,921	3.6
Guamanian or Chamorro	332	--	Mexican	126,719	2.4
Samoan	333	--	Puerto Rican	30,267	0.6
Other Pacific Islander[2]	507	--	Cuban	2,491	--
Other race	84,842	1.6	Other Hispanic or Latino	33,444	0.6

[1]Other Asian alone, or two or more Asian categories.

[2]Other Pacific Islander alone, or two or more Native Hawaiian and Other Pacific Islander categories.

[3]The total population of the categories adds to more than 100 percent because individuals may report more than one race.

Source: U.S. Census Bureau, *Profile of General Demographic Characteristics: 2000 Census of Population and Housing, Wisconsin*, 2001.

WISCONSIN ASIAN POPULATION
1940 – 2000

	Total[1]	Asian Indian	Chinese	Filipino	Hmong	Japanese	Korean	Laotian	Vietnamese
1940	388	NA	290	75	NA	23	NA	NA	NA
1950	1,119	NA	590	NA	NA	529	NA	NA	NA
1960	2,836	NA	1,010	401	NA	1,425	NA	NA	NA
1970	6,557	NA	2,700	1,209	NA	2,648	NA	NA	NA
1980	22,043	3,902	4,835	3,036	NA	2,123	2,900	NA	1,699
1990	53,583	6,914	7,354	3,690	16,373	2,765	5,618	3,622	2,494
2000	90,393[2]	12,665	11,184	5,158	33,791	2,868	6,800	4,469	3,891

NA – Not available.

[1]Includes Native Hawaiian, other Pacific Islanders until 2000, and all other Asians not identified in the detailed categories.

[2]Also includes those listed in two or more Asian categories.

Sources: U.S. Department of Commerce, Bureau of the Census, 1970 Census of Population, *Characteristics of the Population, Wisconsin*; 1980 Census of Population, *Characteristics of the Population, General Social and Economic Characteristics*; 1990 Census of Population, *General Population Characteristics, Wisconsin*, Table 3, June 1992; *Profiles of General Demographic Characteristics, 2000 Census of Population and Housing, Wisconsin*, 2001.

WISCONSIN INDIANS
Wisconsin Indian Population, 1900 – 2000

Year	Total	Male	Female
1900	8,372	4,321	4,051
1910	10,142	5,231	4,911
1920	9,611	4,950	4,661
1930	11,548	5,951	5,597
1940	12,265	6,354	5,911
1950	12,196	6,274	5,922
1960	14,297	7,195	7,102
1970	18,924	9,251	9,673
1980	29,320	14,489	14,831
1990	38,986	19,240	19,746
2000	47,228*	23,462	23,766

*For the first time in the 2000 Census, individuals were allowed to select more than one race. Total includes those who selected "American Indian" alone.

Source: U.S. Census Bureau, *Profiles of General Demographic Characteristics, 2000 Census of Population and Housing, Wisconsin,* 2001.

Wisconsin Indian Reservations: Population and Acreage

Reservation Total/ County Detail	Tribe	2000 Reservation Population			June 2003 Acreage Ownership Status[1]		
		Total	Indian	% Indian	Total	Tribal	Individual
Bad River	Chippewa	1,411	1,096	77.68%	56,338.62	21,378.35	34,959.27
Ho-Chunk Nation	Ho-Chunk Nation	960	827	86.15	5,525.49	2,118.07	3,407.42
Lac Courte Oreilles ...	Chippewa	2,900	2,150	74.14	47,998.25	23,592.52	24,405.73
Lac du Flambeau	Chippewa	2,995	1,778	59.37	44,946.54	30,553.87	14,377.61
Menominee[2]	Menominee	3,225	3,070	95.19	236,548.42	230,420.42	6,128.00
Oneida (West)	Oneida	21,321	3,288	15.42	6,645.93	6,216.35	429.59
Potawatomi (Wisconsin)	Potawatomi	531	482	90.77	12,280.18	11,560.18	400.00
Red Cliff	Chippewa	1,078	928	86.09	7,982.35	6,200.62	1,767.08
St. Croix	Chippewa	641	561	87.52	2,064.74	2,064.74	0.00
Sokaogon	Chippewa	392	332	84.69	1,731.01	1,731.01	0.00
Stockbridge-Munsee ..	Mahican/Munsee	1,527	769	50.36	16,280.29	16,124.67	155.62
TOTAL		37,276	15,567	41.73%	438,341.82	351,960.80	86,030.32

[1]Figures do not include off-reservation public domain acreage.

[2]Public Law 93-107, the Menominee Restoration Act, effective on December 22, 1973, repealed the Menominee Termination Act of June 17, 1954 (P.L. 83-399) and acknowledged the Menominee Indian Tribe of Wisconsin as a federally recognized Indian tribe.

Sources: U.S. Census Bureau, *Profiles of General Demographic Characteristics, 2000 Census of Population and Housing, Wisconsin,* 2001; U.S. Bureau of Indian Affairs, departmental data, May 2003; Menominee Indian Tribe of Wisconsin, tribal data, May 2003. Acreage ownership totals calculated by the Wisconsin Legislative Reference Bureau.

Wisconsin Indian Land Holding in Acres
By County, February 2003

County	Total Holdings	Tribal Land	Individual Land
Adams	121.35	0.34	121.01
Ashland	53,869.12	20,998.35	32,869.77
Barron	81.11	81.11	0.00
Bayfield	7,982.35	6,200.62	1,767.08
Brown	2,368.50	2,193.45	175.05
Burnett	1,183.43	1,183.43	0.00
Clark	640.24	20.00	620.24
Crawford	193.20	80.00	113.20
Dane	4.45	4.45	0.00
Douglas	516.20	0.00	516.20
Forest	13,831.69	13,151.69	360.00
Iron	16,483.34	11,989.15	4,494.19
Jackson	1,200.61	415.29	785.32
Juneau	393.85	83.00	310.85
La Crosse	92.30	0.00	92.30
Marathon	200.00	0.00	200.00
Marinette	40.00	0.00	40.00
Milwaukee	19.50	19.50	0.00
Monroe	445.50	52.50	393.00
Oconto	120.00	120.00	0.00
Oneida	355.41	176.07	179.34
Outagamie	4,277.43	4,022.89	254.54
Polk	851.80	851.80	0.00
Sauk	88.27	88.27	0.00
Sawyer	47,926.65	23,520.92	24,405.73
Shawano	16,688.29	16,207.17	481.12
Vilas	30,577.29	18,768.65	11,793.58
Vernon	1,200.00	1,200.00	0.00
Washburn	20.00	20.00	0.00
Wood	537.72	91.72	446.00

Note: Total holdings include government land.

Source: U.S. Bureau of Indian Affairs, departmental data, May 2003.

Tribal Chairpersons and Mailing Addresses
May 2005

Tribe and Chairperson	Tribal Mailing Address
Bad River Band (Lake Superior Chippewa) Donald Moore	P.O. Box 39, Odanah 54861-0039, (715) 682-7111
Forest County Potawatomi Tribe Harold Frank	P.O. Box 340, Crandon 54520-0346, (715) 478-7200
Ho-Chunk Nation George R. Lewis (president)	P.O. Box 667, W9814 Airport Rd., Black River Falls 54615-0667, (715) 284-9343
Lac Courte Oreilles Band (Lake Superior Chippewa) Louis Taylor	13394 W. Trepania Road, Hayward 54843-2186, (715) 634-8934
Lac du Flambeau Band (Lake Superior Chippewa) Victoria Doud	P.O. Box 67, Lac du Flambeau 54538-0067, (715) 588-3303
Menominee Tribe Michael Chapman	P.O. Box 910, Keshena 54135-0910, (715) 799-5114
Oneida Tribe Cristina Danforth	P.O. Box 365, Oneida 54155, (920) 869-1600
Red Cliff Band (Lake Superior Chippewa) Ray DePerry	88385 Pike Rd., Hwy 13, Bayfield 54814-0529, (715) 779-3700
St. Croix Band (Lake Superior Chippewa) David Merrill	24663 Angelina Avenue, Webster 54893, (715) 349-2195
Sokaogon Chippewa Community Sandra Rachal	3051 Sand Lake Rd., Crandon 54520, (715) 478-2604
Stockbridge-Munsee Band, Mohican Nation Roger Chicks	N8476 MoHeConuch Rd., Bowler 54416-9801, (715) 793-4111

Sources: Great Lakes Inter-Tribal Council, www.glitc.org [May 2005], and individual tribal Web sites.

WISCONSIN VOTING AGE POPULATION BY RACE AND COUNTY
2000 Census and 2004 Estimate

County	2004 Total[1]	2000 Total[2]	White	Black/ African American	American Indian and Alaska Native	Asian	Native Hawaiian and Other Pacific Islander	Other	More Than One	Hispanic Origin[3] (of any race)
Adams	16,396	15,761	14,482	34	72	39	3	31	99	148
Ashland	12,649	12,582	11,249	20	1,089	37	8	37	142	110
Barron	34,756	33,583	32,980	39	229	88	11	72	164	229
Bayfield	11,737	11,313	10,307	4	835	20	1	28	118	41
Brown	175,641	167,551	156,000	1,798	3,334	2,498	49	2,727	1,249	5,302
Buffalo	10,511	10,343	10,238	9	25	27	3	7	34	48
Burnett	12,774	12,209	11,560	30	456	25	8	17	113	63
Calumet	31,613	29,014	28,301	72	98	323	3	93	122	248
Chippewa	43,757	40,593	39,980	45	121	236	5	42	164	148
Clark	24,057	23,494	23,148	25	94	65	3	111	73	244
Columbia	40,834	39,247	38,242	411	135	118	11	140	190	521
Crawford	12,920	12,731	12,416	173	27	31	2	17	65	69
Dane	348,588	330,269	299,370	10,861	1,041	10,823	112	4,268	3,796	9,871
Dodge	66,437	64,634	61,377	2,051	278	182	19	460	267	1,447
Door	22,694	21,789	21,425	27	124	51	3	57	102	172
Douglas	33,404	33,085	31,814	173	548	162	9	46	333	168
Dunn	31,937	30,553	29,693	92	83	403	4	96	182	212
Eau Claire	73,680	71,322	68,798	291	338	1,211	18	180	486	547
Florence	4,022	3,924	3,863	6	19	10	1	3	22	11
Fond du Lac	74,502	72,779	70,520	687	275	418	12	501	394	1,209
Forest	7,623	7,488	6,679	82	631	13	4	16	63	48
Grant	38,545	37,829	37,217	205	45	174	4	44	140	187
Green	25,834	24,739	24,419	41	44	51	—	62	122	190
Green Lake	14,672	14,491	14,254	16	30	30	3	99	59	234
Iowa	17,233	16,609	16,446	19	16	44	1	15	68	49
Iron	5,599	5,527	5,457	3	25	7	3	1	31	28
Jackson	14,935	14,497	13,081	417	732	21	8	158	80	273
Jefferson	58,531	56,625	53,639	158	166	239	10	792	360	1,911
Juneau	19,004	18,134	17,648	42	188	64	3	87	102	198
Kenosha	113,799	109,075	98,672	4,583	397	987	37	3,100	1,299	6,391
Kewaunee	15,455	14,970	14,795	18	33	18	1	35	70	101
La Crosse	83,602	81,856	78,623	621	287	1,630	15	186	497	603
Lafayette	11,871	11,748	11,668	11	12	17	3	13	24	54
Langlade	16,053	15,683	15,437	16	75	36	2	23	94	95
Lincoln	22,588	22,100	21,793	27	83	61	2	38	96	109
Manitowoc	62,807	61,790	60,035	149	265	743	19	301	274	776
Marathon	95,124	92,118	88,632	192	313	2,384	14	187	396	565
Marinette	33,805	33,181	32,674	44	162	84	8	57	154	193
Marquette	11,728	11,345	11,600	532	149	32	16	41	127	323
Menominee	2,819	2,786	487	2	2,263	—	1	14	19	50
Milwaukee	691,828	692,339	496,391	140,938	4,494	15,397	299	24,612	10,208	49,981
Monroe	30,643	29,398	28,549	118	245	110	12	225	142	448
Oconto	27,951	26,487	26,004	21	185	49	2	44	169	131
Oneida	29,324	28,573	28,050	100	160	74	10	38	141	130
Outagamie	122,068	116,523	110,855	585	1,602	1,764	32	853	753	1,971
Ozaukee	62,374	60,308	58,732	553	103	573	11	164	250	636
Pepin	5,569	5,304	5,250	3	9	10	2	5	25	18
Pierce	29,154	27,808	27,361	63	63	118	7	67	128	182
Polk	32,331	30,484	29,953	35	263	63	4	42	124	179
Portage	52,313	51,005	49,449	123	178	784	19	178	274	574
Price	12,148	12,052	11,884	7	61	30	3	10	57	68
Racine	140,159	137,880	118,057	12,718	498	919	46	4,297	1,345	9,042
Richland	13,542	13,412	13,254	14	28	25	—	23	68	81
Rock	114,287	111,913	103,716	4,409	310	836	44	1,671	955	3,663
Rusk	11,659	11,544	11,299	69	41	29	9	31	66	63
St. Croix	52,291	45,538	44,740	141	101	226	12	91	227	277
Sauk	43,384	40,854	40,018	82	289	93	4	202	166	542
Sawyer	12,935	12,295	10,486	46	1,577	30	3	41	112	77
Shawano	31,161	30,231	28,159	33	1,631	73	10	81	244	211
Sheboygan	85,928	83,877	79,285	990	282	1,723	17	1,008	566	2,300
Taylor	14,480	14,348	14,207	4	23	29	—	18	67	61
Trempealeau	20,720	20,166	19,966	21	26	26	2	53	72	149
Vernon	20,969	20,360	20,170	6	29	36	2	42	76	95
Vilas	17,431	16,688	15,416	32	1,120	25	2	23	70	99
Walworth	73,269	69,548	67,786	599	160	449	21	1,543	547	3,749
Washburn	12,771	12,221	11,969	13	121	16	2	12	88	75
Washington	90,616	86,165	84,568	292	199	444	25	278	357	876
Waukesha	275,072	265,864	256,676	1,505	553	3,686	65	1,927	1,452	5,738
Waupaca	39,498	38,526	37,867	38	141	84	7	164	153	384
Waushara	18,963	17,639	17,280	39	48	45	3	181	114	502
Winnebago	123,281	119,420	114,521	1,408	559	1,540	25	694	673	1,836
Wood	56,665	56,170	54,804	109	324	578	5	123	227	358
STATE	4,119,320	3,994,307	3,635,741	189,140	30,560	53,286	1,143	52,943	32,106	117,682

Note: The voting age population is 18 and older.
[1]Wisconsin Department of Administration estimate. [2]Population totals include corrections made by the U.S. Census Bureau through 10/10/2004. Race and ethnicity data have not been adjusted. Population estimates are based on the corrected totals. [3]Includes all persons who identified themselves as Hispanic, regardless of race.
Sources: U.S. Department of Commerce, Census Bureau, P.L. 94-171 Redistricting File, as processed by the Wisconsin Legislative Technology Services Bureau, March 2001; Wisconsin Department of Administration, Division of Housing and Intergovernmental Relations, Demographic Services Center, *Final Population Estimates for Wisconsin Counties*, January 1, 2004.

WISCONSIN VITAL STATISTICS
1910 – 2003

Year	Marriages Number	Marriages Rate[3]	Divorces, Annulments Number[4]	Divorces, Annulments Rate[3]	Live Births Number	Live Births Rate[3]	Total Deaths[1] Number	Total Deaths[1] Rate[3]	Infant Deaths Number	Infant Deaths Rate[5]	Fetal Deaths[2] Number	Fetal Deaths[2] Rate[6]	Maternal Deaths Number	Maternal Deaths Rate[7]
1910	18,528	7.9	1,189	0.5	51,435	22.0	28,213	12.1	5,621	109.3	1,414	26.8	255	49.6
1915	17,833	7.2	1,721	0.7	58,014	23.3	26,676	10.7	4,520	77.9	1,711	28.6	291	50.2
1920	22,294	8.4	2,425	0.9	59,269	22.4	29,859	11.3	4,566	77.0	1,673	27.5	338	57.0
1925	16,385	5.8	2,467	0.9	58,024	20.7	29,380	10.5	3,861	66.5	1,712	28.7	294	50.7
1930	15,328	5.2	2,553	0.9	56,643	19.2	30,488	10.4	3,149	55.6	1,683	28.9	298	52.6
1935	21,075	6.9	3,543	1.2	52,402	17.2	30,404	10.0	2,413	46.0	1,257	23.4	193	36.8
1940	23,379	7.5	3,599	1.1	56,324	17.9	31,457	10.0	2,030	36.0	1,209	21.0	151	26.8
1945	25,269	8.5	6,393	2.2	61,577	20.9	31,776	10.7	1,890	30.7	1,141	18.2	81	13.2
1950	29,081	8.4	4,845	1.4	82,364	23.9	33,573	9.7	2,098	25.5	1,241	14.8	35	4.3
1955	25,543	7.0	4,720	1.3	92,333	25.2	35,250	9.6	2,175	23.6	1,233	13.2	22	2.4
1960	24,573	6.2	3,672	0.9	99,493	25.1	38,121	9.6	2,173	21.8	1,341	13.3	27	2.7
1965	28,410	6.7	5,232	1.2	82,919	19.7	40,146	9.5	1,829	22.1	1,042	12.4	13	1.6
1970	34,415	7.8	8,930	2.0	77,455	17.5	40,820	9.2	1,308	16.9	817	10.4	6	0.8
1975	35,888	7.8	13,187	2.9	65,145	14.3	39,916	8.8	881	13.5	530	8.1	3	0.5
1980	41,113	8.7	17,589	3.7	74,763	15.9	40,801	8.7	763	10.2	549	7.3	5	0.7
1985	40,014	8.4	16,596	3.5	73,647	15.4	41,434	8.7	674	9.2	471	6.4	4	0.5
1990	38,934	8.0	17,727	3.6	72,636	14.8	42,655	8.7	611	8.4	443	6.1	3	0.4
1991	37,765	7.6	18,480	3.7	72,039	14.6	43,117	8.7	607	8.4	423	5.8	4	0.6
1992	37,069	7.4	18,487	3.7	70,662	14.2	42,179	8.5	513	7.3	457	6.4	4	0.4
1993	36,415	7.2	17,527	3.5	69,760	13.8	44,466	8.8	552	7.9	401	5.7	3	0.3
1994	36,375	7.2	17,569	3.5	68,265	13.4	44,420	8.7	537	7.9	438	6.4	2	0.3
1995	36,354	7.1	17,313	3.4	67,493	13.2	45,037	8.8	493	7.3	403	5.9	1	0.1
1996	36,186	7.0	17,218	3.3	67,076	13.0	45,107	8.7	492	7.3	416	6.2	2	0.3
1997	35,546	6.8	17,289	3.3	66,490	12.7	44,860	8.6	431	6.5	361	5.4	2	0.3
1998	34,946	6.7	17,484	3.3	67,379	12.8	45,890	8.7	488	7.2	401	5.9	6	0.3
1999	35,754	6.8	17,302	3.3	68,181	12.9	46,571	8.8	456	6.7	353	5.2	6	0.9
2000	36,100	6.7	17,388	3.2	69,289	12.9	46,405	8.7	457	6.6	414	5.9	5	0.7
2001	34,790	6.5	17,457	3.3	69,012	12.7	46,537	8.6	491	7.1	375	5.4	4	0.6
2002	34,241	6.3	17,471	3.2	68,510	12.6	46,893	8.6	471	6.9	379	5.5	5	0.7
2003	34,220	6.3	17,150	3.1	69,999	12.7	46,040	8.4	454	6.5	344	4.9	9	0.1

[1] Excludes fetal deaths (20 weeks gestation and over).
[2] A fetal death report is not used for induced abortions.
[3] Per 1,000 population.
[4] Pre-1960 data includes legal separations.
[5] Per 1,000 live births.
[6] Per 1,000 deliveries (live births plus stillbirths of 20 weeks or more gestation).
[7] Per 10,000 live births.

Sources: Wisconsin Department of Health and Family Services, *Vital Statistics 1994*, August 1995, and previous issues; *Wisconsin Births and Infant Deaths, 2003*, October 2004, and previous issues; *Wisconsin Deaths, 2003*, October 2004, and previous issues; *Wisconsin Marriages and Divorces, 2003*, June 2004, and previous issues.

RESIDENT LIVE BIRTHS AND DEATHS IN WISCONSIN
By County, 1980 – 2003

County	Live Births						Deaths					
	1980	1985	1990	1995	2000	2003	1980	1985	1990	1995[1]	2000	2003
Adams	179	170	175	167	158	161	136	178	182	185	226	239
Ashland	279	248	202	239	224	208	219	196	214	218	206	191
Barron	654	628	579	550	466	540	411	432	433	450	442	474
Bayfield	219	193	155	135	141	111	146	159	151	152	153	127
Brown	2,802	2,917	3,169	2,962	3,212	3,364	1,181	1,310	1,349	1,482	1,591	1,565
Buffalo	236	227	176	165	163	150	129	147	145	121	123	145
Burnett	167	160	143	171	136	138	168	128	159	179	183	193
Calumet	546	514	491	488	513	640	205	221	242	235	252	235
Chippewa	903	867	704	633	673	681	456	495	498	534	533	497
Clark	641	514	464	448	496	532	316	345	355	323	307	348
Columbia	667	650	610	607	616	646	436	440	450	532	508	485
Crawford	293	239	230	215	183	224	167	176	180	178	178	175
Dane	4,685	4,984	5,305	5,023	5,555	5,725	1,928	2,112	2,078	2,397	2,512	2,657
Dodge	1,186	1,146	985	947	994	963	678	711	765	810	848	919
Door	412	400	325	254	232	265	262	245	311	311	315	290
Douglas	702	590	540	493	513	501	457	422	440	455	454	450
Dunn	537	501	417	444	483	470	240	305	271	289	280	262
Eau Claire	1,117	1,201	1,208	1,118	1,116	1,110	646	618	658	664	639	687
Florence[2]	55	63	26	36	36	37	52	39	44	66	63	53
Fond du Lac	1,512	1,368	1,270	1,119	1,151	1,209	824	807	771	867	908	866
Forest[2]	140	156	132	137	114	122	104	118	122	109	131	109
Grant	867	743	661	561	540	584	454	476	493	465	495	496
Green	483	471	418	390	402	397	311	303	270	316	322	324
Green Lake	262	266	241	192	219	231	208	204	201	248	243	246
Iowa	345	319	318	296	263	308	204	205	195	191	195	189
Iron[2]	84	76	68	63	40	53	93	75	97	87	84	92
Jackson	276	240	217	189	233	231	179	176	187	187	219	212
Jefferson	973	1,004	873	852	931	980	605	576	541	579	608	620
Juneau	347	339	277	308	275	285	221	227	230	271	264	311
Kenosha	1,826	1,910	2,043	2,040	2,151	2,160	1,093	1,034	1,131	1,229	1,222	1,266
Kewaunee	323	303	237	218	224	255	166	179	184	193	189	171
La Crosse	1,349	1,394	1,416	1,267	1,234	1,247	768	798	836	869	888	875
Lafayette	289	271	227	176	174	173	139	147	172	147	144	156
Langlade	287	259	232	228	209	212	207	234	220	252	220	236
Lincoln	406	363	343	320	281	284	284	279	281	298	333	294
Manitowoc	1,338	1,228	1,072	898	894	867	779	779	774	819	852	751
Marathon	1,930	1,812	1,685	1,585	1,520	1,546	853	827	875	907	924	946
Marinette[2]	662	592	431	454	457	458	446	424	491	478	470	524
Marquette[2]	167	158	148	121	146	165	134	152	149	141	174	169
Menominee[2]	111	132	128	92	93	90	36	37	42	45	36	34
Milwaukee	15,841	16,296	17,013	15,067	14,846	14,793	9,278	9,143	9,282	9,200	9,063	8,614
Monroe	607	600	591	529	602	624	339	376	384	383	414	415
Oconto	469	451	398	388	383	392	300	304	272	331	357	329
Oneida	423	437	371	352	316	301	316	348	363	375	431	355
Outagamie	2,340	2,320	2,273	2,056	2,289	2,255	895	923	993	1,026	1,109	1,147
Ozaukee	992	960	945	934	869	874	437	436	497	541	583	620
Pepin	128	94	90	83	79	79	107	82	93	72	73	90
Pierce	507	492	477	403	412	481	234	225	237	235	244	228
Polk	506	506	529	470	454	477	319	360	352	380	376	419
Portage	927	876	913	788	805	772	360	375	398	438	404	417
Price	242	225	185	184	125	123	211	220	196	198	207	202
Racine	2,980	2,641	2,697	2,512	2,650	2,539	1,393	1,328	1,438	1,534	1,616	1,492
Richland	275	267	219	196	201	205	184	189	186	200	185	180
Rock	2,256	2,189	2,166	1,963	2,075	2,055	1,205	1,204	1,277	1,268	1,335	1,308
Rusk	222	216	213	192	148	170	135	170	157	183	168	170
St. Croix	835	741	840	725	908	1,018	303	334	375	438	444	464
Sauk	654	690	670	670	755	730	433	459	485	484	485	507
Sawyer	219	203	176	196	182	157	155	136	171	194	183	189
Shawano	528	488	525	456	470	479	414	399	418	444	476	445
Sheboygan	1,588	1,507	1,401	1,336	1,437	1,376	954	982	908	957	1,083	992
Taylor	379	354	289	221	247	242	159	143	195	191	176	172
Trempealeau	373	370	369	315	322	338	314	296	300	338	298	318
Vernon	408	409	332	351	390	409	325	289	290	311	330	286
Vilas	228	240	201	205	155	186	204	215	244	254	251	240
Walworth	1,026	1,009	996	952	1,102	1,160	626	662	651	710	826	788
Washburn	226	198	181	168	163	183	136	175	167	194	198	173
Washington	1,442	1,383	1,349	1,440	1,490	1,489	562	583	650	687	795	892
Waukesha	3,841	3,727	4,046	4,120	4,357	4,311	1,648	1,800	1,906	2,316	2,795	2,743
Waupaca	697	656	667	619	567	596	618	610	620	658	634	711
Waushara	243	247	245	240	225	247	214	238	223	242	243	268
Winnebago	1,901	2,028	1,936	1,838	1,926	1,745	1,099	1,095	1,094	1,271	1,194	1,315
Wood	1,198	1,211	1,039	923	878	870	583	599	646	704	695	672
STATE	74,758	73,647	72,661	67,493	69,289	69,999	40,801	41,434	42,655	45,036	46,405	46,040

[1]The total for 1995 includes one death with an unknown county of residence.

[2]Since nearly all births and deaths occur in hospitals, the numbers for Florence, Forest, Iron, Marinette, Marquette, and Menominee Counties are small because they have no hospitals. Caution must be used in making inferences based on this data.

Sources: Wisconsin Department of Health and Family Services, Division of Health, *Vital Statistics 1993,* August 1994, and previous issues; Division of Health Care Financing, *Wisconsin Births and Infant Deaths, 2003,* October 2004, and previous issues; and Division of Health Care Financing, *Wisconsin Deaths, 2003,* October 2004, and previous issues.

MARRIAGES AND DIVORCES, BY STATE OF OCCURRENCE
1970 – 2002
(In Thousands)

State	Marriages[1]						Divorces[2]					
	1970	1980	1990	2000	2001	2002[3]	1970	1980	1990	2000[3]	2001[3]	2002[3]
Alabama	47.0	49.0	43.3	45.0	42.2	42.7	15.1	26.9	25.3	23.5	23.4	24.6
Alaska	3.4	5.3	5.7	5.6	5.1	5.5	1.7	3.4	2.9	2.7	2.6	2.6
Arizona	18.5	30.2	37.0	38.7	40.0	36.2	12.7	19.9	25.1	21.6	21.1	25.9
Arkansas	23.3	25.2	35.7	41.1	38.4	37.8	9.3	21.8	16.8	17.9	17.1	16.9
California	172.4	218.4	236.7	196.9	224.2	217.9	112.9	134.0	NA	NA	NA	NA
Colorado	25.0	34.1	31.5	35.6	36.5	35.6	10.4	18.1	18.4	20.0	21.0	21.1
Connecticut	25.0	25.9	27.8	19.4	18.6	16.2	5.8	11.9	10.3	6.5	9.7	9.9
Delaware	4.3	4.4	5.6	5.1	5.2	4.9	1.7	2.3	3.0	3.2	3.1	2.4
District of Columbia	7.3	5.2	4.7	2.8	3.5	3.0	2.3	4.7	3.3	1.5	1.2	1.4
Florida	69.2	110.6	142.3	141.9	151.3	159.3	37.2	71.4	81.7	81.9	84.6	86.6
Georgia	63.9	69.4	64.4	56.0	51.3	58.4	18.6	33.6	35.7	30.7	30.6	31.5
Hawaii	10.6	11.7	18.1	25.0	24.0	25.3	2.6	4.4	5.2	4.6	4.5	4.6
Idaho	10.9	13.1	15.0	14.0	14.7	14.4	3.6	6.6	6.6	6.9	7.2	7.0
ILLINOIS	115.5	110.7	NA	85.5	89.8	83.2	36.5	50.5	NA	39.1	39.7	36.9
Indiana	55.2	57.8	54.3	48.1	48.2	43.9	15.2	NA	NA	NA	NA	NA
IOWA	24.6	27.5	24.8	20.3	20.9	18.1	7.2	11.8	11.1	9.4	9.3	8.6
Kansas	22.4	24.9	23.4	22.2	20.3	19.8	8.8	13.4	12.6	10.6	8.7	10.3
Kentucky	36.3	34.3	51.3	39.7	36.6	36.6	10.7	17.0	21.8	21.6	22.0	21.1
Louisiana	35.4	41.7	41.2	40.5	37.5	35.6	5.1	NA	NA	NA	NA	NA
Maine	11.0	14.3	11.8	11.3	11.0	10.9	3.9	6.2	5.3	6.4	6.0	5.0
Maryland	52.2	46.0	46.1	40.0	37.5	38.0	9.3	16.3	16.1	17.0	15.9	16.4
Massachusetts	47.4	49.0	47.8	37.0	40.0	36.5	11.0	16.5	16.8	16.0	14.8	16.7
MICHIGAN	89.7	89.6	76.1	66.4	66.5	65.2	30.0	40.8	40.2	39.4	38.9	37.8
MINNESOTA	31.3	37.8	33.7	33.4	33.0	31.8	8.3	15.1	15.4	14.8	16.0	15.6
Mississippi	26.3	28.0	24.3	19.7	18.7	19.0	8.2	13.5	14.4	14.4	15.1	14.2
Missouri	50.1	55.5	49.3	43.7	42.2	41.9	17.9	27.8	26.4	26.5	23.8	22.9
Montana	6.9	8.4	7.0	6.6	6.4	6.3	3.0	5.0	4.1	2.1	2.3	2.5
Nebraska	15.7	14.2	12.5	13.0	13.6	13.0	3.7	6.5	6.4	6.2	6.3	6.3
Nevada	97.6	115.4	NA	144.3	146.1	123.3	9.1	13.7	13.3	18.1	13.2	20.9
New Hampshire	10.0	9.3	10.6	11.6	10.6	11.0	2.4	5.2	5.3	7.1	6.1	5.9
New Jersey	56.6	55.0	58.0	50.4	54.1	51.4	10.8	25.9	23.6	25.6	28.5	29.2
New Mexico	12.4	16.3	13.2	14.5	13.9	14.7	4.4	10.4	7.7	9.2	9.0	8.1
New York	161.2	141.3	169.3	133.9	145.5	134.3	26.4	54.2	57.9	62.8	54.1	71.6
North Carolina	48.3	46.3	52.1	65.6	61.1	61.0	13.7	28.2	34.0	36.9	34.9	37.3
North Dakota	5.3	6.1	4.8	4.6	4.1	4.6	1.0	2.1	2.3	2.0	1.7	1.8
Ohio	90.1	99.5	95.8	88.5	82.3	80.4	39.3	58.2	51.0	49.3	45.6	46.0
Oklahoma	39.0	46.5	33.2	NA	NA	NA	16.8	24.2	24.9	NA	NA	NA
Oregon	17.3	23.1	25.2	26.0	26.0	24.9	9.6	17.9	15.9	16.7	16.5	16.2
Pennsylvania	94.5	95.4	86.8	73.2	71.4	69.6	22.6	34.8	40.1	37.9	38.0	37.1
Rhode Island	7.5	7.1	8.1	8.0	8.6	8.3	1.7	3.6	3.8	3.1	3.3	3.3
South Carolina	57.9	53.9	55.8	42.7	40.1	36.4	5.8	13.8	16.1	14.4	13.8	13.3
South Dakota	11.0	8.9	7.7	7.1	6.7	6.8	1.4	2.8	2.6	2.7	2.5	2.6
Tennessee	45.4	58.8	66.6	88.2	77.7	76.5	16.6	30.1	32.3	33.8	28.8	31.5
Texas	139.5	187.1	182.8	196.4	194.9	192.6	51.2	97.2	95.1	85.2	78.6	84.0
Utah	11.7	17.1	19.0	24.1	23.2	22.7	3.9	8.0	8.8	9.7	9.7	9.6
Vermont	4.5	5.2	6.1	6.1	6.0	6.0	1.0	2.5	2.6	2.5	2.4	2.6
Virginia	52.0	60.2	71.3	62.4	63.4	63.2	11.9	23.6	27.3	30.2	30.2	30.8
Washington	41.3	46.6	48.6	40.9	42.2	38.1	17.9	28.4	28.8	27.2	26.3	28.0
West Virginia	15.9	17.4	13.2	15.7	14.2	14.9	5.6	9.9	9.7	9.3	9.3	9.9
WISCONSIN	34.4	40.9	41.2	36.1	34.9	34.3	8.9	17.9	17.8	17.6	17.3	17.7
Wyoming	4.5	6.8	4.8	4.9	5.0	4.7	1.8	4.0	3.1	2.8	2.9	2.7

NA – Not available.

[1]Data represent marriages performed or licenses issued in the state. [2]Data includes reported annulments. [3]Preliminary data.

Sources: National Center for Health Statistics, *National Vital Statistics Report,* February 22, 2001, and previous issues; and *Table 3: Provisional Number of Marriages and Divorces: Each State, December 2001 and 2002 and Cumulative Figures, 2000-2002,* and previous issues, at: http://www.cdc.gov/nchs [May 2005].

WISCONSIN DEATHS AND DEATH RATES – 2003

	Total		Males		Females	
Age Group	Deaths	Rate*	Deaths	Rate*	Deaths	Rate*
Under 1 year	454	648.6	246	688.9	207	603.7
1-4 years	85	31.4	46	33.1	39	29.6
5-9 years	52	14.6	28	15.4	24	13.8
10-14 years	74	18.6	46	22.5	28	14.4
15-19 years	284	69.4	196	93.5	88	44.0
20-24 years	343	84.8	277	134.3	66	33.3
25-29 years	280	83.4	209	121.0	71	43.6
30-34 years	321	90.7	220	122.2	101	58.1
35-39 years	500	125.2	317	157.8	183	92.2
40-44 years	805	177.9	503	222.1	302	133.6
45-49 years	1,219	282.9	762	352.1	457	213.2
50-54 years	1,528	406.0	957	504.9	571	305.7
55-59 years	1,955	656.2	1,186	801.6	769	512.8
60-64 years	2,266	992.2	1,345	1,213.8	921	783.4
65-69 years	2,922	1,587.0	1,721	1,975.0	1,201	1,238.4
70-74 years	4,207	2,524.3	2,384	3,148.4	1,823	2,004.4
75-79 years	5,975	4,046.7	3,252	5,161.9	2,723	3,216.8
80-84 years	7,311	6,639.7	3,544	8,585.3	3,767	5,472.9
85-89 years	7,500	10,661.0	3,068	13,462.0	4,432	9,318.8
90-94 years	5,315	18,461.3	1,646	21,601.0	3,669	17,331.1
95 years and over	2,644	34,248.7	542	32,650.6	2,102	34,686.5
ALL AGES	46,040	837.3	22,495	826.9	23,544	847.5

*Per 100,000 population in that group.

Source: Wisconsin Department of Health and Family Services, Bureau of Health Information and Policy, *Wisconsin Deaths, 2003,* October 2004.

WISCONSIN POPULATION, BY AGE GROUP, 2000 and 2003

	Population of Group		Male		Female	
Age Group	2000 Census	2003	2000	2003	2000	2003
Under 5 years	342,340	339,186	175,041	173,750	167,299	165,436
5-9 years	379,484	354,070	194,506	181,093	184,978	172,977
10-14 years	403,074	395,957	206,665	203,065	196,409	192,892
15-19 years	407,195	407,493	208,785	208,566	198,410	198,927
20-24 years	357,292	402,362	182,372	205,338	174,920	197,024
25-29 years	333,913	334,026	170,011	171,856	163,902	162,170
30-34 years	372,255	352,298	188,414	179,179	183,841	173,119
35-39 years	435,255	397,446	217,663	199,974	217,592	197,472
40-44 years	440,267	450,325	221,424	225,359	218,843	224,966
45-49 years	397,693	428,774	200,621	215,395	197,072	213,379
50-54 years	334,613	374,564	168,086	188,665	166,527	185,899
55-59 years	252,742	296,514	124,363	147,261	128,379	149,253
60-64 years	204,999	227,297	99,580	110,284	105,419	117,013
65-69 years	182,119	183,240	85,771	86,729	96,348	96,511
70-74 years	173,188	165,872	78,610	75,359	94,578	90,513
75-79 years	146,675	146,950	61,121	62,695	85,554	84,255
80-84 years	104,946	109,585	38,757	41,083	66,189	68,502
85 years and over	95,625	106,340	27,251	31,913	68,374	74,427
STATE	5,363,675	5,472,299	2,649,041	2,707,564	2,714,634	2,764,735
Median age	36.0	37.0	35.0	35.8	37.1	38.2

Source: U.S. Census Bureau, Population Division, *Annual Estimates of the Population by Sex and Age for Wisconsin: April 1, 2000 to July 1, 2003,* September 30, 2004.

WISCONSIN POST OFFICES
2005

Post Office and County[1]	ZIP Code	Post Office and County[1]	ZIP Code
		Blair, Trempealeau	54616
Abbotsford, Clark	54405	Blanchardville, Lafayette	53516
Abrams, Oconto	54101	Blenker, Wood	54415
Adams, Adams	53910	Bloom City, Richland	54634
Adell, Sheboygan	53001	Bloomer, Chippewa	54724
Afton, Rock	53501	Bloomington, Grant	53804
Albany, Green	53502	Blue Mounds, Dane	53517
Algoma, Kewaunee	54201	Blue River, Grant	53518
Allenton, Washington	53002	Bonduel, Shawano	54107
Alma, Buffalo	54610	Boscobel, Grant	53805
Alma Center, Jackson	54611	Boulder Junction, Vilas	54512
Almena, Barron	54805	Bowler, Shawano	54416
Almond, Portage	54909	Boyceville, Dunn	54725
Altoona, Eau Claire	54720	Boyd, Chippewa	54726
Alvin, Florence	54542	Brandon, Fond du Lac	53919
Amberg, Marinette	54102	Brantwood, Price	54513
Amery, Polk	54001	Briggsville, Marquette	53920
Amherst, Portage	54406	Brill, Barron	54818
Amherst Junction, Portage	54407	Brillion, Calumet	54110
Aniwa, Marathon	54408	Bristol, Kenosha	53104
Antigo, Langlade	54409	Brodhead, Green	53520
Appleton, Outagamie	54911[2]	Brokaw, Marathon	54417
Arbor Vitae, Oneida	54568	Brookfield, Waukesha	53045[2]
Arcadia, Trempealeau	54612	Brooklyn, Green	53521
Arena, Iowa	53503	Brooks, Adams	53952
Argonne, Forest	54511	Brownsville, Dodge	53006
Argyle, Lafayette	53504	Browntown, Green	53522
Arkansaw, Pepin	54721	Bruce, Rusk	54819
Arkdale, Adams	54613	Brule, Douglas	54820
Arlington, Columbia	53911	Brussels, Door	54204
Armstrong Creek, Forest	54103	Bryant, Langlade	54418
Arpin, Wood	54410	Buffalo City, Buffalo	54622
Ashippun, Dodge	53003	Burlington, Racine	53105
Ashland, Ashland	54806	Burnett, Dodge	53922
Athelstane, Marinette	54104	Butler, Waukesha	53007
Athens, Marathon	54411	Butte des Morts, Winnebago	54927
Auburndale, Wood	54412	Butternut, Ashland	54514
Augusta, Eau Claire	54722		
Avalon, Rock	53505	Cable, Bayfield	54821
Avoca, Iowa	53506	Cadott, Chippewa	54727
		Caledonia, Racine	53108
Babcock, Wood	54413	Cambria, Columbia	53923
Bagley, Grant	53801	Cambridge, Dane	53523
Baileys Harbor, Door	54202	Cameron, Barron	54822
Baldwin, St. Croix	54002	Campbellsport, Fond du Lac	53010
Balsam Lake, Polk	54810	Camp Douglas, Juneau	54618
Bancroft, Portage	54921	Camp Lake, Kenosha	53109
Bangor, La Crosse	54614	Canton, Barron	54868
Baraboo, Sauk	53913	Caroline, Shawano	54928
Barnes, Douglas	54873	Cascade, Sheboygan	53011
Barneveld, Iowa	53507	Casco, Kewaunee	54205
Barron, Barron	54812	Cashton, Monroe	54619
Barronett, Barron	54813	Cassville, Grant	53806
Bassett, Kenosha	53101	Cataract, Monroe	54620
Bay City, Pierce	54723	Catawba, Price	54515
Bayfield, Bayfield	54814	Cato, Manitowoc	54230
Bay View, Milwaukee (Milwaukee)[3]	53207	Cavour, Forest	54511
Bear Creek, Outagamie	54922	Cazenovia, Richland	53924
Beaver, Marinette	54114	Cecil, Shawano	54111
Beaver Dam, Dodge	53916	Cedarburg, Ozaukee	53012
Beetown, Grant	53802	Cedar Grove, Sheboygan	53013
Beldenville, Pierce	54003	Centuria, Polk	54824
Belgium, Ozaukee	53004	Chaseburg, Vernon	54621
Belleville, Dane	53508	Chelsea, Taylor	54451
Belmont, Lafayette	53510	Chetek, Barron	54728
Beloit, Rock	53511[2]	Chili, Clark	54420
Benet Lake, Kenosha	53102	Chilton, Calumet	53014
Bennett, Douglas	54873	Chippewa Falls, Chippewa	54729
Benoit, Bayfield	54816	Clam Falls, Polk	54837
Benton, Lafayette	53803	Clam Lake, Ashland	54517
Berlin, Green Lake	54923	Clayton, Polk	54004
Big Bend, Waukesha	53103	Clear Lake, Polk	54005
Big Falls, Waupaca	54926	Cleveland, Manitowoc	53015
Birchwood, Washburn	54817	Clinton, Rock	53525
Birnamwood, Shawano	54414	Clintonville, Waupaca	54929
Black Creek, Outagamie	54106	Clyman, Dodge	53016
Black Earth, Dane	53515	Cobb, Iowa	53526
Black River Falls, Jackson	54615	Cochrane, Buffalo	54622

Post Office and County[1]	ZIP Code	Post Office and County[1]	ZIP Code
Colby, Clark	54421	Elk Mound, Dunn	54739
Coleman, Marinette	54112	Ellison Bay, Door	54210
Colfax, Dunn	54730	Ellsworth, Pierce	54011
Colgate, Washington	53017	Elm Grove, Waukesha	53122
Collins, Manitowoc	54207	Elmwood, Pierce	54740
Coloma, Waushara	54930	Elroy, Juneau	53929
Columbus, Columbia	53925	Elton, Langlade	54430
Combined Locks, Outagamie	54113	Embarrass, Waupaca	54933
Comstock, Barron	54826	Endeavor, Marquette	53930
Conover, Vilas	54519	Ephraim, Door	54211
Conrath, Rusk	54731	Ettrick, Trempealeau	54627
Coon Valley, Vernon	54623	Eureka, Winnebago	54934
Cornell, Chippewa	54732	Evansville, Rock	53536
Cornucopia, Bayfield	54827	Exeland, Sawyer	54835
Cottage Grove, Dane	53527		
Couderay, Sawyer	54828	**F**airchild, Eau Claire	54741
Crandon, Forest	54520	Fairwater, Fond du Lac	53931
Crivitz, Marinette	54114	Fall Creek, Eau Claire	54742
Cross Plains, Dane	53528	Fall River, Columbia	53932
Cuba City, Grant	53807	Fence, Florence	54120
Cudahy, Milwaukee	53110	Fennimore, Grant	53809
Cumberland, Barron	54829	Fenwood, Marathon	54426
Curtiss, Clark	54422	Ferryville, Crawford	54628
Cushing, Polk	54006	Fifield, Price	54524
Custer, Portage	54423	Fish Creek, Door	54212
Cutler, Juneau	54618	Florence, Florence	54121
		Fond du Lac, Fond du Lac	54935[2]
Dairyland, Burnett	54830	Fontana, Walworth	53125
Dale, Outagamie	54931	Footville, Rock	53537
Dallas, Barron	54733	Forest Junction, Calumet	54123
Dalton, Green Lake	53926	Forestville, Door	54213
Danbury, Burnett	54830	Fort Atkinson, Jefferson	53538
Dane, Dane	53529	Fountain City, Buffalo	54629
Darien, Walworth	53114	Fox Lake, Dodge	53933
Darlington, Lafayette	53530	Francis Creek, Manitowoc	54214
Deerbrook, Langlade	54424	Franksville, Racine	53126
Deerfield, Dane	53531	Frederic, Polk	54837
Deer Park, St. Croix	54007	Fredonia, Ozaukee	53021
DeForest, Dane	53532	Freedom, Outagamie	54131
Delafield, Waukesha	53018	Fremont, Waupaca	54940
Delavan, Walworth	53115	Friendship, Adams	53934
Dellwood, Adams	53927	Friesland, Columbia	53935
Delta, Bayfield	54856		
Denmark, Brown	54208	**G**alesville, Trempealeau	54630
De Pere, Brown	54115	Galloway, Marathon	54432
Deronda, Polk	54001	Gays Mills, Crawford	54631
De Soto, Vernon	54624	Genesee Depot, Waukesha	53127
Dickeyville, Grant	53808	Genoa, Vernon	54632
Dodge, Trempealeau	54625	Genoa City, Walworth	53128
Dodgeville, Iowa	53533	Germantown, Washington	53022
Dorchester, Clark	54425	Gile, Iron	54525
Dousman, Waukesha	53118	Gillett, Oconto	54124
Downing, Dunn	54734	Gilman, Taylor	54433
Downsville, Dunn	54735	Gilmanton, Buffalo	54743
Doylestown, Columbia	53928	Gleason, Lincoln	54435
Dresser, Polk	54009	Glenbeulah, Sheboygan	53023
Drummond, Bayfield	54832	Glen Flora, Rusk	54526
Dunbar, Marinette	54119	Glen Haven, Grant	53810
Durand, Pepin	54736	Glenwood City, St. Croix	54013
		Glidden, Ashland	54527
Eagle, Waukesha	53119	Goodman, Marinette	54125
Eagle River, Vilas	54521	Gordon, Douglas	54838
Eastman, Crawford	54626	Gotham, Richland	53540
East Troy, Walworth	53120	Grafton, Ozaukee	53024
Eau Claire, Eau Claire	54703[2]	Grand Chute, Outagamie (Appleton)[3]	54911
Eau Galle, Dunn	54737	Grand Marsh, Adams	53936
Eden, Fond du Lac	53019	Grand View, Bayfield	54839
Edgar, Marathon	54426	Granton, Clark	54436
Edgerton, Rock	53534	Grantsburg, Burnett	54840
Edgewater, Sawyer	54834	Gratiot, Lafayette	53541
Egg Harbor, Door	54209	Green Bay, Brown	54303[2]
Eland, Marathon	54427	Greenbush, Sheboygan	53026
Elcho, Langlade	54428	Greendale, Milwaukee	53129
Elderon, Marathon	54429	Greenfield, Milwaukee (Milwaukee)[3]	53220
Eldorado, Fond du Lac	54932	Green Lake, Green Lake	54941
Eleva, Trempealeau	54738	Greenleaf, Brown	54126
Elkhart Lake, Sheboygan	53020	Green Valley, Shawano	54127
Elkhorn, Walworth	53121	Greenville, Outagamie	54942

Post Office and County[1]	ZIP Code	Post Office and County[1]	ZIP Code
Greenwood, Clark	54437	Kimberly, Outagamie	54136
Gresham, Shawano	54128	King, Waupaca	54946
Gurney, Iron	54559	Kingston, Green Lake	53939
		Knapp, Dunn	54749
Hager City, Pierce	54014	Knowles, Dodge	53048
Hales Corners, Milwaukee	53130	Kohler, Sheboygan	53044
Hamburg, Marathon	54411	Krakow, Shawano	54137
Hammond, St. Croix	54015		
Hancock, Waushara	54943	**L**ac du Flambeau, Vilas	54538
Hannibal, Taylor	54439	La Crosse, La Crosse	54601[2]
Hanover, Rock	53542	Ladysmith, Rusk	54848
Harshaw, Oneida	54529	La Farge, Vernon	54639
Hartford, Washington	53027	Lake Delton, Sauk	53940
Hartland, Waukesha	53029	Lake Geneva, Walworth	53147
Hatley, Marathon	54440	Lake Mills, Jefferson	53551
Haugen, Barron	54841	Lake Nebagamon, Douglas	54849
Haven, Sheboygan (Sheboygan)[3]	53083	Lake Tomahawk, Oneida	54539
Hawkins, Rusk	54530	Lakewood, Oconto	54138
Hawthorne, Douglas	54842	Lancaster, Grant	53813
Hayward, Sawyer	54843	Land O'Lakes, Vilas	54540
Hazel Green, Grant	53811	Lannon, Waukesha	53046
Hazelhurst, Oneida	54531	Laona, Forest	54541
Heafford Junction, Lincoln	54532	La Pointe, Ashland	54850
Helenville, Jefferson	53137	Larsen, Winnebago	54947
Herbster, Bayfield	54844	La Valle, Sauk	53941
Hewitt, Wood	54441	Lebanon, Dodge	53047
High Bridge, Ashland	54846	Lena, Oconto	54139
Highland, Iowa	53543	Leopolis, Shawano	54948
Hilbert, Calumet	54129	Lily, Langlade	54491
Hiles, Forest	54511	Lime Ridge, Sauk	53942
Hillpoint, Sauk	53937	Linden, Iowa	53553
Hillsboro, Vernon	54634	Little Chute, Outagamie	54140
Hingham, Sheboygan	53031	Little Suamico, Oconto	54141
Hixton, Jackson	54635	Livingston, Grant	53554
Holcombe, Chippewa	54745	Lodi, Columbia	53555
Hollandale, Iowa	53544	Loganville, Sauk	53943
Holmen, La Crosse	54636	Lomira, Dodge	53048
Honey Creek, Walworth	53138	Lone Rock, Richland	53556
Horicon, Dodge	53032	Long Lake, Florence	54542
Hortonville, Outagamie	54944	Loretta, Sawyer	54896
Howards Grove, Sheboygan	53083	Lowell, Dodge	53557
Hubertus, Washington	53033	Loyal, Clark	54446
Hudson, St. Croix	54016	Lublin, Taylor	54447
Humbird, Clark	54746	Luck, Polk	54853
Hurley, Iron	54534	Luxemburg, Kewaunee	54217
Hustisford, Dodge	53034	Lyndon Station, Juneau	53944
Hustler, Juneau	54637	Lynxville, Crawford	54626
		Lyons, Walworth	53148
Independence, Trempealeau	54747		
Ingram, Rusk	54526	**M**adison, Dane	53714[2]
Iola, Waupaca	54945	Maiden Rock, Pierce	54750
Irma, Lincoln	54442	Malone, Fond du Lac	53049
Iron Belt, Iron	54536	Manawa, Waupaca	54949
Iron Ridge, Dodge	53035	Manchester, Green Lake	53946
Iron River, Bayfield	54847	Manitowish Waters, Vilas	54545
Ixonia, Jefferson	53036	Manitowoc, Manitowoc	54220[2]
		Maple, Douglas	54854
Jackson, Washington	53037	Maplewood, Door	54226
Janesville, Rock	53545[2]	Marathon, Marathon	54448
Jefferson, Jefferson	53549	Marengo, Ashland	54855
Jim Falls, Chippewa	54748	Maribel, Manitowoc	54227
Johnson Creek, Jefferson	53038	Marinette, Marinette	54143
Juda, Green	53550	Marion, Waupaca	54950
Jump River, Taylor	54434	Markesan, Green Lake	53946
Junction City, Portage	54443	Marquette, Green Lake	53947
Juneau, Dodge	53039	Marshall, Dane	53559
		Marshfield, Wood	54449
Kansasville, Racine	53139	Mason, Bayfield	54856
Kaukauna, Outagamie	54130	Mather, Juneau	54641
Kellnersville, Manitowoc	54215	Mattoon, Shawano	54450
Kendall, Monroe	54638	Mauston, Juneau	53948
Kennan, Price	54537	Mayville, Dodge	53050
Kenosha, Kenosha	53140[2]	Mazomanie, Dane	53560
Keshena, Menominee	54135	McFarland, Dane	53558
Kewaskum, Washington	53040	McNaughton, Oneida	54543
Kewaunee, Kewaunee	54216	Medford, Taylor	54451
Kiel, Manitowoc	53042	Mellen, Ashland	54546
Kieler, Grant	53812	Melrose, Jackson	54642

Post Office and County[1]	ZIP Code	Post Office and County[1]	ZIP Code
Menasha, Winnebago	54952	Norwalk, Monroe	54648
Menomonee Falls, Waukesha	53051[2]		
Menomonie, Dunn	54751	Oak Creek, Milwaukee	53154
Mequon, Ozaukee	53092	Oakdale, Monroe	54649
Mercer, Iron	54547	Oakfield, Fond du Lac	53065
Merrill, Lincoln	54452	Oconomowoc, Waukesha	53066
Merrillan, Jackson	54754	Oconto, Oconto	54153
Merrimac, Sauk	53561	Oconto Falls, Oconto	54154
Merton, Waukesha	53056	Odanah, Ashland	54861
Middle Inlet, Marinette	54114	Ogdensburg, Waupaca	54962
Middleton, Dane	53562	Ogema, Price	54459
Mikana, Barron	54857	Ojibwa, Sawyer	54862
Milan, Marathon	54411	Okauchee, Waukesha	53069
Milladore, Wood	54454	Omro, Winnebago	54963
Millston, Jackson	54643	Onalaska, La Crosse	54650
Milltown, Polk	54858	Oneida, Outagamie	54155
Milton, Rock	53563	Ontario, Vernon	54651
Milwaukee, Milwaukee	53201[2]	Oostburg, Sheboygan	53070
Mindoro, La Crosse	54644	Oregon, Dane	53575
Mineral Point, Iowa	53565	Orfordville, Rock	53576
Minocqua, Oneida	54548	Osceola, Polk	54020
Minong, Washburn	54859	Oshkosh, Winnebago	54901[2]
Mishicot, Manitowoc	54228	Osseo, Trempealeau	54758
Modena, Buffalo	54755	Owen, Clark	54460
Mondovi, Buffalo	54755	Oxford, Marquette	53952
Monico, Oneida	54501		
Monona, Dane (Madison)[3]	53713	Packwaukee, Marquette	53953
Monroe, Green	53566	Palmyra, Jefferson	53156
Montello, Marquette	53949	Pardeeville, Columbia	53954
Montfort, Grant	53569	Park Falls, Price	54552
Monticello, Green	53570	Patch Grove, Grant	53817
Montreal, Iron	54550	Pearson, Langlade	54462
Moquah, Ashland	54806	Pelican Lake, Oneida	54463
Morrisonville, Dane	53571	Pell Lake, Walworth	53157
Mosinee, Marathon	54455	Pembine, Marinette	54156
Mountain, Oconto	54149	Pence, Iron	54550
Mount Calvary, Fond du Lac	53057	Pepin, Pepin	54759
Mount Hope, Grant	53816	Peshtigo, Marinette	54157
Mount Horeb, Dane	53572	Pewaukee, Waukesha	53072
Mount Sterling, Crawford	54645	Phelps, Vilas	54554
Mukwonago, Waukesha	53149	Phillips, Price	54555
Muscoda, Grant	53573	Phlox, Langlade	54464
Muskego, Waukesha	53150	Pickerel, Langlade	54465
		Pickett, Winnebago	54964
Nashotah, Waukesha	53058	Pigeon Falls, Trempealeau	54760
Navarino, Shawano	54107	Pine River, Waushara	54965
Necedah, Juneau	54646	Pittsville, Wood	54466
Neenah, Winnebago	54956[2]	Plain, Sauk	53577
Neillsville, Clark	54456	Plainfield, Waushara	54966
Nekoosa, Wood	54457	Platteville, Grant	53818
Nelma, Forest	54542	Plover, Portage	54467
Nelson, Buffalo	54756	Plum City, Pierce	54761
Nelsonville, Portage	54458	Plymouth, Sheboygan	53073
Neopit, Menominee	54150	Poplar, Douglas	54864
Neosho, Dodge	53059	Portage, Columbia	53901
Neshkoro, Marquette	54960	Port Edwards, Wood	54469
Newald, Forest	54511	Porterfield, Marinette	54159
New Auburn, Chippewa	54757	Port Washington, Ozaukee	53074
New Berlin, Waukesha	53186[2]	Port Wing, Bayfield	54865
Newburg, Washington	53060	Poskin, Barron	54812
New Franken, Brown	54229	Potosi, Grant	53820
New Glarus, Green	53574	Potter, Calumet	54160
New Holstein, Calumet	53061	Pound, Marinette	54161
New Lisbon, Juneau	53950	Powers Lake, Kenosha	53159
New London, Waupaca	54961	Poynette, Columbia	53955
New Munster, Kenosha	53152	Poy Sippi, Waushara	54967
New Post, Sawyer	54828	Prairie du Chien, Crawford	53821
New Richmond, St. Croix	54017	Prairie du Sac, Sauk	53578
Newton, Manitowoc	53063	Prairie Farm, Barron	54762
Niagara, Marinette	54151	Prentice, Price	54556
Nichols, Outagamie	54152	Prescott, Pierce	54021
North Fond du Lac, Fond du Lac		Presque Isle, Vilas	54557
(Fond du Lac)[3]	54935	Princeton, Green Lake	54968
North Freedom, Sauk	53951	Pulaski, Brown	54162
North Lake, Waukesha	53064	Pulcifer, Oconto	54124
North Prairie, Waukesha	53153		
North Woods Beach, Sawyer	54843	Racine, Racine	53401[2]
Northfield, Jackson	54635		

Post Office and County[1]	ZIP Code	Post Office and County[1]	ZIP Code
Radisson, Sawyer	54867	South Wayne, Lafayette	53587
Randolph, Dodge	53956	Sparta, Monroe	54656
Random Lake, Sheboygan	53075	Spencer, Marathon	54479
Readfield, Waupaca	54969	Spooner, Washburn	54801
Readstown, Vernon	54652	Springbrook, Washburn	54875
Redgranite, Waushara	54970	Springfield, Walworth	53176
Reedsburg, Sauk	53959	Spring Green, Sauk	53588
Reedsville, Manitowoc	54230	Spring Valley, Pierce	54767
Reeseville, Dodge	53579	Stanley, Chippewa	54768
Rewey, Iowa	53580	Star Lake, Vilas	54561
Rhinelander, Oneida	54501	Star Prairie, Polk	54026
Rib Lake, Taylor	54470	Stetsonville, Taylor	54480
Rice Lake, Barron	54868	Steuben, Crawford	54657
Richfield, Washington	53076	Stevens Point, Portage	54481
Richland Center, Richland	53581	Stiles, Oconto	54139
Ridgeland, Dunn	54763	Stitzer, Grant	53825
Ridgeway, Iowa	53582	Stockbridge, Calumet	53088
Ringle, Marathon	54471	Stockholm, Pepin	54769
Rio, Columbia	53960	Stoddard, Vernon	54658
Rio Creek, Kewaunee	54201	Stone Lake, Sawyer	54876
Ripon, Fond du Lac	54971	Stoughton, Dane	53589
River Falls, Pierce	54022	Stratford, Marathon	54484
Roberts, St. Croix	54023	Strum, Trempealeau	54770
Rochester, Racine	53167	Sturgeon Bay, Door	54235
Rock Falls, Dunn	54764	Sturtevant, Racine	53177
Rockfield, Washington	53022	Suamico, Brown	54173
Rockland, La Crosse	54653	Sullivan, Jefferson	53178
Rock Springs, Sauk	53961	Summit Lake, Langlade	54485
Rosendale, Fond du Lac	54974	Sun Prairie, Dane	53590
Rosholt, Portage	54473	Superior, Douglas	54880
Rothschild, Marathon	54474	Suring, Oconto	54174
Royalton, Waupaca	54975	Sussex, Waukesha	53089
Rubicon, Dodge	53078		
Rudolph, Wood	54475	Taylor, Jackson	54659
		Theresa, Dodge	53091
St. Cloud, Fond du Lac	53079	Thiensville, Ozaukee	53092
St. Croix Falls, Polk	54024	Thorp, Clark	54771
St. Francis, Milwaukee	53235	Three Lakes, Oneida	54562
St. Germain, Vilas	54558	Tigerton, Shawano	54486
St. Nazianz, Manitowoc	54232	Tilleda, Shawano	54978
Salem, Kenosha	53168	Tipler, Florence	54542
Sanborn, Ashland	54806	Tisch Mills, Manitowoc	54240
Sand Creek, Dunn	54765	Tomah, Monroe	54660
Sarona, Washburn	54870	Tomahawk, Lincoln	54487
Sauk City, Sauk	53583	Tony, Rusk	54563
Saukville, Ozaukee	53080	Townsend, Oconto	54175
Saxeville, Waushara	54976	Trego, Washburn	54888
Saxon, Iron	54559	Trempealeau, Trempealeau	54661
Sayner, Vilas	54560	Trevor, Kenosha	53179
Scandinavia, Waupaca	54977	Tripoli, Oneida	54564
Schofield, Marathon	54476	Tunnel City, Monroe	54662
Seneca, Crawford	54654	Turtle Lake, Barron	54889
Sextonville, Richland	53584	Twin Lakes, Kenosha	53181
Seymour, Outagamie	54165	Two Rivers, Manitowoc	54241
Sharon, Walworth	53585		
Shawano, Shawano	54166	Union Center, Juneau	53962
Sheboygan, Sheboygan	53081[2]	Union Grove, Racine	53182
Sheboygan Falls, Sheboygan	53085	Unity, Marathon	54488
Sheldon, Rusk	54766	Upson, Iron	54565
Shell Lake, Washburn	54871		
Sherwood, Calumet	54169	Valders, Manitowoc	54245
Shiocton, Outagamie	54170	Van Dyne, Fond du Lac	54979
Shorewood, Milwaukee (Milwaukee)[3]	53211	Vernon, Waukesha (Waukesha)[3]	53186
Shullsburg, Lafayette	53586	Verona, Dane	53593
Silver Cliff, Marinette	54104	Vesper, Wood	54489
Silver Lake, Kenosha	53170	Victory, Vernon	54624
Sinsinawa, Grant	53824	Viola, Vernon	54664
Siren, Burnett	54872	Viroqua, Vernon	54665
Sister Bay, Door	54234		
Slinger, Washington	53086	Wabeno, Forest	54566
Sobieski, Oconto	54171	Waldo, Sheboygan	53093
Soldiers Grove, Crawford	54655	Wales, Waukesha	53183
Solon Springs, Douglas	54873	Walworth, Walworth	53184
Somers, Kenosha	53171	Warrens, Monroe	54666
Somerset, St. Croix	54025	Wascott, Douglas	54838
South Byron, Fond du Lac	53006	Washburn, Bayfield	54891
South Milwaukee, Milwaukee	53172	Washington Island, Door	54246
South Range, Douglas	54874		

Post Office and County[1]	ZIP Code	Post Office and County[1]	ZIP Code
Waterford, Racine	53185	Whitewater, Walworth	53190
Waterloo, Jefferson	53594	Wild Rose, Waushara	54984
Watertown, Jefferson	53094[2]	Willard, Clark	54493
Waubeka, Ozaukee	53021	Williams Bay, Walworth	53191
Waukau, Winnebago	54980	Wilmot, Kenosha	53192
Waukesha, Waukesha	53186[2]	Wilson, St. Croix	54027
Waumandee, Buffalo	54622	Wilton, Monroe	54670
Waunakee, Dane	53597	Winchester, Vilas	54557
Waupaca, Waupaca	54981	Wind Lake, Racine	53185
Waupun, Dodge	53963	Windsor, Dane	53598
Wausau, Marathon	54403[2]	Winnebago, Winnebago	54985
Wausaukee, Marinette	54177	Winneconne, Winnebago	54986
Wautoma, Waushara	54982	Winter, Sawyer	54896
Wauwatosa, Milwaukee (Milwaukee)[3]	53210	Wisconsin Dells, Columbia	53965
Wauzeka, Crawford	53826	Wisconsin Rapids, Wood	54494[2]
Webb Lake, Burnett	54830	Withee, Clark	54498
Webster, Burnett	54893	Wittenberg, Shawano	54499
Wentworth, Douglas	54874	Wonewoc, Juneau	53968
West Allis, Milwaukee (Milwaukee)[3]	53214	Woodford, Lafayette	53599
West Bend, Washington	53095[2]	Woodland, Dodge	53099
West Lima, Vernon	54639	Woodman, Grant	53827
West Milwaukee, Milwaukee (Milwaukee)[3]	53214	Woodruff, Oneida	54568
West Salem, La Crosse	54669	Woodville, St. Croix	54028
Westboro, Taylor	54490	Woodworth, Kenosha	53194
Westby, Vernon	54667	Wyeville, Monroe	54660
Westfield, Marquette	53964	Wyocena, Columbia	53969
Weston, Marathon	54476		
Weyauwega, Waupaca	54983	Yellow Lake, Burnett	54830
Weyerhaeuser, Rusk	54895	Yuba, Richland	54634
Wheeler, Dunn	54772		
Whitehall, Trempealeau	54773	Zachow, Shawano	54182
White Lake, Langlade	54491	Zenda, Walworth	53195
Whitelaw, Manitowoc	54247		

[1]Does not include stations. Many of these locations no longer have post offices but their names may be used for addressing mail.

[2]Indicates multicoded city. To determine last 2 digits of ZIP code for any specific city street, consult the local post office. The ZIP code given is the general delivery ZIP code for the city.

[3]Post office is located in the city shown in parenthesis. ZIP code is listed as "acceptable" on USPS website.

Sources: U.S. Postal Service, *2004 National Five-Digit ZIP Code And Post Office Directory*, 2004, and http://www.usps.com

HIGHLIGHTS OF SOCIAL SERVICES IN WISCONSIN

Public Welfare — According to the U.S. Census Bureau, during 2001-02, almost $279.6 billion was spent nationally by state and local governments on a variety of public welfare programs. Wisconsin spent $5.6 billion, or $1,022 per capita, which ranked it 17th among the states and close to the national average of $970.91. New York's per capita expenditure was highest at $1,699 and Nevada the lowest at $517. State and local welfare expenditures represented $34.08 per $1,000 of personal income in Wisconsin, ranking it 22nd among the states, while Mississippi ($50.31) and Rhode Island ($50.27) ranked highest, and Nevada lowest ($16.84).

Participation in Wisconsin Works (W-2), a program providing job subsidies to employers and cash and noncash benefits, such as job assistance and subsidized child care, to participants if they meet certain work requirements, continues to increase. The average monthly caseload for W-2 during 2003 was reported as 10,829 households with a statewide average monthly payment of $548.09. The caseload increased to 12,060 households during 2004 with an average monthly payment of $569.54 per household. Average monthly payments ranged from a low of $428.42 in Iron County to a high of $729.23 in Jefferson County. Among the counties with larger populations, the counties with the lowest average monthly payments were Brown ($487.11), La Crosse ($494.90), and Racine ($497.48); the highest payments for high population counties were Milwaukee ($577.45), Waukesha ($564.17), and Walworth ($556.16).

Medical Assistance and BadgerCare — Medical assistance expenditures in Wisconsin in calendar year 2004 totaled over $3.9 billion, about 7.7% higher than in 2003. The largest proportion of total combined Medical Assistance and BadgerCare benefits in fiscal year 2003-04 was spent on nursing home care (falling to 23%) and health maintenance organization (HMO) care (rising to 21%). Expenditures for drugs continue to rise as a proportion of medical assistance payments, to 13.3% of the total for 2003-04, while the proportion accounted for by home care payments has declined slightly, to 15.1%.

A county breakdown of medical assistance for 2004 shows average expenditures of $4,170 per recipient for 945,010 people, or 17.1% of the population of Wisconsin. The counties with the greatest percentage of recipients were Menominee (42.09%), Ashland (27.88%), Sawyer (27.74%), and Milwaukee (27.02%). The counties with the smallest proportion of recipients were Ozaukee (5.48%), Waukesha (5.73%), and Washington (8.34%). The highest average expenditures per recipient were in Waupaca ($6,412) and Jefferson ($5,938) counties; Menominee ($2,642) and Waushara ($2,777) counties were lowest.

Institutions — From 2003 to 2004, the average daily adult corrections population increased from 21,511 to 22,011. In 2004, a daily average of 56,126 persons were on probation, and 12,335 on parole. Overall, more than 90,000 people are under the control of the Department of Corrections.

A per inmate state expenditure for corrections of $40,096 ranked Wisconsin 15th among the states in 2003. As of June 30, 2004, Wisconsin had an incarceration rate of 394 persons per 100,000 population. Louisiana (814), Texas (704), Oklahoma (684), Mississippi (682), South Carolina (555), Alabama (554), and Georgia (551) had the highest rates. Maine (149), Minnesota (169), New Hampshire (188), North Dakota (189), Massachusetts (234), Vermont (236), Utah (239), Washington (264), West Virginia (272), and Iowa (292) had the lowest rates.

The total average daily number of persons in Wisconsin's care and treatment facilities declined slightly from 1,895 in 2003 to 1,877 in 2004.

The number of youths under the supervision of the state's juvenile corrections division declined from 770 in 2003 to 664 in 2004.

The following tables present selected data. Consult footnoted sources for more detailed information about corrections and social services.

STATE AND LOCAL PUBLIC WELFARE EXPENDITURES
State Fiscal Years 2001-02

State	Amount (in thousands)			Per Capita*		Per $1,000 Personal Income*	
	Total	State	Local	Amount	Rank	Amount	Rank
Alabama	$4,161,953	$4,110,058	$51,895	$929.24	25	$36.62	18
Alaska	1,034,937	1,028,749	6,188	1,613.35	2	49.52	3
Arizona	3,286,119	2,779,969	506,150	603.94	49	22.87	46
Arkansas	2,592,774	2,577,745	15,029	958.06	24	40.83	12
California	35,559,242	23,014,323	12,544,919	1,015.92	19	30.94	28
Colorado	2,823,132	2,283,219	539,913	627.22	48	18.38	49
Connecticut	3,471,835	3,361,839	109,996	1,003.83	20	23.48	44
Delaware	659,394	659,038	356	818.16	33	25.18	37
District of Columbia	1,462,362	---	1,462,362	2,569.35	---	55.97	---
Florida	12,500,047	11,873,673	626,374	748.88	41	25.40	36
Georgia	6,159,345	6,012,846	146,499	720.90	44	24.96	38
Hawaii	1,141,298	1,111,750	29,548	919.91	27	31.05	27
Idaho	1,034,938	1,003,118	31,820	770.55	38	30.47	30
ILLINOIS	9,861,010	9,429,426	431,584	783.46	36	23.92	40
Indiana	5,312,531	4,804,551	507,980	862.86	32	30.92	29
IOWA	2,682,250	2,572,934	109,316	913.62	29	32.74	24
Kansas	2,002,967	1,963,003	39,964	738.62	42	25.58	35
Kentucky	4,816,404	4,762,386	54,018	1,177.66	8	46.29	7
Louisiana	3,362,348	3,310,858	51,490	751.16	40	29.68	33
Maine	1,791,700	1,761,629	30,071	1,383.67	5	49.36	5
Maryland	4,737,003	4,625,372	111,631	869.09	31	23.86	42
Massachusetts	5,731,241	5,664,638	66,603	892.47	30	22.94	45
MICHIGAN	9,837,380	9,068,702	768,678	979.50	22	32.57	25
MINNESOTA	7,473,369	6,071,269	1,402,100	1,487.30	4	44.83	9
Mississippi	3,236,353	3,213,913	22,440	1,128.93	11	50.31	1
Missouri	5,519,734	5,377,144	142,590	973.58	23	34.29	20
Montana	670,968	643,020	27,948	737.03	43	29.79	32
Nebraska	1,702,873	1,647,165	55,708	985.71	21	34.14	21
Nevada	1,120,376	1,003,929	116,447	516.91	50	16.84	50
New Hampshire	1,029,934	878,680	151,254	808.17	34	23.69	43
New Jersey	6,608,168	5,662,876	945,292	770.61	37	19.56	47
New Mexico	2,076,590	2,028,295	48,502	1,121.35	12	45.34	8
New York	32,503,209	23,328,217	9,174,992	1,698.69	1	47.79	6
North Carolina	7,657,145	6,521,666	1,135,479	921.90	26	33.19	23
North Dakota	663,785	625,824	37,961	1,047.13	16	39.56	15
Ohio	12,278,304	9,723,455	2,554,849	1,076.22	14	36.99	17
Oklahoma	3,191,774	3,156,200	35,574	914.63	28	35.43	19
Oregon	4,045,141	3,795,606	249,535	1,149.07	10	40.28	14
Pennsylvania	14,486,426	12,160,406	2,326,020	1,175.00	9	38.11	16
Rhode Island	1,666,668	1,659,392	7,276	1,560.07	3	50.27	2
South Carolina	4,373,722	4,360,120	13,602	1,065.78	15	41.84	10
South Dakota	604,844	592,694	12,150	795.39	35	29.85	31
Tennessee	6,458,267	6,319,314	138,953	1,115.46	13	40.41	13
Texas	14,903,225	14,606,999	296,226	685.62	46	23.89	41
Utah	1,595,137	1,573,411	21,726	687.92	45	27.63	34
Vermont	756,815	756,196	619	1,227.78	6	41.48	11
Virginia	4,673,802	3,622,277	1,051,525	641.32	47	19.52	48
Washington	6,198,479	6,151,140	47,339	1,021.66	18	31.25	26
West Virginia	2,139,275	2,135,874	3,401	1,185.27	7	49.40	4
WISCONSIN	5,559,624	4,135,984	1,423,640	1,022.05	17	34.08	22
Wyoming	381,266	372,135	9,131	764.32	39	24.74	39
UNITED STATES	$279,597,690	$239,903,027	$39,694,663	$970.91		$31.53	

*Per capita amounts and ranks calculated by the Wisconsin Legislative Reference Bureau.

Source: U.S. Department of Commerce, Census Bureau, Governments Division, at: http://www.census.gov/govs/www/
estimate02.html [March 21, 2005] and U.S. Department of Commerce, Bureau of Economic Analysis, Regional Economic
Analysis Division, at: http://www.bea.doc.gov/bea/regional/spi [March 22, 2005].

WISCONSIN WORKS (W-2) EXPENDITURES, BY COUNTY
Calendar Years 2003 and 2004

County	2003 Average Monthly Caseload	2003 Average Monthly Payment	2003 Total Expenditures	2004 Average Monthly Caseload	2004 Average Monthly Payment	2004 Total Expenditures
Adams[1]	7	$560.42	$122,973	8	$579.40	$1,708,347
Ashland[2]	7	452.29	130,080	7	559.64	193,601
Barron	15	541.66	329,441	13	555.54	348,762
Bayfield	7	527.11	152,970	7	587.14	112,719
Brown	114	472.92	1,846,679	142	487.11	2,094,035
Buffalo	4	545.36	139,602	5	583.84	80,973
Burnett	2	557.58	52,391	1	570.50	46,306
Calumet	8	531.63	305,890	6	504.74	198,155
Chippewa	16	509.44	679,733	20	510.71	421,362
Clark	22	521.41	199,065	19	673.83	286,253
Columbia	16	510.48	459,967	17	603.73	343,724
Crawford	4	542.33	160,051	5	537.21	94,310
Dane[3]	425	536.05	7,713,345	415	542.93	6,464,378
Dodge[3]	44	555.29	845,628	41	---	---
Door	4	455.63	217,922	10	564.62	185,442
Douglas	31	588.76	971,035	34	615.96	650,890
Dunn	24	533.62	529,956	35	579.23	555,516
Eau Claire	48	533.72	1,075,575	52	506.16	818,391
Florence[4]	2	603.17	119,904	---	493.94	188,491
Fond du Lac	68	501.11	1,313,433	90	534.11	1,141,156
Forest[5]	11	560.33	1,002,914	8	587.92	880,639
Grant[6]	7	559.05	1,049,410	7	522.28	669,147
Green[6]	4	---	---	12	---	---
Green Lake	8	525.62	211,070	7	571.94	193,432
Iowa[6]	3	---	---	4	---	---
Iron	1	512.50	92,652	2	428.42	80,512
Jackson[7]	11	502.10	1,118,068	9	528.61	911,257
Jefferson	18	557.13	344,475	19	729.23	357,816
Juneau[7]	12	---	---	11	---	---
Kenosha	340	525.98	5,468,440	269	544.17	4,535,783
Kewaunee[4]	3	503.44	126,029	2	---	---
La Crosse	42	523.63	760,296	57	494.90	650,544
Lafayette[6]	3	---	---	3	---	---
Langlade[5]	15	---	---	13	---	---
Lincoln[5]	9	513.65	259,270	12	---	---
Manitowoc[8]	3	504.61	245,499	6	501.47	984,860
Marathon	82	537.00	1,768,258	68	514.03	1,487,637
Marinette	8	551.56	529,944	5	613.92	300,506
Marquette[3]	5	552.25	138,477	5	---	---
Menominee[4]	3	495.06	159,517	5	---	---
Milwaukee	8,435	552.91	107,950,397	9,632	577.45	110,519,654
Monroe[7]	26	---	---	29	---	---
Oconto	6	448.16	385,789	7	493.84	387,694
Oneida[5]	17	---	---	14	---	---
Outagamie	55	570.33	1,214,475	46	525.18	1,020,350
Ozaukee[9]	10	478.26	287,792	16	539.14	614,059
Pepin	1	383.00	78,433	2	535.19	49,020
Pierce[10]	8	502.61	100,649	8	562.50	357,122
Polk	9	679.54	436,858	4	535.69	252,664
Portage[1]	23	549.54	547,139	36	---	---
Price[2]	6	417.85	224,013	6	---	---
Racine	184	488.66	3,437,508	183	497.48	3,336,389
Richland[6]	10	---	---	7	---	---
Rock	164	535.37	3,189,659	167	520.88	2,173,427
Rusk	3	401.87	66,931	2	653.57	55,182
St. Croix[10]	7	535.33	283,846	9	---	---
Sauk[3]	14	575.05	414,043	9	---	---
Sawyer[11]	2	495.20	115,758	2	600.81	188,767
Shawano	14	541.55	384,600	15	518.86	269,358
Sheboygan[8]	45	568.57	889,915	62	---	---
Taylor	6	430.31	170,399	9	508.27	134,371
Trempealeau	9	599.06	270,416	13	540.65	196,426
Vernon	6	482.99	122,411	7	537.30	117,950
Vilas[5]	5	---	---	4	---	---
Walworth	35	567.24	713,297	41	556.16	531,441
Washburn[11]	4	563.89	106,684	2	---	---
Washington[9]	27	568.29	613,411	25	---	---
Waukesha	91	569.22	2,485,295	101	564.17	1,562,626
Waupaca	17	479.12	325,221	19	593.42	282,383
Waushara	14	473.28	228,309	12	682.23	199,568
Winnebago	57	540.57	1,508,613	71	526.06	1,127,724
Wood[1]	64	572.71	1,234,816	53	---	---
TOTAL[12]	10,829	$548.09	$158,479,047	12,060	$569.54	$150,361,117

[1]For 2004, Adams County data include Portage and Wood Counties in PAW Consortium. [2]For 2004, Ashland County data include Price County in Ashland Consortium. [3]For 2004, Dane County data include Dodge, Marquette, and Sauk Counties in Capital Consortium. [4]For 2004, Florence County data include Florence, Kewaunee, and Menominee Counties in FSC Bay Consortium. [5]For 2003 and 2004, Forest County FSC Northern Consortium includes Langlade, Oneida, and Vilas Counties, plus Lincoln County in 2004. [6]For 2003 and 2004, Grant County data include Green, Iowa, Lafayette, and Richland Counties in S/W Consortium. [7]For 2003 and 2004, Jackson County data include Juneau and Monroe Counties in Workforce Connections Consortium. [8]For 2004, Manitowoc County data include Sheboygan County in Lakeshore Consortium. [9]For 2004, Ozaukee County data include Washington County in WOW Consortium. [10]For 2004, Pierce County data include St. Croix County in Workforce Connections Consortium. [11]For 2004, Sawyer County data include Washburn County. [12]Includes Oneida Tribe, which ended its participation in Wisconsin Works effective May 1, 2003.

Source: Wisconsin Department of Workforce Development, departmental data, July 2005.

BADGERCARE AND MEDICAL ASSISTANCE IN WISCONSIN
By Type of Service, Fiscal Years 1999-2000 – 2003-04
(In Millions)

Fiscal Year	Nursing Care				Hospitals				Physicians and Clinics		Drugs		Home Care		Managed Care (HMO)[1]		Other Non-Institutional Fee-for-Service		Total Provider Payments[2,3]	
	Nursing Homes		State Centers		Inpatient		Outpatient													
	Amount	% of Total	Amount	% of Total	Amount	% of Total	Amount	% of Total	Amount	% of Total	Amount	% of Total	Amount	% of Total	Amount	% of Total	Amount	% of Total	Amount	Annual % Change
1999-2000	$906.3	29.8%	$135.9	4.5%	$270.6	8.9%	$55.3	1.8%	$63.2	2.1%	$336.5	11.1%	$498.8	16.4%	$394.4	13.0%	$251.8	8.3%	$3,044.0	--
2000-01	916.2	27.8	115.3	3.5	297.8	9.0	58.7	1.8	72.4	2.2	373.6	11.4	522.2	15.9	523.6	15.9	280.1	8.5	3,291.8	8.1%
2001-02	980.6	26.5	126.9	3.4	333.2	9.0	69.6	1.9	78.7	2.1	432.5	11.7	528.4	14.3	681.8	18.4	319.2	8.6	3,700.9	12.4
2002-03	990.6	25.7	123.9	3.2	332.0	8.6	75.6	2.0	85.2	2.2	494.7	12.9	592.6	15.4	657.9	17.1	334.5	8.7	3,849.2	4.0
2003-04	972.2	23.0	143.0	3.4	323.3	7.7	80.8	1.9	104.0	2.5	560.6	13.3	636.4	15.1	887.1	21.0	354.4	8.4	4,224.3	9.7

Note: Enrollments in BadgerCare began in July 1999, and expenditures for the program are included in the Medical Assistance figures above. Medical Assistance expenditure data prior to BadgerCare can be found in previous *Blue Books*.

[1]Includes payments to HMOs for low-income families and payments to Family Care CMOs, PACE/WPP, and I-Care.

[2]Does not include offsetting recoveries and collections, such as estate recoveries, drug rebates, etc.

[3]Total includes expenditures not listed separately.

Source: Wisconsin Department of Health and Family Services, departmental data, June 2005, and Wisconsin Legislative Fiscal Bureau. Percentages calculated by Wisconsin Legislative Reference Bureau.

MEDICAL ASSISTANCE IN WISCONSIN
Calendar Years 2003 and 2004

County	Recipients 2003	Recipients 2004	2004 as % of County Population	Expenditures 2003	Expenditures 2004	2004 Per Recipient Amount	Rank
Adams	4,032	4,305	20.79%	$13,439,422	$16,136,654	$3,748.35	55
Ashland	4,499	4,731	27.88	16,956,489	18,214,400	3,850.01	46
Barron	9,476	10,155	21.82	34,721,663	37,809,685	3,723.26	58
Bayfield	2,669	2,742	17.61	9,456,852	10,528,602	3,839.75	48
Brown	29,099	32,298	13.58	104,246,222	117,456,224	3,636.64	61
Buffalo	1,988	2,117	15.09	8,683,170	10,327,276	4,878.26	13
Burnett	3,214	3,313	20.20	11,916,601	12,728,517	3,841.99	47
Calumet	3,572	3,926	8.85	11,729,517	12,695,530	3,233.71	69
Chippewa	10,410	11,227	18.88	44,536,570	46,073,513	4,103.81	37
Clark	5,774	6,236	18.14	23,856,898	26,883,514	4,311.02	30
Columbia	5,829	6,525	11.95	24,021,593	26,741,135	4,098.26	38
Crawford	3,262	3,439	19.65	12,272,973	14,037,678	4,081.91	40
Dane	39,581	44,655	9.91	211,806,570	226,741,654	5,077.63	10
Dodge	9,497	10,506	11.90	43,653,805	47,285,452	4,500.80	19
Door	3,219	3,642	12.51	12,463,443	13,809,854	3,791.83	52
Douglas	9,241	9,665	22.11	36,788,837	40,987,992	4,240.87	33
Dunn	6,724	7,445	17.84	23,369,492	26,104,818	3,506.36	63
Eau Claire	15,205	17,137	17.81	64,033,452	68,950,143	4,023.47	42
Florence	857	892	17.11	2,990,400	3,903,409	4,376.02	27
Fond du Lac	12,119	13,720	13.77	66,520,885	68,762,760	5,011.86	12
Forest	2,031	2,142	21.00	8,611,029	9,709,310	4,532.82	17
Grant	6,733	7,239	14.32	33,261,416	37,413,632	5,168.34	8
Green	4,108	4,537	12.90	17,145,341	19,717,980	4,346.04	29
Green Lake	2,769	3,003	15.52	11,005,941	11,513,956	3,834.15	49
Iowa	2,584	2,819	11.93	9,660,036	11,797,022	4,184.83	35
Iron	1,411	1,522	21.91	5,901,617	6,888,123	4,525.70	18
Jackson	3,759	4,051	20.59	13,011,717	14,853,056	3,666.52	59
Jefferson	8,156	9,364	11.95	49,997,188	55,599,281	5,937.56	2
Juneau	4,712	5,236	20.56	18,250,189	20,488,771	3,913.06	43
Kenosha	26,778	29,093	18.64	93,563,551	108,713,736	3,736.77	57
Kewaunee	2,137	2,410	11.55	9,172,881	11,322,840	4,698.27	14
La Crosse	16,225	17,757	16.20	84,705,016	89,220,582	5,024.53	11
Lafayette	2,020	2,350	14.41	6,345,886	8,158,709	3,471.79	64
Langlade	4,409	4,697	22.13	16,256,582	17,760,375	3,781.22	53
Lincoln	4,255	4,621	15.27	17,806,067	20,329,179	4,399.30	24
Manitowoc	10,032	11,186	13.27	45,566,669	51,422,247	4,597.02	16
Marathon	17,910	19,373	14.91	62,231,167	67,182,429	3,467.84	65
Marinette	7,030	7,592	17.17	35,715,384	39,224,371	5,166.54	9
Marquette	2,497	2,749	18.26	7,650,595	8,989,057	3,269.94	68
Menominee	1,872	1,943	42.09	6,121,956	5,133,980	2,642.30	72
Milwaukee	247,045	253,786	27.02	1,048,693,679	1,086,329,490	4,280.49	32
Monroe	7,413	7,801	18.30	25,084,429	27,641,740	3,543.36	62
Oconto	4,829	5,305	14.08	17,103,653	19,834,347	3,738.80	56
Oneida	6,520	6,842	18.14	27,564,777	30,014,108	4,386.74	25
Outagamie	15,574	17,081	10.12	62,886,397	68,997,154	4,039.41	41
Ozaukee	4,081	4,668	5.48	20,691,890	24,760,203	5,304.24	4
Pepin	1,123	1,256	16.60	5,879,724	6,936,852	5,522.97	3
Pierce	3,902	4,500	11.65	15,382,843	17,500,047	3,888.90	44
Polk	6,268	6,565	14.96	26,075,799	29,345,780	4,470.03	21
Portage	8,617	9,739	14.13	42,251,208	42,666,165	4,380.96	26
Price	3,395	3,638	22.80	13,755,825	15,654,534	4,303.06	31
Racine	29,275	31,127	16.22	113,505,221	118,852,739	3,818.32	51
Richland	3,094	3,397	18.77	17,064,540	17,724,325	5,217.64	6
Rock	27,736	29,649	19.06	90,992,405	99,938,259	3,370.71	67
Rusk	3,613	3,707	23.90	13,932,372	15,400,168	4,154.35	36
St. Croix	6,432	7,125	9.82	29,382,597	31,809,261	4,464.46	22
Sauk	7,046	7,884	13.46	28,514,357	34,379,857	4,360.71	28
Sawyer	4,436	4,724	27.74	14,371,143	14,932,516	3,160.99	70
Shawano	6,061	6,705	15.99	25,219,815	30,114,340	4,491.33	20
Sheboygan	12,644	14,233	12.33	57,366,584	63,123,322	4,435.00	23
Taylor	3,409	3,659	18.41	12,217,809	14,144,690	3,865.73	45
Trempealeau	4,588	4,912	17.69	23,296,967	25,641,232	5,220.12	5
Vernon	4,369	4,754	16.43	17,845,910	19,909,529	4,187.95	34
Vilas	2,705	2,836	12.91	9,523,911	10,871,552	3,833.41	50
Walworth	11,238	12,813	13.20	42,248,828	46,857,847	3,657.06	60
Washburn	4,081	4,317	25.75	13,833,044	14,854,533	3,440.94	66
Washington	8,990	10,307	8.34	43,778,546	47,664,625	4,624.49	15
Waukesha	19,450	21,377	5.73	102,104,728	111,390,740	5,210.78	7
Waupaca	8,324	8,628	16.23	60,581,243	55,322,825	6,412.01	1
Waushara	4,075	4,288	17.29	11,254,088	11,909,243	2,777.34	71
Winnebago	18,698	20,481	12.65	73,437,892	83,855,232	4,094.29	39
Wood	12,150	13,190	17.30	44,016,783	49,636,436	3,763.19	54
STATE	887,138	945,010	17.08%	$3,659,682,632	$3,941,009,707	$4,170.34	

Note: State totals include categories not separately displayed, as well as some duplication of recipients if they resided in more than one county during the year.

Sources: Wisconsin Department of Health and Family Services, Division of Health Care Financing, departmental data; Department of Administration, Intergovernmental Relations Bureau, Demographic Services Center, *County Population Estimates, January 1, 2004*. Percentages and rankings calculated by Wisconsin Legislative Reference Bureau.

PRISON POPULATION AND CORRECTIONAL EXPENDITURES
By State, 1970 – 2004

State	Total confined as of Dec. 31[1]				Prison Population (as of 6/30/2004)		State Corrections Expenditures 2003		
	1970	1980	1990	2003	Total	Rate[2]	Total (in thousands)	Per Inmate Amount	Rank
Alabama	3,790	6,543	15,665	27,913	26,521	554	$356,928	$12,787	50
Alaska[3]	NA	822	2,622	4,527	4,515	367	182,046	40,213	14
Arizona[6]	1,461	4,372	14,261	31,170	31,631	506	731,041	23,453	39
Arkansas	NA	2,911	6,766	13,084	13,477	487	305,803	23,372	40
California	25,033	24,569	97,309	164,487	166,053	457	5,690,346	34,595	23
Colorado[5]	2,066	2,629	7,671	19,671	19,756	429	723,572	36,784	21
Connecticut[3]	1,568	4,308	10,500	19,846	20,018	379	615,670	31,022	29
Delaware[3]	596	1,474	3,471	6,794	6,973	487	206,085	30,333	30
District of Columbia[3]	1,423	3,145	8,637	--	--	--	--	--	--
Florida	9,187	20,735	44,387	82,012	84,733	489	2,141,271	26,109	38
Georgia[6]	5,113	12,178	22,345	47,208	48,625	551	1,271,565	26,935	36
Hawaii[3]	228	985	2,533	5,828	5,946	320	135,034	23,170	41
Idaho	411	817	1,961	5,887	6,312	454	164,813	27,996	35
ILLINOIS[5]	6,381	11,899	27,516	43,418	44,379	349	1,369,510	31,542	28
Indiana	4,137	6,683	12,736	23,069	23,760	380	654,475	28,370	33
IOWA	1,747	2,481	3,967	8,546	8,611	292	294,911	34,509	24
Kansas[5]	1,902	2,494	5,777	9,132	9,152	335	336,268	36,823	20
Kentucky	2,849	3,588	9,023	16,622	17,763	413	474,334	28,537	32
Louisiana	4,196	8,889	18,599	36,047	36,745	814	619,414	17,184	48
Maine	516	814	1,523	2,013	2,014	149	107,345	53,326	2
Maryland	5,186	7,731	17,848	23,791	23,727	416	1,050,389	44,151	10
Massachusetts[4]	2,053	3,185	8,273	10,232	10,365	234	1,049,512	102,572	1
MICHIGAN	9,079	15,124	34,267	49,358	48,591	480	1,678,957	34,016	26
MINNESOTA	1,585	2,001	3,176	7,865	8,613	169	403,527	51,307	3
Mississippi	1,730	3,902	8,375	20,589	20,429	682	295,629	14,359	49
Missouri	3,413	5,726	14,943	30,303	30,775	536	656,273	21,657	43
Montana	260	739	1,425	3,620	3,800	410	103,384	28,559	31
Nebraska	1,001	1,446	2,403	4,040	4,042	227	182,378	45,143	8
Nevada	690	1,839	5,322	10,543	10,971	468	216,356	20,521	45
New Hampshire	244	326	1,342	2,434	2,441	188	95,637	39,292	16
New Jersey[5]	5,704	5,884	21,128	27,246	28,107	323	1,294,773	47,522	6
New Mexico	742	1,279	3,187	6,223	6,341	319	264,845	42,559	11
New York	12,059	21,815	54,895	65,198	64,596	336	2,535,996	38,897	17
North Carolina	5,969	15,513	18,411	33,560	34,917	358	942,711	28,090	34
North Dakota	147	253	483	1,239	1,266	189	44,526	35,937	22
Ohio[5]	9,185	13,489	31,822	44,778	44,770	391	1,686,179	37,656	19
Oklahoma[5]	3,640	4,796	12,285	22,821	24,767	684	533,090	21,310	44
Oregon[5]	1,800	3,177	6,492	12,715	13,219	366	533,090	41,926	13
Pennsylvania	6,289	8,171	22,290	40,890	40,692	328	1,359,531	33,248	27
Rhode Island[3]	NA	813	2,392	3,527	3,701	187	159,095	45,108	9
South Carolina	2,726	7,862	17,319	23,719	24,173	555	426,300	17,973	47
South Dakota	391	635	1,341	3,026	3,101	402	79,858	26,391	37
Tennessee	3,268	7,022	10,388	25,403	25,834	439	558,669	21,992	42
Texas	14,331	29,892	50,042	166,911	169,110	704	3,201,068	19,178	46
Utah	491	932	2,496	5,763	5,802	239	261,283	45,338	7
Vermont[3]	162	480	1,049	1,944	2,033	236	81,767	42,061	12
Virginia	4,648	8,920	17,593	35,067	35,472	474	1,194,241	34,056	25
Washington	2,864	4,399	7,995	16,148	16,559	264	786,781	48,723	4
West Virginia	938	1,257	1,565	4,758	4,980	272	182,064	38,265	18
WISCONSIN[7]	2,973	3,980	7,362	22,614	22,614	394	906,725	40,096	15
Wyoming	231	534	1,110	1,872	1,923	382	89,551	47,837	5
UNITED STATES	174,968	302,313	706,288	1,468,530	1,494,216	486	$39,187,839	$26,685	

NA – Not available.

[1]Except where noted otherwise, total confined refers to prisoners under a state's jurisdiction, whether in the state's custody in its own institutions or in the custody of a local jail, another state's prison, or other correctional facility, including private institutions. The figure also includes federal prisoners located in the state. Jail inmates under the jurisdiction of local authorities are not included. District of Columbia inmates sentenced to more than one year are now under the responsibility of the Federal Bureau of Prisons.

[2]Number of state and federal prisoners with a sentence of more than one year per 100,000 state residents. Rates for states with integrated systems are likely to be overstated compared to states that do not include jails in total population counts.

[3]Prisons and jails form one integrated system. Data include total jail and prison population.

[4]An estimated 6,200 inmates sentenced to more than one year but held in local jails or houses of correction are excluded from the population count included in the incarceration rate. Adding them to the population count would reduce the average expenditure per inmate but not change the Commonwealth's ranking.

[5]"Sentenced to more than 1 year" includes some inmates "sentenced to 1 year or less."

[6]Population figures are based on custody counts.

[7]Custody counts exclude inmates held in non-Wisconsin DOC facilities under contract.

Sources: U.S. Department of Justice, Office of Justice Programs, Bureau of Justice Statistics, "Prison and Jail Inmates at Midyear 2004" [April 24, 2005]; U.S. Department of Commerce, U.S. Census Bureau, "State Government Finances: 2003" [April 2005]. Per inmate averages calculated by Wisconsin Legislative Reference Bureau.

STATE CORRECTIONS AND DHFS INSTITUTIONS
Population, 1970 – 2004

Institutions	2004 Avg. Pop.	Rated Cap.[1]	1970	1980	1990	2000	2002	2003
STATE CORRECTIONS POPULATION								
Maximum Security								
Assessment and Evaluation[2]	1,135	934	--	--	--	--	1,076	1,110
Columbia Correctional Institution	815	541	--	--	477	808	805	816
Dodge Correctional Institution[2]	353	261	--	88	551	1,377	363	351
Green Bay Correctional Institution	1,069	749	755	658	832	1,002	1,021	1,042
Wisconsin Secure Program Facility	426	426	--	--	--	101	325	381
Waupun Correctional Institution	1,233	882	954	1,087	1,126	1,225	1,212	1,216
Maximum/Medium	5,031	3,793	1,709	1,833	2,986	4,513	4,802	4,916
Taycheedah Correctional Institution (women)	668	653	141	123	203	644	597	630
Medium Security								
Fox Lake Correctional Institution	1,024	691	553	570	785	1,112	972	1,016
Jackson Correctional Institution	970	837	--	--	--	971	975	973
Kettle Moraine Correctional Institution	1,174	783	293	368	542	1,233	1,168	1,170
New Lisbon Correctional Institution[3]	110	950	--	--	--	--	--	--
Oshkosh Correctional Institution	2,030	1,494	--	--	444	1,859	1,895	1,921
Prairie du Chien Correctional Institution[4]	386	326	--	--	--	297	304	304
Racine Correctional Institution	1,503	1,021	--	--	--	1,414	1,413	1,459
Racine Youthful Offender Correctional Facility	439	400	--	--	--	395	393	395
Red Granite Correctional Institution	975	990	--	--	--	--	893	966
Stanley	1,482	1,500	--	--	--	--	--	587
Minimum Security	10,093	8,992	846	938	1,771	7,281	8,013	8,791
Chippewa Valley Correctional Treatment Center[3]	63	450	--	--	--	--	--	--
Fox Lake	274	288	--	--	--	--	276	275
Oakhill Correctional Institution	591	300	--	198	368	564	586	591
Sturtevant Transitional Facility[3]	80	150	--	--	--	--	--	--
Wis. Correctional Center System[5]	2,121	1,570	390	276	1,071	1,816	1,953	2,037
Detention Facility	3,129	2,758	390	474	1,439	2,380	2,815	2,903
Milwaukee Secure Detention Facility	1,001	396	--	--	--	--	464	929
Contract Facilities								
Federal Contract[6]	25	--	--	--	--	--	140	27
In-State[7]	305	--	--	--	--	--	289	195
Corrections Corporation of America[8]	1,759	--	--	--	--	--	3,602	3,120
Other Adults	2,089	--	--	--	78	4,665	4,031	3,342
Community Residential Confinement	--	--	--	--	48	--	--	--
Division of Intensive Sanctions	--	--	--	--	--	412	--	--
Parole and mandatory release[9]	12,335	--	4,329	3,045	4,217	8,951	10,037	11,014
Probation	56,126	--	4,530	16,797	25,907	55,046	56,040	56,211
Juvenile Corrections[10]	68,461	--	8,859	19,842	30,172	64,409	66,077	67,225
Ethan Allen School	322	342	365	306	320	438	401	378
Lincoln Hills School	263	298	--	245	252	330	329	304
Southern Oaks Girls School	70	57	--	--	--	87	87	79
Youth Leadership Training Center[11]	--	--	--	--	--	40	10	--
SPRITE Program	9	12	--	--	--	9	9	9
Juvenile Correctional Camp System	--	--	81	24	--	--	--	--
	664	709	446	575	572	904	836	770
Juvenile Aftercare	178	--	--	--	--	--	250	250
TOTAL POPULATION	91,314		12,391	23,785	37,221	84,796	87,885	89,756
MENTAL HEALTH INSTITUTIONS (MHI)								
Mendota MHI	224	246	522	202	266	238	230	232
Winnebago MHI	266	290	574	310	266	279	277	272
Mendota Juvenile Treatment Center	29	29	--	--	--	43	33	29
Sand Ridge Secure Treatment Center	212	250	--	--	--	72	170	199
Central State Hospital	--	--	258	154	--	--	--	--
Wisconsin Resource Center	379	380	--	--	161	421	382	371
CENTERS FOR DEVELOPMENTALLY DISABLED (CDD)								
Central Wisconsin CDD	349	408	1,070	731	606	380	364	354
Northern Wisconsin CDD	157	189	1,421	676	495	189	184	173
Southern Wisconsin CDD	261	315	1,207	735	576	274	267	265
TOTAL POPULATION	1,877	2,107	5,052	2,808	2,370	1,896	1,907	1,895

[1]For Department of Corrections, "operating capacity" is defined as the original design capacity of the institution, based on industry standards, plus modifications and expansions. It excludes beds and multiple bunking that were instituted to accommodate crowding. Department of Health and Family Services Care and Treatment Facilities' capacity is "staffed capacity" based on staffing and other budgetary resources rather than number of beds. [2]Dodge Correctional Institution serves as the assessment and evaluation center for sentenced adult felons. Operating capacity is 934 (includes 30 for females) for reception and 261 institutional. ADP includes 69 women in 2002, 70 women in 2003, and 72 women in 2004. [3]New Lisbon and Chippewa Valley opened April 2004. Sturtevant opened December 2003. [4]Prairie du Chien was designed as a juvenile institution for boys, but currently houses 15-21 year-old males and minors convicted in adult courts. [5]Includes 563 women in 2002, 612 women in 2003, and 594 women in 2004. Capacity includes 470 for women. [6]Includes 62 women in 2001. [7]Includes 31 women in 2002 and 100 women in 2001. [8]CCA prisons holding Wisconsin prisoners are located in Minnesota and Oklahoma. Includes 63 women in 2001. [9]Parole data through 1991 included juveniles; figures from 1992 to date do not include juvenile cases. [10]Juvenile incarceration has been administered by the Department of Corrections since July 1, 1996. [11]Youth Leadership Training Camp program, formerly at Camp Douglas and closed in February 2002, is now part of the program at Lincoln Hills.
Sources: Wisconsin Department of Corrections, *Fiscal Year Summary Report of Population Movement for 1991* and previous issues, and departmental data, June 2005 and prior years; Wisconsin Department of Health and Family Services, departmental data, June 2005 and prior years.

HIGHLIGHTS OF STATE AND LOCAL FINANCE IN WISCONSIN

Revenues and Expenditures — In the 2003-04 fiscal year, Wisconsin state government received total revenues of $41.6 billion from all sources, including federal and nontax revenue, and its expenditures totaled $33.9 billion. $21.7 billion of these expenditures were general fund and the remaining $12.2 billion were from special funds (such as the conservation and transportation funds), federal funding, pension and retirement funds, and other sources.

Of the total state budget allocations of $47.9 billion for the 2003-05 biennium, state operations accounted for 34.0% ($16.3 billion) and local assistance for 37.7% ($18.0 billion). The remaining 28.4% ($13.6 billion) comprised aids to individuals and organizations.

For the 2003-04 fiscal year, two state agencies accounted for about 36.7% of total state expenditures. The largest expenditure total was $6.6 billion (20.0%) by the Department of Health and Family Services. Expenditures by the Department of Public Instruction, including state aids to local schools, were $5.5 billion (16.7%). Shared revenue and tax relief of $1.9 billion accounted for 5.9%.

Total state tax revenues for 2003-04 were just over $11.9 billion, including about $10.7 billion in general purpose revenue. These collections were about $0.6 billion higher than during fiscal year 2002-03. Revenue from income taxes totaled a little over $5.9 billion, about $5.3 billion of which was individual income taxes and $651 million in corporation income taxes, while sales and excise taxes were about $4.3 billion.

State-Local Finances — In 2001-02, Wisconsin ranked 17th nationally in total per capita state and local government general revenues ($5,984, or slightly more than the U.S. average of $5,851). In total direct general state and local government per capita expenditures, Wisconsin ranked 14th ($6,250 compared to the U.S. average of $6,011).

Wisconsin returned slightly more than $1.4 billion to local units of government in property tax relief and shared revenue in fiscal year 2005 ($469.3 million as school levy credits and about $951.7 million in shared revenue).

Property Taxes — General property taxes levied in Wisconsin in 2003 totaled almost $7.7 billion for a net amount of about $7.2 billion after state property tax relief. Milwaukee County had the highest effective (full value equalized) net tax rate ($25.13 per $1,000) and Vilas County the lowest ($11.28 per $1,000). Residential taxpayers paid almost 70% of the total, compared to about 19% commercial and 3% manufacturing.

State-Federal Finances — Federal tax receipts from Wisconsin in fiscal year 2004 totaled over $34.7 billion, with the largest amount generated by individual income and employment taxes ($30.4 billion). Federal expenditures in Wisconsin – including grants to state and local government, salaries and wages, direct payments to individuals, procurement, and other programs – amounted to $5,525 per resident. This distribution, on a per capita basis, ranked Wisconsin 48th among the states in federal funds received, with only Minnesota ($5,451) and Nevada ($5,193) lower. Alaska was the highest at $12,244 per person.

Direct federal aid to Wisconsin in 2003-04 totaled $6.92 billion, and about 53% of that applied to health and family services. Local units of government received almost $1.24 billion for all functions.

Indebtedness — Total outstanding state government debt in Wisconsin, as of May 31, 2005, amounted to $4.91 billion, of which $3.8 billion was tax-supported and $1.11 billion was revenue-supported. Total state indebtedness at the end of 2003 constituted 1.33% of state-assessed valuation and amounted to $876.17 per capita. Local debt in 2003 totaled almost $11.9 billion. Among state political subdivisions, school district debt ($5.02 billion) was largest, followed by city debt ($3.34 billion).

The following tables present selected data. Consult footnoted sources for more detailed information about state and local finance.

STATE BUDGET ALLOCATIONS
By Type of Revenue Source
Fiscal Years 2003-04 and 2004-05

Revenue Type and Allocation	2003-04	2004-05	2003-05 Total	% of Total – All Sources
GENERAL PURPOSE REVENUE	**$10,673,036,500**	**$11,767,851,700**	**$22,440,888,200**	**46.87%**
State operations	2,460,379,700	2,572,272,600	5,032,652,300	10.51
Local assistance	6,590,747,700	6,767,703,200	13,358,450,900	27.90
Aids to individuals and organizations	1,621,909,100	2,427,875,900	4,049,785,000	8.46
PROGRAM REVENUE – TOTAL	**$9,098,338,100**	**$9,042,333,300**	**$18,140,671,400**	**37.89%**
State operations	4,002,722,900	4,112,257,800	8,114,980,700	16.95
Local assistance	1,131,200,900	944,646,000	2,075,846,900	4.34
Aids to individuals and organizations	3,964,414,300	3,985,429,500	7,949,843,800	16.60
Program Revenue – Federal	5,710,050,800	5,509,198,900	11,219,249,700	23.43
State operations	969,608,900	962,453,200	1,932,062,100	4.04
Local assistance	1,043,889,400	855,609,200	1,899,498,600	3.97
Aids to individuals and organizations	3,696,552,500	3,691,136,500	7,387,689,000	15.43
Program Revenue – Service	833,499,900	860,070,200	1,693,570,100	3.54
State operations	593,537,600	607,721,600	1,201,259,200	2.51
Local assistance	62,629,900	62,904,700	125,534,600	0.26
Aids to individuals and organizations	177,332,400	189,443,900	366,776,300	0.77
Program Revenue – Other	2,554,787,400	2,673,064,200	5,227,851,600	10.92
State operations	2,439,576,400	2,542,083,000	4,981,659,400	10.40
Local assistance	24,681,600	26,132,100	50,813,700	0.11
Aids to individuals and organizations	90,529,400	104,849,100	195,378,500	0.41
SEGREGATED REVENUE – TOTAL	**$3,824,478,900**	**$3,471,892,600**	**$7,296,371,500**	**15.24%**
State operations	1,485,214,000	1,637,029,200	3,122,243,200	6.52
Local assistance	1,312,332,600	1,277,841,400	2,590,174,000	5.41
Aids to individuals and organizations	1,026,932,300	557,022,000	1,583,954,300	3.31
Segregated Revenue – Federal	633,682,200	663,188,700	1,296,870,900	2.71
State operations	454,626,200	479,122,300	933,748,500	1.95
Local assistance	173,895,100	178,747,100	352,642,200	0.74
Aids to individuals and organizations	5,160,900	5,319,300	10,480,200	0.02
Segregated Revenue – Local	73,184,000	70,750,700	143,934,700	0.30
State operations	5,989,700	5,989,700	11,979,400	0.03
Local assistance	59,463,800	56,530,500	115,994,300	0.24
Aids to individuals and organizations	7,730,500	8,230,500	15,961,000	0.03
Segregated Revenue – Service	174,894,000	175,319,800	350,213,800	0.73
State operations	174,894,000	175,319,800	350,213,800	0.73
Segregated Revenue – Other	2,942,718,700	2,562,633,400	5,505,352,100	11.50
State operations	849,704,100	976,597,400	1,826,301,500	3.81
Local assistance	1,078,973,700	1,042,563,800	2,121,537,500	4.43
Aids to individuals and organizations	1,014,040,900	543,472,200	1,557,513,100	3.25
FEDERAL REVENUE – TOTAL	**$6,343,733,000**	**$6,172,387,600**	**$12,516,120,600**	**26.14%**
State operations	1,424,235,100	1,441,575,500	2,865,810,600	5.99
Local assistance	1,217,784,500	1,034,356,300	2,252,140,800	4.70
Aids to individuals and organizations	3,701,713,400	3,696,455,800	7,398,169,200	15.45
TOTAL – ALL SOURCES	**$23,595,853,500**	**$24,282,077,600**	**$47,877,931,100**	**100.00%**
State operations	7,948,316,600	8,321,559,600	16,269,876,200	33.98
Local assistance	9,034,281,200	8,990,190,600	18,024,471,800	37.65
Aids to individuals and organizations	6,613,255,700	6,970,327,400	13,583,583,100	28.37

General purpose revenue: general taxes, miscellaneous receipts and revenues collected by state agencies that are paid into the general fund, lose their identity, and are available for appropriation by the legislature.

Program revenue: revenues paid into the general fund and credited by law to an appropriation used to finance a specific program or agency.

Segregated fund revenue: revenues deposited, by law, into funds other than the general fund and available only for the purposes for which such funds were created.

Federal revenue: money received from the federal government (may be disbursed either through a segregated fund or through the general fund).

Service revenue: money transferred between or within state agencies for reimbursement for services rendered or materials purchased.

State operations: amounts budgeted to operate programs carried out by state government.

Local assistance: amounts budgeted as state aids to assist programs carried out by local governmental units in Wisconsin.

Source: Wisconsin Department of Administration, State Budget Office, departmental data, April 2005. Percentages and totals calculated by Wisconsin Legislative Reference Bureau.

WISCONSIN STATE REVENUES – ALL FUNDS
Fiscal Years 2001-02, 2002-03, and 2003-04
(In Thousands)

	2001-02	2002-03	2003-04
TOTAL GENERAL FUND TAX REVENUES*	$10,036,703	$10,217,994	$10,759,514
TOTAL GPR TAX REVENUES*	$10,020,184	$10,199,739	$10,739,319
Income Taxes*	5,482,670	5,578,542	5,927,645
Individual	4,979,662	5,051,997	5,277,119
Corporation	503,008	526,545	650,526
Sales and Excise Taxes*	4,044,078	4,092,672	4,254,759
General Sales and Use	3,695,796	3,737,912	3,899,264
Cigarette	288,769	293,697	291,323
Other Tobacco Products	13,932	15,508	16,101
Liquor and Wine	35,984	36,038	38,470
Malt Beverage (beer)	9,597	9,517	9,601
Public Utility Taxes*	252,237	276,790	269,801
Private Light, Heat, and Power	143,134	147,018	165,436
Municipal Light, Heat, and Power	1,657	1,729	1,813
Telephone	86,638	106,256	81,587
Pipeline	10,260	10,542	10,555
Electric Cooperative	8,586	9,417	8,486
Municipal Electric	1,273	1,233	1,296
Conservation and Regulation	567	552	512
Utility Tax (Refunds) Interest and Penalties	122	43	116
Inheritance, Estate, and Gift Taxes*	82,635	68,702	86,357
Inheritance and Estate	82,631	68,702	86,357
Gift	4	0	0
Miscellaneous Taxes*	158,564	183,033	200,757
Insurance Companies (Premiums)	96,055	114,897	123,621
Real Estate Transfer Fee	51,176	57,384	66,325
Lawsuits (Courts)	10,455	10,567	10,691
Other	878	185	120
PROGRAM TAX REVENUES*	16,519	18,255	20,195
Fire Dues	11,297	13,350	14,768
Pari-mutuel Taxes	2,104	1,916	1,804
County Expo Tax Administration	356	370	385
Baseball Park Administration Fee	365	354	319
Business Trust Regulation Fee	1,692	1,520	2,094
Other	705	745	825
TRANSPORTATION FUND*	887,934	925,087	959,594
Motor Fuel Tax	865,454	902,480	934,605
Air Carrier Tax	5,651	5,446	8,195
Railroad Tax	12,011	12,459	11,923
Aviation Fuel Tax	1,226	1,312	1,348
Other Taxes	3,592	3,390	3,523
CONSERVATION FUND*	65,885	70,923	76,800
2/10 Mill Forestry Mill Tax	62,425	67,063	72,190
Forest Crop Taxes	3,460	3,860	4,610
MEDIATION FUND	3	3	3
PETROLEUM INSPECTION TAX	88,694	93,686	92,563
RECYCLING FUND TEMPORARY SERVICE CHARGES	12,529	15,428	25,543
TOTAL STATE TAX REVENUES	$11,091,748	$11,323,121	$11,914,017
TOTAL DEPARTMENTAL REVENUES*	14,371,347	19,019,880	28,824,413
Intergovernmental Revenue	7,203,159	7,518,310	7,302,464
Licenses and Permits	805,536	845,776	969,210
Charges for Goods and Services	1,747,654	2,587,332	2,784,392
Contributions	1,768,712	2,038,155	2,980,855
Interest and Investment Income	(3,541,516)	2,038,503	9,696,273
Gifts and Donations	337,322	343,153	341,902
Proceeds from Sale of Bonds	785,364	646,000	2,706,057
Other Revenues	3,913,624	2,082,322	1,797,449
Other Transactions	1,351,492	920,329	245,811
TRANSFERS	1,307,220	939,406	847,007
TOTAL REVENUES	$26,770,315	$31,282,407	$41,585,437

*Total of subsequent detail.

Source: Wisconsin Department of Administration, *2004 Annual Fiscal Report,* October 15, 2004.

WISCONSIN STATE EXPENDITURES BY AGENCY
Fiscal Years 2002-03 and 2003-04

Agency	2002-03		2003-04	
	Amount	Percent	Amount	Percent
Administration, Department of*	$416,979,375	1.31%	$1,980,905,067	6.02%
Adolescent Pregnancy Prevention and Pregnancy Services Board*	581,517	0.00+	--	--
Aging and Long-Term Care, Board on	1,665,556	0.01	1,687,545	0.01
Agriculture, Trade and Consumer Protection, Department of	72,297,488	0.23	70,186,771	0.21
Arts Board	3,319,963	0.01	3,129,124	0.01
Child Abuse and Neglect Prevention Board	2,471,002	0.01	2,567,512	0.01
Commerce, Department of	228,543,454	0.72	287,807,586	0.87
Corrections, Department of	1,004,308,193	3.16	986,734,527	3.00
District Attorneys (DOA)	42,243,867	0.13	43,654,473	0.13
Educational Communications Board	14,423,625	0.05	13,233,735	0.04
Electronic Government, Department of*	125,826,108	0.40	--	--
Elections Board	1,790,985	0.01	1,598,317	0.00+
Employee Trust Funds, Department of	3,787,884,323	11.92	4,136,292,854	12.57
Employment Relations Commission	2,727,766	0.01	2,725,626	0.01
Employment Relations, Department of*	6,495,263	0.02	--	--
Employment Relations, Office of State*	--	--	5,614,343	0.02
Environmental Improvement Program (DOA)	159,547,483	0.50	149,199,289	0.45
Ethics Board	672,460	0.00+	634,141	0.00+
Financial Institutions, Department of	15,176,426	0.05	13,830,981	0.04
Governor, Office of the	3,304,194	0.01	3,156,245	0.01
Health and Family Services, Department of*	6,671,262,840	21.00	6,584,549,062	20.01
Higher Educational Aids Board	73,507,597	0.23	80,706,226	0.25
Historical Society, State	18,125,441	0.06	16,856,091	0.05
Insurance, Office of the Commissioner of	72,446,387	0.23	65,132,450	0.20
Investment Board	16,402,481	0.05	19,081,903	0.06
Justice, Department of	86,961,867	0.27	82,178,126	0.25
Lieutenant Governor, Office of the	417,087	0.00+	374,348	0.00+
Lower Wisconsin State Riverway Board	152,713	0.00+	163,999	0.00+
Medical College of Wisconsin, Inc.	7,628,095	0.02	5,502,148	0.02
Military Affairs, Department of	60,568,938	0.19	62,680,663	0.19
Natural Resources, Department of	521,320,279	1.64	433,514,460	1.32
Personnel Commission	780,455	0.00+	89,198	0.00+
Public Defender, Office of the	66,097,174	0.21	80,906,739	0.25
Public Instruction, Department of	5,352,230,024	16.85	5,488,535,128	16.68
Public Lands, Board of Commissioners of	1,383,500	0.00+	1,483,192	0.00+
Public Service Commission	19,559,049	0.06	20,665,512	0.06
Regulation and Licensing, Department of	11,509,185	0.04	11,080,967	0.03
Revenue, Department of	406,642,278	1.28	438,689,365	1.33
Secretary of State, Office of the	673,345	0.00+	628,974	0.00+
State Fair Park Board	19,264,115	0.06	22,494,325	0.07
TEACH Wisconsin Board*	66,503,769	0.21	--	--
Technical College System Board	177,701,643	0.56	175,849,387	0.53
Tobacco Control Board*	16,949,605	0.05	--	--
Tourism, Department of	14,319,001	0.05	13,573,361	0.04
Transportation, Department of	2,283,862,551	7.19	1,957,671,040	5.95
Treasurer, Office of the State	2,652,759	0.01	9,748,120	0.03
University of Wisconsin System	3,439,322,984	10.83	3,647,964,152	11.08
Veterans Affairs, Department of	422,748,111	1.33	306,072,447	0.93
Workforce Development, Department of	2,076,298,629	6.54	1,977,532,573	6.01
TOTAL EXECUTIVE	$27,797,550,950	87.50%	$29,206,682,091	88.74%
TOTAL JUDICIAL	110,052,974	0.34	111,239,028	0.33
TOTAL LEGISLATIVE	61,219,698	0.19	59,302,088	0.18
Shared Revenue/Tax Relief	1,339,719,141	4.22	1,945,399,588	5.91
Miscellaneous Appropriations	1,312,217,153	4.13	116,113,694	0.35
Program Supplements	25,944,041	0.08	44,395,080	0.13
Public Debt	705,482,725	2.22	630,948,266	1.92
Building Commission	9,695,486	0.03	5,736,073	0.02
BUILDING PROGRAM	408,241,886	1.28	791,678,647	2.41
GRAND TOTAL	$31,770,124,053	100.00%	$32,911,494,555	100.00%

*"Negative expenditures" during 2003-04 for entities that were eliminated are combined with the expenditures for the state agencies that absorbed the functions. The former Adolescent Pregnancy Prevention and Pregnancy Services Board and Tobacco Control Board functions are now in the Department of Health and Family Services. The responsibilities of the Department of Electronic Government and the TEACH Wisconsin Board are now in the Department of Administration. The Department of Employment Relations is now the Office of State Employment Relations.

Source: Wisconsin Department of Administration, State Controller's Office, *Appendix to Annual Fiscal Report*, October 2003 and October 2004. Agency percentages calculated by Wisconsin Legislative Reference Bureau.

WISCONSIN TRANSPORTATION FUND REVENUES AND EXPENDITURES[1]
Fiscal Years 2002-03 and 2003-04

	2002-03		2003-04	
	State Funds	Federal, Local, and Agency Funds	State Funds	Federal, Local, and Agency Funds
OPENING BALANCE	$129,651,842	($675,111,119)	$113,824,572	($776,667,607)
REVENUES				
Motor fuel taxes	$902,478,327	---	$934,604,657	---
Vehicle registration	268,337,395	---	301,345,516	---
Drivers license fees	29,819,421	---	29,936,470	---
Motor carrier fees	2,689,498	---	2,088,172	---
Other motor vehicle fees	22,482,269	---	21,825,084	---
Overweight/oversize permits	4,327,215	---	4,468,123	---
Investment earnings	3,692,268	---	2,714,286	---
Aeronautical taxes and fees	7,306,329	---	9,924,474	---
Railroad property taxes	12,459,264	---	11,923,899	---
Dealers' licenses	869,235	---	750,105	---
Miscellaneous	30,997,822	$2,277,139	7,744,129	$3,034,543
Service center operations	---	20,610,110	---	19,880,850
State and local highway facilities – Federal	---	510,969,149	---	518,893,680
State and local highway facilities – Local	---	69,712,722	---	64,940,856
Major highway development – Revenue bonds	---	136,980,925	---	184,656,179
Highway administration and planning – Federal	---	4,713,444	---	4,530,861
Aeronautics – Federal	---	41,800,452	---	50,311,769
Aeronautics – Local	---	25,195,280	---	32,356,234
Railroad assistance – Federal	---	5,548,164	---	1,542,242
Railroad assistance – Local	---	4,958,800	---	5,130,116
Railroad passenger service – Federal	---	3,578,078	---	8,444,663
Railroad passenger service – Local	---	324,692	---	792,326
Transit assistance – Federal	---	24,398,168	---	24,950,954
Transit assistance – Local	---	582,371	---	662,263
Congestion mitigation air quality – Federal	---	3,568,122	---	3,973,310
Congestion mitigation air quality – Local	---	889,745	---	1,689,588
Surface transportation grants – Federal	---	2,120,374	---	1,410,162
Surface transportation grants – Local	---	503,731	---	374,682
Transportation enhancement activities – Federal	---	7,623,039	---	6,248,846
Transportation enhancement activities – Local	---	3,162,689	---	698,385
Transportation facilities economic assistance and development – Local	---	(35,811)	---	128,750
Transportation planning grants	---	803,990	---	808,860
Multimodal transportation studies – Federal	---	386,733	---	32,327
General administration and planning – Federal	---	25,150,844	---	26,687,763
General administration and planning – Local	---	1,304,032	---	1,064,307
Administrative facilities – Revenue bonds	---	5,760,000	---	3,314,193
Highway safety – Federal	---	2,686,988	---	1,911,467
Gifts and grants	---	387,003	---	123,955
TOTAL REVENUES	$1,285,459,043	$905,960,973	$1,327,324,915	$968,594,131
TOTAL AVAILABLE	$1,415,110,885	$230,849,854	$1,441,149,487	$191,926,524

WISCONSIN TRANSPORTATION FUND
REVENUES AND EXPENDITURES[1]
Fiscal Years 2002-03 and 2003-04–Continued

	2002-03		2003-04	
EXPENDITURES	State Funds	Federal, Local, and Agency Funds	State Funds	Federal, Local, and Agency Funds
Local Assistance				
Highway aids	$382,748,763	---	$389,528,317	---
Local bridge and highway improvement	34,431,211	$124,152,136	25,733,196	$144,777,114
Mass transit	104,031,400	17,411,456	106,119,408	21,852,379
Railroads	1,868,346	(96,743)	1,826,268	375,892
Aeronautics	14,074,247	88,465,513	9,849,623	67,051,559
Highway safety	---	2,315,748	---	1,814,116
Multimodal transportation studies	1,538,250	176,400	(71,083)	---
Rail passenger service	397,564	6,551,142	1,012,350	12,432,436
Surface transportation grants	---	2,179,012	---	1,060,465
Harbors	90,562	---	55,338	---
Transportation planning grants to local governmental units	---	994,240	---	---
Transportation enhancement activities	---	15,717,454	---	13,862,720
Public Instruction – General equalization aids	---	---	40,000,000	---
Shared revenue and municipal aid	---	---	230,000,000	---
Total Local Assistance	$539,180,343	$257,866,358	$804,053,417	$263,226,681
Aids to Individuals and Organizations				
Transportation facilities economic assistance and development	$1,541,148	$375,971	$4,479,802	($690,797)
Railroad crossings	3,918,803	3,945,835	4,480,053	6,220,498
Elderly and disabled	879,446	1,426,762	456,637	2,059,783
Freight rail	2,766,692	(2,370,000)	(104,172)	3,030,834
Total Aids to Individuals and Organizations	$9,106,089	$3,378,568	$9,312,320	$10,620,318
State Operations				
Highway improvements	$320,033,058	$521,231,814	$63,587,627	$437,244,714
Major highway development – Revenue bonds	---	149,950,338	---	189,841,533
Highway maintenance, repair, and traffic operations	196,338,772	8,753,861	166,023,550	728,719
Highway administration and planning	17,564,867	4,557,636	18,224,972	4,049,193
Traffic enforcement and inspection	53,004,272	5,096,032	54,058,262	6,093,685
General administration and planning	55,620,095	16,627,826	54,986,706	14,212,280
Administrative facilities – Revenue bonds	---	5,923,760	---	3,135,800
Vehicle registration and drivers licensing	74,084,036	621,946	74,181,162	672,976
Vehicle inspection and maintenance	7,809,535	3,754,800	7,750,457	6,321,700
Debt repayment and interest	4,684,559	---	6,611,407	---
Service centers	---	16,797,083	---	18,059,201
Congestion mitigation air quality	---	7,971,855	---	9,325,128
Miscellaneous	7,278,018	4,985,584	1,195,819	800,359
Total State Operations	$736,417,212	$746,272,535	$446,619,962	$690,485,288
Transfers				
Conservation fund	$16,582,669	---	$17,497,710	---
General fund[2]	---	---	103,683,900	---
Total Transfers	$16,582,669	0	$121,181,610	0
TOTAL EXPENDITURES	$1,301,286,313	$1,007,517,461	$1,381,167,309	$964,332,287
UNRESERVED FUND BALANCE	$113,824,572	($776,667,607)	$59,982,178	($772,405,763)

[1]The Transportation Fund is a multipurpose special revenue fund created to provide resources for transportation related facilities and modes with revenues derived from users of transportation facilities. Transportation facilities and major highway projects are also funded with revenue bonds.

[2]Transfer to the general fund required by 2003 Wisconsin Act 33 (2003-05 biennial budget act).

Source: Wisconsin Department of Administration, Bureau of Financial Operations, *2004 Annual Fiscal Report (Budgetary Basis)* Appendix.

WISCONSIN CONSERVATION FUND
REVENUES, EXPENDITURES AND BALANCES
Fiscal Years 1999-2000 – 2003-04

	1999-2000	2000-01	2001-02	2002-03	2003-04
OPENING CASH BALANCE	$54,721,799	$62,236,240	$55,242,837	$40,521,057	$22,913,012
REVENUES	205,822,905	211,013,810	217,255,388	230,335,769	234,076,587
User fees (licenses, registration)	79,657,097	79,435,959	80,983,195	80,518,675	91,022,359
Forestry mill tax	53,312,623	57,226,371	62,507,745	67,063,094	72,189,588
Federal aids	24,492,738	26,255,098	30,271,993	37,025,736	26,425,275
Motor fuel tax formula	14,353,522	17,569,751	16,202,509	20,800,718	21,147,710
Severance tax	4,748,627	1,339,803	3,459,695	3,859,905	4,610,242
Other revenues (sales, services)	29,258,298	29,186,828	23,830,251	21,067,641	18,681,413
EXPENDITURES	197,678,464	217,507,090	231,977,168	247,943,755	228,896,029
Land management – state	63,851,035	67,513,760	73,431,021	80,986,487	76,923,406
Land management – federal	6,438,538	8,376,400	6,585,224	6,596,082	8,411,268
Enforcement/science – state	17,866,940	22,463,690	20,112,462	22,126,883	20,035,522
Enforcement/science – federal	4,961,788	6,025,977	5,723,864	5,908,960	5,465,792
Water management – state	16,471,802	19,081,813	19,848,117	20,728,513	19,542,407
Water management – federal	4,669,849	4,534,503	4,018,207	4,060,084	4,095,346
Conservation aids – state	23,932,179	21,183,529	29,995,186	28,720,052	24,503,633
Conservation aids – federal	950,574	1,246,463	1,268,468	1,730,262	1,820,296
Environmental aids – state	2,227,782	4,276,268	2,905,418	3,055,285	2,736,567
Development/debt service – state ...	6,634,967	7,351,042	9,860,459	12,300,815	14,117,341
Development/debt service – federal ..	2,011,062	2,889,352	2,025,606	9,173,151	4,646,964
Administrative services – state	24,186,216	25,888,808	27,799,749	16,531,910	15,267,898
Administrative services – federal	3,025,586	5,079,318	5,555,301	5,926,469	5,615,766
CAER management – state*	12,777,831	13,299,044	14,785,699	14,683,151	14,007,620
CAER management – federal*	2,136,800	1,386,732	485,181	979,319	709,948
Other activities – state	5,535,515	6,910,391	7,577,206	14,436,332	10,996,255
TRANSFER TO GENERAL FUND ...	---	500,000	---	59	57,916
FUND BALANCE	$62,866,240	$55,242,960	$40,521,057	$22,913,012	$28,035,654

*CAER – Customer Assistance and External Relations.

Note: The Conservation Fund is a segregated fund that provides funding for many activities of the Wisconsin Department of Natural Resources, including fish and wildlife management, forestry, parks and recreation, law enforcement, administrative activities, and a portion of the Wisconsin Conservation Corps program.

Source: Wisconsin Department of Administration, Bureau of Financial Operations, *State of Wisconsin 2004 Annual Fiscal Report (Budgetary Basis) Appendix*, and previous issues.

WISCONSIN STATE REVENUES AND EXPENDITURES
Fiscal Years 1975-76 – 2003-04
(In Thousands)

Fiscal Year	General Fund[1]		Other Funds[2]		Total-All Funds		Net Surplus[3]
Ending 6/30	Revenues	Expenditures	Revenues	Expenditures	Revenues	Expenditures	(or deficit)
1975	2,966,532	3,148,968	1,252,422	924,455	4,218,954	4,073,423	78,120
1980	4,900,275	5,027,130	2,481,324	1,809,840	7,381,599	6,836,970	72,627
1985	7,160,174	7,237,716	4,908,582	2,743,287	12,068,756	9,981,002	314,084
1990	9,418,918	9,464,483	5,483,442	3,287,809	14,902,360	12,752,292	306,452
1995	13,259,772	13,094,450	9,823,810	4,963,553	23,083,582	18,058,003	400,881
1996	13,804,399	13,648,601	10,038,961	5,057,062	23,843,360	18,705,663	581,690
1997	14,669,320	14,932,404	12,741,438	5,144,002	27,410,758	20,076,406	386,558
1998	15,701,212	15,509,615	13,896,719	6,071,649	29,597,931	21,581,264	533,240
1999	16,252,539	16,098,587	11,847,678	6,864,567	28,100,217	22,963,154	737,748
2000	18,185,980	18,333,634	14,687,330	8,111,005	32,873,310	26,444,639	574,416
2001	19,285,734	19,448,417	2,990,770	8,719,341	22,276,504	28,167,758	445,999
2002	20,850,074	21,248,608	5,920,241	10,395,514	26,770,315	31,644,122	44,469
2003	20,683,921	20,956,485	10,598,486	11,025,745	31,282,407	31,982,230	(163,608)
2004	22,040,940	21,716,332	19,544,497	12,177,401	41,585,437	33,893,733	127,369

[1]Includes general purpose revenue (GPR), program revenue, and federal funding.
[2]Includes special revenue funds (such as conservation and transportation), federal funding, debt service, capital projects, pension and retirement funds, trust and agency funds, and others.
[3]Unappropriated (unreserved) balance of the general fund for the fiscal year.
Source: Wisconsin Department of Administration, Bureau of Financial Operations, *2004 State of Wisconsin Annual Fiscal Report*, and previous issues.

WISCONSIN STATE AIDS BY COUNTY
Calendar Year 2003

County	Health and Human Services	Transportation	Recycling and Sanitation	Public Housing	Conservation	Public Safety	Total State Aids
Adams	$4,367,431	$2,841,201	$141,108	$5,000	$313,726	$245,648	$8,132,593
Ashland	5,274,796	3,884,461	115,406	----	419,703	578,288	10,891,988
Barron	10,865,392	5,714,574	111,928	557,781	314,021	368,245	18,323,068
Bayfield	5,800,769	4,609,677	66,265	11,500	629,646	258,648	11,623,574
Brown	50,563,315	15,138,860	1,144,377	309,438	1,054,567	1,479,752	74,370,225
Buffalo	3,354,830	2,018,260	140,529	----	362,867	158,201	6,156,060
Burnett	4,129,837	3,308,535	119,104	301,417	388,901	406,724	8,791,680
Calumet	7,238,339	2,945,447	183,716	212,219	242,572	291,527	11,357,384
Chippewa	12,626,409	6,109,607	422,334	658,647	1,334,067	532,824	22,260,382
Clark........	9,772,678	4,995,578	126,659	----	347,009	340,340	15,846,967
Columbia	13,251,035	5,480,267	247,927	361,330	331,043	509,213	21,118,556
Crawford	5,125,558	3,144,602	46,113	6,750	135,060	77,935	8,902,849
Dane	134,146,932	23,848,687	2,158,049	97,500	1,432,894	2,635,268	193,755,309
Dodge	14,178,109	8,107,446	369,266	390,808	424,932	437,049	24,875,484
Door	6,105,497	2,879,274	115,466	----	1,582,770	155,986	11,543,333
Douglas	16,714,195	5,291,831	200,458	527,759	126,999	894,559	25,099,717
Dunn	9,293,315	6,289,912	240,683	133,380	330,121	292,693	17,909,878
Eau Claire	23,292,419	6,717,099	663,082	100,323	227,949	813,407	34,287,556
Florence	1,891,258	1,114,441	102,340	----	220,996	198,360	3,704,477
Fond du Lac ..	15,737,141	7,898,601	322,101	1,009,138	549,208	389,840	26,846,892
Forest	1,746,523	2,000,261	113,552	140,429	115,823	538,303	4,948,141
Grant	12,189,363	5,561,789	188,570	279,371	222,778	923,639	20,754,544
Green	7,685,527	3,365,749	185,160	161,669	242,799	325,864	12,424,241
Green Lake ...	4,077,438	2,411,524	69,128	241,979	200,652	298,533	7,550,187
Iowa	1,705,863	3,285,466	80,292	----	213,009	47,865	5,580,201
Iron	2,448,688	1,567,208	106,832	434,680	424,533	188,031	5,436,732
Jackson	7,592,968	3,121,714	118,023	30,782	866,969	118,729	12,122,152
Jefferson	16,985,455	7,542,272	407,970	----	159,323	799,230	27,075,277
Juneau	5,815,193	3,595,278	82,203	106,000	216,289	286,766	10,552,410
Kenosha	53,652,507	6,873,402	666,862	546,527	363,065	1,456,394	67,439,244
Kewaunee	4,510,735	2,599,417	94,385	851,500	719,431	373,640	9,254,525
La Crosse	17,027,294	7,129,907	733,025	338,584	209,222	662,270	29,405,148
Lafayette	3,748,767	2,571,441	62,344	356,278	304,788	102,109	7,801,257
Langlade	3,669,573	3,016,060	128,869	232,000	283,439	332,147	8,068,747
Lincoln	6,358,774	3,929,840	103,057	----	288,106	273,786	11,873,429
Manitowoc ...	21,099,888	8,205,628	531,643	1,208,865	464,784	674,657	33,901,201
Marathon	15,581,564	20,706,392	539,181	1,840,344	681,864	718,118	42,795,288
Marinette	9,464,526	5,726,079	155,826	1,044,991	1,122,406	648,981	18,802,078
Marquette	3,371,167	1,748,522	113,172	----	235,510	259,752	5,866,242
Menominee ...	3,698,905	419,701	103,236	----	155,615	182,799	5,147,354
Milwaukee ...	217,615,689	51,780,003	4,626,468	806,131	----	6,550,081	358,014,860
Monroe	8,812,254	3,983,206	214,380	138,651	274,375	683,977	15,344,519
Oconto	8,720,966	4,905,441	254,546	12,098	419,693	157,561	14,766,114
Oneida	5,508,616	5,070,001	180,843	45,049	426,251	619,283	12,815,897
Outagamie ...	28,512,787	11,313,239	808,564	548,771	603,300	775,312	45,870,337
Ozaukee	11,491,336	7,697,354	187,755	----	407,574	798,058	21,128,592
Pepin	3,467,260	1,209,260	90,060	94,630	223,953	199,794	5,398,430
Pierce	7,432,860	3,644,108	280,834	513,831	291,833	352,083	13,040,804
Polk	8,359,335	5,079,157	192,167	282,704	614,935	674,882	15,727,669
Portage	27,422,297	6,138,599	402,665	----	393,208	613,412	37,229,742
Price	5,397,260	3,140,962	63,571	26,261	341,817	95,742	9,218,082
Racine	53,592,253	12,305,043	712,083	2,886,091	124,256	1,403,735	76,312,185
Richland	3,317,234	2,846,359	179,324	----	434,820	147,223	7,813,084
Rock	19,920,095	10,033,615	688,286	308,414	33,723	685,066	34,697,817
Rusk	6,294,586	3,197,220	99,019	1,045,032	305,915	1,314,170	12,439,366
St. Croix	13,487,763	6,790,188	352,020	852,333	650,181	599,388	23,504,966
Sauk	15,044,725	5,806,974	172,086	----	1,210,260	827,997	25,462,564
Sawyer	5,011,273	3,131,664	60,889	87,541	414,780	508,471	9,398,809
Shawano	8,130,648	5,134,716	125,505	480,712	310,434	464,899	15,292,934
Sheboygan ...	24,423,827	8,690,488	397,561	1,615,515	436,942	469,691	37,901,447
Taylor	5,420,801	3,048,351	34,546	123,851	318,660	485,624	9,482,043
Trempealeau ..	7,914,981	3,099,734	66,947	126,055	1,256,398	197,662	13,134,168
Vernon	6,719,438	3,511,560	197,738	1,058,334	555,591	361,949	12,627,643
Vilas	3,610,791	3,378,981	270,668	103,555	433,928	305,229	8,538,169
Walworth	26,077,407	7,819,712	312,518	199,288	349,525	757,693	36,788,500
Washburn	5,039,824	3,324,581	114,903	229,360	356,946	51,367	9,451,819
Washington ..	21,235,516	9,287,576	354,797	1,044,215	265,973	442,242	33,722,639
Waukesha	50,162,989	22,399,506	1,600,824	542,049	191,084	1,541,844	81,641,519
Waupaca	11,215,484	5,627,192	250,686	485,502	614,351	395,503	20,321,091
Waushara ...	6,596,149	2,637,074	128,408	----	463,752	247,464	10,255,370
Winnebago ...	37,063,536	13,580,187	926,149	836,401	627,959	749,479	57,692,532
Wood	11,686,808	7,804,471	263,433	3,258,793	336,026	347,023	24,413,304
TOTAL ...	$1,230,866,761	$465,132,532	$26,230,484	$30,248,156	$31,947,899	$44,100,024	$2,012,043,385

Note: Table includes state aids to municipalities and county governments. Data do not include state school aids distributed to school districts or state property tax relief. Totals include categories not listed separately.

Source: Wisconsin Department of Revenue, departmental data, June 2005. Categories and county totals computed by Wisconsin Legislative Reference Bureau.

STATE PAYMENTS TO LOCAL UNITS OF GOVERNMENT
Property Tax Relief and Shared Revenue
By County, Fiscal Year 2005

County	School Levy Credits	Shared Revenue Payments	County Total	Per Capita Amount*	Rank
Adams	$1,881,788	$1,387,163	$3,268,951	$157.87	69
Ashland	1,163,147	6,068,895	7,232,042	426.19	1
Barron	3,153,035	7,905,919	11,058,954	237.62	33
Bayfield	1,775,603	1,585,679	3,361,282	215.81	47
Brown	19,190,438	30,775,804	49,966,242	210.08	49
Buffalo	974,750	2,860,983	3,835,733	273.34	20
Burnett	1,983,107	1,259,168	3,242,275	197.72	56
Calumet	2,967,569	4,195,341	7,162,910	161.47	66
Chippewa	4,128,623	11,403,859	15,532,482	261.20	27
Clark	1,767,900	8,519,130	10,287,030	299.28	10
Columbia	4,665,281	6,351,767	11,017,048	201.79	51
Crawford	1,114,626	3,847,844	4,962,470	283.55	15
Dane	52,058,178	27,514,433	79,572,611	176.54	65
Dodge	6,470,515	13,882,673	20,353,188	230.54	37
Door	3,798,356	1,609,440	5,407,796	185.75	63
Douglas	2,722,467	12,290,558	15,013,025	343.48	4
Dunn	2,605,284	8,805,745	11,411,029	273.40	19
Eau Claire	7,650,343	14,867,150	22,517,493	234.04	35
Florence	481,798	351,282	833,080	159.78	68
Fond du Lac	6,677,833	15,218,140	21,895,973	219.82	43
Forest	1,076,442	1,129,564	2,206,006	216.32	45
Grant	2,736,950	12,954,094	15,691,044	310.39	6
Green	3,062,226	4,371,604	7,433,830	211.41	48
Green Lake	1,988,604	3,196,961	5,185,565	268.07	23
Iowa	2,234,924	2,396,528	4,631,452	195.92	57
Iron	717,132	1,385,377	2,102,509	302.61	9
Jackson	1,178,123	3,426,148	4,604,271	233.99	36
Jefferson	6,649,114	10,600,746	17,249,860	220.19	42
Juneau	1,865,650	5,235,335	7,100,985	278.80	16
Kenosha	12,217,042	21,918,297	34,135,339	218.70	44
Kewaunee	1,307,521	4,489,335	5,796,856	277.89	17
La Crosse	7,999,211	20,300,140	28,299,351	258.17	30
Lafayette	1,177,691	4,725,038	5,902,729	361.89	3
Langlade	1,620,064	4,481,285	6,101,349	287.43	12
Lincoln	2,337,227	6,062,833	8,400,060	277.50	18
Manitowoc	5,234,671	17,717,010	22,951,681	272.38	21
Marathon	9,713,772	19,135,243	28,849,015	221.98	40
Marinette	3,558,724	10,067,523	13,626,247	308.26	7
Marquette	1,253,568	1,117,683	2,371,251	157.55	70
Menominee	184,144	729,075	913,219	197.84	55
Milwaukee	65,095,777	330,775,638	395,871,415	421.43	2
Monroe	2,157,935	9,064,775	11,222,710	263.28	25
Oconto	3,244,653	4,902,314	8,146,967	216.22	46
Oneida	5,340,358	2,153,130	7,493,488	198.63	54
Outagamie	12,470,027	24,923,200	37,393,227	221.47	41
Ozaukee	11,918,382	4,471,298	16,389,680	192.46	59
Pepin	565,627	1,493,137	2,058,764	272.04	22
Pierce	2,809,594	5,778,219	8,587,813	222.40	39
Polk	3,673,394	4,583,807	8,257,201	188.22	60
Portage	4,657,670	9,144,566	13,802,236	200.22	53
Price	1,064,801	3,088,841	4,153,642	260.35	28
Racine	13,236,010	37,324,470	50,560,480	263.54	24
Richland	1,304,547	4,104,375	5,408,922	298.87	11
Rock	10,907,830	33,699,179	44,607,009	286.80	13
Rusk	1,284,709	3,859,216	5,143,925	331.61	5
St. Croix	6,471,138	4,401,794	10,872,932	149.93	72
Sauk	5,293,898	5,613,209	10,907,107	186.14	62
Sawyer	2,337,198	985,701	3,322,899	195.15	58
Shawano	2,591,149	5,859,146	8,450,295	201.47	52
Sheboygan	9,015,254	19,157,257	28,172,511	244.03	31
Taylor	1,216,867	3,936,101	5,152,968	259.31	29
Trempealeau	1,754,948	6,771,124	8,526,072	307.08	8
Vernon	1,622,883	5,985,355	7,608,238	263.01	26
Vilas	4,660,633	580,720	5,241,353	238.61	32
Walworth	12,104,781	7,566,513	19,671,294	202.69	50
Washburn	1,661,320	1,484,527	3,145,847	187.68	61
Washington	11,928,205	6,780,697	18,708,902	151.38	71
Waukesha	52,121,575	13,965,890	66,087,465	177.02	64
Waupaca	3,706,531	8,901,435	12,607,966	237.22	34
Waushara	2,136,407	1,859,706	3,996,113	161.09	67
Winnebago	11,090,626	25,073,533	36,164,159	223.42	38
Wood	4,517,633	17,222,587	21,740,220	285.17	14
STATE	**$469,305,801**	**$951,652,252**	**$1,420,958,053**	**$256.82**	

*Per capita calculations are based on 2004 county population estimates, the most recent available at publication time.

Sources: Wisconsin Department of Revenue, Division of State and Local Finance, Bureau of Local Financial Assistance, departmental data, June 2005; Wisconsin Department of Administration, Division of Intergovernmental Relations, Demographic Services Center, *January 1, 2004 Final Population Estimates for Wisconsin Counties.* Per capita amounts and ranks calculated by Wisconsin Legislative Reference Bureau.

SELECTED STATE TAX REVENUES
By State, Per $1,000 Personal Income
Fiscal Year Ending in 2004

State	Total Taxes* Amount	Rank	Sales and Gross Receipts Taxes — General Sales	Selective Sales Taxes — Motor Fuels	Public Utilities	Tobacco	Alcohol	Individual Income	Corporation Net Income	Motor Vehicle	Property
Alabama	$55.74	42	$15.03	$4.25	$4.77	$0.74	$1.09	$17.82	$2.32	$1.51	$1.76
Alaska	57.04	37	NA	1.80	0.18	1.91	1.25	NA	15.04	1.94	2.10
Arizona	58.80	34	28.89	4.11	0.21	1.68	0.34	14.18	3.22	1.09	2.12
Arkansas	78.81	8	30.36	6.40	NA	2.07	0.58	23.80	2.57	1.78	7.35
California	68.20	15	21.09	2.65	0.41	0.86	0.25	28.96	5.51	1.86	1.65
Colorado	42.49	49	11.51	3.60	0.06	0.39	0.19	20.57	1.44	1.25	NA
Connecticut	64.70	22	19.66	2.87	1.23	1.74	0.28	27.16	2.39	1.48	NA
Delaware	79.77	7	NA	3.78	1.19	2.53	0.45	26.23	7.31	1.13	NA
Florida	56.23	41	31.72	3.33	4.58	0.82	1.08	NA	2.46	2.33	0.48
Georgia	54.91	43	18.55	2.85	NA	0.86	0.56	25.74	1.86	1.19	0.25
Hawaii	94.78	1	46.79	2.08	2.45	1.95	1.02	28.79	1.43	2.20	NA
Idaho	70.13	14	17.46	5.77	0.05	1.38	0.18	24.04	2.75	3.03	NA
ILLINOIS	58.37	35	15.85	3.26	3.90	1.74	0.34	18.64	4.74	3.32	0.13
Indiana	63.70	24	25.35	4.27	0.06	1.80	0.21	20.29	3.43	1.97	0.05
IOWA	56.85	38	17.91	3.96	NA	1.04	0.14	21.69	0.99	4.39	NA
Kansas	62.69	26	22.93	5.09	0.01	1.48	1.04	22.73	1.98	2.09	0.68
Kentucky	73.67	10	21.47	4.15	NA	0.18	0.69	24.54	3.32	1.88	3.96
Louisiana	64.44	23	21.52	4.50	0.06	0.81	0.43	17.56	1.90	1.01	0.32
Maine	71.95	11	22.78	5.47	0.21	2.30	0.98	28.81	2.77	2.21	1.13
Maryland	56.45	40	13.50	3.42	0.63	1.25	0.12	24.20	2.05	1.43	2.19
Massachusetts	62.26	29	13.96	2.55	NA	1.59	0.26	32.92	4.85	1.43	0
MICHIGAN	74.46	9	24.43	3.35	0.09	3.07	0.46	20.35	5.70	3.50	8.67
MINNESOTA	80.55	4	22.23	3.54	0	1.04	0.38	31.21	3.48	3.04	3.32
Mississippi	71.62	12	34.70	6.49	0.17	0.78	0.56	14.84	3.41	1.97	0.56
Missouri	51.78	46	16.75	4.13	NA	0.62	0.16	21.12	1.27	1.54	0.13
Montana	65.31	20	NA	7.94	1.13	1.82	0.83	24.33	2.72	6.02	7.39
Nebraska	66.47	16	27.84	5.53	0.06	1.30	0.42	22.69	3.06	1.77	0.04
Nevada	60.76	32	29.04	3.76	0.12	1.65	0.43	NA	NA	1.97	1.70
New Hampshire ...	41.66	50	NA	2.70	1.36	2.08	0.25	1.14	8.47	2.03	10.25
New Jersey	58.36	36	17.42	1.52	2.62	2.16	0.24	20.58	5.28	1.21	0.01
New Mexico	80.28	5	28.95	4.23	0.36	1.06	0.75	20.21	2.77	2.55	1.06
New York	62.36	28	13.67	0.71	1.12	1.37	0.26	33.53	2.78	1.24	NA
North Carolina	66.36	17	17.42	5.09	1.28	0.18	0.85	29.03	3.35	2.06	NA
North Dakota	61.70	30	18.44	5.96	1.71	1.06	0.30	10.74	2.50	2.94	0.07
Ohio	62.62	27	21.96	4.29	0.77	1.55	0.25	24.25	2.95	2.18	0.11
Oklahoma	64.93	21	16.11	4.20	0.21	0.64	0.69	23.43	1.35	5.73	NA
Oregon	56.65	39	NA	3.76	0.10	2.46	0.12	39.64	2.97	4.18	0.15
Pennsylvania	61.26	31	18.79	4.31	2.46	2.37	0.54	17.70	4.06	2.06	0.17
Rhode Island	66.08	18	22.07	3.66	2.43	3.17	0.29	24.69	1.91	1.58	0.04
South Carolina	59.64	33	23.90	4.29	0.40	0.26	1.29	21.38	1.72	1.39	0.10
South Dakota	44.68	48	24.65	5.30	0.08	1.16	0.52	NA	1.98	1.85	NA
Tennessee	53.86	44	33.01	4.70	0.03	0.67	0.52	0.83	3.92	1.68	NA
Texas	45.24	47	22.75	4.29	1.17	0.79	0.89	NA	NA	1.95	NA
Utah	65.91	19	24.49	5.41	0.22	0.97	0.44	26.62	2.28	1.58	NA
Vermont	86.76	2	12.62	4.22	0.53	2.51	0.83	21.11	3.06	3.28	22.01
Virginia	53.78	45	11.25	3.44	0.49	0.06	0.55	28.04	1.59	1.46	0.08
Washington	63.45	25	38.46	4.23	1.61	1.61	0.88	NA	NA	1.74	6.97
West Virginia	79.82	6	21.75	6.59	4.01	2.29	0.18	22.74	3.86	1.86	0.07
WISCONSIN	70.74	13	22.01	5.81	2.08	1.74	0.27	28.52	3.85	2.04	0.59
Wyoming	86.60	3	26.64	4.03	0.17	1.07	0.08	NA	NA	3.03	8.05
UNITED STATES	$61.54		$20.58	$3.48	$1.19	$1.28	$0.48	$20.47	$3.19	$2.00	$1.18

NA – Not available.

*Includes other taxes not listed separately.

Sources: U.S. Census Bureau, Governments Division, "2004 State Government Tax Collections", May 2005, at: http://www.census.gov/govs/www/statetax04.html [June 3, 2005] and U.S. Department of Commerce, Bureau of Economic Analysis, Regional Economic Information System, "Regional Economic Accounts: SA1-3 – Personal Income", 2004 preliminary estimates, March 2005, at: http://www.bea.doc.gov/bea/regional/spi/ [June 3, 2005]. Amounts per $1,000 personal income and rankings calculated by Wisconsin Legislative Reference Bureau.

PER CAPITA STATE AND LOCAL REVENUES
Selected Sources, Fiscal Year 2001-02

State	Total State and Local General Revenue Per Capita						State and Local Taxes Per Capita			
	Total		Federal Sources		State/Local Sources		Total			Individual
	Amount	Rank	Amount	Percent	Amount[1]	Percent	Taxes[2]	Property	Sales	Income
Alabama	$5,298	35	$1,398	26.4%	$3,900	73.6%	$2,169	$329	$1,071	$475
Alaska	11,249	1	2,792	24.8	8,457	75.2	3,230	1,295	485	---
Arizona	4,693	50	1,051	22.4	3,641	77.6	2,651	782	1,302	384
Arkansas	4,897	48	1,346	27.5	3,551	72.5	2,386	371	1,234	578
California	6,478	7	1,379	21.3	5,099	78.7	3,442	864	1,188	945
Colorado	5,789	22	949	16.4	4,840	83.6	3,090	925	1,179	773
Connecticut	6,593	6	1,168	17.7	5,425	82.3	4,373	1,733	1,306	1,065
Delaware	6,947	4	1,190	17.1	5,757	82.9	3,333	496	405	947
District of Columbia	12,260	--	5,030	41.0	7,230	59.0	5,717	1,423	1,657	1,681
Florida	5,195	38	897	17.2	4,299	82.7	2,688	944	1,375	---
Georgia	5,194	39	1,096	21.1	4,099	78.9	2,817	778	1,100	760
Hawaii	6,018	15	1,254	20.8	4,764	79.2	3,434	498	1,818	900
Idaho	4,928	47	1,054	21.4	3,875	78.6	2,450	714	845	627
ILLINOIS	5,490	29	1,010	18.4	4,480	81.6	3,303	1,261	1,103	594
Indiana	5,255	37	1,020	19.4	4,235	80.6	2,758	970	897	669
IOWA	5,749	24	1,236	21.5	4,513	78.5	2,839	981	983	618
Kansas	5,395	30	1,142	21.2	4,253	78.8	2,940	931	1,130	684
Kentucky	5,191	40	1,324	25.5	3,867	74.5	2,636	483	964	855
Louisiana	5,818	21	1,448	24.9	4,370	75.1	2,721	433	1,552	400
Maine	6,224	11	1,465	23.5	4,759	76.5	3,499	1,473	957	827
Maryland	5,939	18	1,089	18.3	4,850	81.7	3,652	995	914	1,405
Massachusetts	6,082	14	963	15.8	5,119	84.2	3,726	1,360	836	1,234
MICHIGAN	5,770	23	1,249	21.6	4,521	78.4	3,051	975	1,019	657
MINNESOTA	6,606	5	1,212	18.3	5,394	81.7	3,673	1,038	1,178	1,083
Mississippi	5,333	33	1,613	30.2	3,720	69.8	2,275	574	1,135	344
Missouri	5,117	44	1,290	25.2	3,826	74.8	2,663	683	1,064	692
Montana	5,625	27	1,746	31.0	3,878	69.0	2,345	936	411	568
Nebraska	5,689	26	1,143	20.1	4,546	79.9	3,079	1,013	1,054	668
Nevada	5,265	36	753	14.3	4,513	85.7	2,967	785	1,771	---
New Hampshire	5,022	46	1,016	20.2	4,006	79.8	2,821	1,701	475	56
New Jersey	6,442	8	1,043	16.2	5,399	83.8	4,037	1,871	1,026	801
New Mexico	5,858	19	1,684	28.7	4,174	71.3	2,629	407	1,250	530
New York	8,122	3	1,889	23.3	6,232	76.7	4,641	1,401	1,174	1,577
North Carolina	5,313	34	1,232	23.2	4,081	76.8	2,716	652	945	874
North Dakota	6,302	9	1,824	28.9	4,478	71.0	2,728	840	1,087	315
Ohio	5,746	25	1,215	21.1	4,531	78.9	3,169	933	943	1,034
Oklahoma	5,178	41	1,265	24.4	3,913	75.6	2,518	425	988	655
Oregon	6,138	13	1,827	29.8	4,311	70.2	2,555	891	252	1,043
Pennsylvania	5,837	20	1,300	22.3	4,537	77.7	3,052	885	916	771
Rhode Island	6,209	12	1,652	26.6	4,556	73.4	3,389	1,368	1,089	770
South Carolina	5,173	42	1,299	25.1	3,874	74.9	2,375	754	834	572
South Dakota	5,131	43	1,513	29.5	3,618	70.5	2,422	878	1,223	---
Tennessee	4,745	49	1,313	27.7	3,432	72.3	2,240	596	1,288	25
Texas	5,024	45	1,055	21.0	3,969	79.0	2,715	1,129	1,318	0
Utah	5,388	31	1,126	20.9	4,262	79.1	2,598	612	1,129	692
Vermont	6,257	10	1,763	28.2	4,494	71.8	3,188	1,336	929	662
Virginia	5,365	32	857	16.0	4,508	84.0	3,043	923	899	923
Washington	5,990	16	1,161	19.4	4,830	80.6	3,216	954	1,974	---
West Virginia	5,601	28	1,661	29.7	3,940	70.3	2,571	499	1,097	573
WISCONSIN	5,984	17	1,187	19.8	4,797	80.1	3,421	1,189	1,047	914
Wyoming	8,487	2	2,378	28.0	6,109	72.1	3,643	1,387	1,385	---
UNITED STATES	$5,851		$1,252	21.4%	$4,599	78.6%	$3,143	$969	$1,125	$705

[1]Includes taxes, charges, and miscellaneous general revenues.

[2]Total taxes also include corporate income, motor vehicle license, and other taxes not listed separately.

Source: U.S. Department of Commerce, U.S. Census Bureau, "State and Local Government Finances, 2002 Census of Governments", Table 1: "State and Local Government Finances by Level of Government and by State: 2001-02", at: http://www.census.gov/govs/www/estimate02.html [June 10, 2005] and "Annual Estimates of the Population for the United States and States, and for Puerto Rico: April 1, 2000 to July 1, 2004 (NST-EST2004-01)", at: http://www.census.gov/popest/states/NST-ann-est.html [May 5, 2005]. Per capita figures, percentages, and rankings calculated by Wisconsin Legislative Reference Bureau.

SELECTED PER CAPITA STATE AND LOCAL GOVERNMENT EXPENDITURES, BY FUNCTION
Fiscal Year 2001-02

State	Direct General Expenditure* Amount	Rank	Education	Public Welfare	Health and Hospitals	Highways	Police and Fire	Corrections	Parks and Natural Resources	Sewerage and Solid Waste
Alabama	$5,491	30	$1,857	$929	$911	$372	$221	$103	$128	$189
Alaska	13,175	1	3,287	1,615	410	1,429	546	274	532	160
Arizona	4,643	50	1,617	604	222	352	321	206	194	163
Arkansas	4,827	49	1,767	958	338	483	204	136	143	125
California	6,734	6	2,196	1,016	599	328	409	258	246	190
Colorado	6,024	20	2,003	628	454	630	333	190	266	132
Connecticut	6,996	4	2,270	1,004	550	354	339	184	143	185
Delaware	6,645	8	2,402	818	405	576	266	304	189	183
District of Columbia	10,944	—	2,081	2,590	983	123	923	308	537	450
Florida	5,220	41	1,546	749	449	403	375	202	254	214
Georgia	5,264	40	2,034	721	566	344	257	207	148	184
Hawaii	6,715	7	1,829	924	528	339	290	127	297	255
Idaho	5,065	46	1,804	771	451	460	240	171	230	180
ILLINOIS	5,866	23	2,062	784	413	451	364	149	252	155
Indiana	5,326	38	1,980	863	467	330	227	137	135	178
IOWA	5,856	24	2,204	914	643	600	211	112	194	152
Kansas	5,483	31	2,028	738	454	563	246	133	156	107
Kentucky	5,279	39	1,682	1,178	353	477	198	147	138	157
Louisiana	5,432	33	1,786	751	809	342	279	173	186	138
Maine	6,124	18	1,920	1,381	385	476	204	112	157	170
Maryland	5,843	25	2,231	871	274	341	341	231	224	170
Massachusetts	6,604	9	2,096	894	495	508	357	175	84	192
MICHIGAN	6,047	12	2,365	980	532	321	265	210	162	196
MINNESOTA	6,952	5	2,242	1,487	391	533	256	129	262	176
Mississippi	5,365	36	1,779	1,129	746	431	221	113	137	82
Missouri	5,114	44	1,859	972	428	435	263	144	125	105
Montana	5,546	28	1,968	737	415	596	233	134	285	116
Nebraska	5,645	27	2,199	986	351	535	228	149	215	104
Nevada	5,427	34	1,697	517	426	586	431	232	275	91
New Hampshire	4,973	48	1,912	807	144	395	259	90	88	120
New Jersey	6,341	12	2,395	770	319	345	364	187	160	252
New Mexico	6,164	16	2,251	1,119	447	616	300	200	222	121
New York	8,414	2	2,492	1,697	679	370	479	243	129	241
North Carolina	5,359	37	1,836	921	732	363	250	141	155	153
North Dakota	6,132	17	2,069	1,047	164	727	163	94	371	102
Ohio	5,876	22	2,070	1,076	478	359	317	159	128	180
Oklahoma	5,205	42	1,979	915	374	443	248	161	141	124
Oregon	6,525	10	2,141	1,148	623	340	326	235	202	208
Pennsylvania	5,947	21	1,971	1,175	418	429	238	199	103	177
Rhode Island	6,321	13	2,040	1,559	280	310	401	147	104	175
South Carolina	5,801	26	2,041	1,065	766	363	232	139	124	113
South Dakota	5,108	45	1,789	795	224	763	187	123	280	90
Tennessee	4,998	47	1,635	1,115	570	306	242	119	119	118
Texas	5,138	43	2,104	686	465	346	240	203	141	124
Utah	5,544	29	2,240	688	370	438	253	162	232	150
Vermont	6,172	15	2,369	1,228	142	588	206	129	158	124
Virginia	5,399	35	2,083	643	438	426	266	191	117	179
Washington	6,370	11	2,121	1,022	661	392	289	189	261	231
West Virginia	5,455	32	1,949	1,185	286	576	140	112	162	102
WISCONSIN	6,250	14	2,310	1,022	383	549	324	216	220	215
Wyoming	7,719	3	2,559	764	1,034	956	328	220	478	159
UNITED STATES	$6,011		$2,065	$971	$508	$401	$314	$190	$181	$175

*Includes amounts for categories not shown separately.

Sources: U.S. Department of Commerce, U.S. Census Bureau, *State and Local Government Finances: 2002 Census of Governments*, at: http://www.census.gov/govs/www/estimate02.html [April 29, 2005], and *National and State Population Estimates*, at: http://www.census.gov/popest/states/NST-ann-est.html [April 29, 2005]. Per capita values and rankings calculated by Wisconsin Legislative Reference Bureau.

STATE PAYMENTS TO OTHER UNITS OF GOVERNMENT
By State and Type of Governmental Unit
2003 State Fiscal Years
(In Thousands)

State	Total	Government Units Receiving Transfers				
		Local Governments Not Elsewhere Classified	General Purpose Local Governments	School Districts	Special Districts	Federal Government*
Alabama	$4,074,005	$25,602	$516,843	$3,531,560	---	---
Alaska	1,091,391	250,698	840,693	---	---	---
Arizona	6,936,753	49,478	3,518,805	3,368,470	---	---
Arkansas	3,210,582	135,631	436,977	2,609,842	$27,076	$1,056
California	84,468,847	1,437,165	37,936,243	40,930,673	1,106,053	3,058,713
Colorado	4,666,350	---	1,598,015	3,037,908	27,680	2,747
Connecticut	3,030,485	172,785	2,836,060	21,640	---	---
Delaware	903,476	---	96,935	805,507	---	1,034
Florida	14,460,722	---	3,758,762	10,701,960	---	---
Georgia	9,016,458	87,613	1,495,219	7,389,085	44,541	---
Hawaii	125,434	23,548	100,671	---	---	1,215
Idaho	1,449,076	112,684	178,937	1,156,840	615	---
ILLINOIS	13,369,662	746,928	4,079,765	7,964,002	575,815	3,152
Indiana	6,760,945	1,105,867	1,514,378	4,134,937	5,763	---
IOWA	3,442,552	220,311	691,788	2,484,619	---	45,834
Kansas	2,925,220	153,211	320,746	2,447,274	3,394	595
Kentucky	3,693,634	2,517	620,581	3,070,536	---	---
Louisiana	4,329,053	379,454	636,844	3,312,755	---	---
Maine	1,051,164	819,605	187,941	---	---	43,618
Maryland	5,358,342	72,510	5,285,832	---	---	---
Massachusetts	6,435,841	217,312	4,613,426	524,861	899,113	181,129
MICHIGAN	19,851,778	295,917	6,684,238	12,815,989	713	54,921
MINNESOTA	9,618,471	154,976	3,250,751	6,038,015	174,729	---
Mississippi	3,665,580	14,877	1,280,210	2,370,493	---	---
Missouri	5,159,094	314,429	604,463	4,202,178	34,488	3,536
Montana	938,000	38,281	213,935	684,637	---	1,147
Nebraska	1,784,749	449,180	201,346	1,084,147	34,120	15,956
Nevada	2,648,660	669	915,663	1,725,066	---	7,262
New Hampshire	1,283,091	1,046,934	235,348	164	645	---
New Jersey	8,997,417	29,102	4,937,206	3,959,781	---	71,328
New Mexico	2,951,328	---	764,866	2,186,462	---	---
New York	40,874,514	805,856	29,242,490	10,197,168	---	629,000
North Carolina	10,356,152	---	10,299,402	---	56,750	---
North Dakota	606,096	501	183,618	410,306	11,671	---
Ohio	15,249,395	2,146,384	3,790,835	9,285,216	24,381	2,579
Oklahoma	3,395,494	172,222	469,750	2,705,722	6,717	41,083
Oregon	4,071,501	115,939	1,185,232	2,731,101	39,229	---
Pennsylvania	11,943,470	129,742	4,351,493	6,995,210	291,317	175,708
Rhode Island	828,198	6,000	755,673	39,369	---	27,156
South Carolina	4,155,920	2,975	1,385,674	2,766,121	1,150	---
South Dakota	514,949	7,845	81,387	425,017	700	---
Tennessee	4,952,923	17,270	4,721,246	190,056	24,351	---
Texas	17,332,957	1,385,337	897,981	15,043,381	6,258	---
Utah	2,165,151	---	194,193	1,970,464	---	494
Vermont	938,085	---	95,511	842,303	---	271
Virginia	8,352,635	---	8,351,582	---	---	1,053
Washington	6,785,341	23,178	1,204,653	5,515,729	21,273	20,508
West Virginia	1,544,758	16,287	143,905	1,384,376	190	---
WISCONSIN	9,478,166	887,175	3,245,586	5,345,405	---	---
Wyoming	952,705	48,871	270,188	632,952	694	---
TOTAL	$382,196,570	$14,122,866	$161,223,886	$199,039,297	$3,419,426	$4,391,095

Note: Intergovernmental transfers are amounts paid to other governments as shared revenues, grants-in-aid, reimbursement for services, etc.

*The Supplemental Security Income (SSI) and Temporary Assistance for Needy Families (TANF) programs account for almost all of the state to federal transfers shown here.

Source: U.S. Department of Commerce, U.S. Census Bureau, *2003 State Government Finance Data*, at http://www.census.gov/ govs/www/state03.html and http://ftp2.census.gov/govs/state/03statecd.txt [June 12, 2005].

FEDERAL TAX RECEIPTS
By State, Fiscal Year 2004
(In Thousands of Dollars)

State[1]	Total	Individual Income and Employment[2]	Corporate Income[3]	Estate and Gift	Excise[4]
Alabama	$18,489,339	$16,205,117	$1,931,414	$215,812	$136,995
Alaska	3,267,127	3,077,947	124,599	9,491	55,091
Arizona	25,344,852	22,687,926	1,894,886	257,350	504,691
Arkansas	20,576,284	14,657,385	5,204,945	140,283	573,670
California	237,931,491	202,345,010	28,252,413	4,273,940	3,060,128
Colorado	34,660,999	30,621,321	2,131,191	342,699	1,565,787
Connecticut	41,909,468	32,560,865	8,107,681	648,351	592,572
Delaware	11,151,222	7,086,221	3,922,315	79,800	62,886
District of Columbia	16,930,784	14,296,490	2,322,763	135,450	176,080
Florida	94,277,725	86,738,693	4,447,784	2,002,469	1,088,779
Georgia	59,083,748	46,401,995	9,195,080	554,287	2,932,387
Hawaii	8,394,777	7,746,147	460,777	80,728	107,125
Idaho	6,479,611	6,134,461	261,352	60,243	23,554
ILLINOIS	108,476,636	86,357,840	17,581,098	1,071,214	3,466,484
Indiana	32,192,435	29,079,537	2,270,997	336,566	505,334
IOWA	14,543,095	12,661,060	1,626,888	136,962	118,185
Kansas	15,897,378	12,954,523	1,036,076	160,416	1,746,363
Kentucky	17,515,169	15,849,995	1,217,679	217,044	230,451
Louisiana	20,340,779	19,133,840	854,664	220,680	131,595
Maine	5,486,728	4,927,343	326,757	105,819	126,809
Maryland	40,893,427	37,772,869	2,361,572	574,030	184,956
Massachusetts	59,060,000	53,699,352	3,955,703	936,010	468,935
MICHIGAN	63,744,637	58,754,149	4,163,750	591,306	235,432
MINNESOTA	58,068,156	48,050,665	8,485,882	310,357	1,221,252
Mississippi	8,951,397	8,005,741	583,703	110,941	251,011
Missouri	38,326,485	32,579,102	4,124,336	447,469	1,175,578
Montana	3,134,044	2,939,876	120,677	31,678	41,812
Nebraska	14,392,629	10,036,235	4,124,398	122,886	109,110
Nevada	13,293,706	11,142,062	1,767,895	313,526	70,223
New Hampshire	7,183,339	6,695,993	355,208	64,475	67,663
New Jersey	91,082,077	77,076,938	11,535,032	851,966	1,618,142
New Mexico	6,050,390	5,740,363	171,491	48,845	89,691
New York	171,948,716	147,210,379	20,399,783	3,058,045	1,280,509
North Carolina	53,979,373	41,910,144	11,251,342	568,124	249,763
North Dakota	2,825,077	2,603,011	158,334	12,339	51,393
Ohio	87,853,784	73,909,457	9,912,042	849,632	3,182,653
Oklahoma	20,418,765	12,843,853	2,303,842	318,840	4,952,230
Oregon	18,880,258	17,140,695	1,262,025	237,639	239,899
Pennsylvania	87,841,245	76,223,055	8,741,526	980,320	1,896,344
Rhode Island	8,544,847	6,949,536	1,493,266	95,163	6,883
South Carolina	15,357,129	14,179,633	839,709	185,873	151,914
South Dakota	3,293,837	3,048,862	174,084	49,266	21,624
Tennessee	36,802,257	32,601,321	3,292,517	305,377	603,042
Texas	152,691,189	118,410,514	17,127,574	1,213,772	15,939,329
Utah	9,593,606	8,677,321	648,792	70,462	197,031
Vermont	3,079,343	2,767,214	226,227	66,282	19,620
Virginia	47,016,582	41,381,186	4,895,573	628,570	111,253
Washington	42,167,997	35,247,916	5,544,468	552,215	823,398
West Virginia	5,226,420	4,818,131	249,566	66,825	91,899
WISCONSIN	34,711,183	30,394,876	3,727,712	304,642	283,954
Wyoming	2,333,993	2,357,056	108,409	33,609	434,919
UNITED STATES[5]	$2,018,502,103	$1,707,496,056	$230,619,359	$25,579,462	$54,807,225

[1] Taxes may be collected in one state from residents of another state for a variety of reasons, and some corporations pay taxes from a principal office, although their operations may be located in several states.

[2] Collections of individual income tax (withheld and not withheld) include old-age, survivors, disability, and hospital insurance (OASDHI) taxes on salaries and wages under the Federal Insurance Contributions Act or FICA, and on self-employment income under the Self-Employment Insurance Contributions Act or SECA. Includes estate and trust income tax collections of $10.7 billion. Collections of individual income tax include Presidential Election Campaign Fund contributions of $55.9 million.

[3] Includes $347.1 million in "unrelated business income" from tax-exempt organizations (Forms 990-T).

[4] Excludes excise taxes collected by the Customs Service and the Alcohol and Tobacco Tax and Trade Bureau.

[5] United States totals include international and undistributed totals not included in state listing for taxes filed by members of armed forces stationed overseas or other U.S. citizens abroad. Also included are returns from residents of Puerto Rico either with income from sources outside Puerto Rico or income earned as U.S. government employees. Corporation taxes include those paid by domestic and foreign businesses with principal offices outside the United States. Detail may not add to totals due to rounding.

Source: U.S. Department of the Treasury, Internal Revenue Service, "IRS Data Book, FY 2004," Publication 55b at: http://www.irs.gov/taxstats/article/0,,id=102174,00.html [May 31, 2005].

PER CAPITA FEDERAL EXPENDITURES
By State, Fiscal Year 2003

State	Total Amount	Rank	Retirement and Disability	Grants	Procurement	Salaries and Wages	Other Direct Payments
Alabama	$8,192.16	9	$2,717.78	$1,477.34	$1,570.28	$716.29	$1,710.47
Alaska	12,243.59	1	1,603.78	4,658.11	2,589.50	2,491.55	900.65
Arizona	6,773.44	26	2,154.13	1,296.43	1,533.29	597.51	1,192.08
Arkansas	6,728.64	28	2,582.22	1,665.95	317.00	491.29	1,672.18
California	6,191.60	36	1,725.71	1,446.52	1,044.11	580.85	1,394.42
Colorado	6,345.02	32	1,840.33	1,321.65	1,129.87	951.30	1,101.87
Connecticut	8,209.05	8	2,167.23	1,543.35	2,435.66	435.30	1,627.52
Delaware	6,190.71	37	2,379.29	1,444.38	299.46	598.31	1,469.28
District of Columbia	61,680.52	--	3,433.26	7,650.50	20,192.09	26,198.83	4,205.84
Florida	6,659.64	30	2,655.35	1,026.09	640.40	572.65	1,765.15
Georgia	5,977.19	40	1,918.99	1,216.07	603.65	922.83	1,315.65
Hawaii	8,960.91	6	2,396.66	1,519.52	1,573.15	2,277.12	1,194.46
Idaho	6,334.08	33	2,096.51	1,360.03	1,120.76	610.56	1,146.23
ILLINOIS	5,770.68	43	1,958.82	1,242.34	452.75	517.85	1,598.93
Indiana	5,733.81	46	2,161.81	1,180.34	532.89	377.43	1,481.35
IOWA	5,961.06	42	2,302.95	1,316.98	376.78	383.58	1,580.77
Kansas	6,685.55	29	2,274.98	1,253.90	741.74	774.16	1,640.77
Kentucky	7,565.42	16	2,469.41	1,611.06	1,243.15	755.84	1,485.96
Louisiana	7,038.24	25	2,126.05	1,739.25	710.51	588.87	1,873.57
Maine	7,632.30	15	2,606.01	1,998.76	1,004.64	680.45	1,342.43
Maryland	10,464.19	3	2,415.44	1,566.93	2,943.57	1,875.38	1,662.86
Massachusetts	7,968.51	11	2,144.09	2,071.73	1,299.07	535.70	1,917.93
MICHIGAN	5,741.09	44	2,186.73	1,286.70	385.32	339.07	1,543.26
MINNESOTA	5,451.26	49	1,902.82	1,366.48	475.53	419.00	1,287.44
Mississippi	7,545.47	17	2,402.72	1,845.87	911.28	683.70	1,701.90
Missouri	7,691.08	14	2,368.08	1,517.24	1,400.94	671.68	1,733.15
Montana	7,729.15	13	2,522.83	2,112.48	541.93	920.38	1,631.54
Nebraska	6,324.35	34	2,274.49	1,444.21	349.69	685.32	1,570.64
Nevada	5,192.58	50	2,100.55	872.31	656.92	545.27	1,017.53
New Hampshire	5,707.26	47	2,203.93	1,448.54	573.37	443.59	1,037.83
New Jersey	6,213.98	35	2,128.68	1,329.06	632.18	481.41	1,642.66
New Mexico	9,994.53	4	2,340.70	2,305.69	3,104.09	1,027.38	1,216.66
New York	7,185.89	22	2,110.76	2,479.12	404.29	444.77	1,746.95
North Carolina	6,157.35	38	2,236.85	1,381.33	451.33	777.98	1,309.86
North Dakota	9,033.36	5	2,283.24	2,425.04	627.20	1,131.36	2,566.52
Ohio	6,112.53	39	2,216.51	1,371.79	572.55	468.87	1,482.81
Oklahoma	7,191.72	21	2,498.19	1,462.51	708.48	954.74	1,567.79
Oregon	5,970.74	41	2,254.22	1,433.65	336.59	500.32	1,445.96
Pennsylvania	7,306.68	19	2,593.69	1,506.09	658.02	514.54	2,034.35
Rhode Island	7,467.11	18	2,355.21	2,076.22	612.44	759.02	1,664.22
South Carolina	6,760.82	27	2,436.79	1,439.30	871.53	690.28	1,322.92
South Dakota	8,114.01	10	2,366.77	2,221.10	498.44	880.85	2,146.85
Tennessee	7,292.74	20	2,352.80	1,550.40	1,287.62	574.70	1,527.23
Texas	6,349.93	31	1,769.96	1,285.01	1,348.34	630.21	1,316.41
Utah	5,741.00	45	1,655.08	1,209.84	1,133.27	870.44	872.38
Vermont	7,176.49	23	2,192.99	2,150.36	914.33	581.55	1,337.26
Virginia	11,163.05	2	2,647.23	1,067.64	4,175.11	1,997.69	1,275.38
Washington	7,073.06	24	2,215.97	1,448.40	1,081.07	939.13	1,388.48
West Virginia	7,858.15	12	3,128.21	1,967.51	367.28	711.96	1,683.40
WISCONSIN	5,525.40	48	2,123.12	1,378.53	366.87	326.20	1,330.69
Wyoming	8,432.05	7	2,298.04	3,224.42	690.26	1,017.93	1,201.40
UNITED STATES*	$6,910.31		$2,167.50	$1,496.00	$1,011.02	$712.81	$1,522.98

*Totals include the 50 states and District of Columbia. U.S. Outlying Areas are excluded.

Source: U.S. Department of Commerce, U.S. Census Bureau, *Consolidated Federal Funds Report for Fiscal Year 2003: State and County Areas*, September 2004. Rankings calculated by Wisconsin Legislative Reference Bureau.

FEDERAL REVENUE DISTRIBUTED
TO STATE AND LOCAL GOVERNMENTS
by State, Fiscal Year 2001-02

	Per Capita		Amount Distributed (in thousands) to			Percent of all
	Amount	Rank	State Government	Local Government	Total	State and Local General Revenue
Alabama	$1,397.74	15	$5,794,984	$468,396	$6,263,380	26.4%
Alaska	2,792.06	1	1,551,339	237,927	1,789,266	24.8
Arizona	1,051.39	41	4,874,813	843,767	5,718,580	22.4
Arkansas	1,346.36	17	3,409,971	235,303	3,645,274	27.5
California	1,379.03	16	40,843,408	7,406,307	48,249,715	21.3
Colorado	949.00	47	3,806,370	462,320	4,268,690	16.4
Connecticut	1,167.78	32	3,685,655	353,702	4,039,357	17.7
Delaware	1,189.71	30	890,855	68,174	959,029	17.1
District of Columbia	5,029.89	--	--	2,840,094	2,840,094	41.0
Florida	896.60	48	12,785,500	2,170,757	14,956,257	17.3
Georgia	1,095.74	37	8,540,902	816,408	9,357,310	21.1
Hawaii	1,253.52	24	1,364,923	182,564	1,547,487	20.8
Idaho	1,053.57	40	1,324,351	90,801	1,415,152	21.4
ILLINOIS	1,010.43	45	10,448,759	2,267,759	12,716,518	18.4
Indiana	1,020.18	43	5,885,522	397,067	6,282,589	19.4
IOWA	1,235.61	26	3,320,315	305,920	3,626,235	21.5
Kansas	1,141.97	35	2,963,516	134,528	3,098,044	21.2
Kentucky	1,323.62	18	5,101,806	311,778	5,413,584	25.5
Louisiana	1,448.46	14	5,994,423	490,383	6,484,806	24.9
Maine	1,464.52	13	1,816,913	83,672	1,900,585	23.5
Maryland	1,089.30	38	5,259,864	667,582	5,927,446	18.3
Massachusetts	963.10	46	5,061,024	1,114,919	6,175,943	15.8
MICHIGAN	1,249.00	25	11,241,287	1,301,791	12,543,078	21.6
MINNESOTA	1,211.54	29	5,282,293	805,798	6,088,091	18.3
Mississippi	1,612.91	11	4,374,145	251,080	4,625,225	30.2
Missouri	1,290.28	22	6,693,283	635,228	7,328,511	25.2
Montana	1,746.41	7	1,418,565	171,837	1,590,402	31.0
Nebraska	1,143.10	34	1,780,050	193,444	1,973,494	20.1
Nevada	752.86	50	1,280,691	351,747	1,632,438	14.3
New Hampshire	1,015.93	44	1,188,622	107,307	1,295,929	20.2
New Jersey	1,043.34	42	8,235,257	713,715	8,948,972	16.2
New Mexico	1,683.71	8	2,759,537	363,985	3,123,522	28.7
New York	1,889.48	3	32,196,997	3,988,632	36,185,629	23.3
North Carolina	1,232.07	27	9,466,152	774,670	10,240,822	23.2
North Dakota	1,824.23	5	1,022,350	133,845	1,156,195	28.9
Ohio	1,214.96	28	12,327,824	1,535,372	13,863,196	21.1
Oklahoma	1,265.12	23	4,043,825	369,168	4,412,993	24.4
Oregon	1,827.24	4	5,625,495	812,374	6,437,869	29.8
Pennsylvania	1,299.95	20	13,685,396	2,340,945	16,026,341	22.3
Rhode Island	1,652.32	10	1,637,228	128,929	1,766,157	26.6
South Carolina	1,298.80	21	5,027,914	304,781	5,332,695	25.1
South Dakota	1,512.64	12	1,045,385	104,908	1,150,293	29.5
Tennessee	1,312.79	19	7,077,747	526,322	7,604,069	27.7
Texas	1,054.85	39	20,672,252	2,242,455	22,914,707	21.0
Utah	1,126.43	36	2,266,508	346,512	2,613,020	20.9
Vermont	1,763.35	6	1,041,012	46,094	1,087,106	28.2
Virginia	857.19	49	5,377,424	857,422	6,234,846	16.0
Washington	1,160.61	33	6,215,948	825,648	7,041,596	19.4
West Virginia	1,661.27	9	2,847,201	151,770	2,998,971	29.7
WISCONSIN	1,186.61	31	5,912,806	542,810	6,455,616	19.8
Wyoming	2,378.21	2	1,112,947	74,236	1,187,183	28.0
UNITED STATES	$1,252.11	--	$317,581,354	$42,952,953	$360,534,307	21.4%

Sources: U.S. Department of Commerce, U.S. Census Bureau, "State and Local Government Finances: 2002 Census of Governments", at: http://www.census.gov/govs/www/estimate02.html [April 29, 2005], and "National and State Population Estimates", at: http://www.census.gov/popest/states/NST-ann-est.html [April 29, 2005]. Per capita amounts, percentages, and rankings calculated by Wisconsin Legislative Reference Bureau.

FEDERAL AIDS TO WISCONSIN
Fiscal Years 2002-03 and 2003-04
(In Thousands)

Agency administering aid	Federal Aid Received by Wisconsin		Disbursed to Local Governments		Aid to Individuals and Organizations	
	2003-04	2002-03	2003-04	2002-03	2003-04	2002-03
Administration, Department of .	$42,189.2	$219,136.0	$95,448.3	$98,530.1	–$4,005.1	$21,202.9
Agriculture, Trade, and Consumer Protection, Department of . . .	6,787.2	6,649.0	---	---	---	---
Arts Board	589.9	625.9	---	---	190.1	190.9
Child Abuse and Neglect Prevention Board	457.6	377.6	---	---	472.3	365.6
Commerce, Department of	72,760.8	38,102.5	80,385.4	31,931.4	20,269.0	211.9
Corrections, Department of	1,691.8	828.2	---	---	---	---
Elections Board	7,026.1	---	---	---	---	---
Electronic Government, Department of*	43.4	415.6	---	---	---	---
Employment Relations, Department of	---	---	---	---	---	---
Environmental Improvement Program/Clean Water (DOA)	87,368.6	75,024.2	87,368.6	75,024.2	---	---
Health and Family Services, Department of	3,696,935.9	3,191,366.7	157,946.4	167,496.1	3,280,409.4	2,942,588.2
Higher Educational Aids Board .	1,429.5	1,457.6	---	---	1,387.3	1,396.4
Historical Society	1,312.2	1,030.4	---	---	---	---
Justice, Department of	12,490.6	11,611.0	6,681.2	5,313.6	908.4	844.2
Military Affairs, Department of .	41,606.8	33,570.1	12,653.9	11,616.6	50.5	669.2
Natural Resources, Department of	56,893.1	64,510.6	4,883.1	6,094.6	---	---
Public Instruction, Department of	603,241.5	515,607.8	505,857.4	452,760.0	47,068.0	44,464.4
Public Lands Board	41.6	---	41.6	---	---	---
Public Service Commission	287.1	249.3	---	---	---	---
Regulation and Licensing, Department of	55.2	---	---	---	---	---
Supreme Court	1,013.4	527.4	---	---	---	---
TEACH Wisconsin*	–298.2	927.1	---	2,175.0	---	---
Technical College System Board	35,493.4	33,430.1	31,045.6	31,061.9	797.0	793.1
Tourism, Department of	20.0	80.5	---	---	---	---
Transportation, Department of . .	648,968.0	632,573.6	193,670.6	161,610.9	7,650.0	3,948.1
University of Wisconsin System	858,550.5	800,428.7	---	---	273,998.4	241,819.0
Veterans Affairs, Department of	1,126.0	700.9	---	---	223.3	164.6
Workforce Development, Department of	739,809.9	861,337.9	60,150.6	59,290.7	507,707.4	514,744.1
TOTAL	$6,917,891.2	$6,490,568.9	$1,236,132.7	$1,102,905.0	$4,137,126.1	$3,773,402.5

Note: Aid is not necessarily disbursed in the same fiscal year in which it is received by the agency. In some cases, aid is received as reimbursement for previous expenditures.

*The Department of Electronic Government and the Technology for Educational Achievement in Wisconsin (TEACH) Board were abolished pursuant to 2003 Wisconsin Act 33, the biennial budget act. Their functions were transferred to the Department of Administration.

Source: Wisconsin Department of Administration, State Controller's Office, *Annual Fiscal Report – Appendix*, October 2003 and October 2004.

STATE AND LOCAL PUBLIC DEBT, BY STATE
State Fiscal Years 2001-02

State	Debt Outstanding at End of Fiscal Year (in thousands)			Per Capita Debt Outstanding		Per Capita Interest	Interest as
	Total	State	Local	Amount	Rank	on Debt	% of Debt
Alabama	$19,056,995	$6,405,164	$12,651,831	$4,252.77	41	$182.86	4.30%
Alaska	8,645,562	5,307,941	3,337,621	13,490.96	1	666.74	4.94
Arizona	26,606,401	4,347,558	22,258,843	4,891.70	26	200.52	4.10
Arkansas	8,753,923	3,002,264	5,751,659	3,233.20	49	153.75	4.76
California	209,299,330	71,262,728	138,036,602	5,981.99	15	248.16	4.15
Colorado	26,718,356	5,419,234	21,299,122	5,939.95	16	279.78	4.71
Connecticut	27,767,247	20,783,595	6,983,652	8,027.52	4	413.14	5.15
Delaware	5,532,722	4,038,455	1,494,267	6,863.53	9	404.81	5.90
District of Columbia . . .	5,436,087	---	5,436,087	9,627.48	—	417.74	4.34
Florida	90,275,844	20,265,599	70,010,245	5,411.85	22	250.36	4.63
Georgia	34,300,600	8,242,834	26,057,766	4,016.59	43	132.52	3.30
Hawaii	8,448,272	5,656,333	2,791,939	6,843.40	10	464.26	6.78
Idaho	3,985,310	2,544,863	1,440,447	2,967.04	50	156.17	5.26
ILLINOIS	80,936,138	34,760,529	46,175,609	6,431.05	13	311.99	4.85
Indiana	24,070,857	9,455,859	14,614,998	3,908.67	44	191.00	4.89
IOWA	9,494,328	3,712,920	5,781,408	3,235.11	48	128.21	3.96
Kansas	12,313,015	2,288,355	10,024,660	4,538.70	35	233.37	5.14
Kentucky	28,993,629	9,038,631	19,954,998	7,088.93	7	364.20	5.14
Louisiana	20,985,667	9,232,827	11,752,840	4,687.40	31	235.48	5.02
Maine	6,346,249	4,321,366	2,024,883	4,890.19	27	253.47	5.18
Maryland	25,663,252	12,308,854	13,354,398	4,716.18	30	251.48	5.33
Massachusetts	65,322,342	45,216,090	20,106,252	10,186.63	3	504.68	4.95
MICHIGAN	54,194,825	21,947,042	32,247,783	5,396.55	23	237.21	4.40
MINNESOTA	32,010,125	6,408,289	25,601,836	6,370.07	14	289.48	4.54
Mississippi	9,933,625	4,159,879	5,773,746	3,464.05	47	173.34	5.00
Missouri	24,244,237	12,692,540	11,551,697	4,268.52	40	182.74	4.28
Montana	3,962,884	2,751,900	1,210,984	4,351.61	39	230.75	5.30
Nebraska	7,905,990	2,215,191	5,690,799	4,579.37	34	148.50	3.24
Nevada	15,772,823	3,667,666	12,105,157	7,274.27	6	311.89	4.29
New Hampshire	7,221,258	5,396,517	1,824,741	5,661.04	18	317.95	5.62
New Jersey	57,590,436	32,093,133	25,497,303	6,714.32	12	277.12	4.13
New Mexico	8,603,278	4,493,374	4,109,904	4,637.53	32	203.67	4.39
New York	197,194,861	89,855,964	107,338,897	10,296.81	2	434.90	4.22
North Carolina	33,460,541	11,128,287	22,332,254	4,025.62	42	161.53	4.01
North Dakota	2,904,992	1,673,109	1,231,883	4,583.46	33	237.02	5.17
Ohio	51,343,613	20,008,613	31,335,000	4,499.72	37	236.15	5.25
Oklahoma	12,508,160	6,477,128	6,031,032	3,585.85	46	149.80	4.18
Oregon	18,827,113	7,667,746	11,159,367	5,343.63	24	209.07	3.91
Pennsylvania	83,809,049	20,982,531	62,826,518	6,798.01	11	328.15	4.83
Rhode Island	7,344,889	5,855,777	1,489,112	6,871.47	8	303.48	4.42
South Carolina	22,872,515	10,115,612	12,756,903	5,570.72	21	282.34	5.07
South Dakota	3,450,753	2,307,536	1,143,217	4,537.77	36	227.25	5.01
Tennessee	21,128,046	3,627,931	17,500,115	3,647.61	45	159.13	4.36
Texas	122,809,828	24,008,384	98,801,444	5,653.39	19	230.14	4.07
Utah	13,249,622	4,729,182	8,520,440	5,711.68	17	183.13	3.21
Vermont	3,027,741	2,283,773	743,968	4,911.18	25	265.43	5.40
Virginia	35,422,294	13,785,231	21,637,063	4,870.00	28	234.49	4.81
Washington	45,560,550	13,552,176	32,008,374	7,509.39	5	253.59	3.38
West Virginia	8,084,701	4,537,449	3,547,252	4,478.49	38	246.96	5.51
WISCONSIN	30,327,288	14,870,092	15,457,196	5,574.49	20	267.81	4.80
Wyoming	2,387,995	1,298,017	1,089,978	4,783.72	29	255.54	5.34
UNITED STATES . . .	$1,686,106,158	$642,202,068	$1,043,904,090	$5,855.73		$261.52	4.47%

Sources: U.S. Department of Commerce, U.S. Census Bureau, *State and Local Government Finances: 2002 Census of Govern-ments*, at: http://www.census.gov/govs/www/estimate02.html and *National and State Population Estimates*, at: http://www.census.gov/popest/states/NST-ann-est.html [May 8, 2005]. Per capita values and rankings calculated by Wisconsin Legislative Reference Bureau.

PUBLIC INDEBTEDNESS IN WISCONSIN

Outstanding State Indebtedness, May 31, 2005
(In Thousands)

| | Tax Supported Debt | | Revenue Supported Debt[2] | | |
| | General Fund | Segregated Funds[3] | Veterans Housing | Other[4] | Total |
Type of Debt[1]					
General Obligations – State of Wisconsin	$3,163,525	$634,848	$357,335	$756,139	$4,911,848

[1]Amendment of the state constitution in April 1969 permitted direct state borrowing. Previously, debt was incurred through public, nonstock, nonprofit building corporations.
[2]Revenue supported debt includes debt that is issued with initial expectation that revenues and other proceeds from the operation of the programs or facilities financed will amortize the debt without recourse to the general fund.
[3]Includes the Transportation Fund and certain administrative facilities for the Wisconsin Department of Natural Resources.
[4]Includes dormitories, food service, and intercollegiate athletic facilities; certain facilities on the State Fair grounds; and capital equipment.
Source: Wisconsin Department of Administration, Division of Executive Budget and Finance, departmental data, June 2005.

Selected Data on State Indebtedness, 1970 – 2003

| | Outstanding State Indebtedness (Dec. 31) | | As Percent of State Assessed Value | Annual Debt Limitation[1,2] | Actual Debt Incurred[1] | Debt as Percent of Limitation |
Calendar Year	Total[1]	Per Capita				
1970	$646,414	$146.31	1.86%	$260,929	$156,810	60.1%
1975	1,078,215	235.47	1.84	439,124	217,600	49.6
1980	1,916,177	407.18	1.77	813,604	123,500	15.2
1985	2,410,628	507.93	1.96	922,661	440,955	47.8
1990	2,781,071	568.49	1.97	1,060,277	484,099	45.7
1991	3,126,390	631.34	2.07	1,131,958	359,716	31.8
1992	3,065,122	612.41	1.92	1,196,903	427,655	35.7
1993	3,104,055	613.93	1.81	1,287,579	129,325	10.0
1994	3,244,079	636.59	1.75	1,387,461	289,810	20.9
1995	3,305,471	643.46	1.64	1,511,536	368,322	24.4
1996	3,468,447	670.36	1.60	1,627,078	353,295	21.7
1997	3,604,798	693.23	1.55	1,748,057	404,310	23.1
1998	3,751,542	718.41	1.51	1,867,462	475,485	25.5
1999	3,942,659	750.92	1.48	1,999,256	482,360	24.1
2000	4,270,718	796.18	1.49	2,147,411	538,795	25.1
2001	4,452,626	824.26	1.42	2,343,628	485,645	20.7
2002	4,682,045	860.67	1.40	2,514,949	481,000	19.1
2003	4,794,398	876.17	1.33	2,705,327	499,030	18.5

[1]In thousands.
[2]An aggregate debt limit is derived for each calendar year through a formula specified in Section 18.05, Wisconsin Statutes.
Source: Wisconsin Department of Administration, Division of State Executive Budget and Finance, departmental data, June 2005.

State Revenue Bond Indebtedness, May 31, 2005
(In Thousands)

Program Funded	Amount Authorized	Amount Issued	Amount Outstanding
Student loans	$295,000	$215,000	---
Veterans mortgage loans	280,000	90,055	---
Transportation facilities and highway projects	2,095,584	2,932,718[1]	$1,432,998
Health education loans	92,000	129,230[2]	---
Property tax deferral loans	10,000		---
Clean water	1,615,955	1,198,025[3]	682,935
Petroleum environmental cleanup	436,000	483,020[4]	348,455
TOTAL	$4,824,539	$5,048,048	$2,464,388

Note: Revenue bonds are issued for purposes and amounts specifically authorized by the legislature. This debt is not a legal obligation of the state and is not subject to existing debt limitations.
[1]Includes $1,023,467,036 par amount of refunding bonds that do not count against the authorization.
[2]Includes $48,002,520 par amount of refunding bonds that do not count against the authorization.
[3]Includes $288,680,000 par amount of refunding bonds that do not count against the authorization.
[4]Includes $95,470,000 par amount of refunding bonds and $550,000 par amount for issuance expenses that do not count against the authorization.
Source: Wisconsin Department of Administration, Division of State Executive Budget and Finance, departmental data, June 2005.

PUBLIC INDEBTEDNESS IN WISCONSIN–Continued
State Authority Indebtedness
(In Thousands)

	Total Outstanding Indebtedness of State Authorities
Wisconsin Health and Educational Facilities Authority	$6,325,813 (6/30/05)
Wisconsin Housing and Economic Development Authority	$1,958,156 (12/31/04)

Source: Data provided by Authorities, June 2005.

Wisconsin Local Governments, 1955 – 2003
(In Millions)

Unit	1955	1965	1975	1985	1995	2000	2002	2003
Counties	$61.7	$192.5	$261.0	$532.5	$1,221.6	$1,449.2	$1,746.1	$1,843.1
Cities	175.4	548.1	598.7	1,320.4	2,082.8	2,797.8	3,115.3	3,335.7
Villages	6.1	22.5	69.8	227.6	418.7	700.0	822.2	917.2
Towns	4.0	9.2	26.2	75.2	193.8	281.0	338.4	332.2
School districts	62.1	336.6	798.7	448.7	2,104.9	4,314.1	4,902.0	5,021.0
Technical College districts[1]	---	---	97.2	64.7	192.8	329.1	389.4	437.7
TOTAL[2]	$309.4	$1,108.8	$1,851.6	$2,669.0	$6,214.5	$9,871.2	$11,313.4	$11,886.9

Note: Long-term indebtedness includes issues maturing more than one year after date of issue that constitute an obligation of the taxable property in the issuing district.

[1]Technical College districts (previously called Vocational, Technical and Adult Education districts) were included within the municipal bonding statute provisions by Chapter 47, Laws of 1967.

[2]Detail does not add to total due to rounding.

Sources: Wisconsin Department of Revenue, Bureau of Local Financial Assistance, *Indebtedness 1981* and previous issues; *County and Municipal Revenues and Expenditures, 2003* and previous issues; departmental data from Wisconsin Department of Revenue, Wisconsin Department of Public Instruction, and the Wisconsin Technical College System Board.

WISCONSIN GENERAL PROPERTY TAX LEVIES
By Type of Property and Municipality, 2003

Type of Property	Towns	Villages	Cities	Total
Real Estate	$2,459,347,487	$1,108,586,083	$3,897,777,971	$7,465,711,541
Residential	1,882,602,491	830,704,980	2,641,527,550	5,354,835,022
Commercial	156,084,413	218,657,277	1,073,651,688	1,448,393,379
Agricultural	41,425,505	549,385	530,426	42,505,317
Manufacturing	26,459,431	54,111,368	178,162,307	258,733,107
Forest lands	146,289,905	1,025,926	442,605	147,758,437
Swamp and waste land	27,701,578	646,785	289,769	28,638,133
Other land and improvements	178,784,161	2,890,359	3,173,623	184,848,144
Personal Property	**33,538,492**	**32,068,733**	**155,988,694**	**221,595,920**
Furniture, fixtures, and equipment ..	9,796,363	14,939,889	82,629,143	107,365,396
Machinery, tools, and patterns	14,161,420	12,329,924	50,561,911	77,053,255
Boats and other watercraft	86,103	50,488	467,980	604,572
All other personal property	9,494,605	4,748,431	22,329,658	36,572,696
Total General Property Taxes	**$2,492,885,967**	**$1,140,654,837**	**$4,053,766,522**	**$7,687,307,326**
Total State Tax Credit	**(174,608,739)**	**(69,964,065)**	**(224,732,208)**	**(469,305,012)**
TOTAL EFFECTIVE TAXES	**$2,318,277,228**	**$1,070,690,772**	**$3,829,034,314**	**$7,218,002,314**

Note: Some column and row totals may not add to total because the Department of Revenue truncates (rather than rounds) amounts under $1 for individual units of government.

Source: Wisconsin Department of Revenue, Division of State and Local Finance, *Town, Village, and City Taxes – 2003: Taxes Levied 2003 – Collected 2004*, 2004.

WISCONSIN GENERAL PROPERTY ASSESSMENTS
AND TAX LEVIES
1900 – 2003

Calendar Year	Full Value Assessment of All Property		Total State and Local Property Taxes Levied		State Property Tax Relief	Average Full Value Tax Rate Per $1,000		Average Net Rate Per $1,000 After State Relief	
	Amount (in millions)	Percent Change	Amount (in millions)	Percent Change	Amount (in millions)	Rate	Percent Change	Rate	Percent Change
1900	$630	—	$19	—	—	$30.75	—	—	—
1910	2,743	—	31	—	—	11.18	—	—	—
1920	4,571	—	96	—	—	21.06	—	—	—
1930	5,896	—	121	—	—	20.49	—	—	—
1940	4,354	—	110	—	—	25.26	—	—	—
1950	9,201	—	226	—	—	24.52	—	—	—
1960	18,844	—	481	—	—	25.55	—	—	—
1970	34,790	—	1,179	—	$140	33.88	—	—	—
1980	108,480	—	2,210	—	309	20.37	—	—	—
1990	141,370	6.1%	4,388	7.6%	319	31.04	1.4%	$28.78	2.0%
1991	150,928	6.8	4,733	7.9	319	31.35	1.0	29.24	1.6
1992	159,587	5.7	5,169	9.2	319	32.39	3.3	30.39	3.9
1993	171,677	7.6	5,438	5.2	319	31.67	-2.2	29.81	-1.9
1994	184,995	7.8	5,572	2.5	319	30.12	-4.9	28.39	-4.8
1995	201,538	8.9	5,739	3.0	319	28.47	-5.5	26.89	-5.3
1996	216,944	7.6	5,378	-6.3	469	24.78	-13.0	22.62	-15.9
1997	233,074	7.4	5,636	4.8	469	24.18	-2.8	22.16	-2.0
1998	248,995	6.8	5,975	6.0	469	23.99	-0.8	22.11	-0.2
1999	266,568	7.1	6,191	3.6	469	23.22	-3.2	21.46	-2.9
2000	286,321	7.4	6,605	6.7	469	23.07	-0.7	21.43	-0.2
2001	312,484	9.1	7,044	6.7	469	22.54	-2.3	21.04	-1.8
2002	335,326	7.3	7,364	4.5	469	21.96	-2.6	20.56	-2.3
2003	360,710	7.6	7,687	4.4	469	21.31	-3.0	20.01	-2.7

Source: Wisconsin Department of Revenue, Division of State and Local Finance, *Town, Village, and City Taxes – 2003: Taxes Levied 2003 – Collected 2004*, 2004, and previous issues. Percentages calculated by Wisconsin Legislative Reference Bureau.

TOTAL MUNICIPAL PROPERTY TAXES LEVIED IN WISCONSIN
1960 – 2003

Year Levied	Total Taxes (in millions)	Percentage of Taxes Levied by Property Type					
		Residential	Commercial	Manufacturing	Agricultural	Personal[1]	Other[2]
1960	$481.4	47.5%	13.5%	10.7%	11.2%	16.5%	0.6%
1965	664.1	48.4	14.4	10.3	10.6	15.8	0.6
1970	1,179.0	47.3	15.2	10.4	9.7	16.9	0.5
1975	1,601.3	50.5	16.8	5.7	10.1	16.2	0.7
1980	2,210.0	57.7	16.2	4.8	12.5	7.5	1.3
1985	3,203.5	58.9	17.7	4.7	12.4	4.8	1.6
1986	3,489.4	59.6	18.3	4.5	11.0	5.1	1.5
1987	3,499.2	60.3	19.0	4.3	9.7	5.2	1.5
1988	3,755.4	60.3	19.9	4.2	9.0	5.3	1.4
1989	4,078.9	60.3	20.1	4.1	8.7	5.4	1.4
1990	4,388.2	60.4	20.2	4.1	8.4	5.5	1.3
1991	4,732.7	60.9	20.2	4.0	8.1	5.5	1.3
1992	5,169.5	61.7	19.8	4.0	7.9	5.4	1.2
1993	5,438.0	62.7	19.5	3.9	7.5	5.2	1.2
1994	5,572.1	63.8	19.2	3.7	7.1	5.0	1.1
1995	5,738.9	64.8	18.8	3.6	6.7	4.9	1.1
1996	5,378.0	65.7	18.9	3.6	3.6	4.6	3.7
1997	5,635.9	66.2	18.7	3.6	3.3	4.5	3.7
1998	5,975.0	66.5	18.7	3.6	2.9	4.5	3.9
1999	6,190.9	67.3	18.8	3.7	2.7	3.5	4.0
2000	6,604.5	67.9	18.9	3.7	1.7	3.4	4.3
2001	7,043.7	68.1	19.0	3.6	1.6	3.4	4.4
2002	7,363.6	69.0	18.9	3.5	0.8	3.2	4.6
2003	7,687.3	69.7	18.8	3.4	0.6	2.9	4.7

[1] An exemption for "Line A" business property was phased in beginning in 1977. "Line A" property was completely exempted by 1981.

[2] Beginning in 1996, "Other" includes agricultural property not considered agricultural land for the purposes of use value assessment.

Sources: Wisconsin Department of Revenue, Division of State and Local Finance, *Town, Village, and City Taxes – 2003: Taxes Levied 2003 – Collected 2004*, 2004 and previous issues. For 1981 and earlier, *Property Tax, 1981* and previous issues. 1960 and 1965 data are from Wisconsin Department of Taxation. Percentages calculated by Wisconsin Legislative Reference Bureau.

GENERAL PROPERTY ASSESSMENTS, TAXES AND RATES
By County, 2003

County	Full Value Assessment[1]	Total Property Tax[2]	State Property Tax Credit[3]	Average Full Value Tax Rate per $1,000[4] Gross	Net
Adams	$1,660,724,200	$32,805,264	$1,881,789	$19.75	$18.62
Ashland	908,068,600	19,868,878	1,163,147	21.88	20.60
Barron	2,839,237,500	55,838,542	3,153,034	19.67	18.56
Bayfield	1,771,672,200	27,939,575	1,775,604	15.77	14.77
Brown	14,465,487,100	317,505,895	19,190,437	21.95	20.62
Buffalo	705,963,100	15,814,508	974,753	22.40	21.02
Burnett	2,026,825,800	29,353,901	1,983,109	14.48	13.50
Calumet	2,396,791,500	53,709,891	2,967,569	22.41	21.17
Chippewa	3,239,643,700	60,784,877	4,128,622	18.76	17.49
Clark	1,359,767,300	30,001,342	1,767,100	22.06	20.76
Columbia	3,587,811,900	73,867,431	4,665,279	20.59	19.29
Crawford	777,455,900	19,886,136	1,114,623	25.58	24.14
Dane	34,696,825,100	783,359,938	52,058,178	22.58	21.08
Dodge	4,508,049,900	104,485,075	6,470,515	23.18	21.74
Door	5,579,066,200	71,781,922	3,798,359	12.87	12.19
Douglas	2,397,987,000	47,738,774	2,722,466	19.91	18.77
Dunn	2,143,903,800	47,209,621	2,605,282	22.02	20.81
Eau Claire	5,177,368,500	108,905,926	7,650,343	21.03	19.56
Florence	409,009,700	8,591,668	481,798	21.01	19.83
Fond du Lac	5,298,866,400	110,804,281	6,677,836	20.91	19.65
Forest	831,263,200	15,395,592	1,076,442	18.52	17.23
Grant	1,863,896,900	42,127,148	2,736,952	22.60	21.13
Green	1,851,534,200	46,792,732	3,062,226	25.27	23.62
Green Lake	1,672,012,300	33,313,218	1,988,605	19.92	18.73
Iowa	1,406,277,700	34,016,081	2,234,923	24.19	22.60
Iron	647,410,200	11,888,597	717,131	18.36	17.26
Jackson	977,312,600	22,248,120	1,178,124	22.76	21.56
Jefferson	4,725,683,300	101,680,478	6,649,116	21.52	20.11
Juneau	1,365,455,200	32,451,886	1,865,648	23.77	22.40
Kenosha	10,106,676,600	223,031,361	12,217,041	22.07	20.86
Kewaunee	1,132,915,500	23,238,597	1,307,520	20.51	19.36
La Crosse	5,620,717,500	131,698,286	7,999,212	23.43	22.01
Lafayette	659,123,000	17,062,873	1,177,689	25.89	24.10
Langlade	1,328,309,600	25,712,573	1,620,063	19.36	18.14
Lincoln	1,887,115,900	37,952,658	2,337,227	20.11	18.87
Manitowoc	4,321,880,200	92,206,370	5,234,672	21.33	20.12
Marathon	7,152,373,100	162,414,253	9,713,770	22.71	21.35
Marinette	2,815,417,500	53,229,474	3,558,724	18.91	17.64
Marquette	1,193,080,700	22,024,686	1,253,567	18.46	17.41
Menominee	220,446,100	4,386,393	184,144	19.90	19.06
Milwaukee	47,266,665,200	1,252,879,246	65,095,776	26.51	25.13
Monroe	1,788,049,100	42,825,262	2,157,936	23.95	22.74
Oconto	2,741,651,900	50,807,007	3,244,654	18.53	17.35
Oneida	4,853,442,900	75,001,905	5,340,358	15.45	14.35
Outagamie	9,937,346,300	211,216,093	12,470,029	21.25	20.00
Ozaukee	8,453,948,600	164,873,095	11,918,380	19.50	18.09
Pepin	400,376,900	9,325,808	565,627	23.29	21.88
Pierce	2,380,732,100	47,152,322	2,809,593	19.81	18.63
Polk	3,438,519,800	59,692,457	3,673,393	17.36	16.29
Portage	3,730,747,700	78,226,730	4,657,669	20.97	19.72
Price	1,145,016,200	21,411,436	1,064,802	18.70	17.77
Racine	10,965,780,800	237,081,550	13,236,009	21.62	20.41
Richland	807,713,300	19,661,178	1,304,549	24.34	22.73
Rock	7,722,415,000	182,655,086	10,907,834	23.65	22.24
Rusk	847,324,400	16,330,356	1,284,707	19.27	17.76
St. Croix	5,936,959,400	104,192,772	6,471,136	17.55	16.46
Sauk	4,617,518,500	91,593,547	5,293,897	19.84	18.69
Sawyer	2,524,236,600	32,395,184	2,337,198	12.83	11.91
Shawano	2,257,868,900	44,108,518	2,591,149	19.54	18.39
Sheboygan	6,665,403,800	155,282,520	9,015,256	23.30	21.94
Taylor	1,039,308,800	22,326,589	1,216,866	21.48	20.31
Trempealeau	1,173,678,300	28,146,041	1,754,947	23.98	22.49
Vernon	1,146,906,500	28,200,521	1,622,884	24.59	23.17
Vilas	4,920,932,600	60,176,754	4,660,633	12.23	11.28
Walworth	9,478,615,400	183,950,090	12,104,781	19.41	18.13
Washburn	1,750,202,400	28,027,727	1,661,320	16.01	15.06
Washington	9,759,743,200	186,198,495	11,928,207	19.08	17.86
Waukesha	37,450,170,400	714,658,302	52,121,579	19.08	17.69
Waupaca	2,943,135,900	61,642,546	3,706,533	20.94	19.69
Waushara	1,953,938,800	36,934,431	2,136,409	18.90	17.81
Winnebago	9,225,241,400	206,248,690	11,090,626	22.36	21.15
Wood	3,657,193,500	80,960,247	4,517,636	22.14	20.90
TOTAL	**$360,710,211,300**	**$7,687,307,326**	**$469,305,012**	**$21.31**	**$20.01**

[1] Reflects actual market value of all taxable general property, as determined by the Wisconsin Department of Revenue independent of locally assessed values, which vary substantially from full value (from less than 35% to more than 125%).

[2] Includes taxes and special charges levied by all units of government and special districts.

[3] Total amount of general property tax credit paid by the state to taxing districts and credited to taxpayers on their tax bills.

[4] A county's average tax rate per $1,000 of assessed valuation (determined by dividing total taxes by equalized value and multiplying by 1,000) is the preferred figure for comparison purposes, rather than the general local property tax rate because the average is based on full market value. Net tax rate per $1,000 reflects the effect of state property tax relief.

Source: Wisconsin Department of Revenue, Division of State and Local Finance, *Town, Village, and City Taxes – 2003: Taxes Levied 2003 – Collected 2004*, 2004.

HIGHLIGHTS OF TRANSPORTATION IN WISCONSIN

Roads — As of January 1, 2004, there were 113,269 miles of roads in Wisconsin. The total included 11,772 miles of state trunk highways, 19,705 miles of county trunk highways, and 79,970 miles of local roads. Eighty-one percent (91,822 miles) of Wisconsin's road system is surfaced at bituminous grade or higher, with the remaining 19% being gravel or soil-surfaced, graded and drained, or unimproved.

Motor Vehicles and Drivers — Over the decades, the total number of motor vehicle registrations has increased from 819,718 in 1930 to 5,170,728 in 2004. Of 3,933,924 drivers licensed in 2003, 668,542 (17%) were 25-34 years old; 803,469 (20.4%) were 35-44 years old; 775,496 (19.7%) were 45-54 years old; 507,559 (12.9%) were 55-64 years old. Of the 589,678 drivers age 65 and older, 56,413 (1.4%) were 85 years and above.

In 2003, 131,191 single- or multi-vehicle traffic crashes were reported, including 748 fatal and 39,413 injury crashes. The 25-34 year old age group had the highest percentage of drivers in crashes with 17.5%, followed by the 35-44 year old group with 17.4%. Of 572 drivers killed in fatal crashes, 520 were tested for blood alcohol content (BAC), and 195 (34.1%) of them registered a BAC of 0.10% or above. Vehicle miles traveled in 2003 totaled 59.6 billion; the fatality rate for that year was 1.40 per 100 million vehicle miles, and the fatal crash rate was 1.23.

Mass Transit — As of March 2005, there were 26 urban bus systems operating in Wisconsin (24 publicly owned and 2 privately owned). There were 10 rural/intercity systems (3 publicly owned and 7 privately contracted). The majority of the publicly owned systems were established in the mid- to late-1970s; only 3 date back to the 1950s. In 43 municipalities, shared-ride taxi service was available.

Statewide urban bus systems showed a decrease in usage in 2003 with 47.7 million revenue miles traveled and 81.6 million revenue passengers.

Air Carriers — In 2004, there were 711 airports operating in Wisconsin. Of these, 99 were publicly owned and 405 privately owned. The remaining 172 specialized facilities included heliports (139), seaplane bases (26), and military/police fields (7). In 2004, certificated air carriers carried 5,244,880 passengers.

Railroads — Since 1920 the number of railroads operating in Wisconsin has decreased from 35 to 11. Over the same period, railroad road mileage declined to 3,417 miles. Rail freight traffic rose from 9.1 billion ton-miles in 1920 to 27.4 billion ton-miles in 2004 and revenue rose from $92,826 million in 1920 to $713,951 million in 2004. Rail passenger traffic dropped drastically from 20.2 million passengers in 1920 to 146,000 in 1994. More recent passenger data are not available.

Harbors — In 2003, Wisconsin reported 10 active lake harbors on Lake Michigan and Lake Superior, which handled 44.5 million short tons of commodities. The Duluth-Superior harbor reported the greatest amount of commerce at 38.3 million tons.

The following tables present selected data. Consult footnoted sources for more detailed information about transportation.

WISCONSIN AIRPORTS
By Type, 1998 – 2004

	Number of Airports						
Type of Airport	1998	1999	2000	2001	2002	2003	2004
Publicly owned airports	97	97	98	98	97	99	99
Scheduled air carrier airports	(9)	(9)	(9)	(9)	(9)	(8)	(8)
All other publicly owned or operated airports	(88)	(88)	(89)	(89)	(88)	(91)	(91)
Privately owned airports open to the public	35	34	38	38	37	35	35
Private use airports	403	419	426	430	407	403	405
Heliports.......................................	115	120	131	126	132	136	139
Seaplane bases	26	27	27	27	27	25	26
Military/police fields and helipads	7	7	7	7	7	7	7
TOTAL	683	704	727	726	700	705	711

Sources: Wisconsin Department of Transportation, *Wisconsin Aviation Activity 2004,* at: http://www.dot.wisconsin.gov/travel/ air/ activity.htm [March 2005] and previous issues; departmental data, March 2005.

WISCONSIN AIRPORT SYSTEM USAGE
1950 – 2004

Year	Certificated Air Carriers[1]		
	Passengers[2]	Tonnage	
		Mail	Cargo
1950	145,049	427	4,483
1955	366,787	731	3,266
1960	561,160	608	5,264
1965	843,215	3,265	10,133
1970	1,483,077	NA	NA
1975	1,906,826	7,314	17,833
1980	2,681,529	9,784	10,451
1985	2,502,782	7,184	5,054
1990	3,488,596	9,380	18,616
1991	3,225,383	8,044	21,305
1992	3,517,446	8,076	24,143
1993	3,595,918	10,080	26,996
1994	3,885,969	12,660	30,125
1995	3,969,886	14,049	33,964
1996	4,114,213	15,571	54,594
1997	4,307,134	NA	NA
1998	4,387,673	NA	NA
1999	4,520,419	NA	117,489
2000	4,659,187	NA	110,875
2001	4,386,021	NA	114,381
2002	4,531,810	NA	117,024
2003	4,850,196	NA	61,258
2004	5,244,880	NA	61,866

NA – Not available.

[1]Certificated air carrier is an airline that holds a valid Certificate of Public Convenience and Necessity, issued by the Civil Aeronautics Board.

[2]Beginning in 1965, the passenger count includes originating, stop-over, and transfer revenue passengers. Prior to that only those revenue passengers boarding aircraft at point of origin were counted.

Source: Wisconsin Department of Transportation, *Wisconsin Aviation Activity 2004*, at: http://www.dot.wisconsin.gov/travel/air/activity.htm [March 2005] and previous issues.

RAILROAD MILEAGE, USAGE AND REVENUE IN WISCONSIN
1920 – 2004

Year	No. of Railroads	Mileage Operated in Wisconsin[1]		Freight Traffic (in thousands)			Passenger Traffic (in thousands)		
		Road[2]	Track[3]	Tons	Ton-Miles[4]	Revenue (in thousands)	Passengers	Miles[5]	Revenue (in thousands)
1920	35	7,546	11,615	100,991	9,052,084	$92,826	20,188	960,569	$28,646
1930	27	7,231	11,583	83,672	6,908,656	78,747	4,799	466,154	14,071
1940	22	6,646	10,484	87,980	6,910,647	69,941	3,952	445,938	8,201
1950	20	6,337	10,000	121,576	10,850,178	141,762	5,575	646,353	14,933
1960	18	6,195	9,625	93,475	9,096,855	134,065	3,127	383,457	9,800
1970	15	5,965	9,127	97,130	13,432,055	191,764	1,463	138,572	4,264
1980[6]	21	5,192	7,990	101,008	14,727,522	453,977	174	1,122	54
1990	15	4,415	6,125	116,099	14,436,776	455,541	112	783	63
1993	13	4,227	5,697	123,691	17,435,929	487,496	152	1,069	87
1994	13	4,208	5,441	131,503	18,908,961	508,056	146	1,012	93
1995	12	4,170	5,403	132,858	20,980,751	573,501	NA	NA	NA
1996	10	4,170	5,420	147,906	21,026,799	575,048	NA	NA	NA
1997	11	3,678	5,056	169,478	27,366,352	629,012	NA	NA	NA
1998	12	3,671	5,049	148,286	21,198,769	576,848	NA	NA	NA
1999	12	3,619	4,997	152,425	21,929,925	574,707	NA	NA	NA
2000	12	3,548	4,956	151,573	21,321,266	580,678	NA	NA	NA
2001	13	3,699	5,107	158,881	25,922,949	700,258	NA	NA	NA
2002	12	3,688	5,095	NA	21,417,016	704,167	NA	NA	NA
2003	11	3,450	4,643	118,387	26,092,960	667,736	NA	NA	NA
2004	11	3,417	4,610	106,719	27,408,816	713,951	NA	NA	NA

NA – Not available.

[1]In order to avoid duplication, mileage shown is exclusive of trackage rights.

[2]Road mileage is the measurement of stone roadbed in miles.

[3]Track mileage is the measurement of track (2 steel rails) on roadbeds in miles.

[4]A ton-mile is the movement of one ton (2,000 pounds) of cargo over the distance of one mile.

[5]Passenger miles are the combination of the number of passengers carried on Wisconsin trains and the miles traveled by the passengers while within Wisconsin boundaries.

[6]Intercity passenger service operated by Amtrak after May 1, 1971.

Source: Office of the Wisconsin Commissioner of Railroads, departmental data, June 2005.

HIGHWAY MILEAGE, BY COUNTY AND SYSTEM
January 1, 2004

County	Total All Systems	State Trunk System	County Trunk System	Local Roads (City, Village, Town)	Other Roads (Parks, Forests)
Adams	1,435.91	91.46	225.27	1,117.98	1.20
Ashland	1,168.90	120.60	93.25	869.47	85.58
Barron	1,986.92	141.78	290.84	1,553.20	1.10
Bayfield	2,187.31	155.05	172.89	1,775.85	83.52
Brown	2,269.89	181.86	355.16	1,706.57	26.30
Buffalo	1,043.29	147.85	318.07	577.37	—
Burnett	1,572.38	106.40	216.85	1,205.07	44.06
Calumet	842.14	100.75	128.33	613.06	—
Chippewa	2,092.07	207.43	480.22	1,383.94	20.48
Clark	2,193.92	156.71	300.92	1,680.20	56.09
Columbia	1,724.71	277.97	356.40	1,090.34	—
Crawford	1,078.07	180.12	132.86	762.09	3.00
Dane	3,968.12	398.86	541.36	3,027.20	0.70
Dodge	2,032.03	239.40	540.61	1,252.02	—
Door	1,247.67	101.88	279.67	866.12	—
Douglas	2,085.06	160.87	337.13	1,493.85	93.21
Dunn	1,742.95	204.56	425.09	1,113.30	—
Eau Claire	1,552.94	147.29	418.99	966.85	19.81
Florence	525.59	66.84	49.18	375.62	33.95
Fond du Lac	1,751.49	229.68	356.58	1,165.04	0.19
Forest	1,057.95	155.70	108.95	772.10	21.20
Grant	2,103.16	257.70	309.91	1,535.55	—
Green	1,246.62	122.15	278.74	845.73	—
Green Lake	700.00	69.98	228.86	401.16	—
Iowa	1,311.84	169.50	358.61	781.62	2.11
Iron	791.56	113.52	66.99	544.28	66.77
Jackson	1,477.78	185.98	231.43	1,024.24	36.13
Jefferson	1,395.67	176.65	257.66	961.08	0.28
Juneau	1,517.64	191.87	234.18	1,075.60	15.99
Kenosha	1,054.47	116.53	262.70	674.91	0.33
Kewaunee	819.44	61.15	211.59	543.02	3.68
La Crosse	1,157.32	157.85	284.90	713.67	0.90
Lafayette	1,147.80	126.11	267.19	753.84	0.66
Langlade	1,148.89	145.12	271.00	725.10	7.67
Lincoln	1,310.48	155.51	267.27	860.45	27.25
Manitowoc	1,650.50	153.07	284.48	1,210.88	2.07
Marathon	3,313.96	274.70	608.95	2,418.33	11.98
Marinette	2,324.17	153.13	338.55	1,608.33	224.16
Marquette	858.29	86.85	237.33	534.11	—
Menominee	453.54	40.68	36.51	79.05	297.30
Milwaukee	2,987.01	251.05	85.92	2,586.38	63.66
Monroe	1,630.64	238.20	343.42	1,043.30	5.72
Oconto	2,008.81	142.55	313.39	1,522.65	30.22
Oneida	1,694.47	160.10	172.95	1,324.65	36.77
Outagamie	1,926.16	185.77	349.05	1,387.84	3.50
Ozaukee	904.51	80.00	151.42	672.30	0.79
Pepin	460.04	47.96	154.80	257.28	—
Pierce	1,280.05	164.98	245.41	868.17	1.49
Polk	1,963.69	159.23	333.20	1,455.55	15.71
Portage	1,862.31	156.26	429.74	1,276.31	—
Price	1,438.61	154.87	218.12	1,048.58	17.04
Racine	1,285.52	159.31	150.67	964.20	11.34
Richland	1,130.66	150.17	296.72	679.77	4.00
Rock	2,028.95	250.91	217.78	1,560.26	—
Rusk	1,238.41	115.42	245.36	856.83	20.80
St. Croix	1,844.54	200.72	335.14	1,299.67	9.01
Sauk	1,799.60	221.15	300.33	1,267.54	10.58
Sawyer	1,512.88	161.33	229.01	1,096.03	26.51
Shawano	1,825.87	183.27	293.42	1,242.89	106.29
Sheboygan	1,537.44	166.52	450.89	920.03	—
Taylor	1,452.36	111.37	242.14	1,076.43	22.42
Trempealeau	1,343.04	176.39	291.73	874.92	—
Vernon	1,645.15	214.01	285.26	1,140.68	5.20
Vilas	1,586.95	133.15	204.44	1,123.06	126.30
Walworth	1,493.89	216.85	199.66	1,077.38	—
Washburn	1,405.76	136.53	199.23	975.86	94.14
Washington	1,465.04	187.31	190.98	1,086.75	—
Waukesha	2,917.43	232.18	391.78	2,291.90	1.57
Waupaca	1,649.97	197.43	342.30	1,110.24	—
Waushara	1,328.26	132.32	333.58	862.36	—
Winnebago	1,508.57	169.72	216.66	1,121.54	0.65
Wood	1,770.35	183.81	324.78	1,240.54	21.22
STATE	113,269.38	11,771.95	19,704.75	79,970.08	1,822.60

Source: Wisconsin Department of Transportation, Division of Transportation Investment Management, departmental data, February 2005.

WISCONSIN ROAD MILEAGE, BY SYSTEM AND SURFACE TYPE
January 1, 2004

Type of Road System	Miles	Percent	Surface Type	Miles	Percent
State trunk highways	11,772	10.4%	Bituminous or higher*	91,822	81.1%
County trunk highways	19,705	17.4	Gravel or soil-surfaced	18,265	16.1
City streets	13,074	11.5	Graded and drained	3,024	2.7
Village streets	5,116	4.5	Unimproved	159	0.1
Town roads	61,780	54.5	TOTAL	113,269	100.0%
Park, forest, and other roads	1,823	1.6			
TOTAL	113,269	100.0%			

Note: Detail may not add to total due to rounding.

*Bituminous or higher includes 3,210 surface types.

Source: Wisconsin Department of Transportation, Division of Transportation Investment Management, departmental data, February 2005.

MOTOR VEHICLES IN WISCONSIN, BY TYPE
1930 – 2004

Fiscal Year (ending June 30)	Total	Autos	Trucks*	Trailers, Semitrailers	Motor Homes	Buses	Motor-cycles	Mopeds
1930	819,718	700,251	115,883	—	—	554	3,030	—
1935	722,797	597,197	116,912	5,634	—	498	2,556	—
1940	874,652	741,583	123,742	5,144	—	675	3,508	—
1945	828,425	676,978	139,591	6,484	—	1,489	3,883	—
1950	1,157,221	921,194	209,083	14,124	—	2,465	10,355	—
1955	1,369,636	1,108,084	227,367	21,643	—	3,337	9,205	—
1960	1,598,693	1,303,679	246,353	31,502	—	5,184	11,975	—
1965	1,867,223	1,517,397	269,771	44,017	—	7,218	28,820	—
1970	2,205,662	1,762,681	317,096	64,065	—	8,178	53,642	—
1975	2,737,164	2,096,694	425,854	91,609	—	11,897	111,110	—
1980	3,417,748	2,509,904	558,840	102,256	17,071	13,775	205,786	10,116
1985	3,372,029	2,310,024	765,852	72,289	17,195	10,325	176,023	20,321
1990	3,834,608	2,456,175	1,045,583	123,061	21,095	15,081	149,268	24,345
1995	4,285,753	2,464,358	1,391,374	207,042	22,554	15,593	161,762	23,070
2000	4,703,294	2,405,408	1,813,385	214,344	24,427	15,587	160,920	17,977
2001	4,860,457	2,413,001	1,913,964	224,833	24,402	16,259	192,305	21,636
2002	4,948,282	2,404,081	2,003,863	237,258	24,774	17,061	183,883	20,158
2003	5,091,716	2,401,816	2,094,464	252,352	25,022	17,555	215,225	24,597
2004	5,170,728	2,387,459	2,167,503	279,843	25,258	14,099	207,586	24,519

*"Trucks" includes minivans and sport utility vehicles.

Sources: Wisconsin Secretary of State, *Biennial Report – 1928-30*; Wisconsin Highway Commission, *Biennial Reports – 1933-35, 1938-40*; Wisconsin Motor Vehicle Department, *Wisconsin Motor Vehicle Registrations – Fiscal Years 1944-45 through 1964-65*; Wisconsin Department of Transportation, *Wisconsin Motor Vehicle Registrations – Fiscal Year 1979-80*, 1980, and previous issues, and *Wisconsin Transportation Facts* (periodical); departmental data, February 2005.

WISCONSIN MOTOR VEHICLE CRASHES
Statistical Summary, 1993 – 2003

Year	Total Licensed Drivers	Crashes[1] Total	Crashes[1] Fatal	Crashes[1] Injury	Persons Killed	Persons Injured	Miles Traveled (in millions)	Fatality Rate[2]	Fatal Crash Rate
1993	3,502,347	142,285	616	41,216	703	60,902	48,805	1.44	1.26
1994	3,554,003	148,325	616	43,775	706	66,403	50,273	1.40	1.23
1995	3,601,619	148,864	656	43,845	739	66,232	51,395	1.44	1.28
1996	3,723,685	136,698	656	43,773	759	66,048	52,639	1.44	1.25
1997	3,672,469	129,954	631	41,962	721	63,166	53,729	1.34	1.17
1998	3,709,957	125,831	628	41,594	709	62,236	56,048	1.26	1.12
1999	3,733,077	130,950	674	41,345	744	61,577	56,960	1.31	1.18
2000	3,667,497	139,510	718	43,145	801	63,890	57,266	1.40	1.25
2001	3,835,549	125,403	684	39,358	764	58,279	57,266	1.33	1.19
2002	3,839,930	129,072	723	39,634	805	57,776	58,745	1.37	1.23
2003	3,933,924	131,191	748	39,413	836	56,882	59,617	1.40	1.23

[1]A motor vehicle crash is defined as an event caused by a single variable or chain of variables. Property damage threshold for a reportable crash was raised from $500 to $1,000, effective January 1, 1996.

[2]Per 100-million vehicle miles traveled.

Source: Wisconsin Department of Transportation, *2003 Wisconsin Traffic Crash Facts,* October 2004, and previous issues.

Fatal Crashes on Wisconsin Highways and Roads, 1993 – 2003

Year	Total	Interstate	State	County	Local
1993	616	38	287	142	149
1994	616	30	281	142	163
1995	656	24	312	152	168
1996	656	37	328	142	149
1997	631	32	303	132	164
1998	628	35	297	156	140
1999	674	41	301	164	168
2000	718	39	311	143	225
2001	684	35	286	167	196
2002	723	44	310	171	198
2003	748	46	317	174	211

Source: Wisconsin Department of Transportation, *2003 Wisconsin Traffic Crash Facts,* October 2004, and previous issues.

Drivers in Fatal Crashes – Age and BAC of Drivers Killed, 2003

Age of Drivers	All Drivers	Drivers Killed	Tests of Drivers Killed Total	Tests of Drivers Killed Negative	Tests of Drivers Killed Positive	Blood Alcohol Concentration (BAC) 0.001-0.049	Blood Alcohol Concentration (BAC) 0.05-0.099	Blood Alcohol Concentration (BAC) 0.10 and over
14 years and under ...	1	0	0	0	0	0	0	0
15 years	3	2	2	2	0	0	0	0
16 years	20	11	10	9	1	0	1	0
17 years	32	12	12	11	1	0	1	0
18 years	42	21	21	13	8	1	1	6
19 years	39	19	17	7	10	0	1	9
20 years	32	17	15	5	10	1	0	9
21 years	40	22	20	5	15	0	0	15
22 years	38	22	22	11	11	1	2	8
23 years	32	19	18	5	13	1	1	11
24 years	31	16	15	4	11	0	1	10
25-34 years	200	91	89	35	54	3	5	46
35-44 years	195	98	90	48	42	3	3	36
45-54 years	198	92	82	44	38	3	2	33
55-64 years	96	51	46	35	11	1	1	9
65-74 years	54	27	23	21	2	0	0	2
75-84 years	61	38	28	27	1	0	0	1
85 and over	15	14	10	10	0	0	0	0
TOTAL	1,175*	572	520	292	228	14	19	195

Note: Drivers include motorcycle and moped drivers.

*Includes 23 of unknown age.

Source: Wisconsin Department of Transportation, *2003 Wisconsin Traffic Crash Facts,* October 2004.

WISCONSIN MOTOR VEHICLE CRASHES–Continued
Motorcycle Crashes, 1993 – 2003

Year	Total Registered Cycles	Cycle Crashes Total	Fatal	Personal Injury	Property Damage	Cyclist Fatalities* Total	No Helmet or Unknown	Helmet
1993	169,499	2,243	41	1,861	341	40	32	8
1994	149,756	2,297	53	1,924	320	57	50	7
1995	168,287	2,057	45	1,709	303	47	43	4
1996	148,975	1,823	48	1,580	195	50	40	10
1997	167,997	1,760	59	1,487	214	63	52	11
1998	157,230	1,989	63	1,691	235	65	51	14
1999	179,494	2,012	61	1,720	231	65	46	17
2000	175,486	2,078	76	1,760	242	78	57	15
2001	201,143	2,285	69	1,928	288	70	53	14
2002	198,495	2,184	73	1,794	317	78	59	15
2003	225,181	2,512	98	2,099	315	100	74	24

*Number of cyclists killed includes both drivers and passengers.
Source: Wisconsin Department of Transportation, *2003 Wisconsin Traffic Crash Facts*, October 2004.

Drivers Involved in Crashes, By Age Group, 2003

Age of Drivers	Total Licensed Drivers Number	Age Group as Percent of Total Drivers	Drivers Involved in Crashes* Number	Percent of Total Drivers in Crashes	Drivers by Type of Crash* Fatal	Injury	Property Damage
14 years and under ..	0	0.0%	177	0.1%	1	62	114
15 years	354	0.0	383	0.2	3	131	249
16 years	40,720	1.0	6,848	3.2	20	2,405	4,423
17 years	57,927	1.5	7,982	3.7	32	2,785	5,165
18 years	65,587	1.7	8,252	3.8	42	2,828	5,382
19 years	66,199	1.7	6,876	3.2	39	2,366	4,471
20 years	68,409	1.7	6,572	3.1	32	2,295	4,245
21 years	71,374	1.8	6,285	2.9	40	2,153	4,092
22 years	72,427	1.8	5,946	2.8	38	2,019	3,889
23 years	73,578	1.9	5,290	2.5	32	1,794	3,464
24 years	72,605	1.8	4,886	2.3	31	1,712	3,143
25-34 years	668,542	17.0	37,558	17.5	200	12,553	24,805
35-44 years	803,469	20.4	37,408	17.4	195	12,510	24,703
45-54 years	775,496	19.7	30,554	14.2	198	10,106	20,250
55-64 years	507,559	12.9	16,553	7.7	96	5,423	11,034
65-74 years	320,568	8.1	8,786	4.1	54	2,829	5,903
75-84 years	212,697	5.4	5,634	2.6	61	1,881	3,692
85 and over	56,413	1.4	1,300	0.6	15	485	800
Unknown	0	0.0	17,665	8.2	23	2,815	14,827
TOTAL	3,933,924	100.0%	214,955	100.0%	1,152	69,152	144,651

*Figure indicates the number of times a driver in this age group was involved in a crash. If a driver had more than one crash, the driver would be counted more than once.
Source: Wisconsin Department of Transportation, *2003 Wisconsin Traffic Crash Facts*, October 2004.

WISCONSIN MOTOR VEHICLE CRASHES–Continued
Possible Contributing Circumstances, 2003

Circumstance by category	All Crashes				Urban Crashes				Rural Crashes			
	Total	Fatal	Injury	Property Damage	Total	Fatal	Personal Injury	Property Damage	Total	Fatal	Personal Injury	Property Damage
DRIVER												
Inattentive driving	25,492	133	9,667	15,692	14,725	17	5,251	9,457	10,767	116	4,416	6,235
Failure to yield right-of-way	23,293	120	9,452	13,721	16,806	33	6,673	10,100	6,487	87	2,779	3,621
Failure to have control	22,705	292	8,526	13,887	9,070	37	2,917	6,116	13,635	255	5,609	7,771
Speed too fast for conditions	16,667	148	5,614	10,905	5,760	16	1,646	4,098	10,907	132	5,968	6,807
Following too closely	10,347	11	3,830	6,506	7,324	1	2,732	4,591	3,023	10	1,098	1,915
Driver condition	8,138	190	4,037	3,911	3,586	42	1,517	2,027	4,552	148	2,520	1,884
Disregarded traffic control	6,382	52	3,035	3,295	5,157	13	2,430	2,714	1,225	39	605	581
Improper turn	4,084	10	874	3,200	2,998	1	581	2,416	1,086	9	293	784
Exceeding speed limit	3,743	139	1,737	1,867	1,991	40	879	1,072	1,752	99	858	795
Unsafe backing	3,136	2	248	2,886	2,040	1	156	1,883	1,096	1	92	1,003
Left of center	2,309	104	1,020	1,185	632	5	231	396	1,677	99	789	789
Improper overtake	2,080	17	519	1,544	1,134	1	237	896	946	16	282	648
Physically disabled	179	2	91	86	99	1	47	51	80	1	44	35
Other	6,193	35	2,040	4,118	4,362	14	1,382	2,966	1,831	21	658	1,152
HIGHWAY												
Snow/ice/wet	27,791	190	8,571	19,030	12,366	34	3,679	8,653	15,425	156	4,892	10,377
Visibility obscured	2,940	12	1,206	1,722	1,864	4	767	1,093	1,076	8	439	629
Construction zone	1,698	10	611	1,077	978	1	334	643	720	9	277	434
Loose gravel	758	6	360	392	102	1	43	58	656	5	317	334
Other debris	500	2	126	372	177	0	47	130	323	2	79	242
Narrow shoulder	276	4	120	152	33	0	12	21	243	4	108	131
Soft shoulder	166	2	69	95	26	0	9	17	140	2	60	78
Low shoulder	155	4	74	77	21	0	11	10	134	4	63	67
Debris from prior crash	130	0	52	78	68	0	29	39	62	0	23	39
Rough pavement	102	1	42	59	45	1	15	29	57	0	27	30
Sign obscured or missing	95	1	41	53	68	0	29	38	27	1	12	15
Narrow bridge	35	0	6	29	7	0	0	7	28	0	6	22
Other	1,270	6	414	850	564	3	154	407	706	3	260	443
VEHICLE												
Brakes	1,384	6	501	877	869	0	322	547	515	6	179	330
Tires	1,378	16	466	896	478	2	133	343	900	14	333	553
Steering	282	0	111	171	153	0	49	104	129	0	62	67
Turn signals	143	1	36	106	43	0	3	40	100	1	33	66
Other disabled	105	3	36	68	61	1	22	39	44	2	14	29
Head lamps	100	1	48	49	61	0	30	30	39	1	18	19
Suspension	83	1	25	57	31	0	7	24	52	1	18	33
Tail lamps	77	0	30	46	16	0	5	11	61	0	25	35
Stop lamps	66	0	24	42	28	0	7	21	38	0	17	21
Disabled from prior crash	63	0	29	33	27	0	11	15	36	0	18	18
Mirrors	52	0	12	40	26	0	8	18	26	0	4	22
Other	1,805	8	358	1,439	898	2	199	697	907	6	159	742

Note: Numbers represent the number of times a possible contributing circumstance was cited and not number of accidents.
Source: Wisconsin Department of Transportation, *2003 Wisconsin Traffic Crash Facts*, October 2004.

TRANSIT SYSTEMS IN WISCONSIN, BY TYPE
March 2005

Urban Bus	Rural/Intercity Bus	Shared Ride Taxi[1]	
Appleton	Adams County Transit[3]	Baraboo	Plover
Bay Area Transit (Ashland)	La Crosse Intercity[3]	Beaver Dam	Portage
Beloit	Marshfield Shuttle[3]	Berlin	Port Washington
Eau Claire	Menominee Indian Reservation	Black River Falls	Prairie du Chien
Fond du Lac	Oneida Indian Reservation	Chippewa Falls	Prairie du Sac
Green Bay	Ozaukee County Express[3]	Clintonville	Reedsburg
Janesville	Racine Commuter[3]	Edgerton	Rhinelander
Kenosha	Rusk County	Fort Atkinson	Ripon
La Crosse	Sawyer County	Grant County	River Falls
Ladysmith	Washington County Express[3]	Hartford	Shawano
Madison		Jefferson	Stoughton
Manitowoc		Lake Mills	Sun Prairie
Merrill		Marinette	Viroqua
Milwaukee County[2]		Marshfield	Washington County
Monona[3]		Mauston	Waterloo/Marshall
Oshkosh		Medford	Watertown
Ozaukee County[3]		Monroe	Waupaca
Racine[2]		Neillsville	Waupun
Rice Lake		New Richmond	West Bend
Sheboygan		Onalaska	Whitewater
Stevens Point		Ozaukee County	Wisconsin Rapids
Superior		Platteville	
Washington County[3]			
Waukesha (city)			
Waukesha County[3]			
Wausau			

[1]Taxi services are privately contracted except for the City of Hartford and Grant County, where they are publicly owned and operated.

[2]Privately managed.

[3]Privately contracted. (Note: The private service in Waukesha County is an inter-urban service.)

Source: Wisconsin Department of Transportation, Division of Transportation Investment Management, departmental data, March 2005.

WISCONSIN URBAN TRANSIT SYSTEMS
USAGE AND REVENUE, 1950 – 2004
(In Thousands)

Year	Revenue Miles	Revenue Passengers	Operating Revenue[1]
1950	53,362	288,996	$22,692
1955	42,807	169,129	23,134
1960	34,950	130,299	20,665
1965	32,330	110,979	20,457
1970	28,371	80,172	22,078
1975	26,119	63,587	22,454
1980	33,943	88,756	29,631
1985	31,829	79,540	39,635
1990	33,685	78,215	39,594
1991	33,820	74,764	45,489
1992	33,941	72,981	45,356
1993	33,954	71,444	46,492
1994	33,996	71,242	48,291
1995	30,734	71,875	50,171
1996	34,306	73,172	54,147
1997	38,222	74,703	55,842
1998	45,064	76,367	57,836
1999	54,585	77,169	58,101
2000[2]	42,447	89,821	58,785
2001	46,755	87,729	60,299
2002	48,322	84,874	64,263
2003	47,753	81,650	NA
2004	NA	NA	NA

NA – Not available.

[1]As recognized by the Wisconsin Department of Transportation.

[2]A revised reporting system was implemented in 2000. Prior data may not be comparable.

Sources: Wisconsin Department of Transportation, Division of Transportation Assistance, Bureau of Transit and Local Roads, departmental data, March 2005.

WISCONSIN HARBOR COMMERCE – 2003
(In Thousands of Short Tons)

Harbors[1]	Total Tonnage[2]	Crude Inedible Materials (except fuels)	Coal and Lignite	Food and Farm Products	Primary Manufactured Goods	Petroleum and Petroleum Products	Manufactured Equipment, Machinery and Products	Chemicals and Related Products	Unknown
LAKE SUPERIOR									
Duluth-Superior	38,295	16,951	17,874	2,910	469	21	2	39	30
Ashland	53	—	53	—	—	—	7	—	—
Bayfield	8	—	—	—	—	—	7	—	—
La Pointe	8	—	—	—	—	—	—	—	—
LAKE MICHIGAN									
Milwaukee	3,002	879	674	277	995	143	17	8	2
Green Bay	2,084	816	763	—	440	43	—	22	—
Port Washington	225	36	189	—	177	—	—	—	—
Manitowoc	383	48	158	—	177	—	—	—	—
Menominee[3]	356	195	20	—	140	—	—	—	—
Detroit Harbor[4]	55	—	—	8	—	40	—	—	7
TOTAL	44,469	18,889	19,767	3,187	2,221	247	33	69	61

Note: Tonnage reported in short tons. One short ton equals 2,000 lbs.

[1]Zero or no commerce reported for the following harbors: Algoma, Cornucopia, Kenosha, Kewaunee, Oconto, Pensaukee, Port Wing, Racine, Sheboygan, Sturgeon Bay, and Two Rivers.

[2]Detail may not add due to rounding.

[3]Includes tonnage handled at Marinette, Wisconsin.

[4]Washington Island.

Source: U.S. Army Corps of Engineers, Navigation Data Center, Water Resources Support Center, *Waterborne Commerce of the United States, Calendar Year 2003,* Part 3, at: http://www.iwr.usace.army.mil/ndc/wcsc/pdf/wcusgl03.pdf [February 04, 2005].

Political Parties

9

Wisconsin political parties: state organizations and current party platforms

Richland County Courthouse

L. Roger Turner

POLITICAL PARTY ORGANIZATION IN WISCONSIN

What Is a Political Party?

A political party is a private, voluntary organization of people with similar political beliefs that vies with other parties for control of government. Political parties help voters select their government officials and create a consensus on the basic principles that direct governmental activities and processes.

Political parties in the United States have traditionally provided an organized framework for the orderly performance of several basic political tasks necessary to representative democracy. Parties act to:

- Provide a stable institution for building coalitions based on shared principles and priorities.
- Recruit and nominate candidates for elective and appointive offices in government.
- Promote the election of the party's slate of candidates.
- Guard the integrity of election procedures and vote canvassing.
- Educate the voters by defining issues, taking policy positions, and formulating programs.

U.S. parties offer a marked contrast to the party apparatus in other nations. In many parts of the world, political parties start out with defined ideologies and programs. Their members are recruited on the basis of these ideas, and there is not a lot of room for disagreement within the ranks. In other cases, parties represent regional interests or ethnic groups. By contrast, parties in the United States are loosely organized groups reflecting a broad spectrum of interests. They are truly populist parties in the sense that they accommodate diversity and are instruments of party activists at the grass roots level. Political ideology, as stated in a party's national platform, is formulated first at the local level and then refined through debate and compromise at meetings representing successively larger geographic areas.

Depending on the time, place, and circumstances, political party labels in the United States may have widely different meanings, and within a single party there may be room for members whose ideologies span a wide political spectrum. Individual Republicans or Democrats, for instance, are often further identified as "liberal", "conservative", "right-wing", "left-wing", or "moderate".

Despite the diversity within a party, specific philosophies are generally associated with the various political parties. In the public's perception, the name of a particular party conjures up a surprisingly distinct set of economic, social, and political principles.

Political Parties in Wisconsin

Throughout its history, the United States has operated with a two-party political structure, rather than single-party or multiparty systems found elsewhere. Although minor parties have always been a part of American politics, few have gained the support necessary to challenge the two dominant parties at the national level. Those that did lasted only briefly, with the predominant exception of the Republican Party, which replaced the Whig Party in the 1850s. The same cannot be said of politics on the state level. In Wisconsin, for example, the Socialist Party regularly sent one or more representatives to the legislature between 1911 and 1937, and the Progressive Party was influential between 1933 and 1947, capturing a plurality of both houses of the 1937 Legislature. Third parties were relatively quiet in Wisconsin in the 1950s, but the last 30 years have seen more activity with more parties officially recognized on the ballot.

Under Wisconsin law, a "recognized political party" is a political party that qualifies for a separate ballot or column on the ballot, based on its receiving a required number of votes at the previous November election or through acquiring the required number of petition signatures. At the beginning of 2005, Wisconsin had five recognized political parties: Constitution, Democrat, Libertarian, Republican, and Wisconsin Green.

The Wisconsin Statutes define a political party in Section 5.02 (13) as a state committee that is legally registered with the state Elections Board and "all county, congressional, legislative, local and other affiliated committees authorized to operate under the same name". It must be a body "organized exclusively for political purposes under whose name candidates appear on a ballot at any election".

The delegates from the political party's local units meet in an annual state convention to draft or amend the party's state platform (a statement of its principles and objectives), select national committee members, elect state officers, consider resolutions, and conduct other party business. Every four years, party delegates from throughout the United States meet in a national convention to nominate their candidates for president and vice president and to adopt a national platform for the next four years. In Wisconsin, the slates of national convention delegates are usually based on the April presidential preference primary vote.

Statutory and Voluntary Organizations

Wisconsin law provides that each major political party must have certain local officers and committees, but over the years, these statutory organizations have been merged within the voluntary party organizations that are governed by their own constitutions and bylaws. The actual power is found in the voluntary structures.

In the case of the majority parties, voluntary organizations are composed of dues-paying members, who are affiliated with Wisconsin chapters of the national political parties. Third parties vary in the amount of regional autonomy and/or national control allowed. Given minor organizational differences, voluntary parties operate to tend to their party's interests, collect money to finance campaigns, maintain cooperation between the various county and congressional district organizations, and act as liaison with national parties. (Currently recognized parties and their voluntary organizations are discussed in the party descriptions that follow this introduction.)

The History of Wisconsin's Political Parties

In *How Wisconsin Voted*, Professor James R. Donoghue divided Wisconsin's political history into four eras. From statehood in 1848 until 1855, the Democratic Party was the dominant political party, and the Whig Party provided major opposition. This was a continuation of the party alignment that had prevailed during the state's territorial period.

The second era was one of Republican domination from 1856 to 1900. The birth of the national Republican Party is attributed to a meeting in Ripon, Wisconsin, in 1854. Its founding was based on the conditions and events that eventually led to the Civil War, and within Wisconsin these same circumstances contributed to the rapid growth of the Republican Party and the demise of the Whigs.

The second era ended at the turn of the century with the election of Governor Robert M. La Follette. The third era, from 1900 to 1945, was a time of great stress and change, encompassing the Great Depression and World Wars I and II. Until 1932, the major political battles usually occurred not between two parties, but between two factions of the Republican Party – the conservative "stalwart" Republicans and the "progressive" (La Follette) Republicans. The Democratic Party was in eclipse, and election contests tended to be decided in Republican primary elections.

The third era also saw the high point of third party influence in Wisconsin. The progressive faction formally split from the Republicans to form its own party in 1934. The new Progressive Party won gubernatorial elections in 1936 and 1942 and a plurality in both houses of the legislature in 1936. Declining popularity, however, led to its dissolution in 1946, and Progressive Party leadership urged its members and supporting voters to return to the Republican Party. The period from 1900 to 1937 was also the time of greatest strength for the Socialists.

The fourth era, from 1945 to the present, witnessed a realignment of the major parties. A resurgence of the Democratic Party ended the long Republican domination, turning the state to a more balanced, two-party, competitive system. In the late 1940s, some former Progressives, Socialists, and others began moving into a moribund Democratic Party. This influx both revitalized the party and made it more liberal. In the following decade, the Democrats worked at uniting their party and building their strength at the polls. Meanwhile, the conservative faction solidified its control of the Republican Party with the departure of more liberal-minded Progressives and addition of conservative Democrats fleeing their former party as it became more liberal.

In the years following World War II, the resurgent Democratic Party began seriously challenging the majority Republicans. Steady Democratic growth culminated in the 1957 election of William Proxmire to the U.S. Senate, the first "new" Democrat to win a major statewide election, followed by the election of Gaylord Nelson as governor in 1958. These elections marked the emergence on Wisconsin's political scene of a Democratic Party fully capable of competing successfully with the long dominant Republicans for public office. During this period, third party and independent candidates usually failed to garner any significant support on a statewide level.

The hallmark of contemporary Wisconsin politics is a highly competitive, two-party, issue-oriented system. At the beginning of the 1995 session, Republicans gained control of both houses for the first time since 1969. In 1993, 1995, and 1997, the majority party in the senate shifted during the session. Democrats controlled the senate in 1999 and 2001, while Republicans retained the control of the assembly they had won in the 1994 elections. For the first time since 1982, a Democrat was elected governor in November 2002.

Of the state's major elected partisan offices in January 2005, the Democrats held the positions of governor, lieutenant governor, secretary of state, and attorney general, as well as holding both U.S. Senate seats and four of the eight congressional seats. Republicans filled the position of state treasurer, held four congressional seats, and controlled both the senate and the assembly.

CONSTITUTION PARTY OF WISCONSIN
(Formerly U.S. Taxpayers Party of Wisconsin)
May 2005
Headquarters

State Headquarters: P.O. Box 994, Appleton 54912-0994, (877) 201-2411.
State Internet Address: http://www.cpow.org
National Office: 23 N. Lime Street, Lancaster, PA 17602, (800) 2-VETO-IRS.
National Internet Address: http://www.constitutionparty.com

State Committee – Officers
Chairman: RANDY W. HAMBY, Appleton.
1st Vice Chairman: TIMOTHY J. FARNESS, Whitewater.
2nd Vice Chairman: JOHN P. CLARK, Westfield.
Secretary: DANIEL M. HOYT, Oshkosh.
Treasurer: WILLIAM HEMENWAY, Pewaukee.
Parliamentarian: vacancy.

National Committee Members
Randy W. Hamby, Appleton

Timothy J. Farness, Whitewater

John P. Clark, Westfield

Daniel M. Hoyt, Oshkosh

William C. Hemenway, Pewaukee

Daniel E. Gibson, Janesville

Mark P. Gabriel, Appleton

National Committee Alternates
Suzanne Hemenway, Pewaukee

Linda Clark, Westfield

José Figueroa, Waldo

State Committee – Congressional District Representatives

1st District
Daniel E. Gibson, Janesville
Glenn Petroski, Kenosha

2nd District
Bob Bellard, Beloit
vacancy

3rd District
vacancy
vacancy

4th District
Joan Tatarsky, Milwaukee
S. Kent Steffke, Milwaukee

5th District
Peter Economou, New Berlin
vacancy

6th District
Todd Brehmer, Potter
José Figueroa, Waldo

7th District
Jim Scholz, Rhinelander
Larry Oftedahl, Barron

8th District
Patrick Risch, Boulder Junction
Mark Gabriel, Appleton

At-Large
James King, Green Bay
Lorraine Decker, La Crosse
3 vacancies

Source: Constitution Party of Wisconsin.

Membership. Individual membership in the Constitution Party of Wisconsin is based on state-wide affiliation. Anyone who is in good standing with the state party and has paid the annual membership fee may attend the state convention and participate in lesser party committees.

Lesser Committees. Members in congressional districts, state senate and assembly districts, and county and election districts may form party committees affiliated with the state committee. The purpose of the lesser committees is to help build the party and aid its candidates seeking election.

State Committee. The Constitution Party of Wisconsin is headed by a state committee composed of 27 members: 6 state officers, 2 representatives elected by the members in each of the 8 congressional districts, and up to 5 at-large members. The state officers are the chairman, first vice chairman, second vice chairman, secretary, treasurer, and parliamentarian. The state chairman serves as the party's executive and is responsible for the day-to-day operations of the party. The officers are elected in odd-numbered years and serve 2-year terms. The congressional district representatives are elected in caucuses prior to the state convention each year.

National Committee. The Constitution Party of Wisconsin is the officially recognized state affiliate of the Constitution Party whose headquarters are in Lancaster, Pennsylvania. The Wisconsin party currently has 7 representatives to the Constitution Party National Committee.

CONSTITUTION PARTY OF WISCONSIN PLATFORM

As Modified and Adopted at the State Party Convention, Beloit, October 11, 2003

[Editor's Note: Due to space limitations, only the state planks are included.]

National Party Planks

The Constitution Party National Platform planks shall serve as the foundation of the Constitution Party of Wisconsin Platform for National Issues. For state and additional perspectives on national concerns, the Constitution Party of Wisconsin shall adopt its own superseding state planks to complement the National Platform planks.

Preamble

The Constitution Party of Wisconsin gratefully acknowledges the blessing of the Lord God as Creator, Preserver, and Ruler of the Universe and of this Nation. It recognizes Jesus Christ as transcendent King over all nations and hereby appeals to Him for aid, comfort, guidance and the protection of His Divine Providence as we work to restore and preserve this nation as a government of the people, by the people, and for the people.

The U.S. Constitution established a republic under God, rather than a democracy.

Our republic is a nation governed by a Constitution, which is rooted in Biblical law, administered by representatives who are constitutionally elected by the citizens.

In a republic governed by Constitutional law rooted in Biblical law, all life, liberty and property are protected because law rules.

We affirm the principles of inherent individual rights upon which these United States of America were founded:

- That each individual is endowed by his Creator with certain unalienable rights; that among these are the rights to life, liberty, property, and the pursuit of the individual's personal interest;

- That the freedoms to own, use, exchange, control, protect, and freely dispose of property is a natural, necessary and inseparable extension of the individual's unalienable rights;

- That the legitimate function of government is to secure these rights through the preservation of domestic tranquility, the maintenance of a strong national defense, and the promotion of equal justice for all;

- That history makes clear that left unchecked, it is the nature of government to usurp the liberty of its citizens and eventually become a major violator of the people's rights; and

- That, therefore, it is essential to bind government with the chains of the Constitution and carefully divide and jealously limit government powers to those assigned by the consent of the governed.

The Constitution Party of Wisconsin calls on all who love liberty and value their inherent rights to join with us in the pursuit of these goals and in the restoration of these founding principles.

Abortion, Euthanasia, and Bio-research

The Constitution Party of Wisconsin calls upon our state officials to fulfill their obligations as lesser magistrates to uphold the U.S. Constitution and the state constitution by taking immediate action to end the practice of abortion in Wisconsin.

We condemn the practice of so-called "assisted suicide" and call upon our state legislators to resist any and all attempts to legalize euthanasia.

In addition we oppose the funding of and support the outlawing of bio-research and technology involving human embryonic or pre-embryonic cells.

Borrowing Money

The CPoW calls upon Congress to refrain from incurring debt, except upon the formal Declaration of War pursuant to Article I, Section 8, and solely for the purpose of financing such a constitutional war for its duration or to fulfill obligations undertaken during and as part of that war, and to refinance the national debt to prevent default.

Census

The CPoW believes that the census, as presently administered, is an unconstitutional invasion of privacy, and that the census is being misused to provide the government with information to support unnecessary spending. We call upon Congress to fund the Census Bureau only to the extent necessary to achieve the Bureau's sole constitutional purpose: enumeration of the citizenry in order to reapportion the legislature. Additionally, the CPoW stands opposed to "statistical sampling" as a means of enumeration.

Citizen Initiative Referenda

The Wisconsin Constitution guarantees the citizens of Wisconsin a republican form of government with democratically elected representation. Citizen referenda constitute a form of pure democracy, which is akin to "mob rule" and is, therefore, inconsistent with the Wisconsin Constitution and the intentions of this nation's founders. The CPoW stands strongly opposed to the adoption of Citizen Initiative Referenda in this state.

Crime

The amount of crime in a society is directly related to the level of moral restraint of its citizens. Government is a reflection of that moral restraint, not its legislator. Increasing the amount of moral restraint in our society is not the responsibility of government, but of those called to that mission; namely the family, and the clergy and their congregations. We call upon these to fulfill their mission, renewing the souls of our citizenry, thereby increasing the amount of moral restraint, which will result in a reduction of crime.

We assert that upon completion of his sentence, the person convicted of a crime shall be fully restored to society with full exercise of all rights of citizenship.

Furthermore, we oppose defendants being charged and tried by both state and federal jurisdictions under different laws for the same alleged criminal act, thus violating the constitutionally secured prohibition against double jeopardy.

Education

Education should be free from any State Government subsidy and government interference. The State Government has no legitimate role in either subsidizing or regulating education. To that end, the CPoW supports amending the Wisconsin Constitution to remove the State of Wisconsin from any role in education.

We support an orderly transition to free market education including Home Education and Private Schools (for profit and non profit) and encourage benevolence to provide effective education for those in need.

Elimination of Elective Offices

The CPoW opposes any proposal to change any state wide (e.g., Secretary of State or State Treasurer) or local offices (e.g., County Clerk or Mayor) currently filled through popular election to appointed positions. Such changes will reduce that officeholder's accountability to the electorate and instead make the office essentially a political patronage position.

Eminent Domain

The Constitution Party of Wisconsin supports the return to the original constitutional meaning of "just compensation" as meaning the owner whose property is being taken is to be "made whole" in the same sense used in tort law litigation, rather than the recent court imposed doctrine of "fair market value."

The CPoW supports the limitation on the use of the nuisance condemnation proceedings to the acquiring of property only in the case of proven owner abandonment.

Family

The CPoW calls upon our national and state officials to oppose any action by the U.S. Courts that would establish any recognition of "same-sex marriage." We also call upon the Wisconsin State Legislature to pass a law defining marriage so no union other than that of one man and one woman may be recognized in Wisconsin, despite any action(s) taken by any other state(s).

We further call upon the Wisconsin State Legislature to repeal the provisions in the Wisconsin State Statutes that allow for "no fault divorce".

Finally, we call upon all state officials to outlaw all acts of sodomy.

Federal Government

Wisconsin is an independent, sovereign republic. As such, the federal government has no authority to trespass on or confiscate property within the state without due process of the law.

Legal Reform and Individual Rights

The content of a man or woman's thoughts is not within the civil magistrate's jurisdictional purview, and is, therefore, not punishable under civil law. The only permissible inquiry in this area is whether or not a defendant intended to commit the crime charged. Attempting to determine whether or not a defendant was motivated to commit a crime because the victim was a member of a certain class of persons is illegitimate. Therefore, the CPoW advocates abolition of all "hate crime" penalty enhancers.

In 1771, John Adams said of the juror: "It is not only his right, but his duty... to find verdict according to his own best understanding, judgment and conscience, though in direct opposition to the direction of the court." We support legal reform measures that will require the courts in all jury trials to inform the jurors that in addition to their responsibility to judge the facts of the case, they have a prerogative right to judge the law, itself.

Additionally, the CPoW opposes using state and national executive power to bring civil suits against private parties to obtain relief properly sought only through criminal process and procedure. These civil actions are initiated to bypass the higher standards of proof required in criminal prosecutions. Examples of such governmental overreaching are the application of civil forfeiture, RICO, and abortion protesting injunction laws. We therefore call for the repeal of all state and national statutes which authorize the executive power to initiate such actions.

Finally, we categorically oppose all efforts to criminalize a person's lawful challenge to, or disapproval or criticism of, any beliefs, speech or conduct.

Light Rail

The CPoW opposes the expenditure of Federal, State or Local tax dollars for the purpose of building a "Light Rail" system in any current state community. If an idea such as this has such great merit, the private sector should construct and operate it. We believe our gas tax dollars are better spent improving and expanding existing roadways.

'No-Quota' Constitutional Amendment

The Constitution Party of Wisconsin, believing that an individual should be allowed to succeed or fail based on his own merits and not because he is a member of a particular cultural subgroup, wholly supports the following amendment to the Constitution of the State of Wisconsin:

Neither the state of Wisconsin nor any of its political subdivisions or agents shall use race, sex, color, ethnicity or national origin as a criterion for either discriminating against, or granting preferential treatment to, any individual or group in the operation of the state's system of public employment, public education or public contracting.

Non-related Legislative Provisions

It is common practice for provisions and amendments to be attached to bills that have no common relationship with the purpose of the bill. This practice results in the passage of laws and expenditures that have not been open to congressional and public scrutiny because of their hidden nature. It also results in presidential approval of provisions which may have been vetoed if allowed to stand on their own merits and not attached to desirable legislation. In addition, this practice aids in the continuance of the loathsome practice of "pork barrel" spending. For this reason the Constitution Party of Wisconsin calls upon Congress and the State Legislature to adopt the following policy:

Every law, or resolution having the force of law, shall relate to but one subject, and that shall be accurately expressed in the title.

Representation

We propose to amend the State Constitution to allow the State Senators to be appointed by the County Board, or elected county wide, and paid by the people of each county, so as to assure each county's interests are represented in the State Legislature.

Smart Growth

The Constitution Party of Wisconsin stands against state directed land use planning. The notion of "Smart Growth" strikes at the very concept of private property. It attempts government control of property by allowing the property owner only title and responsibility for taxes, while imposing draconian legal use restrictions upon land, and relinquishing all other control of it to government bureaucracy.

Social Security

The Constitution Party of Wisconsin advocates phasing out the entire Social Security program, while continuing to meet the obligations already incurred under the system.

State Sovereignty

We demand that our State Legislature repudiate unconstitutional federal government mandates, regulations, programs, and enticements, and that they assert their authority under the Tenth Amendment of the U.S. Constitution to defend the sovereignty of the State of Wisconsin.

Taxes

While it is morally correct and necessary that government exists, the CPoW agrees with George Washington that "it is the government which governs least which governs best". Individual freedom is best safeguarded by keeping local government strong and distant government less powerful. In order to protect that freedom, county and local governments must have greater power with respect to state authority than is presently the case. To reach this end, the system of taxing authority must change.

We, therefore, oppose all progressive taxes and any form of taxes on property, both real or personal, or on compensation paid for services rendered. However, we recognize that provisions must be made for support of state, county, and local governments through taxation.

For the state government, we support user fees and excise taxes. To the degree that these taxes are insufficient to cover the legitimate costs of state government, we will offer a "county-rate tax" in which the responsibility for covering the cost of unmet obligations will be divided among the seventy-two counties in accordance with their proportion of the total population of the State of Wisconsin. Thus, if a county contains 10% of our state's population, it will be responsible for assuming 10% of the annual deficit. The effect of this county rate tax will be to encourage politicians to argue for less rather than more state spending.

For county and local levels, we support the people's freedom to tax themselves by the following means: user fees, excise taxes, flat-rate sales taxes on goods purchased and services rendered, and head taxes.

The Constitution Party of Wisconsin opposes imposing any tax on internet commerce, services or the internet as a whole at either the state, national or both levels.

DEMOCRATIC PARTY OF WISCONSIN
June 2005
Headquarters

State Headquarters: 222 West Washington Avenue, Suite 150, Madison 53703.
Telephone: (608) 255-5172; Fax: (608) 255-8919.
Executive Director: KIM WARKENTIN.
Compliance Director: LARHONDA WELLS.
Membership Director: JOANNA BEILMAN-DULIN.
Political Director: LINDA CHAPPETTO.
Internet Address: http://www.wisdems.org

State Administrative Committee

Chair: JOE WINEKE, Verona.
First Vice Chair: LINDA HONOLD, Milwaukee.
Second Vice Chair: JEF HALL, Oshkosh.
Secretary: ANGELA SUTKIEWICZ, Sheboygan.
Treasurer: ROB FYRST, Madison.
National Committee Members: STAN GRUSZYNSKI, Porterfield; JASON RAE, Rice Lake; MELISSA SCHROEDER, Merrill; PAULA ZELLNER, Shawano.
Legislative Representatives: SENATOR JUDY ROBSON, Beloit; REPRESENTATIVE GARY SHERMAN, Port Wing.
College Democrats President: AWAIS KHALEEL, Madison.
County Chairs Association Chair: STEVE MELLENTHIN, Porterfield.
Milwaukee County Chair: MARTHA LOVE, Milwaukee.
At-Large Members: GWEN CARR, Madison; LYNN DAVIS, Racine; DIAN PALMER, Brookfield; MARIANA STOUT, Oshkosh.
Congressional District Representatives:

1st District
Ray Rivera, chair, Pleasant Prairie
Marilyn Nemeth, Racine

2nd District
Margaret McEntire, chair, Madison
Tim Sullivan, Verona

3rd District
Karen Dahl, chair, Viroqua
Robert Johnson, La Crosse

4th District
Stephanie Findley, chair, Milwaukee
Mario Aguirre-Villa

5th District
Jim Shinners, chair, Wauwatosa
Christine Marshall, Thiensville
6th District
Gordon Hintz, chair, Oshkosh
Jan Banicki, Montello

7th District
Marlys Matuszak, chair, Wausau
Eric Peterson, Amery
8th District
Jack Krueger, chair, Green Bay
Dottie LeClair, Appleton

Source: Democratic Party of Wisconsin.

County Organization. The county organization is the basic unit of the Democratic Party of Wisconsin. In each county, the membership elects the county officers. They include a chairperson, vice chairperson, secretary, and treasurer (or secretary/treasurer). Their terms of office are usually one year, but some county organizations may provide for 2-year terms.

Congressional District Organization. Congressional district organizations function mainly as a base of support for Democratic congressional candidates. They also select representatives to the state administrative committee. An executive committee directs each congressional district organization.

State Convention. The party holds its annual state convention in June. Each year, the convention considers amendments to the state party constitution and other resolutions and party business. State party officers are elected in odd-numbered years, and state party platforms are adopted in even-numbered years. State convention delegates elect Democratic National Committee members every four years.

Each county unit elects delegates to the state convention, and all party members are eligible. The state administrative committee determines the number of delegates that represent each county by using a formula based on the number of party members and the percentage of the vote cast for the Democratic candidate in the most recent U.S. Senate election. In addition to the regular quota, certain Democratic officeholders are automatically delegates to the state convention.

State Officers and Administrative Committee. The Democratic Party of Wisconsin is headed by a state administrative committee, composed of 32 party officials chosen in a variety of ways. Delegates to the state convention elect the 5 party officers and the 4 Democratic National Committee members. The 8 congressional district conventions each select 2 representatives to serve on the state administrative committee in the spring of each odd-numbered year: the district chairperson and an additional representative of the opposite sex. The remaining voting committee members include the County Chairs Association chairperson; the Milwaukee County chairperson; a representative of the College Democrats; 2 state legislative representatives, elected by their house caucuses prior to the beginning of the new legislative term; the immediate past state chairperson and an at-large administrative committee member.

The party officers are the state chairperson, first vice chairperson, second vice chairperson, treasurer, and secretary. The chairperson and first vice chairperson must be of the opposite sex. Party officers are elected in the odd-numbered year for 2-year terms. Democratic National Committee members are elected each presidential election year and serve 4-year terms. The state chairperson and the first vice chairperson are also *ex officio* members of the Democratic National Committee.

Whenever a vacancy occurs, the chairperson, with the concurrence of the entire state administrative committee, appoints a successor to serve until the next annual convention, where the delegates elect an individual to fill the position for the remainder of the unexpired term.

National Committee. The Democratic National Committee is composed of the chairperson and the highest ranking officer of the opposite sex in each recognized state Democratic Party. In Wisconsin these are the chairperson and the first vice chairperson of the state administrative committee. An additional 200 committee memberships are apportioned to the states on the same basis as delegates to the national convention, and other specified members are appointed. Wisconsin's Democratic National Committee members are selected every 4 years at the annual state conventions held in presidential election years.

2004 WISCONSIN DEMOCRATIC PARTY PLATFORM

Adopted at the State Party Convention, Appleton, June 11, 2004

PREAMBLE

The Democratic Party of Wisconsin stands open to all citizens, responds sensitively, promotes outreach to and inclusion of all segments of society, and works actively for open and honest government responsive to the will of the people.

DEMOCRACY, COMMUNITY AND GOVERNMENT

Government must be responsive to the needs and will of the people while respecting rights of minorities.

Government must respect, protect and support freedom of expression, strict separation of government and religion, individuals' privacy, constitutional rights of criminal suspects and the rehabilitated, all other rights under the Bill of Rights, and equal protection of the law for all.

We are committed to equality of rights and opportunities for individuals regardless of race, color, actual or perceived gender, marital or domestic partner status, age, occupation, national origin, disability, physical appearance, living arrangements, sexual orientation, and political or religious preference.

We are committed to the principle that women and men are equal.

We oppose racial and ethnic profiling.

All governments must respect the sovereignty of and abide by treaties with Native American nations.

We encourage initiatives to involve and empower citizens in civic affairs.

All governments must comply with open meetings and public record laws. Public records should be available through the Internet.

The Internet must be affordably available to all citizens without unwarranted intrusion on privacy.

Free libraries with access to uncensored information must be adequately supported.

We oppose consolidation of media ownership.

We support free media time for candidate debate. The Fairness Doctrine should be re-instituted.

We call for full public financing of all election campaigns, reform of campaign finance laws to lessen the influence of money on public policy, and programs to enhance election participation by all citizens. We oppose measures that make voting more difficult.

We reject voting systems that do not leave a verifiable hardcopy record of votes.

We support improvements in government efficiency but hold government accountable for outsourcing. We oppose abuse of limited term employment.

We oppose taxes or legislation imposed under the guise of gubernatorial partial veto, and support a state constitutional amendment assuring that the Legislature approves all taxes and laws.

Government must deal effectively with crime, terrorism, and their causes, while protecting constitutional rights.

We oppose the death penalty.

We support adequate funding for law enforcement.

We support efforts to reduce the nation's crime rate. Education and jobs with decent wages are more effective and economical than imprisonment in dealing with crime.

We support equitable sentencing standards, judges' authority to modify sentences, and alternatives to incarceration.

Minor marijuana offenses should be processed as local ordinance violations.

We support the right to hunt.

We support reasonable firearm regulations to protect the safety of citizens and law enforcement officers. These include requiring safety locks on guns and background checks on all gun purchasers. We support Wisconsin's concealed carry ban.

We advocate strengthening consumer protection laws and returning enforcement authority to the Wisconsin Department of Justice.

We support accurate labeling of food products, including "organic" foods.

Usurious lending should be prohibited.

State revenue sharing should continue. The state must honor its obligation to fund two thirds of school districts' expenses.

Federal and state governments must fully fund mandated programs.

We support the Social Security system, with inflation indexing, but oppose its privatization, and object to misusing its Trust Fund to hide federal deficits.

We support the arts as essential for the spiritual, intellectual and economic health of our communities.

Our wealth should be measured not only by the GNP, but also by broad measures of well being such as the United Nations' Human Development Index.

HUMAN CONCERNS

Government should ensure that everyone can lead a dignified, healthy, secure, fulfilling and useful life: one without abuse or unjust discrimination; with excellent, affordable health care; safe, sanitary, accessible, and affordable housing; access to quality public education; and opportunities for rewarding work, recreation, and meaningful participation in community affairs.

We support individuals' rights to make their own moral, religious, philosophical, and medical decisions.

We support family values: love, commitment, mutual support, protection, stability and nurture for all family members, especially children. Marriage by civil ceremony must be permitted for unmarried couples of marriageable age without regard to sex.

We support the right to choose death with dignity with appropriate safeguards.

Family planning services must be readily accessible, confidential, and available without interference by government or others. We support freedom of reproductive choice, and oppose all measures to interfere with or limit it.

We seek an affordable single-payer health care system that provides universal access, promotes preventive health care, and covers prescription drugs, and all physical and mental illnesses.

We support Badger Care, Wisconsin Senior Care, Medicaid and Medicare with prescribed drug and medical device benefits and oppose undercutting Medicare by HMOs and insurance companies.

We favor enhancing programs for the aging and disabled, including subsidized long term in-home or nursing home care.

Health insurance companies should be required to cover physical and mental illnesses equally, cover pregnancy terminations, and include contraceptives in drug coverage.

We support health education and disease prevention programs, especially for young people, concerning smoking, alcohol, other drugs, pregnancy and STDs.

We favor increasing government support for biomedical research, eliminating prohibitions on human embryonic stem cell research, and permitting therapeutic cloning. We oppose reproductive human cloning.

Non-violent alcohol and other drug offenses can and should be dealt with more effectively and at less cost by treatment, education, rehabilitation, and employment, rather than by imprisonment.

Government must adequately support rural health care, public education, and other social services. We support adequate income and living conditions, and access to health insurance for farmers, migrant workers, and their families.

We advocate a welfare system in which able people are gainfully employed whenever jobs are available, with access to adequate affordable childcare, health insurance, transportation and job training.

We call for additional affordable, quality, licensed daycare centers and government support for adequate pay for licensed childcare givers.

EDUCATION

Quality public education for all is critical for individual wellbeing, economic prosperity, national security, and the health of our democracy.

We oppose public funding of private schools and privatization of public education through vouchers or other means.

Governments should increase funding of public education at all levels. Early childhood and preschool programs should be expanded. State government should increase funding and financial aid for the UW and Technical College Systems. Tuition in these systems must not increase faster than inflation.

Public school teachers must be better paid.

The QEO system must be repealed.

We oppose excessive or discriminatory testing.

We support students' right to participate in post-secondary school governance.

THE ENVIRONMENT

We must preserve Earth's environment. This requires clean air and water, uncontaminated land, wilderness, wildlife, and other natural resources.

We must conserve energy, develop and use renewable energy sources and alternative fuels, and improve automobile fuel efficiency.

Biodiversity must be protected.

We must develop sustainable food production systems.

We must be protected from pollution and unnatural radiation.

Mining must be strictly controlled to prevent environmental damage.

Environmentally threatening activities such as mining, quarrying, fossil fuel extraction, logging and grazing by free-roaming cattle should be banned from wilderness areas and parks.

Soil and water conservation should be improved.

We oppose diversion of Great Lakes water and extraction of groundwater for commercial bottling.

We support a balanced transportation system. Walking and bicycling should be encouraged, and public transportation improved and made affordable and available to all. We support passenger rail and ferries.

Laws to halt global warming and acid rain must be strengthened. Power plant emissions must be controlled.

We support land use plans that encourage compact urban development, reduce sprawl and waste, preserve topsoil, green space, and Wisconsin's rural flavor.

Recycling should be required in order to save energy and landfill space and to reduce waste. Composting, use of recycled packaging, and minimal packaging should be encouraged.

Communities and workers have the right to information and control regarding location and transportation of nearby hazardous substances.

We support prompt polluter-paid cleanup of toxic waste sites and banning of residential development on or near them.

A Public Intervenor's Office should be re-established.

An independent Department of Natural Resources should be restored.

LABOR AND EMPLOYMENT

Our top priority is meaningful full employment.

All workers must have the right to organize, bargain collectively, and strike for fair wages, benefits, and safe working conditions. We support public employees' rights to speedy mediation and binding arbitration of labor disputes.

We favor strengthening OSHA and other safety agencies to ensure enforcement of workers' rights to a safe workplace.

We oppose right-to-work legislation. Hiring strikebreakers must be prohibited.

Workers are entitled to a living wage with benefits.

We support full equity in pay and benefits.

We support equitable ratios of management to labor pay.

We advocate national industrial policies to ensure thriving basic industries. We favor public investment in research and development of new technologies and worker retraining for nonmilitary domestic jobs.

Management and labor should cooperate for competitive success of U.S.-owned businesses.

We oppose American businesses establishing plants in foreign countries with the express purpose of evading taxes, taking advantage of sub-standard wages and circumventing environmental protection laws.

We support tariffs against nations where unfair conditions impede American exports.

Pension funds must be responsibly managed and strictly safeguarded. Employees and retirees must be informed regularly of anticipated retirement benefits. No employer should have access to pension fund assets.

Workers owed wages by a bankrupt business must have first claim to the business' assets.

Businesses must be required to give sufficient notification of job cutbacks and plant closings to help communities and workers adjust.

Unemployment compensation should include health insurance and, in long recessions, automatic extension of benefits.

THE ECONOMY AND TAXES

We support a tax system that treats work and investment income equally, is based on ability to pay, and has a progressive income tax as its core. We must reduce our dependence on regressive levies such as property and sales taxes. Taxation of land should be according to use. Property taxes should not be the primary source of school funding.

The state must equitably fund local units of government, including school districts, and remove revenue caps.

We oppose welfare for big business and the wealthy in the form of handouts, tax breaks, or tax loopholes. We support tax policies that create long-term economic development, good jobs, and environmentally sound development of affordable housing.

We oppose tax cuts for the wealthy that shift wealth inequitably away from middle- and low-income people and fail to spur economic development or job growth.

Deficits weaken the economy and the ability of governments to implement necessary programs. The federal deficit and the state structural deficit should be eliminated.

Businesses must stop avoiding taxation by nominally locating offshore.

We support fair, indexed estate taxes.

Leases for commercial use, or extraction of resources from, public land should be at fair market value and permitted only for environmentally sound activities.

We proudly support our state's cooperatives, which are community owned and operated businesses.

AGRICULTURAL AFFAIRS

We are committed to preserving family farming. We favor policies that allow family farmers and farm-related enterprises in rural communities to succeed.

We support supply policies that enhance family farmers' incomes.

We call for farm subsidies that favor family farms over absentee-owned corporate farms.

We discourage absentee-owned corporate farms.

Foreign ownership of farmland should be discouraged.

Agricultural practices must protect the environment and provide safe, wholesome food supplies. We oppose factory farms.

We call for reducing high levels of processor involvement in agriculture and verifiable price discovery to insure fair prices.

We seek development of fair trade international markets for agricultural products.

Fair and safe electricity delivery to farms must be assured.

FOREIGN AFFAIRS, WAR AND PEACE

Our nation should seek to befriend others, work with them to secure peace and enhance the lives of all, and address the grievances and problems that foster terrorism. America must work with others on overpopulation, environment, hunger, disease, illiteracy, and unemployment, and encourage development of representative government.

Law and diplomacy must replace force in international decision-making. Our nation must strengthen, participate equitably in adequate funding of, cooperate with, and use international institutions such as the UN, its agencies, and the International Criminal Court. Such institutions should be responsible for eliminating international terrorism.

An efficient military ready to defend our country is essential.

We must use military force only as a last resort. Our government must renounce the illegal, destabilizing policy of preemptive force when there is no imminent threat to our nation.

Our country should work with other nations to eliminate nuclear weapons, weapons in space, land mines, chemical and biological weapons, and other weapons-related threats to people and the environment. Nuclear weapons' development must stop. Existing nuclear weapons should be de-alerted and disposed of in agreed, verifiable stages. Ballistic missile defense plans should be abandoned. The international arms trade should be brought under international control. War industries should receive assistance for converting from military manufacturing to the manufacture of peaceful products.

A Department of Peace should be established to support national policies for a safe and peaceful world.

We can best support our military personnel by not placing them in harm's way unnecessarily. We support fully meeting all material and medical, including psychological, needs of our active military and veterans. For those who have served in the military, the Peace Corps, or similar agencies, we support full, lifelong medical care and generous educational, housing, and employment programs.

We support the Universal Declaration of Human Rights and urge U.S. ratification of the treaties that implement it.

Foreign aid should be allocated to meet basic needs and encourage human rights. Our nation must never employ economic sanctions with genocidal effects.

Our country's immigration policies should be fair and applied fairly. We should offer refuge to victims of oppressive regimes without regard to political persuasion.

We support agreements to expand international trade, provided that they do not erode worker compensation, worker safety, environmental standards, or democratic control. We oppose fast-track legislation limiting Congress' trade authority. Our government should block multinational corporations' practices of avoiding U.S. taxes and work for international control of their monopolistic practices.

CONCLUSION

We expect all Democrats to support this Platform as candidates and work to implement it when in office.

WISCONSIN GREEN PARTY
May 2005

Headquarters

State Headquarters: P.O. Box 1701, Madison 53701-1701.
Telephone: (608) 204-7336 or (608) 20-GREEN.
Internet Address: www.wisconsingreenparty.org
E-mail: mail@wisconsingreenparty.org

Coordinating Council

Co-Chairs: JILL BUSSIERE, Kewaunee; vacancy.
Corresponding Secretary: BOB VEITH, Madison.
Recording Secretary: CINDY STIMMLER, Dresser.
Treasurer: GINNY BORMANN, Bristol.
Diversity Caucus: WINSTON F. SEPHUS, JR., Milwaukee.
Lavender Caucus: MIKE LAFOREST, Lafayette County.
Women's Caucus: JESSA THOMPSON, Chaseburg.
Youth Caucus: PAUL SCHMIDT, LUKE TOMBERLIN, Oshkosh.
Council Members:

1st District
  Bill Hensley, Kenosha
  Pete Karas, Racine
2nd District
  Bill Anderson, Madison
  Saul Wolf, Madison
3rd District
  Andrew Posselt, Chaseburg
  vacancy
4th District
  Tommy King, Milwaukee
  Ruth Weill, Milwaukee

5th District
  Tom Depies, Oconomowoc
  Bruce Hinkforth, Oconomowoc
6th District
  David Barnhill, Oshkosh
  Bob Poeschl, Oshkosh
7th District
  Jeff Peterson, Luck
  Doug Stingle, Stevens Point
8th District
  Chris Burkley, Waupaca
  Taku Ronsman, Green Bay

Source: Wisconsin Green Party.

Officers. The officers of the Wisconsin Greens are two spokespersons, a recording secretary, a corresponding secretary, and a treasurer. The spokespersons serve staggered 2-year terms and may not be reelected for successive terms. The other officers serve one-year terms and may be reelected. Elections are held at the fall meeting.

Coordinating Council. The Wisconsin Green Party Coordinating Council includes all of the officers plus two members from each of the eight congressional districts in Wisconsin, as well as a representative from each statewide caucus. The officers and members are elected each fall at the membership meeting.

State Convention. The Wisconsin Greens hold state conventions in the spring and fall of each year. Officers are elected at the fall convention.

2003 WISCONSIN GREEN PLATFORM
Abridged June 2005

"We hold these truths to be self-evident: that we must treat each other with love, respect and fairness, and that we must protect the earth for future generations."

PREAMBLE

Our vision is of a sustainable society in harmony with the environment, one that meets all people's needs for security, self-respect, freedom, creativity, and community. We recognize that personal, cultural, social, economic, political, and ecological problems are interconnected. We reject the current simplistic solutions to these problems. New, creative solutions are needed which allow us to live well and happily.

1. ECOLOGY

Wisconsin is primarily an agricultural and forest products state. Stewardship and ecological responsibility are integral parts of land ownership, whether held by individuals, corporations, land trusts, or as a public heritage. The "public trust doctrine," which holds that public land, water, minerals, forests, and other natural resources are held in trust for the public and used for the common good, must be enforced.

A. Agriculture A sustainable system of agriculture should be based upon the use of crop rotation, unprocessed natural fertilizers, disease resistant indigenous plants, integrated pest management, and crop cultivation.

Subsidies for a change to organic farming methods are mandatory. New and ecologically sound agricultural products should be encouraged. Regionalization of the food production system should be encouraged.

The state must support universities and technical schools in teaching sustainable farming practices.

Reestablish the family farm as an indispensable part of a diverse and healthy agricultural economy.

A state funded farmer retirement system, funded by real estate transfer taxes, subdivision fees and other methods, should be created. This should be combined with state land banking of prime farmland to prevent diversion to non farm use through first-option state acquisition of the land, annuities to retiring farmers, subsidies to beginning farmers and farm land trusts, and restricted farm resale agreements.

Hybridization and genetic engineering must be reexamined to protect species diversity and impacts on human health and the environment. Growth producing hormones and the preventative use of antibiotics in the production of livestock must be eliminated.

B. Forestry The primary tenet of forestry should be sustainability, The forest and all other ecological communities must be maintained in a manner which allows future generations to benefit.

We advocate for sustainable rural communities. Rural communities in forested regions should include ecosystem-based value-added industries. We demand an elimination of government subsidies for the timber industry.

We support city, county and state zoning which would protect forestland from development and protect forest owners from excessive taxes. We support a general moratorium on Wisconsin road building in public forests and limiting construction of roads in privately owned forests.

C. Energy Major government investments and incentives should encourage renewable energy technology and conservation. Wind, solar and biomass need to be included in Wisconsin's energy future.

High-energy efficiency standards should be required in new construction and encouraged for the retrofitting of existing structures.

Fossil fuels should be phased out. Nonrenewable energy production and consumption should be taxed, and the revenue used to cover the hidden costs of fossil fuels and the development of alternatives.

Nuclear power must be phased out. Workers at closing nuclear plants should be retrained and given top priority for jobs at Wisconsin's new wind farms.

Regional high level nuclear waste dumps must not be located in Wisconsin.

New vehicles must have higher average miles per gallon requirements and stricter emission control requirements. Wisconsin should impose "gas guzzler" taxes and renewable fuel and "gas sipper" rebates.

Full consideration should be given to alternatives such as mass transit, light rail, high-speed rail, commuter rail, bicycling and walking. Cost benefit analyses must account for the full social and environmental costs of all transportation alternatives and should encourage compact urban and suburban land use patterns to facilitate public transportation.

An elected, citizen oversight board should set highway policy, in place of the Transportation Projects Commission.

State laws and regulations should support local ownership of utilities. Electric power should be decentralized.

D. Mining There must be moratorium on metallic mining in Wisconsin until its impacts are more fully documented. Mining in wetlands and on state lands must be banned.

Mining of ore deposits must ensure the complete protection of the air, surface and ground waters and wildlife, and with respect for sacred sites and medicines of Native Americans.

Mining companies must have no violations of federal, state or local environmental and workplace safety laws to obtain permits to mine in Wisconsin.

Local units of government may ban mining activities within their jurisdictions by local ordinance. Mining companies should be taxed on the net value of their holdings, not on net profits from extracted ore.

Wisconsin's needs for minerals should be met through recycling.

E. The Natural Environment Commercial practices that pollute or degrade air and water resources must be substituted with nonpolluting alternatives. The use of pollution credits to curb industrial air and water pollution is inadequate.

State initiatives to accelerate conservation and reduce the release of hydrocarbons and other gases that contribute to global warming, to completely eliminate industrial gases that deplete the ozone layer, and to control industrial emissions that contribute to acid rain, must be instituted immediately.

DNR water quality rules must be amended to require absolute non-degradation of existing water bodies. State agencies must inventory the water quality in Wisconsin lakes and rivers and take all measures needed to reduce pollution.

More stringent enforcement and monitoring of surface water pollution by the DNR, and surface water pollution levels that conform to those for groundwater, must be required.

There must be statewide standards for landfill siting and construction. The state must provide educational and material assistance to assist in meeting new standards.

We must respect native prairies, forest and wetland flora and fauna, and support the reintroduction of indigenous plant and animal life where it has dwindled. Drainage of wetlands and development of lake and river shorelines should be severely restricted.

2. ENVIRONMENTAL PROTECTION

A. Pollution Prevention Greens call for the eventual elimination of discharges of toxic substances. Policy priority should be: (1) new technologies for eliminating the toxic chemicals, (2) recycling of toxics in industrial processes, (3) mitigating or controlling discharges (as a last resort).

The Wisconsin Greens support the goal of zero discharge for the Great Lakes.

An acid rain and heavy metal atmospheric deposition tax on cars, and on all industrial and commercial applications that generate pollutants should be implemented. Use of ozone depleting substances must be banned.

The state must support industries' conversion to clean technologies through tax incentives, loans, grants, and assistance with research and development.

B. Waste The focus of waste handling needs to be changed to resource management.

Reuse and recycling of products to reduce the use of virgin materials should be required whenever possible. Non-recyclable products should be heavily taxed, and the revenue used to pay for waste disposal and waste reduction programs.

The recycling tax incidence should fall more directly on those firms generating the waste. The standardization and overall reduction of packaging should be encouraged. State loans and subsidies to businesses should require toxic waste use reduction plans.

The state government must build markets for recyclable and reusable products, and buy such products whenever possible.

All products should be rated and labeled as to their total environmental impact. Economic incentives for the production of toxic wastes need to be removed through "full-cost" pricing.

Deregulation of low-level radioactive waste is unacceptable. High-level waste storage should be only for waste generated in Wisconsin, and should not be sited until the elimination of nuclear power in the state is complete.

Incentives to phase out existing incineration, by substitution of recycling, reuse and source reduction must be implemented. Dilution of toxic incinerator ash must be discontinued. Ash must be classified and disposed of as hazardous waste.

The history and environmental record of a recycling or waste disposal firm should be major criteria in considering bids by municipalities for such services.

C. Pesticides The state should create and maintain a citizen accessible central database of the chemical contents, products used, dosage applied, health effects, and company responsible, for any private or commercial pesticide application.

Pesticides should not be used on or in public property, except as a last resort, after demonstrating the failure of other organic alternatives.

Tax incentives should reward the use of organic pest control methods. Communities in the state should have the right to pass stronger controls on pesticides than those specified in state and federal regulations.

D. Public Right to Protection The public should have an absolute right to know when substances that can harm our health or the health of plants and animals are being handled or transported.

The DNR and State Attorney General must be more vigorous in prosecuting corporate offenses and should hold individuals accountable when appropriate. Corporations that engage in gross violations should be faced with revocation of their corporate charter.

3. POLITICAL REFORM

A. Grassroots Power The Greens support open meetings and open records laws.

The "partial veto" power of governors should be eliminated.

B. Campaign Financing PACs must be eliminated. Limits should be imposed on the money that candidates could spend on campaigns, with the amount determined for each race by the size of constituency of the office being contested. We do not support term limits since they restrict the rights of people to choose their representatives.

C. Conflicts of Interest Governmental decision-making bodies must be free of conflicts of interest that would cause their members to put personal interest above the public good. Ethics laws must be strengthened and rigorously enforced.

D. Third Party Rights Laws must be changed to level the playing field for other parties. Subsidies that favor the current major parties must be eliminated.

The current winner-take-all system of voting stifles the voices of many Americans and ensures the perpetuation of a two-party duopoly. We advocate for the immediate adoption of Instant Runoff Voting and the gradual transition to a system of Proportional Representation.

4. ECONOMICS

A. "Growth" vs. Development Current economics is oriented toward perpetual growth. Economic development is different from unlimited growth. Our society must develop into to a sustainable economy, where the goal is to improve quality of life for people.

Government economists must be required to develop measurements for quality of life, quality of the environment, and long-term effects of policies.

B. Trade "Free" trade agreements sacrifice the sovereignty of our people, giving a small body of international bureaucrats the ability to override our federal, state and local laws on working conditions, discrimination, health and safety, consumer protection, and environmental protection. These agreements reduce the living conditions of people to the lowest common denominator. They rob us of our right to use trade sanctions to pressure other countries to be responsible about environmental protection and human rights.

The exportation of pesticides, and other products prohibited for use in the United States must be banned, as well as the importation of food produced with banned products. Tax policies and tariffs should favor products that were produced in a sustainable way and penalize unsustainable products.

C. Responsible Technology Programs of applied research need citizen oversight to assure that technology applications developed with public support are carefully screened based on the public interest, including: quality, need, safety, durability, and the lifecycle toxicity/environmental cost of the products and processes.

D. True Cost Pricing Greens support taxes and other policies to make the price of goods reflect their true cost, thus making environmentally safe products more competitive in the marketplace.

E. Jobs and Quality of Life Economic development must focus on jobs that are based in the community and that will last. The workplace must accommodate people's human needs.

The minimum wage must be raised to a level that comfortably allows support of a family of four. Health and unemployment benefits must cover everyone who does not work. Part-time and temporary workers must make a living wage and have reasonable health coverage.

Health coverage and other "safety nets" must extend to people who are doing unpaid but important work in society.

Policies must be focused on businesses that have a vested interest in the community where their employees live – especially small businesses.

The Wisconsin Greens support family leave legislation, paid vacation time, job sharing, and involving workers in decision-making, management, and scheduling. Workplace safety regulations are necessary.

The Wisconsin Greens support the right of people to form unions, bargain collectively, and strike. We oppose "union-busting" tactics. The State should assist management in working more closely and cooperatively with unions.

F. Welfare Reform Wisconsin must support investment in areas that have few high-quality jobs. Job development incentives should concentrate on companies that will offer local people a direct stake in the business, through local ownership, worker ownership, and profit sharing.

5. COMMUNITY

A. Community Economics The state should create a development bank that would strengthen community economies through loan guarantees, loan participation, and direct loans to new and small businesses, cooperatives and worker owned firms, organic and beginning farmers, and community land trusts.

B. Rural Communities State tax policies should favor businesses that stay in the community where their employees live. Farmers must receive decent prices for their products, so that they continue to act as an important economic support to small towns.

C. Urban Vision and Revitalization Ecological interdependence and integrity are touchstones of healthy communities – both natural and human. We support the cultural traditions, strong families and initiative and creativity within our cities' many cultural groups that will restore cities to economic, ecological and social health.

What is needed is a coordinated program of public intervention based on ecologically sound reindustrialization programs with worker and management retraining. We support safe neighborhoods. Urban centers in regional watersheds need to become sustainable with clean, renewable energy and safe food produced regionally.

D. Planning State law should require more compact urban and suburban land use patterns by mandating comprehensive state planning goals that include determination of permanent urban growth boundaries in conjunction with local governments, while establishing the primacy of the right to farm.

Local zoning and infrastructure investment planning commissions should be elected, and planners should be accountable to local legislative bodies. Neighborhood planning councils should be created in large cities with the power to veto major projects in their communities.

The state should set guidelines for preservation of prime farmland, wetlands, woodlands, and strict management of urban growth.

6. VIOLENCE AND CRIME

A. The Nonviolent Ethic One of the key values of the Greens is nonviolence. All types of violence must be addressed.

B. Crime & Punishment Greens emphasize that the solutions to violence, poverty, alienation, anger and political inequality are the key to solving the dilemma of crime and punishment.

Crimes against people and communities must be punished through restitution and/or jail time. Alternative sentencing must be emphasized as much as possible for nonviolent offenders. Ex-offenders need to come out into a healthy community that both supports them and holds them accountable. Prisons must be government-run in a humane manner.

Our justice system must attach equal importance to justice for white-collar criminals, including environmental violators of our common property. Corporate executives should be held personally responsible for the consequences of their corporate actions.

Community members must be involved directly in crime control in their own communities through citizen police boards and neighborhood watch programs.

C. Drugs No "war on drugs" can ever be won as long as communities that are overrun with drug abuse and the drug trade have no economic alternatives. Drug abuse of all kinds should be treated as a disease, rather than a criminal offense.

7. TAXATION

A. Fair Taxation Rates Wisconsin Greens support progressive methods of taxation.

A portion of funds from an increase in the motor fuel tax should go for development of alternative transportation.

We favor eliminating tax loopholes for corporations and the wealthy, including the state capital gains deduction and the exemption of manufacturing machinery and equipment from property tax.

The Greens oppose state caps on property taxes. It is the community's right to decide how to control its own spending.

B. Spending Government decisions should be made as close to the people as possible. When money comes to a community from the state and federal government, the people of the local community must have greater say in how that money is spent. State budgets must be independently audited for unnecessary "pork barrel" spending and that spending eliminated. State agencies must be prepared to defend their budgets, and to submit to external audits of their efficiency and effectiveness.

Special tax breaks should only be granted when there will be a benefit to society to justify the cost.

8. EDUCATION

A. Institutional Policy Educational systems must be decentralized with greater input and control at the local level. After-school programs for the children of single or working parents must be available. Parent education programs should be developed.

The Wisconsin Greens support a family's right to educate its children at home. The state and local school districts should assist with home schooling by providing curriculum materials if needed.

The state's educational system should teach principles of sustainable development as part of the curriculum in economics, agriculture, engineering and other fields. The Greens call for creating an "Institute for Sustainable Development," based at one or more of the UW system campuses and involving the UW Extension and the Technical Colleges.

B. Educational Techniques Expansion beyond the traditional concept of the classroom and structure of the school day should be encouraged. Opportunities for learning, and the use of "teachers" from the local community must be developed. Educational experiences can involve community service, fieldwork, political activity, and job training.

Students must be helped to learn interpersonal relations, dealing with emotions, conflict resolution, environmental appreciation, and manual skills. Students should be taught the arts of democracy, including how to be involved politically in their communities. The Wisconsin Greens oppose the use of 'high stakes' standardized tests as the primary determinant for grade advancement, graduation or teacher pay.

C. Funding Educational funding should be sufficient to assure true equality of educational opportunity. The state share in public school costs should be increased. School "choice" programs should be limited to public schools. Funding private or religious schools with public tax dollars is unacceptable.

9. HUMAN & CIVIL RIGHTS

A. Individual Freedom The Wisconsin Greens oppose any attempt by the government to restrict individual freedom, unless a person's actions threaten the safety or welfare of others.

B. Nondiscrimination No one should be treated unfairly or segregated because they are from a particular racial or ethnic background; are young or old, have or don't have a family; are educated or uneducated; who they love or share their household with; what their physical or mental abilities are.

The government must support nondiscrimination in housing and employment.

C. Native American Rights The Wisconsin Greens support full tribal sovereignty. Members of Indian tribes have rights under treaties with the US government.

Public education should foster an understanding of the history of our conflicts and treaties with Wisconsin's tribes and a respect for native cultures. We support the efforts of tribes to protect our state's environmental future.

D.Rights of Lesbian, Gay, Bisexual, and Transgendered Individuals Wisconsin Greens affirm the rights of all individuals to freely choose intimate partners, regardless of their sex, gender or sexual orientation.

Wisconsin Greens support the right of gay, lesbian, bisexual and transgendered people to be treated equally with all other people, in all areas of life, including in housing, employment, civil marriage, benefits, and child custody.

10. HEALTH

A. Health Care System Health care should be a service everyone has access to. When people don't get good health care – especially preventative medicine – all of society pays.

A universal, single-payer system should be funded through state and federal taxes. The system must be designed to minimize bureaucracy and paperwork, and to allow citizens to select health care providers and treatment. The state and federal government should impose cost controls and efficiency requirements to keep costs as low as possible without rationing or denying care.

Regional consumer boards to assure equal access to quality services should be created. Comprehensive health education needs to be offered to all in schools and community centers including information on sex education, AIDS, and substance abuse prevention. People with long-term illness or disabilities must have the right to live at home in their community.

B. Contraception & Abortion Research in contraceptive technologies to make birth control safe, inexpensive and easy to use must be fully supported. Contraceptives need to be made widely available to all people, along with educational programs regarding sexuality and birth control. Safe, legal abortion services must be available.

C. Food and Health Citizens have a right to know what is in the food they eat and to be protected from substances that are toxic. Untested food additives and genetically engineered food should be kept off the market until tested.

The benefits of vegetarianism for the environment, health, the alleviation of world hunger should be taught in all public health education programs. Vegetarian meal options should be made available at all public institutions, including schools.

11. SPIRITUAL AND CULTURAL LIFE

The state government should recognize that cultural activities like art, music, and dance are important to all parts of our society, and should support these activities.

The Greens respect all spiritual traditions and support the freedom of people to worship or not worship as they choose. We support freely chosen individual and group participation in spiritual communion, and the separation of spiritual or religious practices from the activities of government. We encourage the development of all aspects of our being: body, emotions, mind and spirit

LIBERTARIAN PARTY OF WISCONSIN
May 2005

Headquarters

State Headquarters: P.O. Box 20815, Greenfield 53220-0815.

Telephone: (800) 236-9236.

Internet Address: http://www.lpwi.org

State Executive Committee

Chair: Arif Kahn, Fond du Lac.

Vice-Chair: Jeremy Keil, Hales Corners

Secretary: Keith Deschler, Racine.

Treasurer: Markus Rostig, Fond du Lac.

Past Chair: Ed Thompson, Tomah.

At-Large Member: John Gatewood, Madison.

At-Large Member: Jim Maas, Rothschild.

Congressional District Representatives:

1st District: Jim Sewell, Racine	*5th District:* Linda Stanley, Waukesha
2nd District: Stu Seffern, Madison	*6th District:* Jacob Burns, Oshkosh
3rd District: Thomas Peralta, Richland Center	*7th District:* Andy Sutton, Rothschild
4th District: Mike McKenna, Milwaukee	*8th District:* Roy Leyendecker, Green Bay

Source: Libertarian Party of Wisconsin.

State Convention. The Libertarian Party of Wisconsin holds its state convention in the spring of each year to adopt a state party platform and resolutions and conduct other party business. In even-numbered years, the convention selects delegates to the national convention and may endorse candidates for election. In odd-numbered years, it elects party officers and members-at-large to the executive committee.

State Officers and Executive Committee. The party is headed by an executive committee consisting of the 4 party officers, the immediate past state party chair, a representative and alternative from each of the 8 congressional districts, and 2 members-at-large.

The 4 party officers and the 2 members-at-large serve 2-year terms, which begin at the end of the convention at which they are elected. Party officer or member-at-large vacancies are filled by a vote of the committee.

Congressional district members are not assigned fixed terms but generally serve for one year. Congressional district conventions meet annually, although state party members within a congressional district may hold an election at any time. Any vacant congressional district position is filled by a vote of state party members residing within that congressional district. A party member receiving the most votes at a congressional district election becomes a representative when the executive committee accepts his or her credentials.

National Committee. The Libertarian National Committee is composed of the 4 national officers, the immediate past chair, 5 members-at-large, and 9 regional representatives. A state's affiliation with a region is determined by the convention delegates from that state and is often the subject of negotiations before and during the national convention. Members of the Libertarian National Committee are selected at each biennial national convention and serve for 2 years from one national convention to the next. The Libertarian National Committee addresses national issues and serves, but does not control, the state parties.

[**Editor's Note:** The text of the Libertarian Party Platform submitted by party officials is identical to the version printed in the *2003-2004 Wisconsin Blue Book*. Please refer to pp. 875-876 of that edition.]

REPUBLICAN PARTY OF WISCONSIN
June 2005

Headquarters and Staff

State Headquarters: 148 East Johnson Street, Madison 53703.
Telephone: (608) 257-4765; Fax: (608) 257-4141.
Internet Address: http://www.wisgop.org
Executive Director: RICK WILEY.
Member Relations Director: SHERRIE OSEGARD.
Political Director: JILL LATHAM.
Field Director: TOM MOONEY.
Communications Director: CHRISTINE MANGI.
Controller: LESLIE OEHMEN.
Finance Director: KELLEY WILLETT.
Deputy Finance Director: KIM JORNS.
IT Director: BRIAN KIND.
Telemarketing Manager: RICHARD DICKIE.

State Executive Committee

State Chairman: RICHARD GRABER, Shorewood.
Finance Chairman: MICHAEL MARTIN, Antigo.
Vice Chairmen: 1st – BRAD COURTNEY, Whitefish Bay; *2nd* – E.D. COOPER, Mukwonago;
   3rd – DON TAYLOR, Waukesha; *4th* – vacancy; *5th* – KERRI KUESTER, Milwaukee.
Secretary: DAVID ANDERSON, Wausau.
Treasurer: BUCK SCHILLING, Minocqua.
National Committeewoman: MARY BUESTRIN, Mequon.
National Committeeman: TERRY KOHLER, Sheboygan.
Wisconsin African American Council: HATTIE DANIELS-RUSH, Milwaukee.
Wisconsin Heritage Council Chairman: vacancy.
Wisconsin Labor Council Chairman: JOHN RUDIG, Wauwatosa.
Wisconsin Senior Council Chairman: ROD NELSON, Sheboygan.
Immediate Past Chairman: DAVID OPITZ, Port Washington.
Congressional District Chairmen and Vice Chairmen:

1st District
   Robert Trapp, Salem
   Greg Helding, Racine
2nd District
   Kim Babler, Madison
   Regina Schaar, Lake Mills
3rd District
   Gary Arneson, La Crosse
   Jerry Nauman, Norwalk
4th District
   Bob Spindell, Milwaukee
   Doug Haag, Milwaukee

5th District
   Crystal Berg, Hartford
   Curt David, Brookfield
6th District
   Rod Nelson, Sheboygan
   David Vliestra, Sheboygan
7th District
   Bill Johnson, Hayward
   Sean Duffy, Ashland
8th District
   William Ross, Shawano
   Mary Ellen Ramstack, Sturgeon Bay

Source: Republican Party of Wisconsin.

County Organization. County party organizations are the basic building blocks of the Republican Party of Wisconsin. County party leaders are elected in county caucuses prior to April 1 of the odd-numbered year. Each committee has a chairman, first vice chairman, secretary, and treasurer.

Congressional District Organization. Each congressional district has an organization that coordinates the activities of the county organizations in the district, with special emphasis on the election of Republican congressional candidates. The district organization is directed by a committee consisting of district members of the state executive committee and, at minimum, an elected chairman, vice chairman, secretary, and treasurer. Committee officers are elected in odd-numbered years prior to the state convention.

State Officers and Executive Committee. Party leadership is vested in a 32-member state executive committee, consisting of the 11 party officers (including the chairman of the county chairmen's organization and the chairman of the Young Republicans Professionals, who are designated respectively as the third and fifth vice chairmen of the committee); the immediate past state party chairman; the chairman and vice chairman from each of the state's 8 congressional district organizations; and the Wisconsin Republican African American Council, the Wisconsin Heritage Council, the Wisconsin Senior Citizen Council, and the Wisconsin Labor Council. State committee vacancies are filled by the committee.

Five of the 11 party officers – the chairman, first and second vice chairmen, secretary, and treasurer – are selected in odd-numbered years by the state executive committee at an organizational meeting within 30 days following the state convention. Their 2-year terms begin upon adjournment of the organizational meeting. The persons holding those offices and the immediate past state party chairman may not vote in the selection of the new officers.

The national committeeman and committeewoman are included among the 11 state executive committee officers and are elected for 4-year terms by state convention delegates in presidential election years. They serve from the adjournment of one national party convention to the end of the next and must be approved by the assembled delegates at the party's national convention.

The party finance chairman is also included among the 11 party officers. The finance chairman serves at the pleasure of the newly elected state chairman and is appointed with the consent of the committee to a term that continues until a successor is named.

State Convention. The party holds its state convention in May, June, or July of each year to pass resolutions and conduct other party business. In even-numbered years, the convention adopts a state party platform. A national committeeman and committeewoman are selected in those years in which a national party convention is held.

National Convention and National Committee. The Republican National Committee consists of a committeeman, committeewoman, and a chairman from each state, plus American Samoa, Washington, D.C., Guam, Puerto Rico, and the Virgin Islands. Each state and territory has its own method of electing representatives. National committee members serve from convention to convention. The national committee is led by a chairman and cochairman, who serve 2-year terms.

REPUBLICAN PARTY OF WISCONSIN PLATFORM

Adopted at the State Party Convention, La Crosse, May 2004

Preamble

The most important platform of any American political party was adopted 150 years ago when the Republican Party was founded in Ripon, Wisconsin. Our party began its life committing us to the abolition of slavery and advocating the principles of freedom, central to which is the belief that life, liberty and the pursuit of happiness are the inalienable rights of all people.

In this Presidential election year of 2004, we recommit ourselves to the goals and ideals of the Republican Party.

We believe in the equality of all individuals – equality of justice, opportunity and treatment. We believe in the dignity of all people. We believe in the freedom of each individual to peacefully debate the issues of the day, to speak their minds and to worship as they choose. We believe that each individual has the personal responsibility to become the best person that one can be and that we as a society need to help him or her when necessary. We believe that a strong national government is necessary to protect our freedoms but that all governmental decisions should be made at the level closest to those governed by such decisions. Governments, like people, must act responsibly to protect our values and traditions and to encourage individuals in their pursuit of their personal goals.

America is the land of the free and the home of the brave. America is a shining beacon to the rest of the world. This is our country and this is our belief. We are the Republican Party of Wisconsin and we believe in America.

Individual States' Rights

We believe our citizens and the fifty states must continue to vigorously reclaim all power not expressly given to the federal government as guaranteed through the Ninth and Tenth Amendments to the Constitution. We oppose all efforts of an activist judiciary to usurp these powers.

Family Values

We commit ourselves to the values that strengthen our culture and sustain our state and nation: faith, family, personal responsibility, and a belief in the dignity and value of human life. Prosperity with a purpose and compassionate conservatism bind us together in a great enterprise for the future of our children.

We continue to believe that traditional families, homes and communities are the foundation of strength in our society and we reaffirm our commitment to them. Parents should be responsible for the overall sex education of their children and schools should only teach abstinence and monogamy. We specifically pledge to support marriage as a union between one man and one woman only.

Republicans support legislative and judicial efforts that would affirm legal protection for all innocent human beings from conception until natural death and affirm our support for the Human Life Amendment to the U.S. Constitution. We strongly support a ban on human cloning and we oppose all research that relies on the destruction of human life, including the unborn.

Government and the People

Governments are a necessary part of society. They have vital functions in providing us with security and services that would otherwise not be possible. They provide us with the framework for improving our lives and protecting our traditions and freedoms. Governments should exist only to serve the needs of their citizens and must continue to be accountable to them. Our leaders need to be the best people that we have; they need to be scrupulously honest. Governments must limit themselves to only those functions that cannot be fulfilled by other means. They must act with fiscal responsibility to prevent unnecessary taxation, regulation and interference in the lives of our citizens.

Education

Parental involvement is the key to successful education.

Parents must be given the ability to choose where their children go to school, whether public, private or religious, through a comprehensive school choice plan in which funding follows the students. We support expansion of school choice throughout Wisconsin. We also advocate the right of parents to homeschool their children.

Republicans seek policies and programs that will unleash the independence, innovation and creativity of individual teachers, administrators and school boards. We condemn compliance with state and federal mandates as a substitute for local accountability. We will promote local control of public schools while demanding accountability for results and high standards.

We urge Wisconsin's education system to teach the basic skills and traditional family values as defined by the local community, and to use technology to prepare students to compete in the global economy.

Freedom of Religion

We call for an end to governmental discrimination against religion and interference with the free practice of religion.

Growing Wisconsin's Economy

Growing Wisconsin's economy is a high priority for Wisconsin Republicans as we continue to build Wisconsin through economic development and job creation.

Recognizing that Wisconsin taxes are too high, we oppose any net increases in taxes and call for significant tax relief immediately. Because Wisconsin citizens still carry a heavier tax burden than citizens of other states, we call for a State constitutional amendment to limit government growth.

Environment

Republicans believe a balance must be struck between protection of our resources and protection of private property rights. It is the Republican viewpoint that Wisconsin can have a strong economy and protect the environment at the same time. Both private and public interests have a responsibility to preserve the rich heritage that our state has been blessed with, both in its great natural beauty and precious resources.

We support compensation for individuals when their property is taken or its value is reduced by government actions.

Campaign Finance Reform

We support the right of individuals to freely express their political opinions through their financial contributions, with full, prompt disclosure. We insist that neither employers nor unions should force individuals to contribute to political causes against their will. We oppose public financing of all campaigns.

Constitutional Right to Keep and Bear Arms

The Republican Party of Wisconsin is a vigilant supporter of the right of individuals to keep and bear arms embodied in both the Second Amendment to the Constitution of the United States and Article I, Section 25, of the Wisconsin Constitution. We fully endorse the Second Amendment to the Constitution of the United States, support its broad interpretation as an individual right and oppose restrictive legislation. We cannot ignore the clear lessons of history regarding the tyranny and suffering which can fall upon a disarmed and vulnerable people.

Equal Treatment for Everyone

The Republican Party of Wisconsin believes that all human beings are created equal in the eyes of God, that all human beings have inherent civil rights and that government should promote equal opportunity for all. We believe that individuals should be allowed to succeed or fail based upon their own merits, not because they are members of particular subgroups. We therefore support an amendment to the Wisconsin Constitution that would prohibit the state or any of its political subdivisions or agents, from using race, color, ethnicity, national origin, gender, or religion as criterion for discriminating against or granting preferential treatment including the lowering of standards to any individual or group with regard to public education, government employment, or government contracting.

National Defense

America must remain a strong force in the world through example, education and assistance to other governments. It must encourage the development of democracy, equality and respect for humanity throughout the world and, when necessary, it must protect itself and its allies from the forces of evil through military means. To that end we support the continued maintenance of a strong national defense with the most modern of weapons and the best training that can be provided for our troops. We support the continued development of homeland security against attack by all reasonable means that do not infringe upon our constitutional freedoms. We wholeheartedly support our troops abroad and our military and political leaders who direct their efforts.

Republican Leadership

We are fortunate today to have numerous, dedicated Republican political leaders to set the example for us. We are proud of President Bush and our Republican congressional members at the national level and their principled positions on topics of national concern. Our state and local elected Republican leaders continue their example as we pursue Republican principles elsewhere in government.

As we look ahead to the next 150 years of supporting the principles of freedom and democracy in America and the world, we also proudly acknowledge the efforts of Republican volunteers in politics and society. We encourage all like-minded Americans to join us in our quest to defend and improve our country now and in the future.

This platform is dedicated to the memory of all Wisconsin Republicans who have committed themselves to the principles of our party over the last 150 years.

Elections

10

Elections in Wisconsin: June 2003 through June 2005 spring primary, September primary, spring, general, and special election statistics

Dane County Courthouse

Kathleen Sitter, LRB

ELECTIONS IN WISCONSIN

I. The Wisconsin Electorate

History of the Suffrage. When Wisconsin became a state in 1848, suffrage (the right to vote) was restricted to white or Indian males who were citizens of the United States or white male immigrants in the process of being naturalized. To be eligible to vote, these men had to be at least 21 years-of-age and Wisconsin residents for at least one year preceding the election. Wisconsin extended suffrage to male "colored persons" in a constitutional referendum held in November 1849. In 1908, the Wisconsin Constitution was amended to require that voters had to be citizens of the United States. Women's suffrage came with the 19th Amendment to the U.S. Constitution in 1920. (Wisconsin was the second state in the nation to ratify this amendment, on June 10, 1919.) The most recent major suffrage change was to lower the voting age from 21 to 18 years-of-age. This was accomplished by the 26th Amendment to the U.S. Constitution, which was ratified by the states in July 1971.

Size of the Electorate. Because Wisconsin does not currently maintain a statewide register of voters, the exact size of the current electorate is unknown (statewide voter registration is to start with the 2006 spring primary election). It is estimated that in November 2004 there were about 4,126,000 potential voters 18 years-of-age and older. An estimated 73% of eligible voters cast 2,997,007 ballots in the 2004 presidential election (second only to Minnesota in voter turnout).

Age and Residence Requirements. The right to vote in Wisconsin state and local elections is granted to U.S. citizens who are age 18 or older and have resided in the election district or ward for 10 days prior to the election. Residence for purposes of voting is statutorily defined as "the place where the person's habitation is fixed, without any present intent to move, and to which, when absent, the person intends to return."

Voter Registration. Beginning with the 2006 spring primary, with limited exceptions, voter registration will be required for all voters prior to voting. Voters registering in Wisconsin do not have to record a political party affiliation.

State law permits registration on election day at the proper polling place, and it also provides for advance registration by mail or in person with the municipal clerk, the county register of deeds, or the city board of election commissioners in the case of residents of the City of Milwaukee. Municipal officials may designate other locations, such as fire stations or libraries for registration, or conduct door-to-door registration drives. In addition, high school students and staff may register at public high schools or, in some cases, private high schools designated by the municipal clerk.

II. A Capsule View of Elections

The Wisconsin Statutes, Chapters 5 through 12, provide for four regularly scheduled elections: the spring primary, the spring election, the September primary, and the general election in November.

The spring primary on the third Tuesday in February of each year is followed by the spring election on the first Tuesday in April. The September primary is held on the second Tuesday in September in even-numbered years. It is followed by the general election on the first Tuesday after the first Monday in November.

Nonpartisan officials are chosen in the spring. These include the state superintendent of public instruction, judicial officers, county board members, county executives, and municipal and school district officers.

Partisan officials, chosen in the fall, include all other county administrative officials, members of the legislature, state constitutional officers (except for the state superintendent), and members of the U.S. Congress. Not all of these offices are filled at each election because their terms vary from two to six years.

In presidential election years, the presidential preference primary vote is held at the spring primary in February, and the vote for U.S. President occurs at the general election in November. In some elections, referendum questions allow Wisconsin voters to advise the state legislature or local government on matters of public policy or to ratify a proposed law, ordinance, or amendment to the Wisconsin Constitution.

Primary Elections

Until 1905, Wisconsin candidates for public office were selected through caucuses or conventions composed of delegates, eligible voters, or members of a political party. Since then, candidates have been chosen in primary elections, but the nominating caucus remains an optional method of selecting candidates for town and village offices. Aspirants must file a declaration of candidacy to run in a primary election, and they usually are required to file nomination papers signed by a specified number of persons eligible to vote in the jurisdiction or district in which they seek office.

Nonpartisan February Spring Primary. A nonpartisan primary election must be held in February if three or more candidates run for one of the offices on the April ballot and no caucus is held to nominate candidates. The two persons receiving the highest number of votes for the specific office in the primary are nominated to run as finalists in the nonpartisan election.

Partisan September Primary. The purpose of the September partisan primary is to select a party's nominees for the general election in November. In a partisan primary, the voter may vote on the ballot of only one political party (unlike the general election where it is possible to select any party's candidate for a particular office). Frustrated voters often object that their choices are limited because they are not permitted to vote for candidates of more than one party. What they need to understand is that the primary is a nominating device for the political parties; its purpose is to nominate the candidates that one political party will support against the nominees of the other parties in the general election.

Most states have a closed primary system that requires voters to publicly declare their party affiliation before they can receive the primary ballot of that party. Wisconsin's "open primary" law does not require voters to make a public declaration of their party preference. Instead, the voter is given the primary ballots of all parties but, once inside the voting booth, may cast only one party's ballot.

Candidates must appear on the primary ballot, even if unopposed, in order to be nominated by their respective parties. The candidate receiving the largest number of party votes for an office becomes the party's nominee in the November election. (In the case of a special election, which is held at a time other than the general election to fill a vacated partisan office, a primary is not held if there is no more than one candidate for a party's nomination.)

Elections

Nonpartisan April Spring Election. The officials chosen in the spring nonpartisan election are the state superintendent of public instruction; judicial officers; county executive (if the county elects one); county supervisor; town, village, and city officers; and school board members. Because the terms of office vary, not all offices are filled each year. The only nonpartisan officers elected on a statewide basis are the state superintendent of public instruction and justices of the supreme court; all others are elected from the county, circuit, district, or municipality represented.

The governor is authorized to fill vacancies that occur in nonpartisan state elective offices by appointment. Gubernatorial appointments strongly influence the composition of the Wisconsin judiciary, because many of the state's justices and judges who are appointed to the bench are later elected to office by the voters.

Partisan November General Election. In November, Wisconsin voters select their federal, state, and county partisan officials on a ballot listing the winners of the September primary election plus "independent" candidates who are either unaffiliated or affiliated with minor parties that are not recognized for separate ballot status. "Write-in" votes may be cast for persons whose names do not appear on the ballot.

The general election ballot includes a broad range of offices. The constitutional offices of governor, lieutenant governor, secretary of state, state treasurer, and attorney general are filled through a statewide vote. These officers are elected for 4-year terms in the even-numbered years that alternate with the U.S. presidential election.

Candidates for congressional representative and for representative to the state assembly are included on every general election ballot, because the terms for these offices are two years. Wisconsin's 33 state senators are elected for 4-year terms, with the odd-numbered senate districts electing their senators in the years when a gubernatorial election is held and even-numbered senate districts electing their senators in the presidential election years. U.S. senators, who serve 6-year terms, are also chosen at the appropriate general election.

The state's 72 counties elect certain partisan officers for 4-year terms at each general election. Clerks of circuit court, coroners, and sheriffs are elected at the general election in which the governor is also elected, while county clerks, district attorneys, registers of deeds, surveyors, and treasurers are elected at the general election in which the president is elected. State law requires all counties either to elect a coroner or appoint a medical examiner. The post of surveyor may be filled by election or appointment at the county's option. (Milwaukee County is required by law to appoint its medical examiner and surveyor.)

Vacancies in the offices of U.S. Senator, U.S. Congressional representative, state senator, and representative to the assembly may be filled only by special election, but vacancies in state constitutional offices and most county offices are filled through appointment by the governor. The exception is that the lieutenant governor constitutionally succeeds the governor in case of a vacancy in that office.

Presidential Preference Vote

Wisconsin conducts its presidential preference vote on the third Tuesday in February of each presidential election year, in conjunction with the nonpartisan spring primary. 1985 Wisconsin Act 304 gave political parties complete freedom to select delegates for their national conventions on any basis they choose, so the vote has no binding effect. It does, however, indicate voter preferences.

A committee, composed of officials of the recognized parties, meets on the second Tuesday in December of the year prior to the presidential preference vote in February to certify to the state Elections Board the list of names to be placed on the ballot. (If a party's candidate for governor received at least 10% of the vote in the previous election, it is considered a "recognized party".) The committee lists the names of all nationally advocated or recognized candidates of the recognized parties and such other names as it chooses. The committee includes each party's state chairperson (or designee), one national committeeman and one committeewoman (designated by the party's state chairperson), the president and the minority leader of the senate (or designees), and the speaker and minority leader of the assembly (or designees). An additional member is elected by the committee to serve as chairperson.

Any person named by the committee as a potential presidential candidate may withdraw from the ballot by filing a disclaimer with the Elections Board. Persons not named may have their names placed on the ballot by filing a nomination petition signed by a specified number of qualified electors.

Presidential Elections

Presidential Electors. On the first Tuesday in October in each presidential election year, the five partisan constitutional state officers, all hold-over senators, and the senate and assembly candidates nominated by each political party at the September primary election meet at the State Capitol to select a slate of presidential electors, who will cast Wisconsin's official ballots for the offices of U.S. President and Vice President. A party selects one elector from each of the Wisconsin congressional districts and two electors at large, and then certifies its list of electors to the Elections Board. After the November presidential election, the party that receives a plurality of the votes statewide sends its electors to the State Capitol on the first Monday after the second Wednesday in December to perform their duties as Wisconsin's electors. They compose Wisconsin's segment of the Electoral College – the group of 538 electors nationwide who actually cast the votes for president and vice president.

Referendum and Recall

Referendum. A "referendum" is simply a question referred to the people for determination through a vote. On the state level, Wisconsin provides for four types of referenda: 1) amendments to the state constitution, 2) measures extending the right of suffrage, 3) ratification of legislation prior to its becoming law, and 4) advisory questions.

The procedure for amending the Wisconsin Constitution requires that two consecutive legislatures must adopt an identically worded amendment proposal and a majority of the voters must ratify the change at a subsequent election.

An advisory referendum gives the legislature a means of asking the voters their opinion on legislative policy. Advisory referenda are usually submitted to the electorate at the April or November elections. Wisconsin county boards may submit advisory or ratifying referenda to county voters. Municipalities also are permitted and sometimes required to submit referendum questions relating to village and city charter ordinances and certain other subjects.

Recall. The Wisconsin Constitution and statutes provide for the removal of elected officers through a process of petition and special election, known as "recall". Officials may be recalled after serving the first year of a term, and no reason need be given for the recall in the case of a state, congressional, legislative, state judicial, or county officer. A petition seeking recall of a city, village, town, or school district official must contain a statement of a reason for the recall. The reason must be related to the official responsibilities of the office, but the petitioners need not provide supporting evidence for the reason.

Following the filing of a successful recall petition, an election is held to fill the vacated office. A recall primary is required whenever two or more persons compete for a nonpartisan office or whenever more than one person competes for the nomination of a political party for a partisan office. Unless the official facing recall resigns, he or she is listed on the recall ballot along with the other candidates who have been nominated.

Prior to 1977, the recall was seldom used. In August of that year, five La Crosse school board members were recalled, and in the following month a county judge was recalled for the first time in Wisconsin history. Attempts to recall state legislators are rare, but on June 4, 1996, a state senator became the first state legislator to be recalled. Since 1996 only one other legislator has been recalled, a state senator defeated in a special recall primary on October 21, 2003.

Mechanics of the Election Process

Certifying candidates, registering voters, and recording and reporting millions of votes is a complex process governed by state law. The state Elections Board determines the format for all national and state ballots, certifies to each county clerk the list of candidates for national and state office, and performs other duties pertaining to elections.

County clerks prepare the ballots for federal, state, and county elections and distribute them to the municipal clerks, except when municipalities use voting machines or electronic voting systems. The law requires every city, village, and town having a population of 7,500 or more to use mechanical voting machines or an electronic voting system, unless otherwise permitted by the state Elections Board.

Municipal clerks supervise registration and elections in their municipalities. In cities or counties with more than 500,000 population, election duties are performed by a city board of election commissioners and a county board of election commissioners. (This provision currently applies only to the City of Milwaukee and Milwaukee County.)

Registration and Voting

The first step in casting a Wisconsin ballot usually is to register to vote. The voter must provide information on name, residence, citizenship, date of birth, age, the voter's driver's license number or last 4 digits of the voter's social security number, if any, length of residence in the ward or election district, and whether the applicant has lost his or her right to vote or is currently registered to vote at any other location. A voter's registration is considered permanent unless the person changes his or her residence, in which case it is necessary to transfer registration to the new residence. Municipalities, however, must cancel the registration of a person who, though eligible, does not vote during a 4-year period and does not respond to a written request to apply for continued registration.

A voter who is unable or unwilling to come to the polling place on election day may vote by absentee ballot. An absentee ballot may be cast by mail or in person at the municipal clerk's office. Every request for an absentee ballot must be made in writing.

On election day, there are usually seven inspectors (election officials) for each polling place. The number may vary, but no polling place may have fewer than three. Any member of the public may be present in any polling place for the purpose of observation and the major parties often designate official polling place observers.

III. Campaign Finance Regulation

Early Reforms. Wisconsin's first attempt to regulate election practices (Chapter 358, Laws of 1897) was passed to stymie the crudest forms of corrupt practices, such as bribery, illegal voting, election fraud, and related corruption. It also required the filing of financial statements that were open to the public.

The current ban on campaign contributions by corporations dates back to 1905 (Chapter 492). Corporations are still prohibited from donating to candidates, political parties, or committees. (Labor organizations were also banned from making such contributions by Chapter 135, Laws of 1935, but the prohibition was repealed by Chapter 429, Laws of 1959.)

The "Corrupt Practices Act" of 1911 (Chapter 650) strengthened and expanded the earlier laws. Central to the act were tightening disclosure provisions. Candidates were required to report all sources of their funding, and they were barred from trading favors, monetary or otherwise, in return for financial support.

1974 Campaign Finance Reforms. The legislature passed sweeping campaign finance reform in Chapter 334, Laws of 1973, which created the current statutory "Chapter 11 – Campaign Finance". The law regulated campaign contributions and expenditures and required central filing of financial reports. It also created the state Elections Board, with representation from the three branches of government and the major political parties, to administer and enforce both election and campaign finance laws. Candidates, individuals, committees, and groups involved in campaigns for state offices and statewide referenda must file detailed campaign finance reports with the board, which supervises the auditing of the reports. The board investigates election law violations and must notify the district attorney, attorney general, or the governor of any facts or evidence that might be grounds for civil action or criminal prosecution. Wisconsin's candidates for federal office are regulated by federal campaign finance laws, but the state board does receive copies of their finance reports. (County and municipal clerks maintain financial statements for campaigns in their respective jurisdictions.)

Regulation of Contributions

Wisconsin regulates campaign finance according to function – contribution or expenditure – with separate dollar limits and reporting requirements.

Contributions are moneys donated directly either to individual candidates or to political committees, with the recipients determining how the money will be spent. The state determines the contribution limits in the case of state or local offices, but candidates running for federal office are subject to the limits set by federal campaign finance laws.

Contributions by candidates from their own personal funds or by individuals and groups acting independently of the candidate cannot be limited because they are considered to be free expression and are protected by the First Amendment. However, independent individuals and groups are required to file reports disclosing the contributions they receive and the expenditures they make.

Individuals. States are free to set their own limits on contributions to candidates for state or local office. Limitations usually pertain to the type of office. Wisconsin also limits the overall amount a single individual is allowed to contribute to all candidates in a calendar year.

Other than a candidate's own contributions to the campaign, no individual may contribute more than the amounts specified to the following candidates or any individuals or voluntary committees supporting them: constitutional officer (governor, lieutenant governor, secretary of state, state treasurer, attorney general, or superintendent of public instruction) or supreme court justice –

$10,000; state senator – $1,000; representative to the assembly – $500; and all other state and local candidates – a maximum of $250 to $3,000 depending upon the office. Furthermore, no individual may make contributions to a combination of candidates or registered groups that exceed a total of $10,000 in any calendar year.

Committees. Wisconsin limits campaign contributions made by political committees. Different limits apply in terms of the amounts a particular type of committee may donate and the amounts a candidate may receive from committees. Committees subject to contribution limits include: 1) the *political action committee (PAC)*, which may be created by but operate separately from a private interest group (such as a trade association or a union) to raise and spend money to elect or defeat particular candidates; 2) the *political party committee*, organized by a formal political party; 3) the *legislative campaign committees*, organized by the respective political parties within the State Senate or the State Assembly; and 4) the candidate's *personal campaign committee*. Any committee that contributes directly to a particular candidate's campaign is subject to specific contribution limits, which vary according to the type of elective office. However, legislative campaign committees and political party committees are allowed to use contributions for party building activities or administrative expenses. PACs may contribute to the political parties and legislative committees in which case the PAC per-candidate limitations do not apply (although other limitations remain applicable).

No committee, other than a political party or legislative campaign committee, may make contributions to a candidate for statewide constitutional office or justice of the supreme court that exceed 4% of the candidate's statutory expenditure level. (Similar limits on contributions apply to candidates for other state and local offices.)

Regulation of Expenditures

Expenditures by the Candidate. Candidates may make campaign expenditures from their own personal funds and the moneys received as contributions from individuals and registered committees, plus any public funding they are awarded. There are no limits on the amount the candidates can spend on their own campaigns, unless they voluntarily accept public funding. There were attempts at the federal and state level in the early 1970s to limit candidates' personal expenditures, but the U.S. Supreme Court in *Buckley v. Valeo* held that this type of financing was protected by the U.S. Constitution as an exercise of free speech.

Expenditures by Independent Committees. Committees are considered to be making independent expenditures if they do not donate to a candidate's campaign organization and they do not coordinate their efforts with a candidate. Independent committees are permitted to spend unlimited amounts promoting or opposing a candidate, but in Wisconsin they are required to file a statement declaring that the money will be spent without consultation or coordination with the candidate. (If the candidate is knowingly involved in the expenditure, the money is viewed as a contribution, and the contributor must adhere to contribution limits.)

Expenditures by Political Party Committees. When a political party makes an expenditure to support its candidate, the expenditure is normally counted as a contribution to that candidate. Candidates are subject to aggregate limitations on the amount they may receive from parties and other committees. In *Colorado Republican Federal Campaign Committee et al. v. Federal Election Commission,* 518 U.S. 604 (1996), the U.S. Supreme Court held, however, that political party committees may make unlimited independent expenditures as long as they are not acting in consultation or coordination with a candidate.

Reporting Requirements

Registration and Reporting. Campaign finance laws are designed to track the flow of dollars received and spent by the candidates. Expenditures from the campaign depository may not be made anonymously, nor may contributions or expenditures be made in a fictitious name. Any anonymous contribution of more than $10 must be donated to a charity or the common school fund.

Generally, all candidates for state office, the four types of committees listed above, and other committees that make contributions or expenditures expressly supporting or opposing state candidates must register and file campaign finance reports with the state Elections Board. These reports must include: the name, address, and total contributions of each contributor who donates more than $20 in a calendar year and give the occupation and principal place of employment of each contributor who makes cumulative contributions of over $100 in a calendar year. Reports must also itemize all contributions, loans, disbursements, or obligations in excess of $20.

Each candidate must appoint one campaign treasurer and designate one campaign depository, such as a numbered bank account, before receiving any contributions or making any expenditures. The candidate and campaign treasurer are then required to file a registration statement regardless of the amount of money they expect to receive or dispense. Unless exempted from reporting, the candidate, or the treasurer acting on the candidate's behalf, must file periodic financial reports. The candidate is considered personally responsible for the accuracy of these reports.

Political party committees or other groups that make or accept contributions or make expenditures amounting to more than $25 per year, and individuals (other than candidates) who accept contributions or make expenditures amounting to more than $25 per year must file registration statements. These statements include such information as the name and address of the registrant, the officers, the campaign depository, and the candidate or referendum question they support or oppose.

Beginning on July 1, 1999, registrants with the state Elections Board who have accepted contributions totaling more than $20,000 within a campaign or biennial period must file their reports electronically. These reports may be viewed on the Internet.

Nonresident committees, groups, or individuals making contributions or expenditures in this state must also file their names and addresses and those of a designated agent in the state with the secretary of state and must also file regular reports, unless a reporting exemption applies.

Disclosure. Candidates and political committees that are subject to state reporting requirements must identify themselves on any mass media communications, such as billboards, handbills, and radio or TV advertisements. This disclosure must contain the words "paid for" followed by the name of the organization responsible for the communication.

IV. Public Campaign Financing

Chapter 107, Laws of 1977, created the Wisconsin Election Campaign Fund in the state treasury as a mechanism for publicly funding campaigns. Under the state's public financing law, each individual who files a state income tax return may specify that $1 shall be set aside for the election fund without increasing the person's tax liability or reducing any refund due. (The $1 contributions are derived from an appropriation created by the legislature to support the campaign fund.)

The public campaign fund is available to candidates for statewide executive and judicial offices, as well as legislative candidates, for use after the primary, provided, in the case of candidates for partisan office, that they obtain a specified number of primary votes and raise a specified amount of private contributions from individuals in amounts limited to $100 or less per individual.

To receive public funding, candidates must agree to accept spending limits and limit personal contributions to their own campaigns. These restrictions are lifted if the candidate's opponent qualifies for a grant but does not accept it and refuses to file a sworn statement affirming adherence to the limits. Money from the campaign fund can be used only for media advertising, printing, graphic arts or advertising services, office supplies, or postage. Other campaign expenses must be financed with contributions from individuals, political parties, PACs, or other committees. Because the spending limits imposed as a condition of acceptance of public funding are low and the amount of money generated for distribution from the fund at any given election is limited, participation in public funding has become rare in competitive races.

4-YEAR TERMS OF OFFICE FOR CERTAIN COUNTY OFFICERS

Amending Article VI, Section 4 and Article VII, Section 12; 2003 AJR 10 (JR 12); 2005 SJR 2 (JR 2); Adopted

Ballot Question: *"4-year terms of office for certain county officers.* Shall section 4 of article VI and section 12 of article VII of the constitution be amended to provide that district attorneys, coroners, elected surveyors, registers of deeds, treasurers, county clerks, and clerks of circuit court be elected to 4-year terms?"

Text of Section:

Section 1. Section 4 (1) of article VI of the constitution is renumbered section 4 (1) (a) of article VI and amended to read:

[Article VI] Section 4 (1) (a) Except as provided in <u>pars. (b) and (c) and</u> sub. (2), coroners, registers of deeds, district attorneys, and all other elected county officers, except judicial officers, sheriffs, and chief executive officers, shall be chosen by the electors of the respective counties once in every 2 years.

Section 2. Section 4 (1) (b) and (c) of article VI of the constitution are created to read:

[Article VI] Section 4 (1) (b) Beginning with the first general election at which the governor is elected which occurs after the ratification of this paragraph, sheriffs shall be chosen by the electors of the respective counties, or by the electors of all of the respective counties comprising each combination of counties combined by the legislature for that purpose, for the term of 4 years and coroners in counties in which there is a coroner shall be chosen by the electors of the respective counties, or by the electors of all of the respective counties comprising each combination of counties combined by the legislature for that purpose, for the term of 4 years.

(c) Beginning with the first general election at which the president is elected which occurs after the ratification of this paragraph, district attorneys, registers of deeds, county clerks, and treasurers shall be chosen by the electors of the respective counties, or by the electors of all of the respective counties comprising each combination of counties combined by the legislature for that purpose, for the term of 4 years and surveyors in counties in which the office of surveyor is filled by election shall be chosen by the electors of the respective counties, or by the electors of all of the respective counties comprising each combination of counties combined by the legislature for that purpose, for the term of 4 years.

Section 3 Section 4 (3) (c) of article VI of the constitution is amended so as in effect to repeal said paragraph:

[Article VI] Section 4 (3) (c) ~~Beginning with the first general election at which the governor is elected which occurs after the ratification of this paragraph, sheriffs shall be chosen by the electors of the respective counties once in every 4 years.~~

Section 4. Section 4 (4) of article VI of the constitution is amended to read:

[Article VI] Section 4 (4) The governor may remove any elected county officer mentioned in this section <u>except a county clerk, treasurer, or surveyor,</u> giving to the officer a copy of the charges and an opportunity of being heard.

Section 5. Section 12 of article VII of the constitution is renumbered section 12 (1) of article VII and amended to read:

[Article VII] Section 12 (1) There shall be a clerk of ~~the~~ circuit court chosen in each county organized for judicial purposes by the qualified electors thereof, who<u>, except as provided in sub. (2),</u> shall hold ~~his~~ office for two years, subject to removal as ~~shall be~~ provided by law<del>; in.</del>

<u>(3)</u> In case of a vacancy, the judge of the circuit court ~~shall have power to~~ <u>may</u> appoint a clerk until the vacancy ~~shall be~~ <u>is</u> filled by an election<del>; the.</del>

<u>(4)</u> The clerk ~~thus elected or appointed~~ <u>of circuit court</u> shall give such security as the legislature ~~may require~~ <u>requires by law.</u>

<u>(5)</u> The supreme court shall appoint its own clerk, and <u>may appoint</u> a clerk of ~~the~~ circuit court ~~may be appointed~~ a <u>to be the</u> clerk of the supreme court.

Section 6. Section 12 (2) of article VII of the constitution is created to read:

[Article VII] Section 12 (2) Beginning with the first general election at which the governor is elected which occurs after the ratification of this subsection, a clerk of circuit court shall be chosen by the electors of each county, for the term of 4 years, subject to removal as provided by law.

COUNTY VOTE FOR CONSTITUTIONAL AMENDMENT
4-Year Terms of Office for Certain County Officers
April 5, 2005

County	Yes	No	County	Yes	No
Adams	2,123	1,060	Marinette	4,693	2,370
Ashland	2,179	790	Marquette	1,370	613
Barron	2,999	1,181	Menominee	208	66
Bayfield	2,803	842	Milwaukee	52,019	16,565
Brown	22,051	6,099	Monroe	4,193	1,111
Buffalo	1,226	272	Oconto	3,918	1,590
Burnett	2,453	700	Oneida	6,396	2,600
Calumet	4,306	1,228	Outagamie	20,249	5,706
Chippewa	5,175	1,451	Ozaukee	7,898	2,347
Clark	5,304	1,900	Pepin	725	260
Columbia	5,144	1,800	Pierce	3,125	1,022
Crawford	1,659	705	Polk	4,347	1,581
Dane	45,833	14,114	Portage	11,704	3,444
Dodge	6,453	2,091	Price	2,114	959
Door	5,140	1,668	Racine	17,529	6,231
Douglas	2,836	786	Richland	1,511	622
Dunn	3,310	984	Rock	11,983	3,223
Eau Claire	8,294	1,892	Rusk	1,848	821
Florence	788	463	St. Croix	9,830	2,956
Fond du Lac	11,517	3,156	Sauk	4,664	1,967
Forest	1,394	719	Sawyer	2,336	905
Grant	4,775	1,560	Shawano	4,529	1,664
Green	4,301	1,263	Sheboygan	15,732	4,456
Green Lake	3,045	1,078	Taylor	1,979	778
Iowa	2,894	1,035	Trempealeau	3,917	1,236
Iron	1,566	748	Vernon	3,493	1,493
Jackson	1,824	748	Vilas	3,432	1,338
Jefferson	6,311	2,263	Walworth	6,682	2,572
Juneau	2,479	867	Washburn	2,454	863
Kenosha	10,975	4,500	Washington	14,634	4,458
Kewaunee	2,299	914	Waukesha	41,087	15,828
La Crosse	14,061	3,519	Waupaca	4,848	1,965
Lafayette	2,229	799	Waushara	3,127	1,166
Langlade	3,750	1,263	Winnebago	17,330	5,920
Lincoln	2,345	865	Wood	10,085	2,876
Manitowoc	11,460	4,042	TOTAL	534,742	177,037
Marathon	11,452	4,100			

Source: Official records of the Elections Board. Scattered votes omitted.

COUNTY VOTE FOR SUPREME COURT JUSTICE
April 5, 2005 Spring Election

County	Ann W. Bradley*	County Total	County	Ann W. Bradley*	County Total
Adams	2,327	2,328	Marinette	5,218	5,223
Ashland	2,053	2,057	Marquette	1,517	1,517
Barron	3,390	3,394	Menominee	176	178
Bayfield	2,715	2,721	Milwaukee	47,448	47,952
Brown	22,130	22,220	Monroe	4,301	4,315
Buffalo	1,164	1,164	Oconto	4,240	4,256
Burnett	2,353	2,355	Oneida	7,337	7,361
Calumet	4,475	4,479	Outagamie	20,921	20,968
Chippewa	5,129	5,133	Ozaukee	7,566	7,594
Clark	5,703	5,710	Pepin	786	786
Columbia	5,791	5,805	Pierce	3,198	3,212
Crawford	1,781	1,782	Polk	5,117	5,122
Dane	45,400	45,656	Portage	11,878	11,927
Dodge	6,750	6,767	Price	2,289	2,290
Door	5,220	5,240	Racine	17,235	17,295
Douglas	2,845	2,850	Richland	1,776	1,786
Dunn	3,362	3,479	Rock	12,276	12,343
Eau Claire	8,078	8,120	Rusk	1,978	1,981
Florence	858	858	St. Croix	10,027	10,089
Fond du Lac	10,877	10,902	Sauk	5,231	5,254
Forest	1,478	1,478	Sawyer	2,431	2,431
Grant	4,971	4,977	Shawano	5,008	5,009
Green	4,449	4,469	Sheboygan	16,911	16,940
Green Lake	3,230	3,235	Taylor	2,152	2,153
Iowa	3,080	3,080	Trempealeau	4,237	4,244
Iron	1,517	1,517	Vernon	3,833	3,835
Jackson	1,999	2,000	Vilas	3,609	3,623
Jefferson	6,746	6,781	Walworth	7,302	7,349
Juneau	2,573	2,574	Washburn	2,614	2,616
Kenosha	11,542	11,587	Washington	14,605	14,649
Kewaunee	2,637	2,640	Waukesha	43,015	43,236
La Crosse	14,357	14,426	Waupaca	5,414	5,418
Lafayette	2,345	2,348	Waushara	3,689	3,695
Langlade	4,378	4,392	Winnebago	17,603	17,715
Lincoln	2,815	2,818	Wood	10,737	10,761
Manitowoc	12,231	12,256	TOTAL	550,478	552,790
Marathon	14,054	14,069			

*Incumbent.

Source: Official records of the Elections Board. County totals include scattered votes.

DISTRICT VOTE FOR COURT OF APPEALS
April 6, 2004 Spring Election

District I

County	Joan F. Kessler	Charles B. Schudson*	County Total
Milwaukee	106,640	102,980	210,655
TOTAL	106,640	102,980	210,655

District II

County	Harry G. Snyder*	County Total	County	Harry G. Snyder*	County Total
Calumet	4,053	4,061	Sheboygan	12,311	12,338
Fond du Lac	7,897	7,910	Walworth	6,709	6,758
Green Lake	1,589	1,597	Washington	11,521	11,552
Kenosha	14,371	14,452	Waukesha	39,643	39,823
Manitowoc	4,760	4,774	Winnebago	17,918	18,056
Ozaukee	7,633	7,693	TOTAL	148,189	148,871
Racine	19,784	19,857			

District IV

County	Charles P. Dykman*	County Total	County	Charles P. Dykman*	County Total
Adams	1,709	1,713	Lafayette	2,282	2,290
Clark	3,321	3,330	Marquette	1,116	1,122
Columbia	4,535	4,555	Monroe	2,922	2,937
Crawford	1,951	1,951	Portage	4,681	4,698
Dane	35,862	36,064	Richland	1,665	1,667
Dodge	8,962	8,989	Rock	16,132	16,234
Grant	3,690	3,697	Sauk	5,278	5,300
Green	1,861	1,874	Vernon	2,550	2,552
Iowa	1,936	1,939	Waupaca	4,531	4,547
Jackson	2,000	2,001	Waushara	1,470	1,472
Jefferson	5,393	5,415	Wood	9,195	9,214
Juneau	3,754	3,760	TOTAL	136,848	137,432
La Crosse	10,052	10,111			

DISTRICT VOTE FOR COURT OF APPEALS
April 5, 2005 Spring Election

District III

County	Gregory A. Peterson*	County Total	County	Gregory A. Peterson*	County Total
Ashland	1,994	1,999	Marinette	5,078	5,081
Barron	3,373	3,375	Menominee	151	152
Bayfield	2,687	2,689	Oconto	4,121	4,131
Brown	21,472	21,534	Oneida	6,951	6,972
Buffalo	1,165	1,166	Outagamie	20,194	20,220
Burnett	2,338	2,341	Pepin	762	762
Chippewa	5,124	5,128	Pierce	3,179	3,186
Door	5,148	5,161	Polk	5,077	5,081
Douglas	2,752	2,757	Price	2,246	2,246
Dunn	3,446	3,482	Rusk	1,957	1,960
Eau Claire	8,471	8,509	St. Croix	9,889	9,927
Florence	837	837	Sawyer	2,410	2,411
Forest	1,472	1,472	Shawano	4,915	4,918
Iron	1,482	1,482	Taylor	2,074	2,077
Kewaunee	2,617	2,620	Trempealeau	4,174	4,177
Langlade	4,033	4,042	Vilas	3,487	3,500
Lincoln	2,655	2,660	Washburn	2,592	2,592
Marathon	13,158	13,164	TOTAL	163,481	163,811

District IV

County	Paul B. Higginbotham*	County Total	County	Paul B. Higginbotham*	County Total
Adams	2,219	2,219	Lafayette	2,286	2,290
Clark	5,549	5,558	Marquette	1,428	1,428
Columbia	5,648	5,664	Monroe	4,143	4,158
Crawford	1,717	1,717	Portage	11,389	11,429
Dane	45,986	46,202	Richland	1,712	1,719
Dodge	6,601	6,608	Rock	12,050	12,111
Grant	4,852	4,857	Sauk	5,136	5,158
Green	4,400	4,414	Vernon	3,734	3,738
Iowa	3,015	3,015	Waupaca	5,280	5,284
Jackson	1,950	1,950	Waushara	3,568	3,575
Jefferson	6,529	6,555	Wood	10,240	10,253
Juneau	2,399	2,400	TOTAL	165,592	166,119
La Crosse	13,761	13,817			

*Incumbent.

Source: Official records of the Elections Board. County totals include scattered votes.

VOTE FOR CIRCUIT JUDGES
February 17, 2004 Spring Primary

Circuit Court	Vote
Lincoln County, Branch 1	
Don Dunphy	1,771
Shawn M. Mutter	1,150
Jay R. Tlusty	3,181
Marathon County, Branch 2	
Philip J. Freeburg	3,367
Greg Huber	10,008
Coleen Kennedy	6,825
Racine County, Branch 4	
Jennifer Bias	4,623
Georgia L. Herrera	11,002
John S. Jude	9,092
Jay Krans Nixon	1,323
Michael J. Piontek	6,410
Rock County, Branch 2	
Alan Bates	6,676
William Hayes	5,381
Barbara W. McCrory	5,686
Kimberly M. Vele	2,362
James D. Wickhem	7,735
Vilas County	
Steven M. Lucareli	1,785
Albert D. Moustakis	1,978
Neal A. Nielsen III*	4,721

February 15, 2005 Spring Primary

Circuit Court	Vote
Kenosha County, Branch 4	
Robert J. Jambois	2,256
Anthony Milisauskas	2,429
Walter W. Stern	957

*Incumbent.

Source: Official records of the Elections Board. Scattered votes omitted.

VOTE FOR CIRCUIT JUDGES
April 6, 2004 Spring Election

Circuit Court	Vote	Circuit Court	Vote
Barron County		Branch 37	
Branch 1		Karen E. Christenson*	163,054
James C. Babler*	4,586	Branch 44	
Brown County		Daniel L. Konkol*	162,052
Branch 3		Branch 45	
Sue E. Bischel*	22,402	Thomas P. Donegan*	162,918
Calumet County		Monroe County	
Donald A. Poppy*	4,188	Branch 2	
Dane County		Michael J. McAlpine*	3,565
Branch 4		Oconto County	
Steven D. Ebert*	35,007	Branch 2	
Branch 14		Richard D. Delforge*	3,316
C. William Foust*	36,848	Pierce County	
Branch 15		Robert W. Wing*	4,127
Stuart A. Schwartz*	35,267	Racine County	
Branch 16		Branch 2	
Sarah B. O'Brien*	36,970	Stephen A. Simanek*	21,139
Branch 17		Branch 4	
James L. Martin*	34,538	Georgia L. Herrera	13,880
Dunn County		John S. Jude	16,272
Branch 1		Rock County	
Bill Stewart*	3,087	Branch 2	
Fond du Lac County		Alan Bates	11,668
Branch 2		James D. Wickhem	10,882
Peter L. Grimm*	8,492	Branch 3	
Branch 4		Michael J. Byron*	16,673
Steven W. Weinke*	8,345	Rusk County	
Iowa County		Frederick A. Henderson*	2,528
William Dyke*	2,492	Sauk County	
Juneau County		Branch 2	
John P. Roemer	3,326	James Evenson*	5,876
Dennis C. Schuh*	2,040	Taylor County	
Kewaunee County		Gary L. Carlson*	2,154
Dennis J. Mleziva*	2,746	Vilas County	
Lincoln County		Albert D. Moustakis	2,159
Branch 1		Neal A. Nielsen III*	4,442
Don Dunphy	2,017	Walworth County	
Jay R. Tlusty	3,008	Branch 2	
Manitowoc County		James L. Carlson*	7,157
Branch 1		Branch 4	
Patrick L. Willis*	5,162	Michael S. Gibbs*	7,144
Marathon County		Washington County	
Branch 1		Branch 2	
Dorothy L. Bain*	16,007	Annette K. Ziegler*	12,067
Branch 2		Waupaca County	
Greg Huber	10,791	Branch 2	
Coleen Kennedy	8,941	John P. Hoffmann*	5,223
Milwaukee County		Winnebago County	
Branch 5		Branch 3	
Mary M. Kuhnmuench*	163,462	Barbara Hart Key*	19,077
Branch 14		Branch 5	
Christopher R. Foley*	169,182	William H. Carver*	12,825
Branch 24		John Jorgensen	12,040
Charles F. Kahn, Jr.*	161,443	Wood County	
Branch 34		Branch 2	
Robert Crawford	72,930	James Mason*	10,459
Glenn H. Yamahiro*	134,795		

April 5, 2005 Spring Election

Circuit Court	Vote	Circuit Court	Vote
Brown County		Branch 10	
Branch 5		Timothy G. Dugan*	46,092
Peter J. Naze*	23,581	Branch 13	
Columbia County		Mary Triggiano*	44,996
Branch 2		Branch 18	
James O. Miller*	5,829	Patricia D. McMahon*	45,687
Dane County		Branch 19	
Branch 1		Dennis R. Cimpl	45,315
Robert A. DeChambeau*	43,141	Branch 25	
Branch 2		John Franke*	45,880
Maryann Sumi*	43,000	Branch 33	
Branch 9		Carl Ashley*	45,345
Richard G. Niess*	37,804	Branch 35	
Koua Vang	15,077	Frederick C. Rosa*	44,980
Eau Claire County		Branch 36	
Branch 2		Jeffrey A. Kremers*	45,050
Eric J. Wahl*	8,503	Branch 47	
Fond du Lac County		John Siefert*	45,128
Branch 5		Oconto County	
Robert Wirtz*	11,645	Branch 1	
Grant County		Michael T. Judge	4,108
Branch 1		John A. Muraski	1,500
Robert P. VanDeHey*	5,093	Outagamie County	
Green Lake County		Branch 1	
W.M. McMonigal*	2,283†	Mark McGinnis	17,997
John B. Selsing	2,201†	Brad Priebe*	9,229
Iron County		Branch 3	
Patrick J. Madden*	1,920	Joseph M. Troy*	22,053
Jefferson County		Portage County	
Branch 4		Branch 1	
Randy R. Koschnick*	6,766	Fred Fleishauer*	12,658
Kenosha County		Racine County	
Branch 4		Branch 3	
Robert J. Jambois	7,395	Emily S. Mueller*	17,971
Anthony Milisauskas	8,829	Branch 5	
La Crosse County		Dennis J. Barry*	19,115
Branch 5		Sheboygan County	
Dale T. Pasell*	14,773	Branch 3	
Langlade County		Gary Langhoff*	17,595
Fred W. Kawalski	3,005	Vernon County	
Jerry D. McCormack	2,250	Michael J. Rosborough*	4,161
Lincoln County		Waukesha County	
Branch 2		Branch 3	
Glenn H. Hartley*	2,863	Ralph M. Ramirez*	43,603
Manitowoc County		Waupaca County	
Branch 3		Branch 1	
Jerome L. Fox	12,623	Philip M. Kirk*	5,797
Marathon County		Waushara County	
Branch 5		Guy Dutcher	2,516
Patrick Brady*	13,367	Joan A. Olson	2,354
Milwaukee County		Winnebago County	
Branch 1		Branch 2	
Maxine A. White*	47,703	Daniel Bissett	8,793
Branch 9		Scott C. Woldt*	14,350
Paul R. Van Grunsven*	45,077		

*Incumbent.

†Recount vote total.

Source: Official records of the Elections Board. Scattered votes omitted.

COUNTY VOTE FOR SUPERINTENDENT OF PUBLIC INSTRUCTION
February 15, 2005 Spring Primary

County	Elizabeth Burmaster*	Todd Stelzel	Gregg Underheim	Paul Yvarra
Adams	353	60	157	36
Ashland	772	68	158	41
Barron	586	68	189	38
Bayfield	920	53	133	45
Brown	6,728	1,397	2,529	724
Buffalo	271	29	55	16
Burnett	528	84	158	47
Calumet	1,362	172	637	100
Chippewa	825	158	318	84
Clark	944	124	274	48
Columbia	1,224	186	408	103
Crawford	413	40	168	18
Dane	24,056	2,873	6,953	2,119
Dodge	1,144	223	708	72
Door	1,173	212	331	94
Douglas	799	61	191	67
Dunn	767	87	228	51
Eau Claire	1,445	110	502	69
Florence	905	264	295	163
Fond du Lac	1,661	341	1,151	134
Forest	271	41	67	20
Grant	913	122	264	66
Green	483	72	168	46
Green Lake	362	58	269	31
Iowa	495	80	117	48
Iron	232	20	50	28
Jackson	354	37	135	14
Jefferson	1,152	167	649	247
Juneau	580	100	240	48
Kenosha	3,467	458	1,091	315
Kewaunee	450	116	202	59
La Crosse	5,894	791	2,230	376
Lafayette	426	46	97	25
Langlade	1,026	166	204	72
Lincoln	518	105	122	35
Manitowoc	4,173	859	1,403	326
Marathon	5,675	1,239	1,359	364
Marinette	1,070	195	404	105
Marquette	307	49	158	22
Menominee	61	4	6	7
Milwaukee	16,881	1,458	7,033	902
Monroe	811	144	238	80
Oconto	839	168	327	109
Oneida	904	129	211	56
Outagamie	8,176	1,272	3,640	608
Ozaukee	1,201	133	1,078	73
Pepin	149	18	20	8
Pierce	481	48	132	35
Polk	673	78	223	62
Portage	1,689	211	358	106
Price	458	51	108	23
Racine	3,207	370	1,508	298
Richland	351	34	133	22
Rock	2,899	210	797	196
Rusk	345	38	81	18
St. Croix	726	70	222	62
Sauk	1,104	128	358	80
Sawyer	478	51	99	32
Shawano	718	106	318	64
Sheboygan	4,822	945	1,996	423
Taylor	435	93	150	43
Trempealeau	492	39	123	25
Vernon	1,125	138	371	55
Vilas	713	117	290	57
Walworth	1,415	197	675	286
Washburn	733	97	164	51
Washington	2,182	492	1,797	219
Waukesha	7,580	1,558	6,180	867
Waupaca	922	99	451	67
Waushara	492	56	300	26
Winnebago	5,028	531	5,453	376
Wood	1,857	314	475	116
TOTAL	144,671	20,728	60,087	11,768

*Incumbent.

Source: Official records of the Elections Board. Scattered votes omitted.

COUNTY VOTE FOR SUPERINTENDENT OF PUBLIC INSTRUCTION
April 5, 2005 Spring Election

County	Elizabeth Burmaster[1]	Gregg Underheim	County Total
Adams	1,858	1,150	3,008
Ashland	2,076	824	2,900
Barron	2,593	1,542	4,136
Bayfield	2,532	982	3,514
Brown	19,456	9,650	29,161
Buffalo	985	444	1,429
Burnett	1,765	1,048	2,815
Calumet	3,673	2,007	5,685
Chippewa	3,966	2,609	6,577
Clark	4,162	2,771	6,938
Columbia	4,203	2,827	7,032
Crawford	1,501	826	2,329
Dane	41,828	20,229	62,109
Dodge	4,755	3,959	8,718
Door	4,828	1,906	6,746
Douglas	2,462	1,078	3,541
Dunn	2,557	1,723	4,281
Eau Claire	6,267	4,208	10,496
Florence	758	401	1,159
Fond du Lac	8,569	6,358	14,939
Forest	1,300	644	1,944
Grant	3,846	2,292	6,145
Green	3,386	2,080	5,476
Green Lake	2,669	1,631	4,302
Iowa	2,505	1,440	3,945
Iron	1,368	685	2,053
Jackson	1,571	1,047	2,618
Jefferson	4,705	4,054	8,778
Juneau	1,967	1,362	3,329
Kenosha	10,769	4,797	15,585
Kewaunee	2,181	1,160	3,344
La Crosse	10,996	6,768	17,817
Lafayette	1,848	1,092	2,940
Langlade	3,032	1,860	4,897
Lincoln	1,940	1,380	3,324
Manitowoc	10,053	5,497	15,552
Marathon	9,922	6,143	16,068
Marinette	4,800	2,205	7,006
Marquette	1,023	926	1,949
Menominee	222	62	286
Milwaukee	48,593	25,339	74,057
Monroe	3,363	1,922	5,289
Oconto	3,796	1,837	5,642
Oneida	5,205	3,663	8,885
Outagamie	17,752	9,590	27,360
Ozaukee	5,474	5,089	10,569
Pepin	636	317	953
Pierce	2,600	1,384	3,988
Polk	3,775	2,098	5,875
Portage	9,735	4,862	14,640
Price	1,791	1,122	2,913
Racine	15,495	8,915	24,430
Richland	1,235	897	2,132
Rock	10,123	5,275	15,438
Rusk	1,641	982	2,623
St. Croix	7,035	4,284	11,354
Sauk	4,240	2,485	6,733
Sawyer	1,966	1,125	3,091
Shawano	4,145	2,117	6,262
Sheboygan	13,025	7,440	20,474
Taylor	1,662	1,105	2,768
Trempealeau	3,023	1,932	4,960
Vernon	3,100	1,858	4,960
Vilas	2,635	1,844	4,495
Walworth	5,887	3,451	9,354
Washburn	2,015	1,041	3,056
Washington	9,605	9,840	19,452
Waukesha	29,386	28,570	58,012
Waupaca	4,387	2,521	6,911
Waushara	2,939	1,634	4,575
Winnebago	14,480	9,852	24,352
Wood	8,098	5,042	13,149
TOTAL	449,739	273,100	723,623
Percent of Total[2]	62.15%	37.74%	

[1] Incumbent.
[2] Percentages do not equal 100%, as scattered votes have been omitted.

Source: Official records of the Elections Board. County totals include scattered votes.

COUNTY VOTE FOR UNITED STATES SENATOR
September 14, 2004 Primary

County	Russ Feingold* (Dem.)	Arif Khan (Lib.)	Russ Darrow (Rep.)	Robert Gerald Lorge (Rep.)	Tim Michels (Rep.)	Bob Welch (Rep.)
Adams	1,132	2	458	54	460	365
Ashland	684	0	217	22	89	187
Barron	1,120	5	938	71	487	656
Bayfield	2,020	0	208	8	86	197
Brown	4,775	29	4,969	1,010	9,583	3,611
Buffalo	384	1	431	56	412	347
Burnett	1,429	2	180	32	80	208
Calumet	670	4	968	210	2,406	790
Chippewa	1,540	5	919	101	1,053	774
Clark	906	1	1,023	244	1,586	806
Columbia	2,142	6	1,267	275	2,113	1,225
Crawford	1,496	0	494	48	327	365
Dane	29,019	81	8,502	2,387	10,126	7,451
Dodge	1,496	6	1,639	289	5,760	1,883
Door	642	4	1,197	385	2,820	891
Douglas	4,943	3	209	19	85	360
Dunn	1,683	6	611	47	446	426
Eau Claire	3,969	21	1,788	167	1,507	1,250
Florence	125	1	118	16	116	101
Fond du Lac	1,900	8	1,583	371	7,360	2,689
Forest	755	1	276	25	254	100
Grant	1,716	14	2,988	306	1,825	1,578
Green	1,664	2	882	66	762	428
Green Lake	249	1	367	131	1,392	1,350
Iowa	914	4	541	132	686	391
Iron	810	0	91	10	101	63
Jackson	799	7	262	47	324	364
Jefferson	1,610	6	2,331	253	3,299	1,449
Juneau	555	14	1,317	209	1,226	844
Kenosha	7,363	33	2,629	133	2,495	1,675
Kewaunee	297	1	274	55	784	352
La Crosse	7,364	24	2,702	152	2,546	1,399
Lafayette	577	4	455	42	312	222
Langlade	811	2	759	156	882	465
Lincoln	731	3	933	187	1,260	585
Manitowoc	5,246	3	1,173	148	2,845	1,061
Marathon	3,828	12	2,814	458	3,744	1,498
Marinette	1,637	7	1,163	145	1,787	658
Marquette	392	3	379	152	882	837
Menominee	357	1	22	4	39	19
Milwaukee	84,285	157	17,411	847	20,717	13,449
Monroe	850	21	643	85	907	508
Oconto	780	7	815	182	1,541	509
Oneida	1,772	6	1,225	100	1,320	664
Outagamie	3,021	25	3,219	1,165	7,686	2,607
Ozaukee	2,626	16	5,091	478	6,759	3,591
Pepin	210	0	88	21	94	56
Pierce	1,932	14	646	60	446	539
Polk	1,602	6	404	54	225	537
Portage	3,521	4	950	140	1,355	593
Price	987	4	280	41	275	277
Racine	5,211	44	3,958	393	5,226	2,846
Richland	694	4	683	59	534	347
Rock	8,591	11	2,687	276	2,666	1,485
Rusk	1,507	4	195	8	151	176
St. Croix	2,122	20	733	46	626	604
Sauk	1,523	11	1,673	422	2,019	1,652
Sawyer	420	0	284	38	208	301
Shawano	790	11	1,402	624	2,699	932
Sheboygan	3,253	12	3,102	367	5,618	2,812
Taylor	337	2	344	49	454	273
Trempealeau	2,353	1	337	20	312	220
Vernon	1,811	3	1,029	83	1,106	658
Vilas	777	2	942	78	999	519
Walworth	1,762	7	2,550	199	2,350	1,623
Washburn	758	2	275	25	172	186
Washington	2,889	17	7,201	484	10,388	4,936
Waukesha	9,603	77	16,391	795	19,973	11,144
Waupaca	747	5	898	1,977	1,705	596
Waushara	474	4	300	131	1,075	1,743
Winnebago	3,324	18	3,106	767	7,683	2,909
Wood	1,633	8	1,149	172	2,018	759
TOTAL	251,915	850	130,088	18,809	183,654	99,971

*Incumbent.

Dem. – Democratic Party; Lib. – Libertarian Party; Rep. – Republican Party.

Source: Official records of the Elections Board. Scattered votes omitted.

COUNTY VOTE FOR UNITED STATES SENATOR
November 2, 2004 General Election

County	Russ Feingold[1] (Dem.)	Arif Khan (Lib.)	Tim Michels (Rep.)	Eugene A. Hem (Ind.)	County Total
Adams	5,765	24	4,505	56	10,350
Ashland	5,852	23	2,726	11	8,612
Barron	12,361	43	10,612	38	23,056
Bayfield	6,331	18	3,039	21	9,409
Brown	62,387	301	58,534	255	121,495
Buffalo	4,190	11	3,144	7	7,355
Burnett	4,815	23	4,115	19	8,972
Calumet	11,590	57	13,275	67	24,989
Chippewa	16,585	61	13,412	124	30,184
Clark	7,979	27	6,982	56	15,047
Columbia	15,893	106	13,249	101	29,359
Crawford	4,938	20	3,319	2	8,279
Dane	194,999	1,139	74,787	471	271,462
Dodge	18,019	104	25,731	145	44,005
Door	9,146	43	8,075	50	17,318
Douglas	17,814	63	6,748	110	24,743
Dunn	13,029	96	9,373	89	22,594
Eau Claire	33,188	195	21,192	130	54,724
Florence	1,183	7	1,430	2	2,622
Fond du Lac	21,515	118	30,853	87	52,586
Forest	2,828	8	2,092	0	4,930
Grant	12,762	47	11,577	19	24,409
Green	10,966	55	7,002	46	18,073
Green Lake	4,042	18	5,989	22	10,083
Iowa	7,530	15	4,948	2	12,495
Iron	2,166	4	1,508	3	3,681
Jackson	5,617	12	3,826	4	9,460
Jefferson	19,684	101	21,725	106	41,626
Juneau	5,980	57	5,850	27	11,918
Kenosha	43,741	306	29,547	215	73,826
Kewaunee	5,781	21	5,393	23	11,218
La Crosse	36,797	210	24,249	145	61,430
Lafayette	4,679	7	3,521	10	8,218
Langlade	5,562	12	5,272	19	10,871
Lincoln	8,877	41	6,601	42	15,566
Manitowoc	21,788	94	21,392	101	43,380
Marathon	37,153	136	30,254	183	67,738
Marinette	10,855	43	10,896	29	21,825
Marquette	3,952	25	4,217	7	8,203
Menominee	1,332	3	298	5	1,638
Milwaukee	312,914	1,328	157,576	866	472,980
Monroe	9,808	66	9,314	45	19,239
Oconto	9,439	37	10,036	46	19,562
Oneida	12,079	59	9,638	29	21,807
Outagamie	45,395	238	42,808	249	88,714
Ozaukee	20,744	125	31,620	83	52,580
Pepin	2,298	9	1,619	4	3,930
Pierce	11,914	85	8,931	95	21,030
Polk	11,660	95	10,265	56	22,078
Portage	23,590	119	14,528	115	38,354
Price	4,835	10	3,683	16	8,548
Racine	54,775	292	45,182	189	100,447
Richland	4,739	18	4,468	5	9,230
Rock	51,336	256	27,699	210	79,538
Rusk	4,415	35	3,337	20	7,809
St. Croix	20,415	241	19,555	348	40,566
Sauk	16,925	109	12,967	97	30,100
Sawyer	4,588	16	4,510	22	9,136
Shawano	9,397	30	10,936	31	20,401
Sheboygan	30,245	130	31,572	137	62,095
Taylor	4,807	21	4,587	29	9,447
Trempealeau	8,370	21	5,396	23	13,811
Vernon	8,597	20	5,856	13	14,486
Vilas	6,758	26	7,000	35	13,822
Walworth	22,210	181	25,235	153	47,790
Washburn	5,000	17	4,235	21	9,275
Washington	25,124	145	46,404	95	71,780
Waukesha	86,775	540	139,979	300	227,650
Waupaca	11,694	36	14,750	51	26,538
Waushara	5,657	16	6,176	37	11,888
Winnebago	45,537	266	41,544	278	87,654
Wood	20,986	86	18,519	115	39,709
TOTAL	1,632,697	8,367	1,301,183	6,662	2,949,743
Percent of Total Vote[2]	55.35%	0.28%	44.11%	0.23%	

Dem. – Democratic Party; Lib. – Libertarian Party; Rep. – Republican Party; Ind. – Independent.

[1]Incumbent.

[2]Percentages do not equal 100% as scattered votes have been omitted.

Source: Official records of the Elections Board. Scattered votes included in county totals.

DISTRICT VOTE FOR MEMBERS OF THE 109TH U.S. CONGRESS
September 14, 2004 Primary

First Congressional District

County	Chet Bell (Dem.)	Jeffrey Chapman Thomas (Dem.)	Don Bernau (Lib.)	Paul Ryan* (Rep.)
Kenosha	2,487	4,192	30	6,085
Milwaukee (part)	1,486	3,456	23	9,002
Racine	1,746	2,862	46	10,636
Rock (part)	3,402	2,017	4	3,387
Walworth (part)	540	779	7	5,522
Waukesha (part)	305	617	7	5,303
TOTAL	9,966	13,923	117	39,935

Second Congressional District

County	Tammy Baldwin* (Dem.)	Ron Greer (Rep.)	Dave Magnum (Rep.)
Columbia	2,010	1,719	3,044
Dane	28,068	10,593	16,893
Green	1,580	699	1,362
Jefferson (part)	927	1,123	2,003
Rock (part)	2,311	1,501	1,901
Sauk (part)	748	1,154	1,533
Walworth (part)	260	175	238
TOTAL	35,904	16,964	26,974

Third Congressional District

County	Ron Kind* (Dem.)	Dale W. Schultz (Rep.)
Buffalo	398	977
Clark (part)	544	1,499
Crawford	1,508	1,134
Dunn	1,673	1,294
Eau Claire	3,684	3,541
Grant	1,619	6,026
Iowa	774	1,461
Jackson	816	739
Juneau	504	3,204
La Crosse	7,061	5,215
Lafayette	511	864
Monroe	814	1,777
Pepin	216	214
Pierce	1,827	1,514
Richland	640	1,434
St. Croix	2,066	1,673
Sauk (part)	638	2,412
Trempealeau	2,403	737
Vernon	1,768	2,515
TOTAL	29,464	38,230

DISTRICT VOTE FOR MEMBERS OF THE 109TH U.S. CONGRESS
September 14, 2004 Primary–Continued

Fourth Congressional District

County	Colin Hudson (Con.)	Tim Carpenter (Dem.)	Matt Flynn (Dem.)	Gwen Moore (Dem.)	Gerald H. Boyle (Rep.)	Corey Hoze (Rep.)
Milwaukee (part)	56	7,801	19,377	48,858	11,720	10,490
TOTAL	56	7,801	19,377	48,858	11,720	10,490

Fifth Congressional District

County	Bryan Kennedy (Dem.)	Gary Kohlenberg (Dem.)	Tim Peterson (Lib.)	F. James Sensenbrenner, Jr.* (Rep.)
Jefferson (part)	171	58	2	867
Milwaukee (part)	8,920	2,988	42	13,100
Ozaukee	1,524	801	19	11,956
Washington	1,843	766	17	16,894
Waukesha (part)	5,292	2,051	103	33,362
TOTAL	17,750	6,664	183	76,179

Sixth Congressional District

County	Jef Hall (Dem.)	Tom Petri* (Rep.)	Carol Ann Rittenhouse (WG)
Adams	819	1,043	1
Calumet (part)	363	2,670	6
Dodge	1,178	6,198	20
Fond du Lac	1,519	9,917	13
Green Lake	132	2,581	2
Jefferson (part)	261	1,908	2
Manitowoc	3,791	3,998	9
Marquette	246	1,789	6
Outagamie (part)	134	539	0
Sheboygan	2,547	9,129	15
Waushara	314	2,657	7
Winnebago	2,450	10,030	139
TOTAL	13,754	52,459	220

DISTRICT VOTE FOR MEMBERS OF THE 109TH U.S. CONGRESS
September 14, 2004 Primary–Continued

Seventh Congressional District

County	Larry Oftedahl (Con.)	David R. Obey* (Dem.)	Mike Miles (WG)
Ashland	0	683	10
Barron	14	1,096	4
Bayfield	2	2,055	6
Burnett	3	1,454	2
Chippewa	1	1,478	5
Clark (part)	0	337	3
Douglas	3	4,963	3
Iron	0	863	1
Langlade (part)	0	593	0
Lincoln	1	718	5
Marathon	2	3,680	10
Oneida (part)	2	958	0
Polk	12	1,578	23
Portage	5	3,362	23
Price	1	956	1
Rusk	1	1,524	1
Sawyer	1	417	6
Taylor	0	326	1
Washburn	6	763	8
Wood	6	1,586	10
TOTAL	60	29,390	112

Eighth Congressional District

County	Dottie Le Clair (Dem.)	Mark Green* (Rep.)
Brown	3,838	16,295
Calumet (part)	135	637
Door	530	4,382
Florence	88	333
Forest	482	540
Kewaunee	242	1,209
Langlade (part)	190	488
Marinette	1,033	3,151
Menominee	171	74
Oconto	566	2,422
Oneida (part)	549	1,518
Outagamie (part)	1,944	10,535
Shawano	569	4,738
Vilas	597	2,113
Waupaca	545	4,068
TOTAL	11,479	52,503

*Incumbent.

Con. - Constitution Party; Dem. – Democratic Party; Lib. – Libertarian Party; Rep. – Republican Party; WG – Wisconsin Green Party

Source: Official records of the Elections Board. Scattered votes omitted.

DISTRICT VOTE FOR MEMBERS OF THE 109TH U.S. CONGRESS
November 2, 2004 General Election

First Congressional District

County	Jeffrey Chapman Thomas (Dem.)	Don Bernau (Lib.)	Paul Ryan[1] (Rep.)	Norman Aulabaugh (Ind.)
Kenosha	27,000	647	43,002	622
Milwaukee (part)	22,507	593	44,208	338
Racine	34,993	696	62,413	542
Rock (part)	12,833	324	26,965	2,040
Walworth (part)	10,889	448	29,988	527
Waukesha (part)	8,028	228	26,796	183
TOTAL	116,250	2,936	233,372	4,252
Percent of Total Vote[2]	32.57%	0.82%	65.37%	1.19%

Second Congressional District

County	Tammy Baldwin[1] (Dem.)	Dave Magnum (Rep.)
Columbia	14,494	14,621
Dane	181,033	88,003
Green	9,849	8,111
Jefferson (part)	12,426	11,882
Rock (part)	22,204	14,248
Sauk (part)	8,525	6,839
Walworth (part)	3,106	2,106
TOTAL	251,637	145,810
Percent of Total Vote[2]	63.27%	36.66%

Third Congressional District

County	Ron Kind[1] (Dem.)	Dale W. Schultz (Rep.)
Buffalo	4,450	2,900
Clark (part)	5,363	3,457
Crawford	5,037	3,210
Dunn	12,853	9,480
Eau Claire	34,264	19,714
Grant	11,083	13,073
Iowa	5,884	6,063
Jackson	6,168	3,217
Juneau	4,831	6,777
La Crosse	38,949	21,906
Lafayette	3,443	4,581
Monroe	10,395	8,711
Pepin	2,355	1,534
Pierce	11,865	9,089
Richland	3,674	5,476
St. Croix	20,821	19,496
Sauk (part)	5,510	8,983
Trempealeau	9,207	4,502
Vernon	8,704	5,697
TOTAL	204,856	157,866
Percent of Total Vote[2]	56.43%	43.49%

DISTRICT VOTE FOR MEMBERS OF THE 109TH U.S. CONGRESS
November 2, 2004 General Election–Continued

Fourth Congressional District

County	Colin Hudson (Con.)	Gwen Moore (Dem.)	Gerald H. Boyle (Rep.)	Tim Johnson (Ind.)	Robert R. Raymond (Ind.)
Milwaukee (part)	897	212,382	85,928	3,733	1,861
TOTAL	897	212,382	85,928	3,733	1,861
Percent of Total Vote[2]	0.29%	69.60%	28.16%	1.22%	0.61%

Fifth Congressional District

County	Bryan Kennedy (Dem.)	Tim Peterson (Lib.)	F. James Sensenbrenner, Jr.[1] (Rep.)
Jefferson (part)	2,127	139	4,376
Milwaukee (part)	42,780	1,521	47,296
Ozaukee	14,706	788	36,157
Washington	17,705	1,231	51,108
Waukesha (part)	52,066	2,870	132,216
TOTAL	129,384	6,549	271,153
Percent of Total Vote[2]	31.77%	1.61%	66.57%

Sixth Congressional District

County	Jef Hall (Dem.)	Tom Petri[1] (Rep.)	Carol Ann Rittenhouse (WG)
Adams	3,999	5,874	302
Calumet (part)	4,721	13,774	388
Dodge	12,711	28,072	1,541
Fond du Lac	12,337	37,950	1,176
Green Lake	2,423	7,169	211
Jefferson (part)	2,774	6,550	325
Manitowoc	14,100	27,166	856
Marquette	2,571	5,031	73
Outagamie (part)	1,886	3,735	158
Sheboygan	19,012	40,099	1,624
Waushara	3,271	7,988	345
Winnebago	27,404	55,212	3,019
TOTAL	107,209	238,620	10,018
Percent of Total Vote[2]	30.12%	67.03%	2.81%

DISTRICT VOTE FOR MEMBERS OF THE 109TH U.S. CONGRESS
November 2, 2004 General Election–Continued
Seventh Congressional District

County	Larry Oftedahl (Con.)	David R. Obey[1] (Dem.)	Mike Miles (WG)
Ashland	59	6,008	224
Barron	1,252	13,608	571
Bayfield	79	6,370	236
Burnett	177	5,514	284
Chippewa	1,413	20,868	1,971
Clark (part)	265	4,057	473
Douglas	828	19,063	1,507
Iron	27	2,459	62
Langlade (part)	153	5,482	428
Lincoln	682	10,859	1,562
Marathon	3,345	44,401	8,298
Oneida (part)	269	8,091	587
Polk	461	12,868	893
Portage	1,313	26,875	3,764
Price	139	5,626	163
Rusk	231	5,200	284
Sawyer	90	4,829	192
Taylor	356	6,417	888
Washburn	211	5,555	257
Wood	1,491	27,156	3,874
TOTAL	12,841	241,306	26,518
Percent of Total Vote[2]	4.56%	85.64%	9.41%

Eighth Congressional District

County	Dottie Le Clair (Dem.)	Mark Green[1] (Rep.)
Brown	35,029	84,641
Calumet (part)	1,678	3,754
Door	5,175	11,860
Florence	743	1,825
Forest	1,510	2,995
Kewaunee	2,910	7,991
Langlade (part)	757	1,905
Marinette	6,596	14,869
Menominee	893	634
Oconto	5,369	13,808
Oneida (part)	3,084	6,856
Outagamie (part)	25,580	54,775
Shawano	5,019	14,112
Vilas	3,941	9,597
Waupaca	7,229	18,448
TOTAL	105,513	248,070
Percent of Total Vote[2]	29.83%	70.13%

Con. – Constitution Party; Dem. – Democratic Party; Lib. – Libertarian Party; Rep. – Republican Party; WG – Wisconsin Green Party; Ind. – Independent.

[1]Incumbent.

[2]Percentages do not equal 100% as scattered votes have been omitted.

Source: Official records of the Elections Board.

COUNTY VOTE FOR STATE SENATORS
Special and September Primary Elections

County or Part	Senate District	Democratic	Vote	Republican	Vote
		October 21, 2003 Special Recall Primary			
Milwaukee (part)	6	Coggs[1]	4,538	No candidate	
		George[1]	2,477		
		September 14, 2004 Primary			
Adams (part)	14	No candidate		Cross	36
				Olsen	65
				Spillner, Sr.	27
(part)	24	Lassa[1]	920	Swank	822
Brown (part)[2]	2	No candidate		Cowles[1]	5,419
(part)	30	Hansen[1]	2,778	Drzewiecki	4,719
				Steffen	4,410
Burnett	10	Bakke	313	Harsdorf[1]	374
		Clausing	649		
		O'Meara Nooney	90		
		Paulaha	64		
Columbia (part)	14	No candidate		Cross	550
				Olsen	827
				Spillner, Sr.	249
(part)	16	Hebl	794	Peterson	1,993
		Miller	755		
Crawford	32	Jacobson	360	Kapanke	1,162
		Pfaff	1,047		
Dane (part)	16	Hebl	5,329	Peterson	7,196
		Miller	7,790		
(part)[3]	26	Risser[1]	8,540	No candidate	
Dodge (part)	18	No candidate		Roessler[1]	425
(part)	20	No candidate		Grothman	257
				Panzer[1]	143
Dunn (part)	10	Bakke	513	Harsdorf[1]	556
		Clausing	452		
		O'Meara Nooney	130		
		Paulaha	28		
Florence	12	Breske[1]	117	Baier	42
				Raduege	34
				Tiffany	244
Fond du Lac (part) ...	14	No candidate		Cross	235
				Olsen	1,234
				Spillner, Sr.	48
(part)	18	No candidate		Roessler[1]	6,614
(part)	20	No candidate		Grothman	1,286
				Panzer[1]	508
Forest	12	Breske[1]	731	Baier	77
				Raduege	63
				Tiffany	470
Green Lake	14	No candidate		Cross	679
				Olsen	2,441
				Spillner, Sr.	121
Kenosha	22	Wirch[1]	7,024	Priebus	5,727
La Crosse	32	Jacobson	1,228	Kapanke	6,036
		Pfaff	6,119		
Langlade	12	Breske[1]	803	Baier	437
				Raduege	299
				Tiffany	1,360
Lincoln	12	Breske[1]	692	Baier	587
				Raduege	446
				Tiffany	1,757
Marathon (part)	12	Breske[1]	175	Baier	35
				Raduege	21
				Tiffany	174
(part)	24	Lassa[1]	7	Swank	16
Marinette (part)	12	Breske[1]	712	Baier	193
				Raduege	149
				Tiffany	1,395
(part)	30	Hansen[1]	740	Drzewiecki	894
				Steffen	848
Marquette (part)	14	No candidate		Cross	494
				Olsen	862
				Spillner, Sr.	459
(part)	24	Lassa[1]	35	Swank	174
Menominee	12	Breske[1]	234	Baier	15
				Raduege	9
				Tiffany	39
Milwaukee (part)	4	Morris-Tatum	7,735	No candidate	
		Taylor	10,042		
		White	3,633		
(part)	6	Coggs[1]	17,362	No candidate	
(part)	8	Morales	7,174	Darling[1]	6,077
(part)	28	No candidate		Lazich[1]	4,936
Monroe (part)	32	Jacobson	56	Kapanke	461
		Pfaff	144		

COUNTY VOTE FOR STATE SENATORS
Special and September Primary Elections–Continued

County or Part	Senate District	Democratic	Vote	Republican	Vote
Oconto (part)[2]	2	No candidate		Cowles[1]	1,028
(part)	12	Breske[1]	180	Baier	100
				Raduege	59
				Tiffany	252
(part)	30	Hansen[1]	337	Drzewiecki	784
				Steffen	476
Oneida	12	Breske[1]	1,625	Baier	911
				Raduege	841
				Tiffany	1,670
Outagamie (part)[2]	2	No candidate		Cowles[1]	2,549
(part)	14	No candidate		Cross	254
				Olsen	126
				Spillner, Sr.	21
Ozaukee (part)	8	Morales	832	Darling[1]	3,575
(part)	20	No candidate		Grothman	9,170
				Panzer[1]	2,727
Pierce	10	Bakke	682	Harsdorf[1]	1,511
		Clausing	805		
		O'Meara Nooney	275		
		Paulaha	95		
Polk (part)	10	Bakke	671	Harsdorf[1]	1,173
		Clausing	862		
		O'Meara Nooney	65		
		Paulaha	45		
Portage (part)	24	Lassa[1]	3,289	Swank	1,708
Racine (part)	22	Wirch[1]	277	Priebus	1,003
(part)	28	No candidate		Lazich[1]	560
Richland (part)	32	Jacobson	46	Kapanke	201
		Pfaff	99		
St. Croix	10	Bakke	1,398	Harsdorf[1]	1,893
		Clausing	670		
		O'Meara Nooney	158		
		Paulaha	179		
Sauk (part)	14	No candidate		Cross	541
				Olsen	869
				Spillner, Sr.	327
(part)	16	Hebl	47	Peterson	78
		Miller	37		
Shawano (part)[2]	2	No candidate		Cowles[1]	3,771
(part)	12	Breske[1]	216	Baier	64
				Raduege	46
				Tiffany	340
(part)	14	No candidate		Cross	0
				Olsen	1
				Spillner, Sr.	0
(part)	30	Hansen[1]	0	Drzewiecki	7
				Steffen	4
Sheboygan (part)	20	No candidate		Grothman	3,825
				Panzer[1]	865
Vernon	32	Jacobson	568	Kapanke	2,731
		Pfaff	1,228		
Vilas	12	Breske[1]	697	Baier	537
				Raduege	861
				Tiffany	1,208
Walworth (part)	22	Wirch[1]	0	Priebus	0
(part)	28	No candidate		Lazich[1]	564
Washington (part)	8	Morales	501	Darling[1]	2,661
(part)	20	No candidate		Grothman	13,194
				Panzer[1]	3,187
Waukesha (part)	4	Morris-Tatum	0	No candidate	
		Taylor	0		
		White	0		
(part)	8	Morales	898	Darling[1]	3,377
(part)	28	No candidate		Lazich[1]	7,130
Waupaca (part)	2	No candidate		Cowles[1]	117
(part)	14	No candidate		Cross	2,215
				Olsen	1,887
				Spillner, Sr.	254
Waushara (part)	14	No candidate		Cross	699
				Olsen	1,912
				Spillner, Sr.	107
(part)	24	Lassa[1]	131	Swank	234
Winnebago (part)	18	No candidate		Roessler[1]	5,964
Wood	24	Lassa[1]	1,545	Swank	2,701

[1]Incumbent.

[2]Votes for Libertarian Party candidate Roy Leyendecker in 2nd SD: Brown – 13, Oconto – 2, Outagamie – 5, Shawano – 6, Waupaca – 2.

[3]Votes for Wisconsin Green Party candidate Tony Schultz in 26th SD: Dane – 424.

Source: Official records of the Elections Board. Scattered votes omitted.

COUNTY VOTE FOR STATE SENATORS
Special and General Elections

County or Part	Senate District	Democratic	Vote	Republican	Vote
		November 18, 2003 Special Recall Election			
Milwaukee (part)	6	Coggs	1,727	No candidate	
		November 2, 2004 General Election			
Adams (part)	14	No candidate		Olsen	768
(part)	24	Lassa[1]	5,755	Swank	3,105
Brown (part)[2]	2	No candidate		Cowles[1]	28,079
(part)	30	Hansen[1]	33,378	Drzewiecki	26,791
Burnett	10	Bakke	2,344	Harsdorf[1]	3,518
Columbia (part)	14	No candidate		Olsen	6,853
(part)	16	Miller	7,814	Peterson	7,240
Crawford	32	Pfaff	3,673	Kapanke	4,562
Dane (part)	16	Miller	49,893	Peterson	31,017
(part)[3]	26	Risser[1]	71,745	No candidate	
Dodge (part)	18	No candidate		Roessler[1]	1,900
(part)	20	No candidate		Grothman	1,033
Dunn (part)	10	Bakke	5,267	Harsdorf[1]	5,391
Florence	12	Breske[1]	1,179	Tiffany	1,418
Fond du Lac (part)	14	No candidate		Olsen	4,731
(part)	18	No candidate		Roessler[1]	28,856
(part)	20	No candidate		Grothman	4,261
Forest	12	Breske[1]	2,901	Tiffany	2,011
Green Lake	14	No candidate		Olsen	7,792
Kenosha	22	Wirch[1]	38,605	Priebus	33,395
La Crosse	32	Pfaff	30,041	Kapanke	30,911
Langlade	12	Breske[1]	6,079	Tiffany	4,766
Lincoln	12	Breske[1]	8,878	Tiffany	6,572
Marathon (part)	12	Breske[1]	1,340	Tiffany	878
(part)	24	Lassa[1]	130	Swank	84
Marinette (part)	12	Breske[1]	4,299	Tiffany	5,354
(part)	30	Hansen[1]	6,277	Drzewiecki	5,449
Marquette (part)	14	No candidate		Olsen	4,561
(part)	24	Lassa[1]	464	Swank	469
Menominee	12	Breske[1]	1,246	Tiffany	260
Milwaukee (part)	4	Taylor	62,689	No candidate	
(part)	6	Coggs[1]	59,463	No candidate	
(part)	8	Morales	26,736	Darling[1]	21,535
(part)	28	No candidate		Lazich[1]	26,068
Monroe (part)	32	Pfaff	1,261	Kapanke	2,117
Oconto (part)[2]	2	No candidate		Cowles[1]	5,536
(part)	12	Breske[1]	1,211	Tiffany	1,128
(part)	30	Hansen[1]	4,549	Drzewiecki	4,488
Oneida	12	Breske[1]	11,552	Tiffany	10,106
Outagamie (part)[2]	2	No candidate		Cowles[1]	15,434
(part)	14	No candidate		Olsen	1,670
Ozaukee (part)	8	Morales	5,226	Darling[1]	10,980
(part)	20	No candidate		Grothman	25,930
Pierce	10	Bakke	7,121	Harsdorf[1]	9,865
Polk (part)	10	Bakke	8,714	Harsdorf[1]	12,841
Portage (part)	24	Lassa[1]	25,626	Swank	10,603
Racine (part)	22	Wirch[1]	3,492	Priebus	5,249
(part)	28	No candidate		Lazich[1]	4,511
Richland (part)	32	Pfaff	599	Kapanke	789
St. Croix	10	Bakke	15,555	Harsdorf[1]	25,089
Sauk (part)	14	No candidate		Olsen	6,800
(part)	16	Miller	440	Peterson	386
Shawano (part)[2]	2	No candidate		Cowles[1]	11,018
(part)	12	Breske[1]	2,164	Tiffany	1,264
(part)	14	No candidate		Olsen	5
(part)	30	Hansen[1]	21	Drzewiecki	38
Sheboygan (part)	20	No candidate		Grothman	11,208
Vernon	32	Pfaff	6,354	Kapanke	8,037
Vilas	12	Breske[1]	6,438	Tiffany	7,362
Walworth (part)	22	Wirch[1]	0	Priebus	0
(part)	28	No candidate		Lazich[1]	3,549
Washington (part)	8	Morales	3,915	Darling[1]	10,544
(part)	20	No candidate		Grothman	32,992
Waukesha (part)	4	Taylor	0	No candidate	
(part)	8	Morales	6,171	Darling[1]	12,672
(part)	28	No candidate		Lazich[1]	39,771
Waupaca (part)	2	No candidate		Cowles[1]	479
(part)	14	No candidate		Olsen	17,446
Waushara (part)	14	No candidate		Olsen	6,922
(part)	24	Lassa[1]	1,269	Swank	792
Winnebago (part)	18	No candidate		Roessler[1]	32,950
Wood	24	Lassa[1]	25,015	Swank	12,873

[1]Incumbent.
[2]Votes for Libertarian Party candidate Roy Leyendecker in 2nd SD: Brown – 3,574, Oconto – 517, Outagamie – 2,415, Shawano – 760, Waupaca – 22.
[3]Votes for Wisconsin Green Party candidate Tony Schultz in 26th SD: Dane – 16,807.
Source: Official records of the Elections Board. Scattered votes omitted.

DISTRICT VOTE FOR STATE SENATORS
Special and September Primary Elections

Senate District	Composed of Assembly Districts	Political Party	Candidates	Vote
		October 21, 2003 Special Recall Primary		
6	16, 17, 18	Dem.	G. Spencer Coggs	4,538
		Dem.	Gary R. George*	2,477
		September 14, 2004 Primary		
2	4, 5, 6	Lib.	Roy Leyendecker	28
		Rep.	Robert L. Cowles*	12,884
4	10, 11, 12	Dem.	Johnnie Morris-Tatum	7,735
		Dem.	Lena C. Taylor	10,042
		Dem.	James White	3,633
6	16, 17, 18	Dem.	Spencer Coggs*	17,362
8	22, 23, 24	Dem.	Jennifer Morales	9,405
		Rep.	Alberta Darling*	15,690
10	28, 29, 30	Dem.	Gary L. Bakke	3,577
		Dem.	Alice Clausing	3,438
		Dem.	Elise O'Meara Nooney	718
		Dem.	Dennis Paulaha	411
		Rep.	Sheila Harsdorf*	5,507
12	34, 35, 36	Dem.	Roger Breske*	6,182
		Rep.	Gary Baier	2,998
		Rep.	William E. Raduege	2,828
		Rep.	Tom Tiffany	8,909
14	40, 41, 42	Rep.	Roger D. Cross	5,703
		Rep.	Luther S. Olsen	10,224
		Rep.	John C. Spillner, Sr.	1,613
16	46, 47, 48	Dem.	Tom Hebl	6,170
		Dem.	Mark Miller	8,582
		Rep.	Eric P. Peterson	9,267
18	52, 53, 54	Rep.	Carol A. Roessler*	13,003
20	58, 59, 60	Rep.	Glenn Grothman	27,732
		Rep.	Mary E. Panzer*	7,430
22	64, 65, 66	Dem.	Robert W. Wirch*	7,301
		Rep.	Reince Priebus	6,730
24	70, 71, 72	Dem.	Julie Lassa*	5,927
		Rep.	Greg Swank	5,655
26	76, 77, 78	Dem.	Fred A. Risser*	8,540
		WG	Tony Schultz	424
28	82, 83, 84	Rep.	Mary Lazich*	13,190
30	88, 89, 90	Dem.	Dave Hansen*	3,855
		Rep.	Gary Drzewiecki	6,404
		Rep.	David Steffen	5,738
32	94, 95, 96	Dem.	Monte L. Jacobson	2,258
		Dem.	Brad Pfaff	8,637
		Rep.	Dan Kapanke	10,591

Dem. – Democratic Party; Lib. – Libertarian Party; Rep. – Republican Party; WG – Wisconsin Green Party.

*Incumbent.

Source: Official records of the Elections Board. Scattered votes omitted.

DISTRICT VOTE FOR STATE SENATORS
Special and General Elections

Senate District	Composed of Assembly Districts	Political Party	Candidates	Vote	Percent of Total Vote[1]
			November 18, 2003 Special Recall Election		
6	16, 17, 18	Dem.	G. Spencer Coggs	1,727	92.65%
			November 2, 2004 General Election		
2	4, 5, 6	Lib.	Roy Leyendecker	7,288	10.73
		Rep.	Robert L. Cowles[2]	60,546	89.13
4	10, 11, 12	Dem.	Lena C. Taylor	62,689	99.16
6	16, 17, 18	Dem.	Spencer Coggs[2]	59,463	99.15
8	22, 23, 24	Dem.	Jennifer Morales	42,048	42.96
		Rep.	Alberta Darling[2]	55,731	56.94
10	28, 29, 30	Dem.	Gary L. Bakke	39,001	40.73
		Rep.	Sheila Harsdorf[2]	56,704	59.21
12	34, 35, 36	Dem.	Roger Breske[2]	47,287	53.47
		Rep.	Tom Tiffany	41,119	46.49
14	40, 41, 42	Rep.	Luther S. Olsen	57,548	99.35
16	46, 47, 48	Dem.	Mark Miller	58,147	60.04
		Rep.	Eric P. Peterson	38,643	39.90
18	52, 53, 54	Rep.	Carol A. Roessler[2]	63,706	98.60
20	58, 59, 60	Rep.	Glenn Grothman	75,424	99.15
22	64, 65, 66	Dem.	Robert W. Wirch[2]	42,097	52.11
		Rep.	Reince Priebus	38,644	47.84
24	70, 71, 72	Dem.	Julie Lassa[2]	58,259	67.57
		Rep.	Greg Swank	27,926	32.39
26	76, 77, 78	Dem.	Fred A. Risser[2]	71,745	80.81
		WG	Tony Schultz	16,807	18.93
28	82, 83, 84	Rep.	Mary Lazich[2]	73,899	99.27
30	88, 89, 90	Dem.	Dave Hansen[2]	44,225	54.55
		Rep.	Gary Drzewiecki	36,766	45.35
32	94, 95, 96	Dem.	Brad Pfaff	41,928	47.39
		Rep.	Dan Kapanke	46,416	52.46

Dem. – Democratic Party; Lib. – Libertarian Party; Rep. – Republican Party; WG – Wisconsin Green Party.
[1]Percentages do not equal 100%, as scattered votes have been omitted.
[2]Incumbent.
Source: Official records of the Elections Board.

COUNTY VOTE FOR REPRESENTATIVES TO THE ASSEMBLY
Special and September Primary Elections

County or Part	Assembly District	Democratic	Vote	Republican	Vote
		June 24, 2003 Special Primary[1]			
Milwaukee (part)	21	Foeckler	1,468	Honadel[2]	1,844
		Sostarich	1,347	Ruetz	300
Portage (part)[3]	71	Hawley	436	Bankson	220
		Higgins	465	Harris	239
		Kieper	327	Szehner	322
		Ladick	454		
		Molepske[2]	863		
		Nealis	237		
		Seiser	828		
		Senski	711		
Waushara (part)[3]	71	Hawley	19	Bankson	34
		Higgins	9	Harris	49
		Kieper	25	Szehner	30
		Ladick	6		
		Molepske[2]	15		
		Nealis	5		
		Seiser	5		
		Senski	7		
		September 14, 2004 Primary			
Adams (part)	42	Henney	75	Hines[2]	121
(part)	72	Schneider[2]	933	Ziegler	842
Ashland[4]	74	Sherman[2]	672	Linton	548
Barron (part)[4]	67	Monette	44	Wood[2]	135
(part)	75	Hubler[2]	1,082	Serio	1,634
Bayfield[4]	74	Sherman[2]	1,947	Linton	544
Brown (part)	1	Hermann	120	Bies[2]	451
(part)	2	No candidate		Lasee[2]	1,900
(part)	3	Fischer	43	Ott[2]	282
(part)	4	Vandeveer	868	Montgomery[2]	3,999
(part)	5	T. Nelson	182	Weber[2]	1,252
(part)	88	Aude	1,038	Krawczyk[2]	2,843
(part)	89	Berman	118	Gard[2]	1,155
		Peterlin	59		
(part)	90	Schaal	1,267	Van Roy	3,585
Buffalo	91	Gronemus[2]	383	Anderson	896
Burnett (part)	28	Wolden	885	Pettis[2]	375
(part)	73	Boyle[2]	407	Brunner	108
		Pukema	159		
Calumet (part)	3	Fischer	371	Ott[2]	2,561
(part)	25	Woznicki	10	No candidate	
		Ziegelbauer[2]	13		
(part)	27	No candidate		Kestell[2]	581
Chippewa (part)[4]	67	Monette	895	Wood[2]	1,292
(part)	68	Xiong	280	Moulton	547
(part)	69	No candidate		Murphy	57
				Suder[2]	416
Clark (part)	69	No candidate		Murphy	792
				Suder[2]	3,309
(part)	92	Taft	25	Musser[2]	47
Columbia (part)[4]	38	Johnson	58	Berg	110
				Counsell	114
				Kleefisch	144
(part)	39	Spadaro	6	Fitzgerald[2]	63
(part)	42	Henney	480	Hines[2]	1,480
(part)[4]	47	Jardine	504	Hahn[2]	1,997
		Yost	1,033	Keating	145
				Pate	414
Crawford	96	Frie	455	Allbaugh	390
		Havlik	223	Nerison	394
		Morga	914	Schmirler	496
Dane (part)	37	Rattmann	269	Ward[2]	404
(part)	43	McIntyre	0	Towns[2]	2
(part)	46	Hebl	3,491	Hutkowski	1,653
				Voegeli	2,105
(part)[4]	47	Jardine	520	Hahn[2]	1,477
		Yost	960	Keating	144
				Pate	244
(part)	48	Dixon	2,369	Long	2,395
		Parisi	5,006		
(part)	76	Berceau[2]	2,809	No candidate	
(part)	77	Black[2]	3,055	No candidate	
(part)	78	Pocan[2]	2,692	Block	960

COUNTY VOTE FOR REPRESENTATIVES TO THE ASSEMBLY
Special and September Primary Elections–Continued

County or Part	Assembly District	Democratic	Vote	Republican	Vote
(part)	79	Menamin	600	Bakken	3,019
		Pope-Roberts[2]	2,910		
(part)[4]	80	Ringhand	326	Davis	592
		Thomson	523		
(part)	81	Travis[2]	2,482	No candidate	
Dodge (part)[4]	38	Johnson	361	Berg	764
				Counsell	1,267
				Kleefisch	1,312
(part)	39	Spadaro	686	Fitzgerald[2]	4,038
(part)	53	Bird	95	Owens[2]	326
		DeDow	38	Spanbauer	192
(part)	59	No candidate		LeMahieu[2]	298
(part)	99	No candidate		Baker	0
				M. Lehman[2]	0
				Pridemore	0
Door	1	Hermann	542	Bies[2]	4,164
Douglas	73	Boyle[2]	3,463	Brunner	497
		Pukema	3,258		
Dunn (part)[5]	29	Plouff[2]	987	Lamb	528
(part)[4]	67	Monette	474	Wood[2]	624
(part)	93	Smith	95	Kreibich[2]	122
		White	47		
Eau Claire (part)	68	Xiong	1,084	Moulton	1,539
(part)	69	No candidate		Murphy	4
				Suder[2]	20
(part)	92	Taft	100	Musser[2]	124
(part)	93	Smith	1,498	Kreibich[2]	2,311
		White	1,228		
Florence[6]	36	Champagne	45	Jones[7]	75
		Crawford	39	Kircher	39
		Runnoe	23	Kluss	26
				Mursau	204
Fond du Lac (part)	27	No candidate		Kestell[2]	469
(part)[8]	41	No candidate		Ballweg	535
				Buchholtz	85
				Gustin	88
				Metoxen	60
				Priske	85
				Sensenbrenner	577
				Slate	118
				Wagner	8
				Zuehls	12
(part)	52	E. Schultz	922	Townsend[2]	4,421
(part)	53	Bird	307	Owens[2]	1,368
		DeDow	71	Spanbauer	973
(part)	59	No candidate		LeMahieu[2]	1,295
Forest[6]	36	Champagne	264	Jones[7]	188
		Crawford	366	Kircher	265
		Runnoe	135	Kluss	171
				Mursau	78
Grant	49	Siss	993	Loeffelholz[2]	4,107
		J. Williams	764	Saint	3,885
Green[4]	80	Ringhand	731	Davis	1,802
		Thomson	1,131		
Green Lake[8]	41	No candidate		Ballweg	859
				Buchholtz	569
				Gustin	234
				Metoxen	233
				Priske	525
				Sensenbrenner	325
				Slate	568
				Wagner	47
				Zuehls	82
Iowa (part)	49	Siss	1	Loeffelholz[2]	12
		J. Williams	6	Saint	7
(part)	51	Miller	560	Freese[2]	1,446
		Reilly	258		
Iron (part)[4]	74	Sherman[2]	742	Linton	207
Jackson (part)	91	Gronemus[2]	51	Anderson	26
(part)	92	Taft	645	Musser[2]	726
Jefferson (part)[3]	31	Woods	252	Nass[2]	974
(part)	37	Rattmann	945	Ward[2]	3,248

COUNTY VOTE FOR REPRESENTATIVES TO THE ASSEMBLY
Special and September Primary Elections–Continued

County or Part	Assembly District	Democratic	Vote	Republican	Vote
(part)[4]	38	Johnson	198	Berg	552
				Counsell	445
				Kleefisch	1,143
(part)	43	McIntyre	31	Towns[2]	39
Juneau[5]	50	Buros	416	Albers[2]	2,781
				Buswell	277
				Deitrich	822
Kenosha (part)	32	Schroeder	101	Guido	67
				Lothian[2]	205
(part)	64	Kreuser[2]	2,638	No candidate	
(part)	65	Steinbrink[2]	2,600	No candidate	
(part)	66	Dunton	1,239	Kerkman	2,124
Kewaunee (part)	1	Hermann	236	Bies[2]	1,094
(part)	2	No candidate		Lasee[2]	45
La Crosse (part)	94	Burke	1,686	Huebsch[2]	2,876
		Seitz	1,049		
(part)	95	Shilling[2]	4,381	No candidate	
Lafayette (part)	49	Siss	49	Loeffelholz[2]	107
		J. Williams	26	Saint	119
(part)	51	Miller	146	Freese[2]	696
		Reilly	373		
(part)[4]	80	Ringhand	11	Davis	38
		Thomson	9		
Langlade (part)	35	Brandt	610	Friske[2]	1,409
(part)[6]	36	Champagne	44	Jones[7]	70
		Crawford	88	Kircher	56
		Runnoe	33	Kluss	46
				Mursau	123
Lincoln	35	Brandt	613	Friske[2]	2,610
Manitowoc (part)	2	No candidate		Lasee[2]	1,334
(part)	25	Woznicki	1,395	No candidate	
		Ziegelbauer[2]	3,362		
(part)	27	No candidate		Kestell[2]	367
Marathon (part)	35	Brandt	73	Friske[2]	176
(part)[6]	36	Champagne	38	Jones[7]	7
		Crawford	28	Kircher	8
		Runnoe	5	Kluss	7
				Mursau	11
(part)	69	No candidate		Murphy	124
				Suder[2]	1,112
(part)	70	Vruwink[2]	7	Mielke	15
(part)	85	Seidel	1,951	Gale	349
				Kamke	1,605
				Marcis	963
				Minnihan	795
(part)	86	Kreager	1,225	Petrowski[2]	2,665
(part)	87	Satterwhite	42	M. Williams[2]	92
Marinette (part)[6]	36	Champagne	408	Jones[7]	281
		Crawford	145	Kircher	170
		Runnoe	245	Kluss	85
				Mursau	1,347
(part)	89	Berman	492	Gard[2]	1,554
		Peterlin	396		
Marquette (part)[8]	41	No candidate		Ballweg	120
				Buchholtz	31
				Gustin	67
				Metoxen	23
				Priske	71
				Sensenbrenner	39
				Slate	31
				Wagner	54
				Zuehls	13
(part)	42	Henney	169	Hines[2]	1,316
(part)	72	Schneider[2]	32	Ziegler	179
Menominee[6]	36	Champagne	53	Jones[7]	8
		Crawford	237	Kircher	22
		Runnoe	9	Kluss	10
				Mursau	25
Milwaukee (part)	7	Krusick[2]	4,329	No candidate	
(part)	8	Colón[2]	1,311	No candidate	
(part)	9	Zepnick[2]	3,159	No candidate	
(part)[3]	10	A. Williams[2]	7,120	No candidate	

COUNTY VOTE FOR REPRESENTATIVES TO THE ASSEMBLY
Special and September Primary Elections–Continued

County or Part	Assembly District	Democratic	Vote	Republican	Vote
(part)	11	Fields	2,793	No candidate	
		Goudy	2,172		
		Malloy	1,173		
(part)[8]	12	Kessler	3,112	No candidate	
		Settle-Robinson	2,496		
(part)	13	Cullen[2]	4,648	Adamczyk	2,408
				W. S. Nelson	2,108
(part)	14	No candidate		Vukmir[2]	3,042
(part)	15	Staskunas[2]	3,252	No candidate	
(part)	16	Young[2]	4,503	No candidate	
(part)	17	Toles[2]	6,754	No candidate	
(part)	18	Grigsby	3,231	No candidate	
		Love	1,128		
		Zaffiro	692		
(part)	19	Richards[2]	5,419	No candidate	
(part)	20	Sinicki[2]	5,007	Schuknecht	2,432
(part)	21	No candidate		Honadel[2]	3,690
(part)	22	Wasserman[2]	5,703	Hintze	3,719
(part)	23	No candidate		Gielow[2]	1,632
(part)	82	No candidate		Stone[2]	4,546
(part)	84	No candidate		Gundrum[2]	695
Monroe (part)[5]	50	Buros	30	Albers[2]	52
				Buswell	64
				Deitrich	11
(part)	92	Taft	493	Musser[2]	1,328
(part)	94	Burke	25	Huebsch[2]	123
		Seitz	20		
(part)	96	Frie	74	Allbaugh	54
		Havlik	63	Nerison	74
		Morga	23	Schmirler	259
Oconto (part)	6	No candidate		Ainsworth[2]	857
				Drengler	370
(part)[6]	36	Champagne	103	Jones[7]	106
		Crawford	65	Kircher	97
		Runnoe	26	Kluss	48
				Mursau	146
(part)	89	Berman	208	Gard[2]	1,045
		Peterlin	102		
Oneida (part)	34	Hallman	441	Meyer[2]	2,369
		Kinnunen	1,257		
(part)	35	Brandt	117	Friske[2]	332
Outagamie (part)	3	Fischer	299	Ott[2]	1,142
(part)	5	T. Nelson	631	Weber[2]	1,990
(part)	6	No candidate		Ainsworth[2]	428
				Drengler	188
(part)	40	Van Handel	40	Hundertmark[2]	324
				J. Schultz	99
(part)	56	No candidate		McCormick[2]	2,828
(part)	57	No candidate		Wieckert[2]	4,115
Ozaukee (part)	23	No candidate		Gielow[2]	3,464
(part)	59	No candidate		LeMahieu[2]	1,023
(part)	60	No candidate		Gottlieb[2]	7,252
Pepin (part)	91	Gronemus[2]	176	Anderson	149
(part)	93	Smith	17	Kreibich[2]	48
		White	14		
Pierce (part)[5]	29	Plouff[2]	164	Lamb	95
(part)	30	Parent	1,364	Rhoades[2]	1,336
(part)	91	Gronemus[2]	215	Anderson	202
(part)	93	Smith	7	Kreibich[2]	16
		White	3		
Polk (part)	28	Wolden	1,479	Pettis[2]	1,144
(part)	75	Hubler[2]	64	Serio	56
Portage (part)	70	Vruwink[2]	557	Mielke	496
(part)	71	Higgins	588	No candidate	
		Molepske[2]	2,714		
(part)	72	Schneider[2]	13	Ziegler	36
(part)	86	Kreager	70	Petrowski[2]	74
Price	87	Satterwhite	898	M. Williams[2]	711
Racine (part)[5]	61	Turner[2]	1,536	No candidate	
(part)[5]	62	J. Lehman[2]	1,622	No candidate	
(part)	63	No candidate		Vos	3,781
(part)	66	Dunton	255	Kerkman	1,018
(part)	83	No candidate		Gunderson[2]	844

COUNTY VOTE FOR REPRESENTATIVES TO THE ASSEMBLY
Special and September Primary Elections–Continued

County or Part	Assembly District	Democratic	Vote	Republican	Vote
Richland (part)	49	Siss	38	Loeffelholz[2]	122
		J. Williams	24	Saint	118
(part)[5]	50	Buros	295	Albers[2]	758
				Buswell	27
				Deitrich	147
(part)	51	Miller	78	Freese[2]	157
		Reilly	22		
(part)	96	Frie	72	Allbaugh	155
		Havlik	73	Nerison	58
		Morga	20	Schmirler	24
Rock (part)	43	McIntyre	1,236	Towns[2]	1,828
(part)	44	Brien	958	Bollerud	1,371
		Murray	1,840		
		Sheridan	2,556		
(part)	45	Benedict	1,472	Brown	1,512
				Murry	847
(part)[4]	80	Ringhand	481	Davis	275
		Thomson	185		
Rusk	87	Satterwhite	1,224	M. Williams[2]	375
St. Croix (part)	28	Wolden	66	Pettis[2]	64
(part)[5]	29	Plouff[2]	1,089	Lamb	808
(part)	30	Parent	826	Rhoades[2]	914
Sauk (part)	42	Henney	429	Hines[2]	1,617
(part)[4]	47	Jardine	31	Hahn[2]	80
		Yost	54	Keating	11
				Pate	7
(part)[5]	50	Buros	306	Albers[2]	1,328
				Buswell	95
				Deitrich	1,136
(part)	51	Miller	447	Freese[2]	850
		Reilly	123		
Sawyer (part)[4]	74	Sherman[2]	364	Linton	607
(part)	87	Satterwhite	26	M. Williams[2]	70
Shawano (part)	5	T. Nelson	8	Weber[2]	69
(part)	6	No candidate		Ainsworth[2]	3,169
				Drengler	1,773
(part)[6]	36	Champagne	84	Jones[7]	78
		Crawford	78	Kircher	89
		Runnoe	19	Kluss	62
				Mursau	196
(part)	40	Van Handel	0	Hundertmark[2]	2
				J. Schultz	0
(part)	85	Seidel	24	Gale	3
				Kamke	19
				Marcis	15
				Minnihan	4
(part)	86	Kreager	25	Petrowski[2]	129
(part)	89	Berman	0	Gard[2]	10
		Peterlin	0		
Sheboygan (part)	26	Van Akkeren[2]	1,733	No candidate	
(part)	27	No candidate		Kestell[2]	2,898
(part)	59	No candidate		LeMahieu[2]	3,834
Taylor (part)	69	No candidate		Murphy	3
				Suder[2]	22
(part)	87	Satterwhite	256	M. Williams[2]	701
Trempealeau	91	Gronemus[2]	2,342	Anderson	690
Vernon	96	Frie	1,165	Allbaugh	572
		Havlik	477	Nerison	1,690
		Morga	314	Schmirler	786
Vilas	34	Hallman	156	Meyer[2]	2,134
		Kinnunen	635		
Walworth (part)[3]	31	Woods	265	Nass[2]	1,330
(part)	32	Schroeder	864	Guido	975
				Lothian[2]	2,597
(part)	43	McIntyre	285	Towns[2]	471
(part)	45	Benedict	48	Brown	54
				Murry	37
(part)	66	Dunton	0	Kerkman	0
(part)	83	No candidate		Gunderson[2]	591
Washburn (part)	73	Boyle[2]	295	Brunner	185
		Pukema	92		
(part)	75	Hubler[2]	430	Serio	345
Washington (part)	23	No candidate		Gielow[2]	0
(part)	24	No candidate		Jeskewitz[2]	2,491

COUNTY VOTE FOR REPRESENTATIVES TO THE ASSEMBLY
Special and September Primary Elections–Continued

County or Part	Assembly District	Democratic	Vote	Republican	Vote
(part)	58	Uhlig	1,185	Karshna	4,259
				Strachota	6,683
(part)	59	No candidate		LeMahieu[2]	2,025
(part)	60	No candidate		Gottlieb[2]	731
(part)	99	No candidate		Baker	222
				M. Lehman[2]	1,446
				Pridemore	2,040
Waukesha (part)[8]	12	Kessler	0	No candidate	
		Settle-Robinson	0	No candidate	
(part)	14	No candidate		Vukmir[2]	2,537
(part)	24	No candidate		Jeskewitz[2]	3,227
(part)[3]	31	Woods	474	Nass[2]	2,337
(part)	33	Byrne	953	Vrakas[2]	5,620
(part)[4]	38	Johnson	375	Berg	300
				Counsell	917
				Kleefisch	1,575
(part)	83	No candidate		Gunderson[2]	3,204
(part)	84	No candidate		Gundrum[2]	4,462
(part)	97	No candidate		Nischke[2]	3,302
(part)	98	No candidate		Jensen[2]	6,722
(part)	99	No candidate		Baker	838
				M. Lehman[2]	1,591
				Pridemore	1,181
Waupaca (part)	6	No candidate		Ainsworth[2]	95
				Drengler	37
(part)	40	Van Handel	520	Hundertmark[2]	3,800
				J. Schultz	859
(part)[8]	41	No candidate		Ballweg	33
				Buchholtz	36
				Gustin	23
				Metoxen	9
				Priske	7
				Sensenbrenner	33
				Slate	2
				Wagner	2
				Zuehls	2
Waushara (part)[8]	41	No candidate		Ballweg	859
				Buchholtz	368
				Gustin	517
				Metoxen	49
				Priske	114
				Sensenbrenner	205
				Slate	141
				Wagner	517
				Zuehls	21
(part)	71	Higgins	47	No candidate	
		Molepske[2]	69		
Winnebago (part)	53	Bird	552	Owens[2]	1,621
		DeDow	496	Spanbauer	1,501
(part)[3,4]	54	Hintz	1,069	Underheim[2]	3,336
(part)	55	No candidate		Kaufert[2]	3,051
(part)	56	No candidate		McCormick[2]	1,619
Wood (part)	69	No candidate		Murphy	16
				Suder[2]	101
(part)	70	Vruwink[2]	852	Mielke	1,544
(part)	72	Schneider[2]	707	Ziegler	1,234

[1]District 21 incumbent Jeff Plale and District 71 incumbent Julie M. Lassa resigned from the Assembly and took office in the Senate on May 8, 2003, following an April 29, 2003 special election.

[2]Incumbent.

[3]Votes for Wisconsin Green Party candidates: 71st AD: Amy Heart: Portage – 102, Waushara – 2; 10th AD: Damien Jones: Milwaukee – 10; 31st AD: Bruce Hinkforth: Jefferson – 1, Walworth – 3, Waukesha – 5; 54th AD: Tony Palmeri: Winnebago – 183.

[4]Votes for Independent candidates: 38th AD: Adam Beardsley: Columbia – 0, Dodge – 8, Jefferson – 1, Waukesha – 16; Andrew Sellinger: Columbia – 0, Dodge – 4, Jefferson – 0, Waukesha – 0; 44th AD: Charles A. Knipp: Rock – 54, Steve Trueblood: Rock – 10; 47th AD: Bill Landgraf: Columbia – 3, Dane – 11, Sauk – 0; 54th AD: Dan Carpenter: Winnebago – 43; 67th AD: Jan Morrow: Barron – 0, Chippewa – 8, Dunn – 4; 74th AD: Eugene Bigboy, Sr.: Ashland – 13, Bayfield – 8, Iron – 2, Sawyer – 2; 80th AD: Patrick J. O'Brien: Dane – 5, Green – 13, Lafayette – 0, Rock – 3.

[5]Votes for Libertarian Party candidates: 29th AD: Craig Mohn: Dunn – 5, Pierce – 7, St. Croix – 61; 50th AD: Tom Kuester: Juneau – 30, Monroe – 8, Richland – 2, Sauk – 29; 61st AD: George Meyers: Racine – 19; 62nd AD: Keith Deschler: Racine – 17.

[6]Recount vote total.

[7]Write-in candidate.

[8]Votes for Constitution Party candidates: 12th AD: Joan Tatarsky: Milwaukee – 10, Waukesha – 0; 41st AD: James E. Tostenson: Fond du Lac – 1, Green Lake – 1, Marquette – 2, Waupaca – 0, Waushara – 11.

Source: Official records of the Elections Board. Scattered votes omitted.

COUNTY VOTE FOR REPRESENTATIVES TO THE ASSEMBLY
Special and General Elections

County or Part	Assembly District	Democratic	Vote	Republican	Vote
		July 22, 2003 Special Election[1]			
Milwaukee	21	Foeckler	4,216	Honadel	6,624
Portage (part)[2]	71	Molepske	2,534	Szehner	2,318
		Seiser[3]	942		
Waushara (part)[2]	71	Molepske	94	Szehner	174
		Seiser[3]	4		
		January 27, 2004 Special Election[4]			
Milwaukee (part)[5]	17	Toles	1,332	No candidate	
		November 2, 2004 General Election			
Adams (part)	42	Henney	519	Hines[6]	685
(part)	72	Schneider[6]	5,321	Ziegler	3,511
Ashland[5]	74	Sherman[6]	5,227	Linton	3,596
Barron (part)[5]	67	Monette	459	Wood[6]	682
(part)	75	Hubler[6]	13,087	Serio	9,126
Bayfield[5]	74	Sherman[6]	5,572	Linton	3,901
Brown (part)	1	Hermann	1,486	Bies[6]	2,148
(part)	2	No candidate		Lasee[6]	11,908
(part)	3	Fischer	481	Ott[6]	1,203
(part)	4	Vandeveer	10,733	Montgomery[6]	17,324
(part)	5	Nelson	3,568	Weber[6]	4,989
(part)	88	Aude	11,093	Krawczyk[6]	13,174
(part)	89	Berman	2,356	Gard[6]	5,172
(part)	90	Schaal	12,944	Van Roy[6]	14,289
Buffalo	91	Gronemus[6]	4,786	Anderson	2,477
Burnett (part)	28	Wolden	2,636	Pettis[6]	3,307
(part)	73	Boyle[6]	1,797	Brunner	1,343
Calumet (part)	3	Fischer	6,409	Ott[6]	12,584
(part)	25	Ziegelbauer[6]	529	No candidate	
(part)	27	No candidate		Kestell[6]	2,973
Chippewa (part)[5]	67	Monette	7,538	Wood[6]	9,738
(part)	68	Xiong	3,293	Moulton	5,250
(part)	69	No candidate		Suder[6]	1,916
Clark (part)	69	No candidate		Suder[6]	10,992
(part)	92	Taft	164	Musser[6]	227
Columbia (part)[5]	38	Johnson	1,202	Kleefisch	1,080
(part)	39	Spadaro	43	Fitzgerald[6]	201
(part)	42	Henney	5,361	Hines[6]	5,104
(part)[5]	47	Yost	6,819	Hahn[6]	8,206
Crawford	96	Frie	3,762	Nerison	4,405
Dane (part)	37	Rattmann	2,529	Ward[6]	1,794
(part)	43	McIntyre	1	Towns[6]	5
(part)	46	Hebl	18,950	Voegeli	13,482
(part)[5]	47	Yost	7,063	Hahn[6]	7,071
(part)	48	Parisi	25,066	Long	8,451
(part)	76	Berceau[6]	27,270	No candidate	
(part)	77	Black[6]	26,338	No candidate	
(part)	78	Pocan[6]	25,674	Block	5,122
(part)	79	Pope-Roberts[6]	21,999	Bakken	14,731
(part)[5]	80	Thomson	4,235	Davis	3,127
(part)	81	Travis[6]	24,938	No candidate	
Dodge (part)[5]	38	Johnson	3,677	Kleefisch	7,801
(part)	39	Spadaro	8,291	Fitzgerald[6]	18,791
(part)	53	Bird	1,021	Owens[6]	1,429
(part)	59	No candidate		LeMahieu[6]	1,012
(part)	99	No candidate		Pridemore	0
Door	1	Hermann	6,294	Bies[6]	10,664
Douglas	73	Boyle[6]	16,149	Brunner	8,296
Dunn (part)[7]	29	Plouff[6]	5,445	Lamb	5,044
(part)[5]	67	Monette	3,986	Wood[6]	4,913
(part)	93	Smith	1,007	Kreibich[6]	1,163
Eau Claire (part)	68	Xiong	10,801	Moulton	11,415
(part)	69	No candidate		Suder[6]	123
(part)	92	Taft	900	Musser[6]	751
(part)	93	Smith	14,092	Kreibich[6]	15,364
Florence	36	Crawford	811	Mursau	1,705
Fond du Lac (part)	27	No candidate		Kestell[6]	2,288
(part)[8]	41	No candidate		Ballweg	4,298
(part)	52	Schultz	8,775	Townsend[6]	17,395
(part)	53	Bird	3,658	Owens[6]	6,192
(part)	59	No candidate		LeMahieu[6]	4,078
Forest	36	Crawford	2,132	Mursau	2,488
Grant	49	Siss	10,674	Loeffelholz[6]	13,750

COUNTY VOTE FOR REPRESENTATIVES TO THE ASSEMBLY
Special and General Elections–Continued

County or Part	Assembly District	Democratic	Vote	Republican	Vote
Green[5]	80	Thomson	7,482	Davis	9,632
Green Lake[8]	41	No candidate		Ballweg	6,910
Iowa (part)	49	Siss	33	Loeffelholz[6]	42
(part)	51	Miller	5,326	Freese[6]	6,753
Iron (part)[5]	74	Sherman[6]	1,697	Linton	2,039
Jackson (part)	91	Gronemus[6]	350	Anderson	122
(part)	92	Taft	4,284	Musser[6]	4,649
Jefferson (part)[2]	31	Woods	2,363	Nass[6]	4,732
(part)	37	Rattmann	9,148	Ward[6]	15,609
(part)[5]	38	Johnson	2,141	Kleefisch	4,919
(part)	43	McIntyre	556	Towns[6]	653
Juneau[7]	50	Buros	3,089	Albers[6]	6,914
Kenosha (part)	32	Schroeder	751	Lothian[6]	912
(part)	64	Kreuser[6]	16,340	No candidate	
(part)	65	Steinbrink[6]	18,522	No candidate	
(part)	66	Dunton	6,679	Kerkman[6]	12,061
Kewaunee (part)	1	Hermann	4,110	Bies[6]	6,210
(part)	2	No candidate		Lasee[6]	427
La Crosse (part)	94	Burke	12,735	Huebsch[6]	17,456
(part)	95	Shilling[6]	22,879	No candidate	
Lafayette (part)	49	Siss	441	Loeffelholz[6]	418
(part)	51	Miller	2,215	Freese[6]	4,570
(part)[5]	80	Thomson	149	Davis	286
Langlade (part)	35	Brandt	4,554	Friske[6]	4,281
(part)	36	Crawford	848	Mursau	1,019
Lincoln	35	Brandt	5,952	Friske[6]	9,381
Manitowoc (part)	2	No candidate		Lasee[6]	9,513
(part)	25	Ziegelbauer[6]	19,739	No candidate	
(part)	27	No candidate		Kestell[6]	2,124
Marathon (part)	35	Brandt	744	Friske[6]	978
(part)	36	Crawford	213	Mursau	177
(part)	69	No candidate		Suder[6]	5,815
(part)	70	Vruwink[6]	134	Mielke	82
(part)	85	Seidel	15,528	Kamke	11,559
(part)	86	Kreager	9,393	Petrowski[6]	19,139
(part)	87	Satterwhite	409	M. Williams[6]	636
Marinette (part)	36	Crawford	3,430	Mursau	6,179
(part)	89	Berman	5,116	Gard[6]	6,848
Marquette (part)[8]	41	No candidate		Ballweg	1,033
(part)	42	Henney	1,794	Hines[6]	3,625
(part)	72	Schneider[6]	424	Ziegler	498
Menominee	36	Crawford	1,246	Mursau	266
Milwaukee (part)	7	Krusick[6]	21,074	No candidate	
(part)	8	Colón[6]	8,815	No candidate	
(part)	9	Zepnick[6]	14,775	No candidate	
(part)[2]	10	A. Williams[6]	21,516	No candidate	
(part)	11	Fields	19,625	No candidate	
(part)[8]	12	Kessler	18,720	No candidate	
(part)	13	Cullen[6]	17,765	Adamczyk	13,428
(part)	14	No candidate		Vukmir[6]	13,433
(part)	15	Staskunas[6]	19,219	No candidate	
(part)	16	Young[6]	18,397	No candidate	
(part)	17	Toles[6]	22,063	No candidate	
(part)	18	Grigsby	17,102	No candidate	
(part)	19	Richards[6]	24,344	No candidate	
(part)	20	Sinicki[6]	17,285	No candidate	
(part)	21	No candidate		Schuknecht	10,905
(part)	22	Wasserman[6]	21,750	Honadel[6]	20,522
(part)	23	No candidate		Hintze	11,495
(part)	82	No candidate		Gielow[6]	7,501
(part)	84	No candidate		Stone[6]	22,482
				Gundrum[6]	3,314
Monroe (part)[7]	50	Buros	242	Albers[6]	398
(part)	92	Taft	5,607	Musser[6]	9,258
(part)	94	Burke	344	Huebsch[6]	595
(part)	96	Frie	956	Nerison	1,423
Oconto (part)	6	No candidate		Ainsworth[6]	5,691
(part)	36	Crawford	1,027	Mursau	1,255
(part)	89	Berman	2,834	Gard[6]	6,154
Oneida (part)	34	Kinnunen	8,825	Meyer[6]	10,320
(part)	35	Brandt	923	Friske[6]	1,303
Outagamie (part)	3	Fischer	5,039	Ott[6]	6,107
(part)	5	Nelson	11,265	Weber[6]	8,942
(part)	6	No candidate		Ainsworth[6]	2,816

COUNTY VOTE FOR REPRESENTATIVES TO THE ASSEMBLY
Special and General Elections–Continued

County or Part	Assembly District	Democratic	Vote	Republican	Vote
(part)	40	Van Handel	868	Hundertmark[6]	1,692
(part)	56	No candidate		McCormick[6]	15,020
(part)	57	No candidate		Wieckert[6]	19,329
Ozaukee (part)	23	No candidate		Gielow[6]	12,142
(part)	59	No candidate		LeMahieu[6]	3,544
(part)	60	No candidate		Gottlieb[6]	22,226
Pepin (part)	91	Gronemus[6]	2,130	Anderson	1,117
(part)	93	Smith	279	Kreibich[6]	321
Pierce (part)[7]	29	Plouff[6]	853	Lamb	1,087
(part)	30	Parent	6,604	Rhoades[6]	8,233
(part)	91	Gronemus[6]	1,979	Anderson	1,773
(part)	93	Smith	123	Kreibich[6]	149
Polk (part)	28	Wolden	10,319	Pettis[6]	11,488
(part)	75	Hubler[6]	567	Serio	333
Portage (part)	70	Vruwink[6]	4,920	Mielke	2,972
(part)	71	Molepske[6]	20,571	No candidate	
(part)	72	Schneider[6]	471	Ziegler	265
(part)	86	Kreager	369	Petrowski[6]	355
Price	87	Satterwhite	4,343	M. Williams[6]	4,132
Racine (part)[7]	61	Turner[6]	17,173	No candidate	
(part)[7]	62	J. Lehman[6]	19,282	No candidate	
(part)	63	No candidate		Vos	23,682
(part)	66	Dunton	2,711	Kerkman[6]	5,773
(part)	83	No candidate		Gunderson[6]	4,670
Richland (part)	49	Siss	575	Loeffelholz[6]	711
(part)[7]	50	Buros	1,755	Albers[6]	2,875
(part)	51	Miller	713	Freese[6]	793
(part)	96	Frie	488	Nerison	793
Rock (part)	43	McIntyre	9,518	Towns[6]	12,049
(part)[5]	44	Sheridan	16,053	Bollerud	5,861
(part)	45	Benedict	15,044	Brown	10,462
(part)[5]	80	Thomson	2,126	Davis	1,532
Rusk	87	Satterwhite	3,784	M. Williams[6]	3,892
St. Croix (part)	28	Wolden	1,141	Pettis[6]	1,485
(part)[7]	29	Plouff[6]	8,279	Lamb	9,870
(part)	30	Parent	6,477	Rhoades[6]	12,307
Sauk (part)	42	Henney	5,219	Hines[6]	4,797
(part)[5]	47	Yost	405	Hahn[6]	401
(part)[7]	50	Buros	2,416	Albers[6]	5,519
(part)	51	Miller	3,949	Freese[6]	4,271
Sawyer (part)[5]	74	Sherman[6]	3,717	Linton	4,598
(part)	87	Satterwhite	250	M. Williams[6]	347
Shawano (part)	5	Nelson	181	Weber[6]	318
(part)	6	No candidate		Ainsworth[6]	10,917
(part)	36	Crawford	1,495	Mursau	1,624
(part)	40	Van Handel	2	Hundertmark[6]	5
(part)	85	Seidel	138	Kamke	108
(part)	86	Kreager	253	Petrowski[6]	544
(part)	89	Berman	12	Gard[6]	42
Sheboygan (part)	26	Van Akkeren[6]	19,810	No candidate	
(part)	27	No candidate		Kestell[6]	16,819
(part)	59	No candidate		LeMahieu[6]	11,190
Taylor (part)	69	No candidate		Suder[6]	128
(part)	87	Satterwhite	3,559	M. Williams[6]	5,643
Trempealeau	91	Gronemus[6]	9,036	Anderson	4,403
Vernon	96	Frie	6,717	Nerison	7,570
Vilas	34	Kinnunen	5,212	Meyer[6]	8,523
Walworth (part)[2]	31	Woods	3,681	Nass[6]	6,686
(part)	32	Schroeder	11,108	Lothian[6]	13,235
(part)	43	McIntyre	2,721	Towns[6]	3,253
(part)	45	Benedict	450	Brown	572
(part)	66	Dunton	0	Kerkman[6]	0
(part)	83	No candidate		Gunderson[6]	3,573
Washburn (part)	73	Boyle[6]	1,914	Brunner	1,670
(part)	75	Hubler[6]	3,442	Serio	2,252
Washington (part)	23	No candidate		Gielow[6]	0
(part)	24	No candidate		Jeskewitz[6]	11,570
(part)	58	Uhlig	9,357	Strachota	21,429
(part)	59	No candidate		LeMahieu[6]	5,727
(part)	60	No candidate		Gottlieb[6]	2,074
(part)	99	No candidate		Pridemore	10,973
Waukesha (part)[8]	12	Kessler	0	No candidate	
(part)	14	No candidate		Vukmir[6]	9,353

COUNTY VOTE FOR REPRESENTATIVES TO THE ASSEMBLY
Special and General Elections–Continued

County or Part	Assembly District	Democratic	Vote	Republican	Vote
(part)	24	No candidate		Jeskewitz[6]	14,598
(part)[2]	31	Woods	3,997	Nass[6]	9,516
(part)	33	Byrne	9,426	Vrakas[6]	24,501
(part)[5]	38	Johnson	2,454	Kleefisch	6,052
(part)	83	No candidate		Gunderson[6]	17,729
(part)	84	No candidate		Gundrum[6]	22,065
(part)	97	No candidate		Nischke[6]	20,047
(part)	98	No candidate		Jensen[6]	27,696
(part)	99	No candidate		Pridemore	15,312
Waupaca (part)	6	No candidate		Ainsworth[6]	500
(part)	40	Van Handel	7,296	Hundertmark[6]	16,643
(part)[8]	41	No candidate		Ballweg	567
Waushara (part)[8]	41	No candidate		Ballweg	6,129
(part)	71	Molepske[6]	1,269	No candidate	
Winnebago (part)	53	Bird	7,362	Owens[6]	8,143
(part)[2,5]	54	Hintz	12,028	Underheim[6]	14,045
(part)	55	No candidate		Kaufert[6]	19,662
(part)	56	No candidate		McCormick[6]	9,912
Wood (part)	69	No candidate		Suder[6]	675
(part)	70	Vruwink[6]	13,066	Mielke	7,568
(part)	72	Schneider[6]	10,860	Ziegler	6,758

[1] Assembly District 21 incumbent Jeff Plale and Assembly District 71 incumbent Julie M. Lassa resigned from the Assembly and took office in the Senate on May 8, 2003, following an April 29, 2003 special election.

[2] Votes for Wisconsin Green Party candidates: 71st AD: Amy Heart: Portage – 996, Waushara – 15; 10th AD: Damien Jones: Milwaukee – 1,538; 31st AD: Bruce Hinkforth: Jefferson – 159, Walworth – 210, Waukesha – 327; 54th AD: Tony Palmeri: Winnebago – 2,653.

[3] Write-in candidate.

[4] Assembly District 17 incumbent G. Spencer Coggs resigned from the Assembly and took office in the Senate on November 25, 2003, following a November 18, 2003 special recall election. No special primary election was held for the 17th Assembly District.

[5] Votes for Independent candidates: 17th AD: Wendell J. Harris: Milwaukee – 316; 38th AD: Adam Beardsley: Columbia – 35, Dodge – 96, Jefferson – 55, Waukesha – 214; Andrew Sellinger: Columbia – 69, Dodge – 343, Jefferson – 75, Waukesha – 78; 44th AD: Charles A. Knipp: Rock – 3,935; Steve Trueblood: Rock – 748; 47th AD: Bill Landgraf: Columbia – 420, Dane – 658, Sauk – 36; 54th AD: Dan Carpenter: Winnebago – 1,157; 67th AD: Jan Morrow: Barron – 16, Chippewa – 1,466, Dunn – 153; 74th AD: Eugene Bigboy, Sr.: Ashland – 49, Bayfield – 37, Iron – 10, Sawyer – 64; 80th AD: Patrick J. O'Brien: Dane – 273, Green – 771, Lafayette – 2, Rock – 123.

[6] Incumbent.

[7] Votes for Libertarian Party candidates: 29th AD: Craig Mohn: Dunn – 250, Pierce – 50, St. Croix – 883; 50th AD: Tom Kuester: Juneau – 1,523, Monroe – 95, Richland – 205, Sauk – 2,078; 61st AD: George Meyers: Racine – 1,980; 62nd AD: Keith Deschler: Racine – 2,195.

[8] Votes for Constitution Party candidates: 12th AD: Joan Tatarsky: Milwaukee – 1,761, Waukesha – 0; 41st AD: James E. Tostenson: Fond du Lac – 591, Green Lake – 1,340, Marquette – 65, Waupaca – 27, Waushara – 1,470.

Source: Official records of the Elections Board. Scattered votes omitted.

DISTRICT VOTE FOR REPRESENTATIVES TO THE ASSEMBLY
Special and September Primary Elections

Assembly District	Political Party	Candidates	Vote
		June 24, 2003 Special Primary[1]	
21	Dem.	Al Foeckler	1,468
	Dem.	Karen Baranek Sostarich	1,347
	Rep.	Mark Honadel	1,844
	Rep.	Jim Ruetz	300
71	Dem.	Gary Hawley	455
	Dem.	Jesse J. Higgins	474
	Dem.	Cynthia L. Kieper	352
	Dem.	Corey Ladick	460
	Dem.	Louis John Molepske, Jr.	878
	Dem.	Neal Nealis	242
	Dem.	Jo Seiser	833
	Dem.	Steve Senski	718
	Rep.	Dennis Patrick Bankson	254
	Rep.	Leo V. Harris	288
	Rep.	Jackie Szehner	352
	WG	Amy Heart	104
		September 14, 2004 Primary	
1	Dem.	Tom Hermann	898
	Rep.	[2]Garey D. Bies	5,709
2	Rep.	[2]Frank Lasee	3,279
3	Dem.	Brad Fischer	713
	Rep.	[2]Al Ott	3,985
4	Dem.	Tracey R. Vandeveer	868
	Rep.	[2]Phil Montgomery	3,999
5	Dem.	Tom Nelson	821
	Rep.	[2]Becky Weber	3,311
6	Rep.	[2]John H. Ainsworth	4,549
	Rep.	J.P. Drengler	2,368
7	Dem.	[2]Peggy Krusick	4,329
8	Dem.	[2]Pedro Colón	1,311
9	Dem.	[2]Josh Zepnick	3,159
10	Dem.	[2]Annette Polly Williams	7,120
	WG	Damien Jones	10
11	Dem.	Jason Fields	2,793
	Dem.	Leonard Goudy	2,172
	Dem.	Jim Malloy	1,173
12	Con.	Joan Tatarsky	10
	Dem.	Frederick P. Kessler	3,112
	Dem.	Rene Settle-Robinson	2,496
13	Dem.	[2]David Cullen	4,648
	Rep.	Matt Adamczyk	2,408
	Rep.	W. Scott Nelson	2,108
14	Rep.	[2]Leah Vukmir	5,579
15	Dem.	[2]Tony Staskunas	3,252
16	Dem.	[2]Leon D. Young	4,503
17	Dem.	[2]Barbara L. Toles	6,754
18	Dem.	Tamara D. Grigsby	3,231
	Dem.	Walt Love	1,128
	Dem.	Jim Zaffiro	692
19	Dem.	[2]Jon Richards	5,419
20	Dem.	[2]Christine M. Sinicki	5,007
	Rep.	Bruce Schuknecht	2,432
21	Rep.	[2]Mark Honadel	3,690
22	Dem.	[2]Sheldon A. Wasserman	5,703
	Rep.	R. Jay Hintze	3,719
23	Rep.	[2]Curt Gielow	5,096
24	Rep.	[2]Sue Jeskewitz	5,718
25	Dem.	Anne-Marie Suchomel Woznicki	1,405
	Dem.	[2]Bob Ziegelbauer	3,375
26	Dem.	[2]Terry Van Akkeren	1,733
27	Rep.	[2]Steve Kestell	4,315
28	Dem.	Charlie Wolden	2,430
	Rep.	[2]Mark L. Pettis	1,583
29	Dem.	[2]Joe Plouff	2,240
	Lib.	Craig Mohn	73
	Rep.	Andy Lamb	1,431
30	Dem.	Tom Parent	2,190
	Rep.	[2]Kitty Rhoades	2,250
31	Dem.	Scott Woods	991
	Rep.	[2]Steve Nass	4,641
	WG	Bruce Hinkforth	9
32	Dem.	Ryan J. Schroeder	965
	Rep.	Joseph C. Guido, Sr.	1,042
	Rep.	[2]Thomas A. Lothian	2,802
33	Dem.	Patrick Byrne	953
	Rep.	[2]Daniel P. Vrakas	5,620
34	Dem.	Tony Hallman	597
	Dem.	Mary Kinnunen	1,892
	Rep.	[2]Dan Meyer	4,503
35	Dem.	Bill Brandt	1,413
	Rep.	[2]Don Friske	4,527

DISTRICT VOTE FOR REPRESENTATIVES TO THE ASSEMBLY
Special and September Primary Elections–Continued

Assembly District	Political Party	Candidates	Vote
36	Dem.	Kathryn D. Champagne	1,039
	Dem.	James W. Crawford	1,046
	Dem.	Roger K. Runnoe	495
	Rep.	[3]Robert M. Jones II	813
	Rep.	Steven Paul Kircher	746
	Rep.	Roy W. Kluss	455
	Rep.	Jeffrey L. Mursau	2,130
37	Dem.	Gary R. Rattmann	1,214
	Rep.	[2]David W. Ward	3,652
38	Dem.	Pam Johnson	992
	Rep.	Kenneth Berg	1,726
	Rep.	Ron Counsell	2,743
	Rep.	Joel Kleefisch	4,174
	Ind.	[4]Adam Beardsley	25
	Ind.	[4]Andrew Sellinger	8
39	Dem.	Vic Spadaro	692
	Rep.	[2]Jeff Fitzgerald	4,101
40	Dem.	Cornelius D. Van Handel	560
	Rep.	[2]Jean Hundertmark	4,126
	Rep.	John Schultz	958
41	Con.	James E. Tostenson	15
	Rep.	Joan Ballweg	2,406
	Rep.	Lance Buchholtz	1,089
	Rep.	Mike Gustin	929
	Rep.	Matt Metoxen	374
	Rep.	Dan Priske	802
	Rep.	Peter Sensenbrenner	1,179
	Rep.	Rich Slate	860
	Rep.	Marv Wagner, Jr.	628
	Rep.	Leon Zuehls	130
42	Dem.	Tim Henney	1,153
	Rep.	[2]J.A. Hines	4,534
43	Dem.	Matt McIntyre	1,552
	Rep.	[2]Debi Towns	2,340
44	Dem.	Thomas Brien	958
	Dem.	Kevin Murray	1,840
	Dem.	Mike Sheridan	2,556
	Rep.	Ty Bollerud	1,371
	Ind.	[4]Charles A. Knipp	54
	Ind.	[4]Steve Trueblood	10
45	Dem.	Chuck Benedict	1,520
	Rep.	Brian Brown	1,566
	Rep.	Chad Murry	884
46	Dem.	Gary Hebl	3,491
	Rep.	Hariah H. Hutkowski	1,653
	Rep.	Nick Voegeli	2,105
47	Dem.	Dan Jardine	1,055
	Dem.	Meagan Yost	2,047
	Rep.	[2]Eugene Hahn	3,554
	Rep.	John Stanley Keating	300
	Rep.	Steven Pate	665
	Ind.	[4]Bill Landgraf	14
48	Dem.	Amy Dixon	2,369
	Dem.	Joseph T. Parisi	5,006
	Rep.	Dan Long	2,395
49	Dem.	Arlene Dorsey Siss	1,081
	Dem.	Justin D. Williams	820
	Rep.	[2]Gabe Loeffelholz	4,348
	Rep.	Ray Saint	4,129
50	Dem.	Will Buros	1,047
	Lib.	Tom Kuester	69
	Rep.	[2]Sheryl Albers	4,919
	Rep.	Craig L. Buswell	463
	Rep.	John M. Deitrich	2,116
51	Dem.	Todd Miller	1,231
	Dem.	Emmett J. Reilly	776
	Rep.	[2]Stephen J. Freese	3,149
52	Dem.	Eric Schultz	922
	Rep.	[2]John Townsend	4,421
53	Dem.	LuAnn Bird	954
	Dem.	Stephen G. DeDow	605
	Rep.	[2]Carol Owens	3,315
	Rep.	Richard J. Spanbauer	2,666
54	Dem.	Gordon Hintz	1,069
	Rep.	[2]Gregg Underheim	3,336
	WG	Tony Palmeri	183
	Ind.	[4]Dan Carpenter	43
55	Rep.	[2]Dean R. Kaufert	3,051
56	Rep.	[2]Terri McCormick	4,447
57	Rep.	[2]Steve Wieckert	4,115
58	Dem.	Dennis A. Uhlig	1,185
	Rep.	Rick Karshna	4,259
	Rep.	Pat Strachota	6,683

DISTRICT VOTE FOR REPRESENTATIVES TO THE ASSEMBLY
Special and September Primary Elections–Continued

Assembly District	Political Party	Candidates	Vote
59	Rep.	[2]Daniel R. LeMahieu	8,475
60	Rep.	[2]Mark Gottlieb	7,983
61	Dem.	[2]Robert L. Turner	1,536
	Lib.	George Meyers	19
62	Dem.	[2]John Lehman	1,622
	Lib.	Keith Deschler	17
63	Rep.	Robin J. Vos	3,781
64	Dem.	[2]Jim Kreuser	2,638
65	Dem.	[2]John P. Steinbrink	2,600
66	Dem.	David Dunton	1,494
	Rep.	[2]Samantha J. Kerkman	3,142
67	Dem.	Jeff W. Monette	1,413
	Rep.	[2]Jeff Wood	2,051
	Ind.	[4]Jan Morrow	12
68	Dem.	Joe Bee Xiong	1,364
	Rep.	Terry Moulton	2,086
69	Rep.	Diane L. Murphy	996
	Rep.	[2]Scott Suder	4,980
70	Dem.	[2]Amy Sue Vruwink	1,416
	Rep.	Daniel Mielke	2,055
71	Dem.	Jesse J. Higgins	635
	Dem.	[2]Louis John Molepske, Jr.	2,783
72	Dem.	[2]Marlin D. Schneider	1,685
	Rep.	Thomas P. Ziegler	2,291
73	Dem.	[2]Frank Boyle	4,165
	Dem.	Dick Pukema	3,509
	Rep.	Larry E. Brunner	790
74	Dem.	[2]Gary E. Sherman	3,725
	Rep.	Barb Linton	1,906
	Ind.	[4]Eugene Bigboy, Sr.	25
75	Dem.	[2]Mary Hubler	1,576
	Rep.	Chris Serio	2,035
76	Dem.	[2]Terese Berceau	2,809
77	Dem.	[2]Spencer Black	3,055
78	Dem.	[2]Mark Pocan	2,692
	Rep.	James Block	960
79	Dem.	Bob Menamin	600
	Dem.	[2]Sondy Pope-Roberts	2,910
	Rep.	Keith Bakken	3,019
80	Dem.	Janis Ringhand	1,549
	Dem.	Gof Thomson	1,848
	Rep.	Brett H. Davis	2,707
	Ind.	[4]Patrick J. O'Brien	21
81	Dem.	[2]Dave Travis	2,482
82	Rep.	[2]Jeff Stone	4,546
83	Rep.	[2]Scott L. Gunderson	4,639
84	Rep.	[2]Mark Gundrum	5,157
85	Dem.	Donna J. Seidel	1,975
	Rep.	Ed Gale	352
	Rep.	Sarah L. Kamke	1,624
	Rep.	Bill Marcis	978
	Rep.	Linda Minnihan	799
86	Dem.	Tom Kreager	1,320
	Rep.	[2]Jerry J. Petrowski	2,868
87	Dem.	Mary Satterwhite	2,446
	Rep.	[2]Mary Williams	1,949
88	Dem.	Dan Aude	1,038
	Rep.	[2]Judy Krawczyk	2,843
89	Dem.	Bruce J. Berman	818
	Dem.	Don Peterlin	557
	Rep.	[2]John G. Gard	3,764
90	Dem.	Helen Schaal	1,267
	Rep.	[2]Karl Van Roy	3,585
91	Dem.	[2]Barbara Gronemus	3,167
	Dem.	David Anderson	1,963
92	Dem.	Michael B. Taft	1,263
	Rep.	[2]Terry M. Musser	2,225
93	Dem.	Jeff Smith	1,617
	Dem.	Howard White	1,292
	Rep.	[2]Rob Kreibich	2,497
94	Dem.	Vicki Burke	1,711
	Dem.	Mark Seitz	1,069
	Rep.	[2]Mike Huebsch	2,999
95	Dem.	[2]Jennifer Shilling	4,381
96	Dem.	Gail A. Frie	1,766
	Dem.	Betty Havlik	836
	Dem.	Miguel Morga	1,271
	Rep.	Todd R. Allbaugh	1,171
	Rep.	Lee A. Nerison	2,216
	Rep.	Judy Schmirler	1,565
97	Rep.	[2]Ann M. Nischke	3,302
98	Rep.	[2]Scott R. Jensen	6,722

DISTRICT VOTE FOR REPRESENTATIVES TO THE ASSEMBLY
Special and September Primary Elections–Continued

Assembly District	Political Party	Candidates	Vote
99	Rep.	Deb Baker	1,060
	Rep.	[2]Michael Lehman	3,037
	Rep.	Don Pridemore	3,221

Con. – Constitution Party; Dem. – Democratic Party; Lib. – Libertarian Party; Rep. – Republican Party; WG – Wisconsin Green Party; Ind. – Independent.

[1]District 21 incumbent Jeff Plale and District 71 incumbent Julie M. Lassa resigned from the Assembly and took office in the Senate on May 8, 2003, following an April 29, 2003 special election.

[2]Incumbent.

[3]Write-in candidate.

[4]All independent candidates shall appear on the general election ballot regardless of the number of votes received by such candidates at the September primary [Section 8.16 (1), Wisconsin Statutes].

Source: Official records of the Elections Board. Scattered votes omitted.

DISTRICT VOTE FOR REPRESENTATIVES TO THE ASSEMBLY
Special and General Elections

Assembly District	Party	Candidates	Vote	Percent of Total Vote[1]
		July 22, 2003 Special Election[2]		
21	Dem.	Al Foeckler	4,216	38.82%
	Rep.	Mark Honadel	6,624	60.99
71	Dem.	Louis John Molepske, Jr.	2,628	37.09
		[3]Jo Seiser	946	13.35
	Rep.	Jackie Szehner	2,492	35.17
	WG	Amy Heart	1,011	14.27
		January 27, 2004 Special Election[4]		
17	Dem.	Barbara L. Toles	1,332	79.38
	Ind.	Wendell J. Harris	316	18.83
		November 2, 2004 General Election		
1	Dem.	Tom Hermann	11,890	38.43
	Rep.	[5]Garey D. Bies	19,022	61.48
2	Rep.	[5]Frank Lasee	21,848	99.36
3	Dem.	Brad Fischer	11,929	37.47
	Rep.	[5]Al Ott	19,894	62.49
4	Dem.	Tracey R. Vandeveer	10,733	38.21
	Rep.	[5]Phil Montgomery	17,324	61.67
5	Dem.	Tom Nelson	15,014	51.28
	Rep.	[5]Becky Weber	14,249	48.67
6	Rep.	[5]John H. Ainsworth	19,924	99.42
7	Dem.	[5]Peggy Krusick	21,074	98.91
8	Dem.	[5]Pedro Colón	8,815	98.70
9	Dem.	[5]Josh Zepnick	14,775	98.72
10	Dem.	[5]Annette Polly Williams	21,516	93.04
	WG	Damien Jones	1,538	6.65
11	Dem.	Jason Fields	19,625	99.37
12	Con.	Joan Tatarsky	1,761	8.56
	Dem.	Frederick P. Kessler	18,720	90.98
13	Dem.	[5]David Cullen	17,765	56.84
	Rep.	Matt Adamczyk	13,428	42.96
14	Rep.	[5]Leah Vukmir	22,786	98.65
15	Dem.	[5]Tony Staskunas	19,219	98.69
16	Dem.	[5]Leon D. Young	18,397	99.11
17	Dem.	[5]Barbara L. Toles	22,063	99.35
18	Dem.	Tamara D. Grigsby	17,102	99.18
19	Dem.	[5]Jon Richards	24,344	98.31
20	Dem.	[5]Christine M. Sinicki	17,285	61.20
	Rep.	Bruce Schuknecht	10,905	38.61
21	Rep.	[5]Mark Honadel	20,522	98.52
22	Dem.	[5]Sheldon A. Wasserman	21,750	65.36
	Rep.	R. Jay Hintze	11,495	34.54
23	Rep.	[5]Curt Gielow	19,643	98.71
24	Rep.	[5]Sue Jeskewitz	26,168	99.56
25	Dem.	[5]Bob Ziegelbauer	20,268	99.50
26	Dem.	[5]Terry Van Akkeren	19,810	99.40
27	Rep.	[5]Steve Kestell	24,204	99.69
28	Dem.	Charlie Wolden	14,096	46.39
	Rep.	[5]Mark L. Pettis	16,280	53.58
29	Dem.	[5]Joe Plouff	14,577	45.87
	Lib.	Craig Mohn	1,183	3.72
	Rep.	Andy Lamb	16,001	50.35
30	Dem.	Tom Parent	13,081	38.89
	Rep.	[5]Kitty Rhoades	20,540	61.07
31	Dem.	Scott Woods	10,041	31.68
	Rep.	[5]Steve Nass	20,934	66.06
	WG	Bruce Hinkforth	696	2.20
32	Dem.	Ryan J. Schroeder	11,859	45.56
	Rep.	[5]Thomas A. Lothian	14,147	54.35
33	Dem.	Patrick Byrne	9,426	27.76
	Rep.	[5]Daniel P. Vrakas	24,501	72.16
34	Dem.	Mary Kinnunen	14,037	42.68
	Rep.	[5]Dan Meyer	18,843	57.29
35	Dem.	Bill Brandt	12,173	43.28
	Rep.	[5]Don Friske	15,943	56.69
36	Dem.	James W. Crawford	11,202	42.85
	Rep.	Jeffrey L. Mursau	14,713	56.29
37	Dem.	Gary R. Rattmann	11,677	40.13
	Rep.	[5]David W. Ward	17,403	59.80
38	Dem.	Pam Johnson	9,474	31.26
	Rep.	Joel Kleefisch	19,852	65.50
	Ind.	[6]Adam Beardsley	400	1.32
	Ind.	[6]Andrew Sellinger	565	1.86
39	Dem.	Vic Spadaro	8,334	30.49
	Rep.	[5]Jeff Fitzgerald	18,992	69.47
40	Dem.	Cornelius D. Van Handel	8,166	30.80
	Rep.	[5]Jean Hundertmark	18,340	69.17
41	Con.	James E. Tostenson	3,493	15.53
	Rep.	Joan Ballweg	18,937	84.19
42	Dem.	Tim Henney	12,893	47.54
	Rep.	[5]J.A. Hines	14,211	52.40

DISTRICT VOTE FOR REPRESENTATIVES TO THE ASSEMBLY
Special and General Elections–Continued

Assembly District	Party	Candidates	Vote	Percent of Total Vote[1]
43	Dem.	Matt McIntyre	12,796	44.40
	Rep.	[5]Debi Towns	15,960	55.38
44	Dem.	Mike Sheridan	16,053	60.27
	Rep.	Ty Bollerud	5,861	22.00
	Ind.	[6]Charles A. Knipp	3,935	14.77
	Ind.	[6]Steve Trueblood	748	2.81
45	Dem.	Chuck Benedict	15,494	58.31
	Rep.	Brian Brown	11,034	41.52
46	Dem.	Gary Hebl	18,950	58.41
	Rep.	Nick Voegeli	13,482	41.56
47	Dem.	Meagan Yost	14,287	45.96
	Rep.	[5]Eugene Hahn	15,678	50.43
	Ind.	[6]Bill Landgraf	1,114	3.58
48	Dem.	Joseph T. Parisi	25,066	74.75
	Rep.	Dan Long	8,451	25.20
49	Dem.	Arlene Dorsey Siss	11,723	43.85
	Rep.	[5]Gabe Loeffelholz	14,921	55.81
50	Dem.	Will Buros	7,502	27.67
	Lib.	Tom Kuester	3,901	14.39
	Rep.	[5]Sheryl Albers	15,706	57.93
51	Dem.	Todd Miller	12,203	42.67
	Rep.	[5]Stephen J. Freese	16,387	57.31
52	Dem.	Eric Schultz	8,775	33.51
	Rep.	[5]John Townsend	17,395	66.43
53	Dem.	LuAnn Bird	12,041	43.27
	Rep.	[5]Carol Owens	15,764	56.65
54	Dem.	Gordon Hintz	12,028	40.20
	Rep.	[5]Gregg Underheim	14,045	46.94
	WG	Tony Palmeri	2,653	8.87
	Ind.	[6]Dan Carpenter	1,157	3.87
55	Rep.	[5]Dean R. Kaufert	19,662	98.30
56	Rep.	[5]Terri McCormick	24,932	99.47
57	Rep.	[5]Steve Wieckert	19,329	98.66
58	Dem.	Dennis A. Uhlig	9,357	30.38
	Rep.	Pat Strachota	21,429	69.57
59	Rep.	[5]Daniel R. LeMahieu	25,551	99.74
60	Rep.	[5]Mark Gottlieb	24,300	99.60
61	Dem.	[5]Robert L. Turner	17,173	89.49
	Lib.	George Meyers	1,980	10.32
62	Dem.	[5]John Lehman	19,282	89.55
	Lib.	Keith Deschler	2,195	10.19
63	Rep.	Robin J. Vos	23,682	99.37
64	Dem.	[5]Jim Kreuser	16,340	99.96
65	Dem.	[5]John P. Steinbrink	18,522	99.04
66	Dem.	David Dunton	9,390	34.44
	Rep.	[5]Samantha J. Kerkman	17,834	65.41
67	Dem.	Jeff W. Monette	11,983	41.39
	Rep.	[5]Jeff Wood	15,333	52.96
	Ind.	[6]Jan Morrow	1,635	5.65
68	Dem.	Joe Bee Xiong	14,094	45.74
	Rep.	Terry Moulton	16,665	54.09
69	Rep.	[5]Scott Suder	19,649	99.44
70	Dem.	[5]Amy Sue Vruwink	18,120	63.03
	Rep.	Daniel Mielke	10,622	36.95
71	Dem.	[5]Louis John Molepske, Jr.	21,840	99.28
72	Dem.	[5]Marlin D. Schneider	17,076	60.73
	Rep.	Thomas P. Ziegler	11,032	39.23
73	Dem.	[5]Frank Boyle	19,860	63.65
	Rep.	Larry E. Brunner	11,309	36.24
74	Dem.	[5]Gary E. Sherman	16,213	53.14
	Rep.	Barb Linton	14,134	46.33
	Ind.	[6]Eugene Bigboy, Sr.	160	0.52
75	Dem.	[5]Mary Hubler	17,096	59.34
	Rep.	Chris Serio	11,711	40.65
76	Dem.	[5]Terese Berceau	27,270	99.30
77	Dem.	[5]Spencer Black	26,338	99.16
78	Dem.	[5]Mark Pocan	25,674	83.21
	Rep.	James Block	5,122	16.60
79	Dem.	[5]Sondy Pope-Roberts	21,999	59.86
	Rep.	Keith Bakken	14,731	40.09
80	Dem.	Gof Thomson	13,992	47.02
	Rep.	Brett H. Davis	14,577	48.98
	Ind.	[6]Patrick J. O'Brien	1,169	3.93
81	Dem.	[5]Dave Travis	24,938	99.45
82	Rep.	[5]Jeff Stone	22,482	99.08
83	Rep.	[5]Scott L. Gunderson	25,972	99.68
84	Rep.	[5]Mark Gundrum	25,379	99.51
85	Dem.	Donna J. Seidel	15,666	57.29
	Rep.	Sarah L. Kamke	11,667	42.67
86	Dem.	Tom Kreager	10,015	33.31
	Rep.	[5]Jerry J. Petrowski	20,038	66.64
87	Dem.	Mary Satterwhite	12,345	45.72
	Rep.	[5]Mary Williams	14,650	54.26

DISTRICT VOTE FOR REPRESENTATIVES TO THE ASSEMBLY
Special and General Elections–Continued

Assembly District	Party	Candidates	Vote	Percent of Total Vote[1]
88	Dem.	Dan Aude	11,093	45.67
	Rep.	[5]Judy Krawczyk	13,174	54.24
89	Dem.	Bruce J. Berman	10,318	36.15
	Rep.	[5]John G. Gard	18,216	63.81
90	Dem.	Helen Schaal	12,944	47.49
	Rep.	[5]Karl Van Roy	14,289	52.42
91	Dem.	[5]Barbara Gronemus	18,281	64.87
	Rep.	David Anderson	9,892	35.10
92	Dem.	Michael B. Taft	10,955	42.37
	Rep.	[5]Terry M. Musser	14,885	57.57
93	Dem.	Jeff Smith	15,501	47.63
	Rep.	[5]Rob Kreibich	16,997	52.23
94	Dem.	Vicki Burke	13,079	41.96
	Rep.	[5]Mike Huebsch	18,051	57.91
95	Dem.	[5]Jennifer Shilling	22,879	98.60
96	Dem.	Gail A. Frie	11,923	45.64
	Rep.	Lee A. Nerison	14,191	54.32
97	Rep.	[5]Ann M. Nischke	20,047	99.14
98	Rep.	[5]Scott R. Jensen	27,696	99.35
99	Rep.	Don Pridemore	26,285	99.57

Con. – Constitution Party; Dem. – Democratic Party; Lib. – Libertarian Party; Rep. – Republican Party; WG – Wisconsin Green Party; Ind. – Independent.

[1]Percentages do not equal 100%, as scattered votes have been omitted.

[2]District 21 incumbent Jeff Plale and District 71 incumbent Julie M. Lassa resigned from the Assembly and took office in the Senate on May 8, 2003, following an April 29, 2003 special election.

[3]Write-in candidate.

[4]Assembly District 17 incumbent G. Spencer Coggs resigned from the Assembly and took office in the Senate on November 25, 2003, following a November 18, 2003 special recall election. No special primary election was held for the 17th Assembly District.

[5]Incumbent.

[6]All independent candidates shall appear on the general election ballot regardless of the number of votes received by such candidates at the September primary [Section 8.16(1), Wisconsin Statutes].

Source: Official records of the Elections Board. Scattered votes omitted.

REPUBLICAN PRESIDENTIAL PREFERENCE VOTE, BY COUNTY
February 17, 2004

		Choices on Ballot	
County	Total*	George W. Bush	Uninstructed Delegation
Adams	535	530	5
Ashland	366	348	11
Barron	582	576	4
Bayfield	364	361	3
Brown	5,797	5,752	34
Buffalo	212	208	2
Burnett	599	593	4
Calumet	991	983	8
Chippewa	656	650	4
Clark	527	520	5
Columbia	1,563	1,552	8
Crawford	418	411	5
Dane	19,395	19,179	174
Dodge	1,942	1,926	16
Door	1,342	1,333	8
Douglas	429	422	4
Dunn	516	510	3
Eau Claire	1,752	1,741	9
Florence	92	90	1
Fond du Lac	2,457	2,442	14
Forest	190	190	0
Grant	903	895	4
Green	476	474	2
Green Lake	414	412	1
Iowa	460	455	3
Iron	226	220	5
Jackson	633	628	4
Jefferson	1,611	1,595	12
Juneau	643	637	3
Kenosha	3,223	3,185	35
Kewaunee	533	530	3
La Crosse	2,105	2,090	11
Lafayette	356	353	2
Langlade	471	465	6
Lincoln	1,162	1,156	5
Manitowoc	2,825	2,799	19
Marathon	3,622	3,583	34
Marinette	716	709	4
Marquette	383	382	1
Menominee	15	14	1
Milwaukee	35,519	35,206	253
Monroe	535	529	3
Oconto	817	813	3
Oneida	774	757	15
Outagamie	4,239	4,205	30
Ozaukee	2,553	2,531	16
Pepin	150	149	0
Pierce	753	743	10
Polk	656	644	8
Portage	1,067	1,043	13
Price	342	339	3
Racine	6,478	6,412	56
Richland	434	422	4
Rock	4,899	4,849	37
Rusk	330	323	7
St. Croix	1,448	1,436	9
Sauk	1,563	1,541	18
Sawyer	612	606	2
Shawano	1,035	1,023	7
Sheboygan	3,337	3,330	5
Taylor	480	473	5
Trempealeau	393	392	0
Vernon	565	561	3
Vilas	2,994	2,966	27
Walworth	1,874	1,849	22
Washburn	464	461	2
Washington	3,588	3,563	22
Waukesha	13,582	13,503	63
Waupaca	1,342	1,329	11
Waushara	486	481	5
Winnebago	4,072	4,024	40
Wood	1,545	1,531	9
TOTAL	160,428*	158,933	1,184

*Scattered vote included in county total.

Source: Official records of the Elections Board.

DEMOCRATIC PRESIDENTIAL PREFERENCE VOTE, BY COUNTY
February 17, 2004

		Choices on Ballot				
County	Total*	Carol Moseley Braun	Wesley K. Clark	Howard Dean	John Edwards	Dick Gephardt
Adams	2,994	10	43	354	1,089	5
Ashland	2,400	8	38	368	424	11
Barron	4,067	2	44	577	1,162	6
Bayfield	2,869	4	41	512	562	8
Brown	26,542	36	519	4,742	9,490	27
Buffalo	1,518	4	13	276	483	4
Burnett	1,845	1	25	328	413	6
Calumet	4,811	7	80	747	1,902	10
Chippewa	6,134	5	83	1,000	2,542	11
Clark	3,713	5	76	648	1,420	6
Columbia	8,060	9	152	1,325	3,011	11
Crawford	2,600	1	27	332	780	13
Dane	125,363	157	1,765	25,978	41,560	126
Dodge	8,824	18	122	1,561	3,366	19
Door	4,808	10	113	767	1,611	7
Douglas	5,830	9	80	1,484	890	12
Dunn	4,106	6	78	842	1,148	2
Eau Claire	13,197	15	205	2,718	4,474	24
Florence	366	0	7	43	91	0
Fond du Lac	9,949	24	119	1,669	4,055	18
Forest	1,052	2	21	118	373	2
Grant	5,396	8	60	742	1,829	14
Green	4,130	8	53	628	1,627	4
Green Lake	1,826	1	31	246	732	6
Iowa	3,489	3	52	536	1,230	4
Iron	1,027	0	13	134	243	1
Jackson	3,374	4	67	506	1,262	13
Jefferson	8,997	15	117	1,597	3,572	9
Juneau	2,955	5	51	396	1,063	3
Kenosha	17,783	41	303	3,217	5,655	28
Kewaunee	2,521	4	37	445	1,003	6
La Crosse	14,554	18	216	2,477	5,792	21
Lafayette	2,114	1	30	297	787	4
Langlade	2,457	6	61	399	800	6
Lincoln	4,761	10	80	814	1,583	9
Manitowoc	13,420	26	237	2,175	5,133	17
Marathon	17,195	26	287	3,694	5,529	48
Marinette	4,327	9	65	592	1,499	11
Marquette	2,015	1	20	310	711	2
Menominee	303	0	9	42	55	1
Milwaukee	189,135	605	2,997	34,016	58,384	269
Monroe	3,937	8	72	636	1,551	5
Oconto	4,022	5	88	607	1,457	4
Oneida	5,118	4	83	714	1,778	11
Outagamie	19,022	20	310	2,985	7,240	40
Ozaukee	11,752	16	102	2,415	4,593	16
Pepin	825	3	12	152	237	1
Pierce	3,687	8	42	696	852	11
Polk	3,611	8	44	543	839	10
Portage	10,935	9	152	2,657	3,139	12
Price	2,214	7	32	330	699	4
Racine	27,248	77	471	5,187	9,708	41
Richland	2,406	3	34	335	872	3
Rock	24,600	66	338	3,421	9,235	40
Rusk	2,170	1	43	352	759	4
St. Croix	5,659	11	77	1,044	1,318	16
Sauk	8,711	15	132	1,327	3,164	17
Sawyer	2,128	5	44	290	632	4
Shawano	4,107	7	103	630	1,494	8
Sheboygan	16,013	30	228	2,848	6,339	30
Taylor	2,342	4	46	396	899	3
Trempealeau	3,358	7	45	462	1,206	9
Vernon	3,730	4	60	522	1,354	6
Vilas	5,565	11	123	933	1,873	12
Walworth	8,756	11	129	1,614	3,113	15
Washburn	2,249	2	35	342	587	4
Washington	13,222	18	129	2,635	5,480	10
Waukesha	51,286	55	642	10,645	21,409	56
Waupaca	5,111	7	112	797	1,790	10
Waushara	2,346	3	33	349	872	6
Winnebago	19,673	29	341	3,614	6,773	35
Wood	9,734	12	174	1,715	3,566	16
TOTAL	828,364	1,590	12,713	150,845	284,163	1,263

*Scattered vote included in county total.

Source: Official records of the Elections Board.

DEMOCRATIC PRESIDENTIAL PREFERENCE VOTE, BY COUNTY
February 17, 2004–Continued

		Choices on Ballot				
John F. Kerry	Dennis J. Kucinich	Lyndon H. LaRouche, Jr.	Joe Lieberman	Al Sharpton	Uninstructed Delegation	County
1,392	62	5	14	11	5	.... Adams
1,254	239	10	15	24	5	.... Ashland
2,061	154	8	15	27	8	.... Barron
1,421	271	7	18	17	3	.... Bayfield
10,501	854	36	135	172	19	.... Brown
674	47	4	6	3	2	.... Buffalo
1,011	24	3	14	14	5	.... Burnett
1,873	123	2	21	36	7	.... Calumet
2,276	146	11	21	22	10	.... Chippewa
1,420	74	7	13	27	10	.... Clark
3,206	240	14	33	51	5	.... Columbia
1,264	139	7	17	14	3	.... Crawford
45,777	7,604	179	622	1,289	202	.... Dane
3,368	212	18	31	89	14	.... Dodge
2,016	198	7	20	45	8	.... Door
3,089	187	11	25	32	9	.... Douglas
1,754	227	6	10	24	4	.... Dunn
5,082	523	17	53	71	9	.... Eau Claire
212	5	3	1	3	1	.... Florence
3,678	224	36	38	76	4	.... Fond du Lac
514	8	4	2	8	0	.... Forest
2,549	128	9	11	37	2	.... Grant
1,634	128	8	8	26	3	.... Green
699	75	2	12	14	1	.... Green Lake
1,464	170	8	6	13	2	.... Iowa
587	27	1	5	14	1	.... Iron
1,406	70	8	10	21	4	.... Jackson
3,244	310	18	22	66	19	.... Jefferson
1,329	61	11	6	17	8	.... Juneau
7,701	324	130	104	241	24	.... Kenosha
920	74	5	13	12	1	.... Kewaunee
5,007	821	23	70	83	15	.... La Crosse
920	47	8	1	10	5	.... Lafayette
1,113	27	9	11	16	6	.... Langlade
2,094	85	13	27	37	5	.... Lincoln
5,298	286	32	100	83	21	.... Manitowoc
7,113	265	37	94	83	16	.... Marathon
2,020	77	8	13	23	4	.... Marinette
896	54	3	3	13	1	.... Marquette
188	2	1	0	3	1	.... Menominee
76,901	5,160	395	926	9,015	279	.... Milwaukee
1,514	110	5	10	19	5	.... Monroe
1,718	81	10	17	24	7	.... Oconto
2,315	129	13	24	38	7	.... Oneida
7,648	503	41	85	118	19	.... Outagamie
4,000	357	9	66	157	15	.... Ozaukee
384	29	2	3	1	1	.... Pepin
1,875	131	7	23	25	14	.... Pierce
2,019	82	23	15	18	7	.... Polk
4,374	464	18	32	52	15	.... Portage
1,056	61	3	7	14	1	.... Price
10,338	510	60	148	640	47	.... Racine
1,027	104	4	5	10	8	.... Richland
10,552	498	58	133	218	28	.... Rock
877	80	4	10	14	24	.... Rusk
2,939	142	6	53	36	16	.... St. Croix
3,568	376	7	29	57	13	.... Sauk
1,006	100	9	14	19	4	.... Sawyer
1,718	87	13	14	27	2	.... Shawano
5,896	349	27	92	141	25	.... Sheboygan
908	47	3	7	22	4	.... Taylor
1,461	126	10	14	11	4	.... Trempealeau
1,463	267	13	13	17	6	.... Vernon
2,379	92	10	54	61	12	.... Vilas
3,422	290	18	31	92	13	.... Walworth
1,168	62	12	19	15	2	.... Washburn
4,433	302	18	42	139	11	.... Washington
16,270	1,252	61	219	611	35	.... Waukesha
2,175	152	14	16	32	3	.... Waupaca
977	75	4	11	13	3	.... Waushara
7,980	589	21	105	139	34	.... Winnebago
3,972	154	10	52	39	10	.... Wood
328,358	27,353	1,637	3,929	14,701	1,146	.... TOTAL

2004 DEMOCRATIC NATIONAL CONVENTION DELEGATES
July 26-29, 2004 – Boston

Delegate	Address	Delegate	Address
For Howard Dean			
Pledged Leaders and Elected Officials		**Fourth Congressional District**	
Jon Erpenbach	Middleton	Terri Gabriel	Milwaukee
Peg Lautenschlager	Fond du Lac	Michael Lowrey	Milwaukee
First Congressional District		**Fifth Congressional District**	
Marianne Olson	Kenosha	Renee Crawford	Shorewood
Second Congressional District		**Sixth Congressional District**	
Ann Batiza	Madison	Robert Jome	Manitowoc
Kathleen Falk	Madison	**Seventh Congressional District**	
Steven Singh	Madison	Mary Thurmaier	Stevens Point
Michael Tate (alternate)	Madison	**Eighth Congressional District**	
Russell Wallace	Madison	Mary Goulding	Green Bay
Third Congressional District			
Robert Johnson	La Crosse		
For John Edwards			
Pledged Leaders and Elected Officials		**Fourth Congressional District**	
Jennifer Shilling	La Crosse	Rita Czukas	Milwaukee
Lena Taylor	Milwaukee	George McKinney	Milwaukee
First Congressional District		Kelly McMahon	Milwaukee
William Cobb	Kenosha	Martin Schreiber	Milwaukee
Gail Gabrelian	Franklin	Peggy West	Milwaukee
Second Congressional District		**Fifth Congressional District**	
Bryan Brooks	Sun Prairie	Bryan Kennedy (alternate)	Glendale
Dave Cieslewicz	Madison	Robert Lehmann	Waukesha
Terrance Craney (alternate)	Baraboo	Iva Richards	Waukesha
Constance Palmer-Smalley	Madison	**Sixth Congressional District**	
Nehna Rauf	Madison	Irene Klein	Chilton
Paulette Timm (alternate)	Mazomanie	Keith Wilhelm	Manitowoc
Scott Tyre	Middleton	**Seventh Congressional District**	
Third Congressional District		Amy Sue Vruwink	Milladore
Karen Dahl	Viroqua	David Wille	Marshfield
Mark Meyer	La Crosse	**Eighth Congressional District**	
Robert Miller	Alma	Jane Rufe	Appleton
		Donsia Strong-Hill	Oneida
		Daniel Weidner	Bonduel
For John F. Kerry			
Pledged Leaders and Elected Officials		**Fourth Congressional District**	
Spencer Coggs	Milwaukee	Milton Bond, Jr.	Milwaukee
Jim Kreuser	Kenosha	Paula Dorsey	Milwaukee
Melissa Schroeder	Merrill	Patrick Kehoe	Milwaukee
Add-Ons		Martha Love	Milwaukee
Tom Barrett	Milwaukee	Harold Moore	Milwaukee
Barbara Lawton	Algoma	Jennifer Morales	Milwaukee
First Congressional District		Dawn Marie Sass (alternate)	Milwaukee
Timothy Daley (alternate)	Union Grove	Victoria Toliver	Milwaukee
Lynn Davis	Racine	**Fifth Congressional District**	
Jeanne Sanchez-Bell	Kenosha	Carol Lers	Pewaukee
Ryan Schroeder	Delavan	Christine Marshall	Mequon
Second Congressional District		Larry Nelson	Waukesha
Jessica Doyle	Madison	Dian Palmer	Brookfield
Don Eggert	Madison	**Sixth Congressional District**	
Robert Fyrst (alternate)	Madison	Joan Kaeding	Oshkosh
Judith Karofsky (alternate)	Madison	Thomas Kitchen	Fond du Lac
George Lewis	Madison	Angela Sutkiewicz (alternate)	Sheboygan
Nathan Timm	Mazomanie	**Seventh Congressional District**	
Margaret Walker	Stoughton	Marjorie Bunce (alternate)	Chippewa Falls
Third Congressional District		Ned Grossnickle	Mosinee
Margaret Baecker	Independence	Gary Hawley	Stevens Point
Jill Berke	River Falls	Jolene Plautz	Merrill
Veronica Burke (alternate)	Onalaska	**Eighth Congressional District**	
Jerry LaPoint	Eau Claire	Kathy Groat	Appleton
Richard Trussoni (alternate)	Chaseburg	Jack Krueger	Green Bay
		Steven Toney (alternate)	New London
Unpledged Delegates			
At-Large		**Congressional Delegation (Automatic)**	
Elizabeth Burmaster	Madison	Tammy Baldwin	Madison
DNC Members (Automatic)		Jim Doyle	Madison
Stan Gruszynski	Porterfield	Russ Feingold	Middleton
Linda Honold	Milwaukee	Ron Kind	La Crosse
Ken Opin	Madison	Gerald Kleczka	Milwaukee
Mary Rasmussen	Boyceville	Herb Kohl	Milwaukee
Tim Sullivan	Verona	Dave Obey	Wausau
Paula Zellner	Shawano		

Source: Democratic Party of Wisconsin.

2004 REPUBLICAN NATIONAL CONVENTION DELEGATES
August 30-September 2, 2004 – New York

Delegate	Address	Delegate	Address

For George W. Bush

Delegate	Address	Delegate	Address
Delegates at Large		**Fourth Congressional District**	
Saied Assef	Green Bay	Thomas P. Burant (alternate)	Milwaukee
Jan Baldock	West Bend	Rose Ann Dieck (alternate)	Greendale
James Barry (alternate)	Milwaukee	Rick Graber	Milwaukee
Duane Bluemke (alternate)	Oconomowoc	Doug Haag (alternate)	Milwaukee
Brad Courtney	Milwaukee	Patrick Prudlow	Milwaukee
Sedgwick Daniels	Milwaukee	Robert Spindell	Milwaukee
Hattie Daniels-Rush	Milwaukee	**Fifth Congressional District**	
George French (alternate)	De Pere	Crystal Berg	Hartford
Robert Gonzalez	Milwaukee	Mary Buestrin	Mequon
Jon Hammes	Mequon	E.D. Cooper	Mukwonago
Brian Hayes (alternate)	Madison	Terence Dittrich	Milwaukee
Nancy Hernandez (alternate)	Milwaukee	Kathy Kiernan	Richfield
James R. Klauser	Pewaukee	Kerri Kuester	Milwaukee
Scott Klug	Madison	Stephanie Southwell (alternate)	Mequon
Kathy Lochner (alternate)	De Pere	Don Taylor	Waukesha
Virginia Marschman (alternate)	Waukesha	Cathy Waller (alternate)	Waukesha
Michael Martin (alternate)	Antigo	Gus Wirth, Jr. (alternate)	Cedarburg
Gerard Randall	Milwaukee	**Sixth Congressional District**	
Pamela Reeves (alternate)	Pewaukee	Karen Church	Grand Marsh
Fran Rudig (alternate)	Wauwatosa	Charles Church (alternate)	Grand Marsh
James Sensenbrenner	Menomonee Falls	Terry Kohler	Kohler
Leniwati M. Siker (alternate)	Milwaukee	Drew MacEwen	Sheboygan
Tommy Thompson	Washington, D.C.	Rod Nelson	Sheboygan
Scott Walker (alternate)	Milwaukee	Carl Toepel (alternate)	Sheboygan
Gerald Whitburn (alternate)	Merrill	**Seventh Congressional District**	
Bob Wood	Washington, D.C.	Dave Anderson	Wausau
First Congressional District		Rachel Campos (alternate)	Ashland
Steve King (alternate)	Milton	Sandy Ermeling (alternate)	Wausau
John Knuteson	Racine	Bill Johnson	Hayward
Second Congressional District		Pat Rasmussen	Schofield
Margery Buckeridge (alternate)	Evansville	Mary Willett (alternate)	Phillips
Pierre Charles, Jr.	Beloit	**Eighth Congressional District**	
Angela Frozena (alternate)	Madison	Diane Campbell (alternate)	Williams Bay
Terry Grosenheider	Madison	Gail Chimenti	De Pere
Bridget O'Connell	Bristol	Barbara Hartwig (alternate)	Green Bay
Elizabeth Orella (alternate)	Fitchburg	Virginia Jesse (alternate)	Shawano
Phil Prange (alternate)	Madison	Sonja Maas (alternate)	Bowler
Carol Skorupan	Madison	Darlene Ross	Shawano
Third Congressional District		Norbert Waterstreet	Luxemburg
Gary Arneson	La Crosse		
Laurie Forcier	Eau Claire		
Linda Hansen (alternate)	Prairie du Chien		
Dean Knudson (alternate)	Hudson		
Maripat Krueger (alternate)	Menomonie		
Dennis Shaw	Menomonie		

Source: Republican Party of Wisconsin.

COUNTY VOTE FOR PRESIDENT AND VICE PRESIDENT
November 2, 2004 General Election

County	John F. Kerry John Edwards (Dem.)	Michael Badnarik Richard V. Campagna (Lib.)	George W. Bush[1] Dick Cheney[1] (Rep.)	David Cobb Patricia LaMarche (WG)	Walter F. Brown Mary Alice Herbert (Ind.)[2]	James Harris Margaret Trowe (Ind.)[3]	Ralph Nader Peter Miguel Camejo (Ind.)[4]
Adams	5,447	10	4,890	10	2	2	79
Ashland	5,805	17	3,313	8	1	0	55
Barron	11,696	32	12,030	14	3	3	126
Bayfield	5,845	14	3,754	12	0	1	70
Brown	54,935	268	67,173	91	44	9	668
Buffalo	3,998	13	3,502	13	0	0	62
Burnett	4,499	16	4,743	9	0	0	43
Calumet	10,290	48	14,721	20	4	1	161
Chippewa	14,751	58	15,450	31	8	1	198
Clark	6,966	22	7,966	19	2	3	132
Columbia	14,300	66	14,956	15	4	6	158
Crawford	4,656	23	3,680	12	2	0	57
Dane	181,052	742	90,369	331	27	19	1,465
Dodge	16,690	78	27,201	39	3	5	283
Door	8,367	51	8,910	24	2	4	118
Douglas	16,537	32	8,448	25	3	5	125
Dunn	12,039	55	10,879	11	7	2	151
Eau Claire	30,068	158	24,653	101	10	8	371
Florence	993	3	1,703	1	0	0	18
Fond du Lac	19,216	98	33,291	56	6	9	297
Forest	2,509	7	2,608	0	1	3	24
Grant	12,864	45	12,208	19	3	0	112
Green	9,575	32	8,497	24	6	0	101
Green Lake	3,605	21	6,472	10	0	0	55
Iowa	7,122	16	5,348	6	0	1	44
Iron	1,956	7	1,884	4	0	0	25
Jackson	5,249	18	4,387	9	2	1	47
Jefferson	17,925	86	23,776	29	5	3	240
Juneau	5,734	52	6,473	18	1	3	73
Kenosha	40,107	217	35,587	76	18	9	366
Kewaunee	5,175	33	5,970	12	0	2	78
La Crosse	33,170	129	28,289	107	15	5	348
Lafayette	4,402	8	3,929	8	1	0	37
Langlade	4,751	12	6,235	5	0	0	64
Lincoln	7,484	41	8,024	23	0	2	112
Manitowoc	20,652	74	23,027	50	6	14	300
Marathon	30,899	129	36,394	68	9	6	505
Marinette	10,190	51	11,866	10	0	4	128
Marquette	3,785	25	4,604	7	0	0	36
Menominee	1,412	2	288	1	0	1	6
Milwaukee	297,653	963	180,287	319	72	142	2,232
Monroe	8,973	58	10,375	9	5	1	114
Oconto	8,534	43	11,043	22	1	1	126
Oneida	10,464	63	11,351	16	2	1	135
Outagamie	40,169	230	48,903	85	11	5	519
Ozaukee	17,714	108	34,904	25	4	2	245
Pepin	2,181	4	1,853	2	2	0	22
Pierce	11,176	41	10,437	32	7	4	148
Polk	11,173	53	12,095	31	1	1	134
Portage	21,861	104	16,546	95	11	0	299
Price	4,349	26	4,312	10	1	0	56
Racine	48,229	245	52,456	62	41	20	459
Richland	4,501	21	4,836	10	9	25	38
Rock	46,598	161	33,151	46	4	3	409
Rusk	3,820	24	3,985	10	4	2	74
St. Croix	18,784	99	22,679	30	3	2	202
Sauk	15,708	59	14,415	19	3	0	184
Sawyer	4,411	12	4,951	6	0	3	62
Shawano	8,657	26	12,150	13	4	3	130
Sheboygan	27,608	128	34,458	49	4	12	323
Taylor	3,829	16	5,582	15	4	1	87
Trempealeau	8,075	21	5,878	10	0	1	71
Vernon	7,924	19	6,774	16	5	0	87
Vilas	5,713	24	8,155	11	1	1	76
Walworth	19,177	125	28,754	43	13	5	278
Washburn	4,705	18	4,762	10	2	1	60
Washington	21,234	121	50,641	43	7	5	341
Waukesha	73,626	453	154,926	115	27	15	966
Waupaca	10,792	39	15,941	17	6	3	162
Waushara	5,257	11	6,888	10	1	3	66
Winnebago	40,943	240	46,542	103	19	7	611
Wood	18,950	100	20,592	49	6	8	336
TOTAL	1,489,504	6,464	1,478,120	2,661	471	411	16,390
Percent of Total[5]	49.70%	0.22%	49.32%	0.09%	0.02%	0.01%	0.55%

Dem. – Democratic Party; Lib. – Libertarian Party; Rep. – Republican Party; WG – Wisconsin Green Party; Ind. – Independent.

Note: Only 4 parties qualified for ballot status according to Section 5.62, Wisconsin Statutes. Other candidates were listed as "independent" although they indicated a name of party or statement of principle to the Election Board as footnoted.

[1]Incumbent. [2]Socialist Party of Wisconsin. [3]The Socialist Workers Party. [4]The Better Life. [5]Percentages do not equal 100%, as scattered votes have been omitted.

Source: Official records of the Elections Board.

VOTE FOR PRESIDENT AND VICE PRESIDENT
BY WARD, November 2, 2004 General Election

District	John F. Kerry John Edwards (Dem.)	George W. Bush[1] Dick Cheney[1] (Rep.)
ADAMS COUNTY		
Adams		
Wards 1 & 2	350	324
Adams, city		
Wards 1 - 5	490	350
Big Flats	290	210
Colburn	64	54
Dell Prairie		
Wards 1 & 2	411	356
Easton		
Wards 1 & 2	264	228
Friendship, vil.	175	142
Jackson	256	294
Leola	55	94
Lincoln	99	88
Monroe	147	127
New Chester		
Wards 1 & 2	268	159
New Haven	188	210
Preston		
Wards 1 - 3	396	297
Quincy		
Wards 1 & 2	419	287
Richfield	43	43
Rome		
Wards 1 - 5	848	1,008
Springville		
Wards 1 & 2	324	312
Strongs Prairie		
Wards 1 & 2	358	303
Wisconsin Dells, city		
Ward 5	2	4
TOTAL	5,447	4,890
ASHLAND COUNTY		
Agenda	127	148
Ashland	211	110
Ashland, city		
Ward 1	271	231
Ward 2	256	99
Ward 3	251	144
Ward 4	264	190
Ward 5	266	153
Ward 6	253	120
Ward 7	377	130
Ward 8	262	133
Ward 9	241	109
Ward 10	268	143
Ward 11	298	115
Butternut, vil.		
Wards 1 & 2	132	75
Chippewa	127	97
Gingles		
Wards 1 & 2	349	125
Gordon	112	99
Jacobs	216	225
La Pointe	173	67
Marengo		
Wards 1 & 2	136	71
Mellen, city		
Wards 1 - 3	274	148
Morse		
Wards 1 & 2	165	138
Peeksville	45	62
Sanborn		
Wards 1 & 2	469	87
Shanagolden	48	37
White River		
Wards 1 - 3	214	257
TOTAL	5,805	3,313
BARRON COUNTY		
Almena		
Wards 1 - 3	248	245
Almena, vil.	151	150
Arland	148	166
Barron		
Wards 1 & 2	141	318
Barron, city		
Wards 1 - 7	752	809
Bear Lake	182	162
Cameron, vil.		
Wards 1 & 2	368	403
Cedar Lake	259	348
Chetek		
Wards 1 - 3	519	560
Chetek, city		
Wards 1 - 4	636	520
Clinton		
Wards 1 & 2	172	221

District	John F. Kerry John Edwards (Dem.)	George W. Bush[1] Dick Cheney[1] (Rep.)
Crystal Lake	248	204
Cumberland	268	253
Cumberland, city		
Wards 1 - 5	669	529
Dallas		
Wards 1 & 2	135	167
Dallas, vil.	75	101
Dovre	179	199
Doyle	117	158
Haugen, vil.	93	66
Lakeland		
Wards 1 & 2	284	266
Maple Grove		
Wards 1 - 3	195	295
Maple Plain	250	222
New Auburn, vil.		
Ward 2	4	5
Oak Grove		
Wards 1 & 2	264	219
Prairie Farm		
Wards 1 & 2	173	135
Prairie Farm, vil.	140	121
Prairie Lake		
Wards 1 & 2	390	420
Rice Lake		
Wards 1 - 4	767	882
Rice Lake, city		
Wards 1 - 4	445	377
Wards 5 - 8	606	590
Wards 9 - 13	561	576
Wards 14 - 17	556	580
Sioux Creek	143	202
Stanfold	190	163
Stanley		
Wards 1 - 3	549	777
Sumner		
Wards 1 & 2	190	172
Turtle Lake	170	134
Turtle Lake, vil.		
Ward 1	286	146
Vance Creek	173	169
TOTAL	11,696	12,030
BAYFIELD COUNTY		
Ashland, city		
Ward 12	0	0
Barksdale	264	200
Barnes	309	266
Bayfield	310	174
Bayfield, city		
Wards 1 - 4	256	115
Bayview	181	141
Bell	123	73
Cable	254	287
Clover	102	65
Delta	118	96
Drummond	194	138
Eileen		
Wards 1 & 2	228	188
Grand View	196	135
Hughes	142	121
Iron River		
Wards 1 & 2	440	291
Kelly	126	103
Keystone	120	73
Lincoln	105	89
Mason	94	85
Mason, vil.	31	21
Namakagon	119	125
Orienta	46	32
Oulu	185	124
Pilsen	114	50
Port Wing	198	105
Russell		
Wards 1 & 2	460	100
Tripp	56	57
Washburn	220	117
Washburn, city		
Wards 1 - 4	854	383
TOTAL	5,845	3,754
BROWN COUNTY		
Allouez, vil.		
Wards 1 & 2	872	829
Wards 3 & 14	1,014	1,176
Wards 5 & 6	920	1,471
Wards 7 - 9	783	1,130
Ashwaubenon, vil.		
Wards 1 & 2	649	636
Wards 3 & 4	695	773

VOTE FOR PRESIDENT AND VICE PRESIDENT
BY WARD, November 2, 2004 General Election—Continued

District	John F. Kerry John Edwards (Dem.)	George W. Bush[1] Dick Cheney[1] (Rep.)	District	John F. Kerry John Edwards (Dem.)	George W. Bush[1] Dick Cheney[1] (Rep.)
Wards 5 & 6	703	928	Pittsfield		
Wards 7 & 8	622	1,008	Wards 1 – 4	559	934
Ward 9	248	369	Pulaski, vil.		
Ward 10	483	655	Wards 1 – 3 & 6	574	708
Wards 11 & 12	620	996	Rockland		
Bellevue, vil.			Wards 1 & 2	363	666
Wards 1 – 6	1,416	1,750	Scott		
Wards 7 – 10	1,313	2,101	Wards 1 – 4	921	1,119
De Pere, city			Ward 5	33	37
Wards 1 – 3	1,262	1,880	Suamico, vil.		
Wards 4 – 7	1,294	1,600	Wards 1 – 3 & 10	790	1,431
Wards 8 – 10	1,331	1,386	Ward 7	222	528
Wards 11 – 14	1,267	1,872	Wards 4 – 6, 8 & 9	1,035	1,902
Ward 15	2	2	Wrightstown		
Denmark, vil.			Wards 1 – 3	483	679
Wards 1 – 3	512	566	Wrightstown, vil.		
Eaton			Wards 1 & 2	456	691
Wards 1 & 2	391	465	TOTAL	54,935	67,173
Glenmore					
Wards 1 & 2	250	423	**BUFFALO COUNTY**		
Green Bay			Alma	99	83
Wards 1 & 2	434	626	Alma, city		
Green Bay, city			Wards 1 & 2	290	215
Ward 1	522	632	Belvidere	126	122
Ward 2	624	591	Buffalo	220	215
Ward 3	522	709	Buffalo, city	352	273
Ward 4	540	539	Canton	92	63
Ward 5	588	794	Cochrane, vil.	137	120
Ward 6	484	369	Cross	108	96
Ward 7	692	817	Dover	125	97
Ward 8	625	721	Fountain City, city		
Ward 9	394	602	Wards 1 & 2	290	205
Ward 10	483	682	Gilmanton	135	111
Ward 11	454	458	Glencoe	112	144
Ward 12	380	318	Lincoln	64	47
Ward 13	459	335	Maxville	73	91
Ward 14	624	484	Milton	184	125
Ward 15	682	474	Modena	85	95
Ward 16	582	385	Mondovi		
Ward 17	442	295	Wards 1 & 2	128	139
Ward 18	438	178	Mondovi, city		
Ward 19	422	192	Wards 1 – 3	700	652
Ward 20	434	347	Montana	69	73
Ward 21	580	377	Naples	174	190
Ward 22	436	376	Nelson	164	163
Ward 23	426	350	Nelson, vil.	127	65
Ward 24	428	282	Waumandee	144	118
Ward 25	434	258	TOTAL	3,998	3,502
Ward 26	216	121			
Ward 27	542	386	**BURNETT COUNTY**		
Ward 28	697	694	Anderson	86	139
Ward 29	571	497	Blaine	67	49
Ward 30	603	560	Daniels	185	223
Ward 31	326	272	Dewey	175	131
Ward 32	742	676	Grantsburg		
Ward 33	714	741	Wards 1 – 3	247	320
Ward 34	509	437	Grantsburg, vil.		
Ward 35	430	423	Wards 1 & 2	298	407
Ward 36	390	254	Jackson	276	279
Ward 37	515	320	La Follette		
Ward 38	494	495	Wards 1 & 2	145	142
Ward 39	460	323	Lincoln	88	96
Ward 40	488	430	Meenon		
Ward 41	490	466	Wards 1 – 3	286	293
Ward 42	492	647	Oakland		
Ward 43	539	697	Wards 1 & 2	325	261
Ward 44	543	607	Roosevelt	65	62
Ward 45	665	611	Rusk		
Ward 46	567	775	Wards 1 & 2	153	128
Ward 47	483	442	Sand Lake	186	115
Ward 48	513	925	Scott		
Ward 49	373	729	Wards 1 & 2	196	256
Ward 50	7	13	Siren		
Hobart, vil.			Wards 1 – 3	278	240
Wards 1 – 7	1,196	2,019	Siren, vil.		
Holland			Wards 1 & 2	216	214
Wards 1 & 2	323	497	Swiss		
Howard, vil.			Wards 1 & 2	278	193
Wards 1 – 8	1,600	2,118	Trade Lake		
Wards 9 – 16	1,897	2,980	Wards 1 & 2	225	325
Humboldt			Union	116	114
Wards 1 & 2	302	413	Webb Lake	117	150
Lawrence			Webster, vil.	199	158
Wards 1 – 3	507	1,023	West Marshland		
Ledgeview			Wards 1 & 2	63	102
Wards 1 – 4	838	1,527	Wood River		
Morrison			Wards 1 & 2	229	346
Wards 1 & 2	295	625	TOTAL	4,499	4,743
New Denmark					
Wards 1 – 3	396	528			

VOTE FOR PRESIDENT AND VICE PRESIDENT
BY WARD, November 2, 2004 General Election—Continued

District	John F. Kerry John Edwards (Dem.)	George W. Bush[1] Dick Cheney[1] (Rep.)
CALUMET COUNTY		
Appleton, city		
Ward 12	74	77
Ward 13	236	333
Ward 14	292	366
Ward 40	460	522
Ward 42	429	683
Ward 43	451	508
Ward 44	378	435
Ward 45	185	199
Ward 46	15	50
Ward 47	2	16
Ward 48	0	0
Brillion		
Wards 1 & 2	261	534
Brillion, city		
Wards 1 – 4	664	1,017
Brothertown		
Wards 1 & 2	303	464
Charlestown		
Wards 1 & 2	171	298
Chilton		
Wards 1 & 2	196	407
Chilton, city		
Wards 1 & 2	445	519
Wards 3 & 4	428	486
Harrison		
Wards 1 – 3, 6 & 8	1,100	1,540
Wards 4, 5 & 7	851	1,572
Ward 9	3	0
Hilbert, vil.		
Wards 1 & 2	217	384
Kaukauna, city		
Ward 13	2	9
Kiel, city		
Wards 7 & 8	96	71
Menasha, city		
Wards 11 & 15	353	499
New Holstein		
Wards 1 & 2	286	332
Ward 3	73	110
New Holstein, city		
Wards 1 – 5	887	927
Potter, vil.	52	103
Rantoul		
Wards 1 & 2	153	255
Sherwood, vil.		
Wards 1 – 7	533	961
Stockbridge		
Wards 1 – 3	319	498
Stockbridge, vil.	186	215
Woodville		
Wards 1 & 2	189	331
TOTAL	10,290	14,721
CHIPPEWA COUNTY		
Anson		
Wards 1 – 3	446	631
Arthur	145	198
Auburn	186	154
Birch Creek	146	172
Bloomer	217	274
Bloomer, city		
Wards 1 – 4	825	917
Boyd, vil.	176	158
Cadott, vil.		
Wards 1 & 2	336	354
Chippewa Falls, city		
Ward 1	547	428
Ward 2	439	489
Ward 3	567	559
Ward 4	463	381
Ward 5	412	383
Ward 6	508	394
Ward 7	446	415
Cleveland	185	230
Colburn	175	225
Cooks Valley	179	190
Cornell, city		
Wards 1 – 4	328	380
Delmar	216	223
Eagle Point		
Wards 1 – 4	765	998
Eau Claire, city		
Wards 16 & 40	598	375
Edson	218	201
Estella	100	131
Goetz		
Wards 1 & 2	181	181
Hallie		
Wards 1 & 2	56	41
Howard	194	178
Lafayette		
Wards 1 – 7	1,567	1,666
Lake Hallie, vil.		
Wards 1 – 5	1,435	1,377
Lake Holcombe		
Wards 1 & 2	260	352
New Auburn, vil.		
Ward 1	120	143
Ruby	109	99
Sampson	195	289
Sigel		
Wards 1 & 2	238	250
Stanley, city		
Wards 1 – 4	429	508
Tilden		
Wards 1 – 3	363	406
Wheaton		
Wards 1 – 3	744	813
Woodmohr		
Wards 1 – 3	237	287
TOTAL	14,751	15,450
CLARK COUNTY		
Abbotsford, city		
Ward 2	98	147
Ward 3	98	132
Ward 4	105	166
Beaver		
Wards 1 & 2	116	166
Butler	20	27
Colby	142	153
Colby, city		
Ward 2	77	135
Ward 3	91	132
Ward 4	81	101
Curtiss, vil.	34	36
Dewhurst	82	100
Dorchester, vil.		
Ward 1	165	195
Eaton		
Wards 1 & 2	118	141
Foster	43	24
Fremont		
Wards 1 & 2	200	289
Grant		
Wards 1 & 2	180	210
Granton, vil.	104	89
Green Grove	118	149
Greenwood, city		
Ward 1	142	140
Ward 2	120	133
Hendren	132	104
Hewett		
Wards 1 & 2	96	97
Hixon		
Wards 1 & 2	142	112
Hoard		
Wards 1 & 2	112	157
Levis		
Wards 1 & 2	120	107
Longwood		
Wards 1 & 2	125	131
Loval		
Wards 1 & 2	112	162
Loyal, city		
Wards 1 – 3	289	374
Lynn		
Wards 1 & 2	133	183
Mayville		
Wards 1 & 2	168	231
Mead	71	49
Mentor	116	137
Neillsville, city		
Ward 1	126	141
Ward 2	119	146
Ward 3	141	117
Ward 4	115	120
Ward 5	97	129
Owen, city		
Ward 1	88	89
Ward 2	81	59
Ward 3	71	73
Pine Valley		
Wards 1 & 2	239	405
Reseburg		
Wards 1 & 2	120	97
Seif	61	46

VOTE FOR PRESIDENT AND VICE PRESIDENT
BY WARD, November 2, 2004 General Election—Continued

District	John F. Kerry John Edwards (Dem.)	George W. Bush[1] Dick Cheney[1] (Rep.)	District	John F. Kerry John Edwards (Dem.)	George W. Bush[1] Dick Cheney[1] (Rep.)
Sherman	149	193	Wisconsin Dells, city		
Sherwood	84	67	Wards 1 – 3 & 6	650	536
Stanley, city			Wyocena		
Ward 5	0	0	Wards 1 – 3	426	485
Thorp	173	132	Wyocena, vil.	176	165
Thorp, city			TOTAL	14,300	14,956
Ward 1	64	67			
Ward 2	93	85	CRAWFORD COUNTY		
Ward 3	90	59	Bell Center, vil.	47	19
Ward 4	54	44	Bridgeport	250	252
Ward 5	110	90	Clayton		
Ward 6	37	34	Wards 1 – 3	283	192
Unity	156	189	De Soto, vil.		
Unity, vil.			Ward 2	34	12
Ward 2	29	45	Eastman		
Warner			Wards 1 & 2	176	193
Wards 1 & 2	117	126	Eastman, vil.	102	98
Washburn			Ferryville, vil.	81	39
Wards 1 & 2	56	93	Freeman	225	184
Weston			Gays Mills, vil.	216	114
Wards 1 & 2	157	183	Haney	103	59
Withee	154	159	Lynxville, vil.	50	36
Withee, vil.	131	122	Marietta	135	145
Worden			Mount Sterling, vil.	60	45
Ward 1	68	131	Prairie du Chien	252	217
Ward 2	34	23	Prairie du Chien, city		
York	202	193	Ward 1	248	236
TOTAL	6,966	7,966	Wards 2 & 3	183	173
			Wards 4 & 5	238	201
COLUMBIA COUNTY			Ward 6	294	174
Arlington			Wards 7 & 8	303	229
Wards 1 & 2	239	215	Ward 9	296	221
Arlington, vil.	185	190	Scott	154	94
Caledonia			Seneca	233	208
Wards 1 & 2	376	406	Soldiers Grove, vil.	175	132
Cambria, vil.	172	253	Steuben, vil.	31	28
Columbus	143	199	Utica	227	149
Columbus, city			Wauzeka		
Wards 1 – 8	1,268	1,260	Wards 1 & 2	87	99
Courtland			Wauzeka, vil.	173	131
Wards 1 & 2	82	214	TOTAL	4,656	3,680
Dekorra					
Wards 1 – 4	646	715	DANE COUNTY		
Doylestown, vil.	66	82	Albion		
Fall River, vil.			Wards 1 & 2	640	413
Wards 1 & 2	294	327	Belleville, vil.		
Fort Winnebago			Wards 1 & 2	693	351
Wards 1 & 2	233	303	Berry		
Fountain Prairie			Wards 1 & 2	414	336
Wards 1 & 2	240	267	Black Earth	177	134
Friesland, vil.	51	157	Black Earth, vil.		
Hampden	141	188	Wards 1 & 2	442	270
Leeds			Blooming Grove		
Wards 1 & 2	259	223	Wards 1 – 3	689	406
Lewiston			Blue Mounds	321	209
Wards 1 & 2	262	416	Blue Mounds, vil.	254	155
Lodi			Bristol		
Wards 1 – 5	953	919	Wards 1 – 3	928	1,012
Lodi, city			Brooklyn, vil.		
Wards 1 – 4	937	669	Ward 1	223	120
Lowville			Burke		
Wards 1 & 2	300	319	Wards 1 – 4	955	876
Marcellon			Cambridge, vil.		
Wards 1 & 2	216	344	Wards 2 & 3	413	305
Newport	182	191	Christiana		
Otsego	202	199	Wards 1 & 2	392	329
Pacific			Cottage Grove		
Wards 1 – 3	762	883	Wards 1 – 5	1,262	1,129
Pardeeville, vil.			Cottage Grove, vil.		
Wards 1 – 3	540	554	Wards 1 – 7	1,533	1,219
Portage, city			Cross Plains		
Wards 1 & 2	230	193	Wards 1 & 2	538	413
Wards 3 & 4	259	211	Cross Plains, vil.		
Wards 5 & 6	339	371	Wards 1 – 4	1,193	826
Wards 7 & 8	281	253	Dane	255	276
Wards 9 & 10	287	188	Dane, vil.	216	202
Wards 11 & 12	290	273	Deerfield		
Wards 13 & 14	248	185	Wards 1 & 2	468	356
Wards 15 & 16	106	88	Deerfield, vil.		
Wards 17 & 18	278	249	Wards 1 & 2	623	446
Poynette, vil.			DeForest, vil.		
Wards 1 – 3	683	529	Wards 1 – 8	2,071	1,800
Randolph	80	344	Dunkirk		
Randolph, vil.			Wards 1 – 3	705	533
Ward 3	59	188	Dunn		
Rio, vil.	321	231	Wards 1 & 7	488	383
Scott	115	240	Wards 2 – 6	1,438	1,064
Springvale	145	168	Edgerton, city		
West Point			Ward 7	2	4
Wards 1 & 2	578	566			

VOTE FOR PRESIDENT AND VICE PRESIDENT
BY WARD, November 2, 2004 General Election—Continued

District	John F. Kerry John Edwards (Dem.)	George W. Bush[1] Dick Cheney[1] (Rep.)	District	John F. Kerry John Edwards (Dem.)	George W. Bush[1] Dick Cheney[1] (Rep.)
Fitchburg, city			Ward 79	676	235
Wards 1 – 3	1,732	787	Ward 80	529	194
Wards 4 & 6	1,125	709	Ward 81	1,081	564
Ward 5	580	174	Ward 82	1,156	651
Wards 7 – 9	2,010	1,373	Ward 83	1,256	945
Wards 10 – 12	1,819	1,134	Ward 84	842	249
Ward 13	0	0	Ward 85	1,027	350
Madison			Ward 86	1,310	681
Ward 1	293	47	Ward 87	1,167	553
Wards 2 – 4 & 6	636	145	Ward 88	364	130
Wards 5, 7 – 11	1,260	251	Ward 89	454	236
Madison, city			Ward 90	699	346
Ward 1	1,380	566	Ward 91	987	656
Ward 2	1,465	781	Ward 92	1,203	768
Ward 3	857	406	Ward 93	1,409	690
Ward 4	843	482	Ward 94	535	217
Ward 5	916	533	Ward 95	491	213
Ward 6	957	553	Ward 96	1,359	483
Ward 7	1,150	505	Ward 97	268	145
Ward 8	1,123	414	Ward 98	1,370	576
Ward 9	569	190	Ward 99	1,714	1,198
Ward 10	1,116	318	Ward 100	0	4
Ward 11	1,650	511	Ward 101	0	0
Ward 12	861	116	Ward 102	17	14
Ward 13	366	71	Ward 103	0	0
Ward 14	910	225	Ward 104	0	0
Ward 15	491	147	Ward 105	2	0
Ward 16	379	154	Ward 106	0	0
Ward 17	995	496	Ward 107	1	4
Ward 18	655	380	Ward 108	39	13
Ward 19	1,289	540	Ward 109	0	0
Ward 20	343	129	Ward 110	39	33
Ward 21	279	66	Ward 111	0	0
Ward 22	695	306	Ward 112	1	0
Ward 23	631	151	Ward 113	1	8
Ward 24	961	366	Ward 114	0	0
Ward 25	1,763	889	Ward 115	0	0
Ward 26	212	84	Ward 116	0	0
Ward 27	1,074	320	Ward 117	0	0
Ward 28	196	42	Ward 118	0	0
Ward 29	210	78	Ward 119	0	0
Ward 30	789	243	Ward 120	0	0
Ward 31	738	177	Ward 121	0	0
Ward 32	1,594	184	Ward 122	0	2
Ward 33	2,284	204	Ward 123	0	0
Ward 34	2,577	153	Ward 124	0	0
Ward 35	1,536	80	Ward 125	0	0
Ward 36	350	48	Ward 126	0	0
Ward 37	1,441	178	Ward 127	0	0
Ward 38	1,203	108	Ward 128	0	0
Ward 39	1,978	229	Ward 129	0	0
Ward 40	1,494	367	Ward 130	0	0
Ward 41	1,165	261	Ward 131	0	0
Ward 42	1,813	609	**Maple Bluff, vil.**		
Ward 43	1,249	273	Wards 1 & 2	536	485
Ward 44	2,325	552	**Marshall, vil.**		
Ward 45	1,649	878	Wards 1 – 6	958	757
Ward 46	1,598	451	**Mazomanie**		
Ward 47	1,048	443	Wards 1 & 2	363	249
Ward 48	1,408	634	**Mazomanie, vil.**		
Ward 49	720	191	Wards 1 & 2	580	311
Ward 50	1,925	484	**McFarland, vil.**		
Ward 51	885	150	Wards 1 – 7	2,568	1,835
Ward 52	1,422	231	**Medina**		
Ward 53	474	65	Wards 1 & 2	370	382
Ward 54	763	278	**Middleton**		
Ward 55	100	19	Wards 1 – 5	1,669	1,795
Ward 56	1,086	355	**Middleton, city**		
Ward 57	414	79	Wards 1 & 9	953	489
Ward 58	443	106	Wards 2 – 4	2,316	1,182
Ward 59	796	307	Wards 5 – 7 & 10	2,746	1,230
Ward 60	351	145	Ward 8	648	567
Ward 61	1,762	567	**Monona, city**		
Ward 62	744	395	Wards 1 – 5	1,848	855
Ward 63	392	100	Wards 6 – 10	1,701	776
Ward 64	1,417	333	**Montrose**		
Ward 65	1,300	193	Wards 1 & 2	443	255
Ward 66	1,390	247	**Mount Horeb, vil.**		
Ward 67	1,863	474	Wards 1 – 6	2,140	1,430
Ward 68	703	103	**Oregon**		
Ward 69	1,172	332	Wards 1 – 4	1,137	865
Ward 70	1,483	260	**Oregon, vil.**		
Ward 71	788	131	Wards 1, 5 – 8	1,706	1,179
Ward 72	1,112	351	Wards 2 – 4	988	663
Ward 73	1,114	344	**Perry**	288	162
Ward 74	1,383	390	**Pleasant Springs**		
Ward 75	1,701	592	Wards 1 – 4	1,012	872
Ward 76	733	327	**Primrose**	310	117
Ward 77	421	180	**Rockdale, vil.**	85	43
Ward 78	975	437			

VOTE FOR PRESIDENT AND VICE PRESIDENT
BY WARD, November 2, 2004 General Election—Continued

District	John F. Kerry John Edwards (Dem.)	George W. Bush[1] Dick Cheney[1] (Rep.)
Roxbury		
Wards 1 & 2	504	493
Rutland		
Wards 1 & 2	706	503
Shorewood Hills, vil.		
Wards 1 & 2	1,023	221
Springdale		
Wards 1 & 2	599	508
Springfield		
Wards 1 – 3	847	725
Stoughton, city		
Wards 1 – 3	1,064	607
Wards 4 & 5	1,025	531
Wards 6 – 8	1,088	624
Wards 9 & 10	1,057	941
Sun Prairie		
Wards 1 – 3	637	628
Sun Prairie, city		
Wards 1 – 4, 18, 19, 22 & 25	1,799	1,445
Wards 5 – 9	1,839	1,513
Wards 10 – 13 & 20	1,541	1,017
Wards 14 – 17	2,048	2,240
Wards 21, 23, 26 – 28	3	2
Ward 24	0	0
Vermont	389	180
Verona		
Wards 1 – 3	691	599
Verona, city		
Wards 1 – 4	1,451	1,234
Wards 5 – 8	1,574	1,034
Vienna		
Wards 1 & 2	356	404
Waunakee, vil.		
Wards 1 – 7	1,208	1,210
Wards 8 – 14	1,780	1,699
Westport		
Wards 1 – 4	1,443	1,271
Windsor		
Wards 1 – 7	1,621	1,622
York	202	217
TOTAL	**181,052**	**90,369**
DODGE COUNTY		
Ashippun		
Wards 1 – 3	382	1,049
Beaver Dam		
Wards 1 – 5	859	1,090
Beaver Dam, city		
Wards 1, 3 & 5	804	695
Wards 2 & 6	621	541
Wards 4 & 10	494	471
Wards 7, 12 & 13	749	712
Wards 8 & 14	475	491
Wards 9 & 11	601	697
Brownsville, vil.	88	257
Burnett		
Wards 1 & 2	197	358
Calamus		
Wards 1 & 2	214	274
Chester		
Wards 1 & 2	93	302
Clyman		
Wards 1 & 2	129	301
Clyman, vil.	87	128
Columbus, city		
Ward 9	0	0
Elba		
Wards 1 & 2	247	356
Emmet		
Wards 1 & 2	206	470
Fox Lake		
Wards 1 – 4	237	483
Fox Lake, city		
Wards 1 – 3	357	403
Hartford, city		
Ward 16	0	0
Herman		
Wards 1 & 2	133	574
Horicon, city		
Wards 1 – 6	900	1,068
Hubbard		
Wards 1 – 3	352	641
Hustisford		
Wards 1 – 3	237	573
Hustisford, vil.		
Wards 1 & 2	196	403
Iron Ridge, vil.	163	336
Juneau, city		
Wards 1 – 3	428	654

District	John F. Kerry John Edwards (Dem.)	George W. Bush[1] Dick Cheney[1] (Rep.)
Kekoskee, vil.	54	68
Lebanon		
Wards 1 & 2	318	622
Leroy		
Wards 1 & 2	162	410
Lomira		
Wards 1 & 2	155	493
Lomira, vil.		
Wards 1 – 3	425	789
Lowell		
Wards 1 & 2	214	397
Lowell, vil.	60	108
Mayville, city		
Wards 1 – 7	1,057	1,545
Neosho, vil.	105	246
Oak Grove		
Wards 1 – 3	225	420
Portland		
Wards 1 & 2	264	330
Randolph, vil.		
Wards 1 & 2	198	486
Reeseville, vil.	161	196
Rubicon		
Wards 1 – 3	295	966
Shields	109	202
Theresa		
Wards 1 & 2	155	493
Theresa, vil.		
Wards 1 – 3	242	421
Trenton		
Wards 1 – 3	213	512
Watertown, city		
Wards 1 – 7	1,694	2,797
Waupun, city		
Wards 1 & 2	383	633
Wards 3 & 8	92	174
Wards 4 & 6	132	247
Wards 5 & 7	264	572
Westford		
Wards 1 & 2	340	436
Williamstown	124	311
TOTAL	**16,690**	**27,201**
DOOR COUNTY		
Baileys Harbor		
Wards 1 & 2	429	351
Brussels		
Wards 1 & 2	226	350
Claybanks	129	125
Egg Harbor		
Ward 1	284	248
Wards 2 & 3	152	147
Egg Harbor, vil.	103	114
Ephraim, vil.	122	135
Forestville		
Wards 1 & 2	280	318
Forestville, vil.	128	135
Gardner	319	378
Gibraltar		
Wards 1 & 2	426	335
Jacksonport	235	265
Liberty Grove		
Wards 1 – 3	708	712
Nasewaupee		
Wards 1 – 3	556	696
Sevastopol		
Wards 1 – 3	794	947
Sister Bay, vil.	314	313
Sturgeon Bay		
Wards 1 & 2	246	297
Sturgeon Bay, city		
Wards 1 & 2	344	256
Wards 3 & 4	379	274
Wards 5 & 6	372	433
Wards 7 & 8	306	347
Wards 9 & 10	386	360
Wards 11 & 12	336	303
Wards 13 & 14	281	366
Wards 15 – 17	18	29
Wards 18, 19 & 25	20	19
Wards 20, 21 & 24	22	31
Wards 22 & 23	0	0
Union	249	294
Washington	203	332
TOTAL	**8,367**	**8,910**
DOUGLAS COUNTY		
Amnicon		
Wards 1 & 2	413	234
Bennett	205	167

VOTE FOR PRESIDENT AND VICE PRESIDENT
BY WARD, November 2, 2004 General Election—Continued

District	John F. Kerry John Edwards (Dem.)	George W. Bush[1] Dick Cheney[1] (Rep.)
Brule	263	111
Cloverland	87	54
Dairyland	73	50
Gordon	242	209
Hawthorne		
Wards 1 & 2	351	270
Highland	103	90
Lake Nebagamon, vil.		
Wards 1 & 2	397	341
Lakeside	216	161
Maple		
Wards 1 & 2	327	101
Oakland		
Wards 1 & 2	472	232
Oliver, vil.	170	50
Parkland		
Wards 1 & 2	510	198
Poplar, vil.	146	197
Solon Springs	310	238
Solon Springs, vil.	220	129
Summit		
Wards 1 & 2	462	170
Superior		
Wards 1 – 3	788	517
Superior, city		
Wards 1 – 5	1,155	496
Wards 6 – 8	1,127	417
Wards 9 – 12	1,060	480
Wards 13 – 19	1,067	503
Wards 20 – 24	1,118	584
Wards 25 – 27	785	326
Wards 28 – 31	927	432
Wards 32 – 37	1,026	422
Wards 38 – 43	1,027	616
Wards 44 – 47	925	290
Superior, vil.	279	127
Wascott	286	236
TOTAL	16,537	8,448
DUNN COUNTY		
Boyceville, vil.	301	226
Colfax		
Wards 1 – 3	280	256
Colfax, vil.		
Wards 1 & 2	306	263
Downing, vil.	67	43
Dunn		
Wards 1 – 3	439	373
Eau Galle	213	263
Elk Mound		
Wards 1 – 3	303	443
Elk Mound, vil.	255	203
Grant	116	130
Hay River		
Wards 1 & 2	175	139
Knapp, vil.	87	151
Lucas	213	211
Menomonie		
Wards 1 – 4	905	770
Menomonie, city		
Wards 1 & 2	920	716
Wards 3 & 4	876	564
Wards 5 & 7	998	689
Ward 6	439	368
Wards 8 & 9	775	545
Wards 10 & 11	783	678
New Haven	177	169
Otter Creek	120	157
Peru	65	68
Red Cedar		
Wards 1 – 3	479	643
Ridgeland, vil.	94	45
Rock Creek	278	258
Sand Creek	141	194
Sheridan	141	120
Sherman	221	276
Spring Brook		
Wards 1 – 3	372	473
Stanton	212	230
Tainter		
Wards 1 – 3	665	717
Tiffany		
Wards 1 – 3	191	180
Weston		
Wards 1 & 2	159	157
Wheeler, vil.	94	55
Wilson	179	106
TOTAL	12,039	10,879

District	John F. Kerry John Edwards (Dem.)	George W. Bush[1] Dick Cheney[1] (Rep.)
EAU CLAIRE COUNTY		
Altoona, city		
Wards 1 – 7, 9 – 11	1,476	1,225
Wards 8, 12 & 13	445	332
Augusta, city		
Wards 1 – 5	349	379
Bridge Creek		
Wards 1 & 2	278	328
Brunswick		
Wards 1 & 2	512	475
Clear Creek		
Wards 1 & 2	205	226
Drammen	235	205
Eau Claire, city		
Ward 1	740	370
Ward 2	741	285
Ward 3	1,230	508
Ward 4	447	459
Ward 5	853	410
Ward 6	537	252
Ward 7	397	327
Ward 8	634	496
Ward 9	49	20
Ward 10	346	230
Ward 11	655	620
Ward 12	714	516
Ward 13	360	365
Ward 14	674	480
Ward 15	688	622
Ward 17	719	801
Ward 18	900	921
Ward 19	365	181
Ward 20	1,487	996
Ward 21	517	333
Ward 22	275	202
Ward 23	1,029	738
Ward 24	185	76
Ward 25	586	645
Ward 26	315	279
Ward 27	326	267
Ward 28	404	445
Ward 29	714	415
Ward 30	816	601
Ward 31	1,147	538
Ward 32	165	105
Ward 33	71	60
Ward 34	461	296
Ward 35	66	36
Ward 36	444	286
Ward 37	290	287
Ward 38	306	368
Ward 39	260	240
Fairchild	71	78
Fairchild, vil.	141	79
Fall Creek, vil.		
Wards 1 & 2	348	375
Lincoln		
Wards 1 & 2	251	325
Ludington	265	291
Otter Creek	98	154
Pleasant Valley		
Wards 1 – 4	819	1,012
Seymour		
Wards 1 – 4	918	916
Union		
Wards 1 – 3	748	709
Washington		
Wards 1 – 8, 10 – 12	1,607	1,849
Wards 9 & 13	288	430
Wilson	101	99
TOTAL	30,068	24,653
FLORENCE COUNTY		
Aurora		
Wards 1 – 3	238	320
Commonwealth		
Wards 1 – 3	77	173
Fence	45	70
Fern	42	77
Florence		
Wards 1 – 7	422	766
Homestead	90	145
Long Lake	50	68
Tipler	29	84
TOTAL	993	1,703
FOND DU LAC COUNTY		
Alto		
Wards 1 & 2	94	521

VOTE FOR PRESIDENT AND VICE PRESIDENT
BY WARD, November 2, 2004 General Election—Continued

District	John F. Kerry John Edwards (Dem.)	George W. Bush[1] Dick Cheney[1] (Rep.)
Ashford		
Wards 1 – 3	308	699
Auburn		
Wards 1 – 3	368	945
Brandon, vil.	146	333
Byron		
Wards 1 & 2	275	697
Calumet		
Wards 1 – 4	300	570
Campbellsport, vil.		
Wards 1 – 4	401	691
Eden	158	475
Eden, vil.	132	280
Eldorado		
Wards 1 – 3	241	588
Empire		
Wards 1 – 3	480	1,233
Fairwater, vil.	66	113
Fond du Lac		
Wards 1 – 3	518	1,071
Fond du Lac, city		
Ward 1	530	573
Ward 2	617	897
Ward 3	519	604
Ward 4	557	593
Ward 5	555	599
Ward 6	439	530
Ward 7	523	633
Ward 8	587	770
Ward 9	636	1,029
Ward 10	756	1,085
Ward 11	620	803
Ward 12	680	1,092
Ward 13	689	988
Ward 14	494	954
Ward 15	400	723
Ward 16	181	204
Forest		
Wards 1 & 2	165	553
Friendship		
Wards 1 – 4	515	846
Kewaskum, vil.		
Ward 5	0	0
Lamartine		
Wards 1 – 3	286	713
Marshfield		
Wards 1 & 2	185	442
Metomen	136	264
Mount Calvary, vil.	141	208
North Fond du Lac, vil.		
Wards 1 – 7	813	1,113
Oakfield	102	286
Oakfield, vil.		
Wards 1 & 2	172	418
Osceola		
Wards 1 & 2	295	854
Ripon		
Wards 1 & 2	277	544
Ripon, city		
Wards 1 – 3	389	522
Wards 4 – 6	523	574
Wards 7 & 8	430	452
Wards 9 – 11	437	507
Rosendale	111	287
Rosendale, vil.	153	420
St. Cloud, vil.	100	223
Springvale	125	285
Taycheedah		
Wards 1 – 5	813	1,667
Waupun		
Wards 1 & 2	208	605
Waupun, city		
Wards 9 & 10	313	752
Wards 11 & 12	257	463
TOTAL	19,216	33,291
FOREST COUNTY		
Alvin		
Wards 1 & 2	49	68
Argonne		
Wards 1 & 2	116	166
Armstrong Creek	146	118
Blackwell	99	56
Caswell	21	38
Crandon		
Wards 1 & 2	165	176
Crandon, city		
Wards 1 – 4	431	496
Freedom	91	123
Hiles	130	127

District	John F. Kerry John Edwards (Dem.)	George W. Bush[1] Dick Cheney[1] (Rep.)
Laona		
Wards 1 – 3	351	344
Lincoln		
Wards 1 – 3	269	252
Nashville		
Ward 1	46	94
Ward 2	112	144
Ward 3	147	53
Ward 4	2	10
Popple River	25	21
Ross	47	45
Wabeno		
Wards 1 – 5	262	277
TOTAL	2,509	2,608
GRANT COUNTY		
Bagley, vil.	126	73
Beetown	153	173
Bloomington		
Wards 1 & 2	66	110
Bloomington, vil.	201	159
Blue River, vil.	99	111
Boscobel		
Wards 1 & 2	118	116
Boscobel, city		
Wards 1 – 4	698	548
Cassville		
Wards 1 & 2	105	94
Cassville, vil.		
Wards 1 & 2	260	183
Castle Rock	64	72
Clifton	69	82
Cuba City, city		
Wards 1 – 5	605	428
Dickeyville, vil.		
Wards 1 & 2	320	264
Ellenboro		
Wards 1 & 2	95	152
Fennimore		
Wards 1 & 2	82	152
Fennimore, city		
Wards 1 – 6	605	602
Glen Haven	97	122
Harrison	120	161
Hazel Green		
Wards 1 & 2	384	266
Hazel Green, vil.		
Wards 1 & 2	349	237
Hickory Grove		
Wards 1 & 2	58	116
Jamestown		
Wards 1 – 3	555	540
Lancaster, city		
Wards 1 – 8	965	1,066
Liberty	104	163
Lima	152	189
Little Grant	44	72
Livingston, vil.		
Ward 1	141	164
Marion	117	125
Millville	55	30
Montfort, vil.		
Ward 1	183	124
Mount Hope		
Wards 1 & 2	50	56
Mount Hope, vil.		
Wards 1 & 2	40	45
Mount Ida	98	155
Muscoda		
Wards 1 & 2	132	162
Muscoda, vil.		
Wards 1 & 2	327	260
North Lancaster	106	169
Paris		
Wards 1 & 2	185	181
Patch Grove		
Wards 1 & 2	65	81
Patch Grove, vil.		
Wards 1 & 2	52	31
Platteville		
Wards 1 & 2	314	420
Platteville, city		
Wards 1 – 4	824	632
Wards 5 – 7	831	607
Wards 8 – 10	676	702
Wards 11 – 13	839	635
Potosi		
Wards 1 & 2	213	186
Potosi, vil.	220	180

VOTE FOR PRESIDENT AND VICE PRESIDENT
BY WARD, November 2, 2004 General Election—Continued

District	John F. Kerry John Edwards (Dem.)	George W. Bush[1] Dick Cheney[1] (Rep.)
Smelser		
Wards 1 & 2	237	234
South Lancaster		
Wards 1 – 3	128	204
Tennyson, vil.	92	102
Waterloo	131	135
Watterstown	74	91
Wingville	79	83
Woodman	25	60
Woodman, vil.	27	27
Wyalusing	109	76
TOTAL	12,864	12,208
GREEN COUNTY		
Adams	150	110
Albany		
Wards 1 & 2	253	211
Albany, vil.		
Wards 1 & 2	324	207
Belleville, city		
Ward 3	71	41
Brodhead, city		
Ward 1	141	133
Ward 2	129	118
Ward 3	127	129
Ward 4	142	109
Ward 5	122	91
Ward 6	128	104
Brooklyn		
Wards 1 & 2	337	275
Brooklyn, vil.		
Ward 2	144	80
Browntown, vil.	70	67
Cadiz	203	222
Clarno		
Wards 1 & 2	230	349
Decatur		
Wards 1 – 3	436	496
Exeter		
Wards 1 & 2	580	368
Jefferson		
Wards 1 – 3	250	363
Jordan	136	193
Monroe		
Wards 1 & 2	288	359
Monroe, city		
Ward 1	246	265
Ward 2	284	262
Ward 3	278	342
Ward 4	282	275
Ward 5	289	214
Ward 6	233	187
Ward 7	274	198
Ward 8	321	274
Ward 9	261	175
Ward 10	250	212
Monticello, vil.		
Wards 1 & 2	350	259
Mount Pleasant		
Wards 1 & 2	181	153
New Glarus		
Wards 1 & 2	369	325
New Glarus, vil.		
Wards 1 & 2	394	206
Wards 3 & 4	372	235
Spring Grove	194	251
Sylvester	230	296
Washington	225	156
York	281	187
TOTAL	9,575	8,497
GREEN LAKE COUNTY		
Berlin		
Wards 1 & 2	205	433
Berlin, city		
Wards 1 – 6, 8 – 10	1,043	1,438
Brooklyn		
Wards 1 – 3	421	791
Green Lake		
Wards 1 – 3	213	591
Green Lake, city		
Wards 1 – 6	276	392
Kingston		
Wards 1 & 2	85	235
Kingston, vil.	40	131
Mackford	61	237
Manchester	96	306
Markesan, city		
Wards 1 – 3	201	528

District	John F. Kerry John Edwards (Dem.)	George W. Bush[1] Dick Cheney[1] (Rep.)
Marquette		
Wards 1 & 2	76	193
Marquette, vil.	19	56
Princeton		
Wards 1 – 4	370	517
Princeton, city		
Wards 1 – 4	322	374
St. Marie	78	133
Seneca	99	117
TOTAL	3,605	6,472
IOWA COUNTY		
Arena		
Wards 1 & 2	550	327
Arena, vil.	228	160
Avoca, vil.	146	128
Barneveld, vil.		
Wards 1 & 2	378	223
Blanchardville, vil.		
Ward 2	53	37
Brigham		
Wards 1 – 3	344	231
Clyde		
Wards 1 – 3	118	78
Cobb, vil.	137	129
Dodgeville		
Wards 1 – 3	506	398
Dodgeville, city		
Wards 1 & 2	369	313
Wards 3 & 4	289	254
Wards 5 & 6	268	228
Wards 7 & 8	321	268
Eden	98	95
Highland		
Wards 1 & 2	208	191
Highland, vil.	244	194
Hollandale, vil.	126	39
Linden		
Wards 1 – 3	176	198
Linden, vil.	164	94
Livingston, vil.		
Ward 2	3	1
Mifflin		
Wards 1 & 2	137	183
Mineral Point		
Wards 1 & 2	223	249
Mineral Point, city		
Ward 1	191	164
Ward 2	215	170
Wards 3 & 4	267	143
Wards 5 & 6	189	106
Montfort, vil.		
Ward 2	23	24
Moscow		
Wards 1 & 2	214	132
Muscoda, vil.		
Ward 3	13	11
Pulaski	109	80
Rewey, vil.	71	50
Ridgeway		
Wards 1 & 2	206	121
Ridgeway, vil.	203	140
Waldwick	169	119
Wyoming	166	70
TOTAL	7,122	5,348
IRON COUNTY		
Anderson	25	16
Carey	55	59
Gurney	59	33
Hurley, city		
Ward 1	151	100
Ward 2	138	118
Ward 3	107	66
Ward 4	127	78
Kimball	165	137
Knight	87	51
Mercer		
Ward 1	106	192
Ward 2	121	154
Ward 3	108	151
Ward 4	80	123
Montreal, city		
Ward 1	155	132
Ward 2	126	64
Oma	90	112
Pence	59	51
Saxon	111	97

VOTE FOR PRESIDENT AND VICE PRESIDENT
BY WARD, November 2, 2004 General Election—Continued

District	John F. Kerry John Edwards (Dem.)	George W. Bush[1] Dick Cheney[1] (Rep.)	District	John F. Kerry John Edwards (Dem.)	George W. Bush[1] Dick Cheney[1] (Rep.)
Sherman	86	150	Palmyra, vil.		
TOTAL	1,956	1,884	Wards 1 & 2	380	548
			Sullivan		
JACKSON COUNTY			Wards 1 – 3	448	799
Adams			Sullivan, vil.	131	235
Wards 1 – 4	410	380	Sumner	250	246
Albion			Waterloo	183	295
Wards 1 – 4	328	312	Waterloo, city		
Alma			Wards 1 – 5	790	796
Wards 1 & 2	211	296	Watertown		
Alma Center, vil.	150	111	Wards 1 & 2	406	721
Bear Bluff	9	53	Watertown, city		
Black River Falls, city			Ward 8	150	219
Wards 1 – 4	1,015	756	Wards 9 & 10	345	933
Brockway			Wards 11 & 12	408	605
Wards 1 – 6	536	266	Wards 13 & 14	442	768
City Point	50	69	Wards 15 & 16	580	888
Cleveland	106	135	Wards 17 & 18	541	985
Curran	115	73	Whitewater, city		
Franklin	122	79	Wards 9 – 11	743	599
Garden Valley	96	117	Wards 14 & 15	0	2
Garfield	156	136			
Hixton			TOTAL	17,925	23,776
Wards 1 & 2	150	159			
Hixton, vil.	127	111	JUNEAU COUNTY		
Irving			Armenia	158	186
Wards 1 & 2	223	161	Camp Douglas, vil.	110	172
Knapp	63	97	Clearfield		
Komensky	121	22	Wards 1 & 2	163	213
Manchester	169	215	Cutler	65	105
Melrose			Elroy, city		
Wards 1 & 2	108	107	Wards 1 – 5	400	320
Melrose, vil.	151	150	Finley	11	32
Merrillan, vil.	167	107	Fountain	147	146
Millston	50	54	Germantown		
North Bend	128	111	Wards 1 & 2	372	400
Northfield	172	144	Hustler, vil.	55	50
Springfield			Kildare	156	144
Wards 1 & 2	159	99	Kingston	8	14
Taylor, vil.	157	67	Lemonweir		
			Wards 1 – 4	436	413
TOTAL	5,249	4,387	Lindina		
			Wards 1 & 2	166	229
JEFFERSON COUNTY			Lisbon		
Aztalan			Wards 1 & 2	238	251
Wards 1 & 2	370	480	Lyndon		
Cambridge, vil.			Wards 1 & 2	368	251
Ward 1	24	27	Lyndon Station, vil.	153	92
Cold Spring			Marion	126	135
Wards 1 & 2	167	309	Mauston, city		
Concord			Wards 1 – 10	870	902
Wards 1, 2 & 4	399	699	Necedah		
Ward 3	32	84	Wards 1 – 3	378	697
Farmington			Necedah, vil.	201	253
Wards 1 & 2	336	535	New Lisbon, city		
Fort Atkinson, city			Wards 1 – 6	278	383
Ward 1	325	415	Orange	108	174
Ward 2	388	351	Plymouth		
Ward 3	365	328	Wards 1 & 2	139	182
Ward 4	392	310	Seven Mile Creek		
Ward 5	358	253	Wards 1 & 2	75	102
Ward 6	289	280	Summit	126	195
Ward 7	346	270	Union Center, vil.	84	49
Ward 8	367	368	Wisconsin Dells, city		
Ward 9	320	361	Ward 7	0	0
Hebron			Wonewoc		
Wards 1 & 2	218	398	Wards 1 & 2	136	204
Ixonia			Wonewoc, vil.	207	179
Wards 1, 3 & 4	429	1,156			
Ward 2	139	362	TOTAL	5,734	6,473
Jefferson					
Wards 1 & 2	152	336	KENOSHA COUNTY		
Wards 3 – 5	296	386	Brighton		
Jefferson, city			Wards 1 – 3	280	561
Wards 1 – 8	1,728	1,756	Bristol		
Johnson Creek, vil.			Wards 1 – 4 & 8	501	967
Wards 1 & 2	434	596	Wards 5 & 7	259	360
Koshkonong			Ward 6	201	385
Wards 1 – 5	885	1,118	Genoa City, vil.		
Lac la Belle, vil.			Ward 4	0	0
Ward 2	0	1	Kenosha, city		
Lake Mills			Ward 1	697	402
Wards 1 & 2	577	693	Ward 2	817	498
Lake Mills, city			Ward 3	711	339
Wards 1 – 4	1,347	1,445	Ward 4	772	412
Milford			Ward 5	864	678
Wards 1 & 2	255	347	Ward 6	781	557
Oakland			Ward 7	840	706
Wards 1 – 4	966	956	Ward 8	967	548
Palmyra			Ward 9	1,161	780
Wards 1 & 2	224	517	Ward 10	783	681
			Ward 11	803	405

VOTE FOR PRESIDENT AND VICE PRESIDENT
BY WARD, November 2, 2004 General Election—Continued

District	John F. Kerry John Edwards (Dem.)	George W. Bush[1] Dick Cheney[1] (Rep.)	District	John F. Kerry John Edwards (Dem.)	George W. Bush[1] Dick Cheney[1] (Rep.)
Ward 12	793	390	West Kewaunee		
Ward 13	668	258	Wards 1 – 3	292	393
Ward 14	435	108	TOTAL	5,175	5,970
Ward 15	508	158			
Ward 16	621	168	LA CROSSE COUNTY		
Ward 17	849	529	Bangor	124	195
Ward 18	631	420	Bangor, vil.		
Ward 19	697	239	Wards 1 & 2	375	355
Ward 20	755	232	Barre		
Ward 21	907	617	Wards 1 & 2	253	357
Ward 22	514	347	Burns	216	337
Ward 23	645	315	Campbell		
Ward 24	822	576	Wards 1 – 6	1,345	1,152
Ward 25	818	690	Ward 7	28	15
Ward 26	867	638	Farmington		
Ward 27	931	737	Wards 1 – 3	540	451
Ward 28	801	757	Greenfield		
Ward 29	1,018	807	Wards 1 – 3	486	562
Ward 30	656	631	Hamilton		
Ward 31	866	580	Wards 1 – 3	541	778
Ward 32	714	483	Holland		
Ward 33	677	536	Wards 1 – 4	763	1,036
Ward 34	931	1,089	Holmen, vil.		
Ward 35	0	0	Wards 1 – 10	1,688	1,803
Ward 36	34	48	La Crosse, city		
Ward 37	2	0	Ward 1	981	715
Ward 38	0	1	Ward 2	887	595
Ward 39	13	27	Ward 3	799	419
Ward 40	25	10	Ward 4	975	552
Ward 41	1	1	Ward 5	1,302	938
Ward 42	0	1	Ward 6	1,387	768
Ward 43	3	8	Ward 7	1,111	500
Ward 44	1	2	Ward 8	1,204	806
Ward 45	0	0	Ward 9	1,115	804
Ward 46	1	0	Ward 10	1,109	677
Ward 47	0	0	Ward 11	955	438
Ward 48	0	0	Ward 12	939	461
Ward 49	0	0	Ward 13	883	493
Paddock Lake, vil.			Ward 14	1,097	739
Wards 1 – 5	642	902	Ward 15	931	738
Paris			Ward 16	938	704
Wards 1 & 2	390	577	Ward 17	1,128	787
Pleasant Prairie, vil.			Ward 18	0	4
Wards 1 – 3	934	950	Ward 19	2	3
Wards 4 & 5	541	702	Ward 20	0	0
Wards 6 & 7	911	902	Ward 21	0	0
Wards 8 – 11	1,176	1,449	Medary		
Wards 12 & 13	965	1,147	Wards 1 & 2	413	458
Randall			Onalaska		
Wards 1 – 5	610	1,026	Wards 1 – 7	1,452	1,774
Salem			Onalaska, city		
Wards 1 – 15	1,799	2,820	Wards 1 – 4	1,530	1,997
Silver Lake, vil.			Wards 5 – 8 & 13	1,377	1,248
Wards 1 – 3	494	664	Wards 9 – 12	1,496	1,552
Somers			Rockland, vil.	141	140
Wards 1 – 4	802	891	Shelby		
Wards 5 – 7 & 12	917	749	Wards 1, 4 – 6	945	1,006
Ward 8	180	156	Wards 2 & 3	522	582
Wards 9 – 11	548	574	Washington	166	143
Twin Lakes, vil.			West Salem, vil.		
Wards 1 – 7	915	1,281	Wards 1 – 6	1,026	1,207
Wheatland			TOTAL	33,170	28,289
Wards 1 – 5	642	1,115			
TOTAL	40,107	35,587	LAFAYETTE COUNTY		
			Argyle		
KEWAUNEE COUNTY			Wards 1 & 2	128	114
Ahnapee	270	280	Argyle, vil.	238	158
Algoma, city			Belmont		
Wards 1 – 7	883	757	Wards 1 & 2	131	172
Carlton			Belmont, vil.	216	238
Wards 1 & 2	297	319	Benton		
Casco			Wards 1 & 2	127	128
Wards 1 & 2	246	390	Benton, vil.	304	173
Casco, vil.	125	181	Blanchard	96	57
Franklin	272	282	Blanchardville, vil.		
Kewaunee, city			Ward 1	270	105
Wards 1 – 5	844	756	Cuba City, city		
Lincoln	249	259	Wards 6 & 7	75	49
Luxemburg			Darlington		
Wards 1 & 2	308	526	Wards 1 & 2	182	244
Luxemburg, vil.			Darlington, city		
Wards 1 & 2	431	701	Wards 1 – 6	675	523
Montpelier			Elk Grove	93	117
Wards 1 – 3	328	451	Fayette	80	114
Pierce			Gratiot	136	188
Wards 1 & 2	244	224	Gratiot, vil.	75	46
Red River			Hazel Green, vil.		
Wards 1 – 3	386	451	Ward 3	9	4
			Kendall	78	103
			Lamont	93	80

VOTE FOR PRESIDENT AND VICE PRESIDENT
BY WARD, November 2, 2004 General Election—Continued

District	John F. Kerry John Edwards (Dem.)	George W. Bush[1] Dick Cheney[1] (Rep.)	District	John F. Kerry John Edwards (Dem.)	George W. Bush[1] Dick Cheney[1] (Rep.)
Monticello	29	44	Wilson	87	94
New Diggings	126	132	TOTAL	7,484	8,024
Seymour	76	108			
Shullsburg	96	84	**MANITOWOC COUNTY**		
Shullsburg, city			Cato		
Wards 1 – 3	432	202	Wards 1 & 2	324	584
South Wayne, vil.	95	123	Centerville	160	245
Wayne	94	147	Cleveland, vil.		
White Oak Springs	22	34	Wards 1 & 2	426	446
Willow Springs	160	203	Cooperstown		
Wiota	266	239	Wards 1 & 2	309	434
TOTAL	4,402	3,929	Eaton	181	302
			Francis Creek, vil.	153	202
LANGLADE COUNTY			Franklin		
Ackley	119	158	Wards 1 & 2	286	437
Ainsworth	157	150	Gibson		
Antigo			Wards 1 & 2	359	412
Wards 1 & 2	344	513	Kellnersville, vil.	91	92
Antigo, city			Kiel, city		
Ward 1	210	218	Wards 1 – 6	846	993
Ward 2	202	243	Kossuth		
Ward 3	206	221	Wards 1 – 3	550	619
Ward 4	204	200	Liberty		
Ward 5	197	200	Wards 1 & 2	256	525
Ward 6	147	231	Manitowoc		
Ward 7	204	283	Wards 1 – 3	271	322
Ward 8	206	236	Manitowoc, city		
Ward 9	198	271	Wards 1 & 2	872	697
Elcho			Wards 3, 4 & 21	937	878
Wards 1 – 3	380	449	Wards 5 & 6	780	575
Evergreen	136	168	Wards 7 & 8	636	480
Langlade			Wards 9 & 10	899	679
Wards 1 & 2	128	157	Wards 11 & 12	843	1,036
Neva	241	312	Wards 13, 14, 23 & 27	837	692
Norwood			Wards 15 & 16	935	1,094
Wards 1 & 2	166	348	Wards 17, 18, 22, 24 – 26,		
Parrish	27	36	28 – 30 & 32	804	786
Peck	86	119	Wards 19, 20 & 31	857	1,249
Polar			Manitowoc Rapids		
Wards 1 & 2	204	403	Wards 1 – 5	558	952
Price			Maple Grove	151	315
Wards 1 & 2	68	76	Maribel, vil.	68	121
Rolling			Meeme		
Wards 1 & 2	310	473	Wards 1 & 2	365	498
Summit	39	52	Mishicot		
Upham	193	296	Wards 1 – 4	308	402
Vilas	41	78	Mishicot, vil.		
White Lake, vil.	78	83	Wards 1 & 2	367	424
Wolf River			Newton		
Wards 1 & 2	260	261	Wards 1 – 4	471	858
TOTAL	4,751	6,235	Reedsville, vil.		
			Wards 1 & 2	313	336
LINCOLN COUNTY			Rockland		
Birch			Wards 1 & 2	203	317
Wards 1 & 2	141	136	St. Nazianz, vil.	200	192
Bradley			Schleswig		
Wards 1 – 4	734	846	Wards 1 – 3	488	670
Corning	214	239	Two Creeks	110	156
Harding	100	119	Two Rivers		
Harrison			Wards 1 – 4	565	567
Wards 1 – 4	231	285	Two Rivers, city		
King	281	294	Wards 1 – 3	852	762
Merrill			Wards 4, 5, 10 & 11	992	942
Wards 1 – 5	725	898	Wards 6 & 7	777	652
Merrill, city			Wards 8 & 9	849	541
Ward 1	317	309	Valders, vil.	213	301
Ward 2	311	340	Whitelaw, vil.	190	242
Ward 3	278	260	TOTAL	20,652	23,027
Ward 4	278	288			
Ward 5	282	257	**MARATHON COUNTY**		
Ward 6	341	297	Abbotsford, city		
Ward 7	303	292	Ward 1	91	102
Ward 8	286	272	Athens, vil.		
Pine River			Wards 1 & 2	246	305
Wards 1 – 3	476	568	Bergen	230	213
Rock Falls			Berlin	169	370
Wards 1 & 2	139	208	Bern	118	117
Russell	192	164	Bevent		
Schley			Wards 1 & 2	390	224
Wards 1 & 2	210	263	Birnamwood, vil.		
Scott			Ward 2	8	3
Wards 1 & 2	354	429	Brighton	112	151
Skanawan	106	121	Brokaw, vil.	43	46
Somo	38	33	Cassel	213	240
Tomahawk			Cleveland	255	411
Wards 1 & 2	126	108	Colby, city		
Tomahawk, city			Ward 1	110	111
Wards 1 – 6	934	904	Day		
			Wards 1 & 2	181	338

VOTE FOR PRESIDENT AND VICE PRESIDENT
BY WARD, November 2, 2004 General Election—Continued

District	John F. Kerry John Edwards (Dem.)	George W. Bush[1] Dick Cheney[1] (Rep.)
Dorchester, vil.		
Ward 2	0	2
Easton		
Wards 1 & 2	254	407
Eau Pleine	167	237
Edgar, vil.		
Wards 1 & 2	365	395
Ward 3	0	0
Elderon	175	159
Elderon, vil.	47	46
Emmet	248	238
Fenwood, vil.	33	67
Frankfort	142	179
Franzen	141	144
Green Valley	135	206
Guenther	91	104
Halsey	123	155
Hamburg	176	275
Harrison	70	124
Hatley, vil.		
Ward 1	123	123
Ward 2	3	1
Hewitt	121	198
Holton		
Wards 1 & 2	168	248
Hull	133	211
Johnson	160	242
Knowlton		
Wards 1 & 2	305	366
Ward 3	171	251
Kronenwetter, vil.		
Wards 1 – 4	809	1,055
Wards 5 – 8	642	767
Maine		
Wards 1 – 4	588	802
Marathon		
Wards 1 & 2	248	404
Marathon City, vil.		
Wards 1 – 3	355	500
Marshfield, city		
Wards 21, 22 & 26	95	124
Wards 28 – 32	22	20
McMillan		
Wards 1 – 3	448	714
Mosinee		
Wards 1 – 3	514	686
Mosinee, city		
Wards 1, 2 & 6	473	488
Wards 3 – 5	630	627
Norrie	254	258
Plover	139	188
Reid		
Wards 1 & 2	411	294
Rib Falls	193	337
Rib Mountain		
Wards 1 – 10	1,778	2,662
Rietbrock	216	241
Ringle		
Wards 1 & 2	415	472
Rothschild, vil.		
Wards 1 & 2	442	477
Wards 3 & 4	425	501
Wards 5 & 6	461	548
Schofield, city		
Wards 1 & 2	265	277
Wards 3 & 4	324	313
Spencer		
Wards 1 & 2	277	400
Spencer, vil.		
Wards 1 – 4	445	514
Stettin		
Wards 1 & 2	251	474
Wards 3 & 4	253	396
Stratford, vil.		
Wards 1 & 2	255	483
Texas		
Wards 1 & 2	475	513
Unity, vil.		
Ward 1	51	68
Wausau		
Wards 1 – 3	549	760
Wausau, city		
Ward 1	476	439
Ward 2	456	440
Ward 3	241	258
Ward 4	398	299
Ward 5	59	59
Ward 6	63	116
Ward 7	51	80
Ward 8	342	192
Ward 9	352	264
Ward 10	334	210
Ward 11	407	418
Ward 12	354	304
Ward 13	361	336
Ward 14	461	603
Ward 15	447	593
Ward 16	491	392
Ward 17	429	386
Ward 18	410	322
Ward 19	399	377
Ward 20	476	553
Ward 21	364	506
Ward 22	52	59
Ward 23	318	225
Ward 24	362	244
Ward 25	384	292
Ward 26	323	266
Ward 27	438	400
Ward 28	331	259
Ward 29	50	40
Ward 30	0	0
Ward 31	0	0
Ward 32	0	0
Ward 33	0	1
Ward 34	2	3
Ward 35	4	9
Ward 36	2	2
Ward 37	0	0
Ward 38	0	0
Ward 39	0	0
Ward 40	0	1
Ward 41	0	0
Ward 42	0	0
Ward 43	0	0
Ward 44	2	11
Ward 45	0	0
Ward 46	0	0
Weston	131	193
Weston, vil.		
Wards 1 & 2	472	619
Wards 3 & 6	644	839
Wards 4 & 5	554	851
Wards 7, 8 & 11	641	829
Wards 9 & 10	436	497
Wien	162	235
TOTAL	30,899	36,394
MARINETTE COUNTY		
Amberg	217	257
Athelstane		
Wards 1 & 2	149	167
Beaver		
Wards 1 – 3	253	391
Beecher		
Wards 1 – 3	142	220
Coleman, vil.	164	223
Crivitz, vil.	242	285
Dunbar		
Wards 1 & 2	110	578
Goodman	207	185
Grover		
Wards 1 – 3	351	549
Lake		
Wards 1 & 2	270	362
Marinette, city		
Ward 1	386	327
Ward 2	350	326
Ward 3	338	343
Ward 4	438	317
Ward 5	381	259
Ward 6	346	240
Ward 7	389	330
Ward 8	354	329
Middle Inlet		
Wards 1 & 2	216	245
Niagara	209	253
Niagara, city		
Wards 1 – 3	443	394
Pembine		
Wards 1 & 2	234	296
Peshtigo		
Wards 1 – 5	1,064	1,218
Peshtigo, city		
Wards 1 – 3 & 8	337	402
Wards 4 – 6	248	320
Ward 7	81	79
Porterfield		
Wards 1 – 3	496	555

VOTE FOR PRESIDENT AND VICE PRESIDENT
BY WARD, November 2, 2004 General Election—Continued

District	John F. Kerry John Edwards (Dem.)	George W. Bush[1] Dick Cheney[1] (Rep.)
Pound		
Wards 1 – 4	251	503
Pound, vil.	50	123
Silver Cliff		
Wards 1 & 2	125	159
Stephenson		
Wards 1 – 3	430	440
Wards 4 – 6	354	458
Wagner	164	218
Wausaukee		
Wards 1 – 4	285	385
Wausaukee, vil.	116	130
TOTAL	10,190	11,866
MARQUETTE COUNTY		
Buffalo		
Wards 1 & 2	267	289
Crystal Lake	133	196
Douglas	222	273
Endeavor, vil.	97	120
Harris	208	284
Mecan	200	238
Montello		
Wards 1 – 3	294	334
Montello, city		
Wards 1 – 4	319	428
Moundville		
Wards 1 & 2	108	168
Neshkoro		
Wards 1 & 2	170	208
Neshkoro, vil.	112	130
Newton		
Wards 1 & 2	96	177
Oxford		
Wards 1 & 2	215	286
Oxford, vil.	132	139
Packwaukee		
Wards 1 – 3	403	361
Shields	126	185
Springfield	216	242
Westfield		
Wards 1 & 2	209	260
Westfield, vil.		
Wards 1 & 2	258	286
TOTAL	3,785	4,604
MENOMINEE COUNTY		
Menominee		
Wards 1, 3 – 5	1,129	261
Ward 2	283	27
TOTAL	1,412	288
MILWAUKEE COUNTY		
Bayside, vil.		
Wards 1 & 4	429	329
Wards 2 & 5	667	441
Wards 3 & 7	513	482
Brown Deer, vil.		
Wards 1 – 9	3,679	3,343
Cudahy, city		
Wards 1 – 3	1,188	980
Wards 4 – 6	1,077	852
Wards 7 – 9	793	600
Ward 10	489	393
Wards 11 & 12	502	476
Wards 13 & 14	557	395
Ward 15	775	749
Fox Point, vil.		
Wards 1 – 4	1,014	1,051
Wards 5 – 9	1,387	1,070
Franklin, city		
Wards 1 – 4	1,108	1,569
Wards 5 – 8	1,131	1,964
Wards 9 – 12	1,329	1,589
Wards 13 – 16	1,248	2,013
Wards 17 – 20	1,150	2,099
Wards 21 – 24	1,256	1,848
Glendale, city		
Ward 1	452	299
Wards 2 & 8	915	573
Wards 3 & 9	751	652
Wards 4 & 10	852	582
Wards 5 & 11	859	635
Wards 6 & 12	864	594
Ward 7	269	223
Greendale, vil.		
Wards 1 & 2	568	1,122
Wards 3 & 4	926	1,160
Wards 5 & 6	739	1,015
Wards 7 & 8	744	986

District	John F. Kerry John Edwards (Dem.)	George W. Bush[1] Dick Cheney[1] (Rep.)
Wards 9 & 10	795	1,062
Greenfield, city		
Ward 1	544	562
Ward 2	552	549
Ward 3	424	441
Ward 4	482	411
Ward 5	475	471
Ward 6	419	528
Ward 7	507	674
Ward 8	530	519
Ward 9	517	647
Ward 10	394	597
Ward 11	415	760
Ward 12	366	594
Ward 13	317	359
Ward 14	470	446
Ward 15	291	277
Ward 16	331	375
Ward 17	481	388
Ward 18	448	550
Ward 19	614	692
Ward 20	557	637
Ward 21	454	423
Hales Corners, vil.		
Wards 1 – 3	598	1,005
Wards 4 – 6	576	904
Wards 7 – 9	578	957
Milwaukee, city		
Ward 1	947	267
Ward 2	687	25
Ward 3	896	52
Ward 4	450	42
Ward 5	616	54
Ward 6	608	71
Ward 7	709	92
Ward 8	590	148
Ward 9	772	126
Ward 10	786	188
Ward 11	696	35
Ward 12	797	37
Ward 13	708	34
Ward 14	683	28
Ward 15	1,352	117
Ward 16	824	45
Ward 17	1,409	68
Ward 18	950	40
Ward 19	847	32
Ward 20	612	134
Ward 21	678	163
Ward 22	619	61
Ward 23	561	141
Ward 24	550	148
Ward 25	668	183
Ward 26	870	240
Ward 27	997	314
Ward 28	531	118
Ward 29	614	99
Ward 30	730	183
Ward 31	852	238
Ward 32	800	131
Ward 33	897	143
Ward 34	533	144
Ward 35	796	117
Ward 36	1,037	308
Ward 37	1,124	781
Ward 38	772	473
Ward 39	1,204	845
Ward 40	1,180	493
Ward 41	1,056	235
Ward 42	1,063	521
Ward 43	792	369
Ward 44	1,323	598
Ward 45	689	306
Ward 46	742	286
Ward 47	688	234
Ward 48	830	126
Ward 49	776	308
Ward 50	589	267
Ward 51	1,251	381
Ward 52	1,045	400
Ward 53	905	296
Ward 54	1,628	773
Ward 55	607	396
Ward 56	912	515
Ward 57	885	220
Ward 58	1,248	878
Ward 59	771	448
Ward 60	692	434
Ward 61	448	254
Ward 62	536	508

VOTE FOR PRESIDENT AND VICE PRESIDENT
BY WARD, November 2, 2004 General Election—Continued

District	John F. Kerry John Edwards (Dem.)	George W. Bush[1] Dick Cheney[1] (Rep.)	District	John F. Kerry John Edwards (Dem.)	George W. Bush[1] Dick Cheney[1] (Rep.)
Ward 63	248	73	Ward 153	248	185
Ward 64	559	170	Ward 154	767	245
Ward 65	399	109	Ward 155	727	227
Ward 66	412	60	Ward 156	823	134
Ward 67	599	48	Ward 157	851	206
Ward 68	315	49	Ward 158	801	147
Ward 69	305	40	Ward 159	1,021	151
Ward 70	610	77	Ward 160	616	44
Ward 71	842	84	Ward 161	609	91
Ward 72	618	63	Ward 162	832	132
Ward 73	416	63	Ward 163	576	77
Ward 74	717	149	Ward 164	677	11
Ward 75	681	206	Ward 165	872	41
Ward 76	569	446	Ward 166	836	16
Ward 77	685	405	Ward 167	738	16
Ward 78	529	169	Ward 168	868	26
Ward 79	525	181	Ward 169	864	28
Ward 80	573	185	Ward 170	967	61
Ward 81	439	290	Ward 171	1,154	81
Ward 82	522	316	Ward 172	1,373	78
Ward 83	462	203	Ward 173	697	13
Ward 84	527	403	Ward 174	580	12
Ward 85	382	328	Ward 175	454	19
Ward 86	391	506	Ward 176	574	6
Ward 87	320	426	Ward 177	625	9
Ward 88	516	425	Ward 178	510	15
Ward 89	547	447	Ward 179	851	19
Ward 90	417	428	Ward 180	1,130	22
Ward 91	337	434	Ward 181	547	15
Ward 92	783	686	Ward 182	244	142
Ward 93	403	510	Ward 183	313	241
Ward 94	469	540	Ward 184	599	626
Ward 95	844	133	Ward 185	399	315
Ward 96	544	118	Ward 186	369	434
Ward 97	789	35	Ward 187	359	346
Ward 98	621	25	Ward 188	748	735
Ward 99	831	18	Ward 189	558	466
Ward 100	829	17	Ward 190	628	627
Ward 101	927	49	Ward 191	434	481
Ward 102	518	117	Ward 192	764	798
Ward 103	1,056	168	Ward 193	492	630
Ward 104	502	33	Ward 194	300	367
Ward 105	933	129	Ward 195	314	353
Ward 106	599	40	Ward 196	737	762
Ward 107	619	25	Ward 197	569	749
Ward 108	764	17	Ward 198	709	605
Ward 109	1,105	24	Ward 199	479	510
Ward 110	1,097	418	Ward 200	933	766
Ward 111	480	55	Ward 201	538	178
Ward 112	725	12	Ward 202	367	133
Ward 113	885	139	Ward 203	355	117
Ward 114	566	85	Ward 204	336	84
Ward 115	1,075	74	Ward 205	253	64
Ward 116	668	31	Ward 206	307	79
Ward 117	1,009	115	Ward 207	364	94
Ward 118	702	116	Ward 208	279	77
Ward 119	457	171	Ward 209	426	99
Ward 120	787	216	Ward 210	335	113
Ward 121	442	78	Ward 211	363	157
Ward 122	622	61	Ward 212	437	110
Ward 123	783	133	Ward 213	271	81
Ward 124	731	137	Ward 214	162	87
Ward 125	646	226	Ward 215	356	170
Ward 126	603	245	Ward 216	432	414
Ward 127	874	104	Ward 217	480	456
Ward 128	1,076	98	Ward 218	528	407
Ward 129	744	53	Ward 219	423	323
Ward 130	656	33	Ward 220	666	425
Ward 131	443	13	Ward 221	577	373
Ward 132	364	96	Ward 222	492	400
Ward 133	255	89	Ward 223	507	422
Ward 134	403	138	Ward 224	483	484
Ward 135	512	231	Ward 225	486	414
Ward 136	550	209	Ward 226	537	258
Ward 137	504	249	Ward 227	258	205
Ward 138	693	313	Ward 228	609	565
Ward 139	256	79	Ward 229	608	516
Ward 140	486	169	Ward 230	541	709
Ward 141	374	139	Ward 231	928	904
Ward 142	570	242	Ward 232	768	657
Ward 143	307	195	Ward 233	417	424
Ward 144	548	358	Ward 234	418	395
Ward 145	506	452	Ward 235	589	258
Ward 146	438	447	Ward 236	737	354
Ward 147	711	247	Ward 237	597	270
Ward 148	568	392	Ward 238	668	394
Ward 149	1,052	385	Ward 239	524	309
Ward 150	734	160	Ward 240	600	262
Ward 151	492	185	Ward 241	397	230
Ward 152	1,268	321	Ward 242	418	291

VOTE FOR PRESIDENT AND VICE PRESIDENT
BY WARD, November 2, 2004 General Election—Continued

District	John F. Kerry John Edwards (Dem.)	George W. Bush[1] Dick Cheney[1] (Rep.)	District	John F. Kerry John Edwards (Dem.)	George W. Bush[1] Dick Cheney[1] (Rep.)
Ward 243	434	217	Wards 11 & 12	826	453
Ward 244	405	233	South Milwaukee, city		
Ward 245	456	220	Wards 1 & 2	813	818
Ward 246	320	152	Wards 3 & 4	691	652
Ward 247	338	236	Wards 5 & 6	713	575
Ward 248	376	295	Wards 7 & 8	768	634
Ward 249	465	276	Wards 9 & 10	879	873
Ward 250	564	366	Wards 11 & 12	759	687
Ward 251	639	344	Wards 13 & 14	761	680
Ward 252	652	333	Wards 15 & 16	824	764
Ward 253	664	329	Wauwatosa, city		
Ward 254	458	271	Ward 1	575	510
Ward 255	625	511	Ward 2	648	588
Ward 256	552	428	Ward 3	633	617
Ward 257	431	337	Ward 4	795	749
Ward 258	791	227	Ward 5	822	1,026
Ward 259	751	335	Ward 6	259	355
Ward 260	427	44	Ward 7	613	705
Ward 261	805	374	Ward 8	291	436
Ward 263	404	281	Ward 9	623	855
Ward 264	1,049	585	Ward 10	735	736
Ward 265	638	247	Ward 11	639	616
Ward 266	473	206	Ward 12	524	696
Ward 267	862	444	Ward 13	341	361
Ward 268	488	386	Ward 14	697	700
Ward 269	1,058	402	Ward 15	818	653
Ward 270	648	126	Ward 16	683	864
Ward 271	1,047	343	Ward 17	504	861
Ward 272	683	153	Ward 18	377	552
Ward 273	905	898	Ward 19	654	776
Ward 275	838	345	Ward 20	656	1,066
Ward 276	1,089	518	Ward 21	218	291
Ward 277	520	338	Ward 22	576	720
Ward 278	589	344	Ward 23	487	737
Ward 279	611	166	Ward 24	578	700
Ward 280	400	270	West Allis, city		
Ward 281	319	146	Ward 1	605	495
Ward 282	468	316	Ward 2	475	344
Ward 283	435	342	Ward 3	489	453
Ward 284	442	407	Ward 4	413	372
Ward 285	368	437	Ward 5	463	451
Ward 286	392	421	Ward 6	425	397
Ward 287	300	605	Ward 7	378	419
Ward 288	458	429	Ward 8	503	581
Ward 289	689	426	Ward 9	438	465
Ward 290	319	81	Ward 10	475	402
Ward 291	217	99	Ward 11	544	519
Ward 292	417	162	Ward 12	517	577
Ward 293	208	105	Ward 13	544	633
Ward 294	210	110	Ward 14	499	546
Ward 295	460	220	Ward 15	465	471
Ward 296	560	273	Ward 16	416	475
Ward 297	499	20	Ward 17	501	529
Ward 298	774	30	Ward 18	468	542
Ward 299	875	22	Ward 19	672	642
Ward 300	650	31	Ward 20	370	391
Ward 301	606	22	Ward 21	479	530
Ward 302	821	48	Ward 22	508	533
Ward 303	738	66	Ward 23	493	521
Ward 304	586	55	Ward 24	394	445
Ward 305	590	66	Ward 25	477	579
Ward 306	656	45	Ward 26	472	586
Ward 307	507	92	Ward 27	443	441
Ward 308	428	48	Ward 28	503	539
Ward 309	613	44	Ward 29	565	579
Ward 310	648	51	Ward 30	633	830
Ward 311	874	540	Ward 31	527	567
Ward 312	699	613	Ward 32	350	361
Ward 313	670	44	Ward 33	416	514
Ward 314	592	21	Ward 34	0	0
Oak Creek, city			Ward 35	115	129
Wards 1 – 3	1,209	1,445	West Milwaukee, vil.		
Wards 4 – 6	1,208	1,422	Wards 1, 2 & 5	500	369
Wards 7 – 9	1,426	1,784	Wards 3, 4 & 6	569	431
Wards 10 – 12	1,180	1,420	Whitefish Bay, vil.		
Wards 13 – 15	1,309	2,048	Wards 1 & 2	628	838
Wards 16 – 18	1,451	1,689	Wards 3 & 4	624	676
River Hills, vil.			Wards 5 & 6	705	768
Ward 1	110	94	Wards 7 & 8	780	643
Wards 2 & 3	395	591	Ward 9	425	360
St. Francis, city			Ward 10	512	418
Wards 1 – 4	751	674	Wards 11 & 12	837	764
Wards 5 – 8	892	676			
Wards 9 – 12	1,026	927	TOTAL	297,653	180,287
Shorewood, vil.					
Wards 1 & 2	951	549	MONROE COUNTY		
Wards 3 & 4	1,309	584	Adrian	132	237
Wards 5 & 6	883	477	Angelo		
Wards 7 & 8	979	406	Wards 1 – 3	317	341
Wards 9 & 10	906	412			

VOTE FOR PRESIDENT AND VICE PRESIDENT
BY WARD, November 2, 2004 General Election—Continued

District	John F. Kerry / John Edwards (Dem.)	George W. Bush[1] / Dick Cheney[1] (Rep.)
Byron		
Wards 1 & 2	300	329
Cashton, vil.		
Wards 1 & 2	270	227
Clifton	98	129
Glendale	130	167
Grant	86	139
Greenfield	150	224
Jefferson	119	138
Kendall, vil.	127	99
La Grange		
Wards 1 – 3	443	562
Lafayette		
Wards 1 & 2	46	80
Leon	229	317
Lincoln	164	285
Little Falls		
Wards 1 & 2	318	343
Melvina, vil.	25	21
New Lyme	40	46
Norwalk, vil.	119	113
Oakdale	149	171
Oakdale, vil.	60	57
Portland	180	190
Ridgeville	102	129
Scott	9	45
Sheldon	81	128
Sparta		
Wards 1 – 4	641	794
Sparta, city		
Wards 1 – 6	655	758
Wards 7 – 12	734	735
Wards 13 – 17	537	539
Tomah		
Wards 1 & 2	281	386
Tomah, city		
Wards 1 – 16	1,851	1,995
Warrens, vil.	61	85
Wellington		
Wards 1 & 2	146	119
Wells	118	142
Wilton		
Wards 1 – 3	118	132
Wilton, vil.	109	129
Wyeville, vil.	28	44
TOTAL	**8,973**	**10,375**
OCONTO COUNTY		
Abrams		
Wards 1 – 4	427	552
Bagley	68	112
Brazeau		
Wards 1 – 3	340	449
Breed	182	223
Chase		
Wards 1 – 4	540	831
Doty		
Ward 1	56	81
Ward 2	27	30
Gillett		
Wards 1 & 2	156	429
Gillett, city		
Wards 1 – 4	302	349
How		
Wards 1 – 3	89	218
Lakewood	240	333
Lena		
Wards 1 & 2	166	236
Lena, vil.	124	141
Little River		
Wards 1 & 2	264	280
Little Suamico		
Wards 1 – 7	836	1,367
Maple Valley		
Wards 1 & 2	145	242
Morgan	224	325
Mountain		
Wards 1 & 2	228	250
Oconto		
Wards 1 – 3	338	416
Oconto, city		
Wards 1 – 8	1,122	1,060
Oconto Falls		
Wards 1 & 2	263	387
Oconto Falls, city		
Wards 1 – 5	605	696
Pensaukee		
Wards 1 – 3	318	397
Pulaski, vil.		
Ward 5	0	0
Riverview		
Wards 1 & 2	291	210
Spruce		
Wards 1 & 2	213	233
Stiles		
Wards 1 – 3	335	446
Suring, vil.	100	175
Townsend	313	331
Underhill	222	244
TOTAL	**8,534**	**11,043**
ONEIDA COUNTY		
Cassian		
Wards 1 & 2	268	366
Crescent		
Wards 1 – 3	686	579
Enterprise	88	118
Hazelhurst		
Wards 1 & 2	333	450
Lake Tomahawk		
Wards 1 & 2	313	377
Little Rice	121	118
Lynne	57	54
Minocqua		
Wards 1 – 6	1,230	1,827
Monico	67	109
Newbold		
Wards 1 – 4	742	889
Ward 5	50	50
Nokomis		
Wards 1 & 2	464	404
Pelican		
Wards 1 – 5	800	748
Piehl	30	25
Pine Lake		
Wards 1 – 4	920	795
Rhinelander, city		
Wards 1 & 2	288	191
Wards 3 & 4	246	207
Wards 5 – 7	290	193
Wards 8 & 9	255	171
Wards 10 & 11	299	260
Wards 12 – 14	211	178
Wards 15 – 17	246	191
Wards 18 – 20	317	231
Schoepke	149	114
Stella	188	158
Sugar Camp		
Wards 1 & 2	451	643
Three Lakes		
Wards 1 – 3	609	989
Woodboro	245	277
Woodruff		
Wards 1 – 3	501	639
TOTAL	**10,464**	**11,351**
OUTAGAMIE COUNTY		
Appleton, city		
Ward 1	653	490
Ward 2	216	157
Ward 3	985	544
Ward 4	210	238
Ward 5	198	267
Ward 6	445	565
Ward 7	692	754
Ward 8	339	317
Ward 9	531	516
Ward 10	367	471
Ward 11	304	358
Ward 15	350	304
Ward 16	795	816
Ward 17	300	534
Ward 18	623	669
Ward 19	609	595
Ward 20	326	297
Ward 21	370	123
Ward 22	629	696
Ward 23	475	473
Ward 24	734	738
Ward 25	411	387
Ward 26	407	231
Ward 27	305	264
Ward 28	562	498
Ward 29	655	800
Ward 30	382	462
Ward 31	312	804
Ward 32	334	739
Ward 33	424	678
Ward 34	166	160

VOTE FOR PRESIDENT AND VICE PRESIDENT
BY WARD, November 2, 2004 General Election—Continued

District	John F. Kerry John Edwards (Dem.)	George W. Bush[1] Dick Cheney[1] (Rep.)
Ward 35	337	440
Ward 36	355	460
Ward 37	220	231
Ward 50	0	0
Ward 51	0	0
Ward 52	0	0
Ward 53	0	2
Ward 54	3	5
Ward 55	1	4
Ward 56	0	0
Bear Creek, vil.	86	84
Black Creek		
Wards 1 & 2	284	376
Black Creek, vil.		
Wards 1 & 2	287	385
Bovina		
Wards 1 & 2	274	322
Buchanan		
Wards 1 – 5 & 10	1,013	1,505
Wards 6 – 9	526	772
Center		
Wards 1 – 5	640	1,354
Cicero		
Wards 1 & 2	252	323
Combined Locks, vil.		
Wards 1 – 4	759	884
Dale		
Wards 1 – 4	478	942
Deer Creek		
Wards 1 & 2	114	172
Ellington		
Wards 1 – 4	500	944
Freedom		
Wards 1 – 7	1,225	1,780
Grand Chute		
Ward 1	355	614
Wards 2, 4 & 5	955	1,219
Ward 3	429	608
Wards 6 – 8	912	1,275
Wards 9 & 11	737	952
Ward 10	220	382
Wards 12 & 13	765	1,074
Greenville		
Wards 1 – 8	1,512	2,971
Hortonia		
Wards 1 & 2	212	440
Hortonville, vil.		
Wards 1 – 3	515	852
Howard, vil.		
Ward 17	0	0
Kaukauna		
Wards 1 & 2	275	371
Kaukauna, city		
Wards 1 – 3	944	774
Wards 4 – 6	989	896
Wards 7 & 8	1,035	761
Wards 9 – 12	952	762
Kimberly, vil.		
Wards 1 – 5	1,187	1,140
Wards 6 & 7	555	593
Liberty	172	272
Little Chute, vil.		
Wards 1, 4, 9 & 10	928	1,030
Wards 2, 8, 12 & 13	251	242
Ward 3	49	59
Wards 5 & 11	441	491
Wards 6 & 7	930	990
Ward 14	0	0
Maine	160	245
Maple Creek	140	220
New London, city		
Wards 1 & 2	337	352
Nichols, vil.	49	68
Oneida		
Wards 1 – 5	1,028	933
Osborn		
Wards 1 & 2	227	339
Seymour		
Wards 1 & 2	217	411
Seymour, city		
Wards 1 – 6	661	968
Shiocton, vil.	211	195
Vandenbroek		
Wards 1 & 2	343	449
Wrightstown, vil.		
Ward 3	13	25
TOTAL	40,169	48,903

District	John F. Kerry John Edwards (Dem.)	George W. Bush[1] Dick Cheney[1] (Rep.)
OZAUKEE COUNTY		
Bayside, vil.		
Ward 6	46	33
Belgium		
Wards 1 – 3	279	620
Belgium, vil.		
Wards 1 & 2	306	772
Cedarburg		
Wards 1, 2 & 10	249	619
Wards 3 & 4	272	671
Wards 5 & 6	276	819
Wards 7 – 9	274	731
Cedarburg, city		
Wards 1 & 2	284	644
Wards 3 & 4	336	760
Wards 5 & 6	470	609
Wards 7 & 8	318	563
Wards 9 & 10	390	629
Wards 11 & 12	333	652
Wards 13 & 14	371	683
Fredonia		
Wards 1 – 3	331	905
Fredonia, vil.		
Wards 1 & 2	349	869
Grafton		
Wards 1, 2 & 6	376	980
Wards 3 – 5 & 7	394	932
Grafton, vil.		
Wards 1 & 2	258	659
Wards 3 & 4	341	586
Ward 5	306	610
Wards 6 – 8	525	1,134
Wards 9 – 11	402	865
Wards 12 & 13	356	777
Mequon, city		
Wards 1, 18 & 20	364	835
Ward 2	134	478
Wards 3 – 5	606	1,433
Ward 6	426	654
Ward 7	289	624
Wards 8, 9 & 21	739	1,259
Wards 10 & 11	624	1,169
Wards 12 & 13	666	1,134
Wards 14 & 15	725	1,205
Wards 16, 17 & 19	562	1,199
Newburg, vil.		
Ward 3	12	44
Port Washington		
Wards 1 & 2	323	627
Port Washington, city		
Ward 1	374	570
Wards 2 & 3	353	474
Wards 4 & 5	304	404
Ward 6	335	513
Wards 7 & 8	422	590
Wards 9 & 10	365	525
Ward 11	392	507
Saukville		
Ward 1	84	242
Wards 2 – 5	242	614
Saukville, vil.		
Wards 1, 6 & 7	290	600
Wards 2 – 5 & 8	420	729
Thiensville, vil.		
Wards 1 & 2	345	741
Wards 3 & 4	476	612
TOTAL	17,714	34,904
PEPIN COUNTY		
Albany	161	135
Durand		
Wards 1 & 2	175	210
Durand, city		
Wards 1 – 3	532	550
Frankfort		
Wards 1 & 2	127	75
Lima		
Wards 1 & 2	180	158
Pepin		
Wards 1 & 2	234	167
Pepin, vil.		
Wards 1 & 2	357	158
Stockholm	62	73
Stockholm, vil.	43	13
Waterville		
Wards 1 & 2	216	200
Waubeek	94	114
TOTAL	2,181	1,853

VOTE FOR PRESIDENT AND VICE PRESIDENT
BY WARD, November 2, 2004 General Election—Continued

District	John F. Kerry John Edwards (Dem.)	George W. Bush[1] Dick Cheney[1] (Rep.)
PIERCE COUNTY		
Bay City, vil.	127	76
Clifton		
Wards 1 & 2	521	632
Diamond Bluff	152	153
El Paso		
Wards 1 & 2	221	166
Ellsworth		
Wards 1 & 2	309	366
Ellsworth, vil.		
Wards 1 – 4	828	750
Elmwood, vil.	278	172
Gilman	285	245
Hartland	214	284
Isabelle	71	72
Maiden Rock	167	162
Maiden Rock, vil.	45	27
Martell		
Wards 1 & 2	314	366
Oak Grove		
Wards 1 & 2	455	609
Plum City, vil.	153	168
Prescott, city		
Wards 1 – 4	1,076	1,078
River Falls		
Wards 1 – 3	701	741
River Falls, city		
Wards 3 & 4	363	248
Wards 5 – 7	1,016	709
Wards 8 – 10	956	710
Wards 11 & 12	952	760
Rock Elm	152	138
Salem		
Wards 1 & 2	168	136
Spring Lake		
Wards 1 & 2	186	148
Spring Valley, vil.		
Wards 1 & 2	350	309
Trenton		
Wards 1 & 2	521	525
Trimbelle		
Wards 1 & 2	441	512
Union	154	175
TOTAL	11,176	10,437
POLK COUNTY		
Alden		
Wards 1 – 3	701	878
Amery, city		
Wards 1 & 2	370	357
Ward 3	119	111
Wards 4 & 5	327	300
Apple River		
Wards 1 & 2	324	309
Balsam Lake		
Wards 1 & 2	373	466
Balsam Lake, vil.	276	265
Beaver	213	208
Black Brook		
Wards 1 & 2	282	438
Bone Lake	207	200
Centuria, vil.	195	201
Clam Falls	180	139
Clayton	266	246
Clayton, vil.	116	97
Clear Lake		
Wards 1 & 2	188	258
Clear Lake, vil.		
Wards 1 & 2	274	269
Dresser, vil.	199	200
Eureka		
Wards 1 & 2	369	485
Farmington		
Wards 1 & 2	386	538
Frederic, vil.		
Wards 1 & 2	309	263
Garfield		
Wards 1 – 3	387	473
Georgetown		
Wards 1 & 2	341	218
Johnstown	159	110
Laketown	270	300
Lincoln		
Wards 1 – 4	597	681
Lorain	66	87
Luck		
Wards 1 & 2	275	249
Luck, vil.		
Wards 1 & 2	352	263
McKinley	94	109

District	John F. Kerry John Edwards (Dem.)	George W. Bush[1] Dick Cheney[1] (Rep.)
Milltown		
Wards 1 & 2	313	318
Milltown, vil.	249	185
Osceola		
Wards 1 – 4	550	836
Osceola, vil.		
Wards 1 – 3	580	665
St. Croix Falls		
Wards 1 – 3	280	392
St. Croix Falls, city		
Wards 1 – 3	569	579
Sterling	191	197
Turtle Lake, vil.		
Ward 2	31	12
West Sweden		
Wards 1 & 2	195	193
TOTAL	11,173	12,095
PORTAGE COUNTY		
Alban	313	172
Almond	176	206
Almond, vil.	95	132
Amherst		
Wards 1 & 2	416	387
Amherst, vil.	292	259
Amherst Junction, vil.	110	80
Belmont	175	182
Buena Vista		
Wards 1 & 2	345	299
Carson		
Wards 1 & 2	416	376
Dewey	310	252
Eau Pleine	250	251
Grant		
Wards 1 & 2	383	381
Ward 3	165	187
Hull		
Wards 1 – 8	1,796	1,462
Junction City, vil.	119	92
Lanark		
Wards 1 & 2	399	418
Linwood		
Wards 1 & 2	404	288
Milladore, vil.		
Ward 2	2	2
Nelsonville, vil.	63	37
New Hope	315	167
Park Ridge, vil.	176	167
Pine Grove		
Wards 1 & 2	211	210
Plover		
Wards 1 & 4	263	321
Wards 2 & 3	381	388
Plover, vil.		
Wards 1 – 9	2,878	2,727
Rosholt, vil.	148	111
Sharon		
Wards 1 – 3	731	459
Stevens Point, city		
Wards 1 & 2	924	387
Wards 3 & 4	963	561
Wards 5 & 6	996	622
Wards 7 & 8	702	400
Wards 9 & 10	702	407
Wards 11 & 12	716	631
Wards 13 & 14	862	545
Wards 15 & 16	826	594
Wards 17 & 18	761	381
Wards 19 & 20	647	381
Wards 21 & 22	867	564
Stockton		
Wards 1 – 4	922	691
Whiting, vil.		
Wards 1 – 4	641	369
TOTAL	21,861	16,546
PRICE COUNTY		
Catawba	81	60
Catawba, vil.	49	19
Eisenstein		
Ward 1	132	123
Ward 2	66	99
Elk		
Ward 1	65	59
Ward 2	32	62
Ward 3	244	284
Emery	109	72
Fifield		
Ward 1	213	196
Ward 2	68	109

VOTE FOR PRESIDENT AND VICE PRESIDENT
BY WARD, November 2, 2004 General Election—Continued

District	John F. Kerry John Edwards (Dem.)	George W. Bush[1] Dick Cheney[1] (Rep.)	District	John F. Kerry John Edwards (Dem.)	George W. Bush[1] Dick Cheney[1] (Rep.)
Flambeau	145	144	Ward 13	338	237
Georgetown	42	43	Ward 14	850	654
Hackett			Ward 15	803	542
Ward 1	32	43	Ward 16	785	504
Ward 2	17	21	Ward 17	699	334
Harmony	77	68	Ward 18	906	722
Hill	64	143	Ward 19	630	144
Kennan	90	71	Ward 20	724	77
Kennan, vil.	55	32	Ward 21	790	560
Knox			Ward 22	715	692
Ward 1	94	91	Ward 23	903	648
Ward 2	30	11	Ward 24	924	630
Lake			Ward 25	791	630
Ward 1	160	152	Ward 26	807	430
Ward 2	221	182	Ward 27	912	849
Ogema			Ward 28	745	863
Ward 1	183	209	Ward 29	793	649
Ward 2	36	29	Ward 30	744	458
Park Falls, city			Ward 31	727	503
Ward 1	213	103	Ward 32	841	412
Ward 2	145	101	Ward 33	726	494
Ward 3	57	48	Ward 34	805	805
Ward 4	80	73	Raymond		
Ward 5	96	66	Wards 1 – 5	794	1,536
Ward 6	76	90	Rochester		
Ward 7	128	83	Wards 1 – 5	436	1,052
Phillips, city			Rochester, vil.		
Ward 1	66	70	Wards 1 & 2	174	415
Ward 2	84	80	Sturtevant, vil.		
Ward 3	128	90	Wards 1 – 6	1,118	1,228
Ward 4	41	30	Union Grove, vil.		
Ward 5	117	110	Wards 1 – 7	794	1,562
Prentice			Waterford		
Ward 1	64	115	Wards 1 – 10	999	2,338
Ward 2	24	48	Waterford, vil.		
Prentice, vil.	182	180	Wards 1 – 7	859	1,718
Spirit	63	113	Wind Point, vil.		
Worcester			Wards 1 – 3	431	842
Ward 1	166	189	Yorkville		
Ward 2	157	203	Wards 1 – 5	627	1,165
Ward 3	115	136	**TOTAL**	48,229	52,456
Ward 4	42	62	**RICHLAND COUNTY**		
TOTAL	4,349	4,312	Akan	106	115
			Bloom	113	156
RACINE COUNTY			Boaz, vil.	48	21
Burlington			Buena Vista		
Wards 1 – 8	736	1,424	Wards 1 & 2	416	418
Wards 9 – 12	542	907	Cazenovia, vil.		
Burlington, city			Ward 1	118	52
Wards 1 – 8	1,058	1,393	Dayton	189	197
Wards 9 – 16	1,021	1,846	Eagle	106	182
Caledonia			Forest	91	94
Wards 1 – 3	931	1,497	Henrietta	143	119
Wards 4, 20 & 21	599	1,076	Ithaca	148	181
Wards 5, 6 & 18	832	1,197	Lone Rock, vil.		
Wards 7 – 9 & 19	1,213	1,338	Wards 1 & 2	255	168
Wards 10 – 12, 16 & 17	1,591	2,351	Marshall	130	209
Wards 13 – 15	922	1,230	Orion	134	173
Dover			Richland		
Wards 1 – 8	677	1,246	Wards 1 – 4	249	465
Elmwood Park, vil.	138	198	Richland Center, city		
Mount Pleasant, vil.			Ward 1	124	126
Wards 1, 16 – 18 & 20	1,404	1,559	Ward 2	81	104
Wards 2, 3 & 11	1,102	965	Ward 3	115	108
Wards 4 & 5	634	765	Ward 4	79	64
Wards 6 & 8	616	862	Ward 5	108	137
Wards 7, 10 & 12	1,072	1,241	Ward 6	103	133
Ward 9	289	460	Ward 7	115	130
Wards 13 & 15	423	579	Ward 8	108	110
Ward 14	211	326	Ward 9	105	146
Wards 19, 21 & 23	780	922	Ward 10	162	142
Ward 22	311	196	Ward 11	85	115
Mukwonago, vil.			Ward 12	129	137
Ward 10	0	0	Richwood		
North Bay, vil.	65	111	Wards 1 & 2	203	115
Norway			Rockbridge		
Wards 1 – 11	1,425	3,179	Wards 1 – 3	190	205
Racine, city			Sylvan		
Ward 1	136	78	Wards 1 – 4	117	122
Ward 2	685	161	Viola, vil.		
Ward 3	592	98	Ward 2	130	92
Ward 4	612	44	Westford		
Ward 5	353	109	Wards 1 & 2	149	114
Ward 6	725	376	Willow	127	166
Ward 7	679	170	Yuba, vil.	25	20
Ward 8	866	239	**TOTAL**	4,501	4,836
Ward 9	534	170			
Ward 10	502	197			
Ward 11	479	42			
Ward 12	284	211			

VOTE FOR PRESIDENT AND VICE PRESIDENT
BY WARD, November 2, 2004 General Election—Continued

District	John F. Kerry John Edwards (Dem.)	George W. Bush[1] Dick Cheney[1] (Rep.)	District	John F. Kerry John Edwards (Dem.)	George W. Bush[1] Dick Cheney[1] (Rep.)
ROCK COUNTY			Newark		
Avon	147	169	Wards 1 & 2	420	538
Beloit			Orfordville, vil.		
Wards 1 – 3	592	637	Wards 1 & 2	416	311
Wards 4 & 5	561	293	Plymouth		
Wards 6 – 9	942	1,110	Wards 1 & 2	361	336
Beloit, city			Porter	362	251
Ward 1	340	218	Rock		
Ward 2	450	337	Wards 1 – 7	971	591
Ward 3	552	332	Spring Valley	201	209
Ward 4	421	365	Turtle		
Ward 5	562	394	Wards 1 & 4	150	218
Ward 6	373	178	Wards 2 & 3	452	670
Ward 7	471	262	Union		
Ward 8	338	249	Wards 1 & 2	641	469
Ward 9	329	120	TOTAL	46,598	33,151
Ward 10	381	224			
Ward 11	186	59	RUSK COUNTY		
Ward 12	399	111	Atlanta	176	184
Ward 13	523	182	Big Bend	152	131
Ward 14	496	58	Big Falls	37	52
Ward 15	838	157	Bruce, vil.		
Ward 16	462	171	Wards 1 & 2	209	203
Ward 17	255	149	Cedar Rapids	10	15
Ward 18	262	174	Conrath, vil.	33	16
Ward 19	426	278	Dewey	120	196
Ward 20	533	309	Flambeau		
Ward 21	412	285	Wards 1 – 3	230	327
Ward 22	318	371	Glen Flora, vil.	24	18
Ward 23	481	540	Grant		
Ward 24	153	165	Wards 1 & 2	188	212
Bradford	227	325	Grow	86	138
Brodhead, city			Hawkins	54	50
Ward 7	2	2	Hawkins, vil.	92	73
Center	365	295	Hubbard	49	62
Clinton	173	283	Ingram, vil.	40	14
Clinton, vil.			Ladysmith, city		
Wards 1 – 3	479	572	Wards 1 – 14	834	767
Edgerton, city			Lawrence	49	90
Wards 1 – 6	1,658	899	Marshall		
Evansville, city			Wards 1 & 2	104	141
Wards 1 – 8	1,453	883	Murry	74	74
Footville, vil.	237	158	Richland		
Fulton			Wards 1 & 2	67	45
Wards 1 – 4	1,088	846	Rusk		
Harmony			Wards 1 & 2	178	155
Wards 1 – 5	779	710	Sheldon, vil.	59	66
Janesville			South Fork	36	36
Wards 1 – 5	1,011	916	Strickland	92	65
Ward 6	12	6	Stubbs	195	155
Janesville, city			Thornapple		
Ward 1	842	598	Wards 1 & 2	180	250
Ward 2	879	429	Tony, vil.	34	27
Ward 3	772	478	True	78	96
Ward 4	789	440	Washington	96	124
Ward 5	1,016	1,102	Weyerhaeuser, vil.		
Ward 6	592	503	Wards 1 & 2	89	42
Ward 7	1,025	652	Wilkinson	15	23
Ward 8	812	509	Willard	120	116
Ward 9	699	485	Wilson	20	22
Ward 10	861	696	TOTAL	3,820	3,985
Ward 11	773	723			
Ward 12	828	761	ST. CROIX COUNTY		
Ward 13	912	627	Baldwin	252	302
Ward 14	720	429	Baldwin, vil.		
Ward 15	671	282	Wards 1 – 5	789	851
Ward 16	647	277	Cady	191	279
Ward 17	806	403	Cylon	158	190
Ward 18	859	505	Deer Park, vil.	60	68
Ward 19	800	463	Eau Galle		
Ward 20	921	459	Wards 1 & 2	274	332
Ward 21	892	422	Emerald		
Ward 22	786	316	Wards 1 & 2	201	193
Ward 23	751	446	Erin Prairie	159	204
Ward 24	696	705	Forest	165	176
Ward 25	17	9	Glenwood	205	193
Ward 26	67	36	Glenwood City, city		
Ward 27	3	3	Wards 1 & 2	330	271
Johnstown	234	233	Hammond	323	553
La Prairie			Hammond, vil.		
Wards 1 & 2	261	260	Wards 1 & 2	494	481
Lima			Hudson		
Wards 1 & 2	321	310	Wards 1 – 11	1,674	2,656
Magnolia	237	176	Hudson, city		
Milton			Wards 1 – 14	3,059	3,228
Wards 1 – 5	853	760	Kinnickinnic		
Milton, city			Wards 1 – 3	472	543
Wards 1 – 4	856	668	New Richmond, city		
Wards 5 – 8	739	601	Wards 1 – 6	890	750
			Wards 7 – 13	880	978

VOTE FOR PRESIDENT AND VICE PRESIDENT
BY WARD, November 2, 2004 General Election—Continued

District	John F. Kerry / John Edwards (Dem.)	George W. Bush[1] / Dick Cheney[1] (Rep.)
North Hudson, vil.		
Wards 1 – 6	934	1,237
Pleasant Valley	131	129
Richmond		
Wards 1 – 3	571	736
River Falls, city		
Wards 1 & 2	757	624
Roberts, vil.		
Wards 1 & 2	348	430
Rush River	147	152
St. Joseph		
Wards 1 – 7	919	1,293
Somerset		
Wards 1, 3 – 5	737	957
Ward 2	76	142
Somerset, vil.		
Wards 1 & 2	453	558
Spring Valley, vil.		
Ward 3	0	2
Springfield	247	241
Stanton		
Wards 1 & 2	244	298
Star Prairie		
Wards 1 – 5	729	954
Star Prairie, vil.	175	178
Troy		
Wards 1 – 7	1,081	1,573
Warren		
Wards 1 & 2	345	536
Wilson, vil.	57	47
Woodville, vil.		
Wards 1 & 2	257	344
TOTAL	18,784	22,679
SAUK COUNTY		
Baraboo		
Wards 1 – 4	457	591
Baraboo, city		
Ward 1	155	96
Ward 2	185	153
Ward 3	370	226
Ward 4	131	127
Ward 5	246	148
Ward 6	290	223
Ward 7	258	194
Ward 8	147	119
Ward 9	143	147
Ward 10	337	314
Ward 11	196	208
Ward 12	222	196
Ward 13	174	138
Ward 14	179	130
Bear Creek	214	120
Cazenovia		
Ward 2	8	3
Dellona		
Wards 1 & 2	375	377
Delton		
Wards 1 – 4	537	521
Excelsior		
Wards 1 – 3	402	459
Fairfield		
Wards 1 & 2	356	292
Franklin		
Wards 1 – 3	197	176
Freedom	109	147
Greenfield	306	314
Honey Creek	208	238
Ironton	139	170
Ironton, vil.	49	48
La Valle		
Wards 1 & 2	322	405
La Valle, vil.	112	92
Lake Delton, vil.		
Wards 1 – 3	646	522
Lime Ridge, vil.	68	36
Loganville, vil.	52	92
Merrimac	297	321
Merrimac, vil.	133	116
North Freedom, vil.	159	168
Plain, vil.	220	225
Prairie du Sac		
Wards 1 – 3	315	341
Prairie du Sac, vil.		
Wards 1 – 5	1,055	795
Reedsburg		
Wards 1 – 4	280	360
Reedsburg, city		
Wards 1 – 3 & 13	489	426
Wards 4, 6, 11 & 14	536	595
Wards 7, 8, 10 & 15	583	634
Wards 5, 9, 12 & 16	388	398
Rock Springs, vil.	113	97
Sauk City, vil.		
Wards 1 – 4	1,044	697
Spring Green		
Wards 1 – 4	564	442
Spring Green, vil.		
Wards 1 & 2	512	340
Sumpter		
Wards 1 – 3	233	174
Troy	229	198
Washington	158	222
West Baraboo, vil.		
Wards 1 & 2	283	255
Westfield		
Wards 1 & 2	126	179
Winfield		
Wards 1 & 2	209	207
Wisconsin Dells, city		
Ward 4	28	22
Woodland	164	181
TOTAL	15,708	14,415
SAWYER COUNTY		
Bass Lake		
Wards 1 – 4	717	532
Couderay		
Wards 1 & 2	100	59
Couderay, vil.	35	19
Draper	57	80
Edgewater	153	212
Exeland, vil.	59	51
Hayward		
Wards 1 – 6	786	988
Hayward, city		
Ward 1	121	105
Ward 2	104	119
Ward 3	135	154
Ward 4	142	188
Hunter		
Wards 1 & 2	230	214
Lenroot		
Wards 1 – 3	347	456
Meadowbrook	24	62
Meteor	26	59
Ojibwa	68	79
Radisson		
Wards 1 & 2	92	131
Radisson, vil.	65	62
Round Lake		
Wards 1 & 2	299	391
Sand Lake	267	292
Spider Lake	127	165
Weirgor	92	116
Winter		
Wards 1 & 2	284	340
Winter, vil.	81	77
TOTAL	4,411	4,951
SHAWANO COUNTY		
Almon		
Wards 1 & 2	123	174
Angelica		
Wards 1 – 3	353	569
Aniwa	104	173
Aniwa, vil.	53	71
Bartelme	304	79
Belle Plaine		
Wards 1 – 3	361	674
Birnamwood		
Wards 1 & 2	163	185
Birnamwood, vil.		
Ward 1	179	146
Bonduel, vil.		
Wards 1 & 2	247	477
Bowler, vil.	77	71
Cecil, vil.	97	164
Eland, vil.	85	48
Fairbanks		
Wards 1 & 2	94	210
Germania	111	94
Grant		
Wards 1 & 2	178	325
Green Valley		
Wards 1 & 2	217	288
Gresham, vil.	110	145
Hartland	119	291

VOTE FOR PRESIDENT AND VICE PRESIDENT
BY WARD, November 2, 2004 General Election—Continued

District	John F. Kerry / John Edwards (Dem.)	George W. Bush[1] / Dick Cheney[1] (Rep.)
Herman		
Wards 1 & 2	138	366
Hutchins	72	222
Lessor		
Wards 1 & 2	275	365
Maple Grove		
Wards 1 & 2	198	322
Marion, city		
Ward 4	2	7
Mattoon, vil.	77	117
Morris		
Wards 1 & 2	120	131
Navarino	111	133
Pella	155	305
Pulaski, vil.		
Ward 4	20	40
Red Springs	269	199
Richmond		
Wards 1 – 3	348	741
Seneca	122	170
Shawano, city		
Wards 1 & 2	265	361
Wards 3 & 4	251	342
Wards 5 & 6	270	348
Wards 7 & 8	266	305
Wards 9 & 10	327	420
Wards 11 & 12	310	392
Tigerton, vil.	165	196
Washington		
Wards 1 & 2	408	645
Waukechon		
Wards 1 & 2	173	318
Wescott		
Wards 1 – 5	890	1,031
Wittenberg		
Wards 1 & 2	194	251
Wittenberg, vil.		
Wards 1 & 2	256	239
TOTAL	8,657	12,150

SHEBOYGAN COUNTY

District	John F. Kerry / John Edwards (Dem.)	George W. Bush[1] / Dick Cheney[1] (Rep.)
Adell, vil.	92	198
Cascade, vil.	140	250
Cedar Grove, vil.		
Wards 1 & 2	240	951
Elkhart Lake, vil.		
Wards 1 – 3	307	377
Glenbeulah, vil.	111	140
Greenbush		
Wards 1 – 4	348	579
Herman		
Wards 1 – 3	405	642
Holland		
Wards 1 – 4	341	1,179
Howards Grove, vil.		
Wards 1 – 3	716	1,002
Kohler, vil.		
Wards 1 – 3	480	912
Lima		
Wards 1 – 4	498	1,298
Lyndon		
Wards 1 & 2	301	613
Mitchell		
Wards 1 & 2	245	459
Mosel	227	293
Oostburg, vil.		
Wards 1 – 4	246	1,497
Plymouth		
Wards 1 – 4	687	1,144
Plymouth, city		
Wards 1 – 3	459	547
Wards 4 & 5	500	583
Wards 6 – 8	622	774
Wards 9 & 10	430	618
Random Lake, vil.		
Wards 1 & 2	304	642
Rhine		
Wards 1 – 3	590	836
Russell	57	177
Scott		
Wards 1 & 2	279	759
Sheboygan		
Wards 1, 3 & 4	732	1,045
Ward 2	301	286
Wards 5 – 7	868	1,098
Sheboygan, city		
Ward 1	831	791
Ward 2	837	884
Ward 3	662	534
Ward 4	742	441
Ward 5	679	356
Ward 6	846	725
Ward 7	817	548
Ward 8	1,006	846
Ward 9	927	809
Ward 10	922	664
Ward 11	889	618
Ward 12	871	573
Ward 13	1,058	983
Ward 14	1,000	838
Ward 15	842	611
Ward 16	630	400
Ward 17	0	0
Ward 18	0	0
Ward 19	0	0
Ward 20	1	3
Ward 21	0	0
Ward 22	0	0
Ward 23	3	0
Sheboygan Falls		
Wards 1 & 2	414	607
Sheboygan Falls, city		
Wards 1, 2 & 9	731	994
Wards 3 & 4	510	542
Wards 5 – 8	586	565
Ward 10	97	89
Sherman		
Wards 1 & 2	252	648
Waldo, vil.	84	183
Wilson		
Wards 1 – 4	845	1,306
TOTAL	27,608	34,458

TAYLOR COUNTY

District	John F. Kerry / John Edwards (Dem.)	George W. Bush[1] / Dick Cheney[1] (Rep.)
Aurora	80	102
Browning		
Wards 1 & 2	146	298
Chelsea	131	261
Cleveland	42	94
Deer Creek		
Wards 1 & 2	109	234
Ford	69	85
Gilman, vil.	120	126
Goodrich	85	173
Greenwood	136	183
Grover	35	99
Hammel		
Wards 1 & 2	156	234
Holway	113	154
Jump River	80	69
Little Black		
Wards 1 & 2	252	339
Lublin, vil.	48	28
Maplehurst		
Wards 1 & 2	84	92
McKinley	75	104
Medford		
Wards 1 – 3	391	840
Medford, city		
Wards 1 & 2	215	233
Wards 3 & 4	161	239
Wards 5 & 6	171	231
Wards 7 & 8	145	203
Molitor	68	97
Pershing	63	24
Rib Lake		
Wards 1 & 2	164	255
Rib Lake, vil.	209	213
Roosevelt	126	80
Stetsonville, vil.	136	147
Taft	78	99
Westboro	141	246
TOTAL	3,829	5,582

TREMPEALEAU COUNTY

District	John F. Kerry / John Edwards (Dem.)	George W. Bush[1] / Dick Cheney[1] (Rep.)
Albion		
Wards 1 & 2	201	150
Arcadia		
Wards 1 – 3	469	353
Arcadia, city		
Wards 1 – 3	563	398
Blair, city		
Wards 1 – 3	388	201
Burnside		
Wards 1 & 2	194	67
Caledonia	212	254
Chimney Rock	85	45
Dodge	142	95
Eleva, vil.	240	112

VOTE FOR PRESIDENT AND VICE PRESIDENT
BY WARD, November 2, 2004 General Election—Continued

District	John F. Kerry John Edwards (Dem.)	George W. Bush[1] Dick Cheney[1] (Rep.)	District	John F. Kerry John Edwards (Dem.)	George W. Bush[1] Dick Cheney[1] (Rep.)
Ettrick			**Cloverland**	256	396
Wards 1 & 2	405	304	**Conover**		
Ettrick, vil.	156	112	Wards 1 – 3	329	479
Gale			**Eagle River, city**		
Wards 1 & 2	365	414	Wards 1 – 5	256	431
Galesville, city			**Lac du Flambeau**		
Wards 1 – 3	401	369	Wards 1 – 3	933	650
Hale			**Land O'Lakes**	220	404
Wards 1 – 3	339	191	**Lincoln**		
Independence, city			Wards 1 – 4	640	1,011
Wards 1 – 3	386	183	**Manitowish Waters**	212	348
Lincoln			**Phelps**		
Wards 1 & 2	245	120	Wards 1 & 2	324	528
Osseo, city			**Plum Lake**		
Wards 1 – 4	489	408	Wards 1 & 2	133	226
Pigeon			**Presque Isle**	223	330
Wards 1 & 2	257	133	**St. Germain**		
Pigeon Falls, vil.	155	79	Wards 1 & 2	502	882
Preston			**Washington**		
Wards 1 – 3	231	179	Wards 1 – 3	395	631
Strum, vil.			**Winchester**	141	210
Wards 1 & 2	377	188			
Sumner	229	228	TOTAL	5,713	8,155
Trempealeau					
Wards 1 – 3	477	460	**WALWORTH COUNTY**		
Trempealeau, vil.			**Bloomfield**		
Wards 1 & 2	431	370	Wards 1 – 7	874	1,152
Unity			**Burlington, city**		
Wards 1 & 2	154	120	Ward 17	0	0
Whitehall, city			**Darien**		
Wards 1 – 4	484	345	Wards 1 – 6	317	531
TOTAL	8,075	5,878	Darien, vil.		
			Wards 1 & 2	265	386
VERNON COUNTY			**Delavan**		
Bergen			Wards 1 – 6	1,111	1,631
Wards 1 – 3	419	390	**Delavan, city**		
Chaseburg, vil.	66	87	Wards 1 – 11	1,559	1,824
Christiana			**East Troy**		
Wards 1 & 2	270	232	Wards 1 – 6	719	1,738
Clinton			East Troy, vil.		
Wards 1 & 2	143	119	Wards 1 – 6	711	1,467
Coon			**Elkhorn, city**		
Wards 1 & 2	254	185	Wards 1 – 3, 6, 10, 12 & 13	735	937
Coon Valley, vil.	223	220	Wards 4, 5, 7 – 9, 11 & 15 .	803	1,304
De Soto, vil.			Ward 14	19	26
Ward 1	68	58	**Fontana, vil.**		
Forest	139	132	Wards 1 – 4	367	675
Franklin	220	304	**Geneva**		
Genoa			Wards 1 – 8	760	1,251
Wards 1 & 2	246	159	**Genoa City, vil.**		
Genoa, vil.	100	58	Wards 1 – 3	416	709
Greenwood	110	121	**La Grange**		
Hamburg			Wards 1 – 3	460	930
Wards 1 & 2	266	264	**Lafayette**		
Harmony	194	170	Wards 1 – 4	332	765
Hillsboro			**Lake Geneva, city**		
Wards 1 & 2	182	186	Wards 1, 2, 7, 8 & 12	748	866
Hillsboro, city			Wards 3 – 6, 9 – 11, 13 & 14	683	860
Wards 1 – 4	335	315	**Linn**		
Jefferson			Wards 1, 2 & 4	353	626
Wards 1 – 4	347	264	Wards 3 & 5	90	164
Kickapoo	174	102	**Lyons**		
La Farge, vil.	251	127	Wards 1 – 6	729	1,221
Liberty	64	74	**Mukwonago, vil.**		
Ontario, vil.	112	92	Ward 9	7	15
Readstown, vil.	120	103	**Richmond**		
Stark			Wards 1 – 3	446	630
Wards 1 & 2	122	80	**Sharon**	178	321
Sterling	129	193	**Sharon, vil.**		
Stoddard, vil.	269	178	Wards 1 & 2	338	374
Union			**Spring Prairie**		
Wards 1 & 2	114	96	Wards 1 – 4	376	902
Viola, vil.			**Sugar Creek**		
Ward 1	42	65	Wards 1 – 5	691	1,261
Viroqua			**Troy**		
Wards 1 – 4	480	444	Wards 1 – 3	470	965
Viroqua, city			**Walworth**		
Wards 1 – 9	1,259	1,133	Wards 1 – 4	255	672
Webster	207	120	Walworth, vil.		
Westby, city			Wards 1 – 3	462	767
Wards 1 – 5	703	474	**Whitewater**		
Wheatland	193	107	Wards 1 – 3	334	534
Whitestown	103	122	**Whitewater, city**		
TOTAL	7,924	6,774	Wards 1 & 2	708	676
			Wards 3 & 4	769	485
VILAS COUNTY			Wards 5 & 6	825	682
Arbor Vitae			Wards 7 & 8	719	497
Wards 1 – 4	850	1,183	Ward 12	3	0
Boulder Junction			Ward 13	0	0
Wards 1 & 2	299	446			

VOTE FOR PRESIDENT AND VICE PRESIDENT
BY WARD, November 2, 2004 General Election—Continued

District	John F. Kerry / John Edwards (Dem.)	George W. Bush[1] / Dick Cheney[1] (Rep.)
Williams Bay, vil.		
Wards 1 – 4	545	910
TOTAL	19,177	28,754
WASHBURN COUNTY		
Barronett		
Wards 1 & 2	133	99
Bashaw		
Wards 1 – 3	260	327
Bass Lake	111	166
Beaver Brook		
Wards 1 – 3	184	208
Birchwood		
Wards 1 & 2	123	232
Birchwood, vil.	132	141
Brooklyn	73	102
Casey	165	142
Chicog		
Wards 1 & 2	117	75
Crystal		
Wards 1 & 2	82	88
Evergreen		
Wards 1 & 2	338	336
Frog Creek	35	50
Gull Lake	58	48
Long Lake	254	205
Madge		
Wards 1 – 3	186	159
Minong		
Wards 1 & 2	291	261
Minong, vil.	145	113
Sarona	105	114
Shell Lake, city		
Ward 1	176	192
Ward 2	216	181
Spooner		
Wards 1 – 3	199	228
Spooner, city		
Ward 1	131	126
Ward 2	173	137
Ward 3	146	156
Ward 4	131	132
Ward 5	149	113
Springbrook	136	110
Stinnett	46	61
Stone Lake	127	163
Trego		
Wards 1 – 3	283	297
TOTAL	4,705	4,762
WASHINGTON COUNTY		
Addison		
Wards 1 – 6	499	1,581
Barton		
Wards 1 – 4	495	1,113
Erin		
Wards 1 – 4	633	1,833
Farmington		
Wards 1 – 4	453	1,641
Germantown	44	126
Germantown, vil.		
Wards 1, 7, 15 – 17	899	2,485
Wards 2, 4 – 6	950	1,673
Wards 3, 8 – 10 & 18	839	1,872
Wards 11 – 14	755	1,951
Hartford		
Wards 1 – 4 & 6	500	1,291
Ward 5	149	371
Hartford, city		
Wards 1 – 8, 18, 24, 25, 29, 32 & 36	847	1,687
Wards 9 – 11, 23 & 31	623	1,274
Wards 12 – 15, 17, 19 – 22, 26 – 28, 30, 33 & 35	701	1,270
Jackson		
Wards 1 – 5	535	1,826
Jackson, vil.		
Wards 1 – 11	884	2,320
Kewaskum		
Wards 1 & 2	195	510
Kewaskum, vil.		
Wards 1 – 4 & 6	553	1,264
Milwaukee, city		
Ward 262	0	0
Newburg, vil.		
Wards 1 & 2	151	411
Polk		
Wards 1 – 4, 6 & 7	545	1,460
Ward 5	95	343
Richfield		
Ward 1	219	717
Wards 2 – 4	400	1,136
Ward 5	135	345
Wards 6, 12 & 13	412	1,077
Wards 7 & 11	299	718
Ward 8	195	510
Wards 9 & 10	228	748
Slinger, vil.		
Wards 1 – 8 & 10	709	1,588
Ward 9	0	18
Trenton		
Wards 1, 2, 5 – 7	585	1,566
Wards 3 & 4	158	445
Wayne		
Wards 1 – 3	246	886
West Bend		
Wards 1 – 9	902	2,229
West Bend, city		
Wards 1 & 12	764	1,379
Wards 2, 3 & 5	638	1,183
Wards 4, 11, 22 & 29	582	1,010
Wards 6, 7, 24 & 31	662	1,503
Wards 8 – 10	724	1,552
Wards 13 – 15	654	1,285
Wards 16, 18 & 21	524	1,099
Wards 17, 19, 20, 23, 25 & 26	853	1,345
Ward 27	0	0
Wards 28 & 34	0	0
Ward 30	0	0
Ward 32	0	0
Ward 33	0	0
TOTAL	21,234	50,641
WAUKESHA COUNTY		
Big Bend, vil.		
Wards 1 – 3	213	532
Brookfield		
Wards 1 & 4	282	585
Wards 2 & 8	203	317
Wards 3 & 6	398	834
Wards 5 & 7	261	614
Wards 9 & 10	239	417
Brookfield, city		
Ward 1	377	699
Ward 2	406	814
Ward 3	434	839
Ward 4	374	852
Ward 5	367	852
Ward 6	313	909
Ward 7	244	654
Ward 8	293	586
Ward 9	311	726
Ward 10	226	554
Ward 11	306	909
Ward 12	297	897
Ward 13	242	776
Ward 14	220	495
Ward 15	254	540
Ward 16	207	602
Ward 17	426	1,044
Ward 18	294	700
Ward 19	414	911
Ward 20	368	957
Ward 21	249	452
Ward 22	274	608
Ward 23	232	516
Ward 24	466	736
Butler, vil.		
Wards 1 – 3	459	669
Chenequa, vil.	67	349
Delafield		
Wards 1, 2, 5 & 6	417	1,428
Wards 3 & 4	219	908
Wards 7 & 8	221	644
Wards 9 – 11	370	952
Delafield, city		
Wards 1 – 7	1,329	2,845
Dousman, vil.		
Wards 1 & 2	391	751
Eagle		
Wards 1 – 4	580	1,464
Eagle, vil.		
Wards 1 & 2	257	802
Elm Grove, vil.		
Wards 1 – 4	628	1,690
Wards 5 – 8	661	1,352

VOTE FOR PRESIDENT AND VICE PRESIDENT
BY WARD, November 2, 2004 General Election—Continued

District	John F. Kerry John Edwards (Dem.)	George W. Bush[1] Dick Cheney[1] (Rep.)	District	John F. Kerry John Edwards (Dem.)	George W. Bush[1] Dick Cheney[1] (Rep.)
Genesee			**Oconomowoc, city**		
Wards 1, 4 & 5	436	1,123	Wards 1 – 3	736	1,308
Wards 2, 3 & 9	398	1,019	Wards 4 – 6 & 14	572	1,116
Wards 6 – 8 & 10	526	1,366	Wards 7 – 9, 17 – 19	587	1,247
Hartland, vil.			Wards 10 – 13, 15 & 16	817	1,639
Wards 1 – 7	885	1,930	Oconomowoc Lake, vil.	92	325
Wards 8 – 13	667	1,443	**Ottawa**		
Lac la Belle, vil.			Wards 1 – 5	771	1,602
Ward 1	50	171	**Pewaukee, city**		
Lannon, vil.			Ward 1	322	836
Wards 1 & 2	208	400	Wards 2 & 3	351	791
Lisbon			Ward 4	151	446
Wards 1, 9, 10 & 12	585	1,495	Ward 5	353	785
Wards 2, 3 & 11	494	993	Ward 6	257	764
Ward 4	111	258	Ward 7	235	588
Wards 5 – 7	481	1,187	Ward 8	370	787
Ward 8	126	447	Ward 9	161	405
Menomonee Falls, vil.			Ward 10	275	990
Wards 1 & 2	490	945	**Pewaukee, vil.**		
Wards 3, 9 & 10	831	1,489	Wards 1 – 5	867	1,946
Wards 4, 8 & 11	735	1,190	Wards 6 – 9	701	1,157
Wards 5, 6 & 13	713	1,151	**Summit**		
Wards 7 & 12	563	1,046	Wards 1 – 3	446	1,046
Wards 14, 15 & 21	869	1,751	Wards 4 – 6	464	1,189
Wards 16 & 17	429	974	**Sussex, vil.**		
Wards 18, 25 & 26	485	1,204	Wards 1, 2, 4 & 5	651	1,244
Ward 19	246	461	Wards 3, 10, 11 & 13	510	1,228
Wards 20 & 22	617	1,367	Wards 6 – 9	562	1,495
Wards 23 & 29	599	1,068	Wards 12, 14 & 15	3	8
Ward 24	149	352	**Vernon**		
Ward 27	210	470	Wards 1, 6 – 10	854	2,014
Ward 28	260	485	Wards 2 – 5	560	1,326
Merton			**Wales, vil.**		
Wards 1 – 3	433	1,437	Wards 1 – 3	510	1,098
Wards 4 – 6	426	1,151	**Waukesha**		
Wards 7 – 9	320	1,447	Wards 1 & 4	253	531
Merton, vil.			Wards 2 & 5	305	624
Wards 1 – 3	273	1,074	Ward 3	188	433
Milwaukee, city			Ward 6	208	317
Ward 274	0	0	Wards 7 & 8	232	654
Mukwonago			Wards 9 & 10	293	697
Wards 1, 2, 4 – 10	1,161	3,056	Wards 11 & 12	266	661
Ward 3	122	358	**Waukesha, city**		
Mukwonago, vil.			Ward 1	379	612
Wards 1 – 8	1,138	2,435	Ward 2	486	798
Muskego, city			Ward 3	455	516
Wards 1 – 3	651	1,242	Ward 4	400	691
Wards 4 – 6	664	1,355	Ward 5	372	439
Wards 7 – 9	647	1,311	Ward 6	360	430
Wards 10 & 11	619	1,157	Ward 7	325	494
Wards 12 & 13	620	1,418	Ward 8	410	589
Wards 14 & 15	546	1,463	Ward 9	272	465
Wards 16 & 17	603	1,473	Ward 10	249	355
Nashotah, vil.			Ward 11	289	633
Wards 1 & 2	230	682	Ward 12	339	743
New Berlin, city			Ward 13	264	684
Ward 1	403	603	Ward 14	32	43
Ward 2	493	845	Ward 15	318	556
Ward 3	426	751	Ward 16	313	450
Ward 4	242	324	Ward 17	362	519
Ward 5	524	872	Ward 18	170	226
Ward 6	267	455	Ward 19	355	458
Ward 7	242	456	Ward 20	546	561
Ward 8	167	309	Ward 21	396	346
Ward 9	357	616	Ward 22	481	375
Ward 10	446	685	Ward 23	191	295
Ward 11	176	415	Ward 24	471	521
Ward 12	176	414	Ward 25	450	837
Ward 13	352	648	Ward 26	544	839
Ward 14	313	877	Ward 27	455	764
Ward 15	356	710	Ward 28	321	419
Ward 16	233	505	Ward 29	260	383
Ward 17	242	548	Ward 30	341	371
Ward 18	466	738	Ward 31	359	495
Ward 19	446	655	Ward 32	466	866
Ward 20	356	754	Ward 33	434	923
Ward 21	353	685	Ward 34	265	439
Ward 22	502	803	Ward 35	237	400
Ward 23	298	755	Ward 36	655	1,567
Ward 24	380	732	Ward 37	384	636
Ward 25	226	473	Ward 38	481	575
Ward 26	226	510	Ward 39	10	16
Ward 27	7	30	Ward 40	2	0
Ward 28	8	6	Ward 41	0	1
North Prairie, vil.			Ward 42	0	0
Wards 1 – 3	345	835	Ward 43	0	0
Oconomowoc			Ward 44	0	0
Wards 1, 2 & 4	500	1,314	Ward 45	0	0
Wards 3, 6 & 7	470	1,251	Ward 46	19	18
Wards 5, 8 & 9	377	1,081	Ward 47	1	1

VOTE FOR PRESIDENT AND VICE PRESIDENT
BY WARD, November 2, 2004 General Election—Continued

District	John F. Kerry John Edwards (Dem.)	George W. Bush[1] Dick Cheney[1] (Rep.)
Ward 48	2	0
Ward 49	0	0
Ward 50	1	0
Ward 51	0	0
Ward 52	0	0
Ward 53	0	0
Ward 54	0	0
Ward 55	1	0
TOTAL	73,626	154,926
WAUPACA COUNTY		
Bear Creek	147	256
Big Falls, vil.	18	21
Caledonia		
Wards 1 & 2	303	601
Clintonville, city		
Wards 1 – 7	932	1,232
Dayton		
Wards 1 – 4	610	1,044
Dupont		
Wards 1 & 2	112	210
Embarrass, vil.	70	122
Farmington		
Wards 1, 2 & 6	446	699
Wards 3 – 5	442	608
Fremont	132	235
Fremont, vil.	130	303
Harrison	143	135
Helvetia		
Wards 1 & 2	124	232
Iola		
Wards 1 & 2	227	331
Iola, vil.		
Wards 1 – 3	322	380
Larrabee		
Wards 1 & 2	262	436
Lebanon		
Wards 1 & 2	349	479
Lind		
Wards 1 & 2	266	509
Little Wolf		
Wards 1 – 3	212	512
Manawa, city		
Wards 1 – 3	269	360
Marion, city		
Wards 1 – 3	237	364
Matteson	188	323
Mukwa		
Wards 1 & 4	285	343
Wards 2, 3 & 5	385	537
New London, city		
Wards 3, 4 & 8	334	417
Wards 5, 9 & 10	319	334
Wards 6 & 7	376	376
Wards 11 & 12	289	262
Ogdensburg, vil.	46	63
Royalton		
Wards 1 – 3	239	542
St. Lawrence		
Wards 1 & 2	154	227
Scandinavia		
Wards 1 & 2	281	358
Scandinavia, vil.	89	95
Union	151	252
Waupaca		
Wards 1 & 2	198	458
Waupaca, city		
Wards 1 – 12	1,189	1,515
Weyauwega	104	214
Weyauwega, city		
Wards 1 – 3	347	455
Wyoming	65	101
TOTAL	10,792	15,941
WAUSHARA COUNTY		
Aurora	191	330
Berlin, city		
Ward 7	11	39
Bloomfield		
Wards 1 & 2	178	384
Coloma		
Wards 1 & 2	168	215
Coloma, vil.	84	132
Dakota		
Wards 1 – 3	192	349
Deerfield		
Wards 1 & 2	170	252
Hancock	118	188
Hancock, vil.	112	86

District	John F. Kerry John Edwards (Dem.)	George W. Bush[1] Dick Cheney[1] (Rep.)
Leon		
Wards 1 – 3	389	441
Lohrville, vil.	118	76
Marion		
Wards 1 – 4	496	692
Mount Morris		
Wards 1 & 2	311	394
Oasis	94	138
Plainfield	107	148
Plainfield, vil.		
Wards 1 & 2	186	216
Poysippi	183	340
Redgranite, vil.		
Wards 1 & 2	294	191
Richford		
Wards 1 & 2	78	166
Rose	162	153
Saxeville		
Wards 1 & 2	276	319
Springwater		
Wards 1 – 3	375	418
Warren	158	179
Wautoma		
Wards 1 & 2	276	451
Wautoma, city		
Wards 1 – 4	351	418
Wild Rose, vil.		
Wards 1 & 2	179	173
TOTAL	5,257	6,888
WINNEBAGO COUNTY		
Algoma		
Wards 1 – 12	1,114	2,006
Appleton, city		
Ward 38	159	170
Ward 39	62	43
Ward 41	0	0
Ward 49	0	2
Black Wolf		
Wards 1 – 3	605	988
Clayton		
Wards 1 – 4	702	1,320
Menasha		
Ward 1	294	421
Ward 2	715	1,034
Wards 3 & 4	547	647
Wards 5 & 6	726	1,207
Wards 7, 8, 10 & 13	1,114	1,148
Wards 9, 11 & 12	828	744
Menasha, city		
Wards 1 & 2	1,043	793
Wards 3, 4, 7, 12 & 13	1,142	931
Wards 5 & 6	1,082	843
Wards 8 – 10 & 14	890	848
Neenah		
Wards 1 – 5	777	1,049
Neenah, city		
Wards 1 – 4	1,024	1,012
Wards 5 – 8	1,055	914
Wards 9 – 12	1,011	1,372
Wards 13 – 16	971	1,088
Wards 17 – 20	1,028	956
Wards 21 – 24	1,201	1,309
Wards 25, 26 & 31	36	45
Wards 27 & 28	2	3
Wards 29 & 32	3	2
Ward 30	0	0
Nekimi		
Wards 1 & 2	317	604
Nepeuskun	170	261
Omro		
Wards 1 – 3	483	760
Omro, city		
Wards 1 – 7	765	917
Oshkosh		
Wards 1 – 6	624	971
Oshkosh, city		
Ward 1	527	512
Ward 2	601	661
Ward 3	426	481
Ward 4	308	343
Ward 5	76	92
Ward 6	59	61
Ward 7	470	489
Ward 8	539	641
Ward 9	465	364
Ward 10	737	553
Ward 11	665	531
Ward 12	657	486
Ward 13	824	695

VOTE FOR PRESIDENT AND VICE PRESIDENT
BY WARD, November 2, 2004 General Election—Continued

District	John F. Kerry / John Edwards (Dem.)	George W. Bush[1] / Dick Cheney[1] (Rep.)	District	John F. Kerry / John Edwards (Dem.)	George W. Bush[1] / Dick Cheney[1] (Rep.)
Ward 14	651	548	Grand Rapids		
Ward 15	802	580	Wards 1 – 13	2,037	2,540
Ward 16	374	271	Hansen	168	241
Ward 17	739	705	Hewitt, vil.	178	249
Ward 18	428	324	Hiles	39	66
Ward 19	524	387	Lincoln		
Ward 20	584	460	Wards 1 & 2	340	511
Ward 21	362	313	Marshfield	184	248
Ward 22	602	489	Marshfield, city		
Ward 23	470	551	Wards 1 – 4, 10, 11, 13, 14,		
Ward 24	606	697	20, 23 & 24	2,258	2,647
Ward 25	212	277	Wards 5 – 7, 15 – 17 & 27	1,329	1,515
Ward 26	622	633	Wards 8, 9, 12, 18, 19 & 25	897	981
Ward 27	555	537	Milladore	188	165
Ward 28	617	924	Milladore, vil.		
Ward 29	534	741	Ward 1	68	72
Ward 30	429	625	Nekoosa, city		
Ward 31	625	652	Ward 1	180	133
Ward 32	822	623	Ward 2	125	103
Ward 33	461	599	Wards 3 & 5	164	216
Ward 34	0	0	Wards 4 & 6	171	132
Ward 35	0	5	Pittsville, city		
Ward 36	0	0	Wards 1 – 3	203	234
Poygan			Port Edwards		
Wards 1 & 2	293	426	Wards 1 – 3	351	340
Rushford			Port Edwards, vil.		
Wards 1 & 2	344	517	Wards 1 – 3	488	553
Utica			Remington	75	106
Wards 1 & 2	286	549	Richfield		
Vinland			Wards 1 & 2	287	433
Wards 1 – 3	512	716	Rock	185	276
Winchester			Rudolph		
Wards 1 & 2	381	663	Wards 1 & 2	360	294
Winneconne			Rudolph, vil.	147	110
Wards 1 – 3	532	990	Saratoga		
Winneconne, vil.			Wards 1 – 6	1,435	1,366
Wards 1 – 4	479	917	Seneca		
Wolf River			Wards 1 – 3	310	312
Wards 1 & 2	253	506	Sherry	219	188
TOTAL	**40,943**	**46,542**	Sigel		
			Wards 1 – 4	314	325
WOOD COUNTY			Vesper, vil.	137	184
Arpin			Wisconsin Rapids, city		
Wards 1 – 3	208	226	Wards 1 – 3	654	480
Arpin, vil.	82	62	Wards 4 – 6	670	567
Auburndale	171	243	Wards 7 – 9	613	646
Auburndale, vil.	158	213	Wards 10 – 12	716	602
Biron, vil.	267	240	Wards 13 – 15	668	612
Cameron	102	190	Wards 16 – 20	697	705
Cary	91	163	Wards 21 – 23	663	681
Cranmoor	30	67	Wood	206	266
Dexter	117	89	**TOTAL**	**18,950**	**20,592**

Note: Other presidential and vice presidential candidates received the following votes: Michael Badnarik and Richard V. Campagna (Libertarian Party) – 6,464; David Cobb and Patricia LaMarche (Wisconsin Green Party) – 2,661; Walter F. Brown and Mary Alice Herbert (Independent) – 471; James Harris and Margaret Trowe (Independent) – 411; Ralph Nader and Peter Miguel Camejo (Independent) – 16,390.

All municipalities are towns, unless noted as a village (vil.) or city.

Source: Official records of the Elections Board. Scattered votes omitted.

Wisconsin
State Symbols

11

Wisconsin state symbols: origin and descriptions of the official state symbols as specified by law

Oneida County Courthouse

L. Roger Turner

WISCONSIN STATE SYMBOLS

(See front and back endpapers)

Over the years the Wisconsin Legislature has officially recognized a wide variety of state symbols. In order of adoption, Wisconsin has designated an official seal, coat of arms, motto, flag, song, flower, bird, tree, fish, state animal, wildlife animal, domestic animal, mineral, rock, symbol of peace, insect, soil, fossil, dog, beverage, grain, dance, ballad, waltz, and fruit. (The "Badger State" nickname, however, remains unofficial.) These symbols provide a focus for expanding public awareness of Wisconsin's history and diversity.

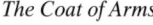

The Coat of Arms

The Great Seal

Seal and coat of arms. Article XIII, Section 4, of the Wisconsin Constitution requires the legislature to provide a "great seal" to be used by the secretary of state to authenticate all of the governor's official acts except laws. The seal consists of the coat of arms, described below, with the words "Great Seal of the State of Wisconsin" centered above and a curved line of 13 stars, representing the 13 original United States, centered below, surrounded by an ornamental border. A modified "lesser seal" serves as the seal of the secretary of state.

The coat of arms is an integral part of the state seal and also appears on the state flag. It contains a sailor with a coil of rope and a "yeoman" (usually considered a miner) with a pick, who jointly represent labor on water and land. These two figures support a quartered shield with symbols for agriculture (plow), mining (pick and shovel), manufacturing (arm and hammer), and navigation (anchor). Centered on the shield is a small U.S. coat of arms and the U.S. motto, "E pluribus unum" ("out of many, one"), referring to the union of U.S. states, to symbolize Wisconsin's loyalty to the Union. At the base, a cornucopia, or horn of plenty, stands for prosperity and abundance, while a pyramid of 13 lead ingots represents mineral wealth and the 13 original United States. Centered over the shield is a badger, the state animal, and the state motto "Forward" appears on a banner above the badger.

The history of the seal is inextricably entwined with that of the coat of arms. An official seal was created in 1836, when Wisconsin became a territory, and was revised in 1839. When Wisconsin achieved statehood in 1848, a new seal was prepared. This seal was changed in 1851 at the instigation of Governor Nelson Dewey and slightly modified to its current design in 1881 when Dewey's seal wore out and had to be recast. (See "Motto" below.) Chapter 280, Laws of 1881, provided the first precise statutory description of the great seal and coat of arms in what ultimately became Sections 1.07 and 14.45 of the statutes.

Motto: "Forward". The motto, "Forward", was introduced in the 1851 revision of the state seal and coat of arms. Governor Dewey had asked University of Wisconsin Chancellor John H. Lathrop to design a new seal. It is alleged the motto was selected during a chance meeting between Governor Dewey and Edward Ryan (later chief justice of the Wisconsin Supreme Court) when the governor went to New York City, carrying the Lathrop design to the engraver. Ryan objected to the Latin motto, "Excelsior", which Lathrop proposed. According to tradition, Dewey and Ryan sat down on the steps of a Wall Street bank, designed a new seal and chose "Forward" on the spot. It is officially recognized in Section 1.07 of the statutes.

Flag. An official design for Wisconsin's state flag was initially provided by the legislature in 1863. Noting that a flag had not been adopted and that Civil War regiments in the field were requesting flags, the legislature formed a 5-member joint select committee to report "a description for a proper state flag." This action resulted in the adoption of 1863 Joint Resolution 4, which provided a design for a state flag that was substantially the same as the regimental flags already in use by Wisconsin troops.

It was not until 1913, however, that language concerning flag specifications was added to the Wisconsin Statutes. Chapter 111, Laws of 1913, created a state flag provision, specifying a dark blue flag with the state coat of arms centered on each side. That provision has become Section 1.08 of the statutes.

The 1913 design remained unchanged until the enactment of Chapter 286, Laws of 1979, which culminated years of legislative efforts to alter or replace Wisconsin's flag so it would be more distinctive and recognizable. The most significant changes made by the 1979 act were adding the word "Wisconsin" and the statehood date "1848" in white letters, centered respectively above and below the coat of arms.

Song: "On, Wisconsin!" The music for "On, Wisconsin!" was composed in 1909 by William T. Purdy with the idea of entering it in a contest for the creation of a new University of Minnesota football song. ("Minnesota" would have replaced "On, Wisconsin" in the opening lines.) Carl Beck persuaded Purdy to dedicate the song to the University of Wisconsin football team instead, and Beck collaborated with the composer by writing the lyrics. The song was introduced at the Madison campus in November 1909. It was later acclaimed by world-famous composer and bandmaster John Philip Sousa as the best college song he had ever heard.

Lyrics more in keeping with the purposes of a state song were subsequently written in 1913 by Judge Charles D. Rosa and J. S. Hubbard, editor of the *Beloit Free Press*. Rosa and Hubbard were among the delegates from many states convened in 1913 to commemorate the centennial of the Battle of Lake Erie. Inspired by the occasion, they provided new, more solemn words to the already well-known football song.

Although "On, Wisconsin!" was widely recognized as Wisconsin's song, the state did not officially adopt it until 1959. Representative Harold W. Clemens discovered that Wisconsin was one of only ten states without an official song. He introduced a bill to give the song the status he thought it deserved. On discovering that many different lyrics existed, an official text for the first verse was incorporated in Chapter 170, Laws of 1959, and it is contained in Section 1.10 of the statutes:

> On, Wisconsin! On, Wisconsin! Grand old badger state!
> We, thy loyal sons and daughters, Hail thee, good and great.
> On, Wisconsin! On, Wisconsin! Champion of the right,
> 'Forward', our motto — God will give thee might!

Flower: wood violet *(Viola papilionacea)*. In 1908, Wisconsin school children nominated four candidates for state flower: the violet, wild rose, trailing arbutus, and white water lily. On Arbor Day 1909, the final vote was taken, and the violet won. Chapter 218, Laws of 1949, which created Section 1.10, named the wood violet Wisconsin's official flower.

Bird: robin *(Turdus migratorius)*. In 1926-27, Wisconsin school children voted to select a state bird. The robin received twice as many votes as those given any other bird. Chapter 218, Laws of 1949, which created Section 1.10, officially made the robin the state bird.

Tree: sugar maple *(Acer saccharum)*. A favorite state tree was first selected by a vote of Wisconsin school children in 1893. The maple tree won, followed by oak, pine, and elm. Another vote was conducted in 1948 among school children by the Youth Centennial Committee. In that election, the sugar maple again received the most votes, followed by white pine and birch. The 1949 Legislature, in spite of efforts by white pine advocates, named the sugar maple the official state tree by enacting Chapter 218, Laws of 1949, which created Section 1.10.

Fish: muskellunge *(Esox masquinongy masquinongy Mitchell).* Members of the legislature attempted to adopt the muskellunge as the state fish as early as 1939. The trout was a very distant alternative suggestion. In 1955, the legislature unanimously passed Chapter 18 to amend Section 1.10 and designate the muskellunge as Wisconsin's official fish.

Animals: badger *(Taxidea taxus),* **white-tailed deer** *(Odocoileus virginianus),* **dairy cow** *(Bos taurus).* Although the *badger* has been closely associated with Wisconsin since territorial days, it was not declared the official state animal until 1957. Over the years its likeness had been incorporated in the state coat of arms, the seal, the flag, and even State Capitol architecture, as well as being immortalized in the song, "On, Wisconsin!" ("Grand old badger state!"). "Bucky Badger" has long been the mascot of the UW-Madison. In 1957, a bill to establish the badger as state animal was introduced at the request of four Jefferson County elementary school students who discovered from a historical society publication that the badger had not been given the official status most people assumed. Serious opposition developed, however, when a faction from Wisconsin's northern counties introduced a bill to make the *white-tailed deer* the official animal, citing the state's large native deer population, the animal's physical attributes, and the considerable economic benefits derived from the annual deer hunt. The legislature reached a compromise by adding two official animals to Section 1.10. In Chapter 209, Laws of 1957, it named the badger the "state animal", and Chapter 147 designated the white-tailed deer as the state "wildlife animal".

The *dairy cow* was added to Section 1.10 as Wisconsin's official "domestic animal" by Chapter 167, Laws of 1971, in recognition of the animal's many contributions to the state. This action was termed a logical and long overdue step, consistent with the state's promoting itself as *America's Dairyland,* the slogan placed on state automobile license plates by Chapter 115, Laws of 1939. 1972 Executive Order 32 designated Wisconsin's first official dairy cow, but the Secretary of the Department of Agriculture, Trade and Consumer Protection is now required to establish an annual rotation among Wisconsin's remaining purebreds. The Brown Swiss was selected for 2005, followed by the Jersey in 2006.

Badger nickname. History, rather than the law, explains Wisconsin's unofficial nickname as the "Badger State". During the lead-mining boom that began just prior to 1830 in southwestern Wisconsin, the name was first applied to miners who were too busy digging the "gray gold" to build houses. Like badgers, they moved into abandoned mine shafts and makeshift burrows for shelter. Although "badgers" had a somewhat derogatory connotation at first, it gradually gained acceptance as an apt description of the hardworking and energetic settlers of the Wisconsin Territory.

Mineral and rock: galena (lead sulphide) and **red granite.** Chapter 14, Laws of 1971, amended Section 1.10 to make galena the official state mineral and red granite the state rock. The proposal was introduced at the request of the Kenosha Gem and Mineral Society to promote geological awareness. Galena met the criteria for selection, as set by the Wisconsin Geological Society, including abundance, uniqueness, economic value, historical significance, and native nature. Red granite is an igneous rock composed of quartz and feldspar. It is mined in several sections of the state and was selected as the state rock because of its economic importance.

Symbol of peace: mourning dove *(Zenaidura macroura corolinensis linnaus).* Various individuals and organizations concerned with conservation and wildlife long sought a protected status for the dove. Concluding an effort that stretched over a decade, the mourning dove was added to Section 1.10 of the statutes as Wisconsin's official symbol of peace and removed from the statutory definition of game birds by Chapter 129, Laws of 1971.

Insect: honey bee *(Apis mellifera).* The honey bee was designated as the official state insect when Section 1.10 was amended by Chapter 326, Laws of 1977. The bill was introduced at the request of the third grade class of Holy Family School of Marinette and the Wisconsin Honey Producers Association. Attempts to allow all elementary school pupils in the state to decide the selection by popular ballot were unsuccessful. Other contenders for the title were the monarch butterfly, dragonfly, ladybug, and mosquito.

Soil: Antigo Silt Loam *(Typic glossoboralf).* An official state soil was created by 1983 Wisconsin Act 33 to remind Wisconsinites of their soil stewardship responsibilities. Advocates argued that soil, a natural resource that took 10,000 years to produce, is essential to Wisconsin's economy and is also the foundation of life. Selected to represent the more than 500 major soil types in Wisconsin, Antigo Silt Loam is a productive, level, silty soil of glacial origin, subsequently enriched by organic matter from prehistoric forests. The soil, named after a Wisconsin city, is found chiefly in Wisconsin and stretches in patches across the north central part of the state. It is a versatile soil that supports dairying, potato growing, and timber. The amendment to Section 1.10 was the result of a successful drive led by Professor Francis D. Hole, UW-Madison soil scientist.

Fossil: trilobite *(Calymene celebra)*. 1985 Wisconsin Act 162 amended Section 1.10 to designate the trilobite as the official state fossil. Pronounced "TRY-loh-bite", the Latin term describes the 3-lobed anatomy of this small invertebrate body divided by furrows into segments. The trilobite is an extinct marine arthropod with multiple sets of paired, jointed legs. Its head and tapering body were armored in an exoskeleton that was repeatedly molted as the animal grew. Trilobites flourished in the warm, shallow salt water sea that periodically covered Wisconsin territory hundreds of millions of years ago. Their fossil remains average 1 to 2 inches in length. The largest complete specimen is 14 inches, while incomplete parts indicate some were possibly much longer (over 30 inches). Trilobite fossils are abundant and distinctive enough to be easily recognized. Good specimens are preserved in rock formations throughout most of Wisconsin.

The Wisconsin Geological Society proposed the fossil to symbolize Wisconsin's ancient past and encourage interest in the state's rich geological heritage. A major rival for recognition as state fossil was the mastodon, a large prehistoric, elephant-like creature.

Dog: American water spaniel. 1985 Wisconsin Act 295 amended Section 1.10 to name the American water spaniel as Wisconsin's official state dog. Enactment of the law was the culmination of years of effort by eighth grade students of Lyle Brumm at Washington Junior High School in New London. The American water spaniel is said to be one of only five dog breeds indigenous to the United States and the only one native to Wisconsin. A New London area physician, Dr. Fred J. Pfeifer, is generally credited with developing and standardizing the breed and working to secure United Kennel Club registration for it in 1920. American Kennel Club recognition followed in 1940. The American water spaniel was developed as a practical, versatile hunting dog that combined certain physical attributes with intelligence and a good disposition. No flashy show animal, the American water spaniel is described as an unadorned, utilitarian dog that earns its keep as an outstanding hunter, watchdog, and family pet.

Beverage: milk. The Wisconsin Legislature designated milk as the official state beverage in 1987 Wisconsin Act 279. This action recognized Wisconsin's position as the nation's leading milk-producing state and the contribution of milk to the state's economy. World Dairy Expo and various Wisconsin dairy production and dairy cattle associations supported the amendment of Section 1.10.

Grain: corn *(Zea mays)*. 1989 Wisconsin Act 162 amended Section 1.10 to designate corn as the official state grain. During legislative debate, sponsors claimed designating corn as the state grain would draw attention to its importance as a cash crop in Wisconsin and make people more aware of corn's many uses, including livestock feed, sweeteners, ethanol fuel, and biodegradable plastics.

Dance: polka. 1993 Wisconsin Act 411 amended Section 1.10 to name the polka as the state dance. The bill was introduced at the request of a second grade class from Charles Lindbergh Elementary School in Madison and supported by several groups, including the Wisconsin Polka Boosters, Inc., and the Wisconsin Folk Museum. Supporters documented the polka heritage of Wisconsin and provided evidence that the polka is deeply ingrained in Wisconsin cultural traditions.

Ballad: "Oh Wisconsin, Land of My Dreams". "Oh Wisconsin, Land of My Dreams" was designated the Wisconsin state ballad by 2001 Wisconsin Act 16 in Section 1.10 (1m). The ballad was the work of Shari Sarazin of Mauston who set to music a poem written in the 1920s by her grandmother Erma Barrett of Juneau County. The words to this ballad are:

Oh Wisconsin, land of beauty, with your hillsides and your plains, with your jackpine and your birch tree, and your oak of mighty frame.

Land of rivers, lakes and valleys, land of warmth and winter snows, land of birds and beasts and humanity, Oh Wisconsin, I love you so.

Oh Wisconsin, land of my dreams. Oh Wisconsin, you're all I'll ever need. A little heaven here on earth could you be? Oh Wisconsin, land of my dreams.

In the summer, golden grain fields; in the winter, drift of white snow; in the springtime, robins singing; in the autumn, flaming colors show.

Oh I wonder who could wander, or who could want to drift for long, away from all your beauty, all your sunshine, all your sweet song?

Oh Wisconsin, land of my dreams. Oh Wisconsin, you're all I'll ever need. A little heaven here on earth could you be? Oh Wisconsin, land of my dreams.

Oh Wisconsin, land of my dreams. And when it's time, let my spirit run free in Wisconsin, land of my dreams.

Waltz: "The Wisconsin Waltz". 2001 Wisconsin Act 16 created Section 1.10 (1r) and designated "The Wisconsin Waltz" as the state waltz. The music and lyrics were written by Eddie Hansen, a Waupaca native and one-time theater organist. The words to this waltz are:

Music from heaven throughout the years; the beautiful Wisconsin Waltz.

Favorite song of the pioneers; the beautiful Wisconsin Waltz.

Song of my heart on that last final day, when it is time to lay me away. One thing I ask is to let them play the beautiful Wisconsin Waltz.

My sweetheart, my complete heart, it's for you when we dance together; the beautiful Wisconsin Waltz.

I remember that September, before love turned into an ember, we danced to the Wisconsin Waltz.

Summer ended, we intended that our lives then would both be blended, but somehow our planning got lost.

Memory now sings a dream song, a faded love theme song; the beautiful Wisconsin Waltz.

Fruit: cranberry *(vaccinium macrocarpon)*. 2003 Wisconsin Act 174 created Section 1.10 (3)(r) and designated the cranberry as the state fruit. The legislation was the culmination of a class project by fifth grade students from Trevor Grade School in Kenosha County who decided that the cranberry rather than the cherry was the best candidate for Wisconsin's state fruit. Wisconsin leads the nation in cranberry production, accounting for over half of the nation's output. Cranberries are grown in 20 of Wisconsin's 72 counties, primarily in the central part of the state.

Alphabetical
Index

12

Racine County Courthouse

L. Roger Turner

ALPHABETICAL INDEX

T

Wisconsin Symbols *continued*

Antigo Silt Loam
STATE SOIL

Honey Bee
STATE INSECT

Red Granite
STATE ROCK

Galena
STATE MINERAL

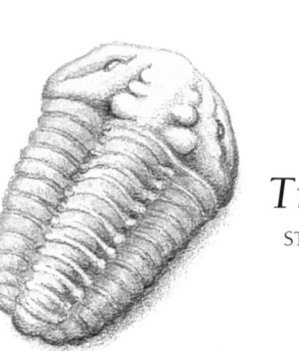

Trilobite
STATE FOSSIL

American Water Spaniel
STATE DOG

Corn
STATE GRAIN